THE BANTAM NEW COLLEGE GERMAN & ENGLISH DICTIONARY

The Best Low-Priced Dictionary You Can Own

With more entries than any other compact paper-bound dictionary—including thousands of new words—*The Bantam New College German & English Dictionary* is the most complete budget dictionary available today.

Whether you need it at home, the office, school, or in the library, this one indispensable, authoritative volume will prove its value over and over again, every time you use it.

THE BANTAM NEW COLLEGE DICTIONARY SERIES

John C. Traupman, Author

JOHN C. TRAUPMAN received his B.A. in German and in Latin at Moravian College and his M.A. and Ph.D. in Classics at Princeton University. He is chairman of the Department of Classical Languages at St. Joseph's University (Philadelphia). He served as president of the Philadelphia Classical Society, of the Pennsylvania Classical Association, and of the Classical and Modern Language League. He has published widely in learned journals and is the author of *The New College Latin & English Dictionary* (Bantam Books, 1966) and an associate editor of *The Scribner-Bantam English Dictionary* (Scribner's, 1977; Bantam Books, 1979).

Edwin B. Williams, General Editor

EDWIN B. WILLIAMS (1891–1975), A.B., A.M., Ph.D., Doct. d'Univ., LL.D., L.H.D., was chairman of the Department of Romance Languages, dean of the Graduate School, and provost of the University of Pennsylvania. He was a member of the American Philosophical Society and the Hispanic Society of America. Among his many lexicographical works are *The Williams Spanish and English Dictionary* (Scribner's, formerly Holt) and *The Bantam New College Spanish and English Dictionary*. He created and coordinated the Bantam series of original dictionaries—English, French, German, Italian, Latin, and Spanish.

THE BANTAM NEW COLLEGE
GERMAN & ENGLISH
DICTIONARY

JOHN C. TRAUPMAN, Ph.D.
St. Joseph's University, Philadelphia

BANTAM BOOKS
TORONTO • NEW YORK • LONDON • SYDNEY • AUCKLAND

THE BANTAM NEW COLLEGE
GERMAN & ENGLISH DICTIONARY

A Bantam Book / February 1981

2nd printing .... August 1983	*4th printing .. December 1984*
3rd printing ...... June 1984	*5th printing .. February 1986*

ISBN 0-553-25953-9

Published simultaneously in the United States and Canada

CONTENTS

I wish to express my appreciation to the many persons on whose help I relied in researching and compiling this Dictionary. I am particularly indebted to Edwin B. Williams, Walter D. Glanze, Donald Reis, Rudolf Pillwein, and Helmut Kreitz.

J. C. T.

HOW TO USE
THIS DICTIONARY

HINWEISE FÜR
DEN BENUTZER

All entry words are treated in a fixed order according to the parts of speech and the functions of verbs. On the German-English side: past participle, adjective, adverb, pronoun, preposition, conjunction, interjection, transitive verb, reflexive verb, reciprocal verb, intransitive verb, impersonal verb, auxiliary verb, substantive; on the English-German side: adjective, substantive, pronoun, adverb, preposition, conjunction, transitive verb, intransitive verb, auxiliary verb, impersonal verb, interjection.

Alle Stichwörter werden in einheitlicher Reihenfolge gemäß der Wortart und der Verbfunktion behandelt. Im deutsch-englischen Teil: Partizip Perfekt, Adjektiv, Adverb, Pronomen, Präposition, Konjunktion, Interjektion, transitives Verb, reflexives Verb, reziprokes Verb, intransitives Verb, unpersönliches Verb, Hilfsverb, Substantiv; im englisch-deutschen Teil: Adjektiv, Substantiv, Pronomen, Adverb, Präposition, Konjunktion, transitives Verb, intransitives Verb, Hilfsverb, unpersönliches Verb, Interjektion.

The order of meanings within an entry is as follows: first, the more general meanings; second, the meanings with usage labels; third, the meanings with subject labels in alphabetical order; fourth, illustrative phrases in alphabetical order.

Die verschiedenen Bedeutungen sind innerhalb eines Stichwortartikels in folgender Anordnung gegeben: zuerst die allgemeinen Bedeutungen; dann die Bedeutungen mit Bezeichnung der Sprachgebrauchsebene; dann die Bedeutungen mit Bezeichnung des Sachgebietes, in alphabetischer Reihenfolge; zuletzt die Anwendungsbeispiele, in alphabetischer Reihenfolge.

Subject and usage labels (printed in roman and in parentheses) refer to the preceding entry word or illustrative phrase in the source language (printed in boldface), e.g.,

Die Bezeichnungen der Sprachgebrauchsebene und des Sachgebiets (in Antiqua und in Klammern) beziehen sich auf das vorangehende Stichwort oder Anwendungsbeispiel in der Ausgangssprache (halbfett gedruckt), z.B.

mund′tot *adj*—**j-n m. machen** (fig) silence s.o.
Pinke [′pɪŋkə] *f* (—;) (coll) dough

Words in parentheses and in roman coming after a meaning serve to clarify that meaning, e.g.,

Kursiv gedruckte Wörter in Klammern, die nach einer Bedeutung stehen, sollen diese Bedeutung illustrieren, z.B.

überschau′en *tr* look over, survey; overlook (*a scene*)

Words in parenthese and in roman type coming after or before a meaning are optional additions to the word in the target language, e.g.,	In Antiqua gedruckte Wörter in Klammern, die nach oder vor einer Bedeutung stehen, sind wahlfreie Erweiterungen des Wortes der Zielsprache, z.B.

Tanne ['tanə] *f* (–;–n) fir (tree)
Pap′rikaschote *f* (green) pepper

Meaning discriminations are given in the source language and are in italics, e.g.,	Bedeutungsdifferenzierungen sind in der Ausgangssprache angegeben und kursiv gedruckt, z.B.

überrei′zen *tr* overexcite; (*Augen, Nerven*) strain
earn [ʌrn] *tr* (*money*) verdienen; (*interest*) einbringen

Since vocabulary entries are not determined on the basis of etymology, homographs are listed as a single entry.	Da die Etymologie bei der Anführung der Stichwörter unberücksichtigt bleibt, sind gleichgeschriebene Wörter als ein und dasselbe Stichwort verzeichnet.

The entry word is represented within the entry by its initial letter followed by a period (if the entry word contains more than three letters), provided the form is identical. The same applies to a word that follows the parallels. The entry word is not abbreviated within the entry when associated with suspension points, e.g.,	Innerhalb eines Stichwortartikels wird das Stichwort (wenn es mehr als drei Buchstaben enthält) durch seinen Anfangsbuchstaben angegeben, vorausgesetzt, daß die betreffende Form mit dem Stichwort identisch ist. Das Gleiche gilt für ein Wort, das nach dem Vertikalstrichen steht. Wenn ein Stichwort innerhalb eines Stichwortartikels in Verbindung mit Auslassungspunkten angegeben ist, wird es nicht abgekürzt, z.B.

weder . . . noch

Parallels are used (a) to separate parts of speech, (b) to separate transitive, reflexive, reciprocal, intransitive, impersonal, and auxiliary verbs, (c) to separate verbs taking HABEN from those taking SEIN, (d) to indicate a change in pronunciation of the entry word, depending on the meaning, e.g.,	Es ist der Zweck der Vertikalstriche, (a) Wortarten voneinander zu trennen, (b) transitive, reflexive, reziproke, intransitive, unpersönliche Verben und Hilfsverben zu trennen, (c) Verben mit dem Hilfsverb HABEN von Verben mit dem Hilfsverb SEIN zu trennen, (d) verschiedene Aussprachen des Stichwortes je nach Bedeutung anzuzeigen, z.B.

bow [baʊ] *s* Verbeugung *f*; (naut) Bug *m* . . .
‖ [bo] *s* (*weapon*) Bogen *m*; . . .

(e) to show change from a strong verb to a weak verb and vice versa, (f) to show a change in the case governed by	(e) den Wechsel von einem starken zu einem schwachen Verb und umgekehrt anzuzeigen, (f) den Wechsel in einem

viii

a preposition where the entry word is a preposition, (g) to show a shift of accent, e.g.,

von einer Präposition regierten Fall anzuzeigen, wo das Stichwort selbst eine Präposition ist, (g) unterschiedliche Stellungen des Akzents anzuzeigen, z.B.

ü′bergießen *tr* ... || **übergie′ßen** *tr* ...

The centered period in the English word on the German-English side marks the point at which the following letters are dropped before irregular plural endings are added. The centered period in the entry word on the English-German side marks the point at which the following letters are dropped before irregular plural endings are added to nouns and inflections are added to verbs. The centered period in the phonetic spelling indicates diaeresis, e.g.,

Der auf Mitte stehende Punkt im Stichwort des deutsch-englischen Teils zeigt die Stelle an, wo die nachfolgenden Buchstaben abzutrennen sind, bevor unregelmäßige Pluralendungen angefügt werden können. Der auf Mitte stehende Punkt im Stichwort des englisch-deutschen Teils zeigt die Stelle an, wo die nachfolgenden Buchstaben abzutrennen sind, bevor unregelmäßige Pluralendungen an Hauptwörter and Flexionen an Verben angefügt werden können. Der auf Mitte stehende Punkt in der Lautschrift zeigt Diärese an, z.B.

befähigt [bə′fɛ·ıçt]

On the German-English and the English-German side, in the case of a transitive verb, the meaning discrimination in parentheses before the target word is always the object of the verb. On the German-English side, in the case of an intransitive verb, the meaning discrimination in parentheses before the target word is always the subject of the verb. On the English-German side, the suggested subject of a verb is prefaced by the words "said of".

Im deutsch-englischen und im englisch-deutschen Teil ist die bei transitiven Verben in Klammern vor dem Wort in der Zielsprache angegebene Bedeutungsdifferenzierung immer das Objekt des Verbs. Im deutsch-englischen Teil ist bei intransitiven Verben die vor dem Wort in der Zielsprache angegebene Bedeutungsdifferenzierung immer das Subjekt des Verbs. Im englisch-deutschen Teil stehen vor dem beabsichtigten Subjekt eines Verbs die Worte "said of."

Inflections are generally not shown for compound entry words, since the inflections have been shown where the components are entry words. However, when the last component of a compound noun on the German-English side has various inflections depending on meaning, the inflection is shown for the compound, e.g.,

Bei zusammengesetzten Stichwörtern ist die Flexion im Allgemeinen nicht angegeben, da sie unter den als Stichwörter angeführten Teilen des Kompositums angegeben ist. Falls jedoch der letzte Teil eines deutschen Kompositums je nach der Bedeutung verschieden flektiert wird, ist die Flexion für das Kompositum angegeben, z.B.

Ton′band *n* (–[e]s;⸚er) ...

German verbs are regarded as reflexive regardless of whether the reflexive pronoun is the direct or indirect object of the verb.

Deutsche Verben gelten als reflexiv ohne Rücksicht darauf, ob das Reflexivpronomen das direkte oder indirekte Objekt des Verbs ist.

On the English-German side, when the pronunciation of an entry word is not given, stress in the entry word is shown as follows: a high-set primary stress mark ′ follows the syllable that receives the primary stress, and a high-set secondary stress mark ′ follows the syllable that receives the secondary stress. When the pronunciation of an entry word *is* provided [given in brackets], a high-set primary stress mark ‵ *precedes* the syllable that receives the primary stress, and a *low*-set secondary stress mark ‚ *precedes* the syllable that receives the secondary stress.

On the German-English side, when the pronunciation of an entry word is not given, a high-set primary stress mark ′ follows the syllable of the entry word that receives the primary stress. When the pronunciation of the entry *is* provided [given in brackets], a high-set primary stress mark ‵ *precedes* the syllable that receives the primary stress. (Because opinions on the system of secondary stress in German differ widely, secondary stress marks are not employed in this Dictionary.)

Wo die Aussprache des Stichwortes im englisch-deutschen Teil nicht angegeben ist, wird die Betonung des Stichwortes folgendermaßen angedeutet: Das stärkere, obere graphische Zeichen ′ steht nach der Silbe mit dem Haupttonakzent, und das schwächere, obere Zeichen ′ steht nach der Silbe mit dem Nebentonakzent. Wo hingegen die Aussprache des Stichwortes im englisch-deutschen Teil [in eckigen Klammern] angegeben ist, steht das stärkere, obere Zeichen ‵ *vor* der Silbe mit dem Haupttonakzent und das schwächere, *untere* Zeichen ‚ *vor* der Silbe mit dem Nebentonakzent.

Wo die Aussprache das Stichwortes im deutsch-englischen Teil nicht angegeben ist, steht das starke Zeichen ′ nach der Stichwortsilbe mit dem Haupttonakzent. Wo hingegen die Aussprache des Stichwortes im deutsch-englischen Teil [in eckigen Klammern] angegeben ist, steht das starke Zeichen ‵ *vor* der Silbe mit dem Haupttonakzent. (Wegen der widersprüchlichen Theorien, die die Frage des Nebentonakzents im Deutschen umgeben, wendet dieses Wörterbuch keine Nebentonakzente für die deutschen Wörter an.)

Proper nouns and general abbreviations are listed in their alphabetical position in the main body of the Dictionary.

Eigennamen und allgemeine Abkürzungen sind in den beiden Hauptteilen des Wörterbuches in alphabetischer Reihenfolge angegeben.

This Dictionary contains approximately 75,000 "entries." As entries are counted (a) nonindented boldface headwords and (b) elements that could have been set nonindented as separate headwords, too, but that for reasons of style and typography are grouped under the nonindented headwords, namely, separate parts of speech and boldface idioms and phrases.

Dieses Wörterbuch enthält ungefähr 75.000 "Stichwörter." Die folgenden Elemente gelten als Stichwörter: (a) die nicht eingerückten fettgedruckten Wörter am Anfang eines Stichwortartikels und (b) Elemente, die man auf dieselbe Weise hatte drucken können, die aber aus Stil- und Typographiegründen eingerückt wurden, nämlich die unterschiedlichen Wortarten und die fettgedruckten Redewendungen.

PART ONE

German-English

GERMAN—ENGLISH

A

A, a [α] *invar n* A, a; (mus) A; **das A und O** the beginning and the end; (*das Wichtigste*) the most important thing

Aal [αl] *m* (-[e]s;-e) eel; (nav) torpedo

aal'glatt' *adj* (fig) sly as a fox

Aas [αs] *n* (-es;-e) carrion; (sl) louse

ab [αp] *adv* off; away; down; on, e.g., **von heute ab** from today on; (theat) exit, exeunt, e.g., **Hamlet ab exit Hamlet; ab und zu** now and then || *prep* (*dat*) from, e.g., **ab Frankfurt** from Frankfurt; minus, e.g., **ab Skonto** minus discount

ab'ändern *tr* alter; (*völlig*) change; (*mildern*) modify; (parl) amend

Ab'änderung *f* (-;-en) alteration; change; modification; (parl) amendment

Ab'änderungsantrag *m* (parl) (proposed) amendment

ab'arbeiten *tr* work off || *ref* work hard

Ab'art *f* variety, type

ab'arten *intr* (SEIN) deviate from type

Ab'bau *m* (-[e]s;) demolition; reduction; cutback; layoff; (chem) decomposition; (min) exploitation

ab'bauen *tr* demolish; (*Maschinen, Fabriken*) dismantle; (*Steuern, Preise, Truppen*) reduce; (*Zelt*) take down; (*Lager*) break; (*Angestellte*) lay off; (chem) decompose; (min) work, exploit

ab'beißen §53 *tr* bite off || *intr* take a bite

ab'bekommen §99 *tr* (*seinen Teil*) get; (*Schmutz*) get out; (*Deckel*) get off; **du wirst was a.!** you're going to get it!

ab'berufen §122 *tr* (dipl) recall

ab'bestellen *tr* cancel

ab'betteln *tr*—**die ganze Straße a.** beg up and down the street; **j-m etw a.** chisel s.th. from s.o.

ab'biegen §57 *tr* bend, twist off; (*Gefahr*) avert; (*Plan*) thwart; **das Gespräch a.** change the subject || *intr* (SEIN) branch off; (fig) get off the track; **in e-e Seitenstraße a.** turn down a side street; **nach links a.** turn left; **von e-r Straße a.** turn off a road

Ab'bild *n* picture, image

ab'bilden *tr* represent

Ab'bildung *f* (-;-en) illustration, figure

ab'binden §59 *tr* untie; (*Kalb*) wean; (*Arm*) apply a tourniquet to; (surg) tie off || *intr* (*Zement*) set

Ab'bitte *f* apology; **A. tun wegen** apologize for

ab'bitten §60 *tr* apologize for || *intr* apologize

ab'blasen §61 *tr* blow off; (fig) call off || *intr* (mil) sound the retreat

ab'blättern *intr* (SEIN) shed leaves; (*Farben, Haut*) flake, peel

ab'blenden *tr* dim; (cin) fade out; (phot) stop down || *intr* (aut) dim the lights; (nav) darken ship; (phot) stop down the lens

Ab'blendlicht *n* (aut) low-beam lights

ab'blitzen *intr* (SEIN) be unsuccessful; **j-n a. lassen** snub s.o.

ab'blühen *intr* stop blooming || *intr* (SEIN) fade

ab'böschen *tr* slope; (*Mauer*) batter

ab'brausen *tr* hose down || *ref* shower off || *intr* (SEIN) (coll) roar off

ab'brechen §64 *tr* break off; (*Belagerung*) raise; (*Gebäude*) demolish; (*Zelt*) take down; (sport) call; **das Lager a.** break camp || *intr* (SEIN) (& fig) break off

ab'bremsen *tr* slow down; (*Streik*) prevent; (*Motoren*) (aer) rev || *intr* put on the brakes; (aer) fishtail

ab'brennen §97 *tr* burn off; (*Feuerwerk*) set off; (*Geschütz*) fire; (chem) distil out; (metal) refine; (naut) bream; **ich bin vollkommen abgebrannt** (coll) I'm dead broke || *intr* (SEIN) burn down

ab'bringen §65 *tr* (*Fleck*) remove; (*gestrandetes Schiff*) refloat; **davon a. zu** (*inf*) dissuade from (*ger*); **vom rechten Weg a.** lead astray; **vom Thema a.** throw off; **von der Spur a.** throw off the scent; **von e-r Gewohnheit a.** break of the habit

ab'bröckeln *intr* crumble; (*Farbe*) peel (off); (*Preis, Aktie*) go slowly down; (*Mitglieder*) fall off

Ab'bruch *m* (-[e]s Zweiges, der Beziehungen) breaking off; (e-s Gebäudes) demolition; (*Schaden*) damage; **A. des Spiels** (sport) calling of the game; **A. tun** (*dat*) harm, spoil; **auf A. verkaufen** sell at demolition value; (*Maschinen*) sell for junk

ab'brühen *tr* (culin) scald

ab'brummen *tr* (*Strafe*) (coll) serve, do || *intr* (SEIN) (coll) clear out

ab'buchen *tr* (*abschreiben*) write off; (acct) debit

ab'bürsten *tr* brush off

ab'büßen *tr* atone for; **e-e Strafe a.** serve time; **er hat es schwer a. müssen** (coll) he had to pay for it dearly

Abc [αbe'tse] *n* (-;-) ABC's

Abc'-Schütze *m* (-n;-n) pupil

ab'danken *tr* dismiss; (*pensionieren*)

retire || *intr* resign; (*Herrscher*) abdicate; (mil) get a discharge

ab'decken *tr* uncover; (*Tisch*) clear; (*Bett*) turn down; (*Vieh*) skin; (*e-e Schuld*) pay back; (mil) camouflage; (phot) mask

ab'dichten *tr* seal (off); (*Loch*) plug up; (*mit weichem Material*) pack; (naut) caulk

ab'dienen *tr* (*Schuld*) work off; (mil) serve (*one's term*)

ab'drehen *tr* twist off; (*Gas, Licht, Wasser*) turn off || *intr* turn away

ab'dreschen §67 *tr* thrash

Ab'druck *m* (-s;-e) reprint; offprint; copy; (*Abguß*) casting; (phot, typ) proof || *m* (-s;-e) impression, imprint

ab'drucken *tr* print

ab'drücken *tr* (*abformen*) mold; (*Gewehr*) fire; (*Pfeil*) shoot; (*umarmen*) hug; **den Hahn a.** pull the trigger || *ref* leave an impression || *intr* pull the trigger

ab'duschen *ref* shower off

Abend ['abənt] *m* (-s;-e) evening; **am A.** in the evening; **bunter A.** social; (telv) variety show; **des Abends in the evening(s)**; **zu A. essen** eat dinner

A'bendblatt *n* evening paper

A'bendbrot *n* supper, dinner

A'benddämmerung *f* twilight, dusk

A'bendessen *n* supper, dinner

abendfüllend ['abəntfYlənt] *adj* full-length (*movie*)

A'bendgesellschaft *f* party (*in the evening*)

A'bendland *n* West, Occident

abendländisch ['abəntlendiʃ] *adj* occidental

a'bendlich *adj* evening || *adv* evenings

A'bendmahl *n* supper; **das Heilige A.** Holy Communion

abends ['abənts] *adv* in the evening

Abenteuer ['abəntɔɪ·ər] *s* (-s;-) adventure; **galantes A.** (love) affair

a'benteuerlich *adj* adventurous; (*Unternehmen*) risky

aber ['abər] *adv* yet, however; (before adjectives and adverbs) really, indeed; **a. und abermals** over and over again; **hundert und a. hundert** hundreds and hundreds of || *conj* but || *interj*—**aber, aber! now, now!** || **Aber** *n* (-s;-s) but; **hier gibt es kein A.!** no ifs and buts

A'berglaube *m* superstition

abergläubisch ['abərglɔɪbɪʃ] *adj* superstitious

ab'erkennen §97 *tr*—**j-m etw a.** deny s.o. s.th.; (jur) dispossess s.o. of s.th.

Ab'erkennung *f* (-;-en) denial; (jur) dispossession

abermalig ['abərmalɪç] *adj* repeated

abermals ['abərmals] *adv* once more

ab'ernten *tr* reap, harvest

ab'fahren §71 *tr* cart away; (*Strecke*) cover; (*Straße*) wear out; (*Reifen*) wear down || *intr* (SEIN) depart; drive off

Ab'fahrt *f* departure

Ab'fall *m* (*der Blätter*) falling; (*Bö-*

---

schung) steep slope; (*von e–m Glauben*) falling away; (*von e–r Partei*) defection; (*Sinken*) drop, decrease; **Abfälle** garbage, trash; chips, shavings

ab'fallen §72 *intr* (SEIN) fall off; (*von e–r Partei*) defect; (*vom Glauben*) fall away; (*abnehmen*) decrease, fail; (*Kunden*) stay away; (sport) fall behind; **a. gegen** compare badly with; **es wird etw für dich a.** there'll be s.th. in it for you; **körperlich a.** lose weight; **steil a.** drop away

abfällig ['apfelɪç] *adj* disparaging

Ab'fallprodukt *n* by-product

ab'fangen §73 *tr* catch; (*Angriff*) foil; (*Brief*) intercept; (aer) pull out of a dive; (*U-Boot*) (nav) trim; (sport) catch (up with); **j-m die Kunden a.** steal s.o.'s customers

ab'färben *intr* (*Farben*) run; (*Stoff*) fade; **a. auf** (*acc*) stain; (fig) rub off on

ab'fassen *tr* compose, draft; (*erwischen*) catch

Ab'fassung *f* (-;-en) wording; composition

ab'faulen *intr* (SEIN) rot away

ab'fegen *tr* sweep off, whisk off

abfertigen ['apfertɪgən] *tr* get ready for sending off; (*Gepäck*) check; (*Zollgüter*) clear; (*Kunden*) wait on; (*abweisen*) snub; (*verwaltungsmäßig*) (adm) process;

Ab'fertigung *f* (-;-en) dispatch; snub; **zollamtliche A.** clearance

ab'feuern *tr* fire; (rok) launch

ab'finden §59 *tr* (*Gläubiger*) satisfy; (*Partner*) buy off; (*entschädigen*) (*für*) compensate (for) || *ref*—**sich a. lassen** settle for a lump-sum payment; **sich a. mit** put up with; come to terms with

Ab'findung *f* (-;-en) satisfaction; lump-sum settlement

Ab'findungsvertrag *m* lump-sum settlement

abflachen ['apflaxən] *tr* level; (*abschrägen*) bevel || *ref* flatten out

abflauen ['apflau·ən] *intr* (SEIN) slack off; (*Interesse*) flag; (*Preis*) go down; (st. exch.) ease off

ab'fliegen §57 *intr* (SEIN) take off

ab'fließen §76 *intr* (SEIN) flow off, drain off

Ab'flug *m* takeoff, departure

Ab'fluß *m* discharge; drain, gutter, gully; **See ohne A.** lake without outlet

Ab'flußrinne *f* drainage ditch

Ab'flußrohr *n* drainpipe; soil pipe; (*vom Dach*) downspout

ab'fordern *tr*—**j-m etw a.** demand s.th. from s.o.

ab'fragen *tr*—**j-n etw a.** question s.o. about s.th.; quiz s.o. on s.th.

ab'fressen §70 *tr* eat up; crop, chew off; (*Metall*) corrode

ab'frieren §77 *intr* (SEIN) be nipped by the frost; abgefroren frostbitten

Abfuhr ['apfur] *f* (-;-en) removal; (*Abweisung*) (coll) cold shoulder, snub

ab'führen *tr* lead away; (*festnehmen*) arrest; (*fencing*) defeat || *intr* cause the bowels to move

Abführmittel ['apfyrmɪtəl] *n* laxative

ab'füllen *tr* (*Wein, Bier*) bottle

Ab'gabe *f* (*Auslieferung*) delivery; (*Verkauf*) sale; (*Steuer*) tax; (*Zoll*) duty; (*der Wahlstimme*) casting; (*e-s Urteils*) pronouncing; (*e-r Meinung*) expressing; (fb) pass; **Abgaben** taxes, fees

ab'gabenfrei *adj* tax-free, duty-free

abgabenpflichtig ['apgabənpfliçtiç] *adj* taxable, subject to duty

Ab'gang *m* departure; (*von e-m Amt*) retirement; (*von der Schule*) dropping out; graduation; (*Verlust*) loss; (*Abnahme*) decrease; (gym) finish; (pathol) discharge; (pathol) miscarriage; (theat) exit; **guten A. haben** sell well

abgängig ['apgɛnɪç] *adj* lost, missing; (com) marketable

Ab'gangsprüfung *f* final examination

Ab'gangspunkt *m* point of departure

Ab'gas *n* (aut) exhaust; (indust) waste gas

ab'geben §80 *tr* (*Paß*) hand over; (*Gepäck*) check; (*abliefern*) deliver; (*Schulheft*) hand in; (*Urteil*) pass; (*Meinung*) express; (*Gutachten*) give; (*Amt*) lay down; (*gute Ernte*) yield; (*Schuß*) fire; (*Wahlstimme*) cast; (*Waren*) sell, let go; (*sich eignen als*) act as, serve as; be cut out to be; (elec) deliver; (fb) pass; (phys) give off; **e-e Offerte a.** (jur) make an offer; **e-n Narren a.** play the fool; **er würde e-n guten Vater a.** he would make a good father; **j-m eins a.** (coll) let s.o. have it; **j-m von etw a.** share s.th. with s.o. || *ref*—**sich a.** not bother with; associate with; spend time on

abgebrannt ['apgəbrant] *adj* (coll) broke

abgebrüht ['apgəbryt] *adj* (fig) hardened

abgedroschen ['apgədrɔʃən] *adj* trite, hackneyed; (*Witz*) stale

abgefeimt ['apgəfaɪmt] *adj* cunning; out-and-out

abgegriffen ['apgəgrifən] *adj* well-thumbed

abgehackt ['apgəhakt] *adj* jerky

abgehärmt ['apgəhɛrmt] *adj* careworn, drawn

ab'gehen §82 *intr* (SEIN) leave, depart; (*Brief*) go off; (*Knopf*) come off; (*Schuß*) go off; (*Farbe*) fade; (*Seitenweg*) branch off; (*vom Gesprächsgegenstand*) digress, go off; (*vom rechten Wege*) stray; (*aus e-m Amt*) resign, retire; (*von der Bühne*) retire; (*von der Schule*) drop out; graduate; (com) sell; (theat) exit; **bei Barzahlung gehen fünf Prozent ab** you get a five-percent reduction for paying cash; **davon kann ich nicht a.** I must insist on it; **er geht mir sehr ab** I miss him a lot; **nicht a. von** stick to; **reißend a.** sell like hotcakes; || *ref*—**sich** [dat] **nichts a.**

lassen deny oneself nothing || *impers*—**es geht ihm nichts ab** he lacks for nothing; **es gehen mir zehn Dollar ab** I am ten dollars short; **es ist alles glatt abgegangen** everything went well

ab'gehend *adj* (*Post, Beamte*) outgoing; (*Zug*) departing

abgekämpft ['apgəkɛmpft] *adj* exhausted

abgekartet ['apgəkartət] *adj* (*Spiel*) fixed; **abgekartete Sache** put-up job

abgeklappert ['apgəklapərt] *adj* hackneyed

abgeklärt ['apgəklɛrt] *adj* mellow, wise

abgelebt ['apgəlept] *adj* decrepit

abgelegen ['apgəlegən] *adj* out-of-the-way, outlying

ab'gelten §83 *tr* meet, satisfy

abgemacht ['apgəmaxt] *adj* settled || *interj* agreed!

abgemagert ['apgəmagərt] *adj* emaciated

abgemessen ['apgəmesən] *adj* measured; (*genau*) exact; (*Rede*) deliberate; (*Person*) stiff, formal

abgeneigt ['apgənaɪkt] *adj* reluctant; (dat) averse to; **ich bin durchaus nicht a.** (coll) I don't mind if I do

Ab'geneigtheit *f* (–;) aversion

abgenutzt ['apgənʊtst] *adj* worn out

Abgeordnete ['apgə-ɔrdnətə] §5 *mf* delegate; (pol) representative; deputy (*member of the Bundestag*); (Brit) Member of Parliament

Ab'geordnetenhaus *n* House of Representatives; (Brit) House of Commons

abgerissen ['apgərɪsən] *adj* torn; (*zerlumpt*) ragged; (*ohne Zusammenhang*) incoherent, disconnected

Abgesandte ['apgəzantə] §5 *mf* envoy

abgeschieden ['apgəʃidən] *adj* secluded; (*verstorben*) deceased, late

Ab'geschiedenheit *f* (–;) seclusion

abgeschliffen ['apgəʃlifən] *adj* polished

abgeschlossen ['apgəʃlɔsən] *adj* isolated; (*Leben*) secluded; (*Ausbildung*) completed

abgeschmackt ['apgəʃmakt] *adj* tactless, tasteless; (fig) insipid

absehen ['apgəze-ən] *adj*—**a. davon, daß** not to mention that; **a. von** aside from, except for

abgespannt ['apgəʃpant] *adj* tired out

abgestanden ['apgəʃtandən] *adj* stale

abgestorben ['apgəʃtɔrbən] *adj* (*Pflanze, Gewebe*) dead; (*Glied*) numb

abgestumpft ['apgəʃtʊmpft] *adj* blunt; (*Kegel*) truncated; (fig) dull; (gegen) indifferent (to)

abgetakelt ['apgətakəlt] *adj* (*Person*) seedy; (*Schiff*) unrigged

abgetan ['apgətan] *adj* settled

abgetragen ['apgətragən] *adj* threadbare

abgetreten ['apgətretən] *adj* worndown

ab'gewinnen §52 *tr* win; **e-r Sache Geschmack a.** acquire a taste for s.th.; **e-r Sache Vergnügen a.** derive pleasure from s.th.; **j–m e–n Vorteil a.** gain an advantage over s.o.

abgewirtschaftet ['apgəvɪrt/aftət] *adj* run-down

ab'gewöhnen *tr*—**ich kann es mir nicht a.** I can't get it out of my system; **j–m etw a.** break s.o. of s.th.

abgezehrt ['apgətsert] *adj* emaciated

ab'gießen §76 *tr* pour off; (*Statue*) cast; (chem) decant; (culin) strain off

Ab'glanz *m* reflection

ab'gleiten §86 *intr* (SEIN) slip off; (an *dat*) glance off (*s.th.*); (aer, aut) skid; (st. exch.) decline

Ab'gott *m* idol

Abgötterei [apgøtə'raɪ] *f* (–;–en) idolatry; **A. treiben** worship idols; **mit j–m A. treiben** idolize s.o.

abgöttisch ['apgøtɪ/] *adj* idolatrous || *adv*—**a. lieben** idolize

Ab'gottschlange *f* boa constrictor

ab'graben §87 *tr* (*Bach*) divert; (*Feld*) drain; (*Hügel*) level

ab'grämen *ref* eat one's heart out

ab'grasen *tr* (*Wiese*) graze on; (fig) scour, search

ab'greifen §88 *tr* wear out (*by constant handling*); (*Buch*) thumb

ab'grenzen *tr* mark off, demarcate; delimit; (fig) differentiate

Ab'grund *m* abyss; precipice

abgründig ['apgryndɪç] *adj* precipitous; (fig) deep, unfathomable

ab'gucken *tr* (coll) copy, crib; (coll) **pick up a habit from** || *intr* (coll) copy, crib

Ab'guß *m* (sculp) cast; **A. in Gips** plaster cast

ab'hacken *tr* chop off; (*Baum*) chop down

ab'haken *tr* unhook, undo; (in e–r *Liste*) check off; (telp) take off (*the receiver*)

ab'halftern *tr* unharness; (fig) sack

ab'halten §90 *tr* hold off; (*Vorlesung*) give; (*Regen*) keep out; (*Versammlung, Parade*) hold; (von) keep (from)

Ab'haltung *f* (–;–en) hindrance; (e–r *Versammlung*) holding; (e–s *Festes*) celebration

ab'handeln *tr* (*Thema*) treat; (erörtern) discuss; **er läßt sich nichts a.** he won't come down (in price); **etw vom Preise a.** get s.th. off the price (by bargaining)

abhanden [ap'handən] *adv*—**a. kommen** get lost; **a. sein** be missing

Ab'handlung *f* (–;–en) essay; (*Vortrag in e–m gelehrten Verein*) paper; (*Doktorarbeit*) thesis, dissertation; (*mündlich*) discourse, discussion

Ab'hang *m* slope

ab'hängen *tr* (*vom Haken*) take off; (e–n *Verfolger*) shake off; (rr) uncouple || *intr* (telp) hang up; **a. von** depend on; be subject to (*s.o.'s approval*)

abhängig ['apheŋɪç] *adj* (*Stellung*) subordinate; (*Satz*) dependent; (*Rede*) indirect; (*Kasus*) oblique; (von) dependent (on), contingent (upon)

Ab'hängigkeit *f* (–;–en) dependence; (gram) subordination; **gegenseitige A.** interdependence

ab'härmen *ref* pine away; **sich a. wegen** (or **über** *acc*) fret about

ab'härten *tr* harden; (gegen) inure (to) || *ref* (gegen) become hardened (to)

ab'hauen §93 *tr* cut off; chop off || **§109** *intr* (SEIN) (coll) scram, get lost

ab'häuten *tr* skin, flay

ab'heben §94 *tr* lift off; (*Rahm*) skim; (*Geld*) withdraw; (*Dividende*) collect; (*Haut*) (surg) strip off || *ref* become airborne; (von) contrast (with)

Ab'hebung *f* (–;–en) lifting; (*vom Bankkonto*) withdrawal; (cards) cutting

Ab'hebungsformular *n* withdrawal slip

ab'heften *tr* (*Briefe*) file; (sew) tack

ab'heilen *intr* (HABEN & SEIN) heal up

ab'helfen §96 *intr* (dat) (an *e–m Unrecht*) redress; (e–r *Schwierigkeit*) remove; (e–m *Mangel*) relieve; **dem ist nicht abzuhelfen** that can't be helped

ab'hetzen *tr* drive hard, work to death; (hunt) hunt down || *ref* rush; tire oneself out

Ab'hilfe *f* remedy, redress; **A. schaffen** take remedial measures; **A. schaffen für** remedy, redress

ab'hobeln *tr* plane (down)

abhold ['apholt] *adj* (dat) ill-disposed (towards), averse (to)

Abholdienst ['apholdinst] *m* pickup service

ab'holen *tr* fetch, call for, pick up

ab'holzen *tr* clear (of trees), deforest

Abhörapparat ['aphørəparat] *m* (mil, nav) listening device

ab'horchen *tr* overhear; (med) sound; (rad, telp) monitor

ab'hören *tr* overhear, eavesdrop on; (*Studenten*) quiz; (*Schallplatte, Tonband*) listen to; (mil) intercept; (telp) monitor

Ab'hörgerät *n* bugging device

Ab'hörraum *m* (rad, telv) control room

Ab'irrung *f* (–;–en) deviation; (opt) aberration

Abitur [abɪ'tur] *n* (–s;–e) final examination (at end of *junior college*); **das A. bestehen** graduate

Abiturient –in [abɪturɪ'ent(ɪn)] **§7** *mf* graduate (of a *junior college*)

Abitur'zeugnis *n* diploma (from senior high school or *junior college*)

ab'jagen *tr* drive hard; **j–m etw a. recover** s.th. from s.o. || *ref* run one's head off

abkanzeln ['apkantsəln] *tr* (coll) give (*s.o.*) a good talking to

ab'kauen *tr* chew off || *ref*—**sich** [*dat*] **die Nägel a.** bite one's nails

ab'kaufen *tr*—**j–m etw a.** buy s.th. from s.o.

Abkehr ['apker] *f* (–;) turning away; estrangement; (*Verzicht*) renunciation

ab'kehren *tr* turn away, avert; (mit *dem Besen*) sweep off || *ref* turn away; become estranged

ab'klappern *tr* (coll) scour, search

ab'klatschen *tr* imitate slavishly; make an exact copy of; (*beim Tanzen*) cut in on; (*typ*) pull (*a proof*)

ab'klingen §142 *intr* (SEIN) (*Farbe*) fade; (*Töne*) die away; (*Schmerz*) ease off

ab'klopfen *tr* beat off, knock off; (*Teppich*) beat; (*med*) tap, percuss ‖ *intr* stop the music (*with the rap of the baton*)

ab'knabbern *tr* (coll) nibble off

ab'knallen *tr* fire off; (sl) bump off

ab'knicken *tr* snap off ‖ *intr* (SEIN) snap off

ab'knipsen *tr* pinch off, snip off; (*Film*) use up

ab'knöpfen *tr* unbutton; **j-m Geld a.** squeeze money out of s.o.

ab'knutschen *tr* (coll) pet

ab'kochen *tr* boil; (*Obst*) stew; (*Milch*) scald ‖ *intr* cook out

ab'kommandieren *tr* detach, detail

ab'kommen §99 *intr* (SEIN) (von) get away (from); (*Mode*) go out of style; (naut) become afloat (again); **auf zwei Tage a.** get away for two days; **gut** (or **schlecht**) **a.** (sport) get off to a good (or bad) start; **hoch** (or **tief**) **a.** aim too high (or low); **vom Kurs a.** go off course; **vom Boden a.** become airborne; **vom Thema a.** get off the subject; **vom Wege a.** lose one's way, stray; **von der Wahrheit a.** deviate from the truth; **von e-r Ansicht a.** change one's views ‖ **Ab-kommen** *n* (-s;-) (com, pol) agree-ment; (jur) settlement

abkömmlich ['apkœmlıç] *adj*—**a. sein** be able to get away

Abkömmling ['apkœmlıŋ] *m* (-s;-e) descendant, scion

ab'koppeln *tr* uncouple

ab'kratzen *tr* scratch off; (*Schuhe*) scuff up ‖ *intr* (*sterben*) (sl) croak; (*abhauen*) (sl) beat it; **kratz ab!** drop dead!

ab'kriegen *tr* (coll) get off or out

ab'kühlen *tr*, *ref* & *intr* cool off

Abkunft ['apkunft] *f* (-;) lineage

ab'kürzen *tr* shorten; (*Inhalt*) abridge; (*Wort*) abbreviate; (math) reduce

Ab'kürzung *f* (-;-en) shortening; abridgement; abbreviation; (*kürzerer Weg*) shortcut

ab'küssen *tr* smother with kisses

ab'laden §103 *tr* unload; (*Schutt*) dump

Ab'ladeplatz *m* dump; (mil) unloading point

Ab'lage *f* (*für Kleider*) cloakroom; (*Lagerhaus*) depot, warehouse; (*ab-gelegte Akten*) files; (mil) dump

ab'lagern *tr* (*Wein*, *usw.*) age; (geol) deposit ‖ *ref* (geol) be deposited ‖ *intr*—**a. lassen** age, season

Ab'laß *m* (-lasses;-lässe) outlet, drain; (com) deduction; (eccl) indulgence

ab'lassen §104 *tr* leave off; (*Bier*) tap; (*Dampf*) let off; (*Teich*, *Faß*) drain; (*Waren*) sell; **etw vom Preise a.** knock s.th. off the price; **j-m etw billig a.** (com) let s.o. have s.th. cheaply ‖ *intr* desist, stop; **a. von** let go of, give up

Ablativ ['ablatif] *m* (-s;-e) ablative

Ab'lauf *m* overflow; (*e-r Frist*, *e-s Vertrags*) expiration; (*der Ereig-nisse*) course; (sport) start

ab'laufen §105 *tr* (*Strecke*) run; (*Stadt*) scour; (*Schuhe*) wear out; **j-m den Rang a.** get the better of s.o.; outrun s.o. ‖ *intr* (SEIN) run away; (*Zeit*) expire; (*ausfallen*) turn out; (com) fall due; (sport) start

Ab'laut *m* ablaut

Ab'leben *n* demise, decease

ab'lecken *tr* lick (off)

ab'legen *tr* (*Last*, *Waffen*) lay down; (*ausziehen*) take off; (*Schwert*) lay aside; (*die alte Haut*) slough; (*Kar-ten*) discard; (*Akten*, *Dokumente*) file; (*Briefe*) sort; (*Namen*) drop, stop using; (*Sorgen*, *Kummer*) put away; (*Prüfung*, *Gelübde*, *Eid*) take; (*Predigt*) deliver; (*Gewohnheit*) give up; (*Rechenschaft*) render, give; **Bekenntnis a.** make a confession; **die Maske a.** (fig) throw off all dis-guise; **die Trauer a.** come out of mourning; **ein volles Geständnis a.** come clean; **Probe a.** furnish proof; **seine Fehler a.** mend one's ways; **Zeugnis a.** (für or gegen) testify (for or against) ‖ *intr* take off one's coat or hat and coat); **bitte, legen Sie ab!** please take your things off

Ab'leger *m* (-s;-) (bot) shoot; (com) subsidiary; (hort) slip, cutting

ab'lehnen *tr* refuse, turn down; (*An-trag*) reject; (*Zeugen*) challenge; (*Erbschaft*) renounce; **durch Ab-stimmung a.** vote down

ab'lehnend *adj* negative

Ab'lehnung *f* (-;-en) refusal

ab'leiern *tr* recite mechanically

ab'leisten *tr* (*Eid*) take; **den Militär-dienst a.** (mil) serve one's time

ab'leiten *tr* lead away; (*Herkunft*) trace back; (*Fluß*, *Blitz*) divert; (*Wasser*) drain off; (*Wärme*) con-duct; (chem) derive; (elec) shunt; (gram, math) derive; **abgeleitetes Wort** derivative ‖ *ref* (aus, von) be derived (from)

Ab'leitung *f* (-;-en) (*e-s Flusses*) di-version; (*des Wassers*) drainage; (elec, phys) conduction; (gram, math) derivation; (phys) convection

ab'lenken *tr* turn away, divert; (*Ge-fahr*, *Verdacht*) ward off; (fencing) parry; (opt, phys) deflect

Ab'lenkung *f* (-;-en) diversion; dis-traction; (opt) refraction

ab'lernen *tr*—**j-m etw a.** learn s.th. from s.o.

ab'lesen §107 *tr* read off; (*Zähler*) read; (*Obst*) pick; **es j-m vom Ge-sicht a.**, **daß** tell by looking at s.o. that

ab'leugnen *tr* deny, disown; (*Glauben*) renounce

Ab'leugnung *f* (-;-en) denial, dis-avowal

ab'liefern *tr* deliver, hand over, sur-render

Ab'lieferung *f* (-;-en) delivery; (*der Schußwaffen*) surrender

ab'liegen §108 *intr* (*Wein*) mature; (*Obst*) ripen ‖ *intr* (SEIN) be remote
ab'löschen *tr* extinguish; (*Stahl*) temper; (*Tinte*) blot; (*Kalk*) slake
ab'lösen *tr* loosen, detach; (*Posten*) relieve; (*Schuld*) discharge; (*Pfand*) redeem; (*Haut*) peel off ‖ *ref* (*bei*) take turns (at)
Ab'lösung *f* (-;-en) loosening; relief; discharge
ab'machen *tr* undo, untie; (*erledigen*) settle, arrange; (*Vertrag*) conclude; (*Rechnung*) close
Ab'machung *f* (-;-en) settlement
abmagern ['apmagərn] *intr* (SEIN) grow thin, thin down
Ab'magerung *f* (-;) emaciation
ab'mähen *tr* mow
ab'malen *tr* portray; (fig) depict
Ab'marsch *m* departure
ab'marschieren *intr* (SEIN) march off
Ab'mattung *f* (-;) fatigue
ab'melden *tr* (*Besuch*) (coll) call off; **der ist bei mir abgemeldet** (coll) I've had it with him; **j-n bei der Polizei a.** give notice to the police that s.o. is leaving town ‖ *ref* (mil) report off duty
ab'messen §70 *tr* measure (off); (*Worte*) weigh; (*Land*) survey
ab'montieren *tr* dismantle; (*Geschütz*) disassemble; (*Reifen*) take off ‖ *ref* (aer) (coll) disintegrate in the air
ab'mühen *ref* exert oneself, slave
ab'murksen *tr* (sl) do in
ab'nagen *tr* gnaw (off); (*Knochen*) pick
Ab'nahme *f* (-;-n) (*Verminderung*) (an *dat*) reduction (in), drop (in); (*des Gewichts*) loss; (*des Mondes*) waning; (*des Tages*) shortening; (*e-s Eides*) administering; (*e-r Rechnung*) auditing; (indust) final inspection; (surg) amputation; **A. der Geschäfte** decline in business; **A. e-r Parade** reviewing of the troops; **A. finden** be sold; **in A. geraten** decline, wane
ab'nehmen §116 *tr* take off, remove; (*Wäsche*) take down; (*Schnurrbart*) shave off; (*wegnehmen*) take away; (*Hörer*) lift, unhook; (*Strom*) use; (*Obst*) pick; (*Eid*) administer; (*Waren*) purchase; (*Rechnung*) audit; (*prüfen*) inspect and pass; (*Verband*) remove; (phot) take; (surg) amputate; **aus Berichten a.** gather from reports; **das kann ich dir nicht a.** I can't accept what you are saying; **die Parade a.** inspect the troops; **j-m die Arbeit a.** take the work off s.o.'s shoulders; **j-m die Beichte a.** hear s.o.'s confession; **j-m die Maske a.** unmask s.o., expose s.o.; **j-m die Verantwortung a.** relieve s.o. of responsibility; **j-m ein Versprechen a.** make s.o. make a promise; **j-m zuviel a.** charge s.o. too much ‖ *intr* diminish; (*Preise*) drop; (*Wasser*) recede; (*Kräfte*) fail; (*Mond*) be on the wane; **an Dicke a.** taper; **an Gewicht a.** lose weight; **an Kräften a.** lose strength ‖ **Abnehmen**

n (-s;) decrease; **im A. sein** be on the decrease
Ab'nehmer **-in** §6 *mf* buyer, consumer; (*Kunde*) customer; (*Hehler*) fence
Ab'neigung *f* (-;-en) (gegen, vor *dat*) aversion (to, for), dislike (of)
abnorm [ap'nɔrm] *adj* abnormal
Abnormität [apnɔrmɪ'tet] *f* (-;-en) abnormity, monstrosity
ab'nötigen *tr* (*dat*) extort (from)
ab'nutzen, ab'nützen *tr* wear out ‖ *ref* wear out, become worn out
Ab'nutzung *f* (-;-en) wear and tear; (*Abrieb*) abrasion; (mil) attrition
Ab'öl *n* (-s;-e) used oil
Abonnement [abɔn(ə)'mã] *n* (-s;-s) (auf *acc*) subscription (to)
Abonnements'karte *f* commutation ticket
Abonnent **-in** [abɔ'nent(ɪn)] §7 *mf* subscriber
abonnieren [abɔ'nirən] *tr* subscribe to; **abonniert sein auf** (*acc*) have a subscription to ‖ *intr* (auf *acc*) subscribe (to)
ab'ordnen *tr* delegate, deputize
Ab'ordnung *f* (-;-en) delegation
Abort [a'bɔrt] *m* (-[e]s;-e) toilet ‖ [a'bɔrt] *m* (-s;-e) abortion
ab'passen *tr* measure, fit; (*abwarten*) watch for; (*auflauern*) waylay
ab'pfeifen §88 *tr* (sport) stop
ab'pflücken *tr* pluck (off)
ab'placken, ab'plagen *ref* work oneself to death, slave
ab'platzen *intr* (SEIN) come loose
Abprall ['apral] *m* rebound; (*Geschoß*) richochet
ab'prallen *intr* (SEIN) rebound; ricochet
ab'pressen *tr* extort
ab'putzen *tr* clean (off); (*polieren*) polish; (*Mauer*) roughcast, plaster
ab'raten §63 *intr*—**j-m von etw a.** advise s.o. against s.th.
Ab'raum *m* (-es;) rubble; (min) overburden
ab'räumen *tr* clear away; (*Tisch*) clear
ab'reagieren *tr* (*Spannung, Erregung*) work off ‖ *ref* (coll) calm down
ab'rechnen *tr* subtract; (*Spesen*) account for; (com) deduct ‖ *intr* settle accounts
Ab'rechnung *f* (-;-en) (von *Konten*) settlement; (*Abzug*) deduction; **A. halten** balance accounts
Ab'rede *f* agreement, arrangement; **in A. stellen** deny
ab'reden *intr*—**j-m von etw a.** dissuade s.o. from s.th.
ab'reiben *tr* rub off; (*Körper*) rub down
Ab'reise *f* departure
ab'reisen *intr* (SEIN) (nach) depart (for)
ab'reißen §53 *tr* tear off; (*Haus*) tear down; (*Kleid*) wear out ‖ *intr* (SEIN) tear off
ab'richten *tr* (*Tier*) train; (*Pferd*) break in; (*Brett*) dress
Ab'richter **-in** §6 *mf* trainer
ab'riegeln *tr* (*Tür*) bolt; (mil) seal off

ab'ringen §142 *tr*—*j-m etw a.* wrest s.th. from s.o.

ab'rinnen §121 *intr* (SEIN) run off, run down

Ab'riß *m* summary, outline; (*Skizze*) sketch

ab'rollen *tr & ref* unroll, unwind || *intr* (SEIN) unroll, unwind

ab'rücken *tr* push away, move back || *intr* (SEIN) clear out; (fig) dissociate oneself; (mil) march off

Ab'ruf *m* recall; **auf A.** on call

ab'rufen §122 *tr* call away; (*Zug*) call out, announce

ab'runden *tr* round off

ab'rupfen *tr* pluck (off)

ab'rüsten *tr & intr* disarm

Ab'rüstung *f* (–;) disarmament

ab'rutschen *intr* (SEIN) slip (off)

absacken ['apzakən] *intr* (SEIN) sink; (*Flugzeug*) pancake

Ab'sage *f* cancellation; (*Ablehnung*) refusal

ab'sagen *tr* cancel || *intr* decline; (*dat*) renounce, repudiate

ab'sägen *tr* saw off

ab'sahnen *tr* (& fig) skim (off)

Ab'satz *m* stop, pause, break; (*Zeileneinrückung*) indentation; (*Abschnitt*) paragraph; (*des Schuhes*) heel; (*der Treppen*) landing; (*Vertrieb*) market, sale(s); **ohne A.** without a break

ab'satzfähig *adj* marketable

Ab'satzgebiet *n* territory (*of a salesman*)

Ab'satzmarkt *m* (com) outlet

Ab'satzstockung *f* slump in sales

ab'saugen *tr* suck off; (*Teppich*) vacuum

Ab'saugventilator *m* exhaust fan

ab'schaben *tr* scrape off

ab'schaffen *tr* abolish, do away with; (*Mißbrauch*) redress; (*Diener*) dismiss

ab'schälen *tr* peel

ab'schalten *tr* switch off

ab'schätzen *tr* (*Wert*) estimate; (*für die Steuer*) assess, appraise

abschätzig ['apʃɛtsɪç] *adj* disparaging

Ab'schaum *m* (–[e]s;) (& fig) scum

ab'scheiden §112 *tr* part, sever; (physiol) excrete; (physiol) secrete || *intr* (SEIN) pass away, pass on

Ab'scheu *m* (–[e]s;) (vor *dat*, gegen) abhorrence (of), disgust (at)

ab'scheuern *tr* scrub off, scour; (*Haut*) scrape; (*abnutzen*) wear out

abscheu'lich *adj* atrocious

ab'schicken *tr* send away; (*Post*) mail

ab'schieben §130 *tr* shove off; deport

Abschied ['apʃit] *m* (–[e]s;–e) (*Weggang*) departure; (*Entlassung*) dismissal; (mil) discharge; **A. nehmen von** take leave of; (*e-m Amt*) resign, retire from

Ab'schiedsfeier *f* farewell party

Ab'schiedsrede *f* valediction

Ab'schiedsschmaus *m* farewell dinner

ab'schießen §76 *tr* (*Gewehr*) fire, shoot; (*Flugzeug*) shoot down; (*Panzer*) knock out; (rok) launch; **j-n a.** bring about s.o.'s downfall

ab'schinden §167 *tr* skin || *ref* slave

ab'schirmen *tr* screen (off); (gegen) guard (against)

ab'schlachten *tr* butcher; (fig) massacre

Ab'schlag *m* discount; (golf) tee shot; **auf A.** in part payment, on account

ab'schlagen §132 *tr* knock off; (*Baum*) fell; (*Angriff*) repel; (*Bitte*) refuse; **das Wasser a.** pass water || *intr* (golf) tee off

abschlägig ['apʃlɛgɪç] *adj* negative; **a. bescheiden** turn down

Ab'schlagszahlung *f* installment

ab'schleifen §88 *tr* grind off; (fig) refine, polish || *ref* become refined

ab'schleppen *tr* drag away, tow away

Ab'schleppwagen *m* tow truck

ab'schleudern *tr* fling off, catapult

ab'schließen §76 *tr* lock (up); (*Straße*) close off; (*Rechnung*) close, settle; (*Bücher*) balance; (*Vertrag*) conclude; (*Rede*) wind up; (*Wette*) wager || *ref* seclude oneself, shut oneself off || *intr* conclude

ab'schließend *adj* definitive; (*Worte*) concluding || *adv* definitively; (*schließlich*) in conclusion

Ab'schluß *m* completion; (*e-s Vertrags*) conclusion; (*Geschäft*) transaction, deal; (*Verkauf*) sale; (*Rechnungs-, Konto-, Buch-*) closing; (mach) seal

ab'schmeicheln *tr*—*j-m etw a.* coax s.th. out of s.o.

ab'schmelzen §133 *tr* (*Erz*) smelt; (*Schnee*) melt || *intr* (SEIN) melt

ab'schmieren *tr* copy carelessly; (coll) beat up; (aut) lubricate || *intr* (SEIN) (aer) (coll) crash

ab'schnallen *tr* unbuckle, unstrap

ab'schnappen *intr* (SEIN) (coll) stop dead; (coll) die

ab'schneiden §106 *tr* cut (off); (*Hecke*) trim; **den Weg. a.** take a shortcut; **j-m das Wort a.** cut s.o. short; **j-m die Ehre a.** steal s.o.'s good name || *intr*—**gut a.** do well

Ab'schnitt *m* cut, cutting; (*Teilstück*) part, section; (*im Scheckbuch*) stub; (*Kapitel*) section, paragraph; (math) segment; (mil) sector

ab'schnüren *tr* untie; (surg) ligature; **j-m den Atem a.** choke s.o.

ab'schöpfen *tr* skim off

ab'schrägen *tr & ref* slant, slope

ab'schrauben *tr* unscrew

ab'schrecken §134 *tr* scare off; (*abbringen*) deter

ab'schreiben §62 *tr* copy; (*Schularbeit*) crib; (*uneinbringliche Forderung*) write off; (*Literaturwerk*) plagiarize; (*Wert*) depreciate || *intr* send a refusal

Ab'schreiber –in §6 *mf* plagiarist

Ab'schreibung *f* (–;–en) write-off

ab'schreiten §86 *tr* pace off; (mil) review; **die Front a.** review the troops

Ab'schrift *f* copy, transcript; (com, jur) duplicate

ab'schriftlich *adj & adv* in duplicate

ab'schuften *ref* work oneself to death

ab'schürfen *ref*—**sich** [*dat*] **die Haut a.** skin oneself

Ab'schürfung *f* (–;–en) abrasion
Ab'schuß *m* (*e–r Waffe*) firing; (*e–r Rakete*) launching; (*e–s Panzers*) knocking out; (*e–s Flugzeugs*) downing, kill; (hunt) kill
abschüssig ['apʃʏsɪç] *adj* sloping; (*steil*) steep
Ab'schußrampe *f* launch pad
ab'schütteln *tr* shake off
ab'schwächen *tr* weaken; (*vermindern*) diminish, reduce; (*Farben*) tone down ‖ *ref* (*Preis*) decline
ab'schweifen *intr* (SEIN) stray, digress
Ab'schweifung *f* (–;–en) digression
ab'schwellen §119 *intr* (SEIN) go down; (*Lärm, Gesang*) die down
ab'schwenken *intr* (SEIN) swerve
ab'schwören *intr* (*dat*) (*dem Glauben*) deny; (*dem Trunk*) swear off
ab'segeln *intr* (SEIN) set sail
absehbar ['apzebar] *adj* foreseeable
ab'sehen §138 *tr* foresee; **es abgesehen haben auf** (*acc*) be out to get ‖ *intr*—a. von disregard; refrain from
ab'seifen *tr* soap down
abseits ['apzaɪts] *adv* aside; (sport) offside ‖ *prep* (*genit*) off
ab'senden §140 *tr* send (off), dispatch; (*Post*) mail; (*befördern*) forward
Ab'sender –in §6 *mf* sender, dispatcher
Ab'sendung *f* (–;–en) sending, dispatching; mailing, shipping
ab'sengen *tr* singe off
Absentismus [apzɛn'tɪsmʊs] *m* (–;) absenteeism
ab'setzen (*Betrag*) deduct; (*Last*) set down; (*entwöhnen*) wean; (*Beamten*) remove; (*König*) depose; (*Fallschirmtruppen, Passagiere*) drop; (com) sell; (typ) set up ‖ *ref* settle, set; (mil) disengage ‖ *intr* stop, pause
Absetzung *f* (–;–en) dismissal
Ab'sicht *f* intention, purpose; **in der A.** with the intention; **mit A.** on purpose; **ohne A.** unintentionally
ab'sichtlich *adj* intentional ‖ *adv* on purpose, intentionally
ab'sitzen §144 *tr* (*Strafzeit*) serve, do ‖ *intr* (SEIN) (*vom Pferde*) dismount; **a. lassen** (chem) let settle
absolut [apzo'lut] *adj*
absolvieren [apzɔl'virən] *tr* absolve; (*Studien*) finish; (*Hochschule*) graduate from; (*Prüfung*) pass
abson'derlich *adj* peculiar, strange
ab'sondern *tr* separate, segregate; (*Kranken*) isolate; (physiol) secrete ‖ *ref* keep aloof
absorbieren [apzɔr'birən] *tr* absorb
ab'speisen *tr* feed; **j–n mit schönen Worten a.** put s.o. off with polite words
abspenstig ['apʃpɛnstɪç] *adj*—a. **machen** lure away; **j–m a. werden** desert s.o.
ab'sperren *tr* shut off, block off; (*Tür*) lock; (*Strom*) cut off; (*Gas*) turn off
ab'spielen *tr* play through to the end; (*Schallplatte, Tonband*) play; (*Tonbandaufnahme*) play back ‖ *ref* take place
ab'sprechen §64 *tr* dispute, deny; (*ab-*

machen) arrange; **j–m das Recht a. zu** (*inf*) dispute s.o.'s right to (*inf*)
ab'sprechend *adj* (*Urteil*) unfavorable; (*Kritik*) adverse; (*tadelnd*) disparaging
ab'springen §142 *intr* (SEIN) jump down, jump off; (*Ball*) rebound; (*Glasur*) chip; (*abschweifen*) digress; (aer) bail out, jump; **a. von** quit, desert
Ab'sprung *m* jump; (*ins Wasser*) dive; (*des Balles*) rebound
ab'spulen *tr* unwind, unreel
ab'spülen *tr* rinse (off)
ab'stammen *intr* (SEIN) (**von**) be descended (from); (**von**) be derived (from)
Abstammung *f* (–;–en) descent, extraction; (gram) derivation
Ab'stand *m* distance; (*räumlich und zeitlich*) interval; **A. nehmen von** refrain from; **A. zahlen** pay compensation
abstatten ['apʃtatən] *tr* (*Besuch*) pay; (*Bericht*) file; (*Dank*) give, return
ab'stauben *tr* dust off; (sl) swipe
ab'stechen §64 *tr* (*töten*) stab; (*Rasen*) cut; (*Hochofen*) tap; (*Karten*) trump ‖ *intr*—**gegen** (or von) etwa a. contrast with s.th.
Ab'stecher *m* (–s;–) side trip; (*Umweg*) detour; (fig) digression
ab'stecken *tr* (*Haar*) unpin, let down; (*Kleid*) pin, fit; (surv) mark off
ab'stehen §146 *intr* (*entfernt sein*) (**von**) be, stand away (from); (*Ohren, usw.*) stick out ‖ *intr* (HABEN & SEIN) (**von**) refrain (from)
ab'steigen §148 *intr* (SEIN) get down, descend; **in e–m Gasthof a.** stay at a hotel
ab'stellen *tr* (*Last*) put down; (*Radio, Gas, usw.*) turn off; (*Motor*) switch off; (*Auto*) park; (*Mißstand*) redress; (mil) detach, assign; **a. auf** (*acc*) gear to
Ab'stellraum *m* storage room
ab'stempeln *tr* stamp
ab'sterben §149 *intr* (SEIN) die off; (*Pflanzen*) wither; (*Glieder*) get numb
Abstieg ['apʃtik] *m* (–[e]s;) descent
ab'stimmen *tr* tune; (com) balance; **a. auf** (*acc*) (fig) atune (to) ‖ *intr* (*über acc*) vote (on)
Abstinenzler –in [apstɪ'nɛntslər(ɪn)] §6 *mf* teetotaler
ab'stoppen *tr* stop; (sport) clock
ab'stoßen §150 *tr* push off; (*Waren*) get rid of, sell; (*Schulden*) pay off; (*Geweih*) shed; (fig) disgust, sicken; (phys) repel ‖ *ref*—**sich** [*dat*] **die Hörner a.** (fig) sow one's wild oats ‖ *intr* (SEIN) shove off
ab'stoßend *adj* repulsive
abstrakt [ap'strakt] *adj* abstract
ab'streichen *tr* (*abwischen*) wipe off; (*Rasiermesser*) strop; (*abhaken*) check off; (bact) swab; (com) deduct
ab'streifen *tr* (*Handschuh, usw.*) take off; (*Haut*) slough off; (*Gewohnheit*) break ‖ *intr* (SEIN) deviate, stray
ab'streiten §86 *tr* contest, dispute

Ab'strich m (*beim Schreiben*) downstroke; (*Abzug*) cut; (bact) swab

ab'stufen tr (*Gelände*) terrace; (*Farben*) shade off

abstumpfen ['ap∫tumpfən] tr blunt

Ab'sturz m fall; (*Abhang*) precipice; (aer) crash

abstürzen intr (SEIN) fall down; (aer) crash

ab'suchen tr (*Gebiet*) scour, comb

Ab'szeß [ap'stses] m (-szesses; -szesse) abscess

Abt [apt] m (-[e]s;∸e) abbot

ab'takeln tr unrig; (coll) sack, fire

ab'tasten tr probe; (rad) scan

Abtei [ap'taɪ] f (-;-en) abbey

Ab'teil m compartment

ab'teilen tr divide, partition

Ab'teilung f (-;-en) department, division; (*im Krankenhaus*) ward; (arti) battery; (mil) detachment, unit

Ab'teilungsleiter -in §6 mf department head, section head

Ab'teilungszeichen n hyphen

Äbtissin [ep'tɪsɪn] f (-;-nen) abbess

ab'tönen tr tone down, shade off

ab'töten tr (*Bakterien*) kill; (*das Fleisch*) mortify

Abtrag ['aptrak] m (-[e]s;∸e)—j-m A. leisten compensate s.o.; j-m A. tun hurt s.o.

ab'tragen §132 tr carry away; (*Gebäude*) raze; (*Kleid*) wear out; (*Schuld*) pay

abträglich ['aptrεklɪç] adj detrimental

ab'treiben §62 tr drive away; (*Leibesfrucht*) abort ‖ intr (SEIN) drift away; **vom Kurs a.** drift off course

Ab'treibung f (-;-en) abortion

ab'trennen tr separate, detach; (*Glied*) sever; (*Genähtes*) unstitch

ab'treten §152 tr wear out (*by walking*); (*aufgeben*) cede, turn over ‖ intr (SEIN) retire, resign; (theat) exit

Ab'treter m (-s;-) doormat

Ab'tretung f (-;-en) (*von Grundeigentum*) transfer; (pol) cession

ab'trocknen tr dry ‖ intr (SEIN) dry

ab'tropfen intr (SEIN) trickle, drip

ab'trudeln intr (SEIN) go into a tailspin; (coll) toddle off, saunter off

abtrünnig ['aptrynɪç] adj unfaithful; (eccl) apostate; **a. werden** defect

Ab'trünnigkeit f (-;-) desertion, defection; (eccl) apostasy

ab'tun §154 tr (*ablegen*) take off; (*beiseite schieben*) get rid of; (*töten*) kill; (*erledigen*) settle; **a. als** dismiss as; **kurz a.** make short work of; **mit e-m Achselzucken a.** shrug off

ab'urteilen tr pass final judgment on

ab'verlangen tr—j-m etw a. demand s.th. of s.o.

ab'wägen §156 tr weigh

ab'wälzen tr roll away; (*Schuld*) shift

ab'wandeln tr (*Thema*) vary; (*Hauptwort*) (gram) decline; (*Zeitwort*) (gram) conjugate

ab'wandern intr (SEIN) wander off; (*Bevölkerung*) migrate; (*Arbeitskräfte*) drift away

Ab'wanderung f (-;-en) exodus, migration

Ab'wandlung f (-;-en) variation; (*e-s Hauptwortes*) declension; (*e-s Zeitwortes*) conjugation

ab'warten tr wait for; (*Anweisung*) await; **das bleibt abzuwarten!** that remains to be seen! **s-e Zeit a.** bide one's time ‖ intr wait and see

abwärts ['apvεrts] adv down, downwards; **mit ihm geht es a.** (coll) he's going downhill

ab'waschen §158 tr wash (off)

ab'wechseln tr & intr alternate

ab'wechselnd adj alternate

Ab'wechs(e)lung f (-;-en) variation; (*Mannigfaltigkeit*) variety; (*Zerstreuung*) diversion, entertainment

Ab'weg m wrong way; **auf Abwege führen** mislead; **auf Abwege geraten** go wrong

Ab'wehr f (-;-en) defense; (*e-s Stoßes, usw.*) warding off; (mil) counter-espionage service

ab'wehren tr ward off, avert

ab'weichen §85 intr (SEIN) deviate, diverge; (*verschieden sein*) differ

Ab'weichung f (-;-en) deviation; difference; (math) divergence

ab'weiden tr graze on

ab'weisen §118 tr refuse, turn down; (*Angriff*) repel; (*Berufung*) deny

ab'weisend adj (gegen) unfriendly (to)

Ab'weisung f (-;-en) refusal; (jur) denial; (mil) repulse

ab'wenden tr turn away, turn aside; (*Augen*) avert; (*Aufmerksamkeit*) divert; (*Krieg, Gefahr*) prevent ‖ §140 & 120 ref (von) turn away (from)

ab'werfen §160 tr throw off; (*Bomben*) drop; (*Blätter, Geweih*) shed; (*Gewinn*) bring in, yield; (*Zinsen*) bear; (*Karten*) discard; (*Joch*) shake off

ab'werten tr devaluate

Ab'wertung f (-;-en) devaluation

abwesend ['apvezənt] adj absent, missing; (fig) absent-minded

Ab'wesenheit f (-;) absence; (fig) absent-mindedness

ab'wickeln tr unwind, unroll; (*Geschäfte*) transact; (*Schulden*) settle; (*Aktiengesellschaft*) liquidate ‖ ref unwind; (fig) develop **sich gut a.** (com) turn out well

ab'wiegen §57 tr weigh

ab'wischen tr wipe off, wipe clean

Abwurf ['apvurf] m drop(ping); (*Bomben*) release; (*Ertrag*) yield

ab'würgen tr wring the neck of; (aut) stall

ab'zahlen tr pay off

ab'zählen tr count off

Ab'zahlung f (-;-en) payment in installments; (*Rate*) installment; **auf A. on terms**

Ab'zahlungsgeschäft n deferred-payment system

ab'zapfen tr (*Bier*) tap; (*Blut*) draw

Ab'zehrung f emaciation; consumption

Ab'zeichen n distinguishing mark; badge; (mil) decoration

ab'zeichnen tr copy, draw, sketch;

(*Dokument*) initial ‖ *ref* become apparent; (*gegen*) stand out (against)
Ab′ziehbild *n* decal
ab′ziehen §163 *tr* pull off; (*Kunden*) lure away; (*Reifen*) take off; (*Bett*) strip; (*vom Preise*) deduct, knock off; (*vervielfältigen*) run off; (*Abziehbild*) transfer; (*Schlüssel vom Loch*) take out; (*Rasiermesser*) strop; (*Wein*) draw; (*Truppen*) withdraw; (*Aufmerksamkeit*) divert; (arith) deduct; (phot) print; (typ) pull ‖ *intr* (SEIN) depart; (*abmarschieren*) march off; (*Rauch*) disperse
Ab′zug *m* (*e-r Summe*) deduction; (*Rabatt*) rebate, allowance; (*Skonto*) discount; (*am Gewehr*) trigger; (*Weggang*) departure; (*für Wasser*) outlet; (*für Rauch*) escape; (mil) withdrawal; (phot) print; (typ) proof sheet
abzüglich [′aptsyklɪç] *prep* (*genit or acc*) less, minus
Ab′zugsbogen *m* proof sheet
Ab′zugspapier *n* duplicating paper; (phot) printing paper
Ab′zugsrohr *n* drainpipe
ab′zweigen *tr* divert ‖ *intr* (SEIN) branch off
ach [ax] *interj* oh!; ah!; **ach so!** oh, I see!; **ach was!** nonsense!; **ach wo!** of course not!
Achse [′aksə] *f* (*-;-n*) axis; (*am Wagen*) axle; (mach) shaft; **auf der A.** on the move; **per A.** by truck; by rail
Achsel [′aksəl] *f* (*-;-n*) shoulder; **auf die leichte A. nehmen** make light of; **mit den Achseln zucken** shrug one's shoulders; **über die Achseln ansehen** look down on
Ach′selbein *n* shoulder blade
Ach′selgrube *f*, **Ach′selhöhle** *f* armpit
Ach′selträger –in §6 *mf* opportunist
acht [axt] *adj* eight; **alle a. Tage** once a week; **in a. Tagen** within a week; **über a. Tage** a week from today ‖ **Acht** *f* (*-;-n*) eight ‖ *f* (*-;*) (*Bann*) outlawry; (*Obacht*) care, attention; **in die A. erklären** outlaw; (fig) ostracize; **sich in a. nehmen vor** (*dat*) watch out for
achtbar [′axtbar] *adj* respectable
achte [′axtə] §9 *adj* & *pron* eight
achteckig [′axtɛkɪç] *adj* octagonal
Achtel [′axtəl] *n* (*-s;-*) eighth (part)
achten [′axtən] *tr* (*beachten*) respect; (*schätzen*) esteem; (*erachten*) consider ‖ *intr*—**a. auf** (*acc*) pay attention to; **a. darauf, daß** see to it that
ächten [′ɛçtən] *tr* outlaw, proscribe; (*gesellschaftlich*) ostracize
ach′tenswert *adj* respectable
achter(n) [′axtər(n)] *adv* aft, astern
acht′geben §80 *intr* (auf *acc*) pay attention (*to*); **gib acht!** watch out!
acht′los *adj* careless
Acht′losigkeit *f* (*-;*) carelessness
acht′sam *adj* [′axtzam] cautious; (auf *acc*) attentive (to); (auf *acc*) careful (of)
Acht′samkeit *f* (*-;*) carefulness

achttägig [′axttɛgɪç] *adj* eight-day; eight-day old; one-week
Ach′tung *f* (*-;*) attention; (vor *dat*) respect (for); **A.!** watch out!; (mil) attention!
ach′tungsvoll *adj* respectful; (*als Briefschluß*) Yours truly
acht′zehn *adj* & *pron* eighteen ‖ **Achtzehn** *f* (*-;-en*) eighteen
acht′zehnte §9 *adj* & *pron* eighteenth
achtzig [′axtsɪç] *adj* eighty
achtziger [′axtsɪgər] *invar adj* of the eighties; **die a. Jahre** the eighties ‖ **Achtziger –in** §6 *mf* octogenarian
achtzigste [′axtsɪçstə] §9 *adj* eightieth
ächzen [′ɛçtsən] *intr* groan, moan
Acker [′akər] *m* (*-s;⸚*) soil, (arable) land, field; (*Maß*) acre
Ackerbau (Ak′kerbau) *m* farming
ackerbautreibend [′akərbautraɪbənt] *adj* agricultural
Ackerbestellung (Ak′kerbestellung) *f* cultivation, tilling
Ackerland (Ak′kerland) *n* arable land
ackern [′akərn] *tr* & *intr* plow
addieren [a′dirən] *tr* & *intr* add
Addiermaschine [a′dirmaʃinə] *f* adding machine
Addition [adɪ′tsjon] *f* (*-;-en*) addition
ade [a′de] *interj* farewell!; bye-bye!
Adel [′adəl] *m* (*-s;*) nobility, noble birth; (*edle Gesinnung*) noble-mindedness
ad(e)lig [′ad(ə)lɪç] *adj* noble, titled; nobleman's ‖ **Ad(e)lige** §5 *m* nobleman ‖ §5 *f* noblewoman
A′delstand *m* nobility
Ader [′adər] *f* (*-;-n*) vein
adieu [a′djø] *interj* adieu!
Adjektiv [′atjektif] *n* (*-s;-e*) adjective
Adjutant –in [atju′tant(ɪn)] §7 *mf* adjutant; (*e-s Generals*) aide(-de-camp)
Adler [′adlər] *m* (*-s;-*) eagle
Ad′lernase *f* aquiline nose
Admiral [atmi′ral] *m* (*-[e]s;-e*) admiral
Admiralität [atmiralɪ′tet] *f* (*-;*) admiralty
adoptieren [adɔp′tirən] *tr* adopt
Adoption [adɔp′tsjon] *f* (*-;-en*) adoption
Adoptiv– [adɔp′tif] *comb. fm.* adoptive
Adressat –in [adre′sat(ɪn)] §7 *mf* addressee; (*e-r Warensendung*) consignee
Adresse [a′dresə] *f* (*-;-n*) address; **an die falsche A. kommen** (fig) bark up the wrong tree; **per A.** care of
adressieren [adre′sirən] *tr* address; (*Waren*) consign
adrett [a′dret] *adj* smart, neat
Advent [at′vent] *m* (*-s;-e*) Advent
Adverb [at′verp] *n* (*-[e]s;-ien* [-ɪ-ən]) adverb
Advokat –in [atvo′kat(ɪn)] §7 *mf* lawyer
Affäre [a′ferə] *f* (*-;-n*) affair
Affe [′afə] *m* (*-n;-n*) ape, monkey; **e-n Affen haben** (sl) be drunk
Affekt [a′fekt] *m* (*-[e]s;-e*) emotion; (*Leidenschaft*) passion
affektiert [afek′tirt] *adj* affected

Affektiert'heit *f* (-;-en) affectation

äffen ['ɛfən] *tr* ape, mimic

Af'fenliebe *f* doting

Af'fenpossen *pl* monkeyshines

Af'fenschande *f* crying shame

Af'fentheater *n* farce, joke

affig ['afɪç] *adj* affected; (geckenhaft) foppish

Äffin ['ɛfɪn] *f* (-;-nen) female ape, female monkey

Afrika ['afrɪka] *n* (-s;) Africa

afrikanisch [afrɪ'kanɪʃ] *adj* African

After ['aftər] *m* (-s;-) anus

AG, A.G., A.-G. *abbr* (Aktiengesellschaft) stock company

ägäisch [ɛ'ge·ɪʃ] *adj* Aegean

Agende [a'gendə] *f* (-;-n) memo pad

Agent -in [a'gent(ɪn)] §7 *mf* agent, representative; (Geheim-) secret agent

Agentur [agen'tur] *f* (-;-en) agency

aggressiv [agre'sif] *adj* aggressive

Ägide [ɛ'gidə] *f* (-;-n) aegis

Agio ['aʒɪ·o] *n* (-s;-s) premium

Agitation [agɪta'tsjon] *f* (-;-en) agitation, rabble-rousing

Agi·tator [agɪ'tatər] *m* (-s;-tatoren [ta'torən] (& mach) agitator

agitatorisch [agɪta'torɪʃ] *adj* inflammatory

agitieren [agɪ'tirən] *intr* agitate

Agraffe [a'grafə] *f* (-;-n) clasp

agrarisch [a'grarɪʃ] *adj* agrarian

Ägypten [ɛ'gyptən] *n* (-s;) Egypt

Ägypter -in [ɛ'gyptər(ɪn)] §6 *mf* Egyptian

ägyptisch [ɛ'gyptɪʃ] *adj* Egyptian

ah [a] *interj* ah!

Ahle ['alə] *f* (-;-n) awl, punch

Ahn [an] *m* (-(e)s & -en;-en) ancestor

ahnden ['andən] *tr* (strafen) punish; (rächen) avenge

Ahn'dung *f* (-;) revenge

ähneln ['ɛnəln] *intr* (dat) resemble

ahnen ['anən] *tr* have a premonition of, suspect; (erfassen) divine

Ah'nentafel *f* family tree

ähnlich ['ɛnlɪç] *adj* alike; (dat) similar (to), analagous (to): das sieht ihm ä. that's just like him; j-m ä sehen look like s.o.

Ähn'lichkeit *f* (-;-en) (mit) resemblance (to)

Ah'nung ['anʊŋ] *f* (-;-en) (Vorgefühl) presentiment, hunch; (böse) misgiving; (Argwohn) suspicion; keine A. haben have no idea

ah'nungslos *adj* unsuspecting

ah'nungsvoll *adj* full of misgivings

Ahorn ['ahorn] *m* (-(e)s;-e) maple

Ähre ['ɛrə] *f* (-;-n) (Korn) ear; (e-r Blume) spike; Ähren lesen glean

Ais ['a·ɪs] *n* (-;-) (mus) A sharp

Akade·mie [akadə'mi] *f* (-;-mien ['mi·ən]) academy; university

Akademiker -in [aka'demɪkər(ɪn)] §6 *mf* university graduate

akademisch [aka'demɪʃ] *adj* academic; university

Akazie [a'katsjə] *f* (-;-n) acacia

akklimatisieren [aklɪmatɪ'zirən] *tr* acclimate || *ref* become acclimated

Akkord [a'kort] *m* (-(e)s;-e) chord; (Vereinbarung) accord; (com) settlement; im A. arbeiten do piecework

Akkord'arbeit *f* piecework

Akkordeon [a'kordə·ɔn] *n* (-s;-s) accordion

akkreditieren [akredɪ'tirən] *tr* accredit; open an account for

Akkreditiv [akredɪ'tif] *n* (-[e]s;-e) (Beglaubigungsschreiben) credentials; (com) letter of credit

Akkumula·tor [akumu'latər] *m* (-s; -toren ['torən]) storage battery

akkurat [aku'rat] *adj* accurate

Akkusativ ['akuzatif] *m* (-[e]s;-e) accusative (case)

Akrobat [akro'bat] §7 *m* acrobat

Akrobatik [akro'batɪk] *f* (-;) acrobatics

Akrobatin [akro'batɪn] §7 *f* acrobat

Akt [akt] *m* (-[e]s;-e) act, action; (paint) nude; (theat) act

Akte ['aktə] *f* (-;-n) document; record, file; (jur) instrument; zu den Akten legen file; (fig) shelve

Ak'tendeckel *m* file folder

Ak'tenklammer *f* paper clip

Ak'tenmappe *f* brief case, portfolio

ak'tenmäßig *adj* documentary

Ak'tenschrank *m* file cabinet

Ak'tentasche *f* brief case

Ak'tenzeichen *n* file number

Aktie ['aktsjə] *f* (-;-n) stock

Ak'tienbesitzer -in §6 *mf* stockholder

Ak'tienbörse *f* stock exchange

Ak'tiengesellschaft *f* corporation

Ak'tieninhaber -in §6 *mf* stockholder

Ak'tienmakler -in §6 *mf* stockbroker

Ak'tienmarkt *m* stock market

Ak'tienschein *m* stock certificate

Aktion [ak'tsjon] *f* (-;-en) action; (Unternehmung) campaign, drive; (polizeiliche) raid; (mil) operation; Aktionen activity

Aktionär -in [aktsjo'ner(ɪn)] §8 *mf* stockholder

aktiv [ak'tif] *adj* active; (Bilanz) favorable; (chem) activated; (gram) active; a. werden become a member (of a student club) || Aktiv *n* (-s;) (gram) active voice

Aktiva [ak'tiva] *pl* assets; A. und Passiva assets and liabilities

Aktiv'posten *m* asset

aktuell [aktu'el] *adj* current, topical || Aktuelle *pl* (journ) newsbriefs

Akustik [a'kustɪk] *f* (-;) acoustics

akustisch [a'kustɪʃ] *adj* acoustic(al)

akut [a'kut] *adj* acute

Akzent [ak'tsent] *m* (-[e]s;-e) accent (mark); (Nachdruck) emphasis; (phonet) stress

akzentuieren [aktsentu'irən] *tr* accent; (fig) stress, accentuate

akzeptieren [aktsep'tirən] *tr* accept

Alabaster [ala'bastər] *m* (-s;) alabaster

Alarm [a'larm] *m* (-[e]s;-e) alarm; A. blasen (or schlagen) (mil & fig) sound the alarm; blinder A. false alarm

Alarm'anlage *f* alarm system; warning system (in civil defense)

alarm'bereit *adj* on the alert

Alarm'bereitschaft f (state of) readiness; in A. on the alert
alarmieren [alar'mirən] tr alert; alarm
Alaun [a'laun] m (-s;-e) alum
Alaun'stift m steptic pencil
Albanien [al'bɑnjən] n (-s;) Albania
albanisch [al'bɑnɪʃ] adj Albanian
albern ['albərn] adj silly
Al·bum ['album] n (-s;-ben [bən]) album
Alchimist [alçı'mɪst] §7 m alchemist
Alge ['algə] f (-;-n) alga; seaweed
Algebra ['algebra] f (-;) algebra
algebraisch [alge'brɑ.ɪʃ] adj algebraic
Algerien [al'gerjən] n (-s;) Algeria
algerisch [al'gerɪʃ] adj Algerian
Algier ['alʒir] n (-s;) Algiers
Alibi ['ɑlibɪ] n (-s;-s) alibi
Alimente [alɪ'mentə] pl child support
alimentieren [alɪmen'tirən] tr pay alimony to; (Kind) support
Alkohol ['alkohol] m (-s;-e) alcohol
al'koholfrei adj non-alcoholic
Alkoholiker –in [alko'holikər(ın)] §6 mf alcoholic
alkoholisch [alko'holɪʃ] adj alcoholic
all [al] adj all; (jeder) every; (jeder beliebige) any; alle beide both (of them); alles Gute! take care!; (im Brief) best wishes; alle zehn Minuten every ten minutes; alle zwei Tage every other day; auf alle Fälle in any case || indef pron each, each one; everyone, everything; all; aller und jeder each and every one; in allem all told; vor allem above all, first of all
alle ['alə] adv all gone; a. machen finish off; a. sein be all gone; a. werden run low
Allee [a'le] f (-;-n) (tree-lined) avenue; (tree-lined) walk
Allego·rie [alego'ri] f (-;-rien ['ri·ən]) allegory
allegorisch [ale'gorɪʃ] adj allegoric(al)
allein [a'laɪn] adj alone || adv alone; only; however; no fewer than, no less than; schon a. der Gedanke the mere thought
Allein'berechtigung f exclusive right
Allein'flug m solo flight
Allein'handel m monopoly
Allein'herrschaft f autocracy
Allein'herrscher –in §6 mf autocrat
allei'nig adj (ausschließlich) sole, exclusive; (einzig) only
allein'stehend adj alone in the world; (unverheiratet) single; (Gebäude) detached
Allein'verkauf m, **Allein'vertrieb** m franchise
al'lemal adv every time; ein für a. once and for all
al'lenfalls adv if need be; (vielleicht) possibly; (höchstens) at most
allenthalben ['alənt'halbən] adv everywhere
al'lerart invar adj all kinds of
al'lerbe'ste §9 adj very best; aufs b. in the best possible manner
al'lerdings' adv (gewiß) certainly (strong affirmative answer); (zugestehend) admittedly, I must admit

al'lerer'ste §9 adj very first, first ... of all
Aller·gie [alɛr'gi] (-;-gien ['gi·ən]) allergy
allergisch [a'lergɪʃ] adj allergic
al'lerhand' invar adj all kinds of; (viel) a lot of || indef pron —das ist a.! that's great!; das ist doch a.! the nerve!
Allerhei'ligen invar n All Saints' Day
allerlei ['alər'laɪ] invar adj all kinds of || **Allerlei** n (-s;-s) hotchpotch; (mus) medley
al'lerlet'zte §9 adj very last, last of all; latest
al'lerlieb'ste ['alər'lipstə] §9 adj dearest ... of all; (Kind) sweet
al'lermei'ste §9 adj most; am allermeisten most of all; chiefly
al'lernäch'ste §9 adj very next
al'lerneu'este §9 adj latest, newest
Allersee'len invar n All Souls' Day
allesamt [alə'zamt] adv all together
al'lezeit adv always
All'gegenwart f omnipresence
all'gemein adj general, universal
All'gemeinheit f universality; (Öffentlichkeit) public
Allheil'mittel n cure-all
Allianz [alɪ'ants] f (-;-en) alliance
alliieren [alɪ'irən] ref—sich a. mit ally oneself with
alliiert [alɪ'irt] adj allied || **Alliierte** §5 mf ally
alljähr'lich adj annual, yearly
All'macht f omnipotence
allmäch'tig adj omnipotent, almighty
allmählich [al'melɪç] adj gradual
allnäch'tlich adj nightly
allseitig ['alzaɪtɪç] adj all-round || adv from all sides, on all sides
All'tag m daily routine
alltäg'lich adj daily; (fig) everyday
all'tags adv daily; (wochentags) weekdays
All'tags- comb.fm. everyday; (fig) commonplace
All'tagsmensch m common man
All'tagswort n (-[e]s;⸗er) household word
allwissend [al'vɪsənt] adj omniscient
allwö'chentlich adj & adv weekly
allzu– comb.fm. all too
all'zumal adv one and all, all together
all'zusammen adv all together
Alm [alm] f (-;-en) Alpine meadow
Almanach ['almanax] m (-[e]s;-e) almanac
Almosen ['almozen] n (-s;-) alms
Alp [alp] m (-[e]s;-e) elf, goblin; (Alptraum) nightmare
Alp'druck m (-[e]s;⸗e), **Alp'drücken** n (-s;) nightmare
Alpen ['alpən] pl Alps
Alphabet [alfa'bet] n (-[e]s;-e) alphabet
alphabetisch [alfa'betɪʃ] adj alphabetical
alpin [al'pin] adj alpine
als [als] adv as, like || conj than; when, as; but, except; als ob as if
alsbald' adv presently, immediately
alsdann' adv then, thereupon

also ['alzo] *adv* so, thus; therefore, consequently; na a.! well then!

alt [alt] *adj* (älter ['ɛltər], älteste ['ɛltəstə] §9) *adj* old; (*bejahrt*) aged; (*gebraucht*) second-hand; (*abgestanden*) stale; (*antik*) antique; (*Sprache*) ancient || **Alt** *m* (-[e]s;-e) contralto || **Alte** §5 *m* (coll) old man; **die Alten** the ancients; **mein Alter** (coll) my husband || **Alte** §5 *f* (coll) old woman; **meine Alte** (coll) my wife

Altan [al'tɑn] *m* (-[e]s;-e), **Altane** [al'tɑnə] *f* (-;-n) balcony, gallery

Altar [al'tɑr] *m* (-[e]s;-̈e) altar

alt'bewährt *adj* long-standing

Alt'eisen *n* scrap iron

Alt'eisenhändler *m* junk dealer

Alter ['altər] *n* (-s;-) age; (*Greisen-*) old age; (*Zeit-*) epoch; (*Dienst-*) seniority; **er ist in meinem A. he** is my age; **im A. von** at the age of; **mittleren Alters** middle-aged

altern ['altərn] *intr* (SEIN) age

Alternative [alterna'tivə] *f* (-;-n) alternative

Al'tersgrenze *f* age limit; (*für Beamte*) retirement age

Al'tersheim *n* home for the aged

Al'tersrente *f* old-age pension

al'tersschwach *adj* decrepit; senile

Al'tersschwäche *f* (feebleness of) old age

Al'tersversorgungskasse *f* old-age pension fund

Altertum ['altərtum] *n* (-s;) antiquity

altertümlich ['altərtymlıç] *adj* ancient; (*Möbel*) antique; (*veraltet*) archaic

Al'tertumsforscher -in §6 *mf* archaeologist; (*Antiquar*) antiquarian

Al'tertumskunde *f*, **Al'tertumswissenschaft** *f* study of antiquity; classical studies

althergebracht ['alt'hergəbraxt] *adj* long-standing, traditional

alther'kömmlich *adj* ancient, traditional

Altist [al'tıst] §7 *m* alto (*singer*)

Altistin [al'tıstın] §7 *f* contralto (*female singer*)

alt'klug *adj* precocious

ältlich ['ɛltlıç] *adj* elderly

Alt'meister *m* past master; (sport) ex-champion

alt'modisch *adj* old-fashioned

Alt'stadt *f* old (part of the) city

Alt'stadtsanierung *f* urban renewal

Alt'stimme *f* alto; contralto (*female voice*)

altväterlich ['altfetərlıç], **altväterisch** ['altfetərıʃ] *adj* old-fashioned; old-time

Alt'warenhändler -in §6 *mf* second-hand dealer

Altweibersommer [alt'varbərzomər] *m* Indian summer; (*Spinnweb*) gossamer

Aluminium [alu'minjum] *n* (-s;) aluminum

am [am] *contr* an dem

amalgamieren [amalga'mirən] *tr* amalgamate

Amateur [ama'tør] *m* (-s;-e) amateur

Amazone [ama'tsonə] *f* (-;-n) Amazon

Am-boß ['ambɔs] *m* (-bosses;-bosse) anvil

ambulant [ambu'lant] *adj* ambulatory || *adv*—a. Behandelte out-patient

Ambulanz [ambu'lants] *f* (-;-en) out-patient clinic; (*Krankenwagen*) ambulance

Ameise ['ɑmaɪzə] *f* (-;-n) ant

Amerika [a'merika] *n* (-s;) America

Amerikaner -in [amerı'kɑnər(ın)] §6 *mf* American

amerikanisch [amerı'kɑnıʃ] *adj* American

Ami ['ami] *m* (-s;-s) (sl) Yank || *f* (-;-s) American cigarette

Amme ['amə] *f* (-;-n) nurse, wet-nurse

Amnes-tie [amnes'ti] *f* (-;-tien ['ti-ən]) amnesty

amnestieren [amnes'tirən] *tr* pardon

A-mor ['ɑmɔr] *m* (-s;-moren ['morən]) (myth) Cupid

Amortisation [amɔrtiza'tsjon] *f* (-;-en) amortization

Amortisations'kasse *f* sinking fund

amortisieren [amɔrtı'zirən] *tr* amortize

Ampel ['ampəl] *f* (-;-n) hanging lamp; (*Verkehrs-*) traffic light

Ampere [am'per] *n* (-s;-) ampere

Amphibie [am'fibjə] *f* (-;-n) amphibian

Amphi'bienpanzerwagen *m* amphibious tank

Amphitheater [am'fite-atər] *n* (-s;-) amphitheater

Ampulle [am'pulə] *f* (-;-n) phial

Amputation [amputa'tsjon] *f* (-;-en) amputation

amputieren [ampu'tirən] *tr* amputate

Amputierte [ampu'tirtə] §5 *mf* amputee

Amsel ['amzəl] *f* (-;-n) blackbird

Amt [amt] *n* (-[e]s;-̈er) office; (*Pflicht*) duty, function; (dipl) post; (eccl) divine service; (telp) exchange

amtieren [am'tirən] *intr* be in office, hold office; (eccl) officiate

amt'lich *adj* official

Amts- *comb.fm.* official, of (an) office

Amts'antritt *m* inauguration

Amts'befugnis *f* competence

Amts'bereich *m* jurisdiction

Amts'bewerber -in §6 *mf* office seeker

Amts'bezirk *m* jurisdiction

Amts'blatt *n* official bulletin

Amts'eid *m* oath of office

Amts'enthebung *f* dismissal

Amts'führung *f* administration

amts'gemäß *adj* official || *adv* officially

Amts'gericht *n* district court

Amts'gerichtsrat *m* (official rank of) district-court judge

Amts'geschäfte *pl* official duties

Amts'gewalt *f* (official) authority

Amts'handlung *f* official act

Amts'niederlegung *f* resignation

Amts'schimmel *m* bureaucracy; (coll) red tape

Amts'siegel *n* seal of office

Amts′sprache ƒ official language; (coll) officialese, gobbledygook

Amts′tracht ƒ robes

Amts′träger –in §6 mƒ officeholder

Amts′verletzung ƒ misconduct in office

Amts′weg m—auf dem Amtswege through official channels

Amts′zeichen n (telp) dial tone

Amulett [amu′lɛt] n (-[e]s;-e) amulet

amüsant [amy′zant] adj amusing

amüsieren [amy′zirən] tr amuse, entertain || ref amuse oneself; (sich gut unterhalten) enjoy oneself

an [an] adv on; onward || prep (dat) at, against, on, upon, by, to; (Grad, Maß) in; an sich per se; an und für sich properly speaking; es ist an dir zu (inf) it's up to you to (inf) || prep (acc) at, on, upon, against, to

analog [ana′lok] adj analogous

Analo•gie [analo′gi] ƒ (-;-gien [′gi•ən]) analogy

Analphabet –in [analfa′bet(ɪn)] §7 mƒ illiterate

Analphabetentum [analfa′betəntum] n (-s;), **Analphabetismus** [analfabe′tɪsmʊs] m (-;) illiteracy

analphabetisch [analfa′betɪʃ] adj illiterate

Analyse [ana′lyzə] ƒ (-;-n) analysis; (gram) parsing; durch A. analytically

analysieren [analy′zirən] tr analyze; (gram) parse

Analy•sis [a′nalyzɪs] ƒ (-;-sen [ana′lyzən]) (math) analysis

Analytiker –in [ana′lytikər(ɪn)] §6 mƒ analyst

analytisch [ana′lytɪʃ] adj analytic(al)

Anämie [ane′mi] ƒ (-;) anemia

anämisch [an′emɪʃ] adj anemic

Ananas [′ananas] ƒ (-;-se) pineapple

Anarchie [anar′çi] ƒ (-;) anarchy

anästhesieren [aneste′zirən] tr anesthetize

Anästheti•kum [anes′tetɪkʊm] n (-s; -ka [ka]) anesthetic

an′atmen tr breathe on

Anato•mie [anato′mi] ƒ (-;-mien [′mi•ən]) anatomy

anatomisch [ana′tomɪʃ] adj anatomical

an′backen §50 tr bake gently || intr (HABEN & SEIN) cake on

an′bahnen tr pave the way for

anbandeln [′anbandəln] intr—a. mit flirt with

An′bau m (-[e]s) cultivation || m (-[e]s;-bauten) annex, new wing

an′bauen tr cultivate; (Gebäudeteil) add on

An′baufläche ƒ (arable) acreage

An′baumöbel pl sectional furniture

An′beginn m outset

an′behalten §90 tr keep (garment) on

anbei [an′bai] adv enclosed (herewith)

an′beißen §53 tr bite into, take the first bite of || intr nibble at the bait; (fig) bite

an′belangen tr—was mich anbelangt as far as I am concerned, as for me

an′bellen tr bark at

anberaumen [′anbəraumən] tr schedule

an′beten tr (& fig) worship

An′betracht m—in A. (genit) in consideration of, in view of

an′betteln tr bum, chisel

An′betung ƒ (-;) worship

an′betungswürdig adj adorable

an′bieten §58 tr offer || ref offer one's services

an′binden §59 tr tie (up) || intr—mit j–m a. pick a quarrel with s.o.

an′blasen §61 tr blow at, blow on

An′blick m look, view, sight

an′blicken tr look at; (besehen) view; (mustern) eye

an′blinzeln tr wink at

an′brechen §64 tr (Vorräte) break into; (Flasche, Kiste) open || intr (SEIN) (Tag) dawn; (Nacht) come on

an′brennen §97 tr light || intr (SEIN) catch fire; (Speise) burn

an′bringen §65 tr bring, fetch; (befestigen) (an acc) attach (to): (Bitte) make; (Klage) (Geld) invest; (Tochter) marry off; (Waren) sell, get rid of; (Bemerkung) insert; (Licht, Lampe) install; (Geld) (coll) blow

An′bruch m break; bei A. der Nacht at nightfall; bei A. des Tages at daybreak

an′brüllen tr roar at

Andacht [′andaxt] ƒ (-;-en) devotion; (Gottesdienst) devotions

andächtig [′andɛçtiç] adj devout

an′dauern intr continue, last; (hartnäckig sein) persist

An′denken n (-s;-) remembrance; souvenir; zum A. an (acc) in remembrance of

andere [′andərə] §9 adj & pron other; (folgend) next; ein anderer another; another one; kein anderer no one else

ändern [′endərn] tr change; (Wortlaut) modify || ref change

andernfalls [′andərn′fals] adv (or) else

anders [′andərs] adj else; (als) different (from); a. werden change || adv otherwise differently

an′dersartig adj of a different kind

anderseits [′andər′zaits] adv on the other hand

an′derswo adv somewhere else

anderthalb [′andərt′halp] invar one and a half

Än′derung ƒ (-;-n) change, variation; modification

Än′derungsantrag m amendment

anderwärts [′andər′verts] adv elsewhere

anderweitig [′andər′vaitiç] adj other, further || adv otherwise; elsewhere

an′deuten tr indicate, suggest; (anspielen) hint at, allude to; (zu verstehen geben) imply, intimate

an′deutungsweise adv by way of suggestion

an′dichten tr—j–m etw a. impute s.th. to s.o.

An′drang m rush; crowd; heavy traffic; (von Arbeit) pressure

an′drehen tr turn on; j–m etw a. palm s.th. off on s.o.

an'drohen *tr*—j—m etw a. threaten s.o. with s.th.

an'drücken *tr*—etw a. an (*acc*) press s.th. against

an'eignen *ref*—sich [*dat*] a. appropriate; (*Gewohnheit*) acquire; (*Meinungen*) adopt; (*Sprache*) master; (*widerrechtlich*) appropriate, usurp

aneinan'der *adv* together

aneinan'dergeraten §63 *intr* (SEIN) come to blows

Anekdote [anek'dotə] *f* (-;-n) anecdote

an'ekeln *tr* disgust, nauseate

an'empfehlen §147 *tr* recommend

An'erbieten *n* (-s;-) offer, proposal

an'erkennbar *adj* recognizable

an'erkennen §97 *tr* (als) recognize (as); (als) acknowledge (as); (*Schuld*) admit; (*billigen*) approve; (*lobend*) appreciate; (*Anspruch*) allow; nicht a. repudiate, disown; (sport) disallow

An'erkennung *f* (-;-en) acknowledgement; recognition; appreciation; admission; lobende A. honorable mention

anfachen ['anfaxən] *tr* (*Feuer*) fan; (*Gefühle*) inflame; (*Haß*) stir up

an'fahren §71 *tr* (*herbeibringen*) carry, convey; (*anstoßen*) run into; (fig) snap at; (naut) run afoul of || *intr* (SEIN) drive up; (*losfahren*) start off

An'fall *m* attack

an'fallen §72 *tr* attack, assail || *intr* (SEIN) accumulate, accrue

anfällig ['anfeliç] *adj* (für) susceptible (to)

An'fang *m* beginning, start; von A. an from the very beginning

an'fangen §73 *tr & intr* begin, start

Anfänger—in ['anfeŋər(ın)] §6 *mf* beginner; (*Neuling*) novice

anfänglich ['anfeŋlıç] *adj* initial

an'fangs *adv* at the start, initially

An'fangsbuchstabe *m* initial (letter)

An'fangsgründe *pl* rudiments, elements

an'fassen *tr* take hold of; (*behandeln*) handle, touch || *intr* lend a hand

an'faulen *intr* (SEIN) begin to rot

anfechtbar ['anfeçtbar] *adj* debatable, questionable; (jur) contestable

an'fechten §74 *tr* (*Richtigkeit*) contest; (*beunruhigen*) trouble; (jur) challenge

An'fechtung *f* (-;-en) (eccl) temptation; (jur) challenge

an'fertigen *tr* make, manufacture

an'feuchten *tr* moisten, wet

an'feuern *tr* inflame; (sport) cheer

an'flehen *tr* implore

an'fliegen §57 *tr* (aer) approach

An'flug *m* (*Anzeichen*) suggestion, trace; (*oberflächliche Kenntnis*) smattering; (*dünner Überzug*) film; A. von Bart down; leichter A. von slight case of

an'fordern *tr* call for, demand; (mil) requisition

an'fragen *intr* (über *acc*, wegen, nach) ask (about *s.th.*); (bei) inquire (of *s.o.*)

an'fressen §70 *tr* gnaw; (*Metall*) corrode

anfreunden ['anfrɔındən] *ref* (mit) make friends (with)

an'frieren §77 *intr* (SEIN) begin to freeze; a. an (*acc*) freeze onto

an'fügen *tr* (an *acc*) join (to)

an'fühlen *tr & ref* feel

Anfuhr ['anfur] *f* (-;-en) delivery

an'führen *tr* lead; (*Worte*) quote; (*Grund*) adduce; (*täuschen*) take in, fool; (mil) lead, command

An'führer —in §6 *mf* leader; (mil) commander; (pol) boss

an'führung *f* quotation

An'führungszeichen *n* quotation mark

an'füllen *tr & ref* fill up

An'gabe *f* (*Erklärung*) statement; (*beim Zollamt*) declaration; (coll) showing off; Angaben data; directions; nähere Angaben machen give particulars; wer hat die A.? whose serve is it?

an'geben §80 *tr* (*mitteilen*) state; (*bestimmen*) appoint; (*anzeigen*) inform against; (*vorgeben*) pretend; (*Preis*) quote || *intr* (coll) show off; (cards) deal first; (tennis) serve

An'geber —in §6 *mf* informer; (*Prahler*) show-off

angeblich ['angeplıç] *adj* alleged

an'geboren *adj* innate, natural

An'gebot *n* offer; (*bei Auktionen*) bid; A. und Nachfrage supply and demand

angebracht ['angəbraxt] *adj* advisable; es für a. halten zu (*inf*) see fit to (*inf*); gut a. appropriate; schlecht a. ill-timed

angegossen ['angəgosən] *adj*—wie a. sitzen fit like a glove

angeheiratet ['angəharratət] *adj* related by marriage

angeheitert ['angəhartərt] *adj* tipsy

an'gehen §82 *tr* charge, attack; (*Problem*) tackle; das geht dich gar nichts an that's none of your business; j—n um etw a. approach s.o. for s.th. || *intr* (SEIN) begin; (*zulässig sein*) be allowable; (*leidlich sein*) be tolerable; das geht nicht an that won't do

an'gehend *adj* future, prospective

an'gehören *intr* (*dat*) be a member (of)

Angehörige ['angəhørigə] §5 *mf* member; nächste Angehörigen next of kin; seine Angehörigen his relatives

Angeklagte ['angəklaktə] §5 *mf* defendant; (*wenn verhaftet*) suspect

Angel ['aŋəl] *f* (-;-n) fishing tackle; (*e-r Tür*) hinge; aus den Angeln heben (& fig) unhinge

an'gelangen *intr* (SEIN) (an *dat*, bei) arrive (at)

an'gelegen *adj*—sich [*dat*] etw a. sein lassen make s.th. one's business

An'gelegenheit *f* (-;-en) affair, business

angelehnt ['angəlent] *adj* ajar

An'gelgerät *n* fishing tackle

An'gelhaken *m* fish(ing) hook

angeln ['aŋəln] *intr* (nach) fish (for)

An'gelpunkt *m* pivot, central point

An'gelrute *f* fishing rod

angelsächsisch [ˈaŋəlzɛksɪʃ] *adj* Anglo-Saxon

Anʹgelschnur *f* fishing line

angemessen [ˈangəmɛsən] *adj* suitable (*ausreichend*) adequate; (*annehmbar*) reasonable; (*Benehmen*) proper; (*dat*) in keeping (with); **für a. halten** think fit

angenehm [ˈangənem] *adj* pleasant; **sehr a!** pleased to meet you!

angeregt [ˈangərɛkt] *adj* lively

angeschlagen [ˈangəʃlagən] *adj* chipped; (*Boxer*) groggy; (*mil*) hard-hit

angesehen [ˈangəze·ən] *adj* respected; (*ausgezeichnet*) distinguished

Anʹgesicht *n* countenance, face; **von A.** by sight

anʹgesichts *prep* (*genit*) in the presence of; (*fig*) in view of

angestammt [ˈangəʃtamt] *adj* hereditary

Angestellte [ˈangəʃtɛltə] §5 *mf* employee; **die Angestellten** the staff

angetan [ˈangətan] (*mit*) clad (in); **a. sein von** have a liking for; **ganz danach a. zu** (*inf*) very likely to (*inf*)

angetrunken [ˈangətruŋkən] *adj* tipsy

angewandt [ˈangəvant] *adj* applied

angewiesen [ˈangəvizən] *adj*—**a. sein auf** (*acc*) have to rely on

anʹgewöhnen *tr*—**j-m etw a.** accustom s.o. to s.th.

Anʹgewohnheit *f* (-;-en) habit

anʹgleichen §85 *tr* adapt, adjust

Angler –in [ˈaŋlər(ɪn)] §6 *mf* fisher

anʹgliedern *tr* link, attach; (*Gesellschaft*) affiliate

anʹgreifen §88 *tr* (*anfassen*) handle; (*Vorräte*) draw on, dip into; (*Körper*) affect; (*mil*) attack

anʹgreifend *adj* aggressive, offensive

Anʹgreifer –in §6 *mf* aggressor

anʹgrenzen *intr* (an *acc*) be adjacent (to), border (on)

Anʹgriff *m* attack

Anʹgriffskrieg *m* war of aggression

anʹgriffslustig *adj* aggressive

Angst [aŋst] *f* (-;⸚e) fear, anxiety

ängstigen [ˈɛŋstɪgən] *tr* alarm ‖ *ref* (*vor*) be afraid (of); (*um*) be alarmed (about)

ängstlich [ˈɛŋstlɪç] *adj* uneasy, jittery; (*besorgt*) anxious; (*sorgfältig*) scrupulous; (*schüchtern*) timid

Angstʹzustände *pl* jitters

anʹhaben §89 *tr* have on; **j-m etw a. have s.th. on.** s.o.; **j-m etw a. können** be able to harm s.o.

anʹhaften *intr* (*dat*) stick (to)

anʹhaken *tr* check off; (an *acc*) hook (onto)

anʹhalten §90 *tr* stop; (*Atem, Ton*) hold; ‖ *intr* stop; (*andauern*) continue, last

anʹhaltend *adj* continuous

Anʹhalter *m*—**per A. fahren** hitch-hike

Anʹhaltspunkt *m* clue, lead

Anʹhang *m* (-[e]s;⸚e) appendix; (*Gefolgschaft*) following; (*jur*) codicil

anʹhängen §92 & §109 *tr* (*Hörer*) hang up; (*hinzufügen*) add on; **j-m e-e Krankheit a.** infect s.o. with a disease; **j-m e-n Prozeß a.** bring suit

against s.o.; **j-m etw a.** pin s.th. on s.o. ‖ §92 *intr* (an *dat*) adhere (to)

Anʹhänger –in §6 *mf* follower ‖ *m* (*Schmuck*) pendant; (aut) trailer

anhänglich [ˈanhɛŋlɪç] *adj* (an *acc*) attached (to), devoted (to)

Anhängsel [ˈanhɛŋzəl] *m* (-s;-) appendage, adjunct

anʹhauchen *tr* breathe on

anʹhäufen *tr* & *ref* pile up

Anʹhäufung *f* (-;-en) accumulation

anʹheben §94 *tr* lift (up); (*Lied*) strike up; (aut) jack up

anʹheften *tr* fasten; (*annähen*) stitch

anʹheilen *tr* & *intr* heal up

anheimʹfallen §72 *intr* (SEIN) (*dat*) devolve (upon)

anheimʹstellen *tr* (*dat*) leave (to)

Anʹhöhe *f* rise, hill

anʹhören *tr* listen to, hear ‖ *ref* —**sich gut a.** sound good

Anilin [aniˈlin] *n* (-s;) aniline

Animierʹdame *f* B-girl

animieren [aniˈmirən] *tr* encourage

Anis [aˈnis] *m* (-es;-e) anise

anʹkämpfen *intr* (gegen) struggle (against)

Anʹkauf *m* purchase

anʹkaufen *tr* purchase

Anker [ˈaŋkər] *m* (-s;-) anchor; (elec) armature; **vor A. gehen** drop anchor

ankern [ˈaŋkərn] *intr* anchor

Anʹklage *f* accusation, charge; (jur) indictment; **A. erheben** prefer charges; **die A. vertreten** be counsel for the prosecution; **unter A. stellen** indict

anʹklagen *tr* (*wegen*) accuse (of), charge (with), indict (for)

Anʹkläger –in §6 *mf* accuser; (jur) prosecutor

Anʹklageschrift *f* (bill of) indictment

anʹklammern *tr* (an *acc*) clip (to) ‖ *ref* (an *acc*) cling (to)

Anʹklang *m* (an *acc*) reminiscence (of), trace (of); **A. finden** be well received, catch on

anʹkleben *tr* (an *acc*) paste (on), stick (on) ‖ *intr* (HABEN & SEIN) stick

anʹkleiden *tr* & *ref* dress

anʹklingeln *tr* ring, call up ‖ *intr*—**bei j-m a.** ring s.o.'s doorbell

anʹklopfen *intr* (an *acc*) knock (on)

anʹknipsen *tr* switch on

anʹknüpfen *tr* tie, attach; (*Gespräch*) start ‖ *intr* (an *acc*) link up (with)

anʹkommen §99 *intr* (SEIN) (in *dat*) arrive (at); (bei) be well received (by); (bei) get a job (with); **es darauf a. lassen** take one's chances; **es kommt ganz darauf an, ob** it (all) depends on whether

Ankömmling [ˈankœmlɪŋ] *m* (-s;-e) newcomer, arrival

anʹkündigen *tr* announce, proclaim; **j-m etw a.** notify s.o. of s.th.

Anʹkündigung *f* (-;-en) announcement

Ankunft [ˈankunft] *f* (-;⸚e) arrival

anʹkurbeln *tr* crank up; **die Wirtschaft a.** prime the economy

anʹlachen *tr* laugh at

Anʹlage *f* (*Anordnung*) plan, layout;

(*Bau*) construction; (*Errichtung*) installation; (*Fabrik*) plant, works; (*Garten*) park, grounds; (*Fähigkeit*) ability, aptitude (*im Brief*) enclosure; in der A. enclosed

An'lagekapital *n* invested capital; permanent assets

an'langen *tr*—was mich anlangt as far as I'm concerned || *intr* (SEIN) arrive

An-laß ['anlas] *m* (-lasses;-lässe) occasion; (*Grund*) reason, motive; A. geben zu give rise to; ohne allen A. without any reason

an'lassen §104 *tr* (*Kleid*) keep on; (*Motor*) start (up); (*Wasser*) turn on; (*Pumpe*) prime; (*Stahl*) temper; j–n hart a. rebuke s.o. sharply || *ref* sich gut a. shape up

Anlasser ['anlasər] *m* (-s;-) starter

anläßlich ['anlɛslɪç] *prep* (*genit*) on the occasion of

An'lauf *m* run, start

an'laufen §105 *tr* run at; (*Hafen*) put into || *intr* (SEIN) (*Motor*) start up; (*Brille*) fog up; (*Metall*) tarnish; (*anwachsen*) accumulate; (*Schulden*) mount up; (*Film*) start, come on; angelaufen kommen come running up; ins Rollen a. (fig) get rolling; rot a. blush

an'legen *tr* (an *acc*) put (on), lay (on); (*Garten*; *Geld*) lay out; (*Kapital*) invest; (*Leitung*) install; (*Verband*) apply; (*Kolonie*) found || *ref*—sich a. mit have a run-in with || *intr* put ashore; moor

An'legeplatz *m* pier

an'lehnen *tr* (an *acc*) lean (against); (*Tür*) leave ajar || *ref* (an *acc*) lean (against); (fig) be based (on), rely (on)

Anleihe ['anlaɪ-ə] *f* (-;-n) loan

an'leiten *tr* (zu) guide (to); a. in (*dat*) instruct in

An'leitung *f* (-;-en) guidance; (*Lehre*) instruction

an'lernen *tr* train, break in

an'liegen §108 *intr* (*passen*) fit; (an *dat*) lie near, be adjacent (to); eng a. fit tight; j–m a. pester s.o. || **An'liegen** *n* (-s;-) request; ein A. an j–n haben have a request to make of s.o.

an'liegend *adj* adjacent; (*Kleid*) tight-fitting; (*im Brief*) enclosed

an'locken *tr* lure (on)

an'machen *tr* (*Licht*) switch on; (*Feuer*) light; (*zubereiten*) prepare; (an *acc*) attach (to)

an'malen *tr* paint

an'marschieren *intr* (SEIN) approach

anmaßen ['anmasən] *ref*—sich [*dat*] etw a. usurp s.th.; sich [*dat*] a., etw zu sein pretend to be s.th.

an'maßend *adj* arrogant

An'meldeformular *n* registration form

an'melden *tr* announce; report; (*Anspruch, Berufung*) file; (*Konkurs*) declare; (*Patent*) apply for; (educ) register; (sport) enter || *ref* (bei) make an appointment (with); (zu) enroll (in); (mil) report in

an'merken *tr* note down; j–m etw a. notice s.th. in s.o.

an'messen §70 *tr*—j–m etw a. measure s.o. for s.th.

An'mut *f* (-;) charm, attractiveness

an'mutig *adj* charming

an'nageln *tr* (an *acc*) nail (to)

an'nähen *tr* (an *acc*) sew on (to)

annähernd ['anne-ərnt] *adj* approximate

An'näherung *f* (-;-en) approach

An'näherungsversuch *m* (romantic) pass; attempt at reconciliation

an'näherungsweise *adv* approximately

An'nahme *f* (-;-n) acceptance; (*Vermutung*) assumption

annehmbar ['annembar] *adj* acceptable

an'nehmen §116 *tr* accept, take; (*vermuten*) assume, suppose, guess; (*Glauben*) embrace; (*Gewohnheit*) acquire; (*Gesetz*) pass; (*Kind*) adopt; (*Arbeiter*) hire; (*Farbe, Gestalt*) take on; (*Titel*) assume; etw als erwiesen a. take s.th. for granted || *ref* (*genit*) take care of

annektieren [anɛk'tirən] *tr* annex

Annexion [anɛ'ksjon] *f* (-;-en) annexation

Annonce [a'nõsə] *f* (-;-n) advertisement

annoncieren [anɔ̃'sirən] *tr* advertise

anöden ['anøːdən] *tr* bore to death

anonym [anɔ'nyːm] *adj* anonymous

an'ordnen *tr* arrange; (*befehlen*) order

an'packen *tr* grab hold of, seize; (*Problem*) tackle

an'passen *tr* fit; (*Worte*) adapt; || *ref* (dat or an *acc*) adapt oneself (to)

an'passungsfähig *adj* adaptable

an'pflanzen *tr* plant, cultivate

an'pflaumen *tr* (coll) kid

anpöbeln ['anpøːbəln] *tr* mob

an'pochen *tr* (an *acc*) knock (on)

An'prall *m* impact; (*e-s Angriffs*) brunt

an'prallen *intr* (SEIN) (gegen, an *acc*) collide (with), run (into)

an'preisen *tr* praise; j–m etw a. recommend s.th. to s.o.

An'probe *f* fitting, trying on

an'probieren *tr* try on

an'pumpen *tr*—j–n a. um hit s.o. for

an'quatschen *tr* talk the ears off

an'raten §63 *tr* advise, recommend

an'rechnen *tr* charge; hoch a. appreciate; j–m etw a. charge s.o. for s.th.

An'recht *n* (auf *acc*) right (to)

An'rede *f* address

an'reden *tr* address, speak to

an'regen *tr* stimulate; suggest

An'reiz *m* incentive

an'reizen *tr* stimulate; spur on

an'rennen §97 *intr* (SEIN) (gegen) run (into); angerannt kommen come running

an'richten *tr* (*Schaden*) cause, do; (culin) prepare

anrüchig ['anryçɪç] *adj* disreputable

an'rücken *intr* SEIN) approach

An'ruf *m* (telephone) call

an'rufen §122 *tr* call; (*Gott*) invoke; (*Schiff*) hail; (jur) appeal to; (mil) challenge; (telp) call up

an'rühren *tr* touch; (*Thema*) touch on; (*mischen*) stir

An'sage *f* announcement

an'sagen *tr* announce; (*Trumpf*) declare

An'sager **–in** §6 *mf* announcer

an'sammeln *tr* gather; (*anhäufen*) amass; (*Truppen*) concentrate || *ref* gather; (*Zinsen*) accumulate

ansässig ['anzɛsɪç] *adj* residing; a. **werden** (or **sich a. machen**) settle || **Ansässige** §5 *mf* resident

An'satz *m* start; (*Mundstück*) mouthpiece; (*Spur*) trace; (*in e-r Rechnung*) charge; (*Schätzung*) estimate; (geol) deposit; (mach) attachment; (math) statement

an'saugen §125 *tr* suck in; (*Pumpe*) prime

an'schaffen *tr* procure; (*kaufen*) get, purchase; **Kinder a.** (coll) have kids

an'schalten *tr* switch on

an'schauen *tr* look at

an'schaulich *adj* graphic

An'schauung *f* outlook, opinion; (*Vorstellung*) perception; (*Auffassung*) conception; (*Erkenntnis*) intuition; (*Betrachtung*) contemplation

An'schauungsbild *n* mental image

An'schauungsmaterial *n* visual aids

An'schein *m* appearance

an'scheinend *adj* apparent, seeming

an'scheinlich *adv* apparently

an'schicken *ref* get ready

an'schieben §130 *tr* give (*s.th.*) a push

anschirren ['anʃɪrən] *tr* harness

An'schlag *m* (an *acc*, gegen) striking (against); (*Anprall*) impact; (*Attentat*) attempt; (*Bekanntmachung*) notice; (*e-r Uhr*) stroke; (*e-r Taste*) hitting; (*Berechnung*) calculation; (*e-s Gewehrs*) firing position; (*Komplott*) plot; (mach) stop (*for arresting motion*); (mus) touch; (tennis) serve; **A. spielen** play tag

An'schlagbrett *n* bulletin board

an'schlagen §132 *tr* (an *acc*) fasten (to); (*Plakat*) post; (*Gewehr*) level; (*Tasse, usw.*) chip; (*Taste*) hit; (*einschätzen*) estimate; (*Gegner*) (box) have in trouble; **e-n anderen Ton a.** (fig) change one's tune || *ref* bump oneself || *intr* (*Wellen*) (an *acc*) beat against; (*Hund*) let out a bark; (*Arznei*) work

An'schlagzettel *m* notice; poster

an'schließen §76 *tr* padlock; (*anketten*) chain; (*verbinden*) connect; (*anfügen*) join; (com) affiliate; (elec) plug in || *ref* (dat, an *acc*) join, side with || *intr* (*Kleid*) be tight

an'schließend *adj* (an *acc*) subsequent (to); adjacent (to) || *adv* next, then

An'schluß *m* connection; (pol) annexation, union; **sie sucht A.** (coll) she is looking for a man

An'schlußbahn *f* (rr) branch line

An'schlußdose *f* (elec) receptacle

An'schlußschnur *f* (elec) cord

An'schlußzug *m* connection, connecting train

an'schmachten *tr* make eyes at

an'schmiegen *ref* (an *acc*) nestle up (to); (*Kleid*) (an *acc*) cling (to)

anschmiegsam ['anʃmiːkzam] *adj* accommodating; cuddly

an'schmieren *tr* smear; (coll) bamboozle

an'schnallen *tr* buckle || *ref* fasten one's seat belt

an'schnauzen *tr* snap at, bawl out

an'schneiden §106 *tr* cut into; (*Thema*) take up

An'schnitt *m* first cut

an'schrauben *tr* (an *acc*) screw on (to)

an'schreiben §62 *tr* write down; (*Spielstand*) mark; (dat) charge (to): (com) write to; **etw a. lassen** buy s.th. on credit

An'schreiber **–in** §6 *mf* scorekeeper

An'schreibetafel *f* scoreboard

an'schreien §135 *tr* yell at

An'schrift *f* address

An'schriftenmaschine *f* addressograph

anschuldigen ['anʃuldɪgən] *tr* accuse

an'schwärzen *tr* blacken, disparage

an'schwellen *tr* cause to swell; (*Unkosten, usw.*) swell || §119 *intr* (SEIN) swell up, puff up; increase

an'schwemmen *tr* wash (*s.th.*) ashore; (geol) deposit

an'sehen §138 *tr* look at; (fig) regard || **Ansehen** *n* (**–s;–**) appearance; (*Achtung*) reputation; (*Geltung*) prestige, authority; **von A.** by sight; of high repute

ansehnlich ['anzeːnlɪç] *adj* good-looking; (*beträchtlich*) considerable; (*eindrucksvoll*) imposing

An'sehung *f* (**–;**) **–in A.** (*genit*) in consideration of

anseilen ['anzaɪlən] *tr* rope together

an'setzen *tr* (an *acc*) put (on), apply (to): (*zum Kochen*) put on; (*Frist, Preis*) set; (*abschätzen*) rate; (*berechnen*) charge; (*Knospen*) put forth || *intr* begin; (*fett werden*) get fat

An'sicht *f* view; (*Meinung*) opinion; **zur A.** on approval

an'sichtig *adj*—a. **werden** (*genit*) catch sight of

An'sichtspostkarte *f* picture postcard

An'sichtssache *f* matter of opinion

An'sichtsseite *f* frontal view, façade

An'sichtssendung *f* article(s) sent on approval

ansiedeln *tr* & *ref* settle

An'siedler **–in** §6 *mf* settler

An'siedlung *f* (**–;–en**) settlement

An'sinnen *n* (**–s;–**) unreasonable demand

an'spannen *tr* stretch; (*Pferd*) hitch up; (fig) exert, strain

An'spannung *f* (**–;–en**) exertion, strain

an'speien §135 *tr* spit on

an'spielen *tr* (cards) lead with || *intr* (auf *acc*) allude (to); (mus) start playing; (sport) kick off, serve, break

An'spielung *f* (**–;–en**) allusion, hint

an'spitzen *tr* sharpen (*to a point*)

An'sporn *m* spur, stimulus

an'spornen *tr* spur

An'sprache *f* (an *acc*) address (to); **e–e A. halten** deliver an address

an'sprechen §64 *tr* speak to, address; (*Ziel, Punkt*) make out; **a. als** regard as; **j–n a. um** ask s.o. for || *intr* (dat) appeal to, interest; (auf *acc*) respond (to)

an'sprechend adj appealing
an'springen §142 tr leap at ‖ intr (SEIN) (Motor) start (up); **angesprungen kommen** come skipping along
an'spritzen tr sprinkle, squirt
An'spruch m claim; **A. haben auf** (acc) be entitled to; **A. machen** (or **erheben**) **auf** (acc), in **A. nehmen** demand, require, claim; **große Ansprüche stellen** ask too much
an'spruchslos adj unpretentious
an'spruchsvoll adj pretentious; (wählerisch) choosey, hard to please
an'spucken tr spit on
an'spülen tr wash ashore; (geol) deposit
an'stacheln tr goad on
Anstalt ['anˌʃtalt] f (-;-en) institution, establishment; **Anstalten treffen zu** make preparations for
An'stand m (Schicklichkeit) decency; (Bedenken) hesitation; (Einwendung) objection; (hunt) blind
anständig ['anˌʃtendɪç] adj decent
An'standsbesuch m formal call
An'standsdame f chaperone
An'standsgefühl n tact
an'standshalber adv out of politeness, out of human decency
an'standslos adv without fuss
an'starren tr stare at, gaze at
anstatt [anˈʃtat] prep (genit) instead of
an'stauen tr dam up ‖ ref pile up
an'staunen tr gaze at (in astonishment)
an'stecken tr stick on; (Ring) put on; (anzünden) set on fire; (Zigarette, Feuer) light; (pathol) infect ‖ ref become infected
an'steckend adj infectious; (durch Berührung) contagious
An'steckung f (-;-en) infection; (durch Berührung) contagion
an'stehen §146 intr (nach) line up (for); (zögern) hesitate; **j-m gut a.** fit s.o. well, become s.o.
an'steigen §148 intr (SEIN) rise, ascend; (zunehmen) increase, mount up
an'stellen tr (an acc) place (against); (beschäftigen) hire; (Versuch, usw.) (Vergleich) draw; (Heizung, Radio) turn on ‖ ref (nach) line up (for); **sich a., als ob** act as if; **stell dich nicht so dumm an!** don't play dumb!
anstellig ['anˌʃtelɪç] adj skilful
An'stellung f (-;-en) hiring; job
an'steuern tr steer for
Anstieg ['anˌʃtik] m (-[e]s;-e) rise; (e-s Weges) grade
an'stieren tr stare at, glower at
an'stiften tr instigate
An'stifter -in §6 mf instigator
an'stimmen tr (Lied) strike up; (Geheul) let out
An'stoß m impact; (Antrieb) impulse; (Ärgernis) offense; (sport) kickoff; **den A. geben zu** start
an'stoßen §150 tr bump against; (Ball) kick off; (Wagen) give a push; (mit dem Ellbogen) nudge, poke ‖ intr clink glasses; **a. an** (acc) adjoin; **bei j-m a.** shock s.o.; **mit den Gläsern a.** clink glasses; **mit der Zunge a.** lisp ‖

intr (SEIN)—**mit dem Kopf a. an** (acc) bump one's head against
an'stoßend adj adjoining
anstößig ['anˌʃtøsɪç] adj shocking
an'strahlen tr beam on; (fig) beam at; (mit Scheinwerfern) floodlight
an'streben tr strive for
an'streichen §85 tr paint; (Fehler) underline; (anhaken) check off
An'streicher m house painter
an'streifen tr brush against, graze
an'strengen tr exert; (Geist) tax; **e-n Prozeß a.** file suit ‖ intr be a strain
an'strengend adj strenuous, trying
An'strengung f (-;-en) exertion, effort
An'strich m (Farbe) paint; (Überzug) coat (of paint); (fig) tinge
An'sturm m assault, charge
antarktisch [antˈarktɪʃ] adj antarctic
an'tasten tr touch, finger
An'teil m share, portion; (Quote) quota; (st. exch.) share; **A. nehmen an** (dat) take part in; (fig) sympathize with
an'teilmäßig adj proportional
An'teilnahme f (-;) (an dat) participation (in); (Mitleid) sympathy
Antenne [anˈtenə] f (-;-n) antenna, aerial; (ent) antenna, feeler
Antibioti·kum [antibiˈotikum] n (-s; -ka [ka]) antibiotic
antik [anˈtik] adj ancient; classical ‖ **Antike** f (-;-n) (classical) antiquity; (Kunstwerk) antique
Anti'kenhändler -in §6 mf antique dealer
Antilope [antiˈlopə] f (-;-n) antelope
Antipa·thie [antipaˈti] f (-;-thien ['ti-ən]) antipathy
an'tippen tr & intr tap
Antiqua [anˈtikva] f (-;) roman (type)
Antiquar -in [antiˈkvar(ɪn)] §8 mf antique dealer; second-hand bookdealer
Antiquariat [antikvaˈrjat] n (-[e]s;-e) second-hand bookstore
antiquarisch [antiˈkvarɪʃ] adj second-hand
Antiquität [antikviˈtet] f (-;-en) antique
Antlitz ['antlɪts] m (-es;-e) (Bib, poet) countenance
Antrag ['antrak] m (-[e]s;⁼e) (Angebot) offer; (Vorschlag) proposal; (Gesuch) application; (pol) motion
an'tragen §132 tr offer; (vorschlagen) propose ‖ intr—**a. auf** (acc) make a motion for; propose, suggest
An'tragsformular n application form
Antragsteller -in ['antrakˌʃtelər(-ɪn)] §6 mf applicant; (parl) mover
an'treffen §151 tr meet; find at home
an'treiben §62 tr drive on, urge on; (Schiff) propel; (anreizen) egg on ‖ intr (SEIN) wash ashore
an'treten §152 tr (Amt, Erbschaft) enter (upon); (Reise) set out on; (Motorrad) start up ‖ intr (SEIN) take one's place; (mil) fall in; (sport) enter
An'trieb m (-s;-e) (Beweggrund) motive; (Anreiz) incentive; (mech) drive, impetus; **aus eigenem A.** on

one's own initiative; **neuen A. ver-**
leihen (*dat*) give fresh impetus to

An'tritt *m* (-[e]s;-e) beginning, start;
(*e-s Amtes*) entrance upon

an'tun §154 *tr* (*Kleid*) put on; **j-m**
etw a. do s.th. to s.o.

Antwort ['antvɔrt] *f* (-;-en) answer

antworten ['antvɔrtən] *intr* (auf *acc*)
reply (to), answer; **j-m a.** answer s.o.

an'vertrauen *tr* entrust; (*mitteilen*)
tell, confide

an'verwandt *adj* related || **Anver-**
wandte §5 *mf* relative

an'wachsen §155 *intr* (SEIN) begin to
grow; grow together; (*Wurzel schla-*
gen) take root; (*zunehmen*) increase

Anwalt ['anvalt] *m* (-[e]s;⸚e) attorney

An'waltschaft *f* legal profession, bar

an'wandeln *tr*—**mich wandelte die Lust**
an zu (*inf*) I got a yen to (*inf*); **was**
wandelte dich an? what got into
you?

An'wandlung *f* (-;-en) impulse, sudden feeling; (*von Zorn*) fit

An'wärter **-in** §6 *mf* candidate; (mil)
cadet, officer candidate

Anwartschaft ['anvart/aft] *f* (-;) expectancy; (*Aussicht*) prospect

an'wehen *tr* blow on || *intr* (SEIN)
drift

an'weisen §118 *tr* (*beauftragen*) instruct; (*zuteilen*) assign; (*Geld*) remit

An'weisung *f* (-;-en) instruction; assignment; (fin) money order

anwendbar ['anventbar] *adj* (auf *acc*)
applicable (to); (**für, zu**) that can be
used (for)

an'wenden §140 *tr* (auf *acc*) apply
(to); (**für, zu**) use (for)

An'wendung *f* (-;-en) application;
use

an'werben §149 *tr* recruit

an'werfen §160 *tr* (*Motor*) start up

An'wesen *n* estate, property; presence

anwesend ['anvezənt] *adj* present ||
Anwesende §5 *mf* person present;
verehrte Anwesende! ladies and
gentlemen!

An'wesenheit *f* (-;) presence

an'wurzeln *ref* & *intr* (SEIN) take root;
wie angewurzelt rooted to the spot

An'zahl *f* (-;) number, quantity

an'zahlen *tr* pay down || *intr* make a
down payment

an'zapfen *tr* tap

An'zeichen *n* indication, sign; (*Vorbe-*
deutung) omen; (pathol) symptom

Anzeige ['antsaigə] *f* (-;-n) (*Ankündi-*
gung) announcement, notice; (*Re-*
klame) ad; (med) advice; **kleine**
Anzeigen classified ads

an'zeigen *tr* announce; notify; (*Symp-*
tome, Fieber) show, indicate; (*bei*
der Polizei) report, inform against;
(*inserieren*) advertise

An'zeigenvermittlung *f* advertising
agency

an'zetteln *tr* (*Verschwörung*) hatch

an'ziehen §163 *tr* pull; (& fig) attract;
(*Kleid*) put on; (*e-e Person*) dress;
(*Riemen, Schraube*) tighten; (*Bremse*)
apply; (*Beispiele, Quellen*) quote ||

intr pull, start pulling; (*Preis*) go up;
(chess) go first

An'ziehung *f* (-;-en) attraction; (*Zitat*)
quotation

An'ziehungskraft *f* appeal; (& phys)
attraction; (astr) gravitation

An'zug *m* suit; (mil) uniform; **in A.**
sein (*Armee*) be approaching;
(*Sturm*) be gathering; (*Gefahr*) be
imminent

anzüglich ['antsyliç] *adj* offensive; **a.**
werden become personal

an'zünden *tr* set on fire; (*Feuer*) light

an'zweifeln *tr* doubt, question

apart [a'part] *adj* charming; (coll)
cute

Apathie [apa'ti] *f* (-;) apathy

apathisch [a'pati∫] *adj* apathetic

Apfel ['apfəl] *m* (-s;⸚) apple

Ap'felkompott *n* stewed apples

Ap'felmus *n* applesauce

Ap'felsaft *m* apple juice

Apfelsine [apfəl'zinə] *f* (-;-n) orange

Ap'feltorte *f* apple tart; **gedeckte A.**
apple pie

Ap'felwein *m* cider

Apostel [a'pɔstəl] *m* (-s;-) apostle

Apostroph [apo'strof] *m* (-[e]s;-e)
apostrophe

Apotheke [apo'tekə] *f* (-;-n) pharmacy

Apotheker **-in** [apo'tekər(ın)] §6 *mf*
druggist

Apothe'kerwaren *pl* drugs

Apparat [apa'rat] *m* (-[e]s;-e) apparatus, device; (phot) camera; (rad,
telv) set; (telp) telephone; **am A.!**
speaking

Appell [a'pɛl] *m* (-[e]s;-e) appeal;
(mil) roll call; (mil) inspection

appellieren [apɛ'lirən] *intr* (& jur)
(an *acc*) appeal (to)

Appetit [ape'tit] *m* (-[e]s;-e) appetite

Appetit'brötchen *n* canapé

appetit'lich *adj* appetizing; (*Mädchen*)
attractive

applaudieren [aplau'dirən] *tr* & *intr*
applaud

Applaus [a'plaus] *m* (-es;-e) applause

Appretur [apre'tur] *f* (-;-en) (tex)
finish

Aprikose [aprı'kozə] *f* (-;-n) apricot

April [a'prıl] *m* (-[s];-e) April

Aquarell [akva'rɛl] *n* (-[e]s;-e) watercolor; watercolor painting

Aqua·rium [a'kvarjum] *n* (-s;-rien
[rı-ən]) aquarium

Äqua·tor [e'kvatɔr] *m* (-s;-toren
['torən]) equator

Ära ['era] *f* (-;Ären ['erən]) era

Araber **-in** ['arabər(ın)] §6 *mf* Arab

Arabien [a'rabjən] *n* (-s;) Arabia

arabisch [a'rabı∫] *adj* Arabian; (*Zif-*
fer) Arabic

Arbeit ['arbait] *f* (-;-en) work

arbeiten ['arbaitən] *tr* & *intr* work

Arbeiter ['arbaitər] *m* (-s;-) worker;
A. und Unternehmer *pl* labor and
management

Ar'beiterausstand *m* walkout, strike

Ar'beitergewerkschaft *f* labor union

Arbeiterin ['arbaitərın] *f* (-;-nen)
working woman, working girl

Ar'beiterschaft *f* (-;) working class
Arbeitertum ['arbaɪtərtum] *n* (-s;) working class, workers
Ar'beitgeber -in §6 *mf* employer
Ar'beitnehmer -in §6 *mf* employee
arbeitsam ['arbaɪtzam] *adj* industrious
Ar'beitsanzug *m* overalls; (mil) fatigue clothes, fatigues
Ar'beitseinkommen *n* earned income
Ar'beitseinstellung *f* work stoppage
ar'beitsfähig *adj* fit for work
Ar'beitsgang *m* process; operation (*single step of a process*)
Ar'beitsgemeinschaft *f* team; (educ) workshop
Ar'beitsgerät *n* equipment, tools
Ar'beitskommando *n* (mil) work detail
Ar'beitskraft *f* labor force; Arbeitskräfte personnel
Ar'beitslager *n* work camp
Ar'beitsleistung *f* (work) quota; (*e-r Maschine, Fabrik*) output
Ar'beitslohn *m* wages, pay
ar'beitslos *adj* unemployed
Ar'beitslosenunterstützung *f* unemployment compensation
Ar'beitslosigkeit *f* unemployment
Ar'beitsmarkt *m* labor market
Ar'beitsminister *m* secretary of labor
Ar'beitsministerium *n* department of labor
Ar'beitsnachweis *m*, Ar'beitsnachweisstelle *f* employment agency
Ar'beitsniederlegung *f* walkout, strike
ar'beitsparend *adj* labor-saving
Ar'beitspause *f* break, rest period
Arbeitspferd *n* (& *fig*) workhorse
Ar'beitsplatz *m* job, place of employment
Ar'beitsrecht *n* labor law
Ar'beitsscheu *adj* work-shy, lazy
Ar'beitsschicht *f* shift
Ar'beitsstätte *f* place of employment; workshop; yard
Ar'beitsstelle *f* job, position
Ar'beitstag *m* workday
Ar'beitsvermittlung *f* employment agency
Ar'beitsversäumnis *n* absenteeism
Ar'beitszeug *n* tools
Ar'beitszimmer *n* study; workroom
archaisch [ar'çaɪʃ] *adj* archaic
Archäologe [arçɛo'logə] *m* (-n;-n) archaeologist
Archäologie [arçɛolɔ'gi] *f* (-;) archaeology
Archäologin [arçɛo'logɪn] *f* (-;-nen) archaeologist
archäologisch [arçɛo'logɪʃ] *adj* archaeological
Architekt -in [arçɪ'tɛkt(ɪn)] §7 *mf* architect
Architektur [arçɪtɛk'tur] *f* (-;-en) architecture
Ar-chiv [ar'çif] *n* (-[e]s;-chive ['çivə]) archives; (*für Zeitungen*) morgue
Areal [are'ɑl] *n* (-s;-e) area
Are-na [a'rena] *f* (-;-nen [nən]) arena
arg [ark] *adj* (ärger ['ergər]; ärgste ['erkstə] §9) bad, evil, wicked; (coll) awful; (*schlimm*) grave; (*Raucher*)

heavy ǁ Arg *n* (-s;) malice, cunning ǁ Arge §5 *m* Evil One ǁ §5 *n* evil
Argentinien [argen'tinjən] *n* (-s;) Argentina
Argentinier -in [argen'tinjər(ɪn)] §6 *mf* Argentinean
Ärger ['ergər] *m* (-s;) irritation; mit j–m A. haben have trouble with s.o.
är'gerlich *adj* (auf *acc* or über *acc*) annoyed (at); irritating, annoying
ärgern ['ergərn] *tr* annoy ǁ *ref* (über *acc*) be annoyed (at)
Ärgernis ['ergərnɪs] *n* (-ses;-se) scandal, offense; (*Mißstand*) nuisance
Arg'list *f* craft, cunning
arg'listig *adj* crafty, cunning
arg'los *adj* guileless; (*nichtsahnend*) unsuspecting
Argwohn ['arkvon] *m* (-s;) suspicion
argwöhnen ['arkvønən] *tr* suspect
argwöhnisch ['arkvønɪʃ] *adj* suspicious
Arie ['arjə] *f* (-;-n) aria
Arier -in ['arjər(ɪn)] §6 Aryan
arisch ['arɪʃ] *adj* Aryan
Aristokrat [arɪstɔ'krɑt] *m* (-en;-en) aristocrat
Aristokra-tie [arɪstɔkra'ti] *f* (-;-tien ['ti-ən]) aristocracy
Aristokratin [arɪstɔ'krɑtɪn] *f* (-;-nen) aristocrat
Arithmetik [arɪt'metɪk] *f* (-;) arithmetic
Arktis ['arktɪs] *f* (-;) Arctic
arktisch ['arktɪʃ] *adj* arctic
arm [arm] *adj* (ärmer ['ermər], ärmste ['ermstə] §9 (an *dat*) poor in) ǁ Arm *m* (-[e]s;-e) arm; (*e-s Flusses*) branch
Armatur [arma'tur] *f* (-;-en) armature; Armaturen fittings, mountings
Arma'tu/renbrett *n* instrument panel; (aut) dashboard
Arm'band *n* (-[e]s;-er) bracelet; watchband; (*Armabzeichen*) brassard
Arm'banduhr *f* wrist watch
Arm'binde *f* brassard; (med) sling
Ar-mee [ar'me] *f* (-;-meen ['me-ən]) army
Ärmel ['erməl] *m* (-s;-) sleeve
Är'melaufschlag *m* cuff
Är'melkanal *m* English Channel
är'mellos *adj* sleeveless
Armen- [armən] *comb.fm.* for the poor
Ar'menhaus *n* poorhouse
Armenien [ar'menjən] *n* (-s;) Armenia
armenisch [ar'menɪʃ] *adj* Armenian
Ar'menpflege *f* public assistance
Ar'menunterstützung *f* public assistance, welfare
Ar'menviertel *n* slums
Armes'tin/dermiene *f* hangdog look
Arm'lehne *f* arm, armrest
Arm'leuchter *m* candelabrum
ärmlich ['ermlɪç] *adj* poor, humble
arm'selig *adj* poor, wretched; (*kläglich*) paltry
Armut ['armut] *f* (-;) poverty
Arm'zeichen *n* semaphore
Aro-ma [a'roma] *n* (-s;-men [mən], -mata [mata]) aroma
aromatisch [aro'mɑtɪç] *adj* aromatic
Arrest [a'rest] *m* (-[e]s;-e) arrest;

(in der Schule) detention; *(jur)* impounding, seizure

Arsch [arʃ] *m* (-es;⁼e) *(sl)* ass

Arsch/backe *f* *(sl)* buttock

Arsch/kriecher *m* *(sl)* brown-noser

Arsch/lecker *m* *(sl)* brown-noser

Arsen [ar'zen] *n* (-s;) arsenic

Arsenal [arze'nɑl] (-s;-e) arsenal

Art [art] *f* (-;-en) sort, kind; nature; *(Rasse)* race, breed; species; *(Weise)* manner; *(Verfahren)* procedure; *(Muster)* model; **das ist keine Art!** that's no way to behave!

art/eigen *adj* true to type

arten ['artən] *intr* (SEIN)—a. nach take after

Arterie [ar'terjə] *f* (-;-n) artery

artig ['artɪç] *adj* *(brav)* good, well-behaved; *(höflich)* polite

Artikel [ar'tikəl] (-s;-) (com, gram, journ) article

Artillerie [artɪlə'ri] *f* (-;) artillery

Artillerie/aufklärer *m* artillery spotter

Artischocke [artɪ'ʃɔkə] *f* (-;-n) artichoke

Artist –in [ar'tɪst(ɪn)] §7 *mf* artist; *(beim Zirkus)* performer

Arznei [arts'naɪ] *f* (-;-en) medicine, medication, drug

Arznei/kraut *n* herb, medicinal plant

Arznei/kunde *f*, Arznei/kunst *f* pharmaceutics; pharmacology

Arznei/mittel *n* medication

Arzt [artst] *m* (-[e]s;⁼e) doctor

Ärztin ['ɛrtstɪn] *f* (-;-nen) doctor

ärztlich ['ɛrtstlɪç] *adj* medical

As [as] *n* (Asses; Asse) ace ‖ *n* (-;-) (mus) A flat

Asbest [as'bɛst] *m* (-[e]s;-e) asbestos

asch/bleich *adj* ashen, pale

Asche ['aʃə] *f* (-;-n) ash(es), cinders

Aschen– *comb.fm.* ash; cinder; funerary

A/schenbahn *f* cinder track

A/schenbecher *m* ashtray

Aschenbrödel ['aʃənbrødəl] *n* (-s;-) Cinderella; drudge

Aschermittwoch [aʃər'mɪtvɔx] *m* (-s; -e) Ash Wednesday

asch/fahl *adj* ashen, pale

äsen ['ɛzən] *intr* graze, feed

asiatisch [azɪ'atɪʃ] *adj* Asiatic

Asien ['ɑzjən] *n* (-s;) Asia

Asket [as'ket] *m* (-en;-en) ascetic

asketisch [as'ketɪʃ] *adj* ascetic

Asphalt [as'falt] *m* (-[e]s;-e) asphalt

asphaltieren [asfal'tirən] *tr* asphalt

Asphalt/pappe *f* tar paper

aß[as] *pret* of essen

Assistent –in [asɪs'tent(ɪn)] §7 *mf* assistant

Assistenz [asɪs'tents] *f* (-;-en) assistance

Assistenz/arzt *m*, Assistenz/ärztin *f* intern

Ast [ast] *m* (-es;⁼e) bough, branch; *(im Holz)* knot, knob

ästhetisch [ɛs'tetɪʃ] *adj* esthetic(al)

Asthma ['astma] *n* (-s;) asthma

ast/rein *adj* free of knots; **nicht ganz a.** (coll) not quite kosher

Astrologe [astro'logə] *m* (-n;-n) astrologer

Astrologie [astrolo'gi] *f* (-;) astrology

Astronaut [astro'naut] *m* (-en;-en) astronaut

Astronom [astro'nom] *m* (-en;-en) astronomer

Astronomie [astrono'mi] (-;) astronomy

astronomisch [astro'nomɪʃ] *adj* astronomic(al)

Astrophysik [astrofy'zik] *f* (-;) astrophysics

Asyl [a'zyl] *n* (-[e]s;-e) asylum, sanctuary; *(Obdach)* shelter; **ohne A.** homeless

Atelier [ate'lje] *n* (-s;-s) studio

Atem ['ɑtəm] *m* (-s;) breath

A/tembeklemmung *f* shortness of breath

A/temholen *n* (-s;) respiration

a/temlos *adj* breathless

A/temnot *f* breathing difficulty

A/tempause *f* breathing spell

a/temraubend *adj* breath-taking

A/temzug *m* breath

Atheismus [ate'ɪsmus] *m* (-;) atheism

Atheist –in [ate'ɪst(ɪn)] §7 *mf* atheist

Äther ['ɛtər] *m* (-s;) ether

Athlet [at'let] *m* (-en;-en) athlete

Athletik [at'letɪk] *f* (-;) athletics

Athletin [at'letɪn] *f* (-;-nen) athlete

athletisch [at'letɪʃ] *adj* athletic

Atlantik [at'lantɪk] *m* (-s;) Atlantic

At-las ['atlas] *m* (-;) (myth) Atlas ‖ *m* (-lasses; -lanten ['lantən] & -lasse) atlas ‖ *m* (- & -lasses;-lasse) satin

atmen ['atmən] *tr* & *intr* breathe

Atmosphäre [atmo'sfɛrə] *f* (-;-n) (& fig) atmosphere

atmosphärisch [atmo'sfɛrɪʃ] *adj* atmospheric; **atmosphärische Störungen** (rad) static

At/mung *f* (-;) breathing

Atom [a'tom] *n* (-s;-e) atom

Atom– *comb. fm.* atom, atomic

Atom/abfall *m* fallout; atomic waste

atomar [ato'mar] *adj* atomic

Atom/bau *m* atomic structure

atom/betrieben *adj* atomic-powered

Atom/bombe *f* atomic bomb

Atom/bombenversuch *m* atomic test

Atom/-Epoche *f* atomic age

Atom/kern *m* atomic nucleus

Atom/müll *m* atomic waste

Atom/regen *m* fallout

Atom/schutt *m* atomic waste

ätsch [etʃ] *interj* (to express gloating) serves you right!, good for you!

Attentat [aten'tat] *n* (-s;-e) attempt *(on s.o.'s life)*; assassination

Attentäter –in [aten'tetər(ɪn)] §6 *mf* assailant, would-be assassin; assassin

Attest [a'test] *n* (-es;-e) certificate

attestieren [ates'tirən] *tr* attest (to)

Attrappe [a'trapə] *f* (-;-n) dummy

Attribut [atrɪ'but] *n* (-[e]s;-e) attribute; (gram) attributive

atzen ['atsən] *tr* feed

ätzen ['etsən] *tr* corrode; (med) cauterize (typ) etch

ät/zend *adj* corrosive; caustic

Au [au] *f* (-;-en) (poet) mead, meadow

au *interj* owl, ouch!; oh!
Aubergine [ober'ʒin(ə)] *f* (-;-n) eggplant
auch [aux] *adv* also, too; (*selbst*) even
Audienz [au'djents] *f* (-;-en) audience; (*jur*) hearing
auf [auf] *adv* up; **auf und ab** up and down; **von Kind auf** from childhood on || *prep* (*dat*) on, upon; **auf der ganzen Welt** in the whole world; **auf der Universität** at the university || *prep* (*acc*) on; up; to; **auf den Bahnhof gehen** go to the station; **auf deutsch** in German; **drei aufs Dutzend** three to a dozen; **es geht auf vier Uhr zu** it's going on four; **Monat auf Monat** verging month after month passed || *interj* get up! || **Auf** *n*—**das Auf und Nieder** the ups and downs
auf'arbeiten *tr* (*Rückstände*) catch up on; (*verbrauchen*) use up; (*erneuern*) renovate; (*mach*) recondition || *ref* work one's way up
auf'atmen *intr* breathe a sigh of relief
aufbauschen ['aufbarzən] *tr* lay out
Auf'bau *m* (-[e]s;) construction; structure; organization; (*Anlage*) arrangement, setup; (*chem*) synthesis || *m* (-[e]s;-ten) structure; (*aer*) framework; (*aut*) body; (*naut*) superstructure
auf'bauen *tr* erect; (*Organization*) establish; (*chem*) synthesize; (*mach*) assemble || *ref*—**er baute sich vor mir auf** he planted himself in front of me; **sich** [*dat*] **e-e Existenz a.** make a life for oneself
auf'bäumen *ref* rear; (fig) rebel
auf'bauschen *tr* puff up; (fig) exaggerate
auf'begehren *intr* flare up; (gegen) protest (against), rebel (against)
auf'behalten §90 *tr* keep on; keep open
auf'bekommen §99 *tr* (*Tür*) get open; (*Knoten*) loosen; (*Hausaufgabe*) be assigned
auf'bereiten *tr* prepare, process
auf'bessern *tr* (*Gehalt*) improve, raise
auf'bewahren *tr* keep, store; **das Gepäck a. lassen** check one's baggage
auf'bieten §58 *tr* summon; (*Brautpaar*) announce the banns of; (mil) call up
auf'binden §58 *tr* tie up; (*lösen*) untie; **j-m etw a.** put s.th. over on s.o.
auf'blähen *tr* inflate, distend
auf'blasen §61 *tr* inflate || *ref* get puffed up
auf'bleiben §62 *intr* (SEIN) (*Tür*) stay open; (*wachen*) stay up
auf'blenden *intr* turn on the high beam
auf'blicken *intr* glance up
auf'blitzen *intr* (HABEN & SEIN) flash
auf'blühen *intr* (SEIN) begin to bloom
auf'bocken *tr* (aut) jack up
auf'brauchen *tr* use up
auf'brausen *intr* (HABEN & SEIN) bubble, seethe; (*Wind*) roar; (fig) flare up
auf'brausend *adj* effervescent; irascible
auf'brechen §64 *tr* break up; break open; (hunt) eviscerate || *intr* (SEIN)

burst open; (*fortgehen*) (nach) set out (for)
auf'bringen §65 *tr* bring up; (*Geld, Truppen*) raise; (*Schiff*) capture; (*Kraft*) gather; (*Mut*) get up; (*erzürnen*) infuriate
Auf'bruch *m* departure
auf'brühen *tr* bring to a boil
auf'bügeln *tr* iron, press; refresh (*one's knowledge of s.th.*)
auf'bürden ['aufbYrdən] *tr*—**j-m etw a.** saddle s.o. with s.th.
auf'decken *tr* uncover; (*Bett*) turn down; (*Tischtuch*) spread
auf'drängen *tr* force open; **j-m etw a.** force s.th. on s.o.
auf'drehen *tr* turn up; (*Uhr*) wind; (*Hahn*) turn on; (*Schraube*) unscrew; (*Strick*) untwist || *intr* (*Wagen*) increase speed; (coll) step on it, get a move on
auf'dringlich *adj* pushy; (*Farben*) gaudy
Auf'druck *m* print, imprint
auf'drücken *tr* impress, imprint, affix; (*öffnen*) squeeze open
aufeinan'der *adv* one after the other
Aufeinan'derfolge *f* succession; series
aufeinan'derfolgen *intr* (SEIN) follow one another
aufeinan'derfolgend *adj* successive
Aufenthalt ['aufenthalt] *m* (-[e]s;-e) holdup, delay; ohne A. nonstop
Auf'enthaltsgenehmigung *f* residence permit
Auf'enthaltsort *m* (*Wohnsitz*) residence; (*Verbleib*) whereabouts
Auf'enthaltsraum *m* lounge
auf'erlegen *tr* impose || *ref*—**sich** [*dat*] **die Pflicht a. zu** (*inf*) make it one's duty to (*inf*); **sich** [*dat*] **Zwang a.** müssen have to restrain oneself
auf'erstehen §146 *intr* (SEIN) rise (from the dead)
Auf'erstehung *f* (-;) resurrection
auf'erwecken *tr* raise from the dead
auf'erziehen §163 *tr* bring up, raise
auf'essen §70 *tr* eat up
auf'fädeln *tr* (*Perlen*) string
auf'fahren §71 *tr* (*Fahrzeuge*) park; (*Geschütze*) bring up; (*Wein, Speisen*) serve up || *intr* (SEIN) rise, mount; (*im Auto*) pull up; (*in Erregung*) jump (up); (arti) move into position; **a. auf** (*acc*) run into
Auf'fahrt *f* ascent; (*Zufahrt*) driveway
auf'fallen §72 *intr* (SEIN) be conspicuous; **j-m a.** strike s.o.
auf'fallend, auf'fällig *adj* striking; noticeable; (*Farben*) loud, gaudy
auf'fangen §73 *tr* (*Ball, Worte*) catch; (*Briefe, Nachrichten*) intercept
auf'fassen *tr* comprehend; (*deuten*) interpret; (*Perlen*) string
Auf'fassung *f* (-;-en) understanding; interpretation; (*Meinung*) view
auf'finden §59 *tr* find (*after searching*)
auf'fliegen §57 *intr* (SEIN) fly up; (*Tür*) fly open; (*scheitern*) fail; a. lassen break up (*e.g., a gang*)
auf'fordern *tr* call upon, ask
Auf'forderung *f* (-;-en) invitation; (jur) summons

auf/frischen tr freshen up, touch up

auf/führen tr (Bau) erect; (Schauspiel) present; (eintragen) enter; (Zeugen) produce; (anführen) cite; (mil) post; einzeln a. itemize || ref behave, act

Auf/führung f (-;-en) erection; performance; entry; specification; behavior

auf/füllen tr fill up

Auf/gabe f task, job; (e-s Briefes) mailing; (des Gepäcks) checking; (e-r Bestellung) placing; (e-s Amtes, e-s Geschäfts) giving up; (educ) homework; (jur) waiver; (math) problem; (mil) assignment

auf/gabeln tr (& coll) pick up

Auf/gang m ascent; (Treppe) stairs; (astr) rising

auf/geben §80 tr give up; (Amt) resign; (Post) mail; (Gepäck) check in; (Anzeige) place; (Preis) quote; (Arbeit) assign; (Telegramm) send

auf/geblasen adj (fig) uppity

Auf/gebot n public notice; (eccl) banns; (mil) call-up

auf/gebracht adj angry, irate

auf/gedonnert adj (coll) dolled up

auf/gehen §82 intr (SEIN) rise; (Tür) open; (Pflanzen) come up; (arith) go into; genau a. come out exactly

auf/geklärt adj enlightened

auf/geknöpft adj (coll) chatty

auf/gekratzt adj (coll) chipper

Auf/geld n surcharge; premium

auf/gelegt adj (zu) disposed (to)

auf/geräumt adj (fig) good-humored

auf/geschlossen adj open-minded; (für) receptive (to)

auf/geschmissen adj (coll) stuck

auf/gestaut adj pent-up

auf/geweckt adj smart, bright

auf/geworfen adj (Lippen) pouting; (Nase) turned-up

auf/gießen §76 tr (auf acc) pour (on); (Tee, Kaffee) make, brew

auf/graben §87 tr dig up

auf/greifen §88 tr pick up; (Dieb) catch; (fig) take up

auf/haben §98 tr (Hut) have on; (Tür, Mund) have open; (Aufgabe) have to do

auf/hacken tr hoe up

auf/haken tr unhook

auf/halten §90 tr hold up; (Tür) hold open; (anhalten) stop, delay || ref stay; (wohnen) live; sich über etw a. find fault with s.th.

Auf/hängeleine f clothesline

auf/hängen §92 tr hang up; j-m etw a. push s.th. on s.o.; (Wertloses) palm s.th. off on s.o.

auf/häufen tr & ref pile up

auf/heben §94 tr lift up, pick up; (bewahren) preserve; (ungültig machen) cancel; (Gesetz) repeal; (ausgleichen) cancel out, offset; (Strafe, Belagerung) lift; gut aufgehoben sein be in good hands

auf/heitern tr cheer up || ref cheer up; (Gesicht) brighten; (Wetter) clear up

auf/hellen ref & intr brighten

auf/hetzen tr incite, egg on

auf/holen tr hoist; (Verspätung) make up for || intr catch up

auf/horchen intr prick up one's ears

auf/hören intr stop, quit

auf/jauchzen intr shout for joy

auf/kaufen tr buy up; (Markt) corner

auf/klären tr clear up; enlighten; (mil) reconnoitre || ref clear up; (Gesicht) light up, brighten

Auf/klärer m (-s;-) (aer) reconnaissance plane; (mil) scout

Auf/klärung f (-;-en) explanation; enlightenment; (mil) reconnaissance

Auf/klärungsbuch n sex-education book

Auf/klärungsspähtrupp m reconnaissance patrol

auf/kleben tr (auf acc) paste (onto)

auf/klinken tr unlatch

auf/knacken tr crack open

auf/knöpfen tr unbutton

auf/knüpfen tr (lösen) untie; (hängen) (coll) string up

auf/kochen tr & intr boil

auf/kommen §99 intr (SEIN) come up, rise; (Gedanke) occur; (Mode) come into fashion; (Schiff) appear on the horizon; a. für answer for; (Kosten) defray; a. gegen stand up against, cope with; a. von recover from || Aufkommen n (-s;) rise; recovery

auf/krempeln tr roll up

auf/kreuzen intr (coll) show up

auf/kriegen tr see aufbekommen

auf/lachen intr burst out laughing

auf/laden §103 tr load up; (Batterie) charge || ref—sich [dat] etw a. saddle oneself with s.th.

Auf/lage f edition, printing; (e-r Zeitung) circulation; (Steuer) tax; (Stütze) rest, support

auf/lassen §104 tr leave open; (Fabrik, Bergwerk) abandon

auf/lauern intr (dat) lie in wait (for)

Auf/lauf m gathering, crowd; (Tumult) riot; (com) accumulation; (culin) soufflé

auf/laufen §105 intr (SEIN) rise; (anwachsen) accrue; (Schiff) get stranded; (Panzer) get stuck

auf/leben intr (SEIN) revive

auf/lecken tr lick up

auf/legen tr (auf acc) put (on); (Steuer) impose; (Hörer) hang up; (Buch) publish; (Karten) lay on the table; (Liste) make available for inspection; (Anleihe) float; (Faß Bier) put on || intr (telp) hang up

auf/lehnen tr (auf acc) lean (on) || ref (auf acc) lean (on); (gegen) rebel (against)

Auf/lehnung f (-;-en) rebellion; resistance

auf/lesen §107 tr pick up, gather

auf/liegen §108 intr (auf dat) lie (on); (zur Ansicht) be displayed

auf/lockern tr loosen; (Eintönigkeit, Vortrag) break (up)

auf/lösbar adj soluble; solvable

auf/lösen tr untie; (öffnen) loosen; (entwirren) disentangle; (Versammlung) break up; (Heer) disband; (Ehe) dissolve; (Verbindung) sever; (Firma) liquidate; (Rätsel) solve;

(*zerlegen*) break down; dissolve; (*entziffern*) decode; **ganz aufgelöst** all out of breath

Auf'lösung *f* (-;-en) solution; disentanglement; (*e-r Versammlung, Ehe*) breakup; (*Zerfall*) disintegration; (*von Beziehungen*) severance; (com) liquidation

auf'machen *tr* open (up); (*Geschäft*) open; (*Dampf*) get up; (coll) do up (*e.g., big, tastefully*) || *ref* (*Wind*) rise; (**nach**) set out (for)

Auf'machung *f* (-;-en) layout, format; (*Kleidung*) outfit

Auf'marsch *m* parade; (mil) concentration; (*zum Gefecht*) (mil) deployment

auf'marschieren *intr* (SEIN) parade; (*strategisch*) assemble; (*taktisch*) deploy

auf'merken *tr* (auf *acc*) pay attention (to)

aufmerksam ['aufmɛrkzam] *adj* (auf *acc*) attentive (to)

Auf'merksamkeit *f* (-;) attention

auf'möbeln *tr* (coll) dress up; (*anherrschen*) (sl) chew out; (*aufmuntern*) (coll) pep up || *ref* (coll) doll up

auf'muntern *tr* cheer up

Auf'nahme *f* (-;-n) taking up; (*Empfang*) reception; (*Zulassung*) admission; (*von Beziehungen*) establishment; (*Inventur*) stock-taking; (electron) recording; (phot) photograph

Auf'nahmeapparat *m* camera; recorder

Auf'nahmegerät *n* camera; recorder

Auf'nahmeprüfung *f* entrance exam

auf'nehmen §116 *tr* take up; (*erfassen*) grasp; (*Diktat*) take down; (*Gast*) receive; (*Inventar*) take; (*Geld*) borrow; (*Anleihe*) float; (*Spur*) pick up; (*Beziehungen*) establish; (*eintragen*) enter; (*durch Tonband, Schallplatte*) record; (geog) map out; (phot) take

auf'opfern *tr* offer up, sacrifice

auf'päpeln *tr* spoon-feed

auf'passen *intr* pay attention; look out; **paß auf!** watch out!

auf'pflanzen *tr* set up; (*Seitengewehr*) fix

auf'platzen *intr* (SEIN) burst (open)

auf'polieren *tr* polish up

auf'prägen *tr* (auf *acc*) (& fig) impress (on)

auf'prallen *intr* (auf *acc*) crash (into)

auf'pumpen *tr* pump up

auf'putschen *tr* incite; (coll) pep up

auf'putzen *tr* dress up; clean up || *ref* dress up

auf'raffen *tr* pick up || *ref* stand up; (fig) pull oneself together

auf'ragen *intr* tower, stand high

auf'räumen *tr* (*Zimmer*) straighten up; (*wegräumen*) clear away || *intra—a.* **mit** do away with, get rid of

Auf'räumungsarbeiten *pl* clearance

auf'rechnen *tr* add up; (acct) balance

auf'recht *adj* upright, erect

auf'rechterhalten §90 *tr* maintain

auf'regen *tr* excite, stir up; (*unruhig machen*) disturb, upset

Auf'regung *f* (-;-en) excitement

---

auf'reiben §62 *tr* rub off; (*wundreiben*) rub sore; (*vertilgen*) destroy; (*Heer*) grind up; (*Kräfte*) sap; (*Nerven*) fray || *ref* worry onself to death

auf'reibend *adj* wearing, exhausting

auf'reihen *tr* string, thread

auf'reißen §53 *tr* tear open; (*Straße*) tear up; (*Tür*) fling open; (*Augen*) open wide; (*zeichnen*) sketch || *intr* (SEIN) split open, crack

auf'reizen *tr* provoke, incite; (*stark erregen*) excite

auf'reizend *adj* provoking, annoying; (*Rede*) inflammatory; (*Anblick*) sexy

auf'richten *tr* erect, set up; (*trösten*) comfort || *ref* sit up

auf'richtig *adj* upright, sincere

Auf'richtigkeit *f* sincerity

auf'riegeln *tr* unbolt

Auf'riß *m* front view

auf'rollen *tr* roll up; (*entfalten*) unroll

auf'rücken *intr* (SEIN) advance; (**zu**) be promoted (to)

Auf'ruf *m* (*Aufschrei*) outcry; (*Aufforderung*) call; (mil) call-up

auf'rufen §122 *tr* call on; (*appellieren an*) appeal to; (*Banknoten*) call in

Auf'ruhr *m* uproar; (*Tumult*) riot

auf'rühren *tr* stir up

aufrührerisch ['aufryrərɪʃ] *adj* inflammatory, rebellious; (mil) mutinous

auf'runden *tr* round out

auf'rüsten *tr* & *intr* arm; rearm

Auf'rüstung *f* (-;-en) rearmament

auf'rütteln *tr* wake up (*by shaking*)

auf'sagen *tr* recite; (*ein Ende machen mit*) terminate

auf'sammeln *tr* gather up

aufsässig ['aufzesɪç] *adj* hostile; (*widerspenstig*) rebellious

Auf'satz *m* superstructure; (*auf dem Tische*) centerpiece; (*Schularbeit*) essay, composition; (*in der Zeitung*) article; (golf) tee; (mil) gun sight

auf'saugen §125 *tr* suck up; absorb

auf'schauen *intr* look up

auf'scheuchen *tr* scare up

auf'scheuern *tr* scrape

auf'schichten *tr* stack (up), pile (up)

auf'schieben §130 *tr* push up; (*Tür*) push open; (*verschieben*) postpone

auf'schließen §76 *intr* (SEIN) shoot up

Auf'schlag *m* (auf *acc*) striking (upon), impact (on); (*an Kleidung*) cuff, lapel; (*Steuer-*) surtax; (*Preis-*) price hike; (tennis) service, serve

auf'schlagen §132 *tr* (*öffnen*) open; (*Ei*) crack; (*Karte, Ärmel*) turn up; (*Zelt*) pitch; (*Wohnung*) take up; (*Preis*) raise; (*Knie, usw.*) bruise; (*Ball*) serve || *intr* (SEIN) (*Tür*) fly open; (*Flugzeug*) crash; (*Ball*) bounce; (tennis) serve

auf'schließen §76 *tr* unlock, open || *ref* (*dat*) pour out one's heart (to) || *intr* (mil) close ranks

auf'schlitzen *tr* slit open

Auf'schluß *m* information; (chem) decomposition

auf'schlußreich *adj* informative

auf'schnallen *tr* buckle; unbuckle

auf'schnappen *tr* snap up; (*Nachricht*) pick up

Auf'schneidemaschine *f* meat slicer
auf'schneiden §106 *tr* cut open;
(*Fleisch*) slice || *intr* (coll) talk big
Auf'schneider *m* boaster
Auf'schnitt *m*—kalter A. cold cuts
auf'schnüren *tr* untie, undo
auf'schrauben *tr* unscrew; (*auf acc*)
screw (on)
auf'schrecken §134 *tr* startle; (*Wild*)
scare up || *intr* (SEIN) be startled
Auf'schrei *m* scream, yell; (fig) outcry
auf'schreiben §62 *tr* write down
auf'schreien §135 *intr* scream, yell
Auf'schrift *f* inscription; (*Anschrift*)
address; (*e-r Flasche*) label
Auf'schub *m* deferment, postponement; (*Verzögerung*) delay; (jur) stay
auf'schürfen *tr* scrape; (*Bein*) skin
auf'schwellen §119 *intr* (SEIN) swell
up; (*Fluß*) rise
auf'schwemmen *tr* bloat
auf'schwingen §142 *ref* (& fig) soar;
sich a., etw zu tun bring oneself to
do s.th.
Auf'schwung *m* (& fig) upswing
auf'sehen §138 *intr* look up || **Aufse-
hen** *n* (–s;) sensation, stir
auf'sehenerregend *adj* sensational
Auf'seher –in §6 *mf* supervisor; (*im
Museum*) guard; (*im Geschäft*) floorwalker
auf'sein §139 *intr* (SEIN) be up; (*Tür*)
be open
auf'setzen *tr* put on; (*aufrichten*) set
up; (*schriftlich*) compose, draft ||
ref sit up || *intr* (aer) touch down ||
(rok) splash down
Auf'sicht *f* inspection, supervision
Auf'sichtsbeamte *m*, **Auf'sichtsbeam-
tin** *f* inspector, supervisor
Auf'sichtsbehörde *f* control board
Auf'sichtsdame *f* floorwalker
Auf'sichtsherr *m* floorwalker
Auf'sichtsrat *m* board of trustees;
(*Mitglied*) trustee
auf'sitzen §144 *intr* (SEIN) sit up; (auf
dat) sit (on), rest (on); **j—m a.** be
taken in by s.o.; **j—n a.** lassen stand
s.o. up
auf'spannen *tr* stretch, spread; (*Regenschirm*) open
auf'sparen *tr* save (up)
auf'speichern *tr* store (up)
auf'sperren *tr* unlock; (*Augen, Tür*)
open wide
auf'spielen *tr* strike up || *ref* (mit)
show off (with) || *intr* play dance
music
auf'spießen *tr* spear, pierce
auf'sprengen *tr* force open; (*mit
Sprengstoff*) blow up
auf'springen §142 *intr* (SEIN) jump up;
(*Tür*) fly open; (*Ball*) bounce;
(*Haut*) chap, crack
auf'spritzen *tr* (*Farbe*) spray on; (sl)
shoot up || *intr* (SEIN) squirt up
auf'sprudeln *intr* (SEIN) bubble (up)
auf'spulen *tr* wind up
auf'spüren *tr* track down, ferret out
auf'stacheln *tr* goad; (fig) stir up
auf'stampfen *intr*—mit dem Fuß a.
stamp one's foot
Auf'stand *m* insurrection, uprising

aufständisch ['auf,tendɪʃ] *adj* insur-
gent || **Aufständischen** *pl* insurgents
auf'stapeln *tr* stack up, pile up
auf'stechen §64 *tr* puncture; (surg)
lance
auf'stecken *tr* (*Flagge*) plant; (*Haar*)
pin up; (coll) give up; **j—m ein Licht
a.** enlighten s.o.
auf'stehen §146 *intr* (HABEN) stand
open || *intr* (SEIN) stand up, get up;
(gegen) revolt (against)
auf'steigen §148 *intr* (SEIN) climb;
(*Reiter*) mount; (*Rauch*) rise; (*Gewitter*) come up; (*Tränen*) well up;
a. auf (*acc*) get on
auf'stellen *tr* set up, put up; (*Beispiel*)
set; (*Behauptung*) make; (*Wach-
posten*) post; (*Bauten*) erect; (*Leiter*)
raise; (*Waren*) display; (*Maschine*)
assemble; (als *Kandidaten*) nominate;
(*Regel, Problem*) state; (*Lehre*) propound; (*Rekord*) set; (*Liste*) make
out; (*Rechnung*) draw up, make out;
(*Stühle*) arrange; (*Falle*) set; (*Bedingungen, Grundsätze*) lay down;
(*Beweis*) furnish || *ref* station one-
self
Auf'stellung *f* (–;–en) erection; assertion; list, schedule; (mil) formation;
(pol) nomination; (sport) lineup
auf'stemmen *tr* pry open || *ref* prop
oneself up
Auf'stieg *m* climb; (*Steigung*) slope;
(fig) advancement
auf'stöbern *tr* ferret out; (fig) unearth
auf'stoßen §150 *tr* push open || *ref*—
sich [*dat*] das Knie a. skin one's
knee || *intr* (HABEN) (sl) belch || *intr*
(HABEN & SEIN) bump, touch; (*Schiff*)
touch bottom || *intr* (SEIN)—**j—m a.**
strike s.o., cross s.o.'s mind
auf'streichen §85 *tr* (*Butter*) spread
auf'streuen *tr* (auf *acc*) sprinkle (on)
Auf'strich *m* upstroke; (auf *Brot*)
spread
auf'stützen *tr* prop up
auf'suchen *tr* search for; (*nachschlagen*) look up; (*Ort*) visit; (*aufsam-
meln*) pick up; (*Arzt*) go to see
auf'tauchen *intr* (SEIN) turn up, appear; (*Frage*) crop up; (*U-Boot*) surface; (*Gerücht*) arise
auf'tauen *tr* & *intr* (SEIN) thaw
auf'teilen *tr* divide up
Auftrag ['auftrak] *m* (–[e]s;–̈e) (*Anweisung*) orders, instructions; (*Bestellung*) order, commission; (*Sendung*)
mission; in A. von on behalf of
auf'tragen §132 *tr* instruct, order;
(*Speise*) serve; (*Farben, Butter*) put
on; (*Kleidungsstück*) wear out;
(surv) plot; **j—m etw a.** impose s.th.
on s.o. || *intr*—**dick** (or **stark**) **a.** (sl)
put it on thick
Auf'traggeber –in §6 *mf* employer;
(*Besteller*) client, customer
Auf'tragsformular *n* order blank
auf'tragsgemäß, auf'trag(s)mäßig *adv*
as ordered, according to instructions
auf'treffen §151 *intr* (SEIN) strike
Auf'treffpunkt *m* point of impact
auf'treiben §62 *tr* (*Staub; Geld*) raise;

(*Wild*) flush; (*aufblähen*) distend; (*Teig*) cause to rise

auf'trennen *tr* rip, undo, unstitch

auf'treten §152 *tr* (*Tür*) kick open ‖ *intr* (SEIN) step, tread; (*erscheinen*) appear; (*handeln*) act, behave; (*eintreten*) occur, crop up; (*pathol*) break out; (*theat*) enter ‖ **Auftreten** *n* (-s;) appearance; occurrence; behavior; **sicheres A.** poise

Auf'trieb *m* drive; buoyancy; (aer & fig) lift; (agr) cattle drive; **j-m A. geben** encourage s.o.

Auf'tritt *m* (*Streit*) scene, row; (theat) entrance (*of an actor*); (theat) scene

auf'trumpfen *intr* play a higher trump; **gegen j-n a.** go to s.o. better

auf'tun §154 *tr* & *ref* open

auf'türmen *tr* & *intr* pile up

auf'wachen *intr* (SEIN) awaken, wake up

auf'wachsen §155 *intr* (SEIN) grow up

auf'wallen *intr* (SEIN) boil, seethe; (fig) surge, rise up

Auf'wallung *f* (-;-en) (fig) outburst

Aufwand ['aufvant] *m* (-[e]s;⁻e) (an *dat*) expenditure (of); (*Prunk*) show

auf'wärmen *tr* warm up; (fig) drag up

Auf'wartefrau *f* cleaning woman

auf'warten *intr* (*dat*) wait on; **a. mit** oblige with, offer

Auf'wärter -in §6 *mf* attendant ‖ *f* cleaning woman

aufwärts ['aufverts] *adv* upward(s)

Auf'wärtshaken *m* (box) uppercut

Auf'wartung *f* (-;) attendance; (*bei Tisch*) service; (*Besuch*) call; **j-m seine A. machen** pay one's respects to s.o.

Aufwasch ['aufvaʃ] *m* (-es;) washing; dirty dishes

auf'waschen §158 *tr* & *intr* wash up

auf'wecken *tr* wake (up)

auf'weichen *tr* soften; soak ‖ *intr* (SEIN) become soft; become sodden

auf'weisen §118 *tr* produce, show

auf'wenden §140 *tr* spend, expend; **Mühe a.** take pains

auf'werfen §160 *tr* throw up; (*Tür*) fling open; (*Graben*) dig; (*Frage*) raise ‖ *ref*—**sich a.** zu set oneself up as

auf'wickeln *tr* wind up; (*Haar*) curl; (*loswickeln*) unwind

aufwiegeln ['aufvi:gəln] *tr* instigate

Aufwiegler -in ['aufvi:glər(ɪn)] §6 *mf* instigator

aufwieglerisch ['aufvi:glərɪʃ] *adj* inflammatory

Auf'wind *m* updraft

auf'winden §59 *tr* wind up; (*Anker*) weigh ‖ *ref* coil up

auf'wirbeln *tr* (*Staub*) raise; **viel Staub a.** (coll) make quite a stir

auf'wischen *tr* wipe up

auf'wühlen *tr* dig up; (*Wasser*) churn up; (fig) stir up

auf'zählen *tr* enumerate, itemize

auf'zäumen *tr* bridle

auf'zehren *tr* consume

auf'zeichnen *tr* make a sketch of; (*notieren*) write down, record

aufzeigen *tr* point out

auf'ziehen §163 *tr* pull up; (*öffnen*) pull open; (*Uhr*) wind; (*Saite*) put on; (*Perlen*) string; (*Kind*) bring up; (*Tier*) breed; (*Pflanzen*) grow; (*Flagge, Segel*) hoist (*Anker*) weigh; (*Veranstaltung*) arrange, organize; (coll) kid ‖ *intr* (SEIN) approach, pull up

Auf'zucht *f* breeding, raising

Auf'zug *m* elevator; (*e-r Uhr*) winder; (*Aufmarsch*) parade, procession; (gym) chin-up; (theat) act

auf'zwingen §142 *tr*—**j-m etw a.** force s.th. on s.o.; **j-m seinen Willen a.** impose one's will on s.o.

Augapfel ['aukapfəl] *m* eyeball; (fig) apple of the eye

Auge ['augə] *n* (-s;-n) eye; (*auf Würfeln*) dot; (*hort*) bud; (typ) face

äugeln ['ɔɪgəln] *intr*—**ä. mit** wink at

Augen- ['augən] *comb.fm.* eye, of the eye(s), in the eye(s); visual; (anat) ocular, optic(al)

Au'genblick *m* moment, instant

au'genblicklich *adj* momentary; (*sofortig*) immediate, instantaneous

Au'genblicksmensch *m* hedonist; impulsive person

Au'genbraue *f* eyebrow

Au'genbrauenstift *m* eyebrow pencil

au'genfällig *adj* conspicuous, obvious

Au'genhöhle *f* eye socket

Au'genlicht *n* eyesight

Au'genlid *n* eyelid

Au'genmaß *n* sense of proportion; **ein gutes A. haben** have a keen eye; **nach dem A.** by eye

Au'genmerk *n* attention

Au'gennerv *m* optic nerve

Au'genschein *m* inspection; (*Anschein*) appearances; **in A. nehmen** inspect

au'genscheinlich *adj* obvious

Au'genstern *m* pupil; iris

Au'gentäuschung *f* optical illusion

Au'gentrost *m* sight for sore eyes

Au'genwasser *n* eyewash

Au'genweide *f* sight for sore eyes

Au'genwimper *f* eyelash

Au'genwinkel *m* corner of the eye

Au'genzeuge *m*, **Au'genzeugin** *f* eyewitness

-äugig [ɔɪgɪç] *comb.fm.* -eyed

August [au'gust] *m* (-[e]s & -;-e) August

Auktion [auk'tsjon] *f* (-;-en) auction

Auktio·nator [auktsjo'nator] *m* (-s; -natoren [na'torən]) auctioneer

auktionieren [auktsjo'nirən] *tr* auction off, put up for auction

Au·la ['aula] *f* (-;-s & -len [lən]) auditorium

aus [aus] *adv* out; **von ... aus** from, e.g., **vom Fenster aus** from the window ‖ *prep* (*dat*) out of, from; because of

aus'arbeiten *tr* elaborate; finish ‖ *ref* work out, take physical exercise

Aus'arbeitung *f* (-;-en) elaboration; (*schriftlich*) composition; (*körperlich*) workout; (tech) finish

aus'arten *intr* (SEIN) get out of hand; (in *acc*) degenerate (into)

aus'atmen *tr* exhale

aus'baden *tr* (coll) take the rap for
aus'baggern *tr* dredge
Aus'bau *m* (-[e]s;) completion; expansion, development
aus'bauen *tr* complete; (*erweitern*) expand, develop
aus'bedingen *tr* stipulate
aus'bessern *tr* repair; (*Kleid*) mend; (*Bild*) retouch
aus'beulen *tr* take the dents out of
Aus'beute *f* (*Ertrag*) output; (*Gewinn*) profit, gain
ausbeuten ['ausbɔɪtən] *tr* exploit
aus'biegen §57 *tr* bend out ‖ *intr* (SEIN) curve; (*dat*, *vor dat*) make way (for)
aus'bilden *tr* develop; (*lehren*) train, educate; (mil) drill ‖ *ref* train
Aus'bilder *m* (mil) drill instructor
aus'bitten §60 *ref—sich* [*dat*] etw a. ask for s.th.; insist on s.th.
aus'bleiben §62 *intr* (SEIN) stay out; stay away; be missing
aus'bleichen §85 *tr* & *intr* (SEIN) bleach; fade
aus'blenden *tr* (cin, rad) fade-out
Aus'blick *m* (auf *acc*) view (of); (fig) outlook
aus'bohren *tr* bore (out), drill (out)
aus'borgen *ref—sich* [*dat*] etw a. von borrow s.th. from
aus'brechen §64 *tr* break off ‖ *intr* (SEIN) (aus) break out (of)
aus'breiten *tr* & *ref* spread; extend
aus'brennen §97 *tr* burn out, gut; (*Sonne*) parch; (med) cauterize ‖ *intr* (SEIN) burn out; (*Haus*) be gutted
Aus'bruch *m* outbreak; (*e-s Vulkans*) eruption; (*e-s Gefangenen*) breakout; (*des Gelächters*) outburst
aus'brüten *tr* incubate; hatch
Ausbuchtung ['ausbuxtuŋ] *f* (-;-en) bulge
ausbuddeln ['ausbudəln] *tr* (coll) dig out
aus'bügeln *tr* iron out
Aus'bund *m* (von) very embodiment (of)
ausbürgern ['ausbyrgərn] *tr* expatriate
aus'bürsten *tr* brush out
Aus'dauer *f* perseverance
aus'dauern *intr* persevere, persist
aus'dauernd *adj* persevering; (bot) perennial
aus'dehnen *tr* & *ref* stretch, expand; (*Organ*) dilate
aus'denken §66 *tr* think out; think up; nicht auszudenken inconceivable
aus'deuten *tr* interpret, explain
aus'dienen *intr* serve one's time
aus'dorren *intr* (SEIN) dry up; wither
aus'dörren *tr* dry up, parch
aus'drehen *tr* turn out; turn off
Aus'druck *m* expression
aus'drücken *tr* squeeze out; (fig) express
ausdrücklich ['ausdrʏklɪç] *adj* express, explicit
aus'druckslos *adj* expressionless
aus'druckvoll *adj* expressive
Aus'druckweise *f* way of speaking
aus'dünsten *tr* exhale, give off ‖ *intr* evaporate; (*schwitzen*) sweat

auseinan'der *adv* apart; separately
auseinan'derfallen §72 *intr* (SEIN) fall apart
auseinan'dergehen §82 *intr* (SEIN) part; (*Versammlung*) break up; (*Meinungen*) differ; (*Wege*) branch off; (*auseinanderfallen*) come apart
auseinan'derhalten §90 *tr* keep apart
auseinan'derlaufen §105 *intr* (SEIN) (*Menge*) disperse; (*Wege*) diverge
auseinan'dernehmen §116 *tr* take apart
auseinan'dersetzen *tr* explain ‖ *ref—sich mit etw a.* come to grips with s.th.; *sich mit j—m a.* have it out with s.o.; (*gütlich*) come to an understanding with s.o.
Auseinan'dersetzung *f* explanation; (*Erörterung*) discussion, controversy; (*Übereinkommen*) arrangement
aus'erkoren *adj* chosen; predestined
aus'erlesen *adj* choice ‖ §107 *tr* choose, select
aus'ersehen §138 *tr* destine
aus'erwählen *tr* pick out, choose
aus'fahren §71 *tr* (*Straße, Gleis*) wear out; (aer) let down; **den Motor a.** (coll) open it up; **die Kurve a.** not cut the corner ‖ *intr* (SEIN) drive out; (naut) put to sea; (rr) pull out
Aus'fahrt *f* departure; exit; (*Spazierfahrt*) ride, drive; (*Torweg*) gateway
Aus'fall *m* falling out; (*Ergebnis*) result; (*Verlust*) loss; (fencing) lunge; (mach) breakdown; (mil) sally
aus'fallen §72 *intr* (SEIN) fall out; (*nicht stattfinden*) fail to take place; (*ausgelassen werden*) be omitted; (*versagen*) go out of commission; (*Ergebnis*) turn out; (mil) sortie
aus'fallend *adj* aggressive, insulting
aus'fechten §74 *tr* (*Kampf*) fight; (*Streit*) settle (by fighting)
aus'fegen *tr* sweep (out)
aus'fertigen *tr* finish; (*Paß*) issue; (*Scheck*) write out; (*Schriftstück*) draw up, draft; **doppelt a.** draw up in duplicate
aus'findig *adj—a.* **machen** find out; (*aufspüren*) trace
aus'fliegen §57 *intr* (SEIN) fly out; (*wegfliegen*) fly away; (*von Hause wegziehen*) leave home; go on a trip
aus'fließen §76 *intr* (SEIN) flow out
Aus'flucht *f* evasion; **Ausflüchte machen** dodge, beat around the bush
aus'flüchten *tr* align
Aus'flug *m* trip, outing
Ausflügler ['ausflyglər] *m* (-s;-) tourist, vacationer
Aus'fluß *m* outflow; (*Eiter*) discharge; (*Ergebnis*) outcome; (*Mündung*) outlet
aus'folgen *tr* hand over
aus'forschen *tr* investigate; sound out
aus'fragen *tr* interrogate, quiz
aus'fressen §70 *tr* empty (by eating); (chem) corrode; (geol) erode; **was hast du denn ausgefressen?** (coll) what were you up to?
Ausfuhr ['ausfur] *f* (-;-en) export
Aus'fuhrabgabe *f* export duty
ausführbar ['ausfyrbar] *adj* feasible

aus′führen *tr* carry out; export, ship; (*Auftrag*) fill; (*darlegen*) explain

Aus′fuhrhändler –in §6 *mf* exporter

ausführlich ['ausfy:rlɪç] *adj* detailed ‖ *adv* in detail, in full

Aus′führung *f* (–;–en) carrying out, performance; (*Qualität*) workmanship; (*Darlegung*) explanation; (*e-s Gesetzes, Befehls*) implementation; (*Fertigstellung*) completion; (*e-s Verbrechens*) perpetrations; (*typ*) type, model; copy

Aus′fuhrwaren *pl* exports

aus′füllen *tr* fill out; (*Zeit*) occupy; (*Lücke; Stellung*) fill

Aus′gabe *f* (*Verteilung*) distribution; (*von Geldern*) expenditure; (*von Briefen*) delivery; (*e-s Buches*) edition; (*von Aktien*) issue

Aus′gang *m* exit; (*Auslaß*) outlet; (*Ergebnis*) result; (*Ende*) close, end; (aer) gate

Aus′gangspunkt *m* starting point

Aus′gangssprache *f* source language

aus′geben §80 *tr* give out, distribute; (*Aktien; Befehl*) issue; (*Geld*) spend; (*Briefe*) deliver; (*Karten*) deal ‖ *ref*—sich a. für pass oneself off as

ausgebeult ['ausgəbɔɪlt] *adj* baggy

Aus′geburt *f* figment

aus′gedehnt *adj* extensive

aus′gedient *adj* retired; (educ) emeritus

aus′gefallen *adj* (fig) eccentric, odd

aus′gefeilt *adj* (fig.) flawless

aus′geglichen *adj* (*Person*) well-balanced; (*Styl*) balanced

aus′gehen §82 *intr* (SEIN) go out; (*Vorräte, Geld, Geduld*) run out; (*Haar*) fall out; (*Farbe*) fade; a. auf (*acc*) aim at, be bent on; a. von proceed from; die Sache ging von ihm aus it was his idea; frei a. get off scot-free; gut a. turn out well; leer a. come away empty-handed; wenn wir davon a., daß going on the assumption that

Aus′gehverbot *n* curfew

aus′gekocht *adj* (*Lügner*) out-and-out; (*Verbrecher*) hardened

aus′gelassen *adj* boisterous

aus′geleiert *adj* trite; worn-out; (*Gewinde*) stripped

aus′gemacht *adj* settled; downright

ausgenommen *prep* (*acc*) except; niemand a. bar none

aus′gepicht *adj* inveterate

aus′gerechnet *adv* just, of all ...; a. Sie! you of all people!

aus′geschlossen *adj* out of the question, impossible

Ausgesiedelte ['ausgəzidəltə] §5 *mf* evacuee, displaced person

aus′gestalten *tr* make arrangements for

aus′gesucht *adj* choice

aus′gezeichnet *adj* excellent

ausgiebig ['ausgibɪç] *adj* abundant; (*ergiebig*) productive

aus′gießen §76 *tr* pour out, pour away

Aus′gleich *m* (–s;–e) (*Ersatz*) compensation; (*Vergleich*) compromise; (acct) settlement; (tennis) deuce

aus′gleichen §85 *tr* level, smooth out; (*Konten*) balance; (*Verlust*) compensate for ‖ *ref* cancel one another out

Ausgleichs– *comb.fm.* balancing, compensating

Aus′gleichung *f* (–;–en) equalization; settlement; compensation

aus′gleiten §86 *intr* (SEIN) slip

aus′graben §87 *tr* dig out, dig up; (*Leiche*) exhume; (archeol) excavate

aus′greifen §88 *intr* reach out; weit ausgreifend far-reaching

Ausguck ['ausgʊk] *m* (–s;–e) lookout

aus′gucken *intr* (nach) be on the lookout (for)

Aus′guß *m* sink; (*Tülle*) nozzle

aus′haken *tr* unhook

aus′halten §90 *tr* endure, stand ‖ *intr* persevere, stick it out

aus′handeln *tr* get by bargaining

aushändigen ['aushɛndɪgən] *tr* hand over, surrender

Aus′hang *m* notice, shingle

Aus′hängeschild *n* (–[e]s;–er) sign board, shingle; (fig) front, cover

aus′harren *intr* hold out, last

aus′hauchen *tr* breathe out, exhale

aus′heben §94 *tr* lift out; (*Tür*) lift off its hinges; (*Truppen*) recruit

aushecken ['aushɛkən] *tr* (fig) hatch

aus′heilen *tr* heal completely ‖ *intr* (SEIN) heal up

aus′helfen §96 *intr* (*dat*) help out

Aus′hilfe *f* (temporary) help; (temporary) helper; makeshift

Aushilfs– *comb.fm.* temporary, emergency

Aus′hilfsarbeit *f* part-time work

Aus′hilfslehrer –in §6 *mf* substitute teacher

aus′hilfsweise *adv* temporarily

aus′höhlen *tr* hollow out

aus′holen *tr* (*ausfragen*) sound out ‖ *intr* (beim Schwimmen) stroke; mit dem Arm a. raise the arm (before striking); weit a. start from the beginning

aus′horchen *tr* sound out, pump

aus′hülsen *tr* (*Bohnen, usw.*) shell

aus′hungern *tr* starve (out)

aus′husten *tr* cough up

aus′kehlen *tr* groove

Aus′kehlung *f* (–;–en) groove

aus′kehren *tr* sweep (out)

aus′kennen §97 *ref* know one's way; (in e–m Fach) be well versed

Aus′klang *m* end, close

aus′klappen *tr* pull out (a fold-away bed)

aus′kleiden *tr* line, panel; (*ausziehen*) undress ‖ *ref* undress

aus′klopfen *tr* beat the dust out of

ausklügeln ['ausklygəln] *tr* figure out (ingeniously)

aus′kneifen §88 *intr* (SEIN) beat it

aus′knipsen *tr* (coll) switch off

ausknobeln ['ausknobəln] *tr* figure out

aus′kochen *tr* boil out; boil clean

aus′kommen §99 *intr* (SEIN) come out, get out; (*ausreichen*) manage ‖ Aus′kommen *n* (–s) livelihood

auskömmlich ['auskœmlɪç] *adj* adequate

aus′kosten *tr* relish

aus′kramen ['auskrɑmən] *tr* (aus Schubladen) drag out; (fig) show off

aus/kratzen *tr* scratch out; (surg) curette

aus/kriechen §102 *intr* (SEIN) be hatched

aus/kugeln *ref—sich* [*dat*] **den Arm** a. dislocate the shoulder

aus/kundschaften *tr* explore; (mil) scout

Auskunft ['auskunft] *f* (–;–e) information, piece of information

Auskunftei [auskunf'taɪ] *f* (–;–en) private detective agency

Aus/kunftschalter *m* information desk

aus/kuppeln *tr* uncouple; (*die Kupplung*) release || *intr* disengage the clutch

aus/lachen *tr* laugh at || *ref* have a good laugh

aus/laden §103 *tr* unload; (*Gast*) put off || *intr* project, jut out || **Ausladen** *n* (–s;) unloading; projection

Aus/lage *f* (*von Geld*) outlay; (*Unkosten*) expenses; (*von Waren*) display; (*Schaufenster*) display window

Aus/land *n* foreign country, foreign countries; **im A. leben** live abroad; **ins A. gehen** go abroad

Ausländer –in ['auslendər(ɪn)] §6 *mf* foreigner, alien

aus/ländisch *adj* foreign, alien

Auslands— *comb.fm.* foreign

Aus·laß ['auslas] *m* (–lasses;–lässe) outlet

aus/lassen §104 *tr* let out; (*weglassen*) omit; (*Wut*) (*an dat*) vent (on) || *ref* express one's opinion

Aus/lassung *f* omission; (*Bemerkung*) remark

Aus/lassungszeichen *n* (gram) apostrophe; (typ) caret

Aus/lauf *m* sailing; room to run

aus/laufen §105 *intr* (SEIN) run out; (*Schiff*) put to sea; (*Farbe*) run; **a. in** (*acc*) end in; (*Straße*) run into

Aus/läufer *m* (geol) spur; (hort) runner

aus/leben *tr* live out || *ref* make the most of one's life || *intr* die

aus/lecken *tr* lick clean

aus/leeren *tr* empty || *ref* have a bowel movement

aus/legen *tr* lay out; (*Waren*) display; (*erklären*) construe; (*Geld*) advance; (*Fußboden*) cover (*with carpeting*); (*Minen*) lay; (*Schlinge*) set; **falsch a.** misconstrue, misinterpret

Aus/leger –in §6 *mf* interpreter || *m* outrigger; (*e–s Krans*) boom

aus/leihen §81 *tr* lend (out) || *ref—sich* [*dat*] etw a. borrow s.th.

aus/lernen *intr* finish one's apprenticeship; **man lernt nie aus** one never stops learning

Aus/lese *f* pick, choice

aus/lesen §107 *tr* pick out; (*Buch*) finish reading

aus/liefern *tr* deliver, turn over; (*verteilen*) distribute; (*Verbrecher*) extradite; **j–m ausgeliefert sein** be at s.o.'s mercy

aus/liegen §108 *intr* (SEIN) be on display

aus/löffeln *tr* spoon out; **etw a. zu ha-**

ben have to face the consequences of s.th.

aus/löschen *tr* (*Feuer*) extinguish; (*Licht*) put out; (*Schreiben*) erase

aus/losen *tr* draw lots for

aus/lösen *tr* loosen, release; (*Gefangegen*) ransom; (*Pfand*) redeem

Aus/löser *m* (–s;–) release

aus/loten *tr* (naut & fig) plumb

aus/lüften *tr* air, ventilate

aus/machen *tr* (*Feuer*) put out; (*sichten*) make out; (*betragen*) amount to; (*Fleck*) remove; (*Licht*) turn out; (*bilden*) constitute; (*vereinbaren*) agree upon; **es macht nichts aus** it doesn't matter

aus/malen *tr* paint || *ref—sich* [*dat*] etw a. picture s.th.

aus/marschieren *intr* (SEIN) march out

Aus/maß *n* measurement; dimensions; **in großem A.** on a large scale; (fig) to a great extent

ausmergeln ['ausmergərln] *tr* exhaust

ausmerzen ['ausmertsən] *tr* reject; (*ausrotten*) eradicate

aus/messen §70 *tr* measure; survey

aus/misten *tr* (*Stall*) clean; (fig) clean up

aus/mustern *tr* discard; (mil) discharge

Aus/nahme *f* (–;–) exception

Aus/nahmezustand *m* state of emergency

aus/nahmslos *adj & adv* without exception

aus/nahmsweise *adv* by way of exception

aus/nehmen §116 *tr* take out; (*Fisch, Huhn*) clean; (*ausschließen*) exclude; (sl) clean out (of money) || *ref—sich gut a.* look good

aus/nutzen, aus/nützen *tr* utilize; (*Gelegenheit*) take advantage of

aus/packen *tr* unpack; (*Geheimnis*) disclose || *intr* (coll) unburden oneself, open up

aus/pfeifen §88 *tr* hiss (off the stage)

aus/plappern *tr* blurt out, blab out

aus/plaudern *tr* blab out

aus/plündern *tr* ransack; (coll) clean out (of money)

aus/polstern *tr* stuff, pad

aus/posaunen *tr* (coll) broadcast

aus/probieren *tr* try out, test

Aus/puff *m* (–e]s;–e) exhaust

Aus/puffleitung *f* (aut) manifold

Aus/puffrohr *n* exhaust pipe

Aus/pufftopf *m* (aut) muffler

aus/pumpen *tr* pump out; **ausgepumpt** (coll) exhausted

aus/putzen *tr* (*reinigen*) clean out; (*schmücken*) adorn || *ref* dress up

aus/quartieren *tr* put out (*of s.o.'s room*)

aus/radieren *tr* erase

aus/rangieren *tr* (coll) scrap

aus/rauben *tr* rob, ransack

aus/räumen *tr* (*Schrank*) clear out; (*Möbel*) remove; (med) clean out

aus/rechnen *tr* figure out

aus/recken *tr* stretch || *ref—sich* [*dat*] **den Hals** a. crane one's neck

Aus/rede *f* evasion, excuse

aus/reden *tr—j—m* etw a. talk s.o. out

of s.th. || *ref* make excuses || *intr* finish speaking

aus'reiben §62 *tr* rub out; (mach) ream

aus'reichen *tr* suffice, be enough

aus'reichend *adj* sufficient

Aus'reise *f* departure; way out

aus'reißen §53 *tr* tear out || *ref*—er reißt sich [*dat*] dabei kein Bein aus he's not exactly killing himself || *intr* (SEIN) run away

Aus'reißer *m* runaway

aus'renken *tr* dislocate

aus'richten *tr* straighten; (in e-e Linie bringen) align; (vollbringen) accomplish; (Botschaft, Gruß) convey

aus'roden *tr* root out; (Wald) clear

aus'rollen *tr* roll out || *intr* (SEIN) (aer) taxi to a standstill

ausrotten ['ausrotən] *tr* root out; (Volk, Tierrasse) exterminate; (Übel) eradicate

aus'rücken *tr* (Kupplung) disengage || *intr* (SEIN) march off; run away

Aus'ruf *m* outcry; (öffentlich) proclamation; (gram) interjection

aus'rufen §122 *tr* call out; exclaim; a. als (or zum) proclaim

Aus'rufungszeichen *n* exclamation point

aus'ruhen *ref & intr* rest

aus'rupfen *tr* pluck

aus'rüsten *tr* equip, fit out; arm

aus'rutschen *intr* (SEIN) slip (out)

Aus'saat *f* sowing; (& fig) seed(s)

aus'säen *tr* sow; (fig) disseminate

Aus'sage *f* statement; (gram) predicate; (jur) affidavit

aus'sagen *tr* state || *intr* give evidence, make a statement

Aus'sagesatz *m* declarative sentence

Aus'sageweise *f* (gram) mood

Aus'satz *m* leprosy

Aussätzige ['auszetsɪgə] §5 *mf* leper

aus'saugen §125 *tr* suck dry; (fig) bleed white

Aus'sauger –in §6 *mf* (coll) bloodsucker

aus'schalten *tr* (Licht, Radio, Fernseher) turn off; (fig) shut out

Aus'schalter *m* circuit breaker

Aus'schank *m* sale of alcoholic drinks; (Knelpe) bar, taproom

aus'scharren *tr* dig up

Aus'schau *f*—A. halten nach be on the lookout for

aus'schauen *intr*—a. nach look out for; look like; gut schaust du aus! what a mess you are!

aus'scheiden §112 *tr* eliminate; (physiol) excrete, secrete || *intr* (SEIN) retire, resign; (sport) drop out; das scheidet aus! that's out!

Aus'scheidung *f* (–;–en) elimination; retirement; (physiol) excretion, secretion

Aus'scheidungskampf *m* elimination bout

aus'schelten §83 *tr* scold, berate

aus'schenken *tr* pour (drinks)

aus'scheren *intr* (aus) veer away (from)

aus'schiffen *tr* disembark; (Ladung) unload || *ref* disembark

aus'schimpfen *tr* scold, take to task

aus'schirren *tr* unharness

aus'schlachten *tr* cut up; (Flugzeuge, usw.) cannibalize; (ausnutzen) make the most of

aus'schlafen §131 *tr* sleep off || *ref & intr* get enough sleep

Aus'schlag *m* rash; (e–s Zeigers) deflection; den A. geben turn the scales

aus'schlagen §132 *tr* knock out; (Feuer) beat out; (Metall) hammer out; (Innenraum) line; (Angebot) refuse || *intr* bud; sprout; (Pferd) kick; (Pendel) swing; (Zeiger) move || *intr* (SEIN) turn out

aus'schlaggebend *adj* decisive

aus'schließen §76 *tr* lock out; (von der Schule) expel; (ausscheiden) exclude; (sport) disqualify

aus'schließlich *adj* exclusive, sole || *adv* exclusively, only || *prep* (genit) exclusive of

aus'schlürfen *tr* sip

aus'schmieren *tr* grease; (mit) smear (with); (fig) pull a fast one on; (mas) point

aus'schmücken *tr* adorn, decorate; (Geschichte) embellish

aus'schnaufen *intr* get one's wind

aus'schneiden §106 *tr* cut out; tief ausgeschnitten low-cut, low-necked

Aus'schnitt *m* cut; (Zeitungs–) clipping; (Kleid–) neckline; (literarisch) extract; (geom) sector

aus'schreiben §62 *tr* write out (in full); finish writing; (ankündigen) announce; (Formular) fill out; (Rezept) make out

aus'schreiten §86 *tr* pace off || *intr* (SEIN) walk briskly

Aus'schreitung *f* (–;–en) excess

Aus'schuß *m* waste, scrap; (Komitee) committee

Aus'schußware *f* (indust) reject

aus'schütten *tr* pour out, spill; (Dividende) pay || *ref*—sich vor Lachen a. split one's sides laughing

aus'schwärmen *intr* (SEIN) swarm out; (Truppen) deploy

aus'schwatzen *tr* blab out, blurt out

aus'schweifend *adj* (Phantasie) wild; (liederlich) wild, dissolute

Aus'schweifung *f* (–;–en) excess; curve; digression

aus'schwemmen *tr* rinse out; wash out

aus'schwenken *tr* rinse

aus'schwitzen *tr* sweat out; exude

aus'sehen §138 *intr* look; nach j–m a. look out for s.o.; nach Regen a. look like rain; wie sieht er aus? what does he look like? || **Aussehen** *n* (–s;) look(s); appearance(s)

außen ['ausən] *adv* outside; nach a. out(wards)

außen–, **Außen–** *comb.fm.* external; outer; exterior; outdoor; foreign

Au'ßenaufnahme *f* (phot) outdoor shot

Au'ßenbahn *f* (sport) outside lane

Au'ßenfläche *f* outer surface

Au'ßenminister *m* Secretary of State; (Brit) Foreign Secretary

Au'ßenpolitik *f* foreign policy

Au'ßenseite *f* outside

Außenseiter ['ausənzaɪtər] m (-s;-) dark horse, long shot; (Einzelgänger) loner; (Nichtfachmann) layman

Außenstelle ['ausənʃtɛlə] f branch office

Außenstände ['ausənʃtɛndə] pl accounts receivable

außer ['ausər] prep (genit)—a. Landes abroad ‖ prep (dat) outside, out of; except, but; besides, in addition to; **a. Hause** not at home; **a. sich sein** be beside oneself

au'ßeramtlich adj unofficial, private

außerdem ['ausərdem] adv also, besides; moreover, furthermore

au'ßerdienstlich adj unofficial, private; (mil) off duty

äußere ['ɔɪsərə] §9 adj outer, exterior, external ‖ **Äußere** §5 n exterior

au'ßerehelich adj extra-marital; (Kind) illegitimate

au'ßergewöhnlich adj extraordinary

außerhalb ['ausərhalp] prep (genit) outside, out of

äußerlich ['ɔɪsərlɪç] adj external, outward; (oberflächlich) superficial

Äu'ßerlichkeit f superficiality; (Formalität) formality; **Äußerlichkeiten** externals; formalities

äußern ['ɔɪsərn] tr express ‖ ref (über acc) express one's views (about); (in dat) be manifested (in)

au'ßerordentlich adj extraordinary; **außerordentlicher Professor** associate professor

äußerst ['ɔɪsərst] adj outermost; (fig) extreme, utmost ‖ adv extremely, highly ‖ **Äußerste** §5 n extremity, extreme(s); **aufs Ä.** to the utmost; **bis zum Äußersten** to extremes; **to the bitter end**

außerstande ['ausərʃandə] adj unable

Äu'ßerung f (-;-en) (Ausdruck) expression; (Bemerkung) remark

aus'setzen tr set out, put out; (an der Küste) maroon; (Kind; dem Wetter) expose; (Boot) lower; (Wachen) post; (Belohnung) hold out, promise; (Tätigkeit) discontinue; **auszusetzen haben** (an dat) find fault with ‖ intr stop, halt

Aus'sicht f (auf acc) view (of); (fig) (auf acc) hope (of); **in A. nehmen** consider, plan

aus'sichtslos adj hopeless

Aus'sichtspunkt m vantage point

aus'sichtsreich adj promising

Aus'sichtsturm m lookout tower

aussichtsvoll adj promising

aus'sieben tr sift out; (fig) screen

aus'siedeln tr evacuate by force

Aus'siedlung f (-;-en) forced evacuation

aus'sinnen §121 tr think up, devise

aussöhnen ['auszønən] tr reconcile

aus'sondern tr (trennen) separate; (auswählen) single out; (physiol) excrete

aus'spähen tr spy out ‖ intr (nach) keep a lookout (for), reconnoiter

aus'spannen tr stretch; extend; (Zugtiere) unhitch ‖ intr relax

Aus'spannung f (-;) relaxation

aus'speien §135 tr spit out

aus'sperren tr lock out, shut out

aus'spielen tr (Karten) lead with; (Preis) play for ‖ intr lead off

aus'spionieren tr spy out

Aus'sprache f pronunciation; (Erörterung) discussion, talk

aus'sprechen §64 tr pronounce; (deutlich) articulate; (ausdrücken) express ‖ ref (über acc) speak one's mind (about); (für; gegen) declare oneself (for; against); **sich mit j-m über etw a.** talk s.th. over with s.o. ‖ intr finish speaking

Aus'spruch m statement

aus'spülen tr rinse

aus'spüren tr trace (down)

aus'staffieren tr fit out, furnish

aus'stampfen tr stamp out

Aus'stand m walkout

aus'ständig adj on strike, striking; (fin) in arrears, outstanding

ausstatten ['ausʃtatən] tr furnish, equip; (Tochter) give a dowry to

Aus'stattung f (-;-en) furnishings; equipment; trousseau

aus'stechen §64 tr cut out; (Auge) poke out; (fig) outdo

aus'stehen §146 tr endure, stand ‖ intr still be expected, be overdue

aus'steigen §148 intr (SEIN) get out, get off

aus'stellen tr exhibit; (Wache) post; (Quittung, Scheck) make out; (Paß) issue

Aus'stellung f (-;-en) exhibit; issuance; criticism

Aus'stellungsdatum n date of issue

aus'sterben §149 intr (SEIN) die out

Aus'steuer f hope chest, dowry

aus'stopfen tr stuff, pad

Aus'stoß m (indust) output

aus'stoßen §150 tr knock out; (vertreiben) eject; (Seufzer, Schrei, Fluch) utter; (Torpedo) launch; (math) eliminate; (phonet) elide; (phys) emit

Aus'stoßrohr n torpedo tube

Aus'stoßung f (-;-en) ejection; utterance; (gram) elision

Aus'stoßzahlen pl (indust) production figures

aus'strahlen tr & intr radiate

aus'strecken tr & ref stretch out

aus'streichen §85 tr cross out; (glätten) smooth out; (Bratpfanne) grease

aus'streuen tr strew, scatter, spread

aus'strömen tr & intr (SEIN) pour out

aus'studieren tr study thoroughly

aus'suchen tr pick out

Aus'tausch m exchange

aus'tauschbar adj exchangeable; interchangeable

aus'tauschen tr exchange; interchange

Aus'tauschstoff m substitute

aus'teilen tr distribute, deal out

Auster ['austər] f (-;-n) oyster

aus'tilgen tr exterminate, wipe out

aus'toben tr give vent to ‖ (Person) let one's hair down; (Kinder) raise a rumpus; (Gewitter) stop raging

aus'tollen ref make a racket

Austrag ['austrak] m (-[e]s;-)—bis zum A. der Sache until the matter is decided; zum A. bringen bring to a head; (jur) settle; **zum A. kommen** come up for a decision

aus'tragen §132 tr carry out; (*Briefe*) deliver; (*Kleider*) wear out; (*Meisterschaft*) decide; (*Klatschereien*) spread; (acct) cancel

Aus'träger m deliveryman

Australien [aus'traljən] n (-s;) Australia

Australier -in [aus'traljər(ın)] §6 mf Australian

aus'treiben §62 tr drive out; exorcise

aus'treten §152 tr (*Feuer*) tread out; (*Schuhe, Treppen*) wear out || intr (SEIN) step out; (*Blut*) come out; (coll) go to the bathroom; **a. aus** leave (*school, a company, club*)

aus'trinken §143 tr drink up, drain

Aus'tritt m withdrawal

aus'trocknen tr & intr (SEIN) dry up

aus'tüfteln tr puzzle out

aus'üben tr (*Aufsicht, Macht*) exercise; (*Beruf*) practice; (*Pflicht*) carry out; (*Einfluß, Druck*) exert; (*Verbrechen*) commit; **ausübende Gewalt** executive power

Aus'verkauf m clearance sale

aus'verkaufen tr sell out; close out

aus'wachsen §155 tr outgrow

Aus'wahl f choice, selection

aus'wählen tr select, pick out

Aus'wanderer -in §6 mf emigrant

aus'wandern intr (SEIN) emigrate

auswärtig ['ausvertıç] adj out-of-town; (*ausländisch*) foreign

auswärts ['ausverts] adv outward(s); out, away from home; (*außer der Stadt*) out of town; (*im Ausland*) abroad

Aus'wärtsspiel n away game

aus'wechselbar adj interchangeable

aus'wechseln tr exchange, interchange; (*ersetzen*) replace

Aus'weg m way out; escape

Ausweich- comb.fm. evasive; alternate; substitute; emergency; reserve

aus'weichen §85 intr (SEIN) (dat) make way (for), get out of the way (of); (dat) evade; **a. auf** (acc) switch to

aus'weichend adj evasive

Aus'weichklausel f escape clause

Aus'weichlager n emergency store

Aus'weichstelle f passing zone

Aus'weichstraße f bypass

Aus'weichziel n secondary target

aus'weinen ref have a good cry || intr stop crying

Ausweis ['ausvais] m (-s;-e) identification (card); (com) statement

aus'weisen §118 tr expel; (*aus Besitz*) evict; (*verbannen*) banish, deport; (*zeigen*) show || ref prove one's identity

Aus'weispapiere pl identification papers

Aus'weisung f (-;-en) expulsion; eviction; deportation

aus'weiten tr & ref widen, expand

auswendig ['ausvendıç] adj outer || adv outside; outwardly; by heart

aus'werfen §160 tr throw out; (*Graben*) dig; (*Summe*) allocate; (*Lava*) eject; (*Blut, Schleim*) spit up; (angl) cast

aus'werten tr evaluate; (*ausnützen*) utilize; (*Statistik*) interpret

aus'wickeln tr unwrap

aus'wiegen §57 tr weigh out

aus'wirken tr knead || ref take effect; **sich a. auf** (acc) affect; **sich** [dat] **etw bei** j—m **a.** obtain s.th. from s.o.

Aus'wirkung f (-;-en) effect

aus'wischen tr wipe out; wipe clean; **j—m eins a.** play a dirty joke on s.o.

aus'wittern tr & intr weather

aus'wringen §142 tr wring out

Aus'wuchs m outgrowth; (pathol) tumor

Aus'wurf m throwing out; (fig) scum; (mach) ejection

aus'zacken tr indent; (*wellenförmig*) scallop

aus'zahlen tr pay out; pay off || ref— **es zahlt sich nicht aus** it doesn't pay

aus'zählen tr count out

aus'zanken tr scold

aus'zehren tr consume, waste

Aus'zehrung f (-;) consumption

aus'zeichnen tr mark, tag; (*ehren*) honor; (fig) distinguish

Aus'zeichnung f (-;-en) labeling; decoration, honor; distinction

aus'ziehen §163 tr pull out; (*Kleid*) take off; (*Stelle*) excerpt; (*Zeichnung*) ink in; (chem) extract || ref undress || intr (SEIN) set out; (*aus e-r Wohnung*) move out

aus'zischen tr hiss off the stage

Aus'zug m departure; moving; excerpt; (*Abriß*) summary; (Bib) Exodus; (chem) extract; (com) statement

aus'zugsweise adv in summary form

aus'zupfen tr pluck out

authentisch [au'tentıʃ] adj authentic

Auto ['auto] n (-s;-s) auto(mobile)

Au'tobahn f superhighway

Au'tobus m bus

Autodidakt [autodı'dakt] m (-en;-en) self-educated person

Au'todroschke f taxi

Au'tofahrer -in §6 mf motorist

Au'tofahrschule f driving school

Au'tofahrt f car ride, drive

Au'tofalle f speed trap

Autogramm [auto'gram] n (-[e]s;-e) autograph

Autogramm'jäger -in §6 mf autograph hound

Au'tokino n drive-in movie

Au'tokolonne f motorcade

Autokrat [auto'krat] m (-en;-en) autocrat

autokratisch [auto'kratıʃ] adj autocratic

Automat [auto'mat] m (-en;-en) vending machine; (Musik-) jukebox; (*Spiel-*) slot machine

Automa'tenrestaurant n automat

automatisch [auto'matıʃ] adj automatic

Automobil [automo'bil] n (-[e]s;-e) automobile

autonom [auto'nom] adj autonomous

Autonomie [autono'mi] f (-;) autonomy

Au·tor ['autor] m (-s;-toren ['torən]) author

Autoreparatur'werkstatt f auto repair shop, garage
Autorin [aʊˈtoːrɪn] f (-;-nen) authoress
autorisieren [aʊtɔrɪˈziːrən] tr authorize
autoritär [aʊtɔriˈtɛːr] adj authoritarian
Autorität [aʊtɔriˈtɛːt] f (-;-en) authority
Au'toschlosser m automobile mechanic
Au'toschuppen m carport

Au'tounfall m automobile accident
avancieren [avãˈsiːrən] intr (SEIN) advance; (zu) be promoted (to)
avisieren [aviˈziːrən] tr advise, notify
Axt [akst] f (-;̈e) ax
Azalee [atsaˈleːə] f (-;-n) azalea
Azetat [atseˈtat] n (-[e]s;-e) acetate
Azeton [atseˈton] n (-s;) acetone
Azetylen [atsetyˈlen] n (-s;) acetylene
azurn [aˈtsurn] adj azure, sky-blue

B

B, b [beː] invar n B, b; (mus) B flat
babbeln [ˈbabəln] intr babble
Baby [ˈbeːbi] n (-s;-s) baby
Babysitter [ˈbeːbɪzɪtər] m (-s;-) babysitter
Bach [bax] m (-[e]s;̈e) brook, creek
Backe [ˈbakə] f (-;-n) cheek; jaw (of a vise); (mach) die
backen [ˈbakən] §50 (& pret **backte**) tr bake; (in der Pfanne) fry || (pret backte; pp gebacken) intr bake || §109 intr (HABEN & SEIN) cake; stick
Backenbart (Bak'kenbart) m side whiskers
Backenstreich (Bak'kenstreich) m slap
Backenzahn (Bak'kenzahn) m molar; kleiner (or vorderer) B. bicuspid
Bäcker [ˈbɛkər] m (-s;-) baker
Bäckerei [bɛkəˈraɪ] f (-;-en) bakery
Back'fett n shortening
Back'fisch m fried fish; (fig) teenager
Back'fischalter n teens (of girls)
Back'form f cake pan
Back'hähnchen n fried chicken
Back'hendel n (Aust) fried chicken
Back'huhn n fried chicken
Back'obst n dried fruit
Back'ofen m baking oven
Back'pfeife f slap in the face, smack
Back'pflaume f prune
Back'pulver n baking powder
Back'stein m brick
Back'trog m kneading trough
Back'waren pl baked goods
Back'werk n pastries
Bad [bat] n (-[e]s;̈er) bath; bathroom; (Badeort) spa
Ba'deanstalt f public baths; public pool
Ba'deanzug m swim suit
Ba'dehaube f bathing cap
Ba'dehose f bathing trunks
Ba'dekappe f bathing cap
Ba'demantel m bathrobe
baden [ˈbadən] tr & ref bathe || intr take a bath; b. gehen go swimming
Ba'deort m bathing resort; spa
Ba'destrand m bathing beach
Ba'detuch n bath towel
Ba'dewanne f bathtub
Badende [ˈbadəndə] §5 mf bather
Ba'dewärter m §6 mf lifeguard; bathhouse attendant
Ba'dezimmer n bathroom
baff [baf] adj dumbfounded

Bagage [baˈgaːʒə] f (-;) (fig) rabble; (mil) baggage
Bagatelle [bagaˈtɛlə] f (-;-n) trifle
Bagatell'sache f petty offense
bagatellisieren [bagatɛlɪˈziːrən] tr minimize, make light of
Bagger [ˈbagər] m (-s;-) dredge
baggern [ˈbagərn] tr & intr dredge
bähen [ˈbeːən] intr bleat
Bahn [ban] f (-;-en) way, path; (aer) runway; (astr) orbit; (aut) lane; (rr) railroad; (sport) course, track; (Eis-) (sport) rink; auf die schiefe B. geraten go astray; B. brechen (dat) pave the way (for); mit der B. fahren travel by train
bahn'brechend adj pioneering, epoch-making
Bahn'brecher -in §6 mf pioneer
Bahn'damm m railroad embankment
bahnen [ˈbanən] tr—e-n Weg. b. clear a path, open up a path
Bahn'fahrt f train trip
bahn'frei adj free on board, f.o.b.
Bahn'hof m railroad station
Bahn'hofshalle f concourse
Bahn'hofsvorsteher m stationmaster
Bahn'linie f railroad line
Bahn'schranke f (rr) barrier
Bahn'steig m (rr) platform
Bahn'strecke f (rr) line, track
Bahn'übergang m railroad crossing
Bahn'wärter m (rr) signalman
Bahre [ˈbarə] f (-;-n) stretcher; bier
Bahr'tuch n pall
Bai [baɪ] f (-;-en) bay
Baiser [beˈze] m & n (-s;-s) meringue cookie
Baisse [ˈbɛsə] f (-;-n) (com) slump
Bais'sestimmung f downward trend
Baissier [bɛsˈje] m (-s;-s) (st.exch.) bear
Bajonett [bajoˈnɛt] n (-s;-e) bayonet
Bake [ˈbakə] f (-;-n) beacon
Bakterie [bakˈterjə] f (-;-n) bacterium
Bakte'rienforscher -in §6 mf bacteriologist
Bakte'rienkunde f bacteriology
Balance [baˈlãsə] f (-;) balance
balancieren [balãˈsiːrən] tr & intr balance
bald [balt] adv (eher [ˈeːər]; eheste [ˈeːəstə] §9 soon; (beinahe) nearly
baldig [ˈbaldɪç] adj speedy; (Antwort) early

baldigst ['baldıgst] *adv* very soon; at the earliest possible moment

Balg [balk] *m* (-[e]s;⸚e) skin, pelt; (*Hülse*) shell, husk; Bälge bellows; j-m den B. abziehen fleece s.o. || *m & n* (-[e]s;⸚er) (coll) brat

balgen ['balgən] *ref* roll around; romp; (*raufen*) scuffle || Balgen *m* (-s;-) (phot) bellows

Balgerei [balgə'raɪ] *f* (-;-en) scuffle

Balken ['balkən] *m* (-s;-) beam, rafter

Bal'kenwerk *n* framework

Balkon [bal'kon] *m* (-s;-e) balcony

Ball [bal] *m* (-[e]s;⸚e) ball; (*Tanz*) ball

Ballade [ba'ladə] *f* (-;-n) ballad

Ballast [balast] *m* (-[e]s;-e) ballast; (fig) drag; (coll) padding

ballen ['balən] *tr*—die Faust b. clench one's fist || *ref* form a cluster || Ballen *m* (-s;-) (anat) ball; (com) bale; (pathol) bunion

ballern ['balərn] *intr* (coll) bang away

Ballett [ba'lɛt] *n* (-[e]s;-e) ballet

Ballistik [ba'lıstık] *f* (-;) ballistics

Ballon [ba'lon] *m* (-s;-s) balloon

Ball'saal *m* ballroom

Ball'schläger *m* (sport) bat

Ball'spiel *n* ball game

Bal'lung *f* (-;-en) (mil) massing (of troops)

Balsam ['balzam] *m* (-s;-e) balm, balsam; (fig) balm

balsamieren [balza'mirən] *tr* embalm

balzen ['baltsən] *intr* perform a mating dance

Bambus ['bambus] *m* (-;- & -ses;-se) bamboo

Bam'busrohr *n* bamboo, bamboo cane

banal [ba'nal] *adj* banal

Banane [ba'nanə] *f* (-;-n) banana

Banause [ba'nauzə] *m* (-;-n) philistine

banausisch [ba'nauzıʃ] *adj* narrow-minded

Band [bant] *m* (-[e]s;⸚e) volume; (*Einband*) binding || *n* (-[e]s;⸚er) bond, tie; Bande chains, shackles || *n* (-[e]s;⸚er) (*e-s Hutes, usw.*) band; (*Bindfaden*) string; (*zum Schmuck*) ribbon; tape; (anat) ligament; (electron) recording tape; (rad) band; am laufenden B. continuously

Bandage [ban'daʒə] *f* (-;-n) bandage

bandagieren [banda'ʒirən] *tr* bandage

Bande ['bandə] *f* (-;-n) band, gang, crew; (billiards) cushion

Ban'denkrieg *m* guerilla war(fare)

Ban'denmitglied *n* gangster; (mil) guerilla

Ban'denunwesen *n* gangsterism; partisan activities

bändigen ['bɛndıgən] *tr* tame; (fig) subdue, overcome, master

Bandit [ban'dit] *m* (-en;-en) bandit

Band'maß *n* tape measure

Band'säge *f* band saw

Band'scheibe *f* (anat) disk

Band'scheibenquetschung *f* slipped disk

Band'wurm *m* tapeworm

bang(e) [baŋ(ə)] *adj* scared, anxious; (*Gefühl*) disquieting; j-m b. machen scare s.o. || Bange *f* (-;) fear

Bangigkeit ['baŋıçkaıt] *f* (-;) fear

Bank [baŋk] *f* (-;⸚e) bench; pew; (geol) layer, bed || *f* (-;-en) bank

Bank'anweisung *f* check

Bank'ausweis *m* bank statement

Bank'einlage *f* bank deposit

Bankett [baŋ'kɛt] *n* (-s;-e) banquet

bank'fähig *adj* negotiable

Bank'guthaben *n* bank balance

Bank'halter -in §6 *mf* banker (in games)

Bankier [baŋk'je] *m* (-s;-s) banker

Bank'konto *n* bank account

bank'mäßig *adj* by check

bankrott [baŋk'rot] *adj* bankrupt || *m* (-[e]s;-e) bankruptcy

Bank'verkehr *m* banking (activity)

Bank'wesen *n* banking

Bann [ban] *m* (-[e]s;-e) ban; (*Zauber*) spell; (eccl) excommunication

bannen ['banən] *tr* banish; (*Geister*) exorcize; (eccl) excommunicate

Banner ['banər] *n* (-s;-) banner; standard

Ban'nerträger *m* standard-bearer

Bann'fluch *m* anathema

Bann'kreis *m* spell; in j-s B. geraten come under s.o.'s spell

Bann'meile *f* (fig) city limits

Bann'ware *f* contraband

bar [bar] *adj* bare; (*rein*) pure, sheer; (fin) cash || *adv* cash || *prep* (genit) devoid of, lacking || Bar *f* (-;-s) bar, taproom

Bär [ber] *m* (-en;-en) bear; (astr) Dipper; j-m e-n B. aufbinden tell s.o. a fish story

Bar- *comb.fm.* cash

Baracke [ba'rakə] *f* (-;-n) barrack; (wooden) hut

Barbar -in [bar'bar(ın)] §7 *mf* barbarian

Barbarei [barba'raı] *f* (-;-en) barbarism; (*Grausamkeit*) brutality

barbarisch [bar'barıʃ] *adj* barbarous; barbaric, primitive

bärbeißig ['bɛrbaısıç] *adj* surly

Bar'bestand *m* cash on hand

Bar'betrag *m* amount in cash

Barbier [bar'bir] *m* (-s;-e) barber

barbieren [bar'birən] *tr* shave; (fig) fleece

Barett [ba'rɛt] *n* (-[e]s;-e) beret

barfuß ['barfus] *adv* barefoot

barfüßig ['barfysıç] *adj* barefooted

barg [bark] *pret* of bergen

Bar'geld *n* cash

barhäuptig ['barhɔıptıç] *adj* bareheaded

Bar'hocker *m* bar stool

Bariton ['barıton] *m* (-s;-e) baritone

Barkasse [bar'kasə] *f* (-;-n) launch

Bärme ['bɛrmə] *f* (-;) yeast, leaven

barmherzig [barm'hɛrtsıç] *adj* merciful

Bar'mittel *pl* cash

barock [ba'rok] *adj* baroque || Barock *m & n* (-s;) baroque; baroque period

Barometer [barə'metər] *n* (-s;-) barometer

Baron [ba'ron] *m* (-s;-e) baron

Baronin [ba'ronın] *f* (-;-nen) baroness

Barre ['barə] f (-;-n) bar

Barren ['barən] m (-s;-) bar; ingot; (gym) parallel bars

Barriere [bar'jerə] f (-;-n) barrier

barsch [barʃ] adj gruff, rude || Barsch m (-es;-e) (ichth) perch

Barschaft ['barʃaft] f (-;) cash

barst [barst] pret of bersten

Bart [bart] m (-[e]s;∺) beard; (e-r Katze) whiskers; (e-s Fisches) barb; der B. ist ab! the jig is up!; sich [dat] e-n B. wachsen lassen grow a beard

bärtig ['bertɪç] adj bearded

bart'los adj beardless

Bar'verlust m straight loss

Basalt [ba'zalt] m (-[e]s;-e) basalt

Basar [ba'zar] m (-s;-e) bazaar

Ba•sis ['bazɪs] f (-;-sen [zən]) basis; (archit, math, mil) base

Baß [bas] m (Basses;Bässe) (mus) bass

Baß'geige f bass viol, contrabass

Bassin [ba'sɛ̃] n (-s;-s) reservoir; swimming pool; (naut) dock, basin

Baß'schlüssel m bass clef

Baß'stimme f bass (voice), basso

basta ['basta] interj—und damit b.! and that's that!

Bastard ['bastart] m (-[e]s;-e) bastard; (bot) hybrid

Bastei [bas'taɪ] f (-;-en) bastion

basteln ['bastəln] intr tinker

Bast'ler –in §6 mf hobbyist

bat [bat] pret of bitten

Bataillon [batal'jon] n (-s;-e) battalion

Batte•rie [batə'ri] f (-;-rien ['ri·ən] battery

Bau [bau] m (-[e]s;) erection, construction, building; (Bauart) structure, design; (Körper-) build; er ist beim Bau he is in the building trade; er ist vom Bau (coll) he's in the racket; im Bau under construction || m (-[e]s;-ten) building; auf dem Bau at the construction site || m (-[e]s;-e) burrow, hole; (min) mine –bau m comb.fm. –construction, –building; –culture; –mining

Bau'abnahme f building inspection

Bau'arbeiter m construction worker

Bau'art f build; structure; type, mode

Bauch [baux] m (-[e]s;∺e) belly, stomach; (Leib) bowels; (coll) potbelly

Bauch– comb.fm. abdominal

bauchig ['bauxɪç] adj bulging; convex

Bauch'klatscher m belly flop

Bauch'laden m vendor's tray

Bauch'landung f belly-landing

Bauch'redner –in §6 mf ventriloquist

Bauch'speicheldrüse f pancreas

Bauch'weh n stomach ache, bellyache

bauen ['bau·ən] tr build; erect; make, manufacture; (ackern) till; (anbauen) grow || intr build; (an dat) work (at); (auf acc) depend (on), trust

Bauer ['bau·ər] m (-s & -n;-n) farmer; (cards) jack; (chess) pawn || m (-s;-) builder || m & n (-s;-) birdcage

Bäuerchen ['bɔɪ·ərçən] n (-s;-) small farmer; (baby's) burp

Bäuerin ['bɔɪ·ərɪn] f (-;-nen) farmer's wife

bäuerisch ['bɔɪ·ərɪʃ] adj boorish

Bau'erlaubnis f building permit

bäuerlich ['bɔɪ·ərlɪç] adj rural

Bau'ernbursche m country lad

Bau'erndirne f country girl

Bauernfänger ['bau·ərnfɛŋər] m (-s;-) confidence man

Bau'erngut n, Bau'ernhof m farm

Bau'fach n architecture

bau'fällig adj dilapidated

Bau'genhemigung f building permit

Bau'gerüst n scaffold(ing)

Bau'gewerbe n building trade

Bau'gewerkschule f school of architecture and civil engineering

Bau'grundstück n building site

Bau'holz n lumber

Bau'kasten m building set

Bau'kunst f architecture

bau'lich adj architectural; structural; in gutem baulichen Zustand in good repair

Baum [baum] m (-[e]s;∺e) tree; (mach) shaft, axle; (naut) boom

Bau'meister m building contractor, builder; architect

baumeln ['bauməln] intr dangle

bäumen ['bɔɪmən] ref rear

Baum'garten m orchard

Baum'grenze f timber line

Baum'krone f treetop

Baum'schere f pruning shears

Baum'schule f nursery (of saplings)

Baum'stamm m tree trunk

baum'stark' adj strong as an ox

Baum'wolle f cotton

Baum'wollkapsel f cotton boll

Baum'wollsamt m velveteen

Bau'plan m ground plan

Bau'platz m building lot

Bau'rat m (-[e]s;∺e) building inspector

Bausch [bauʃ] m (-[e]s;∺e) pad, wad; (e-s Segels) bulge, belly; in B. und Bogen wholesale

bauschen ['bau·ʃən] tr, ref & intr bulge, swell

bauschig ['bauʃɪç] adj puffy; baggy

Bau'schule f school of architecture and civil engineering

Bau'sparkasse f building and loan association

Bau'stahl m structural steel

Bau'stein m building stone; brick

Bau'stelle f building site; road construction

Bau'stoff m building material

Bau'techniker m construction engineer

Bau'unternehmer m contractor

Bau'unternehmung f building firm, building contractors

Bau'werk n building, edifice

Bau'wesen n building industry

Bau'zaun m hoarding

Bau'zeichnung f blueprint

Bayer –in ['baɪ·ər(ɪn)] §6 mf Bavarian

bayerisch ['baɪ·ərɪʃ] adj Bavarian

Bayern ['baɪ·ərn] n (-s;) Bavaria

Bazillenträger [ba'tsɪləntreɡər] m germ carrier

Bazil·lus [ba'tsɪlus] *m* (-;-len [lən]) bacillus

be– [bə] *insep pref*

beabsichtigen [bə'apzɪçtɪgən] *tr* intend; (**mit**) mean (by)

beach'ten *tr* pay attention to; (*merken*) note, notice; (*befolgen*) observe; (*berücksichtigen*) consider

beach'tenswert *adj* noteworthy

Beach'tung *f* (-;) attention; notice; observance; consideration

Beamte [bə'amtə] *m* (-n;-n) official

Beam'tenherrschaft *f* bureaucracy

Beam'tenlaufbahn *f* civil service career

Beamtentum [bə'amtəntum] *n* (-[e]s;) officialdom, bureaucracy

Beamtin [bə'amtɪn] *f* (-;-nen) official

beäng'stigen *tr* make anxious, alarm

beanspruchen [bə'an/pruxən] *tr* claim; (*Zeit, Raum*) require; **zu stark beansprucht werden** be worked too hard

beanstanden [bə'an/tandən] *tr* object to, find fault with; (*Waren*) reject; (*Wahl*) contest; (*Recht*) challenge

Bean'standung *f* (-;-en) objection; complaint

bean'tragen *tr* propose; (**bei**) apply for (**to**)

beant'worten *tr* answer

Beant'wortung *f* (-;-en) answer

bear'beiten *tr* work; (*Land*) cultivate; (*Buch, Text*) revise; (*Wörterbuch*) compile; (*für die Bühne*) adapt; (*ein Manuskript*) prepare; (*Thema; Kunden*) work on; (*Person*) try to influence; (*chem*) treat; (*Auftrag*) (*com*) handle; (*Fall*) (*jur*) handle; (*metal*) machine, tool; (*mus*) arrange

bearg'wöhnen *tr* be suspicious of

beaufsichtigen [bə'aufzɪçtɪgən] *tr* supervise; (*Arbeiten*) superintend; (*Kinder*) look after; (*educ*) proctor; **streng b.** keep a sharp eye on

beauf'tragen *tr* commission, appoint; (**mit**) entrust (**with**)

Beauftragte [bə'auftraktə] §5 *mf* representative; (*com*) agent

bebau'en *tr* cultivate; (*Gelände*) build up

beben ['bebən] *intr* (**vor**) tremble (**with**), shake (**with**); (*Erde*) quake

bebrillt [bə'brɪlt] *adj* bespectacled

Becher ['beçər] *m* (-s;-) cup, mug

bechern ['beçərn] *intr* (**coll**) booze

Becken ['bekən] *n* (-s;-) basin, bowl; (*anat*) pelvis; (*mus*) cymbal

bedacht [bə'daxt] *adj* (**auf** *acc*) intent (**on**); **auf alles b. sein** think of everything; **darauf b. sein zu** (*inf*) be anxious to (*inf*) || **Bedacht** *m—***B. nehmen auf** (*acc*) take into consideration; **mit B.** deliberately; with caution

bedächtig [bə'deçtɪç], **bedachtsam** [bə'daxtzam] *adj* cautious, deliberate

bedan'ken *ref—***ich würde mich bestens b., wenn** (iron) I would be most indignant if; **sich b. bei j—m für** thank s.o. for

Bedarf [bə'darf] *m* (-[e]s;) demand; requirement; (**an** *dat*) need (**of**); **bei B. if** required; **den B. decken** meet the demand; **nach B. as** required;

seinen B. decken an (*dat*) get one's supply of

Bedarfs'artikel *pl* needs, supplies

Bedarfs'fall *m—***im B. in** case of need

Bedarfs'güter *pl* consumer goods

Bedarfs'haltestelle *f* optional bus or trolley stop

Bedarfs'träger *m* consumer

bedauerlich [bə'dau·ərlɪç] *adj* regrettable

bedau'erlicherweise *adv* unfortunately

bedauern [bə'dau·ərn] *tr* pity, feel sorry for; regret, deplore || **Bedauern** *n* (-s;) (**über** *acc*) regret (**over**); (*Mitleid*) (**mit**) pity (**for**)

bedau'ernswert *adj* pitiful, pitiable

bedecken (bedek'ken) *tr* cover; **bedeckt** overcast

Bedeckung (**Bedek'kung**) *f* (-;-en) cover; escort; (*mil*) escort; (*nav*) convoy

beden'ken §66 *tr* consider; (*beachten*) bear in mind; (*im Testament*) provide for || *ref* deliberate, think a matter over; **sich e–s anderen b.** change one's mind || **Bedenken** *n* (-s;-) (*Erwägung*) consideration, reflection; (*Einwand*) objection; (*Zweifel*) doubt, scruple

bedenk'lich *adj* (*ernst*) serious, critical; (*gefährlich*) risky; (*heikel*) ticklish; (*Charakter*) questionable

bedeu'ten *tr* mean; **das hat nichts zu b.** that doesn't matter; **j–m b., daß** make it clear to s.o. that

bedeu'tend *adj* important; (*beträchtlich*) considerable

bedeutsam [bə'dɔɪtzam] *adj* significant; (*Blick*) meaningful

Bedeu'tung *f* (-;-en) meaning; (*Wichtigkeit*) importance

bedeu'tungsvoll *adj* significant

bedie'nen *tr* wait on, serve; (*Maschine*) operate || *ref* (*genit*) make use of; **bedienen Sie sich** help yourself || *intr* wait on people; (*cards*) follow suit

Bedie'nung *f* (-;) service; servants; waitresses

Bedienungs– *comb.fm.* control

Bedie'nungsanweisung *f* instructions

Bedie'nungsmannschaft *f* gun crew

bedingen [bə'dɪŋən] *tr* condition, stipulate; (*in sich schließen*) imply; **bedingt** conditioned, conditional

bedin'gungsweise *adv* conditionally

bedrän'gen *tr* press hard; (*beunruhigen*) pester; **bedrängte Lage** state of distress; **bedrängte Verhältnisse** financial difficulties

Bedrängnis [bə'drenɪs] *f* (-;-se) distress; **in ärgster B.** in dire straits

bedro'hen *tr* threaten, menace

bedroh'lich *adj* threatening

bedrucken (bedruk'ken) *tr* print on; (*Stoff*) print

bedrücken (bedrük'ken) *tr* oppress

bedür'fen §69 *intr* (*genit*) require

Bedürfnis [bə'dyrfnɪs] *n* (-ses;-se) need, requirement; (*Wunsch*) desire; **Bedürfnisse** necessities; **das dringende B. haben zu** (*inf*) have the urge to (*inf*)

Bedürf'nisanstalt *f* comfort station
bedürf'nislos *adj* having few needs
bedürftig [bə'dʏrftɪç] *adj* needy; **b. sein** (*genit*) be in need of
Beefsteak ['bifstɛk] *n* (-s;-s) steak; **Deutsches B.** hamburger
beehren [bə'erən] *tr* honor || *ref—sich b. zu* (*inf*) have the honor of (*ger*)
beei'len *ref* hurry (up)
beein'drucken *tr* impress
beeinflussen [bə'aɪnflʊsən] *tr* influence
Beein'flussung *f* (-;) (*genit*) influence (on), effect (on); (pol) lobbying
beeinträchtigen [bə'aɪntrɛçtɪgən] *tr* (*Ruf*) damage; (*Wert*) detract from; (*Rechte*) encroach upon; (*Aussichten*) hurt, spoil
been'den, been'digen *tr* end, conclude; (*Arbeit*) complete
beengen [bə'ɛŋən] *tr* confine, cramp; **sich beengt fühlen** feel cramped; (fig) feel restricted
beer'ben *tr—j—n b.* inherit s.o.'s estate
beerdigen [bə'erdɪgən] *tr* bury, inter
Beer'digung *f* (-;-en) burial
Beere ['berə] *f* (-;-n) berry
Beet [bet] *n* (-[e]s;-e) (agr) bed
befähigen [bə'fe·ɪgən] *tr* enable, qualify
befähigt [bə'fe·ɪçt] *adj* able, capable
Befä'higung *f* (-;-en) qualification; (*Fähigkeit*) ability
befahl [bə'fal] *pret* of **befehlen**
befahrbar [bə'farbar] *adj* (*Weg*) passable; (*Wasser*) navigable
befah'ren §71 *tr* travel; (*Meer*) sail; (*Fluß*) navigate; (*Küste*) sail along; (*Schacht*) go down into
befal'len §72 *tr* strike, attack; infest
befan'gen *adj* embarrassed; (*schüchtern*) shy; (*voreingenommen*) prejudiced; (*parteiisch*) partial
befas'sen *tr* touch, handle || *ref—sich b. mit* concern oneself with
befehden [bəfedən] *tr* make war on
Befehl [bə'fel] *m* (-s;-e) order, command; **auf B.** (*genit*) by order of
befeh'len §51 *tr* order, command; **was b. Sie?** what is your pleasure?
befehligen [bə'feligən] *tr* command, be in command of
Befehls'form *f* imperative mood
Befehlshaber [bə'felshabər] *m* (-s;-) (mil) commanding officer; (nav) commander in chief; **oberster B.** supreme commander
befehlshaberisch [bə'felshabərɪʃ] *adj* imperious
Befehls'stelle *f* command post
befe'stigen *tr* (*an dat*) fasten (to), attach (to); (mil) fortify
Befe'stigung *f* (-;-en) fortification
befeuchten [bə'fɔɪçtən] *tr* moisten, wet
befeu'ern *tr* (aer, naut) mark with lights; (mil) fire on, shoot at
befin'den §59 *tr* deem || *ref* be, feel || **Befinden** *n* (-s;) judgment, view; (state of) health; **je nach B.** according to taste
befindlich [bə'fɪntlɪç] *adj* present, to

be found; **all die im Hafen befindlichen Schiffe** the ships (present) in the harbor; **b. sein** happen to be
beflecken (beflck'ken) *tr* stain, taint
beflissen [bə'flɪsən] *adj* (*genit*) keen (on), interested (in) || **Beflissene** §5 *mf* (*genit*) student (of)
befohlen [bə'folən] *pp* of **befehlen**
befol'gen *tr* obey, comply with
Befol'gung *f* (-;) observance
beför'dern *tr* ship; (*spedieren*) forward; (*im Rang*) promote; (*fördern*) further
Beför'derungsmittel *n* means of transportation
befra'gen *tr* question, interrogate; poll; (*um Rat*) consult
befrakt [bə'frakt] *adj* in tails
befrei'en *tr* free; liberate; (*vom Militärdienst*) exempt; (*von e-r Aufgabe*) excuse; (*von Sorgen, e-r Last*) relieve
Befrei'ung *f* (-;-en) freeing; liberation; exemption; rescue
befremden [bə'frɛmdən] *tr* surprise, astonish; strike as odd || **Befremden** *n* (-s;) surprise, astonishment
befreunden [bə'frɔɪndən] *ref—sich mit etw b.* reconcile oneself to s.th.; **sich mit j—m b.** make friends with s.o.
befrieden [bə'fridən] *tr* pacify
befriedigen [bə'fridɪgən] *tr* satisfy
befrie'digend *adj* satisfactory
befristen [bə'frɪstən] *tr* set a time limit on
Befri'stung *f* (-;-en) time limit
befruchten [bə'frʊxtən] *tr* (*Land*) make fertile; (*schwängern*) impregnate; (*Ei*) fertilize; **künstlich b.** inseminate; (bot) pollinate
befugt [bə'fukt] *adj* authorized
befüh'len *tr* feel, touch
Befund *m* (-[e]s;-e) findings, facts
befürch'ten *tr* fear, be afraid of
Befürch'tung *f* (-;-en) apprehension
befürworten [bə'fyrvərtən] *tr* support; (*anraten*) recommend
begabt [bə'gapt] *adj* gifted, talented
Bega'bung *f* (-;-en) aptitude; (natural) gift, talent
Bega'bungsprüfung *f* intelligence test
begann [bə'gan] *pret* of **beginnen**
begatten [bə'gatən] *tr* mate with || *ref* copulate, mate
bege'ben §80 *tr* (*Anleihen*) float, place; (*Wertpapiere*) sell || *ref* go; occur; **es begab sich** (Bib) it came to pass; **sich an die Arbeit b.** set to work; **sich auf die Flucht b.** take to flight; **sich auf die Reise b.** set out on a trip; **sich b.** (*genit*) renounce; **sich in Gefahr b.** expose oneself to danger
Bege'benheit *f* (-;-en) event, incident
begegnen [bə'gegnən] *intr* (SEIN) (*dat*) meet, come upon; (*Schwierigkeiten, Feind*) encounter; (*Gefahr*) face
bege'hen §82 *tr* walk on; walk along; (*Verbrechen, Irrtum*) commit; (*Fest*) celebrate
Begehr [bə'ger] *m & n* (-s;) desire; request; (econ) demand
begehren [bə'gerən] *tr* wish for; crave;

(Bib) covet; etw von j-m b. ask s.o. for s.th. || intr (nach) yearn (for)

begeh'renswert adj desirable

begehr'lich adj covetous

begehrt [bə'gert] adj in demand

begeistert [bə'gaɪstərt] adj enthusiastic

Begei'sterung f (-;) enthusiasm

Begier [bə'gir] f (-;) var of **Begierde**

Begierde [bə'girdə] f (-;-n) desire; (fleshly) appetite; eagerness; craving

begierig [bə'giriç] adj eager; (Augen) hungry; (nach, auf acc) desirous (of); b. zu (inf) eager to (inf)

begie'ßen §76 tr water; (culin) baste; das wollen wir b. we want to celebrate it (by drinking)

Beginn [bə'gɪn] m (-[e]s;) beginning; (Ursprung) origin

beginnen [bə'gɪnən] §52 tr & intr begin

beglaubigen [bə'glaubɪgən] tr certify, authenticate; (Gesandten) accredit

Beglau'bigung f (-;) authentication; accreditation

Beglau'bigungsschreiben n (dipl) credentials

beglei'chen §85 tr balance; (Rechnung) pay in full; (Streit) settle

begleiten [bə'glaɪtən] tr accompany; escort; see (e.g., off, home); hinaus b. see to the door

Beglei'ter -in §6 mf companion

Begleit'erscheinung f concomitant

Begleit'musik f background music

Begleit'schreiben s covering letter

Beglei'tung f (-;-en) company; escort; (Gefolge) retinue; (mus) accompaniment

beglück'wünschen tr (zu) congratulate (on)

Beglück'wünschung f (-;-en) congratulation

begnadet [bə'gnadət] adj highly gifted

begnadigen [bə'gnadɪgən] tr pardon; (pol) grant amnesty to

Begna'digung f (-;-en) pardon; amnesty

begnügen [bə'gnygən] ref (mit) content oneself (with), be satisfied (with)

begonnen [bə'gɔnən] pp of **beginnen**

begra'ben §87 tr bury

Begräbnis [bə'grepnɪs] n (-ses;-se) burial; funeral

Begräb'nisfeier f funeral

Begräb'nisstätte f burial place

begradigen [bə'gradɪgən] tr straighten; (tech) align

begrei'fen §88 tr touch, handle; (verstehen) grasp; (enthalten) comprise

begreif'lich adj understandable

begreif'licherweise adv understandably

begren'zen tr bound; limit, restrict

Begren'zung f (-;-en) limitation

Begriff [bə'grɪf] m (-[e]s;-e) idea, notion; (Ausdruck) term; (philos) concept; im B. sein zu (inf) to be at the point of (ger)

begriffen [bə'grɪfən] adj—b. sein in (dat) be in the process of

begrün'den tr found, establish; (Behauptung) substantiate, prove

Begrün'der -in §6 mf founder

Begrün'dung f (-;-en) establishment; proof; (Grund) ground, reason

begrüßen tr greet; welcome

begünstigen [bə'gynstɪgən] tr favor; (fördern) promote, support; (jur) aid and abet

Begün'stiger m (-s;-) accessory after the fact

Begünstigte [bə'gynstɪçtə] §5 mf (ins) beneficiary

Begün'stigung f (-;-en) promotion, encouragement; support, backing; (jur) aiding and abetting

begut'achten tr give an expert opinion on; b. lassen obtain expert opinion on

begütert [bə'gytərt] adj well-to-do

begütigen [bə'gytɪgən] tr appease

behaart [bə'hart] adj hairy

behäbig [bə'hebɪç] adj comfort-loving; (beleibt) portly

behaftet [bə'haftət] adj afflicted

behagen [bə'hagən] intr (dat) please, suit || **Behagen** n (-s;) pleasure

behaglich [bə'haklɪç] adj pleasant; (traulich) snug, cozy

behal'ten §90 tr keep, retain; **Recht b.** turn out to be right

Behälter [bə'heltər] m (-s;-) container; box; (für Öl, usw.) tank

behan'deln tr treat; deal with; handle

behän'gen §92 tr hang; deck out

beharren [bə'harən] intr remain (unchanged); (in dat) persevere (in); (auf dat) persist (in), stick (to)

beharrlich [bə'harlɪç] adj steadfast

behau'en §93 tr hew

behaupten [bə'hauptən] tr declare, assert; (festhalten) maintain, retain; allege || ref stand one's ground; (Preise) remain steady

behausen [bə'hauzən] tr lodge, house

Behau'sung f (-;-en) dwelling

behe'ben §94 tr (Schwierigkeiten) remove; (Zweifel) dispel; (Schaden) repair; (Lage) remedy; (Geld) withdraw; (Schmerzen) eliminate

beheimatet [bə'haɪmatət] adj—b. sein in (dat) reside in; come from

Behelf [bə'helf] m (-[e]s;-e) expedient; makeshift

behel'fen §96 ref (mit) make do (with)

Behelfs— comb.fm. temporary

behelfs'mäßig adj temporary, makeshift

behelligen [bə'helɪgən] tr bother

Behel'ligung f (-;-en) bother, trouble

behende [bə'hendə] adj agile, quick; (gewandt) handy; (geistig) smart

beherbergen [bə'herbergən] tr take in, put up (as guest)

beherr'schen tr (Land) rule; (Sprache) master; (Gefühle) control; (überragen) tower over; **den Luftraum b.** (mil) have air supremacy

Beherr'scher -in §6 mf ruler || m master || f mistress

beherzigen [bə'hertsɪgən] tr take to heart, remember

beherzt [bə'hertst] adj courageous

behe'xen tr bewitch; (fig) captivate

behilflich [bə'hɪlflɪç] adj helpful

behin'dern tr hinder; hamper; block

behor'chen tr overhear

Behörde [bə'hørdə] *f* (-;-n) authority, board; *die Behörden* the authorities

behördlich [bə'hørtlɪç] *adj* official

behü'ten *tr* (vor *dat*) protect (against); **Gott behüte!** God forbid!

behutsam [bə'hutzam] *adj* wary

bei [baɪ] *prep* (*dat*) (*Ort*) by, beside, at, with, in; (*in Anschriften*) in care of, c/o; (*Zeit, Umstände*) at, by, during, on; (*Zustände, Eigenschaften*) at, while, in; **bei mir haben** have on me; **bei meiner Ehre** upon my honor; **bei Schiller** in the works of Schiller; **bei uns** at our house; **bei weitem** by far

bei'behalten §90 *tr* retain, keep

Bei'blatt *n* supplement

bei'bringen §65 *tr* obtain, procure; (*Beweise, Zeugen*) produce; (*Arznei, Gift*) administer; (*Wunde, Niederlage, Schlag, Verluste*) inflict; **j-m die Nachricht schonend b.** break the news gently to s.o.; **j-m etw b.** teach s.o. s.th., make s.th. clear to s.o.

Beichte ['baɪçtə] *f* (-;-n) confession

beichten ['baɪçtən] *tr* (eccl) confess

Beicht'kind *n* (eccl) penitent

Beicht'stuhl *m* (eccl) confessional

beide ['baɪdə] *adj* both; two || *pron* both; two; **keiner von beiden** neither of them

beiderlei ['baɪdər'laɪ] *invar adj* both kinds of

beiderseitig ['baɪdər'zaɪtɪç] *adj* bilateral; (*gemeinsam*) mutual

beiderseits ['baɪdər'zaɪts] *adv* on both sides; mutually, reciprocally || *prep* (*genit*) on both sides of

beieinan'der *adv* together; **gut b. sein** (coll) be in good shape

Bei'fahrer -in §6 *mf* relief driver; passenger (*next to the driver*)

Bei'fall *m* approval; applause

bei'fällig *adj* approving; (*Bericht*) favorable || *adv* approvingly

Bei'fallklatschen *n* clapping, applause

Bei'fallsgeschrei *n* loud cheering

Bei'fallsruf *m* cheer

Bei'film *m* (cin) second feature

bei'folgend *adj* enclosed

bei'fügen *tr* add; (*e-m Brief*) enclose

bei'fügend *adj* (gram) attributive

Bei'fügung *f* (-;-en) addition, enclosure; (gram) attributive

Bei'gabe *f* extra; funerary gift

bei'geben §80 *tr* add; assign || *intr* give in; **klein b.** knuckle under

Bei'geschmack *m* taste, flavor; tinge

Bei'hilfe *f* aid; (*Stipendium*) grant; (*Unterstützung*) subsidy; allowance; (jur) aiding and abetting

bei'kommen § 99 *intr* (SEIN) (*dat*) get the better of; (*dat*) reach; **e-r Schwierigkeit b.** overcome

Beil [baɪl] *n* (-[e]s;-e) hatchet

Bei'lage *f* (*im Brief*) enclosure; (*e-r Zeitung*) supplement; **Fleisch mit B.** meat and vegetables

beiläufig ['baɪloɪfɪç] *adj* incidental; casual || *adv* by the way, incidentally; **b. erwähnen** mention in passing

bei'legen *tr* add; (*Titel*) confer; (*Wichtigkeit*) attach; (*Streit*) settle; etw

e-m Brief b. enclose s.th. in a letter

Bei'leid *n* (-s;) condolence(s)

bei'liegen §108 *intr—e-m Brief b.** be enclosed in a letter; **j-m b.** lie with s.o

beim *abbr* bei dem

bei'messen §70 *tr* attribute, impute

bei'mischen *tr* mix in

Bein [baɪn] *n* (-[e]s;-e) leg; (*Knochen*) bone; (fig) foot; **j-m ein B. stellen** trip s.o.

beinahe ['baɪna·ə], [baɪ'na·e] *adv* almost, nearly

Bei'name *m* appellation; (*Spitzname*) nickname

Bein'bruch *m* fracture, broken leg

Bein'schiene *f* (surg) splint; (sport) shin guard

Bein'schützer *m* (sport) shin guard

Bein'stellen *n* (sport) tripping

bei'ordnen *tr* assign, appoint (*s.o.*) as assistant; (*dat*) place (*s.th.*) on a level (with)

beipflichten ['baɪpflɪçtən] *intr* (*dat*) agree with (*s.o.*), agree to (*s.th.*)

Bei'programm *n* (cin) second feature

Bei'rat *m* (-s;⸚e) adviser, counselor; (*Körperschaft*) advisory board

beir'ren *tr* mislead

beisammen [baɪ'zamən] *adv* together

Beisam'mensein *n* (-s;) being together; gathering, reunion; **geselliges B.** social; informal reception

Bei'satz *m* addition; (*bei Legierung*) alloy; (gram) appositive

Bei'schlaf *m* sexual intercourse

bei'schließen §76 *tr* enclose

Bei'schluß *m—unter B. von allen Dokumenten** with all documents attached

bei'schreiben §62 *tr* write in the margin; add as a postscript

Bei'schrift *f* postscript

Bei'sein *n* (-s;) presence

beisei'te *adv* aside; **b. schaffen** remove; (coll) do (*s.o.*) in

bei'setzen *tr* bury, inter

Bei'sitzer *m* associate judge

Bei'spiel *n* example; **zum B.** for example

bei'spielhaft *adj* exemplary

bei'spiellos *adj* unparalleled

bei'spielsweise *adv* by way of example

bei'springen §142 *intr* (*dat*) come to the aid of

beißen ['baɪsən] §53 *tr & intr* bite

bei'ßend *adj* biting; stinging, pungent, acrid; sarcastic; (*Reue*) bitter

Beiß'korb *m* muzzle

Beiß'zahn *m* (anat) incisor

Beiß'zange *f* pincers, nippers

Bei'stand *m* aid, support; (*Person*) assistant

bei'stehen §146 *intr* (*dat*) stand by, back, support

Bei'steuer *f* contribution

bei'steuern *tr* contribute

bei'stimmen *intr* (*dat*) agree with

Bei'stimmung *f* (-;) approval

Bei'strich *m* comma

Beitrag ['baɪtrak] *m* (-[e]s;⸚e) contribution; (*e-s Mitglieds*) dues

bei'tragen §132 *tr & intr* contribute
bei'treiben §62 *tr* collect; (*Abgaben*) exact; (*mil*) commandeer, requisition
bei'treten §152 *intr* (SEIN) (*dat*) join; (*j-s Meinung*) concur in
Bei'tritt *m* joining; concurrence
Bei'wagen *m* (aut) sidecar
Bei'werk *n* (-[e]s;) accessories
bei'wohnen *intr* (*dat*) attend; (*e-m Ereignis*) be witness to; (*j-m*) have intercourse with (*s.o.*)
Bei'wort *n* (-[e]s;≃er) epithet; (gram) adjective
Beize ['baftsǝ] *f* (-;-n) corrosive; (wood) stain; (*Falken-*) falconry; (culin) marinade
beizeiten [baɪ'tsaɪtǝn] *adv* on time; (*frühzeitig*) early
beizen ['baɪtsǝn] *tr* (*ätzen*) corrode; (*Holz*) stain; (*Wunde*) cauterize; (hunt) go hawking
bejahen [bǝ'ja-ǝn] *tr* say 'yes' to
beja'hend *adj* affirmative
bejahrt [bǝ'jart] *adj* aged
bekämp'fen *tr* fight, oppose
bekannt [bǝ'kant] *adj* known; familiar; (*berühmt*) well-known || Bekannte §5 *mf* acquaintance
Bekannt'gabe *f* announcement
bekannt'geben §80 *tr* announce
bekannt'lich *adv* as is well known
bekannt'machen *tr* announce; (*Gesetz*) promulgate
Bekannt'machung *f* (-;-en) publication, announcement; (*Plakat*) poster
Bekannt'schaft *f* (-;) acquaintance; (coll) acquaintances
bekeh'ren *tr* convert || *ref* (zu) become a convert (to)
Bekehrte [bǝ'kertǝ] §5 *mf* convert
beken'nen §97 *tr* (*Sünde*) confess; (*zugestehen*) admit; Farbe b. follow suit; (fig) put one's cards on the table || *ref*—sich schuldig b. plead guilty; sich zu e-r Religion b. profess a religion; sich zu e-r Tat b. own up to a deed; sich zu j-m b. stand by s.o., believe in s.o.
Bekennt'nis *n* (eccl) confession; (*Konfession*) denomination
bekla'gen *tr* deplore; (*Tod*) mourn || *ref* (über *acc*) complain (about), find fault (with)
bekla'genswert *adj* deplorable
Beklagte [bǝ'klaktǝ] §5 *mf* defendant
beklat'schen *tr* applaud
bekle'ben *tr* paste; (*mit Etiketten*) label; e-e Mauer mit Plakaten b. paste posters on a wall
beklei'den *tr* clothe, dress; (*Mauer*) face, cover; (*Amt*) hold
beklem'men *tr* stifle, oppress
Beklem'mung *f* (-;-en) worry, anxiety; Beklemmungen claustrophobia
beklommen [bǝ'klɔmǝn] *adj* uneasy
bekom'men §99 *tr* get; obtain; receive; (*Schnupfen*) catch; (*Risse*) develop || *intr* (*dat*) do good; j-m schlecht b. do s.o. harm; wohl bekomm's! to your health!
bekömmlich [bǝ'kœmlɪç] *adj* digestible; (*gesund*) healthful; (*zuträglich*) wholesome

beköstigen [bǝ'kœstɪgǝn] *tr* board, feed || *ref*—sich selbst b. do one's own cooking
bekräf'tigen *tr* (*Vorschlag*) support; (*bestätigen*) substantiate; mit e-m Eid b. seal with an oath
bekrän'zen *tr* wreath, crown
bekreu'zen, bekreu'zigen *ref* cross oneself, make the sign of the cross
bekrie'gen *tr* make war on
bekrit'teln *tr* criticize, pick at
bekrit'zeln *tr* scribble on, doodle on
beküm'mern *tr* worry, trouble || *ref* (um) concern onself (with), bother (about)
beküm'mert *adj* (über *acc*) worried (about)
bekunden [bǝ'kundǝn] *tr* manifest, show; (*öffentlich*) state publicly
bela'den §103 *tr* load; (fig) burden
Belag [bǝ'lak] *m* (-[e]s;≃) covering; coat(ing); flooring; layer; surface
bela'gern *tr* besiege, beleaguer
Bela'gerung *f* (-;-en) siege
Belang [bǝ'laŋ] *m* (-[e]s;e) importance, consequence; Belange interests
belan'gen *tr* (jur) sue; was mich belangt as far as I am concerned
belang'los *adj* unimportant
bela'sten *tr* load (down); (*Grundstück*) encumber; (fig) burden; (acct) charge; (jur) incriminate
belästigen [bǝ'lestɪgǝn] *tr* annoy, bother; (*mit Fragen*) pester; (*unabsichtlich*) inconvenience
Bela'stung *f* (-;-en) load; encumbrance; (fig) burden; (acct) debit; die Zeiten größter B. the peak hours
Bela'stungsprobe *f* (fig) acid test
Bela'stungszeuge *m* witness for the prosecution
belau'fen §105 *ref*—sich b. auf (*acc*) amount to, come to
belau'schen *tr* overhear
bele'ben *tr* animate; (*Getränk*) spike; wieder b. revive
belebt [bǝ'lept] *adj* animated, lively
Bele'bungsmittel *n* stimulant
Beleg [bǝ'lek] *m* (-s;-e) (*Beweisstück*) evidence; (*Unterlage*) voucher; (*Beispiel*) example; (jur) exhibit
bele'gen *tr* cover; (*Platz*) take, occupy; (*bemannen*) man; (*beweisen*) verify; (*Vorlesung*) register for; ein Brötchen mit Schinken b. make a ham sandwich; mit Beispielen b. exemplify; mit Fliesen b. tile; mit Steuern b. tax; mit Teppichen b. carpet || *ref* become coated
Beleg'schaft *f* (-;-en) crew; personnel; shift
Beleg'schein *m* voucher; receipt
Beleg'stelle *f* reference
belegt [bǝ'lekt] *adj* (*Platz*) reserved; (*Zunge*) coated; (*Stimme*) husky; (telp) busy; belegtes Brot sandwich
beleh'ren *tr* instruct || *ref*—sich b. lassen listen to reason
beleh'rend *adj* instructive
Beleh'rung *f* (-;-en) instruction; (*Lehre*) lesson; (*Rat*) advice; zu Ihrer B. for your information

beleibt [bə'laɪpt] adj stout
beleidigen [bə'laɪdɪɡən] tr offend
belei'digend adj offensive
bele'sen adj well-read
beleuch'ten tr light (up), illuminate;
  (fig) throw light on
Beleuch'ter m (aer) pathfinder; (theat)
  juicer
Beleuch'tung f (-;-en) lighting, illumination; (fig) elucidation
Beleuch'tungskörper m lighting fixture
Belgien ['bɛlɡjən] n (-s) Belgium
Belgier –in ['bɛlɡjər(ɪn)] §6 mf Belgian
belgisch ['bɛlɡɪʃ] adj Belgian
belichten [bə'lɪçtən] tr (phot) expose
Belich'tung f (-;-en) exposure
belie'ben intr please || impers (dat)—
  wenn es Ihnen beliebt if you please
  || Belieben n (-s) liking; es steht in
  Ihrem B. it's up to you; nach B. as
  you like
beliebig [bə'libɪç] adj any (you please)
  || adv as ... as you please
beliebt [bə'lipt] adj favorite; (bel)
  popular (with)
Beliebt'heit f (-;) popularity
belie'fern tr supply, furnish
bellen ['bɛlən] intr bark
belob(ig)en [bə'lob(ɪɡ)ən] tr praise;
  commend; (mil) cite
beloh'nen tr reward
belü'gen §111 tr lie to, deceive
belustigen [bə'lustɪɡən] tr amuse
bemächtigen [bə'mɛçtɪɡən] intr (genit)
  seize, get hold of; (mil) seize
bemä'keln tr criticize, carp at
bema'len tr paint; decorate
bemängeln [bə'mɛŋəln] tr criticize
bemannen [bə'manən] tr man
Beman'nung f (-;-en) (nav) crew
bemänteln [bə'mɛntəln] tr gloss over;
  (Fehler, Fehltritt) cover up
bemei'stern tr master || ref control
  oneself; (genit) get hold of
bemerk'bar adj perceptible
bemer'ken tr notice; (äußern) remark
bemer'kenswert adj remarkable
Bemer'kung f (-;-en) note; remark
bemes'sen §70 tr measure; proportion
bemit'leiden tr pity, feel sorry for
bemittelt [bə'mɪtəlt] adj well-to-do
bemogeln [bə'moɡəln] tr cheat
bemü'hen tr trouble, bother; bemüht
  sein zu (inf) take pains to (inf) ||
  ref bother, exert oneself; sich für
  j–n b. intervene for s.o.; sich um
  etw b. make an effort to obtain s.th.;
  sich um j–n b. attend to s.o.; sich
  zu j–m b. go to s.o.
Bemü'hung f (-;-en) bother; effort
bemüßigt [bə'mysɪçt] adj—sich b. fühlen zu (inf) feel obliged to (inf)
bemu'stern tr—ein Angebot b. (com)
  send samples of an offer
bemuttern [bə'mutərn] tr mother
benachbart [bə'naxbart] adj neighboring; (Fachgebiet) related, allied
benachrichtigen [bə'naxrɪçtɪɡən] tr
  notify; put on notice
Benach'richtigung f (-;-en) notification; notice
benachteiligen [bə'naxtaɪlɪɡən] tr

place at a disadvantage, handicap;
  discriminate against
benebelt [bə'nebəlt] adj covered in
  mist; (fig) groggy
benedeien [bene'daɪ·ən] tr bless
beneh'men §116 tr—j–m etw b. take
  s.th. away from s.o. || ref behave ||
  Benehmen n (-s) behavior
beneiden [bə'naɪdən] tr—j–n um etw
  b. begrudge s.o. s.th.
benei'denswert adj enviable
benen'nen §97 tr name, term
Bengel ['bɛŋəl] m (-s;-) rascal
benommen [bə'nomən] adj dazed
benö'tigen tr need
benutz'bar adj usable
benut'zen, benüt'zen tr use, make use
  of
Benut'zerkarte f library card
Benzin [bent'sin] n (-s;-e) gasoline
Benzin'behälter m gas tank
beobachten [bə'obaxtən] tr observe;
  (polizeilich) keep under surveillance;
  (med) keep under observation
Beob'achtung f (-;-en) observation;
  (e–s Gesetzes) observance
beor'dern tr order (to go to a place)
bepacken (bepak'ken) tr load (down)
bepflan'zen tr plant
bequem [bə'kvem] adj comfortable;
  cozy; (Stellung) soft; (Raten, Lösung)
  easy; (faul) lazy; b. zur Hand haben
  have handy
berappen [bə'rapən] tr (coll) shell out
bera'ten §63 tr (über acc) advise (on);
  discuss || ref & intr (über acc) con-
  fer (about), deliberate (on)
bera'tend adj advisory, consulting
beratschlagen [bə'rat/laɡən] intr (über
  acc) consult (on); mit j–m b. consult
  s.o., confer with s.o.
berat'schlagend adj advisory
Bera'tung f (-;-en) advice; (jur, med)
  consultation; in B. sein be under consideration
Bera'tungsstelle f counseling center
berau'ben tr (genit) rob (of); (genit)
  dispossess (of); (genit) deprive (of);
  (genit) bereave (of)
berech'nen tr calculate, figure out;
  (schätzen) estimate; (com) charge
berech'nend adj calculating
Berech'nung f (-;-en) calculation
berechtigen [bə'rɛçtɪɡən] tr authorize;
  justify, warrant; (zu) entitle (to)
Berech'tigung f (-;-en) right, authorization; justification; (zu) title (to)
bereden [bə'redən] tr talk over, discuss; j–n zu etw b. talk s.o. into s.th.
  || ref—sich mit j–m über etw b. con-
  fer with s.o. on s.th.
beredsam [bə'retzam] adj eloquent
beredt [bə'ret] adj eloquent
Bereich m & n (-[e]s;-e) region;
  range; (fig) field, sphere; es fällt
  nicht in meinen B. it's not within my
  province
bereichern [bə'raɪçərn] tr enrich
berei'fen tr cover with frost; (aut) put
  tires on
berei'nigen tr (Streit, Konto) settle;
  (Mißverständnis) clear up
berei'sen tr tour

bereit [bə'raɪt] *adj* ready
bereiten [bə'raɪtən] *tr* prepare; (*Kaffee*) make; (*Freude*) give
Bereit'schaft *f* (-;) readiness; team, squad; (mil) alert
bereit'stellen *tr* make available
Berel'tung *f* (-;-en) preparation; (*Herstellung*) manufacture
bereit'willig *adj* ready, willing
bereu'en *tr* rue, regret
Berg [bɛrk] *m* (-[e]s;-e) mountain; (*Hügel*) hill; **über alle Berge sein** be off and away; **zu Berge stehen** stand on end
bergab' *adv* downhill, down the mountain
bergauf' *adv* uphill; up the mountain
Berg'bahn *f* mountain railroad
Berg'bau *m* (-[e]s;) mining
Berg'bewohner —in §6 *mf* mountaineer
bergen ['bɛrgən] §54 *tr* rescue; (*enthalten*) hold; (*Gefahr*) involve; (*Segel*) take in; (naut) salvage; (poet) conceal; (rok) recover || *ref*—in sich b. involve
bergig ['bɛrgɪç] *adj* mountainous
Berg'kessel *m* gorge
Berg'kette *f* mountain range
Berg'kluft *f* ravine, gully
Berg'kristall *m* rock crystal, quartz
Berg'land *n* hill country
Berg'mann *m* (-[e]s;-leute) miner
Berg'predigt *f* Sermon on the Mount
Berg'recht *n* mining law
Berg'rücken *m* ridge
Berg'rutsch *m* landslide
Berg'schlucht *f* gorge, ravine
Berg'spitze *f* mountain peak
Berg'steiger —in §6 *mf* mountain climber
Berg'steigerei *f* mountain climbing
Berg'sturz *m* landslide
Ber'gung *f* (-;-en) rescue; (naut) salvage; (rok) recovery
Ber'gungsarbeiten *pl* salvage operations
Ber'gungsschiff *n* salvage vessel; (rok) recovery ship
Berg'wacht *f* mountain rescue service
Berg'werk *n* mine
Berg'wesen *n* mining
Bericht [bə'rɪçt] *m* (-[e]s;-e) report
berichten [bə'rɪçtən] *tr* & *intr* report
Berichterstatter —in [bə'rɪçtər/tatər (ɪn)] §6 *mf* reporter; correspondent; (rad) commentator
Bericht'erstattung *f* (-;) reporting
berichtigen [bə'rɪçtɪgən] *tr* rectify; (*Text*) emend; (*Schuld*) pay off
berie'chen §102 *tr* sniff at; (fig) size up || *recip* (coll) sound each other out
Berlin [bɛr'lin] *n* (-s;) Berlin
Bernstein ['bɛrn/taɪn] *m* amber
bersten ['bɛrstən] §55 *intr* (SEIN) (vor *dat*) burst (with)
berüchtigt [bə'rʏçtɪçt] *adj* notorious
berücken (berük'ken) *tr* captivate
berücksichtigen [bə'rʏkzɪçtɪgən] *tr* (*erwägen*) consider; (*in Betracht ziehen*) make allowance for
Berück'sichtigung *f* (-;-en) consideration

Beruf' *m* (-[e]s;-e) vocation; profession; (*Gewerbe*) trade; (*Tätigkeit*) occupation; (*Laufbahn*) career
beru'fen *adj* called; authorized || §122 *tr* call; (*ernennen*) appoint; (*Geister*) conjure up || *ref*—sich auf ein Gesetz b. quote a law (*in support*); sich auf j—n b. use s.o.'s name as a reference
beruf'lich *adj* professional; vocational
Berufs— *comb.fm.* professional; vocational
Berufs'diplomat *m* career diplomat
Berufs'genossenschaft *f* professional association; trade association
Berufs'heer *n* regular army
Berufs'schule *f* vocational school
Berufs'sportler —in §6 *mf* professional
berufs'tätig *adj* working
Beru'fung *f* (-;-en) call; vocation; appointment; (jur) appeal; **B. einlegen** (jur) appeal; **unter B. auf** (*acc*) referring to
Beru'fungsgericht *n* appellate court
beru'hen *intr* (auf *dat*) be based (on); (auf *dat*) be due (to); **e-e Sache auf sich b. lassen** let a matter rest
beruhigen [bə'ru·ɪgən] *tr* calm; appease
beru'higend *adj* soothing; reassuring
Beru'higung *f* (-;) calming; appeasement, pacification; reassurance; (*der Lage*) stabilization; **zu meiner großen B.** much to my relief
Beru'higungsmittel *n* sedative
berühmt [bə'rymt] *adj* (wegen) famous (for)
Berühmt'heit *f* (-;-en) renown; (*berühmte Persönlichkeit*) celebrity
berüh'ren *tr* touch; (*erwähnen*) touch on; (*wirken auf*) affect; (*Zug*) pass through || *ref* come in contact, meet
Berüh'rung *f* (-;-en) touch; contact
besä'en *tr* sow; (*bestreuen*) strew; **mit Sternen besät** star-spangled
besa'gen *tr* say; (*bedeuten*) mean
besagt [bə'zakt] *adj* aforesaid
besänftigen [bə'zɛnftɪgən] *tr* calm; appease || *ref* calm down
Besatz' *m* trimming
Besat'zung *f* (-;-en) garrison; occupation; army of occupation; (aer, nav) crew
Besat'zungsarmee *f* army of occupation
Besat'zungsbehörde *f* military government
besau'fen §124 *ref* (coll) get drunk
beschä'digen *tr* damage || *ref* injure oneself
beschaf'fen *tr*—**ich bin eben so b.** that's the way I am; **übel b. sein** be in bad shape || *tr* get, procure; (*Geld*) raise
Beschaf'fenheit *f* (-;-en) quality, property; (*Zustand*) state; (*Art*) nature; (*Anlage*) design
Beschaf'fung *f* (-;-en) procuring; (*Erwerb*) acquisition
beschäftigen [bə'ʃɛftɪgən] *tr* occupy; keep busy; (*anstellen*) employ; **beschäftigt sein bei** work for (*a company*); **beschäftigt sein mit** be busy with

beschä/men *tr* shame, make ashamed; beschämt sein be ashamed

Beschau/ *f* inspection

beschau/en *tr* look at; inspect

beschau/lich *adj* contemplative

Bescheid [bə'ʃaɪt] *m* (-[e]s;-e) answer; (*Anweisung*) instructions, directions; (*Auskunft*) information; (*jur*) decision; B. hinterlassen bei leave word with; B. wissen be well-informed; j-m B. geben (or sagen) give s.o. information or directions

beschei/den *adj* modest; (*Preise*) moderate; (*Auswahl*) limited; (*einfach*) simple, plain ‖ §112 *tr* inform; (*beordern*) order, direct; (*vorladen*) summon; (*zuteilen*) allot; abschlägig b. turn down; es ist mir beschieden it fell to my lot ‖ *ref* be satisfied

Beschei/denheit *f* (-;) modesty

bescheinigen [bə'ʃaɪnɪgən] *tr* (*Empfang*) acknowledge; (*bezeugen*) certify

Beschei/nigung *f* (-;-en) acknowledgement; certification; (*Schein*) certificate; (*im Brief*) to whom it may concern

beschei/ßen §53 *tr* (sl) cheat

beschen/ken j-n b. mit present s.o. with

bescheren [bə'ʃeːrən] *tr* give gifts to

Besche/rung *f* (-;-en) distribution of gifts (especially at Christmas); e-e schöne B. (coll) a nice mess

beschicken (beschik/ken) *tr* (mit Waren) supply; (*Messe*) exhibit at, send exhibits to; (*Kongreß*) send delegates to; (*Hochofen*) feed, charge

beschie/ßen §76 *tr* shoot up; (mil, phys) bombard

beschimp/fen *tr* insult, call (s.o.) names

beschir/men *tr* shield, protect

beschla/fen *tr* (e-e Frau) sleep with; (e-e Sache) sleep on

Beschlag/ *m* (-s;⸚e) hardware; (Huf-) horse shoes; (auf Fensterscheiben) steam, vapor; (Überzug) thin coating; in B. nehmen confiscate; (Schiff) seize; (Gehalt) attach

beschla/gen *adj*—b. in (dat) well-versed in ‖ §132 *tr* cover, coat; (Metallverzierungen) fit, mount; (Pferd) shoe ‖ *ref & intr* steam up; (Mauer) sweat; (Metall) oxidize

beschlagnahmen [bə'ʃlaːknaːmən] *tr* confiscate; (Schuldnervermögen) attach; (mil) requisition; (naut) seize

beschlei/chen §85 *tr* stalk, creep up on

beschleunigen [bə'ʃlɔɪnɪgən] *tr* accelerate, speed up

Beschleu/niger *m* (-s;-) accelerator

beschlie/ßen §76 *tr* end, wind up; (sich entschließen) decide

Beschluß/ *m* conclusion; decision; resolution; (jur) decree; unter B. under lock and key; zum B. in conclusion

beschluß/fähig *adj*—b. sein have a quorum; beschlußfähige Anzahl quorum

beschmie/ren *tr* smear, coat; grease

beschmut/zen *tr* soil, dirty

beschnei/den §106 *tr* clip, trim; (fig) curtail; (surg) circumcise

beschneit [bə'ʃnaɪt] *adj* snow-covered

beschönigen [bə'ʃøːnɪgən] *tr* (Fehler) whitewash, cover up, gloss over

beschrän/ken *tr* limit

beschränkt/ *adj* limited; (Verhältnisse) straitened; (geistig) dense

beschrei/ben §62 *tr* describe; use up (in writing)

Beschrei/bung *f* (-;-en) description

beschrei/ten §86 *tr* walk on; den Rechtsweg b. take legal action

beschriften [bə'ʃrɪftən] *tr* inscribe; (Kisten) mark; (mit Etikett) label

Beschrif/tung *f* (-;-en) inscription; lettering; (erläuternde) caption

beschuldigen [bə'ʃʊldɪgən] *tr* (genit) accuse (of), charge (with)

beschummeln [bə'ʃʊməln] *tr* (coll) (um) cheat (out of)

Beschuß/ *m* test firing

beschüt/zen *tr* protect, defend

beschwat/zen *tr* gossip about; j-n dazu b. zu (inf) talk s.o. into (ger)

Beschwerde [bə'ʃveːrdə] *f* (-;-n) trouble; (Klage, Krankheit) complaint

beschweren [bə'ʃveːrən] *tr* burden ‖ *ref* (über acc) complain (about)

beschwer/lich *adj* troublesome

beschwichtigen [bə'ʃvɪçtɪgən] *tr* appease; (Hunger) satisfy; (Gewissen) soothe

beschwin/deln *tr* swindle (out of)

beschwingt [bə'ʃvɪŋt] *adj* lively

beschwipst [bə'ʃvɪpst] *adj* tipsy, high

beschwö/ren *tr* swear to; (Geister) conjure up; (bitten) implore, entreat

Beschwö/rungsformel *f* incantation

beseelen [bə'zeːlən] *tr* inspire, animate

beseelt/ *adj* animated; (von Hoffnungen) filled; (Spiel) inspired

bese/hen §138 *tr* look at; inspect

beseitigen [bə'zaɪtɪgən] *tr* eliminate, remove, clear away; (Übel, Fehler) redress; (Schwierigkeit) overcome; (töten) do away with; (pol) purge

Besen ['beːzən] *m* (-s;-) broom

Be/senstiel *m* broomstick

besessen [bə'zɛsən] *adj* (von) obsessed (by); (vom Teufel) possessed

Beses/senheit *f* (-;-en) obsession; (vom Teufel) possession

beset/zen *tr* occupy; (mit Juwelen) set off; (Amt, Rolle) fill; (Hut) trim

besetzt/ *adj* (Platz, Abort) occupied; (Stelle) filled; (Kleid) trimmed, set off; (telp) busy

Besetzt/zeichen *n* (telp) busy signal

Beset/zung *f* (-;-en) decoration; (e-r Stelle) filling; (mil) occupation; (theat) cast

besichtigen [bə'zɪçtɪgən] *tr* view; tour; inspect; (mil) inspect, review

Besich/tigung *f* (-;-en) sightseeing; inspection; (mil) inspection, review

besie/deln *tr* colonize; populate

besie/geln *tr* seal

besie/gen *tr* defeat; (Widerstand) overcome; (Gefühle) master

besin/nen §121 *ref* consider; (auf acc) think (of); sich anders b. change one's mind; sich e-s Besseren b. think better of it

besinn'lich adj reflective

Besin'nung f (-;) consciousness; reflection; j-n zur B. bringen bring s.o. to his senses

besin'nungslos adj unconscious; (unüberlegt) senseless

Besitz' m (-es;-e) possession; in B. nehmen take possession of

besitz'anzeigend adj possessive

besit'zen §144 tr own, possess

Besit'zer –in 86 mf possessor, owner

Besitz'ergreifung f (-;-en) occupancy; seizure

Besitz'stand m ownership; (fin) assets

Besitztum [bə'zɪtstum] n (-s;⸚er) possession

Besit'zung f (-;-en) possession, property; (Landgut) estate

besoffen [bə'zɔfən] adj (coll) soused

besohlen [bə'zolən] tr sole

besolden [bə'zoldən] tr pay

Besol'dung f (-;-en) pay, salary

beson'dere §9 adj particular, special

Beson'derheit f (-;-en) peculiarity; (com) specialty

beson'ders adv especially; separately

besonnen [bə'zɔnən] adj prudent; (bedacht) considerate; level-headed

besor'gen tr take care of; (beschaffen) procure, get; (befürchten) fear

Besorgnis [bə'zɔrknɪs] f (-;-se) concern; (Furcht) fear

besorg'niserregend adj alarming

besorgt [bə'zɔrkt] adj (um) worried (about), anxious (for)

Besor'gung f (-;-en) care; procurement; (Auftrag) errand; Besorgungen machen run errands

bespre'chen §64 tr discuss; (Buch) review; e-e Schallplatte b. make a recording || ref confer

Bespre'cher –in 83 mf reviewer, critic

bespren'gen tr sprinkle

besprit'zen tr splash; spray

besser ['bɛsər] adj & adv better

bessern ['bɛsərn] tr better, improve || ref improve

Bes'serung f (-;-en) improvement; baldige B. speedy recovery

Bes'serungsanstalt f reform school

Bestand' m (-[e]s;⸚e) existence; (Vorrat) stock, inventory; (Kassen-) cash on hand; (Baum-) stand; B. an (dat) number of; B. an kampffähigen Truppen effective strength; B. haben, von B. sein have endurance, be lasting

bestän'dig adj constant, steady

Bestands'aufnahme f inventory

Bestand'teil m component; ingredient

bestär'ken tr strengthen, fortify

bestätigen [bə'ʃtɛtɪgən] tr confirm; (Zeugnis) corroborate; (Empfang) acknowledge; (Vertrag) ratify || ref prove true, come true

bestatten [bə'ʃtatən] tr bury, inter

Bestat'tungsinstitut n funeral home

bestau'ben, bestäuben (bə'ʃtɔrbən) tr cover with dust; sprinkle; (bot) pollinate

beste ['bɛstə] §9 adj best; am besten

best (of all); auf dem besten Weg sein zu be well on the way to; aufs b. in the best way; der erste b. anybody

beste'chen §64 tr bribe; (fig) impress

beste'chend adj fascinating, charming

bestech'lich adj open to bribery

Beste'chung f (-;-) bribery

Beste'chungsgeld n bribe

Besteck [bə'ʃtɛk] n (-[e]s;-e) kit; (Tisch-) single service; (aer, naut) reckoning, position; (med) set of instruments

bestecken (bestek'ken) tr stick; (culin) garnish

beste'hen §146 tr undergo; (Prüfung) pass || intr exist, be; (gegen) hold one's own (against); (in e-r Prüfung) pass; b. auf (dat) insist on; b. aus consist of; b. in (dat) consist in

beste'hend adj existing, extant; present

besteh'len §147 tr (um) rob (of)

bestei'gen §148 tr climb; (Schiff) board; (Pferd) mount; (Thron) ascend

Bestell'buch n order book

bestel'len tr order; (Zimmer) reserve; (Zeitung) subscribe to; (ernennen) appoint; (Briefe) deliver; (Feld) till; (kommen lassen) send for

Bestell'zettel m order slip

be'stenfalls adv at best

besteu'ern tr tax

bestialisch [bɛst'jɑlɪʃ] adj beastly

Bestie ['bɛstjə] f (-;-n) beast

bestim'men tr determine; (Zeit, Preis) set; (ernennen) appoint; (Begriff) define; (gram) modify; (math) find; j-n b. zu (or für) destine s.o. for; talk s.o. into || intr decree; b. in (dat) have a say in; b. über (acc) dispose of

bestimmt' adj determined; definite; particular || adv definitely

Bestim'mung f (-;-en) determination; (e-r Zeit, e-s Preises) setting; destination; mission, goal; (e-s Begriffs) definition; (Schicksal) fate; (Vorschrift) regulation; (e-s Vertrags) provision; (gram) modifier; mit B. nach (naut) heading for; seiner B. übergeben dedicate, open

bestra'fen tr punish

bestrah'len tr irradiate; (med) give radiation treatment to

bestre'ben ref strive, endeavor || Bestreben n (-s;) tendency

Bestre'bung f (-;-en) effort

bestrei'chen §85 tr spread; (mit Feuer) rake; mit Butter b. butter

bestrei'ken tr strike

bestrei'ten §86 tr contest; fight; (Ausgaben) defray; (Recht) challenge; (leugnen) deny; e-e Unterhaltung allein b. do all the talking

bestreu'en tr (mit) strew (with)

bestricken (bestrik'ken) tr (fig) charm

besticken (bə'ʃtʏkən) tr arm, equip

bestür'men tr storm; (fig) bombard

Bestür'mung f (-;-en) storming

bestür'zen tr dismay

Besuch [bə'zux] m (-[e]s;-e) visit; (Besucher) visitor(s), company;

(*genit*) visit (to); **auf B. gehen** pay a visit

besu'chen *tr* visit; (*Gasthaus, usw.*) frequent; (*Schule, Versammlung*) attend; (*Kino*) go to

Besu'cher –in §6 *mf* visitor, caller

Besuchs'zeit *f* visiting hours

besudeln *tr* soil, stain

betagt [bə'takt] *adj* advanced in years

beta'sten *tr* finger, touch, handle

betätigen [bə'tɛtɪgən] *tr* set in operation; (*Maschine*) operate; (*Bremse*) apply ‖ *ref*—**sich nützlich b.** make oneself useful; **sich politisch b.** be active in politics

betäuben [bə'tɔɪbən] *tr* deafen; stun; (*Schmerz*) deaden; (*durch Rauschgift*) drug, dope; (*med*) anesthetize

Betäu'bungsmittel *n* drug; painkiller; (*med*) anesthetic

Bete ['betə] *f* (-;-n) beet

beteiligen [bə'taɪlɪgən] *tr* (**an** *dat*, **bei**) give (*s.o.*) a share (in) ‖ *ref* (**an** *dat*) participate (in)

Betei'ligung *f* (-;-en) participation; (*Teilhaberschaft*) partnership; (*Teilnehmerzahl*) attendance

beten ['betən] *tr & intr* pray

beteuern [bə'tɔɪ-ərn] *tr* affirm

betiteln [bə'titəln] *tr* entitle

Beton [be'tɔn] *m* (-s;) concrete

betonen [bə'tonən] *tr* (*Silbe*) stress, accent; (*nachdrücklich*) emphasize

betonieren [betə'nirən] *tr* cement

Betonmisch'maschine *f* cement mixer

betören [bə'tørən] *tr* infatuate

Betracht' *m* (-[e]s;) consideration; **außer B. lassen** rule out; **es kommt nicht in B.** it is out of the question; **in B. ziehen** take into account, consider

betrachten [bə'traxtən] *tr* look at; consider

beträchtlich [bə'trɛçtlɪç] *adj* considerable

Betrach'tung *f* (-;-en) observation; consideration; meditation; **Betrachtungen anstellen über** (*acc*) reflect on

Betrag [bə'trak] *m* (-[e]s;≃e) amount; **über den B. von** in the amount of

betra'gen §132 *tr* amount to ‖ *ref* behave ‖ **Betragen** *n* (-s;) behavior

betrau'en *tr* entrust

betrau'ern *tr* mourn for

Betreff' [bə'trɛf] *m* (-[e]s;) (*am Briefanfang*) re; **in B.** (*genit*) in regard to

betref'fen §151 *tr* befall; (*berühren*) affect, hit; (*angehen*) concern; **betrifft** (*acc*) re; **was das betrifft** as far as that is concerned; **was mich betrifft** I for one

betreffs [bə'trɛfs] *prep* (*genit*) concerning

betrei'ben §62 *tr* carry on; (*leiten*) manage; (*Beruf*) practice; (*Studien*) pursue; (*Maschine*) operate

betre'ten §152 *tr* embarrassed ‖ §152 *tr* step on; set foot on or in; (*Raum*) enter; (*unbefugt*) trespass on

betreuen [bə'trɔɪ-ən] *tr* look after

Betrieb [bə'trip] *m* (-s;-e) operation,

running; (*Unternehmen*) business; (*Anlage*) plant; (*Werkstatt*) workshop; (fig) rush, bustle; **aus dem B. ziehen** take out of service; **außer B.** out of order; **großer B.** hustle and bustle; **in vollem B.** in full swing

betriebsam [bə'tripzam] *adj* enterprising, active

Betrieb'samkeit *f* (-;) hustle

betriebs'fähig *adj* in working order

betriebs'fertig *adj* ready for use

Betriebs'ingenieur *m* production engineer

Betriebs'kosten *pl* operating costs

Betriebs'leiter *m* superintendent

Betriebs'material *n* (rr) rolling stock

Betriebs'prüfer –in §6 *mf* auditor

Betriebs'ruhe *f*—**heute B.** (public sign) closed today

Betriebs'stoff *m* fuel

Betriebs'störung *f* breakdown

Betriebs'wirtschaft *f* industrial management

betrin'ken §143 *ref* get drunk

betroffen [bə'trɔfən] *adj* shocked, stunned; (*heimgesucht*) afflicted

betrü'ben *tr* sadden, distress

betrüb'lich *adj* sad, distressing

betrübt [bə'trypt] *adj* sad, sorrowful

Betrug [bə'truk] *m* (-[e]s;) fraud, swindle; **frommer B.** white lie

betrü'gen §111 *tr* cheat, swindle

Betrüger(r) [bətryge'raɪ] *f* (-;-en) deceit, cheating

betrü'gerisch *adj* deceitful; fraudulent

betrunken [bə'truŋkən] *adj* drunk

Bett [bɛt] *n* (-[e]s;-en) bed

Bett'decke *f* bedspread

Bettelei [bɛtə'laɪ] *f* (-;) begging

betteln ['bɛtəln] *intr* (**um**) beg (for)

betten ['bɛtən] *tr* put to bed ‖ *ref* make onself a bed; bed down

Bett'genosse *m* bedfellow

Bett'gestell *n* bedstead

Bett'himmel *m* canopy (*over a bed*)

bettlägerig ['bɛtlɛgərɪç] *adj* bedridden

Bett'laken *n* bed sheet

Bettler –in ['bɛtlər(ɪn)] §6 *mf* beggar

Bett'stelle *f* bedstead

Bettuch (**Bett'tuch**) *n* sheet

Bett'tung *f* (-;) bedding; (mil) emplacement; (rr) bed

Bett'vorleger *m* bedside rug

Bett'wäsche *f* bed linen

Bett'zeug *n* bedding

betupfen [bə'tupfən] *tr* dab (at); (surg) swab

beugen ['bɔɪgən] *tr* bend; (fig) humble; (gram) inflect ‖ *ref* bend; bow

Beu'gung *f* (-;-en) bending; bowing; (gram) inflection

Beule ['bɔɪlə] *f* (-;-n) lump; (*Geschwür*) boil; (*kleiner Blechschaden*) dent

beunruhigen [bə'unru-ɪgən] *tr* make uneasy, worry, disturb

Beun'ruhigung *f* (-;-en) anxiety, uneasiness; disturbance

beurkunden [bə'urkundən] *tr* authenticate

beurlauben [bə'urlaubən] *tr* grant leave of absence to; (*vom Amt*) suspend; (mil) furlough; **sich b. lassen**

ask for time off || *ref* (bei) take one's leave (of)

beur'teilen *tr* evaluate; (nach) judge (by); **falsch b.** misjudge

Beute ['bɔɪtə] *f* (–;) booty, loot; **zur B. fallen** (*dat*) fall prey to

Beutel ['bɔɪtəl] *m* (–s;–) bag, pouch; purse; (billiards) pocket

beu'telig *adj* baggy

Beu'tezug *m* raid

bevölkern [be'fœlkərn] *tr* populate

Bevöl'kerung *f* (–;–en) population

bevollmächtigen [be'fɔlmɛçtɪgən] *tr* authorize; (*jur*) give (*s.o.*) power of attorney

Bevoll'mächtigte §5 *mf* authorized agent; proxy; (*pol*) plenipotentiary

bevor [bə'for] *conj* before; **bevor ... nicht** until

bevormunden [be'formundən] *tr* treat in a patronizing manner

bevor'raten *tr* stock; stockpile

bevorrechtet [bə'fɔrreçtət] *adj* privileged

bevor'stehen §146 *intr* be imminent, be on hand; **bevorstehend** forthcoming; **j–m b.** be in store for s.o.

bevorzugen [bə'fortsugən] *tr* prefer

bevor'zugt *adj* preferential; high-priority; privileged; favorite

bewa'chen *tr* guard, watch over

bewach'sen §155 *tr* overgrow, cover

Bewa'chung *f* (–;–en) guard, custody

bewaff'nen *tr* arm

Bewaff'nung *f* (–;) armament, arms

Bewahr'anstalt *f* detention home

bewah'ren *tr* keep, preserve; (**vor** *dat*) save (from), protect (against)

bewäh'ren *tr* prove || *ref* prove one's worth; **sich nicht b.** prove a failure

Bewah'rer –in §6 *mf* keeper

bewahrheiten [bə'varhaitən] *tr* verify || *ref* come true

bewährt [bə'vert] *adj* tried, trustworthy

Bewah'rung *f* (–;) preservation

Bewäh'rung *f* (–;–en) testing, trial; (*jur*) probation

Bewäh'rungsfrist *f* (*jur*) probation; **j–m B. zubilligen** put s.o. on probation

Bewäh'rungsprobe *f* test

bewaldet [bə'valdət] *adj* woody

bewältigen [bə'veltɪgən] *tr* (*Hindernis*) overcome; (*Lehrstoff*) master

bewandert [bə'vandərt] *adj* experienced

Bewandtnis [bə'vantnɪs] *f* (–;) circumstances, situation

bewäs'sern *tr* water, irrigate

bewegen [bə'vegən] *tr* move, stir || *ref* move, stir; (*von der Stelle*) budge; (*Temperatur*) vary; (*exerzieren*) take exercise; (*astr*) revolve || §56 *tr* prompt, induce

Beweg'grund *m* motive; incentive

beweg'lich *adj* movable; (*behend*) agile; (*Geist*) versatile; (*Zunge*) glib

Beweg'lichkeit *f* (–;) mobility; agility; versatility

bewegt [bə'vekt] *adj* agitated; (*ergreifend*) stirring; (*Stimme*) trembling; (*Unterhaltung*) lively; (*Leben*) eventful; (*unruhig*) turbulent

Bewe'gung *f* (–;–en) movement; mo-

tion; move; (*Gebärde*) gesture; (*fig*) emotion; **in B. setzen** set in motion

Bewe'gungsfreiheit *f* room to move; (*fig*) leeway, freedom of action

bewe'gungslos *adj* motionless

beweh'ren *tr* arm; (*Beton*) reinforce

beweihräuchern [bə'vairɔiçərn] *tr* (*fig*) flatter; (*eccl*) incense

bewei'nen *tr* mourn, shed tears over

Beweis [bə'vais] *m* (–es;–e) (**für**) proof (of), evidence (of)

beweisen [bə'vaizən] §118 *tr* prove, demonstrate; (*bestätigen*) substantiate

Beweis'führung *f* argumentation

Beweis'grund *m* argument

Beweis'kraft *f* cogency, force

beweis'kräftig *adj* convincing

Beweis'last *f* burden of proof

Beweis'stück *n* exhibit

bewen'den *intr*—es dabei b. lassen leave it at that || **Bewenden** *n*—**damit hat es sein B.** there the matter rests

bewer'ben §149 *ref*—**sich b. um** apply for; (*kandidieren*) run for; (*Vertrag*) bid for; (*Preis*) compete for; (*Frau*) court

Bewer'ber –in §6 *mf* applicant; candidate; bidder; competitor || *m* suitor

Bewer'bungsformular *n* application form

Bewer'bungsschreiben *n* written application

bewer'fen §160 *tr* pelt; (*Mauer*) plaster

bewerkstelligen [bə'verkʃtɛlɪgən] *tr* manage, bring off

bewer'ten *tr* (auf *acc*) value (at), appraise (at); **b. mit fünf Punkten** give five points to (*e.g., a performance*); **zu hoch b.** overrate

Bewer'tung *f* (–;–en) valuation

bewilligen [bə'vilɪgən] *tr* approve, grant

Bewil'ligung *f* (–;–en) approval; permit

bewillkommnen [bə'vilkɔmnən] *tr* welcome

bewir'ken *tr* cause, occasion, effect

bewir'ten *tr* entertain

bewirt'schaften *tr* (*Acker*) cultivate; (*Betrieb*) manage; (*Mangelware*) ration

Bewir'tung *f* (–;) hospitality

bewitzeln [bə'vitsəln] *tr* poke fun at

bewog [bə'vok] *pret* of **bewegen**

bewogen [bə'vogən] *pp* of **bewegen**

bewoh'nen *tr* inhabit, occupy

Bewoh'ner –in §6 *mf* (*e–s Landes*) inhabitant; (*e–s Hauses*) occupant

bewölken [bə'vœlkən] *tr* cloud || *ref* cloud over, get cloudy

bewölkt' *adj* cloudy, overcast

Bewöl'kung *f* (–;) clouds

bewun'dern *tr* admire

bewun'dernswert, bewun'dernswürdig *adj* admirable

bewußt [bə'vust] *adj* conscious; **die bewußte Sache** the matter in question

bewußt'los *adj* unconscious

Bewußt'sein *n* consciousness; **bei B. sein** be conscious

Bewußt'seinspaltung *f* schizophrenia

bezah'len *tr* pay; (*Gekauftes*) pay for

Bezah'lung *f* (-;-en) payment; (*Lohn*) pay
bezäh'men *tr* tame; (fig) control
bezau'bern *tr* bewitch; (fig) fascinate
bezeich'nen *tr* (*zeichnen*) mark; (*bedeuten*) signify; (*benennen*) designate; (*kennzeichnen*) characterize; (*zeigen*) point out
bezeich'nend *adj* characteristic
Bezeich'nung *f* (-;-en) marking, mark; (*Name*) name; (*Ausdruck*) term
bezei'gen *tr* show, manifest, express
bezeu'gen *tr* attest; (jur) testify to
bezichtigen [bə'tsɪçtɪgən] *tr* accuse
bezieh'bar *adj* (*Ware*) obtainable; (*Wohnung*) ready for occupancy; (auf acc) referable (to)
bezie'hen §163 *tr* (*Polstermöbel*) cover; (*Wohnung*) move into; (*Universität*) go to; (*geliefert bekommen*) get; (*Gehalt*) draw; (*auf acc*) relate (to), refer (to); **das Bett frisch b.** change the bed linens; **die Stellung b.** (mil) occupy the position; **die Wache b.** (mil) go on guard duty || *ref* become overcast; **sich auf j-n b.** use s.o.'s name as a reference
Bezie'hung *f* (-;-en) relation, connection, respect; **in B. auf** (acc) in respect to; **in guten Beziehungen stehen zu** be on good terms with
bezie'hungslos *adj* unrelated; irrelevant
bezie'hungsweise *adv* respectively
Bezie'hungssatz *m* relative clause
Bezie'hungswort *n* (-[e]s; ̈er) (gram) antecedent
beziffern [bə'tsɪfərn] *tr* (auf acc) estimate (at) || *ref*—**sich b. auf** (acc) amount to, number
Bezirk [bə'tsɪrk] *m* (-s;-e) district, ward, precinct; (*Bereich*) sphere
Bezug' *m* (-[e]s; ̈e) cover, case; (*von Waren*) purchase; (*von Zeitungen*) subscription; (*Auftrag*) order; **Bezüge** earnings; **B. nehmen auf** (acc) refer to; **in B. auf** (acc) in reference to
bezüglich [bə'tsyklɪç] *adj* (auf acc) relative (to); **bezügliches Fürwort** relative pronoun || *prep* (genit) concerning, as to, with regard to
Bezugnahme [bə'tsuknamə] *f*—**unter B. auf** (acc) with reference to
Bezugs'anweisung *f* delivery order
bezugs'berechtigt *adj* entitled to receive || **Bezugsberechtigte** §5 *mf* (ins) beneficiary
bezwecken [bə'tsvɛkən] *tr* aim at, have in mind; (mit) intend (by)
bezwei'feln *tr* doubt, question
bezwin'gen §142 *tr* conquer; (fig) control, master
Bibel ['biːbəl] *f* (-;-n) Bible
Bi'belforscher –**in** §6 *mf* Jehovah's Witness
Biber ['biːbər] *m* (-s;-) beaver
Bibliothek [bɪblɪ·ɔ'teːk] *f* (-;-en) library
Bibliothekar –**in** [bɪblɪ·ɔte'kar(ɪn)] §8 *mf* librarian
biblisch ['biːblɪʃ] *adj* biblical
bieder ['biːdər] *adj* honest; (*leichtgläubig*) gullible

Bie'dermann *m* (-[e]s; ̈er) honest man
biegen ['biːgən] §57 *tr* bend; (gram) inflect || *ref*—**sich vor Lachen b.** double up with laughter || *intr* (SEIN) bend; **um die Ecke b.** go around the corner
biegsam ['biːkzam] *adj* flexible
Bie'gung *f* (-;-en) bend, bending; (gram) inflection
Biene ['biːnə] *f* (-;-n) bee
Bie'nenfleiß *m*—**mit B. arbeiten** work like a bee
Bie'nenhaus *n* beehive
Bie'nenkorb *m* beehive
Bie'nenstich *m* bee sting; (culin) almond pastry
Bie'nenstock *m* beehive
Bie'nenzucht *f* beekeeping
Bier [biːr] *n* (-[e]s;-e) beer
bie'ten ['biːtən] §58 *tr* offer; **b. auf** (acc) bid for || *ref* present itself; **das läßt er sich nicht b.** he won't stand for it
Bigamie [bɪga'mi] *f* (-;) bigamy
bigott [bɪ'gɔt] *adj* bigoted
Bigotterie [bɪgɔtə'ri] *f* (-;) bigotry
Bilanz [bɪ'lants] *f* (acct) balance; (acct) balance sheet
Bilanz'abteilung *f* auditing department
bilanzieren [bɪlan'tsirən] *intr* balance
Bild [bɪlt] *n* (-es;-er) picture; image; (*Bildnis*) portrait; (*in e-m Buch*) illustration; (*Vorstellung*) idea; (rhet) metaphor, figure of speech; **im Bilde sein** be in the know
Bild'band *m* (-[e]s; ̈e) picture book || *n* (-[e]s;-er) (telv) video tape
Bild'bandgerät *n* video tape recorder
Bild'betrachter *m* slide viewer
Bildchen ['bɪltçən] *n* (-s;-) small picture; (cin) frame
Bild'einstellung *f* (-;-en) focusing
bilden ['bɪldən] *tr* form, fashion, create; (*entwerfen*) design; (*gründen*) establish; (*Geist*) educate, develop; (*Gruppe*) constitute || *ref* form, be produced; develop; educate oneself
bil'dend *adj* instructive; **bildende Künste** fine arts, plastic arts
bil'derreich *adj* (*Buch*) richly illustrated; (*Sprache*) picturesque, ornate
Bil'derschrift *f* picture writing
Bil'dersprache *f* imagery
Bil'derstürmer *m* iconoclast
Bild'frequenz *f* camera speed
Bild'funk *m* television
bild'haft *adj* pictorial; graphic
Bildhauer ['bɪlthau·ər] *m* (-s;-) sculptor
Bildhauerei ['bɪlthau·ərai] *f* (-;) sculpture
Bildhauerin ['bɪlthau·ərɪn] *f* (-;-nen) sculptress
bild'hübsch *adj* pretty as a picture
Bild'karte *f* photographic map; (cards) face card
bild'lich *adj* pictorial; figurative
Bildner –**in** ['bɪldnər(ɪn)] §6 *mf* sculptor || *m* (fig) molder || *f* sculptress
Bildnis ['bɪltnɪs] *n* (-ses;-se) portrait
Bild'röhre *f* picture tube, TV tube
bildsam ['bɪltzam] *adj* plastic; (fig) pliant

Bild′säule f statue
Bild′schirm m television screen
bild′schön adj very beautiful
Bild′schriftzeichen n hieroglyph
Bild′seite f head, obverse
Bild′signal n video signal
Bild′stock m wayside shrine
Bild′streifen m filmstrip; (journ) comic strip
Bild′sucher m (phot) viewfinder
Bild′teppich m tapestry
Bild′ton′kamera f sound-film camera
Bil′dung f (-;-en) formation; shape; education, culture
Bil′dungsanstalt f educational institution
Bild′werfer m projector
Bild′werk n sculpture; imagery
Billard [′bɪljart] n (-s;-) billiards
Bil′lardkugel f billiard ball
Bil′lardloch n pocket
Bil′lardstab, Bil′lardstock m cue
Billett [bɪl′jet] m (-s;-e) ticket
Billett′ausgabe f, Billett′schalter m ticket office; (theat) box office
billig [′bɪlɪç] adj cheap; (Preis) low; (Ausrede, Trost) poor
billigen [′bɪlɪgən] tr approve
Bil′ligung f (-;) approval
Billion [bɪl′jon] f (-;-en) trillion; (Brit) billion
bimbam [′bɪm′bam] interj ding-dong || Bimbam m—heiliger B.! holy smokes!
bimmeln [′bɪməln] intr (coll) jingle; (telp) ring
Bimsstein [′bɪms/taɪn] m (-s;-e) pumice stone
Binde [′bɪndə] f (-;-n) band; (Krawatte) tie; (Armschlinge) sling; (für Frauen) sanitary napkin; (med) bandage
Bin′deglied n link; (fig) bond, tie
binden [′bɪndən] §59 tr bind, tie
Bin′destrich m hyphen; mit B. schreiben hyphenate
Bin′dewort n (-[e]s;-er) conjunction
Bind′faden m string, twine; es regnet Bindfäden it's raining cats and dogs
Bin′dung f (-;-en) binding; tie, bond; obligation; (mus) ligature
binnen [′bɪnən] prep (genit & dat) within; b. kurzem before long
Binnen- comb.fm. inner; internal; inland; domestic, home
Bin′nengewässer n inland water
Bin′nenhandel m domestic trade
Bin′nenland n inland; interior; im B. inland
Binse [′bɪnzə] f (-;-n) rush, reed; in die Binsen gehen (coll) go to pot
Bin′senwahrheit f truism
Biochemie [bi·oçe′mi] f (-;) biochemistry
Biogra·phie [bi·ogra′fi] (-;-phien [′fi·ən]) biography
biographisch [bi·o′grafɪʃ] adj biographic(al)
Biologie [bi·olo′gi] f (-;) biology
biologisch [bi·o′logɪʃ] adj biological
Biophysik [bi·ofy′zik] f (-;) biophysics
Birke [′bɪrkə] f (-;-n) birch
Birma [′bɪrma] n (-s;) Burma

Birne [′bɪrnə] f (-;-n) pear; (elec) bulb; (Kopf) (sl) bean
bis [bɪs] prep (acc) (zeitlich) till, until; (örtlich) up to, to; bis an (acc) up to; bis auf (acc) except for; bis nach as far as || conj until, till
Bisamratte [′bizamratə] f (-;-n) muskrat
Bischof [′bɪ/ɔf] m (-;⁼e) bishop
bischöflich [′bɪ/øflɪç] adj episcopal
Bi′schofsamt n episcopate
Bi′schofsmütze f miter
Bi′schofssitz m episcopal see
Bi′schofsstab m crosier
bisher [bɪs′her] adv till now
bisherig [bɪs′herɪç] adj former, previous; (Präsident) outgoing
Biskuit [bɪs′kvit] m & n (-[e]s;-e) biscuit
bislang′ adv till now
biß [bɪs] pret of beißen || Biß m (Bisses; Bisse) bite; sting
bißchen [′bɪsçən] n (also used as invar adj & adv) bit, little bit
Bissen [′bɪsən] m (-s;-) bit, morsel
bissig [′bɪsɪç] adj biting, snappish
Bistum [′bɪstum] n (-s;⁼er) bishopric
bisweilen [bɪs′vaɪlən] adv sometimes
Bitte [′bɪtə] f (-;-n) request; e-e B. einlegen bei intercede with
bitten [′bɪtən] §60 tr ask || intr b. für intercede for; b. um ask for; wie bitte? I beg your pardon? || interj please!; you are welcome!
bitter [′bɪtər] adj bitter
bit′terböse adj (coll) furious
Bit′terkeit f (-;) bitterness
bit′terlich adv bitterly; deeply
Bit′tersalz n Epsom salts
Bittgang [′bɪtgaŋ] m (-[e]s;⁼e) (eccl) procession
Bittsteller [′bɪt/telər] m (-s;-) petitioner, suppliant
Biwak [′bivak] n (-s;-s) bivouac
biwakieren [biva′kirən] intr bivouac
bizarr [bɪ′tsar] adj bizarre
blähen [′ble·ən] tr inflate, distend || ref swell || intr cause gas
blaken [′blakən] intr smolder
Blamage [bla′maʒə] f (-;-n) disgrace
blamieren [bla′mirən] tr embarrass || ref make a fool of oneself
blank [blaŋk] adj bright; (Schuh) shiny; (bloß) bare; (Schwert) drawn; (sl) broke; blanke Waffe side arms; b. ziehen draw one's sword
Blankett [blaŋ′ket] n (-s;-e) blank
blanko [′blaŋko] adv—b. lassen leave blank; b. verkaufen sell short
Blan′koscheck m blank check
Blan′kovollmacht f blanket authority
Blank′vers m blank verse
Bläschen [′blesçən] n (-s;-) small blister; small bubble
Blase [′blazə] f (-;-n) blister; bubble; (coll) gang; (anat) bladder; Blasen werfen (Farbe) blister; Blasen ziehen (Haut) blister
Bla′sebalg m pair of bellows
blasen [′blazən] tr blow; (Instrument) play || intr blow
Bla′senleiden n bladder trouble
Bläser [′blezər] m (-s;-) blower

blasiert [bla'zirt] *adj* blasé
blasig ['blazɪç] *adj* blistery; bubbly
Blas'instrument *n* wind instrument
Blaspheme·mie [blasfe'mi] *f* (-;-mien ['mi·ən]) blasphemy
blasphemieren [blasfe'mirən] *intr* blaspheme
Blas'rohr *n* blowpipe; peashooter
blaß [blas] *adj* pale; **keine blasse Ahnung** not the foggiest notion
Blässe ['blesə] *f* (-;) paleness, pallor
Blatt [blat] *n* (-s;⁻er) leaf; (*Papier-*) sheet; (*Gras-*) blade
Blatter ['blatər] *f* (-;-n) pustule; **die Blattern** smallpox
blätterig ['bletərɪç] *adj* leafy; scaly
blättern ['bletərn] *intr*—**in e-m Buch b.** page through a book
Blat'ternarbe *f* pockmark
Blät'terwerk *n* foliage
Blatt'gold *n* gold leaf, gold foil
Blatt'laus *f* aphid
Blatt'pflanze *f* house plant
blättrig ['bletrɪç] *adj var of* **blätterig**
Blatt'zinn *n* tin foil
blau [blau] *adj* (& *fig*) blue; (*coll*) drunk; **blaues Auge** black eye; **keinen blauen Dunst haben** (*coll*) not have the foggiest notion; **mit e-m blauen Auge davonkommen** (*coll*) get off easy || **Blau** *n* (-s;-s) blue; blueness
blau'äugig *adj* blue-eyed
Blau'beere *f* blueberry
Bläue ['blɔɪ·ə] *f* (-;) blue; blueness
bläuen ['blɔɪ·ən] *tr* dye blue
bläulich ['blɔɪlɪç] *adj* bluish
blau'machen *intr* (*coll*) take off from work
Blech [bleç] *n* (-[e]s;-e) sheet metal; (*sl*) baloney; (*mus*) brass
Blech'büchse *f* tin can
blechen ['bleçən] *tr* (*coll*) pay out || *intr* (*coll*) cough up the dough
Blech'instrument *n* brass instrument
blecken ['blekən] *tr*—**die Zähnen b.** bare one's teeth
Blei [blaɪ] *n* (-[e]s;) lead
Bleibe ['blaɪbə] *f* (-;-n) place to stay
bleiben ['blaɪbən] §62 *intr* (SEIN) remain, stay; **am Leben b.** survive; **bei etw b.** stick to s.th.; **dabei bleibt es!** that's final!; **für sich b.** keep to oneself; **sich** [*dat*] **gleich b.** never change; **und wo bleibe ich?** (*coll*) and where do I come in?
blei'bend *adj* lasting, permanent
bleich [blaɪç] *adj* pale || **Bleiche** *f* (-;) bleaching; paleness
blei'chen *tr* bleach; make pale || *intr* (SEIN) bleach; (*verblassen*) fade
Bleich'gesicht *n* paleface
Bleich'mittel *n* bleach
bleiern ['blaɪ·ərn] *adj* leaden
Blei'soldat *m* tin soldier
Blei'stift *m* pencil
Bleistiftspitzer ['blaɪʃtɪftʃpɪtsər] *m* (-s;-) pencil sharpener
Blende ['blendə] *f* (-;) window blind; shutter; (*phot*) diaphragm
blen'den *tr* blind; (*bezaubern*) dazzle
blen'dend *adj* fabulous
Blen'der *m* (-s;-) (*coll*) fourflusher

Blendling ['blentlɪŋ] *m* (-s;-e) (*Mischling*) mongrel; (*bot*) hybrid
Blick [blɪk] *m* (-[e]s;-e) glance, look; (*auf acc*) view (of)
blicken [blɪk'kən] *intr* (**auf** *acc*, **nach**) glance (at), look (at); **sich b. lassen** show one's face
Blick'fang *m* (*coll*) eye catcher
blieb [blip] *pret of* **bleiben**
blies [blis] *pret of* **blasen**
blind [blɪnt] *adj* (**für, gegen**) blind (to); (*Spiegel*) clouded; (*trübe*) dull; (*Alarm*) false; (*Patrone*) blank; **blinder Passagier** stowaway
Blind'band *m* (-[e]s;-e) (*typ*) dummy
Blind'boden *m* subfloor
Blind'darm *m* appendix
Blind'darmentzündung *f* appendicitis
Blind'darmoperation *f* appendectomy
Blin'denheim *n* home for the blind
Blin'denhund *m* Seeing-Eye dog
Blin'denschrift *f* braille
Blind'flug *m* blind flying
Blind'gänger *m* (*mil*) dud
Blind'landung *f* instrument landing
blindlings ['blɪntlɪŋs] *adv* blindly
Blind'schreiben *n* touch typing
blinken ['blɪŋkən] *intr* blink, twinkle; (*Sonne*) shine; (*mil*) signal
Blin'ker *m*, **Blink'licht** *n* (*aut*) blinker
blinzeln ['blɪntsəln] *intr* blink, wink
Blitz [blɪts] *m* (-es;-e) lightning; (*fig & phot*) flash
Blitz'ableiter *m* lightning rod
blitz'blank *adj* shining; spick and span
Blitz'krieg *m* blitzkrieg
Blitz'licht *n* (*phot*) flash
Blitz'lichtaufnahme *f* (*phot*) flash shot
Blitz'lichtbirne *f* (*phot*) flash bulb
Blitz'lichtgerät *n* flash gun
Blitz'lichtröhre *f* (*phot*) electronic flash, flash tube
Blitz'schlag *m* stroke of lightning
blitz'schnell *adj* quick as lightning
Blitz'strahl *m* flash of lightning
Block [blɔk] *m* (-s;-e) block, log; (*Stück Seife*) cake; (*von Schokolade*) bar; (*von Löschpapier*) pad; (*geol*) boulder; (*metal*) ingot; (*pol*) bloc
Blockade [blɔ'kadə] *f* (-;-n) blockade
Blocka'debrecher *m* blockade runner
blocken [blɔk'kən] *tr* (*sport*) block
Block'haus *n* log cabin
blockieren [blɔ'kirən] *tr* block up; (*mil*) blockade
Block'kalender *m* tear-off calendar
Block'schrift *f* block letters
blöd(e) ['blød(ə)] *adj* stupid, idiotic; feeble-minded; (*schüchtern*) shy
Blöd'heit *f* (-;) stupidity, idiocy
Blö'digkeit *f* (-;) shyness
Blöd'sinn *m* idiocy; nonsense
blöd'sinnig *adj* idiotic || *adv* idiotically; (*sehr*) (*coll*) awfully
blöken ['bløkən] *intr* bleat; (*Kuh*) moo
blond [blɔnt] *adj* blond, fair || **Blonde** §5 *m* blond || *f* blonde
blondieren [blɔn'dirən] *tr* bleach
Blondine [blɔn'dinə] *f* (-;-n) blonde
bloß [blos] *adj* bare; (*nichts als*) mere *adv* only; barely
Blöße ['bløsə] *f* bareness; nakedness; (*fig*) weak point

bloß'legen *tr* lay bare
bloß'stellen *tr* expose
blühen ['blyːən] *intr* blossom, bloom; (*Backen*) be rosy; (fig) flourish
Blume ['bluːmə] *f* (-;-n) flower; (*des Weins*) bouquet; (*des Biers*) head
Blu'menbeet *n* flower bed
Blu'menblatt *n* petal
Blu'mengewinde *n* garland, festoon
Blu'menhändler –in §6 *mf* florist
Blu'menkelch *m* calyx
Blu'menkohl *m* cauliflower
Blu'menstaub *m* pollen
Blu'mentopf *m* flowerpot
Bluse ['bluːzə] *f* (-;-n) blouse
Blut [bluːt] *n* (-[e]s;) blood; **bis aufs B.** almost to death; **B. lecken** taste blood; **heißes B.** hot temper
Blut'andrang *m* (pathol) congestion
blut'arm *adj* anemic
Blut'armut *f* anemia
Blut'bahn *f* bloodstream
Blut'bild *n* blood count
blut'dürstig *adj* bloodthirsty
Blüte ['blyːtə] *f* (-;-n) blossom, flower, bloom; (fig) prime
Blut'egel *m* leech
bluten ['bluːtən] *intr* bleed
Blü'tenblatt *n* petal
Blü'tenstaub *m* pollen
Blut'erguß *m* bruise
Blu'terkrankheit *f* hemophilia
Blü'tezeit *f* blooming period; (fig) heyday
Blut'farbstoff *m* hemoglobin
Blut'gerinnsel *n* blood clot
Blut'hund *m* bloodhound
blutig ['bluːtɪç] *adj* bloody
blut'jung *adj* very young, green
Blut'körperchen *n* corpuscle
Blut'kreislauf *m* blood circulation
blut'leer, blut'los *adj* bloodless
Blut'pfropfen *m* blood clot
Blut'probe *f* blood test
Blut'rache *f* blood feud
Blut'rausch *m* mania to kill
blutrünstig ['bluːtrʏnstɪç] *adj* gory
Blut'sauger *m* bloodsucker, leech
Blut'schande *f* incest
blutschänderisch ['bluːtʃɛndərɪʃ] *adj* incestuous
Blut'spender –in §6 *mf* blood donor
blut'stillend *adj* coagulant
Blut'sturz *m* hemorrhage
Bluts'verwandte §5 *mf* blood relation
Blut'übertragung *f* blood transfusion
blut'unterlaufen *adj* bloodshot
Blut'vergießen *n* (-s;) bloodshed
blut'voll *adj* lively, vivid
Blut'wasser *n* lymph
Blut'zeuge *m*, **Blut'zeugin** *f* martyr
Bö [bøː] *f* (-;-en) gust, squall
Bob [bɔb] *m* (-s;-s) bobsled
Bock [bɔk] *m* (-[e]s; ̈e) buck; ram; he-goat; (*Kutsch-*) driver's seat; (tech) horse; **B. springen** play leapfrog; **e–n B. schießen** pull a boner
bockbeinig ['bɔkbainɪç] *adj* stubborn
bocken ['bɔkən] *intr* buck; (*sich aufbäumen*) rear; (*ausschlagen*) kick; (*brunsten*) be in heat; (aut) hesitate
bockig ['bɔkɪç] *adj* thickheaded
Bock'sprung *m* caper; leapfrog

Boden ['boːdən] *m* (-s; ̈) (*Erd-*) ground, soil; (*Meeres-*) bottom; (*Fuß-*) floor; (*Dach-*) attic; (*Trocken-*) loft; **B. fassen** get a firm footing; **zu B. drücken** crush
Bo'denertrag *m* (agr) yield
Bo'denfenster *n* dormer window
Bo'denfläche *f* floor space; (agr) acreage
Bo'denfliese *f* floor tile
Bodenfräse ['boːdənfrɛːzə] *f* (-;-n) Rototiller
Bo'denhaftung *f* roadability
Bo'denkammer *f* attic
bo'denlos *adj* bottomless; (fig) unmitigated
Bo'denmannschaft *f* (aer) ground crew
Bo'denreform *f* agrarian reform
Bo'densatz *m* grounds, sediment
Bodenschätze ['boːdənʃɛtsə] *pl* mineral resources
Bo'densee *m* (-s;) Lake Constance
bo'denständig *adj* native, indigenous
bog [boːk] *pret* of biegen
Bogen ['boːgən] *m* (-s; ̈) bow; (*Kurve*) curve; (*Papier-*) sheet; (*beim Schilaufen*) turn; (*beim Eislaufen*) circle; (archit) arch; (math) arc; **den B. raushaben** have the hang of it; **den B. überspannen** (fig) go too far; **e–n großen B. um j–n machen** give s.o. wide berth
Bo'genfenster *n* bow window
bo'genförmig *adj* arched
Bo'gengang *m* arcade; archway
Bo'genschießen *n* (-s;) archery
Bo'genschütze *m* archer
Bo'gensehne *f* bowstring
Bohle ['boːlə] *f* (-;-n) plank
Böhme ['bøːmə] *m* (-n;-n) Bohemian
Böhmen ['bøːmən] *n* (-s;) Bohemia
Bohne ['boːnə] *f* (-;-n) bean; **blaue Bohnen** bullets; **grüne Bohnen** string beans
Boh'nermasse *f* polish; floor polish
bohnern ['boːnərn] *tr* wax, polish
Boh'nerwachs *n* floor wax
Bohr- [boːr] *comb.fm.* drill, drilling, bore, boring
bohren ['boːrən] *tr* drill, bore
Bohrer *m* (-s;-) drill; (ent) borer
Bohr'insel *f* offshore drilling platform
Bohr'presse *f* drill press
Bohr'turm *m* derrick
böig ['bøːɪç] *adj* gusty; (aer) bumpy
Boje ['boːjə] *f* (-;-n) buoy
Böller ['bœlər] *m* (-s;-) mortar
böllern ['bœlərn] *intr* fire a mortar
Bollwerk ['bɔlvɛrk] *n* (-s;-e) bulwark
Bolzen ['bɔltsən] *m* (-s;-) bolt; dowel
Bombardement [bɔmbardə'mɑ̃] *n* (-s; -s) bombardment
bombardieren [bombar'diːrən] *tr* bombard
Bombe ['bɔmbə] *f* (-;-n) bomb, bombshell; (coll) smash hit
Bomben- *comb.fm.* bomb, bombing; huge
Bom'benabwurf *m* bombing; **gezielter B.** precision bombing
Bom'benerfolg *m* (theat) smash hit
bom'benfest *adj* bombproof
Bom'benflugzeug *m* bomber

Bom'bengeschäft n (coll) gold mine
Bom'benpunktzielwurf m precision
  bombing
Bom'benreihenwurf m stick bombing
Bom'bensache f (coll) humdinger
Bom'benschacht m bomb bay
Bom'benschütze m bombardier
Bom'bentrichter m bomb crater
Bom'benzielanflug m bombing run
Bom'benzielgerät n bombsight
Bon [bõ] m (-s;-s) sales slip; (Gut-
  schein) credit note
Bonbon [bõ'bõ] m & n (-s;-s) piece
  of candy; Bonbons candy
Bonbonniere [bõbɔni'erə] f (-;-n) box
  of candy
Bonze ['bontsə] m (-;-n) (coll) big
  shot, bigwig; (pol) boss
Boot [bot] n (-[e]s;-e) boat
Boots'mann m (-es;-leute) boatswain;
  (nav) petty officer
Bord [bɔrt] m (-[e]s;-e) edge; bookshelf;
  (naut) board, side; an B. aboard, on
  board; von B. gehen leave the ship
Bordell [bɔr'dɛl] n (-s;-e) brothel
Bord'karte f boarding pass
Bord'schütze m aerial gunner
Bord'schwelle f curb
Bord'stein m curb
Bord'waffen pl (aer, mil) armament
Bord'wand f ship's side
Borg [bɔrk] m (-s;) borrowing; auf B.
  on credit; on loan
borgen ['bɔrgən] tr (von, bei) borrow
  (from); loan out, lend
Borke ['bɔrkə] f (-;-n) bark
Born [bɔrn] m (-es; -e) (poet) foun-
  tain
borniert [bɔr'nirt] adj narrow-minded
Borsäure ['bɔrzɔɪrə] f (-;) boric acid
Börse ['bœrzə] f (-;-n) purse; stock
  exchange
Bör'senkurs m market price; quotation
Bör'senmakler –in §6 mf stockbroker
Bör'senmarkt m stockmarket
Bör'sennotierung f (st.exch.) quotation
Bör'senpapiere pl stocks, shares, securities
Borste ['bɔrstə] f (-;-n) bristle
borstig ['bɔrstɪç] adj birstly; (fig)
  crusty
Borte ['bɔrtə] f (-;-n) trim; braid;
  (Saum) hem
bös [bøs] var of böse
bös'artig adj nasty; (Tier) vicious;
  (pathol) malignant
Böschung ['bœʃʊŋ] f (-;-en) slope;
  (e-s Flusses) bank; (rr) embankment
böse ['bøzə] adj bad, evil, nasty; angry
  || Böse §5 mf wicked person || m
  devil || n evil; harm
Bösewicht ['bøzəvɪçt] m (-s;-e) villain
boshaft ['boshaft] adj malicious; wicked; (tückisch) spiteful
bossieren [bɔ'sirən] tr emboss
bös'willig adj malicious, willful
bot [bot] pret of bieten
Botanik [bo'tanɪk] f (-;) botany
Botaniker –in §6 mf botanist
botanisch [bo'tanɪʃ] adj botanic(al)
Bote ['botə] m (-n;-n) messenger
Bo'tengang m errand
Botin ['botɪn] f (-;-nen) messenger

Bot'schaft f (-;-en) message, news;
  (Amt) embassy; (Auftrag) mission
Botschafter –in ['bot/aftər(ɪn)] §6 am-
  bassador
Bottich ['bɔtɪç] m (-s;-e) tub; vat
Bouillon (bul'jõ] f (-;-s) bouillon
Bowle ['bolə] f (-;-n) punch
boxen ['bɔksən] tr & intr box
Bo'xer m (-s;-) boxer
Box'kampf m boxing match
Boykott [bɔɪ'kɔt] m (-s;-e) boycott
boykottieren [bɔɪkɔ'tirən] tr boycott
brach [brax] pret of brechen || adj
  fallow
brachte ['braxtə] pret of bringen
brackig ['brakɪç] adj brackish
Branche ['brãʃə] f (-;-n) line of busi-
  ness; (com) branch
Brand [brant] m (-[e]s;ᵉe) burning;
  fire; (coll) thirst; (agr) blight;
  (pathol) gangrene in B. geraten
  catch fire; in B. setzen (or stecken)
  set on fire
Brand'blase f blister
Brand'bombe f incendiary bomb
Brand'brief m urgent letter
Brand'direktor m fire chief
branden ['brandən] intr surge, break
Brand'fackel f firebrand
brandig ['brandɪç] adj (agr) blighted;
  (pathol) gangrenous
Brand'mal n brand; (fig) moral stigma
brand'marken tr stigmatize
Brand'mauer f fire wall
brandschatzen ['brant/atsən] tr sack
Brand'stifter –in §6 mf arsonist
Bran'dung f (-;) breakers
Bran'dungswelle f breaker
Brand'wunde f burn
Brand'zeichen n brand
brannte ['brantə] pret of brennen
Branntwein ['brantvain] m brandy
Brasilien [bra'ziljən] n (-s;) Brazil
Bratapfel ['brat/apfəl] m baked apple
braten ['bratən] §63 tr & intr roast;
  (im Ofen) bake; (auf dem Rost)
  broil, grill; (in der Pfanne) fry ||
  Braten m (-s;-) roast
Bra'tensoße f gravy
Brat'fisch m fried fish
Brat'huhn n broiler
Brat'kartoffeln pl fried potatoes
Brat'pfanne f frying pan, skillet
Bratsche ['brat/ə] f (-;-n) viola
Bräu [brɔɪ] m & n (-[e]s;-e) brew
Brauch [braux] m (-[e]s;ᵉe) custom
brauchbar ['brauxbar] adj useful
brauchen ['brauxən] tr need; (Zeit)
  take; (gebrauchen) use
Brauchtum ['brauxtum] n (-s;) tradi-
  tion
Braue ['brauə] f (-;-n) eyebrow
brauen ['brau-ən] tr brew
Brau'er m (-s;-) brewer
Brauerei [brau-ə'rai] f (-;-en), Brau'-
  haus n brewery
braun [braun] adj brown; (Pferd) bay
Bräune ['brɔɪnə] f (-;) brown; sun
  tan; (pathol) diphtheria
bräunen ['brɔɪnən] tr tan; (culin)
  brown || ref & intr tan
bräunlich ['brɔɪnlɪç] adj brownish
Braus [braus] m (-es;) noise; revelry

Brause ['brauzə] f (-;-n) soda, soft drink; (Duschbad) shower; (an Gieß-kannen) nozzle
Brau'sebad n shower
Brau'sekopf m hothead
Brau'selimonade f soda, soft drink
brau'sen tr spray, water ‖ intr bubble; (toben) roar ‖ intr (SEIN) rush
Braut [braut] f (-;²e) fiancée; bride
Braut'ausstattung f trousseau
Braut'führer m usher
Bräutigam ['brɔɪtɪgam] m (-s;-e) fiancé; bridegroom
Braut'jungfer f (-;-n) bridesmaid; er-ste B. maid of honor
Braut'kleid n bridal gown
Braut'leute pl engaged couple
bräutlich ['brɔɪtlɪç] adj bridal; nuptial
Braut'schatz m dowry
Braut'werber -in §6 mf matchmaker
Braut'werbung f courting
Braut'zeit f period of engagement
Braut'zeuge m best man
brav [braf] adj well-mannered, good, honest
Brav'heit f good behavior
Bravour [bra'vur] f (-;) bravado
Brech'eisen n crowbar, jimmy
brechen ['brɛçən] §64 tr break; (Pa-pier) fold; (Steine) quarry; (Blumen) pick; (coll) vomit; (opt) refract; die Ehe b. commit adultery ‖ ref break; (opt) be refracted ‖ intr (SEIN) break; (coll) vomit
Brech'reiz m nausea
Brech'stange f crowbar
Bre'chung f (-;-en) (opt) refraction
Brei [braɪ] m (-s;-e) paste; pap, gruel; zu B. schlagen beat to a pulp
breit [braɪt] adj broad, wide
breitbeinig ['braɪtbaɪnɪç] adv with legs outspread
breit'drücken tr flatten (out)
Brei'te f (-;-n) width; latitude
Brei'tengrad m degree of latitude
breit'machen ref take up (too much) room; (fig) throw one's weight around
breit'schlagen §132 tr (coll) persuade
breitschulterig ['braɪtʃultərɪç] adj broad-shouldered
breitspurig ['braɪtʃpurɪç] adj (coll) pompous; (rr) broad-gauge
breit'treten §152 tr belabor
Breit'wand f (cin) wide screen
Bremsbelag ['brɛmsbəlak] m brake lining
Bremse ['brɛmzə] f (-;-n) brake; (ent) horsefly
bremsen ['brɛmzən] tr brake; (fig) curb; (atom phys) slow down ‖ intr brake
Brem'ser m (-s;-) brakeman
Brems'flüssigkeit f brake fluid
Brems'fußhebel m brake pedal
Brems'klotz m wheel chock
Bremsleuchte ['brɛmslɔɪçtə] f, Brems'-licht n (aut) brake light
Brems'rakete f (rok) retrorocket
Brems'schuh m brake shoe
brems'sicher adj skidproof
Brems'spur f skid mark
Brems'wagen m (rr) caboose

Brems'weg m braking distance
Brennapparat ['brɛnaparat] m still
brennbar ['brɛnbar] adj inflammable, combustible
brennen §97 tr burn; (Branntwein) dis-til; (Kaffee) roast; (Haar) curl; (Ziegel) fire ‖ intr burn; smart
Bren'ner m (-s;-) burner; distiller
Brennerei [brɛnə'raɪ] f (-;-en) distil-lery
Brenn'holz n firewood
Brenn'material n fuel
Brenn'ofen m kiln
Brenn'punkt m focus; im B. stehen be the focal point
Brenn'schere f curler
Brenn'schluß m (rok) burnout
Brenn'spiegel m concave mirror
Brenn'stoff m fuel
brenzlig ['brɛntslɪç] adj (Geruch) burnt; (Situation) precarious
Bresche ['brɛʃə] f (-;-n) breach; e-e B. schlagen make a breach
Brett [brɛt] n (-[e]s;-er) board; plank; (für Bücher, Geschirr) shelf; Bretter (coll) skis; (theat) stage; Schwarzes B. bulletin board
Bret'terbude f shack
Bret'terverschlag m wooden partition
Brett'säge f ripsaw
Brezel ['brɛtsəl] f (-;-n) pretzel
Brief [brif] m (-[e]s;-e) letter; Briefe wechseln correspond
Brief'ausgabe f mail delivery
Briefbeschwerer ['brifbəʃverər] m (-s; -) paperweight
Brief'bestellung f mail delivery
Brief'beutel m mail bag
Brief'bogen m piece of notepaper
Brief'bote m mailman, postman
Briefchen ['brifçən] n (-s;-) note; B. Streichhölzer book of matches
Brief'einwurf m slot in a mailbox; let-terdrop; mailbox
Brief'fach n pigeonhole; post-office box
Brief'freund -in §8 mf pen pal
Brief'hülle f envelope
Brief'kasten m mailbox
Brief'klammer f paper clip
Brief'kopf m letterhead
Brief'kurs m (st.exch.) selling price
brief'lich adj written; brieflicher Ver-kehr correspondence ‖ adv by letter
Brief'mappe f folder
Brief'marke f postage stamp
Brief'markenautomat m stamp ma-chine
Brief'ordner m ring binder
Brief'papier n stationery; note paper
Brief'porto n postage
Brief'post f first-class mail
Brief'schaften pl correspondence
Brief'stempel m postmark
Brief'tasche f billfold, wallet
Brief'taube f carrier pigeon
Brief'träger m mailman, postman
Brief'umschlag m envelope
Brief'verkehr m correspondence
Brief'waage f postage scales
Brief'wahl f absentee ballot
Brief'wechsel m correspondence
briet [brit] pret of braten

Brigade [brɪ'gɑdə] *f* (-;-n) brigade
Briga′degeneral *m* brigadier general; (Brit) brigadier
Brikett [brɪ'kɛt] *n* (-[e]s;-s) briquette
brillant [brɪl'jant] *adj* brilliant || **Brillant** *m* (-en;-en) precious stone (esp. diamond)
Brille ['brɪlə] *f* (-;-n) eyeglasses; (*für Pferde*) blinkers; (*Toilettenring*) toilet seat; **B. mit doppeltem Brennpunkt** bifocals
Bril′lenbügel *m* sidepiece (*of glasses*)
Bril′lenfassung *f* eyeglass frame
Bril′lenschlange *f* cobra
bringen ['brɪŋən] §65 *tr* bring, take; **an sich b.** acquire; **es mit sich b., daß** bring it about that; **es zu etw b.** achieve s.th.; **etw hinter sich b.** get s.th. over and done with; **etw über sich** (or **übers Herz**) **b.** be able to bear s.th.; **j-n auf etw b.** put s.o. on to s.th.; **j-n außer sich b.** enrage s.o.; **j-n dazu b. zu** (*inf*) get s.o. to (*inf*); **j-m um etw b.** deprive s.o. of s.th.; **j-n zum Lachen b.** make s.o. laugh; **unter die Leute b.** circulate
brisant [brɪ'zant] *adj* high-explosive
Brise ['brizə] *f* (-;-n) breeze
Britannien [brɪ'tanjən] *n* (-s;) Britain
Brite ['brɪtə] *m* (-n;-n) Briton, Britisher; **die Briten** the British
Britin ['brɪtɪn] *f* (-;-nen) Briton, British woman
britisch ['brɪtɪʃ] *adj* British
Broché [brɔ'ʃe] *n* (-s;) broché; brocaded fabric
Bröckchen ['brœkçən] *n* (-s;-) bit; morsel, crumb; fragment
bröck(e)lig ['brœk(ə)lɪç] *adj* crumbly
bröckeln ['brœkəln] *tr & intr* crumble
brocken ['brɔkən] *tr*—**Brot in die Suppe b.** break bread into the soup || **Brocken** *m* (-s;-) piece, bit; lump; **Brocken** *pl* scraps, bits and pieces; **harter B.** (coll) tough job
brockenweise (**brok′kenweise**) *adv* bit by bit
brodeln ['brodəln] *intr* bubble, simmer
Brokat [brɔ'kat] *m* (-[e]s;-e) brocade
Brombeere ['brɔmberə] *f* (-;-n) blackberry
Bromid [bro'mit] *n* (-[e]s;-e) bromide
Bronchitis [brɔn'çitɪs] *f* (-;) bronchitis
Bronze ['brɔ̃sə] *f* (-;-n) bronze
Brosche ['brɔʃə] *f* (-;-n) brooch
broschieren [brɔ'ʃirən] *tr* stitch; brocade; **broschiert** with stapled binding
Broschüre [brɔ'ʃyrə] *f* (-;-n) brochure
Brösel ['brøzəl] *m* (-s;-) crumb
Brot [brot] *n* (-[e]s;-e) bread; loaf; **geröstetes B.** toast
Brot′aufstrich *m* spread
Brötchen ['brøtçən] *n* (-s;-) roll
Brot′erwerb *m* livelihood, living
Brot′geber *m*, **Brot′herr** *m* employer
Brot′kasten *m* breadbox
brot′los *adj* unemployed; unprofitable
Brot′neid *m* professional jealousy
Brot′röster *m* toaster
Brot′schnitte *f* slice of bread
Brot′studium *n* bread-and-butter courses
Brot′zeit *f* breakfast

Bruch [brux] *m* (-[e]s;-̈e) breaking; break, crack; breakage; (aer) crash; (geol) fault; (math) fraction; (min) quarry; (pathol) hernia; (surg) fracture; **B. machen** crash-land; **in die Brüche gehen** go to pot; **zu B. gehen** break || [brux] *m & n* (-s;-̈e) bog
Bruch′band *n* (-s;-̈er) (surg) truss
Bruch′bude *f* shanty
brüchig ['brYçɪç] *adj* fragile, brittle
Bruch′landung *f* crash landing
Bruch′rechnung *f* fractions
Bruch′stück *n* fragment, chip; **Bruchstücke** (fig) scraps, snatches
bruch′stückhaft *adj* fragmentary
Bruch′teil *m* fraction; **im B. e-r Sekunde** in a split second
Bruch′zahl *f* fractional number
Brücke ['brYkə] *f* (-;-n) bridge; (*Teppich*) small (narrow) rug; (gym) backbend
Brückenkopf (**Brük′kenkopf**) *m* bridgehead
Brückenpfeiler (**Brük′kenpfeiler**) *m* pier of a bridge
Brückenwaage (**Brük′kenwaage**) *f* platform scale
Brückenzoll (**Brük′kenzoll**) *m* bridge toll
Bruder ['brudər] *m* (-s;-̈) brother; (*Genosse*) companion; (eccl) lay brother
brüderlich ['brydərlɪç] *adj* brotherly
Brüderschaft ['brydər'ʃaft] *f* (-;-en) brotherhood; fraternity
Brühe ['bry.ə] *f* (-;-n) broth; (*Fleisch-*) gravy; **in der B. stecken** be in a jam
brühen ['bry.ən] *tr* boil; scald
brüh′heiß′ *adj* piping hot
Brüh′kartoffeln *pl* potatoes boiled in broth
Brüh′würfel *m* bouillon cube
brüllen ['brylən] *tr & intr* roar, bellow; (*Sturm*) howl; (*Ochse*) low; **b. vor Lachen** roar with laughter
Brummbär ['brumbɛr] *m* (-en;-en) grouch
brummen ['brumən] *tr* mumble; grumble; growl || *intr* mumble; grumble; growl; (*summen*) buzz, hum; (*Orgel*) boom; (*im Gefängnis*) do time, do a stretch
brummig ['brumɪç] *adj* grouchy
brünett [bry'nɛt] *adj* brunet(te) || **Brünette** §5 brunette
Brunft [brunft] *f* (-;) rut
Brunft′zeit *f* rutting season
Brunnen ['brunən] *m* (-s;-) well; (*Spring-*) spring
Brunnenkresse ['brunənkrɛsə] *f* (-;-n) watercress
Brunst [brunst] *f* (-;) rut, heat; (fig) ardor, passion
brunsten ['brunstən] *intr* be in heat
brünstig ['brYnstɪç] *adj* in heat; (fig) passionate
brüsk [brusk] *adj* brusque
brüskieren [brus'kirən] *tr* snub
Brust [brust] *f* (-;-̈e) breast, chest
Brust′bein *n* breastbone, sternum
Brust′bild *n* portrait; (sculp) bust
brüsten ['brYstən] *ref* show off

Brust′fellentzündung f pleurisy
Brust′kasten m, **Brust′korb** m thorax
Brust′schwimmen n breast stroke
Brust′stück n (culin) brisket
Brust′ton m —**im B. der Überzeugung** with utter conviction
Brust′umfang m chest measurement; (bei Frauen) bust measurement
Brü′stung f (-;-en) balustrade
Brust′warze f nipple
Brust′wehr f breastwork
Brut [brut] f (-;-en) brood; (pej) scum
brutal [bru′tal] adj brutal
Brut′apparat m, **Brut′ofen** m incubator
brüten [′brytən] tr hatch; (fig) plan || intr incubate; **b. auf** (dat) (fig) sit on; **b. über** (dat) brood over; pore over
brutto [′bruto] adj (com) gross
Brut′tosozialprodukt n gross national product
Bube [′bubə] m (-n;-n) boy; (Schurke) rascal; (cards) jack
Bu′benstreich m, **Bu′benstück** n prank; dirty trick
bübisch [′bybɪʃ] adj rascally
Buch [bux] n (-[e]s;-″er) book; (cards) straight
Buch′besprechung f book review
Buchbinderei [′buxbɪndəraɪ] f (-;-en) bookbindery; (Gewerbe) bookbinding
Buch′binderleinwand f buckram
Buch′deckel m book cover
Buch′drama n closet drama
Buch′druck m printing, typography
Buch′drucker m printer
Buch′druckerei f print shop; (Gewerbe) printing
Buche [′buxə] f (-;-n) beech
Buchecker [′buxɛkər] f (-;-n) beechnut
buchen [′buxən] tr book, reserve; (com) enter
Bücher- [byçər] comb.fm. book
Bü′cherabschluß m balancing of books
Bü′cherausgabe f circulation desk
Bü′cherbrett n bookshelf
Bücherei [byçə′raɪ] f (-;-en) library
Bü′cherfreund m bibliophile
Bü′chergestell n bookrack, bookcase
Bü′cherregal n bookshelf; bookcase
Bü′cherrevision f audit
Bü′cherrevisor m auditor; accountant
Bü′cherschrank m bookcase
Bü′cherstütze f book end
Buch′führung f bookkeeping, accounting
Buch′halter -in §6 mf bookkeeper
Buch′haltung f bookkeeping; accounting department
Buch′händler -in §6 mf book dealer
Buch′handlung f bookstore
Büchlein [′byçlaɪn] n (-s;-) booklet
Buch′macher m bookmaker
Buch′prüfer -in §6 mf auditor
Buchsbaum [′buksbaum] m boxwood
Buchse [′buksə] f (-;-n) (mach) bushing
Büchse [′byksə] f (-;-n) box, case; (Dose) can; (Gewehr) rifle
Büch′senfleisch n canned meat

Büch′senöffner m can opener
Buchstabe [′bux/tabə] m (-n;-n) letter
buchstabieren [bux/ta′birən] tr & intr spell
buchstäblich [′bux/teplɪç] adj literal
Bucht [buxt] f (-;-en) bay
Buch′umschlag m book jacket
Bu′chung f (-;-en) booking; (acct) entry
Buckel [′bukəl] m (-s;-) hump; (coll) back; **B. haben** be hunchback; **e-n B. machen** arch its back
buck(e)lig [′buk(ə)lɪç] adj hunchbacked || **Buck(e)lige** §5 mf hunchback
bücken [′bykən] tr & ref bow (down)
Bückling [′byklɪŋ] m (-s;-e) bow
Bude [′budə] f (-;-n) booth, stall; (coll) shanty; (coll) hole in the wall
Budget [by′dʒe] n (-s;-s) budget
Büfett [by′fe], [by′fet] n (-s;-s) buffet, sideboard; counter; (Schanktisch) bar; **kaltes B.** cold buffet
Büffel [′byfəl] m (-s;-) buffalo
Büffelei [byfə′laɪ] f (-;-en) cramming
büffeln [′byfəln] intr (für) cram (for)
Bug [buk] m (-[e]s;-e) (aer) nose; (naut) bow; (zool) shoulder, withers
Bügel [′bygəl] m (-s;-) handle; (Kleider-) coat hanger; (Steig-) stirrup; (e-r Säge) frame
Bü′gelbrett n ironing board
Bü′geleisen n iron, flatiron
Bü′gelfalte f crease
bü′gelfrei adj drip-dry
bügeln [′bygəln] tr iron, press
Bü′gelsäge f hacksaw
bugsieren [buk′sirən] tr tow
Buhldirne [′buldɪrnə] f (-;-n) bawd
buhlen [′bulən] intr have an affair; **um j-s Gunst b.** curry favor with s.o.
Bühne [′bynə] f (-;-n) stage; platform
Büh′nenanweisung f stage direction
Büh′nenaussprache f standard pronunciation
Büh′nenausstattung f, **Büh′nenbild** n set
Büh′nenbildner -in §6 mf stage designer
Büh′nendeutsch n standard German
Büh′nendichter -in §6 mf playwright
Büh′nendichtung f drama, play
Büh′nenkünstler m actor
Büh′nenkünstlerin f actress
Büh′nenleiter -in §6 mf stage manager
Büh′nenstück n play, stage play
buk [buk] pret of backen
Bukarest [′bukarɛst] n (-s;) Bucharest
Bulette [bu′letə] f (-;-n) meatball
Bulgarien [bul′garjən] n (-s;) Bulgaria
Bullauge [′bulaugə] n (-s;-en) porthole
Bulldogge [′buldɔgə] f (-;-n) bulldog
Bulle [′bulə] m (-n;-n) bull; brawny fellow; (sl) cop || f (-;-n) (eccl) bull
bullern [′bulərn] intr bubble, boil; (Feuer) roar; (Sturm) rage
Bummel [′buməl] m (-s) stroll
Bummelei [bumə′laɪ] f (-;-en) dawdling; loafing; sloppiness
bummelig [′buməlɪç] adj slow; sloppy
bummeln [′buməln] intr loaf; dawdle; (Autos) crawl || intr (SEIN) stroll

Bum′melstreik m slowdown

Bum′melzug m (coll) slow train, local

Bummler [′bʊmlər] m (-s;-) loafer, bum; slowpoke; gadabout

Bums [bʊms] m (-es;-e) thud, thump, bang || *interj* boom!; bang!

bumsen [′bʊmsən] *intr* thud, thump, bump; (sl) have intercourse

Bums′lokal n (coll) dive, joint

Bund [bʊnt] m (-[e]s;-ꞏe) union, federation; (*Schlüssel*) ring; (*Rand an Hose*) waistband; (*Ehe*-) bond; (mach) flange; (mus) fret; (pol) federal government; **im Bunde mit** with the cooperation of || n (-[e]s;- & -e) bunch, bundle

Bündel [′byndəl] n (-s;-) bunch, bundle; (phys) beam

Bundes- *comb.fm.* federal

Bun′desgenosse m ally, confederate

Bun′desgerichtshof m federal supreme court

Bun′deslade f ark of the covenant

bun′desstaatlich adj state; federal

Bun′destag m lower house

bündig [′byndɪç] adj binding; (*überzeugend*) convincing; (*treffend*) succinct; **b. liegen** be flush

Bündnis [′byntnɪs] n (-ses;-se) agreement, pact, alliance

Bunker [′bʊŋkər] m (-;-) bin; (agr) silo; (aer) air-raid shelter; (mil) bunker; (nav) submarine pen

bunt [bʊnt] adj colored; (*mehrfarbig*) multicolored; (*gefleckt*) dappled; (*gemischt*) varied, motley; (*Farbe*) bright, gay; (*Wiese*) gay with flowers; **bunter Abend** variety show; **buntes Durcheinander** complete muddle

Bunt′metall n nonferrous metal

Bunt′stift m colored pencil, crayon

Bürde [′byrdə] f (-;-n) burden

Burg [bʊrk] f (-;-en) fortress, stronghold; citadel; castle

Bürge [′byrgə] m (-;-n) bondsman, guarantor, surety; **B. sein für** (or **als B. haften für**) stand surety for (s.o.); vouch for (s.th.)

bürgen [′byrgən] *intr*—**b. für** put up bail for (s.o.); vouch for (s.th.)

Bürger -in [′byrgər(ɪn)] §6 mf citizen; member of the middle class; commoner

Bür′gerkrieg m civil war

bür′gerlich adj civic; civil; middleclass; (*nicht überfeinert*) plain

Bür′germeister m mayor

Bür′gerrecht n civil rights

Bür′gerschaft f (-;) citizens

Bür′gersteig m sidewalk

Bürgschaft [′byrkʃaft] f (-;-en) security, guarantee; (jur) bail; **gegen B. freilassen** release on bail

Büro [by′ro] n (-s;-s) office

Büro′angestellte §5 mf clerk

Büro′bedarf m office supplies

Büro′klammer f paper clip

Büro′kraft f office worker; **Bürokräfte** office personnel

Bürokrat [byro′krat] m (-en;-en) bureaucrat

Bürokra-tie [byrokra′ti] f (-;-tien [′tiꞏən]) bureaucracy; (fig) red tape

bürokratisch [byro′kratɪʃ] adj bureaucratic

Bursch(e) [′bʊrʃ(ə)] m (-[e]n;-[e]n) boy, fellow; (mil) orderly; **ein übler B.** a bad egg

burschikos [bʊrʃi′kos] adj tomboyish; devil-may-care

Bürste [′byrstə] f (-;-n) brush; (coll) crewcut

bürsten [′byrstən] tr brush

Bürzel [′byrtsəl] m (-s;-) rump (*of bird*)

Bus [bʊs] m (-ses;-se) bus

Busch [bʊʃ] m (-es;-ꞏe) bush; forest

Büschel [′byʃəl] m & n clump, bunch, cluster; (*Haar*-) tuft; (elec) brush

Busch′holz n boxwood

buschig [′bʊʃɪç] adj bushy; shaggy

Busch′klepper m bushwacker

Busch′messer n machete

Busch′werk n bushes, brush

Busen [′buzən] m (-s;-) bosom, breast; (*Bucht*) bay, gulf; (fig) bosom

Bussard [′bʊsart] m (-s;-e) buzzard

Buße [′busə] f (-n;-n) penance; (*Sühne*) atonement; (*Strafgeld*) fine

büßen [′bysən] tr atone for, pay for

Büßer -in [′bysər(ɪn)] §6 mf penitent

Busserl [′bʊsərl] n (-s;-n) kiss

buß′fertig adj repentant

Bussole [bʊ′solə] f (-;-n) compass

Büste [′bystə] f (-;-n) bust

Bü′stenhalter m brassière, bra

Blüte [′bytə] f (-;-n) tub; vat

Butter [′bʊtər] f (-;) butter

But′terbrot n bread and butter

But′terdose f butter dish

But′termilch f buttermilk

buttern [′bʊtərn] butter || *intr* make butter

byzantinisch [bytsan′tiniʃ] adj Byzantine

Byzanz [by′tsants] n (-′;) Byzantium

bzw. *abbr* (beziehungsweise) respectively

C

C, c [tse] *invar* n C, c; (meteor) centigrade; (mus) C

Café [ka′fe] n (-s;-s) café; coffee shop

Camping [′kɛmpɪŋ] n (-s;-s) camping

Canaille [ka′naljə] f (-;-n) scoundrel

Cäsar [′tsezar] m (-s;) Caesar

Cellist -in [tʃɛ′lɪst(ɪn)] §7 mf cellist

Cello [′tʃɛlo] n (-s;-s) cello

Cellophan [tsɛlo′fan] n (-s;) cellophane

Celsius [′tsɛlzjʊs] centigrade

Cembalo [′tʃɛmbalo] n (-s;-s) harpsichord

Ces [tsɛs] n (-;-) (mus) C flat

Champagner [ʃam'panjər] *m* (-s;-) champagne

Champignon ['ʃampɪnjõ] *m* (-s;-s) mushroom

Chance ['ʃãsə] *f* (-;-n) chance

Chaos ['ka·ɔs] *n* (-;) chaos

chaotisch [ka'otɪʃ] *adj* chaotic

Charak·ter [ka'raktər] *m* (-s;-tere ['terə]) character; (mil) honorary rank

Charak'terbild *n* character sketch

Charak'tereigenschaft *f* trait

charak'terfest *adj* of a strong character

charakterisieren [karakteri'zirən] *tr* characterize

Charakteristik [karakte'rɪstɪk] *f* (-; -en) characterization

Charakteristi·kum [karakte'rɪstɪkum] *n* [-s;-ka [ka]) characteristic

charakteristisch [karakte'rɪstɪʃ] *adj* (für) characteristic (of)

charak'terlich *adj* of character || *adv* in character

charak'terlos *adj* wishy-washy

Charak'terzug *m* characteristic, trait

Charge ['ʃarʒə] *f* (-;-n) (metal) charge; (mil) rank; **Chargen** (mil) non-coms

charmant [ʃar'mant] *adj* charming

Charme [ʃarm] *m* (-s;) charm, grace

Chas·sis [ʃa'si] *n* (-sis ['si[s]]; -sis ['sis]) chassis

Chaus·see [ʃɔ'se] *f* (-;-seen ['se·ən]) highway

Chef [ʃef] *m* (-s;-s) chief, head; (com) boss; (culin) chef; **C. des Generalstabs** chief of staff; **C. des Heeresjustizwesens** judge advocate general

Chemie [çe'mi] *f* (-;) chemistry; **technische C.** chemical engineering

Chemie'faser *f* synthetic fiber

Chemikalien [çemi'kaljən] *pl* chemicals

Chemiker -in ['çemɪkər(ɪn)] §6 *mf* chemist; student of chemistry

chemisch ['çemɪʃ] *adj* chemical; **chemische Reinigung** dry cleaning

Chemotechniker -in [çemo'tɛçnɪkər-(ɪn)] §6 *mf* chemical engineer

Chiffre ['ʃɪfər] *f* (-;-n) cipher; code; (*in Anzeigen*) box number

Chif'freschrift *f* code

chiffrieren [ʃɪ'frirən] *tr* code

China ['çina] *n* (-s;) China

Chinese [çɪ'nezə] *m* (-n;-n;), **Chinesin** [çɪ'nezɪn] *f* (-;-nen) Chinese

chinesisch [çɪ'nezɪʃ] *adj* Chinese

Chinin [çɪ'nin] *n* (-s;) quinine

Chirurg [çɪ'rurg] *m* (-en;-en) surgeon

Chirurgie [çɪrur'gi] *f* (-;) surgery

chirurgisch [çɪ'rurgɪʃ] *adj* surgical

Chlor [klor] *n* (-s;) chlorine

chloren ['klorən] *tr* chlorinate

Chlorid [klo'rit] *n* (-[e]s;-e) chloride

Chloroform [kloro'form] *n* (-s;) chloroform

chloroformieren [klorofor'mirən] *tr* chloroform

Cholera ['kolera] *f* (-;) cholera

cholerisch [ko'lerɪʃ] *adj* choleric

Chor [kor] *m* (-s;ːe) choir; chorus

Choral [ko'ral] *m* (-s;ːe) Gregorian chant; (Prot) hymn

Chor'altar *m* high altar

Chor'anlage *f* (archit) choir

Chor'bühne *f* choir loft

Choreograph -in [kore·o'graf(ɪn)] §7 *mf* choreographer

Chor'hemd *n* surplice

Chor'stuhl *m* choir stall

Christ [krɪst] *m* (-s;) Christ || *m* (-en; -en) Christian

Christ'abend *m* Christmas Eve

Christ'baum *m* Christmas tree

Chri'stenheit *f* (-;) Christendom

Christentum ['krɪstəntum] *n* (-s;) Christianity

Christin ['krɪstɪn] *f* (-;-nen) Christian

Christ'kind *m* Christ child

christ'lich *adj* Christian

Christ'nacht *f* Holy Night

Chri·stus ['krɪstus] *m* (-sti [sti];) Christ; **nach Christi Geburt** A.D.; **vor Christus** B.C.

Chri'stusbild *n* crucifix; picture of Christ

Chrom [krom] *n* (-s;) chromium, chrome

chromatisch [kro'matɪʃ] *adj* chromatic

Chromosom [kromo'zom] *n* (-s;-en) chromosome

Chronik ['kronɪk] *f* (-;-en) chronicle

chronisch ['kronɪʃ] *adj* chronic

Chronist -in [kro'nɪst(ɪn)] §7 *mf* chronicler

Chronolo·gie [kronolo·'gi] *f* (-;-gien ['gi·ən]) chronology

chronologisch [krono'logɪʃ] *adj* chronological

circa ['tsɪrka] *adv* approximately

Cis [tsɪs] *n* (-;-) (mus) C sharp

Clique ['klɪka] *f* (-;-n) clique

Cocktail ['kɔktel] *m* (-s;-s) cocktail

Conferencier [kõferã'sje] *m* (-s;-s) master of ceremony

Couch [kautʃ] *f* (-;-es) couch

Countdown ['kauntdaun] *m* (-s;-s) (rok) countdown

Couplet [ku'ple] *n* (-s;-s) song (*in a musical*)

Coupon [ku'põ] *m* (-s;-s) coupon

Courage [ku'raʒə] *f* (-;) courage

Courtage [kur'taʒə] *f* (-;-n) brokerage

Cousin [ku'zẽ] *m* (-s;-s) cousin

Cousine [ku'zina] *f* (-;-n) cousin

Cowboy ['kaubɔɪ] *m* (-s;-s) cowboy

creme [krem] *adj* cream-colored || **Creme** ['krem(ə)] *f* (-;-s) cream; custard

Crew [kru] *f* (-;) crew; (nav) cadets (*of the same year*)

Cut [kœt] *m* (-s;-s) cutaway

D

D, d [de] *invar n* D, d; (mus) D
da [da] *adv* there; then; in that case, **da und da** at such and such a place; **wieder da** back again ‖ *conj* since, because; when
dabei [da'baɪ] *adv* nearby; besides, moreover; at that; at the same time; (*trotzdem*) yet; **d. bleiben** stick to one's point; **d. sein** be present, take part; **d. sein zu** (*inf*) be on the point of (*ger*); **es ist nichts d.** there's nothing to it
da capo [da'kapo] *interj* encore!
Dach [dax] *n* (−[e]s;̈−er) roof; (fig) shelter; **unter D. und Fach** under cover
Dach′boden *m* attic
Dach′decker *m* roofer
Dach′fenster *n* dormer window; skylight
Dach′first *m* ridge of a roof
Dach′geschoß *n* top floor
Dach′gesellschaft *f* holding company
Dach′kammer *f* attic room
Dach′luke *f* skylight
Dach′organisation *f* parent company
Dach′pappe *f* roofing paper
Dach′pfanne *f* roof tile
Dach′rinne *f* rain gutter; eaves
Dach′röhre *f* downspout
Dachs [daks] *m* (−es;−e) badger; **ein frecher D.** a young whippersnapper
Dachs′hund *m* dachshund
Dach′sparren *m* rafter
Dach′stube *f* attic, garret
Dach′stuhl *m* roof framework
dachte ['daxtə] *pret* of denken
Dach′traufe *f* rain gutter
Dach′werk *n* roof
Dach′ziegel *m* roof tile
dadurch [da'durç] *adv* through it; thereby; by this means; **dadurch, daß** by (*ger*)
dafür [da'fyr] *adv* for it or them; in its place; that's why; therefore
Dafür′halten *n*—**nach meinem D.** in my opinion
dagegen [da'gegən] *adv* against it or them; in exchange for it or them; in comparison; on the other hand; etw **d. haben** have an objection; **ich bin d.** I'm against it
daheim [da'haɪm] *adv* at home
daher [da'her] *adv* from there; therefore; (*bei Verben der Bewegung*) along ‖ ['daher] *adv* that's why
dahin [da'hɪn] *adv* there, to that place; (*vergangen*) gone; (*bei Verben der Bewegung*) along; **bis d.** that far, up to there; until then; **es steht mir bis d.** I'm fed up with it
da′hinauf *adv* up there
da′hinaus *adv* out there
dahin′geben §80 *tr* give away; give up
dahin′gehen §82 *intr* (SEIN) walk along; pass; (*sterben*) pass away; **dahingehend, daß** to the effect that
dahingestellt [da'hɪŋgə'ʃtelt] *adj*—**d.**

sein lassen, ob leave the question open whether
dahin′leben *intr* exist from day to day
dahin′raffen *tr* carry off
dahin′scheiden §112 *intr* (SEIN) pass on
dahin′schwinden *intr* (SEIN) dwindle away; fade away; pine away
dahin′stehen §146 *impers*—**es steht dahin** it is uncertain
dahin′ten *adv* back there
dahin′ter *adv* behind it or them
dahinterher′ *adv*—**d. sein, daß** be insistent that
dahin′terkommen §99 *intr* (SEIN) find out about it; get behind the truth of it
dahin′tersetzen *tr* put (*s.o.*) to work on it
dahin′welken §113 *intr* (SEIN) fade away
dahin′ziehen §163 *intr* (SEIN) move along
Dakapo [da'kapo] *n* (−s;−s) encore
da′lassen §104 *tr* leave behind
dalli ['dalɪ] *interj*—**mach d.!** step on it!
damalig ['damalɪç] *adj* of that time
damals ['damals] *adv* then, at that time
Damast [da'mast] *m* (−es;−e) damask
Dame ['damə] *f* (−;−n) lady; (*beim Tanz*) partner; (cards, chess) queen; (checkers) king; **e-e D. machen** crown a checker; **meine D.!** madam!; **meine Damen und Herrn!** ladies and gentlemen!
Da′mebrett *n* checkerboard
Da′menbinde *f* sanitary napkin
Da′mendoppelspiel *n* (tennis) women's doubles
Da′meneinzelspiel *n* (tennis) women's singles
Da′mengesellschaft *f* hen party
da′menhaft *adj* ladylike
Da′menhemd *n* chemise
Da′menschneider **−in** §6 *mf* dressmaker
Da′menwäsche *f* lingerie
Da′mespiel *n* checkers
damisch ['damɪʃ] *adj* dopey
damit [da'mɪt] *adv* with it or them; by it; thereby; **d. hat's noch Zeit** that can wait; **es ist nichts d.** it is useless ‖ *conj* in order that, to
dämlich ['demlɪç] *adj* dopey
Damm [dam] *m* (−[e]s;̈−e) dam; dike; embankment; causeway; breakwater; pier; (fig) barrier; (anat) perineum; **auf dem D. sein** feel up to it; **wieder auf dem D. sein** be on one's feet again
Dämmer ['demər] *m* (−s;) (poet) twilight
dämmerig ['demərɪç] *adj* dusky, dim
Däm′merlicht *n* dusk, twilight
dämmern ['demərn] *intr* dawn, grow light; (*am Abend*) grow dark, become twilight

Däm'merung *f* (-;-en) (*Morgenrot*) dawn; (*am Abend*) dusk, twilight
Dämmplatte ['dɛmplatə] *f* acoustical tile
Dämmstoff ['dɛmʃtəf] *m* insulation
Damm'weg *m* causeway
Dämon ['dɛmon] *m* (-s; Dämonen [dɛ'monən] demon
dämonisch [dɛ'moniʃ] *adj* demonical
Dampf [dampf] *m* (-[e]s;╧e) steam; vapor; (*Angst*) (coll) fear; (*Hunger*) (coll) hunger; (vet) broken wind; **D. dahinter machen** (coll) step on it
dampfen ['dampfən] *intr* steam ‖ *intr* (SEIN) steam along, steam away
dämpfen ['dɛmpfən] *tr* (*dünsten*) steam; (*Lärm*) muffle; (*Farben, Gefühle, Lichter*) subdue; (*Stoß*) absorb; (*Begeisterung*) dampen; **mit gedämpfter Stimme** under one's breath
Dampfer ['dampfər] *m* (-s;-) steamer
Dämpfer ['dɛmpfər] *m* (-s;-) (culin) steamer, boiler; (mach) baffle; (mus) mute; (*beim Klavier*) (mus) damper; **e-n D. aufsetzen** (dat) put a damper on
Dampf'heizung *f* steam heat
Dampf'kessel *m* steam boiler, boiler
Dampf'maschine *f* steam engine
Dampf'schiffahrtslinie *f* steamship line
Dämp'fungsfläche *f* (aer) stabilizer
Dampf'walze *f* steam roller
Damspiel ['dam'piːl] *n* var of **Dame-spiel**
danach [da'nax] *adv* after it or them; accordingly; according to it or them; afterwards; **d. fragen** ask about it; **d. streben** strive for it; **d. sieht er auch aus** that's just what he looks like
Däne ['dɛnə] *m* (-n;-n) Dane
daneben [da'nebən] *adv* next to it or them ‖ *adv* in addition
dane'begehen §82 *intr* (SEIN) go amiss
dane'benhauen *intr* miss; (fig) be wrong
Dänemark ['dɛnəmark] *n* (-s;) Denmark
dang [daŋ] *pret* of **dingen**
daniederliegen [da'nidərligən] §108 *intr* (fig) be down; **d. an** (dat) be laid up with
Dänin ['dɛnin] *f* (-;-nen) Dane
dänisch ['dɛniʃ] *adj* Danish
dank [daŋk] *prep* (dat) thanks to ‖ **Dank** *m* (-[e]s;) thanks; gratitude; **Gott sei D.!** thank God!, thank heaven!
dankbar ['daŋkbar] *adj* thankful; (*lohnend*) rewarding, profitable
Dank'barkeit *f* (-;) gratitude
danken ['daŋkən] *intr* (dat) thank; **danke!** thanks!; (*bei Ablehnung*) no, thanks!; **danke schön!** thank you!; **nichts zu d.!** you are welcome!
dan'kenswert *adj* meritorious; rewarding
dank'sagen *intr* return thanks
Danksagung ['daŋkzaguŋ] *f* (-;) thanksgiving
Dank'sagungstag *m* Thanksgiving Day

Dank'schreiben *n* letter of thanks
dann [dan] *adv* then; **d. und wann** now and then
dannen ['danən] *adv*—**von d.** away
daran [da'ran] *adv* on, at, by, in, onto it or them; **das ist alles d.!** that's great!; **er ist gut d.** he's well off; **er tut gut d. zu** (inf) he does well to (inf); **es ist nichts d.** there's nothing to it; **ich will wissen, wie ich d. bin** I want to know where I stand; **jetzt bin ich d.** it's my turn; **nahe d. sein zu** (inf) be on the point of (ger); **was liegt d.?** what does it matter?
daran'gehen §82 *intr* (SEIN) go about it; **d. gehen zu** (inf) proceed to (inf)
daran'setzen *tr*—**alles d. zu** (inf) do one's level best to (inf)
darauf [da'rauf] *adv* on it or them; after that; **d. kommt es an** that's what matters; **gerade d. zu** straight towards; **gleich d.** immediately afterwards; **ich lasse es d. ankommen** I'll risk it
daraufhin [darauf'hin] *adv* thereupon
daraus [da'raus] *adv* of it, from it; from that; from them; hence; **d. wird nichts!** nothing doing!; **es wird nichts d.** nothing will come of it
darben ['darbən] *intr* live in poverty
darbieten ['darbitən] §58 *tr* present
Dar'bietung *f* (-;-en) presentation; (theat) performance
dar'bringen §65 *tr* present, offer
Dardanellen [darda'nelən] *pl* Dardanellen
darein [da'rain] *adv* into it or them
darein'reden *intr* interrupt; **er redet mir in alles d.** he interferes in all that I do
darin [da'rin] *adv* in it or them
dar'legen *tr* explain; state
Dar'legung *f* (-;-en) explanation
Darlehen ['darle(ə)n] *n* (-s;-) loan
Dar'leh(e)nskasse *f* loan association
Darm [darm] *m* (-[e]s;╧e) intestine, gut; (*Wursthaut*) skin
Darm— *comb.fm.* intestinal
Darm'entzündung *f* enteritis
Darm'fäule *f* dysentery
dar'stellen *tr* describe; show, depict, portray; represent; mean; plot, chart; (indust) produce; (theat) play the part of
Dar'steller -in §6 *mf* performer
Dar'stellung *f* (-;-en) representation; portrayal; account, version; (indust) production; (theat) performance
dar'tun §154 *tr* prove; demonstrate
darüber [da'rybər] *adv* over it or them; (*querüber*) across it; (*betreffs*) about that; **d. hinaus** beyond it; moreover; **ich bin d. hinweg** I've gotten over it
darum [da'rum] *adv* around it or them; (*deshalb*) therefore; per weiß d. he's aware of it; **es ist mir nur d. zu tun, daß** all I ask is that
darunter [da'runtər] *adv* below it or them; among them; (*weniger*) less; **d. leiden** suffer from it; **zehn Jahre und d.** ten years and under
das [das] §1 *def art* the ‖ §1 *dem adj* & *dem pron* this, that; **das und das**

such and such ‖ §11 *rel pron* which, that, who

da′sein §139 *intr* (SEIN) be there; be present; exist; **es ist schon alles mal dagewesen** there's nothing new under the sun; **noch nie dagewesen** unprecedented ‖ **Dasein** *n* (-s;) being, existence, life

Da′seinsberechtigung *f* raison d'être

daselbst [da′zɛlpst] *adv* just there; ibidem; **wohnhaft d.** address as above

dasjenige [′dasjenɪgə] §4,3 *dem adj* that ‖ *dem pron* the one

daß [das] *conj* that; **daß du nicht vergißt!** be sure not to forget!; **daß er doch käme!** I wish he'd come; **es sei denn, daß** unless

dasselbe [das′zɛlbə] §4,3 *dem adj & dem pron* the same

da′stehen §146 *intr* stand there; **einzig d.** be unrivaled; **gut d.** be well-off; **wie stehe ich nun da!** how foolish I look now!

Daten [′datən] *pl* data

Da′tenverarbeitung *f* data processing

datieren [da′tirən] *tr & intr* date

Dativ [′datif] *m* (-s;-e) dative (case)

dato [′dato] *adv*—**bis d.** to date

Dattel [′datəl] *f* (-;-n) (bot) date

Da·tum [′datum] *n* (-s;-ten [tən]) date; **Daten** data, facts; **heutigen Datums** of today; **neueren Datums** of recent date; **welches D. haben wir heute?** what's today's date?

Daube [′daubə] *f* (-;-n) (barrel) stave

Dauer [′dauər] *f* (-;) length, duration; permanence; **auf die D.** in the long run; **für die D. von** for a period of; **von D. sein** last, endure

Dau′erauftrag *m* standing order

Dau′erbelastung *f* constant load

Dau′erertrag *m* constant yield

Dau′erfeuer *n* (mil) automatic fire

Dau′erflug *m* endurance flight

Dau′ergeschwindigkeit *f* cruising speed

dau′erhaft *adj* lasting, durable; *(Farbe)* fast

Dau′erkarte *f* season ticket; (rr) commutation ticket

Dau′erlauf *m* (long-distance) jogging

dauern [′dauərn] *tr*—**er dauert mich** I feel sorry for him ‖ *intr* last, continue; **die Fahrt dauert fünf Stunden** the trip takes five hours; **es wird nicht lange d., dann** it won't be long before; **lange d.** take a long time

Dau′erplissee *n* permanent pleat

Dau′erprobe *f* endurance test

Dau′erschmierung *f* self-lubrication

Dau′erstellung *f* permanent job

Dau′erton *m* (telp) dial tone

Dau′erversuch *m* endurance test

Dau′erwelle *f* permanent wave

Dau′erwirkung *f* lasting effect

Dau′erwurst *f* hard salami

Dau′erzustand *m* permanent condition; **zum D. werden** get to be a regular thing

Daumen [′daumən] *m* (-s;-) thumb; **D. halten** keep your fingers crossed!; **die D. drehen** twiddle one's thumbs; **über den D. peilen** (or **schätzen**) give a rough estimate of

Dau′menabdruck *m* thumb print

Dau′menindex *m* thumb index

Daune [′daunə] *f* (-;-n) downy feather; **Daunen** down

Dau′nenbett *n* feather bed

Davit [′devɪt] *m* (-s;-s) (naut) davit

davon [da′fɔn] *adv* of it or them; from it or them; about it or them; away

davon′kommen §99 *intr* (SEIN) escape

davon′laufen §105 *intr* (SEIN) run away; ‖ **Davonlaufen** *n*—**es ist zum D.** (coll) it's enough to drive you insane

davon′machen *ref* take off, go away

davon′tragen §132 *tr* carry off; win

davor [da′for] *adv* in front of it or them; of it or them; from it or them

dawider [da′vidər] *adv* against it

dazu [da′tsu] *adv* thereto; to it or them; in addition to that; for that purpose; about it or them; with it or them

dazu′gehörig *adj* belonging to it; proper, appropriate

da′zumal *adv* at that time

dazu′tun §154 *tr* add ‖ **Dazutun** *n*—**ohne sein D.** without any effort on his part

dazwischen [da′tsvɪʃən] *adv* in between; among them

dazwi′schenfahren §71 *intr* (SEIN) jump in to intervene

dazwi′schenfunken *intr* (coll) butt in

dazwi′schenkommen §99 *intr* (SEIN) intervene

Dazwischenkunft [da′tsvɪʃənkunft] *f* (-;) intervention

dazwi′schentreten §152 *intr* (SEIN) intervene

Debatte [de′batə] *f* (-;-n) debate, discussion; **zur D. stehen** be under discussion; **zur D. stellen** open to discussion

debattieren [deba′tirən] *tr & intr* debate, discuss

Debet [′debet] *n* (-s;) debit; **im D. stehen** be on the debit side

Debüt [de′by] *n* (-s;-s) debut

Debütantin [deby′tantɪn] *f* (-;-nen) debutante

debütieren [deby′tierən] *intr* make one's debut

Dechant [de′çant] *m* (-en;-en) (educ; R.C.) dean

dechiffrieren [deʃɪf′rirən] *tr* decipher

Deck [dek] *n* (-s;-s) deck

Deck′anstrich *m* final coat

Deck′bett *n* feather bed

Deck′blatt *n* overlay

Decke [′dekə] *f* (-;-n) cover, covering; *(Bett-)* blanket; *(Tisch-)* tablecloth; *(Zimmer-)* ceiling; *(Schicht)* layer; **mit j-m unter e-r D. stecken** be in cahoots with s.o.; **sich nach der D. strecken** make the best of it

Deckel [′dekəl] *m* (-s;-) lid, cap; *(Buch-)* cover; **j-m eins auf den D. geben** (coll) chew s.o. out

decken [′dekən] *tr* cover; *(Tisch)* set; **das Tor d.** guard the goal ‖ *ref* coincide ‖ *intr* cover

Deckenbeleuchtung (Dek′kenbeleuchtung) *f* (-;) ceiling lighting

Deckenlicht (Dek'kenlicht) *n* ceiling light; skylight; (aut) dome light

Deck'farbe *f* one-coat paint

Deck'konto *n* secret account

Deck'mantel *m* pretext, pretense

Deck'name *m* pseudonym; alias; (mil) code name, cover name

Deck'offizier *m* (nav) warrant officer

Deck'plane *f* awning; tarpaulin

Deckung (Dek'kung) *f* (-;-e) covering; protection; roofing; (box) defense; (com) security, surety; collateral

deckungsgleich (dek'kungsgleich) *adj* congruent

defekt [de'fekt] *adj* defective || **Defekt** *m* (-[e]s;-e) defect

defensiv [defen'zif] *adj* defensive || **Defensive** [defen'zivə] *f* (-;-n) defensive

definieren [defi'nirən] *tr* define

definitiv [defini'tif] *adj* (endgültig) definitive; (bestimmt) definite

Defizit ['defɪtsɪt] *n* (-s;-e) deficit

Degen ['degən] *m* (-s;-) sword; (poet) warrior; (typ) compositor

degradieren [degra'dirən] *tr* demote

Degradie'rung *f* (-;-en) demotion

dehnbar ['denbar] *adj* elastic; (Metall) ductile; (fig) vague, loose

dehnen ['denən] *tr* stretch; extend; expand; (Worte) drawl out; (Vokal) lengthen; (mus) sustain || *ref* stretch out; expand

Deh'nung *f* (-;-en) extension; expansion; dilation; (ling) lengthening

Deich [daɪç] *m* (-[e]s;-e) dike; (Damm) bank, embankment

Deichsel ['daɪksəl] *f* (-;-n) pole

deichseln ['daɪksəln] *tr* (coll) manage

dein [daɪn] §2 poss adj your, thy

deinerseits ['daɪnər'zaɪts] *adv* on your part

deinesgleichen ['daɪnəs'glaɪçən] *invar pron* your own kin, your equals, the likes of you

deinethalben ['daɪnət'halbən], **deinetwegen** ['daɪnət'vegən], **deinetwillen** ['daɪnət'vɪlən] *adv* for your sake; because of you, on your account

deinige ['daɪnɪgə] poss pron yours

Dekan [de'kan] *m* (-s;-e) dean

deklamieren [dekla'mirən] *tr & intr* declaim; recite

Deklination [deklɪna'tsjon] *f* (-;-en) declension

deklinieren [deklɪ'nirən] *tr* decline

dekolletiert [dekolə'tirt] *adj* low-necked; (Dame) bare-necked

Dekorateur [dekora'tør] *m* (-s;-e) decorator, interior decorator

Dekoration [dekora'tsjon] *f* (-;-en) decoration; (theat) scenery

dekorieren [deko'rirən] *tr* decorate

Dekret [de'kret] *n* (-[e]s;-e) decree

delikat [delɪ'kat] *adj* delicate; (lecker) delicious

Delikt [de'lɪkt] *n* (-[e]s;-e) offense

Delle ['delə] *f* (-;-n) dent; dip

Delphin [del'fin] *m* (-s;-e) dolphin

Delta ['delta] *n* (-s;-s) delta

dem [dem] §1 def art, dem adj & dem pron || §11 rel pron

Demagoge [dema'gogə] *m* (-n;-n) demagogue

Dementi [de'menti] *n* (-s;-s) official denial

dementieren [demen'tirən] *tr* deny (officially)

dem'entsprechend *adj* corresponding || *adv* correspondingly, accordingly

dem'gegenüber *adv* in contrast

dem'gemäß *adv* accordingly

dem'nach *adv* therefore; accordingly

dem'nächst *adv* soon, before long; (theat) (public sign) coming soon

demobilisieren [demobɪlɪ'zirən] *tr & intr* demobilize

Demokrat [demo'krat] *m* (-en;-en) democrat

Demokra·tie [demokra'ti] *f* (-;-tien ['ti·ən]) democracy

Demokratin [demo'kratɪn] *f* (-;-nen) democrat

demokratisch [demo'kratɪʃ] *adj* democratic

demolieren [demo'lirən] *tr* demolish

Demonstrant –in [demon'strant(ɪn)] §7 *mf* demonstrator

demonstrieren [demon'strirən] *tr & intr* demonstrate

Demontage [demon'taʒə] *f* (-;) dismantling

demontieren [demon'tirən] *tr* dismantle

demselben [dem'zelbən] §4,3 dem adj & dem pron

Demut ['demut] *f* (-;) humility

demütig ['demytɪç] *adj* humble

demütigen ['demytɪgən] *tr* humble; (beschämen) humiliate

De'mütigung *f* (-;-en) humiliation

de'mutsvoll *adj* submissive

dem'zufolge *adv* accordingly

den [den] §1 def art, dem adj & dem pron || §11 rel pron

denen ['denən] §11 rel pron to whom

Denkarbeit ['deŋkarbaɪt] *f* (-;) brainwork

Denkart ['deŋkart] *f* var of **Denkungsart**

Denkaufgabe ['deŋkaufgabə] *f* brain twister, problem

denkbar ['deŋkbar] *adj* conceivable; (vorstellbar) imaginable

denken ['deŋkən] §66 *tr* think, consider; was d. Sie zu tun? what do you intend to do? || *ref*—bei sich (or für sich) d. think to oneself; denke dir e–e Zahl think of a number; d. Sie sich in ihre Lage imagine yourself in her place; sich [dat] etw d. imagine s.th.; was denkst du dir eigentlich? what do you think you're doing? || *intr* think; das gibt mir zu d. that set me thinking; d. an (acc) think about

denk'faul *adj* mentally lazy

Denk'fehler *m* fallacy, false reasoning

Denk'mal *n* (-s;-e & ·er) monument

Denk'schrift *f* (pol) memorandum

Denkungsart ['deŋkuŋsart] *f* way of thinking, mentality

Denk'weise *f* way of thinking, mentality

denk'würdig *adj* memorable

Denk'zettel _m_—**j-m** e-n **D. geben** teach s.o. a lesson

denn [dɛn] _adv_ then; **es sei denn, daß** unless || _conj_ for

dennoch ['dɛnɔx] _adv_ nevertheless, all the same, (but) still

Dentist –in [dɛn'tɪst(ɪn)] §7 _mf_ dentist

Denunziant –in [denun'tsjant(ɪn)] §7 _mf_ informer

denunzieren [denun'tsirən] _tr_ denounce

Depesche [de'pɛʃə] _f_ (–;–n) dispatch

De·ponens [de'ponɛns] _n_ (–;–ponenzien [po'nɛntsjən]) (gram) deponent

deponieren [depo'nirən] _tr_ (com) deposit

deportieren [dɛpɔr'tirən] _tr_ deport

Depot [de'po] _n_ (–s;–s) depot; warehouse; storage; safe; safe deposit

Depp [dɛp] _m_ (–s;–e) (coll) dope

Depression [deprɛ'sjon] _f_ (–;–en) depression

der [der] §1 _def art_ the || §1 _dem adj & dem pron_ this, that; **der und der** such and such, so and so || §11 _rel pron_ who, which, that; (to) whom that

der'art _adv_ so, in such a way; (coll) that

der'artig _adj_ such, of that kind

derb [dɛrp] _adj_ coarse; tough; rude

Derb'heit _f_ (–;–en) coarseness; toughness; crude joke

dereinst' _adv_ some day

deren ['derən] §11 _rel pron_ whose

derenthalben ['derənt'halbən], **derentwegen** ['derənt'vegən], **derentwillen** ['derənt'vrlən] _adv_ for her sake, for their sake

dergestalt ['dergə'ʃtalt] _adv_ so

dergleichen ['der'glaɪçən] _invar dem adj_ such; similar; **of that kind** || _invar dem pron_ such a thing; **und d. und die like;** **und d. mehr** and so on

derjenige ['derjenɪgə] §4,3 _dem adj_ that || _dem pron_ the one; he

dermaßen [der'masən] _adv_ so, in such a way

derselbe [der'zɛlbə] §4,3 _dem adj & dem pron_ the same

derweilen ['der'varlən] _adv_ meanwhile

derzeit ['der'tsart] _adv_ at present

derzeitig ['der'tsartɪç] _adj_ present; then, of that time

des [dɛs] _n_ (–;–) (mus) D flat

Desaster [de'zastər] _n_ (–s;–) disaster

Deserteur [dezɛr'tør] _m_ (–s;–e) deserter

desertieren [dezɛr'tirən] _intr_ (SEIN) desert

desgleichen ['des'glaɪçən] _invar dem pron_ such a thing || _invar rel pron_ the likes of which || _adv_ likewise

deshalb ['deshalp] _adv_ therefore

Desinfektion [desɪnfɛk'tsjon] _f_ (–;–en) disinfection

Desinfektions'mittel _n_ disinfectant

desinfizieren [desɪnfɪr'tsirən] _tr_ disinfect

Despot [des'pot] _m_ (–en;–en) despot

despotisch [des'potɪʃ] _adj_ despotic

Dessin [de'sɛ̃] _n_ (–s;–s) design

destillieren [dɛstɪ'lirən] _tr_ distill

desto ['dɛsto] _adv_ the; **d. besser** the better, all the better

deswegen ['des'vegən] _adv_ therefore

Detail [de'taɪ(l)] _n_ (–s;–s) detail; (com) retail

Detail'geschäft _n_ retail store

Detail'händler –in §6 _mf_ retail dealer

detaillieren [deta'jirən] _tr_ relate in detail; specify; itemize

Detek·tiv [detɛk'tif] _m_ (–s;–tive ['tivə]) private investigator; (coll) private eye

detonieren [deto'nirən] _intr_ detonate; **etw. d. lassen** detonate s.th.

deuchte ['dɔɪçtə] _pret_ of dünken

Dentelei [dɔrtə'laɪ] _f_ (–;–en) quibble

deuteln ['dɔrtəln] _intr_ (an dat) quibble (about), split hairs (over)

deuten ['dɔrtən] _tr_ interpret; **falsch d. misinterpret** || _intr_ (auf acc) (& fig) point (to)

deutlich ['dɔɪtlɪç] _adj_ clear, distinct

deutsch [dɔɪtʃ] _adj_ German || **Deutsche** §5 _mf_ German

Deu'tung _f_ (–;–en) interpretation

Devise [de'vizə] _f_ (–;–n) motto; **Devisen** foreign currency

Devi'senbestand _m_ foreign-currency reserve

Devi'senbilanz _f_ balance of payments

Devi'senkurs _m_ rate of exchange

Dezember [de'tsɛmbər] _m_ (–s;–) December

dezent [de'tsɛnt] _adj_ unobtrusive; (Licht, Musik) soft; (anständig) decent

Dezernat [detsɛr'nat] _n_ (–[e]s;–e) (administrative) department

dezimal [detsɪ'mal] _adj_ decimal || **Dezimale** [detsɪ'malə] _f_ (–;–n) decimal

Dezimal'bruch _m_ decimal fraction

Dezimal'zahl _f_ decimal

dezimieren [detsɪ'mirən] _tr_ decimate

Dia ['di·a] _n_ (–s;–s) (coll) slide

Diadem [di·a'dem] _n_ (–s;–e) diadem

Diagnose [di·a'gnozə] _f_ (–;–n) diagnosis

diagnostizieren [di·agnɔstɪ'tsirən] _tr_ diagnose

diagonal [di·ago'nal] _adj_ diagonal || **Diagonale** _f_ (–;–n) diagonal

Diagramm [di·a'gram] _n_ (–[e]s;–e) diagram; graph

Diakon [di·a'kon] _m_ (–s;–e & –en;–en) deacon

Dialekt [di·a'lɛkt] _m_ (–[e]s;–e) dialect

dialektisch [di·a'lɛktɪʃ] _adj_ dialectical

Dialog [di·a'lok] _m_ (–s;–e) dialogue

Diamant [di·a'mant] _m_ (–en;–en) diamond

Diaposi·tiv [di·apozɪ'tif] _n_ (–s;–tive ['tivə]) slide, transparency

Diät [di'ɛt] _f_ (–;–en) diet (under medical supervision); **Diäten** daily allowance; **diät leben** be on a diet

Diät– _comb.fm._ dietary

diätetisch [dɪɛ'tetɪʃ] _adj_ dietetic

dich [dɪç] §11 _pers pron_ you, thee || _reflex pron_ yourself, thyself

dicht [dɪçt] _adj_ dense; thick; heavy; leakproof; tight || **Dichte** ['dɪçtə] _f_ (–;–en) density

dichten ['dɪçtən] *tr* tighten; caulk; compose, write || *intr* write poetry
Dichter ['dɪçtər] *m* (-s;-) (important) writer; poet
Dichterin ['dɪçtərɪn] *f* (-;-nen) poetess
dichterisch ['dɪçtərɪʃ] *adj* poetic(al)
dicht/gedrängt *adj* tightly packed
dicht/halten §90 *intr* keep mum
Dicht/heit *f* (-;), **Dich/tigkeit** *f* (-;) density; compactness; tightness
Dich/kunst *f* poetry
dicht/machen *tr* (coll) close up
Dich/tung *f* (-;-en) gasket; packing; imagination; fiction; poetry; poem;
Dich/tungsring *m*, **Dich/tungsscheibe** *f* washer; gasket
dick [dɪk] *adj* thick; fat; big; (*Luft, Freunde*) close; **dicke Luft!** (coll) cheese it!; **sich d. tun** talk big || **Dicke** *f* (-s) thickness, stoutness
Dick/darm *m* (anat) colon
dickfellig ['dɪkfɛlɪç] *adj* thick-skinned
dick/flüssig *adj* viscous
Dickicht ['dɪkɪçt] *n* (-[e]s;-e) thicket
Dick/kopf *m* thick head
dickköpfig ['dɪkkœpfɪç] *adj* thick-headed
dickleibig ['dɪklaɪbɪç] *adj* stout, fat
Dick/schädel *m* thick head
dick/schädelig ['dɪkʃɛdəlɪç] *adj* thick-headed
die [di] §1 *def art* the || §1 *dem adj & dem pron* this, that; **die und die** such and such || §11 *rel pron* who, which, that
Dieb [dip] *m* (-[e]s;-e) thief
Dieberei [dibə'raɪ] *f* (-;-en) thievery; (*Diebstahl*) theft
Diebesbande ['dibəsbandə] *f* pack of thieves
Diebin ['dibɪn] *f* (-;-nen) thief
diebisch ['dibɪʃ] *adj* thievish || *adv*—**sich d. freuen** be tickled pink
Diebstahl ['dip/tal] *m* (-[e]s;-e) theft, larceny; **leichter D.** petty larceny; **schwerer D.** grand larceny
diejenige ['dijənɪgə] §4,3 *dem adj* that || *dem pron* the one; she
Diele ['dilə] *f* (-;-n) floorboard; (*breiter Flur*) entrance hall; **Dielen** flooring
dienen ['dinən] *intr* (*dat*) serve; **damit ist mir nicht gedient** that doesn't help me any; **womit kann ich d.?** may I help you?
Diener -in ['dinər(ɪn)] §6 *mf* servant
die/nerhaft *adj* servile
dienern ['dinərn] *intr* bow and scrape
Die/nerschaft *f* (-;) domestics, help
dienlich ['dinlɪç] *adj* useful
Dienst [dinst] *m* (-es;-e) service; job; employment; (adm, mil) grade; **außer D.** retired; **im. D.** on duty; **j-m e-n D. tun** do s.o. a favor
Dienstag ['dinstak] *m* (-[e]s;-e) Tuesday
Dienst/alter *n* seniority
dienstbar ['dinstbar] *adj* subservient
Dienst/barkeit *f* (-;) servitude, bondage; (jur) easement
dienst/beflissen *adj* eager to serve || *adv* eagerly

Dienst/bote *m* servant, domestic
Dienst/boteneingang *m* service entrance
Dienst/eid *m* oath of office
dienst/eifrig *adj* eager to serve || *adv* eagerly
Dienst/einteilung *f* work schedule; (mil) duty roster
Dienst/fahrt *f* official trip
dienst/frei *adj*—**d. haben** be off duty
Dienst/gebrauch *m*—**nur zum D.** for official use only
Dienst/gespräch *n* business call
Dienst/grad *m* (mil) rank, grade; (nav) rating
dienst/habend *adj* on duty
Dienst/herr *m* employer; (hist) lord
Dienst/leistung *f* service
dienst/lich *adj* official || *adv* officially; on official business
Dienst/mädchen *n* maid
Dienst/pflicht *f* official duty; compulsory military service
Dienst/plan *m* work schedule; (mil) duty roster
Dienst/sache *f* official business
dienst/tauglich *adj* fit for active service
diensttuend ['dinsttu-ənt] *adj* on duty; active; in charge
Dienst/weg *m* official channels
Dienst/wohnung *f* official residence
dies [dis] *dem adj & dem pron* var of **dieses**
diese ['dizə] §3 *dem adj* this || *dem pron* this one
dieselbe [di'zɛlbə] §4,3 *dem adj & dem pron* the same
Dieselmotor ['dizəlmotor] *m* diesel engine
dieser ['dizər] §3 *dem adj* this || *dem pron* this one
dieses ['dizəs] §3 *dem adj* this || *dem pron* this one
diesig ['dizɪç] *adj* hazy, misty
dies/jährig *adj* this year's
dies/mal *adv* this time
diesseits ['diszaɪts] *prep* (*genit*) on this side of
Dietrich ['ditrɪç] *m* (-s;-e) skeleton key; (*Einbrecherwerkzeug*) picklock
Differential [dɪferen'tsjal] *n* (-s;-e) (aut, math) differential
Differential- comb.fm. (econ, elec, mach, math, phys) differential
Differenz [dɪfe'rents] *f* (-;-en) difference
Diktaphon [dɪkta'fon] *n* (-[e]s;-e) dictaphone
Diktat [dɪk'tat] *n* (-s;-e) dictation; **nach D. schreiben** take dictation
Diktator [dɪk'tator] *m* (-s;-tatoren) [ta'toren] dictator
diktatorisch [dɪkta'torɪʃ] *adj* dictatorial
Diktatur [dɪkta'tur] *f* (-;-en) dictatorship
diktieren [dɪk'tirən] *tr & intr* dictate
Dilettant -in [dɪle'tant(ɪn)] §7 *mf* dilettante, amateur
Diner [di'ne] *n* (-s;-s) dinner
Ding [dɪŋ] *n* (-[e]s;-e) thing; **ein D. drehen** (coll) pull a job
dingen ['dɪŋən] §109 & §142 *tr* hire

ding'fest adj—j-n d. machen arrest s.o.

ding'lich adj real

Dings [dɪŋs] n (-s;) (coll) thing, doodad, thingamajig

Dings'bums m & n (-;) var of Dingsda

Dings'da mfn (-s;) what-d'ye-call-it

Diözese [dɪˈøˀtseːzə] f (-;-n) diocese

Diphtherie [dɪftəˈriː] f (-;) diphtheria

Dipl.-Ing. abbr (Diplom-Ingenieur) engineer holding a degree

Diplom [dɪˈploːm] n (-s;-e) diploma

Diplom- comb.fm. holding a degree

Diplomat [dɪploˈmaːt] m (-en;-en) diplomat

Diplomatie [dɪplomaˈtiː] f (-;) diplomacy

Diplomatin [dɪploˈmaːtɪn] f (-;-nen) diplomat

diplomatisch [dɪploˈmaːtɪʃ] adj diplomatic

dir [diːr] §11 pers pron to or for you, to or for thee || reflex pron to or for yourself, to or for thyself

direkt [dɪˈrɛkt] adj direct

Direktion [dɪrɛkˈtsjoːn] f (-;) direction; (Verwaltung) management

Direk·tor [dɪˈrɛktoːr] m (-s;-toren [ˈtoːrən]) director; (e-r Bank) president; (e-r Schule) principal; (e-s Gefängnisses) warden

Direktorat [dɪrɛktoˈraːt] n (-[e]s;-e) directorship

Direktorin [dɪrɛkˈtoːrɪn] f (-;-nen) director; (educ) principal

Direkto·rium [dɪrɛkˈtoːriˌum] n (-s; -rien [riˌən]) board of directors; executive committee

Direktrice [dɪrɛkˈtriːsə] f (-;-n) directress, manager

Dirigent -in [dɪrɪˈgɛnt(ɪn)] §7 mf (mus) conductor

dirigieren [dɪrɪˈgiːrən] tr direct, manage; (mus) conduct

Dirnd(e)l [ˈdɪrndəl] n (-s;-) girl; (Tracht) dirndle

Dirne [ˈdɪrnə] f (-;-n) girl; (pej) prostitute

Dis [dɪs] n (-;-) D sharp

disharmonisch [dɪsharˈmoːnɪʃ] adj discordant

Diskont [dɪsˈkɔnt] m (-[e]s;-e) discount

diskontieren [dɪskɔnˈtiːrən] tr discount

Diskothek [dɪskoˈteːk] f (-;-en) discotheque

diskret [dɪsˈkreːt] adj discreet

Diskretion [dɪskreˈtsjoːn] f (-;) discretion

Diskussion [dɪskuˈsjoːn] f (-;-en) discussion

diskutieren [dɪskuˈtiːrən] tr discuss || intr—d. über (acc) discuss

disponieren [dɪspoˈniːrən] intr (über acc) dispose (of)

Disposition [dɪspoˈtsjoːn] f (-;-en) disposition; arrangement; disposal

Distanz [dɪsˈtants] f (-;-en) distance

distanzieren [dɪsˈtanˈtsiːrən] tr (mit) beat (by, e.g., one meter) || ref (von) dissociate oneself (from)

distanziert' adj (fig) detached

Distel [ˈdɪstəl] f (-;-n) thistle

Dis'telfink m goldfinch

Distrikt [dɪsˈtrɪkt] m (-[e]s;-e) district

Disziplin [dɪstsɪˈpliːn] f (-;-en) discipline

disziplinarisch [dɪstsɪpliˈnaːrɪʃ] adj disciplinary

dito [ˈdiːto] adv ditto || Dito n (-s;-s) ditto

Dividend [dɪvɪˈdɛnt] m (-en;-en), Dividende [dɪvɪˈdɛndə] f (-;-n) dividend

dividieren [dɪvɪˈdiːrən] tr divide

Division [dɪvɪˈzjoːn] f (-;-en) division

Diwan [ˈdiːvan] m (-s;-e) divan

D-Mark [ˈdeːmark] f (-;-) mark (monetary unit of West Germany)

doch [dɔx] adv yet; of course

Docht [dɔxt] m (-[e]s;-e) wick

Dock [dɔk] n (-[e]s;-s & -e) dock

docken [ˈdɔkən] tr & intr (naut, rok) dock

Dogge [ˈdɔgə] f (-;-n) mastiff; deutsche D. Great Dane

Dog·ma [ˈdɔgma] n (-s;-men [mən]) dogma

Dohle [ˈdoːlə] f (-;-n) jackdaw

Dok·tor [ˈdɔktoːr] m (-s;-toren [ˈtoːrən]) doctor

Dok'torarbeit f dissertation

Dok'torvater m adviser (for a doctoral dissertation)

Dokument [dokuˈmɛnt] n (-[e]s;-e) document; (jur) instrument, deed

Dokumentarfilm [dokumenˈtarfɪlm] m documentary

dokumentarisch [dokumenˈtarɪʃ] adj documentary

Dolch [dɔlç] m (-[e]s;-e) dagger

Dolch'stoß m (pol) stab in the back

Dollar [ˈdɔlar] m (-s;-) dollar

dolmetschen [ˈdɔlmɛtʃən] tr & intr interpret

Dol'metscher -in §6 mf interpreter

Dom [doːm] m (-[e]s;-e) cathedral; dome

Domäne [doˈmɛːnə] f (-;-n) domain

Domino [ˈdoːmino] n (-s;-s) domino

Donau [ˈdonau] f (-;) Danube

Donner [ˈdɔnər] m (-s;-) thunder

Don'nerkeil m thunderbolt

donnern [ˈdɔnərn] intr thunder

Don'nerschlag m clap of thunder

Don'nerstag m (-[e]s;-e) Thursday

Don'nerwetter n thunderstorm; zum D.! confound it! || interj geez!

doof [doːf] adj (coll) goofy

dopen [ˈdoːpən] tr dope (a racehorse)

Doppel [ˈdɔpəl] n (-s;-) duplicate; (tennis) doubles

Doppel- comb.fm. double, two, bi-, twin

Dop'pelbelichtung f double exposure

Dop'pelbild n (telv) ghost

Dop'pelbruch m compound fracture

Dop'pelehe f bigamy

Dop'pelgänger m double; second self

Dop'pellaut m diphthong

doppeln [ˈdɔpəln] tr double

Dop'pelprogramm n double feature

Dop'pelpunkt m (typ) colon

doppelreihig [ˈdɔpəlraɪˌɪç] adj double-breasted

Dop'pelrendezvous n double date

dop′pelseitig adj reversible; (Lungenentzündung) double
Dop′pelsinn m double entendre
dop′pelsinnig adj ambiguous
Dop′pelspiel n (fig) double-dealing; (sport) double-header; (tennis) doubles
doppelt [′dɔpəlt] adj double; **doppelter Boden** false bottom; **ein doppeltes Spiel spielen** mit doublecross; in **doppelter Ausführung** in duplicate || adv twice; **ein Buch d. haben** have two copies of a book
Dop′pelverdiener –in §6 mf moonlighter
Dop′pelvokal m diphthong
doppelzüngig [′dɔpəltsʏŋıç] adj two-faced
Dorf [dɔrf] n (−[e]s;⁻er) village
Dorf′bewohner –in §6 mf villager
Dörfchen [′dœrfçən] n (−s;−) hamlet
Dorn [dɔrn] m (−[e]s;−en) thorn; tongue (of a buckle); (mach) pin; (sport) spike
Dorn′busch m briar, bramble
dornig [′dɔrnıç] adj thorny
Dornröschen [′dɔrnrøsçən] n (−s;) Sleeping Beauty
Dörr- [dœr] comb.fm. dried
dorren [′dɔrən] intr (SEIN) dry (up)
dörren [′dœrən] tr dry
Dorschlebertran [′dɔrʃlebərtran] m (−[e]s;) cod-liver oil
dort [dɔrt] adv there, over there
dort′her adv from there
dort′hin adv there, to that place
dor′tig adj in that place, there
Dose [′dozə] f (−;−n) can; box
dösen [′døzən] intr doze
Do′senöffner m can opener
dosieren [do′zirən] tr prescribe (the correct dosage of)
Dosie′rung f (−;−en) dosage
Do·sis [′dozıs] f (−;−sen [zən]) dose
dotieren [do′tirən] tr endow; **ein Preis mit 100 Mark dotiert** a prize worth 100 marks
Dotter [′dɔtər] m & n (−s;−) yolk
Double [′dubəl] m & n (−s;−s) (cin, theat) stand-in
Dozent –in [do′tsent(ın)] §7 (university) instructor, lecturer
Drache [′draxə] m (−n;−n) dragon; (böses Weib) battle-ax
Drachen [′draxən] m (−n;−s) kite
Dra′chenfliegen n (−s;) hang gliding
Draht [drat] m (−[e]s;⁻e) wire; **auf D. sein** (coll) be on the beam
drahten [′dratən] tr telegraph, wire
draht′haarig adj wire-haired
Draht′hindernis n (mil) wire entanglement, barbed wire
drahtig [′dratıç] adj wiry
draht′los adj wireless
Draht′seil n cable
Draht′seilbahn f cable car, funicular
Draht′zaun m wire fence
drall [dral] adj plump; (Faden) sturdy || **Drall** m (−[e]s;) rifling
Dra·ma [′drama] n (−s;−men [mən]) drama
Dramatiker –in [dra′matıkər(ın)] §6 mf dramatist, playwright

dramatisch [dra′matıʃ] adj dramatic
dran [dran] adv var of **daran**
drang [draŋ] pret of **dringen** || **Drang** m (−[e]s;⁻e) pressure; urge
drängeln [′drɛŋəln] tr & intr shove
drängen [′drɛŋən] tr & intr push, shove; (drücken) press || ref crowd, crowd together; force one's way
Drangsal [′draŋzal] f (−;−e) distress, anguish; hardship
drangsalieren [draŋza′lirən] tr vex
drastisch [′drastıʃ] adj drastic
drauf [drauf] adv var of **darauf**
Drauf′gänger m (−s;−) go-getter
drauf′gehen §82 intr (SEIN) go down the drain
drauflos′ adv—**d. arbeiten an** (dat) work away at
drauflos′gehen §82 intr (SEIN)—**d. auf** (acc) make straight for
drauflos′reden intr ramble on
drauflos′schlagen §132 intr (auf acc) let fly (at)
draußen [′drausən] adv outside; out of doors; (in der Fremde) abroad
drechseln [′drɛksəln] tr work (on a lathe); (fig) embellish
Dreck [drɛk] m (−[e]s;) dirt; mud; excrement; (Abfälle) trash
dreckig [′drɛkıç] adj dirty; muddy
Dreh- [dre] comb.fm. revolving, rotary
Dreh′arbeiten pl (cin) shooting
Dreh′aufzug m dumb waiter
Dreh′bank f (−;⁻e) lathe
drehbar [′drebar] adj revolving
Dreh′buch n (mov) script, scenario
drehen [′dre·ən] tr turn; (Zigaretten) roll; (coll) wangle; (cin) shoot || ref turn; rotate
Dreh′kreuz n turnstile
Dreh′orgel f hurdy-gurdy
Dreh′orgelspieler m organ grinder
Dreh′punkt m fulcrum; (fig) pivotal point
Dreh′scheibe f potter's wheel; (rr) turntable
Dreh′stuhl m swivel chair
Dre′hung f (−;−en) turn
Dreh′zahl f revolutions per minute
Dreh′zahlmesser m tachometer
drei [drai] adj & pron three || **Drei** f (−;−en) three; (educ) C
dreidimensional [′draidimenzjonal] adj three-dimensional
Dreieck [′drai·ɛk] n (−[e]s;−e) triangle
drei′eckig adj triangular
drei′fach adj threefold, triple
dreifältig [′draifɛltıç] adj threefold, triple
Dreifaltigkeit [′draifaltıçkait] f (−;) Trinity
Drei′fuß m tripod
Dreikäsehoch [′drai′kezəhoç] m (−s;−) (coll) shrimp, runt
drei′mal adv three times, thrice
Drei′rad n tricycle
Drei′sprung m hop, step, and jump
dreißig [′draisıç] adj & pron thirty || **Dreißig** f (−;− & −en) thirty
dreißiger [′draisıgər] invar adj of the thirties, in the thirties
dreißigste [′draisıçstə] §9 adj & pron thirtieth

dreist [draɪst] *adj* brazen, bold
dreistimmig ['draɪ/tɪmɪç] *adj* for three voices
drei'zehn *adj & pron* thirteen || Dreizehn *f* (-;-) thirteen
drei'zehnte §9 *adj & pron* thirteenth
dreschen ['drɛ/ən] §67 *tr* thresh; (coll) thrash
Dresch'flegel *m* flail
Dresch'tenne *f* threshing floor
dressieren [drɛ'siːrən] *tr* train; (*Pferd*) break in
Dressur [drɛ'suːr] *f* (-;-) training
dribbeln ['drɪbəln] *intr* (sport) dribble
drillen ['drɪlən] *tr* drill; train
Drillich ['drɪlɪç] *m* (-s;-e) denim
Dril'lichanzug *m* dungarees; (mil) fatigue uniform, fatigues
Dril'lichhosen *pl* dungarees, jeans
Drilling ['drɪlɪŋ] *m* (-s;-e) triplet
drin [drɪn] *adv* var of darin
dringen ['drɪŋən] §142 *intr* (auf *acc*) press (for), insist (on); (in *acc*) pressure, urge || *intr* (SEIN) (aus) break forth (from); (durch) penetrate, pierce; (durch) force one's way (through); (in *acc*) penetrate (into), get (into); in die Öffentlichkeit d. leak out; in j-n d. press the point with s.o.; d. bis zu get as far as
drin'gend *adj* urgent; (*Gefahr*) imminent; (*Verdacht*) strong
dring'lich *adj* urgent
Dring'lichkeit *f* (-;-en) urgency; priority
Drink [drɪŋk] *m* (-s;-s) alcoholic drink
drinnen ['drɪnən] *adv* inside
dritt [drɪt] *adv*—zu d. the three of
dritte ['drɪtə] §9 *adj & pron* third; in Dritter a disinterested person; (com, jur) a third party
Drittel ['drɪtəl] *n* (-s;-) third (*part*)
drittens ['drɪtəns] *adv* thirdly
dritt'letzt *adj* third from last
droben ['droːbən] *adv* above; up there
Droge ['droːɡə] *f* (-;-n) drug
Droge-rie [droːɡə'riː] *f* (-;-rien ['riːən]) drugstore
Drogist -in [droː'ɡɪst(ɪn)] §7 *mf* druggist
Droh'brief *m* threatening letter
drohen ['droːən] *intr* (*dat*) threaten
dro'hend *adj* threatening; impending
Drohne ['droːnə] *f* (-;-n) drone
dröhnen ['drøːnən] *intr* boom, roar; (*Kopf, Motor*) throb
Dro'hung *f* (-;-en) threat
drollig ['drɔlɪç] *adj* amusing, funny
Dromedar [droːme'daːr] *n* (-s;-e) dromedary
drosch [drɔʃ] *pret* of dreschen
Droschke ['drɔʃkə] *f* (-;-n) cab, hackney; taxi
Drosch'kenkutscher *m* coachman
Drossel ['drɔsəl] *f* (-;-n) thrush; (aut) throttle
Dros'selhebel *m* (aut) throttle
drosseln ['drɔsəln] *tr* (coll) curb, cut; (aut) throttle; (elec) choke
drüben ['dryːbən] *adv* over there
Druck [drʊk] *m* (-[e]s;-̈e) (& fig) pressure; (*der Hand*) squeeze; (phys)

compression, pressure || *m* (-[e]s-e) printing; print, type; (tex) print
Druck'anzug *m* (aer) pressurized suit
Druck'bogen *m* (printed) sheet
druck'dicht *adj* pressurized
Drückeberger ['drykəbɛrɡər] *m* (-s;-) shirker; absentee; (mil) goldbrick
drucken ['drʊkən] *tr* print
drücken ['drykən] *tr* press; squeeze; imprint; (*Preise*) lower; (cards) discard; die Stimmung d. be a kill-joy; j-m die Hand d. shake hands with s.o. || *intr* (*Schuh*) pinch
Druck'entlastung *f* decompression
Drucker ['drʊkər] *m* (-s;-) printer
Drücker ['drykər] *m* (-s;-) push button; (e-s *Schlosses*) latch, latch key; (e-s *Gewehrs*) trigger
Druckerei [drʊkə'raɪ] *f* (-;-en) print shop, press
Druckerschwärze (Druk'kerschwärze) *f* printer's ink
Druck'fehler *m* misprint
druck'fertig *adj* ready for the press
druck'fest *adj* pressurized
Druck'kabine *f* pressurized cabin
Druck'knopf *m* push button; (am *Kleid*) snap
Druck'knopfbetätigung *f* push-button control
Druck'luft *f* compressed air
Druckluft- *comb.fm.* pneumatic, air
Druck'luftbremse *f* air brake
Druck'lufthammer *m* jackhammer
Druck'messer *m* pressure gauge
Druck'sache *f* printed matter; Drucksachen (com) literature
Druck'schrift *f* type; block letters; publication, printed work; leaflet
drucksen ['drʊksən] *intr* hem and haw
drum [drʊm] *adv* var of darum
Drüse ['dryːzə] *f* (-;-n) gland
Drüsen- *comb.fm.* glandular
Dschungel ['dʒʊŋəl] *m* (-s;-) jungle
du [duː] §11 *per pron* you, thou
Dübel ['dyːbəl] *m* (-s;-) dowel
Dublette [du'blɛtə] *f* (-;-n) duplicate; imitation stone
ducken ['dʊkən] *tr* (den *Kopf*) duck; (coll) take down a peg or two || *ref* duck
Duckmäuser ['dʊkmɔɪzər] *m* (-s;-) pussyfoot
dudeln ['duːdəln] *tr* hum || *intr* hum, drone; (mus) play the bagpipe
Dudelsack ['duːdəlzak] *m* bagpipe
Duell [du'ɛl] *n* (-s;-e) duel
duellieren [du-ɛ'liːrən] *recip* duel
Duett [du'ɛt] *n* (-[e]s;-e) duet
Duft [dʊft] *m* (-[e]s;-̈e) fragrance
duften ['dʊftən] *intr* be fragrant
duf'tend *adj* fragrant
duftig ['dʊftɪç] *adj* flimsy, dainty
dulden ['dʊldən] *tr* (*ertragen*) bear; (*leiden*) suffer; (*zulassen*) tolerate || *intr* suffer
duldsam ['dʊldzam] *adj* tolerant
Duld'samkeit *f* (-;) tolerance
dumm [dʊm] *adj* stupid, dumb; foolish
Dumm'heit *f* (-;-en) stupidity; foolishness; (*Streich*) foolish prank
Dumm'kopf *m* dunderhead
dumpf [dʊmpf] *adj* dull, muffled;

(*schwül*) muggy; (*moderig*) musty, moldy; (*Ahnung*) vague

dumpfig ['dumpfɪç] *adj* musty, moldy; muggy

Düne ['dynə] *f* (-;-n) sand dune

Dung [duŋ] *m* (-[e]s;) dung; (*künstlicher*) fertilizer

düngen ['dyŋən] *tr* manure; fertilize

Dünger ['dyŋər] *m* (-s;) var of **Dung**

dunkel ['duŋkəl] *adj* dark; vague; obscure ‖ **Dunkel** *n* (-s;) darkness

Dünkel ['dyŋkəl] *m* (-s;) conceit

dün'kelhaft *adj* conceited

Dun'kelheit *f* (-;) darkness; obscurity

Dun'kelkammer *f* (phot) darkroom

Dun'kelmann *m* (-[e]s;⁻er) shady character

dünn [dyn] *adj* thin

Dunst [dunst] *m* (-es;⁻e) vapor, mist, haze; (*Rauch*) smoke; (*Dampf*) steam; **in D. und Rauch aufgehen** (fig) go up in smoke; **sich in (blauen) D. auflösen** vanish in thin air

dünsten ['dynstən] *tr & intr* stew; steam

dunstig ['dunstɪç] *adj* steamy; (*Wetter*) misty, hazy

Duplikat [duplɪ'kat] *n* (-[e]s;-e) duplicate; copy

Dur [dur] *invar n* (mus) major

durch [durç] *adv* throughout; **d. und d.** through and through ‖ *prep* (*acc*) through, by, by means of

durch'arbeiten *tr* work through ‖ *ref* (**durch**) work one's way (through); elbow one's way (through)

durchaus' *adv* throughout; entirely; quite, absolutely; **d. nicht** by no means

durch'backen §50 *tr* bake through and through

durch'blättern *tr* thumb through

durch'bleuen *tr* beat up

Durch'blick *m* vista

durch'blicken *intr* be apparent; (**durch**) look (through); **d. lassen** intimate

durchblutet [durç'blutət] *adj* supplied with blood

durch'bohren *tr* bore through ‖ **durchboh'ren** *tr* pierce

durch'braten §63 *tr* roast thoroughly

durchbre'chen §64 *tr* break through; (*Vorschriften*) violate; (mil) breach ‖ **durch'brechen** *tr* cut (*a hole*); break in half ‖ *intr* (SEIN) break through

durch'brennen §97 *tr* burn through; (*e-e Sicherung*) blow ‖ *intr* (SEIN) run away; (*Sicherung*) blow

durch'bringen §65 *tr* get through; (*Gesetz*) pass; (*Geld*) spend; (med) pull (*a patient*) through ‖ *ref* support oneself; **sich ehrlich d.** make an honest living

Durch'bruch *m* breakthrough; (*Öffnung*) breach, gap; (*der Zähne*) cutting

durch'denken §66 *tr* think through ‖ **durchden'ken** *tr* think out, think over

durch'drängen *ref* push one's way through

durch'drehen *tr* grind; (*Wäsche*) put

through the wringer ‖ *intr* (SEIN) (coll) go mad

durchdrin'gen §142 *tr* penetrate; pervade, imbue ‖ **durch'dringen** *intr* (SEIN) get through; penetrate

durch'drucken *tr* (parl) push through

durchdrungen [durç'druŋən] *adj* imbued

durchei'len *tr* rush through ‖ **durch'eilen** *intr* (SEIN) (durch) rush through

durcheinan'der *adj & adv* in confusion ‖ **Durcheinander** *n* (-s;-) mess, muddle

durcheinan'derbringen §65 *tr* muddle

durcheinan'dergeraten §63 *intr* (SEIN) get mixed up

durcheinan'derlaufen §105 *intr* (SEIN) mill about

durcheinan'derreden *intr* speak all at once

durcheinan'derwerfen §160 *tr* throw into confusion, turn upside down

durchfah'ren §71 *tr* travel through; (*Gedanke, Schreck*) strike ‖ **durch'fahren** §71 *intr* (SEIN) go through without stopping

Durch'fahrt *f* passage; **keine D.!** no thoroughfare

Durch'fahrtshöhe *f* clearance

Durch'fall *m* diarrhea; (coll) flop; (educ) flunk, failure

durch'fallen §72 *intr* (SEIN) fall through; (educ) flunk; (theat) flop

durch'fechten §74 *tr* fight through

durch'finden §59 *ref* find one's way

durchflech'ten *tr* interweave

durchfor'schen *tr* examine, make an exhaustive study of

Durchfor'schung *f* exploration; search; thorough research

durch'fressen §70 *tr* eat through; corrode ‖ *ref* (bei) sponge (on); (**durch**) work one's way (through)

Durchfuhr ['durçfur] *f* (-;-en) transit

durchführbar ['durçfyrbar] *adj* feasible

durch'führen *tr* lead through or across; (*Auftrag*) carry out; (*Gesetz*) enforce

Durch'gang *m* passage; aisle; (fig) transition; (astr, com) transit; **D. verboten!** no thoroughfare, no trespassing

Durch'gänger *m* (-s;-) runaway

Durch'gangslager *n* transit camp

Durch'gangsverkehr *m* through traffic

Durch'gangszug *m* through train

durch'geben §80 *tr* pass on

durch'gebraten *adj* (culin) well done

durch'gehen §82 *tr* (SEIN) go through; (*durchlesen*) go over ‖ *intr* (SEIN) go through; (*Pferd*) bolt; (*heimlich davonlaufen*) run away; abscond; (*Vorschlag*) pass

durch'gehend(s) *adv* generally; (*durchaus*) throughout

durchgeistigt [durç'gaɪstɪçt] *adj* highly intellectual

durch'greifen §88 *intr* reach through; (fig) take drastic measures

durch'greifend *adj* vigorous; drastic

durch'halten §90 *tr* keep up ‖ *intr* hold out, stick it out

durch'hauen §93 *tr* chop through;

knock a hole through; (coll) thrash, beat

durch'hecheln *tr* (coll) run down

durch'helfen §96 *intr* (*dat*) (**durch**) help (through) || *ref* get by, manage

durch'kämmen *tr* (& fig) comb through

durch'kochen *tr* boil thoroughly

durch'kommen §99 *intr* (SEIN) come through; (*durch Krankheit*) pull through; (*sich durchhelfen*) get by; (*educ*) pass

durchkreu'zen *tr* cross; (*durchstreichen*) cross out; (fig) frustrate

Durch'laß ['dʊrçlas] *m* (–lasses;–lässe) passage; outlet; culvert

durch'lassen §104 *tr* let through, let pass; (*Licht*) transmit; (educ) pass

durchlässig ['dʊrçlɛsɪç] *adj* permeable

Durch'laßschein *m* pass

durchlau'fen §105 *tr* run through; look through; (*Schule*) go through; **seine Bahn d.** run its course || **durch'laufen** §105 *ref*—**sich** [*dat*] **die Schuhe d.** wear out one's shoes || §105 *intr* (SEIN) run through

durchle'ben *tr* live through

durch'lesen §107 *tr* read over, peruse

durchleuch'ten *tr* illuminate; (*Gesicht*) light up; (*Ei*) test; X-ray

durch'liegen §108 *ref* develop bedsores || **Durchliegen** *n* (–s;) bedsores

durchlo'chen *tr* punch

durch'löchern *tr* perforate; pierce; (*mit Kugeln*) riddle

durch'machen *tr* go through, undergo

Durch'marsch *m* marching through; (coll) diarrhea, runs

Durch'messer *m* diameter

durchnäs'sen *tr* soak, drench

durch'nehmen §116 *tr* (*in der Klasse*) do, have

durch'pausen *tr* trace

durch'peitschen *tr* whip soundly; (*Gesetzentwurf*) rush through

durchque'ren *tr* cross, traverse

durch'rechnen *tr* check, go over

Durch'reise *f* passage; **auf seiner D.** on his way through

durch'reisen *intr* (SEIN) travel through

Durch'reisende §5 *mf* transient, transit passenger

durch'reißen §53 *tr* tear in half || *intr* (SEIN) tear, break, snap

Durch'sage *f* special announcement

durch'sagen *tr* announce

durchschau'en *tr* (fig) see through || **durch'schauen** *intr* look through

durch'scheinen §128 *intr* shine through; show through; be seen

durch'scheuern *tr* rub through

durchschie'ßen §76 *tr* shoot through, riddle; (typ) lead || **durch'schießen** §76 *intr* (**durch**) shoot (through) || *intr* (SEIN) dash through

Durch'schlag *m* carbon copy; (*Sieb*) (large) strainer, separator; (elec) breakdown; (tech) punch

durchschla'gen §132 *tr* penetrate || **durch'schlagen** §132 *tr* knock a hole through; (*Holz*) split; (*Fensterscheibe*) smash; (*Nagel*) drive through; (*Kartoffeln, Früchte*) strain; (*mit Kohlepapier*) make a carbon copy of

|| *ref* fight one's way through; (*sich durchhelfen*) manage || *intr* come through; penetrate; take effect; show up || *intr* (SEIN) (*Sicherung*) blow

durch'schlagend *adj* effective; striking

Durch'schlagpapier *n* carbon paper

durch'schleichen §85 *ref* & *intr* (SEIN) creep through

durchschleu'sen *tr* pass (*a ship*) through a lock; (*Passagiere, Rekruten, usw.*) process; (fig) sneak (*s.o.*) through

durch'schneiden §106 *tr* cut through; cut in half || **durchschnei'den** §106 *tr* cut through, cut across || *ref* cross, intersect

Durch'schnitt *m* cutting through; average; cross section; **der große D. der Menschen** the majority of people; **im D.** on an average

durch'schnittlich *adj* average || *adv* on the average

Durchschnitts– *comb.fm.* average; mean

Durch'schnittsmensch *m* average person

durch'schreiben §62 *tr* make a carbon copy of

durch'sehen §138 *tr* look over, examine; (*flüchtig anschauen*) scan; (*Papiere, Post*) check || *intr* see through

durch'seihen *tr* filter; percolate

durchset'zen *tr* intersperse; penetrate || **durch'setzen** *tr* carry through; **d., daß** bring it about that, succeed in (ger) || *ref* get one's way

Durch'sicht *f* examination, inspection; (*auf acc*) view (of)

durch'sichtig *adj* transparent; clear

durch'sickern *intr* (SEIN) seep out; (*Wahrheit, Gerücht*) leak out

durch'sieben *tr* sift

durch'sprechen §64 *tr* talk over

durchste'chen §64 *tr* pierce || **durch'stechen** §64 *tr* (*Nadel*) stick through

durch'stehen §146 *tr* go through

durchstö'bern *tr* rummage through

durch'stoßen §150 *tr* push (*s.th.*) through; (*Tür*) knock down; (*Scheibe*) smash in; (*Ellbogen*) wear through; (mil) penetrate || **durchsto'ßen** §150 *tr* break through || **durch'stoßen** §150 *intr* (SEIN) break through

durchstrei'chen §85 *tr* roam through || **durch'streichen** §85 *tr* cross out

durchstrei'fen *tr* wander through

durchsu'chen *tr* go through, search

durch'treten §152 *tr* (*Sohle*) wear a hole in; (*Gashebel*) floor || *intr* (SEIN) go through, pass through

durchtrieben [dʊrç'triːbən] *adj* sly

durchwa'chen *tr* remain awake through

durchwach'sen *adj* streaky

durch'wählen *tr* & *intr* dial direct

durchwan'dern *tr* travel or walk through || **durch'wandern** *intr* (SEIN) (**durch**) walk (through), hike (through)

durchwe'ben *tr* interweave

durch'weg(s) *adv* throughout

durchwei'chen, durch'weichen *tr* soak

durchwüh'len *tr* burrow through; (*Ge-*

päck, Schränke) rummage through ‖
durch'wühlen _ref_ burrow through;
(fig) work one's way through

durch'wursteln _ref_ muddle through

durchzie'hen §163 _tr_ pass through,
cross; (_Zimmer_) permeate, fill;
streak; (sew) interweave ‖ **durch'-
ziehen** §163 _tr_ pull through ‖ _intr_
(SEIN) pass through; flow through

durchzucken (durchzuk'ken) _tr_ flash
through the mind of

Durch'zug _m_ passage; (_Luftzug_) draft

durch'zwängen _tr_ force through ‖ _ref_
squeeze through

dürfen ['dyrfən] §69 _aux_ be allowed;
be likely; **darf ich?** may I?; **ich darf
nicht** I must not; **man darf wohl erwarten** it is to be expected

durfte ['durftə] _pret_ of **dürfen**

dürftig ['dyrftɪç] _adj_ needy; poor,
wretched, miserable, scanty

dürr [dyr] _adj_ dry; (_Boden_) arid, barren; (_Holz_) dead, dry; (_Mensch_)
skinny ‖ **Dürre** ['dyrə] _f_ (–;) dry-
ness; barrenness; leanness; drought

Durst [durst] _m_ (–[e]s;) (nach) thirst
(for); **D. haben** be thirsty

dursten ['durstən], **dürsten** ['dyr-
stən] _intr_ be thirsty; (**nach**) thirst
(for)

durstig ['durstɪç] _adj_ thirsty

Dusche ['du/ə] _f_ (–;–n) shower

duschen ['du/ən] _intr_ take a shower

Düse ['dyzə] _f_ (–;–n) nozzle, jet

Dusel ['duzəl] _m_ (–s;–) (coll) fluke

Düsen– _comb.fm._ jet

Dü'senantrieb _m_ jet propulsion

Dü'senjäger _m_ jet fighter

düster ['dystər] _adj_ gloomy; sad; dark
‖ **Düster** _n_ (–s;) gloom; darkness

Dutzend ['dutsənt] _n_ (–s;– & –e) dozen

dut'zendmal _adv_ a dozen times

dut'zendweise _adv_ by the dozen

Duzbruder ['dutsbrudər] _m_ buddy

duzen ['dutsən] _tr_ say du to, be on intimate terms with

Dynamik [dy'namɪk] _f_ (–s;) dynamics

dynamisch [dy'namɪ/] _adj_ dynamic

Dynamit [dyna'mit] _n_ (–s;–e) dyna-
mite

Dynamo ['dynamo] _m_ (–s;–s) dynamo

Dyna·stie [dynas'ti] _f_ (–;–stien
['sti·ən] dynasty

D'–Zug _m_ through train, express

E

E, e [e] _invar n_ E, e; (mus) E

Ebbe ['ebə] _f_ (–;–n) ebb tide

eben ['ebən] _adj_ even, level, flat; **zu
ebener Erde** on the ground floor ‖
adv just; a moment ago; exactly
‖ _interj_ exactly!; that's right!

E'benbild _n_ image, exact likeness

ebenbürtig ['ebənbyrtɪç] _adj_ of equal
rank, equal

ebenda ['ebən'da] _adv_ right there;
(_beim Zitieren_) ibidem

ebendersel'be §4,3 _adv_ self-same

ebendes'wegen _adv_ for that very reason

Ebene ['ebənə] _f_ (–;–n) plain; (fig)
level; (geom) plane

e'benerdig _adj_ ground-floor

e'benfalls _adv_ likewise, too

E'benholz _n_ ebony

E'benmaß _n_ right proportions

ebenmäßig _adj_ well-proportioned

e'benso _adv_ just as; likewise

e'bensogut _adv_ just as well

e'bensoviel _adv_ just as much

e'bensowenig _adv_ just as little

Eber ['ebər] _m_ (–s;–) boar

E'beresche _f_ mountain ash

ebnen ['ebnən] _tr_ level, even; smooth

Echo ['eço] _n_ (–s;–s) echo

echoen ['eço·ən] _intr_ echo

echt [eçt] _adj_ genuine, real, true

Eck [ek] _n_ (–[e]s;–e) corner; end

Eck– _comb.fm._ corner; end

Ecke ['ekə] _f_ (–;–n) corner; edge

Ecker ['ekər] _f_ (–;–n) beechnut

eckig ['ekɪç] _adj_ angular; (fig) awkward; **eckige Klammer** bracket

Eck'stein _m_ cornerstone; (cards) dia-
monds

Eck'stoß _m_ (fb) corner kick

Eck'zahn _m_ canine tooth

Eclair [e'kler] _n_ (–s;–s) éclair

edel ['edəl] _adj_ noble; (_Metall_) precious; (_Pferd_) thoroughbred; **edle
Teile** vital organs

e'deldenkend _adj_ noble-minded

e'delgesinnt _adj_ noble-minded

E'del·mann _m_ (–[e]s;–leute) noble

e'delmütig _adj_ noble-minded

E'delstahl _m_ high-grade steel

E'delstein _m_ precious stone, gem

E'delweiß _n_ (–[e]s;–e) edelweiss

Edikt [e'dɪkt] _n_ (–[e]s;–e) edict

Edle ['edlə] §5 _mf_ noble

Efeu ['efɔɪ] _m_ (–s;–e) ivy

Effekt [e'fɛkt] _m_ (–[e]s;–e) effect

Effekten [e'fɛktən] _pl_ property; effects; (fin) securities, stocks

Effek'tenmakler _–in_ §6 _mf_ stock broker

Effekthascherei [efɛktha/ə'raɪ] _f_ (–;)
showiness

effektiv [efɛk'tif] _adj_ effective; (_wirk-
lich_) actual

Effektiv'lohn _m_ take-home pay

Effet [e'fe] _n_ (–s;) spin, English

egal [e'gal] _adj_ equal; all the same

Egge ['egə] _f_ (–;–n) harrow

eggen ['egən] _tr_ harrow

Ego ['ego] _n_ (–s;) ego

Egoismus [ego'ɪsmus] _m_ (–;) egoism

Egoist –in [ego'ɪst(ɪn)] §7 _mf_ egoist

egoistisch [ego'ɪstɪ/] _adj_ egoistic

Egotist –in [ego'tɪst(ɪn)] §7 _mf_ egotist

eh [e] _adv_ (Aust) somehow, anyway

ehe ['e·ə] _conj_ before ‖ **Ehe** _f_ (–;–n)
marriage; matrimony

E'hebrecher _m_ (–s;–) adulterer

E'hebrecherin f (-;-nen) adulteress
e'hebrecherisch adj adulterous
E'hebruch m adultery, infidelity
ehedem ['e·ə'dem] adv formerly
E'hefrau f wife
E'hegatte m spouse
E'hegattin f spouse
E'hegelöbnis n marriage vow
E'hehälfte f (coll) better half
E'heleute pl married couple
e'helich adj marital; (Kind) legitimate
e'helos adj unmarried, single
E'helosigkeit f (-;) celibacy
ehemalig ['e·əmɑlɪç] adj former; ex-; (verstorben) late
ehemals ['e·əmɑls] adv formerly
E'hemann m husband
E'hepaar m married couple
eher ['e·ər] adv sooner; rather
E'hering m wedding band
ehern ['e·ərn] adj brass; (fig) unshakable
E'hescheidung f divorce
E'hescheidungsklage f divorce suit
E'heschließung f marriage
E'hestand m married state, wedlock
ehestens ['e·əstəns] adv at the earliest; as soon as possible
E'hestifter –in §6 mf matchmaker
E'heversprechen n promise of marriage
Ehrabschneider –in ['erapʃnaɪdər(ɪn)] §6 mf slanderer
ehrbar ['erbɑr] adj honorable, respectable
Ehr'barkeit f (-;) respectability
Ehre ['erə] f (-;-n) honor; glory
ehren ['erən] tr honor; Sehr geehrter Herr Dear Sir
eh'renamtlich adj honorary
Eh'rendoktor m honorary doctor
Eh'renerklärung f apology
eh'renhaft adj honorable
ehrenhalber ['erənhalbər] invar adj— Doktor e. Doctor honoris causa
Eh'renmitglied n honorary member
Eh'renrechte pl—bürgerliche E. civil rights
Eh'rensache f point of honor
eh'renvoll adj honorable, respectable
eh'renwert adj honorable
Eh'renwort n word of honor; auf E. entlassen put on parole
ehrerbietig ['ererbiːtɪç] adj respectful, reverent, deferential
Ehrerbietung ['ererbiːtuŋ] f (-;), Ehrfurcht ['erfʊrçt] f (-;) respect, reverence; (vor dat) awe (for)
ehrfürchtig ['erfʏrçtɪç], ehrfurchtsvoll ['erfʊrçtsfɔl] adj respectful
Ehr'gefühl n sense of honor
Ehr'geiz m ambition
ehr'geizig adj ambitious
ehrlich ['erlɪç] adj honest; sincere; fair; j–n e. machen restore s.o.'s good name
Ehr'lichkeit f (-;) honesty; candor
ehr'los adj dishonorable; (Frau) of easy virtue; infamous
Ehr'losigkeit f (-;) dishonesty; infamy
ehrsam ['erzɑm] adj respectable
Ehr'sucht f (-;) ambition
ehr'süchtig adj ambitious

Ehr'verlust m loss of civil rights
ehr'würdig adj venerable; (eccl) reverend
ei [aɪ] interj oh!; ah!; ei,ei! oho!; ei je! oh dear!; ei was! nonsense! || Ei n (-[e]s;-er) egg
Eiche ['aɪçə] f (-;-n) oak
Eichel ['aɪçəl] f (-;-n) acorn; (cards) club
eichen ['aɪçən] adj oak || tr gauge
Ei'chenlaub n oak leaf cluster
Eichhörnchen ['aɪçhœrnçən] n (-s;-), Eichkätzchen ['aɪçketsçən] n (-s;-) squirrel
Eichmaß ['aɪçmɑs] n gauge; standard
Eid [aɪt] m (-[e]s;-e) oath
Eid'bruch m perjury
eid'brüchig adj perjured
Eidechse ['aɪdeksə] f (-;-n) lizard
Eiderdaunen ['aɪdərdaʊnən] pl eider down
eidesstattlich ['aɪdəsʃtatlɪç] adj in lieu of an oath, solemn
eid'lich adj sworn || adv under oath
Ei'dotter m egg yolk
Ei'erkrem f custard
Ei'erkuchen m omelet; pancake
Ei'erlandung f three-point landing
Ei'erlikör m eggnog
Ei'erschale f eggshell
Ei'erstock m ovary
Eifer ['aɪfər] m (-;) zeal, eagerness
Eiferer –in ['aɪfərər(ɪn)] §6 mf zealot
Ei'fersucht f jealousy
ei'fersüchtig adj (auf acc) jealous (of)
eifrig ['aɪfrɪç] adj zealous; ardent
Eigelb n (-[e]s;-e) egg yolk
eigen ['aɪgən] adj own; of (my, your, etc.) own; (dat) peculiar (to), characteristic (of) || invar pron—etw mein e. nennen call s.th. my own
ei'genartig adj peculiar; odd, queer
Eigenbrötler ['aɪgənbrøtlər] m (-s;-) (coll) lone wolf, loner; crank
Ei'gengewicht n dead weight
eigenhändig ['aɪgənhendɪç] adj & adv with or in one's own hand
Ei'genheit f (-;-en) peculiarity
Ei'genliebe f self-love, egotism
Ei'genlob n self-praise
ei'genmächtig adj arbitrary, highhanded
Ei'genname m proper name
Ei'gennutz m self-interest
ei'gennützig adj selfish
eigens ['aɪgəns] adv expressly
Ei'genschaft f (-;-en) quality, property; in seiner E. als in his capacity as
Ei'genschaftswort n (-[e]s;-̈er) adjective
Ei'gensinn m stubbornness
ei'gensinnig adj stubborn
eigentlich ['aɪgəntlɪç] adj actual || adv actually, really
Eigentum ['aɪgəntum] n (-[e]s;-̈er) property, possession; ownership
Eigentümer –in ['aɪgəntymər(ɪn)] §6 mf (legal) owner || m proprietor || f proprietress
eigentümlich ['aɪgəntymlɪç] adj odd; (dat) peculiar (to)
Ei'gentümlichkeit f (-;-en) peculiarity

Ei′gentumsrecht n ownership, title

Ei′genwechsel m promissory note

ei′genwillig adj independent; (Stil) original

eignen [′aɪgnən] ref (für) be suited (to); (als) be suitable (as); (zu) be cut out (for)

Eig′nung f (-;-en) qualification, aptitude

Ei′gnungsprüfung f aptitude test

Eilbrief [′aɪlbrif] m special delivery

Eile [′aɪlə] f (-;) hurry; E. haben or in E. sein be in a hurry

eilen [′aɪlən] ref hurry (up) || intr be urgent || intr (SEIN) hurry; eilt! (Briefaufschrift) urgent! || impers— es eilt mir nicht damit I'm in no hurry about it

eilends [′aɪlənts] adv hurriedly

Eilgut [′aɪlgut] n express freight

eilig [′aɪlɪç] adj quick, hurried; urgent || adv hurriedly; es e. haben be in a hurry

Eilpost [′aɪlpost] f special delivery

Eilzug [′aɪltsuk] m (rr) limited

Eimer [′aɪmər] m (-s;-) bucket, pail

ein [aɪn] §2,1 indef art a, an || §2,1 num adj one || adv in; ein und aus in and out; nicht ein und aus wissen not know which way to turn || einer indef pron & num pron see einer

ein-, Ein- comb.fm. one-, single

einan′der invar recip pron each other; (unter mehreren) one another

ein′arbeiten tr train (for a job); (in acc) work (into) || ref (in acc) become familiar (with), get the hang (of)

einarmig [′aɪnarmɪç] adj one-armed

einäschern [′aɪnɛʃərn] tr reduce to ashes, incinerate; (Leiche) cremate

ein′atmen tr & intr inhale

ein′äugig adj one-eyed

einbahnig [′aɪnbanɪç] adj single-lane; single-line; one-way

Ein′bahnstraße f one-way street

ein′balsamieren tr embalm

Ein′band m (-[e]s;-̈e) binding; cover

ein′bauen tr build in, install

einbegriffen [′aɪnbəgrɪfən] adj included, inclusive

ein′behalten §90 tr retain; (Lohn) withhold

ein′berufen §122 tr call, convene; (mil) call up, draft || **Einberufene** §5 mf draftee

Ein′berufung f (-;-en) (mil) induction

ein′betten tr embed

ein′beziehen §163 tr include

ein′bilden ref—sich [dat] etw e. imagine s.th.

ein′binden §59 tr (bb) bind

ein′blenden tr (cin) fade in

Ein′blick m view; (fig) insight

ein′brechen §64 tr break in || intr (SEIN) collapse; (Nacht) fall; (Kälte) set in; (Dieb) break in

Ein′brecher -in §6 mf burglar

ein′bringen §65 tr break in; earn; yield

Ein′bruch m break-in, burglary; invasion; E. der Nacht nightfall

Ein′bruchsdiebstahl m burglary

ein′bruchssicher adj burglarproof

einbürgern [′aɪnbyrgərn] tr naturalize || ref (fig) take root, become accepted

Ein′bürgerung f (-;) naturalization

Ein′buße f loss, forfeiture

ein′büßen tr lose, forfeit

ein′dämmen tr check, contain

ein′decken tr cover || ref (mit) stock up (on)

Eindecker [′aɪndɛkər] m (-s;-) monoplane

ein′deutig adj unequivocal, clear

eindeutschen [′aɪndɔɪtʃən] tr Germanize

ein′drängen ref squeeze in; interfere

ein′dringen §142 intr (SEIN) penetrate, come in; e. auf (acc) crowd in on; e. in (acc) rush into; penetrate; infiltrate; (mil) invade

ein′dringlich adj urgent

Eindringling [′aɪndrɪŋlɪŋ] m (-s;-e) intruder, interloper; gate-crasher

Ein′druck m imprint; impression

ein′drücken tr press in; crash, flatten; imprint; (Fenster) smash in

Ein′druckskunst f impressionism

ein′drucksvoll adj impressive

ein′engen tr narrow; (fig) limit

einer [′aɪnər] §2,4 indef pron & num pron one || **Einer** m (-s;-) (math) unit

einerlei [′aɪnərlaɪ] invar adj (nur attributiv) one kind of; (nur prädikativ) all the same || **Einerlei** n (-;) monotony

einerseits [′aɪnərzaɪts], **einestells** [′aɪnəstaɪls] adv on the one hand

ein′fach adj single; simple || adv simply

einfädeln [′aɪnfɛdəln] tr thread; (fig) engineer

ein′fahren §71 tr (Auto) break in; (Ernte) bring in; (aer) retract || ref get driving experience; die Sache hat sich gut eingefahren it's off to a good start || intr (SEIN) drive in; (rr) arrive

Ein′fahrt f entrance; gateway

Ein′fall m inroad; (fig) idea; (mil) invasion

ein′fallen §72 intr (SEIN) fall in; cave in, collapse; (in die Rede) interrupt; join in; e. in (acc) invade; j-m e. occur to s.o.; sich [dat] etw e. lassen take s.th. into one's head; think up s.th.; sich [dat] nicht e. lassen not dream of; was fällt dir ein? what's the idea?

ein′fallslos adj unimaginative

ein′fallsreich adj imaginative

Ein′falt f simplicity; simple-mindedness

einfältig [′aɪnfɛltɪç] adj (pej) simple

Ein′faltspinsel m sucker, simpleton

ein′farbig adj one-colored; plain

ein′fassen tr edge, trim; (einschließen) enclose; (Edelstein) set

Ein′fassung f (-;-en) border; mounting

ein′fetten tr grease

ein′finden §59 ref show up

ein′flechten tr plait; (Haar) braid; (fig) insert

ein′fliegen §57 tr (Truppen) fly in;

(*Flugzeug*) flight-test || *intr* (SEIN) fly in

ein′fließen §76 *intr* (SEIN) flow in; e. in (*acc*) flow into; **einige Bemerkungen e. lassen** slip in a few remarks

ein′flößen *tr* infuse, instill

Ein′fluß *m* influx; (fig) influence

ein′flußreich *adj* influential

ein′förmig *adj* monotonous

einfried(ig)en [′aɪnfriːd(ɪg)ən] *tr* enclose, fence in

ein′frieren §77 *tr* (& fin) freeze || *intr* (SEIN) freeze (up) || **Einfrieren** *n* (-s) (fin) freeze

ein′fügen *tr* insert, fit || *ref* fit in; (in *acc*) adapt oneself (to)

ein′fühlen *ref* (in *acc*) relate (to)

Einfuhr [′aɪnfuːr] *f* (-;-en) importation; **Einfuhren** imports

ein′führen *tr* import; introduce; (in *ein Amt*) install

Ein′führung *f* (-;-en) introduction

Ein′fuhrwaren *pl* imports

Ein′fuhrzoll *m* import duty

ein′füllen *tr*—e. in (*acc*) pour into

Ein′gabe *f* petition; application

Ein′gang *m* entrance; entry; beginning; introduction; (*von Waren*) arrival; **Eingänge** (com) incoming goods; incoming mail; (fin) receipts

ein′geben §80 *tr* suggest, prompt; (med) administer, give

eingebildet [′aɪngəbɪldət] *adj* imaginary; self-conceited

eingeboren [′aɪngəboːrən] *adj* native; only-begotten; (*Eigenschaft*) innate || **Eingeborene** §5 *mf* native

Ein′gebung *f* (-;-en) suggestion; (*höhere*) inspiration

eingedenk [′aɪngədɛŋk] *adj* (genit) mindful (of)

ein′gefallen *adj* (*Backen, Augen*) sunken

eingefleischt [′aɪngəflaɪʃt] *adj* inveterate

ein′gefroren *adj* icebound

ein′gehen §82 *tr* (HABEN & SEIN) enter into; (*Verpflichtungen*) incur; (*Wette, Geschäft*) make; (*Chance*) take; (*Versicherung*) take out; **e-n Vergleich e.** come to an agreement || *intr* (SEIN) come in; arrive; (*aufhören*) come to an end; fizzle out; (*Stoff*) shrink; (bot, zool) die off; (com) close down; **e. auf** (*acc*) go into, consider; consent to; **e. lassen** drop, discontinue; **es geht mir nicht ein, daß** I can't accept the fact that

ein′gehend *adj* thorough

eingelegt [′aɪngəleːkt] *adj* inlaid

Eingemachte [′aɪngəmaxtə] §5 *n* (-n;) preserves

eingemeinden [′aɪngəmaɪndən] *tr* (*Vorort*) incorporate

eingenommen [′aɪngənɔmən] *adj* prejudiced; **von sich e.** self-conceited

eingeschnappt [′aɪngəʃnapt] *adj* (coll) peeved

eingeschneit [′aɪngəʃnaɪt] *adj* snowed in

Eingesessene [′aɪngəzɛsənə] §5 *mf* resident

Ein′geständis *n* (-ses;-se) confession

ein′gestehen §146 *tr* confess, admit

Eingeweide [′aɪngəvaɪdə] *pl* viscera; intestines; (*von Vieh*) entrails

Eingeweihte [′aɪngəvaɪtə] §5 *mf* insider

ein′gewöhnen *tr* (in *acc*) accustom (to) || *ref* (in *acc*) become accustomed (to)

eingewurzelt [′aɪngəvurtsəlt] *adj* deep-rooted

ein′gießen §76 *tr* pour in, pour out

eingleisig [′aɪnglaɪzɪç] *adj* single-track

ein′gliedern *tr* integrate; annex

ein′graben §87 *tr* bury; engrave || *ref* burrow; (mil) dig in

ein′greifen §88 *intr* take action; interfere; (in *j-s Rechte*) encroach; (mach) mesh, be in gear || **Eingreifen** *n* (-s;) interference; (mach) meshing

Ein′griff *m* interference; encroachment; (mach) meshing; (surg) operation

ein′hacken *tr*—e. auf (*acc*) peck at; (fig) pick at

ein′haken *tr* (in *acc*) hook (into) || *ref* —sich bei j-m e. link arms with s.o. || *intr* (fig) cut in

Ein′halt *m* (-[e]s;) stop, halt; **E. gebieten** (*dat*) put a stop to

ein′halten §90 *tr* stick to; (*Verabredung*) keep; (*Zahlungen*) keep up; **die Zeit e.** be punctual || *intr* stop

ein′händigen *tr* hand over

ein′hängen §92 *tr* (*Türe*) hang; (in *acc*) hook (into); (telp) hang up || *ref*—sich bei j-m e. link arms with s.o. || *intr* (telp) hang up

ein′heften *tr* sew in; baste on

ein′heimisch *adj* domestic; local; home-grown; **e. in** (*dat*) native to

einheimsen [′aɪnhaɪmzən] *tr* reap

Einheit [′aɪnhaɪt] *f* (-;-en) oneness, unity; (math, mil) unit

ein′heitlich *adj* uniform

Einheits- comb.fm. standard, uniform; unit; united

ein′heizen *intr* start a fire; **j-m tüchtig e.** (fig) burn s.o. up

einhellig [′aɪnhɛlɪç] *adj* unanimous

ein′holen *tr* bring in; (*Flagge*) haul down; (*Segel*) hawl down; (*im Wettlauf*) catch up with; (*Erkundigungen*) lauf catch up with; (*Erkundigungen*) make; (*Rat, Nachricht, Erlaubnis*) get; (*Verlust*) make good; (*abholen und geleiten*) escort; (*Schiff, Tau*) tow in || *intr* shop

Ein′horn *n* (myth) unicorn

ein′hüllen *tr* wrap up; enclose

einig [′aɪnɪç] *adj* united; of one mind; **sich** [*dat*] **e. sein** be in agreement

einige [′aɪnɪgə] §9 *indef adj & indef pron* some

einigen [′aɪnɪgən] *tr* unite || *ref* come to terms, agree

einigermaßen [′aɪnɪgərmaːsən] *adv* to some extent; (*ziemlich*) somewhat

ein′niggehen §82 *intr* (SEIN) concur

Ei′nigkeit *f* (-;) unity; harmony; agreement

Ei'nigung f (-;-en) unification; agreement, understanding

ein'impfen tr—j-m Impfstoff e. inoculate s.o. with vaccine; j-m e., daß (fig) drive it into s.o. that

ein'jagen tr (dat) put (e.g., a scare) into

ein'jährig adj one-year-old; (bot) annual

ein'kassieren tr collect

Ein'kauf m purchase; Einkäufe machen go shopping

ein'kaufen tr purchase; e. gehen go shopping

Ein'käufer –in §6 mf shopper

Ein'kaufspreis m purchase price

Ein'kehr f—E. bei sich halten search one's conscience; E. halten stop off

ein'kehren intr (SEIN) stay overnight; (im Gasthaus) stop off, stay

ein'keilen tr wedge in

ein'kerben tr notch, cut a notch in

einkerkern ['aınkɛrkərn] tr imprison

einkesseln ['aınkɛsəln] tr encircle

ein'klagen tr sue for (a bad debt)

ein'klammern tr bracket, put in parentheses

Ein'klang m unison; accord

Ein'klebebuch n scrap book

ein'kleben tr (in acc) paste (into)

ein'kleiden tr clothe; vest; (mil) issue uniforms to

ein'klemmen tr jam in, squeeze in

ein'klinken tr & intr engage, catch

ein'knicken tr fold

ein'kochen tr thicken (by boiling); can || intr thicken

ein'kommen §99 intr (SEIN)—bei j-m um etw e. apply to s.o. for s.th. || Einkommen n (-s;) income, revenue

Ein'kommensteuer f income tax

Ein'kommensteuererklärung f income-tax return

Ein'kommenstufe f income bracket

ein'kreisen tr encircle

Einkünfte ['aınkʏnftə] pl revenue

ein'kuppeln tr let out the clutch

ein'laden §103 tr load; invite

Ein'ladung f (-;-en) invitation

Ein'lage f (-;-n) (im Brief) enclosure; (im Schuh) insole; arch support; (Zwischenfutter) padding; (Kapital–) investment; (Sparkassen–) deposit; (beim Spiel) bet; (culin) solids (in soup); (dent) temporary filling; (mus) musical extra

ein'lagern tr store, store up

Ein·laß ['aınlas] m (–lasses;) admission; admittance; (tech) intake

ein'lassen §104 tr let it, admit; (tech) (in acc) sink (into) || ref (auf acc, in acc) let oneself get involved (in)

Ein'laßkarte f admission ticket

Ein'lauf m incoming mail; (e–s Schiffes) arrival; j-m e–n E. machen give s.o. an enema

ein'laufen §105 intr (SEIN) come in, arrive; (Stoff) shrink; das Badewasser e. lassen run the bath; j-m das Haus e. keep running to s.o.'s house || ref warm up (by running)

ein'leben ref (in acc) accustom oneself (to)

Ein'legearbeit f inlaid work

ein'legen tr put in; (Fleisch, Gurken) pickle; (Geld) deposit; (in e–n Brief) enclose; (Film, Kassette) insert; (Veto) interpose; (Beschwerde) lodge; (Protest) enter; (Berufung) (jur) file; Busse e. put on extra buses

ein'leiten tr introduce; (Buch) write a preface to; (beginnen, eröffnen) start, open; ein Verfahren e. gegen institute proceedings against s.o.

Ein'leitung f (-;-en) introduction; initiation

ein'lenken intr (fig) give in

ein'leuchten intr be evident; (coll) sink in

ein'liefern tr deliver; (ins Gefängnis) put, commit; ins Krankenhaus e. take to the hospital

ein'lösen tr ransom; redeem; (Scheck) cash

ein'machen tr can, preserve

ein'mal adv once; (künftig) one day; auf e. suddenly; all at the same time; einmal...einmal now...now; nicht e. (unstressed) not even; (stressed) not even once

Ein'maleins' n multiplication table

ein'malig adj unique

Einmann– comb.fm. one-man

Ein'marsch m entry

ein'marschieren intr (SEIN) march in

ein'mauern tr wall in

ein'mengen ref, ein'mischen ref (in acc) meddle (with), interfere (with)

Ein'mischung f (-;-en) interference

einmotorig ['aınmo·torɪç] adj single-engine

einmummen ['aınmumən] ref bundle up

ein'münden intr (in acc) empty (into); (Straßen) run (into)

Ein'mündung f (-;-en) (e–s Flusses) mouth; (e–r Straße) junction

ein'mütig adj unanimous

ein'nähen tr sew in; (Kleid) take in

Ein'nahme f (-;-n) taking; capture; (fin) receipts; Einnahmen income

ein'nehmen §116 tr take; capture; (Essen) eat; (Geld) earn; (Steuern) collect; (Stellung) fill; (sew) take in; e-e Haltung e. assume an attitude; e-e hervorragende Stelle e. rank high; j-n für sich e. captivate s.o.; j-n gegen sich e. prejudice s.o. against oneself; seinen Platz e. take one's seat

ein'nicken intr (SEIN) doze off

ein'nisten ref (in dat) settle (in); (fig) find a home (at)

Ein'öde f desert, wilderness

ein'ordnen tr put in its place; file; classify || ref fit into place; (sich anstellen) get in line; sich rechts (or links) e. get into the right (or left) lane

ein'packen tr pack up

ein'passen tr (in acc) fit (into)

ein'pauken tr—j-m etw e. drum s.th. into s.o.'s head

ein'pferchen tr pen up; (fig) crowd together

ein'pflanzen *tr* plant; implant

ein'pökeln *tr* pickle; salt

ein'prägen *tr* imprint, impress

ein'quartieren *tr* billet, quarter

ein'rahmen *tr* frame

ein'rammen *tr* ram in, drive in

ein'räumen *tr* (*Recht, Kredit*) grant; (*zugeben*) concede, admit; **e. in** (*acc*) put into

ein'rechnen *tr* include, comprise

Ein'rede *f* objection; (*jur*) plea

ein'reden *tr*—**j-m etw e.** talk s.o. into s.th; **das lasse ich mir nicht e.** I can't believe that || *intr*—**auf j-n e.** badger s.o.

ein'reiben §62 *tr* rub

ein'reichen *tr* hand in, file; (*Rechnung*) present; (*Abschied*) tender; (*Gesuch*) submit; (*Beschwerde, Klage*) file

ein'reihen *tr* file; rank; enroll; (*Bücher*) shelve || *ref* fall into place; fall in line

ein'reihig *adj* single-breasted

Ein'reise *f* entry

ein'reißen §53 *tr* tear; demolish || *intr* (SEIN) tear; (fig) spread

ein'renken *tr* (*Knochen*) set; (fig) set right

ein'richten *tr* arrange; establish; (*Wohnung*) furnish; (surg) set || *ref* settle down; economize, make ends meet; (auf *acc*) make arrangements (for); (*nach*) adapt oneself (to)

Ein'richtung *f* (-;-en) setup; establishment; furniture; equipment

Ein'richtungsgegenstand *m* piece of furniture, piece of equipment

ein'rosten *intr* (SEIN) get rusty

ein'rücken *tr* (*Zeile*) indent; (*Anzeige*) put in || *intr* (SEIN) march in; **in j-s Stelle e.** succeed s.o.; **zum Militär e.** enter military service

Ein'rückung *f* (-;-en) indentation

ein'rühren *tr* (in *acc*) stir (into)

eins [aɪns] *pron* one; one o'clock; **es ist mir eins** it's all the same to me || **Eins** *f* (-;-en) one; (*auf Würfeln*) ace; (educ) A

einsam ['aɪnzam] *adj* lonely, lonesome

ein'sammeln *tr* gather; (*Geld*) collect

Ein'satz *m* insert, insertion; (*Wette*) bet; (*Risiko*) risk; (*Verwendung*) use; (*für Flaschen*) deposit; (aer) sortie; (mil) action; (mus) starting in, entry; **im E. stehen** be in action; **im vollen E.** in full operation; **unter E. seines Lebens** at the risk of one's life; **zum E. bringen** employ, use; (*Maschinen*) put into operation; (*Polizei*) call out; (mil) throw into action

ein'satzbereit *adj* combat-ready

Ein'satzstück *n* insert

ein'saugen *tr* suck in; (fig) imbibe

ein'säumen *tr* (sew) hem

ein'schalten *tr* insert; (elec) switch on, turn on || *ref* intervene

ein'schärfen *tr*—**j-m etw e.** impress s.th. on s.o.

ein'schätzen *tr* appraise, value

ein'schenken *tr* pour

ein'schicken *tr* send in

ein'schieben §130 *tr* push in; insert

ein'schießen §76 *tr* (*Gewehr*) test; (*Geld*) contribute; (*Brot in den Ofen*) shove; (fb) score || *ref* (auf *acc*) zero in (on)

ein'schiffen *tr* & *intr* embark

Ein'schiffung *f* (-;-en) embarkation

ein'schlafen §131 *intr* (SEIN) fall asleep; (*Glied*) go to sleep

ein'schläf(e)rig *adj* single (bed)

einschläfern ['aɪnʃlefərn] *tr* lull to sleep; (vet) put to sleep

Ein'schlag *m* striking; impact; explosion; (*Umschlag*) wrapper; (fig) admixture, element; (golf) putt; (sew) tuck; (tex) weft, woof

ein'schlagen §132 *tr* (*Nagel*) drive in; (*zerbrechen*) smash, bash in; (*einwickeln*) wrap; (*Weg*) take; (*Laufbahn*) enter upon; (*Pflanzen*) stick in the ground; (golf) putt; **die Richtung e. nach** go in the direction of || *intr* (*Blitz*) strike; (*Erfolg haben*) be a success; smack at, fail

einschlägig ['aɪnʃlegɪç] *adj* relevant

Ein'schlagpapier *n* wrapping paper

ein'schleichen §85 *ref* (in *acc*) creep (into), slip (into); (in j-s *Gunst*) worm one's way

ein'schleppen *tr* tow in; (*e-e Krankheit*) bring in (from abroad)

ein'schleusen *tr* (*Schmuggelwaren*) sneak in; (*Spionen*) insert

ein'schließen §76 *tr* lock up; (in e-m *Brief*) enclose; (fig) include; (mil) encircle, surround

ein'schließlich *adv* inclusive(ly) || *prep* (*genit*) inclusive of

ein'schlummern *intr* (SEIN) doze off

Ein'schluß *m* encirclement; **mit E.** (*genit*) including

ein'schmeicheln *ref* (bei) ingratiate oneself (with)

ein'schmeichelnd *adj* ingratiating

ein'schmuggeln *tr* smuggle in

ein'schnappen *intr* (SEIN) snap shut; (fig) take offense

ein'schneidend *adj* (fig) incisive

Ein'schnitt *m* cut, incision; (*Kerbe*) notch; (geol) gorge; (pros) caesura

ein'schnüren *tr* tie up; pinch

ein'schränken *tr* (auf *acc*) restrict (to), confine (to); (*Ausgaben*) cut; (*Behauptung*) qualify || *ref* economize

Ein'schränkung *f* (-;-en) restriction; **ohne jede E.** without reservation

ein'schreibebrief *m* registered letter

ein'schreiben §62 *tr* enroll; (*Brief*) register; (*eintragen*) enter; **e-n Brief e. lassen** send a letter by registered mail || *ref* register

ein'schreiten §86 *intr* (SEIN) step in, intervene; (gegen) take action (against)

ein'schrumpfen *intr* (SEIN) shrivel up

ein'schüchtern *tr* intimidate, overawe

Ein'schüchterung *f* (-;) intimidation

ein'schulen *tr* enroll in school

Ein'schuß *m* hit (*of a bullet*)

ein'schütten *tr* pour in

ein'segnen *tr* (*neues Gebäude*) consecrate; (*konfirmieren*) confirm

ein'sehen §138 *tr* inspect; (*Akten*) consult; (fig) realize; (mil) observe ||

Einsehen *n*—ein E. haben show (some) consideration

ein'seifen *tr* soap; (coll) softsoap

ein'seitig *adj* one-sided

ein'senden §140 *tr* send in, submit

Ein'sender –in §6 *mf* sender

ein'senken *tr* (in *acc*) sink (into)

ein'setzen *tr* insert, put in; (*Geld*) bet; (*Leben*) risk; (*Polizei*) call out; (*Truppen*) commit; (*Kräfte*) muster; (*Einfluß*) use; (*Beamten*) install; (*ernennen*) appoint; (*einpflanzen*) plant; (*Artillerie, Tanks, Bomber*) employ; (*Edelsteine*) mount || *ref* (für) stand up (for) || *intr* set in, begin; (mus) come in

Ein'sicht *f* inspection; (fig) insight

ein'sichtig *adj* understanding

ein'sichtsvoll *adj* understanding

ein'sickern *intr* (SEIN) seep in; (mil) infiltrate

Einsiedelei [aɪnzidə'laɪ] *f* (–;–en) hermitage

Einsiedler –in ['aɪnzidlər(ɪn)] §6 *mf* hermit, recluse

einsilbig ['aɪnzɪlbɪç] *adj* monosyllabic; (fig) taciturn

ein'sinken §143 *intr* (SEIN) sink in; (*Erdboden*) subside

ein'sparen *tr* economize on, save

ein'sperren *tr* lock up

ein'springen §142 *intr* (SEIN) jump in; (für) substitute (for); (tech) catch

ein'spritzen *tr* inject

Ein'spritzung *f* (–;–en) injection

Ein'spruch *m* objection; (jur) appeal

einspurig ['aɪnʃpurɪç] *adj* single-track

einst [aɪnst] *adv* once; (*künftig*) someday; e. wie jezt (now) as ever

Ein'stand *m* (tennis) deuce

ein'stecken *tr* insert, put in; stick in, pocket; (*Schwert*) sheathe; (*hinnehmen*) take; (coll) lock up, jail

ein'stehen §146 *intr* (SEIN) für vouch (for), stand up (for); für die Folgen e. take the responsibility

ein'steigen §148 *intr* (SEIN) get in; alle e.! all aboard!

Ein'steigkarte *f* (aer) boarding pass

Ein'steigloch *n* manhole

einstellbar ['aɪnʃtelbar] *adj* adjustable

ein'stellen *tr* put in; (*Arbeiter*) hire; (*Gerät*) set, adjust; (*beenden*) stop, quit; (*Sender*) tune in on; (*Fernglas, Kamera*) focus; die Arbeit e. go on strike; etw bei j–m e. leave s.th. at s.o.'s house; in die Garage e. put into the garage; zum Heeresdienst e. induct || *ref* show up, turn up; sich e. auf (*acc*) attune oneself to

Ein'stellung *f* (–;–en) adjustment; setting; focusing; stoppage; (*der Feindseligkeiten, Zahlungen*) suspension; hiring; (aut) timing; (mil) induction; E. des Feuers cease-fire; geistige E. mental attitude

einstig ['aɪnstɪç] *adj* former; (*verstorben*) late; (*künftig*) future

ein'stimmen *intr* join in; e. in (*acc*) agree to, consent to

einstimmig ['aɪnʃtɪmɪç] *adj* unanimous

ein'studieren *tr* study; rehearse

ein'stufen *tr* classify

ein'stürmen *intr* (SEIN) (auf *acc*) rush (at); (mil) charge

Ein'sturz *m* (–es;) collapse

ein'stürzen *intr* (SEIN) collapse; e. auf (*acc*) (fig) overwhelm

einstweilen ['aɪnstvaɪlən] *adv* for the present; temporarily

einstweilig ['aɪnstvaɪlɪç] *adj* temporary

Ein'tänzer *m* gigolo

ein'tauschen *tr* trade in; e. gegen exchange for

ein'teilen *tr* divide; (*austeilen*) distribute; (*einstufen*) classify; (*Geld, Zeit*) budget; (*Arbeit*) plan

eintönig ['aɪntønɪç] *adj* monotonous

Ein'tönigkeit *f* (–;) monotony

Ein'topf *m*, Ein'topfgericht *n* one-dish meal

Ein'tracht *f* (–;) harmony, unity

einträchtig ['aɪntreçtɪç] *adj* harmonious

Eintrag ['aɪntrak] *m* (–[e]s;–e) entry; E. tun (*dat*) hurt

ein'tragen §132 *tr* enter, register; (*Gewinn*) bring in, yield; j–m etw e. bring down s.th. on s.o. || *ref* register

einträglich ['aɪntreklɪç] *adj* profitable, lucrative

Ein'tragung *f* (–;–en) entry

ein'treffen §151 *intr* (SEIN) arrive; (in Erfüllung gehen) come true

ein'treiben §62 *tr* drive in; (*Geld*) collect || *intr* (SEIN) drift in, sail in

ein'treten §152 *tr* smash in || *ref*—sich [*dat*] in Nagel e. step on a nail || *intr* (SEIN) enter; (*geschehen*) occur; (*Fieber*) develop; (*Fall, Not*) arise; (*Dunkelheit*) fall; e. für stand up for, champion; e. in (*acc*) join, enter

Ein'tritt *m* (–s;) entry; (*Einlaß*) admittance; (*Anfang*) beginning, onset; (rok) re-entry; E. frei free admission; E. verboten no admittance

Ein'trittsgeld *n* admission fee

Ein'trittskarte *f* admission ticket

ein'trocknen *intr* (SEIN) dry up

ein'trüben *ref* become overcast

ein'tunken *tr* (in *acc*) dip (into)

ein'üben *tr* practice; train, coach

ein'verleiben *tr* incorporate

Einvernahme ['aɪnfernamə] *f* (–;–n) interrogation

Ein'vernehmen *n* (–s;) agreement; sich mit j–m ins E. setzen try to come to an understanding with s.o.

einverstanden ['aɪnferʃtandən] *adj* in agreement || *interj* agreed!

Ein'verständnis *n* agreement; approval

ein'wachsen *tr* wax || *intr* (SEIN) (in *acc*) grow (into)

Ein'wand *m* (–s;–e) objection

Ein'wanderer –in §6 *mf* immigrant

ein'wandern *intr* (SEIN) immigrate

Ein'wanderung *f* (–;) immigration

ein'wandfrei *adj* unobjectionable; (tadellos) flawless; (*Alibi, Zustand*) perfect; (*Quelle*) unimpeachable

einwärts ['aɪnverts] *adv* inward(s)

Einweg– *comb.fm.* disposable

ein'weichen *tr* soak

ein'weihen *tr* consecrate, dedicate; e. in (*acc*) initiate into; let in on

Ein'weihung f (-;-en) dedication; initiation

ein'weisen §118 tr install; (Verkehr) direct; **e. in** (acc) assign to; **j–n in seine Pflichten e.** brief s.o. in his duties; **j–n ins Krankenhaus e.** have s.o. admitted to the hospital

ein'wenden §140 tr—**etw e. gegen** raise an objection to; **nichts einzuwenden haben gegen** have no objections to

Ein'wendung f (-;-en) objection

ein'werfen §160 tr throw in; (Fenster) smash; (Brief) mail; (Münze) insert; (fig) interject

ein'wickeln tr wrap (up); (fig) trick

ein'willigen intr (**auf** acc) agree (to)

ein'wirken intr (**auf** acc) have an effect (on), exercise influence (on)

Ein'wirkung f (-;-en) effect, influence

Ein'wohner –in §6 mf inhabitant

Ein'wurf m (Schlitz) slot; (e–r Münze) insertion; (Einwand) objection

ein'wurzeln ref take root

Ein'zahl f (-;) singular

ein'zahlen tr pay in; (**in** e–e Kasse) deposit

Ein'zahlung f (-;-en) payment; deposit

Ein'zahlungsschein m deposit slip

einzäunen [ˈaɪntsɔɪnən] tr fence in

Einzel [ˈaɪntsəl] n (-s;-) singles

Einzel- comb.fm. individual; single; isolated; detailed; retail

Ein'zelbild n (cin) frame; (phot) still

Ein'zelfall m individual case

Ein'zelgänger m (coll) lone wolf

Ein'zelhaft f solitary confinement

Ein'zelhandel m retail trade

Ein'zelheit f (-;-en) item; detail, particular; **wegen näherer Einzelheiten** for further particulars

einzellig [ˈaɪntsɛlɪç] adj single-cell

einzeln [ˈaɪntsəln] adj single; particular, individual; separate

Ein'zelperson f individual

Ein'zelspiel n singles (match)

Ein'zelwesen n individual

Ein'zelzimmer n single room; (im Krankenhaus) private room

ein'ziehen §163 tr draw in; retract; (Flagge) hawl down; (Segel) take in; (Münzen) call in; (eintreiben) collect; (mil) draft ‖ intr (SEIN) move in; **e. in** (acc) enter; penetrate

einzig [ˈaɪntsɪç] adj & adv only; **e. darstellen** be unique ‖ indef pron—**ein einziger** one only; **kein einziger** not a single one

ein'zigartig adj unique; extraordinary

Ein'zug m entry; moving in; (Beginn) start; (typ) indentation; **seinen E. halten** make one's entry

ein'zwängen tr (**in** acc) squeeze (into)

Eis [aɪs] n (-es;-) ice; (Speise-) ice cream ‖ [ˈeˑɪs] n (-;-s) (mus) E sharp

Eis'bahn f ice-skating rink

Eis'bär m polar bear

Eis'bein n (culin) pigs feet

Eis'berg m iceberg

Eis'beutel m (med) ice pack

Eis'blume f window frost

Eis'creme f ice cream

Eis'diele f ice cream parlor

Eisen [ˈaɪzən] n (-s;-) iron; **altes E.** scrap iron; **heißes E.** (fig) hot potato; **zum alten E. werfen** (fig) scrap

Ei'senbahn f railroad; **mit der E.** by train, by rail

Ei'senbahndamm m railroad embankment

Ei'senbahner m (-s;-) railroader

Ei'senbahnknotenpunkt m railroad junction

Ei'senblech n sheet iron

Ei'senerz n iron ore

Ei'senhütte f ironworks

Ei'senwaren pl hardware, ironware

Ei'senwarenhandlung f hardware store

Ei'senzeit f iron age

eisern [ˈaɪzərn] adj iron; (Fleiß) unflagging; (Rationen) emergency

Eis'glätte f icy road conditions

eis'grau adj hoary

eisig [ˈaɪsɪç] adj icy; icy-cold

Eis'kappe f ice cap

Eis'kunstlauf m figure skating

Eis'lauf m ice skating

Eis'laufbahn f ice-skating rink

eis'laufen §105 intr ice-skate

Eis'läufer –in §6 mf skater

Eis'meer n—**Nördliches E.** Arctic Ocean; **Südliches E.** Antarctic Ocean

Eis'pickel m ice axe

Eis'schnellauf m speed skating

Eis'scholle f ice floe

Eis'schrank m icebox

Eis'vogel m kingfisher

Eis'würfel m ice cube

Eis'würfelschale f ice-cube tray

Eis'zapfen m icicle

Eis'zeit f ice age, glacial period

eitel [ˈaɪtəl] adj (nutzlos) vain, empty; (selbstgefällig) vain; ‖ invar adj pure ‖ adv merely

Eitelkeit f (-;) vanity

Eiter [ˈaɪtər] m (-s;) pus

Ei'terbeule f boil, abscess

eitern [ˈaɪtərn] intr fester, suppurate

Eiterung f (-;-en) festering

eitrig [ˈaɪtrɪç] adj pussy

Ei'weiß n (-es;-e) egg white; albumen

Ekel [ˈeːkəl] m (-s;) (**vor** dat) disgust (at) ‖ n (-s;) (coll) pest

ekelerregend [ˈeːkələregənt] adj sickening, nauseating

e'kelhaft adj disgusting

ekeln [ˈeːkəln] impers—**es ekelt mir** or **mich** I am disgusted ‖ ref (**vor** dat) feel disgusted (at)

eklig [ˈeːklɪç] adj disgusting, revolting; nasty, beastly

Ekzem [ɛkˈtseːm] n (-s;-e) eczema

elastisch [eˈlastɪʃ] adj elastic

Elch [ɛlç] m (-[e]s;-e) elk, moose

Elefant [eleˈfant] m (-en;-en) elephant

Elefan'tentreiber m mahout

Elefan'tenzahn m elephant's tusk

elegant [eleˈgant] adj elegant

Eleganz [eleˈgants] f (-;) elegance

Elektriker [eˈlɛktrɪkər] m (-s;-) electrician

elektrisch [eˈlɛktrɪʃ] adj electric(al)

elektrisieren [elɛktrɪˈziːrən] tr electrify

Elektrolyse [elɛktroˈlyːzə] f (-;-) electricity

Elektrizitäts– *comb.fm.* electric, electro–

Elektro– [elɛktrə] *comb.fm.* electrical, electro–

Elektrode [elɛk'trodə] *f* (–;–n) electrode

Elek'trogerät *n* electrical appliance

Elektrizität [elɛktrɪtsɪ'tet] *f* (–;) electricity

Elek·tron [ɛ'lektrɔn] *n* (–s;–tronen ['tronən]) electron

Elektronen– [elɛktronən–] *comb.fm.* electronic

Elektronik [elɛk'tronɪk] *f* (–;) electronics

Elektrotechnik *f* (–;) electrical engineering

Elektrotech'niker *m* (–s;–) electrical engineer

Element [ele'ment] *n* (–[e]s;–e) element; (elec) cell

elementar [elemen'tar] *adj* elementary

Elementar'buch *n* primer

Elen ['elen] *m & n* (–s;–) elk

elend ['elɛnt] *adj* miserable ‖ **Elend** *n* (–[e]s) misery; extreme poverty; **das graue E.** the blues

E'lendsviertel *n* slums

elf [elf] *adj & pron* eleven ‖ **Elf** *f* (–;–e) eleven

Elfe ['elfə] *m* (–n;–n), *f* (–;–n) elf

Elfenbein ['elfənbaɪn] *n* (–s;) ivory

elfte ['elftə] §9 *adj & pron* eleventh

Elftel ['elftəl] *n* (–s;–) eleventh (*part*)

Elite [ɛ'litə] *f* (–;) elite, flower

Ellbogen ['elbogən] *m* (–s;–) elbow

Ell'bogenfreiheit *f* elbowroom

Elsaß ['elzas] *n* (–;) Elsace

elsässisch ['elzesɪʃ] *adj* Alsatian

Elster ['elstər] *f* (–;–n) magpie

elterlich ['eltərlɪç] *adj* parental

Eltern ['eltərn] *pl* parents; **nicht von schlechten E.** (coll) terrific

El'ternbeirat *m* Parent-Teacher Association

El'ternhaus *n* home

el'ternlos *adj* orphaned; **elternlose Zeugung** spontaneous generation

El'ternschaft *f* parenthood

El'ternteil *m* parent

Email [e'maj] *n* (–s;), **Emaille** [e'maljə] *f* (–;) enamel

Email'geschirr *n* enamelware

Email'lack *m* enamel paint

emaillieren [ema(l)'jirən] *tr* enamel

Email'waren *pl* enamelware

emanzipieren [emantsɪ'pirən] *tr* emancipate

Embargo [em'bargo] *n* (–s;–s) embargo

Embo·lie [embo'li] *f* (–;–lien ['li·ən]) embolism

Embry·o ['embry·o] *m* (–s;–onen ['onən]) embryo

Emigrant –in [emɪ'grant(ɪn)] §7 *mf* emigrant

Emission [emɪ'sjon] *f* (–;–en) emission; (fin) issuance; (rad) broadcasting

empfahl [em'pfal] *pret* of **empfehlen**

Empfang [em'pfaŋ] *m* (–[e]s;–e) reception; (*Erhalten*) receipt; (*im Hotel*) reception desk

empfangen [em'pfaŋən] §73 *tr* receive; (*Kind*) conceive

Empfänger –in (em'pfeŋər(ɪn)] §6 *mf* receiver, recipient; addressee

empfänglich [em'pfeŋlɪç] *adj* (**für**) susceptible (to)

Empfängnis [em'pfeŋnɪs] *f* (–;) conception

empfäng'nisverhütend *adj* contraceptive; **empfängnisverhütendes Mittel** contraceptive

Empfäng'nisverhütung *f* contraception

Empfangs'chef *m* desk clerk

Empfangs'dame *f* receptionist; (*im Restaurant*) hostess

Empfangs'schein *m* (com) receipt

empfehlen [em'pfelən] §147 *tr* recommend; **e. Sie mich** (*dat*) remember me to ‖ *ref* say goodbye

empfeh'lenswert *adj* commendable

Empfeh'lung *f* (–;–en) recommendation; (*Gruß*) compliments

empfinden [em'pfɪndən] §59 *tr* feel

empfindlich [em'pfɪntlɪç] *adj* sensitive; delicate, touchy; (*Kälte*) bitter; (gegen) susceptible (to)

Empfind'lichkeit *f* (–;–en) sensitivity, touchiness; susceptibility

empfindsam [em'pfɪntzam] *adj* sensitive, touchy; sentimental

Empfind'samkeit *f* (–;–en) sensibility; sentimentality

Empfin'dung *f* (–;–en) sensation; feeling, sentiment

empfin'dunglos *adj* numb; (fig) callous

Empfin'dungswort *n* (gram) interjection

Emphysem [emfy'zem] *n* (–s;) emphysema

empor [em'por] *adv* up, upwards

empören [em'pørən] *tr* anger, shock ‖ *ref* rebel, revolt; (mil) mutiny

empor'fahren §71 *intr* (SEIN) jump up

empor'kommen §99 *intr* (SEIN) rise up; (*in der Welt*) get ahead

Emporkömmling [em'pørkœmlɪŋ] *m* (–s;–e) upstart, parvenu

empor'ragen *intr* tower, rise

empor'steigen §148 *intr* (SEIN) rise

empor'streben *intr* (SEIN) rise, soar; (fig) aspire

Empö'rung *f* (–;–en) revolt; (über *acc*) indignation (at)

emsig ['emzɪç] *adj* industrious, busy

Em'sigkeit *f* (–;) industry; activity

End– [ent] *comb.fm.* final, ultimate

Ende ['endə] *n* (–s;–n) end; ending; outcome; **letzten Endes** in the final analysis; **zu E. gehen** end; **zu E. sein** be over

enden ['endən] *tr & intr* end; **nicht e. wollend** unending

End'ergebnis *n* final result, upshot

End'gerade *f* (–;) home stretch

end'gültig *adj* final, definitive

endigen ['endɪgən] *tr & intr* end; **e. auf** (*acc*) terminate in

Endivie [en'divjə] *f* (–;–n) endive

End'lauf *m* (sport) final heat

end'lich *adj* final; limited, finite ‖ *adv* finally, at last

end'los *adj* endless

End'runde *f* final round, finals

End'station f final stop, terminus
End'summe f sum total
End'termin m final date; closing date
En'dung f (-;-en) ending
Ener·gie [enɛr'gi] f (-;-gien ['gi·ən])
energy
energisch [e'nɛrgiʃ] adj energetic
eng [ɛŋ] adj narrow; tight; (Freunde)
close; (innig) intimate; **im engeren
Sinne** strictly speaking
engagieren [ãga'zirən] tr engage, hire
|| ref commit oneself
Enge ['ɛŋə] f (-;-n) narrowness; tight-
ness; (Meer-) strait; (fig) tight spot
Engel ['ɛŋəl] m (-s;-) angel
en'gelhaft adj angelic
eng'herzig adj stingy; petty
England ['ɛŋlant] n (-s;) England
Engländer ['ɛŋlɛndər] m (-s;-) Eng-
lishman; **die E.** the English
Engländerin ['ɛŋlɛndərɪn] f (-;-nen)
Englishwoman
englisch ['ɛŋlɪʃ] adj English
Eng'paß m pass, defile; (fig) bottleneck
engros [ã'gro] adv wholesale
engstirnig ['ɛŋʃtɪrnɪç] adj narrow-
minded
Enkel ['ɛŋkəl] m (-s;-) grandson
Enkelin ['ɛŋkəlɪn] f (-;-nen) grand-
daughter
En'kelkind n grandchild
enorm [e'nɔrm] adj enormous
Ensemble [ã'sãbl(ə)] n (-s;-s) (mus)
ensemble; (theat) company, cast
ent- [ent] insep pref
entarten [ent'artən] intr (SEIN) degenerate
entartet [ent'artət] adj degenerate;
(fig) decadent
entäu'ßern ref (genit) divest oneself of
entbehren [ent'berən] tr lack, miss;
do without; spare; dispense with
entbehr'lich adj dispensable; needless,
superfluous
Entbeh'rung f (-;-en) privation, need
entbin'den §59 tr release, absolve;
(Frau) deliver || intr give birth
Entbin'dung f (-;-en) dispensation;
(Niederkünft) delivery, childbirth
Entbin'dungsanstalt f maternity hospital
entblät'tern tr defoliate || ref defoliate;
(coll) strip
entblößen [ent'bløsən] tr bare; un-
cover; (mil) expose || ref strip; re-
move one's hat
entbren'nen §97 intr (SEIN) flare up
entdecken (entdek'ken) tr discover ||
ref—**sich** j-m e. confide in s.o.
Entdeckung (Entdek'kung) f (-;-en)
discovery
Ente ['ɛntə] f (-;-n) duck; (coll) hoax
enteh'ren tr dishonor; (Mädchen) violate, deflower
enteh'rend adj disgraceful
Enteh'rung f (-;-en) disgrace; rape
enteig'nen tr dispossess
enteisen [ent'aizən] tr defrost; deice
enter'ben tr disinherit
Enterich ['ɛntərɪç] m (-s;-e) drake
entern ['ɛntərn] tr (naut) board
entfachen [ent'faxən] tr kindle; (fig)
provoke

entfah'ren §71 intr (SEIN) (dat) slip
out (on)
entfal'len §72 intr (SEIN) (dat) slip
(from); **auf j-n e.** fall to s.o.'s share;
entfällt not applicable
entfal'ten tr unfold; display; (mil) de-
ploy || ref unfold; develop
entfernen [ent'fɛrnən] tr remove || ref
withdraw, move away; deviate
entfernt [ent'fɛrnt] adj distant; **nicht
weit davon e. zu** (inf) far from (ger)
Entfer'nung f (-;-en) removal; range;
distance; absence
Entfer'nungsmesser m (phot) range
finder
entfes'seln tr unleash
entflam'men tr inflame || intr (SEIN)
ignite; flash; (fig) flare up
entflech'ten tr disentangle; (Kartell)
break up; (mil) disengage
entflie'hen §75 intr (SEIN) flee, escape;
(Zeit) fly
entfremden [ent'fremdən] tr alienate
entfrosten [ent'frɔstən] tr defrost
entfüh'ren tr abduct; kidnap; (Flugzeug) hijack; (hum) steal
Entfüh'rer -in §6 mf abductor, kidnaper; (aer) hijacker
Entfüh'rung f (-;-en) abduction; kidnaping; (aer) hijacking
entge'gen prep (dat) contrary to; in the
direction of, towards
entge'gengehen §82 intr (SEIN) (dat)
go to meet; (dat) face, confront
entge'gengesetzt adj contrary, opposite
entge'genhalten §90 tr hold out; point
out, say in answer
entge'genkommen §99 intr (SEIN) (dat)
approach; (dat) come to meet; (dat)
meet halfway || **Entgegenkommen** n
(-s;) courtesy
entge'genkommend adj on-coming;
(fig) accommodating
entge'genlaufen §105 intr (SEIN) (dat)
run towards; (dat) run counter to
entge'gennehmen §116 tr accept, receive
entge'gensehen §138 intr (dat) look forward to; (dat) await; (dat) face
entge'gensetzen tr put up, offer
entge'genstehen §146 intr (dat) oppose
entge'genstellen tr set in opposition ||
ref (dat) oppose, resist
entge'genstrecken tr (dat) stretch out
(toward)
entge'gentreten §152 intr (SEIN) (dat)
walk toward; (fig) (dat) confront
entgegnen [ent'gegnən] tr & intr reply
Entgeg'nung f (-;-en) reply
entge'hen §82 intr (SEIN) (dat) escape,
elude; **sich** [dat] **etw e. lassen** let
s.th. slip by
Entgelt [ent'gelt] n (-[e]s;) compensation, payment
entgel'ten §83 tr pay for
entgeistert [ent'gaistərt] adj aghast
entgleisen [ent'glaizən] intr (SEIN)
jump the track; (fig) make a slip
Entglei'sung f (-;-en) derailment;
(fig) slip
entglei'ten §86 intr (SEIN) (dat) slip
away (from)
entgräten [ent'gretən] tr bone (a fish)

enthaaren [ɛnt'haːrən] *tr* remove the hair from
Enthaa'rungsmittel *n* hair remover
enthal'ten §90 *tr* contain; comprise || *ref* (*genit*) refrain (from); **sich der Stimme e.** (*parl*) abstain
enthaltsam [ɛnt'haltzam] *adj* abstinent
Enthalt'samkeit *f* (-;) abstinence
Enthal'tung *f* (-;-en) abstention
enthär'ten *tr* (*Wasser*) soften
enthaupten [ɛnt'hauptən] *tr* behead
enthäuten [ɛnt'hɔɪtən] *tr* skin
enthe'ben §94 *tr* (*genit*) exempt (from), relieve (of); (*e-s Amtes*) remove (*from office*)
enthei'ligen *tr* desecrate, profane
enthül'len *tr* unveil; reveal, expose
Enthül'lung *f* (-;-en) unveiling; (*fig*) exposé
enthül'sen *tr* shell; (*Mais*) husk
Enthusiasmus [ɛntuzɪ'asmus] *m* (-;) enthusiasm
enthusiastisch [ɛntuzɪ'astɪʃ] *adj* enthusiastic
entjungfern [ɛnt'juŋfərn] *tr* deflower
entkei'men *tr* sterilize; (*Milch*) pasteurize || *intr* (SEIN) sprout
entkernen [ɛnt'kɛrnən] *tr* (*Obst*) pit
entklei'den *tr* undress; (*genit*) strip (of), divest (of) || *ref* undress
Entklei'dungsnummer *f* striptease act
Entklei'dungsrevue *f* striptease show
entkom'men §99 *intr* (SEIN) (*dat*) escape (from) || **Entkommen** *n* (-s;) escape
entkor'ken *tr* uncork, open
entkräften [ɛnt'krɛftən] *tr* weaken; (*Argument*) refute
entla'den §103 *tr* unload; (*Batterie*) discharge || *ref* (*Gewehr*) go off; (*Sturm*) break; (*elec*) discharge; **sein Zorn entlud sich** he vented his anger
Entla'dung *f* (-;-en) unloading; discharge; explosion; **zur E. bringen** detonate
entlang' *adv* along || *prep* (*dat* or *acc* or **an** *dat*; or after *genit* or *dat*) along
entlarven [ɛnt'larfən] *tr* expose
entlas'sen §104 *tr* dismiss, fire; set free; (*mil*) discharge
Entlas'sungspapiere *pl* discharge papers
entla'sten *tr* unburden; (**von**) relieve (of); (*jur*) exonerate
Entla'stungsstraße *f* bypass
Entla'stungszeuge *m* witness for the defense
entlauben [ɛnt'laubən] *tr* defoliate
entlaubt' *adj* leafless
entlau'fen §105 *intr* (SEIN) (*dat*) run away (from); (*mit e-m Liebhaber*) elope
entlausen [ɛnt'lauzən] *tr* delouse
entledigen [ɛnt'leːdɪgən] *tr* (*genit*) release (from) || *ref* (*genit*) get rid (of), rid oneself (of)
entlee'ren *tr* empty; drain
entle'gen *adj* distant, remote
entleh'nen *tr* borrow
entlei'hen §81 *tr* borrow
entlo'ben *ref* break the engagement
entlocken (entlok'ken) *tr* elicit
entloh'nen *tr* pay, pay off
entlüf'ten *tr* ventilate

entmannen [ɛnt'manən] *tr* castrate
entmilitarisieren [ɛntmɪlɪtarɪ'ziːrən] *tr* demilitarize
entmutigen [ɛnt'muːtɪgən] *tr* discourage
entneh'men §116 *tr* (*dat*) take (from); (*Geld*) (**aus**) withdraw (from); (*dat* or **aus**) infer (from), gather (from)
entnerven [ɛnt'nɛrfən] *tr* enervate
entpuppen [ɛnt'pupən] *ref* emerge from the cocoon; **sich e. als** (*fig*) turn out to be
enträtseln [ɛnt'rɛtsəln] *tr* solve; (*Schriftzeichen*) decipher
entrei'ßen §53 *tr* (*dat*) wrest (from)
entrich'ten *tr* pay
entrin'nen §121 *intr* (SEIN) escape (from)
entrol'len *tr* unroll; unfurl || *ref* unroll || *intr* (SEIN) roll down
entrüsten [ɛnt'rystən] *tr* anger || *ref*—**sich e. über** (*acc*) become incensed at; be shocked at
Entrü'stung *f* (-;) anger, indignation
entsa'gen *intr* (*dat*) renounce, forego; **dem Thron e.** abdicate
Entsatz' *m* (-es;) (*mil*) relief
entschä'digen *tr* compensate; reimburse
Entschä'digung *f* (-;) compensation
Entschä'digungsanspruch *m* damage claim
entschär'fen *tr* defuse
Entscheid [ɛnt'ʃaɪt] *m* (-[e]s;-e) (*jur*) decision
entschei'den §112 *tr, ref & intr* decide
entschei'dend *adj* decisive
Entschei'dung *f* (-;-en) decision
Entschei'dungsbefugnis *f* jurisdiction
Entschei'dungskampf *m* (*sport*) finals
Entschei'dungsspiel *n* (*cards*) rubber game; (*sport*) finals
Entschei'dungsstunde *f* moment of truth
entschei'dungsvoll *adj* critical
entschieden [ɛnt'ʃiːdən] *adj* decided; decisive; firm, resolute
entschla'fen §131 *intr* (SEIN) fall asleep; (*sterben*) pass away, die
entschlei'ern *tr* unveil; (*fig*) reveal
entschlie'ßen §76 *ref* (**zu**) decide (on)
Entschlie'ßung *f* (-;-en) (*parl*) resolution
entschlossen [ɛnt'ʃlɔsən] *adj* resolute
entschlüp'fen *intr* (SEIN) slip away (from); (*dat*) slip out (on)
Entschluß' *m* resolve, decision
entschlüs'seln *tr* decipher
Entschluß'kraft *f* will power
entschulden [ɛnt'ʃuldən] *tr* free of debt
entschuldigen [ɛnt'ʃuldɪgən] *tr* excuse; exculpate || *ref* apologize; **es läßt sich e.** it's excusable; **sich e. lassen** beg to be excused; **sich mit Unwissenheit e.** plead ignorance
entschul'digend *adj* apologetic
Entschul'digung *f* (-;-en) excuse; apology; **ich bitte um E. I** beg your pardon
Entschul'digungsgrund *m* excuse
entseelt [ɛnt'zeːlt] *adj* lifeless, dead
entsen'den §140 *tr* send off
entset'zen *tr* horrify; (*mil*) relieve ||

ref (über *acc*) be horrified (at) || **Ent-setzen** *n* (-s;) horror
entsetz'lich *adj* horrible, appalling || *adv* (coll) awfully
Entset'zung *f* (-;) dismissal; (mil) relief
entsi'chern *tr* take (*a gun*) off safety
entsie'geln *tr* unseal
entsin'nen §121 *ref* (*genit*) recall
entspan'nen *tr* & *ref* relax
Entspan'nung *f* (-;) relaxation; (pol) detente
entspre'chen §64 *intr* (*dat*) correspond (to); (*dat*) meet, suit; (*dat*) be equivalent (to); (*dat*) answer (*a description*)
entspre'chend *adj* corresponding; adequate; equivalent || *adv* accordingly || *prep* (*dat*) according to
entsprin'gen §142 *intr* (SEIN) rise, originate; (*entlaufen*) escape
entstaatlichen [ent'ʃtatlɪçən] *tr* free from state control, denationalize
entstam'men *intr* (SEIN) (*dat*) descend (from), originate (from)
entste'hen §146 *intr* (SEIN) originate
Entste'hung *f* (-;) origin
entstel'len *tr* disfigure; deface; (*Tatsachen*) distort
enttäu'schen *tr* disappoint
entthronen [ent'tronən] *tr* dethrone
entvölkern [ent'fœlkərn] *tr* depopulate
entwach'sen §155 *intr* (SEIN) (*dat*) outgrow
entwaff'nen *tr* disarm
entwar'nen *intr* sound the all-clear
entwäs'sern *tr* drain; dehydrate
entweder [ent'vedər] *conj*—**entweder ... oder** either ... or
entwei'chen §85 *intr* (SEIN) escape
entwei'hen *tr* desecrate, profane
entwen'den *tr* steal
entwer'fen §160 *tr* sketch; draft
entwer'ten *tr* (*Geld*) depreciate; (*Briefmarke*) cancel; (*Karten*) punch
entwickeln (entwik'keln) *tr* develop; evolve; (mil) deploy || *ref* develop
Entwick'lung *f* (-;-en) development; evolution; (mil) deployment
Entwick'lungsland *n* developing country
Entwick'lungslehre *f* theory of evolution
entwin'den §59 *tr* (*dat*) wrest (from) || *ref* extricate oneself
entwirren [ent'vɪrən] *tr* & *ref* unravel
entwi'schen *intr* (SEIN) escape; (*dat* or *aus*) slip away (from)
entwöhnen [ent'vønən] *tr* wean; **j-n e.** (*genit*) break s.o. of || *ref* (*genit*) give up
Entwurf' *m* (-s;̈-e) sketch; draft
entwur'zeln *tr* uproot
entzau'bern *tr* disenchant
entzie'hen §163 *tr* (*dat*) withdraw (from), take away (from); (chem) extract; **j-m das Wort e.** (parl) rule s.o. out of order || *ref* (*dat*) shirk, elude
Entzie'hungsanstalt *f* rehabilitation center
entziffern [ent'tsɪfərn] *tr* decipher
entzücken (entzük'ken) *tr* delight

Entzückung (Entzük'kung) *f* (-;-en) delight, rapture
Entzug' *m* (-[e]s;) deprivation
entzündbar [ent'tsyntbar] *adj* inflammable
entzün'den *tr* set on fire; (fig) inflame || *ref* catch fire; (pathol) become inflamed
Entzün'dung *f* (-;) kindling; (pathol) inflammation
entzwei' *adv* in two, apart
entzwei'brechen §64 *tr* & *intr* break in two, snap
entzweien [ent'tsvar-ən] *tr* divide
Enzykli·ka [en'tsyklɪka] *f* (-;-ken [kən]) encyclicle
Enzyklopä·die [entsyklɔpe'di] *f* (-;-dien ['di·ən]) encyclopedia
Enzym [en'tsym] *n* (-[e]s;-e) enzyme
Epaulette [epɔ'leta] *f* (-;-n) epaulet
ephemer [ɛfe'mer] *adj* ephemeral
Epide·mie [epɪde'mi] *f* (-;-mien ['mi·ən] epidemic
epidemisch [epɪ'demɪʃ] *adj* epidemic
Epigramm [epɪ'gram] *n* (-s;-e) epigram
Epik ['epɪk] *f* (-;) epic poetry
Epilog [epɪ'lok] *m* (-s;-e) epilogue
episch ['epɪʃ] *adj* epic
Episode [epɪ'zodə] *f* (-;-n) episode
Epoche [e'pɔxə] *f* (-;-n) epoch
Epos ['epɔs] *n* (-; **Epen** ['epən]) epic
Equipage [ek(v)ɪ'paʒə] *f* (-;-n) carriage; (naut) crew; (sport) team
Equipe [ɛ'k(v)ɪp(ə)] *f* (-;-n) team; group
er [er] §11 *pers pron* he; it
er- [er] *insep pref*
erach'ten *tr* think || **Erachten** *n* (-s;) opinion; **meines Erachtens** in my opinion
erar'beiten *tr* acquire (*by working*)
Erb- [erp] *comb.fm.* hereditary
Erb'anfall *m* inheritance
Erb'anlage *f* (biol) gene
erbarmen [er'barmən] *tr* move to pity || *ref* (*genit*) pity; **erbarme Dich unser** have mercy on us || **Erbarmen** *n* (-s;) pity, mercy
erbar'menswert, erbar'menswürdig *adj* pitiable
erbärmlich [er'bermlɪç] *adj* pitiful; wretched, miserable || *adv* awfully
erbar'mungslos *adj* pitiless
erbau'en *tr* erect; (fig) edify || *ref* (an *dat*) be edified (by)
Erbau'er *m* (-s;-) builder
erbau'lich *adj* edifying
Erbau'ung *f* (-;) building; edification
Erbau'ungsbuch *n* book of devotions
erb'berechtigt *adj* eligible as heir
Erbe ['erbə] *m* (-n;-n) heir; (ohne **Leibliche Erben** without issue || *n* (-s;) inheritance, heritage; **väterliches E.** patrimony
erbe'ben *intr* (SEIN) tremble
erb'eigen *adj* hereditary
erben ['erbən] *tr* inherit
erbet'teln *tr* get (by begging)
erbeuten [er'bɔɪtən] *tr* capture
Erb'feind *m* traditional enemy
Erb'folge *f* succession
erbie'ten §58 *ref* volunteer

Erbin ['ɛrbɪn] f (-;-nen) heiress
erbit'ten §60 ref—sich [dat] etw e. ask for s.th., request s.th.
erbittern [ɛr'bɪtərn] tr embitter
Erb'krankheit f hereditary disease
erblassen [ɛr'blasən] intr (SEIN) turn pale
Erblasser –in ['ɛrplasər(ɪn)] §6 mf testator
erbleichen [ɛr'blaɪçən] §85 & §109 intr (SEIN) turn pale; (poet) die
erb'lich adj hereditary
Erb'lichkeit f (-;) heredity
erblicken (erblik'ken) tr spot, see
erblinden [ɛr'blɪndən] intr (SEIN) go blind
Erblin'dung f (-;) loss of sight
Erb'onkel m (coll) rich uncle
erbre'chen §64 tr break open || ref vomit
erbrin'gen §65 tr produce
Erb'schaft f (-;-en) inheritance
Erbse ['ɛrpsə] f (-;-n) pea
Erb'stück n heirloom
Erb'sünde f original sin
Erb'tante f (coll) rich aunt
Erb'teil m share (in an inheritance)
Erd– [ɛrt] comb.fm. earth, of the earth; geo–; ground
Erd'anschluß m (elec) ground
Erd'arbeiten pl excavation work
Erd'bahn f orbit of the earth
Erd'ball m globe
Erd'beben n (-s;–) earthquake
Erd'bebenmesser m seismograph
Erd'beere f strawberry
Erd'boden m ground, earth; dem E. gleichmachen raze (to the ground)
Erde ['ɛrdə] f (-;-n) earth; ground, soil, land; (elec) ground wire; zu ebener E. on the ground floor
erden ['ɛrdən] tr (elec) ground
erden'ken §66 tr think up
erdenk'lich adj imaginable
Erd'gas n natural gas
Erd'geschoß n ground floor
erdich'ten tr fabricate, think up
Erdich'tung f (-;-en) fabrication
erdig ['ɛrdɪç] adj earthy
Erd'innere §5 n interior of the earth
Erd'klumpen m clod
Erd'kreis m earth, world
Erd'kugel f globe, sphere; world
Erd'kunde f geography
Erd'leitung f (elec) ground wire
Erd'nuß f peanut
Erd'nußbutter f peanut butter
Erd'öl n petroleum, oil; auf E. stoßen strike oil
erdolchen [ɛr'dɔlçən] tr stab
Erd'reich n soil
erdreisten [ɛr'draɪstən] ref have the nerve, have the audacity
Erd'rinde f crust of the earth
erdros'seln tr strangle
erdrücken (erdrük'ken) tr crush to death
erdrückend (erdrük'kend) adj overwhelming
Erd'rutsch m land slide
Erd'schicht f stratum
Erd'spalte f fissure; chasm
Erd'teil m continent

erdul'den tr suffer
ereifern [ɛr'aɪfərn] ref get excited
ereignen [ɛr'aɪgnən] ref happen, occur
Ereignis [ɛr'aɪgnɪs] n (-ses;-se) event, occurrence
ereig'nislos adj uneventful
ereig'nisvoll adj eventful
Erektion [erɛk'tsjon] f (-;-en) erection
Eremit [ere'mit] m (-en;-en) hermit
erer'ben tr inherit
erfah'ren adj experienced || §71 tr find out; (erleben) experience; (Pflege) receive
Erfah'rung f (-;-en) experience
erfas'sen tr grasp; understand; include; register, list
erfin'den §59 tr invent
Erfin'der –in m §6 mf inventor
erfinderisch [ɛr'fɪndərɪʃ] adj inventive
Erfin'dung f (-;-en) invention
Erfin'dungsgabe f inventiveness
erfle'hen tr obtain (by entreaty)
Erfolg [ɛr'fɔlk] m (-[e]s;-e) success; (Wirkung) result
erfol'gen intr (SEIN) ensue; occur
erfolg'los adj unsuccessful || adv in vain
erfolg'reich adj successful
Erfolgs'mensch m go-getter
erfolg'versprechend adj promising
erforderlich [ɛr'fɔrdərlɪç] adj required, necessary
erfor'derlichenfalls adv if need be
erfordern [ɛr'fɔrdərn] tr require
Erfordernis [ɛr'fɔrdərnɪs] n (-ses;-se) requirement; exigency
erfor'schen tr investigate; (Land) explore
Erfor'scher –in §6 mf explorer
Erfor'schung f (-;-en) investigation; exploration
erfra'gen tr ask for; find out
erfreu'en tr delight || ref (an dat) be delighted (at); sich e. (genit) enjoy
erfreulich [ɛr'frɔɪlɪç] adj delightful; (Nachricht) welcome, good
erfreut [ɛr'frɔɪt] adj (über acc) glad (about); e. zu (inf) pleased to (inf)
erfrie'ren §77 intr (SEIN) freeze to death; (Pflanzen) freeze
Erfrie'rung f (-;-en) frostbite
erfrischen [ɛr'frɪʃən] tr refresh
Erfri'schung f (-;-en) refreshment
erfül'len tr fill; fulfill; (Aufgabe) perform; (Bitte) comply with; (Hoffnungen) live up to || ref materialize
Erfül'lung f (-;) fulfillment; accomplishment; in E. gehen come true
erfunden [ɛr'fundən] adj made-up
ergänzen [ɛr'gɛntsən] tr complete; complement; (Statue) restore
ergän'zend adj complementary
ergattern [ɛr'gatərn] tr (coll) dig up
ergau'nern tr—etw von j-m e. cheat s.o. out of s.th.
erge'ben adj devoted || §80 tr yield; amount to; show || ref surrender; (dat) devote oneself (to); (aus) result (from); sich dem Trunk e. take to drinking; sich e. in (acc) resign oneself to
Erge'benheit f (-;) devotion; resignation

ergebenst [er'ge:bənst] *adv* respectfully

Ergebnis [er'ge:pnɪs] *n* (-ses;-se) result, outcome; (*Punktzahl*) score

Erge'bung *f* (-;) submission, resignation; (mil) surrender

erge'hen §82 *intr* (SEIN) come out, be published; e. lassen issue, publish; **etw über sich e. lassen** put up with s.th.; Gnade vor Recht e. lassen show leniency || *ref* take a stroll; **sich e. in** (*acc*) indulge in; **sich e. über** (*acc*) expatiate on || *impers*—es ist ihm gut ergangen things went well for him || **Ergehen** *n* (-s;) state of health

ergiebig [er'gi:bɪç] *adj* productive, fertile; rich, abundant

ergie'ßen §76 *ref* flow; pour out

ergötzen [er'gœtsən] *tr* amuse || *ref* (**an** *dat*) take delight (in)

ergötz'lich *adj* delightful

ergrau'en *intr* (SEIN) turn gray

ergrei'fen §88 *tr* seize; (*Verbrecher*) apprehend; (*Gemüt*) move; (*Beruf, Waffen*) take up; (*Maßnahmen*) take

Ergrei'fung *f* (-;) seizure

ergriffen [er'grɪfən] *adj* moved; **e. von** seized with

Ergriffenheit *f* (-;) emotion

ergrün'den *tr* get to the bottom of

Erguß' *m* discharge; (fig) flood of words

erha'ben *adj* elevated, lofty; **erhabene Arbeit** relief work; **e. sein über** (*acc*) be above

Erhalt' *m* (-es;) receipt

erhal'ten §90 *tr* get, receive; keep, keep up, maintain; conserve; (*Familie*) support; (*Gesundheit*) preserve; Betrag dankend e. (stamped on bills) paid; **gut e.** well preserved; **noch e. sein** survive || *ref* survive; (von) subsist (on)

erhältlich [er'hɛltlɪç] *adj* obtainable

Erhal'tung *f* (-;) preservation; maintenance; support; (*der Energie, usw.*) conservation

erhän'gen *tr* hang

erhär'ten *tr* harden; (fig) substantiate || *intr* (SEIN) harden

erha'schen *tr* catch; **e-n Blick von ihr e.** catch her eye

erhe'ben §94 *tr* raise; (*erhöhen*) elevate; (*preisen*) exalt; (*Steuern*) collect; (*Anklage*) bring; (math) raise || *ref* get up, rise, start; arise

erheblich [er'he:plɪç] *adj* considerable

Erhe'bung *f* (-;-en) elevation; promotion; uprising, revolt; **Erhebungen machen** make inquiries

erheitern [er'haɪtərn] *tr* amuse || *ref* cheer up

erhellen [er'hɛlən] *tr* light up; (fig) shed light on || *ref* grow light(er); light up || *impers*—es erhellt it appears

erhitzen [er'hɪtsən] *tr* heat; (fig) inflame || *ref* grow hot; get angry

erhöhen [er'hø:ən] *tr* raise; (fig) heighten || *ref* increase; be enhanced

Erhö'hung *f* (-;-en) rise

erho'len *ref* recover; relax

Erho'lung *f* (-;-en) recovery; relaxation; recreation

erho'lungsbedürftig *adj* in need of rest

Erho'lungsheim *n* convalescent home

erhö'ren *tr* (*Gebet*) hear; (*Bitte*) grant

erinnerlich [er'ɪnərlɪç] *adj*—das ist **mir nicht e.** it slipped my mind; **soviel mir e. ist** as far as I can remember

erinnern [er'ɪnərn] *tr* (**an** *acc*) remind (of) || *ref* (**an** *acc*) remember

Erin'nerung *f* (-;-en) recollection, remembrance; (*Mahnung*) reminder; **zur E. an** (*acc*) in memory of

Erin'nerungsvermögen *n* memory

erkalten [er'kaltən] *intr* (SEIN) cool off; (fig) grow cool

erkälten [er'kɛltən] *ref* catch cold

Erkäl'tung *f* (-;-en) cold

erkennbar [er'kɛnbar] *adj* recognizable

erkennen [er'kɛnən] §97 *tr* make out; recognize; detect; realize; **j—n e. für** (com) credit s.o. with; **sich zu e. geben** disclose one's identity; **zu e. geben, daß** indicate that || *intr*—**auf e-e Geldstrafe e.** impose a fine; **gegen j—n e.** judge against s.o.

erkenntlich [er'kɛntlɪç] *adj* grateful

Erkennt'lichkeit *f* (-;) gratitude

Erkenntnis [er'kɛntnɪs] *f* (-;-se) insight, judgment, realization, knowledge; (philos) cognition || *n* (-ses; -se) decision, finding

Erker ['ɛrkər] *m* (-s;-) (archit) oriel

Er'kerfenster *n* bay window

erklären [er'kle:rən] *tr* explain, account for; (*aussprechen*) state

Erklä'rer *-in* §6 *mf* commentator

erklär'lich *adj* explicable

Erklä'rung *f* (-;-en) explanation; statement; commentary; (jur) deposition

erklin'gen §142 *intr* (SEIN) sound; (*widerhallen*) resound

erkor (er'kor) *pret of* erkiesen

erkoren [er'korən] *adj* chosen

erkranken [er'kraŋkən] *intr* (SEIN) get sick; (*Pflanzen*) become diseased

erkühnen [er'ky:nən] *ref* dare, venture

erkunden [er'kundən] *tr & intr* reconnoiter

erkundigen [er'kundɪgən] *ref* inquire

Erkun'digung *f* (-;-en) inquiry

Erkun'dung *f* (-;) reconnaissance

erlahmen [er'la:mən] *intr* (SEIN) tire; (*Kraft*) give out

erlangen [er'laŋən] *tr* reach; (*sich verschaffen*) get; **wieder e.** recover

Er-laß' [er'las] *m* (-lasses;-lässe) remission; exemption; edict, order

erlas'sen §104 *tr* release; (*Schulden*) cancel; (*Strafe*) remit; (*Sünden*) pardon; (*Verordnung*) issue; **e. Sie es mir zu** (*inf*) allow me not to (*inf*), don't ask me to (*inf*)

erläßlich [er'lɛslɪç] *adj* pardonable

erlauben [er'laubən] *tr* allow || *ref*—**sich** [*dat*] **e. zu** (*inf*) take the liberty to (*inf*); **sich** [*dat*] **nicht e.** not be able to afford

Erlaubnis [er'laupnɪs] *f* (-;-se) permission

Erlaub'nisschein *m* permit, license

erlaucht [er'lauxt] *adj* illustrious

erläutern [er'lɔɪtərn] *tr* explain

Erläu'terung *f* (-;-en) explanation

Erle ['ɛrlə] f (-;-n) (bot) alder

erle'ben tr live to see; experience

Erlebnis [ɛr'lepnɪs] n (-ses;-se) experience, adventure; occurrence

erledigen [ɛr'ledɪgən] tr settle; (Post, Einkäufe, Gesuch) attend to, take care of; j—n e. (coll) do s.o. in

erledigt [ɛr'ledɪçt] adj (& fig) finished; (Stellung) open; (coll) bushed

erle'gen tr pay down; (töten) kill

erleichtern [ɛr'laɪçtərn] tr lighten; make easy; (Not) relieve, ease

Erleich'terung f (-;) alleviation

erler'nen tr learn

erle'sen adj choice || §107 tr choose

erleuch'ten tr light up; enlighten

erlie'gen §108 intr (SEIN) (dat) succumb (to), fall victim (to)

erlogen [ɛr'logən] adj false

Erlös [ɛr'løs] m (-es;) proceeds

erlosch [ɛr'lɔʃ] pret of **erlöschen**

erloschen [ɛr'lɔʃən] pp of **erlöschen**

erlöschen [ɛr'lœʃən] §110 intr (SEIN) go out; (Vertrag) expire; (fig) become extinct

erlö'sen tr redeem; free; get (by sale)

Erlö'ser m (-s;-) deliverer; (relig) Redeemer

Erlö'sung f (-;) redemption

ermächtigen [ɛr'mɛçtɪgən] tr authorize

Ermäch'tigung f (-;-en) authorization

ermah'nen tr admonish

Ermah'nung f (-;-en) admonition

ermangeln [ɛr'maŋəln] intr (genit) lack; es an nichts e. lassen spare no pains; nicht e. zu (inf) not fail to (inf)

Erman'gelung f—in E. (genit) in default of

ermä'ßigen tr reduce

ermatten [ɛr'matən] tr tire || intr (SEIN) tire; grow weak; slacken

Ermat'tung f (-;) fatigue

ermes'sen §70 tr judge, estimate; realize; e. aus infer from || **Ermessen** n (-s;) judgment, opinion; nach freiem E. at one's discretion

ermitteln [ɛr'mɪtəln] tr ascertain || intr conduct an investigation

Ermitt'lung f (-;-en) ascertainment; **Ermittlungen** investigation

Ermitt'lungsausschuß m fact-finding committee

Ermitt'lungsbeamte m investigator

Ermitt'lungsverfahren n judicial inquiry

ermöglichen [ɛr'møklɪçən] tr enable, make possible

ermorden [ɛr'mɔrdən] tr murder

ermüden [ɛr'mydən] tr tire || intr (SEIN) tire, get tired

Ermü'dung f (-;) fatigue

ermuntern [ɛr'muntərn] tr cheer up; encourage || ref cheer up

Ermun'terung f (-;) encouragement

ermutigen [ɛr'mutɪgən] tr encourage

ernäh'ren tr nourish; (fig) support

Ernäh'rer -in §6 mf supporter

Ernäh'rung f (-;) nourishment; support; (physiol) nutrition

ernen'nen §97 tr nominate, appoint

erneuern [ɛr'nɔɪ.ərn] tr renew; reno-

vate; (Gemälde) restore; (Öl) change; (Reifen) retread; (mach) replace

erneu'ert adj repeated || adv anew

Erneu'erung f (-;-en) renewal; renovation; restoration; replacement

erniedrigen [ɛr'nidrɪgən] tr lower; (demütigen) humble; (im Rang) degrade || ref humble oneself; debase oneself

ernst [ɛrnst] adj earnest; serious || **Ernst** m (-[e]s;) seriousness; im E. in earnest

Ernst'fall m—im E. in case of emergency; (mil) in case of war

ernst'haft adj earnest, serious

ernst'lich adj earnest; serious

Ernte ['ɛrntə] f (-;-n) harvest; crop

ernten ['ɛrntən] tr reap, harvest

ernüch'tern tr sober; disillusion || ref sober up; be disillusioned

Ero'berer -in §6 mf conqueror

erobern [ɛr'obərn] tr conquer

Ero'berung f (-;-en) conquest

eröff'nen tr open; (feierlich) inaugurate; disclose || ref open; present itself; sich j—m e. unburden oneself to s.o.

Eröff'nung f (-;-en) (grand) opening; inauguration; announcement

erörtern [ɛr'œrtərn] tr discuss

erotisch [ɛ'rotɪʃ] adj erotic

Erpel ['ɛrpəl] m (-s;-) drake

erpicht [ɛr'pɪçt] adj—e. auf (acc) keen on, dead set on, hell bent on

erpres'sen tr extort; (Person) blackmail

Erpres'sung f (-;-en) extortion; blackmail

erpro'ben tr test, try out

erquicken [ɛr'kvɪkən] tr refresh

erquick'lich adj refreshing; agreeable

erra'ten §63 tr guess

errech'nen tr calculate

erregbar [ɛr'rekbar] adj excitable; irritable

erregen [ɛr'regən] tr excite; cause || ref get excited, get worked up

Erre'gung f (-;) excitation; agitation; excitement; E. öffentlichen Ärgernisses disorderly conduct

erreichbar [ɛr'raɪçbar] adj reachable; available

errei'chen tr reach, attain; get to; (Zug, Bus) catch; e., daß bring it about that

erret'ten tr save, rescue

Erret'tung f (-;-en) rescue; (relig) Salvation

errich'ten tr erect; found

errin'gen §142 tr get; attain, achieve

errö'ten intr (SEIN) redden; blush

Errungenschaft [ɛr'ruŋənʃaft] f (-;-en) achievement; acquisition

Ersatz' m (-es;) substitute; replacement; compensation; (mil) recruitment

Ersatz- comb.fm. substitute, replacement; spare; alternative; recruiting

Ersatz'mann m substitute; alternate

Ersatz'stück n, **Ersatz'teil** n spare part, spare

erschaf'fen §126 tr create

Erschaf'fer -in §6 mf creator

Erschaf'fung f (-;-en) creation

erschal'len §127 *intr* (SEIN) begin to sound; ring out; resound

erschau'ern *intr* shudder

erschei'nen §128 *intr* (SEIN) appear; (*Buch*) come out, be published

Erschei'nung *f* (-;-en) appearance; apparition; phenomenon

erschie'ßen §76 *tr* shoot (dead)

Erschie'ßung *f* (-;-en) shooting, execution

Erschie'ßungskommando *n* firing squad

erschlaffen [er'ʃlafən] *tr* relax; enervate ‖ *intr* (SEIN) relax; weaken

erschla'gen §132 *tr* slay; **wie e. sein** dead tired

erschlie'ßen §76 *tr* open up; develop; **e. aus** infer from; derive from ‖ *ref* **—sich j-m e.** unburden oneself to s.o.

erschöp'fen *tr* exhaust; (*fig*) deplete

erschrak [er'ʃrak] *pret* of **erschrecken**

erschrecken (erschre'cken) *tr* startle; shock ‖ *ref* get scared ‖ §134 *intr* (SEIN) be startled

erschreckend (erschre'ckend) *adj* terrifying; alarming; dreadful

erschüt'ten *tr* shake; upset; move deeply

Erschüt'terung *f* (-;-en) tremor; vibration; deep feeling; concussion

erschweren [er'ʃverən] *tr* make more difficult; hamper, impede

erschwin'deln *tr—etw von j-m e.** cheat s.o. out of s.th.

erschwin'gen §142 *tr* afford

erschwing'lich *adj* within one's means

erse'hen §138 *tr* (aus) gather (from)

erseh'nen *tr* long for

ersetzbar [er'zetsbar] *adj* replaceable

erset'zen *tr* replace; (*Schaden*) compensate for; (*Kräfte*) renew; **j-m etw e.** reimburse s.o. for s.th.; **sie ersetzte ihm die Eltern** she was mother and father to him

ersetz'lich *adj* replaceable

ersicht'lich *adj* evident

ersin'nen §121 *tr* think up

erspa'ren *tr* save

Ersparnis [er'ʃparnɪs] *f* (-;-se) (an *dat*) saving (in)

ersprießlich [er'ʃprislɪç] *adj* useful

erst [erst] *adv* first; at first; just; only; not until; **e. recht** really; **e. recht nicht** most certainly not

erstar'ren *intr* (SEIN) grow stiff; (*Finger*) grow numb; (*Blut*) congeal; (*Zement*) set; (*fig*) run cold; **vor Schreck e.** be paralyzed with fear

erstatten [er'ʃtatən] *tr* refund, repay; (*Bericht*) file; **Meldung e.** report

Erstat'tung *f* (-;-en) refund; reimbursement; compensation

Erst'aufführung *f* primiere

erstau'nen *tr* astonish ‖ *intr* (SEIN) (über *acc*) be astonished (at) ‖ **Erstaunen** *n* (-s;) astonishment; **in E. setzen** astonish

erstaun'lich *adj* astonishing

Erst'ausfertigung *f* original

erste ['erstə] §9 *adj* first; **der erste beste** the first that comes along; **fürs e.** for the time being; **zum ersten, zum zweiten, zum dritten** going, going, gone

erste'chen §64 *tr* stab

erste'hen §146 *tr* buy, get ‖ *intr* (SEIN) rise; (*Städte*) spring up

erstei'gen §148 *tr* climb

erstel'len *tr* provide, supply; erect

erstens ['erstəns] *adv* first; in the first place

erst'geboren *adj* first-born

ersticken [er'ʃtɪkən] *tr* choke, stifle, smother; **im Keim e.** nip in the bud ‖ *intr* (SEIN) choke; **in Arbeit e.** be snowed under

erstklassig ['erstklasɪç] *adj* first-class

Erstling ['erstlɪŋ] *m* (-s;-e) first-born child; (*fig*) first fruits

Erstlings— comb.fm. first

Erst'lingsausstattung *f* layette

erstmalig ['erstmalɪç] *adj* first

erstre'ben *tr* strive for

erstrecken (erstre'cken) *ref* extend

ersu'chen *tr* request, ask

ertappen [er'tapən] *tr* surprise, catch

ertei'len *tr* give; confer; (*Auftrag*) place; (*Audienz, Patent*) grant

ertö'nen *intr* (SEIN) sound; resound

ertö'ten *tr* (fig) stifle

Ertrag [er'trak] *m* (-[e]s;-̈e) yield; proceeds; produce

ertra'gen §132 *tr* stand, bear

erträglich [er'treklɪç] *adj* bearable

ertränken [er'treŋkən] *tr* drown

erträu'men *tr* dream of

ertrin'ken §143 *intr* (SEIN) drown

ertüchtigen [er'tʏçtɪgən] *tr* train

erübrigen [er'ybrɪgən] *tr* save; (*Zeit*) spare ‖ *ref* be superfluous

erwa'chen *intr* (SEIN) wake up

erwach'sen *adj* adult ‖ §155 *intr* (SEIN) grow, grow up; arise ‖ **Erwachsene** §5 *mf* adult, grown-up

erwä'gen §156 *tr* weigh, consider

Erwä'gung *f* (-;-en) consideration

erwäh'len *tr* choose

erwäh'nen *tr* mention

erwäh'nenswert *adj* worth mentioning

Erwäh'nung *f* (-;) mention

erwär'men *tr* warm, warm up

erwar'ten *tr* expect, await; **etw zu e. haben** be in for s.th.

Erwar'tung *f* (-;-en) expectation

erwar'tungsvoll *adj* expectant

erwecken (erwek'ken) *tr* wake; (*Hoffnungen*) raise; (*Gefühle*) awaken; **den Anschein e.** give the impression

erweh'ren *ref* (genit) ward off; (*genit*) refrain from; (*der Tränen*) hold back

erwei'chen *tr* soften; (fig) move, touch; **sich e. lassen** relent

erwei'sen §118 *tr* prove; show; (*Achtung*) show; (*Dienst*) render; (*Ehre, Gunst*) do ‖ *ref—sich e. als* prove

erweitern [er'vaitərn] *tr & ref* widen; (*vermehren*) increase; extend, expand

Erwerb [er'verp] *m* (-[e]s;-̈e) acquisition; (*Verdienst*) earnings; (*Unterhalt*) living

erwer'ben §149 *tr* acquire; gain; (*verdienen*) earn; (*kaufen*) purchase

erwerbs'behindert *adj* disabled

Erwerbs'betrieb *m* business enterprise

erwerbs'fähig *adj* capable of earning a living

erwerbs'los *adj* unemployed

Erwerbs'quelle f source of income
Erwerbs'sinn m acquisitiveness
erwerbs'tätig adj gainfully employed
erwerbs'unfähig adj unable to earn a living
Erwerbs'zweig m line of business
Erwer'bung f (-;-en) acquisition
erwidern [er'vidərn] tr reply; reciprocate, return
Erwi'derung f (-;-en) reply; return; retaliation
erwir'ken tr secure, obtain
erwi'schen tr catch; ihn hat's erwischt! (coll) he's had it!
erwünscht [er'vyn∫t] adj desired; welcome; (wünschenswert) desirable
erwür'gen tr strangle
Erz [erts] n (-es;-e) ore; brass; bronze
Erz-, erz– comb.fm. ore; bronze; utterly; (fig) arch-
erzählen [er'tselən] tr tell, narrate
Erzäh'lung f (-;-en) story, narrative
Erz'bischof m archbishop
Erz'engel m archangel
erzeu'gen tr beget; manufacture; produce; generate
Erzeugnis [er'tsɔɪknɪs] n (-ses;-se) product; produce
Erzeu'gung f (-;-en) production; manufacture
erzie'hen §163 tr bring up, rear; (geistig) educate
Erzieher [er'tsiər] m (-s;-) educator; private tutor
Erzieherin [er'tsi-ərɪn] f (-;-nen) educator; governess
erzieherisch [er'tsi-ərɪ∫] adj educational, pedagogical
Erzie'hung f (-;) upbringing; education; (Lebensart) breeding
Erzie'hungslehre f (educ) education
Erzie'hungswesen n educational system
erzie'len tr achieve, reach; (Gewinn) realize; (sport) score
Erz'lager n ore deposit
Erz'probe f assay
erzür'nen tr anger || ref get angry
erzwin'gen §142 tr force; wring, obtain by force; (Gehorsam) exact
es [es] adv (as expletive) there; es gibt there is, there are || §11 pers pron it; he; she || Es n (-;-) (mus) E flat; (psychol) id
Esche ['e∫ə] f (-;-n) ash tree
Esel ['ezəl] m (-s;-) donkey, ass
Eselei [eze'laɪ] f (-;-en) foolish act, foolish remark
E'selsbrücke f (educ) pony
E'selsohr n dog's-ear
eskalieren [eska'lirən] tr & intr escalate
Eskimo ['eskimo] m (-s;-s) Eskimo
Espe ['espə] f (-;-n) (bot) aspen
eßbar ['esbar] adj edible, eatable
Eßbesteck ['esbə'∫tek] n knife, fork, and spoon
Esse ['esə] f (-;-n) chimney; forge
essen ['esən] §70 tr & intr eat; zu Mittag e. eat lunch || Essen n (-s;) eating; food, meal
Essenz [e'sents] f (-;-en) essence
Eßgeschirr ['esgə'∫ɪr] n (-s;) tableware; table service; (mil) mess kit

Eßgier ['esgir] f (-;) gluttony
Essig ['esɪç] m (-s;-e) vinegar
Es'siggurke f pickle, gherkin
Es'sigsäure f acetic acid
Eßlöffel ['eslœfəl] m (-s;-) tablespoon
Eßnapf ['esnapf] m dinner pail
Eßsaal ['eszal] m dining room
Eßstäbchen ['es∫tepçən] n chopstick
Eßwaren ['esvarən] pl food, victuals
Eßzimmer ['estsɪmər] n (-s;-) dining room
Estland ['estlant] n (-s;) Estonia
Estrade [es'tradə] f (-;-n) dais
etablieren [eta'blirən] tr establish
Etablissement [etablɪs(ə)'mã] n (-s; -s) establishment
Etage [e'taʒə] f (-;-n) floor, story
Eta'genbett n bunk bed
Eta'genwohnung f apartment
Etappe [e'tapə] f (-;-n) (Teilstrecke) leg, stage; (mil) rear eschelon, rear
Etat [e'ta] m (-s;-s) budget
Etats'jahr n fiscal year
etepetete [etəpe'tetə] adj overly particular
Ethik ['etɪk] f (-;) ethics
ethisch ['etɪ∫] adj ethical
ethnisch ['etnɪ∫] adj ethnic
Ethnologie [etnolo'gi] f (-;) ethnology
Etikett [etɪ'ket] n (-s;-e) tab, label
Etikette [etɪ'ketə] f (-;) etiquette
etikettieren [etɪke'tirən] tr label
etliche ['etlɪçə] adj & pron a few
Etui [e'tvi] n (-s;-s) case (for spectacles, cigarettes, etc.)
etwa ['etva] adv about, around; perhaps; by chance; for example
etwaig [et'va-ɪç] adj eventual
etwas ['etvas] adj some, a little || adv somewhat || pron something; anything || Etwas n—ein gewißes E. a certain something
euch [ɔɪç] pers pron you; to you || reflex pron yourselves
euer ['ɔɪ-ər] adj your
Eukalyptus [ɔɪka'lyptus] m (-;- & -ten [tən]) eucalyptus
Eule ['ɔɪlə] f (-;-n) owl
Euphorie [ɔɪfo'ri] f (-;) euphoria
euphorisch [ɔɪ'forɪ∫] adj euphoric
eurige ['ɔɪrɪgə] §2,5 pron yours
Europa [ɔɪ'ropa] n (-s;) Europe
Europäer –in [ɔɪro'pe-ər(ɪn)] §6 mf European
europäisch [ɔɪro'pe-ɪ∫] adj European
Euter ['ɔɪtər] n (-s;-) udder
evakuieren [evaku'irən] tr evacuate
evangelisch [evan'gelɪ∫] adj evangelical; Protestant
Evangelist [evangə'lɪst] m (-en;-en) Evangelist
Evange-lium [evan'geljum] n (-s;-lien [ljən]) gospel
eventuell [eventu'el] adj eventual || adv possibly
ewig ['evɪç] adj eternal; perpetual
E'wigkeit f (-;-en) eternity
e'wiglich adv forever
exakt [e'ksakt] adj exact
Exa·men [e'ksamən] n (-s;-s & -mina [mina]) examination
examinieren [eksamɪ'nirən] tr examine
exekutiv [ekseku'tif] adj executive

Exempel [ɛˈksɛmpəl] n (-s;-) example; **ein E. statuieren an** (dat) make an example of

Exemplar [ɛksɛmˈplɑr] n (-s;-e) sample, specimen; (e-s Buches) copy

exerzieren [ɛksɛrˈtsirən] tr & intr exercise

Exil [ɛˈksil] n (-s;-e) exile

Existenz [ɛksɪˈstɛnts] f (-;-en) existence; livelihood; personality

Existenz/minimum n living wage

existieren [ɛksɪsˈtirən] intr exist

exklusiv [ɛksluˈzif] adj exclusive

Exkommunikation [ɛkskɔmunɪkɑˈtsjon] f (-;-en) excommunication

exkommunizieren [ɛkskɔmunɪˈtsirən] tr excommunicate

Exkrement [ɛkskreˈmɛnt] n (-[e]s;-e) excrement

exmittieren [ɛksmɪˈtirən] tr evict

exotisch [ɛˈksotɪʃ] adj exotic

expedieren [ɛkspeˈdirən] tr send, ship

Expedition [ɛkspedɪˈtsjon] f (-;-en) forwarding; (mil) expedition

Experiment [ɛksperɪˈmɛnt] n (-[e]s; -e) experiment

experimentieren [ɛksperɪmɛnˈtirən] intr experiment

explodieren [ɛksploˈdirən] intr (SEIN) explode; blow up

Explosion [ɛksploˈzjon] f (-;-en) explosion

exponieren [ɛkspoˈnirən] tr expose; (darlegen) expound, set forth

Export [ɛksˈpɔrt] m (-[e]s;-e) export

exportieren [ɛkspɔrˈtirən] tr export

Ex-preß [ɛksˈprɛs] m (-presses; -presse) express

Expreß/zug m express train

extra [ˈɛkstrɑ] adv extra; (coll) on purpose, for spite

Ex/trablatt n (journ) extra

extrahieren [ɛkstraˈhirən] tr extract

Extrakt [ɛksˈtrakt] m (-[e]s;-e) extract; (aus Büchern) excerpt

extravagant [ɛkstravaˈgant] adj luxurious; wild, fantastic

Extravaganz [ɛkstravaˈgants] f (-;-en) luxury

extrem [ɛksˈtrem] adj extreme || **Extrem** n (-s;-e) extreme

Exzellenz [ɛkstseˈlɛnts] f (-;-en) Excellency

exzentrisch [ɛksˈtsɛntrɪʃ] adj eccentric

Ex-zeß [ɛksˈtsɛs] m (-zesses;-zesse) excess

F

F, f [ɛf] invar n F, f; (mus) F

Fabel [ˈfɑbəl] f (-;-n) fable; story; (e-s Dramas) plot

fa/belhaft adj fabulous

fabeln [ˈfɑbəln] intr tell stories

Fabrik [faˈbrik] f (-;-en) factory, mill

Fabrik/anlage f manufacturing plant

Fabrikant -in [fabrɪˈkant(ɪn)] §7 mf manufacturer, maker

Fabrikat [fabrɪˈkat] n (-[e]s;-e) product; brand, make

Fabrikation [fabrɪkaˈtsjon] f (-;-) manufacture, manufacturing

Fabrikations/fehler m flaw, defect

Fabrikations/nummer f serial number

Fabrik/marke f trademark

fabrik/mäßig adj mass

Fabrik/nummer f serial number

Fabrik/waren pl manufactured goods

Fabrik/zeichen n trademark

fabrizieren [fabrɪˈtsirən] tr manufacture

fabulieren [fabuˈlirən] tr make up || intr tell yarns

fabulös [fabuˈløs] adj fabulous

Facette [faˈsɛtə] f (-;-n) facet

Fach [fax] n (-[e]s;⁺er) compartment; (im Schreibtisch) pigeonhole; (Bücherbrett) shelf; (fig) field, department; line, business; (educ) subject; **vom F. sein** be an expert

Fach/arbeiter -in §6 mf specialist

Fach/arzt m, **Fach/ärztin** f (med) specialist

Fach/ausbildung f professional training

Fach/ausdruck m technical term

fächeln [ˈfɛçəln] tr fan

Fächer [ˈfɛçər] m (-s;-) fan

Fä/cherpalme f palmetto

Fach/gebiet n field, line; department

fach/gemäß adj expert, professional

Fach/gelehrte §5 mf expert

Fach/genosse m colleague

Fach/kenntnisse pl specialized knowledge

Fach/kreis m experts, specialists

fach/kundig adj expert, experienced

fach/lich adj professional; technical, specialized

Fach/mann m (-es;⁺er & -leute) expert, specialist

fachmännisch [ˈfaxmɛnɪʃ] adj expert

Fach/schule f vocational school

Fachsimpelei [faxzɪmpəˈlaɪ] f (-;-en) shoptalk

fachsimpeln [ˈfaxzɪmpəln] intr talk shop

Fach/werk n framework; specialized book

Fach/zeitschrift f technical journal

Fackel [ˈfakəl] f (-;-n) torch

fackeln [ˈfakəln] intr flare; (fig) hesitate, dilly-dally

Fackelschein (**Fak/kelschein**) m torchlight

Fackelzug (**Fak/kelzug**) m torchlight procession

fade [ˈfɑdə] adj stale; (fig) dull

Faden [ˈfɑdən] m (-s;⁺) (& fig) thread; filament; (naut) fathom; **keinen guten F. lassen an** (dat) tear apart

Fa/denkreuz n crosshairs

Fa/dennudeln pl vermicelli

fadenscheinig [ˈfɑdənʃaɪnɪç] *adj* threadbare

Fagott [faˈgɔt] *n* (-[e]s;-e) bassoon

fähig [ˈfɛːɪç] *adj* capable, able

Fähigkeit *f* (-;-en) ability; talent

fahl [fɑl] *adj* pale; faded, washed-out

fahnden [ˈfɑndən] *intr* (nach) search (for), hunt (for)

Fahndung *f* (-;-en) search, hunt

Fahne [ˈfɑnə] *f* (-;-n) flag; pennant; (mil) colors; (typ) galley proof

Fahnenabzug *m* galley proof

Fahneneid *m* (mil) swearing in

Fahnenflucht *f* desertion

fahnenflüchtig *adj*—**f. werden** desert || **Fahnenflüchtige** §5 *mf* deserter

Fahnenmast *m* flagpole

Fahnenträger **-in** §6 *mf* standard bearer

Fähnrich [ˈfɛnrɪç] *m* (-s;-e) officer cadet; **F. zur See** midshipman

Fahrbahn [ˈfɑrbɑn] *f* (traffic) lane

fahrbar [ˈfɑrbɑr] *adj* passable; navigable; mobile

fahrbereit [ˈfɑrbərɑɪt] *adj* in running order

Fahrbereitschaft *f* (-;-en) motor pool

Fähre [ˈfɛrə] *f* (-;-n) ferry

fahren [ˈfɑrən] §71 *tr* haul; (*lenken*) drive; (*Boot*) sail || *intr* (SEIN) go; travel, drive; ride; **es fuhr mir durch den Sinn** it flashed across my mind; **f. lassen** run (*a boat, train*); let go; (fig) abandon, renounce; **gut f. bei** do well in; **mit der Hand f. über** (*acc*) run one's hand over; **rechts f.** (public sign) keep right; **was ist in ihn gefahren?** what's gotten into him?

fahrenlassen §104 *tr* let go of

Fahrer **-in** §6 *mf* driver

Fahrerflucht *f* hit-and-run case

Fahrgast [ˈfɑrgast] *m* passenger

Fahrgeld [ˈfɑrgelt] *n* fare

Fahrgelegenheit [ˈfɑrgəleːgənhaɪt] *f* transportation (facilities)

Fahrgestell [ˈfɑrgəʃtel] *n* (-[e]s;-e) (aer) landing gear; (aut) chassis

fahrig [ˈfɑrɪç] *adj* fidgety

Fahrkarte [ˈfɑrkartə] *f* ticket

Fahrkartenausgabe *f*, **Fahrkartenschalter** *m* ticket window

fahrlässig [ˈfɑrlesɪç] *adj* negligent; **fahrlässige Tötung** involuntary manslaughter

Fahrlässigkeit *f* (-;) negligence

Fahrlehrer **-in** [ˈfɑrleːrər(ɪn)] §6 *mf* driving instructor

Fahrnis [ˈfɑrnɪs] *f* (-;-se) movables

Fährnis [ˈfɛrnɪs] *f* (-;-se) (poet) danger

Fahrplan [ˈfɑrplɑn] *m* schedule

fahrplanmäßig *adj* scheduled || *adv* on schedule, on time

Fahrpreis [ˈfɑrprɑɪs] *m* fare

Fahrprüfung [ˈfɑrpryːfʊŋ] *f* driver's test

Fahrrad [ˈfɑrrɑd] *n* bicycle

Fahrrinne [ˈfɑrrɪnə] *f* channel

Fahrschein [ˈfɑrʃɑɪn] *m* ticket

Fahrstuhl [ˈfɑrʃtuːl] *m* elevator; (med) wheel chair

Fahrstuhlführer **-in** §6 *mf* elevator operator

Fahrstuhlschacht *m* elevator shaft

Fahrstunde [ˈfɑrʃtʊndə] *f* driving lesson

Fahrt [fɑrt] *f* (-;-en) ride, drive; trip; **auf F. gehen** go hiking; **F. verlieren** lose speed; **freie F. haben** have the green light; **in F. kommen** pick up speed; (fig) swing into action; **in F. sein** (coll) be keyed up; (coll) be on the warpath; (naut) be under way

Fährte [ˈfɛrtə] *f* (-;-n) track, scent

Fahrtunterbrechung *f* (-;-en) stopover

Fahrwasser [ˈfɑrvasər] *n* navigable water; (& fig) wake

Fahrwerk [ˈfɑrverk] *n* see **Fahrgestell**

Fahrzeug [ˈfɑrtsɔɪk] *n* vehicle; vessel; craft

Fahrzeugpark *m* (aut) fleet; (rr) rolling stock

fair [fer] *adj* fair

Fairneß [ˈfernes] *f* (-;) fairness

Fäkalien [feˈkɑljən] *pl* feces

faktisch [ˈfaktɪʃ] *adj* actual, factual

Faktor [ˈfaktor] *m* (-s;-toren [ˈtoːrən]) factor; foreman; (com) agent

Faktura [fakˈtuːra] *f* (-;-ren [rən]) invoice

Fakultät [fakʊlˈtɛt] *f* (-;-en) (educ) department, school

Falbe [ˈfalbə] *adj* claybank (*horse*)

Falke [ˈfalkə] *m* (-;-n) falcon; (pol) hawk

Falkenjagd *f* falconry

Falkner [ˈfalknər] *m* (-s;-) falconer

Fall [fal] *m* (-[e]s;⁻e) fall, drop; downfall; case; **auf alle Fälle** in any case; **auf keinen F.** in no case; **auf jeden F.** in any case; **gesetzt den F.** supposing; **im besten F.** at best; **im schlimmsten F.** if worst comes to worst; **von F. zu F.** according to circumstances; **zu F. bringen** (fig) ruin; (parl) defeat; **zu F. kommen** (fig) collapse

Fallbrücke *f* drawbridge

Falle [ˈfalə] *f* (-;-n) (& fig) trap; (fig) pitfall; (*Bett*) (coll) sack

fallen [ˈfalən] §72 *intr* (SEIN) fall, drop; (*Schuß*) be heard; (mil) fall in battle; **j-m ins Wort f.** interrupt s.o. || **Fallen** *n* (-s;) fall, drop; (fig) downfall

fällen [ˈfelən] *tr* (*Bäume*) fell; (*Urteil*) pass; (chem) precipitate

Fallensteller [ˈfalənʃtelər] *m* (-s;-) trapper

Fallgrube *f* trap, pit; (fig) pitfall

fällig [ˈfelɪç] *adj* due; payable

Fälligkeit *f* (-;-en) due date

Fallobst *n* windfall

Fallrohr *n* soil pipe; (*e-r Dachrinne*) down spout

falls [fals] *conj* in case, if

Fallschirm *m* parachute

Fallschirmabsprung *m* parachute jump

Fallschirmjäger *m* paratrooper

Fallschirmspringer **-in** §6 *mf* parachutist, sky diver

Fallstrick *m* snare

Fallsucht *f* (pathol) epilepsy

fallsüchtig *adj* (pathol) epileptic

Falltür *f* trapdoor

falsch [falʃ] *adj* false; (*verkehrt*) wrong; (*unecht*) counterfeit; **falsches Spiel** double-dealing ‖ *adv* wrongly; **f. gehen** (horol) be off; **f. schreiben** misspell; **f. schwören** perjure oneself; **f. singen** sing off key; **f. spielen** cheat; **f. verbunden** wrong number ‖ **Falsch** m—**ohne F.** without guile

fälschen [ˈfɛlʃən] *tr* falsify; (*Geld*) counterfeit; (*Urkunde*) forge

Fäl'scher –in §6 *mf* forger; counterfeiter

Falsch'geld n counterfeit money

Falsch'heit *f* (-;-en) falsity; deceitfulness

fälschlich [ˈfɛlʃlɪç] *adv* falsely

Falsch'münzer m counterfeiter

Falsch'spieler –in §6 *mf* card sharp

Fäl'schung *f* (-;-en) falsification; forgery; fake

Faltboot [ˈfaltboʔt] n collapsible boat

Falte [ˈfaltə] *f* (-;-n) fold; (*Plissee*) pleat, crease; (*Runzel*) wrinkle

fälteln [ˈfɛltəln] *tr* pleat

falten [ˈfaltən] *tr* fold; wrinkle

Fal'tenrock m pleated skirt

Falter [ˈfaltər] m (-s;-) butterfly; (*Nacht–*) moth

faltig [ˈfaltɪç] *adj* creased; wrinkled

Falz [falts] m (-es;-e) fold; (*Kerbe*) notch; (carp) rabbet

familiär [famɪˈljɛr] *adj* intimate; familiar

Familie [faˈmiljə] *f* (-;-n) family

Fami'lienangehörige §5 *mf* member of the family

Fami'lienanschluß m—**F. haben** live as one of the family

Fami'lienname m last name

Fami'lienstand m marital status

Fami'lienstück n family heirloom

Fami'lienzuwachs m addition to the family

famos [faˈmoːs] *adj* excellent, swell

Fan [fɛn] m (-s;-s) (sport) fan

Fanatiker –in [faˈnaːtɪkər(ɪn)] §6 *mf* fanatic; (sport) fan

fanatisch [faˈnaːtɪʃ] *adj* fanatic

fand [fant] *pret* of **finden**

Fanfare [fanˈfaːrə] *f* (-;-n) (mus) fanfare

Fang [faŋ] m (-[e]s;ᵘe) capture; (*Fisch–*) haul, catch; (*Falle*) trap; (*Kralle*) claw

Fang'arm m tentacle

Fang'eisen n steel trap

fangen [ˈfaŋən] §73 *tr* catch; trap; (*Ohrfeige*) get ‖ *ref* get caught ‖ **Fangen n—F. spielen** play catch

Fang'frage *f* loaded question

Fang'messer n hunting knife

Fang'zahn m fang; tusk

Farb– [farp] *comb.fm.* color

Farb'abzug m (phot) color print

Farb'aufnahme *f* color photograph

Farb'band n (-[e]s;ᵘer) typewriter ribbon

Farbe [ˈfarbə] *f* (-;-n) color; dye; (*zum Malen*) paint; (*Gesichts–*) complexion; (cards) suit; **F. bekennen** folow suit; (fig) lay one's cards on the table

färben [ˈfɛrbən] *tr* color, dye, tint ‖

ref take on color; change color; **sich rot f.** turn red; blush

farb'enprächtig *adj* colorful

Fär'ber –in §6 *mf* dyer

Farb'fernsehen n color television

Farb'film m color film

farbig [ˈfarbɪç] *adj* colored; colorful

Farb'kissen n ink pad

Farb'körper m pigment

farb'los *adj* colorless

Farb'spritzpistole *f* paint sprayer

Farb'stift m colored pencil; crayon

Farb'stoff m dye

Farb'ton m tone, hue, shade

Fär'bung *f* (-;-en) coloring; hue

Farm [farm] *f* (-;-en) farm

Farmer –in [ˈfarmər(ɪn)] §6 *mf* farmer

Farn [farn] m (-[e]s;-e) fern

Farn'kraut n fern

Fasan [faˈzaːn] m (-s;-e & -en) pheasant

Fasching [ˈfaʃɪŋ] m (-s;) carnival

Faschismus [faˈʃɪsmus] m (-;) fascism

Faschist –in [faˈʃɪst(ɪn)] §7 *mf* fascist

Faselei [faːzəˈlaɪ] *f* (-;-en) drivel

Faselhans [ˈfaːzəlhans] m (-ᵉ;-e & ᵘe) blabberer; scatterbrain

faseln [ˈfaːzəln] *intr* talk nonsense

Faser [ˈfaːzər] *f* (-;-n) fiber; (*im Holz*) grain; (*Fädchen*) thread, string

Fa'serholzplatte *f* fiberboard

fasern [ˈfaːzərn] *tr* unravel ‖ *ref* fray ‖ *intr* unravel

Fa'serschreiber m felt pen

Faß [fas] n (Fasses;Fässer) barrel, keg; (*Bütte*) vat, tub

Fassade [faˈsaːdə] *f* (-;-n) façade

faßbar [ˈfasbar] *adj* comprehensible

Faß'bier n draft beer

fassen [ˈfasən] *tr* (packen) seize; (*erwischen*) apprehend; (*begreifen*) grasp; (*für Edelsteine*) mount; (*enthalten können*) hold, seat; (*Essen*) (mil) draw; **e-n Gedanken f.** form an idea; **in Worte f.** put into words; **j-n bei der Ehre f.** appeal to s.o.'s honor; **Tritt fassen** fall in step ‖ *ref* get hold of oneself; **in sich f.** include; **sich f. an** (*acc*) put one's hand to, touch; **sich in Geduld f.** exercise patience; **sich kurz f.** be brief ‖ *intr* take hold; (nach) grab (for); **es ist nicht zu f.** it is incomprehensible

Faß'hahn m tap, faucet

faß'lich *adj* conceivable

Fasson [faˈsoŋ] *f* (-;-en) style, cut

Fas'sung *f* (-;-en) composure; (*schriftlich*) draft; (*für Edelsteine*) setting, mounting; (*Brillenrand*) frame; (*Wortlaut*) wording; (*Lesart*) version; (elec) socket; **aus der F. bringen** upset; **außer F. sein** be beside onself

Fas'sungskraft *f* comprehension

fas'sungslos *adj* disconcerted, shaken

Fas'sungsvermögen n capacity; (*geistliches*) (powers of) comprehension

fast [fast] *adv* almost, nearly

fasten [ˈfastən] *intr* fast ‖ **Fasten n** (-s;) fasting

Fa'stenzeit *f* Lent, Lenten season

Fast'nacht *f* carnival

Fast'tag m day of fasting, fast day

faszinieren [fastsɪ'nirən] *tr* fascinate
fatal [fa'tɑl] *adj* disastrous; (*unangenehm*) unpleasant
fauchen ['fauxən] *intr* hiss; (*Person*) snarl; (*Katze*) spit
faul [faul] *adj* rotten; lazy; bad, nasty; (*verdächtig*) fishy; (*Ausrede, Witz*) lame, poor; (sport) foul || **Faul** *n* (-s;-s) (sport) foul
Fäule ['fɔɪlə] *f* (-;-) rot, decay
faulen ['faulən] *intr* rot, decay
faulenzen ['faulɛntsən] *intr* loaf
Faulenzer ['faulɛntsər] *m* (-s;-) loafer; (*Liegestuhl*) chaise longue; (*Linienblatt*) ruled sheet of paper
Faul'heit *f* (-;) laziness
faulig ['faulɪç] *adj* rotten, putrid
Fäulnis ['fɔɪlnɪs] *f* (-;) rot; **in F. übergehen** begin to rot
Faul'pelz *m* (coll) loafer
Faust [faust] *f* (-;-̈e) fist; **auf eigene F.** on one's own
faust'dick' *adj* (coll) whopping
Faust'handschuh *m* mitten
Faust'kampf *m* boxing match
Fäustling ['fɔɪstlɪŋ] *m* (-[e]s;-e) mitten
Faust'schlag *m* punch, blow
Favorit –in [favo'rit(ɪn)] §7 *mf* favorite
Faxen ['faksən] *pl* antics; faces; **F. machen** fool around; make a fuss; **F. schneiden** make faces
Fazit ['fatsɪt] *n* (-s;-e & -s) result; **das F. ziehen** sum it up
Feber ['febər] *m* (-[s];-) (Aust) February
Februar ['febru·ɑr] *m* (-[s];-e) February
fechten ['fɛçtən] §74 *intr* fence; fight; (*betteln*) beg
Feder ['fedər] *f* (-;-n) feather; pen; quill; (mach) spring; **F. und Nut** (carp) tongue and groove
Fe'derball *m* shuttlecock
Fe'derballspiel *n* badminton
Fe'derbett *n* feather bed
Fe'derbusch *m* plume
Fe'derdecke *f* feather quilt
Federfuchser ['fedərfuksər] *m* (-s;-) scribbler; hack writer
fe'derführend *adj* in charge
Fe'dergewicht *n* featherweight division
Federgewichtler ['fedərgəvɪçtlər] *m* (-s;-) featherweight (boxer)
Fe'derhubtor *n* overhead door
Fe'derkernmatratze *f* innerspring mattress
Fe'derkiel *m* quill
Fe'derkraft *f* springiness; tension
Fe'derkrieg *m* paper war, war of words
fe'derleicht' *adj* light as a feather
Fe'derlesen *n—ohne viel Federlesen(s)* without much ado
Fe'dermesser *n* penknife
federn ['fedərn] *tr* fit with springs || *intr* be springy; (*Vogel*) moult; (gym) bounce
Fe'derring *m* lock washer
Fe'derstrich *m* stroke of the pen
Fe'derung *f* (-;) (aut) suspension
Fe'derzug *m* stroke of the pen
Fee [fe] *f* (-;Feen) ['fe·ən] fairy

Feg(e)feuer ['feg(ə)fɔɪ·ər] *n* (-s;) purgatory
fegen ['fegən] *tr* sweep; (*Laub*) tear off || *intr* (SEIN) tear along
Fehde ['fedə] *f* (-;-n) feud
Feh'dehandschuh *m* gauntlet
fehl [fel] *adj—f. am Ort* out of place || **Fehl** *m* (-[e]s;-e) blemish; fault
fehl– *comb.fm.* wide of the mark; mis–, incorrectly, wrongly || **Fehl–** *comb.fm.* missing; vain, unsuccessful; incorrect, wrong; faulty; negative
Fehl'anzeige *f* negative report
Fehl'ball *m* (tennis) fault
fehlbar ['felbar] *adj* fallible
Fehl'betrag *m* shortage, deficit
Fehl'bitte *f* vain request; **e-e F. tun** meet with a refusal
fehlen ['felən] *tr* miss || *intr* be absent; be missing; be lacking; fail, be unsuccessful; sin, err; (dat) miss, e.g., **er fehlt mir sehr** I miss him very much; (dat) lack, e.g., **ihm fehlt die Zeit** he lacks the time; **was fehlt Ihnen?** what's wrong with you? || *impers—es fehlte nicht viel, und ich wäre gefallen* I came close to falling
Fehler ['felər] *m* (-s;-) mistake, error; flaw, imperfection; blunder
feh'lerfrei *adj* faultless, flawless
feh'lerhaft *adj* faulty
feh'lerlos *adj* faultless, flawless
Fehl'geburt *f* miscarriage
fehl'gehen §82 *intr* (SEIN) go wrong; (*Schuß*) miss
Fehl'gewicht *n* short weight
fehl'greifen §88 *intr* miss one's hold; (fig) make a mistake
Fehl'griff *m* mistake, blunder
Fehl'leistung *f* (Freudian) slip
fehl'leiten *tr* (& fig) misdirect
Fehl'schlag *m* miss; failure, disappointment; (baseball) foul
Fehl'schluß *m* false inference; fallacy
Fehl'spruch *m* miscarriage of justice
Fehl'start *m* false start
Fehl'tritt *m* false step; (fig) slip
Fehl'wurf *m* (beim Würfeln) crap
fehl'zünden *intr* backfire
feien ['faɪ·ən] *tr—gefeit sein gegen be* immune to; **j–n f. gegen** make s.o. immune to
Feier ['faɪ·ər] *f* (-;-n) celebration; ceremony
Fei'erabend *m* closing time
fei'erlich *adj* solemn
Fei'erlichkeit *f* (-;-en) solemnity; **Feierlichkeiten** festivities; ceremonies
feiern ['faɪ·ərn] *tr* celebrate, observe; honor || *intr* rest from work
Fei'erstunde *f* commemorative ceremony
Fei'ertag *m* holiday; holy day
feig [faɪk] *adj* cowardly
feige ['faɪgə] *adj* cowardly || **Feige** *f* (-;-n) fig
Feig'heit *f* (-;) cowardice
feig'herzig *adj* faint-hearted
Feigling ['faɪklɪŋ] *m* (-s;-e) coward
feil [faɪl] *adj* for sale
feil'bieten §58 *tr* offer for sale
Feile ['faɪlə] *f* (-;-n) file

Feile ['faɪlən] *tr* file

feilschen ['faɪlʃən] *intr* (um) haggle (over), dicker (about)

Feilspäne ['faɪlʃpenə] *pl* filings

fein [faɪn] *adj* fine; delicate; fancy

feind [faɪnt] *adj* hostile ‖ **Feind** *m* (-[e]s;-e) enemy, foe

Feind— *comb.fm.* enemy, hostile; against the enemy

Feind'fahrt *f* (nav) operation against the enemy

Feind'flug *m* (aer) combat mission

Feindin ['faɪndɪn] *f* (-;-nen) enemy

feind'lich *adj* hostile

Feind'schaft *f* (-;-en) enmity

feind'selig *adj* hostile

Feind'seligkeit *f* (-;-en) hostility, animosity; hostile action

fein'fühlend, fein'fühlig *adj* sensitive

Fein'gefühl *n* sensitivity

Fein'heit *f* (-;-en) fineness, fine quality; delicacy; subtlety

Fein'mechanik *f* precision engineering

Feinschmecker ['faɪnʃmɛkər] *m* (-s;-) gourmet, epicure

fein'sinnig *adj* sensitive; subtle

feist [faɪst] *adj* fat, plump

Feld [fɛlt] *n* (-[e]s;-er) field; panel, compartment; (checkers, chess) square; **auf dem Felde in the field(s); auf freiem Felde in the open; aufs F. gehen go to (work in) the fields; das F. behaupten stand one's ground; ins F. ziehen take the field**

Feld'bau *m* agriculture

Feld'becher *m* collapsible drinking cup

Feld'bett *n* army cot; camping cot

Feld'blume *f* wild flower

Feld'bluse *f* army jacket

feld'dienstfähig *adj* fit for active duty

Feld'flasche *f* canteen

Feld'geistliche *m* (-n;-n) army chaplain

Feld'gendarm *m* military police

Feld'gendarmerie *f* military police

Feld'geschrei *n* battle cry

Feld'geschütz *n* field gun, field piece

Feld'herr *m* general; commander in chief

Feld'lager *n* bivouac, camp

Feld'lazarett *n* evacuation hospital

Feld'lerche *f* skylark

Feld'marschall *m* field marshal

feld'marschmäßig *adj* with full field pack

Feld'messer *m* surveyor

Feld'meßkunst *f* (-;) surveying

Feld'mütze *f* (mil) overseas cap

Feld'postamt *n* army post office

Feld'schlacht *f* battle

Feld'stecher *m* field glasses

Feldwebel ['fɛltvebəl] *m* (-s;-) sergeant

Feld'zeichen *n* ensign, standard

Feld'zug *m* campaign

Feige ['faɪgə] *f* (-;-n) fig

Fell [fɛl] *n* (-[e]s;-e) pelt, skin; fur; **ein dickes F. haben be thick-skinned**

Fels [fɛls] *m* (-es & -en;-en) rock; cliff; **zackige Felsen crags**

Fels'block *m* boulder

Felsen ['fɛlzən] *m* (-s;-) rock; cliff

fel'senfest *adj* firm as a rock

Fel'sengebirge *n* Rocky Mountains

Fel'senklippe *f* cliff

Fel'senriff *n* reef

felsig ['fɛlzɪç] *adj* rocky

Fenster ['fɛnstər] *n* (-s;-) window

Fen'sterbrett *n* window sill

Fen'sterflügel *m* casement

Fen'sterladen *m* window shutter

Fen'sterleder *n* chamois

Fen'sterplatz *m* (rr) window seat

Fen'sterrahmen *m* window frame; sash

Fen'sterrosette *f* rose window

Fen'sterscheibe *f* windowpane

Ferien ['ferjən] *pl* vacation; (parl) recess

Fe'rienreisende §5 *mf* vacationer

Fe'rienstimmung *f* holiday spirit

Ferkel ['fɛrkəl] *n* (-s;-) piglet

Ferkelei [fɛrkə'laɪ] *f* (-;-en) obscenity

fern [fɛrn] *adj* far, distant; (*entlegen*) remote; (*weit fort*) far away

Fern'amt *n* long-distance exchange

Fern'anruf *m* long-distance call

Fern'aufklärung *f* long-range reconnaissance

Fern'bedienung *f* remote control

fern'bleiben §62 *intr* (SEIN) (*dat*) stay away (from) ‖ **Fernbleiben** *n* (-s;) absence; absenteeism

Fern'blick *m* distant view, vista

Ferne ['fɛrnə] *f* (-;-n) distance

ferner ['fɛrnər] *adj* remote, distant ‖ *adv* further; moreover

Fern'fahrer *m* long-distance trucker

Fern'fahrt *f* long-distance trip

Fern'gang *m* (aut) overdrive

Fern'geschoß *n* long-range missile

Fern'geschütz *n* long-range gun

Fern'gespräch *n* long-distance call; toll call

Fern'glas *n* binoculars

fern'halten §90 *tr* & *ref* keep away

Fern'heizung *f* heating from a central heating plant

Fern'kursus *m* correspondence course

Fern'laster *m* long-distance truck

fern'lenken *tr* guide by remote control

Fern'lenkrakete *f* guided missile

Fern'lenkung *f* (-;-en) remote control

Fern'lenkwaffe *f* guided missile

Fern'licht *n* (aut) high beam

fern'liegen §108 *impers*—**es liegt mir fern zu** (*inf*) I'm far from (ger)

Fernmelde— [fɛrnmɛldə] *comb.fm.* communications, signal

Fern'meldetruppen *pl* signal corps

Fern'meldewesen *n* telecommunications system

fern'mündlich *adj* & *adv* by telephone

Fern'objektiv *n* telephoto lens

Fernost— *comb.fm.* Far Eastern

fern'östlich *adj* Far Eastern

Fern'rohr *n* telescope

Fern'rohraufsatz *m* telescopic gun sight

Fern'ruf *m* telephone call; telephone number

Fern'schnellzug *m* long-distance express

Fern'schreiber *m* teletype, telex

Fernseh— [fɛrnze] *comb.fm.* television

Fern'sehansager -in §6 *mf* television announcer

Fern'sehapparat *m* television set

Fern'sehbildröhre f picture tube
fern'sehen §138 intr watch television || **Fernsehen** n (-s;) television
Fern'seher m (-s;-) television set; television viewer
Fern'sehgerät n television set
Fern'sehkanal m television channel
Fern'sehschau f television show
Fern'sehsendung f telecast
Fern'sehtellnehmer -in §6 mf televiewer
Fern'sehübertragung f telecast
Fern'sicht f view, vista; panorama
fern'sichtig adj far-sighted
Fernsprech- [fernʃpreç] comb.fm. telephone
Fern'sprechauftragsdienst m answering service
Fern'sprechautomat m pay phone
Fern'sprecher m telephone
Fern'sprechzelle f telephone booth
fern'stehen §146 intr (dat) have no personal contact (with); (dat) not be close (to)
Fern'stehende §5 mf outsider; disinterested observer
fern'steuern tr guide by remote control
Fern'studium n correspondence course
Ferse ['fɛrzə] f (-;-n) heel
Fer'sengeld n—F. geben take to one's heels
fertig ['fɛrtɪç] adj finished; ready; (kaputt) ruined, done for
fertig-, Fertig- comb.fm. final; finished; finishing; prefabricated
fer'tigbringen §65 tr finish, get done; bring about; es glatt f. zu (inf) be capable of (ger); es nicht f., ihm das zu sagen not have the heart to tell him that
fertigen ['fɛrtɪgən] tr manufacture
Fer'tigkeit f (-;-en) skill
Fer'tigrasen m sod
fer'tigstellen tr complete; get ready
Fer'tigung f (-;-en) manufacture; production; copy, draft
Fes [fɛs] n (mus) F flat
fesch [fɛʃ] adj smart, chic
Fessel ['fɛsəl] f (-;-n) fetter, bond; (anat) ankle; (vet) fetlock
Fes'selballon m captive balloon
fesseln ['fɛsəln] tr chain, tie; (bezaubern) captivate, arrest; (mil) contain; ans Bett gefesselt confined to bed, bedridden
fes'selnd adj fascinating, gripping; (Personalität) magnetic
fest [fɛst] adj firm; solid; tight; stationary; steady; (Preis, Kost, Einkommen, Gehalt) fixed; (Schlaf) sound; (mil) fortified; feste Straße improved road || **Fest** n (-es;-e) feast; festival
fest'backen intr (SEIN) cake (on)
fest'besoldet adj with a fixed salary
fest'binden §59 tr (an dat) tie (to)
Fest'essen n banquet
fest'fahren §71 tr run aground || ref come to a standstill
fest'halten §90 tr hold on to || ref (an dat) cling (to), hold on (to)
festigen ['fɛstɪgən] tr strengthen; consolidate || ref grow stronger

Fe'stigkeit f (-;-en) firmness; steadiness; strength
Fe'stigung f (-;) strengthening; consolidation; stabilization
Fest'land n continent
fest'legen tr fix, determine, set; (Anordnung) lay down; (fin, naut) tie up; j-n f. auf (acc) pin s.o. down on || ref (auf acc) commit oneself (to)
fest'lich adj festive
Fest'lichkeit f (-;-en) festivity
fest'liegen §108 intr be stranded
fest'machen tr fix; (fig) settle || intr (naut) moor
Fest'mahl n feast
Fest'nahme f (-;-n) arrest
fest'nehmen §116 tr arrest, apprehend
Fest'rede f ceremonial speech
Fest'saal m grand hall, banquet hall
fest'schnallen tr buckle up || ref fasten one's seat belt
Fest'schrift f homage volume
fest'setzen tr fix, set || ref settle down (in a town, etc.)
fest'sitzen intr fit tight; be stuck
Fest'spiel n play for a festive occasion; Festspiele (mus, theat) festival
fest'stehen §146 intr stand firm; (Tatsache) be certain || impers—es steht fest it is a fact
fest'stehend adj stationary; (Achse) fixed; (Tatsache) established
feststellbar ['fɛst|tɛlbar] ascertainable
Fest'stellbremse f hand brake
fest'stellen tr ascertain; (unbeweglich machen) lock, secure; (Tatbestand) find out, establish; (angeben) state; (Schaden) assess; (Kurs) (fin) set, fix
Fest'stellschraube f set screw
Fest'tag m feastday; holiday
Fe'stung f (-;-en) fortress
Fe'stungsgraben m moat
Fest'wagen m float
Fest'wert m standard value; (math, phys) constant
Fest'wiese f fairground
fest'ziehen §163 tr pull tight
Fest'zug m procession
Fetisch ['fetɪʃ] m (-[e]s;-e) fetish
fett [fɛt] adj fat; (Boden, Milch, Gemisch) rich; (Zeiten, Leben) of plenty || **Fett** n (-[e]s;-e) fat; (Schmalz) lard; (Pflanzen-) shortening; (Schmier-) grease
Fett'auge n speck of fat
Fett'druck m boldface type
fetten ['fɛtən] tr grease, lubricate
Fett'fleck m grease spot
fettig ['fɛtɪç] adj fatty, greasy, oily
Fett'kloß m (coll) fatso
Fett'kohle f bituminous coal
fettleibig ['fɛtlaɪbɪç] adj stout
Fettnäpfchen ['fɛtnɛpfçən] n—bei j-m ins F. treten hurt s.o.'s feelings; ins F. treten put one's foot in it
Fett'presse f (aut) grease gun
Fett'spritze f (aut) grease gun
Fett'sucht f obesity
Fett'wanst m (sl) fatso
Fetzen ['fɛtsən] m (-s;-) rag; bit; scrap; (Aust) dishcloth; daß die F. fliegen violently
feucht [fɔɪçt] adj moist, damp, humid

feuchten ['fɔɪçtən] tr moisten, dampen
Feuch'tigkeit f (-;) moisture, dampness, humidity
feudal [fɔɪ'dal] adj feudal; (fig) magnificent
Feudalismus [fɔɪda'lɪsmus] m (-;) feudalism
Feuer ['fɔɪ-ər] n (-s;-) fire
Feu'eralarm m fire alarm
Feu'eralarmübung f fire drill
feu'erbeständig adj fireproof
Feu'erbestattung f cremation
Feu'erbrand m firebrand
Feu'ereifer m enthusiasm, zeal
Feu'ereinstellung f cease-fire
feu'erfest adj fireproof
Feu'erfliege f firefly
feu'erflüssig adj molten
feu'ergefährlich adj inflammable
Feu'erhahn m hydrant, fireplug
Feu'erhaken m poker
Feu'erherd m fireplace
Feu'erkampf m fire fight, gun battle
Feu'erkraft f (mil) fire power
Feu'erleiter f fire ladder; (Nottreppe) fire escape
Feu'erlinie f firing line
Feu'erlöscher m fire extinguisher
Feu'ermelder m fire alarm
Feu'ermeldung f fire alarm
feuern ['fɔɪ-ərn] tr fire; (coll) fire, sack || intr fire, shoot
Feu'erprobe f ordeal by fire; acid test
Feu'ersalve f fusillade
Feu'erschneise f firebreak
Feu'erspritze f fire engine
Feu'erstein m flint
Feu'ertaufe f baptism of fire
Feu'erversicherung f fire insurance
Feu'erwache f firehouse
Feu'erwalze f (mil) creeping barrage
Feu'erwehr f fire department
Feu'erwehrmann m (-[e]s;-er & -leute) fireman
Feu'erwerk n fireworks
Feu'erwerkskörper m firecracker
Feu'erzange f fire tongs
Feu'erzeug n cigarette lighter
Feu'erzeugbenzin n lighter fluid
feurig ['fɔɪrɪç] adj fiery; ardent
Fiasko [fɪ'asko] n (-s;-s) fiasco
Fibel ['fibəl] f (-;-n) primer; (archeol) fibula
Fiber ['fibər] f (-;-n) fiber
Fichte ['fɪçtə] f (-;-n) spruce; pine
Fich'tennadel f pine needle
fidel [fɪ'del] adj jolly, cheerful
Fieber ['fibər] n (-s;-) fever; das F. messen take the temperature
fie'berhaft adj feverish
fieberig ['fibərɪç] adj feverish
fie'berkrank adj running a fever
fiebern ['fibərn] intr be feverish
Fie'berphantasie f delirium
Fie'bertabelle f temperature chart
Fiedel ['fidəl] f (-;-n) fiddle
Fie'delbogen m fiddlestick
fiel [fil] pret of fallen
Figur [fɪ'gur] f (-;-en) figure; (cards) face card
figürlich [fɪ'gyrlɪç] adj figurative
fiktiv [fɪk'tif] adj fictitious
Filet [fɪ'le] n (-s;-s) (culin) fillet

Filiale [fɪ'ljalə] f (-;-n) branch
Filia'lengeschäft n chain store
Filigran [fɪlɪ'gran] n (-s;-e), Fili-gran'arbeit f filigree
Film [fɪlm] m (-s;-e) film; (cin) movie
Film'atelier n motion-picture studio
Film'empfindlichkeit f film speed
Film'kulisse f (cin) movie set
Film'leinwand f movie screen
Film'probe f screen test
Film'regisseur m (cin) director
Film'wesen n motion-picture industry
Filter ['fɪltər] m & n (-s;-) filter
Fil'teranlage f filtration plant
Fil'terkaffee m drip-grind coffee
Fil'termundstück n filter tip
filtern ['fɪltərn] tr filter, strain
filtrieren [fɪl'triran] tr filter
Filz [fɪlts] m (-es;-e) felt; (coll) miser, skinflint
Filz'schreiber m felt pen
Fimmel ['fɪməl] f (-;-s) craze, fad
-fimmel m comb.fm. mania for
Finanz [fɪ'nants] f (-;-en) finance
Finanz- comb.fm. financial, fiscal
Finanz'amt n internal revenue service
Finanz'ausschuß m (adm) ways and means committee
Finanzen [fɪ'nantsən] pl finances
finanziell [fɪnan'tsjel] adj financial
finanzieren [fɪnan'tsiran] tr finance
Finanz'minister m secretary of the treasury
Finanz'ministerium n treasury department
Finanz'wesen n finances
Finanz'wirtschaft f public finances
Findelkind ['fɪndəlkɪnt] n foundling
finden ['fɪndən] §59 tr find; f. Sie nicht? don't you think so? || ref be found; ach, das wird sich schon f. oh, we'll see about that; es fanden sich there were; es findet sich it happens, it turns out; sich f. in (acc) resign oneself to; sie haben sich gefunden they were united || intr find one's way
findig ['fɪndɪç] adj resourceful
Findling ['fɪntlɪŋ] m (-s;-e) foundling; (geol) boulder
fing [fɪŋ] pret of fangen
Finger ['fɪŋər] m (-s;-) finger
Fin'gerabdruck m fingerprint
fin'gerfertig adj deft
Fin'gerhut m thimble; (bot) foxglove
fingern ['fɪŋərn] tr finger
Fin'gerspitze f finger tip; bis in die Fingerspitzen through and through
Fin'gerspitzengefühl n sensitivity
Fin'gersprache f sign language
Fingerzeig ['fɪŋərtsaɪk] m (-s;-e) hint
fingieren [fɪŋ'giran] tr feign
fingiert [fɪŋ'girt] adj fictitious
Fink [fɪŋk] m (-en;-en) finch
Finne ['fɪnə] m (-n;-n) Finn || f (-;-n) fin; (Ausschlag) pimple
Fin'nenausschlag m acne
Finnin ['fɪnɪn] f (-;-nen) Finn
finnisch ['fɪnɪʃ] adj Finnish
Finnland ['fɪnlant] n (-s;) Finland
finster ['fɪnstər] adj dark; gloomy
Finsternis ['fɪnstərnɪs] f (-;) darkness; gloom

Finte ['fɪntə] f (-;-n) feint; trick
Firlefanz ['fɪrləfants] m (-es;) junk;
F. treiben fool around
Fir·ma ['fɪrma] f (-;-men [mən]) firm
Firmament [fɪrma'mɛnt] n (-[e]s;-e)
firmament
firmen ['fɪrmən] tr (Cath) confirm
Fir'menschild n (com) name plate
Fir'menwert m (com) good will
Firmling ['fɪrmlɪŋ] m (-s;-e) (Cath)
person to be confirmed
Fir'mung f (-;-en) (Cath) confirma-
tion
Fir·nis ['fɪrnɪs] m (-ses;-se) varnish;
mit F. streichen varnish
firnissen ['fɪrnɪsən] tr varnish
First [fɪrst] m (-es;-e) (archit) ridge
(of roof); (poet) mountain ridge
Fis [fɪs] n (-;-) (mus) F sharp
Fisch [fɪʃ] m (-es;-e) fish
fischen ['fɪʃən] tr fish for, catch ‖ intr
(nach) fish (for)
Fi'scher m (-s;-) fisherman
Fischerei [fɪʃə'raɪ] f (-;-en) fishing;
fishery; fishing trade
Fi'schergerät n fishing tackle
Fisch'fang m catch, haul
Fisch'gräte f fishbone
Fisch'grätenmuster n (tex) herringbone
Fisch'händler -in §6 mf fishmonger
fischig ['fɪʃɪç] adj fishy
Fisch'kunde f ichthyology
Fisch'laich m spawn, fish eggs
Fisch'otter m & f otter
Fisch'rogen m roe
Fisch'schuppe f scale (of a fish)
Fisch'zug m (& fig) catch
fiskalisch [fɪs'kɑːlɪʃ] adj fiscal
Fis·kus ['fɪskus] m (-;-kusse & -ken
[kən]) treasury
Fistelstimme ['fɪstəlʃtɪmə] f falsetto
Fittich ['fɪtɪç] m (-es;-e) (poet) wing
fix [fɪks] adj (Idee, Preis) fixed;
(flink) smart, sharp; fix und fertig
all set; all in; done for; fix und
fertig mit through with; mach fix!
make it snappy!
fixen ['fɪksən] intr sell short
fixieren [fɪ'ksiːrən] tr fix, decide upon;
stare fixedly at; (phot) fix
Fixier'mittel n (phot) fixer
flach [flax] adj flat, level; shallow;
(Relief) low; (fig) dull
Fläche ['flɛçə] f (-;-n) surface; plain;
expanse; facet; (geom) area
Flä'cheninhalt m (geom) area
Flä'chenraum m surface area
flach'fallen §72 intr (SEIN) (coll) fall
flat, flop
Flach'heit f (-;) flatness; shallowness
Flach'land n lowland
Flach'relief n low relief, bas-relief
Flach'rennen n flat racing
Flachs [flaks] m (-es;-e) flax
flachsen ['flaksən] intr (coll) kid
flächse(r)n ['flɛksə(r)n] adj flaxen
Flach'zange f pliers
flackern ['flakərn] intr flicker; (Stim-
me) quaver, shake
Flagge ['flagə] f (-;-n) flag (esp. for
signaling or identification)
Flag'genmast m flagpole
Flag'genstange f flagstaff

Flagg'schiff n flagship
Flak [flak] abbr (Flugzeugabwehr-
kanone) anti-aircraft gun
Flak'feuer n flak
Flakon [fla'kõ] m & n (-s;-s) perfume
bottle
Flamme ['flamə] f (-;-n) flame
flammen ['flamən] intr blaze; be in
flames
flam'mend adj passionate
Fla'mmenwerfer m flame thrower
Flandern ['flandərn] n (-s;) Flanders
flandrisch ['flandrɪ] adj Flemish
Flanell [fla'nɛl] m (-s;-e) flannel
Flanke ['flaŋkə] f (-;-n) flank
Flan'kenfeuer n (mil) enfilade; mit F.
bestreichen enfilade
flankieren [flaŋ'kiːrən] tr flank
Flansch [flanʃ] m (-es;-e) flange
Flasche ['flaʃə] f (-;-n) bottle; (coll)
flop; (mach) pulley
Fla'schengranate f Molotov cocktail
Fla'schenzug m block and tackle; (coll)
pulley
Flaschner ['flaʃnər] m (-s;-) plumber
flatterhaft ['flatərhaft] adj fickle
flattern ['flatərn] intr flutter, flap
flau [flau] adj stale; (schwach) feeble,
faint; (fade) dull, lifeless; (com)
slack; (phot) overexposed; mir ist
f. (im Magen) I feel queezy
Flaum [flaum] m (-[e]s;) down; (am
Gesicht, am Pfirsich) fuzz
flaumig ['flaumɪç] adj downy, fluffy
Flause ['flauzə] f (-;-n) fib; Flausen
funny ideas, nonsense
Flaute ['flautə] f (-;-n) (com) slack
period; (naut) dead calm
fläzen ['flɛtsən] ref sprawl out
Flechse ['flɛksə] f (-;-n) (dial) sinew,
tendon
Flechte ['flɛçtə] f (-;-n) plait; (bot)
lichen; (pathol) ringworm
flechten ['flɛçtən] §74 tr braid, plait;
(Körbe) weave
Fleck [flɛk] m (-[e]s;-e & -en) spot;
blemish; (Flicken, Landstück) patch
Flecken ['flɛkən] m (-s;-) spot; piece
of land; (Markt-) market town
fleckenlos ['flɛkənloːs] adj spotless
Fleck'fieber n spotted fever
fleckig ['flɛkɪç] adj spotty; splotchy
fleddern ['flɛdərn] tr (sl) rob
Fledermaus ['fleːdərmaus] f bat
Flegel ['fleːgəl] m (-s;-) flail; (coll)
lout, boor
Flegelei [fleːgə'laɪ] f (-;) rudeness
fle'gelhaft adj uncouth, boorish
Fle'geljahre pl awkward age
flehen ['fleːən] intr plea; zu j-m f.
implore s.o. ‖ Flehen n (-s;-) sup-
plication
Fleisch [flaɪʃ] n (-es;) flesh; meat;
sich ins eigene F. schneiden cut one's
own throat; wildes F. proud flesh
Fleisch'bank f (-;-e) meat counter
Fleisch'beil n cleaver
Fleisch'beschau f meat inspection
Fleisch'brühe f broth
Flei'scher m (-s;-) butcher
Flei'scheslust f lust
Fleisch'farbe f flesh color
fleisch'fressend adj carnivorous

Fleisch'hacker (-s;-) m, **Fleisch'hauer** m (-s;-) butcher

fleischig ['flaɪʃɪç] adj fleshy; meaty

fleisch'lich adj carnal

Fleisch'markt m meat market

Fleisch'pastete f meat pie

Fleisch'saft m meat juice, gravy

Fleisch'salat m diced-meat salad

Fleisch'speise f meat course

Fleisch'spieß m skewer

Fleischwerdung ['flaɪʃverdʊŋ] f (-;) incarnation

Fleisch'wolf m meat grinder

Fleisch'wunde f flesh wound, laceration

Fleisch'wurst f pork sausage

Fleiß [flaɪs] m (-es;) diligence, industry; **mit F.** intentionally

fleißig ['flaɪsɪç] adj diligent, hardworking

flektieren [flɛk'tiːrən] tr inflect

fletschen ['flɛtʃən] tr bare (teeth)

Flexion [flɛk'sjoːn] f (-;-en) (gram) inflection

flicken ['flɪkən] tr patch, repair || **Flicken** m (-s;-) patch

Flick'schuster m cobbler

Flick'werk n patchwork; hotchpotch; (Pfuscherei) bungling job

Flick'zeug n repair kit

Flieder ['fliːdər] m (-s;-) lilac

Fliege ['fliːgə] f (-;-n) fly; (coll) bow tie

fliegen ['fliːgən] §57 tr fly, pilot || intr (SEIN) fly; (coll) get sacked; **in die Luft f.** blow up

Flie'genfenster n window screen

Flie'gengewicht n flyweight division

Fliegengewichtler ['fliːgəngəvɪçtlər] m (-s;-) flyweight (boxer)

Flie'gengitter n screen

Flie'genklappe f, **Flie'genklatsche** f fly swatter

Flie'genpilz m toadstool

Flie'ger m (-s;-) flyer

Flieger- comb.fm. air-force; air, aerial; flying; airman's

Flie'gerabwehr f anti-aircraft defense

Flie'geralarm m air-raid alarm

Flie'gerangriff m air raid

Flie'gerheld m (aer) ace

Flie'gerhorst m air base

Flie'gerin f (-;-nen) flyer

Flie'gerschaden m air-raid damage

fliehen ['fliːən] §75 tr run away from; avoid || intr (SEIN) flee

Flieh'kraft f (-;) centrifugal force

Fliese ['fliːzə] f (-;-n) tile

Flie'senleger m tiler, tile man

Fließband ['fliːsbant] n (-[e]s;-er) assembly line

fließen ['fliːsən] §76 intr (SEIN) flow

flie'ßend adj (Wasser) running; (fig) fluent

Fließheck ['fliːshɛk] n (aut) fastback

Fließpapier ['fliːspapiːr] n blotting paper

flimmern ['flɪmərn] intr glimmer; glisten, shimmer; flicker

flink [flɪŋk] adj nimble, quick; **mach mal f.!** get a move on!

Flinte ['flɪntə] f (-;-n) shotgun; gun

Flin'tenlauf m gun barrel

flirren ['flɪrən] intr shimmer

Flirt [flɪrt] m (-s;-s) flirtation; boyfriend, girlfriend

flirten ['flɪrtən] intr flirt

Flitter ['flɪtər] m (-s;-) sequins; (Scheinglanz) flashiness

Flit'terglanz m flashiness

Flit'tergold n gold tinsel

Flit'terkram m trinkets

Flit'terstaat m flashy clothes

Flit'terwochen pl honeymoon

flitzen ['flɪtsən] intr (SEIN) flit

flocht [flɔxt] pret of flechten

Flocke ['flɔkə] f (-;-n) flake; tuft

flog [floːk] pret of fliegen

floh [floː] pret of fliehen || **Floh** m (-s;-e) flea; **j-m e-n F. ins Ohr setzen** put a bug in s.o.'s ear

Floh'hüpfspiel n tiddlywinks

Flor [floːr] m (-s;-e) bloom || m (-s;-e & -e) gauze; (tex) nap, pile

Flor'band n (-[e]s;-er) crepe; mourning band

Florett [flo'rɛt] n (-s;-e) foil

florieren [flo'riːrən] intr flourish

Floskel ['flɔskəl] f (-;-n) rhetorical ornament, flowery phrase

Floß [floːs] n (-es;-e) raft

Flosse ['flɔsə] f (-;-n) fin; (aer) stabilizer

flößen ['fløːsən] tr float

Flöte ['fløːtə] f (-;-n) flute; (cards) flush

flöten ['fløːtən] tr play on the flute || intr play the flute; **f. gehen** (fig) go to the dogs

flott [flɔt] adj afloat; brisk, lively; gay; chic, dashing

Flotte ['flɔtə] f (-;-n) fleet

Flot'tenstützpunkt m naval base

flott'gehend adj (com) brisk, lively

Flottille [flɔ'tɪljə] f (-;-n) flotilla

flott'machen tr set afloat; (fig) get going again

Flöz [fløːts] n (-es;-e) (min) seam

Fluch [fluːx] m (-[e]s;-e) curse

fluchen ['fluːxən] intr curse

Flucht [fluxt] f (-;-en) flight; escape; straight line, alignment; (Häuser-) row; (Spielraum) space, leeway; (Zimmer-) suite; **außerhalb der F. out of line; in die F. schlagen** put to flight

flüchten ['flʏçtən] ref (an acc, in acc) take refuge (in), have recourse (to) || intr (SEIN) flee; escape; (vor dat) run away (from)

flüchtig ['flʏçtɪç] adj fugitive; fleeting; cursory, superficial; hurried; (chem) volatile; **f. sein** to be on the run; **f. werden** escape, flee

Flüch'tigkeitsfehler m oversight, slip

Flüchtling ['flʏçtlɪŋ] m (-s;-) fugitive; refugee

Flücht'lingslager n refugee camp

Flug [fluːk] m (-[e]s;-e) flight

Flug'abwehr f anti-aircraft defense

Flugabwehr- comb.fm. anti-aircraft

Flug'anschluß m plane connection

Flug'aufgabe f, **Flug'auftrag** m (aer) mission

Flug'bahn f line of flight; trajectory

Flug'blatt n leaflet, flyer

Flügel ['flygəl] *m* (-s;-) wing; (*e-r Doppeltür*) leaf; (mus) grand piano
Flü'geladjutant *m* aide-de-camp
Flü'gelfenster *n* casement window
Flü'gelmutter *f* wing nut
Flü'gelschlag *m* flap of the wings
Flü'gelschraube *f* thumb screw
Flü'gelschraubenmutter *f* wing nut
Flü'geltür *f* folding door
Flug'gast *m* (aer) passenger
flügge ['flygə] *adj* (*Vogel*) fledged (fig) ready to go on one's own
Flug'gesellschaft *f* airline company
Flug'hafen *m* airport
Flug'hafenbefeuerung *f* airport lights
Flug'kapitän *m* captain, pilot
Flug'karte *f* plane ticket; aeronautical chart
flug'klar *adj* ready for take-off
Flug'körper *m* missile; space vehicle
Flug'leitung *f* air-traffic control
Flug'linie *f* air route; airline
Flug'meldesystem *n* air-raid warning system
Flug'motor *m* aircraft engine
Flug'ortung *f* (aer) navigation
Flug'plan *m* flight schedule
Flug'platz *m* airfield, airport
Flug'post *f* air mail
Flug'preis *m* air fare
flugs [fluks] *adv* quickly; at once
Flug'schein *m* plane ticket
Flug'schneise *f* air lane
Flug'schrift *f* pamphlet
Flug'strecke *f* flying distance
Flug'stützpunkt *m* air base
flug'tauglich, flug'tüchtig *adj* airworthy
Flug'techniker -in §6 *mf* aeronautical engineer
Flug'verbot *n* (aer) grounding
Flug'verkehr *m* air traffic
Flug'wesen *n* aviation; aeronautics
Flug'wetter *n* flying weather
Flug'zeug *n* airplane, aircraft
Flug'zeugabwehrgeschütz *n*, **Flug'zeugabwehrkanone** *f* anti-aircraft gun
Flug'zeugführer *m* pilot; **zweiter F.** co-pilot, second officer
Flug'zeugführerschein *m* pilot's license
Flug'zeuggeschwader *n* (consisting of 3 squadrons of 9 planes each)
Flug'zeugkreuzer *m*, **Flug'zeugmutterschiff** *n* seaplane tender, seaplane carrier
Flug'zeugrumpf *m* fuselage
Flug'zeugstaffel *f* squadron (consisting of 9 planes)
Flug'zeugträger *m* aircraft carrier
Flug'zeugwerk *n* aircraft factory
Flunder ['flundər] *f* (-;-n) flounder
Flunkerei [fluŋkə'raɪ] *m* (-s;-) fibber
flunkern ['fluŋkərn] *intr* fib
Flunsch [fluntʃ] *m* (-es;-e) face; **e-n F. ziehen** (or **machen**) make a face
Fluor ['flu·ər] *n* (-s;) fluorine
Fluoreszenz [flu·ɔres'tsents] *f* (-;) fluorescence; fluorescent light
Fluorid [flu·ɔ'riːt] *n* (-[e]s;-e) fluoride
Flur [fluːr] *m* (-[e]s;-e) entrance hall; hallway || *f* (-;-en) open farmland; meadow; community farmland

Flur'garderobe *f* hallway closet
Fluß [flus] *m* (Flusses; Flüsse) river; flow; (metal) fusion; (phys) flux
flußab'wärts *adv* downstream
flußauf'wärts *adv* upstream
Fluß'bett *n* riverbed, channel
Flüßchen ['flʏsçən] *n* (-s;-) rivulet
flüssig ['flʏsɪç] *adj* liquid; fluid; (Gelder) ready; **f. machen** convert into cash || *adv* fluently
Flüs'sigkeit *f* (-;-en) liquid, fluid; (fig) fluency; (fin) liquidity
Flüs'sigkeitsmaß *n* liquid measure
Fluß'pferd *n* hypopotamus
flüstern ['flʏstərn] *tr & intr* whisper
Flü'sterparole *f* rumor
Flut [fluːt] *f* (-;-en) flood; waters; high tide
fluten ['fluːtən] *tr* flood || *intr* (SEIN) flow, pour
Flut'grenze *f* high-water mark
Flut'licht *n* floodlight
Flut'linie *f* high-water mark
Flut'wasser *n* tidewater
Flut'welle *f* tidal wave
Flut'zeit *f* flood tide, high tide
focht [fɔxt] *pret* of fechten
Focksegel ['fɔkzeːgəl] *n* (-s;-) foresail
fohlen ['foːlən] *intr* foal || **Fohlen** *n* (-s;-) foal
Folge ['fɔlgə] *f* (-;-n) sequence; consequence; succession; series; (*e-s Romans*) continuation; (*e-r Zeitschrift*) number; **die Folgen tragen** take the consequences; **in der F.** subsequently
folgen ['fɔlgən] *intr* (dat) obey || *intr* (SEIN) (dat) follow; (dat) succeed; (aus) ensue (from)
folgendermaßen ['fɔlgəndərmaːsən] *adv* in the following manner, as follows
fol'genschwer *adj* momentous, grave
fol'gerichtig *adj* logical, consistent
folgern ['fɔlgərn] *tr* infer, conclude
Fol'gerung *f* (-;-en) inference, conclusion
Fol'gesatz *m* (gram) result clause
fol'gewidrig *adj* inconsistent
Fol'gezeit *f*—**in der F.** in subsequent times
folglich ['fɔlklɪç] *adv* consequently
folgsam ['fɔlkzaːm] *adj* obedient
Foliant [fol'jant] *m* (-en;-en) folio
Folie ['foːljə] *f* (-;-n) (metal) foil
Folter ['fɔltər] *f* (-;-n) torture; rack; **auf die F. spannen** put to the rack; (fig) keep in suspense
Fol'terbank *f* (-;ᵕe) rack
foltern ['fɔltərn] *tr* torture
Fol'terqual *f* torture
Fol'terverhör *n* third degree
Fön [føːn] *m* (-[e]s;-e) hand hairdryer
Fond [fõ] *m* (-s;-s) background; rear, back; (culin) gravy
Fonds [fõ] *m* (-s [fõs];-s [fõs]) fund
Fontäne [fɔn'tɛːnə] *f* (-;-n) fountain
foppen ['fɔpən] *tr* tease; bamboozle
Fopperei [fɔpə'raɪ] *f* (-;-en) teasing
forcieren [fɔr'siːrən] *tr* force; speed up
Förderband ['fœdərbant] *n* (-;ᵕer) conveyor belt

För'derer m (-s;-) promoter; patron

för'derlich adj useful; (dat) conducive (to)

fordern ['fɔrdərn] tr demand; (Recht) claim; (zum Zweikampf) challenge; (vor Gericht) summon

fördern ['fœrdərn] tr promote, back; (Kohle) produce; **förderndes Mitglied** social member; **zutage f.** bring to light

For'derung f (-;-en) demand, claim; debt; (zum Zweikampf) challenge

För'derung f (-;-en) promotion; support; encouragement; (min) output

Forelle [fo'rɛlə] f (-;-n) trout

Forke ['fɔrkə] f (-;-n) pitchfork

Form [fɔrm] f (-;-en) form; shape; mold; condition; (gram) voice; **die F. wahren** keep up appearances

formal [fɔr'mal] adj formal

Formalität [fɔrmali'tɛt] f (-;-en) formality

Format [fɔr'mat] n (-[e]s;-e) size, format; distinction, stature

Formel ['fɔrməl] f (-;-n) formula

for'melhaft adj (Wendung, Gebet) set

formell [fɔr'mɛl] adj formal

formen ['fɔrmən] tr form, shape, mold

For'menlehre f morphology

Form'fehler m defect; flaw; (jur) irregularity

formieren [fɔr'mirən] tr & ref line up

-förmig [fœrmɪç] comb.fm. -shaped

förmlich ['fœrmlɪç] adj formal || adv virtually; literally; formally

form'los adj shapeless; informal; unconventional; rude; (chem) amorphous

form'schön adj well-shaped, beautiful

Formular [fɔrmu'lar] n (-s;-e) form, blank

formulieren [fɔrmu'lirən] tr formulate; word, phrase

Formulie'rung f (-;-en) formulation; wording

form'vollendet adj perfectly shaped

forsch [fɔrʃ] adj dashing || adv briskly

forschen ['fɔrʃən] intr do research; (nach) search (for)

For'scher -in §6 mf researcher; scholar; explorer

For'schung f (-;-en) research

For'schungsanstalt f research center

Forst [fɔrst] m (-[e]s;-e) forest

Förster ['fœrstər] m (-s;-) forester; forest ranger

Forst'fach n forestry

Forst'mann m (-s;-leute) forester

Forst'revier n forest range

Forst'wesen n, **Forst'wirtschaft** f forestry

fort [fɔrt] adv away; gone, lost; (weiter) on; (vorwärts) forward; **ich muß f.** I must be off; **in e-m f.** continuously; **und so f.** and so forth || **Fort** [fɔr] n (-s;-s) (mil) fort

fortan' adv from now on, henceforth

Fort'bestand m continued existence

fort'bestehen §146 intr continue

fort'bewegen §56 tr move along || ref get about

fort'bilden ref continue one's studies

Fort'bildung f continuing education

fort'bleiben §62 intr (SEIN) stay away

Fort'dauer f continuance

fort'dauern intr continue; last

fort'fahren §71 tr hawl away; continue (to say); **f. zu** (inf) continue to (inf), go on (ger) || intr continue, go on || intr (SEIN) drive off, leave

Fort'fall m omission; discontinuation; **in F. kommen** be discontinued

fort'fallen §72 intr (SEIN) drop out; be omitted; be discontinued

fort'führen tr lead away; continue; (Geschäft) carry on; (Linie) extend

Fort'gang m departure; continuation; progress

fort'gehen §82 intr (SEIN) go away

fort'geschritten adj advanced; late

fort'gesetzt adj incessant

fort'kommen §99 intr (SEIN) go on, make progress; get away; **in der Welt f.** get ahead in the world || **Fortkommen** n (-s;) progress

fort'lassen §104 tr allow to go; omit

fort'laufen §105 intr (SEIN) run away

fort'laufend adj continuing; (Nummer) consecutive

fort'leben intr live on

fort'pflanzen tr propagate; spread || ref reproduce; propagate; spread

Fort'pflanzung f (-;) propagation

fort'reißen §53 tr tear away; **j-n mit sich f.** sweep s.o. off his feet; **sich f. lassen** be caried away

fort'schaffen tr remove

fort'scheren ref (coll) scram

fort'schreiten §86 intr (SEIN) progress, advance

Fort'schritt m progress; improvement

fort'schrittlich adj progressive

fort'setzen tr continue; resume

Fort'setzung f (-;-en) continuation; sequel; installment; **F. folgt** to be continued

fort'während adj continual; lasting, permanent || adv all the time, always

Fossil [fɔ'sil] n (-s;-ien [jən]) fossil

foul [faul] adj foul, dirty || **Foul** n (-s;-) (sport) foul; **ein F. begehen an** (dat) commit a foul against

foulen ['faulən] tr (sport) foul

Foyer [fwa'je] n (-s;-s) foyer; (im Hotel) lobby

Fracht [fraxt] f (-;-en) freight, cargo

Fracht'brief m bill of lading

Frachter ['fraxtər] m (-s;-) freighter

Fracht'gut n freight, goods

Fracht'raum m cargo compartment; cargo capacity

Fracht'stück n package

Frack [frak] m (-[e]s;-e & -s) tails

Frack'schoß m coattail

Frage ['fragə] f (-;-n) question; **außer F. stehen** be out of the question; **e-e F. stellen** ask a question; **in F. stellen** call in question; **kommt nicht in F.!** nothing doing!

Fra'gebogen m questionnaire

fragen ['fragən] tr ask; **j-n f. nach** ask s.o. about; **j-n nach der Zeit f.** ask s.o. the time; **j-n f. um** ask s.o. for || ref wonder; **es fragt sich, ob** the question is whether || intr ask

Fra'gesatz m interrogative sentence; **abhängiger F.** indirect question
Fragesteller ['frɑːɡəʃtɛlər] m (-s;-) questioner
Fra'gewort n (-es;̈-er) interrogative
Fra'gezeichen n question mark
fraglich ['frɑːklɪç] adj questionable
fraglos ['frɑːkloːs] adv unquestionably
Fragment [frɑˈɡmɛnt] n (-[e]s;-e) fragment
frag'würdig adj questionable
Fraktion [frakˈtsjoːn] f (-;-en) (chem) fraction; (pol) faction
fraktionell [fraktsoˈnɛl] adj factional
Fraktur [frakˈtuːr] f (-;-en) fracture; Gothic type, Gothic lettering; **mit j-m F. reden** talk turkey with s.o.
frank [frɑŋk] adv—**f. und frei** quite frankly
Franke ['frɑŋkə] m (-n;-n) Franconian; (hist) Frank
Franken ['frɑŋkən] m (-[e]s;-) (Swiss) franc || n (-s;) Franconia
frankieren [frɑŋˈkiːrən] tr frank, put postage on
Fränkin ['frɛŋkɪn] f (-;-nen) Frank
franko ['frɑŋko] adv postage paid; **f. Berlin** freight paid to Berlin; **f. verzollt** free of freight and duty
Frank'reich n (-s;) France
Franse ['frɑnzə] f (-;-n) fringe
fransen ['frɑnzən] intr fray
Franzband ['frɑntsbant] m (-[e]s;̈-e) leather binding
Franz'branntwein m rubbing alcohol
Franzose [frɑnˈtsoːzə] m (-;-n) Frenchman; **die Franzosen** the French
Französin [frɑnˈtsøːzɪn] f (-;-nen) Frenchwoman
französisch [frɑnˈtsøːzɪʃ] adj French
frappant [frɑˈpant] adj striking
frappieren [frɑˈpiːrən] tr strike, astonish; (Wein) put on ice
fräsen ['frɛːzən] tr mill
fraß [frɑs] pret of **fressen** || **Fraß** m (-es;) fodder, food; (pel) garbage
Fratz [frats] m (-es;-e) brat
Fratze ['fratsə] f (-;-n) grimace; (coll) face; **e-e F. schneiden** make a face
frat'zenhaft adj grotesque
Frau [frau] f (-;-en) woman; lady; wife; (vor Namen) Mrs; **zur F. geben** give in marriage
Frauen- comb.fm. of women
Frau'enarzt m, **Frau'enärztin** f gynecologist
Frau'enheld m ladykiller
Frau'enkirche f Church of Our Lady
Frau'enkleidung f women's wear
Frau'enklinik f women's hospital
Frau'enleiden n gynecological disorder
Frau'enzimmer n (pej) woman, female
Fräulein ['frɔɪlaɪn] n (-s;-) young lady; (vor Namen) Miss
frau'lich adj womanly
frech [frɛç] adj brazen; fresh, smart
Frech'dachs m smart aleck
Frech'heit f (-;-en) impudence
Fregatte [freˈɡatə] f (-;-n) frigate
frei [frai] adj free; (Feld) open; (offen) frank; **auf freien Fuß setzen** release; **auf freier Strecke** (rr) outside the station; **die freien Berufe**

the professions; **freie Fahrt** (public sign) resume speed; **freies Spiel haben** have a free hand; **frei werden** (chem) be released; **ich bin so frei** thank you, I will have some; **sich frei machen** take off one's clothes || **Freie §5** n—**im Freien** out of doors; **ins Freie** out of doors, into the open
Frei'bad n outdoor swimming pool
Frei'bank f (-;̈-e) cheap-meat counter
frei'beruflich adj freelance
Frei'betrag m allowable deduction
Frei'brief m charter; (fig) license
Freier ['fraiər] m (-s;-) suitor
Frei'frau f baroness
Frei'gabe f release
frei'geben §80 tr release; **für den Verkehr f.** open to traffic || intr—**j-m f.** give s.o. (time) off
freigebig ['fraigeːbɪç] adj generous
Frei'gebigkeit f (-;) generosity
Frei'geist m freethinker
frei'geistig adj open-minded
frei'gestellt adj optional
frei'haben intr be off
Frei'hafen m free port
frei'halten §90 tr keep open; **j-n f. pay the tab for s.o.**
Frei'heit f (-;-en) freedom; **dichterische F.** poetic license
Frei'heitskrieg m war of liberation
Frei'heitsstrafe f imprisonment
Frei'herr m baron
Frei'karte f free ticket; (theat) complimentary ticket
Frei'korps n volunteer corps
frei'lassen §104 tr release, set free
Frei'lauf m coasting
frei'legen tr lay open, expose
frei'lich adv of course
Freilicht- comb.fm. open-air
frei'machen tr (Platz) vacate; (Straße) clear; (Brief) stamp; **den Arm f.** roll up one's sleeves || ref undress
Frei'marke f postage stamp
Frei'maurer m Freemason
Frei'maurerei f freemasonry
Frei'mut m frankness
frei'mütig adj frank, outspoken
frei'schaffend adj freelance
Frei'sinn m (pol) liberalism
frei'sinnig adj (pol) liberal
frei'sprechen §64 tr acquit
Frei'spruch m acquittal
frei'stehen §146 intr—**es steht Ihnen frei zu** (inf) you are free to (inf)
frei'stehend adj free-standing; (Gebäude) detached
Frei'stelle f scholarship
frei'stellen tr exempt; **j-m etw f.** leave it to s.o.'s discretion
Frei'stoß m (fb) free kick
Frei'tag m Friday
Frei'tod m suicide
Frei'treppe f outdoor stairway
Frei'wild n (& fig) fair game
frei'willig adj voluntary || **Freiwillige §5** mf (& mil) volunteer
Frei'zeichen n (telp) dial tone
Frei'zeit f spare time, leisure
Frei'zeitgestaltung f planning one's leisure time
freizügig ['fraitsyːɡɪç] adj unhampered

fremd [frɛmt] *adj* foreign; strange; someone else's; *(Name)* assumed
fremd'artig *adj* strange, odd
Fremde ['frɛmdə] *mf* foreigner; stranger || *f—aus der F.* from abroad; *in der F.* far from home; *in die F. gehen* go far from home; go abroad
Frem'denbuch *n* visitors' book
Frem'denführer –in §6 *mf* tour guide; *(Buch)* guidebook
Frem'denheim *n* boarding house
Frem'denlegion *f* foreign legion
Frem'denverkehr *m* tourism
Frem'denzimmer *n* guest room; spare room
Fremd'herrschaft *f* foreign domination
Fremd'körper *m* foreign body; *(pol)* alien element
fremdländisch ['frɛmtlɛndɪʃ] *adj* foreign
Fremdling ['frɛmtlɪŋ] *m* (-s;-) stranger
Fremd'sprache *f* foreign language
Fremd'wort *n* (-es;¨er) foreign word
frequentieren [frekvɛn'tirən] *tr* frequent
Frequenz [fre'kvɛnts] *f* (-;-en) frequency; *(Besucherzahl)* attendance
Freske ['frɛskə] *f* (-;-n), **Fres·ko** ['frɛsko] *n* (-s;-ken [kən]) fresco
Freßbeutel ['frɛsbɔɪtəl] *m* feed bag
Fresse ['frɛsə] *f* (-;-n) (sl) puss
fressen ['frɛsən] §70 *tr (von Tieren)* eat; feed on; (sl) devour; *(ätzen)* corrode, pit; (tech) freeze || *ref—sich satt f.* stuff oneself || *intr* (sl) eat; *(an dat)* gnaw (at)
Fresserei [frɛsə'raɪ] *f* (-;) gluttony
Freude ['frɔɪdə] *f* (-;-n) joy, pleasure
Freu'denbotschaft *f* glad tidings
Freu'denfeier *f*, **Freu'denfest** *n* celebration, happy occasion
Freu'denhaus *n* brothel
Freu'denmädchen *n* prostitute
freudig ['frɔɪdɪç] *adj* joyful, happy
freud'los *adj* joyless, sad
freuen ['frɔɪən] *tr* please || *ref* be happy; *(an dat)* be delighted (by); *(auf acc)* look forward (to); *(über acc)* be glad (about) || *impers—es freut mich* I am glad
Freund [frɔɪnt] *m* (-[e]s;-e) friend; boyfriend; *F. der Musik* music lover
Freundin ['frɔɪndɪn] *f* (-;-nen) friend; girlfriend
freund'lich *adj* friendly; cheerful
Freund'lichkeit *f* (-;) friendliness
Freund'schaft *f* (-;-en) friendship
Frevel ['frefəl] *m* (-s;-) outrage; crime; sacrilege
fre'velhaft *adj* wicked
freveln ['frefəln] *intr* commit an outrage; *am Gesetz f.* violate the law
Fre'veltat *f* outrage
Friede ['fridə] *m* (-ns;), **Frieden** ['fridən] *m* (-s;) peace
Frie'densrichter *m* justice of the peace
Frie'densschluß *m* conclusion of peace
Frie'densstifter –in §6 *mf* peacemaker
Frie'densverhandlungen *pl* peace negotiations
Frie'densvertrag *m* peace treaty

friedfertig ['fritfɛrtɪç] *adj* peaceable
Friedhof ['frithof] *m* cemetery
friedlich ['fritlɪç] *adj* peaceful
friedliebend ['fritlibənt] *adj* peace-loving
frieren ['frirən] §77 *intr* be cold; freeze || *impers—es friert mich* I'm freezing
Fries [fris] *m* (-es;-e) frieze
Frikadelle [frika'dɛlə] *f* (-;-n) meatball
frisch [frɪʃ] *adj* fresh; *(kühl)* cool; *(munter)* brisk || *adv* freshly; *f. gestrichen* (public sign) wet paint; *f. zu!* on with it! || **Frische** *f* (-;) freshness; coolness; briskness
Frisch'haltepackung *f* vacuum package
Friseur [fri'zǿr] *m* (-s;-e) barber
Friseur'laden *m* barbershop
Friseur'sessel *m* barber chair
Friseuse [fri'zøzə] *f* (-;-n) hairdresser
frisieren [fri'zirən] *tr (Dokumente)* doctor; (aut) soup up; *j-m die Haare f.* do s.o.'s hair
Frisier'haube *f* hair dryer; hair net
Frisier'kommode *f*, **Frisier'tisch** *m* dresser
Frist [frɪst] *f* (-;-en) time, period, term; (com, jur) grace; *die F. einhalten* meet the deadline
fristen ['frɪstən] *tr—das Leben f.* eke out a living
Frisur [fri'zur] *f* (-;-en) hairstyle
frivol [fri'vol] *adj* frivolous
froh [fro] *adj* glad, happy, joyful
froh'gelaunt *adj* cheerful
fröhlich ['frølɪç] *adj* gay, merry
froh'locken *intr* rejoice
Froh'sinn *m* good humor
fromm [from] *adj* pious, devout
Frömmelei [frœmə'laɪ] *f* (-;-en) sanctimoniousness; sanctimonious act
frommen ['frɔmən] *intr* (dat) profit
Frömmigkeit ['frœmɪçkaɪt] *f* (-;) piety
Frömmler –in ['frœmlər-ɪn] §6 *mf* hypocrite
Fron [fron] *f* (-;) drudgery; (hist) forced labor
frönen ['frønən] *intr* (dat) gratify
Fron'leichnam *m* Corpus Christi
Front [front] *f* (-;-en) (& mil) front
Front'abschnitt *m* (mil) sector
fror [fror] *pret of* **frieren**
Frosch [froʃ] *m* (-es;¨e) frog; *(Feuerwerkkörper)* firecracker; *sei kein F.!* don't be a party pooper
Frost [frost] *m* (-es;¨e) frost
Frost'beule *f* chilblain
frösteln ['frœstəln] *intr* feel chilly
Frosterfach ['frostərfax] *n* freezer compartment *(of refrigerator)*
frostig ['frostɪç] *adj* frosty; chilly
Frost'schutzmittel *n* antifreeze
Frottee [fro'te] *m & n* (-s;-s) terry cloth
frottieren [fro'tirən] *tr* rub down
Frottier'tuch *n* Turkish towel
Frucht [fruxt] *f* (-;¨e) fruit; foetus
fruchtbar ['fruxtbar] *adj* fruitful
frucht'bringend *adj* productive
Frücht'tebecher *m* fruit cup *(as dessert)*
fruchten ['fruxtən] *intr* bear fruit; have effect; be of use

Frucht'folge f rotation of crops
Frucht'knoten m (bot) pistil
frucht'los adj fruitless
Frucht'saft m fruit juice
Frucht'wechsel m rotation of crops
frugal [fru'gal] adj frugal
früh [fry] adj early || adv early; in the morning; **von f. bis spät** from morning till night || **Frühe** f (-;) early morning; **in aller F.** very early
früher ['fry-ər] adj earlier; former || adv earlier; sooner; formerly
frühestens ['fry-əstəns] adv at the earliest
Früh'geburt f premature birth
Früh'jahr n, **Frühling** ['fryliŋ] m (-s; -e) spring
Früh'lingsmüdigkeit f spring fever
früh'reif adj precocious
Früh'schoppen m eye opener (beer, wine)
Früh'stück n breakfast; **zweites F.** lunch
frühstücken ['fry/tykən] intr eat breakfast
früh'zeitig adj & adv (too) early
Fuchs [fuks] m (-es;ᵉe) fox; (Pferd) sorrel, chestnut; (educ) freshman
Fuchsie ['fuksjə] f (-n) fuchsia
fuchsig ['fuksɪç] adj red; (fig) furious, wild
Fuchs'jagd f fox hunt(ing)
fuchs'rot adj sorrel
Fuchs'schwanz m foxtail; (bot) amaranth; (carp) hand saw (with tapered blade)
fuchs'teufelswild adj hopping mad
Fuge ['fugə] f (-;-n) joint; (mus) fugue; **aus allen Fugen gehen** come apart; go to pieces, go to pot
fügen ['fygən] tr join; (verhängen) decree; (carp) joint || ref give in; **es fügte sich** it so happened
fügsam ['fyksɑm] adj compliant; (Haar) manageable
Fü'gung f (-;-en) (gram) construction; **F. des Himmels, F. Gottes** divine providence; **F. des Schicksals** stroke of fate; **göttliche F.** divine providence
fühlbar ['fylbɑr] adj tangible; noticeable; **sich f. machen** make itself felt
fühlen ['fylən] tr feel, touch; sense || ref feel; feel big || intr—**f. mit** feel for (s.o.); **f. nach** feel for, grope for
-fühlig [fylɪç] comb.fm. -feeling
Füh'lung f (-;) touch, contact; **F. nehmen mit** get in touch with
fuhr [fur] pret of **fahren**
Fuhre ['furə] f (-;-n) wagon load
führen ['fyrən] tr lead; guide; (Artikel) carry, sell; (Besprechungen) hold, conduct; (Bücher) keep; (Geschäft) run, manage; (Krieg) carry on; (Sprache) use; (Titel) bear; (Truppen) command; (Waffe) wield; (Fahrzeug) drive; (aer) pilot; **den Beweis f.** prove; **die Aufsicht f. über** (acc) superintend; **j-m den Haushalt f.** keep house for s.o. || ref conduct oneself || intr lead; (sport) be in the lead
Füh'rer -in §6 mf leader, guide; (aer)

pilot; (aut) driver; (com) manager; (sport) captain
Füh'rerschaft f (-;) leadership
Füh'rerschein m driver's license
Füh'rerscheinentzug m suspension of driver's license
Führhund ['fyrhunt] m Seeing Eye dog
Fuhr'park m (aut) fleet
Füh'rung f (-;-en) guidance; leadership; management; guided tour; behavior; (mil) command; (sport) lead
Füh'rungskraft f executive; **die Führungskräfte** management; (pol) authorities; **untere F.** junior executive
Füh'rungsschicht f (com) management
Füh'rungsspitze f top echelon
Fuhr'unternehmen n trucking
Fuhr'werk n cart, wagon; vehicle
Füllbleistift ['fylblaɪ/trft] m mechanical pencil
Fülle ['fylə] f (-;) fullness; abundance; wealth; (Körper-) plumpness
füllen ['fylən] tr fill || ref fill up || **Füllen** n (-s;-) foal, colt, filly
Fül'ler m (-s;-) fountain pen
Füll'federhalter m fountain pen
Füll'horn n cornucopia
Füllsel ['fylzəl] n (-s;-) stopgap; (beim Schreiben) padding; (culin) stuffing
Fül'lung f (-;-en) (Zahn-) filling; (Tür-) panel; (culin) stuffing
Fund [funt] m (-[e]s;-e) find; discovery
Fundament [fundɑ'ment] n (-[e]s;-e) foundation
fundamental [fundɑmen'tɑl] adj fundamental
Fund'büro n lost-and-found department
Fund'grube f (fig) mine, storehouse
fundieren [fun'dirən] tr lay the foundations of; found; establish; (Schuld) fund; **fundiertes Einkommen** unearned income; **gut fundiert** well-established
fünf [fynf] adj & pron five || **Fünf** f (-;-en) five
Fünf'eck n pentagon
fünfte ['fynftə] §9 adj & pron fifth
Fünftel ['fynftəl] n (-s;-) fifth (part)
fünf'zehn adj & pron fifteen || **Fünfzehn** f (-;-en) fifteen
fünf'zehnte §9 adj & pron fifteenth
Fünf'zehntel n (-s;-) fifteenth (part)
fünfzig ['fynftsɪç] adj fifty
fünf'ziger invar adj of the fifties; **die f. Jahre** the fifties
fünfzigste ['fynftsɪçstə] §9 adj & pron fiftieth
fungieren [fuŋ'girən] intr function; **f. als** function as, act as
Funk [fuŋk] m (-s;) radio
Funk'amateur m (rad) ham
Funk'bastler -in §6 mf (rad) ham
Fünkchen ['fyŋçən] n (-s;-) small spark; **kein F.** (fig) not an ounce
Funke ['fuŋkə] m (-ns;-n), **Funken** ['fuŋkən] m (-s;-) spark
funkeln ['fuŋkəln] intr sparkle; (Sterne) twinkle
fun'kelnagelneu' adj brand-new

funken ['funkən] tr radio, broadcast || intr spark
Fun'ker m (-s;-) radio operator
Funk'feuer n (aer) radio beacon
Funk'leitstrahl m radio beam
Funk'meßanlage f radar installation
Funk'meßgerät n radar
Funk'netz n radio network
Funk'peilung f radio direction finding
Funk'spruch m radiogram
Funk'streifenwagen m squad car
Funktionär –in [fuŋktsjə'nɛr(ɪn)] §8 mf functionary
für [fyr] prep (acc) for || Für n—das Für und Wider the pros and cons
Für'bitte f intercession
Furche ['furçə] f (-;-n) furrow; (Runzel) wrinkle; (Wagenspur) rut
furchen ['furçən] tr furrow; wrinkle
Furcht [furçt] f (-;) fear, dread
furchtbar ['furçtbar] adj terrible
fürchten ['fyrçtən] tr fear, be afraid of || ref (vor dat) be afraid (of)
fürchterlich ['fyrçtərlɪç] adj terrible, awful
furcht'erregend adj awe-inspiring
furcht'los adj fearless
furchtsam ['furçtzam] adj timid, shy
Furie ['furjə] f (-;-n) (myth) Fury
Furnier [fur'nir] n (-s;-e) veneer
Furore [fu'rorə] f (-;) & n (-s;) stir; F. machen cause a stir, be a big hit
Für'sorge f care; welfare
Für'sorgeamt n welfare department
Fürsorger –in ['fyrzorgər(ɪn)] §6 mf social worker; welfare officer
fürsorglich ['fyrzorklɪç] adj thoughtful
Für'sprache f intercession; F. einlegen intercede
Für'sprecher –in §6 mf intercessor
Fürst [fyrst] m (-en;-en) prince
Fürstentum ['fyrstəntum] n (-s;ᵉer) principality
Fürstin ['fyrstɪn] f (-;-nen) princess
fürst'lich adj princely
Furt [furt] f (-;-en) ford
Furunkel [fu'runkəl] m (-s;-) boil
Für'wort n (-[e]s;ᵉer) pronoun

Furz [furts] m (-es;ᵉe) (vulg) fart
Fusel ['fuzəl] m (-s;) (coll) booze
Fusion [fu'sjon] f (-;-en) (com) merger
Fuß [fus] m (-es;ᵉe) foot; auf freien Fuß setzen set free; zu Fuß on foot; zu Fuß gehen walk
Fuß'abdruck m footprint
Fuß'ball m soccer; football
Fuß'bank f (-;ᵉe) footstool
Fuß'bekleidung f footwear
Fuß'boden m floor; flooring
Fussel ['fusəl] f (-;-n) fuzz
fußen ['fusən] intr—f. auf (dat) be based on; rely on
Fuß'fall m prostration
fuß'fällig adv on one's knees
fuß'frei adj ankle-length
Fuß'freiheit f leg room
Fuß'gänger m (-s;-) pedestrian
Fuß'gelenk n ankle joint
Fuß'gestell n pedestal
–füßig [fysɪç] comb.fm. –footed
Fuß'knöchel m ankle
Fuß'leiste f baseboard, washboard
Füßling ['fyslɪŋ] m (-s;-e) foot (of stocking, sock, etc.)
Fuß'note f footnote
Fuß'pfad m footpath
Fuß'pilz m athlete's foot
Fuß'spur f footprint(s)
Fuß'stapfe f footstep
Fuß'steg m footbridge; footpath
Fuß'steig m footpath; sidewalk
Fuß'tritt m step; (Stoß) kick
futsch [futʃ] adj (coll) gone; (coll) ruined
Futter ['futər] n (-s;) fodder, feed; (e-s Mantels) lining
Futteral [futə'ral] n (-s;-e) case
Fut'terkrippe f crib; (sl) gravy train
Fut'terkrippensystem n (pol) spoils system
futtern ['futərn] intr (coll) eat heartily
füttern ['fytərn] tr feed; (Kleid, Mantel, Pelz) line
Fut'terneid m jealousy
Fut'terstoff m lining
Fut'tertrog m feed trough

G

G, g [ge] invar n G, g; (mus) G
gab [gap] pret of geben
Gabardine [gabar'dinə] m (-s;-) (tex) gabardine
Gabe ['gabə] f (-;-n) gift; donation; talent; (med) dose; milde G. alms
Gabel ['gabəl] f (-;-n) fork; (arti) bracket; (telp) cradle
Ga'belbein n wishbone
Ga'belbissen m tidbit
Ga'belfrühstück n brunch
gabelig ['gabəlɪç] adj forked
gabeln ['gabəln] tr pick up with a fork || ref divide, branch off
Ga'belstapler m forklift
Ga'belung f (-;-en) fork (in the road)

gackeln ['gakəln], gackern ['gakərn], gacksen ['gaksən] intr cackle, cluck
Gage ['gaʒə] f (-;-n) salary, pay
gähnen ['gɛnən] intr yawn
gaffen ['gafən] intr gape; stare
Gala ['gala] invar f gala, Sunday best
galant [ga'lant] adj courteous; galantes Abenteuer love affair
Galanterie [galantə'ri] f (-;-rien ['ri·ən]) courtesy; flattering word
Galaxis [ga'laksɪs] f (-;-xien [ksjən]) galaxy
Galeere [ga'lerə] f (-;-n) galley
Galerie [galə'ri] f (-;-rien ['ri·ən]) gallery
Galgen ['galgən] m (-s;-) gallows

Gal′genfrist *f* (coll) brief respite

Gal′genhumor *m* grim humor

Gal′genstrick *m*, **Gal′genvogel** *m* (coll) good-for-nothing

gälisch [′gɛlɪʃ] *adj* Gaelic

Galle [′galə] *f* (-;) gall, bile; (fig) bitterness

Gal′lenblase *f* gall bladder

Gal′lenstein *m* gallstone

Gallert [′galərt] *n* (-[e]s;-e), **Gallerte** [ga′lertə] *f* (-;-n) gelatine; jelly

gallig [′galɪç] *adj* bitter; grouchy

Gallone [ga′lonə] *f* (-;-n) gallon

Galopp [ga′lɔp] *m* (-[e]s;-s & -e) gallop; **im G. reiten** gallop; **in gestrecktem G.** at full gallop; **in kurzem G.** at a canter

galoppieren [galɔ′pirən] *intr* (SEIN) gallop

galt [galt] *pret of* **gelten**

galvanisieren [galvani′zirən] *tr* galvanize; electroplate

Gambe [′gambə] *f* (-;-n) bass viol

gammeln [′gaməln] *intr* bum around

Gammler [′gamlər] *m* (-s;-) hippie

Gamsbart [′gamsbart] *m* goatee

gang [gaŋ] *adj*—**g. und gäbe** customary ‖ **Gang** *m* (-[e]s;ֿe) walk, gait; (*e-r Maschine*) running, operation; (*im Hause*) hallway; (*zwischen Reihen*) aisle; (*Botengang*) errand; (*Röhre*) conduit; (*e-r Schraube*) thread; (anat) duct, canal; (aut) gear; (box) round; (culin) course; (min) vein, lode; (min) gallery; (mus) run; **außer G. setzen** stop; (aut) put in neutral; **erster G.** low gear; **es ist etw im G.** there is s.th. afoot; **im G. sein** be in operation; be in progress; **in G. bringen** (or setzen) set in motion; **in vollem G.** in full swing

Gang′art *f* gait

gangbar [′gaŋbar] *adj* passable; (*Münze*) current; (com) marketable

Gängelband [′gɛŋəlbant] *n*—**am G. führen** (fig) lead by the nose, dominate

-gänger [gɛŋər] *comb.fm.*, e.g., Fußgänger pedestrian

gängig [′gɛŋɪç] *adj see* gangbar

Gang′schaltung *f* (aut) gear shift

Gangster [′gɛŋstər] *m* (-s;-s) gangster

Ganove [ga′novə] *m* (-;-n) crook

Gans [gans] *f* (-;ֿe) goose

Gänseblümchen [′gɛnzəblymçən] *n* (-s;-) daisy

Gänsehaut [′gɛnzəhaut] *f* (coll) goose flesh, goose pimples

Gänseklein [′gɛnzəklain] *n* (-s;) (culin) giblets

Gänsemarsch [′gɛnzəmarʃ] *m* single file

Gänserich [′gɛnzərɪç] *m* (-s;-e) gander

ganz [gants] *adj* whole; all; total; intact; **im ganzen** in all ‖ *adv* entirely, quite; **g. und gar** completely; **g. und gar nicht** not at all ‖ **Ganze** §5 *n* whole; **aufs G. gehen** go all the way

Ganz′aufnahme *f* full-length photograph

Gänze [′gɛntsə] *f* (-;)—**in G.** in its entirety; **zur G.** entirely

Ganz′fabrikat *n* finished product

Ganz′leinenband *m* (-[e]s;ֿe) cloth-bound volume

gänzlich [′gɛntslɪç] *adj* entire, total

ganz′seitig *adj* full-page

ganz′tägig *adj* full-time

gar [gar] *adj* (culin) well done; (metal) refined ‖ *adv* quite, very; (*sogar*) even; **gar nicht** not at all

Garage [ga′raʒə] *f* (-;-n) garage

Garan-tie [garan′ti] *f* (-;-tien [′ti·ən]) guarantee

garantieren [garan′tirən] *tr* guarantee ‖ *intr*—**g. dafür, daß** guarantee that

Garaus [′garaus] *m* (-;) finishing blow

Garbe [′garbə] *f* (-;-n) sheaf, shock

Garde [′gardə] *f* (-;-n) guard

Gardenie [gar′denjə] *f* (-;-n) gardenia

Garderobe [gardə′robə] *f* (-;-n) wardrobe; (*Kleiderablage*) cloakroom; (theat) dressing room

Gardero′benmarke *f* hat or coat check

Gardero′benständer *m* coatrack, hatrack

Garderobiere [gardəro′bjerə] *f* (-;-n) cloakroom attendant

Gardine [gar′dinə] *f* (-;-n) curtain

Gardi′nenhalter *m* tieback

Gardi′nenpredigt *f* (coll) dressing down

Gardi′nenstange *f* curtain rod

gären [′gɛrən] §78 *intr* ferment; bubble

Gärmittel [′gɛrmɪtəl] *n* ferment; leaven

Garn [garn] *n* (-[e]s;-e) yarn; thread; snare; (fig) trap; (fig) yarn

Garnele [gar′nelə] *f* (-;-n) shrimp

garnieren [gar′nirən] *tr* garnish; trim

Garnison [garni′zon] *f* (-;-en) garrison

Garnitur [garni′tur] *f* (-;-en) trimming; set (*of matching objects*); (mach) fittings, mountings; (mil) uniform

garstig [′garstɪç] *adj* ugly; nasty

Garten [′gartən] *m* (-s;ֿe) garden

Gar′tenanlage *f* gardens, grounds

Gar′tenarbeit *f* gardening

Gar′tenarchitekt *m* landscape gardener

Gar′tenbau *m* gardening; horticulture

Gar′tenlaube *f* arbor

Gar′tenmesser *n* pruning knife

Gärtner [′gɛrtnər] *m* (-s;-) gardener

Gärtnerei [gɛrtnə′rai] *f* (-;-en) gardening; truck farm; nursery

Gä′rung *f* (-;) fermentation

Gas [gas] *n* (-es;-e) gas; **Gas geben** step on the gas

Gas′anstalt *f* gasworks

gas′artig *adj* gaseous

Gas′behälter *m* gas tank

gas′förmig *adj* gaseous

Gas′hebel *m* (aut) accelerator

Gas′heizung *f* gas heat(ing)

Gas′herd *m* gas range

Gas′krieg *m* chemical warfare

Gas′leitung *f* gas main

Gas′messer *m* gas meter

Gasse [′gasə] *f* (-;-n) side street; **über die G. verkaufen** sell takeouts

Gas′senhauer *m* popular song

Gas′senjunge *m* urchin

Gast [gast] m (-[e]s;≃e) guest; boarder; (com) customer; (theat) guest performer; **zu Gast bitten** invite

Gäste buch ['gɛstəbux] n guest book; visitors' book

Gast freund m guest friend

gast freundlich adj hospitable

Gast freundschaft f hospitality

Gast geber m host

Gast geberin f hostess

Gast haus n, **Gast hof** m inn

Gast hörer -in §6 mf (educ) auditor

gastieren [gas'tirən] intr (telv, theat) appear as a guest

gast lich adj hospitable

Gast mahl n feast; banquet

Gast professor m visiting professor

Gast rolle f guest performance; **e-e G. geben** pay a flying visit

Gast spiel n (theat) guest performance

Gast stätte f restaurant

Gast stube f dining room

Gast wirt m innkeeper

Gast wirtschaft f restaurant

Gas uhr f gas meter

Gas werk n gas works

Gas zähler m gas meter

Gatte ['gatə] m (-n;-n) husband; **Gatten** married couple

Gatter ['gatər] n (-s;-) grating; latticework; iron gate

Gattin ['gatɪn] f (-;-nen) wife

Gattung ['gatuŋ] f (-;-en) kind, type, species; family; (biol) genus

Gat tungsname m generic name; (gram) common noun

Gau [gau] m (-[e]s;-e) district

Gaukelbild ['gaukəlbɪlt] n illusion

gaukeln ['gaukəln] intr flit, flutter; perform hocus-pocus

Gau kelspiel n, **Gau kelwerk** n sleight of hand; delusion

Gaul [gaul] m (-[e]s;≃e) horse; nag

Gaumen ['gaumən] m (-s;-) palate

Gauner ['gaunər] m (-s;-) rogue; swindler

Gaunerei [gaunə'rai] f (-;-en) swindling, cheating

gaunern ['gaunərn] intr swindle

Gau nersprache f thieves' slang

Gaze ['gazə] f (-;-n) gauze; cheesecloth

Gazelle [ga'tselə] f (-;-n) gazelle

Geächtete [gə'ɛçtətə] §5 mf outlaw

Geächze [gə'ɛçtsə] n (-s) moaning

geartet [gə'artət] adj—**anders g. sein** be of a different disposition

Gebäck [gə'bɛk] n (-s) baked goods, cookies

geballt [gə'balt] adj concentrated; dense; (Schnee) hardened; (Faust) clenched; (Stil) succinct

gebannt [gə'bant] adj spellbound

gebar [gə'bar] pret of **gebären**

Gebärde [gə'bɛrdə] f (-;-n) gesture

gebärden [gə'bɛrdən] ref behave

Gebär denspiel n gesticulation

gebaren [gə'barən] ref behave, act ‖ **Gebaren** n (-s) behavior

gebären [gə'bɛrən] §79 tr bear ‖ **Gebären** n (-s) childbirth; labor

Gebär mutter f (anat) uterus

Gebär mutterkappe f diaphragm

Gebäude [gə'bɔrdə] n (-s;-) building

gebefreudig ['gebəfrɔrdɪç] adj openhanded

Gebein [gə'bain] n (-[e]s;-e) bones; **Gebeine** bones; mortal remains

Gebell [gə'bɛl] n (-[e]s;), **Gebelle** [gə'bɛlə] n (-s;) barking

geben ['gebən] §80 tr give; yield; (Gelegenheit) afford; (Laut) utter; (Karten) deal; **Feuer g.** give (s.o.) a light; (mil) open fire; **viel g. auf** (acc) set great store by; **von sich g.** utter; throw up; (Rede) deliver; (chem) give off ‖ ref give; (Kopfweh, usw.) get better; **sich g. als** pretend to be; **sich gefangen g.** surrender ‖ impers—**es gibt** there is, there are; **es wird Regen geben** it's going to rain

Ge ber -in §6 mf giver, donor

Gebet [gə'bet] n (-[e]s;-e) prayer

gebeten [gə'betən] pp of **bitten**

Gebiet [gə'bit] n (-[e]s;-e) district, territory; (Fläche) area; (Fach) line; (Bereich) field, sphere

gebieten [gə'bitən] §58 tr (Stillschweigen) impose; (Ehrfurcht) command; (verlangen) demand; **j-m g.,** **etw zu tun** order s.o. to do s.th. ‖ intr (über acc) have control (over); (dat) control

Gebieter [gə'bitər] m (-s;-) master; ruler; commander; governor

Gebieterin [gə'bitərɪn] f (-;-nen) mistress; (des Hauses) lady

gebieterisch [gə'bitərɪʃ] adj imperious

Gebilde [gə'bɪldə] n (-s;-) shape, form; structure; (geol) formation

gebildet [gə'bɪldət] adj educated

Gebirge [gə'bɪrgə] n (-s;-) mountain range, mountains; **festes G.** bedrock

gebirgig [gə'bɪrgɪç] adj mountainous

Gebirgs- [gəbɪrks] comb.fm. mountain

Gebirgs bewohner -in §6 mf mountaineer

Gebirgs kamm m, **Gebirgs rücken** m mountain ridge

Gebirgs zug m mountain range

Ge biß [gə'bɪs] n (-bisses;-bisse) teeth; false teeth; (am Zaum) bit

gebissen [gə'bɪsən] pp of **beißen**

Gebläse [gə'blezə] n (-s;-) bellows; blower; (aut) supercharger

geblieben [gə'blibən] pp of **bleiben**

Geblök [gə'bløk] n (-[e]s;) bleating

geblümt [gə'blymt] adj flowered

Geblüt [gə'blyt] n (-[e]s;) (& fig) blood

geboren [gə'borən] pp of **gebären** ‖ adj born; native; **geborene** nee

geborgen [gə'bɔrgən] pp of **bergen** ‖ adj safe

Gebor genheit f (-;) safety, security

geborsten [gə'bɔrstən] pp of **bersten**

Gebot [gə'bot] n (-[e]s;-e) order, command; commandment; (Angebot) bid

geboten [gə'botən] pp of **bieten** ‖ adj requisite; **dringend g.** imperative

Gebr. abbr. (Gebrüder) Brothers

gebracht [gə'braxt] pp of **bringen**

gebrannt [gə'brant] pp of **brennen**

Gebräu [gə'brɔɪ] n (-[e]s;-e) brew

Gebrauch [gə'braux] m (-s;⁼e) use; usage; (Sitte) custom

gebrauchen [gə'brauxən] tr use, employ

gebräuchlich [gə'brɔɪçlɪç] adj usual; in use; (gemein) common

Gebrauchs′anweisung f directions

Gebrauchs′fertig adj ready for use; (Kaffee, usw.) instant

Gebrauchs′graphik f commercial art

Gebrauchs′gut n commodity

Gebrauchs′muster n registered pattern

gebraucht [gə'brauxt] adj second-hand

Gebraucht′wagen m used car

Gebrechen [gə'breçən] n (-s;-) physical disability, infirmity

gebrech′lich adj frail, weak; rickety

gebrochen [gə'brɔxən] pp of brechen

Gebrüder [gə'brydər] pl brothers

Gebrüll [gə'bryl] n (-[e]s;) roaring; bellowing; lowing

Gebühr [gə'byr] f (-;-en) charge, fee; due, what is due; nach G. deservedly; über G. excessively; zu ermäßigter G. at a reduced rate

gebühren [gə'byrən] intr (dat) be due to || impers ref—es gebührt sich it is proper

gebüh′rend adj due; (entsprechend) appropriate || adv duly

gebüh′renfrei adj free of charge

gebüh′renpflichtig adj chargeable

gebunden [gə'bundən] pp of binden || adj bound; (Hitze) latent; (Preise) controlled; (Kapital) tied-up; an (acc) (chem) combined with; gebundene Rede verse

Geburt [gə'burt] f (-;-en) birth

Gebur′tenbeschränkung f birth control

Gebur′tenregelung f birth control

Gebur′tenrückgang m decline in births

gebürtig [gə'byrtɪç] adj native

Geburts′anzeige f announcement of birth; registration of birth

Geburts′fehler n congenital defect

Geburts′helfer –in §6 mf obstetrician || f midwife

Geburts′hilfe f obstetrics

Geburts′mal n birth mark

Geburts′recht n birthright

Geburts′schein m birth certificate

Geburts′tag m birthday

Geburts′tagskind n person celebrating his or her birthday

Geburts′wehen pl labor pains

Geburts′zange f forceps

Gebüsch [gə'byʃ] n (-es;-e) thicket, underbrush; clump of bushes

Geck [gek] m (-en;-en) dude

geckenhaft [gek'kenhaft] adj flashy

gedacht [gə'daxt] pp of denken

Gedächtnis [gə'deçtnɪs] n (-ses;) memory; aus dem G. by heart; im G. behalten bear in mind; zum G. (genit or an acc) in memory of

Gedächt′nisfeier f lapse of memory

Gedächt′nisrede f memorial address

gedämpft [gə'dempft] adj muffled; hushed, quiet; (Licht, Stimme) subdued; (culin) stewed

Gedanke [gə'dankə] m (-ns;-n) thought; notion, idea; etw in Ge-

danken tun do s.th. absent-mindedly; in Gedanken sein be preoccupied; sich [dat] Gedanken machen über (acc) worry about

Gedan′kenblitz m (iron) brain wave

Gedan′kenfolge f, **Gedan′kengang** m train of thought

gedan′kenlos adj thoughtless; absent-minded; irresponsible

Gedan′kenpunkt m suspension point

Gedan′kenstrich m (typ) dash

Gedan′kenübertragung f telepathy

gedank′lich adj mental; intellectual

Gedärme [gə'dermə] pl intestines

Gedeck [gə'dek] n (-[e]s;-e) cover; table setting; menu

gedeihen [gə'daɪ·ən] §81 intr (SEIN) thrive; succeed || Gedeihen n (-s;) prosperity; success

Gedenk- [gədenk] comb.fm. memorial; commemorative

gedenken [gə'denkən] §66 intr (genit) think of, be mindful of; remember; mention; g. zu (inf) intend to (inf) || Gedenken n (-s;) memory

gedeucht [gə'dɔɪçt] pp of dünken

Gedicht [gə'dɪçt] n (-[e]s;-e) poem; (fig) dream

gediegen [gə'digən] adj (Gold) solid; (Silber) sterling; (Arbeit) excellent; (Kenntnisse) thorough; (Möbel) solidly made; (Charakter) sterling; (coll) very funny

gedieh [gə'di] pret of gedeihen

gediehen [gə'di·ən] pp of gedeihen

Gedränge [gə'drenə] n (-s;-) pushing; crowd; difficulties; (fb) scrimmage

gedrängt [gə'drent] adj crowded, packed; (Sprache) concise

gedroschen [gə'drɔʃən] pp of dreschen

gedrückt [gə'drykt] adj depressed

gedrungen [gə'druŋən] pp of dringen || adj compact; stocky; squat; (Sprache) concise

Geduld [gə'dult] f (-;) patience

gedulden [gə'duldən] ref wait (patiently)

geduldig [gə'duldɪç] adj patient

Geduld′spiel n puzzle

gedungen [gə'duŋən] pp of dingen

gedunsen [gə'dunzən] adj bloated

gedurft [gə'durft] pp of dürfen

geehrt [gə'ert] adj—Sehr geehrte Herren! Dear Sirs; Sehr geehrter Herr X! Dear Mr. X

geeignet [gə'aɪgnət] adj suitable, right; qualified; appropriate

Gefahr [gə'far] f (-;-en) danger; (Wagnis) risk; G. laufen zu (inf) run the risk of (ger)

gefährden [gə'ferdən] tr jeopardize

gefährlich [gə'ferlɪç] adj dangerous

gefahr′los adj safe

Gefährt [gə'fert] n (-[e]s;-e) carriage

Gefährte [gə'fertə] m (-n;-n), **Gefährtin** [gə'fertɪn] f (-;-nen) companion; spouse

Gefälle [gə'felə] n (-s;-) pitch; slope

gefallen [gə'falən] adj fallen; (mil) killed in action || §72 ref—sich g. in (dat) take pleasure in || intr please; das gefällt mir I like this; das lasse ich mir nicht g. I won't stand for this || **Gefallen** *m* (-;-) favor || *n* (-s;) (an *dat*) pleasure (in); **j-m etw zu G. tun** do s.th. to please s.o.; **nach G.** as one pleases; at one's descretion

gefällig [gə'fɛliç] *adj* pleasing; obliging; kind; **j-m g. sein** do s.o. a favor; **Kaffee g.?** would you care for coffee?; **was ist g.?** what can I do for you?; **würden Sie so g. sein zu** (*inf*)? would you be so kind as to (*inf*)?

Gefäl'ligkeit *f* (-;-en) favor

gefälligst [gə'fɛliçst] *adv* if you please; please

gefangen [gə'faŋən] *pp* of **fangen** || *adj* captive; **g. nehmen** take prisoner || **Gefangene** §5 *mf* captive, prisoner

Gefan'genenlager *n* prison camp; (mil) prisoner-of-war camp

Gefan'gennahme *f* (-;) capture; arrest

gefan'gennehmen §116 *tr* take prisoner

Gefan'genschaft *f* (-;) captivity; imprisonment; **in G. geraten** be taken prisoner

gefan'gensetzen *tr* imprison

Gefängnis [gə'fɛŋnis] *n* (-ses;-se) prison, jail; imprisonment

Gefäng'nisdirektor *m* warden

Gefäng'nisstrafe *f* prison term

Gefäng'niswärter **-in** §6 *mf* guard

Gefäß [gə'fɛs] *n* (-es;-e) vessel; jar

gefaßt [gə'fast] *adj* calm, composed; **g. auf** (*acc*) ready for

Gefecht [gə'fɛçt] *n* (-[e]s;-e) fight, battle, action

Gefechts'auftrag *m* (mil) objective

Gefechts'kopf *m* warhead

Gefechts'lage *f* tactical situation

Gefechts'stand *m* command post

gefeit [gə'fart] *adj* (gegen) immune (from), proof (against)

Gefieder [gə'fidər] *n* (-s;-) plumage

gefleckt [gə'flɛkt] *adj* spotted

geflissentlich [gə'flisəntliç] *adj* intentional, willful

geflochten [gə'flɔxtən] *pp* of **flechten**

geflogen [gə'flogən] *pp* of **fliegen**

geflohen [gə'flo·ən] *pp* of **fliehen**

geflossen [gə'flɔsən] *pp* of **fließen**

Geflügel [gə'flygəl] *n* (-s;) fowl; (*Federvieh*) poultry

Geflü'gelmagen *m* gizzard

Geflunker [gə'fluŋkər] *n* (-s;) (coll) fibbing

Geflüster [gə'flystər] *n* (-s;) whisper

Gefolge [gə'fɔlgə] *n* (-s;-) retinue; **in seinem G.** in its wake

Gefolgschaft [gə'fɔlkʃaft] *f* (-;-en) allegiance; followers

gefräßig [gə'frɛsiç] *adj* gluttonous

Gefrä'ßigkeit *f* (-;) gluttony

Gefreite [gə'fraɪtə] §5 *m* private first class; lance corporal (Brit)

gefressen [gə'frɛsən] *pp* of **fressen**

Gefrieranlage [gə'friranlagə] *f* **Gefrierapparat** [gə'friraparat] *m* freezer

gefrieren [gə'frirən] §77 *intr* (SEIN) freeze

Gefrie'rer *m* (-s;-) freezer; deepfreeze

Gefrier'fach *n* freezing compartment

Gefrier'punkt *m* freezing point

Gefrier'schutz *m*, **Gefrier'schutzmittel** *n* antifreeze

gefroren [gə'frorən] *pp* of **frieren** || **Gefrorene** §5 *n* ice cream

Gefüge [gə'fygə] *n* (-s;-) structure, make-up; arrangement; texture

gefügig [gə'fygiç] *adj* pliant, pliable

Gefühl [gə'fyl] *n* (-[e]s;-e) feeling; feel; touch; sense; sensation

gefühl'los *adj* numb; callous

gefühls-, Gefühls- [gəfyls] *comb.fm.* of the emotions; emotional; sentimental; (anat) sensory

gefühls'betont *adj* emotional

Gefühlsduselei [gə'fylsduzəlaɪ] *f* (-;) sentimentalism, mawkishness

gefühls'selig *adj* mawkish

gefühl'voll *adj* sensitive; tender-hearted || *adv* with feeling

gefunden [gə'fundən] *pp* of **finden**

gefurcht [gə'furçt] *adj* furrowed

gegangen [gə'gaŋən] *pp* of **gehen**

gegeben [gə'gebən] *pp* of **geben** || *adj* given; (*Umstände*) existing; **gegebene Methode** best approach; **zu gegebener Zeit** at the proper time

gege'benfalls *adv* if necessary

gegen [gegən] *prep* (*acc*) towards; against; about, approximately; compared with; contrary to; in exchange for

gegen-, Gegen- *comb.fm.* anti-; counter-; contrary; opposite; back; in return

Ge'genantwort *f* rejoinder

Ge'genbeschuldigung *f* countercharge

Ge'genbild *n* counterpart

Gegend ['gegənt] *f* (-;-en) neighborhood, vicinity; region, district

gegeneinan'der *adv* against one another; towards one another

Ge'gengerade *f* back stretch

Ge'gengewicht *n* counterbalance; (am Rad) (aut) weight; **das G. halten** (*dat*) counterbalance

Ge'gengift *n* antidote

Ge'genkandidat **-in** §7 *mf* rival candidate

Ge'genklage *f* countercharge; counterclaim

Ge'genmittel *n* (gegen) remedy (for), antidote (against)

Ge'genrede *f* reply, rejoinder

Ge'gensatz *m* contrast; opposite, antithesis; (*Widerspruch*) opposition

gegensätzlich ['gegənzɛtsliç] *adj* contrary, opposite, antithetical

Ge'genschlag *m* counterplot

ge'genseitig *adj* mutual, reciprocal

Ge'genstand *m* object, thing; subject

gegenständlich ['gegənʃtɛntliç] *adj* objective; (fa) representational; (log) concrete

ge'genstandslos *adj* baseless; without purpose; irrelevant; (fa) non-representational

Ge'genstoß *m* (box) counterpunch; (mil) counterthrust

Ge'genstück *n* counterpart

Ge'genteil *n* contrary, opposite; **im G.** on the contrary

ge'genteilig *adj* contrary, opposite

gegenü'ber *prep* (*dat*) opposite to; across from; with regard to; compared with

gegenü'berstellen *tr* (*dat*) place opposite to; (*dat*) confront with; (*dat*)
contrast with

Gegenü'berstellung *f* confrontation;
comparison; (*auf e-r Wache*) line-up

Gegenwart ['gegɔnvart] *f* (-;) present;
present time; (*gram*) present tense

gegenwärtig ['gegɔnvertiç] *adj* present,
current || *adv* at present; nowadays

Ge'genwehr *f* defense, resistance

Ge'genwind *m* head wind

Ge'genwirkung *f* (auf *acc*) reaction
(to)

ge'genzeichnen *tr* countersign

Ge'genzug *m* countermove

geglichen [gɔ'gliçɔn] *pp* of gleichen

geglitten [gɔ'glitɔn] *pp* of gleiten

Gegner –in ['gegnɔr(ɪn)] §6 *mf* oppo-
nent, rival || *m* (mil) enemy

gegnerisch ['gegnɔrɪʃ] *adj* adverse;
antagonistic; opposing; (mil) enemy

gegolten [gɔ'goltɔn] *pp* of gelten

gegoren [gɔ'gorɔn] *pp* of gären

gegossen [gɔ'gosɔn] *pp* of gießen

gegriffen [gɔ'grifɔn] *pp* of greifen

Gehabe [gɔ'habɔ] *n* (-;) affectation

gehaben [gɔ'habɔn] *ref* fare; gehab
dich nicht so! stop putting on!; gehab dich wohl! farewell!

Gehackte [gɔ'haktɔ] §5 *n* hamburger

Gehalt [gɔ'halt] *m* (-[e]s;-e) contents;
capacity; standard; **G. an** (*dat*) per-
centage of || *n* (-[e]s;-er) salary

Gehalts'stufe *f* salary bracket

Gehalts'zulage *f* increment, raise

gehalt'voll *adj* substantial; profound

Gehänge [gɔ'heŋɔ] *n* (-s;-) slope; pendant; festoon; (*e-s Degens*) belt

gehangen [gɔ'haŋɔn] *pp* of hängen

gehässig [gɔ'hesɪç] *adj* spiteful, nasty

Gehäuse [gɔ'hɔizɔ] *n* (-s;-) case, box;
housing; (*e-r Schnecke*) shell; (*e-s
Apfels*) core

Gehege [gɔ'hegɔ] *n* (-s;-) enclosure

geheim [gɔ'haim] *adj* secret; **streng g.**
top-secret

geheim'halten §90 *tr* keep secret

Geheimnis [gɔ'haimnis] *n* (-ses;-se)
secret, mystery

geheim'nisvoll *adj* mysterious

Geheim'schrift *f* code; coded message

Geheim'tinte *f* invisible ink

Geheim'vorbehalt *m* mental reservation

Geheiß [gɔ'hais] *n* (-es) bidding

gehen ['ge·ɔn] §82 *intr* (SEIN) go;
walk; leave; (*Teig*) rise; (*Maschine*)
work; (*Uhr*) go; (*Ware*) sell; (*Wind*)
blow; **das geht nicht** that will not do;
das geht schon it will be all right;
sich g. lassen take it easy; **wieviel
Zoll g. auf einen Fuß?** how many
inches make a foot? || *impers*—**es
geht mir gut** I am doing well; **es
geht nichts über** (*acc*) there is nothing like; **es geht um...** is at stake;
wie geht es Ihnen? how are you?

geheuer [gɔ'hɔi·ɔr] *adj*—**mir war nicht
recht g. zumute** I didn't feel quite
at ease; **nicht g.** spooky; suspicious;

Geheul [gɔ'hɔil] *n* (-s;) howling; loud
sobbing

Gehilfe [gɔ'hilfɔ] *m* (-n;-n), Gehilfin
[gɔ'hilfin] *f* (-;-nen) assistant

Gehirn [gɔ'hirn] *n* (-[e]s;-e) brains,
mind; (anat) brain; **sein G. anstrengen** rack one's brain

Gehirn– *comb.fm.* brain; cerebral

Gehirn'erschütterung *f* concussion

Gehirn'schlag *m* (pathol) stroke

Gehirn'wäsche *f* brainwashing

gehoben [gɔ'hobɔn] *pp* of heben || *adj*
(*Stellung*) high; (*Stil*) lofty; **gehobene
Stimmung** high spirits

Gehöft [gɔ'hœft] *n* (-[e]s;-e) farm

geholfen [gɔ'holfɔn] *pp* of helfen

Gehölz [gɔ'hœlts] *n* (-es;-e) grove;
thicket

Gehör [gɔ'hør] *n* (-s;) hearing; ear

Gehör– *comb.fm.* of hearing; auditory

gehorchen [gɔ'hɔrçɔn] *intr* (dat) obey

gehören [gɔ'hørɔn] *ref* be proper, be
right || *intr* (dat or zu) belong to;
(in *acc*) go into, belong in

gehörig [gɔ'hørɪç] *adj* proper, due;
(*dat* or zu) belonging to || *adv* prop-
erly; duly; thoroughly

Gehörn [gɔ'hœrn] *n* (-s;-e) horns; Ge-
hörne sets of horns

gehorsam [gɔ'hɔrzam] *adj* obedient ||
adv obediently; **gehorsamst** respect-
fully || Gehorsam *m* (-s;) obedience

Gehor'samverweigerung *f* disobedience

gehren ['gerɔn] *tr* (carp) miter

Gehrlade ['gerladɔ] *f* (-;-n) miter box

Gehrock ['gerɔk] *m* Prince Albert

Geh'rung *f*—auf G., nach der G. on
the slant; auf G. verbinden miter

Geh'rungslade *f* (-;-n) miter box

Gehsteig ['geʃtaik] *m* sidewalk

Gehweg ['gevek] *m* sidewalk; footpath

Gehwerk ['geverk] *n* clockwork, works

Geier ['gai·ɔr] *m* (-s;-) vulture; **zum
Geier!** what the devil!

Geifer ['gaifɔr] *m* (-s;) drivel; froth,
slaver, foam; (fig) venom

geifern ['gaifɔrn] *intr* slaver

Geige ['gaigɔ] *f* (-;-n) violin, fiddle

geigen ['gaigɔn] *intr* play the violin

Gei'genbogen *m* bow, fiddlestick

Gei'genharz *n* rosin

Gei'ger –in §6 *mf* violinist

geil [gail] *adj* lustful; in heat; (*Boden*)
rich; (*üppig*) luxuriant

Geisel ['gaizɔl] *f* (-;-n) hostage

Geiser ['gaizɔr] *m* (-s;-) geyser

Geiß [gais] *f* (-;-en) she-goat

Geißel ['gaisɔl] *f* (-;-n) scourge

geißeln ['gaisɔln] *tr* scourge; (fig)
castigate

Geist [gaist] *m* (-es;-er) spirit; (*Gespenst*) ghost; (*Verstand*) mind, intellect; **im Geiste** in one's imagination; in spirit

Gei'sterbeschwörung *f* (-;) necromancy

Gei'sterstadt *f* ghost town

Gei'sterstunde *f* witching hour

geistes– [gaistɔs] *comb.fm.* spiritually;
mentally, intellectually || Geistes-
comb.fm. spiritual; mental, intellectual

gei'stesabwesend *adj* absent-minded

Gei'stesanlagen *pl* natural gift

Gei'stesarbeit *f* brainwork

Gei'stesarmut *f* dullness, stupidity

Gei'stesblitz m brain wave; aphorism

Gei'stesflug m flight of the imagination

Gei'stesfreiheit f intellectual freedom

Gei'stesfrucht f brainchild

Gei'stesgegenwart f presence of mind

gei'stesgegenwärtig adj mentally alert

geistesgestört ['gaistəsgəʃtørt] adj mentally disturbed

Gei'steshaltung f mentality

gei'steskrank adj insane

gei'stesschwach adj feeble-minded

Gei'stesstörung f mental disorder

Gei'stes- und Natur'wissenschaften pl arts and sciences

Gei'stesverfassung f frame of mind

gei'stesverwandt adj (mit) spiritually akin (to); (mit) congenial (with)

Gei'stesverwirrung f derangement

Gei'steswissenschaften pl humanities

gei'steswissenschaftlich adj humanistic

Gei'steszustand m state of mind

geistig ['gaistiç] adj mental, intellectual; spiritual

geist'lich adj spiritual; (Orden) religious; (kirchlich) sacred, ecclesiastical; der geistliche Stand holy orders; the clergy ‖ **Geistliche** §5 m clergyman

Geist'lichkeit f (-;) clergy

geist'los adj spiritless; dull; stupid

geist'reich adj witty; ingenious

Geiz [gaits] m (-es;) stinginess; avarice

geizen ['gaitsən] intr—g. mit be sparing with; nicht g. mit show freely

Geiz'hals m (coll) tightwad

geizig ['gaitsiç] adj stingy, miserly

Geiz'kragen m (coll) tightwad

Gejammer [gə'jamər] n (-s;) wailing

gekannt [gə'kant] pp of kennen

Geklapper [gə'klapər] n (-s;) rattling

Geklatsche [gə'klatʃə] n (-s;) clapping; gossiping

Geklirr [gə'klɪr] n (-[e]s;) rattling

geklommen [gə'kləmən] pp of klimmen

geklungen [gə'kluŋən] pp of klingen

gekniffen [gə'knɪfən] pp of kneifen

gekonnt [gə'kənt] pp of können

Gekreisch [gə'kraɪʃ] n (-es;) screaming; screeching

Gekritzel [gə'krɪtsəl] n (-s;) scribbling

gekrochen [gə'krəxən] pp of kriechen

Gekröse [gə'krøzə] n (-s;) tripe

gekünstelt [gə'kynstəlt] adj affected

Gelächter [gə'lɛçtər] n (-s;) laughter

Gelage [gə'lagə] n (-s;) carousing

Gelände [gə'lɛndə] n (-s;-) terrain; site, lot; (educ) campus; (golf) fairway

Gelän'delauf m crosscountry running

Gelän'depunkt m landmark

Geländer [gə'lɛndər] n (-s;-) railing; guardrail; banister; parapet

gelang [gə'laŋ] pret of gelingen

gelangen [gə'laŋən] intr (SEIN) (an acc, in acc, zu) attain, reach

gelassen [gə'lasən] pp of lassen ‖ adj composed, calm

Gelatine [ʒela'tinə] f (-;) gelatin

geläufig [gə'ləifiç] adj fluent; (gemein) common; (Zunge) glib

gelaunt [gə'launt] adj—gut gelaunt in good humor; zu etw g. sein be in the mood for s.th.

Geläut [gə'ləit] n (-es;), **Geläute** [gə'ləitə] n (-s;) ringing; chimes

gelb [gɛlp] adj yellow ‖ **Gelb** n (-s;) yellow

gelb'lich adj yellowish

Gelb'sucht f jaundice

Geld [gɛlt] n (-[e]s;) money; bares G. cash

Geld- comb.fm. money, financial

-geld n comb.fm. money; fee(s); tax, toll; allowance

Geld'anlage f investment

Geld'anleihe f loan

Geld'anweisung f money order; draft

Geld'ausgabe f expense; expenditure

Geld'beutel m pocketbook

Geld'bewilligung f (parl) appropriation

Geld'buße f fine

Geld'einlage f deposit

Geld'einwurf m coin slot

Geld'entwertung f inflation

Geld'erwerb m moneymaking

Geld'geber m investor; mortgagee

Geld'gier f avarice

Geld'mittel pl funds, resources

Geld'onkel m sugar daddy

Geld'schein m bank note, bill

Geld'schrank m safe

Geld'schublade f till (of cash register)

Geld'sendung f remittance

Geld'sorte f (fin) denomination

Geld'spende f contribution, donation

Geld'strafe f fine

Geld'stück n coin

Geld'überhang m surplus (of money)

Geld'währung f currency; monetary standard

Geld'wechsel m money exchange

Geld'wesen n financial system, finance

Gelee [ʒe'le] m & n (-s;-s) jelly

gelegen [gə'legən] pp of liegen ‖ adj located; convenient; opportune; du kommst mir gerade g. you're just the person I wanted to see; es kommt mir gerade gelegen that suits me just fine; mir ist daran g. zu (inf) I'm anxious to (inf); was ist daran g.? what of it?

Gele'genheit f (-;-en) occasion; opportunity, chance; (com) bargain

Gelegenheits- comb.fm. occasional

Gele'genheitsarbeit f odd job

Gele'genheitskauf m good bargain

gele'gentlich adj occasional; casual; chance ‖ adv occasionally ‖ prep (genit) on the occasion of

gelehrig [gə'leriç] adj teachable; intelligent

gelehrsam [gə'lerzam] adj erudite

gelehrt [gə'lert] adj learned, erudite ‖ **Gelehrte** §5 mf scholar

Geleise [gə'laizə] n (-s;-) rut; (rr) track; totes G. blind alley, deadlock

Geleit [gə'lait] n (-[e]s;-e) escort; freies (or sicheres) G. safe-conduct; j-m das G. geben escort s.o., accompany s.o.; zum G. forward

geleiten [gə'laitən] tr escort, accompany; j-n zur Tür g. see s.o. to the door

Geleit'zug m convoy

Geleit'zugsicherung f convoy escort

Gelenk [gə'lɛŋk] n (-[e]s;-e) joint

Gelenk'entzündung f arthritis

gelenkig [gə'lɛŋkɪç] adj jointed; flexible; agile

gelernt [gə'lɛrnt] adj skilled

Gelichter [gə'lɪçtər] n (-s;) riffraff

Geliebte [gə'liptə] §6 mf beloved, sweetheart

geliehen [gə'li·ən] pp of leihen

gelieren [ʒe'lirən] intr jell, gel

gelinde [gə'lɪndə] adj soft; gentle, mild || adv gently, mildly; g. gesagt to put it mildly

gelingen [gə'lɪŋən] §142 intr (SEIN) succeed || impers (SEIN)—es gelingt mir I succeed || **Gelingen** n (-s;) success

gelitten [gə'lɪtən] pp of leiden

gell [gɛl] adj shrill || interj say!

gellen ['gɛlən] intr ring out; yell

gel'lend adj shrill, piercing

geloben [gə'lobən] tr solemnly promise, vow; take the vow of || ref—sich [dat] g. vow to oneself

gelogen [gə'logən] pp of lügen

gelt [gɛlt] interj say!

gelten ['gɛltən] §83 tr be worth; wenig g. mean little || intr be valid; (Münze) be legal tender; (Gesetz) be in force; (Grund) hold true; (Regel) apply; (Mittel) be allowable; (beim Spiel) count; g. als or für have the force of; be ranked as; pass for, be considered; g. lassen acknowledge as correct; j-m g. be aimed at s.o. || impers—es gilt (acc) be at stake; be a matter of; be worth (s.th.); es gilt mir gleich, ob it's all the same to me whether; es gilt zu (inf) it is necessary to (inf); jetzt gilt's! here goes!

Gel'tung f (-;) validity; value, importance; **zur G. bringen** make the most of; **zur G. kommen** show off well

Gel'tungsbedürfnis n need for recognition

Gelübde [gə'lʏpdə] n (-s;-) vow

gelungen [gə'lʊŋən] pp of gelingen || adj successful; (Wendung) well-turned; funny

Gelüst [gə'lʏst] n (-[e]s;-e) desire

gelüsten [gə'lʏstən] impers—es gelüstet mich nach I could go for

gemach [gə'max] adv slowly, by degrees || **Gemach** n (-[e]s;ᵘer) room; apartment; chamber

gemächlich [gə'mɛçlɪç] adj leisurely; comfortable

Gemahl [gə'mal] m (-[e]s;-e) husband

Gemahlin [gə'malɪn] f (-;-nen) wife

Gemälde [gə'mɛldə] n (-s;-) painting

gemäß [gə'mɛs] prep (dat) according to

gemäßigt [gə'mɛsɪçt] adj moderate

gemein [gə'maɪn] adj common; mean, vile; **sich g. machen mit** associate with || **Gemeine** §5 m (mil) private

Gemeinde [gə'maɪndə] f (-;-n) community; municipality; (eccl) parish

Gemein'deabgaben pl local taxes

Gemein'deanleihen pl municipal bonds

Gemein'dehaus n town hall

gemein'frei adj in the public domain

gemein'gefährlich adj constituting a public danger, dangerous

gemein'gültig adj generally accepted

Gemein'heit f (-;-en) meanness; dirty trick; vulgarity

gemein'hin adv commonly, usually

Gemein'kosten pl overhead

Gemein'nutz m public interest

gemein'nützig adj non-profit

Gemein'platz m platitude

gemeinsam [gə'maɪnzam] adj common, joint; mutual

Gemein'schaft f (-;-en) community; close association

gemein'schaftlich adj common, joint; mutual

Gemein'schaftsanschluß m (telp) party line

Gemein'schaftsarbeit f teamwork

Gemein'schaftsgeist m esprit de corps

Gemein'sinn m public spirit

gemein'verständlich adj popular; g. darstellen popularize

Gemein'wesen n community

Gemein'wohl n commonweal

Gemenge [gə'mɛŋə] n (-s;) mixture; (Kampfgewühl) scuffle, melee

gemessen [gə'mɛsən] pp of messen || adj deliberate; precise; dignified; g. an (dat) compared with

Gemetzel [gə'mɛtsəl] n (-s;-) massacre

gemieden [gə'midən] pp of meiden

Gemisch [gə'mɪʃ] n (-es;-e) mixture

Gemischt'warenhandlung f general store

Gemme ['gɛmə] f (-;-n) gem

gemocht [gə'maxt] pp of mögen

gemolken [gə'mɔlkən] pp of melken

Gemse ['gɛmzə] f (-;-n) chamois

Gemunkel [gə'mʊŋkəl] n (-s;-) gossip, whispering

Gemurmel [gə'mʊrməl] n (-s;) murmur

Gemüse [gə'myzə] n (-s;-) vegetable; vegetables

Gemü'sebau m (-[e]s;) vegetable gardening

Gemü'sekonserven pl canned vegetables

gemüßigt [gə'mysɪçt] adj—sich g. fühlen feel compelled

gemußt [gə'mʊst] pp of müssen

Gemüt [gə'myt] n (-[e]s;-er) mind; disposition; person, soul; warmth of feeling; **j-m etw zu Gemüte führen** bring s.th. home to s.o.

gemütlich [gə'mytlɪç] adj good-natured, easy-going; (Wohnung) cosy

Gemüt'lichkeit f (-;) easy-going nature; cosiness

Gemüts'art f disposition, nature

Gemüts'bewegung f emotion

gemüts'krank adj melancholy

Gemüts'mensch m warm-hearted person

Gemüts'ruhe f—in (aller) G. in peace and quiet

Gemüts'stimmung f mood

Gemüts'verfassung f state of mind

Gemüts'zustand m frame of mind

gemüt'voll adj emotional

gen [gen] prep (acc) (poet) towards || Gen [gen] n (-s;-e) (biol) gene

genannt [gə'nant] pp of nennen

genau [gə'nau] adj exact; fussy

genau'genommen adv strictly speaking

Genau'igkeit f (-;) exactness, accuracy; meticulousness

Gendarm [ʒã'darm] m (-en;-en) policeman

Gendarme·rie [ʒãdarmə'ri] f (-;-rien ['ri·ən]) rural police; rural police station

Genealo·gie [gene·alə'gi] f (-;-gien ['gi·ən]) genealogy

genehm [gə'nem] adj agreeable; acceptable; (dat) convenient (for)

genehmigen [gə'nemigən] tr grant; approve; sich [dat] etw g. (coll) treat oneself to s.th.; genehmigt O.K.

Geneh'migung f (-;-en) grant; approval; permission; permit

geneigt [gə'naikt] adj sloping; (zu) inclined (to); (dat) well-disposed (towards)

Geneigt'heit f inclination; good will

General [gene'ral] m (-[e]s;-e & =e) general

General'feldmarschall m field marshal

General'inspekteur m chief of the joint chiefs of staff

Generalität [generalɪ'tet] f (-;) body of generals

General'konsul m consul general

General'leutnant m lieutenant general; (aer) air marshal

General'major m major general

General'nenner m common denominator

General'probe f dress rehearsal

General'stabskarte f strategic map

General'vollmacht f full power of attorney

Generation [genera'tsjon] f (-;-en) generation

generell [gene'rel] adj general, blanket

genesen [gə'nezən] §84 intr (SEIN) convalesce; (von) recover (from)

Gene'sung f (-;-en) convalescence

Gene'sungsheim n convalescent home

genetisch [ge'netɪʃ] adj genetic

Genf [genf] n (-s;) Geneva

Gen'forscher -in §6 mf genetic engineer

Gen'forschung f (-;) genetic engineering

genial [ge'njal] adj brilliant, gifted

Genick [gə'nɪk] n (-s;-e) nape of the neck

Genick'bruch m broken neck

Genick'schlag m (box) rabbit punch

Genie [ʒe'ni] n (-s;-s) (man of) genius

genieren [ʒe'nirən] tr bother; embarrass || ref feel embarrassed

genießbar [gə'nisbar] adj edible; drinkable; (fig) agreeable

genießen [gə'nisən] §76 tr enjoy; eat; drink

Genie'streich m stroke of genius

Genitalien [genɪ'taljən] pl genitals

Geni·tiv ['genɪtif] m (-s;-tive ['tivə]) genitive

genommen [gə'nɔmən] pp of nehmen

genoß [gə'nɔs] pret of genießen

Genosse [gə'nɔsə] m (-n;-n) companion, buddy; (pol) comrade

-genosse m comb.fm. fellow-, -mate

Genos'senschaft f (-;-en) association; cooperative

Genossin [gə'nɔsɪn] f (-;-nen) companion, buddy; (pol) comrade

genug [gə'nuk] invar adj & adv enough

Genüge [gə'nygə] f—j—m G. tun give s.o. satisfaction; zur G. enough; only too well

genügen [gə'nygən] intr suffice, do || ref—sich [dat] g. lassen an (dat) be content with

genü'gend adj sufficient

genügsam [gə'nykzam] adj easily satisfied; frugal

genug'tun §154 intr (dat) satisfy

Genugtuung [gə'nuktu·uŋ] f (-;) satisfaction

Ge·nuß [gə'nus] m (-nusses;-nüsse) enjoyment; pleasure; (Nutznießung) use; (von Speisen) consumption

Genuß'mittel n semi-luxury (as coffee, tobacco, etc.)

genuß'reich adj thoroughly enjoyable

genuß'süchtig adj pleasure-seeking

Geographie [ge·ogra'fi] f (-;) geography

geographisch [ge·o'grafɪʃ] adj geographical

Geologe [ge·o'logə] m (-n;-n) geologist

Geologie [ge·olo'gi] f (-;) geology

Geometer [ge·o'metər] m (-s;-) surveyor

Geometrie [ge·ome'tri] f (-;) geometry

Geophysik [ge·ofy'zik] f (-;) geophysics

Geopolitik [ge·opoli'tik] f (-;) geopolitics

Georgine [ge·or'ginə] f (-;-n) dahlia

Gepäck [gə'pek] n (-[e]s;) luggage

Gepäck'abfertigung f luggage check-in; luggage counter

Gepäck'ablage f luggage rack

Gepäck'anhänger m tag; luggage trailer

Gepäck'aufbewahrung f baggage room

Gepäck'netz n baggage rack (net type)

Gepäck'raum m luggage compartment

Gepäck'schein m luggage check

Gepäck'träger m porter; (aut) roof rack

Gepäck'wagen m (rr) baggage car

gepanzert [gə'pantsart] adj armored

gepfeffert [gə'pfefərt] adj peppered; (Worte) sharp; (Preis) exorbitant

Gepfeife [gə'pfaifə] n (-s;) whistling

gepfiffen [gə'pfifən] pp of pfeifen

geplogen [gə'pflogən] pp of pflegen

Gepflo'genheit f (-;-en) custom, practice

Geplänkel [gə'plenkəl] n (-s;) skirmish; (fig) exchange of words

Geplapper [gə'plapər] n (-s;) jabber

Geplärr [gə'pler] n (-s;) bawling

Geplauder [gə'plaudər] n (-s;) small talk, chat

Gepolter [gə'poltər] n (-s;) rumbling

Gepräge [gə'pregə] n (-s;) impression; stamp, character

Gepränge [gə'preŋə] n (-s;) pomp

gepriesen [gə'pri:zən] *pp* of **preisen**

gequollen [gə'kvɔlən] *pp* of **quellen**

gerade [gə'ra:də] *adj* straight; even; direct; (*Haltung*) erect; (*aufrichtig*) straightforward || *adv* straight; exactly; just; just now || **Gerade** *f* (–;–n) straight line; straightaway; (box) straight; **rechte G.** straight right

gerade(n)wegs [gə'ra:də(n)ve:ks] *adv* immediately, straightaway

geradezu' *adv* downright

Geranie [ge'ra:njə] *f* (–;–n) geranium

gerannt [gə'rant] *pp* of **rennen**

Gerassel [gə'rasəl] *n* (–s;) clanking

Gerät [gə'rɛt] *n* (–[e]s;–e) device, instrument; tool; (rad, telv) set

geraten [gə'ra:tən] *pp* of **raten** || *adj* successful; (*ratsam*) advisable || §63 *intr* (SEIN) (*gut, schlecht, usw.*) turn out; **außer sich g.** be beside oneself; **g. an** (*acc*) come by; **g. auf** (*acc*) get into; get on to; **g. hinter** (*acc*) get behind; find out about; **g. in** (*acc*) get into, fall into; **g. nach** take after; **g. über** (*acc*) come across; **in Bewegung g.** begin to move; **in Brand g.** catch fire; **ins Schleudern g.** begin to skid; **ins Stocken g.** come to a standstill

Gerä'teschuppen *m* tool shed

Geratewohl [gə'ra:təvol] *n* (–s;)—**aufs G.** at random

geraum [gə'raum] *adj* considerable

geräumig [gə'rɔimiç] *adj* spacious

Geräusch [gə'rɔiʃ] *n* (–[e]s;–e) noise

gerben ['gɛrbən] *tr* tan

Gerberei [gɛrbə'rai] *f* (–;–en) tannery

gerecht [gə'rɛçt] *adj* just, fair; justified; **g. werden** (*dat*) do justice to

Gerech'tigkeit *f* (–;) justice; fairness

Gerede [gə're:də] *n* (–s;) talk; hearsay

gereichen [gə'raiçən] *intr*—**es gereicht ihm zur Ehre** it does him justice; **es gereicht ihm zum Vorteil** it is to his advantage; **es gereicht mir zur Freude** it gives me pleasure

gereizt [gə'raitst] *adj* irritable; irritated

gereuen [gə'rɔi·ən] *tr* cause (*s.o.*) regret || *ref*—**sich keine Mühe g. lassen** spare no trouble || *impers*—**es gereut mich** I regret

Geriatrie [gɛri·a'tri:] *f* (–;) geriatrics

Gericht [gə'riçt] *n* (–[e]s;–e) court; courthouse; judgment; (culin) dish; **das Jüngste G.** the Last Judgment

gericht'lich *adj* legal, judicial, court

Gerichtsbarkeit [gə'riçtsbarkait] *f* (–;) jurisdiction

Gerichts'bote *m* (jur) bailiff

Gerichts'hof *m* law court; **Oberster G.** Supreme Court

Gerichts'medizin *f* forensic medicine

Gerichts'saal *m* courtroom

Gerichts'schreiber –in §6 *mf* (jur) clerk

Gerichts'stand *m* (jur) venue

Gerichts'verhandlung *f* hearing; trial

Gerichts'vollzieher *m* (jur) marshal

Gerichts'wesen *n* judicial system

gerieben [gə'ri:bən] *pp* of **reiben** || *adj* cunning, smart

Geriesel [gə'ri:zəl] *n* (–s;) purling

gering [gə'riŋ] *adj* slight, trifling; small; (*niedrig*) low; (*ärmlich*) poor; (*minderwertig*) inferior; **nicht im geringsten** not in the least

gering'achten *tr* think little of

gering'fügig *adj* insignificant

gering'schätzen *tr* look down on

Gering'schätzung *f* contempt, disdain

gerinnen [gə'rinən] §121 *intr* coagulate, clot; (*Milch*) curdle

Gerinnsel [gə'rinzəl] *n* (–s;–) clot

Gerippe [gə'ripə] *n* (–s;–) skeleton; (*Gerüst*) framework

gerippt [gə'ript] *adj* ribbed; (*Säule*) fluted; (*Stoff*) corded

gerissen [gə'risən] *pp* of **reißen** || *adj* sly

geritten [gə'ritən] *pp* of **reiten**

gern(e) ['gɛrn(ə)] *adv* gladly; **g. haben** or **mögen** like; **ich rauche g.** I like to smoke

gerochen [gə'rɔxən] *pp* of **riechen**

Geröll [gə'rœl] *n* (–s;) pebbles

geronnen [gə'rɔnən] *pp* of **gerinnen** & **rinnen**

Gerste ['gɛrstə] *f* (–;–n) barley

Ger'stenkorn *n* grain of barley; (pathol) sty

Gerte ['gɛrtə] *f* (–;–n) switch, rod

Geruch [gə'rux] *m* (–[e]s;–e) smell

geruch'los *adj* odorless

Gerücht [gə'rүçt] *n* (–[e]s;–e) rumor

geruhen [gə'ru·ən] *intr* deign

geruhsam [gə'ru:zam] *adj* quiet; relaxed

Gerümpel [gə'rүmpəl] *n* (–s;) junk

gerungen [gə'rυŋən] *pp* of **ringen**

Gerüst [gə'ryst] *n* (–s;–e) scaffold; (*Tragewerk*) frame; (fig) outline

Ges [gɛs] *n* (–;–) (mus) G flat

gesamt [gə'zamt] *adj* entire, total

gesamt–, Gesamt– comb.fm. total, overall; all–; joint; collective

gesandt [gə'zant] *pp* of **senden**

Gesandt'e §5 *mf* envoy

Gesandt'schaft *f* (–;–en) legation

Gesang [gə'zaŋ] *m* (–[e]s;–e) singing; song; (lit) canto

Gesang'verein *m* glee club

Gesäß [gə'zɛs] *n* (–es;–e) buttocks; (coll) behind

Geschäft [gə'ʃɛft] *n* (–[e]s;–e) business; deal, bargain; shop, store

Geschäftemacherei [gə'ʃɛftəmaxərai] *f* (–;) commercialism

geschäftig [gə'ʃɛtiç] *adj* busy

Geschäf'tigkeit *f* (–;) hustle, bustle

geschäft'lich *adj* business || *adv* on business

Geschäfts'abschluß *m* contract; deal

Geschäfts'aufsicht *f* receivership

Geschäfts'bedingungen *pl* terms

geschäfts'führend *adj* managing; executive; **geschäftsführende Regierung** caretaker government

Geschäfts'führer –in §6 *mf* manager

Geschäfts'haus *n* firm; office building

Geschäfts'inhaber –in §6 *mf* proprietor

geschäfts'kundig *adj* with business experience

Geschäfts'lokal *n* business premises; (*Laden*) shop; (*Büro*) office

Geschäfts'mann *m* (–[e]s;–leute) businessman

geschäfts'mäßig *adj* business-like
Geschäfts'ordnung *f* rules of procedure; zur G.! point of order!
Geschäfts'reise *f* business trip
Geschäfts'schluß *m* closing time
Geschäfts'stelle *f* office; branch
Geschäfts'träger *m* agent, representative; (pol) chargé d'affaires
geschäfts'tüchtig *adj* sharp
Geschäfts'verbindung *f* business connections
Geschäfts'verkehr *m* business transactions
Geschäfts'viertel *n* business district
Geschäfts'wert *m* (com) good will
Geschäfts'zweig *m* line of business
geschah [gə'ʃaː] *pret* of geschehen
geschehen [gə'eːən] §138 *intr* (SEIN) happen; take place; be done; das geschieht dir recht! serves you right! || Geschehen (*n* -s;) events
Geschehnis [gə'ʃenɪs] *n* (-ses;-se) event
gescheit [gə'ʃaɪt] *adj* clever; bright; sensible; er ist wohl nicht ganz g. he's not all there
Geschenk [gə'ʃɛŋk] *n* (-[e]s;-e) gift
Geschichte [gə'ʃɪçtə] *f* (-;-n) story; history; (coll) affair, thing
geschicht'lich *adj* historical
Geschichts'forscher -in §6 *mf*, Geschichts'schreiber -in §6 *mf* historian
Geschick [gə'ʃɪk] *n* (-[e]s;-e) fate, destiny; dexterity, skill
Geschick'lichkeit *f* (-;) skillfulness
geschickt [gə'ʃɪkt] *adj* skillful
geschieden [gə'ʃiːdən] *pp* of scheiden
geschienen [gə'ʃiːnən] *pp* of scheinen
Geschirr [gə'ʃɪr] *n* (-[e]s;-e) dishes; china; pot; (*e-s Pferdes*) harness
Geschirr'schrank *m* kitchen cabinet
Geschirrspülmaschine [gə'ʃɪrʃpylmaʃinə] *f* dishwasher
Geschirr'tuch *n* dishtowel
geschissen [gə'ʃɪsən] *pp* of scheißen
Geschlecht [gə'ʃlɛçt] *n* (-[e]s;-er) sex; race; family, line; generation; (gram) gender
geschlecht'lich *adj* sexual
Geschlechts'krankheit *f* venereal disease
Geschlechts'teile *pl* genitals
Geschlechts'trieb *m* sexual instinct
Geschlechts'verkehr *m* intercourse
Geschlechts'wort *n* (-[e]s;ˬ) (gram) article
geschlichen [gə'ʃlɪçən] *pp* of schleichen
geschliffen [gə'ʃlɪfən] *pp* of schleifen || *adj* (*Glas*) cut; (*fig*) polished
geschlissen [gə'ʃlɪsən] *pp* of schleißen
geschlossen [gə'ʃlɔsən] *pp* of schließen || *adj* closed; enclosed; (*Front*) united; (*Gesellschaft*) private; (ling) close; (telv) closed-circuit || *adv* unanimously; g. hinter j-m stehen be solidly behind s.o.
geschlungen [gə'ʃluŋən] *pp* of schlingen
Geschmack [gə'ʃmak] *m* (-s;ˬe & ˬer) taste
Geschmacks'richtung *f* vogue

geschmeidig [gə'ʃmaɪdɪç] *adj* pliant; flexible; lithe; (*Haar*) manageable
Geschmeiß [gə'ʃmaɪs] *n* (-es;) vermin; rabble
geschmissen [gə'ʃmɪsən] *pp* of schmeißen
geschmolzen [gə'ʃmɔltsən] *pp* of schmelzen
Geschnatter [gə'ʃnatər] *n* (-s;) cackle
geschniegelt [gə'ʃniːgəlt] *adj* spruce
geschnitten [gə'ʃnɪtən] *pp* of schneiden
geschnoben [gə'ʃnoːbən] *pp* of schnauben
geschoben [gə'ʃoːbən] *pp* of schieben
gescholten [gə'ʃɔltən] *pp* of schelten
Geschöpf [gə'ʃœpf] *n* (-[e]s;-e) creature
geschoren [gə'ʃoːrən] *pp* of scheren
Ge-schoß [gə'ʃɔs] *n* (-schosses; -schosse) shot; missile; shell; floor, story
Geschoß'bahn *f* trajectory
geschossen [gə'ʃɔsən] *pp* of schießen
geschraubt [gə'ʃraʊbt] *adj* affected; (*Stil*) stilted
Geschrei [gə'ʃraɪ] *n* (-[e]s;) shouting
Geschreibsel [gə'ʃraɪpsəl] *n* (-s;) scribbling, scrawl
geschrieben [gə'ʃriːbən] *pp* of schreiben
geschrie(e)n [gə'ʃriːən] *pp* of schreien
geschritten [gə'ʃrɪtən] *pp* of schreiten
geschunden [gə'ʃundən] *pp* of schinden
Geschütz [gə'ʃyts] *n* (-es;-e) gun
Geschütz'bedienung *f* gun crew
Geschütz'legierung *f* gun metal
Geschütz'stand *m* gun emplacement
Geschwader [gə'ʃvadər] *n* (-s;-) (aer) group (*consisting of 27 aircraft*); (nav) squadron
Geschwätz [gə'ʃvɛts] *n* (-es;) chatter
geschweige [gə'ʃvaɪgə]—g. denn let alone, much less
geschwiegen [gə'ʃviːgən] *pp* of schweigen
geschwind [gə'ʃvɪnt] *adj* quick
Geschwin'digkeit *f* (-;-en) speed; velocity; mit der G. von at the rate of
Geschwin'digkeitsbegrenzung *f* speed limit
Geschwin'digkeitsmesser *m* speedometer
Geschwind'schritt *m* (mil) double time
Geschwister [gə'ʃvɪstər] *pl* brother and sister, brothers, sisters, brothers and sisters; siblings
geschwollen [gə'ʃvɔlən] *pp* of schwellen || *adj* turgid
geschwommen [gə'ʃvɔmən] *pp* of schwimmen
geschworen [gə'ʃvoːrən] *pp* of schwören || Geschworene §5 *mf* juror; die Geschworenen the jury
Geschwo'renengericht *n* jury
Geschwulst [gə'ʃvulst] *f* (-;ˬe) swelling; tumor
geschwunden [gə'ʃvundən] *pp* of schwinden
geschwungen [gə'ʃvuŋən] *pp* of schwingen
Geschwür [gə'ʃvyr] *n* (-s;-e) ulcer

Geselle [gə'zɛlə] *m* (-n;-n) journeyman; companion; lad, fellow

gesellen [gə'zɛlən] *ref*—**sich zu j-m g.** join s.o.

gesellig [gə'zɛlɪç] *adj* gregarious, sociable

Gesell'schaft *f* (-;-en) society; company; (pej) bunch; (com) company; **j-m G. leisten** keep s.o. company

Gesell'schafter -in §6 *mf* companion; shareholder; (com) partner

gesell'schaftlich *adj* social

Gesell'schaftsspiel *n* party game

Gesell'schaftswissenschaft *f* social science; sociology

gesessen [gə'zɛsən] *pp* of **sitzen**

Gesetz [gə'zɛts] *n* (-es;-e) law

Gesetz'buch *n* legal code

Gesetz'entwurf *m* (parl) bill

Gesetzes- [gəzɛtsəs] *comb.fm.* legal, of law

Geset'zesantrag *m*, **Geset'zesvorlage** *f* (parl) bill

gesetz'gebend *adj* legislative

Gesetz'geber -in §6 *mf* legislator

Gesetz'gebung *f* (-;-en) legislation

gesetz'lich *adj* legal

gesetz'los *adj* lawless

gesetz'mäßig *adj* legal; legitimate

Gesetz'sammlung *f* code of laws

gesetzt [gə'zɛtst] *adj* sedate; (*Alter*) mature; **g. den Fall, daß** assuming that || *adv* in a dignified manner

gesetz'widrig *adj* illegal, unlawful

Gesicht [gə'zɪçt] *n* (-[e]s;-er) face; sight; eyesight; (*Aussehen*) look

Gesichts'farbe *f* complexion

Gesichts'kreis *m* horizon; outlook

Gesichts'punkt *m* point of view, angle

Gesichts'spannung *f* face lift

Gesichts'zug *m* feature

Gesims [gə'zɪms] *n* (-es;-e) molding

Gesindel [gə'zɪndəl] *n* (-s;) rabble; **lichtscheues G.** shady characters

gesinnt [gə'zɪnt] *adj* disposed; -minded

Gesinnung [gə'zɪnʊŋ] *f* (-;-en) mind; character; convictions

gesin'nungslos *adj* without definite convictions

gesin'nungsmäßig *adv* according to one's convictions

gesin'nungstreu, gesin'nungstüchtig *adj* staunch

gesittet [gə'zɪtət] *adj* polite; civilized

gesoffen [gə'zɔfən] *pp* of **saufen**

gesogen [gə'zogən] *pp* of **saugen**

gesonnen [gə'zɔnən] *pp* of **sinnen** || *adj*—**g. sein zu** (*inf*) have a mind to (*inf*), be inclined to (*inf*)

gesotten [gə'zɔtən] *pp* of **sieden**

Gespann [gə'ʃpan] *n* (-[e]s;-e) team; pair, combination

gespannt [gə'ʃpant] *adj* stretched; tense; (*Aufmerksamkeit*) close; (*Beziehungen*) strained; **ich bin g.** (coll) I wonder, I am anxious to know

Gespenst [gə'ʃpɛnst] *n* (-[e]s;-er) ghost, specter

gespen'sterhaft *adj* ghostly; spooky

gespenstisch [gə'ʃpɛnstɪʃ] *adj* ghostly

gespie(e)n [gə'ʃpi(ə)n] *pp* of **speien**

Gespiele [gə'ʃpilə] *m* (-n;-n), **Gespielin** [gə'ʃpilɪn] *f* (-;-nen) playmate

Gespinst [gə'ʃpɪnst] *n* (-es;-e) yarn; (*Gewebe*) web

gesponnen [gə'ʃpɔnən] *pp* of **spinnen**

Gespött [gə'ʃpœt] *n* (-[e]s;) ridicule; laughing stock

Gespräch [gə'ʃprɛç] *n* (-[e]s;-e) conversation; (telp) call; **Gespräche** (pol) talks; **G. mit Voranmeldung** person-to-person call

gesprächig [gə'ʃprɛçɪç] *adj* talkative

gespreizt [gə'ʃpraɪtst] *adj* outspread; affected || *adv*—**g. tun** act big

gesprenkelt [gə'ʃprɛŋkəlt] *adj* spotted

gesprochen [gə'ʃprɔçən] *pp* of **sprechen**

gesprossen [gə'ʃprɔsən] *pp* of **sprießen**

gesprungen [gə'ʃprʊŋən] *pp* of **springen**

Gestade [gə'ʃtadə] *f* (-s;-) (river) bank; (sea)shore

Gestalt [gə'ʃtalt] *f* (-;-en) shape; figure; (*Wuchs*) stature

gestalten [gə'ʃtaltən] *tr* shape; form; arrange || *ref* take shape; turn out

Gestal'tung *f* (-;-en) formation; development; arrangement; design

gestanden [gə'ʃtandən] *pp* of **stehen**

geständig [gə'ʃtɛndɪç] *adj*—**g. sein** admit one's guilt

Geständnis [gə'ʃtɛntnɪs] *n* (-ses;-se) confession, admission

Gestank [gə'ʃtaŋk] *m* (-[e]s;) stench

Gestapo [gə'ʃtapo] *f* (-;) (Geheime Staatspolizei) secret state police

gestatten [gə'ʃtatən] *tr* permit, allow

Geste ['gɛstə] *f* (-;-n) gesture

gestehen [gə'ʃte-ən] §146 *tr* admit

Gestein [gə'ʃtaɪn] *n* (-[e]s;-e) rock

Gestell [gə'ʃtɛl] *n* (-[e]s;-e) frame; rack; mounting; (coll) beanpole

Gestel'lungsbefehl *m* (mil) induction orders

gestern ['gɛstərn] *adv* yesterday; **g. abend** last evening, last night

gestiefelt [gə'ʃtifəlt] *adj* in boots

gestiegen [gə'ʃtigən] *pp* of **steigen**

gestikulieren [gɛstiku'lirən] *intr* gesticulate

Gestirn [gə'ʃtɪrn] *n* (-[e]s;-e) star; (*Sternbild*) constellation

gestirnt [gə'ʃtɪrnt] *adj* starry

gestoben [gə'ʃtobən] *pp* of **stieben**

Gestöber [gə'ʃtøbər] *n* (-s;-) snow flurry

gestochen [gə'ʃtɔxən] *pp* of **stechen**

gestohlen [gə'ʃtolən] *pp* of **stehlen**

gestorben [gə'ʃtɔrbən] *pp* of **sterben**

gestoßen [gə'ʃtosən] *pp* of **stoßen**

Gesträuch [gə'ʃtrɔɪç] *n* (-[e]s;) bushes, shrubbery

gestreift [gə'ʃtraɪft] *adj* striped

gestrichen [gə'ʃtrɪçən] *pp* of **streichen**

gestrig ['gɛstrɪç] *adj* yesterday's

gestritten [gə'ʃtrɪtən] *pp* of **streiten**

Gestrüpp [gə'ʃtryp] *n* (-[e]s;) underbrush

gestunken [gə'ʃtʊŋkən] *pp* of **stinken**

Gestüt [gə'ʃtyt] *n* (-[e]s;-e) stud farm

Gestüt'hengst *m* stallion, studhorse

Gesuch [gə'zux] *n* (-[e]s;-e) request; application; (jur) petition

gesucht [gə'zuxt] *adj* wanted; in demand; studied; (*Vergleich*) farfetched

Gesudel [gə'zudəl] *n* (-s;) messy job

Gesumme [gə'zumə] n (-s;) humming

gesund [gə'zunt] adj healthy; sound; wholesome; g. werden get well

Gesund'beter –in §6 mf faith healer

Gesund'brunnen m mineral spring

gesunden [gə'zundən] intr (SEIN) get well again, recover

Gesund'heit f (-;) health; auf Ihre G.! to your health!; G.! (God) bless you!

Gesund'heitslehre f hygiene

Gesund'heitspflege f hygiene

Gesund'heitsrücksichten pl—aus G. for reasons of health

Gesund'heitswesen n public health

gesungen [gə'zuŋən] pp of singen

gesunken [gə'zuŋkən] pp of sinken

Getäfel [gə'tefəl] n (-s;) wainscoting

getä'felt adj inlaid

getan [gə'tan] pp of tun

Getöse [gə'tøzə] n (-s;) din, noise

getragen [gə'tragən] pp of tragen || adj solemn

Getrampel [gə'trampəl] n (-s;) trample

Getränk [gə'treŋk] n (-[e]s;-e) drink

getrauen [gə'trau·ən] ref dare

Getreide [gə'traidə] n (-s;-) grain

getreu [gə'trɔɪ] adj faithful, true

getreu'lich adv faithfully

Getriebe [gə'tribə] n (-s;-) hustle and bustle; (adm) machinery; (aut) transmission

getrieben [gə'tribən] pp of treiben

getroffen [gə'trɔmən] pp of treffen

getrogen [gə'trogən] pp of trügen

getrost [gə'trost] adj confident

getrunken [gə'truŋkən] pp of trinken

Getto ['geto] n (-s;-s) ghetto

Getue [gə'tu·ə] n (-s;) fuss

Getümmel [gə'tyməl] n (-s;) turmoil

getupft [gə'tupft] adj polka-dot

Geviert [gə'firt] n (-[e]s;-e) square

Gewächs [gə'veks] n (-es;-e) growth; plant

gewachsen [gə'vaksən] adj—g. sein (dat) be equal to, be up to

Gewächs'haus n greenhouse, hothouse

gewagt [gə'vakt] adj risky; off-color

gewählt [gə'velt] adj choice; refined

gewahr [gə'var] adj—g. werden (genit) become aware of

Gewähr [gə'ver] f (-;) guarantee

gewahren [gə'varən] tr notice

gewähren [gə'verən] tr grant

gewähr'leisten tr guarantee, ensure

Gewähr'leistung f (-;-en) guarantee

Gewahrsam [gə'varzam] m (-[e]s) safekeeping, custody || n (-[e]s;-e) prison

Gewährs'mann m (-[e]s;"er & -leute) informant, source

Gewährs'pflicht f warranty

Gewalt [gə'valt] f (-;-en) force; violence; authority; (Aufsicht) control

Gewalt'haber m (-s;-) ruler; tyrant

Gewalt'herrschaft f tyranny

Gewalt'herrscher m tyrant

gewal'tig adj powerful; huge; (coll) awful || adv terribly

Gewalt'kur f drastic measure; (coll) crash program

gewalt'los adj nonviolent

Gewalt'marsch m forced march

Gewalt'mensch m brute, tyrant

gewaltsam [gə'valtzam] adj violent; forcible; drastic || adv by force

Gewalt'samkeit f (-;) violence

Gewalt'streich m bold stroke

Gewalt'tat f act of violence

gewalt'tätig adj violent, brutal

Gewalt'verbrechen n felony

Gewalt'verbrecher –in §6 mf felon

Gewand [gə'vant] n (-[e]s;"er) robe; appearance, guise; (eccl) vestment

gewandt [gə'vant] pp of wenden || adj agile; clever

gewann [gə'van] pret of gewinnen

gewärtig [gə'vertiç] adj—g. sein (genit) be prepared for

Gewäsch [gə've/] n (-es;) nonsense

Gewässer [gə'vesər] n (-s;-) body of water; waters

Gewebe [gə'vebə] n (-s;-) tissue; (tex) fabric

geweckt [gə'vekt] adj bright, sharp

Gewehr [gə'ver] n (-[e]s;-e) rifle

Geweih [gə'vai] n (-[e]s;-e) antlers

Gewerbe [gə'verbə] n (-s;-) trade, business; calling, profession; industry

Gewer'bebetrieb m business enterprise

Gewer'beschule f trade school

gewerblich [gə'verpliç] adj industrial; commercial, business

gebwerbs'mäßig adj professional

Gewerkschaft [gə'verk/aft] f (-;-en) labor union

gewerk'schaftlich adj union || adv—sich g. organisieren unionize

Gewerk'schaftsbeitrag m union dues

gewesen [gə'vezən] pp of sein

gewichen [gə'viçən] pp of weichen

Gewicht [gə'viçt] n (-[e]s;-e) (& fig) weight

gewichtig [gə'viçtiç] adj weighty

gewiegt [gə'vigt] adj experienced, smart, shrewd

gewiesen [gə'vizən] pp of weisen

gewillt [gə'vilt] adj willing

Gewimmel [gə'viməl] n (-s;) swarm; (Menschen–) throng

Gewimmer [gə'vimər] n (-s;) whimpering; whining

Gewinde [gə'vində] n (-s;-) thread (of a screw); (Kranz) garland; skein

Gewinn [gə'vin] m (-[e]s;-e) winnings; profit; (Vorteil) advantage

Gewinn'anteil m dividend

Gewinn'aufschlag m (com) markup

Gewinn'beteiligung f profit sharing

gewinn'bringend adj profitable

gewinnen [gə'vinən] §121 tr win, gain; reach || intr win; make a profit; improve; g. an (dat) gain in; g. von or durch profit by

gewin'nend adj engaging

Gewinn'spanne f margin of profit

Gewinn'sucht f greed; profiteering

Gewinsel [gə'vinzəl] n (-s;) whimpering

Gewirr [gə'vir] n (-[e]s;-e) tangle; entanglement; maze

gewiß [gə'vis] adj sure, certain || adv certainly; aber g.! of course!

Gewissen [gə'visən] n (-s;-) conscience

gewis'senhaft *adj* conscientious

gewis'senlos *adj* unscrupulous

Gewis'sensbisse *pl* pangs of conscience

Gewis'sensnot *f* moral dilemma

gewis'sermaßen *adv* to some extent; so to speak

Gewiß'heit *f* (-;-en) certainty

gewiß'lich *adv* certainly

Gewitter [gə'vɪtər] *n* (-s;-) thunderstorm

gewittern [gə'vɪtərn] *impers*—es gewittert a storm is brewing

Gewit'terregen *m* thundershower

gewitzigt [gə'vɪtsɪçt] *adj*—g. sein to have learned from experience

gewitzt [gə'vɪtst] *adj* bright, smart

gewoben [gə'voːbən] *pp* of weben

gewogen [gə'voːgən] *pp* of wägen & wiegen || *adj* well disposed

Gewo'genheit *f* (-;) favorable attitude

gewöhnen [gə'vøːnən] *tr* (an *acc*) accustom (to) || *ref* (an *acc*) get used (to)

Gewohnheit [gə'voːnhaɪt] *f* (-;-en) habit, custom

gewohn'heitsmäßig *adj* habitual

Gewohn'heitsmensch *m* creature of habit

gewöhnlich [gə'vøːnlɪç] *adj* usual; normal; common, ordinary

gewohnt [gə'voːnt] *adj* usual; g. sein (*acc*) to be used to

Gewölbe [gə'vœlbə] *n* (-s;-) vault; arch

gewölbt [gə'vœlpt] *adj* vaulted

Gewölk [gə'vœlk] *n* (-[e]s;) clouds

gewonnen [gə'vonən] *pp* of gewinnen

geworben [gə'vorbən] *pp* of werben

geworden [gə'vordən] *pp* of werden

geworfen [gə'vorfən] *pp* of werfen

gewrungen [gə'vrʊŋən] *pp* of wringen

Gewühl [gə'vyːl] *n* (-[e]s;) milling crowd

gewunden [gə'vʊndən] *pp* of winden

gewürfelt [gə'vyrfəlt] *adj* checkered

Gewürm [gə'vyrm] *n* (-[e]s;-) vermin

Gewürz [gə'vyrts] *n* (-[e]s;-e) spice

Gewürz'nelke *f* clove

gewußt [gə'vʊst] *pp* of wissen

Geysir ['gaɪzɪr] *m* (-s;-) geyser

gezackt [gə'tsakt] *adj* jagged; (bot) serrated

gezähnt [gə'tsɛnt] *adj* toothed; (*Rand*) perforated; (bot) dentated

Gezänk [gə'tsɛŋk] *n* (-[e]s;) squabbling

Gezeiten [gə'tsaɪtən] *pl* tides

Gezeiten- *comb.fm.* tidal

Gezeter [gə'tseːtər] *n* (-s;) yelling

geziehen [gə'tseɪ.ən] *pp* of zeihen

geziemen [gə'tsiːmən] *intr* (*dat*) be proper for || *impers ref*—es geziemt sich für j-n it is right for s.o.

geziert [gə'tsiːrt] *adj* affected, phoney

Gezisch [gə'tsɪʃ] *n* (-es;) hissing

gezogen [gə'tsoːgən] *pp* of ziehen

Gezücht [gə'tsʏçt] *n* (-[e]s;-e) riffraff

Gezwitscher [gə'tsvɪtʃər] *n* (-s;) chirping

gezwungen [gə'tsvʊŋən] *pp* of zwingen || *adj* forced; (*Stil*) labored || *adv* stiffly

Gicht [gɪçt] *f* (-;-en) gout

Giebel ['giːbəl] *m* (-s;-) gable

Gier [gir] *f* (-;) greed

gierig ['gɪrɪç] *adj* (nach) greedy (for)

Gießbach ['gisbax] *m* torrent

gießen ['gisən] §76 *tr* pour; (*Blumen, usw.*) water; (metal) cast, found || *impers*—es gießt it is pouring

Gießer ['gisər] *m* (-s;-) foundryman

Gießerei [gisə'raɪ] *f* (-;-en) foundry

Gieß'form *f* casting mold; (typ) matrix

Gieß'kanne *f* sprinkling can

Gift [gɪft] *n* (-[e]s;-e) poison

giftig ['gɪftɪç] *adj* poisonous; malicious

Gigant [gɪ'gant] *m* (-en;-en) giant

Gilde ['gɪldə] *f* (-;-n) guild

Gimpel ['gɪmpəl] *m* (-s;-) (coll) sucker

ging [gɪŋ] *pret* of gehen

Gipfel ['gɪpfəl] *m* (-s;-) top; peak

Gip'felkonferenz *f* summit meeting

Gips [gɪps] *m* (-es;-e) gypsum; plaster of Paris; (surg) cast

Gips'arbeit *f* plastering

Gips'diele *f* plasterboard

gipsen ['gɪpsən] *tr* plaster

Gips'verband *m* (surg) cast

Giraffe [gɪ'rafə] *f* (-;-n) giraffe

girieren [ʒɪ'riːrən] *tr* endorse

Girlande [gɪr'landə] *f* (-;-n) garland

Giro ['ʒiːro] *n* (-s;-s) endorsement

girren ['gɪrən] *intr* coo

Gis [gɪs] *n* (-;-) (mus) G sharp

Gischt [gɪʃt] *m* (-es;) foam; spray

Gitarre [gɪ'tarə] *f* (-;-n) guitar

Gitter ['gɪtər] *n* (-s;-) grating, grille; bars; lattice; railing; trellis; (electron) grid

Git'terbett *n* baby crib

Git'ternetz *n* grid (on *map*)

Git'tertor *n* wrought-iron gate

Git'terwerk *n* latticework

Glacéhandschuhe [gla'sehant∫u.ə] *pl* (& fig) kid gloves

Gladiator [gladi'atər] *m* (-s;-atoren [a'torən]) gladiator

Glanz [glants] *m* (-es;) shine; polish; luster; brilliance

glänzen ['glɛntsən] *tr* polish || *intr* shine; durch Abwesenheit g. be conspicuous by one's absence

glän'zend *adj* bright; glossy; polished; (fig) splendid, brilliant

Glanz'leder *n* patent leather

Glanz'licht *n* (paint) highlight

glanz'los *adj* dull; lackluster

Glanz'punkt *m* highlight

Glanz'stück *n* master stroke

glanz'voll *adj* brilliant, splendid

Glanz'zeit *f* heyday, golden age

Glas [glas] *n* (-es;er) glass

Glaser ['glazər] *m* (-s;-) glazier

gläsern ['glezərn] *adj* glass; glassy

Glas'hütte *f* glassworks

glasieren [gla'ziːrən] *tr* glaze; (*Kuchen*) frost, ice

glasig ['glazɪç] *adj* glassy; vitreous

Glas'jalousie *f* jalousie window

Glas'scheibe *f* pane of glass

Glasur [gla'zur] *f* (-;-en) enamel (on *pots*); glaze; (culin) icing

glatt [glat] *adj* smooth; (*eben*) even; (*poliert*) glossy; (*schlüpfrig*) slippery; (*Absage*) flat; (*Lüge*) downright || *adv* smoothly; directly; entirely

Glätte ['glɛtə] *f* (–;) smoothness; slipperiness; (*Politur*) polish

Glatt'eis *n* sheet of ice; **bei G. fahren** drive in icy conditions

glätten ['glɛtən] *tr* smooth; smooth out ‖ *ref* smooth out; become calm

glatt'streichen §85 *tr* smooth out

glatt'weg *adv* outright, point-blank

glattzüngig ['glatsyŋɪç] *adj* smoothtalking

Glatze ['glatsə] *f* (–;–n) bald head

glatz'köpfig *adj* baldheaded

Glaube ['glaubə] *m* (–ns;), **Glauben** ['glaubən] *m* (–s;) belief; faith

glauben ['glaubən] *tr* believe; (*annehmen*) suppose ‖ *intr* (*dat*) believe; **g. an** (*acc*) believe in; **j–m aufs Wort glauben take** s.o.'s word

Glau'bensbekenntnis *n* profession of faith; creed

Glau'benslehre *f* Christian doctrine

Glau'benssatz *m* dogma

gläubig ['glɔIbɪç] *adj* believing ‖ **Gläubige** §5 *mf* believer ‖ **Gläubiger** –in §6 *mf* creditor

glaublich ['glaublɪç] *adj* credible

glaub'würdig *adj* credible; reliable; plausible

Glaukom [glau'kom] *n* (–s;–e) glaucoma

gleich [glaIç] *adj* (*dat*) like; (an *dat*) equal (in); **es ist mir ganz g.** it's all the same to me ‖ *adv* equally; immediately

gleichaltrig ['glaIçaltrɪç] *adj* of the same age

gleich'artig *adj* similar, homogeneous

gleich'bedeutend *adj* synonymous

Gleich'berechtigung *f* (pol) equality

gleichen ['glaIçən] §85 *intr* (*dat*) resemble, look like, be like

glei'chermaßen *adv* equally, likewise

gleich'falls *adv* likewise; as well

gleich'förmig *adj* uniform; regular; monotonous

gleich'gesinnt *adj* like-minded

Gleich'gewicht *n* equilibrium

gleich'gültig *adj* indifferent; **es ist mir g.** it's all the same to me

Gleich'heit *f* (–;–en) equality; (*Ähnlichkeit*) likeness

gleich'klang *m* consonance; unison

gleich'kommen §99 *intr* (SEIN) (*dat*) equal; (*dat*) be tantamount to

gleich'laufend *adj* (mit) parallel (to)

gleich'machen *tr* make equal; standardize; **dem Erdboden g.** raze

Gleich'maß *n* regularity; evenness; balance, equilibrium; proportion

gleich'mäßig *adj* symmetrical; regular

Gleich'mut *m* equanimity, calmness

gleich'mütig *adj* calm

gleichnamig ['glaIçnamɪç] *adj* of the same name; (phys) like

Gleichnis ['glaIçnɪs] *n* (–ses;–se) parable; figure of speech; simile

Gleich'richter *m* (elec) rectifier

gleichsam ['glaIçzam] *adv* so to speak; more or less, practically

gleichschenklig ['glaIçʃɛŋklɪç] *adj* isosceles

Gleich'schritt *m*—**im G.** in cadence; **im G. marsch!** forward, march!

gleich'seitig *adj* equilateral

gleich'setzen *tr* (*dat* or **mit**) equate (with)

Gleich'setzung *f* (–;), **Gleich'stellung** *f* (–;) equalization

Gleich'strom *m* direct current

gleich'tun §154 *tr*—**es j–m g.** emulate s.o.

Glei'chung *f* (–;–en) (math) equation

gleichviel' *adv*—**g. wer** not matter who

gleich'wertig *adj* evenly matched

gleichwohl' *adv* nevertheless

gleich'zeitig *adj* simultaneous

gleich'ziehen §163 *intr* (mit) catch up (with or to)

Gleis [glais] *n* (–es;–e) (rr) track

Gleitboot ['glaitbot] *n* hydrofoil

gleiten ['glaitən] §86 *intr* (SEIN) glide; slip, slide

Gleitfläche ['glaitflɛçə] *f* (aer) hydroplane

Gleitflugzeug ['glaitfluktsɔIk] *n* (aer) glider

Gleitschutz– *comb.fm.* skid-proof

Gleit'zeit *f* flexitime

Gletscher ['glɛtʃər] *m* (–s;–) glacier

glich [glɪç] *pret of* gleichen

Glied [glit] *n* (–[e]s;–er) limb; member; joint; link; (anat) penis; (log, math) term; (mil) rank, file

glie'derlahm *adj* paralyzed

gliedern ['glidərn] *tr* arrange; plan; divide, break down ‖ *ref* (in *acc*) consist of

Glie'derung *f* (–;–en) arrangement; construction; division; organization

Gliedmaßen ['glitmasən] *pl* limbs

glimmen ['glɪmən] *intr* §136 & §109 *intr* glimmer; glow

Glim'mer *m* (–s;) glimmer; (min) mica

glimpflich ['glɪmpflɪç] *adj* gentle; (*Strafe*) light, lenient

glitschen ['glɪtʃən] *intr* (SEIN) slip

glitschig ['glɪtʃɪç] *adj* slippery

glitt [glɪt] *pret of* gleiten

glitzern ['glɪtsərn] *intr* glitter

global [glo'bal] *adj* global

Glo-bus ['globus] *m* (–bus & –busses; –busse & –ben [bən]) globe

Glöckchen ['glœkçən] *n* (–s;–) small bell

Glocke ['glɔkə] *f* (–;–n) bell; (e–s *Rocks*) flare

Glockenspiel (Glok'kenspiel) *n* carillon

Glockenstube (Glok'kenstube) *f*, **Glockenturm** (Glok'kenturm) *m* belfry

Glockenzug (Glok'kenzug) *m* bell rope

Glöckner ['glœknər] *m* (–s;–) bell ringer; sexton

glomm [glom] *pret of* glimmen

Glorie ['glorjə] *f* (–;–n) glory

Glo'rienschein *m* halo

glorreich ['glorraIç] *adj* glorious

glotzäugig ['glotsɔIgɪç] *adj* popeyed

glotzen ['glotsən] *intr* stare, goggle

Glück [glYk] *n* (–[e]s;) luck; fortune; happiness; **auf gut G.** at random; **zum G.** luckily

glucken ['glukən] *intr* cluck

glücken ['glYkən] *intr* (SEIN) succeed ‖ *impers*—**es glückt mir** I succeed

gluckern ['glukərn] *intr* gurgle

glück'lich adj lucky, fortunate; happy; (günstig) auspicious

glück'licherweise adv fortunately

glück'selig adj blissful; blessed; joyful

Glück'seligkeit f (-;) bliss; joy

glucksen ['gluksən] intr gurgle; chuckle

Glücks'fall m stroke of luck; windfall

Glücks'güter pl earthly possessions

Glücks'hafen m raffle drum

Glücks'pilz m (coll) lucky dog

Glücks'spiel n game of chance

Glücks'topf m grab bag

glück'verheißend adj auspicious

Glück'wunsch m good wishes, congratulations

Glück'wunschkarte f greeting card

Glühbirne ['glybırnə] f light bulb

glühen ['gly·ən] tr make red-hot; (metal) anneal || intr glow

glü'hendheiß adj red-hot

Glüh'faden ['glyfadən] m filament

Glüh'wurm ['glyvurm] m firefly

Glut [glut] f (-;) embers; fire; scorching heat; (fig) ardor

Glyzerin [glytsə'rin] n (-s) glycerine

GmbH abbr (Gesellschaft mit beschränkter Haftung) Inc.; Ltd. (Brit)

Gnade ['gnadə] f (-;-n) grace; favor; mercy; von eigenen Gnaden self-styled

Gna'denbeweis m token of favor

Gna'denbrot n—bei j-m das G. essen to live on s.o.'s charity

Gna'denfrist f grace, e.g., e-e G. von zwei Monaten two months' grace

Gna'dengesuch n plea for mercy

Gna'denstoß m coup de grâce, deathblow

gnädig ['gnedıç] adj gracious, kind; merciful; gnädige Frau madam; Sehr verehrte gnädige Frau Dear Madam

Gold [gɔlt] n (-[e]s) gold

Gold'blech n gold foil

Gold'fink m (orn) goldfinch

goldig ['gɔldıç] adj (coll) cute

Gold'plombe f (dent) gold filling

Gold'schmied m goldsmith

Gold'schnitt m gilt edging

Golf [gɔlf] m (-[e]s;-e) gulf; bay || n (-s) golf

Golf'platz m golf course

Golf'schläger m golf club

Gondel ['gɔndəl] f (-;-n) gondola

Gon'delführer m gondolier

gönnen ['gœnən] tr not begrudge; allow; j-m etw nicht g. begrudge s.o. s.th.

Gön'ner –in §6 mf patron

gön'nerhaft adj patronizing

Gön'nerschaft f (-;) patronage

gor [gor] pret of gären

Gorilla [go'rıla] m (-s;-s) gorilla

goß [gɔs] pret of gießen

Gosse ['gɔsə] f (-;-n) gutter

Gote ['gotə] m (-n;-n) Goth

gotisch ['gotıʃ] adj Gothic

Gott [gɔt] m (-[e]s;⁀er) god; God

gottbegnadet ['gɔtbəgnadət] adj gifted

gott'ergeben adj resigned to God's will

Got'tesdienst m divine service; Mass

got'tesfürchtig adj God-fearing

Got'tesgabe f godsend

got'teslästerlich adj blasphemous

Got'teslästerung f blasphemy

Got'tesurteil n ordeal

gott'gefällig adj pleasing to God

Gott'heit f (-;-en) deity, divinity

Göttin ['gœtın] f (-;-nen) goddess

göttlich ['gœtlıç] adj godlike, divine; (fig) heavenly

gottlob' interj thank goodness!

Gott'mensch m God incarnate

gott'selig adj godly

gott'verlassen adj godforsaken

Götze ['gœtsə] m (-n;-n) idol

Göt'zenbild n idol

Göt'zendiener –in §6 mf idolater

Göt'zendienst m idolatry

Gouvernante [guver'nantə] f (-;-n) governess

Gouverneur [guver'nør] m (-s;-e) governor

Grab [grap] n (-[e]s;⁀er) grave; tomb

graben ['grabən] §87 tr dig; burrow || Graben m (-s;⁀) ditch; trench; moat

Grab'geläute n death knell

Grab'gesang m funeral dirge

Grab'hügel m burial mound

Grab'inschrift f epitaph

Grab'mal n tombstone; tomb, sepulcher

Grab'stätte f burial place

Grab'stelle f burial plot

Grad [grat] m (-[e]s;-e) degree; grade; (mil) rank

grade ['gradə] adv var of gerade

Grad'einteilung f gradation

Grad'messer m graduated scale; (fig) yardstick

grad'weise adv by degrees

Graf [graf] m (-en;-en) count; earl (Brit)

Gräfin ['grefın] f (-;-nen) countess

gräflich ['greflıç] adj count's; earl's

Graf'schaft f (-;-en) county

gram [gram] adj—j-m g. sein be cross with s.o. || Gram m (-[e]s) grief

grämen ['gremən] tr sadden, distress || ref (über acc) grieve (over)

grämlich ['gremlıç] adj glum; crabby

Gramm [gram] n (-s;- & -e) gram

Grammatik [gra'matık] f (-;-en) grammar

grammatisch [gra'matıʃ] adj grammatical

Gran [gran] n (-[e]s;) (fig) bit, jot

Granat [gra'nat] m (-[e]s;-e) garnet

Granat'apfel m pomegranate

Granate [gra'natə] f (-;-n) (artil) shell; (mil) grenade

Granat'feuer n shelling

Granat'hülse f shell case

Granat'splitter m shrapnel

Granat'werfer m (mil) mortar

grandios [grandi'os] adj grandiose

Granit [gra'nit] m (-[e]s;-e) granite

Graphik ['grafık] f (-;-en) graphic arts; print; engraving; woodcut

graphisch ['grafıʃ] adj graphic

Graphit [gra'fit] m (-[e]s;) graphite

Gras [gras] n (-es;⁀er) grass

grasen ['grazən] intr graze

Gras'halm m blade of grass

Grashüpfer ['grashypfer] m (-s;-) grasshopper

grasig ['graːzɪç] adj grassy
Gras'mäher m lawn mower; grass cutter
Gras'mähmaschine f lawn mower
Gras'narbe f sod, turf
grassieren [gra'siːrən] intr rage
gräßlich ['grɛslɪç] adj grisly
Gras'weide f pasture
Grat [graːt] m (-[e]s;-e) ridge; edge
Gräte ['grɛːtə] f (-;-n) fishbone
Gratifikation [gratifika'tsjoːn] f (-;
-en) bonus
grätig ['grɛːtɪç] adj full of fishbones;
(mürrisch) crabby
gratis ['graːtɪs] adv gratis; g. und
franko (coll) for free
Gratulation [gratula'tsjoːn] f (-;-en)
congratulations
gratulieren [gratu'liːrən] intr—j-m g.
zu congratulate s.o. on
grau [grau] adj gray; (Vorzeit) re-
mote || Grau n (- & -s;-s) gray
Grau'bär m grizzly bear
grauen ['grau-ən] intr dawn || impers
—es graut day is breaking; es graut
mir vor (dat) I shudder at || Grauen
n (-s;) (vor dat) horror (of)
grau'enhaft, grau'envoll adj horrible
gräulich ['grɔɪlɪç] adj grayish
Graupe ['graupə] f (-;-n) peeled barley
graupeln ['graupəln] impers—es grau-
pelt it is sleeting || Graupeln pl sleet
Graus [graus] m (-es;) dread, horror
grausam ['grauzam] adj cruel; (coll)
awful
Grau'schimmel m gray horse
grausen ['grauzən] impers—es graust
mir vor (dat) I shudder at
grausig ['grauzɪç] adj gruesome
Graveur [gra'vøːr] m (-s;-e) engraver
gravieren [gra'viːrən] tr engrave
gravie'rend adj aggravating
gravitätisch [gravi'tɛːtɪʃ] adj stately
Grazie ['graːtsjə] f (-;-n) grace, charm
graziös [gra'tsjøːs] adj graceful
Greif [graɪf] m (-[e]s;-e) griffin
greifbar ['graɪfbar] adj tangible; at
hand
greifen ['graɪfən] §88 tr grasp; seize;
(Note) strike || intr (Anker) catch;
(Zahnrad) engage; ans Herz g. touch
deeply; an j-s Ehre g. attack s.o.'s
honor; g. in (acc) reach into; g. nach
reach for; try to seize; g. zu reach
for; (fig) resort to; um sich g. grope
about; (Feuer) spread; zu den Waffen g. take up arms
Greis [graɪs] m (-es;-e) old man
Grei'senalter n old age
grei'senhaft adj aged; senile
Greisin ['graɪzɪn] f (-;-nen) old lady
grell [grɛl] adj (Ton) shrill; (Farbe,
Kleider) flashy; (Licht) glaring
Gre•mium ['greːmjum] n (-s;-mien
[mjən]) group, body; committee;
corporation
Grenze ['grɛntsə] f (-;-n) boundary;
frontier; borderline; limit
grenzen ['grɛntsən] intr (an acc) adjoin, border (on); (fig) verge (on)
gren'zenlos adj limitless
Grenz'fall m borderline case

Grenz'linie f boundary line
Grenz'sperre f ban on border traffic;
frontier barricade
Grenz'stein m boundary stone
Greuel ['grɔɪ-əl] m (-s;-) abhorrence;
horror, abomination
Greu'eltat f atrocity
greulich ['grɔɪlɪç] adj horrible
Griebs ['griːps] m (-es;-e) core
Grieche ['griːçə] m (-n;-n) Greek
Grie'chenland n (-s;) Greece
Griechin ['griːçɪn] f (-;-nen) Greek
griechisch ['griːçɪʃ] adj Greek
Griesgram ['griːsgram] m (-[e]s;-e)
(coll) grouch
Grieß [griːs] m (-es;-e) grit; gravel
Grieß'mehl n farina
Griff [grɪf] pret of greifen || Griff m
(-[e]s;-e) grip; handle; hilt; (mus)
touch
Grill [grɪl] m (-s;-s) grill; broiler
Grille ['grɪlə] f (-;-n) cricket; (fig)
whim
grillen ['grɪlən] tr grill; broil
gril'lenhaft adj whimsical
Grimasse [grɪ'masə] f (-;-n) grimace
Grimm [grɪm] m (-[e]s;) anger, fury
grimmig ['grɪmɪç] adj furious
Grind [grɪnt] m (-[e]s;-e) scab
grinsen ['grɪnzən] intr grin
Grippe ['grɪpə] f (-;-n) grippe
grob [groːp] adj coarse, rough; crude
Grobian ['groːbjan] m (-s;-e) boor
gröblich ['grøːplɪç] adj gross
grölen ['grøːlən] intr shout raucously
Groll [grɔl] m (-[e]s;) resentment
grollen ['grɔlən] intr rumble; (über
acc) be resentful (about); j-m g.
have a grudge against s.o.
Grönland ['grøːnlant] n (-s;) Green-
land
Gros [groːs] n (-ses;-) gross || [gro]
n (-;-) bulk; (mil) main forces
Groschen ['grɔʃən] m (-s;-) (Aust)
penny (one hundredth of a shilling)
groß [groːs] adj big, large; tall; great
groß'artig adj grand; magnificent
Groß'aufnahme f (phot) close-up
groß'äugig adj wide-eyed
Groß'betrieb m big company
Großbritan'nien n Great Britain
Größe ['grøːsə] f (-;-n) size, greatness;
celebrity; (astr) magnitude; (math)
quantity
Groß'eltern pl grandparents
Groß'enkel m great-grandson
Groß'enkelin f great-granddaughter
großenteils ['groːsəntaɪls] adv largely
Größenwahn ['grøːsənvaːn] f megalo-
mania
Groß'grundbesitz m large estate
Groß'handel m wholesale trade; im G.
kaufen buy wholesale
Großhandels—comb.fm. wholesale
Groß'händler -in §6 mf wholesaler
Groß'handlung f (-;-en) wholesale
business
groß'herzig adj big-hearted
Grossist [grɔ'sɪst] m (-en;-en) whole-
saler
groß'jährig adj of legal age
Groß'maul n bigmouth
Groß'mut m magnanimity

groß'mütig *adj* big-hearted
Groß'mutter *f* grandmother
Groß'onkel *m* great-uncle
Groß'schreibung *f* capitalization
Groß'segel *n* main sail
Groß'sprecher *m* braggart
großspurig ['grosʃpurɪç] *adj* pompous
Groß'stadt *f* large city (*with over 100,000 inhabitants*)
Großstädter ['grosʃtetər] *m* (-s;-) (coll) city slicker
Groß'tat *f* achievement
Groß'teil *m* major part
größtenteils ['grøstəntaɪls] *adv* mainly
groß'tun §154 *intr* brag; put on the dog
Groß'vater *m* grandfather
Groß'wild *n* big game
groß'ziehen §163 *tr* bring up, raise
großzügig ['grostsygɪç] *adj* broad-minded, liberal; generous; large-scale
grotesk [gro'tesk] *adj* grotesque
Grotte ['grotə] *f* (-;-n) grotto
grub [grup] *pret of* graben
Grübchen ['grypçən] *n* (-s;-) dimple
Grube ['grubə] *f* (-;-n) pit; mine
Grübelei [grybə'laɪ] *f* (-;-en) brooding
grübeln ['grybəln] *intr* brood
Gruben- [grubən] *comb.fm.* mine, miner's
Gruft [gruft] *f* (-;̈e) tomb, vault
grün [gryn] *adj* green; Grüne Minna (sl) paddy wagon || Grün *n* (-s;) green
Grün'anlage *f* public park
Grund [grunt] *m* (-[e]s;̈e) ground; land; bottom; foundation, basis; cause, ground; auf G. von on the strength of; G. und Boden property; im Grunde genommen after all; in G. und Boden outright
-grund *m comb.fm.* bottom of; -ground; grounds for, reasons for
Grund'anstrich *m* first coat
Grund'ausbildung *f* (mil) basic training
Grund'bedeutung *f* primary meaning
Grund'begriff *m* fundamental principle
Grund'besitz *m* real estate
Grund'buch *n* land register
grund'ehr'lich *adj* thoroughly honest
gründen ['gryndən] *tr* found; g. auf (*acc*) base on || *ref* (auf *acc*) be based (on)
Gründer -in ['gryndər(ɪn)] §6 *mf* founder
grund'falsch' *adj* absolutely false
Grund'farbe *f* primary color
Grund'fläche *f* area; (geom) base
grundieren [grun'dirən] *tr* prime; size
Grundier'farbe *f* primer coat
Grundier'schicht *f* primer coat
Grund'kapital *n* capital stock
Grund'lage *f* basis, foundation
grund'legend *adj* basic, fundamental
Grund'legung *f* founding, foundation
gründlich ['gryntlɪç] *adj* thorough
Grund'linie *f* (geom) base; Grundlinien basic features, outlines
Gründon'nerstag *m* Holy Thursday
Grund'riß *m* floor plan; outline

Grund'satz *m* principle
grundsätzlich ['gruntzetslɪç] *adj* basic || *adv* as a matter of principle
Grund'schule *f* primary school
Grund'stein *m* cornerstone
Grund'stellung *f* position of attention; die G. einnehmen come to attention
Grund'steuer *f* real-estate tax
Grund'stoff *m* raw material; (chem) element
Grund'strich *m* downstroke
Grund'stück *n* lot, property
Grund'ton *m* (fig) prevailing mood; (mus) keynote; (paint) ground shade
Grün'dung *f* (-;-en) foundation
grund'verschie'den *adj* entirely different
Grund'wasserspiegel *m* water table
Grund'zahl *f* cardinal number
Grund'zug *m* main feature; Grundzüge fundamentals, essentials
Grüne ['grynə] *n*—ins G. into the country
grün'lich *adj* greenish
Grün'schnabel *m* know-it-all
Grünspan ['grynʃpan] *m* (-[e]s;) verdigris
Grün'streifen *m* grass strip; (auf der Autobahn) median strip
grunzen ['gruntsən] *tr & intr* grunt
Gruppe ['grupə] *f* (-;-n) group; (mil) squad
Grup'penführer *m* group leader; (hist) lieutenant general (*of S.S. troops*); (mil) squad leader
gruppieren [gru'pirən] *tr & ref* group
Gruppie'rung *f* (-;-en) grouping
gruselig ['gruzəlɪç] *adj* creepy
gruseln ['gruzəln] *intr*—j-n g. machen give s.o. the creeps || *ref* have a creepy feeling || *impers*—es gruselt mir (or mich) it gives me the creeps
Gruß [grus] *m* (-es;̈e) greeting; salute; greetings, regards; mit freundlichem Gruß, Ihr ... Sincerely yours
grüßen ['grysən] *tr* greet; salute, grüß Gott! hello!; j-n g. lassen send best regards to s.o.
Grütze ['grytsə] *f* (-;-n) groats; (coll) brains
gucken ['gukən] *intr* look; peep
Guck'loch *n* peephole
Guerilla [ge'rɪlja] *m* (-s;-s) guerilla
Gulasch ['gula ʃ] *n* (-[e]s;) goulash
gültig ['gyltɪç] *adj* valid; legal
Gummi ['gumi] *m & n* (-s;-s) gum; rubber
gum'miartig *adj* gummy; rubbery
Gum'miband *n* (-[e]s;̈er) rubber band; elastic
Gum'mibaum *m* rubber plant
Gum'mibonbon *m & n* gumdrop
gummieren [gu'mirən] *tr* gum; rubberize
Gum'miknüppel *m* truncheon; billy club
Gummilinse *f* (phot) zoom lens
Gum'mimantel *m* mackintosh
Gum'mireifen *m* tire
Gum'mischuhe *pl* rubbers
Gum'mizelle *f* padded cell
Gunst [gunst] *f* favor, goodwill; kindness, good turn

Gunst'bezeigung f expression of good-will

günstig ['gʏnstɪç] adj favorable; (Bedingungen) easy

Günstling ['gʏnstlɪŋ] m (-s;-e) favorite; (pej) minion

Gurgel ['gurgəl] f (-;-n) gullet

gurgeln ['gurgəln] intr gurgle; gargle

Gurke ['gurkə] f (-;-n) cucumber

Gurt [gurt] m (-[e]s;-e) belt, strap

Gürtel ['gʏrtəl] m (-s;-) girdle; belt; (geog) zone

gürten ['gʏrtən] tr gird

Guß [gus] m (Gusses; Güsse) gush; (Regen) downpour; (Gießen) casting; (culin) icing; (typ) font

gut [gut] adj good; es ist schon gut it's all right; mach's gut! so long || adv well || Gut n (-[e]s;-er) good; possessions; estate; (com) commodity; **Güter** goods; assets

Gut'achten n (-s;-) expert opinion

gut'artig adj good-natured; (pathol) benign

gut'aussehend adj good-looking

Gut'dünken n (-s;) judgment; discretion; nach G. at will, as one pleases; (culin) to taste

Gute ['gutə] §5 n good; alles G! best of everything!; sein Gutes haben have its good points

Güte ['gytə] f (-;) goodness

Güter- [gytər] comb.fm. freight; property; (com) of goods

Gü'terabfertigung f freight office

Gü'terbahnhof m (rr) freight yard

gut'erhalten adj in good condition

Gü'terwagen m freight car; **geschlossener G.** boxcar; **offener G.** gondola car

Gü'terzug m freight train

gut'gelaunt adj good-humored

gut'gesinnt adj well-disposed

gut'haben §89 tr have to one's credit || **Guthaben** n (-s;-) credit balance

gut'heißen §95 tr approve of

gut'herzig adj good-hearted

gütig ['gytɪç] adj kind, good

gütlich ['gytlɪç] adj amicable

gut'machen tr—wieder g. make good for

gut'mütig adj good-natured

gut'sagen intr—für j-n g. vouch for s.o.

Gut'schein m coupon; credit note

gut'schreiben §62 tr—j-m e-n Betrag g. credit s.o. with a sum

Gut'schrift f credit entry; credit item

Gut'schriftsanzeige f credit note

Guts'herr m landowner

gut'tun §154 intr do good; behave

gut'willig adj willing, obliging

Gymnasiast -in [gʏm'nazjast(ɪn)] §7 mf high school student

Gymna•sium [gʏm'nazjum] n (-s;-sien [zjən]) high school (with academic course)

Gymnastik [gʏm'nastɪk] f (-;) gymnastics

Gynäkologe [gʏnɛko'logə] m (-n;-n), **Gynakologin** [gʏnɛko'login] f (-; nen) gynecologist

Gynäkologie [gʏnɛkɔlɔ'gi] f (-;) gynecology

H

H, h [ha] invar n H, h; (mus) B

Haar [har] n (-[e]s;-e) hair; (tex) nap, pile; aufs H. exactly; um ein H. by a hair's breadth

Haar'büschel n tuft of hair

haaren ['harən] intr lose hair

Haarfärbmittel ['harfɛrpmɪtəl] n hair dye

Haar'feder f hairspring

haar'genau' adj exact, precise

haarig ['harɪç] adj hairy

haar'klein adj (coll) in detail

Haar'locke f lock of hair

Haar'nadel f hairpin

haar'scharf' adj razor-sharp

Haar'schneider m barber

Haar'schnitt m haircut

Haar'spange f barrette

Haarspray ['harspre] m (-s;-s) hair spray

haar'sträubend adj hair-raising

Haar'teil m hair piece

Haar'tolle f loose curl

Haar'tracht f hairdo

Haar'trockner m, **Haar'trockenhaube** f hair dryer

Haar'wäsche f shampoo

Haar'wasser n hair tonic

Haar'wickler m curler; hair roller

Haar'zwange f tweezers

Hab [hap] invar n—Hab und Gut possessions

Habe ['habə] f (-;) possessions

haben ['habən] §89 tr & aux have || **Haben** n (-s;) credit side

Habe'nichts m (-es;-e) have-not

Hab'gier f greed, avarice

hab'haft adj—h. werden (genit) get hold of; (Diebes) apprehend

Habicht ['habɪçt] m (-[e]s;-e) hawk

Ha'bichtsnase f aquiline nose

Habilitation [habɪlɪta'tsjon] f (-;-en) accreditation as a university lecturer

habilitieren [habɪlɪ'tirən] ref be accredited as a university lecturer

Hab'seligkeiten pl belongings

Hab'sucht f greed, avarice

hab'süchtig adj greedy, avaricious

Hackbeil ['hakbaɪl] n cleaver

Hacke ['hakə] f (-;-n) heel; hoe; pick; pickax; hatchet; mattock

hacken ['hakən] tr hack, chop; peck || intr (nach) peck (at)

Häckerling ['hɛkərlɪŋ] m (-s;) chaff

Hackfleisch ['hakflaɪ/] n ground meat

Häcksel ['hɛksəl] n (-s;) chaff

Hader ['haːdər] *m* (-s;) strife ‖ *m* (-s; -n) rag

hadern ['haːdərn] *intr* quarrel

Hafen ['haːfən] *m* (-s;ː) harbor; port; (fig) haven

Ha'fenamt *n* port authority

Ha'fenanlagen *pl* docks

Ha'fenarbeiter *m* longshoreman

Ha'fendamm *m* jetty, mole

Ha'fensperre *f* blockade

Ha'fenstadt *f* seaport

Ha'fenviertel *n* dock area, waterfront

Hafer ['haːfər] *m* (-s;-) oats; **ihn sticht der H.** he's feeling his oats

Ha'fergrütze *f*, **Ha'fermehl** *m* oatmeal

Hafner ['haːfnər] *m* (-s;-) potter

Haft [haft] *f* (-;) arrest; custody; imprisonment; **in H.** under arrest; in custody; **in prison**

haftbar ['haftbaːr] *adj* (jur) liable

Haft'befehl *m* warrant for arrest

haften ['haftən] *intr* (an *dat*) cling (to), stick (to); **h. für** vouch for; (jur) be held liable for; (jur) put up bail for

Haft'fähigkeit *f*, **Haft'festigkeit** *f* adhesion

Häftling ['heftlɪŋ] *m* (-s;-e) prisoner

Haft'lokal *n* (mil) guardhouse

Haft'pflicht *f* liability

haft'pflichtig (**für**) *adj* liable (for)

Haft'pflichtversicherung *f* liability insurance

Haft'richter *m* (jur) magistrate

Haft'schale *f* contact lens

Haf'tung *f* (-;-en) liability

Hag [haːk] *m* (-[e]s;-e) enclosure; (*Hain*) grove; (*Buschwerk*) bushes

Hagedorn ['haːgədɔrn] *m* hawthorn

Hagel ['haːgəl] *m* (-s;) hail

Ha'gelkorn *n* hailstone

hageln ['haːgəln] *intr* (SEIN) (fig) rain down ‖ *impers*—es hagelt it is hailing

Ha'gelschauer *m* hailstorm

hager ['haːgər] *adj* gaunt, haggard

Hagestolz ['haːgə/tɔlts] *m* (-es;-e) confirmed bachelor

Häher ['heːər] *m* (-s;-) (orn) jay

Hahn [haːn] *m* (-[e]s;ːe) rooster; (*Wasser-*) faucet; **den H. spannen** cock the gun; **H. im Korbe sein** rule the roost

Hähnchen ['heçən] *n* (-s;-) young rooster

Hah'nenkamm *m* cockscomb

Hah'nenkampf *m* cock fight

Hah'nenschrei *m* crow of the cock

Hahnrei ['haːnraɪ] *m* (-s;-e) cuckold

Hai [haɪ] *m* (-[e]s;-e), **Hai'fisch** *m* shark

Hain [haɪn] *m* (-[e]s;-e) grove

Haiti [ha'iti] *n* (-s;) Haiti

Häkelarbeit ['heːkəlarbaɪt] *f* crocheting

häkeln ['heːkəln] *tr* & *intr* crochet ‖ **Häkeln** *n* (-s;) crocheting

Haken ['haːkən] *m* (-s;-) hook; (*Spange*) clasp; (fig) snag, hitch

Ha'kenkreuz *n* swastika

Ha'kennase *f* hooknose

halb [halp] *adj* & *adv* half

halb-, Halb- *comb.fm.* half-, semi-

Halb'blut *n* half-breed

-halber [halbər] *comb.fm.* for the sake of; owing to

halb'fett *adj* (typ) bold

Halb'franzband *m* (bb) half leather

halb'gar *adj* (culin) (medium) rare

Halb'gott *m* demigod

Halbheit ['halphaɪt] *f* (-;) halfhalf

Halb'kugel *f* hemisphere

halbieren [hal'biːrən] *tr* halve, bisect

Halb'insel *f* peninsula

Halb'kettenfahrzeug *n* half-track

Halb'kugel *f* hemisphere

halb'lang *adj* half-length; **halblange Ärmel** half sleeves

halb'laut *adj* low ‖ *adv* in a low voice

Halb'leiter *m* (elec) semiconductor

halb'mast *adv* at half-mast; **auf h.** at half-mast

Halb'messer *m* radius

halbpart ['halppart] *adv*—**mit j-m h. machen** go fifty-fifty with s.o.

Halb'schuh *m* low shoe

Halb'schwergewicht *n* light-heavyweight division

Halb'schwergewichtler *m* light-heavyweight

halb'stündig *adj* half-hour

halb'stündlich *adj* half-hourly ‖ *adv* every half hour

Halb'vers *m* hemistich

halbwegs ['halpveːks] *adv* halfway

Halb'welt *f* demimonde

halbwüchsig ['halpvyːksɪç] *adj* teenage ‖ **Halbwüchsige** §5 *mf* teenager

Halb'zug *m* (mil) section

Halde ['haldə] *f* (-;-n) slope; (*Schutt-*) slag pile

half [half] *pret* of **helfen**

Hälfte ['helftə] *f* (-;-n) half

Halfter ['halftər] *f* (-;-n) holster ‖ *n* (-s;-) halter

Hall [hal] *m* (-[e]s;-e) sound; clang

Halle ['halə] *f* (-;-n) hall; (*e-s Hotels*) lobby; (aer) hangar; (rr) concourse

hallen ['halən] *intr* sound, resound

Hal'lenbad *n* indoor pool

Hallo [ha'loː] *n* (-s;) hullabaloo ‖ *interj* (to attract attention) hey!; (telp) hello

Halm [halm] *m* (-[e]s;-e) stem, stalk; blade (*of grass*)

Hals [hals] *m* (-es;ːe) neck; throat; **H. über Kopf** head over heels

Hals'abschneider *m* cutthroat

hals'abschneiderisch *adj* cutthroat

Hals'ader *f* jugular vein

Hals'ausschnitt *m* neckline, neck

Hals'band *n* (-[e]s;ːer) necklace, choker; (*e-s Hundes*) collar

halsbrecherisch ['halsbreçərɪʃ] *adj* breakneck

Hals'entzündung *f* sore throat

Hals'kette *f* necklace, chain

Hals'kragen *m* collar

Hals'krause *f* frilled collar

hals'starrig *adj* stubborn

Hals'weh *n* sore throat

halt [halt] *adv* just, simply ‖ *interj* stop!; (mil) halt! ‖ **Halt** *m* (-[e]s;-e) hold; foothold; support; stability; stop, halt

haltbar ['haltbaːr] *adj* durable; tenable

halten ['haltən] §90 *tr* hold; keep; detain; (*Rede*) deliver; (*Vorlesung*) give; (*feiern*) celebrate; **es h. mit** do with; **have an affair with; etw auf sich h.** have self-respect; **j-n h. für** take s.o. for; **viel h. von** think highly of || *ref* keep, last; hold ones own; **an sich h.** restrain oneself; **auf sich h.** be particular about one's appearance; **sich an etw h.** (fig) stick to s.th.; **sich an j-n h.** hold s.o. liable; **sich gesund h.** keep healthy; **sich links h.** keep to the left || *intr* stop; last; **h. auf** (*acc*) pay attention to; **h. nach** head for; **h. zu** stick by; **was das Zeug hält** with might and main
Hal'ter *m* (*-s;-*) holder; rack; owner
Hal'teriemen *m* strap (*on bus or trolley*)
Hal'testelle *f* bus stop, trolley stop; (rr) stop
Hal'teverbot *n* (public sign) no stopping
-haltig [haltıç] *comb.fm.* containing
halt'los *adj* without support; helpless; unprincipled
halt'machen *intr* stop, halt
Hal'tung *f* (*-;-en*) pose, posture; attitude
Halte'zeichen *n* stop sign
Halunke [ha'luŋkə] *m* (*-;-n*) rascal
hämisch ['hemɪʃ] *adj* spiteful, malicious
Hammel ['haməl] *m* (*-s;-e & ⁚*) wether; (coll) mutton-head; (culin) mutton
Ham'melkeule *f* leg of mutton
Hammer ['hamər] *m* (*-s;⁚*) hammer; gavel; **unter den H. kommen** be auctioned off
hämmern ['hemərn] *tr & intr* hammer
Hämorrhoiden [hemɔrɔ'idən] *pl* hemorroids, piles
Hampelmann ['hampəlman] *m* (*-[e]s; ⁚er*) jumping jack
hamstern ['hamstərn] *tr* hoard
Hand [hant] *f* (*-;⁚e*) hand; **an H. von** with the help of; **auf eigene H.** of one's own accord; **aus erster H.** (*bei Verkauf*) one-owner; **aus erster H. haben** hear first-hand; **aus erster H. kaufen** buy directly; **bei der H.** at hand, handy; **die letzte H.** finishing touches; **die öffentliche H.** the state, public authorities; **es liegt auf der H.** it is obvious; **H. ans Werk legen** get down to work; **H. aufs Herz!** cross my heart!; **Hände hoch!** hands up!; **H. und Fuß haben** make sense; **in die H. (or Hände) bekommen** get one's hands on; **j-m an die H. gehen** lend s.o. a hand; **j-m die H. drücken** shake hands with s.o.; **j-m etw an (die) H. geben** quote s.o. a price on s.th.; **j-m zur H. gehen** lend s.o. a hand; **unter der H.** underhandedly; unofficially; **von der H. weisen** reject; **zu Händen Herrn X** Attention Mr. X; **zur H.** at hand, handy
Hand'arbeit *f* manual labor; needlework
Hand'aufheben *n*, **Hand'aufhebung** *f* show of hands

Hand'ausgabe *f* abridged edition
Hand'bedienung *f* manual control
Hand'betrieb *m*—**mit** (or **für**) **H.** hand-operated
Hand'bibliothek *f* reference library
hand'breit *adj* wide as a hand || **Hand'breit** *f* (*-;-*) hand's breadth
Hand'bremse *f* (aut) hand brake
Hand'buch *n* handbook, manual
Händedruck ['hendədruk] *m* handshake
Händeklatschen ['hendəklatʃən] *n* clapping
Handel ['handəl] *m* (*-s;⁚*) trade; deal, bargain; business; affair; **e-n H. eingehen** conclude a deal; **e-n H. treiben** carry on business; **H. und Gewerbe** trade and industry; **Händel suchen** pick a quarrel; **im H. sein** be on the market; **in den H. bringen** put on the market
-handel *m comb.fm.* –trade, –business
handeln ['handəln] *intr* act; take action; proceed; **gegen das Gesetz h.** go against the law; **gut an j-m h.** treat s.o. well; **h. über** (*acc*) or **von** deal with; **h. mit** do business with; **im großen h.** do wholesale business || *impers ref*—**es handelt sich um** it is a matter of; **darum handelt es sich nicht** that's not the point
Han'delsabkommen *n* trade agreement
Han'delsartikel *m* commodity
Han'delsbetrieb *m* commercial enterprise; business; firm
Han'delsbilanz *f* balance of trade; **aktive H.** favorable balance of trade
Han'delsdampfer *m* (naut) merchantman
han'delseinig *adj*—**h. werden mit** come to terms with
Han'delsgärtner *m* truck farmer
Han'delskammer *f* chamber of commerce
Han'delsmarine *f* merchant marine
Han'delsmarke *f* trademark
Han'delsminister *m* secretary of commerce
Han'delsministerium *n* department of commerce
Han'delsplatz *m* trade center
Han'delsschiff *n* merchantman
Han'delssperre *f* trade embargo
händelsüchtig ['hendəlzYçtıç] *adj* quarrelsome
Han'delsvertrag *m* commercial treaty
Han'delswert *m* trade-in value
Han'delszeichen *n* trademark
Hand'exemplar *n* desk copy
Hand'fertigkeit *f* manual dexterity
Hand'fessel *f* handcuff
hand'fest *adj* sturdy; well-founded
Hand'fläche *f* palm of the hand
Hand'geld *n* advance payment; deposit
Hand'gelenk *n* wrist; **aus** (or **mit**) **dem H.** (coll) easy as pie
hand'gemein *adj*—**h. werden** come to blows
Hand'gemenge *n* scuffle
Hand'gepäck *n* hand luggage
Hand'gepäckschließfach *n* locker
Hand'granate *f* hand grenade
hand'greiflich *adj* tangible; obvious;

j-m etw h. machen make s.th. clear to s.o.; h. werden come to blows

Hand'griff m grip; handle; keinen H. tun not lift a finger

Hand'habe f (-;-n) handle; pretext; occasion; er hat keine H. gegen mich he has nothing on me

hand'haben tr handle; (Maschine) operate; (Rechtspflege) administer; (fig) manage

–händig [hendıç] comb.fm. -handed

Hand'karren m hand cart, push cart

Hand'koffer m suitcase; attaché case

Handlanger ['hantlaŋər] m (-s;-) handyman; (pej) underling

Händler –in ['hendlɐ(ın)] §6 mf dealer, merchant; storekeeper

Hand'lesekunst f palmistry

Hand'leserin f (-;-nen) palm reader

hand'lich adj handy

Hand'lung f (-;-en) deed; act, action

–handlung f comb.fm. business; shop

Hand'lungsgehilfe m clerk, salesman

Hand'lungsweise f conduct

Hand'pflege f manicure

Hand'pflegerin f (-;-nen) manicurist

Hand'rücken m back of the hand

Hand'schaltung f manual shift

Hand'schelle f handcuff

Hand'schlag m handshake

Hand'schreiben n hand-written letter

Hand'schrift f handwriting; manuscript; (sl) slap, box on the ear

Hand'schriftenkunde f paleography

hand'schriftlich adj hand-written

Hand'schuh m glove

Hand'schuhfach n (aut) glove compartment

Hand'streich m (mil) raid

Hand'tasche f handbag, purse

Hand'tuch n towel; schmales H. (sl) beanpole

Hand'tuchhalter m towel rack

Hand'umdrehen n—im. H. in a jiffy

Hand'voll f (-;-) handful

Hand'werk n craft, trade; j-m ins H. pfuschen (sl) stick one's nose in s.o. else's business

Hand'werker m craftsman

Hand'werkszeug n tool kit

Hand'wörterbuch n pocket dictionary

Hand'wurzel f wrist

Hand'zettel m handbill

hanebüchen ['hanəbyçən] adj (coll) incredible; (coll) monstrous

Hanf [hanf] m (-[e]s;) hemp

Hang [haŋ] m (-[e]s;:e) slope; hillside; (fig) inclination, tendency

Hangar ['haŋgar] m (-s;-s) hangar

Hängebacken ['heŋəbakən] pl jowls

Hängebauch ['heŋəbaux] m potbelly

Hängebrücke ['heŋəbrykə] f suspension bridge

Hängematte ['heŋəmatə] f hammock

hängen ['heŋən] tr hang || ref—sich an j-n h. hang on to s.o.; sich ans Telephon h. be on the telephone || §92 intr hang; cling, stick

hän'genbleiben §62 intr (SEIN) stick; be detained, get stuck; (an dat) get caught (on); (educ) stay behind

Hans [hans] m (-' & -ens;) Johnny, Jack

Hans'dampf m (-[e]s;-e) busybody; H. in allen Gassen jack-of-all trades

Hänselei [henzə'laı] f (-;-en) teasing

hänseln ['henzəln] tr tease

Hans'narr m fool

Hans'wurst m (-es;-e & :e) clown

Hantel ['hantəl] f (-;-n) dumbbell

hantieren [han'tirən] intr (an acc) be busy (with); mit etw h. handle s.th.

hapern ['hapərn] impers—bei mir hapert es an (dat) (or mit) I am short of; bei mir hapert es in (dat) (or mit) I am weak in; damit hapert's that's the hitch

Happen ['hapən] m (-s;-) morsel; mouthful; (fig) good opportunity; fetter H. (coll) big hawl

happig ['hapıç] adj greedy; (Preis) steep

Härchen ['herçən] n (-s;-) tiny hair

Harem ['harem] m (-s;-s) harem

Häre·sie [here'zi] f (-;-sien ['zi·ən]) heresy

Häretiker [he'retikər] m (-s;-) heretic

Harfe ['harfə] f (-;-n) harp

Harke ['harkə] f (-;-n) rake

harken ['harkən] tr & intr rake

Harm [harm] m (-[e]s;) harm; grief

härmen ['hermən] ref (um) grieve (over)

harm'los adj harmless

Harmo·nie [harmo'ni] f (-;-nien ['ni·ən]) harmony

harmonieren [harmo'nirən] intr harmonize

Harmoni·ka [har'monıka] f (-;-kas & -ken [kən]) accordion; harmonica

harmonisch [har'monıʃ] adj harmonious

Harn [harn] m (-[e]s;-e) urine; H. lassen pass water

Harn'blase f (anat) bladder

harnen ['harnən] intr urinate

Harn'glas n urinal

Harn'grieß m (pathol) gravel

Harnisch ['harnıʃ] m (-es;-e) armor; in H. geraten über (acc) fly into a rage over; j-n in H. bringen get s.o. hopping mad

Harn'leiter m (anat) ureter; (surg) catheter

Harn'röhre f urethra

harn'treibend adj diuretic

Harpune [har'punə] f (-;-n) harpoon

harpunieren [harpu'nirən] tr harpoon

harren ['harən] intr tarry; hope; (genit or auf acc) wait (for)

harsch [harʃ] adj harsh || Harsch m (-es;), Harsch'schnee m crushed snow

hart [hart] adj hard; severe || adv—h. an (dat) close to, hard by

Härte ['hertə] f (-;) hardness; severity

härten ['hertən] tr, ref & intr harden

Hart'faserplatte f fiber board

Hart'geld n coins

hartgesotten ['hartgəzotən] adj hard-boiled; (Verbrecher) hardened

hart'herzig adj hard-hearted

hart'köpfig adj thick-headed

hart'leibig adj constipated

Hart'leibigkeit f (-;) constipation

hart'löten tr braze

hartnäckig ['hartnɛkɪç] *adj* stubborn

Hart'platz *m* (tennis) hard court

Harz [harts] *n* (—es;-e) resin; rosin

harzig [hartsɪç] *adj* resinous

Hasardspiel [ha'zart/pil] *n* gambling game; gamble

haschen ['haʃən] *tr* snatch, grab || *intr* (nach) try to catch, snatch (at)

Hase ['hazə] *m* (—n;-n) hare; alter H. old-timer, veteran

Ha'selnuß ['hazəlnʊs] *f* hazelnut

Hasenfuß *m* (coll) coward

Ha'senherz *n* (coll) yellow belly

Ha'senmaus *f* chinchilla

Hasenpanier [hazənpanir] *n*—das H. ergreifen take to ones heels

ha'senrein *adj*—nicht ganz h. (fig a) a bit fishy, rather shady

Ha'senscharte *f* harelip

Haspe ['haspə] *f* (—;-n) hasp

Haspel ['haspəl] *f* (—;-n) & *m* (—s;-) reel, spool; winch, windlass

haspeln ['haspəln] *tr* reel, spool

Haß [has] *m* (Hasses) hatred

hassen ['hasən] *tr* hate

has'senswert, has'senswürdig *adj* hateful

häßlich ['hɛslɪç] *adj* ugly; nasty

Hast [hast] *f* (—;) haste

hasten ['hastən] *intr* be in a hurry, act quickly || *intr* (SEIN) hasten, rush

hastig ['hastɪç] *adj* hasty

hätscheln ['hɛt/əln] *tr* caress, cuddle; (*verzärteln*) coddle, spoil

hatte ['hatə] *pret* of haben

Haube ['haubə] *f* (—;-n) cap; (aer) cowling; (aut) hood; (orn) crest

Haubitze [hau'bɪtsə] *f* (—;-n) howitzer

Hauch [haux] *m* (—[e]s;-e) breath; breeze; (*Schicht*) thin layer; (*Spur*) trace

hauch'dünn *adj* paper-thin

hauchen ['hauxən] *tr* whisper; (ling) aspirate || *intr* breathe

Hauch'laut *m* (ling) aspirate

Haue ['hauə] *f* (—;-n) hoe; adze; H. kriegen get a spanking

hauen ['hau.ən] §93 *tr* hack, cut; strike; (*Baum*) fell; (*Stein*) hew || §109 *tr* beat (up) || *intr*—h. nach lash out at; um sich h. flail

Hauer ['hau.ər] *m* (—s;-) tusk

häufeln ['hɔɪfəln] *tr* hill

häufen ['hɔɪfən] *tr* & *ref* pile up

Haufen ['haufən] *m* (—s;-) pile, heap

Hau'fenwolke *f* cumulus cloud

häufig ['hɔɪfɪç] *adj* frequent || *adv* frequently

Häu'figkeit *f* (—;) frequency

Häu'fung *f* (—;-en) accumulation

Haupt [haupt] *n* (—[e]s;-er) head; top; chief, leader aufs H. schlagen vanquish

Haupt- *comb.fm.* head; chief; major; most important; prime; primary, leading

Haupt'altar *m* high altar

haupt'amtlich *adj* full-time

Haupt'bahnhof *m* main train station

Haupt'darsteller *m* leading man

Haupt'darstellerin *f* leading lady

Häuptel ['hɔɪptəl] *n* (—s;-) head

Haupt'fach *n* (educ) major

Haupt'farbe *f* primary color

Haupt'feldwebel *m* first sergeant

Haupt'film *m* (cin) feature

Haupt'gefreite §5 *m* private first class; lance corporal (Brit); seaman; airman second class

Haupt'geschäftsstelle *f* head office

Haupt'gewinn *m* first price

Haupt'haar *n* hair (*on the head*)

Häuptling ['hɔɪptlɪŋ] *m* (—s;-e) chief

häuptlings ['hɔɪptlɪŋs] *adv* head first

Haupt'linie *f* (rr) trunk line

Haupt'mann *m* (—[e]s;-leute) captain

Haupt'masse *f* bulk

Haupt'mast *m* mainmast

Hauptnenner ['hauptnɛnər] *m* (—s;-) (math) common denominator

Haupt'probe *f* dress rehearsal

Haupt'quartier *n* headquarters; Großes H. general headquarters

Haupt'rolle *f* leading role, lead

Haupt'sache *f* main thing; (jur) point at issue

haupt'sächlich *adj* main, principal

Haupt'satz *m* (gram) main clause; (phys) principle, law

Haupt'schalter *m* master switch

Haupt'schiff *n* (archit) nave

Haupt'schlagader *f* aorta

Haupt'schlüssel *m* master key, pass key

Haupt'schriftleiter *m* editor in chief

Haupt'spaß *m* great fun; great joke

Haupt'stadt *f* capital

Haupt'straße *f* main street; highway

Haupt'strecke *f* (rr) main line

Haupt'stütze *f* mainstay

Haupt'ton *m* primary accent

Haupt'treffer *m* first prize; jackpot

Haupt'verkehr *m* peak-hour traffic

Haupt'verkehrsstraße *f* main artery

Haupt'verkehrszeit *f* rush hour

Haupt'wort *n* (—[e]s;-er) noun

Haus [haus] *n* (—es;-er) house; ein großes H. führen do a lot of entertaining; H. und Hof house and home; öffentliches H. brothel; nach Hause home; sich zu Hause fühlen feel at home; von zu Hause from home

Haus'angestellte §5 *mf* domestic

Haus'apotheke *f* medicine cabinet

Haus'arbeit *f* housework; (educ) homework

Haus'arzt *m* family doctor

Haus'aufgabe *f* homework

haus'backen *adj* homemade; (*Frau*) plain; (fig) provincial

Haus'bedarf *m* household needs; für den H. for the home

Haus'brand *m* domestic fuel

Haus'bursche *m* porter

Haus'diener *m* porter

hausen ['hauzən] *intr* reside; (coll) make a mess; schlimm h. wreak havoc

Häuserblock ['hɔɪzərblɔk] *m* block of houses

Häusermakler -in ['hɔɪzərmaklər(ɪn)] §6 *mf* realtor

Haus'flur *m* entrance hall; hallway

Haus'frau *f* housewife; landlady

Haus'freund *m* friend of the family; (coll) wife's lover

Haus'gebrauch *m* family custom; household use
Haus'gehilfin *f* domestic
Haus'genosse *m*, **Haus'genossin** *f* occupant of the same house
Haus'gesinde *n* domestics
Haus'glocke *f* doorbell
Haus'halt *m* household; budget; **den H. führen** keep house
haus'halten §90 *intr* keep house; economize
Haushälter **-in** ['haushɛltər(ɪn)] §6 *mf* housekeeper
haushälterisch ['haushɛltərɪʃ] *adj* economical
Haus'haltsausschuß *m* ways and means committee
Haus'haltsgerät *n* household utensil
Haus'haltsjahr *n* fiscal year
Haus'haltsplan *m* budget
Haus'haltung *f* housekeeping; household; family budget; management
Haus'haltungslehre *f* home economics
Haus'herr *m* master of the house; landlord
Haus'herrin *f* lady of the house; landlady
haus'hoch' *adj* very high; vast
Haus'hofmeister *m* steward
hausieren [hau'zirən] *intr*—**mit etw h.** peddle s.th.; **go around telling everyone about s.th.**
Hausierer [hau'zirər] *m* (-s;-) door-to-door salesman
Haus'lehrer **-in** §6 *mf* private tutor
häuslich ['hɔɪslɪç] *adj* home, domestic; homey; thrifty
Häus'lichkeit *f* (-;) family life; home
Haus'mädchen *n* maid
Haus'meister *m* caretaker, janitor
Haus'mittel *n* home remedy
Haus'mutter *f* mother of the family
Haus'pflege *f* home nursing
Haus'schlüssel *m* front-door key
Haus'schuh *m* slipper
Hausse ['hosə] *f* (-;-n) (econ., st. exch.) boom
Haus'sespekulant *m* (st. exch.) bull
Haussier [hos'je] *m* (-s;-) (st. exch.) bull
haussieren [ho'sirən] *tr* raise ‖ *intr* (fin) go up, rise
Haus'stand *m* household
Haus'suchungsbefehl *m* search warrant
Haus'tier *n* domestic animal; pet
Haus'vater *m* father of the family
Haus'verwalter *m* superintendent
Haus'wesen *n* household
Haus'wirt *m* landlord
Haus'wirtin *f* landlady
Haus'wirtschaft *f* housekeeping
haus'wirtschaftlich *adj* domestic; household
Haus'wirtschaftslehre *f* home economics
Haus'zins *m* house rent
Haut [haut] *f* (-;̈e) skin; hide; **aus der H. fahren** fly off the handle
Haut'abschürfung *f* skin abrasion
Haut'arzt *m* dermatologist
Haut'ausschlag *m* rash
Häutchen ['hɔɪtçən] (-s;-) membrane; pellicle; film

häuten ['hɔɪtən] *tr* skin ‖ *ref* slough the skin
haut'eng *adj* skin-tight
Haut'farbe *f* complexion
Haut'plastik *f* skin graft
Haut'reizung *f* skin irritation
Haut'transplantation *f*, **Haut'verpflanzung** *f* skin grafting
havariert [hava'rirt] *adj* damaged
H'-Bombe *f* H-bomb
Hebamme ['hepamə] *f* (-;-n) midwife
Hebebaum ['hebəbaum] *m* lever
Hebebühne ['hebəbynə] *f* car lift
Hebeeisen ['hebə-aɪzən] *n* crowbar
Hebel ['hebəl] *m* (-s;-) lever
heben ['hebən] §94 *tr* lift, raise; (steigern) increase; (fördern) further; (aut) jack up ‖ *ref* rise
Heber ['hebər] *m* (-s;-) siphon; (aut) jack
Hebeschiff ['hebəʃɪf] *n* salvage ship
Hebräer **-in** [he'bre-ər(ɪn)] §6 *mf* Hebrew
hebräisch [he'bre-ɪʃ] *adj* Hebrew
He'bung *f* (-;-en) lifting; increase; improvement; (mus, pros) stress
Hecht [hɛçt] *m* (-[e]s;-e) (ichth) pike
hechten ['hɛçtən] *intr* dive
Hecht'sprung *m* flying leap; jacknife dive
Heck [hek] *n* (-[e]s;-e & -s) stern; (aer) tail; (aut) rear
Heck'antrieb *m* (aut) rear drive
Hecke ['hekə] *f* (-;-n) hedge; brood, hatch
hecken ['hekən] *tr & intr* breed
Heckenhüpfen (Hek'kenhüpfen) *n* (-s;) (aer) hedgehopping
Heckenschütze (Hek'kenschütze) *m* sniper
Heck'fenster *n* (aut) rear window
Heck'licht *n* (aer, aut) tail light
Heck'motor *m* rear engine
Heck'pfennig *m* lucky penny
Heck'schütze *m* (aer) tail gunner
heda ['heda] *interj* hey there!
Heer [her] *n* (-[e]s;-e) army; host
Heeres- [heres] *comb.fm.* army
Hee'resbericht *m* official army communiqué
Hee'resdienst *m* military service
Hee'resdienstvorschriften *pl* army regulations
Hee'resgeistliche §5 *m* army chaplain
Hee'resmacht *f* armed forces; army
Hee'reszug *m* (mil) campaign
Heer'lager *n* army camp; (pol) faction
Heer'schar *f* host, legion
Heer'zug *m* (mil) campaign
Hefe ['hefə] *f* (-;-n) yeast; dregs
He'feteig *m* leavened dough
Heft [heft] *n* (-[e]s;-e) haft, handle; notebook; (e-r Zeitschrift) issue
heften ['heftən] *tr* fasten together; sew, stitch; tack, baste; (Blick) fix ‖ *ref* (an acc) stick close (to)
heftig ['heftɪç] *adj* violent; (Regen) heavy; (Fieber) high; **h. werden** lose one's temper
Heft'klammer *f* paper clip; staple
Heft'maschine *f* stapler
Heft'stich *m* (sew) tack
Heft'zwecke *f* thumbtack

hegen ['heːgən] *tr* (*Wild*) preserve; (*Zweifel, Gedanken*) have; **h. und pflegen** lavish care on

Hehl [heːl] *n* (-[e]s;) secret

hehlen ['heːlən] *intr* receive stolen goods

Hehl'ler -in §6 *mf* fence

hehr [heːr] *adj* sublime, noble

Heide ['haɪdə] *m* (-n;-n) heathen; (Bib) gentile || *f* (-;-n) heath

Hei'dekraut *n* heather

Heidelbeere ['haɪdəlbeːrə] *f* blueberry

Hei'denangst *f* (coll) jitters

Hei'dengeld *n* (coll) piles of money

Hei'denlärm *m* hullabaloo

hei'denmäßig *adv*—**h. viel** tremendous amount of

Hei'denspaß *m* (coll) great fun

Heidentum ['haɪdəntum] *n* (-s;) heathendom

heidi [har'diː] *adj* gone; lost; **h. gehen** get lost; be all gone || *interj* quick!

Heidin ['haɪdɪn] *f* (-;-nen) heathen

heidnisch ['haɪdnɪʃ] *adj* heathen

heikel ['haɪkəl] *adj* particular, fastidious; (*Sache*) ticklish

heil [haɪl] *adj* safe, sound; undamaged || Heil *n* (-[e]s;) welfare, benefit; salvation || Heil *interj* hail!

Heiland ['haɪlant] *m* (-[e]s;) Saviour

Heil'anstalt *f* sanitarium

Heil'bad *n* spa

heilbar ['haɪlbar] *adj* curable

heil'bringend *adj* beneficial, healthful

Heilbutt ['haɪlbut] *m* (-[e]s;-e) (ichth) halibut

heilen ['haɪlən] *tr* heal || *intr* (HABEN & SEIN) heal

Heil'gehilfe *m* male nurse

Heil'gymnastik *f* physical therapy

heilig ['haɪlɪç] *adj* holy, sacred || Heilige §5 *mf* saint

Hei'ligabend *m* Christmas Eve

heiligen ['haɪlɪgən] *tr* hallow

Hei'ligenschein *m* halo

Hei'ligkeit *f* (-;) holiness, sanctity

hei'ligsprechen §64 *tr* canonize

Heiligtum ['haɪlɪçtum] *n* (-[e]s;⸚er) sanctuary; shrine; sacred relic

Hei'ligung *f* (-;) sanctification

Heil'kraft *f* healing power

Heil'kraut *n* medicinal herb

Heil'kunde *f* medical science

heil'los *adj* wicked; (coll) awful

Heil'mittel *n* remedy; medicine

Heil'mittellehre *f* pharmacology

heilsam ['haɪlzam] *adj* healthful

Heils'armee *f* Salvation Army

Heil'stätte *f* sanitarium

Heil'lung *f* (-;-en) cure

heim [haɪm] *adv* home || Heim *n* (-[e]s;-e) home; (*Alters-*) old-age home

Heimat ['haɪmat] *f* (-;-en) home; hometown; homeland

hei'matlich *adj* native

hei'matlos *adj* homeless

Hei'matort *m* hometown, home village

Hei'matstadt *f* hometown, native city

heim'begeben §80 *ref* head home

Heimchen ['haɪmçən] *n* (-s;-) cricket

Heim'computer *m* home computer

Heim'fahrt *f* homeward journey

heim'finden §59 *intr* find one's way home

Heim'gang *m* going home; passing on

heimisch ['haɪmɪʃ] *adj* local; locally-produced; domestic; **heimische Sprache** vernacular; **h. werden** settle down; become established; **sich h. fühlen** feel at home

Heimkehr ['haɪmker] *f* (-;) homecoming

heim'kehren *intr* (SEIN) return home

Heim'kunft *f* homecoming

heim'leuchten *intr* (sl) (*dat*) tell (*s.o.*) where to get off

heim'lich *adj* secret

Heim'lichkeit *f* (-;-en) secrecy; (*Geheimnis*) secret

Heim'reise *f* homeward journey

heim'suchen *tr* afflict, plague

Heim'tücke *f* treachery

heim'tückisch *adj* treacherous

heimwärts ['haɪmverts] *adv* homeward

Heim'weh *n* homesickness; nostalgia

heim'zahlen *tr*—**j-m etw h.** (coll) pay s.o. back for s.th.

Heini ['haɪni] *m* (-s;) Harry; guy

Heinzelmännchen ['haɪntsəlmɛnçən] *pl* (myth) little people

Heirat ['haɪrat] *f* (-;-en) marriage

heiraten ['haɪratən] *tr* & *intr* marry

Hei'ratsantrag *m* marriage proposal

hei'ratsfähig *adj* marriageable

Hei'ratsgut *n* dowry

Hei'ratskandidat *m* eligible bachelor

Hei'ratsurkunde *f* marriage certificate

Hei'ratsvermittler -in §6 *mf* marriage broker

heischen ['haɪʃən] *tr* demand; beg

heiser ['haɪzər] *adj* hoarse

heiß [haɪs] *adj* hot; (fig) ardent

heißen ['haɪsən] §95 *tr* call; ask, bid; mean || *intr* be called; **das heißt** that is, i.e.; **wie h. Sie?** what is your name?

heiß'geliebt *adj* beloved

heiter ['haɪtər] *adj* cheerful; hilarious; serene; (*Wetter*) clear

Heiz- [haɪts] *comb.fm.* heating

Heiz'anlage *f* heating system

Heiz'apparat *m* heater

heizen ['haɪtsən] *tr* heat; **den Ofen mit Kohle h.** burn coal in the stove || *intr* give off heat; heat; turn on the heating; light the fire (or stove)

Hei'zer *m* (-s;) boilerman; (naut) stoker; (rr) fireman

Heiz'faden *m* (elec) filament

Heiz'kissen *n* heating pad

Heiz'körper *m* radiator; heater

Heiz'material *n* fuel

Heiz'platte *f* hot plate

Heiz'raum *m* boiler room

Heiz'schlange *f* heating coil

Hei'zung *f* (-;) heating; (coll) central heating; radiator

Hei'zungskessel *m* boiler

Hei'zungsrohr *n* radiator pipe

Held [hɛlt] *m* (-en;-en) hero

Hel'denalter *n* heroic age

Hel'dengedicht *n* epic

Hel'dengeist *m* heroism

hel'denhaft *adj* heroic

Hel'denmut *m* heroism

hel'denmütig adj heroic

Hel'dentat f heroic deed, exploit

Heldentum ['hɛldəntum] n (-[e]s;) heroism

Heldin ['hɛldɪn] f (-;-nen) heroine

helfen ['hɛlfən] intr (dat) help; **es hilft nichts** it's of no use

Hel'fer –in §6 mf helper

Hel'fershelfer m accomplice

Helikopter [hɛli'kɔptər] m (-s;-) helicopter

hell [hɛl] adj clear; bright; lucid; (Haar) fair; (Bier) light; (Wahnsinn, usw.) sheer || **Helle** §5 f brightness; lightness; clarity || n light; **ein Helles** a glass of light beer

hellenisch [hɛ'leniʃ] adj Hellenic

Heller ['hɛlər] m (-s;-) penny

hellhörig ['hɛlhørɪç] adj having sharp ears; **h. werden** prick up one's ears

hellicht ['hɛlɪçt] adj—**hellichter Tag** broad daylight

Hel'ligkeit f (-;-en) brightness; (astr) magnitude

hell'sehen §138 intr be clairvoyant || **Hellsehen** n (-s;) clairvoyance

Hell'seher –in §6 mf clairvoyant; (coll) mind reader

hell'sichtig adj clear-sighted

hell'wach adj wide awake

Helm [hɛlm] m (-[e]s;-e) helmet; (archit) dome, spire; (naut) helm

Helm'busch m crest, plume

Hemd [hɛmt] n (-[e]s;-en) shirt

Hemd'brust f dickey, shirt front

Hemd'hose f union suit

hemmen ['hɛmən] tr slow up; stop; **gehemmt** inhibited

Hemmnis ['hɛmnɪs] n (-ses;-se) hindrance

Hemmschuh ['hɛm/u] m (fig) hindrance; (rr) brake

Hem'mung f (-;-en) inhibition

hem'mungslos adj uninhibited

Hengst [hɛŋst] m (-es;-e) stallion

Henkel ['hɛŋkəl] m (-s;-) handle

henken ['hɛŋkən] tr hang (s.o.)

Henker ['hɛŋkər] m (-s;-) hangman

Henne ['hɛnə] f (-;-n) hen

her [her] adv hither, here; ago

herab [hɛ'rap] adv down, downwards

herab– comb.fm. down; down here

herab'drücken tr press down; force down; **die Kurse h.** bear the market

herab'lassen §104 ref condescend

Herab'lassung f (-;) condescension

herab'sehen §138 intr (auf acc) look down (on)

herab'setzen tr put down; reduce; belittle, disparage

herab'steigen §148 intr (SEIN) climb down; (vom Pferd) dismount

herab'würdigen tr demean

Heraldik [he'raldɪk] f (-;) heraldry

heran [he'ran] adv near; up

heran'arbeiten ref (an acc) work one's way (towards)

heran'bilden tr (zu) train (as)

heran'brechen §64 intr (SEIN) (Tag) dawn, break; (Nacht) fall, come on

heran'gehen §82 intr (SEIN) go close; **h. an** (acc) approach, go up to

heran'kommen §99 intr (SEIN) come near; **h. an** (acc) approach; get at; **h. bis an** (acc) reach as far as

heran'machen ref—**h. an** (acc) apply oneself to; approach

heran'nahen intr (SEIN) approach

heran'wachsen §155 intr (SEIN) (zu) grow up (to be)

heran'wagen ref (an acc) dare to approach

heran'ziehen §163 tr pull closer; call on for help; (Quellen) consult; (zur Beratung) call in; (Pflanzen) grow; (Nachwuchs) train || intr (SEIN) approach

herauf [hɛ'rauf] adv up, up here; upstairs

herauf'arbeiten ref work one's way up

herauf'bemühen ref take the trouble to come up (or upstairs)

herauf'beschwören §137 tr conjure up; (verursachen) bring on, provoke

herauf'kommen §99 intr (SEIN) come up

herauf'setzen tr raise, increase

herauf'steigen §148 intr (SEIN) climb up; (Tag) dawn

herauf'ziehen §163 tr pull up || intr (SEIN) move upstairs; (Sturm) come up

heraus [hɛ'raus] adv out, out here

heraus'bekommen §99 tr (aus) get out (of); (Wort) utter; (Geld) get back in change; (Problem) figure out

heraus'bringen §65 tr bring out; (Wort) utter; (Lösung) work out; (Buch) publish; (Fabrikat) bring out

heraus'drücken tr squeeze out; (die Brust) throw out

heraus'fahren §71 intr (SEIN) drive out; (aus dem Bett) jump up; (Bemerkung) slip out

heraus'finden §59 tr find out || ref (aus) find one's way out (of)

heraus'fordern tr challenge, call on

heraus'fordernd adj defiant || adv defiantly; **sich h. anziehen** dress provocatively

Heraus'forderung f (-;-en) challenge

heraus'fühlen tr sense

Heraus'gabe f surrender; (e-s Buches) publication; (jur) restitution

heraus'geben §80 tr surrender; give back; (Buch) publish || intr (dat) give (s.o.) his change; **h. auf** (acc) give change for

Heraus'geber m publisher; (Redakteur) editor

heraus'greifen §88 tr single out

heraus'haben §89 tr have (s.th.) figured out; **er hat den Bogen heraus** (coll) he has the knack of it

heraus'halten §90 tr hold out || ref (aus) keep out (of)

heraus'hängen §92 tr & intr hang out

heraus'kommen §99 intr (SEIN) come out

heraus'lesen §107 tr pick out; deduce; **zu viel aus e-m Gedicht h.** read too much into a poem

heraus'machen tr (Fleck) get out || tr (Kinder) turn out well; (Geschäft) make out well

heraus'nehmen §116 tr take out || ref

—**sich** [*dat*] **zu viel** (or **Freiheiten**) **h.** take liberties

heraus′platzen *intr* (SEIN)—**mit etw h.** blurt out s.th.

heraus′putzen *ref* dress up

heraus′reden *ref* (**aus**) talk one's way out (of)

heraus′rücken *tr* move out (here); (coll) (*Geld*) shell out ‖ *intr* (SEIN) —**mit dem Geld h.** shell out money; **mit der Sprache h.** reveal it, admit it

heraus′schälen *ref* become apparent

heraus′stehen §146 *intr* protrude

heraus′steigen §148 *intr* (SEIN) (**aus**) climb out (of), step out (of)

heraus′stellen *tr* put out; **groß h.** give a big build-up to; **klar h.** present clearly ‖ *ref* emerge, come to light; **sich h. als** prove to be

heraus′streichen §85 *tr* delete; (fig) praise

heraus′suchen *tr* pick out

heraus′treten §152 *intr* (SEIN) come out, step out; bulge, protrude

heraus′winden §59 *ref* extricate oneself

heraus′wirtschaften *tr* manage to save; (*Profit*) manage to make

heraus′ziehen §163 *tr* pull out

herb [herp] *adj* harsh; (*sauer*) sour; (*zusammenziehend*) tangy; (*Wein*) dry; (*Worte*) bitter; (*Schönheit*) austere ‖ **Herbe** *f* (**-;**) harshness; tang; bitterness; austerity

herbei′ *adv* here (*toward the speaker*)

herbei- *comb.fm.* up, along, here (*toward the speaker*)

herbei′bringen §65 *tr* bring along

herbei′eilen *intr* (SEIN) hurry here

herbei′führen *tr* bring here; cause

herbei′kommen §99 *intr* (SEIN) come up

herbei′lassen §104 *ref* condescend

herbei′rufen §122 *tr* call over; summon

herbei′schaffen *tr* bring here; procure; (*Geld*) raise

herbei′sehnen *tr* long for

herbei′strömen *intr* (SEIN) come flocking, flock

herbei′winken *tr* beckon (*s.o.*) to come over

herbei′wünschen *tr* long for, wish for

Herberge [′herbergə] *f* (**-;-n**) lodging, shelter; hostel; (obs) inn

her′beten *tr* say mechanically

Herb′heit *f* (**-;**), and **Herb′igkeit** *f* (**-;**) harshness; tang; bitterness; austerity

her′bringen §65 *tr* bring here

Herbst [herpst] *m* (**-es;-e**) autumn

herbst′lich *adj* autumn, fall

Herd [hert] *m* (**-[e]s;-e**) hearth, fireplace; home; kitchen range; center

Herde [′herdə] *f* (**-;-n**) herd, flock

herein [he′rain] *adv* in, in here; **h.!** come in!

herein- *comb.fm.* in, in here (*toward the speaker*)

herein′bemühen *tr* ask (*s.o.*) to come in ‖ *ref* trouble oneself to come in

herein′bitten §60 *tr* invite in

Herein′fall *m* disappointment, letdown

herein′fallen §72 *intr* (SEIN) fall in; **h. auf** (*acc*) fall for; **h. in** (*acc*) fall into

herein′legen *tr* fool, take in

herein′platzen *intr* (SEIN) burst in

her′fallen §72 *intr* (SEIN)—**h. über** (*acc*) fall upon, attack

her′finden §59 *ref & intr* find one's way here

Her′gang *m* background details

her′geben §80 *tr* hand over; give up ‖ *ref*—**sich h. zu** be a party to

her′halten §90 *tr* hold out, extend ‖ *intr*—**h. müssen** (*Person*) be the victim; (*Sache*) have to do (*as a make-shift*)

Hering [′herɪŋ] *m* (**-s;-e**) herring; **sitzen wie die Heringe** be packed in like sardines

her′kommen §99 *intr* (SEIN) come here; (*Wort*) originate; **wo kommst du denn her?** where have you come from? ‖ **Herkommen** *n* (**-s;-**) origin; custom, tradition, convention

herkömmlich [′herkœmlɪç] *adj* customary, usual; traditional, conventional

Herkunft [′herkunft] *f* (**-;**) origin; birth, family

her′laufen §105 *intr* (SEIN) walk here; **hinter j-m h.** follow s.o.

her′leiten *tr* derive; deduce, infer

Her′leitung *f* (**-;-en**) derivation

her′machen *tr*—**viel h. von** make a fuss over ‖ *ref*—**sich h. über** (*acc*) attack; (fig) tackle

Hermelin [hermə′lin] *m* (**-s;-e**) ermine ‖ *n* (**-s;-e**) (zool) ermine

hermetisch [her′metɪʃ] *adj* hermetic

hernach′ *adv* afterwards

her′nehmen §116 *tr* get; **j-n scharf h.** give s.o. a good talking-to

hernie′der *adv* down, down here

Heroin [hero′in] *n* (**-s;**) (pharm) heroin

Heroine [hero′inə] *f* (**-;-n**) heroine

heroisch [he′ro·ɪʃ] *adj* heroic

Heroismus [hero′ɪsmus] *m* (**-;**) heroism

Herold [′herolt] *m* (**-[e]s;-e**) herald

Heros [′heros] *m* (**-;** **Heroen** [he′ro·ən]) hero

Herr [her] *m* (**-n;-en**) lord; master; gentleman; (*als Anrede*) Sir; (*vor Eigennamen*) Mr.; (*Gott*) Lord; **meine Herren!** gentlemen!

her′reichen *tr* hand, pass

Herren- [′herən] *comb.fm.* man's, men's; gentlemen's

Her′renabend *m* stag party

Her′renbegleitung *f*—**in H.** accompanied by a gentleman

Her′rendoppel *n* (tennis) men's doubles

Her′reneinzel(spiel) *n* (tennis) men's singles

Her′renfahrer *m* (aut) owner-driver

Her′renfriseur *m* barber

Her′rengesellschaft *f* male company; stag party

Her′rengröße *f* men's size

Her′rengut *n* domain, manor

Her′renhaus *n* mansion; House of Lords

Her′renhof *m* manor

Her′renleben *n* life of Riley

her'renlos *adj* ownerless

Her'renmensch *m* born leader

Her'renschnitt *m* woman's very short hairstyle

Her'renzimmer *n* study

Herr'gott *m* Lord, Lord God

her'richten *tr* arrange; get ready

Herrin ['herɪn] *f* (–;-nen) lady

herrisch ['herɪʃ] *adj* masterful

herr'lich *adj* splendid

Herr'lichkeit *f* (–;-en) splendor

Herr'schaft *f* (–;-en) rule, domination; mastery; control; lord, master; estate; **meine Herrschaften!** ladies and gentlemen!

herr'schaftlich *adj* ruler's; gentleman's; high-class

herrschen ['herʃən] *intr* rule; prevail; exist

Herr'scher –in §6 *mf* ruler

Herrschsucht ['herʃzʊçt] *f* (–;) thirst for power; bossiness

herrsch'süchtig *adj* power-hungry; autocratic; domineering

her'rühren *intr*—h. **von** come from, originate with

her'sagen *tr* recite, say

her'schaffen *tr* get (here)

her'stammen *intr*—h. **von** come from, be descended from; (gram) be derived from

her'stellen §2 *tr* put here; (erzeugen) produce; **fabrikmäßig h.** mass-produce; **Verbindung h.** establish contact; (telp) put a call through

Her'steller *m* (–s;-) manufacturer

Her'stellung *f* (–;-en) production

Her'stellungsbetrieb *m* factory

Her'stellungsverfahren *n* manufacturing process

herüber [he'rybər] *adv* over, over here, in this direction (toward the speaker)

herum [he'rʊm] *adv* around; about

herum'bringen §65 *tr* bring around; (Zeit) spend

herum'drehen *tr, ref & intr* turn around

herum'fragen *intr* make inquiries

herumfuchteln [he'rʊmfʊxtəln] *intr*—**mit den Händen h.** wave one's hands about

herum'führen *tr* show around

herum'greifen §88 *intr*—h. **um** reach around

herum'hacken *intr*—h. **auf** (dat) pick on, criticize

herum'kauen *intr* (an *dat*, auf *dat*) chew away (on)

herum'kommen §99 *intr* (SEIN) get around; h. **um** get around; evade

herum'lungern *intr* loaf around

herum'reiten §86 *intr* (SEIN) ride around; h. **auf** (dat) harp on (s.th.); pick on (s.o.)

herum'schnüffeln *intr* snoop around

herum'streichen §85 *intr* (SEIN) prowl about

herum'streiten §86 *ref* squabble

herum'treiben §62 *tr* drive around || *ref* roam around, knock about

Herum'treiber *m* (–s;-) loafer, tramp

herum'ziehen §163 *tr* pull around; h. **um** draw (s.th.) around || *ref*—sich h. **um** surround || *intr* (SEIN) wander

around; run around; h. **um** march around

herunter [he'rʊntər] *adv* down, down here (towards the speaker); downstairs; **den Berg h.** down the mountain; **ins Tal h.** down into the valley

herun'terbringen §65 *tr* bring down; (fig) lower, reduce

herun'tergehen §82 *intr* (SEIN) go down; (Preis, Temperatur) fall, drop

herun'terhandeln *tr* (Preis) beat down

herun'terhauen §93 *tr* chop off; (Brief) dash off; **j–m eins h.** clout s.o.

herun'terkommen §99 *intr* (SEIN) come down; come downstairs; deteriorate

herun'terlassen §104 *tr* let down, lower

herun'terleiern *tr* drone

herun'terlesen §107 *tr* (Liste) read down; rattle off

herun'termachen *tr* take down; turn down; (coll) chew out; (coll) pan

herun'terschießen §76 *tr* shoot down

herun'tersein §139 *intr* (SEIN) be run-down

herun'terwirtschaften *tr* ruin (through mismanagement)

herun'terwürgen *tr* choke down

hervor [her'for] *adv* out; forth

hervor'bringen §65 *tr* bring out; engender, produce; (Wort) utter

hervor'dringen §142 *intr* (SEIN) emerge

hervor'gehen §82 *intr* (SEIN)—h. **aus** come from; emerge from; **to have been trained at**

hervor'heben §94 *tr* highlight

hervor'holen *tr* produce

hervor'kommen §99 *intr* (SEIN) come out

hervor'lugen *intr* peep out

hervor'ragen *intr* jut out; be prominent; h. **über** (acc) tower over

hervor'ragend *adj* prominent

hervor'rufen §122 *tr* evoke, cause; (Schauspieler) recall

hervor'stechen §64 *tr* stick out; be conspicuous; be prominent

hervor'treten §152 *intr* (SEIN) emerge; come to the fore; become apparent; (Augen) bulge; (Ader) protrude

hervor'tun §154 *ref* distinguish oneself

hervor'wagen *ref* dare to come out; **sich mit e–r Antwort h.** venture an answer

hervor'zaubern *tr* produce by magic; **ein Essen h.** whip up a meal

Herweg ['hervek] *m* way here; way home

Herz [herts] *n* (–ens;-en) heart; (als Anrede) darling; (cards) heart(s); **ich bringe es nicht übers H. zu** (inf) I haven't the heart to (inf); **sich** [dat] **ein H. fassen** get up the courage; **seinem Herzen Luft machen** give vent to one's feelings

Herz- comb.fm. heart, cardiac

Herz'anfall *m* heart attack

Herz'beschwerden *pl* heart trouble

Herz'blume *f* (bot) bleeding heart

herzen ['hertsən] *tr* hug, embrace

Her'zensgrund *m* bottom of one's heart

her'zensgut *adj* good-hearted

Her'zenslust *f*—**nach H.** to one's heart's content

herz'ergreifend *adj* moving, touching

Herz'geräusch *n* heart murmur

herz'haft *adj* hearty

herzig ['hertsɪç] *adj* sweet, cute

–herzig *comb.fm.* **–hearted**

Herzinfarkt ['hertsɪnfarkt] *m* (–[e]s; –e) cardiac infarction

herz'innig *adj* heartfelt

herz'inniglich *adv* sincerely

Herz'klappe *f* cardiac valve

Herz'klopfen *n* palpitations

Herz'kollaps *m* heart failure

herz'lich *adj* cordial; sincere || *adv* very; **h. wenige** precious few

herz'los *adj* heartless

Herzog ['hertsok] *m* (–[e]s;-ë) duke

Herzogin ['hertsogɪn] *f* (–;-nen) duchess

Herzogtum ['hertsoktum] *n* (–[e]s;-ër) dukedom; duchy

Herz'schlag *m* heartbeat; heart failure

Herz'stück *n* heart, central point

Herz'verpflanzung *f* heart transplant

Herz'weh *n* (& *fig*) heartache

Hetzblatt ['hetsblat] *n* scandal sheet

Hetze ['hetsə] *f* (–;-n) hunting; hurry, rush; vicious campaign; baiting

hetzen ['hetsən] *tr* hunt; bait; rush; (*fig*) hound; **e–n Hund auf j–n h.** sic a dog on s.o. || *ref* rush || *intr* stir up trouble; **h. gegen** conduct a vicious campaign against || *intr* (SEIN) race, dash

Het'zer –**in** §6 *mf* agitator

Hetz'hund *m* hound, hunting dog

Hetz'jagd *f* hunt; baiting; hurry

Hetz'rede *f* inflammatory speech

Heu [hoɪ] *n* (–[e]s) hay

Heu'boden *m* hayloft

Heuchelei [hoɪçə'laɪ] *f* (–;-en) hypocrisy; piece of hypocrisy

heucheln ['hoɪçəln] *tr* feign || *intr* be hypocritical

Heuch'ler –**in** §6 *mf* hypocrite

heuchlerisch ['hoɪçlərɪç] *adj* hypocritical

heuen ['hoɪ·ən] *intr* make hay

heuer ['hoɪ·ər] *adv* this year

heuern ['hoɪ·ərn] *tr* hire

Heu'fieber *n* hayfever

Heu'gabel *f* pitchfork

heulen ['hoɪlən] *intr* bawl; (*Wind*) howl

heurig ['hoɪrɪç] *adj* this year's || **Heurige** §5 *m* new wine

Heu'schnupfen *m* (–s;) hayfever

Heuschober ['hoɪ/obər] *m* (–s;-) haystack

Heu'schrecke *f* (–;-n) locust

heute ['hoɪtə] *adv* today; **h. abend** this evening; **h. früh** (or **h. morgen**) this morning; **h. vor acht Tagen** a week ago today; **h. in acht Tagen** today a week

heutig ['hoɪtɪç] *adj* today's; present-day; **am heutigen Tage** (or **der heutige Tag** or **mit dem heutigen Tag**) today

heutzutage ['hoɪttsutagə] *adv* nowadays

Hexe ['heksə] *f* (–;-n) witch; hag

hexen ['heksən] *intr* practice witchcraft

He'xenkessel *m* chaos, inferno

He'xenmeister *m* wizard; sorcerer

He'xenschuß *m* lumbago

Hexerei [heksə'raɪ] *f* (–;) witchcraft

Hiatus [hɪ'atus] *m* (–;-) (& pros) hiatus

Hibis·kus [hɪ'bɪskus] *m* (–;-ken [kən]) hibiscus

hieb [hip] *pret* of **hauen** || **Hieb** *m* (–[e]s;-e) blow, stroke; **Hiebe** thrashing

hieb'-undstich'fest *adj* (*fig*) watertight

Hieb'wunde *f* gash

hielt [hilt] *pret* of **halten**

hier [hir] *adv* here

hieran' *adv* at (by, in, on, to) it or them

Hierar·chie [hɪ·erar'çi] *f* (–;-chien ['çi·ən]) hierarchy

hierauf' *adv* on it, on them; then

hieraus' *adv* out of it (or them); from this (or these)

hierbei' *adv* near here; here; in this case; in connection with this

hierdurch' *adv* through it (or them); through here; hereby

hierfür' *adv* for it (or them)

hierge'gen *adv* against it

hierher' *adv* hither, here

hier'herum *adv* around here

hierhin' *adv* here; **bis h.** up to here

hierin' *adv* herein, in this

hiermit' *adv* herewith, with it

hiernach' *adv* after this, then; about this; according to this

Hieroglyphe [hɪ·ero'glyfə] *f* (–;-n) hieroglyph

hierorts ['hirorts] *adv* in this town

hierü'ber *adv* over it (or them); about it (or this)

hierzu' *adv* to it; in addition to it; concerning this

hiesig ['hizɪç] *adj* local

hieß [his] *pret* of **heißen**

Hilfe ['hɪlfə] *f* (–;-n) help, aid; **zu H. nehmen** make use of

Hil'feleistung *f* assistance

Hil'feruf *m* cry for help

hilf'los *adj* helpless

hilf'reich *adj* helpful

Hilfs– [hɪlfs] *comb.fm.* auxiliary

Hilfs'arbeiter –**in** §6 *mf* unskilled laborer

Hilfs'arzt *m*, **Hilf'ärztin** *f* intern

hilfs'bedürftig *adj* needy

hilfs'bereit *adj* ready to help

Hilfs'dienst *m* help, assistance

Hilfs'gerät *n* labor-saving device

Hilfs'kraft *f* assistant, helper; (*mach*) auxiliary power

Hilfs'kraftbremse *f* power brake

Hilfs'kraftlenkung *f* power steering

Hilfs'lehrer –**in** §6 *mf* student teacher

Hilfs'maschine *f* auxiliary engine

Hilfs'mittel *n* aid, device; remedy; financial aid

Hilfs'quellen *pl* material; sources

Hilfs'rakete *f* booster rocket

Hilfs'schule *f* school for the mentally slow

Hilfs'truppen pl auxiliaries

Hilfs'werk n welfare organization

Hilfs'zeitwort n (-[e]s;⸚er) (gram) auxiliary (verb)

Himbeere ['hɪmbeːrə] f (-;-n) raspberry

Himmel ['hɪməl] m (-s;-) sky, skies; heaven(s); firmament; (eccl) baldachin; ach du lieber H.! good heavens!; aus heiterem H. out of the blue; in den H. heben praise to the skies

himmelan' adv skywards; heavenwards

him'melangst invar adj—mir wird h. I feel frightened to death

Him'melbett n canopy bed

him'melblau adj sky-blue

Him'melfahrt f ascension; assumption

Him'melfahrtstag m Ascension Day

Him'melreich n kingdom of heaven

Himmels- comb.fm. celestial

him'melschreiend adj atrocious

Him'melsgegend f region of the sky; point of the compass

Him'melskörper m celestial body

Him'melsrichtung f point of the compass; direction

Him'melsschrift f skywriting

Him'melswagen m (astr) Great Bear

Him'melszelt n canopy of heaven

himmelwärts ['hɪməlverts] adv skywards; heavenwards

himmlisch ['hɪmlɪʃ] adj heavenly, celestial; divine; (coll) gorgeous

hin [hɪn] adv there (away from the speaker); ganz hin (coll) bushed; (coll) quite carried away; hin ist hin what's done is done; hin und her up and down, back and forth; hin und wieder now and then; vor sich hin to oneself

hinab' adv down

hinan' adv up; bis an etw h. up to s.th., as far as s.th.

hinauf' adv up, up there; upstairs; den Fluß h. up the river

hinauf'reichen tr hand (s.th.) up || intr reach up

hinauf'schrauben tr (Preis) jack up

hinauf'setzen tr raise, increase

hinauf'steigen §148 tr (SEIN) (Treppe, Berg) climb || intr (SEIN) climb up; (Temperatur) rise

hinaus' adv out, out there; auf viele Jahre h. for many years to come

hinaus'beißen §53 tr (coll) edge out

hinaus'gehen §82 intr (SEIN) go out; h. auf (acc) look out over; lead to; drive at, imply; h. über (acc) exceed

hinaus'kommen §99 intr (SEIN) come out; es kommt auf eins (or aufs gleiche) hinaus it amounts to the same thing; h. über (acc) get beyond

hinaus'laufen §105 intr (SEIN) run out; es läuft aufs eins (or aufs gleiche) hinaus it amounts to the same thing

hinaus'schieben §130 tr push out; (Termin, usw.) postpone

hinaus'werfen §160 tr throw out; fire

hinaus'wollen §162 intr want to go out; h. auf (acc) be driving at; hoch h. aim high, be ambitious

hinaus'ziehen §163 tr prolong || ref

take longer than expected || intr (SEIN) go out; move out

Hin'blick m—im H. auf (acc) in view of

hin'bringen §65 tr bring (there); take (there); (Zeit) pass

hinderlich ['hɪndərlɪç] adj in the way

hindern ['hɪndərn] tr block; h. an (dat) prevent from (ger)

Hindernis ['hɪndərnɪs] n (-ses;-se) hindrance; obstacle

Hin'dernisbahn f obstacle course

Hin'dernislauf m (sport) hurdles

Hin'dernisrennen n steeplechase; hurdles

hindurch' adv through; den ganzen Sommer h. throughout the summer

hinein' adv in, in there

hinein'arbeiten ref—sich h. in (acc) work one's way into

hinein'denken §66 ref—sich h. in (acc) imagine oneself in

hinein'geraten §63 intr (SEIN)—h. in (acc) get into, fall into

hinein'leben intr—in den Tag h. live for the moment

hinein'tun §154 tr put in

Hin'fahrt f journey there, out-bound passage

hin'fallen §72 intr (SEIN) fall down

hinfällig ['hɪnfelɪç] adj frail; (Gesetz) invalid

hinfort' adv henceforth

hing [hɪŋ] pret of hängen

Hin'gabe f (an acc) devotion (to)

hin'geben §80 tr give up || ref (dat) abandon oneself (to)

Hin'gebung f (-;) devotion

hinge'gen adv on the other hand

hin'gehen §82 intr (SEIN) go there; pass

hin'halten §90 tr hold out; (Person) keep waiting, string along; den Kopf h. (fig) take the rap

hinken ['hɪnkən] intr limp; der Vergleich hinkt that's a poor comparison || intr (SEIN) limp

hin'länglich adj sufficient

hin'legen tr put down || ref lie down

hin'nehmen §116 tr accept; take, put up with

hin'raffen tr snatch away

hin'reichen tr (dat) pass to, hand to || intr reach; suffice

hin'reißen §53 tr enchant, carry away

hin'richten tr execute; h. auf (acc) direct towards

Hin'richtung f (-;-en) execution

Hin'richtungsbefehl m death warrant

hin'setzen tr put down || ref sit down

Hin'sicht f respect, way; in H. auf (acc) regarding, in regard to

hin'sichtlich prep (genit) regarding

hin'stellen tr put there; put down

hintan'setzen, hintan'stellen tr put last, consider last

hinten ['hɪntən] adv at the back, in the rear; h. im Zimmer at the back of the room; nach h. to the rear; backwards; von h. from the rear

hinter ['hɪntər] prep (dat) behind; h. j-m her sein be after s.o. || prep (acc) behind; h. etw kommen find out about s.th., get to the bottom of s.th.

Hin'terachse *f* rear axle

Hin'terbacke *f* buttock

Hin'terbein *n* hind leg; **sich auf die Hinterbeine setzen** strain oneself

Hinterbliebene ['hɪntərblibənə] §5 *mf* survivor (*of a deceased*); **H. pl** next-of-kin

hinterbrin'gen §65 *tr*—**j-m etw h.** let s.o. in on s.th.

Hin'terdeck *n* quarter deck

hinterdrein [hɪntər'draɪn] *adv* after; subsequently, afterwards

hin'tere §9 *adj* back, rear ‖ **Hintere** §5 *m* (coll) behind

hintereinan'der *adv* one behind the other; in succession; one after the other

Hin'terfuß *m* hind foot

Hin'tergaumen *m* soft palate, velum

Hin'tergedanke *m* ulterior motive

hinterge'hen §82 *tr* deceive

Hin'tergrund *m* background

Hin'terhalt *m* ambush

hinterhältig ['hɪntərhɛltɪç] *adj* underhanded

Hin'terhand *f* hind quarters (*of horse*)

Hin'terhaus *n* rear building

hinterher' *adv* behind; afterwards

Hin'terhof *m* backyard

Hin'terkopf *m* back of the head

Hin'terland *n* hinterland

hinterlas'sen §104 *tr* leave behind

Hinterlas'senschaft *f* (–;–en) inheritance

Hin'terlauf *m* hind leg

hinterle'gen *tr* deposit

Hinterle'gung *f* (–;–en) deposit

Hin'terlist *f* deceit; trick, ruse

Hin'termann *m* (–[e]s;⁼er) instigator; wheeler-dealer; (pol) backer

Hintern ['hɪntərn] *m* (–s;–) (coll) behind

Hin'terradantrieb *m* rear-wheel drive

hinterrücks ['hɪntərrʏks] *adv* from behind; (fig) behind one's back

Hin'tertreffen *n*—**ins H. geraten** fall behind; **im H. sein** be at a disadvantage

hintertrei'ben §62 *tr* frustrate

Hintertrei'bung *f* (–;–en) frustration

Hin'tertreppe *f* backstairs

Hin'tertür *f* backdoor

Hinterwäldler ['hɪntərvɛltlər] *m* (–s;–) hillbilly

hin'terwäldlerisch *adj* hillbilly

hinterzie'hen §163 *tr* evade

Hinterzie'hung *f* (–;) tax evasion

hinü'ber *adv* over, over there; across

hinun'ter *adv* down

hinun'tergehen §82 *tr* (SEIN) (*Treppe*) go down ‖ *intr* (SEIN) go down

hinweg [hɪn'vɛk] *adv* away; **über etw h. over** s.th., across s.th. ‖ **Hinweg** ['hɪnvɛk] *m* way there

hinweg'kommen §99 *intr* (SEIN)—**h. über** (*acc*) get over

hinweg'sehen §138 *intr*—**h. über** (*acc*) look over; overlook, ignore

hinweg'setzen *ref*—**sich h. über** (*acc*) ignore, disregard

hinweg'täuschen *tr* mislead, blind

Hinweis ['hɪnvaɪs] *m* (–es;–e) reference; hint; announcement

hin'weisen §118 *tr*—**j-n h. auf** (*acc*) point s.th. out to s.o. ‖ *intr*—**h. auf** (*acc*) point to; point out

hin'werfen §160 *tr* throw down; (coll) dash off, jot down

hin'wirken *intr*—**h. auf** (*acc*) work toward(s)

hin'ziehen §163 *tr* attract protract ‖ *ref* drag on; **sich h. an** (*dat*) run along; **sich h. bis zu** extend to

hin'zielen *intr*—**h. auf** (*acc*) aim at

hinzu' *adv* there, thither; in addition

hinzu'fügen *tr* add

hinzu'kommen §99 *intr* (SEIN) come (upon the scene); be added; **es kamen noch andere Gründe hinzu** besides, there were other reasons

hinzu'setzen *tr* add

hinzu'treten §152 *intr* (SEIN) (zu) walk up (to); **es traten noch andere Gründe hinzu** besides, there were other reasons

hinzu'tun §154 *tr* add

hinzu'ziehen §163 *tr* (*Arzt*) call in

Hirn [hɪrn] *n* (–[e]s;–e) brain; brains; **sein H. anstrengen** rack one's brains

Hirn– *comb.fm.* brain; cerebral; intellectual

Hirn'anhang *m* pituitary gland

Hirn'gespinst *n* figment of the imagination

Hirn'hautentzündung *f* meningitis

hirn'los *adj* brainless

Hirn'rinde *f* (anat) cortex

Hirn'schale *f* cranium

hirn'verbrannt *adj* (coll) crazy

Hirsch [hɪrʃ] *m* (–es;–e) deer, stag

Hirsch'fänger *m* hunting knife

Hirsch'kalb *n* fawn, doe

Hirsch'kuh *f* hind

Hirsch'leder *n* deerskin, buckskin

Hirt [hɪrt] *m* (–en;–en) shepherd –**hirte** [hɪrtə] *m* (–n;–n) –herd

Hir'tenbrief *m* (eccl) pastoral letter

Hirtin ['hɪrtɪn] *f* (–;–nen) shepherdess

His [hɪs] *n* (–;) (mus) B sharp

hissen ['hɪsən] *tr* hoist

Historie [hɪs'torjə] *f* (–;–n) history; story

Historiker –in [hɪs'torɪkər(ɪn)] §6 *mf* historian

historisch [hɪs'torɪʃ] *adj* historical

Hitze ['hɪtsə] *f* (–;–n) heat

hit'zebeständig *adj* heat-resistant

Hit'zeferien *pl* school holiday (*because of hot weather*)

Hit'zeschild *m* (rok) heat shield

Hit'zewelle *f* heat wave

hitzig ['hɪtsɪç] *adj* hot-tempered

Hitz'kopf *m* hothead

hitz'köpfig *adj* hot-headed

Hitz'schlag *m* heatstroke

hob [hop] *pret* of **heben**

Hobel ['hobəl] *m* (–s;–) (carp) plane

Ho'belbank *f* carpenter's bench

hobeln ['hobəln] *tr* (carp) plane

hoch [hox], (hohe ['ho·ə] §9) *adj* (höher ['hø·ər]; höchste ['høçstə] §9) high; noble; (*Alter*) advanced; **das ist mir zu h.** that's beyond me; **hohes Gericht!** your honor!; members of the jury!; **in höchster Not** in dire need ‖ *adv* high; highly, very; (math) to the ... power ‖ **Hoch** *n* (-s;-s) (*Trinkspruch, Heilruf*) cheer; (meteor) high

hoch— *comb.fm.* up; upwards; highly, very; high, as high as

hoch'achten *tr* esteem

Hoch'actung *f* (-;) esteem; **mit vorzüglicher H., Ihr ... or Ihre ...** Very truly yours, Respectfully yours

hoch'achtungsvoll *adj* respectful ‖ *adv* **—h., Ihr ... or Ihre ...** Very truly yours, Respectfully yours

Hoch'amt *n* (eccl) High Mass

Hoch'antenne *f* outdoor antenna

hoch'arbeiten *ref* work one's way up

hoch'aufgeschossen *adj* tall, lanky

Hoch'bahn *f* el, elevated train

Hoch'bauingenieur *m* structural engineer

hoch'bäumen *ref* rear up

Hoch'behälter *m* water tower; reservoir

Hochbeiner ['hɔxbaɪnər] *m* (-s;-) (ent) daddy-long-legs

hoch'beinig *adj* long-legged

hoch'betagt *adj* advanced in years

Hoch'betrieb *m* bustle, big rush

Hoch'blüte *f* high bloom; (fig) heyday

hoch'bringen §65 *tr* restore to health; (*Geschäft*) put on its feet; **es h.** (sport) get a high score

Hoch'burg *f* fortress, citadel

hoch'denkend *adj* noble-minded

hoch'deutsch *adj* High German

Hoch'druck *m* high pressure; (fig) great pressure; (meteor) high; **mit H.** (fig) full blast

Hoch'druckgebiet *n* (meteor) high, high-pressure area

Hoch'ebene *f* plateau

hoch'fahrend *adj* high-handed

hoch'fein *adj* very refined; high-grade

Hoch'flut *m* high tide; (fig) deluge

Hoch'form *f* top form

hochfrequent ['hɔxfrekvent] *adj* high-frequency

Hoch'frequenz *f* high-frequency

Hoch'frisur *f* upsweep

Hoch'gefühl *n* elation

hoch'gemut *adj* cheerful

Hoch'genuß *m* great pleasure

Hoch'gericht *n* place of execution

hoch'gesinnt *adj* noble-minded

hoch'gespannt *adj* (*Hoffnungen*) high; (elec) high-voltage

hoch'gestellt *adj* high-ranking

Hoch'glanz *m* high polish, high gloss

Hoch'haus *n* high rise (building)

hoch'herzig *adj* generous

hoch'jagen *tr* (*Wild*) ferret out; (*Motor*) race; (coll) blow up

hochkant ['hɔxkant] *adv* on end

Hoch'konjunktur *f* (econ) boom

Hoch'land *n* highlands; plateau

Hoch'leistung *f* (-;-en) high output; (sport) first-class performance

Hochleistungs— *comb.fm.* high-powered; high-capacity; high-speed; heavy-duty

Hoch'mut *m* haughtiness, pride

hoch'mütig *adj* haughty, proud

hochnäsig ['hɔxnɛzɪç] *adj* snooty

Hoch'ofen *m* blast furnace

hoch'ragend *adj* towering

hoch'rappeln *ref* (coll) get on one's feet again, pick up again

hoch'rollen *tr* roll up

Hoch'ruf *m* cheer

Hoch'saison *f* height of the season

Hoch'schule *f* university, academy

Hoch'schüler –in §6 *mf* university student

Hoch'seefischerei *f* deep-sea fishing

hoch'selig *adj* late, of blessed memory

Hoch'spannung *f* high voltage

Hoch'spannungsleitung *f* high-tension line

hoch'spielen *tr* play up; put into the limelight

Hoch'sprache *f* standard language; (die) deutsche H. standard German

höchst *adv* see hoch

Höchst— *comb.fm.* maximum, top

Hochstapelei [hɔxʃtapəˈlaɪ] *f* (-;) false pretenses; fraud

Hochstapler ['hɔxʃtaplər] *m* (-s;) confidence man; imposter, swindler

Hoch'start *m* (sport) standing start

Höchst'belastung *f* (-;-en) maximum load; (elec) peak load

höchstens ['hœçstəns] *adv* at best, at the very most

Höchst'form *f* (sport) top form

Höchst'frequenz *f* ultrahigh frequency

Höchst'geschwindigkeit *f* top speed; zulässige H. speed limit

Höchst'leistung *f* (-;-en) maximum output; highest achievement; (sport) record

Hoch'straße *f* overpass

Hoch'ton *m* (ling) primary stress

hoch'tönend *adj* bombastic

hochtourig ['hɔxtuːrɪç] *adj* high-revving

hoch'trabend *adj* pompous

Hoch'–und Tief'bau *m* (-[e]s;) civil engineering

hoch'verdient *adj* of great merit

Hoch'verrat *m* high treason

Hoch'verräter –in §6 *mf* traitor

Hoch'wasser *n* flood(s); **der Fluß führt H.** the river is swollen

hoch'wertig *adj* high-quality

Hoch'wild *n* big game

Hoch'würden *pl* (*als Anrede*) Reverend; **Seine H. ... the Reverend ...**

Hoch'zeit *f* wedding

hoch'zeitlich *adj* bridal; nuptial

Hoch'zeitsfeier *f* wedding ceremony; wedding reception

Hoch'zeitspaar *n* newly-weds

Hoch'zeitsreise *f* honeymoon

Hocke ['hɔkə] *f* (-;-n) crouch

hocken ['hɔkən] *ref & intr* squat; (coll) sit down

Hocker ['hɔkər] *m* (-s;-) stool

Höcker ['hœkər] *m* (-s;-) hump; bump

höckerig ['hœkərɪç] *adj* hunchbacked; (*Weg*) bumpy

Hockey ['hɔki] *n* (-s;) hockey

Ho'ckeyschläger *m* hockey stick

Hode ['hoːdə] *f* (-;-n) testicle

Ho'densack *m* (anat) scrotum

Hof [hoːf] *m* (-[e]s;-e) courtyard;

yard; barnyard; (e-s Königs) court; (astr) halo; corona; e-m Mädchen den Hof machen court a girl

Hoffart ['hɔfart] f (-;) haughtiness

hoffärtig ['hɔfɛrtɪç] adj haughty

hoffen ['hɔfən] tr—das Beste h. hope for the best || intr (auf acc) hope (for); auf j-n h. put one's hopes in s.o

hoffentlich ['hɔfəntlɪç] adv as I hope; h. kommt er bald I hope he comes soon

Hoffnung ['hɔfnʊŋ] f (-;-en) hope

hoff'nungslos adj hopeless

hoff'nungsvoll adj hopeful; promising

Hof'hund m watchdog

hofieren [hɔ'firən] tr court

höfisch ['hø:fɪʃ] adj court, courtly

höflich ['hø:flɪç] adj polite, courteous

Höf'lichkeit f (-;-en) politeness, courtesy

Höf'lichkeitsformel f complimentary close (in a letter)

Höfling ['hø:flɪŋ] m (-[e]s;-e) courtier

Hof'meister m steward; tutor

Hof'narr m court jester

Hof'staat m royal household; retinue

hohe ['ho:ə] adj see hoch

Höhe ['hø:ə] f (-;-en) height; altitude; (Anhöhe) hill; (mus) pitch; auf der H. in good shape; das ist die H.! that's the limit!; in der H. von in the amount of; in die H. up; in die H. fahren jump up; wieder in die H. bringen (com) put back on its feet

Hoheit ['ho:haɪt] f (-;-en) sovereignty; (als Titel) Highness

Ho'heitsbereich m (pol), **Ho'heitsgebiet** n (pol) territory

Ho'heitsgewässer pl territorial waters

Ho'heitsrechte pl sovereign rights

ho'heitsvoll adj regal, majestic

Ho'heitszeichen n national emblem

Hö'henmesser m altimeter

Hö'henruder n (aer) elevator

Hö'hensonne f ultra-violet lamp

Hö'henstrahlen pl cosmic rays

Hö'henzug m mountain range

Ho'hepriester m high priest

Hö'hepunkt m climax; height; acme

höher ['hø:ər] adj see hoch

hohl [ho:l] adj hollow

Höhle ['hø:lə] f (-;-n) cave; grotto; lair, den; hollow, cavity; socket

Höh'lenmensch m caveman

hohl'geschliffen adj hollow-ground

Hohl'heit f (-;) hollowness

Hohl'maß n dry measure; liquid measure

Hohl'raum m hollow, cavity

Hohl'saum m hemstitch

Hohl'weg m defile, narrow pass

Hohn [ho:n] m (-[e]s;) scorn; sarcasm; etw j-m Hohn tun do s.th. in defiance of s.o

höhnen ['hø:nən] intr jeer; sneer

höhnisch ['hø:nɪʃ] adj scornful

hohn'sprechen §64 intr (dat) treat with scorn; defy; make a mockery of

Höker -in ['hø:kər(ɪn)] §6 mf huckster

hold [hɔlt] adj kindly; lovely; sweet

hold'selig adj lovely, sweet

holen ['ho:lən] tr fetch; get; (Atem, Luft) draw; h. lassen send for; sich [dat] etw h. (coll) catch s.th.

Holland ['hɔlant] n (-s;) Holland

Holländer ['hɔlɛndər] m (-s;-) Dutchman

Holländerin ['hɔlɛndərɪn] f (-;-nen) Dutch woman

holländisch ['hɔlɛndɪʃ] adj Dutch

Hölle ['hœlə] f (-;) hell

Höl'lenangst f mortal fear

höllisch ['hœlɪʃ] adj hellish

Holm [hɔlm] m (-[e]s;-e) islet; (Stiel) handle; (aer) spar; (gym) parallel bar

holp(e)rig ['hɔlp(ə)rɪç] adj bumpy

holpern ['hɔlpərn] intr jolt, bump along; (beim Lesen) stumble

Holunder [hɔ'lʊndər] m (-s;-) (bot) elder

Holz [hɔlts] n (-es;¨er) wood; lumber; timber, trees; ins H. gehen go into the woods

Holz'apfel m crab apple

Holz'arbeit f woodwork; lumbering

Holz'arbeiter m woodworker; lumberjack

holz'artig adj woody

Holz'blasinstrumente pl wood winds

Holz'brei m wood pulp

holzen ['hɔltsən] tr fell; deforest; (coll) spank || intr cut wood

hölzern ['hœltsərn] adj wooden; (fig) clumsy

Holzfäller ['hɔltsfɛlər] m (-s;-) lumberjack, logger

Holz'faser f wood fiber; wood pulp; grain; gegen die H. against the grain

Holz'faserstoff m wood pulp

Holzhacker ['hɔltshakər] m (-s;-), **Holzhauer** ['hɔltshau̯ər] m (-s;-) lumberjack; wood chopper

holzig ['hɔltsɪç] adj woody, wooded; (Gemüse) stringy

Holz'knecht m lumberjack

Holz'kohle f charcoal

Holz'nagel m wooden peg

Holz'platz m lumber yard

holz'reich adj wooded

Holz'schnitt m woodcut; wood engraving

Holz'schuh m wooden shoe

Holz'schuppen m woodshed

Holz'wolle f excelsior

Homi-lie [homɪ'li:] f (-;-lien ['li:ən]) homily

homogen [homo'ge:n] adj homogeneous

Homosexualität [homozɛksu̯alɪ'tɛt] f (-;) homosexuality

homosexuell [homozɛksu̯'ɛl] adj homosexual || **Homosexuelle** §5 mf homosexual

Honig ['ho:nɪç] m (-s;) honey

Ho'nigkuchen m gingerbread

ho'nigsüß adj sweet as honey

Ho'nigwabe f honeycomb

Honorar [hono'ra:r] n (-s;-e) fee

Honoratioren [honoratsɪ'o:rən] pl dignitaries

honorieren [hono'ri:rən] tr give an honorarium to; pay royalties to; (Scheck) honor

Hopfen ['hɔpfən] m (-s;) hops

hopp [hɔp] *interj* up!; quick!; **hopp, los!** get going!

hoppla ['hɔpla] *interj* whoops!; **jetzt aber h.!** come on!; look sharp!

hops [hɔps] *adj*—**h. gehen** go to pot; **h. sein** be done for

hopsasa ['hɔpsasa] *interj* upsy-daisy

hopsen ['hɔpsən] *intr* (SEIN) hop

Hop'ser *m* (-s;-) hop

Hörapparat ['høraparat] *m* hearing aid

hörbar ['hørbar] *adj* audible

hörbehindert ['hørbəhɪndərt] *adj* hard of hearing

Hörbericht ['hørbərɪçt] *m* radio report; radio commentary

horchen ['hɔrçən] *intr* listen; eavesdrop

Hor'cher –*in* §6 *mf* eavesdropper

Horch'gerät *n* sound detector; (nav) hydrophone

Horch'posten *m* (mil) listening post

Horde ['hɔrdə] *f* (-;-n) horde

hören ['hørən] *tr* hear; listen to; (*Vorlesung*) attend || *intr* hear; **h. auf** (acc) pay attention to, obey

Hö'rer *m* (-s;-) listener; member of an audience; student; (telp) receiver

Hö'rerbrief *m* letter from a listener

Hö'rerkreis *m* listeners

Hö'rerschaft *f* (-;-en) audience; (educ) enrollment

Hör'folge *f* radio serial

Hör'gerät *n* hearing aid

hörig ['hørɪç] *adj* in bondage || **Hörige** §5 *mf* serf, thrall

Horizont [hɔrɪ'tsɔnt] *m* (-[e]s;-e) horizon

horizontal [hɔrɪtsɔn'tal] *adj* horizontal || **Horizontale** §5 *f* horizontal line

Horn [hɔrn] *n* (-[e]s;¨er) horn; (mil) bugle; (mus) horn, French horn

Hörnchen ['hœrnçən] *n* (-s;-) crescent roll

Horn'haut *f* (anat) cornea

Hornisse [hɔr'nɪsə] *f* (-;-n) hornet

Hornist [hɔr'nɪst] *m* (-en;-en) bugler

Horn'ochse *f* (coll) dumb ox

Horoskop [hɔrɔ'skop] *n* (-[e]s;-e) horoscope

horrend [hɔ'rɛnt] *adj* (coll) terrible

Hör'rohr *n* stethescope

Hör'saal *m* lecture room

Hör'spiel *n* radio play

Horst [hɔrst] *m* (-[e]s;-e) (eagle's) nest

Hort [hɔrt] *m* (-[e]s;-e) hoard, treasure; (place of) refuge; protector

Hör'weite *f*—**in H.** within earshot

Hose ['hozə] *f* (-;-n), **Hosen** ['hozən] *pl* pants, trousers; (*Unterhose*) shorts; panties; **sich auf die Hosen setzen** buckle down

Ho'senboden *m* seat (of trousers)

Ho'senklappe *f*, **Ho'senlatz** *m* fly

Ho'senrolle *f* (theat) male role

Ho'senträger *pl* suspenders

Hospitant [hɔspɪ'tant] *m* (-en;-en) (educ) auditor

hospitieren [hɔspɪ'tirən] *intr* (educ) audit a course

Hospiz [hɔs'pits] *n* (-es;-e) hospice

Hostie ['hɔstjə] *f* (-;-n) host, wafer

Hotel [hɔ'tɛl] *n* (-s;-s) hotel

Hotel'boy *m* bellboy, bellhop

Hotel'diener *m* hotel porter

Hotel'fach *n*, **Hotel'gewerbe** *n* hotel business

Hub [hup] *m* (-[e]s;¨e) (mach) stroke

hübsch [hypʃ] *adj* pretty; handsome; (coll) good-sized

Hubschrauber ['hupʃraubər] *m* (-s;-) helicopter

huckepack ['hukəpak] *adv* piggyback

hudeln ['hudəln] *intr* be sloppy

Huf [huf] *m* (-[e]s;-e) hoof

Huf'eisen *n* horseshoe

Huf'schlag *m* hoofbeat

Hüfte ['hyftə] *f* (-;-n) hip; **die Arme in die Hüften gestemmt** with arms akimbo

Hüft'gelenk *n* hip joint

Hüft'gürtel *m*, **Hüft'halter** *m* garter belt

Hügel ['hygəl] *m* (-s;-) hill; mound

hügelab' *adv* downhill

hügelauf' *adv* uphill

hügelig ['hygəlɪç] *adj* hilly

Huhn [hun] *n* (-[e]s;¨er) fowl; hen, chicken

Hühnchen ['hynçən] *n* (-s;-) young chicken; **ein H. zu rupfen haben mit** (fig) have a bone to pick with

Hüh'nerauge *n* (pathol) corn

Hüh'nerdraht *m* chicken wire

Hüh'nerhund *m* bird dog

Huld [hult] *f* (-;) grace, favor

huldigen ['huldɪgən] *intr* (dat) pay homage to

Hul'digung *f* (-;) homage

Hul'digungseid *m* oath of allegiance

huld'reich, huld'voll *adj* gracious

Hülle ['hylə] *f* (-;-n) cover; case; wrapper; envelope; (-s *Buches*) jacket; (fig) cloak; **in H. und Fülle** in abundance; **sterbliche H.** mortal remains

hüllen ['hylən] *tr* cover; veil; wrap

Hülse ['hylzə] *f* (-;-n) pod, hull; cartridge case, shell case

Hül'senfrucht *f* legume

human [hu'man] *adj* humane

humanistisch [huma'nɪstɪʃ] *adj* humanistic; classical

humanitär [humanɪ'ter] *adj* humanitarian

Humanität [humanɪ'tet] *f* (-;) humanity; humaneness

Humanitäts'duselei *f* sentimental humanitarianism

Humanitäts'verbrechen *n* crime against humanity

Hummel ['huməl] *f* (-;-n) bumblebee

Hummer ['humər] *m* (-s;-) lobster

Humor [hu'mor] *m* (-s;) humor

humoristisch [humo'rɪstɪʃ] *adj* humorous

humpeln ['humpəln] *intr* (SEIN) hobble

Hund [hunt] *m* (-[e]s;-e) dog

Hündchen ['hyntçən] *n* (-s;-) small dog; puppy

Hun'deangst *f*—**e–e H. haben** (coll) be scared stiff

Hun'dearbeit *f* drudgery

Hun'dehütte *f* doghouse

Hun'dekälte *f* severe cold

Hun′demarke *f* dog tag
hun′demü′de *adj* (coll) dog-tired
hundert ['hundərt] *invar adj & pron* hundred || **Hundert** *n* (-s;-e) hundred; **drei von H.** three percent; **im H.** by the hundred || *f* (-;-en) hundred
hun′dertfach *adj* hundredfold
Hundertjahr′feier *f* centennial
Hun′dertsatz *m* percentage
hundertste ['hundərtstə] §9 *adj & pron* hundredth
Hun′deschau *f* dog show
Hun′dezwinger *m* dog kennel
Hündin ['hyndɪn] *f* (-;-nen) bitch
hündisch ['hyndɪʃ] *adj* (*Benehmen*) servile; (*Angst*) deadly
hunds′gemein *adj* beastly
hunds′miserabel *adj* (sl) lousy
Hunds′stern *m* Dog Star
Hunds′tage *pl* dog days
Hüne ['hynə] *m* (-n;-n) giant
hü′nenhaft *adj* gigantic
Hunger ['huŋər] *m* (-s;) hunger; **H. haben** be hungry
Hun′gerkur *f* starvation diet
Hun′gerlohn *m* starvation wages
hungern ['huŋərn] *intr* be hungry; go without food; **h. nach** yearn for || *impers*—**es hungert mich** I am hungry
Hun′gersnot *f* famine
Hun′gertod *m* death from starvation
Hun′gertuch *n*—**am H. nagen** go hungry; live in poverty
hungrig ['huŋrɪç] *adj* hungry; (*Jahre*) lean
Hunne ['hunə] *m* (-n;-n) (hist) Hun
Hupe ['hupə] *f* (-;-n) (aut) horn
hupen ['hupən] *intr* blow the horn
hüpfen ['hypfən], **hupfen** ['hupfən] *intr* (SEIN) hop, jump
Hürde ['hyrdə] *f* (-;-n) hurdle
Hure ['hurə] *f* (-;-n) whore
huren ['hurən] *intr* whore around
hurtig ['hurtɪç] *adj* nimble, swift
huschen ['huʃən] *intr* (SEIN) scurry
hüsteln ['hystəln] *intr* clear the throat
husten ['hustən] *tr* cough up || *intr* cough; **h. auf** (*acc*) (coll) not give a rap about

Hut [hut] *m* (-[e]s;-̈e) hat || *f* (-;) protection, care; **auf der Hut sein** be on guard
hüten ['hytən] *tr* guard, protect; tend; **das Bett h.** be confined to bed; **das Haus h.** stay indoors; **Kinder h.** baby-sit || *ref* (**vor** *dat*) be on guard (against), beware (of); **ich werde mich schön h.** (coll) I'll do no such thing
Hü′ter –in §6 *mf* guardian
Hut′krempe *f* brim of a hat
hut′los *adj* hatless
Hütte ['hytə] *f* (-;-n) hut; cabin; doghouse; glassworks; (Bib) tabernacle; (metal) foundry
Hüt′tenkunde *f*, **Hüt′tenwesen** *n* metallurgy
Hyäne [hy'ɛnə] *f* (-;-n) hyena
Hyazinthe [hya'tsɪntə] *f* (-;-n) hyacinth
Hydrant [hy'drant] *m* (-en;-en) hydrant
Hydraulik [hy'draulɪk] *f* (-;) hydraulics; hydraulic system
hydraulisch [hy'draulɪʃ] *adj* hydraulic
hydrieren [hy'drirən] *tr* hydrogenate
Hygiene [hy'gjenə] *f* (-;) hygiene
hygienisch [hy'gjenɪʃ] *adj* hygienic
Hymne ['hymnə] *f* (-;-n) hymn; anthem
Hyperbel [hy'pɛrbəl] *f* (-;-n) (geom) hyperbola; (rhet) hyperbole
Hypnose [hyp'nozə] *f* (-;-n) hypnosis
hypnotisch [hyp'notɪʃ] *adj* hypnotic
Hypothese [hfilpo'tezə] *f* (-;-n) hypothesis
Hypochonder [hypo'xɔndər] *m* (-s;-) hypochondriac
Hypothek [hypo'tek] *f* (-;-en) mortgage
Hypothe′kengläubiger *m* mortgagee
Hypothe′kenschuldner *m* mortgagor
Hypothese [hypo'tezə] *f* (-;-n) hypothesis
hypothetisch [hypo'tetɪʃ] *adj* hypothetical
Hysterektomie [hysterekto'mi] *f* (-;) hysterectomy
Hysterie [hystɛ'ri] *f* (-;) hysteria
hysterisch [hys'teriʃ] *adj* hysterical

I

I, i [i] *invar n* I, i
iah ['i'a] *interj* heehaw!
iahen ['i'a-ən] *intr* heehaw, bray
iberisch [i'beriʃ] *adj* Iberian
ich [ɪç] §11 *pers pron* I
ichbezogen ['ɪçbətsogən] *adj* self-centered, egocentric
Ich′sucht *f* egotism
ideal [ide'al] *adj* ideal || **Ideal** *n* (-s;-e) deal
idealisieren [ide-alɪ'zirən] *tr* idealize
Idealismus [ide-a'lɪsmus] *m* (-;) idealism
Idealist –in [ide-a'lɪst(ɪn)] §7 *mf* idealist

idealistisch [ide-a'lɪstɪʃ] *adj* idealistic
I-dee [i'de] *f* (-;-deen ['de-ən]) idea
Iden ['idən] *pl* Ides
identifizieren [identifi'tsirən] *tr* identify || *ref*—**i. mit** identify with
identisch [i'dentɪʃ] *adj* identical
Identität [identi'tet] *f* (-;-en) identity
Ideolo·gie [ide-olo'gi] *f* (-;-gien ['gi-ən]) ideology
Idiom [i'djom] *n* (-s;-e) idiom, dialect, language
idiomatisch [idjo'matɪʃ] *adj* idiomatic
Idiosynkra·sie [idjozynkra'zi] *f* (-;-sien ['zi-ən]) idiosyncrasy
Idiot [i'djot] *m* (-en;-en) idiot

Idio·tie [ɪdjɔ'ti] f (-;-tien ['ti·ən]) idiocy

Idiotin [ɪdjotɪn] f (-;-nen) idiot

Idol [ɪ'dol] n (-s;-e) idol

idyllisch [ɪ'dylɪʃ] adj idyllic

Igel ['igəl] m (-s;-) hedgehog

Ignorant [ɪgno'rant] m (-en;-en) ignoramus

ignorieren [ɪgno'rirən] tr ignore

ihm [im] §11 pers pron (dative of er and es) (to) him; (to) it

ihn [in] §11 pers pron (accusative of er) him

ihnen ['inən] §11 pers pron (dative of sie) (to) them ‖ **Ihnen** §11 pers pron (dative of Sie) (to) you

ihr [ir] §2,2 poss adj her; their ‖ §11 pers pron (dative of sie) (to) her ‖ **Ihr** §2,2 poss adj your

ihrerseits ['irərzaits] adv on her (or their) part; **Ihrerseits** on your part

ihresgleichen ['irəsglaiçən] pron the likes of her (or them); her (or their) equal(s); **Ihresgleichen** the likes of you; your equal(s)

ihrethalben ['irət'halbən] adv var of ihretwegen

ihretwegen ['irət'vegən] adv because of her (or them); for her (or their) sake; **Ihretwegen** because of you, for your sake

ihretwillen ['irət'vilən] adv var of ihretwegen

ihrige ['irigə] §2,5 poss pron hers; theirs; **Ihrige** yours

Ikone [i'konə] f (-;-n) icon

illegal [ile'gal] adj illegal

illegitim [ilegi'tim] adj illegitimate

illuminieren [ilumi'nirən] tr illuminate

Illusion [ilu'zjon] f (-;-en) illusion

illustrieren [ilus'trirən] tr illustrate

Illustrierte [ilus'trirtə] §5 f (illustrated) magazine

Iltis ['iltis] m (-ses;-se) polecat

im [im] contr in dem

Image ['imidʒ] n (-s;-s) (fig) image

imaginär [imagi'nɛr] adj imaginary

Im·biß ['imbis] m (-bisses;-bisse) snack

Im'bißhalle f luncheonette

Im'bißstube f snack bar

Imi·tator [imi'tator] m (-s;-tatoren [ta'torən]) imitator; impersonator

Imker ['imkər] m (-s;-) beekeeper

immateriell [imate'rjel] adj immaterial, spiritual

immatrikulieren [imatriku'lirən] tr & intr register; **sich i. lassen** get registered

immens [i'mens] adj immense

immer ['imər] adv always; **auf i. und ewig** for ever and ever; **für i.** for good; **i. langsam!** steady now!; **i. mehr** more and more; **i. wieder** again and again; **noch i.** still; **nur i. zu!** keep trying!; **was auch i.** whatever

immerdar' adv (Lit) forever

immerfort' adv all the time

im'mergrün adj evergreen ‖ **Immergrün** n (-s;-e) evergreen

immerhin' adv after all, anyhow

immerwäh'rend adj perpetual

immerzu' adv all the time, constantly

Immobilien [imo'biljən] pl real estate

Immobi'lienmakler **-in** §6 mf real-estate broker

immun [i'mun] adj (gegen) immune (to)

immunisieren [imuni'zirən] tr immunize

Imperativ [impera'tif] m (-s;-e) (gram) imperative

Imperfek·tum [imper'fektum] n (-s;-ta [ta]) (gram) imperfect

Imperialismus [imperi·a'lismus] m (-;) imperialism

impfen ['impfen] tr vaccinate; inoculate

Impfling ['impflin] m (-s;-e) person to be vaccinated or inoculated

Impf'schein m vaccination certificate

Impf'stoff m vaccine

Imp'fung f (-;-en) vaccination; inoculation

imponieren [impo'nirən] intr (dat) impress

Import [im'port] m (-[e]s;-e) import

importieren [impor'tirən] tr import

imposant [impo'zant] adj imposing

imprägnieren [impreg'nirən] tr waterproof; creosote

Impresario [impre'zarjo] m (-s;-s) agent, business manager

Impres·sum [im'presum] n (-s;-sen [sən]) (journ) masthead

imstande [im'standə] adv—**i. sein zu** (inf) be in a position to (inf)

in [in] prep (position) (dat) in, at; (direction) (acc) in, into

Inangriffnahme [in'angrifnamə] f (-;) starting; putting into action

Inanspruchnahme [in'an·pruxnamə] f (-;) laying claim; demands; utilization

In'begriff m essence; embodiment

in'begriffen adj included

Inbrunst ['inbrunst] f (-;) ardor

inbrünstig ['inbrynstiç] adj ardent

indem [in'dem] conj while, as; by (ger)

Inder **-in** ['indər(in)] §6 mf Indian (inhabitant of India)

indes [in'des], **indessen** [in'desən] adv meanwhile; however ‖ conj while; whereas

Indianer **-in** [in'djanər(in)] §6 mf Indian (of North America)

Indien ['indjən] n (-s;) India

Indio ['indi·o] m (-s;-s) Indian (of Central or South America)

indisch ['indiʃ] adj Indian

indiskret [indis'kret] adj indiscreet

indiskutabel [indisku'tabəl] adj out of the question

individuell [individu'el] adj individual

Individu·um [indi'vidu·um] n (-s;-en [ən]) individual; (pej) character

Indizienbeweis [in'ditsjənbevais] m (piece of) circumstantial evidence

Indossament [indosa'ment] n (-[e]s; -e) indorsement

Indossant [indo'sant] m (-en;-en) indorser

indossieren [indo'sirən] tr indorse

industrialisieren [industri·ali'zirən] tr industrialize

Indus·trie [ɪndus'triː] f (-;-trien ['triːən]) industry
Industrie'anlage f industrial plant
Industrie'betrieb m industrial establishment
Industrie'kapitän m tycoon
industriell [ɪndustri'el] adj industrial || **Industrielle** §5 m industrialist
ineinan'der adv into one another; **i. übergehen** merge
ineinan'derfügen tr dovetail
ineinan'dergreifen §88 intr mesh
ineinan'derpassen intr dovetail
infam [ɪn'fam] adv (coll) frightfully
Infante·rie [ɪnfantə'riː] f (-;-rien ['riːən]) infantry
Infanterist [ɪnfantə'rɪst] m (-en;-en) infantryman
infantil [ɪnfan'til] adj infantile
Infektion [ɪnfɛk'tsjon] f (-;-en) infection
Infini·tiv [ɪnfɪni'tif] m (-s;-tive ['tivə]) infinitive
infizieren [ɪnfi'tsirən] tr infect
infolge [ɪn'folgə] prep (genit) in consequence of, owing to; according to
infolgedes'sen adv consequently
Information [ɪnforma'tsjon] f (-;-en) (piece of) information
informieren [ɪnfor'mirən] tr inform
infrarot [ɪnfra'rot] adj infrared || **Infrarot** n (-s;-) infrared
Ingenieur [ɪnʒen'jør] m (-s;-e) engineer
Ingenieur'bau m (-[e]s;) civil engineering
Ingenieur'wesen n engineering
ingeniös [ɪngə'njøs] adj ingenious
Ingrimm ['ɪngrɪm] m inner rage
Ingwer ['ɪŋvər] m (-s;) ginger
Ing'werplätzchen n gingersnap
Inhaber -in ['ɪnhabər(ɪn)] §6 mf owner; bearer; occupant; holder
inhaftieren [ɪnhaf'tirən] tr arrest
Inhalierapparat [ɪnha'lirapaːrat] m (med) inhalator
inhalieren [ɪnha'lirən] tr & intr inhale
Inhalt ['ɪnhalt] m (-[e]s;-e) contents; subject matter; (geom) area; volume
In'haltsangabe f summary; list of contents
in'haltsarm, in'haltsleer adj empty
in'haltsreich adj substantive; (Leben) full
in'haltsschwer adj pregnant with meaning; momentous
In'haltsverzeichnis n table of contents
in'haltsvoll adj full of meaning
inhibieren [ɪnhi'birən] tr inhibit
Initiative [ɪnɪtsja'tivə] f (-;-en) initiative
Injektion [ɪnjɛk'tsjon] f (-;-en) injection
Injektions'nadel f hypodermic needle
injizieren [ɪnji'tsirən] tr inject
Inkasso [ɪn'kaso] n (-s;-s) bill collecting
Inkas'sobeamte m bill collector
inklusive [ɪnklu'zivə] adj inclusive || prep (genit) including
inkonsequent ['ɪnkonzekvent] adj inconsistent; illogical
Inkraft'treten n going into effect

In'land n (-[e]s;) home country; interior
Inländer -in ['ɪnlendər(ɪn)] §6 mf native
inländisch ['ɪnlendɪʃ] adj home, domestic; inland
In'landspost f domestic mail
Inlett ['ɪnlet] n (-[e]s;-e) bedtick
in'liegend adj enclosed
inmit'ten prep (genit) in the middle of, among
innehaben ['ɪnəhabən] §89 tr (Amt) hold; (Wohnung) occupy, own
innehalten ['ɪnəhaltən] §90 intr stop
innen ['ɪnən] adv inside; indoors; **nach i.** inwards; **tief i.** deep down
Innen- comb.fm. inner, internal; inside, interior; home, domestic
In'nenarchitekt -in §7 mf interior decorator
In'nenaufnahme f (phot) indoor shot
In'nenhof m quadrangle
In'nenleben n inner life
In'nenminister m Secretary of the Interior; Secretary of State for Home Affairs (Brit)
In'nenpolitik f domestic policy
In'nenraum m interior (of building)
In'nenstadt f center of town, inner city
inner- ['ɪnər] comb.fm. internal; intra-
innere ['ɪnərə] §9 adj inner, internal; inside; inward; domestic || **Innere** §5 n inside, interior
in'nerhalb adv on the inside; **i. von** within || prep (genit) inside, within
in'nerlich adj inner, inward || adv inwardly; mentally; emotionally
In'nerlichkeit f (-;-en) introspection; inner quality
innerste ['ɪnərstə] §9 adj innermost
innesein ['ɪnəzaɪn] §139 intr (SEIN) (genit) be aware of
innewerden ['ɪnəverdən] §159 intr (SEIN) (genit) become aware of
innig ['ɪnɪç] adj close; deep, heartfelt || adv deeply
In'nigkeit f (-;) intimacy; deep feeling; tender affection
Innung ['ɪnuŋ] f (-;-en) guild
inoffiziell ['ɪnofitsjel] adj unofficial
ins contr in das
Insasse ['ɪnzasə] m (-n;-n), **Insassin** ['ɪnsasɪn] f (-;-nen) occupant; (e-s Gefängnisses) inmate; (e-s Autos) passenger
insbesondere [ɪnsbə'zondərə] adv in particular, especially
In'schrift f inscription
Insekt [ɪn'zekt] n (-[e]s;-en) insect
Insek'tenbekämpfungsmittel n insecticide
Insek'tenkunde f entomology
Insek'tenstich m insect bite
Insektizid [ɪnzektɪ'tsit] n (-[e]s;-e) insecticide
Insel ['ɪnzəl] f (-;-n) island
Inserat [ɪnzə'rat] n (-es;-e) classified advertisement, ad
inserieren [ɪnzə'rirən] tr insert || intr (in dat) advertise (in)
insgeheim [ɪnsgə'haɪm] adv secretly
insgemein [ɪnsgə'maɪn] adv as a whole; in general, generally

insgesamt [ɪnsgə'zamt] *adv* in a body, as a unit; in all, altogether

inso'fern' *adv* to this extent || **insofern'** *conj* in so far as

insoweit' *adv* & *conj* var of **insofern**

Inspek·tor [ɪn'spektɔr] *m* (-s;-toren ['torən]) inspector

inspirieren [ɪnspɪ'rirən] *tr* inspire

inspizieren [ɪnspɪ'sirən] *tr* inspect

Installation [ɪnstala'tsjon] *f* (-;-en) installation

installieren [ɪnsta'lirən] *tr* install

instand [ɪn'ʃtant] *adv*—**i.** halten keep in good condition; **i. setzen** repair

Instand/haltung *f* upkeep, maintenance

inständig [ɪn'ʃtendɪç] *adj* insistent

Instand/setzung *f* repair, renovation

Instanz [ɪn'ʃtants] *f* (-;-en) (adm) authority; **e-e höhere I. anrufen** appeal to a higher court; **Gericht der ersten I.** court of primary jurisdiction; **Gericht der zweiten I.** court of appeal; **höchste I.** court of final appeal

Institut [ɪnstɪ'tut] *n* (-[e]s;-e) institute

instruieren [ɪnstru'irən] *tr* instruct

Instruktion [ɪnstruk'tsjon] *f* (-;-en) instruction

Instrument [ɪnstru'ment] *n* (-[e]s;-e) instrument

Instrumentalist –**in** [ɪnstrumenta'lɪst (ɪn)] §7 *mf* instrumentalist

Insulaner –**in** [ɪnzu'lanər(ɪn)] §6 *mf* islander

insular [ɪnzu'lar] *adj* insular

Insulin [ɪnzu'lin] *n* (-s;) insulin

inszenieren [ɪnstse'nirən] *tr* stage

Intellekt [ɪnte'lekt] *m* (-[e]s;) intellect

intellektuell [ɪntelektu'el] *adj* intellectual || **Intellektuelle** §5 *mf* intellectual

intelligent [ɪntelɪ'gent] *adj* intelligent

Intelligenzler [ɪntelɪ'gentslər] *m* (-s;-) (pej) egghead

Intendant [ɪnten'dant] *m* (-en;-en) (theat) director

intensiv [ɪnten'zif] *adj* intense; intensive

–**intensiv** *comb.fm.*, e.g., **lohnintensive Güter** goods of which wages constitute a high proportion of the cost

interessant [ɪntere'sant] *adj* interesting

Interesse [ɪnte'resə] *n* (-s;-n) (an *dat*, **für**) interest (in)

interes'selos *adj* uninterested

Interes'sengemeinschaft *f* community of interest; (com) syndicate

Interessent –**in** [ɪntere'sent(ɪn)] §7 *mf* interested party

interessieren [ɪntere'sirən] *tr* (für) interest (in) || *ref*—**sich i. für** be interested in

interimistisch [ɪnterɪ'mɪstɪʃ] *adj* provisional

intern [ɪn'tern] *adj* internal

Internat [ɪnter'nat] *n* (-[e]s;-e) boarding school

international [ɪnternatsjo'nal] *adj* international

Internat(s)/schüler –**in** §6 *mf*, **Interne** [ɪn'ternə] §5 *mf* boarding student

internieren [ɪnter'nirən] *tr* intern

Internist –**in** [ɪnter'nɪst(ɪn)] §7 *mf* (med) internist

Interpret [ɪnter'pret] *m* (-en;-en) interpreter; exponent

interpunktieren [ɪnterpuŋk'tirən] *tr* punctuate

Interpunktion [ɪnterpuŋk'tsjon] *f* (-;-en) punctuation

Interpunktions'zeichen *n* punctuation mark

Intervall [ɪnter'val] *n* (-s;-e) interval

intervenieren [ɪnterve'nirən] *intr* intervene

Interview ['ɪntervju] *n* (-s;-s) interview

interviewen [ɪnter'vju·ən] *tr* interview

intim [ɪn'tim] *adj* intimate

Intimität [ɪntimɪ'tet] *f* (-;-en) intimacy

intolerant [ɪntole'rant] *adj* intolerant

intonieren [ɪntə'nirən] *tr* intone

intransitiv ['ɪntransitif] *adj* intransitive

intravenös [ɪntrave'nøs] *adj* intravenous

intrigant [ɪntrɪ'gant] *adj* intriguing, scheming || **Intragant** –**in** §7 *mf* intriguer, schemer

Intrige [ɪn'trigə] *f* (-;-n) intrigue

introspektiv [ɪntrospek'tif] *adj* introspective

Introvertierte [ɪntrover'tirtə] §5 *mf* introvert

invalide [ɪnva'lidə] *adj* disabled || **Invalide** §5 *mf* invalid

Invalidität [ɪnvalidɪ'tet] *f* (-;) disability

Invasion [ɪnva'zjon] *f* (-;-en) invasion

Inventar [ɪnven'tar] *n* (-s;-e) inventory

Inventur [ɪnven'tur] *f* (-;-en) stock taking; **I. machen** take stock

inwärts ['ɪnverts] *adv* inwards

inwendig ['ɪnvendɪç] *adj* inward, inner

inwiefern' *adv* how far; in what way

inwieweit' *adv* var of **inwiefern**

In'zucht *f* inbreeding

inzwi'schen *adv* meanwhile

Ion [i'on] *n* (-s;-en) (phys) ion

ionisieren [i·onɪ'zirən] *tr* ionize

Irak [i'rak] *m* (-s;) Iraq

Iraker –**in** [i'rakər(ɪn)] §6 *mf* Iraqi

irakisch [i'rakɪʃ] *adj* Iraqi

Iran [i'ran] *m* (-s;) Iran

Iraner –**in** [i'ranər(ɪn)] §6 *mf* Iranian

iranisch [i'ranɪʃ] *adj* Iranian

irden ['ɪrdən] *adj* earthen

irdisch ['ɪrdɪʃ] *adj* earthly, worldly || **Irdische** §5 *n* earthly nature

Ire ['irə] *m* (-n;-n) Irishman; **die Iren** the Irish

irgend ['ɪrgənt] *adv*—**i. etwas** something, anything; **i. jemand** someone, anyone; **nur i.** possibly

ir'gendein *adj* some, any || **ingendeiner** *indef pron* someone, anyone

ir'gendeinmal *adv* at some time or other

ir'gendwann *adv* at some time or other

ir'gendwelcher *adj* any; any kind of

ir'gendwer *indef pron* someone

ir'gendwie *adv* somehow or other

ir'gendwo *adv* somewhere or other; anywhere

ir'gendwoher *adv* from somewhere or other

ir'gendwohin *adv* somewhere or other

Irin ['ɪrɪn] *f* (-;-nen) Irish woman

Iris ['ɪrɪs] *f* (-;-) (anat, bot) iris

irisch ['ɪrɪ] *adj* Irish

Irland ['ɪrlant] *n* (-s;) Ireland

Iro•nie [ɪro'ni] *f* (-;-nien ['ni•ən]) irony

ironisch [ɪ'roniʃ] *adj* ironic(al)

irre ['ɪrə] *adj* stray; confused; mad; **i. werden** go astray; get confused; **i. werden an** (*dat*) lose faith in ‖ **Irre** §5 *mf* lunatic ‖ *f* maze; wrong track; **in die I. führen** put on the wrong track; **in die I. gehen** go astray

ir'refahren §71 *intr* (SEIN) lose one's way, go wrong

ir'reführen *tr* mislead

ir'regehen §82 *intr* (SEIN) lose one's way; (fig) go wrong

ir'remachen *tr* confuse; **j–n i. an** (*dat*) make s.o. lose faith in

irren ['ɪrən] *intr* go astray; err ‖ *ref* (in *dat*) be mistaken (about); **sich in der Straße i.** take the wrong road; **sich in der Zeit i.** misjudge the time

Ir'renanstalt *f*, Ir'renhaus *n* insane asylum

Ir'renhäusler ['ɪrənhɔɪzlər] *m* (-s;-) inmate of an insane asylum

ir'rereden *intr* rave; talk deliriously

Irrfahrt ['ɪrfart] *f* odyssey

Irrgang ['ɪrgaŋ] *m* winding path

Irrgarten ['ɪrgartən] *m* labyrinth

Irrglaube ['ɪrglaubə] *m* heresy

irrgläubig ['ɪrglɔɪbɪç] *adj* heretical

irrig ['ɪrɪç] *adj* mistaken

Irri•gator [ɪrɪ'gator] *m* (-s;-gatoren [ga•torən]) douche

irritieren [ɪrɪ'tirən] *tr* irritate; (coll) confuse

Irrlehre ['ɪrlerə] *f* false doctrine

Irrlicht ['ɪrlɪçt] *n* jack-o'-lantern

Irrsinn ['ɪrzɪn] *m* insanity

irr'sinnig *adj* insane

Irrtum ['ɪrtum] *n* (-s;-er) error

irrtümlich ['ɪrtymlɪç] *adj* erroneous

Irrweg ['ɪrvek] *m* wrong track

Irrwisch ['ɪrvɪʃ] *m* (-es;-e) jack-o'-lantern; (coll) fireball

Islam [ɪs'lam] *m* (-s;) Islam

Island ['ɪslant] *n* (-s;) Iceland

Iso•lator [ɪzo'lator] *m* (-s;-latoren [la'torən]) (elec) insulator

Isolier– [ɪzo'lir] *comb.fm.* isolation; insulating; insulated

Isolier'band *n* (-[e]s;-er) friction tape

isolieren [ɪzo'lirən] *tr* (Kranke) isolate; (abdichten) insulate

Isolier'haft *f* solitary confinement

Insolier'station *f* isolation ward

Isolie'rung *f* (-;-en) isolation; (elec) insulation

Isotop [ɪzo'top] *n* (-[e]s;-e) isotope

Israel ['ɪsra•el] *n* (– & –s;) Israel

Israeli [ɪsra'eli] *m* (-s;-s) Israeli

israelisch [ɪsra'eliʃ] *adj* Israeli

Israelit –in [ɪsra•e'lit(ɪn)] §7 *mf* Israelite

israelitisch [ɪsra•e'litɪʃ] *adj* Israelite

Ist– [ɪst] *comb.fm.* actual

Ist–'Bestand *m* actual stock; (fin) actual balance; (mil) actual stockpile

Ist–'Stand *m*, Ist–'Stärke *f* (mil) effective strength

Italien [ɪ'taljən] *n* (-s;) Italy

Italiener –in [ɪtal'jenər(ɪn)] §6 *mf* Italian

italienisch [ɪtal'jeniʃ] *adj* Italian

J

J, j [jot] *invar n* J, j

ja [ja] *adv* yes; indeed, certainly; of course ‖ **Ja** *n* (-s;-s) yes

Jacht [jaxt] *f* (-;-en) yacht

Jacke ['jakə] *f* (-;-n) jacket, coat

Jackenkleid (Jak'kenkleid) *n* lady's two-piece suit

Jackett [ʒa'ket] *n* (-s;-e) jacket

Jagd [jakt] *f* (-;-en) hunt(ing); **auf die J. gehen** go hunting; **J. machen auf** (*acc*) hunt for

Jagd'abschirmung *f* (aer) fighter screen

Jagd'aufseher *m* gamewarden

jagdbar ['jaktbar] *adj* in season, fair (game)

Jagd'bomber *m* (aer) fighter-bomber

Jagd'flieger *m* fighter pilot

Jagd'flugzeug *n* (aer) fighter plane

Jagd'gehege *n* game preserve

Jagd'geleit *n* (aer) fighter escort

Jagd'hund *m* hunting dog, hound

Jagd'rennen *n* steeplechase

Jagd'revier *n* hunting ground

Jagd'schein *m* hunting license

Jagd'schutz *m* (aer) fighter protection

Jagd'verband *m* (aer) fighter unit

Jagd'wild *n* game; game bird

jagen ['jagən] *tr* hunt; pursue; chase; (fig) follow close on; **in die Luft j.** blow up ‖ *intr* go hunting; **j. nach** pursue ‖ *intr* (SEIN) rush

Jäger ['jegər] *m* (-s;-) hunter; (aer) fighter plane; (mil) rifleman

Jägerei [jegə'rar] *f* (-;) hunting

Jä'gerlatein *n* (coll) fish story

Jaguar ['jagu•ar] *m* (-s;-s) jaguar

jäh [je] *adj* sudden; steep ‖ **Jähe** *f* (-;) suddenness; steepness

jählings ['jelɪŋs] *adv* suddenly; steeply

Jahr [jar] *n* (-[e]s;-e) year

jahraus' –j. jahrein year in year out, year after year

Jahr'buch *n* almanac; yearbook; annual

jahrelang ['jarəlaŋ] *adj* long-standing ‖ *adv* for years

jähren ['jerən] *ref* be a year ago

Jahres– [jarəs] *comb.fm.* annual, yearly, of the year

Jah'resfeier *f* anniversary
Jah'resfrist *f* period of a year
Jah'resrente *f* annuity
Jah'restag *m* anniversary
Jah'reszahl *f* date, year
Jah'reszeit *f* season
jah'reszeitlich *adj* seasonal
Jahr'gang *m* age group; class, year; crop; vintage; er gehört zu meinem J. he was born in the same year as I
Jahrhun'dert *n* century
–jährig [jerɪç] *comb.fm.* –year-old
jährlich ['jerlɪç] *adj* yearly, annual
Jahr'markt *m* fair
Jahr'marktplatz *m* fairground
Jahrtau'send *n* millennium
Jahrzehnt [jɑr'tsent] *n* (–[e]s;–e) decade
Jäh'zorn *m* fit of anger; hot temper
jäh'zornig *adj* quick-tempered
Jalou•sie [ʒalu'zi] *f* (–;–sien ['zi•ən]) louvre; Venetian blind
Jammer ['jamər] *m* (–s;) misery; wailing; es ist ein J., daß it's a pity that
Jam'merlappen *m* (pej) jellyfish
jämmerlich ['jemərlɪç] *adj* miserable; pitiful; (*Anblick*) sorry
jammern ['jamərn] *tr* move to pity || *intr* (über *acc*, um) moan (about); j. nach (or um) whimper for
Jam'merschade *adj* deplorable
Jänner ['jenər] *m* (–s & –;–) (Aust) January
Januar ['janu•ɑr] *m* (–s & –;–e) January
Japan ['japan] *n* (–s;) Japan
Japaner –in [ja'panər(ɪn)] §6 *mf* Japanese
japanisch [ja'panɪʃ] *adj* Japanese
jappen ['japən] *intr* pant, gasp
Jasager ['jazɑgər] *m* (–s;–) yes-man
jäten ['jetən] *tr* weed; das Unkraut j. pull out weeds || *intr* weed
Jauche ['jauxə] *f* (–;–n) liquid manure; (sl) slop
jauchen ['jauxən] *tr* manure
Jau'chegrube *f* cesspool
jauchzen ['jauxtsən] *intr* rejoice; vor Freude j. shout for joy || Jauchzen *n* (–s) jubilation
Jauch'zer *m* (–s;–) shout of joy
jawohl [ja'vol] *interj* yes, indeed!
Ja'wort *n* (–[e]s;) consent
Jazz [dʒez], [jats] *m* (–;) jazz
je [je] *adv* ever; denn je than ever; je länger, je (or desto) besser the longer the better; je nach according to, depending on; je nachdem, ob according to whether; je Pfund per pound; je zwei two each; two by two, in twos; seit je always
Jeans [dʒɪnz] *pl* jeans
jedenfalls ['jedənfals] *adv* at any rate; ich j. I for one
jeder ['jedər] §3 *indef adj* each, every || *indef pron* each one, everyone
jederlei ['jedər'laɪ] *invar adj* every kind of
je'dermann *indef pron* everyone, everybody
je'derzeit *adv* at all times, at any time
je'desmal *adv* each time, every time
jedoch [je'dɔx] *adv* however

jeglicher ['jeklɪçər] §3 *indef adj* each, every || *indef pron* each one, everyone
je'her *adv*—von j. since time immemorial
Jelän'gerjelie'ber *m & n* honeysuckle
jemals ['jemals] *adv* ever
jemand ['jemant] *indef pron* someone, somebody; anyone, anybody
jener ['jenər] §3 *dem adj* that || *dem pron* that one
jenseitig ['jenzaɪtɪç] *adj* opposite, beyond, otherworldly
Jenseits ['jenzaɪts] *prep* (*genit*) on the other side of; beyond || Jenseits *n* (–;) beyond
jetzig ['jetsɪç] *adj* present, current
jetzt [jetst] *adv* now
jeweilig ['jevaɪlɪç] *adj* at that time
jeweils ['jevaɪls] *adv* at that time
jiddisch ['jɪdɪʃ] *adj* Yiddish
Joch [jɔx] *n* (–[e]s;–[e]) yoke; yoke of oxen; (*e–r Brücke*) span; (*e–s Berges*) saddleback
Joch'bein *n* cheekbone
Joch'brücke *f* pile bridge
Jockei ['dʒɔki] *m* (–s;–s) jockey
Jod [jot] *n* (–s;) iodine
jodeln ['jodəln] *intr* yodel
Jodler –in ['jodlər(ɪn)] §6 *mf* yodeler || *m* yodel
Jodtinktur ['jottɪŋktur] *f* (–;) (pharm) iodine
Johannisbeere [jo'hanɪsberə] *f* currant
johlen ['jolən] *intr* yell, boo
jonglieren [ʒɔŋ'(g)lirən] *tr & intr* juggle
Journalist –in [ʒurna'lɪst(ɪn)] §7 *mf* journalist
jovial [jo'vjɑl] *adj* jovial
Jubel ['jubəl] *m* (–s;) jubilation
Ju'belfeier *f*, Ju'belfest *n* jubilee
Ju'beljahr *n* jubilee year
jubeln ['jubəln] *intr* rejoice; shout for joy
Jubiläum [jubɪ'le•um] *n* (–s;–en [ən]) jubilee
juche [jux'he] *interj* hurray!
juchei [jux'haɪ] *interj* hurray!
juchzen ['juxtsən] *intr* shout for joy
jucken ['jukən] *tr* itch; scratch || *ref* scratch || *intr* itch || *impers*—es juckt mich I feel itchy; es juckt mir (or mich) in den Fingern zu (*inf*) I am itching to (*inf*); es juckt sie in den Beinen she is itching to dance
Jude ['judə] *m* (–n;–n) Jew
Ju'denschaft *f* (–;) Jewry
Ju'denstern *m* star of David
Judentum ['judəntum] *n* (–s;) Judaism; das J. the Jews
Jüdin ['jydɪn] *f* (–;–nen) Jewish woman
jüdisch ['jydɪʃ] *adj* Jewish
Jugend ['jugənt] *f* (–;) youth
Ju'gendalter *n* youth; adolescence
Ju'gendgericht *n* juvenile court
Ju'gendherberge *f* youth hostel
Ju'gendkriminalität *f* juvenile delinquency
jugendlich ['jugəntlɪç] *adj* youthful || Jugendliche §5 *mf* youth, teenager
Ju'gendliebe *f* puppy love
Ju'gendstrich *m* youthful prank

Jugoslawien [jugo'slavjən] n (-s;) Yugoslavia

jugoslawisch [jugo'slavi∫] adj Yugoslav

Juli ['juli] m (-[s];-s) July

jung [juŋ] adj (jünger ['jyŋər]; jüngste ['jyŋstə] §9) young; (Erbsen) green; (Wein) new ‖ **Junge** §5 m boy ‖ n newly born; young

jungen ['juŋən] intr produce young

jun'genhaft adj boyish

Jünger ['jyŋər] m (-s;-) disciple

Jungfer ['juŋfər] f (-;-n) maiden; virgin

jüngferlich ['jyŋfərliç] adj maidenly

Jung'fernfahrt f maiden voyage

Jung'fernhäutchen n hymen

Jung'fernkranz m bridal wreath

Jung'fernschaft f virginity

Jung'frau f virgin

jungfräulich ['juŋfrɔɪliç] adj maidenly; virgin

Jung'fräulichkeit f virginity

Jung'geselle m bachelor

Jung'gesellenstand m bachelorhood

Jung'gesellin f single girl

Jüngling ['jyŋliŋ] m (-s;-e) young man

jüngst [jyŋst] adv recently

jüng'ste adj see jung

Juni ['juni] m (-[s];-s) June

Junker ['juŋkər] m (-s;-) young nobleman; nobleman

Jura ['jura] pl—**J. studieren** study law

Jurist –in [ju'rɪst(ɪn)] §7 mf lawyer; (educ) law student

Juristerei [jurɪstə'raɪ] f (-;) jurisprudence

juristisch [ju'rɪstɪ∫] adj legal, law; **juristische Person** legal entity, corporation

just [just] adv just, precisely

justieren [jus'tirən] tr adjust

Justiz [jus'tits] f (-;) justice; administration of justice

Justiz'irrtum m miscarriage of justice

Justiz'minister m minister of justice; attorney general; Lord Chancellor (Brit)

Jutesack ['jutəzak] m gunnysack

Juwel [ju'vel] n (-s;-en) jewel, gem; Juwelen jewelry

Juwe'lenkästchen n jewel box

Juwelier –in [juve'lir(ɪn)] §6 mf jeweler

Juwelier'waren pl jewelry

Jux [juks] m (-es;-e) spoof, joke; **aus Jux** as a joke; **sich** [dat] **e-n Jux mit j–m machen** play a joke on s.o.

K

K, k [ka] invar n K, k

Kabale [ka'balə] f (-;-n) intrigue

Kabarett [kaba'rɛt] n (-[e]s;-e) cabaret; floor show; (drehbare Platte) lazy Suzan

Kabel ['kabəl] n (-s;-) cable

Ka'belgramm n (-s;-e) cablegram

Kabeljau ['kabəljau] m (-s;-e) codfish

kabeln ['kabəln] tr cable

Kabine [ka'binə] f (-;-n) cabin; booth; (aer) cockpit

Kabinett [kabi'nɛt] n (-s;-e) closet; small room; (& pol) cabinet

Kabriolett [kabrio'lɛt] n (-[e]s;-e) (aut) convertible

Kachel ['kaxəl] f (-;-n) glazed tile

kacken ['kakən] intr (sl) defecate

Kadaver [ka'davər] m (-s;-) cadaver

Kada'vergehorsam m blind obedience

Kadenz [ka'dɛnts] f (-;-en) cadence

Kader ['kadər] m (-s;-) cadre

Kadett [ka'dɛt] m (-en;-en) cadet

Käfer ['kefər] m (-s;-) beetle

Kaffee ['kafe] m (-s;-s) coffee

Kaf'feebohne f coffee bean

Kaf'feeklatsch m coffee klatsch

Kaf'feemaschine f coffee maker

Kaf'feepflanzung f, **Kaf'feeplantage** f coffee plantation

Kaf'feesatz m coffee grounds

Kaf'feetante f coffee fiend

Käfig ['kefiç] m (-[e]s;-e) cage

kahl [kal] adj bald; (Baum) bare; (Landschaft) bleak, barren

kahl'köpfig adj bald-headed

Kahm [kam] m (-[e]s;-e) mold; scum

kahmig ['kamiç] adj moldy; scummy

Kahn [kan] m (-[e]s;ːe) boat; barge

Kai [kaɪ], [ke] m (-s;-s) quay, wharf

Kaiser ['kaɪzər] m (-s;-) emperor

Kaiserin ['kaɪzərɪn] f (-;-nen) empress

kai'serlich adj imperial

Kai'serreich n, **Kaisertum** ['kaɪzərtum] n (-[e]s;ːer) empire

Kai'serschnitt m Caesarian operation

Kai'serzeit f (hist) Empire

Kajüte [ka'jytə] f (-;-n) (naut) cabin

Kajü'tenjunge m cabin boy

Kajü'tentreppe f (naut) companionway

Kakao [ka'ka.o] m (-s;-) cocoa; **j–n durch den K. ziehen** pull s.o.'s leg

Kaktee [kak'te.ə] f (-;-n), **Kaktus** ['kaktus] m (-;-se) cactus

Kalauer ['kalau-ər] m (-s;-) pun

Kalb [kalp] n (-[e]s;ːer) calf

Kalbe ['kalbə] f (-;-n) heifer

kalbern ['kalbərn] intr be silly

Kalb'fell n calfskin

Kalb'fleisch n veal

Kalbs'braten m roast veal

Kalbs'kotelett n veal cutlet

Kalbs'schnitzel n veal cutlet

Kaleidoskop [kalaɪdo'skop] n (-s;-e) kaleidoscope

Kalender [ka'lendər] m (-s;-) calendar

Kali ['kali] n (-s;) potash

Kaliber [ka'libər] n (-s;-) caliber

kalibrieren [kali'brirən] tr calibrate; gauge

Kaliko ['kaliko] m (-s;-s) calico

Kalium ['kaljum] n (-s;) potassium

Kalk [kalk] *m* (-[e]s;-e) lime; calcium

kalken ['kalkən] *tr* whitewash; lime

kalkig ['kalkıç] *adj* limy

Kalk'ofen *m* limekiln

Kalk'stein *m* limestone

Kalk'steinbruch *m* limestone quarry

Kalkül [kal'kyl] *m & n* (-s;-e) calculation; (math) calculus

kalkulieren [kalku'lirən] *tr* calculate

Kal·mar ['kalmar] *m* (-s;-mare ['marə]) squid

Kalo·rie [kalo'ri] *f* (-;-rien ['ri·ən]) calorie

Kalotte [ka'lɔtə] *f* (-;-n) skullcap

kalt [kalt] *adj* (kälter ['kɛltər]; kälteste ['kɛltəstə] §9) cold

kaltblütig ['kaltblytıç] *adj* cold-blooded

Kälte ['kɛltə] *f* (-;) cold, coldness

käl'tebeständig *adj* cold-resistant

Käl'tegrad *m* degree below freezing

kälten ['kɛltən] *tr* chill

Käl'tewelle *f* (meteor) cold wave

Kalt'front *f* cold front

kalt'herzig *adj* cold-hearted

kalt'machen *tr* (sl) bump off

kaltschnäuzig ['kalt/nɔytsıç] *adj* (coll) callous; (coll) cool, unflappable

kalt'stellen *tr* render harmless

kam [kam] *pret* of **kommen**

Kambodscha [kam'bɔtʒa] *n* (-s;) Cambodia

kambodschanisch [kambo'dʒanıʃ] *adj* Cambodian

Kamel [ka'mel] *n* (-[e]s;-e) camel

Kamel'garn *n* mohair

Kamera ['kamera] *f* (-;-s) camera

Kamerad [kamə'rat] *m* (-en;-en), **meradin** [kamə'radın] *f* (-;-nen) comrade

Kamerad'schaft (-;-en) comradeship

Kamin [ka'min] *m* (-s;-e) chimney; fireplace

Kamin'platte *f* hearthstone

Kamin'sims *n* mantelpiece

Kamm [kam] *m* (-[e]s;⸚e) comb; (e·s Gebirges) ridge; (e·r Welle) crest

kämmen ['kɛmən] *tr* comb; (Wolle) card

Kammer ['kamər] *f* (-;-n) chamber; (adm) board; (anat) ventricle

Kämmerer ['kɛmərər] *m* (-s;-) chamberlain; (Schatzmeister) treasurer

Kam'mermusik *f* chamber music

Kamm'garn *n* (tex) worsted

Kamm'rad *n* cogwheel

Kampagne [kam'panjə] *f* (-;-n) campaign

Kämpe ['kɛmpə] *m* (-n;-n) warrior

Kampf [kampf] *m* (-[e]s;⸚e) fight

Kampf'bahn *f* (sport) stadium, arena

kämpfen ['kɛmpfən] *tr & intr* fight

Kampfer ['kampfər] *m* (-s;) camphor

Kämpfer -in ['kɛmpfər(ın)] §6 *mf* fighter

kämpferisch ['kɛmpfərıʃ] *adj* fighting

kampf'erprobt *adj* battle-tested

kampf'fähig *adj* fit to fight; (mil) fit for active service

Kampf'hahn *m* gamecock; (fig) scrapper

Kampf'handlung *f* (mil) action

Kampf'müdigkeit *f* combat fatigue

Kampf'parole *f* (pol) campaign slogan

Kampf'platz *m* battleground

Kampf'raum *m* battle zone

Kampf'richter *m* referee, umpire

Kampf'schwimmer *m* (nav) frogman

Kampf'spiel *n* (sport) competition

Kampf'staffel *f* tactical squadron

kampf'unfähig *adj* disabled; **k. machen** put out of action

Kampf'veranstalter *m* (sport) promotor

Kampf'verband *m* combat unit

Kampf'wert *m* fighting efficiency

Kampf'ziel *n* (mil) objective

kampieren [kam'pirən] *intr* camp

Kanada ['kanada] *n* (-s;) Canada

Kanadier -in [ka'nadjər(ın)] §6 *mf* Canadian || *m* canoe

kanadisch [ka'nadıʃ] *adj* Canadian

Kanaille [ka'naljə] *f* (-;-n) bum; (Pöbel) riffraff

Kanal [ka'nal] *m* (-s;⸚e) canal; (für Abwasser) drain, sewer; (agr) irrigation ditch; (anat, elec) duct; (geol, telv) channel

Kanalisation [kanalıza'tsjon] *f* (-;) drainage; sewerage system

Kanalräumer [ka'nalrɔymər] *m* (-s;-) sewer worker

Kanal'wähler *m* (telv) channel selector

Kanapee ['kanape] *n* (-s;-s) sofa

Kanarienvogel [ka'narjənfogəl] *m* canary

Kandare [kan'darə] *f* (-;-n) bit, curb; **j-n an die K. nehmen** take s.o. in hand

Kanda'renkette *f* curb chain

Kandelaber [kande'labər] *m* (-s;-) candelabrum

Kandidat -in [kandı'dat(ın)] §7 *mf* candidate

Kandidatur [kandıda'tur] *f* (-;-en) candidacy

kandideln [kan'didəln] *ref* get drunk

kandidieren [kandı'dirən] *intr* be a candidate, run for office

Kandis ['kandıs] *m* (-;) rock candy

Kaneel [ka'nel] *m* (-s;-e) cinnamon

Känguruh ['kɛŋguru] *n* (-s;-s) kangaroo

Kaninchen [ka'nınçən] *n* (-s;-) rabbit

Kanister [ka'nıstər] *m* (-s;-) canister

Kanne [ka'nə] *f* (-;-n) can; pot; jug

Kannelüre [kanə'lyrə] *f* (-;-n) (archit) flute

Kannibale [kanı'balə] *m* (-n;-n), **Kannibalin** [kanı'balın] *f* (-;-nen) cannibal

kannte ['kantə] *pret* of **kennen**

Ka·non ['kanɔn] *m* (-s;-s) (Maßstab; Gebet der Messe) canon; (mus) round || *m* (-s;-nones ['nonəs] canon (of Canon Law)

Kanone [ka'nonə] *f* (-;-n) (arti) gun; (hist) canon; (coll) expert; **unter aller K.** indescribably bad

Kano'nenboot *n* gunboat

Kano'nenrohr *n* gun barrel; **heiliges K.!** holy smokes!

kanonisieren [kanɔnı'zirən] *tr* canonize

Kante ['kantə] *f* (-;-n) edge

kanten ['kantən] *tr* set on edge; (*beim Schifahren*) cant ‖ **Kanten** *m* (-s;-) end of a loaf, crust

Kanthaken ['kanthakən] *m* grappling hook

kantig ['kantıç] *adj* angular; squared

Kantine [kan'tinə] *f* (-;-n) canteen; (mil) post exchange

Kanton [kan'ton] *m* (-s;-e) canton

Kan·tor ['kantor] *m* (-s;-toren ['torən]) choir master; organist

Kanu [ka'nu] *n* (-s;-s) canoe

Kanzel ['kantsəl] *f* (-;-n) pulpit; (aer) cockpit

Kanzlei [kants'laı] *f* (-;-en) office; chancellery

Kanzlei'papier *n* official foolscap

Kanzlei'sprache *f* legal jargon

Kanzler ['kantslər] *m* (-s;-) chancellor

Kap [kap] *n* (-s;-s) cape, headland

Kapaun [ka'paun] *m* (-s;-e) capon

Kapazität [kapatsı'tet] *f* (-;-en) capacity; (*Könner*) authority

Kapelle [ka'pelə] *f* (-;-n) chapel; (mus) band

Kapell'meister *m* band leader; orchestra conductor

kapern ['kapərn] *tr* capture; (coll) nab

kapieren [ka'pirən] *tr* get, understand ‖ *intr* get it; **kapiert?** got it?

kapital [kapı'tal] *adj* excellent ‖ **Kapital** *n* (-s;-e & -ien [jən]) (fin) capital; **K. schlagen aus** capitalize on; **K. und Zinsen** principal and interest

Kapital'anlage *f* investment

Kapital'ertragssteuer *f* tax on unearned income

kapitalisieren [kapıtalı'zirən] *tr* (fin) capitalize

Kapitalismus [kapıta'lısmus] *m* (-s;) capitalism

Kapitalist -in [kapıta'lıst(ın)] *m* §7 capitalist

Kapital'verbrechen *n* capital offense

Kapitän [kapı'ten] *m* (-s;-e) captain, skipper; **K. zur See** (nav) captain

Kapitän'leutnant *m* (nav) lieutenant

Kapitel [ka'pıtəl] *n* (-s;-) chapter

Kapitell [kapı'tel] *n* (-s;-e) (archit) capital

kapitulieren [kapıtu'lirən] *intr* capitulate, surrender; reenlist

Kaplan [ka'plan] *m* (-s;⸗e) chaplain; (R.C.) assistant (pastor)

Kapo ['kapo] *m* (-s;-s) prisoner overseer; (mil) (coll) N.C.O.

Kappe ['kapə] *f* (-;-n) cap; hood, cover; **etw auf seine eigene K. nehmen** take the responsibility for s.th.

Käppi ['kepı] *n* (-s;-s) garrison cap

Kaprice [ka'prisə] *f* (-;-n) caprice

Kapriole [kaprı'olə] *f* (-;-n) caper

kaprizieren [kaprı'tsirən] *ref*—**sich k. auf** (acc) be dead set on

kapriziös [kaprı'tsjøs] *adj* capricious

Kapsel ['kapsəl] *f* (-;-n) capsule; (*e-r Flasche*) cap; (*e-s Sprengkörpers*) detonator

kaputt [ka'put] *adj* (sl) broken; (sl) ruined; (sl) exhausted; (sl) dead

kaputt'gehen §82 *intr* (SEIN) get ruined

kaputt'machen *tr* ruin

Kapuze [ka'putsə] *f* (-;-n) hood; (eccl) cowl

Kapuziner [kapu'tsinər] *m* (-s;-) Capuchin

Kapuzi'nerkresse *f* Nasturtium

Karabiner [kara'binər] *m* (-s;-) carbine

Karabi'nerhaken *m* snap

Karaffe [ka'rafə] *f* (-;-n) carafe

Karambolage [karambo'laʒə] *f* (-;-n) (coll) collision

karambolieren [karambo'lirən] *intr* (coll) collide

Karamelle [kara'melə] *f* (-;-n) caramel

Karat [ka'rat] *n* (-[e]s;) carat

-karätig [karetıç] *comb.fm.* –*carat*

Karawane [kara'vanə] *f* (-;-n) caravan

Karbid [kar'bit] *n* (-[e]s;-e) carbide

Karbolsäure [kar'bolzɔırə] *f* (-;) carbolic acid

Karbon [kar'bon] *n* (-s;) (geol) carbon

Karbunkel [kar'buŋkəl] *n* (-s;-) carbuncle

Kardinal- [kardınal] *comb.fm.* cardinal, principal ‖ **Kardinal** *m* (-s;⸗e) (eccl, orn) cardinal

Karenzzeit [ka'rentstsaıt] *f* (ins) waiting period

Karfreitag [kar'fraıtak] *m* Good Friday

karg [kark] *adj* (karger & kärger ['kergər]; kargste & kärgste ['kerstə] §9) (*ärmlich*) meager; (*Boden*) poor; (*Landschaft*) bleak

kargen ['kargən] *intr* be sparing

Karg'heit *f* (-;) bleakness; meagerness; frugality

kärglich ['kerlıç] *adj* meager, poor

kariert [ka'rirt] *adj* checked, squared

Karikatur [karıka'tur] *f* (-;-en) caricature; cartoon

karikieren [karı'kirən] *tr* caricature

Karl [karl] *m* (-s;) Charles; **Karl der Große** Charlemagne

Karmeliter [karme'litər] *m* (-s;-) Carmelite Friar

Karmelitin [karme'litın] *f* (-;-nen) Carmelite nun

karmesinrot [karme'zinrot], **karminrot** [kar'minrot] *adj* crimson

Karneval ['karnəval] *m* (-s;-s & -e) carnival

Karnickel [kar'nıkəl] *n* (-s;-) (coll) rabbit; (*Sündenbock*) (coll) scapegoat; (*Einfaltspinsel*) simpleton

Karo ['karo] *n* (-s;-s) diamond; check, square; (cards) diamond(s)

Karosse [ka'rosə] *f* (-;-n) state carriage

Karosse·rie [karosə'ri] *f* (-;-rien ['ri·ən]) (aut) body

Karotte [ka'rotə] *f* (-;-n) carrot

Karpfen ['karpfən] *m* (-s;-) carp

Karre ['karə] *f* (-;-n), **Karren** ['karən] *m* (-s;-) cart; wheelbarrow; **die alte K.** the old rattletrap

Karriere [ka'rjerə] *f* (-;-n) career; gallop; **K. machen** get ahead

Karte ['kartə] *f* (-;-n) card; ticket; (*Landkarte*) map; (*Speise-*) menu

Kartei [kar'taı] *f* (-;-en) card file

Kartei'karte *f* index card

Kartell [kar'tɛl] n (-s;-e) cartel

Kar'tenkunststück n card trick

Kartenlegerin ['kartənleːgərɪn] f (-; -nen) fortuneteller

Kar'tenstelle f ration board

Kartoffel [kar'tɔfəl] f (-;-n) potato

Kartof'felbrei m mashed potatoes

Kartoffelpuffer [kar'tɔfəlpufər] m (-s; -) potato pancake

Karton [kar'tɔŋ] m (-s;-s) cardboard; carton; (paint) cartoon

Kartonage [kartə'naːʒə] f (-;-n) cardboard box

kartoniert [kartə'niːrt] adj (bb) softcover

Karton'papier n (thin) cardboard

Kartothek [kartə'teːk] f (-;-en) card index; card filing system

Kartothek'ausgabe f loose-leaf edition

Karussell [karu'sɛl] n (-s;-e) merry-go-round

Karwoche ['karvɔxə] f Holy Week

Karzer ['kartsər] m (-s;-) (educ) detention room; **K. bekommen** get a detention

Kaschmir ['kaʃmɪr] m (-s;-e) cashmere

Käse ['keːzə] m (-s;-) cheese; (sl) baloney

Kaserne [ka'zɛrnə] f (-;-n) barracks

käsig ['keːzɪç] adj cheesy; (Gesichtsfarbe) pasty

Kasino [ka'ziːno] n (-s;-) casino; (mil) officer's mess

Kas'pisches Meer ['kaspiʃəs] n Caspian Sea

Kassa ['kasa] f—per **K. in cash**

Kassa- comb.fm. cash, spot

Kasse ['kasə] f (-;-n) money box; till; cash register; cashiers desk; (Bargeld) cash; (adm) finance department; (educ) bursars office; (sport) ticket window; (theat) box office; **gegen** (or **per**) **K.** cash, for cash; **gut bei K. sein** (coll) be flush

Kas'senabschluß m balancing of accounts

Kas'senbeamte m cashier; teller

Kas'senbeleg m sales slip

Kas'senbestand m cash on hand

Kas'senerfolg m (theat) hit

Kas'senführer –in §6 mf cashier

Kas'senschalter m teller's window

Kas'senschrank m safe

Kas'senzettel m sales slip

Kasserolle [kasə'rɔlə] f (-;-n) casserole

Kassette [ka'sɛtə] f (-;-n) base, box; (cin, phot) cassette

kassieren [ka'siːrən] tr (Geld) take in; get; (Urteil) annul; (coll) confiscate; (coll) arrest; (mil) break

Kassie'rer –in §6 mf cashier; teller

Kastagnette [kastan'jɛtə] f (-;-n) castanet

Kastanie [kas'taːnjə] f (-;-n) chestnut

Kästchen ['kɛstçən] n (-s;-) case, box

Kaste ['kastə] f (-;-n) caste

kastelen [kas'taɪ·ən] tr & ref mortify; **sein Leib k.** mortify the flesh

Kastell [kas'tɛl] n (-s;-e) small fort

Kasten ['kastən] m (-s;: & -) chest, case, box; cupboard, cabinet; (Auto)

(coll) crate; (Boot) (coll) tub; (Gefängnis) (coll) jug

Ka'stengeist m snobbishness

Ka'stenwagen m (aut) panel truck; (rr) boxcar

Ka'stenwesen n caste system

Kastrat [kas'traːt] m (-en;-en) eunuch

kastrieren [kas'triːrən] tr castrate

Katakomben [kata'kɔmbən] pl catacombs

Katalog [kata'loːk] m (-[e]s;-e) catalogue

katalogisieren [kataloːgɪ'ziːrən] tr catalogue

Katapult [kata'pult] m & n (-[e]s;-e) catapult

katapultieren [katapul'tiːrən] tr catapult

Katarakt [kata'rakt] m (-[e]s;-e) cataract, rapids; (pathol) cataract

Katasteramt [ka'tastəramt] n landregistry office

katastrophal [katastro'faːl] adj catastrophic, disastrous

Katastrophe [kata'stroːfə] f (-;-n) catastrophe, disaster

Katastro'phengebiet m disaster area

Kategorie [kategoː'riː] f (-;-rien ['riːən] category

kategorisch [kate'goːrɪʃ] adj categorical

Kater ['kaːtər] m (-s;-) tomcat; (coll) hangover

Katheder [ka'teːdər] n & m (-s;-) teacher's desk

Kathe'derblüte f teacher's blunder

Kathedrale [kate'draːlə] f (-;-n) cathedral

Kathode [ka'toːdə] f (-;-n) cathode

Katholik –in [katoː'liːk(ɪn)] §7 mf Catholic

katholisch [ka'toːlɪʃ] adj Catholic

Kattun [ka'tuːn] m (-s;-e) calico

Kätzchen ['kɛtsçən] n (-s;-) kitten

Katze ['katsə] f (-;-n) cat; **für die K.** (coll) for the birds

kat'zenartig adj cat-like, feline

Kat'zenauge n reflector

Kat'zenbuckel m cat's arched back; **vor j-m K. machen** lick s.o.'s boots

kat'zenfreundlich adj overfriendly

Kat'zenjammer m hangover; blues

Kat'zenkopf m (coll) cobblestone; (box) rabbit punch

Kat'zensprung m stone's throw

Kauderwelsch ['kaudərvɛlʃ] n (-es;) gibberish

kauen ['kau·ən] tr chew

kauern ['kau·ərn] ref & intr cower

Kauf [kauf] m (-[e]s;:-e) purchase; **in K. nehmen** (fig) take, put up with; **leichten Kaufes davonkommen** get off cheaply; **zum K. stehen** be for sale

Kauf'auftrag m (com) order

kaufen ['kaufən] tr purchase, buy

Käufer –in ['kɔifər(ɪn)] §6 mf buyer

Kauf'haus n department store

Kauf'kraft f purchasing power

käuflich ['kɔiflɪç] adj for sale; (bestechlich) open to bribes

Kauf'mann m (-[e]s;-leute) businessman; salesman

kaufmännisch ['kaufmenɪʃ] *adj* commercial, business
Kauf′mannsdeutsch *n* business German
Kauf′zwang *m* obligation to buy
Kaugummi ['kaugumɪ] *m* chewing gum
kaukasisch [kau'kazɪʃ] *adj* Caucasian
Kaulquappe ['kaulkvapə] *f* (-;-n) tadpole, polliwog
kaum [kaum] *adv* hardly, scarcely
Kautabak ['kautabak] *m* chewing tobacco
Kaution [kau'tsjon] *f* (-;-en) (jur) bond; (*Bürgschaft*) (jur) bail; **gegen K.** on bail
Kautschuk ['kaut/uk] *m* (-s;-e) rubber
Kauz [kauts] *m* (-es;-e) owl; (sl) crackpot
Kavalier [kava'lir] *m* (-s;-e) cavalier; gentleman; beau
Kavalkade [kaval'kadə] *f* (-;-n) cavalcade
Kavalle′rie [kavalə'ri] *f* (-;-rien ['ri-ən]) cavalry
Kavallerist [kavalə'rɪst] *m* (-en;-en) cavalryman, trooper
Kaviar ['kavjar] *m* (-[e]s;-e) caviar
keck [kek] *adj* bold; impudent; cheeky
Kegel ['kegəl] *m* (-s;-) tenpin; (geom) cone; **K. schieben** bowl
Ke′gelbahn *f* bowling alley
kegeln ['kegəln] *intr* bowl
Keg′ler -in §6 *mf* bowler
Kehle ['kelə] *f* (-;-n) throat
kehlig ['kelɪç] *adj* throaty
Kehlkopf ['kelkɔpf] *m* larynx
Kehl′kopfentzündung *f* laryngitis
Kehre ['kerə] *f* (-;-n) turn, bend
kehren ['kerən] *tr* sweep; (*wenden*) turn; **alles zum besten k.** make the best of it; **j-m den Rücken k.** turn one's back on s.o. || *ref* turn; **in sich gekehrt sein** be lost in thought; **sich an nichts k.** not care about anything; **sich k. an** (*acc*) heed || *intr* sweep
Kehricht ['kerɪçt] *m & n* (-[e]s;) sweepings: trash, rubbish
Keh′richteimer *m* trash can
Keh′richtschaufel *f* dustpan
Kehr′maschine *f* street cleaner
Kehr′reim *m* refrain, chorus
Kehr′seite *f* reverse; (fig) seamy side
kehrtmachen ['kertmaxən] *intr* turn around; (mil) about-face
Kehrt′wendung *f* about-face
keifen ['kaifən] *intr* nag
Keiferei [kaifə'rai] *f* (-;-en) nagging; squabble
Keil [kail] *m* (-[e]s;-e) wedge
keilen ['kailən] *tr* wedge; (coll) recruit || *recip* scrap
Kellerei [kailə'rai] *f* (-;-en) scrap
keil′förmig *adj* wedge-shaped; tapered
Keil′hammer *m* sledgehammer
Keil′hose *f* tapered trousers
Keil′schrift *f* cuneiform writing
Keim [kaim] *m* (-[e]s;-e) germ; embryo; (fig) seeds; (bot) bud, sprout; **im K. ersticken** nip in the bud; **im K. vorhanden** at an embryonic stage; **Keime treiben** germinate
keimen ['kaimən] *intr* germinate;

sprout || **Keimen** *n*—**zum K. bringen** cause to germinate
keim′frei *adj* germ-free, sterile
Keimling ['kaimlɪŋ] *m* (-s;-e) embryo; sprout; seedling
keimtötend ['kaimtøtənt] *adj* germicidal; antiseptic, sterilizing
Keim′zelle *f* germ cell, sex cell
kein [kain] §2,2 *adj* no, not any
keiner ['kainər] §2,4 *indef pron* none; no one, nobody, not one; **k. von beiden** neither of them
keinerlei ['kainər'lai] *invar adj* no... of any kind, no...whatsoever
keineswegs ['kainəs'veks] *adv* by no means, not at all
Keks [keks] *m & n* (-es;-e) biscuit, cracker; cookie
Kelch [kelç] *m* (-[e]s;-e) cup; (bot) calyx; (eccl) chalice
Kelch′blatt *n* (bot) sepal
Kelle ['kelə] *f* (-;-n) ladle; (hort, mas) trowel
Keller ['kelər] *m* (-s;-) cellar
Kel′lergeschoß *n* basement
Kel′lergewölbe *n* underground vault
Kellner ['kelnər] *m* (-s;-) waiter
Kellnerin ['kelnərɪn] *f* (-;-nen) waitress
Kelte ['keltə] *m* (-n;-n) Celt
Kelter ['keltər] *f* (-;-n) wine press
keltern ['keltərn] *tr* press
Keltin ['keltɪn] *f* (-;-nen) Celt
keltisch ['keltɪʃ] *adj* Celtic
kennbar ['kenbar] *adj* recognizable
kennen ['kenən] §97 *tr* be acquainted with, know
Ken′nenlernen *tr* get to know, meet
Ken′ner -in §6 *mf* expert
Ken′nerblick *m* knowing glance
Ken′ner -in §6 *mf* expert
Kennkarte ['kenkartə] *f* identity card
kenntlich ['kentlɪç] *adj* identifiable, recognizable; conspicuous
Kenntnis ['kentnɪs] *f* (-;-se) knowledge; **gute Kenntnisse haben in** (*dat*) be well versed in; **j-n von etw in K. setzen** apprise s.o. of s.th.; **Kenntnisse** knowledge; skills; know-how; **oberflächliche Kenntnisse** a smattering; **von etw K. nehmen** take note of s.th.; **zur K. nehmen** take note of s.th.
Kennwort ['kenvɔrt] *n* (-[e]s;-̈er) code word; (mil) password
Kennzeichen ['kentsaiçən] *n* distinguishing mark; hallmark; criterion; (aer) marking; (aut) license number
kennzeichnen ['kentsaiçnən] *tr* characterize; identify; brand
Kennziffer ['kentsɪfər] *f* code number
kentern ['kentərn] *intr* (SEIN) capsize
Keramik [ke'ramik] *f* (-;) ceramics; pottery
keramisch [ke'ramɪʃ] *adj* ceramic
Kerbe ['kerbə] *f* (-;-n) notch, groove
kerben ['kerbən] *tr* notch, nick; make a groove in; serrate
Kerbholz ['kerphɔlts] *n*—**etw auf dem K. haben** have a crime chalked up against one
Kerbtier ['kerptir] *n* insect
Kerker ['kerkər] *m* (-s;-) jail

Kerl [kɛrl] m (-s;-e) fellow, guy; (*Mädchen*) lass

Kern [kɛrn] m (-[e]s;-e) kernel; (*im Obst*) pit, stone, pip; hard core; (*e-s Problems*) crux; (phys) nucleus

Kern– comb.fm. core; central, basic; through and through; (phys) nuclear

Kern'aufbau m nuclear structure

kern'deutsch' adj German through and through

Kern'energie f nuclear energy

Kern'fächer pl core curriculum

kern'gesund' adj perfectly sound

Kern'holz n heartwood

kernig ['kɛrnɪç] adj full of seeds; robust, vigorous

kern'los adj seedless

Kern'physik f nuclear physics

Kern'punkt m gist, crux; focal point

Kern'schußweite f—auf K. at point-blank range

Kern'spaltung f nuclear fission

Kern'truppen pl crack troops

Kern'verschmelzung f nuclear fusion

Kern'waffe f nuclear weapon

Kerosin [kero'zin] n (-s;) kerosene

Kerze ['kɛrtsə] f (-;-n) candle; (aut) plug

ker'zengera'de adj straight as an arrow || adv bolt upright

Kessel ['kɛsəl] m (-s;-) kettle; cauldron; boiler; (geog) basin-shaped valley; (mil) pocket

Kes'selpauke f kettledrum

Kes'selraum m boiler room

Kes'selschmied m boilermaker

Kes'selwagen m (aut) tank truck; (rr) tank car

Kette ['kɛtə] f (-;-n) chain; (e-s Panzers) track

ketten ['kɛtən] tr (an acc) chain (to)

Ket'tengeschäft n chain store

Ket'tenglied n chain link

Ket'tenhund m watch dog

Ket'tenrad n sprocket

Ket'tenraucher –in §6 mf chain smoker

Ket'tenstich m chain stitch, lock stitch

Ketzer –in ['kɛtsər(ɪn)] §6 mf heretic

Ketzerei [kɛtsə'raɪ] f (-;-en) heresy

ketzerisch ['kɛtsərɪʃ] adj heretical

keuchen ['kɔɪçən] intr pant, gasp

Keuch'husten m (-s;) whooping cough

Keule ['kɔɪlə] f (-;-n) club; (culin) leg, drumstick

keusch [kɔɪʃ] adj chaste

Keusch'heit f (-;) chastity

KG abbr (**Kommanditgesellschaft**) Ltd.

Khaki ['kaki] n (-s) (tex) khaki

kichern ['kɪçərn] intr giggle

kicken ['kɪkən] tr (fb) kick

Kicker ['kɪkər] m (-s;-) soccer player

Kiebitz ['kibɪts] m (-[e]s;-e) (orn) lapwing; (*Zugucker*) kibitzer

kiebitzen ['kibɪtsən] intr kibitz

Kiefer ['kifər] m (-s;-) jaw(bone) || f (-;-n) pine; gemeine K. Scotch pine

Kiel [kil] m (-[e]s;-e) (*Feder*) quill; (naut) keel

Kiel'raum m bilge

Kiel'wasser n wake

Kieme ['kimə] f (-;-n) gill

Kien ['kin] m (-[e]s;-e) pine cone

Kien'span m pine torch

Kiepe ['kipə] f (-;-n) basket (*carried on one's back*)

Kies [kis] m (-es;-e) gravel

Kiesel ['kizəl] m (-s;-) pebble

Kilo ['kilo] n (-s;-s & -) kilogram

Kilogramm [kilo'gram] n (-s;-e & -) kilogram

Kilometer [kilo'metər] m & n (-s;-) kilometer

Kilome'terfresser m (coll) speedster

Kilowatt ['kilo'vat] n (-s;-) kilowatt

Kimm [kɪm] m (-es;-e) horizon || f (-;-e) (naut) bilge

Kimme ['kɪmə] f (-;-n) notch; groove; (e-s Gewehrs) sight

Kind [kɪnt] n (-[e]s;-er) child; baby

Kinder– [kɪndər] comb.fm. child's, children's

Kinderei [kɪndə'raɪ] f (-;-en) childish behavior, childish prank

Kin'derfrau f nursemaid

Kin'derfräulein n governess

Kin'derfürsorge f child welfare

Kin'dergarten m nursery school, playschool

Kin'dergärtnerin f nursery school attendant

Kin'dergeld n see **Kinderzulage**

Kin'derheilkunde f pediatrics

Kin'derheim n children's home

Kin'derhort m day nursery

Kin'derlähmung f polio

kin'derleicht adj easy as pie

Kin'derlied n nursery rhyme

kin'derlos adj childless

Kin'dermädchen n nursemaid

Kin'derpuder m baby powder

Kin'derreim m nursery rhyme

Kin'derschreck m bogeyman

Kin'dersportwagen m stroller

Kin'derstube f nursery; (*Erziehung*) upbringing

Kin'derstuhl m highchair

Kin'derwagen m baby carriage

Kin'derzulage f family allowance (*paid by the employer*)

Kin'desalter n childhood; infancy

Kin'desannahme f adoption

Kin'desbeine pl—von **Kindesbeinen** an from childhood on

Kin'desentführer –in §6 mf kidnaper

Kin'desentführung f, **Kin'desraub** m kidnaping

Kind'heit f (-;) childhood

kindisch ['kɪndɪʃ] adj childish

kindlich ['kɪntlɪç] adj childlike

Kinetik [kɪ'netɪk] f (-;) kinetics

kinetisch [kɪ'netɪʃ] adj kinetic

Kinkerlitzchen ['kɪŋkərlɪtsçən] pl trifles; gimmicks

Kinn [kɪn] n (-[e]s;-e) chin

Kinn'backen m jawbone

Kinn'haken m (box) uppercut

Kinn'kette f curb chain

Kino ['kino] n (-s;-s) movie theater

Ki'nobesucher –in §6 mf moviegoer

Ki'nokamera f movie camera

Ki'nokasse f box office

Kiosk [kɪ'ɔsk] m (-[e]s;-e) stand

Kipfel ['kɪpfəl] n (-s;-) (Aust) (culin) crescent roll

Kippe ['kɪpə] *f* (-;-n) edge; (*Zigarettenstummel*) butt; **auf der K. stehen** stand on edge; (fig) be touch and go
kippen ['kɪpən] *tr* tilt, tip over; dump || *intr* (SEIN) tilt; overturn
Kipper ['kɪpər] *m* (-s;-) dump truck
Kirche ['kɪrçə] *f* (-;-n) church
Kirchen- [kɪrçən] *comb.fm.* church, ecclesiastical
Kir'chenbann *m* excommunication; **in den K. tun** excommunicate
Kir'chenbau *m* (-[e]s;) building of churches
Kir'chenbesuch *m* church attendance
Kir'chenbuch *n* parish register
Kir'chendiener *m* sacristan, sexton
Kir'chengut *n* church property
Kir'chenlied *n* hymn
Kir'chenschändung *f* desecration of a church
Kir'chenschiff *n* (archit) nave
Kir'chenspaltung *f* schism
Kir'chenstaat *m* Papal States
Kir'chenstuhl *m* pew
Kir'chentag *m* Church congress
Kirchgang ['kɪrçgaŋ] *m* going to church
Kirch'gänger -in §6 *mf* church-goer
Kirch'hof *m* churchyard
kirch'lich *adj* church, ecclesiastical
Kirch'spiel *n* parish
Kirch'turm *m* steeple
Kirch'turmpolitik *f* (pej) parochialism
Kirch'turmspitze *f* spire
Kirchweih ['kɪrçvai] *f* (-;-en) church picnic
Kirch'weihe *f* dedication of a church
Kirch'weihfest *n* church picnic
Kirsch [kɪrʃ] *m* (-es;-) cherry brandy
Kirsche ['kɪrʃə] *f* (-;-n) cherry
Kirsch'wasser *n* cherry brandy
Kissen ['kɪsən] *n* (-s;-) cushion, pillow; (*Polster*) pad
Kis'senbezug *m* pillowcase
Kiste ['kɪstə] *f* (-;-n) box, crate, case; (aer) crate; (aut) rattletrap; (naut) tub
Kitsch [kɪtʃ] *m* (-es;) kitsch
kitschig ['kɪtʃɪç] *adj* trashy; mawkish
Kitt [kɪt] *m* (-[e]s;-e) putty; cement; **der ganze Kitt** the whole caboodle
Kittchen ['kɪtçən] *n* (-s;-) (coll) jail
Kittel ['kɪtəl] *m* (-s;-) smock, coat; (Aust) skirt
Kit'telkleid *n* house dress
kitten ['kɪtən] *tr* putty; cement, glue; (fig) patch up
Kitzel ['kɪtsəl] *m* (-s;) tickle; (fig) itch
kitzeln ['kɪtsəln] *tr* tickle
kitzlig ['kɪtslɪç] *adj* ticklish
Kladderadatsch [kladəra'datʃ] *m* (-es;) crash, bang; mess, muddle
klaffen ['klafən] *intr* gape, yawn
kläffen ['klɛfən] *intr* yelp
Klafter ['klaftər] *f* (-; & -n), *m* & *n* (-s;-) fathom; (*Holz*-) cord
klagbar ['klakbar] *adj* (jur) actionable
Klage ['klagə] *f* (-;-n) complaint; (jur) (civil) suit
Kla'gelied *n* dirge, threnody
klagen ['klagən] *tr*—j—m seinen Kummer k. pour out one's troubles to s.o.

|| *intr* complain; **auf Scheidung k.** sue for divorce; **k. über** (acc) complain about; **k. um** lament
Kläger -in ['klɛgər(ɪn)] §6 *mf* (jur) plaintiff
Kla'geweib *n* hired mourner
kläglich ['klɛklɪç] *adj* plaintive, pitiful; (*Zustand*) sorry; (*Ergebnis, Ende*) miserable
klaglos ['klaklos] *adv* uncomplainingly
klamm [klam] *adj* (erstarrt) numb; (*feuchtkalt*) clammy; **k. an Geld** (coll) short of dough || **Klamm** *f* (-;-en) gorge
Klammer ['klamər] *f* (-;-n) clamp; clip; paper clip; (*Schließe*) clasp; clothespin; hair clip, bobby pin; **eckige K.** bracket; **runde K.** parenthesis
klammern ['klamərn] *tr* clamp; clasp || *ref*—sich k. an (acc) cling to
Klamotte [kla'mɔtə] *f* (-;-n)—alte K. oldy; (aer, aut) old crate; **Klamotten** things, clothes
Klampfe ['klampfə] *f* (-;-n) guitar
klang [klaŋ] *pret of* klingen || **Klang** *m* (-[e]s;-e) tone, sound
Klang'farbe *f* timbre
klang'getreu *adj* high-fidelity
Klang'regler *m* (rad) tone-control knob
Klang'taste *f* tone-control push button
klang'voll *adj* sonorous
Klappe ['klapə] *f* (-;-n) flap; (*Mund*) (sl) trap; (anat, mach) valve; **in die K. gehen** (sl) hit the sack
klappen ['klapən] *tr* flip || *intr* flap, fold || *impers*—es klappt (coll) it clicks, it turns out well
Klapper ['klapər] *f* (-;-n) rattle
klap'perdürr *adj* skinny
Klap'pergestell *n* (coll) beanpole; (*Kiste*) (coll) rattletrap
klappern ['klapərn] *intr* rattle, clatter; (*Zähne*) chatter
Klap'perschlange *f* rattlesnake
Klap'perstorch *m* stork
Klappflügel ['klapflygəl] *m* (aer) folding wing (*of carrier plane*)
Klappmesser ['klapmɛsər] *n* jackknife
klapprig ['klaprɪç] *adj* rickety
Klappstuhl ['klapʃtul] *m* folding chair
Klapptisch ['klaptɪʃ] *m* drop-leaf table
Klapptür ['klaptyr] *f* trap door
Klaps [klaps] *m* (-es;-e) smack, slap; **e-n K. kriegen** (sl) go nuts
klapsen ['klapsən] *tr* smack, slap
Klaps'mühle *f* (coll) booby hatch
klar [klar] *adj* clear; **klar zum Start** ready for take-off
Kläranlage ['klɛranlagə] *f* sewage-disposal plant
klären ['klɛrən] *tr* clear; (*Mißverständnis*) clear up || *ref* become clear
Klar'heit *f* (-;) clearness, clarity
Klarinette [klarɪ'nɛtə] *f* (-;-n) clarinet
klar'legen, **klar'stellen** *tr* clear up
Klärung ['klɛrʊŋ] *f* (-;) clarification
Klasse ['klasə] *f* (-;-n) class; (educ) grade, class
Klas'senarbeit *f* test
Klas'senaufsatz *m* composition (*written in class*)
klas'senbewußt *adj* class-conscious

Klas′seneinteilung f classification
Klas′senkamerad –in §7 mf classmate
Klas′sentreffen n (–s;–) class reunion
klassifizieren [klasıfı′tsirən] tr classify
Klassifizie′rung f (–;–en) classification
–**klassig** [klasıç] comb.fm. –class, –grade
Klassik [′klasık] f (–;) classical antiquity, classical period
Klas′siker –in §6 mf classical author
klassisch [′klasıʃ] adj classic(al)
Klatsch [klatʃ] m (–es;) clap; gossip
Klatsch′base f gossipmonger; tattletale
Klatsch′blatt n scandal sheet
Klatsche [′klatʃə] f (–;–n) fly swatter; tattletale; (educ) pony
klatschen [′klatʃən] tr smack, slap; **dem Lehrer etw k.** tattletale to the teacher about s.th.; **j–m Beifall k.** applaud s.o. || intr clap; (Regen) patter; (fig) gossip; **in die Hände (or mit den Händen) k.** clap the hands
Klatscherei [klatʃə′raı] f (–;–en) gossip
klatsch′naß adj soaking wet
Klatsch′spalte f glossip column
klauben [′klaubən] tr pick
Klaue [′klau·ə] f (–;–n) claw, talon; (Spalthuf) hoof; (coll) scrawl
klauen [′klau·ən] tr (coll) snitch
Klause [′klauzə] f (–;–n) hermitage; (Schlucht) defile; (coll) den, pad
Klausel [′klauzəl] f (–;–n) clause; (Abmachung) stipulation
Klausner [′klausnər] m (–s;–) hermit
Klausur [klau′zur] f (–;–en) seclusion; (educ) final examination
Klausur′arbeit f final examination
Klaviatur [klavja′tur] f (–;–en) keyboard
Klavier [kla′vir] n (–[e]s;–e) piano
Klavier′auszug m piano score
Klebemittel [′klebəmıtəl] n (–s;–) adhesive, glue
kleben [′klebən] tr & intr stick
Kleberolle [′klebərələ] f roll of gummed tape
Klebestreifen [′klebəʃtraıfən] m adhesive tape; Scotch tape (trademark)
Klebezettel [′klebətsetəl] m label, sticker
klebrig [′klebrıç] adj sticky
Klebstoff [′klep/tɔf] m adhesive
Klecks [kleks] m (–es;–e) stain; dab
klecksen [′kleksən] tr splash || intr make blotches
Kleckser –in [′kleksər(ın)] §6 mf scribbler; dauber
Klee [kle] m (–s;) clover
Klee′blatt n cloverleaf; (fig) trio
Kleid [klaıt] n (–[e]s;–er) garment; dress; robe; **Kleider** clothes
kleiden [′klaıdən] tr dress; **j–n gut k.** look good on s.o.
Klei′derablage f cloakroom; (Kleiderständer) clothes rack
Klei′derbestand m wardrobe
Klei′derbügel m coat hanger
Klei′dersack m (mil) duffle bag
Klei′derschrank m clothes closet
Klei′derständer m clothes rack
kleidsam [′klaıtzam] adj well-fitting, becoming

Klei′dung f (–;) clothing
Kleie [′klaı·ə] f (–;–n) bran
klein [klaın] adj small, little; short; **ein k. wenig** a little bit || **Kleine** §5 m little boy || f little girl || n little one
Klein′anzeigen pl classified ads
Klein′arbeit f detailed work
Klein′asien n Asia Minor
Klein′bahn f narrow-gauge railroad
Klein′bauer m small farmer
Klein′betrieb m small business
Kleinbild– comb.fm. (phot) 35mm
klein′bürgerlich adj lower middle-class
Klein′geld n change
klein′gläubig adj of little faith
Klein′handel m retail business
Klein′händler –in §6 mf retailer
Klein′hirn n (anat) cerebellum
Klein′holz n kindling; **K. aus j–m machen** (coll) beat s.o. to a pulp
Klei′nigkeit f small object; trifle, minor detail; small matter
Klei′nigkeitskrämer m fusspot
kleinkalibrig [′klaınkalıbrıç] adj small-bore
Klein′kind n infant
Klein′kinderbewahranstalt f day care center
Klein′kram m odds and ends; details
klein′laut adj subdued
klein′lich adj stingy; (Betrag) paltry; (engstirnig) narrow-minded, pedantic
Klein′mut m despondency; faintheartedness
klein′mütig adj despondent; faint-hearted
Klei′nod [′klaınot] n (–[e]s;–node & –nodien [′nodjən] jewel, gem
klein′schneiden §106 tr chop up
Klein′schreibmaschine f portable typewriter
Kleister [′klaıstər] m (–s;–) paste
Klemme [′klemə] f (–;–n) clamp, clip; (coll) tight spot, fix; (elec) terminal; (surg) clamp
klemmen [′klemən] tr tuck, put; (stehlen) pinch, swipe || ref—sich [dat] **den Finger k.** smash one's finger; **sich hinter die Arbeit k.** get down to business; **sich k. hinter** (acc) get after || intr be stuck
Klempner [′klempnər] m (–s;–) tinsmith; plumber
Klempnerei [klempnə′raı] f (–;) plumbing
Kleptomane [klepto′manə] §5 mf kleptomaniac
klerikal [klerı′kal] adj clerical
Kleriker [′klerıkər] m (–s;–) clergyman, priest
Klerus [′klerus] m (–s;) clergy
Klette [′kletə] f (–;–n) (bot) burr; (coll) pain in the neck
Klet′tergarten m training area (for mountain climbing)
klettern [′kletərn] intr (SEIN) climb
Klet′terpflanze f (bot) creeper
Klet′terrose f rambler
Klet′tertour f climbing expedition
Klient [klı′ent] m (–en;–en) client
Klientel [klı·en′tel] f (–;–en) clientele (of a lawyer)

Klientin [klɪ'entɪn] *f* (-;-nen) client
Klima ['klima] *n* (-s;-s) climate
Kli'maanlage *f* air conditioner
kli'magerecht *adj* air-conditioned
klimatisch [klɪ'matɪʃ] *adj* climatic
klimatisieren [klimati'zirən] *tr* air-condition
Klimatisie'rung *f* (-;) air conditioning
Klimbim [klɪm'bɪm] *m* (-s;) (coll) junk; (coll) racket; (coll) fuss
klimmen ['klɪmən] §164 *intr* (SEIN) climb
klimpern ['klɪmpərn] *intr* jingle; (*auf der Gitarre*) strum; **mit den Wimpern k.** flutter one's eyelashes
Klinge ['klɪŋə] *f* (-;-n) blade; sword, saber; **über die K. springen lassen** put to the sword
Klingel ['klɪŋəl] *f* (-;-n) bell
Klin'gelbeutel *m* collection basket
Klin'gelknopf *m* doorbell button
klingeln ['klɪŋəln] *intr* ring, tinkle; (*Vers, Reim*) jingle || *impers*—**es klingelt** the doorbell is ringing; there goes the (school) bell; the phone is ringing
kling'klang *interj* ding-dong!
Klinik ['klinɪk] *f* (-;-en) teaching hospital (*of a university*); private hospital; nursing home
klinisch ['klinɪʃ] *adj* clinical; hospital
Klinke ['klɪŋkə] *f* (-;-n) door handle; (telp) jack; **Klinken putzen** beg or peddle from door to door
Klippe ['klɪpə] *f* (-;-n) rock, reef
klirren ['klɪrən] *intr* rattle, clang; (*Gläser*) clink; (*Waffen*) clash
Klischee [klɪ'ʃe] *n* (-s;-s) cliché
Klistier [klɪs'tir] *n* (-s;-e) enema
klistieren [klɪs'tirən] *tr* give an enema to
klitschig ['klɪtʃɪç] *adj* doughy
Klo [klo] *n* (-s;-s) (coll) john
Kloake [klo'akə] *f* (-;-n) sewer
Kloben ['klobən] *m* (-s;-) pulley; (*Holz*) block; (*Schraubenstock*) vise
klobig ['klobɪç] *adj* clumsy; bulky
klomm [klɔm] *pret* of **klimmen**
klopfen ['klɔpfən] *tr* (*Nagel*) drive; (*Teppich*) beat; (*Fleisch*) pound || *intr* knock; (*Herz*) beat, pound; (*Motor*) ping; **j-m auf die Schulter k.** pat s.o. on the back || *impers*—**es klopft s.o.** is knocking
klopffest ['klɔpffest] *adj* antiknock
Klöppel ['klœpəl] *m* (-s;-) bobbin; (*e-r Glocke*) clapper; (mus) mallet
klöppeln ['klœpəln] *tr* make (*lace*) with bobbins
Klops [klɔps] *m* (-es;-e) meatball
Klosett [klo'zet] *n* (-s;-e & -s) (flush) toilet
Klosett'becken *n* toilet bowl
Klosett'brille *f* toilet seat
Klosett'deckel *m* toilet-seat lid
Klosett'papier *n* toilet paper
Kloß [klos] *m* (-es;-e) dumpling; **e-n K. im Hals haben** have a lump in one's throat
Kloster ['klostər] *n* (-s;-̈) monastery, convent
Kloster- *comb.fm.* monastic
Klo'sterbruder *m* lay brother, friar

Klo'sterfrau *f* nun
klösterlich ['kløstərlɪç] *adj* monastic
Klotz [klɔts] *m* (-es;-̈e) block; toy building block; (coll) blockhead; **ein K. am Bein** (coll) a drag; **wie ein K. schlafen** sleep like a log
klotzig ['klɔtsɪç] *adj* clumsy; uncouth || *adv*—**k. reich** filthy rich
Klub [klup] *m* (-s;-s) club
Klub'jacke *f* blazer
Klub'sessel *m* easy chair
Kluft [kluft] *f* (-;-̈e) gorge, ravine; (fig) gulf; (poet) chasm || *f* (-;) outfit, uniform
klug [kluk] *adj* (klüger ['klygər]; klügste ['klygstə] §9) clever, bright; wise; **aus Schaden k. werden** learn the hard way; **nicht k. werden können aus** be unable to figure out
klügeln ['klygəln] *intr* quibble
Klug'heit *f* (-;) cleverness; intelligence; wisdom
klüglich ['klyklɪç] *adv* wisely
Klug'redner *m* wise guy, know-it-all
Klumpen ['klumpən] *m* (-s;-) lump, clod; (*Haufen*) heap; (min) nugget
Klumpfuß ['klumpfus] *m* clubfoot
klumpig ['klumpɪç] *adj* lumpy
Klüngel ['klyŋəl] *m* (-s;-) clique
knabbern ['knabərn] *intr* nibble
Knabe ['knabə] *m* (-n;-n) boy
Kna'benalter *n* boyhood
kna'benhaft *adj* boyish
knack [knak] *interj* crack!; snap!; click!
knacken ['knakən] *tr* crack || *intr* crack; (*Schloß*) click; (*Feuer*) crackle
Knacks [knaks] *m* (-es;-e) crack; snap; click; **e-n K. kriegen** get a crack; **e-n K. weg haben** be badly hit; **sich [dat] e-n K. holen** suffer a blow
Knack'wurst *f* pork sausage; smoked sausage
Knall [knal] *m* (-[e]s;-e) crack, bang; **K. und Fall** on the spot, at once
Knallblättchen ['knalbletçən] *n* (-s;-) cap (*for a toy pistol*)
Knall'bonbon *m* & *n* noise maker
Knall'büchse *f* popgun
Knall'dämpfer *m* silencer
Knall'effekt *m* big surprise
knall'rot *adj* fiery red
knapp [knap] *adj* (eng) close, tight; (*Mehrheit*) bare; (*Zeit*) short; (*Stil*) concise; **k. werden** run short, run low
Knappe ['knapə] *m* (-n;-n) (hist) squire; (min) miner
Knapp'heit *f* (-;) closeness, tightness; shortage; conciseness
Knapp'schaft *f* (-;-en) miner's union
Knapp'schaftskasse *f* miner's insurance
knarren ['knarən] *intr* creak
Knaster ['knastər] *m* (-s;-) tobacco
knattern ['knatərn] *intr* crackle; (*Maschinengewehr*) rattle || *intr* (SEIN) put-put along
Knäuel ['knɔɪəl] *m* & *n* (-s;-) (*Garn*) ball; (*Menschen*) throng
Knauf [knauf] *m* (-[e]s;-̈e) knob
Knauser -in ['knauzər(ɪn)] §6 *mf* tightwad

Knauserei [knauzəˈraɪ] *f* (-;) stinginess

knauserig [ˈknauzərɪç] *adj* stingy

knausern [ˈknauzərn] *intr* be stingy

knautschen [ˈknautʃən] *tr* crumple ‖ *intr* crumple; (coll) wimper

Knebel [ˈkneːbəl] *m* (-s;-) gag

Kne'belbart *m* handlebar moustache

knebeln [ˈkneːbəln] *tr* gag; (fig) muzzle

Kne'belpresse *f* tourniquet

Kne'belung *f—K.* der Presse muzzling of the press

Knecht [knɛçt] *m* (-[e]s;-e) servant; farmhand; serf; slave

knechten [ˈknɛçtən] *tr* enslave; oppress

knechtisch [ˈknɛçtɪʃ] *adj* servile

Knecht'schaft *f* (-;) servitude

kneifen [ˈknaɪfən] §88 & §109 *tr* pinch ‖ §88 *intr* (*Kleid*) be too tight; back out, back down; (fencing) retreat; k. vor (*dat*) shirk, dodge

Kneif'zange [ˈknaɪftsaŋə] *f* (pair of) pincers

Kneipe [ˈknaɪpə] *f* (-;-n) saloon

kneipen [ˈknaɪpən] *intr* (coll) booze

Knei'penwirt *m* saloon keeper

Kneiperei [knaɪpəˈraɪ] *f* (-;-en) drinking bout

kneten [ˈkneːtən] *tr* knead; massage

Knick [knɪk] *m* (-[e]s;-e) bend; (*Bruch*) break; (*Falte*) fold, crease

knicken [ˈknɪkən] *tr* bend; break; fold; (*Hoffnungen*) dash ‖ *intr* (SEIN) snap

Knicker [ˈknɪkər] *m* (-s;-) tightwad

Knicks [knɪks] *m* (-es;-e) curtsy

knicksen [ˈknɪksən] *intr* curtsy

Knie [kniː] *n* (-s;- [ˈkniː-ə]) knee

Knie'beuge *f* knee bend

Knie'beugung *f* genuflection

knie'fällig *adj* on one's knees

knie'frei *adj* above-the-knee

Knie'freiheit *f* legroom

Knie'kehle *f* hollow of the knee

knien [ˈkniː-ən] *intr* kneel

Knie'scheibe *f* kneecap

Knie'schützer *m* (sport) kneepad

kniff [knɪf] *pret* of kneifen ‖ **Kniff** *m* (-[e]s;-e) crease, fold; (*Kunstgriff*) knack

kniff(e)lig [ˈknɪf(ə)lɪç] *adj* tricky

kniffen [ˈknɪfən] *tr* crease, fold

Knigge [ˈknɪgə] *m* (-s) (fig) Emily Post

knipsen [ˈknɪpsən] *tr* (*Karte*) punch; (phot) snap ‖ *intr* (coll) take a picture; mit den Fingern k. snap one's fingers

Knirps [knɪrps] *m* (-es;-e) (coll) shrimp

knirschen [ˈknɪrʃən] *intr* crunch; mit den Zähnen k. gnash one's teeth

knistern [ˈknɪstərn] *intr* crackle; (*Seide*) rustle

knitterfest [ˈknɪtərfest] *adj* wrinkleproof

knittern [ˈknɪtərn] *tr* wrinkle; crumple

knobeln [ˈknoːbəln] *intr* play dice; an e-m Problem k. puzzle over a problem

Knoblauch [ˈknoːblaux] *m* (-[e]s;) garlic

Knöchel [ˈknœçəl] *m* (-s;-) knuckle, joint; ankle

Knochen [ˈknɔxən] *m* (-s;-) bone

Kno'chenbruch *m* fracture

Kno'chengerüst *n* skeleton

Kno'chenmark *n* marrow

Kno'chenmühle *f* (coll) sweat shop

knöchern [ˈknœçərn] *adj* bone; bony

knochig [ˈknɔxɪç] *adj* bony

Knödel [ˈknøːdəl] *m* (-s;-) dumpling; e-n K. im Hals haben have a lump in one's throat

Knolle [ˈknɔlə] *f* (coll) bulbous nose; (bot) tuber

Knollen [ˈknɔlən] *m* (-s;-) lump; (coll) bulbous nose

knollig [ˈknɔlɪç] *adj* bulbous

Knopf [knɔpf] *m* (-[e]s;-e) button; knob; (e-r *Stechnadel*) head; alter K. old fogey

knöpfen [ˈknœpfən] *tr* button

Knopf'loch *n* buttonhole

knorke [ˈknɔrkə] *adj* (coll) super

Knorpel [ˈknɔrpəl] *m* (-s;-) cartilage

Knorren [ˈknɔrən] *m* (-s;-) knot, gnarl

knorrig [ˈknɔrɪç] *adj* gnarled, knotty

Knospe [ˈknɔspə] *f* (-;-n) bud

knospen [ˈknɔspən] *intr* bud

knoten [ˈknoːtən] *tr* & *intr* knot ‖ **Knoten** *m* (-s;-) knot; (*Schwierigkeit*) snag; (*Haarfrisur*) chignon; (*Seemeile*) knot; (astr, med, phys) node; (theat) plot

Kno'tenpunkt *m* intersection, interchange; (rr) junction

knotig [ˈknoːtɪç] *adj* knotty

Knuff [knuf] *m* (-[e]s;-e) (coll) poke

knuffen [ˈknufən] *tr* (coll) poke

knüllen [ˈknylən] *tr* crumple

Knüller [ˈknylər] *m* (-s;-) (coll) hit

knüpfen [ˈknypfən] *tr* tie, knot; (*Teppich*) weave; (*Bündnis*) form; (*befestigen*) fasten; k. an (acc) tie in with ‖ *ref—*sich k. an (acc) to be tied in with

Knüppel [ˈknypəl] *m* (-s;-) cudgel; (e-s *Polizisten*) blackjack; (aer) control stick

knurren [ˈknurən] *intr* growl, snarl; (*Magen*) rumble; (fig) grumble

knurrig [ˈknurɪç] *adj* grumpy

knusprig [ˈknusprɪç] *adj* crisp; (*Mädchen*) attractive

Knute [ˈknuːtə] *f* (-;-n) whip; (*Gewalt*) power; (*Gewaltherrschaft*) tyranny

knutschen [ˈknuːtʃən] *tr*, *recip* & *intr* (coll) neck, pet

Knüttel [ˈknytəl] *m* (-s;-) cudgel

Knüt'telvers *m* doggerel

k.o. [ˈkaˈoː] *adj* knocked out ‖ *adv—*k.o. schlagen knock out ‖ **K.O.** *m* (-[s];-s) knockout

Koalition [ko-alɪˈtsjoːn] *f* (-;-en) coalition

Kobalt [ˈkoːbalt] *n* (-es;) cobalt

Koben [ˈkoːbən] *m* (-s;-) pigsty

Kobold [ˈkoːbɔlt] *m* (-[e]s;-e) goblin

Kobolz [koˈbɔlts] *m—*e-n K. schießen do a somersault

Koch [kɔx] *m* (-[e]s;-e) cook

Koch'buch *n* cookbook

kochen [ˈkɔxən] *tr* & *intr* cook; boil

Kocher [ˈkɔxər] *m* (-s;-) cooker; boiler

Köcher ['kœçər] m (-s;-) quiver; golf bag
Koch'fett n shortening
Koch'geschirr n (mil) mess kit
Koch'herd m kitchen range
Köchin ['kœçɪn] f (-;-nen) cook
Koch'löffel m wooden spoon
Koch'salz n table salt
Köder ['kødər] m (-s;-) bait; lure
ködern ['kødərn] tr bait; lure
Kodex ['kodeks] m (-es;-e) codex; (jur) code
kodifizieren [kodifɪ'tsirən] tr codify
Koffein [kofe'in] n (-s;) caffeine
Koffer ['kɔfər] m (-s;-) suitcase; trunk; case (for portable items)
Kof'ferfernseher m portable television
Kof'fergerät n (rad, telv) portable set
Kof'ferraum m (aut) trunk
Kof'ferschreibmaschine f portable typewriter
Kognak ['kɔnjak] m (-s;-s) cognac
Kohl [kol] m (-s;) cabbage; nonsense
Kohle ['kolə] f (-;-n) coal; (Holzkohle) charcoal
Kohlehydrat ['koləhydrat] n (-[e]s; -e) carbohydrate
kohlen ['kolən] tr & intr carbonize
Koh'lenbergbau m coal mining
Koh'lenbergwerk n coal mine
Koh'lendioxyd n carbon dioxide
Koh'lenoxyd n carbon monoxide
Koh'lenrevier n coal field
Koh'lensäure f carbonic acid
Koh'lenstoff m carbon
Koh'lenwagen m coal truck; (rr) coal car
Koh'lepapier n carbon paper
Koh'leskizze f charcoal sketch
kohl'ra'benschwarz' adj jet black
Koitus ['ko·ɪtus] m (-;) coitus
Koje ['kojə] f (-;-n) bunk, berth
Kojote [ko'jotə] m (-;-n) coyote
Kokain [koka'in] n (-s;) cocaine
Kokerei [kokə'raɪ] f (-;-en) coking plant
kokett [ko'ket] adj flirtatious || **Kokette** f (-;-n) flirt
kokettieren [koke'tirən] intr flirt
Kokon [ko'kõ] m (-s;-s) cocoon
Kokosnuß ['kokosnus] f coconut
Kokospalme ['kokospalmə] f coconut palm, coconut tree
Koks [koks] m (-es;-e) coke; (coll) nonsense; (Geld) (coll) dough
Kolben ['kɔlbən] m (-s;-) butt; (Keule) mace; (Löt-) soldering iron; (aut) piston; (chem) flask; (culin) cob; (elec) bulb
Kol'benhub m piston stroke
Kol'benring m piston ring
Kol'benstange f piston rod
Kolchose [kɔl'çozə] f (-;-n) collective farm
Kolibri ['kolibrɪ] m (-s;-s) humming bird
Kolik ['kolɪk] f (-;-en) colic
Kolkrabe ['kɔlkrabə] m (-n;-n) raven
Kollaborateur [kɔlabora'tør] m (-s;-) collaborator (with the enemy)
kollaborieren [kɔlabo'rirən] intr collaborate
Kollaps [kɔ'laps] m (-es;-e) collapse

kollationieren [kɔlatsjo'nirən] tr collate
Kol·leg [kɔ'lek] n (-s;-s & -legien ['legjən]) lecture; course of lectures; theological college
Kollege [kɔ'legə] m (-n;-n) colleague
Kolleg'heft n lecture notes
Kollegin [kɔ'legɪn] f (-;-nen) colleague
Kollekte [kɔ'lektə] f (-;-n) collection; (eccl) collect
Kollektion [kɔlek'tsjon] f (-;-en) collection
kollektiv [kɔlek'tif] adj collective || **Kollektiv** n (-s;-e) collective
Koller ['kɔlər] m (-s;) rage, temper
kollern ['kɔlərn] ref roll about; (vor Lachen) double over || intr (Puter) gobble; (Magen) rumble || intr (SEIN) roll
kollidieren [kɔlɪ'dirən] intr (SEIN) collide
Kollier [kɔ'lir] n (-s;-s) necklace
Kollision [kɔlɪ'zjon] f (-;-en) collision
Köln [kœln] n (-s;) Cologne
Kölnischwasser [kœlnɪʃ'vasər] n cologne
kolonial [kolo'njal] adj colonial
Kolonial'waren pl groceries
Kolonial'warengeschäft n grocery store
Kolo·nie [kolo'ni] f (-;-nien ['ni·ən]) colony
Kolonnade [kolo'nadə] f (-;-n) colonnade
Kolonne [ko'lɔnə] f (-;-n) column; (mil) convoy (of vehicles)
kolorieren [kolo'rirən] tr color
Kolorit [kolo'rit] n (-[e]s;-e) coloring
Ko·loß [ko'lɔs] m (-losses;-losse) colossus; giant
kolossal [kolo'sal] adj colossal
Kolportage [kɔlpor'taʒə] f (-;-n) trashy literature; spreading of rumors
kolportieren [kɔlpor'tirən] tr peddle; (Gerüchte) spread
Kolumnist -in [kolum'nɪst(ɪn)] §7 mf columnist
Kombi ['kɔmbi] m (-s;-s) (coll) station wagon
Kombination [kɔmbɪna'tsjon] f (-; -en) combination; (Flieger-) flying suit; (e-s Monteurs) coveralls; sport suit; reasoning, deduction; conjecture
kombinieren [kɔmbɪ'nirən] tr combine || intr reason
Kom'biwagen m station wagon
Kombüse [kɔm'byzə] f (-;-n) (naut) galley, kitchen
Komik ['komɪk] f (-;) humor
Komiker ['komɪkər] m (-s;-) comedian
Komikerin ['komɪkərɪn] f (-;-nen) comedienne
komisch ['komɪʃ] adj funny
Komitee [komɪ'te] n (-s;-s) committee
Komma ['kɔma] n (-s;-s) comma; (Dezimalzeichen) decimal point
Kommandant [kɔman'dant] m (-en; -en) commanding officer; commandant

Kommandantur [kɔmandan'tur] *f* (-;
-en) headquarters

Kommandeur [kɔman'dør] *m* (-s;-e)
commanding officer, commander

kommandieren [kɔman'dirən] *tr* command, order; be in command of;
(mil) detail; (mil) detach ‖ *intr* command, be in command

Kommanditgesellschaft [kɔman'ditgəzel∫aft] *f* limited partnership; **K. auf
Aktien** partnership limited by shares

Kommando [kɔ'mando] *n* (-s;-s) command, order; (mil) command; (mil)
detachment, detail; **K. zurück!** as
you were!

Komman'dobrücke *f* (nav) bridge

Komman'doraum *m* control room

Komman'dostab *m* baton

Komman'dostand *m*, **Komman'dostelle**
f command post; (nav) bridge

Komman'dotruppe *f* commando unit

Komman'doturm *m* conning tower;
control tower (*of an aircraft carrier*)

kommen ['kɔmən] §99 *intr* (SEIN)
come; (*geschehen*) happen; **auf etw
[acc] k.** hit on s.th.; **auf jeden k. drei
Mark** each one gets three marks; **das
kommt bloß daher, daß** that's entirely due to; **dazu k.** get around to
it; get hold of it; **hinter etw [acc] k.**
find s.th. out; **j—m grob k.** be rude
to s.o.; **k. lassen** send for; **nichts k.
lassen auf** (*acc*) defend; **so weit k.,
daß** reach the point where; **ums
Leben k.** lose one's life; **wenn Sie
mir so k.** if you talk like that to me;
weit k. get far; **wieder zu sich k.**
come to, regain consciousness; **wie
kam er denn dazu?** how come he did
it? **wie komme ich zum Bahnhof?**
how do I get to the train station?

Kommentar [kɔmen'tar] *m* (-s;-e)
commentary; **kein K.!** no comment!

Kommen·tator [kɔmen'tator] *m* (-s;
-tatoren [ta'torən]) commentator

kommentieren [kɔmen'tirən] *tr* comment on

Kommers [kɔ'mers] *m* (-es;-e) drinking party

Kommers'buch *n* students' song book

kommerziell [kɔmer'tsjel] *adj* commercial

Kommilitone [kɔmili'tonə] *m* (-n;-n)
fellow student

Kom·mis [kɔ'mi] *m* (-mis ['mis];
-mis ['mis]) clerk

Kom·miß [kɔ'mis] *m* (-misses;) (coll)
army; (coll) army life

Kommissar [kɔmi'sar] *m* (-s;-e) commissioner; (pol) commissar

kommissarisch [kɔmi'sari∫] *adj* provisional, temporary

Kommission [kɔmi'sjon] *f* (-;-en)
commission, board; **in K.** (com) on
consignment; on a commission basis

Kommissionär [kɔmisjo'ner] *m* (-s;-e)
agent; wholesale bookseller

Kommissions'gebühr *f* (com) commission

kommissions'weise *adv* on a commission basis

Kommiß'stiefel *m* army boot

kommod [kɔ'mot] *adj* comfortable

Kommode [kɔ'modə] *f* (-;-n) bureau,
chest of drawers

kommunal [kɔmu'nal] *adj* municipal,
local

Kommunal'politik *f* local politics

Kommune [kɔ'munə] *f* (-;-n) municipality; **die K.** the Commies

Kommunikant –in [kɔmuni'kant(in)]
§7 *mf* communicant

Kommunion [kɔmu'njon] *f* (-;-en)
Communion

Kommuniqué [kɔmyni'ke] *n* (-s;-s)
communiqué

Kommunismus [kɔmu'nismus] *m* (-;)
communism

Kommunist –in [kɔmu'nist(in)] §7 *mf*
communist

kommunistisch [kɔmu'nisti∫] *adj* communist(ic)

Komödiant [kɔmø'djant] *m* (-en;-en)
comedian; (pej) ham

Komödie [kɔ'mødjə] *f* (-;-n) comedy;
K. spielen (coll) put on an act

Kompagnon [kɔmpan'jõ] *m* (-s;-s)
(business) partner; associate

kompakt [kɔm'pakt] *adj* compact

Kompa·nie [kɔmpa'ni] *f* (-;-nien
['ni-ən]) company

Kompanie'chef *m* company commander

komparativ [kɔmpara'tif] *adj* comparative ‖ **Komparativ** *m* (-s;-e)
comparative

Komparse [kɔm'parzə] *m* (-n;-n)
(theat) extra

Kom·paß ['kɔmpas] *m* (-passes;
-passe) compass

Kompen·dium [kɔm'pendjum] *n* (-s;
-dien [djən]) compendium

Kompensation [kɔmpenza'tsjon] *f* (-;
-en) compensation

Kompensations'geschäft *n* fair-value
exchange

kompensieren [kɔmpen'zirən] *tr* compensate for, offset

Kompetenz [kɔmpe'tents] *f* (-;-en)
(jur) jurisdiction

komplementär [kɔmplemen'ter] *adj*
complementary

Komplet [kõ'ple] *n* (-s;-s) dress with
matching coat

komplett [kɔm'plet] *adj* complete;
everything included

komplex [kɔm'pleks] *adj* complex ‖
Komplex *m* (-es;-e) complex

Komplice [kɔm'plitsə] *m* (-n;-n) accomplice

komplizieren [kɔmpli'tsirən] *tr* complicate

Komplott [kɔm'plɔt] *n* (-[e]s;-e) plot

Komponente [kɔmpo'nentə] *f* (-;-n)
component

komponieren [kɔmpo'nirən] *tr* compose

Komponist –in [kɔmpo'nist(in)] §7 *mf*
composer

Komposition [kɔmpozi'tsjon] *f* (-;-en)
composition

Komposi·tum [kɔm'pozitum] *n* (-s;
-ta [ta] & -ten [tən]) compound
(word)

Kompott [kɔm'pɔt] *n* (-[e]s;-e) stewed fruit

Kompres·sor [kɔm'prɛsər] m (-s; -soren ['soːrən]) compressor; (aut) supercharger

komprimieren [kɔmpri'miːrən] tr compress

Kompro·miß [kɔmpro'mɪs] m (-misses; -misse) compromise

kompromittieren [kɔmprɔmɪ'tiːrən] tr compromise

kondensieren [kɔndɛn'ziːrən] tr, ref & intr (SEIN) condense

Kondensmilch [kɔn'dɛnsmɪlç] f evaporated milk

Kondens/streifen [kɔn'dɛnsʃtraɪfən] m contrail

Konditorei [kɔndito'raɪ] f (-; -en) pastry shop

Konfekt [kɔn'fɛkt] n (-[e]s; candy, chocolates; fancy cookies

Konfektion [kɔnfɛk'tsjoːn] f (-;) ready-made clothes; manufacture of ready-made clothes

Konfektionär [kɔnfɛktsjo'nɛːr] m (-s; -e) clothing manufacturer; clothing retailer

konfektionieren (kɔnfɛktsjo'niːrən] tr manufacture (clothes)

Konferenz [kɔnfe'rɛnts] f (-; -en) conference

konferieren [kɔnfe'riːrən] intr confer, hold a conference

Konfession [kɔnfe'sjoːn] f (-; -en) religious denomination; (eccl) confession; confession of faith, creed

konfessionell [kɔnfɛsjo'nɛl] adj denominational

konfessions/los adj nondenominational

Konfessions/schule f denominational school, parochial school

konfirmieren [kɔnfɪr'miːrən] tr (eccl) (Prot) confirm

konfiszieren [kɔnfɪs'tsiːrən] tr confiscate

Konfitüre [kɔnfi'tyːrə] f (-; -n) jam

Konflikt [kɔn'flɪkt] m (-[e]s; -e) conflict

konform [kɔn'fɔrm] adj concurring; mit j-m k. gehen agree with s.o.

Konfrontation [kɔnfrɔnta'tsjoːn] f (-; -en) confrontation

konfrontieren [kɔnfrɔn'tiːrən] tr confront

konfus [kɔn'fuːs] adj confused, puzzled

Kongruenz [kɔngru'ɛnts] f (-;) (geom) congruence; (gram) agreement

König ['køːnɪç] m (-[e]s; -e) king

Königin ['køːnɪgɪn] f (-; -nen) queen

kö/niglich adj kingly, royal

Kö/nigreich n kingdom

Kö/nigsadler m golden eagle

Kö/nigsrose f (bot) peony

Kö/nigsschlange f boa constrictor

kö/nigstreu adj royalist

Kö/nigswürde f kingship

Königtum ['køːnɪçtuːm] n (-s;) royalty, kinship; monarchy

konisch ['koːnɪʃ] adj conical

konjugieren [kɔnju'giːrən] tr conjugate

Konjunktion [kɔnjuŋk'tsjoːn] f (-; -en) conjunction

Konjunktiv [kɔnjuŋk'tiːf] m (-s; -e) subjunctive mood

Konjunktur [kɔnjuŋk'tuːr] f (-; -en) economic situation; business trend; (Hochstand) boom

konkav [kɔn'kaːf] adj concave

konkret [kɔn'kreːt] adj concrete

Konkurrent -in [kɔnku'rɛnt(ɪn)] §7 mf competitor

Konkurrenz [kɔnku'rɛnts] f (-; -en) competition; K. machen (dat) compete with

konkurrenz/fähig adj competitive

konkurrieren [kɔnku'riːrən] intr compete

Konkurs [kɔn'kurs] m (-es; -e) bankruptcy; in K. gehen (or geraten) go bankrupt; K. anmelden declare bankruptcy

Konkurs/masse f bankrupt company's assets

können ['kœnən] §100 tr able to do; know; ich kann nichts dafür I can't help it || intr—ich kann nicht hinein I can't get in || mod aux be able to; know how to; be allowed; das kann sein that may be; ich kann nicht sehen I can't see || Können n (-s;) ability

Könner ['kœnər] m (-s;-) expert

konnte ['kɔntə] pret of können

konsequent [kɔnze'kvɛnt] adj consistent

Konsequenz [kɔnze'kvɛnts] f (-; -en) consistency; (Folge) consequence

konservativ [kɔnzɛrva'tiːf] adj conservative

Konservato·rium [kɔnzɛrva'toːrjum] n (-s;-rien [rjən]) conservatory

Konserve [kɔn'zɛrvə] f (-; -n) canned food

Konser/venbüchse f, **Konser/vendose** f can

Konser/venfabrik f cannery

Konser/venöffner m can opener

konservieren [kɔnzɛr'viːrən] tr preserve

Konservie/rung f (-;) preservation

Konsisto·rium [kɔnzɪs'toːrjum] n (-s; -rien [rjən]) (eccl) consistory

Konsole [kɔn'zoːlə] f (-; -n) bracket; (archit) console

konsolidieren [kɔnzoli'diːrən] tr consolidate

Konsonant [kɔnzo'nant] m (-en;-en) consonant

Konsorte [kɔn'zɔrtə] m (-n;-n) (pej) accomplice; (fin) member of a syndicate

Konsor·tium [kɔn'zɔrtjum] n (-s;-tien [tjən]) (fin) syndicate

konstant [kɔn'stant] adj constant || **Konstante** §5 f (math, phys) constant

konstatieren [kɔnsta'tiːrən] tr ascertain; state; (med) diagnose

konsterniert [kɔnstɛr'niːrt] adj stunned

konstituieren [kɔnstitu'iːrən] tr constitute || ref be established; sich als Ausschuß k. form a committee of the whole

konstitutionell [kɔnstitutsjo'nɛl] adj constitutional

konstruieren [kɔnstru'iːrən] tr construct; (entwerfen) design; (gram) construe

Konsul ['kɔnzul] m (-s;-n) consul

konsularisch [kɔnzu'lɑːrɪʃ] *adj* consular

Konsulat [kɔnzu'lɑːt] *n* (-[e]s;-e) consulate; (hist) consulship

Konsulent –in [kɔnzu'lɛnt(ɪn)] §7 *mf* (jur) counsel

konsultieren [kɔnzul'tirən] *tr* consult

Konsum [kɔn'zuːm] *m* (-s;-s) cooperative store; (com) consumption

Konsument –in [kɔnzu'mɛnt(ɪn)] §7 *mf* consumer

Konsum'güter *pl* consumer goods

konsumieren [kɔnzu'mirən] *tr* consume

Konsum'verein *m* cooperative society

Kontakt [kɔn'takt] *m* (-[e]s;-e) contact

Kontakt'glas *n*, **Kontakt'schale** *f* contact lens

Konteradmiral ['kɔntəratmirɑːl] *m* rear admiral

Konterfei [kɔntər'faɪ] *n* (-s;-e) portrait, likeness

kontern ['kɔntərn] *tr* counter

Kontinent ['kɔntinənt] *m* (-[e]s;-e) continent

Kontingent [kɔntɪŋ'gɛnt] *n* (-[e]s;-e) quota; (mil) contingent

Kon·to ['kɔnto] *n* (-s;-s & -ten [tən]) account

Kon'toauszug *m* bank statement

Kontor [kɔn'toːr] *n* (-s;-e) (com) office

Kontorist –in [kɔnto'rɪst(ɪn)] §7 *mf* clerk (*in an office*)

Kontrahent [kɔntra'hɛnt] *m* (-en;-en) contracting party; dueller

kontrahieren [kɔntra'hirən] *tr & intr* contract

Kontrakt [kɔn'trakt] *m* (-[e]s;-e) contract

Kontrapunkt ['kɔntrapuŋkt] *m* (mus) counterpoint

konträr [kɔn'trɛr] *adj* contrary

Kontrast [kɔn'trast] *m* (-[e]s;-e) contrast

konstrastieren [kɔntras'tirən] *intr* contrast

Kontrast'regelung *f* (telv) contrast button

Kontroll– [kɔn'trɔl] *comb.fm.* checking; control

Kontroll'abschnitt *m* stub (*of ticket*)

Kontrolle [kɔn'trɔlə] *f* (-;-n) control; check, inspection

Kontrolleur [kɔntrɔ'løːr] *m* (-s;-e) inspector, supervisor; (aer) air-traffic controller; (indust) timekeeper

kontrollieren [kɔntrɔ'lirən] *tr* control; check, inspect; (*Bücher*) audit

Kontroll'kasse *f* cash register

Kontroll'leuchte *f* (aut) warning light (*on dashboard*)

Kontroll'turm *m* (aer) control tower

Kontroverse [kɔntro'vɛrzə] *f* (-;-n) controversy

Kontur [kɔn'tuːr] *f* (-;-en) contour

Konvent [kɔn'vɛnt] *m* (-[e]s;-e) convent; monastery; (*Versammlung*) convention

Konvention [kɔnvɛn'tsjoːn] *f* (-;-en) convention

konventionell [kɔnvɛntsjo'nɛl] *adj* conventional

Konversation [kɔnvɛrza'tsjoːn] *f* (-;-en) conversation

Konversations'lexikon *n* encyclopedia; **wandelndes K.** (coll) walking encyclopedia

konvertieren [kɔnvɛr'tirən] *tr* convert || *intr* be converted

Konvertit –in [kɔnvɛr'tit(ɪn)] §7 *mf* convert

konvex [kɔn'vɛks] *adj* convex

Konvikt [kɔn'vɪkt] *n* (-s;-e) minor seminary

Konvoi ['kɔnvɔɪ] *m* (-s;-s) convoy

Konvolut [kɔnvo'luːt] *n* (-[e]s;-e) bundle, roll

Konzentration [kɔntsɛntra'tsjoːn] *f* (-;-en) concentration

Konzentrations'lager *n* concentration camp

konzentrieren [kɔntsɛn'trirən] *tr & ref* (**auf** *acc*) concentrate (*on*)

konzentrisch [kɔn'tsɛntrɪʃ] *adj* concentric

Konzept [kɔn'tsɛpt] *n* (-[e]s;-e) rough draft; **aus dem K. bringen** confuse, throw off; **aus dem K. kommen** lose one's train of thought

Konzept'papier *n* scribbling paper

Konzern [kɔn'tsɛrn] *m* (-s;-e) (com) combine

Konzert [kɔn'tsɛrt] *n* (-[e]s;-e) concert

Konzert'flügel *m* grand piano

Konzession [kɔntsɛ'sjoːn] *f* (-;-en) concession; license

konzessionieren [kɔntsɛsjo'nirən] *tr* (com) license

Kon·zil [kɔn'tsiːl] *n* (-[e]s;-e & -zilien ['tsiljan]) (eccl) council

konziliant [kɔntsi'ljant] *adj* conciliatory; understanding

konzipieren [kɔntsi'pirən] *tr* conceive

koordinieren [kɔ·ɔrdi'nirən] *tr* coordinate

Kopf [kɔpf] *m* (-[e]s;ːe) head; **aus dem Kopfe** by heart; **j–m über den K. wachsen** be taller than s.o.; (fig) be too much for s.o.; **mit dem K. voran** head first; **seinen eigenen K. haben** have a mind of one's own; **seinen K. lassen müssen** lose one's life

Kopf'bedeckung *f* headgear, head wear

Kopf'brett *n* headboard

köpfen ['kœpfən] *tr* behead; (*Baum*) top; (fb) head

Kopf'ende *n* head (*of bed, etc.*)

Kopf'geld *n* reward (*for capture of criminal*)

Kopf'haut *f* scalp

Kopf'hörer *m* headset, earphones

–köpfig [kœpfɪç] *comb.fm.* –headed; –man

Kopf'kissen *n* pillow

Kopf'kissenbezug *m* pillowcase

kopf'lastig *adj* top-heavy

Kopf'lehne *f* headrest

Kopf'rechnen *n* (-s;) mental arithmetic

Kopf'salat *m* head lettuce

kopf'scheu *adj* (*Pferd*) nervous; (*Person*) shy; **k. werden** become alarmed

Kopf'schmerzen *pl* headache

Kopf'schuppen *pl* dandruff

Kopf'sprung *m* dive; **e–n K. machen** dive

Kopf'stand *m* handstand; **e–n K. machen** (aer) nose over

Kopf'stärke *f* (mil) strength

kopf'stehen §146 *intr* stand on one's head; (fig) be upside down

Kopf'steinpflaster *n* cobblestones

Kopf'steuer *f* poll tax

Kopf'stimme *f* falsetto

Kopf'stoß *m* butt; (fb) header

Kopf'tuch *n* kerchief, babushka

kopfü'ber *adv* head over heels

kopfun'ter *adv*—**kopfüber k.** head over heels

Kopf'weh *n* headache

Kopf'wellenknall *m* sonic boom

Ko·pie [ko'pi] *f* (–;–pien ['pi·ən]) copy, duplicate; (phot) print

kopieren [ko'pirən] *tr* copy; (phot) print

Kopier'maschine *f* copier, photocopying machine

Kopier'papier *n* tracing paper; carbon paper; (phot) printing paper

Kopier'stift *m* indelible pencil

Koppel ['kɔpəl] *f* (–;–n) leash; (*Gehege*) enclosure, paddock ‖ *n* (–s;–) (mil) belt

koppeln ['kɔpəln] *tr* tie together, yoke; (fig) tie in; (elec) connect; (rad, rr) couple; (rok) dock ‖ **Koppeln** *n* (–s;) (aer, naut) dead reckoning; (rok) docking

Kopplungsgeschäft ['kɔplʊŋsgəʃɛft] *n* package deal

Koralle [ko'ralə] *f* (–;–n) coral

Korb [kɔrp] *m* (–[e]s;ⁱe) basket; **j–m den K. geben** (fig) give s.o. the brush-off

Korb'ball *m* basketball

Körbchen ['kœrpçən] *n* (–s;–) little basket; (*e–s Büstenhalters*) cup

Korb'flasche *f* demijohn

Korb'geflecht *n* wickerwork

Korb'möbel *pl* wicker furniture

Korb'weide *f* (bot) osier

Kordel ['kɔrdəl] *f* (–;–n) cord

Kordon [kɔr'dõ] *m* (–s;–s) cordon; (*Ordensband*) ribbon

Korea [ko're·a] *n* (–s;) Korea

koreanisch [kore'anɪʃ] *adj* Korean

Korinthe [ko'rɪntə] *f* (–;–n) currant

Kork [kɔrk] *m* (–[e]s;–e) cork

Korken ['kɔrkən] *m* (–s;–) cork, stopper

Korkenzieher ['kɔrkəntsi·ər] *m* (–s;–) corkscrew

Korn [kɔrn] *n* (–[e]s;ⁱer) grain; seed; (*am Gewehr*) bead; (*Getreide*) rye; (*e–r Münze*) fineness; (phot) graininess; **j–n aufs K. nehmen** draw a bead on s.o.

Korn'ähre *f* ear of grain

Korn'branntwein *m* whiskey

Kornett [kɔr'nɛt] *n* (–[e]s;–e) (mus) cornet

körnig ['kœrnɪç] *adj* granular

Korn'kammer *f* granary; (fig) breadbasket

koronar [koro'nar] *adj* coronary

Körper ['kœrpər] *m* (–s;–) body; (geom, phys) solid

Kör'perbau *m* (–[e]s;) build, physique

kör'perbehindert *adj* physically handicapped

Kör'perbeschaffenheit *f* constitution

Körperchen [kœrpərçən] *n* (–s;–) corpuscle

Kör'perfülle *f* plumpness, corpulence

Kör'pergeruch *m* body odor

Kör'perhaltung *f* posture, bearing

Kör'perkraft *f* physical strength

kör'perlich *adj* physical; (*stofflich*) corporeal

Kör'perpflege *f* personal hygiene

Kör'perpuder *m* talcum powder

Kör'perschaft *f* (–;–en) body (*of persons*); corporation

Kör'perverletzung *f* bodily injury

Korporation [kɔrpora'tsjon] *f* (–;–en) corporation

Korps [kor] *n* (– [kors];– [kors]) corps

Korps'geist *m* esprit de corps

Korps'student *m* member of a fraternity

korrekt [kɔ'rɛkt] *adj* correct, proper

Korrek·tor [kɔ'rɛktɔr] *m* (–s;–toren ['torən]) proofreader

Korrektur [kɔrɛk'tur] *f* (–;–en) correction; proofreading

Korrektur'bogen *m* page proof

Korrektur'fahne *f* galley proof

Korrelat [kɔrɛ'lat] *n* (–[e]s;–e) correlative

Korrespondent –in [kɔrɛspɔn'dɛnt(ɪn)] §7 *mf* correspondent

Korrespondenz [kɔrɛspɔn'dɛnts] *f* (–;–en) correspondence

Korrespondenz'karte *f* (Aust) postcard

Korridor ['kɔrridɔr] *m* (–s;–e) corridor

korrigieren [kɔrri'girən] *tr* correct

korrodieren [kɔrro'dirən] *tr & intr* corrode

Korse ['kɔrzə] *m* (–n;–n) Corsican

Korsett [kɔr'zɛt] *n* (–[e]s;–e & –s) corset

Korsika ['kɔrzika] *n* (–;) Corsica

Korvette [kɔr'vɛtə] *f* (–;–n) corvette

Kosak [ko'zak] *m* (–en;–en) Cossack

K.-o.-Schlag [ka'o/lak] *m* knockout punch

kosen [kozən] *tr* fondle, caress

Kosename ['kozənamə] *m* pet name

Kosmetik [kɔs'metɪk] *f* (–;) beauty treatment; **chirugische K.** cosmetic surgery, plastic surgery

Kosme'tikartikel *m* cosmetic

Kosmeti·kum [kɔs'metikum] *n* (–s;–ka [ka]) cosmetic

kosmisch ['kɔsmɪʃ] *adj* cosmic

kosmopolitisch [kɔsmopo'litɪʃ] *adj* cosmopolitan

Kosmos ['kɔsmɔs] *m* (–;) cosmos

Kost [kɔst] *f* (–;) food, board

kostbar ['kɔstbar] *adj* valuable; costly

Kost'barkeit *f* (–;–en) costliness; (fig) precious thing

kosten [kɔstən] *tr* cost; taste, sip ‖ **Kosten** *pl* costs; **auf K.** (*genit*) at the expense of; **auf seine K. kommen** get one's money's worth; **sich in K. stürzen** go to great expense

Ko'stenanschlag *m* estimate

Ko'stenaufwand *m* expenditure, outlay

Ko'stenberechnung *f* cost accounting

Ko'stenersatz m, **Ko'stenerstattung** f reimbursement of expenses

ko'stenlos adj free of charge

Ko'stenvoranschlag m estimate

Kost'gänger -in §6 mf boarder

köstlich ['kœstlɪç] adj delicious; delightful || adv—**sich k. amüsieren** have a grand time

Kost'probe f sample (to taste)

kostspielig ['kɔst'piːlɪç] adj expensive

Kostüm [kɔs'tyːm] n (-s;-e) costume; woman's suit; fancy dress

kostümieren [kɔsty'miːrən] tr & ref dress up

Kostüm'probe f dress rehearsal

Kot [koːt] m (-[e]s;) mud, dirt; (tierischer) dirt, dung; excrement

Kotelett [kotə'lɛt] n (-[e]s;-e & -s) pork chop; cutlet

Köter ['køːtər] m (-s;-) mut, mongrel

Kot'flügel m (aut) fender

kotig ['koːtɪç] adj muddy, dirty

kotzen ['kɔtsən] intr (sl) puke || **Kotzen** n—**es ist zum K.** it's enough to make you throw up

Krabbe ['krabə] f (-;-n) crab; shrimp; (niedliches Kind) little darling

krabbeln ['krabəln] tr & intr tickle || intr (SEIN) crawl

Krach [krax] m (-[e]s;-s & -e) crash, bang; (Lärm) racket; (Streit) row; (fin) crash; **K. machen** kick up a row

krachen ['kraxən] intr crash, crack

krächzen ['krɛçtsən] intr croak, caw

kraft [kraft] prep (genit) by virtue of || **Kraft** f (-;ːe) strength, power, force; **außer K. setzen** repeal; **in K. sein** be in force; **in K. treten** come into force

Kraft'anlage f (elec) power plant

Kraft'anstrengung f strenuous effort

Kraft'aufwand m effort

Kraft'ausdruck m swear word; **Kraftausdrücke** strong language

Kraft'brühe f concentrated broth

Kraft'fahrer -in §6 mf motorist

Kraft'fahrzeug n motor vehicle

kräftig ['krɛftɪç] adj strong, powerful; (Speise) nutritious || adv hard; heartily

kräftigen ['krɛftɪgən] tr strengthen

Kraft'leistung f feat of strength

kraft'los adj powerless; weak

Kraft'meier m (coll) bully; (coll) muscle man

Kraft'probe f test of strength

Kraft'protz m (coll) powerhouse

Kraft'rad n motorcycle

Kraft'stoff m fuel

Kraft'stoffleitung f fuel line

kraftstrotzend ['kraft/trɔtsənt] adj strapping

Kraft'übertragung f (aut) transmission

Kraft'wagen m motor vehicle

Kraft'werk n generating plant

Kraft'wort n (-[e]s;ːer) swear word

Kragen ['kraːgən] m (-s;-) collar

Krähe ['krɛːə] f (-;-n) crow

krähen ['krɛːən] intr crow

Krähenfüße ['krɛːənfyːsə] pl crow's feet (wrinkles)

Krakeel [kra'keːl] m (-s;-e) (coll) rumpus; (lauter Streit) brawl

krakeelen [kra'keːlən] intr (coll) kick up a storm

Kralle ['kralə] f (-;-n) claw

Kram [kraːm] m (-[e]s;) (coll) things, stuff; (coll) business, affairs

kramen ['kraːmən] intr rummage

Krämer -in ['krɛːmər(ɪn)] §6 mf shopkeeper || m (pej) philistine

Krä'merseele f philistine

Kram'laden m general store

Krampe ['krampə] f (-;-n) staple

Krampf [krampf] m (-[e]s;ːe) cramp, spasm; convulsion; (Unsinn) nonsense

Krampf'ader f varicose vein

krampf'artig adj spasmodic

krampf'haft adj convulsive

Kran [kraːn] m (-[e]s;ːe & -e) (mach) crane

Kranich ['kraːnɪç] m (-s;-e) (orn) crane

krank [kraŋk] adj sick, ill || **Kranke** §5 mf patient

-krank comb.fm. suffering from

kränkeln ['krɛŋkəln] intr be sickly

kranken ['kraŋkən] intr—**k. an** (dat) suffer from

kränken ['krɛŋkən] tr hurt, offend || ref (über acc) feel hurt (at)

Kran'kenanstalt f hospital

Kran'kenbahre f stretcher

Kran'kenbett n sickbed

Kran'kenfahrstuhl m wheel chair

Kran'kengeld n sick benefit

Kran'kenhaus n hospital; **ins K. einweisen** hospitalize

Kran'kenkasse f medical insurance plan

Kran'kenlager n sickbed

Kran'kenpflege f nursing

Kran'kenpfleger -in §6 mf nurse

Kran'kenrevier n (mil) sick quarters; (nav) sick bay

Kran'kensaal m hospital ward

Kran'kenschwester f nurse

Kran'kenstube f infirmary

Kran'kenstuhl m wheel chair

Kran'kenurlaub m sick leave

Kran'kenversicherung f health insurance

Kran'kenwagen m ambulance

krank'feiern intr (coll) play sick

krank'haft adj morbid, pathological

Krank'heit f (-;-en) sickness, disease

Krank'heitsbericht m medical bulletin

Krank'heitserscheinung f symptom

kränklich ['krɛŋklɪç] adj sickly

Kränk'lichkeit f (-;) poor health

Kränkung ['krɛŋkʊŋ] f (-;-en) offense

Kran'wagen m (aut) wrecker, tow truck

Kranz [krants] m (-[e]s;ːe) wreath

Kränzchen ['krɛntsçən] n (-s;-) small wreath; ladies' circle; informal dance

kränzen ['krɛntsən] tr wreathe

Krapfen ['krapfən] m (-s;-) doughnut

kraß [kras] adj crass, gross

Krater ['kraːtər] m (-s;-) crater

Kratzbürste ['krats'byrstə] f wire brush; (fig) stand-offish woman

Krätze ['krɛtsə] f (-;) itch, scabies

kratzen ['kratsən] tr & intr scratch

Krat'zer m (-s;-) scratch; scraper

krauen ['krau-ən] *tr* scratch gently

kraus [kraus] *adj (Haar)* frizzy; *(Gedanken)* confused; **die Stirn k. ziehen** knit one's brows

Krause ['krauzə] *f (-;-n)* ruffle

kräuseln ['krɔɪzəln] *tr & ref* curl

Krau'seminze *f (bot)* spearmint

Kraus'haar *n* frizz

Kraut [kraut] *n (-[e]s;ᵉer)* herb, plant; leafy top; *(Kohl)* cabbage; **ins K. schießen** run wild

Krawall [kra'val] *m (-[e]s;-e)* riot; *(coll)* rumpus

Krawatte [kra'vatə] *f (-;-n)* necktie

Krawat'tenhalter *m* tie clip

kraxeln ['kraksəln] *intr* (SEIN) climb

Kreatur [krea'tur] *f (-;-en)* creature

Krebs [kreps] *m (-es;-e)* crawfish, crab; *(pathol)* cancer

krebs'artig *adj (pathol)* cancerous

Kredenz [kre'dɛnts] *f (-;-en)* buffet, credenza, sideboard

kredenzen [kre'dɛntsən] *tr (Wein)* serve

Kredit [kre'dit] *m (-[e]s;-e)* credit

Kredit'bank *f* commercial bank

kreditieren [kredi'tirən] *tr* credit || *intr* give credit

Kredit'karte *f* credit card

Kredit'würdigkeit *f* trustworthiness; *(com)* credit rating

Kreide ['kraɪdə] *f (-;-n)* chalk, piece of chalk, crayon

kreieren [kre'irən] *tr* create

Kreis [kraɪs] *m (-es;-e)* circle; *(Bereich)* field; *(Bezirk)* district; *(adm)* county; *(elec)* circuit

Kreis'abschnitt *m* segment

Kreis'amt *n* district office

Kreis'ausschnitt *m* sector

Kreis'bahn *f* orbit

Kreis'bogen *m (geom)* arc

kreischen ['kraɪʃən] *intr* shriek

Kreisel ['kraɪzəl] *m (-s;-)* gyroscope; top *(toy)*

Krei'selbewegung *f* gyration

Krei'selhorizont *m* artificial horizon

kreiseln ['kraɪzəln] *intr* spin, rotate, gyrate; spin the top

Krei'selpumpe *f* centrifugal pump

kreisen ['kraɪzən] *intr* circle; revolve; *(Blut)* circulate

kreis'förmig *adj* circular

Kreis'lauf *m* circulation; cycle

Kreis'laufstörung *f* circulatory disorder

kreis'rund *adj* circular

Kreis'säge *f* circular saw, buzz saw

kreißen ['kraɪsən] *intr* be in labor

Kreißsaal ['kraɪssal] *m* delivery room

Kreis'stadt *f* (rural) county seat

Kreis'umfang *m* circumference

Kreis'verkehr *m* traffic circle

Krem [krem] *f (-;-s) & m (-s;-s)* cream

Kreml ['kreməl] *m (-[e]s;)* Kremlin

Krempe ['krempə] *f (-;-n)* brim, rim

Krempel ['krempəl] *m (-s;)* *(coll)* stuff, junk || *f (-;-n)* (tex) card

Kren [kren] *m (-[e]s;)* horseradish

krepieren [kre'pirən] *intr* (SEIN) *(Tiere)* die; *(Granate)* explode, burst; *(sl)* kick the bucket

Krepp [krep] *m (-s;-s)* crepe

Kreta ['kreta] *n (-s;)* Crete

Kretonne [kre'tonə] *f (-;-n)* cretonne

kreuz [krɔɪts] *adv—k. und quer* crisscross || **Kreuz** *n (-es;-e)* cross; *(anat)* small of the back; *(cards)* club(s)

Kreuz'abnahme *f* deposition

Kreuz'band *n (-[e]s;ᵉer)* mailing wrapper *(for newspapers, etc.)*

kreuz'brav' *adj (coll)* very honest; *(coll)* very well-behaved

kreuzen ['krɔɪtsən] *tr* cross || *recip* cross; interbreed || *intr* cruise

Kreuzer ['krɔɪtsər] *m (-s;-)* penny; *(nav)* cruiser

Kreuz'fahrer *m* crusader

Kreuz'fahrt *f* cruise; *(hist)* crusade

Kreuz'feuer *n* crossfire

kreuz'fidel' *adj* very cheerful

Kreuz'gang *m (archit)* cloister(s)

kreuzigen ['krɔɪtsɪgən] *tr* crucify

Kreu'zigung *f (-;-en)* crucifixion

Kreuz'otter *f* adder

Kreuz'ritter *m* crusader; Knight of the Teutonic Order

Kreuz'schiff *n* transept *(of church)*

Kreuz'schlitzschraubenzieher *m* Phillips screwdriver

Kreu'zung *f (-;-en)* intersection; crossbreeding; hybrid; *(rr)* crossing

Kreuz'verhör *n* cross-examination; **j-n ins K. nehmen** cross-examine s.o.

Kreuz'verweis *m* cross reference

Kreuz'weg *m* crossroad; *(eccl)* stations of the cross

Kreuz'worträtsel *n* crossword puzzle

Kreuz'zeichen *n (eccl)* sign of the cross; *(typ)* dagger

Kreuz'zug *m* crusade

kribbelig ['krɪbəlɪç] *adj* irritable; *(nervös)* edgy, on edge

kribbeln ['krɪbəln] *intr* tickle

kriechen ['kriçən] §102 *intr* (SEIN) creep, crawl

kriecherisch ['kriçərɪʃ] *adj* fawning

Kriechtier ['kriçtir] *n* reptile

Krieg [krik] *m (-[e]s;-e)* war

kriegen ['krigən] *tr (coll)* get, catch

Krie'ger *m (-s;-)* warrior

kriegerisch ['krigərɪʃ] *adj* warlike; *(Person)* belligerent

krieg'führend *adj* warring

Kriegs'akademie *f* war college

Kriegs'bemalung *f* war paint

Kriegs'berichter *m*, **Kriegs'berichterstatter** *m* war correspondent

Kriegs'dienst *m* military service

Kriegs'dienstverweigerer *m* conscientious objector

Kriegs'einsatz *m (mil)* action

Kriegs'entschädigung *f* reparations

Kriegs'fall *m—im K.* in case of war

Kriegs'flotte *f* fleet; naval force

Kriegs'fuß *m—mit j-m auf K. stehen** be at loggerheads with s.o.

Kriegs'gebiet *n* war zone

Kriegs'gefangene §5 *mf* prisoner of war

Kriegs'gericht *n* court martial

Kriegsgewinnler ['kriksgəvɪnlər] *m (-s;-)* war profiteer

Kriegs'hafen *m* naval base

Kriegs'hetzer *m* warmonger

Kriegs'kamerad m fellow soldier
Kriegs'lazarett n base hospital
Kriegs'list f stratagem
Kriegs'marine f navy
Kriegs'ministerium n war department
Kriegs'opfer n war victim
Kriegs'pfad m warpath
Kriegs'rat m council of war
Kriegs'recht n martial law
Kriegs'rüstung f arming for war; war production
Kriegs'schauplatz m theater of war
Kriegs'schuld f war debt; war guilt
Kriegs'teilnehmer m combatant; (ehemaliger) ex-serviceman, veteran
Kriegs'verbrechen n war crime
Kriegs'versehrte §5 m disabled veteran
kriegs'verwendungsfähig adj fit for active duty
Kriegs'wesen n warfare, war
Kriegs'zug m (mil) campaign
Kriegs'zustand m state of war
Krim [krɪm] f (-;) Crimea
Krimi ['krimi] m (-s;-s) & (-;-) (coll) murder mystery; (telv) thriller
kriminal [krɪmɪ'nɑl] adj criminal
Kriminal- comb.fm. criminal, crime
Kriminal'beamte m criminal investigator
Kriminal'roman m detective novel
Kriminal'stück n (telv) thriller
kriminell [krɪmɪ'nɛl] adj criminal ||
Kriminelle §5 mf criminal
Krimskrams ['krɪmskrams] m (-es;) (coll) junk
Kripo ['kripo] abbr (Kriminalpolizei) crime squad
Krippe ['krɪpə] f (-;-n) crib, manger; day nursery (for infants up to 3 years)
Krise ['krizə] f (-;-n) crisis
kriseln ['krizəln] impers—es kriselt there's a crisis, trouble is brewing
Kristall [krɪs'tal] m (-s;-e) crystal
Kristalleuchter (Kristall'leuchter) m crystal chandelier
Kristall'glas n crystal
kristallisieren [krɪstali'zirən] ref & intr crystallize
Kristall'zucker m granulated sugar
Krite-rium [krɪ'terjum] n (-s;-rien [rjən]) criterion
Kritik [krɪ'tik] f (-;-en) criticism; critique; unter aller K. abominable
Kritikaster [krɪti'kastər] m (-s;-) (pej) faultfinder
Kritiker -in ['kritɪkər(ɪn)] §6 mf critic; reviewer
kritik'los adj uncritical
kritisch ['kritɪʃ] adj critical
kritisieren [krɪti'zirən] tr criticize; (werten) review
Krittelei [krɪtə'laɪ] f (-;-en) faultfinding; petty criticism
kritteln ['krɪtəln] intr (an dat) find fault (with), grumble (about)
Kritzelei [krɪtsə'laɪ] f (-;-en) scribbling, scrawling; scribble, scrawl
kritzeln ['krɪtsəln] tr & intr scribble
kroch [krɔx] pret of kriechen
Krokodil [krɔkə'dil] n (-[e]s;-e) crocodile
Krokus ['krokus] m (-;- & -se) crocus

Krone ['kronə] f (-;-n) crown
krönen ['krønən] tr crown
Kronerbe ['kronɛrbə] m, Kronerbin ['kronɛrbɪn] f heir apparent
Kronleuchter ['kronlɔɪçtər] m chandelier
Kronprinz ['kronprɪnts] m crown prince
Kronprinzessin ['kronprɪntsesɪn] f crown princess
Krö'nung f (-;-en) coronation
Kropf [krɔpf] m (-[e]s;⸚e) crop (of bird); (pathol) goiter
Kröte ['krøtə] f (-;-n) toad; Kröten (coll) coins, coppers
Krücke ['krykə] f (-;-n) crutch
Krückstock ['kryk/tɔk] m walking stick
Krug [kruk] m (-[e]s;⸚e) jar, jug; mug; pitcher; (Wirtshaus) tavern
Krume ['krumə] f (-;-n) crumb; topsoil
Krümel ['kryməl] m (-s;-) crumb
krümeln ['kryməln] tr & intr crumble
krumm [krum] adj (krummer & krümmer ['krymər]; krummste & krümmste ['krymstə] §9) bent, stooping; crooked
krumm'beinig adj bowlegged
krümmen ['krymən] tr bend, curve || ref (vor Schmerzen) writhe; (vor Lachen) double up; (Wurm) wriggle; (Holz) warp; (Fluß, Straße) wind
Krümmer ['krymər] m (-s;-) (tech) elbow
krumm'nehmen §116 tr (coll) take the wrong way, take amiss
Krumm'stab m (eccl) crozier
Krüm'mung f (-;-en) bend, curve; winding
krumpeln ['krumpəln] tr & intr (coll) crumple, crease
Krüppel ['krypəl] m (-s;-) cripple; zum K. machen cripple
krüp'pelhaft adj deformed
krüp'pelig adj crippled; stunted
Kruste ['krustə] f (-;-n) crust
Kru'stentier n crustacean
krustig ['krustɪç] adj crusty
Kruzifix [krutsi'fɪks] n (-es;-e) crucifix
Krypta ['krypta] f (-;-ten [tən]) crypt
Kübel ['kybəl] m (-s;-) tub; bucket
Kü'belwagen m jeep
kubieren [ku'birən] tr (math) cube
Kubik- [kubik] comb.fm. cubic
Kubik'maß n cubic measure
kubisch ['kubiʃ] adj cubic
Kubismus [ku'bismus] m (-;) cubism
Küche ['kyçə] f (-;-n) kitchen; (culin) cuisine
Kuchen ['kuxən] m (-s;-) cake, pie
Ku'chenblech n cookie sheet
Kü'chenchef m chef
Kü'chendienst m (mil) K.P.
Ku'chenform f cake pan
Kü'chengerät n kitchen utensil
Kü'chengeschirr n kitchen utensils
Kü'chenherd m kitchen range, stove
Kü'chenmaschine f electric kitchen appliance
Kü'chenmeister m chef

Kü'chenzettel *m* menu

Küchlein ['kyçlaın] *n* (-s;-) chick; (culin) small cake

Kuckuck ['kukuk] *m* (-s;-e) cuckoo; zum K. gehen (coll) go to hell

Kufe ['kufə] *f* (-;-n) vat; (*Schlitten*-) runner

Küfer ['kyfər] *m* (-s;-) cooper

Kugel ['kugəl] *f* (-;-n) ball; sphere; (*Geschoß*) bullet; (sport) shot

ku'gelfest *adj* bulletproof

ku'gelförmig *adj* spherical

Ku'gelgelenk *n* (mach) ball-and-socket joint; (anat) socket joint

Ku'gellager *n* ball bearing

kugeln ['kugəln] *tr* roll ǁ *ref* roll around; sich vor Lachen k. double over with laughter ǁ *intr* (SEIN) roll

Ku'gelregen *m* hail of bullets

ku'gelrund *adj* round; (coll) tubby

Ku'gelschreiber *m* ball-point pen

Ku'gelstoßen *n* (sport) shot put

Kuh [ku] *f* (-;⁻e) cow

Kuh'dorf *n* hick town

Kuh'fladen *m* cow dung

Kuh'handel *m* (pol) horse trading

Kuh'haut *f* cowhide; das geht auf keine K. but that's a long story

kühl [kyl] *adj* cool

Kühl'anlage *f* refrigerator; cooling system; cold storage (room)

Kühle ['kylə] *f* (-;) cool, coolness

kühlen ['kylən] *tr* cool; (*Wein*) chill

Küh'ler *m* (-s;-) cooler; (aut) radiator

Küh'lerverschluß *m* radiator cap

Kühl'mittel *n* coolant

Kühl'schrank *m* refrigerator

Kühl'truhe *f* freezer

Kühl'wagen *m* refrigerator truck; (rr) refrigerator car

Kuh'magd *f* milkmaid

Kuh'mist *m* cow dung

kühn [kyn] *adj* bold, daring

Kühn'heit *f* (-;) boldness, daring

Kuhpocken ['kupɔkən] *pl* cowpox

Kuh'stall *m* cowshed, cow barn

Kujon [ku'jon] *m* (-s;-e) (pej) louse

kujonieren [kujo'nirən] *tr* bully

Küken ['kykən] *n* (-s;-) chick

Kukuruz ['kukuruts] *m* (-es;) (Aust) corn

kulant [ku'lant] *adj* obliging; generous

Kuli ['kuli] *m* (-s;-s) coolie

kulinarisch [kuli'narıʃ] *adj* culinary

Kulisse [ku'lısə] *f* (-;-n) (theat) wing; hinter den Kulissen behind the scenes; Kulissen scenery

Kulis'senfieber *n* stage fright

kullern ['kulərn] *intr* (SEIN) roll

kulminieren [kulmi'nirən] *intr* culminate

Kult [kult] *m* (-[e]s;-e] cult

kultivieren [kulti'virən] *tr* cultivate

Kultur [kul'tur] *f* (-;-en) culture, civilization; (agr) cultivation; (bact, chem) culture

Kultur'austausch *m* cultural exchange

kulturell [kultu'rel] *adj* cultural

Kultur'erbe *n* cultural heritage

Kultur'film *m* educational film

Kultur'geschichte *f* history of civilization; cultural history

Kultur'volk *n* civilized people

Kul·tus ['kultus] *m* (-;-te [tə]) cult

Kümmel ['kyməl] *m* (-s;-) caraway seed; caraway brandy

Küm'melbrot *n* seeded rye bread

Kummer ['kumər] *m* (-s;) grief, sorrow; worry, concern, trouble; j-m großen K. bereiten cause s.o. a lot of worry; sich [*dat*] K. machen über (*acc*) worry about

kümmerlich ['kymərlıç] *adj* wretched; (*dürftig*) needy

Kümmerling ['kymərlıŋ] *m* (-s;-e) stunted animal; stunted plant

kümmern ['kymərn] *tr* trouble, worry; concern ǁ *ref*—sich k. um worry about; take care of; sich nicht k. um not bother about; neglect

Kümmernis ['kymərnıs] *f* (-;-se) worry, trouble

kum'mervoll *adj* grief-stricken

Kumpan [kum'pan] *m* (-s;-e) companion; buddy

Kumpel ['kumpəl] *m* (-s;-) buddy, sidekick; (min) miner

kund [kunt] *adj* known

kündbar ['kyntbar] *adj* (*Vertrag*) terminable; (fin) redeemable

Kunde ['kundə] *m* (-n;-n) customer; übler K. (fig) tough customer ǁ *f* (-;) news, information; lore

-kunde *f comb.fm.* -ology; -graphy; science of; guide to, study of

Kun'dendienst *m* customer service; warranty service

Kun'denkreis *m* clientele

kund'geben §80 *tr* make known, announce

Kundgebung ['kuntgebuŋ] *f* (-;-en) manifestation; (pol) rally

kundig ['kundıç] *adj* well-informed; k. sein (*genit*) know

-kundig *comb.fm.* well versed in; able to

kündigen ['kyndıgən] *tr* (*Vertrag*) give notice to terminate; (*Wohnung*) give notice to vacate; (*Stellung*) give notice of quitting; (*Kapital*) call in; (*Hypothek*) foreclose on; j-m fristlos k. (coll) sack s.o. ǁ *intr* (*dat*) given notice to, release

Kün'digung *f* (-;-en) (*seitens des Arbeitnehmers*) resignation; (*seitens des Arbeitgebers*) notice (*of termination*); mit monatlicher K. subject to a month's notice

Kün'digungsfrist *f* period of notice

kund'machen *tr* make known, announce

Kund'machung *f* (-;-en) announcement

Kund'schaft *f* (-;) clientele, customer(s); (mil) reconnaissance

kundschaften ['kuntʃaftən] *intr* go on reconnaissance, scout

Kund'schafter *m* (-s;-) scout, spy

kund'tun §154 *tr* make known, announce

kund'werden §159 *intr* (SEIN) become known

künftig ['kynftıç] *adj* future, to come, next ǁ *adv* in the future, from now on

künf'tighin' *adv* from now on, hereafter

Kunst [kʊnst] *f* (-;-̈e) art; skill; das ist keine K. it's easy

Kunstbanause [ˈkʊnstbanauzə] *m* (-n; -n) philistine

Kunst'dünger *m* chemical fertilizer

Künstelei [kʏnstəˈlaɪ] *f* (-;-en) affectation

Kunst'faser *f* synthetic fiber

Kunst'fehler *m*—ärztlicher K. malpractice

kunst'fertig *adj* skillful, skilled

Kunst'flieger *m* stunt pilot

Kunst'flug *m* stunt flying

Kunst'freund –in §8 *mf* art lover; patron of the arts

Kunst'gegenstand *m* objet d'art

kunst'gerecht *adj* skillful; expert

Kunst'gewerbe *n* arts and crafts

Kunst'glied *n* artificial limb

Kunst'griff *m* trick

Kunst'händler –in §6 *mf* art dealer

Kunst'kenner –in §6 *mf* art connoisseur

Kunst'laufen *n* figure skating

Künstler –in [ˈkʏnstlər(ɪn)] §6 *mf* artist; performer

künstlerisch [ˈkʏnstlərɪʃ] *adj* artistic

künstlich [ˈkʏnstlɪç] *adj* artificial; (chem) synthetic

Kunst'liebhaber –in §6 *mf* art lover

kunst'los *adj* unaffected

Kunst'maler –in §6 *mf* painter, artist

Kunst'pause *f* pause for effect

kunst'reich *adj* ingenious

Kunst'reiter *m* equestrian

Kunst'seide *f* rayon

Kunst'springen *n* (sport) diving

Kunst'stoff *m* plastic material; synthetic material; (tex) synthetic fiber

Kunststoff- *comb.fm.* plastic; plastics

Kunst'stopfen *n* invisible mending

Kunst'stück *n* trick, feat

Kunst'tischler *m* cabinet maker

Kunstverständige [ˈkʊnstfɛrʃtɛndɪgə] §5 *mf* art expert

kunst'voll *adj* elaborate, ornate

Kunst'werk *n* work of art

kunterbunt [ˈkʊntərbʊnt] *adj* chaotic

Kupfer [ˈkʊpfər] *n* (-s) copper

kupfern [ˈkʊpfərn] *adj* copper

kupieren [kuˈpiːrən] *tr* (*Schwanz, Ohren*) cut off; (*Spielkarten*) cut; (*Fahrkarten*) punch

Kuppe [ˈkʊpə] *f* (-;-n) top, summit

Kuppel [ˈkʊpəl] *f* (-;-n) cupola

Kuppelei [kʊpəˈlaɪ] *f* (-s) procuring

kuppeln [ˈkʊpəln] *tr* couple, connect ‖ *intr* be a pimp; be a procuress; (aut) operate the clutch

Kuppler [ˈkʊplər] *m* (-s;-) pimp

Kupplerin [ˈkʊplərɪn] *f* (-;-nen) procuress

Kupplung [ˈkʊplʊŋ] *f* (-;-en) (aut) clutch; (rr) coupling

Kur [kur] *f* (-;-en) cure (*at a spa*); j–n in die Kur nehmen give s.o. a talking to

Kuratel [kuraˈtel] *f* (-;-en) guardianship; j–n unter K. stellen appoint a guardian for s.o.

Ku·rator [kuˈratɔr] *m* (-s;-ratoren [raˈtoːrən]) (*e-s Museums*) curator; (educ) trustee; (jur) guardian

Kurato·rium [kuraˈtoːrjʊm] *n* (-s;-rien [rjən]) (educ) board of trustees

Kurbel [ˈkʊrbəl] *f* (-;-n) crank, handle, winch

Kurbelei [kʊrbəˈlaɪ] *f* (-;-en) shooting a film; (aer) dogfight

Kur'belgehäuse *n* (aut) crankcase

kurbeln [ˈkʊrbəln] *tr* crank; (*Film*) shoot ‖ *intr* engage in a dogfight

Kur'belstange *f* (mach) connecting rod

Kur'belwelle *f* (mach) crankshaft

Kürbis [ˈkʏrbɪs] *m* (-ses;-se) pumpkin; (*Kopf*) (sl) bean

küren [ˈkyːrən] §165 & §109 *tr* elect

Kurfürst [ˈkʊrfʏrst] *m* (-en;-en) elector (*of the Holy Roman Empire*)

Kur'haus *n* spa; hotel

Kurie [ˈkuːrjə] *f* (-;-n) (eccl) curia

Kurier [kuˈriːr] *m* (-s;-e) courier

kurieren [kuˈriːrən] *tr* cure

kurios [kuˈrjoːs] *adj* odd, curious

Kuriosität [kurjozɪˈtɛt] *f* (-;-en) quaintness; curio, curiosity

Kur'ort *m* health resort, spa

Kurpfuscher [ˈkʊrpfuʃər] *m* (-s;-) quack

Kurrentschrift [kuˈrɛntʃrɪft] *f* cursive script

Kurs [kʊrs] *m* (-es;-e) (educ) course; (fin) rate of exchange; (fin) circulation; (naut) course; (st. exch.) price; außer K. setzen take out of circulation; hoch im K. stehen be at a premium; (fig) rate high; zum Kurse von at the rate of

Kurs'bericht *m* (st. exch.) market report

Kurs'buch *n* (rr) timetable

Kürschner [ˈkʏrʃnər] *m* (-s;-) furrier

Kurs'entwicklung *f* price trend

Kurs'gewinn *m* (st. exch.) gain

kursieren [kʊrˈziːrən] *intr* circulate

Kursive [kʊrˈziːvə] *f* (-;), **Kursivschrift** [kʊrˈzɪf/rɪft] *f* (-s) italics

Kurs'stand *m* (st. exch.) price level

Kur·sus [ˈkʊrzʊs] *m* (-;-se [zə]) (educ) course

Kurs'veränderung *f* (fin) change in exchange rates; (naut) change of course; (pol) change of policy; (st. exch.) price change

Kurs'wert *m* (st. exch.) market value

Kurve [ˈkʊrvə] *f* (-;-n) curve; in die K. gehen (aer) bank

kurz [kʊrts] *adj* (kürzer [ˈkʏrtsər]; kürzeste [ˈkʏrtsəstə] §9) short, brief; auf das kürzeste very briefly; binnen kurzem within a short time; in kurzem before long; k. und gut in a word; seit kurzem for the last few days or weeks; über k. oder lang sooner or later; zu k. kommen (coll) get the short end of it ‖ *adv* shortly; briefly; curtly

kurzatmig [ˈkʊrtsatmɪç] *adj* shortwinded; (*Pferd*) broken-winded

Kürze [ˈkʏrtsə] *f* (-;) shortness; brevity; in K. shortly; briefly

kürzen [ˈkʏrtsən] *tr* shorten; (*Gehalt*) cut; (math) reduce

kurzerhand' *adv* offhand

Kurz'fassung *f* abridged version

Kurz'film *m* (cin) short

kurzfristig ['kurtsfrɪstɪç] *adj* short-term

Kurz'geschichte *f* short story

kurzlebig ['kurtslebɪç] *adj* short-lived

kürzlich ['kʏrtslɪç] *adj* lately, recently

Kurz'meldung *f* news flash

Kurz'nachrichten *pl* news summary

kurz'schließen §76 *tr* short-circuit

Kurz'schluß *m* short circuit

Kurz'schlußbrücke *f* (elec) jumper

Kurz'schrift *f* shorthand

kurz'sichtig *adj* near-sighted; (fig) short-sighted

Kurz'streckenlauf *m* sprint

Kurz'streckenläufer **-in** §6 *mf* sprinter

kurzum' *adv* in short, in a word

Kür'zung *f* (-;-en) reduction; curtailment; (*e-s Buches*) abridgment

Kurz'waren *pl* sewing supplies

kurz'weg *adv* bluntly, flatly

Kurzweil ['kurtsvail] *f* (-;) pastime

kurzweilig ['kurtsvailɪç] *adj* amusing

kusch [kuʃ] *interj* lie down! (*to a dog*)

kuschen ['kuʃən] *ref* lie down; crouch || *intr* lie down; crouch, cringe; (*Person*) knuckle under, submit

Kusine [ku'zinə] *f* (-;-n) female cousin

Kuß [kus] *m* (**Kusses; Küsse**) kiss; **kalter K.** popsicle

küssen ['kʏsən] *tr & intr* kiss

Kuß'hand *f*—**j**—**m e**—**e K. zuwerfen** throw s.o. a kiss; **mit K. with** pleasure

Küste ['kʏstə] *f* (-;-n) coast, shore

Kü'stenfahrer *m* coasting vessel

Kü'stenfischerei *f* inshore fishing

Kü'stengewässer *n* coastal waters

Kü'stenlinie *f* coastline, shoreline

kü'stennah *adj* offshore; coastal

Kü'stenschiffahrt *f* coastal shipping

Kü'stenstreife *f* shore patrol

Küster ['kʏstər] *m* (-s;-) sexton

Kustos ['kustos] *m* (-; **Kustoden** [kus-'todən]) custodian

Kutsche ['kutʃə] *f* (-;-n) coach

Kut'scher *m* (-s;-) coachman

kutschieren [ku'tʃirən] *intr* drive a coach || *intr* (SEIN) ride in a coach

Kutte ['kutə] *f* (-;-n) (eccl) cowl

Kutteln ['kutəln] *pl* tripe

Kutter ['kutər] *m* (-s;-) (naut) cutter

Kuvert [ku'vert] *n* (-s;-s) & (-[-e]s;-e) envelope; table setting

kuvertieren [kuver'tirən] *tr* put into an envelope

Kux [kuks] *m* (-es;-e) mining share

Kyklon [ky'klon] *m* (-s;-e) cyclone

Kyniker ['kynikər] *m* (-s;-) (philos) cynic

L

L, l [ɛl] *invar n* L, l

laben ['labən] *tr* refresh

Labial [la'bjal] *m* (-s;-e) labial

labil [la'bil] *adj* unstable

Labor [la'bor] *n* (-s;-s) (coll) lab

Laborant [labo'rant] (ɪn) §7 *mf* laboratory technician

Laborato·rium [labora'torjum] *n* (-s; **rien** [rjən]) laboratory

laborieren [labo'rirən] *intr* experiment; **l. an** (*dat*) suffer from

Labsal ['lapzal] *n* (-[e]s;-e) refreshment

La'bung *f* (-;-en) refreshment

Labyrinth [laby'rint] *n* (-[e]s;-e) labyrinth

Lache ['laxə] *f* (-;-n) puddle, pool; laugh; **e-e gellende L. anschlagen** break out in laughter

lächeln ['lɛçəln] *intr* (über *acc*) smile (at) || **Lächeln** *n* (-s;) smile; **höhnisches L.** sneer

lachen ['laxən] *intr* laugh; **daß ich nicht lache!** don't make me laugh! || **Lachen** *n* (-s;) laugh, laughter; **du hast gut L.!** you can laugh!

lächerlich ['lɛçərlɪç] *adj* ridiculous; **l. machen** ridicule; **sich l. machen** make a fool of oneself

lachhaft ['laxhaft] *adj* ridiculous

Lachkrampf ['laxkrampf] *m* fit of laughter

Lachs [laks] *m* (-es;-e) salmon

Lachsalve ['laxzalvə] *f* (-;-n) peal of laughter

Lachs'schinken *m* raw, lightly smoked ham

Lack [lak] *m* (-[e]s;-e) lacquer, varnish

Lackel ['lakəl] *m* (-s;-) (coll) dope

lackieren [la'kirən] *tr* lacquer, varnish; (*Autos*) paint

Lack'leder *n* patent leather

Lackmuspapier ['lakmuspapir] *n* litmus paper

Lack'schuhe *pl* patent-leather shoes

Lade ['ladə] *f* (-;-n) box, case; (*Schublade*) drawer

La'dearbeiter *m* loader

La'debaum *m* derrick

La'defähigkeit *f* loading capacity

La'dehemmung *f* jamming (*of a gun*); **L. haben** jam

La'deklappe *f* tailgate

La'deluke *f* (naut) hatch

laden ['ladən] §103 *tr* load; (*Gast*) invite; (elec) charge; (jur) summon; **geladen sein** (coll) be burned up || **Laden** *m* (-s;-) store, shop; (*Fenster-*) shutter; **den L. schmeißen** pull it off, lick it

La'dendieb *m*, **La'dendiebin** *f* shoplifter

La'dendiebstahl *m* shoplifting

La'denhüter *m* drug on the market

La'deninhaber **-in** §6 *mf* shopkeeper

La'denkasse *f* till

La'denmädchen *n* salesgirl

La'denpreis *m* retail price

La'denschluß *m* closing time

La′denschwengel m (pej) stupid shop clerk
La′dentisch m counter
La′derampe f loading platform
La′deschein m bill of lading
La′destock m ramrod
La′destreifen m cartridge clip
La′dung f (-;-en) loading; load; (Güter) freight; (elec) charge; (jur) summons; (mil) charge; (naut) cargo
Lafette [la′fetə] f (-;-n) gun mount
Laffe [′lafə] m (-n;-n) jazzy dresser
lag [lɑk] pret of liegen
Lage [′lɑgə] f (-;-n) site, location; situation; (Zustand) condition, state; (Haltung) posture; (Schicht) layer, deposit; (Salve) volley; (Bier) round; (bb) quire; (mil) position; (mus) pitch; mißliche L. predicament; versetzen Sie sich in meine L. put yourself in my position
Lager [′lɑgər] n (-s;-) bed; (e-s Wildes) lair; (Stapelplatz) dump; (Partei) side, camp; (von Waffen) cache; (Vorrat) stock; (Warenlager) stockroom; (geol) stratum, vein; (mach) bearing; (mil) camp; auf L. in stock; (fig) up one's sleeve; ein L. halten von keep stock of
La′geraufnahme f inventory
La′gerbier n lager beer
La′gerfähigkeit f shelf life
La′gerfeuer n campfire
La′gergebühr f storage charges
La′gerhalter m stock clerk
La′gerhaus n warehouse
Lagerist –in [lɑgə′rɪst(ɪn)] §7 mf warehouse clerk
La′gerleben n camp life
lagern [′lɑgərn] tr lay down; (Waren) stock, store; (altern) season; (mach) mount on bearings || ref lie down, rest || intr lie down, rest; (Waren) be stored; (Wein) season; (geol) be deposited; (mil) camp
La′gerort m, **La′gerplatz** m resting place; (Stapelplatz) dump; (mil) camp site
La′gerraum m storeroom, stockroom
La′gerstand m stock on hand, inventory
La′gerstätte f, **La′gerstelle** f resting place; (geol) deposit; (mil) camp site
La′gerung f (-;-en) storage; (Alterung) seasoning; (geol) stratification
La′gervorrat m stock, supply
Lagune [la′gunə] f (-;-n) lagoon
lahm [lɑm] adj lame; paralyzed || Lahme §5 mf paralytic
lahmen [′lɑmən] intr be lame, limp
lähmen [′lɛmən] tr paralyze; (Verkehr) tie up; (fig) cripple
lahm′legen tr cripple, paralyze; (mil) neutralize
Läh′mung f (-;-en) paralysis
Laib [laɪp] m (-[e]s;-e) loaf
Laich [laɪç] m (-[e]s;-e) spawn
laichen [′laɪçən] intr spawn
Laie [′laɪə] m (-n;-n) layman; **Laien** laity
Lai′enbruder m lay brother
lai′enhaft adj layman's
Lakai [la′kaɪ] m (-en;-en) lackey

Lake [′lɑkə] f (-;-n) brine, pickle
Laken [′lɑkən] n (-s;-) sheet
lakonisch [la′konɪʃ] adj laconic
Lakritze [la′krɪtsə] f (-;-n) licorice
Lakune [la′kunə] f (-;-n) lacuna
lallen [′lalən] tr & intr stammer
lamellenförmig [la′mɛlənfœrmɪç] adj laminate
lamentieren [lamen′tirən] intr wail
Lametta [la′meta] n (-s;) tinsel
Lamm [lam] n (-[e]s;¨er) lamb
Lamm′braten m roast lamb
Lämmerwolke [′lɛmərvolkə] f cirrus
Lamm′fleisch n (culin) lamb
lamm′fromm′ adj meek as a lamb
Lampe [′lampə] f (-;-n) lamp; light
Lam′penfieber n stage fright
Lam′penschirm m lamp shade
Lampion [lam′pjõ] m (-s;-s) Chinese lantern
lancieren [lã′sirən] tr launch, promote; (Kandidaten) (pol) groom
Land [lant] n (-[e]s;¨er & -e) land; (Ackerboden) ground, soil; (Staat) country; (Provinz) state; (Gegensatz: Stadt) country; ans L. ashore; auf dem Lande in the country; aufs L. into the country; aus aller Herren Ländern from everywhere; über Landes gehen go abroad; zu Lande by land
Land′arbeiter m farm hand
Land′armee f land forces
Land′bau m farming, agriculture
Land′besitz m landed property
Land′besitzer –in §6 m landowner
Landebahn [′landəban] f runway
Landedeck [′landədɛk] n flight deck
Land′edel·mann m (-es;-leute) country gentleman
Landefeuer [′landəfɔɪ·ər] n runway lights
land′einwärts adv inland
Landekopf [′landəkɔpf] m beachhead
landen [′landən] tr & intr (SEIN) land
Land′enge f isthmus, neck of land
Landeplatz [′landəplats] m wharf; (aer) landing field
Länderei [lɛndə′raɪ] f (-;-en) or **Ländereien** pl lands, estates
Länderkunde [′lɛndərkundə] f geography
Landes– [landəs] comb.fm. national, native, of the land
Lan′desaufnahme f land survey
Lan′desbank f national bank
Lan′desbeschreibung f topography
lan′deseigen adj state-owned
Lan′deserzeugnis n domestic product
Lan′desfarben pl national colors
Lan′desfürst m sovereign
Lan′desgesetz n law of the land
Lan′desherr m sovereign
Lan′desherrschaft f, **Lan′deshoheit** f sovereignty
Lan′dessprache f vernacular
Lan′destracht f national costume
Lan′destrauer f public mourning
lan′desüblich adj customary
Lan′desvater m sovereign
Lan′desverrat m high treason
Lan′desverräter –in §6 mf traitor
Lan′desverteidigung f national defense

Land/flucht f rural exodus
land/flüchtig adj exiled, fugitive
Land/friedensbruch m disturbance of the peace
Land/gericht n district court, superior court
Land/gewinnung f land reclamation
Land/gut n country estate
Land/haus n country house
Land/jäger m rural policeman; (culin) sausage
Land/junker m country squire
Land/karte f map
Land/kreis m rural district
land/läufig adj customary
Ländler ['lɛntlər] m (-s;-) waltz
Land/leute pl country folk
ländlich ['lɛntliç] adj rural, rustic
Land/luft f country air
Land/macht f land forces
Land/mann m (-[e]s;-leute) farmer
Land/marke f landmark (for travelers and sailors)
Land/maschinen pl farm machinery
Land/messer m surveyor
Land/partie f outing, picnic
Land/plage f nation-wide plague; (coll) big nuisance
Land/rat m regional governor
Land/ratte f (fig) landlubber
Land/recht n common law
Land/regen m steady rain
Land/rücken m ridge
Land/schaft f (-;-en) landscape, scenery; (Bezirk) district, region
land/schaftlich adj scenic; regional
Landser ['lantsər] m (-s;-) G.I.
Lands/knecht m mercenary
Lands/mann m (-[e]s;-leute) fellow countryman
Land/spitze f promontory
Land/straße f highway
Land/streicher m (-s;-) tramp, hobo
Land/strich m tract of land
Land/sturm m home guard
Land/tag m state assembly
landumschlossen ['lantumʃlɔsən] adj landlocked
Lan/dung f (-;-en) landing
Lan/dungsboot n landing craft
Lan/dungsbrücke f jetty, pier
Lan/dungsgestell n landing gear
Lan/dungssteg m gangplank
Land/vermessung f surveying
Land/volk n country folk
Land/weg m overland route
Land/wehr f militia, home guard
Land/wirt m farmer
Land/wirtschaft f agriculture; L. betreiben farm
land/wirtschaftlich adj farm, agricultural
Land/zunge f spit of land
lang [laŋ] adj (länger ['lɛŋər]; längste ['lɛŋstə] §9) long; (Person) tall || adv—die ganze Woche l. all week; e-e Stunde l. for an hour
langatmig ['laŋatmɪç] adj long-winded
lang/beinig adj long-legged
lange ['laŋə] adv long, a long time; es ist noch l. nicht fertig it is far from ready; schon l. her long ago; schon l. her, daß a long time since;

so l. bis until; so l. wie as long as; wie l.? how long?
Länge ['lɛŋə] f (-;-n) length; long syllable; (geog) longitude; (pros) quantity; auf die L. in the long run; der L. nach lengthwise; in die L. ziehen drag out
langen ['laŋən] tr reach, hand; j-m eine l. (coll) give s.o. a smack || intr be enough; l. nach reach for || impers—es langt mir l I have enough; jetzt langt's mir aber! I've had it!
Län/gengrad m degree of longitude
Län/genkreis m meridian
Län/genmaß n linear measure
Lan/geweile f boredom; sich [dat] die L. vertreiben (coll) kill time
Lang/finger m pickpocket
langfingerig ['laŋfɪŋərɪç] adj (fig) thievish
langfristig ['laŋfrɪstɪç] adj long-term
lang/jährig adj long-standing
Lang/lauf m crosscountry skiing
langlebig ['laŋlebɪç] adj long-lived
Lang/lebigkeit f (-;) longevity
lang/legen ref lie down, stretch out
länglich ['lɛŋlɪç] adj oblong
läng/lichrund adj oval, elliptical
Lang/mut f patience
lang/mütig adj patient
Lang/mütigkeit f patience
längs [lɛŋs] prep (genit or dat) along
langsam ['laŋzam] adj slow
Lang/spielplatte f long-playing record
längst [lɛŋst] adv long since, long ago
längstens ['lɛŋstəns] adv at the latest; (höchstens) at the most
Langstrecken— comb.fm. long-range; (sport) long-distance
langweilen ['laŋvailən] tr bore || ref feel bored
Lang/weiler m (-s;-) slowpoke
langweilig ['laŋvailɪç] adj boring
langwierig ['laŋviːrɪç] adj lengthy
Lanolin [lano'lin] n (-s;) lanolin
Lanze ['lantsə] f (-;-n) lance, spear
Lan/zenstechen n (-s;) jousting
Lanzette [lan'tsetə] f (-;-n) lancet
Lappalie [la'paljə] f (-;-n) trifle
Lappen ['lapən] m (-s;-) rag; washrag; (Flicken) patch; (anat) lobe
läppisch ['lɛpɪʃ] adj silly, trifling
Lappland ['laplant] n (-s;) Lapland
Lärche ['lɛrçə] f (-;-n) (bot) larch
Lärm [lɛrm] m (-[e]s;) noise; L. schlagen (fig) make a fuss
lärmen ['lɛrmən] intr make noise
lär/mend adj noisy
Larve ['larfə] f (-;-n) mask; larva
las [las] pret of lesen
lasch [laʃ] adj limp; (Speise) insipid
Lasche ['laʃə] f (-;-n) (Klappe) flap; (Schuh-) tongue; (rr) fishplate
lasieren [la'ziːrən] tr glaze
lassen ['lasən] §104 tr let; (erlauben) allow; (bewirken) have, make; leave (behind, undone, open, etc.); den Film entwickeln l. have the film developed; etw fallen l. drop s.th.; ich kann es nicht l. I can't help it; j-n warten l. keep s.o. waiting; kommen l. send for; laß den Lärm! stop

the noise!; **laß es!** cut it out!; **laßt uns gehen** let us go; **sein Leben l.** lose one's life; **sein Leben l. für** sacrifice one's life for || *rej*—**das läßt sich denken** I can imagine; **das läßt sich hören!** now you're talking!; **es läßt sich nicht beschreiben** it defies description; **es läßt sich nicht leugnen, daß** it cannot be denied that; **sich** [*dat*] **Zeit l.** take one's time

lässig ['lɛsɪç] *adj* (*faul*) lazy; (*träge*) sluggish; (*nachlässig*) remiss

Läs'sigkeit *f* (–;) laziness; negligence

läßlich ['lɛslɪç] *adj* venial

Last [last] *f* (–;-en) load, weight; (*Bürde*) burden; (*Hypotek*) encumbrance; (*aer, naut*) cargo, freight; **j–m etw zur L. legen** blame s.o. for s.th.; **L. der Beweise** weight of evidence; **ruhende L.** dead weight; **zur L. fallen** (*dat*) become a burden for

Last'auto *n* truck

lasten ['lastən] *intr* (auf *dat*) weigh (on)

la'stenfrei *adj* unencumbered

La'stensegler *m* transport glider

Laster ['lastər] *m* (–s;-) (coll) truck || *n* (–s;-) vice

Lästerer -in ['lɛstərər(ɪn)] §6 *mf* slanderer; blasphemer

la'sterhaft *adj* vicious

La'sterleben *n* life of vice

lästerlich ['lɛstərlɪç] *adj* slanderous; blasphemous

Lästermaul ['lɛstərmaul] *n* scandalmonger

lästern ['lɛstərn] *tr* slander; blaspheme

Lä'sterung *f* (–;-en) slander; blasphemy

lästig ['lɛstɪç] *adj* troublesome; **j–m l. fallen** bother s.o.

Last'kahn *m* barge

Last'kraftwagen *m* truck

Last'schrift *f* (acct) debit

Last'tier *n* beast of burden

Last'träger *m* porter

Last'wagen *m* truck

Last'zug *m* tractor-trailer (*consisting of several trailers*)

Lasur [la'zur] *f* (–;) glaze

Latein [la'taɪn] *n* (–s;) Latin

lateinisch [la'taɪnɪʃ] *adj* Latin

Laterne [la'tɛrnə] *f* (–;-n) lantern; lamp

Latrine [la'trinə] *f* (–;-n) latrine

Latri'nenparole *f* scuttlebut

Latsche ['latʃə] *f* (–;-n) (coll) slipper || ['lat/ə] *f* (–;-n) (bot) dwarf pine

latschen ['latʃən] *intr* (SEIN) shuffle along

Latte ['latə] *f* (–;-n) lath

Lat'tenkiste *f* crate

Lat'tenzaun *m* picket fence

Lattich ['latɪç] *n* (–[e]s;-e) lettuce

Latz [lats] *m* (–es;̈-e) bib; (*Klappe*) flap; (*Schürzenlatz*) pinafore

Lätzchen ['lɛtsçən] *n* (–s;-) bib

lau [lau] *adj* lukewarm; (*Wetter*) mild; (fig) half-hearted

Laub [laup] *n* (–[e]s;) foliage

Laub'baum *m* deciduous tree

Laube ['laubə] *f* (–;-n) arbor; (*Säulen-*

gang) portico; (*Bogengang*) arcade; (theat) box

Lau'bengang *m* arcade

Laub'säge *f* fret saw

Laub'sägearbeit *f* fretwork

Laub'werk *n* foliage

Lauer ['lau.ər] *f* (–;) ambush; **auf der L. liegen** lie in wait

lauern ['lau.ərn] *intr* lurk; **l. auf** (*acc*) lie in wait for, watch for

lau'ernd *adj* (*Blick*) wary; (*Gefahr*) lurking

Lauf [lauf] *m* (–[e]s;̈-e) running; run; (*e-s Flusses*) course; (*Strömung*) current; (*Wettlauf*) race; (*e-s Gewehrs*) barrel; (astr) path, orbit; **den Dingen freien L. lassen** let things take their course; **im Laufe der Zeit** in the course of time; **im vollen Laufe** at full speed

Lauf'bahn *f* career; (astr) orbit; (sport) lane

Lauf'bursche *m* errand boy; office boy

laufen ['laufən] §105 *intr* (SEIN) run; (*zu Fuß gehen*) walk; (*leck sein*) leak; (*Zeit*) pass; **die Dinge l. lassen** let things slide; **j–n l. lassen** let s.o. go; (*straflos*) let s.o. off

lau'fend *adj* (*ständig*) steady; (*Jahr, Preis*) current; (*Nummern*) consecutive; (*Wartung, Geschäft*) routine; (*Meter, usw.*) running; **auf dem laufenden** up to date; **laufendes Band** conveyor belt; assembly line

Läufer ['loɪfər] *m* (–s;-) runner; (*Teppich*) runner; (chess) bishop; (fb) halfback; (mach) rotor; (mus) run

Lauferei ['laufə'raɪ] *f* (–;-en) running around

Lauf'feuer *n* (–s;) wildfire

Lauf'fläche *f* tread (on tire)

Lauf'gewicht *n* sliding weight

Lauf'gitter *n* playpen

Lauf'graben *m* trench

läufig ['loɪfɪç] *adj* in heat

Läu'figkeit *f* (–;) heat

Lauf'junge *m* errand boy; office boy

Lauf'kran *m* (mach) traveling crane

Lauf'kunde *m* chance customer

Lauf'masche *f* run (in stocking)

lauf'maschenfrei *adj* runproof

Lauf'paß *m* (coll) walking papers; (coll) brush-off

Lauf'planke *f* gangplank

Lauf'rad *n* (*e-r Turbine*) rotor; (aer) landing wheel

Lauf'schritt *m* double-quick time

Lauf'steg *m* footbridge

Laufställchen ['laufʃtɛlçən] *n* (–s;-) playpen

Lauf'zeit *f* rutting season; (*e-s Vertrags*) term; (cin) running time; (mach) (service) life

Lauge ['laugə] *f* (–;-n) lye; (*Salzlauge*) brine; (*Seifenlauge*) suds

Lau'gensalz *n* alkali

lau'gensalzig *adj* alkaline

Laune ['launə] *f* (–;-n) mood, humor; (*Grille*) whim

lau'nenhaft *adj* capricious

launig ['launɪç] *adj* humorous, witty

lau'nisch *adj* moody

Laus [laus] *f* (–;̈-e) louse

Laus′bub *m* rascal

lauschen [′lauʃən] *intr* listen; eavesdrop; **l. auf** (*acc*) listen to

Lau′scher –in §6 *mf* eavesdropper

lauschig [′lauʃɪç] *adj* cosy, peaceful

Lau′sebengel *m*, **Lau′sejunge** *m*, **Lau′sekerl** *m* (coll) rascal, brat

lausen [′lauzən] *tr* pick lice from; **ich denke, mich laust der Affe** (coll) I couldn't believe my eyes

lausig [′lauzɪç] *adj* lousy

laut [laut] *adj* loud; (*lärmend*) noisy; **l. werden** become public; **l. werden lassen** divulge || *prep* (*genit & dat*) according to; (com) as per; **l. Bericht** according to the report || **Laut** *m* (–[e]s; –e) sound

Laute [′lautə] *f* (–; –n) lute

lauten [′lautən] *intr* sound; (*Worte*) read, go, say; **das Urteil lautet auf Tod** the sentence is death

läuten [′lɔɪtən] *tr & intr* ring, toll || *impers*—**es läutet** the bell is ringing || **Läuten** *n* (–s;) toll

lauter [′lautər] *adj* pure; (*aufrecht*) sincere || *invar adj* (*nichts als*) nothing but

Lau′terkeit *f* (–;) purity; sincerity

läutern [′lɔɪtərn] *tr* purify; (*Metall, Zucker*) refine; (*veredeln*) ennoble

Laut′gesetz *n* phonetic law

Laut′lehre *f* phonetics, phonology

laut′lich *adj* phonetic

Laut′los *adj* soundless

Laut′malerei *f* onomatopoeia

Laut′schrift *f* phonetic spelling

Laut′sprecher *m* loudspeaker

Laut′sprecheranlage *f* public address system

Laut′sprecherwagen *m* sound truck

Laut′stärke *f* volume

Laut′stärkeregler *m* volume control

Laut′system *n* phonetic system

Laut′zeichen *n* phonetic symbol

lau′warm *adj* lukewarm

Lava [′lava] *f* (–;) lava

Lavendel [la′vɛndəl] *m* (–s;) (bot) lavender

laven′delfarben *adj* lavender

lavieren [la′virən] *intr* (fig) maneuver; (naut) tack

Lawine [la′vinə] *f* (–;–n) avalanche

lax [laks] *adj* lax

Lax′heit *f* (–;) laxity

Laxiermittel [la′ksirmɪtəl] *n* laxative

Layout [′le·aut] *n* (–s;–s) layout

Lazarett [latsa′rɛt] *n* (–[e]s;–e) (mil) hospital

Lebedame [′lebədamə] *f* woman of leisure

Lebehoch [lebə′hox] *n* (–s;–s) cheer; toast; **ein dreimaliges L.** three cheers

Lebemann [′lebəman] *m* playboy

leben [′lebən] *tr & intr* live || **Leben** *n* (–s;–) life; existence; **am L. bleiben** survive; **am L. erhalten** keep alive; **ins L. rufen** bring into being; **sein L.** lang all his life; **ums L. kommen** lose one's life

lebendig [le′bɛndɪç] *adj* living, alive; (*lebhaft*) lively; (*Darstellung*) vivid

Le′bensalter *n* age, period of life

Le′bensanschauung *f* outlook on life

Le′bensart *f* manners

Le′bensaufgabe *f* mission in life

Le′bensbaum *m* (bot) arbor vitae

Le′bensbedingungen *pl* living conditions

Le′bensbeschreibung *f* biography

Le′bensdauer *f* life span

Le′benserwartung *f* life expectancy

le′bensfähig *adj* viable

Le′bensfrage *f* vital question

Le′bensgefahr *f* mortal danger

Le′bensgefährlich *adj* perilous

Le′bensgefährte *m*, **Le′bensgefährtin** *f* life companion, spouse

le′bensgroß *adj* life-size

Le′benshaltung *f* standard of living

Le′benshaltungskosten *pl* cost of living

Le′bensinteressen *pl* vital interests

Le′benskraft *f* vitality

Le′benskünstler *m*—**er ist ein L.** nothing can get him down

lebenslänglich [′lebənslɛŋlɪç] *adj* life

Le′benslauf *m* curriculum vitae

Le′bensmittel *pl* groceries

Le′bensmittelgeschäft *n* grocery store

Le′bensmittelkarte *f* food ration card

Le′bensmittellieferant *m* caterer

le′bensmüde *adj* weary of life

le′bensnotwendig *adj* vital, essential

Le′bensprozeß *m* vital function

Le′bensstandard *m* standard of living

Le′bensstellung *f* lifetime job; tenure

Le′bensstil *m* life style

Le′bensunterhalt *m* livelihood

le′bensuntüchtig *adj* impractical

Le′bensversicherung *f* life insurance

Le′benswandel *m* conduct; life

Le′bensweise *f* way of life

Le′bensweisheit *f* worldly wisdom

le′benswichtig *adj* vital, essential

Le′benszeichen *n* sign of life

Le′benszeit *f* lifetime; **auf L.** for life

Leber [′lebər] *f* (–s;–n) liver; **frei von der L. weg reden** speak frankly

Le′berfleck *m* mole

Leberkäs [′lebərkɛs] *m* (–es;) meat loaf (*made with liver*)

Le′bertran *m* cod-liver oil

Lebewesen [′lebəvezən] *n* living being

Lebewohl [lebə′vol] *n* (–[e]s;–e) farewell

lebhaft [′lephaft] *adj* lively; full of life; (*Farbe*) bright; (*Straße*) busy; (*Börse*) brisk; (*Interesse*) keen

Lebkuchen [′lepkuxən] *m* gingerbread

leblos [′leplos] *adj* lifeless

Lebtag [′leptak] *m*—**mein L.** in all my life

Lebzeiten [′leptsaɪtən] *pl*—**zu meinen L.** in my lifetime

lechzen [′lɛçtsən] *intr* (nach) thirst (for)

leck [lɛk] *adj* leaky || **Leck** *n* (–[e]s;–e) leak; **ein L. bekommen** spring a leak

lecken [′lɛkən] *tr* lick || *intr* leak; (naut) have sprung a leak

lecker [′lɛkər] *adj* dainty; (*köstlich*) delicious

Leckerbissen (Lek′kerbissen) *m* delicacy, dainty

Leckerei [lɛkə′raɪ] *f* (–;–en) daintiness; sweets

leckerhaft (lek′kerhaft) *adj* dainty

Leckermaul (Lek'kermaul) n—ein L. sein have a sweet tooth

Leder ['leder] n (-s;) leather

ledern ['ledern] adj leather; (fig) dull, boring

ledig ['ledɪç] adj single; (Kind) illegitimate; **l.** (genit) free of; **lediger Stand** single state; celibacy

le'diglich adv merely, only

leer [ler] adj empty, void; (fig) vain || **Leere** f (-;) emptiness, void; vacuum || n—**der Schlag ging ins L.** the blow missed; **ins L. starren** stare into space

leeren ['lerən] tr empty

Leer'gut n empties (bottles, cases)

Leer'lauf m (aut) idling, idle; (Gang) (aut) neutral

leer'laufen §105 intr (SEIN) idle

leer'stehend adj unoccupied, vacant

Leer'taste f (typ) space bar

legal [le'gɑl] adj legal

legalisieren [legalɪ'zirən] tr legalize

Legat [le'gɑt] m (-en;-en) legate || n (-[e]s;-e) legacy, bequest

legen ['legən] tr lay, put; **auf die Kette l.** chain, tie up; **j-m ans Herz l.** recommend warmly to s.o.; **Nachdruck l. auf** (acc) emphasize; **Wert l. auf** (acc) attach importance to || ref lie down; go to bed; (Wind) die down; **die Krankheit hat sich ihm auf die Lungen gelegt** his sickness affected his lungs

legendär [le'gɑt] adj legendary

Legende [le'gendə] f (-;-n) legend

legieren [le'girən] tr alloy

Legie'rung f (-;-en) alloy

Legion [le'gjon] f (-;-en) legion

Legionär [legjo'ner] m (-s;-e) legionnaire, legionary

legislativ [legɪsla'tif] adj legislative || **Legislative** [legɪsla'tivə] f (-;-n) legislature

Legis·lator [legɪs'lɑtor] m (-s;-latoren [la'torən]) legislator

Legislatur [legɪsla'tur] f (-;-en) legislature

legitim [legɪ'tim] adj legitimate

Legitimation [legɪtɪma'tsjon] f (-;-en) proof of identity

legitimieren [legɪtɪ'mirən] tr legitimize; (berechtigen) authorize || ref prove one's identity

Lehen ['le-ən] n (-s;-) (hist) fief

Le'hensherr m liege lord

Le'hens·mann m (-[e]s;-leute) vassal

Lehm [lem] m (-[e]s;-e) clay, loam

lehmig ['lemɪç] adj clayey, loamy

Lehne ['lenə] f (-;-n) support; (e-s Stuhls) arm, back; (Abhang) slope

lehnen ['lenən] tr, ref & intr lean

Lehnsessel ['lenzesəl] m, **Lehnstuhl** ['len/tul] m armchair, easy chair

Lehn'wort ['lenvort] n (-[e]s;≈er) loan word

Lehramt ['leramt] n teaching profession; professorship

Lehranstalt ['leran/talt] f educational institution

Lehrbrief ['lerbrif] m apprentice's diploma

Lehrbube ['lerbubə] m apprentice

Lehrbuch ['lerbux] n textbook

Lehrbursche ['lerbur/ə] m apprentice

Lehre ['lerə] f (-;-n) doctrine, teaching; (Wissenschaft) science; (Theorie) theory; (Unterweisung) instruction; (Warnung) lesson; (e-r Fabel) moral; (Richtschnur) rule, precept; (e-s Lehrlings) apprenticeship; (tech) gauge; **in der L. sein** be serving one's apprenticeship

lehren ['lerən] tr teach, instruct

Lehrer -in ['lerər(ɪn)] §6 mf teacher

Leh'rerbildungsanstalt f teacher's college

Leh'rerkollegium n teaching staff

Lehrfach ['lerfax] n subject

Lehrfilm ['lerfɪlm] m educational film

Lehrgang ['lergaŋ] m (educ) course

Lehrgedicht ['lergədɪçt] n didactic poem

Lehrgegenstand ['lergegən/tant] m (educ) subject

Lehrgeld ['lergelt] n—**L. zahlen** (fig) learn the hard way

lehrhaft ['lerhaft] adj didactic

Lehrjunge ['lerjuŋə] m apprentice

Lehrkörper ['lerkörpər] m teaching staff; faculty (of a university)

Lehrling ['lerlɪŋ] m (-s;-e) apprentice

Lehrmädchen ['lermetçən] n girl apprentice

Lehrmeister ['lermaɪstər] m master, teacher, instructor

Lehrmittel ['lermɪtəl] n teaching aid

Lehrplan ['lerplan] m curriculum

lehrreich ['lerraɪç] adj instructive

Lehrsaal ['lerzɑl] m lecture hall

Lehrsatz ['lerzats] m (eccl) dogma; (math) theorem

Lehrspruch ['ler/prux] m maxim

Lehrstelle ['ler/telə] f position as an apprentice

Lehrstoff ['ler/tɔf] m subject matter

Lehrstuhl ['ler/tul] m (educ) chair

Lehrstunde ['ler/tundə] f lesson

Lehrzeit ['lertsaɪt] f apprenticeship

Leib [laɪp] m (-[e]s;-er) body; (Bauch) belly, abdomen; (Taille) waist; (Mutterleib) womb; **am ganzen L. zittern** tremble all over; **bleib mir nur damit vom Leibe!** (coll) don't bother me with that; **e-n harten L. haben** be constipated; **gesegneten Leibes** with child; **L. und Leben** life and limb; **mit L. und Seele** through and through; **sich** [dat] **j-n vom Leibe halten** keep s.o. at arm's length; **zu Leibe gehen** (dat) tackle (s.th.), attack (s.o.)

Leib'arzt m personal physician

Leib'binde f sash

Leibchen ['laɪpçən] n (-s;-) bodice; vest

leib'eigen adj in bondage || **Leibeigene** §5 mf serf

Leib'eigenschaft f (-;) serfdom, bondage

Lei'besbeschaffenheit f (-;-en) constitution

Lei'beserbe m (-n;-n) offspring

Lei'beserziehung f physical education

Lei'besfrucht f fetus

Lei'beskräfte pl—**aus Leibeskräften**

schreien scream at the top of one's lungs
Lei′besübungen pl physical education
Lei′besvisitation f body search
Leib′garde f bodyguard
Leibgardist [ˈlaɪpgardɪst] m (-en;-en) bodyguard
Leib′gericht n favorite dish
leibhaft(ig) [ˈlaɪphaft(ɪç)] adj incarnate, real
leib′lich adj bodily, corporal; **leiblicher Vetter** first cousin; **sein leiblicher Sohn** his own son
Leib′rente f annuity for life
Leib′schmerzen pl, **Leib′schneiden** n abdominal pains
Leibstandarte [ˈlaɪpʃtandartə] f (-;-n) (hist) SS bodyguard
Leib′wache f bodyguard
Leib′wäsche f underwear
Leiche [ˈlaɪçə] f (-;-n) corpse, body; carcass; (dial) funeral
Leichenbegängnis [ˈlaɪçənbɛgɛŋnɪs] n (-ses;-se) funeral, interment
Leichenbeschauer [ˈlaɪçənbəʃau·ər] m (-s;-) coroner
Leichenbestatter [ˈlaɪçənbəʃtatər] m (-s;-) undertaker
Lei′chenbittermiene f woe-begone look
Leichenfledderer [ˈlaɪçənfledərər] m (-s;-) body stripper
Lei′chengift n ptomaine poison
lei′chenhaft adj corpse-like
Lei′chenhalle f mortuary
Lei′chenöffnung f autopsy
Lei′chenräuber m body snatcher
Lei′chenrede f eulogy
Lei′chenschau f post mortem
Lei′chenschauhaus n morgue
Lei′chenstarre f rigor mortis
Lei′chenträger m pallbearer
Lei′chentuch n shroud
Lei′chenverbrennung f cremation
Lei′chenwagen m hearse
Lei′chenzug m funeral cortege
Leichnam [ˈlaɪçnam] m (-[e]s;-e) corpse
leicht [laɪçt] adj light; (nicht schwierig) easy; (gering) slight; **leichten Herzens** light-heartedly
Leicht′atletik f track and field
Leicht′bauweise f lightweight construction
Leicht′benzin n cleaning fluid
leichtbeschwingt [ˈlaɪçtbəʃvɪŋt] adj gay
leicht′blütig adj light-hearted
leicht′entzündlich adj highly flammable
Leichter [ˈlaɪçtər] m (-s;-) (naut) lighter
leicht′fertig adj frivolous, flippant; careless
leicht′flüchtig adj highly volatile
leicht′flüssig adj fluid
Leicht′gewicht n lightweight division
Leichtgewichtler [ˈlaɪçtgəvɪçtlər] m (-s;-) lightweight boxer
leicht′gläubig adj gullible
leicht′hin′ adv lightly, casually
Leich′tigkeit f (-;) ease
leichtlebig [ˈlaɪçtlebɪç] adj easygoing
Leicht′sinn m frivolity, irresponsibility;

(Sorglosigkeit) carelessness; (Unbedachtsamkeit) imprudence
leicht′sinnig adj frivolous, irresponsible
leicht′verdaulich adj easy to digest
leicht′verderblich adj perishable
leid [laɪt] adj—er tut mir l. I feel sorry for him; **es tut mir l., daß I** am sorry that; **es ist (or tut) mir l.** um I feel sorry for, I regret; **ich bin es l.** I'm fed up with it ‖ **Leid** n (-[e]s;) (Betrübnis) sorrow; (Schaden) harm; (Unrecht) wrong; **j-m ein L. antun** harm s.o.
Leideform [ˈlaɪdefɔrm] f (gram) passive voice
leiden [ˈlaɪdən] §106 tr suffer; (ertragen) stand ‖ intr (an dat) suffer (from) ‖ **Leiden** n (-s;-) suffering; (Krankheit) ailment
Lei′denschaft f (-;-en) passion
lei′denschaftlich adj passionate
lei′denschaftslos adj dispassionate
Lei′densgefährte m, **Lei′densgefährtin** f fellow sufferer
Lei′densgeschichte f tale of woe; (relig) Passion
Lei′densweg m way of the cross
leider [ˈlaɪdər] adv unfortunately
leiderfüllt [ˈlaɪterfʏlt] adj sorrowful
leidig [ˈlaɪdɪç] adj tiresome
leidlich [ˈlaɪtlɪç] adv tolerable; (halbwegs gut) passable ‖ adv so-so
leidtragend [ˈlaɪttragənt] adj in mourning ‖ **Leidtragende** §5 mf mourner; **er ist der L. dabei** he is the one that suffers for it
Leid′wesen n—**zu meinem L.** to my regret
Leier [ˈlaɪ·ər] f (-;-n) (mus) lyre
Lei′erkasten m hand organ, hurdygurdy
Lei′ermann m (-[e]s;ᵘer) organ grinder
leiern [ˈlaɪ·ərn] tr (winden) crank; (Gebete, Verse) drone ‖ intr drone
Leih- [laɪ] comb.fm. loan, rental
Leih′amt n, **Leih′anstalt** f loan office
Leih′bibliothek f rental library
leihen [ˈlaɪ·ən] tr lend, loan out; (entleihen) (von) borrow (from)
Leih′gebühr f rental fee
Leih′haus n pawnshop
Leim [laɪm] m (-[e]s;-e) glue; birdlime; **aus dem L. gehen** fall apart; **j-m auf den L. gehen** be taken in by s.o.
leimen [ˈlaɪmən] tr glue; (betrügen) take in, fool
Leim′farbe f distemper
leimig [ˈlaɪmɪç] adj gluey
Lein [laɪn] m (-[e]s;-e) flax
Leine [ˈlaɪnə] f (-;-n) line, cord; (Hunde-) leash
Leinen [ˈlaɪnən] n (-s;-) linen
Lei′neneinband m (-[e]s;ᵘe) (bb) cloth binding
Lei′nenschuh m sneaker, canvas shoe
Lei′nenzeug n linen fabric
Lein′öl n linseed oil
Lein′tuch n sheet
Lein′wand f linen cloth; canvas; (cin) screen
leise [ˈlaɪzə] adj soft, low; (sanft) gentle; (gering) faint; (Schlaf) light

lei'sestellen *tr* (rad) turn down
Lei'setreter *m* (-s;-) pussyfoot
Leiste ['laɪstə] *f* (-;-n) (*Rand*) border; (anat) groin; (carp) molding
leisten ['laɪstən] *tr* do, perform, accomplish; (*Dienst*) render; (*Eid*) take; (*Abbitte, Hilfe, Widerstand*) offer; **Bürgschaft l. für** put up bail for; **Folge l.** (*dat*), **Gehorsam l.** (*dat*) obey; **Genüge l.** (*dat*) satisfy; **j-m Gesellschaft l.** keep s.o. company; **sich** [*dat*] **etw l. können** be able to afford s.th. || **Leisten** *m* (-s;-) last; **alles über e-n L. schlagen** (fig) be undiscriminating
Lei'stenbruch *m* hernia, rupture
Lei'stung *f* (-;-en) performance; efficiency; ability; feat, achievement; (*Ergebnis*) result; (*Erzeugung*) production; (*Abgabe, Ausstoß*) output; (*Beitrag*) contribution; (*Dienstleistungen*) services rendered; (elec) power, wattage; (indust) output, production; (insur) benefits; (mach) capacity
Lei'stungsanreiz *m* incentive
lei'stungsfähig *adj* (*Person*) efficient; (*Motor*) powerful; (*Fabrik*) productive; (phys) efficient
Lei'stungsfähigkeit *f* efficiency; proficiency; (*e-s Autos*) performance; (*e-s Motors*) power; (mach) output
lei'stungsgerecht *adj* based on merit
Lei'stungsgrenze *f* peak of performance
Leis'tungslohn *m* pay based on performance
Lei'stungszulage *f* bonus
Leit- [laɪt] *comb.fm.* leading, dominant, guiding
Leit'artikel *m* editorial
Leit'bild *n* (good) example, ideal
leiten ['laɪtən] *tr* lead, guide; (*Verkehr*) route; (*Betrieb*) direct, run; (*Versammlung*) preside over; (arti) direct; (elec, mus, phys) conduct
Lei'ter *m* (-s;-) leader; director; (educ) principal; (elec, mus) conductor || *f* (-;-n) ladder
Lei'terin *f* (-;-nen) leader; director
Leit'faden *m* manual, guide
Leit'fähigkeit *f* conductivity
Leit'gedanke *m* main idea, main theme
Leit'hammel *m* (fig) boss, leader
Leit'motiv *n* keynote; (mus) leitmotiv
Leit'satz *m* basic point
Leit'spruch *m* motto
Leit'stelle *f* head office
Leit'stern *m* polestar, lodestar
Lei'tung *f* (-;-en) direction, guidance; (*Beaufsichtigung*) management; (*Rohr*) pipeline; (*für Gas, Wasser*) main; (elec) lead; (phys) conduction; (telp) line; **e-e lange L. haben** be rather dense; **L. besetzt!** line is busy!
Lei'tungsdraht *m* (elec) lead
Lei'tungsmast *m* telephone pole
Lei'tungsnetz *n* (elec) power lines
Lei'tungsrohr *n* pipe, main
Lei'tungsvermögen *n* conductivity
Lei'tungswasser *n* tap water
Leit'werk *n* (aer) tail assembly
Leit'zahl *f* code number

Lektion [lɛk'tsjon] *f* (-;-en) lesson; (fig) lecture, rebuke
Lek·tor ['lɛktər] *m* (-s;-toren ['torən]) lecturer; (*e-s Verlags*) reader
Lektüre [lɛk'tyrə] *f* (-;) reading matter, literature
Lende ['lɛndə] *f* (-;-n) loin; (*Hüfte*) hip
Len'denbraten *m* roast loin, sirloin
len'denlahm *adj* stiff; (*Ausrede*) lame
Len'denschurz *m* loincloth
Len'denstück *n* tenderloin, sirloin
lenkbar ['lɛŋkbar] *adj* manageable; steerable, maneuverable; **lenkbares Luftschiff** dirigible
lenken ['lɛŋkən] *tr* guide, control; (*Wagen*) drive; (*wenden*) turn; (*steuern*) steer; **Aufmerksamkeit l. auf** (*acc*) call attention to
Len'ker **-in** §6 *mf* ruler; (aut) driver
Lenkrad ['lɛŋkrat] *n* steering wheel
Lenksäule ['lɛŋkzɔɪlə] *f* steering column
Lenkstange ['lɛŋk/taŋə] *f* handlebar; (aut) connecting rod
Len'kung *f* (-;-en) guidance, control; (aut) steering mechanism
Lenz [lɛnts] *m* (-es;-e) (fig) prime of life; (poet) spring
Lenz'pumpe *f* bilge pump
Lepra ['lepra] *f* (-;) leprosy
Lerche ['lɛrçə] *f* (-;-n) (orn) lark
lernbegierig ['lɛrnbəgiriç] *adj* eager to learn, studious
lernen ['lɛrnən] *tr & intr* learn; study
Lesart ['lezart] *f* version
lesbar ['lezbar] *adj* legible; readable
Lesbierin ['lɛsbi·ərin] *f* (-;-nen) lesbian
lesbisch ['lɛsbɪʃ] *adj* lesbian; **lesbische Liebe** lesbianism
Lese ['lezə] *f* (-;-n) gathering, picking; (*Wein-*) vintage
Lese- ['lezə] *comb.fm.* reading; lecture
Le'sebrille *f* reading glasses
Le'sebuch *n* reader
Le'sehalle *f* reading room
lesen ['lezən] §107 *tr* read; gather; (*Messe*) say || *intr* read; lecture; **l. über** (*acc*) lecture on
le'senswert *adj* worth reading
Le'seprobe *f* specimen from a book; (theat) reading rehearsal
Le'ser **-in** §6 *mf* reader; picker
Le'seratte *f* (coll) bookworm
le'serlich *adj* legible
Le'serzuschrift *f* letter to the editor
Le'sestoff *m* reading matter
Le'sezeichen *n* bookmark
Le'sung *f* (-;-en) reading
Lette ['lɛtə] *m* (-n;-n), **Lettin** ['lɛtin] *f* (-;-nen) Latvian
lettisch ['lɛtɪʃ] *adj* Latvian
Lettland ['lɛtlant] *n* (-[e]s;) Latvia
letzte ['lɛtstə] §9 *adj* last; (*endgültig*) final, ultimate; (*neueste*) latest; (*Ausweg*) last; **bis ins l.** to the last detail; **in den letzten Jahren** in recent years; **in der letzten Zeit** lately; **letzten Endes** in the final analysis || **Letzte** §5 *pron* last, last one; **am Letzten** on the last of the month; **sein Letztes hergeben** do one's ut-

most; **zu guter Letzt** finally, last but not least

letztens ['lɛtstəns] adv lately

letztere ['lɛtstərə] §5 mfn latter

letzthin [lɛtst'hɪn] adv lately

letztlich ['lɛtstlɪç] adv lately, recently; in the final analysis

letztwillig ['lɛtstvɪlɪç] adj testamentary

Leucht– [lɔɪçt] comb.fm. luminous; illuminating

Leucht'bombe f flare bomb

Leuchte ['lɔɪçtə] f (–;–n) light, lamp; lantern; (fig) luminary

leuchten ['lɔɪçtən] intr shine

leuch'tend adj shining, bright; luminous

Leuchter ['lɔɪçtər] m (–s;–) candlestick; chandelier

Leucht'farbe f luminous paint

Leucht'feuer n (aer) flare; (naut) beacon

Leucht'käfer m lightning bug

Leucht'körper m light bulb; light fixture

Leucht'kugel n tracer bullet; flare

Leucht'pistole f Very pistol

Leucht'rakete f (aer) flare

Leucht'reklame f neon sign

Leucht'röhre f fluorescent lamp

Leucht'spurgeschoß n tracer bullet

Leucht'turm m lighthouse

Leucht'zifferblatt n luminous dial

leugnen ['lɔɪgnən] tr deny; disclaim

Leukoplast [lɔɪko'plast] n (–[e]s;–e) adhesive tape

Leumund ['lɔɪmʊnt] m (–[e]s;) reputation

Leu'mundszeugnis n character reference

Leute ['lɔɪtə] pl people, persons, men; (Dienstleute) servants

Leu'teschinder m oppressor; slave driver

Leutnant ['lɔɪtnant] m (–s;–s) lieutenant

Leut'priester m secular priest

leut'selig adj affable

Lexikograph [lɛksiko'graf] m (–en;–en) lexicographer

Lexikon ['lɛksikɔn] n (–s;–s) encyclopedia

Libanon ['libanɔn] n (–s;) Lebanon

Libelle [li'bɛlə] f (–;–n) dragonfly; (carp) level

liberal [libe'ral] adj liberal

Liberalismus [libera'lɪsmʊs] m (–s;) liberalism

Libyen ['liby·ən] n (–s;) Libya

licht [lɪçt] adj light, bright; (durchsichtig) clear ‖ **Licht** n (–[e]s;–er) light; (Kerze) candle

licht'beständig adj non-fading

Licht'bild n photograph

Licht'bildervortrag m illustrated lecture

licht'blau adj light-blue

Licht'blick m (fig) bright spot

Licht'bogen m (elec) arc

Licht'bogenschweißung f arc welding

Licht'brechung f (–;–en) refraction of light

Licht'druck m phototype

licht'durchlässig adj translucent

licht'echt adj non-fading

licht'empfindlich adj sensitized; **l. machen** sensitize

Licht'empfindlichkeit f (phot) speed

lichten ['lɪçtən] tr clear; thin; (Anker) weigh

lichterloh ['lɪçtərlo] adv ablaze; **l. brennen** be ablaze

Licht'hof m (archit) light well, inner court; (phot) halo

Licht'kegel m beam of light

Licht'maschine f generator, dynamo

Licht'pause f blueprint

Licht'punkt m (fig) ray of hope

Licht'schacht m light well

Licht'schalter m light switch

licht'scheu adj—**lichtscheues Gesindel** shady characters

Licht'schirm m lamp shade

Licht'seite f (fig) bright side

Licht'spiele pl, **Licht'spielhaus** n, **Licht'spieltheater** n movie theater

licht'stark adj (Objektiv) high-powered; (phot) high-speed

Lich'tung f (–;–en) clearing

Lid [lit] n (–[e]s;–er) eyelid

Lid'schatten m eye shadow

lieb [lip] adj dear; (nett) nice; **der liebe Gott** the good Lord; **es ist mir l., daß** I am glad that; **seien Sie so l. und** please; **sich lieb Kind machen bei** ingratiate oneself with

lieb'äugeln intr—**l. mit** (& fig) flirt with

Liebchen ['lipçən] n (–s;–) darling

Liebe ['libə] f (–;) (zu) love (for, of)

liebedienerisch ['libədinəriʃ] adj fawning

Liebelei [libə'laɪ] f (–;–en) flirtation

lieben ['libən] tr love, be fond of

lie'bend adj loving ‖ adv—**l. gern** gladly ‖ **Liebende** §5 mf lover

lie'benswert adj lovable

lie'benswürdig adj lovable; charming; **das ist sehr l. von Ihnen** that's very kind of you

lieber ['libər] adv rather, sooner; **l. haben** prefer

Liebes– [libəs] comb.fm. love, of love

Lie'besdienst m favor, good turn

Lie'beserlebnis n romance

Lie'besgabe f charitable gift

Lie'beshandel m love affair

Lie'besmahl n love feast

Lie'besmühe f—**verlorene L.** wasted effort

Lie'bespaar n couple (of lovers)

Lie'bespfand n token of love

Lie'bestrank m love potion

Lie'besbewerben n advances

lie'bevoll adj loving, affectionate

Lieb'frauenkirche f Church of Our Lady

lieb'gewinnen §121 tr grow fond of

lieb'haben §89 tr love, be fond of

Liebhaber ['liphabər] m (–s;–) lover, beau; amateur; fan, buff; **erster L.** leading man

lieb'kosen tr caress, fondle

lieb'lich adj lovely, sweet; charming

Liebling ['liplɪŋ] m (–s;–e) darling; (Haustier) pet; (Günstling) favorite

Lieblings– comb.fm. favorite

Lieb'lingsgedanke *m* pet idea
Lieb'lingswunsch *m* dearest wish
lieb'los *adj* unkind
lieb'reich *adj* kind, affectionate
Lieb'reiz *m* charm, attractiveness
lieb'reizend *adj* charming
Lieb'schaft *f* (-;-en) love affair
liebste ['lipstə] §9 *adj* favorite; **am liebsten trinke ich Wein** I like wine best of all
Lied [lit] *n* (-[e]s;-er) song; **er weiß ein L. davon zu singen** he can tell you all about it; **geistliches L.** hymn
liederlich ['lidərlɪç] *adj* dissolute; (*unordentlich*) disorderly
lief [lif] *pret of* **laufen**
Lieferant -in [lifə'rant(ɪn)] §7 *mf* supplier; (*Verteiler*) distributor; (*von Lebensmitteln*) caterer
Lieferauto ['lifərauto] *n* delivery truck
lieferbar ['lifərbar] *adj* available, deliverable
Liefergebühr ['lifərgə'byr] *f* delivery charge
liefern ['lifərn] *tr* deliver; (*beschaffen*) supply, furnish; (*Ertrag*) yield; **ich bin geliefert** (coll) I'm done for
Lieferschein ['lifərʃain] *m* delivery receipt
Lie'ferung *f* (-;-en) delivery, shipment; supply; (*e-s Werkes*) installment, number; **zahlbar bei L.** cash on delivery
Lieferwagen ['lifərvagən] *m* delivery truck
Liege ['ligə] *f* (-;-n) couch
Lie'gekur *f* rest cure
liegen ['ligən] §108 *intr* lie, be situated; **gut auf der Straße l.** hug the road; **l. an** (*dat*) lie near; (fig) be due to; **wie die Sache jetzt liegt** as matters now stand ‖ *impers*—**es liegt an ihm zu** (*inf*) it's up to him to (*inf*); **es liegt auf der Hand it is** obvious; **es liegt mir nichts daran** it doesn't matter to me; **es liegt mir (sehr viel) daran** it matters (a great deal) to me
lie'genbleiben §62 *intr* (SEIN) stay in bed; (*Waren*) remain unsold; (*stekkenbleiben*) have a breakdown; (*Arbeit*) be left undone
lie'genlassen §104 *tr* let lie; leave alone; (*Arbeit*) leave undone
Lie'genschaft *f* (-;-en) real estate
Lie'gestuhl *m* deck chair
Lie'gestütz *m* (gym) pushup
lieh [li] *pret of* **leihen**
ließ [lis] *pret of* **lassen**
Li-ga ['liga] *f* (-;-gen [gən]) league
Liguster [lɪ'gustər] *m* (-s;-) privet
liieren [lɪ'irən] *ref*—**sich l. mit** ally oneself with
Likör [lɪ'kør] *m* (-s;-e) liqueur
lila ['lila] *adj* lilac
Lilie ['liljə] *f* (-;-n) lily
Limonade [limo'nadə] *f* (-;-n) soft drink, soda
lind [lɪnt] *adj* mild, gentle
Linde ['lɪndə] *f* (-;-n) (bot) linden
lindern ['lɪndərn] *tr* alleviate; (*Übel*) mitigate; (*mildern*) soften

Lindwurm ['lɪntvurm] *m* dragon
Lineal [line'al] *n* (-s;-e) ruler
Linguist -in [lɪŋgu'ıst(ɪn)] §7 *mf* linguist
Linie ['linjə] *f* (-;-n) line; **auf gleicher L. mit** on a level with; **in erster L.** in the first place
Li'nienpapier *n* lined paper
Li'nienrichter *m* (sport) linesman
Li'nienschiff *n* ship of the line
li'nientreu *adj*—**l. sein** follow the party line
linieren [lɪ'nirən] *tr* line, rule
linke ['lɪŋkə] §9 *adj* left; (*Seite*) wrong, reverse ‖ §5 **Linke** *m* (box) left ‖ §5 *f* left side; left hand; **die L.** (pol) the left
linkisch ['lɪŋkɪʃ] *adj* clumsy, awkward
links [lɪŋks] *adv* left; to the left; on the left; (*verkehrt*) inside out; **l. liegenlassen** bypass, ignore; **links um!** left, face!
links'drehend *adj* counterclockwise
linksgängig ['lɪŋksgɛnıç] *adj* counterclockwise
Linkshänder ['lɪŋkshendər] *m* (-s;-) left-hander
links'läufig *adj* counterclockwise
links'stehend *adj* (pol) leftist
Linnen ['lɪnən] *n* (-s;) linen
Linse ['lɪnzə] *f* (-;-n) (bot) lentil; (opt) lens
Lippe ['lɪpə] *f* (-;-n) lip; **e-e L. riskieren** (fig) speak out of turn
Lip'penbekenntnis *n* lip service
Lip'penlaut *m* labial
Lip'penstift *m* lipstick
liquid [lɪ'kvit] *adj* (*Geldmittel*) liquid; (*Gesellschaft*) solvent
Liquidation [lɪkvɪda'tsjon] *f* (-;-en) liquidation; (*Kostenrechnung*) bill
liquidieren [lɪkvɪ'dirən] *tr* liquidate; (*Geschäft*) wind up; (*Honorar*) charge
lispeln ['lɪspəln] *tr & intr* lisp; (*flüstern*) whisper
Lissabon [lɪsa'bon] *n* (-s;) Lisbon
List [lɪst] *f* (-;-en) cunning; trick
Liste ['lɪstə] *f* (-;-n) list; **schwarze L.** blacklist
Li'stenwahl *f* block voting
listig ['lɪstɪç] *adj* cunning, sly
Litanei [lɪta'nai] *f* (-;-en) litany
Litauen ['litau-ən] *n* (-s;) Lithuania
litauisch ['litau-ɪʃ] *adj* Lithuanian
Liter ['litər] *m & n* (-s;-) liter
literarisch [lɪtə'rarıʃ] *adj* literary
Literatur [lɪtera'tur] *f* (-;-en) literature
Litfaßsäule ['lɪtfaszorlə] *f* advertising pillar
Litur-gie [lɪtur'gi] *f* (-;-gien ['gi-ən]) liturgy
Litze ['lɪtsə] *f* (-;-n) cord; (elec) strand
Li-vree [lɪ'vre] *f* (-;-vreen ['vre-ən]) uniform, livery
Lizenz [li'tsents] *f* (-;-en) license
Lob [lop] *n* (-[e]s;) praise
loben ['lobən] §109 *tr* praise
lo'benswert *adj* praiseworthy
Lobhudelei [lophudə'lai] *f* (-;-en) flattery

lob′hudeln tr heap praise on

löblich ['lØplɪç] adj commendable

lob′preisen tr extol, praise

Lob′rede f panegyric

Loch [lɔx] n (-es;ːer) hole

Loch′bohrer m auger

lochen ['lɔxən] tr punch, perforate

Locher ['lɔxər] m (-s;-) punch

löcherig ['lœçərɪç] adj full of holes

Loch′karte f punch card

Lo′chung f (-;-en) perforation

Locke ['lɔkə] f (-;-n) lock, curl

locken ['lɔkən] tr allure, entice; decoy; (*Hund*) whistle to

locker ['lɔkər] adj loose; (*nicht straff*) slack; spongy; (*moralisch*) loose

lockern ['lɔkərn] tr loosen

lockig ['lɔkɪç] adj curly, curled

Lock′mittel n, **Lock′speise** f (& fig) bait

Lockspitzel ['lɔk′pɪtsəl] m stoolpigeon

Lo′ckung f (-;-en) allurement

Lock′vogel m (& fig) decoy

Loden ['lodən] m (-s;-) coarse woolen cloth

lodern ['lodərn] intr blaze; (fig) glow

Löffel ['lœfəl] m (-s;-) spoon; (*culin*) spoonful; (*coll & hunt*) ear; **über den L. balbieren** hoodwink

Löf′felbagger m power shovel

löffeln ['lœfəln] tr spoon out

log [lok] pret of lügen

Logbuch ['lɔkbux] n logbook

Loge ['loʒə] f (-;-n) (*der Freimaurer*) lodge; (*theat*) box

Lo′genbruder m freemason

Logierbesuch [lo′ʒirbəzux] m houseguest(s)

logieren [lo′ʒirən] intr (**bei**) stay (**with**)

Logik ['logɪk] f (-;) logic

Logis [lo′ʒi] invar lodgings

logisch ['logɪʃ] adj logical

Lohe ['lo·ə] f (-;-n) blaze, flame

Lohgerber ['logerbər] m (-s;-) tanner

Lohn [lon] m (-[e]s;ːe) pay, wages; (fig) reward

Lohn′abbau m wage cut

lohnen ['lonən] tr compensate, reward; (*Arbeiter*) pay; **j-m etw l.** reward s.o. for s.th.; **|| ref** be worthwhile

löhnen ['lØnən] tr pay, pay wages to

Lohn′erhöhung f raise, wage increase

Lohn′gefälle n wage differential

Lohn′herr m employer

lohn′intensiv adj with high labor costs

Lohn′liste f payroll

Lohn′satz m pay rate

Lohn′stopp m wage freeze

Lohn′tag m payday

Lohn′tüte f pay envelope

Löh′nung f (-;-en) payment

lokal [lo′kal] adj local **|| Lokal** n (-[e]s;-e) locality, premises; (*Wirtshaus*) restaurant, pub, inn

lokalisieren [lokalɪ′zirən] tr localize

Lokalität [lokalɪ′tet] f (-;-en) locality

Lokomotive [lokomo′tivə] f (-;-n) locomotive

Lokomotiv′führer m (rr) engineer

Lokus ['lokus] m (-;-se) (coll) john

Lorbeer ['lɔrbər] m (-s;-en) laurel

los [los] adj loose; **es ist etw los** there is s.th. going on; **es ist nichts los** there is nothing going on; **etw los haben** have s.th. on the ball; **j-n** (or **etw**) **los sein** be rid of s.o. (or s.th.); **los!** go on!; scram!; (*spricht*) fire away!; (*mach schnell*) let's go!; (sport) play ball!; **mit ihm ist nicht viel los** he's no great shakes; **was ist los?** what's the matter? **|| Los** n (-[e]s;-e) lot; (*Lotterie-*) ticket; (*Anteil*) portion; (*Schicksal*) fate; **das Große Los** first prize; **das Los ziehen** draw lots; **die Lose sind gefallen** the die is cast

los- comb.fm. un-, e.g., **losmachen** undo

los′arbeiten tr extricate **|| ref** get loose, extricate oneself **|| intr** (**auf** acc) work away (at)

losbar ['lØsbar] adj solvable

los′binden §59 tr loosen, untie

los′brechen §64 tr break off **|| intr** (SEIN) break loose

Löschblatt ['lœʃblat] n blotter

Löscheimer ['lœʃaɪmər] m fire bucket

löschen ['lœʃən] tr put out; (*Durst*) quench; (*Schuld*) cancel; (*Schrift*) blot; (*Bandaufnahme*) erase; (*Firma*) liquidate; (*Hypotek*) pay off; (naut) unload

Lö′scher m (-s;-) blotter; (*Feuer-*) fire extinguisher

Löschgerät ['lœʃgəret] n fire extinguisher

Löschmannschaft ['lœʃmanʃaft] f fire brigade

Löschpapier ['lœʃpapir] n blotting paper

Lö′schung f (-;-en) extinction; (*Tilgung*) cancellation; (naut) unloading

los′drehen tr unscrew, twist off

los′drücken tr fire **|| intr** pull the trigger

lose ['lozə] §9 adj loose

Lösegeld ['lØzəgelt] n ransom

loseisen ['losaɪzən] tr—**Geld l. von** wangle money out of; **j-n l. aus** get s.o. out of; **j-n l. von** get s.o. away from **|| ref** (**von**) worm one's way (out of)

losen ['lozən] intr draw lots

lösen ['lØzən] tr loosen, untie; (*abtrennen*) sever; (*Bremse*) release; (*Fahrkarte*) buy; (*loskaufen*) ransom; (*lossprechen*) absolve; (*Rätsel*) solve; (*Schuß*) fire; (*Verlobung*) break off **|| ref** come loose, come undone; dissolve; (*sich befreien*) free oneself

los′fahren §71 intr (SEIN) drive off; **l. auf** (acc) head for; rush at; attack (verbally)

los′gehen §82 intr (SEIN) (coll) begin; (*Gewehr*) go off; (*sich lösen*) come loose; **auf j-n l.** attack s.o.

los′haken tr unhook

los′kaufen tr ransom

los′ketten tr unchain

los′kommen §99 intr (SEIN) come loose, come off; **ich komme nicht davon los** I can't get over it; **l. von** get away from; get rid of

los′lachen intr burst out laughing

los'lassen §104 *tr* let go; release; den Hund l. auf (*acc*) sic the dog on

los'legen *intr* (coll) start up, let fly; (*reden*) (coll) open up; leg los! (coll) fire away!

löslich ['løsliç] *adj* soluble

los'lösen *tr* detach

los'machen *tr* undo, untie; (*freimachen*) free || *ref* disengage onself

los'platzen *intr* (SEIN) burst out laughing; l. mit blurt out

los'reißen §53 *tr & ref* break loose

los'sagen *ref*—**sich l. von** renounce

los'schlagen §132 *tr* knock off; (*verkaufen*) dispose of, sell cheaply || *intr* open the attack; l. auf (*acc*) let fly at

los'schnallen *tr* unbuckle

los'schrauben *tr* unscrew

los'sprechen §64 *tr* absolve

los'steuern *intr*—**l. auf** (*acc*) head for

Lo'sung *f* (-;-en) (*Kot*) dung; (mil) password; (pol) slogan

Lö'sung *f* (-;-en) solution

Lö'sungsmittel *n* solvent; thinner

los'werden §159 *tr* (SEIN) get rid of

los'ziehen §163 *intr* (SEIN) set out, march away; l. auf (*acc*) talk about, run down

Lot [lot] *n* (-[e]s;-e) plummet; plumb line; (*Lötmetall*) solder; (geom) perpendicular; im Lot perpendicular; (fig) in order; ins Lot bringen (fig) set right

Löteisen ['løtaɪzən] *n* soldering iron

loten ['lotən] *tr* (naut) plumb || *intr* (naut) take soundings

löten ['løtən] *tr* solder

Lötkolben ['løtkɔlbən] *m* soldering iron

Lötlampe ['løtlampə] *f* blowtorch

Lötmetall ['løtmetal] *n* solder

lot'recht *adj* perpendicular

Lotse ['lotsə] *m* (-n;-n) (aer) air traffic controller; (naut) pilot

lotsen ['lotsən] *tr* (*Flugzeuge*) guide in; (naut) pilot

Lotte·rie [lotə'ri] *f* (-;-rien ['ri·ən]) lottery, sweepstakes

Lotterie'los *n* lottery ticket

lotterig ['lotəriç] *adj* sloppy

Lotterleben ['lotərlebən] *n* dissolute life

Lotto ['lɔto] *n* (-s;-s) state-owned numbers game

Löwe ['løvə] *m* (-n;-n) lion

Lö'wenanteil *m* lion's share

Lö'wenbändiger **-in** §6 *mf* lion tamer

Lö'wengrube *f* lion's den

Lö'wenmaul *n* (bot) snapdragon

Lö'wenzahn *m* (bot) dandelion

Löwin ['løvɪn] *f* (-;-nen) lioness

loyal [lo·a'jal] *adj* loyal

Luchs [luks] *m* (-es;-e) lynx

Lücke ['lykə] *f* (-;-n) gap, hole; (*Mangel*) deficiency; (*im Gesetz*) loophole; (*Zwischenraum*) interval; auf L. stehend staggered

Lückenbüßer ['lykənbysər] *m* (-s;-) stop-gap

lückenhaft (lük'kenhaft) *adj* defective, fragmentary

Luder ['ludər] *n* (-s;-) carrion; (coll)

cad; (*Weibsbild*) slut; das arme L.! the poor thing!; dummes L.! fathead!

Lu'derleben *n* dissolute life

ludern ['ludərn] *intr* lead a dissolute life

Luft [luft] *f* (-;̈e) air; (*Atem*) breath; (*Brise*) breeze; die L. ist rein the coast is clear; es ist dicke L. there is trouble brewing; es liegt etw in der L. (fig) there's s.th. in the air; frische L. schöpfen get a breath of fresh air; in die L. fliegen be blown up; in die L. gehen blow one's top; in die L. sprengen blow up; j-n an die L. setzen give s.o. the air; nach L. schnappen gasp for breath; seinem Zorn L. machen give vent to one's anger; tief L. holen take a deep breath

Luft'alarm *m* air-raid alarm

Luft'angriff *m* air raid

Luft'ansicht *f* aerial view

Luft'aufklärung *f* air reconnaissance

Luft'bild *n* aerial photograph

Luft'bremse *f* air brake

Luft'brücke *f* airlift

Lüftchen ['lyftçən] *n* (-s;-) gentle breeze

luft'dicht *adj* airtight

Luft'druck *m* atmospheric pressure; (*e-r Explosion*) blast; (aut) air pressure

Luft'druckbremse *f* air brake

Luft'druckmesser *m* barometer

Luft'druckprüfer *m* tire gauge

Luft'düse *f* air nozzle, air jet

lüften ['lyftən] *tr* air, ventilate; den Hut l. tip one's hat

Luft'fahrt *f* aviation

Luft'fahrzeug *n* aircraft

Luft'flotte *f* air force

luft'förmig *adj* gaseous

Luft'hafen *m* airport

Luft'heizung *f* hot-air heating

Luft'herrschaft *f* air supremacy

Luft'hülle *f* atmosphere

luftig ['luftɪç] *adj* airy; (*windig*) windy; (*Person*) flighty; (*Kleidung*) loosely woven, light

Luftikus ['luftikus] *m* (-;-se) light-headed person

Luft'klappe *f* air valve

luft'krank *adj* airsick

Luft'kurort *m* mountain resort

Luft'landetruppen *pl* airborne troops

luft'leer *adj* vacuous; luftleerer Raum vacuum

Luft'linie *f* beeline; fünfzig Kilometer L. 50 kilometers as the crow flies

Luft'loch *n* vent; (aer) air pocket

Luft'parade *f* flyover

Luft'post *f* airmail

Luft'raum *m* atmosphere; air space

Luft'reifen *m* tire

Luft'reklame *f* sky writing

Luft'röhre *f* (anat) windpipe

Luft'schiff *n* airship

Luft'schiffahrt *f* aviation

Luft'schloß *n* castle in the air

Luft'schutz *m* air-raid protection

Luft'schutzkeller *m* air-raid shelter

Luft'schutzwart *m* air-raid warden

Luft'spiegelung *f* mirage

Luft'sprung m caper
Luft'streitkräfte pl air force
Luft'strom m air current
Luft'strudel m (aer) wash
luft'tüchtig adj air-worthy
Lüf'tung f (-s) airing, ventilation
Luft'veränderung f change of climate
Luft'verkehrsgesellschaft f, **Luft'verkehrslinie** f airline
Luft'vermessung f aerial survey
Luft'verpestung f (-s), **Luft'verschmutzung** f (-s), **Luft'verunreinigung** f (-s) air pollution
Luft'waffe f air force
Luft'warnung f air-raid warning
Luft'weg m air route; **auf dem Luftwege** by air
Luft'widerstand m (phys) air resistance
Luft'zug m draft
Lug [luk] m (-[e]s;) lie; **Lug und Trug** pack of lies
Lüge ['lygə] f (-;-n) lie; **fromme L.** white lie; **j-n Lügen strafen** prove s.o. a liar
lugen ['lugən] intr peep
lügen ['lygən] §111 tr—**das Blaue vom Himmel herunter l.** lie like mad || intr lie, tell a lie
Lügendetek·tor ['lygəndetektər] m (-s; -toren ['torən]) lie detector
Lü'gengeschichte f cock-and-bull story
Lü'gengespinst n, **Lü'gengewebe** n tissue of lies
lü'genhaft adj (Person) dishonest, lying; (Nachricht) untrue
Lügner –in ['lygnər(ın)] §6 mf liar
lügnerisch ['lygnərıʃ] adj dishonest
Luke ['lukə] f (-;-n) (am Dach) dormer window; (naut) hatch
Lümmel ['lYməl] m (-s;-) lout
Lump [lump] m (-en;-en) scoundrel
lumpen ['lumpən] intr lead a wild life; **sich nicht l. lassen** (coll) be generous || **Lumpen** m (-s;-) rag
Lum'pengeld n measly sum; **für ein L.** dirtcheap
Lum'pengesindel n mob, rabble
Lum'penhändler m ragman
Lum'penkerl m (coll) bum
Lum'penpack n rabble, riffraff
Lumperei [lumpə'raɪ] f (-;-en) shady deal; dirty trick; (Kleinigkeit) trifle
lumpig ['lumpıç] adj ragged; shabby

Lunge ['lunə] f (-;-n) lung
Lungen– comb.fm. pulmonary
Lun'genentzündung f pneumonia
Lun'genflügel m lung
lun'genkrank adj consumptive || **Lungenkranke** §5 mf consumptive
Lun'genschwindsucht f tuberculosis
lungern ['luŋərn] intr (HABEN & SEIN) loiter about, lounge about
Lunte ['luntə] f (-;-n) fuse; **L. riechen** smell a rat
Lupe ['lupə] f (-;-n) magnifying glass; **unter die L. nehmen** examine closely
lüpfen ['lYpfən] tr lift gently
Lust [lust] f (-;ˑe) pleasure; (Verlangen) desire; (Wollust) lust; **L. haben zu** (inf) feel like (ger); **mit L. und Liebe** with heart and soul
Lust'barkeit f (-;-en) amusement, entertainment
Lüster ['lYstər] m (-s;-) luster
lüstern ['lYstərn] adj (nach) desirous (of); lustful; (Bilder, Späße) lewd
Lü'sternheit f (-s) greediness; lustfulness; lewdness
Lust'fahrt f pleasure ride
lustig ['lustıç] adv gay, jolly; (belustigend) amusing; **du bist vielleicht l.!** you must be joking!; **l. sein** have a gay time; **sich l. machen über** (acc) poke fun at
Lüstling ['lYstlıŋ] m (-s;-e) lecher
lust'los adj listless; (Börse) inactive
Lustmolch ['lustmolç] m (-[e]s;-e) sex fiend
Lust'mord m sex murder
Lust'reise f pleasure trip
Lust'seuche f venereal disease
Lust'spiel n comedy
lust'wandeln intr (SEIN) stroll
Lutheraner –in [lutə'ranər(ın)] §6 mf Lutheran
lutherisch ['lutərıʃ] adj Lutheran
lutschen ['lutʃən] tr & intr suck
Lut'scher m (-s;-) nipple, pacifier
Luxus ['luksus] m (-;) luxury
Lu'xusausgabe f deluxe edition
Luzerne [lu'tsernə] f (-;-n) alfalfa
Lymphe ['lYmfə] f (-;-n) lymph
lynchen ['lYnçən] tr lynch
Lyrik ['lyrık] f (-s) lyric poetry
lyrisch ['lyrıʃ] adj lyric(al)
Lyze·um [ly'tse·um] n (-s;-en [ən]) girls' high school

M

M, m [ɛm] invar n M, m
M abbr (Mark) (fin) mark
Maar [mar] n (-[e]s;-e) crater lake
Maat [mat] m (-[e]s;-e) (naut) mate
Machart ['maxart] f make, type
Mache ['maxə] f (-s) (coll) make-believe; **er hat es schon in der M.** he is working on it
machen ['maxən] tr make; (tun) do; (bewirken) produce; (verursachen) cause; (Prüfung, Reise, Spaziergang)

take; (Begriff) form; (Besuch) pay; (Freude) give; (Holz) chop; (Konkurrenz) offer; **das macht mir zu schaffen** that causes me trouble; **das macht nichts** it doesn't matter; never mind; **das macht Spaß** that's fun; **Dummheiten m.** behave foolishly; **Ernst m.** be in earnest; **gemacht!** right!; **O.K.!** **Geschäfte m.** do business; **Geschichten m.** make a fuss; **Hochzeit m.** get married; **ich mache**

Spaß I'm joking; **mach dir nichts daraus!** don't worry about it; **mach's gut!** so long!; **wieviel macht es?** how much is it? ‖ *ref* make progress, do all right; **sich auf den Weg m.** set out; **sich** [*dat*] **etw m. lassen** have s.th. made to order; **sich m. an** (*acc*) get down to; **sich** [*dat*] **nichts daraus m.** not care for (or about) ‖ *intr*—**laß mich nur m.!** just leave it to me; **mach, daß . . . !** see to it that . . . !; **m. in** (*dat*) deal in; dabble in; **mach schon** (or zu)! get going!; **nichts zu m.!** (coll) nothing doing! no dice!

Machenschaften ['maxənʃaftən] *pl* intrigues

Macher ['maxər] *m* (-s;-) instigator; (coll) big shot

Macht [maxt] *f* (-;-e) might, power; (*Kraft*) force, strength; **aus eigener M.** on one's own responsibility; **an der Macht** in power; **an die M. kommen** come to power

Macht'balance *f* balance of power

Macht'befugnis *f* authority

Machthaber ['maxthabər] *m* (-s;-) ruler; dictator

machthaberisch ['maxthabərɪʃ] *adj* dictatorial

mächtig ['mɛçtɪç] *adj* mighty, powerful; (*riesig*) huge

macht'los *adj* powerless

Macht'losigkeit *f* (-;) impotence

Macht'politik *f* power politics

Macht'vollkommenheit *f* absolute power; **aus eigener M.** on one's own authority

Macht'wort *n* (-[e]s;-e)—**ein M. sprechen** put one's foot down

Machwerk ['maxverk] *n* bad job

Mädchen ['mɛtçən] *n* (-s;-) girl; maid

mäd'chenhaft *adj* girlish; maidenly

Mäd'chenhandel *m* white slavery

Mäd'chenname *m* maiden name; girl's name

Made ['madə] *f* (-;-n) maggot

Mädel ['mɛdəl] *n* (-s;-) (coll) girl

madig ['madɪç] *adj* wormy

Magazin [maga'tsin] *n* (-s;-e) warehouse; (*Zeitschrift; Fernsehprogramm; am Gewehr*) magazine

Magd [makt] *f* (-;-e) maid; (poet) maiden

Magen ['magən] *m* (-s;- & -) stomach; **auf nüchternen M.** on an empty stomach

Ma'genbeschwerden *pl* stomach trouble

Ma'gengrube *f* pit of the stomach

Ma'gensaft *m* gastric juice

Ma'genweh *n* stomach ache

mager ['magər] *adj* lean; (*Ernte*) poor

Magie [ma'gi] *f* (-;) magic

Magier -in ['magjər(ɪn)] §6 *mf* magician

magisch ['magɪʃ] *adj* magic(al)

Magister [ma'gɪstər] *m* (-s;-) (coll) school teacher; **M. der freien Künste** Master of Arts

Magistrat [magɪs'trat] *m* (-[e]s;-e) city council; (hist) magistracy

Magnat [mag'nat] *m* (-en;-en) magnate

Magnet [mag'net] *m* (-[e]s;-e) or (-en;-en) magnet

magnetisch [mag'netɪʃ] *adj* magnetic

magnetisieren [magneti'zirən] *tr* magnetize

Magnetismus [magne'tɪsmus] *m* (-;) magnetism

Mahagoni [maha'goni] *n* (-s;) mahogany

Mahd [mat] *f* (-;-en) mowing

Mähdrescher ['mɛdreʃər] *m* (agr) combine

mähen ['me·ən] *tr* mow; (*Getreide*) reap

Mä'her *m* (-s;-) mower; reaper

Mahl [mal] *n* (-[e]s;-er) meal

mahlen ['malən] (pp **gemahlen**) *tr* grind ‖ *intr* spin

Mahl'zahn *m* molar

Mahl'zeit *f* meal; **prost M.!** that's a nice mess!

Mähmaschine ['memaʃinə] *f* reaper; (*Rasen-*) lawn mower

Mähne ['menə] *f* (-;-n) mane

mahnen ['manən] *tr* (an *acc*) remind (of); (an *acc*) warn (about or of)

Mahnmal ['manmal] *n* (-s;-e) monument

Mah'nung *f* (-;-en) admonition; (com) reminder, notice

Mähre ['merə] *f* (-;-n) old nag

Mähren ['merən] *n* (-s;) Moravia

Mai [mai] *m* (-[e]s;-e) May

Mai'baum *m* maypole

Mai'blume *f* lily of the valley

Maid [mait] *f* (-;-en) (poet) maiden

Mai'glöckchen *n* lily of the valley

Mai'käfer *m* June bug

Mailand ['mailant] *n* (-[e]s;) Milan

Mais [mais] *m* (-es;) Indian corn

Maische ['maiʃə] *f* (-;) mash

Mais'hülse *f* corn husk

Mais'kolben *m* corncob

Majestät [majes'tet] *f* (-;-en) majesty

majestätisch [majes'tetɪʃ] *adj* majestic

Major [ma'jor] *m* (-s;-e) major

Majoran [majo'ran] *m* (-s;-e) marjoram

majorenn [majo'ren] *adj* of age

Majorität [majorɪ'tet] *f* (-;-en) majority

Makel ['makəl] *m* (-s;-) spot, stain

Mäkelei [mekə'lai] *f* (-;-en) carping

mäkelig ['mekəlɪç] *adj* critical; (*im Essen*) picky

ma'kellos *adj* spotless; (fig) impeccable

mäkeln ['mekəln] *intr* (an *dat*) carp (at), find fault (with)

Makkaroni [maka'roni] *pl* macaroni

Makler -in ['maklər(ɪn)] §6 *mf* agent, broker

Mäkler -in ['meklər(ɪn)] §6 *mf* faultfinder

Mak'lergebühr *f* brokerage

Makrele [ma'krelə] *f* (-;-n) mackerel

Makrone [ma'kronə] *f* (-;-n) macaroon

Makulatur [makula'tur] *f* (-;) waste

mal [mal] *adv* (coll) once; (arith) times; **komm mal her!** come here once!; **zwei mal drei** two times three; **zwei mal Spinat** two (orders of) spinach || **Mal** n (-[e]s;-e) mark, sign; (*Mutter-*) birthmark, mole; (*Fleck*) stain; time; **dieses Mal** this time; **manches liebe Mal** many a time; **mit e-m Male** all at once

Malbuch ['malbux] n coloring book

malen ['maːlən] tr & intr paint

Ma'ler -in §6 mf painter

Malerei [maːlə'raɪ] f (-;-en) painting

malerisch ['maːlərɪʃ] adj picturesque

Ma'lerleinwand f canvas

Malkunst ['maːlkunst] f art of painting

Malstrom ['maːlʃtroːm] m maelstrom

malträtieren [maltrɛ'tiːrən] tr maltreat

Malve ['malvə] f (-;-n) mallow

Malz [malts] n (-es;) malt

Malz'bonbon m cough drop

Mal'zeichen n multiplication sign

Mama [ma'maː], ['mama] f (-;-s) mom, ma

Mamsell [mam'zɛl] f (-;-en) miss; (*Wirtschafterin*) housekeeper

man [man] indef pron one, they, people, you; **man hat mir gesagt** I have been told

manch [manç] invar adj—**manch ein** many a || **mancher** §3 adj many a; **manche** pl some, several || pron many a person; many a thing

mancherlei ['mançərlaɪ] invar adj all sorts of, various

Manchester [man'ʃɛstər] m (-s;) corduroy

manch'mal adv sometimes

Mandant -in [man'dant(ɪn)] §7 mf client

Mandarine [manda'riːnə] f (-;-n) tangerine

Mandat [man'daːt] n (-[e]s;-e) mandate

mandatieren [manda'tiːrən] tr mandate

Mandel ['mandəl] f (-;-n) almond; (*15 Stück*) fifteen; (anat) tonsil

Man'delentzündung f tonsilitis

Mandoline [mando'liːnə] f (-;-n) mandolin

Mandschurei [mantʃu'raɪ] f (-;) Manchuria

Mangan [maŋ'gaːn] n (-s;) manganese

Mangel ['maŋəl] m (-s;:) lack, deficiency; (*Knappheit*) shortage; (*Fehler*) shortcoming; **aus M. an** (*dat*) for lack of; **M. haben an** (*dat*) be deficient in; **M. leiden an** (*dat*) be short of || f (-;-n) mangle

Mangel- comb.fm. in short supply

Man'gelberuf m undermanned profession

man'gelhaft adj defective; faulty; unsatisfactory, deficient

Man'gelkrankheit f nutritional deficiency

mangeln ['maŋəln] tr (*Wäsche*) mangle || intr (an dat) be short of, lack || impers—**es mangelt mir an** (*dat*) I lack

Mängelrüge ['mɛŋəlryːgə] f (-;-n) (com) complaint (*about a shipment*)

mangels ['maŋəls] prep (genit) for want of, for lack of

Ma·nie [ma'niː] f (-;-nien ['niːən) mania

Manier [ma'niːr] f (-;-en) manner

manieriert [mani'riːrt] adj affected

Manieriert'heit f (-;-en) mannerism

manier'lich adj mannerly, polite

Manifest [mani'fɛst] n (-es;-e) (aer, naut) manifest; (pol) manifesto

Maniküre [mani'kyːrə] f (-;-n) manicure; manicurist

maniküren [mani'kyːrən] tr manicure

manipulieren [manɪpu'liːrən] tr manipulate

manisch ['maːnɪʃ] adj maniacal

Manko ['maŋko] n (-s;-s) deficit; (com) shortage

Mann [man] m (-[e]s;:er) man; (*Gatte*) husband; **an den M. bringen** manage to get rid of; **der M. aus dem Volke** the man in the street; **seinen M. stehen** hold one's own

mannbar ['manbar] adj marriageable

Mann'barkeit f (-;) puberty; marriageable age (*of girls*)

Männchen ['mɛnçən] n (-s;-) little man; (*Ehemann*) hubby; (zool) male; **M. machen** sit on its hind legs

Männerchor ['mɛnərkoːr] m men's choir

Mannesalter ['manəsaltər] n manhood

Manneszucht ['manəstsuxt] f discipline

mann'haft adj manly, valiant

mannigfaltig ['manɪçfaltɪç] adj manifold

Man'nigfaltigkeit f (-;) diversity

männlich ['mɛnlɪç] adj male; (fig) manly; (gram) masculine

Männ'lichkeit f (-;) manhood; virility

Mannsbild ['mansbɪlt] n (-[e]s;-er) (pej) man

Mann'schaft f (-;-en) crew; (sport) team, squad; **Mannschaften** (mil) enlisted men

Mann'schaftsführer -in §6 mf (sport) captain

Mann'schaftswagen m (mil) personnel carrier

Mannsleute ['manslɔɪtə] pl menfolk

mannstoll ['manstɔl] adj man-crazy

Manns'tollheit f (-;) nymphomania

Mann'weib n mannish woman

Manometer [mano'meːtər] n pressure gauge

Manöver [ma'nøːvər] n (-s;-) maneuver

manövrieren [manø'vriːrən] intr maneuver

manövrier'fähig adj maneuverable

Mansarde [man'zardə] f (-;-n) attic

manschen ['manʃən] tr & intr splash

Manschette [man'ʃɛtə] f (-;-n) cuff

Manschet'tenknopf m cuff link

Mantel ['mantəl] m (-s;:) overcoat; (*Fahrrad-*) tire; (*e-s Kabels*) sheathing; (*Geschoß-*) jacket, case; (geol, orn) mantle

manuell [manu'ɛl] adj manual

Manufaktur [manufak'tuːr] f (-;-en) manufacture

Manufaktur'waren pl manufactured goods

Manuskript [manu'skrɪpt] n (-[e]s;-e) manuscript

Mappe ['mapə] f (-;-n) briefcase; (*Aktendeckel*) folder

Märchen ['mɛrçən] n (-s;-) fairy tale

mär'chenhaft adj legendary; (fig) fabulous

Mär'chenland n fairyland

Marchese [mar'keːzə] m (-;-n) marquis

Marder ['mardər] m (-s;-) marten; (fig) thief

Margarine [marga'riːnə] f (-;) margarine

Marienbild [ma'riːənbɪlt] n image of the Virgin

Marienfäden [ma'riːənfeːdən] pl gossamer(s)

Marienglas [ma'riːənglas] n mica

Marienkäfer [ma'riːənkeːfər] m ladybug

Marine [ma'riːnə] f (-;-n) (Kriegs-) navy; (Handels-) merchant marine

mari'neblau adj navy-blue

Mari'neflugzeug n seaplane

Mari'neinfanterie f marines

Mari'neminister m secretary of the navy

Mari'neoffizier –in §6 mf naval officer

Mari'nesoldat m marine

marinieren [mari'niːrən] tr marinate

Marionette [mariə'netə] f (-;-n) puppet

Marionet'tentheater n puppet show

Mark [mark] f (-;-) (fin) mark; (hist) borderland, march || n (-[e]s;-) marrow; (im Holz) pith; **bis ins M. to the quick; er hat M.** (fig) he has guts; **j-m durch M. und Bein gehen** (fig) go right through s.o.

markant [mar'kant] adj (einprägsam) marked; (außergewöhnlich) striking; (Geländepunkt) prominent

Marke ['markə] f (-;-n) mark; (Brief-) stamp; (Handelszeichen) trademark; (Sorte) brand; (Fabrikat) make; (Spiel-) counter

mark'erschütternd adj piercing

Marktenderei [marktendə'raɪ] f (-;-en) post exchange, PX

Marketing ['markıtıŋ] n (-s;) (com) marketing

markieren [mar'kiːrən] tr mark; (spielen) pretend to be

Markise [mar'kiːzə] f (-;-n) awning

Mark'stein m landmark

Markt [markt] m (-[e]s;ːe) market; (Jahrmarkt) fair

Markt'bude f booth, stall

markten ['marktən] intr (um) bargain (for)

markt'fähig adj marketable

Markt'flecken m market town

marktgängig ['marktgɛŋɪç] adj marketable

Markt'platz m market place

Markt'schreier m quack

Marmelade [marmə'laːdə] f (-;-n) jam

Marmor ['marmɔr] m (-s;-e) marble

Mar'morbruch m marble quarry

marmorn ['marmɔrn] adj marble

marode [ma'roːdə] adj (coll) tired out

Marodeur [marɔ'døːr] m (-s;-e) marauder

marodieren [marɔ'diːrən] intr maraud

Marone [ma'roːnə] f (-;-n) chestnut

Maroquin [marɔ'kɛ̃] m (-s;) morocco

Marotte [ma'rɔtə] f (-;-n) whim

marsch [marʃ] interj march!; be off!; **m., m.!** on the double || **Marsch** m (-es; ːe) march; **in M. setzen** get

going; **j-m den M. blasen** (coll) chew s.o. out; **(sich) in M. setzen** set out

Marschall ['marʃal] m (-s;ːe) marshal

Mar'schallstab m marshal's baton

Marsch'gepäck n full field pack

marschieren [mar'ʃiːrən] intr (SEIN) march

Marsch'kompanie f replacement company

Marsch'lied n marching song

Marsch'verpflegung f field rations

Marter ['martər] f (-;-n) torture

martern ['martərn] tr torture, torment

Mar'terpfahl m stake

Märtyrer –in ['mɛrtyrər(ɪn)] §6 mf martyr

Märtyrertum ['mɛrtyrərtum] n (-s;) martyrdom

März [mɛrts] m (-[es];-e) March

Masche ['maʃə] f (-;-n) mesh; stitch; (fig) trick

Ma'schendraht m chicken wire; screen; wire mesh

ma'schenfest adj runproof

Maschine [ma'ʃiːnə] f (-;-n) machine; (aer) airplane

maschinell [maʃɪ'nel] adj mechanical || adv by machine

Maschi'nenantrieb m—**mit M.** machine-driven

Maschi'nenbau m (-[e]s;) mechanical engineering

Maschi'nengewehr n machine gun

Maschi'nengewehrschütze m machine gunner

maschi'nenmäßig adj mechanical

Maschi'nenpistole f tommy gun

Maschi'nenschaden m engine trouble

Maschi'nenschlosser m machinist

maschi'nenschreiben tr type || **Maschinenschreiben** n (-s;) typing; typewritten letter

Maschi'nenschrift f typescript

Maschi'nensprache f computer language

Maschinerie [maʃinə'riː] f (-;) (& fig) machinery

Maschinist –in [maʃɪ'nıst(ɪn)] §7 mf machinist

Masern ['maːzərn] pl measles

Maserung ['maːzərʊŋ] f (-;) grain (in wood)

Maske ['maskə] f (-;-n) mask; (fig) disguise; (theat) make-up

Ma'skenball m masquerade

Maskerade [maskə'raːdə] f (-;-n) masquerade

maskieren [mas'kiːrən] tr mask

Maskotte [mas'kɔtə] f (-;-n) mascot

maskulin [masku'liːn] adj masculine

Maskuli·num [masku'liːnum] n (-s;-na [na]) masculine noun

maß [mas] pret of **messen** || **Maß** n (-es;-e) measure; (Messung) measurement; (Ausdehnung) extent, dimension; (Verhältnis) rate, proportion; (Grad) degree; (Mäßigung) moderation; **das Maß ist voll!** I've had it!; **das Maß überschreiten** go too far; **er hat sein gerütteltes Maß an Kummer gehabt** he had his full share of trouble; **in gewissem Maße** to a certain extent; **in hohem Maße**

highly; **j—m Maß nehmen zu** take s.o.'s measurements for; **Maß halten** observe moderation; **mit Maße in** moderation; **nach Maß angefertigt** custom-made; **ohne Maß und Ziel** without limit; **weder Maß noch Ziel kennen** know no bounds; zweierlei **Maß** double standard ‖ *f* (-;- & -e) quart (*of beer*), stein

massakrieren [masa'krirən] *tr* massacre

Maß'anzug *m* tailor-made suit

Maß'arbeit *f* work made to order

Masse ['masə] *f* (-;-n) mass; bulk; (*Menge*) volume; (*Volk*) crowd; (*Hinterlassenschaft*) estate; (elec) ground; **die breite M.** the masses; **the rank and file; e–e Masse . . .** (coll) lots of

Maß'einheit *f* unit of measure

Masseleisen ['masəlaɪzən] *n* pigiron

Massen– *comb.fm.* mass, bulk, wholesale

Mas'senabsatz *m* wholesale selling

Mas'senangriff *m* mass attack

Mas'senanziehung *f* gravitation

mas'senhaft *adj* in large quantities

Maß'gabe *f*—**mit der M., daß** with the understanding that; **nach M.** (*genit*) in proportion to; according to; (jur) as provided in

maß'gebend, maßgeblich ['masgepliç] *adj* standard; authoritative; (*Kreise*) leading, influential; **das ist nicht maßgebend für** that is no criterion for

maß'gerecht *adj* to scale

maß'halten §90 *intr* observe moderation

maß'haltig *adj* precise

massieren [ma'sirən] *tr* massage; (*Truppen*) mass

massig ['masɪç] *adj* bulky; solid; (*Person*) stout ‖ *adv*—**m. viel** (coll) very much

mäßig ['mesɪç] *adj* moderate; frugal; (*Leistung*) mediocre

mäßigen ['mesɪgən] *tr* moderate, tone down ‖ *ref* control oneself

Mä'ßigkeit *f* moderation; frugality; temperance

Mä'ßigung *f* (-;) moderation

massiv [ma'sif] *adj* massive; solid

Maß'krug *m* beer mug, stein

Maß'liebchen *n* daisy

maß'los *adj* immoderate ‖ *adv* extremely

Maß'nahme *f* (-;-n), **Maß'regel** *f* (-;-n) measure, step, move

maß'regeln *tr* reprimand

Maß'schneider *m* custom tailor

Maß'stab *m* ruler; (fig) yardstick, standard; (*auf Landkarten*) scale; **jeden M. verlieren** lose all sense of proportion

maß'voll *adj* moderate; (*Benehmen*) discreet

Mast [mast] *m* (-es;-en & -e) pole; (naut) mast ‖ *f* (-;) (*Schweinfutter*) mast

Mast'baum *m* (naut) mast

Mast'darm *m* rectum

mästen ['mestən] *tr* fatten

Mast'korb *m* masthead, crow's nest

Material [materɪ'ɑl] *n* (-s;-ien [ɪ-ən]) material

Materialismus [materɪ·a'lɪsmʊs] *m* (-;) materialism

materialistisch [materɪ·a'lɪstɪʃ] *adj* materialistic

Material'waren *pl* (Aust) medical supplies

Materie [ma'terɪ·ə] *f* (-;-n) matter

materiell [materɪ'el] *adj* material; (*Schwierigkeiten*) financial; (*Recht*) substantive

Mathe ['matə] *f* (-;) (coll) math

Mathematik [matema'tik] *f* (-;) mathematics

Mathematiker –in [mate'mɑtɪkər(ɪn)] §6 *mf* mathematician

mathematisch [mate'mɑtɪʃ] *adj* mathematical

Matratze [ma'tratsə] *f* (-;-n) mattress

Mätresse [me'tresə] *f* (-;-n) mistress

Matrize [ma'tritsə] *f* (-;-n) stencil; (*Stempel*) die, matrix

Matrone [ma'tronə] *f* (-;-n) matron

matro'nenhaft *adj* matronly

Matrose [ma'trozə] *m* (-n;-n) sailor

Matro'senanzug *m* sailor's uniform

Matro'senjacke *f* (nav) peacoat

Matsch [matʃ] *m* (-es;) (*Brei*) mush; (*Schlamm*) mud; (*halbgetauter Schnee*) slush

matschig ['matʃɪç] *adj* mushy; muddy; slushy

matt [mat] *adj* dull; weak; limp; (*Glas, Birne*) frosted; (*Börse*) slack; (*erschöpft*) exhausted; (*Kugel*) spent; (*Licht*) dim; (*Metall*) tarnished; (phot) matt; **m. machen** dull; tarnish; **m. setzen** checkmate

Matte ['matə] *f* (-;-n) mat; (*Wiese*) Alpine meadow; (poet) mead

Matt'glas *n* frosted glass

Matt'gold *n* dull gold

Matt'heit *f* dullness; fatigue

matt'herzig *adj* faint-hearted

Mat'tigkeit *f* (-;) fatigue

Matura [ma'tura] *f* (-;) (Aust) final examination (*before graduation*)

Mätzchen ['metsçən] *n* (-s;-) trick; **M. machen** play tricks; put on airs

Mauer ['mau·ər] *f* (-;-n) wall

Mau'erblümchen *n* (fig) wallflower

Mau'erhaken *m* mortar

mauern ['mau·ərn] *tr* build (*in stone or brick*)

Mau'erstein *m* brick

Mau'erwerk *n* brickwork; masonry

Mau'erziegel *m* brick

Maul [maul] *n* (-[e]s;⸗er) mouth; maw; **halt's M.!** (sl) shut up!

Maul'affe *m* gaping fool

Maul'beerbaum *m* mulberry tree

Maul'beere *f* mulberry

maulen ['maulən] *intr* gripe

Maul'esel *m* mule

maul'faul *adj* too lazy to talk

Maul'held *m* braggart

Maul'korb *m* muzzle

Maul'schelle *f* slap in the face

Maul'sperre *f* lock jaw

Maul'tier *n* mule

Maul'trommel *f* Jew's-harp

Maul'– und Klau'enseuche *f* hoof and mouth disease
Maul'werk *n*—**ein großes M. haben** have the gift of gab
Maul'wurf *m* (zool) mole
Maul'wurfshaufen *m*, **Maul'wurfshügel** *m* molehill
Maure ['maurə] *m* (-n;-n) Moor
Maurer ['maurər] *m* (-s;-) mason; bricklayer
Mau'rerkelle *f* trowel
Mau'rerpolier *m* bricklayer foreman
Maus [maus] *f* (-;¨e) mouse
Mäuschen ['mɔɪsçən] *n* (-s;-) little mouse; (fig) pet, darling; wench
Mau'sefalle *f* mousetrap
mausen ['mauzən] *tr* pilfer, swipe ‖ *intr* catch mice
Mauser ['mauzər] *f* (-;) molting season; **in der M. sein** be molting
mausern ['mauzərn] *ref* molt
mau'setot *adj* dead as a doornail
mausig ['mauzɪç] *adj*—**sich m. machen** put on airs, be stuck-up
Mauso•leum [mauzo'le•um] *n* (-s; -leen ['le•ən]) mausoleum
Maxime [ma'ksimə] *f* (-;-n) maxim
Mayonnaise [majɔ'nɛzə] *f* (-;) mayonnaise
Mechanik [me'çanɪk] *f* (-;-en) mechanics; (*Triebwerk*) mechanism
Mechaniker [me'çanɪkər] *m* (-s;-) mechanic
mechanisch [me'çanɪʃ] *adj* mechanical; power-
mechanisieren [meçanɪ'zirən] *tr* mechanize
Mechanis•mus [meça'nɪsmus] *m* (-; -men [mən]) mechanism; (*Uhrwerk*) works
Meckerer ['mɛkərər] *m* (-s;-) (coll) grumbler
meckern ['mɛkərn] *intr* bleat; (coll) grumble
Medaille [me'daljə] *f* (-;-n) medal
Medaillon [medal'jõ] *n* (-s;-s) medallion; locket
Medikament [medɪka'mɛnt] *n* (-s;-e) medication
Meditation [medɪta'tsjon] *f* (-;-en) meditation
meditieren [medɪ'tirən] *intr* meditate
Medizin [medɪ'tsin] *f* (-;-en) medicine
Medizinalassistant [medɪtsɪ'nalassɪstant(ɪn)] §7 *mf* intern
Medizinalbeamte [medɪtsɪ'nalbə·amtə] *m* health officer
Medizinalbehörde[medɪtsɪ'nalbəhørdə] *f* board of health
Mediziner –in [medɪ'tsinər(ɪn)] §6 *mf* physician; medical student
medizinisch [medɪ'tsinɪʃ] *adj* medical, medicinal; medicated; **medizinische Fakultät** medical school
Meer [mer] *n* (-[e]s;-e) sea; **am Meere** at the seashore; **übers M.** overseas
Meer'busen *m* bay, gulf
Meer'enge *f* straits
Meeres– [merəs] *comb.fm.* sea, marine
Mee'resarm *m* inlet
Mee'resboden *m* bottom of the sea
Mee'resbucht *f* bay

Mee'resgrund *m* bottom of the sea
Mee'reshöhe *f* sea level
Mee'reskÜste *f* seacoast
Mee'resleuchten *n* phosphorescence
Mee'resspiegel *m* sea level
meer'grün *adj* sea-green
Meer'rettich *m* horseradish
Meer'schaum *m* meerschaum
Meer'schwein *n* porpoise
Meer'schweinchen *n* guinea pig
Meer'ungeheuer *n* sea monster
Meer'weib *n* mermaid
Mehl [mel] *n* (-[e]s) (*grobes*) meal; (*feines*) flour; (*Staub*) dust, powder
Mehl'kloß *m* dumpling
Mehl'speise *f* pastry; pudding
Mehl'suppe *f* gruel
Mehl'tau *m* mildew
mehr [mer] *invar adj & adv* more; **immer m.** more and more; **kein Wort m.!** not another word!; **m. oder weniger** more or less, give or take; **nicht m.** no more, no longer; **nie m.** never again ‖ **Mehr** *n* (-s;) majority; (*Zuwachs*) increase; (*Überschuß*) surplus
Mehr'arbeit *f* extra work; (*Überstunden*) overtime
Mehr'aufwand *m*, **Mehr'ausgabe** *f* additional expenditure
Mehr'betrag *m* surplus; extra charge
mehr'deutig *adj* ambiguous
mehren ['merən] *tr & ref* increase
mehrere ['merərə] *adj & pron* several
mehr'fach *adj* manifold; repeated, multiple
mehr'farbig *adj* multicolored
Mehr'gebot *n* higher bid
Mehr'gepäck *n* excess luggage
Mehr'gewicht *n* excess weight
Mehr'heit *f* (-;-en) majority; (pol) plurality
Mehr'heitsbeschluß *m*, **Mehr'heitsentscheidung** *f* plurality vote
mehr'jährig *adj* (bot) perennial
Mehr'kosten *pl* extra charges
Mehr'ladegewehr *n* repeater
Mehr'leistung *f* increased performance; (ins) extended benefits
mehrmalig ['mermalɪç] *adj* repeated
mehrmals ['mermals] *adv* several times, on several occasions; repeatedly
Mehr'porto *n* additional postage
Mehr'preis *m* extra charge
mehr'seitig *adj* multilateral; many-sided; (*Brief*) of many pages
mehrsilbig ['merzilbɪç] *adj* polysyllabic
mehrsprachig ['mer/praxɪç] *adj* polyglot
mehrstöckig ['mer/tœkɪç] *adj* multistory
mehrstufig ['mer/tufɪç] *adj* multistage
Meh'rung *f* (-;) increase, multiplication
Mehr'verbrauch *m* increased consumption
Mehr'wertsteuer *f* added value tax
Mehr'zahl *f* majority; (gram) plural
meiden ['maɪdən] §112 *tr* avoid, shun
Meier ['maɪ·ər] *m* (-s;-) tenant farmer; dairy farmer
Meierei [maɪ·ə'raɪ] *f* (-;-en) dairy

Mei′ergut *n*, **Mei′erhof** *m* dairy farm

Meile ['maɪlə] *f* (-;-n) mile

mei′lenweit *adj* extending for miles, miles and miles of ‖ *adv* far away; **m. auseinander** miles apart

Mei′lenzahl *f* mileage

mein [maɪn] §2,2 *poss adj* my ‖ §2,4,5 *pron* mine; **das Meine** my share; my due; **die Meinen** my family

Meineid ['maɪnaɪt] *m* (-[e]s;) perjury; **e-n M. schwören** (or **leisten**) commit perjury

meineidig ['maɪnaɪdɪç] *adj* perjured; **m. werden** perjure oneself

meinen ['maɪnən] *tr* think; *(im Sinne haben)* mean, intend; **das will ich m.** I should think so; **die Sonne meint es heute gut** the sun is very warm today; **es ehrlich m.** have honorable intentions; **es gut m.** mean well; **ich meinte dich im Recht** I thought you were in the right; **m. das ernst** (or **im Ernst**)? do you really mean it?; **was m. Sie damit?** what do you mean by that?; **was m. Sie dazu?** what do you think of that? ‖ *intr* think; **m. Sie?** do you think so?; **Sie nicht auch?** don't you agree?; **wie m. Sie?** I beg your pardon?

meinerseits ['maɪnər zaɪts] *adv* for my part

meinesgleichen ['maɪnəs glaɪçən] *pron* people like me, the likes of me

meinethlben ['maɪnət halbən], **meinetwegen** ['maɪnət veːgən] *adv* for my sake, on my account; for all I care

meinetwillen ['maɪnət vɪlən] *adv*—**um m.** for my sake, on my behalf

meinige ['maɪnɪgə] §2,5 *pron* mine

Mei′nung *f* (-;-en) opinion; **anderer M. mit j-m sein über** *(acc)* disagree with s.o. about; **der M. sein** be of the opinion; **geteilter M. sein** be of two minds; **j-m die** (or **seine**) **M. sagen** give s.o. a piece of one's mind; **meiner M. nach** in my opinion; **vorgefaßte M.** preconceived idea

Mei′nungsäußerung *f* expression of opinion

Mei′nungsaustausch *m* exchange of views

Mei′nungsbefragung *f*, **Mei′nungsforschung** *f* public opinion poll

Mei′nungsumfrage *f* public opinion poll

Mei′nungsverschiedenheit *f* difference of opinion, disagreement

Meise ['maɪzə] *f* (-;-n) titmouse

Meißel ['maɪsəl] *m* (-s;-) chisel

meißeln ['maɪsəln] *tr & intr* chisel

meist [maɪst] *adj* most; **am meisten** most; **das meiste** the most; **die meisten Menschen** most people; **die meiste Zeit** most of the time; **die meiste Zeit des Jahres** most of the year ‖ *adv* usually, generally

Meist′begünstigungsklausel *f* most-favored nation clause

Meist′bietende §5 *mf* highest bidder

meistens ['maɪstəns] *adv* mostly

Meister ['maɪstər] *m* (-s;-) master; boss; *(im Betrieb)* foreman; *(sport)* champion

mei′sterhaft *adj* masterly

Meisterin ['maɪstərɪn] *f* (-;-nen) master's wife; *(sport)* champion

mei′sterlich *adj* masterly

meistern ['maɪstərn] *tr* master

Mei′sterschaft *f* (-;-en) mastery; *(sport)* championship

Mei′sterstück *n*, **Mei′sterwerk** *n* masterpiece

Mei′sterzug *m* master stroke

Melancholie [melaŋko'liː] *f* (-;) melancholy

melancholisch [melaŋ'koːlɪʃ] *adj* melancholy

Melasse [me'lasə] *f* (-;-n) molasses

Meldeamt ['meldə amt] *n*. **Meldebüro** ['meldəbyro] *n* registration office

Meldefahrer ['meldəfaːrər] *m* (mil) dispatch rider

Meldegänger ['meldəgɛŋər] *m* (mil) messenger, runner

melden ['meldən] *tr* report; *(polizeilich)* turn *(s.o.)* in; **den Empfang m.** *(genit)* acknowledge the receipt of; **er hat nichts zu m.** he has nothing to say in the matter; **gemeldet werden zu** (sport) be entered in; **j-m m. lassen, daß** send s.o. word that ‖ *ref* report; *(Alter)* begin to show; *(Gläubiger)* come forward; *(Kind)* cry; *(Magen)* growl; *(polizeilich)* register; *(Winter)* set in; *(telp)* answer; **sich auf e-e Anzeige m.** answer an ad; **sich krank m.** (mil) go on sick call; **sich m. zu** apply for; *(freiwillig)* volunteer for; (mil) enlist in; (sport) enter; **sich zum Dienst m.** (mil) report for duty; **sich zum Wort m.** ask to speak; *(in der Schule)* hold up the hand

Mel′der *m* (-s;-) (mil) runner

Meldezettel ['meldətsetəl] *m* registration form

Mel′dung *f* (-;-en) report; message, notification; *(Bewerbung)* application

Melkeimer ['melkaɪmər] *m* milk pail

melken ['melkən] §113 *tr* milk

Melo·die [melo'diː] *f* (-;-dien ['diːən]) melody

melodisch [me'loːdɪʃ] *adj* melodious

Melone [me'loːnə] *f* (-;-n) melon; (coll) derby

Meltau ['meltau] *m* (-[e]s;) honeydew

Membran [mem'braːn] *f* (-;-en), **Membrane** [mem'braːnə] *f* (-;-n) membrane

Memme ['memə] *f* (-;-n) coward

Memoiren [memo'aːrən] *pl* memoirs

memorieren [memo'riːrən] *tr* memorize

Menge ['meŋə] *f* (-;-n) quantity, amount; crowd; **e-e M.** a lot of

mengen ['meŋən] *tr* mix ‖ *ref* *(unter acc)* mingle (with); *(in acc)* meddle (in)

Men′genlehre *f* (math) theory of sets

men′genmäßig *adj* quantitative

Mengsel ['meŋzəl] *n* (-s;-) hodgepodge

Mennige ['menɪgə] *f* (-;) rust-preventive paint

Mensch [menʃ] *m* (-en;-en) human being, man; person, individual; **die Menschen** the people; **kein M.** no one ‖ *n* (-es; -er) hussy, slut

Menschen– [men/ən] *comb.fm.* man, of men; human
Men′schenalter *n* generation, age
Men′schenfeind –in §8 *mf* misanthropist
Men′schenfresser *m* cannibal
Men′schenfreund –in §8 *mf* philanthropist
men′schenfreundlich *adj* philanthropic, humanitarian
Men′schengedenken *n*—seit M. since time immemorial
Men′schengeschlecht *n* mankind
Men′schengewühl *n* milling crowd
Men′schenglück *n* human happiness
Men′schenhandel *m* slave trade
Men′schenhaß *m* misanthropy
Men′schenjagd *f* manhunt
Men′schenkenner –in §6 *mf* judge of human nature
Men′schenkind *n* human being; **armes M.** poor soul
men′schenleer *adj* deserted
Men′schenliebe *f* philanthropy
Men′schenmaterial *n* manpower
men′schenmöglich *adj* humanly possible
Men′schenraub *m* kidnaping
Men′schenräuber –in §6 *mf* kidnaper
Men′schenrechte *pl* human rights
men′schenscheu *adj* shy, unsociable
Men′schenschinder *m* oppressor, slave driver
Men′schenschlag *m* race
Men′schenseele *f* human soul; **keine M. not a living soul**
Men′schenskind *interj* man alive!
Men′schensohn *m* (Bib) Son of man
men′schenunwürdig *adj* degrading
Men′schenverächter –in §6 *mf* cynic
Men′schenverstand *m*—guter M. common sense
Men′schenwürde *f* human dignity
men′schenwürdig *adj* decent
Mensch′heit *f* (–;) mankind, humanity
mensch′lich *adj* human; (*human*) humane
Mensch′lichkeit *f* (–;) humanity
Menschwerdung [′men/verduŋ] *f* (–;) incarnation
Menstruation [mentru·a′tsjon] *f* (–;-en) menstruation
Mensur [men′zur] *f* (–;-en) measure; (*Meßglas*) measuring glass; students' duel
Mentalität [mentali′tet] *f* (–;) mentality
Menuett [menu′ɛt] *n* (–[e]s;-e) minuet
Meridian [meri′djan] *m* (–s;-e) (astr) meridian
merkbar [′merkbar] *adj* noticeable
Merkblatt [′merkblat] *n* instruction sheet
Merkbuch [′merkbux] *n* notebook
merken [′merkən] *tr* notice; realize; **etw m. lassen** show s.th., betray s.th.; **man merkte es sofort an ihrem Ausdruck, daß** one noticed immediately by her expression that ‖ *ref*—**m. Sie sich** [*dat*], **was ich sage!** mark my word!; **sich** [*dat*] **etw m. bear s.th. in mind; sich** [*dat*] **nichts m. lassen** not give oneself away ‖ *intr*—**m. auf** (*acc*) pay attention to, heed
merk′lich *adj* noticeable

Merkmal [′merkmal] *n* (–[e]s;-e) mark, feature, characteristic
Merkur [mer′kur] *m & n* (–s;) mercury
Merk′wort *n* (–[e]s;-er) catchword; (theat) cue
merk′würdig *adj* remarkable; (*seltsam*) curious, strange
merkwürdigerweise [′merkvvrdigər-vaizə] *adv* strange to say
Merk′würdigkeit *f* (–;-en) strange thing
Merk′zeichen *n* mark
meschugge [me′/ugə] *adj* (coll) nuts
Mesner [′mesnər] *m* (–s;-) sexton
Meß– [mes] *comb.fm.* measuring; (eccl) mass
Meß′band *n* (–[e]s;-er) measuring tape
meßbar [′mesbar] *adj* measurable
Meß′buch *n* (relig) missal
Meß′diener *m* acolyte
Messe [′mesə] *f* (–;-n) fair; (eccl) mass; (nav) officers' mess
messen [′mesən] §70 *tr* measure; (*Zeit*) time, clock; (*mustern*) size up ‖ *ref* —**sich m. mit** cope with; (*geistig*) match with; **sich nicht m. können mit** be no match for ‖ *intr* measure
Messer [′mesər] *m* (–s;-) gauge; meter ‖ *n* (–s;-) knife; (surg) scalpel; **bis aufs M. to the death**
Mes′serheld *m* (coll) cutthroat
mes′serscharf *adj* razor-sharp
Mes′serschmied *m* cutler
Messerschmiedewaren [′mesər/midəva-rən] *pl* cutlery
Mes′serschneide *f* knife edge
Meß′gewand *n* (eccl) vestment; chasuble
Meß′hemd *n* (eccl) alb
Messias [me′si·as] *invar m* Messiah
Messing [′mesiŋ] *n* (–s;) brass
messingen [′mesiŋən] *adj* brass
Meß′opfer *n* sacrifice of the mass
Mes′sung *f* (–;-en) measurement
Metall [me′tal] *n* (–s;-e) metal
Metall′baukasten *m* erector set
metallen [me′talən], **metallisch** [me-′talɪʃ] *adj* metallic
Metall′säge *f* hacksaw
Metallurgie [metalur′gi] *f* (–;) metallurgy
metall′verarbeitend *adj* metal-processing
Metall′waren *pl* hardware
Metapher [me′tafər] *f* (–;-n) metaphor
Meteor [mete′or] *m* (–s;-e) meteor
Meteorologe [mete·oro′logə] *m* (–n;-n) meteorologist
Meteorologie [mete·orolo′gi] *f* (–;) meteorology
Meteorologin [mete·oro′login] *f* (–;-nen) meteorologist
meteorologisch [mete·oro′logiʃ] *adj* meteorological
Meteor′stein *m* meteorite, aerolite
Meter [′metər] *m & n* (–s;-) meter
Me′termaß *n* tape measure
Methode [me′todə] *f* (–;-n) method
methodisch [me′todɪʃ] *adj* methodical
Metrik [′metrɪk] *f* (–;) metrics
metrisch [′metrɪʃ] *adj* metrical

Metropole [metro'po:lə] f (-;-n) metropolis

Mette ['mɛtə] f (-;-n) matins

Mettwurst ['mɛtvurst] f soft sausage

Metzelei [mɛtsə'laɪ] f (-;-en) massacre, slaughter

metzeln ['mɛtsəln] tr massacre

Metzger ['mɛtsgər] m (-s;-) butcher

Metzgerei [mɛtsgə'raɪ] f (-;-en) butcher shop

Meuchelmord ['mɔɪçəlmɔrt] m assassination

Meuchelmörder –in ['mɔɪçəlmœrdər (ɪn)] §6 mf assassin

meucheln ['mɔɪçəln] tr murder

meuchlerisch ['mɔɪçlərɪʃ] adj murderous

meuchlings ['mɔɪçlɪŋs] adv treacherously

Meute ['mɔɪtə] f (-;-n) pack (of hounds); (fig) horde, gang

Meuterei [mɔɪtə'raɪ] f (-;-en) mutiny

meuterisch ['mɔɪtərɪʃ] adj mutinous

meutern ['mɔɪtərn] intr mutiny

Mexikaner –in [mɛksɪ'kɑnər(ɪn)] §6 mf Mexican

mexikanisch [mɛksɪ'kɑnɪʃ] adj Mexican

Mexiko ['mɛksɪko] n (-s;) Mexico

miauen [mɪ'au.ən] intr meow

mich [mɪç] §11 pers pron me || §11 reflex pron myself

mied [mit] pret of meiden

Mieder ['midər] n (-s;-) bodice

Mie'derwaren pl foundation garments

Mief [mif] n (-s;) foul air

Miene ['minə] f (-;-n) mien; facial expression; M. machen zu (inf) make a move to (inf); ohne die M. zu verziehen without flinching

mies [mis] adj (coll) miserable, lousy

Mies'macher m (-s;-) alarmist

Miet- [mit] comb.fm. rental, rented; rent

Miet'auto n rented car

Miete ['mitə] f (-;-n) rent; (Zins) rental; (Erd-) pit (for storing vegetables); in M. geben rent out; in M. nehmen rent; kalte M. rent not including heat; zur M. wohnen live in a rented apartment (or home)

mieten ['mitən] tr rent, hire; (Flugzeug) charter

Miet'entschädigung f allowance for house rent

Mie'ter –in §6 mf tenant

Miet'ertrag m rent, rental

Miet'kontrakt m lease

Mietling ['mitlɪŋ] m (-s;-e) hireling

Miets'haus n apartment building

Miets'kaserne f tenement house

Miet'vertrag m lease

Miet'wagen m rented car

Miet'wohung f apartment

Miet'zins m rent

Mieze ['mitsə] f (-;-n) pussy

Migräne [mɪ'grɛnə] f (-;-n) migraine

Mikrobe [mɪ'kro:bə] f (-;-n) microbe

Mikrofilm ['mikrofɪlm] m microfilm

Mikrophon [mikro'fon] n (-s;-e) microphone

Mikroskop [mikro'skop] n (-s;-e) microscope

mikroskopisch [mikro'skopɪʃ] adj microscopic

Milbe ['mɪlbə] f (-;-n) (ent) mite

Milch [mɪlç] f (-;) milk

Milch'bart m sissy

Milch'brot n, **Milch'brötchen** n French roll

Milch'bruder m foster brother

Milch'drüse f mammary gland

Milch'eimer m milk pail

Milch'geschäft n creamery, dairy

Milch'glas m milk glass

milchig ['mɪlçɪç] adj milky

Milch'mädchen n milkmaid

Milch'mädchenrechnung f oversimplification

Milch'mixgetränk n milkshake

Milch'pulver n powdered milk

Milch'reis m rice pudding

Milch'schwester f foster sister

Milch'straße f Milky Way

Milch'tüte f carton of milk

Milch'wirtschaft f dairy

Milchzähne ['mɪlçtsɛnə] pl baby teeth

mild [mɪlt] adj mild; (nicht streng) lenient; (Stiftung) charitable; (Wein) smooth; (Lächeln) faint || **Milde** f (-;) mildness; leniency; kindness

mildern ['mɪldərn] tr soften, alleviate; mildernde Umstände extenuating circumstances

Mil'derung f (-;) softening, alleviation, mitigation

mild'herzig, mild'tätig adj charitable

Militär [mɪlɪ'tɛr] n (-s;) military, army; zum M. gehen join the army || m (-s;-s) professional soldier

Militär'dienst m military service

Militär'geistliche §5 m chaplain

Militär'gericht n military court

militärisch [mɪlɪ'tɛrɪʃ] adj military

Militarismus [mɪlɪta'rɪsmus] m (-;) militarism

Miliz [mɪ'lɪts] f (-;-en) militia

Miliz'soldat m militiaman

Milliardär –in [mɪljar'dɛr(ɪn)] §8 mf multimillionaire

Milliarde [mɪl'jardə] f (-;-n) billion

Milligramm [mɪlɪ'gram] n milligram

Millimeter [mɪlɪ'metər] n & m millimeter

Millime'terpapier n graph paper

Million [mɪl'jon] f (-;-en) million

Millionär –in [mɪljo'nɛr(ɪn)] §8 mf millionaire

millionste [mɪl'jonstə] §9 adj & pron millionth

Milz [mɪlts] f (-;) spleen

Mime ['mimə] m (-n;-n) mime

Mimiker –in [mɪ'mikər(ɪn)] §6 mf mimic

Mimose [mɪ'mozə] f (-;-n) mimosa

minder ['mɪndər] adj lesser, smaller; (geringer) minor, inferior || adv less; m. gut inferior; nicht m. likewise

min'derbedeutend adj less important

min'derbegabt adj less talented

min'derbemittelt adj of moderate means

Min'derbetrag m shortage, deficit

Min'derheit f (-;-en) minority

min'derjährig adj underage || **Minderjährige** §5 mf minor

mindern ['mɪndərn] tr lessen, diminish
Min'derung f (-;-en) diminution
min'derwertig adj inferior
Min'derwertigkeit f inferiority
Min'derwertigkeitskomplex m inferiority complex
Min'derzahl f minority
Mindest- [mɪndəst] comb.fm. minimum
mindeste ['mɪndəstə] §9 adj least; (kleinste) smallest; nicht die mindesten Aussichten not the slightest chance; nicht im mindesten not in the least; zum mindesten at the very least
mindestens ['mɪndəstəns] adv at least
Min'destgebot n lowest bid
Min'destlohn m minimum wage
Mine ['mɪnə] f (-;-n) (im Bleistift) lead; (mil, min) mine; alle Minen springen lassen (fig) pull out all the stops
Minenleger ['mɪnənlegər] m (-s;-) minelayer
Minenräumboot ['mɪnənrɔɪmboːt] n minesweeper
Mineral [mɪnə'raːl] n (-s;-e & -ien [jən]) mineral
mineralisch [mɪnə'raːlɪʃ] adj mineral
Mineralogie [mɪnəralɔ'giː] f (-;) mineralogy
Miniatur [mɪnja'tuːr] f (-;-en) miniature
minieren [mɪ'niːrən] tr (fig) undermine; (mil) mine
minimal [mɪnɪ'maːl] adj minimal
Minirock ['mɪnɪrɔk] m miniskirt
Minister [mɪ'nɪstər] m (-s;-) minister, secretary
Ministe•rium [mɪnɪs'teːrjum] n (-s; -rien [rjən]) ministry, department
Mini'sterpräsident m prime minister
Mini'sterrat m (-[e]s;-̈e) cabinet
Ministrant [mɪnɪs'trant] m (-en;-en) altar boy, acolyte
Minne ['mɪnə] f (-;) (obs) love
Min'nesänger m minnesinger; troubadour
minorenn [mɪnə'ren] adj underage
minus ['mɪnus] adv minus || Minus n (-;-) minus; (com) deficit
Minute [mɪ'nuːtə] f (-;-n) minute
Minu'tenzeiger m minute hand
-minutig [mɪnuːtɪç] comb.fm. -minute
Minze ['mɪntsə] f (-;-n) (bot) mint
mir [mɪr] §11 pers pron me, to me, for me; mir ist kalt I am cold; mir nichts, dir nichts suddenly; von mir aus for all I care || §11 reflex pron myself, to myself, for myself
Mirabelle [mɪra'belə] f (-;-n) yellow plum
Mirakel [mɪ'raːkəl] n (-s;-) miracle
Mira'kelspiel n miracle play
Mischehe ['mɪʃ-eːə] f mixed marriage
mischen ['mɪʃən] tr mix, blend; (cards) shuffle
Mischling ['mɪʃlɪŋ] m (-es;-e) halfbreed; mongrel
Mischmasch ['mɪʃmaʃ] m (-es;-e) hodgepodge
Mischpult ['mɪʃpult] n (rad, telv) master console

Mischrasse ['mɪʃrasə] f cross-breed
Mi'schung f (-;-en) mixture, blend
Misere [mɪ'zeːrə] f (-;-n) misery
Miß-, miß- [mɪs] comb.fm. mis-, dis-, amiss; bad, wrong, false
mißach'ten tr disregard; (geringschätzen) slight
mißartet [mɪs'artət] adj degenerate
miß'behagen intr (dat) displeasure || Mißbehagen n (-s;) displeasure
miß'bilden tr misshape, deform
Miß'bildung f (-;-en) deformity
miß'billigen tr disapprove
Miß'billigung f (-;-en) disapproval
Miß'brauch m abuse; (falsche Anwendung) misuse
mißbrau'chen tr abuse; misuse
mißbräuchlich ['mɪsbrɔɪçlɪç] adj improper
mißdeu'ten tr misinterpret
missen ['mɪsən] tr miss; do without
Miß'erfolg m failure, flop
Miß'ernte f bad harvest
Missetat ['mɪsətat] f misdeed; (Verstoß) offense; (Verbrechen) felony; (Sünde) sin
Missetäter –in ['mɪsətetər(ɪn)] §6 mf wrongdoer; offender; felon; sinner
mißfal'len §72 intr (dat) displease || Mißfallen n (-s;) displeasure
miß'fällig adj displeasing; (anstößig) shocking; (verächtlich) disparaging
miß'farben, miß'farbig adj discolored
Miß'geburt f freak
mißgelaunt ['mɪsgəlaunt] adj in bad humor, sour
Miß'geschick n (-s;) mishap; misfortune
Miß'gestalt f deformity; monster
miß'gestaltet adj deformed, misshapen
mißgestimmt ['mɪsgəʃtɪmt] adj grumpy
mißglücken ['mɪsglük'kən] intr (SEIN) fail, not succeed
mißgön'nen tr begrudge
Miß'griff m mistake
Miß'gunst f grudge, jealousy
mißhan'deln tr mistreat
Miß'heirat f mismarriage
Mißhelligkeit ['mɪshelɪçkart] f (-;-en) friction, disagreement
Mission [mɪ'sjon] f (-;-en) mission
Missionar [mɪsjo'nar] m, Missionär [mɪsjo'neːr] m (-s;-e) missionary
Miß'klang m dissonance; (fig) sour note
Miß'kredit m discredit, disrepute
mißlang [mɪs'laŋ] pret of mißlingen
miß'lich adj awkward; (gefährlich) dangerous; (bedenklich) critical
miß'liebig adj unpopular
mißlingen [mɪs'lɪŋən] §142 intr (SEIN) go wrong, misfire, prove a failure || Mißlingen n (-s;) failure
Miß'mut m bad humor; discontent
miß'mutig adj sullen; discontented
mißra'ten §63 intr (SEIN) go wrong, misfire; mißratene Kinder spoiled children
Miß'stand m bad state of affairs; Mißstände abschaffen remedy abuses
Miß'stimmung f dissension; (Mißmut) bad humor
Miß'ton m dissonance; (fig) sour note

miß'trau'en *intr* (*dat*) mistrust, distrust ‖ **Miß'trauen** *n* (**–s;**) mistrust
mißtrauisch ['mɪstrau·ɪʃ] *adj* distrustful
Miß'vergnügen *n* displeasure
miß'vergnügt *adj* cross; discontented
Miß'verhältnis *n* disproportion
Miß'verständnis *n* misunderstanding
miß'verstehen §146 *tr & intr* misunderstand
Miß'wirtschaft *f* mismanagement
Mist [mɪst] *m* (**–es;**) dung, manure; (*Schmutz*) dirt; (fig) mess, nonsense; **M. machen** (coll) blow the job; (*Spaß machen*) (coll) horse around; **viel M. verzapfen** talk a lot of nonsense
Mist'beet *n* hotbed
Mistel ['mɪstəl] *f* (**–;–n**) mistletoe
misten ['mɪstən] *tr* (*Stall*) muck; (*Acker*) fertilize
Mist'fink *m* (coll) dirty brat
Mist'haufen *m* manure pile
mistig ['mɪstɪç] *adj* dirty; (*sehr unangenehm*) very unpleasant
mit [mɪt] *adv* along; also, likewise; simultaneously ‖ *prep* (*dat*) with; **mit 18 Jahren** at the age of eighteen
Mit'angeklagte §5 *mf* codefendant
Mit'arbeit *f* cooperation, collaboration
mit'arbeiten *intr* cooperate, collaborate; **m. an** (*dat*) contribute to
Mit'arbeiter **–in** §6 *mf* co-worker
Mit'arbeiterstab *m* staff
mit'bekommen §99 *tr* receive when leaving; (*verstehen*) get, catch
mit'benutzen *tr* use jointly
Mit'bestimmung *f* share in decision making
mit'bewerben *ref* (um) compete (for)
Mit'bewerber **–in** §6 *mf* competitor
mit'bringen §65 *tr* bring along
Mitbringsel ['mɪtbrɪŋzəl] *n* (**–s;–**) little present
Mit'bürger **–in** §6 *mf* fellow citizen
Mit'eigentümer **–in** §6 *mf* co-owner
miteinan'der *adv* together
mit'empfinden §59 *tr* sympathize with
Mit'erbe *m*, **Mit'erbin** *f* coheir
Mitesser ['mɪtesər] *m* (**–s;–**) pimple, blackhead
mit'fahren §71 *intr* (SEIN) ride along; **j–n m. lassen** give s.o. a lift
mit'fühlen *tr* share, sympathize with
mit'fühlend *adj* sympathetic
mit'gehen §82 *intr* (SEIN) (mit) go along (with)
Mit'gift *f* dowry
Mit'giftjäger *m* fortune hunter
Mit'glied *n* member; **M. auf Lebenszeit** life member
Mit'gliederversammlung *f* general meeting
Mit'gliederzahl *f* membership
Mit'gliedsbeitrag *m* dues
Mit'gliedschaft *f* (**–;–en**) membership
Mit'gliedskarte *f* membership card
Mit'gliedstaat *m* member nation
Mit'haftung *f* joint liability
mit'halten §90 *intr* be one of a party; **ich halte mit** I'll join you
mit'helfen §96 *intr* help along, pitch in

Mit'helfer **–in** §6 *mf* assistant
Mit'herausgeber **–in** §6 *mf* coeditor
Mit'hilfe *f* assistance
mithin' *adv* consequently
mit'hören *tr* listen in on; (*zufällig*) overhear; (rad, telp) monitor
Mit'inhaber **–in** §6 *mf* copartner
Mit'kämpfer **–in** §6 *mf* fellow fighter
mit'klingen §142 *intr* resonate
mit'kommen §99 *intr* (SEIN) come along; (fig) keep up
mit'kriegen *tr* (coll) see **mitbekommen**
Mit'läufer **–in** §6 *mf* (pol) fellow traveler
Mit'laut *m* consonant
Mit'leid *n* compassion, pity
Mit'leidenschaft *f*—**j–n in M. ziehen** affect s.o.
mit'leidig *adj* compassionate; pitiful
Mit'leidsbezeigung *f* condolences
mit'leidslos *adj* pitiless
mit'leidsvoll *adj* full of pity
mit'machen *tr* participate in, join in on; (*ertragen*) suffer, endure
Mit'mensch *m* fellow man
mit'nehmen §116 *tr* take along; (*erschöpfen*) wear out, exhaust; (*abholen*) pick up; (*Ort, Museum*) visit, take in; **j–n arg m.** treat s.o. roughly
mitnichten [mɪt'nɪçtən] *adv* by no means, not at all
mit'rechnen *tr* include ‖ *intr* count
mit'reden *tr*—**ein Wort mitzureden haben bei** have a say in ‖ *intr* join in a conversation
Mit'reisende §5 *mf* travel companion
mit'reißen §53 *tr* (& fig) carry away
mit'reißend *adj* stirring
mitsamt [mɪt'zamt] *prep* (*dat*) together with
mit'schreiben §62 *intr* take notes
Mit'schuld *f* (an *dat*) complicity (in)
mit'schuldig *adj* (an *dat*) accessory (to) ‖ **Mitschuldige** §5 *mf* accomplice
Mit'schüler **–in** §6 *mf* schoolmate
mit'singen §142 *intr* sing along
mit'spielen *intr* play along; (fig) be involved; **j–m arg** (or **übel**) **m.** play s.o. dirty
Mit'spieler **–in** §6 *mf* partner
Mit'spracherecht *n* right to share in decision making
mit'sprechen §64 *tr* say with (*s.o.*) ‖ *intr* be involved; (an e–r Entscheidung beteiligt sein) share in decision making
Mit'tag *m* noon; (poet) South; **M. machen** stop for lunch; **zu M. essen** eat lunch
Mittag– *comb.fm.* midday, noon
Mit'tagbrot *n*, **Mit'tagessen** *n* lunch
mit'täglich *adj* midday, noontime
mittags ['mɪtaks] *adv* at noon
Mit'tagskreis *m*, **Mit'tagslinie** *f* meridian
Mit'tagsruhe *f* siesta
Mit'tagsstunde *f* noon; lunch hour
Mit'tagstisch *m* lunch table; lunch; **gut bürgliche M.** good home cooking
Mit'tagszeit *f* noontime; lunch time
Mit'täter **–in** §6 *mf* accomplice
Mit'täterschaft *f* complicity

Mitte ['mɪtə] *f* (-;-n) middle, midst; (*Mittelpunkt*) center; **ab durch die M.!** (coll) scram!; **aus unserer M.** from among us; **die goldene M.** the golden mean; **die richtige M. treffen** hit a happy medium; **er ist M. Vierzig** he is in his mid-forties; **in die M. nehmen** take by both arms; (sport) sandwich in; **j-m um die M. fassen** put one's arms around s.o.'s waist

mit′teilbar *adj* communicable

mit′teilen *tr* tell; (*im Vertrauen*) intimate; **ich muß Ihnen leider m., daß** I regret to inform you that

mitteilsam ['mɪttaɪlzam] *adj* communicative

Mit′teilung *f* (-;-en) communication; information; (*amtliche*) communiqué; (*an die Presse*) release

mittel ['mɪtəl] *adj* medium, average ‖ **Mittel** *n* (-s;-) middle; means; (*Heil-*) remedy; (*Maßnahme*) measure; (*Ausweg*) expedient; (*Durchschnitt*) average; (math) mean; (phys) medium; **im M. on the average; ins M. treten** (or **sich ins M. legen**) intervene, intercede; **letztes M. last resort; mit allen Mitteln** by every means; **Mittel** *pl* resources, means; funds; **M. und Wege** ways and means; **M. zum Zweck** means to an end; **sicheres M.** reliable method

Mit′telalter *n* Middle Ages

mittelalterlich ['mɪtəlaltərlɪç] *adj* medieval

Mit′telamerika *n* Central America

mittelbar ['mɪtəlbar] *adj* indirect

Mit′telgang *m* center aisle

Mit′telgebirge *n* highlands

Mit′telgewicht *n* (box) middleweight class

Mittelgewichtler ['mɪtəlgəvɪçtlər] *m* (-s;-) middleweight boxer

Mit′telgröße *f* medium size

mit′telhochdeutsch *adj* Middle High German ‖ **Mittelhochdeutsch** *n* (-es;) Middle High German

Mit′tellage *f* central position; (mus) middle range

mittelländisch ['mɪtəllendɪʃ] *adj* Mediterranean

Mit′telläufer *m* (fb) center halfback

mit′tellos *adj* penniless, destitute

Mit′telmaß *n* medium; balance; average

mitt′telmäßig *adj* medium, mediocre; (*leidlich*) indifferent, so–so

Mit′telmäßigkeit *f* mediocrity

Mit′telmast *m* mainmast

Mit′telmeer *n* Mediterranean

Mit′telohr *n* middle ear

Mit′telpreis *m* average price

Mit′telpunkt *m* center

mittels ['mɪtəls] *prep* (*genit*) by means of

Mit′telschiff *n* (archit) nave

Mit′telschule *f* secondary school

Mit′tels·mann *m* (-[e]s;″er & -leute) go-between; (com) middleman

Mit′telsorte *f* medium quality

Mit′telsperson *f* see **Mittelsmann**

Mit′telstand *m* middle class

Mit′telstürmer *m* (fb) center forward

Mit′telweg *m* middle course; **der goldene M.** the golden mean; **e–n M. einschlagen** steer a middle course

Mit′telwort *n* (-[e]s;″er) (gram) participle

mitten ['mɪtən] *adv*—**m. am Tage in** broad daylight; **m. auf dem Wege** well on the way; **m. auf die Straße;** right in the middle of the street; **m. aus** from the midst of, from among; **m. darin** right in the very center (of it, of them); **m. entzwei brechen** break right in two; **m. im Winter** in the dead of winter; **m. in der Luft** in midair; **m. ins zwanzigste Jahrhundert** well into the twentieth century

Mitternacht ['mɪtərnaxt] *f* midnight

mitternächtig ['mɪtərnɛçtɪç], **mitternächtlich** ['mɪtərnɛçtlɪç] *adj* midnight

Mittler –in ['mɪtlər(ɪn)] §6 *mf* mediator; (com) middleman

mittlere ['mɪtlərə] §9 *adj* middle, central; (*durchschnittlich*) average; (*mittelmäßig*) medium; (math) mean; **der Mittlere Osten** the Middle East; **in mittleren Jahren sein** be middle-aged; **von mittlerer Größe** medium-sized

mitt′lerweile *adv* in the meantime

mittschiffs ['mɪtʃɪfs] *adv* amidships

Mittwoch ['mɪtvox] *m* (-[e]s;-e) Wednesday

mitun′ter *adv* now and then

mit′unterzeichnen *tr* & *intr* countersign

mit′verantwortlich *adj* jointly responsible

Mit′verantwortung *f* joint responsibility

Mit′verschworene §5 *mf* co-conspirator

Mit′welt *f* present generation; our (his, etc.) contemporaries

mit′wirken *intr* (an *dat* or bei) cooperate (in)

Mit′wirkung *f* cooperation

Mit′wissen *n*—**ohne mein M.** without my knowledge

Mitwisser –in ['mɪtvɪsər(ɪn)] §6 *mf* accessory; one in the know

mit′zählen *tr* include ‖ *intr* count along

mixen ['mɪksən] *tr* mix

Mixgetränk ['mɪksgətrɛŋk] *n* mixed drink

Mixtur [mɪks′tur] *f* (-;-en) mixture

Möbel ['møbəl] *n* (-s;-) piece of furniture; **Möbel** *pl* furniture

Mö′belstück *n* piece of furniture

Möbeltransporteur ['møbəltranspɔrtør] *m* (-s;-e) mover

Mö′belwagen *m* moving van

mobil [mo′bil] *adj* movable; (*flink*) chipper; (mil) mobile

Mobiliar [mobɪ′ljar] *n* (-[e]s;) furniture

Mobilien [mo′biljən] *pl* movables

mobilisieren [mobɪlɪ′zirən] *tr* mobilize

Mobilisierung [mobɪlɪ′zirʊŋ] *f* (-;) mobilization

mobil'machen tr mobilize

Mobilmachung [mo'bilmaxuŋ] f (-;) mobilization

möblieren [mø'bliːrən] tr furnish; **möbliert wohnen** (coll) live in a furnished room; **neu m.** refurnish

mochte ['mɔxtə] pret of mögen

Mode ['moːdə] f (-;-n) fashion, style

Mo'debild n fashion plate

Modell [mo'del] n (-[e]s;-e) model; (Muster) pattern; (fig) prototype; **M. stehen zu** (dat) model for

modellieren [mode'liːrən] tr fashion, shape

Modell'puppe f mannequin

modeln ['moːdəln] tr fashion, shape; (nach) model (on) ‖ ref—zu alt sein, um sich m. zu lassen be too old to change

Mo'dengeschäft n dress shop

Mo'denschau f fashion show

Mo'denzeitung f fashion magazine

Moder ['moːdər] m (-;) mold; mustiness; (Schlamm) mud

Mo'derduft m, **Mo'dergeruch** m musty smell

moderig ['moːdərɪç] adj moldy, musty

modern [mo'dern] adj modern ‖ ['moːdərn] intr rot, decay ‖ **Modern** n (-s;) decay

modernisieren [modernɪ'ziːrən] tr modernize; bring up to date

Mo'deschmuck m costume jewelry

Mo'deschriftsteller –in §6 mf popular writer

Mo'dewaren pl (com) novelties

modifizieren [modifi'tsiːrən] tr modify

modisch ['moːdɪʃ] adj fashionable

Modistin [mo'dɪstɪn] f (-;-nen) milliner

modrig ['moːdrɪç] adj moldy

Mo·dus ['moːdus] m (-;-di [di]) mode, manner; (gram) mood

mogeln ['moːgəln] intr cheat ‖ **Mogeln** n (-s;) cheating

mögen ['møːgən] §114 tr like, care for; **ich mag lieber I** prefer ‖ mod aux may; can; care to; **er mag nicht nach Hause gehen** he doesn't care to go home; **ich möchte lieber bleiben** I'd rather stay; **ich möchte wissen I** should like to know; **mag kommen was da will** come what may; **wer mag das nur sein?** who can that be?; **wie mag das geschehen sein?** how could this have happened?

möglich ['møːklɪç] adj possible; (ausführbar) feasible; **sein möglichstes tun** do one's utmost ‖ **Mögliche** §5 n possibility; **er muß alles Mögliche bedenken** he must consider every possibility; **im Rahmen des Möglichen** within the realm of possibility

möglichenfalls ['møːklɪçənfals], **möglicherweise** ['møːklɪçərvaɪzə] adv possibly, if possible

Mög'lichkeit f (-;-en) possibility; potentiality; **ist es die M.!** well, I never!; **finanzielle Möglichkeiten** financial means; **nach M.** as far as possible

möglichst ['møːklɪçst] adv as ... as possible

Mohn [moːn] m (-[e]s;-e) poppyseed; (bot) poppy

Mohn'samen m poppyseed

Mohr [moːr] m (-en;-en) Moor

Möhre ['møːrə] f (-;-n) carrot

Mohr'rübe f carrot

Mokka ['mɔka] m (-s;-s) mocha (coffee)

Molch [mɔlç] m (-[e]s;-e) salamander

Mole ['moːlə] f (-;-n) mole, breakwater

Molekül [mole'kyːl] n (-s;-e) molecule

molekular [moleku'laːr] adj molecular

Molke ['mɔlkə] f (-;) whey

Molkerei [mɔlkə'raɪ] f (-;-en) dairy

Moll [mɔl] invar n (mus) minor

mollig ['mɔlɪç] adj plump; (Frau) buxom; (behaglich) snug, cozy

Moll'tonart f (mus) minor key

Moment [mo'ment] m (-[e]s;-e) moment ‖ n (-[e]s;-e) momentum; (Antrieb) impulse, impetus; (Faktor) factor, point; (Beweggrund) motive

momentan [momen'taːn] adj momentary

Moment'aufnahme f snapshot; (Bewegungsaufnahme) action shot

Monarch [mo'narç] m (-en;-en) monarch

Monar·chie [monar'çi] f (-;-chien ['çi·ən]) monarchy

Monat ['moːnat] m (-[e]s;-e) month

monatelang ['moːnatəlaŋ] adj lasting for months ‖ adv for months

mo'natlich adj monthly

Mo'natsbinde f sanitary napkin

Mo'natsfluß m menstruation

mo'natsweise adv monthly

Mönch [mœnç] m (-[e]s;-e) monk, friar

Mönchs'kappe f monk's cowl

Mönchs'kloster n monastery

Mönchs'kutte f monk's habit

Mönchs'orden m monastic order

Mönchs'wesen n monasticism

Mond [moːnt] m (-[e]s;-e) moon; **abnehmender M.** waning moon; **zunehmender M.** waxing moon

mondän [mɔn'dɛːn] adj sophisticated

Mond'fähre f (rok) lunar lander

Mond'finsternis f lunar eclipse

mond'hell adj moonlit

Mond'jahr n lunar year

Mond'kalb n (fig) born fool

Mond'schein m moonlight

Mond'sichel f crescent moon

Mond'sucht f lunacy; somnambulism

mond'süchtig adj moonstruck

Moneten [mo'neːtən] pl (coll) dough

monieren [mo'niːrən] tr criticize; remind

Monogramm [mono'gram] n (-s;-e) monogram

Monolog [mono'loːk] m (-s;-e) monologue

Monopol [mono'poːl] n (-s;-e) monopoly

monopolisieren [monopolɪ'ziːrən] tr monopolize

monoton [mono'toːn] adj monotonous

Monotonie [monoto'niː] f (-;) monotony

Monsterfilm ['mɔnstərfɪlm] *m* (cin) spectacular

Monstranz [mɔn'strants] *f* (-;-en) monstrance

monströs [mɔn'strøs] *adj* monstrous

Monstrosität [mɔnstrɔzi'tet] *f* (-;-en) monstrosity

Mon·strum ['mɔnstrum] *n* (-;-stra [stra]) monster

Monsun [mɔ'zun] *m* (-s;-e) monsoon

Montag ['mɔntak] *m* (-[e]s;-e) Monday

Montage [mɔn'taʒə] *f* (-;-n) mounting, fitting; (mach) assembly

Monta'gebahn *f*, **Monta'geband** *n* assembly line

Monta'gehalle *f* assembly room

montags ['mɔntaks] *adv* Mondays

Montan- [mɔntan] *comb.fm.* mining

Monteur [mɔn'tør] *m* (-s;-e) assemblyman, mechanic

Monteur'anzug *m* coveralls

montieren [mɔn'tirən] *tr* mount, fit; (*zusammenbauen*) assemble; (*einrichten*) install; (*aufstellen*) set up

Montur [mɔn'tur] *f* (-;-en) uniform

Moor [mor] *n* (-[e]s;-e) swamp

Moor'bad *n* mud bath

moorig ['mɔrɪç] *adj* swampy

Moos [mos] *n* (-es;) moss; (*Geld*) (coll) dough

Mop [mɔp] *m* (-s;-s) mop

Moped ['mɔped] *n* (-s;-s) motor bike, moped

moppen ['mɔpən] *tr* mop

mopsen ['mɔpsən] *tr* (coll) swipe || *ref* be bored stiff; be upset

Moral [mo'ral] *f* (-;) morality; (*Nutzwendung*) moral; (mil) morale

moralisch [mo'ralɪʃ] *adj* moral

moralisieren [mɔralɪ'zirən] *intr* moralize

Moralität [mɔrali'tet] *f* (-;) morality

Morast [mo'rast] *m* (-es;-e & ⁼e) mire; morass, quagmire

Mord [mɔrt] *m* (-[e]s;-e) murder

Mord'anschlag *m* murder attempt; (pol) assassination attempt

Mord'brennerei *f* arson and murder

Mord'bube *m* murderer, assassin

morden ['mɔrdən] *tr* & *intr* murder

Mörder -in ['mœrdər(ɪn)] §6 murderer

mörderisch ['mœrdərɪç] *adj* murderous; (coll) awful, terrible

mord'gierig *adj* bloodthirsty

Mord'kommission *f* homicide squad

mord'lustig *adj* bloodthirsty

Mords- [mɔrts] *comb.fm.* huge; terrible, awful; fantastic, incredible

Mords'angst *f* mortal fear

Mords'geschichte *f* tall story

Mords'geschrei *n* loud shouting

Mords'kerl *m* (coll) great guy

mords'mäßig *adv* (coll) awfully

Mords'spektakel *n* awful din

Mord'tat *f* murder

Mord'waffe *f* murder weapon

Mores ['mores] *pl*—j—n M. lehren teach s.o. manners

morgen ['mɔrgən] *adv* tomorrow; **m. abend** tomorrow evening (or night); **m. früh** tomorrow morning; **m. in**

acht Tagen (or **über acht Tage**) a week from tomorrow; **m. mittag** tomorrow noon || **Morgen** *m* (-s;-) morning; acre; **des Morgens** in the morning || *n* (-;) tomorrow

Mor'genblatt *n* morning paper

Mor'gendämmerung *f* dawn, daybreak

mor'gendlich *adj* morning

Mor'gengabe *f* wedding present

Mor'gengrauen *n* dawn, daybreak

Mor'genland *n* Orient

Morgenländer -in ['mɔrgənlendər(ɪn)] §6 *mf* Oriental

Mor'genrock *m* house robe

Mor'genrot *n*, **Mor'genröte** *f* dawn, sunrise; (fig) dawn, beginning

morgens ['mɔrgəns] *adv* in the morning

Mor'genstern *m* morning star

Mor'genstunde *f* morning hour

Mor'genzeitung *f* morning paper

morgig ['mɔrgɪç] *adj* tomorrow's

Morphium ['mɔrfjum] *n* (-s;) morphine

morsch [mɔrʃ] *adj* rotten; (*baufällig*) dilapidated; (*brüchig*) brittle; (fig) decadent

Morsealphabet ['mɔrzə·alfabet] *n* Morse code

Mörser ['mœrzər] *m* (-s;-) (& mil) mortar

Mör'serkeule *f* pestle

Mörtel ['mœrtəl] *m* (-s;-) mortar; plaster; **mit M. bewerfen** roughcast

Mör'telkelle *f* trowel

Mör'teltrog *m* hod

Mosaik [mɔza'ik] *n* (-s;-en) mosaic

mosaisch [mɔ'zaɪʃ] *adj* Mosaic

Moschee [mɔ'ʃe] *f* (-;-n) mosque

Moskau ['mɔskau] *n* (-s;) Moscow

Moslem ['mɔslem] *m* (-s;-s) Moslem

moslemisch [mɔs'lemɪʃ] *adj* Moslem

Most [mɔst] *m* (-es;-e) must, grape juice; new wine

Mostrich ['mɔstrɪç] *m* (-[e]s;-e) mustard

Motel [mo'tel] *n* (-s;-s) motel

Motiv [mo'tif] *n* (-[e]s;-e) (*Beweggrund*) motive; (mus, paint) motif

motivieren [mɔti'virən] *tr* justify

Mo·tor ['mɔtor] , [mo'tor] *m* (-s; -toren ['torən] & -tore ['torə]) motor

Mo'tordefekt *m* motor trouble

Mo'torhaube *f* (aer) cowl; (aut) hood

-motorig [motorɪç] *comb.fm.* -motor, -engine

Mo'torpanne *f* (aut) breakdown

Mo'torpflug *m* tractor plow

Mo'torrad *n* motorcycle

Mo'torradfahrer -in §6 *mf* motorcyclist

Mo'torrasenmäher *m* power mower

Mo'torroller *m* motor scooter

Mo'torsäge *f* power saw

Mo'torschaden *m* engine trouble

Motte ['mɔtə] *f* (-;-n) moth

mot'tenfest *adj* mothproof

Mot'tenkugel *f* mothball

Motto ['mɔto] *n* (-s;-s) motto

moussieren [mu'sirən] *intr* fizz; (*Wein*) sparkle

Möwe ['møvə] *f* (-;-n) sea gull

Mucke ['mʊkə] *f* (-;-n) whim; (dial) gnat; **Mucken haben** have moods

Mücke ['mʏkə] *f* (-;-n) gnat; mosquito; (dial) fly

Mucker ['mʊkər] *m* (-s;-) hypocrite; bigot; grouch; (coll) awkward guy

Muckerei [mʊkə'raɪ] *f* (-;) hypocrisy

muckerhaft ['mʊkərhaft] *adj* hypocritical, bigoted

Mucks [mʊks] *m* (-es;-e) faint sound; **keinen M. mehr!** not another sound!

mucksen ['mʊksən] *ref & intr* stir, say a word; **nicht gemuckst!** stay pat!

müde ['mydə] *adj* tired; **zum Umfallen m.** ready to drop

Müdigkeit *f* (-;) weariness

Muff [mʊf] *m* (-[e]s;-e) (*Handwärmer*) muff; (*Schimmel*) mold; musty smell

Muffe ['mʊfə] *f* (-;-n) (mach) sleeve

muffeln ['mʊfəln] *intr* sulk, be grouchy; (*anhaltend kauen*) munch; mumble

muffig ['mʊfɪç] *adj* musty; (*Person*) sulky; (*Luft*) stale, frowzy

Mühe ['my·ə] *f* (-;-n) trouble, pains; (*Anstrengung*) effort; **geben Sie sich keine M.!** don't bother; **j-m M. machen** cause s.o. trouble; **mit M.** with difficulty; **mit M. und Not** barely; **nicht der M. wert** not worthwhile; **sich** [*dat*] **große M. machen** go to great pains; **verlorene M.** wasted effort

mü/helos *adj* easy, effortless

muhen ['mu·ən] *intr* moo, low

mühen ['my·ən] *ref* take pains

mü/hevoll *adj* hard, troublesome

Mühewaltung ['my·əvaltʊŋ] *f* (-;) trouble, efforts; **für Ihre M. dankend, verbleiben wir ...** thanking you for your cooperation, we remain ...

Mühle ['mylə] *f* (-;-n) mill

Mühlrad ['mylrat] *n* water wheel

Mühlstein ['mylʃtaɪn] *m* millstone

Muhme ['mumə] *f* (-;-n) aunt; cousin

Mühsal ['myzal] *f* (-;-e) trouble

mühsam ['myzam] *adj* wearisome; (*Leben*) hard; (*Arbeit*) painstaking || *adv* with effort, with difficulty

mühselig ['myzelɪç] *adj* (*Arbeit*) hard; (*Leben*) miserable, tough

Mulatte [mu'latə] *m* (-n;-n), **Mulattin** [mu'latɪn] *f* (-;-nen) mulatto

Mulde ['mʊldə] *f* (-;-n) trough; (geol) depression, basin

Mull [mʊl] *m* (-[e]s;) gauze

Müll [mʏl] *m* (-[e]s;) dust, ashes; (*Abfälle*) trash, garbage

Müll/abfuhr *f* garbage disposal

Müll/abfuhrwagen *m* garbage truck

Müll/eimer *m* trash can, garbage can

Müller ['mʏlər] *m* (-s;-) miller

Müllerin ['mʏlərɪn] *f* (-;-nen) miller's wife; miller's daughter

Müll/fahrer *m* garbage man

Müll/haufen *m* scrap heap

Müll/platz *m* garbage dump

Müll/schaufel *f* dustpan

Mulm [mʊlm] *m* (-[e]s;) rotten wood

mul/mig *adj* rotten; dusty; (*Luft*) sticky; (*Lage*) ticklish

Multiplikation [mʊltɪplɪka'tsjon] *f* (-;) multiplication

multiplizieren [mʊltɪplɪ'tsirən] *tr* multiply

Mumie ['mumjə] *f* (-;-n) mummy

Mumm [mʊm] *m* (-s;) (coll) drive, grit

Mummelgreis ['mʊməlgraɪs] *m* (coll) old fogey

mummeln ['mʊməln] *tr & intr* mumble

Mund [mʊnt] *m* (-[e]s;:er) mouth; **den M. aufreißen** brag; **den M. halten** shut up; **den M. vollnehmen** talk big; **e-n losen M. haben** answer back; **sich** [*dat*] **den Mund verbrennen** put one's foot into it; **wie auf den M. geschlagen** dumbfounded

Mund/art *f* dialect

Mündel ['mʏndəl] *m & n* (-s;-) & *f* (-;-n) ward

Mündelgelder ['mʏndəlgɛldər] *pl* trustfund

mün/delsicher *adj* gilt-edged; absolutely safe

munden ['mʊndən] *intr* taste good

münden ['mʏndən] *intr*—**m. in** (*acc*) empty into, flow into

mund/faul *adj* too lazy to talk

mund/gerecht *adj* palatable

Mund/geruch *m* halitosis

Mund/harmonika *f* mouth organ

Mund/höhle *f* oral cavity

mündig ['mʏndɪç] *adj* of age

Mün/digkeit *f* (-;) majority, full age

mündlich ['mʏntlɪç] *adj* oral, verbal

Mund/pflege *f* oral hygiene

Mund/sperre *f* lockjaw

Mund/stück *n* mouthpiece; (*Zigaretten-*) tip; (*Düse*) nozzle

mund/tot *adj*—**j-n m. machen** (fig) silence s.o.

Mund/tuch *n* table napkin

Mün/dung *f* (-;-s Flusses) mouth; (*e-r Feuerwaffe*) muzzle

Mün/dungsfeuer *n* muzzle flash

Mün/dungsweite *f* (arti) bore

Mund/vorrat *m* provisions

Mund/wasser *n* mouthwash

Mund/werk *n* (fig) mouth, tongue

Mund/winkel *m* corner of the mouth

Munition [mʊni'tsjon] *f* (-;) ammunition

Munitions/lager *n* ammunition dump

munkeln ['mʊŋkəln] *tr & intr* whisper

Münster ['mʏnstər] *n* (-s;-) cathedral

munter ['mʊntər] *adj* awake; (*lebhaft*) lively; (*rüstig*) vigorous; gay

Münz- [mʏnts] *comb.fm.* monetary; of the mint; coin; coinage; coin-operated

Münz/anstalt *f* mint

Münze ['mʏntsə] *f* (-;-n) coin; change; (*Münzanstalt*) mint; (*Denkmünze*) medal; **bare M.** hard cash; **für bare Münze nehmen** take at face value

Münz/einheit *f* monetary unit

Münz/einwurf *m* coin slot

münzen ['mʏntsən] *tr* coin, mint; **das ist auf ihn gemünzt** that is meant for him || **Münzen** *n* (-s;) mintage, coinage

Münz/fälscher *m* counterfeiter

Münz/fernsprecher *m* public telephone

Münz′kunde f numismatics
Münz′wesen n monetary system
Münz′wissenschaft f numismatics
mürb [mʏrp], **mürbe** ['mʏrbə] adj (Fleisch) tender; (sehr reif) mellow; (gut durchgekocht) well done; (Gebäck) crisp and flaky; (brüchig) brittle; (erschöpft) worn out; (mil) demoralized; **j-n mürbe machen** (fig) break s.o. down; **mürbe werden** soften, give in
Murks [mʊrks] m (-es) bungling job
murksen ['mʊrksən] intr bungle
Murmel ['mʊrməl] f (-;-n) marble
murmeln ['mʊrməln] tr & intr murmur
Mur′meltier n ground hog, woodchuck
murren ['mʊrən] intr grumble
mürrisch ['mʏrɪʃ] adj grouchy, crabby
Mus [mus] n (-es;-e) purée; sauce
Muschel ['mʊʃəl] f (-;-n) mussel; (Schale) shell; (anat) concha
Muse ['muzə] f (-;-n) (myth) Muse
Muse·um [mu'ze·ʊm] n (-s;-en) museum
Musik [mu'zik] f (-) music
Musikalien [muzi'kaljən] pl music book
musikalisch [muzi'kalɪʃ] adj musical
Musikant [muzi'kant] m (-en;-en) musician
Musikan′tenknochen m funny bone
Musik′automat m, **Musikbox** ['mjuzɪkbɔks] f (-;-en) juke box
Musiker -in ['muzɪkər(ɪn)] §6 mf musician
Musik′hochschule f conservatory
Musik′kapelle f band
Musik′korps n military band
Musik′pavillon m bandstand
Musik′schrank m, **Musik′truhe** f radio-phonograph console
Musi·kus ['muzɪkʊs] m (-;-zi [tsi]) (hum) musician
Musik′wissenschaft f musicology
musisch ['muzɪʃ] adj artistic
musizieren [muzi'tsirən] intr play music
Muskat [mus'kat] m (-[e]s;-e) nutmeg
Muskateller [muska'telər] m (-s;) muscatel
Muskat′nuß f nutmeg
Muskel ['mʊskəl] m (-s;-n) muscle
Mus′kelkater m (coll) charley horse
Mus′kelkraft f brawn
Mus′kelriß m torn muscle
Mus′kelschwund m muscular distrophy
Mus′kelzerrung f pulled muscle
Muskete [mus'ketə] f (-;-n) musket
Muskulatur [muskula'tur] f (-;-en) muscles, muscular system
muskulös [musku'løs] adj muscular
Muß [mus] invar n must, necessity
Muße ['musə] f (-;) leisure; **mit M. at leisure**
Muß′ehe f shotgun wedding
Musselin [musə'lin] m (-s;-e) muslin
müssen ['mʏsən] intr—**ich muß nach Hause** I must go home ‖ mod aux—**ich muß** (inf) I must, I have to (inf); **ich muß nicht** I don't have to; **muß das wirklich sein?** is it really neecessary?; **sie hätten hier sein m.**

they ought to have been here; **sie müssen bald kommen** they are bound to come soon
müßig ['mysɪç] adj idle; (unnütz) unprofitable; (zwecklos) useless; (überflüssig) superfluous
Mü′ßiggang m idleness
Müßiggänger m loafer
mußte ['mʊstə] pret of müssen
Muster ['mʊstər] n (-s;-) pattern; (Probestück) sample; (Vorbild) example, model; **das M. e-r Hausfrau** a model housewife; **nach dem M. von** along the lines of; **sich** [dat] **ein M. nehmen an** (dat) model oneself on
Mu′sterbeispiel n typical example
Mu′sterbild n ideal, paragon
Mu′stergatte m model husband
Mu′stergattin f model wife
mu′stergültig adj model, ideal
Mu′stergut n model farm
mu′sterhaft adj model, ideal
Mu′sterknabe m (pej) sissy
Mu′sterkollektion f (kit of) samples
mustern ['mʊstərn] tr examine, eye, size up; (mil) inspect, review
Mu′sterprozeß m test case
Mu′sterschüler -in §6 mf model pupil
Mu′sterstück n specimen, sample
Mu′sterstudent -in §7 mf model student
Mu′sterung f (-;-en) inspection; examination; (mil) review
Mu′sterungsbescheid m induction notice
Mu′sterungskommission f draft board
Mu′sterwerk n standard work
Mu′sterwort n (-[e]s;∺er) (gram) paradigm
Mut [mut] m (-[e]s;) courage; **den Mut sinken lassen** lose heart; **guten Mutes sein** feel encouraged; **j-m den Mut nehmen** discourage s.o.; **nur Mut!** cheer up!
Mutation [muta'tsjon] f (-;-en) (biol) mutation, sport
Mütchen ['mytçən] n—**sein M. kühlen an** (dat) take it out on
mutieren [mu'tirən] intr (Stimme) change
mutig ['mutɪç] adj courageous, brave
-mütig [mytɪç] comb.fm. -minded, -feeling
mut′los adj discouraged
Mut′losigkeit f (-;) discouragement
mutmaßen ['mutmasən] tr suppose, conjecture
mutmaßlich ['mutmasliç] adj supposed, alleged; **mutmaßlicher Erbe** heir presumptive ‖ adv presumably
Mut′maßung f (-;-en) conjecture, guesswork; **Mutmaßungen anstellen** conjecture
Mutter ['mutər] f (-;∺) mother; **werdende M.** expectant mother ‖ f (-;-n) nut
Mut′terboden m rich soil
Mütterchen ['mytərçən] n (-s;-) mummy; little old lady
Mut′tererde f rich soil; native soil
Mut′terfürsorge f maternity welfare
Mut′terkuchen m (anat) placenta

Mut′terleib m womb

Mütterlich ['mʏtərlıç] adj motherly, maternal; m. verwandt related on the mother's side

mut′terlos adj motherless

Mut′termal n birthmark

Mut′terpferd n mare

Mut′terschaf n ewe

Mut′terschaft f (-;) motherhood, maternity

Mut′terschlüssel m (mach) wrench

mut′terseelenallein′ adj all alone

Muttersöhnchen ['mutərzøːnçən] n (-s;-) mamma's boy

Mut′tersprache f mother tongue

Mut′terstelle f—bei j-m die M. vertreten be a mother to s.o.

Mut′terstute f mare

Mut′tertier n (zool) dam

Mut′terwitz m common sense

Mutti ['mutı] f (-;-s) (coll) mom

mut′voll adj courageous

Mut′wille m mischievousness

mut′willig adj mischievous, willful

Mütze ['mʏtsə] f (-;-n) cap

Myriade [mʏrɪ'aːdə] f (-;-n) myriad

Myrrhe ['mʏrə] f (-;-n) myrrh

Myrte ['mʏrtə] f (-;-n) myrtle

Mysterienspiel [mʏs'teːrjən/piːl] n (theat) mystery play

mysteriös [mʏste'rjøːs] adj mysterious

Myste-rium [mʏs'teːrjum] n (-s;-rien [rjən]) mystery

mystifizieren [mʏstifɪ'tsiːrən] tr mystify; (täuschen) hoax

Mystik ['mʏstɪk] f (-;) mysticism

My′stiker –in §6 mf mystic

mystisch ['mʏstɪʃ] adj mystic(al)

Mythe ['mʏtə] f (-;-n) myth

mythisch ['mʏtɪʃ] adj mythical

Mytholo-gie [mʏtoloˈgiː] f (-;-gien ['giːən]) mythology

mythologisch [mʏtoˈloːgɪʃ] adj mythological

My-thus ['mʏtus] m (-s;-then [tən]) myth

N

N, n [ɛn] invar n N, n

na [na] interj well!; **na also!** there you are!; **na, so was!** don't tell me!; **na, und ob! I'll say!; na, warte!** just you wait!

Nabe ['naːbə] f (-;-n) hub

Nabel ['naːbəl] m (-s;-) navel

Na′belschnur f umbilical cord

nach [nax] adv after; n. und n. little by little; n. wie vor now as ever || prep (dat) (Zeit) after; (Reihenfolge) after, behind; (Ziel, Richtung) to, towards, for; (Art, Maß, Vorbild, Richtschnur) according to, after

Nach-, nach- comb.fm. subsequent, additional, supplementary; post-; over, over again, re–; after

nach′äffen tr ape, imitate

nachahmen ['naxaːmən] tr imitate, copy

Nach′ahmer –in §6 mf imitator

Nach′ahmung f (-;-en) imitation, copy

nach′arbeiten tr copy; (ausbessern) touch up; (Versäumtes) make up for

nach′arten intr (SEIN) (dat) take after

Nachbar ['naxbar] m (-s & -n;-n), **Nachbarin** ['naxbarın] f (-;-nen) neighbor

nach′barlich adj neighborly; neighboring

Nach′barschaft f (-;-en) neighborhood; gute N. halten be on friendly terms with neighbors

Nach′bau m (-s) imitation, duplication; licensed manufacture; unerlaubter N. illegal manufacture

Nach′behandlung f (med) follow-up treatment

nach′bestellen tr reorder, order more of

Nach′bestellung f (-;-en) repeat order

nach′beten tr & intr repeat mechanically

nach′bezahlen tr pay afterwards; pay the rest of || intr pay afterwards

Nach′bild n copy

nach′bilden tr copy

Nach′bildung f (-;-en) copying; (Kopie) copy, reproduction; (Modell) mock-up; (Attrappe) dummy

nach′bleiben §62 intr (SEIN) remain behind; (educ) stay in; hinter j-m n. lag behind s.o.

nach′blicken intr (dat) look after

nach′brennen §97 intr smolder || **Nach′brennen** n (-s;) (rok) afterburn

Nach′brenner m (aer) afterburner

nach′datieren tr postdate

nachdem [nax'deːm] adv afterwards; je n. as the case may be, it all depends || conj after, when; je n. according to how, depending on how

nach′denken §66 intr think it over; n. über (acc) think over, reflect on || **Nachdenken** n (-s;) reflection; bei weiterem N. on second thought

nach′denklich adj reflective, thoughtful; (Buch) thought-provoking; (abwesend) lost in thought

Nach′dichtung f (-;-en) free poetical rendering

nach′drängen intr (SEIN) (dat) crowd after; pursue

nach′dringen §142 intr be in hot pursuit; (dat) pursue

Nach′druck m (Betonung) stress, emphasis; energy; (Raubdruck) pirated edition; (typ) reprint; mit N. emphatically; N. verboten all rights reserved

nach′drucken tr reprint

nach′drücklich adj emphatic; n. betonen emphasize

nach′dunkeln intr get darker

nach′eifern intr (dat) emulate

nach/eilen intr (SEIN) (dat) hasten after, rush after

nacheinan/der adv one after another

nach/empfinden §59 tr have a feeling for; j–m etw n. sympathize with s.o. about s.th.

Nachen ['naxən] m (-s;-) (poet) boat

nach/erzählen tr repeat, retell

Nachfahr ['naxfar] m (-s;-en) descendant

nach/fahren §71 intr (SEIN) (dat) drive after, follow

nach/fassen tr (mil) get a second helping of || intr (econ) do a follow-up

Nach/folge f succession

nach/folgen intr (dat) succeed, follow; follow in the footsteps of

nach/folgend adj following, subsequent

Nach/folger –in §6 mf follower; successor

nach/fordern tr charge extra; claim subsequently

nach/forschen intr (dat) investigate

Nach/frage f inquiry; (com) demand

nach/fragen intr (nach) ask (about)

Nach/frist f time extension

nach/fühlen tr—j–m etw n. sympathize with s.o. about s.th.

nach/füllen tr refill, fill up

nach/geben §80 tr give later; (beim Essen) give another helping of; j–m nichts an Eifer n. not be outdone by s.o. in zeal || intr give way, give; (schlaff werden) slacken, give; (dat) give in to, yield to

nach/geboren adj younger; posthumous

Nach/gebühr f postage due

nach/gehen §82 intr (SEIN) (dat) follow; (Geschäften) attend to; (untersuchen) investigate, check on

nachgemacht ['naxgəmaxt] adj false, imitation; (künstlich) artificial

nachgeordnet ['naxgə‧ordnət] adj subordinate

nach/gerade adv by now; (allmählich) gradually; (wirklich) really

Nach/geschmack m aftertaste, bad taste

nachgewiesenermaßen ['naxgəvizənər‧masən] adv as has been shown (or proved)

nachgiebig ['naxgibɪç] adj elastic, yielding, compliant; (nachsichtig) indulgent; (st. exch.) declining

nach/gießen §76 tr fill up, refill || intr add more

nach/glühen tr (tech) temper || intr smolder

nach/grübeln intr (dat or über acc) mull (over), ponder (on)

Nach/hall m echo, reverberation

nach/hallen intr echo, reverberate

nachhaltig ['naxhaltɪç] adj lasting

nach/hängen §92 intr (dat) give free rein to || impers—es hängt mir nach I still feel the effects of it

nach/helfen §96 intr (dat) help along

nach/her adv afterwards, later, then; bis n.! so long!

nachherig ['naxherɪç] adj later

Nach/hilfe f assistance, help

Nach/hilfelehrer –in §6 mf tutor

Nach/hilfestunde f tutoring lesson

Nach/hilfeunterricht m tutoring

nach/hinken intr (dat) lag behind

Nachholbedarf ['naxholbədarf] m backlog of unsatisfied demands

nach/holen tr make up for

Nach/hut f (mil) rear guard

nach/jagen tr—j–m etw n. send s.th. after s.o. || intr (SEIN) (dat) pursue

Nach/klang m echo; (fig) reminiscence

nach/klingen §142 intr reecho, resound

Nachkomme ['naxkɔmə] m (-n;-n) off‧spring, descendant

nach/kommen §99 intr (SEIN) (dat) follow; join (s.o.) later; (Vorschriften, e–m Gesetz) obey; (e–m Versprechen) keep; (e–r Pflicht) live up to

Nach/kommenschaft f (-;) posterity

Nachkömmling ['naxkœmlɪŋ] m (-s; -e) offspring, descendant

Nach/laß ['naxlas] m (-lasses;-lässe) remission; (am Preis) reduction; (Erbschaft) estate; **literarischer N.** unpublished works

nach/lassen §104 tr leave behind; (lockern) slacken; j–m 15% vom Preise n. give s.o. a fifteen percent reduction in price || intr (sich lockern) slacken; (sich vermindern) diminish; (milder werden) relent; (Regen) let up; (Kräfte) give out; (Wind, Sturm) die down; (schlechter werden) get worse

Nach/laßgericht n probate court

nach/lässig adj careless, negligent

Nach/lässigkeit f carelessness, negligence

nach/laufen §105 intr (SEIN) (dat) run after, pursue

nach/leben intr (dat) live up to || **Nach‧leben** n afterlife

Nach/lese f gleanings

nach/lesen §107 tr glean; (Stelle im Buch) reread, look up

nach/liefern tr deliver subsequently

nach/machen tr imitate; (fälschen) counterfeit; j–m alles n. imitate s.o. in everything

nach/malen tr copy

nachmalig ['naxmalɪç] adj later

nachmals ['naxmals] adv afterwards

nach/messen §70 tr measure again

Nach/mittag m afternoon

nach/mittags adv in the afternoon

Nach/mittagsvorstellung f matinée

Nach/nahme f (-;) C.O.D.

Nach/name m last name, family name

nach/plappern tr repeat mechanically

Nach/porto n postage due

nachprüfbar ['naxpryfbar] adj verifiable

nach/prüfen tr verify, check out

nach/rechnen tr (acct) check

Nach/rede f epilogue; j–n in üble N. bringen bring s.o. into bad repute; üble N. spread; üble N. verbreiten spread nasty rumors

nach/reden tr—j–m etw n. say s.th. behind s.o.'s back

Nachricht ['naxrɪçt] f (-;-en) news; (Bericht) report; (kurzer Bericht) notice; (Auskunft) information; e–e N. verbreiten spread the news; geben Sie mir von Zeit zu Zeit N.! keep me advised; **Nachrichten** (rad, telv) news, news report; **Nachrichten einholen** make inquiries; **Nachrichten einziehen** gather information; **zur N.!** for your information

Nach′richtenabteilung f (mil) intelligence section

Nach′richtenagentur f news agency

Nach′richtenbüro n news room; news agency

Nach′richtendienst m news service; (mil) army intelligence

Nach′richtensatellit m communications satellite

Nach′richtensendung f newscast

Nach′richtenwesen n communications

nach′rücken intr (SEIN) (im Rang) move up; (mil) (dat) follow up; **j-m n.** move up into s.o.'s position

Nach′ruf m obituary

nach′rufen §122 tr (dat) call after

Nach′ruhm m posthumous fame

nach′rühmen tr—j-m etw n. say s.th. nice about s.o.

nach′sagen tr—j-m etw n. repeat s.th. after s.o.; say s.th behind s.o.'s back; **das lasse ich mir nicht n.** I won't let that be said of me

Nach′satz m concluding clause

nach′schaffen tr replace

nach′schauen intr (dat) gaze after

nach′schicken tr forward

Nachschlagebuch [′nɑx/lɑgəbux] n reference book

nach′schlagen §132 tr look up; (Buch) consult ‖ intr (box) counter

Nachschlagewerk [′nɑx/lɑgəverk] n reference work

Nach′schlüssel m skeleton key

nach′schreiben §62 tr copy; take down from dictation

Nach′schrift f postscript

Nach′schub m (mil) supply, fresh supplies; (mil) supply lines

Nach′schublinie f (mil) supply line

Nach′schubstützpunkt m (mil) supply base

Nach′schubweg m supply line

nach′sehen §138 tr (nachschlagen) look up; (nachprüfen) check; (acct) audit; (mach) overhaul; **j-m vieles n.** overlook much in s.o. ‖ intr (dat) gaze after ‖ **Nachsehen** n—**das N. haben** get the short end

nach′senden §140 tr send after, forward

nach′setzen intr (dat) run after

Nach′sicht f patience; **mit j-m N. üben** have patience with s.o.

nach′sichtig, nach′sichtsvoll adj lenient, considerate

Nach′silbe f suffix

nach′sinnen §121 intr (über acc) reflect (on), muse (over)

nach′sitzen intr be kept in after school

Nach′sommer m Indian summer

Nach′speise f dessert

Nach′spiel n (fig) sequel

nach′spüren intr (dat) track down

nächst [neçst] §9 (dat) next to

nächst′beste §9 adj second-best

nächstdem′ adv thereupon

nächste [′neçstə] §9 adj (super of

nahe) next; (Weg) shortest; (Beziehungen) closest ‖ **Nächste** §5 mf neighbor, fellow man, fellow creature

nach′stehen §146 intr (dat) be inferior to

nach′stehend adj following ‖ adv (mentioned) below

nach′stellen tr (Schraube) reset, adjust; (Uhr) set back ‖ intr (dat) be after; (e-m Mädchen) run after

Nach′stellung f (-;-en) persecution; ambush; (gram) postposition

nächsten [′neçstən] adv one of these days, before long; next time

Näch′stenliebe f charity

nächst′liegend adj nearest

nach′stöbern intr rummage about

nach′stoßen §150 intr (SEIN) (dat) (mil) follow up

nach′streben intr (dat) strive after; (e-r Person) emulate

nach′strömen, nach′strümen, nach′stürzen intr (SEIN) (dat) crowd after

nach′suchen tr search for ‖ intr—n. um apply for

Nach′suchung f (-;-en) search, inquiry; petition

Nacht [naxt] f (-;¨e) night; **bei N. und Nebel** under cover of night

Nacht′ausgabe f final (edition)

Nach′teil m disadvantage

nach′teilig adj disadvantageous

Nacht′essen n supper

Nacht′eule f night owl

Nacht′falter m (ent) moth

Nacht′geschirr n chamber pot

Nacht′gleiche f equinox

Nacht′hemd n nightgown

Nachtigall [′naxtigal] f (-;-n) nightingale

nächtigen [′neçtigən] intr pass the night

Nach′tisch m dessert

Nacht′klub m, **Nacht′lokal** n nightclub

Nacht′lager n accommodations for the night

nächtlich [′neçtliç] adj night, nightly

Nacht′mal n supper

Nacht′musik f serenade

nach′tönen intr resound; (Note) linger

Nacht′quartier n accommodations for the night

Nachtrag [′naxtrak] m (-[e]s;¨e) supplement, addition

nach′tragen §132 tr add; **j-m etw n.** carry s.th. after s.o.; (fig) hold s.th. against s.o.

nachträgerisch [′naxtregəriʃ] adj resentful, vindictive

nachträglich [′naxtrekliç] adj supplementary; (später) subsequent

Nachtrags- comb.fm. supplementary

Nach′trupp m (-s;) rear guard

nachts [naxts] adv at night

Nacht′schicht f night shift

nacht′schlafend adj—**bei** (or zu) **nachtschlafender Zeit** late at night

Nacht′schwärmer, -in §6 mf reveler

Nacht′tisch m night table

Nacht′topf m chamber pot

nach′tun §154 tr—j-m etw n. imitate s.o. in s.th.

Nacht′wache f night watch, vigil

Nacht′wächter m night watchman

Nachtwandler –in [ˈnaxtvandlər(ɪn)] §6 *mf* sleepwalker, somnambulist

Nacht′zeug *n* overnight things

Nach′urlaub *m* extended leave

nach′wachsen §155 *intr* (SEIN) grow again

Nach′wahl *f* special election

Nachwehen [ˈnaxve·ən] *pl* afterpains; (fig) painful consequences

nach′weinen *tr*—keine Tränen n. (dat) waste no tears over ‖ *intr* (dat;-t) cry over

Nachweis [ˈnaxvaɪs] *m* (-es;-e) proof; den N. bringen (or führen) furnish proof

nach′weisbar *adj* demonstrable

nach′weisen §118 *tr* point, show; (beweisen) prove; (begründen) substantiate; (verweisen) refer to

nach′weislich *adj* demonstrable

Nach′welt *f* posterity

nach′wiegen §57 *tr* verify the weight of

nach′wirken *intr* have an aftereffect

Nach′wirkung *f* (-;-en) aftereffect

Nach′wort *n* (-[e]s;-e) epilogue

Nach′wuchs *m* younger generation; younger set; children

nach′zählen *tr & intr* pay extra

nach′zählen *tr* count over, check

nach′zeichnen *tr* draw a copy of ‖ *intr* copy

nach′ziehen §163 *tr* drag; tow; (Linien) trace; (Schraube) tighten ‖ *intr* (SEIN) (dat) follow after

nach′zoteln *intr* (SEIN) (coll) trot after

Nachzügler –in [ˈnaxtsyklər(ɪn)] §6 *mf* straggler; latecomer

Nackedei [ˈnakədaɪ] *m* (-[e]s;-e) naked child; nude

Nacken [ˈnakən] *m* (-s;-) nape of the neck

nackend [ˈnakənt] *adj* var of nackt

Nackenschlag (Nak′kenschlag) *m* rabbit punch; (fig) hard blow

–nackig [nakɪç] *comb.fm.* –necked

nackt [nakt] *adj* nude, bare; (Tatsache) hard; sich n. ausziehen strip bare

Nackt′heit *f* (-;) nudity, nakedness

Nadel [ˈnadəl] *f* (-;-n) needle; pin; wie auf Nadeln sitzen be on pins and needles

Na′delbaum *m* coniferous tree

Na′delkissen *n* pin cushion

Nadelöhr [ˈnadəløːr] *n* (-s;-e) eye of a needle

Na′delstich *m* pinprick; (sew) stitch

Nagel [ˈnagəl] *m* (-s;-̈) nail; an den N. hängen (fig) shelve; an den Nägeln kauen bite one's nails

Na′gelhaut *f* cuticle

nageln [ˈnagəln] *tr & intr* nail

na′gelneu′ *adj* brand-new

nagen [ˈnagən] *tr* gnaw; das Fleisch vom Knochen n. pick the meat off the bone ‖ *intr* (an dat) gnaw (at); nibble (at); (fig) (an dat) rankle

Nagetier [ˈnagətiːr] *n* rodent

Nah- [na] *comb.fm.* close-range, short-range

Näh- [nɛ] *comb.fm.* sewing, needlework

Näh′arbeit *f* sewing, needlework

Näh′aufnahme *f* (phot) close-up

---

nahe [ˈnaːə] *adj* (näher [ˈnɛ·ər]; nächste [ˈnɛçstə] §9) near, close; nearby; (bevorstehend) forthcoming; (Gefahr) imminent ‖ *adv*—j—m zu n. treten hurt s.o.'s feelings; n. an. (dat or acc), n. bei close to; n. daran sein zu (inf) be on the point of (ger)

Nähe [ˈnɛ·ə] *f* (-;-n) nearness; vicinity; in der N. close by

na′hebei *adv* nearby

na′hebringen §65 *tr* drive home

na′hegehen §82 *intr* (SEIN) (dat) affect, touch, grieve

na′hekommen §99 *intr* (SEIN) approach; (dat) come near to; der Wahrheit n. get at the truth

na′helegen *tr* suggest

na′heliegen §108 *intr* be close by; be obvious; be easy

na′heliegend *adj* obvious

nahen [ˈnaːən] *ref & intr* (SEIN) approach; (dat) draw near to

nähen [ˈnɛ·ən] *tr & intr* sew, stitch

näher [ˈnɛ·ər] *adj* (comp of nahe) nearer; bei näherer Betrachtung upon further consideration ‖ *adv* closer; immer n. kommen close in; treten Sie n.! this way, please! ‖ Nähere §5 n details, particulars; das N. auseinandersetzen explain fully; Näheres erfahren learn further particulars; sich des Näheren entsinnen remember all particulars; wenn Sie Näheres wissen wollen if you want details

Näherin [ˈnɛ·ərɪn] *f* (-;-nen) seamstress

nähern [ˈnɛ·ərn] *ref* approach; (dat) draw near to, approach

Nä′herungswert *m* approximate value

na′hestehen §146 *intr* (dat) share the view of

na′hetreten §152 *intr* (SEIN) (dat) come into close contact with

na′hezu *adv* almost, nearly

Näh′garn *n* thread

Näh′kampf *m* hand-to-hand fighting; (box) in-fighting

nahm [nɑm] *pret* of nehmen

Näh′maschine *f* sewing machine

–nahme [nɑmə] *f* (-;-n) *comb.fm.* taking

Nähr- [nɛr] *comb.fm.* nutritive

Nähr′boden *m* rich soil; (fig) breeding ground; (biol) culture medium

nähren [ˈnɛrən] *tr* nourish, feed; (Kind) nurse ‖ *ref* make a living; sich n. von subsist on ‖ *intr* be nutritious

nahrhaft [ˈnɑrhaft] *adj* nourishing, nutritious, nutritive

Nähr′mittel *pl* (Teigwaren) noodles; (Hülsenfrüchte) beans and peas

Nahrung [ˈnɑrʊŋ] *f* (-;) nourishment; (Kost) diet; (Unterhalt) livelihood

Nah′rungsmittel *pl* food

Nah′rungsmittelvergiftung *f* food poisoning

Nah′rungssorgen *pl* difficulty in making ends meet

Nähr′wert *m* nutritive value

Näh′stube *f* sewing room

Naht [nɑt] *f* (-;-ᵉe) seam

Nah'verkehr m local traffic

Näh'zeug n sewing kit

naiv [na'if] adj naive

Name ['namə] m (-ns;-n), **Namen** ['namən] m (-s;-) name

na'menlos adj nameless; (*unsäglich*) indescribable

namens ['naməns] adv named, called || prep (*genit*) in the name of, on behalf of

Na'mensschild n nameplate

Na'menstag m name day

Na'mensvetter m namesake

namentlich ['naməntlɪç] adj—**namentliche Abstimmung** roll-call vote || adv by name, individually; (*besonders*) especially

Na'menverzeichnis n index of names; nomenclature

namhaft ['namhaft] adj distinguished; (*beträchtlich*) considerable; **n. machen** name, specify

nämlich ['nemlɪç] adv namely, that is; (coll) you know, you see

nannte ['nantə] pret of **nennen**

manu [na'nu] interj gee!

Napf [napf] m (-[e]s;=e) bowl

Narbe ['narbə] f (-;-n) scar; (*des Leders*) grain; (agr) topsoil

narbig ['narbɪç] adj scarred

Narkose [nar'kozə] f (-;-n) anesthesia

Narkoti-kum [nar'kotıkʊm] n (-s;-ka [ka]) narcotic, dope

markotisch [nar'kotɪʃ] adj narcotic

Narr [nar] m (-en;-en) fool; (hist) jester; **j—n zum Narren halten** make a fool of s.o.

Närrchen ['nerçən] n (-s;-) silly little goose

marren ['narən] tr make a fool of

Narrenfest ['narənfest] n masquerade

Narrenhaus ['narənhaʊs] n madhouse

Narrenkappe ['narənkapə] f cap and bells

narrensicher ['narənzɪçər] adj (coll) foolproof

Narren(s)possen ['narən(s)posən] pl horseplay; **laß die N.!** stop horsing around!

Narr'heit f (-;-en) folly

närrisch ['nerɪʃ] adj foolish; (*verrückt*) crazy; (*Kauz*) eccentric; **n. sein auf** (*acc*) be crazy about

Narzisse [nar'tsɪsə] f (-;-n) (bot) narcissus; **gelbe N.** daffodil

naschen ['naʃən] tr nibble at || intr (an dat, von) nibble (on); **gern n.** have a sweet tooth

Näscher –in ['neʃər(ɪn)] §6 mf nibbler

Näscherei [neʃə'raɪ] f (-;-en) snack

naschhaft ['naʃhaft] adj sweet-toothed

Naschkatze ['naʃkatsə] f nibbler

Naschmaul ['naʃmaʊl] n nibbler

Naschwerk ['naʃverk] n sweets, tidbits

Nase ['nazə] f (-;-n) nose; **auf der N. liegen** be laid up in bed; **aufgeworfene N.** turned-up nose; **das sticht ihm in die N.** it annoys him; he's itching to have it; **daß du die N. im Gesicht behältst!** keep your shirt on!; **dem Kind die N. putzen** wipe the child's nose; **die N. läuft ihm blau an** his nose is getting red; **die N. rüm-** **pfen über** (*acc*) turn up one's nose at; **die N. voll haben von** be fed up with; **e–e tüchtige N. voll bekommen** (or **einstecken müssen**) get chewed out; **faß dich an deine eigene N.!** mind your own business!; **feine N. für** flair for; **immer der N. nach!** follow your nose!; **in der N. bohren** poke one's nose; **j–m e–e lange N. machen** thumb one's nose at s.o.; **j–m e–e N. drehen** outwit s.o.; **j–m die Würmer aus der N. ziehen** worm it out of s.o.; **j–m etw auf die N. binden** divulge s.th. to s.o.; **j–m in die N. fahren** (or **steigen**) annoy s.o.; **j–n an der N. herumführen** lead s.o. by the nose; **man kann es ihm an der N. ansehen** it's written all over his face; **mit langer N. abziehen** be the loser; **pro N. per head; sich** [dat] **die N. begießen** wet one's whistle

näseln ['nezəln] intr speak through the nose || **Näseln** n (-s;) nasal twang

nä'selnd adj nasal

Na'senbein n nasal bone

Na'senbluten n (-s;) nosebleed

na'senlang adv—**alle n.** constantly

Na'senlänge f—**um e–e N.** by a nose

Na'senlaut m (phonet) nasal

Na'senloch n nostril

Na'senrücken m bridge of the nose

Na'senschleim m mucus

Na'senschleimhaut f mucous membrane

Nasenspray ['nazənspre] m (-s;-s) nose spray

Na'sentropfen m nose drop

na'seweis adj fresh, wise || **Naseweis** m (-es;-e) wise guy

Na'seweisheit f freshness

nasführen ['nasfyrən] tr lead by the nose; (*foppen*) fool

Nashorn ['nashorn] n (-[e]s;=er) rhinoceros

naß [nas] adj nasser ['nasər] or nässer ['nesər]; **nasseste** ['nasəstə] or **nässeste** ['nesəstə] §9) wet; (*feucht*) moist || **Naß** n (Nasses;) (poet) liquid

Nassauer ['nasaʊ·ər] m (-s;-) sponger, chiseler

nassauern ['nasaʊ·ərn] intr (coll) sponge

Nässe ['nesə] f (-;) wetness; moisture

nässen ['nesən] tr wet; moisten || intr ooze

naß'forsch adj rash, bold

naß'kalt adj raw, cold and damp

Nation [na'tsjon] f (-;-en) nation

national [natsjo'nal] adj national

National'hymne f national anthem

nationalisieren [natsjonalı'zirən] tr nationalize

Nationalismus [natsjona'lɪsmʊs] m (-s;) nationalism

Nationalität [natsjonalɪ'tet] f (-;-en) nationality; ethnic minority

National'sozialismus m national socialism, Nazism

National'sozialist –in §7 mf national socialist, Nazi

National'tracht f national costume

Nativität [natıvı'tet] f (-;-en) horoscope

Natrium ['nɑtrɪ·um] n (-s;) sodium
Natter ['natər] f (-;-n) adder, viper
Natur [na'tur] f (-;-en) nature; (Körperbeschaffenheit) constitution; (Gemütsart) disposition; (Art) character; (Person) creature; **von N. by nature**
Natura [na'tura] f—**in N. in kind**
Naturalien [natu'raljən] pl produce
naturalisieren [naturalɪ'ziːrən] tr naturalize || ref—**sich n. lassen become naturalized**
Natur'anlage f disposition
Natur'arzt m naturopath
Naturell [natu'rɛl] n (-[e]s;-e) nature, temperament
Natur'erscheinung f phenomenon
Natur'forscher –in §6 mf naturalist
Natur'gabe f natural gift, talent
natur'gemäß adv naturally
Natur'geschichte f natural history
Natur'gesetz n natural law
natur'getreu adj life-like
Natur'kunde f, Natur'lehre f natural science
natürlich [na'tyrlɪç] adj natural; (echt) real; (ungezwungen) natural; **das geht aber nicht mit natürlichen Dingen zu there is s.th. fishy about it; das geht ganz n. zu there is nothing strange about it** || adv naturally, of course
Natur'mensch m primitive man; nature enthusiast
Natur'philosoph m natural philosopher
Natur'recht n natural right
Natur'schutz m preservation of natural beauty
Natur'schutzgebiet n wildlife preserve
Natur'schutzpark m national park
Natur'spiel n freak of nature
Natur'theater n outdoor theater
Natur'trieb m instinct
Natur'verehrung f natural religion
Natur'volk n primitive people
natur'widrig adj contrary to nature
Natur'wissenschaft f natural science
Natur'wissenschaftler –in §6 mf scientist
naturwüchsig [na'turvyksɪç] adj unspoiled by civilization
Natur'zustand m natural state
nautisch ['nautɪʃ] adj nautical
Navigation [naviga'tsjon] f (-;) navigation
navigieren [navi'giːrən] intr navigate
Nazi ['natsi] m (-s;-s) Nazi
Nazismus [na'tsimus] m (-;) Nazism
nazistisch [na'tsɪstɪʃ] adj Nazi
Nebel ['nebəl] m (-s;-) fog, mist; (Dunst) haze
Ne'belbank f (-;̈e) fog bank
Ne'belfeld n patch of fog
Ne'belferne f hazy distance; (fig) dim future
Ne'belfleck m (astr) nebula
ne'belhaft adj foggy, hazy; (Ferne) dim
Ne'belhorn n foghorn
nebeln ['nebəln] intr be foggy
Ne'belscheinwerfer m (aut) fog light
Ne'belschicht f fog bank
Ne'belschirm m smoke screen
Ne'belvorhang m smoke screen
neben ['nebən] prep (dat & acc) by,

beside; side by side with, alongside, close to, next to; (verglichen mit) compared with; (außer) besides, aside from; in addition to; extra
Neben– comb.fm. secondary, accessory, by–, side–, subordinate
Ne'benabsicht f ulterior motive
Ne'benaltar m side altar
Ne'benamt n additional duties
nebenan' adv close by; next-door
Ne'benanschluß m (telp) extension; (telp) party line
Ne'benarbeit f extra work
Ne'benarm m tributary, branch
Ne'benausgaben pl incidentals, extras
Ne'benausgang m side exit
Ne'benbahn f (rr) branch line
Ne'benbedeutung f (-;-en) secondary meaning
nebenbei' adv close by; (außerdem) besides, on the side; (beiläufig) incidentally
Ne'benberuf m sideline, side job
ne'benberuflich adj sideline, sparetime
Ne'benbeschäftigung f sideline
Nebenbuhler –in ['nebənbuːlər(ɪn)] §6 mf competitor, rival
ne'benbuhlerisch adj rival
Ne'bending n secondary matter
nebeneinan'der adv side by side; neck and neck; (gleichzeitig) simultaneously; **n. bestehen coexist**
Nebeneinan'derleben n coexistence
nebeneinan'derstellen tr juxtapose
Ne'beneingang m side entrance
Ne'beneinkünfte pl, Ne'beneinnahmen pl extra income
Ne'benerzeugnis n by-product
Ne'benfach n (educ) minor; **als N. studieren minor in**
Ne'benflügel m (archit) wing
Ne'benfluß m tributary
Ne'benfrage f side issue
Ne'benfrau f concubine
Ne'bengang m side aisle
Ne'bengasse f side street, alley
Ne'bengebäude n annex, wing
Ne'bengedanke m ulterior motive
Ne'bengericht n side dish
Ne'bengeschäft n (com) branch
Ne'bengleis n (rr) siding, sidetrack
Ne'benhandlung f (-;-en) subplot
nebenher' adv on the side; besides; along
nebenhin' adv incidentally, by the way
Ne'benkosten pl incidentals, extras
Ne'benlinie f (rr) branch line
Ne'benmann m (-[e]s;̈er) neighbor
Ne'benprodukt n by-product
Ne'benpunkt m minor point
Ne'benrolle f supporting role
Ne'bensache f side issue
ne'bensächlich adj subordinate; incidental; (unwesentlich) unimportant
Ne'bensächlichkeit f unimportance; triviality
Ne'bensatz m subordinate clause
Ne'benschaltung f (-;-en) (elec) shunt
Ne'benschluß m (elec) shunt
Ne'benspesen pl additional charges
ne'benstehend adj marginal, in the margin || Nebenstehende §5 mf bystander

Ne′benstelle f branch; (telp) extension
Ne′benstraße f side street
Ne′bentisch m next table
Ne′bentür f side door
Ne′benverdienst m extra pay; side job
Ne′benvorstellung f side show
Ne′benweg m side road
Ne′benwirkung f (-; -en) side effect
Ne′benzimmer n adjoining room
Ne′benzweck m secondary aim
neblig [′neblɪç] adj foggy, misty
nebst [nepst] prep (dat) including
necken [′nekən] tr & recip tease, kid
Neckerei [nekə′raɪ] f (-; -en) teasing
meckisch [′nekɪʃ] adj fond of teasing; (coll) cute
nee [ne] adv (dial) no
Neffe [′nefə] m (-n; -n) nephew
Negation [nega′tsjon] f (-; -en) negation
negativ [nega′tif] adj negative ‖ **Negativ** n (-s; -e) negative
Neger –in [′negər(ɪn)] §6 mf black, Negro
Negligé [neglɪ′ʒe] n (-s; -s) negligee
nehmen [′nemən] §116 tr take; (weg-) take away; (anstellen) take on, hire; (Anwalt) retain; (Hindernis) clear, take; (Kurve) negotiate; (Schaden) suffer; **Anfang n.** begin; **Anstand n.** hesitate; **an sich n.** pocket, misappropriate; collect; retrieve; **Anstoß n. an** (dat) take offense at; **auf sich n.** assume, take upon oneself; **das Wort n.** begin to speak; **den Mund voll n.** (coll) talk big; **die Folgen auf sich n.** bear the consequences; **ein Ende n.** come to an end; **ein gutes Ende n.** turn out all right; **er versteht es, die Kunden richtig zu n.** he knows how to handle customers; **etw genau n.** take s.th. literally; **ich lasse es mir nicht n. zu** (inf) I insist on (ger); **im Grunde genommen** basically; **in Angriff n.** begin; **in Arbeit n.** start making; **in die Hand n.** pick up; (fig) take in hand; **j–m etw n.** take s.th. away from s.o.; **deprive** s.o. of s.th.; **kein Ende n.** go on endlessly; **man nehme zwei Eier, usw.** (im Kochbuch) take two eggs, etc.; **n. Sie bitte Platz!** please sit down; **n. wir den Fall, daß** let's suppose that; **Rücksicht n. auf** (acc) show consideration for; **sich** [dat] **das Leben n.** take one's life; **sich** [dat] **nichts von seinen Rechten n. lassen** insist on one's rights; **streng genommen** strictly speaking; **Stunden n.** take lessons; **Urlaub n.** take a vacation; (mil) go on furlough; **wie man's nimmt** it all depends; **zu Hilfe n.** use; **zur Ehe n.** marry; **zu sich** [dat] **n.** put into one's pocket; (Speise) eat; (Kind) take charge of
Neid [naɪt] m (-es;) envy; **blasser** (or **gelber**) **N.** pure envy; **vor N. vergehen** die of envy
neiden [′naɪdən] tr—**j–m etw n.** envy s.o. for s.th.
Neid′hammel m envious person
nel′dig adj (dial) var of neidisch
neidisch [′naɪdɪʃ] adj (auf acc) envious (of)

neid′los adj free of envy
Neid′nagel m hangnail
Neige [′naɪgə] f (-; -n) slope; (Abnahme) decline; (Überbleibsel) sediment, dregs; **zur N. gehen** (Geld, Vorräte) run low; (Sonne) go down; (Tag, Jahr) draw to a close
neigen [′naɪgən] tr incline, bend; **geneigt** sloping; (fig) friendly, favorable ‖ ref (vor dat) bow (to); (Abhang) slope; **sich zum Ende n.** draw to a close ‖ intr—n. zu be inclined to
Nel′gung f (-; -en) slope, incline; (des Hauptes) bowing; (e–s Schiffes) list; (in der Straße) dip; (Gefälle) gradient; (Hang) inclination; (Anlage) tendency; (Vorliebe) taste, liking; (Zuneigung) affection; **e–e N. nach rechts haben** lean towards the right; **N. fassen zu** take (a fancy) to
nein [naɪn] adv no ‖ **Nein** n (-s;) no
Nein′stimme f (parl) nay
Nekrolog [nekrə′lok] m (-[e]s;-e) obituary
Nektar [′nektar] m (-s;) nectar
Nelke [′nelkə] f (-; -n) carnation; (Gewürz) clove
Nel′kenöl n oil of cloves
Nel′kenpfeffer m allspice
Nemesis [′nemezɪs] f (-;) Nemesis
nennbar [′nenbar] adj mentionable
nennen [′nenən] §97 tr name, call; (erwähnen) mention; (benennen) term ‖ ref be called, be named
nen′nenswert adj worth mentioning
Nenner [′nenər] m (-s;-) (math) denominator; **auf e–n gemeinsamen N. bringen** reduce to a common denominator
Nennform [′nenform] f (gram) infinitive
Nenngeld [′nengelt] n entry fee
Nen′nung f (-;) naming; mentioning
Nennwert [′nenvert] m face value
Neologis-mus [ne-ɔlɔ′gɪsmus] m (-; -men [mən]) neologism
Neon [′ne-ɔn] n (-s;) neon
Ne′onlicht n neon light
Nepotismus [nepɔ′tɪsmus] m (-;) nepotism
neppen [′nepən] tr (coll) gyp, clip
Nepplokal [′neplɔkal] n (sl) clip joint
Neptun [nep′tun] m (-s;) Neptune
Nerv [nerf] m (-s;-en) nerve; **die Nerven behalten** keep cool; **die Nerven verlieren** lose one's head; **j–m auf die Nerven gehen** get on s.o.'s nerves; **mit den Nerven herunter sein** be a nervous wreck
Nerven-, nerven- [nerfən] comb.fm. nervous, neuro–, of nerves
Ner′venarzt m, **Ner′venärztin** f neurologist
ner′venaufreibend adj nerve-racking
Ner′venberuhigungsmittel n sedative
Ner′venbündel n (fig) bundle of nerves
Ner′venentzündung f neuritis
Ner′venfaser f nerve fiber
Ner′venheilanstalt f mental institution
Ner′venheilkunde f neurology
Ner′venkitzel m thrill, suspense
Ner′venknoten m ganglion
ner′venkrank adj neurotic

Ner'venkrieg m war of nerves
Ner'venlehre f neurology
Ner'vensäge f (coll) pain in the neck
Ner'venschmerz m neuralgia
Ner'venschwäche f nervousness
Ner'venzentrum n (fig) nerve center
Ner'venzusammenbruch m nervous breakdown
nervig ['nɛrvɪç], ['nɛrfɪç] adj sinewy
nervös [nɛr'vøs] adj nervous
Nervosität [nɛrvozɪ'tet] f (-;) nervousness
Nerz [nɛrts] m (-es;-e) (zool) mink
Nerz'mantel m mink coat
Nessel ['nɛsəl] f (-;-n) nettle; sich in die Nesseln setzen (fig) get oneself into hot water
Nest [nɛst] n. (-es;-er) nest; (Schlupfwinkel) hideout; small town; dead town; (Bett) (coll) bed
nesteln ['nɛstəln] tr lace, tie || intr —n. an (dat) fiddle with, fuss with
Nesthäkchen ['nɛsthɛkçən] n (-s;-), Nestküken ['nɛstkykən] n (-s;-) baby (of the family)
nett [nɛt] adj nice; (sauber) neat; (niedlich) cute; das kann ja n. werden! (iron) that's going to be just dandy!
netto ['nɛto] adv net; clear
Net'togewicht n net weight
Net'togewinn m clear profit
Net'tolohn m take-home pay
Net'topreis m net price
Netz [nɛts] n (-es;-e) net; network; grid
netzen ['nɛtsən] tr wet, moisten
Netz'haut f retina
Netz'werk n netting, webbing
neu [nɔɪ] adj new; (frisch) fresh; (unlängst geschehen) recent; aufs neue anew; neuere Geschichte modern history; neuere Sprachen modern languages; von neuem all over again || adv newly; recently; anew; afresh || Neue f,m,n newcomer || §5 n— was gibt es Neues? what's new?
Neu-, neu- comb.fm. new-, newly; re-; neo-
Neu'anlage f new installation; (fin) reinvestment
Neu'anschaffung f recent acquisition
neu'artig adj novel; modern
Neu'aufführung f (-;-en) (theat) revival
Neu'ausgabe f new edition, republication; (Neudruck) reprint
Neu'bau m (-[e]s;-bauten) new building
neu'bearbeiten tr revise
Neubelebung ['nɔɪbəlebʊŋ] f (-;-en) revival
Neu'bildung f (-;-en) new growth; (gram) neologism
Neu'druck m reprint
neuerdings ['nɔɪərdɪŋs] adv recently; (vom neuem) anew
Neuerer -in ['nɔɪ·ərər(ɪn)] §6 mf innovator
Neuerung ['nɔɪ·ərʊŋ] f (-;-en) innovation
neuestens ['nɔɪ·əstəns] adv recently
Neu'fassung f revision

Neufundland [nɔɪ'fʊntlant] n (-s;) Newfoundland
neu'gebacken adj fresh-baked; brand-new
neu'geboren adj new-born
neu'gestalten tr reorganize
Neu'gier f, Neugierde ['nɔɪgɪrdə] f (-;) curiosity, inquisitiveness
neu'gierig adj curious, nosey
Neu'gründung f (-;-en) reestablishment
Neu'gruppierung f (-;-en) regrouping; reshuffling
Neu'heit f (-;-en) novelty
neu'hochdeutsch adj modern High German
Neu'igkeit f (-;-en) news, piece of news
Neu'jahr n New Year
Neu'land n virgin soil; (fig) new ground
neu'lich adv lately
Neuling ['nɔɪlɪŋ] m (-[e]s;-e) beginner
neu'modisch adj fashionable; newfangled
neun [nɔɪn] invar adj & pron nine || Neun f (-;-en) nine
Neunmalkluge ['nɔɪnmalklugə] §5 mf wiseacre
neunte ['nɔɪntə] §9 adj & pron ninth
Neuntel ['nɔɪntəl] n (-s;-) ninth
neun'zehn invar adj & pron nineteen || Neunzehn f (-;-en) nineteen
neun'zehnte §9 adj & pron nineteenth
neunzig ['nɔɪntsɪç] invar adj & pron ninety || Neunzig f (-;-en) ninety
neunziger ['nɔɪntsɪgər] invar adj of the nineties; die n. Jahre the nineties || Neunziger -in §6 mf nonagenarian
neunzigste ['nɔɪntsɪçstə] §9 adj & pron ninetieth
Neu'ordnung f (-;-en) reorganization
Neural'gie [nɔɪral'gi] f (-;-gien ['gi·ən]) neuralgia
Neu'regelung f (-;-en) rearrangement
Neu-ron ['nɔɪrɔn] n (-s;-ronen ['ronən]) neuron
Neurose [nɔɪ'rozə] f (-;-n) neurosis
Neurotiker -in [nɔɪ'rotikər(ɪn)] §6 mf neurotic
neurotisch [nɔɪ'rotɪʃ] adj neurotic
Neusee'land n (-s;) New Zealand
Neu'silber n German silver
Neusprachler -in ['nɔɪ/praxlər(ɪn)] §6 mf modern-language teacher
Neu'stadt f new section of town
Neu'steinzeit f neolithic age
neu'steinzeitlich adj neolithic
neutral [nɔɪ'tral] adj neutral
neutralisieren [nɔɪtralɪ'zirən] tr neutralize
Neutralität [nɔɪtralɪ'tet] f (-;) neutrality
Neu-tron ['nɔɪtrɔn] n (-;-tronen ['trɔnən]) neutron
Neu-trum ['nɔɪtrʊm] n (-s;-tra [tra] & -tren [trən]) (gram) neuter
neuvermählt ['nɔɪfɛrmelt] adj newly married || Neuvermählte §5 pl newlyweds
Neu'zeit f recent times
Nibelung ['nibəlʊŋ] m (-s;) (myth)

(King) Nibelung ‖ *m* (-en;-en) Nibelung

nicht [nɪçt] *adv* not; **auch...nicht** not ...either; **n. doch!** please don't; **n. einmal** not even, not so much as; **n. mehr** no longer, no more; **n. um die Welt** not for the world; **n. wahr?** isn't it so?, no?, right?

Nicht-, nicht- *comb.fm.* in-, im-, un-, non-

Nicht'achtung *f* disregard, disrespect; **N. des Gerichts** contempt of court

nicht'amtlich *adj* unofficial

Nicht'angriffspakt *m* nonaggression pact

Nicht'annahme *f* nonacceptance

Nichte ['nɪçtə] *f* (-;-n) niece

Nicht'einmischung *f* noninterference

Nicht'eisenmetall *n* nonferrous metal

nichtig ['nɪçtɪç] *adj* invalid; void; (*eitel*) vain; (*vergänglich*) transitory; **für n. erklären** annul

Nich'tigkeit *f* (-;-en) invalidity; futility; (*Kleinigkeit*) trifle; **Nichtigkeiten** trivia

Nich'tigkeitserklärung *f* annulment

Nicht'kämpfer *m* noncombatant

nicht'öffentlich *adj* private; (*Sitzung*) closed

nicht'rostend *adj* rustproof; (*Stahl*) stainless

nichts [nɪçts] *indef pron* nothing; gar **n.** nothing at all; **n. als** nothing but; **n. mehr davon!** not another word about it!; **n. und wieder n.** absolutely nothing; **soviel wie n.** next to nothing; **um n.** for nothing, to no avail; **weiter n.?** is that all?; **wenn es weiter n. ist!** if it's nothing worse than that ‖ **Nichts** *n* (-s;) nothingness; nonentity; (*Leere*) void; (*Kleinigkeit*) trifle; **vor dem N. stehen** be faced with utter ruin

nichtsdestowe'niger *adv* nevertheless

Nichts'könner *m* incompetent person; ignoramus

Nichts'nutz *m* good-for-nothing

nichts'nutzig *adj* good-for-nothing

nichts'sagend *adj* insignificant; (*Antwort*) vague; noncommittal; (*Gesicht*) vacuous; (*Redensart*) trite

Nichts'tuer -in §6 *mf* loafer

Nichts'wisser -in §6 *mf* ignoramus

nichts'würdig *adj* contemptible

Nicht'zutreffende §5 *n*—**Nichtzutreffendes streichen!** delete if not applicable

Nickel ['nɪkəl] *n* (-s;-) (metal) nickel

nicken ['nɪkən] *intr* nod; (*schlummern*) nap

Nickerchen ['nɪkərçən] *n* (-s;-) nap

nie [ni] *adv* never, at no time

nieder ['nidər] *adj* low; (*gemein*) base ‖ *adv* down

nie'derbrechen §64 *tr & intr* (SEIN) break down

nie'derbrennen §97 *tr & intr* (SEIN) burn down

nie'derdeutsch *adj* Low German ‖ **Niederdeutsch** §5 *n* Low German ‖ **Niederdeutsche** §5 *mf* North German

nie'derdonnern *tr* (coll) shout down ‖ *intr* go (or come) crashing down

Nie'derdruck *m* low pressure

nie'derdrücken *tr* press down (fig) weigh down; (*unterdrücken*) oppress; (*entmutigen*) depress

nie'derfallen §72 *intr* (SEIN) fall down

Nie'derfrequenz *f* low frequency; audio frequency

Nie'dergang *m* descent; (*der Sonne*) setting; (fig) decline, fall

nie'dergehen §82 *intr* (SEIN) go down; (*Flugzeug*) land; (*Regen*) fall; (*Vorhang*) drop

nie'dergeschlagen *adj* dejected

nie'derhalten §90 *tr* hold down, keep down

nie'derholen *tr* lower, haul down

Nie'derholz *n* underbrush

nie'derkämpfen *tr* (& fig) overcome

nie'derkommen §99 *intr* (SEIN) (mit) give birth (to)

Niederkunft ['nidərkunft] *f* (-;) confinement, childbirth

Nie'derlage *f* defeat; (*Lager*) warehouse; (*Filiale*) branch

Niederlande, die ['nidərlandə] *pl* The Netherlands, Holland

Niederländer ['nidərlendər] *m* (-s;-) Dutchman

niederländisch ['nidərlendɪʃ] *adj* Dutch

nie'derlassen §104 *tr* let down ‖ *ref* sit down, recline; (*Wohnsitz nehmen*) settle; (*ein Geschäft eröffnen*) set oneself up in business; (*Vogel, Flugzeug*) land

Nie'derlassung *f* (-;-en) settlement, colony; establishment; (*e-r Bank*) branch; (com) plant

nie'derlegen *tr* lay down, put down; (*Amt*) resign; (*Geschäft*) give up; (*Krone*) abdicate; (*schriftlich*) set down in writing; **die Arbeit n.** go on strike ‖ *ref* lie down; go to bed

nie'dermachen *tr* butcher, massacre

nie'dermähen *tr* mow down

nie'dermetzeln *tr* butcher, massacre

Nie'derschlag *m* (Bodensatz) sediment; (box) knockdown; (chem) precipitate; (meteor) precipitation; **radioaktiver N.** fallout

nie'derschlagen §132 *tr* knock down; (*Augen*) cast down; (*Aufstand*) put down; (*vertuschen*) hush up; (*Verfahren*) quash; (*Forderung*) waive; (*Hoffnungen*) dash; (chem) precipitate

nie'derschmettern *tr* knock to the ground; (fig) crush

nie'derschreiben §62 *tr* write down

nie'dersetzen *tr* set down ‖ *ref* sit down

nie'dersinken §143 *intr* (SEIN) sink down

nie'derstimmen *tr* vote down

Nie'dertracht *f* nastiness, meanness

nie'derträchtig *adj* nasty; underhand

Nie'derung *f* (-;-en) low ground, depression

niederwärts ['nidərverts] *adv* downward

nie'derwerfen §160 *tr* knock down; (*Aufstand*) put down ‖ *ref* fall down

Nie'derwild *n* small game

niedlich ['nitlɪç] *adj* nice, cute

Niednagel ['nitnagəl] *m* hangnail

niedrig ['niːdrɪç] *adj* low; (*Herkunft*) humble; (*gemein*) mean, base

niemals ['niːmals] *adv* never

niemand ['niːmant] *indef pron* no one, nobody

Nie'mandsland *n* no man's land

Niere ['niːrə] *f* (-;-n) kidney; **das geht mir an die Nieren** (fig) that cuts me deep

nieseln ['niːzəln] *impers*—**es nieselt** it is drizzling

Nie'selregen *m* drizzle

niesen ['niːzən] *intr* sneeze

Niet [niːt] *m* (-[e]s;-e) rivet

Niete ['niːtə] *f* (-;-n) rivet; (*in der Lotterie*) blank; (*Versager*) flop

nieten ['niːtən] *tr* rivet

niet-/ und na'gelfest *adj* nailed down

Nihilismus [nihi'lɪsmʊs] *m* (-;) nihilism

Nikotin [nikoˈtiːn] *n* (-s;) nicotine

nikotin'arm *adj* low in nicotine

Nil [niːl] *m* (-s;) Nile

Nil'pferd *n* hippopotamus

Nimbus ['nɪmbʊs] *m* (-;-se) halo; aura; (*Ansehen*) prestige; (meteor) nimbus

nimmer ['nɪmər] *adv* never; (dial) no more

nim'mermehr *adv* never more; by no means

Nippel ['nɪpəl] *m* (-s;-) (mach) nipple

nippen ['nɪpən] *tr & intr* sip

Nippsachen ['nɪpzaxən] *pl* knicknacks

nirgends ['nɪrgənts] *adv* nowhere

nirgendwo ['nɪrgəntvoː] *adv* nowhere

Nische ['niːʃə] *f* (-;-n) niche

nisten ['nɪstən] *intr* nest

Nitrat [ni'traːt] *n* (-[e]s;-e) nitrate

Nitrid [ni'triːt] *n* (-[e]s;-e) nitride

Nitroglyzerin [nitroglytsə'riːn] *n* (-s;) nitroglycerin

Niveau [ni'voː] *n* (-s;-s) level; **N. haben** have class; **unter dem N. sein** be substandard

Niveau'übergang *m* (rr) grade crossing

nivellieren [nivɛ'liːrən] *tr* level

nix [nɪks] *indef pron* (dial) nothing ||
Nix *m* (-[e]s;-e) water sprite

Nixe ['nɪksə] *f* (-;-n) water nymph

nobel ['noːbəl] *adj* noble; elegant; (*freigebig*) generous

noch [nɔx] *adv* still, yet; even; else; **heute n.** this very day; **n. besser** even bettter; **n. dazu** over and above that; **n. einer** one more, still another; **n. einmal** once more; **n. einmal so viel** twice as much; **n. etwas** one more thing; **n. etwas?** anything else?; **n. heute** even today; **n. immer** still; **n. nicht** not yet; **n. nie** never before; **n. und n.** (coll) over and over; **sei es n. so klein** now matter how small it is; **was denn n. alles?** what next? **wer kommt n.?** who else is coming?

noch'mal *adv* once more

nochmalig ['nɔxmaːlɪç] *adj* repeated

nochmals ['nɔxmals] *adv* once more

Nocke ['nɔkə] *f* (-;-n) (mach) cam

Nockenwelle (**Nok'kenwelle**) *f* camshaft

Nockerl ['nɔkərl] *n* (-s;- & -n) (Aust) dumpling

Nomade [noˈmaːdə] *m* (-n;-n) nomad

nominell [nomɪ'nɛl] *adj* nominal

nominieren [nomɪ'niːrən] *tr* nominate

Nonne ['nɔnə] *f* (-;-n) nun

Non'nenkloster *n* convent

Noppe ['nɔpə] *f* (-;-n) (tex) nap

Nord [nɔrt] *m* (-[e]s;); North; (poet) north wind

Norden ['nɔrdən] *m* (-s;) North; **im N. von** north of

nordisch ['nɔrdɪʃ] *adj* northern; (*Rasse*) Nordic; (*skandinavisch*) Norse

nördlich ['nœrtlɪç] *adj* northern

Nord'licht *n* northern lights

nordwärts ['nɔrtvɛrts] *adv* northward

Nörgelei [nœrgə'laɪ] *f* (-;-en) griping

nörgelig ['nœrgəlɪç] *adj* nagging

nörgeln ['nœrgəln] *intr*—**n. an** (*dat*) gripe about, kick about

Norm [nɔrm] *f* (-;-en) norm, standard

normal [nɔr'maːl] *adj* normal, standard

normalisieren [nɔrmalɪ'ziːrən] *tr* normalize

Normal'zeit *f* standard time

Normanne [nɔr'manə] *m* (-n;-n) Norman

normen ['nɔrmən], **normieren** [nɔr'miːrən] *tr* normalize, standardize

Norwegen ['nɔrveːgən] *n* (-s;) Norway

Norweger **–in** [nɔr'veːgər(ɪn)] §6 *mf* Norwegian

norwegisch [nɔr'veːgɪʃ] *adj* Norwegian

Not [noːt] *f* (-;-e) need, want; (*Notlage*) necessity; (*Gefahr*) distress; (*Dringlichkeit*) emergency; **es hat keine Not** there's no hurry about it; **es tut not** it is necessary; **in der Not** in a pinch; **in Not geraten** fall upon hard times; **j-m große Not machen** give s.o. a lot of trouble; **j-m seine Not klagen** cry on s.o.'s shoulders; **mit knapper Not** narrowly; **mit Not** scarcely; **Not haben zu** (*inf*) be scarcely able to (*inf*); **Not leiden** suffer want; **ohne Not** needlessly; **seine liebe Not haben mit** have a lot of trouble with; **sie haben Not auszukommen** they have difficulty making ends meet; **zur Not** if need be, in a pinch

Nota ['noːta] *f* (-;-s) note; **etw in N. geben** place an order for s.th.; **etw in N. nehmen** make a note of s.th.

Notar **–in** [noˈtaːr(ɪn)] §8 *mf* notary public

Notariat [nota'rjaːt] *n* (-[e]s;-e) notary office

notariell [nota'rjɛl] *adv*—**n. beglaubigen** notarize

Not'ausgang *m* emergency exit

Not'ausstieg *m* escape hatch

Not'behelf *m* makeshift, stopgap

Not'bremse *f* (rr) emergency brake

Notdurft ['noːtdʊrft] *f* (-;) want; necessities of life; **seine N. verrichten** relieve oneself

not'dürftig *adj* scanty, poor; hard up; (*behelfsmäßig*) temporary

Note ['noːtə] *f* (-;-n) note; (*Banknote*) bill; (*Eigenart*) tint; (educ) mark; (mus) note; **in Noten setzen** set to music; **nach Noten** (fig) thoroughly; **persönliche Note** personal touch; **wie nach Noten** like clock-work

No'tenblatt n sheet music

No'tenbuch n, **No'tenheft** n music book

No'tenlinie f (mus) line

No'tenschlüssel m (mus) clef

No'tenständer m music stand

No'tensystem n (mus) staff

Not'fall m emergency

notfalls ['notfals] adv if necessary

notgedrungen ['notgədruŋən] adj com-pulsory ‖ adv of necessity

notieren [no'tiran] tr note down; jot down; (Preise) quote

Notie'rung f (-;-en) noting; (st. exch.) quotation

nötig ['nøtiç] adj necessary; **das habe ich nicht n.!** I don't have to stand for that!; **n. haben** need

nötigen ['nøtigən] tr urge; (zwingen) force ‖ ref—**lassen Sie sich nicht n.!** don't wait to be asked; **sich genötigt sehen zu** (inf) feel compelled to (inf)

nö'tigenfalls adv in case of need

Nö'tigung f (-;) compulsion; urgent request; (jur) duress

Notiz [no'tits] f (-;-en) notice; (Ver-merk) note, memorandum; **keine N. nehmen von** take no notice of; **sich** [dat] **Notizen machen** jot down notes

Notiz'block m scratch pad

Not'lage f predicament; emergency

Not'landung f emergency landing

Not'lüge f white lie

Not'maßnahme f emergency measure

Not'nagel m (fig) stopgap

notorisch [no'tori∫] adj notorious

Not'pfennig m savings; **sich e-n N. auf-sparen** save up for a rainy day

Not'ruf m (telp) emergency

Not'signal n distress signal

Not'stand m state of emergency

Not'standsgebiet n disaster area

Not'treppe f fire escape

Not'wehr f—**aus N.** in self-defense

notwendig ['notvendiç] adj necessary

Not'wendigkeit f (-;-en) necessity

Not'zeichen n distress signal

Not'zucht f rape

not'züchtigen tr rape, ravish

Nougat ['nugat] m & n (-s;-s) nougat

Novelle [no'velə] f (-;-n) short story; (parl) amendment, rider

November [no'vembər] m (-s;-) No-vember

Novität [novi'tet] f (-;-en) novelty

Novize [no'vitsə] m (-n;-n), **Novizin** [no'vitsɪn] f (-;-nen), novice

Noviziat [novi'tsjat] n (-[e]s;-e) novi-tiate

Nu [nu] invar m—**im Nu** in a jiffy

Nuance [ny'ãsə] f (-;-n) nuance

nüchtern ['nɪçtərn] adj fasting; not having had breakfast; (Magen) empty; (nicht betrunken) sober; (leidenschaftslos) cool; (geistlos) dry, dull; (unsentimental) matter-of-fact

Nudel ['nudəl] f (-;-n) noodle; **e-e komische N.** (coll) a funny person

Nu'delholz n rolling pin

nudeln ['nudəln] tr force-feed

Nugat ['nugat] m (-s;-s) nougat

nuklear [nukle'ar] adj nuclear

Nukle·on ['nukle·ɔn] n (-s;-onen [-'onən]) nucleon

null [nul] adj null; **n. und nichtig** null and void; **n. und nichtig machen** an-nul ‖ **Null** f (-;-en) naught; zero; (fig) nobody; **in N. Komma nichts** in less than no time, in no time

Null'punkt m zero; freezing point; **auf dem N. angekommen sein** hit bot-tom

Numera·le [nume'ralə] n (-s;-lien [ljən] & -lia [lja]) numeral

numerieren [nume'riron] tr number; **numerierten Platz** reserved seat

numerisch [nu'meri∫] adj numerical

Nummer ['numər] f (-;-n) number; (Größe) size; (e-r Zeitung) issue; **auf N. Sicher sitzen** (sl) be in jail; **bei j-m e-e gute N. haben** (coll) be in good with s.o.; **e-e bloße N.** a mere figurehead; **er ist e-e N.** he's quite a character; **laufende N.** serial number; **N. besetzt!** line is busy!

Num'mernfolge f numerical order

Num'mernscheibe f (telp) dial

Num'mernschild n (aut) license plate

nun [nun] adv now; **nun?** well?; **nun aber** now; **nun also!** well now!; **nun gut!** all right then!; **nun und nim-mer(mehr)** never more; **von nun ab** from now on; **wenn er nun käme?** what if he came?

nun'mehr adv now; from now on

nur [nur] adv only, merely, but; (lauter) nothing but; **nicht nur ... sondern auch** not only ... but also; **nur daß** except that; **nur eben** scarcely; (zeitlich) a moment ago; **nur zu!** go to it!; **wenn nur** if only, provided that

Nürnberg ['nʏrnberk] n (-s;) Nurem-berg

nuscheln ['nu∫əln] intr (coll) mumble

Nuß [nus] f (-; Nüsse) nut

nuß'braun adj nut-brown; (Augen) hazel

Nuß'kern m kernel

Nußknacker ['nusknakər] m (-s;-) nutcracker

Nuß'schale f nutshell

Nüster ['nystər] f (-;-n) nostril

Nut [nut] f (-;-en), **Nute** ['nutə] f (-;-n) groove, rabbet

Nutte ['nutə] f (-;-n) whore

nutz [nuts] adj useful; **zu nichts n. sein** be good for nothing ‖ **Nutz** m (-es;) use; benefit; profit; **zu j-s N. und Frommen** for s.o.'s benefit

Nutz'anwendung f utilization

nutzbar ['nutsbar] adj useful; **sich** [dat] **etw n. machen** utilize s.th.

nutz'bringend adj useful, profitable

nütze ['nytsə] adj useful; **nichts n.** of no use; **zu nichts n. sein** be good for nothing

Nutz'effekt m efficiency

nutzen ['nutsən], **nützen** ['nʏtsən] tr make use of; **das kann mir viel (wenig, nichts) n.** this can do me much (little, no) good; **was nützt das**

alles? what's the good of all this? ‖ *intr* do good ‖ *impers*—es nützt nichts it's no use ‖ **Nutzen** *m* (-s;-) use; benefit; (*Gewinn*) profit; (*Vorteil*) advantage; von N. sein be of use

Nutz/fahrzeug *n* commercial vehicle
Nutz/garten *m* vegetable garden
Nutz/holz *n* lumber
Nutz/leistung *f* (mech) output

nützlich ['nʏtslɪç] *adj* useful
nutz/los *adj* useless
Nutz/losigkeit *f* (-;) uselessness
Nutz/schwelle *f* break-even point
Nut/zung *f* (-;) use
Nylon ['naɪlɔn] *n* (-s;) nylon
Nymphe ['nʏmfə] *f* (-;-n) nymph
Nymphomanin [nʏmfoˈmanɪn] *f* (-; -nen) nymphomaniac

O

O, o [o] *invar n* O, o
Oase [oˈazə] *f* (-;-n) oasis
ob [ɔp] *prep* (*dat*) above; (*genit*) on account of ‖ *conj* whether; als ob as if; **na ob!** rather!; **und ob!** and how!
Obacht ['obaxt] *f* (-;)—**in O. nehmen** take care of; **O.!** watch out!; **O. geben auf** (*acc*) pay attention to; take care of
Obdach ['ɔpdax] *n* (-[e]s;) shelter
ob/dachlos *adj* homeless
Obduktion [ɔpdukˈtsjon] *f* (-;-en) autopsy
obduzieren [ɔpduˈtsirən] *tr* perform an autopsy on
O-Beine ['obaɪnə] *pl* bow legs
O/-beinig *adj* bowlegged
Obelisk [obeˈlɪsk] *m* (-en;-en) obelisk
oben ['obən] *adv* above; (*in der Höhe*) up; (*im Himmelsraum*) on high; (*im Hause*) upstairs; (*auf der Spitze*) at the top; (*auf der Oberfläche*) on the surface; (*Aufschrift auf Kisten*) this side up; **da o.** up there; **nach o. gehen** go up, go upstairs; **o. am Tische sitzen** sit at the head of the table; **o. auf** (*dat*) at the top of, on the top of; **von o.** from above; **von o. bis unten** from top to bottom; from head to foot; **von o. herab** (fig) condescendingly; **wie o. angegeben** as stated above
obenan/ *adv* at the top, at the head
obenauf/ *adv* on top; **immer o. sein** be always in top spirits
obendrein [obənˈdraɪn] *adv* on top of it, into the bargain
o/benerwähnt, o/bengenannt *adj* above-mentioned
o/bengesteuert *adj* (aut) overhead
obenhin/ *adv* superficially; perfunctorily
obenhinaus/ *adv*—**o. wollen** have big ideas
o/ben-oh/ne *adj* (coll) topless
o/benstehend *adj* given above
Ober ['obər] *m* (-s;-) (coll) waiter; **Herr O.!** waiter!
Ober- *comb.fm.* upper, higher; superior; chief, supreme; head; southern
O/berägypten *n* Upper Egypt
O/berarm *m* upper arm
O/beraufseher *m* inspector general; superintendent
O/beraufsicht *f* superintendence

O/berbau *m* (-[e]s;-ten) superstructure
O/berbefehl *m* supreme command; **O. führen** have supreme command
O/berbefehlshaber *m* commander in chief
O/berbegriff *m* wider concept
O/berdeck *n* upper deck
O/berdeckomnibus *m* double-decker bus
o/berdeutsch *adj* of southern Germany
obere ['obərə] §9 *adj* higher, upper; chief, superior; supreme ‖ **Obere** §5 *m* (eccl) father superior ‖ *n* top
o/berfaul *adj* (fig) fishy
O/berfeldwebel *m* sergeant first class
O/berfläche *f* surface
o/berflächlich *adj* superficial
O/bergefreite §5 *m* corporal
O/bergeschoß *n* upper floor
O/bergewalt *f* supreme authority
o/berhalb *prep* (*genit*) above
O/berhand *f* (fig) upper hand; **die O. gewinnen über** (*acc*) get the better of
O/berhaupt *n* head, chief
O/berhaus *n* upper house
O/berhaut *f* epidermis
O/berhemd *n* shirt, dress shirt
O/berherr *m* sovereign
O/berherrschaft *f* sovereignty; supremacy
O/berhirte *m* prelate
O/berhofmeister *m* Lord Chamberlain
O/berhoheit *f* supreme authority
Oberin ['obərɪn] *f* (-;-nen) mother superior; (med) head nurse
O/beringenieur *m* chief engineer
o/berirdisch *adj* above-ground; overhead
O/berkellner *m* head waiter
O/berkiefer *m* upper jaw
O/berkleidung *f* outer wear
O/berkommando *n* general headquarters
O/berkörper *m* upper part of the body
O/berland *n* highlands
Oberländer -in ['obərlendər(ɪn)] §6 *mf* highlander
o/berlastig *adj* top-heavy
O/berleder *n* uppers
O/berlehrer -in §6 *mf* secondary school teacher, high school teacher
O/berleitung *f* supervision; (elec) overhead line (*of trolley, etc.*)
O/berleutnant *m* first lieutenant

O'berlicht n skylight
O'berliga f (sport) upper division
O'berlippe f upper lip
O'berpostamt n general post office
O'berprima f senior class
Obers ['obərs] m (-;) (Aust) cream
O'berschenkel m thigh
O'berschicht f upper layer; (der Be-völkerung) upper classes; geistige O. intelligentsia
O'berschule f high school
O'berschwester f (med) head nurse
O'berseite f topside, right side
Oberst ['obərst] m (-en;-en) colonel
O'berstaatsanwalt m attorney general
oberste ['obərstə] §9 adj (super of obere) uppermost, highest, top ‖ Oberste §5 mf senior, chief
O'berstimme f treble, soprano
O'berstleutnant m lieutenant colonel
O'berstock m upper floor
O'berwasser n—O. haben (fig) have the upper hand
O'berwelt f upper world
O'berwerk n upper manual (of organ)
obgleich' conj though, although
Ob'hut f (-;) care, protection
obig ['obɪç] adj above, above-mentioned
Objekt [ɔp'jɛkt] n (-[e]s;-e) object
objektiv [ɔpjɛk'tif] adj objective; (un-parteiisch) impartial ‖ Objektiv n (-s;-e) objective lens
Objektivität [ɔpjɛktɪvɪ'tɛt] f (-;) objectivity; impartiality
Objekt'träger m slide (of microscope)
Oblate [ɔ'blatə] f (-;-n) wafer; (eccl) host
obliegen [ɔp'ligən] §108 intr (dat) apply oneself to, devote oneself to; (dat) be incumbent upon ‖ impers—es obliegt mir zu (inf) it's up to me to (inf)
Ob'liegenheit f (-;-en) obligation
obligat [ɔblɪ'gat] adj obligatory; (uner-läßlich) indispensable; (unvermeid-lich) inevitable
Obligation [ɔblɪga'tsjon] f (-s;-en) bond; obligation
obligatorisch [ɔblɪga'torɪʃ] adj obligatory
Ob·mann ['ɔpman] m (-[e]s;⁻er & -leute) chairman; (jur) foreman
Oboe [ɔ'bo·ə] f (-;-n) oboe
Obrigkeit ['obrɪçkaɪt] f (-;-en) authority; (coll) authorities
o'brigkeitlich adj government(al)
obschon' conj though, although
Observato·rium [ɔpzɛrva'torjum] n (-s;-rien) [rjən] observatory
obsiegen ['ɔpzigən] intr be victorious; (dat) triumph over
obskur [ɔps'kur] adj obscure
Obst [ɔpst] n (-es;) (certain kinds of) fruit (mainly central-European, e.g., apples, plums; but not bananas, oranges); O. und Südfrüchte European and (sub)tropical fruit
Obst'garten m orchard
Obst'kern m stone; seed, pip
Obstruktion [ɔpstruk'tsjon] f (-;-en) obstruction; (pol) filibuster; O. trei-ben filibuster

obszön [ɔps'tsøn] adj obscene
Obszönität [ɔpstsønɪ'tɛt] f (-;-en) obscenity
ob'walten, obwal'ten intr exist; pre-vail; hold sway
obwohl' conj though, although
Ochse ['ɔksə] m (-n;-n) ox
ochsen ['ɔksən] intr (educ) cram
O'chsenfleisch n beef
O'chsenfrosch m bullfrog
öde ['ødə] adj bleak ‖ Öde f (-;-n) wasteland; (fig) bleakness
Ödem [ø'dem] n (-s;-e) edema
oder ['odər] conj or
Öd·land ['ødlant] n (-[e]s;-ländereien [lendə'raɪ-ən]) wasteland
Ofen ['ofən] m (-s;⁻) stove; (Back-) oven; (Hoch-) furnace; (Brenn-, Dürr-) kiln
O'fenklappe f damper
O'fenrohr n stovepipe
O'fenröhre f warming oven
offen ['ɔfən] adj open; (öffentlich) public; (fig) frank, open
offenbar ['ɔfənbar] adj obvious, mani-fest
offenbaren [ɔfən'barən] tr reveal
Offenba'rung f (-;-en) revelation
Of'fenheit f (-;) openness
of'fenherzig adj forthright; (Kleid) (hum) low-cut
of'fenkundig adj well-known; (offen-sichtlich) obvious; (Beweis) clear
of'fensichtlich adj obvious
offensiv [ɔfɛn'zif] adj offensive ‖ Of-fensive [ɔfɛn'zivə] f (-;-n) offen-sive
öffentlich ['œfəntlɪç] adj public; (Dienst) civil; öffentliches Haus brothel
Öf'fentlichkeit f (-;) public; publicity; an die Ö. treten appear in public; im Licht der Ö. in the limelight; in aller Ö. in public; sich in die Ö. flüchten rush into print
offerieren [ɔfə'rirən] tr offer
Offerte [ɔ'fɛrtə] f (-;-n) offer
Offerto·rium [ɔfɛr'torjum] n (-s;-rien [rjən] offertory
Offiziant [ɔfɪ'tsjant] m (-en;-en) of-ficiating priest
offiziell [ɔfɪ'tsjɛl] adj official
Offizier -in [ɔfɪ'tsir(ɪn)] §6 mf officer
Offiziers'anwärter -in §6 mf officer candidate
Offiziers'bursche m orderly
Offiziers'deck n quarter deck
Offiziers'kasino n officers' club
Offiziers'patent n officer's commission
Offizin [ɔfɪ'tsin] f (-;-en) drugstore; (Druckerei) print shop, press
offiziös [ɔfɪ'tsjøs] adj semiofficial
öffnen ['œfnən] tr & ref open
Öff'ner m (-s;-) opener
Öff'nung f (-;-en) opening
oft [ɔft], öfter(s) ['œftər(s)] adv often
oftmals ['ɔftmals] adv often(times)
oh [o] interj oh!, O!
Oheim ['ohaɪm] m (-s;-e) uncle
Ohm [om] m (-s;-e) (poet) uncle ‖ n (-s;-) (elec) ohm
ohne ['onə] prep (acc) without; o. daß (ind) without (ger); o. mich! count

me out!; **o. weiteres** right off; **o. zu** (*inf*) without (*ger*)

ohnedies' *adv* anyhow, in any case

ohneglei'chen *adj* unequaled

ohnehin' *adv* anyhow, as it is

Ohnmacht ['onmaxt] *f* (-;) faint, unconsciousness; helplessness; **in O. fallen** (or **sinken**) faint, pass out

ohnmächtig ['onmɛçtɪç] *adj* unconscious; helpless; **o. werden** faint

Ohr [or] *n* (-[e]s;-en) ear; (*im Buch*) dog-ear; **die Ohren spitzen** prick up the ears; **es dick hinter den Ohren haben** be sly; **ganz Ohr sein** be all ears; **j-m in den Ohren liegen** keep dinning it into s.o.'s ears; **j-n hinter die Ohren hauen** box s.o.'s ears; **j-n übers Ohr hauen** cheat s.o.; **sich aufs Ohr legen** take a nap; **zum e-n Ohr hinein, zum anderen wieder hinaus** in one ear and out the other

Öhr [ør] *n* (-[e]s;-e) eye (*of needle*); ax hole, hammer hole

ohrenbetäubend *adj* earsplitting

Oh'renklingen *n* ringing in the ears

Oh'rensausen *n* buzzing in the ear

Oh'renschmalz *n* earwax

Oh'renschmaus *m* treat for the ears

Ohrenschützer *m* earmuff

Ohr'feige *f* (-;-n) box on the ear

ohrfeigen ['orfaɪgən] *tr* box on the ear

Ohrläppchen ['ørlɛpçən] *n* (-s;-) earlobe

Ohr'muschel *f* auricle

okkult [ɔ'kult] *adj* occult

Ökologie [økolo'gi] *f* (-;) ecology

ökologisch [øko'logiʃ] *adj* ecological

Ökonom [øko'nom] *m* (-en;-en) economist

Ökono-mie [økonə'mi] (-;-mien ['mi-ən]) economy; economics

ökonomisch [øko'nomiʃ] *adj* economical

Oktav [ɔk'taf] *n* (-s;-e) octavo

Oktave [ɔk'tavə] *f* (-;-n) octave

Oktober [ɔk'tobər] *m* (-s;-) October

oktroyieren [ɔktrwa'jirən] *tr* impose

Okular [oku'lar] *n* (-s;-e) eyepiece

okulieren [oku'lirən] *tr* inoculate

Ökumene [øku'menə] *f* (-;) ecumenism

ökumenisch [øku'meniʃ] *adj* ecumenical

Okzident ['ɔktsɪdɛnt] *m* (-s;) Occident

Öl [øl] *n* (-[e]s;-e) oil; **Öl ins Feuer gießen** (fig) add fuel to the fire

Öl'baum *m* olive tree

Öl'berg *m* Mount of Olives

Oleander [ole'andər] *m* (-s;-) oleander

ölen ['ølən] *tr* oil; (mach) lubricate

Öl'götze *m* (coll) dummy, lout

Öl'heizung *f* oil heat

ölig ['ølɪç] *adj* oily

Oligar-chie [ɔligar'çi] *f* (-;-chien ['çi·ən]) oligarchy

Olive [o'livə] *f* (-;-n) olive

Oli'venöl *n* olive oil

Öl'leitung *f* pipeline

Öl'quelle *f* oil well

Öl'schlick *m* oil slick

Öl'stand *m* (aut) oil level

Öl'standanzeiger *m* oil gauge

Öl'standmesser *m* (aut) oil gauge; dip stick

Ö'lung *f* (-;-en) oiling; anointing; **die Letzte Ö.** extreme unction

Olymp [o'lymp] *m* (-s;) Mt. Olympus

Olympiade [əlym'pjadə] *f* (-;-n) olympiad

olympisch [o'lympiʃ] *adj* Olympian; Olympic; **die Olympischen Spiele** the Olympics

Öl'zweig *m* olive branch

Oma ['oma] *f* (-;-s) (coll) grandma

Omelett [ɔm(ə)'lɛt] *n* (-[e]s;-e & -s) omelette

O·men ['omen] *n* (-s;-mina [mina])

ominös [ɔmi'nøs] *adj* ominous

Omnibus ['ɔmnibus] *m* (ses;-se) bus

Onanie [ona'ni] *f* (-;) masturbation

ondulieren [ɔndu'lirən] *tr* (Haar) wave

Onkel ['ɔnkəl] *m* (-s;- & -s) uncle; **der große O.** (coll) the big toe

Opa ['opa] *m* (-s;-s) (coll) grandpa

Oper ['opər] *f* (-;-n) opera

Operateur [opera'tør] *m* (-s;-s) operator; (cin) projectionist; (surg) operating surgeon

Operation [opera'tsjon] *f* (-;-en) operation

Operations'gebiet *n* theater of operations

Operations'saal *m* operating room

operativ [opera'tif] *adj* surgical; operational, strategic

operieren [ope'rirən] *tr* operate on; **sich o. lassen** undergo an operation

O'pernglas *n*, **O'perngucker** *m* opera glasses

O'pernhaus *n* opera house, opera

Opfer ['ɔpfər] *n* (-s;-) sacrifice; victim; **zum O. fallen** (dat) fall victim to

op'ferfreudig *adj* self-sacrificing

Op'fergabe *f* offering

Op'ferkasten *m* poor box

Op'ferlamm *n* sacrificial lamb; **Lamb of God;** (fig) victim

Op'fermut *m* spirit of sacrifice

opfern ['ɔpfərn] *tr* sacrifice, offer up

Op'ferstock *m* poor box

Op'fertier *n* victim

Op'fertod *m* sacrifice of one's life

Op'fertrank *m* libation

Op'ferung *f* (-;-en) offering, sacrifice

op'ferwillig *adj* willing to make sacrifices

opponieren [ɔpo'nirən] *intr* (dat) oppose

opportun [ɔpɔr'tun] *adj* opportune

optieren [ɔp'tirən] *intr*—**o. für** opt for

Optik ['ɔptik] *f* (-;) optics

Optiker -in ['ɔptikər(ɪn)] §6 *mf* optician

optimistisch [ɔpti'mistiʃ] *adj* optimistic

optisch ['ɔptiʃ] *adj* optic(al)

Orakel [o'rakəl] *n* (-s;-) oracle

ora'kelhaft *adj* oracular

orange [o'rãʒə] *adj* orange ‖ **Orange** *f* (-;-n) orange

oran'genfarben, oran'genfarbig *adj* orange-colored

oratorisch [ɔra'toriʃ] *adj* oratorical

Orchester [ɔr'kɛstər] *n* (-s;-) orchestra

orchestral [ɔrçɛs'traːl] *adj* orchestral

orchestrieren [ɔrkɛs'triːrən] *tr* orchestrate

Orchidee [ɔrçi'deːə] *f* (-;-n) orchid

Orden ['ɔrdən] *m* (-s;-) medal, decoration; (eccl) order

Or'densband *n* (-[e]s;-̈er) ribbon

Or'densbruder *m* monk, friar

Or'denskleid *n* (eccl) habit

Or'densschwester *f* nun, sister

ordentlich ['ɔrdəntlɪç] *adj* orderly; (*aufgeräumt*) tidy; (*anständig*) decent, respectable; (*regelrecht*) regular; (*tüchtig*) sound; (*Frühstück*) solid; (*Mitglied*) active; (*Professor*) full; **e-e ordentliche Leistung a pretty good job; in ordentlichem Zustand** in good condition || *adv* thoroughly, properly; (*sehr*) (coll) awfully, very; really

Order ['ɔrdər] *f* (-;-n) (com, mil) order

ordinär [ɔrdi'nɛr] *adj* ordinary; vulgar; rude

Ordina·rius [ɔrdi'narjus] *m* (-;-rien [rjən]) professor; (eccl) ordinary

Ordinär'preis *m* retail price

ordinieren [ɔrdi'niːrən] *tr* ordain || *intr* (med) have office hours

ordnen ['ɔrdnən] *tr* arrange; (*regeln*) put in order; (*säubern*) tidy up

Ord'nung *f* (-;-en) order, arrangement; classification; system; class; rank; regulation; (mil) formation; **aus der O. bringen** disturb; **in bester O. in** tiptop shape; **in O. bringen** set in order; **in O. sein** be all right; **nicht in O. sein** be out of order; be wrong; be out of sorts

ord'nungsgemäß *adv* duly

Ord'nungsliebe *f* tidiness, orderliness

ord'nungsmäßig *adj* orderly, regular || *adv* duly

Ord'nungsruf *m* (parl) call to order

Ord'nungssinn *m* sense of order

Ord'nungsstrafe *f* fine

ord'nungswidrig *adj* irregular, illegal

Ord'nungszahl *f* ordinal number

Ordonnanz [ɔrdɔ'nants] *f* (-;-en) (mil) orderly

Organ [ɔr'gaːn] *n* (-s;-e) organ

Organisation [ɔrganiza'tsjoːn] *f* (-;-en) organization

organisch [ɔr'gaːnɪʃ] *adj* organic; (*Gewebe*) structural || *adv* organically

organisieren [ɔrgani'ziːrən] *tr* organize; (mil) scrounge || *ref* unionize; **organisierter Arbeiter** union worker

Organis·mus [ɔrga'nɪsmʊs] *m* (-;-men [mən]) organism

Organist –**in** [ɔrga'nɪst(ɪn)] §7 *mf* organist

Orgas·mus [ɔr'gasmʊs] *m* (-;-men [mən]) orgasm

Orgel ['ɔrgəl] *f* (-;-n) organ

Or'gelzug *m* organ stop

Orgie ['ɔrgjə] *f* (-;-n) orgy

Orient ['oːrjɛnt] *m* (-s;) Orient

Orientale [ɔrjɛn'taːlə] *m* (-n;-n) Orientalin [ɔrjɛn'taːlɪn] *f* (-;-nen) Oriental

orientalisch [ɔrjɛn'taːlɪʃ] *adj* oriental

orientieren [ɔrjɛn'tiːrən] *tr* orient; (fig) inform, instruct; (mil) brief

Orientie'rung *f* (-;-en) orientation; information, instruction; **die O. verlieren** lose one's bearings

Orientie'rungssinn *m* sense of direction

original [ɔrigi'naːl] *adj* original || **Original** *n* (-s;-e) original; (typ) copy

Original'ausgabe *f* first edition

Originalität [ɔriginali'tɛt] *f* (-;) originality

Original'sendung *f* live broadcast

originell [ɔrigi'nɛl] *adj* original

Orkan [ɔr'kaːn] *m* (-[e]s;-e) hurricane

Ornament [ɔrna'mɛnt] *n* (-[e]s;-e) ornament

Ornat [ɔr'naːt] *m* (-[e]s;-e) robes

Ort [ɔrt] *m* (-[e]s;-e) place, spot; (*Örtlichkeit*) locality; (*Dorf*) village; **am Ort sein** be appropriate; **an allen Orten** everywhere; **an Ort und Stelle** on the spot; **an Ort und Stelle gelangen** reach one's destination; **höheren Ortes** at higher levels; **vor Ort** on location; **vor Ort arbeiten** (min) work at the face || *m* (-[e]s;-̈er) position, locus

Örtchen ['œrtçən] *n* (-s;-) toilet

orten ['ɔrtən] *tr* get the bearing on, locate || *intr* take a bearing

orthodox [ɔrto'dɔks] *adj* orthodox

Orthographie [ɔrtogra'fiː] *f* (-;) orthography

Orthopäde [ɔrto'pɛːdə] *m* (-n;-n), **Orthopädin** [ɔrto'pɛːdɪn] *f* (-;-nen) orthopedist

orthopädisch [ɔrto'pɛːdɪʃ] *adj* orthopedic

örtlich ['œrtlɪç] *adj* local, topical

Ört'lichkeit *f* (-;-en) locality

Orts-, orts- [ɔrts] *comb.fm.* local

Orts'amt *n* (telp) local exchange

Orts'angabe *f* address

orts'ansässig *adj* resident || **Ortsansässige** §5 *mf* resident

Orts'behörde *f* local authorities

Orts'beschreibung *f* topography

Ort'schaft *f* (-;-en) place; (*Dorf*) village

orts'fremd *adj* nonlocal, out-of-town

Orts'gespräch *n* (telp) local call

Orts'kenntnis *f* familiarity with a place

orts'kundig *adj* familiar with the locality

Orts'name *m* place name

Orts'sinn *m* sense of direction

Orts'veränderung *f* change of scenery

Orts'verkehr *m* local traffic

Orts'zeit *f* local time

Orts'zustellung *f* local delivery

Or'tung *f* (-;-en) (aer, naut) taking of bearings, navigation

Öse ['øːzə] *f* (-;-n) loop, eye; (*des Schuhes*) eyelet

Ost [ɔst] *m* (-es;-e) East; (poet) east wind

Ost- *comb.fm.* eastern, East

Osten ['ɔstən] *m* (-s;) East; **der Ferne O.** the Far East; **der Nahe O.** the Near East; **nach O.** eastward

ostentativ [ɔstenta'tiːf] *adj* ostentatious

Oster- [ostər] *comb.fm.* Easter
O'sterei *n* Easter egg
O'sterfest *n* Easter
O'sterhase *m* Easter bunny
O'sterlamm *m* paschal lamb
Ostern ['ostərn] *n* (–;–) & *pl* Easter
Österreich ['østəraıç] *n* (–s;) Austria
Österreicher **–in** ['østəraıçər(ın)] §6 *mf* Austrian
österreichisch ['østəraıçıʃ] *adj* Austrian
O'sterzeit *f* Eastertide
Ost'front *f* eastern front
Ost'gote *m* Ostrogoth
östlich ['œstlıç] *adj* eastern, easterly; Oriental; **ö. von** east of
Ost'mark *f* East-German mark
Ost'see *f* Baltic Sea
ostwärts ['ostverts] *adv* eastward

Otter ['ɔtər] *m* (–s;–) otter ‖ *f* (–;–n) (*Schlange*) adder
Ouvertüre [uvɛr'tyrə] *f* (–;–n) (mus) overture
oval [o'val] *adj* oval ‖ **Oval** *n* (–s;–e) oval
Ovar [o'var] *n* (–s;–e & –ien [jən] ovary
Overall ['ovərol] *m* (–s;–s) overalls
Oxyd [ɔ'ksyt] *n* (–[e]s;–e) oxide
Oxydation [ɔksyda'tsjon] *f* (–;) oxidation
oxydieren [ɔksy'dirən] *tr & intr* (SEIN) oxidize
Ozean ['otse·an] *m* (–s;–e) ocean; **der Große** (or **Stille**) **O.** the Pacific
Ozeanographie [otse·anogra'fi] *f* (–;) oceanography
Ozon [o'tson] *n* (–s;) ozone

P

P, p [pe] *invar n* P, p
paar [par] *adj* even ‖ *invar adj*—**ein p.** a couple of, a few ‖ **Paar** *n* (–[e]s; –e) pair, couple; **zu Paaren treiben** rout
paaren ['parən] *tr* match, mate ‖ *ref* mate
paarig ['parıç] *adj* in pairs
paar'laufen §105 *intr* (SEIN) skate as a couple
paar'mal *adv*—**ein p.** a couple of times
Paa'rung *f* (–;) pairing, matching; (*Begattung*) mating
Paa'rungszeit *f* mating season
paar'weise *adv* in pairs, two by two
Pacht [paxt] *f* (–;–en) lease; (*Geld*) rent; **in P. geben** lease out; **in P. nehmen** lease, rent
Pacht'brief *m* lease
pachten ['paxtən] *tr* take a lease on
Pächter **–in** ['pɛçtər(ın)] §6 *mf* tenant
Pacht'ertrag *m*, **Pacht'geld** *n* rent
Pacht'gut *n*, **Pacht'hof** *m* leased farm
Pacht'kontrakt *m* lease
Pach'tung *f* (–;–en) leasing; leasehold
Pacht'vertrag *m* lease
Pacht'zeit *f* term of lease
Pacht'zins *m* rent
Pack [pak] *m* (–[e]s;–e & ⸚e) pack; (*Paket*) parcel; (*Ballen*) bale ‖ *n* (–[e]s;) rabble; **ein P. von Lügnern** a pack of liars
Päckchen ['pɛkçən] *n* (–s;–) small package; (*Zigaretten-*) pack
packen ['pakən] *tr* pack, pack up; (*fassen*) seize, grab; (*fig*) grip, thrill; **pack dich!** scram! ‖ **Packen** *m* (–s;–) pack; (*Ballen*) bale ‖ *n* (–s;) packing
Pack'esel *m* (fig) drudge
Pack'papier *n* wrapping paper
Pack'pferd *n* packhorse
Pack'tier *n* pack animal
Packung (**Pak'kung**) *f* (–;–en) packing; (*Paket*) packet; **P. Zigaretten** pack of cigarettes

Pack'wagen *m* (rr) baggage car
Pädadoge [peda'gogə] *m* (–n;–n) pedagogue
Pädagogik [peda'gogık] *f* (–;) pedagogy
pädagogisch [peda'gogıʃ] *adj* pedagogical, educational
Paddel ['padəl] *n* (–s;–) paddle
Pad'delboot *n* canoe
paddeln ['padəln] *intr* paddle, canoe
Pädiatrie [pedɪ·a'tri] *f* (–;) pediatrics
paff [paf] *interj* bang!
paffen ['pafən] *tr & intr* puff
Page ['paʒə] *m* (–n;–n) page
Pa'genfrisur *f*, **Pa'genkopf** *m* pageboy
Pagode [pa'godə] *f* (–;–n) pagoda
Pair [per] *m* (–s;–s) peer
Pak [pak] *f* (–;– & –s) (Panzerabwehrkanone) antitank gun
Paket [pa'ket] *n* (–[e]s;–e) parcel; (*Bücher-, Post-*) bundle
Paket'adresse *f* gummed label
Paket'post *f* parcel post
Pakt [pakt] *m* (–[e]s;–e) pact
paktieren [pak'tirən] *intr* make a pact
Paläontologie [pale·ontolo'gi] *f* (–;) paleontology
Palast [pa'last] *m* (–es;⸚e) palace
palast'artig *adj* palatial
Palästina [pale'stina] *n* (–s;) Palestine
Palette [pa'letə] *f* (–;–n) palette
Palisade [palı'zadə] *f* (–;–n) palisade
Palme ['palmə] *f* (–;–n) palm tree; palm branch; **j–n auf die P. bringen** (coll) drive s.o. up the wall
Palm'wedel *m*, **Palm'zweig** *m* palm branch
Pampelmuse ['pampəlmuzə] *f* (–;–n) grapefruit
Pamphlet [pam'flet] *n* (–[e]s;–e) lampoon
Panama ['panama] *n* (–s;) Panama
Paneel [pa'nel] *n* (–s;–e) panel
paneelieren [pane'lirən] *tr* panel
Panier [pa'nir] *n* (–s;–e) slogan
panieren [pa'nirən] *tr* (culin) bread

Panik ['pɑnɪk] f (-;) panic
panisch ['pɑnɪʃ] adj panic-stricken
Panne ['panə] f (-;-n) breakdown; (Reifenpanne) blowout; (fig) mishap
Panora·ma [pano'rama] n (-s;-men [mən]) panorama
panschen ['panʃən] tr adulterate, water down || intr splash about; mix
Panther ['pantər] m (-s;-) panther
Pantine [pan'tinə] f (-;-n) clog
Pantoffel [pan'tɔfəl] m (-s;-n) slipper; unter dem P. stehen be henpecked
Pantof'felheld m henpecked husband
Panzer ['pantsər] m (-s;-) armor; armor plating; (mil) tank; (zool) shell
Pan'zerabwehrkanone f antitank gun
pan'zerbrechend adj armor-piercing
Pan'zerfalle f tank trap
Pan'zerfaust f bazooka
Pan'zergeschoß n, **Pan'zergranate** f armor-piercing shell
Pan'zerhandschuh m gauntlet
Pan'zerhemd n coat of mail
Pan'zerkreuzer m battle cruiser
panzern ['pantsərn] tr armor || ref arm oneself
Pan'zerschrank m safe
Panzerspähwagen ['pantsər/pevagən] m (mil) armored car
Pan'zersperre f antitank obstacle
Pan'zerung f (-;-en) armor plating
Pan'zerwagen m armored car
Papagei [papa'gaɪ] m (-en;-en) & (-[e]s;-e) parrot
Papier [pa'pir] n (-[e]s;-e) paper
Papier'bogen m sheet of paper
Papier'brei m paper pulp
papieren [pa'pirən] adj paper
Papier'fabrik f paper mill
Papier'format n size of paper
Papier'korb m wastebasket
Papier'krieg m (fig) red tape
Papier'mühle f paper mill
Papier'schlange f paper streamer
Papier'tüte f paper bag
Papier'waren pl stationery
Papp [pap] m (-[e]s;-e) (Brei) pap; (Kleister) paste
Papp- [pap] comb.fm. sticky; cardboard
Papp'band m (-[e]s;ᵘe) paperback
Papp'deckel m piece of cardboard
Pappe ['papə] f (-;-) cardboard
Pappel ['papəl] f (-;-n) poplar
päppeln ['pepəln] tr feed lovingly
pappen ['papən] tr paste, glue || intr stick
Pap'penstiel m (coll) trifle; das ist keinen P. wert (coll) this isn't worth a thing
papperlapapp [papərla'pap] interj nonsense!
pap'pig adj sticky
Papp'karton m, **Papp'schachtel** f cardboard box, cardboard carton
Papp'schnee m sticky snow (for skiing)
Paprika ['paprɪka] m (-s) paprika
Pap'rikaschote f (green) pepper
Papst [papst] m (-es;ᵘe) pope
päpstlich ['pepstlɪç] adj papal
Papsttum ['papsttum] n (-s;) papacy
Papy·rus [pa'pyrus] m (-;-ri [ri]) papyrus

Parabel [pa'rabəl] f (-;-n) parable; (geom) parabola
Parade [pa'radə] f (-;-n) parade; (fencing) parry; (mil) review; (fb) save
Para'deanzug m (mil) dress uniform
Paradeiser [para'daɪzər] m (-s;-) (Aust) tomato
Para'depferd n (fig) show-off
Para'deplatz m parade ground
Para'deschritt m goose step
paradieren [para'dirən] intr parade; (fig) show off
Paradies [para'dis] n (-es;-e) paradise
Paradies'apfel m tomato
paradox [para'dɔks] adj paradoxical || **Paradox** n (-es;-e) paradox
Paraffin [para'fin] n (-s;) paraffin
Paragraph [para'graf] m (-en & -s; -en) paragraph; (jur) section
parallel [para'lel] adj parallel || **Parallele** f (-;-n) parallel
Paralyse [para'lyzə] f (-;-n) paralysis
paralysieren [paraly'zirən] tr paralyze
Paralytiker -in [para'lytɪkər(ɪn)] §6 mf paralytic
Paranuß f ['paranus] f Brazil nut
Parasit [para'zit] m (-en;-en) parasite
parat [pa'rat] adj ready
Pardon [par'dɔ̃] m (-s;) pardon; keinen P. geben (mil) given no quarter
Parenthese [paren'teza] f (-;-n) parenthesis
Parfüm [par'fym] n (-[e]s;-e) perfume
Parfüme·rie [parfymə'ri] f (-;-rien ['ri-ən]) perfume shop
parfümieren [parfy'mirən] tr perfume
pari ['pari] adv at par || **Pari** m (-[s];) par; auf P. at par
Paria ['parja] m (-s;-s) pariah
parieren [pa'rirən] tr (Pferd) rein in; (Hieb) parry || intr (dat) obey
Pa'rikurs m (com) parity
Paris [pa'ris] n (-;) Paris
Pariser -in [pa'rizər(ɪn)] §6 mf Parisian
Parität [pari'tet] f (-;) equality; (fin, st. exch.) parity
paritätisch [pari'tetɪʃ] adj on a footing of equality
Park [park] m (-s;-s & -e) park
Park'anlage f park; **Parkanlagen** grounds
parken ['parkən] tr & intr park
Parkett [par'ket] n (-[e]s;-e) (Fußboden) parquet; (theat) parquet
Parkett'fußboden m parquet flooring
Park'licht n parking light
Park'platz m parking lot
Park'platzwärter m parking lot attendant
Park'uhr f parking meter
Parlament [parla'ment] n (-[e]s;-e) parliament
Parlamentär [parlamen'ter] m (-s;-e) truce negotiator
parlamentarisch [parlamen'tarɪʃ] adj parliamentary
parlamentieren [parlamen'tirən] intr (coll) parley
Paro·die [paro'di] f (-;-dien ['di-ən]) parody
parodieren [paro'dirən] tr parody

Parole [pa'rolə] f (-;-n) (mil) pass-word; (pol) slogan

Partei [par'taɪ] f (-;-en) party; (Mieter) tenant(s); (jur, pol) party; (sport) side; j-s P. ergreifen or P. nehmen für j-n side with s.o.

Partei'bonze m (pol) party boss

Partei'gänger -in §6 mf (pol) party sympathizer

Partei'genosse m, **Partei'genossin** f party member

Partei'grundsatz m party plank

parteiisch [par'taɪ·ɪʃ] adj partial, bi-ased; (pol) partisan

partei'lich adj partisan

Partei'lichkeit f (-;) partiality

partei'los adj (pol) independent || **Parteilose** §5 mf independent

Partei'losigkeit f (-;) impartiality; political independence

Partei'nahme f (-;) taking sides

Partei'programm n party platform

Partei'tag m party rally

Partei'zugehörigkeit f party affiliation

Parterre [par'ter] n (-s;-s) ground floor; (theat) parterre

Par·tie [par'ti] f (-;-tien ['ti·ən]) part; (Gesellschaft) party; (Spiel) game; (Ausflug) outing; (com) lot; (theat) role; e-e gute P. machen (coll) marry rich; ich bin mit von der P.! count me in!

partiell [par'tsjɛl] adj partial || adv partly, partially

Partikel [par'tikəl] f (-;-n) particle

Partisan -in [partɪ'zan(ɪn)] §7 mf partisan

Partitur [partɪ'tur] f (-;-en) (mus) score

Partizip [partɪ'tsip] n (-s;-ien [jən]) participle

Partner -in ['partnər(ɪn)] §6 mf partner

Part'nerschaft f (-;-en) partnership

Parzelle [par'tselə] f (-;-n) lot

parzellieren [partse'lirən] tr parcel out, allot

paschen ['paʃən] tr smuggle || intr smuggle; (würfeln) play dice

Paß [pas] m (Passes; Pässe) pass; passport; (geog) mountain pass

passabel [pa'sabəl] adj tolerable

Passage [pa'saʒə] f (-;-n) passage; (mus) run

Passagier [pasa'ʒir] m (-s;-e) passenger; **blinder P.** stowaway

Passagier'dampfer m passenger liner

Passagier'gut n luggage

Passah ['pasa] n (-s;), **Pas'sahfest** n Passover

Paß'amt n passport office

Passant -in [pa'sant(ɪn)] §7 mf passer-by

Paß'ball m (sport) pass

Paß'bild n passport photograph

passen ['pasən] ref be proper || intr fit; (dat) suit; (cards, fb) pass; p. auf (acc) watch for, wait for; p. zu suit, fit; sie p. zueinander they are a good match

pas'send adj suitable; convenient; (Kleidungsstück) matching; für p. halten think it proper

Paß'form f—e-e gute P. haben be form-fitting

passierbar [pa'sirbar] adj passable

passieren [pa'sirən] tr pass, cross; (culin) sift, sieve || intr (SEIN) happen

Passier'schein m pass, permit

Passion [pa'sjon] f (-;-en) passion

passioniert [pasjo'nirt] adj ardent

Passions'spiel n passion play

passiv [pa'sif] adj passive; (Handels-bilanz) unfavorable; passives Wahl-recht eligibility || **Passiv** n (-s;-e) (gram) passive

Passiva [pa'siva] pl, **Passiven** [pa'sivən] pl debts, liabilities

Paß'kontrolle f passport inspection

Paste ['pastə] f (-;-n) paste

Pastell [pa'stɛl] n (-s;-e) pastel; crayon

pastell'farben adj pastel

Pastell'stift m crayon

Pastete [pas'tetə] f (-;-n) meat pie, fish pie

pasteurisieren [pastœrɪ'zirən] tr pas-teurize

Pastille [pa'stɪlə] f (-;-n) lozenge

Pa·stor ['pastor] m (-s;-storen ['torən]) pastor, minister, vicar

Pate ['patə] m (-n;-n) godfather || f (-;-n) godmother

Pa'tenkind n godchild

patent [pa'tɛnt] adj neat; smart; ein patenter Kerl quite a fellow || **Patent** n (-[e]s;-e) patent; (mil) commis-sion; P. angemeldet patent pending

Patent'amt n patent office

patentieren [patɛn'tirən] tr patent

Pater ['patər] m (-s; Patres ['patres]) (eccl) Father

pathetisch [pa'tetɪʃ] adj impassioned; solemn

Pathologe [pato'logə] m (-n;-n) path-ologist

Pathologie [patolo'gi] f (-;) pathology

Pathologin [pato'login] f (-;-nen) pathologist

Patient -in [pa'tsjɛnt(ɪn)] §7 mf pa-tient

Patin ['patɪn] f (-;-nen) godmother

Patriarch [patrɪ'arç] m (-en;-en) pa-triarch

Patriot -in [patrɪ'ot(ɪn)] §7 mf patriot

patriotisch [patrɪ'otɪʃ] adj patriotic

Patrize [pa'tritsə] f (-;-n) die, stamp

Patrizier -in [pa'tritsjər(ɪn)] §6 mf patrician

Patron [pa'tron] m (-s;-e) patron; (pej) guy

Patronat [patro'nat] n (-[e]s;-e) pa-tronage

Patrone [pa'tronə] f (-;-n) cartridge

Patro'nengurt m cartridge belt

Patro'nenhülse f cartridge case

Patronin [pa'tronɪn] f (-;-nen) pa-troness

Patrouille [pa'truljə] f (-;-n) patrol

patrouillieren [patru'ljirən] tr & intr patrol

Patsche ['patʃə] f (-;-en) (Pfütze) pud-dle; (coll) jam, scrape; in der P. lassen leave in a lurch; in e-e P. geraten get into a jam

patschen ['patʃ ən] *tr* slap ‖ *intr* splash; **in die Hände p.** clap hands

patsch/naß *adj* soaking wet

patzig ['patsɪç] *adj* snappy, sassy

Pauke ['paukə] *f* (-;-n) kettledrum; **j-m e-e P. halten** give s.o. a lecture

pauken ['paukən] *tr* (educ) cram ‖ *intr* beat the kettledrum; (educ) cram

Pau'ker *m* (-s;-) (coll) martinet

pausbackig ['pausbakɪç], **pausbäckig** ['pausbɛkɪç] *adj* chubby-faced

pauschal [pau'ʃal] *adj* (*Summe*) flat

Pauschal'betrag *m* flat rate

Pauscha•le [pau'ʃalə] *n* (-s;-lien [ljən]) lump sum

Pauschal'preis *m* package price

Pauschal'reise *f* all-inclusive tour

Pauschal'summe *f* flat sum

Pause ['pauzə] *f* (-;-n) pause; (*Pauszeichnung*) tracing; (educ) recess, break; (mus) rest; (theat) intermission; **e-e P. machen** take a break

pausen ['pauzən] *tr* trace

pau'senlos *adj* continuous

Pau'senzeichen *n* (rad) station identification

pausieren [pau'zirən] *intr* pause; rest

Pauspapier ['pauzpapir] *n* tracing paper

Pavian ['pavjan] *m* (-s;-e) baboon

Pavillon ['pavɪljɔ] *m* (-s;-s) pavilion

Pazifik [pa'tsifɪk] *m* (-s) Pacific

pazifisch [pa'tsifɪʃ] *adj* Pacific

Pazifist –in [patsɪ'fɪst(ɪn)] §7 *mf* pacifist

Pech [pɛç] *n* (-[e]s;-e) pitch; **P. haben** (coll) have tough luck

Pech/fackel *f* torch

Pech/kohle *f* bituminous coal

pech/ra'benschwarz *adj* pitch-black

pech/schwarz *adj* pitch-dark

Pech/strähne *f* streak of bad luck

Pech/vogel *m* (coll) unlucky fellow

Pedal [pe'dal] *n* (-s;-e) pedal

Pedant [pe'dant] *m* (-en;-en) pedant

pedantisch [pe'dantɪʃ] *adj* pedantic

Pegel ['pegəl] *m* (-s;-) water gauge

Pe'gelstand *m* water level

Peil– [paɪl] *comb.fm.* direction-finding, sounding

peilen ['paɪlən] *tr* take the bearings of; (*Tiefe*) sound; **über den Daumen p.** (coll) estimate roughly ‖ *intr* take bearings

Pei/lung *f* (-;-en) bearings; taking of bearings; sounding

Pein [paɪn] *f* (-;) pain, torment

peinigen ['paɪnigən] *tr* torment

pein/lich *adj* painful; embarrassing; (*genau*) painstaking; (*sorgfältig*) scrupulous ‖ *adv* scrupulously; carefully

Peitsche ['paɪtʃə] *f* (-;-n) whip; **mit der P. knallen** crack the whip

peitschen ['paɪtʃən] *tr* whip

Peit'schenhieb *m* whiplash

Peit'schenknall *m* crack of the whip

Pelerine [pelə'rinə] *f* (-;-n) cape

Pelikan ['pelɪkan] *m* (-s;-e) pelican

Pelle ['pelə] *f* (-;-n) peel, skin

pellen ['pelən] *tr* peel, skin

Pellkartoffeln ['pelkartɔfəln] *pl* potatoes in their jackets

Pelz [pɛlts] *m* (-es;-e) fur; (*Fell*) pelt; fur coat

Pelz/besatz *m* fur trimming

Pelz/futter *n* fur lining

Pelz/händler –in §6 *mf* furrier

pel/zig *adj* furry; (*Gefühl im Mund*) cottony

Pelz/tier *n* fur-bearing animal

Pelz/tierjäger *m* trapper

Pelz/werk *n* furs

Pendel ['pendəl] *n* (-s;-) pendulum

pendeln ['pendəln] *intr* swing, oscillate; (*zwischen zwei Orten*) commute

Pen/deltür *f* swinging door

Pen/delverkehr *m* commuter traffic; shuttle service

Pen/delzug *m* shuttle train

Pendler ['pendlər] *m* (-s;-) commuter

Penizillin [penɪtsɪ'lin] *n* (-s;) penicillin

Pension [pen'zjon] *f* (-;-en) pension, retirement pay; (*Fremdenhaus*) boarding house; (*Unterkunft und Verpflegung*) room and board; (*Pensionat*) girls' boarding school; **in P. gehen** go on pension

Pensionär [penzjo'ner] *m* (-s;-e) pensioner; boarder

Pensionat [penzjo'nat] *n* (-[e]s;-e) girls boarding school

pensionieren [penzjo'nirən] *tr* put on pension; (mil) retire on half pay; **sich p. lassen** retire

Pensions/kasse *f* pension fund

Pensions/preis *m* price of room and board

Pen•sum ['penzum] *n* (-s;-sen [zən] & –sa [za]) task, assignment; quota

per [per] *prep* (acc) per, by, with; (*zeitlich*) by, until; **per Adresse** care of, c/o; **per sofort** at once

perfekt [per'fekt] *adj* perfect; concluded ‖ **Perfekt** *n* (-[e]s;-e) perfect

Pergament [perga'ment] *n* (-[e]s;-e) parchment

Periode [per'jodə] *f* (-;-n) period

periodisch [per'jodɪʃ] *adj* periodic

Periphe•rie [perɪfe'ri] *f* (-;-rien ['ri•ən]) periphery

Periskop [perɪ'skop] *n* (-s;-e) periscope

Perle ['perlə] *f* (-;-n) pearl; (*aus Glas*) bead; (*Tropfen*) drop, bead; (*Bläschen*) bubble; (fig) gem

perlen ['perlən] *intr* sparkle

Per/lenauster *f* pearl oyster

Per/lenkette *f*, **Per/lenschnur** *f* pearl necklace, string of pearls

Perlhuhn ['perlhun] *n* guinea fowl

perlig ['perlɪç] *adj* pearly

Perl/muschel *f* pearl oyster

Perlmutt ['perlmut] *n* (-s;), **Perl/mutter** *f* mother of pearl

perplex [per'pleks] *adj* perplexed

Persenning [per'zenɪŋ] *f* (-;-en) tarpaulin

Persien ['perzjən] *n* (-s;) Persia

persisch [perzɪʃ] *adj* Persian

Person [per'zon] *f* (-;-en) person; (theat) character; **ich für meine P.** I for one; **klein von P.** small of stature

Personal [perzo'nal] *n* (-s;) personnel

Personal/akte *f* personal file, dossier

Personal'angaben *pl* personal data
Personal'aufzug *m* passenger elevator
Personal'ausweis *m* identity card
Personal'chef *m* personnel manager
Personalien [perzə'naljən] *pl* personal data, particulars
Personal/pronomen *n* personal pronoun
Perso'nengedächtnis *n* good memory for names
Perso'nenkraftwagen *m* passenger car
Perso'nenschaden *m* personal injury
Perso'nenverzeichnis *n* list of persons; (theat) dramatis personae, cast
Perso'nenwagen *m* passenger car
Perso'nenzug *m* passenger train; (rr) local
personifizieren [perzonɪfɪ'tsirən] *tr* personify
persönlich [per'zønlɪç] *adj* personal ǁ *adv* personally, in person
Persön'lichkeit *f* (-;-en) personality
Perspektiv [perspɛk'tif] *n* (-s;-e) telescope
Perücke [pe'rʏkə] *f* (-;-n) wig
pervers [pɛr'vɛrs] *adj* perverse
pessimistisch [pɛsɪ'mɪstɪʃ] *adj* pessimistic
Pest [pɛst] *f* (-;) plague
pest'artig *adj* pestilential
Pestilenz [pɛstɪ'lɛnts] *f* (-;-en) pestilence
Petersilie [petər'ziljə] *f* (-;) parsley
Petroleum [pe'trole·um] *n* (-s;) petroleum
Petschaft ['petʃaft] *n* (-s;-e) seal
Petting ['pɛtɪŋ] *n* (-s;) petting
petto ['peto]—**in p. haben** have in reserve; (coll) have up one's sleeve
Petunie [pe'tunjə] *f* (-;-n) petunia
Petze ['petsə] *f* (-;-n) tattletale
petzen ['petsən] *intr* tattle, squeal
Pfad [pfat] *m* (-[e]s;-e) path, track
Pfadfinder ['pfatfɪndər] *m* (-s;-) boy scout
Pfadfinderin ['pfatfɪndərɪn] *f* (-;-nen) girl scout
Pfaffe ['pfafə] *m* (-n;-n) (pej) priest
Pfahl [pfal] *m* (-[e]s;⸚e) stake; post
Pfahl'bau *m* (-[e]s;-bauten) lake dwelling
Pfahl'werk *n* palisade, stockade
Pfahl'wurzel *f* taproot
Pfahl'zaun *m* palisade, stockade
Pfälzer **-in** ['pfɛltsər(ɪn)] §6 *mf* inhabitant of the Palatinate
Pfand [pfant] *n* (-[e]s;⸚er) pledge; deposit; (*Bürgschaft*) security, pawn (*auf Immobilien*) mortgage; **zum Pfande geben** (or **setzen**) pawn, mortgage
pfändbar ['pfɛntbar] *adj* (jur) attachable
Pfand'brief *m* mortgage papers
pfänden ['pfɛndən] *tr* attach, impound
Pfand'geber *m* mortgagor
Pfand'gläubiger *m* mortgagee
Pfand'haus *n*, **Pfand'leihe** *f* pawnshop
Pfand'leiher **-in** §6 *mf* pawnbroker
Pfand'recht *n* lien
Pfand'schein *m* pawn ticket
Pfand'schuldner *m* mortgagor
Pfän'dung *f* (-;-en) attachment, confiscation

Pfanne ['pfanə] *f* (-;-n) pan; (anat) socket; **etw auf der P. haben** (fig) have s.th. up one's sleeve; **in die P. hauen** (fig) make mincemeat of
Pfan'nenstiel *m* panhandle
Pfann'kuchen *m* pancake; **Berliner P.** doughnut
Pfarr- [pfar] *comb.fm.* parish, parochial
Pfarr'amt *n* rectory
Pfarr'bezirk *m* parish
Pfarr'dorf *n* parish seat
Pfarre ['pfarə] *f* (-;-n) parish; (*Pfarrhaus*) rectory
Pfarrei [pfa'raɪ] *f* (-;-en) parish; (*Pfarrhaus*) rectory
Pfarrer ['pfarər] *m* (-s;-) pastor
Pfarr'gemeinde *f* parish
Pfarr'haus *n* rectory
Pfarr'kind *n* parishioner
Pfarr'kirche *f* parish church
Pfarr'schule *f* parochial school
Pfau [pfau] *m* (-[e]s;-en) peacock
Pfau'enhenne *f* peahen
Pfeffer ['pfefər] *m* (-s;) pepper
pfefferig ['pfefərɪç] *adj* peppery
Pfef'ferkorn *n* peppercorn
Pfef'ferkuchen *m* gingerbread
Pfef'ferminze *f* (bot) peppermint
Pfef'ferminzplätzchen *n* peppermint cookie
pfeffern ['pfefərn] *tr* pepper
Pfef'fernuß *f* ginger nut
Pfeife ['pfaɪfə] *f* (-;-n) whistle; (*Orgel-*) pipe; (*zum Rauchen*) (tobacco) pipe
pfeifen ['pfaɪfən] *tr* whistle; **ich pfeife ihm was** he can whistle for it ǁ *intr* whistle; (*Schiedsrichter*) blow the whistle; (*Maus*) squeak; (*Vogel*) sing; (*dat*) whistle for or to; **auf dem letzten Loche p.** be on one's last legs; **ich pfeife darauf!** I couldn't care less!
Pfei'fenkopf *m* pipe bowl
Pfei'fenrohr *n* pipestem
Pfeifer **-in** §6 *mf* whistler; (mus) piper, fife player
Pfeif'kessel *m*, **Pfeif'topf** *m* whistling kettle
Pfeil [pfaɪl] *m* (-[e]s;-e) arrow, dart; **P. und Bogen** bow and arrow
Pfei'ler *m* (-s;-) (& fig) pillar; (*e-r Brücke*) pier
pfeil'gera'de *adj* straight as an arrow
pfeil'schnell' *adj* swift as an arrow ǁ *adv* like a shot
Pfeil'schütze *m* archer
Pfeil'spitze *f* arrowhead
Pfennig ['pfɛnɪç] *m* (-[e]s;-e & -) pfennig, penny (*one hundredth of a mark*)
Pfennigfuchser ['pfɛnɪçfuksər] *m* (-s; -) penny pincher
Pferch [pfɛrç] *m* (-[e]s;-e) fold, pen
pferchen ['pfɛrçən] *tr* herd together, pen in
Pferd [pfert] *n* (-[e]s;-e) horse; **zu Pferde** on horseback
Pferde- [pfɛrdə] *comb.fm.* horse
Pfer'deapfel *m* horse manure
Pfer'debremse *f* horsefly
Pfer'dedecke *f* horse blanket

Pfer'defuß m (*Kennzeichen des Teufels*) cloven hoof; (pathol) clubfoot
Pfer'degeschirr n harness
Pfer'degespann n team of horses
Pfer'deknecht m groom
Pfer'dekoppel f corral
Pfer'delänge f (*beim Rennen*) length
Pfer'derennbahn f race track
Pfer'derennen n horse racing
Pfer'destärke f horsepower
Pfer'dezucht f horse breeding
pfiff [pfɪf] *pret* of **pfeifen** ‖ **Pfiff** m (-[e]s;-e) whistle; **den P. heraushaben** (fig) know the ropes
Pfifferling ['pfɪfərlɪŋ] m (-s;-e) (bot) chanterelle; **keinen P. wert** not worth a thing
pfiffig ['pfɪfɪç] *adj* shrewd, sharp
Pfiffikus ['pfɪfɪkʊs] m (-;-), (-ses;-se) (coll) sly fox
Pfingsten ['pfɪŋstən] n (-s;) Pentecost
Pfingst'rose f (bot) peony
Pfingst'son'ntag m Whitsunday
Pfirsich ['pfɪrzɪç] m (-[e]s;-e) peach
Pflanze ['pflantsə] f (-;-n) plant
pflanzen ['pflantsən] tr plant
Pflan'zenfaser f vegetable fiber
Pflan'zenfett n vegetable shortening
pflan'zenfressend adj herbivorous
Pflan'zenkost f vegetable diet
Pflan'zenkunde f botany
Pflan'zenleben n plant life, vegetation
Pflan'zenlehre f botany
Pflan'zenöl n vegetable oil
Pflan'zenreich n vegetable kingdom
Pflan'zensaft m sap, juice
Pflan'zenschutzmittel n pesticide
Pflan'zenwelt f flora
Pflan'zer -in §6 mf planter
pflanz'lich adj vegetable
Pflanz'schule f, **Pflanz'stätte** f nursery; (fig) hotbed
Pflan'zung f (-;-en) plantation
Pflaster ['pflastər] n (-s;-) pavement; (*Fleck*) patch; (med) Band-Aid; **als P.** (fig) in compensation; **ein teueres P.** (fig) an expensive place; **P. treten** (fig) pound the sidewalks
Pflasterer ['pflastərər] m (-s;-) paver
pfla'stermüde adj tired of walking the streets
pflastern ['pflastərn] tr pave
Pfla'sterstein m paving stone; (*Kopfstein*) cobblestone
Pfla'stertreter m (-s;-) loafer
Pfla'sterung f (-;) paving
Pflaume ['pflaumə] f (-;-n) plum; (*spitze Bemerkung*) dig
pflaumen ['pflaumən] intr (coll) tease
pflau'menweich adj (fig) spineless
Pflege ['pflegə] f (-;-n) care; (*Wartung*) tending; (*e-s Gartens, der Künste*) cultivation; **gute P. haben** be well cared for; **in P. nehmen** take charge of
Pflegebefohlene ['pflegəbəfoːlənə] §5 mf charge; fosterchild
Pfle'geeltern pl foster parents
Pfle'geheim n nursing home
Pfle'gekind n foster child
pflegen ['pfleːgən] tr take care of, look after; (*Kranken*) nurse; (*Garten, Kunst*) cultivate; (*Freundschaft*) fos-

ter; **Gesellkeit p.** lead an active social life; **Umgang p. mit** associate with ‖ *intr*—**p. zu** (*inf*) be wont to (*inf*), be in the habit of (*ger*); **sein Vater pflegte zu sagen** his father used to say; **sie pflegt morgens zeitig aufzustehen** she usually gets up early in the morning ‖ *intr* (*pp* **gepflegt & gepflogen**) (*genit*) carry on; **der Liebe p.** enjoy the pleasures of love; **der Ruhe p.** take a rest; **Rats p. mit** consult with
Pfle'ger -in §6 m/ nurse; (jur) guardian
Pfle'gesohn m foster son
Pfle'gestelle f foster home
Pfle'getocher f foster daughter
Pfle'gevater m foster father
pfleglich ['pfleːklɪç] adj careful
Pflegling ['pfleːklɪŋ] m (-s;-e) foster child; (*Pflegebefohlener*) charge
Pflegschaft ['pfleːkʃaft] f (-;-en) (jur) guardianship
Pflicht [pflɪçt] f (-;-en) duty; **sich seiner P. entziehen** evade one's duty
pflicht'bewußt adj conscientious
Pflicht'bewußtsein n conscientiousness
Pflicht'eifer m zeal
pflicht'eifrig adj zealous
Pflicht'erfüllung f performance of duty
Pflicht'fach n (educ) required course
Pflicht'gefühl n sense of duty
pflicht'gemäß adj dutiful
-pflichtig [pflɪçtɪç] comb.fm. obligated, e.g., **schulpflichtig** obligated to attend school
pflicht'schuldig adj duty-bound
pflicht'treu adj dutiful, loyal
pflicht'vergessen adj forgetful of one's duty; (*untreu*) disloyal
Pflicht'vergessenheit f dereliction of duty; disloyalty
Pflicht'verletzung f, **Pflicht'versäumnis** n neglect of duty
Pflock [pflɔk] m (-[e]s;ᵉe) peg; e-n **P. zurückstecken** (fig) come down a peg
pflog [pfloːk] pret of **pflegen**
pflücken ['pflʏkən] tr pluck, pick
Pflug [pfluːk] m (-[e]s;ᵉe) plow
pflügen ['pflyːgən] tr & intr plow
Pflug'schar f plowshare
Pforte ['pfɔrtə] f (-;-n) gate
Pförtner -in ['pfœrtnər(ɪn)] §6 m/ gatekeeper ‖ m doorman; (anat) pylorus
Pfosten ['pfɔstən] m (-s;-) post; (carp) jamb
Pfote ['pfoːtə] f (-;-n) paw; **j–m eins auf die Pfoten geben** rap s.o.'s knuckles
Pfriem [pfriːm] m (-[e]s;-e) awl
Pfropf [pfrɔpf] m (-[e]s;-e) stopper, plug, cork
pfropfen ['pfrɔpfən] tr cork, plug; (*stopfen*) cram; (hort) graft ‖ **Pfropfen** m (-s;-) stopper, plug, cork
Pfropf'fenzieher m corkscrew
Pfropf'reis n (hort) graft
Pfründe ['pfrʏndə] f (-;-n) benefice; (*ohne Seelsorge*) sinecure; **fette P.** (fig) cushy, well-paying job
Pfuhl [pfuːl] m (-[e]s;-e) pool, puddle; (fig) pit

Pfühl [pfyl] *m* (-[e]s;-e) (poet) cushion
pfui ['pfu·ɪ] *interj* phooey!; **p. über dich!** shame on you!
Pfund [pfunt] *n* (-[e]s;-e) pound
pfundig ['pfundɪç] *adj* (coll) great
–**pfündig** [pfyndɪç] *comb.fm.* –pound
Pfundskerl ['pfuntskerl] *m* (coll) great guy
pfund'weise *adv* by the pound
Pfuscharbeit ['pfuʃʼarbaɪt] *f* bungling
pfuschen ['pfu·ʃən] *tr & intr* bungle; **j-m ins Handwerk p.** meddle in s.o.'s business
Pfuscherei [pfu·ʃə'raɪ] *f* (-;-en) bungling
Pfütze ['pfytsə] *f* (-;-n) puddle
Phänomen [fenoʼmen] *n* (-s;-e) phenomenon
phänomenal [fenəmeʼnal] *adj* phenomenal
Phanta·sie [fanta'zi] *f* (-;-sien ['zi·ən]) imagination
Phantasie'gebilde *n* daydream
phantasieren [fanta'zirən] *intr* daydream; (mus) improvise; (pathol) be delirious
phantasie'voll *adj* imaginative
Phantast –in [fan'tast(ɪn)] §7 *mf* visionary
phantastisch [fan'tastɪʃ] *adj* fantastic
Phantom [fan'tom] *n* (-s;-e) phantom
Pharisäer [farɪ'ze·ər] *m* (-s;-) Pharisee; (fig) pharisee
pharmazeutisch [farma'tsɔɪtɪʃ] *adj* pharmaceutical
Pharmazie [farma'tsi] *f* (-;) pharmacy
Phase ['fazə] *f* (-;-n) phase
Philantrop –in [fɪlan'trop(ɪn)] §7 *mf* philanthropist
philanthropisch [fɪlan'tropɪʃ] *adj* philanthropic
Philister [fɪ'lɪstər] *m* (-s;-) Philistine
Phiole [fɪ'olə] *f* (-;-n) vial, phial
Philologe [fɪlo'logə] *m* (-n;-n) philologist
Philologie [fɪlolo'gi] *f* (-;) philology
Philologin [fɪlo'login] *f* (-;-nen) philologist
Philosoph [fɪlo'zof] *m* (-en;-en) philosopher
Philoso·phie [fɪlozo'fi] *f* (-;-fien ['fi·ən]) philosophy
philosophieren [fɪlozo'firən] *intr* philosophize
philosophisch [fɪlo'zofɪʃ] *adj* philosophic(al)
Phlegma ['flegma] *n* (-s;) indolence
Phonetik [fo'netɪk] *f* (-s;) phonetics
phonetisch [fo'netɪʃ] *adj* phonetic
Phönix ['fønɪks] *m* (-[e]s;-e) phoenix
Phönizien [fø'nitsjən] *n* (-s;) Phoenicia
Phönizier –in [fø'nitsjər(ɪn)] §6 *mf* Phoenician
Phosphor ['fosfor] *m* (-s;) phosphorus
phos'phorig *adj* phosphorous
Photo ['foto] *n* (-s;-) photo
Pho'toapparat *m* camera
photogen [foto'gen] *adj* photogenic
Photograph [foto'graf] *m* (-en;-en) photographer
Photogra·phie [fotogra'fi] *f* (-;-fien ['fi·ən]) photography

photographieren [fotogra'firən] *tr & intr* photograph; **sich p. lassen** have one's photograph taken
Photographin [foto'grafin] *f* (-;-nen) photographer
photographisch [foto'grafɪʃ] *adj* photographic
Photokopie *f* photocopy
photokopie'ren *tr* photocopy
Pho'tozelle *f* photoelectric cell
Phrase ['frazə] *f* (-;-n) phrase; (fig) platitude; **das sind nur Phrasen** that's just talk
phra'senhaft *adj* empty, trite; windy
Physik [fy'zik] *f* (-;) physics
physikalisch [fyzɪ'kalɪʃ] *adj* physical
Physiker –in ['fysɪkər(ɪn)] §6 *mf* physicist
Physiogno·mie [fyzjogno'mi] *f* (-;-mien ['mi·ən]) physiognomy
Physiologie [fyzjolo'gi] *f* (-;) physiology
physiologisch [fyzjo'logɪʃ] *adj* physiological
physisch ['fyzɪʃ] *adj* physical
Pianino [pɪ·a'nino] *n* (-s;-s) small upright piano
Pianist –in [pɪ·a'nɪst(ɪn)] §7 *mf* pianist
picheln ['pɪçəln] *tr & intr* tipple
pichen ['pɪçən] *tr* pitch, cover with pitch
Pichler –in ['pɪçlər(ɪn)] §6 *mf* tippler
Picke ['pɪkə] *f* (-;-n) pickax
Pickel ['pɪkəl] *m* (-s;-) pimple; (*Picke*) pickax; (*Eispicke*) ice ax
Pickelhaube (**Pik'kelhaube**) *f* spiked helmet
Pickelhering (**Pik'kelhering**) *m* pickled herring
pickelig (**pik'kelig**) *adj* pimply
picken ['pɪkən] *tr & intr* peck
picklig ['pɪklɪç] *adj* var of pickelig
Picknick ['pɪknɪk] *n* (-s;-s) picnic
pieken ['pikən] *tr* sting; (coll) prick
piekfein ['pik'faɪn] *adj* tiptop
pieksauber ['pik'zaubər] *adj* spick and span
piepen ['pipən] *intr* chirp; (*Maus*) squeal; **bei dir piept's wohl?** are you quite all there? ‖ **Piepen** *n*— **das ist zum P.!** that's ridiculous
Pier [pir] *m* (-s;-e) pier
piesacken ['pizakən] *tr* (coll) pester
Pietät [pɪ·e'tet] *f* (-;) piety
pietät'los *adj* irreverent
pietät'voll *adj* reverent(ial)
Pigment [pɪg'ment] *n* (-[e]s;-e) pigment
Pik [pik], [pik] *m* (-s;-s & -e) (*Bergspitze*) peak ‖ *n* (-s;-) (coll) grudge; **e-n Pik auf j-n haben** hold a grudge against s.o. ‖ *n* (-s;-e) (cards) spade(s)
pikant [pi'kant] *adj* piquant, pungent; (*Bermerkung*) suggestive
Pikante·rie [pɪkantə'ri] *f* (-;-rien ['ri·ən]) piquancy; spicy story, suggestive remark
Pike ['pikə] *f* (-;-n) pike, spear; **von der P. auf dienen** (fig) rise through the ranks
pikiert [pɪ'kirt] *adj* (**über** *acc*) piqued (at)

Pikkolo ['pɪkɔlo] m (-s;-s) apprentice waiter; (mus) piccolo
Pik'koloflöte f (mus) piccolo
Pilger ['pɪlgər] m (-s;-) pilgrim
Pil'gerfahrt f pilgrimage
Pilgerin ['pɪlgərɪn] f (-;-nen) pilgrim
pilgern ['pɪlgərn] intr (SEIN) go on a pilgrimage, make a pilgrimage
Pille ['pɪlə] f (-;-n) pill; P. danach morning-after pill
Pilot -in [pɪ'lot(ɪn)] §7 mf pilot
Pilz [pɪlts] m (-es;-e) fungus; mushroom
pimp(e)lig ['pɪmp(ə)lɪç] adj sickly, delicate; (verweichlicht) effeminate
Pinguin [pɪŋgu'in] m (-s;-e) penguin
Pinie ['pinjə] f (-;-n) umbrella pine
Pinke ['pɪŋkə] f (-;) (coll) dough
Pinkel ['pɪŋkəl] m (-s;-) (coll) dude
pinkeln ['pɪŋkəln] intr (sl) pee
Pinne ['pɪnə] f (-;-n) pin; tack; (naut) tiller
Pinscher ['pɪnʃər] m (-s;-) terrier
Pinsel ['pɪnzəl] m (-s;-) brush; (fig) simpleton, dope
Pinselei [pɪnzə'laɪ] f (-;-en) daubing; (schlechte Malerei) daub
pinseln ['pɪnzəln] tr & intr paint
Pinzette [pɪn'tsetə] f (-;-n) pair of tweezers, tweezers
Pionier [pɪ·ə'nir] m (-s;-e) (fig) pioneer; (mil) engineer
Pionier'arbeit f (fig) spadework
Pionier'truppe f (mil) engineers
Pirat [pɪ'rat] m (-en;-en) pirate
Piraterie [pɪratə'ri] f (-;) piracy
Pirol [pɪ'rol] m (-s;-e) oriole
Pirsch [pɪrʃ] f (-;) hunt
pirschen ['pɪrʃən] intr stalk game
Pirsch'jagd f hunt
Pistazie [pɪs'tatsjə] f (-;-n) pistachio
Piste ['pɪstə] f (-;-n) beaten track; ski run; toboggan run; (aer) runway
Pistole [pɪs'tolə] f (-;-n) pistol
Pisto'lentasche f holster
pitsch(e)naß ['pɪtʃ(ə)'nas] adj soaked to the skin
pittoresk [pɪtɔ'resk] adj picturesque
Pkw., PKW abbr (Personenkraftwagen) passenger car
placieren [pla'sirən] tr place
placken ['plakən] tr pester, plague || ref toil, drudge
Plackerei [plakə'raɪ] f (-;) drudgery
plädieren [ple'dirən] intr plead
Plädoyer [pledwa'je] f (-;-s) plea
Plage ['plagə] f (-;-n) trouble, bother; torment; (Seuche) plague
Pla'gegeist m pest, pain in the neck
plagen ['plagən] tr trouble, bother; (mit Fragen, usw.) pester
Plagiat [pla'gjat] n (-[e]s;-e) plagiarism
Pla'giator [pla'gjatɔr] m (-s;-giatoren [gja'torən]) plagiarist
Plakat [pla'kat] n (-[e]s;-e) poster
Plakat'träger m sandwich man
Plakette [pla'ketə] f (-;-n) plaque
plan [plan] adj plain, clear; (eben) level || Plan m (-[e]s;ꞋꞋe) plan; (Stadt-) map; (poet) battlefield; auf den P. treten appear on the scene
Plane ['planə] f (-;-n) tarpaulin

Plänemacher ['plenəmaxər] m (-s;-) schemer
planen ['planən] tr plan
Pläneschmied ['plenə/mit] m schemer
Planet [pla'net] m (-en;-en) planet
Planeta·rium [plane'tarjum] n (-s; -rien [rjən]) planetarium
Planeten– [planetən] comb.fm. planetary
Plane'tenbahn f planetary orbit
plan'gemäß adv according to plan
planieren [pla'nirən] tr level, grade
Planier'raupe f bulldozer
Planimetrie [planime'tri] f (-;) plane geometry
Planke ['plaŋkə] f (-;-n) plank
Plänkelei [plɛŋkə'laɪ] f (-;-en) skirmish, skirmishing
plänkeln ['plɛŋkəln] intr skirmish
plan'los adj aimless; indiscriminate
plan'mäßig adj systematic; fixed, regular; (Verkehr) scheduled || adv according to plan
planschen ['planʃən] intr splash
Plantage [plan'taʒə] f (-;-n) plantation
Pla'nung f (-;) planning
plan'voll adj systematic, methodical
Plan'wagen m covered wagon
Plan'wirtschaft f planned economy
Plapperei [plapə'raɪ] f (-;) chatter
Plappermaul ['plapərmaʊl] n chatterbox
plappern ['plapərn] intr chatter; prattle
plärren ['plɛrən] intr (coll) bawl
Plas·ma ['plasma] n (-s;-men [men]) plasma
Plastik ['plastɪk] f (-;-en) (Bildwerk) sculpture; (surg) plastic surgery || n (-s;) plastic
plastisch ['plastɪʃ] adj plastic; (anschaulich) graphic
Platane [pla'tanə] f (-;-n) sycamore
Plateau [pla'to] n (-s;-s) plateau
Plateau'schuhe pl platform shoes
Platin [pla'tin] n (-s;) platinum
platin'blond adj platinum-blonde
Platoniker [pla'tonikər] m (-s;-) Platonist
platonisch [pla'toniʃ] adj Platonic
plätschern ['pletʃərn] intr splash; (Bach) babble
platt [plat] adj flat; (nichtssagend) trite; (coll) flabbergasted
Plättbrett ['pletbret] n ironing board
platt'deutsch adj Low German
Platte ['platə] f (-;-n) plate; top, surface; slab; (Präsentierteller) tray; (Speise) dish; (fig) pate, bean; (mus) record; (phot) plate
Plätteisen ['pletaɪzən] n flatiron
plätten ['pletən] tr & intr iron
Plat'tenjockey m disc jockey
Plat'tenspieler m record player
Plat'tenteller m turntable
Plat'tenwechsler m record changer
Platt'form f platform
Platt'fuß m (aut) flat; **Plattfüße** flat feet
platt'füßig adj flat-footed
Platt'heit f (-;-en) flatness; (fig) banality

plattieren [pla'tirən] tr plate
Plättwäsche ['plɛtvɛʃə] f ironing
Platz [plats] m (-es;ᵉe) place; spot; locality; square; (Sitz) seat; (Raum) room, space; (Stellung) position; (sport) ground, field; (tennis) court; **auf die Plätze, fertig, los!** on your marks, get set, go! **fortified position; freier P.** open space; **immer auf dem Platze sein** be always on the alert; **nicht am P. sein** be out of place; be irrelevant; **P. da!** make way; **P. greifen** (fig) take effect, gain ground; **P. machen** make room; **P. nehmen** sit down; **seinen P. behaupten** stand one's ground
Platz'anweiser –in §6 mf usher
Plätzchen ['plɛtsçən] n (-s;-) little place; little square; (Süßware) candy wafer; (Gebäck) cookie, cracker
platzen ['platsən] intr (SEIN) burst; split; crack; (Granate) explode; (Luftreifen) blow out; (fig) come to nothing; **da platzte ihm endlich der Kragen** he finally blew his top; **der Wechsel ist geplatzt** the check bounced
Platz'karte f reserved-seat ticket
Platz'kommandant m commandant
Platz'konzert n open-air concert
Platz'patrone f blank cartridge; **mit Platzpatronen schießen** fire blanks
Platz'regen m cloudburst
Platz'runde f (aer) circuit of a field
Platz'wechsel m change of place; (sport) change in lineup
Platz'wette f betting on a horse to finish in first, second, or third place, bet to place
Plauderei [plaudə'raɪ] f (-;-en) chat; small talk
Plau'derer –in §6 mf talker, chatterer
plaudern ['plaudərn] intr chat, chatter; **aus der Schule p.** tell tales out of school
Plaudertasche ['plaudərtaʃə] f chatterbox
Plauderton ['plaudərton] m conversational tone
plausibel [plau'zibəl] adj plausible
plauz [plauts] interj crash!
pleite ['plaɪtə] adj (coll) broke || adv —p. gehen go broke || Pleite f (-;) (coll) bankruptcy; **P. machen** (coll) go broke
Plenarsitzung [ple'narzɪtsuŋ] f (-;-en) plenary session
Plenum ['plenum] n (-s;) plenary session
Pleuelstange ['plɔɪəlʃtaŋə] f (mach) connecting rod
Plexiglas ['plɛksɪglas] n (-es;) plexiglass
Plinse ['plɪnzə] f (-;-n) pancake; fritter
Plissee [plɪ'se] n (-s;-s) pleat
Plissee'rock m pleated skirt
plissieren [plɪ'sirən] tr pleat
Plombe ['plɔmbə] f (-;-n) lead seal; (dent) filling
plombieren [plɔm'birən] tr seal with lead; (dent) fill

plötzlich ['plœtslɪç] adj sudden || adv suddenly, all of a sudden
plump [plump] adj (unförmig) shapeless; (schwerfällig) heavy, slow; (derb) coarse; (unbeholfen) ungainly; (taktlos) tactless, blunt
plumps [plumps] interj plop! thump!
plumpsen ['plumpsən] intr (HABEN & SEIN) plop, flop
Plunder ['plundər] m (-s;) junk
plündern ['plyndərn] tr & intr plunder
Plural ['plural] m (-s;-e) plural
plus [plus] adv plus || Plus n (-;-) plus; (Überschuß) surplus; (Vorteil) advantage, edge
Plus'pol m (elec) positive pole
Plutokrat [pluto'krat] m (-en;-en) plutocrat
Plutonium [plu'tonjum] n (-s;) plutonium
pneumatisch [pnɔɪ'matɪʃ] adj pneumatic
Pöbel ['pøbəl] m (-s;) mob, rabble
pö'belhaft adj rude, rowdy
Pö'belherrschaft f mob rule
pochen ['pɔxən] tr (min) crush || intr knock; (Herz) pound; **p. an** (dat) knock on; **p. auf** (acc) pound on; (fig) insist on
Pochmühle ['pɔxmylə] f, Pochwerk ['pɔxvɛrk] n crushing mill
Pocke ['pɔkə] f (-;-n) pockmark; Pocken (pathol) smallpox
Pockennarbe [Pok'kennarbe] f pockmark
pockennarbig (pok'kennarbig) adj pockmarked
Podest [pɔ'dɛst] m & n (-es;-e) pedestal; (Treppenabsatz) landing; podium
Po'dium ['podjum] n (-s;-dien [djən]) podium, platform
Poesie [poe'zi] f (-;) poetry
Poet [po'et] m (-en;-en) poet
Poetik [po'etik] f (-;) poetics
poetisch [po'etɪʃ] adj poetic
Pointe [po'ɛ̃tə] f (-;) point (of joke)
Pokal [po'kal] m (-s;-e) goblet; (sport) cup
Pökel ['pøkəl] m (-s;) brine
Pö'kelfleisch n salted meat
Pö'kelhering m pickled herring
pökeln ['pøkəln] tr pickle, salt
Poker ['pokər] n (-s;) poker
Pol [pol] m (-s;-e) pole
Polar– [polar] comb.fm. polar
polarisieren [polarɪ'zirən] tr polarize
Polarität [polarɪ'tɛt] f (-;-en) polarity
Polar'kreis m polar circle; **nördlicher P.** Arctic Circle; **südlicher P.** Antarctic Circle
Polar'licht n polar lights
Polar'stern m polestar
Polar'zone f frigid zone
Pole ['polə] m (-n;-n) Pole
Polemik [po'lemɪk] f (-;) polemics
polemisch [po'lemɪʃ] adj polemical
Polen ['polən] n (-s;) Poland
Police [po'lisə] f (-;-n) (ins) policy
Polier [po'lir] m (-s;-e) foreman
polieren [po'lirən] tr polish
Polin ['polɪn] f (-;-nen) Pole
Politik [polɪ'tik] f (-;-en) policy; (Staatsangelegenheiten) politics

Politiker –in [po'litɪkər(ɪn)] §6 *mf* politician

Politi•kum [po'litɪkum] *n* (-s;-ka [ka]) political issue, political matter

politisch [po'litɪʃ] *adj* political

politisieren [polɪtɪ'zirən] *intr* talk politics

Politur [polɪ'tur] *f* (-;-en) polish

Polizei [polɪ'tsaɪ] *f* (-;) police

Polizei′aufgebot *n* posse

Polizei′aufsicht *f*—unter P. stehen have to report periodically to the police

Polizei′beamte §5 *m* police officer

Polizei′büro *n*, **Polizei′dienststelle** *f* police station

Polizei′knüppel *m* billy club

Polizei′kommissar *m* police commissioner

polizei′lich *adj* police

Polizei′präsident *m* chief of police

Polizei′revier *n* police station

Polizei′spion *m*, **Polizei′spitzel** *m* stoolpigeon

Polizei′streife *f* raid; police patrol

Polizei′streifenwagen *m* squad car

Polizei′stunde *f* closing time; curfew

Polizei′wache *f* police station

polizei′widrig *adj* against police regulations

Polizist [polɪ'tsɪst] *m* (-en;-en) policeman

Polizistin [polɪ'tsɪstɪn] *f* (-;-nen) policewoman

Polizze [po'lɪtsə] *f* (-;-n) (Aust) insurance policy

Polka ['polka] *f* (-;-s) polka

polnisch ['polnɪʃ] *adj* Polish

Polo ['polo] *n* (-s;) (sport) polo

Polster ['polstər] *m & n* (-s;-) cushion

Pol′stergarnitur *f* living-room suite

Pol′stermöbel *pl* upholstered furniture

polstern ['polstərn] *tr* upholster

Pol′stersessel *m* upholstered chair

Pol′sterstuhl *m* padded chair

Pol′sterung *f* (-;) padding, stuffing

Polterabend ['poltərabənt] *m* eve of the wedding day

Poltergeist ['poltərgaɪst] *m* poltergeist

poltern ['poltərn] *intr* make noise; (*rumpeln*) rumble; (*zanken*) bluster

Polyp [po'lyp] *m* (-en;-en) (pathol, zool) polyp; (*Polizist*) (sl) cop

Polytechni•kum [poly'teçnɪkum] *n* (-s; -ka [ka]) polytechnic institute

Pomade [po'madə] *f* (-;-n) pomade

Pomeranze [pomə'rantsə] *f* (-;-n) bitter orange

Pommern ['pomərn] *n* (-s;) Pomerania

Pommes frites [pom'frɪt] *pl* French fries

Pomp [pomp] *m* (-es;) pomp

Pompadour ['pompadur] *m* (-s;-e & -s) lady's string-drawn bag

pomp′haft, pompös [pom'pøs] *adj* pompous

pontifikal [pontɪfɪ'kal] *adj* pontifical

Pontifikat [pontɪfɪ'kat] *n* (-s;) pontificate

Pontius ['pontsjus] *m*—von P. zu Pilatus geschickt werden (coll) get the run-around

Pony ['poni] *m* (-s;-s) (*Damenfrisur*) pony ‖ *n* (-s;-s) (*Pferd*) pony

Popo [po'po] *m* (-s;-s) (coll) backside

populär [popu'ler] *adj* popular

Popularität [popularɪ'tet] *f* (-;) popularity

Pore ['porə] *f* (-;-n) pore

porig ['porɪç] *adj* porous

Pornofilm ['pornofɪlm] *m* (coll) smoker, pornographic movie

Pornoladen ['pornoladən] *m* (coll) porn shop

Pornographie [pornogra'fi] *f* (-;) pornography

porös [po'røs] *adj* porous

Porphyr ['porfyr] *m* (-s;) porphyry

Porree ['pore] *m* (-s;-s) (bot) leek

Portal [por'tal] *n* (-s;-e) portal

Portemonnaie [portmo'ne] *n* (-s;-s) wallet

Portier [por'tje] *m* (-s;-s) doorman

Portion [por'tsjon] *f* (-;-en) portion; (culin) serving, helping; **halbe P.** (coll) half pint; **zwei Portionen Kaffee** two cups of coffee

Por•to ['porto] *n* (-s;-ti [ti]) postage

Por′togebühren *pl* postage

Por′tokasse *f* petty cash

Porträt [por'tret] *n* (-s;-s), (-[e]s;-e) portrait

porträtieren [portre'tirən] *tr* portray

Portugal ['portugal] *n* (-s;) Portugal

Portugiese [portu'gizə] *m* (-n;-n), **Portugiesin** [portu'gizɪn] *f* (-;-nen) Portuguese

portugiesisch [portu'gizɪʃ] *adj* Portuguese

Porzellan [portsə'lan] *n* (-s;-e) porcelain; china; **Meißener Porzellan** Dresden china

Porzellan′brennerei *f* porcelain factory

Posament [poza'ment] *n* (-[e]s;-en) trimming, lace

Posaune [po'zaunə] *f* (-;-n) trombone

posaunen [po'zaunən] *intr* play the trombone

Pose ['pozə] *f* (-;-n) pose

posieren [po'zirən] *intr* pose

Position [pozɪ'tsjon] *f* (-;-en) position

Positions′lampe *f* **Positions′licht** *n* (aer, naut) navigation light

positiv [pozɪ'tif] *adj* (*bejahend*) affirmative; (*Kritik*) favorable; (elec, math, med) positive ‖ *adv* in the affirmative; (coll) for certain ‖ **Positiv** *m* (-s;-e) (gram) positive degree ‖ *n* (-s;-e) (mus) small organ; (phot) positive

Positur [pozɪ'tur] *f* (-;-en) posture, attitude; **sich in P. setzen** (or **stellen** or **werfen**) strike a pose

Posse ['posə] *f* (-;-n) (theat) farce

Possen ['posən] *m* (-s;-) trick, practical joke; **j-m einen P. spielen** play a practical joke on s.o.; **laß die P.!** cut out the nonsense; **P. treiben** (or **reißen**) crack jokes

pos′senhaft *adj* farcical, comical

Possenreißer ['posənraɪsər] *m* (-s;-) joker

Pos′senspiel *n* farce, burlesque

possierlich [po'sirlɪç] *adj* funny

Post [post] *f* (-;-en) mail; (*Postgebäude*) post office

postalisch [pos'talɪʃ] *adj* postal

Postament [pɔsta'mɛnt] n (-[e]s;-e) pedestal
Post'amt n post office
Post'anweisung f money order
Post'auto n mail truck
Post'beamte m postal clerk
Post'beutel m mailbag
Post'bote m mailman
Post'direktor m postmaster
Posten ['pɔstən] m (-s;-) post; (*Stellung*) position; (acct) entry, item; (com) line, lot; (mil) guard, sentinel; **auf dem P. sein** (fig) be on guard; **auf verlorenem P. kämpfen** (coll) play a losing game; **nicht recht auf dem P. sein** be out of sorts; **P. aufstellen** post sentries; **P. stehen** stand guard; **ruhiger P.** (mil) soft job
Po'stenjäger –in §6 mf job hunter
Po'stenkette f line of outposts
Post'fach n post-office box
Post'gebühr f postage
posthum [pɔst'hum] adj posthumous
postieren [pɔs'tirən] tr post, place
Postille [pɔs'tilə] f (-;-n) devotional book
Post'karte f post card
Post'kasten m mail box
Post'kutsche f stagecoach
post'lagernd adj general-delivery || adv general delivery
Postleitzahl ['pɔstlaɪttsal] f zip code
Post'minister m postmaster general
Post'nachnahme f (-;-n) C.O.D.
Post'sack m mailbag
Post'schalter m post-office window
Post'scheck m postal check
Postschließfach ['pɔst/lisfax] n post-office box
Postskript [pɔst'skrɪpt] n (-[e]s;-e) postscript
Post'stempel m postmark
Post'überweisung f money order
post'wendend adj & adv by return mail
Post'wertzeichen n postage stamp
Post'wesen n postal system
potent [pɔ'tɛnt] adj potent
Potential [pɔtɛn'tsjal] n (-s;-e) potential
Potenz [pɔ'tɛnts] f (-;-en) potency; (math) power; **dritte P.** (math) cube; **zweite P.** (math) square
potenzieren [pɔtɛn'tsirən] tr raise to a higher power; (fig) intensify
Pottasche ['pɔta/ə] f (-;) potash
Pottwal ['pɔtval] m sperm whale
potz [pɔts] interj—**p. Blitz!** holy smoke!
potztau'send interj holy smoke!
poussieren [pu'sirən] tr (coll) flirt with; (coll) butter up || intr flirt
Pracht [praxt] f (-;) splendor, magnificence
Pracht'ausgabe f deluxe edition
Pracht'exemplar n beauty, beaut
prächtig ['prɛçtɪç] adj splendid
Pracht'kerl m (coll) great guy
Pracht'stück n (coll) beauty, beaut
pracht'voll adj gorgeous
Pracht'zimmer n stateroom (*in palace*)
Prädikat [prɛdɪ'kat] n (-[e]s;-e) title; (educ) mark, grade; (gram) predicate

Prädikatsnomen [prɛdɪ'katsnomən] n (-s;-s) (gram) complement
Präfix [prɛ'fiks] n (-es;-e) prefix
Prag [prak] n (-s;) Prague
Prägeanstalt ['prɛgə-anstalt] f mint
prägen ['prɛgən] tr stamp, coin || ref —**das hat sich mir tief in das Gedächtnis geprägt** that made a lasting impression on me
Prä'gestempel m (mach) die
pragmatisch [prag'matɪʃ] adj pragmatic
prägnant [prɛ'gnant] adj pithy, terse
Prä'gung f (-;-en) coining, minting; (fig) coinage
prahlen ['pralən] intr (**mit**) brag (about); (**mit**) show off (with)
Prah'ler m (-s;-) braggart; show-off
Prahlerei [pralə'raɪ] f (-;-en) bragging, boasting; (*Prunken*) showing off
Prah'lerin f (-;-nen) braggart; show-off
prahlerisch ['pralərɪʃ] adj bragging
Prahlhans ['pralhans] m (-es;ᵉe) braggart
Prahm [pram] m (-[e]s;-e) flat-bottomed lighter
Praktik ['praktɪk] f (-;-en) practice; (*Kniff*) trick
Praktikant –in [prakti'kant(ɪn)] §7 mf student in on-the-job training
Praktiker ['praktɪkər] m (-s;-) practical person
Prakti·kum ['praktɪkum] n (-s;-ka [ka]) practical training
Praktikus ['praktɪkus] m (-;-se) old hand
praktisch ['praktɪʃ] adj practical; **praktischer Arzt** general practitioner
praktizieren [prakti'tsirən] tr practice; **etw in die Tasche p.** manage to slip s.th. into the pocket
Prälat [prɛ'lat] m (-en;-en) prelate
Praline [pra'linə] f (-;-n) chocolate
prall [pral] adj (*straff*) tight; (*Brüste*) full; (*Backen*) chubby; (*Arme, Beine*) shapely; (*Sonne*) blazing || **Prall** m (-[e]s;-e) impact; collision
prallen ['pralən] intr (SEIN) bounce, rebound; (*Sonne*) beat down
Prämie ['prɛmjə] f (-;-n) award, prize; premium; bonus
prämiieren [prɛmi'irən] tr award a prize to
prangen ['praŋən] intr shine; look beautiful
Pranger ['praŋər] m (-s;-) pillory
Pranke ['praŋkə] f (-;-n) claw
pränumerando [prɛnumə'rando] adv in advance, beforehand
Präparat [prɛpa'rat] n (-[e]s;-e) preparation
präparieren [prɛpa'rirən] tr prepare
Präposition [prɛpozi'tsjon] f (-;-en) preposition
Prä·rie [prɛ'ri] f (-;-rien ['ri·ən]) prairie
Präsens ['prɛzens] n (-; Präsentia [prɛ'zentsɪ·a]) (gram) present
präsent [prɛ'zent] adj present || **Präsent** n (-s;-e) present, gift
präsentieren [prɛzen'tirən] tr present
Präsentier'teller m tray

Präsenzstärke [prɛ'zɛnts/tɛrkə] *f* effective strength

Präservativ [prɛzɛrva'tif] *m* (-s;-e) prophylactic, condom

Präsident [prɛzɪ'dɛnt] *m* (-en;-en) president

Präsidenten- [prɛzɪdɛntən] *comb.fm.* presidential

Präsident/schaft *f* (-;-en) presidency

präsidieren [prɛzɪ'diːrən] *intr* preside

Präsi-dium [prɛ'ziːdjʊm] *n* (-s;-dien [djən]) presidency; chairmanship

prasseln ['prasəln] *intr* crackle; (*Regen*) patter

prassen ['prasən] *intr* lead a dissipated life

Prasserei [prasə'raɪ] *f* (-;) luxurious living, high life

Prätendent [prɛtɛn'dɛnt] *m* (-en;-en) (*auf acc*) pretender (to)

Pra-xis ['praksɪs] *f* (-;-xen [ksən]) practice; experience; doctor's office; law office; (jur) clientele; (med) patients

Präzedenzfall [prɛtsɛ'dɛntsfal] *m* precedent

präzis [prɛ'tsɪs] *adj* precise

Präzision [prɛtsi'zjoːn] *f* (-;) precision

predigen ['preːdɪgən] *tr & intr* preach

Prediger ['preːdɪgər] *m* (-s;-) preacher

Predigt ['preːdɪçt] *f* (-;-en) sermon

Preis [praɪs] *m* (-es;-e) price, rate, cost; (poet) praise, glory; **äußerster P.** (coll) rock-bottom price; **um jeden P.** (fig) at all costs; **um keinen P.** (fig) on no account; **zum P. von** at the rate of

Preis/aufgabe *f* project in a competition

Preis/aufschlag *m* extra charge

Preis/ausschreiben *n* competition

Preisdrückerei ['praɪsdrʏkəraɪ] *f* (-;-en) price cutting

Preiselbeere ['praɪzəlbeːrə] *f* cranberry

preisen ['praɪzən] *tr* praise

Preis/ermäßigung *f* price reduction

Preis/frage *f* question in a competition; question of price (coll) sixty-four-dollar question

Preis/gabe *f* abandonment, surrender

preis/geben §80 *tr* abandon, surrender; (*Geheimnis*) betray; **j-n dem Spott p.** hold s.o. up to ridicule

preisgekrönt ['praɪsgəkrøːnt] *adj* prize-winning

Preis/gericht *n* jury

Preis/grenze *f* price limit; **obere P.** ceiling; **untere P.** minimum price

preis/günstig *adj* worth the money

Preis/lage *f* price range

Preis/niveau *n* price level

Preis/notierung *f* rate of exchange

Preis/richter *m* judge (*in competition*)

Preis/schießen *n* shooting competition

Preis/schild *n* price tag

Preis/schlager *m* bargain price

Preis/schrift *f* prize-winning essay

Preis/stopp *m* price freezing

Preis/sturz *m* drop in prices

Preis/träger -in §6 *mf* prize winner

Preistreiberei [praɪstraɪbə'raɪ] *f* (-;) price rigging

Preis/überwachung *f* price control

Preis/verzeichnis *n* price list

preis/wert, preis/würdig *adj* worth the money, reasonable

Preis/zuschlag *m* markup

prekär [pre'kɛːr] *adj* precarious

Prellbock ['prɛlbɔk] *m* (-(e)s;-e) buffer

prellen ['prɛlən] *tr* bump; bounce; toss up (*in a blanket*); (um) cheat (out of) ‖ *ref*—**sich** [*dat*] **den Arm p.** bruise one's arm

Prel/ler *m* (-s;-) bump; ricochet; bilker, cheat

Prellerei [prɛlə'raɪ] *f* (-;-en) (act of) cheating

Prell/schuß *m* ricochet

Prell/stein *m* curbstone

Prel/lung *f* (-;-en) bruise

Premier [prə'mje] *m* (-s;-s) premier

Premiere [prə'mjeːrə] *f* (-;-n) (theat) premiere, first night, opening

Premier/minister *m* prime minister

Presbyterianer -in [prɛsbytə'rjaːnər (ɪn)] §6 *mf* Presbyterian

presbyterianisch [prɛsbytə'rjaːnɪʃ] *adj* Presbyterian

preschen ['prɛʃən] *intr* charge

pressant [prɛ'sant] *adj* pressing

Presse ['prɛsə] *f* (-;-n) (& journ) press; (educ) cram class

Pres/seagentur *f* press agency

Pres/seamt *n* public-relations office

Pres/seausweis *m* press card

Pres/sebericht *m* press report

Pres/sechef *m* press secretary

Pres/sekonferenz *f* press conference

Pres/semeldung *f* news item

Pres/sestelle *f* public-relations office

Pres/severtreter *m* reporter; public-relations officer

Preßkohle ['prɛskoːlə] *f* briquette

Preßluft ['prɛsluft] *f* compressed air

Preß/lufthammer *m* jackhammer

Preuße ['prɔɪsə] *m* (-n;-n) Prussian

Preußen ['prɔɪsən] *n* (-s;) Prussia

Preußin ['prɔɪsɪn] *f* (-;-nen) Prussian

preußisch ['prɔɪsɪʃ] *adj* Prussian

prickeln ['prɪkəln] *intr* tingle

Priem [priːm] *m* (-(e)s;-e) plug (*of tobacco*)

priemen ['priːmən] *intr* chew tobacco

pries [priːs] *pret* of **preisen**

Priester ['priːstər] *m* (-s;-) priest

Prie/steramt *n* priesthood

Priesterin ['priːstərɪn] *f* (-;-nen) priestess

prie/sterlich *adj* priestly

Prie/sterrock *m* cassock

Priestertum ['priːstərtuːm] *n* (-s;) priesthood

Prie/sterweihe *f* (eccl) ordination

prima ['priːma] *invar adj* first-class; terrific, swell

primär [prɪ'mɛːr] *adj* primary ‖ *adv* primarily

Primat [prɪ'maːt] *m & n* (-(e)s;-e) primacy, priority ‖ *m* (-en;-en) primate

Primel ['priːməl] *f* (-;-n) primrose

primitiv [prɪmi'tiːf] *adj* primitive

Prinz [prɪnts] *m* (-en;-en) prince

Prinzessin [prɪn'tsɛsɪn] *f* (-;-nen) princess

Prinz/gemahl *m* prince consort

Prin·zip [prɪn'tsip] *n* (-s;-zipien ['tsipjən]) principle
prinzipiell [prɪntsɪ'pjel] *adj* in principle, fundamentally
Prinzi'pienreiter *m* (coll) pedant
prinz'lich *adj* princely
Pri·or ['pri·or] *m* (-s;-oren ['orən]) (eccl) prior
Priorität [pri·ɔrɪ'tet] *f* (-;-en) priority
Prise ['prizə] *f* (-;-n) pinch (*of salt, etc.*); (nav) prize
Pris·ma ['prɪsma] *n* (-s;-men [mɛn]) prism
privat [prɪ'vat] *adj* private; personal
Privat'adresse *f*, **Privat'anschrift** *f* home address
Privat'dozent –in §7 *mf* non-salaried university lecturer
Privat'druck *m* private printing
Privat'eigentum *n* private property
Privat'gespräch *n* (telp) personal call
privatim [prɪ'vatɪm] *adv* privately; confidentially
privatisieren [prɪvatɪ'zirən] *intr* in §6 financially independent
Privat'lehrer –in §6 *mf* tutor
Privat'recht *n* civil law
privat'rechtlich *adj* (jur) civil
Privi·leg [prɪvɪ'lek] *n* (-[e]s;-legien ['legjən]) privilege
privilegiert [prɪvɪle'girt] *adj* privileged
probat [pro'bat] *adj* tried, tested
Probe ['probə] *f* (-;-n) (*Versuch*) trial, experiment; (*Prüfung*) test; (*Muster*) sample; (*Beweis*) proof; (theat) rehearsal; **auf die P. stellen** put to the test; **auf (or zur) P.** on approval
Pro'beabdruck *m*, **Pro'beabzug** *m* (typ) proof
Pro'bebild *n* (phot) proof
Pro'bebogen *m* proof sheet
Pro'bedruck *m* (typ) proof
Pro'befahrt *f* road test, trial run
Pro'beflug *m* test flight
Pro'belauf *m* trial run; dry run
Pro'besendung *f* sample sent on approval
Pro'bestück *n* sample, specimen
pro'beweise *adv* on trial; on approval
Pro'bezeit *f* probation period
probieren [pro'birən] *tr* try out, test; try, taste; (metal) assay
Probier'glas *n* test tube
Probier'stein *m* touch-stone
Problem [pro'blem] *n* (-s;-e) problem
Produkt [pro'dʊkt] *n* (-[e]s;-e) product; (*des Bodens*) produce
Produktion [prodʊk'tsjon] *f* (-;-en) production; (indust) output
produktiv [prodʊk'tif] *adj* productive
Produzent [produ'tsɛnt] *m* (-en;-en) (& cin) producer
produzieren [produ'tsirən] *tr* produce || *ref* perform; (pej) show off
profan [pro'fan] *adj* profane
profanieren [profa'nirən] *tr* profane
Profession [profe'sjon] *f* (-;-en) profession
Professional [profesjo'nal] *m* (-s;-e) (sport) professional
professionell [profesjo'nel] *adj* professional
Profes·sor [pro'fɛsor] *m* (-s;-soren ['sorən]), **Professorin** [profe'sorɪn] *f* (-;-nen) professor; **außerordentlicher P.** associate professor; **ordentlicher P.** full professor
Professur [profe'sur] *f* (-;-en) professorship
Profi ['profi] *m* (-s;-s) (coll) pro
Profil [pro'fil] *n* (-s;-e) profile; (aut) tread; **im P.** in profile
profiliert [profi'lirt] *adj* outstanding
Profit [pro'fit] *m* (-[e]s;-e) profit
profitabel [profi'tabəl] *adj* profitable
Profit'gier *f* profiteering
profitieren [profi'tirən] *tr & intr* profit
Prognose [pro'gnozə] *f* (-;-n) (med) prognosis; (meteor) forecast
Programm [pro'gram] *n* (-s;-e) program; (pol) platform
programmieren [progra'mirən] *tr* (data proc) program
Projekt [pro'jekt] *n* (-[e]s;-e) project
Projektil [projek'til] *n* (-s;-e) projectile
Projektion [projek'tsjon] *f* (-;-en) projection
Projektions'apparat *m*, **Projektions'gerät** *n*, **Projek·tor** [pro'jektor] *m* (-s;-toren ['torən]) projector
projizieren [proji'tsirən] *tr* project
proklamieren [prokla'mirən] *tr* proclaim
Prokura [pro'kura] *f* (-;) power of attorney; **per P.** by proxy
Prolet [pro'let] *m* (-en;-en) (pej) cad
Proletariat [proleta'rjat] *n* (-[e]s;-e) proletariat
Proletarier –in [prole'tarjər(ɪn)] §6 *mf* proletarian
proletarisch [prole'tarɪʃ] *adj* proletarian
Prolog [pro'lok] *m* (-[e]s;-e) prologue
prolongieren [prolɔŋ'girən] *tr* extend; (cin) hold over
Promenade [promə'nadə] *f* (-;-n) avenue; (*Spaziergang*) promenade
promenieren [promə'nirən] *intr* stroll
prominent [promi'nɛnt] *adj* prominent
Promotion [promo'tsjon] *f* (-;-en) awarding of the doctor's degree
promovieren [promo'virən] *intr* attain a doctor's degree
prompt [prɔmpt] *adj* prompt, quick
Prono·men [pro'nomən] *n* (-s;-mina [mina]) pronoun
Propaganda [propa'ganda] *f* (-;) propaganda
propagieren [propa'girən] *tr* propagate
Propeller [pro'pelər] *m* (-s;-) propeller
Prophet [pro'fet] *m* (-en;-en) prophet
Prophetin [pro'fetɪn] *f* (-;-nen) prophetess
prophetisch [pro'fetɪʃ] *adj* prophetic
prophezeien [profe'tsai·ən] *tr* prophesy
Prophezei'ung *f* (-;-en) prophecy
Proportion [propor'tsjon] *f* (-;-en) proportion
proportional [proportsjo'nal] *adj* proportional
proportioniert [proportsjo'nirt] *adj* proportionate
Propst [propst] *m* (-es;-̈e) provost

Prosa ['proza] f (-;) prose

prosaisch [pro'za·ɪʃ] adj prosaic

prosit ['prozɪt] interj to your health! || **Prosit** n (-s;-s) toast

Prospekt [pro'spekt] m (-[e]s;-e) prospect, view; brochure, folder

prostituieren [prɔstɪtu'irən] tr prostitute

Prostituierte [prɔstɪtu'irtə] §5 f prostitute

protegieren [prote'girən] tr patronize; (schützen) protect

Protektion [protek'tsjon] f (-;) pull, connections

Protest [pro'test] m (-es;-e) protest

Protestant -in [protes'tant(ɪn)] §7 mf Protestant

protestantisch [protes'tantɪʃ] adj Protestant

protestieren [protes'tirən] tr & intr protest

Protokoll [proto'kɔl] n (-s;-e) protocol; record, minutes; **P. führen** take the minutes; **zu P. nehmen** take down

Protokoll'führer -in §6 mf recording secretary; (jur) clerk

protokollieren [protoko'lirən] tr record

Pro·ton ['proton] n (-s;-tonen ['tonən]) (phys) proton

Protz [prɔts] m (-en;-en) show-off

protzen ['prɔtsən] intr show off

prot'zenhaft, protzig ['prɔtsɪç] adj show-offish

Prozedur [protse'dur] f (-;-en) procedure; (jur) proceeding

Prozent [pro'tsent] n (-[e]s;-e) per cent

Prozent'satz m percentage

Pro·zeß [pro'tses] m (-zesses;-zesse) process; (jur) case, suit; (jur) proceedings; **e-en P. anstrengen** (or **führen**) gegen sue; **kurzen P. machen mit** make short work of

Prozeß'akten pl (jur) record

Prozeß'führer -in §6 mf litigant

prozessieren [protse'sirən] intr go to court; **p. gegen** sue

Prozession [protse'sjon] f (-;-en) procession

Prozeß'kosten pl (jur) court costs

Prozeß'vollmacht f power of attorney

prüde ['prydə] adj prudish

prüfen ['pryfən] tr test; (nachprüfen) check, verify; (untersuchen) examine; (kosten) taste; (acct) audit

Prüfer -in §6 mf examiner; (acct) auditor

Prüfling ['pryflɪŋ] m (-s;-e) examinee

Prüfstein ['pryfʃtaɪn] m touchstone

Prü'fung f (-;-en) test; examination; check, verification; (acct) audit; (jur) review

Prü'fungsarbeit f test paper

Prü'fungsausschuß m, **Prü'fungskommission** f examining board

Prügel ['prygəl] m (-s;-) stick, cudgel; **Prügel** pl whipping

Prügelei [prygə'laɪ] f (-;-en) brawl; free-for-all

Prü'gelknabe m whipping boy, scapegoat

prügeln ['prygəln] tr beat, whip || ref have a fight

Prü'gelstrafe f corporal punishment

Prunk [prʊŋk] m (-[e]s;) pomp, show

prunken ['prʊŋkən] intr show off

Prunk'gemach n stateroom

prunk'haft adj showy

Prunk'sucht f ostentatiousness

prunk'süchtig adj ostentatious

prunk'voll adj gorgeous

Prunk'zimmer n stateroom

prusten ['prustən] intr snort

Psalm [psalm] m (-s;-en) psalm

Psalter ['psaltər] m (-s;-) psalter

Pseudonym [psɔɪdo'nym] n (-s;-e) pseudonym

Psychiater (psyçɪ'atər] m (-s;-) psychiatrist

Psychiatrie [psyçɪ·a'tri] f (-;) psychiatry

psychiatrisch [psyçɪ'atrɪʃ] adj psychiatric

psychisch ['psyçɪʃ] adj psychic(al)

Psychoanalyse [psyço·ana'lyzə] f (-;) psychoanalysis

Psychoanalytiker -in [psyço·ana'lytɪkər(ɪn)] §6 mf psychoanalyst

Psychologe [psyço'logə] m (-n;-n) psychologist

Psychologie [psyçolo'gi] f (-;) psychology

Psychologin [psyço'login] f (-;-nen) psychologist

psychologisch [psyço'logɪʃ] adj psychological

Psychopath -in [psyço'pat(ɪn)] §7 mf psychopath

Psychose [psy'çozə] f (-;-n) psychosis

Psychotherapie [psyçotera'pi] f (-;) psychotherapy

Pubertät [puber'tet] f (-;) puberty

publik [pub'lik] adj public

Publi·kum ['publikum] n (-s;-ka [ka]) public; (theat) audience

publizieren [publɪ'tsirən] tr publish

Publizist -in [publɪ'tsɪst(ɪn)] §7 mf (journ) writer on public affairs; teacher or student of journalism

Publizität [publɪtsɪ'tet] f (-;) publicity

Pudel ['pudəl] m (-s;-) poodle; **des Pudels Kern** (fig) gist of the matter

Pu'delmütze f fur cap; woolen cap

pu'delnaß adj (coll) soaking wet

Puder ['pudər] m (-s;) powder

Pu'derdose f powder box; compact

Pu'derquaste f powder puff

Pu'derzucker m powdered sugar

Puff [puf] m (-[e]s;=e & -e) (Stoß) poke; (Knall) pop; (Bausch) puff; || m (-s;-s) (coll) brothel

Puff'ärmel m puffed sleeve

puffen ['pufən] tr poke; (coll) prod || intr puff; (knallen) pop, bang away

Puffer ['pufər] m (-s;-) buffer; popgun; (culin) potato pancake

Puf'ferbatterie f booster battery

Puf'ferstaat m buffer state

Puff'mais m popcorn

Puff'reis m (-es;) puffed rice

Pulli ['puli] m (-s;-s) (coll) sweater

Pullover [pu'lovər] m (-s;-) sweater

Puls [puls] m (-es;-e) pulse

Puls'ader f artery

pulsieren [pul'zirən] intr pulsate

Puls'schlag m pulse beat

Pult [pult] n (-[e]s;-e) desk
Pulver ['pulfər] n (-s;-) powder; (*Schieß-*) gunpowder; (coll) dough
pul'verig adj powdery
pulverisieren [pulfərɪ'zirən] tr pulverize
Pul'verschnee m powdery snow
Pummel ['puməl] m (-s;-) butterball (*chubby child*)
pummelig ['puməlɪç] adj (coll) chubby
Pump [pump] m—auf P. (coll) on tick
Pumpe ['pumpə] f (-;-n) pump
pumpen ['pumpən] tr pump; (coll) give on tick; (coll) get on tick ‖ intr pump
Pum'penschwengel m pump handle
Pumpernickel ['pumpərnɪkəl] m (-s; -) pumpernickel
Pump'hosen f pair of knickerbockers
Punkt [puŋkt] m (-[e]s;-e) point; (*Tüpfelchen*) dot; (*Stelle*) spot; (*Einzelheit*) item; (gram) period; **der tote P.** a deadlock; **dunkler P.** (fig) skeleton in the closet; **nach Punkten siegen** win on points; **P. sechs Uhr** at six o'clock sharp; **springender P.** crux; **strittiger P.** point at issue; **wunder P.** (fig) sore spot
Punkt'gleichheit f (sport) tie
punktieren [puŋk'tirən] tr dot, stipple; **punktierte Linie** dotted line
pünktlich ['pyŋktlɪç] adj punctual
Punkt'sieg m (box) winning on points
punktum ['puŋktum] interj—und damit p.! and that's it!; period!
Punkt'zahl f (sport) score
Punsch [pun/] m (-es;) punch (*drink*)
Punze ['puntsə] f (-;-n) punch, stamp
punzen ['puntsən] tr punch, stamp
Pupille [pu'pɪlə] f (-;-n) (anat) pupil
Puppe ['pupə] f (-;-n) doll; puppet; (*Schneider-*) dummy; (zool) pupa
Pup'penspiel n puppet show
Pup'penwagen m doll carriage
pur [pur] adj pure, sheer

Püree [py're] n (-s;-s) mashed potatoes; puree
purgieren [pur'girən] tr & intr purge
Purpur ['purpur] m (-s;) purple
pur'purfarben adj purple
purpurn [purpurn] adj purple
Purzelbaum ['purtsəlbaum] m somersault; **e-en P. schlagen** do a somersault
purzeln ['purtsəln] intr (SEIN) tumble
pusselig ['pusəlɪç] adj fussy
Puste ['pustə] f (-;) (coll) breath
Pustel ['pustəl] f (-;-n) pustule
pusten ['pustən] tr—**ich puste dir was!** (coll) you may whistle for it! ‖ intr puff, pant
Pu'sterohr n peashooter
Pute ['putə] f (-;-n) turkey (hen)
Puter ['putər] m (-s;-) turkey (cock)
Putsch [put/] m (-es;-e) putsch, uprising
Putz [puts] m (-es;) finery; trimming; ornaments; plaster
putzen ['putsən] tr (*reinigen*) clean; (*Schuhe*) polish; (*Zähne*) brush; (*Person*) dress; (*schmücken*) adorn ‖ ref dress; **sich** [dat] **die Nase p.** blow one's nose
Put'zer m (-s;-) cleaner; (mil) orderly
Putzerei [putsə'raɪ] f (-;-en) (Aust) dry cleaner's; (Aust) laundry
Putz'frau f cleaning woman
putzig ['putsɪç] adj funny
Putz'lappen m cleaning cloth
Putz'mittel n cleaning agent
Putz'wolle f cotton waste
Putz'zeug n cleaning things
Pygmäe [pyg'mɛ·ə] m (-n;-n) pygmy
Pyjama [pɪ'dʒama] m (-s;-s) pajamas
Pyramide [pyra'midə] f (-;-n) pyramid; (mil) stack
Pyrenäen [pyra'nɛ·ən] pl Pyrenees
Pyrotechnik [pyro'teçnɪk] f (-;) pyrotechnics
Pythonschlange ['pyton/laŋə] f python

Q

Q, q [ku] invar n Q, q
quabbelig ['kvabəlɪç] adj flabby; quivering, jelly-like
quabbeln ['kvabəln] intr quiver
Quackelei [kvakə'laɪ] f (-;-en) silly talk; (*unnützes Zeug*) rubbish
Quacksalber ['kvakzalbər] m (-s;-) quack
Quader ['kvadər] m (-s;-) ashlar
Quadrant [kva'drant] m (-en;-en) quadrant
Quadrat [kva'drat] n (-[e]s;-e) square; **e-e Zahl ins Q. erheben** square a number; **zwei Fuß im Q.** two feet square
quadratisch [kva'dratɪ/] adj square; quadratic
Quadrat'meter n square meter
Quadrat'wurzel f square root
quadrieren [kva'drirən] tr square

quaken ['kvakən] intr (Ente) quack; (*Frosch*) croak
quäken ['kvekən] intr bawl
Qual [kval] f (-;-en) torment, agony
quälen ['kvelən] tr torment; worry; (*ständig bedrängen*) pester ‖ ref—**sich mit e-r Arbeit q.** slave at a job; **sich umsonst q.** labor in vain; **sich zu Tode q.** worry oneself to death
Quälgeist ['kvelgaɪst] m pest
Qualifikation [kvalɪfɪka'tsjon] f (-; -en) qualification
qualifizieren [kvalɪfɪ'tsirən] tr & ref (zu) qualify (for)
Qualität [kvalɪ'tet] f (-;-en) quality
Qualitäts- comb.fm. high-quality, high-grade, quality
Qualle ['kvalə] f (-;-n) jellyfish
Qualm [kvalm] m (-[e]s;) smoke; vapor

qualmen ['kvalmən] *tr* smoke || *intr* smoke; (coll) smoke like a chimney
qual'mig *adj* smoky
qual'voll *adj* agonizing
Quantentheorie ['kvantəntə·ori] *f* quantum theory
Quantität [kvantı'tɛt] *f* (–;-en) quantity
Quan·tum ['kvantum] *n* (–s;-ten [tən]) quantum; quantity; (*Anteil*) portion
Quappe ['kvapə] *f* (–;-n) tadpole
Quarantäne [kvaran'tɛnə] *f* (–;-n) quarantine
Quark [kvark] *m* (–[e]s) curds; cottage cheese; (fig) nonsense
Quark'käse *m* cottage cheese
quarren ['kvarən] *intr* (*Frosch*) croak; (fig) groan
Quart [kvart] *n* (–s;-e) quart; quarto || *f* (–;-en) (mus) fourth
Quartal [kvar'tɑl] *n* (–s;-e) quarter (*of a year*)
Quartals'abrechnung *f* (fin) quarterly statement
Quartals'säufer *m* periodic drunkard
Quart'band *m* (–[e]s;-e) quarto volume
Quarte ['kvartə] *f* (–;-n) (mus) fourth
Quartett [kvar'tɛt] *n* (–[e]s;-e) quartet
Quart'format *n* quarto
Quartier [kvar'tir] *n* (–s;-e) (*Stadtviertel*) quarter; (*Unterkunft*) quarters; (mil) quarters, billet
Quartier'meister *m* (mil) quartermaster
Quarz [kvarts] *m* (–es;-e) quartz
quasseln ['kvasəln] *tr* (coll) talk || *intr* talk nonsense
Quast [kvast] *m* (–[e]s;-e) brush
Quaste ['kvastə] *f* (–;-n) tassel
Quatsch [kvatʃ] *m* (–es) (coll) baloney
quatschen ['kvatʃən] *intr* chatter; talk nonsense; (*durch Schlamm*) slog
Quecksilber ['kvɛkzılbər] *n* mercury
queck'silbrig *adj* fidgety
Quell [kvɛl] *m* (–[e]s;-e) (poet) var of Quelle
Quelle ['kvɛlə] *f* (–;-n) fountainhead; source; spring
quellen ['kvɛlən] §119 *tr* cause to swell; soak || *intr* (sein) spring, gush; (*Tränen*) well up; (*anschwellen*) swell; ihm quollen die Augen fast aus dem Kopf his eyes almost popped out
Quel'lenangabe *f* citation; bibliography
quel'lenmäßig *adj* according to the best authorities, authentic
Quel'lenmaterial *n* source material
Quel'lenstudium *n* original research

Quell'fluß *m* source
Quell'gebiet *n* headwaters
Quell'wasser *n* spring water
Quengelei [kvɛŋə'lai] *f* (–;-en) nagging
quengeln ['kvɛŋəln] *intr* nag
quer [kver] *adj* cross, transverse || *adv* crosswise; q. über (*acc*) across
Quer'balken *m* crossbeam
Quere ['kverə] *f* (–;) diagonal direction; j–m in die Q. kommen run across s.o.; (fig) disturb s.o.
queren ['kverən] *tr* traverse, cross
querfeldein' *adv* cross-country
Quer'kopf *m* contrary person
quer'köpfig *adj* contrary
Quer'pfeife *f* (mus) fife
Quer'ruder *n* (aer) aileron
Quer'schiff *n* (archit) transept
Quer'schläger *m* ricochet
Quer'schnitt *m* cross section
Quer'treiber *m* schemer, plotter
querü'ber *adv* straight across
Querulant –in [kveru'lant(ın)] §7 *mf* grumbler, grouch
Quetsche ['kvetʃə] *f* (–;-n) squeezer; (pej) joint
quetschen ['kvetʃən] *tr* squeeze, pinch; bruise; (*zerquetschen*) crush, mash
Quetsch'kartoffeln *pl* mashed potatoes
Quet'schung *f* (–;-en) bruise, contusion
Quetsch'wunde *f* bruise
quick [kvik] *adj* brisk, lively
quick'lebendig *adj* (coll) very lively
quieken ['kvikən] *intr* squeal, squeak
quietschen ['kvitʃən] *intr* (*Tür*) creak; (*Ferkel*) squeal; (*Bremsen*) screetch
Quintessenz ['kvintesents] *f* (–;) quintessence
Quintett [kvin'tɛt] *n* (–[e]s;-e) quintet
Quirl [kvirl] *m* (–[e]s;-e) (fig) fidgeter; (culin) whisk, mixer
quirlen ['kvirlən] *tr* beat, mix
quitt [kvit] *adj* even, square
Quitte ['kvitə] *f* (–;-n) quince
quittieren [kvi'tirən] *tr* give a receipt for; (*aufgeben*) quit
Quit'tung *f* (–;-en) receipt
Quiz [kvis] *n* (–;) quiz
quoll [kvɔl] *pret* of quellen
Quotation [kvota'tsjon] *f* (–;-en) (st. exch.) quotation
Quote ['kvotə] *f* (–;-en) quota
Quotient [kvo'tsjent] *m* (–en;-en) quotient
quotieren [kvo'tirən] *tr* quote

R

R, r [er] *invar n* R, r
Rabatt [ra'bat] *m* (–[e]s;-e) reduction, discount
Rabatt'marke *f* trading stamp
Rabatz [ra'bats] *m*—R. machen (coll) raise Cain
Rab·bi ['rabi] *m* (–[s];-s & –binen

['binən]), **Rabbiner** [ra'binər] *m* (–s;-) rabbi
Rabe ['rabə] *m* (–n;-n) raven; weißer R. (fig) rare bird
Ra'benaas *n* (coll) beast
Ra'benmutter *f* hard-hearted mother
ra'benschwarz' *adj* jet-black

rabiat [ra'bjat] *adj* rabid, raving

Rache ['raxə] *f* (-;) revenge

Rachen ['raxən] *m* (-s;-) throat; mouth; (fig) jaws

rächen ['reçən] *tr* avenge ‖ *ref* (an *dat*) avenge oneself (on)

Ra'chenhöhle *f* pharynx

Ra'chenkatarrh *m* sore throat

Rä'cher –in §6 *mf* avenger

Rachgier ['raxgir] *f* revengefulness

rach'gierig, rach'süchtig *adj* vengeful

Rad [rat] *n* (-[e]s;-er) wheel; bike; ein Rad schlagen turn a cartwheel; (*Pfau*) fan the tail

Radar ['radar], [ra'dar] *n* (-s;) radar

Ra'dargerät *n* radar

Ra'darschirm *m* radarscope

Radau [ra'dau] *m* (-s;-) (coll) row

Radau'macher *m* rowdy

Rädchen ['retçən] *n* (-s;-) little wheel

Rad'dampfer *m* river boat

radebrechen ['radəbreçən] §64 *tr* murder (*a language*)

radeln ['radəln] *intr* (SEIN) (coll) ride a bike

Rädelsführer ['redəlsfyrər] *m* ringleader

rädern ['redərn] *tr* torture; wie gerädert sein (coll) be bushed

Räderwerk ['redərverk] *n* gears; (fig) clockwork

rad'fahren §71 *intr* (SEIN) ride a bicycle

radieren [ra'dirən] *tr* erase; etch

Radie'rer *m* (-s;-) eraser; etcher

Radier'gummi *m* eraser

Radier'kunst *f* art of etching

Radier'messer *n* scraper, eraser

Radie'rung *f* (-;-en) erasure; etching

Radieschen [ra'disçən] *n* (-s;-) radish

radikal [radɪ'kal] *adj* radical ‖ Radikale §5 *mf* radical, extremist

Radio ['radjo] *n* (-s;-s) radio; im R. on the radio; R. hören listen to the radio

Ra'dioamateur *m* (rad) ham

Ra'dioapparat *m*, Ra'diogerät *n* radio set

Radiologe [radjo'logə] *m* (-n;-n) radiologist

Radiologie [radjolo'gi] *f* (-;) radiology

Ra'dioröhre *f* radio tube

Ra'diosender *m* radio transmitter

Radium ['radjum] *n* (-s;) radium

Ra·dius ['radjus] *m* (-;-dien [djən]) radius

Rad'kappe *f* hubcap

Rad'kranz *m* rim

Radler –in ['radlər(ɪn)] §6 *mf* cyclist

Rad'nabe *f* hub

Rad'rennen *n* bicycle race

–rädrig [redrɪç] *comb.fm.* –wheeled

rad'schlagen §132 *intr* turn a cartwheel

Rad'spur *f* rut, track

Rad'stand *m* wheelbase

Rad'zahn *m* cog

raffen ['rafən] *tr* snatch up, gather up; (sew) take up

Raffgier ['rafgir] *f* rapacity

raffgierig ['rafgirɪç] *adj* rapacious

Raffine·rie [rafinə'ri] *f* (-;-rien ['ri-ən]) refinery

raffinieren [rafɪ'nirən] *tr* refine

raffiniert [rafɪ'nirt] *adj* refined; (fig) shrewd, cunning

Raffzahn ['raftsan] *m* canine tooth

ragen ['ragən] *intr* tower, loom

Ragout [ra'gu] *n* (-s;-s) (culin) stew

Rahe ['ra·ə] *f* (-;-n) (naut) yard

Rahm [ram] *m* (-[e]s;) cream

Rahmen ['ramən] *m* (-s;-) frame; (Gefüge) framework; (Bereich) scope, limits; (fig) setting; (aut) chassis; aus dem R. fallen be out of place; e-n R. abgeben für form a setting for; im R. (genit) in the course of; im R. von (or genit) within the scope of; within the framework of

Rah'menerzählung *f* story within a story

rahmig ['ramɪç] *adj* creamy

Rakete [ra'ketə] *f* (-;-n) rocket

Rake'tenabschußrampe *f* launch pad

Rake'tenbunker *m* silo

Rake'tenstart *m* rocket launch

Rake'tenwerfer *m* rocket launcher

Rake'tenwesen *n* rocketry

Rakett [ra'ket] *n* (-[e]s;-e & -s) (tennis) racket

Rammbär ['rambɛr] *m*, Rammbock ['rambɔk] *m*, Ramme ['ramə] *f* (-;-n) rammer; pile driver

rammeln ['raməln] *tr* shove; (zusammenpressen) pack; (belegen) copulate with ‖ *intr* copulate

rammen ['ramən] *tr* ram; (Beton) tamp

Rampe ['rampə] *f* (-;-n) ramp; (rok) launch pad; (rr) platform; (theat) apron

Ram'penlicht *n* footlights; (fig) limelight

Ramsch [ramʃ] *m* (-es;) odds and ends; junk; (com) rummage

Ramsch'verkauf *m* rummage sale

Ramsch'waren *pl* junk

Rand [rant] *m* (-[e]s;-er) edge, border; (e-s Druckseite) margin; am Rande bemerken note in passing; außer R. und Band completely out of control; bis zum Rande to the brim; e-n R. hinterlassen leave a ring (e.g., from a wet glass); Ränder unter den Augen circles under the eyes

Rand'auslöser *m* (typ) margin release

Rand'bemerkung *f* marginal note; (fig) snide remark

rändeln ['rendəln], ländern ['rendərn] *tr* border, edge; (Münzen) mill

Rand'gebiet *n* borderland; (e-r Stadt) outskirts

rand'los *adj* rimless

Rand'staat *m* border state

Ranft [ranft] *m* (-[e]s;-e) crust

rang [raŋ] *pret of* ringen ‖ Rang *m* (-[e]s;-e) rank; (theat) balcony; j-m den R. ablaufen (fig) run rings around s.o.

Rang'abzeichen *n* insignia of rank

Rang'älteste §5 *mf* ranking officer

Range ['raŋə] *m* (-n;-n) & *f* (-;-n) brat

Rangier'bahnhof *m* (rr) marshaling yard

rangieren [rɑ̃'ʒirən] *tr* rank; (rr) shunt, switch ‖ *intr* rank

Rang'ordnung f order of precedence
Rang'stufe f rank
rank [raŋk] adj slender
Ranke ['raŋkə] f (-;-n) tendril
Ränke ['reŋkə] pl schemes; **R. schmieden** scheme
ranken ['raŋkən] ref & intr creep, climb; **sich r. um** wind around
rän'kevoll adj scheming
rann [ran] pret of rinnen
rannte ['rantə] pret of rennen
Ranzen ['rantsən] m (-s;-) knapsack; school bag; (Bauch) belly; (mil) field pack
ranzig ['rantsɪç] adj rancid
rapid [ra'pit], **rapide** [ra'pidə] adj rapid
Rappe ['rapə] m (-n;-n) black horse
rar [rar] adj rare, scarce
Rarität [rarɪ'tet] f (-;-en) rarity
rasant [ra'zant] adj grazing, point-blank (fire); (fig) impetuous
Rasanz [ra'zants] f (-;) flat trajectory; (fig) impetuosity
rasch [raʃ] adj quick; (hastig) hasty
rascheln ['raʃəln] intr rustle
Rasch'heit f (-;) haste, speed
rasen ['razən] intr rage, rave || intr (SEIN) rush; (aut) speed || **Rasen** m (-s;-) lawn, grass
ra'send adj raging, raving; wild, mad; (Hunger) ravenous; (Wut) towering; (Tempo) break-neck; **r. werden** see red
Ra'sendecke f turf
Ra'senmäher m lawn mower
Ra'senplatz m lawn
Ra'sensprenger m lawn sprinkler
Raserei [razə'raɪ] f (-;) rage, madness; (aut) reckless driving
Rasier- [razir] comb.fm. shaving, razor
Rasier'apparat m safety razor
rasieren [ra'zirən] tr & ref shave
Rasier'klinge f razor blade
Rasier'messer n straight razor
Rasier'napf m shaving mug
Rasier'pinsel m shaving brush
Rasier'wasser n after-shave lotion
Rasier'zeug n shaving outfit
Raspel ['raspəl] f (-;-n) rasp; (culin) grater
raspeln ['raspəln] tr rasp; grate
Rasse ['rasə] f (-;-n) race; (Zucht) breed, blood, stock; (fig) good breeding
Rassel ['rasəl] f (-;-n) rattle
rasseln ['rasəln] intr rattle; **durchs Examen r.** (coll) flunk the exam
Rassen- [rasən] comb.fm. racial
Ras'senfrage f racial problem
Ras'senhaß m racism, race hatred
Ras'senkreuzung f miscegenation; crossbreeding
Ras'senkunde f ethnology
ras'senmäßig adj racial
Ras'senmerkmal n racial characteristic
Ras'sentrennung f segregation
Ras'senunruhen pl racial disorders
Ras'sepferd n thoroughbred (horse)
ras'serein adj racially pure; thoroughbred
Ras'sevieh n purebred cattle

rassig ['rasɪç] adj racy; thoroughbred
rassisch ['rasɪʃ] adj racial
Rast [rast] f (-;-en) rest; station, stage; (mach) notch, groove; (mil) halt; **e-e R. machen** take a rest
rasten ['rastən] intr rest; (mil) halt
rast'los adj restless
Rast'losigkeit f (-;) restlessness
Rast'platz m, **Rast'stätte** f resting place
Rast'tag m day of rest
Rasur [ra'zur] f (-;-en) shave
Rat [rat] m (-[e]s; Ratschläge ['rat-ʃlegə] advice, piece of advice, counsel; (Beratung) deliberation; (Ausweg) means, solution; **auf e-n Rat hören** listen to reason; **sich** [dat] **keinen Rat mehr wissen** be at one's wits' end; **zu Rate ziehen** consult (a person, dictionary, etc.) || m -[e]s; =e) council, board; (Person) councilor, alderman; advisor; (jur) counsel
Rate ['ratə] f (-;-n) installment; **auf Raten** on the installment plan
raten ['ratən] §63 tr guess; (Rätsel) solve; **das will ich dir nicht geraten haben!** you had better not!; **geraten!** you guessed it!; **j-m etw r.** advise s.o. about s.th.; **komm nicht wieder. das rate ich dir!** take my advice and don't come back! || intr guess; give advice; (dat) advise; **gut r.** take a good guess; **hin und her r.** make random guesses; **j-m gut r.** give s.o. good advice; **j-m zu etw r.** recommend s.th. to s.o. || **Raten** n (-s;) guesswork; advice
ra'tenweise adv by installments
Ra'tenzahlung f payment in installments; **auf R.** on the installment plan
Räterepublik ['retərepublik] f Soviet Union, Soviet State
Rat'geber –in §6 mf adviser, counselor
Rat'haus n city hall
ratifizieren [ratɪfɪ'tsirən] tr ratify
Ratifizie'rung f (-;-en) ratification
Ration [ra'tsjon] f (-;-en) ration
rational [ratsjo'nal] adj rational
rationalisieren [ratsjonalɪ'zirən] tr streamline (operations in industry)
rationell [ratsjo'nel] adj rational
rationieren [ratsjo'nirən] tr ration
rätlich ['retlɪç] adj advisable
rat'los adj helpless, perplexed
ratsam ['ratzam] adj advisable
Ratsche ['ratʃə] f (-;-n) rattle; (coll) chatterbox; (tech) ratchet
ratschen ['ratʃən] intr make noise with a rattle; (coll) chat
Rat'schlag m advice, piece of advice
rat'schlagen §132 intr deliberate, consult
Rat'schluß m decision, decree, resolution
Rätsel ['retsəl] n (-s;-) puzzle; (fig) riddle, enigma, mystery
rät'selhaft adj puzzling; mysterious
Ratte ['ratə] f (-;-n) rat
Rat'tenschwanz m rat tail; (fig) tangle; (coll) whole string (of questions, etc.); (Haarzopf) (coll) pigtail
rattern ['ratərn] intr rattle
ratzekahl ['ratsə'kal] adj (Person)

completely bald; (*Landschaft*) completely barren || *adv* completely

Raub [raup] *m* (-[e]s;) robbery; plunder; (*Beute*) prey, spoils; **zum Raube fallen** fall prey, fall victim

Raub- *comb.fm.* predatory, rapacious

Raub′bau *m* (-[e]s;) excessive exploitation (*of natural resources*)

rauben ['rauben] *tr*—**j–m etw r.** rob s.o. of s.th.; **e–m Mädchen die Unschuld r.** seduce a girl; **e–n Kuß r.** steal a kiss || *intr* rob

Räuber ['rɔɪbər] *m* (-s;) robber; **R. und Gendarm spielen** play cops and robbers

Räu′berbande *f* gang of robbers

Räu′berhauptmann *m* gang leader

räuberisch ['rɔɪbərɪʃ] *adj* predatory

Raub′fisch *m* predatory fish

Raub′gesindel *n* gang of robbers

Raub′lust *f* rapacity

raub′gierig *adj* rapacious

Raub′lust *f* rapacity

Raub′mord *m* murder with robbery

Raub′mörder *m* robber and murderer

Raub′schiff *n* corsair, pirate ship

Raub′tier *n* beast of prey

Raub′überfall *m* holdup, robbery

Raub′vogel *m* bird of prey

Raub′zug *m* plundering raid

Rauch [raux] *m* (-[e]s;) smoke

rauchen ['rauxən] *tr & intr* smoke

Raucher ['rauxər] *m* (-s;) smoker

Räucher- [rɔɪxər] *comb.fm.* smoked

Rau′cherabteil *n* smoking section

Räu′cherfaß *n* (eccl) censer

Räu′cherhering *m* smoked herring

Rau′cherhusten *m* cigarette cough

Räu′cherkammer *f* smokehouse

räuchern ['rɔɪxərn] *tr* smoke, cure; (*desinzieren*) fumigate

Räu′cherschinken *m* smoked ham

Räu′cherung *f* (-;) smoking; fumigation

Rau′cherwagen *m* (rr) smoker

Rauch′fahne *f* trail of smoke

Rauch′fang *m* (*über dem Herd*) hood; (*im Schornstein*) flue

Rauch′fleisch *n* smoked meat

rauchig ['rauxɪç] *adj* smoky

rauch′los *adj* smokeless

Rauch′schleier *m* (mil) smoke screen

Rauch′waren *pl* (*Pelze*) furs; (*Tabakwaren*) tobacco supplies

Räude ['rɔɪdə] *f* (-;) mange

räudig ['rɔɪdɪç] *adj* mangy; **räudiges Schaf** (fig) black sheep

Raufbold ['raufbɔlt] *m* (-[e]s;-e) roughneck, bully

Raufe ['raufə] *f* (-;-n) hayrack

raufen ['raufən] *tr* tear, pull out || *recip & intr* fight, brawl, scuffle

Rauferei [raufə′raɪ] *f* (-;-en) fight, scuffle

Rauf′handel *m* fight, scuffle

rauf′lustig *adj* scrappy, belligerent

rauh [rau] *adj* rough; (*Hals*) hoarse; (*Behandlung*) harsh; **rauhe Wirklichkeit** hard facts

Rauh′bein *n* (fig) roughneck, churl

rauh′beinig *adj* tough, churlish

Rauh′heit *f* (-;) roughness; hoarseness

rauhen ['rau·ən] *tr* roughen

Rauh′futter *n* roughage

rauh′haarig *adj* shaggy, hirsute

Rauh′reif *m* hoarfrost

Raum [raum] *m* (-[e]s;ˑe) room, space; (*Zimmer*) room; (*Bereich*) area; (*e–s Schiffes*) hold; **am Rande R. lassen** (typ) leave a margin; **freier R.** open space; **gebt R.!** make way! **luftleerer R.** vacuum; **R. bieten für accommodate; R. einnehmen** take up space; **R. geben** (*dat*) give way to; comply with

Raum′anzug *m* space suit

Räumboot ['rɔɪmbot] *n* minesweeper

Raum′dichte *f* (phys) density by volume

räumen ['rɔɪmən] *tr* clear; (*Wohnung*) vacate; (*Minen*) clear; (mil) evacuate; **den Saal r.** clear the room; **das Lager r.** (com) clear out the stock; **j–n aus dem Wege r.** (fig) finish s.o. off

Raum′ersparnis *f* economy of space; **der R. wegen** to save space

Raum′fahrer *m* spaceman

Raum′fahrt *f* space travel

Raum′flug *m* space flight

Raum′gestaltung *f* interior decorating

Raum′inhalt *m* volume, capacity

Raum′kunst *f* interior decorating

Raum′lehre *f* geometry

räumlich ['rɔɪmlɪç] *adj* spatial

Räum′lichkeit *f* (-;-en) room

Raum′mangel *m* lack of space

Raum′medizin *f* space medicine

Raum′meter *n* cubic meter

Raum′schiff *n* space ship

Raum′schiffart *f* space travel

Raum′schiffkapsel *f* space capsule

Raum′sonde *f* unmanned space explorer

Raum′ton *m* stereophonic sound

Räu′mung *f* (-;-en) clearing, removal; (com) clearance; (mil) evacuation

Räu′mungsausverkauf *m* clearance sale

Räu′mungsbefehl *m* eviction notice; (mil) evacuation order

raunen ['raunən] *tr & intr* whisper

raunzen ['rauntsən] *intr* grumble

Raupe ['raupə] *f* (-;-n) (ent, mach) caterpillar

Rau′penfahrzeug *n* full-track vehicle

Rau′penkette *f* caterpillar track

Rau′penschlepper *m* caterpillar tractor

Rausch [rau] *m* (-es;ˑe) drunkenness; (fig) intoxication, ecstasy; **e–n R. haben** be drunk; **sich** [*dat*] **e–n R. antrinken** get drunk

rauschen ['rau·ʃən] *intr* (*Blätter, Seide*) rustle; (*Bach*) murmur; (*Brandung, Sturm*) roar || *intr* (SEIN) strut; rush

rau′schend *adj* rustling; (*Fest*) uproarious; (*Beifall*) thunderous

Rausch′gift *n* drug, dope

Rausch′gifthandel *m* drug traffic

Rausch′giftschieber *m* in §6 *mf* pusher

Rausch′giftsucht *f* drug addiction

Rausch′giftsüchtige §5 *mf* dope addict

Rausch′gold *n* tinsel

räuspern ['rɔɪspərn] *ref* clear one's throat

Rausschmeißer ['raus/maɪsər] *m* (-s;-) (coll) bouncer

Raute ['rautə] *f* (-;-n) (cards) diamond; (geom) rhombus

Rayon [rɛ'jõ] *m* (-s;-s) (*Bezirk*) district, region; (*im Warenhaus*) department

Raz·zia ['ratsja] *f* (-;-zien [tsjən]) police raid

Reagenzglas [rea'gɛntsglas] *n* test tube

reagieren [rea'girən] *intr* (auf *acc*) react (to)

Reaktion [re·ak'tsjon] *f* (-;-en) reaction

reaktionär [re·aktsjo'nɛr] *adj* reactionary || **Reaktionär** *m* (-s;-e) reactionary

Reak·tor [re'aktor] *m* (-s;-toren ['torən]) (phys) reactor

real [re'al] *adj* real

Real'gymnasium *n* high school (*where modern languages, mathematics, or sciences are stressed*)

Realien [re'aljən] *pl* real facts, realities; exact sciences

realisieren [re·alɪ'zirən] *tr* realize

Realist –in [re·a'lɪst(ɪn)] §7 *mf* realist

realistisch [re·a'lɪstɪ/] *adj* realistic

Realität [re·alɪ'tɛt] *f* (-;-en) reality; Realitäten real property

Real'lexikon *n* encyclopedia

Real'lohn *m* purchasing power of wages

Real'schule *f* non-classical secondary school

Rebe ['rebə] *f* (-;-n) vine; tendril

Rebell [re'bɛl] *m* (-en;-en) rebel

rebellieren [rebe'lirən] *intr* rebel

Rebellin [re'bɛlɪn] *f* (-;-nen) rebel

Rebellion [rebɛl'jon] *f* (-;-en) rebellion

rebellisch [re'bɛlɪ/] *adj* rebellious

Re'bensaft *m* (poet) juice of the grape

Rebhuhn ['rephun] *n* partridge

Rebstock ['rep/tɔk] *m* vine

rechen ['reçən] *tr* rake || **Rechen** *m* (-s;-) rake; grate

Re'chenaufgabe *f* arithmetic problem

Re'chenautomat *m* computer

Re'chenbrett *n* abacus

Re'chenbuch *n* arithmetic book

Re'chenexemplar *n* arithmetic problem

Re'chenkunst *f* arithmetic

Re'chenmaschine *f* calculator

Re'chenpfennig *m* counter

Re'chenschaft *f* (-;) account; **j–n zur R. ziehen** call s.o. to account

Re'chenschaftsbericht *m* report

Re'chenschieber *m* slide rule

rechnen ['reçnən] *tr* reckon, calculate, figure out || *intr* reckon, calculate; **falsch r.** miscalculate; **r. auf** (*acc*) count on; **r. mit** be prepared for; expect; take into account; **r. zu** be counted among || **Rechnen** *n* (-s;) arithmetic; calculation

Rech'ner –in [–ər] *m* (-s;-) calculator, computer; **er ist ein guter R.** he is good at numbers

rechnerisch ['reçnərɪ/] *adj* arithmetical

Rech'nung *f* (-;-en) calculation; account; bill; (*Warenrechnung*) invoice; (*im Restaurant*) check; **auf j–s R.**

account; **auf R. kaufen** buy on credit; **auf seine R. kaufen** get one's money's worth; **außer R. lassen** overlook; **das geht auf meine R.** this is on me; **die R. begleichen** settle an account (or bill); **j–m in R. stellen** charge to s.o.'s account; **in R. ziehen** take into account; **R. tragen** (*dat*) make allowance for

Rech'nungsabschluß *m* closing of accounts

Rech'nungsauszug *m* (com) statement

Rech'nungsführer –in §6 *mf* accountant

Rech'nungsführung *f* accounting

Rech'nungsjahr *n* fiscal year

Rech'nungsprüfer –in §6 *mf* auditor

Rech'nungswesen *n* accounting

recht [reçt] *adj* right; (*richtig*) correct; (*echt*) real; (*gerecht*) all right, right; (*geziemend*) suitable, proper; **es ist mir nicht r.** I don't like it; **es ist schon r.** that's all right; **mir soll's r. sein** I don't mind; **zur rechten Zeit** at the right moment || *adv* right; quite; (*sehr*) very; **das kommt mir gerade r.** that comes in handy; **erst r.** all the more; **es j–m r. machen** please s.o.; **es geschieht ihm r.** it serves him right; **j–m r. geben** agree with s.o.; **nun erst r.** now less than ever; **r. daran tun zu** (*inf*) do right to (*inf*); **r. haben** be right || **Recht** *n* (-[e]s;-e) right; (*Vorrecht*) privilege; (jur) law; **alle Rechte vorbehalten** all rights reserved; **die Rechte studieren** study law; **mit R.** with good reason; **R. sprechen** dispense justice; **sich** [*dat*] **selbst R. verschaffen** take the law into one's hands; **von Rechts wegen** by rights; **wieder zu seinem Rechte kommen** come into one's own again; **zu R. bestehen** be justified || **Rechte** §5 *mf* right person; **an den Rechten kommen** meet one's match; **du bist mir der R.!** you're a fine fellow! || *f* right hand; (box) right; **die R.** (pol) the right || *n* right; **er dünkt sich** [*dat*] **was Rechtes** he thinks he's somebody; **nach dem Rechten sehen** look after things

Recht'eck *n* rectangle, oblong

recht'eckig *adj* rectangular

recht'fertigen *tr* justify, vindicate

Recht'fertigung *f* (-;-en) justification

recht'gläubig *adj* orthodox

rechthaberisch ['reçthabərɪ/] *adj* dogmatic

recht'lich *adj* legal, lawful; (*ehrlich*) honest, honorable

Recht'lichkeit *f* (-;) legality; (*Redlichkeit*) honesty

recht'los *adj* without rights

recht'mäßig *adj* legal; legitimate

Recht'mäßigkeit *f* (-;) legality; legitimacy

rechts [reçts] *adv* on the right; right, to the right

Rechts– *comb.fm.* legal

Rechts'angelegenheit *f* legal matter

Rechts'anspruch *m* legal claim

Rechts'anwalt *m* lawyer, attorney

Rechts'ausdruck *m* legal term
Rechts'auskunft *f* legal advice
Rechts'außen *m* (-;-) (fb) right wing
recht'schaffen *adj* honest
Recht'schaffenheit *f* (-;) honesty
Recht'schreibung *f* orthography
Rechts'fall *m* case, legal case
Rechts'gang *m* legal procedure
Rechts'gefühl sense of justice
Rechts'gelehrsamkeit *f* jurisprudence
Rechts'grund *m* legal grounds; (*An-
spruch*) title, claim
rechts'gültig *adj* legal, valid
Rechts'gültigkeit *f* legality
Rechts'gutachten *n* legal opinion
Rechts'handel *m* lawsuit
rechtshändig ['reçtshendɪç] *adj* right-
handed
rechts'herum *adv* clockwise
Rechts'kraft *f* legal force
rechts'kräftig *adj* valid
Rechts'lage *f* legal status
Rechts'lehre *f* jurisprudence
Rechts'mittel *n* legal remedy
Rechts'pflege *f* administration of jus-
tice
Recht'sprechung *f* (-;) administration
of justice; die R. (coll) the judiciary
Rechts'schutz *m* legal protection
Rechts'spruch *m* verdict
Rechts'streit *m* legal dispute; pending
case; difference of opinion in the
interpretation of the law
rechtsum' *interj* (mil) right face!
rechts'ungültig *adj* illegal, invalid
rechts'verbindlich *adj* legally binding
Rechtsverdreher -in ['reçtsferdre-
ər(ɪn)] §6 *mf* pettifogger
Rechts'verletzung *f* (-;-en) violation of
the law; infringement of another's
rights
Rechts'weg *m* recourse to the law; auf
dem Rechtswege by the courts; den
R. beschreiten take legal action
Rechts'wissenschaft *f* jurisprudence
Reck [rek] *n* (-[e]s;-e) horizontal bar
recken ['rekən] *tr* stretch; den Hals r.
crane one's neck
Redakteur [redak'tør] *m* (-s;-e) editor
Redaktion [redak'tsjon] *f* (-;-en) edi-
torship; (*Arbeitskräfte*) editorial
staff; (*Arbeitsraum*) editorial office
redaktionell [redaktsjo'nel] *adj* editorial
Redaktions'schluß *m* press time, deadline
Rede ['redə] *f* (-;-n) speech; (*Gespräch*) conversation; (*Gerücht*) rumor; das ist nicht der R. wert that
is not worth mentioning; davon kann
keine R. sein that's out of the question; die in R. stehende Person the
person in question; e-e R. halten
give a speech; es geht die R., daß
it is rumored that; gebundene R.
verse; gehobene R. lofty language;
j-m in die R. fallen interrupt s.o.;
j-m R. und Antwort stehen explain
oneself to s.o.; j-n zur R. stellen take
s.o. to task; keine R.! absolutely
not!; lose Reden führen engage in
loose talk; ungebundene R. prose

Re'defigur *f* figure of speech
Re'defluß *m* flow of words
Re'defreiheit *f* freedom of speech
Re'degabe *f* eloquence, fluency
re'degewandt *adj* fluent; (iron) glib
Re'degewandtheit *f* fluency, eloquence
Re'dekunst *f* eloquence
reden ['redən] *tr* speak, talk || *ref*—
mit sich r. lassen listen to reason;
sich heiser r. talk oneself hoarse;
von sich r. machen cause a lot of
talk || *intr* speak, talk; converse; du
hast gut r.! it's easy for you to talk;
j-m ins Gewissen r. appeal to s.o.'s
conscience; j-m nach dem Munde r.
humor s.o.; mit j-m deutsch r. (fig)
talk turkey to s.o.
Re'densart *f* phrase, expression; idiom
Rederei [redə'raɪ] *f* (-;-en) empty talk
Re'deschwall *m* verbosity
Re'deteil *m* part of speech
Re'deweise *f* style of speaking
Re'dewendung *f* phrase, expression
redigieren [redɪ'girən] *tr* edit
redlich ['retlɪç] *adj* upright, honest ||
adv—es r. meinen mean well; sich r.
bemühen make an honest effort
Red'lichkeit *f* (-;) honesty, integrity
Redner -in ['rednər(ɪn)] §6 *mf* speaker
Red'nerbühne *f* podium, platform
Red'nergabe *f* (gift of) eloquence
rednerisch ['rednərɪʃ] *adj* rhetorical
Redoute [re'dutə] *f* (-;-n) masquerade;
(mil) redoubt
redselig ['retzelɪç] *adj* talkative
Reduktion [reduk'tsjon] *f* (-;-en) reduction
reduplizieren [reduplɪ'tsirən] *tr* redu-
plicate
reduzieren [redu'tsirən] *tr* (auf *acc*)
reduce (to)
Reede ['redə] *f* (-;-n) (naut) road-
stead
Reeder ['redər] *m* (-s;-) shipowner
Reederei [redə'raɪ] *f* (-;-en) shipping
company; shipping business
reell [re'el] *adj* honest; (*Preis*) fair;
(*Geschäft*) sound || *adv*—r. bedient
werden get one's money's worth
Reep [rep] *n* (-[e]s;-e) (naut) rope
Referat [refə'rat] *n* (-[e]s;-e) report;
(*Vortrag*) paper; ein R. halten give
a paper
Referendar [referen'dar] *m* (-s;-e)
junior lawyer; in-service teacher
Referent -in [refe'rent(ɪn)] §7 *mf*
reader of a paper; (*Berichterstatter*)
reporter; (*Gutachter*) official adviser
Referenz [refe'rents] *f* (-;-en) reference; j-n als R. angeben give s.o.
as a reference; über gute Referenzen
verfügen have good references
referieren [refe'rirən] *intr* (über *acc*)
give a report (on); (über *acc*) read
a paper (on)
reffen ['refən] *tr* (naut) reef
reflektieren [reflek'tirən] *tr* reflect ||
intr reflect; r. auf (*acc*) reflect on;
(com) think of buying
Reflek•tor [re'flektor] *m* (-s;-toren
[•'torən] reflector
Reflex [re'fleks] *m* (-es;-e) reflex
Reflex'bewegung *f* reflex action

Reflexion [refle'ksjon] *f* (-;-en) reflection

reflexiv [refle'ksif] *adj* reflexive

Reform [re'form] *f* (-;-en) reform

Reformation [reforma'tsjon] *f* (-;-en) reformation

Refor·mator [refor'mator] *m* (-s; [ma'toren]) reformer

Reform'haus *n* health-food store

reformieren [refor'miren] *tr* reform

Reform'kost *f* health food

Refrain [re'frɛ̃] *m* (-s;-s) refrain; **den R. mitsingen** join in the refrain

Regal [re'gal] *n* (-s;-e) shelf

Regat·ta [re'gata] *f* (-;-ten [tən]) regatta

rege ['regə] *adj* brisk, lively

Regel ['regəl] *f* (-;-n) rule, regulation; (pathol) menstruation; **in der R. as a rule**

re'gellos *adj* irregular; disorderly

Re'gellosigkeit *f* (-;-en) irregularity

re'gelmäßig *adj* regular

Re'gelmäßigkeit *f* regularity

regeln ['regəln] *tr* regulate; arrange; control

re'gelrecht *adj* regular; downright

Re'gelung *f* (-;-en) regulation; control

re'gelwidrig *adj* against the rules; (sport) foul

regen ['regən] *tr & ref* move, stir ‖ **Regen** *m* (-s;-) rain; **vom R. unter die Traufe kommen** jump out of the frying pan into the fire

re'genarm *adj* rainless, dry

Re'genbö *f* rain squall

Re'genbogen *m* rainbow

Re'genbogenhaut *f* (anat) iris

re'gendicht *adj* rainproof

Re'genfall *m* rainfall

re'genfest *adj* rainproof

Re'genguß *m* downpour

Re'genhaut *f* oilskin coat

Re'genmantel *m* raincoat

Re'genmenge *f* amount of rainfall

Re'genmesser *m* rain gauge

Re'genpfeifer *m* (orn) plover

Re'genschauer *m* shower

Re'genschirm *m* umbrella

Regent **–in** [re'gent(ɪn)] §7 *mf* regent

Re'gentag *m* rainy day

Re'gentropfen *m* raindrop

Re'genumhang *m* cape

Re'genwetter *n* rainy weather

Re'genwurm *m* earthworm

Re'genzeit *f* rainy season

Re·gie [re'ʒi] *f* (-;-gien ['ʒi·ən]) management, administration; (com) state monopoly; (cin, theat) direction

Regie'assistent **–in** §7 *mf* (cin, theat) assistant director

Regie'pult *n* (rad) control console

Regie'raum *m* (rad) control room

regieren [re'giren] *tr* govern, rule; (gram) govern, take ‖ *intr* reign; (fig) predominate

Regie'rung *f* (-;-en) government, rule; administration; reign

Regie'rungsanleihe *f* government loan

Regie'rungsantritt *m* accession

Regie'rungsbeamte §5 *m* government official

Regie'rungssitz *m* seat of government

Regie'rungszeit *f* reign; administration

Regime [re'ʒim] *n* (-s;-s) regime

Regiment [regɪ'ment] *n* (-[e]s;-e) rule, government ‖ *n* (-[e]s;-er) (mil) regiment

Regiments- *comb.fm.* regimental

Regiments'kommandeur *m* regimental commander

Region [re'gjon] *f* (-;-en) region

regional [regjo'nal] *adj* regional

Regisseur [reʒɪ'sør] *m* (-s;-e) (cin, theat) director

Register [re'gɪstər] *n* (-s;-) file clerk; (Inhaltsverzeichnis) index; (Orgel-) stop

Regi·strator [regɪs'trator] *m* (-s; -stratoren [stra'toren]) registrar

Registratur [regɪstra'tur] *f* (-;-en) registry; filing cabinet

registrieren [regɪs'triren] *tr* register; (Betrag) ring up

Registrier'kasse *f* cash register

Registrie'rung *f* (-;-en) registration

Reglement [reglə'mã] *n* (-s;-s) regulation(s), rule(s)

Regler ['reglər] *m* (-s;-) regulator; (mach) governor

reglos ['reklos] *adj* motionless

regnen ['regnən] *impers* —**es regnet** it is raining; **es regnet Bindfäden** it's raining cats and dogs; **es regnete Püffe** blows came thick and fast

regnerisch ['regnərɪʃ] *adj* rainy

Re·greß [re'gres] *m* (-gresses;-gresse) recourse, remedy; **R. nehmen zu** have recourse to

regsam ['rekzam] *adj* lively; quick

regulär [regu'ler] *adj* regular

regulierbar [regu'lirbar] *adj* adjustable

regulieren [regu'liren] *tr* regulate; adjust

Regung ['regun] *f* (-;-en) motion, stirring; emotion; impulse

Reh [re] *n* (-[e]s;-e) deer

rehabilitieren [rehabilɪ'tiren] *tr* rehabilitate

Rehabilitie'rung *f* (-;-en) rehabilitation

Reh'bock *m* roebuck

Reh'braten *m* roast venison

Reh'kalb *n* fawn

Reh'keule *f* leg of venison

Rehkitz ['rekɪts] *n* (-es;-e) fawn

Reh'leder *n* doeskin

Reibahle ['raɪpalə] *f* (-;-n) reamer

Reibe ['raɪbə] *f* (-;-n) (coll) grater

Reibeisen ['raɪpaɪzən] *n* (culin) grater

reiben ['raɪbən] §62 *tr* rub; grate; grind ‖ *ref* —**sich r. an** (dat) take offense at ‖ *intr* rub

Reiberei [raɪbə'raɪ] *f* (-;-en) (coll) friction, squabble

Rei'bung *f* (-;-en) friction

rei'bungslos *adj* frictionless; (fig) smooth

reich [raɪç] *adj* wealthy; (an *dat*) rich (in); (Fang) big; (Phantasie) fertile; (Mahlzeit) lavish ‖ **Reich** *n* (-[e]s; -e) empire, realm; kingdom

reichen ['raɪçən] *tr* reach; hand, pass ‖ *intr* reach, extend; do, manage; **das reicht!** that will do!

reich'haltig *adj* rich; abundant

reich′lich adj plentiful, abundant || adv pretty, fairly

Reichs′kanzlei f chancellery

Reichs′kanzler m chancellor

Reichs′mark f reichsmark

Reichs′tag m (hist) diet; (hist) Reichstag (lower house)

Reichtum [′raɪçtum] n (–s;-̈er) riches

Reich′weite f reach, range

reif [raɪf] adj ripe; (fig) mature || **Reif** m (–[e]s;-) frost

Reife [′raɪfə] f (–;) ripeness; (fig) maturity

reifen [′raɪfən] intr (SEIN) ripen; mature || impers—es reift there is frost || Reifen m (–s;-) tire; hoop

Rei′fendruckmesser m tire gauge

Rei′fenpanne f, **Rei′fenschaden** m flat tire, blowout

Rei′feprüfung f final examination (as prerequisite for entering university)

Rei′fezeugnis n high school diploma

reif′lich adj careful

Reigen [′raɪgən] m (–s;-) square dance

Reihe [′raɪə] f (–;-n) row, string; set, series; rank, file; turn; **an der R. sein** be next; **an die R. kommen** get one's turn; **aus der R. tanzen** (fig) go one's own way; **die R. ist an mir** it's my turn; **nach der R.** in succession

reihen [′raɪən] tr range, rank; (Perlen) string

Rei′hendorf n one-street village

Rei′henfabrikation f assembly-line production

Rei′henfolge f succession, sequence

Rei′henhaus n row house

Rei′henschaltung f (elec) series connection

reih′enweise adv in rows

Reiher [′raɪ-ər] m (–s;-) heron

Reim [raɪm] m (–[e]s;-e) rhyme

reimen [′raɪmən] tr (auf acc) make rhyme (with) || ref rhyme; (fig) make sense; (auf acc) go (with) || intr rhyme

reim′los adj unrhymed, blank

rein [raɪn] adj pure; (sauber) clean; (klar) clear; (Gewinn) net; (Wahrheit) simple; (Wahnsinn) sheer, absolute; **etw ins reine bringen** clear up s.th.; **etw ins reine schreiben** write (or type) a final copy of s.th.; **mit j–m ins reine kommen** come to an understanding with s.o. || adv quite, downright; **r. alles** almost everything || Rein f (–;-en) pan

Reindl [′raɪndəl] n (–s;- & –n) pan

Rei′nemachen n (–s;) housecleaning

Rein′ertrag m clear profit

Rein′fall m flop, disappointment

Rein′gewicht n net weight

Rein′gewinn m net profit

Rein′heit f (–;) purity; cleanness

reinigen [′raɪnɪgən] tr clean, cleanse; (fig) purify, refine

Rei′nigung f (–;-en) cleaning; purification; dry cleaning

Rei′nigungsanstalt f dry cleaner's

Rei′nigungsmittel n cleaning agent

Reinmachefrau [′raɪnmaxəfrau] f cleaning woman

Rein′schrift f final copy

reinweg [′raɪn′vɛk] adv (coll) flatly, absolutely

rein′wollen adj all-wool

Reis [raɪs] m (–es;) rice || n (–es;-er) twig; (fig) scion

Reis′brei m rice pudding

Reise [′raɪzə] f (–;-n) trip, tour; (aer) flight; (naut) voyage; **auf der R. while traveling; auf Reisen sein** be traveling

Rei′sebericht m travelogue

Rei′sebeschreibung f travel book

Rei′sebüro n travel agency

rei′sefertig adj ready to leave

Rei′seführer m guidebook

Rei′segefährte m, **Rei′segefährtin** f travel companion

Rei′segenehmigung f travel permit

Rei′segepäck n luggage; (rr) baggage

Rei′segesellschaft f tour operator(s); travel group

Rei′sehandbuch n guidebook

Rei′seleiter –in §6 mf courier, guide

rei′selustig adj fond of traveling

reisen [′raɪzən] intr (SEIN) travel

Reisende [′raɪzəndə] §5 mf traveler

Rei′sepaß m passport

Rei′seplan m itinerary

Rei′seprospekt m travel folder

Rei′seroute f itinerary

Rei′sescheck m traveler's check

Rei′seschreibmaschine f portable typewriter

Rei′sespesen pl travel expenses

Rei′setasche f overnight bag, flight bag

Rei′seziel n destination

Reisig [′raɪzɪç] n (–s;) brushwood

Rei′sigbündel n faggot

Reisige [′raɪzɪgə] §5 m cavalryman

Reißaus [raɪs′aus] n—**R. nehmen** (coll) take to one's heels

Reißbrett [′raɪsbret] n drawing board

reißen [′raɪsən] §53 tr tear, rip; (ziehen) pull, yank; (wegschnappen) wrest, snatch || intr tear; pull, tug; break, snap; (sich spalten) split, burst; **das reißt ins Geld** this is running into money; **mir reißt die Geduld** I am losing all patience || ref—**an sich r.** seize; (com) monopolize; **die Führung an sich r.** take the lead; **sich an e–m Nagel r.** scratch oneself on a nail; **sich um etw r.** scramble for s.th. || Reißen n (–s;) tearing; bursting; sharp pains; rheumatism

rei′ßend adj rapid; (Schmerz) sharp; (Tier) rapacious; **reißenden Absatz finden** (coll) sell like hotcakes

Reißer [′raɪsər] m (–s;-) bestseller; (cin) box-office hit; (com) good seller

Reißfeder [′raɪsfedər] f drawing pen

Reißleine [′raɪslaɪnə] f rip cord

Reißnagel [′raɪsnagəl] m thumbtack

Reißschiene [′raɪsʃinə] f T-square

Reißverschluß [′raɪsfɛrʃlus] m zipper

Reißzahn [′raɪstsan] m canine tooth

Reißzeug [′raɪstsɔɪk] n mechanical-drawing tools

Reißzwecke [′raɪstsvɛkə] f thumbtack

Reit- [raɪt] comb.fm. riding

Reit′anzug m riding habit

Reit'bahn f riding ring

reiten ['raɪtən] §86 tr ride; **e-n Weg r.** ride along a road; **ihn reitet der Teufel** (coll) he is full of the devil; **krumme Touren r.** (coll) pull shady deals; **Prinzipien r.** (fig) stick rigidly to principles; **über den Haufen r.** knock down ‖ intr (SEIN) go horseback riding; **geritten kommen** come on horseback; **vor Anker r.** ride at anchor

Rei'ter –in §6 mf rider

Rei'terstandbild n equestrian statue

Reit'gerte f riding crop

Reit'hose f riding breeches

Reit'knecht m groom

Reit'kunst f horsemanship

Reit'peitsche f riding crop

Reit'pferd n saddle horse

Reit'schule f riding academy

Reit'stiefel m riding boot

Reit'weg m bridle path

Reiz [raɪts] m (–es;–e) charm, appeal; (Erregung) irritation; (physiol, psychol) stimulus; **e-n R. ausüben auf** (acc) attract; **sie läßt ihre Reize spielen** she turns on the charm

reizbar ['raɪtsbar] adj irritable; (empfindlich) sensitive, touchy

reizen ['raɪtsən] tr (entzünden, ärgern) irritate; (locken) allure; (anziehen) attract; (anregen) excite, stimulate; (aufreizen) provoke; (Appetit) whet ‖ intr (cards) bid ‖ impers—**es reizt mich zu** (inf) I'm itching to (inf)

rei'zend adj charming, cute, sweet; (pathol) irritating

Reiz'entzug m sensory deprivation

Reiz'husten m (–s) constant cough

reiz'los adj unattractive; (Kost) bland

Reiz'mittel n stimulant; (fig) incentive

Reiz'stoff m irritant

Rei'zung f (–;–en) irritation; (Lokkung) allurement; (Anregung) stimulation; (Aufreizung) provocation

reiz'voll adj charming, attractive, fascinating; (verlockend) tempting

rekeln ['rekəln] ref (coll) lounge

Reklamation [reklama'tsjon] f (–;–en) complaint, protest

Reklame [re'klamə] f (–;–n) advertisement, ad; publicity; **R. machen für** advertise

Rekla'mebüro n advertising agency

Rekla'mefeldzug m advertising campaign

reklamieren [rekla'mirən] tr claim ‖ intr (gegen) protest (against); (wegen) complain (about)

rekognoszieren [rekɔs'tsirən] tr & intr reconnoiter

Rekonvaleszent –in [rekɔnvales'tsent (ɪn)] §7 mf convalescent

Rekonvaleszenz [rekɔnvales'tsents] f (–;) convalescence

Rekord [re'kɔrt] m (–[e]s;–e) record

Rekord'ernte f bumper crop, record crop

Rekordler –in [re'kɔrtlər(ɪn)] §6 mf (coll) record holder

Rekord'versuch m attempt to break the record

Rekrut [re'krut] m (–en;–en) recruit

Rekru'tenausbildung f basic training

Rekru'tenaushebung f recruitment

rekrutieren [rekru'tirən] tr recruit ‖ ref—**sich r. aus** be recruited from

Rek·tor ['rektor] m (–s;–toren ['torən]) principal; (e-r Universität) president

Relais [rə'le] n (–lais ['le(s)];–lais ['les]) relay

relativ [rela'tif] adj relative

Relegation [relega'tsjon] f (–;–en) expulsion

relegieren [rele'girən] tr expel

Relief [re'ljef] n (–s;–s & –e) relief

Religion [reli'gjon] f (–;–en) religion

Religions'ausübung f practice of religion

Religions'bekenntnis n religious denomination

religiös [reli'gjøs] adj religious

Reling ['relɪŋ] f (–s;–s) (naut) rail

Reliquie [re'likvjə] f (–;–n) relic

Reli'quienschrein m reliquary

remis [rə'mi] adj (cards) tied ‖ **Remis** n (–;–) (chess) tie, draw

remittieren [remɪ'tirən] tr (Geld) remit; (Waren) return ‖ intr (Fieber) go down

rempeln ['rempəln] tr bump, jostle ‖ intr (fb) block

Remter ['remtər] m (–s;–) refectory; assembly hall

Ren [ren] (–s;–e) reindeer

Renaissance [renɛ'sãs] f (–;–n) renaissance

Rendite [ren'ditə] f (–;–n) return

Renn– [ren] comb.fm. race, racing

Renn'bahn f race track; (aut) speedway

Renn'boot n racing boat

rennen ['renən] §97 tr run; **j–m den Degen durch den Leib r.** run s.o. through with a sword; **über den Haufen r.** run over; **zu Boden r.** knock down ‖ intr (SEIN) run; race ‖ **Rennen** n (–s;–) running; race; (Einzelrennen) heat; **das R. machen** win the race; **totes R.** dead heat, tie

Ren'ner m (–s;–) (good) race horse

Renn'fahrer m (aut) race driver

Renn'pferd n race horse

Renn'platz m race track; (aut) speedway

Renn'rad n racing bicycle, racer

Renn'sport m racing

Renn'strecke f race track; distance (to be raced); (aut) speedway

Renn'wagen m racing car, racer

Renommee [renɔ'me] n (–s;–s) reputation

renommieren [renɔ'mirən] intr (mit) brag (about), boast (about)

renommiert' adj (wegen) renowned (for)

Renommist [renɔ'mɪst] m (–en;–en) braggart

renovieren [reno'virən] tr renovate; redecorate

rentabel [ren'tabəl] adj profitable

Rentabilität [rentabɪli'tet] f (–;–en) (e-r Investition) return; (fin) productiveness

Rente ['rɛntə] *f* (-;-n) income, revenue; pension; annuity
Ren'tenbrief *m* annuity bond
Ren'tenempfänger -in §6 *mf* pensioner
Rentier [rɛn'tje] *m* (-s;-s) person of independent means ‖ ['rɛntir] *n* (-s; -s) reindeer
rentieren [rɛn'tirən] *ref* pay
Rentner -in ['rɛntnər(ɪn)] §6 *mf* person on pension
Reparatur [repara'tur] *f* (-;-en) repair
Reparatur'werkstatt *f* repair shop; (aut) garage
reparieren [repa'rirən] *tr* repair, fix
Reportage [repɔr'taʒə] *f* (-;-n) report; coverage
Reporter -in [re'pɔrtər(ɪn)] §6 *mf* reporter
Repräsentant -in [reprɛzen'tant(ɪn)] §7 *mf* representative
repräsentieren [reprɛzen'tirən] *tr* represent ‖ *intr* be a socialite
Repressalie [reprɛ'saljə] *f* (-;-n) reprisal
Reprise [re'prizə] *f* (-;-n) (cin) rerun; (mus) repeat; (theat) revival
reproduzieren [reprodu'tsirən] *tr* reproduce
Reptil [rep'til] *n* (-s;-ien [jən] & -e) reptile
Republik [repu'blik] *f* (-;-en) republic
Republikaner -in [republi'kanər(ɪn)] §6 *mf* republican
republikanisch [republi'kanɪʃ] *adj* republican
Requisit [rekvi'zit] *n* (-[e]s;-en) requisite; **Requisiten** (theat) props
Reservat [rezer'vat] *f* (-[e]s;-e) reservation
Reserve [re'zɛrvə] *f* (-;-n) reserve
Reser'vebank *f* (-;-e) (sport) bench
Reser'vereifen *m* spare tire
Reser'veteil *m* spare part
Reser'vetruppen *pl* (mil) reserves
reservieren [rezer'virən] *tr* reserve
Reservie'rung *f* (-;-en) reservation
Residenz [rezi'dɛnts] *f* (-;-en) residence
Residenz'stadt *f* capital
residieren [rezi'dirən] *intr* reside
resignieren [rezɪg'nirən] *intr* resign
Respekt [re'spɛkt] *m* (-[e]s) respect
respektabel [respɛk'tabəl] *adj* respectable
respektieren [respɛk'tirən] *tr* respect
respekt'los *adj* disrespectful
respekt'voll *adj* respectful
Ressort [re'sɔr] *n* (-s;-s) department
Rest [rɛst] *m* (-es;-e & -er) rest; (Stoff-) remnant; (Zahlungs-) balance; (Bodensatz) residue; (math) remainder; **irdische** (or **sterbliche**) **Reste** earthly (or mortal) remains; **j-m den R. geben** (coll) finish s.o. off
Rest'auflage *f* remainders
Restaurant [rɛsto'rã] *n* (-s;-s) restaurant
Restauration [rɛstaura'tsjon] *f* (-;-en) restoration; (Aust) restaurant
Rest'bestand *m* remainder
Rest'betrag *m* balance, remainder
Re'steverkauf *m* remnant sale

rest'lich *adj* remaining
rest'los *adj* complete
Resultat [rezul'tat] *n* (-[e]s;-e) result; upshot; (sport) score
retten ['rɛtən] *tr* save, rescue
Ret'ter *m* (-s;-) rescuer; (*Heiland*) Savior
Rettich ['rɛtɪç] *m* (-s;-e) radish
Ret'tung *f* (-;-en) rescue; salvation
Ret'tungsaktion *f* rescue operation
Ret'tungsboot *n* lifeboat
Ret'tungsfloß *n* life raft
Ret'tungsgürtel *m* life preserver
Ret'tungsleine *f* life line
ret'tungslos *adj* irretrievable
Ret'tungsmannschaft *f* rescue party
Ret'tungsring *m* life preserver
Ret'tungsstation *f* first-aid station
retuschieren [retu'ʃirən] *tr* retouch
Reue ['rɔɪə] *f* (-;) remorse
reu'elos *adj* remorseless, impenitent
reuen ['rɔɪən] *tr*—**die Tat reut mich** I regret having done it; **die Zeit reut mich** I regret wasting the time ‖ *impers*—**es reut mich, daß I regret that,** I am sorry that
reu'evoll *adj* repentant, contrite
Reugeld ['rɔɪgɛlt] *n* forfeit
Revanche [re'vãʃə] *f* (-;) revenge
Revan'chekrieg *m* punitive war
revan'chelustig *adj* vengeful
Revan'chepartie *f* (sport) return game
revanchieren [revã'ʃirən] *ref* (an *dat*) take revenge (on); **sich für e-n Dienst r.** return a favor
Revers [re'vɛrs] *m* (-es;-e) (*e-r Münze*) reverse; (*Erklärung*) statement ‖ [re'ver] *m* (Aust) & *n* (-s;-) lapel; cuff
revidieren [revi'dirən] *tr* revise; (*nachprüfen*) check; (com) audit
Revier [re'vir] *n* (-s;-e) district; quarter; hunting ground; police station; (mil) sick quarters
Revier'stube *f* (mil) sickroom
Revision [revi'zjon] *f* (-;-en) revision; (com) audit; (jur) appeal
Re'visor [re'vizɔr] *m* (-s;-visoren [vi'zorən]) reviser; (com) auditor
Revolte [re'vɔltə] *f* (-;-n) revolt
revoltieren [revɔl'tirən] *intr* revolt
Revolution [revolu'tsjon] *f* (-;-en) revolution
revolutionär [revolutsjo'nɛr] *adj* revolutionary ‖ **Revolutionär -in** §8 *mf* revolutionary
Revolver [re'vɔlvər] *m* (-s;-) revolver
Revol'verblatt *n* (coll) scandal sheet
Revol'verschnauze *f* (coll) lip, sass
Re'vue [re'vy] *f* (-;-vuen [vy·ən]) review; (theat) revue
Rezensent -in [retsen'zɛnt(ɪn)] §7 *mf* reviewer, critic
rezensieren [retsen'zirən] *tr* review
Rezension [retsen'zjon] *f* (-;-en) review
Rezept [re'tsɛpt] *n* (-[e]s;-e) (culin) recipe; (med) prescription
rezitieren [retsi'tirən] *tr* recite
Rhabarber [ra'barbər] *m* (-s;) rhubarb
Rhapso·die [rapso'di] *f* (-;-dien ['di·ən]) rhapsody

Rhein [raɪn] m (-[e]s;) Rhine
Rhesusfaktor ['rezuːsfaktɔr] m (-s;)
Rh factor
Rhetorik [reˈtoːrɪk] f (-;) rhetoric
rhetorisch [reˈtoːrɪʃ] adj rhetorical
rheumatisch [rɔɪˈmaːtɪʃ] adj rheumatic
Rheumatismus [rɔɪmaˈtɪsmus] m (-;)
rheumatism
rhythmisch ['rʏtmɪʃ] adj rhythmical
Rhyth·mus ['rʏtmus] m (-;-men
[mən]) rhythm
Richtbeil ['rɪçtbaɪl] n executioner's ax
Richtblei ['rɪçtblaɪ] n plummet
richten ['rɪçtən] tr arrange, adjust;
put in order; (lenken) direct; (Waffe, Fernrohr) (auf acc) point (at),
aim (at); (Bitte, Brief, Frage, Rede)
(an acc) address (to); (Augenmerk,
Streben) (auf acc) concentrate (on),
focus (on); (Bett) make; (Essen) prepare; (ausbessern) fix; (gerade biegen) straighten; (jur) judge, sentence; (mil) dress; zugrunde r. ruin
|| ref (auf acc, gegen) be directed
(at); das richtet sich ganz danach, ob
it all depends on whether; sich [dat]
die Haare r. do one's hair; sich r.
nach follow the example of; sich
selbst r. commit suicide || intr judge,
sit in judgment
Richter m (-s;-) judge
Richteramt n judgeship
Richterin f (-;-nen) judge
Richterkollegium n (jur) bench
richterlich adj judicial
Richterspruch m judgment; sentence
Richterstand m judiciary
Richterstuhl m tribunal, bench
richtig ['rɪçtɪç] adj right, correct;
(echt) real, genuine; (genau) exact;
(Zeit) proper || adv right, really,
downright; die Uhr geht r. the clock
keeps good time; und r., da kam sie!
and sure enough, there she was!
richtiggehend adj (Uhr) keeping good
time; (fig) regular
Richtigkeit f (-;) correctness; accuracy
richtigstellen tr rectify
Richtlinien ['rɪçtliːnjən] pl guidelines
Richtlot ['rɪçtloːt] n plumbline
Richtmaß ['rɪçtmaːs] n standard, gauge
Richtplatz ['rɪçtplats] m place of execution
Richtpreis ['rɪçtpraɪs] m standard price
Richtschnur ['rɪçtʃnuːr] f plumbline;
(fig) guiding principle
Richtschwert ['rɪçtʃvɛrt] n executioner's sword
Richtstätte ['rɪçtʃtɛtə] f place of execution
Richtung f (-;-en) direction; (Weg)
course; (Entwicklung) trend; (Einstellung) slant, view
Richtungsanzeiger m (aut) direction
signal
Richtwaage ['rɪçtvaːgə] f level
rieb [riːp] pret of reiben
riechen ['riːçən] §102 tr smell; (fig)
stand; kein Pulver r. können have no
guts || intr smell; r. an (dat) sniff at;
r. nach smell of
Riechsalz ['riːçzalts] n smelling salts

rief [riːf] pret of rufen
Riefe ['riːfə] f (-;-n) groove; (archit)
flute
Riege ['riːgə] f (-;-n) (gym) squad
Riegel ['riːgəl] m (-s;-) bolt; (Seife)
cake; (Schokolade) bar
riegeln ['riːgəln] tr bolt, bar
Riemen ['riːmən] m (-s;-) strap;
(Leib-, Trieb-) belt; (Ruder) oar;
(e-s Gewehrs) sling
Riemenscheibe f pulley
Ries [riːs] n (-es;-e) ream (of one thou-
sand sheets)
Riese ['riːzə] m (-;-n) giant
rieseln ['riːzəln] intr (HABEN & SEIN)
trickle; (Bach) purl || impers—es
rieselt it is drizzling
Rieselregen m drizzle
Riesenbomber m superbomber
Riesenerfolg m smash hit
riesengroß adj gigantic
riesenhaft adj gigantic
Riesenrad n Ferris wheel
Riesenschlange f boa constrictor
Riesentanne f (bot) sequoia
riesig ['riːzɪç] adj gigantic, huge || adv
(coll) awfully
Riesin ['riːzɪn] f (-;-nen) giant
riet [riːt] pret of raten
Riff [rɪf] n (-[e]s;-e) reef
Rille ['rɪlə] f (-;-n) groove; small fur-
row; (archit) flute
Rimesse [rɪˈmɛsə] f (-;-n) (com) re-
mittance
Rind [rɪnt] n (-[e]s;-er) head of cat-
tle; Rinder cattle
Rinde ['rɪndə] f (-;-n) rind; (Baum-)
bark; (Brot-) crust; (anat) cortex
Rinderbraten m roast beef
Rinderbremse f horsefly
Rinderherde f herd of cattle
Rinderhirt m cowboy
Rindfleisch n beef
Rindsleder n cowhide
Rindslendenstück n rump steak, ten-
derloin
Rindsrückenstück n sirloin of beef
Rindvieh n cattle; (sl) idiot
Ring [rɪŋ] m (-[e]s;-e) ring; (Kreis)
circle; (Kettenglied) link; (Kartell)
combine; (astr) halo
Ringel ['rɪŋəl] m (-s;) small ring;
(Locke) ringlet, curl
Ringelblume f marigold
ringeln ['rɪŋəln] tr & ref curl
Ringelreihen m ring-around-the-rosy
Ringelspiel n merry-go-round
ringen ['rɪŋən] §142 tr wrestle;
(Wäsche, Hände) wring; (heraus-
winden) wrest || intr wrestle; (fig)
struggle
Ringer m -in §6 mf wrestler
Ringkampf m wrestling match
Ringmauer f town wall, city wall
Ringrichter m (box) referee
rings [rɪŋs] adv around; r. um all
around
Ringschlüssel m socket wrench
ringsherum', rings'um', rings'umher'
adv all around
Rinne ['rɪnə] f (-;-n) groove; (Strom-
bett) channel; (Leitung) duct;
(Gosse) gutter; (Erdfurche) furrow

rinnen ['rɪnən] §121 *intr* (SEIN) run, flow; trickle || *intr* (HABEN) leak
Rinnsal ['rɪnzal] *n* (-[e]s;-e) little stream
Rinn'stein *m* gutter; (*Ausgußbecken*) sink; (*unterirdisch*) culvert
Rippchen ['rɪpçən] *n* (-s;-) cutlet
Rippe ['rɪpə] *f* (-;-n) rib; (*Schokolade*) bar; (*archit*) groin
rippen ['rɪpən] *tr* rib, flute
Rip'penfellentzündung *f* pleurisy
Rip'penstoß *m* nudge (in the ribs)
Rip'penstück *n* loin end
Risi·ko ['rizɪko] *n* (-s;-s & -ken [kən]) risk; **ein R. eingehen** take a risk
riskant [rɪs'kant] *adj* risky
riskieren [rɪs'kirən] *tr* risk
riß [rɪs] *pret of* **reißen** || **Riß** *m* (-sses; Risse) tear, rip; (*Bruch*) fracture; (*Lücke*) gap; (*Kratzer*) scratch; (*Spalt*) split, cleft; (*Spaltung*) fissure; (*Sprung*) crack; (*Zeichnung*) sketch; (eccl) schism; (geol) crevasse
rissig ['rɪsɪç] *adj* torn; cracked; split; (*Haut*) chapped
Rist [rɪst] *m* (-es;-e) wrist; (*des Fußes*) instep
ritt [rɪt] *pret of* **reiten** || **Ritt** *m* (-[e]s; -e) ride
Ritter ['rɪtər] *m* (-s;-) knight; cavalier; **zum R. schlagen** knight
Rit'tergut *n* manor
Rit'terkreuz *n* (mil) Knight's Cross (*of the Iron Cross*)
rit'terlich *adj* knightly; (fig) chivalrous
Rit'terlichkeit *f* (-;) chivalry
Rit'terzeit *f* age of chivalry
rittlings ['rɪtlɪŋs] *adv*—**r. auf** (*dat or acc*) astride
Ritual [rɪtu'al] *n* (-s;-e & -ien [jən]) ritual
rituell [rɪtu'el] *adj* ritual
Ri·tus ['ritus] *m* (-;-ten [tən]) rite
Ritz [rɪts] *m* (-es;-e), **Ritze** ['rɪtsə] *f* (-;-n) crack, crevice; (*Schlitz*) slit; (*Schramme*) scratch
ritzen ['rɪtsən] *tr* scratch; (*Glas*) cut
Rivale [rɪ'valə] *m* (-n;-n), **Rivalin** [rɪ'valɪn] *f* (-;-nen) rival
rivalisieren [rɪvalɪ'zirən] *intr* be in rivalry; **r. mit** rival
Rivalität [rɪvalɪ'tet] *f* (-;-en) rivalry
Rizinusöl ['ritsɪnusøl] *n* castor oil
Robbe ['robə] *f* (-;-n) seal
robben ['robən] *intr* (HABEN & SEIN) (mil) crawl (*using one's elbows*)
Rob'benfang *m* seal hunt
Robe ['robə] *f* (-;-n) robe, gown
Roboter ['robotər] *m* (-s;-) robot
robust [ro'bust] *adj* robust
roch [rox] *pret of* **riechen**
röcheln ['rœçəln] *tr* gasp out || *intr* rattle (*in one's throat*)
rochieren [ro'xirən] *intr* (chess) castle
Rock [rok] *m* (-[e]s;-e) skirt; jacket
Rock'schoß *m* coattail
Rodel ['rodəl] *m* (-s;-) & *f* (-;-n) toboggan; (*mit Steuerung*) bobsled
Ro'delbahn *f* toboggan slide
rodeln ['rodəln] *intr* (HABEN & SEIN) toboggan
Ro'delschlitten *m* toboggan; bobsled

roden ['rodən] *tr* root out; (*Wald*) clear; (*Land*) make arable
Rogen ['rogən] *m* (-s;) roe, spawn
Roggen ['rogən] *m* (-s;) rye
roh [ro] *adj* raw; crude; (*Steine*) unhewn; (*Dielen*) bare; (fig) uncouth, brutal
Roh'bau *m* (-[e]s;-ten) rough brickwork
Roh'diamant *m* uncut diamond
Roh'einnahme *f* gross receipts
Roh'eisen *n* pig iron
Ro'heit *f* (-;) rawness, raw state; crudeness; brutality
Roh'entwurf *m* rough sketch
Roh'gewicht *n* gross weight
Roh'gewinn *m* gross profit
Roh'gummi *m* crude rubber
Roh'haut *f* rawhide
Roh'kost *f* uncooked vegetarian food
Rohling ['rolɪŋ] *m* (-s;-e) blank; slug; (fig) thug, hoodlum
Roh'material *n* raw material
Roh'öl *n* crude oil
Rohr [ror] *n* (-[e]s;-e) reed, cane; (*Röhre*) pipe, tube; (*Kanal*) duct, channel; (*Gewehrlauf*) barrel
Rohr'anschluß *m* pipe joint
Rohr'bogen *m* elbow
Röhre ['rørə] *f* (-;-n) tube, pipe; (electron) tube
Röh'renblitz *m* electronic flash
Röh'renblitzgerät *n* electronic flash unit
Rohr'leger *m* pipe fitter
Rohr'leitung *f* pipeline, main
Rohr'schäftung *f* sleeve joint
Rohr'schelle *f* pipe clamp
Rohr'zange *f* pipe wrench
Rohr'zucker *m* cane sugar
Roh'stoff *m* raw material
Rolladen (**Roll'laden**) *m* sliding shutter; sliding cover
Rollbahn ['rolban] *f* (aer) runway; (mil) road leading up to the front
Röllchen ['rœlçən] *n* (-s;-) caster
Rolldach ['roldax] *n* (aut) sun roof
Rolle ['rolə] *f* (-;-n) roll; (*Walze*) roller; (*Flaschenzug*) pulley; (*Spule*) spool, reel; (*unter Möbeln*) caster; (*Mangel*) mangle; (*Liste*) list, register; (theat) role; **aus der R. fallen** (fig) misbehave; **spielt keine R.!** never mind!, forget it!
rollen ['rolən] *tr* roll; (*auf Rädern*) wheel; (*Wäsche*) mangle; || *ref* curl up || *intr* (HABEN & SEIN) roll; (*Flugzeug*) taxi; (*Geschütze*) roar || **Rollen** *n*—**ins. R. kommen** get going
Rol'lenbesetzung *f* (theat) cast
Rol'lenlager *n* roller bearing
Rol'lenzug *m* block and tackle
Rol'ler *m* (-s;-) scooter; motor scooter
Roll'feld *n* (aer) runway
Roll'kragen *m* turtleneck
Roll'mops *m* pickled herring
Rollo ['rolo] *n* (-s;-s) (coll) blind, shade
Roll'schuh *m* roller skate; **R. laufen** roller-skate
Roll'schuhbahn *f* roller-skating rink
Roll'stuhl *m* wheelchair
Roll'treppe *f* escalator

Roll'wagen m truck
Rom [rom] n (-s;) Rome
Roman [ro'mɑn] m (-s;-e) novel
Roman'folge f serial
roman'haft adj fictional
romanisch [ro'mɑniʃ] adj (Sprache) Romance; (archit) Romanesque
Romanist –in [romɑ'nist(in)] §7 mf scholar of Romance languages
Roman'schriftsteller –in §6 mf novelist
Romantik [ro'mɑntik] f (-;) Romanticism
romantisch [ro'mɑntiʃ] adj romantic
Romanze [ro'mɑntsə] (-;-n) romance
Römer –in ['rømər(in)] §6 mf Roman
römisch ['rømiʃ] adj Roman
rö'misch-katho'lisch adj Roman Catholic
röntgen ['rœntgən] tr x-ray
Rönt'genapparat m x-ray machine
Rönt'genarzt m, **Rönt'genärztin** f radiologist
Rönt'genaufnahme f, **Rönt'genbild** n x-ray
Rönt'genstrahlen pl x-rays
rosa ['roza] adj pink || **Rosa** n (-s;- & -s) pink
Rose ['rozə] f (-;-n) rose
Ro'senkohl m Brussels sprouts
Ro'senkranz m (eccl) rosary
ro'senrot adj rosy, rose-colored
Ro'senstock m rosebush
rosig ['roziç] adj (& fig) rosy; (Laune) happy
Rosine [ro'zinə] f (-;-n) raisin
Roß [ros] n (Rosses; Rosse) horse; (sl) jerk; (poet) steed
Rost [rost] m (-es;) rust; mildew || m (-es;-e) grate; grill; **auf dem R. braten** grill
Rost'braten m roast beef
Röstbrot ['røstbrot] n toast
rosten ['rostən] intr rust
rösten ['røstən] tr (auf dem Rost) grill; (in der Pfanne) roast; (Brot) toast; (Mais) pop; (Kaffee) roast
Rö'ster m (-s;-) roaster; toaster
Rost'fleck m rust stain
rost'frei adj rust-proof; (Stahl) stainless
rostig ['rostiç] adj rusty, corroded
rot [rot] adj (röter ['røtər]; röteste ['røtəstə] §9) red || **Rot** n (-es) red; (Schminke) rouge
Rotation [rotɑ'tsjon] f (-;-en) rotation
Rotations'maschine f rotary press
rotbäcklg ['rotbɛkıç] adj red-cheeked
Rot'dorn m (bot) pink hawthorn
Röte ['røtə] f (-;) red(ness); blush
Röteln ['røtəln] pl German measles
rotieren [ro'tirən] intr rotate
Rotkäppchen ['rotkɛpçən] n (-s;) Little Red Riding Hood
Rotkehlchen ['rotkelçən] n (-s;-) robin
rötlich ['røtliç] adj reddish
Ro-tor ['rotor] m (-s;-toren ['torən]) (aer) rotor; (elec) armature
Rot'schimmel m roan (horse)
Rot'tanne f spruce
Rotte ['rotə] f (-;-n) gang, mob
Rotz [rots] m (-es;-e) (sl) snot
rot'zig adj (sl) snotty

Rouleau [ru'lo] n (-s;-s) window shade
Route ['rutə] f (-;-n) route
Routine [ru'tinə] f (-;) routine; practice, experience
routiniert [ruti'nirt] adj experienced
Rübe ['rybə] f (-;-n) beet; **gelbe R.** carrot; **weiße R.** turnip
Rubin [ru'bin] m (-s;-e) ruby
Rubrik [ru'brik] f (-;-en) rubric; heading; (Spalte) column
ruchbar ['ruxbar] adj known, public
ruchlos ['ruxlos] adj wicked
Ruck [ruk] m (-[e]s;-e) jerk; yank; jolt; **auf e-n R.** at once; **mit e-m R.** in one quick move
Rück-, rück- [ryk] comb.fm. re-, back, rear; return
Rück'ansicht f rear view
Rück'antwort f reply; **Postkarte mit R.** prepaid reply postcard
rück'bezüglich adj (gram) reflexive
Rück'bleibsel n remainder
rücken ['rykən] tr move, shove || intr (SEIN) move; (Platz machen) move over; (marschieren) march; **höher r.** be promoted; **näher r.** approach || **Rücken** m (-s;-) back; (Rückseite) rear; (der Nase) bridge
Rückendeckung (Rük'kendeckung) f (fig) backing, support
Rückenlehne (Rük'kenlehne) f back rest
Rückenmark (Rük'kenmark) n spinal cord
Rückenschwimmen (Rük'kenschwimmen) n backstroke
Rückenwind (Rük'kenwind) m tail wind
Rückenwirbel (Rük'kenwirbel) m (anat) vertebra
rück'erstatten tr reimburse, refund
Rück'fahrkarte f, **Rück'fahrschein** m round-trip ticket
Rück'fahrt f return trip
Rück'fall m relapse
rück'fällig adj habitual, relapsing
rück'federnd adj resilient
Rück'flug m return flight
Rück'frage f further question
Rück'führung f repatriation
Rück'gabe f return, restitution
Rück'gang m return; regression; (der Preise) drop; (econ) recession
rückgängig ['rykgeniç] adj retrogressive; dropping; **r. machen** cancel
rück'gewinnen §121 tr recover
Rück'grat n backbone, spine
Rück'griff m (auf acc) recourse (to)
Rück'halt m backing; (mil) reserves; **e-n R. an j-m haben** have s.o.'s backing; **ohne R.** without reservation
rück'haltlos adj frank, unreserved || adv without reserve
Rück'handschlag m (tennis) back-hand stroke
Rück'kauf m repurchase
Rück'kehr f return; (fig) comeback
Rück'kopplung f (electron) feedback
Rück'lage f reserves, savings
Rück'lauf m reverse; (mil) recoil
Rück'läufer m letter returned to sender
rückläufig ['ryklɔifiç] adj retrograde

Rück'licht n (aut) taillight
rücklings ['ryklɪŋs] adv backwards
Rück'nahme f withdrawal, taking back
Rück'porto n return postage
Rück'prall m bounce, rebound, recoil
Rück'reise f return trip
Ruck'sack m knapsack
Rück'schau m—R. halten auf (acc) look back on
Rück'schlag m back stroke; (e-s Balles) bounce; (fig) setback
Rück'schluß m conclusion, inference
Rück'schritt m backward step; (fig) falling off, retrogression
Rück'seite f back; reverse; wrong side
Rück'sicht f regard, respect, consideration; aus R. auf (acc) out of consideration for; in (or mit) R. auf (acc) in regard to; ohne R. auf (acc) irrespective of; R. nehmen auf (acc) take into account, show consideration for
rück'sichtlich prep (genit) considering
rück'sichtslos adj inconsiderate; reckless; ruthless
rück'sichtsvoll adj considerate
Rück'sitz m (aut) rear seat
Rück'spiegel m (aut) rear-view mirror
Rück'spiel n return match
Rück'sprache f discussion; conference; R. nehmen mit consult with
Rück'stand m arrears; (Satz) sediment; (Rest) remainder; (von Aufträgen, usw.) backlog; (chem) residue
rück'ständig adj behind, in arrears; (Geld) outstanding; (Raten) delinquent; (altmodisch) backward
Rück'stau m back-up water
Rück'stelltaste f backspace key
Rück'stoß m repulsion; recoil, kick
Rückstrahler ['rykstralər] m (-s;-) reflector
Rück'strahlung f reflection
Rück'tritt m resignation
Rück'trittbremse f coaster brake
Rück'umschlag m return envelope
rückwärts ['rykverts] adv backward(s)
Rück'wärtsgang m (aut) reverse
Rück'weg m way back, return
ruck'weise adv by fits and starts
rück'wirken intr react
rück'wirkend adj retroactive
Rück'wirkung f (-;-en) reaction; repercussion
rück'zahlen tr repay, refund
Rück'zug m withdrawal; retreat; zum R. blasen sound the retreat
Rück'zugsgefecht n running fight
rüde ['rydə] adj rude, coarse || **Rüde** m (-n;-n) male (wolf, fox, etc.)
Rudel ['rudəl] n (-s;-) herd; flock; (von Wölfen, U-Booten) wolf pack
Ruder ['rudər] n (-s;-) (aer, naut) rudder; (naut) oar
Ru'derblatt n blade of an oar
Ru'derboot n rowboat
Ru'derer -in §6 mf rower
Ru'derklampe f oarlock
rudern ['rudərn] tr & intr row
Ru'derschlag m stroke of the oar
Ru'dersport m (sport) crew
Ruf [ruf] m (-[e]s;-e) call; shout, yell; (Berufung) vocation; (Nach-

rede) reputation; appointment; (com) credit
rufen ['rufən] §122 tr call; shout; r. lassen send for || intr call; shout
Ruf'mord m character assassination
Ruf'name m first name
Ruf'nummer f telephone number
Ruf'weite f—in R. within earshot
Ruf'zeichen n (rad) station identification; (telp) call sign
Rüge ['rygə] f (-;-n) reprimand
rügen ['rygən] tr reprimand
Ruhe ['ru·ə] f (-;) rest; quiet, calm; (Frieden) peace; (Stille) silence; immer mit der R.! (coll) take it easy!
ru'hebedürftig adj in need of rest
Ru'hegehalt n pension
Ru'hekur f rest cure
ru'helos adj restless
ruhen ['ru·ən] intr rest; sleep
Ru'hepause f pause, break
Ru'heplatz m resting place
Ru'hestand m retirement
Ru'hestätte f resting place
Ru'hestörer -in §6 mf disturber of the peace
Ru'hetag m day of rest, day off
Ru'hezeit f leisure
ruhig ['ru·ɪç] adj still, quiet; calm
Ruhm [rum] m (-[e]s;) glory, fame
rühmen ['rymən] tr praise || ref (genit) boast (about)
rühmlich ['rymlɪç] adj praiseworthy
ruhm'los adj inglorious
ruhmredig ['rumredɪç] adj vainglorious
ruhm'reich adj glorious
ruhm'voll adj famous, glorious
ruhm'würdig adj praiseworthy
Ruhr [rur] f (-;) dysentery; **Ruhr** (river)
Rührei ['ryrar] n scrambled egg
rühren ['ryrən] tr stir; touch, move; (Trommel) beat; alle Kräfte r. exert every effort || ref stir, move; get a move on; rührt euch! (mil) at ease! || intr stir, move; r. an (acc) touch; (fig) mention; r. von originate in
rührig ['ryrɪç] adj active; agile
Rührlöffel ['ryrlœfəl] m ladle
rührselig ['ryrzelɪç] adj sentimental
Rührstück ['ryrʃtyk] n soap opera
Rüh'rung f (-;-en) emotion
Ruin [ru'in] m (-s;) ruin; decay
Ruine [ru'inə] f (-;-n) ruins; (fig) wreck
rui'nenhaft adj ruinous
ruinieren [ru·ɪ'nirən] tr ruin
Rülps [rylps] m (-es;-e) belch
rülpsen ['rylpsən] intr belch
Rülp'ser m (-s;-) belch
Rum [rum] m (-s;-s) rum
Rumäne [ru'menə] m (-n;-n) Rumanian
Rumänien [ru'menjən] n (-s;) Rumania
Rumänin [ru'menɪn] f (-;-nen) Rumanian
rumänisch [ru'menɪʃ] adj Rumanian
Rummel ['rum

əl] m (-s;) junk; racket; hustle and bustle; auf den R. gehen go to the fair; den ganzen R. kaufen (coll) buy the works
Rum'melplatz m amusement park, fair
Rumor [ru'mor] m (-s;) noise, racket

Rumpel ['rumpəl] f (-;-n) scrub board

Rum'pelkammer f storage room, junk room

Rum'pelkasten m (aut) jalopy

rumpeln ['rumpəln] tr (Wäsche) scrub || intr rumble, rattle

Rumpf [rumpf] m (-[e]s;ːe) trunk, body; torso; (aer) fuselage; (naut) hull

rümpfen ['rympfən] tr—die Nase r. über (acc) turn up one's nose at

rund [runt] adj round; (Absage) flat || adv around; about, approximately; r. um around

Rund'blick m panorama

Rund'brief m circular letter

Runde ['rundə] f (-;-n) round; (box) round; (beim Rennsport) lap

runden ['rundən] tr make round; round off || ref become round

Rund'erlaß m circular

rund'erneuern tr (aut) retread; runderneuerter Reifen m retread

Rund'fahrt f sightseeing tour

Rund'flug m (aer) circuit

Rund'frage f questionnaire, poll

Rund'funk m radio; im R. on the radio

Rund'funkansage f radio announcement

Rund'funkansager –in §6 mf radio announcer

Rund'funkgerät n radio set

Rund'funkgesellschaft f broadcasting company

Rund'funkhörer –in §6 mf listener

Rund'funknetz n radio network

Rund'funksender m broadcasting station

Rund'funksendung f radio broadcast

Rund'funksprecher –in §6 mf announcer

Rund'funkwerbung f (rad) commercial

Rund'gang m tour; stroll

rund'heraus' adv plainly, flatly

rundherum' adv all around

rund'lich adj round; (dick) plump

Rund'reise f sightseeing tour

Rund'schau f panorama; (journ) news in brief

Rund'schreiben n circular letter

rundweg ['runt'vɛk] adv bluntly, flatly

Runzel ['runtsəl] f (-;-n) wrinkle

runzelig ['runtseliç] adj wrinkled

runzeln ['runtsəln] tr wrinkle; die Brauen r. knit one's brows; die Stirn r. frown || ref wrinkle

Rüpel ['rypəl] m (-s;-) boor

rüpelhaft adj rude, boorish

rupfen ['rupfən] tr pluck; (fig) fleece

ruppig ['rupiç] adj shabby; (fig) rude

Ruprecht ['ruprɛçt] m (-s;)—Knecht R. Santa Claus

Ruß [rus] m (-es;) soot

Russe ['rusə] m (-n;-n) Russian

Rüssel ['rysəl] m (-s;-) snout; (Elephanten-) trunk; (coll) snoot; (ent) proboscis

rußig ['rusiç] adj sooty

Russin ['rusin] f (-;-nen) Russian

russisch ['rusi] adj Russian

Rußland ['ruslant] n (-s;) Russia

Rüst- [ryst] comb.fm. scaffolding; armament, munition

rüsten ['rystən] tr arm, equip; prepare || ref get ready || intr (zu) get ready (for); zum Krieg r. mobilize

Rüster ['rystər] f (-;-n) elm

rüstig ['rystiç] adj vigorous; alert

Rüst'kammer f armory, arsenal

Rü'stung f (-;-en) preparation; equipment; armament; mobilization; armor; implements; (archit) scaffolding

Rü'stungsbetrieb m munitions factory

Rü'stungsfertigung f war production

Rü'stungsindustrie f war industry

Rü'stungskontrolle f arms control

Rü'stungsmaterial n war materiel

Rü'stungsstand m state of preparedness

Rüst'zeug n kit; (fig) knowledge

Rute ['rutə] f (-;-n) rod; twig; tail; (anat) penis

Rutsch [rut] m (-es;-e) slip, slide

Rutsch'bahn f slide; chute

Rutsche ['rutə] f (-;-n) slide; chute

rutschen ['rutən] intr (SEIN) slip, slide; (aut) skid

rutschig ['rutiç] adj slippery

rütteln ['rytəln] tr shake; jolt; (Getreide) winnow; (aus dem Schlafe) rouse || intr—r. an (acc) cause to rattle; (fig) try to undermine

S

S, s [ɛs] invar n S, s

SA abbr (mil) (Sturmabteilung) storm troopers

Saal [zal] m (-[e]s; Säle ['zɛlə]) hall

Saat [zat] f (-;-en) seed; (Säen) sowing; (Getreide auf dem Halm) crop(s); die S. bestellen sow

Saat'bestellung f sowing

Saat'kartoffel f seed potato

Sabbat ['zabat] m (-s;-e) Sabbath

Sabberei [zabə'rar] f (-;-en) drooling; (Geschwätz) drivel

sabbern ['zabərn] intr drool, drivel

Säbel ['zebəl] m (-s;) saber; mit dem S. rasseln (pol) rattle the saber

sä'belbeinig adj bowlegged

säbeln ['zebəln] tr (coll) hack

Sä'belrasseln n (pol) saber rattling

Sabotage [zabo'taʒə] f (-;-n) sabotage

Saboteur [zabo'tør] m (-s;-e) saboteur

sabotieren [zabo'tirən] tr sabotage

Saccharin [zaxa'rin] n (-s;) saccharin

Sach- [zax] comb.fm. of facts, factual

Sach'anlagevermögen n tangible fixed assets

Sach'bearbeiter –in §6 mf specialist

Sach'beschädigung f property damage
Sach'bezüge pl compensation in kind
Sach'buch n nonfiction (work)
Sach'darstellung f statement of facts
sach'dienlich adj relevant, pertinent
Sache ['zaxə] f (-;-n) thing, matter; cause; (jur) case; bei der S. sein be on the ball; **beschlossene S.** foregone conclusion; **die S. der Freiheit** the cause of freedom; **große S.** big affair; **gute S.** good cause; **heikle S.** delicate point; **in eigner S.** on one's own behalf; **in Sachen X gegen Y** (jur) in the case of X versus Y; **meine sieben Sachen** all my belongings; **nicht bei der S. sein** not be with it; **nicht zur S. gehörig** irrelevant; **von der S. abkommen** get off the subject; **zur S.!** come to the point! (parl) question!
sach'gemäß adj proper, pertinent || adv in a suitable manner
Sach'kenner –in §6 mf expert
Sach'kenntnis f, **Sach'kunde** f expertise
sach'kundig adj expert || **Sach'kundige** §5 mf expert
Sach'lage f state of affairs, circumstances
Sach'leistung f payment in kind
sach'lich adj (treffend) to the point; (gegensätzlich) objective; (tatsächlich) factual; (unparteilich) impartial; (nüchtern) matter-of-fact || adv to the point
sächlich ['zɛçliç] adj (gram) neuter
Sach'lichkeit f (-;) objectivity; reality; impartiality; matter-of-factness
Sach'register n index
Sach'schaden m property damage
Sach'schadenersatz m indemnity (for property damage)
Sachse ['zaksə] m (-n;-n) Saxon
Sachsen ['zaksən] n (-s;) Saxony
sächsisch ['zɛksiʃ] adj Saxon
sacht(e) ['zaxt(ə)] adj soft, gentle; (langsam) slow || adv gingerly; **immer sacht!** easy does it!
Sach'verhalt m facts of the case
Sach'vermögen n real property
sach'verständig adj experienced || **Sachverständige** §5 mf expert
Sach'wert m actual value; **Sachwerte** material assets
Sach'wörterbuch n encyclopedia
Sack [zak] m (-[e]s;=e) sack, bag; pocket; **j–n in den S. stecken** (coll) be way above s.o.; **mit S. und Pack** bag and baggage
Säckel ['zɛkəl] m (-s;-) little bag; pocket; purse
sacken ['zakən] tr bag || refl be baggy || intr (SEIN) sag; (archit) settle; (naut) founder
Sack'gasse f blind alley, dead end; (fig) stalemate, dead end
Sack'leinwand f burlap
Sack'pfeife f bagpipe
Sack'tuch n handkerchief
Sadist –in ['za'dɪst(ɪn)] §7 mf sadist
sadistisch [za'dɪstɪʃ] adj sadistic
säen ['zɛ·ən] tr & intr sow
Saffian ['zafjɑn] m (-s;) morocco

Safran ['zafrɑn] m (-s;-e) saffron
Saft [zaft] m (-[e]s;=e) juice; sap; (culin) gravy
saftig ['zaftɪç] adj juicy; (Witze) spicy
saft'los adj juiceless; (fig) wishy-washy
saft'reich adj juicy, succulent
Sage ['zɑgə] f (-;-n) legend, saga
Säge ['zɛgə] f (-;-n) saw
Sä'geblatt n saw blade
Sä'gebock m sawhorse, sawbuck
Sä'gefisch m sawfish
Sä'gemehl n sawdust
sagen ['zɑgən] tr say; (mitteilen) tell; **das hat nichts zu s.** that's neither here nor there; **das will nicht s.** that is not to say; **gesagt, getan** no sooner said than done; **j–m s. lassen** send s.o. word; **laß dir gesagt sein** let it be a warning to you; **sich** [dat] **nichts s. lassen** not listen to reason
sägen ['zɛgən] tr saw || intr saw; (coll) snore, cut wood
sa'genhaft adj legendary
Sägespäne ['zɛgəʃpɛnə] pl sawdust
Sä'gewerk n sawmill
sah [za] pret of sehen
Sahne ['zɑnə] f (-;) cream
Saison [sɛˈzõ] f (-;-s) season
Saison– comb.fm. seasonal
saison'bedingt, saison'mäßig adj seasonal
Saite ['zartə] f (-;-n) string, chord
Sai'teninstrument n string instrument
Sakko ['zako] m & n (-s;-s) suit coat
Sak'koanzug m sport suit
Sakrament [zakra'ment] n (-[e]s;-e) sacrament; **das S. des Altars** the Eucharist || interj (sl) dammit!
Sakrileg [zakrɪ'lek] n (-s;-e) sacrilege
Sakristan [zakrɪs'tɑn] m (-s;-e) sacristan
Sakristei [zakrɪs'tar] f (-;-en) sacristy
Säkular– [zekular] comb.fm. secular; centennial
säkularisieren [zekularɪ'zirən] tr secularize
Salami [za'lɑmi] f (-;-s) salami
Salat [za'lɑt] m (-[e]s;-e) salad; lettuce; **gemischter S.** tossed salad
Salat'soße f salad dressing
salbadern [zal'bɑdərn] intr talk hypocritically, put on the dog
Salbe ['zalbə] f (-;-n) salve
salben ['zalbən] tr put salve on; anoint
Sal'bung f (-;-en) anointing
sal'bungsvoll adj unctuous
saldieren [zal'dirən] tr (com) balance
Sal'do ['zaldo] m (-s;-s & di [di]) (acct) balance; **e–n S. aufstellen** (or **ziehen**) strike a balance; **e–n S. ausweisen** show a balance
Saline [za'linə] f (-;-n) saltworks
Salmiak [zal'mjak] m (-s;) ammonium chloride, sal ammoniac
Salmiak'geist m ammonia
Salon [za'lõ] m (-s;-s) salon; parlor, living room
salon'fähig adj (Aussehen) presentable; (Ausdruck) fit for polite company
Salon'held m, **Salon'löwe** m ladies' man
salopp [za'lop] adj sloppy; (ungezwungen) casual
Salpeter [zal'petər] m (-s;) saltpeter

salpeterig [zal'petəriç] *adj* nitrous
Salpe'tersäure *f* nitric acid
Salto ['zalto] *m* (-s;-s) somersault
Salut [za'lut] *m* (-[e]s;-e) salute; S. schießen fire a salute
salutieren [zalu'tirən] *tr & intr* salute
Salve ['zalvə] *f* (-;-n) volley, salvo
Salz [zalts] *n* (-es;-e) salt
Salz'bergwerk *n* salt mine
Salz'brühe *f* brine
salzen ['zaltsən] *tr* salt
Salz'faß *n* salt shaker
Salz'fleisch *n* salted meat
Salz'gurke *f* pickle
salz'haltig *adj* saline
Salz'hering *m* pickled herring
salzig ['zaltsıç] *adj* salty; saline
Salz'kartoffeln *pl* boiled potatoes
Salz'lake *f* brine
Salz'säure *f* hydrochloric acid, muriatic acid
Salz'sole *f* brine
Salz'werk *n* salt works
Samariter –in [zama'ritər(ın)] §6 *mf* Samaritan
Same ['zamə] *m* (-ns;-n), Samen ['zamən] *m* (-s;-) seed; (biol) semen
Sa'menkorn *n* grain of seed
Sa'menstaub *m* pollen
Samentierchen ['zaməntirçən] *n* (-s;-) spermatozoon
samig ['zemıç] *adj* (culin) thick, creamy
Sämischleder ['zemı/ledər] *n* chamois
Sämling ['zemlıŋ] *m* (-s;-e) seedling
Sammel- [zaməl] *comb.fm.* collecting, collective
Sam'melbatterie *f* storage battery
Sam'melbecken *n* reservoir; storage tank
Sam'melbegriff *m* collective noun
Sam'melbüchse *f* poor box
Sam'mellinse *f* convex lens
sammeln ['zaməln] *tr* gather; collect; (*Aufmerksamkeit, Truppen*) concentrate || *ref* gather; compose oneself; sich wieder s. (mil) reassemble
Sam'melname *m* collective noun
Sam'melplatz *m* collecting point; meeting place; (mil) rendezvous
Sam'melverbindung *f* conference call
Sam'melwerk *n* compilation
Sammler ['zamlər] *m* (-s;-) collector; compiler; (elec) storage cell
Samm'lung *f* (-;-en) collection; (*Zusammenstellung*) compilation; (*Fassung*) composure; concentration
Samstag ['zamstak] *m* (-[e]s;-e) Saturday
samt [zamt] *adv—s. und sonders* each and everyone, without exception || *prep* (*dat*) together with || Samt *m* (-[e]s;-e) velvet
samt'artig *adj* velvety
sämtlich ['zemtlıç] *adj* all, complete || *adv* all together
Sanato•rium [zana'torjum] *n* (-s;-rien [rjən]) sanitarium
Sand [zant] *m* (-[e]s;-e) sand; im Sande verlaufen (fig) peter out
Sandale [zan'dələ] *f* (-;-n) sandal
Sand'bahn *f* (sport) dirt track
Sand'bank *f* (-;ᵘe) sandbank

Sand'boden *m* sandy soil
Sand'düne *f* sand dune
Sand'grube *f* sand pit
sandig ['zandıç] *adj* sandy
Sand'kasten *m* sand box
Sand'korn *n* grain of sand
Sand'mann *m* (-[e]s;) (fig) sandman
Sand'papier *n* sandpaper; mit S. abschleifen sand, sandpaper
Sand'sack *m* sandbag
Sand'stein *m* sandstone
Sand'steingebäude *n* brownstone
sand'strahlen *tr* sandblast
Sand'sturmgebiet *n* dust bowl
sandte ['zantə] *pret* of senden
Sand'torte *f* sponge cake
Sand'uhr *f* hour glass
Sand'wüste *f* sandy desert
sanft [zanft] *adj* soft, gentle
Sänfte ['zenftə] *f* (-;-n) sedan chair
Sanft'mut *f* gentleness, meekness
sanft'mütig *adj* gentle, meek, mild
sang [zaŋ] *pret* of singen || Sang *m* (-[e]s;ᵘe) song; mit S. und Klang (fig) with great fanfare
sang- *und* klang'los *adv* unceremoniously
Sänger ['zeŋər] *m* (-s;-) singer
Sän'gerchor *m* glee club
Sängerin ['zeŋərın] *f* (-;-nen) singer
Sanguiniker [zaŋ'gwinıkər] *m* (-s;-) optimist
sanguinisch [zaŋ'gwini/] *adj* sanguine
sanieren [za'nirən] *tr* cure; improve the sanitary conditions of; disinfect; (fin) put on a firm basis
Sanie'rung *f* (-;-en) restoration; reorganization
sanitär [zanı'ter] *adj* sanitary
Sanitäter [zanı'tetər] *m* (-s;-) first-aid-man; (mil) medic
Sanitäts- [zanıtets] *comb.fm.* first-aid, medical
Sanitäts'korps *n* army medical corps
Sanitäts'soldat *m* medic
Sanitäts'wache *f* first-aid station
Sanitäts'wagen *m* ambulance
Sanitäts'zug *m* hospital train
sank [zaŋk] *pret* of sinken
Sanka ['zaŋka] *m* (-s;-s) (Sanitätskraftwagen) field ambulance
Sankt [zaŋkt] *invar mf* Saint
Sanktion [zaŋk'tsjon] *f* (-;-en) sanction
sanktionieren [zaŋktsjo'nirən] *tr* sanction
sann [zan] *pret* of sinnen
Saphir ['zafır] *m* (-s;-e) sapphire
sapperment [zapər'ment] *interj* the deuce!
Sardelle [zar'delə] *f* (-;-n) anchovy
Sardine [zar'dinə] *f* (-;-n) sardine
Sardinien [zar'dinjən] *n* (-s;) Sardinia
sardinisch [zar'dini/] *adj* Sardinian
Sarg [zark] *m* (-[e]s;ᵘe) coffin
Sarg'tuch *n* pall
Sarkasmus [zar'kasmus] *m* (-;) sarcasm
sarkastisch [zar'kastı/] *adj* sarcastic
Sarkophag [zarko'fak] *m* (-s;-e) sarcophagus
saß [zas] *pret* of sitzen
Satan ['zatan] *m* (-s;-e) Satan

satanisch [za'tanɪʃ] *adj* satanic(al)
Satellit [zate'lit] *m* (-en;-en) satellite
Satin [sa'tɛ̃] *m* (-s;-s) satin
Satire [za'tirə] *f* (-;-n) satire
Satiriker -in [za'tirikər(ɪn)] §6 *mf* satirist
satirisch [za'tirɪʃ] *adj* satirical
satt [zat] *adj* satisfied; satiated; (*Farben*) deep, rich; (chem) saturated; **etw s. bekommen** (or **haben**) be fed up with s.th.; **ich bin s.** I've had enough; **sich s. essen** eat one's fill
Sattel ['zatəl] *m* (-s;⸚) saddle
sat'telfest *adj* (fig) well-versed
Sat'telgurt *m* girth
satteln ['zatəln] *tr* saddle
Sat'telschlepper *m* semi-trailer
Sat'teltasche *f* saddlebag
Satt'heit *f* (-;) saturation; (*der Farben*) richness
sättigen ['zetɪgən] *tr* satisfy, satiate; saturate
Sät'tigung *f* (-;) satiation; saturation
Sattler ['zatlər] *m* (-s;-) harness maker
sattsam ['zatzam] *adv* sufficiently
saturieren [zatu'rirən] *tr* saturate
Satz [zats] *m* (-es;⸚e) sentence; clause; phrase; (*Behauptung*) proposition; (*Bodensatz*) grounds; sediment; (*Betrag*) amount; (*Tarif*) rate; (*Gebühr*) fee; (*Garnitur*) set; (*Sprung*) leap; (*Wette*) stake; (*Menge*) batch; (math) theorem; (mus) movement; (tennis) set; (typ) typesetting, composition; **e-n S. machen** jump; **e-n S. aufstellen** set down an article of faith; **einfacher S.** simple sentence; **hauptwörtlicher S.** substantive clause; **in S. gehen** go to press; **verkürzter S.** phrase; **zum S. von** at the rate of; **zusammengesetzter S.** compound sentence
Satz'aussage *f* gram) predicate
Satz'bau *m* (-[e]s;) (gram) construction
Satz'gefüge *n* complex sentence
Satz'gegenstand *m* (gram) subject
Satz'lehre *f* syntax
Satz'teil *m* (gram) part of speech
Sat'zung *f* (-;-en) rule, regulation; (*Vereins-*) bylaw; statute
sat'zungsgemäß, **sat'zungsmäßig** *adj* statutory, according to the bylaws
Satz'zeichen *n* punctuation mark
Sau [zau] *f* (-;⸚e) sow; (pej) pig; **wie e-e gesengte Sau fahren** drive like a maniac
Sau'arbeit *f* (coll) sloppy work; (coll) tough job; (coll) dirty job
sauber ['zaubər] *adj* clean; exact
säuberlich ['zɔɪbərlɪç] *adj* clean, neat; (*anständig*) decent
sau'bermachen *tr* clean, clean up
säubern ['zɔɪbərn] *tr* clean; (*freimachen*) clear; (*Buch*) expurgate; (mil) mop up; (pol) purge
Säu'berungsaktion *f* (mil) mopping-up operation; (pol) purge
Sau'borste *f* hog bristle
Sauce ['zosə] *f* (-;-n) sauce; gravy; (*Salat-*) dressing
sau'dumm *adj* (coll) awfully dumb
sauer ['zau·ər] *adj* sour

Sau'erbraten *m* braised beef soaked in vinegar
Sauerei [zau·ə'raɪ] *f* (-;-en) filth, filthy joke
Sau'erkohl *m*, **Sau'erkraut** *n* sauerkraut
säuerlich ['zɔɪ·ərlɪç] *adj* sourish, acidulous; (*Lächeln*) forced
säuern ['zɔɪ·ərn] *tr* sour; (*Teig*) leaven || *intr* turn sour, acidify
Sau'erstoff *m* (-[e]s;) oxygen
Sau'erstoffflasche *f* oxygen tank
Sau'erteig *m* leaven
Sau'ertopf *m* (coll) sourpuss
Sau'erwasser *n* sparkling water
Saufaus ['zaufaus] *m* (-;-), **Saufbold** ['zaufbɔlt] *m* (-[e]s;-e), **Saufbruder** ['zaufbrudər] *m* (coll) booze hound
saufen ['zaufən] §124 *tr* drink, guzzle || *intr* drink; (sl) booze
Säufer -in ['zɔɪfər(ɪn)] §6 *mf* drunkard
Saufgelage ['zaufgəlagə] *n* booze party
Sau'fraß *m* terrible food, slop
Säugamme ['zɔɪkamə] *f* wet nurse
saugen ['zaugən] §109 & §125 *tr* suck || *ref—sich* [*dat*] **etw aus den Fingern s.** invent s.th., make up s.th.
säugen ['zɔɪgən] *tr* suckle, nurse
Sauger ['zaugər] *m* (-s;-) sucker; nipple; pacifier
Säuger ['zɔɪgər] *m* (-s;-), **Säugetier** ['zɔɪgətir] *n* mammal
Saug'flasche *f* baby bottle
Säugling ['zɔɪklɪŋ] *m* (-s;-e) baby
Säug'lingsausstattung *f* layette
Säug'lingsheim *n* nursery
Sau'glück *n* (coll) dumb luck
Saug'napf *m* suction cup
Saug'pumpe *f* suction pump
Saug'watte *f* absorbent cotton
Saug'wirkung *f* suction
Sau'hund *m* (sl) louse, dirty dog
Sau'igel *m* (sl) dirty guy
sauigeln ['zau·igəln] *intr* (sl) tell dirty jokes
Sau'kerl *m* (sl) cad, skunk
Säule ['zɔɪlə] *f* (-;-n) column; (& fig) pillar; (elec) dry battery; (phys) pile
Säu'lenfuß *m* base of a column
Säu'lengang *m* colonnade, peristyle
Säu'lenhalle *f* portico, gallery
Säu'lenkapitell *n*, **Säu'lenknauf** *m*, **Säu'lenkopf** *m* (archit) capital
Säu'lenschaft *m* shaft of a column
Säu'lenvorbau *m* portico, (front) porch
Saum [zaum] *m* (-[e]s;⸚e) seam, hem; (*Rand*) border; (*e-r Stadt*) outskirts
säumen ['zɔɪmən] *tr* hem; border; (*Straßen*) line || *intr* tarry
Sau'mensch *n* (vulg) slut
säumig ['zɔɪmɪç] *adj* tardy
Säumnis ['zɔɪmnɪs] *f* (-;-nisse) dilatoriness; (*Verzug*) delay; (*Nichterfüllung*) default
Saum'pfad *m* mule track
Saum'tier *n* beast of burden
Sau'pech *n* (coll) rotten luck
Säure ['zɔɪrə] *f* (-;-n) sourness; acidity; tartness; (chem) acid
Sauregur'kenzeit *f* slack season
Säu'remesser *m* (aut) battery tester
Saures ['zaurəs] *n—*gib ihm S. (coll) give it to 'im!

Saus [zaus] *m*—**in S. und Braus leben** live high

säuseln [ˈzɔɪzəln] *intr* rustle; **mit säuselnder Stimme** in whispers

sausen [ˈzauzən] *intr* (*Wind, Kugel*) whistle; (*Wasser*) gush || *intr* (SEIN) rush, whiz || *impers*—**mir saust es in den Ohren** my ears are ringing || **Sausen** *n* (-s;) rush and roar; humming, ringing (*in the ears*)

Sau′stall *m* pigsty; (fig) terrible mess

Sau′wetter *n* (coll) nasty weather

Sau′wirtschaft *f* (coll) helluva mess

sau′wohl *adj* (coll) in great shape

Saxophon [zaksoˈfoːn] *n* (-s;-e) saxophone

Schabe [ˈʃabə] *f* (-;-n) cockroach

Schabeisen [ˈʃapaɪzən] *n* scraper

schaben [ˈʃabən] *tr* scrape; grate, rasp

Scha′ber *m* (-s;-) scraper

Schabernack [ˈʃabərnak] *m* (-[e]s;-e) practical joke

schäbig [ˈʃeːbɪç] *adj* shabby; (fig) mean

Schablone [ʃaˈbloːnə] *f* (-;-n) (*Muster*) pattern, model; (*Matrize*) stencil; (*mechanische Arbeit*) routine; **nach der S.** mechanically

schablo′nenhaft, schablo′nenmäßig *adj* mechanical; (*Arbeit*) routine

Schach [ʃax] *n* (-[e]s;-) chess; **in S. halten** (fig) keep in check; **S. bieten** (or **geben**) check; (fig) defy; **S. dem König!** check!

Schach′brett *n* chessboard

Schacher [ˈʃaxər] *m* (-s;) haggling; **S. treiben** haggle, huckster

Schach′feld *n* (chess) square

Schach′figur *f* chessman; (fig) pawn

schach′matt′ *adj* checkmated; (fig) beat

Schach′partie *f*, **Schach′spiel** *n* game of chess

Schacht [ʃaxt] *m* (-[e]s;ːe) shaft; manhole

Schacht′deckel *m* manhole cover

Schachtel [ˈʃaxtəl] *f* (-;-n) box; (*von Zigaretten*) pack; (fig) frump

Schach′zug *m* (chess & fig) move

schade [ˈʃaːdə] *adj* too bad

Schädel [ˈʃeːdəl] *m* (-s;-) skull; **mir brummt** (or **dröhnt**) **der S.** my head is throbbing

Schä′delbruch *m*, **Schä′delfraktur** *f* skull fracture

Schä′delhaut *f* scalp

Schä′delknochen *m* cranium

Schä′dellehre *f* phrenology

schaden [ˈʃaːdən] *intr* do harm; (dat) harm, damage; **das wird ihr nichts s.** it serves her right; **ein Versuch kann nichts s.** there's no harm in trying || *impers*—**es schadet nichts** it doesn't matter || **Schaden** *m* (-s;ː) damage, injury; (*Verlust*) loss; (*Nachteil*) disadvantage; **er will deinen S. nicht** he means you no harm; **j-m S. zufügen** inflict loss on s.o.; (coll) give s.o. a black eye; **mit S. verkaufen** sell at a loss; **S. nehmen** come to grief; **zu meinem S.** to my detriment

Scha′denersatz *m* compensation, damages; (*Wiedergutmachung*) reparation; **S. leisten** pay damages; make amends

Scha′denersatzklage *f* damage suit

Scha′denfreude *f* gloating

scha′denfroh *adj* gloating, malicious

Scha′denversicherung *f* comprehensive insurance

schadhaft [ˈʃathaft] *adj* damaged; (*Material*) faulty; (*Zähne*) decayed; (*baufällig*) dilapidated

schädigen [ˈʃeːdɪɡən] *tr* inflict financial damage on; (*benachteiligen*) wrong; (*Ruf*) damage; (*Rechte*) infringe on

Schä′digung *f* (-;) damage

schädlich [ˈʃeːtlɪç] *adj* harmful; (*nachteilig*) detrimental; (*verderblich*) noxious; (*Speise*) unwholesome

Schädling [ˈʃeːtlɪŋ] *m* (-s;-e) (*Person*) parasite; (ent) pest; **Schädlinge vermin**

Schäd′lingsbekämpfung *f* pest control

schadlos [ˈʃaːtloːs] *adj*—**sich an j-m s. halten** make s.o. pay (*for an injury done to oneself*); **sich für etw s. halten** compensate oneself for s.th., make up for s.th.

Schaf [ʃaf] *n* (-[e]s;-e) sheep; (fig) blockhead, dope

Schaf′bock *m* ram

Schäfchen [ˈʃeːfçən] *n* (-s;-) lamb; (*Wolken*) fleecy clouds

Schäf′chenwolke *f* fleecy cloud

Schäfer [ˈʃeːfər] *m* (-s;-) shepherd

Schä′ferhund *m* sheep dog; **deutscher S.** German shepherd

Schaf′fell *n* sheepskin

schaffen [ˈʃafən] §109 *tr* do; get; put; manage, manage to do; (*erreichen*) accomplish; (*liefern*) supply; (*erschaffen*) bring, cause; (*wegbringen*) take; **auf die Seite s.** put aside; (betrügerisch) embezzle; **ich schaffe es noch, daß** I'll see to it that; **Rat s.** know what to do; **vom Halse s.** get off one's neck || §126 *tr* create; produce; **wie geschaffen sein für** cut out for || §109 *intr* do; (*arbeiten*) work; **j-m viel zu s. machen** cause s.o. a lot of trouble; **sich zu s. machen** be busy, putter around

schaf′fend *adj* working; (*schöpferisch*) creative; (*produktiv*) productive

Schaf′fensdrang *m* creative urge

Schaf′fenskraft *f* creative power

Schaffner [ˈʃafnər] *m* (-s;-) (rr) conductor

Schaf′fung *f* (-;-en) creation

Schaf′hirt *m* shepherd

Schaf′pelz *m* sheepskin coat

Schaf′pferch *m* sheepfold

Schafs′kopf *m* (sl) mutton-head

Schaf′stall *m* sheepfold

Schaft [ʃaft] *m* (-[e]s;ːe) shaft; (e-r Feder) stem; (e-s Gewehrs) stock; (e-s Ankers) shank; (bot) stem, stalk

Schaft′stiefel *m* high boot

Schaf′zucht *f* sheep raising

Schakal [ʃaˈkal] *m* (-s;-e) jackal

schäkern [ˈʃeːkərn] *intr* joke around; flirt

schal [ʃal] *adj* stale; insipid; (fig) flat || **Schal** *m* (-s;-e & -s) scarf; shawl

Schale [ˈʃaːlə] *f* (-;-n) bowl; (*Tasse*) cup; (von Obst) peel, skin; (*Hülse*) shell; (*Schote*) pod; (*Rinde*) bark;

(Waagschale) scale; (zool) shell; **sich in S. werfen** (coll) doll up

schälen [ˈʃɛlən] *tr* peel; *(Mais)* husk; *(Baumrinde)* bark ‖ *ref* peel off

Scha′lentier *n* (zool) crustacean

Schalk [ʃalk] *m* (-[e]s;-e & ²e) rogue

schalk′haft *adj* roguish

Schall [ʃal] *m* (-[e]s;-e & ²e) sound; *(Klang)* ring; *(Lärm)* noise

Schall′boden *m* sounding board

Schall′dämpfer *m (an Schußwaffen)* silencer; (aut) muffler; (mus) soft pedal

schall′dicht *adj* soundproof

Schall′dose *f* (electron) pickup

Schall′druck *m* sonic boom

Schallehre (Schall′lehre) *f* acoustics

schallen [ˈʃalən] *intr* sound, resound

Schall′grenze *f* sound barrier

Schall′mauer *f* sound barrier

Schall′meßgerät *n* sonar

Schall′pegel *m* sound level

Schall′platte *f* phonograph record

Schall′plattenaufnahme *f* recording

Schall′wand *f* baffle

Schall′welle *f* sound wave

Schalotte [ʃaˈlɔtə] *f* (-;-n) (bot) scallion

schalt [ʃalt] *pret of* **schelten**

Schalt- *comb.fm.* switch; connecting; breaking; shifting

Schalt′bild *n* circuit diagram

Schalt′brett *n* switchboard; control panel; (aut) dashboard

Schalt′dose *f* switch box

schalten [ˈʃaltən] *tr* switch; *(anlassen)* start; *(Gang)* (aut) shift ‖ *intr* switch; *(regieren)* be in command; (aut) shift gears; **s. und walten mit** do as one pleases with

Schal′ter *m* (-s;-) switch; *(Ausschalter)* circuit breaker; *(für Kundenverkehr)* window, ticket window

Schal′terdeckel *m* switch plate

Schalt′hebel *m* (aut) gearshift; (elec) switch lever

Schalt′jahr *n* leap year

Schalt′kasten *m* switch box

Schalt′pult *n* (rad, telv) control desk

Schalt′tafel *f* switchboard, instrument panel; (aut) dashboard

Schalt′uhr *f* timer

Schal′tung *f* (-;-en) switching; (elec) connection; (elec) circuit

Schaluppe [ʃaˈlupə] *f* (-;-n) sloop

Scham [ʃam] *f* (-;) shame; (anat) genitals

Scham′bein *n* (anat) pubis

schämen [ˈʃɛmən] *ref (über acc)* feel ashamed (of)

Scham′gefühl *n* sense of shame

Scham′haar *n* pubic hair

scham′haft *adj* modest, bashful

scham′los *adj* shameless

Schampun [ʃamˈpun] *n* (-s;-s) shampoo

schampunieren [ʃampuˈnirən] *tr* shampoo

scham′rot *adj* blushing; **s. werden** blush

Scham′teile *pl* genitals

Schand- [ʃant] *comb.fm.* of shame

schandbar [ˈʃantbar] *adj* shameful; infamous

Schande [ˈʃandə] *f* (-;) shame, disgrace

schänden [ˈʃɛndən] *tr* disgrace; *(entweihen)* desecrate; *(Mädchen)* rape

Schän′der *m* (-s;-) violator; rapist

Schand′fleck *m* stain; (fig) blemish; (fig) good-for-nothing; **der S. der Familie** the disgrace of the family

schändlich [ˈʃɛntlɪç] *adj* shameful, disgraceful; scandalous ‖ *adv* (coll) awfully

Schand′mal *n* stigma

Schand′tat *f* shameful deed, crime

Schän′dung *f* (-;-en) desecration; disfigurement; rape

Schank [ʃaŋk] *m* (-[e]s;²e) bar, saloon

Schank′bier *n* draft beer

Schank′erlaubnis *f*, **Schank′gerechtigkeit** *f*, **Schank′konzession** *f* liquor license

Schank′stätte *f* bar, tavern

Schank′tisch *m* bar

Schank′wirt *m* bartender

Schank′wirtschaft *f* bar, saloon

Schanzarbeit [ˈʃantsarbait] *f* earthwork; **Schanzarbeiten** entrenchments

Schanze [ˈʃantsə] *f* (-;-n) entrenchments, trenches; (naut) quarter-deck; (sport) take-off ramp *(of ski jump)*

Schanz′gerät *n* entrenching tool

Schar [ʃar] *f* (-;-en) group, bunch; crowd; *(von Vögeln)* flock, flight

Scharade [ʃaˈradə] *f* (-;-n) charade

scharen [ˈʃarən] *ref (um)* gather (around)

scharf [ʃarf] *adj* (**schärfer** [ˈʃɛrfər], **schärfste** [ˈʃɛrfstə] §9) sharp; *(Tempo)* fast; *(Bemerkung)* cutting; *(Blick)* hard; *(Brille)* strong; *(Fernrohr)* powerful; *(Geruch)* pungent; *(Munition)* live; *(Pfeffer, Senf)* hot; *(streng)* severe; *(genau)* exact; *(Ton)* shrill; *(wahrnehmend)* keen; **s. machen** sharpen; **s. sein auf** (acc) be keen on ‖ *adv* hard; fast; **j–n s. nehmen** be very strict with s.o.; **s. ansehen** look hard at; **s. geladen** loaded; **s. schießen** shoot with live ammunition; **s. umreißen** define clearly

Scharf′blick *m* (fig) sharp eye

Schärfe [ˈʃɛrfə] *f* (-;-n) sharpness; keenness; pungency; severity; accuracy

Scharf′einstellung *f* (phot) focusing

schärfen [ˈʃɛrfən] *tr* sharpen, whet; make pointy; (fig) intensify

scharf′kantig *adj* sharp-edged

scharf′machen *tr* stir up; *(Bomben)* arm; *(Zünder)* activate

Scharf′macher *m* demagogue, agitator

Scharf′richter *m* executioner

Scharf′schütze *m* (mil) sharpshooter

scharf′sichtig *adj* sharp-eyed; (fig) clear-sighted

Scharf′sinn *m* sagacity, acumen

scharf′sinnig *adj* sharp, sagacious

Scharlach [ˈʃarlax] *m* (-s;-e) scarlet; (pathol) scarlet fever

schar′lachfarben *adj* scarlet

schar′lachrot *adj* scarlet

Scharlatan [ˈʃarlatan] *m* (-s;-e) charlatan, quack

scharmant [ʃarˈmant] *adj* charming

Scharmützel [ʃarˈmʏtsəl] *n* (-s;-) skirmish

Scharnier [ʃarˈniːr] *n* (-s;-e) hinge; joint

Schärpe [ˈʃɛrpə] *f* (-;-n) sash

Scharre [ˈʃarə] *f* (-;-n) scraper

Scharreisen [ˈʃaraɪzən] *n* scraper

scharren [ˈʃarən] *tr* scrape, paw || *intr* scrape; (an *acc*) scratch (on); **auf den Boden s.** paw the ground; **mit den Füßen s.** scrape the feet (*in disapproval*)

Scharte [ˈʃartə] *f* (-;-n) nick, dent; (*Kerbe*) notch; (*Kratzer*) scratch; (*Riß*) crack; (*Bergsattel*) gap; (fig) mistake; **e-e S. auswetzen** (fig) make amends

Scharteke [ʃarˈteːkə] *f* (-;-n) worthless old book; (fig) frump

schartig [ˈʃartɪç] *adj* jagged; notched

Schatten [ˈʃatən] *m* (-s;-) shade; shadow; **in den S. stellen** throw into the shade

Schat'tenbild *n* silhouette; (fig) phantom

Schat'tendasein *n* shadowy existence

Schat'tengestalt *f* shadowy figure

schat'tenhaft *adj* shadowy

Schat'tenriß *m* silhouette

Schat'tenseite *f* shady side; dark side; (fig) seamy side

schattieren [ʃaˈtiːrən] *tr* shade; (*schraffieren*) hatch; (*abtönen*) tint

Schattie'rung *f* (-;-en) shading; (*Farbton*) shade, tint

schattig [ˈʃatɪç] *adj* shadowy; shady

Schatulle [ʃaˈtulə] *f* (-;-n) cash box; (*für Schmuck*) jewelry box; (hist) private funds (*of a prince*)

Schatz [ʃats] *m* (-es;-̈e) treasure; (*Vorrat*) store; (fig) sweetheart

Schatz'amt *n* treasury department

Schatz'anweisung *f* treasury bond

schätzbar [ˈʃɛtsbar] *adj* valuable

schätzen [ˈʃɛtsən] *tr* (*Grundstücke, Häuser, Schaden*) estimate, appraise; (*urteilen, vermuten*) guess; (*achten*) esteem, value; (*würdigen*) appreciate; **er schätzte mich auf 20 Jahre** he took me for 20 years old; **zu hoch s.** overestimate, overrate; **zu s. wissen** appreciate || *ref—sich* [*dat*] es zu Ehre **s.** consider it an honor; **sich glücklich s.** consider oneself lucky || *recip—sie s. sich nicht* there's no love lost between them

schät'zenswert *adj* valuable

Schät'zer –in §6 *mf* appraiser; (*zur Besteuerung*) assessor

Schatz'kammer *f* treasury; (fig) storehouse

Schatz'meister –in §6 *mf* treasurer

Schät'zung *f* (-;-en) estimate; (*Meinung*) estimation; (*Hochachtung*) esteem; (*Hochschätzung*) appreciation; (*zur Besteuerung*) assessment

schät'zungsweise *adv* approximately

Schät'zungswert *m* estimated value; assessed value; (*des Schadens*) appraisal

Schatz'wechsel *m* treasury bill

Schau [ʃau] *f* (-;-en) view; (*Ausstel-*
lung) exhibition, show; (mil) review; (telv) show; **zur S. stehen** be on display; **zur S. stellen** put on display; **zur S. tragen** feign

Schau'bild *n* diagram, chart

Schauder [ˈʃaudər] *m* (-s;-) shudder, shiver; (*Schrecken*) horror, terror

schauderbar [ˈʃaudərbar] *adj* terrible

schau'dererregend *adj* horrifying

schau'derhaft *adj* horrible, awful

schaudern [ˈʃaudərn] *intr* (vor *dat*) shudder (at) || *impers—es schaudert mich* I shudder

schauen [ˈʃau·ən] *tr* look at; (*beobachten*) observe || *intr* look

Schauer [ˈʃau·ər] *m* (-s;-) shower, downpour; (*Schauder*) shudder, chill; thrill; (*Anfall*) fit, attack; **einzelne S.** scattered showers

Schau'erdrama *n* (theat) thriller

schau'erlich *adj* dreadful, horrible

schauern [ˈʃau·ərn] *intr* shudder || *impers—es schauert* it is pouring; **es schauert mich (or mir) vor** (*dat*) I shudder at; **I shiver with**

Schau'erroman *m* thriller

Schaufel [ˈʃaufəl] *f* (-;-n) shovel; scoop; (*Rad—*) paddle; (*Turbinen—*) blade, vane

schaufeln [ˈʃaufəln] *tr* shovel; (*Grab*) dig || *intr* shovel

Schau'felrad *n* paddle wheel

Schau'fenster *n* display window; **die S. ansehen** go window-shopping

Schau'fensterauslage *f* window display

Schau'fensterbummel *m* window-shopping

Schau'fensterdekoration *f* window dressing

Schau'fliegen *n* stunt flying

Schau'flug *m* air show

Schau'gepränge *n* pageantry

Schau'gerüst *n* grandstand

Schau'kampf *m* (box) exhibition fight

Schau'kasten *m* showcase

Schaukel [ˈʃaukəl] *f* (-;-n) swing

Schau'kelbrett *n* seesaw

schaukeln [ˈʃaukəln] *tr* swing; rock || *intr* swing; rock; sway

Schau'kelpferd *n* rocking horse

Schau'kelreck *n* trapeze

Schau'kelstuhl *m* rocking chair

Schau'loch *n* peephole

Schaum [ʃaum] *m* (-[e]s;-̈e) foam, froth; (*Abschaum*) scum; (*Geifer*) slaver; **zu S. schlagen** whip; **zu S. werden** (fig) come to nothing

Schaum'bad *n* bubble bath

schäumen [ˈʃɔɪmən] *intr* foam; (*Wein*) sparkle; (*aus Wut*) fume, boil

Schaum'gummi *n & m* foam rubber

Schaum'haube *f* head (*on beer*)

schaumig [ˈʃaumɪç] *adj* foamy

Schaum'krone *f* whitecap (*on wave*)

Schaum'modell *n* mock-up

Schaum'wein *m* sparkling wine

Schau'platz *m* scene, theater

Schau'prozeß *m* mock trial

schaurig [ˈʃaurɪç] *adj* horrible

Schau'spiel *n* play, drama; spectacle

Schau'spieler *m* actor

Schau'spielerin *f* actress

schau'spielerisch *adj* theatrical

schauspielern [ˈʃauʃpiːlərn] *intr* act; (*schwindeln*) act, make believe
Schau′spielhaus *n* theater
Schau′spielkunst *f* dramatic art
Schau′stück *n* show piece; (*Muster*) sample
Scheck [ʃɛk] *m* (-s;-s & -e) check; e–n S. ausstellen an (*acc*) über (*acc*) write out a check to (*s.o.*) in the amount of; e–n S. einlösen cash a check; e–n S. sperren lassen stop payment on a check; offener S. blank check
Scheck′abschnitt *m* check stub
Scheck′formular *n* blank check
Scheck′heft *n* check book
scheckig [ˈʃɛkɪç] *adj* dappled
Scheck′konto *n* checking account
scheel [ʃeːl] *adj* squinting; squint-eyed; (fig) envious, jealous
Scheffel [ˈʃɛfəl] *m* (-s;-) bushel
scheffeln [ˈʃɛfəln] *tr* amass
Scheibe [ˈʃaɪbə] *f* (-;-n) disk; sheet; plate; (*Glas*-) pane; (*Honig*-) honeycomb; (*Ziel*-) target; (*Schnitte*-) slice; (astr) orb, disk; (mach) washer; (telp) dial
Schei′benbremse *f* disk brake
Schei′benkönig *m* top marksman
Schei′benschießen *n* target practice
Schei′benwäscher *m* windshield washer
Schei′benwischer *m* windshield wiper
Scheide [ˈʃaɪdə] *f* (-;-n) sheath; border, boundary; (anat) vagina
Schei′debrief *m* farewell letter
Schei′degruß *m* goodbye
scheiden [ˈʃaɪdən] §112 *tr* separate, divide; (*zerlegen*) decompose; (*Ehe*) dissolve; (*Eheleute*) divorce; (chem) analyze; (chem) refine ‖ *ref* part; sich s. lassen get a divorce ‖ *intr* (SEIN) part; depart; (aus dem Amt) resign, retire
schei′dend *adj* (*Tag*) closing; (*Sonne*) setting
Schei′dewand *f* partition
Schei′deweg *m* fork, crossroad; (fig) moment of decision
Schei′dung *f* (-;-en) separation; (*Ehe*-) divorce
Schein [ʃaɪn] *m* (-[e]s;-e) shine; (*Licht*) light; (*Schimmer*) gleam, glitter; (*Strahl*) flash; (*Erscheinung*) appearance; (*Anschein*) pretense, show; (*Urkunde*) certificate, papers, license, ticket; (*Geldschein*) bill; (*Quittung*) receipt; dem Scheine nach apparently; den äußeren S. wahren save face; sich [*dat*] den S. geben make believe; zum S. pro forma
Schein- *comb.fm.* sham, mock, make-believe
scheinbar [ˈʃaɪnbaːr] *adj* seeming, apparent; likely; (*vorgeblich*) make-believe
Schein′bild *n* illusion; phantom
scheinen [ˈʃaɪnən] §128 *intr* shine; seem, appear ‖ *impers*—es scheint it seems
Schein′grund *m* pretext
schein′heilig *adj* sanctimonious, hypocritical
Schein′tod *m* suspended animation

Schein′werfer *m* flashlight; (aer) beacon; (aut) headlight
Scheit [ʃaɪt] *n* (-[e]s;-e) piece of chopped wood; Holz in Scheite hakken chop wood
Scheitel [ˈʃaɪtəl] *m* (-s;-) apex, top; top of the head; (*des Haares*) part; e–n S. ziehen make a part
scheiteln [ˈʃaɪtəln] *tr & ref* part
Schei′telpunkt *m* (fig) summit; (astr) zenith; (math) vertex
Schei′telwinkel *m* opposite angle
Scheiterhaufen [ˈʃaɪtərhaufən] *m* funeral pile; auf dem S. sterben die at the stake
scheitern [ˈʃaɪtərn] *intr* (SEIN) run aground, be wrecked; (*Plan*) miscarry ‖ Scheitern *n* (-s;) shipwreck; (fig) failure
Schelle [ˈʃɛlə] *f* (-;-n) bell; (*Fessel*) handcuff; (*Ohrfeige*) box on the ear
schellen [ˈʃɛlən] *tr & intr* ring
Schel′lenkappe *f* cap and bells
Schellfisch [ˈʃɛlfɪʃ] *m* haddock
Schelm [ʃɛlm] *m* (-[e]s;-e) rogue; (Lit) knave; armer S. poor devil
Schel′menstreich *m* prank
schelmisch [ˈʃɛlmɪʃ] *adj* roguish, impish
Schelte [ˈʃɛltə] *f* (-;-n) scolding
schelten [ˈʃɛltən] *tr & intr* scold
Scheltwort [ˈʃɛltvɔrt] *n* (-[e]s;-e & =er) abusive word; word of reproof
Sche•ma [ˈʃeːma] *n* (-s;-s & -mata [mata] & -men [mən]) scheme; diagram; (*Muster*) pattern, design
Schemel [ˈʃeːməl] *m* (-s;-) stool
Schemen [ˈʃeːmən] *m* (-s;-) phantom, shadow
sche′menhaft *adj* shadowy
Schenk [ʃɛŋk] *m* (-en;-en) bartender
Schenke [ˈʃɛŋkə] *f* (-;-n) bar, tavern
Schenkel [ˈʃɛŋkəl] *m* (-s;-) thigh; (e–s Winkels) side; (e–r Schere) blade; (e–s Zirkels) leg
schenken [ˈʃɛŋkən] *tr* give, offer; pour (out); (*Aufmerksamkeit*) pay; (*Schuld*) remit; das ist geschenkt that's dirt cheap; das kann ich mir s. I can pass that up; das kannst du dir s.! keep it to yourself! j–m Beifall s. applaud s.o.; j–m das Leben s. grant s.o. pardon
Schenk′stube *f* taproom, barroom
Schenk′tisch *m* bar
Schen′kung *f* (-;-en) donation
Schenk′wirt *m* bartender
scheppern [ˈʃɛpərn] *intr* (coll) rattle
Scherbe [ˈʃɛrbə] *f* (-;-n), **Scherben** [ˈʃɛrbən] *m* (-s;-) broken piece; potsherd; in Scherben gehen go to pieces
Scher′bengericht *n* ostracism
Scherbett [ʃɛrˈbɛt] *m* (-[e]s;-e) sherbe(r)t
Schere [ˈʃeːrə] *f* (-;-n) (pair of) scissors; shears; (*Draht*-) cutter; (zool) claw
scheren [ˈʃeːrən] *tr* bother; was schert dich das? what's that to you? ‖ §129 *tr* cut, clip, trim; (*Schafe*) shear; ‖ §109 *ref*—scher dich ins Bett! off to bed with you!; scher dich zum Teu-

fel! the devil with you!; **sich um etw s.** trouble oneself about s.th.

Schererei [ʃerəˈraɪ] f (-;-en) trouble

Scherflein [ˈʃerflaɪn] n (-s;-) bit; **sein S. beitragen** contribute one's bit

Scherz [ʃerts] m (-es;-e) joke; **im (or zum) S.** for fun; **S. treiben mit** make fun of

scherzen [ˈʃertsən] intr joke, kid

scherz'haft adj joking, humorous

Scherz'name m nickname

scherz'weise adv in jest, as a joke

scheu [ʃɔɪ] adj shy; **s. machen** frighten; startle || **Scheu** f (-;) shyness

Scheuche [ˈʃɔɪçə] f (-;-n) scarecrow

scheuchen [ˈʃɔɪçən] tr scare (away)

scheuen [ˈʃɔɪ.ən] tr shun; shrink from; fear; (Mühen, Kosten) spare; **ohne die Kosten zu s.** regardless of expenses || ref (vor dat) be afraid (of); **ich s. mich zu** (inf) I am reluctant to (inf) || intr—s. **vor** (dat) shy at

Scheuer [ˈʃɔɪ.ər] f (-;-n) barn

Scheu'erbürste f scrub brush

Scheu'erfrau f scrubwoman

Scheu'erlappen m scrub rag

scheuern [ˈʃɔɪ.ərn] tr scrub, scour; (reiben) rub

Scheu'erpulver n scouring powder

Scheu'klappe f blinder (for horses)

Scheune [ˈʃɔɪnə] f (-;-n) barn

Scheu'nendrescher m—er **ißt wie ein S.** (coll) he eats like a horse

Scheusal [ˈʃɔɪzal] n (-s;-e) monster

scheußlich [ˈʃɔɪslɪç] adj dreadful, atrocious; (coll) awful, rotten

Scheuß'lichkeit f (-;-en) hideousness; (Tat) atrocity

Schi [ʃiː] m (-s;- & -er) ski; **Schi fahren** (or laufen) ski

Schicht [ʃɪçt] f (-;-en) layer, film; (Farb-) coat; (Arbeiter-) shift; (Gesellschafts-) class; (geol) stratum; (phot) emulsion; **Leute aus allen Schichten** people from all walks of life; **S. machen** (coll) knock off from work

Schicht'arbeit f shift work

schichten [ˈʃɪçtən] tr arrange in layers; laminate; (Holz) stack (up); (in Klassen einteilen) classify; (geol) stratify; (Ladung) (naut) stow

Schich'tenaufbau m, **Schich'tenbildung** f (geol) stratification

-schichtig [ʃɪçtɪç] comb.fm. -layer, -ply

Schicht'linie f contour

Schicht'linienplan m contour map

Schicht'meister m shift foreman

schicht'weise adv in layers; in shifts

schick [ʃɪk] adj chic, swank || **Schick** m (-[e]s;) stylishness; (Geschick) skill; (Geschmack) tact, taste; **S. haben für** have a knack for

schicken [ˈʃɪkən] tr send || ref—**sich s. für** (or **zu**) be suitable for; **sich s. in** (acc) adapt oneself to; resign oneself to || intr—**nach j-m s.** send for s.o. || impers—**es schickt sich** it is proper; (sich ereignen) come to pass

schick'lich adj proper; decent

Schick'lichkeit f (-;) propriety

Schick'lichkeitsgefühl n sense of propriety

Schicksal [ˈʃɪkzal] n (-[e]s;-e) destiny, fate

Schick'salsgefährte m fellow sufferer

Schick'salsglaube m fatalism

Schick'salsgöttinnen pl (myth) Fates

Schick'salsschlag m stroke of fate

Schickung [Schik'kung] f (-;-en) (divine) dispensation

Schiebe- [ʃibə] comb.fm. sliding, push

Schie'beleiter f extension ladder

schieben [ˈʃibən] §130 tr push, shove; traffic in; **auf die lange Bank s.** put off; **e-e ruhige Kugel s.** have a cushy job; **Kegel s.** bowl; **Wache s.** (mil) pull guard duty || ref move, shuffle || intr shuffle along; profiteer

Schieber [ˈʃibər] m (-s;-) slide valve; (Riegel) bolt; (am Schornstein) damper; (fig) racketeer

Schie'bergeschäft f (com) racket

Schiebertum [ˈʃibərtum] n (-s;) (com) racketeering

Schie'betür f sliding door

schied [ʃiːt] pret of scheiden

Schieds- [ʃits] comb.fm. of arbitration

Schieds'gericht n board of arbitration; **an ein S. verweisen** refer to arbitration

Schieds'mann m (-[e]s;-er) arbitrator

Schieds'richter m arbitrator; (sport) referee, umpire

schieds'richterlich adj of an arbitration board || adv by arbitration

Schieds'spruch m decision; **e-n S. fällen** render a decision

schief [ʃiːf] adj (abfallend) slanting; (krumm) crooked; (einseitig) lopsided; (geneigt) inclined; (Winkel) oblique; (falsch) false, wrong; **auf die schiefe Ebene geraten** (fig) go downhill; **schiefe Lage** (fig) tight spot; **schiefes Licht** (fig) bad light || adv at an angle; awry; obliquely; wrong; **s. ansehen** look askance at; **s. halten** tip, tilt; **s. nehmen** take amiss

Schiefer [ˈʃifər] m (-s;-) slate; (Splitter) splinter

Schie'ferbruch m slate quarry

Schie'feröl n shale oil

Schie'fertafel f (educ) slate

schief'gehen §82 intr (SEIN) go wrong

schief'treten §152 tr—**die Abstätze s.** wear down the heels

schieläugig [ˈʃiːlɔɪgɪç] adj squint-eyed; cross-eyed

schielen [ˈʃiːlən] intr squint; **s. nach** squint at; leer at

schie'lend adj squinting; cross-eyed; furtive

schien [ʃiːn] pret of scheinen

Schienbein [ˈʃiːnbaɪn] n shinbone, tibia

Schien'beinschützer m shinguard

Schiene [ˈʃiːnə] f (-;-n) (rr) rail, track; (surg) splint; **aus den Schienen springen** jump the track

schienen [ˈʃiːnən] tr put in splints

Schie'nenbahn f track, rails; streetcar; railroad

Schie'nenfahrzeug n rail car

Schie'nengleis n track

schier [ʃir] adj sheer || adv almost

Schierling [ˈʃirlɪŋ] m (-s;-e) (bot) hemlock

Schieß- [ʃis] comb.fm. shooting

Schieß′baumwolle f guncotton

Schieß′bedarf m ammunition

Schieß′bude f shooting gallery

Schieß′eisen n (hum) shooting iron

schießen [ˈʃisən] §76 tr shoot, fire; e-n Bock s. (coll) pull a boner; ein Tor s. make a goal || intr (auf acc) shoot (at); aus dem Hinterhalt s. snipe; gut s. be a good shot; scharf s. shoot with live ammunition || intr (SEIN) shoot up; spurt; zig. fly; das Blut schoß ihm ins Gesicht his face got red; in Samen s. go to seed; ins Kraut s. sprout || Schießen n (-s;) shooting; das ist ja zum s.! (coll) that's a riot!

Schießerei [ʃisəˈrai] f (-;-en) gun fight; pointless firing

Schieß′gewehr n firearm

Schieß′hund m (hunt) pointer

Schieß′lehre f ballistics

Schieß′platz m firing range

Schieß′prügel m (hum) shooting iron

Schieß′pulver n gunpowder

Schieß′scharte f loophole

Schieß′scheibe f target

Schieß′stand m shooting gallery; (mil) firing range, rifle range

Schieß′übung f firing practice

Schi′fahrer -in §6 mf skier

Schiff [ʃɪf] n (-[e]s;-e) ship; (archit) nave; (typ) galley

Schiffahrt (Schiff′fahrt) f navigation

Schiffahrtslinie (Schiff′fahrtslinie) f steamship line

Schiffahrtsweg (Schiff′fahrtsweg) m shipping lane

schiffbar [ˈʃɪfbar] adj navigable

Schiff′bau m (-[e]s;) shipbuilding

Schiff′bruch m shipwreck

schiff′brüchig adj shipwrecked

Schiff′brücke f pontoon bridge; (naut) bridge

Schiffchen [ˈʃɪfçən] n (-s;-) little ship; (mil) overseas cap; (tex) shuttle

schiffen [ˈʃɪfən] intr (vulg) pee || impers—es schifft (vulg) it's pouring

Schiffer [ˈʃɪfər] m (-s;-) seaman; skipper; (Schiffsführer) navigator

Schif′ferklavier n (coll) concertina

Schiffs′journal n log, logbook

Schiffs′junge m cabin boy

Schiffs′küche f galley

Schiffs′ladung f cargo

Schiffs′luke f hatch

Schiffs′mannschaft f crew

Schiffs′ortung f dead reckoning

Schiffs′raum m hold; tonnage

Schiffs′rumpf m hull

Schiffs′schraube f propeller

Schiffs′tau n hawser

Schiffs′taufe f christening of a ship

Schiffs′werft f shipyard, dockyard

Schiffs′winde f winch, capstan

Schiffs′zimmermann m ship's carpenter; (bei e-r Werft) shipwright

Schikane [ʃɪˈkanə] f (-;-n) chicanery; mit allen Schikanen with all the frills; (aut) fully loaded

schikanieren [ʃɪkaˈnirən] tr harass

schikanös [ʃɪkaˈnøs] adj annoying

Schi′langlauf m cross-country skiing

Schi′lauf m skiing

schi′laufen §105 intr (SEIN) ski || Schilaufen n (-s;) skiing

Schi′läufer -in §6 mf skier

Schild [ʃɪlt] m (-[e]s;-e) shield; (heral) coat of arms; etw im Schilde führen have s.th. up one's sleeve || n (-[e]s;-er) sign; road sign; nameplate; (e-s Arztes, usw.) shingle; (Etikett) label; (Mützenschirm) visor, shade

Schild′bürger m (fig) dunce

Schild′bürgerstreich m boner

Schild′drüse f thyroid gland

Schilderhaus [ˈʃɪldərhaus] n sentry box

Schil′dermaler m sign painter

schildern [ˈʃɪldərn] tr depict, describe

Schil′derung f (-;-en) description

Schild′kröte f tortoise, turtle

Schildpatt [ˈʃɪltpat] n (-[e]s;) tortoise shell, turtle shell

Schilf [ʃɪlf] n (-[e]s;-e) reed

Schilf′rohr n reed

Schi′lift m ski lift

Schiller [ˈʃɪlər] m (-s;) luster; iridescence

schillern [ˈʃɪlərn] intr be iridescent

Schil′lerwein m bright-red wine

Schilling [ˈʃɪlɪŋ] m (-s;- & -e) shilling; (Aust) schilling

Schimäre [ʃɪˈmerə] f (-;-n) chimera

Schimmel [ˈʃɪməl] m (-s;-) white horse; mildew, mold

schimmelig [ˈʃɪməlɪç] adj moldy

schimmeln [ˈʃɪməln] intr (HABEN & SEIN) get moldy

Schimmer [ˈʃɪmər] m (-s;) glimmer

schimmern [ˈʃɪmərn] intr glimmer

schimmlig [ˈʃɪmlɪç] adj moldy

Schimpanse [ʃɪmˈpanzə] m (-n;-n) chimpanzee

Schimpf [ʃɪmpf] m (-[e]s;-e) insult, abuse

schimpfen [ˈʃɪmpfən] tr scold, abuse || intr be abusive; (über acc or auf acc) curse (at), swear (at)

schimpf′lich adj disgraceful

Schimpf′name m nickname; j-m Schimpfnamen geben call s.o. names

Schimpf′wort n (-[e]s;-e & ″er) swear word

Schindaas [ˈʃɪntas] n carrion

Schindel [ˈʃɪndəl] f (-;-n) shingle

schindeln [ˈʃɪndəln] tr shingle

schinden [ˈʃɪndən] §167 tr skin; torment; oppress; exploit; Eindruck s. try to make an impression; Eintrittsgeld s. crash the gate; Zeilen s. pad the writing; Zigaretten s. bum cigarettes || ref break one's back

Schin′der m (-s;-) slave driver

Schinderei [ʃɪndəˈrai] f (-;-en) drudgery, grind

Schindluder [ˈʃɪntludər] n carrion; mit j-m S. treiben treat s.o. outrageously

Schindmähre [ˈʃɪntmerə] f old nag

Schinken [ˈʃɪŋkən] m (-s;-) ham; (hum) tome; (hum) huge painting

Schinnen [ˈʃɪnən] pl dandruff

Schippe ['∫ɪpə] *f* (-;-n) shovel, scoop; (cards) spade(s); **e-e S. machen** (or **ziehen**) pout; **j-n auf die S. nehmen** (coll) pull s.o.'s leg

schippen ['∫ɪpən] *tr & intr* shovel

Schirm [∫ɪrm] *m* (-[e]s;-e) screen; umbrella; x-ray screen; lampshade; visor; (fig) protection, shelter; (hunt) blind

Schirm'bild *n* x-ray

Schirm'bildaufnahme *f* x-ray

Schirm'dach *n* lean-to

schirmen ['∫ɪrmən] *tr* protect

Schirm'futteral *n* umbrella case

Schirm'herr *m* protector, patron

Schirm'herrin *f* protectress, patroness

Schirm'herrschaft *f* protectorate; patronage

Schirm'ständer *m* umbrella stand

Schir'mung *f* (-;-en) (elec) shielding

schirren ['∫ɪrən] *tr* harness

Schis·ma ['∫ɪsma] *n* (-;-mata [mata] & -men [mən] schism

Schi'sprung *m* ski jump

Schi'stock *m* ski pole

schizophren [sçɪtso'fren] *adj* schizophrenic

Schizophrenie [sçɪtsofre'ni] *f* (-;) schizophrenia

schlabbern ['∫labərn] *tr* lap up || *intr* (geifern) slobber; (fig) babble

Schlacht [∫laxt] *f* (-;-en) battle; **die S. bei** the battle of

schlachten ['∫laxtən] *tr* slaughter

Schlach'tenbummler *m* camp follower; (sport) fan

Schlächter ['∫leçtər] *m* (-s;-) butcher

Schlacht'feld *n* battlefield

Schlacht'flieger *m* combat pilot; close-support fighter

Schlacht'geschrei *n* battle cry

Schlacht'haus *n* slaughterhouse

Schlacht'kreuzer *m* heavy cruiser

Schlacht'opfer *n* sacrifice; (fig) victim

Schlacht'ordnung *f* battle array

Schlacht'roß *n* (hist) charger

Schlacht'ruf *m* battle cry

Schlacht'schiff *n* battleship

Schlach'tung *f* (-;-en) slaughter

Schlacke ['∫lakə] *f* (-;-n) cinder; lava; (metal) slag, dross

schlackig ['∫lakɪç] *adj* sloppy (weather)

Schlaf [∫laf] *m* (-[e]s;) sleep

Schlaf'abteil *n* sleeping compartment

Schlaf'anzug *m* pajamas

Schläfchen ['∫lefçən] *n* (-s;-) nap; **ein S. machen** take a nap

Schläfe ['∫lefə] *f* (-;-n) temple

schlafen ['∫lafən] §131 *tr* sleep || *intr* sleep; **sich s. legen** go to bed

Schla'fenszeit *f* bedtime

Schläfer -in ['∫lefər(ɪn)] §6 *mf* sleeper

schläfern ['∫lefərn] *impers*—**es schläfert mich** I'm sleepy

schlaff [∫laf] *adj* slack; limp; flabby; (locker) loose

Schlaf'gelegenheit *f* sleeping accommodations

Schlaf'kammer *f* bedroom

Schlaf'krankheit *f* sleeping sickness

schlaf'los *adj* sleepless

Schlaf'losigkeit *f* (-;) sleeplessness

Schlaf'mittel *n* sleeping pill

Schlaf'mütze *f* nightcap; (fig) sleepyhead

schläfrig ['∫lefrɪç] *adj* sleepy, drowsy

Schläf'rigkeit *f* (-;) sleepiness, drowsiness

Schlaf'rock *m* housecoat

Schlaf'saal *m* dormitory

Schlaf'sack *m* sleeping bag

Schlaf'stätte *f*, **Schlaf'stelle** *f* place to sleep

Schlaf'stube *f* bedroom

Schlaf'trunk *m* (hum) nightcap

schlaf'trunken *adj* still half-asleep

Schlaf'wagen *m* (rr) sleeping car

schlaf'wandeln *intr* (SEIN) walk in one's sleep

Schlafwandler -in ['∫lafvandlər(ɪn)] §6 *mf* sleepwalker

Schlaf'zimmer *n* bedroom

Schlag [∫lak] *m* (-[e]s;⸚e) blow; stroke; (Puls-) beat; (Faust-) punch; (Hand-) slap; (Donner-) clap; (Tauben-) loft; (Art, Sorte) kind, sort, breed; (e-s Taues) coil; (der Vögel) song; (vom Pferd) kick; (e-r Kutsche) door; (Holz-) cut; (Pendel-) swing; (agr) field; (elec) shock; (mil) scoop, ladleful; (pathol) stroke; **ein S. ins Wasser** a vain attempt; **Leute seines Schlages** the likes of him; **S. zwölf Uhr** at the stroke of twelve; **von gutem S.** of the right sort

Schlag'ader *f* artery

Schlag'anfall *m* (pathol) stroke

schlag'artig *adj* sudden, surprise; (heftig) violent || *adv* all of a sudden; with a bang

Schlag'baum *m* barrier

Schlag'besen *m* eggbeater

Schlag'bolzen *m* firing pin

Schlägel ['∫legəl] *m* (-s;-) sledge hammer

schlagen ['∫lagən] §132 *tr* hit; strike; beat; (besiegen) defeat; (strafen) spank; (Alarm) sound; (Brücke) build; (Eier) beat; (Geld) coin; (Holz) fell; (Saiten) strike; (Schlacht) fight; **die Augen zu Boden s.** cast down the eyes; **durch ein Sieb s.** strain, sift; **e-e geschlagene Stunde** (coll) a solid hour; **in die Flucht s.** put to flight; **in Fesseln s.** put in chains; **in Papier s.** wrap in paper; **Wurzel s.** take root; **zu Boden s.** knock down || *ref* come to blows; fight a duel; fence; **sich gut s.** stand one's ground; **sich s. zu side with;** **um sich s.** flail about || *intr* strike; beat; (Pferd) kick; (Vogel) sing; **mit den Flügeln s.** flap the wings; **nach j-m s.** take a swing at s.o.; (fig) be like s.o., take after s.o.

schla'gend *adj* striking, impressive; convincing; **schlagende Verbindung** dueling fraternity; **schlagende Wetter** firedamp

Schla'ger *m* (-s;-) (tolle Sache) hot item; (mus, theat) hit

Schläger ['∫legər] *m* (-s;-) beater; hitter; batter; baseball bat; golf club; tennis racket; eggbeater; mallet; (Singvogel) warbler; (Raufbold) bully

Schlägerei [ʃlɛgəˈraɪ] *f* (-;-en) fight, fighting; brawl

Schla'gerpreis *m* rock-bottom price

Schla'gersänger -in §6 *mf* pop singer

schlag'fertig *adj* quick with an answer; (*Antwort*) ready

Schlag'holz *n* club, bat

Schlag'instrument *n* percussion instrument

Schlag'kraft *f* striking power

schlag'kräftig *adj* (*Armee*) powerful; (*Beweis*) conclusive

Schlag'licht *n* strong light; glare

Schlag'loch *n* pothole

Schlag'mal *n* (baseball) home plate

Schlag'ring *m* brass knuckles

Schlag'sahne *f* whipped cream

Schlag'schatten *m* deep shadow

Schlag'seite *f* (naut) list; **S. haben** have a list; (hum) be drunk

Schlag'uhr *f* striking clock

Schlag'weite *f* striking distance

Schlag'welle *f* breaker, comber

Schlag'wetter *pl* (min) firedamp

Schlag'wort *n* (-[e]s;-̈er & -e) slogan; key word, subject (*in cataloguing*); (*Phrasendrescherei*) claptrap

Schlag'wörterkatalog *m* (libr) subject index

Schlag'zeile *f* headline

Schlag'zeug *n* percussion instruments

Schlaks [ʃlaks] *m* (-es;-e) lanky person

schlaksig [ˈʃlaksɪç] *adj* lanky

Schlamassel [ʃlaˈmasəl] *m* & *n* (-s;-) (coll) jam, pickle, mess

Schlamm [ʃlam] *m* (-[e]s;-e) mud, slime; (*im Motor*) sludge; (fig) mire

Schlamm'bad *n* mud bath

schlämmen [ˈʃlɛmən] *tr* dredge; (metal) wash

schlammig [ˈʃlamɪç] *adj* muddy

Schlampe [ˈʃlampə] *f* (-;-n) frump; (sl) slut

Schlamperei [ʃlampəˈraɪ] *f* (-;-en) slovenliness; untidiness, mess

schlampig [ˈʃlampɪç] *adj* sloppy

schlang [ʃlaŋ] *pret* of schlingen

Schlange [ˈʃlaŋə] *f* (-;-n) snake; queue, waiting line; (*Wasserschlauch*) hose; **Schlange stehen** nach line up for

schlängeln [ˈʃlɛŋəln] *ref* wind; (*Fluß*) meander; (*sich krümmen*) squirm; wriggle; (fig) worm one's way

Schlan'genbeschwörer -in §6 *mf* snake charmer

Schlan'genlinie *f* wavy line

schlank [ʃlaŋk] *adj* slender, slim; **im schlanken Trabe** at a fast clip

Schlank'heit *f* (-;) slenderness

Schlank'heitskur *f*—e—e **S. machen** diet

schlankweg [ˈʃlaŋkvɛk] *adv* flatly; downright

schlapp [ʃlap] *adj* slack, limp; flabby; (*müde*) washed out || **Schlappe** *f* (-;-n) setback; (*Verlust*) loss

schlappen [ˈʃlapən] *intr* flap; shuffle along || **Schlappen** *m* (-s;-) slipper

schlappern [ˈʃlapərn] *tr* lap up

schlapp'machen *intr* (*zusammenbrechen*) collapse; (*ohnmächtig werden*) faint; (*nicht durchhalten*) call it quits

Schlapp'schwanz *m* (coll) weakling, sissy; (*Feigling*) coward

Schlaraffenland [ʃlaˈrafənlant] *n* paradise

Schlaraffenleben [ʃlaˈrafənlebən] *n* life of Riley

schlau [ʃlau] *adj* sly; clever

Schlauch [ʃlaux] *m* (-[e]s;-̈e) hose; tube; (fig) souse; (aut) inner tube; (educ) pony

Schlauch'boot *n* rubber dinghy

schlauchen [ˈʃlauxən] *tr* drive hard; (mil) drill mercilessly

Schlauch'ventil *n* (aut) valve

Schläue [ˈʃlɔɪ·ə] *f* (-;) slyness

schlau'erweise *adv* prudently

Schlaufe [ˈʃlaufə] *f* (-;-n) loop

Schlau'kopf *m*, **Schlau'meier** *m* sly fox

schlecht [ʃlɛçt] *adj* bad, poor; **mir wird s.** I'm getting sick; **schlechter werden** get worse; **s. werden** go bad || *adv* poorly; **die Uhr geht s.** the clock is off; **s. daran sein** be badly off; **s. und recht** somehow; **s. zu sprechen sein auf** (*acc*) have it in for

schlechterdings [ˈʃlɛçtərdɪŋs] *adv* utterly, absolutely

schlecht'gelaunt *adj* in a bad mood

schlecht'hin *adv* simply, downright

schlecht'machen *tr* talk behind the back of

schlechtweg [ˈʃlɛçtvɛk] *adv* simply, downright

schlecken [ˈʃlɛkən] *tr* lick || *intr* eat sweets, nibble

Schleckerei [ʃlɛkəˈraɪ] *f* (-;-en) sweets

schleckern [ˈʃlɛkərn] *intr* have a sweet tooth || *impers*—**mich schleckert es nach** I have a yen for

Schlegel [ˈʃlegəl] *m* (-s;-) sledge hammer; (*Holz*-) mallet; (culin) leg; (mus) drumstick

schleichen [ˈʃlaɪçən] §85 *ref* & *intr* (SEIN) sneak

schlei'chend *adj* creeping; furtive; (*Krankheit*) lingering; (*Gift*) slow

Schlei'cher *m* (-s;-) sneak, hypocrite

Schleicherei [ʃlaɪçəˈraɪ] *f* (-;-en) sneaking; underhand dealing

Schleich'gut *n* contraband

Schleich'handel *m* underhand dealing; smuggling; black-marketing

Schleich'weg *m* secret path; **auf Schleichwegen** in a roundabout way

Schleier [ˈʃlaɪ·ər] *m* (-s;-) veil; haze; gauze

schlei'erhaft *adj* hazy; mysterious; (fig) veiled; **das ist mir s.** I don't know what to make of it

Schleif- [ʃlaɪf] *comb.fm.* sliding; grinding, abrasive

Schleif'bürste *f* (elec) brush

Schleife [ˈʃlaɪfə] *f* (-;-n) (*am Kleid, im Haar*) bow; (*in Schnüren*) slipknot; (*e-r Straße*) hairpin curve; (*e-s Flusses*) bend; (*Wende*-) loop; (*mit langen Bändern*) streamer; (*Rutschbahn*) slide, chute; (aer) loop

schleifen [ˈʃlaɪfən] *tr* drag; (*Kleid*) trail along; demolish; raze; (mus) slur || §88 *tr* grind; whet; polish; (*Glas, Edelstein*) cut; (mil) drill hard || §109 *intr* drag, trail

Schleif'mit'tel *n* abrasive
Schleif'papier *n* sandpaper
Schleif'rad *n* emery wheel
Schleif'stein *m* whetstone
Schleim [ʃlaɪm] *m* (-[e]s;-e) slime; mucus, phlegm
Schleim'haut *f* mucous membrane
schleimig [ˈʃlaɪmɪç] *adj* slimy; mucous
schließen [ˈʃlaɪsən] §53 *tr* split; slit; (*Federkiele*) strip ‖ *intr* wear out
Schlemm [ʃlɛm] *m* (-s;-e) (cards) slam
schlemmen [ˈʃlɛmən] *intr* carouse; gorge oneself; live high
Schlem'mer **-in** §6 *mf* glutton, guzzler; gourmet
schlem'merhaft *adj* gluttonous; (*üppig*) plentiful, luxurious
Schlem'merlokal *n* gourmet restaurant
Schlempe [ˈʃlɛmpə] *f* (-;-n) slop
schlendern [ˈʃlɛndərn] *intr* (SEIN) stroll
Schlendrian [ˈʃlɛndrɪ·an] *m* (-s;) routine
schlenkern [ˈʃlɛŋkərn] *tr* dangle, swing ‖ *intr* dangle; **mit den Armen s.** swing the arms
Schlepp- [ʃlɛp] *comb.fm.* towing, drag
Schlepp'dampfer *m* tugboat
Schlepp'dienst *m* towing service
Schleppe [ˈʃlɛpə] *f* (-;-n) train
schleppen [ˈʃlɛpən] *tr* drag; lug, tote; (*aer, naut*) tow ‖ *ref* drag along; **sich mit etw s.** be burdened with s.th.
Schlep'penkleid *n* dress with a train
Schlep'per *m* (-s;-) hauler; tractor; tugboat; tender, lighter
Schlepp'fischerei *f* trawling
Schlepp'netz *n* dragnet, dredge; trawling net
Schlepp'netzboot *n* trawler
Schlepp'schiff *n* tugboat
Schlepp'tau *n* towline; **ins S. nehmen** take in tow
Schleuder [ˈʃlɔɪdər] *f* (-;-n) sling, slingshot; (*aer*) catapult; (*mach*) centrifuge
schleudern [ˈʃlɔɪdərn] *tr* fling; sling; (*aer*) catapult ‖ *intr* (*aut*) skid; (*com*) undersell
Schleu'derpreis *m* cutrate price
Schleu'dersitz *m* (*aer*) ejection seat
schleunig [ˈʃlɔɪnɪç] *adj* speedy ‖ *adv* in all haste; (*sofort*) at once
schleunigst [ˈʃlɔɪnɪçst] *adv* as soon as possible; right away
Schleuse [ˈʃlɔɪzə] *f* (-;-n) lock, sluice, sluice way; drain, sewer
schleusen [ˈʃlɔɪzən] *tr* (*fig*) maneuver
schlich [ʃlɪç] *pret* of **schleichen** ‖ **Schlich** [ʃlɪç] *m* (-[e]s;-e) trick; **alle Schliche kennen** know all the ropes; **j-m auf die Schliche** (or **hinter j-s Schliche) kommen** be on to s.o.
schlicht [ʃlɪçt] *adj* smooth; plain
schlichten [ˈʃlɪçtən] *tr* smooth; (*fig*) settle, arbitrate
Schlich'ter **-in** §6 *mf* arbitrator
Schlich'tung *f* (-;-en) arbitration; settlement
schlief [ʃliːf] *pret* of **schlafen**
Schließe [ˈʃliːsə] *f* (-;-n) clasp; pin
schließen [ˈʃliːsən] §76 *tr* shut, close; lock; end, conclude; (*Betrieb*) shut

down; (*Bücher*) balance; (*Konto, Klammer*) close; (*Bündnis*) form; (*Frieden; Rede*) conclude; (*Kompromiß*) reach; (*Heirat*) form; (*Geschäft, Handel*) strike; (*Versammlung*) adjourn; (*Wette*) make; (*Reihen*) (*mil*) close; **ans Herz s.** press to one's heart; **aus etw. s., daß** conclude from s.th. that; **den Zug s.** (*mil*) bring up the rear; **e-n Vergleich s.** come to an agreement; **ins Herz s.** take a liking to; **kurz s.** (*elec*) short ‖ *ref* shut, close; **in sich s.** comprise, include; (*bedeuten*) imply; (*umfassen*) involve; **von sich auf andere s.** judge others by oneself ‖ *intr* shut, close; end
Schließ'fach *n* post office box; safe-deposit box
schließlich [ˈʃliːslɪç] *adj* final, eventual ‖ *adv* finally
schliff [ʃlɪf] *pp* of **schleifen** ‖ **Schliff** *m* (-[e]s;-e) polish; (*e-s Diamanten*) cut; (*fig*) polish; (*mil*) rigorous training
schlimm [ʃlɪm] *adj* bad; (*bedenklich*) serious; (*traurig*) sad; (*wund*) sore; (*eklig*) nasty; **am schlimmsten** worst; **immer schlimmer** worse and worse; **s. daran sein** be badly off
schlimmstenfalls [ˈʃlɪmstənfals] *adv* at worst
Schlinge [ˈʃlɪŋə] *f* (-;-n) loop; coil; (*fig*) trap, difficulty; (*bot*) tendril; (*hunt*) snare; (*surg*) sling; **in die S. gehen** (*fig*) fall into a trap
Schlingel [ˈʃlɪŋəl] *m* (-s;-) rascal; **fauler S.** lazybones
schlingen [ˈʃlɪŋən] §142 *tr* tie; twist; wind; wrap; gulp ‖ *ref* wind, coil; climb, creep ‖ *intr* gulp down food
Schlingerbewegung [ˈʃlɪŋərbəveɡuŋ] *f* (*naut*) roll
schlingern [ˈʃlɪŋərn] *intr* (*naut*) roll
Schlinggewächs [ˈʃlɪŋɡəvɛks] *n*, **Schlingpflanze** [ˈʃlɪŋpflantsə] *f* climber
Schlips [ʃlɪps] *m* (-es;-e) necktie
Schlitten [ˈʃlɪtən] *m* (-s;-) sled; (*an der Schreibmaschine*) carriage
schlit'tenfahren §71 *intr* go sleigh riding; **mit j-m s.** make life miserable for s.o.
schlittern [ˈʃlɪtərn] *intr* (HABEN & SEIN) slide; (*Wagen*) skid
Schlittschuh [ˈʃlɪtʃu] *m* ice skate; **S. laufen** skate, go ice-skating
Schlitt'schuhläufer **-in** §6 *mf* ice skater
Schlitz [ʃlɪts] *m* (-es;-e) slit, slot; (*Hosen-*) fly
schlitz'äugig *adj* slit-eyed, sloe-eyed
schlitzen [ˈʃlɪtsən] *tr* slit; rip
Schloß [ʃlɔs] *n* (Schlosses; Schlösser) castle; country mansion; lock; snap, clasp; **hinter S. und Riegel** behind bars; **unter S. und Riegel** under lock and key
Schloße [ˈʃlɔsə] *f* (-;-n) hailstone
Schlosser [ˈʃlɔsər] *m* (-s;-) mechanic; locksmith
Schloß'graben *m* moat
Schlot [ʃlot] *m* (-[e]s;-e & ⁓e) chimney, smokestack; (*fig*) louse

Schlot′baron m (coll) tycoon
Schlot′feger m chimney sweep
schlotterig [′ʃlɔtərɪç] adj loose, dangling; wobbly; (liederlich) slovenly
schlottern [′ʃlɔtərn] intr fit loosely; (baumeln) dangle; (zittern) tremble; (wackeln) wobble
Schlucht [ʃlʊçt] f (–;–en) gorge; ravine
schluchzen [′ʃlʊxtsən] intr sob
Schluck [ʃlʊk] m (–[e]s;–e) gulp; sip
Schluck′auf m (–s;) hiccups
schlucken [′ʃlʊkən] tr & intr gulp
Schlucker [′ʃlʊkər] m (–s;–)—**armer S.** (coll) poor devil
schlucksen [′ʃlʊksən] intr have the hiccups
schluderig [′ʃlʊdərɪç] adj slipshod
schludern [′ʃlʊdərn] intr do slipshod work
Schlummer [′ʃlʊmər] m (–s;) slumber
Schlum′merlied n lullaby
schlummern [′ʃlʊmərn] intr slumber
schlum′mernd adj latent
Schlum′merrolle f cushion
Schlund [ʃlʊnt] m (–[e]s;–e) gullet; pharynx; (e–s Vulcans) crater; (fig) abyss
Schlund′röhre f esophagus
Schlupf [ʃlʊpf] m (–[e]s;–e) hole; (elec, mach) slip
schlüpfen [′ʃlʏpfən] intr (SEIN) slip; sneak
Schlüp′fer m (–s;–) (pair of) panties; (pair of) bloomers
Schlupf′jacke f sweater
Schlupf′loch n hiding place; loophole
schlüpfrig [′ʃlʏpfrɪç] adj slippery; (obszön) off-color
Schlupf′winkel m hiding place; haunt
schlurfen [′ʃlʊrfən] intr (SEIN) shuffle
schlürfen [′ʃlʏrfən] tr slurp; lap up
Schluß [ʃlʊs] m (Schlusses; Schlüsse) end, close; (Ablauf) expiration; (Folgerung) conclusion; **S. damit!** time!; cut it out!; **S. folgt** to be concluded; **S. machen mit** put an end to; knock off from (work); break up with (s.o.); **zum S.** in conclusion
Schluß′effekt m upshot
Schlüssel [′ʃlʏsəl] m (–s;–) key; wrench; quota; code key; (fig) key, clue
Schlüs′selbein n collarbone, clavicle
Schlüs′selblume f cowslip; **helle S.** primrose
Schlüs′selbrett n keyboard
Schlüs′selbund m bunch of keys
schlüs′selfertig adj ready for occupancy
Schlüs′selloch n keyhole
Schluß′ergebnis n final result
Schluß′folge f, **Schluß′folgerung** f conclusion, deduction
Schluß′formel f complimentary close
schlüssig [′ʃlʏsɪç] adj determined; logical; (Beweis) conclusive; **sich** [dat] **noch nicht s. sein, ob** be undecided whether
Schluß′licht n (aut) taillight
Schluß′linie f (typ) dash
Schluß′rennen n (sport) final heat
Schluß′runde f (sport) finals
Schluß′schein m sales agreement

Schluß′verkauf m clearance sale
Schmach [ʃmɑx] f (–;) disgrace, shame; insult; humiliation
schmachten [′ʃmɑxtən] intr (vor dat) languish (with); **s. nach** long for
Schmachtfetzen [′ʃmɑxtfetsən] m sentimental song or book; melodrama
schmächtig [′ʃmɛçtɪç] adj scrawny
Schmachtriemen [′ʃmɑxtrimən] m—**den S. enger schnallen** (fig) tighten one's belt
schmach′voll adj disgraceful; humiliating
schmackhaft [′ʃmakhaft] adj tasty
schmähen [′ʃme·ən] tr revile, abuse; speak ill of
schmählich [′ʃmɛlɪç] adj disgraceful, scandalous; humiliating
Schmährede [′ʃmerədə] f abuse; diatribe
Schmähschrift [′ʃmeʃrɪft] f libel
schmähsüchtig [′ʃmezʏçtɪç] adj abusive
Schmä′hung f (–;–en) abuse; slander
schmal [ʃmɑl] adj narrow; slim; meager
schmälern [′ʃmelərn] tr curtail; belittle
Schmal′spurbahn f narrow-gauge railroad
Schmalz [ʃmalts] n (–[e]s;) lard, grease; (fig) schmaltz
schmalzen [′ʃmaltsən] tr lard, grease
schmalzig [′ʃmaltsɪç] adj greasy; fatty; (fig) schmaltzy
schmarotzen [ʃma′rɔtsən] intr (bei) sponge (on)
Schmarot′zer m (–s;–) sponger; (zool) parasite
schmarotzerisch [ʃma′rɔtsərɪʃ] adj sponging; (zool) parasitic(al)
Schmarre [′ʃmarə] f (–;–n) scar; scratch
schmarrig [′ʃmarɪç] adj scary
Schmatz [ʃmats] m (–es;–e) hearty kiss
schmatzen [′ʃmatsən] tr (coll) kiss loudly || intr smack one's lips
Schmaus [ʃmaus] m (–es;–e) feast; treat
schmausen [′ʃmauzən] intr (von) feast (on)
schmecken [′ʃmɛkən] tr taste, sample; (fig) stand || intr taste good; **s. nach** taste like
Schmeichelei [ʃmaiçə′lai] f (–;–en) flattery; coaxing
schmeichelhaft [′ʃmaiçəlhaft] adj flattering
schmeicheln [′ʃmaiçəln] ref—**sich** [dat] **s. zu** (inf) pride oneself on (ger) || intr be flattering; (dat) flatter
Schmeich′ler m in §6 mf flatterer
schmeichlerisch [′ʃmaiçlərɪʃ] adj flattering; complimentary; fawning
schmeißen [′ʃmaisən] §53 tr (coll) throw; (coll) manage; **e–e Runde Bier s.** set up a round of beer || ref—**mit Geld um sich s.** throw money around
Schmelz [ʃmelts] m (–es;–e) enamel; glaze; melodious ring; (fig) bloom
schmelzen [′ʃmeltsən] §133 tr melt; smelt || intr (SEIN) melt; (fig) soften

schmel′zend *adj* mellow; melodious
Schmelzerei [ˌʃmɛltsə′raɪ] *f* (-;-en) foundry
schmelz′flüssig *adj* molten
Schmelz′hütte *f* foundry
Schmelz′käse *m* soft cheese
Schmelz′ofen *m* smelting furnace
Schmelz′punkt *m* melting point
Schmelz′tiegel *m* crucible, melting pot
Schmer [ʃmer] *m & n* (-[e]s;) fat, grease
Schmer′bauch *m* (coll) potbelly
Schmerz [ʃmɛrts] *m* (-es;-en) pain, ache; **mit Schmerzen** (coll) anxiously, impatiently
schmerzen [′ʃmɛrtsən] *tr & intr* hurt
schmer′zend *adj* aching, sore
Schmer′zensgeld *n* damages (*for pain or anguish*)
Schmer′zenskind *n* problem child
schmerz′haft *adj* painful, aching
schmerz′lich *adj* painful, severe
schmerz′lindernd *adj* soothing
schmerz′los *adj* painless
Schmerz′schwelle *f* threshold of pain
Schmetterling [′ʃmɛtərlɪŋ] *m* (-s;-e) butterfly
Schmet′terlingsstil *m* (sport) butterfly
schmettern [′ʃmɛtərn] *tr* smash; **zu Boden s.** knock down || *intr* (Trompete) blare; (Vogel) warble
Schmied [ʃmit] *m* (-[e]s;-e) smith
Schmiede [′ʃmidə] *f* (-;-n) forge; blacksmith shop
Schmie′deeisen *n* wrought iron
Schmie′dehammer *m* sledge hammer
schmieden [′ʃmidən] *tr* forge; hammer; (Pläne, usw.) devise, concoct
schmiegen [′ʃmigən] *tr*—**das Kinn (die Wange) in die Hand s.** prop one's chin (or cheek) in one's hand || *ref* (**an** *acc*) snuggle up (to); **sich s. und biegen vor** (*dat*) bow and scrape before
schmiegsam [′ʃmikzam] *adj* flexible
Schmier- [ʃmir] *comb.fm.* grease, lubricating; smearing
Schmiere [′ʃmirə] *f* (-;-n) grease; lubricant; salve; (Schmutz) muck; (fig) mess; (fig) spanking; (theat) barnstormers; **S. stehen** be the lookout man
schmieren [′ʃmirən] *tr* grease, lubricate; smear; (Butter) spread; (Brot) butter; (bestechen) bribe; **j-m e-e s.** (coll) paste s.o.; **wie geschmiert** like greased lightning || *ref*—**sich** [*dat*] **die Kehle s.** (coll) wet one's whistle || *intr* scribble
Schmie′renkomödiant –in §7 *mf* (theat) barnstormer, ham
Schmiererei [ʃmirə′raɪ] *f* (-;-en) greasing; smearing; scribbling
Schmier′fink *m* scrawler; (Schmutzkerl) dirty fellow
Schmier′geld *n* (coll) bribe; (coll) hush money; (pol) slush fund
schmierig [′ʃmirɪç] *adj* smeary, greasy, oily; (Geschäfte) dirty
Schmier′käse *m* cheese spread
Schmier′mittel *n* lubricant
Schmier′pistole *f*, **Schmier′presse** *f* grease gun
Schmie′rung *f* (-;-en) lubrication

Schminke [′ʃmɪŋkə] *f* (-;-n) rouge; make-up
schminken [′ʃmɪŋkən] *tr* apply make-up to; rouge; **die Lippen s.** put on lipstick || *ref* put on make-up
Schminkunterlage [′ʃmɪŋkʊntərlagə] *f* base
Schmirgel [′ʃmɪrgəl] *m* (-s;) emery
Schmir′gelleinen *n*, **Schmir′gelleinwand** *f* emery cloth
Schmir′gelpapier *n* emery paper
Schmir′gelscheibe *f* emery wheel
Schmiß [ʃmɪs] *m* (Schmisses; Schmisse) (coll) stroke, blow; (coll) gash; (coll) dueling scar; (coll) zip
schmissig [′ʃmɪsɪç] *adj* (coll) snazzy
schmollen [′ʃmɔlən] *intr* pout, sulk
schmolz [′ʃmɔlts] *pret* of **schmelzen**
Schmorbraten [′ʃmorbratən] *m* braised meat
schmoren [′ʃmorən] *tr* braise, stew || *intr* (fig) swelter; **laß ihn s.!** let him stew!
schmuck [ʃmʊk] *adj* nice, cute; smart, dapper; (sauber) neat || **Schmuck** *m* (-[e]s;) ornament; decoration; trimmings; trinket(s); jewelry
schmücken [′ʃmʏkən] *tr* adorn; decorate, trim; (Aufsatz) embellish || *ref* spruce up, dress up
Schmuck′kästchen *n* jewel box
schmuck′los *adj* unadorned, plain
Schmuck′waren *pl* jewelry
Schmuddel [′ʃmʊdəl] *m* (-s;-) slob
schmuddelig [′ʃmʊdəlɪç] *adj* dirty
Schmuggel [′ʃmʊgəl] *m* (-s;), **Schmuggelei** [ʃmʊgə′laɪ] *f* (-;-en) smuggling
schmuggeln [′ʃmʊgəln] *tr & intr* smuggle
Schmug′gelware *f* contraband
Schmuggler –in [′ʃmʊglər(ɪn)] §6 *mf* smuggler
schmunzeln [′ʃmʊntsəln] *intr* grin || **Schmunzeln** *n* (-s;) big grin
Schmutz [ʃmʊts] *m* (-es;) dirt, filth; (Zote) smut
schmutzen [′ʃmʊtsən] *tr & intr* soil
Schmutz′fink *m* (coll) slob
Schmutz′fleck *m* stain, smudge, blotch
schmut′zig *adj* dirty
Schnabel [′ʃnabəl] *m* (-s;⸚) beak, bill; **halt den S.!** (sl) shut up!
Schna′belhieb *m* peck
schnäbeln [′ʃnebəln] *tr & intr* peck; (fig) kiss
Schnalle [′ʃnalə] *f* (-;-n) buckle; (vulg) whore
schnallen [′ʃnalən] *tr* buckle, fasten
schnalzen [′ʃnaltsən] *intr*—**mit den Fingern s.** snap one's fingers; **mit der Zunge s.** click one's tongue
schnapp [ʃnap] *interj* snap!
schnappen [′ʃnapən] *tr* snap; grab; (Dieb) nab || *intr* snap; **ins Schloß s.** snap shut; **mit den Fingern s.** snap one's fingers; **nach Luft s.** gasp for air; **s. nach** snap at
Schnapp′messer *n* jackknife
Schnapp′schuß *m* (phot) snapshot
Schnaps [ʃnaps] *m* (-es;⸚e) hard liquor
Schnaps′brennerei *f* distillery
Schnaps′bruder *m* (coll) booze hound

Schnaps'idee f (coll) crazy idea
schnarchen ['ʃnarçən] intr snore
Schnarre ['ʃnarə] f (-;-n) rattle
schnarren ['ʃnarən] intr rattle; (Säge) buzz; (Insekten) drone, buzz
schnattern ['ʃnatərn] intr (Enten) cackle; (Zähne) chatter; (fig) gab
schnauben ['ʃnaubən] intr pant, puff; (Pferd) snort; **nach Rache s.** breathe revenge; **vor Wut s.** fume with rage || ref blow one's nose
schnaufen ['ʃnaufən] intr pant; wheeze
Schnau'fer m (-s;-) (coll) deep breath
Schnauzbart ['ʃnautsbart] m mustache
Schnauze ['ʃnautsə] f (-;-n) snout, muzzle; spout; (sl) snoot; (sl) big mouth
Schnauzer ['ʃnautsər] m (-s;-) schnauzer
schnauzig ['ʃnautsɪç] adj rude
Schnecke ['ʃnɛkə] f (-;-n) snail; (Nacht-) slug; (e-r Säule) volute; spiral; (anat) cochlea; (mach) worm; (e-r Violine) (mus) scroll
Schneckenhaus (Schnek'kenhaus) n snail shell
Schneckentempo (Schnek'kentempo) n (fig) snail's pace
Schnee [ʃne] m (-s;) snow; whipped egg white
Schnee'besen m eggbeater
Schnee'brett n snow slide, avalanche
Schnee'brille f snow goggles
Schnee'decke f blanket of snow
Schnee'flocke f snowflake
Schnee'gestöber n snow flurry
schneeig ['ʃne·ɪç] adj snowy
Schnee'matsch m slush
Schnee'pflug m snowplow
Schnee'schaufel f, **Schnee'schippe** f snow shovel
Schnee'schläger m eggbeater
Schnee'schmelze f thaw
Schnee'treiben n blizzard
schneeverweht ['ʃnefervet] adj snow-bound
Schnee'verwehung f snowdrift
Schnee'wehe f snowdrift
Schneewittchen ['ʃnevɪtçən] n (-s;) Snow White
Schneid [ʃnart] m (-[e]s;) (coll) pluck; (Mut) (coll) guts
Schneid'brenner m cutting torch
Schneide ['ʃnardə] f (-;-n) (cutting) edge; (e-s Hobels) blade; **auf des Messers S.** (fig) on the razor's edge
Schnei'debrett n cutting board
Schnei'demaschine f cutter, slicer
Schnei'demühle f sawmill
schneiden ['ʃnardən] §106 tr cut; (Baum) prune; (Fingernägel) pare; (Hecke) trim; (nicht grüßen) snub; (surg) operate on; (tennis) slice; **Gesichter s.** make faces; **klein s.** cut up || ref (fig) be mistaken; (fig) be disappointed; (math) intersect; **sich in den Finger s.** cut one's finger || intr cut
Schnei'der (-s;-) m cutter; tailor
Schneiderei [ʃnardə'raɪ] f (-;-en) tailoring; (Werkstatt) tailorshop
Schnei'derin f (-;-nen) dressmaker

schneidern ['ʃnardərn] tr make || intr do tailoring; be a dressmaker
Schnei'derpuppe f dummy
Schnei'dezahn m incisor
schneidig ['ʃnardɪç] adj sharp-edged; energetic; smart, sharp
schneien ['ʃnar·ən] impers—**es schneit** it is snowing
Schneise ['ʃnarzə] f (-;-n) lane (between rows of trees)
schnell [ʃnɛl] adj fast, quick
Schnellauf (Schnell'lauf) m race; sprint; speed skating
Schnell'bahn f high-speed railroad
Schnelle ['ʃnɛlə] f (-;-n) speed; (Strom-) rapids; **auf die S.** (coll) in a hurry, very briefly
schnellen ['ʃnɛlən] tr let fly || intr (SEIN) spring, jump up; (Preise) shoot up; **mit dem Finger s.** snap one's fingers
Schnell'gang m (aut) overdrive
Schnell'hefter m (-s;-) folder, file
Schnell'imbiß m snack
Schnell'kraft f elasticity
schnellstens ['ʃnɛlstəns] adv as fast as possible
Schnell'verfahren n quick process; (jur) summary proceeding
Schnell'zug m express train
Schneppe ['ʃnɛpə] f (-;-n) spout; (sl) prostitute
schneuzen ['ʃnɔɪtsən] ref blow one's nose
schniegeln ['ʃnigəln] ref dress up; **geschniegelt und gebügelt** dressed to kill
schnipfeln ['ʃnɪpfəln] tr & intr snip
Schnippchen ['ʃnɪpçən] n—**j-m ein S. schlagen** (coll) pull a fast one on s.o.; outwit s.o.
Schnippel ['ʃnɪpəl] m & n (-s;-) chip
schnippeln ['ʃnɪpəln] tr & intr snip
schnippen ['ʃnɪpən] intr—**mit den Fingern s.** (coll) snap one's fingers
schnippisch ['ʃnɪpɪʃ] adj fresh || adv pertly; **s. erwidern** snap back
schnitt [ʃnɪt] pret of schneiden ||
Schnitt m (-[e]s;-e) cut, incision; (Kerbe) notch; (Schnitte) slice; (Quer-) profile, cross section; (Durch-) average; (e-s Anzuges) cut, style; (Gewinn) cut; (agr) reaping; (bb) edge; (cin) editing; (geom) intersection; **weicher Schnitt** (cin) dissolve
Schnitt'ansicht f sectional view
Schnitt'ball m (tennis) slice
Schnitt'blumen pl cut flowers
Schnitt'bohnen pl string beans
Schnittchen ['ʃnɪtçən] n (-s;-) thin slice; sandwich
Schnitte ['ʃnɪtə] f (-;-n) slice
Schnit'ter –in §6 mf reaper, mower
Schnitt'fläche f (geom) plane
Schnitt'holz n lumber
schnittig ['ʃnɪtɪç] adj smart-looking; (aut) streamlined
Schnitt'lauch ['ʃnɪtlaux] m (-[e]s;) (bot) chive
Schnitt'linie f (geom) secant
Schnitt'meister m (cin) editor

Schnitt′muster n pattern (of dress, etc.)

Schnitt′punkt m intersection

Schnitt′waren pl dry goods

Schnitt′wunde f cut, gash

Schnitz [ʃnɪts] m (-es;-e) cut; slice; chop; chip

Schnitzel [′ʃnɪtsəl] n (-s;-) chip; slice; shred; (Abfälle) parings; (culin) cutlet

schnitzeln [′ʃnɪtsəln] tr cut up; shred; (Holz) whittle

schnitzen [′ʃnɪtsən] tr carve

Schnit′zer m (-s;-) carver; (Fehler) blunder; grober S. boner

Schnitzerei [ʃnɪtsə′raɪ] f (-;-en) wood carving, carved work

schnob [ʃnop] pret of **schnauben**

schnodderig [′ʃnɔdərɪç] adj brash

schnöde [′ʃnøːdə] adj vile; disdainful; (Gewinn) filthy

Schnorchel [′ʃnɔrçəl] m (-s;-) snorkel

Schnörkel [′ʃnœrkəl] m (-s;-) (beim Schreiben) flourish; (fig) frills; (archit) scroll

schnorren [′ʃnɔrən] tr (coll) chisel, bum ‖ intr (coll) sponge, chisel

Schnösel [′ʃnøːzəl] m (-s;-) wise guy

schnüffeln [′ʃnyfəln] intr snoop around; (an dat) sniff (at)

Schnüff′ler -in §6 mf (coll) snoop

Schnuller [′ʃnʊlər] m (-s;-) pacifier

Schnultze [′ʃnʊltsə] f (-;-n) (coll) tear-jerker

schnultzig [′ʃnʊltsɪç] adj (coll) corny, mawkish

schnupfen [′ʃnʊpfən] tr snuff ‖ intr take snuff ‖ **Schnupfen** m (-s;-) cold; **den S. bekommen** catch a cold

Schnupftabak [′ʃnʊpftabak] m snuff

schnuppe [′ʃnʊpə] adj—das ist mir s. it's all the same to me ‖ **Schnuppe** f (-;-n) shooting star; (e-r Kerze) snuff

Schnur [ʃnuːr] f (-;-̈e & -en) string; (Band) braid; (elec) flexible cord; **nach der S.** regularly

Schnür′band [′ʃnyːrbant] n (-[e]s;-̈er) shoestring; corset lace

Schnür′chen [′ʃnyːrçən] n (-s;-) string; **etw am S. haben** have at one's fingertips; **wie am S.** like clockwork

schnüren [′ʃnyːrən] tr tie; lace; (Perlen) string ‖ ref put on a corset

schnur′gerade adj straight ‖ adv straight, as the crow flies

schnurr [ʃnʊr] interj purr!; buzz!

Schnurrbart [′ʃnʊrbart] m mustache

schnurren [′ʃnʊrən] intr (Katze) purr; (Rad) whir; (Maschine) hum; (schnorren) sponge, chisel

schnurrig [′ʃnʊrɪç] adj funny; queer

Schnürschuh [′ʃnyːrʃu] m oxford shoe

Schnürsenkel [′ʃnyːrzeŋkəl] m shoestring

schnurstracks [′ʃnuːrʃtraks] adv right away; directly; **s. entgegengesetzt** diametrically opposite; **s. losgehen auf** (acc) make a beeline for

schob [ʃop] pret of **schieben**

Schober [′ʃoːbər] m (-s;-) stack

Schock [ʃɔk] m (-[e]s;-s) shock ‖ n (-[e]s;-e) threescore

schockant [ʃɔ′kant] adj shocking

schockieren [ʃɔ′kiːrən] tr shock

schofel [′ʃoːfəl] adj mean; miserable; (schäbig) shabby; (geizig) stingy

Schöffe [′ʃœfə] m (-n;-n) juror

Schokolade [ʃokɔ′laːdə] f (-;-n) chocolate

schokoladen [ʃokɔ′laːdən] adj chocolate

Schokola′dentafel f chocolate bar

scholl [ʃɔl] pret of **schallen**

Scholle [′ʃɔlə] f (-;-n) clod; sod; stratum; ice floe; (ichth) sole; **heimatliche S.** native soil

schon [ʃon] adv already; as early as; yet, as yet; (sogar) even; (bloß) the bare, the mere; **ich komme s.!** all right, I'm coming!; **s. am folgenden Tage** on the very next day; **s. der Gedanke** the mere thought; **s. früher** before now; **s. gut!** all right!; **s. immer** always; **s. lange** long since, for a long time; **s. wieder** again

schön [ʃøn] adj beautiful; nice; (Künste) fine; (Mann) handsome; (Summe) nice round; (Geschlecht) fair; **schönen Dank!** many thanks!; **schönen Gruß an** (acc) best regards to ‖ adv nicely; **der Hund macht s.** the dog sits up and begs; **s. warm** nice and warm

schonen [′ʃoːnən] tr spare; take it easy on; treat with consideration ‖ ref take care of oneself

scho′nend adj careful; considerate

schön′färben tr gloss over

Schon′frist f period of grace

Schon′gang m (aut) overdrive

Schön′heit f (-;-en) beauty

Schön′heitsfehler m flaw

Schön′heitskönigin f beauty queen

Schön′heitspflege f beauty treatment

schön′tun §154 intr (dat) flatter; (dat) flirt (with)

Scho′nung f (-;-en) care, careful treatment; mercy; consideration; tree nursery; wild-game preserve

scho′nungslos adj unsparing; merciless; relentless

scho′nungsvoll adj considerate

Schon′zeit f (hunt) closed season

Schopf [ʃɔpf] m (-[e]s;-̈e) tuft of hair; (orn) crest

schöpfen [′ʃœpfən] tr draw; bail; scoop, ladle; (frische Luft) breathe; (Mut) take; **Verdacht s.** become suspicious; **wieder Atem** (or **Luft**) **s.** (fig) breathe freely again

Schöp′fer m (-s;-) creator; author; composer; painter; sculptor; dipper, ladle

schöpferisch [′ʃœpfərɪʃ] adj creative

Schöp′ferkraft f creative power

Schöpf′kelle f scoop

Schöpf′löffel m ladle

Schöp′fung f (-;-en) creation

Schoppen [′ʃɔpən] m (-s;-) pint; glass of beer, glass of wine

schor [ʃor] pret of **scheren**

Schorf [ʃɔrf] m (-[e]s;-e) scab

Schornstein [′ʃɔrnʃtaɪn] m chimney; smokestack

Schorn′steinfeger m chimney sweeper

Schoß [ʃos] m (Schosses; Schosse)

sprout ‖ [ʃos] *m* (-es;-̈e) lap; womb;
(fig) bosom; **die Hände in den S.
legen** cross one's arms; (fig) be idle
Schößling ['ʃœslɪŋ] *m* (-s;-e) shoot
Schote ['ʃotə] *f* (-;-n) pod, shell
Schotte ['ʃotə] *m* (-n;-n) Scotchman
‖ *f* (-;-n) (naut) bulkhead
Schotter ['ʃotər] *m* (-s;-) gravel; macadam, crushed stone; (rr) ballast
Schottin ['ʃotɪn] *f* (-;-nen) Scotch-
woman
schottisch ['ʃotɪʃ] *adj* Scotch
schraffieren [ʃra'firən] *tr* hatch
schräg [ʃrek] *adj* oblique; (*abfallend*)
slanting, sloping; diagonal ‖ *adv*
obliquely; **s. gegenüber von** diagonally across from; **s. geneigt** sloping
Schräg'linie *f* diagonal
schrak [ʃrak] *pret of* **schrecken**
Schramme ['ʃramə] *f* (-;-n) scratch,
abrasion; scar
schrammen ['ʃramən] *tr* scratch; skin
Schrank [ʃraŋk] *m* (-[e]s;-̈e) closet
Schranke ['ʃraŋkə] *f* (-;-n) barrier;
(fig) bounds, limit; (jur) bar; (rr)
gate; (sport) starting gate
schran'kenlos *adj* boundless; exagger-
ated
Schran'kenwärter *m* (rr) signalman
Schrank'fach *n* compartment
Schrank'koffer *m* wardrobe trunk
Schrapnell [ʃrap'nɛl] *n* (-s;-e & -s)
shrapnel, piece of shrapnel
Schraubdeckel ['ʃraupdekəl] *m* screw-
on cap
Schraube ['ʃraubə] *f* (-;-n) screw;
bolt; (aer, naut) propeller
schrauben ['ʃraubən] *tr* screw; **in die
Höhe s.** raise ‖ *ref*—**sich in die
Höhe s.** circle higher and higher
Schrau'benflügel *m* propeller blade
Schrau'bengang *m*, **Schrau'bengewinde**
n thread (of a screw)
Schrau'benmutter *f* (-;-n) nut
Schrau'benschlüssel *m* wrench; ver-
stellbarer S. monkey wrench
Schrau'benstrahl *m*, **Schrau'benstrom**
m (aer) slipstream
Schraubenzieher ['ʃraubəntsi·ər] *m*
(-s;-) screwdriver
Schraubstock ['ʃraupʃtɔk] *m* vice
Schrebergarten ['ʃrebərgartən] *m* gar-
den plot (*at edge of town*)
Schreck [ʃrek] *m* (-[e]s;-e) var of
Schrecken
Schreck'bild *n* frightful sight; boogey-
man
schrecken ['ʃrekən] *tr* frighten, scare
‖ **Schrecken** *m* (-s;-) fright, fear
Schreckensbotschaft (Schrek'kensbot-
schaft) *f* alarming news
Schreckensherrschaft (Schrek'kensherr-
schaft) *f* reign of terror
Schreckenskammer (Schrek'kenskam-
mer) *f* chamber of horrors
Schreckensregiment (Schrek'kensregi-
ment) *n* reign of teror, terrorism
Schreckenstat (Schrek'kenstat) *f* atrocity
schreck'haft *adj* timid
schreck'lich *adj* frightful, terrible
Schrecknis ['ʃreknɪs] *n* (-ses;-se) horror

Schreck'schuß *m* warning shot
Schreck'sekunde *f* reaction time
Schrei [ʃraɪ] *m* (-[e]s;-e) cry, shout;
letzter S. latest fashion
Schreib- [ʃraɪp] *comb.fm.* writing
Schreib'art *f* style; spelling
Schreib'bedarf *m* stationery
Schreib'block *m* writing pad, note pad
schreiben ['ʃraɪbən] §62 *tr* write; spell;
type; **ins Konzept s.** make a rough
draft of; **ins reine s.** make a clean
copy; **Noten s.** copy music ‖ *ref*
spell one's name ‖ *intr* write; spell;
type ‖ **Schreiben** *n* (-s;-) writing;
(com) letter
Schrei'ber *m* (-s;-) writer; clerk; re-
cording instrument, recorder
schreib'faul *adj* too lazy to write
Schreib'feder *f* pen
Schreib'fehler *m* slip of the pen
Schreib'heft *n* copybook, exercise book
Schreib'mappe *f* portfolio
Schreib'maschine *f* typewriter; **mit der
S. geschrieben** typed; **S. schreiben**
type
Schreib'maschinenfarbband *n* (-[e]s;
-̈er) typewriter ribbon
Schreib'maschinenschreiber -in §6 *mf*
typist
Schreib'maschinenschrift *f* typescript
Schreib'materialien *pl*, **Schreib'papier**
n stationery
Schreib'schrift *f* (typ) script
Schreib'stube *f* (mil) orderly room
Schreib'tisch *m* desk
Schrei'bung *f* (-;-en) spelling
Schreib'unterlage *f* desk pad
Schreib'waren *pl* stationery
Schreib'warenhandlung *f* stationery
store
Schreibweise *f* style; spelling
Schreib'zeug *n* writing materials
schreien ['ʃraɪ·ən] §135 *tr* cry, shout,
scream, howl ‖ *ref*—**sich heiser s.**
shout oneself hoarse; **sich tot s.** yell
one's lungs out ‖ *intr* cry, shout,
scream, howl; (*Esel*) bray; (*Eule*)
screech; (*Schwein*) squeal; **s. nach**
clamor for; **s. über** (*acc*) cry out
against; **s. vor** (*dat*) shout for (*joy*);
cry out in (*pain*); roar with (*laughter*) ‖ **Schreien** *n* (-s;) shouting; **das
ist zum S.!** that's a scream!
schrei'end *adj* shrill; (*Farbe*) loud;
(*Unrecht*) flagrant
Schrei'hals *m* (coll) crybaby
Schrei'krampf *m* crying fit
Schrein [ʃraɪn] *m* (-[e]s;-e) reliquary
Schreiner ['ʃraɪnər] *m* (-s;-) carpenter; cabinetmaker
schreiten ['ʃraɪtən] §86 *intr* (SEIN)
step; stride; (*bei Abstimmung*) s. proceed to vote; **zur Tat s.** proceed to
act
schrie [ʃri] *pret of* **schreien**
schrieb [ʃrip] *pret of* **schreiben**
Schrift [ʃrɪft] *f* (-;-en) writing; handwriting; letter, character; document;
book; publication; periodical; (*auf
Münzen*) legend; (typ) type, font;
die Heilige S. Holy Scripture; **nach
der S. sprechen** speak standard German

Schrift′art f type, font
Schrift′auslegung f exegesis
Schrift′bild n type face
Schrift′deutsch n literary German
Schrift′führer -in §6 mf secretary
Schrift′leiter -in §6 mf editor
schrift′lich adj written || adv in writing; s. wiedergeben transcribe
Schrift′satz m (jur) brief; (typ) composition
Schrift′setzer m typesetter
Schrift′sprache f literary language
Schriftsteller -in [′ʃrɪft/tɛlər(ɪn)] §6 mf writer, author
Schrift′stück n piece of writing; document
Schrifttum [′ʃrɪftum] n (-s;) literature
Schrift′verkehr m, Schrift′wechsel m correspondence
Schrift′zeichen n letter, character
schrill [ʃrɪl] adj shrill
schrillen [′ʃrɪlən] intr ring loudly
schritt [ʃrɪt] pret of schreiten ||
Schritt m (-[e]s;-e) step; pace; stride; (e-r Hose) crotch; (fig) step
Schritt′macher m pacemaker
schritt′weise adv gradually; step by step
schroff [ʃrɔf] adj steep; rugged; rude, uncouth; rough, harsh; (Ablehnung, Widerspruch) flat
schröpfen [′ʃrœpfən] tr (fig) milk, fleece; (med) bleed, cup
Schrot [ʃrot] m & n (-[e]s;-e) scrap; (Getreide) crushed grain, grits; (zum Schießen) buckshot
Schrot′brot n whole grain bread
Schrot′flinte f shotgun
Schrot′korn n, Schrot′kugel f pellet
Schrott [ʃrɔt] m (-[e]s;) scrap metal
Schrott′platz m junk yard
schrubben [′ʃrubən] tr scrub
Schrulle [′ʃrulə] f (-;-n) (coll) nutty idea
schrul′lenhaft, schrullig [′ʃrulɪç] adj whimsical
schrumpelig [′ʃrumpəlɪç] adj crumpled; wrinkled, shriveled
schrumpeln [′ʃrumpəln] intr shrivel
schrumpfen [′ʃrumpfən] intr (SEIN) shrink; shrivel; (path) atrophy
Schub [ʃup] m (-[e]s;ːe) shove, push; batch; (phys) thrust
Schub′fach n drawer
Schub′karre f, Schub′karren m wheelbarrow
Schub′kasten m drawer
Schub′kraft f thrust
Schub′lade f drawer
Schub′leistung f thrust
Schubs [ʃups] m (-es;-e) (coll) shove
schubsen [′ʃupsən] tr & intr shove
Schub′stange f (aut) connecting rod
schüchtern [′ʃʏçtərn] adj shy, bashful
schuf [ʃuf] pret of schaffen
Schuft [ʃuft] m (-[e]s;-e) cad
schuften [′ʃuftən] intr drudge, slave
Schufterei [ʃuftə′raɪ] f (-;) drudgery; (Schuftigkeit) meanness
schuftig [′ʃuftɪç] adj (fig) rotten
Schuh [ʃu] m (-[e]s;-e) shoe; boot
Schuh′band n (-[e]s;ːer) shoestring

Schuhflicker [′ʃuflɪkər] m (-s;-) shoe repairman, shoemaker
Schuh′krem m shoe polish
Schuh′laden m shoe store
Schuh′leisten m last
Schuh′löffel m shoehorn
Schuh′macher m shoemaker
Schuhplattler [′ʃuplatlər] m (-s;-) Bavarian folk dance
Schuh′putzer m shoeshine boy
Schuh′sohle f sole
Schuhspanner [′ʃuʃpanər] m (-s;-) shoetree
Schuh′werk n footwear
Schuh′wichse f shoe polish
Schuh′zeug n footwear
Schul- [ʃul] comb.fm. school
Schul′amt n school board
Schul′arbeit f homework; (Aust) classroom work
Schul′aufsicht f school board
Schul′bank m (-;ːe) school desk
Schul′behörde f school board; board of education
Schul′beispiel n (fig) test case
Schul′besuch m attendance at school
Schul′bildung f schooling, education
schuld [ʃult] adj at fault, to blame ||
Schuld f (-;-en) debt; fault; guilt
schuld′bewußt adj conscious of one's guilt
schulden [′ʃuldən] tr owe
schuld′haft adj culpable || Schuld′haft f imprisonment for debt
Schul′diener m school janitor
schuldig [′ʃuldɪç] adj guilty; responsible; j-m etw s. sein owe s.o. s.th. ||
Schuldige §5 mf culprit; guilty party
Schul′digkeit f (-;-en) duty, obligation; seine S. tun do one's duty
Schul′direktor -in §7 mf principal
schuld′los adj innocent
Schuld′losigkeit f (-;) innocence
Schuldner -in [′ʃuldnər(ɪn)] §6 mf debtor
Schuld′schein m promissory note, IOU
Schuld′spruch m verdict of guilty
Schuld′verschreibung f promissory note, IOU; (Obligation) bond
Schule [′ʃulə] f (-;-n) school; auf der S. in school; S. machen (fig) set a precedent; von der S. abgehen quit school
schulen [′ʃulən] tr train; (pol) indoctrinate
Schüler [′ʃylər] m (-s;-) pupil (in grammar school or high school); trainee; (Jünger) disciple
Schü′leraustausch m student exchange
Schülerin [′ʃylərɪn] f (-;-nen) pupil
Schul′film m educational film
Schul′flug m training flight
schul′frei adj—schulfreier Tag holiday; s. haben have off
Schul′gelände n school grounds; campus
Schul′geld n tuition
Schul′gelehrsamkeit f book learning
Schul′hof m schoolyard, playground
Schul′kamerad m school chum
Schul′lehrer -in §6 mf schoolteacher
Schul′mappe f schoolbag
Schul′meister m schoolmaster; pedant
schul′meistern intr criticize

Schul'ordnung f school regulation
Schul'pflicht f compulsory school attendance
schul'pflichtig adj of school age; **schulpflichtiges Alter** school age
Schul'plan m curriculum
Schul'ranzen m schoolbag
Schul'rat m (-[e]s;-̈e) (educ) superintendent
Schul'reise f field trip
Schul'schiff n training ship
Schul'schluß m close of school
Schul'schwester f teaching nun
Schul'stunde f lesson, period
Schul'tasche f schoolbag
Schulter ['ʃʊltər] f (-;-n) shoulder
Schul'terblatt n shoulder blade
schul'terfrei adj off-the-shoulder; (trägerfrei) strapless
schultern ['ʃʊltərn] tr shoulder
Schul'terstück n epaulet
Schul'unterricht m instruction; schooling; **im S.** in school
Schul'wesen n school system
Schul'zeugnis n report card
Schul'zimmer n classroom
Schul'zwang m compulsory education
schummeln ['ʃʊməln] intr (coll) cheat
schund [ʃʊnt] pret of **schinden** ‖ **Schund** m (-[e]s;) junk, trash
Schund'literatur f trashy literature
Schund'roman m dime novel
Schupo ['ʃupo] m (-s;-s) (Schutzpolizist) policeman, copy ‖ f (-;) (Schutzpolizei) police
Schuppe [ʃʊpə] f (-;-n) scale; **Schuppen** dandruff
schuppen ['ʃʊpən] tr scale; scrape ‖ **Schuppen** m (-s;-) shed; (aer) hangar; (aut) garage
schuppig ['ʃʊpɪç] adj scaly, flaky
Schups [ʃʊps] m (-es;-e) shove
schupsen ['ʃʊpsən] tr shove
Schüreisen ['ʃyraɪzən] n poker
schüren ['ʃyrən] tr poke, stir; (fig) stir up, foment
schürfen ['ʃyrfən] tr scratch, scrape; dig for ‖ intr (nach) prospect (for)
schurigeln ['ʃurigəln] tr (coll) bully
Schurke ['ʃʊrkə] m (-n;-n) bum, punk
Schur'kenstreich m, **Schur'kentat** f, **Schurkerei** [ʃʊrkə'raɪ] f (-;-en) mean trick
schurkisch ['ʃʊrkɪʃ] adj mean, low-down
Schürze ['ʃyrtsə] f (-;-n) apron
schürzen ['ʃyrtsən] tr tuck up; tie
Schür'zenband n (-[e]s;-̈er) apron
Schür'zenjäger m skirt chaser, wolf
Schuß [ʃus] m (Schusses; Schüsse) shot; (Ladung) round; (Schußwunde) gunshot wound; (rasche Bewegung) rush; (Brot) batch; (bot) shoot; (culin) dash; (sport) shot; **blinder S.** blank; **e-n S. abgeben** fire a shot; **ein S. ins Blaue** a wild shot; **ein S. ins Schwarze** a bull's-eye; **im S. haben** have under control; **im vollen S.** in full swing; **in S. bekommen** get going; **in S. bringen** get (s.th.) going; **j-m vor den S. kommen** come within s.o.'s range; (fig) come across s.o.; **scharfer S.**

live round; **weit vom S.** out of harm's way
Schüssel ['ʃysəl] f (-;-n) bowl; (fig) dish
schuß'fest, schuß'sicher adj bulletproof
Schuß'waffe f firearm
Schuß'weite f range
Schuster ['ʃustər] m (-s;-) shoemaker; (fig) bungler
schustern ['ʃustərn] intr bungle
Schutt [ʃut] m (-es;) rubbish; rubble
Schutt'abladeplatz m dump
Schüttboden ['ʃytbodən] m granary
Schüttelfrost ['ʃytəlfrost] m shivers
schütteln ['ʃytəln] tr shake; **j-m die Hand s.** shake hands with s.o.
schütten ['ʃytən] tr pour, spill ‖ impers **—es schüttet** it is pouring
Schutz [ʃuts] m (-es;) protection, defense; (Obdach) shelter; (Deckung) cover; (Schirm) screen; (Schutzgeleit) safeguard; **zu S. und Trutz** defensive and offensive
Schutz'brille f safety goggles
Schütze ['ʃytsə] m (-n;-n) marksman, shot; (astr) Sagittarius; (mil) rifleman ‖ f (-;-n) sluice gate
schützen ['ʃytsən] tr (gegen) protect (against), defend (against); (vor dat) preserve (from) ‖ **Schützen** m (-s;-) (tex) shuttle
schüt'zend adj protective; tutelary
Schutz'engel m guardian angel
Schüt'zengraben m (mil) foxhole
Schüt'zenkompanie f rifle company
Schüt'zenkönig m crack shot
Schüt'zenloch n (mil) foxhole
Schüt'zenmine f anti-personnel mine
Schutz'geleit n escort; safe conduct; (aer) air cover; (nav) convoy
Schutz'glocke f (aer) umbrella
Schutz'gott m, **Schutz'göttin** f tutelary deity
Schutz'haft f protective custody
Schutzheilige §5 mf patron saint
Schutz'herr m protector; patron
Schutz'herrin f protectress; patroness
Schutz'impfung f immunization
Schutz'insel f traffic island
Schützling ['ʃytslɪŋ] m (-s;-e) ward
schutz'los adj defenseless
Schutz'mann m (-[e]s;-̈er & -leute) policeman
Schutz'marke f trademark
Schutz'mittel n preservative; preventive
Schutz'patron –in §8 mf patron saint
Schutz'polizei f police
Schutz'polizist m policeman, cop
Schutz'scheibe f (aut) windshield
Schutz'staffel f SS troops
Schutz'umschlag m dust jacket
Schutz- und-Trutz-'Bündnis f defensive and offensive alliance
Schutz'waffe f defensive weapon
Schutz'zoll m protective tariff
Schwabe ['ʃvabə] m (-n;-n) Swabian
Schwaben ['ʃvabən] n (-s;) Swabia
Schwäbin ['ʃvebɪn] f (-;-nen) Swabian
schwäbisch ['ʃvebɪʃ] adj Swabian; **das Schwäbische Meer** Lake Constance
schwach [ʃvax] adj (schwächer ['ʃvɛçər]; schwächste ['ʃvɛçstə] §9)

weak; (*Hoffnung, Ton, Licht*) faint; (*unzureichend*) scanty; sparse; (*armselig*) poor

Schwäche ['∫veçə] *f* (–;–n) weakness

Schwach'kopf *m* dunce; sap, dope

schwächlich ['∫veçlıç] *adj* feeble, delicate

Schwächling ['∫veçlıŋ] *m* (–s;–e) weakling

schwach'sinnig *adj* feeble-minded || **Schwachsinnige** §5 *mf* dimwit, moron

Schwach'strom *m* low-voltage current

Schwaden ['∫vadən] *m* (–s;–) swath; cloud (*of smoke, etc.*)

Schwadron [∫va'dron] *f* (–;–en) squadron

schwadronieren [∫vadrɔ'nirən] *intr* (coll) brag

schwafeln ['∫vafəln] *intr* talk nonsense

Schwager ['∫vagər] *m* (–s;⁼) brother-in-law

Schwägerin ['∫vegərın] *f* (–;–nen) sister-in-law

Schwalbe ['∫valbə] *f* (–;–n) swallow

Schwal'bennest *n* (aer) gun turret

Schwal'benschwanz *m* (*Frack*) tails; (carp) dovetail

Schwall [∫val] *m* (–[e]s;–e) flood; (*von Worten*) torrent

schwamm [∫vam] *pret of* **schwimmen** || **Schwamm** *m* (–[e]s;⁼e) sponge; mushroom; fungus; dry rot; **S. darüber!** skip it!

schwammig ['∫vamıç] *adj* spongy

Schwan [∫van] *m* (–[e]s;⁼e) swan

schwand [∫vant] *pret of* **schwinden**

schwang [∫vaŋ] *pret of* **schwingen**

schwanger ['∫vaŋər] *adj* pregnant

schwängern ['∫veŋərn] *tr* make pregnant; (fig) impregnate

Schwan'gerschaft *f* (–;–en) pregnancy

Schwan'gerschaftsverhütung *f* contraception

schwank [∫vaŋk] *adj* flexible; unsteady || **Schwank** *m* (–[e]s;⁼e) prank; joke; funny story; (theat) farce

schwanken ['∫vaŋkən] *intr* stagger; (*schaukeln*) rock; (*schlingern*) roll; (*stampfen*) pitch; (*Flamme*) flicker; (*pendeln*) oscillate; (*vibrieren*) vibrate; (*wellenartig*) undulate; (*zittern*) shake; (*Preise*) fluctuate; (*zögern*) vacillate, hesitate

Schwanz [∫vants] *m* (–es;⁼e) tail; (*Gefolge*) train; (vulg) pecker; **kein S.** not a living soul; **mit dem S. wedeln** (or **wippen**) wag its tail

schwänzeln ['∫ventsəln] *intr* wag its tail; **s. um** fawn on

schwänzen ['∫ventsən] *tr*—**die Schule s.** play hooky from school; **e-e Stunde s.** cut a class || *intr* play hooky

schwappen ['∫vapən] *intr* slosh around; **s. über** (*acc*) spill over

schwapps [∫vaps] *interj* slap!; splash!

Schwäre ['∫verə] *f* (–;–n) abscess

schwären ['∫verən] *intr* fester

Schwarm [∫varm] *m* (–[e]s;⁼e) swarm; flock, herd; (*von Fischen*) school; (fig) idol; (fig) craze; (aer) flight of five aircraft; **sie ist mein S.** (coll) I have a crush on her

schwärmen ['∫vermən] *intr* swarm; stray; daydream; go out on the town; **s. für** (or **über** *acc* or **von**) rave about

Schwär'mer *m* (–s;–) enthusiast; reveler; daydreamer; firecracker; (religious) fanatic; (ent) hawk moth

Schwärmerei [∫vermə'raı] *f* (–;–en) enthusiasm; daydreaming; revelry; fanaticism

schwärmerisch ['∫vermorı∫] *adj* enthusiastic; gushy; fanatic; fanciful

Schwarte ['∫vartə] *f* (–;–n) rind, skin; (coll) old book

schwarz [∫varts] *adj* black; dark; (*ungesetzlich*) illegal; (*schmutzig*) dirty; (*düster*) gloomy; (*von der Sonne*) tanned; **schwarze Kunst** black magic; **schwarzes Brett** bulletin board || *adv* illegally

Schwarz'arbeit *f* moonlighting; non-union work; illicit work

Schwarz'brenner *m* moonshiner

Schwärze ['∫vertsə] *f* (–;–n) blackness; darkness; printer's ink

schwärzen ['∫vertsən] *tr* darken; blacken

schwarz'fahren §71 *intr* (SEIN) drive without a license; ride without a ticket

Schwarz'fahrer –in §6 *mf* unlicensed driver; rider without a ticket

Schwarz'fahrt *f* joy ride; ride without a ticket

Schwarz'handel *m* black-marketing

Schwarz'händler –in §6 *mf* black marketeer; (*mit Eintrittskarten*) scalper

schwärzlich ['∫vertslıç] *adj* blackish

Schwarz'markt *m* black market

Schwarz'seher –in §6 *mf* pessimist

Schwarz'sender *m* illegal transmitter

schwatzen ['∫vatsən], **schwätzen** ['∫vetsən] *tr* (coll) talk || *intr* (coll) yap, talk nonsense; (coll) gossip

Schwät'zer –in §6 *mf* windbag; gossip

schwatz'haft *adj* talkative

Schwatz'maul *n* blabber mouth

Schwebe ['∫vebə] *f* (–;) suspense; **in der S. sein** be undecided; be pending

Schwe'bebahn *f* cablecar

Schwe'beflug *m* hovering, soaring

schweben ['∫vebən] *intr* (HABEN & SEIN) be suspended, hang; float; (*Hubschrauber*) hover; (*Segelflugzeug*) soar; glide; (fig) waver, be undecided; **in Gefahr s.** be in danger; **in Ungewißheit s.** be in suspense

Schwede ['∫vedə] *m* (–n;–n) Swede

Schweden ['∫vedən] *n* (–s;) Sweden

Schwedin ['∫vedın] *f* (–;–nen) Swede

schwedisch ['∫vedı∫] *adj* Swedish

Schwefel ['∫vefəl] *m* (–s;) sulfur

Schwe'felsäure *f* sulfuric acid

Schweif [∫vaıf] *m* (–[e]s;–e) tail; (fig) train

schweifen ['∫vaıfən] *tr* curve; (*spülen*) rinse || *intr* (SEIN) roam, wander

Schweigegeld ['∫vaıgəgelt] *n* hush money

schweigen ['∫vaıgən] §148 *intr* be silent, keep silent; (*aufhören*) stop; **ganz zu s. von** to say nothing of; **s. zu** to make no reply to

schwei'gend adj silent || adv in silence
schweigsam ['ʃvaɪkzəm] adj taciturn
Schwein [ʃvaɪn] n (-[e]s;-e) pig, hog; **S. haben** be lucky, have luck
Schwei'nebraten m roast pork
Schwei'nefleisch n pork
Schwei'nehund m (pej) filthy swine
Schwei'nekoben m pigsty, pig pen
Schweinerei [ʃvaɪnə'raɪ] f (-;-en) mess; dirty business
Schwei'nerippchen pl pork chops
Schwei'newirtschaft f dirty mess
Schweins'kotelett n pork chop
Schweiß [ʃvaɪs] m (-es;) perspiration
schweißen ['ʃvaɪsən] tr weld || intr begin to melt, fuse; (hunt) bleed
Schwei'ßer m §6 mf welder
Schweißfüße ['ʃvaɪsfysə] pl sweaty feet
schweißig ['ʃvaɪsɪç] adj sweaty; (hunt) bloody
Schweiß'perle f bead of sweat
Schweiz [ʃvaɪts] f (-;)—**die S.** Switzerland
Schwei'zer m Swiss; dairyman
schweizerisch ['ʃvaɪtsərɪʃ] adj Swiss
schwelen ['ʃvelən] intr smolder
schwelgen ['ʃvelgən] intr feast; **s. in** (dat) (fig) revel in; wallow in
Schwelgerei [ʃvelgə'raɪ] f (-;-en) feasting, carousing
schwelgerisch ['ʃvelgərɪʃ] adj riotous; luxurious
Schwelle ['ʃvelə] f (-;-n) doorstep; (fig) verge; (psychol) threshold; (rr) railroad tie
schwellen ['ʃvelən] §119 tr swell || intr (SEIN) swell; (Wasser) rise; (anwachsen) increase
Schwel'lung f (-;-en) swelling
Schwemme ['ʃvemə] f (-;-n) watering place; (coll) taproom; (com) glut
schwemmen ['ʃvemən] tr wash off, rinse; (Vieh) water; (Holz) float
Schwengel ['ʃveŋəl] m (-s;-) pump handle; (e-r Glocke) hammer
schwenkbar ['ʃveŋkbɑr] adj rotating
schwenken ['ʃveŋkən] tr swing; shake; (drohend) brandish; (Hut) wave; (spülen) rinse || intr (SEIN) turn; swivel, pivot; (Geschütz) traverse; (mil) wheel; (pol) change sides
Schwen'kung f (-;-en) turn; wheeling, traversing; (fig) change of mind
schwer [ʃver] adj heavy; difficult, hard; serious; (schwerfällig) ponderous; (Strafe) severe; (Wein) strong; (Speise) rich; (unbeholfen) clumsy; (Kompanie) heavy-weapons; **drei Pfund s. sein** weigh three pounds; **schweres Geld bezahlen** pay a stiff price || adv hard; with difficulty; (coll) very
Schwere ['ʃverə] f (-;) weight; seriousness; (des Weines) body; difficulty; significance; (phys) gravity
schwe'relos adj weightless
schwer'fällig adj heavy; clumsy, slow
Schwer'gewicht n heavyweight class; (Nachdruck) emphasis
Schwergewichtler -in ['ʃvergəvɪçtlər (ɪn)] §6 mf (sport) heavyweight
schwer'hörig adj hard of hearing

Schwer'industrie f heavy industry
Schwer'kraft f gravity
schwer'lich adv hardly
Schwer'mut f melancholy, depression
schwer'mütig adj melancholy, depressed
schwer'nehmen §116 tr take hard
Schwer'punkt m center of gravity; crucial point, focal point
Schwert [ʃvert] n (-[e]s;-er) sword
Schwer'verbrecher -in §6 mf felon
schwer'verdient adj hard-earned
schwer'wiegend adj weighty
Schwester ['ʃvestər] f (-;-n) sister; nurse; nun
Schwe'sternhelferin f nurse's aide
schwieg [ʃvik] pret of schweigen
Schwieger- ['ʃvigər] comb.fm. -in-law
Schwie'germutter f mother-in-law
Schwie'gersohn m son-in-law
Schwie'gertochter f daughter-in-law
Schwie'gervater m father-in-law
Schwiele ['ʃvilə] f (-;-n) callus
schwielig ['ʃvilɪç] adj callous
schwierig ['ʃvirɪç] adj hard, difficult
Schwie'rigkeit f (-;-en) difficulty
Schwimm- [ʃvɪm] comb.fm. swimming
Schwimm'anstalt f, **Schwimm'bad** n, **Schwimm'bassin** n, **Schwimm'becken** n swimming pool
schwimmen ['ʃvɪmən] §136 intr (HABEN & SEIN) swim; float
Schwimm'gürtel m life belt
Schwimm'haut f web
Schwimm'hose f bathing trunks
Schwimm'kraft f buoyancy
Schwimm'panzer m amphibious tank
Schwimm'weste f life jacket
Schwindel ['ʃvɪndəl] m (-s;-) dizziness; swindle, gyp; (Unsinn) bunk; (pathol) vertigo; **der ganze S.** the whole caboodle
Schwin'delanfall m dizzy spell
Schwin'delfirma f fly-by-night
schwin'delhaft adj fraudulent, bogus
schwindelig ['ʃvɪndəlɪç] adj dizzy
schwindeln ['ʃvɪndəln] tr swindle || intr fib || impers—**mir schwindelt** I feel dizzy
Schwin'delunternehmen n fly-by-night
schwinden ['ʃvɪndən] §59 intr (SEIN) dwindle; decline; (Farbe) fade
Schwind'ler -in §6 mf swindler; fibber
schwindlig ['ʃvɪntlɪç] adj dizzy
Schwindsucht ['ʃvɪntzuçt] f tuberculosis
Schwinge ['ʃvɪŋə] f (-;-n) wing; fan; winnow; (poet) pinion
schwingen ['ʃvɪŋən] §142 tr swing; wave; brandish; (agr) winnow; (tex) swingle || ref vault; soar || intr swing; sway; oscillate; vibrate
Schwin'ger m (-s;-) oscillator; (box) haymaker
Schwin'gung f (-;-en) oscillation; vibration; swinging
Schwips [ʃvɪps] m—**e-n S. haben** (coll) be tight, be tipsy
schwirren ['ʃvirən] intr (HABEN & SEIN) whiz, whir; buzz; (Gerüchte) fly
Schwitzbad ['ʃvɪtsbɑt] n Turkish bath
schwitzen ['ʃvɪtsən] tr & intr sweat

schwoll [ʃvɔl] *pret of* **schwellen**
schwor [ʃvoːr] *pret of* **schwören**
schwören [ˈʃvøːrən] §137 *tr & intr* swear; **auf** j-n (or etw) s. swear by s.o. (or s.th.)
schwul [ʃvuːl] *adj* (vulg) homosexual
schwül [ʃvyːl] *adj* sultry, muggy
Schwulität [ʃvuːliˈtɛt] *f* (-;-en) trouble
Schwulst [ʃvulst] *m* (-es;̈e) bombast
schwülstig [ˈʃvylstɪç] *adj* bombastic
schwummerig [ˈʃvumərɪç] *adj* (coll) shaky
Schwund [ʃvunt] *m* (-[e]s;) dwindling; shrinkage; loss; leakage; (*des Haares*) falling out; (rad) fading; (pathol) atrophy
Schwung [ʃvuŋ] *m* (-[e]s;̈e) swing; vault; (*Tatkraft*) zip, go; (*der Phantasie*) flight; **in S. bringen** start; **S. bekommen** gather momentum
schwung'haft *adj* brisk, lively
Schwung'kraft *f* centrifugal force; (fig) zip, pep; (phys) momentum
Schwung'rad *n* (mach) flywheel
schwung'voll *adj* enthusiastic, lively
schwur [ʃvuːr] *pret of* **schwören** ‖ **Schwur** *m* (-[e]s;̈e) oath
Schwur'gericht *n* jury
sechs [zɛks] *invar adj & pron* six ‖ **Sechs** *f* (-;-en) six
Sechs'eck *n* hexagon
Sechser [ˈzɛksər] *m* (-s;-) six; (*in der Lotterie*) jackpot
Sechsta'gerennen *n* six-day bicycle race
sechste [ˈzɛkstə] §9 *adj & pron* sixth
Sechstel [ˈzɛkstəl] *n* (-s;-) sixth
sech'zehn *invar adj & pron* sixteen ‖ **Sech'zehn** *f* (-;-en) sixteen
sech'zehnte §9 *adj & pron* sixteenth
Sech'zehntel *n* (-s;-) sixteenth
sechzig [ˈzɛçtsɪç] *invar adj & pron* sixty ‖ **Sechzig** *f* (-;-en) sixty
sechziger [ˈzɛçtsɪgər] *invar adj* of the sixties; **die J. Jahre** the sixties ‖ **Sechziger** *m* (-s;-) sexagenarian
sechzigste [ˈzɛçtsɪçstə] §9 *adj & pron* sixtieth
See [zeː] *m* (Sees; Seen [ˈzeː-ən] lake ‖ *f* (See; Seen [ˈzeː-ən]) sea; ocean; **an der See** at the seashore; **an die See gehen** go to the seashore; **auf See** at sea; **in See gehen** (or stechen) put out to sea; **in See sein** be in open water; **Kapitän zur See** navy captain; **zur See gehen** go to sea
See'bad *n* seashore resort
See'bär *m* (fig) sea dog
see'fähig *adj* seaworthy
See'fahrer *m* seafarer
See'fahrt *f* seafaring; voyage
see'fest *adj* seaworthy; **s. werden** get one's sea legs
See'gang *m* —**hoher** (or **schwerer** or **starker**) **S.** heavy seas
See'hafen *m* seaport
See'handel *m* maritime trade
See'hund *m* (zool) seal
See'jungfer *f*, **See'jungfrau** *f* mermaid
See'kadett *m* naval cadet
See'karte *f* (naut) chart
see'krank *adj* seasick
See'krebs *m* lobster
Seele [ˈzeːlə] *f* (-;-n) soul; mind; (*Ein-*

wohner) inhabitant, soul; (*-s Geschützes*) bore; (*-s Kabels*) core
See'lenangst *f* mortal fear
See'lenfriede *m* peace of mind
See'lenheil *n* salvation
See'lennot *f* mental distress
See'lenpein *f*, **See'lenqual** *f* mental anguish
See'lenruhe *f* peace of mind; composure
see'lensgut *adj* good-hearted
seelisch [ˈzeːlɪʃ] *adj* mental, psychic
Seel'sorge *f* (-;) ministry
Seel'sorger *m* (-s;-) minister, pastor
See'macht *f* sea power
See'mann *m* (-[e]s;-leute) seaman
See'meile *f* nautical mile
See'möwe *f* sea gull
See'not *f* (naut) distress
See'ratte *f* (fig) old salt
See'raub *m* piracy
See'räuber *m* pirate; corsair
See'räuberei *f* piracy
See'recht *n* maritime law
See'reise *f* voyage; cruise
See'sperre *f* naval blockade
See'stadt *f* seaport town; coastal town
See'straße *f* shipping lane
See'streitkräfte *pl* naval forces
See'tang *m* seaweed
see'tüchtig *adj* seaworthy
See'warte *f* oceanographic institute
See'weg *m* sea route; **auf dem S. by sea**
See'wesen *n* naval affairs
Segel [ˈzeːgəl] *n* (-s;-) sail
Se'gelboot *n* sailboat; (sport) yacht
Se'gelfliegen *n* gliding
Se'gelflieger *-in* §6 *mf* glider pilot
Se'gelflug *m* glide, gliding
Se'gelflugzeug *n* glider
Se'gelleinwand *f* sailcloth, canvas
segeln [ˈzeːgəln] *intr* (HABEN & SEIN) sail; (aer) glide
Se'gelschiff *n* sailing vessel
Se'gelsport *m* sailing
Se'geltuch *n* sailcloth, canvas
Se'geltuchhülle *f*, **Se'geltuchplane** *f* tarpaulin
Segen [ˈzeːgən] *m* (-s;-) blessing
se'gensreich *adj* blessed, blissful
Segler [ˈzeːglər] *m* (-s;-) yachtsman; (aer) glider; (naut) sailing vessel
segnen [ˈzeːgnən] *tr* bless
Seh- [zeː] *comb.fm.* visual, of vision
sehen [ˈzeː-ən] §138 *tr & intr* see; look; **s. auf** (*acc*) look at; take care of; face (*a direction*); **s. nach** look for, look around for; **schlecht s.** have poor eyes ‖ **Sehen** *n* (-s;) sight; eyesight, vision; **vom S.** by sight
se'henswert *adj* worth seeing
Se'henswürdigkeit *f* object of interest; **Sehenswürdigkeiten** sights
Seher [ˈzeː-ər] *m* (-s;-) seer, prophet
Se'hergabe *f* gift of prophecy
Seh'feld *n* field of vision
Seh'kraft *f* eyesight
Sehne [ˈzeːnə] *f* (-;-n) tendon, sinew; (*Bogen-*) string; (geom) secant
sehnen [ˈzeːnən] *ref*—**sich s. nach** long for, crave ‖ **Sehnen** *n* (-s;) longing
Seh'nerv *m* optic nerve

sehnig ['zeniç] *adj* sinewy; *(Fleisch)* stringy

sehnlich ['zenliç] *adj* longing; ardent

Sehnsucht ['zenzuçt] *f* (-;) yearning

sehr [zer] *adv* very; very much

Seh'rohr *n* periscope

Seh'vermögen *n* sight, vision

Seh'weite *f* visual range; **in S.** within sight

seicht [zaiçt] *adj* (& *fig*) shallow

Seide ['zaidə] *f* (-;-n) silk

seiden ['zaidən] *adj* silk, silky

Sei'denatlas *m* satin

Sei'denpapier *n* tissue paper

Sei'denraupe *f* silkworm

Sei'denspinnerei *f* silk mill

Sei'denstoff *m* silk cloth

seidig ['zaidiç] *adj* silky

Seife ['zaifə] *f* (-;-n) soap

Sei'fenblase *f* soap bubble

Sei'fenbrühe *f* soapsuds

Sei'fenflocken *pl* soap flakes

Sei'fenlauge *f* soapsuds

Sei'fenpulver *n* soap powder

Sei'fenschale *f* soap dish

Sei'fenschaum *m* lather

seifig ['zaifiç] *adj* soapy

seihen ['zai.ən] *tr* strain, filter

Sei'her *m* (-s;-) strainer, filter

Seil [zail] *n* (-[e]s;-e) rope; cable

Seil'bahn *f* cable railway; cable car

seil'springen *intr* jump rope

Seil'tänzer -in *§6 mf* ropewalker

sein [zain] *§139 intr* (SEIN) be; exist; **es ist mir, als wenn** I feel as if; **es sei denn, daß** unless; **lassen Sie das s.!** stop it!; **wenn dem so ist** if that is the case; **wie dem auch sein mag** however that may be ‖ *aux* (to form compound past tenses of intransitive verbs of motion, change of condition, etc.) have, e.g., **ich bin gegangen** I have gone, I went ‖ *§2,2 poss adj* his; its; one's; her ‖ *§2,4,5 poss pron* his; hers; **die Seinen** his family; **er hat das Seine getan** he did his share; **jedem das Seine** to each his own ‖ **Sein** *n* (-s;) being; existence; reality

seinerseits ['zainər'zaits] *adv* for his part

seinerzeit ['zainər'tsait] *adv* in its time; in those days; in due time

seinesgleichen ['zainəs'glaiçən] *pron* people like him, the likes of him

seinethalben ['zainət'halbən], seinetwegen ['zainət'vegən] *adv* for his sake; on his account; *(von ihm aus)* for all he cares

seinetwillen ['zainət'vilən] *adv*—**um s.** for his sake, on his behalf

Seinige ['zainigə] *§2,5 pron* his; das S. his property, his own; his due; his share; **die Seinigen** his family

seit [zait] *prep (dat)* since; for; **s. e-m Jahr** for one year; **s. einiger Zeit** for some time past; **s. kurzem** lately; **s. langem** for a long time; **s. wann** since when ‖ *conj* since

seitdem [zait'dem] *adv* since that time ‖ *conj* since

Seite ['zaitə] *f* (-;-n) side; page; direction; *(Quelle)* source; (*mil*) flank

Sei'tenansicht *f* side view, profile

Sei'tenbau *m* (-[e]s;-ten) annex

Sei'tenblick *m* side glance

Sei'tenflosse *f* (aer) horizontal stabilizer

Sei'tenflügel *m* (archit) wing

Sei'tengang *m* side aisle

Sei'tengeleise *n* sidetrack

Sei'tenhieb *m* snide remark, dig

sei'tenlang *adj* pages of

Sei'tenriß *m* profile

sei'tens *prep (genit)* on the part of

Sei'tenschiff *n* (archit) aisle

Sei'tenschwimmen *n* sidestroke

Sei'tensprung *m* (fig) escapade

Sei'tenstück *n* (fig) counterpart

Sei'tenwind *m* cross wind

seither [zait'her] *adv* since then

–seitig [zaitiç] *comb.fm.* –sided

seit'lich *adj* lateral

seitwärts ['zaitverts] *adv* sideways, sidewards; aside

Sekretär –in [zekre'ter(in)] *§8 mf* secretary

Sekt [zekt] *m* (-[e]s;-e) champagne

Sekte ['zektə] *f* (-;-n) sect

Sek·tor ['zektor] *m* (-s;-toren ['torən]) sector; (fig) field

Sekundant [zekun'dant] *m* (-en;-en) (box) second

sekundär [zekun'der] *adj* secondary

Sekunde [ze'kundə] *f* (-;-n) second

Sekun'denbruchteil *m* split second

Sekun'denzeiger *m* second hand

Sekurit [zeku'rit] *n* (-s;) safety glass

selber ['zelbər] *invar pron* (coll) var of selbst

selbst [zelpst] *invar pron* self; in person, personally; *(sogar)* even; by oneself; **ich s.** I myself; **von s.** voluntarily; spontaneously; automatically ‖ *adv* even; **s. ich** even I; **s. wenn** even if, even when

Selbst'achtung *f* self-respect

selbständig ['zelp/tendiç] *adj* independent

Selbst'bedienung *f* self-service

Selbst'beherrschung *f* self-control

Selbst'beobachtung *f* introspection

Selbst'bestimmung *f* self-determination

Selbst'betrug *m* self-deception

selbst'bewußt *adj* self-confident

Selbst'binder *m* necktie; (agr) combine

Selbst'erhaltung *f* self-preservation

selbst'gebacken *adj* homemade

selbst'gefällig *adj* complacent, smug

Selbst'gefühl *n* self-confidence

selbst'gemacht *adj* homemade

selbst'gerecht *adj* self-righteous

Selbst'gespräch *n* soliloquy

selbst'gezogen *adj* home-grown

selbst'herrlich *adj* high-handed

Selbst'herrschaft *f* autocracy

Selbst'herrscher *m* autocrat

Selbst'kosten *pl* production costs

Selbst'kostenpreis *m* factory price; **zum S. abgeben** sell at cost

Selbstlader ['zelpstladər] *m* (-s;-) automatic (weapon)

Selbst'laut *m* vowel

selbst'los *adj* unselfish

Selbst'mord *m* suicide

selbst'sicher *adj* self-confident

Selbst'steuer *n* automatic pilot

Selbst'sucht f egotism, selfishness
selbst'süchtig adj egotistical
selbst'tätig adj automatic
Selbst'täuschung f self-deception
Selbstüberhebung [ˈzɛlpstybərhebʊŋ] f (-;) self-conceit, presumption
Selbst'verbrennung f spontaneous combustion; self-immolation
Selbst'verlag m—im S. printed privately
Selbst'verleugnung f self-denial
Selbst'versorger m (-s;-) self-supporter
selbst'verständlich adj obvious; natural ‖ adv of course
Selbst'verständlichkeit f foregone conclusion, matter of course
Selbst'verteidigung f self-defense
Selbst'vertrauen n self-confidence
Selbst'verwaltung f autonomy
Selbst'wähler m (-s;-) dial telephone
Selbst'zucht f self-discipline
Selbst'zufrieden adj self-satisfied
Selbst'zufriedenheit f self-satisfaction
Selbst'zweck m end in itself
selig [ˈzeliç] adj blessed; (verstorben) late; (fig) ecstatic; (fig) tipsy; **seligen Angedenkens** of blessed memory; **s. werden** attain salvation, be saved
Se'ligkeit f (-;) happiness; salvation
Se'ligpreisung f (Bib) beatitude
se'ligsprechen §64 tr beatify
Sellerie [ˈzɛləri] m (-s;) & f (-;) celery (bulb)
selten [ˈzɛltən] adj rare, scarce ‖ adv seldom, rarely
Selterswasser [ˈzɛltərsvasər] n seltzer, soda water
seltsam [ˈzɛltzam] adj odd, strange
Semester [zeˈmɛstər] n (-s;-) semester
Semikolon [ˈzemikɔlɔn] n semicolon
Seminar [zemiˈnar] n (-s;-e) seminary; (educ) seminar
Seminarist [zeminaˈrɪst] m (-en;-en) seminarian
semitisch [zeˈmɪtiʃ] adj Semitic
Semmel [ˈzɛməl] f (-;-n) roll
Senat [zeˈnat] m (-[e]s;-e) senate
Se·nator [zeˈnator] m (-s;-natoren [naˈtoːrən]) senator
Sende- [ˈzɛndə] comb.fm. transmitting, transmitter, broadcasting
senden [ˈzɛndən] tr & intr transmit, broadcast; telecast ‖ §120 & §140 tr send ‖ intr—s. nach send for
Sen'der m (-s;-) (rad, telv) transmitter; (rad) broadcasting station
Sen'deraum m broadcasting studio
Sen'dezeichen n station identification
Sen'dezeit f air time
Sen'dung f (-;-en) sending; (fig) mission; (com) shipment; (rad) broadcast; (telv) telecast
Senf [zɛnf] m (-[e]s;-e) mustard
sengen [ˈzɛŋən] tr singe, scorch
seng(e)rig [ˈzɛŋ(ə)rɪç] adj burnt; (fig) suspicious, fishy
senil [zeˈnil] adj senile
Senilität [zeniliˈtɛt] f (-;) senility
senior [ˈzenjor] adj senior
Senkblei [ˈzɛŋkblaɪ] n plummet; (naut) sounding lead
Senke [ˈzɛŋkə] f (-;-n) depression
senken [ˈzɛŋkən] tr lower; sink; (Kopf)

bow ‖ ref sink, settle; dip, slope; (Mauer) sag
Senkfüße [ˈzɛŋkfysə] pl flat feet, fallen arches
Senk'fußeinlage f arch support
Senkgrube [ˈzɛŋkgrubə] f cesspool
Senkkasten [ˈzɛŋkkastən] m caisson
senkrecht [ˈzɛŋkrɛçt] adj vertical; (geom) perpendicular
Sen'kung f (-;-en) sinking; depression; dip, slope; sag; (der Preise) lowering
Sensation [zɛnzaˈtsjon] f (-;-en) sensation
sensationell [zɛnzatsjoˈnɛl] adj sensational
Sensations'blatt n (pej) scandal sheet
Sensations'lust f sensationalism
Sensations'meldung f, **Sensations'nachricht** f (journ) scoop
Sensations'presse f yellow journalism
Sense [ˈzɛnzə] f (-;-n) scythe
sensibel [zɛnˈzibəl] adj sensitive; (Nerven) sensory
Sensibilität [zɛnzibiliˈtɛt] f (-;) sensitivity, sensitiveness
sentimental [zɛntimɛnˈtal] adj sentimental
separat [zepaˈrat] adj separate
September [zɛpˈtɛmbər] m (-[s];) September
Serenade [zereˈnadə] f (-;-n) serenade
Serie [ˈzerjə] f (-;-n) series; line
Se'rienanfertigung f, **Se'rienbau** m, **Se'rienfabrikation** f, **Se'rienherstellung** f mass production
se'rienmäßig adj—**serienmäßige Herstellung** mass production ‖ adv—**s. herstellen** mass-produce
Se'riennummer f serial number
Se'rienproduktion f mass production
seriös [zeˈrjøs] adj serious; reliable
Se·rum [ˈzerum] n (-s;-ren [rən] & -ra [ra]) serum
Service [ˈzɔrvɪs] m (Services [ˈzɔrvɪs(əs)];) (Kundendienst) service ‖ [zɛrˈvis] n (Services [zɛrˈvis]; Service [zɛrˈvis(ə)]) (Tafelgeschirr) service
Servierbrett [zɛrˈvirbrɛt] n tray
servieren [zɛrˈvirən] tr serve; **es ist serviert!** dinner is ready! ‖ intr wait at table
Serviertisch [zɛrˈvirtiʃ] m sideboard
Servierwagen [zɛrˈvirvagən] m serving cart
Serviette [zɛrˈvjɛtə] f (-;-n) napkin
Servo- [zɛrvə] comb.fm. booster, auxiliary, servo, power, automatic
Ser'vobremsen pl power brakes
Ser'vokupplung f automatic transmission
Ser'volenkung f power steering
Servus [ˈzɛrvus] interj (Aust) hello!; (coll) so long!
Sessel [ˈzɛsəl] m (-s;-) easy chair
Ses'sellift m chair lift
seßhaft [ˈzɛshaft] adj settled; **sich s. machen** settle down
Setzei [ˈzɛtsaɪ] n fried egg
setzen [ˈzɛtsən] tr set, put, place; seat; (beim Spiel) bet; (Denkmal) erect; (Frist) fix; (Junge) breed; (Fische) stock; (Pflanzen) plant; (mus) com-

pose; (typ) set ‖ *ref* sit down; (*Kaffee*) settle ‖ *intr* set type; **s. auf** (*acc*) bet on ‖ *intr* (SEIN)—**s. über** (*acc*) jump over

Set'zer *m* (-s;-) typesetter, compositor

Setz'fehler *m* typographical error

Seuche ['zɔɪçə] *f* (-;-n) epidemic

seufzen ['zɔɪftsən] *intr* sigh

Seuf'zer *m* (-s;-) sigh

Sex [zɛks] *m* (-es;) sex

Sex-Appeal ['zɛks ə'pil] *m* (-s;) sex appeal

Sex'-Bombe *f* (coll) sex pot

Sexual- [zɛksu̇al] *comb.fm.* sex

sexuell [zɛksu̇'ɛl] *adj* sexual

Sexus ['zɛksus] *m* (-;-) sex

sezieren [ze'tsirən] *tr* dissect

Shampoo [ʃam'pu] *n* (-s;-s) shampoo

Sibirien [zɪ'birjən] *n* (-s;) Siberia

sich [zɪç] §11 *reflex pron* oneself; himself; herself; itself; themselves; **an (und für) s.** in itself; **außer s. sein** be beside oneself ‖ *recip pron* each other, one another

Sichel ['zɪçəl] *f* (-;-n) sickle

sicher ['zɪçər] *adj* sure; positive; reliable; (**vor** *dat*) safe (from), secure (from) ‖ *adv* surely, certainly

Si'cherheit *f* (-;-en) safety, security; (*Gewißheit*) certainty; (*Zuverlässigkeit*) reliability; (*im Auftreten*) assurance; (com) security; (jur) bail

Si'cherheitsgurt *m*, **Si'cherheitsgürtel** *m* (aer, aut) seat belt

Si'cherheitsnadel *f* safety pin

Si'cherheitspolizei *f* security police

Si'cherheitsspielraum *m* margin of safety, leeway

si'cherlich *adv* surely, certainly

sichern ['zɪçərn] *tr* secure; fasten; guarantee; (*Gewehr*) put on safety

Si'cherstellung *f* safekeeping; guarantee

Si'cherung *f* (-;-en) protection; guarantee; (*an Schußwaffe*) safety catch; (elec) fuse; **durchgebrannte S.** blown fuse

Si'cherungskasten *m* fuse box

Sicht [zɪçt] *f* (-;) sight; (*Aussicht*) view; (*Sichtigkeit*) visibility; **auf kurze S.** short-range; **auf S.** at sight

sichtbar ['zɪçtbar] *adj* visible

sichten ['zɪçtən] *tr* sight; (fig) sift

sichtig ['zɪçtɪç] *adj* clear

sicht'lich *adj* visible

Sicht'vermerk *m* visa

sickern ['zɪkərn] *intr* (HABEN & SEIN) trickle, seep, leak

sie [zi] §11 *pers pron* she, her; it; they, them ‖ §11 **Sie** *pers pron* you

Sieb [zip] *n* (-[e]s;-e) sieve, colander; screen; (rad) filter

sieben ['zibən] *invar adj & pron* seven ‖ *tr* sift, strain; (fig) screen; (rad) filter ‖ **Sieben** *f* (-;-en) seven

siebente ['zibəntə] §9 *adj & pron* seventh

Siebentel ['zibəntəl] *n* (-s;-) seventh

siebte ['ziptə] §9 *adj & pron* seventh

Siebtel ['ziptəl] *n* (-s;-) seventh

siebzehn ['ziptsen] *invar adj & pron* seventeen ‖ **Siebzehn** *f* (-;-en) seventeen

siebzehnte ['ziptsentə] §9 *adj & pron* seventeenth

Siebzehntel ['ziptsentəl] *n* (-s;-) seventeenth

siebzig ['ziptsɪç] *invar adj & pron* seventy ‖ **Siebzig** *f* (-;-en) seventy

siebziger ['ziptsɪgər] *invar adj* of the seventies; **die s. Jahre** the seventies ‖ **Siebziger** *m* (-s;-) septuagenarian

siebzigste ['ziptsɪçstə] §9 *adj & pron* seventieth

siech [ziç] *adj* sickly

siechen ['ziçən] *intr* be sickly

Siechtum ['ziçtum] *n* (-s;) lingering illness

siedeheiß ['zidə'haɪs] *adj* piping hot

siedeln ['zidəln] *intr* settle

sieden ['zidən] §141 *tr & intr* boil

Siedepunkt ['zidəpʊŋkt] *m* boiling point

Siedler –in ['zidlər(ɪn)] §6 *mf* settler

Sied'lerstelle *f* homestead

Sied'lung *f* (-;-en) settlement; colony; housing development

Sieg [zik] *m* (-[e]s;-e) victory

Siegel ['zigəl] *n* (-s;-) seal

siegeln ['zigəln] *tr* seal

Sie'gelring *m* signet ring

siegen ['zigən] *intr* win, be victorious

Sie'ger –in §6 *mf* winner, victor; **zweiter Sieger** runner-up

Sieges- [zigəs] *comb.fm.* victory, of victory, triumphal

Sie'gesbogen *m* triumphal arch

sieg'reich *adj* victorious

Signal [zɪg'nal] *n* (-s;-e) signal

signalisieren [zɪgnalɪ'zirən] *tr* signal

Silbe ['zɪlbə] *f* (-;-n) syllable

Sil'bentrennung *f* syllabification

Silber ['zɪlbər] *n* (-s;) silver

silbern ['zɪlbərn] *adj* silver, silvery

Sil'berzeug *n* silver, silverware

Silhouette [zɪlu'ɛtə] *f* (-;-n) silhouette

Silo ['zilo] *m* (-s;-s) silo

Silvester [zɪl'vɛstər] *m* (-s;-), **Silve'sterabend** *m* New Year's Eve

simpel ['zɪmpəl] *adj* simple ‖ **Simpel** *m* (-s;-) simpleton

Sims [zɪms] *m & n* (-es;-e) ledge; (*Fenster-*) sill; (*Kamin-*) mantelpiece

Simulant –in [zɪmu'lant(ɪn)] §7 *mf* faker; (mil) goldbrick

simulieren [zɪmu'lirən] *tr* simulate, fake ‖ *intr* loaf

simultan [zɪmul'tan] *adj* simultaneous

Sinfo-nie [zɪnfo'ni] *f* (-;-nien ['ni·ən]) symphony

singen ['zɪŋən] §142 *tr & intr* sing

Singsang ['zɪŋzaŋ] *m* (-[e]s;) singsong

Sing'spiel *n* musical comedy, musical

Sing'stimme *f* vocal part

Singular ['zɪŋgular] *m* (-s;-e) singular

sinken ['zɪŋkən] §143 *intr* (SEIN) sink slump, sag; (*Preise*) drop; **s. lassen** lower; (*Mut*) lose

Sinn [zɪn] *m* (-[e]s;-e) sense; mind; meaning; liking, taste

Sinn'bild *n* emblem, symbol

sinn'bildlich *adj* symbolic(al) ‖ *adv* symbolically; **s. darstellen** symbolize

sinnen ['zɪnən] §121 *tr* plan; plot ‖ *intr* (**auf** *acc*) plan, plot; (**über** *acc*)

think (about) ‖ **Sinnen** *n* (-s;) reflection, meditation, reverie
Sin'nenlust *f* sensuality
Sin'nenmensch *m* sensualist
Sin'nenwelt *f* material world
Sin'nesänderung *f* change of mind
Sin'nesart *f* character, disposition
Sin'nestäuschung *f* illusion, hallucination, mirage
sinn'lich *adj* sensual; material
sinn'los *adj* senseless
sinn'reich *adj* ingenious, bright
sinn'verwandt *adj* synonymous
sinn'voll *adj* meaningful; sensible
Sintflut ['zɪntfluːt] *f* deluge, flood
Sippe ['zɪpə] *f* (-;-n) kin; clan
Sipp'schaft *f* (-;-en) clique, set
Sirup ['ziːrup] *m* (-s;-e) syrup
Sitte ['zɪtə] *f* (-;-n) custom; habit; usage; **die Sitten** the morals
Sit'tenbild *n*, **Sit'tengemälde** *n* description of the manners (*of an age*)
Sit'tengesetz *n* moral law
Sit'tenlehre *f* ethics
Sit'tenlos *adj* immoral
Sit'tenpolizei *f* vice squad
sit'tenrein *adj* chaste
Sit'tenrichter *m* censor
sit'tenstreng *adj* puritanical, prudish
Sittich ['zɪtɪç] *m* (-s;-e) parakeet
sittlich ['zɪtlɪç] *adj* moral, ethical
Sittlichkeit *f* (-;) morality
Sitt'lichkeitsverbrechen *n* indecent assault
sittsam ['zɪtzam] *adj* modest, decent
Situation [zɪtu·a'tsjoːn] *f* (-;-en) situation
situiert [zɪtu'iːrt] *adj*—**gut s.** well-to-do
Sitz [zɪts] *m* (-es;-e) seat; residence; (*e-s Kleides*) fit; (eccl) see
sitzen ['zɪtsən] §144 *intr* sit; dwell; (*Vögel*) perch; (*Kleider*) fit; (*Hieb*) hit home; (coll) be in jail
sit'zenbleiben §62 *intr* (SEIN) remain seated; (*beim Tanzen*) be a wallflower; (*bei der Heirat*) remain unmarried; (educ) stay behind, flunk
sit'zenlassen §104 *tr* leave, abandon; (*Mädchen*) jilt
Sitz'gelegenheit *f* seating accommodation
Sitz'ordnung *f* seating arrangement
Sitz'platz *m* seat
Sitz'streik *m* sit-down strike
Sitz'ung *f* (-;-en) session
Sitz'ungsbericht *m* minutes
Sitz'ungsperiode *f* session; (jur) term
Sizilien [zi'tsiːljən] *n* (-s;) Sicily
Ska·la ['skaːla] *f* (-;-len [lən]) scale
Skandal [skan'daːl] *m* (-s;-e) scandal
skandalös [skanda'løːs] *adj* scandalous
Skandinavien [skandi'naːvjən] *n* (-s;) Scandinavia
Skelett [ske'lɛt] *n* (-[e]s;-e) skeleton
Skepsis ['skɛpsɪs] *f* (-;) skepticism
Skeptiker -in ['skɛptɪkər(ɪn)] §6 *mf* skeptic
skeptisch ['skɛptɪʃ] *adj* skeptical
Ski [/i] *m* (-s; **Skier** ['iːər]) ski
Skizze ['skɪtsə] *f* (-;-n) sketch
skizzieren [skɪ'tsiːrən] *tr & intr* sketch
Sklave ['sklaːvə] *m* (-n;-n) slave

Sklaverei [sklaːvə'raɪ] *f* (-;) slavery
sklavisch ['sklaːvɪʃ] *adj* slavish
Skonto ['skɔnto] *m & n* (-s;-s) discount
Skrupel ['skruːpəl] *m* (-s;-) scruple
skru'pellos *adj* unscrupulous
skrupulös [skrupu'løːs] *adj* scrupulous
Skulptur [skulp'tuːr] *f* (-;-en) sculpture
Slalom ['slaːlɔm] *m & n* (-s;-s) slalom
Slawe ['slaːvə] *m* (-n;-n), **Slawin** ['slaːvɪn] *f* (-;-nen) Slav
slawisch ['slaːvɪʃ] *adj* Slavic
Smaragd [sma'rakt] *m* (-[e]s;-e) emerald
Smoking ['smoːkɪŋ] *m* (-s;-s) tuxedo
so [zo] *adv* so; this way, thus; so ein such a; **so oder so** by hook or by crook; **so...wie so...als...**
sobald' *conj* as soon as
Socke ['zɔkə] *f* (-;-n) sock
Sockenhalter (Sok'kenhalter) *m* garter
Soda ['zoːda] *f* (-;) & *n* (-s;) soda
sodann' *adv* then
Sodbrennen ['zoːtbrɛnən] *n* (-s;) heartburn
soeben [zo'eːbən] *adv* just now, just
Sofa ['zoːfa] *n* (-s;-s) sofa
sofern' *conj* provided, if
soff [zɔf] *pret of* **saufen**
sofort' *adv* at once, right away
sofortig [zo'fɔrtɪç] *adj* immediate
sog [zoːk] *pret of* **saugen** ‖ **Sog** *m* (-[e]s;) suction; undertow; (aer) wash
sogar' *adv* even
so'genannt *adj* so-called; would-be
sogleich' *adv* at once, right away
Sohle ['zoːlə] *f* (-;-n) sole; bottom
Sohn [zoːn] *m* (-[e]s;ᴗe) son
solang *ge conj* as long as
solch [zɔlç] *adj* such
Sold [zɔlt] *m* (-[e]s;-e) pay
Soldat [zɔl'daːt] *m* (-en;-en) soldier
Söldner ['zœldnər] *m* (-s;-) mercenary
Sole ['zoːlə] *f* (-;-n) brine
solid [zo'liːt] *adj* solid; sound; reliable; steady; respectable; (*Preis*) reasonable; (com) sound, solvent
solide [zo'liːdə] *adj* var of **solid**
Solist -in [zo'lɪst(ɪn)] §7 *mf* soloist
Soll [zɔl] *n* (-s;-e) quota; (acct) debit side; **S. und Haben** debit and credit
Soll— *comb.fm.* estimated; debit
sollen ['zɔlən] §145 *mod* (*inf*) be obliged to (*inf*), have to (*inf*); (*inf*) be supposed to (*inf*); (*inf*) be said to (*inf*)
Soll'wert *m* face value
solo ['zoːlo] *adv* (mus) solo ‖ **So·lo** *n* (-s;-s & -li [li]) solo
somit' *adv* so, consequently
Sommer ['zɔmər] *m* (-s;-) summer
Som'merfrische *f* health resort; **in die S. fahren** go to the country
Sommerfrischler ['zɔmərfrɪʃlər] *m* (-s;-) vacationer
som'merlich *adj* summery
Som'mersprosse *f* freckle
sonach' *adv* consequently, so
Sonate [zo'naːtə] *f* (-;-n) sonata
Sonde ['zɔndə] *f* (-;-n) probe
Sonder— ['zɔndər] *comb.fm.* special, extra; separate

sonderbar ['zɔndərbar] adj strange, odd; peculiar

son'derlich adj special, particular

Sonderling ['zɔndərlɪŋ] m (-s;-e) odd person, strange character

sondern ['zɔndərn] tr separate; sever; part; sort out; classify || conj but

Son'derrecht n privilege

Son'derung f (-;-en) separation; sorting, sifting; classifying

Son'derverband m (mil) task force

Son'derzug m (rr) special

sondieren [zɔn'dirən] tr probe; (fig) sound out; (naut) sound

Sonnabend ['zɔnabɛnt] m (-s;-e) Saturday

Sonne ['zɔnə] f (-;-n) sun

sonnen ['zɔnən] tr sun || ref sun oneself

Son'nenaufgang m sunrise

Son'nenbad n sun bath

Son'nenblende f (aut) sun visor; (phot) lens shade

Sonnenbrand m sunburn

Son'nenbräune f suntan

Son'nenbrille f (pair of) sun glasses

Son'nendach n awning

Son'nenenergie f solar energy

Son'nenfinsternis f eclipse of the sun

Son'nenfleck m sunspot

Son'nenjahr n solar year

son'nenklar' adj sunny; (fig) clear as day

Son'nenlicht n sunlight

Son'nenschein m sunshine

Son'nenschirm m parasol

Son'nensegel n awning

Son'nenseite f sunny side

Son'nenstich m sunstroke

Son'nenstrahl m sunbeam

Son'nensystem n solar system

Son'nenuhr f sundial

Son'nenuntergang m sunset

son'nenverbrannt adj sunburnt, tanned

Son'nenwende f solstice

sonnig ['zɔnɪç] adj sunny

Sonntag ['zɔntak] m (-s;-e) Sunday

sonn'tags adv on Sundays

Sonn'tagsfahrer m §6 mf Sunday driver

Sonn'tagskind n person born under a lucky star

Sonn'tagsstaat m Sunday clothes

sonor [zə'nor] adj sonorous

sonst [zɔnst] adv otherwise; else; (ehemals) formerly; s. etw something else; s. keiner no one else; s. nichts nothing else; s. noch was? anything else?; wie s. as usual; wie s. was (coll) like anything

sonstig ['zɔnstɪç] adj other

sonst'wer pron someone else

sonst'wie adv in some other way

sonst'wo adv somewhere else

Sopran [zo'pran] m (-s;-e) soprano; treble

Sopranist –in [zopra'nɪst(ɪn)] §7 mf soprano

Sorge ['zɔrgə] f (-;-n) care; worry; außer S. sein be at ease; keine S.! don't worry; sich [dat] Sorgen machen über (acc) or um be worried about

sorgen ['zɔrgən] intr—dafür s., daß take care that, see to it that; s. für take care of || ref be uneasy; sich s. über (acc) grieve over; sich s. um be worried about

sor'genfrei adj carefree; untroubled

Sor'genkind n problem child

sor'genlos adj carefree

sor'genvoll adj uneasy, anxious

Sor'gerecht n (für) custody (of)

Sorgfalt ['zɔrkfalt] f (-;) care, carefulness; accuracy

sorgfältig ['zɔrkfɛltɪç] adj careful

sorglich ['zɔrklɪç] adj careful

sorglos ['zɔrklos] adj careless; thoughtless; carefree

sorgsam ['zɔrkzam] adj careful; cautious

Sorte ['zɔrtə] f (-;-n) sort, kind

sortieren [zɔr'tirən] tr sort out

Sortiment [zɔrtɪ'mɛnt] n (-[e]s;-e) assortment

Soße ['zosə] f (-;-n) sauce; gravy

sott [zɔt] pret of sieden

Souffleur [zu'flør] m (-s;-s), **Souffleuse** [zu'fløzə] f (-;-n) prompter

soufflieren [zu'flirən] intr (dat) prompt

Soutane [zu'tanə] f (-;-n) cassock

Souvenir [zuva'nir] n (-s;-s) souvenir

souverän [zuvə'ren] adj sovereign || **Souverän** m (-s;-e) sovereign

Souveränität [zuvərəni'tet] f (-;) sovereignty

soviel' adv so much; noch einmal s. twice as much || conj as far as

soweit' conj as far as

sowie' conj as well as

sowieso' adv in any case, anyhow

Sowjet [zɔv'jet] m (-s;-s) Soviet

sowjetisch [zɔv'jetɪʃ] adj Soviet

sowohl' conj—sowohl...als auch as well as the, both...and

sozial [zo'tsjal] adj social

Sozial'fürsorge f social welfare

sozialisieren [zotsjali'zirən] tr nationalize

Sozialismus [zotsja'lɪsmus] m (-;) socialism

Sozialist –in [zotsja'lɪst(ɪn)] §7 mf socialist

sozialistisch [zotsja'lɪstɪʃ] adj socialistic

Sozial'wissenschaft f social science

Soziologie [zotsjolo'gi] f (-;) sociology

Sozius ['zotsjus] m (-;-se) associate, partner; (auf dem Motorrad) rider

sozusa'gen adv so to speak, as it were

Spachtel ['ʃpaxtəl] m (-s;-) & f (-;-n) spatula; putty knife

Spach'telmesser n putty knife

Spagat [ʃpa'gat] m (-[e]s;-e) (gym) split; (dial) string

spähen ['ʃpe·ən] intr peer; spy

Spä'her m (-s;-) lookout; (mil) scout

Spä'herblick m searching glance

Spähtrupp ['ʃpetrup] m reconnaissance squad

Späh'wagen m reconnaissance car

Spalier [ʃpa'lir] n (-s;-e) trellis; double line (of people)

Spalt [ʃpalt] m (-[e]s;-e) split; crack; slit; (geol) cleft

Spalte ['ʃpaltə] f (-;-n) split; crack; slit; (typ) column

spalten ['ʃpaltən] tr (pp gespaltet or gespalten) split; slit; crack; (Holz) chop

Spal'tung f (-;-en) split; (der Meinungen) division; (chem) decomposition; (eccl) schism; (phys) fission

Span [ʃpan] m (-[e]s;ᵉe) chip; splinter; Späne shavings

Span'ferkel n suckling pig

Spange ['ʃpaŋə] f (-;-n) clasp; hair clip; (Schnalle) buckle

Spanien ['ʃpanjən] n (-s;) Spain

Spanier -in ['ʃpanjər(in)] §6 mf Spaniard

spanisch ['ʃpanɪʃ] adj Spanish; das kommt mir s. vor (coll) that's Greek to me; spanischer Pfeffer paprika; spanische Wand folding screen

spann [ʃpan] pret of spinnen || Spann m (-s;-e) instep

Spanne ['ʃpanə] f (-;-n) span; (com) margin

spannen ['ʃpanən] tr stretch; strain; make tense; (Bogen) bend; (Feder) tighten; (Flinte) cock; (Erwartungen) raise; (Pferde) hitch; straff s. tighten; || intr be (too) tight; s. auf (acc) wait eagerly for; listen closely to

span'nend adj tight; exciting

Spann'kraft f tension; elasticity; (fig) resiliency

spann'kräftig adj elastic

Span'nung f (-;-en) stress; strain; pressure; close attention; suspense; excitement; strained relations; (elec) voltage

Spar- [ʃpar] comb.fm. savings

Spar'buch n bank book, pass book

Spar'büchse f piggy bank

sparen ['ʃparən] tr & intr save

Spar'flamme f pilot light

Spargel ['ʃpargəl] m (-s;-) asparagus

Spar'kasse f savings bank

Spar'konto n savings account

spärlich ['ʃperlɪç] adj scanty; scarce; sparse; frugal; (Haar) thin || adv poorly; scantily; sparsely

Sparren ['ʃparən] m (-s;-) rafter

sparsam ['ʃparzam] adj thrifty

Spaß [ʃpas] m (-es;ᵉe) joke; fun; aus S. in fun; S. beiseite! all joking aside; S. haben an (dat) enjoy; S. machen be joking; be fun; viel S.! have fun!; zum S. for fun

spaß'haft, spaßig ['ʃpasɪç] adj funny, facetious

Spaß'macher m joker

Spaßverderber ['ʃpasverderbər] m (-s;-) (coll) kill-joy

Spaß'vogel m joker

spät [ʃpet] adj late; wie s. ist es? what time is it? || adv late

Spaten ['ʃpatən] m (-s;-) spade

später ['ʃpetər] adv later

späterhin ['ʃpetərhɪn] adv later on

spätestens ['ʃpetəstəns] adv at the latest

Spät'jahr n autumn, fall

Spatz [ʃpats] m (-es & -en;-en) sparrow

spazieren [ʃpa'tsirən] intr (SEIN) stroll, take a walk

spazie'renfahren §71 intr (SEIN) go for a drive

spazie'renführen tr walk (e.g., a dog)

spazie'rengehen §82 intr (SEIN) go for a walk

Spazier'fahrt f drive

Spazier'gang m stroll, walk; e-n S. machen take a walk

Spazier'gänger -in §6 mf stroller

Spazier'weg m walk

Specht [ʃpeçt] m (-[e]s;-e) woodpecker

Speck [ʃpek] m (-[e]s;-e) fat; bacon; (beim Wal) blubber

Speck'bauch m (coll) potbelly

speckig ['ʃpekɪç] adj greasy, dirty

spedieren [ʃpe'dirən] tr dispatch, ship

Spediteur [ʃpedi'tœr] m (-s;-e) shipper; furniture mover

Spedition [ʃpedi'tsjon] f (-;-en) shipment; moving company, movers

Speer [ʃper] m (-[e]s;-e) spear; (sport) javelin

Speiche ['ʃpaɪçə] f (-;-n) spoke

Speichel ['ʃpaɪçəl] m (-s;) saliva

Spei'chellecker m brown-noser

speicheln ['ʃpaɪçəln] intr drool

Speicher ['ʃpaɪçər] m (-s;-) warehouse; grain elevator; attic, loft

speichern ['ʃpaɪçərn] tr store

speien ['ʃpaɪ-ən] §135 tr vomit; spit; (Feuer) belch; (Wasser) spurt || intr vomit, throw up; spit

Speise ['ʃpaɪzə] f (-;-n) food; meal; (Gericht) dish

Spei'seeis n ice cream

Spei'sekammer f pantry

Spei'sekarte f menu

speisen ['ʃpaɪzən] tr feed; (fig) supply || intr eat; auswärts s. dine out

Spei'senfolge f menu

Spei'sereste pl leftovers

Spei'serohr n (mach) feed pipe

Spei'seröhre f esophagus

Spei'sesaal m dining room

Spei'seschrank m cupboard

Spei'sewagen m (rr) diner

Spei'sezimmer n dining room

Spektakel [ʃpek'takəl] m (-s;-) noise, racket

Spekulant -in [ʃpeku'lant(in)] §7 mf speculator

Spekulation [ʃpekula'tsjon] f (-;-en) speculation; venture

spekulieren [ʃpeku'lirən] intr speculate, reflect; (fin) speculate

Spelunke [ʃpe'luŋkə] f (-;-n) (coll) drive, joint

Spende ['ʃpendə] f (-;-n) donation

spenden ['ʃpendən] tr give; donate; (Sakramente) administer; (Lob) bestow; j-m Trost s. comfort s.o.

spendieren [ʃpen'dirən] tr—j-m etw s. treat s.o. to s.th.

Sperling ['ʃperlɪŋ] m (-s;-e) sparrow

Sperr- [ʃper] comb.fm. barrage; barred

Sperr'baum m barrier, bar

Sperre ['ʃperə] f (-;-n) shutting; close; blockade; embargo; barricade; catch; lock; (rr) gate

sperren ['ʃperən] tr shut; (Gas, Licht) cut off; (Straße) block off; cordon

off; (*blockieren*) blockade; (*mit Schloß*) lock; (*verriegeln*) bolt; (*Konto, Gelder*) freeze; (*Scheck*) stop payment on; (*verbieten*) stop; (sport) block; (sport) suspend; (typ) space || *intr* jam, be stuck
Sperr'feuer n barrage
Sperr'gebiet n restricted area
Sperr'holz n plywood
sperrig [ˈʃpɛrɪç] *adj* bulky
Sperr'sitz m (*im Kino*) rear seat; (*im Zirkus*) front seat
Sperr'stunde f closing time; curfew
Sper'rung f (-;-en) stoppage; blocking; blockade; embargo; suspension (*of telephone service, etc.*)
Spesen [ˈʃpezən] pl costs, expenses
Spezi [ˈʃpetsi] m (-s;-s) (coll) buddy
spezial [ʃpeˈtsjaːl] *adj* special
Spezial'arzt m, **Spezial'ärztin** f specialist
Spezial'fach n specialty
Spezial'geschäft n specialty shop
spezialisieren [ʃpetsjaliˈziːrən] *ref* (auf *acc*) specialize (in)
Spezialist -in [ʃpetsjaˈlɪst(ɪn)] §7 *mf* specialist
Spezialität [ʃpetsjaliˈtɛt] f (-;-en) specialty
speziell [ʃpeˈtsjɛl] *adj* special
spezifisch [ʃpeˈtsifɪʃ] *adj* specific
Sphäre [ˈsfeːrə] f (-;-n) sphere
sphärisch [ˈsfeːrɪʃ] *adj* spherical
Spickaal [ˈʃpɪkaːl] m smoked eel
spicken [ˈʃpɪkən] *tr* lard; (fig) bribe
spie [ʃpiː] *pret* of speien
Spiegel [ˈʃpiːgəl] m (-s;-) mirror
Spie'gelbild n reflection (*in mirror*)
spie'gelblank' *adj* spick and span
Spie'gelei n fried egg
spie'gelglatt' *adj* glassy
spiegeln [ˈʃpiːgəln] *tr* reflect; mirror || *ref* be reflected || *intr* shine
Spiel [ʃpiːl] n (-[e]s;-e) game; play; set (*of chessmen or checkers*); (cards) deck; (mach) play; (mus) playing; (sport) match; (theat) acting, performance; auf dem S. stehen be at stake; aufs S. setzen risk; bei etw im S. sein be at the bottom of s.th.; leichtes S. haben mit have an easy time with; S. der Natur freak of nature
Spiel'art f (biol) variety
Spiel'automat m slot machine
Spiel'bank f (-;-en) gambling table; gambling casino
Spiel'dose f music box
spielen [ˈʃpiːlən] *tr & intr* play
Spielerei [ʃpiːləˈraɪ] f (-;-en) fooling around; child's play
Spiel'ergebnis n (sport) score
spielerisch [ˈʃpiːlərɪʃ] *adj* playful
Spiel'feld n (sport) playing field
Spiel'film m feature film
Spiel'folge f program
Spiel'gefährte m, **Spiel'gefährtin** f playmate
Spiel'karten pl (playing) cards
Spiel'leiter m (cin, theat) director
Spiel'marke f chip, counter
Spiel'plan m program
Spiel'platz m playground; playing field

Spiel'raum m (fig) elbowroom; (mach) play
Spiel'sachen pl toys
Spiel'tisch m gambling table
Spiel'verderber m kill-joy
Spiel'verlängerung f overtime
Spiel'waren pl toys
Spiel'zeug n toy(s)
Spieß [ʃpiːs] m (-es;-e) spear, pike; (sl) top kick; (culin) spit; den S. umdrehen gegen turn the tables on
Spieß'bürger m Philistine, lowbrow
spieß'bürgerlich *adj* narrow-minded
spießen [ˈʃpiːsən] *tr* spear; spit
Spie'ßer m (-s;-) Philistine, lowbrow
Spieß'gesell m accomplice
Spießruten [ˈʃpiːsruːtən] pl—S. laufen run the gauntlet
spinal [ʃpiˈnaːl] *adj* spinal; spinale Kinderlähmung infantile paralysis
Spinat [ʃpiˈnaːt] m (-[e]s;-e) spinach
Spind [ʃpɪnt] m & n (-[e]s;-e) wardrobe; (mil) locker
Spindel [ˈʃpɪndəl] f (-;-n) spindle; (*Spinnrocken*) distaff
spin'deldürr' *adj* skinny, scrawny
Spinne [ˈʃpɪnə] f (-;-n) spider
spinnen [ˈʃpɪnən] *tr* spin; Ränke s. hatch plots || *intr* purr; (*im Gefängnis sitzen*) do time; (sl) be looney
Spin'nengewebe n spider web
Spin'ner m (-s;-) spinner; (sl) nut
Spinnerei [ʃpɪnəˈraɪ] f (-;-en) spinning; spinning mill
Spinn'faden m spider thread; **Spinnfäden** gossamer
Spinn'gewebe n (-s;-) cobweb
Spinn'rad n spinning wheel
Spinn'webe f (-;-n) (Aust) cobweb
Spion [ʃpiˈoːn] m (-[e]s;-e) spy
Spionage [ʃpiˈoˈnaːʒə] f (-;-) spying, espionage
Spiona'geabwehr f counterintelligence
spionieren [ʃpiˈoˈniːrən] *intr* spy
Spirale [ʃpiˈraːlə] f (-;-n) spiral
Spirituosen [ʃpirituˈoːzən] pl liquor
Spiritus [ˈʃpiːrɪtus] m (-;-se) alcohol
Spital [ʃpiˈtaːl] n (-s;-̈er) hospital
spitz [ʃpɪts] *adj* pointed; sharp; (*Winkel*) acute
Spitz'bart m goatee
Spitz'bube m rascal; thief; swindler
Spitze [ˈʃpɪtsə] f (-;-n) point; tip; top, summit; (tex) lace; an der S. liegen be in the lead; auf die S. treiben carry to extremes
Spitzel [ˈʃpɪtsəl] m (-s;-) spy; stool pigeon; plain-clothes man
spitzen [ˈʃpɪtsən] *tr* point; sharpen; (*Ohren*) prick up; den Mund s. purse the lips || *ref*—sich s. auf (*acc*) look forward to || *intr* be on one's toes
Spitzen— *comb.fm.* top; peak; leading; topnotch; maximum; (tex) lace
Spit'zenform f (sport) top form
Spit'zenleistung f top performance
Spit'zenmarke f (com) top brand
Spit'zer m (-s;-) pencil sharpener
spitz'findig *adj* subtle; sharp
Spitz'hacke f, **Spitz'haue** f pickax
spitzig [ˈʃpɪtsɪç] *adj* pointed; (& fig) sharp

Spitz′marke f (typ) heading
Spitz′name m nickname; pet name
Spitz′nase f pointed nose
spleißen [′ʃplaɪsən] §53 tr splice
spliß [ʃplɪs] pret of **spleißen**
Splitter [′ʃplɪtər] m (-s;-) splinter; chip; fragment
split′ternackt′ adj stark-naked
Split′terpartei f splinter party
split′tersicher adj shatterproof
spontan [ʃpɔn′tan] adj spontaneous
Spore [′ʃporə] f (-;-n) spore
Sporn [ʃpɔrn] m (-[e]s; **Sporen** [′ʃporən]) spur; (fig) stimulus; (aer) tail skid; (naut) ram
spornen [′ʃpɔrnən] tr spur
Sport [ʃpɔrt] m (-[e]s;-e) sport(s); **S. ausüben** (or **treiben**) play sports
Sport′freund –**in** §8 mf sports fan
Sport′hose f shorts, trunks
Sport′jacke f sport jacket, blazer
Sport′kleidung f sportswear
Sportler –**in** [′ʃpɔrtlər(ɪn)] §6 mf athlete
sport′lich adj sportsmanlike; (Figur) athletic; (Kleidung) sport
Sport′wagen m sports car; (Kinderwagen) stroller
Sport′wart m trainer
Spott [ʃpɔt] m (-[e]s;-e) mockery; scorn
Spott′bild n caricature
spott′bil′lig adj dirt-cheap
Spott′drossel f mockingbird
Spöttelei [ʃpœtə′laɪ] f (-;-en) mockery
spötteln [′ʃpœtəln] intr scoff (at), ridicule; **das spottet jeder Beschreibung** that defies description
Spötterei [ʃpœtə′raɪ] f (-;-en) mockery
Spott′gebot n (com) ridiculous offer
spöttisch [′ʃpœtɪʃ] adj mocking, satirical; sneering
Spott′name m nickname
Spott′schrift f satire
sprach [ʃprax] pret of **sprechen**
Sprach- comb.fm. speech; grammatical; linguistic; philological
Sprache [′ʃpraxə] f (-;-n) language, tongue; speech; diction; style; idiom
Sprach′eigenheit f, **Sprach′eigentümlichkeit** f idiom, idiomatic expression
Sprach′fehler m speech defect
Sprach′forschung f linguistics
Sprach′führer m phrase book
Sprach′gebrauch m usage
Sprach′gefühl n feeling for a language
sprach′gewandt adj fluent
sprach′kundig adj proficient in languages
Sprach′lehre f grammar
Sprach′lehrer –**in** §6 mf language teacher
sprach′lich adj grammatical; linguistic
sprach′los adj speechless
Sprach′rohr n megaphone; (fig) mouthpiece
Sprach′schatz m vocabulary
Sprach′störung f speech defect
Sprach′wissenschaft f philology; linguistics
sprang [ʃpraŋ] pret of **springen**
Sprech- [ʃprɛç] comb.fm. speaking
Sprech′art f way of speaking

Sprech′bühne f legitimate theater
sprechen [′ʃprɛçən] §64 tr speak; talk; (Gebet) say; (Urteil) pronounce; **speak to**, see || intr (über acc, von) speak (about), talk (about); **er ist nicht zu s.** he's not available
Spre′cher –**in** §6 mf speaker, talker
Sprech′fehler m slip of the tongue
Sprech′funkgerät n walkie-talkie
Sprech′probe f audition
Sprech′sprache f spoken language
Sprech′stunde f office hours
Sprech′stundenhilfe f receptionist
Sprech′zimmer n office (of doctor, etc.)
Spreize [′ʃpraɪtsə] f (-;-n) prop, strut; (gym) split
spreizen [′ʃpraɪtsən] tr spread, stretch out || ref sprawl out; (fig) boast (of); **sich s. gegen** resist
Spreng- [ʃprɛŋ] comb.fm. high-explosive
Sprengel [′ʃprɛŋəl] m (-s;-) diocese; parish
sprengen [′ʃprɛŋən] tr break, burst; (mit Sprengstoff) blow up; (Tür) force; (Versammlung) break up; (Mine) set off; (bespritzen) sprinkle; (Garten) water || intr (SEIN) gallop
Spreng′kommando n bomb disposal unit
Spreng′kopf m warhead
Spreng′körper m, **Spreng′stoff** m explosive
Spreng′wagen m sprinkling truck
Sprenkel [′ʃprɛŋkəl] m (-s;-) speck
sprenkeln [′ʃprɛŋkəln] tr speckle
Spreu [ʃprɔɪ] f (-;) chaff
Sprichwort [′ʃprɪçvɔrt] n (-[e]s;⸚er) proverb, saying
sprichwörtlich [′ʃprɪçvœrtlɪç] adj proverbial
sprießen [′ʃprisən] §76 intr (SEIN) sprout
Springbrunnen [′ʃprɪŋbrunən] m (-s;-) fountain
springen [′ʃprɪŋən] §142 intr (SEIN) jump; dive; burst; (Eis) crack; (coll) rush, hurry
Sprin′ger m (-s;-) jumper; (chess) knight; (sport) diver
Spring′insfeld m (-[e]s;-e) (coll) live wire
Spring′kraft f (& fig) resiliency
Spring′seil n jumping rope
Sprint [ʃprɪnt] m (-s;-s) sprint
Sprit [ʃprɪt] m (-[e]s;-e) alcohol; (coll) gasoline
Spritze [′ʃprɪtsə] f (-;-n) squirt; (Feuerwehr) fire engine; (med) injection, shot; (med) syringe
spritzen [′ʃprɪtsən] tr squirt; splash; (sprühen) spray; (sprengen) sprinkle; (Wein) mix with soda water; (med) inject || intr spurt, spout || impers—**es spritzt** it is drizzling || intr (SEIN) dash, flit
Spritz′tour f (coll) side trip
spröde [′ʃprødə] adj brittle; (Haut) chapped; (fig) prudish, coy
sproß [ʃprɔs] pret of **sprießen** || **Sproß** m (Sprosses; Sprosse) offspring, descendant; (bot) shoot

Sprosse ['ʃprɔsə] f (-;-n) rung; prong
sprossen ['ʃprɔsən] intr (HABEN & SEIN) sprout
Sprößling ['ʃprœslɪŋ] m (-s;-e) offspring, descendant; (bot) sprout
Spruch [ʃprux] m (-[e]s;∸e) saying; motto; text, passage; (jur) sentence; (jur) verdict; **e-n S. fällen** give the verdict
Spruch'band n (-[e]s;∸er) banderole
Sprudel ['ʃprudəl] m (-s;-) mineral water
sprudeln ['ʃprudəln] intr bubble
sprühen ['ʃpry·ən] tr emit ‖ intr spray; sparkle; (fig) flash ‖ impers—**es sprüht** it is drizzling
Sprüh'regen m drizzle
Sprüh'teufel m (coll) spitfire
Sprung [ʃpruŋ] m (-[e]s;∸e) jump; crack; (sport) dive
Sprung'brett n diving board; (fig) stepping stone
Spucke ['ʃpukə] f (-;) (coll) spit
spucken ['ʃpukən] tr spit ‖ intr spit; (Motor) sputter
Spuk [ʃpuk] m (-[e]s;-e) ghost, spook; (Lärm) racket; (Alptraum) nightmare
spuken ['ʃpukən] intr linger on ‖ impers—**es spukt hier** this place is haunted
spuk'haft adj spooky
Spülabort ['ʃpylabɔrt] m flush toilet
Spül'becken n sink
Spule ['ʃpulə] f (-;-n) spool, reel; (elec) coil
Spüle ['ʃpylə] f (-;-n) wash basin
spulen ['ʃpulən] tr reel, wind
spülen ['ʃpylən] tr wash, rinse; (Abort) flush; **an Land s.** wash ashore ‖ intr flush the toilet; undulate
Spü'ler m (-s;-) dishwasher
Spülicht ['ʃpylɪçt] n (-[e]s;-e) dishwater; swill, slop
Spül'maschine f dishwasher
Spül'mittel n detergent
Spülwasser n dishwater
Spund [ʃpunt] m (-[e]s;∸e) bung, plug; (carp) feather, tongue
Spur [ʃpur] f (-;-en) trace; track, rut; (hunt) scent; **S. Salz** pinch of salt
spürbar ['ʃpyrbar] adj perceptible
spüren ['ʃpyrən] tr trace; track, trail; (fühlen) feel; (wahrnehmen) perceive
spur'los adj trackless ‖ adv without a trace
Spür'nase f (coll) good nose
Spür'sinn m flair
Spur'weite f (aut) tread; (rr) gauge
sputen ['ʃputən] ref hurry up
SS ['ɛs'ɛs] f (-;) (Schutzstaffel) S.S.
Staat [ʃtat] m (-[e]s;-en) state; government; (Aufwand) show; (Putz) finery
Staats— comb.fm. state; government; national; public; political
Staatsangehörigkeit ['ʃtatsangəhøriç-kait] f (-;) nationality
Staats'anwalt m district attorney
Staats'bauten pl public works
Staats'beamte m civil servant

Staats'bürger –in §6 mf citizen
Staats'bürgerkunde f civics
Staats'bürgerschaft f citizenship
Staats'dienst m civil service
staats'eigen adj state-owned
Staats'feind m public enemy
staats'feindlich adj subversive
Staats'form f form of government
Staats'gewalt f supreme power
Staats'hoheit f sovereignty
staats'klug adj politic, diplomatic
Staats'klugheit f statecraft
Staats'kunst f statesmanship
Staats'mann m (-[e]s;∸er) statesman
staats'männisch adj statesmanlike
Staats'oberhaupt n head of state
Staats'papiere pl government bonds
Staats'recht n public law
Staats'streich m coup d'état
Staats'wirtschaft f political economy
Staats'wissenschaft f political science
Stab [ʃtap] m (-[e]s;∸e) staff; rod; bar; (e-r Jalousie) slat; (eccl) crozier; (mil) staff; (mil) headquarters; (mus, sport) baton
stab'hochspringen §142 intr (SEIN) pole-vault
stabil [ʃta'bil] adj stable, steady
stabilisieren [ʃtabɪli'zirən] tr stabilize
stach [ʃtax] pret of stechen
Stachel ['ʃtaxəl] m (-s;-n) prick; quill; (bot) thorn; (ent) sting
Sta'chelbeere f gooseberry
Sta'cheldraht m barbed wire
stachelig ['ʃtaxəlɪç] adj prickly; (& fig) thorny
Sta'chelschwein n porcupine
Sta·dion ['ʃtadjɔn] n (-s;-dien [djən]) stadium
Sta·dium ['ʃtadjum] n (-s;-dien [djən]) stage
Stadt [ʃtat] f (-;∸e) city, town
Städtchen ['ʃtetçən] n (-s;-) town
Städtebau ['ʃtetəbau] m (-[e]s;) city planning
Stadt'gemeinde f township
Stadt'gespräch n talk of the town
städtisch ['ʃtetɪʃ] adj municipal
Stadt'plan m map of the city
Stadt'rand m outskirts
Stadt'rat m (-[e]s;∸e) city council; (Person) city councilor
Stadt'teil m Stadt'viertel n quarter (of the city)
Stafete [ʃta'fetə] f (-;-n) courier; (sport) relay
Staffel ['ʃtafəl] f (-;-n) step, rung; (Stufe) degree; (aer) squadron (of nine aircraft); (sport) relay team
Staffelei [ʃtafə'lai] f (-;-en) easel
Staf'felkeil m (aer) V-formation
Staf'fellauf m relay race
staffeln ['ʃtafəln] tr graduate; (Arbeitszeit, usw.) stagger
stahl [ʃtal] pret of stehlen ‖ **Stahl** m (-[e]s;∸e) steel
Stahl'beton m reinforced concrete
stählen ['ʃtelən] tr temper; (fig) steel
Stahl'kammer f steel vault
Stahlspäne ['ʃtalʃpenə] pl steel wool
stak [ʃtak] pret of stecken
Stalag ['ʃtalak] n (-s;-s) (Stammlager) main camp (for P.O.W.'s)

Stall [ʃtal] m (-[e]s;⸚e) stable; shed
Stall'knecht m groom
Stamm [ʃtam] m (-[e]s;⸚e) stem; stalk; trunk; stock, race; tribe; breed
Stamm'aktie f common stock
Stamm'baum m family tree; pedigree
stammeln ['ʃtaməln] tr & intr stammer
Stamm'eltern pl ancestors
stammen ['ʃtamən] intr (SEIN) (aus, von) come (from); (von) date (from); (gram) (von) be derived (from)
Stamm'gast m regular customer
stämmig ['ʃtɛmɪç] adj stocky; husky
Stamm'kneipe f favorite bar
Stamm'kunde m, Stamm'kundin f regular customer
Stamm'personal n skeleton staff
Stamm'tisch m reserved table
Stammutter (Stamm'mutter) f ancestress
Stamm'vater m ancestor
stampfen ['ʃtampfən] tr tamp, pound; (Kartoffeln) mash; (Boden) paw || intr stamp the ground; (durch Schnee) trudge; (naut) pitch
stand [ʃtant] pret of stehen || Stand m (-[e]s;⸚e) stand; footing, foothold; level, height; condition; status, rank; class, caste; booth; profession; trade; (sport) score; seinen S. behaupten hold one's ground
Standard ['ʃtandart] m (-s;-s) standard
Standarte [ʃtan'dartə] f (-;-n) banner; standard
Stand'bild n statue
Ständchen ['ʃtɛntçən] n (-s;-) serenade; j-m ein S. bringen serenade s.o.
Ständer ['ʃtɛndər] m (-s;-) stand, rack; pillar; stud; (mach) column
Stan'desamt n bureau of vital statistics
stan'desamtlich adj & adv before a civil magistrate
stan'desgemäß adj according to rank
Stan'desperson f dignitary
stand'fest adj stable, steady, sturdy
stand'haft adj steadfast
stand'halten §90 intr hold out; (dat) withstand
ständig ['ʃtɛndɪç] adj permanent; steady, constant
Stand'licht n parking light
Stand'ort m position; station; (mil) base; (mil) garrison
Stand'pauke f (coll) lecture
Stand'punkt m standpoint
Stand'recht n martial law
Stand'uhr f grandfather's clock
Stange ['ʃtaŋə] f (-;-n) pole; rod, bar; perch, roost; e-e S. Zigaretten a carton of cigarettes; von der S. ready-made (clothes)
stank [ʃtaŋk] pret of stinken
stänkern ['ʃtɛŋkərn] intr (coll) stink; (coll) make trouble
Stanniol [ʃta'njol] n (-s;-e), Stanniol'papier n tinfoil
Stanze ['ʃtantsə] f (-;-n) stanza; punch, die, stamp
stanzen ['ʃtantsən] tr (mach) punch
Stapel ['ʃtapəl] m (-s;-) stack; depot;

stock; (naut) slip; (tex) staple; auf S. liegen be in drydock; vom S. laufen lassen launch
Sta'pellauf m launching
stapeln ['ʃtapəln] tr stack, pile up
Sta'pelplatz m lumberyard; depot
stapfen ['ʃtapfən] intr (SEIN) slog
Star [ʃtar] m (-[e]s;-e) (orn) starling; (pathol) cataract; grauer S. cataract; grüner S. glaucoma || m (-s;-s) (cin, theat) star
starb [ʃtarp] pret of sterben
stark [ʃtark] adj (stärker ['ʃtɛrkər]; stärkste ['ʃtɛrkstə] §9) strong; stout; (Erkältung) bad; (Familie) big; (Kälte) severe; (Frost, Verkehr) heavy; (Wind) high; (Stunde) full || adv much; hard; very
Stärke ['ʃtɛrkə] f (-;-n) strength; force; stoutness; thickness; might; violence; intensity; (Anzahl) number; (fig) forte; (chem) starch
stärken ['ʃtɛrkən] tr strengthen; (Wäsche) starch || ref take some refreshment
Stark'strom m high-voltage current
Stär'kung f (-;-en) strengthening; refreshment; (Imbiß) snack
starr [ʃtar] adj stiff, rigid; fixed; inflexible; obstinate; dumbfounded; numb || adv—s. ansehen stare at
starren ['ʃtarən] intr (auf acc) stare (at); s. von be covered with
Starr'kopf m stubborn fellow
starr'köpfig adj stubborn
Starr'krampf m (-es;) tetanus
Starr'sinn m (-[e]s;) stubbornness
Start [ʃtart] m (-[e]s;-s & -e) start; (aer) take-off; (rok) launching
Start'bahn f (aer) runway
starten ['ʃtartən] tr start; launch || intr (SEIN) start; (aer) take off; (rok) lift off, be launched
Start'rampe f (rok) launch pad
Station [ʃta'tsjon] f (-;-en) station; (med) ward; freie S. free room and board
statisch ['ʃtatɪʃ] adj static
Statist -in [ʃta'tɪst(ɪn)] §7 mf (cin) extra; (theat) supernumerary
Statistik [ʃta'tɪstɪk] f (-;-en) statistic; (Wissenschaft) statistics
statistisch [ʃta'tɪstɪʃ] adj statistical
Stativ [ʃta'tif] n (-s;-e) stand; (phot) tripod
statt [ʃtat] prep (genit) instead of; s. zu (inf) instead of (ger) || Statt f (-;) place, stead; an Kindes S. annehmen adopt
Stätte ['ʃtɛtə] f (-;-n) place, spot; (Wohnung) abode; room
statt'finden §59 intr take place
statt'haft adj admissible; legal
Statthalter ['ʃtathaltər] m (-s;-) governor
statt'lich adj stately; imposing
Statue ['ʃtatu-ə] f (-;-n) statue
statuieren [ʃtatu'irən] tr establish; ein Exempel s. an (dat) make an example of
Statur [ʃta'tur] f (-;-en) stature
Statut [ʃta'tut] n (-[e]s;-en) statute; Statuten bylaws

Stau [ʃtau] m -[e]s;-e dammed-up water; updraft; (aut) tie-up
Staub [ʃtaup] m -[e]s; dust
Stau'becken n reservoir
stauben ['ʃtaubən] intr make dust
stäuben ['ʃtɔibən] tr dust; sprinkle, powder; (Flüssigkeit) spray ‖ intr make dust; throw off spray
staubig ['ʃtaubɪç] adj dusty
staub'saugen tr & intr vacuum
Staub'sauger m vacuum cleaner
Staub'wedel m feather duster
Staub'zucker m powdered sugar
stauchen ['ʃtauçən] tr knock, jolt; compress; (sl) chew out
Stau'damm m dam
Staude ['ʃtaudə] f -;-n perennial
stauen ['ʃtau·ən] tr dam up; (Waren) stow away; (Blut) stanch ‖ ref be blocked, jam up
Stau'er m -s;- stevedore
staunen ['ʃtaunən] intr (über acc) be astonished (at) ‖ **Staunen** n -s; astonishment
stau'nenswert adj astonishing
Staupe ['ʃtaupə] f -s; (vet) distemper
Stau'see m reservoir
Stau'ung f -;-en damming up; blockage; (Engpaß) bottleneck; (Verkehrs-) jam-up; (pathol) congestion
stechen ['ʃteçən] §64 prick; sting, bite; (mit e-r Waffe) stab; (Torf) cut; (Star) remove; (Kontrolluhr) punch; (Wein) draw; (Näherei) stitch; (gravieren) engrave; (cards) trump; (cards) take (a trick) ‖ intr sting, bite; (Sonne) be hot; (cards) be trump; j–m in die Augen s. catch s.o.'s eye ‖ impers—es sticht mich in der Brust I have a sharp pain in my chest
ste'chend adj (Blick) piercing; (Geruch) strong; (Schmerz) sharp, stabbing
Stech'karte f timecard
Stech'schritt m goosestep
Stech'uhr f time clock
Steckbrief ['ʃtɛkbrif] m warrant for arrest
steck'brieflich adv—s. verfolgen put out a "wanted" notice for
Steckdose ['ʃtɛkdozə] f (elec) outlet
stecken ['ʃtɛkən] tr & intr stick ‖ **Stecken** m -s;- stick
steckenbleiben (**steck'kenbleiben**) §62 intr (SEIN) get stuck
Steckenpferd (**Stek'kenpferd**) hobbyhorse; (fig) hobby
Stecker (**Stek'ker**) m -s;- (elec) plug
Steck'kontakt m (elec) plug
Steck'nadel f pin
Steg [ʃtek] m -[e]s;-e footpath; footbridge; (e-r Brille, Geige) bridge; (Landungs-) jetty; (naut) gangplank
Steg'reif m—aus dem S. extempore
stehen ['ʃte·ən] §146 tr—e–m Maler Modell s. sit for a painter; Schlange s. stand in line; Schmiere s. (coll) be a lookout; Wache s. stand guard ‖ intr (HABEN & SEIN) stand; be; (gram) occur, be used; (Kleider) fit; das steht bei Ihnen that depends on you; gut s. (dat) fit, suit; gut s. mit be on good terms with; wie steht's? (coll) how is it going?
ste'henbleiben §62 intr (SEIN) stop
ste'henlassen §104 tr leave standing; (nicht anrühren) leave alone; (Fehler) leave uncorrected; (vergessen) forget; (culin) allow to stand or cool
Ste'her m -s;- long-distance cyclist
Stehlampe ['ʃtelampə] f floor lamp
Stehleiter ['ʃtelaitər] f stepladder
stehlen ['ʃtelən] §147 tr & intr steal
Stehplatz ['ʃteplats] m standing room
steif [ʃtaif] adj stiff; rigid; (Lächeln) forced; (förmlich) formal; (starr) numb
steifen ['ʃtaifən] tr stiffen; (Wäsche) starch
Steig [ʃtaik] m -[e]s;-e path
Steig'bügel m stirrup
steigen ['ʃtaigən] §148 tr (Treppen) climb ‖ intr (SEIN) climb; rise; go up; (Nebel) lift; (Blut in den Kopf) rush ‖ **Steigen** n -s; rise; increase
steigern ['ʃtaigərn] tr raise, increase; (verstärken) enhance; (gram) compare ‖ ref increase, go up
Stei'gerung f -;-en rising; increase; intensification; (gram) comparison
Stei'gerungsgrad m (gram) degree of comparison
Stei'gung f -;-en rise; (Hang) slope; (e-s Propellers) pitch
steil [ʃtail] adj steep
Stein [ʃtain] m -[e]s;-e stone; rock; (horol) jewel; (pathol) stone
stein'alt' adj old as the hills
Stein'bruch m quarry
Stein'druck m lithography; (Bild) lithograph
steinern ['ʃtainərn] adj stone
Stein'gut n earthenware
steinig ['ʃtainɪç] adj stony, rocky
steinigen ['ʃtainigən] tr stone
Stein'kohle f hard coal
Stein'metz m stonemason
stein'reich' adj (coll) filthy rich
Stein'salz n rock salt
Stein'schlag m (public sign) falling rocks
Stein'wurf m stone's throw
Stein'zeit f stone age
Steiß [ʃtais] m -es;-e buttocks
Stelldichein ['ʃteldiçain] n -[s]; -[s]) (coll) date
Stelle ['ʃtelə] f -;-n place, spot; position; job; agency, department; quotation; (math) digit; an S. von in place of; auf der S. on the spot; auf der S. treten (fig & mil) mark time; freie (or offene) S. opening; zur S. sein be on hand
stellen ['ʃtelən] tr put, place; set; stand; (ein-) regulate, adjust; (anordnen) fix, arrange; (Frage) ask; (Horoskop) cast; (Diagnose) give; (Falle, Wecker) set; (Kaution) put up; (Zeugen) produce; e–n Antrag s. make a motion; in Dienst s. appoint; put into service ‖ ref place oneself; stand; give oneself up; der Preis stellt sich auf...the price is...; sich s., als ob act as if

Stel'lenangebot n help wanted

Stel'lenbewerber –in §6 mf applicant

Stel'lengesuch n situation wanted

Stel'lenjagd f job hunting

Stel'lennachweis m, Stel'lenvermittlungsbüro n employment agency

stel'lenweise adv here and there

–stellig [ʃtɛlɪç] comb.fm. –digit

Stell'schraube f set screw

Stel'lung f (–;–en) position; situation; job; standing; status; rank; posture; (mil) line, position; (mil) emplacement; S. nehmen zu express one's opinion on; (erklären) explain; (beantworten) answer

Stel'lungnahme f (–;–n) attitude, point of view; (Erklärung) comment; (Gutachten) opinion; (Bericht) report; (Beantwortung) answer; (Entscheidung) decision; sich [dat] e–e S. vorbehalten not commit oneself

Stel'lungsgesuch n (job) application

stel'lungslos adj jobless

stell'vertretend adj acting

Stell'vertreter –in §6 mf representative; deputy; proxy; substitute

Stell'vertretung f (–;–en) representation; substitution; in S. by proxy

Stelzbein ['ʃtɛltsbaɪn] n wooden leg

Stelze ['ʃtɛltsə] f (–;–n) stilt

stelzen ['ʃtɛltsən] intr (SEIN) stride

Stemmeisen ['ʃtɛmaɪzən] n crowbar

stemmen ['ʃtɛmən] tr support; (Gewicht) lift; (Loch) chisel || ref—sich s. gegen oppose

Stempel ['ʃtɛmpəl] m (–s;–) stamp; prop; (Kolben) piston; (bot) pistil

Stem'pelkissen n ink pad, stamp pad

stempeln ['ʃtɛmpəln] tr stamp || intr—s. gehen (coll) collect unemployment insurance

Stengel ['ʃtɛŋəl] m (–s;–) stalk

Steno ['ʃteno] f (–;) stenography

Stenograf [ʃteno'graf] m (–en;–en) stenographer

Stenographie [ʃtenogra'fi] f (–;) stenography, shorthand

stenographieren [ʃtenogri'firən] tr take down in shorthand || intr do shorthand

Stenographin [ʃteno'grafɪn] f (–;–nen) stenographer

Stenotypistin [ʃtenoty'pɪstɪn] f (–;–nen) stenographer

Step [ʃtɛp] m (–s;–) tap dance; S. tanzen tap-dance

Steppdecke ['ʃtɛpdekə] f comforter

Steppe ['ʃtɛpə] f (–;–n) steppe

steppen ['ʃtɛpən] tr quilt || intr tap-dance || Steppen n (–s;) tap-dancing

Sterbe– ['ʃtɛrbə] comb.fm. dying, death

Ster'befall m death

Ster'begeld n death benefit

Ster'behilfe f euthanasia

sterben ['ʃtɛrbən] §149 intr (SEIN) (an dat) die (of)

sterb'lich adj mortal || adv—s. verliebt in (acc) head over heals in love with

Sterb'lichkeit f (–;) mortality

Sterb'lichkeitsziffer f death rate

stereotyp [stere·o'typ] adj stereotyped

steril [ʃte'ril] adj sterile

sterilisieren [ʃterili'zirən] tr sterilize

Stern [ʃtern] m (–[e]s;–e) star; (typ) asterisk

Stern'bild n constellation

Stern'blume f aster

Sterndeuter ['ʃterndɔɪtər] m (–s;–) astrologer

Sterndeuterei [ʃterndɔɪtə'raɪ] f (–;) astrology

Ster'nenbanner n Stars and Stripes

stern'ha'gelvoll' adj (sl) dead drunk

stern'hell' adj starlit

Stern'himmel m starry sky

Stern'kunde f astronomy

Stern'schuppe f shooting star

Stern'warte f observatory

stet [ʃtet], stetig ['ʃtetɪç] adj steady

stets [ʃtets] adv constantly, always

Steuer ['ʃtɔɪ·ər] f (–;–n) tax; duty || n (–s;–) rudder, helm; (aer) controls; (aut) steering wheel; am S. at the helm; (aut) behind the wheel

Steu'eramt n tax office

Steu'erbord n (naut) starboard

Steu'erebung f levy of taxes

Steu'ererhebung f levy of taxes

Steu'ererklärung f tax return

Steu'erflosse f vertical stabilizer

Steu'erhinterziehung f tax evasion

Steu'erjahr n fiscal year

Steu'erknüppel m control stick

Steu'ermann m (–[e]s;⁻er & –leute) helmsman

steuern ['ʃtɔɪ·ərn] tr steer; control; regulate; (aer, naut) pilot; (aut) drive || intr (dat) curb, check

steu'erpflichtig adj taxable; dutiable

Steu'errad n steering wheel

Steu'erruder n rudder, helm

Steu'ersatz m tax rate

Steu'ersäule f (aer) control column; (aut) steering column

Steu'erstufe f tax bracket

Steu'erung f (–;–en) steering; (Bekämpfung) control; (Verhinderung) prevention; (aer) piloting; (aut) steering mechanism

Steu'erveranlagung f tax assessment

Steu'erwerk n (aer) controls

Steu'erzahler –in §6 mf tax payer

Steu'erzuschlag m surtax

Steven ['ʃtevən] m (–s;–) (naut) stem

Stewar·deß ['st(j)u·ərdes] f (–;–dessen [desən]) (aer) stewardess

stibitzen [ʃti'bɪtsən] tr snitch

Stich [ʃtɪç] m (–[e]s;–e) prick; (Messer–) stab; (Insekten–) sting, bite; (Stoß) thrust; (Seitenstechen) sharp pain; (Kupfer–) engraving; (cards) trick; (naut) knot; (sew) stitch; im S. lassen abandon

Sticheleí [ʃtɪçə'laɪ] f (–;–en) taunt

sticheln ['ʃtɪçəln] intr—gegen j–n s. (fig) needle s.o.

Stich'flamme f flash

stich'haltig adj valid, sound

Stich'probe f spot check

Stich'tag m effective date; due date

Stich'wahl f run-off election

Stich'wort n (–[e]s;⁻er) key word; dictionary entry || n (–[e]s;–e) (theat) cue

Stich'wunde f stab wound

sticken ['ʃtɪkən] tr embroider || intr embroider

Stickerei [ʃtɪkə'raɪ] *f* (-;-en) embroidery

Stick/husten *m* whooping cough

stickig ['ʃtɪkɪç] *adj* stuffy, close

Stick/stoff *m* nitrogen

stieben ['ʃtibən] §130 *intr* (HABEN & SEIN) fly; (*Menge*) disperse

Stief [ʃtif] *comb.fm.* step-

Stief/bruder *m* stepbrother

Stiefel ['ʃtifəl] *m* (-s;-) boot

Stie/felknecht *m* bootjack

Stief/mutter *f* stepmother

Stief/mütterchen *n* (bot) pansy

Stief/vater *m* stepfather

stieg [ʃtik] *pret of* steigen

Stiege ['ʃtigə] *f* (-;-n) staircase

Stiel [ʃtil] *m* (-[e]s;-e) handle; (bot) stalk

stier [ʃtir] *adj* staring, glassy || **Stier** *m* (-[e]s;-e) bull; (astr) Taurus

stieren ['ʃtirən] *intr* (auf *acc*) stare (at)

Stier/kampf *m* bullfight

stieß [ʃtis] *pret of* stoßen

Stift [ʃtɪft] *m* (-[e]s;-e) pin; peg; pencil; crayon; (*Zwecke*) tack; (coll) apprentice || *n* (-[e]s;-e & -er) charitable foundation or institution

stiften ['ʃtɪftən] *tr* (*gründen*) found; (*spenden*) donate; (*verursachen*) cause; (*Unruhe*) stir up; (*Frieden*) make; (*Brand*) start; (*e-e Runde Bier*) set up

Stif/ter -in §6 *mf* founder; donor; (fig) author, cause

Stif/tung *f* (-;-en) foundation; donation; grant; **fromme S.** religious establishment; **milde S.** charitable institution

Stif/tungsfest *n* founder's day

Stil [ʃtil] *m* (-[e]s;-e) style

stil/gerecht *adj* in good taste

stilisieren [ʃtili'zirən] *tr* word

stilistisch [ʃti'lɪstɪʃ] *adj* stylistic

still [ʃtɪl] *adj* still; calm; silent; (com) slack; **im stillen** in secret; **Stiller Ozean** Pacific Ocean || **Stille** *f* (-;) stillness; silence

still/bleiben §62 *intr* (SEIN) keep still

Stilleben (Still/leben) *n* still life

stillegen (still/legen) *tr* (*Betrieb*) shut down; (*Verkehr*) stop; (*Schiff*) put into mothballs

stillen ['ʃtɪlən] *tr* still; (*Hunger*) appease; (*Durst*) quench; (*Blut*) stanch; (*Begierde*) gratify

stilliegen (still/liegen) §108 *intr* lie still; (*Betrieb*) lie idle; (*Verkehr*) be at a standstill

still/schweigen §148 *intr* be silent; **s. zu** acquiesce in || **Stillschweigen** *n* (-s;) silence; secrecy

still/schweigend *adj* silent; (fig) tacit

Still/stand *m* standstill; (*Sackgasse*) stalemate, deadlock

still/stehen §146 *intr* stand still; (*Betrieb*) be idle; (mil) stand at attention; **stillgestanden!** (mil) attention!

Stil/möbel *pl* period furniture

stil/voll *adj* stylish

Stimm- [ʃtɪm] *comb.fm.* vocal; voting

Stimm/abgabe *f* vote, voting

Stimm/band *n* (-[e]s;ᵉer) vocal cord

Stimm/block *m* (parl) bloc

Stimm/bruch *m* change of voice

Stimme ['ʃtɪmə] *f* (-;-n) voice; vote

stimmen ['ʃtɪmən] *tr* make feel (*happy, etc.*); (mus) tune || *intr* be right; vote; (mus) be in tune

Stim/menrutsch *m* (pol) landslide

Stimm/enthaltung *f* abstention

Stimm/gabel *f* tuning fork

Stimm/recht *n* right to vote, suffrage

Stim/mung *f* (-;-en) tone; (*Laune*) mood; (mil) morale; (mus) tuning; (st.exch.) trend

stim/mungsvoll *adj* cheerful

Stimm/zettel *m* ballot

stinken ['ʃtɪŋkən] §143 *intr* stink

Stink/tier *n* skunk

Stipen-dium ['ʃtɪ'pendjum] *n* (-s;-dien [djən]) scholarship, grant

stippen ['ʃtɪpən] *tr* (coll) dunk

Stippvisite ['ʃtɪpvizitə] *f* (-;-n) short visit

Stirn [ʃtɪrn] *f* (-;-en), **Stirne** ['ʃtɪrnə] *f* (-;-n) forehead, brow; (fig) insolence, gall; **die S.** runzeln frown

Stirn/runzeln *n* (-s;) frown(ing)

stob [ʃtop] *pret of* stieben

stöbern ['ʃtøbərn] *tr* (*Wild*) flush; (*aus dem Bett*) yank || *intr* poke around; browse; (*Schnee*) drift

stochern ['ʃtoxərn] *intr* poke around; **im Essen s.** pick at one's food; **im Feuer s.** stoke the fire; **in den Zähnen s.** pick one's teeth

Stock [ʃtok] *m* (-[e]s;ᵉe) stick; cane; wand; baton; stem; vine; tree stump; cleaning rod; beehive; massif; story, floor; **im ersten S.** on the second floor

Stock-, stock- *comb.fm.* thoroughly

stock/blind *adj* stone-blind

stock/dun/kel *adj* pitch-dark

Stöckel ['ʃtœkəl] *m* (-s;-) high heel

stocken ['ʃtokən] *intr* stop; (*Geschäft*) slack off; (*Blut*) coagulate; (*in der Rede*) get stuck; (*Milch*) curdle; (*Stimme*) falter; (*schimmeln*) get moldy; (*Unterhandlungen*) become deadlocked; (*Verkehr*) get tied up; (*zögern*) hesitate || **Stocken** *n* (-s;) stopping; hesitation; **ins S. bringen** tie up

stock/fin/ster *adj* pitch-black

Stock/fleck *m* mildew

stock/fleckig *adj* mildewy

stockig ['ʃtokɪç] *adj* moldy

-stöckig ['ʃtœkɪç] *comb.fm.* -story

stock/nüch/tern *adj* dead-sober

stock/steif *adj* stiff as a board

stock/taub *adj* stone-deaf

Stockung (Stok/kung) *f* (-;-en) stoppage; (*des Verkehrs*) tie-up; (*des Blutes*) congestion; (*Unterbrechung*) interruption; (*Verlangsamung*) slow-down; (*Zeitverlust*) delay; (*Pause*) pause; (*Zögern*) hesitation; (*der Unterhandlungen*) deadlock

Stock/werk *n* story, floor

Stoff [ʃtof] *m* (-[e]s;-e) stuff, matter; fabric; material; cloth; subject, topic; (chem) substance

stoff/lich *adj* material

Stoff/rest *m* (tex) remnant

Stoff'wechsel m metabolism

stöhnen ['ʃtøːnən] intr groan, moan

Stolle ['ʃtɔlə] f (-;-n) fruit cake

Stollen ['ʃtɔlən] m (-s;-) fruit cake; tunnel; (Pfosten) post; (Stütze) prop

stolpern ['ʃtɔlpərn] intr (SEIN) stumble, trip

stolz [ʃtɔlts] adj (auf acc) proud (of) || **Stolz** m (-es;) pride

stolzieren ['ʃtɔl'tsiːrən] intr (SEIN) strut; (Pferd) prance

stopfen ['ʃtɔpfən] tr stuff, cram; (Pfeife) fill; (Strumpf) darn; (mus) mute; j—m den Mund s. shut s.o. up || intr be filling; cause constipation

Stopf'garn n darning yarn

Stoppel ['ʃtɔpəl] f (-;-n) stubble

stoppelig ['ʃtɔpəlɪç] adj stubbly

stoppeln ['ʃtɔpəln] tr glean; (fig) patch

stoppen ['ʃtɔpən] tr stop; clock, time || intr stop

Stopp'licht n tail light; stoplight

Stopp'uhr f stopwatch

Stöpsel ['ʃtœsəl] m (-s;-) stopper, cork; (coll) squirt; (elec) plug

stöpseln ['ʃtœpsəln] tr plug; cork

Storch [ʃtɔrç] m (-[e]s;⸚e) stork

stören ['ʃtøːrən] tr disturb, bother; (Pläne) cross; (Vergnügen) spoil; (mil) harass; (rad) jam

Störenfried ['ʃtøːrənfriːt] m (-[e]s;-e) pain in the neck

störrig ['ʃtœrɪç], **störrisch** ['ʃtœrɪʃ] adj stubborn

Stö'rung f (-;-en) disturbance, trouble; breakdown; interruption; annoyance; intrusion; (rad) static; (rad) jamming

Stoß [ʃtoːs] m (-es;⸚e) push, shove; hit, blow; nudge, poke; (Einschlag) impact; (Erschütterung) shock; (Fecht-) pass; (Feuer-) burst (of fire); (Fuß-) kick; (Haufen) pile, bundle; (Rück-) recoil; (Saum) seam, hem; (Schwimm-) stroke; (Trompeten-) blast; (Wind-) gust; (mil) thrust; (orn) tail

Stoß'dämpfer m shock absorber

Stößel ['ʃtøsəl] m (-s;-) pestle

stoßen ['ʃtoːsən] §150 tr push, shove; hit, knock; kick; punch; jab, nudge, poke; ram; pound; pulverize; oust || ref bump oneself; sich s. an (dat) take offense at; take exception to || intr kick; (mit den Hörnern) butt; (Gewehr) recoil, kick; (Wagen) jolt (Schiff) toss; in die Trompete s. blow the trumpet; s. auf (acc) swoop down on || intr (SEIN)—s. an (acc) bump against; adjoin; be next-door to; s. auf (acc) run into; come across; (naut) dash against; s. durch (mil) smash through; vom Lande s. shove off; zu j—m s. side with s.o.

Stoß'stange f (aut) bumper

Stoß'trupp m assault party; **Stoßtruppen** shock troops; commandos, rangers

Stoß'zahn m tusk

stottern ['ʃtɔtərn] tr stutter, stammer || intr stutter, stammer; (aut) sputter

stracks [ʃtraks] adv immediately; (geradeaus) straight ahead

Straf- [ʃtraf] comb.fm. penal; criminal

Straf'anstalt f penal institution

Straf'arbeit f (educ) extra work

Straf'aufschub m reprieve

strafbar ['ʃtraːfbar] adj punishable

Strafe ['ʃtraːfə] f (-;-n) punishment; penalty; (Geld-) fine; bei S. von under pain of; zur S. as punishment

strafen ['ʃtraːfən] tr punish

straff [ʃtraf] adj tight; (Seil) taut; (gespannt) tense; (aufrecht) erect; (fig) strict; s. spannen tighten

straf'fällig adj punishable; culpable

Straf'geld n fine

Straf'gesetzbuch n penal code

sträflich ['ʃtrɛːflɪç] adj culpable

Sträfling ['ʃtrɛːflɪŋ] m (-s;-e) convict

straf'los adj unpunished

Straf'porto n postage due

Straf'predigt f talking-to, lecture

Straf'raum m (sport) penalty box

Straf'recht n criminal law

Straf'stoß m (sport) penalty kick

Straf'umwandlung f (jur) commutation

Straf'verfahren n criminal proceedings

Strahl [ʃtraːl] m (-[e]s;-en) ray; beam; flash; jet; (geom) radius

Strahl'antrieb m jet propulsion

strahlen ['ʃtraːlən] intr beam, shine

Strahl'motor m, **Strahl'triebwerk** n jet engine

Strah'lung f (-;-en) radiation

Strähne ['ʃtrɛːnə] f (-;-n) strand; lock; hank, skein

strähnig ['ʃtrɛːnɪç] adj wispy

stramm [ʃtram] adj tight; (kräftig) strapping; (Zucht) strict; (Arbeit) hard; (Soldat) smart; (Mädel) buxom || adv—s. stehen stand at attention

stramm'ziehen §163 tr draw tight

strampeln ['ʃtrampəln] intr kick

Strand [ʃtrant] m (-[e]s;⸚e) beach, seashore, shore

stranden ['ʃtrandən] intr (SEIN) be beached, run aground, be stranded

Strand'gut n flotsam, jetsam

Strand'gutjäger –in §6 mf beachcomber

Strand'korb m hooded beach chair

Strand'schirm m beach umbrella

Strang [ʃtraŋ] m (-[e]s;⸚e) rope; (Strähne) hank; (Zugseil) trace; (rr) track; wenn alle Stränge reißen (fig) if worse comes to worst

Strapaze [ʃtra'paːtsə] f (-;-n) fatigue; exertion, strain

strapazieren [ʃtrapa'tsiːrən] tr tire out; (Kleider) wear hard

strapazier'fähig adj heavy-duty

strapaziös [ʃtrapa'tsjøːs] adj tiring

Straße ['ʃtraːsə] f (-;-n) street; road; highway; (Meerenge) strait

Stra'ßenanzug m business suit

Stra'ßenbahn f streetcar, trolley; trolley line

Stra'ßenbahnwagen m streetcar

Stra'ßendirne f streetwalker

Stra'ßengraben m ditch, gutter

Stra'ßenhändler –in §6 mf street vendor

Stra'ßenjunge m urchin

Stra'ßenkarte f street map

Stra'ßenkreuzung f intersection

Stra'ßenlage f (aut) roadability

Stra'ßenrennen n drag race

Stra'ßenrinne f gutter

Stra'ßenschild n street sign

Stra'ßensperrung f (public sign) road closed

Stra'ßenstreife f highway patrol

strategisch [ʃtra'teːgɪʃ] adj strategic

sträuben ['ʃtrɔɪbən] tr ruffle ‖ ref bristle, stand on end; **sich s. gegen** resist, struggle against

Strauch [ʃtraux] m (-[e]s;˙-er) shrub

straucheln ['ʃtrauxəln] intr (SEIN) stumble, trip; (fig) go wrong

Strauß [ʃtraus] m (-[e]s;˙-e) bouquet ‖ m (-[e]s;-e) ostrich

Strebe ['ʃtreːbə] f (-;-n) prop, strut

Stre'bebogen m flying buttress

streben ['ʃtreːbən] intr (nach) strive (after); (nach) tend (toward) ‖ Streben n (-s;-) striving; pursuit; (Hang) tendency; (Anstrengung) endeavor

Stre'ber m (-s;-) go-getter, eager beaver; social climber; (in der Schule) grind

strebsam ['ʃtreːpzam] adj zealous

Streb'samkeit f (-;) zeal; industry

Strecke ['ʃtrekə] f (-;-n) stretch; extent; distance; stage, leg; (geom) straight line; (hunt) bag; (rr) section; **zur S. bringen** catch up with; (box) defeat; (hunt) bag

strecken ['ʃtrekən] tr stretch; (Metalle) laminate; (Wein) dilute; (fig) make last; **die Waffen s.** lay down one's arms ‖ ref stretch (oneself)

Streich [ʃtraɪç] m (-[e]s;-e) blow; (fig) trick, prank

streicheln ['ʃtraɪçəln] tr stroke; pat

streichen ['ʃtraɪçən] §85 tr stroke; (Butter, usw.) spread; (an-) paint; (Geige) play; (Messer) whet; (Rasiermesser) strop; (Streichholz) strike; (Flagge, Segel) lower; (Ärmel) roll down; (Ziegel) make; (mit Ruten) flog; delete; (sport) scratch ‖ intr—mit der Hand s. über (acc) pass one's hand over ‖ intr (SEIN) stretch, extend; wander; pass, move; rush

Streich'holz n match

Streich'holzbrief m matchbook

Streich'instrument n stringed instrument

Streich'orchester n string band

Streich'riemen m razor strop

Streif [ʃtraɪf] m (-[e]s;-e) streak, stripe; strip

Streif'band n (-[e]s;˙-er) wrapper

Streife ['ʃtraɪfə] f (-;-n) raid; (Runde) beat; (mil) patrol

streifen ['ʃtraɪfən] tr stripe; streak; graze; skim over; (abziehen) strip; (grenzen an) verge on; (Thema) touch on ‖ intr (SEIN) roam; (mil) patrol; **s. an** (acc) brush against; (fig) verge on; **s. über** (acc) scan ‖ Streifen m (-s;-) stripe; streak; strip; slip; (cin) movie

Strei'fendienst m patrol duty

Strei'fenwagen m patrol car, squad car

streifig ['ʃtraɪfɪç] adj striped

Streif'licht n flash, streak of light; **S. werfen auf** (acc) shed light on

Streif'wunde f scratch

Streif'zug m exploratory trip, looksee

Streik [ʃtraɪk] m (-[e]s;-s) strike, walkout; **wilder S.** wildcat strike

streiken ['ʃtraɪkən] intr go on strike

Strei'kende §5 mf striker

Streik'posten m picket; **S. stehen** picket

Streit [ʃtraɪt] m (-[e]s;-e) fight; argument, quarrel; (jur) litigation

Streit'axt f battle-ax; **die S. begraben** (fig) bury the hatchet

streitbar ['ʃtraɪtbar] adj belligerent

streiten ['ʃtraɪtən] §86 recip & intr quarrel

Streit'frage f point at issue

streitig ['ʃtraɪtɪç] adj controversial; at issue

Streit'kräfte pl (mil) forces, troops

streit'lustig adj belligerent, scrappy

Streit'objekt n bone of contention

Streit'punkt m issue, point at issue

streit'süchtig adj quarrelsome

streng [ʃtreŋ] adj severe, stern; austere; strict; (Geschmack) sharp ‖ Strenge f (-;) severity, sternness; austerity; strictness; sharpness

streng'genommen adv strictly speaking

streng'gläubig adj orthodox

Streu [ʃtrɔɪ] f (-;-en) straw bed

Streu'büchse f shaker

streuen ['ʃtrɔɪ.ən] tr strew, sprinkle; (ausbreiten) spread; (verbreiten) scatter ‖ intr spread, scatter

strich [ʃtrɪç] pret of streichen ‖ Strich m (-[e]s;-e) stroke; line; (Streif) stripe; (Landstrich) tract; (carp) grain; (tex) nap; (typ) dash; **auf den S. gehen** walk the streets (as prostitute); **gegen den S. gehen** go against the grain; (fig) rub the wrong way

Strich'mädchen n streetwalker

Strich'punkt m semicolon

Strich'regen m local shower

strich'weise adv here and there

Strick [ʃtrɪk] m (-[e]s;-e) rope, cord; (fig) rogue, good-for-nothing

stricken ['ʃtrɪkən] tr & intr knit

Strick'garn n knitting yarn

Strick'jacke f cardigan

Strick'kleid n knitted dress

Strick'leiter f rope ladder

Strick'waren pl knitwear

Strick'zeug n knitting things

Striemen ['ʃtriːmən] m (-s;-) stripe, streak; (in der Haut) weal

Strippe ['ʃtrɪpə] f (-;-n) string; strap; shoestring; (telp) line

stritt [ʃtrɪt] pret of streiten

strittig ['ʃtrɪtɪç] adj controversial

Stroh [ʃtroː] n (-[e]s;) straw

Stroh'dach n thatched roof

Stroh'halm m straw; drinking straw

Stroh'mann m (-[e]s;˙-er) scarecrow; (cards) dummy

Stroh'puppe f scarecrow

Stroh'sack m straw mattress; **heiliger S.!** holy smokes!

Strolch [ʃtrɔlç] m (-[e]s;-e) bum

strolchen ['ʃtrɔlçən] intr bum around

Strom [ʃtroːm] m (-[e]s;˙-e) river; stream; (von Worten) torrent; (& elec) current

stromab′wärts *adv* downstream
stromauf′wärts *adv* upstream
Strom′ausfall *m* (elec) power failure
strömen [′ʃtrøːmən] *intr* (HABEN & SEIN) stream; (*Regen*) pour (down)
Stro′mer *m* (-s;-) (coll) tramp
Strom′kreis *m* (elec) circuit
strom′linienförmig *adj* streamlined
Strom′richter *m* (elec) converter
Strom′schnelle *f* rapids
Strom′spannung *f* voltage
Strom′stärke *f* (elec) amperage
Strö′mung *f* (-;-en) current; trend
Strom′unterbrecher *m* circuit breaker
Strom′wandler *m* (elec) transformer
Strom′zähler *m* electric meter
Strophe [′ʃtroːfə] *f* (-;-n) stanza
strotzen [′ʃtrɔtsən] *intr*—s. **von** or **vor** (*dat*) abound in, teem with
Strudel [′ʃtruːdəl] *m* (-s;-) eddy, whirlpool; (fig) maelstrom; (culin) strudel
strudeln [′ʃtruːdəln] *intr* eddy, whirl
Struktur [ʃtrʊk′tuːr] *f* (-;-en) structure; (tex) texture
Strumpf [ʃtrʊmpf] *m* (-[e]s;⸚e) stocking
Strumpf′band *n* (-[e]s;⸚er), **Strumpfhalter** *m* garter
Strumpf′waren *pl* hosiery
struppig [′ʃtrʊpɪç] *adj* shaggy, unkempt
Stube [′ʃtuːbə] *f* (-;-n) room
Stu′benmädchen *n* chambermaid
stu′benrein *adj* housebroken
Stubsnase [′ʃtʊpsnaːzə] *f* snub nose
Stuck [ʃtʊk] *m* (-[e]s;) stucco
Stück [ʃtyk] *n* (-[e]s;-e) piece; lot; plot; stretch distance; (*Butter*) pat; (*Zucker*) lump; (*Seife*) cake; (*Vieh*) head; (mus) piece, number; (theat) play, show; **pro S.** apiece
stückeln [′ʃtykəln] *tr* cut or break into small pieces; piece together
stück′weise *adv* piecemeal
Stück′werk *n* patchwork
Student [ʃtu′dɛnt] *m* (-en;-en) college student
Studen′tenheim *n* dormitory
Studen′tenverbindung *f* fraternity
Studentin [ʃtu′dɛntɪn] *f* (-;-nen) college student, coed
Studie [′ʃtuːdjə] *f* (-;-n) (Lit) essay; (paint) study, sketch
Stu′diengang *m* (educ) course
Stu′dienplan *m* curriculum
Stu′dienrat *m* (-[e]s;⸚e) high school teacher
Stu′dienreferendar –in §8 *mf* practice teacher
Stu′dienreise *f* (educ) field trip
studieren [ʃtu′diːrən] *tr* & *intr* study (*at college*); examine
studiert [ʃtu′diːrt] *adj* college-educated; (*gekünstelt*) affected
Studier′zimmer *n* study
Stu-dium [′ʃtuːdjʊm] *n* (-s;-dien [djən]) study (*at college*); studies
Stufe [′ʃtuːfə] *f* (-;-n) step, stair; (*e-r Leiter*) rung; (*Grad*) stage; (*Niveau*) level; stage; (mus) interval
Stu′fenfolge *f* graduation; succession
Stu′fenleiter *f* stepladder; (fig) gamut
stu′fenweise *adv* by degrees

Stuhl [ʃtuːl] *m* (-[e]s;⸚e) chair; (*Stuhlgang*) stool, feces; **der Heilige S.** the Holy See
Stuhl′bein *n* leg of a chair
Stuhl′drang *m* urgent call of nature
Stuhl′gang *m* stool, feces; **S. haben** have a bowel movement
Stuhl′lehne *f* back of a chair
Stulpe [′ʃtʊlpə] *f* (-;-n) cuff
Stülpnase [′ʃtʏlpnaːzə] *f* snub nose
stumm [ʃtʊm] *adj* dumb; mute; (*schweigend*) silent; (gram) mute
Stummel [′ʃtʊməl] *m* (-s;-) (e-s *Armes, Baumes, e-r Zigarette*) stump
Stümper [′ʃtʏmpər] *m* (-s;-) bungler
Stümperei [ʃtʏmpə′raɪ] *f* (-;-en) bungling
stüm′perhaft *adj* bungling
stümpern [′ʃtʏmpərn] *tr* & *intr* bungle
stumpf [ʃtʊmpf] *adj* blunt; (& fig) obtuse ‖ **Stumpf** *m* (-[e]s;⸚e) stump
Stumpf′sinn *m* apathy, dullness
stumpf′sinnig *adj* dull, stupid
Stunde [′ʃtʊndə] *f* (-;-n) hour; (educ) class, lesson, period
stunden [′ʃtʊndən] *tr* grant postponement of
Stun′dengeld *n* tutoring fee
Stun′dengeschwindigkeit *f* miles per hour
Stun′denkilometer *pl* kilometers per hour
stun′denlang *adv* for hours
Stun′denlohn *m* hourly wage(s)
Stun′denplan *m* roster, schedule
stun′denweise *adv* by the hour
Stun′denzeiger *m* hour hand
–stündig [′ʃtʏndɪç] *comb.fm.* –hour
stündlich [′ʃtʏntlɪç] *adj* hourly
Stun′dung *f* (-;-en) period of grace
Stunk [ʃtʊŋk] *m* (-[e]s;) stink; **S. machen** (sl) raise a stink
Stups [ʃtʊps] *m* (-es;-e) nudge
stupsen [′ʃtʊpsən] *tr* nudge
Stups′nase *f* snub nose
stur [ʃtuːr] *adj* stubborn; (*Blick*) fixed
Sturm [ʃtʊrm] *m* (-[e]s;⸚e) storm; gale
Sturm′abteilung *f* storm troopers
stürmen [′ʃtʏrmən] *tr* storm ‖ *intr* rage, roar ‖ *intr* (SEIN) rush ‖ *impers* —es stürmt it is stormy
Stürmer [′ʃtʏrmər] *m* (-s;-) (fb) forward
stürmisch [′ʃtʏrmɪʃ] *adj* stormy; impetuous ‖ *adv*—**nicht so s.!** not so fast!
Sturm′schritt *m* (mil) double time
Sturm′trupp *m* assault party
Sturm′welle *f* (mil) assault wave
Sturm′wind *m* gale, hurricane
Sturz [ʃtʊrts] *m* (-es;⸚e) fall, sudden drop; overthrow; collapse; (archit) lintel; (aut) camber; (com) slump
Sturz′bach *m* torrent
Sturz′bomber *m* dive bomber
Stürze [′ʃtʏrtsə] *f* (-;-n) lid
stürzen [′ʃtʏrtsən] *tr* throw down; upset, overturn; overthrow; (*tauchen*) plunge; **nicht s.!** this side up! ‖ *ref* rush; plunge ‖ *intr* (SEIN) fall, tumble; rush; (*Tränen*) pour; (aer) dive
Sturz′flug *m* (aer) dive
Sturz′helm *m* crash helmet

Sturz'regen m downpour
Sturz'see f heavy seas
Stute ['ʃtuta] f (-;-n) mare
Stütze ['ʃtytsə] f (-;-n) support, prop; (fig) help, support
stutzen ['ʃtutsən] tr cut short; (Flügel) clip; (Bäume) prune; (Ohren) crop; (Bart) trim || intr stop short; be startled; (Pferd) shy
stützen ['ʃtytsən] tr support; prop; shore up; (fig) support || ref—sich s. auf (acc) lean on; (fig) depend on
Stutzer ['ʃtutsər] m (-s;-) car coat; (coll) snazzy dresser
Stutz'flügel m baby grand piano
stutzig ['ʃtutsɪç] adj suspicious
Stütz'pfeiler m abutment
Stütz'punkt m footing; (mil) base; (phys) fulcrum
Subjekt [zup'jekt] n (-[e]s;-e) (coll) guy, character; (gram) subject
subjektiv [zupjek'tif] adj subjective
Substantiv [zupstan'tif] n (-[e]s;-e) (gram) substantive, noun
Substanz [zup'stants] f (-;-en) substance
subtil [zup'til] adj subtle
subtrahieren [zuptra'hirən] tr subtract
Subtraktion [zuptrak'tsjon] f (-;-en) subtraction
Subvention [zupven'tsjon] f (-;-en) subsidy
Such- [zux] comb.fm. search
Such'anzeige f want ad
Such'büro n, **Such'dienst** m missing-persons bureau
Suche ['zuxə] f (-;-en) search; auf der S. nach in search of, in quest of
suchen ['zuxən] tr search for, look for; (erstreben) seek; want, desire; (in der Zeitung) advertise for; (Gefahr) court; das Weite s. run away || intr search; nach etw s. look for s.th.
Sucht [zuxt] f (-;-e) passion, mania; (nach) addiction (to)
süchtig ['zyçtɪç] adj addicted || Süchtige §5 mf addict
Sud [zut] m (-[e]s;-e) brewing; brew
Süd [zyt] m (-[e]s) south
sudelhaft ['zudəlhaft], **sudelig** ['zudəlɪç] adj slovenly, sloppy
sudeln ['zudəln] tr & intr mess up
Süden ['zydən] m (-s;) south
Sudeten [zu'detən] pl Sudeten mountains (along northern border of Czechoslovakia)
Süd'früchte pl (tropical and subtropical) fruit (e.g., bananas, oranges)
süd'lich adj south, southern, southerly; s. von south of || adv south
Südost' m, **Süd'o'sten** m southeast
südöst'lich adj southeast(ern)
Süd'pol m (-s;) South Pole
südwärts ['zytverts] adv southward
Südwest' m, **Süd'we'sten** m southwest
süffig ['zyfɪç] adj tasty
suggerieren [zuge'rirən] tr suggest
suggestiv [zuges'tif] adj suggestive
Suggestiv'frage f leading question
suhlen ['zulən] ref wallow
Sühne ['zynə] f (-;) atonement
sühnen ['zynən] tr atone for, expiate
Sülze ['zyltsə] f (-;-n) jellied meat

summarisch [zu'marɪʃ] adj summary
Summe ['zumə] f (-;-n) sum, total
summen ['zumən] tr hum || intr hum; buzz
Sum'mer m (-s;-) buzzer
summieren [zu'mirən] tr sum up, total || ref run up, pile up
Summton ['zumton] m (telp) dial tone
Sumpf [zumpf] m (-[e]s;-e) swamp
sumpfig ['zumpfɪç] adj swampy, marshy
Sünde ['zyndə] f (-;-n) sin
Sün'denbock m scapegoat
Sün'deneriaß m absolution
Sün'denfall m original sin
Sün'der m (-s;-) sinner
Sünd'flut ['zyntflut] f Deluge
sünd'haft, sündig ['zyndɪç] adj sinful
sündigen ['zyndɪgən] intr sin
Superlativ ['zuperlatif] m (-s;-e) (gram) superlative
Su'permarkt m supermarket
Suppe ['zupə] f (-;-n) soup
Sup'penschüssel f tureen
surren ['zurən] intr buzz
Surrogat [zuro'gat] n (-[e]s;-e) substitute
suspendieren [zuspen'dirən] tr suspend
süß [zys] adj sweet || **Süße** f (-;) sweetness
süßen ['zysən] tr sweeten
Sü'ßigkeit f (-;-en) sweetness; Süßigkeiten sweets, candy
süß'kartoffel f sweet potato
süß'lich adj sweetish; (fig) mawkish
Süß'stoff m artificial sweetener
Süß'waren pl sweets, candy
Süß'wasser n fresh water
Symbol [zym'bol] n (-s;-e) symbol
Symbolik [zym'bolɪk] f (-;) symbolism
symbolisch [zym'bolɪʃ] adj symbolic(al)
Symme·trie [zyme'tri] f (-;-trien) ['tri·ən]) symmetry
symmetrisch [zy'metrɪʃ] adj symmetrical
Sympa·thie [zympa'ti] f (-;-thien ['ti·ən]) liking
sympathisch [zym'patɪʃ] adj likeable; er ist mir s. I like him
sympathisieren [zympatɪ'zirən] intr—s. mit sympathize with; like
Sympho·nie [zymfo'ni] f (-;-nien ['ni·ən]) symphony
Symptom [zymp'tom] n (-s;-e) symptom
symptomatisch [zympto'matɪʃ] adj (für) symptomatic (of)
Synagoge [zyna'gogə] f (-;-n) synagogue
synchronisieren [zynkronɪ'zirən] tr synchronize
Syndikat [zyndɪ'kat] n (-[e]s;-e) syndicate
Syndi·kus ['zyndɪkus] m (-;-kusse & -ki [ki]) corporation lawyer
synonym [zyno'nym] adj synonymous || Synonym n (-s;-e) synonym
Syntax ['zyntaks] f (-;) syntax
synthetisch [zyn'tetɪʃ] adj synthetic
Syrien ['zyrjən] n (-s;) Syria

System [zɪs'tem] *n* (-s;-e) system
systematisch [zɪste'mɑtɪʃ] *adj* systematic
Szene ['stsenə] *f* (-;-n) scene; in S.

setzen stage; sich in S. setzen put on an act
Sze'nenaufnahme *f* (cin) take
Szenerie [stenə'ri] *f* (-;) scenery

T

T, t [te] *invar n* T, t
Tabak [ta'bak], ['tɑbak] *m* (-[e]s;-e) tobacco
Tabaks'beutel *m* tobacco pouch
Tabak'trafik *f* (Aust) cigar store
Tabak'waren *pl* tobacco products
tabellarisch [tabe'lɑrɪʃ] *adj* tabular
tabellarisieren [tabelɑrɪ'zirən] *tr* tabulate
Tabelle [ta'bɛlə] *f* (-;-n) table, chart; graph
Tabernakel [taber'nakəl] *m & n* (-s;-) tabernacle
Tablett [ta'blet] *n* (-[e]s;-e) tray
Tablette [ta'bletə] *f* (-;-n) tablet, pill
tabu [ta'bu] *adj* taboo || Tabu *n* (-s; -s) taboo
Tachometer [taxo'metər] *n* speedometer
Tadel ['tɑdəl] *m* (-s;-) scolding; (*Schuld*) blame; (educ) demerit
ta'dellos *adj* blameless; flawless
tadeln ['tɑdəln] *tr* scold, reprimand; blame, find fault with
Tafel ['tɑfəl] *f* (-;-n) (*Tisch, Diagramm*) table; (*Anschlag-*) billboard; (*Glas-*) pane; (*Holz-, Schalt-*) panel; (*Mahlzeit*) meal, dinner; (*Metall-*) sheet, plate; (*Platte*) slab; (*Schiefer-*) slate; (*Schreib-*) tablet; (*Schokolade*) bar; (*Wand-*) blackboard; bei T. at dinner; die T. decken set the table; offene T. halten have open house
Ta'felaufsatz *m* centerpiece
Ta'felbesteck *n* knife, fork, and spoon
ta'felförmig *adj* tabular
Ta'felgeschirr *n* table service
Ta'felland *n* tableland, plateau
Ta'felmusik *f* dinner music
tafeln ['tɑfəln] *intr* dine, feast
täfeln ['tɛfəln] *tr* (*Wand*) wainscot, panel; (*Fußboden*) parquet
Ta'felöl *n* salad oil
Ta'felservice *n* tableware
Tä'felung *f* (-;-en) inlay; paneling
Taft [taft] *m* (-[e]s;-e) taffeta
Tag [tak] *m* (-[e]s;-e) day; daylight; am Tage by day; am Tage nach the day after; an den Tag bringen bring to light; bei Tage by day, in the daytime; den ganzen Tag all day long; e-n Tag um den andern every other day; e-s Tages someday; es wird Tag day is breaking; guten Tag! hello!; how do you do?; (*bei Verabschiedung*) good day!; goodby!; Tag der offenen Tür open house; unter Tage (min) underground, below the surface
tagaus', tagein' *adv* day in and day out
Tage- [tagə] *comb.fm.* day-, daily

Ta'geblatt *n* daily, daily paper
Ta'gebuch *n* diary, journal
Ta'gegeld *n* per diem allowance
ta'gelang *adv* for days
Ta'gelohn *m* daily wage
Tagelöhner –in ['tagəlønər(ɪn)] §6 *mf* day laborer
tagen ['tɑgən] *intr* dawn; (*beraten*) meet; (jur) be in session
Ta'gesanbruch *m* daybreak
Ta'gesangriff *m* (aer) daylight raid
Ta'gesbefehl *m* (mil) order of the day
Ta'gesbericht *m* daily report
Ta'geseinnahme *f* daily receipts
Ta'gesgespräch *n* topic of the day
ta'geshell' *adj* as light as day
Ta'geskasse *f* (theat) box office
Ta'gesleistung *f* daily output
Ta'geslicht *n* daylight
Ta'geslichtaufnahme *f* (phot) daylight shot
Ta'gesordnung *f* agenda; (coll) order of the day
Ta'gespreis *m* market price
Ta'gespresse *f* daily press
Ta'gesschau *f* (telv) news
Ta'geszeit *f* time of day; daytime; zu jeder T. at any hour
Ta'geszeitung *f* daily paper
ta'geweise *adv* by the day
Ta'gewerk *n* day's work
-tägig [tegɪç] *comb.fm.* -day
täglich ['teklɪç] *adj* daily
tags [taks] *adv* —t. darauf the following day; t. zuvor the day before
Tag'schicht *f* day shift
tags'über *adv* during the day, in the daytime
Tagung ['tɑguŋ] *f* (-;-en) convention, conference, meeting
Ta'gungsort *m* meeting place
Taifun [tai'fun] *m* (-s;-e) typhoon
Taille ['taljə] *f* (-;-n) waist; (*Mieder*) bodice
Takel ['tɑkəl] *n* (-s;-) tackle
Takelage [takə'lɑʒə] *f* (-;-n) rigging
takeln ['tɑkəln] *tr* rig
Ta'kelwerk *n* var of Takelage
Takt [takt] *m* (-[e]s;-e) tact; (mach) stroke; (mus) time, beat; (mus) bar; den T. schlagen mark time; im T. in time; in step; T. halten mark time
takt'fest *adj* keeping good time; (fig) reliable
Taktik ['taktɪk] *f* (-;-en) (& fig) tactics
Tak'tiker *m* (-s;-) tactician
taktisch ['taktɪʃ] *adj* tactical
takt'los *adj* tactless
Takt'messer *m* metronome
Takt'stock *m* baton

Takt′strich m (mus) bar
takt′voll adj tactful
Tal [tɑl] n (-[e]s;⁻er) valley
Talar [ta′lɑr] m (-s;-e) robe, gown
Tal′boden m valley floor
Talent [ta′lɛnt] n (-[e]s;-e) talent
talentiert [talɛn′tirt] adj talented
Tal′fahrt f descent
Talg [talk] m -[e]s;-e) suet; tallow
Talg/kerze f, **Talg/licht** n tallow candle
Talisman [′tɑlɪsman] m (-s;-e) talisman
Talk(um)puder [′talk(ʊm)pudər] m talcum powder
Talmi [′talmi] n (-s;) (fig) imitation
Tal′sperre f dam
Tamburin [tambu′rin] n (-s;-e) tambourine
Tampon [tã′põ] m (-s;-s) (med) tampon
Tamtam [tam′tam] n (-s;-s) gong; (fig) fanfare, drum beating
Tand [tant] m (-[e]s;) trifle; bauble
tändeln [′tɛndəln] intr trifle; flirt
Tang [taŋ] m (-[e]s;-e) seaweed
Tangente [taŋ′gɛntə] f (-;-n) (geom) tangent
tangieren [taŋ′girən] tr concern
Tango [′taŋgo] m (-s;-s) tango
Tank [taŋk] m (-[e]s;-e & -s) tank
tanken [′taŋkən] intr get gas; refuel
Tan′ker m, **Tank′schiff** n tanker
Tank′stelle f gas (or service) station
Tank′wagen m tank truck; (rr) tank car
Tankwart [′taŋkvart] m (-[e]s;-e) gas station attendant
Tanne [′tanə] f (-;-n) fir (tree)
Tan′nenbaum m fir tree
Tan′nenzapfen m fir cone
Tante [′tantə] f (-;-n) aunt; T. Meyer (coll) john
Tantieme [tã′tjemə] f (-;-n) dividend; (com) royalty
Tanz [tants] m (-es;⁻e) dance
Tanz′bein n—das T. schwingen (coll) cut a rug
Tanz′diele f dance hall
tänzeln [′tɛntsəln] intr (HABEN & SEIN) skip about; (Pferd) prance
tanzen [′tantsən] tr & intr dance
Tänzer –in [′tɛntsər(ɪn)] §6 mf dancer
Tanz′fläche f dance floor
Tanz′kapelle f dance band
Tanz′lokal n dance hall
Tanz′saal m ballroom
Tanz′schritt m dance step
Tanz′stunde f dancing lesson
Tapete [ta′petə] f (-;-n) wallpaper
Tape′tenpapier n wallpaper (in rolls)
Tape′tentür f wallpapered door
Tapezierarbeit [tape′tsirarbaɪt] f paperhanging
tapezieren [tape′tsirən] tr wallpaper
Tapezie′rer m (-s;-) paperhanger
tapfer [′tapfər] adj brave, valiant
Ta′pferkeit f (-;) bravery, valor
tappen [′tapən] intr (HABEN & SEIN) grope about; t. nach grope for
täppisch [′tɛpɪʃ] adj clumsy
tapsen [′tapsən] intr (SEIN) clump along

Tara [′tɑra] f (-;) (com) tare
Tarif [ta′rif] m (-s;-e) tariff; price list; wage scale; postal rates
Tarif′lohn m standard wages
Tarif′verhandlung f collective bargaining
Tarif′vertrag m wage agreement
Tarn– [tarn] comb.fm. camouflage
tarnen [′tarnən] tr camouflage
Tarn′kappe f (myth) magic cap (rendering wearer invisible)
Tar′nung f (-;) camouflage
Tasche [′taʃə] f (-;-n) pocket; handbag; pocketbook; schoolbag; flight bag; pouch; briefcase
Ta′schenausgabe f pocket edition
Ta′schenbuch n paperback
Ta′schendieb m pickpocket
Ta′schendiebstahl m pickpocketing
Ta′schengeld n pocket money
Ta′schenlampe f flashlight
Ta′schenmesser n pocketknife
Ta′schenrechner m pocket calculator
Ta′schenspieler –in §6 mf magician
Ta′schenspielerei f sleight of hand
Ta′schentuch n handkerchief
Ta′schenuhr f pocket watch
Ta′schenwörterbuch n pocket dictionary
Tasse [′tasə] f (-;-n) cup
Tastatur [tasta′tur] f (-;-en) keyboard
Taste [′tastə] f (-;-n) key
tasten [′tastən] tr feel, touch; (telg) send ‖ ref feel one's way ‖ intr (nach) grope (for)
Tastsinn [′tastzɪn] m sense of touch
tat [tɑt] pret of **tun** ‖ **Tat** f (-;-en) deed, act; (Verbrechen) crime; auf frischer Tat ertappen catch redhanded; in der Tat in fact; in die Tat umsetzen implement
Tat′bestand m facts of the case
Tat′bestandsaufnahme f factual statement
tatenlos [′tɑtənlos] adj inactive
Ta′tenlosigkeit f (-;) inactivity
Täter –in [′tɛtər(ɪn)] §6 mf doer, perpetrator; culprit
Tat′form f (gram) active voice
tätig [′tɛtɪç] adj active; busy; t. sein bei be employed by
tätigen [′tɛtɪgən] tr conclude
Tä′tigkeit f (-;-en) activity; occupation, job, profession
Tä′tigkeitsbericht m progress report
Tä′tigkeitsfeld n field, line
Tä′tigung f (-;-en) transaction
Tat′kraft f energy, strength; vigor
tat′kräftig adj energetic; vigorous
tätlich [′tɛtlɪç] adj violent; tätliche Beleidigung (jur) assault and battery; t. werden gegen assault ‖ adv –t. beleidigen (jur) assault
Tät′lichkeit f (-;-en) (act of) violence; es kam zu Tätlichkeiten it came to blows
Tat′ort m scene of the crime
tätowieren [teto′virən] tr tattoo
Tätowie′rung f (-;-en) tattoo
Tat′sache f fact
Tat′sachenbericht m factual report
tat′sächlich adj actual, real, factual
tätscheln [′tɛtʃəln] tr pet, stroke

Tatterich ['tatərɪç] m (-s;) shakes

Tatze ['tatsə] f (-;-n) paw

Tau [tau] m (-[e]s;) dew || n (-[e]s; -e) rope; (naut) hawser

taub [taup] adj deaf; (betäubt) numb; (unfruchtbar) barren; (Gestein) not containing ore; (Nuß) hollow; (Ei) unfertile; (Hafer) wild; t. gegen deaf to; t. vor Kälte numb with cold

Taube ['taubə] f (-;-n) pigeon; (pol) dove

Tau'benhaus n, Tau'benschlag m dove-cote

Taub'heit f (-;) deafness; numbness

taub'stumm adj deaf and dumb || Taub-stumme §5 mf deaf-mute

Tauchboot ['tauxbot] n submarine

tauchen ['tauxən] tr dip, duck, immerse || intr (HABEN & SEIN) dive, plunge; (naut) submerge, dive

Tau'cher -in §6 mf (& orn) diver

Tau'cheranzug m diving suit

Tau'chergerät n aqualung

Tau'cherglocke f diving bell

Tauch'krankheit f bends

Tauch'schwimmer m (nav) frogman

tauen ['tau·ən] tr thaw, melt; (schleppen) tow || intr (HABEN & SEIN) thaw || impers—es taut dew is falling || impers (HABEN & SEIN)—es taut it is thawing || Tauen n (-s;) thaw

Tauf- [tauf] comb.fm. baptismal

Tauf'becken n baptismal font

Tauf'buch n parish register

Taufe ['taufə] f (-;-n) baptism, christening

taufen ['taufən] tr baptize, christen

Täufer ['tɔɪfər] m—Johannes der T. John the Baptizer

Täufling ['tɔɪflɪŋ] m (-s;-e) child (or person) to be baptized

Tauf'name m Christian name

Tauf'pate m godfather

Tauf'patin f godmother

Tauf'schein m baptismal certificate

taugen ['taugən] intr be of use; zu etw t. be good for s.th.

Taugenichts ['taugənɪçts] m (-es;-e) good-for-nothing

tauglich ['tauklɪç] adj (für, zu) good (for), fit (for), suitable (for); (mil) able-bodied; t. zu (inf) able to (inf)

Taumel ['tauməl] m (-s;) giddiness; (Überschwang) ecstasy

taumelig ['tauməlɪç] adj giddy; reeling

taumeln ['tauməln] intr (SEIN) reel, stagger; be giddy; be ecstatic

Tausch [tauʃ] m (-es;-e) exchange

tauschen ['tauʃən] tr (gegen) exchange (for) || intr—mit j-m t. exchange places with s.o.

täuschen ['tɔɪʃən] tr deceive, fool; (betrügen) cheat; (Erwartungen) disappoint || ref be mistaken

täu'schend adj deceptive, illusory; (Ähnlichkeit) striking

Tausch'geschäft n exchange, swap

Tausch'handel m barter; T. treiben barter

Täu'schung f (-;-en) deception, deceit; fraud; optische T. optical illusion

Täu'schungsangriff m (mil) feint attack

Täu'schungsmanöver n feint

Tausch'wert m trade-in value

tausend ['tauzənt] invar adj & pron thousand || Tausend m—ei der T.! (or potz T.!) holy smokes! || f (-; -en) thousand || n (-s;-e) thousand

Tau'sendfuß m, Tausendfüß(l)er ['tauzəntfys(l)ər] m (-s;-) centipede

tausendste ['tauzəntstə] §9 adj & pron thousandth

Tausendstel ['tauzəntstəl] n (-s;-) thousandth

Tau'tropfen m dewdrop

Tau'werk n (naut) rigging

Tau'wetter n thaw

Tau'ziehen n tug of war

Taxameter [taksa'metər] m taxi meter

Taxe ['taksə] f (-;-n) tax; (Schätzung) appraisal; (Gebühr) fee; (Taxi) taxi

Taxi ['taksi] n (-s;-s) taxi, cab

taxieren [ta'ksirən] tr appraise; rate

Taxifahrer -in §6 mf taxi driver

Ta'xistand m taxi stand

Taxus ['taksus] m (-;-) (bot) yew

Team [tim] n (-s;-s) team

Technik ['tɛçnɪk] f (-;-en) technique; workmanship; technology

Tech'niker -in §6 mf technician; engineer

Techni-kum ['tɛçnɪkum] n (-s;-ka [ka] & -ken [kən]) technical school; school of engineering

technisch ['tɛçnɪʃ] adj technical; technische Angelegenheit technicality; technische Hochschule technical institute

Technologie [tɛçnɔlo'gi] f (-;) technology

technologisch [tɛçno'logɪʃ] adj technological

Tee [te] m (-s;-s) tea

Tee'gebäck n tea biscuit, cookie

Tee'kanne f teapot

Tee'kessel m teakettle

Tee'löffel m teaspoon; teaspoonful

Teenager ['tinedʒər] m (-s;-) teenager

Teer [ter] m (-[e]s;-e) tar

Teer'decke f tar surface, blacktop

teeren ['terən] tr tar

Teer'pappe f tar paper

Tee'satz m tealeaves

Teich [taɪç] m (-[e]s;-e) pond, pool

Teig [taɪk] m (-[e]s;-e) dough

teigig ['taɪgɪç] adj doughy

Teig'mulde f kneading trough

Teig'waren pl noodles; pastries

Teil [taɪl] m & n (-[e]s;-e) part; piece; portion; (Abschnitt) section; (jur) party; der dritte T. von one third of; edle Teile des Körpers vital parts; zu gleichen Teilen fifty-fifty; zum größten T. for the most part; zum T. partly, in part

Teil- comb.fm. partial

teilbar ['taɪlbar] adj divisible

Teilchen ['taɪlçən] n (-s;-) particle

teilen ['taɪlən] tr divide; (mit) share (with) || ref (Weg) divide; (Ansichten) differ; sich t. in (acc) share (in), share (in)

teil'haben §89 intr (an dat) participate (in), share in

Teilhaber -in ['taɪlhabər(ɪn)] §6 mf participant; (com) partner

Teil'haberschaft f (-;-en) partnership

–teilig [taɪlɪç] *comb.fm.* –piece
Teil′nahme *f* (–;) participation; sympathy; interest
teilnahmslos [′taɪlnamslos] *adj* indifferent; apathetic
Teil′nahmslosigkeit *f* (–;) indifference; apathy
teilnahmsvoll [′taɪlnamsfəl] *adj* sympathetic; (*besorgt*) solicitous
teil′nehmen §116 *intr* (an *dat*) participate (in), take part (in); (an *dat*) attend; (fig) (an *dat*) sympathize (with)
Teil′nehmer –in §6 *mf* participant; (*Mitglied*) member; (sport) competitor; (telp) customer, party
teils [taɪls] *adv* partly
Teil′strecke *f* section, stage
Tei′lung *f* (–;–en) division; partition; separation; (*Grade*) graduation, scale; (*Anteile*) sharing
teil′weise *adv* partly
Teil′zahlung *f* partial payment; auf T. kaufen buy on the installment plan
Teint [tẽ] *m* (–s;–s) complexion
Telefon [tele′fon] *n* (–s;–e) telephone
Telegramm [tele′gram] *n* (–s;–e) telegram
Telegraph [tele′graf] *m* (–en;–en) telegraph
Telegra′phenstange *f* telegraph pole
telegraphieren [telegra′firən] *tr & intr* telegraph; (*nach Übersee*) cable
Teleobjektiv [′tele-objektif] *n* telephoto lens
Telephon [tele′fon] *n* (–s;–e) telephone, phone; ans T. gehen answer the phone
Telephon′anruf *m* telephone call
Telephon′anschluß *m* telephone connection
Telephon′gespräch *n* telephone call
Telephon′hörer *m* receiver
telephonieren [telefo′nirən] *intr* telephone; mit j–m t. phone s.o.
telephonisch [tele′foni∫] *adj* telephone || *adv* by telephone
Telephonist –in [telefo′nɪst(ɪn)] §7 *mf* telephone operator
Telephon′vermittlung *f* telephone exchange
Telephon′zelle *f* telephone booth
Telephon′zentrale *f* telephone exchange
Teleskop [tele′skop] *n* (–s;–e) telescope
Television [televi′zjon] *f* (–;) television
Teller [′telər] *m* (–s;–) plate
Tel′lereisen *n* trap
Tel′lermine *f* antitank mine
Tel′lertuch *n* dishtowel
Tempel [′tempəl] *m* (–s;–) temple
Temperament [tempəra′ment] *n* (–[e]s;–e) temperament; enthusiasm; er hat kein T. he has no life in him; hitziges T. hot temper
temperament′los *adj* lifeless, boring
temperament′voll *adj* lively, vivacious
Temperatur [tempəra′tur] *f* (–;–en) temperature
Temperenzler [tempe′rentslər] *m* (–s; –) teetotaler
temperieren [tempe′rirən] *tr* temper; cool; air-condition; (mus) temper

Tem·po [′tempo] *n* (–s;–s & pl pi [pi]) tempo; speed; (mus) movement
Tem·pus [′tempus] *n* (–; –pora [pəra]) (gram) tense
Tendenz [ten′dents] *f* (–;–en) tendency
Tender [′tendər] *m* (–;–;–) (nav, rr) tender
Tenne [′tenə] *f* (–;–n) threshing floor
Tennis [′tenɪs] *n* (–;) tennis
Ten′nisplatz *m* tennis court
Ten′nisschläger *m* tennis racket
Ten′nistournier *n* tennis tournament
Tenor [′tenor] *m* (–s;) (*Wortlaut*) tenor, purport || [te′nor] *m* (–[e]s; ⸚e) tenor
Teppich [′tepɪç] *m* (–s;–e) rug, carpet
Teppichkehrmaschine [′tepɪçkerma-jinə] *f* carpet sweeper
Termin [ter′min] *m* (–s;–e) date, time, day; deadline; (com) due date; er hat heute T. he is to appear in court today; äußerster T. deadline
termin′gemäß *adv* on time, punctually
Termin′geschäft *n* futures
Termin′kalender *m* appointment book; (jur) court calendar
Terminologie [terminolo′gi] *f* (–; –gien [′gi-ən]) terminology
termin′weise *adv* (com) on time
Terpentin [terpen′tin] *m* (–s;) terpentine
Terrain [te′rɛ̃] *n* (–s;–s) ground; (*Grundstück*) lot; (mil) terrain; T. gewinnen (fig & mil) gain ground
Terrasse [te′rasə] *f* (–;–n) terrace
terras′senförmig *adj* terraced
Terrine [te′rinə] *f* (–;–n) tureen
Territo·rium [terɪ′torjum] *n* (–s;–rien [rjən]) territory
Terror [′teror] *m* (–s;) terror
terrorisieren [terori′zirən] *tr* terrorize
Terrorist –in [tero′rɪst(ɪn)] §7 *mf* terrorist
Terz [terts] *f* (–;–en) (mus) third
Terzett [ter′tset] *n* (–[e]s;–e) trio
Test [test] *m* (–[e]s;–e & –s) test
Testament [testa′ment] *n* (–[e]s;–e) will; (eccl) Testament
testamentarisch [testamen′tarɪ∫] *adj* testamentary || *adv* by will; t. bestimmen will
Testaments′vollstrecker –in §6 *mf* executor
testen [′testən] *tr* test
teuer [′tɔɪ-ər] *adj* dear, expensive; (*Preis*) high
Teu′erung *f* (–;–en) rise in price
Teu′erungswelle *f* rise in prices
Teu′erungszulage *f* cost-of-living increase
Teufel [′tɔɪfəl] *m* (–s;) devil; des Teufels sein to be mad; wer zum T.? who the devil?
Teufelei [tɔɪfə′laɪ] *f* (–;–en) deviltry
Teufelsbanner [′tɔɪfəlsbanər] *m* (–s;–) exorcist
Teu′felskerl *m* helluva fellow
teuflisch [′tɔɪflɪ∫] *adj* devilish
Teutone [tɔɪ′tonə] *m* (–n;–n) Teuton
teutonisch [tɔɪ′toni∫] *adj* Teutonic
Text [tekst] *m* (–[e]s;–e) text, words; (cin) script; (mus) libretto; (typ) double pica; aus dem T. kommen

lose the train of thought; j—m den T. lesen give s.o. a lecture

Text'buch n (mus) libretto

Texter –in ['tekstər(ɪn)] §6 mf ad writer, ad man; (mus) lyricist

Textil- [tekstil] comb.fm. textile

Textilien [teks'tiljən] pl, **Textil'waren** pl textiles

text'lich adj textual

Theater [te'ɑtər] n (-s;–) theater; T. machen (fig) make a fuss; T. spielen (fig) make believe, put on

Thea'terbesucher –in §6 mf theater-goer

Thea'terdichter –in §6 mf playwright

Thea'terkarte f theater ticket

Thea'terkasse f box office

Thea'terprobe f rehearsal

Thea'terstück n play

Thea'terzettel n program

theatralisch [te·a'trɑlɪʃ] adj theater; (fig) theatrical

Theke ['tekə] f (-;-n) counter; bar

The·ma ['tema] n (-s;-men [mən] & -mata [mata]) theme, subject

Theologe [te·o'logə] m (-n;-n) theologian

Theologie [te·olo'gi] f (-;) theology

theologisch [te·o'logɪʃ] adj theological

theoretisch [te·o'retɪʃ] adj theoretic(al)

Theo·rie [te·o'ri] f (-;-rien ['ri·ən]) theory

Thera·pie [tera'pi] f (-;-pien ['pi·ən]) therapy

Thermalbad [ter'mɑlbɑt] n thermal bath

Thermometer [termo'metər] n thermometer

Thermome'terstand m thermometer reading

Thermosflasche ['termosflaʃə] f thermos bottle

Thermostat [termo'stɑt] m (-[e]s;-e) & (-en;-en) thermostat

These ['tezə] f (-;-n) thesis

Thrombose [trom'bozə] f (-;-n) thrombosis

Thron [tron] m (-[e]s;-e) throne

Thron'besteigung f accession to the throne

Thron'bewerber m pretender to the throne

Thron'folge f succession to the throne

Thron'folger m successor to the throne

Thron'himmel m canopy, baldachin

Thron'räuber m usurper

Thunfisch ['tunfɪʃ] m tuna

Tick [tɪk] m (-[e]s;-s & -e) tic; (fig) eccentricity; e–n T. auf j–n haben have a grudge against s.o.; e–n T. haben (coll) be balmy

ticken ['tɪkən] intr tick

ticktack ['tɪk'tak] adv ticktock || Ticktack n (-s;) ticktock

tief [tif] adj deep; profound; (niedrig) low; (Schlaf) sound; (Farbe) dark; (äußerst) extreme; aus tiefstem Herzen from the bottom of one's heart; im tiefsten Winter in the dead of winter || adv deeply; zu t. singen be flat || Tief n (-[e]s;-e) (meteor) low

Tief'angriff m low-level attack

Tief'bau m (-[e]s;) underground engineering; underground work

tief'betrübt adj deeply grieved

Tief'druckgebiet n (meteor) low

Tiefe ['tifə] f (-;-n) depth; profundity

Tief'ebene f lowlands, plain

teif'empfunden adj heartfelt

Tie'fenanzeiger m (naut) depth gauge

Tie'fenschärfe f (phot) depth of field

Tief'flug m low-level flight

Tief'gang m (fig) depth; (naut) draft

tief'gekühlt adj deep-freeze

tief'greifend adj far-reaching; radical; deep-seated

Tief'kühlschrank m deep freeze

Tief'land n lowlands

tief'liegend adj low-lying; deep-seated; (Augen) sunken

Tief'punkt m (& fig) low point

Tief'schlag m (box) low blow

Tiefsee- [tifze] comb.fm. deep-sea

tief'sinnig adj pensive; melancholy

Tief'stand m low level

Tiegel ['tigəl] m (-s;-) saucepan; (zum Schmelzen) crucible; (typ) platen

Tier [tir] n (-[e]s;-e) animal; (& fig) beast; großes (or hohes) T. (coll) big shot, big wheel

Tier'art f species (of animal)

Tier'arzt m veterinarian

Tier'bändiger –in §6 mf wild-animal tamer

Tier'garten m zoo

Tier'heilkunde f veterinary medicine

tierisch ['tirɪʃ] adj animal (fig) brutish, bestial

Tier'kreis m zodiac

Tier'kreiszeichen n sign of the zodiac

Tier'quälerei f cruelty to animals

Tier'reich n animal kingdom

Tier'schutzverein m society for the prevention of cruelty to animals

Tier'wärter m keeper (at zoo)

Tier'welt f animal kingdom

Tiger ['tigər] m (-s;-) tiger

Tigerin ['tigərɪn] f (-;-nen) tigress

tilgen ['tɪlgən] tr wipe out; (ausrotten) eradicate; (Schuld) pay off; (Sünden) expiate; (streichen) delete

Til'gung f (-;-en) eradication, extinction; payment; deletion

Til'gungsfonds m sinking fund

Tingeltangel ['tɪŋəltaŋəl] m & n (-s;-) honky-tonk

Tinktur [tɪŋk'tur] f (-;-en) tincture

Tinte ['tɪntə] f (-;-n) ink; in der T. sitzen (coll) be in a pickle

Tin'tenfaß n inkwell

Tin'tenfisch m cuttlefish

Tin'tenfleck m, **Tin'tenklecks** m ink spot

tin'tenstift m indelible pencil

Tip [tɪp] m (-s;-s) tip, hint

Tippelbruder ['tɪpəlbrudər] m tramp

tippeln ['tɪpəl] intr (SEIN) (coll) tramp; (coll) toddle

tippen ['tɪpən] tr type || intr type; tap; (wetten) bet; an j–n nicht t. können not be able to come near s.o. (in performance); daran kannst du nicht t. that's beyond your reach; t. auf (acc) predict || ref—sich an die Stirn t. tap one's forehead

Tippfehler ['tɪpfelər] *m* typographical error

Tippfräulein ['tɪpfrɔɪlaɪn] *n* (coll) typist

tipptopp ['tɪp'tɔp] *adj* tiptop

Tirol [tɪ'rol] *n* (-s) Tyrol

Tiroler -in [tɪ'rolər(ɪn)] §6 *mf* Tyrolean

tirolerisch [tɪ'rolərɪʃ] *adj* Tyrolean

Tisch [tɪʃ] *m* (-es;-e) table; (*Mahlzeit*) meal, dinner, supper; **bei T.** during the meal; **nach T.** after the meal; **reinen T. machen** make a clean sweep of it; **unter den T. fallen** be ignored; **vom grünen T.** armchair; bureaucratic; **vor T.** before the meal; **zu T., bitte!** dinner is ready

Tisch′aufsatz *m* centerpiece

Tisch′besen *m* crumb brush

Tisch′besteck *n* knife, fork, and spoon

Tisch′blatt *n* leaf of a table

Tisch′decke *f* tablecloth

Tisch′gast *m* dinner guest

Tisch′gebet *n*—**T. sprechen** say grace

Tisch′gesellschaft *f* dinner party

Tisch′glocke *f* dinner bell

Tisch′karte *f* name plate

Tisch′lampe *f* table lamp; desk lamp

Tischler ['tɪʃlər] *m* (-s;-) cabinet maker

Tisch′platte *f* table top

Tisch′rede *f* after-dinner speech

Tisch′tennis *n* Ping-Pong

Tisch′tuch *n* tablecloth

Tisch′zeit *f* mealtime, dinner time

Tisch′zeug *n* table linen and tableware

Titan [tɪ'tɑn] *m* (-en;-en) Titan || *n* (-s;) (chem) titanium

titanisch [tɪ'tɑnɪʃ] *adj* titanic

Titel ['tital] *m* (-s;-) title; (*Anspruch*) claim; **e-n T. innehaben** (sport) hold a title

Ti′telbild *n* frontispiece; (*e-r Illustrierten*) cover picture

Ti′telblatt *n* title page

Ti′telkampf *m* (box) title bout

Ti′telrolle *f* title role

titulieren [titu'lirən] *tr* title

Toast [tost] *m* (-es;-e & -s) toast

toasten ['tostən] *tr* (*Brot*) toast || *intr* propose a toast, drink a toast; **auf j-n t.** toast s.o.

toben ['tobən] *intr* rage; (*Kinder*) raise a racket || **Toben** *n* (-s;) rage, raging; racket, noise

Tob′sucht *f* frenzy, madness

tob′süchtig *adj* raving, mad; frantic

Tochter ['tɔxtər] *f* (-;-̈) daughter

Toch′terfirma *f*, **Toch′tergesellschaft** *f* (com) subsidiary, affiliate

Tod [tot] *m* (-es;-e) death; (*jur*) decease; **des Todes sein** be a dead man; **sich** [*dat*] **den Tod holen** catch a death of a cold

tod′ernst′ *adj* dead serious

Todes– [todəs] *comb.fm.* of death; deadly

To′desanzeige *f* obituary

To′desfall *m* death

To′desgefahr *f* mortal danger

To′deskampf *m* death struggle

To′deskandidat *m* one at death's door

To′desstoß *m* coup de grâce

To′desstrafe *f* death penalty; **bei T. on pain of death**

To′destag *m* anniversary of death

To′desursache *f* cause of death

To′desurteil *n* death sentence

Tod′feind –**in** §8 *mf* mortal enemy

todgeweiht ['totgəvaɪt] *adj* doomed

tödlich ['tø:tlɪç] *adj* deadly, fatal

tod′müde *adj* dead tired

tod′schick′ *adj* (coll) very chic

tod′si′cher *adj* (coll) dead sure

Tod′sünde *f* mortal sin

Toilette [twa'lɛtə] *f* (-;-n) toilet

Toilet′tentisch *m* dressing table

tolerant [tole'rant] *adj* (gegen) tolerant (toward)

Toleranz [tole'rants] *f* (-;-en) toleration; (mach) tolerance

tolerieren [tole'rirən] *tr* tolerate

toll [tɔl] *adj* mad, crazy; fantastic, terrific; **das wird noch toller kommen** the worst is yet to come; **er ist nicht so t.** (coll) he's not so hot; **es zu t. treiben** carry it a bit too far; **t. nach** crazy about

tollen ['tɔlən] *intr* (HABEN & SEIN) romp about

Toll′haus *n* (fig) bedlam

Toll′heit *f* (-;) madness

Toll′kopf *m* (coll) crackpot

toll′kühn *adj* foolhardy, rash

Toll′wut *f* rabies

Tolpatsch ['tolpatʃ] *m* (-es;-e), **Tölpel** ['tœlpal] *m* (-s;-) (coll) clumsy ox

töl′pelhaft *adj* clumsy

Tomate [to'matə] *f* (-;-n) tomato

Ton [ton] *m* (-[e]s;-e) tone; sound; tint, shade; (*Betonung*) accent, stress; (fig) fashion; **den Ton angeben** (fig) set the tone; (mus) give the keynote; **e-n anderen Ton anschlagen** change one's tune; **große Töne reden** talk big; **guter Ton** (fig) good taste; **hast du Tö′ne!** can you beat that! || *m* (-s;-e) clay

Ton′abnehmer *m* (electron) pickup

ton′angebend *adj* leading

Ton′arm *m* pickup arm

Ton′art *f* type of clay; (mus) key

Ton′atelier *n* (cin) sound studio

Ton′band *n* (-[e]s;-̈er) (cin) sound track; (electron) tape

Ton′bandgerät *n* tape recorder

tönen ['tønən] *tr* tint, shade || *intr* sound; (*läuten*) ring

tönern ['tønərn] *adj* clay, of clay

Ton′fall *m* intonation, accent

Ton′farbe *f* timbre

Ton′film *m* sound film

Ton′folge *f* melody

Ton′frequenz *f* audio frequency

Ton′geschirr *n* earthenware

Ton′höhe *f*, **Ton′lage** *f* pitch

Ton′leiter *f* (mus) scale

ton′los *adj* voiceless; unstressed

Ton′malerei *f* onomotopoeia

Ton′meister *m* sound engineer

Tonnage [to'naʒə] *f* (-;-n) (naut) tonnage

Tonne ['tonə] *f* (-;-n) barrel; ton

Ton′silbe *f* accented syllable

Ton′spur *f* groove (*of record*)

Ton′streifen *m* (cin) sound track

Tonsur [tɔn'zur] f (-;-en) tonsure
Ton'taube f clay pigeon
Ton'taubenschießen n trapshooting
Tö'nung f (-;-en) tint; (phot) tone
Ton'verstärker m amplifier
Ton'waren pl earthenware
Topas [to'pas] m (-es;-e) topaz
Topf [tɔpf] m (-[e]s;⸚e) pot
Topf'blume f potted flower
Töpfer ['tœpfər] m (-s;-) potter
Töpferei [tœpfə'raɪ] f (-;-en) potter's shop
Töp'ferscheibe f potter's wheel
Töp'ferwaren pl pottery
Topf'lappen m potholder
Topf'pflanze f potted plant
Topp [tɔp] m (-s;-e) (naut) masthead || topp interj it's a deal
Tor [tor] m (-en;-en) fool || n (-[e]s;-e) gate; gateway; (sport) goal
Torbogen m archway
Torf [tɔrf] m (-[e]s;) peat
Tor'flügel m door (of double door)
Torf'moos n peat moss
Tor'heit f (-;-en) foolishness, folly
Tor'hüter m gatekeeper; (sport) goalie
töricht ['tørɪçt] adj foolish, silly
Törin ['tørɪn] f (-;-nen) fool
torkeln ['tɔrkəln] intr (HABEN & SEIN) (coll) stagger
Tor'latte f (sport) crossbar
Tor'lauf m slalom
Tor'linie f (sport) goal line
Tornister [tɔr'nɪstər] m (-s;-) knapsack; school bag; (mil) field pack
torpedieren [tɔrpe'dirən] tr torpedo
Torpedo [tɔr'pedo] m (-s;-s) torpedo
Tor'pfosten m doorpost; (fb) goal post
Tor'schluß m—kurz vor T. (fig) at the eleventh hour
Torte ['tɔrtə] f (-;-n) cake; pie
Tortur [tɔr'tur] f (-;-en) torture
Tor'wächter m, Torwart ['tɔrvart] m (-[e]s;-e) (sport) goalie
Tor'weg m gateway
tosen ['tozən] intr (HABEN & SEIN) rage, roar || Tosen n (-s;) rage, roar
tot [tot] adj dead; (Kapital) idle; (Wasser) stagnant; toter Punkt dead center; (fig) snag; totes Rennen dead heat; tote Zeit dead season
total [to'tal] adj total; all-out
totalitär [totali'tɛr] adj totalitarian
tot'arbeiten ref work oneself to death
Tote ['totə] §5 mf dead person
töten ['tøtən] tr kill; (Nerv) deaden
To'tenacker m churchyard
To'tenbett n deathbed
to'tenblaß' adj deathly pale
To'tenblässe f deathly pallor
to'tenbleich' adj deathly pale
To'tengräber m gravedigger
To'tengruft f crypt
To'tenhemd n shroud, winding sheet
To'tenklage f lament
To'tenkopf m skull
To'tenkranz m funeral wreath
To'tenmaske f death mask
To'tenmesse f requiem
To'tenreich n (myth) underworld
To'tenschau f coroner's inquest
To'tenschein m death certificate
To'tenstadt f necropolis

To'tenstarre f rigor mortis
To'tenstille f dead silence
To'tenwache f wake
tot'geboren adj stillborn
Tot'geburt f stillbirth
tot'lachen ref die laughing
Toto ['toto] m (-s;-s) football pool
tot'schießen §76 tr shoot dead
Tot'schlag m manslaughter
tot'schlagen §132 tr strike dead; (Zeit) kill
tot'schweigen §148 tr hush up; keep under wraps || intr hush up
tot'stellen ref feign death, play dead
tot'treten §152 tr trample to death
Tö'tung f (-;-en) killing
Tour [tur] f (-;-en) tour; turn; (Umdrehung) revolution; auf die krumme T. by hook or by crook; auf die langsame T. very leisurely; auf höchsten Touren at full speed; (fig) full blast; auf Touren bringen (aut) rev up; auf Touren kommen pick up speed; (fig) get worked up; auf Touren sein (coll) be in good shape
Tou'renzahl f revolutions per minute
Tourismus [tu'rɪsmus] m (-;) tourism
Tourist [tu'rɪst] m (-en;-en) tourist
Touri'stenverkehr m, Touristik [tu'rɪstɪk] f (-;) tourism
Touristin [tu'rɪstɪn] f (-;-nen) tourist
Tour·nee [tur'ne] f (-;-neen ['ne·ən]) (mus, theat) tour
Trab [trap] m (-[e]s;) trot; im T. at a trot
Trabant [tra'bant] m (-en;-en) satellite
traben ['trabən] intr (HABEN & SEIN) trot
Tra'ber m (-s;-) trotter
Tra'berwagen m sulky
Trab'rennen n harness racing
Tracht [traxt] f (-;-en) costume; (Last) load; (Ertrag) yield
trachten ['traxtən] intr—t. nach strive for; t. zu (inf) endeavor to (inf)
trächtig ['trɛçtɪç] adj pregnant
Tradition [tradɪ'tsjon] f (-;-en) tradition
traditionell [tradɪtsjo'nɛl] adj traditional
traf [traf] pret of treffen
Trafik [tra'fɪk] f (-;-en) (Aust) cigar store
träg [trek] adj var of träge
Tragbahre ['trakbarə] f (-;-n) stretcher, litter
Trag'balken ['trakbalkən] m supporting beam; girder; joist
Tragband ['trakbant] n (-[e]s;⸚er) strap; shoulder strap
tragbar ['trakbar] adj portable; (Kleid) wearable; (fig) bearable
Trage ['tragə] f (-;-n) litter
träge ['tregə] adj lazy; slow; inert
tragen ['tragən] §132 tr carry; bear; endure; support; (Kleider) wear, have on; (hervorbringen) produce, yield; (Bedenken) have; (Folgen) take; (Risiko) run; (Zinsen) yield; bei sich t. have on one's person; getragen sein von be based on; zur Schau t. show off || ref dress; sich

gut t. wear well || intr (Stimme) carry; (Schußwaffe) have a range; (Baum, Feld) bear, yield; (Eis) be thick enough
Träger ['trɛgər] m (-s;-) carrier; porter; (Inhaber) bearer; shoulder strap; (archit) girder, beam
Trä'gerflugzeug n carrier plane
trä'gerlos adj strapless
tragfähig ['trakfɛ·ɪç] adj strong enough, capable of carrying; trag'fähige Grundlage (fig) sound basis
Trag'fähigkeit f (-;-en) capacity, load limit; (naut) tonnage
Tragfläche ['trakflɛçə] f, **Tragflügel** ['trakflygəl] m airfoil
Träg'heit ['trɛkhaɪt] f (-;) laziness; (phys) inertia
Traghimmel ['trakhɪməl] m canopy
Tragik ['tragɪk] f (-;) tragedy
tragisch ['tragɪʃ] adj tragic
Tragödie [tra'gødjə] f (-;-n) tragedy
Tragriemen ['trakrimən] m strap
Tragsessel ['trakzɛsəl] m sedan chair
Tragtasche ['traktaʃə] f shopping bag
Tragtier ['traktir] n pack animal
Tragweite ['trakvaɪtə] f range; (Bedeutung) significance, moment
Tragwerk ['trakvɛrk] n (aer) airfoil
Trainer ['trɛnər] m (-s;-) coach
trainieren [trɛ'nirən] tr & intr train; coach
Training ['trɛnɪŋ] n (-s;) training
Trai'ningsanzug m sweat suit
traktieren [trak'tirən] tr treat; treat rougly
Trak·tor ['traktor] m (-s;-toren ['torən]) tractor
trällern ['trɛlərn] tr & intr hum
trampeln ['trampəln] tr trample
Tram'pelpfad m beaten path
Tran [tran] m (-[e]s;-e) whale oil; im T. sein be drowsy; be under the influence of alcohol
tranchieren [trã'ʃirən] tr carve
Träne ['trɛnə] f (-;-n) tear
tränen ['trɛnən] intr water
Trä'nengas n tear gas
trank [traŋk] pret of trinken || **Trank** m (-[e]s;-̈e) drink, beverage; potion
Tränke ['trɛŋkə] f (-;-n) watering hole
tränken ['trɛŋkən] tr give (s.o.) a drink; (Tiere) water; soak
Transfor·mator [transfor'mator] m (-s; -matoren [ma'torən] transformer
transformieren [transfor'mirən] tr transform; step up; step down
Transfusion [transfu'zjon] f (-;-en) transfusion
Tran·sistor [tran'zɪstor] m (-s;-sistoren [zɪs'torən]) transistor
transitiv [tranzi'tif] adj transitive
Transmission [transmɪ'sjon] f (-;-en) transmission
transparent [transpa'rɛnt] adj transparent || **Transparent** n (-[e]s;-e) transparency; (Spruchband) banderol
transpirieren [transpi'rirən] intr perspire
Transplantation [transplanta'tsjon] f (-;-en) (surg) transplant
Transport [trans'port] m (-[e]s;-e) transportation

transportabel [transpor'tabəl] adj transportable
Transporter [trans'portər] m (-s;-) troopship; transport plane
transport'fähig adj transportable
transportieren [transpor'tirən] tr transport, ship
Transport'unternehmen n carrier
Trapez [tra'pets] n (-es;-e) trapeze; (geom) trapezoid
trappeln ['trapəln] intr (SEIN) clatter; (Kinder) patter
Trassant [tra'sant] m (-en;-en) (fin) drawer
Trassat [tra'sat] m (-en;-en) drawee
trassieren [tra'sirən] tr trace, lay out; e-n Wechsel t. auf (acc) write out a check to
trat [trat] pret of treten
Tratsch [tratʃ] m (-es;) gossip
tratschen ['tratʃən] intr gossip
Tratte ['tratə] f (-;-n) (fin) draft
Trau- [trau] comb.fm. wedding, marriage
Traube ['traubə] f (-;-n) grape; bunch of grapes; (fig) bunch
Trau'bensaft m grape juice
Trau'benzucker m glucose
trauen ['trau·ən] tr (Brautpaar) marry; sich t. lassen get married || ref dare || intr (dat) trust (in), have confidence (in)
Trauer ['trau·ər] f (-;) grief, sorrow; mourning; (Trauerkleidung) mourning clothes; T. anlegen put on mourning clothes; T. haben be in mourning
Trau'eranzeige f obituary
Trau'erbotschaft f sad news
Trau'erfall m death
Trau'erfeier f funeral ceremony
Trau'erflor m mourning crepe
Trau'ergefolge n, **Trau'ergeleit** n funeral procession
Trau'ergottesdienst m funeral service
Trau'erkloß m (coll) sad sack
Trau'ermarsch m funeral march
trauern ['trau·ərn] intr (um) mourn (for); (um) wear mourning (for)
Trau'erspiel n tragedy
Trau'erweide f weeping willow
Trau'erzug m funeral cortege
Traufe ['traufə] f (-;-n) eaves
träufeln ['trɔɪfəln] tr & intr drip
Trauf'rinne f rain gutter
Trauf'röhre f rain pipe
traulich ['traulɪç] adj intimate; cozy
Traum [traum] m (-[e]s;-̈e) dream; (fig) daydream, reverie
Traum'bild n vision, phantom
Traum'deuter -in §6 mf interpreter of dreams
träumen ['trɔɪmən] tr & intr dream
Träu'mer m (-s;-) dreamer
Träumerei [trɔɪmə'raɪ] f (-;-en) dreaming; daydream
Träumerin ['trɔɪmərɪn] f (-;-nen) dreamer
träumerisch ['trɔɪmərɪʃ] adj dreamy; absent-minded
Traum'gesicht n vision, phantom
traum'haft adj dream-like
traurig ['traurɪç] adj sad
Trau'ring m wedding ring (or band)

Trau'schein *m* marriage certificate

traut [traut] *adj* dear; cozy; intimate

Trau'ung *f* (-;-en) marriage ceremony; kirchliche T. church wedding; standesamtliche T. civil ceremony

Trau'zeuge *m* best man

Trecker ['trɛkər] *m* (-s;-) tractor

Treff [trɛf] *n* (-s;-s) (cards) club(s)

treffen ['trɛfən] §151 *tr* hit; (*begegnen*) meet; (*betreffen*) concern || *ref* meet; assemble; sich t. mit meet with || *intr* hit home; (box) land, connect || Treffen *n* (-s;-) meeting; (mil) encounter; (sport) meet

tref'fend *adj* pertinent; to the point; (*Ähnlichkeit*) striking

Tref'fer *m* (-s;-) hit; winner; prize

treff'lich *adj* excellent

Treff'punkt *m* rendezvous, meeting place

Treib- [traɪp] *comb.fm.* moving; driving

treiben ['traɪbən] §62 *tr* drive; propel; chase, expel; (*Beruf*) pursue; (*Blätter, Blüten*) put forth; (*Geschäft*) run, carry on; (*Metall*) work; (*Musik, Sport*) go in for; (*Sprachen*) study; (*Pflanzen*) force; es zu weit t. go too far; was treibst du denn? (coll) what are you doing? || *intr* blossom; sprout; (*Teig*) ferment || *intr* (SEIN) drift, float || Treiben *n* (-s;) doings, activity; drifting, floating

Treib'haus *n* hothouse

Treib'holz *n* driftwood

Treib'kraft *f* driving force

Treib'mine *f* floating mine

Treib'rakete *f* booster rocket

Treib'riemen *m* drive belt

Treib'sand *m* drifting sand; quicksand

Treib'stange *f* connecting rod

Treib'stoff *m* fuel; propellant

Treib'stoffbehälter *m* fuel tank

trennbar ['trɛnbar] *adj* separable

trennen ['trɛnən] *tr* separate; sever; (*Naht*) undo; (*Ehe*) dissolve; (elec, telp) cut off || *ref* part; separate; (*Weg*) branch off

Tren'nung *f* (-;-en) separation; parting; dissolution

Tren'nungsstrich *m* dividing line; hyphen

Trense ['trɛnzə] *f* (-;-n) snaffle

Treppe ['trɛpə] *f* (-;-n) stairs, stairway; flight of stairs; die T. hinaufgefallen (coll) be kicked upstairs; zwei Treppen hoch wohnen live two flights up

Trep'penabsatz *m* landing

Trep'penflucht *f* flight of stairs

Trep'pengeländer *n* banister

Trep'penhaus *n* staircase

Trep'penläufer *m* stair carpet

Trep'penstufe *f* step, stair

Tresor [tre'zor] *m* (-s;-e) safe; vault

Tresse ['trɛsə] *f* (-;-n) (mil) stripe

treten ['tretən] §152 *tr* tread; tread on; trample; (*Fußhebel*) work; (*Orgel*) pump; mit Füßen t. (fig) trample under foot || *intr* (SEIN) step, walk; tread; an j-s Stelle t. succeed s.o.; auf der Stelle t. (mil) mark time; in

Kraft t. go into effect; j—m zu nahe t. offend s.o.; t. in (*acc*) enter (into)

Tretmühle ['tretmylə] *f* treadmill

treu [trɔɪ] *adj* loyal, faithful, true

Treu'bruch *m* breach of faith

Treue ['trɔɪ.ə] *f* (-;) loyalty, fidelity; allegiance; j—m die T. halten remain loyal to s.o.

Treu'eid *m* oath of allegiance

Treu'hand *f* (jur) trust

Treuhänder –in ['trɔɪhɛndər(ɪn)] §6 *mf* trustee

Treu'handfonds *m* trust fund

treu'herzig *adj* trusting; sincere

treu'los *adj* unfaithful; (gegen) disloyal (to)

Tribüne [trɪ'bynə] *f* (-;-n) rostrum; (mil) reviewing stand; (sport) grandstand

Tribut [trɪ'but] *m* (-[e]s;-e) tribute

Trichter ['trɪçtər] *m* (-s;-) funnel; (*Bomben-*) crater, pothole; (mus) bell (*of wind instrument*); auf den T. kommen (coll) catch on

Trick [trɪk] *m* (-s;-s & -e) trick

Trick'film *m* animated cartoon

trieb [trip] *pret* of treiben || Trieb *m* (-[e]s;-e) sprout, shoot; urge, drive; instinct

Trieb'feder *f* (horol) mainspring

Trieb'kraft *f* motive power

trieb'mäßig *adj* instinctive

Trieb'werk *n* motor, engine

triefäugig ['trifɔɪgɪç] *adj* bleary-eyed

triefen ['trifən] §153 *intr* drip; (*Augen*) water; (*Nase*) run

triezen ['tritsən] *tr* (coll) tease

Trift [trɪft] *f* (-;-en) pasture land; cattle track; log-running

triftig ['trɪftɪç] *adj* cogent; valid

Trigonometrie [trigonome'tri] *f* (-;) trigonometry

Trikot [tri'ko] *m & n* (-s;-s) knitted cloth; (sport) trunks, tights

Triller ['trɪlər] *m* (-s;-) trill; (mus) quaver

trillern ['trɪlərn] *intr* trill; (*Vogel*) warble

Tril'lerpfeife *f* whistle

Trink- [trɪŋk] *comb.fm.* drinking

trinkbar ['trɪŋkbar] *adj* drinkable

Trink'becher *m* drinking cup

trinken ['trɪŋkən] §143 *tr & intr* drink

Trin'ker –in §6 *mf* drinker

trink'fest *adj* able to hold one's liquor

Trink'gelage *n* drinking party

Trink'geld *n* tip, gratuity

Trink'glas *n* drinking glass

Trink'halm *m* straw

Trink'spruch *m* toast

Trink'wasser *n* drinking water

Trio ['tri.o] *n* (-s;-s) trio

trippeln ['trɪpəln] *intr* (SEIN) patter

Tripper ['trɪpər] *m* (-s;) gonorrhea

trist [trɪst] *adj* dreary

tritt [trɪt] *pret* of treten || *m* (-[e]s; -e) step; kick; pace; footstep; footprint; small stepladder; pedal; j—m e–n T. versetzen give s.o. a kick

Tritt'brett *n* running board

Tritt'leiter *f* stepladder

Triumph [tri'umf] *m* (-[e]s;-e) triumph

Triumph'bogen *m* triumphal arch

triumphieren [trɪ·umˈfirən] *intr* triumph

Triumph'zug *m* triumphal procession

trocken [ˈtrɔkən] *adj* dry; arid; trok-kenes Brot plain bread

Trockenbagger (Trok'kenbagger) *m* (mach) excavator

Trockendock (Trok'kendock) *n* dry-dock

Trockenei (Trok'kenei) *n* dehydrated eggs

Trockeneis (Trok'keneis) *n* dry ice

Trockenhaube (Trok'kenhaube) *f* hair drier

Trockenheit (Trok'kenheit) *f* (-;) dry-ness, aridity

trockenlegen (trok'kenlegen) *tr* (Sumpf) drain; (Säugling) change (the diapers of)

Trockenmaß (Trok'kenmaß) *n* dry measure

Trockenmilch (Trok'kenmilch) *f* pow-dered milk

Trockenschleuder (Trok'kenschleuder) *f* spin-drier, clothes drier

Trockenübung (Trok'kenübung) *f* dry run

trocknen [ˈtrɔknən] *tr* dry || *intr* (SEIN) dry, dry up

Troddel [ˈtrɔdəl] *f* (-;-n) tassel

Trödel [ˈtrødəl] *m* (-s;) secondhand goods; old clothes; junk; (fig) nui-sance, waste of time

Trö'delkram *m* junk

trödeln [ˈtrødəln] *intr* waste time

Tröd'ler –in §6 *mf* secondhand dealer

troff [trɔf] *pret* of triefen

trog [trok] *pret* of trügen Trog *m* (-[e]s;ːe) trough

Trommel [ˈtrɔməl] *f* (-;-n) drum

Trom'melfell *n* drumhead; (anat) ear-drum

trommeln [ˈtrɔməln] *tr & intr* drum

Trom'melschlag *m* drumbeat

Trom'melschlegel *m*, Trom'melstock *m* drumstick

Trom'melwirbel *m* drum roll

Trommler [ˈtrɔmlər] *m* (-s;-) drum-mer

Trompete [trɔmˈpetə] *f* (-;-n) trumpet

trompeten [trɔmˈpetən] *intr* blow the trumpet; (Elefant) trumpet

Trompe'ter –in §6 *mf* trumpeter

Tropen [ˈtropən] *pl* tropics

Tropf [trɔpf] *m* (-[e]s;ːe) simpleton; armer T. poor devil

tröpfeln [ˈtrœpfəln] *tr & intr* drip || *intr* (SEIN) trickle || *impers*—es tröpfelt it is sprinkling

tropfen [ˈtrɔpfən] *tr & intr* drip || *intr* (SEIN) trickle || Tropfen *m* (-s;-) drop; ein T. auf den heißen Stein a drop in the bucket

trop'fenweise *adv* drop by drop

Trophäe [troˈfɛ·ə] *f* (-;-n) trophy

tropisch [ˈtropiʃ] *adj* tropical

Troß [trɔs] *m* (Trosses; Trosse) (coll) load, baggage; (coll) hangers-on

Trosse [ˈtrɔsə] *f* (-;-n) cable; (naut) hawser

Trost [trost] *m* (-es;) consolation, comfort; geringer T. cold comfort;

wohl nicht bei T. sein not be all there

trösten [ˈtrøstən] *tr* console, comfort || *ref* cheer up; feel consoled

tröstlich [ˈtrøstlɪç] *adj* comforting

trost'los *adj* disconsolate; bleak

Trost'preis *m* consolation prize

trost'reich *adj* comforting

Trö'stung *f* (-;-en) consolation

Trott [trɔt] *m* (-[e]s;ːe) trot; (coll) routine

Trottel [ˈtrɔtəl] *m* (-s;-) (coll) dope

trotten [ˈtrɔtən] *intr* (SEIN) trot

Trottoir [troˈtwar] *n* (-s;-e & -s) side-walk

trotz [trɔts] *prep* (genit) in spite of; t. alledem for all that || Trotz *m* (-es;) defiance; j–m T. bieten defy s.o.

trotz'dem *adv* nevertheless || *conj* al-though

trotzen [ˈtrɔtsən] *intr* be stubborn; (schmollen) sulk; (dat) defy

trotzig [ˈtrɔtsɪç] *adj* defiant; sulky; obstinate

Trotz'kopf *m* defiant child (or adult)

trüb [tryp], trübe [ˈtrybə] *adj* turbid, muddy; (Wetter) dreary; (glanzlos) dull; (Erfahrung) sad

Trubel [ˈtrubəl] *m* (-s;) bustle

trüben [ˈtrybən] *tr* make turbid, muddy; dim; dull; disturb, trouble (Freude, Stimmung) spoil || *ref* grow cloudy; become muddy; become strained

Trübsal [ˈtrypzal] *f* (-;-en) distress, misery; T. blasen be in the dumps

trüb'selig *adj* gloomy, sad

Trüb'sinn *m* (-[e]s;) gloom

trüb'sinnig *adj* gloomy

Trü'bung *f* (-;) muddiness; blurring

trudeln [ˈtrudəln] *intr* go into a spin || Trudeln *n* (-s;) spin; ins T. kom-men (aer) go into a spin

trug [truk] *pret* of tragen || Trug *m* (-[e]s;) deceit; fraud; delusion

Trug'bild *n* phantom; illusion

trügen [ˈtrygən] §111 *tr & intr* deceive

trügerisch [ˈtrygərɪʃ] *adj* deceptive, illusory; (verräterisch) treacherous

Trug'schluß *m* fallacy

Truhe [ˈtru·ə] *f* (-;-n) trunk, chest

Trulle [ˈtrulə] *f* (-;-n) slut

Trümmer [ˈtrymər] *pl* ruins; rubble

Trumpf [trumpf] *m* (-[e]s;ːe) trump

Trunk [truŋk] *m* (-[e]s;ːe) drinking; im T. when drunk

trunken [ˈtruŋkən] *adj* drunk; t. vor (dat) elated with

Trunkenbold [ˈtruŋkənbɔlt] *m* (-[e]s; -e) drunkard

Trun'kenheit *f* (-;) drunkenness; T. am Steuer (jur) drunken driving

trunk'süchtig *adj* alcoholic || Trunk-süchtige §5 *mf*

Trupp [trup] *m* (-s;-s) troop, gang; (mil) detail, detachment

Truppe [ˈtrupə] *f* (-;-n) (mil) troop; (theat) troupe; Truppen (mil) troops

Trup'peneinheit *f* unit

Trup'penersatz *m* reserves

Trup'pengattung *f* branch of service

Trup'penschau *f* (mil) review, parade

Trup′pentransporter m (aer) troop carrier; (nav) troopship
Trup′penübung f field exercise
Trup′penverband m unit; task force
Trup′penverbandplatz m (mil) first-aid station
Trust [trʊst] m (-[e]s;-e & -s) (com) trust
Truthahn [′truthɑn] m turkey (cock)
Truthenne [′truthɛnə] f turkey (hen)
trutzig [′trʊtsɪç] adj defiant
Tscheche [′tʃɛçə] m (-n;-n), **Tschechin** [′tʃɛçɪn] f (-;-nen) Czech
tschechisch [′tʃɛçɪʃ] adj Czech
Tschechoslowakei [tʃɛçəsləva′kaɪ] f (-;)—die T. Czechoslovakia
Tube [′tubə] f (-;-n) tube; **auf die T. drücken** (aut) step on it
Tuberkulose [tubɛrku′lozə] f (-;) tuberculosis
Tuch [tux] n (-[e]s;-e) cloth; fabric ‖ n (-[e]s;-er) kerchief; shawl; scarf
tuchen [′tuxən] adj cloth, fabric
Tuch′fühlung f—T. haben mit (mil) stand shoulder to shoulder with; T. halten mit keep in close touch with
Tuch′seite f right side (of cloth)
tüchtig [′tʏçtɪç] adj able, capable, efficient; sound, thorough; excellent; good; (Trinker) hard; t. in (dat) good at; t. zu qualified for ‖ adv very much; hard; soundly, thoroughly; (sl) awfully
Tüch′tigkeit f (-;) ability, efficiency; soundness, thoroughness; excellency
Tuch′waren pl dry goods
Tücke [′tʏkə] f (-;-n) malice; **mit List und T.** by cleverness
tückisch [′tʏkɪʃ] adj insidious
tüfteln [′tʏftəln] intr—t. an (dat) (coll) puzzle over
Tugend [′tugənt] f (-;-en) virtue
Tugendbold [′tugəntbəlt] m (-[e]s;-e) (pej) paragon of virtue
tu′gendhaft adj virtuous
Tulpe [′tʊlpə] f (-;-n) tulip
tummeln [′tʊməln] tr (Pferd) exercise ‖ ref hurry; (Kinder) romp about
Tum′melplatz m playground; (fig) arena
Tümmler [′tʏmlər] m (-s;-) dolphin; (Taube) tumbler
Tumor [′tumɔr] m (-s; Tumoren [tu′morən]) tumor
Tümpel [′tʏmpəl] m (-s;-) pond
Tumult [tu′mʊlt] m (-[e]s;-e) uproar; uprising
tun [tun] §154 tr do; make; take; **dazu tun** add to it; **e-n Zug tun** take a swig; **es zu tun bekommen mit** have trouble with; **j-n in ein Internat tun** send s.o. to a boarding school ‖ intr do; be busy; **alle Hände voll zu tun haben** have one's hands full; **es ist mir darum zu tun** I am anxious about it; **groß tun** talk big; **mir ist sehr darum zu tun zu** (inf) it is very important for me to (inf); **nur so tun, als ob** pretend that; **spröde tun** be prudish; **stolz tun** be proud; **weh tun** hurt; **zu t. haben** be busy; have one's work cut out; **zu tun haben mit** have trouble with ‖ impers—**es tut mir**

leid I am sorry; **es tut nichts** it doesn't matter ‖ **Tun** n (-s;) doings; action; **Tun und Treiben** doings
Tünche [′tʏnçə] f (-;-n) whitewash
tünchen [′tʏnçən] tr whitewash
Tunichtgut [′tunɪçtgut] m (- & -[e]s; -e) good-for-nothing
Tunke [′tʊŋkə] f (-;-n) sauce; gravy
tunken [′tʊŋkən] tr dip, dunk
tunlichst [′tunlɪçst] adv—**das wirst du t. bleiben lassen** you had better leave it alone
Tunnel [′tunəl] m (-s;- & -s) tunnel
Tüpfchen [′tʏpfçən] n (-s;-) dot
Tüpfel [′tʏpfəl] m & n (-s;-) dot
tupfen [′tʊpfən] tr dab; dot ‖ **Tupfen** m (-s;-) dot, spot
Tür [tyr] f (-;-en) door
Tür′angel f door hinge
Tür′anschlag m doorstop
Turbine [tʊr′binə] f (-;-n) turbine
Turboprop [′turbɔprɔp] m (-s;-s) turboprop
Tür′drücker m latch
Tür′flügel m door (of double door)
Tür′griff m door handle; door knob
Türke [′tʏrkə] m (-n;-n) Turk
Türkei [tʏr′kaɪ] f (-;)—**die T.** Turkey
Türkin [′tʏrkɪn] f (-;-nen) Turk
Türkis [tʏr′kis] m (-es;-e) turquoise
türkisch [′tʏrkɪʃ] adj Turkish
türkisen [tʏr′kizən] adj turquoise
Tür′klingel f doorbell
Tür′klinke f door handle
Turm [tʊrm] m (-[e]s;-e) tower; steeple; turret; (chess) castle
Türmchen [′tʏrmçən] n (-s;-) turret
türmen [′tʏrmən] tr & ref pile up ‖ intr (SEIN) run away, bolt
turm′hoch adj towering ‖ adv (by) far
Turm′spitze f spire
Turm′springen n high diving
Turn- [tʊrn] comb.fm. gymnastic, gym, athletic
turnen [′tʊrnən] intr do exercises ‖ **Turnen** n (-s;) gymnastics
Tur′ner -in §6 mf gymnast
turnerisch [′tʊrnərɪʃ] adj gymnastic
Turn′gerät n gymnastic apparatus
Turn′halle f gymnasium, gym
Turn′hemd n gym shirt
Turn′hose f trunks
Turnier [tʊr′nir] n (-s;-e) tournament
Turn′schuhe pl sneakers
Tür′pfosten m doorpost
Tür′rahmen m doorframe
Tür′schild n doorplate
Tür′schwelle f threshold
Tusche [′tuʃə] f (-;-n) (paint) wash; **chinesische T.** India ink
tuscheln [′tuʃəln] intr whisper
Tute [′tutə] f (-;-n) (aut) horn
Tüte [′tytə] f (-;-n) paper bag; paper cone; ice cream cone
tuten [′tutən] intr blow the horn; (coll) blare away
Twen [tvɛn] m (-s;-s) young man (in his twenties)
Typ [typ] m (-s;-en) type; (Bauart) model
Type [′typə] f (-;-n) type; (coll) strange character
Ty′pennummer f model number

Typhus ['tyfus] _m_ (-;) typhoid
typisch ['typɪʃ] _adj_ (für) typical (of)
Tyrann [ty'ran] _m_ (-en;-en) tyrant
Tyrannei [tyra'naɪ] _f_ (-;-en) tyranny

tyrannisch [ty'ranɪʃ] _adj_ tyrannical
tyrannisieren [tyranɪ'zirən] _tr_ tyrannize, oppress
Tz ['tetset] _n_—bis ins Tz thoroughly

U

U, u [u] _invar n_ U, u
u.A.w.g. _abbr_ (um Antwort wird gebeten) R.S.V.P.
U-Bahn ['uban] _f_ (Untergrundbahn) subway
übel ['ybəl] _adj_ evil; (_schlecht_) bad; (_unwohl_) queasy, sick; (_Geruch, usw._) nasty, foul; er ist ein übler Geselle he's a bad egg; **mir ist** ü. I feel sick; **ü. daran sein** have it rough || _adv_ badly; **est steht ü. mit things** don't look good for; **ü. auslegen** misconstrue; **ü. deuten** misinterpret; **ü. ergehen** fare badly; **ü. gelaunt** in bad humor || **Übel** _n_ (-s;-) evil; ailment
ü/belgelaunt _adj_ ill-humored
ü/belgesinnt _adj_ evil-minded
U/belkeit _f_ (-;) nausea
ü/belnehmen §116 _tr_ take amiss; take offense at, resent
ü/belnehmend _adj_ resentful
ü/belriechend _adj_ foul-smelling
U/belstand _m_ evil; bad state of affairs
U/beltat _f_ misdeed, crime, offense
U/beltäter -in §6 _mf_ wrongdoer; criminal
ü/belwollen §162 _intr_ (dat) be ill-disposed towards || **Übelwollen** _n_ (-s;) ill will, malevolence
ü/belwollend _adj_ malevolent
üben ['ybən] _tr_ practice, exercise; (_e-e Kunst_) cultivate; (_Handwerk_) pursue; (_Gewalt_) use; (_Verrat_) commit; (mil) drill; (sport) train; **Barmherzigkeit ü. an** (dat) have mercy on; **Gerechtigkeit ü. gegen** be fair to; **Nachsicht ü. gegen** be lenient towards; **Rache ü. an** (dat) take revenge on || _ref_—**sich im Schifahren ü.** practice skiing
über ['ybər] _adv_—**j—m ü. sein in** (dat) be superior to s.o. in; **ü. und ü.** over and over || _prep_ (dat) over; above, on top of || _prep_ (acc) by way of, via; (_bei, während_) during; (_nach_) past; over; across; (_betreffend_) about, concerning; **Briefe ü. Briefe** letter after letter; **ein Scheck ü. 10 DM** a check for 10 marks; **es geht nichts ü.** there is nothing better than; **heute übers Jahr** a year from today; **ü. Gebühr** more than was due; **ü. kurz oder lang** sooner or later; **ü. Land** crosscountry
überall/ _adv_ everywhere, all over
überallher/ _adv_ from all sides
überallhin/ _adv_ in every direction
U/berangebot _n_ over-supply
überan/strengen _tr_ overexert, strain || _ref_ overexert oneself, strain oneself

überar/beiten _tr_ revise, touch up || _ref_ —**sich ü.** overwork oneself
Überar/beitung _f_ (-;-en) revision, touching up; revised text
ü/beraus _adv_ extremely, very
überbacken (überbak/ken) §50 _tr_ bake lightly
U/berbau _m_ (-[e]s; -e & -ten [tən]) superstructure
ü/berbeanspruchen _tr_ overwork
ü/berbelasten _tr_ overload
ü/berbelegt _adj_ overcrowded
ü/berbelichten _tr_ (phot) overexpose
ü/berbetonen _tr_ overemphasize
überbie/ten §58 _tr_ outbid; (fig) outdo
Überbleibsel ['ybərblaɪpsəl] _n_ (-s;-) remains; leftovers
Überbien/dung _f_ (cin) dissolve
U/berblick _m_ survey; (fig) synopsis
überblicken (überblik/ken) _tr_ survey
überbrin/gen §65 _tr_ deliver; convey
Überbrin/ger -in §6 _mf_ bearer
überbrücken (überbrük/ken) _tr_ (& fig) bridge
Überbrückung (Überbrük/kung) _f_ (-;-en) bridging; (rr) overpass
Überbrückungs— _comb.fm._ emergency, stop-gap
überdachen [ybər'daxən] _tr_ roof over
überdau/ern _tr_ outlast
überdecken (überdek/ken) _tr_ cover
überden/ken §66 _tr_ think over
überdies/ _adv_ moreover, besides
überdre/hen _tr_ (Uhr) overwind
U/berdruck _m_ excess pressure
U/berdruckanzug _m_ space suit
U/berdruckkabine _f_ pressurized cabin
Über•druß ['ybərdrus] _m_ (-drusses;) boredom; (Übersättigung) satiety; (Ekel) disgust; **bis zum U.** ad nauseam
überdrüssig ['ybərdrysɪç] _adj_ (genit) sick of, disgusted with
ü/berdurchschnittlich _adj_ above the average
U/bereifer _m_ excessive zeal
ü/bereifrig _adj_ overzealous
überei/len _tr_ precipitate; rush || _ref_ be in too big a hurry; act rashly
übereilt [ybər'aɪlt] _adj_ hasty, rash
übereinan/der _adv_ one on top of the other
übereinan/derschlagen §132 _tr_ cross
überein/kommen §99 _intr_ (SEIN) come to an agreement || **Übereinkommen** _n_ (-s;-) agreement
Überein/kunft _f_ agreement
überein/stimmen _intr_ be in agreement; concur; (Farben, usw.) harmonize
Überein/stimmung _f_ agreement; accord; (Gleichförmigkeit) conformity;

(Einklang) harmony; **in Ü. mit** in line with

ü'berempfindlich *adj* oversensitive

überfah'ren §71 *tr* run over, run down; *(Fluß, usw.)* cross; **ein Signal ü.** go through a traffic light; **ü. werden** (coll) be taken in || **ü'berfahren** §71 *tr (über e-n Fluß, usw.)* take across || *intr* (SEIN) drive over, cross

Ü'berfahrt *f* crossing

Ü'berfall *m* surprise attack, assault; *(Raubüberfall)* holdup; *(Einfall)* raid

überfal'len §72 *tr (räuberisch)* hold up; assault; (mil) surprise; (mil) invade, raid; **ü. werden** be overcome *(by sleep)*; be seized *(with fear)*

ü'berfällig *adj* overdue

Ü'berfallkommando *n* riot squad

überflie'gen §57 *tr* fly over; *(Buch)* skim through

überflie'ßen §76 *intr* (SEIN) overflow

überflügeln [ybər'flygəln] *tr* outflank; (fig) outstrip

Ü'berfluß *m* abundance; excess; **im Ü. vorhanden sein** be plentiful

ü'berflüssig *adj* superfluous

überflu'ten *tr* overflow, flood, swamp || **ü'berfluten** *intr* (SEIN) overflow

überfor'dern *tr* demand too much of; overwork

Ü'berfracht *f* excess luggage

überfüh'ren *tr* carry across; *(Leiche)* transport in state || **überfüh'ren** *tr* (genit) convince of; (genit) convict of

Überfüh'rung *f* (–;–en) overpass; *(e-s Verbrechers)* conviction

Ü'berfülle *f* superabundance

überfül'len *tr* stuff, jam, pack

Ü'bergabe *f* delivery; (& mil) surrender

Ü'bergang *m* passage; crossing; transition; (jur) transfer; (mil) desertion; (paint) blending; (rr) crossing

Ü'bergangsbeihilfe *f* severance pay

Ü'bergangsstadium *n* transition stage

Ü'bergangszeit *f* transitional period

überge'ben §80 *tr* hand over; give up; *(einreichen)* submit; (& mil) surrender; **dem Verkehr ü.** open to traffic || *ref* vomit, throw up

überge'hen §82 *tr* omit; overlook; **mit Stillschweigen ü.** pass over in silence || **ü'bergehen** §82 *intr* (SEIN) go over, cross; *(sich verändern)* (in *acc*) change (into); **auf j–n ü.** devolve upon s.o.; **in andere Hände ü.** change hands; **in Fäulnis ü.** become rotten

Ü'bergewicht *n* overweight; (fig) preponderance; **das Ü. bekommen** become top-heavy; (fig) get the upper hand

ü'bergießen §76 *tr* spill || **übergie'ßen** §76 *tr* pour over, pour on; *(Braten)* baste; **mit Zuckerguß ü.** (culin) ice

übergrei'fen §88 *intr* (auf *acc*) spread (to); (auf *acc*) encroach (on)

Ü'bergriff *m* encroachment

ü'bergroß *adj* huge, colossal; oversize

ü'berhaben §89 *tr* have left; *(Kleider)* have on; (fig) be fed up with

überhand'nehmen §116 *intr* get the upper hand; run riot

(Gewehr) sling over the shoulders || *intr* overhang, project

überhäu'fen *tr* overwhelm, swamp

überhaupt' *adv* really; anyhow; *(besonders)* especially; *(überdies)* besides; at all; **ü. kein** no...whatever; **ü. nicht** not at all; **wenn ü.** if...at all; **if...really**

überheblich [ybər'heplɪç] *adj* arrogant

überhei'zen, übzerhit'zen *tr* overheat

überhöhen [ybər'hø·ən] *tr (Kurve)* bank; *(Preise)* raise too high

ü'berholen *tr* take across; **die Segel ü.** shift sails || *intr* (naut) heel || **überho'len** *tr* outdistance, outrun; *(ausbessern)* overhaul; *(Fahrzeug)* pass; (fig) outstrip

überholt [ybər'holt] *adj* obsolete, out of date; *(repariert)* reconditioned

überhö'ren *tr* not hear, miss; ignore; misunderstand

ü'berirdisch *adj* supernatural

überkandidelt ['ybərkandidəlt] *adj* (coll) nutty, wacky

ü'berkippen *intr* (SEIN) tilt over

überkle'ben *tr* paper over; **ü. mit** cover with

Ü'berkleid *n* outer garment; overalls

ü'berklug *adj* (pej) wise, smart

ü'berkochen *intr* (SEIN) boil over

überkom'men *adj* traditional || §99 *tr* overcome || *intr* (SEIN) be handed down to

überla'den *adj* overdone || §103 *tr* overload

Ü'berlandbahn *f* interurban trolley line

Ü'berlandleitung *f* (elec) high-tension line; (telp) long-distance line

überlas'sen §104 *tr* yield, leave, relinquish; entrust; (com) sell; **das bleibt ihm ü.** he is free to do as he pleases || *ref (dat)* give way to

Ü'berlast *f* overload; overweight

überla'sten *tr* overload

überlau'fen *adj* overcrowded; (fig) swamped || §105 *tr* overrun; *(belästigen)* pester; **Angst überlief ihn** fear came over him || **ü'berlaufen** §105 *intr* (SEIN) run over, overflow; boil over; (fig & mil) desert; **die Galle läuft mir über** (fig) my blood boils || *impers*—**mich überläuft es kalt** I shudder

Ü'berläufer –in §6 *mf* (mil) deserter; (pol) turncoat

ü'berlaut *adj* too noisy

überle'ben *tr* outlive, survive || *ref* go out of style

überle'bend *adj* surviving || **Überlebende** §5 *mf* survivor

ü'berlebensgroß *adj* bigger than life

überlebt [ybər'lept] *adj* antiquated

überle'gen *adj* (dat) superior (to); (an *dat*) superior (in) || *tr* consider, think over || *ref*—**sich** [*dat*] **anders ü.** change one's mind; **sich** [*dat*] **ü.** consider, think over || *intr* think it over || **ü'berlegen** *tr* lay across; *(Mantel)* put on

Überle'genheit *f* (–;) superiority

überlegt' *adj* well considered; (jur) willful

Überle'gung f (-;-en) consideration

überle'sen §107 tr read over, peruse

überlie'fern tr deliver; hand down, transmit; (mil) surrender

Überlie'ferung f (-;-en) delivery; (fig) tradition; (mil) surrender

überli'sten tr outwit, outsmart

überma'chen tr bequeath

Ü'bermacht f superiority; (fig) predominance

ü'bermächtig adj overwhelming; predominant

überma'len tr paint over

übermannen [ybər'manən] tr overpower

Ü'bermaß n excess; **bis zum Ü.** to excess

ü'bermäßig adj excessive || adv excessively; overly

ü'bermensch m superman

ü'bermenschlich adj superhuman

übermitteln [ybər'mɪtəln] tr transmit, convey, forward

Übermitt'lung f (-;-en) transmission, conveyance, forwarding

ü'bermorgen adv the day after tomorrow

übermüdet [ybər'mydət] adj overtired

Ü'bermut m exuberance, mischievousness

ü'bermütig adj exuberant; haughty

ü'bernächste §9 adj next but one; **am übernächsten Tag** the day after tomorrow; **ü. Woche** week after next

übernach'ten intr spend the night

Übernach'tung f (-;-en) accommodations for the night; spending the night

Ü'bernahme f taking over, takeover

ü'bernatürlich adj supernatural

überneh'men §116 tr take over; assume; undertake; take upon oneself; accept, receive || **ü'bernehmen** §116 tr (Mantel, Schal) put on; (Gewehr) shoulder || **überneh'men** §116 ref overreach oneself; **sich beim Essen ü.** overeat

ü'berordnen tr place over, set over

ü'berparteilich adj nonpartisan

Ü'berproduktion f overproduction

überprü'fen tr examine again, check; verify; (Personen) screen

Überprü'fung f (-;-en) checking; checkup

überquellen §119 intr (SEIN) (Teig) run over; **überquellende Freude** irrepressible joy

überqueren [ybər'kverən] tr cross

überra'gen tr tower over; (fig) surpass

überraschen [ybər'raʃən] tr surprise

Überra'schung f (-;-en) surprise

überrech'nen tr count over

überre'den tr persuade; **j-n zu etw ü.** talk a person into s.th.

Überre'dung f (-;-en) persuasion

ü'berreich adj (an dat) abounding (in) || adv—**ü. ausgestattet** well equipped

überrei'chen tr hand over, present

ü'berreichlich adj superabundant

ü'berreif adj overripe

überrei'zen tr overexcite; (Augen, Nerven) strain

überreizt adj overwrought

überren'nen §97 tr overrun; (fig) overwhelm

Ü'berrest m rest, remainder; **irdische Überreste** mortal remains

Ü'berrock m topcoat, overcoat

überrum'peln tr take by surprise

Überrum'pelung f (-;-en) surprise

überrun'den tr (sport) lap

übersät [ybər'zet] adj (fig) strewn, dotted

übersät'tigen tr stuff; cloy; (chem) saturate, supersaturate

Übersät'tigung f (chem) supersaturation

Überschall– comb.fm. supersonic

überschat'ten tr overshadow

überschät'zen tr overestimate

Ü'berschau f survey

überschau'en tr look over, survey; overlook (a scene)

überschla'fen §131 tr (fig) sleep on

Ü'berschlag m rough estimate; (aer) loop; (gym) somersault

überschla'gen adj lukewarm || §132 tr skip, omit; estimate roughly; consider || ref go head over heels; do a somersault; (Auto) overturn; (Boot) capsize; (Flugzeug) do a loop; (beim Landen) nose over; (Stimme) break; (fig) (vor dat) outdo oneself (in) || **ü'berschlagen** §132 tr (Beine) cross; flip over; **ü. in** (acc) (fig) change suddenly to

ü'berschnappen intr (SEIN) (Stimme) squeak; (coll) flip one's lid

überschnei'den §106 ref (Linien) intersect; (& fig) overlap

überschrei'ben §62 tr sign over

überschrei'en §135 tr shout down || ref strain one's voice

überschrei'ten §86 tr cross, step over; (Kredit) overdraw; (Gesetz) violate, transgress; (fig) exceed, overstep

Ü'berschrift f heading, title

Ü'berschuh m overshoe

Ü'berschuß m surplus, excess; profit

ü'berschüssig adj surplus, excess

überschüt'ten tr shower; (& fig) overwhelm, flood

Ü'berschwang m (-[e]s;) rapture

überschwem'men tr flood, inundate

Überschwem'mung f (-;-en) flood, inundation

überschwenglich ['ybərʃvɛnlɪç] adj effusive, gushing

Ü'bersee f (-;) overseas

Ü'berseedampfer m ocean liner

Ü'berseehandel m overseas trade

übersehbar [ybər'zebar] adj visible at a glance

überse'hen §138 tr survey, look over; (nicht bemerken) overlook; (absichtlich) ignore; (erkennen) realize

übersen'den §140 tr send, forward; transmit; (Geld) remit

Übersen'dung f (-;-en) forwarding; transmission; consignment

ü'bersetzen tr ferry across || **übersetzen** tr translate

Überset'zung f (-;-en) translation; (mach) gear, transmission

Ü'bersicht f survey, review; (Abriß) abstract; (Zusammenfassung) sum-

ü'bersichtlich *adj* clear; (*Gelände*) open

Ü'bersichtsplan *m* general plan

ü'bersiedeln *intr* (SEIN) move; emigrate

ü'bersinnlich *adj* transcendental

überspan'nen *tr* span; cover; overstrain; (*fig*) exaggerate

überspannt [ybər'∫pant] *adj* eccentric; extravagant

Überspannt'heit *f* (-;-en) eccentricity

Überspan'nung *f* (-;-en) overstraining; (*fig*) exaggeration; (*elec*) excess voltage

überspie'len *tr* outplay; outwit; (*Tonbandaufnahme*) transcribe; (*Schüchternheit*) hide

überspitzt [ybər'∫pıtst] *adj* oversubtle

übersprin'gen §142 *tr* jump; (*auslassen*) omit, skip ‖ **ü'berspringen** §142 *intr* (SEIN) jump

ü'bersprudeln *intr* (SEIN) bubble over

ü'berständig *adj* leftover; (*Bier*) flat; (*Obst*) overripe

überste'hen §146 *tr* stand, endure; (*Krankheit, usw.*) get over; (*Operation*) pull through; (*überleben*) survive ‖ **ü'berstehen** §146 *intr* jut out

überstei'gen §148 *tr* climb over; (*Hindernisse*) overcome; (*Erwartungen*) exceed ‖ **ü'bersteigen** §148 *intr* (SEIN) step over

überstim'men *tr* vote down, defeat

überstrah'len *tr* shine upon; (*verdunkeln*) outshine, eclipse

überstrei'chen §85 *tr* paint over

ü'berstreifen *tr* slip on

überströ'men *tr* flood, inundate ‖ **ü'berströmen** *intr* (SEIN) overflow

Ü'berstunde *f* hour of overtime; **Überstunden machen** work overtime

überstür'zen *tr* rush, hurry ‖ *ref* be in too big a hurry; act rashly; (*Ereignisse*) follow one another rapidly

überstürzt [ybər'∫tʏrtst] *adj* hasty

überteuern [ybər'tɔɪ-ərn] *tr* overcharge

übertölpeln [ybər'tœpəln] *tr* dupe

übertö'nen *tr* drown out

Übertrag ['ybərtrak] *m* (-[e]s;-e) (acct) carryover, balance

übertragbar [ybər'trakbar] *adj* transferable; (pathol) contagious

übertra'gen *adj* figurative, metaphorical ‖ §132 *tr* carry over, transfer; (*Amt, Titel*) confer; (*Aufgabe*) assign; (*Vollmacht*) delegate; (*Kurzschrift*) transcribe; (in *acc*) translate (into); (acct) transfer; (pathol) spread, communicate; (rad) broadcast, transmit; (*mit Relais*) relay; (telv) televise

Übertra'gung *f* (-;-en) carrying over; transfer; assignment; delegation; conferring; transcription; translation; copy; (pathol) spread; (rad) broadcast; relay; (telv) televising

übertref'fen §151 *tr* surpass, outdo

übertrei'ben §62 *tr* overdo; exaggerate; (theat) overact

Übertrei'bung *f* (-;-en) overdoing; exaggeration; (theat) overacting

übertre'ten §152 *tr* (*Gesetz*) transgress, break ‖ *ref*—**sich** [*dat*] **den Fuß ü.** sprain one's ankle ‖ **ü'bertreten** §152 *intr* (SEIN) (sport) go off sides; **ü. zu** (fig) go over to; (relig) be converted to

Übertre'tung *f* (-;-en) violation

Ü'bertritt *m* change, going over; (relig) conversion

übervölkern [ybər'fœlkərn] *tr* overpopulate

Übervöl'kerung *f* (-;) overpopulation

ü'bervoll *adj* brimful; crowded

übervorteilen [ybər'fortaılən] *tr* take advantage of, get the better of

überwa'chen *tr* watch over; supervise; (*kontrollieren*) inspect, check; (*polizeilich*) shadow; (rad, telv) monitor

Überwa'chung *f* (-;-en) supervision; inspection; control; surveillance

Überwa'chungsausschuß *m* watchdog committee

überwältigen [ybər'vɛltıgən] *tr* overpower (fig) overwhelm

überwei'sen §118 *tr* (*Geld*) send; (*zu e-m Spezialisten*) refer

Überwei'sung *f* (-;-en) sending, remittance; referral

ü'berweltlich *adj* otherworldly

ü'berwerfen §160 *tr* throw over ‖ **überwer'fen** §160 *ref* (mit) have a run-in (with)

überwie'gen §57 *tr* outweigh ‖ *intr* prevail, preponderate ‖ **Überwiegen** *n* (-s) prevalence, preponderance

überwie'gend *adj* prevailing; (*Mehrheit*) vast ‖ *adv* predominantly

überwin'den §59 *tr* conquer, overcome ‖ *ref*—**sich ü. zu** (inf) bring oneself to (inf)

überwin'tern [ybər'vıntərn] *intr* pass the winter; (bot) survive the winter

überwu'chern *tr* overrun; (fig) stifle

Ü'berwurf *m* wrap; shawl

Ü'berzahl *f* numerical superiority; majority

überzah'len *tr* & *intr* overpay

überzäh'len *tr* count over, recount

überzählig ['ybərtsɛlıç] *adj* surplus

überzeu'gen *tr* convince ‖ *ref*—**ü. Sie sich selbst davon!** go and see for yourself!

Überzeu'gung *f* (-;-en) conviction

überzie'hen §163 *tr* cover; (*mit Farbe*) coat; (*Bett*) put fresh linen on; (*Konto*) overdraw; **ein Land mit Krieg ü.** invade a country ‖ **ü'berziehen** §163 *tr* (*Mantel, usw.*) slip on; **j-m eins ü.** (coll) give s.o. a whack

ü'berzieher *m* (-s;-) overcoat

überzuckern (überzuk'kern) *tr* (& fig) sugarcoat

Ü'berzug *m* coat, film; (*Decke*) cover; (*Hülle*) case; (*Kissen*) pillow case; (*Kruste*) crust; (*Schale, Rinde*) skin

üblich ['yplıç] *adj* usual, customary

U'-Boot *n* (Unterseeboot) submarine

U'-Bootbunker *m* submarine pen

U'-Bootjäger *m* (aer) antisubmarine aircraft; (nav) subchaser

U'-Bootortungsgerät *n* sonar

U'-Bootrudel *n* (nav) wolf pack

übrig ['ybrıç] *adj* left (over), remaining, rest (of); **die übrigen** the others, the rest; **ein übriges tun** do more than is necessary; **etw ü. haben für** have a soft spot for; **im übrigen** for the rest, otherwise

ü/brigbehalten §90 *tr* keep, spare

ü/brigbleiben §62 *intr* (SEIN) be left (over) ‖ *impers*—**es blieb mir nichts anderes ü. als zu** (*inf*) I had no choice but to (*inf*)

übrigens ['ybrigəns] *adv* moreover; after all; by the way

ü/briglassen §104 *tr* leave, spare

Übung ['ybuŋ] *f* (–;–en) exercise; practice; (*Gewohnheit*) use; (*Ausbildung*) training; (mil) drill

Ü/bungsbeispiel *n* practical example

Ü/bungsbuch *n* composition book; workbook

Ü/bungsgelände *n* training ground; (*für Bomben*) target area

Ü/bungshang *m* (sport) training slope

Ü/bungsheft *n* composition book; workbook

Ufer ['ufər] *n* (–s;–) (*e-s Flusses*) bank; (*e-s Meers*) shore

U/ferdamm *m* embankment, levee

u/ferlos *adj* fruitless

Uhr [ur] *f* (–;–en) clock; watch; o'clock; **um wieviel Uhr?** at what time; **um zwölf Uhr** at twelve o'clock; **wieviel Uhr ist es?** what time is it?

Uhr/armband *n* (–[e]s;–er) watchband

Uhr/feder *f* watch spring

Uhr/glas *n* watch crystal

Uhr/macher *m* watchmaker

Uhr/werk *n* works, clockwork

Uhr/zeiger *m* hand

Uhr/zeigerrichtung *f*—**entgegen der U.** counterclockwise; **in der U.** clockwise

Uhr/zeigersinn *m*—**im U.** clockwise

Uhu ['uhu] *m* (–s;–s) owl

Ukraine [u'krainə] *f* (–;)—**die U.** the Ukraine

ukrainisch [u'krainiʃ] *adj* Ukrainian

UK-Stellung [u'ka/teluŋ] *f* (–;–en) military deferment

Ulk [ulk] *m* (–[e]s;–e) joke, fun

ulken ['ulkən] *intr* (coll) make fun

ulkig ['ulkiç] *adj* funny

Ulme ['ulmə] *f* (–;–n) elm

Ultima-tum [ulti'matum] *n* (–s;–ten [tən] & –ta [ta]) ultimatum

Ultra-, ultra- [ultra] *comb.fm.* ultra-

Ul/trakurzfrequenz *f* ultrashort frequency

ultramontan [ultramon'tan] *adj* strict Catholic

ul/trarot *adj* infrared

Ultraschall— *comb.fm.* supersonic

ul/traviolett *adj* ultraviolet

um [um] *adv*—**deine Zeit ist um** your time is up; **je…um so the…the**; **um so besser** all the better; **um so weniger** all the less; **um und um** round and round ‖ *prep* (*acc*) around, about; for; at; **um die Hälfte mehr** half as much again; **um die Wette laufen** race; **um ein Jahr älter** one year older; **um etw eintauschen exchange for s.th.; um jeden Preis** at any price; **um…Uhr** at…o'clock; **um…zu** (*inf*) in order to (*inf*)

um/ackern *tr* plow up, turn over

um/adressieren *tr* readdress

um/ändern *tr* change (around)

Um/änderung *f* (–;–en) change, alteration

um/arbeiten *tr* rework; (*Metall*) recast; (*Buch*) revise; (*Haus*) remodel; (*berichtigen*) emend, correct; (*verbessern*) improve

umar/men *tr* embrace, hug

Umar/mung *f* (–;–en) embrace, hug

Um/bau *m* (–[e]s;–e & –ten) rebuilding; alterations, remodeling; reorganization

um/bauen *tr* remodel; reorganize ‖ **umbau/en** *tr* build around; **umbauter Raum** floor space

um/besetzen *tr* (*Stellungen*) switch around; (pol) reshuffle; (theat) recast

um/biegen §47 *tr* bend (over); bend up, bend down

um/bilden *tr* remodel; reconstruct; (adm) reorganize, (pol) reshuffle

Um/bildung *f* (–;–en) remodeling; reconstruction; reorganization; reshuffling

um/binden §59 *tr* (*Schürze, usw.*) put on ‖ **umbin/den** §59 *tr* (*verletztes Glied, usw.*) bandage

um/blättern *tr* turn ‖ *intr* turn the page(s)

um/brechen §64 *tr* (*Bäume, usw.*) knock down; (*Acker*) plow up ‖ **umbre/chen** *tr* make into page proof

um/bringen §65 *tr* kill

Um/bruch *m* upheaval; (typ) page proof

um/buchen *tr* transfer to another account; book for another date

um/denken §66 *tr* rethink

um/dirigieren *tr* redirect

um/disponieren *tr* rearrange

umdrän/gen *tr* crowd around

um/drehen *tr* turn around; (*Hals*) wring; (*j-s Worte*) twist ‖ *ref* turn around ‖ *intr* turn around

Umdre/hung *f* (–;–en) turn; revolution

um/drucken *tr* reprint; (typ) transfer

umeinan/der *adv* around each other

um/erziehen §163 *tr* reeducate

um/fahren §71 *tr* run down ‖ **umfah/ren** §71 *tr* drive around; sail around

um/fallen §72 *intr* (SEIN) fall over, fall down; collapse; give in

Um/fang *m* circumference; perimeter; (*Bereich*) range; (*Ausdehnung*) extent; (*des Leibes*) girth; (fig) scope; (mus) range; **im großen U.** on a large scale

umfan/gen §73 *tr* surround; embrace

um/fangreich *adj* extensive; (*körperlich*) bulky; (*geräumig*) spacious

umfas/sen *tr* embrace; clasp; comprise; cover; include; contain; (mil) envelop

umfas/send *adj* comprehensive; extensive

Umfas/sung *f* (–;–en) embrace; clasp; enclosure, fence; (mil) envelopment

Umfas'sungsmauer f enclosure
umflat'tern tr flutter around
umflech'ten §74 tr braid
umflie'gen §57 tr fly around ‖ **um'flie-gen** §57 intr (SEIN) (coll) fall down
umflie'ßen §76 tr flow around
um'formen tr reshape; (elec) convert
Um'former m (-s;-) (elec) converter
Um'frage f inquiry, poll; **öffentliche U.** public opinion poll
umfrieden [um'fri:dən] tr enclose
Um'gang m round, circuit; revolution, rotation; (Zug) procession; association, company; (archit) gallery; **ge-schlechtlicher U.** sexual intercourse; **schlechter U.** bad company; **U. mit j-m haben** (or **pflegen**) associate with s.o.
umgänglich ['umgɛnlɪç] adj sociable
Um'gangsformen pl social manners
Um'gangssprache f colloquial speech
um'gangssprachlich adj colloquial
umgar'nen tr (fig) trap
umge'ben §80 tr surround
Umgebung [um'ge:buŋ] f (-;-en) surroundings, environs, neighborhood; company, associates; background, environment
Umgegend ['umge:gənt] f (-;) (coll) neighborhood
umgehen §82 tr go around; evade; by-pass; (mil) outflank ‖ **um'gehen** §82 intr (SEIN) go around; (Gerücht) circulate; **an** (or **in**) **e-m Ort u.** haunt a place; **mit dem Gedanken** (or **Plan**) **u. zu** (inf) be thinking of (ger); **u. mit etw** deal with, handle; manage; be occupied with; hang around with
um'gehend adj immediate; **mit umge-hender Post** by return mail; **umge-hende Antwort erbeten!** please an-swer at your earliest convenience ‖ adv immediately
Umge'hung f (-;-en) going around; bypassing; (fig) evasion; (mil) flank-ing movement
Umge'hungsstraße f bypass
umgekehrt ['umgəke:rt] adj reverse; contrary ‖ adv on the contrary; vice versa; upside down; inside out
um'gestalten tr alter; remodel
um'graben §87 tr dig up
umgren'zen tr fence in; (fig) limit
Umgren'zung f (-;-en) enclosure; (fig) limit, boundary
um'gruppieren tr regroup; (pol) re-shuffle
um'gucken ref look around
um'haben §89 tr have on, be wearing
Um'hang m wrap; cape; shawl
um'hängen tr put on; (Gewehr) sling; (Bild) hang elsewhere
Um'hängetasche f shoulder bag
um'hauen §93 tr cut down; (coll) bowl over
umher' adv around, about
umher'blicken tr look around
umher'fuchteln intr gesticulate
umher'schweifen, umher'streifen intr (SEIN) rove, roam about
umhin' adv—**ich kann nicht u.** I can't do otherwise; **ich kann nicht u. zu** (inf) I can't help (ger)

umhül'len tr wrap up, cover; envelop
Umhül'lung f (-;-en) wrapping
Umkehr ['umke:r] f (-;) return; change; conversion; (elec) reversal
um'kehren tr turn around; overturn; (Tasche) turn out; (elec) reverse; (gram, math, mus) invert ‖ intr (SEIN) turn back, return
Um'kehrung f (-;-en) overturning; re-versal; conversion; inversion
um'kippen tr upset ‖ intr (SEIN) tilt over
umklam'mern tr clasp; cling to; (mil) envelop; **einander u.** (box) clinch
Umklam'merung f (-;-en) embrace; (box) clinch; (mil) envelopment
umklei'den tr clothe ‖ ref change around ‖ **um'kleiden** tr change the clothes of
Um'kleideraum m dressing room
um'kommen §99 intr (SEIN) perish; (Essen) spoil
Um'kreis m circuit; vicinity; (geom) circumference; **5 km im U.** within a radius of 5 km
umkrei'sen tr circle, revolve around
um'krempeln (Ärmel) roll up; völ-lig u. (coll) change completely
um'laden §103 tr reload; transship
Um'lauf m circulation; (Umdrehung) revolution, rotation; (Flugblatt) cir-cular; (Rundschreiben) circular let-ter; **in U. setzen** circulate
Um'laufbahn f orbit
um'laufen §105 tr run down ‖ intr (SEIN) circulate ‖ **umlau'fen** §105 tr walk around
Um'laut m (-es;-e) umlaut, vowel mu-tation; mutated vowel
umlegbar ['umle:kba:r] adj reversible
um'legen tr lay down; turn down; (an-ders legen) shift; (Kragen) put on; (gleichmäßig verteilen) apportion; (coll) knock down; (vulg) lay
um'leiten tr detour, divert
Um'leitung f (-;-en) detour
um'lenken tr turn back
um'lernen tr relearn, learn anew
um'liegend adj surrounding
ummau'ern tr wall in
um'modeln tr remodel
umnachtet [um'naxtət] adj deranged
Umnach'tung f (-;)—**geistige U.** men-tal derangement
um'nähen tr hem
umne'beln tr fog; (fig) dull; **umnebelter Blick** glassy eyes
um'nehmen §116 tr put on
um'packen tr repack
um'pflanzen tr transplant ‖ **umpflan'-zen** tr—**etw mit Blumen u.** plant flowers around s.th.
um'pflügen tr plow up, turn over
um'rahmen tr frame
umranden [um'randən] tr edge, border
Umran'dung f (-;-en) edging, edge
umran'ken tr twine around; **mit Efeu umrankt** ivy-clad
um'rechnen tr convert; **umgerechnet auf** (acc) expressed in
Um'rechnungskurs m rate of exchange
Um'rechnungstabelle f conversion table
Um'rechnungswert m exchange value

um'reißen §53 *tr* pull down; knock down || **umrei'ßen** §53 *tr* outline
umrin'gen *tr* surround
Um'riß *m* outline
Um'rißzeichnung *f* sketch
um'rühren *tr* stir, stir up
um'satteln *tr* resaddle || *intr* change jobs; (educ) change one's course or major; (pol) switch parties
Um'satz *m* turnover, sales
Um'satzsteuer *f* sales tax
umsäu'men *tr* enclose, hem in
um'schalten *tr* switch; (*Strom*) convert || *intr* (auf *acc*) switch back (to)
Um'schalter *m* (elec) switch; (typ) shift key
Um'schaltung *f* (-;-en) switching; shifting
Um'schau *f* look around; **U. halten** have a look around
um'schauen *ref* look around
um'schichten *tr* regroup, reshuffle
umschichtig ['um,ɪçtɪç] *adv* alternately
umschif'fen *tr* circumnavigate; (*ein Kap*) double
Um'schlag *m* (sudden) change, shift; envelope; (*e-s Buches*) cover, jacket; cuff; hem; transshipment; (med) compress
um'schlagen §132 *tr* knock down; (*Ärmel*) roll up; (*Bäume*) fell; (*Saum*) turn up; (*Seite*) turn; (*umladen*) transship || *intr* (SEIN) (*Laune, Wetter*) change; (*Wind*) shift; (*kentern*) capsize
Um'schlagpapier *n* wrapping paper
umschlie'ßen §76 *tr* surround, enclose
umschlin'gen §142 *tr* clasp; embrace; wind around
um'schmeißen §53 *tr* (coll) throw over
um'schnallen *tr* buckle on
um'schreiben §62 *tr* rewrite; (*abschreiben*) transcribe; (*Wechsel*) reendorse; **u. auf** (*acc*) transfer to || **umschrei'ben** §62 *tr* circumscribe; paraphrase
Um'schreibung *f* (-;-en) transcription; transfer || **Umschrei'bung** *f* (-;-en) paraphrase
Um'schrift *f* transcription; (*e-r Münze*) legend
um'schulen *tr* retrain
um'schütteln *tr* shake (up)
um'schütten *tr* spill; pour into another container
umschwär'men *tr* swarm around; (fig) idolize
Um'schweif *m* digression; **ohne Umschweife** point-blank; **Umschweife machen** beat around the bush
umschweifig ['um,vaifɪç] *adj* roundabout
um'schwenken *intr* wheel around; (fig) change one's mind
Um'schwung *m* change; (*Drehung*) revolution; (*Umkehrung*) reversal; (*der Gesinnung*) revulsion
umse'geln *tr* sail around; (*Kap*) double
Umse'gelung *f* (-;-en) circumnavigation
um'sehen §138 *ref* (nach) look around (for); (fig) (nach) look out (for)

um'sein §139 *intr* (SEIN) (*Zeit*) be up; (*Ferien*) be over
um'setzen *tr* shift; transplant; (*Nährstoffe*) assimilate; (*Schüler*) switch around; (*Ware*) sell; (*verwandeln*) convert; (mus) transpose; **Geld in** (*acc*) spend money on; **in die Tat u.** translate into action || *ref*—**sich u. in** (*acc*) (biochem) be converted into
Um'sicht *f* (-;) circumspection
umsichtig ['umzɪçtɪç] *adj* circumspect
um'siedeln *tr* & *intr* (SEIN) resettle
Um'siedlung *f* (-;-en) resettlement
umsonst' *adv* for nothing, gratis; (*vergebens*) in vain
um'spannen *tr* (*Wagenpferde*) change; (elec) transform || **umspan'nen** *tr* span; encompass; include
Um'spanner *m* (-s;-) (elec) transformer
um'springen §142 *intr* (SEIN) (*Wind*) shift; **mit j-m rücksichtslos u.** (coll) treat s.o. thoughtlessly
Um'stand *m* circumstance; factor; fact; (*Einzelheit*) detail; (*Aufheben*) fuss; **in anderen Umständen** (coll) pregnant; **sich** [*dat*] **Umstände machen** go to the trouble; **Umstände machen** be formal; **unter Umständen** under certain conditions
umständehalber ['um,tɛndəhalbər] *adv* owing to circumstances
umständlich ['um,tɛntlɪç] *adj* detailed; (*förmlich*) formal; (*zu genau*) fussy; (*verwickelt*) complicated; (*Erzählung*) long-winded, round-about
Um'standskleid *n* maternity dress
Um'standskrämer *m* fusspot
Um'standswort *n* (-[e]s;-er) adverb
um'stehend *adj* (*Seite*) next || **Umstehende** §5 *mf* bystander
um'steigen §148 *intr* (SEIN) transfer
um'stellen *tr* put into a different place, shift; (*Möbel*) rearrange; (auf *acc*) convert (to) || *ref* (auf *acc*) adjust (to) || **umstel'len** *tr* surround
Um'stellung *f* (-;-en) change of position, shift; conversion; readjustment
um'stimmen *tr* tune to another pitch; make (*s.o.*) change his mind
um'stoßen §150 *tr* knock down; (*Pläne*) upset; (*Vertrag*) annul; (*Urteil*) reverse
umstricken (umstrik/ken) *tr* ensnare
umstritten [um'trɪtən] *adj* contested; controversial
Um'sturz *m* overthrow
um'stürzen *tr* overturn; overthrow; (*Mauer*) tear down; (*Plan*) change, throw out || *intr* (SEIN) fall down
Umstürzler **-in** ['um/tyrtslər(ɪn)] §6 *mf* revolutionary, subversive
umstürzlerisch ['um/tyrtslərɪʃ] *adj* revolutionary; subversive
Um'tausch *m* exchange
um'tauschen *tr* (gegen) exchange (for)
um'tun §154 *tr* (*Kleider*) put on || *ref* —**sich u. nach** look around for
um'wälzen *tr* roll around; (fig) revolutionize || *ref* roll around
umwäl'zend *adj* revolutionary
Umwäl'zung *f* (-;-en) revolution

umwandelbar ['ʊmvandəlbɑr] *adj* (com) convertible

um'wandeln *tr* change; (elec, fin) convert; (jur) commute

Um'wandlung *f* (-;-en) change; (elec, fin) conversion; (jur) commutation

um'wechseln *tr* exchange; (fin) convert

Um'weg *m* detour; **auf Umwegen** indirectly

um'wehen *tr* knock down ‖ **umwe'hen** *tr* blow around

Um'welt *f* environment

Um'weltverschmutzung *f* ecological pollution

um'wenden §140 *tr* turn over ‖ *ref* & *intr* turn around

umwer'ben §149 *tr* court, go with

um'werfen §160 *tr* throw down; upset; (*Plan*) ruin; (*Kleider*) throw about one's shoulders

umwickeln (umwik'keln) *tr* (*mit Band*) tape

umwin'den *tr* wreathe

umwölken [ʊm'vœlkən] *ref* & *intr* cloud over

umzäunen [ʊm'tsɔɪnən] *tr* fence in

um'ziehen §163 *ref* change one's clothes ‖ *intr* (SEIN) move ‖ **umzie'hen** §163 *ref*—**der Himmel hat sich umzogen** the sky has become overcast

umzingeln [ʊm'tsɪŋəln] *tr* encircle

Um'zug *m* procession, parade; (*Wohnungswechsel*) moving; (pol) march

un- [ʊn] *comb.fm.* un-, in-, ir-, non-

unabän'derlich *adj* unalterable

un'abhängig *adj* (von) independent (of) ‖ **Unabhängige** §5 *mf* (pol) independent

Un'abhängigkeit *f* independence

unabkömm'lich *adj* unavailable; indispensable; (mil) essential (*on the homefront*); **ich bin augenblicklich u.** I can't get away at the moment

unablässig ['ʊnapleːsɪç] *adj* incessant

unablösbar [ʊnap'løːsbɑr], **unablöslich** [ʊnap'løːslɪç] *adj* unpayable

unabseh'bar *adj* unforeseeable; immense

unabsetz'bar *adj* irremovable

unabsicht'lich *adj* unintentional

unabwendbar [ʊnap'vɛntbɑr] *adj* inevitable

un'achtsam *adj* careless, inattentive

un'ähnlich *adj* dissimilar, unlike

unanfecht'bar *adj* indisputable

un'angebracht *adj* out of place

un'angefochten *adj* undisputed

un'angemessen *adj* improper; inadequate; unsuitable

un'angenehm *adj* unpleasant, disagreeable; awkward

un'annehmbar *adj* unacceptable

Un'annehmlichkeit *f* unpleasantness, annoyance, inconvenience; **Unannehmlichkeiten** trouble

un'ansehnlich *adj* unsightly; (*unscheinbar*) plain, inconspicuous

un'anständig *adj* indecent; obscene

un'antastbar *adj* unassailable

un'appetitlich *adj* unappetizing; (*ekelhaft*) unsavory

Un'art *f* bad habit; (*Ungezogenheit*)

naughtiness; (*schlechte Manieren*) bad manners

un'artig *adj* ill-behaved, naughty

un'aufdringlich *adj* unostentatious; unobtrusive

un'auffällig *adj* inconspicuous

unauffindbar ['ʊnauffɪntbɑr] *adj* not to be found

unaufgefordert ['ʊnaufgəfordərt] *adj* unasked, uncalled for ‖ *adv* spontaneously

unaufhaltbar ['ʊnaufhaltbɑr], **unaufhaltsam** ['ʊnaufhaltzɑm] *adj* irresistible; relentless

unaufhörlich ['ʊnaufhøːrlɪç] *adj* incessant

un'aufmerksam *adj* inattentive

un'aufrichtig *adj* insincere

unaufschiebbar ['ʊnauf/ʃipbɑr] *adj* not to be postponed, urgent

unausbleiblich ['ʊnausblaɪplɪç] *adj* inevitable

unausführbar ['ʊnausfyːrbɑr] *adj* unfeasible, impracticable

unausgeglichen ['ʊnausgəglɪçən] *adj* uneven; (fig) unbalanced

unauslöschbar ['ʊnauslœ/bɑr], **unauslöschlich** ['ʊnauslœ/lɪç] *adj* inextinguishable; (*Tinte*) indelible

unaussprechlich ['ʊnaus/preçlɪç] *adj* unspeakable, ineffable

unausstehlich ['ʊnaus/teːlɪç] *adj* intolerable, insufferable

unbändig ['ʊnbɛndɪç] *adj* wild

un'barmherzig *adj* unmerciful

un'beabsichtigt *adj* unintentional

un'beachtet *adj* unobserved, unnoticed

unbeanstandet ['ʊnbə-an/tandət] *adj* unopposed, unhampered

unbearbeitet ['ʊnbə-arbaɪtət] *adj* unworked; (*roh*) raw; (*Land*) untilled; (mach) unfinished

umbebaut ['ʊnbəbaut] *adj* uncultivated; (*Gelände*) undeveloped

unbedacht ['ʊnbədaxt] *adj* thoughtless

un'bedenklich *adj* unhesitating; unswerving; unobjectionable, harmless ‖ *adv* without hesitation

un'bedeutend *adj* unimportant; slight

un'bedingt *adj* unconditional, unqualified; implicit

un'befahrbar *adj* impassable

un'befangen *adj* unembarrassed; (*unparteiisch*) impartial; natural, unaffected

unbefleckt ['ʊnbəflɛkt] *adj* immaculate

un'befriedigend *adj* unsatisfactory

un'befriedigt *adj* unsatisfied

un'befugt *adj* unauthorized; (jur) incompetent ‖ **Unbefugte** §5 *mf* unauthorized person

un'begabt *adj* untalented

unbegreif'lich *adj* incomprehensible

un'begrenzt *adj* unlimited

un'begründet *adj* unfounded

Un'behagen *n* discomfort, uneasiness

un'behaglich *adj* uncomfortable

unbehelligt ['ʊnbəhɛlɪçt] *adj* undisturbed, unmolested

unbehindert ['ʊnbəhɪndərt] *adj* unhindered; unrestrained

unbeholfen ['ʊnbəhɔlfən] *adj* clumsy

unbeirrbar ['ʊnbə·ɪrbar] *adj* unwavering

unbeirrt ['ʊnbə·ɪrt] *adj* unswerving

un'bekannt *adj* unknown; unfamiliar; unacquainted; (*Ursache*) unexplained ǁ **Unbekannte** §5 *mf* stranger ǁ *f* (math) unknown quantity

unbekümmert ['ʊnbəkymərt] *adj* (**um**) unconcerned (about)

un'beladen *adj* unloaded

unbelastet ['ʊnbəlastət] *adj* unencumbered; (*Wagen*) unloaded; carefree

un'belebt *adj* inanimate; (*Straße*) quiet; (com) slack

unbelichtet ['ʊnbəlɪçtət] *adj* (*Film*) unexposed

un'beliebt *adj* unpopular, disliked

unbemannt ['ʊnbəmant] *adj* unmanned

un'bemerkbar *adj* imperceptible

un'bemittelt *adj* poor

un'benommen *adj*—**es bleibt Ihnen u. zu** (*inf*) you are free to (*inf*); **es ist mir u., ob** it's up to me whether

unbenutzbar ['ʊnbənʊtsbar] *adj* unusable

unbenutzt ['ʊnbənʊtst] *adj* unused

un'bequem *adj* inconvenient; uncomfortable

unberechenbar ['ʊnbəreçənbar] *adj* incalculable; unpredictable

un'berechtigt *adj* unauthorized; unjustified

unbeschadet ['ʊnbəʃadət] *prep* (*genit*) without prejudice to

unbeschädigt ['ʊnbəʃedɪçt] *adj* unhurt; undamaged

un'bescheiden *adj* pushy

unbescholten ['ʊnbəʃɔltən] *adj* of good reputation

un'beschränkt *adj* unlimited; absolute

unbeschreiblich ['ʊnbəʃraɪplɪç] *adj* indescribable

unbesehen ['ʊnbəze·ən] *adv* sight unseen

un'besetzt *adj* unoccupied, vacant

unbesiegbar ['ʊnbəzikbar] *adj* invincible

unbesoldet ['ʊnbəzɔldət] *adj* unsalaried

un'besonnen *adj* thoughtless; careless; rash

un'besorgt *adj* unconcerned; carefree

un'beständig *adj* unsteady, inconstant; (*Preise*) fluctuating; (*Wetter*) changeable; (*Person*) fickle, unstable

unbestätigt ['ʊnbəʃtetɪçt] *adj* unconfirmed

un'bestechlich *adj* incorruptible

un'bestimmt *adj* indeterminate; vague; (*unsicher*) uncertain; (*unentschieden*) undecided; (gram) indefinite

unbestraft ['ʊnbəʃtraft] *adj* unpunished

unbestreit'bar *adj* indisputable

unbestritten ['ʊnbəʃtrɪtən] *adj* undisputed, uncontested

unbeteiligt ['ʊnbətaɪlɪçt] *adj* uninterested; indifferent; impartial

un'beträchtlich *adj* trifling, slight

unbeugsam ['ʊnbɔɪkzam] *adj* inflexible

unbewacht ['ʊnbəvaxt] *adj* unguarded

unbewaffnet ['ʊnbəvafnət] *adj* unarmed; (*Auge*) naked

un'beweglich *adj* immovable; motionless

unbewiesen ['ʊnbəvizən] *adj* unproved

unbewohnt ['ʊnbəvont] *adj* uninhabited

un'bewußt *adj* unconscious; involuntary

unbezähmbar [ʊnbə'tsembar] *adj* untamable; (fig) uncontrollable

Un'bilden *pl*—**U. der Witterung** inclement weather

Un'bildung *f* lack of education

un'billig *adj* unfair

unbotmäßig ['ʊnbotmesɪç] *adj* unruly; insubordinate

unbrauch'bar *adj* useless, of no use

un'bußfertig *adj* unrepentant

un'christlich *adj* unchristian

und [ʊnt] *conj* and; **und? so what? und wenn** even if

Un'dank *m* ingratitude

un'dankbar *adj* ungrateful; thankless

Un'dankbarkeit *f* ingratitude

undatiert ['ʊndatirt] *adj* undated

undenk'bar *adj* unthinkable

undenklich [ʊn'dɛŋklɪç] *adj*—**seit undenklichen Zeiten** from time immemorial

un'deutlich *adj* unclear, indistinct

un'deutsch *adj* un-German

un'dicht *adj* not tight; leaky

Un'ding *n* nonsense, absurdity

un'duldsam *adj* intolerant

undurchdring'lich *adj* (**für**) impervious (to); **undurchdringliche Miene** poker face

undurchführ'bar *adj* not feasible

un'durchlässig *adj* (**für**) impervious (to)

un'durchsichtig *adj* opaque; (*Beweggründe*) hidden; (*Machenschaften*) shady

un'eben *adj* uneven; bumpy; **nicht u.!** (coll) not bad!

un'echt *adj* false, spurious; artificial, imitation; (*Farbe*) fading

un'edel *adj* ignoble; (*Metall*) base

un'ehelich *adj* illegitimate

Un'ehre *f* dishonor

un'ehrenhaft *adj* dishonorable

un'ehrerbietig *adj* disrespectful

un'ehrlich *adj* dishonest; underhand

un'eigennützig *adj* unselfish

un'einig *adj* disunited; at odds

Un'einigkeit *f* disagreement

uneinnehm'bar *adj* impregnable

un'eins *adj* at odds, at variance

un'empfänglich *adj* (**für**) insusceptible (to)

un'empfindlich *adj* (**gegen**) insensitive (to); (**gegen**) insensible (to)

unend'lich *adj* endless; infinite; **auf u. einstellen** (phot) set at infinity ǁ *adv* endlessly; infinitely; **u. viele** an endless number of

unentbehr'lich *adj* indispensable

unentrinnbar [ʊnɛnt'rɪnbar] *adj* inescapable

un'entschieden *adj* undecided; (*schwankend*) indecisive; (sport) tie ǁ **Unentschieden** *n* (**-s;-**) (sport) tie

Un'entschiedenheit *f* indecision

un'entschlossen *adj* irresolute

Un'entschlossenheit f indecision

unentschuld'bar adj inexcusable

unentwegt ['unentvekt] adj staunch; unswerving || adv continuously; untiringly || **Unentwegte** §5 mf die-hard

unentwirrbar ['unentvɪrbɑr] adj inextricable

unerbittlich [uner'bɪtlɪç] adj inexorable; (Tatsache) hard

un'erfahren adj inexperienced

unerfindlich [uner'fɪntlɪç] adj incomprehensible, mysterious

unerforschlich [uner'fɔrʃlɪç] adj inscrutable

unerfreulich ['unerfrɔɪlɪç] adj unpleasant

unerfüllbar [uner'fylbɑr] adj unattainable

un'ergiebig adj unproductive

un'ergründlich adj unfathomable

un'erheblich adj insignificant; (für) irrelevant (to)

unerhört [uner'hørt] adj unheard-of, unprecedented; outrageous || **un'erhört** adj (Bitte) unanswered

un'erkannt adj unrecognized || adv incognito

unerklär'lich adj inexplicable

unerläßlich [uner'lɛslɪç] adj indispensable

un'erlaubt adj illicit, unauthorized

un'erledigt adj unsettled, unfinished

unermeßlich [uner'mɛslɪç] adj immense

unermüdlich [uner'mydlɪç] adj untiring; (Person) indefatigable

unerquicklich [uner'kvɪklɪç] adj unpleasant

unerreich'bar adj unattainable, out of reach

unerreicht ['unerraɪçt] adj unrivaled

unersättlich [uner'zɛtlɪç] adj insatiable

unerschlossen ['uner'ʃlɔsən] adj undeveloped; (Boden) unexploited

unerschöpflich [uner'ʃøpflɪç] adj inhaustible

unerschrocken ['unerʃrɔkən] adj intrepid, fearless

unerschütterlich [uner'ʃytərlɪç] adj unshakable; imperturbable

unerschwing'lich adj unattainable; beyond one's means; exorbitant

unersetz'bar, unersetz'lich adj irreplaceable; (Schaden) irreparable

unerträg'lich adj intolerable

unerwähnt ['unervent] adj unmentioned; u. lassen pass over in silence

unerwartet ['unervartət] adj unexpected, sudden

unerweis'lich adj unprovable

un'erwünscht adj undesired; unwelcome

unerzogen ['unertsogən] adj ill-bred

un'fähig adj incapable, unable; unqualified, inefficient

Un'fähigkeit f inability; inefficiency

Un'fall m accident, mishap

Un'fallflucht f hit-and-run offense

Un'fallstation f first-aid station

Un'falltod m accidental death

Un'fallversicherung f accident insurance

Un'fallziffer m accident rate

unfaß'bar, unfaß'lich adj incomprehensible; inconceivable

unfehl'bar adj infallible; unfailing

Unfehl'barkeit f infallibility

un'fein adj coarse; indelicate

un'fern adj near; u. von not far from || prep (genit) not far from

un'fertig adj not ready; not finished; immature

Unflat ['unflɑt] m (-s;) dirt, filth

unflätig ['unfletɪç] adj dirty, filthy

un'folgsam adj disobedient

Un'folgsamkeit f disobedience

unförmig ['unfœrmɪç] adj shapeless

un'förmlich adj informal

unfrankiert ['unfraŋkirt] adj unfranked, unstamped

un'frei adj not free; unstamped || adv —u. schicken send c.o.d.

un'freiwillig adj involuntary

un'freundlich adj unfriendly, unkind

Un'friede m dissension, discord

un'fruchtbar adj unfruitful, sterile; (fig) fruitless

Unfug ['unfuk] m (-[e]s;) nuisance, disturbance; mischief; misdemeanor; U. treiben cause mischief

ungang'bar adj impassable; unsalable

Ungar ['uŋgar] m (-;-n), **Ungarin** ['uŋgarɪn] f (-;-nen) Hungarian

ungarisch ['uŋgarɪʃ] adj Hungarian

Ungarn ['uŋgarn] n (-s;) Hungary

un'gastlich adj inhospitable

ungeachtet ['uŋgə-axtət] adj not esteemed || prep (genit) regardless of

ungeahnt ['uŋgə-ɑnt] adj unexpected

ungebärdig ['uŋgəberdɪç] adj unruly

ungebeten ['uŋgəbetən] adj unbidden

ungebeugt ['uŋgəbɔɪkt] adj unbowed; (gram) uninflected

un'gebildet adj uneducated

un'gebräuchlich adj unusual; (veraltet) obsolete

un'gebraucht adj unused

Un'gebühr f indecency, impropriety

un'gebührlich adj indecent, improper

ungebunden ['uŋgəbundən] adj unbound; (ausschweifend) loose, dissolute; (frei) unrestrained; **ungebundene Rede** prose

ungedeckt ['uŋgədekt] adj uncovered; (Tisch) unset; (Haus) roofless; (Kosten) unpaid; (Scheck) overdrawn

Un'geduld f impatience

un'geduldig adj impatient

un'geeignet adj unfit, unsuitable; unqualified

ungefähr ['uŋgəfer] adj approximate || adv approximately, about; **nicht von u.** on purpose

ungefährdet ['uŋgəferdət] adj safe, unendangered

un'gefährlich adj not dangerous

un'gefällig adj discourteous

un'gefüge adj monstrous; clumsy

un'gefügig adj unyielding, inflexible

ungefüttert ['uŋgəfytərt] adj unlined

un'gehalten adj (Versprechen) unkept, broken; (über acc) indignant (at)

ungeheißen ['uŋgəhaɪsən] adv of one's own accord

ungehemmt ['uŋgəhemt] adj unchecked

ungeheuer ['ʊngəhɔɪ·ər] *adj* huge; monstrous ‖ *adv* tremendously ‖ **Ungeheuer** *n* (-s;-) monster

un'geheuerlich *adj* monstrous ‖ *adv* (coll) tremendously

ungehobelt ['ʊngəhobəlt] *adj* unplaned; (fig) uncouth

un'gehörig *adj* improper; (*Stunde*) ungodly

Un'gehörigkeit *f* (-;-en) impropriety

un'gehorsam *adj* disobedient ‖ **Ungehorsam** *m* (-s;) disobedience

un'gekünstelt *adj* unaffected, natural

un'gekürzt *adj* unabridged

un'gelegen *adj* inconvenient

Un'gelegenheiten *pl* inconvenience

un'gelehrig *adj* unteachable

un'gelenk *adj* clumsy; stiff

un'gelernt *adj* (coll) unskilled

Un'gemach *n* discomfort; trouble

un'gemein *adj* uncommon

un'gemütlich *adj* uncomfortable; (*Zimmer*) dreary; (*Person*) disagreeable

un'genannt *adj* anonymous

un'genau *adj* inaccurate, inexact

ungeniert ['ʊnʒenirt] *adj* informal ‖ *adv* freely

ungenieß'bar *adj* inedible; undrinkable; (& fig) unpalatable

un'genügend *adj* insufficient; **u. bekommen** get a failing grade

ungepflastert ['ʊngəpflastərt] *adj* unpaved, dirt

un'gerade *adj* uneven; crooked; (*Zahl*) odd

un'geraten *adj* spoiled

un'gerecht *adj* unjust, unfair

Un'gerechtigkeit *f* injustice

ungereimt ['ʊngəraimt] *adj* unrhymed; (*unvernünft*) absurd; **ungereimtes Zeug reden** talk nonsense

un'gern *adv* unwillingly, reluctantly

ungerührt ['ʊngəryrt] *adj* (fig) unmoved

un'geschehen *adj* undone; **u. machen** undo

ungescheut ['ʊngəʃɔɪt] *adv* without fear

Un'geschick *n*, **Un'geschicklichhkeit** *f* awkwardness

un'geschickt *adj* awkward, clumsy

ungeschlacht ['ʊngəʃlaxt] *adj* uncouth

ungeschliffen ['ʊngəʃlɪfən] *adj* unpolished; (*Messer*) blunt; (*Edelstein*) uncut; (fig) rude

ungeschminkt ['ʊngəʃmɪŋkt] *adj* without makeup; (*Wahrheit*) unvarnished

un'gesellig *adj* unsociable

un'gesetzlich *adj* illegal

ungesittet ['ʊngəzɪtət] *adj* unmannerly; uncivilized

ungestört ['ʊngəʃtørt] *adj* undisturbed

ungestraft ['ʊngəʃtraft] *adj* unpunished ‖ *adv* scot-free

ungestüm ['ʊngəʃtym] *adj* impetuous, violent ‖ **Ungestüm** *n* (-[e]s;) impetuosity, violence

un'gesund *adj* unhealthy; unwholesome

ungeteilt ['ʊngətailt] *adj* undivided

un'getreu *adj* disloyal, untrue

ungetrübt ['ʊngətrypt] *adj* cloudless, clear; (fig) untroubled

Ungetüm ['ʊngətym] *n* (-[e]s;-e) monster

ungeübt ['ʊngə·ypt] *adj* untrained; (*Arbeiter*) inexperienced

un'gewandt *adj* unskillful; clumsy

un'gewiß *adj* uncertain; **j-n im ungewissen lassen** keep s.o. in suspense

Un'gewißheit *f* uncertainty

Un'gewitter *n* storm

un'gewöhnlich *adj* unusual

un'gewohnt *adj* unusual; (*genit*) unaccustomed (to)

ungezählt ['ʊngətsɛlt] *adj* countless

Ungeziefer ['ʊngətsifər] *n* (-s;) vermin, bugs

ungeziemend ['ʊngətsimənt] *adj* improper; (*frech*) impudent

un'gezogen *adj* rude; naughty

ungezügelt ['ʊngətsygəlt] *adj* unbridled

un'gezwungen *adj* unforced; natural, easy-going

Un'glaube *m* disbelief, unbelief

un'gläubig *adj* incredulous; (*heidnisch*) infidel ‖ **Ungläubige** §5 *mf* infidel

unglaub'lich *adj* incredible

un'glaubwürdig *adj* untrustworthy; incredible

un'gleich *adj* uneven, unequal; (*unähnlich*) unlike, dissimilar; (*Zahl*) odd ‖ *adv* much, by far

un'gleichartig *adj* heterogeneous

un'gleichförmig *adj* unequal; irregular

Un'gleichheit *f* inequality; difference; dissimilarity; unevenness

un'gleichmäßig *adj* disproportionate

Unglimpf ['ʊnglɪmpf] *m* (-[e]s;-e) harshness; wrong, insult

un'glimpflich *adj* harsh

Un'glück *n* (-s;) bad luck; (*Unfall*) accident; disaster, calamity

un'glücklich *adj* unlucky; unfortunate; unhappy

un'glücklicherweise *adv* unfortunately

Un'glücksbote *m* bearer of bad news

Un'glücksbringer *m* (-s;-) jinx

un'glückselig *adj* miserable; disastrous

Un'glücksfall *m* accident, misfortune

Un'glücksmensch *m* unlucky person

Un'glücksrabe *m*, **Un'glücksvogel** *m* unlucky fellow

Un'gnade *f* (-;) disfavor, displeasure

un'gnädig *adj* ungracious; **etw u. aufnehmen** take s.th. amiss

un'gültig *adj* null and void, invalid; **für u. erklären** nullify, void

Un'gültigkeit *f* invalidity

Un'gültigkeitserklärung *f* annulment

Un'gunst *f* disfavor; **zu meinen Ungunsten** to my disadvantage

un'günstig *adj* unfavorable, bad, adverse

un'gut *adj* unkind; **nichts für u.!** no offense!; **ungutes Gefühl** misgivings

un'haltbar *adj* not durable; untenable

un'handlich *adj* unwieldy, unhandy

Un'heil *n* disaster; mischief; **U. anrichten** cause mischief; **U. heraufbeschwören** ask for trouble

unheil'bar *adj* incurable; irreparable

un'heilvoll *adj* ominous; disastrous

un'heimlich *adj* uncanny; sinister

un'höflich *adj* impolite, uncivil

Un'höflichkeit f impoliteness
un'hold adj unkind || Unhold m (-[e]s; -e) fiend
un'hörbar adj inaudible
un'hygienisch adj unsanitary
Uni ['uni] f (-;-s) (Universität) (coll) university
uniform [uni'form] adj uniform || Uniform f (-;-en) uniform
Uni-kum ['unikum] n (-s;-s & -ka [ka]) unique example; (coll) queer duck
un'interessant adj uninteresting
un'interessiert adj (an dat) uninterested (in)
Union [un'jon] f (-;-en) union
universal [univer'zal] adj universal
Universal'mittel n panacea, cure-all
Universal'schlüssel m monkey wrench
Universität [universi'tet] f (-;-en) university
Universitäts'auswahlmannschaft f varsity (team)
Universum [uni'verzum] n (-s;) universe
Unke ['unkə] f (-;-n) toad
unken ['unkən] intr (coll) be a prophet of doom
um'kenntlich adj unrecognizable; u. machen disguise
Un'kenntnis f (-;) ignorance
Un'kenruf m croak
un'keusch adj unchaste
un'kindlich adj precocious; (Verhalten) disrespectful
un'kirchlich adj secular, worldly
un'klar adj unclear; muddy; misty; im unklaren sein über (acc) be in the dark about
Un'klarheit f obscurity
un'kleidsam adj unbecoming
un'klug adj unwise, imprudent
Un'klugheit f imprudence; foolish act
un'kontrollierbar adj unverifiable
un'körperlich adj incorporeal
Un'kosten pl expenses, costs; overhead; sich in U. stürzen go to great expense
Un'kraut n weed, weeds; U. jäten pull weeds
Un'krautvertilgungsmittel n weed killer
un'kündbar adj binding; (Darlehen) irredeemable; (Stellung) permanent
un'kundig adj (genit) ignorant (of), unacquainted (with)
unlängst ['unlɛŋst] adv recently, the other day
un'lauter adj unfair
un'leidlich adj intolerable
un'lenksam adj unruly
unles'bar, unle'serlich adj illegible
unleugbar ['unlɔıkbar] adj indisputable, undeniable
un'lieb adj disagreeable; es ist mir u. I am sorry
un'logisch adj illogical
unlös'bar adj (Problem) unsolvable; (untrennbar) inseparable; (chem) insoluble
unlös'lich adj (chem) insoluble
Un'lust f reluctance; listlessness
un'lustig adj reluctant; listless

un'manierlich adj impolite
un'männlich adj unmanly
Un'maß n excess; im U. to excess
un'maßgeblich adj unauthoritative; irrelevant; nach meiner unmaßgeblichen Meinung in my humble opinion
un'mäßig adj immoderate; excessive
Un'menge f (coll)—e-e U. von lots of
Un'mensch m brute, monster
un'menschlich adj inhuman, brutal
Un'menschlichkeit f brutality
un'marklich adj imperceptible
un'methodisch adj unmethodical
un'mißverständlich adj unmistakable
un'mittelbar adj direct, immediate
un'möbliert adj unfurnished
un'modern adj outmoded
un'möglich, unmög'lich adj impossible
Un'möglichkeit f impossibility
Un'moral f immorality
un'moralisch adj immoral
un'mündig adj underage
un'musikalisch adj unmusical
Un'mut m (über acc) displeasure (at)
un'mutig adj displeased, annoyed
unnachahmlich ['unnaxamlıç] adj inimitable
un'nachgiebig adj unyielding
un'nachsichtig adj unrelenting, inexorable; strict
unnahbar [un'nabar] adj inaccessible
un'natürlich adj unnatural
un'nennbar adj inexpressible
un'nötig adj unnecessary
unnütz ['unnyts] adj useless; vain
un'ordentlich adj disorderly; untidy
Un'ordnung f disorder; mess; in U. bringen throw into disorder
un'organisch adj inorganic
un'paar, un'paarig adj unpaired, odd
un'parteiisch, un'parteilich adj impartial, disinterested
Un'parteilichkeit f impartiality
un'passend adj unsuitable; (unschicklich) improper; (unzeitgemäß) untimely
un'passierbar adj impassable
unpäßlich ['unpeslıç] adj indisposed, ill
un'patriotisch adj unpatriotic
un'persönlich adj impersonal
un'politisch adj nonpolitical
un'populär adj unpopular
un'praktisch adj impractical; (unerfahren) unskillful
Un'rast f restlessness
Un'rat m (-[e]s;) garbage; dirt; U. wittern (coll) smell a rat
un'rätlich, un'ratsam adj inadvisable
um'recht adj wrong || Unrecht n (-[e]s;) —im U. sein be in the wrong; j-m U. geben decide against s.o.; mit (or zu) U. wrongly; unjustly; illegally
un'redlich adj dishonest
Un'redlichkeit f dishonesty
un'reell adj unfair
un'regelmäßig adj irregular
Un'regelmäßigkeit f irregularity
un'reif adj unripe, green; (fig) immature
Un'reife f unripeness; immaturity
un'rein adj unclean; (& fig) impure;

ins u. schreiben make a rough copy of

Un′reinheit f uncleanness; (& fig) impurity

un′reinlich adj dirty

un′rentabel adj unprofitable

un′rettbar adj irrecoverable

un′richtig adj incorrect, wrong

un′ritterlich adj unchivalrous

Un′ruh f (−;−en) (horol) balance wheel

Un′ruhe f restlessness; uneasiness; (Aufruhr) commotion, riot; (Störung) disturbance; (Besorgnis) anxiety

un′ruhig adj restless; uneasy; (laut) noisy; (Pferd) restive; (Meer) choppy; (nervös) jumpy

un′rühmlich adj inglorious

Un′ruhstifter −in §6 mf agitator, troublemaker; (Wirrkopf) screwball

uns [ʊns] pers pron us; to us || reflex pron ourselves; **wir sind doch unter uns** we are by ourselves || recip pron each other, one another; **wir sehen uns später** we'll meet later

un′sachgemäß adj inexpert

un′sachlich adj subjective; personal

unsagbar [ʊn′zakbar], **unsäglich** [ʊn′zeːklɪç] adj unspeakable; (fig) immense

un′sauber adj unclean; (unlauter) unfair, dirty

un′schädlich adj harmless

un′scharf adj (Apparat) out of focus; (Bild) blurred; (Begriff) poorly defined

un′schätzbar adj inestimable, invaluable

un′scheinbar adj inconspicuous, insignificant

un′schicklich adj unbecoming; indecent

Un′schicklichkeit f impropriety

un′schlüssig adj indecisive

Un′schlüssigkeit f indecision, hesitation

un′schmackhaft adj insipid, unpalatable

un′schön adj unlovely; plain, homely; (Angelegenheit) unpleasant

Un′schuld f innocence; **ich wasche meine Hände in U.** I wash my hands of it

un′schuldig adj innocent; (keusch) chaste; harmless; **sich für u. erklären** (jur) plead not guilty

un′schwer adj not difficult

Un′segen m adversity; (Fluch) curse

un′selbständig adj dependent, helpless

un′selig adj unfortunate; (Ereignis) fatal

unser [′ʊnzər] §2,3 poss adj our || §2,4 poss pron ours || pers pron us; of us; **erinnerst du dich unser noch?** do you still remember us?; **es waren unser vier** there were four of us

unseresgleichen [′ʊnzərəs′glaɪçən] pron people like us; the likes of us

unserige [′ʊnzərɪgə] §2,5 pron ours

unserthalben [′ʊnzərt′halbən], **unsertwegen** [′ʊnzərt′veːgən] adv for our sake, on our behalf, on our account

un′sicher adj unsafe; shaky; precarious

Un′sicherheit f unsafeness; shakiness; insecurity; precariousness

un′sichtbar adj invisible

Un′sinn m (−[e]s;) nonsense, rubbish; **U. machen** fool around

un′sinnig adj nonsensical

Un′sitte f bad habit

un′sittlich adj immoral, indecent

Un′sittlichkeit f immorality

un′solid(e) adj unsolid; (Person) loose; (Firma) unreliable, shaky

unsortiert [′ʊnzərtirt] adj unsorted

un′sozial adj antisocial

un′sportlich adj unsportsmanlike

unsrerseits [′ʊnzər′zaɪts] adv as for us, for our part

unsrige [′ʊnzrɪgə] §2,5 poss pron ours

un′ständig adj impermanent, temporary

un′statthaft adj inadmissible; forbidden

unsterb′lich adj immortal

Unsterb′lichkeit f immortality

Un′stern m unlucky star; (fig) disaster

un′stet adj unsteady; restless; changeable

un′stillbar adj unappeasable; (Durst) unquenchable; (Hunger) unsatiable

unstimmig [′ʊn/tɪmɪç] adj discrepant; inconsistent

Un′stimmigkeit f (−;−en) discrepancy; inconsistency; (Widerspruch) disagreement

un′sträflich adj blameless; guileless

un′streitig adj indisputable

Un′summe f enormous sum

un′symmetrisch adj asymmetrical

un′sympathisch adj unpleasant; **er ist mir u.** I don't like him

un′tadelhaft adj blameless; flawless

Un′tat f crime

un′tätig adj inactive

un′tauglich adj unfit, unsuitable; useless; (Person) incompetent; **u. machen** disqualify

un′teilbar adj indivisible

unten [′ʊntən] adv below; beneath; downstairs; **da u.** down there; **er ist bei ihnen u. durch** they are through with him; **nach u.** downstairs; downwards; **tief u.** far below; **u. am Berge** at the foot of the mountain; **u. an der Seite** at the bottom of the page; **von u. her** from underneath

unter [′ʊntər] prep (dat) under, below; beneath, underneath; (zwischen) among; (während) during; **ganz u. uns gesagt** just between you and me; **u. aller Kritik** beneath contempt; **u. anderem** among other things; **u. diesem Gesichtspunkt** from this point of view; **u. Null** below zero; **was versteht man unter...?** what is meant by...? || prep (acc) under, below; beneath, underneath; among || **Unter** m (−s;−) (cards) jack

Unter−, unter− comb.fm. under−, sub−; lower

Un′terabteilung f subdivision

Un′terarm m forearm

Un′terart f subspecies

Un′terausschuß m subcommittee

Un′terbau m (−[e]s;−ten) foundation

un'terbelichten *tr* underexpose
un'terbewußt *adj* subconscious
Un'terbewußtsein *n* subconscious
unterbie'ten §58 *tr* undercut, undersell; underbid
un'terbinden §59 *tr* tie underneath || **unterbin'den** §59 *tr* (*Verkehr*) tie up; (*Blutgefäß*) tie off; (*verhindern*) prevent; (*Angriff*) neutralize
Unterbin'dung *f* stoppage; (surg) ligature
unterblei'ben §62 *intr* (SEIN) remain undone; not take place; be discontinued; **das muß u.** that must be stopped
unterbre'chen §64 *tr* interrupt; (*einstellen*) suspend; (*Schweigen, Stille, Kontakt*) break; (*Verkehr*) hold up; (telp) disconnect; **die Reise in München u.** have a stopover in Munich || *ref* stop short
Unterbre'cher *m* (elec) circuit breaker
Unterbre'chung *f* interruption; disconnection; (*e-r Fahrt*) stopover
unterbrei'ten *tr* submit
un'terbringen §65 *tr* provide a place for; find room for; (*Gäste*) accommodate, put up; (*Stapeln*) store; (*Anleihe*) place; (*Geld*) invest; (*Pferde*) stable; (*Wagen*) park; (*Truppe*) billet; **e-n Artikel bei e-r Zeitung u.** have an article published in a newspaper; **j-n auf e-m Posten** (or **in e-r Stellung) u.** find s.o. a job, place s.o.
Un'terbringung *f* (–;-en) accommodations, housing; billet; storage; investment; placement
Un'terbringungsmöglichkeiten *pl* accommodations
unterdes [untər'des], **unterdessen** [untər'desən] *adv* meanwhile
Un'terdruck *m* low pressure
unterdrücken (unterdrük'ken) *tr* suppress; (*Aufstand*) quell; (*bedrücken*) oppress; (*ersticken*) stifle; (*Seufzer*) repress
Un'terdruckgebiet *n* low-pressure area
Unterdrückung (Unterdrük'kung) *f* (–;) oppression; suppression
untere ['untərə] §9 *adj* lower, inferior
untereinan'der *adv* among one another; mutually; reciprocally
unterentwickelt ['untərentvikəlt] *adj* underdeveloped
unterernährt ['untərernert] *adj* undernourished
Un'terernährung *f* (–;) undernourishment
Un'terfamilie *f* subfamily
unterfer'tigen *tr* sign
Unterführung *f* (–;-en) underpass
unterfüt'tern *tr* line
Un'tergang *m* setting; (fig) decline, fall; (naut) sinking
unterge'ben *adj* (dat) subject (to), inferior (to) || **Untergebene** §5 *mf* subordinate
un'tergehen §82 *intr* (SEIN) go down, sink; (fig) perish; (astr) set
untergeordnet ['untərgə-ərdnət] *adj* subordinate || **Untergeordnete** §5 *mf* subordinate

Un'tergeschoß *n* ground floor; (*Kellergeschoß*) basement
Un'tergestell *n* undercarriage
Un'tergewand *n* underwear
un'tergliedern *tr* subdivide
untergra'ben §87 *tr* undermine
Un'tergrund *m* subsoil
Un'tergrundbahn *f* subway
Un'tergrundbewegung *f* underground movement
un'terhalb *prep* (genit) below
Un'terhalt *m* (–[e]s;) support; maintenance, upkeep; livelihood
un'terhalten §90 *tr* hold under || **unterhal'ten** §90 *tr* maintain; support; (*Briefwechsel*) keep up; (*Feuer*) feed; entertain, amuse || *ref* enjoy oneself, have a good time; amuse oneself; **sich u. mit** talk with
unterhaltsam [untər'haltzam] *adj* entertaining, amusing, enjoyable
Un'terhaltsbeitrag *m* alimony; (*für Kinder*) support
Unterhaltsberechtigte ['untərhaltsbə-reçtigtə] §5 *mf* dependent
Un'terhaltskosten *pl* living expenses
Unterhal'tung *f* (–;-en) entertainment, amusement; (*Gespräch*) conversation; (*Aufrechterhaltung*) upkeep; (*Unterstützung*) support
Unterhal'tungskosten *pl* maintenance cost, maintenance
Unterhal'tungslektüre *f* light reading
unterhan'deln *intr* negotiate
Un'terhändler **–in** §6 *mf* negotiator; (*Vermittler*) mediator
Unterhand'lung *f* (–;-en) negotiation
Un'terhaus *n* (parl) lower house
Un'terhemd *n* undershirt
unterhöh'len *tr* undermine
Un'terholz *n* undergrowth, underbrush
Un'terhose *f* shorts; panties; **in Unterhosen zeigen** (coll) debunk
un'terirdisch *adj* underground, subterranean; (myth) of the underworld
Un'terjacke *f* vest
unterjo'chen *tr* subjugate
Unterjo'chung *f* (–;) subjugation
Un'terkiefer *m* lower jaw
Un'terkinn *n* double chin
Un'terkleid *n* slip
Un'terkleidung *f* (–;) underwear
un'terkommen §99 *intr* (SEIN) find accommodations; find employment || **Unterkommen** *n* (–;s) accommodations; (*Stellung*) job
Un'terkörper *m* lower part of the body
un'terkriegen *tr* (coll) get the better of; **er läßt sich nicht u.** he won't knuckle under
Unterkunft ['untərkunft] *f* (–;-̈e) accommodations; apartment; (*Obdach*) shelter, place to stay; (mil) quarters; **U. und Verpflegung** room and board
Un'terlage *f* foundation; base; pad; desk pad; rubber pad (*for a bed*); (*Teppich-*) underpad; (*Beleg*) voucher; (*Urkunde*) document; (archit) support; (geol) substratum; **keine Unterlagen haben** have nothing to go on; **Unterlagen** documentation; data
Un'terland *n* lowland

Unterlaß ['ʊntərlas] *m*—**ohne U.** without letup

unterlas/sen §104 *tr* omit; neglect; skip; stop, cut out

Unterlas/sung *f* (–;-en) omission; neglect; failure

Unterlas/sungssünde *f* sin of omission

unterlau/fen *adj*—**blau u.** black-and-blue; **mit Blut u.** bloodshot ‖ **un/ter-laufen** §105 *intr* (SEIN) (*Fehler*) slip in

un/terlegen *tr* lay under, put under; (*Bedeutung, Sinn*) attach; **der Musik Worte u.** set words to music ‖ **unter-le/gen** *adj* defeated; (*dat*) inferior (to) ‖ **Unterlegene** §5 *mf* loser

Unterle/genheit *f* (–;) inferiority

Unterlegring ['ʊntərlekrɪŋ] *m*, **Unter-legscheibe** ['ʊntərlek/aɪbə] *f* washer

Un/terleib *m* abdomen

Unterleibs– *comb.fm.* abdominal

unterlie/gen §108 *intr* (SEIN) (*dat*) be beaten (by), lose (to); **e-m Rabatt u.** be subject to discount ‖ *impers* (SEIN)—**es unterliegt keinem Zweifel, daß** there is no doubt that

Un/terlippe *f* lower lip

untermale/len *tr* put the primer on; **mit Musik u.** accompany with music

untermau/ern *tr* support

Un/termiete *f* (–;) subletting; **in U. ab-geben** sublet; **in U. wohnen bei** sublet from

Un/termieter –in §6 *mf* subtenant

unterminie/ren *tr* (fig) undermine

unterneh/men §116 *tr* undertake; (*ver-suchen*) attempt; **Schritte u.** (fig) take steps ‖ **Unternehmen** *n* (–;-) undertaking; venture; enterprise; (mil) operation

unterneh/mend *adj* enterprising

Unterneh/mensberater *m* management consultant

Unterneh/mer –in §6 *mf* entrepreneur; (*Arbeitgeber*) employer; (*Bau–*) contractor

Unterneh/mung *f* (–;-en) undertaking; enterprise, business; (mil) operation

Unterneh/mungsgeist *m* initiative

unterneh/mungslustig *adj* enterprising

Un/teroffizier *m* noncommissioned officer, N.C.O.

un/terordnen *tr* (*dat*) subordinate (to) ‖ *ref* (*dat*) submit (to)

unterre/den *ref* (mit) confer (with)

Unterre/dung *f* (–;-en) conference

Unterricht ['ʊntərrɪçt] *m* (–[e]s;-e) instruction, lessons

unterrich/ten *tr* instruct; **u. von** (or **über** *acc*) inform (of, about)

Un/terrichtsfach *n* subject, course

Un/terrichtsfilm *m* educational film; (mil) training film

Un/terrichtsministerium *n* department of public instruction

Un/terrichtsstunde *f* (educ) period

Un/terrichtswesen *n* education; teaching

Un/terrock *m* slip

untersa/gen *tr* forbid, prohibit

Un/tersatz *m* saucer; support; (*Gestell*) stand; (archit) socle; (log) minor premise

unterschät/zen *tr* underrate, underestimate; undervalue

unterschei/den §112 *tr* distinguish ‖ *ref* (von) differ (from)

Unterschei/dung *f* (–;-en) difference, distinction

Un/terschenkel *m* shank

un/terschieben §130 *tr* shove under; (*statt genit*) substitute (for); (*dat*) impute (to), foist (on)

Unterschied ['ʊntərʃit] *m* (–[e]s;-e) difference, distinction; **zum U. von** as distinct from, unlike

un/terschiedlich *adj* different; varying

un/terschiedslos *adj* indiscriminate

unterschla/gen §132 *tr* embezzle; (*Nachricht*) suppress; (*Brief*) intercept

Unterschla/gung *f* (–;-en) embezzlement; suppression; interception

Unterschlupf ['ʊntərʃlʊpf] *m* (–[e]s;) shelter; hide-out

unterschrei/ben §62 *tr* sign; (fig) subscribe to, agree to

Un/terschrift *f* signature

Un/terseeboot *n* submarine

unterseeisch ['ʊntərze-ɪʃ] *adj* submarine

Un/terseekabel *n* transoceanic cable

Un/terseite *f* underside

untersetzt [ʊntər'zɛtst] *adj* stocky

Un/tersetzung *f* (–;-en) (mech) reduction

un/tersinken §143 *intr* (SEIN) go down

Un/terstand *m* (mil) dugout

unterste ['ʊntərstə] §9 *adj* lowest, bottom

unterste/hen §146 *ref* dare; **untersteh dich!** don't you dare! ‖ *intr* (*dat*) be under (*s.o.*) ‖ **un/terstehen** §146 *intr* take shelter

un/terstellen *tr* place under; (*Auto*) put into the garage ‖ *ref* take cover ‖ **unterstel/len** *tr* assume, suppose; (*dat*) impute (to); (mil) (*dat*) put under the command (of)

Unterstel/lung *f* (–;-en) assumption; imputation

unterstrei/chen §85 *tr* underline

unterstüt/zen *tr* support, back; help

Unterstüt/zung *f* (–;-en) support, backing; assistance; (*Beihilfe durch Geld*) relief; (ins) benefit

untersu/chen *tr* examine, inspect; investigate; study, do research on; (chem) analyze

Untersu/chung *f* (–;-en) examination; inspection; investigation; study, research; (chem) analysis

Untersu/chungsausschuß *m* fact-finding committee

Untersu/chungsgericht *n* court of inquiry

Untersu/chungshaft *f* (jur) detention

Untersu/chungsrichter *m* examining judge

Untertagebau [ʊntər'tagəbau] *m* (–[e]s;) mine

Untertan ['ʊntərtan] *m* (–s & -en;-en) subject

untertänig [ʊntər'tɛnɪç] *adj* submissive

Un/tertasse *f* saucer; **fliegende U.** flying saucer

un'tertauchen *tr* submerge; duck ‖ *intr* (SEIN) dive; (fig) disappear ‖ **Unter-tauchen** *n* (-s;) dive; disappearance
Un'terteil *m* & *n* lower part, bottom
untertei'len *tr* subdivide
Untertei'lung *f* (-;-en) subdivision
Un'tertitel *m* subtitle; caption
Un'terton *m* undertone
un'tertreten §152 *intr* (SEIN) take cover
un'tervermieten *tr* sublet
Un'tervertrag *m* subcontract
unterwan'dern *tr* infiltrate
Un'terwäsche *f* underwear
Unterwasser- *comb.fm.* underwater, submarine
Un'terwasserbombe *f* depth charge
Un'terwasserhorchgerät *n* hydrophone
Un'terwasserortungsgerät *n* sonar
unterwegs [ʊntər'veks] *adv* on the way; (com) in transit
unterwei'sen §118 *tr* instruct
Unterwei'sung *f* (-;-en) instruction
Un'terwelt *f* underworld; (myth) lower world
unterwer'fen §160 *tr* subjugate; (*dat*) subject (to) ‖ *ref* (*dat*) submit to, subject oneself to; **sich** [*dat*] **ein Volk u.** subjugate a people
Unterwer'fung *f* (-;) subjugation; submission
unterworfen [ʊntər'vɔrfən] *adj* subject
unterwür'fig ['ʊntərvʏrfɪç] *adj* submissive, subservient
unterzeich'nen *tr* sign
Unterzeich'ner –in §6 *mf* signer; signatory
Unterzeichnete [ʊntər'tsaɪçnətə] §5 *mf* undersigned
Unterzeich'nung *f* (-;-en) signing; signature
un'terziehen §163 *tr* put on underneath ‖ unterzie'hen §163 *tr* (*dat*) subject (to) ‖ *ref*—**sich der Mühe u. zu** (*inf*) take the trouble to (*inf*); **sich e-r Operation u.** have an operation; **sich e-r Prüfung u.** take an examination
un'tief *adj* shallow ‖ Untiefe *f* (-;-n) shoal
Un'tier *n* (& fig) monster
untilg'bar *adj* inextinguishable; (*Tinte*) indelible; (*Anleihe*) irredeemable
untrag'bar *adj* unbearable; (*Kleidung*) unwearable; (*Kosten*) prohibitive
untrenn'bar *adj* inseparable
un'treu *adj* unfaithful ‖ Untreue *f* unfaithfulness; infidelity
untröst'lich *adj* inconsolable
untrüg'lich *adj* unerring, infallible
untüch'tig *adj* incapable; inefficient
Un'tugend *f* bad habit, vice
un'überlegt *adj* thoughtless; rash
unüber'sehbar *adj* vast, huge; incalculable ‖ *adv* very
unübersetz'bar *adj* untranslatable
un'übersichtlich *adj* unclear; (*Kurve*) blind
unübersteig'bar, unübersteig'lich *adj* insurmountable
unübertreff'lich *adj* unsurpassable
unübertroffen [ʊnybər'trɔfən] *adj* unsurpassed
unüberwind'lich *adj* invincible; (*Schwierigkeiten*) insurmountable

unumgäng'lich *adj* indispensable
unumschränkt ['ʊnʊm/rɛŋkt] *adj* unlimited; (pol) absolute
unumstößlich ['ʊnʊm/tøslɪç] *adj* irrefutable; (*unwiderruflich*) irrevocable
unumwunden ['ʊnʊmvʊndən] *adj* blunt
un'unterbrochen *adj* continuous
unverän'derlich *adj* unchangeable, invariable
unverant'wortlich *adj* irresponsible
unveräu'ßerlich *adj* inalienable
unverbesserlich [ʊnfɛr'bɛsərlɪç] *adj* incorrigible
unverbind'lich *adj* without obligation; (*Verhalten*) proper, formal; (*Antwort*) noncommittal
un'verblümt *adj* blunt, plain
unverbürgt [ʊnfɛr'byrkt] *adj* unwarranted; (*Nachricht*) unconfirmed
un'verdächtig *adj* unsuspected
un'verdaulich *adj* indigestible
unverderbt ['ʊnfɛrdɛrpt], unverdorben ['ʊnfɛrdɔrbən] *adj* unspoiled
unverdient ['ʊnfɛrdint] *adj* undeserved
un'verdrossen *adj* indefatigable
unverdünnt ['ʊnfɛrdʏnt] *adj* undiluted
unverehelicht ['ʊnfɛrə-əlɪçt] *adj* unmarried, single
un'vereinbar *adj* incompatible; contradictory
unverfälscht ['ʊnfɛrfɛl/t] *adj* genuine; (*Wein*) undiluted
un'verfänglich *adj* innocent
un'verfroren *adj* brash
un'vergänglich *adj* imperishable
un'vergeßlich *adj* unforgettable
un'vergleichbar *adj* incomparable
unvergleichlich ['ʊnfɛrglaɪçlɪç] *adj* incomparable
un'verhältnismäßig *adj* disproportionate
un'verheiratet *adj* unmarried
unvergolten ['ʊnfɛrgɔltən] *adj* unrewarded
unverhofft ['ʊnfɛrhɔft] *adj* unhoped-for
unverhohlen ['ʊnfɛrholən] *adj* unconcealed; (fig) open
un'verkäuflich *adj* unsalable
unverkennbar ['ʊnfɛrkɛnbar] *adj* unmistakable
unverkürzt ['ʊnfɛrkʏrtst] *adj* unabridged
unverlangt ['ʊnfɛrlaŋt] *adj* unsolicited
un'verletzbar, un'verletzlich *adj* undamageable; (fig) inviolable
unverletzt ['ʊnfɛrlɛtst] *adj* safe and sound, unharmed; (*Sache*) undamaged
unvermeid'lich *adj* inevitable
unvermindert ['ʊnfɛrmɪndərt] *adj* undiminished
unvermittelt ['ʊnfɛrmɪtəlt] *adj* sudden
Un'vermögen *n* inability; impotence
un'vermögend *adj* poor; impotent
unvermutet ['ʊnfɛrmutət] *adj* unexpected
un'vernehmlich *adj* imperceptible
Un'vernunft *f* unreasonableness; folly
un'vernünftig *adj* unreasonable; foolish
un'verschämt *adj* brazen, shameless

un'verschuldet [ˈʊnferʃʊldət] *adj* un-encumbered; (*unverdient*) unde-served

un'versehens *adv* unawares, suddenly

unversehrt [ˈʊnferzeːrt] *adj* undamaged (*Person*) unharmed

unversichert [ˈʊnferzɪçərt] *adj* unin-sured

unversiegbar [ˈʊnferˈzikbar] **unversieg-lich** [ˈʊnferˈziklɪç] *adj* inexhaustible

unversiegelt [ˈʊnferzigəlt] *adj* unsealed

un'versöhnlich *adj* irreconcilable

unversorgt [ˈʊnferzorkt] *adj* unpro-vided for

Un'verstand *m* lack of judgment

un'verständig *adj* foolish

un'verständlich *adj* incomprehensible

unversucht [ˈʊnferzuːxt] *adj* untried

unverträglich [ˈʊnferˈtrɛːklɪç] *adj* unsocial; quarrel-some; incompatible, contradictory

un'verwandt *adj* steady, unflinching

unverwelklich [ˈʊnferˈvelklɪç] *adj* un-fading

un'verwendbar *adj* unusable

unverweslich [ˈʊnferˈveːzlɪç] *adj* incor-ruptible

unverwindbar [ˈʊnferˈvɪntbar] *adj* ir-reparable; (*Enttäuschung*) lasting

un'verwundbar *adj* invulnerable

unverwüstlich [ˈʊnferˈvyːstlɪç] *adj* in-destructible; (*Stoff*) durable; (*fig*) irrepressible

unverzagt [ˈʊnfertsakt] *adj* undaunted

un'verzeihlich *adj* unpardonable

unverzerrt [ˈʊnfertsert] *adj* undistorted

unverzinslich [ˈʊnfertsɪnslɪç] *adj* (fin) without interest

unverzüglich [ˈʊnfertsyklɪç] *adj* prompt, immediate ‖ *adv* without delay

unvollendet [ˈʊnfɔlendət] *adj* unfin-ished

un'vollkommen *adj* imperfect

Un'vollkommenheit *f* imperfection

un'vollständig *adj* incomplete; (*gram*) defective

un'vorbereitet *adj* unprepared; (*Rede*) extemporaneous ‖ *adv* extempore

un'voreingenommen *adj* unbiased

un'vorhergesehen *adj* unforeseen

un'vorsätzlich *adj* unintentional

un'vorsichtig *adj* incautious; careless

un'vorteilhaft *adj* disadvantageous; unprofitable; (*Kleid*) unflattering

un'wahr *adj* untrue

un'wahrhaftig *adj* untruthful

Un'wahrheit *f* untruth, falsehood

un'wahrnehmbar *adj* imperceptible

un'wahrscheinlich *adj* unlikely, improb-able

unwan'delbar *adj* unchangeable

unwegsam [ˈʊnvekzam] *adj* impass-able

unweigerlich [ʊnˈvaigərlɪç] *adj* un-hesitating; (*Folge*) necessary ‖ *adv* without fail

un'weit *adj*—u. von not far from ‖ *prep* (*genit*) not far from

Un'wesen *n* mischief; **sein U. treiben** be up to one's old tricks

un'wesentlich *adj* unessential; unim-portant; (*für*) immaterial (to)

Un'wetter *n* storm

un'wichtig *adj* unimportant

unwiederbringlich [ʊnviːdər ˈbrɪŋlɪç] *adj* irretrievable, irreparable

un'widerleg'bar *adj* irrefutable

un'widerruf'lich *adj* irrevocable

un'widersteh'lich *adj* irresistible

Un'wille *m*, **Un'willen** *m* indignation, displeasure; reluctance

un'willig *adj* (über *acc*) indignant (at), displeased (at); **u. zu** (*inf*) reluctant to (*inf*)

un'willkommen *adj* unwelcome

un'willkürlich *adj* involuntary

un'wirklich *adj* unreal

un'wirksam *adj* ineffective; inefficient; (chem) inactive; (jur) null and void

Un'wirksamkeit *f* ineffectiveness; inef-ficiency; (chem) inactivity

unwirsch [ˈʊnvɪrʃ] *adj* surly

un'wirtlich *adj* inhospitable

un'wirtschaftlich *adj* uneconomical

un'wissend [ˈʊnvɪsənt] *adj* ignorant

Unwissenheit [ˈʊnvɪsənhait] *f* (–;) ig-norance

un'wissenschaftlich *adj* unscientific

un'wissentlich *adv* unwittingly

un'wohl *adj* sickish; **ich fühle mich u.** I don't feel well

un'wohnlich *adj* uninhabitable; (*un-behaglich*) uncomfortable

un'würdig *adj* unworthy

Un'zahl *f* (von) huge number (of)

unzähl'bar, **unzählig** [ʊnˈtseliç] *adj* countless, innumerable

un'zart *adj* indelicate

Unze [ˈʊntsə] *f* (–;–n) ounce

Un'zeit *f* wrong time

un'zeitgemäß *adj* out-of-date

un'zeitig *adj* untimely; (*Obst*) unripe

unzerbrech'lich *adj* unbreakable

unzerstör'bar *adj* indestructible

unzertrennlich [ʊntser ˈtrenlɪç] *adj* in-separable

unziemend [ˈʊntsimənt], **un'ziemlich** *adj* unbecoming, unseemly

Un'zucht *f* unchastity; lewdness

un'züchtig *adj* unchaste; lewd

un'zufrieden *adj* dissatisfied

un'zugänglich *adj* inaccessible; aloof

un'zulänglich *adj* inadequate

un'zulässig *adj* inadmissible; (*Beein-flussung, Einmischung*) undue

un'zurechnungsfähig *adj* unaccountable

un'zureichend *adj* inadequate

un'zusammenhängend *adj* incoherent

un'zuträglich *adj* (dat) bad (for)

un'zutreffend *adj* not applicable

un'zuverlässig *adj* unreliable

un'zweckmäßig *adj* inappropriate; un-suitable; impractical

un'zweideutig *adj* unambiguous

un'zweifelhaft *adj* undoubted

üppig [ˈʏpɪç] *adj* luxurious, plush; (*Mahl*) sumptuous; (*Pflanzenwuchs*) luxuriant; (*sinnlich*) voluptuous

Ur-, **ur-** [ur] *comb.fm.* original; very

ur'alt *adj* very old, ancient

Uran [uˈran] *n* (–s;) uranium

Ur'aufführung *f* world première

urbar [ˈʊrbar] *adj* arable; **u. machen** reclaim

Urbarmachung [ˈʊrbarmaxuŋ] *f* (–;) reclamation

Ur'bewohner *pl* aborigines
Ur'bild *n* prototype; original
ur'deutsch *adj* hundred-percent German
ur'eigen *adj* one's very own; original
Ur'einwohner *pl* aborigines
Ur'eltern *pl* ancestors
Ur'enkel *m* great-grandson
Ur'geschichte *f* prehistory
Ur'großmutter *f* great-grandmother
Ur'großvater *m* great-grandfather
Urheber **-in** ['urhebər(ın)] §6 *mf* originator, author
Ur'heberrecht *n* copyright
Ur'heberschaft *f* (-;-e) authorship
Urin [u'rin] *m* (-s;) urine
urinieren [urɪ'nirən] *intr* urinate
ur'ko'misch *adj* very funny
Urkunde ['urkundə] *f* (-;-n) document; deed; (*Vertrag*) instrument
Ur'kundenmaterial *n* documentation
urkundlich ['urkuntlɪç] *adj* documentary; (*verbürgt*) authentic
Urlaub ['urlaup] *m* (-[e]s;-e) vacation; (mil) furlough
Ur'lauber **-in** §6 *mf* vacationer
Ur'laubsschein *m* (mil) pass
Ur'laubstag *m* day off
Urne ['urnə] *f* (-;-n) urn; ballot box; zur U. gehen go to the polls
Ur'nengang *m* balloting

ur'plötz'lich *adj* sudden || *adv* all of a sudden
Ur'sache *f* cause, reason; **keine U.!** don't mention it!
ur'sächlich *adj* causal
Ur'schleim *m* (-es;) protoplasm
Ur'schrift *f* original text, original
Ur'sprung *m* origin, source; beginning; (*Ursache*) cause
ursprünglich ['urʃprʏŋlɪç] *adj* original
Ur'stoff *m* primary matter; (chem) element
Ur'teil *n* judgment; (*Ansicht*) view, opinion; (jur) verdict; (*Strafmaß*) (jur) sentence
urteilen ['urtaɪlən] *intr* judge; **u. nach** judge by
Ur'teilskraft *f* discernment
Ur'teilsspruch *m* verdict; sentence
Ur'text *m* original text
Ur'tier *n* protozoon
Ur'volk *n* aborigines
Ur'wald *m* virgin forest; jungle
ur'weltlich *adj* primeval
urwüchsig ['urvyksɪç] *adj* original; (fig) rough
Ur'zeit *f* remote antiquity
Utensilien [uten'ziljən] *pl* utensils
Uto-pie [uto'pi] *f* (-;-pien ['pi·ən]) utopia; pipe dream
uzen ['utsən] *tr* tease, kid

V

V, v [fau] *invar n* V, v
vag [vak] *adj* vague
Vagabund [vaga'bunt] *m* (-en;-en) vagabond, tramp, bum
vagabundieren [vagabun'dirən] *intr* (HABEN & SEIN) bum around
vage ['vagə] *adj* vague
vakant [va'kant] *adj* vacant
Vakanz [va'kants] *f* (-;-en) vacancy
Vaku-um ['vaku·um] *n* (-s;-ua [u·a]) vacuum
Vakzine [vak'tsinə] *f* (-;-n) vaccine
vakzinieren [vaktsi'nirən] *tr* vaccinate
Valet [va'let] *n* (-s;-s) farewell
Valu-ta [va'luta] *f* (-;-ten [tən]) value; (foreign) currency
Vampir ['vampir] *m* (-s;-e) vampire
Vandale [van'dalə] *m* (-n;-n) Vandal; (fig) vandal
Vanille [va'nɪljə] *f* (-;) vanilla
Variante [varɪ'antə] *f* (-;-n) variant
Varietät [varɪ·e'tet] *f* (-;-en) variety
Varieté [varɪ·e'te] *n* (-s;-s) vaudeville; vaudeville stage
variieren [varɪ'irən] *tr & intr* vary
Vase ['vazə] *f* (-;-n) vase
Vaselin [vaze'lin] *n* (-s;-e), **Vaseline** [vaze'linə] *f* (-;-n) vaseline
Vater ['fatər] *m* (-s;⁻) father
Va'terland *n* (native) country
vaterländisch ['fatərlendɪʃ] *adj* national || *adv*—v. gesinnt patriotic
Va'terlandsliebe *f* patriotism
väterlich ['fetərlɪç] *adj* fatherly

väterlicherseits ['fetərlɪçər'zaɪts] *adv* on the father's side
Va'terliebe *f* paternal love
Va'terschaft *f* (-;) fatherhood
Va'terschaftsklage *f* paternity suit
Va'tersname *m* family name, last name
Va'terstadt *f* home town
Va'terstelle *f*—**bei j-m V. vertreten** be a father to s.o.
Vaterun'ser *n* (-s;-) Lord's Prayer
Vati ['fati] *m* (-s;-s) dad, daddy
Vatikan [vatɪ'kan] *m* (-s;) Vatican
v. Chr. *abbr* (**vor Christus**) B.C.
Vegetarier **-in** [vege'tarjər(ɪn)] §6 *mf* vegetarian
Vegetation [vegeta'tsjon] *f* (-;) vegetation
vegetieren [vege'tirən] *intr* vegetate
Veilchen ['faɪlçən] *n* (-s;-) (bot) violet
Vene ['venə] *f* (-;-n) (anat) vein
Venedig [ve'nedɪç] *n* (-s;) Venice
venerisch [ve'nerɪʃ] *adj* venereal; **venerisches Leiden** venereal disease
Ventil [ven'til] *n* (-s;-e) valve; (bei der Orgel) stop; (fig) outlet
Ventilation [ventɪla'tsjon] *f* (-;) ventilation
Venti-lator [ventɪ'lator] *m* (-s;-latoren [la'torən]) ventilator; fan
ver- [fer] *pref* up, e.g., **verbrauchen** use up; away, e.g., **verjagen** chase away; mis-, wrongly, e.g., **verstellen** misplace, **verdrehen** turn the wrong

way; (to form verbs from other parts of speech) **verwirklichen** realize, **vergöttern** deify; (to express a sense opposite that of the simple verb) **verlernen** forget, **verkaufen** sell; (to indicate consumption or waste through the action of the verb) **verschreiben** use up in writing; (to indicate intensification or completion) **verhungern** die of hunger; (to indicate cessation of action) **vergären** cease to ferment; (to indicate conversion to another state) **verflüssigen** liquify

verabfolgen [fer'apfɔlgən] *tr* hand over; deliver; (*Arznei*) give, administer

verabreden [fer'apredən] *tr* agree upon; **schon anderweitig verabredet sein** have a prior engagement ‖ *ref* make an appointment

Verab'redung *f* (-;-en) agreement; appointment

verabreichen [fer'apraiçən] *tr* give

verabsäumen [fer'apzɔimən] *tr* var of **versäumen**

verabscheuen [fer'apʃɔi·ən] *tr* detest, loath, abhor

verab'scheuenswert, verab'scheuenswürdig detestable

verabschieden [fer'apʃidən] *tr* dismiss; (*Beamte*) put on pension; (*Gesetz*) pass; (mil) disband ‖ *ref* (**von**) take leave (of), say goodbye (to)

Verab'schiedung *f* (-;-en) dismissal; pensioning; (mil) disbanding; (parl) passing, enactment

verach'ten *tr* despise; **nicht zu v.** not to be sneezed at

verächtlich [fer'ɛçtlɪç] *adj* contemptuous; (*verachtungswert*) contemptible

Verach'tung *f* (-;) contempt

veralbern [fer'albərn] *tr* tease

verallgemeinern [feralgə'mainərn] *tr & intr* generalize

Verallgemei'nerung *f* (-;-en) generalization

veralten [fer'altən] *intr* become obsolete; (*Kleider*) go out of style

veraltet [fer'altət] *adj* obsolete; out of date, old-fashioned

Veran·da [ve'randa] *f* (-;-den [dən]) veranda, porch

veränderlich [fer'endərlɪç] *adj* changeable; (math) variable

Verän'derlichkeit *f* (-;-en) changeableness; fluctuation; instability

verän'dern [fer'endərn] *tr* change; vary ‖ *ref* change; look for a new job

Verän'derung *f* (-;-en) change

verängstigt [fer'ɛŋstɪçt] *adj* intimidated

verankern [fer'aŋkərn] *tr* anchor, moor

Veran'kerung *f* (-;-en) anchorage, mooring

veranlagen [fer'anlɑgən] *tr* (*zu e-r Steuer*) assess; **gut veranlagt** highly talented; **künstlerisch veranlagt** artificially inclined; **schlecht veranlagt** poorly endowed

Veran'lagung *f* (-;-en) talents; disposition; (fin) assessment

veran'lassen *tr* cause, occasion, make; (*bereden*) induce

Veran'lassung *f* (-;-en) cause, occasion; **auf V. von** at the suggestion of; **ohne jede V.** without provocation; **V. geben zu** give rise to

veranschaulichen [fer'anʃaulɪçən] *tr* make clear, illustrate

veran'schlagen §132 *tr* rate, value; (*im voraus berechnen*) estimate; **zu hoch v.** overrate

Veran'schlagung *f* (-;) estimate

veranstalten [fer'anʃtaltən] *tr* organize, arrange; (*Empfang*) give; (*Sammlung*) take up; (*Versammlung*) hold

Veran'stalter –in §6 *mf* organizer

Veran'staltung *f* (-;-en) organization, arrangement; affair; performance, show; meeting; (sport) event, meet

veran'tworten *tr* answer for, account for; (*verteidigen*) defend ‖ *ref* defend oneself, justify oneself

verantwortlich [fer'antvɔrtlɪç] *adj* responsible, answerable; **für etw v.** zeichnen sign for s.th.

Verant'wortlichkeit *f* (-;) responsibility; (jur) liability

Verant'wortung *f* (-;-en) responsibility; (*Rechtfertigung*) justification; **auf eigene V.** at one's own risk; **die V. abwälzen auf** (*acc*) pass the buck to; **zur V. ziehen** call to account

Verant'wortungsbewußtsein *n* sense of responsibility

verant'wortungsfreudig *adj* willing to assume responsibility

verant'wortungsvoll *adj* responsible

veräppeln [fer'ɛpəln] *tr* (coll) tease

verar'beiten *tr* manufacture, process; (*zu*) make (into); (*verdauen*) digest; (fig) assimilate

verar'beitend *adj* manufacturing

Verar'beitung *f* (-;-en) manufacturing; digestion; (fig) assimilation

verargen [fer'argən] *tr*—**j-m etw v.** blame s.o. for s.th.

verär'gern *tr* annoy

verarmen [fer'armən] *intr* (SEIN) grow poor

verästeln [fer'ɛstəln] *ref* branch out

verausgaben [fer'ausgabən] *tr* pay out ‖ *ref* run short of money

veräußern [fer'ɔisərn] *tr* sell

Verb [verp] *n* (-s;-en) verb

verbal [ver'bal] *adj* verbal

Verband [fer'bant] *m* (-[e]s;:e) association, union, federation; (aer, nav) formation; (mil) unit; (surg) bandage, dressing; **sich aus dem V. lösen** (aer) peel off

Verband'kasten *m* first-aid kit

Verband'päckchen *n* first-aid pack

Verband'platz *m* first-aid station

Verband'stoff *m* bandage, dressing

verbannen [fer'banən] *tr* banish, exile

Verbannte [fer'bantə] §5 *mf* exile

Verban'nung *f* (-;-en) banishment; place of exile

verbarrikadie'ren *tr* barricade

verbau'en *tr* (*Gelände*) build up; use up (*in building*); (*Geld*) spend (*in building*); build poorly; **j-m den Weg v. zu** bar s.o.'s way to

verbei′ßen §53 *tr* swallow, suppress ‖ *ref* (in *acc*) stick (to)

verber′gen §54 *tr* & *ref* hide

verbes′sern *tr* improve; correct; (*Aufsatz*) grade; (*Gesetz*) amend; (*Tatsache*) rectify ‖ *ref* improve; better oneself

Verbes′serung *f* (–;–en) improvement; correction; amendment

verbeu′gen *ref* bow

Verbeu′gung *f* (–;–en) bow; curtsy

verbeulen [fer′bɔɪlən] *tr* dent; batter

verbie′gen §57 *tr* bend ‖ *ref* warp

verbie′ten §58 *tr* forbid

verbil′den *tr* spoil; educate badly

verbil′ligen *tr* reduce the price of

Verbil′ligung *f* (–;–en) reduction

verbin′den §59 *tr* tie, tie up; join, unite; (*verketten*) link; (*zu Dank verpflichten*) obligate; (chem) combine; (med) bandage; (telp) (**mit**) connect (with), put through (to); **j–m die Augen v.** blindfold s.o. ‖ *ref* unite

verbindlich [fer′bɪntlɪç] *adj* obliging; binding; **verbindlichsten Dank!** thank you ever so much!

Verbind′lichkeit *f* (–;–en) obligation; commitment; polite way; (*e–s Vertrags*) binding force

Verbin′dung *f* (–;–en) union; association; alliance; combination; contact; touch; (*Fuge, Gelenk*) joint; (chem) compound; (educ) fraternity; (mach, rr, telp) connection; (mil) liaison; **die V. verlieren mit** lose touch with; **e–e V. eingehen** (chem) form a compound; **er hat gute Verbindungen** he has good connections; **in V. mit** in conjunction with; **sich in V. setzen mit** get in touch with; **unmittelbare V.** (telp) direct call

Verbin′dungsbahn *f* connecting train

Verbin′dungsleitung *f* (telp) trunk line

Verbin′dungslinie *f* line of communication

Verbin′dungsoffizier *m* liaison officer

Verbin′dungspunkt *m*, **Verbin′dungsstelle** *f* joint, juncture

Verbin′dungsstück *n* joint, coupling

verbissen [fer′bɪsən] *adj* dogged, grim; (*Zorn*) suppressed; **v. sein in** (*dat*) stick doggedly to

Verbis′senheit *f* (–;) doggedness, grimness

verbitten [fer′bɪtən] §60 *ref*—**sich** [*dat*] **etw v.** not stand for s.th.

verbittern [fer′bɪtərn] *tr* embitter

Verbit′terung *f* (–;) bitterness

verblassen [fer′blasən] *intr* (SEIN) grow pale; (fig) fade

verblättern [fer′blɛtərn] *tr*—**die Seite v.** lose the page

Verbleib [fer′blaɪp] *m* (–[e]s;) whereabouts

verblei′ben §62 *intr* (SEIN) remain, be left; (**bei**) persist (in); **wir sind so verblieben, daß** we finally agreed that

verblei′chen §85 *intr* (SEIN) fade

verblen′den *tr* blind; dazzle; (*Mauer*) face; (*Fenster*) wall up

Verblen′dung *f* (–;–en) blindness, infatuation; (archit) facing

verblichen [fer′blɪçən] *adj* faded

verblödet [fer′blødət] *adj* idiotic

verblüffen [fer′blʏfən] *tr* dumbfound, flabbergast; bewilder, perplex

Verblüff′fung *f* (–;) bewilderment

verblü′hen *intr* (SEIN) wither; fade

verblümt [fer′blʏmt] *adj* euphemistic

verblu′ten *ref* & *intr* (SEIN) bleed to death

verbocken [fer′bɔkən] *tr* bungle

verboh′ren *ref*—**sich v. in** (*acc*) stick stubbornly to

verbohrt [fer′bort] *adj* stubborn; odd

verbolzen [fer′bɔltsən] *tr* bolt

verbor′gen *adj* secret; latent; hidden ‖ *tr* lend out ‖ **Verborgene** §5 *n*—**im Verborgenen** in secret, on the sly

Verbor′genheit *f* (–;) secrecy; concealment; seclusion

Verbot [fer′bot] *n* (–[e]s;–e) prohibition; (jur) injunction

verboten [fer′botən] *adj* forbidden; **Eintritt v.!** no admittance; **Plakatankleben v.!** post no bills!; **Stehenbleiben v.!** no loitering

verbrämen [fer′bremən] *tr* trim; edge; (fig) sugar-coat

verbrannt [fer′brant] *adj* burnt; torrid; **Politik der verbrannten Erde** scorched-earth policy

Verbrauch′ *m* (–[e]s;) use, consumption

verbrau′chen *tr* use up, consume; waste; (*abnutzen*) wear out

Verbrau′cher *m* (–s;–) consumer; (*Benützer*) user; (*Kunde*) customer

Verbrau′chergenossenschaft *f* co-op

Verbrauchs′güter *pl* consumer goods

verbraucht′ *adj* used up, consumed; worn out; (*Geld*) spent; (*Luft*) stale

verbre′chen §64 *tr* commit, do ‖ **Verbrechen** *n* (–s;–) crime

Verbre′cher *m* (–s;–) criminal

Verbre′cheralbum *n* rogues' gallery

Verbre′cherin *f* (–;–nen) criminal

verbrecherisch [fer′breçərɪʃ] *adj* criminal

Verbre′cherkolonie *f* penal colony

verbreiten [fer′braɪtən] *tr* spread; (*Frieden, Licht*) shed ‖ *ref* spread; **sich v. über** (*acc*) expatiate on

verbreitern [fer′braɪtərn] *tr* & *ref* widen, broaden

Verbrei′terung *f* (–;) widening, broadening

Verbrei′tung *f* (–;) spreading; dissemination; diffusion

verbren′nen §97 *tr* burn; scorch; (*bräunen*) tan; (*Leichen*) cremate ‖ *ref* burn oneself; **sich** [*dat*] **die Finger v.** (& fig) burn one's fingers

Verbren′nung *f* (–;–en) burning, combustion; cremation; (*Brandwunde*) burn

Verbren′nungskraftmaschine *f*, **Verbren′nungsmotor** *m* internal combustion engine

Verbren′nungsraum *m* combustion chamber

verbrin′gen §65 *tr* spend, pass; (*wegbringen*) take away

verbrüdern [fer′brydərn] *ref* (**mit**) fraternize (with)

Verbrü′derung f (-;) fraternizing

verbrü′hen tr scald

verbu′chen tr book; **etw als Erfolg v.** chalk s.th. up as a success

Ver-bum ['verbum] n (-s;-ba [ba]) verb

verbunden [fer'bundən] adj connected; **falsch v.!** sorry, wrong number!; **untereinander v.** interconnected; **zu Dank v.** obligated

verbünden [fer'byndən] ref—**sich mit j–m v.** ally oneself with s.o.

Verbun′denheit f (-;) connection, ties; solidarity, union

Verbündete [fer'byndətə] §5 mf ally

verbür′gen tr guarantee, vouch for || ref—**sich v. für** vouch for

verbürgt [fer'byrkt] adj authenticated

verbüßen [fer'bysən] tr atone for, pay for; **seine Strafe v.** serve one's time

verchromen [fer'kromən] tr chromeplate

Verchro′mung f (-;-en) chromeplating

Verdacht [fer'daxt] m (-[e]s;) suspicion; **in V. kommen** come under suspicion; **V. hegen gegen** have suspicions about; **V. schöpfen** get suspicious

verdächtig [fer'deçtiç] adj suspicious; (genit) suspected (of)

verdächtigen [fer'deçtigən] tr cast suspicion on; (genit) suspect (of)

Verdäch′tigung f (-;-en) insinuation

verdammen [fer'damən] tr condemn; damn

Verdammnis [fer'damnɪs] f (-;) damnation, perdition

verdammt′ adj (sl) damn || interj (sl) damn it!

verdamp′fen tr & intr (SEIN) evaporate

Verdamp′fung f (-;) evaporation

verdan′ken tr—**j–m etw v.** be indebted to s.o. for s.th.

verdarb [fer'darp] pret of **verderben**

verdattert [fer'datərt] adj (coll) shook up

verdauen [fer'dau·ən] tr digest

verdaulich [fer'dauliç] adj digestible

Verdau′ung f (-;) digestion

Verdau′ungsbeschwerden pl **Verdau′-ungsstörung** f indigestion

Verdau′ungswerkzeug n digestive track

Verdeck [fer'dek] n (-[e]s;-e) hood (of baby carriage); (aut) convertible top; (naut) deck

verdecken (verdek′ken) tr cover; hide

verden′ken §66 tr—**j–m etw v.** blame s.o. for s.th.

Verderb [fer'derp] m (-[e]s;) ruin, decay

verderben [fer'derbən] §149 tr spoil; ruin; (Magen) upset; (verführen) corrupt || intr (SEIN) spoil, go bad; (fig) go to pot || **Verderben** (-s;) ruin; **j–n ins V. stürzen** ruin s.o.

verderblich [fer'derplɪç] adj ruinous; (Lebensmittel) perishable

Verderbnis [fer'derpnɪs] f (-;) depravity

verderbt′ [fer'derpt] adj depraved

Verderbt′heit f (-;) depravity

verdeutlichen [fer'dɔɪtlɪçən] tr make plain, explain

verdeutschen [fer'dɔɪtʃən] tr translate into (or express in) German

verdich′ten tr condense, thicken || ref condense; solidify; thicken; (Nebel, Rauch) grow thicker; (Verdacht) become stronger, grow

verdicken [fer'dɪkən] tr & ref thicken

verdie′nen tr deserve; (Geld) earn

Verdienst [fer'dinst] m (-es;-e) earnings; gain, profit || n (-es;-e) merit; deserts; **es ist dein V.,** daß it is owing to you that; **nach V.** deservedly; **nach V. behandelt werden** get one's due; **sich [dat] als (or zum) V. anrechnen** take credit for it; **V. um** services to

Verdienst′ausfall m loss of wages

verdienst′lich adj meritorious

Verdienst′spanne f margin of profit

verdienst′voll adj meritorious

verdient [fer'dint] adj—**sich um j–n v. machen** serve s.o. well

verdol′metschen tr translate orally; interpret

Verdol′metschung f (-;) oral translation; interpretation

verdonnern [fer'dɔnərn] tr (coll) condemn

verdop′peln tr & ref double

verdorben [fer'dɔrbən] adj spoiled; (Luft) foul; (Magen) upset; (moralisch) depraved

verdorren [fer'dɔrən] intr (SEIN) dry up, wither

verdrän′gen tr push aside, crowd out; dislodge; (phys) displace; (psychol) repress, inhibit

Verdrän′gung f (-;-en) (phys) displacement; (psychol) repression, inhibition

verdre′hen tr twist; (Augen) roll; (Glied) sprain; (fig) distort; **j–m den Kopf v.** make s.o. fall in love with one

verdreht′ adj twisted; (fig) distorted; (fig) (verrückt) cracked

verdreifachen [fer'drafaxən] tr triple

verdre′schen §67 tr (coll) spank

verdrießen [fer'drisən] §76 tr bother, annoy, get down; **laß es dich nicht v.!** don't let it get you down; **sich keine Mühe v. lassen** spare no pains || impers—**es verdrießt mich, daß** it bothers me that

verdrießlich [fer'drislɪç] adj glum; tiresome, depressing; annoyed

verdroß [fer'drɔs] pret of **verdrießen**

verdro′ßen adj cross; (mürrisch) surly; (lustlos) listless

verdrucken (verdruk′ken) tr misprint

verdrücken (verdrük′ken) tr wrinkle; (coll) eat up, polish off || ref (coll) sneak away

Ver-druß [fer'drus] m (-drusses; -drusse) annoyance, vexation; **j–m etw zum V. tun** do s.th. to spite s.o.

verduften [fer'duftən] intr (SEIN) lose its aroma; (coll) take off, scram

verdummen [fer'dumən] tr make stupid || intr (SEIN) become stupid

verdunkeln [fer'duŋkəln] tr darken; obscure; (Glanz) dull; (fig) cloud; (astr) eclipse; (mil) black out || ref darken; (Himmel) cloud over

Verdun′kelung *f* (-;-en) darkening; (astr) eclipse; (mil) blackout
verdünnen [fer′dynən] *tr* thin; dilute; (*Gase*) rarefy
verdun′sten *intr* (SEIN) evaporate
Verdun′stung *f* (-;) evaporation
verdur′sten *intr* (SEIN) die of thirst
verdutzen [fer′dutsən] *tr* bewilder
veredeln [fer′edəln] *tr* ennoble; (*verfeinen*) refine; (*Rohstoff*) process; (*Boden*) enrich; (*Pflanze, Tier*) improve
Vere′delung *f* (-;) refinement; processing; enrichment; improvement
verehelichen [fer′e·əlıçən] *ref* get married
verehren [fer′erən] *tr* revere; worship; (fig) adore; **j–m etw v.** present s.o. with s.th.
Vereh′rer –in §6 *mf* worshiper; (*Liebhaber*) admirer
verehrt [fer′ert] *adj*—Sehr verehrte gnädige Frau! Dear Madam; Sehr verehrter Herr! Dear Sir; Verehrte Anwesende (or Gäste)! Ladies and Gentlemen!
Vereh′rung *f* (-;) reverence, veneration; worship, adoration
vereiden [fer′ardən], **vereidigen** [fer′ardıgən] *tr* swear in
Verein [fer′ain] *m* (-[e]s;-e) society
vereinbar [fer′ainbar] *adj* compatible
vereinbaren [fer′ainbarən] *tr* agree to, agree upon || *ref*—das läßt sich mit meinen Grundsätzen nicht v. that is inconsistent with my principles
Verein′barkeit *f* (-;) compatibility
Verein′barung *f* (-;) agreement, arrangement; terms; **nur nach V.** by appointment only
vereinen [fer′ainən] *tr* unite, join
vereinfachen [fer′ainfaxən] *tr* simplify
Verein′fachung *f* (-;-en) simplification
vereinheitlichen [fer′ainhaitlıçən] *tr* standardize
vereinigen [fer′ainıgən] *tr* unite, join; (*verbinden*) combine; (*verschmelzen*) merge; (*versammeln*) assemble || *ref* unite, join; (*Flüsse*) meet; **sich v. mit** team up with; **sich v. lassen mit** be compatible with, square with
Verei′nigten Staa′ten *pl* United States
Verein′igung *f* (-;-en) union; combination; society, association
vereinnahmen [fer′ainnamən] *tr* take in
vereinsamen [fer′ainzamən] *intr* (SEIN) become lonely; become isolated
Verein′samung *f* (-;) loneliness; isolation
Vereins′meier –in §6 *mf* (coll) joiner
vereinzeln [fer′aintsəln] *tr* isolate
verein′zelt *adj* isolated; sporadic
vereisen [fer′aizən] *tr* (surg) freeze || *intr* (SEIN) become covered with ice; (aer) ice up
vereiteln [fer′aitəln] *tr* frustrate; baffle
verekeln [fer′ekəln] *tr—j–m etw v.** spoil s.th. for s.o.
veren′den *intr* (SEIN) die
verengen [fer′eŋən] *tr & ref* narrow
verer′ben *tr* bequeath, leave; (*über-*

mitteln) hand down; (*Krankheit*) transmit || *ref* run in the family
Verer′bung *f* (-;-en) inheritance; transmission; heredity
Verer′bungslehre *f* genetics
verewigen [fer′evigən] *tr* perpetuate
verewigt [fer′evıçt] *adj* late, deceased
verfah′ren *adj* bungled, messed up || §71 *tr* bungle; (*Geld, Zeit*) spend (on travel) || *ref* lose one's way, take a track || *intr* (SEIN) proceed; act || wrong turn; (fig) be on the wrong
Verfahren *n* (-s;-) procedure, method; system; (chem) process; (jur) proceedings, case
Verfall *m* (-[e]s;) deterioration, decay; decline, downfall; (*Fristablauf*) expiration; (*von Wechseln*) maturity; **in V. geraten** become delapidated
verfal′len *adj* delapidated; **e–m Rauschgift v. sein** be addicted to a drug || §72 *intr* (SEIN) decay, go to ruin, decline; (*ablaufen*) expire; (*Kranker*) waste away; (*Recht*) lapse; (*Pfand*) be forfeited; (*Wechsel*) mature
Verfall′tag *m* due date; date of maturity
verfäl′schen *tr* falsify; (*Geld*) counterfeit; (*Wein*) adulterate; (*Urkunde*) forge
Verfäl′schung *f* (-;-en) falsification; forging; adulteration
verfan′gen §73 *tr* become entangled || *intr* (bei) have an effect (on)
verfänglich [fer′feŋlıç] *adj* (*Frage*) loaded; (*Situation*) awkward
verfär′ben *ref* change color
verfas′sen *tr* compose, write
Verfas′ser –in §6 *mf* author
Verfas′sung *f* (-;-en) constitution; (*Zustand*) condition; frame of mind, mood
verfas′sungsgemäß, verfas′sungsmäßig *adj* constitutional
verfas′sungswidrig *adj* unconstitutional
verfau′len *intr* (SEIN) rot
verfech′ten §74 *tr* defend, stand up for
Verfech′ter *m* (-s;-) champion
verfeh′len *tr* (*Abzweigung, Ziel, Zug*) miss; (*Wirkung*) fail to achieve, not have; **ich werde nicht v. zu** (inf) I will not fail to (inf) || *recip*—**wir haben uns verfehlt** we missed each other
verfehlt [fer′felt] *adj* wrong
Verfeh′lung *f* (-;-en) offense; mistake
verfeinden [fer′faindən] *recip* become enemies
verfeinern [fer′fainərn] *tr* refine, improve || *ref* become refined, improve
verfertigen [fer′fertıgən] *tr* manufacture, make
Verfer′tigung *f* (-;) manufacture
verfilmen [fer′filmən] *tr* adapt to the screen, make into a movie
Verfil′mung *f* (-;-en) film version
verfilzen [fer′filtsən] *ref* get tangled
verfinstern [fer′finstərn] *ref* get dark
verflachen [fer′flaxən] *tr* flatten || *ref & intr* (SEIN) flatten out
verflech′ten §74 *tr* interweave; (fig) implicate, involve
verflie′gen §57 *ref* (aer) lose one's

bearings ‖ *intr* (SEIN) fly away; (*Zeit*) fly; evaporate; (fig) vanish
verflie′ßen §76 *intr* (SEIN) flow off; (*Frist*) run out, expire; (*Farben*) blend; (*Begriffe, Grenzen*) overlap
verflixt [fer′flɪkst] *adj* (sl) darn
verflossen [fer′flɔsən] *adj* past; former
verflu′chen *tr* curse, damn
verflucht′ *adj* (sl) damn ‖ *interj* (sl) damn it!
verflüchtigen [fer′flʏçtɪgən] *tr* volatilize ‖ *ref* evaporate; (fig) disappear
verflüssigen [fer′flʏsɪgən] *tr & ref* liquefy
Verfolg [fer′fɔlk] *m* (–s;) course; **im V.** (*genit*) in pursuance of
verfol′gen *tr* pursue; follow up; persecute; haunt; (hunt) track; (jur) prosecute; **j–n steckbrieflich v.** send out a warrant for the arrest of s.o.
Verfol′ger –in §6 *mf* pursuer; persecutor
Verfol′gung *f* (–;–en) pursuit; persecution; (jur) prosecution
Verfol′gungswahn *m*, **Verfol′gungswahnsinn** *m* persecution complex
verfrachten [fer′fraxtən] *tr* ship; (coll) bundle off
Verfrach′ter –in §6 *mf* shipper
verfrühen [fer′fry.ən] *ref* be too early
verfügbar [fer′fykbar] *adj* available, at one's disposal
verfü′gen *tr* decree, order ‖ *ref—sich v. nach* betake oneself to ‖ *intr—v. über* (*acc*) have at one's disposal, have control over
Verfü′gung *f* (–;–en) decree, order; disposal; einstweilige **V.** (jur) injunction; **j–m zur V. stehen** be at s.o.'s disposal; **j–m zur V. stellen** put at s.o.'s disposal; letztwillige **V.** last will and testament
verfüh′ren *tr* mislead; (*zum Irrtum*) lead; (*verlocken*) seduce
Verfüh′rer –in §6 *mf* seducer
verführerisch [fer′fyrərɪʃ] *adj* seductive, tempting
Verfüh′rung *f* (–;–en) seduction
vergaffen [fer′gafən] *ref* (coll) (**in** *acc*) fall in love (with)
vergammeln [fer′gaməln] *intr* (SEIN) (coll) go to the dogs
vergangen [fer′gaŋən] *adj* past; (*Schönheit*) faded
Vergan′genheit *f* (–;) past; background; (gram) past tense
vergänglich [fer′gɛŋlɪç] *adj* transitory
vergasen [fer′gazən] *tr* gas
Verga′ser *m* (–s;–) carburetor
vergaß [fer′gas] *pret* of **vergessen**
verge′ben §80 *tr* forgive (*s.th.*); give away; (*Chance*) miss, pass up; (*Amt, freie Stelle*) fill; (*Auftrag*) place; (*Karten*) misdeal; (*verleihen*) confer; **v. sein** have a previous engagement; be engaged (*to a man*) ‖ *ref—sich* [*dat*] *etw* **v.** compromise on s.th. ‖ *intr* (*dat*) forgive (*s.o.*)
verge′bens [fer′gebəns] *adv* in vain
vergeb′lich [fer′geplɪç] *adj* vain, futile
Verge′bung *f* (–;) forgiveness; bestowal
vergegenwärtigen [fer′gegənvɛrtɪgən] *ref—sich* [*dat*] *etw.* **v.** visualize s.th.

verge′hen §82 *ref—sich an j–m* **v.** offend s.o.; (*sexuell*) violate s.o. ‖ *intr* (SEIN) pass, go away; fade ‖ **Vergehen** *n* (–s;–) offense, misdemeanor
vergel′ten §83 *tr* requite; **vergelt's Gott!** (coll) thank you!
Vergel′tung *f* (–;) repayment; retaliation, reprisal
Vergel′tungswaffe *f* V-1 or V-2
vergesellschaften [fergə′zelʃaftən] *tr* socialize; nationalize
vergessen [fer′gesən] §70 *tr* forget
Verges′senheit *f* (–;)—**in V. geraten** fall (or sink) into oblivion
vergeßlich [fer′geslɪç] *adj* forceful
Vergeß′lichkeit *f* (–;) forgetfulness
vergeuden [fer′gɔɪdən] *tr* waste
Vergeu′dung *f* (–;) waste, squandering
vergewaltigen [fergə′valtɪgən] *tr* do violence to; (*Mädchen*) rape
Vergewal′tigung *f* (–;–en) rape
vergewerkschaften [fergə′verkʃaftən] *tr* unionize
vergewissern [fergə′vɪsərn] *ref* (*genit*) make sure of, ascertain
vergie′ßen §76 *tr* spill; (*Tränen*) shed
vergiften [fer′gɪftən] *tr* (& fig) poison; (*verseuchen*) contaminate ‖ *ref* take poison
Vergif′tung *f* (–;–en) poisoning; contamination
vergipsen [fer′gɪpsən] *tr* plaster
Vergißmeinnicht [fer′gɪsmaɪnnɪçt] *n* (–[e]s;–e) forget-me-not
vergittern [fer′gɪtərn] *tr* bar up
Vergleich [fer′glaɪç] *m* (–[e]s;–e) comparison; (*Verständigung*) agreement; (*Ausgleich*) settlement; **e–n V. anstellen zwischen** make a comparison between; **e–n V. treffen** reach a settlement, come to an agreement
vergleichbar [fer′glaɪçbar] *adj* comparable
verglei′chen [fer′glaɪçən] §85 *tr* (mit) compare (with, to) ‖ *ref* (mit) come to an agreement (with)
Vergleichs′grundlage *f* basis for comparison
vergleichs′weise *adv* by way of comparison
Verglei′chung *f* (–;–en) comparison; matching; contrasting
verglü′hen *intr* (SEIN) cease to glow
vergnügen [fer′gnygən] *tr* amuse, delight ‖ *ref* enjoy oneself, amuse oneself ‖ **Vergnügen** *n* (–s;–) delight, pleasure; **mit V.** with pleasure; **V. finden an** (*dat*) take delight in; **viel V.!** (coll) have fun!; **zum V. for** fun
vergnügt [fer′gnykt] *adj* cheerful, gay; (**über** *acc*) delighted (with)
Vergnü′gung *f* (–;–en) pleasure, amusement
Vergnü′gungspark *m* amusement park
Vergnü′gungsreise *f* pleasure trip
Vergnü′gungssteuer *f* entertainment tax
vergnü′gungssüchtig *adj* pleasure-loving
vergolden [fer′gɔldən] *tr* gild
Vergol′dung *f* (–;) gilding
vergönnen [fer′gœnən] *tr* not begrudge
vergöttern [fer′gœtərn] *tr* deify; (fig) idolize
vergra′ben §87 *tr* (& fig) bury

vergrämen [fɛr'grɛmən] *tr* annoy, anger

vergrämt [fɛr'grɛmt] *adj* haggard

vergrei'fen §88 *ref* (mus) hit the wrong note; **sich v. an** (*dat*) lay violent hands on; (*fremdem Gut*) encroach on; (*Geld*) misappropriate; (*Mädchen*) assault; **sich im Ausdruck v.** express oneself poorly

vergreisen [fɛr'graizən] *intr* (SEIN) age; become senile

vergriffen [fɛr'grɪfən] *adj* sold out; (*Buch*) out of print

vergröbern [fɛr'grøbərn] *tr* roughen || *ref* become coarser

vergrößern [fɛr'grøsərn] *tr* enlarge; increase; (*ausdehnen*) expand; (opt) magnify || *ref* become larger

Vergrö'ßerung *f* (-;-en) enlargement; increase; expansion; (opt) magnification

Vergrö'ßerungsapparat *m* (phot) enlarger

Vergrö'ßerungsglas *m* magnifying glass

Vergünstigung [fɛr'gʏnstɪguŋ] *f* (-; -en) privilege; (*bevorzugte Behandlung*) preferential treatment

vergüten [fɛr'gytən] *tr* make good; (*Stahl*) temper; **j–m etw v.** reimburse (or compensate) s.o. for s.th.

Vergü'tung *f* (-;-en) reimbursement, compensation; tempering

verhaften [fɛr'haftən] *tr* apprehend

Verhaf'tung *f* (-;-en) apprehension

verhal'ten *adj* (*Atem*) bated; (*Stimme*) low || §90 *tr* hold back; (*Atem*) hold; (*Lachen*) suppress; (*Stimme*) keep down; **den Schritt v.** slow down; (*stehenbleiben*) stop || *ref* behave, act; be; **A verhält sich zu B wie X zu Y A to B as X is to Y**; **sich anders v.** be different; **sich ruhig v.** keep quiet || *impers ref*—**wenn es sich so verhält** if that's the case || **Verhalten** *n* (-s;) conduct, behavior; attitude

Verhältnis [fɛr'hɛltnɪs] *n* (-ses;-se) proportion, ratio; (*Beziehung*) relation; (*Liebes–*) love affair; **aus kleinen Verhältnissen** of humble birth; **bei sonst gleichen Verhältnissen** other things being equal; **das steht in keinem V. zu** that is all out of proportion to; **Verhältnisse** circumstances, conditions; matters; means

verhält'nismäßig *adj* proportionate || *adv* relatively, comparatively

Verhält'nismaßregeln *pl* instructions

Verhält'niswahl *f* proportional representation

verhält'niswidrig *adj* disproportionate

Verhält'niswort *n* (-[e]s;-̈er) preposition

verhan'deln *tr* discuss; (*Waren*) sell || *intr* negotiate; argue; (*beraten*) confer; (jur) plead a case; **gegen j–n wegen etw v.** (jur) try s.o. for s.th.

Verhand'lung *f* (-;-en) negotiation; discussion; proceedings, trial

verhangen [fɛr'haŋən] *adj* overcast

verhän'gen *tr* (*Fenster*) put curtains on; (*Strafe*) impose; (*Untersuchung*) order; (*Belagerungszustand*) pro-claim; **mit verhängtem Zügel** at full speed

Verhängnis [fɛr'hɛŋnɪs] *n* (-ses;-se) destiny, fate; (*Unglück*) disaster

verhäng'nisvoll *adj* fateful; disastrous

verhärmt [fɛr'hɛrmt] *adj* haggard

verharren [fɛr'harən] *intr* (HABEN & SEIN) remain; (**auf** *dat*, **in** *dat*, **bei**) stick (to)

verhärten [fɛr'hɛrtən] *tr & ref* harden

verhaßt [fɛr'hast] *adj* hated, hateful

verhätscheln [fɛr'hɛt∫əln] *tr* pamper

Verhau [fɛr'hau] *m* (-[e]s;-e) barb-wire entanglement

verhau'en §93 *tr* lick, beat up; (*Kind*) spank; (*Auftrag, Ball, usw.*) muff || *ref* make a blunder

verheddern [fɛr'hedərn] *ref* get tangled up

verheeren [fɛr'herən] *tr* devastate

verhee'rend *adj* terrible; (coll) awful

Verhee'rung *f* (-;) devastation

verhehlen [fɛr'helən] *tr* conceal

verhei'len *intr* (SEIN) heal up

verheimlichen [fɛr'haimlɪçən] *tr* keep secret, conceal

Verheim'lichung *f* (-;) concealment

verhei'raten *tr* marry; (*Tocher*) give away || *ref* (**mit**) get married (to)

Verhei'ratung *f* (-;) marriage

verhei'ßen §95 *tr* promise

Verhei'ßung *f* (-;) promise

verhei'ßungsvoll *adj* promising

verhel'fen §96 *intr*—**j–m zu etw v.** help s.o. to acquire s.th.

verherrlichen [fɛr'herlɪçən] *tr* glorify

Verherr'lichung *f* (-;) glorification

verhet'zen *tr* instigate

verhexen [fɛr'heksən] *tr* bewitch, hex

verhimmeln [fɛr'hɪməln] *tr* praise to the skies; (*Schauspieler*) idolize

verhin'dern *tr* prevent

Verhin'derung *f* (-;) prevention; **im Falle seiner V.** in case he's unavailable

verhohlen [fɛr'holən] *adj* hidden

verhöh'nen *tr* jeer at; make fun of

Verhöh'nung *f* (-;) jeering; ridicule

Verhör [fɛr'hør] *n* (-s;-e) interrogation, questioning, hearing

verhö'ren *tr* interrogate, question || *ref* hear wrong

verhudeln [fɛr'hudəln] *tr* (coll) bungle

verhüllen [fɛr'hylən] *tr* cover, veil; wrap up; disguise

Verhül'lung *f* (-;-en) cover; disguise

verhun'gern *intr* (SEIN) starve to death

verhunzen [fɛr'huntsən] *tr* (coll) botch

verhü'ten *tr* prevent, avert

verinnerlicht [fɛr'ɪnərlɪçt] *adj* introspective

verir'ren *ref* lose one's way; (*Augen, Blick*) wander; (*fig*) make a mistake

verirrt [fɛr'ɪrt] *adj* stray

verja'gen *tr* chase away

verjähren [fɛr'jɛrən] *intr* (SEIN) fall under the statute of limitations

verjubeln [fɛr'jubəln] *tr* squander

verjüngen [fɛr'jʏŋən] *tr* rejuvenate; reduce in scale; taper || *ref* be rejuvenated; taper, narrow

Verjün'gung *f* (-;) rejuvenation; tapering; scaling down

verkatert [fɛr'katərt] *adj* suffering from a hangover

Verkauf' *m* (-[e]s;-̈e) sale

verkau'fen *tr* sell

Verkäu'fer -in §6 *mf* seller; salesclerk; vendor || *m* salesman || *f* salesgirl, saleswoman

verkäuf'lich *adj* salable

Verkaufs'anzeige *f* for-sale ad

Verkaufs'automat *m* vending machine

Verkaufs'leiter -in §6 *mf* sales manager

Verkaufs'schlager *m* good seller

Verkaufs'steigerung *f* sales promotion

Verkaufs'vertrag *m* agreement of sale

Verkehr [fɛr'ker] *m* (-s;) traffic; commerce; company, association; (*sexuell*) intercourse; (aer, rr) service; (fin) circulation

verkeh'ren *tr* reverse, invert; turn upside down; convert, change; (*Sinn, Worte*) twist || *intr* (*Fahrzeug*) run, run regularly; **mit j-m geschlechtlich v. have** intercourse with s.o.; **mit j-m v. associate** with s.o.

Verkehrs'ader *f* main artery

Verkehrs'ampel *f* traffic light

Verkehrs'andrang *m* heavy traffic

Verkehrs'betrieb *m* public transportation company

Verkehrs'delikt *n* traffic violation

Verkehrs'flugzeug *n* airliner

Verkehrs'insel *f* traffic island

Verkehrs'mittel *n* means of transportation

Verkehrs'ordnungen *pl* traffic regulations

Verkehrs'polizist -in §7 *mf* traffic cop

verkehrs'reich *adj* crowded, congested

verkehrs'stark *adj* busy

Verkehrs'stockung *f*, **Verkehrs'störung** *f* traffic jam

Verkehrs'unfall *m* traffic accident

Verkehrs'unternehmen *n* transportation company

Verkehrs'vorschrift *f* traffic regulation

Verkehrs'wesen *n* traffic, transportation

Verkehrs'zeichen *n* traffic sign

verkehrt [fɛr'kert] *adj* reversed; upside down; inside out; wrong

verken'nen §97 *tr* misunderstand; (*Person*) misjudge, mistake

verketten [fɛr'kɛtən] *tr* chain together; (fig) link

Verket'tung *f* (-s;) chaining; (fig) concatenation; (fig) coincidence

verkit'ten *tr* cement; putty; seal, bond

verkla'gen *tr* accuse; (jur) sue

Verklagte [fɛr'klaktə] §5 *mf* defendant

verklat'schen *tr* (coll) slander; (educ) squeal on

verkle'ben *tr* glue, cement; **v. mit** cover with

verklei'den *tr* disguise, dress up; (*täfeln*) panel; line, face; (mil) camouflage

Verklei'dung *f* (-s;-en) disguise; paneling; lining, facing; (mil) camouflage

verkleinern [fɛr'klainərn] *tr* lessen, diminish; (fig) disparage; (math) reduce; **maßstäblich v. scale down**

Verklei'nerung *f* (-s;-en) diminution, reduction; (fig) detraction

Verklei'nerungsform *f* diminutive

verklin'gen §142 *intr* (SEIN) die away

verkloppen [fɛr'klɔpən] *tr* (coll) beat up

verknacken [fɛr'knakən] *tr* (coll) sentence

verknallt [fɛr'knalt] *adj*—**in j-n v. sein** (coll) have a crush on s.o.

verknappen [fɛr'knapən] *intr* (SEIN) run short, run low

Verknap'pung *f* (-s;) shortage

verknei'fen §88 *ref*—**sich** [*dat*] **etw v.** deny oneself s.th.

verkniffen [fɛr'knifən] *adj* wry

verknip'sen *tr* (*Film*) waste

verknöchern [fɛr'knœçərn] *intr* (SEIN) ossify; (*Glieder*) become stiff

verknöchert [fɛr'knœçərt] *adj* pedantic; (*Junggeselle*) inveterate

verknoten [fɛr'knotən] *tr* snarl, tie up

verknüp'fen *tr* tie together; (fig) connect, combine, relate

verknusen [fɛr'knuzən] *tr* (coll) stand

verkohlen [fɛr'kolən] *tr* carbonize; char; **j-n v.** (coll) pull s.o.'s leg

verkom'men *adj* decayed; degenerate; (*Gebäude*) squalid || §99 *intr* (SEIN) decay, spoil; (fig) go to the dogs; **v. zu** degenerate into

Verkom'menheit *f* (-s;) depravity

verkop'peln *tr* couple; (*Interessen*) (com) consolidate

verkorken [fɛr'kɔrkən] *tr* cork up

verkorksen [fɛr'kɔrksən] *tr* (coll) bungle || *ref*—**sich** [*dat*] **den Magen v.** (coll) upset one's stomach

verkörpern [fɛr'kœrpərn] *tr* embody, personify; (*Rolle*) play

Verkör'perung *f* (-s;-en) embodiment, incarnation

verkra'chen *ref*—**sich mit j-m v.** have an argument with s.o. || *intr* (SEIN) (coll) go bankrupt

verkrampft [fɛr'krampft] *adj* cramped

verkrie'chen §102 *ref* hide; (& fig) crawl into a hole; **neben ihm kannst du dich v.!** you're no match for him!

verkrümeln [fɛr'kryməln] *tr* crumble || *ref* (fig) disappear

verkrüm'men *tr & ref* bend

Verkrüm'mung *f* (-s;) bend, crookedness; curvature

verkrüppeln [fɛr'krypəln] *tr* cripple || *intr* (SEIN) become crippled; (*verkümmern*) become stunted

verkrustet [fɛr'krustət] *adj* caked

verküh'len *ref* catch a cold

verküm'mern *intr* (SEIN) become stunted; (pathol) atrophy

Verküm'merung *f* (-s;) atrophy

verkünden [fɛr'kyndən], **verkündigen** [fɛr'kyndɪgən] *tr* announce, proclaim; (*Urteil*) pronounce

Verkün'digung *f* (-s;-en) announcement, proclamation; pronouncement; **Mariä Verkündigung** (feast of the) Annunciation

verkup'peln *tr* couple; (*Mädchen, Mann*) procure; (*Tochter*) sell into prostitution

verkür'zen *tr* shorten; abridge; (*beschränken*) curtail; (*Zeit*) pass

Verkür'zung *f* (-;-en) shortening; abridgement; curtailment

verla'chen *tr* laugh at

verla'den §103 *tr* load, ship

Verlag [fɛr'lɑk] *m* (-[e]s;-e) publisher; **im V. von** published by

verla'gern *tr* shift; (*aus Sicherheitsgründen*) evacuate || *ref* shift

Verla'gerung *f* (-;-en) shift, shifting; evacuation

Verlags'anstalt *f* publisher

Verlags'buchhandlung *f* publisher and dealer

Verlags'recht *n* copyright

verlangen [fɛr'laŋən] *tr* demand, require; want, ask || *intr*—**v. nach** ask for; long for || **Verlangen** *n* (-s;) demand; request; wish; claim; (*Sehnsucht*) longing, yearning; **auf V. upon** demand, upon request

verlängern [fɛr'lɛŋərn] *tr* lengthen; prolong, extend; **seinen Paß v. lassen** have one's passport renewed

Verlän'gerung *f* (-;-en) lengthening; prolongation, extension; (sport) overtime

Verlän'gerungsschnur *f* extension cord

verlangsamen [fɛr'laŋzamən] *tr* slow down

verläppern [fɛr'lɛpərn] *tr* (coll) fritter away

Ver·laß [fɛr'las] *m* (-lasses;) reliance; **es ist kein V. auf ihn** you can't rely on him

verlas'sen *adj* abandoned, deserted; lonesome || §104 *tr* leave; forsake, desert || *ref*—**sich v. auf** (*acc*) rely on

Verlas'senheit *f* (-;) loneliness

verläßlich [fɛr'lɛslɪç] *adj* reliable

verlästern [fɛr'lɛstərn] *tr* slander

Verlä'sterung *f* (-;-en) slander

Verlaub [fɛr'laup] *m*—**mit V. with** your permission; **mit V. zu sagen** if I may say so

Verlauf' *m* (-[e]s;) course; **e-n guten V. haben** turn out well; **nach V. von** after a lapse of

verlau'fen §105 *intr* (SEIN) (*Zeit*) pass, lapse; (*ablaufen*) turn out, come off; (*vorgehen*) proceed, run || *ref* lose one's way; (*Wasser*) run off; (*Menschenmenge*) disperse

verlau'ten *intr* (SEIN) become known, be reported; **kein Wort davon v. lassen** not breathe a word about it; **wie verlautet** as reported || *impers*—**es verlautet** it is reported

verle'ben *tr* spend, pass

verlebt [fɛr'lept] *adj* haggard

verle'gen *adj* embarrassed; confused; **v. um** (*e-e Antwort*) at a loss for; (*Geld*) short of || *tr* move, shift; transfer; misplace; (*Buch*) publish; (*Geleise, Kabel, Rohre*) lay; (*sperren*) block; (*vertagen*) postpone || *ref*—**sich v. auf** (*acc*) apply onself to; devote oneself to; resort to

Verle'genheit *f* (-;) embarrassment; difficulties; predicament; **in V. bringen** embarrass

Verle'ger *m* (-s;-) publisher

Verle'gung *f* (-;-en) move, shift; transfer; postponement; (*von Kabeln, usw.*) laying

verleih'den *tr* spoil, take the joy out of

Verleih [fɛr'laɪ] *m* (-s;-e) rental service

verlei'hen §81 *tr* lend out, loan; rent out; (*Gunst*) grant; (*Titel*) confer; (*Auszeichnung*) award

Verlei'her **-in** §6 *mf* lender; grantor; (*von Filmen*) distributor

Verlei'hung *f* (-;-en) lending out; rental; grant; bestowal

verlei'ten *tr* mislead; (*zur Sünde, zum Trunk*) lead; (jur) suborn

verler'nen *tr* unlearn, forget

verle'sen §107 *tr* read out; (*Namen*) read off; (*Salat*) clean; (*Gemüse*) sort out || *ref* misread

verletzen [fɛr'lɛtsən] *tr* (& fig) injure, hurt; (*kränken*) offend; (*Gesetz*) break; (*Recht*) violate

verlet'zend *adj* offensive

Verletzte [fɛr'lɛtsə] §5 *mf* injured party

Verlet'zung *f* (-;-en) injury; offense; (*e-s Gesetzes*) breaking; (*e-s Rechtes*) violation

verleug'nen *tr* deny; (*Kind*) disown; (*Glauben*) renounce || *ref*—**sich selbst v.** act contrary to one's nature; **sich vor Besuchern v. lassen** refuse to see visitors

Verleug'nung *f* (-;-en) denial; renunciation; disavowal

verleumden [fɛr'lɔɪmdən] *tr* slander

verleumderisch [fɛr'lɔɪmdərɪʃ] *adj* slanderous, libelous

Verleum'dung *f* (-;-en) slander

verlie'ben *ref*—**sich in j-n v.** fall in love with s.o.

verliebt [fɛr'lipt] *adj* in love

verlieren [fɛr'lirən] §77 *tr* lose || *ref* lose one's way; disappear; disperse

Verlies [fɛr'lis] *n* (-es;-e) dungeon

verlo'ben *ref* (mit) become engaged (to)

Verlöbnis [fɛr'løpnɪs] *n* (-ses;-se) engagement

Verlobte [fɛr'lopta] §5 *m* fiancé; **die Verlobten** the engaged couple || *f* fiancée

Verlo'bung *f* (-;-en) engagement

verlocken (verlok'ken) *tr* lure, tempt; (*verführen*) seduce

verlockend (verlok'kend) *adj* tempting

Verlockung (Verlok'kung) *f* (-;-en) allurement, temptation

verlogen [fɛr'logən] *adj* dishonest

verlohn'nen *impers ref*—**es verlohnt sich nicht** it doesn't pay || *impers*—**es verlohnt der Mühe nicht** it is not worth the trouble

verlor [fɛr'lor] *pret* of **verlieren**

verloren [fɛr'lorən] *pp* of **verlieren** || *adj* lost; (*hilflos*) forlorn; (*Ei*) poached; **der verlorene Sohn** the prodigal son

verlo'rengeben §80 *tr* give up for lost

verlo'rengehen §82 *intr* (SEIN) be lost

verlö'schen §110 *tr* extinguish; (*Schrift*) erase || *intr* (SEIN) (*Licht, Kerze*) go out; (*Zorn*) cease verlo'sen *tr* raffle off, draw lots for

verlö'ten *tr* solder; e–n v. (coll) belt one down

verlottern [fer'lɔtərn] *intr* (coll) go to the dogs

verlumpen [fer'lumpən] *tr* (coll) blow, squander || *intr* (coll) go to the dogs

Verlust [fer'lust] *m* (–[e]s;–e) loss; in V. geraten get lost; Verluste (mil) casualties

Verlust'liste *f* (mil) casualty list

verma'chen *tr* bequeath, leave

Vermächtnis [fer'mɛçtnɪs] *n* (–ses;–se) bequest, legacy

vermäh'len [fer'mɛlən] *tr* marry || *ref* (mit) get married (to)

Vermäh'lung *f* (–;–en) marriage, wedding

vermah'nen *tr* admonish, warn

Vermah'nung *f* (–;–en) admonition

vermaledeien [fermale'daɪ.ən] *tr* curse

vermanschen [fer'manʃən] *tr* (coll) make a mess of

vermasseln [fer'masəln] *tr* (coll) bungle, muff

vermassen [fer'masən] *intr* (SEIN) lose one's individuality

vermauern [fer'mav.ərn] *tr* wall up

vermehren [fer'merən] *tr* & *ref* increase; (an Zahl) multiply; vermehrte Auflage enlarged edition

vermei'den *tr* avoid

vermeidlich [fer'martlɪç] *adj* avoidable

Vermei'dung *f* (–;) avoidance

vermei'nen *tr* suppose; presume, allege

vermeintlich [fer'marntlɪç] *adj* supposed, alleged; (erdacht) imaginary

vermel'den *tr* (poet) announce

vermen'gen *tr* mix, mingle; confound || *ref* (mit) meddle (with)

Vermerk [fer'merk] *m* (–[e]s;–e) note

vermer'ken *tr* note, record

vermes'sen *adj* daring, bold || §70 *tr* measure; (Land) survey || *ref* measure wrong; sich v. zu (inf) have the nerve to (inf)

Vermes'sung *f* (–;–en) surveying

vermie'ten *tr* rent out; lease out

Vermie'ter –in §6 *mf* (jur) lessor || *m* landlord || *f* landlady

vermindern [fer'mɪndərn] *tr* diminish, lessen; (beschränken) reduce, cut || *ref* diminish, decrease

Vermin'derung *f* (–;–en) diminution, decrease; reduction, cut

verminen [fer'minən] *tr* (mil) mine

vermi'schen *tr* & *ref* mix

Vermi'schung *f* (–;–en) mixture

vermissen [fer'mɪsən] *tr* miss

vermißt [fer'mɪst] *adj* (mil) missing in action || Vermißte §5 *mf* missing person

vermitteln [fer'mɪtəln] *tr* negotiate; arrange, bring about; (beschaffen) get, procure || *intr* mediate; intercede

vermittels [fer'mɪtəls] *prep* (genit) by means of, through

Vermitt'ler –in §6 *mf* mediator, gobetween; (com) agent

Vermitt'lung *f* (–;–en) negotiation; mediation; procuring; providing; intercession; (Mittel) means; agency;

brokerage; (telp) exchange; durch gütige V. (genit) through the good offices of

Vermitt'lungsamt *n* (telp) exchange

Vermitt'lungsgebühr *f*, Vermitt'lungsprovision *f* commission; brokerage

vermo'dern *intr* (SEIN) rot, decay

vermöge [fer'møgə] *prep* (genit) by virtue of

vermö'gen §114 *tr* be able to do; j–n v. zu (inf) induce s.o. to (inf); sie vermag bei ihm viel (or wenig) she has great (or little) influence with him; v. zu (inf) be able to (inf), have the power to (inf) || Vermögen *n* (–s;–) ability; capacity; power; fortune, means; property; (fin) capital, assets; nach bestem V. to the best of one's ability

vermö'gend *adj* well-to-do, well-off

Vermö'genslage *f* financial situation

Vermö'genssteuer *f* property tax

vermorscht [fer'mɔrʃt] *adj* rotten

vermottet [fer'mɔtət] *adj* moth-eaten

vermummen [fer'mumən] *tr* disguise || *ref* disguise oneself

vermuten [fer'mutən] *tr* suppose, presume

vermutlich [fer'mutlɪç] *adj* presumable || *adv* presumably, I suppose

Vermu'tung *f* (–;–en) guess, conjecture

vernachlässigen [fer'nɔxlesɪgən] *tr* neglect

Vernach'lässigung *f* (–;) neglect

verna'geln *tr* nail up; board up

vernä'hen *tr* sew up

vernarben [fer'narbən] *intr* (SEIN) heal up

vernarren [fer'narən] *ref*—sich v. in (acc) be crazy about, be stuck on

verna'schen *tr* spend on sweets; (Mädchen) make love to

vernebeln [fer'nebəln] *tr* (mil) screen with smoke; (fig) hide, cover over

vernehmbar [fer'nembar] *adj* perceptible

verneh'men §116 *tr* perceive; (erfahren) hear, learn; (jur) question; sich v. lassen be heard, express an opinion || Vernehmen *n* (–s;–)—dem V. nach reportedly, according to the report

vernehmlich [fer'nemlɪç] *adj* perceptible, audible; distinct

Verneh'mung *f* (–;–en) interrogation

vernei'gen *ref* bow; curtsy

Vernei'gung *f* (–;–en) bow; curtsy

verneinen [fer'naɪnən] *tr* say no to; reject, refuse; disavow

vernei'nend *adj* negative

Vernei'nung *f* (–;–en) negation; denial

vernichten [fer'nɪçtən] *tr* destroy, annihilate; (Hoffnung) dash

vernich'tend *adj* (Kritik) scathing; (Niederlage) crushing

Vernich'tung *f* (–;) destruction

vernickeln [fer'nɪkəln] *tr* nickel-plate

vernie'ten *tr* rivet

Vernunft [fer'nunft] *f* (–;) reason; good sense, senses; die gesunde V. common sense; V. annehmen listen to reason; zur V. bringen bring to one's senses

Vernunft'ehe *f* marriage of convenience

vernunft'gemäß *adj* reasonable

vernünftig [fer'nynftiç] *adj* rational; reasonable; sensible, level-headed

vernunft'los *adj* senseless

vernunft'mäßig *adj* rational; reasonable

veröden [fer'ø̷dən] *intr* (SEIN) become desolate

veröffentlichen [fer'œfəntliçən] *tr* publish; announce

Veröf'fentlichung *f* (-;-en) publication; announcement

verord'nen *tr* decree; (med) prescribe

Verord'nung *f* (-;-en) decree, order; (med) prescription

verpach'ten *tr* farm out; lease, rent out

Verpäch'ter –in §6 *mf* lessor

verpacken (verpak'ken) *tr* pack up

Verpackung (Verpak'kung) *f* (-;-en) packing (material); wrapping

verpas'sen *tr* (*Gelegenheit, Anschluß, usw.*) miss; **j-m e-n Anzug v.** fit s.o. with a suit; **j-m e-e v.** (coll) give s.o. a smack

verpatzen [fer'patsən] *tr* (coll) make a mess of

verpesten [fer'pestən] *tr* infect, contaminate

verpet'zen *tr* (coll) squeal on

verpfän'den *tr* pawn; mortgage; **sein Wort v.** give one's word of honor

verpflan'zen *tr* (bot, surg) transplant

Verpflan'zung *f* (-;-en) (bot, surg) transplant

verpfle'gen *tr* feed; (mil) supply

Verpfle'gung *f* (-;) feeding; board; (mil) rations, supplies

verpflichten [fer'pfliçtən] *tr* obligate, bind; **zu Dank v.** put under obligation

Verpflich'tung *f* (-;-en) obligation; commitment; (jur) liability

verpfuschen [fer'pfuʃən] *tr* (coll) botch, bungle, muff

verplap'pern *ref* blab out a secret

verplau'dern *tr* waste in chatting

verpönt [fer'pø̷nt] *adj* taboo

verprü'geln *tr* (coll) wallop, thrash

verpuf'fen *intr* (SEIN) fizzle; (fig) fizzle out

verpulvern [fer'pulfərn] *tr* (coll) waste, fritter away

verpum'pen *tr* (coll) loan

verpusten [fer'pustən] *ref* (coll) catch one's breath

Verputz [fer'puts] *m* (-es;-e) finishing coat (of plaster)

verput'zen *tr* plaster; (*aufessen*) polish off; (coll) stand

verquicken [fer'kvikən] *tr* interrelate

verquollen [fer'kvɔlən] *adj* (*Augen*) swollen; (*Gesicht*) puffy; (*Holz*) warped

verrammeln [fer'raməln] *tr* barricade

verramschen [fer'ramʃən] *tr* (coll) sell dirt-cheap

verrannt [fer'rant] *adj*—**v. sein in** (*acc*) be stuck on

Verrat' *m* (-[e]s;) betrayal; treason

verra'ten §63 *tr* betray

Verräter –in [fer'retər(in)] §6 *mf* traitor; betrayer

verräterisch [fer'retəriʃ] *adj* treacherous; (*Spur, usw.*) telltale

verrau'chen *tr* spend on smokes

verräu'chern *tr* fill with smoke

verrech'nen *tr* (*ausgleichen*) balance; (*Scheck*) deposit; (fin) clear || *ref* miscalculate; (fig) be mistaken

Verrech'nung *f* (-;-en) miscalculation; (fin) clearing; **nur zur V.** for deposit only

Verrech'nungsbank *f*, **Verrech'nungskasse** *f* clearing house

verrecken [fer'rekən] *intr* (SEIN) die; (sl) croak; **verrecke!** drop dead!

verreg'nen *tr* spoil with too much rain

verrei'sen *intr* (SEIN) go on a trip; **v. nach** depart for

verreist [fer'raist] *adj* out of town

verren'ken *tr* wrench, dislocate || *ref*—**sich** [*dat*] **den Arm v.** wrench one's arm; **sich** [*dat*] **den Hals v.** (coll) crane one's neck

Verren'kung *f* (-;-en) dislocation

verrich'ten *tr* do; (*Gebet*) say; **seine Notdurft v.** ease oneself

Verrich'tung *f* (-;-en) performance; task, duty

verrie'geln *tr* bolt, bar

verringern [fer'riŋərn] *tr* diminish, reduce || *ref* diminish; be reduced

Verrin'gerung *f* (-;-en) diminution; reduction

verrin'nen §121 *intr* (SEIN) run off; (*Zeit*) pass

verro'sten *intr* (SEIN) rust

verrotten [fer'rɔtən] *intr* (SEIN) rot

verrucht [fer'ruxt] *adj* wicked

verrücken (verrük'ken) *tr* move, shift

verrückt [fer'rykt] *adj* crazy; **v. auf etw** crazy about s.th.; **v. nach j-m** crazy about s.o. || **Verrückte** §5 *mf* lunatic

Verrückt'heit *f* (-;-en) craziness, madness; crazy action or act

Verruf' *m* (-[e]s;) discredit, disrepute

verru'fen *adj* disreputable

verrüh'ren *tr* stir thoroughly

verrut'schen *intr* (SEIN) slip

Vers [fers] *m* (-es;-e) verse

versa'gen *tr* refuse; **versagt sein** have a previous engagement || *ref*—**sich** [*dat*] **etw v.** deny oneself s.th.; **ich kann es mir nicht v. zu** (*inf*) I can't refrain from (*ger*) || *intr* fail; (*Beine, Stimme, usw.*) give out; (*Gewehr*) misfire; (*Motor*) fail to start; **bei e-r Prüfung v.** flunk a test || **Versagen** *n* (-s;-) failure, flop; misfire

Versa'ger *m* (-s;-) failure, flop; (*Patrone*) dud

versal'zen *tr* oversalt; (fig) spoil

versam'meln *tr* gather together, assemble; convoke || *ref* gather, assemble

Versamm'lung *f* (-;-en) assembly, meeting

Versand [fer'zant] *m* (-[e]s;) shipment; mailing

Versand'abteilung *f* shipping department

versanden [fer'zandən] *intr* (SEIN) silt up; (fig) bog down

Versand'geschäft n, **Versand'haus** n mail-order house

versäu'men tr (Gelegenheit, Schule, Zug) miss; (Geschäft, Pflicht) neglect; **v. zu** (inf) fail to (inf)

Versäumnis [fer'zɔɪmnɪs] f (-;-se), n (-ses;-se) omission, neglect; (educ) absence; (jur) default

verschaf'fen tr get, obtain || ref—**sich** [dat] etw v. get; **sich** [dat] **Geld v.** raise money; **sich** [dat] **Respekt v.** gain respect

verschämt [fer'ʃemt] adj bashful, coy

Verschämt'heit f (-;) bashfulness

verschandeln [fer'ʃandəln] tr deface

verschan'zen tr fortify || ref entrench oneself; **sich v. hinter** (dat) (fig) hide behind

Verschan'zung f (-;-en) entrenchment

verschär'fen tr intensify; aggravate; **verschärfter Arrest** detention on a bread-and-water diet || ref get worse

verschei'den §112 intr (SEIN) pass away

verschen'ken tr give away

verscher'zen ref—**sich** [dat] **etw v.** throw away, lose (frivolously)

verscheu'chen tr scare away

verschicken (verschik'ken) tr send away; (deportieren) deport

verschie'bebahnhof m marshaling yard

verschie'ben §130 tr postpone; shift; displace; black-market; (rr) shunt, switch || ref shift

Verschie'bung f (-;-en) postponement; shift, shifting

verschieden [fer'ʃidən] adj different, various; distinct

verschie'denartig adj of a different kind

verschiedenerlei [fer'ʃidənərlaɪ] invar adj different kinds of

Verschie'denheit f (-;-en) difference; variety, diversity

verschiedentlich [fer'ʃidəntlɪç] adv repeatedly; at times, occasionally

verschie'ßen §76 tr (Schießvorrat) use up, expend || intr (SEIN) (Farbe) fade

verschif'fen tr ship

Verschif'fung f (-;) shipment

verschim'meln intr (SEIN) get moldy

verschla'fen adj sleepy, drowsy || §131 tr miss by sleeping; (Zeit) sleep away || intr oversleep

Verschla'fenheit f (-;) sleepiness

Verschlag' m partition; crate

verschla'gen adj sly; (lau) lukewarm || §132 tr partition off; board up; (Kisten) nail shut; (Seite im Buch) lose; (naut) drive off course; (tennis) misserve; **j-m den Atem v.** take s.o.'s breath away; **j-m die Sprache** (or **Rede, Stimme**) **v.** make s.o. speechless; **v. werden auf** (acc) (or in acc) be driven to || impers—**es verschlägt nichts** it doesn't matter

verschlammen [fer'ʃlamən] intr (SEIN) silt up

verschlampen [fer'ʃlampən] tr ruin (through neglect); (verlegen) misplace || intr get slovenly

verschlechtern [fer'ʃleçtərn] tr make worse || ref get worse, deteriorate

Verschlech'terung f (-;) deterioration

verschleiern [fer'ʃlaɪ.ərn] tr veil; (Tatsachen) cover up; (Stimme) disguise; (mil) screen; **die Bilanz v.** juggle the books || ref cloud up

verschleiert [fer'ʃlaɪ.ərt] adj hazy; (Stimme) husky; (Augen) misty

Verschlei'erung f (-;) coverup; camouflaging; (jur) suppression of evidence

verschlei'fen §88 tr slur, slur over

Verschleiß [fer'ʃlaɪs] m (-es;) wear and tear; (Aust) retail trade

verschlei'ßen §53 tr wear out; (Aust) retail || ref wear out

verschleiß'fest adj durable

verschlep'pen tr drag off; abduct; (im Krieg) displace; (Verhandlungen) drag out; (Seuche) spread; (verzögern) delay

verschleu'dern tr waste, squander; (Waren) sell dirt-cheap

verschlie'ßen §76 tr shut; lock; put under lock and key || ref (dat) close one's mind to

verschlimmern [fer'ʃlɪmərn] tr make worse; (fig) aggravate || ref get worse

verschlin'gen §142 tr devour, wolf down; (verflechten) intertwine

verschlissen [fer'ʃlɪsən] adj frayed

verschlossen [fer'ʃlɔsən] adj shut; (fig) reserved, tight-lipped

verschlucken (verschluk'ken) tr swallow || ref swallow the wrong way

verschlungen [fer'ʃluŋən] adj (Weg) winding; (fig) intricate

Ver·schluß' m (-schlusses;-schlüsse) fastener; (Schnapp-) catch; (Schloß-) lock; (e-r Flasche) stopper; (Stöpsel) plug; (Plombe) seal; (e-s Gewehrs) breechlock; (phot) shutter; **unter V.** under lock and key

verschlüsseln [fer'ʃlʏsəln] tr code

Verschluß'laut m (ling) stop, plosive

verschmach'ten intr (SEIN) pine away; **vor Durst v.** be dying of thirst

verschmä'hen tr disdain

verschmel'zen §133 tr & intr (SEIN) fuse, merge; blend

Verschmel'zung f (-;-en) fusion; (com) merger

verschmer'zen tr get over

verschmie'ren tr smear; soil, dirty; (verwischen) blur

verschmitzt [fer'ʃmɪtst] adj crafty

verschmut'zen tr dirty || intr (SEIN) get dirty

verschnap'pen ref give oneself away

verschnau'fen ref & intr stop for breath

verschnei'den §106 tr clip, trim; cut wrong; castrate; (Branntwein, Wein) blend

verschneit [fer'ʃnaɪt] adj snow-covered

Verschnitt' m (-[e]s;) blend

verschnup'fen tr annoy; **verschnupft sein** have a cold; (coll) be annoyed

verschnü'ren tr tie up

verschollen [fer'ʃɔlən] adj missing, never heard of again; (jur) presumed dead

verscho'nen tr spare; **j-n mit etw v.** spare s.o. s.th.

verschönern [fer'ʃønərn] tr beautify

verschossen [fɛr'ʃɔsən] *adj* faded, discolored; (in *acc*) (coll) be madly in love (with)

verschränken [fɛr'ʃrɛŋkən] *tr* fold (one's arms)

verschrau'ben *tr* screw tight

verschrei'ben §62 *tr* use up (in *writing*); (jur) make over; (med) prescribe || *ref* make a mistake (in *writing*)

Verschrei'bung *f* (–;-en) prescription

verschrei'en §135 *tr* decry

verschrien [fɛr'ʃri·ən] *adj*—**v. sein als** have the reputation of being

verschroben [fɛr'ʃrobən] *adj* eccentric

Verschro'benheit *f* (–;-en) eccentricity

verschrotten [fɛr'ʃrɔtən] *tr* scrap

verschüt'tern *tr* intimidate

verschul'den *tr* encumber with debts; **etw v.** be guilty of s.th.; be the cause of s.th. || **Verschulden** *n* (–s;) fault

verschuldet [fɛr'ʃuldət] *adj* in debt

Verschul'dung *f* (–;-en) indebtedness; encumbrance

verschüt'ten *tr* spill; (*ausfüllen*) fill up; (*Person*) bury alive

verschwägert [fɛr'ʃvɛgərt] *adj* related by marriage

verschwei'gen §148 *tr* keep secret; **j–m etw v.** keep s.th. from s.o.

Verschwei'gung *f* (–;) concealment

verschwei'ßen *tr* weld (together)

verschwenden [fɛr'ʃvɛndən] *tr* (an *acc*) waste (on; squander (on)

Verschwen'der –in §6 *mf* spendthrift

verschwenderisch [fɛr'ʃvɛndərɪʃ] *adj* wasteful; lavish, extravagant

Verschwen'dung *f* (–;) waste; extravagance

verschwiegen [fɛr'ʃvigən] *adj* discreet; reserved, reticent

Verschwie'genheit *f* (–;) discretion; reticence; secrecy

verschwim'men §136 *intr* (SEIN) become blurred; (fig) fade

verschwin'den §59 *intr* (SEIN) disappear; **ich muß mal v.** (coll) I have to go (to the toilet); **v. lassen** put out of the way; spirit off || **Verschwinden** *n* (–s;) disappearance

verschwistert [fɛr'ʃvɪstərt] *adj* closely related

verschwit'zen *tr* sweat up; (coll) forget

verschwollen [fɛr'ʃvɔlən] *adj* swollen

verschwommen [fɛr'ʃvɔmən] *adj* hazy, indistinct; (*Bild*) blurred

Verschwom'menheit *f* (–;) haziness

verschwö'ren §137 *tr* forswear || *ref* (gegen) plot (against); **sich zu etw v.** plot s.th.

Verschwö'rer –in §6 *mf* conspirator

Verschwö'rung *f* (–;-en) conspiracy

verse'hen §138 *tr* (Amt, Stellung) hold; (Dienst, Pflicht) perform; (Haushalt, usw.) look after; (mit) provide (with); (eccl) administer the last rites to; **j–s Dienst v.** fill in for s.o.; **mit e–m Saum v.** hem; **mit Giro v.** endorse; **mit Unterschrift v.** sign || *ref* make a mistake; **ehe man es sich versieht** before you know it; **sich v.** (genit) expect || **Versehen** *n* (–s;–) mistake, slip; oversight; **aus V.** by mistake

versehentlich [fɛr'ze·əntlɪç] *adv* by mistake, erroneously, inadvertently

versehren [fɛr'zerən] *tr* injure

Versehrte [fɛr'zertə] §5 *mf* disabled person

versen'den §140 *tr* send, ship; **ins Ausland v.** export

versen'gen *tr* scorch; (Haar) singe

versen'ken *tr* sink; submerge; lower; (Kabel) lay; (Schraube) countersink; (naut) scuttle || *ref*—**sich v. in** (acc) become engrossed in

Versen'kung *f* (–;-en) sinking; (theat) trapdoor; **in der V. verschwinden** (fig) vanish into thin air

versessen [fɛr'zesən] *adj*—**v. auf** (acc) crazy about, obsessed with

verset'zen *tr* move, shift; (Pflanze) transplant; (Schulkind) promote; (Beamte) transfer; (Schlag) deal, give; (verpfänden) pawn; (vermischen) mix; (Metall) alloy; (erwidern) reply; (vergeblich warten lassen) (coll) stand up; (mus) transpose; **in Angst v.** terrify; **in Erstaunen v.** amaze; **in den Ruhestand v.** retire; **in Zorn v.** anger || *ref*—**v. Sie sich in meine Lage** put yourself in my place

Verset'zung *f* (–;-en) moving, shifting; transplanting; transfer; mixing; alloying; (educ) promotion

Verset'zungszeichen *n* (mus) accidental

verseuchen [fɛr'zɔɪçən] *tr* infect, contaminate

Verseu'chung *f* (–;) infection; contamination

Vers'fuß *m* (pros) foot

versicherbar [fɛr'zɪçərbar] *adj* insurable

versichern [fɛr'zɪçərn] *tr* assure; assert, affirm; insure || *ref* (genit) assure oneself of

Versicherte [fɛr'zɪçərtə] §5 *mf* insured

Versi'cherung *f* (–;-en) assurance; affirmation; insurance

Versi'cherungsanstalt *f* insurance company

Versi'cherungsbeitrag *m* premium

versi'cherungsfähig *adj* insurable

Versi'cherungsgesellschaft *f* insurance company

Versi'cherungsleistung *f* insurance benefit

Versi'cherungsmathematiker –in §6 *mf* actuary

Versi'cherungsnehmer –in §6 *mf* insured

versi'cherungspflichtig *adj* subject to mandatory insurance

Versi'cherungspolice *f*, **Versi'cherungsschein** *m* insurance policy

Versi'cherungsträger *m* underwriter

Versi'cherungszwang *m* compulsory insurance

versickern (versik'kern) *intr* (SEIN) seep out, trickle away

versie'geln *tr* seal (up); (jur) seal off

Versie'gelung *f* (–;) sealing (off)

versie'gen *intr* (SEIN) dry up

versil'bern *tr* silver-plate; (coll) sell

Versil'berung *f* (–;) silver-plating

versin'ken §143 *intr* (SEIN) **(in** *acc***)** sink (into); (fig) **(in** *acc***)** lapse (into)

versinnbildlichen [fɛr'zɪnbɪltlɪçən] *tr* symbolize

Version [ver'zjon] *f* (-;-en) version

versippt [fɛr'zɪpt] *adj* **(mit)** related (to)

versklaven [fɛr'sklavən] *tr* enslave

Vers'kunst *f* versification

Vers'macher –in §6 *mf* versifier

Vers'maß *n* meter

versoffen [fɛr'zɔfən] *adj* (coll) drunk

versohlen [fɛr'zolən] *tr* (coll) give (*s.o.*) a good licking

versöhnen [fɛr'zønən] *tr* **(mit)** reconcile (with) ‖ *ref* become reconciled

versöhnlich [fɛr'zønlɪç] *adj* conciliatory

Versöh'nung *f* (-;) reconciliation

Versöh'nungstag *m* Day of Atonement

versonnen [fɛr'zɔnən] *adj* wistful

versor'gen *tr* look after; provide for; **(mit)** supply (with), provide (with)

Versor'ger –in §6 *m* provider, breadwinner

Versor'gung *f* (-;) providing, supplying; (*Unterhalt*) maintenance; (*Alters- und Validen-*) social security

Versor'gungsbetrieb *m* public utility

Versor'gungstruppen *pl* service troops

Versor'gungswege *pl* supply lines

verspan'nen *tr* guy, brace

verspäten [fɛr'ʃpetən] *ref* come late; (rr) be behind schedule

verspätet [fɛr'ʃpetət] *adj* belated, late

Verspä'tung *f* (-;-en) lateness, delay; **mit e–r Stunde V.** one hour behind schedule; **V. haben** be late

verspei'sen *tr* eat up

verspekulie'ren *tr* lose on a gamble ‖ *ref* lose all through speculation

versper'ren *tr* bar, block, obstruct; (*Tür*) lock

verspie'len *tr* lose, gamble away ‖ *intr* **—bei j–m v.** lose favor with s.o.

verspielt [fɛr'ʃpilt] *adj* playful; frivolous

versponnen [fɛr'ʃpɔnən] *adj*—**in Gedanken versponnen** lost in thought

verspot'ten *tr* mock, deride

Verspot'tung *f* (-;) mockery, derision

verspre'chen §64 *tr* promise ‖ *ref* make a mistake in speaking; **ich verspreche mir viel davon** I expect a lot from that ‖ **Versprechen** *n* (-s;-) promise; slip of the tongue

Verspre'chung *f* (-;-en) promise

verspren'gen *tr* scatter, disperse

Versprengte [fɛr'ʃprɛŋtə] §5 *mf* (mil) straggler

verspritz'zen *tr* squirt, spatter

versprü'hen *tr* spray

verspü'ren *tr* feel, sense

verstaatlichen [fɛr'ʃtatlɪçən] *tr* nationalize

Verstaat'lichung *f* (-;) nationalization

verstädtern [fɛr'ʃtetərn] *tr* urbanize

Verstäd'terung *f* (-;) urbanization

Verstand' *m* (-[e]s;) understanding; intellect; intelligence, brains; (*Vernunft*) reason; (*Geist*) mind; senses; sense; **den V. verlieren** lose one's

mind; **gesunder V.** common sense; **klarer V.** clear head; **nicht bei V. sein** be out of one's mind

Verstan'deskraft *f* intellectual power

verstan'desmäßig *adj* rational

Verstan'desmensch *m* matter-of-fact person

verstän'dig *adj* intelligent; sensible; reasonable; wise

verständigen [fɛr'ʃtendɪgən] *tr* **(von)** inform (about), notify (of) ‖ *ref*— **sich v. mit** make oneself understood to; come to an understanding with

Verstän'digung *f* (-;) understanding; information; communication; (telp) quality of reception

verständlich [fɛr'ʃtentlɪç] *adj* understandable, intelligible; **sich v. machen** make oneself understood

Verständnis [fɛr'ʃtentnɪs] *n* (-ses;-e) **(für)** understanding (of), appreciation (for)

verständ'nislos *adj* uncomprehending

verständ'nisinnig *adj* with deep mutual understanding; (*Blick*) knowing

verständ'nisvoll *adj* understanding; appreciative; (*Blick*) knowing

verstär'kern *tr* stink up

verstär'ken *tr* strengthen; (*steigern*) intensify; (elec) boost; (mil) reinforce; (rad) amplify

Verstär'ker *m* (-s;-) (rad) amplifier

Verstär'kung *f* (-;-en) strengthening; intensification; (mil) reinforcement; (rad) amplification

verstatten [fɛr'ʃtatən] *tr* permit

verstau'ben *intr* (SEIN) get dusty

verstäu'ben *intr* atomize

verstaubt [fɛr'ʃtaupt] *adj* dusty; (fig) antiquated

verstau'chen *tr* sprain

Verstau'chung *f* (-;-en) sprain

verstau'en *tr* stow away

Versteck [fɛr'ʃtek] *m* (-[e]s;-e) hiding place; hideout; **V. spielen** play hide-and-seek

verstecken (verstek'ken) *tr & ref* hide

versteckt [fɛr'ʃtekt] *adj* hidden, veiled; (*Absicht*) ulterior

verste'hen §146 *tr* understand, see; make out; realize; (*Sprache*) know; **e–n Spaß v.** take a joke; **ich verstehe es zu** (*inf*) I know how to (*inf*); **falsch v.** misunderstand; **verstanden?** get it? **v. Sie mich recht!** don't get me wrong!; **was v. Sie unter** (*dat*)? what do you mean by? ‖ *ref*—**(das) versteht sich!** that's understood!; **das versteht sich von selbst!** that goes without saying; **sich gut v. mit** get along well with; **sich v. auf** (*acc*) be skilled in; **sich zu etw v.** (*sich zu etw entschließen*) bring oneself to do s.th.; (*in etw einwilligen*) agree to s.th. ‖ *recip* understand each other

verstei'fen *tr* stiffen; strut, brace, reinforce ‖ *ref* stiffen; **sich v. auf** (*acc*) insist on

verstei'gen §148 *ref* lose one's way in the mountain; **sich dazu v., daß** go so far as to (*inf*)

Verstei'gerer *m* (-s;-) auctioneer

verstei'gern *tr* auction off

Verstei′gerung f (-;-en) auction
verstei′nern intr (SEIN) become petrified; (fig) be petrified
verstell′bar adj adjustable
verstel′len tr (regulieren) adjust; (versperren) block; (Stimme, usw.) disguise; (Weiche) throw; (Verkehrsampel) switch; (Zeiger e-r Uhr) move; misplace; j-m den Weg v. block s.o.'s way || ref put on an act
Verstel′lung f (-;-en) adjusting; disguise
versteu′ern tr pay taxes on
Versteu′erung f (-;) paying of taxes
verstiegen [fɛr′ʃtigən] adj (Idee, Plan) extravagant, fantastic
verstim′men tr put out of tune; (fig) put out of humor
verstimmt [fɛr′ʃtɪmt] adj out of tune; (Magen) upset; v. über (acc) upset over
Verstim′mung f (-;) bad humor; (zwischen zweien) bad feeling, bad blood
verstockt [fɛr′ʃtɔkt] adj stubborn; (Verbrecher) hardened; (eccl) impenitent
Verstockt′heit f (-;) stubbornness; (eccl) impenitence
verstohlen [fɛr′ʃtolən] adj furtive
verstop′fen tr stop up, clog; (Straße) block, jam; (Leib) constipate
Verstop′fung f (-;) stopping up, clogging; congestion; (pathol) constipation
verstorben [fɛr′ʃtɔrbən] adj late, deceased || **Verstorbene** §5 mf deceased
verstört [fɛr′ʃtørt] adj shaken, bewildered, distracted
Verstört′heit f (-;) bewilderment
Verstoß′ m (gegen) violation (of), offense (against)
versto′ßen §150 tr disown || intr—v. gegen violate, break
verstre′ben tr prop, brace
verstrei′chen §85 tr (Butter) spread; (Risse) plaster up || intr (SEIN) pass, elapse; (Gelegenheit) slip by; (Frist) expire
verstreu′en tr scatter, disperse, strew
verstricken (verstrik′ken) tr use up in knitting; (fig) involve, entangle || ref get entangled
verstümmeln [fɛr′ʃtyməln] tr mutilate; (Funkspruch) garble
Verstüm′melung f (-;-en) mutilation; (rad) garbling
verstummen [fɛr′ʃtumən] intr (SEIN) become silent; (vor Erstaunen) be dumbstruck; (Geräusch) cease
Versuch [fɛr′zux] m (-[e]s;-e) try, attempt; (Probe) test, trial; (wissenschaftlich) experiment; e-n V. machen mit have a try at
versu′chen tr try; tempt; (kosten) taste
Versuchs′anstalt f research institute
Versuchs′ballon m (& fig) trial balloon
Versuchs′flieger m test pilot
Versuchs′flug m test flight
Versuchs′kaninchen n (fig) guinea pig
Versuchs′reihe f series of tests
versuchs′weise adv by way of a test; on approval
Versu′chung f (-;-en) temptation

versumpfen [fɛr′zumpfən] intr (SEIN) become marshy; (coll) go to the dogs
versün′digen ref (an dat) sin (against)
versunken [fɛr′zuŋkən] adj sunk; v. in (acc) (fig) lost in
versü′ßen tr sweeten
verta′gen tr & ref (auf acc) adjourn (till), recess (till)
Verta′gung f (-;-en) adjournment
vertändeln [fɛr′tɛndəln] tr trifle away
vertäuen [fɛr′tɔɪ·ən] tr (naut) moor
vertau′schen tr (gegen) exchange (for)
Vertau′schung f (-;-en) exchange
verteidigen [fɛr′taɪdɪgən] tr defend
Vertei′diger -in §6 mf defender; (Befürworter) advocate; (jur) counsel for the defense || m (fb) back
Vertei′digung f (-;-en) defense
Vertei′digungsbündnis n defensive alliance
Vertei′digungsminister m secretary of defense
Vertei′digungsministerium n department of defense
Vertei′digungsschrift f written defense
Vertei′digungsstellung f defensive position
vertei′len tr distribute; (zuteilen) allot; (über e-e große Fläche) scatter; (steuerlich) spread out; (Rollen) (theat) cast || ref spread out
Vertei′ler m (-s;-) distributer; (Anschriftenliste) mailing list; (von Durchschlägen) distribution; (aut) distributor
Vertei′lung f (-;-en) distribution; allotment; (theat) casting
verteuern [fɛr′tɔɪ·ərn] tr raise the price of
verteufelt [fɛr′tɔɪfəlt] adj devilish; a devil of a
vertiefen [fɛr′tifən] tr make deeper; (fig) deepen || ref—sich v. in (acc) become absorbed in
Vertie′fung f (-;-en) deepening; (Höhlung) hollow, depression; (Nische) niche; (Loch) hole; (fig) absorption
vertiert [fɛr′tirt] adj bestial
vertikal [vɛrtɪ′kal] adj vertical || **Vertikale** f (-;-n) vertical
vertil′gen tr exterminate, eradicate; (aufessen) (coll) eat, polish off
Vertil′gung f (-;) extermination
vertip′pen tr type incorrectly || ref make a typing error
verto′nen tr set to music
Verto′nung f (-;-en) musical arrangement
vertrackt [fɛr′trakt] adj (coll) odd, strange; (coll) blooming
Vertrag [fɛr′trak] m (-[e]s;-̈e) contract, agreement; (dipl) treaty
vertra′gen §132 tr stand, take; tolerate || recip agree, be compatible; (Farben) harmonize; (Personen) get along
vertrag′lich adj contractual (adv) by contract, as stipulated; sich v. verpflichten zu (inf) contract to (inf)
verträglich [fɛr′trɛklɪç] adj sociable, personable; (Speise) digestible
Vertrags′bruch m breach of contract
vertragsbrüchig [fɛr′traksbryçɪç] adj —v. werden break a contract

vertrags'gemäß *adj* contractual

vertrags'widrig *adj* contrary to the terms of a contract or treaty

vertrau'en *intr* (*dat*) trust; **v. auf** (*acc*) trust in, have confidence in || **Vertrauen** *n* (**-s**;) trust, confidence; **ganz im V.** just between you and me; **im V.** confidentially

vertrau'enerweckend *adj* inspiring confidence

Vertrau'ensbruch *m* breach of trust

Vertrau'ens·mann *m* **-[e]s;꞊er & -leute)** confidential agent; (*Vertrauter*) confidant; (*Sprecher*) spokesman; (*Gewährsmann*) informant

Vertrau'ensposten *m*, **Vertrau'ensstellung** *f* position of trust

vertrau'ensvoll *adj* confident; trusting

Vertrau'ensvotum *n* vote of confidence

vertrau'enswürdig *adj* trustworthy

vertrauern [fɛr'trau·ərn] *tr* spend in mourning

vertraulich [fɛr'trauliç] *adj* confidential; intimate

Vertrau'lichkeit *f* (**-;-en**) intimacy, familiarity; **sich** [*dat*] **Vertraulichkeiten herausnehmen** take liberties

verträu'men *tr* dream away

verträumt [fɛr'trɔimt] *adj* dreamy

vertraut [fɛr'traut]*adj* familiar; friendly, intimate || **Vertraute** §5 *mf* intimate friend || *m* confidant || *f* confidante

Vertraut'heit *f* (**-;**) familiarity

vertrei'ben §62 *tr* drive away, expel; (*aus dem Hause*) chase out; (*aus dem Lande*) banish; (*Ware*) sell, market; (*Zeit*) pass, kill

Vertrei'bung *f* (**-;**) expulsion

vertre'ten §152 *tr* represent; substitute for; (*Ansicht, usw.*) advocate || *ref* —**sich** [*dat*] **den Fuß v.** sprain one's ankle; **sich** [*dat*] **die Beine v.** (coll) stretch one's legs

Vertre'ter **-in** §6 *mf* representative; substitute; (*Bevollmächtigte*) proxy; (*im Amt*) deputy; (*Fürsprecher*) advocate; (com) agent

Vertre'tung *f* (**-;-en**) representation; substitution; (com) agency; (pol) mission; **in V. by proxy; in V.** (genit) signed for

Vertrieb' *m* **-[e]s;-e**) sale, turnover; retail trade; sales department

Vertriebs'abkommen *n* franchise agreement

Vertriebs'abteilung *f* sales department

Vertriebs'kosten *pl* distribution costs

Vertriebs'leiter **-in** §6 *mf* sales manager

Vertriebs'recht *n* franchise

vertrin'ken §143 *tr* drink up

vertrock'nen *intr* (SEIN) dry up

vertrödeln [fɛr'trødəln] *tr* fritter away

vertrö'sten *tr* string along; **auf später v.** put off till later

vertun' §154 *tr* waste || *ref* (coll) make a mistake

vertu'schen *tr* hush up

verübeln [fɛr'ybəln] *tr* take (*s.th.*) the wrong way; **j-m etw v.** blame s.o. for s.th.

verü'ben *tr* commit, perpetrate

verul'ken *tr* (coll) kid

verunehren [fɛr'uneran] *tr* dishonor

veruneinigen [fɛr'unainɪgən] *tr* disunite || *recip* fall out, quarrel

verunglimpfen [fɛr'unglɪmpfən] *tr* slander, defame

verunglücken [fɛr'unglykən] *intr* (SEIN) have an accident; (coll) fail

Verunglückte [fɛr'unglykta] §5 *mf* victim, casualty

verunreinigen [fɛr'unraɪnɪgən] *tr* soil, dirty; (*Luft, Wasser*) pollute

Verun'reinigung *f* (**-;**) pollution

verunstalten [fɛr'un/taltən] *tr* disfigure, deface

veruntreuen [fɛr'untrɔi·ən] *tr* embezzle

Verun'treuung *f* (**-;**) embezzlement

verunzieren [fɛr'untsirən] *tr* mar

verursachen [fɛr'urzaxən] *tr* cause

verur'teilen *tr* condemn; sentence

Verur'teilung *f* (**-;-en**) condemnation; sentence

vervielfachen [fɛr'filfaxən] *tr* multiply || *ref* increase considerably

vervielfältigen [fɛr'filfɛltigən] *tr* multiply; duplicate; mimeograph; (*nachbilden*) reproduce

Verviel'fältigung *f* (**-;-en**) duplication; mimeographing; reproduction; (phot) printing

Verviel'fältigungsapparat *m* duplicator

vervollkommnen [fɛr'fɔlkəmnən] *tr* improve on, perfect

Vervoll'kommnung *f* (**-;**) improvement, perfection

vervollständigen [fɛr'fɔl/tendɪgən] *tr* complete

Vervoll'ständigung *f* (**-;**) completion

verwach'sen *adj* overgrown; deformed; hunchbacked; **mit etw v. sein** (fig) be attached to s.th. || *intr* (SEIN) grow together; become deformed; (*Wunde*) heal up; **zu e-r Einheit v.** form a whole

Verwach'sung *f* (**-;-en**) deformity

verwackelt [fɛr'vakəlt] *adj* (phot) blurred

verwah'ren *tr* keep; **v. vor** (*dat*) protect against || *ref*—**sich v. gegen** protest against

verwahrlosen [fɛr'varlozən] *tr* neglect || *intr* (SEIN) (*Gebäude*) deteriorate; (*Kinder*) run wild; (*Personen*) go to the dogs

verwahrlost [fɛr'varlost] *adj* uncared-for; (*Person*) unkempt; (*sittlich*) degenerate; (*Garten*) overgrown with weeds

Verwahr'losung *f* (**-;**) neglect

Verwah'rung *f* (**-;**) care, safekeeping, custody; (fig) protest; **etw in V. nehmen** take care of s.th.; **j-m in V. geben** entrust to s.o.'s care

verwaisen [fɛr'vaizən] *intr* (SEIN) become an orphan, be orphaned

verwaist [fɛr'vaist] *adj* orphaned; (fig) deserted

verwalten [fɛr'valtən] *tr* administer, manage

Verwal'ter **-in** §6 *mf* administrator, manager

Verwal'tung *f* (**-;-en**) administration; management

Verwal'tungsapparat *m* administrative machinery

Verwal'tungsbeamte *m* civil service worker; administrative official

Verwal'tungsdienst *m* civil service

Verwal'tungsrat *m* advisory board; (*e-r Aktiengesellschaft*) board of directors; (*e-s Instituts*) board of trustees

verwan'deln *tr* change, turn, convert; (*Strafe*) commute ‖ *ref* change, turn

Verwand'lung *f* (-;-en) change, transformation; (jur) commutation

verwandt [fer'vant] *adj* (mit) related (to); (*Wissenschaften*) allied; (*Wörter*) cognate; (*Seelen*) kindred ‖ **Verwandte §5** *mf* relative, relation

Verwandt'schaft *f* (-;-en) relationship; relatives; (chem) affinity

verwandt'schaftlich *adj* kindred

Verwand'schaftsgrad *m* degree of relationship

verwanzt [fer'vantst] *adj* (coll) full of bugs, lousy

verwar'nen *tr* warn, caution

Verwar'nung *f* (-;-en) warning, caution

verwa'schen *adj* washed-out, faded; (*verschwommen*) vague, fuzzy

verwäs'sern *tr* dilute; (fig) water down

verwe'ben §94 *tr* interweave

verwe'chseln *tr* confuse, get (*various items*) mixed up; (*Hüte, Mäntel*) take by mistake ‖ **Verwechseln** *n* (-s;)—**sie sehen sich zum V. ähnlich** they are as alike as two peas

Verwechs'lung *f* (-;-en) mix-up

verwegen [fer'vegən] *adj* bold, daring

verwe'hen *tr* (*Blätter*) blow away; (*Spur*) cover up (with snow) ‖ *intr* (SEIN) be blown in all directions; (*Spur*) be covered up; (*Worte*) drift away

verweh'ren *tr*—**j—m etw v.** refuse s.o. s.th.; prevent s.o. from getting s.th.

Verwe'hung *f* (-;-en) (snow)drift

verweichlichen [fer'vaɪçlɪçən] *tr* make effeminate; (*Kind*) coddle ‖ *ref* & *intr* become effeminate; grow soft

verweichlicht [fer'vaɪçlɪçt] *adj* effeminate; soft, flabby

Verweich'lichung *f* (-;) effeminacy

verwei'gern *tr* refuse, deny, turn down

Verwei'gerung *f* (-;-en) refusal

verweilen [fer'vaɪlən] *intr* linger, tarry; (fig) dwell

verweint [fer'vaɪnt] *adj* red with tears

Verweis [fer'vaɪs] *m* (-es;-e) reprimand, rebuke; (*Hinweis*) reference

verwei'sen §118 *tr* banish; (*Schüler*) expel; **j—m etw v.** reprimand s.o. for s.th.; **j—n an j—n v.** refer s.o. to s.o.; **j—n auf etw v.** refer s.o. to s.th.

Verwei'sung *f* (-;-en) banishment; expulsion; (*an acc*) referral (to); (*auf acc*) reference (to)

verwel'ken *intr* (SEIN) wither, wilt

verweltlichen [fer'veltlɪçən] *tr* secularize

verwendbar [fer'vɛntbɑr] *adj* applicable; available; usable

Verwend'barkeit *f* (-;) availability; usefulness

verwen'den §140 *tr* use, employ; (auf acc, für) apply (to); **Zeit und Mühe v. auf** (*acc*) spend time and effort on ‖ *ref*—**sich bei j—m v. für** intercede with s.o. for

Verwen'dung *f* (-;-en) use, employment; application; **keine V. haben für** have no use for; **vielseitige V.** versatility

verwen'dungsfähig *adj* usable

verwer'fen §160 *tr* reject; (*Plan*) discard; (*Berufung*) turn down; (*Klage*) dismiss; (*Urteil*) overrule ‖ *ref* (*Holz*) warp; (geol) fault

verwerf'lich *adj* objectionable

Verwer'fung *f* (-;-en) rejection; warping; (geol) fault

verwer'ten *tr* utilize

Verwer'tung *f* (-;-en) utilization

verwesen [fer'vezən] *intr* (SEIN) rot

verweslich [fer'vezlɪç] *adj* perishable

Verwe'sung *f* (-;) decay

verwet'ten *tr* lose (*in betting*)

verwich'sen *tr* (coll) clobber

verwickeln (verwik'keln) *tr* snarl, entangle; complicate; (fig) involve ‖ *ref*—**sich v. in** (*acc*) get entangled in; (fig) get involved in

Verwick'lung *f* (-;-en) snarl, tangle; involvement; complexity; complication

verwil'dern *intr* become overgrown; (*Person*) become depraved; (*Kind*) run wild, go wild

verwildert [fer'vildərt] *adj* wild, savage; weed-grown

verwin'den §59 *tr* get over; (*Verlust*) recover from

verwir'ken *tr* forfeit; (*Strafe*) incur ‖ *ref*—**sich** [*dat*] **j—s Gunst v.** lose favor with s.o.

verwirklichen [fer'vɪrklɪçən] *tr* realize, make come true ‖ *ref* come true

Verwirk'lichung *f* (-;) realization

Verwir'kung *f* (-;-en) forfeiture

verwirren [fer'vɪrən] *tr* throw into disorder; (*Haar*) muss up; confuse

verwirrt [fer'vɪrt] *adj* confused

Verwir'rung *f* (-;-en) confusion; **in V. geraten** become confused

verwirt'schaften *tr* squander

verwi'schen *tr* wipe out; (*teilweise*) blur; (*verschmieren*) smear; (*Spuren*) cover ‖ *ref* become blurred

verwit'tern *intr* (SEIN) become weatherbeaten; (*zerfallen*) crumble away

verwittert [fer'vɪtərt] *adj* weatherbeaten

verwitwet [fer'vɪtvət] *adj* widowed

verwöhnen [fer'vønən] *tr* pamper, spoil

verworfen [fer'vorfən] *adj* depraved

Verwor'fenheit *f* (-;) depravity

verworren [fer'vorən] *adj* confused

verwundbar [fer'vuntbɑr] *adj* vulnerable

verwun'den *tr* wound

verwunderlich [fer'vundərlɪç] *adj* remarkable, astonishing

verwun'dern *tr* astonish ‖ *ref* (*über acc*) be astonished (at), wonder (at)

Verwun'derung *f* (-;) astonishment; **j—n in V. setzen** astonish s.o.

verwundet [fer'vundət] *adj* wounded

|| **Verwundete** §5 *mf* wounded person

verwunschen [fɛr'vʊnʃən] *adj* enchanted

verwün'schen *tr* damn, curse; (*in Märchen*) bewitch, put a curse on

verwünscht [fɛr'vʏnʃt] *adj* confounded, darn || *interj* darn it!

Verwün'schung *f* (–;–en) curse

verwurzelt [fɛr'vʊrtsəlt] *adj* deeply rooted

verwüsten [fɛr'vystən] *tr* devastate

Verwü'stung *f* (–;–en) devastation

verzagen [fɛr'tsagən] *intr* (SEIN) lose heart, despair; **v. an** (*dat*) give up on

verzagt [fɛr'tsakt] *adj* despondent

Verzagt'heit *f* (–;) despondency

verzäh'len *ref* miscount

verzärteln [fɛr'tsɛrtəln] *tr* pamper

verzau'bern *tr* bewitch, charm; **v. in** (*acc*) change into

Verzehr [fɛr'tser] *m* (–[e]s;) consumption

verzeh'ren *tr* consume; (*Geld*) spend; (*Mahlzeit*) eat || *ref* (**in** *dat*, **vor** *dat*) pine away (with); (**nach**) yearn (for)

verzeh'rend *adj* (*Blick*) longing; (*Fieber*) wasting; (*Leidenschaft*) burning

Verzeh'rung *f* (–;) consumption

verzeich'nen *tr* draw wrong; make a list of; register; catalogue; (*opt*) distort

Verzeichnis [fɛr'tsaɪçnɪs] *n* (–ses;–se) list; catalogue; (*im Buch*) index; (*Inventar*) inventory; (*Tabelle*) table; (*telp*) directory

verzeihen [fɛr'tsaɪ·ən] §81 *tr* forgive, pardon (*s.th.*); condone || *intr* (*dat*) forgive, pardon (*s.o.*)

verzeihlich [fɛr'tsaɪlɪç] *adj* pardonable

Verzei'hung *f* (–;) pardon

verzer'ren *tr* distort; contort

Verzer'rung *f* (–;–en) distortion; contortion; grimace

verzetteln [fɛr'tsɛtəln] *tr* fritter away; catalogue || *ref* spread oneself too thin

Verzicht [fɛr'tsɪçt] *m* (–[e]s) renunciation; **V. leisten auf** (*acc*) waive

verzichten [fɛr'tsɪçtən] *intr*—**v. auf** (*acc*) do without; (*verabsäumen*) pass up; (*aufgeben*) give up, renounce; (*Rechte*) waive

verzieh [fɛr'tsi] *pret* of **verzeihen**

verzie'hen §163 *tr* distort; (*Kind*) spoil; **den Mund v.** make a face; **ohne e–e Miene zu v.** without batting an eye || *ref* disappear; (*Schmerz*) go away; (*Menge, Wolken*) disperse; (*Holz*) warp; (*durch Druck*) buckle; (*coll*) sneak off

verzie'ren *tr* decorate

Verzie'rung *f* (–;–en) decoration; (*Schmuck*) ornament

verzinsen [fɛr'tsɪnzən] *tr* pay interest on; **e–e Summe zu 6% v.** pay 6% interest on a sum || *ref* yield interest; **sich mit 6% v.** yield 6% interest

verzinslich [fɛr'tsɪnslɪç] *adj* bearing interest || *adv*—**v. anlegen** put out at interest

Verzin'sung *f* (–;) interest

verzog [fɛr'tsok] *pret* of **verziehen**

verzogen [fɛr'tsogən] *adj* distorted; (*Kind*) spoiled; (*Holz*) warped

verzö'gern *tr* delay; put off, postpone || *ref* be late

Verzö'gerung *f* (–;–en) delay; postponement

verzollen [fɛr'tsɔlən] *tr* pay duty on; (*naut*) clear; **haben Sie etw zu v.?** do you have anything to declare?

verzückt [fɛr'tsʏkt] *adj* ecstatic

Verzückung [fɛr'tsykʊŋ] *f* (–;) ecstasy

Verzug' *m* (–[e]s;) delay; (*in der Leistung*) default; **in V. geraten mit** fall behind in; **ohne V.** without delay

verzwei'feln *intr* (HABEN & SEIN) (**an** *dat*) despair (of) || **Verzweifeln** *n*—**es ist zum V.** it's enough to drive one to despair

verzweifelt [fɛr'tsvaɪfəlt] *adj* desperate

Verzweif'lung *f* (–;) despair

verzweigen [fɛr'tsvaɪgən] *ref* branch out

verzweigt [fɛr'tsvaɪkt] *adj* having many branches; (*fig*) complex

verzwickt [fɛr'tsvɪkt] *adj* (coll) tricky, ticklish

Vestibül [vɛstɪ'byl] *n* (–s;–e) vestibule; (*theat*) lobby

Veteran [vete'ran] *m* (–en;–en) veteran, ex-serviceman

Veterinär –in [vetɛrɪ'nɛr(ɪn)] §8 *mf* veterinarian

Veto ['veto] *n* (–s;–s) veto

Vetter ['fɛtər] *m* (–s;–) cousin

Vet'ternwirtschaft *f* nepotism

Vexierbild [vɛ'ksirbɪlt] *n* picture puzzle

vexieren [vɛ'ksirən] *tr* tease; pester

V-förmig ['faufœrmɪç] *adj* V-shaped

vibrieren [vɪ'brirən] *intr* vibrate

Vieh [fi] *n* (–[e]s) livestock; cattle; animal, beast

Vieh'bestand *m* livestock

Vieh'bremse *f* horsefly

viehisch ['fi·ɪʃ] *adj* brutal

Vieh'tränke *f* water hole

Vieh'wagen *m* (rr) cattle car

Vieh'weide *f* cow pasture

Vieh'zucht *f* cattle breeding

Vieh'züchter –in §6 *mf* rancher

viel [fil] *adj* much; many; a lot of || *adv* much; a lot || *pron* much; many

viel'beschäftigt *adj* very busy

viel'deutig *adj* ambiguous

Viel'eck *n* polygon

vielerlei ['filər'laɪ] *invar adj* many kinds of

viel'fach *adj* multiple; manifold || *adv* (coll) often

Vielfach– *comb.fm.* multiple

viel'fältig *adj* manifold, various

Viel'fältigkeit *f* (–;) multiplicity; variety

vielleicht' *adv* maybe, perhaps

vielmalig ['filmalɪç] *adj* oft repeated

vielmals ['filmals] *adv* frequently; **danke v.!** many thanks!

vielmehr' *adv* rather, on the contrary

viel'sagend *adj* suggestive

viel'seitig *adj* many-sided, versatile

vielstufig ['fil'ʃtufɪç] *adj* multistage

viel'teilig *adj* of many parts

viel'versprechend *adj* very promising

vier [fir] *adj* four; **unter vier Augen** confidentially ‖ *pron* four; **auf allen vieren** on all fours ‖ **Vier** *f* (-;-en) four

vier'beinig *adj* four-legged

Vier'eck *n* quadrangle

vier'eckig *adj* quadrangular

viererlei ['fɪrər'laɪ] *invar adj* four different kinds of

vier'fach, **vier'fältig** *adv* fourfold, quadruple

Vierfüßer ['fɪrfysər] *m* (-s;-) quadruped

vierhändig ['fɪrhendɪç] *adv—v.* **spielen** (mus) play a duet

Vierlinge ['fɪrlɪŋə] *pl* quadruplets

vier'mal *adv* four times

vierschrötig ['fɪr'ʃrøtɪç] *adj* stocky

vierstrahlig ['fɪr'ʃtraɪç] *adj* four-engine (jet)

viert [fɪrt] *pron—zu* **v.** in fours; **wir gehen zu v.** the four of us are going

Viertakter ['fɪrtaktər] *m* (-s;-), **Viertaktmotor** ['fɪrtaktmotor] *m* four-cycle engine

Vierte ['fɪrtə] §9 *adj & pron* fourth

vier'teilen *tr* quarter

Viertel ['fɪrtəl] *n* (-s;-) quarter; fourth (*part*); (*Stadtteil*) quarter, section

Vierteljahr' *n* quarter (*of a year*)

vierteljäh'rig, **vierteljähr'lich** *adj* quarterly

vierteln ['fɪrtəln] *tr* quarter

Vier'telnote *f* (mus) quarter note

Viertelpfund' *n* quarter of a pound

Viertelstun'de *f* quarter of an hour

viertens ['fɪrtəns] *adv* fourthly

vier'zehn *invar adj & pron* fourteen ‖ **Vierzehn** *f* (-;-en) fourteen

vier'zehnte §9 *adj & pron* fourteenth

Vier'zehntel *n* (-s;-) fourteenth (*part*)

vierzig ['fɪrtsɪç] *invar adj & pron* forty ‖ **Vierzig** *f* (-;-en) forty

vierziger ['fɪrtsɪgər] *invar adj* of the forties; **die v. Jahre** the forties

vierzigste ['fɪrtsɪçstə] §9 *adj & pron* fortieth

Vikar [vɪ'kar] *m* (-s;-e) vicar

Vil-la ['vɪla] *f* (-;-len [lən]) villa

violett [vɪ-o'let] *adj* violet

Violine [vɪ-o'linə] *f* (-;-n) violin

Violin'schlüssel *m* treble clef

Viper ['vipər] *f* (-;-n) viper

viril [vɪ'ril] *adj* virile

virtuos [vɪrtu'os] *adj* masterly ‖ **Virtuose** [vɪrtu'ozə] *m* (-;-n), **Virtuosin** [vɪrtu'ozɪn] *f* (-;-nen) virtuoso

Vi-rus ['virus] *n* (-;-ren [rən]) virus

Visage [vɪ'zaʒə] *f* (-;-n) (coll) mug

Visier [vɪ'zir] *n* (-s;-e) visor; (*am Gewehr*) sight

visieren [vɪ'zirən] *tr* (*eichen*) gauge; (*Paß*) visa

Vision [vɪ'zjon] *f* (-;-en) vision

visionär [vɪzjo'ner] *adj* visionary ‖ **Visionär** *m* (-s;-e) visionary

Visitation [vɪzɪta'tsjon] *f* (-;-en) inspection; search

Visite [vɪ'zitə] *f* (-;-n) formal call; **Visiten machen** (med) make the rounds

Visi'tenkarte *f* calling card

visuell [vɪzu'el] *adj* visual

Vi-sum ['vizum] *n* (-s;-sa [za]) visa

vital [vɪ'tal] *adj* energetic

Vitalität [vɪtalɪ'tet] *f* (-;) vitality

Vitamin [vɪta'min] *n* (-s;-e) vitamin

Vitamin'mangel *m* vitamin deficiency

Vitrine [vɪ'trinə] *f* (-;-n) showcase

Vize- [fitsə-], [vitsə] *comb.fm.* vice-

Vi'zekönig *m* viceroy

Vlies [flis] *n* (-es;-e) fleece

Vogel ['fogəl] *m* (-s;⸚) bird; (coll) chap, bird; **den V. abschießen** (coll) bring down the house; **du hast e-n V.!** (coll) you're cuckoo!

Vo'gelbauer *n* birdcage

Vogelbeerbaum ['fogəlberbaum] *m* mountain ash

vo'gelfrei *adj* outlawed

Vo'gelfutter *n* birdseed

Vo'gelkunde *f* ornithology

Vo'gelmist *m* bird droppings

vögeln ['føgəln] *tr & intr* (vulg) screw

Vo'gelperspektive *f,* **Vo'gelschau** *f* bird's-eye view

Vo'gelpfeife *f* bird call

Vo'gelscheuche *f* scarecrow

Vo'gelstange *f* perch

Vogel-Strauß'-Politik *f* burying one's head in the sand; **V. betreiben** bury one's head in the sand

Vo'gelstrich *m,* **Vo'gelzug** *m* migration of birds

Vöglein ['føglaɪn] *n* (-s;-) little bird

Vogt [fokt] *m* (-[e]s;⸚e) (obs) steward; (obs) governor, prefect, magistrate

Vokabel [vo'kabəl] *f* (-;-n) vocabulary word

Vokal [vo'kal] *m* (-s;-e) vowel

Volk [fɔlk] *n* (-[e]s;⸚er) people, nation; lower classes; (von Bienen) swarm; (von Rebhühnern) covey

Völker- [fœlkər] *comb.fm.* international

Völ'kerbund *m* League of Nations

Völ'kerfriede *m* international peace

Völ'kerkunde *f* ethnology

Völ'kermord *m* genocide

Völ'kerrecht *n* international law

Völ'kerschaft *f* (-;-en) tribe

Völ'kerwanderung *f* barbarian invasions

volk'reich *adj* populous

Volks'abstimmung *f* plebiscite

Volks'aufwiegler *m* rabble rouser

Volks'ausdruck *m* household expression

Volks'befragung *f* public opinion poll

Volks'begehren *n* national referendum

Volks'bibliothek *f* free library

Volks'charakter *m* national character

Volks'deutsche §5 *mf* German national

Volks'dichter *m* popular poet

volks'eigen *adj* state-owned

Volks'entscheid *m* referendum

Volks'feind *m* public enemy

Volks'gunst *f* popularity

Volks'haufen *m* crowd, mob

Volks'herrschaft *f* democracy

Volks'hochschule *f* adult evening school

Volks'justiz *f* lynch law

Volks'küche f soup kitchen
Volks'kunde f folklore
Volks'lied n folksong
volks'mäßig adj popular
Volks'meinung f popular opinion
Volks'menge f populace, crowd of people
Volks'musik f popular music
Volks'partei f people's party
Volks'republik f people's republic
Volks'schule f grade school
Volks'sitte f national custom
Volks'sprache f vernacular
Volks'stamm m tribe; race
Volks'stimme f popular opinion
Volks'stimmung f mood of the people
Volks'tracht f national costume
Volkstum ['fɔlkstum] n (-s;) nationality
volkstümlich ['fɔlkstymlɪç] adj national; popular
Volks'verführer –in §6 mf demagogue
Volks'versammlung f public meeting
Volks'vertreter –in §6 mf representative
Volks'wirt m political economist
Volks'wirtschaft f national economy
Volks'wirtschaftslehre f (educ) political economy
Volks'wohl n public good
Volks'wohlfahrt f public welfare
Volks'zählung f census
voll [fɔl] adj full, filled; whole, entire; (Tageslicht) broad; (coll) drunk; **aus dem vollen schöpfen** have unlimited resources; **j–n für v. ansehen** (or **nehmen**) take s.o. seriously || adv fully, in full; **v. und ganz** fully
vollauf' adv—**das genügt v.** that's quite enough; **v. beschäftigt** plenty busy; **v. zu tun haben** have plenty to do
Voll'beschäftigung f full employment
Voll'besitz m full possession
Voll'blut n, **Voll'blutpferd** n thoroughbred
vollblütig ['fɔlblytɪç] adj full-blooded
vollbrin'gen §65 tr achieve
vollbusig ['vɔlbuzɪç] adj big-breasted
Voll'dampf m full steam; **mit V.** (fig) at full blast, full speed
vollenden [fɔl'ɛndən] tr bring to a close, finish, complete; (vervollkommnen) perfect; **er hat sein Leben vollendet** (poet) he died
vollendet [fɔl'ɛndət] adj perfect
vollends ['fɔlents] adv completely
Vollen'dung f (-;) finishing, completing; (Vollkommenheit) perfection
Völlerei [fœlə'raɪ] f (-;) gluttony
voll'führen tr carry out, execute
voll'füllen tr fill up
Voll'gas n full throttle
Voll'gefühl n—**im V.** (genit) fully conscious of
Voll'genuß m full enjoyment
vollgepfropft ['fɔlgəpfrɔpft] adj jammed, packed
voll'gießen §76 tr fill up
völlig ['fœlɪç] adj full, complete
voll'jährig adj of age
Voll'jährigkeit f legal age, majority
vollkom'men, voll'kommen adj perfect || adv (coll) absolutely

Vollkom'menheit f (-;) perfection
Voll'kornbrot n whole-grain bread
Voll'kraft f full vigor, prime
voll'machen tr fill up; (coll) dirty
Voll'macht f full authority; (jur) power of attorney; **in V. for...** (prefixed to the signature of another at end of letter)
Voll'matrose m able-bodied seaman
Voll'milch f whole milk
Voll'mond m full moon
Voll'pension f full board and lodging
voll'saftig adj juicy, succulent
voll'schenken tr fill up
voll'schlagen §132 ref—**sich** [dat] **den Bauch v.** (coll) stuff oneself
voll'schlank adj well filled out
Voll'sitzung f plenary session
Voll'spur f (rr) standard-gauge track
voll'ständig adj full; complete, entire || adv completely, quite
Voll'ständigkeit f (-;) completeness
voll'stopfen tr stuff, cram
vollstrecken (vollstrek'ken) tr (Urteil) carry out; (Testament) execute; **ein Todesurteil an j–m v.** execute s.o.
Vollstreckung (Vollstrek'kung) f. (-;) execution
voll'tanken tr (aut) fill up || intr (aut) fill it up
volltönend ['fɔltønənt] adj (Stimme) rich; (Satz) well-rounded
Voll'treffer m direct hit
Voll'versammlung f plenary session
Voll'waise f (full) orphan
voll'wertig adj of full value; complete, perfect
vollzählig ['fɔltselɪç] adj complete; **sind wir v.?** are we all here? || adv in full force
vollzie'hen §163 tr execute, carry out, effect; (Vertrag) ratify; (Ehe) consummate || ref take place
vollzie'hend adj executive
Vollzie'hung f, **Vollzug'** m execution, carrying out
Vollzugs'ausschuß m executive committee
Volontär –in [vɔlɔn'tɛr(ɪn)] §8 mf volunteer; trainee
volontieren [vɔlɔn'tirən] intr work as a trainee
Volt [vɔlt] n (-[e]s;-) (elec) volt
Volu·men [vo'lumən] n (-s;- & -mina [mina]) (Band; Rauminhalt) volume
vom [fɔm] abbr **von dem**
von [fɔn] prep (dat) (beim Passiv) by; **für den Genitiv** of; (räumlich, zeitlich) from; (über) about, of; **von...an** from...on; **von Holz** (made) of wood; **von Kindheit auf** from earliest childhood; **von mir aus** as far as I am concerned; **von selbst** automatically
voneinan'der adv from each other; of each other; apart
vonnöten [fɔn'nøtən] invar adj—**v. sein** be necessary
vonstatten [fɔn'tatən] adv—**gut v. gehen** go well; **v. gehen** take place
vor [for] prep (dat) (örtlich) in front of, before; (zeitlich) before, prior to; (Abwehr) against, from; (wegen) of,

with, for; **etw vor sich haben** face s.th.; **heute vor acht Tagen** today a week ago; **vor sich gehen** take place, occur; **vor sich hin** to oneself ‖ *prep* (*acc*) in front of

vorab′ *adv* in advance

Vor′abend *m*—**am V.** (*genit*) on the eve of

Vor′ahnung *f* (coll) hunch, idea

voran′ *adv* in front, out ahead ‖ *interj* go ahead!, go on!

voran′gehen §82 *intr* (SEIN) go on ahead, take the lead; (fig) set an example; **die Arbeit geht gut voran** the work is coming along well

voran′kommen §99 *intr* (SEIN) make progress; **gut v.** come along well

Vor′anschlag *m* rough estimate

Vor′anzeige *f* preliminary announcement; (cin) preview of coming attractions

Vor′arbeit *f* preliminary work

vor′arbeiten *intr* do the work in advance; do the preliminary work

vorauf′ *adv* ahead, in front

voraus′ *adv* in front; (*dat*) ahead (of) ‖ **vor′aus** *adv*—**im v.** in advance

Voraus′abteilung *f* (mil) vanguard

voraus′bedingen §142 *tr* stipulate beforehand

voraus′bestellen *tr* reserve

voraus′bestimmen *tr* predetermine

voraus′bezahlen *tr* pay in advance

voraus′eilen *intr* (SEIN) rush ahead

vorausgesetzt [fɔˈrausɡəzɛtst] *adj*—**v., daß** provided that

Voraus′sage *f* prediction; prophecy; (*des Wetters*) forecast; (*Wink*) tip

voraus′sagen *tr* predict; prophesy; (*Wetter*) forecast

Voraus′sagung *f* var of Voraussage

voraus′schauen *intr* look ahead

voraus′schicken *tr* send ahead; (fig) mention beforehand

voraus′sehen §138 *tr* foresee

voraus′setzen *tr* presume, presuppose

Voraus′setzung *f* assumption; prerequisite; premise

Voraus′sicht *f* foresight

voraus′sichtlich *adj* probable, presumable ‖ *adv* probably, presumably, the way it looks

Voraus′zahlung *f* advance payment

Vor′bau *m* (-[e]s;-ten) projection; balcony, porch

vor′bauen *tr* build out ‖ *intr* (*dat*) take precautions against

vor′bedacht *adj* premeditated ‖ **Vorbedacht** *m* (-[e]s;)—**mit V.** on purpose; **ohne V.** unintentionally

vor′bedeuten *tr* forebode

Vor′bedeutung *f* (-;-en) foreboding, omen, portent

Vor′bedingung *f* (-;-en) precondition

Vorbehalt [ˈforbəhalt] *m* (-[e]s;-e) reservation; proviso; **mit allem V. hinnehmen!** take it for what it's worth!; **mit** (*or* **unter**) **dem V., daß** with the proviso that; **stiller** (*or* **innerer**) **V.** mental reservation; **unter V. aller Rechte** all rights reserved

vor′behalten §90 *tr* reserve; **Änderungen v.!** subject to change without

notice ‖ *ref*—**sich** [*dat*] **etw v.** reserve s.th. for oneself

vor′behaltlich *prep* (*genit*) subject to

vor′behaltlos *adj* unreserved, unconditional

vorbei′ *adv* over, past, gone; **es ist drei Uhr v.** it's past three o'clock; **v. an** (*dat*) past, by; **v. ist v.** done is done; **v. können** be able to pass

vorbei′eilen *intr* (SEIN)—**an j-m v.** rush past s.o.

vorbei′fahren §71 *intr* (SEIN) drive by

vorbei′fliegen §57 *intr* (SEIN) fly past

vorbei′fließen §76 *intr* (SEIN) flow by

vorbei′gehen §82 *intr* (SEIN) pass; **an j-m v.** pass by s.o. ‖ **Vorbeigehen** *n*—**im V.** in passing

vorbei′gelingen §142 *intr* (SEIN) fail

vorbei′kommen §99 *intr* (SEIN) pass by; (coll) stop in

vorbei′lassen §104 *tr* let pass

Vorbei′marsch *m* parade

vorbei′marschieren *intr* (SEIN) march by

Vor′bemerkung *f* (-;-en) preliminary remark; (parl) preamble

vorbenannt [ˈforbənant] *adj* aforementioned

vor′bereiten *tr* prepare ‖ *ref* (**auf** *acc*, **für**) get ready (for)

vor′bereitend *adj* preparatory

Vor′bereitung *f* (-;-en) preparation

Vor′bericht *m* preliminary report

Vor′besprechung *f* (-;-en) preliminary discussion

vor′bestellen *tr* order in advance; (*Zimmer, usw.*) reserve

Vor′bestellung *f* (-;-en) advance order; reservation

vor′bestraft *adj* previously convicted

vor′beten *tr* keep repeating ‖ *intr* lead in prayer

vor′beugen *ref* bend forward ‖ *intr* (*dat*) prevent

vor′beugend *adj* preventive

Vor′beugung *f* (-;-en) prevention

Vor′beugungsmittel *n* preventive

Vor′bild *n* model; (*Beispiel*) example

vor′bildlich *adj* exemplary, model

Vor′bildung *f* (-;-en) educational background

Vor′bote *m* forerunner; (fig) harbinger

vor′bringen §65 *tr* bring forward, produce; (*Gründe*) give; (*Plan*) propose; (*Klagen*) prefer; (*Wunsch*) express

vor′buchstabieren *tr* spell out

Vor′bühne *f* apron, proscenium

vor′datieren *tr* antedate

vordem [forˈdem] *adv* formerly

Vorder- [fordər] *comb.fm.* front, fore-

Vor′derachse *f* front axle

Vor′derarm *m* forearm

Vor′derbein *n* foreleg

vordere [ˈfordərə] §9 *adj* front

Vor′derfront *f* front; (fig) forefront

Vor′derfuß *m* front foot

Vor′dergrund *m* foreground

vor′derhand *adv* for the time being

vor′derlastig *adj* (aer) nose-heavy

Vor′derlauf *m* (hunt) foreleg

Vor′dermann *m* (-[e]s;-er) man in front; **j-n auf V. bringen** (coll) put s.o. straight; **V. halten** keep in line

Vor′derpfote f front paw
Vor′derrad n front wheel
Vor′derradantrieb m front-wheel drive
Vor′derreihe f front row; front rank
Vor′dersicht f front view
Vor′derseite f front side, front; (e–r Münze) obverse, heads
Vor′dersitz m front seat
vorderste [′fɔrdərstə] §9 adj farthest front
Vor′dersteven m (naut) stem
Vor′derteil m & n front section; (naut) prow
Vor′dertür f front door
Vor′derzahn m front tooth
Vor′derzimmer n front room
vor′drängen tr & ref press forward
vor′dringen §142 intr (SEIN) forge ahead, advance
vor′dringlich adj urgent
Vor′druck m printed form, blank
vor′ehelich adj premarital
vor′eilig adj hasty, rash
Vor′eiligkeit f (–;) haste, rashness
vor′eingenommen adj biased, prejudiced
Vor′eingenommenheit f (–;-en) bias, prejudice
vor′eltern pl ancestors, forefathers
vor′enthalten §90 tr—j–m etw v. withhold s.th. from s.o.
Vor′entscheidung f (–;-en) preliminary decision
vor′erst adv first of all; for the time being, for the present
vorerwähnt [′forervent] adj aforesaid
Vorfahr [′forfɑr] m (–en;-en) forebear
vor′fahren §71 intr (SEIN) (bei) drive up (to)
Vor′fahrt f, **Vor′fahrt(s)recht** n right of way
Vor′fall m incident; event
vor′fallen §72 intr (SEIN) happen
Vor′feld n (aer) apron (of airport); (mil) approaches
Vor′finden §59 tr find there
Vor′freude f anticipation
Vor′frühling m early spring
vor′fühlen intr—bei j–m v. feel s.o. out, put out feelers to s.o.
Vorführdame [′forfyrdɑmə] f mannequin
vor′führen tr bring forward, produce; display, demonstrate; (Kleider) model; (Film) show; (Stück) (theat) present
Vor′führer –in §6 mf projectionist
Vor′führung f (–;-en) production; demonstration; showing; show, performance
Vor′gabe f points, handicap
Vor′gaberennen n handicap (race)
Vor′gabespiel n handicap
Vor′gang m event, incident, phenomenon; (Verfahren) process, procedure; (Präzedenzfall) precedent; (in den Akten) previous correspondence
Vor′gänger –in §6 mf predecessor
Vor′garten m front yard
vor′geben §80 tr pretend; give as an excuse; j–m zehn Punkte v. give s.o. ten points odds ‖ intr—j–m v. give

s.o. odds ‖ **Vorgeben** n (–s;–) pretext
Vor′gebirge n foothills; (Kap) cape
vorgeblich [′forgeplɪç] adj ostensible
vorgefaßt [′forgəfast] adj preconceived
Vor′gefühl n inkling; banges V. misgivings; **im V. von** or genit in anticipation of
vor′gehen §82 intr (SEIN) advance; go first; act; take action, proceed; (sich ereignen) go on, happen; (Uhr) be fast; (dat) take precedence (over); die Arbeit geht vor work comes first; was geht hier vor? what's going on here? ‖ **Vorgehen** n (–s;) advance; action, proceeding; gemeinschaftliches V. concerted action
vorgelagert [′forgəlɑgərt] adj offshore
Vor′gelände n foreground
vorgenannt [′forgənant] adj aforementioned
Vor′gericht n appetizer
Vor′geschichte f previous history; (Urgeschichte) prehistory
vor′geschichtlich adj prehistoric
Vor′geschmack m foretaste
Vorgesetzte [′forgəzetstə] §5 mf superior; boss; (mil) senior officer
vor′gestern adv day before yesterday
vor′gestrig adj of the day before yesterday
vorgetäuscht [′forgətɔɪʃt] adj make-believe
vor′greifen §88 intr (dat) anticipate
Vor′griff m anticipation
vor′gucken intr (Unterkleid) show
vor′haben §89 tr have in mind, plan; intend to do; (ausfragen) question; (schelten) scold; (Schürze) (coll) have on ‖ **Vorhaben** n (–s;–) intention, plan; project
Vor′halle f entrance hall; lobby
vor′halten §90 tr—j–m etw v. hold s.th. in front of s.o.; (fig) reproach s.o. with s.th. ‖ intr last
Vor′haltung f (–;-en) reproach; j–m Vorhaltungen machen über (acc) reproach s.o. for
Vor′hand f (cards) forehand; (tennis) forehand stroke; die V. haben (cards) lead off
vorhanden [for′handən] adj present, at hand, available; (com) in stock; v. sein exist
Vorhan′densein n existence; presence
Vor′hang m (–[e]s;⸗e) curtain; (theat) (coll) curtain call; Eiserner V. iron curtain
Vorhängeschloß [′forhɛŋəʃlos] n padlock
Vor′hangstange f curtain rod
Vor′hangstoff m drapery material
Vor′haut f foreskin
Vor′hemd n dicky, shirt front
vor′her adv before, previously; (im voraus) in advance
vorher′bestellen tr reserve
vorher′bestimmen tr predetermine; (eccl) predestine
Vorher′bestimmung f predestination
vorher′gehend, vorherig [for′herɪç] adj preceding, previous; prior
Vor′herrschaft f predominance

vor'herrschen *intr* predominate, prevail

vor'herrschend *adj* predominant, prevailing

Vorher'sage *f* prediction; forecast

vorher'sagen *tr* predict, foretell; (*Wetter*) forecast

vorhin' *adv* a little while ago

vor'historisch *adj* prehistoric

Vor'hof *m* front yard; (anat) auricle

Vor'hut *f* (mil) vanguard

vorige ['forɪgə] §9 *adj* previous, former; **voriges Jahr** last year

Vor'jahr *n* preceding year

vor'jährig *adj* last year's

Vor'kammer *f* (anat) auricle; (aut) precombustion chamber

Vor'kampf *m* (box) preliminary bout; (sport) heat

Vor'kämpfer –in §6 *mf* pioneer

Vorkehrung ['forkeruŋ] *f* (–;-en) precaution; **Vorkehrungen treffen** take precautions

Vor'kenntnis *f* (von) basic knowledge (of); **Vorkenntnisse** rudiments, basics; **Vorkenntnisse nicht erforderlich** no previous experience necessary

vor'knöpfen *ref*—**sich** [*dat*] **j-n** v. (coll) chew s.o. out

Vor'kommando *n* (mil) advance party

vor'kommen §99 *intr* (SEIN) happen; (*Fall*) come up; (*als Besucher*) be admitted; (*scheinen*) seem, look; (*sich finden*) be found; (*zu Besuch*) call on || *ref*—**er kam sich** [*dat*] **dumm vor** he felt silly || *impers*—**es kommt dir nur so vor** you are just imagining it; **es kommt mir vor it** seems to me || **Vorkommen** *n* (–s;–) occurrence; (min) deposit

Vorkommnis ['forkɔmnɪs] *n* (–ses;–se) event, occurrence

Vorkriegs— *comb.fm.* prewar

vor'laden §103 *tr* (jur) summon; (*unter Strafandrohung*) (jur) subpoena

Vor'ladung *f* (–;-en) (jur) summons; (*unter Strafandrohung*) (jur) subpoena

Vor'lage *f* submission, presentation; proposal; (*Muster*) pattern; bedside carpet; (fb) forward pass; (parl) bill

vor'lassen §104 *tr* let go ahead; (*Auto*) let pass; (*zulassen*) admit

Vor'lauf *m* (sport) qualifying heat

Vor'läufer –in §6 *mf* forerunner

vor'läufig *adj* preliminary; temporary || *adv* provisionally; temporarily, for the time being

vor'laut *adj* forward, fresh

Vor'leben *n* past life, former life

Vorlegebesteck ['forlegəbəʃtɛk] *n* carving set

Vorlegegabel ['forlegəgabəl] *f* carving fork

Vorlegelöffel ['forlegəlœfəl] *m* serving spoon

Vorlegemesser ['forlegəmesər] *n* carving knife

vor'legen *tr* put forward; propose; (*Ausweis, Paß*) show; (*Essen*) serve; (*zur Prüfung, usw.*) submit, present; **den Ball v.** (fb) pass the ball; **ein scharfes Tempo v.** (coll) speed it up;

j-m e-e Frage v. ask s.o. a question || *ref* lean forward

Ver'leger *m* (–s;–) throw rug

Vorlegeschloß ['forlegəʃlɔs] *n* padlock

vor'lesen §107 *tr*—**j-m etw v.** read s.th. to s.o.

Vor'lesung *f* (–;-en) reading; lecture; **e-e V. halten über** (*acc*) give a lecture on

Vor'lesungsverzeichnis *n* university catalogue

vor'letzte §9 *adj* second last; (gram) penultimate

Vor'liebe *f* preference

vorliebnehmen [for'lipneman] §116 *intr* take pot luck; **v. mit** put up with

vor'liegen §108 *intr* be present; exist; be under consideration; **dem Richter v.** be up before the judge; **heute liegt nichts vor** there's nothing doing today; **mir liegt e-e Beschwerde vor** I have a complaint here; **was liegt gegen ihn vor?** what is the charge against him?

vor'liegend *adj* present, at hand

vor'lügen §111 *tr*—**j-m etw v. über** (*acc*) tell s.o. lies about

vor'machen *tr*—**du kannst mir doch nichts v.** you can't put anything over on me; **j-m etw v.** show s.o. how to do s.th. || *ref*—**er läßt sich** [*dat*] **nichts v.** he's nobody's fool; **sich** [*dat*] **selbst etw v.** fool oneself

Vor'macht *f* leading power; supremacy

Vor'machtstellung *f* (position of) supremacy

vormalig ['formalɪç] *adj* former

vormals ['formals] *adv* formerly

Vor'marsch *m* advance

vor'merken *tr* note down; reserve; **sich v. lassen für** put in for

Vor'mittag *m* forenoon, morning

vor'mittags *adv* in the forenoon

Vor'mund *m* guardian

Vor'mundschaft *f* (–;-en) guardianship

vor'mundschaftlich *adj* guardian's

Vor'mundschaftsgericht *n* orphans' court

vorn [forn] *adv* in front; ahead; **ganz v.** all the way up front; **nach v.** forward; **nach v. heraus wohnen** live in the front part of the house; **nach v. liegen** face the front; **von v.** from the front; **von v. anfangen** begin at the beginning

Vor'nahme *f* undertaking

Vor'name *m* first name

vorne ['fornə] *adv* (coll) var of **vorn**

vornehm ['fornem] *adj* distinguished, high-class; **vornehme Welt** high society; **vornehmste Aufgabe** principal task || *adv*—**v. tun** put on airs

vor'nehmen §116 *tr* (*umbinden*) put on; undertake, take up; (*Änderungen*) make; **wieder v.** resume || *ref*—**sich** [*dat*] **ein Buch v.** take up a book; **sich** [*dat*] **etw v.** decide upon s.th.; **sich** [*dat*] **j-n v.** take s.o. to task; **sich** [*dat*] **v. zu** (*inf*) make up one's mind to (*inf*); **sich** [*dat*] **zuviel v.** bite off more than one can chew

vor'nehmheit *f* (–;) distinction, high rank; distinguished bearing

vor′nehmlich *adv* especially
vor′neigen *ref* bend forward
vorn′herein *adv*—**von v.** from the first
vornweg [ˈfɔrnvɛk], (fɔrnˈvɛk) *adv*—**er ist weit v.** he is way out in front; **mit dem Kopf v.** head first; **mit dem Mund v. sein** be fresh
Vor′ort *m* suburb
Vorort– *comb.fm.* suburban
Vor′ortbahn *f* (rr) suburban line
Vor′ortzug *m* commuter train
Vor′platz *m* front yard; (*Diele*) entrance hall; (*Vorfeld*) (aer) apron
Vor′posten *m* (mil) outpost
Vor′rang *m* precedence; priority; preeminence; **den V. vor j–m haben** have precedence over s.o.
Vor′rat *m* (–[e]s;–̈e) (**an** *dat*) stock (of), supply (of); **auf V. kaufen** buy in quantity; **e–n V. anlegen an** (*dat*) stock
vorrätig [ˈfɔrretɪç] *adj* in stock
Vor′ratskammer *f* pantry, storeroom
Vor′ratsraum *m* storeroom
Vor′ratsschrank *m* pantry
Vor′raum *m* anteroom
vor′rechnen *tr*—**j–m etw v.** figure out s.th. for s.o.; **j–m seine Fehler v.** enumerate s.o.'s mistakes to s.o.
Vor′recht *n* privilege, prerogative
Vor′rede *f* preface, introduction
vor′reden *tr*—**j–m etw v.** try to make s.o. believe s.th.
Vor′redner –in §6 *mf* previous speaker
Vor′richtung *f* (–;–en) preparation; (*Gerät*) device, appliance, mechanism; (mach) fixture
vor′rücken *tr* move forward ‖ *intr* (SEIN) (*Truppen*) advance; (*Polizei*) move in; (*im Dienst*) be promoted
Vor′runde *f* (sport) play-offs
vors [fɔrs] *abbr* **vor das**
vor′sagen *tr*—**j–m etw v.** recite s.th. to s.o. ‖ *intr* (aut) prompt
Vor′sager –in §6 *mf* prompter
Vor′satz *m* purpose, intention; (jur) premeditation; **den V. fassen zu** (*inf*) make up one's mind to (*inf*); **mit V. on** purpose; **seinen V. ausführen** gain one's ends
Vor′satzblatt *n* (bb) end paper
Vor′satzgerät *n* adapter
vorsätzlich [ˈfɔrzɛtslɪç] *adj* deliberate; (*Mord*) premeditated
Vor′schau *f* (cin) preview
vor′schieben §130 *tr* push forward; offer as an excuse; (fig) plead; **den Riegel v.** (*dat*) (fig) prevent; **Truppen v.** move troops forward
vor′schießen §76 *tr* (*Geld*) (coll) advance ‖ *intr* (SEIN) dart ahead
Vor′schiff *n* (naut) forecastle
Vor′schlag *m* proposal; (*Angebot*) offer; (*Anregung*) suggestion; (*Empfehlung*) recommendation; (mus) grace note; (parl) motion; **in V. bringen** propose; (parl) move
vor′schlagen §132 *tr* propose; suggest; recommend; **zur Wahl v.** nominate
Vor′schlagsliste *f* slate of candidates
Vor′schlußrunde *f* (sport) semifinal
vor′schnell *adj* rash, hasty
vor′schreiben §62 *tr* prescribe, order;

specify; write out; **ich lasse mir nichts v.** I take orders from no one
vor′schreiten §86 *intr* (SEIN) step forward; advance
Vor′schrift *f* order, direction; regulation; (med) prescription
vor′schriftmäßig *adj* & *adv* according to regulations
vor′schriftswidrig *adj* & *adv* against regulations
Vor′schub *m* assistance; (mach) feed; **V. leisten** (*dat*) encourage; (jur) aid and abet
Vor′schule *f* prep school; (*Elementarschule*) elementary school
Vor′schuß *m* (*Geld*–) advance; (jur) retainer
vor′schützen *tr* pretend, plead
Vor′schützung *f* (–;) pretense
vor′schweben *intr*—**mir schwebte etw anderes vor** I had s.th. else in mind; **das schwebt mir dunkel vor** I have a dim recollection of it
vor′schwindeln *tr*—**j–m etw v.** fool s.o. about s.th.
vor′sehen §138 *tr* schedule, plan; provide; (fin) earmark; **das Gesetz sieht vor, daß** the law provides that ‖ *ref* be careful, take care; **sich mit etw v.** provide oneself with s.th.; **sich v. vor** (*dat*) be on one's guard against
Vor′sehung *f* (–;) Providence
vor′setzen *tr* put forward; (*Silbe*) prefix; **j–m etw v.** set s.th. before s.o. (*to eat*); **j–n v.** set s.o. over s.o.
Vor′sicht *f* caution, care; (*Umsicht*) prudence; **V.!** watch out! (*auf Kisten*) handle with care!; **V., Stufe!** watch your step!
vor′sichtig *adj* cautious, careful
Vor′sichtigkeit *f* (–;) caution
vorsichtshalber [ˈfɔrzɪçtshalbər] *adv* to be on the safe side, as a precaution
Vor′sichtsmaßnahme *f*, **Vor′sichtsmaßregel** *f* precaution
Vor′silbe *f* prefix
vor′singen §142 *tr*—**j–m etw v.** sing s.th. to s.o. ‖ *intr* lead the choir
Vor′sitz *m* chairmanship, chair; presidency; **den V. haben** (or **führen**) **bei** preside over; **unter V. von** presided over by
Vorsitzende [ˈfɔrzɪtsəndə] §5 *mf* chairperson; president
Vor′sorge *f* provision; **V. tragen** (or **treffen**) **für** make provision for, provide for
vor′sorgen *intr* (**für**) provide (for)
vorsorglich [ˈfɔrzɔrklɪç] *adv* as a precaution, just in case
Vor′spann *m* (cin) credits; (*Kurzfilm*) (cin) short
Vor′speise *f* appetizer
vor′spiegeln *tr*—**j–m etw v.** delude s.o. with s.th.; **j–m falsche Tatsachen v.** misrepresent facts to s.o.
Vor′spiegelung *f* (–;) sham; pretense; **V. falscher Tatsachen** misrepresentation of facts
Vor′spiel *n* prelude; (*beim Geschlechtsverkehr*) foreplay; (mus) overture; (theat) curtain raiser; **das**

war nur das V.! (fig) that was only the beginning!

vor'spielen tr—j-m etw v. play s.th. for s.o.

vor'sprechen §64 tr—j-m etw v. pronounce s.th. for s.o.; teach s.o. how to pronounce s.th. || intr—bei j-m v. drop in on s.o.; j-m v. audition before s.o.

vor'springen §142 intr (SEIN) leap forward; (aus dem Versteck) jump out; (vorstehen) stick out, protrude

Vor'sprung m projection; (Sims) ledge; (Vorteil) advantage; (sport) head start; (sport) lead

Vor'stadt f suburb

vor'städtisch adj suburban

Vor'stand m board of directors; executive committee, executive board; (Person) chairman of the board

vor'stehen §146 intr protrude; (dat) be at the head of, direct, manage

Vor'steher m (-s;-) head, director, manager; (educ) principal

Vor'steherdrüse f prostate gland

Vor'steherin f (-;-nen) head, director, manager; (educ) principal

vor'stellen tr place in front, put ahead; (Uhr) set ahead; (einführen) introduce, present; (darstellen) represent; (bedeuten) mean; (hinweisen auf) point out || ref—sich [dat] etw v. imagine s.th., picture s.th.

Vor'stellung f (-;-en) introduction, presentation; (Begriff) idea; (Einspruch) remonstrance, protest; (cin) show; (theat) performance

Vor'stellungsvermögen n imagination

Vor'stoß m (fig & mil) thrust, drive

vor'stoßen §150 tr push forward || intr (SEIN) push forward, advance

Vor'strafe f previous conviction

Vor'strafenregister n previous record

vor'strecken tr stretch out; (Geld) advance

Vor'stufe f preliminary stage

Vor'tag m previous day

vor'täuschen tr pretend, put on

Vor'teil m advantage; profit; (tennis) advantage

vor'teilhaft adj advantageous, profitable

Vortrag ['fortrak] m (-[e]s;⸚e) performance; (Bericht) report; (e-s Gedichtes) recitation; (e-r Rede) delivery; (Vorlesung) lecture; (acct) balance (carried over); (mus) recital; **e-n V. halten über** (acc) give a lecture on

vor'tragen §132 tr perform; present

Vortragende ['fortragəndə] §5 mf performer; speaker; lecturer

Vor'tragsfolge f program

vortrefflich ['fortreflıç] adj excellent

vor'treten §152 intr (SEIN) step forward; (fig) stick out, protrude

Vor'tritt m (-[e]s;) precedence

vorü'ber adv past, by, along; (zeitlich) over, gone by

vorü'bergehen §82 intr (SEIN) pass; (an dat) pass by; (fig) disregard

vorü'bergehend adj passing, transitory || **Vorübergehende** §5 mf passer-by

vorü'berziehen §163 intr (SEIN) march by; (Gewitter) blow over

Vor'übung f warmup

Vor'untersuchung f preliminary investigation

Vor'urteil n prejudice

vor'urteilsfrei, vor'urteilslos adj unprejudiced

Vor'vergangenheit f (gram) past perfect

Vor'verkauf m advance sale; (theat) advance reservation

vor'verlegen tr advance, move up

Vor'wahl f (pol) primary

vor'wählen intr dial the area code

Vor'wählnummer f (telp) area code

Vor'wand m (-[e]s;⸚e) pretext; excuse

vorwärts ['forverts] adv forward, on, ahead || interj go on!

vor'wärtsbringen §65 tr bring forward; (fig) advance

vor'wärtsgehen §82 intr (SEIN) progress

vor'wärtskommen §99 intr (SEIN) go ahead; progress, make headway

vorweg [for'vek] adv beforehand; out in front

Vorweg'nahme f anticipation

vorweg'nehmen §116 tr anticipate; presuppose, assume

vor'weisen §118 tr produce, show

Vor'welt f prehistoric world

vor'weltlich adj primeval

vor'werfen §160 tr—j-m etw v. throw s.th. to s.o.; (fig) throw s.th. up to s.o.

vorwiegend ['forvigant] adj predominant || adv predominantly, chiefly

Vor'wissen n foreknowledge

vor'witzig adj inquisitive; brash

Vor'wort n (-[e]s;⸚e) foreword

Vor'wurf m reproach, blame; (e-s Dramas) subject; **j-m Vorwürfe machen** blame s.o.

vor'wurfslos adj irreproachable

vor'wurfsvoll adj reproachful

vor'zählen tr enumerate

Vor'zeichen n omen; (math) sign; (mus) accidental; **negatives V.** minus sign

vor'zeichnen tr—j-m etw v. draw or sketch s.th. for s.o.

Vor'zeichnung f (-;-en) drawing; (mus) signature

vor'zeigen tr produce, show; (Wechsel) present

Vor'zeiger -in §6 mf bearer

Vor'zeigung f (-;-en) producing, showing; presentation

Vor'zeit f remote antiquity

vor'zeiten adv in days of old

vor'zeitig adj premature

vor'ziehen §163 tr draw forth; pull out; prefer; (mil) move up

Vor'zimmer n anteroom; entrance hall

Vor'zug m preference; (Vorteil) advantage; (Überlegenheit) superiority; (Vorrang) priority; (Vorrecht) privilege; (Vorzüglichkeit) excellence; **e-r Sache den V. geben** prefer s.th.

vorzüglich ['fortsyklıç] adj excellent, first-rate || adv especially

Vor'züglichkeit f (-;) excellence

Vor'zugsaktie f preferred stock

Vor'zugsbehandlung *f* preferential treatment
Vor'zugspreis *m* special price
Vor'zugsrecht *n* priority; privilege
vor'zugsweise *adv* preferably
votieren [vo'tirən] *intr* vote
Votiv- [votif] *comb.jm.* votive
Vo·tum ['votum] *n* (-s;-ten [tən] & -ta [ta]) vote

vulgär [vul'ger] *adj* vulgar
Vulkan [vul'kɑn] *m* (-s;-e) volcano
Vulkan'ausbruch *m* eruption
vulkanisch [vul'kɑnɪʃ] *adj* volcanic
vulkanisieren [vulkɑnɪ'zirən] *tr* vulcanize
Vulkan'schlot *m* volcanic vent
VW *abbr* (Volkswagen) VW
V-Waffe *f* (Vergeltungswaffe) V-1, V-2

W

W, w [ve] *invar n* W, w
Waage ['vɑgə] *f* (-;-n) (pair of) scales; (astr) Libra; (gym) horizontal position; **die beiden Dinge halten sich** [dat] **die W.** the two things balance each other; **die W. halten** (dat) counterbalance; **j-m die W. halten** be a match for s.o.
waa'gerecht, waagrecht ['vɑkreçt] *adj* horizontal, level
Waagschale ['vɑkʃɑlə] *f* scale(s); **in die W. fallen** carry weight; **in die W. werfen** bring to bear
wabbelig ['vabəlɪç] *adj* (coll) flabby
Wabe ['vɑbə] *f* (-;-n) honeycomb
wach [vax] *adj* awake; (lebhaft) lively; (Geist) alert; **ganz w.** wide awake
Wach'ablösung *f* changing of the guard
Wach'dienst *m* guard duty
Wache ['vaxə] *f* (-;-n) guard, watch; (Wachstube) guardroom; (Wachlokal) guardhouse; (Polizei-) police station; (Wachdienst) guard duty; (Posten) guard, sentinel; **auf W.** on guard; **auf W. ziehen** mount guard; **W. schieben** (coll) pull guard duty
wachen ['vaxən] *intr* be awake; **bei j-m w.** sit up with s.o.; **w. über** (acc) watch over, guard
wach'habend *adj* on guard duty
wach'halten §90 *tr* keep awake; (fig) keep alive
Wach'hund *m* watchdog
Wach'lokal *n* guardroom; police station
Wach'mann *m* (-[e]s;-leute) (Aust) policeman
Wach'mannschaft *f* (mil) guard detail
Wacholder [va'xɔldər] *m* (-s;-) juniper
Wachol'derbranntwein *m* gin
Wach'posten *m* sentry
wach'rufen §122 *tr* wake up; (Erinnerung) bring back
Wachs [vaks] *n* (-es;-e) wax
wachsam ['vaxzam] *adj* vigilant
Wach'samkeit *f* (-;) vigilance
Wachs'bohne *f* wax bean
wachsen ['vaksən] *tr* wax || §155 *intr* (SEIN) grow; (an dat) increase (in)
wächsern ['veksərn] *adj* wax; (fig) waxy
Wachs'figurenkabinett *n* wax museum
Wachs'kerze *f*, **Wachs'licht** *n* wax candle
Wachs'leinwand *f* oilcloth

Wach'stube *f* guardroom
Wachs'tuch *n* oilcloth
Wachstum ['vaxstum] *n* (-s;) growth; increase
Wacht [vaxt] *f* (-;-en) guard, watch
Wächte ['veçtə] *f* (-;-n) snow cornice
Wachtel ['vaxtəl] *f* (-;-n) quail
Wach'telhund *m* spaniel
Wächter ['veçtər] *m* (-s;-) guard
Wacht'meister *m* police sergeant
Wacht'traum *m* daydream
Wacht'turm *m* watchtower
wackelig ['vakəlıç] *adj* wobbly; (Zahn) loose; (fig) shaky
Wackelkontakt ['vakəlkɔntakt] *m* (elec) loose connection, poor contact
wackeln ['vakəln] *intr* wobble; shake; (locker sein) be loose
wacker ['vakər] *adj* decent, honest; (tapfer) brave || *adv* heartily
wacklig ['vaklıç] *adj* var of **wackelig**
Wade ['vɑdə] *f* (-;-n) (anat) calf
Wa'denbein *n* (anat) fibula
Wa'denkrampf *m* leg cramp
Wa'denstrumpf *m* calf-length stocking
Waffe ['vafə] *f* (-;-n) weapon; branch of service; **die Waffen strecken** surrender; (fig) give up; **zu den Waffen greifen** take up arms
Waffel ['vafəl] *f* (-;-n) waffle
Waf'fenbruder *m* comrade in arms
waf'fenfähig *adj* capable of bearing arms
Waf'fengang *m* armed conflict
Waf'fengattung *f* branch of service
Waf'fengewalt *f* force of arms
Waf'fenkammer *f* armory
Waf'fenlager *n* ordnance depot; **heimliches W.** cache of arms
waf'fenlos *adj* unarmed
Waf'fenruhe *f* truce
Waf'fenschein *m* gun permit
Waf'fenschmied *m* gunsmith
Waf'fenschmuggel *m* gunrunning
Waf'fen-SS *f* (-;) SS combat unit
Waf'fenstillstand *m* armistice
Wagehals ['vagəhals] *m* daredevil
Wagemut ['vagəmut] *m* daring
wagen ['vagən] *tr* dare; risk || *ref* venture, dare || **Wagen** *m* (-s;-) wagon; (Fahrzeug; Teil e-r Schreibmaschine) carriage; (aut, rr) car; **der Große Wagen** the Big Dipper; **j-m an den W. fahren** (fig) step on s.o.'s toes
wägen ['vegən] *tr* (& fig) weigh
Wa'genabteil *n* (rr) compartment

Wa'genburg f barricade of wagons

Wa'genheber m (aut) jack

Wa'genpark m fleet of cars

Wa'genpflege f (aut) maintenance

Wa'genschlag m car door, carriage door

Wa'genschmiere f (aut) grease

Wa'genspur f wheel track, rut

Wa'genwäsche f car wash

Wagestück ['vagə/tʏk] n hazardous venture, daring deed

Waggon [va'gõ] m (-s;-s) railroad car

waghalsig ['vakhalzɪç] adj foolhardy

Wagnis ['vak015] n (-ses;-se) risk

Wahl [val] f (-;-en) choice, option; (Auswahl) selection; (Alternative) alternative; (pol) election; e-e W. treffen make a choice; vor der W. stehen have the choice

wählbar ['velbar] adj eligible

Wähl'barkeit f (-;) eligibility

Wahl'beeinflussung f interference with the election process

wahl'berechtigt adj eligible to vote

Wahl'beteiligung f election turnout

Wahl'bezirk m ward

wählen ['velən] tr choose; select; (pol) elect; (telp) dial ‖ intr vote

Wäh'ler m (-s;-) voter

Wahl'ergebnis n election returns

Wäh'lerin f (-;-nen) voter

wählerisch ['verlərɪʃ] adj choosy, particular

Wäh'lerschaft f (-;-en) constituency

Wäh'lerscheibe f (telp) dial

Wahl'fach n (educ) elective

wahl'fähig adj eligible for election; having a vote

wahl'frei adj (educ) elective

Wahl'gang m ballot

Wahl'kampf m election campaign

Wahl'kreis m constituency; district

Wahl'leiter m campaign manager

Wahl'liste f (pol) slate, ticket

Wahl'lokal n polling place

Wahl'lokomotive f (coll) vote getter

wahl'los adj indiscriminate

Wahl'parole f campaign slogan

Wahl'programm n (pol) platform

Wahl'recht n right to vote, suffrage

Wahl'rede f campaign speech

Wahl'spruch m motto; (com, pol) slogan

Wahl'urne f ballot box

Wahl'versammlung f campaign rally

wahl'verwandt adj congenial

Wahl'zelle f voting booth

Wahl'zettel m ballot

Wahn [van] m (-[e]s;) delusion; error; folly; madness

Wahn'bild n phantom, delusion

wähnen ['venən] tr fancy, imagine

Wahn'idee f delusion; (coll) crazy idea

Wahn'sinn m (& fig) madness

wahn'sinnig adj (vor dat) mad (with); (coll) terrible ‖ adv madly; (coll) awfully ‖ Wahnsinnige §5 mf lunatic

Wahn'vorstellung f hallucination

Wahn'witz m (& fig) madness

wahn'witzig adj mad; (unverantwortlich) irresponsible

wahr [var] adj true; (wirklich) real; (echt) genuine; nicht w.? right?

wahren ['varən] tr keep; (Anschein) keep up; (vor dat) protect (against)

währen ['verən] intr last

während ['verənt] prep (genit) during; (jur) pending ‖ conj while; whereas

wahr'haben §89 tr admit

wahr'haft, wahr'haftig adj true, truthful; (wirklich) real ‖ adv actually

Wahr'haftigkeit f (-;) truthfulness

Wahr'heit f (-;-en) truth; j-m die W. sagen give s.o. a piece of one's mind

wahr'heitsgemäß, wahr'heitsgetreu adj true, faithful; truthful

Wahr'heitsliebe f truthfulness

wahr'heitsliebend adj truthful

wahr'lich adv truly; (Bib) verily

wahrnehmbar ['varnembar] adj noticeable

wahr'nehmen §116 tr notice; (benutzen) make use of; (Interesse) protect; (Recht) assert

Wahr'nehmung f (-;) observation, perception; (der Interessen) safeguarding

wahr'sagen ref—sich [dat] w. lassen have one's fortune told ‖ intr prophesy; tell fortunes

Wahr'sagerin f (-;-nen) fortuneteller

wahrscheinlich [var'ʃaɪnlɪç] adj probable, likely ‖ adv probably

Wahrschein'lichkeit f (-;) probability

Wahr'spruch m verdict

Wah'rung f (-;) safeguarding

Wäh'rung f (-;-en) currency; standard

Wäh'rungsabwertung f devaluation

Wäh'rungseinheit f monetary unit

Wahr'zeichen n landmark

Waise ['vaɪzə] f (-;-n) orphan

Wai'senhaus n orphanage

Wal [val] m (-[e]s;-e) whale

Wald [valt] m (-[e]s;ᵉ:er) forest, woods

Wald— comb.fm. forest; sylvan; wild

Wald'aufseher m forest ranger

Wald'brand m forest fire

waldig ['valdɪç] adj wooded

Waldung ['valduŋ] f (-;-en) forest

Wald'wirtschaft f forestry

Wal'fang m whaling

Wal'fänger m (-s;-) whaler

walken ['valkən] tr full

Wal'ker m (-s;-) fuller

Wall [val] m (-[e]s;ᵉ:e) mound; embankment; (mil) rampart

Wallach ['valax] m (-[e]s;-e) gelding

wallen ['valən] intr (sieden) boil; (sprudeln) bubble; (Gewand, Haar) flow, fall in waves ‖ intr (SEIN) go on a pilgrimage; travel, wander

wall'fahren insep intr (SEIN) go on a pilgrimage

Wall'fahrer —in §6 mf pilgrim

Wall'fahrt f pilgrimage

Wall'graben m moat

Wal'lung f (-;) simmering, boiling; bubbling; flow; flutter; (Blutandrang) congestion; in W. bringen enrage; in W. geraten fly into a rage; Wallungen hot flashes

Walnuß ['valnus] f walnut

Walroß ['valrɔs] n walrus

Wal'speck m blubber

walten ['valtən] intr rule; hold sway;

Gnade w. lassen show mercy; seines
Amtes w. attend to one's duties

Wal'tran *m* whale oil

Walze ['valtsə] *f* (-;-n) cylinder,
drum; roll, roller; (*der Schreibmaschine*) platen

walzen ['valtsən] *tr* roll

wälzen ['vɛltsən] *tr* roll; (*Bücher*) pore
over; (*Gedanken*) turn over in one's
mind; **die Schuld auf j-n w.** shift the
blame to s.o. else || *ref* roll, toss;
(*im Kot*) wallow; (*im Blut*) welter

Wal'zer *m* (-s;-) waltz

Wäl'zer *m* (-s;-) (coll) thick tome

Walz'werk *n* rolling mill

Wamme ['vamə] *f* (-;-n) dewlap;
(coll) potbelly

Wampe ['vampə] *f* (-;-n) (coll) potbelly

wand [vant] *pret* of **winden** || **Wand** *f*
(-;:-e) wall; partition; (*Fels*-) cliff;
spanische W. folding screen

Wand'apparat *m* (telp) wall phone

Wand'bekleidung *f* wainscot

Wandel ['vandəl] *m* (-s;) change

wandelbar ['vandəlbar] *adj* changeable

Wan'delgang *m*, **Wan'delhalle** *f* lobby

wandeln ['vandəln] *tr* change || *ref* (in
acc) change (into) || *intr* (SEIN)
(poet) wander; (poet) walk

Wan'derer -in §6 *mf* wanderer; hiker

Wan'derlust *f* wanderlust, itch to travel

wandern ['vandərn] *intr* (SEIN) wander; hike; (*Vögel*) migrate

Wan'derniere *f* floating kidney

Wan'derpreis *m* challenge trophy

Wan'derschaft *f* (-;) travels, wander-
ings

Wan'derstab *m* walking stick

Wan'derung *f* (-;-en) hike; migration

Wan'dervogel *m* migratory bird; (coll)
rover

Wand'gemälde *n* mural

Wand'karte *f* wall map

Wand'leuchter *m* sconce

Wand'lung *f* (-;-en) change, transformation; (eccl) consecration

Wand'malerei *f* wall painting

Wand'pfeiler *m* pilaster

Wand'schirm *m* folding screen

Wand'schrank *m* wall shelves

Wand'spiegel *m* wall mirror

Wand'steckdose *f*, **Wand'stecker** *m*
(elec) wall outlet

Wand'tafel *f* blackboard

wandte ['vantə] *pret* of **wenden**

Wand'teppich *m* tapestry

Wange ['vaŋə] *f* (-;-n) cheek

-wangig ['vaŋiç] *comb.fm.* -cheeked

Wan'kelmut *m* fickleness

wan'kelmütig *adj* fickle

wanken ['vaŋkən] *intr* stagger; sway,
rock; (fig) waver

wann [van] *adv* & *conj* when; **w. immer** anytime, whenever

Wanne ['vanə] *f* (-;-n) tub

Wanst [vanst] *m* (-es;:-e) belly,
paunch

-wanstig [vanstiç] *comb.fm.* -bellied

Wanze ['vantsə] *f* (-;-n) bedbug

Wappen ['vapən] *n* (-s;-) coat of
arms

Wap'penkunde *f* heraldry

Wap'penschild *m* escutcheon

wappnen ['vapnən] *ref* arm oneself;
sich mit Geduld w. have patience

war [vɑr] *pret* of **sein**

warb [varp] *pret* of **werben**

ward [vart] *pret* of **sein**

Ware ['vɑrə] *f* (-;-n) ware; article;
commodity; **Waren** goods, merchandise

-waren [vɑrən] *pl comb.fm.* -ware

Wa'renaufzug *m* freight elevator

Wa'renausgabe *f* wrapping department

Wa'renbestand *m* stock

Wa'renbörse *f* commodity market

Wa'renhaus *n* department store

Wa'renlager *n* warehouse; stockroom

Wa'renmarkt *m* commodity market

Wa'renmuster *n*, **Wa'renprobe** *f* sample

Wa'renrechnung *f* invoice

Wa'renzeichen *n* trademark

warf [varf] *pret* of **werfen**

warm [varm] *adj* (**wärmer** ['vɛrmər];
wärmste ['vɛrmstə] §9) warm

Warmblüter ['varmblytər] *m* (-s;-)
warm-blooded animal

warmblütig ['varmblytiç] *adj* warm-
blooded

Wärme ['vɛrmə] *f* (-;) warmth, heat

wär'mebeständig *adj* heatproof

Wär'meeinheit *f* thermal unit; calory

Wär'megrad *m* degree of heat, temperature

wärmen ['vɛrmən] *tr* warm, heat

Wär'meplatte *f*—**elektrische W.** hot-
plate

Wärm'flasche *f* hot-water bottle

warm'halten §90 *tr* keep warm

warm'herzig *adj* warm-hearted

warm'laufen §105 *intr*—**den Motor w.**
lassen let the motor warm up

Warmluft'heizung *f* hot-air heating

Warmwas'serbehälter *m* hot-water tank

Warmwas'serheizung *f* hot-water heating

Warmwas'serspeicher *m* hot-water
tank

Warn- [varn] *comb.fm.* warning

Warn'anlage *f* warning system

warnen ['varnən] *tr* (**vor** *dat*) warn
(of), caution (against)

Warn'gebiet *n* danger zone

Warn'schuß *m* warning shot

Warn'signal *n* warning signal

War'nung *f* (-;-en) warning, caution;
zur W. as a warning

War'nungsschild *n*, **Warn'zeichen** *n*
danger sign

Warschau ['varʃau] *n* (-s;) Warsaw

Warte ['vartə] *f* (-;-n) watchtower,
lookout

War'tefrau *f* attendant; nurse

War'tefrist *f* waiting period

warten ['vartən] *tr* tend, attend to;
(*pflegen*) nurse || *intr* (**auf** *acc*) wait
(for)

Wärter ['vertər] *m* (-s;-) attendant;
(*Pfleger*) male nurse; (*Aufseher*)
caretaker; (*Gefängnis*-) guard; (rr)
signalman

War'teraum *m* waiting room

Wärterin ['vertərɪn] *f* (-;-nen) attendant; nurse

War'tesaal m, **War'tezimmer** n waiting room

War'tung f (–;) maintenance

warum [va'rum] adv why

Warze ['vartsə] f (–;–n) wart; (Brust-) nipple

was [vas] indef pron something; **na, so was!** well, I never! ‖ interr pron what; **ach was!** go on! **was für ein** what kind of, what sort of; **was haben wir gelacht!** how we laughed! ‖ rel pron what; which; that; **was auch immer** no matter what; **was immer** whatever

Wasch– [vaʃ] comb.fm. wash, washing

waschbar ['vaʃbar] adj washable

Wasch'bär m racoon

Wasch'becken n sink

Wasch'benzin n cleaning fluid

Wasch'blau n bluing

Wasch'bütte f washtub

Wäsche ['vɛʃə] f (–;–n) wash, laundry; linen; underwear

Wä'schebeutel m laundry bag

wasch'echt adj washable; (fig) genuine

Wä'scheklammer f clothespin

Wä'schekorb m clothesbasket

Wä'scheleine f clothesline

waschen ['vaʃən] §158 tr wash; launder; (Gold) pan; (Haar) shampoo; (reinigen) purify ‖ ref wash; **sich** [dat] **die Hände w.** wash one's hands ‖ intr wash

Wä'scher ['vɛʃər] m (–s;–) washer; laundryman

Wäscherei [vɛʃə'raɪ] f (–;–en) laundry

Wäscherin ['vɛʃərɪn] f (–;–nen) washerwoman, laundress

Wä'scherolle f mangle

Wä'scheschleuder f spin-drier

Wä'scheschrank m linen closet

Wä'schezeichen n laundry mark

Wasch'frau f laundress

Wasch'haus n laundry

Wasch'korb m clothesbasket

Wasch'küche f laundry

Wasch'lappen m washcloth; (fig) wishy-washy person

Wasch'maschine f washmachine, washer

Wasch'mittel n detergent

Wasch'raum m washroom, lavatory

Wasch'schüssel f wash basin

Wasch'tisch m washstand

Wasch'trog m washtub

Wa'schung f (–;–en) washing; ablution

Wasch'weib n (coll) gossip (woman)

Wasch'zettel m laundry list; (am Schutzumschlag) blurb

Wasser ['vasər] n (–s;–) water; **das W. läuft mir im Mund zusammen** my mouth is watering; **j–m das W. abgraben** pull the rug out from under s.o.; **mit allen Wassern gewaschen** sharp as a needle

was'serabstoßend adj water-repellent

was'serarm adj arid

Was'serball m water polo

Was'serbau m (–[e]s;) harbor and canal construction

Was'serbehälter m water tank; reservoir; cistern

Was'serblase f bubble; (auf der Haut) blister

Was'serbombe f depth charge

Was'serbüffel m water buffalo

Was'serdampf m steam

was'serdicht adj watertight, waterproof

Was'sereimer m bucket

Was'serfall m waterfall, cascade

Was'serfarbe f watercolor

Was'serflasche f water bottle

Was'serflugzeug n seaplane

Was'sergeflügel n waterfowl

Was'sergraben m drain; moat

Was'serhahn m faucet, spigot

Was'serhose f waterspout

wässerig ['vɛsərɪç] adj watery

Was'serjungfer f dragonfly

Was'serkessel m cauldron

Was'serklosett n toilet

Was'serkraftwerk n hydroelectric plant

Was'serkrug m water jug, water pitcher

Was'serkur f spa

Was'serland'flugzeug n amphibian plane

Was'serland'panzerwagen m amphibian tank

Was'serlauf m watercourse

Was'serleitung f water main; aqueduct

Was'sermangel m water shortage

Was'sermann m (–[e]s;) (astr) Aquarius

Was'sermelone f watermelon

wassern ['vasərn] intr land on water; (rok) splash down

wässern ['vɛsərn] tr water; irrigate; (phot) wash ‖ intr (Augen, Mund) water

Was'serratte f water rat; (fig) old salt

Was'serrinne f gutter

Was'serrohr n water pipe

Was'serscheide f watershed, divide

was'serscheu adj afraid of water

Was'serschi m water ski

Was'serschlauch m hose

Wasserspeier ['vasərʃpaɪ·ər] m (–s;–) gargoyle

Was'serspiegel m surface; water level

Was'sersport m aquatics

Was'serstand m water level

Was'serstiefel m rubber boots

Was'serstoff m hydrogen

was'serstoffblond adj peroxide-blond

Was'serstoffbombe f hydrogen bomb

Was'serstrahl m jet of water

Was'serstraße f waterway

Was'sersucht f dropsy

Was'serung f (–;–en) (aer) landing on water; (rok) splashdown

Wäs'serung f (–;) watering; irrigation

Was'serverdrängung f displacement

Was'serversorgung f water supply

Was'servogel m waterfowl

Was'serwaage f (carp) level

Was'serweg m waterway; **auf dem W.** by water

Was'serwerk n waterworks

Was'serzähler m water meter

Was'serzeichen n watermark

wässrig ['vɛsrɪç] adj watery

waten ['vatən] intr (SEIN) wade

Watsche ['vatʃə] f (–;–n) slap

watscheln ['vatʃəln] intr (SEIN) waddle

watschen ['vatʃən] tr slap

Watt [vat] *n* (-s;-) (elec) watt

Watte ['vatə] *f* (-;-en) absorbent cotton; wadding

Wat'tebausch *m* swab

Wat'tekugel *f* cotton ball

Wat'tenmeer *n* shallow coastal waters

Wat'testäbchen *n* Q-tip, cotton swab

wattieren [va'tirən] *tr* pad, wad

Wattie'rung *f* (-;-en) padding, wadding

wauwau ['vau'vau] *interj* bow-wow! ‖ **Wauwau** *m* (-s;-s) bow-wow, doggy

weben ['veːbən] §109 & §94 *tr* & *intr* weave

We'ber *m* (-s;-) weaver

Weberei [veːbə'raɪ] *f* (-;-en) weaving

We'berin *f* (-;-nen) weaver

We'berknecht *m* daddy-long-legs

Webstuhl ['veːp/tuːl] *m* loom

Webwaren ['veːpvarən] *pl* textiles

Wechsel ['vɛksəl] *m* (-s;-) change, shift; (*für Studenten*) allowance; (agr) rotation (*of crops*); (fin) bill of exchange; (hunt) run, beaten track; **gezogener W.** draft; **offener W.** letter of credit; **trockener** (or **eigener**) **W.** promissory note

Wech'selbeziehung *f* correlation

Wechselfälle ['vɛksəlfɛlə] *pl* ups and downs, vicissitudes

Wech'selfieber *n* intermittent fever; malaria

Wech'selfrist *f* period of grace (*before bill of exchange falls due*)

Wech'selgeld *n* change, small change

Wech'selgesang *m* antiphony

Wech'selgespräch *n* dialogue

wech'selhaft *adj* changeable

Wech'selkurs *m* rate of exchange

Wech'selmakler **-in** §6 *mf* bill-broker

wechseln ['vɛksəln] *tr* change; vary; (*austauschen*) exchange; **den Besitzer w.** change hands; **die Zähne w.** get one's second set of teeth; **seinen Wohnsitz w.** move ‖ *intr* change; vary

Wech'selnehmer *m* (fin) payee

Wech'selnotierung *f* foreign exchange rate

Wech'selrichter *m* (elec) vibrator (*producing a.c.*)

wech'selseitig *adj* mutual, reciprocal

Wech'selseitigkeit *f* (-;) reciprocity

Wech'selspiel *n* interplay

Wech'selsprechanlage *f* intercom

Wech'selstrom *m* alternating current

Wech'selstube *f* money-exchange office

Wech'seltierchen *n* amoeba

wech'selvoll *adj* (*Landschaft*) changing; (*Leben*) checkered; (*Wetter*) changeable

wech'selweise *adv* mutually; alternately

Wech'selwirkung *f* interaction

Wech'selwirtschaft *f* crop rotation

wecken ['vɛkən] *tr* wake, awaken, rouse

Wecker (**Wek'ker**) *m* (-s;-) alarm clock

Weck'ruf *m* (mil) reveille

Wedel ['veːdəl] *m* (-s;-) brush, whisk; (*Schwanz*) tail; (eccl) sprinkler

wedeln ['veːdəln] *tr* brush away ‖ *intr*

—**mit dem Fächer w.** fan oneself; **mit dem Schwanz w.** wag its tail

weder ['veːdər] *conj*—**weder...noch** neither...nor

weg [vɛk] *adv* away, off; gone; lost ‖ **Weg** [vɛk] *m* (-[e]s;-e) way, path; road; route, course; (*Art und Weise*) way; (*Mittel*) means; **am Wege** by the roadside; **auf dem besten Wege sein** be well on the way; **auf gütlichem Wege** amicably; **auf halbem Wege** halfway; **aus dem Weg räumen** remove; (fig) bump off; **etw in die Wege leiten** prepare the way for s.th.; introduce s.th.; **j—m aus dem Wege gehen** make way for s.o.; steer clear of s.o.; **Weg und Steg kennen** know every turn in the road

weg'bekommen §99 *tr* (*Fleck*) get out; (*Krankheit*) catch; (*verstehen*) get the hang of; **e—e w.** (coll) get a crack

weg'bleiben §62 *intr* (SEIN) stay away; be omitted

weg'blicken *intr* glance away

weg'bringen §65 *tr* take away; (*Fleck*) get out

Wegebau ['veːgəbau] *m* (-[e]s;) road building

Wegegeld ['veːgəgɛlt] *n* mileage allowance; turnpike toll

wegen ['veːgən] *prep* (genit) because of, on account of; for the sake of; (*mit Rücksicht auf*) in consideration of; (*infolge*) in consequence of; (jur) on (the charge of); **von Amts w.** officially; **von Rechts w.** by right

Wegerecht ['veːgərɛçt] *n* right of way

weg'essen §70 *tr* eat up

weg'fahren §71 *tr* remove ‖ *intr* (SEIN) drive away, leave

weg'fallen §72 *intr* (SEIN) fall away, fall off; (*ausgelassen werden*) be omitted; (*aufhören*) cease; (*abgeschafft werden*) be abolished

weg'fangen §73 *tr* snap away, snatch

weg'fliegen §57 *intr* (SEIN) fly away

weg'fressen §70 *tr* devour

weg'führen *tr* lead away

Weggang ['vɛkgaŋ] *m* departure

weg'geben §80 *tr* give away

weg'gehen §82 *intr* (SEIN) go away; **w. über** (acc) pass over; **wie warme Semmeln w.** go like hotcakes

weg'haben §89 *tr* get rid of; (*Schläge, usw.*) have gotten one's share of; (*verstehen*) catch on to; **der hat eins weg** (sl) he has a screw loose; (sl) he's loaded

weg'jagen *tr* chase away

weg'kehren *tr* sweep away; (*Gesicht*) avert ‖ *ref* turn away

weg'kommen §99 *intr* (SEIN) come away; get away (*verlorengehen*) get lost; **nicht w. über** (acc) not get over

weg'können §100 *intr*—**nicht w.** not be able to get away

Wegkreuzung ['vɛkkrɔɪtsuŋ] *f* (-;-en) crossing, intersection

weg'kriegen *tr* get; (*Fleck*) get out

weg'lassen §104 *tr* leave out; let go; cross out; (gram) elide; (math) cancel

weg'legen *tr* put aside

weg'machen *tr* take away; *(Fleck)* take out

wegmüde ['vekmydə] *adj* travel-weary

weg'müssen §115 *intr* have to go

Wegnahme ['veknɑmə] *f* (-;-n) taking away; confiscation; (mil) capture

weg'nehmen §116 *tr* take away; *(Raum, Zeit)* take up; *(beschlagnahmen)* confiscate; (mil) capture

weg'packen *tr* pack away || *ref* pack off

weg'raffen *tr* snatch away

Wegrand ['vekrant] *m* wayside

weg'räumen *tr* clear away

weg'reißen §53 *tr* tear off, tear away

weg'rücken *tr* move away

weg'schaffen *tr* remove; get rid of

weg'scheren §129 *tr* clip || *ref* scram

weg'scheuchen *tr* scare away

weg'schicken *tr* send away

weg'schleichen §85 *ref & intr* (SEIN) sneak away, steal away

weg'schmeißen §53 *tr* (coll) throw away

weg'schneiden §106 *tr* cut away

weg'sehen §138 *intr* look away; **w. über** *(acc)* shut one's eyes to

weg'setzen *tr* put away || *ref*—**sich w. über** *(acc)* not mind; feel superior to || *intr* (SEIN)—**w. über** *(acc)* jump over

weg'spülen *tr* wash away; (geol) erode

weg'stehlen §147 *ref* slip away

weg'stellen *tr* put aside

weg'stoßen §150 *tr* shove aside

weg'streichen §85 *tr* cross out

weg'treten §152 *intr* (SEIN) step aside; (mil) break ranks; **weggetreten!** (mil) dismissed!; **w. lassen** (mil) dismiss

weg'tun §154 *tr* put away

Wegweiser ['vekvaɪzər] *m* (-s;-) roadsign; *(Buch, Reiseführer)* guide

weg'wenden §120 & §140 *tr & ref* turn away

weg'werfen §160 *tr* throw away || *ref* degrade oneself

weg'werfend *adj* disparaging

weg'wischen *tr* wipe away

weg'zaubern *tr* spirit away

weg'ziehen §163 *tr* pull away || *intr* (SEIN) move; (mil) pull out

weh [ve] *adj* painful, sore; **mir ist weh ums Herz** I am sick at heart || *adv*—**sich** *[dat]* **weh tun** hurt oneself; **weh tun ache** || *interj* woel **weh mir!** woe is me! || **Weh** *n* (-[e]s;-e) pain, ache

wehe ['ve·ə] *adj, adv, & interj* var of **weh** || **Wehe** *f* (-;-n) drift

wehen ['ve·ən] *tr* blow; *(Schnee)* drift || *intr* *(Wind)* blow; *(Fahne, Kerzenflamme)* flutter || **Wehen** *pl* labor, labor pains; (fig) travail

Weh'geschrei *n* wails, wailing

Weh'klage *f* wail

weh'klagen *intr* (über *acc*) wail (over); **w. um** lament for

weh'leidig *adj* complaining, whining; **W. tun** whine

Weh'mut *f* (-;) melancholy; nostalgia

weh'mütig *adj* melancholy; nostalgic

Wehr [ver] *f* (-;-en) weapon; *(Abwehr)* defense, resistance; *(Brüstung)*

parapet; **sich zur W. setzen** offer resistance || **Wehr** *n* (-[e]s;-e) dam

Wehr'dienst *m* military service

wehr'dienstpflichtig *adj* subject to military service

Wehr'dienstverweigerer *m* (-s;-) conscientious objector

wehren ['veran] *tr*—**j-m etw w.** keep s.o. (away) from s.th. || *ref* defend oneself; resist, put up a fight; **sich seiner Haut w.** save one's skin || *intr* *(dat)* resist; *(dat)* check

wehr'fähig *adj* fit for military service

wehr'haft *adj* *(Person)* full of fight; *(Burg)* strong

wehr'los *adj* defenseless

Wehr'macht *f* (hist) German armed forces

Wehr'meldeamt *n* draft board

Wehr'paß *m* service record

Wehr'pflicht *f* compulsory military service; **allgemeine W.** universal military training

wehr'pflichtig *adj* subject to military service

Weib [vaɪp] *n* (-[e]s;-er) woman; wife; **ein tolles W.** a luscious doll

Weibchen ['vaɪpçən] *n* (-s;-) *(Tier)* female; *(Ehefrau)* little woman

Weiberfeind ['vaɪbərfaɪnt] *m* woman-hater

Weiberheld ['vaɪbərhɛlt] *m* ladies' man

Weibervolk ['vaɪbərfɔlk] *n* womenfolk

weibisch ['vaɪbɪʃ] *adj* womanish, effeminate

weib'lich *adj* female; womanly; (& gram) feminine

Weib'lichkeit *f* (-;) womanhood; feminine nature; **die holde W.** (hum) the fair sex

Weibs'bild *n* female; (pej) wench

Weibs'stück *n* (sl) woman

weich [vaɪç] *adj* soft; *(Ei)* soft-boiled; *(zart)* tender; *(schwach)* weak; **w. machen** soften up; **w. werden** (& fig) soften; relent

Weich'bild *n* urban area, outskirts

Weiche ['vaɪçə] *f* (-;-n) (anat) side, flank; (rr) switch; **Weichen stellen** throw the switch

weichen ['vaɪçən] *tr & intr* soften; soak || §85 *intr* (SEIN) yield; give ground; *(Boden)* give way; *(dat)* give in to; **j-m nicht von der Seite w.** not leave s.o.'s side; **nicht von der Stelle w.** not budge from the spot; **von j-m w.** leave s.o.

Weichensteller ['vaɪçənstelər] *m* (-s; -) (rr) switchman

Weich'heit *f* (-;) softness; tenderness

weich'herzig *adj* soft-hearted

Weich'käse *m* soft cheese

weich'lich *adj* soft; tender; flabby; insipid; *(weibisch)* effeminate; *(lässig)* indolent

Weichling ['vaɪçlɪŋ] *m* (-s;-e) weakling

Weich'tier *n* mollusk

Weide ['vaɪdə] *f* (-;-n) pasture; (bot) willow

Wei'deland *n* pasture land

weiden ['vaɪdən] *tr* graze; *(Augen)*

feast || *ref*—**sich w. an** (*dat*) feast
one's eyes on || *intr* graze
Wei′denkorb *m* wicker basket
weidlich [′vaɪtlɪç] *adv* heartily
weidmännisch [′vaɪtmɛnɪʃ] *adj* (hunt)
sportsmanlike
weigern [′vaɪgərn] *ref*—**sich w. zu** (*inf*)
refuse to (*inf*)
Wei′gerung *f* (-;-en) refusal
Weihe [′vaɪə] *f* (-;-n) consecration;
(*e-s Priesters*) ordination
weihen [′vaɪən] *tr* consecrate; (*zum
Priester*) ordain; (*widmen*) dedicate;
dem Tode geweiht doomed to death
|| *ref* devote oneself
Wei′her *m* (-s;-) pond
wei′hevoll *adj* solemn
Weihnachten [′vaɪnaxtən] *n* (-s;) & *pl*
Christmas; **zu W.** for or at Christmas
Weih′nachtsabend *m* Christmas Eve
Weih′nachtsbaum *m* Christmas tree;
(coll) bombing markers
Weih′nachtsbescherung *f* exchange of
Christmas presents
Weih′nachtsfeier *f* Christmas celebra-
tion; (*in Betrieben*) Christmas party
Weih′nachtsfest *n* feast of Christmas
Weih′nachtsgeschenk *n* Christmas pres-
ent
Weih′nachtsgratifikation *f* Christmas
bonus
Weih′nachtslied *n* Christmas carol
Weih′nachtsmann *m* (-[e]s;) Santa
Claus
Weih′nachtsmarkt *m* Christmas fair
(*at which Christmas decorations are
sold*)
Weih′nachtstag *m* Christmas day
Weih′rauch *m* incense
Weih′rauchfaß *n* censer
Weih′wasser *n* holy water
Weih′wedel *m* (eccl) sprinkler
weil [vaɪl] *conj* because, since
weiland [′vaɪlant] *adv* formerly
Weilchen [′vaɪlçən] *n* (-s;) little while
Weile [′vaɪlə] *f* (-;) while
weilen [′vaɪlən] *intr* stay, linger
Wein [vaɪn] *m* (-[e]s;-e) wine;
(*Pflanze*) vine
Wein′bau *m* (-[e]s;) winegrowing
Wein′bauer -in §6 *mf* winegrower
Wein′beere *f* grape
Wein′berg *m* vineyard
Wein′blatt *n* vine leaf
Wein′brand *m* brandy
weinen [′vaɪnən] *tr* (*Tränen*) shed ||
intr cry, weep; **vor Freude w.** weep
for joy; **w. um** cry over
weinerlich [′vaɪnərlɪç] *adj* tearful;
(*Stimme*)) whining
Wein′ernte *f* vintage
Wein′essig *m* wine vinegar
Wein′faß *n* wine barrel
Wein′händler *m* wine merchant
Wein′jahr *n* vintage year
Wein′karte *f* wine list
Wein′keller *m* wine cellar
Wein′kelter *f* wine press
Wein′kenner *m* connoisseur of wine
Wein′krampf *m* crying fit
Wein′laub *n* vine leaves
Wein′lese *f* grape picking
Wein′presse *f* wine press

Wein′ranke *f* vine tendril
Wein′rebe *f* grapevine
wein′selig *adj* tipsy, tight
Wein′stock *m* vine
Wein′traube *f* grape; bunch of grapes
weise [′vaɪzə] *adj* wise || **Weise** §5 *m*
wise man, sage || *f* (-;-n) way;
(*Melodie*) tune; **auf diese W.** in this
way
-weise *comb.fm.* -wise; by, e.g., **dut-
zendweise** by the dozen; -ly, e.g.,
glücklicherweise luckily
weisen [′vaɪzən] §118 *tr* point out,
show; (*aus dem Lande*) banish; (*aus
der Schule*) expel; **j-n w. an** (*acc*)
refer s.o. to; **j-n w. nach** direct s.o.
to; **j-n w. von** order s.o. off (*premises, etc.*); **von der Hand w.** refuse;
weit von der Hand w. have nothing
to do with || *ref*—**von sich w.** refuse
|| *intr*—**w. auf** (*acc*) point to
Weis′heit *f* (-;-en) wisdom; wise saying; **Weisheiten** words of wisdom
Weis′heitszahn *m* wisdom tooth
weis′lich *adv* wisely, prudently
weismachen [′vaɪsmaxən] *tr*—**j-m etw
w.** put s.th. over on s.o.; **mach das
anderen weis!** tell it to the marines!
weiß [vaɪs] *adj* white
weissagen [′vaɪszagən] *tr* foretell
Weiß′blech *n* tin plate, tin
Weiß′blechdose *f* tincan
weiß′bluten *tr* bleed white
Weiß′brot *n* white bread
Weiß′dorn *m* (bot) hawthorn
Weiße [′vaɪsə] *f* (-;-n) whiteness;
(Berlin) ale || §5 *m* white man || *f*
white woman || *n* (*im Auge, im Ei*)
white
weißen [′vaɪsən] *tr* whiten; (*tünchen*)
whitewash
weiß′glühend *adj* white-hot
Weiß′glut *f* white heat, incandescence
Weiß′kohl *m*, **Weiß′kraut** *n* cabbage
weiß′lich *adj* whitish
Weiß′metall *n* pewter; Babbitt metal
Weiß′waren *pl* linens
Weiß′wein *m* white wine
Wei′sung *f* (-;-en) directions, instructions; directive
weit [vaɪt] *adj* far, distant; (*ausgedehnt*) extensive; (*breit*) wide, broad;
(*geräumig*) large; (*Gewissen*) elastic;
(*Herz*) big; (*Kleid*) full, big; (*Meer*)
broad; (*Reise, Weg*) long; (*Welt*)
wide; **bei weitem besser** better by
far; **von weitem** from afar || *adv* far,
way; widely; greatly; **w. besser** far
better
weit′ab′ *adv* (**von**) far away (from)
weit′aus′ *adv* by far
Welt′blick *m* farsightedness
weit′blickend *adj* farsighted
Weite [′vaɪtə] *f* (-;-n) width, breadth;
(*Ferne*) distance; (*Umfang*) size;
(*Ausdehnung*) extent; (*Durchmesser*)
diameter; (fig) range; **in die W.
ziehen** go out into the world
weiten [′vaɪtən] *tr* widen; (*Loch*) en-
large; (*Schuh*) stretch || *ref* widen
weiter [′vaɪtər] *adj* farther; further;
wider; **bis auf weiteres** until further
notice; **des weiteren** furthermore;

ohne weiteres without further ado || *adv* farther; further; furthermore; (*voran*) on; **er kann nicht w.** he can't go on; **nur s. w.!** keep it up!; **und so w.** and so forth, and so on

weiter– *comb.fm.* on; keep on, continue to

wei'terbefördern *tr* forward

Wei'terbestand *m* continued existence

wei'terbestehen §146 *intr* survive

wei'terbilden *tr* develop || *ref* continue one's studies

wei'tererzählen *tr* spread (*rumors*)

wei'terfahren §71 *intr* (SEIN) drive on

wei'tergeben §80 *tr* pass on, relay

wei'tergehen §82 *intr* (SEIN) go on

wei'terhin' *adv* furthermore; again

wei'terkommen §99 *intr* (SEIN) get ahead, make progress

wei'terkönnen §100 *intr* be able to go on; **ich kann nicht weiter** I'm stuck

wei'terleben *intr* live on, survive

wei'termachen *tr & intr* continue || *interj* (mil) as you were!, carry on!

weit'gehend *adj* far-reaching

weit'gereist *adj* widely traveled

weit'greifend *adj* far-reaching

weit'her' *adv*—**von w.** from afar

weit'hergeholt *adj* far-fetched

weit'herzig *adj* broad-minded

weit'hin' *adv* far off

weitläufig ['vaitlɔifiç] *adj* lengthy, detailed; complicated; (*Verwandte*) distant; (*geräumig*) roomy || *adv* at length, in detail

weit'reichend *adj* far-reaching

weitschweifig ['vaitʃvaifiç] *adj* detailed, lengthy; long-winded

weit'sichtig *adj* (& fig) far-sighted

Weit'sprung *m* (sport) long jump

Weit'streckenflug *m* long-distance flight

weit'tragend *adj* long-range; (fig) far-reaching

Weit'winkelobjektiv *n* wide-angle lens

Weizen ['vaitsən] *m* (–s;–) wheat

Wei'zenmehl *n* wheat flour

welch [velç] *interr adj* which || *interr pron* which one; (*in Ausrufen*) what ...!; **mit welcher** (or **mit welch einer**) **Begeisterung arbeitet er!** with what enthusiasm he works! || *indef pron* any; some || *rel pron* who, which, that

welcherlei ['velçər'lai] *invar adj* what kind of; whatever

welk [velk] *adj* withered; (*Haut, Lippen*) wrinkled; (fig) faded

welken ['velkən] *intr* (SEIN) wither; (fig) fade

Wellblech ['velbleç] *n* corrugated iron

Well'blechhütte *f* Quonset hut

Welle ['velə] *f* (–;–n) wave; (*Wellbaum*) shaft; (gym) circle (*around horizontal bar*); (mach) shaft

weilen ['velən] *tr & ref* wave

Wel'lenbereich *m* wave band

Wel'lenberg *m* crest (*of wave*)

Wel'lenbewegung *f* undulation

Wel'lenbrecher *m* breakwater

wel'lenförmig *adj* wavy

Wel'lenlänge *f* wavelength

Wel'lenlinie *f* wavy line

wel'lenreiten §86 *intr* surf; waterski || **Wellenreiten** *n* (–s;) surfing, surfboard riding; waterskiing

Wel'lenreiter –in §6 *mf* surfer; waterskier

Wel'lenreiterbrett *n* surfboard; water ski

Wel'lental *n* trough (*of wave*)

wellig ['veliç] *adj* wavy

Well'pappe *f* corrugated cardboard

Welt [velt] *f* (–;–en) world

Welt'all *n* universe; outer space

Welt'anschauung *f* outlook on life; ideology

Welt'ausmaß *m*—**im W.** on a global scale

Welt'ausstellung *f* world's fair

welt'bekannt, welt'berühmt *adj* world-renowned

Welt'enbummler *m* globetrotter

welt'erfahren *adj* sophisticated

Weltergewicht ['veltərgəviçt] *n* welterweight class

Weltergewichtler ['veltərgəviçtlər] *m* (–s;–) welterweight boxer

welt'erschütternd *adj* earth-shaking

welt'fremd *adj* secluded; innocent

Welt'friede *m* world peace

Welt'geistlicher *m* secular priest

welt'gewandt *adj* worldly-wise

Welt'karte *f* map of the world

welt'klug *adj* worldly-wise

Welt'körper *m* heavenly body

Welt'krieg *m* world war

Welt'kugel *f* globe

Welt'lage *f* international situation

welt'lich *adj* worldly; secular

Welt'macht *f* world power

Welt'mann *m* (–[e]s;–̈er) man of the world

welt'männisch *adj* sophisticated

Welt'meer *n* ocean

Welt'meinung *f* world opinion

Welt'meister –in §6 *mf* world champion

Welt'meisterschaft *f* world championship

Welt'ordnung *f* cosmic order

Welt'postverein *m* postal union

Welt'priester *m* secular priest

Welt'raum *m* (–[e]s;) outer space

Welt'raumfahrer *m* spaceman

Welt'raumfahrt *f* space travel

Welt'raumfahrzeug *n* spacecraft

Welt'raumforschung *f* exploration of outer space

Welt'raumgeschoß *n* space shot

Welt'raumkapsel *f* space capsule

Welt'raumstation *f* space station

Welt'raumstrahlen *pl* cosmic rays

Welt'reich *n* world empire

Welt'reise *f* trip around the world

Welt'rekord *m* world record

Welt'ruf *m* world-wide renown

Welt'ruhm *m* world-wide fame

Welt'schmerz *m* world-weariness

Welt'sicherheitsrat *m* U.N. Security Council

Welt'stadt *f* metropolis (*city with more than one million inhabitants*)

Welt'teil *m* continent

welt'umfassend *adj* world-wide

Welt'weisheit *f* philosophy

wem [vɛm] *interr & rel pron* to whom
Wem'fall *m* dative case
wen [vɛn] *interr & rel pron* whom
Wende ['vɛndə] *f* (-;-n) turn; turning
point; (gym) face vault, front vault
Wen'dekreis *m* (geog) tropic
Wendeltreppe ['vɛndəltrɛpə] *f* spiral
staircase
Wen'demarke *f* (aer) pylon; (sport)
turn post
wenden ['vɛndən] §140 *tr* turn; turn
around; turn over; (Geld, Mühe)
spend ‖ *ref* turn; (Wind, Wetter)
change ‖ *intr* turn, turn around
Wen'depunkt *m* turning point
wendig ['vɛndɪç] *adj* maneuverable;
(Person) versatile, resourceful
Wen'dung *f* (-;-en) turn; change; (Redensart) idiomatic expression
Wen'fall *m* accusative case
wenig ['ven̄ɪç] *adj* little; **ein w.** a little,
a bit of; **wenige** few, a few, some ‖
adv little; not very; seldom ‖ *indef
pron* little; **wenige** few, a few
weniger ['venɪgər] *adj* fewer; less;
(arith) minus
We'nigkeit *f* (-;) fewness; smallness;
pittance; trifle; **meine W.** (coll) poor
little me
wenigste ['venɪçstə] §9 *adj* least; very
few, fewest; **am wenigsten** least of all
wenigstens ['venɪçstəns] *adv* at least
wenn [vɛn] *conj* if, in case; (zeitlich)
when, whenever; **auch w.** even if;
außer w. except when, except if, unless; **w. anders** provided that; **w.
auch** although, even if; **w. schon,
denn schon** go all the way ‖ **Wenn**
n (-;-) if
wenngleich', **wennschon'** *conj* although
Wenzel ['vɛntsəl] *m* (-s;-) (cards)
jack
wer [ver] *interr pron* who, which one;
wer auch immer whoever; **wer da?**
who goes there? ‖ *rel pron* he who,
whoever ‖ *indef pron* somebody,
anybody
Werbe- [verbə] *comb.fm.* advertising;
publicity; commercial
Wer'befernsehen *n* commercial television
Wer'befilm *m* commercial
Wer'befläche *f* advertising space
Wer'begraphik *f* commercial art
Wer'begraphiker –in §6 *mf* commercial artist
werben ['vɛrbən] §149 *tr* (neue Kunden) try to get; (mil) recruit ‖ *intr*
advertise; **für e–n neuen Handelsar-
tikel w.** advertise a new product; **um
ein Mädchen w.** court a girl
Wer'beschrift *f* folder
Wer'bestelle *f* advertising agency
Wer'bung *f* (-;-en) advertising; publicity; courting; recruiting
Werdegang ['verdəgaŋ] *m* career,
background; (Entwicklung) development; (Wachstum) growth; (Ablauf
der Herstellung) process of production
werden ['verdən] §159 *intr* (SEIN) become, grow, get, turn; **w. zu** change
into; **zu nichts w.** come to nought ‖

aux (SEIN) (to form the future) **er
wird gehen** he will go; (to form the
passive) **er wird geehrt** he is being
honored ‖ **Werden** *n* (-s;) becoming,
growing; (Entstehung) evolution;
(Wachstum) growth; **im W. sein** be
in the process of development; be in
the making
wer'dend *adj* nascent; (Mutter) expectant; (Arzt) future
Werder ['verdər] *m* (-s;-) islet
Wer'fall *m* subjective case
werfen ['vɛrfən] §160 *tr* throw, cast;
(Junge) produce; (Blasen) form,
blow; **Falten w.** wrinkle ‖ *ref* (Holz)
warp; **sich hin und her w.** toss; **sich
in die Brust w.** throw out one's chest
‖ *intr* throw; (Tieren) produce young
Werft [vɛrft] *f* (-;-e) shipyard
Werft'halle *f* (aer) repair hangar
Werg [vɛrk] *n* (-[e]s;) oakum, tow
Werk [vɛrk] *n* (-[e]s;-e) work; (Tat)
deed; (Erzeugnis) production; (Lei-
stung) performance; (Unternehmen)
undertaking; (Fabrik) works, plant,
mill; (horol) clockwork; **das ist dein
W.** that's your doing; **gutes W.** good
deed; **im Werke sein** be in the works;
zu Werke gehen go to it
Werk'anlage *f* plant, works
Werk'bank *f* (-;-e) workbench
werk'fremd *adj* (Personen) unauthor-
ized
Werk'meister *m* foreman
Werk'nummer *f* factory serial number
Werks'angehörige §5 *mf* employee
Werk'schutz *m* security force
Werks'kantine *f* factory cafeteria
Werk'statt *f*, **Werk'stätte** *f* workshop
Werk'stattwagen *m* maintenance truck
Werk'stoff *m* manufacturing material
Werk'stück *n* (indust) piece
Werk'tag *m* weekday; working day
werk'tägig *adj* workaday, ordinary
werk'tags *adv* (on) weekdays
werk'tätig *adj* working; practical
Werk'zeug *n* tool
Werk'zeugmaschine *f* machine tool
Wermut ['vermut] *m* (-[e]s;) vermouth; (bot) wormwood
wert [vɛrt] *adj* worth; worthy; esteem-
ed; **etw** [genit or acc] **w. sein** be
worth s.th.; **nicht der Rede w. sein**
not worth mentioning; **nichts w.** good
for nothing; **Werter Herr X** Dear
Mr. X ‖ **Wert** *m* (-[e]s;-e) worth,
value; price, rate; (Wichtigkeit) importance; (chem) valence; **äußerer
W.** face value; **im W. von** valued at;
innerer W. intrinsic value; **Werte**
(com) assets; (phys) data
Wert'angabe *f* valuation
wert'beständig *adj* of lasting value;
(Währung) stable
Wert'bestimmung *f* appraisal
Wert'brief *m* insured letter
werten ['vɛrtən] *tr* (bewerten) value;
(nach Leistung) rate; (auswerten)
evaluate
Wert'gegenstand *m* valuable article;
Wertgegenstände valuables
–wertig [vertɪç] *comb.fm.* –value,
–quality, e.g., **geringwertig** low-qual-

ity; (chem) –valent, e.g., **zweiwertig** bivalent

Wer'tigkeit *f* (–;-en) (chem) valence
wert'los *adj* worthless
Wert'papiere *pl* securities
Wert'sachen *pl* valuables
wert'voll *adj* valuable
Wert'zeichen *n* stamp; (*Briefmarke*) postage stamp; (*Banknote*) bill
Wesen ['vezən] *n* (–s;–) being, creature; entity; (*inneres Sein, Kern*) essence; (*Betragen*) conduct, way; (*Getue*) fuss; (*Natur*) nature, character; **einnehmendes W.** pleasing personality; **höchtes W.** Supreme Being
–wesen *n comb.fm.* system
we'senhaft *adj* real; characteristic
we'senlos *adj* unreal; incorporeal
wesentlich ['vezəntlɪç] *adj* essential; (*beträchtlich*) substantial
Weser ['vezər] *f* (–;) Weser (River)
Wes'fall *m* genitive case
weshalb [ves'halp] *adv* why; wherefore
Wespe ['vespə] *f* (–;-n) wasp
wessen ['vesən] *interr pron* whose
West [vest] *m* (–s;) west; (poet) west wind
Weste ['vestə] *f* (–;-n) vest; **e-e reine W.** a clean slate
Westen ['vestən] *m* (–s;) west; **im W. von** west of; **nach W.** westward
Westfalen [vest'falən] *n* (–s;) Westphalia
westfälisch [vest'felɪç] *adj* Westphalian
West'gote *m* (–n;-n) Visigoth
Westindien [vest'ɪndjən] *n* (–s;) the West Indies
west'lich *adj* west, western; westerly
Westmächte ['vestmeçtə] *pl* Western Powers
westwärts ['vestverts] *adv* westward
weswegen [ves'vegən] *adv* why; wherefore
wett [vet] *adj* even, quits
Wett- *comb.fm.* competitive
Wett'bewerb *m* (–s;-e) competition, contest; (*Treffen*) meet
Wett'bewerber –in §6 *mf* competitor
Wette ['vetə] *f* (–;-n) bet, wager; **e-e W. abschließen** (or **eingehen**) make a bet; **mit j–m um die W. laufen** race s.o.; **was gilt die W.?** what do you bet?
Wett'eifer *m* competitiveness, rivalry
wetteifern ['vetaɪfərn] *insep intr* compete; **w. um** compete for
Wetter ['vetər] *n* (–s;) weather; (min) ventilation; **alle W.!** holy smokes!
wet'terbeständig, wet'terfest *adj* weatherproof
Wet'terglas *n* barometer
wet'terhart *adj* hardy
Wet'terkunde *f* meteorology
Wet'terlage *f* weather conditions
wet'terleuchten *insep impers*—es **wetterleuchtet** there is summer lightning ‖ **Wetterleuchten** *n* (–;) summer lightning, heat lightning
Wet'terverhältnisse *pl* weather conditions
Wet'tervorhersage *f* weather forecast

Wet'terwarte *f* meteorological station
Wet'terwechsel *m* change in the weather
wetterwendisch ['vetərvendɪʃ] *adj* moody
Wett'fahrer –in §6 *mf* racer
Wett'fahrt *f* race
Wett'kampf *m* competition, contest
Wett'kämpfer –in §6 *mf* competitor, contestant
Wett'lauf *m* race, foot race
Wett'läufer –in §6 *mf* runner
wett'machen *tr* make up for
Wett'rennen *n* race
Wett'rudern *n* boat race
Wett'rüsten *n* armaments race
Wett'schwimmen *n* swimming match
Wett'segeln *n* regatta
Wett'spiel *n* game, match
Wett'streit *m* contest, match, game
Wett'zettel *m* betting ticket
wetzen ['vetsən] *tr* whet, sharpen
Wetzstein ['vetstaɪn] *m* whetstone
Whisky ['vɪski] *m* (–s;-s) whiskey
wich [vɪç] *pret* of **weichen**
Wichs [vɪks] *m* (es–;-e) gala; **in vollem W.** in full dress; **sich in W. werfen** dress up
Wichse ['vɪksə] *f* (–;-n) shoepolish ‖ *f* (–;) (coll) spanking
wichsen ['vɪksən] *tr* polish; (coll) spank, beat up
Wicht [vɪçt] *m* (–[e]s;-e) elf; dwarf
Wichtel ['vɪçtəl] *m* (–s;-) dwarf
wichtig ['vɪçtɪç] *adj* important ‖ *adv* —**w. tun** act important
Wich'tigkeit *f* (–;) importance
Wichtigtuer ['vɪçtɪçtu·ər] *m* (–s;-) busybody
wichtigtuerisch ['vɪçtɪçtu·ərɪʃ] *adj* officious
Wicke ['vɪkə] *f* (–;-n) (bot) vetch
Wickel ['vɪkəl] *m* (–s;-) wrapper; curler, roller; (*von Garn*) ball; (med) compress
wickeln ['vɪkəln] *tr* wrap; wind (*Haar*) curl; (*Kind*) diaper; (*Zigaretten*) roll
Widder ['vɪdər] *m* (–s;-) ram; (astr) Ram
wider ['vidər] *prep* (acc) against, contrary to
wider- *comb.fm.* re-, con–, un–, counter-, contra-, anti-, with-
wi'derborstig *adj* stubborn, contrary
widerfah'ren §71 *intr* (SEIN) (dat) befall, happen to
Wi'derhaken *m* barb
Wi'derhall *m* echo, reverberation; (fig) response, reaction
wi'derhallen *intr* echo, resound
Wi'derlager *n* abutment
widerle'gen *tr* refute
wi'derlich *adj* repulsive
wi'dernatürlich *adj* unnatural
widerra'ten §63 *tr*—j–m etw **w.** dissuade s.o. from s.th.
wi'derrechtlich *adj* illegal
Wi'derrede *f* contradiction
Wi'derruf *m* recall; cancellation; retraction; denial; **bis auf W.** until further notice
widerru'fen §122 *tr* revoke; (*Auftrag*)

cancel; (*Befehl*) countermand; (*Behauptung*) retract

Widersacher –in ['vidərzaxər(ın)] §6 *mf* adversary

Wi'derschein *m* reflection

widerset'zen *ref* (*dat*) oppose, resist

widersetz'lich *adj* insubordinate

wi'dersinnig *adj* absurd, nonsensical

widerspenstig ['vidərʃpenstıç] *adj* refractory, contrary; (*Haar*) stubborn

wi'derspiegeln *tr* reflect || *ref* (in *dat*) be reflected (in)

Wi'derspiel *n* contrary, reverse

widerspre'chen §64 *intr* (*dat*) contradict; (*dat*) oppose

widerspre'chend *adj* contradictory

Wi'derspruch *m* contradiction; opposition; **auf heftigen W. stoßen bei** meet with strong opposition from

widersprüchlich ['vidərʃpryçlıç] *adj* contradictory

wi'derspruchsvoll *adj* full of contradictions

Wi'derstand *m* resistance; opposition; (elec) resistance; (elec) resistor

Wi'derstandsnest *n* pocket of resistance

widerste'hen §146 *intr* (*dat*) withstand, resist; (*dat*) be repugnant to

widerstre'ben *intr* (*dat*) oppose, resist; (*dat*) be repugnant to || *impers*—es **widerstrebt mir zu** (*inf*) I hate to (*inf*)

widerstre'bend *adj* reluctant

Wi'derstreit *m* opposition, antagonism; (fig) conflict, clash

widerstrei'ten §86 *intr* (*dat*) clash with

widerwärtig ['vidərvertıç] *adj* nasty

Wi'derwille *m* (gegen) dislike (of, for), aversion (to); (*Widerstreben*) reluctance; **mit W.** reluctantly

wi'derwillig *adj* reluctant, unwilling

widmen ['vıtmən] *tr* dedicate, devote || *ref* (*dat*) devote oneself to

Wid'mung *f* (–;–en) dedication

widrig ['vidrıç] *adj* contrary; (*ungünstig*) unfavorable, adverse

wid'rigenfalls *adv* otherwise, or else

wie [vi] *adv* how; (*vergleichend*) as, such as, like; **so...wie as...as; und wie!** and how!; **wie, bitte?** what did you say?; **wie dem auch sei** be that as it may; **wie wäre es mit...?** how about...?

wieder ['vidər] *adv* again; anew; (*zurück*) back; (*als Vergeltung*) in return

wieder– *comb.fm.* re–

Wie'derabdruck *m* reprint

wiederan'knüpfen *tr* resume

Wiederauf'bau *m* (–[e]s;) rebuilding

wiederauf'bauen *tr* rebuild, reconstruct

wiederauf'erstehen §146 *intr* (SEIN) rise from the dead

Wiederauf'erstehung *f* resurrection

Wiederauf'führung *f* (theat) revival

wiederauf'kommen §99 *intr* (SEIN) (*Kranker*) recover; (*Mode*) come in again

Wiederauf'nahme *f* resumption; (jur) reopening

Wiederauf'nahmeverfahren *n* retrial

Wiederauf'rüstung *f* rearmament

Wie'derbeginn *m* reopening

wie'derbekommen §99 *tr* recover

wie'derbeleben *tr* revive, resuscitate

wie'derbeschaffen *tr* replace

wie'derbringen §65 *tr* bring back; restore, give back

wiederein'bringen §65 *tr* make up for

wiederein'setzen *tr* (in *acc*) reinstate (in); **in Rechte w.** restore to former rights

wiederein'stellen *tr* rehire; (mil) re-enlist

Wie'dereintritt *m* (rok) reentry

wie'derergreifen §88 *tr* recapture

wie'dererhalten §90 *tr* get back

wie'dererkennen §97 *tr* recognize

wie'dererlangen *tr* recover, retrieve

wie'dererstatten *tr* restore; (*Geld*) refund

Wie'dergabe *f* return; reproduction; rendering

wie'dergeben §80 *tr* give back; (*Ton*) reproduce; (*spielen, übersetzen*) render; (*Ehre, Gesundheit*) restore

Wie'dergeburt *f* rebirth

wie'dergenesen §84 *intr* (SEIN) recover

wie'dergewinnen §52 *tr* regain

wiedergut'machen *tr* make good

Wiedergut'machung *f* (–;–en) reparation

wiederher'stellen *tr* restore

wie'derholen *tr* bring back; take back || **wiederho'len** *tr* repeat

wiederholt [vidər'holt] *adv* repeatedly

Wiederho'lung *f* (–;–en) repetition

Wiederho'lungszeichen *n* dittomarks; (mus) repeat

Wie'derhören *n*—**auf W.!** (telp) goodbye!

wie'derimpfen *tr* give (*s.o.*) a booster shot

wiederinstand'setzen *tr* repair

wiederkäuen ['vidərkɔı-ən] *tr* ruminate; (fig) repeat over and over || *intr* chew the cud

Wiederkehr ['vidərker] *f* (–;) return; recurrence; anniversary

wie'derkehren *intr* (SEIN) return; recur

wie'derkommen §99 *intr* (SEIN) come back

Wiederkunft ['vidərkunft] *f* (–;) return

wie'dersehen §138 *tr* see again || *recip* meet again || **Wiedersehen** *n* (–s;) meeting again; **auf W.!** see you!

Wie'dertäufer *m* Baptist

wie'dertun §154 *tr* do again, repeat

wie'derum *adv* again; on the other hand

wie'dervereinigen *tr* reunite; reunify

Wie'dervereinigung *f* reunion; (pol) reunification

wie'derverheiraten *tr* & *recip* remarry

Wie'derverkäufer –in §6 *mf* retailer

Wie'derwahl *f* reelection

wie'derwählen *tr* reelect

wiederzu'lassen §104 *tr* readmit

Wiege ['vigə] *f* (–;–n) cradle

wiegen ['vigən] *tr* (*schaukeln*) rock || *ref*—**sich in den Hüften w.** sway one's hips; **sich w. in** (*acc*) lull oneself into || §57 *tr* & *intr* weigh

Wie'gendruck *m* incunabulum

Wie'genlied *n* lullaby

wiehern ['viˑərn] *intr* neigh; **wiehern-des Gelächter** horselaugh
Wien [vin] *n* (-s;) Vienna
Wiener -in ['vinər(ɪn)] §6 *mf* Viennese
wienerisch ['vinərɪʃ] *adj* Viennese
wies [vis] *pret* of weisen
Wiese ['vizə] *f* (-;-n) meadow
Wiesel ['vizəl] *n* (-s;-) weasel
Wie'senland *n* meadowland
wieso' *adv* why, how come
wieviel' *adj* how much; **w. Uhr ist es?** what time is it? || *adv & pron* how much || **vieviele** *adj & pron* how many
wievielte [vi'filtə] §9 *adj* which; what; **den wievielten haben wir?** (or **der w. ist heute?**) what day of the month is it?
wiewohl' *conj* although
wild [vɪlt] *adj* wild; savage; (*grausam*) ferocious; (*Flucht*) headlong; (**auf** *acc*) wild (about); **wilde Ehe** concubinage; **wilder Streik** wildcat strike || **Wild** *n* (-es;) game
Wild'bach *m* torrent
Wild'braten *m* roast venison
Wildbret ['vɪltbret] *n* (-s;) game; venison
Wild'dieb *m* poacher
Wilde ['vɪldə] §5 *mf* savage; **wie ein Wilder** like a madman
Wild'ente *f* wild duck
Wilderer ['vɪldərər] *m* (-s;-) poacher
wildern ['vɪldərn] *intr* poach
Wild'fleisch *n* game; venison
wild'fremd' *adj* completely strange
Wild'hüter *m* game warden
Wild'leder *n* doeskin, buckskin; chamois; suede
Wildnis ['vɪltnɪs] *f* (-;) wilderness
Wild'schwein *n* wild boar
Wild'wasser *n* rapids
Wildwest'film *m* western
wildwüchsig ['vɪltvyksɪç] *adj* wild
Wille ['vɪlə] *m* (-ns;-n), **Willen** ['vɪlən] *m* (-s;-) will; (*Absicht*) intention; **mit W.** on purpose; **um j-s willen** for s.o.'s sake; **wider Willen** unwillingly; unintentionally; **willens sein zu** (*inf*) be willing to (*inf*)
wil'lenlos *adj* irresolute; unstable
Wil'lensfreiheit *f* free will
Wil'lenskraft *f* will power
wil'lensschwach *adj* weak-willed
wil'lensstark *adj* strong-willed
willfah'ren *intr* (*dat*) comply with
willig ['vɪlɪç] *adj* willing, ready
Wil'ligkeit *f* (-;) willingness
willkom'men *adj* welcome; **j-n w. heißen** welcome s.o. || **Willkommen** *m & n* (-s;) welcome
Willkür ['vɪlkyr] *f* (-;) arbitrariness
will'kürlich *adj* arbitrary
wimmeln ['vɪməln] *intr* (**von**) team (with)
wimmern ['vɪmərn] *intr* whimper
Wimpel ['vɪmpəl] *m* (-s;-) streamer; pennant
Wimper ['vɪmpər] *f* (-;-n) eyelash; **ohne mit der W. zu zucken** without batting an eye
Wim'perntusche *f* mascara

Wind [vɪnt] *m* (-[e]s;-e) wind; flatulence; (*hunt*) scent
Wind'beutel *m* (fig) windbag; (aer) windsock; (culin) cream puff
Winde ['vɪndə] *f* (-;-n) winch, windlass; reel; (naut) capstan
Windel ['vɪndəl] *f* (-;-n) diaper
win'delweich *adj*—**w. schlagen** (coll) beat to a pulp
winden ['vɪndən] §59 *tr* wind; twist, coil; (*Kranz*) weave, make || *ref* wriggle; (*Fluß*) wind; (*vor Schmerzen*) writhe
Wind'fang *m* storm porch
Wind'hose *f* tornado
Wind'hund *m* greyhound; (coll) windbag
windig ['vɪndɪç] *adj* windy; (fig) flighty
Wind'kanal *m* wind tunnel
Wind'licht *n* hurricane lamp
Wind'mühle *f* windmill
Wind'pocken *pl* chicken pox
Wind'sack *m* windsock
Wind'schatten *m* lee
Wind'schutzscheibe *f* windshield
Wind'stärke *f* wind velocity
wind'still *adj* calm || **Windstille** *f* calm
Wind'stoß *m* gust
Wind'strömung *f* air current
Win'dung *f* (-;-en) winding, twisting; (*Kurve*) bend; (*e-r Schlange*) coil; (*e-r Schraube*) thread, worm; (*e-r Muschel*) whorl
Wind'zug *m* air current, draft
Wink [vɪŋk] *m* (-[e]s;-e) sign; (*Zwinkern*) wink; (*mit der Hand*) wave; (*mit dem Kopfe*) nod; (*Hinweis*) hint, tip; **W. mit dem Zaunpfahl** broad hint
Winkel ['vɪŋkəl] *m* (-s;-) corner; (carp) square; (geom) angle; (mil) chevron
winkelig ['vɪŋkəlɪç] *adj* angular; (*Straße*) crooked
Win'kellinie *f* diagonal
Win'kelmaß *n* (carp) square
Win'kelzug *m* subterfuge; evasion
winken ['vɪŋkən] *intr* signal; **mit der Hand** wave; (*mit dem Kopfe*) nod; (*mit dem Auge*) wink; **mit dem Taschentuch w.** wave the handkerchief
Win'ker *m* (-s;-) signalman; (aut) direction signal
winseln ['vɪnzəln] *intr* whimper, whine
Winter ['vɪntər] *m* (-s;-) winter
win'terfest *adj* winterized; (*Pflanzen*) hardy
win'terlich *adj* wintry
Win'terschlaf *m* hibernation; **W. halten** hibernate
Win'tersonnenwende *f* winter solstice
Winzer ['vɪntsər] *m* (-s;-) vinedresser; (*Traubenleser*) grape picker
winzig ['vɪntsɪç] *adj* tiny
Wipfel ['vɪpfəl] *m* (-s;-) treetop
Wippe ['vɪpə] *f* (-;-n) seesaw
wippen ['vɪpən] *intr* seesaw; rock; balance oneself
wir [vir] §11 *pers pron* we
Wirbel ['vɪrbəl] *m* (-s;-) whirl; eddy; whirlpool; (*Trommel-*) roll; (*Violin-*)

peg; (anat) vertebra; **e-n W. machen** (coll) raise Cain

wir'belig ['vɪrbəlɪç] adj whirling; giddy

Wir'belknochen m (anat) vertebra

wir'bellos adj spineless, invertebrate

wirbeln ['vɪrbəln] tr warble || intr whirl; (Wasser) eddy; (Trommel) roll; (Lerche) warble; **mir wirbelt der Kopf** my head is spinning

Wir'belsäule f spinal column, spine

Wir'belsturm m hurricane, typhoon

Wir'beltier n vertebrate

Wir'belwind m whirlwind

wirken ['vɪrkən] tr work, bring about, effect; (Teig) knead; (Teppich) weave; (Pullover) knit; **Gutes w. do good; Wunder w. work wonders** || intr work; be active; function; look, appear; (Worte) tell, hit home; **als Arzt w.** be a doctor; **an e-r Schule (als Lehrer) w.** teach school; **anregend w.** act as a stimulant; **berauschend w. auf** (acc) intoxicate; **beruhigend w. auf** (acc) have a soothing effect on; **gut w.** work well; **lächerlich w.** look ridiculous; **stark w. auf** (acc) touch deeply; **w. auf** (acc) affect, have an effect on; **w. bei** have an effect on; **w. für** work for; **w. gegen** work against, counteract || **Wirken** n (-s;) action, performance; operation

wirk'lich adj real, actual; true || adv really, actually; truly

Wirk'lichkeit f (-;-en) reality; actual fact

Wirk'lichkeitsform f indicative mood

wirksam ['vɪrkzam] adj active; effective; (Hieb) telling; **w. für** good for

Wirk'samkeit f (-;) effectiveness

Wirk'stoff m metabolic substance (vitamin, hormone, or enzyme)

Wir'kung f (-;-en) effect; result; operation, action; influence, impression

Wir'kungsbereich m scope; effective range; (mil) zone of fire

wir'kungsfähig adj active; effective; efficient

Wir'kungskreis m domain, province

wir'kungslos adj ineffective; inefficient

wir'kungsvoll adj effective; efficacious

Wirk'waren pl knitwear

wirr [vɪr] adj confused; (verworren) chaotic; (Haar) disheveled

Wirren ['vɪrən] pl disorders, troubles

Wirr'kopf m scatterbrain

Wirrwarr ['vɪrvar] m (-s;) mix-up, mess

Wirt [vɪrt] m (-[e]s;-e) host; innkeeper; landlord; (biol) host

Wirtin ['vɪrtɪn] f (-;-nen) hostess; innkeeper, innkeeper's wife; landlady

wirt'lich adj hospitable

Wirt'schaft f (-;-en) economy; business; industry and trade; (Haushaltung) housekeeping; (Hauswesen) household; (Gasthaus) inn; (Treiben) goings-on; (Durcheinander) mess; (Umstände) fuss, trouble; **die W. besorgen** (or **führen**) keep house; **gelenkte W.** planned economy

wirtschaften ['vɪrtʃaftən] intr keep

house; economize; (herumhantieren) bustle about; **gut w.** manage well

Wirt'schafter –in §6 mf manager || f housekeeper

Wirt'schaftler –in §6 mf economist; economics teacher

wirt'schaftlich adj economical, thrifty; economic; industrial; (vorteilhaft) profitable

Wirt'schaftsgeld n housekeeping money

Wirt'schaftshilfe f economic aid

Wirt'schaftsjahr n fiscal year

Wirt'schaftslehre f economics

Wirt'schaftspolitik f economic policy

Wirt'schaftsprüfer –in §6 mf certified public accountant, CPA

Wirts'haus n inn, restaurant; bar

wischen ['vɪʃən] tr wipe

Wisch'lappen m dustcloth

Wisch'tuch n dishtowel

wispern ['vɪspərn] tr & intr whisper

Wißbegierde ['vɪsbəgirdə] f (-;) craving for knowledge; curiosity

wissen ['vɪsən] §161 tr & intr know || **Wissen** n (-s;) knowledge; learning; know-how; **meines Wissens** as far as I know

Wis'senschaft f (-;-en) knowledge; science

Wis'senschaftler –in §6 mf scientist

wis'senschaftlich adj scientific; scholarly; learned

Wis'sensdrang m, **Wis'sensdurst** m thirst for knowledge

Wis'sensgebiet n field of knowledge

wis'senswert adj worth knowing

wis'sentlich adj conscious; willful || adv knowingly; on purpose

wittern ['vɪtərn] tr scent, smell

Wit'terung f (-;-en) weather; (hunt) scent; **bei günstiger W.** weather permitting; **e-e feine W. haben** have a good nose

Wit'terungsverhältnisse pl weather conditions

Witwe ['vɪtvə] f (-;-n) widow

Witwer ['vɪtvər] m (-s;-) widower

Witz [vɪts] m (-es;-e) joke; wisecrack; wit; wittiness; **das ist der ganze W.** that's all; **Witze machen** (or **reißen**) crack jokes

Witz'blatt n comics

Witzbold ['vɪtsbɔlt] m (-[e]s;-e) joker

witzig ['vɪtsɪç] adj witty; funny

wo [vo] adv where; **wo auch** (or **wo immer**) wherever; **wo nicht** if not; **wo nur** wherever

woan'ders adv somewhere else

wob [vop] pret of **weben**

wobei' adv whereby; whereat; whereto; at which; in the course of which

Woche ['vɔxə] f (-;-n) week; **heute in e-r W.** a week from today; **in den Wochen sein** be in labor; **in die Wochen kommen** go into labor; **unter der W.** (coll) during the week

Wo'chenbeihilfe f maternity benefits

Wo'chenbett n post-natal period

Wo'chenblatt n weekly (newspaper)

Wo'chenende n weekend

Wo'chengeld n weekly allowance; (für Mütter) maternity benefits wo'chenlang *adj* lasting many weeks ‖ *adv* for weeks

Wo'chenlohn *m* weekly wages

Wo'chenschau *f* (cin) newsreel

wöchentlich ['vœçəntlıç] *adj* weekly ‖ *adv* every week; einmal w. once a week

-wöchig [vœçıç] *comb.fm.* -week

Wöchnerin ['vœçnərɪn] *f* (-;-nen) recent mother

Wodka ['vɔtka] *m* (-s;) vodka

wodurch' *adv* whereby, by which; how

wofern' *conj* provided that; w. nicht unless

wofür' *adv* wherefore, for which; what for; w. halten Sie mich? what do you take me for?

wog [vok] *pret* of wägen & wiegen

Woge ['vogə] *f* (-;-n) billow; Wogen der Erregung waves of excitement

woge'gen *adv* against what; against which; in exchange for what

wogen ['vogən] *intr* billow, surge, heave; (Getreide) wave; hin und her w. fluctuate

woher' *adv* from where; w. wissen Sie das? how do you know this?

wohin' *adv* whereto, where

wohinge'gen *conj* whereas

wohl [vol] *adj* well ‖ *adv* well; (freilich) to be sure, all right; I guess; possibly, probably; perhaps; es sich [dat] w. sein lassen have a good time; nun w.! well!; w. daran tun zu (inf) do well to (inf); w. dem, der happy he who; w. kaum hardly; w. oder übel willy-nilly ‖ Wohl *n* (-[e]s;) good health, well-being; (Wohlfahrt) welfare; (Gedeihen) prosperity; auf Ihr W.! to your health! gemeines W. common good

wohlan' *interj* all right then!

wohlauf' *adj* in good health, well ‖ *interj* all right then!

wohlbedacht ['volbədaxt] *adj* well-thought-out

Wohl'befinden *n* (-;) well-being

Wohl'behagen *n* comfort, contentment

wohl'behalten *adj* safe and sound

wohl'bekannt *adj* well-known

wohl'beschaffen *adj* in good condition

Wohl'ergehen *n* well-being

wohl'erzogen *adj* well-bred

Wohl'fahrt *f* (-;) welfare

Wohl'fahrtsarbeit *f* social work

wohl'feil *adj* cheap

Wohl'gefallen *n* (-s;) pleasure, satisfaction

wohl'gefällig *adj* pleasant, agreeable

wohl'gemeint *adj* well-meant

wohlgemut ['volgəmut] *adj* cheerful

wohl'genährt *adj* well-fed

wohl'geneigt *adj* affectionate

Wohl'geruch *m* fragrance, perfume

wohl'gesinnt *adj* well-disposed

wohl'habend *adj* well-to-do

wohlig ['volıç] *adj* comfortable

Wohl'klang *m* melodious sound

wohl'klingend *adj* melodious

Wohl'leben *n* good living, luxury

wohl'riechend *adj* fragrant

wohl'schmeckend *adj* tasty

Wohl'sein *n* good health, well-being

Wohl'stand *m* prosperity, wealth

Wohl'tat *f* benefit; (Gunst) kindness, good deed; e-e W. sein hit the spot

Wohl'täter -in §6 *mf* benefactor

wohl'tätig *adj* charitable; beneficent

Wohl'tätigkeit *f* charity

wohltuend ['voltu-ənt] *adj* pleasant

wohl'tun §154 *intr* do good; (dat) be pleasant (to)

wohl'unterrichtet *adj* well-informed

wohl'verdient *adj* well-deserved

wohl'verstanden *interj* mark my words!

wohl'weislich *adv* very wisely

wohl'wollen §162 *intr* (dat) be well-disposed towards ‖ Wohlwollen *n* (-s;) good will; (Gunst) favor

Wohn- [von] *comb.fm.* residential; dwelling, living

Wohn'anhänger *m* house trailer

Wohn'block *m* block of apartments

wohnen ['vonən] *intr* live, reside; (als Mieter) room

wohn'haft *adj* residing, living

Wohn'haus *n* dwelling; apartment house

Wohn'küche *f* efficiency apartment

Wohn'laube *f* garden house

wohn'lich *adj* livable; cozy

Wohn'möglichkeit *f* living accommodations

Wohn'ort *m* place of residence; (jur) domicile; ständiger W. permanent address

Wohn'raum *m* living space; room (of a house)

Wohn'sitz *m* place of residence

Woh'nung *f* (-;-en) dwelling, home; apartment; room; accommodations

Woh'nungsamt *n* housing authority

Woh'nungsbau *m* (-[e]s;) housing construction

Woh'nungsfrage *f* housing problem

Woh'nungsinhaber -in §6 *mf* occupant

Woh'nungsmangel *m*, Woh'nungsnot *f* housing shortage

Wohn'viertel *n* residential district

Wohn'wagen *m* mobile home

Wohn'wagenparkplatz *m* trailer camp

Wohn'zimmer *n* living room

wölben ['vœlbən] *tr* vault, arch ‖ *ref* (über dat or acc) arch (over)

Wöl'bung *f* (-;-en) curvature; vault

Wolf [vɔlf] *m* (-[e]s;ːe) wolf; (Fleisch-) meat grinder; (astr) Lupus; (pathol) lupus

Wolfram ['vɔlfram] *n* (-s;) tungsten

Wolke ['vɔlkə] *f* (-;-n) cloud

Wol'kenbildung *f* cloud formation

Wol'kenbruch *m* cloudburst

Wol'kendecke *f* cloudcover

Wol'kenfetzen *m* wispy cloud

Wol'kenhöhe *f* (meteor) ceiling

Wol'kenkratzer *m* (-s;-) skyscraper

Wol'kenwand *f* cloud bank

wolkig ['vɔlkıç] *adj* cloudy, clouded

Wolldecke ['vɔldekə] *f* woolen blanket

Wolle ['vɔlə] *f* (-;-n) wool

wollen ['vɔlən] *adj* woolen, wool ‖ §162 *tr* want, desire; mean, intend; (gern haben) like ‖ *intr* wish, like; dem sei, wie ihm wolle be that as it may; wie Sie w. as you please ‖ *mod aux* want (to), wish (to), intend (to);

be going (to) ‖ **Wollen** *n* (**-s;**) will; volition

Wollfett [ˈvɔlfɛt] *n* lanolin

Wollgarn [ˈvɔlgarn] *n* worsted

wollig [ˈvɔlɪç] *adj* woolly

Wolljacke [ˈvɔljakə] *f* cardigan

Wollsachen [ˈvɔlzaxən] *pl* woolens

Wollstoff [ˈvɔlʃtɔf] *m* woolen fabric

Wollust [ˈvɔlʊst] *f* (**-;-e**) lust

wollüstig [ˈvɔlʏstɪç] *adj* voluptuous; (*geil*) lewd, lecherous

Wollüstling [ˈvɔlʏstlɪŋ] *m* (**-s;-e**) voluptuary

Wollwaren [ˈvɔlvarən] *pl* woolens

womit' *adv* with which; with what; wherewith; **w. kann ich dienen?** (com) can I help you?

womög'lich *adv* possibly, if possible

wonach' *adv* after which, whereupon; according to which

Wonne [ˈvɔnə] *f* (**-;-n**) delight; bliss

Won'negefühl *n* blissful feeling

Won'neschauer *m* thrill of delight

won'netrunken *adj* enraptured

won'nevoll, wonnig [ˈvɔnɪç] *adj* blissful

woran' *adv* at which; at what; **ich weiß nicht, w. ich bin** I don't know where I stand

worauf' *adv* on which; on what; whereupon; **w. warten Sie?** what are you waiting for?

woraus' *adv* out of what, from what; out of which, from which; **w. ist das gemacht?** what is this made of?

worden [ˈvɔrdən] *pp* of **werden**

worin' *adv* in what; in which

Wort [vɔrt] *n* (**-[e]s;-̈er**) word (*individual; literal*) ‖ *n* (**-[e]s;-e**) word (*expression; figurative*); (*Ausspruch*) saying; (*Ehrenwort*) word (*of honor*); **auf ein W.!** may I have a word with you!; **auf mein W.!** word of honor!; **aufs W.** implicitly, to the letter; **das W. ergreifen** begin to speak; (parl) take the floor; **das W. erhalten** (or **haben**) be allowed to speak; (parl) have the floor; **das W. führen** be the spokesman; **hast du Worte!** (coll) can you beat that!; **in Worten** in writing; **j—m das W. erteilen** allow s.o. to speak; **j—m ins W. fallen** cut s.o. short

Wort'art *f* (gram) part of speech

Wort'bedeutungslehre *f* semantics

Wort'beugung *f* declension

Wort'bildung *f* word formation

wort'brüchig *adj*—**w. werden** break one's word

Wörterbuch [ˈvœrtərbux] *n* dictionary

Wörterverzeichnis [ˈvœrtərfɛrtsaɪçnɪs] *n* word index; vocabulary; glossary

Wort'folge *f* word order

Wort'führer –in §6 *mf* spokesman

Wort'gefecht *n* dispute

wort'getreu *adj* literal; verbatim

wort'karg *adj* taciturn

Wortklauber –in [ˈvɔrtklaubər(ɪn)] §6 *mf* quibbler, hairsplitter

Wort'laut *m* wording; (fig) letter

wörtlich [ˈvœrtlɪç] *adj* word-for-word; literal; (*Rede*) direct

wort'los *adv* without saying a word

Wort'register *n* word index

Wort'schatz *m* vocabulary

Wort'schwall *m* flood of words, verbiage

Wort'spiel *n* pun

Wort'stamm *m* stem

Wort'stellung *f* word order

Wort'streit *m*, **Wort'wechsel** *m* argument

worüber [voˈrybər] *adv* over what, over which

worum [voˈrum] *adv* about what, about which

worunter [voˈrʊntər] *adv* under what, under which; among which

wovon' *adv* from what, of what, from which, of which; **w. ist die Rede?** what are they talking about?

wovor' *adv* of what; before which

wozu' *adv* for what; why; to which

Wrack [vrak] *n* (**-[e]s;-e & -s**) (& fig) wreck

Wrack'gut *n* wreckage

wrang [vraŋ] *pret* of **wringen**

wringen [ˈvrɪŋən] §142 *tr* wring

Wringmaschine [ˈvrɪŋmaʃinə] *f* wringer

Wucher [ˈvuxər] *m* (**-s;**) profiteering; **das ist ja W.!** (coll) that's highway robbery!; **W. treiben** profiteer

Wu'cherer –in §6 *mf* profiteer; loan shark

Wu'chergewinn *m* excess profit

wu'cherhaft, wucherisch [ˈvuxərɪʃ] *adj* profiteering, exorbitant

Wu'chermiete *f* excessive rent

wuchern [ˈvuxərn] *intr* grow luxuriantly; (*Wucher treiben*) profiteer

Wu'cherung *f* (**-;-en**) (bot) rank growth; (pathol) growth

Wu'cherzinsen *pl* excessive interest

wuchs [vuks] *pret* of **wachsen** ‖ **Wuchs** *m* (**-es;**) growth; **groß von W.** tall **–wüchsig** [vʏksɪç] *comb.fm.* –growing, –grown

Wucht [vuxt] *f* (**-;-en**) weight, force

wuchten [ˈvuxtən] *tr* lift with effort

wuchtig [ˈvuxtɪç] *adj* heavy; massive

Wühlarbeit [ˈvylarbaɪt] *f* subversive activity

wühlen [ˈvylən] *intr* dig, burrow; (*Schwein*) root about; (*suchend*) rummage about; (pol) engage in subversive activities; **im Geld w.** be rolling in money; **in Schmutz w.** wallow in filth

Wüh'ler –in §6 *mf* subversive, agitator

Wulst [vulst] *m* (**-es;-̈e**) & *f* (**-;-̈e**) bulge; (aut) rim (*of tire*)

wulstig [ˈvulstɪç] *adj* bulging; (*Lippen*) thick

wund [vunt] *adj* sore; (poet) wounded

Wunde [ˈvundə] *f* (**-;-n**) wound; sore

Wunder [ˈvundər] *n* (**-s;-**) wonder; miracle; **W. wirken** work wonders

wunderbar [ˈvundərbar] *adj* wonderful; (& fig) miraculous

Wun'derding *n* marvel

Wun'derdoktor *m* faith healer

Wun'derkind *n* child prodigy

Wun'derkraft *f* miraculous power

wun'derlich *adj* queer, odd

wundern [ˈvundərn] *tr* amaze ‖ *ref*

(**über** *acc*) be amazed (at) ‖ *impers* —**es sollte mich w., wenn** I'd be surprised if; **es wundert mich, daß I am** surprised that

wun'derschön' *adv* lovely, gorgeous

Wun'dertat *f* miracle

Wun'dertäter –in §6 *mf* wonder worker

wundertätig *adj* miraculous

wun'dervoll *adj* wonderful, marvelous

Wun'derwerk *n* (& fig) miracle

wun'derzeichen *n* omen, prodigy

Wund'klammer *f* (surg) clamp

wund'liegen §108 *ref* get bedsores

Wund'mal *n* scar, sore; (relig) wound

wund'reiten §86 *ref* become saddlesore

Wunsch [vunʃ] *m* (-es;⁼e) wish; (**nach**) desire (for); **auf W.** upon request; **ein frommer W.** wishful thinking; **nach W.** as desired

Wünschelrute ['vynʃəlrutə] *f* divining rod

Wün'schelrutengänger *m* dowser

wünschen ['vynʃən] *tr* wish; wish for, desire; **was w. Sie?** (com) may I help you? ‖ *intr* wish, please

wün'schenswert *adj* desirable

Wunsch'form *f* (gram) optative

Wunsch'konzert *n* (rad) request program

wunsch'los *adj* contented ‖ *adv*—**w. glücklich** perfectly happy

wuppdich ['vupdɪç] *interj* zip!, in a flash!; all of a sudden!

wurde ['vurdə] *pret* of **werden**

Würde ['vyrdə] *f* (-;-n) honor; title; dignity; post, office; **akademische W.** academic degree; **unter aller W.** beneath contempt

wür'delos *adj* undignified

Wür'denträger –in §6 *mf* dignitary

wür'devoll *adj* dignified

würdig ['vyrdɪç] *adj* dignified; (genit) worthy (of), deserving (of)

würdigen ['vyrdɪgən] *tr* appreciate, value; (genit) deem worthy (of)

Wurf [vurf] *m* (-[e]s;⁼e) throw, cast, pitch; (fig) hit, success; (zool) litter, brood

Wurf'anker *m* grapnel

Würfel ['vyrfəl] *m* (-s;-) die; cube,

square; (geom) cube; **W. spielen** play dice

Wür'felbecher *m* dice box

würfelig ['vyrfəlɪç] *adj* cube-shaped; (*Muster*) checkered

würfeln ['vyrfəln] *intr* play dice

Wür'felzucker *m* cube sugar

Wurf'geschoß *n* projectile, missile

Wurf'pfeil *m* dart

würgen ['vyrgən] *tr* choke; strangle ‖ *intr* choke; **am Essen w.** gag on food

Wurm [vurm] *m* (-s;⁼er) (& mach) worm

wurmen ['vurmən] *tr* (coll) bug

wurmig ['vurmɪç] *adj* wormy; wormeaten

wurmstichig ['vurmʃtɪçɪç] *adj* wormeaten

Wurst [vurst] *f* (-;⁼e) sausage; **es geht um die W.** now or never; **es ist mir W.** I couldn't care less

Würstchen ['vyrstçən] *n* (-s;-), **Würstel** ['vyrstəl] *n* (-s;-n) hotdog

wursteln ['vurstəln] *intr* muddle along

Würze ['vyrtsə] *f* (-;-n) spice, seasoning; (fig) zest

Wurzel ['vurtsəl] *f* (-;-n) root; **W. fassen** (or **schlagen**) take root

wurzeln ['vurtsəln] *intr* (HABEN & SEIN) take root; **w. in** (dat) be rooted in

würzen ['vyrtsən] *tr* spice, season

würzig ['vyrtsɪç] *adj* spicy; aromatic

Würz'stoff *m* seasoning

wusch [vuʃ] *pret* of **waschen**

wußte ['vustə] *pret* of **wissen**

Wust [vust] *m* (-es) jumble, mess

wüst [vyst] *adj* desert, waste; (roh) coarse; (wirr) confused

Wüste ['vystə] *f* (-;-en) desert

Wüstling ['vystlɪŋ] *m* (-s;-e) debauchee

Wut [vut] *f* (-;) rage, fury; madness

Wut'anfall *m* fit of rage

wüten ['vytən] *intr* rage

wü'tend *adj* (**auf** *acc*) furious (at)

Wüterich ['vytərɪç] *m* (-s;-e) madman; bloodthirsty villain

wut'schäumend *adj* foaming with rage

wut'schnaubend *adj* in a towering rage

Wut'schrei *m* shout of anger

X

X, x [ɪks] *invar n* X, x

X'-Beine *pl* knock-knees

x'-beinig *adj* knock-kneed

x'-beliebig *adj* any, whatever ‖ **X-beliebige** §5 *m*—**jeder X.** every Tom, Dick, and Harry

x'-fach *adj* (coll) hundredfold

x'-mal *adv* umpteen times

X'-Strahlen *pl* x-rays

X'-Tag *m* D-day

x-te ['ɪkstə] §9 *adj* umpteenth; **die x-te Potenz** (math) the nth power

Xylophon [ksylo'fon] *n* (-s;-e) xylophone

Y

Y, y [ypsilon] *invar n* Y, y

Yacht [jaxt] *f* (-;-en) yacht

Yamswurzel ['jamsvurtsəl] *f* (-;-n) (bot) yam

Yankee ['jɛŋki] *m* (-s;-s) Yankee

Yoghurt ['jogurt] *m* & *n* (-s;) yogurt

Yo-Yo ['jo'jo] *n* (-s;-s) yo-yo

Ypsilon ['ypsilon] *n* (-[s];-s) y

Z

Z, z [tset] *invar n* Z, z
Zacke ['tsakə] *f* (-;-n) sharp point; (*Zinke*) prong; (*Fels-*) crag; (*e-s Kamms, e-r Säge*) tooth; (*am Kleid*) scallop
zacken ['tsakən] *tr* notch; scallop ‖ **Zacken** *m* (-s;-) var of Zacke
zackig ['tsakɪç] *adj* toothed; notched; (*Felsen*) jagged; (*spitz*) pointed; (*Kleid*) scalloped; (fig) sharp
zagen ['tsagən] *intr* be faint-hearted
zaghaft ['tsakhaft] *adj* timid
zäh [tse] *adj* tough; (*klebig*) viscous; (*beharrlich*) persistent; (*Gedächtnis*) tenacious; (*halsstarrig*) dogged
zäh′flüssig *adj* viscous
Zäh′flüssigkeit *f* (-;) viscosity
Zä′higkeit *f* (-;) toughness; tenacity; viscosity; doggedness
Zahl [tsal] *f* (-;-en) number; (*Betrag, Ziffer*) figure; **an Z. übertreffen** outnumber; **arabische Z.** Arabic numeral; **der Z. nach** in number; **ganze Z.** integer; **gebrochene Z.** fraction; **gerade Z.** even number; **in roten Zahlen stecken** be in the red; **ungerade Z.** odd number; **wenig an der Z.** few in number
zahlbar ['tsalbar] *adj* payable; **z. bei Lieferung** cash on delivery
zählebig ['tselebɪç] *adj* hardy
zahlen ['tsalən] *tr* pay; (*Schuld*) pay off ‖ *intr* pay
zählen ['tselən] *tr* count; number, amount to ‖ *intr* count; be of importance, count; **nach Tausenden z.** number in the thousands; **z. auf** (*dat*) count on; **z. zu** be numbered among, belong to
Zah′lenangaben *pl* figures
Zah′lenfolge *f* numerical order
zah′lenmäßig *adj* numerical
Zah′ler –in §6 *mf* payer
Zäh′ler (-s;-) counter; recorder; (*für Gas, Elektrizität*) meter; (math) numerator; (parl) teller; (sport) scorekeeper
Zählerableser ['tseləraplezər] *m* (-s;-) meter man
Zahl′karte *f* money-order form
zahl′los *adj* countless, innumerable
Zahl′meister *m* paymaster; (mil) pay officer; (nav) purser
zahl′reich *adj* numerous
Zähl′rohr *n* Geiger counter
Zahl′stelle *f* cashier's window; (*e-r Bank*) branch office
Zahl′tag *m* payday
Zah′lung *f* (-;-en) payment; (*e-r Schuld*) settlement
Zäh′lung *f* (-;-en) counting; computation
Zah′lungsanweisung *f* draft; check; postal money order
Zah′lungsausgleich *m* balance of payments
Zah′lungsbedingungen *pl* (fin) terms
Zah′lungsbestätigung *f* receipt

Zah′lungsbilanz *f* balance of payments; **aktive** (or **passive**) **Z.** favorable (or unfavorable) balance of payments
zah′lungsfähig *adj* solvent
Zah′lungsfähigkeit *f* (-;) solvency
Zah′lungsfrist *f* due date
Zah′lungsmittel *n* medium of exchange; **gesetzliches Z.** legal tender; **bargeldloses Z.** instrument of credit
Zah′lungsschwierigkeiten *pl* financial embarrassment
Zah′lungssperre *f* stoppage of payments
Zah′lungstermin *m* date of payment; (fin) date of maturity
Zah′lungsverzug *m* (fin) default
Zähl′werk *n* meter
Zahl′wort *n* (-[e]s;‐er) numeral
Zahl′zeichen *n* figure, cipher
zahm [tsam] *adj* tame; domesticated
zähmen ['tsemən] *tr* tame; domesticate; (fig) control ‖ *ref* control oneself
Zäh′mung *f* (-;) taming; domestication
Zahn [tsan] *m* (-[e]s;‐e) tooth; (mach) tooth, cog; **j-m auf den Z. fühlen** sound s.o. out; **mit den Zähnen knirschen** grind one's teeth
Zahn′arzt *m*, **Zahn′ärztin** *f* dentist
Zahn′bürste *f* toothbrush
Zahn′creme *f* toothpaste
zahnen ['tsanən] *intr* cut one's teeth
Zahn′ersatz *m* denture
Zahn′fäule *f* tooth decay, caries
Zahn′fleisch *n* gum
Zahn′füllung *f* (dent) filling
Zahn′heilkunde *f* dentistry
Zahn′klammer *f* (-;-n) (dent) brace
Zahn′krem *f* toothpaste
Zahn′krone *f* (dent) crown
Zahn′laut *m* (phonet) dental
Zahn′lücke *f* gap between the teeth
Zahn′paste *f* toothpaste
Zahn′pflege *f* dental hygiene
Zahn′pulver *n* tooth powder
Zahn′rad *n* cog wheel; (*Kettenrad*) sprocket
Zahn′radbahn *f* cog railway
Zahn′schmerz *m* toothache
Zahn′spange *f* (-;-n) (dent) brace
Zahn′stein *m* (dent) tartar
Zahnstocher ['tsan/toxər] *m* (-s;-) toothpick
Zahn′techniker –in §6 *mf* dental technician
Zahn′weh *n* toothache
Zange ['tsaŋə] *f* (-;-en) (pair of) pliers; (pair of) tongs; (*Pinzette*) (pair of) tweezers; (dent, surg, zool) forceps; **j-n in die Z. nehmen** corner s.o. (*with tough questioning*)
Zank [tsaŋk] *m* (-[e]s;) quarrel, fight
Zank′apfel *m* apple of discord
zanken ['tsaŋkən] *tr* scold ‖ *recip & intr* quarrel, fight
zank′haft, zänkisch ['tseŋkɪʃ], **zank′süchtig** *adj* quarrelsome

Zäpfchen ['tsepfçən] *n* (-s;-) little peg; (anat) uvula; (med) suppository

zapfen ['tsapfən] *tr* (*Bier, Wein*) tap ‖ **Zapfen** *m* (-s;-) plug, bung; (*Stift*) stud; (*Drehpunkt*) pivot; (*Eis*-) icicle; (*Tannen*-) cone; (carp) tenon; (mach) pin; (mach) journal

Zap'fenstreich *m* (mil) taps

Zapfhahn ['tsapfhɑn] *m* tap, spigot

Zapfsäule ['tsapfzɔɪlə] *f* (-;-n) (aut) gasoline pump

Zapfstelle ['tsapf/tɛlə] *f* (-;-n) (aut) service station, gas station

Zapfwart ['tsapfvart] *m* (-[e]s;-e) (aut) service station attendant

zappelig ['tsapəlɪç] *adj* fidgety

zappeln ['tsapəln] *intr* fidget; squirm; (*im Wasser*) flounder

Zar [tsɑr] *m* (-en;-en) czar

Zarge ['tsargə] *f* (-;-n) border; frame

zart [tsart] *adj* tender; (*Farbe, Haut*) soft; (*Gesundheit*) delicate

zart'fühlend *adj* tender; sensitive

Zart'gefühl *n* sensitivity; tact

Zart'heit *f* (-;) tenderness

zärtlich ['tsertlɪç] *adj* tender, affectionate

Zärt'lichkeit *f* (-;-en) tenderness; (*Liebkosung*) caress

Zaster ['tsastər] *m* (-s;) (coll) dough

Zauber ['tsaubər] *m* (-s;-) spell; magic; (fig) charm, glamor

Zauber- *comb.fm.* magic

Zauberei [tsaubə'raɪ] *f* (-;-en) magic; witchcraft, sorcery

Zau'berer *m* (-s;-) magician; sorcerer

Zau'berformel *f* incantation, spell

zau'berhaft *adj* magic; enchanting

Zau'berin *f* (-;-nen) sorceress, witch; enchantress

zauberisch ['tsaubərɪʃ] *adj* magic

Zau'berkraft *f* magic power

Zau'berkunst *f* magic

Zau'berkünstler *-in* §6 *mf* magician

Zau'berkunststück *n* magic trick

Zau'berland *n* fairyland

zaubern ['tsaubərn] *tr* produce by magic ‖ *intr* practice magic; do magic tricks

Zau'berspruch *m* incantation, spell

Zau'berstab *m* magic wand

Zau'bertrank *m* magic potion

Zau'berwerk *n* witchcraft

Zau'berwort *n* (-[e]s;-e) magic word

zaudern ['tsaudərn] *intr* procrastinate; hesitate; linger

Zaum [tsaum] *m* (-[e]s;ᵉe) bridle; im Z. halten keep in check

zäumen ['tsɔɪmən] *tr* bridle

Zaun [tsaun] *m* (-[e]s;ᵉe) fence; e-n Streit vom Z. brechen pick a quarrel

Zaun'gast *m* non-paying spectator

Zaun'könig *m* (orn) wren

Zaun'pfahl *m* fence post

zausen ['tsauzən] *tr* tug at; tousle, ruffle ‖ *recip* tug at each other

Zebra ['tsebra] *n* (-s;-s) zebra

Ze'brastreifen *m* zebra stripe; (*auf der Fahrbahn*) passenger crossing

Zech- [tsɛç] *comb.fm.* drinking

Zech'bruder *m* boozehound

Zeche ['tsɛçə] *f* (-;-n) (*Wirtshausrechnung*) check; (min) mine die Z.

prellen (coll) sneak out without paying the bill

zechen ['tsɛçən] *intr* booze

Ze'cher *-in* §6 *mf* heavy drinker

Zech'gelage *n* drinking party

Zechpreller ['tsɛçprɛlər] *m* (-s;-) cheat, bilker

Zech'tour *f* binge; e-e Z. machen go on a binge

Zecke ['tsɛkə] *f* (-;-n) (ent) tick

Zeder ['tsedər] *f* (-;-n) cedar

Zehe ['tse·ə] *f* (-;-n) toe; (*Knoblauch*-) clove

Ze'hennagel *m* toenail

Ze'henspitze *f* tip of the toe; auf den Zehenspitzen (on) tiptoe

zehn [tsen] *invar adj & pron* ten ‖ **Zehn** *f* (-;-en) ten

Zehner ['tsenər] *m* (-s;-) ten; tenmark bill

zehn'fach, zehn'fältig *adj* tenfold

Zehnfin'gersystem *n* touch-type system

Zehn'kampf *m* decathlon

zehn'mal *adv* ten times

zehnte ['tsentə] §9 *adj & pron* tenth ‖ **Zehnte** §5 *mfn* tenth

Zehntel ['tsentəl] *n* (-s;-) tenth (part)

zehren ['tserən] *intr* be debilitating; an den Kräften z. drain one's strength; an der Gesundheit z. undermine one's health; z. an (dat) (fig) gnaw at; z. von live on, live off

Zeh'rung *f* (-;) provisions; expenses

Zeichen ['tsaɪçən] *n* (-s;-) sign; signal; token; (*Merkmal*) distinguishing mark; (*Beweis*) proof; symbol; (astr) sign; (com) brand; (med) symptom; (rad) call sign; er ist seines Zeichens Anwalt he is a lawyer by profession; zum Z., daß as proof that

Zei'chenbrett *n* drawing board

Zei'chenbuch *n* sketchbook

Zei'chengerät *n* drafting equipment

Zei'chenheft *n* sketchbook

Zei'chenlehrer *-in* §6 *mf* art teacher

Zei'chenpapier *n* drawing paper

Zei'chensetzung *f* punctuation

Zei'chensprache *f* sign language

Zei'chentisch *m* drawing board

Zei'chentrickfilm *m* animated cartoon

Zei'chenunterricht *m* drawing lesson

zeichnen ['tsaɪçnən] *tr* draw; sketch; (*entwerfen*) design; (*brandmarken*) brand; (*Anleihe*) take out; (*Aktien*) buy; (*Geld*) pledge; (*Wäsche*) mark; (*Brief*) sign ‖ *intr* draw; sketch; (hunt) leave a trail of blood; z. für sign for

Zeich'ner *-in* §6 *mf* draftsman; (*Mode*-) designer; (*e-r Anleihe*) subscriber

zeichnerisch ['tsaɪçnərɪʃ] *adj* (*Begabung*) for drawing; (*Darstellung*) graphic

Zeich'nung *f* (-;-en) drawing; sketch; design; picture, illustration; diagram; signature; (*e-r Anleihe*) subscription; (*des Holzes*) grain

zeich'nungsberechtigt *adj* authorized to sign

Zeigefinger ['tsaɪgəfɪŋər] *m* index finger

zeigen ['tsaɪgən] *tr* show, indicate;

(*in e-r Rede*) point out; (*zur Schau stellen*) display; (*beweisen*) prove; (*dartun*) demonstrate ‖ *ref* appear, show up; prove to be ‖ *intr* point; **z. auf** (*acc*) point to; **z. nach** point toward ‖ *impers ref*—**es zeigt sich, daß** it turns out that; **es wird sich ja z., ob** we shall see whether

Zei′ger *m* (**-s;-**) pointer; indicator; (*e-r Uhr*) hand

Zeigestock [′tsaɪgəʃtɔk] *m* pointer

Zeile [′tsaɪlə] *f* (**-;-n**) line; (*Reihe*) row

Zeit [tsaɪt] *f* (**-;-en**) time; **auf Z.** (com) on credit, on time; **in der letzten Z.** lately; **in jüngster Z.** quite recently; **mit der Z.** in time, in the course of time; **vor Zeiten** in former times; **zu meiner Z.** in my time; **zu rechter Z.** in the nick of time; on time; **zur Z.** at present; **zur Z.** (*genit*) at the time of

Zeit′abschnitt *m* period, epoch

Zeit′abstand *m* interval of time

Zeit′alter *n* age

Zeit′angabe *f* time; date; exact date and hour; **ohne Z.** undated

Zeit′ansage *f* (rad) (giving of) time

Zeit′aufnahme *f* (phot) time exposure

Zeit′aufwand *m* loss of time; (**für**) time spent (on)

Zeit′dauer *f* term, period of time

Zeit′einteilung *f* timetable; timing

Zei′tenfolge *f* sequence of tenses

Zei′tenwende *f* beginning of the Christian era

Zeit′folge *f* chronological order

Zeit′form *f* tense

Zeit′geist *m* spirit of the times

zeit′gemäß *adj* timely; up-to-date

Zeit′genosse *m*, **Zeit′genossin** *f* contemporary

zeitgenössisch [′tsaɪtgənœsɪʃ] *adj* contemporary

Zeit′geschichte *f* contemporary history

zeitig [′tsaɪtɪç] *adj* early; (*reif*) mature, ripe

zeitigen [′tsaɪtɪgən] *tr* ripen

Zeit′karte *f* commuter ticket

Zeit′lage *f* state of affairs

Zeit′lang *f*—**e-e Z.** for some time

Zeit′lauf *m* course of time

zeit′lebens *adv* during my (his, your, etc.) life

zeit′lich *adj* temporal; chronological ‖ *adv* in time ‖ **Zeitliche** §5 *n*—**das Z. segnen** depart this world

zeit′los *adj* timeless

Zeit′lupe *f* (cin) slow motion

Zeit′mangel *m* lack of time

Zeit′maß *n* (mus) tempo; (pros) quantity

Zeit′nehmer -in §6 *mf* timekeeper

Zeit′ordnung *f* chronological order

Zeit′punkt *m* point of time, moment

Zeitraffer [′tsaɪtrafər] *m* (**-s;**) time-lapse photography

zeit′raubend *adj* time-consuming

Zeit′raum *m* space of time, period

Zeit′rechnung *f* era

Zeit′schaltgerät *n* timer

Zeit′schrift *f* periodical, magazine

Zeit′spanne *f* span (of time)

Zeit′tafel *f* chronological table

Zei′tung *f* (**-;-en**) newspaper; journal

Zei′tungsarchiv *n* (journ) morgue

Zei′tungsartikel *m* newspaper article

Zei′tungsausschnitt *m* newspaper clipping

Zei′tungsbeilage *f* supplement

Zei′tungsdeutsch *n* journalese

Zei′tungsente *f* (journ) hoax, spoof

Zei′tungskiosk *m* newsstand

Zei′tungsmeldung *f*, **Zei′tungsnotiz** *f* newspaper item

Zei′tungspapier *n* newsprint

Zei′tungsverkäufer -in §6 *mf* newsvendor

Zei′tungswesen *n*—**das Z.** the press

Zeit′vergeudung *f* waste of time

zeit′verkürzend *adj* entertaining

Zeit′verlust *m* loss of time

Zeit′vermerk *m* date

Zeit′verschwendung *f* waste of time

Zeit′vertreib *m* pastime

zeitweilig [′tsaɪtvaɪlɪç] *adj* temporary; periodic ‖ *adv* temporarily; at times, from time to time

Zeit′wende *f* beginning of a new era

Zeit′wert *m* current value

Zeit′wort *n* (**-[e]s;-̈er**) verb

Zeit′zeichen *n* time signal

Zeit′zünder *m* time fuse

Zelle [′tsɛlə] *f* (**-;-n**) cell; (aer) fuselage; (telp) booth

Zel′lenlehre *f* cytology

Zellophan [tsɛlo′fɑn] *n* (**-s;**) cellophane

Zellstoff [′tsɛlʃtɔf] *m* cellulose

Zelluloid [tsɛlu′lɔɪt] *n* (**-s;**) celluloid

Zellulose [tsɛlu′lozə] *f* (**-;**) cellulose

Zelt [′tsɛlt] *n* (**-[e]s;-e**) tent

zelten [′tsɛltən] *intr* camp out

Zelt′pfahl *m* tent pole

Zelt′pflock *m* tent peg, tent stake

Zelt′stange *f*, **Zelt′stock** *m* tent pole

Zement [tse′mɛnt] *m* (**-[e]s;**) cement

zementieren [tsemen′tirən] *tr* cement

Zenit [tse′nit] *m* (**-[e]s;**) zenith

zensieren [tsen′zirən] *tr* censor; (educ) mark, grade

Zen·sor [′tsɛnzor] *m* (**-s;-soren** [′zorən]) censor

Zensur [tsen′zur] *f* (**-;-en**) censorship; (educ) grade, mark

Zentimeter [tsɛnti′metər] *m & n* centimeter

Zentner [′tsɛntnər] *m* (**-s;-**) hundredweight

Zent′nerlast *f* (fig) heavy load

zentral [tsen′tral] *adj* central

Zentral′behörde *f* central authority

Zentrale [tsen′tralə] *f* (**-;-n**) central office; telephone exchange, switchboard; (elec) power station

Zentral′heizung *f* central heating

Zen-trum [′tsɛntrum] *m* (**-s;-tren** [trən]) center

Zephir [′tsefɪr] *m* (**-s;-e**) zephyr

Zepter [′tsɛptər] *n* (**-s;-**) scepter

zer- [tser] *pref up, to pieces, apart*

zerbei′ßen §53 *tr* bite to pieces

zerber′sten §53 *intr* (SEIN) split apart

zerbre′chen §64 *tr* break to pieces, shatter, smash ‖ *ref*—**sich** [*dat*] **den**

Kopf z. über (*acc*) rack one's brains over ‖ *intr* (SEIN) shatter

zerbrech'lich *adj* fragile, brittle

zerbröckeln (zerbrök'keln) *tr & intr* (SEIN) crumble

zerdrücken (zerdrük'ken) *tr* crush; (*Kleid*) wrinkle; (*Kartoffeln*) mash

Zeremonie [tseremə'ni] *f* (-;-nien ['ni·ən]) ceremony

zeremoniell [tseremə'njel] *adj* ceremonial ‖ **Zeremoniell** *n* (-s;-e) ceremonial

Zeremo'nienmeister *m* master of ceremonies

zerfah'ren *adj* (*Weg*) rutted; (*zerstreut*) absent-minded; (*konfus*) scatterbrained

Zerfall' *m* (-s;) decay, ruin; disintegration; (*geistig*) decadence

zerfal'len *adj—z.* **sein mit** be at variance with ‖ §72 *intr* (SEIN) fall into ruin; decay; disintegrate; **z. in** (*acc*) divide into; **z. mit** fall out with

zerfa'sern *tr* unravel ‖ *intr* fray

zerfet'zen *tr* tear to shreds

zerflei'schen *tr* mangle; lacerate

zerflie'ßen §76 *intr* (SEIN) melt; (*Farben*) run

zerfres'sen §70 *tr* eat away, chew up; erode, eat a hole in; corrode

zerge'hen §82 *intr* (SEIN) melt

zerglie'dern *tr* dissect; analyze

zerhacken (zerhak'ken) *tr* chop up

zerkau'en *tr* chew well

zerkleinern [tser'klaınərn] *tr* cut into small pieces; chop up

zerklop'fen *tr* pound

zerklüftet [tser'klyftət] *adj* jagged

zerknirscht [tser'knırʃt] *adj* contrite

Zerknir'schung *f* (-;) contrition

zerknit'tern *tr* (*Papier*) crumple; (*Kleider*) rumple

zerknül'len *tr* crumple up

zerko'chen *tr* overcook

zerkrat'zen *tr* scratch up

zerkrü'meln *tr & intr* (SEIN) crumble

zerlas'sen §104 *tr* melt, dissolve

zerlegbar [tser'lekbar] *adj* collapsible; (*chem*) decomposable; (*math*) divisible

zerle'gen *tr* take apart; (*zerstückeln*) cut up; (*Braten*) carve; (*Licht*) dissperse; (*anat*) dissect; (*chem*) break down; (*geom*, *mus*) resolve; (*gram & fig*) analyze; (*mach*) tear down

zerle'sen *adj* well-thumbed

zerlö'chern *tr* riddle with holes

zerlumpt [tser'lumpt] *adj* tattered

zermah'len *tr* grind

zermal'men *tr* crush

zermür'ben *tr* wear down

Zermür'bung *f* (-;) attrition, wear

zerna'gen *tr* gnaw, chew up; (*chem*) corrode

zerplat'zen *intr* (SEIN) burst; explode

zerquet'schen *tr* crush; (*culin*) mash

Zerrbild ['tserbılt] *n* distorted picture; caricature

zerrei'ben §62 *tr* grind, pulverize

zerrei'ßen §95 *tr* tear; tear up; (*zerfleischen*) mangle; (*fig*) split; (*pathol*) rupture; **j—m das Herz z.** break s.o.'s heart ‖ *ref—sich z. für*

(*fig*) knock oneself out for ‖ *intr* (SEIN) tear

zerren ['tserən] *tr* drag; (*Sehne*) pull ‖ *intr* (*an dat*) tug (at)

zerrin'nen §121 *intr* (SEIN) melt away

zerrissen [tser'rısən] *adj* torn

Zer'rung *f* (-;-en) strain, muscle pull

zerrütten [tser'rytən] *tr* disorganize; (*Geist*) unhinge; (*Gesundheit*) undermine; (*Nerven*) shatter; (*Ehe*) wreck

zersä'gen *tr* saw up

zerschel'len *intr* (SEIN) be wrecked; (*Schiff*) break up

zerschie'ßen §76 *tr* shoot up

zerschla'gen *adj* battered, broken; exhausted, beat ‖ §132 *tr* beat up; break to pieces; smash; batter

zerschmel'zen *tr & intr* (SEIN) melt

zerschmet'tern *tr* smash, crush

zerschnei'den §106 *tr* cut up; mince

zerset'zen *tr* decompose; electrolyze; (*fig*) undermine ‖ *ref* decompose, disintegrate

zerspal'ten *tr* split

zersplit'tern *tr* split up; splinter; (*Menge*) disperse; (*Kraft*, *Zeit*) fritter away ‖ *ref* spread oneself thin

zerspren'gen *tr* blow up; (*Kette*) break; (*mil*) rout

zersprin'gen §142 *intr* (SEIN) break, burst; (*Glas*) crack; (*Saite*) snap; (*Kopf*) split; (*vor Wut*) explode; (*vor Freude*) burst

zerstamp'fen *tr* crush, pound; trample

zerstäu'ben *tr* pulverize, spray

Zerstäu'ber *m* (-s;-) sprayer; (*für Parfüm*) atomizer

zerste'chen §64 *tr* sting; bite

zerstie'ben §130 *intr* (SEIN) scatter

zerstö'ren *tr* destroy; (*Fernsprechleitung*) disrupt; (*Leben*, *Ehe*, *usw.*) ruin; (*Illusionen*) shatter

Zerstö'rer *m* (-s;-) (& nav) destroyer

Zerstö'rung *f* (-;-en) destruction; ruin; disruption

Zerstö'rungswerk *n* work of destruction

Zerstö'rungswut *f* vandalism

zersto'ßen §150 *tr* pound, crush

zerstreu'en *tr* scatter, disperse; (*Bedenken*, *Zweifel*) dispel; (*ablenken*) distract; (*Licht*) diffuse ‖ *ref* scatter; amuse oneself

zerstreut' *adj* dispersed; (*Licht*) diffused; (*fig*) absent-minded

Zerstreut'heit *f* (-;) absent-mindedness

Zerstreu'ung *f* (-;) scattering; diffusion; diversion; absent-mindedness

zerstückeln [tser'ʃtykəln] *tr* chop up; (*Körper*) dismember; (*Land*) parcel out

zertei'len *tr* divide; (*zerstreuen*) disperse; (*Braten*, *usw.*) cut up ‖ *ref* divide, separate

Zertifikat [tsertıfı'kat] *n* (-[e]s;-e) certificate

zertren'nen *tr* sever

zertre'ten §152 *tr* trample, squash; (*Feuer*) stamp out

zertrümmern [tser'trymərn] *tr* smash, demolish; (*Atome*) split

zerwüh'len *tr* root up; (*Haar*) dishevel; (*Bett*, *Kissen*) rumple

Zerwürfnis [tser'vʏrfnɪs] *n* (**-ses;-se**) disagreement, quarrel

zerzau'sen *tr* (*Haar*) muss; (*Federn*) ruffle

Zeter ['tsetər] *n* (**-s;**)—**Z. und Mordio schreien** (coll) cry bloody murder

zetern ['tsetərn] *intr* cry out, raise an outcry

Zettel ['tsetəl] *m* (**-s;-**) slip of paper; note; (*Anschlag*) poster; (*zum Ankleben*) sticker; (*zum Anhängen*) tag

Zet'telkartei *f*, **Zet'telkasten** *m*, **Zet'telkatalog** *m* card file

Zeug [tsɔɪk] *n* (**-[e]s;-e**) stuff, material; (*Stoff*) cloth, fabric; (*Sachen*) things; (*Waren*) goods; (*Geräte*) tools; (*Plunder*) junk; **dummes Z.** silly nonsense; **er hat das Z.** he has what it takes

-zeug *n comb.fm.* stuff; tools; equipment; tackle; instrument; things; -wear

Zeuge ['tsɔɪgə] *m* (**-n;-n**) witness; **als Z. aussagen** testify

zeugen ['tsɔɪgən] *tr* beget; (fig) produce, generate || *intr* produce offspring; testify; **z. für** testify in favor of; **z. von** bear witness to

Zeu'genaussage *f* deposition
Zeu'genbank *f* witness stand
Zeu'genbeeinflussung *f* suborning of witnesses
Zeu'genstand *m* witness stand
Zeugin ['tsɔɪgɪn] *f* (**-;-nen**) witness
Zeugnis ['tsɔɪknɪs] *n* (**-ses;-se**) evidence, testimony; proof; (*Schein*) certificate; (educ) report card; **j-m ein Z. ausstellen** (or **schreiben**) write s.o. a letter of recommendation; (**Z. ablegen** testify; **zum Z. dessen** in witness whereof

Zeu'gung *f* (**-;**) procreation; breeding
Zeu'gungstrieb *m* sexual drive
zeu'gungsunfähig *adj* impotent

Zicke ['tsɪkə] *f* (**-;-n**) (pej) old nanny goat; **Zicken machen** (coll) play tricks

Zicklein ['tsɪklaɪn] *n* (**-s;-**) kid
Zickzack ['tsɪktsak] *m* (**-[e]s;-e**) zigzag; **im Z. laufen** run zigzag
Zick'zackkurs *m*—**im Z. fahren** zigzag
Ziege ['tsigə] *f* (**-;-n**) she-goat
Ziegel ['tsigəl] *m* (**-s;-**) brick; (*Dach-*) tile
Zie'gelbrenner *m* brickmaker; tilemaker
Zie'gelbrennerei *f* brickyard; tileworks
Zie'geldach *n* tiled roof
Zie'gelstein *m* brick
Zie'genbart *m* goatee
Zie'genbock *m* billy goat
Zie'genhirt *m* goatherd
Zie'genpeter *m* (pathol) mumps
Zieh- [tsi] *comb.fm.* draw; tow-; foster
Zieh'brunnen *m* well
ziehen ['tsi-ən] §163 *tr* pull; (*Folgerung, Kreis, Linie, Los, Schwert, Seitengewehr, Vorhang, Wechsel*) draw; (*Glocke*) ring; *aus der Tasche* pull out; (*Zahn*) extract, pull; (*züchten*) grow, breed; (*Kinder*) raise; (*beim Schach*) move; (*den*

Hut) tip; (*Graben*) dig; (*Mauer*) build; (*Schiff*) tow; (*Blasen*) raise; (*Vergleich*) make; (*Gewehrlauf*) rifle; (math) extract; **auf Fäden z.** string (*pearls*); **auf Flaschen z.** bottle; **auf seine Seite z.** win over to one's side; **den kürzeren z.** get the short end of it; **die Bilanz z.** balance accounts; **die Stirn kraus z.** knit the brows; **Grimassen z.** make faces; **ins Vertrauen z.** take into confidence; **j-n auf die Seite z.** take s.o. aside; **Nutzen z.** derive benefit; **Wasser z.** leak || *ref* (*Holz*) warp; (*Stoff*) stretch; (geog) extend, run; **an sich** (or **auf sich**) **z.** attract; **sich in die Länge z.** drag on || *intr* ache; (**an** *dat*) pull (on); (theat) (coll) pull them in; **an e-r Zigarette z.** puff on a cigarette || *intr* (SEIN) go; march; (*Vögel*) migrate; (*Wohnung wechseln*) move || *impers*—**es zieht** there is a draft; **es zieht mich nach** I feel drawn to || **Ziehen** *n* (**-s;**) drawing; cultivation; growing; raising; breeding; migration

Zieh'harmonika *f* accordion
Zieh'kind *n* foster child
Zie'hung *f* (**-;-en**) drawing (*of lots*)
Ziel [tsil] *n* (**-[e]s;-e**) aim; mark; goal; (*beim Rennsport*) finish line; (*e-r Reise*) destination; (*beim Schießen*) target; (*Grenze*) limit, boundary; (*Zweck*) end, object; (*des Spottes*) butt; (*Frist*) term; (mil) objective; **auf Z.** (com) on credit; **durchs Z. gehen** pass the finish line; **gegen zwei Jahre Z.** (or **mit zwei Jahren Z.**) with two years to pay; **j-m zwei Jahre Z. gewähren** give s.o. two years to pay; **seinem Ehrgeiz ein Z. setzen** set a limit to one's ambition

Ziel'anflug *m* (aer) bomb run
Ziel'band *n* (**-[e]s;-̈er**) (sport) tape
ziel'bewußt *adj* purposeful; single-minded
zielen ['tsilən] *intr* take aim; **z. auf** (*acc*) or **nach** aim at
Ziel'fernrohr *n* telescopic sight
Ziel'gerade *f* homestretch
Ziel'gerät *n* gunsight; (aer) bombsight
Ziel'landung *f* pinpoint landing
Ziel'linie *f* (sport) finish line
ziel'los *adj* aimless
Ziel'photographie *f* photo finish
Ziel'punkt *m* objective; bull's-eye
Ziel'scheibe *f* target; (fig) butt
Ziel'setzung *f* objective, target
ziel'sicher *adj* steady, unerring
Ziel'sprache *f* target language
zielstrebig ['tsil/trebɪç] *adj* single-minded, determined
Ziel'sucher *m* (rok) homing device
Ziel'vorrichtung *f* gunsight; bombsight
ziemen ['tsimən] *ref* be proper; **sich für j-n z.** become s.o. || *intr* (*dat*) be becoming to

ziemlich ['tsimlɪç] *adj* fit, suitable; (*leidlich*) middling; (*mäßig*) fair; (*beträchtlich*) considerable || *adv* pretty, rather, fairly; (*fast*) almost, practically

Zier [tsir] *f* (–;), **Zierat** ['tsirɑt] *m* (–s;) ornament, decoration

Zierde ['tsirdə] *f* (–;–n) ornament decoration; (fig) credit, honor

zieren ['tsirən] *tr* decorate, adorn || *ref* be affected, be coy; (*beim Essen*) need to be coaxed; **zier dich doch nicht so!** don't be coy!

Zier'leiste *f* trim(ming)

zier'lich *adj* delicate; (*nett*) nice

Zier'pflanze *f* ornamental plant

Zier'puppe *f* glamour girl

Ziffer ['tsifər] *f* (–;–n) digit, figure

Zif'ferblatt *n* face (*of a clock*)

zig [tsɪç] *invar adj* (coll) umpteen

Zigarette [tsɪga'rɛtə] *f* (–;–n) cigarette

Zigaret'tenautomat *m* cigarette machine

Zigaret'tenetui *n* cigarette case

Zigaret'tenspitze *f* cigarette holder

Zigaret'tenstummel *m* cigarette butt

Zigarre [tsɪ'garə] *f* (–;–n) cigar

Zigeuner –in [tsɪ'gɔinər(ɪn)] §6 *mf* gipsy

Zimbel ['tsɪmbəl] *f* (–;–n) cymbal

Zimmer ['tsɪmər] *n* (–s;–) room

Zim'merantenne *f* indoor antenna

Zim'merarbeit *f* carpentry

Zim'merdienst *m* room service

Zim'mereinrichtung *f* furniture

Zim'merer *m* (–s;–) carpenter

Zim'merflucht *f* suite

Zim'mermädchen *n* chambermaid

Zim'mer-mann *m* (–[e]s;–leute) carpenter

zimmern ['tsɪmərn] *tr* carpenter, build || *intr* carpenter

Zim'mervermieter *m* landlord

–zimmrig [tsɪmrɪç] *comb.fm.* –room

zimperlich ['tsɪmpərlɪç] *adj* prudish; fastidious; (*gegen Kälte*) oversensitive

Zimt [tsɪmt] *m* (–[e]s;) cinnamon

Zink [tsɪŋk] *m* & *n* (–[e]s;) zinc

Zinke ['tsɪŋkə] *f* (–;–n) prong; (*e-s Kammes*) tooth; (carp) dovetail

zinken ['tsɪŋkən] *tr* dovetail; (*Karten*) mark || **Zinken** *m* (–s;–) (sl) schnozzle

–zinkig [tsɪŋkɪç] *comb.fm.* –pronged

Zinn [tsɪn] *n* (–[e]s;) tin

Zinne ['tsɪnə] *f* (–;–n) pinnacle; battlement

zinnoberrot [tsɪ'nobərrot] *adj* vermillion

Zins [tsɪns] *m* (–es;–en) interest; (*Miete*) rent; **auf Zinsen anlegen** put out at interest; **j–m mit Zinsen (und Zinseszinsen) heimzahlen** (coll) pay s.o. back in full; **Zinsen berechnen** charge interest

zins'bringend *adj* interest-bearing

Zin'senbelastung *f* interest charge

Zinseszinsen ['tsɪnzəstsɪnzən] *pl* compound interest

zins'frei *adj* rent-free; interest-free

Zins'fuß *m*, **Zins'satz** *m* rate of interest

Zins'schein *m* (interest) coupon; dividend warrant

Zionismus [tsɪ·o'nɪsmus] *m* (–;) Zionism

Zipfel ['tsɪpfəl] *m* (–s;–) tip, point;

edge; (*Ecke*) corner; (*e-r Wurst*) end piece

Zip'felmütze *f* nightcap, tasseled cap

zirka ['tsɪrka] *adv* approximately

Zirkel ['tsɪrkal] *m* (–s;–) circle; (*Reißzeug*) compass; (fig) circle

Zir'kelschluß *m* vicious circle

Zirkon [tsɪr'kon] *m* (–s;–e) zircon

zirkulieren [tsɪrku'lirən] *intr* (SEIN) circulate; **z. lassen** circulate

Zirkus ['tsɪrkus] *m* (–;–se) circus

zirpen ['tsɪrpən] *intr* chirp

zischeln ['tsɪʃəln] *tr* & *intr* whisper

zischen ['tsɪʃən] *intr* hiss; sizzle; (*schwirren*) whiz || **Zischen** *n* (–s;) hissing; sizzle; whiz

Zisch'laut *m* hissing sound; (phonet) sibilant

ziselieren [tsize'lirən] *tr* chase

Zisterne [tsɪs'tɛrnə] *f* (–;–n) cistern

Zitadelle [tsɪta'dɛlə] *f* (–;–n) citadel

Zitat [tsɪ'tɑt] *n* (–[e]s;–e) quotation

Zither ['tsɪtər] *f* (–;–n) zither

zitieren [tsɪ'tirən] *tr* quote; **j–n vor Gericht z.** issue s.o. a summons

Zitronat [tsɪtro'nɑt] *n* (–[e]s;–e) candied lemon peel

Zitrone [tsɪ'tronə] *f* (–;–n) lemon

Zitro'nenlimonade *f* lemonade; (*mit Sodawasser*) lemon soda

Zitro'nenpresse *f* lemon squeezer

Zitro'nensaft *m* lemon juice

Zitro'nensäure *f* citric acid

zitterig ['tsɪtərɪç] *adj* shaky

zittern ['tsɪtərn] *intr* quake, tremble; quiver; (*flimmern*) dance; (**vor** *dat*) shake (with), shiver (with); **beim dem Gedanken an etw** [*acc*] **z.** shudder at the thought of s.th.

Zit'terpappel ['tsɪtərpapəl] *f* aspen

Zitze ['tsɪtsə] *f* (–;–n) teat

zivil [tsɪ'vil] *adj* civil; civilian; (*Preise*) reasonable || **Zivil** *n* (–s;) civilians; **in Z.** in plain clothes

Zivil'courage *f* courage of one's convictions, moral courage

Zivil'ehe *f* civil marriage

Zivilisation [tsɪvɪlɪza'tsjon] *f* (–;–en) civilization

zivilisieren [tsɪvɪlɪ'zirən] *tr* civilize

Zivilist –in [tsɪvɪ'lɪst(ɪn)] §7 *mf* civilian

Zivil'klage *f* (jur) civil suit

Zivil'kleidung *f* civilian clothes

Zivil'person *f* civilian

Zobel ['tsobəl] *m* (–s;–) (zool) sable

Zofe ['tsofə] *f* (–;–n) lady-in-waiting

zog [tsok] *pret* of **ziehen**

zögern ['tsøgərn] *intr* hesitate; delay || **Zögern** *n* (–s;) hesitation; delay

Zögling ['tsøklɪŋ] *m* (–s;–e) pupil

Zölibat [tsølɪ'bɑt] *m* & *n* (–[e]s;) celibacy

Zoll [tsɔl] *m* (–[e]s;ᵘ–e) duty, customs; (*Brückenzoll*) toll; (*Maß*) inch

Zoll'abfertigung *f* customs clearance

Zoll'amt *n* customs office

Zoll'beamte §5 *m* customs official

zollen ['tsɔlən] *tr* give, pay; **j–m Achtung z.** show s.o. respect; **j–m Beifall z.** applaud s.o.; **j–m Dank z.** thank s.o.; **j–m Lob z.** praise s.o.

Zoll'erklärung *f* customs declaration

zoll'frei adj duty-free
Zoll'grenze f customs frontier
–zöllig [tsœlɪç] comb.fm. –inch
Zoll'kontrolle f customs inspection
zoll'pflichtig adj dutiable
Zoll'schein m customs clearance
Zoll'schranke f customs barrier
Zoll'stab m, **Zoll'stock** m foot rule
Zoll'tarif m tariff
Zone ['tsonə] f (-;-n) zone; **blaue Z.** limited-parking area; **Z. der Windstille** doldrums
Zoo [tso] m (- & -s;-s) zoo
Zoologe [tso·o'logə] m (-n;-n) zoologist
Zoologie [tso·olo'gi] f (-;) zoology
Zoologin [tso·o'logɪn] f (-;-nen) zoologist
zoologisch [tso·o'logɪʃ] adj zoological
Zopf [tsɔpf] m (-[e]s;⁻e) plait of hair; pigtail; twisted (bread) roll; **alter Z.** outdated custom
zopfig ['tsɔpfɪç] adj pedantic; old-fashioned
Zorn [tsɔrn] m (-[e]s;) anger, rage
Zorn'anfall m fit of anger
Zorn'ausbruch m outburst of anger
zornig ['tsɔrnɪç] adj (auf acc) angry (at)
zorn'mütig adj hotheaded
Zote ['tsotə] f (-;-n) obscenity; dirty joke; **Zoten reißen** crack dirty jokes; talk dirty
zo'tenhaft, zotig ['tsotɪç] adj obscene, dirty
Zotte ['tsɔtə] f (-;-n) tuft of hair; strand of hair
Zottel ['tsɔtəl] f (-;-n) strand of hair
Zot'telhaar n stringy hair
zottelig ['tsɔtəlɪç] adj stringy (hair)
zotteln ['tsɔtəln] intr (SEIN) (coll) saunter
zottig ['tsɔtɪç] adj shaggy; matted
zu [tsu] adj closed, shut ‖ adv too; **immer zu!** (or **nur zu!**) go on! ‖ prep (dat) at, in, on; to; along with; in addition to; beside, near; **zu Anfang** at the beginning; **zu dritt** in threes; **zu Wasser und zu Lande** by land and by sea
zuallererst [tsu·alər'ɛrst] adv first of all
zuallerletzt [tsu·alər'lɛtst] adv last of all
zuballern ['tsubalərn] tr (coll) slam
zu'bauen tr wall up, wall in
Zubehör ['tsubəhør] m & n (-s;) accessories; fittings; trimmings; **Wohnung mit allem Z.** apartment with all utilities
Zu'behörteil m accessory, attachment, component
zu'beißen §53 intr bite; snap at people
zu'bekommen §99 tr get in addition; (Tür, usw.) manage to close
zu'bereiten tr prepare; (Speise) cook; (Getränk) mix
Zu'bereitung f (-;-en) preparation
zu'billigen tr grant, allow, concede
zu'binden §59 tr tie up; **j-m die Augen z.** blindfold s.o.
zu'bleiben §62 intr (SEIN) remain closed

zu'blinzeln intr (dat) wink at
zu'bringen §65 tr (Zeit) spend; (coll) manage to shut; (tech) feed
Zu'bringer m (-s;-) (tech) feeder
Zu'bringerdienst m shuttle service
Zu'bringerstraße f access road
Zucht [tsuxt] f (-;) breeding; rearing; (Rasse) race, stock; (Pflanzen-) cultivation; (Schul-) education; discipline; training, drill; **Z. halten** maintain discipline
züchten ['tsʏçtən] tr breed; rear, raise; (bot) grow, cultivate
Züch'ter -in §6 mf breeder; grower
Zucht'haus n penitentiary, hard labor; **lebenslängliches Z.** life imprisonment
Zuchthäusler -in ['tsuxthɔɪzlər(ɪn)] §6 mf convict, prisoner at hard labor
Zucht'hengst m studhorse
züchtig ['tsʏçtɪç] adj modest, chaste
züchtigen ['tsʏçtɪgən] tr chastise
zucht'los adj undisciplined
Zucht'losigkeit f (-;) lack of discipline
Zucht'meister m disciplinarian
Zucht'perle f cultured pearl
Züch'tung f (-;) breeding; rearing; growing, cultivation
zucken ['tsukən] tr (Achseln) shrug ‖ intr twitch, jerk; (Blitz) flash; (vor Schmerzen) wince; **mit keiner Wimper z.** not bat an eye; **ohne zu z.** without wincing ‖ impers—**es zuckte mir in den Fingern zu** (inf) my fingers were itching to (inf) ‖ **Zucken** n (-s;) twitch
zücken ['tsʏkən] tr (Schwert) draw
Zucker ['tsukər] m (-s;) sugar
Zuckerdose (Zuk'kerdose) f sugar bowl
Zuckererbse (Zuk'kererbse) f sweet pea
Zuckerguß (Zuk'kerguß) m frosting
Zuckerharnruhr (Zuk'kerharnruhr) f diabetes
Zuckerhut (Zuk'kerhut) m sugar loaf
zuckerig ['tsukərɪç] adj sugary
zuckerkrank (zuk'kerkrank) adj diabetic ‖ **Zuckerkranke** §5 mf diabetic
Zuckerkrankheit (Zuk'kerkrankheit) f diabetes
Zuckerlecken (Zuk'kerlecken) n (-s;) (fig) pushover, picnic
Zuckerrohr (Zuk'kerrohr) n sugar cane
Zuckerrübe (Zuk'kerrübe) f sugar beet
zuckersüß (zuk'kersüß') adj sweet as sugar
Zuckerwerk (Zuk'kerwerk) n, **Zuckerzeug** (Zuk'kerzeug) n candy
Zuckung (Zuk'kung) f (-;-en) twitch, spasm, convulsion
Zu'decke f (coll) bed covering
zu'decken tr cover up
zudem [tsu'dem] adv moreover, besides
zu'denken §66 tr—**j-m etw z.** intend s.th. as a present for s.o.
Zu'drang m crowding, rush
zu'drehen tr turn off; **j-m den Rücken z.** turn one's back on s.o.
zu'dringlich adj obtrusive; **z. werden** make a pass
zu'drücken tr close, shut
zu'eignen tr dedicate
Zu'eignung f (-;-en) dedication

zu'erkennen §97 *tr* confer, award; (*jur*) adjudge, award

zuerst' *adv* first; at first

zu'erteilen *tr* award; confer, bestow

zu'fahren §71 *intr* (SEIN) drive on; **z. auf** (*acc*) drive in the direction of (*s.th.*); rush at (*s.o.*)

Zu'fahrt *f* access

Zu'fahrtsrampe *f* on-ramp

Zu'fahrtsstraße *f* access road

Zu'fall *m* chance; coincidence; accident; **durch Z.** by chance

zu'fallen §72 *intr* (SEIN) close, shut; **j-m z.** fall to s.o.'s share

zufällig ['tsufɛlɪç] *adj* chance, fortuitous; accidental; casual ‖ *adv* by chance; accidentally

zu'fälligerweise *adv* by chance

Zufalls– comb.fm. chance

zu'fassen *intr* set to work; lend a hand; (*e-e Gelegenheit wahrnehmen*) seize the opportunity

Zu'flucht *f* refuge; (fig) recourse; **seine Z. nehmen zu** take refuge in; have recourse to

Zu'fluß *m* influx; (*Nebenfluß*) tributary; (mach) feed

zu'flüstern *intr* (*dat*) whisper to

zufolge [tsu'fɔlgə] *prep* (*genit & dat*) in consequence of; according to

zufrieden [tsu'fridən] *adj* satisfied; **j-n z. lassen** leave s.o. alone

zufrie'dengeben §80 *ref* (mit) be satisfied (with), acquiesce (in)

Zufrie'denheit *f* (–;) satisfaction

zufrie'denstellen *tr* satisfy

zufrie'denstellend *adj* satisfactory

Zufrie'denstellung *f* satisfaction

zu'frieren §77 *intr* (SEIN) freeze up

zu'fügen *tr* add; (*Niederlage*) inflict; (*Kummer, Schaden, Schmerz*) cause

Zufuhr ['tsufur] *f* (–;) supply; importation; supplies; (mach) feed

zu'führen *tr* convey, bring; (*Waren*) supply; (mach) feed

Zu'führung *f* (–;–en) conveyance; supply; importation; (elec) lead; (mach) feed

Zug [tsuk] *m* (–[e]s;⁀e) train; pull, tug; drawing, pulling; (*Spannung*) tension; strain; (*beim Rauchen*) puff; (*beim Atmen*) breath, gasp; (*Schluck*) drink, gulp, swig; (*Luft–*) draft; (*Reihe*) row, line; (*Um–*) procession; parade; (*Kriegs–*) campaign; (*Geleit*) escort; (*von Vögeln*) flock; flight, migration; (*von Fischen*) school; (*Rudel*) pack; (*Trupp*) platoon; (*Gespann*) team, yoke; (*Gesichts–*) feature; (*Charakter–*) trait; characteristic; (*Neigung*) trend, tendency; (*im Gewehrlauf*) groove, rifling; (*Strich*) stroke; (*Schnörkel*) flourish; (*Umriß*) outline; (*beim Brettspiel*) move; **auf dem Zuge** on the march; **auf e-n Zug** in one gulp; at one stroke; at a stretch; **du bist am Zug** (–) it's your move; **e-n guten Zug haben** drink like a fish; **e-n Zug tun** take a puff; make a move; take a drink; **gut im Zuge sein** (or **im besten Zuge sein**) be going strong; **in e-m Zuge** in one

gulp; in one breath; at one stroke; at a stretch; **in großen Zügen** in broad outlines; **in vollen Zügen** thoroughly; **in Zug bringen** start; **nicht zum Zug kommen** not get a chance; **ohne rechten Zug** half-heartedly; **Zug um Zug** in rapid succession

Zu'gabe *f* addition; (theat) encore

Zu'gang *m* access; approach; entrance; (*Zunahme*) increase; (libr) accession

zugänglich ['tsugɛnlɪç] *adj* accessible; (*Person*) affable; (*benutzbar*) available; (*dat, für*) open (to); **nicht z. für** proof against

Zug'artikel *m* (com) popular article

Zug'brücke *f* drawbridge

zu'geben §80 *tr* add; (*erlauben*) allow; (*anerkennen*) admit, concede; (*eingestehen*) confess; (com) throw into the bargain

zugegen [tsu'gegən] *adj* (bei) present (at)

zu'gehen §82 *intr* (SEIN) go on; walk faster; (*sich schließen*) shut; **auf j-n z.** go up to s.o.; **j-m etw z. lassen** send s.th. to s.o.

zu'gehören *intr* (*dat*) belong to

zu'gehörig *adj* (*dat*) belonging to

Zu'gehörigkeit *f* (–;) (zu) membership (in)

Zügel ['tsygəl] *m* (–s;–) rein; bridle; (fig) curb

zü'gellos *adj* (& fig) unbridled; (*ausschweifig*) dissolute

Zü'gellosigkeit *f* (–;) licentiousness

zügeln ['tsygəln] *tr* bridle; (fig) curb

Zu'geständnis *n* admission, concession

zu'gestehen §146 *tr* admit, concede

zu'getan *adj* (*dat*) fond of

Zug'feder *f* tension spring

Zug'führer *m* (mil) platoon leader; (rr) chief conductor

zu'gießen §76 *tr* add

zugig ['tsugɪç] *adj* drafty

zügig ['tsygɪç] *adj* speedy, fast

Zug'klappe *f* damper

Zug'kraft *f* tensile force; (fig) drawing power

zug'kräftig *adj* attractive, popular

zugleich' *adv* at the same time; **z. mit** together with

Zug'luft *f* draft

Zug'maschine *f* tractor

Zug'mittel *n* (fig) attraction, draw

zu'graben §87 *tr* cover up

zu'greifen §88 *intr* grab hold; lend a hand; (fig) go into action; **greifen Sie zu!** (*bei Tisch*) help yourself!; (*bei Reklamen*) don't miss this opportunity!

Zu'griff *m* grip; (fig) clutches

zugrunde [tsu'grundə] *adv—***z. gehen** go to ruin; **z. legen** (*dat*) take as a basis (for); **z. liegen** (*dat*) underlie

Zug'tier *n* draft animal

zu'gucken *intr* (coll) look on

zugunsten [tsu'gunstən] *prep* (*genit*) in favor of; for the benefit of

zugute [tsu'gutə] *adv—***j-m etw z. halten** make allowance to s.o. for s.th.; **j-m z. kommen** stand s.o. in good stead

Zug'verkehr *m* train service

Zug'vogel *m* migratory bird

zu'haben §89 *tr* (*Augen*) have closed; (*Mantel*) have buttoned up || *intr* (*Geschäft*) be closed

zu'halten §90 *tr* keep closed; (*Ohren*) shut || *intr*—z. auf (*acc*) head for

Zuhälter ['tsuhɛltər] *m* (-s;-) pimp

Zuhälterei [tsuhɛlte'raɪ] *f* (-;) pimping

zuhanden [tsu'handən] *prep* (*genit*) (*auf Briefumschlägen*) Attn:

Zuhause [tsu'hauzə] *n* (-s;) home

zu'heilen *intr* (SEIN) heal up

zu'hören *intr* (*dat*) listen (to)

Zu'hörer –in §6 *mf* hearer, listener; die Z. the audience

Zu'hörerschaft *f* (-;) audience

zu'jauchzen, zu'jubeln *intr* cheer

zu'klappen *tr* shut, slam shut

zu'kleben *tr* glue up, paste up

zu'knallen *tr* bang, slam shut

zu'kneifen §88 *tr*—die Augen z. blink; ein Auge z. wink

zu'knöpfen *tr* button up

zu'kommen §99 *intr* (SEIN) (*dat*) reach; (*dat*) be due to; auf j–n z. come up to s.o.; das kommt dir nicht zu you're not entitled to it; j–m etw z. lassen let s.o. have s.th.; send s.th. to s.o. || *impers*—mir kommt es nicht zu zu (*inf*) it's not up to me to (*inf*)

zu'korken *tr* put the cork on

Zu'kost *f* vegetables; trimmings

Zukunft ['tsukunft] *f* (-;) future; (*gram*) future (tense)

zukünftig ['tsukynftɪç] *adj* future || *adv* in the future || **Zukünftige** §5 *m* (coll) fiancé || *f* (coll) fiancée

Zu'kunftsmusik *f* wishful thinking

Zu'kunftsroman *m* science fiction

zu'lächeln *intr* (*dat*) smile at; (*dat*) smile on

Zu'lage *f* extra pay; pay raise

zulande [tsu'landə] *adv*—bei uns z. in my (or our) country

zu'langen *intr* suffice, do; (*bei Tisch*) help oneself

zu'länglich *adj* adequate, sufficient

zu'lassen §104 *tr* admit; (*erlauben*) allow; (*Tür*) leave shut; (*Fahrzeug*) license; (*Zweifel*) admit of

zulässig ['tsulɛsɪç] *adj* permissible; zulässige Abweichung allowance, tolerance

Zu'lassung *f* (-;-en) admission; permission; approval; license

Zu'lassungsprüfung *f* college entrance examination

Zu'lassungsschein *m* registration card

Zu'lauf *m* crowd, rush; Z. haben be popular; (theat) have a long run

zu'laufen §105 *intr* (SEIN) run on; run faster; (*dat*) flock to; auf j–n z. run up to s.o.; spitz z. end in a point

zu'legen *tr* add; etw z. up one's offer || *ref*—sich [*dat*] etw. z. (coll) get oneself s.th.

zuleide [tsu'laɪdə] *adv*—j–m etw z. tun hurt s.o., do s.o. wrong

zu'leiten *tr* (*Wasser*) (*dat*) let in (to); (*dat*) direct (s.o.) (to); (*Schreiben*) (*dat*) pass on (to); auf dem Amtsweg) channel (to); (tech) feed

Zu'leitung *f* (-;-en) feed pipe; (elec) lead-in wire; (elec) conductor

zuletzt [tsu'lɛtst] *adv* last; at last; finally; after all

zuliebe [tsu'libə] *prep* (*dat*) for (s.o.'s) sake

zum [tsum] *abbr* zu dem; es ist zum ...it's enough to make one...

zu'machen *tr* shut; (*Loch*) close up; (*zuknöpfen*) button up

zumal [tsu'mɑl] *adv* especially; z. da all the more because

zu'mauern *tr* wall up

zumindest [tsu'mɪndəst] *adv* at least

zumute [tsu'mutə] *adv*—mir ist gut (or wohl) z. I feel good; mir ist nicht zum Lachen z. I don't feel like laughing

zumuten ['tsumutən] *tr*—j–m etw z. expect s.th. of s.o. || *ref*—sich [*dat*] zuviel z. attempt too much

Zu'mutung *f* (-;-en) imposition

zunächst [tsu'nɛçst] *adv* first, at first; first of all; (*erstens*) to begin with; (*vorläufig*) for the time being || *prep* (*dat*) next to

zu'nageln *tr* nail up, nail shut

zu'nähen *tr* sew up

Zu'nahme *f* (-;-n) increase; growth; rise

Zu'name *m* last name, family name

Zünd– (tsynt] *comb.fm.* ignition

zünden ['tsyndən] *tr* ignite; kindle; (*Sprengstoff*) detonate || *intr* ignite, catch fire; (fig) catch on

Zün'der *m* (-s;–) fuse; detonator

Zünd'flamme *f* pilot light

Zünd'holz *n* match

Zünd'kerze *f* (aut) spark plug

Zünd'nadel *f* firing pin

Zünd'satz *m* primer

Zünd'schlüssel *m* ignition key

Zünd'schnur *f* fuse

Zünd'stein *m* flint

Zünd'stoff *m* fuel

Zün'dung *f* (-;-en) (aut) ignition

zu'nehmen §116 *intr* (an *dat*) increase (in); (*steigen*) rise; grow longer

zu'neigen *tr* (*dat*) tilt toward || *ref* & *intr* (*dat*) incline toward(s); sich dem Ende z. draw to a close

Zu'neigung *f* (-;) (für, zu) liking (for)

Zunft [tsunft] *f* (-;-en) guild

Zunge ['tsuŋə] *f* (-;-n) tongue

zün'geln ['tsyŋəln] *intr* dart out the tongue; (*Flamme*) dart, leap up

Zun'genbrecher *m* tongue twister

zun'genfertig *adj* glib

Zun'genspitze *f* tip of the tongue

zunichte [tsu'nɪçtə] *adv*—z. machen destroy; (*Plan*) spoil; (*Theorie*) explode; z. werden come to nothing

zu'nicken *intr* (*dat*) nod to

zunutze [tsu'nutsə] *adv*—sich etw z. machen utilize s.th.

zuoberst [tsu'obərst] *adv* at the top

zupfen ['tsupfən] *tr* pull; pluck || *intr* (an *dat*) tug (at)

zu'prosten *intr* (*dat*) toast

zur [tsur] *abbr* zu der

zu'rechnen *tr* add; (*dat*) number among, classify with; (*dat*) attribute to

zu'rechnungsfähig *adj* accountable; responsible; of sound mind

Zu'rechnungsfähigkeit *f* responsibility; sound mind

zurecht– [tsu'reçt] *comb.fm.* right, in order; at the right time

zurecht'biegen §57 *tr* straighten out

zurecht'bringen §65 *tr* set right

zurecht'finden §59 *ref* find one's way; (fig) see one's way

zurecht'kommen §99 *intr* (SEIN) come on time; get on, manage; turn out all right; **mit etw nicht z.** make a mess of s.th.; **mit j-m z.** get along with s.o.

zurecht'legen *tr* lay out in order ‖ *ref*—**sich** [*dat*] z. figure out

zurecht'machen *tr & ref* get ready

zurecht'schneiden §106 *tr* cut to size

zurecht'setzen *tr* set right, fix, adjust

zurecht'weisen §118 *tr* reprimand

zu'reden *intr* (*dat*) try to persuade; (*dat*) encourage

zu'reichen *tr* reach, pass ‖ *intr* do

zu'reichend *adj* sufficient

zu'reiten §86 *tr* break in

zu'richten *tr* prepare; cook

zu'riegeln *tr* bolt

zürnen ['tsyrnən] *intr* (*dat*) be angry (with)

zurren ['tsurən] *tr* (naut) lash down

Zurschau'stellung *f* display

zurück [tsu'ryk] *adv* back; backward; behind; **ein paar Jahre z.** a few years ago ‖ *interj* back up!

zurück– *comb.fm.* back; behind; re–

zurück'behalten §90 *tr* keep back

zurück'bekommen §99 *tr* get back

zurück'bleiben §62 *intr* (SEIN) stay behind; fall behind; (*Uhr*) lose time; (**hinter** *dat*) fall short (of)

Zurück'blenden *n* (cin) flashback

zurück'blicken *intr* look back

zurück'bringen §65 *tr* bring back; **z. auf** (*acc*) (math) reduce to

zurück'datieren *tr* antedate

zurück'drängen *tr* force back; repress

zurück'dürfen §69 *intr* be allowed to return

zurück'erobern *tr* reconquer, win back

zurück'erstatten *tr* return; (*Ausgaben*) refund; (*Kosten*) reimburse

zurück'fahren §71 *tr* drive back ‖ *intr* (SEIN) drive back, ride back; (*vor Schreck*) recoil, start

zurück'finden §59 *ref* find one's way back

zurück'fordern *tr* reclaim, demand back

zurück'führen *tr* lead back; trace back; **z. auf** (*acc*) refer to; attribute to

zurück'geben §80 *tr* give back, return

zurück'gehen §82 *intr* (SEIN) go back; (*Fieber, Preise*) drop; (*Geschwulst*) go down; (mil) fall back

zurück'gezogen *adj* secluded

zurück'greifen §88 *intr*—**z. auf** (*acc*) (fig) fall back on

zurück'halten §90 *tr* hold back; **j-n davon z. zu** (*inf*) keep s.o. from (*ger*) ‖ *intr* **mit etw z.** conceal s.th.

zurück'haltend *adj* reserved; shy

Zurück'haltung *f* (–;–en) reserve

zurück'kehren *intr* (SEIN) return

zurück'kommen §99 *intr* (SEIN) return; **z. auf** (*acc*) come back to, revert to; (*hinweisen*) refer to

zurück'können §100 *intr* be able to return

zurück'lassen §104 *tr* leave behind; outstrip, outrun

zurück'legen *tr* (*Kopf*) lean back; (*Geld*) put aside; (*Jahre*) complete; (*Strecke*) cover; (*Ware*) lay away ‖ *ref* lean back

zurück'lehnen *ref* lean back

zurück'liegen §108 *intr* belong to the past ‖ *impers*—**es liegt jetzt zehn Jahre zurück, daß** it's ten years now that

zurück'müssen §115 *intr* have to return

zurück'nehmen §116 *tr* take back; (*widerrufen*) revoke; (*Auftrag*) cancel; (*Vorwurf*) retract; (*Klage*) withdraw; (*Versprechen*) go back on; (*Truppen*) pull back; **das Gas z.** slow down

zurück'prallen *intr* (SEIN) rebound; (*vor Schreck*) start, be startled

zurück'rufen §122 *tr* call back, recall

zurück'schauen *intr* look back

zurück'schicken *tr* send back

zurück'schlagen §132 *tr* beat back, throw back ‖ *intr* strike back

zurück'schrecken *tr* frighten away; (**von**) deter (from) ‖ §109 & §134 *intr* (SEIN) (**von, vor** *dat*) shrink back (from)

zurück'sehnen *ref* yearn to return

zurück'sein §139 *intr* (SEIN) be back; (**in** *dat*) be behind (in)

zurück'setzen *tr* put back; (*im Preis*) reduce; (fig) snub ‖ *ref* sit back

zurück'stecken *tr* put back

zurück'stellen *tr* (*Uhr*) set back; (*Plan*) shelve; (mil) defer

zurück'stoßen §150 *tr* push back; repel

zurück'strahlen *tr* reflect

zurück'streifen *tr* (*Ärmel*) roll up

zurück'treten §152 *intr* (SEIN) step back; (*vom Amt*) resign; (*Wasser, Berge*) recede

zurück'tun §154 *tr* put back

zurück'verfolgen *tr* (*Schritte*) retrace; (fig) trace back

zurück'verweisen §118 *tr* (**an** *acc*) refer back (to); (parl) remand (to)

zurück'weichen §85 *intr* (SEIN) fall back, make way; (*Hochwasser*) recede; (*vor dem Feind*) give ground; **z. vor** (*dat*) shrink from

zurück'weisen §118 *tr* turn back; (*ablehnen*) turn down; (*Angriff*) repel ‖ *intr*—**z. auf** (*acc*) refer to

Zurück'weisung *f* (–;–en) rejection

zurück'wenden §140 *tr & ref* turn back

zurück'werfen §160 *tr* throw back; (*e-n Patienten*) set back; (*Strahlen*) reflect; (*Feind*) hurl back

zurück'wirken *intr* (**auf** *acc*) react (on); (*Gesetz*) be retroactive

zurück'zahlen *tr* pay back; (fin) refund

zurück'ziehen §163 *tr* draw back; (*Antrag*) withdraw; (*Geld*) call in; (*Truppen*) pull back; (sport) scratch ‖ *ref* withdraw; (*schlafengehen*) re-

tire; (mil) pull back || *intr* (SEIN)
move back; (mil) fall back, retreat
Zu′ruf *m* call; cheer; (parl) acclamation
zu′rufen §122 *tr*—j-m etw z. shout
s.th. to s.o.
Zu′sage *f* (-;-n) assent; promise
zu′sagen *tr* promise || *intr* accept an
invitation; (*dat*) please; (*dat*) agree
(with)
zusammen [tsuˈzamən] *adv* together;
in common; at the same time
Zusam′menarbeit *f* cooperation
zusam′menarbeiten *intr* cooperate
zusam′menballen *tr* (*Faust*) clench
zusam′menbeißen §53 *tr*—die Zähne z.
grit one's teeth
zusam′menbinden §59 *tr* tie together
zusam′menbrauen *tr* concoct || *ref*
(*Sturm*) brew
zusam′menbrechen §64 *intr* (SEIN)
break down; collapse
Zusam′menbruch *m* collapse; breakdown
zusam′mendrängen *tr* crowd together
zusam′mendrücken *tr* compress
zusam′menfahren §71 *intr* (SEIN) be
startled; (mit) collide (with)
zusam′menfallen §72 *intr* (SEIN) fall
in, collapse; (*Teig*) fall; (*Person*)
lose weight; (mit) coincide (with)
Zusam′menfall *m* coincidence
zusam′menfalten *tr* fold
zusam′menfassen *tr* (*in sich fassen*)
comprise; (*verbinden*) combine;
(*Macht, Funktionen*) concentrate;
(*Bericht*) summarize
zusam′menfassend *adj* comprehensive;
summary
Zusam′menfassung *f* (-;-en) summary,
résumé
zusam′menfinden §59 *ref* meet
zusam′menfügen *tr* join together;
(*Scherben, Teile*) piece together
zusam′mengehen §82 *intr* (SEIN) go
together; match; close; shrink
zusam′mengehören *intr* belong together
zusam′mengeraten §63 *intr* (SEIN) collide
zusammengewürfelt [tsuˈzaməngevYr-
fəlt] *adj* mixed, motely
Zusam′menhalt *m* cohesion; consistency
zusam′menhalten §90 *tr* hold together;
compare || *intr* stick together
Zusam′menhang *m* connection, relation; context; coherence
zusam′menhängend *adj* coherent; allied
zusam′menklappen *tr* fold up; die
Hacken z. click one's heels || *intr*
(SEIN) collapse
zusam′menkommen §99 *intr* (SEIN)
come together
Zusammenkunft [tsuˈzamənkunft] *f*
(-;ːe) meeting
zusam′menlaufen §105 *intr* (SEIN) run
together; come together; flock;
(*Milch*) curdle; (*Farben*) run; (*einschrumpfen*) shrink up; (geom) converge
zusammenlegbar [tsuˈzamənlekbɑr] *adj*
collapsible
zusam′menlegen *tr* put together; (fal-

ten) fold; (*Geld*) pool; (*vereinigen*)
combine, consolidate || *intr* pool
money
zusam′mennehmen §116 *tr* gather up;
(*Gedanken*) collect; (*Kräfte, Mut*)
muster; alles zusammengenommen
considering everything || *ref* pull oneself together
zusam′menpacken *tr* pack up
zusam′menpassen *tr* & *intr* match
zusam′menpferchen *tr* crowd together
Zusam′menprall *m* collision; (fig) (mit)
impact (on)
zusam′menprallen *intr* collide
zusam′menraffen *tr* collect in haste;
(*ein Vermögen*) amass; (*Kräfte*)
summon up, marshal || *ref* pull oneself together
zusam′menreißen §53 *ref* (coll) pull
oneself together
zusam′menrollen *tr* roll up
zusam′menrotten *ref* band together,
form a gang; (*Aufrührer*) riot
zusam′menrücken *tr* push together ||
intr (SEIN) move closer together
zusam′menschießen *tr* (*Stadt*) shoot
up; (*Menschen*) shoot down; (*Geld*)
pool
zusam′menschlagen §132 *tr* smash up;
(*Absätze*) click; (*Beine, Zeitung*)
fold; (*Hände*) clap; (*zerschlagen*)
beat up; die Hände über den Kopf z.
(fig) throw up one's hands || *intr*
(SEIN)—aneinander z. clash
zusam′menschließen §76 *tr* join; link
together || *ref* join together, unite
Zusam′menschluß *m* union; alliance
zusam′menschmelzen *intr* (SEIN) fuse;
melt away; (fig) dwindle
zusam′menschnüren *tr* tie up
zusam′menschrumpfen *intr* (SEIN)
shrivel; (*Geld*) (coll) dwindle away
zusam′mensetzen *tr* put together;
(*mach*) assemble || *ref* sit down together; sich z. aus consist of
Zusam′mensetzung *f* (-;-en) composition; (*Bestandteile*) ingredients;
(*Struktur*) structure; (chem, gram)
compound
Zusam′menspiel *n* teamwork
zusam′menstauchen *tr* browbeat, chew
out
zusam′menstellen *tr* put together;
(*Liste*) compile; (*Farben*) match;
organize
Zusam′menstoß *m* collision; (*der Meinungen*) clash; (*Treffen*) encounter;
(mil) engagement
zusam′menstoßen §150 *tr* knock together; (*Gläser*) touch || *intr* adjoin;
mit den Gläsern z. clink glasses ||
intr (SEIN) collide; (*Gegner*) clash
zusam′menstückeln *tr* piece together
zusam′menstürzen *intr* (SEIN) collapse
zusam′mentragen §132 *tr* collect
zusam′mentreffen §151 *intr* (SEIN)
meet; coincide || **Zusammentreffen**
n (-;) encounter, meeting; coincidence
zusam′mentreiben §62 *tr* round up;
(*Geld*) scrape up
zusam′mentreten §152 *intr* (SEIN) meet
zusam′menwirken *intr* cooperate; col-

laborate; interact ‖ **Zusammen-wirken** *n* (-s;) cooperation; inter-action

zusam/menzählen *tr* count up, add up

zusam/menziehen §163 *tr* draw to-gether, contract; (*Lippen*) pucker; (*Brauen*) knit; (*Summe*) add up; (*kürzen*) shorten; (*Truppen*) concen-trate ‖ *ref* contract; (*Gewitter*) brew ‖ *intr* (SEIN)—**mit j-m z.** move in with s.o.

Zu/satz *m* addition; (*Ergänzung*) sup-plement; (*Anhang*) appendix; (*Nach-schrift*) postscript; (*Beimischung*) admixture; (*zu e-m Testament*) codi-cil; (parl) rider; **unter Z. von** with the addition of

Zu/satzgerät *n* attachment

zusätzlich ['tsuzetslɪç] *adj* additional, extra ‖ *adv* in addition

zuschanden [tsu'/andən] *adv*—**z. ma-chen** ruin; **z. werden** go to ruin

zu/schauen *intr* look on; (*dat*) watch

Zu/schauer –in §6 *mf* spectator

Zu/schauerraum *m* auditorium

zu/schicken *tr* send (to)

zu/schieben §130 *tr* close, shut; (*Rie-gel*) push forward; **j-m die Schuld z.** push the blame on s.o.

Zu/schlag *m* extra charge; **den Z. er-halten** get the contract (*on a bid*)

zu/schlagen §132 *tr* (*Tür*) slam; (*Buch*) shut; (*auf Auktionen*) knock down; (*hinzurechnen*) add ‖ *intr* hit hard

zu/schließen §76 *tr* shut, lock

zu/schnallen *tr* buckle (up)

zu/schnappen *intr* snap shut; **z. lassen** snap shut

zu/schneiden §106 *tr* cut out; (*Anzug*) cut to size

Zu/schnitt *m* cut; (fig) style

zu/schnüren *tr* lace up

zu/schrauben *tr* screw tight

zu/schreiben §62 *tr* ascribe; (*Bedeu-tung*) attach; (*Grundstück, usw.*) transfer, sign over ‖ *ref*—**er hat es sich** [*dat*] **selbst zuzuschreiben** he has himself to thank for it

Zu/schrift *f* letter, communication

zuschulden [tsu'/ʊldən] *adv*—**sich** [*dat*] **etw. z. kommen lassen** take the blame for s.th.

Zu/schuß *m* subsidy; grant; allowance

zu/schütten *tr* add; (*Graben*) fill up

zu/sehen §138 *intr* look on; (*dat*) watch; **z., daß** see to it that

zusehends ['tsuze·ənts] *adv* visibly

zu/senden §120 & §140 *tr* (*dat*) send to

zu/setzen *tr* add; (*Geld*) lose ‖ *intr* (*dat*) pester; (*dat*) be hard on; (mil) (*dat*) put pressure on

zu/sichern *tr*—**j-m etw z.** assure s.o. of s.th.

Zu/sicherung *f* (-;-en) assurance

zu/siegeln *tr* seal up

Zu/speise *f* side dish

zu/sperren *tr* lock

zu/spielen *tr*—**j-m den Ball z.** pass the ball to s.o.; **j-m etw z.** slip s.th. to s.o.

zu/spitzen *tr* sharpen, make pointy ‖ *ref* (*Lage*) come to a head

zu/sprechen §64 *tr* (& jur) award

Zu/spruch *m* consolation, encourage-ment; (com) customers, clientele

zu/springen §142 *intr* (SEIN) snap shut

Zu/stand *m* state, condition; **gegen-wärtiger Z.** status quo; **in gutem Z.** in good condition; **Zustände state of affairs**

zustande [tsu'/tandə] *adv*—**z. bringen** bring about; put across; get away with; **z. kommen** come about, come off; happen; be realized; (*Gesetz*) pass; (*Vertrag*) be reached

zu/ständig *adj* competent; (*Behörde*) proper; (*verantwortlich*) responsible

Zu/ständigkeit *f* (-;) jurisdiction

zustatten [tsu'/tatən] *adv*—**z. kommen** come in handy

zu/stehen §146 *intr* (*dat*) be due to

zu/stellen *tr* deliver; (jur) serve

Zu/stellung *f* (-;-en) delivery; (jur) serving

zu/steuern *tr* (*Geld*) contribute, kick in ‖ *intr* (dat, **auf** *acc*) head for

zu/stimmen *intr* (*dat*) agree to, approve of (*s.th.*); (*dat*) agree with (*s.o.*)

Zu/stimmung *f* (-;) consent, approval

zu/stopfen *tr* plug up

zu/stoßen §150 *tr* slam ‖ *intr* (SEIN) lunge; (*dat*) happen to

zu/streben *intr* (*dat*) strive for

zutage [tsu'/tagə] *adv* to light; **z. liegen** be evident

Zutaten ['tsutatən] *pl* ingredients

zuteil [tsu'/taɪl] *adv*—**j-m z. werden** fall to s.o.'s share

zu/teilen *tr* allot; ration; award; (*ge-währen*) grant; confer; (mil) assign

Zu/teilung *f* (-;-en) allotment, alloca-tion; rationing; (mil) assignment

zu/tragen §132 *tr* carry; (*Neuigkeiten*) report ‖ *ref* happen

zuträglich ['tsutreklɪç] *adj* advanta-geous; (*Klima*) healthful; (*Nahrung*) wholesome; **j-m z. sein** agree with s.o.

zu/trauen *tr*—**j-m etw z.** give s.o. credit for s.th.; imagine s.o. capable of s.th. ‖ **Zutrauen** *n* (-s;) (zu) con-fidence (in)

zu/traulich *adj* trustful; (*zahm*) tame

zu/treffen §151 *intr* (SEIN) prove right; come true; hold true, be conclusive; **z. auf** (*acc*) apply to

zu/treffend *adj* correct; to the point; (*anwendbar*) applicable

zu/trinken §143 *intr* (*dat*) drink to

Zu/tritt *m* access; admission, entrance; **kein Z.!** no admittance!

zu/tun §154 *tr* close; (*hinzufügen*) add

zu/verlässig *adj* reliable; **von zuverläs-siger Seite** on good authority

Zu/verlässigkeit *f* (-;) reliability

Zuversicht ['tsuferzɪçt] *f* (-;) confi-dence

zu/versichtlich *adj* confident

zuviel [tsu'/fil] *adv* & *indef pron* too much; **einer z.** one too many

zuvor [tsu'/for] *adv* before, previously; first (of all); **kurz z.** shortly before

zuvor- *comb.fm.* beforehand

zuvor/kommen §99 *intr* (SEIN) (*dat*) anticipate; **j-m z.** get the jump on s.o.

zuvor'kommend *adj* obliging; polite

zuvor'tun §154 *tr*—es j—m z. outdo s.o.

Zu'wachs *m* increase; growth; **auf Z.** (big enough) to allow for growth

zu'wachsen §155 *intr* (SEIN) grow together; (*Wunde*) heal up; (*dat*) accrue (to)

Zu'wachsrate *f* rate of increase

zuwege [tsu'vega] *adv*—z. bringen bring about; achieve; finish; **gut z. sein** be fit as a fiddle

zuweilen [tsu'vaɪlən] *adv* sometimes

zu'weisen §118 *tr* assign, allot

zu'wenden §120 & §140 *tr* (*dat*) turn (*s.th.*) towards; (*dat*) give (*s.th.*) to, devote (*s.th.*) to || *ref* (*dat*) devote oneself to, concentrate on

Zu'wendung *f* (-;-en) gift, donation

zuwenig [tsu'veniç] *adv* & *pron* too little

zu'werfen §160 *tr* (*Tür*) slam; (*Blick*) cast; (*Grube*) fill up; j—m etw z. throw s.o. s.th.

zuwider [tsu'vidər] *adj* (*dat*) distasteful (to) || *prep* (*dat*) contrary to

zuwi'derhandeln *intr* (*dat*) go against

Zuwi'derhandlung *f* (-;-en) violation

zu'winken *intr* (*dat*) wave to; beckon to

zu'zahlen *tr* pay extra

zu'zählen *tr* add

zuzeiten [tsu'tsaɪtən] *adv* at times

zu'ziehen §163 *tr* (*Vorhang*) draw; (*Knoten*) tighten; (*Arzt, Experten*) call in || *ref*—**sich** [*dat*] etw z. incur s.th.; contract s.th. || *intr* (SEIN) move in; move (*to a city*)

Zu'ziehung *f*—unter Z. (*genit* or *von*) in consultation with

zuzüglich ['tsutsyklɪç] *prep* (*genit*) plus; including

zwang [tsvaŋ] *pret of* zwingen || Zwang *m* (-[e]s;) coercion, force; restraint; obligation; (*Druck*) pressure; (*jur*) duress; **auf j—n Z. ausüben** put pressure on s.o. || *ref*—**sich** [*dat*] keinen Z. antun (or auferlegen) relax

zwängen ['tsvɛŋən] *tr* force, squeeze || *ref* (*durch*) squeeze (through)

zwang'los *adj* free and easy; informal

Zwang'losigkeit *f* (-;) ease; informality

Zwangs— [tsvaŋs] *comb.fm.* force, compulsory

Zwangs'arbeit *f* hard labor

Zwangs'arbeitslager *n* labor camp

Zwangs'jacke *f* strait jacket

Zwangs'lage *f* tight spot

zwangs'läufig *adj* inevitable

zwangs'mäßig *adj* forced; coercive

Zwangs'maßnahme *f*—zu Zwangsmaßnahmen greifen resort to force

Zwangs'verschleppte §5 *mf* displaced person

Zwangs'verwaltung *f* receivership

Zwangs'vorstellung *f* hallucination

zwangs'weise *adv* by force

Zwangs'wirtschaft *f* (econ) government control, controlled economy

zwanzig ['tsvantsɪç] *invar adj* & *pron* twenty || Zwanzig *f* (-;-en) twenty

zwanziger ['tsvantsɪɡər] *invar adj* of the twenties; **die z. Jahre** the twenties

zwanzigste ['tsvantsɪçstə] §9 *adj* & *pron* twentieth

Zwanzigstel ['tsvantsɪçstəl] *n* (-s;-) twentieth (*part*)

zwar [tsvar] *adv* indeed, no doubt, it is true; **und z.** namely, that is

Zweck [tsvek] *m* (-[e]s;-e) purpose, aim, object, point; **es hat keinen Z.** there's no point to it

zweck'dienlich *adj* serviceable, useful

Zwecke ['tsvekə] *f* (-;-n) tack; thumbtack

zweck'entfremden *tr* misuse

zweck'entsprechend *adj* appropriate

zweck'los *adj* pointless

zweck'mäßig *adj* serving its purpose; (*Möbel*) functional

zwecks [tsveks] *prep* (*genit*) for the purpose of

zwei [tsvar] *adj* & *pron* two; **alle z.** (coll) both; **zu zweien** in twos, two by two, in pairs; **zu zweien hintereinander** in double file || Zwei *f* (-;-en) two

zwei'beinig *adj* two-legged

Zwei'bettzimmer *n* double room

Zweidecker ['tsvaɪdɛkər] *m* (-s;-) biplane

zweideutig ['tsvaɪdɔɪtɪç] *adj* ambiguous; (*Witz*) off-color; (*schlüpfrig*) suggestive

zweierlei ['tsvaɪ·ər'laɪ] *invar adj* two kinds of; **das ist z.** (coll) that's different

zwei'fach, zwei'fältig *adj* twofold, double; **in zweifacher Ausfertigung** in duplicate

Zweifami'lienhaus *n* duplex

zwei'farbig *adj* two-tone

Zweifel ['tsvaɪfəl] *m* (-s;-) doubt; **in Z. stellen** (or ziehen) call into question; **über allen Zweifeln erhaben** beyond reproach

zwei'felhaft *adj* doubtful; questionable; (*Persönlichkeit*) suspicious

zwei'fellos *adj* doubtless

zweifeln ['tsvaɪfəln] *intr* be in doubt; waver, hesitate; **z. an** (*dat*) doubt

Zwei'felsfall *m*—im Z. in case of doubt

Zweif'ler —in §6 *mf* skeptic

Zweig [tsvark] *m* (-[e]s;-e) branch

Zweig'anstalt *f*, Zweig'geschäft *n* (com) branch

Zweig'gesellschaft *f* (com) affiliate

Zweig'niederlassung *f*, Zweig'stelle *f* (com) branch

Zwei'kampf *m* duel, single combat

zwei'mal *adv* twice

zweimalig ['tsvaɪmalɪç] *adj* repeated

zweimotorig ['tsvaɪmotorɪç] *adj* two-engine, twin-engine

zweireihig ['tsvaɪraɪ·ɪç] *adj* (*Sakko*) double-breasted

zwei'schneidig *adj* double-edged

zwei'seitig *adj* bilateral; reversible

zweisprachig ['tsvaɪ'praxɪç] *adj* bilingual

Zweistär'kenglas *n* bifocal lens; (*Brille*) bifocals

zwei'stimmig *adj* for two voices

zweistufig ['tsvaɪ/tufɪç] *adj* (rok) two-stage

zwei'stündig *adj* two-hour

zwei′stündlich *adj & adv* every two hours

zweit [tsvaɪt] *adv*—**zu z.** by twos; **wir sind zu z.** there are two of us

Zwei′taktmotor *m* two-cycle engine

Zweit′ausfertigung *f* duplicate

zweit′beste §9 *adj* second-best

zweite [′tsvaɪtə] §9 *adj & pron* second; another; **aus zweiter Hand** second-hand; **at second hand; zum zweiten** secondly || **Zweite** §5 *mf* (sport) runner-up

zwei′teilig *adj* two-piece; two-part

zweitens [′tsvaɪtəns] *adv* secondly

zweit′klassig *adj* second-class

Zwerchfell [′tsvɛrçfɛl] *n* diaphragm

Zwerg [tsvɛrk] *m* (–[e]s;–e) dwarf

zwer′genhaft *adj* dwarfish

Zwetsche [′tsvɛtʃə] *f* (–;–n), **Zwetschge** [′tsvɛtʃgə] *f* (–;–n) plum

Zwetsch′genwasser *n* plum brandy

zwicken [′tsvɪkən] *tr* pinch

Zwicker (**Zwik′ker**) *m* (–s;–) pince-nez

Zwickmühle [′tsvɪkmylə] *f* (fig) fix

zwie– [tsvi] *comb.fm.* dis–, two–, double

Zwieback [′tsvibak] *m* (–s;–e & –e) zwieback

Zwiebel [′tsvibəl] *f* (–;–n) onion; (*Blumen–*) bulb

Zwie′gespräch *n* dialogue

Zwie′licht *n* twilight

Zwiesel [′tsvizəl] *f* (–;–n) fork (*of tree*)

Zwie′spalt *m* dissension; schism; discrepancy; **im Z. sein mit be at variance with**

zwiespältig [′tsviʃpɛltɪç] *adj* disunited, divided; divergent

Zwie′tracht *f* (–;) discord

Zwilling [′tsvɪlɪŋ] *m* (–s;–e) twin; **eineiige Zwillinge** identical twins

Zwil′lingsbruder *m* twin brother

Zwil′lingsschwester *f* twin sister

Zwinge [′tsvɪŋə] *f* (–;–n) ferrule; clamp; (*Schraubstock*) vise

zwingen [′tsvɪŋən] §142 *tr* force, compel; (*schaffen*) accomplish, swing

zwin′gend *adj* forceful, cogent

Zwin′ger *m* (–s;–) dungeon; cage; dog kennel; bear pit; lists

zwinkern [′tsvɪŋkərn] *intr* blink

Zwirn [tsvɪrn] *m* (–[e]s;–e) thread

Zwirns′faden *m* thread

zwischen [′tsvɪʃən] *prep* (*dat & acc*) between, among

Zwi′schenbemerkung *f* interruption

Zwi′schendeck *n* steerage

Zwi′schending *n* cross, mixture

zwischendurch′ *adv* in between; at times

Zwi′schenergebnis *n* incomplete result

Zwi′schenfall *m* (unexpected) incident

Zwi′schenhändler –**in** §6 *mf* middle-man

Zwi′schenlandung *f* stopover

Zwi′schenlauf *m* (sport) quarterfinal; (sport) semifinal

Zwi′schenpause *f* break, intermission

Zwi′schenraum *m* space, interval

Zwi′schenruf *m* boo; interruption

Zwi′schenrunde *f* (sport) quarterfinal; (sport) semifinal

Zwi′schenspiel *n* interlude

zwi′schenstaatlich *adj* international; interstate

Zwi′schenstation *f* (rr) way station

Zwi′schenstecker *m* (elec) adapter

Zwi′schenstellung *f* (–;–en) intermediate position

Zwi′schenstück *n* insert; (*Verbindung*) connection; (elec) adapter

Zwi′schenstufe *f* intermediate stage

Zwi′schenträger –**in** §6 *mf* gossip

Zwi′schenwand *f* partition wall

Zwi′schenzeit *f* interval, meanwhile

Zwist [tsvɪst] *m* (–es;–e) discord; quarrel; (*Feindschaft*) enmity

Zwi′stigkeit *f* (–;–en) hostility

zwitschern [′tsvɪtʃərn] *tr*—**e–n z.** (coll) have a shot of liquor || *intr* chirp

Zwitter [′tsvɪtər] *m* (–s;–) hermaphrodite

Zwit′terfahrzeug *n* (mil) half-track

zwo [tsvo] *adj & pron* (coll) two

zwölf [tsvœlf] *invar adj & pron* twelve || **Zwölf** *f* (–;–en) twelve

Zwölffin′gerdarm *m* duodenum

zwölfte [′tsvœlftə] §9 *adj & pron* twelfth

Zwölftel [′tsvœftəl] *n* (–s;–) twelfth (part)

Zyklon [tsʏ′klon] *m* (–s;–e), **Zyklone** [tsʏ′klonə] *f* (–;–n) cyclone

Zyk·lus [′tsʏklus] *m* (–;–len [lən]) cycle; (*Reihe*) series, course

Zylinder [tsʏ′lɪndər] *m* (–s;–) cylinder (*e–r Lampe*) chimney; (*Hut*) top hat

zylindrisch [tsʏ′lɪndrɪʃ] *adj* cylindrical

Zyniker [′tsʏnɪkər] *m* (–s;–) cynic; (philos) Cynic

zynisch [′tsʏnɪʃ] *adj* cynical

Zypern [′tsʏpərn] *n* (–s;) Cyprus

Zypresse [tsʏ′prɛsə] *f* (–;–n) cypress

Zyste [′tsʏstə] *f* (–;–n) cyst

GRAMMATICAL EXPLANATIONS

German Pronunciation

All the German letters and their variant spellings are listed below (in column 1) with their IPA symbols (in column 2), a description of their sounds (in column 3), and German examples with phonetic transcription (in column 4).

		VOWELS	
SPELLING	SYMBOL	APPROXIMATE SOUND	EXAMPLES
a	[a]	Like *a* in English *swat*	Apfel ['apfəl], lassen ['lasən], Stadt [ʃtat]
a	[ɑ]	Like *a* in English *father*	Vater ['fatər], laden ['ladən]
aa	[ɑ]	" "	Paar [pɑr], Staat [ʃtat]
ah	[ɑ]	" "	Hahn [hɑn], Zahl [tsɑl]
ä	[ɛ]	Like *e* in English *met*	Äpfel ['epfəl], lässig ['lesɪç], Städte ['ʃtetə]
ä	[e]	Like *e* in English *they* (without the following sound of *y*)	mäßig ['mesɪç], Väter ['fetər]
äh	[e]	" "	ähnlich ['enlɪç], Zähne ['tsenə]
e	[ə]	Like *e* in English *system*	Bitte ['bɪtə], rufen ['rufən]
e	[ɛ]	Like *e* in English *met*	Kette ['kɛtə], messen ['mesən]
e	[e]	Like *e* in English *they* (without the following sound of *y*)	Feder ['fedər], regnen ['regnən]
ee	[e]	" "	Meer [mer], Seele ['zelə]
eh	[e]	" "	Ehre ['erə], zehn [tsen]
i	[ɪ]	Like *i* in English *sin*	bin [bɪn], Fisch [fɪʃ]
i	[i]	Like *i* in English *machine*	Maschine [ma'ʃinə], Lid [lit]
ih	[i]	" "	ihm [im], ihr [ir]
ie	[i]	" "	dieser ['dizər], tief [tif]
o	[ɔ]	Like *o* in English *often*	Gott [gɔt], offen ['ɔfən]
o	[o]	Like *o* in English *note*, but without the diphthongal glide	holen ['holən], Rose ['rozə]
oo	[o]	" "	Boot [bot], Moos [mos]
oh	[o]	" "	Bohne ['bonə], Kohle ['kolə]
ö	[œ]	The lips are rounded for [ə] and held without moving while the sound [ɛ] is pronounced.	Götter ['gœtər], öffnen ['œfnən]

3a

SPELLING	SYMBOL	APPROXIMATE SOUND	EXAMPLES
ö	[ø]	The lips are rounded for [o] and held without moving while the sound [e] is pronounced.	böse ['bøzə], Löwe ['løvə]
öh	[ø]	" "	Röhre ['rørə], Söhne ['zønə]
u	[ʊ]	Like u in English bush	Busch [buʃ], muß [mʊs], Hund [hʊnt]
u	[u]	Like u in English rule	Schule ['ʃulə], Gruß [grus]
uh	[u]	" "	Uhr [ur], Ruhm [rum]
ü	[Y]	The lips are rounded for [ʊ] and held without moving while the sound [ɪ] is pronounced.	Hütte ['hYtə], müssen ['mYsən]
ü	[y]	The lips are rounded for [u] and held without moving while the sound [i] is pronounced.	Schüler ['ʃylər], Grüße ['grysə]
üh	[y]	" "	Mühle ['mylə], kühn [kyn]
y	[Y]	Like ü [Y] above	Mystik ['mYstɪk]
y	[y]	Like ü [y] above	Mythe ['mytə]

DIPHTHONGS

SPELLING	SYMBOL	APPROXIMATE SOUND	EXAMPLES
ai	[aɪ]	Like i in English night	Saite ['zaɪtə], Mais [maɪs]
au	[aʊ]	Like ou in English ouch	kaufen ['kaʊfən], Haus [haʊs]
äu	[ɔɪ]	Like oy in English toy	träumen ['trɔɪmən], Gebäude [gə'bɔɪdə]
ei	[aɪ]	Like i in English night	Zeit [tsaɪt], nein [naɪn]
eu	[ɔɪ]	Like oy in English toy	heute ['hɔɪtə], Eule ['ɔɪlə]

CONSONANTS

SPELLING	SYMBOL	APPROXIMATE SOUND	EXAMPLES
b	[b]	Like b in English boy	Buch [bux], haben ['habən]
b	[p]	Like p in English lap	gelb [gelp], lieblich ['liplɪç]
c	[k]	Like c in English car	Clown [klaʊn], Café [ka'fe]
c	[ts]	Like ts in English its	Cäsar ['tsezar], Centrale [tsen'tralə]
ch	[x]	This sound is made by breathing through a space between the back of the tongue and the soft palate.	auch [aux], Buche ['buxə]
ch	[ç]	This sound is made by breathing through a space left when the front of the tongue is pressed close to the hard palate with the tip of the tongue behind the lower teeth.	ich [ɪç], Bücher ['byçər], Chemie [çe'mi], durch [dʊrç]

4a

SPELLING	SYMBOL	APPROXIMATE SOUND	EXAMPLES
ch	[k]	Like *k* in English *key*	**Charakter** [ka'raktər], **Chor** [kor]
ch	[ʃ]	Like *sh* in English *shall*	**Chef** [ʃef], **Chassis** [ʃa'si]
chs	[ks]	Like *x* in English *box*	**sechs** [zeks], **Wachs** [vaks]
ck	[k]	Like *k* in English *key* When *ck* in a vocabulary entry in this Dictionary has to be divided by an accent mark, the word is first spelled with *ck* and is then repeated in parentheses with the *ck* changed to *kk* in accordance with the principle which requires this change when the division comes at the end of the line, e.g., **Deckenlicht** (Dek'ken-licht).	**wecken** ['vekən], **Ruck** [ruk]
d	[d]	Like *d* in English *door*	**laden** ['ladən], **deutsch** [dɔɪtʃ]
d	[t]	Like *t* in English *time*	**Freund** [frɔɪnt], **Hund** [hunt]
dt	[t]	" "	**verwandt** [fer'vant], **Stadt** [ʃtat]
f	[f]	Like *f* in English *five*	**Fall** [fal], **auf** [auf]
g	[g]	Like *g* in English *go*	**geben** ['gebən], **Regen** ['regən]
g	[k]	Like *k* in English *key*	**Krieg** [krik], **Weg** [vek]
g	[ç]	See **ch** [ç] above	**wenig** ['veniç], **häufig** ['hɔɪfɪç]
h	[h]	Like *h* in English *hat*	**Haus** [haus], **Freiheit** ['fraihait]
j	[j]	Like *y* in English *yet*	**Jahr** [jɑr], **jener** ['jenər]
k	[k]	Like *k* in English *key*	**Kaffee** [ka'fe], **kein** [kain]
l	[l]	This sound is made with the tip of the tongue against the back of the upper teeth and the side edges of the tongue against the side teeth.	**laden** ['ladən], **fahl** [fal]
m	[m]	Like *m* in English *man*	**mehr** [mer], **Amt** [amt]
n	[n]	Like *n* in English *neck*	**Nase** ['nazə], **kaufen** ['kaufən]
n	[ŋ]	Like *n* in English *sink*	**sinken** ['zɪŋkən], **Funke** ['fuŋkə]
ng	[ŋ]	" "	**Finger** ['fɪŋər], **Rang** [raŋ]
p	[p]	Like *p* in English *pond*	**Perle** ['perlə], **Opfer** ['opfər]
ph	[f]	Like *f* in English *five*	**Phase** ['fazə], **Graphik** ['grafɪk]
qu	[kv]	Does not occur in English.	**Quelle** ['kvelə], **bequem** [bə'kvem]
r	[r]	This sound is a trilled sound made by vibrating the tip of the tongue against the upper gums or by vibrating the uvula.	**rufen** ['rufən], **Rede** ['redə]

5a

SPELLING	SYMBOL	APPROXIMATE SOUND	EXAMPLES
s	[s]	Like s in English sock	Glas [glɑs], erst [erst]
s	[z]	Like z in English zest	sind [zɪnt], Eisen ['aɪzən]
sch	[ʃ]	Like sh in English shall	Schuh [ʃu], Schnee [ʃne]
sp	[ʃp]	Does not occur in English in the initial position.	sparen ['ʃpɑrən], Spott [ʃpɒt]
ss	[s]	This spelling is used only in the intervocalic position and when the preceding vowel sound is one of the following: [a], [ɛ], [ɪ], [ɔ], [œ], [ʊ], [ʏ]	Klasse ['klɑsə], essen ['ɛsən], wissen ['vɪsən], Gosse ['gɔsə], Rössel ['rœsəl], Russe ['rʊsə], müssen ['mʏsən]
ß	[s]	This spelling is used instead of ss (a) when in the final position in a word or component, (b) when followed by a consonant, or (c) when intervocalic and preceded by a diphthong or one of the following vowel sounds: [ɑ], [e], [i], [o], [ø], [u], [y]	(a) Fluß [flʊs], Flußufer ['flʊsufər], (b) läßt [lest], (c) dreißig ['draɪsɪç], Straße ['ʃtrɑsə], mäßig ['mesɪç], schießen ['ʃisən], stoßen ['ʃtosən], Stößel ['ʃtøsəl], Muße ['musə], müßig ['mysɪç]
st	[ʃt]	Does not occur in English in the initial position.	Staub [ʃtaʊp], stehen ['ʃte·ən]
t	[t]	Like t in English time	Teller ['telər], Tau [taʊ]
th	[t]	" "	Theater [te'ɑtər], Thema ['tema]
ti+ vowel	[tsj]	Does not occur in English.	Station [stɑ'tsjon], Patient [pɑ'tsjent]
tz	[ts]	Like ts in English its	schätzen ['ʃɛtsən], jetzt [jetst]
v	[f]	Like f in English five	Vater ['fɑtər], brav [brɑf]
v	[v]	Like v in English vat	November [no'vembər], Verb [verp]
w	[v]	" "	Wasser ['vasər], wissen ['vɪsən]
x	[ks]	Like x in English box	Export [eks'pɒrt], Taxe ['taksə]
z	[ts]	Like ts in English its	Zahn [tsɑn], reizen ['raɪtsən]

German Grammar References

§1. Declension of the Definite Article

	SINGULAR			PLURAL
	MASC	FEM	NEUT	MASC, FEM, NEUT
NOM	der	die	das	die
ACC	den	die	das	die
DAT	dem	der	dem	den
GENIT	des	der	des	der

§2. Declension of the Indefinite Article and the Numeral Adjective

1.

	SINGULAR			PLURAL
	MASC	FEM	NEUT	MASC, FEM, NEUT
NOM	ein	eine	ein	
ACC	einen	eine	ein	
DAT	einem	einer	einem	
GENIT	eines	einer	eines	

2. Other words that are declined like **ein** are: **kein** *no, not any* and the possessive adjectives **mein** *my;* **dein** *thy, your;* **sein** *his; her; its;* **ihr** *her; their;* **Ihr** *your;* **unser** *our;* **euer** *your.* Unlike **ein,** they have plural forms, as shown in the following paradigm.

	SINGULAR			PLURAL
	MASC	FEM	NEUT	MASC, FEM, NEUT
NOM	kein	keine	kein	keine
ACC	keinen	keine	kein	keine
DAT	keinem	keiner	keinem	keinen
GENIT	keines	keiner	keines	keiner

3. The **e** of **er** of **unser** and **euer** is generally dropped when followed by an ending, as shown in the following paradigm. And instead of the e of **er** dropping, the e of final **em** and **en** in these words may drop.

	SINGULAR			PLURAL
	MASC	FEM	NEUT	MASC, FEM, NEUT
NOM	unser	uns(e)re	unser	uns(e)re
ACC	uns(e)ren or unsern	uns(e)re	unser	uns(e)re
DAT	uns(e)rem or unserm	uns(e)rer	uns(e)rem or unserm	uns(e)ren or unsern
GENIT	uns(e)res	uns(e)rer	uns(e)res	uns(e)rer

All adjectives that follow these words are declined in the mixed declension.

7a

4. The pronouns **einer** and **keiner**, as well as all the possessive pronouns, are declined according to the strong declension of adjectives. The neuter forms **eines** and **keines** have the variants **eins** and **keins**.

5. When the possessive adjectives are used as possessive pronouns, they are declined according to the strong declension of adjectives. When preceded by the definite article, they are declined according to the weak declension of adjectives. There are also possessive pronouns with the infix **ig** which are always preceded by the definite article and capitalized and are declined according to the declension of adjectives, e.g., **der, die, das Meinige** *mine*.

§3. Declension of the Demonstrative Pronoun

	SINGULAR			PLURAL
	MASC	FEM	NEUT	MASC, FEM, NEUT
NOM	dieser	diese	dieses or dies	diese
ACC	diesen	diese	dieses or dies	diese
DAT	diesem	dieser	diesem	diesen
GENIT	dieses	dieser	dieses	dieser

Other words that are declined like **dieser** are **jeder** *each;* **jener** *that;* **mancher** *many a;* **welcher** *which.* All adjectives that come after these words are declined in the weak declension.

§4. Declension of Adjectives.
Adjectives have three declensions: 1) the strong declension, 2) the weak declension, and 3) the mixed declension. On both sides of this Dictionary, adjectives occurring in the expressions consisting solely of an adjective and a noun are entered in their weak forms.

1. ,The strong declension of adjectives, whose endings are shown in the following table, is used when the adjective is not preceded by **der** or by **dieser** or any of the other words listed in §3 or by **ein** or any of the other words listed in §2.

	SINGULAR			PLURAL
	MASC	FEM	NEUT	MASC, FEM, NEUT
NOM	–er	–e	–es	–e
ACC	–en	–e	–es	–e
DAT	–em	–er	–em	–en
GENIT	–en	–er	–en	–er

2. The weak declension of adjectives, whose endings are shown in the following table, is used when the adjective is preceded by **der** or **dieser** or any of the other words listed in §3.

	SINGULAR			PLURAL
	MASC	FEM	NEUT	MASC, FEM, NEUT
NOM	–e	–e	–e	–en
ACC	–en	–e	–e	–en
DAT	–en	–en	–en	–en
GENIT	–en	–en	–en	–en

3. The **der** component of **derselbe** and **derjenige** is the article **der** and is declined like it, while the –**selbe** and –**jenige** components are declined according to the weak declension of adjectives.

4. The mixed declension of adjectives, whose endings are shown in the following table, is used when the adjective is preceded by **ein** or **kein** or any of the other words listed in §2.

8a

| | SINGULAR | | | PLURAL |
	MASC	FEM	NEUT	MASC, FEM, NEUT
NOM	–er	–e	–es	–en
ACC	–en	–e	–es	–en
DAT	–en	–en	–en	–en
GENIT	–en	–en	–en	–en

§5. Adjectives Used as Nouns. When an adjective is used as a masculine, feminine, or neuter noun, it is spelled with an initial capital letter and is declined as an adjective in accordance with the principles set forth in §4. We have, for example, der or die **Fremde** the foreigner; der or die **Angestellte** *the employee*; **ein Angestellter** *a (male) employee*, **eine Angestellte** *a (female) employee*; **das Deutsche** *German* (i.e., *language*). These nouns are entered on both sides of this Dictionary in the weak form of the adjective and their genitives and plurals are not shown.

§6. Many masculine nouns ending in **–er** and **–ier** have feminine forms made by adding **–in**. The masculine forms have genitives made by adding **s** and remain unchanged in the plural, while the feminine forms remain unchanged in the singular and have plurals made by adding **–nen**. For example:

MASC	FEM
NOM SG **Verkäufer** *salesperson (salesman)*	**Verkäuferin** *salesperson (saleslady)*
GENIT SG **Verkäufers**	Verkäuferin
NOM PL **Verkäufer**	Verkäuferinnen

§7. Many masculine nouns ending in **–at** (e.g., Advokat), or in **–ant** (e.g., Musikant), or in **–ist** (e.g., Artist), or in **–ent** (e.g., Student), or in **–graph** (e.g., Choreograph), or in **–ot** (e.g., Pilot), or in **–et** (e.g., Analphabet), or in **–it** (e.g., Israelit), or in **–ast** (e.g., Phantast), etc., have feminine forms made by adding **–in**. The masculine forms have genitives and plurals made by adding **–en**, while the femine forms remain unchanged in the singular and have plurals made by adding **–nen**. For example:

MASC	FEM
NOM SG **Advokat** *attorney*	**Advokatin** *attorney*
GENIT SG **Advokaten**	Advokatin
NOM PL **Advokaten**	Advokatinnen

§8. Many masculine nouns ending in **–ar** (e.g., Antiquar) or in **–är** (e.g., Milliardär) have feminine forms made by adding **–in**. The masculine forms have genitives made by adding **–(e)s** and plurals made by adding **–e**, while the feminine forms remain unchanged in the singular and have plurals made by adding **–nen**. For example:

MASC	FEM
NOM SG **Antiquar** *antique dealer*	**Antiquarin** *antique dealer*
GENIT SG **Antiquar(e)s**	Antiquarin
NOM PL **Antiquare**	Antiquarinnen

§9. Adjectives are generally given in their uninflected form, the form in which they appear in the predicate, e.g., **billig**, **reich**, **alt**. However, those adjectives which do not occur in an uninflected form are given with the weak ending **–e**, which in the nominative is the same for all genders, e.g., **andere, besondere, beste, hohe.**

9a

§10. Adjectives which denote languages may be used as adverbs. When so used with **sprechen, schreiben, können,** and a few others, they are translated in English by the corresponding noun, and actual and immediate action is implied, e.g., **deutsch sprechen** *to speak German* (i.e., to be speaking German right now). Adjectives which denote languages may be capitalized and used as invariable nouns, and when so used with **sprechen, schreiben, können,** and a few other verbs, general action is implied, e.g., **Deutsch sprechen** *to speak German* (i.e., to know how to speak German, to be a speaker of German).

With other verbs, these adjectives used as adverbs are translated by the corresponding noun preceded by "auf" or "in", e.g., **sich auf (or in) deutsch unterhalten** *to converse in German.*

811. Personal and Reflexive Pronouns

PERSONS		SUBJECT	PERSONAL DIRECT OBJECT	PERSONAL INDIRECT OBJECT	REFLEXIVE DIRECT OBJECT	REFLEXIVE INDIRECT OBJECT
SG						
1		ich *I*	mich *me*	mir *(to) me*	mich *myself*	mir *(to) myself*
2		du *you*	dich *you*	dir *(to) you*	dich *yourself*	dir *(to) yourself*
3	MASC	er *he; it*	ihn *him; it*	ihm *(to) him;* *(to) it*	sich *himself;* *itself*	sich *(to) himself;* *(to) itself*
3	FEM	sie *she; it*	sie *her; it*	ihr *(to) her;* *(to) it*	sich *herself;* *itself*	sich *(to) herself;* *(to) itself*
3	NEUT	es *it; she; he*	es *it; her; him*	ihm *(to) it;* *(to) her* *(to) him*	sich *itself;* *herself;* *himself*	sich *(to) itself;* *(to) herself;* *(to) himself*
PL						
1		wir *we*	uns *us*	uns *(to) us*	uns *ourselves*	uns *(to) ourselves*
2		ihr *you*	euch *you*	euch *(to) you*	euch *yourselves*	euch *(to) yourselves*
3		sie *they*	sie *them*	ihnen *(to) them*	sich *themselves*	sich *(to) themselves*
2 FORMAL SG & PL		Sie *you*	Sie *you*	Ihnen *(to) you*	sich *yourself;* *yourselves*	sich *(to) yourself* *(to) yourselves*

er means *it* when it stands for a masculine noun that is the name of an animal or a thing, as **Hund**, **Tisch**. **sie** means *it* when it stands for a feminine noun that is the name of an animal or a thing, as **Hündin**, **Feder**. **es** means *she* when it stands for a neuter noun that is the name of a female person, as **Fräulein**, **Mädchen**, **Weib**; it means *he* when it stands for a neuter noun that is the name of a male person, as **Söhnchen**, **Söhnlein**. The dative means also *from me*, *from you*, etc., with certain verbs expressing separation such as **entnehmen**.

11a

§12. **Separable and Inseparable Prefixes.** Many verbs can be compounded either with a prefix, which is always inseparable and unstressed, or with a combining form (conventionally called also a prefix), which can be separable and stressed or inseparable and unstressed. Exceptions are indicated by the abbreviations *sep* and *insep*.

1. The inseparable prefixes are be–, emp–, ent–, er–, ge–, ver–, and zer–, e.g., beglei′ten, erler′nen, verste′hen. They are never stressed.

2. The separable prefixes (i.e., combining forms) are prepositions, e.g., auf– as in auf′tragen, adverbs, e.g., vorwärts– as in vor′wärtsbringen, adjectives, e.g., tot– as in tot′schlagen, nouns, e.g., maschine– as in maschi′neschreiben, or other verbs, e.g., stehen– as in ste′henbleiben. They are always stressed except as provided for those listed in the following section.

3. The prefixes (combining forms) durch, hinter, über, um, unter, wider, and wieder, when their meaning is literal, are separable and stressed, e.g. durch′schneiden *cut through, cut in two,* and, when their meaning is figurative or derived, are inseparable and unstressed, e.g., durchschnei′den *cut across, traverse.*

4. A compound prefix is (a) inseparable if it consists of an inseparable prefix plus a separable prefix, e.g., beauf′tragen, (b) separable if it consists of a separable prefix plus an inseparable prefix, e.g.,vor′bereiten—er bereitet etwas vor, and (c) separable if it consists of two separable prefixes, e.g., vorbei′laufen—sie lief vorbei. Although verbs falling under (b) are separable, they do not take –ge– in the past participle, e.g., vor′bereitet (past participle of vorbereiten). But they do take the infix –zu– in the infinitive, e.g., vor′zubereiten. Note that compound prefixes falling under (c) are stressed on the second of the two separable components.

§13. German verbs are regarded as reflexive regardless of whether the reflexive pronoun is the direct or indirect object of the verb.

§14. The declension of German nouns is shown by giving the genitive singular followed by the nominative plural, in parentheses after the abbreviation indicating gender. This is done by presenting the whole noun by a hyphen with which the ending and/or the umlaut may or may not be shown according to the inflection; e.g., Stadt [′tat] *f* (–;″e) means der Stadt and die Städte. If the noun has no plural, the closing parenthesis comes immediately after the semicolon following the genitive singular, e.g., Kleidung [′klaɪdʊŋ] *f* (–;). In loan words in which the ending changes in the plural, the centered period is used to mark off the portion of the word that has to be detached before the portion showing the plural form is added, e.g., Da·tum [′datʊm] *n* (–s;–ten [tən]).

When a vowel is added to a word ending in ß, the ß remains if it is preceded by a diphthong or one of the following vowel sounds: [ɑ], [e], [i], [o], [ø], [y], e.g., Stoß [′tos], plural: Stöße; Strauß, plural: Sträuße, but changes to ss if it is preceded by one of the following vowel sounds: [a], [e], [ɪ], [ɔ], [œ], [ʊ], [ʏ], e.g., Roß [rɔs], plural Rosses. In this Dictionary the inflection of words in which ß does not change is shown in the usual way, e.g., Stoß [′tos] *m* (–es;″e); Strauß [′traus] *m* (–es;″e), while the inflection of words in which ß changes to ss is shown in monosyllables by repeating the full word in its inflected forms, e.g., Roß [rɔs] *n* (Rosses; Rosse) and in polysyllables by marking off with a centered dot the final syllable and then repeating it in its inflected forms, e.g., Ver·laß [fɛr′las] *m* (–lasses;).

§15. When a word ending in a double consonant is combined with a following word beginning with the same single consonant followed by a vowel, the resultant group of three identical consonants is shortened to two, e.g., Schiff combined with Fahrt makes Schiffahrt and Schall combined with Lehre makes

Schallehre.[1] However, when such a compound as a vocabulary entry has to be divided by an accent mark, the word is first spelled with two identical consonants and is then repeated in parentheses with three identical consonants, e.g., **Schiffahrt (Schiff'fahrt)**. Furthermore, when such a compound has to be divided because the first component comes at the end of a line and is followed by a hyphen and the second component begins the following line, the three consonants are used, e.g., **Schiff-fahrt** and **Schall-lehre**.

When the medial group **ck** in a vocabulary entry has to be divided by an accent mark, the word is first spelled with **ck** and is then repeated in parentheses with the **ck** changed to **kk** in accordance with the orthographic principle which requires this change when the division comes at the end of the line, e.g., **Deckenlicht (Dek'kenlicht)**.

---

[1] If the intial consonant of the following word is followed by a consonant instead of a vowel, the group of three identical consonants remains, e.g., **Fetttropfen, Rohstofffrage.**

German Model Verbs

These verbs are models for all the verbs that appear as vocabulary entries in the German-English part of this Dictionary. If a section number referring to this table is not given with an entry, it is understood that the verb is a weak verb conjugated like **loben, reden, handeln,** or **warten.** If a section number is given, it is understood that the verb is a strong, mixed, or irregular verb and that it is identical in all forms with the model referred to in its radical vowel or diphthong and the consonants that follow the radical. Thus **schneiden** is numbered §106 to refer to the model **leiden.** Such words include the model itself, e.g., **denken,** numbered §66 to refer to the model **denken,** compounds of the model, e.g., **bekommen,** numbered §99 to refer to the model **kommen,** and verbs that have the same radical component, e.g., **empfehlen,** numbered §51 to refer to the model **befehlen.**

If a strong or mixed verb in a given function (transitive or intransitive) and/or meaning may be conjugated also as a weak verb, this is indicated by the insertion of the section number of the appropriate weak verb (**loben, handeln, reden,** or **warten**) after the section number of the model strong verb, e.g., **dingen** §142 & §109.

If a strong or mixed verb in a different function is conjugated as a weak verb, this is indicated by dividing the two functions by parallels and showing the conjugation of each by the insertion of the appropriate section numbers, e.g., **hängen** §92 *tr* . . . ‖ §109 *intr.*

If a strong or mixed verb in a different meaning is conjugated as a weak verb, this is indicated by dividing the two meanings by parallels and showing the conjugation of each by the insertion of the appropriate section numbers, e.g., **bewegen** *tr* move, set in motion . . . ‖ §56 *tr* move, induce.

It is understood that verbs with inseparable prefixes, verbs with compound separable prefixes of which the first component is separable and the second inseparable, and verbs ending in –ieren do not take ge in the past participle.

No account is taken here of the auxiliary used in forming compound tenses. The use of SEIN is indicated in the body of the Dictionary.

Alternate forms are listed in parentheses immediately below the corresponding principal part of the model verb.

	INFINITIVE	3D SG PRESENT INDICATIVE	IMPERFECT INDICATIVE	IMPERFECT SUBJUNCTIVE	PAST PARTICIPLE
§50	backen	bäckt	buk	büke	gebacken
§51	befehlen	befiehlt	befahl	beföhle	befohlen
§52	beginnen	beginnt	begann	begönne (begänne)	begonnen
§53	beißen	beißt	biß	bisse	gebissen
§54	bergen	birgt	barg	bärge (bürge)	geborgen
§55	bersten	birst (berstet)	barst	bärste (börste)	geborsten
§56	bewegen	bewegt	bewog	bewöge	bewogen
§57	biegen	biegt	bog	böge	gebogen
§58	bieten	bietet	bot	böte	geboten
§59	binden	bindet	band	bände	gebunden
§60	bitten	bittet	bat	bäte	gebeten
§61	blasen	bläst	blies	bliese	geblasen
§62	bleiben	bleibt	blieb	bliebe	geblieben
§63	braten	brät	briet	briete	gebraten
§64	brechen	bricht	brach	bräche	gebrochen
§65	bringen	bringt	brachte	brächte	gebracht
§66	denken	denkt	dachte	dächte	gedacht
§67	dreschen	drischt	drosch (drasch)	drösche (dräsche)	gedroschen
§68	dünken	dünkt (deucht)	dünkte (deuchte)	dünkte (deuchte)	gedünkt (gedeucht)

	INFINITIVE	3D SG PRESENT INDICATIVE	IMPERFECT INDICATIVE	IMPERFECT SUBJUNCTIVE	PAST PARTICIPLE
§69	dürfen	darf	durfte	dürfte	gedurft (dürfen)
§70	essen	ißt	aß	äße	gegessen
§71	fahren	fährt	fuhr	führe	gefahren
§72	fallen	fällt	fiel	fiele	gefallen
§73	fangen	fängt	fing	finge	gefangen
§74	fechten	ficht	focht	föchte	gefochten
§75	fliehen	flieht	floh	flöhe	geflohen
§76	fließen	fließt	floß	flösse	geflossen
§77	frieren	friert	fror	fröre	gefroren
§78	gären	gärt	gor	göre	gegoren
§79	gebären	gebiert	gebar	gebäre	geboren
§80	geben	gibt	gab	gäbe	gegeben
§81	gedeihen	gedeiht	gedieh	gediehe	gediehen
§82	gehen	geht	ging	ginge	gegangen
§83	gelten	gilt	galt	gälte (gölte)	gegolten
§84	genesen	genest	genas	genäse	genesen
§85	gleichen	gleicht	glich	gliche	geglichen
§86	gleiten	gleitet	glitt	glitte	geglitten
§87	graben	gräbt	grub	grübe	gegraben
§88	greifen	greift	griff	griffe	gegriffen
§89	haben	hat	hatte	hätte	gehabt
§90	halten	hält	hielt	hielte	gehalten

16a

	INFINITIVE	3D SG PRESENT INDICATIVE	IMPERFECT INDICATIVE	IMPERFECT SUBJUNCTIVE	PAST PARTICIPLE
§91	handeln	handelt	handelte	handelte	gehandelt
§92	hängen	hängt	hing	hinge	gehangen
§93	hauen	haut	hieb	hiebe	gehauen
§94	heben	hebt	hob	höbe	gehoben
§95	heißen	heißt	hieß	hieße	geheißen
§96	helfen	hilft	half	hälfe	geholfen
				(hülfe)	
§97	kennen	kennt	kannte	kennte	gekannt
§98	kiesen	kiest	kor	köre	gekoren
§99	kommen	kommt	kam	käme	gekommen
§100	können	kann	konnte	könnte	gekonnt
					(können)
§101	kreischen	kreischt	kreischte	kreischte	gekreischt
			(krisch)	(krische)	(gekrischen)
§102	kriechen	kriecht	kroch	kröche	gekrochen
§103	laden	lädt	lud	lüde	geladen
§104	lassen	läßt	ließ	ließe	gelassen
§105	laufen	läuft	lief	liefe	gelaufen
§106	leiden	leidet	litt	litte	gelitten
§107	lesen	liest	las	läse	gelesen
§108	liegen	liegt	lag	läge	gelegen
§109	loben	lobt	lobte	lobte	gelobt
§110	löschen	lischt	losch	lösche	geloschen
§111	lügen	lügt	log	löge	gelogen

	INFINITIVE	3D SG PRESENT INDICATIVE	IMPERFECT INDICATIVE	IMPERFECT SUBJUNCTIVE	PAST PARTICIPLE
§112	meiden	meidet	mied	miede	gemieden
§113	melken	melkt	molk	mölke	gemolken
§114	mögen	mag	mochte	möchte	gemocht (mögen)
§115	müssen	muß	mußte	müßte	gemußt (müssen)
§116	nehmen	nimmt	nahm	nähme	genommen
§117	pflegen	pflegt	pflog	pflöge	gepflogen
§118	preisen	preist	pries	priese	gepriesen
§119	quellen	quillt	quoll	quölle	gequollen
§120	reden	redet	redete	redete	geredet
§121	rinnen	rinnt	rann	ränne (rönne)	geronnen
§122	rufen	ruft	rief	riefe	gerufen
§123	salzen	salzt	salzte	salzte	gesalzen
§124	saufen	säuft	soff	söffe	gesoffen
§125	saugen	saugt	sog	söge	gesogen
§126	schaffen	schafft	schuf	schüfe	geschaffen
§127	schallen	schallt	scholl	schölle	geschollen
§128	scheinen	scheint	schien	schiene	geschienen
§129	scheren	schert (schiert)	schor	schöre	geschoren
§130	schieben	schiebt	schob	schöbe	geschoben
§131	schlafen	schläft	schlief	schliefe	geschlafen

18a

	INFINITIVE	3d SG PRESENT INDICATIVE	IMPERFECT INDICATIVE	IMPERFECT SUBJUNCTIVE	PAST PARTICIPLE
§132	schlagen	schlägt	schlug	schlüge	geschlagen
§133	schmelzen	schmilzt	schmolz	schmölze	geschmolzen
§134	schrecken	schrickt	schrak	schräke	geschrocken
§135	schreien	schreit	schrie	schrie	geschrie(e)n
§136	schwimmen	schwimmt	schwamm	schwämme (schwömme)	geschwommen
§137	schwören	schwört	schwur (schwor)	schwüre	geschworen
§138	sehen	sieht	sah	sähe	gesehen
§139	sein	ist	war	wäre	gewesen
§140	senden	sendet	sandte	sendete	gesandt
§141	sieden	siedet	sott	sötte	gesotten
§142	singen	singt	sang	sänge	gesungen
§143	sinken	sinkt	sank	sänke	gesunken
§144	sitzen	sitzt	saß	säße	gesessen
§145	sollen	soll	sollte	sollte	gesollt (sollen)
§146	stehen	steht	stand	stände (stünde)	gestanden
§147	stehlen	stiehlt	stahl	stähle (stöhle)	gestohlen
§148	steigen	steigt	stieg	stiege	gestiegen
§149	sterben	stirbt	starb	stürbe	gestorben
§150	stoßen	stößt	stieß	stieße	gestoßen

	INFINITIVE	3D SG PRESENT INDICATIVE	IMPERFECT INDICATIVE	IMPERFECT SUBJUNCTIVE	PAST PARTICIPLE
§151	treffen	trifft	traf	träfe	getroffen
§152	treten	tritt	trat	träte	getreten
§153	triefen	trieft	troff	tröffe	getroffen
§154	tun	tut	tat	täte	getan
§155	wachsen	wächst	wuchs	wüchse	gewachsen
§156	wägen	wiegt	wog	wöge	gewogen
§157	warten	wartet	wartete	wartete	gewartet
§158	waschen	wäscht	wusch	wüsche	gewaschen
§159	werden	wird	wurde (ward)	würde	geworden (worden)
§160	werfen	wirft	warf	würfe	geworfen
§161	wissen	weiß	wußte	wüßte	gewußt
§162	wollen	will	wollte	wollte	gewollt (wollen)
§163	ziehen	zieht	zog	zöge	gezogen
§164	klimmen	klimmt	klomm	klömme	geklommen
§165	küren	kürt	kor	köre	gekoren
§166	schinden	schindet	schund	schünde	geschunden

Die Aussprache des Englischen

Die nachstehenden Lautzeichen bezeichnen fast alle Laute der englischen Sprache:

VOKALE		
LAUTZEICHEN	**UNGEFÄHRER LAUT**	**BEISPIEL**
[æ]	Offener als *ä* in *hätte*	hat [hæt]
[ɑ]	Wie *a* in *Vater* Wie *a* in *Mann*	father [ˈfɑðər] proper [ˈprɑpər]
[ɛ]	Wie *e* in *Fett*	met [mɛt]
[e]	Offener als *eej* in *Seejungfrau*	fate [fet] they [ðe]
[ə]	Wie *e* in *finden*	haven [ˈhevən] pardon [ˈpɑrdən]
[i]	Wie *ie* in *sie*	she [ʃi] machine [məˈʃin]
[ɪ]	Offener als *i* in *bitte*	fit [fɪt] beer [bɪr]
[o]	Offenes *o* mit anschließendem kurzem (halbvokalischem) *u*	nose [noz] road [rod] row [ro]
[ɔ]	Wie *o* in *oft*	bought [bɔt] law [lɔ]
[ʌ]	Wie *er* in *jeder* (umgangssprachlich)	cup [kʌp] come [kʌm] mother [ˈmʌðər]
[ʊ]	Wie *u* in *Fluß*	pull [pʊl] book [bʊk] wolf [wʊlf]
[u]	Wie *u* in *Fluß*	move [muv] tomb [tum]

DIPHTHONGE		
LAUTZEICHEN	**UNGEFÄHRER LAUT**	**BEISPIEL**
[aɪ]	Wie *ei* in *nein*	night [naɪt] eye [aɪ]
[aʊ]	Wie *au* in *Haus*	found [faʊnd] cow [kaʊ]
[ɔɪ]	Wie *eu* in *heute*	voice [vɔɪs] oil [ɔɪl]

KONSONANTEN		
LAUTZEICHEN	**UNGEFÄHRER LAUT**	**BEISPIEL**
[b]	Wie *b* in *bin*	bed [bɛd] robber [ˈrɑbər]

LAUTZEICHEN	UNGEFÄHRER LAUT	BEISPIEL
[d]	Wie d in du	dead [ded] add [æd]
[dʒ]	Wie dsch in Dschungel	gem [dʒem] jail [dʒel]
[ð]	d als Reibelaut ausgesprochen	this [ðɪs] Father ['faðər]
[f]	Wie f in fett	face [fes] phone [fon]
[g]	Wie g in gehen	go [go] get [get]
[h]	Wie h in Haus	hot [hɑt] alcohol ['ælkə‚hɔl]
[j]	Wie j in ja	yes [jes] unit ['junɪt]
[k]	Wie k in kann	cat [kæt] chord [kɔrd] kill [kɪl]
[l]	Wie l in lang, aber mit angehobenem Zungenrücken	late [let] allow [ə'lau]
[m]	Wie m in mehr	more [mor] command [kə'mænd]
[n]	Wie n in Nest	nest [nest] manner ['mænər]
[ŋ]	Wie ng in singen	king [kɪŋ] conquer ['kɑŋkər]
[p]	Wie p in Pech	pen [pen] cap [kæp]
[r]	Im Gegensatz zum deutschen gerollten Zungenspitzen- oder Zäpfchen-r, ist das englische r mit retroflexer Zungenstellung und gerundeten Lippen zu artikulieren.	run [rʌn] far [fɑr] art [ɑrt] carry ['kærɪ]
[s]	Wie s in es	send [send] cellar ['selər]
[ʃ]	Wie sch in Schule	shall [ʃæl] machine [mə'ʃin] nation ['neʃən]
[t]	Wie t in Tee	ten [ten] dropped [drɑpt]
[tʃ]	Wie tsch in deutsch	child [tʃaɪld] much [mʌtʃ] nature ['netʃər]
[θ]	Ist als stimmloser linguadentaler Lispellaut zu artikulieren	think [θɪŋk] truth [truθ]
[v]	Wie w in was	vest [vest] over ['ovər] of [ɑv]
[w]	Ist als Halbvokal zu artikulieren	work [wʌrk] tweed [twid] queen [kwin]
[z]	Ist stimmhaft zu artikulieren wie s in so	zeal [zil] busy ['bɪzi] his [hɪz] winds [wɪndz]
[ʒ]	Wie j in Jalousie	azure ['eʒər] measure ['meʒər]

Aussprache der zusammengesetzten Wörter

Im englisch-deutschen Teil dieses Wörterbuches ist die Aussprache aller einfachen englischen Wörter in einer Neufassung der Lautzeichen des Internationalen Phonetischen Alphabets in eckigen Klammern angegeben.

Außer den mit Präfixen, Suffixen und Wortbildungselementen gebildeten Zusammensetzungen gibt es im Englischen drei Arten von zusammengesetzten Wörtern: (1) zusammengeschriebene, z.B. **bookcase** Bücherregal, (2) mit Bindestrich geschriebene, z.B. **short-circuit** kurzschließen, und (3) getrennt geschriebene, z.B. **post card** Postkarte. Die Aussprache der englischen zusammengesetzten Wörter ist nicht angegeben, sofern die Aussprache der Bestandteile an der Stelle angegeben ist, wo sie als selbständige Stichwörter erscheinen; angegeben ist jedoch die Betonung durch Haupt- und Nebentonakzent und zwar jeweils am Ende der betonten Silben, z.B. book′case′, short′-cir′cuit, post′ card′.

In Hauptwörtern, in denen der Nebenton auf den Bestandteilen **-man** und **-men** liegt, wird der Vokal dieser Bestandteile wie in den Wörtern **man** und **men** ausgesprochen, z.B. **mailman** ['mel,mæn] und **mailmen** ['mel,mɛn]. In Hauptwörtern, in denen diese Bestandteile unbetont bleiben, wird der Vokal beider Bestandteile als schwa ausgesprochen, z.B. **policeman** [pə'lismən] und **policemen** [pə'lismən]. Es gibt Hauptwörter, in denen diese Bestandteile entweder mit dem Nebenton oder unbetont ausgesprochen werden, z.B. **doorman** ['dor,mæn] oder ['dormən] und **doormen** ['dor,mɛn] oder ['dormən]. In diesem Wörterbuch ist die Lautschrift für diese Wörter nicht angegeben, sofern sie für den ersten Bestandteil dort angeführt ist, wo er als Stichwort erscheint; angegeben sind jedoch Haupt- und Nebenton:

> mail′man s (-men′)
> police′man s (-men)
> door′man′ & door′man s (-men′ & -men)

Aussprache des Partizip Perfekt

Bei Wörtern, die auf **-ed** (oder **-d** nach stummem e) enden und nach den nachstehenden Regeln ausgesprochen werden, ist die Aussprache in diesem Wörterbuch nicht angegeben, sofern sie für die endungslose Form dort angegeben ist, wo diese als Stichwort erscheint. Die Doppelschreibung des Schlußkonsonanten nach einfachem betontem Vokal hat keinen Einfluß auf die Aussprache der Endung **-ed**.

Die Endung **-ed** (oder **-d** nach stummem e) der Vergangenheit, des Partizip Perfekt und gewisser Adjektive hat drei verschiedene Aussprachen je nach dem Klang des Konsonanten am Stammende.

1) Wenn der Stamm auf einen stimmhaften Konsonanten mit Ausnahme von [d] ausgeht, nämlich [b], [g], [l], [m], [n], [ŋ], [r], [v], [z], [ʒ], oder auf einen Vokal, wird **-ed** als [d] ausgesprochen.

KLANG DES STAMMENDES	INFINITIV	VERGANGENHEIT UND PARTIZIP PERFEKT
[b]	ebb [eb]	ebbed [ebd]
	rob [rɑb]	robbed [rɑbd]
	robe [rob]	robed [robd]
[g]	egg [eg]	egged [egd]
	sag [sæg]	sagged [sægd]
[l]	mail [mel]	mailed [meld]
	scale [skel]	scaled [skeld]
[m]	storm [storm]	stormed [stormd]
	bomb [bɑm]	bombed [bɑmd]
	name [nem]	named [nemd]
[n]	tan [tæn]	tanned [tænd]
	sign [saɪn]	signed [saɪnd]
	mine [maɪn]	mined [maɪnd]
[ŋ]	hang [hæŋ]	hanged [hæŋd]
[r]	fear [fɪr]	feared [fɪrd]
	care [kɛr]	cared [kɛrd]
[v]	rev [rev]	revved [revd]
	save [sev]	saved [sevd]
[z]	buzz [bʌz]	buzzed [bʌzd]
[ð]	smooth [smuð]	smoothed [smuðd]
	bathe [beð]	bathed [beðd]
[ʒ]	massage [mə'sɑʒ]	massaged [mə'sɑʒd]
[dʒ]	page [pedʒ]	paged [pedʒd]
Klang des Vokals	key [ki]	keyed [kid]
	sigh [saɪ]	sighed [saɪd]
	paw [pɔ]	pawed [pɔd]

2) Wenn der Stamm auf einen stimmlosen Konsonanten mit Ausnahme von [t] ausgeht, nämlich: [f], [k], [p], [s], [θ], [ʃ] oder [tʃ], wird –ed als [t] ausgesprochen.

KLANG DES STAMMENDES	INFINITIV	VERGANGENHEIT UND PARTIZIP PERFEKT
[f]	loaf [lof] knife [naɪf]	loafed [loft] knifed [naɪft]
[k]	back [bæk] bake [bek]	backed [bækt] baked [bekt]
[p]	cap [kæp] wipe [waɪp]	capped [kæpt] wiped [waɪpt]
[s]	hiss [hɪs] mix [mɪks]	hissed [hɪst] mixed [mɪkst]
[θ]	lath [læθ]	lathed [læθt]
[ʃ]	mash [mæʃ]	mashed [mæʃt]
[tʃ]	match [mætʃ]	matched [mætʃt]

3) Wenn der Stamm auf einen Dentallaut ausgeht, nämlich: [t] oder [d], wird –ed als [ɪd] oder [əd] ausgesprochen.

KLANG DES STAMMENDES	INFINITIV	VERGANGENHEIT UND PARTIZIP PERFEKT
[t]	wait [wet] mate [met]	waited ['wetɪd] mated ['metɪd]
[d]	mend [mend] wade [wed]	mended ['mendɪd] waded ['wedɪd]

Es ist zu beachten, daß die Doppelschreibung des Schlußkonsonanten nach einem einfachen betonten Vokal die Aussprache der Endung –ed nicht beeinflußt: **batted** ['bætɪd], **dropped** [drɑpt], **robbed** [rɑbd].

Diese Regeln gelten auch für zusammengesetzte Adjektive, die auf –ed enden. Für diese Adjektive ist nur die Betonung angegeben, sofern die Aussprache der beiden Bestandteile ohne die Endung –ed dort angegeben ist, wo sie als Stichwörter erscheinen, z.B. o'pen-mind'ed.

Es ist jedoch zu beachten, daß bei manchen Adjektiven, deren Stamm auf einen anderen Konsonanten als [d] oder [t] ausgeht, das –ed als [ɪd] ausgesprochen wird; in diesem Fall ist die volle Aussprache in phonetischer Umschrift angegeben, z.B. **blessed** ['blesɪd], **crabbed** ['kræbɪd].

PART TWO

English-German

ENGLISH—GERMAN

A

A, a [e] *s* erster Buchstabe des englischen Alphabets; (mus) A *n*; **A flat** As *n*; **A sharp** Ais *n*

a [e], [ə] *indef art* ein ‖ *prep* pro; **once a year** einmal im Jahr

abandon [ə'bændən] *s*—**with a.** rückhaltlos ‖ *tr* (*forsake*) verlassen; (*give up*) aufgeben; (*a child*) aussetzen; (*a position*) (mil) überlassen; **a. oneself to** sich ergeben (*dat*)

abase [ə'bes] *tr* demütigen

abasement [ə'besmənt] *s* Demütigung *f*

abashed [ə'bæʃt] *adj* fassungslos

abate [ə'bet] *tr* mäßigen ‖ *intr* nachlassen

abbess ['æbɪs] *s* Äbtissin *f*

abbey ['æbi] *s* Abtei *f*

abbot ['æbət] *s* Abt *m*

abbreviate [ə'brivɪ‚et] *tr* abkürzen

abbreviation [ə‚brivɪ'eʃən] *s* Abkürzung *f*

ABC's [‚e‚bi'siz] *spl* Abc *n*

abdicate ['æbdɪ‚ket] *tr* niederlegen; (*a right, claim*) verzichten auf (*acc*) ‖ *intr* abdanken

abdomen ['æbdəmən] *s* Unterleib *m*

abdominal [æb'dɑmɪnəl] *adj* Unterleibs-

abduct [æb'dʌkt] *tr* entführen

abet [ə'bet] *v* (*pret & pp* **abetted;** *ger* **abetting**) *tr* (*a person*) aufhetzen; (*a crime*) Vorschub leisten (*dat*)

abeyance [ə'be‚əns] *s*—**in a.** in der Schwebe

ab‧hor [æb'hɔr] *v* (*pret & pp* **-horred;** *ger* **-horring**) *tr* verabscheuen

abhorrent [æb'hɔrənt] *adj* verhaßt

abide [ə'baɪd] *v* (*pret & pp* **abode** [ə'bod] & **abided**) *intr*—**a. by** (*an agreement*) sich halten an (*acc*); (*a promise*) halten

ability [ə'bɪlɪti] *s* Fähigkeit *f*; **to the best of one's a.** nach bestem Vermögen

abject [æb'dʒekt] *adj* (*servile*) unterwürfig; (*poverty*) äußerst

ablative ['æblətɪv] *s* Ablativ *m*

ablaze [ə'blez] *adj* in Flammen; (**with**) glänzend (vor *dat*); (*excited*) (**with**) erregt (vor *dat*)

able ['ebəl] *adj* fähig, tüchtig; **be a. to** (*inf*) können (*inf*)

able-bodied ['ebəl'badid] *adj* kräftig; (mil) wehrfähig; **a. seaman** Vollmatrose *m*

ably ['ebli] *adv* mit Geschick

abnormal [æb'nɔrməl] *adj* abnorm

abnormality [‚æbnɔr'mælɪti] *s* Ungewöhnlichkeit *f*; (pathol) Mißbildung *f*

abnor/mal psychol/ogy *s* Psychopathologie *f*

aboard [ə'bord] *adv* an Bord; **all a.!** (*a ship*) alles an Bord! (*a bus, plane, train*) alles einsteigen! ‖ *prep* (*a ship*) an Bord (*genit*); (*a bus, train*) in (*dat*)

abode [ə'bod] *s* Wohnsitz *m*

abolish [ə'balɪʃ] *tr* aufheben, abschaffen

abominable [ə'bamɪnəbəl] *adj* abscheulich

aborigines [‚æbə'rɪdʒɪ‚niz] *spl* Ureinwohner *pl*, Urvolk *n*

abort [ə'bɔrt] *tr* (rok) vorzeitig zur Explosion bringen ‖ *intr* fehlgebären; (fig) fehlschlagen

abortion [ə'bɔrʃən] *s* Abtreibung *f*

abortive [ə'bɔrtɪv] *adj* (fig) mißlungen; **prove a.** fehlschlagen

abound [ə'baʊnd] *intr* reichlich vorhanden sein; **a. in** reich sein an (*dat*)

about [ə'baʊt] *adv* umher, herum; (*approximately*) ungefähr, etwa; **be a. to** (*inf*) im Begriff sein zu (*inf*) ‖ *prep* (*around*) um (*acc*); (*concerning*) über (*acc*); (*approximately at*) gegen (*acc*)

about/ face/ *interj* kehrt!

about/-face/ *s*—**do an a.** (fig) umschwenken; **complete a.** (fig) völliger Umschwung *m*

above [ə'bʌv] *adj* obig ‖ *adv* oben, droben ‖ *prep* (*position*) über (*dat*); (*direction*) über (*acc*); (*physically*) oberhalb (*genit*); **a. all** vor allem

above/board/ *adj & adv* ehrlich, redlich

above/-men/tioned *adj* obenerwähnt, obig

abrasion [ə'breʒən] *s* Abschleifen *n*; (*of the skin*) Abschürfung *f*

abrasive [ə'bresɪv] *adj* abschleifend; (*character*) auf die Nerven gehend ‖ *s* Schleifmittel *n*

abreast [ə'brest] *adj & adv* nebeneinander; **keep a. of** Schritt halten mit

abridge [ə'brɪdʒ] *tr* verkürzen

abridgement [ə'brɪdʒmənt] *s* Verkürzung *f*

abroad [ə'brɔd] *adv* im Ausland; (*direction*) ins Ausland; (*out of doors*) draußen

abrogate ['æbrə‚get] *tr* abschaffen

abrupt [ə'brʌpt] *adj* (*sudden*) jäh; (*curt*) schroff; (*change*) unvermittelt; (*style*) abgerissen

abscess ['æbses] *s* Geschwür *n*, Abszeß *m*

abscond [æb'skand] *intr* (**with**) durchgehen (mit)

absence ['æbsəns] *s* Abwesenheit *f*; (*lack*) Mangel *m*; **in the a. of** in Ermangelung von (or *genit*)

ab'sence without' leave' *s* unerlaubte Entfernung *f* von der Truppe

absent ['æbsənt] *adj* abwesend; **be a. fehlen** ‖ [æb'sɛnt] *tr*—**a. oneself** (*stay away*) fernbleiben; (*go away*) sich entfernen

absentee [ˌæbsən'ti] *s* Abwesende *mf*

ab'sent-mind'ed *adj* geistesabwesend

absolute ['æbsəˌlut] *adj* absolut

absolutely ['æbsəˌlutli] *adv* absolut, völlig ‖ [ˌæbsə'lutli] *adv* (coll) ganz bestimmt, jawohl; **a. not!** keine Rede

absolve [æb'sɑlv] *tr* (*from sin, an obligation*) lossprechen; (*sins*) vergeben

absorb [æb'sɔrb] *tr* aufsaugen; (*a shock*) dämpfen; (*engross*) ganz in Anspruch nehmen; **be absorbed in** vertieft sein in (*acc*)

absorbent [æb'sɔrbənt] *adj* aufsaugend

absor'bent cot'ton *s* Verbandswatte *f*

absorb'ing *adj* (fig) packend

abstain [æb'sten] *intr* (*from*) sich enthalten (*genit*); (parl) sich der Stimme enthalten

abstention [æb'stɛnʃən] *s* (*from*) Enthaltung *f* (von); (parl) Stimmenthaltung *f*

abstinence ['æbstɪnəns] *s* Enthaltsamkeit *f*; (*from*) Enthaltung *f* (von)

abstinent ['æbstɪnənt] *adj* enthaltsam

abstract ['æbstrækt] *adj* abstrakt ‖ *s* (*summary*) Abriß *m*; **in the a. an und für sich** (*betrachtet*) ‖ [æb'strækt] *tr* (*the general from the specific*) abstrahieren; (*summarize*) kurz zusammenfassen; (*purloin*) entwenden

abstruse [æb'strus] *adj* dunkel

absurd [æb'sʌrd] *adj* unsinnig

absurdity [æb'sʌrdɪti] *s* Unsinn *m*

abundance [ə'bʌndəns] *s* (of) Fülle *f* (von), Überfluß *m* (an *dat*, von)

abundant [ə'bʌndənt] *adj* reichlich; **a. in** reich an (*dat*)

abuse [ə'bjus] *s* (*misuse*) Mißbrauch *m*; (*insult*) Beschimpfung *f*; (*physical ill-treatment*) Mißhandlung *f* ‖ [ə'bjuz] *tr* mißbrauchen; (*insult*) beschimpfen; (*ill-treat*) mißhandeln; (*a girl*) schänden

abusive [ə'bjusɪv] *adj* mißbräuchlich; (*treatment*) beleidigend; **a. language** Schimpfworte *pl*; **become a.** ausfällig werden

abut [ə'bʌt] *v* (*pret & pp* **abutted;** *ger* **abutting**) *intr*—**a. on** grenzen an (*acc*)

abutment [ə'bʌtmənt] *s* (*of arch*) Strebepfeiler *m*; (*of bridge*) Widerlager *n*

abyss [ə'bɪs] *s* Abgrund *m*

academic [ˌækə'demɪk] *adj* akademisch

academ'ic gown' *s* Talar *m*

academy [ə'kædəmi] *s* Akademie *f*

accede [æk'sid] *intr* beistimmen; **a. to** (*s.o.'s wishes*) gewähren; (*an agreement*) beitreten (*dat*); **a. to the throne** den Thron besteigen

accelerate (æk'seləˌret] *tr & intr* beschleunigen

accelerator [æk'seləˌretər] *s* Gashebel *m*

accent ['æksent] *s* (*stress*) Betonung *f*; (*peculiar pronunciation*) Akzent *m* ‖ [æk'sent] *tr* betonen

ac'cent mark' *s* Tonzeichen *n*, Akzent *m*

accentuate [æk'sentʃuˌet] *tr* betonen

accept [æk'sept] *tr* annehmen; (*one's fate, blame*) auf sich [*acc*] nehmen; (*put up with*) hinnehmen; (*recognize*) anerkennen

acceptable [æk'septəbəl] *adj* annehmbar; (*pleasing*) angenehm; (*welcome*) willkommen

acceptance [æk'septəns] *s* Annahme *f*; (*recognition*) Anerkennung *f*

access ['ækses] *s* Zugang *m*; (*to a person*) Zutritt *m*; (*data proc*) Zugriff *m*

accessible [æk'sesɪbəl] *adj* (to) zugänglich (für)

accession [æk'sɛʃən] *s* (*to an office*) Antritt *m*; **a. to the throne** Thronbesteigung *f*

accessory [æk'sesəri] *adj* (*subordinate*) untergeordnet; (*additional*) zusätzlich ‖ *s* Zubehörteil *n*; (*to a crime*) Teilnehmer –in *mf*; (*after the fact*) Begünstiger –in *mf*; (*before the fact*) Anstifter –in *mf*

ac'cess road' *s* Zufahrtsstraße *f*; (*on a turnpike*) Zubringerstraße *f*

accident ['æksɪdənt] *s* (*mishap*) Unfall *m*; (*chance*) Zufall *m*; **by a.** zufälligerweise; **have an a.** verunglücken

accidental [ˌæksɪ'dentəl] *adj* zufällig; **a. death** Unfalltod *m* ‖ *s* (mus) Versetzungszeichen *n*

acclaim [ə'klem] *s* Beifall *m* ‖ *tr* (e.g., *as king*) begrüßen, akklamieren

acclamation [ˌæklə'meʃən] *s* Beifall *m*

acclimate ['æklɪˌmet] *tr* akklimatisieren ‖ *intr* (to) sich gewöhnen (an *acc*)

accommodate [ə'kɑməˌdet] *tr* (*oblige*) aushelfen (*dat*); (*have room for*) Platz haben für

accom'modating *adj* gefällig

accommodation [əˌkɑmə'deʃən] *s* (*convenience*) Annehmlichkeit *f*; (*adaptation, adjustment*) Anpassung *f*; (*willingness to please*) Gefälligkeit *f*; (*compromise*) Übereinkommen *n*; **accommodations** (*lodgings*) Unterkunft *f*

accompaniment [ə'kʌmpənɪmənt] *s* Begleitung *f*

accompanist [ə'kʌmpənɪst] *s* Begleiter –in *mf*

accompany [ə'kʌmpəni] *v* (*pret & pp* **-nied**) *tr* begleiten

accomplice [ə'kɑmplɪs] *m* Mitschuldige *mf*

accomplish [ə'kɑmplɪʃ] *tr* (*a task*) vollenden; (*a goal*) erreichen

accom'plished *adj* (*skilled*) ausgezeichnet

accomplishment [ə'kɑmplɪʃmənt] *s* (*completion*) Vollendung *f*; (*achievement*) Leistung *f*

accord [ə'kɔrd] *s* Übereinstimmung *f*; **in a. with** übereinstimmend mit; **of**

one's own a. aus eigenem Antriebe
|| tr gewähren || intr übereinstimmen

accordingly [ə'kɔrdɪŋli] adv demgemäß

accord'ing to' prep gemäß (dat), laut (genit or dat), nach (dat)

accordion [ə'kɔrdɪ·ən] s Akkordeon n

accost [ə'kɔst] tr ansprechen

account [ə'kaunt] s Rechnung f; (narrative) Erzählung f; (report) Bericht m; (importance) Bedeutung f; (com) Konto n; **by all accounts** nach allem, was man hört; **call to a.** zur Rechenschaft ziehen; **on a. of** wegen; **on no a.** auf keinen Fall; **render an a. of s.th. to s.o.** j-m Rechenschaft von etw ablegen; **settle accounts with** (coll) abrechnen mit; **take into a.** in Betracht ziehen

accountable [ə'kauntəbəl] adj (explicable) erklärlich; (responsible) (for) verantwortlich (für)

accountant [ə'kauntənt] s Rechnungsführer –in mf, Buchhalter –in mf

account'ing s Rechnungswesen n

accouterments [ə'kutərmənts] spl Ausrüstung f

accredit [ə'krɛdɪt] tr (e.g., an ambassador) beglaubigen; (a school) bestätigen; (a story) als wahr anerkennen; (give credit for) gutschreiben

accrue [ə'kru] intr anwachsen; (said of interest) auflaufen || intr sich anhäufen

accumulation [ə‚kjumjə'leʃən] s Anhäufung f

accuracy ['ækjərəsi] s Genauigkeit f

accurate ['ækjərɪt] adj genau

accursed [ə'kʌrsɪd], [ə'kʌrst] adj verwünscht

accusation [‚ækjə'zeʃən] s Anschuldigung f; (jur) Anklage f

accusative [ə'kjuzətɪv] s Akkusativ m

accuse [ə'kjuz] tr (of) beschuldigen (genit); (jur) (of) anklagen (wegen)

accustom [ə'kʌstəm] tr (to) gewöhnen (an acc); **become accustomed to** sich gewöhnen an (acc)

ace [es] s (aer, cards) As n

acetate ['æsɪ‚tet] s Azetat n; (tex) Azetatseide f

ace'tic ac'id [ə'sitɪk] s Essigsäure f

acetone ['æsɪ‚ton] s Azeton n

acet'ylene torch' [ə'sɛtɪ‚lin] s Schweißbrenner m

ache [ek] s Schmerz m || intr schmerzen; **a. for** (coll) sich sehnen nach

achieve [ə't͡ʃiv] tr erlangen; (success) erzielen; (a goal) erreichen

achievement [ə't͡ʃivmənt] s (something accomplished) Leistung f; (great deed) Großtat f; (heroic deed) Heldentat f; (of one's object) Erreichung f

achieve'ment test' s Leistungsprüfung f

Achil'les' ten'don [ə'krlis] s Achillessehne f

acid ['æsɪd] adj sauer || s Säure f

acidity [ə'sɪdɪti] s Säure f, Schärfe f; (of the stomach) Magensäure f

ac'id test' s (fig) Feuerprobe f

acidy ['æsɪdi] adj säuerlich, säurig

acknowledge [æk'nɑlɪdʒ] tr anerken-

nen; (admit) zugeben; (receipt) bestätigen

acknowledgment [æk'nɑlɪdʒmənt] s Anerkennung f; (e.g., of a letter) Bestätigung f

acme ['ækmi] s Höhepunkt m

acne ['ækni] s (pathol) Akne f

acolyte ['ækə‚laɪt] s Ministrant m

acorn ['ekɔrn] s Eichel f

acoustic(al) [ə'kustɪk(əl)] adj akustisch, Gehör–, Hör–

acous'tical tile' s Dämmplatte f

acoustics [ə'kustɪks] s & spl Akustik f

acquaint [ə'kwent] tr—a. s.o. with s.th. j-m mit etw bekanntmachen, j-m etw mitteilen; **be acquainted with** kennen; **get acquainted with** kennenlernen

acquaintance [ə'kwentəns] s Bekanntschaft f; (person) Bekannte mf

acquiesce [‚ækwɪ'ɛs] intr (in) einwilligen (in acc)

acquiescence [‚ækwɪ'ɛsəns] s (in) Einwilligung f (in acc)

acquire [ə'kwaɪr] tr erwerben, sich [dat] anschaffen; **a. a taste for** Geschmack gewinnen an (dat)

acquisition [‚ækwɪ'zɪʃən] s Anschaffung f

acquisitive [ə'kwɪzɪtɪv] adj gewinnsüchtig

acquit [ə'kwɪt] v (pret & pp acquitted; ger acquitting) tr freisprechen

acquittal [ə'kwɪtəl] s Freispruch m

acre ['ekər] s Acre m

acreage ['ekərɪdʒ] s Fläche f

acrid ['ækrɪd] adj beißend, scharf

acrobat ['ækrə‚bæt] s Akrobat –in mf

acrobatic [‚ækrə'bætɪk] adj akrobatisch; **acrobatics** spl Akrobatik f; (aer) Kunstflug m

acronym ['ækrənɪm] s Akronym n

across [ə'krɔs] adv herüber, hinüber; **a. from** gegenüber (dat); **ten feet a.** zehn Fuß im Durchmesser || prep (quer) über (acc); (on the other side of) jenseits (genit); **come a.** (a person) treffen; (a thing) stoßen auf (acc); **come a. with it!** (say it!) heraus damit!; (give it!) her damit!

across'-the-board' adj allgemein

acrostic [ə'krɔstɪk] s Akrostichon n

act [ækt] s Tat f, Handlung f; (coll) Theater n; (jur) Gesetz n; (telv) Nummer f; (theat) Akt m, Aufzug m; **catch in the act** auf frischer Tat ertappen || tr spielen; || intr (take action) handeln; (function) wirken; (behave) (like) sich benehmen (wie); (theat & fig) Theater spielen; **act as** dienen als; **act as if** so tun, als ob; **act on** (follow) befolgen; (affect) (ein)wirken auf (acc)

act'ing adj stellvertretend; (theat) Bühnen– || s (as an art) Schauspielkunst f

action ['ækʃən] s Tätigkeit f, Tat f; (effect) Wirkung f; (jur) Klage f; (mil) Gefecht n; (tech) Wirkungsweise f; **go into a.** eingreifen; **put out of a.** (mil) außer Gefecht setzen; (tech) außer Betrieb setzen; **see a.** (mil) an der Front kämpfen

activate ['æktɪ‚vet] *tr* aktivieren; (mil) aufstellen
active ['æktɪv] *adj* tätig; (*member*) ordentlich; (gram, mil) aktiv
ac'tive voice' *s* Tätigkeitsform *f*
activist ['æktɪvɪst] *s* Aktivist –in *mf*
activity [æk'tɪvɪti] *s* Tätigkeit *f*
act' of God' *s* höhere Gewalt *f*
act' of war' *s* Angriffshandlung *f*
actor ['æktər] *s* Schauspieler *m*
actress ['æktrɪs] *s* Schauspielerin *f*
actual ['æktʃʊ‚əl] *adj* wirklich
actually ['æktʃʊ‚əli] *adv* (*really*) wirklich; (*as a matter of fact*) eigentlich
actuary ['æktʃʊ‚ɛri] *s* Aktuar –in *mf*
actuate ['æktʃʊ‚et] *tr* in Bewegung setzen; (*incite*) antreiben
acumen [ə'kjumən] *s* Scharfsinn *m*
acupuncture ['ækjə‚pʌŋktʃər] *s* Akupunktur *f*
acute [ə'kjut] *adj* (*stage, appendicitis*) akut; (*pain*) scharf; (*need*) vordringlich; (*vision*) scharf; (*hearing*) fein; (*problem*) brennend; (*shortage*) bedenklich; (*angle*) spitz
A.D. *abbr* n. Chr. (*nach Christus*)
ad [æd] *s* (coll) Anzeige *f*; put an ad in the papers inserieren
adage ['ædɪdʒ] *s* Sprichwort *n*
adamant ['ædəmənt] *adj* unnachgiebig
Ad'am's ap'ple ['ædəmz] *s* Adamsapfel *m*
adapt [ə'dæpt] *tr* (to) anpassen (*dat* or an *acc*); **a. to the stage** für die Bühne bearbeiten; **a. to the screen** verfilmen ‖ *intr* sich anpassen
adaptation [‚ædæp'teʃən] *s* (*adjustment*) (to) Anpassung *f* (an *acc*); (*reworking, rewriting*) (for) Bearbeitung *f* (für)
adapter [ə'dæptər] *s* Zwischenstück *n*; (elec) Zwischenstecker *m*
add [æd] *tr* hinzufügen; (math) addieren; (e.g., 10%) to the price auf den Preis aufschlagen; add up zusammenrechnen ‖ *intr* (math) addieren; **add to** (in *number*) vermehren; (in *size*) vergrößern; **add up** (coll) stimmen; **add up to** betragen
adder ['ædər] *s* Natter *f*, Otter *f*
addict ['ædɪkt] *s* Süchtige *mf* ‖ [ə'dɪkt] *tr*—a. oneself to sich ergeben (*dat*)
addict'ed *adj* ergeben; **a. to drugs** rauschgiftsüchtig
addiction [ə'dɪkʃən] *s* (to) Sucht *f* (nach)
add'ing machine' *s* Addiermaschine *f*
addition [ə'dɪʃən] *s* Hinzufügung *f*, Zusatz *m*; (*to a family, possessions*) Zuwachs *m*; (*to a building*) Anbau *m*; (math) Addition *f*; **in a.** außerdem; **in a. to** außer
additional [ə'dɪʃənəl] *adj* zusätzlich
additive ['ædɪtɪv] *s* Zusatz *m*
address [ə'dres], ['ædres] *s* Adresse *f*, Anschrift *f*; ['ædres] *s* Rede *f*; deliver an a. e–e Rede halten ‖ *tr* (*a letter*) (to) adressieren (an *acc*); (*words, a question*) (to) richten (an *acc*); (*an audience*) e–e Ansprache halten an (*acc*)
adduce [ə'd(j)us] *tr* anführen

adenoids ['ædə‚nɔɪdz] *spl* Polypen *pl*
adept [ə'dept] *adj* (in) geschickt (in *dat*)
adequate ['ædɪkwɪt] *adj* angemessen; (to) ausreichend (für)
adhere [æd'hɪr] *intr* (to) haften (an *dat*); (fig) (to) festhalten (an *dat*)
adherence [æd'hɪrəns] *s* (to) Festhaften *n* (an *dat*); (fig) (to) Festhalten *n* (an *dat*), Beharren *n* (bei)
adherent [æd'hɪrənt] *s* Anhänger –in *mf*
adhesion [æd'hiʒən] *s* (*sticking*) Ankleben *n*; (*loyalty*) Anhänglichkeit *f*; (pathol, phys) Adhäsion *f*
adhesive [æd'hisɪv] *adj* anklebend ‖ *s* Klebemittel *n*, Klebstoff *m*
adhe'sive tape' *s* Heftpflaster *m*
adieu [ə'd(j)u] *s* (adieus & adieux) Lebewohl *n* ‖ *interj* lebe wohl!
adjacent [ə'dʒesənt] *adj* (to) angrenzend (an *acc*); (*angles*) Nebenadjektiv
adjective ['ædʒɪktɪv] *s* Eigenschaftswort *n*, Adjektiv *n*
adjoin [ə'dʒɔɪn] *tr* angrenzen an (*acc*) ‖ *intr* angrenzen, naheliegen
adjoin'ing *adj* angrenzend; **a. rooms** Nebenzimmer *pl*
adjourn [ə'dʒʌrn] *tr* vertagen ‖ *intr* sich vertagen
adjournment [ə'dʒʌrnmənt] *s* Vertagung *f*
adjudge [ə'dʒʌdʒ] *tr* (*a prize*) zusprechen; **a. s.o. guilty** j–n für schuldig erklären
adjudicate [ə'dʒudɪ‚ket] *tr* gerichtlich entscheiden
adjunct ['ædʒʌŋkt] *s* (to) Zusatz *m* (zu)
adjust [ə'dʒʌst] *tr* (to the right position) einstellen; (to an alternate position) verstellen; (*fit*) (to) anpassen (*dat* or an *acc*); (*differences*) ausgleichen; (*an account*) bereinigen; (ins) berechnen ‖ *intr* (to) sich anpassen (*dat* or an *acc*)
adjustable [ə'dʒʌstəbəl] *adj* verstellbar
adjuster [ə'dʒʌstər] *s* (ins) Schadenssachverständiger –in *mf*
adjustment [ə'dʒʌstmənt] *s* (to) Anpassung *f* (*dat* or an *acc*); (of an account) Bereinigung *f*; (ins) Berechnung *f*; (mach) Einstellung *f*
adjutant ['ædʒətənt] *s* Adjutant *m*
ad-lib [‚æd'lɪb] *v* (*pret* & *pp*) –libbed; ger –libbing *tr* & *intr* improvisieren
ad-man ['ædmæn] *s* (–men) Werbefachmann *m*; (*writer*) Werbetexter *m*
administer [æd'mɪnɪstər] *tr* verwalten; (*help*) leisten; (*medicine*) eingeben; (*an oath*) abnehmen; (*punishment*) verhängen; (*a sacrament*) spenden; **a. justice** Recht sprechen ‖ *intr*— **a. to** dienen (*dat*)
administration [æd‚mɪnɪs'treʃən] *s* (*of an institution*) Verwaltung *f*; (*of an official*) Amtsführung *f*; (*government*) Regierung *f*; (*period of government*) Regierungszeit *f*; (*of a president*) Amtszeit *f*; (*of tests*) Durchführung *f*; (*of an oath*) Abnahme *f*; (*of a sacrament*) Spendung *f*; **a. of justice** Rechtspflege *f*

administrator [æd'mınıs‚tretər] s Verwalter –in mf

admiral ['ædmırəl] s Admiral m

admiration [‚ædmı'reʃən] s Bewunderung f

admire [æd'maır] tr (for) bewundern (wegen)

admirer [æd'maırər] s Bewunderer –in mf; (of a woman) Verehrer m

admissible [æd'mısıbəl] adj (& jur) zulässig

admission [æd'mıʃən] s (entry) Eintritt m; (permission to enter) Eintrittserlaubnis f; (entry fee) Eintrittsgebühr f; (of facts) Anerkennung f; (of guilt) Eingeständnis n; (enrollment) (to, into) Aufnahme f (in acc); (to a profession) Zulassung f (zu)

ad·mit [æd'mıt] v (pret & pp -mitted; ger -mitting) tr (hin)einlassen; (to) (a hospital, a society) aufnehmen (in acc); (to) (a profession) zulassen (zu); (accept) anerkennen; (concede) zugeben; (a crime, guilt) eingestehen || intr—a. of zulassen

admittance [æd'mıtəns] s Eintritt m; no a. Eintritt verboten

admittedly [æd'mıtıdlı] adv anerkanntermaßen

admixture [æd'mıkstʃər] s Beimischung f

admonish [æd'manıʃ] tr ermahnen

admonition [‚ædmə'nıʃən] s Ermahnung f

ado [ə'du] s Getue n; much ado about nothing viel Lärm um nichts; without further ado ohne weiteres

adobe [ə'dobi] s Lehmstein m

adolescence [‚ædə'lesəns] s Jugendalter n

adolescent [‚ædə'lesənt] adj jugendlich || s Jugendliche mf

adopt [ə'dapt] tr (a child) adoptieren; (an idea) annehmen

adopt′ed child′ s Adoptivkind n

adoption [ə'dapʃən] s (of a child) Adoption f; (of an idea) Annahme f

adorable [ə'dorəbəl] adj anbetungswürdig; (coll) entzückend

adore [ə'dor] tr anbeten; (coll) entzückend finden

adorn [ə'dorn] tr schmücken

adornment [ə'dornmənt] s Schmuck m

adrenaline [ə'drenəlın] s Adrenalin n

adrift [ə'drıft] adj—be a. treiben; (fig) weder aus noch ein wissen

adroit [ə'droıt] adj geschickt, gewandt

adulation [‚ædjə'leʃən] s Schmeichelei f

adult [ə'dʌlt], ['ædʌlt] adj erwachsen || s Erwachsene mf

adult′ educa′tion s Erwachsenenbildung f

adulterate [ə'dʌltə‚ret] tr verfälschen; (e.g., wine) panschen

adulterer [ə'dʌltərər] s Ehebrecher m

adulteress [ə'dʌltərıs] s Ehebrecherin f

adulterous [ə'dʌltərəs] adj ehebrecherisch

adultery [ə'dʌltərı] s Ehebruch m

advance [æd'væns] s Fortschritt m; (money) Vorschuß m; in a. im voraus; make advances to (e.g., a girl) Annäherungsversuche machen bei || tr vorrücken; (a clock) vorstellen; (money) vorschießen; (a date) aufschieben; (an opinion) vorbringen; (s.o.'s interests) fördern; (in rank) befördern || intr vorrücken

advancement [æd'vænsmənt] s Fortschritt m; (promotion) Beförderung f; (of a cause) Förderung f

advance′ pay′ment s Voraus(be)zahlung f

advantage [æd'væntıdʒ] s Vorteil m; be of a. nützlich sein; take a. of ausnutzen; to a. vorteilhaft

advantageous [‚ædvən'tedʒəs] adj vorteilhaft

advent ['ædvent] s Ankunft f; Advent Advent m, Adventszeit f

adventure [æd'ventʃər] s Abenteuer n

adventurer [æd'ventʃərər] s Abenteurer m

adventuress [æd'ventʃərıs] s Abenteurerin f

adventurous [æd'ventʃərəs] adj (person) abenteuerlustig; (undertaking) abenteuerlich

adverb ['ædvʌrb] s Umstandswort n

adverbial [æd'vʌrbı‚əl] adj adverbial

adversary ['ædvər‚seri] s Gegner –in mf

adverse [æd'vʌrs], ['ædvʌrs] adj ungünstig, nachteilig

adversity [æd'versıtı] s Unglück n, Not f

advertise ['ædvər‚taız] tr Reklame machen für || intr Reklame machen; a. for durch Inserat suchen

advertisement [‚ædvər'taızmənt], [æd'vertısmənt] s Anzeige f, Reklame f

ad′vertising a′gency s Reklamebüro n

ad′vertising campaign′ s Werbefeldzug m

ad′vertising man′ s (solicitor) Anzeigenvermittler m; (writer) Werbetexter m

advice [æd'vaıs] s Rat m, Ratschlag m; a piece of a. ein Rat m; get a. from sich [dat] Rat holen bei; give a. to raten (dat)

advisable [æd'vaızəbəl] adj ratsam

advise [æd'vaız] tr raten (dat); (of) benachrichtigen (von); (on) beraten (über acc); a. s.o. against s.th. j–m von etw abraten

advisement [æd'vaızmənt] s—take under a. in Betracht ziehen

adviser [æd'vaızər] s Berater –in mf

advisory [æd'vaızərı] adj Beratungs-

advi′sory board′ s Beirat m

advocate ['ædvə‚ket] s Fürsprecher –in mf; (jur) Advokat –in mf || tr befürworten

aeon ['i‚ən], ['i‚an] s Äon m

aerial ['erı‚əl] adj Luft- || s Antenne f

aerodynamic [‚erodaı'næmık] adj aerodynamisch || aerodynamics s Aerodynamik f

aeronautic(al) [‚erə'nɔtık(əl)] adj aeronautisch || aeronautics s Aeronautik f, Luftfahrt f

aerosol ['erə‚sol] s Sprühdose f

aerospace ['ɛrəspes] *adj* Raum—

aesthetic [es'θetɪk] *adj* ästhetisch ‖ **aesthetics** *s* Ästhetik *f*

afar [ə'fɑr] *adv*—**a. off** weit weg; **from a.** von weit her

affable ['æfəbəl] *adj* leutselig

affair [ə'fer] *s* Angelegenheit *f*; (*event, performance*) Veranstaltung *f*; (*romantic involvement*) Verhältnis *n*

affect [ə'fekt] *tr* (*influence*) berühren; (*injuriously*) angreifen; (*pretend*) vortäuschen

affectation [,æfek'teʃən] *s* Geziertheit *f*

affect'ed *adj* affektiert

affection [ə'fekʃən] *s* (for) Zuneigung *f* (zu); (*pathol*) Erkrankung *f*

affectionate [ə'fekʃənɪt] *adj* liebevoll

affidavit [,æfɪ'devɪt] *s* (schriftliche) eidesstattliche Erklärung *f*

affiliate [ə'fɪlɪ,et] *s* Zweiggesellschaft *f* ‖ *tr* angliedern ‖ *intr* sich angliedern

affinity [ə'fɪnɪti] *s* Verwandtschaft *f*

affirm [ə'fʌrm] *tr & intr* behaupten

affirmation [,æfər'meʃən] *s* Behauptung *f*

affirmative [ə'fʌrmətɪv] *adj* bejahend ‖ *s* Bejahung *f*; **in the a.** bejahend, positiv

affix [ə'fɪks] *tr* (*a seal*) aufdrücken; (to) befestigen (an *dat*), anheften (an *acc*)

afflict [ə'flɪkt] *tr* plagen; **afflicted with** erkrankt an (*dat*)

affliction [ə'flɪkʃən] *s* Elend *n*, Leiden *n*; (*grief*) Betrübnis *f*

affluence ['æflu‐əns] *s* Wohlstand *m*

affluent ['æflu‐ənt] *adj* wohlhabend

af'fluent socie'ty *s* Wohlstandsgesellschaft *f*

afford [ə'ford] *tr* (*confer*) gewähren; (*time*) erübrigen; (*be able to meet the expense of*) sich [*dat*] leisten

affront [ə'frʌnt] *s* Beleidigung *f* ‖ *tr* beleidigen

afire [ə'faɪr] *adj & adv* in Flammen

aflame [ə'flem] *adj & adv* in Flammen

afloat [ə'flot] *adj* flott, schwimmend; (*awash*) überschwemmt; (*at sea*) auf dem Meer; (*in circulation*) im Umlauf; **keep a.** (& fig) über Wasser halten; **stay a.** (& fig) sich über Wasser halten

afoot [ə'fut] *adj & adv* (on *foot*) zu Fuß; (*in progress*) im Gange

aforesaid [ə'for,sed] *adj* vorerwähnt

afoul [ə'faul] *adj* (*entangled*) verwickelt ‖ *adv*—**run a. of the law** mit dem Gesetz in Konflikt geraten

afraid [ə'fred] *adj* ängstlich; **be a.** (of) (*inf*) sich scheuen zu (*inf*)

afresh [ə'freʃ] *adv* aufs neue

Africa ['æfrɪkə] *s* Afrika *n*

African ['æfrɪkən] *adj* afrikanisch ‖ *s* Afrikaner *–in mf*

aft [æft] *adv* (nach) achtern

after ['æftər] *adj* später; (naut) achter ‖ *adv* nachher, darauf ‖ *prep* nach (*dat*); **a. all** immerhin; **a. that** darauf; **be a. s.o.** hinter j–m her sein ‖ *conj* nachdem

af'ter-din'ner speech' *s* Tischrede *f*

af'tereffect' *s* Nachwirkung *f*; **have an a.** nachwirken

af'terlife' *s* (*later life*) zukünftiges Leben *n*; (*life after death*) Leben *n* nach dem Tode

aftermath ['æftər,mæθ] *s* Nachwirkungen *pl*; (agr) Grummet *n*

af'ternoon' *s* Nachmittag *m*; **in the a.** am Nachmittag, nachmittags; **this a.** heute nachmittag

af'ter-shave' lo'tion *s* Rasierwasser *n*

af'tertaste' *s* Nachgeschmack *m*

af'terthought' *s* nachträglicher Einfall *m*

afterward(s) ['æftərwərd(z)] *adv* später

af'terworld' *s* Jenseits *n*

again [ə'gen] *adv* wieder, noch einmal; **half as much a.** anderthalbmal so viel; **what's his name a.?** wie heißt er doch schnell?

against [ə'genst] *prep* gegen (*acc*); **a. it** dagegen; **a. the rules** regelwidrig; **be up a. it** (coll) in der Klemme sein

age [edʒ] *s* Alter *n*, Lebensalter *n*; (*period of history*) Zeitalter *n*; **at the age of** mit, im Alter von; **come of age** mündig werden; **for ages** e–e Ewigkeit; **of age** volljährig; **of the same age** gleichaltrig; **twenty years of age** zwanzig Jahre alt ‖ *tr* alt machen; (*wine*) ablagern ‖ *intr* altern; (*said of wine*) lagern

aged [edʒd] *adj* alt, e.g., **a. three** drei Jahre alt ‖ ['edʒɪd] *adj* bejahrt

age' lim'it *s* Altersgrenze *f*

agency ['edʒənsi] *s* (*instrumentality*) Vermittlung *f*; (*activity*) Tätigkeit *f*; (adm) Behörde *f*; (com) Agentur *f*

agenda [ə'dʒendə] *s* Tagesordnung *f*

agent ['edʒənt] *s* Handelnde *mf*; (biol, chem) Agens *n*; (com) Agent –in *mf*

agglomeration [ə,glɑmə'reʃən] *s* Anhäufung *f*

aggravate ['ægrə,vet] *tr* erschweren, verschärfen; (coll) ärgern

aggravation [,ægrə'veʃən] *s* Erschwerung *f*, Verschärfung *f*; (coll) Ärger *m*

aggregate ['ægrɪ,get] *adj* gesamt ‖ *s* Aggregat *n*; **in the a.** im ganzen ‖ *tr* anhäufen

aggression [ə'greʃən] *s* Aggression *f*

aggressive [ə'gresɪv] *adj* aggressiv

aggressor [ə'gresər] *s* Aggressor *m*

aggrieved [ə'grivd] *adj* (*saddened*) betrübt; (jur) geschädigt

aghast [ə'gæst] *adj* entsetzt

agile ['ædʒɪl] *adj* flink; (*mind*) rege

agility [ə'dʒɪlɪti] *s* Flinkheit *f*; (*of the mind*) Regsamkeit *f*

agitate ['ædʒɪ,tet] *tr* hin und her bewegen; (fig) beunruhigen ‖ *intr* agitieren

agitator ['ædʒɪ,tetər] *s* Unruhestifter –in *mf*; (*in a washer*) Rührapparat *m*

aglow [ə'glo] *adj & adv* glühend

agnostic [æg'nɑstɪk] *adj* agnostisch ‖ *s* Agnostiker –in *mf*

ago [ə'go] *adv* vor (*dat*), e.g., **a year ago** vor e–m Jahr; **long ago** vor langer Zeit

agog [ə'gɑg] *adv* gespannt, erpicht

agonize ['ægə,naɪz] *intr* sich quälen

ag′onizing adj qualvoll

agony ['ægəni] s Qual f; (death struggle) Todeskampf m

agrarian [ə'grɛrɪ.ən] adj landwirtschaftlich, agrarisch

agree [ə'gri] intr übereinstimmen; a. on (or upon) sich einigen über (acc); a. to zustimmen (dat); a. to (inf) übereinkommen zu (inf); a. with (& gram) übereinstimmen mit; (affect one′s health) bekommen (dat)

agreeable [ə'gri·əbəl] adj angenehm

agreed′ interj abgemacht!, einverstanden!

agreement [ə'grimənt] s Abkommen n, Vereinbarung f; (contract) Vertrag m; (& gram) Übereinstimmung f

agriculture ['ægrɪ͵kʌltʃər] s Landwirtschaft f, Ackerbau m

aground [ə'graund] adv gestrandet; run a. stranden, auf Grund laufen

ahead [ə'hɛd] adj & adv (in the front) vorn; (to the front) nach vorn; (in advance) voraus; (forward) vorwärts; a. of vor (dat); get a. vorwärtskommen; go a. vorangehen; go a.! los!; go a. with fortfahren mit; look a. an die Zukunft denken

ahoy [ə'hɔɪ] interj ahoi!

aid [ed] s Hilfe f, Beihilfe f ‖ tr helfen (dat); aid and abet Vorschub leisten (dat)

aide [ed] s Gehilfe m

aide-de-camp ['eddə'kæmp] s (aides-de-camp) Adjutant m

ail [el] tr schmerzen; what ails you? was fehlt Ihnen? ‖ intr (have pain) Schmerzen haben; (be ill) erkrankt sein

ail′ing adj leidend, kränklich

ailment ['elmənt] s Leiden n

aim [em] s Ziel n; (fig) Ziel n, Zweck m; is your aim good? zielen Sie gut?; take aim zielen ‖ tr (a gun, words) (at) richten auf (acc); aim to (inf) beabsichtigen zu (inf) ‖ intr zielen; aim at (& fig) zielen auf (acc); aim for streben nach

aimless ['emlɪs] adj ziellos, planlos

air [ɛr] s Luft f; (mus) Melodie f; be on the air (an announcer) senden; (a program) gesendet werden; be up in the air (fig) in der Luft hängen; by air per Flugzeug; go off the air die Sendung beenden; go on the air die Sendung beginnen; in the open air im Freien; put on airs groß tun; walk on air sich wie im Himmel fühlen ‖ tr lüften

air′base′ s Flugstützpunkt m

airborne ['ɛr͵bɔrn] adj aufgestiegen; a. troops Luftlandetruppen pl

air′brake′ s Druckluftbremse f

air′-condi′tion tr klimatisieren

air′ condi′tioner s Klimaanlage f

air′ cov′er s Luftsicherung f

air′craft′ s (pl aircraft) Flugzeug n

air′craft car′rier s Flugzeugträger m

air′ cur′rent s Luftströmung f

air′ fare′ s Flugpreis m

air′field′ s Flugplatz m

air′force′ s Luftstreitkräfte pl

air′ing s Lüftung f

air′ lane′ s Flugschneise f

air′lift′ s Luftbrücke f ‖ tr auf dem Luftwege transportieren

air′line(s)′ s Luftverkehrsgesellschaft f

air′line pi′lot s Flugkapitän m

air′lin′er s Verkehrsflugzeug n

air′mail′ s Luftpost f

air′-mail let′ter s Luftpostbrief m

air′-mail stamp′ s Luftpostbriefmarke f

air′plane′ s Flugzeug n

air′ pock′et s Luftloch n

air′ pollu′tion s Luftverunreinigung f

air′port′ s Flughafen m, Flugplatz m

air′ raid′ s Fliegerangriff m

air′-raid drill′ s Luftschutzübung f

air′-raid shel′ter s Luftschutzraum m

air′-raid war′den s Luftschutzwart m

air′-raid warn′ing s Fliegeralarm m

air′ recon′naissance s Luftaufklärung f

air′show′ s Flugvorführung f

air′sick′ adj luftkrank

air′sleeve′, **air′sock′** s Windsack m

air′strip′ s Start- und Landestreifen m

air′ suprem′acy s Luftherrschaft f

air′tight′ adj luftdicht

air′ time′ s (rad, telv) Sendezeit f

air′-traffic control′ s Flugsicherung f

air′waves′ spl Rundfunk m; on the a. im Rundfunk

air′way′ s Luft(verkehrs)linie f

air′wor′thy adj lufttüchtig

airy ['ɛri] adj (room) luftig; (lively) lebhaft; (flippant) leichtsinnig

aisle [aɪl] s Gang m; (archit) Seitenschiff n

ajar [ə'dʒar] adj angelehnt

akimbo [ə'kɪmbo] adj—with arms a. die Arme in die Hüften gestemmt

akin [ə'kɪn] adj verwandt; a. to ähnlich (dat)

alabaster ['ælə͵bæstər] s Alabaster m

alacrity [ə'lækrɪti] s Bereitwilligkeit f

alarm [ə'larm] s Alarm m; (sudden fear) Bestürzung f; (apprehension) Unruhe f ‖ tr alarmieren

alarm′ clock′ s Wecker m

alas [ə'læs] interj o weh!

Albania [æl'benɪ·ə] s Albanien n

Albanian [æl'benɪ·ən] adj albanisch ‖ s Alban(i)er –in m f

albatross ['ælbə͵trɔs] s Albatros m

album ['ælbəm] s Album n

albumen [æl'bjumən] s Eiweiß n

alchemy ['ælkɪmi] s Alchimie f

alcohol ['ælkə͵hɔl] s Alkohol m

alcoholic [͵ælkə'hɔlɪk] adj alkoholisch ‖ s Alkoholiker –in m f

alcove ['ælkov] s Alkoven m

alder ['ɔldər] s (bot) Erle f

al′der·man s (–men) Stadtrat m

ale [el] s Ale n, englisches Bier n

alert [ə'lʌrt] adj wachsam ‖ s (state of readiness) Alarmbereitschaft f; on the a. alarmbereit; (fig) auf der Hut ‖ tr alarmieren

alfalfa [æl'fælfə] s Luzerne f

algae ['ældʒi] spl Algen pl

algebra ['ældʒɪbrə] s Algebra f

Algeria [æl'dʒɪrɪ·ə] s Algerien n

Algerian [æl'dʒɪrɪ·ən] adj algerisch ‖ s Algerier –in m f

Algiers [æl'dʒɪrz] s Algier n

alias ['eɪɪ-əs] *adv* alias, sonst...genannt || *s* Deckname *m*

ali·bi ['ælɪ‚baɪ] *s* (-bis) Alibi *n*; (*excuse*) Ausrede *f*

alien ['eljən], ['eɪɪ-ən] *adj* fremd || *s* Fremde *mf*, Ausländer –in *mf*

alienate ['eljə‚net], ['eɪɪ-ə‚net] *tr* entfremden; (*jur*) übertragen

alight [ə'laɪt] *v* (*pret & pp* **alighted &** **alit** [ə'lɪt]) *intr* aussteigen; (*said of a bird*) (**on**) sich niederlassen (auf *dat* or *acc*); (aer) landen

align [ə'laɪn] *tr* (**with**) ausrichten (nach); (aut) einstellen; **a. oneself** **with** sich anschließen an (*acc*) || *intr* —**a. with** sich ausrichten nach

alignment [ə'laɪnmənt] *s* Ausrichten *n*; (pol) Ausrichtung *f*; **bring into a.** gleichschalten; **out of a.** schlecht ausgerichtet

alike [ə'laɪk] *adj* gleich, ähnlich; **look** **a. sich** [*dat*] ähnlich sehen; (*resemble completely*) gleich aussehen

alimony ['ælɪ‚monɪ] *s* Unterhaltskosten *pl*

alive [ə'laɪv] *adj* lebendig; (*vivacious*) lebhaft; **keep a.** am Leben bleiben; **keep s.o. a.** j–n am Leben erhalten

alka·li ['ælkə‚laɪ] *s* (-lis & -lies) Laugensalz *n*, Alkali *n*

alkaline ['ælkə‚laɪn] *adj* alkalisch

all [ɔl] *adj* all, ganz; **all day long** den ganzen Tag; **all kinds of allerlei; all the time** fortwährend; **for all that** trotzdem || *adv* ganz, völlig; **all along** schon immer; **all at once** auf einmal; **all gone alle; all in** (coll) völlig erschöpft; **all over** (*everywhere*) überall; (*ended*) ganz vorbei; **all right** gut, schön; **all the better** um so besser; **all the same** dennoch; **not be all** **there** (coll) nicht ganz richtig im Kopf sein || *s*—**after all** schließlich; **all in all** im großen und ganzen; **and all gesamt, e.g., he went, family and all er ging mit gesamter Familie; in all insgesamt; not at all überhaupt nicht, gar nicht || *indef pron* alle; (*everything*) alles

all'-around' *adj* vielseitig

allay [ə'le] *tr* beschwichtigen; (*hunger*, *thirst*) stillen

all'-clear' *s* Entwarnung *f*

allege [ə'ledʒ] *tr* behaupten; (*advance as an excuse*) vorgeben

alleged' *adj* angeblich, mutmaßlich

allegiance [ə'lidʒəns] *s* Treue *f*

allegoric(al) [‚ælɪ'gɔrɪk(əl)] *adj* allegorisch

allegory ['ælɪ‚gorɪ] *s* Allegorie *f*

allergic [ə'lʌrdʒɪk] *adj* allergisch

allergy ['ælərdʒɪ] *s* Allergie *f*

alleviate [ə'livɪ‚et] *tr* lindern

alley ['ælɪ] *s* Gasse *f*; (*for bowling*) Kegelbahn *f*

alliance [ə'laɪ-əns] *s* Bündnis *n*

allied' *adj* (*field*) benachbart; (*science*) verwandt; (mil, pol) alliiert

alligator ['ælɪ‚getər] *s* Alligator *m*

all'-inclu'sive *adj* Pauschal–

alliteration [ə‚lɪtə're/ən] *s* Stabreim *m*, Alliteration *f*

all'-know'ing *adj* allwissend

allocate ['ælə‚ket] *tr* zuteilen

al·lot [ə'lat] (*pret & pp* -lotted; *ger* -lotting) *tr* zuteilen, austeilen

all'-out' *adj* vollkommen, total

allow [ə'lau] *tr* erlauben, gestatten; (*admit*) zugeben; (*e.g., a discount*) gewähren; **be allowed to** (*inf*) dürfen (*inf*) || *intr*—**a. for** bedenken

allowable [ə'lau-əbəl] *adj* zulässig

allowance [ə'lau-əns] *s* (*tolerance*) Duldung *f*; (*permission*) Erlaubnis *f*; (*ration*) Zuteilung *f*, Ration *f*; (*pocket money*) Taschengeld *n*; (*discount*) Abzug *m*; (*salary for a particular expense*) Zuschuß *m*, Zulage *f*; (*for groceries*) Wirtschaftsgeld *n*; (*mach*) Toleranz *f*; **make a. for** berücksichtigen

alloy ['ælɔɪ] *s* Legierung *f* || [ə'lɔɪ] *tr* legieren

all'-pow'erful *adj* allmächtig

all' right' *adj*—**be a.** in Ordnung sein || *interj* schon gut!

All' Saints'' Day' *s* Allerheiligen *n*

All' Souls'' Day' *s* Allerseelen *n*

all'spice' *s* Nelkenpfeffer *m*

all'-star' *adj* (sport) aus den besten Spielern bestehend

allude [ə'lud] *intr*—**a. to** anspielen auf (*acc*)

allure [ə'lur] *s* Charme *m* || *tr* anlocken

allurement [ə'lurmənt] *s* Verlockung *f*

allur'ing *adj* verlockend

allusion [ə'luʒən] *s* (**to**) Anspielung *f* (auf *acc*)

al·ly ['ælaɪ], [ə'laɪ] *s* Alliierte *mf*, Verbündete *mf* || [ə'laɪ] *v* (*pret & pp* -lied) *tr*—**a. oneself with** sich verbünden mit

almanac ['ɔlmə‚næk] *s* Almanach *m*

almighty [ɔl'maɪtɪ] *adj* allmächtig

almond ['amənd] *s* Mandel *f*

almost ['ɔlmost], [ɔl'most] *adv* fast

alms [amz] *s & spl* Almosen *n*

aloft [ə'lɔft] *adv* (*position*) oben; (*direction*) nach oben; **raise a.** emporheben

alone [ə'lon] *adj* allein; **let a.** (*not to mention*) geschweige denn; (*not bother*) in Ruhe lassen || *adv* allein

along [ə'lɔŋ] *adv* vorwärts, weiter; **all a.** schon immer; **a. with** zusammen mit; **get a. with** sich gut vertragen mit; **go a. with** mitgehen mit; (*agree with*) sich einverstanden erklären mit || *prep* (*direction*) entlang (*acc*); (*position*) an (*dat*), längs (*genit*)

along'side' *adv* (naut) längsseits; **a. of** im Vergleich zu || *prep* neben (*dat*); (naut) längsseits (*genit*)

aloof [ə'luf] *adj* zurückhaltend || *adv*— **keep a.** (**from**) sich fernhalten (von); **stand a.** für sich bleiben

aloud [ə'laud] *adv* laut

alphabet ['ælfə‚bet] *s* Alphabet *n*

alphabetic(al) [‚ælfə'betɪk(əl)] *adj* alphabetisch

alpine ['ælpaɪn] *adj* alpin, Alpen–

Alps [ælps] *spl* Alpen *pl*

already [ɔl'redɪ] *adv* schon, bereits

Alsace [æl'ses], ['ælsæs] *s* Elsaß *n*

Alsatian [æl'se/ən] *adj* elsässisch || *s*

Elsässer –in *mf;* (*dog*) deutscher Schäferhund *m*

also ['ɔlso] *adv* auch

altar ['ɔltər] *s* Altar *m*

al'tar boy' *s* Ministrant *m*

alter ['ɔltər] *tr* ändern; (*castrate*) kastrieren || *intr* sich ändern

alteration [,ɔltə'refən] *s* Änderung *f*; **alterations** (*in construction*) Umbau *m*

alternate ['ɔltərnɪt] *adj* abwechselnd || *s* Ersatzmann *m* || ['ɔltər,net] *tr* (ab)wechseln; (*e.g., hot and cold compresses*) zwischen (*dat*) und (*dat*) abwechseln || *intr* miteinander abwechseln

al'ternating cur'rent *s* Wechselstrom *m*

alternative [ɔl'tʌrnətɪv] *adj* Ausweich-, Alternativ- || *s* Alternative *f*

although [ɔl'ðo] *conj* obgleich, obwohl

altimeter [æl'tɪmɪtər] *s* Höhenmesser *m*

altitude ['æltɪ,t(j)ud] *s* Höhe *f*

al·to ['ælto] *s* (*-tos*) Alt *m*, Altstimme *f*; (*singer*) Altist *m*

altogether [,ɔltə'gɛðər] *adv* durchaus; (*in all*) insgesamt

altruist ['æltru·ɪst] *s* Altruist –in *mf*

alum ['æləm] *s* Alaun *m*

aluminum [ə'lumɪnəm] *s* Aluminium *n*

alu'minum foil' *s* Aluminiumfolie *f*

alum·na [ə'lʌmnə] *s* (*-nae* [ni]) ehemalige Studentin *f*

alum·nus [ə'lʌmnəs] *s* (*-ni* [naɪ]) ehemaliger Student *m*

always ['ɔlwɪz], ['ɔlwez] *adv* immer

A.M. *abbr* (*ante meridiem*) vormittags; (*amplitude modulation*) Amplitudenmodulation *f*

amalgam [ə'mælgəm] *s* Amalgam *n*; (*fig*) Mischung *f*, Gemenge *n*

amalgamate [ə'mælgə,met] *tr* amalgamieren || *intr* sich amalgamieren

amass [ə'mæs] *tr* aufhäufen, ansammeln

amateur ['æmətʃər] *adj* Amateur– || *s* Amateur *m*, Liebhaber *m*

amaze [ə'mez] *tr* erstaunen

amaz'ing *adj* erstaunlich

Amazon ['æmə,zan] *s* (*river*) Amazonas *m*; (*fig*) Mannweib *n*; (*myth*) Amazone *f*

ambassador [æm'bæsədər] *s* Botschafter –in §6 *mf*; (*fig*) Bote *m*

ambassadorial [æm,bæsə'dorɪ·əl] *adj* Botschafts-

amber ['æmbər] *adj* Bernstein–; (*in color*) bernsteinfarben || *s* Bernstein *m*

ambiguity [,æmbɪ'gju·ɪti] *s* Doppelsinn *m*, Zweideutigkeit *f*

ambiguous [æm'bɪgju·əs] *adj* doppelsinnig, zweideutig

ambit ['æmbɪt] *s* Bereich *m*

ambition [æm'bɪʃən] *s* Ehrgeiz *m*; (*aim, object*) Ambition *f*

ambitious [æm'bɪʃəs] *adj* ehrgeizig

ambivalent [æm'bɪvələnt] *adj* (*chem*) ambivalent; (*psychol*) zwiespältig

amble ['æmbəl] *s* (*of a person*) gemächlicher Gang *m*; (*of a horse*) Paßgang *m* || *intr* schlendern; (*said of a horse*) im Paßgang gehen

ambulance ['æmbjələns] *s* Krankenwagen *m*

ambulatory ['æmbjələ,tori] *adj* gehfähig

ambuscade [,æmbəs'ked] *s* Hinterhalt *m*

ambush ['æmbuʃ] *s* Hinterhalt *m* || *tr* aus dem Hinterhalt überfallen

ameliorate [ə'miljə,ret] *tr* verbessern || *intr* besser werden

amen ['e'men], ['ɑ'men] *s* Amen *n* || *interj* amen!

amenable [ə'menəbəl] *adj* (*docile*) fügsam; a. to (*e.g., flattery*) zugänglich (*dat*); (*e.g., laws*) unterworfen (*dat*)

amend [ə'mend] *tr* (*a law*) (ver)bessern; (*one's ways*) (ab)ändern || *intr* sich bessern

amendment [ə'mendmənt] *s* Änderungsantrag *m*; (*by addition*) Zusatzantrag *m*; (*to the constitution*) Zusatzartikel *m*

amends [ə'mendz] *s & spl* Genugtuung *f*; make a. for wiedergutmachen

amenity [ə'menɪti] *s* (*pleasantness*) Annehmlichkeit *f*; **amenities** (*of life*) Annehmlichkeiten *pl*

America [ə'merɪkə] *s* Amerika *n*

American [ə'merɪkən] *adj* amerikanisch || *s* Amerikaner –in *mf*

Americanize [ə'merɪkə,naɪz] *tr* amerikanisieren

amethyst ['æmɪθɪst] *s* Amethyst *m*

amiable ['emɪ·əbəl] *adj* liebenswürdig

amicable ['æmɪkəbəl] *adj* freundschaftlich, gütlich

amid [ə'mɪd] *prep* inmitten (*genit*)

amidships [ə'mɪd/ɪps] *adv* mittschiffs

amiss [ə'mɪs] *adj* (*improper*) unpassend; (*wrong*) verkehrt; there is s.th. a. etwas stimmt nicht || *adv* verkehrt; go a. danebengehen; take a. übelnehmen

amity ['æmɪti] *s* Freundschaft *f*

ammo ['æmo] *s* (sl) Muni *m*

ammonia [ə'monɪ·ə] *s* (*gas*) Ammoniak *n*; (*solution*) Salmiakgeist *m*

ammunition [,æmjə'nɪʃən] *s* Munition *f*

amnesia [æm'niʒɪ·ə] *s* Amnesie *f*

amnes·ty ['æmnɪsti] *s* Amnestie *f* || *v* (*pret & pp* **-tied**) *tr* begnadigen

amoeba [ə'mibə] *s* Amöbe *f*

among [ə'mʌŋ] *prep* (*position*) unter (*dat*); (*direction*) unter (*acc*); a. other things unter anderem

amorous ['æmərəs] *adj* amourös

amortize ['æmər,taɪz] *tr* tilgen

amount [ə'maunt] *s* (*sum*) Betrag *m*; (*quantity*) Menge *f* || *intr*—a. to betragen

ampere ['æmpɪr] *s* Ampere *n*

amphibian [æm'fɪbɪ·ən] *s* Amphibie *f*

amphibious [æm'fɪbɪ·əs] *adj* amphibisch

amphitheater ['æmfɪ,θi·ətər] *s* Amphitheater *n*

ample ['æmpəl] *adj* (*sufficient*) genügend; (*spacious*) geräumig

amplifier ['æmplɪ,faɪ·ər] *s* Verstärker *m*

ampli·fy ['æmplɪ,faɪ] *v* (*pret & pp* **-fied**) *tr* (*a statement*) erweitern; (*electron, rad, phys*) verstärken amplitude ['æmplɪ‚t(j)ud] *s* Weite *f;* (electron, rad, phys) Amplitude *f*

am'plitude modula'tion *s* Amplitudenmodulation *f*

amputate ['æmpjə‚tet] *tr* amputieren

amputee ['æmpjə'ti] *s* Amputierte *mf*

amuck [ə'mʌk] *adv*—run a. Amok laufen

amulet ['æmjəlɪt] *s* Amulett *n*

amuse [ə'mjuz] *tr* amüsieren, belustigen

amusement [ə'mjuzmənt] *s* Vergnügen *n*

amuse'ment park' *s* Vergnügungspark *m*

amus'ing *adj* amüsant

an [æn], [ən] *indef art* ein

anachronism [ə'nækrə‚nɪzəm] *s* Anachronismus *m*

analogous [ə'næləgəs] *adj* (to) analog (*dat*), ähnlich (*dat*)

analogy [ə'nælədʒi] *s* Analogie *f*

analy•sis [ə'nælɪsɪs] *s* (-ses [‚siz]) Analyse *f;* (of a literary work) Zergliederung *f*

analyst ['ænəlɪst] *s* Analytiker –in *mf*

analytic(al) [‚ænə'lɪtɪk(əl)] *adj* analytisch

analyze ['ænə‚laɪz] *tr* analysieren

anarchist ['ænərkɪst] *s* Anarchist –in *mf*

anarchy ['ænərki] *s* Anarchie *f*

anatomic(al) [‚ænə'tɑmɪk(əl)] *adj* anatomisch

anatomy [ə'nætəmi] *s* Anatomie *f*

ancestor ['ænsestər] *s* Vorfahr *m*, Ahne *m*

ancestral [æn'sestrəl] *adj* angestammt, Ahnen–; (inherited) Erb–, ererbt

ancestry ['ænsestri] *s* Abstammung *f*

anchor ['æŋkər] *s* Anker *m;* cast a. vor Anker gehen; weigh a. den Anker lichten ‖ *tr* verankern ‖ *intr* ankern

anchorage ['æŋkərɪdʒ] *s* Ankerplatz *m*

anchovy ['æntʃovi] *s* Anchovis *f*

ancient ['entʃənt] *adj* (very old) uralt; (civilization) antik ‖ the ancients *spl* die alten Griechen und Römer

an'cient his'tory *s* alte Geschichte *f*

and [ænd], [ənd] *conj* und; and how! und obl and so forth und so weiter

andiron ['ænd‚aɪ·ərn] *s* Kaminbock *m*

anecdote ['ænɪk‚dot] *s* Anekdote *f*

anemia [ə'nimɪ·ə] *s* Anämie *f*

anemic [ə'nimɪk] *adj* anämisch, blutarm

anesthesia [‚ænɪs'θiʒə] *s* Anästhesie *f;* general a. Vollnarkose *f;* local a. Lokalanästhesie *f*

anesthetic [‚ænɪs'θetɪk] *adj* betäubend ‖ *s* Betäubungsmittel *n;* local a. örtliches Betäubungsmittel *n*

anesthetize [æ'nesθɪ‚taɪz] *tr* betäuben

anew [ə'n(j)u] *adv* von neuem, aufs neue

angel ['endʒəl] *s* Engel *m;* (financial backer) Hintermann *m*

angelic(al) [æn'dʒelɪk(əl)] *adj* engelgleich, engelhaft

anger ['æŋgər] *s* Zorn *m* ‖ *tr* erzürnen

angina pectoris [æn'dʒaɪnə'pektɔrɪs] *s* Brustbeklemmung *f*, Herzbräune *f*

angle ['æŋgəl] *s* Winkel *m;* (point of view) Gesichtswinkel *m;* (ulterior motive) Hintergedanken *m;* (side) Seite *f*

angler ['æŋglər] *s* Angler –in *mf*

angry ['æŋgri] *adj* zornig, böse; (wound) entzündet; a. at (s.th.) zornig über (*acc*); a. with (s.o.) zornig auf (*acc*)

anguish ['æŋgwɪʃ] *s* Qual *f*, Pein *f*

angular ['æŋgjələr] *adj* kantig

animal ['ænɪməl] *adj* tierisch, Tier— ‖ *s* Tier *n*

animate ['ænɪmɪt] *adj* belebt; (lively) lebhaft ‖ ['ænɪ‚met] *tr* beleben, beseelen; (make lively) aufmuntern

an'imated cartoon' *s* Zeichentrickfilm *m*

animation [‚ænɪ'meʃən] *s* Lebhaftigkeit *f;* (cin) Herstellung *f* von Zeichentrickfilm

animosity [‚ænɪ'mɑsɪti] *s* Feindseligkeit *f*

anion ['æn‚aɪ·ən] *s* Anion *n*

anise ['ænɪs] *s* Anis *m*

anisette [‚ænɪ'set] *s* Anisett *m*

ankle ['æŋkəl] *s* Fußknöchel *m*

an'kle support' *s* Knöchelstütze *f*

anklet ['æŋklɪt] *s* (ornament) Fußring *m;* (sock) Söckchen *n*

annals ['ænəlz] *spl* Annalen *pl*

anneal [ə'nil] *tr* ausglühen; (the mind) stählen

annex ['æneks] *s* (building) Anbau *m*, Nebengebäude *n;* (supplement) Zusatz *m* ‖ [ə'neks] *tr* annektieren

annexation [‚æneks'eʃən] *s* Einverleibung *f;* (pol) Annexion *f*

annihilate [ə'naɪ·ɪ‚let] *tr* vernichten; (fig) zunichte machen

annihilation [ə‚naɪ·ɪ'leʃən] *s* Vernichtung *f*

anniversary [‚ænɪ'vʌrsəri] *s* Jahrestag *m*

annotate ['ænə‚tet] *tr* mit Anmerkungen versehen

annotation [‚ænə'teʃən] *s* Anmerkung *f*

announce [ə'nauns] *tr* ankündigen, anmelden; (rad) ansagen, melden

announcement [ə'naunsmənt] *s* Ankündigung *f;* (rad) Durchsage *f*

announcer [ə'naunsər] *s* Ansager –in *mf*

annoy [ə'nɔɪ] *tr* ärgern; be annoyed at sich ärgern über (*acc*)

annoyance [ə'nɔɪ·əns] *s* Ärger *m*

annoy'ing *adj* ärgerlich

annual ['ænju·əl] *adj* jährlich, Jahres–; (plant) einjährig ‖ *s* (book) Jahrbuch *n;* (bot) einjährige Pflanze *f*

annuity [ə'n(j)u·ɪti] *s* Jahresrente *f*

an-nul [ə'nʌl] *v* (pret & pp –nulled; ger –nulling) *tr* annullieren

annulment [ə'nʌlmənt] *s* Annullierung *f;* (of marriage) Nichtigkeitserklärung *f*

anode ['ænod] *s* Anode *f*

anoint [ə'nɔɪnt] *tr* salben

anomaly [ə'nɑməli] *s* Anomalie *f*

anonymous [ə'nɑnɪməs] *adj* anonym

another [ə'nʌðər] *adj* (a different) ein anderer; (an additional) noch ein; a. Caesar ein zweiter Cäsar ‖ *pron* (*a different one*) ein anderer; (*an additional one*) noch einer

answer ['ænsər] *s* Antwort *f*; (*to a problem*) Lösung *f* ‖ *tr* (*a person*) antworten (*dat*); (*a question, letter*) beantworten; (*need, description*) entsprechen (*dat*); (*enemy fire*) antworten auf (*acc*); **a. an ad** sich auf e-e Anzeige melden; **a. the door** die Tür öffnen; **a. the telephone** ans Telefon gehen ‖ *intr* antworten; (*telp*) sich melden; **a. back** e-n losen Mund haben; **a. for** verantworten; **a. to** (*a description*) entsprechen (*dat*)

an'swering serv'ice *s* Fernsprechauftragsdienst *m*

ant [ænt] *s* Ameise *f*

antagonism [æn'tægə,nɪzəm] *s* Feindseligkeit *f*

antagonize [æn'tægə,naɪz] *tr* sich [*dat*] zum Gegner machen

antarctic [ænt'ɑrktɪk] *adj* antarktisch ‖ **the Antarctic** *s* die Antarktis

Antarc'tic Cir'cle *s* südlicher Polarkreis *m*

Antarc'tic O'cean *s* südliches Eismeer *n*

ante ['æntɪ] *s* (*cards*) Einsatz *m*; (*com*) Scherflein *n* ‖ *tr* (*cards*) einsetzen ‖ *intr* (*in a joint venture*) sein Scherflein beitragen; (*pay up*) (*coll*) blechen; (*cards*) einsetzen

antecedent [æntɪ'sidənt] *adj* vorhergehend ‖ *s* (*gram*) Beziehungswort *n*; **antecedents** Antezedenzien *pl*

antechamber ['æntɪ,tʃembər] *s* Vorzimmer *n*

antelope ['æntɪ,lop] *s* Antilope *f*

anten·na [æn'tenə] *s* (*-nae* [ni]) (ent) Fühler *m* ‖ *s* (*-nas*) (rad) Antenne *f*

antepenult [,æntɪ'pinʌlt] *s* drittletzte Silbe *f*

anthem ['ænθəm] *s* Hymne *f*

ant'hill' *s* Ameisenhaufen *m*

anthology [æn'θɑlədʒɪ] *s* Anthologie *f*

anthropology [,ænθrə'pɑlədʒɪ] *s* Anthropologie *f*, Lehre *f* vom Menschen

antiaircraft [,æntɪ'er,kræft] *adj* Flak-, Flugabwehr- ‖ *s* Flak *f*

antiair'craft gun' *s* Flak *f*

antibiotic [,æntɪbaɪ'ɑtɪk] *s* Antibiotikum *n*

antibody ['æntɪ,bɑdɪ] *s* Antikörper *m*

anticipate [æn'tɪsɪ,pet] *tr* (*expect*) erwarten; (*remarks, criticism, etc.*) vorwegnehmen; (*trouble*) vorausahnen; (*pleasure*) vorausempfinden; (*s.o.'s wish or desire*) zuvorkommen (*dat*)

anticipation [æn,tɪsɪ'peʃən] *s* Erwartung *f*, Vorfreude *f*

antics ['æntɪks] *spl* Possen *pl*

antidote ['æntɪ,dot] *s* Gegengift *n*

antifreeze ['æntɪ,friz] *s* Gefrierschutzmittel *n*

antiknock [,æntɪ'nɑk] *adj* klopffest ‖ *s* Antiklopfmittel *n*

antipathy [æn'tɪpəθɪ] *s* Abneigung *f*, Antipathie *f*

antiquarian [,æntɪ'kwerɪ·ən] *adj* altertümlich ‖ *s* Altertumsforscher –in *mf*

antiquated ['æntɪ,kwetɪd] *adj* veraltet

antique [æn'tik] *adj* (ur)alt, antik ‖ *s* Antiquität *f*

antique' deal'er *s* Antiquitätenhändler –in *mf*

antique' shop' *s* Antiquitätenladen *m*

antiquity [æn'tɪkwɪtɪ] *s* Altertum *n*, Vorzeit *f*; **antiquities** Antiquitäten *pl*, Altertümer *pl*

antirust [,æntɪ'rʌst] *adj* Rostschutz-

anti-Semitic [,æntɪsɪ'mɪtɪk] *adj* antisemitisch, judenfeindlich

antiseptic [,æntɪ'septɪk] *adj* antiseptisch ‖ *s* Antiseptikum *n*

antitank [,æntɪ'tæŋk] *adj* Panzer-: (*unit*) Panzerjäger-

antitank' mine' *s* Tellermine *f*

antithe·sis [æn'tɪθɪsɪs] *s* (*-ses* [,siz]) Gegensatz *m*, Antithese *f*

antitoxin [,æntɪ'tɑksɪn] *s* Gegengift *n*

antitrust [,æntɪ'trʌst] *adj* Antitrust-

antiwar [,æntɪ'wɔr] *adj* antimilitaristisch

antler ['æntlər] *s* Geweihsprosse *f*; (*pair of*) **antlers** Geweih *n*

antonym ['æntənɪm] *s* Antonym *n*

anus ['enəs] *s* After *m*

anvil ['ænvɪl] *s* Amboß *m*

anxiety [æŋ'zai·ətɪ] *s* (*over*) Besorgnis *f* (um); (*psychol*) Beklemmung *f*

anxious ['æŋk/əs] *adj* (*about*) besorgt (um or wegen); (*for*) gespannt (auf *acc*), begierig (auf *acc*); **I am a. to** (*inf*) es liegt mir daran zu (*inf*)

any ['enɪ] *indef adj* irgendein, irgendwelch; (*a little*) etwas; **any** (*possible*) etwaig; **any** (*you wish*) jeder beliebige; **do you have any money on you?** haben Sie Geld bei sich?; **I do not have any money** ich habe kein Geld ‖ *adv*—**any more** (*e.g., coffee*) noch etwas; (*e.g., apples*) noch ein paar; **not any better** keinwegs besser; **not . . . any longer** nicht mehr; **not . . . any more** nicht mehr

an'ybod'y *indef pron var of* anyone

an'yhow' *adv* sowieso, trotzdem; (*in any event*) jedenfalls

an'yone' *indef pron* (irgend)jemand, irgendeiner; **a. but you** jeder andere als du; **a. else** sonstnochwer; **ask a.** frag wen du willst; **I don't see a.** ich sehe niemand

an'yplace' *adv* (coll) *var of* anywhere

an'ything' *indef pron* (irgend)etwas, (irgend)was; **a. but** alles andere als; **a. else?** noch etwas?, sonst etwas?; **a. you want** was du willst; **not . . . a.** nichts; **not for a. in the world** um keinen Preis

an'ytime' *adv* zu jeder (beliebigen) Zeit; (*at some unspecified time*) irgendwann

an'yway' *adv* sowieso, trotzdem

an'ywhere' *adv* (*position*) irgendwo; (*everywhere*) an jedem beliebigen Ort; (*direction*) irgendwohin; (*everywhere*) an jeden beliebigen Ort; (*to any extent*) einigermaßen, e.g., **a. near correct** einigermaßen richtig; **get a.** (*achieve success*) es zu etwas bringen

apace [ə'pes] *adv* schnell, rasch

apart [ə'pɑrt] *adv* (*to pieces*) auseinander; (*separately*) einzeln, für sich; a. **from** abgesehen von

apartment [ə'pɑrtmənt] *s* Wohnung *f*

apart′ment house′ *s* Apartmenthaus *n*

apathetic [,æpə'θetɪk] *adj* apathisch, teilnahmslos

apathy ['æpəθi] *s* Apathie *f*

ape [ep] *s* Affe *m* ‖ *tr* nachäffen

aperture ['æpərtʃər] *s* Öffnung *f*; (phot) Blende *f*

apex ['epeks] *s* (**apexes** & **apices** ['æpɪ,siz]) Spitze *f*; (fig) Gipfel *m*

aphid ['æfɪd] *s* Blattlaus *f*

aphorism ['æfə,rɪzəm] *s* Aphorismus *m*

apiary ['epɪ,eri] *s* Bienenhaus *n*

apiece [ə'pis] *adv* pro Stück; (*per person*) pro Person

aplomb [ə'plɑm] *s* sicheres Auftreten *n*

apogee ['æpə,dʒi] *s* Erdferne *f*

apologetic [ə,pɑlə'dʒetɪk] *adj* (*remark*) entschuldigend; (*letter, speech*) Entschuldigungs–; **be a.** (*about*) Entschuldigungen vorbringen (für)

apologize [ə'pɑlə,dʒaɪz] *intr* sich entschuldigen; **a. to s.o. for s.th.** sich bei j–m wegen etw entschuldigen

apology [ə'pɑlədʒi] *s* (*excuse*) Entschuldigung *f*; (*apologia*) Verteidigung *f*

apoplec′tic stroke′ [,æpə'plektɪk] *s* Schlaganfall *m*

apoplexy ['æpə,pleksi] *s* Schlaganfall *m*

apostle [ə'pɑsəl] *s* Apostel *m*

apostolic [,æpəs'tɑlɪk] *adj* apostolisch

apostrophe [ə'pɑstrəfi] *s* (gram) Apostroph *m*; (rhet) Anrede *f*

apothecary [ə'pɑθɪ,keri] *s* (*druggist*) Apotheker *m*; (*drugstore*) Apotheke *f*

appall [ə'pɔl] *tr* entsetzen

appall′ing *adj* entsetzlich

appara·tus [,æpə'retəs], [,æpə'rætəs] *s* (**-tus** & **-tuses**) Apparat *m*

apparel [ə'pærəl] *s* Kleidung *f*, Tracht *f*

apparent [ə'pærənt] *adj* (*visible*) sichtbar; (*obvious*) offenbar; (*seeming*) scheinbar

apparition [,æpə'rɪʃən] *s* Erscheinung *f*; (*ghost*) Gespenst *n*

appeal [ə'pil] *s* (*request*) Appell *m*, dringende Bitte *f*; (*to reason, etc.*) Appell *m*; (*charm*) Anziehungskraft *f*; (jur) (**to**) Berufung *f* (an *acc*) ‖ *tr*—**a. a case** Berufung einlegen in e–r Rechtssache ‖ *intr*—**a. to** (*entreat*) dringend bitten; (*be attractive to*) reizen; (jur) appellieren an (*acc*)

appear [ə'pir] *intr* erscheinen; (*seem*) scheinen; (*come before the public*) sich zeigen; (jur) sich stellen; (theat) auftreten; **a. as a guest** (telv) gastieren

appearance [ə'pɪrəns] *s* Erscheinen *n*; (*outward look*) Aussehen *n*; (*semblance*) Anschein *m*; (on the stage) Auftreten *n*; (jur) Erscheinen *n*; **for the sake of appearances** anstandshalber; **to all appearances** allem Anschein nach

appease [ə'piz] *tr* beruhigen; (*hunger*)

stillen; (*pain*) mildern; (dipl) beschwichtigen

appeasement [ə'pizmənt] *s* Beruhigung *f*; (*of hunger*) Stillung *f*; (dipl) Beschwichtigung *f*

appel′late court′ [ə'pelɪt] *s* Berufungsgericht *n*

append [ə'pend] *tr* anhängen; (*a signature*) hinzufügen

appendage [ə'pendɪdʒ] *s* Anhang *m*

appendectomy [,æpən'dektəmi] *s* Blinddarmoperation *f*

appendicitis [ə,pendɪ'saɪtɪs] *s* Blinddarmentzündung *f*, Appendizitis *f*

appen·dix [ə'pendɪks] *s* (**-dixes** & **-dices** [dɪ,siz]) Anhang *m*; (anat) Appendix *m*

appertain [,æpər'ten] *intr* (**to**) gehören (zu), gebühren (*dat*)

appetite ['æpɪ,taɪt] *s* (**for**) Appetit *m* (auf *acc*)

appetizer ['æpɪ,taɪzər] *s* Vorspeise *f*

ap′petizing *adj* appetitlich

applaud [ə'plɔd] *tr* Beifall klatschen (*dat*); (*praise*) billigen ‖ *intr* Beifall klatschen

applause [ə'plɔz] *s* Beifall *m*, Applaus *m*

apple ['æpəl] *s* Apfel *m*

ap′plecart′ *s*—**upset the a.** die Pläne über den Haufen werfen

ap′ple of one′s eye′ *s* Augapfel *m*

ap′ple pie′ *s* gedeckte Apfeltorte *f*

ap′ple-pol′isher *s* (coll) Speichellecker *m*

ap′plesauce′ *s* Apfelmus *n*

ap′ple tree′ *s* Apfelbaum *m*

appliance [ə'plaɪəns] *s* Gerät *n*, Vorrichtung *f*

applicable ['æplɪkəbəl] *adj* (**to**) anwendbar (auf *acc*); **not a.** nicht zutreffend

applicant ['æplɪkənt] *s* Bewerber –in *mf*

application [,æplɪ'keʃən] *s* (*use*) Anwendung *f*; (*for a job*) Bewerbung *f*; (*for a grant*) Antrag *m*; (*zeal*) Fleiß *m*; (med) Anlegen *n*

applica′tion blank′ *s* (*for a job*) Bewerbungsformular *n*; (*for a grant*) Antragsformular *n*

applied′ *adj* angewandt

apply [ə'plaɪ] *v* (*pret* & *pp* **-plied**) *tr* anwenden; (med) anlegen; **a. oneself to** sich befleißigen (*genit*); **a. the brakes** bremsen ‖ *intr* gelten; **a. for** (*a job*) sich bewerben um; (*a grant*) beantragen

appoint [ə'pɔɪnt] *tr* (*a person*) ernennen; (*a time, etc.*) festsetzen

appointment [ə'pɔɪntmənt] *s* Ernennung *f*; (*post*) Stelle *f*; (*engagement*) Verabredung *f*; **by a. only** nur nach Vereinbarung; **have an a. with** (*e.g., a dentist*) bestellt sein zu

appoint′ment book′ *s* Terminkalender *m*

apportion [ə'porʃən] *tr* zumessen

appraisal [ə'prezəl] *s* Abschätzung *f*

appraise [ə'prez] *tr* (ab)schätzen

appraiser [ə'prezər] *s* Schätzer –in *mf*

appreciable [ə'priʃɪ·əbəl] *adj* (*notice-*

able) merklich; (*considerable*) erheblich

appreciate [ə'priʃɪ‚et] *tr* dankbar sein für; (*danger*) erkennen; (*regard highly*) hochschätzen || *intr* (im Werte) steigen

appreciation [ə‚priʃɪ'eʃən] *s* (*gratitude*) Dank *m*. Anerkennung *f*; (*for art*) Verständnis *n*; (*high regard*) Schätzung *f*; (*increase in value*) Wertzuwachs *m*

appreciative [ə'priʃɪ‚ətɪv] *adj* (*of*) dankbar (für)

apprehend [‚æprɪ'hɛnd] *tr* verhaften, ergreifen; (*understand*) begreifen

apprehension [‚æprɪ'hɛnʃən] *s* (*arrest*) Verhaftung *f*; (*fear*) Befürchtung *f*; (*comprehending*) Begreifen *n*

apprehensive [‚æprɪ'hɛnsɪv] *adj* (*of*) besorgt (um)

apprentice [ə'prɛntɪs] *s* Lehrling *m*

appren'ticeship' *s* Lehre *f*; serve an a. in der Lehre sein

apprise, apprize [ə'praɪz] *tr* (*of*) benachrichtigen (von)

approach [ə'protʃ] *s* Annäherung *f*, (*e.g., a road*) Zugang *m*, Zufahrt *f*; *e.g., to a problem*) Behandlung *f*; (*tentative sexual approach*) Annäherungsversuch *m*; (aer) Anflug *m* || *tr* sich nähern (*dat*); (*e.g., a problem*) behandeln; (*perfection*) nahekommen (*dat*); (aer) anfliegen || *intr* sich nähern

approachable [ə'protʃəbəl] *adj* zugänglich

approbation [‚æprə'beʃən] *s* (*approval*) Beifall *m*; (*sanction*) Billigung *f*

appropriate [ə'propɪ‚ɪt] *adj* (to) angemessen (*dat*) || [ə'propɪ‚et] *tr* (*take possession of*) sich [*dat*] aneignen; (*authorize*) bewilligen

approval [ə'pruvəl] *s* (*approbation*) Beifall *m*; (*sanction*) Billigung *f*; meet with s.o.'s a. j–s Beifall finden; **on a.** auf Probe

approve [ə'pruv] *tr* (*sanction*) genehmigen; (*judge favorably*) billigen; (*a bill*) (parl) annehmen || *intr*—**a. of** billigen

approvingly [ə'pruvɪŋli] *adv* beifällig

approximate [ə'præksɪmɪt] *adj* annähernd || [ə'præksɪ‚met] *tr* (*come close to*) nahekommen (*dat*); (*estimate*) schätzen; (*simulate closely*) täuschend nachahmen

approximately [ə'præksɪmɪtli] *adv* ungefähr, etwa

apricot ['eprɪ‚kɑt] *s* Aprikose *f*

ap'ricot tree' *s* Aprikosenbaum *m*

April ['eprɪl] *s* April *m*

A'pril fool' *interj* April, April!

A'pril Fools' Day' *s* der erste April *m*

apron ['eprən] *s* Schürze *f*; (aer) Vorfeld *n*; (theat) Vorbühne *f*

apropos [‚æprə'po] *adj* passend || *adv*—**a. of** in Bezug auf (*acc*)

apse [æps] *s* Apsis *f*

apt [æpt] *adj* (*suited to the occasion*) passend; (*suited to the purpose*) geeignet; (*metaphor*) zutreffend; **be apt to** (*inf*) (*be prone to*) dazu neigen zu

(*inf*); **he is apt to believe it** er wird es wahrscheinlich glauben

aptitude ['æptɪ‚t(j)ud] *s* Eignung *f*

ap'titude test' *s* Eignungsprüfung *f*

aqualung ['ækwə‚lʌŋ] *s* Tauchergerät *n*

aquamarine [‚ækwəmə'rin] *adj* blaugrün || *s* Aquamarin *m*

aquari·um [ə'kwɛrɪ‚əm] *s*. (–ums & –a [ə]) Aquarium *n*

aquatic [ə'kwætɪk] *adj* Wasser– || **aquatics** *spl* Wassersport *m*

aqueduct ['ækwə‚dʌkt] *s* Aquädukt *n*

aq'uiline nose' ['ækwɪ‚laɪn] *s* Adlernase *f*

Arab ['ærəb] *adj* arabisch || *s* Araber *m*

Arabia [ə'rebɪ‚ə] *s* Arabien *n*

Arabic ['ærəbɪk] *adj* arabisch || *s* Arabisch *n*

arable ['ærəbəl] *adj* urbar, Ackerland

arbiter ['arbɪtər] *s* Schiedsrichter *m*

arbitrary ['arbɪ‚trɛri] *adj* (*act*) willkürlich; (*number*) beliebig; (*person, government*) tyrannisch

arbitrate ['arbɪ‚tret] *tr* schlichten || *intr* als Schiedsrichter fungieren

arbitration [‚arbɪ'treʃən] *s* Schlichtung *f*

arbitrator ['arbɪ‚tretər] *s* Schiedsrichter *m*

arbor ['arbər] *s* Laube *f*; (mach) Achse *f*

arbore·tum [‚arbə'ritəm] *s* (–tums & –ta [tə]) Baumgarten *m*

arc [ark] *s* (astr, geom, mach) Bogen *m*; (elec) Lichtbogen *m*

arcade [ar'ked] *s* Bogengang *m*, Arkade *f*

arcane [ar'ken] *adj* geheimnisvoll

arch [artʃ] *adj* (*liar, etc.*) abgefeimt || *s* Bogen *m* || *tr* wölben; (*span*) überwölben || *intr* sich wölben

archaeologist [‚arkɪ'alədʒɪst] *s* Archäolog(e) *m*, Archäologin *f*

archaeology [‚arkɪ'alədʒi] *s* Archäologie *f*

archaic [ar'ke‚ɪk] *adj* (*word*) veraltet; (*manner, notion*) antiquiert

archangel ['ark‚endʒəl] *s* Erzengel *m*

archbishop ['artʃ'bɪʃəp] *s* Erzbischof *m*

archduke ['artʃ'd(j)uk] *s* Erzherzog *m*

archenemy ['artʃ‚enɪmi] *s* Erzfeind *m*

archer ['artʃər] *s* Bogenschütze *m*

archery ['artʃəri] *s* Bogenschießen *n*

archipela·go [‚arkɪ'pelago] *s* (–gos & –goes) Inselmeer *n*; (*group of islands*) Inselgruppe *f*, Archipel *m*

architect ['arkɪ‚tekt] *s* Architekt *m* –in *mf*

architecture ['arkɪ‚tektʃər] *s* Architektur *f*, Baukunst *f*

archives ['arkaɪvz] *spl* Archiv *n*

arch'way' *s* Bogengang *m*, Torbogen *m*

arctic ['arktɪk] *adj* arktisch, nördlich || **the Arctic** *s* die Arktis

Arc'tic Cir'cle *s* nördlicher Polarkreis *m*

arc' weld'ing *s* Lichtbogenschweißung *f*

ardent ['ardənt] *adj* feurig, eifrig

ardor ['ardər] *s* Eifer *m*, Inbrust *f*

arduous ['ardʒu·əs] *adj* mühsam
area ['ɛrɪ·ə] *s* (*surface*) Fläche *f*; (*district*) Gegend *f*; (*field of enterprise*) Bereich *m*, Gebiet *n*; (*of danger*) Zone *f*
arena [ə'rinə] *s* Arena *f*, Kampfbahn *f*
Argentina [ˌɑrdʒən'tinə] *s* Argentinien *n*
argue ['ɑrgju] *tr* erörtern; (*maintain*) behaupten; **a. into** (*ger*) dazu überreden zu (*inf*) || *intr* (*with*) streiten (*mit*); **a. for** (or *against*) *s.th.* für (or *gegen*) etw eintreten; **don't a.!** keine Widerrede!
argument ['ɑrgjəmənt] *s* (*discussion*) Erörterung *f*; (*point*) Beweisgrund *m*; (*disagreement*) Auseinandersetzung *f*; (*theme*) Thema *n*
argumentative [ˌɑrgjə'mɛntətɪv] *adj* streitsüchtig
aria ['ɑrɪ·ə], ['ɛrɪ·ə] *s* Arie *f*
arid ['ærɪd] *adj* trocken, dürr
aridity [ə'rɪdɪti] *s* Trockenheit *f*
arise [ə'raɪz] *v* (*pret* **arose** [ə'roz]; *pp* **arisen** [ə'rɪzən]) *intr* (*come into being*) (*from*) entstehen (aus); (*get out of bed*) aufstehen; (*from a seat*) sich erheben; (*occur*) aufkommen, auftauchen; (*said of an opportunity*) sich bieten; (*stem*) (*from*) stammen (von)
aristocracy [ˌærɪs'tɑkrəsi] *s* Aristokratie *f*
aristocrat [ə'rɪstəˌkræt] *s* Aristokrat –in *mf*
aristocratic [əˌrɪstə'krætɪk] *adj* aristokratisch
arithmetic [ə'rɪθmətɪk] *s* Arithmetik *f*
arithmetical [ˌærɪθ'mɛtɪkəl] *adj* arithmetisch, rechnerisch
ark [ɑrk] *s* Arche *f*
ark' of the cov'enant *s* Bundeslade *f*
arm [ɑrm] *s* Arm *m*; (*of a chair*) Seitenlehne *f*; (*weapon*) Waffe *f*; **keep s.o. at arm's length** sich j-m vom Leibe halten; **take up arms** zu den Waffen greifen; **up in arms** in Aufruhr || *tr* bewaffnen; || *intr* sich bewaffnen
armament ['ɑrməmənt] *s* Kriegsausrüstung *f*, Bewaffnung *f*
ar'maments race' *s* Rüstungswettlauf *m*
armature ['ɑrməˌtʃər] *s* (*of doorbell or magnet*) Anker *m*; (*of a motor or dynamo*) Läufer *m*; (biol) Panzer *m*
arm'chair' *s* Lehnsessel *m*; (*unpadded*) Lehnstuhl *m*
armed' for'ces *spl* Streitkräfte *pl*
armed' rob'bery *s* bewaffneter Raubüberfall *m*
Armenia [ɑr'minɪ·ə] *s* Armenien *n*
armful ['ɑrmˌful] *s* Armvoll *m*
armistice ['ɑrmɪstɪs] *s* Waffenstillstand *m*
armor ['ɑrmər] *s* Panzer *m* || *tr* panzern
ar'mored car' *s* Panzerwagen *m*
armor-piercing ['ɑrmərˌpɪrsɪŋ] *adj* panzerbrechend
ar'mor plat'ing ['pletɪŋ] *s* Panzerung *f*
armory ['ɑrməri] *s* (*large arms storage*) Arsenal *n*; (*arms repair and storage room of a unit*) Waffenkam-

mer *f*; (*arms factory*) Waffenfabrik *f*; (*drill hall*) Exerzierhalle *f*
arm'pit' *s* Achselhöhle *f*
arm'rest' *s* Armlehne *f*
army ['ɑrmi] *adj* Armes–, Heeres– || *s* Armee *f*, Heer *n*; **join the a. zum** Militär gehen
aroma [ə'romə] *s* Aroma *n*, Duft *m*
aromatic [ˌærə'mætɪk] *adj* aromatisch
around [ə'raund] *adv* ringsherum; **be a. in der Nähe sein; get a. viel herumkommen; get a. to** (*inf*) dazukommen zu (*inf*) || *prep* um (*acc*) herum; (*approximately*) etwa; (*near*) bei (*dat*); **a. town in der Stadt**
arouse [ə'rauz] *tr* aufwecken; (fig) erwecken
arraign [ə'ren] *tr* (*accuse*) anklagen; (jur) vor Gericht stellen
arrange [ə'rendʒ] *tr* arrangieren; (*in a certain order*) (an)ordnen; (*a time*) festsetzen; (mus) bearbeiten || *intr*— **a. for** Vorkehrungen treffen für
arrangement [ə'rendʒmənt] *s* Anordnung *f*; (*agreement*) Vereinbarung *f*; (mus) Bearbeitung *f*; **make arrangements to** (*inf*) Vorbereitungen treffen, um zu (*inf*)
array [ə're] *s* (*of troops, facts*) Ordnung *f*; (*large number or quantity*) Menge *f*; (*apparel*) Staat *m* || *tr* ordnen; (*dress up*) putzen
arrears [ə'rɪrz] *spl* Rückstand *m*; **in a. rückständig**
arrest [ə'rɛst] *s* Verhaftung *f*; **make an a. e-e Verhaftung vornehmen; place under a. in Haft nehmen; under a. verhaftet** || *tr* verhaften; (*attention*) fesseln; (*a disease, progress*) hemmen
arrival [ə'raɪvəl] *s* Ankunft *f*; (*of merchandise*) Eingang *m*; (*a person*) Ankömmling *m*
arrive [ə'raɪv] *intr* ankommen; (*said of time, an event*) kommen; **a. at** (*a conclusion, decision*) erlangen
arrogance ['ærəgəns] *s* Anmaßung *f*
arrogant ['ærəgənt] *adj* anmaßend
arrogate ['ærəˌget] *tr* sich [*dat*] anmaßen
arrow ['æro] *s* Pfeil *m*
ar'rowhead' *s* Pfeilspitze *f*
arsenal ['ɑrsənəl] *s* Arsenal *n*
arsenic ['ɑrsɪnɪk] *s* Arsen *n*
arson ['ɑrsən] *s* Brandstiftung *f*
arsonist ['ɑrsənɪst] *s* Brandstifter –in *mf*
art [ɑrt] *s* Kunst *f*
artery ['ɑrtəri] *s* Pulsader *f*; (*highway*) Verkehrsader *f*
artful ['ɑrtfəl] *adj* (*cunning*) schlau, listig; (*skillful*) kunstvoll
arthritic [ɑr'θrɪtɪk] *adj* arthritisch, gichtisch; *s* Arthritiker –in *mf*
arthritis [ɑr'θraɪtɪs] *s* Arthritis *f*
artichoke ['ɑrtɪˌtʃok] *s* Artischocke *f*
article ['ɑrtɪkəl] *s* (*object*) Gegenstand *m*; (com, gram, journ, jur) Artikel *m*
articulate [ɑr'tɪkjəlɪt] *adj* deutlich || [ɑr'tɪkjəˌlet] *tr & intr* deutlich aussprechen
artifact ['ɑrtɪˌfækt] *s* Artefakt *n*
artifice ['ɑrtɪfɪs] *s* Kunstgriff *m*
artificial [ˌɑrtɪ'fɪʃəl] *adj* Kunst–,

künstlich; (emotion, smile) gekünstelt
artillery [ɑr'tɪləri] s Artillerie f
artil/lery-man s (-men) Artillerist m
artisan ['ɑrtɪzən] s Handwerker –in
mf
artist ['ɑrtɪst] s Künstler –in mf
artistic [ɑr'tɪstɪk] adj künstlerisch
artistry ['ɑrtɪstri] s Kunstfertigkeit f
artless ['ɑrtlɪs] adj (lacking art) unkünstlerisch; (made without skill)
stümperhaft; (ingenuous) unbefangen
arts' and crafts' spl Kunstgewerbe n
arts' and sci'ences spl Geistes– und
Naturwissenschaften pl
arty ['ɑrti] adj (coll) gekünstelt
Aryan ['ɛrɪ-ən], ['ɑrjən] adj arisch ||
s Arier –in mf; (language) Arisch n
as [æz], [əz] adv wie; as…as (eben)so
…wie; as far as Berlin bis nach
Berlin; as far as I know soviel ich
weiß; as far back as 1900 schon im
Jahre 1900; as for me was mich betrifft; as if als ob; as long as so-
lange; (with the proviso that) vorausgesetzt, daß; as soon as sobald wie;
as though als ob; as well ebensogut,
auch; as yet bis jetzt || rel pron wie,
was || prep als; as a rule in der
Regel || conj wie; (while) als,
während; (because) da, weil, indem;
as it were sozusagen
asbestos [æs'bɛstəs] adj Asbest– || s
Asbest m
ascend [ə'sɛnd] tr (stairs) hinaufstei-
gen; (a throne, mountain) besteigen
|| intr emporsteigen; (said of a bal-
loon, plane) aufsteigen
ascendancy [ə'sɛndənsi] s Überlegenheit f
ascension [ə'sɛnʃən] s Aufsteigen n
Ascen/sion Day' s Himmelfahrtstag m
ascent [ə'sɛnt] s (on foot) Besteigung
f; (by vehicle) Auffahrt f; (upward
slope) Steigung f; (& fig) Aufstieg m
ascertain [ˌæsər'ten] tr feststellen
ascetic [ə'sɛtɪk] adj asketisch || s
Asket –in mf
ascribe [ə'skraɪb] tr a. to zuschrei-
ben (dat)
aseptic [ə'sɛptɪk] adj aseptisch
ash [æʃ] s Asche f; (tree) Esche f;
ashes Asche f; (mortal remains)
sterbliche Überreste pl
ashamed [ə'ʃemd] adj—be (or feel)
a. (of) sich schämen (genit)
ash/can' s Ascheneimer m
ashen ['æʃən] adj aschgrau
ashore [ə'ʃor] adv (position) am Land;
(direction) ans Land
ash/tray' s Aschenbecher m
Ash' Wednes/day s Aschermittwoch m
Asia ['eʒə], ['eʃə] s Asien n
A'sia Mi'nor s Kleinasien n
aside [ə'saɪd] adv zur Seite; a. from
außer || s (theat) Seitenbemerkung f
asinine ['æsɪˌnaɪn] adj eselhaft
ask [æsk] tr (request) bitten; (demand)
auffordern; (a high price) fordern;
(inquire of) fragen; ask a question
(of s.o.) (j–m) e–e Frage stellen; ask
in hereinbitten; that is asking too
much das ist zuviel verlangt || intr

fragen; **ask for** bitten um; **ask for**
trouble sich [dat] selbst Schwierigkeiten machen
askance [ə'kæns] adv—**look a. at**
schief ansehen
askew [ə'skju] adv schräg
ask/ing s—for the a. umsonst
asleep [ə'slip] adj schlafend; (numb)
eingeschlafen; be a. schlafen; fall a.
einschlafen
asp [æsp] s Natter f
asparagus [ə'spærəgəs] s Spargel m
aspect ['æspɛkt] s Gesichtspunkt m
aspen ['æspən] s Espe f
aspersion [ə'spʌrʒən] s (eccl) Bespren-
gung f; **cast aspersions on** verleumden
asphalt ['æsfɔlt], ['æsfælt] s Asphalt
m || tr asphaltieren
asphyxiate [æs'fɪksɪˌet] tr & intr ersticken
aspirant ['æspɪrənt] s Bewerber –in
mf
aspirate ['æspɪrɪt] s Hauchlaut m ||
['æspɪˌret] tr behauchen
aspire [ə'spaɪr] intr (after, to) streben
(nach); a. to (inf) danach streben zu
(inf)
aspirin ['æspɪrɪn] s Aspirin n
ass [æs] s Esel m; (vulg) Arsch m;
make an ass of oneself (sl) sich
lächerlich machen
assail [ə'sel] tr angreifen, anfallen;
(with questions) bestürmen
assassin [ə'sæsɪn] s Meuchelmörder
–in mf
assassinate [ə'sæsɪˌnet] tr ermorden
assassination [əˌsæsɪ'neʃən] s Meuchelmord m, Ermordung f
assault [ə'sɔlt] s Überfall m; (rape)
Vergewaltigung f; (physical violence)
(jur) tätlicher Angriff m; (threat of
violence) (jur) unmittelbare Bedro-
hung f; (mil) Sturm m || tr (er-
stürmen, anfallen; (jur) tätlich beleidigen
assault' and bat'tery s schwere tätliche
Beleidigung f
assay [ə'se], ['æse] s Prüfung f ||
[ə'se] tr prüfen
assemble [ə'sɛmbəl] tr versammeln;
(mach) montieren || intr sich ver-
sammeln
assembly [ə'sɛmbli] s Versammlung f;
(mach) Montage f; (pol) Unterhaus
n
assem/bly line' s Fließband n
assent [ə'sɛnt] s Zustimmung f || intr
(to) zustimmen (dat)
assert [ə'sʌrt] tr behaupten; a. oneself
sich behaupten
assertion [ə'sʌrʃən] s Behauptung f;
(of rights) Geltendmachung f
assess [ə'sɛs] tr (damage) festsetzen;
(property) (at) (ab)schätzen (auf
acc); **assessed value** Schätzungswert
m
assessment [ə'sɛsmənt] s (of damage)
Festsetzung f; (valuation) Einschät-
zung f; (of real estate) Veranlagung
f
assessor [ə'sɛsər] s Steuereinschätzer
m

asset ['æset] s Vorzug m; (com) Aktivposten m; **assets** Vermögenswerte pl; **assets and liabilities** Aktiva und Passiva pl

assiduous [ə'sɪdʒʊ-əs] adj emsig

assign [ə'saɪn] tr zuweisen; (homework) aufgeben; (transfer) (jur) abtreten; (mil) zuteilen

assignment [ə'saɪnmənt] s Zuweisung f; (homework) Aufgabe f; (task) Auftrag m, Aufgabe f; (transference) (jur) Abtretung f; (to a unit) (mil) Zuteilung f

assimilate [ə'sɪmɪˌlet] tr angleichen || intr sich angleichen

assimilation [ə‚sɪmɪ'leʃən] s Assimilierung f, Angleichung f

assist [ə'sɪst] s (sport) Zuspiel n || tr beistehen (dat) || intr—a. in beistehen bei, behilflich sein bei

assistance [ə'sɪstəns] s Hilfe f

assistant [ə'sɪstənt] adj Hilfs-, Unter- || s (helper) Gehilfe m, Gehilfin f

associate [ə'soʃɪ-ɪt] adj Mit-, beigeordnet; (member) außerordentlich || s (companion) Gefährte m, Gefährtin f; (colleague) Kollege m, Kollegin f; (com) Partner -in mf || [ə'soʃɪˌet] tr verbinden || intr (with) verkehren (mit)

asso′ciate profes′sor s außerordentlicher Professor m

association [ə‚soʃɪ'eʃən] s (connection) Verbindung f; (social intercourse) Verkehr m; (society) Verband m; (suggested ideas, feelings) Assoziation f

assonance ['æsənəns] s Assonanz f

assorted [ə'sɔrtɪd] adj verschieden

assortment [ə'sɔrtmənt] s Sortiment n

assuage [ə'swedʒ] tr (pain) lindern; (hunger) befriedigen; (thirst) stillen

assume [ə's(j)um] tr (a fact as true; a certain shape, property, habit) annehmen; (a duty) auf sich nehmen; (office) antreten; (power) ergreifen; assuming that vorausgesetzt, daß

assumed′ adj (feigned) erheuchelt; a. name Deckname m

assumption [ə'sʌmpʃən] s (supposition) Annahme f; (e.g., of power) Übernahme f

assurance [ə'ʃʊrəns] s Versicherung f

assure [ə'ʃʊr] tr versichern

aster ['æstər] s Aster f

asterisk ['æstəˌrɪsk] s Sternchen n

astern [ə'stʌrn] adv achtern, achteraus

asthma ['æzmə] s Asthma n

astonish [ə'stɑnɪʃ] tr in Erstaunen setzen; **be astonished at** staunen über (acc), sich wundern über (acc)

aston′ishing adj erstaunlich

astonishment [ə'stɑnɪʃmənt] s Erstaunen n, Verwunderung f

astound [ə'staund] tr überraschen

astound′ing adj erstaunlich

astray [ə'stre] adv—go a. a. irregehen; lead a. irreführen

astride [ə'straɪd] adv rittlings || prep (a road) an beiden Seiten (genit); (a horse) rittlings auf (dat)

astringent [ə'strɪndʒənt] adj stopfend || s Stopfmittel n

astrology [ə'strɑlədʒɪ] s Astrologie f

astronaut ['æstrəˌnɔt] s Astronaut m

astronautics [‚æstrə'nɔtɪks] s Raumfahrtwissenschaft f, Astronautik f

astronomer [ə'strɑnəmər] s Astronom –in mf

astronomic(al) [‚æstrə'nɑmɪk(əl)] adj astronomisch

astronomy [ə'strɑnəmɪ] s Astronomie f

astute [ə'st(j)ut] adj scharfsinnig; (cunning) schlau

asunder [ə'sʌndər] adv auseinander

asylum [ə'saɪləm] s (refuge) Asyl n; (for the insane) Irrenhaus n

at [æt], [ət] prep (position) an (dat), auf (dat), in (dat), bei (dat), zu (dat); (direction) auf (acc), gegen (acc), nach (dat), zu (dat); (manner, circumstance) auf (acc), in (dat), bei (dat); (time) um (acc), bei (dat), auf (dat) zu (dat); **at all** (in questions) überhaupt; **at high prices** zu hohen Preisen; **even at that** sogar so

atheism ['eθɪˌɪzəm] s Atheismus m

atheist ['eθɪ-ɪst] s Atheist –in mf

Athens ['æθɪns] s Athen n

athlete ['æθlit] s Sportler –in mf

ath′lete's foot′ s Fußflechte f

athletic [æθ'letɪk] adj athletisch, Sport-, Turn- || **athletics** s Athletik f

Atlantic [æt'læntɪk] adj atlantisch || s Atlantik m

atlas ['ætləs] s Atlas m

atmosphere ['ætməsˌfɪr] s (& fig) Atmosphäre f

atmospheric [‚ætməs'ferɪk] adj atmosphärisch

atom ['ætəm] s Atom n

atomic [ə'tɑmɪk] adj atomisch, atomar, Atom-

atom′ic age′ s Atomzeitalter n

atom′ic bomb′ s Atombombe f

atom′ic pow′er s Atomkraft f; **atomic powers** (pol) Atommächte pl

atomizer ['ætəˌmaɪzər] s Zerstäuber m

atone [ə'ton] intr—a. for büßen

atonement [ə'tonmənt] s Buße f

atrocious [ə'troʃəs] adj gräßlich

atrocity [ə'trɑsɪtɪ] s Greueltat f

atro·phy ['ætrəfɪ] s Verkümmerung f, Atrophie f || v (pret & pp –phied) tr auszehren || intr verkümmern

attach [ə'tætʃ] tr (with glue, stitches, tacks) (to) anheften (an acc); (connect) (to) befestigen (an acc); (importance) (to) beimessen (dat); (a person) (jur) verhaften; (a thing) (jur) beschlagnahmen; (mil) (to) zuteilen (dat); a. oneself to sich anschließen an (acc); **be attached to** festhalten an (dat); (fig) verwachsen sein mit

attaché [‚ætə'ʃe] s Attaché m

attaché′ case′ s Aktenköfferchen n

attachment [ə'tætʃmənt] s Befestigung f; (regard) Zuneigung f (zu); (device) Zusatzgerät n; (of a person) (jur) Verhaftung f; (of a thing) (jur) Beschlagnahme f

attack [ə'tæk] s Angriff m; (pathol)

Anfall *m* || *tr & intr* angreifen; (pathol) überfallen

attain [ə'ten] *tr* erreichen, erzielen || *intr*—a. to erreichen

attainment [ə'tenmənt] *s* Erreichen *n*; **attainments** Fertigkeiten *pl*

attempt [ə'tempt] *s* Versuch *m*; (*assault*) Attentat *n* || *tr* versuchen

attend [ə'tend] *tr* beiwohnen (*dat*); (*school, church*) besuchen; (*accompany*) begleiten; (*a patient*) behandeln || *intr*—a. to nachgehen (*dat*), erledigen

attendance [ə'tendəns] *s* Besuch *m*; (*number in attendance*) Besucherzahl *f*; (med) Behandlung *f*

attendant [ə'tendənt] *s* (*servant, waiter*) Diener –in *mf*; (*keeper*) Wärter –in *mf*; (*at a gas station*) Tankwart *m*; (*escort*) Begleiter –in *mf*

attention [ə'tenʃən] *s* Aufmerksamkeit *f*; Acht *f*; a. Mr. X. zu Händen von Herrn X; **call a.** to hinweisen auf (*acc*); **call s.o.'s a.** to j–n aufmerksam machen auf (*acc*); **pay a.** achtgeben; **pay a.** to achten auf (*acc*); **stand at a.** stillstehen || *interj* (mil) Achtung!

attentive [ə'tentɪv] *adj* aufmerksam

attenuate [ə'tenjʊ͵et] *tr* (*dilute, thin*) verdünnen; (*weaken*) abschwächen

attest [ə'test] *tr* bezeugen || *intr*—a. to bezeugen

attic ['ætɪk] *s* Dachboden *m*; (*as living quarters*) Mansarde *f*

attire [ə'taɪr] *s* Putz *m* || *tr* kleiden

attitude ['ætɪ͵t(j)ud] *s* Haltung *f*; (aer, rok) Lage *f*

attorney [ə'tʌrni] *s* Rechtsanwalt *m*

attor'ney gen'eral *s* (attorneys general) *f* Justizminister *m*

attract [ə'trækt] *tr* anziehen, reizen; (*attention*) erregen

attraction [ə'trækʃən] *s* Anziehungskraft *f*; (*that which attracts*) Anziehungspunkt *m*; (*in a circus, variety show*) Attraktion *f*; (theat) Zugstück *n*

attractive [ə'træktɪv] *adj* reizvoll; (*price, offer*) günstig

attribute ['ætrɪ͵bjut] *s* Attribut *n* || [ə'trɪbjut] *tr* (to) zuschreiben (*dat*)

attrition [ə'trɪʃən] *s* Abnutzung *f*, Verschleiß *m*

attune [ə't(j)un] *tr* (to) abstimmen (auf *acc*)

auburn ['ɔbərn] *adj* kastanienbraun

auction ['ɔkʃən] *s* Auktion *f* || *tr*—a. off versteigern; **be auctioned off** unter den Hammer kommen

auctioneer [͵ɔkʃən'ɪr] *s* Versteigerer –in *mf*

audacious [ɔ'deʃəs] *adj* (*daring*) kühn; (*brazen*) keck

audacity [ɔ'dæsɪti] *s* (*daring*) Kühnheit *f*; (*insolence*) Unverschämtheit *f*

audience ['ɔdɪəns] *s* (*spectators*) Publikum *n*; (*formal hearing*) Audienz *f*; (rad) Zuhörerschaft *f*; (telv) Fernsehpublikum *n*

au'dio fre'quency ['ɔdɪ͵o] *s* Tonfrequenz *f*, Hörfrequenz *f*

au'dio-vis'ual *adj* audiovisuell; **a. aids** Lehrmittel *pl*

audit ['ɔdɪt] *s* Rechnungsprüfung *f* || *tr* prüfen, revidieren; (*a lecture*) als Gasthörer belegen

audition [ɔ'dɪʃən] *s* Hörprobe *f* || *tr* vorspielen (or vorsingen) lassen || *intr* vorspielen, vorsingen

auditor ['ɔdɪtər] *s* (com) Rechnungsprüfer –in *mf*; (educ) Gasthörer –in *mf*

auditorium [͵ɔdɪ'tɔrɪ͵əm] *s* Hörsaal *m*

auger ['ɔgər] *s* Bohrer *m*

augment [ɔg'ment] *tr* (*in size*) vergrößern; (*in number*) vermehren || *intr* sich vergrößern; sich vermehren

augur ['ɔgər] *s* Augur *m* || *intr* weissagen; **a. well for** Gutes versprechen für

augury ['ɔgəri] *s* Weissagung *f*

august [ɔ'gʌst] *adj* erhaben || **August** ['ɔgəst] *s* August *m*

aunt [ænt], [ɑnt] *s* Tante *f*

auricle ['ɔrɪkəl] *s* äußeres Ohr *n*; (*of the heart*) Herzohr *n*

auspices ['ɔspɪsɪz] *spl* Auspizien *pl*

auspicious [ɔs'pɪʃəs] *adj* glückverheißend

austere [ɔs'tɪr] *adj* (*stern*) streng; (*simple*) einfach; (*frugal*) genügsam; (*style*) schmucklos

Australia [ɔ'streljə] *s* Australien *n*

Australian [ɔ'streljən] *adj* australisch || *s* Australier –in *mf*

Austria ['ɔstrɪə] *s* Österreich *n*

Austrian ['ɔstrɪən] *adj* österreichisch || *s* Österreicher –in *mf*; (*dialect*) Österreichisch *n*

authentic [ɔ'θentɪk] *adj* authentisch

authenticate [ɔ'θentɪ͵ket] *tr* (*establish as genuine*) als echt erweisen; (*a document*) beglaubigen

author ['ɔθər] *s* (*of a book*) Autor –in *mf*; (*creator*) Urheber –in *mf*

authoritative [ɔ'θɔrɪ͵tetɪv] *adj* maßgebend

authority [ɔ'θɔrɪti] *s* (*power; expert*) Autorität *f*; (*right*) Recht *n*; (*approval*) Genehmigung *f*; (*source*) Quelle *f*; (*commanding influence*) Ansehen *n*; (*authoritative body*) Behörde *f*; **on one's own a.** auf eigene Verantwortung; **the authorities** die Behörden

authorize ['ɔθə͵raɪz] *tr* autorisieren

au'thorship' *s* Autorschaft *f*

au-to ['ɔto] *s* (–tos) Auto *n*

autobiography [͵ɔtobaɪ'ɑgrəfi] *s* Selbstbiographie *f*

autocratic [͵ɔtə'krætɪk] *adj* autokratisch

autograph ['ɔtə͵græf] *s* Autogramm *n* || *tr* autographieren

automat ['ɔtə͵mæt] *s* Automatenrestaurant *n*

automatic [͵ɔtə'mætɪk] *adj* automatisch || *s* Selbstladepistole *f*

automat'ic transmis'sion *s* Automatik *f*

automation [͵ɔtə'meʃən] *s* Automation *f*

automa-ton [ɔ'tamə͵tan] *s* (–tons & –ta [tə]) Automat *m*

automobile [ˌɔtəmoˈbil] *s* Automobil *n*

automotive [ˌɔtəˈmotɪv] *adj* Auto-

autonomous [ɔˈtɑnəməs] *adj* autonom

autonomy [ɔˈtɑnəmi] *s* Autonomie *f*

autopsy [ˈɔtɑpsi] *s* Obduktion *f*

autumn [ˈɔtəm] *adj* Herbst– ‖ *s* Herbst *m*

autumnal [ɔˈtʌmnəl] *adj* herbstlich

auxiliary [ɔgˈzɪljəri] *adj* Hilfs– ‖ *s* (*helper*) Helfer –in *mf*; (gram) Hilfszeitwort *n*; **auxiliaries** (mil) Hilfstruppen *pl*

avail [əˈvel] *s*—**to no a.** nutzlos; **without a.** vergeblich ‖ *tr* nützen (*dat*); **a. oneself of** sich bedienen (*genit*) ‖ *intr* nützen

available [əˈveləbəl] *adj* vorhanden; (*articles, products*) erhältlich; (*e.g., documents*) zugänglich; **be a.** (*for consultation, etc.*) zu sprechen sein; **make a. (to)** zur Verfügung stellen (*dat*)

avalanche [ˈævəˌlænt ʃ] *s* Lawine *f*

avarice [ˈævərɪs] *s* Habsucht *f*, Geiz *m*

avaricious [ˌævəˈrɪʃəs] *adj* geizig

avenge [əˈvendʒ] *tr* (*a person*) rächen; (*a crime*) ahnden; **a. oneself on** sich rächen an (*dat*)

avenger [əˈvendʒər] *s* Rächer –in *mf*

avenue [ˈævəˌn(j)u] *s* (*wide street*) Straße *f*; (fig) Weg *m*

average [ˈævərɪdʒ] *adj* Durchschnitts– ‖ *s* Durchschnitt *m*; (naut) Havarie *f*; **on the a.** im Durchschnitt ‖ *tr* (*amount to, as a mean quantity*) durchschnittlich betragen; (*find the average of*) den Durchschnitt berechnen von; (*earn on the average*) durchschnittlich verdienen; (*travel on the average*) durchschnittlich zurücklegen

averse [əˈvʌrs] *adj* (to) abgeneigt (*dat*)

aversion [əˈvʌrʒən] *s* (to) Abneigung *f* (gegen)

avert [əˈvʌrt] *tr* abwenden

aviary [ˈevɪˌeri] *s* Vogelhaus *n*

aviation [ˌevɪˈeʃən] *s* Flugwesen *n*

aviator [ˈevɪˌetər] *s* Flieger –in *mf*

avid [ˈævɪd] *adj* gierig

avocation [ˌævəˈkeʃən] *s* Nebenbeschäftigung *f*

avoid [əˈvɔɪd] *tr* (*a person*) meiden; (*a thing*) vermeiden

avoidable [əˈvɔɪdəbəl] *adj* vermeidbar

avoidance [əˈvɔɪdəns] *s* (*of a person*) Meidung *f*; (*of a thing*) Vermeidung *f*

avow [əˈvau] *tr* bekennen, gestehen

avowal [əˈvau‿əl] *s* Bekenntnis *n*

avowed' *adj* (*declared*) erklärt; (*acknowledged*) offen anerkannt

await [əˈwet] *tr* erwarten

awake [əˈwek] *adj* wach, munter ‖ *v* (*pret & pp* **awoke** [əˈwok] & **awaked**) *tr* wecken; (fig) erwecken ‖ *intr* erwachen

awaken [əˈwekən] *tr* wecken; (fig) erwecken ‖ *intr* erwachen

awak'ening *s* Erwachen *n*; **a rude a.** ein unsanftes Erwachen

award [əˈwɔrd] *s* Preis *m*, Prämie *f* ‖ *tr* (to) zuerkennen (*dat*)

aware [əˈwer] *adj*—**be a. of** sich [*dat*] bewußt sein (*genit*)

awareness [əˈwernɪs] *s* Bewußtsein *n*

awash [əˈwɑʃ] *adj* überschwemmt

away [əˈwe] *adj* abwesend; (*on a trip*) verreist; (sport) Auswärts– ‖ *adv* fort, (hin)weg; **do a. with** abschaffen; **make a. with** (*kill*) umbringen

awe [ɔ] *s* (of) Ehrfurcht *f* (vor *dat*); **stand in awe of s.o.** vor j–m Ehrfurcht haben

awesome [ˈɔsəm] *adj* ehrfurchtgebietend

awful [ˈɔfəl] *adj* ehrfurchtgebietend; (coll) furchtbar

awfully [ˈɔfəli] *adv* (coll) furchtbar

awhile [əˈhwaɪl] *adv* eine Zeitlang

awkward [ˈɔkwərd] *adj* ungeschickt; (*situation*) peinlich

awl [ɔl] *s* Ahle *f*, Pfriem *m*

awning [ˈɔnɪŋ] *s* Markise *f*

awry [əˈraɪ] *adv*—**go a.** schiefgehen

ax [æks] *s* Axt *f*, Beil *n*

axiom [ˈæksɪəm] *s* Axiom *n*

axiomatic [ˌæksɪ‿əˈmætɪk] *adj* axiomatisch

axis [ˈæksɪs] *s* (axes [ˈæksiz]) Achse *f*

axle [ˈæksəl] *s* Achse *f*

ay(e) [aɪ] *adv* (*yes*) ja; **aye, aye, sir!** zu Befehl, Herr (*Leutnant, etc.*) ‖ *s* Ja *n*, Jastimme *f*; **the ayes have it** die Mehrheit ist dafür

azalea [əˈzeljə] *s* Azalee *f*

azure [ˈəʒər] *adj* azurblau ‖ *s* Azur *m*

B

B, b [bi] zweiter Buchstabe des englischen Alphabets; (mus) H *n*; **B flat** B *n*; **B sharp** His *n*

babble [ˈbæbəl] *s* Geschwätz *n*; (*of brook*) Geplätscher *n* ‖ *tr* schwätzen ‖ *intr* schwätzen; (*said of a brook*) plätschern

babe [beb] *s* Kind *n*; (*naive person*) Kindskopf *m*; (*pretty girl*) Puppe *f*

baboon [bæˈbun] *s* (zool) Pavian *m*

ba·by [ˈbebi] *s* Baby *n*; (*youngest child*) Nesthäkchen *n* ‖ *v* (*pret & pp* –**bied**) *tr* verzärteln

ba'by bot'tle *s* Saugflasche *f*

ba'by car'riage *s* Kinderwagen *m*

ba'by grand' *s* Stutzflügel *m*

ba'by pow'der *s* Kinderpuder *m*

ba'by-sit' *v* (*pret & pp* –**sat**; *ger* –**sitting**) *intr* Kinder hüten

ba'by-sit'ter *s* Babysitter *m*

ba′by talk′ s Babysprache f
ba′by teeth′ spl Milchzähne pl
baccalaureate [ˌbækəˈlɔrɪ·ɪt] s (*bachelor's degree*) Bakkalaureat n; (*service*) Gottesdienst m bei der akademischen Promotion
bacchanal [ˈbækənəl] s (*devotee*) Bacchantin f; (*orgy*) Bacchanal n
bachelor [ˈbætʃələr] s Junggeselle m
bach′elorhood′ s Junggesellenstand m
Bach′elor of Arts′ s Bakkalaureus m der Geisteswissenschaften
Bach′elor of Sci′ence s Bakkalaureus m der Naturwissenschaften
bacil·lus [bəˈsɪləs] s (-li [laɪ]) Bazillus m, Stäbchenbakterie f
back [bæk] adj Hinter-, Rück- ‖ s (*of a man, animal*) Rücken m, Kreuz n; (*of a hand, book, knife, mountain*) Rücken m; (*of a head, house, door, picture, sheet*) Rückseite f; (*of a fabric*) linke Seite f; (*of a seat*) Rückenlehne f; (*of a coin*) Kehrseite f; (*of clothing*) Rückenteil m; (sport) Verteidiger m; **at the b. of** (*e.g., a room*) hinten in (dat); **b. to b.** (coll) nacheinander; **behind s.o.'s b.** hinter j-s Rücken; **have one's b. to the wall** an die Wand gedrückt sein; **turn one's b. on s.o.** (& fig) j-m den Rücken kehren ‖ adv zurück; **b. and forth** hin und her; **b. home** bei uns (zulande); ‖ tr (*a person*) den Rücken decken (dat); (*a candidate, product*) befürworten; (*a horse*) setzen auf (acc); **b. up** (*a car*) rückwärts laufen lassen; **b. water** rückwärts rudern; das Schiff rückwärts fahren lassen; (fig) sich zurückziehen ‖ intr —**b. down** klein beigeben; **b. down from** abstehen von; **b. out of** zurücktreten von; **b. up** zurückfahren; zurückgehen; (*said of a sewer*) zurückfließen
back′ache′ s Rückenschmerzen pl
back′bit′ing s Anschwärzerei f
back′bone′ s Rückgrat n; (fig) Willenskraft f
back′break′ing adj mühsam
back′ door′ s Hintertür f
back′drop′ s (fig & theat) Hintergrund m
backer [ˈbækər] s Förderer m, Unterstützer m; (com) Hintermann m
back′fire′ s Fehlzündung f ‖ intr fehlzünden; (fig) nach hinten losgehen
back′ground′ adj Hintergrund- ‖ s (& fig) Hintergrund m; (*e.g., of an applicant*) Vorbildung f, Erfahrung f
back′hand′ s (tennis) Ruckhandschlag m
back′hand′ed adj Rückhand-; (*compliment*) zweideutig
back′ing s Unterstützung f; (*material*) versteifende Ausfütterung f
back′lash′ s (& fig) Rückschlag m; (mach) toter Gang m
back′log′ s Rückstand m
back′ or′der s rückständiger Auftrag m
back′ pay′ s rückständiger Lohn m
back′ seat′ s Rücksitz m
back′side′ s Rückseite f; (coll) Gesäß n

back′space′ intr den Wagen zurückschieben
back′space key′ s Rücktaste f
back′spin′ s Rückeffet n
back′stage′ adv hinten auf der Bühne
back′ stairs′ spl Hintertreppe f
back′stop′ s (baseball) Ballfang m
back′ stretch′ s Gegengerade f
back′stroke′ s Rückenschwimmen n
back′swept′ adj pfeilförmig
back′ talk′ s freche Antworten pl
back′track′ intr denselben Weg zurückgehen; (fig) e-n Rückzieher machen
back′up′ s (*stand-by*) Beistand m; (*in traffic*) Verkehrsstauung f
back′up light′ s (aut) Rückfahrscheinwerfer m
backward [ˈbækwərd] adj rückwärts gerichtet, Rück-; (*country*) rückständig; (*in development*) zurückgeblieben; (*shy*) zurückhaltend ‖ adv rückwärts, zurück; (fig) verkehrt; **b. and forward** vor und zurück
backwardness [ˈbækwərdnɪs] s Rückständigkeit f; (*shyness*) Zurückhaltung f
back′wash′ s zurücklaufende Strömung f
back′wa′ter s Rückstau m; (fig) Öde f
back′woods′ spl Hinterwälder pl
back′yard′ s Hinterhof m
bacon [ˈbekən] s Speck m; **bring home the b.** (sl) es schaffen
bacteria [bækˈtɪrɪ·ə] spl Bakterien pl
bacteriological [bækˌtɪrɪ·əˈlɑdʒɪkəl] adj bakteriologisch
bacteriology [bækˌtɪrɪ·əˈlɑdʒi] s Bakteriologie f, Bakterienkunde f
bacteri·um [bækˈtɪrɪ·əm] s (-a [ə]) Bakterie f
bad [bæd] adj schlecht, schlimm; (*unfavorable*; *risk*) zweifelhaft; (*debt*) uneinbringlich; (*check*) ungedeckt; (*blood*) böse; (*breath*) übelriechend; (*language*) anstößig; (*pain*) stark; **bad for** schädlich (dat); **from bad to worse** immer schlimmer; **I feel bad about it** es tut mir leid; **too bad!** schade!
bad′ egg′ s (sl) übler Kunde m
badge [bædʒ] s Abzeichen n
badger [ˈbædʒər] s Dachs m ‖ tr quälen
bad′ luck′ s Unglück n, Pech n
badly [ˈbædli] adv schlecht, übel; (coll) dringend; **b. wounded** schwerverwundet; **be b. off** übel dran sein
badminton [ˈbædmɪntən] s Federballspiel n
bad′-tem′pered adj schlecht gelaunt
baffle [ˈbæfəl] s Sperre f; (*on loudspeaker*) Schallwand f ‖ tr verwirren; (*gas*) drosseln
baf′fling adj verwirrend
bag [bæg] s Sack m; (*for small items*) Tüte f; (*for travel*) Reisetasche f; (sl) Frauenzimmer n; (hunt) Strecke f; **bag and baggage** mit Sack und Pack; **it's in the bag** das haben wir in der Tasche ‖ v (pret & pp bagged; ger bagging) tr einsacken; (hunt) zur Strecke bringen ‖ intr sich bauschen
baggage [ˈbægɪdʒ] s Gepäck n

bag'gage car' *s* Gepäckwagen *m*

bag'gage check' *s* Gepäckschein *m*

bag'gage count'er *s* Gepäckabfertigung *f*

bag'gage room' *s* Gepäckaufbewahrung *f*

baggy ['bægi] *adj* bauschig

bag'pipe' *s* Dudelsack *m;* **play the b.** dudeln

ball [bɛl] *s* Kaution *f;* **be out on b.** gegen Kaution auf freiem Fuß sein; **put up b. for** bürgen für ‖ *tr*—**b. out** (*water*) aussschöpfen; (*fig*) retten; (*jur*) durch Kaution aus der Haft befreien ‖ *intr* Wasser schöpfen; **b. out** (aer) abspringen

bailiff ['belɪf] *s* (agr) Gutsverwalter *m;* (jur) Gerichtsvollzieher *m*

bailiwick ['belɪwɪk] *s* (fig) Spezialgebiet *n;* (jur) Amtsbezirk *m*

bait [bet] *s* (& fig) Köder *m* ‖ *tr* (*traps*) mit Köder versehen; (*lure*) ködern; (*harass*) quälen

bake [bek] *tr* (*bread*) backen; (*meat*) braten; (*in a kiln*) brennen ‖ *intr* backen; (*meat*) braten

baked' goods' *spl* Gebäck *n*, Backwaren *pl*

baked' pota'to *s* gebackene Pellkartoffel *f*

baker ['bekər] *s* Bäcker –in *mf*

bak'er's doz'en *s* dreizehn Stück *pl*

bakery ['bekəri] *s* Bäckerei *f*

bak'ing pow'der *s* Backpulver *n*

bak'ing so'da *s* Backpulver *n*

balance ['bæləns] *s* (*equilibrium*) Gleichgewicht *n;* (*remainder*) Rest *m;* (*scales*) Waage *f;* (*in a bank account*) Bankguthaben *n;* (fig) Fassung *f;* (com) Bilanz *f;* ‖ *tr* balancieren; (*offset*) abgleichen; (*make come out even*) ausgleichen ‖ *intr* balancieren

bal'ance of pay'ments *s* Devisenbilanz *f*

bal'ance of pow'er *s* Gleichgewicht *n* der Kräfte

bal'ance sheet' *s* Bilanz *f*

bal'ance wheel' *s* (horol) Unruh *f*

balcony ['bælkəni] *s* Balkon *m;* (theat) Rang *m*

bald [bɔld] *adj* kahl; (*eagle*) weißköpfig; (fig) unverblümt

bald'head'ed *adj* kahlköpfig

baldness ['bɔldnɪs] *s* Kahlheit *f*

bald' spot' *s* Kahlstelle *f*

bale [bel] *s* Ballen *m* ‖ *tr* in Ballen verpacken

baleful ['belfəl] *adj* unheilvoll

balk [bɔk] *intr* (at) scheuen (vor *dat*)

Balkan ['bɔlkən] *adj* Balkan– ‖ *s*— **the Balkans** die Balkans

balky ['bɔki] *adj* störrisch

ball [bɔl] *s* Ball *m;* (*dance*) Ball *m;* (*of yarn*) Knäuel *m & n;* (*of the foot*) Ballen *m;* **be on the b.** (coll) bei der Sache sein; **have a lot on the b.** (coll) viel auf dem Kasten haben

ballad ['bæləd] *s* Ballade *f*

ball'-and-sock'et joint' *s* Kugelgelenk *n*

ballast ['bæləst] *s* (aer, naut) Ballast *m;* (rr) Schotter *m* ‖ *tr* (aer, naut) mit Ballast beladen; (rr) beschottern

ball' bear'ing *s* Kugellager *n*

ballerina [ˌbælə'rinə] *s* Ballerina *f*

ballet [bæ'le] *s* Ballett *n*

ball' han'dling *s* (sport) Balltechnik *f*

ballistic [bə'lɪstɪk] *adj* ballistisch ‖ **ballistics** *s* Ballistik *f*

balloon [bə'lun] *s* Ballon *m*

ballot ['bælət] *s* Stimmzettel *m* ‖ *intr* abstimmen

bal'lot box' *s* Wahlurne *f*

ball'-point pen' *s* Kugelschreiber *m*

ball'room' *s* Ballsaal *m*, Tanzsaal *m*

ballyhoo ['bælɪ‚hu] *s* Tamtam *n* ‖ *tr* Tamtam machen

balm [bɑm] *s* (& fig) Balsam *m*

balmy ['bɑmi] *adj* mild, lind; **be b.** (coll) e-n Tick haben

baloney [bə'loni] *s* (*sausage*) (coll) Bolognawurst *f;* (sl) Quatsch *m*

balsam ['bɔlsəm] *s* Balsam *m*

Baltic ['bɔltɪk] *adj* baltisch ‖ *s* Ostsee *f*

baluster ['bæləstər] *s* Geländersäule *f*

balustrade ['bæləs‚tred] *s* Brüstung *f*

bamboo [bæm'bu] *s* Bambus *m*, Bambusrohr *n*

bamboozle [bæm'buzəl] *tr* (*cheat*) anschmieren; (*mislead*) irreführen; (*perplex*) verwirren

ban [bæn] *s* Verbot *n;* (eccl) Bann *m;* ‖ *v* (*pret & pp* banned; *ger* banning) *tr* verbieten

banal ['benəl] *adj* banal

banana [bə'nænə] *s* Banane *f;* (*tree*) Bananenbaum *m*

band [bænd] *s* (*e.g., of a hat*) Band *n;* (*stripe*) Steifen *m;* (*gang*) Bande *f;* (mus) Musikkapelle *f;* (rad) Band *n* ‖ *intr*—**b. together** sich zusammenrotten

bandage ['bændɪdʒ] *s* Verband *m* ‖ *tr* verbinden

Band'-Aid' *s* (trademark) Schnellverband *m*

bandit ['bændɪt] *s* Bandit *m*

band'lead'er *s* Kapellmeister *m*

band' saw' *s* Bandsäge *f*

band'stand' *s* Musikpavillon *m*

band'wag'on *s*—**climb the b.** mitlaufen

bane [ben] *s* Ruin *m*

baneful ['benfəl] *adj* verderblich

bang [bæŋ] *s* Knall *m;* **bangs** Ponyfrisur *f;* **with a b.** mit Krach ‖ *tr* knallen lassen; (*a door*) zuschlagen; ‖ *intr* knallen; (*said of a door*) zuschlagen; ‖ *interj* bums! paff!

bang'-up' *adj* (sl) tipptopp, prima

banish ['bænɪʃ] *tr* verbannen

banishment ['bænɪʃmənt] *s* Verbannung *f*

banister ['bænɪstər] *s* Geländer *n*

bank [bæŋk] *s* Bank *f;* (*of a river*) Ufer *n;* (*in a road*) Überhöhung *f;* (aer) Schräglage *f;* (rr) Böschung *f;* ‖ *tr* (*money*) in e-r Bank deponieren; (*a road*) überhöhen; (aer) in Schräglage bringen ‖ *intr* (*a road*) überhöhen; (aer) in Schräglage bringen ‖ *intr* (a) ein Bankkonto haben (bei); (aer) in die Kurve gehen; **b. on** bauen auf (acc)

bank' account' *s* Bankkonto *n*

bank' bal'ance *s* Bankguthaben *n*

bank'book' *s* Sparbuch *n*, Bankbuch *n*

banker ['bæŋkər] *s* Bankier –in *mf*

bank'ing s Bankwesen n

bank' note' s Geldschein m

bank'roll' s Rolle f von Geldscheinen || tr (sl) finanzieren

bankrupt ['bæŋkrʌpt] adj bankrott; go b. Pleite machen || tr bankrott machen

bankruptcy ['bæŋkrʌptsɪ] s Bankrott m

bank' state'ment s Bankausweis m

bank' tell'er s Kassierer –in mf

banner ['bænər] s Fahne f, Banner n

banquet ['bæŋkwɪt] s Bankett n || intr tafeln

banter ['bæntər] s Neckerei f || intr necken

baptism ['bæptɪzəm] s Taufe f

baptismal [bæp'tɪzməl] adj Tauf–

baptis'mal certi'ficate s Taufschein m

bap'tism of fire' s Feuertaufe f

Baptist ['bæptɪst] s Baptist –in mf, Wiedertäufer m

baptistery ['bæptɪstərɪ] s Taufkapelle f

baptize [bæp'taɪz] tr taufen

bar [bar] s Stange f; (of a door, window) Riegel m; (of gold, etc.) Barren m; (of chocolate, soap) Riegel m; (barroom) Bar f; (counter) Schanktisch m; (obstacle) (to) Schranke f (gegen); (jur) Gerichtshof m, Anwaltschaft f; (bar line) (mus) Taktstrich m; (measure) Takt m; (naut) Barre f; be admitted to the bar zur Advokatur zugelassen werden; behind bars hinter Gittern; || prep– bar none ohne Ausnahme || v (pret & pp barred; ger barring) tr (a door) verriegeln; (a window) vergittern; (the way) versperren; bar s.o. from j–n hindern an (dat)

barb [barb] s Widerhaken m; (fig) Stachelrede f; (bot) Bart m

barbarian [bar'berɪ.ən] s Barbar m

barbaric [bar'bærɪk] adj barbarisch

barbarism ['barbə,rɪzəm] s Barbarei f; (gram) Barbarismus m

barbarity [bar'berɪtɪ] s Barbarei f

barbarous ['barbərəs] adj barbarisch

barbecue ['barbɪ,kju] s am Spieß (or am Rost) gebratenes Fleisch n; (grill) Bratrost m; (outdoor meal) Gartengrillfest n || tr am Spieß (or am Rost) braten

barbed' wire' s Stacheldraht m

barbed'-wire entan'glement s Drahtverhau m

barber ['barbər] s Friseur m

bar'ber chair' s Friseursessel m

bar'bershop' s Friseurladen m

bard [bard] s Barde m

bare [ber] (adj) nackt, bloß; (tree, wall) kahl; (facts) nackt; (majority) knapp || tr entblößen; (heart, thoughts) offenbaren; (teeth) fletschen

bare'back' adj & adv sattellos

bare'faced' adj unverschämt

bare'foot' adj & adv barfuß

bare'head'ed adj & adv barhäuptig

barely ['berlɪ] adv kaum, bloß

bar'fly' s Kneipenhocker m

bargain ['bargɪn] s (deal) Geschäft n; (cheap purchase) Sonderangebot n; into the b. obendrein; it's a b.! abge-

macht! || tr—b. away mit Verlust verkaufen || intr handeln; b. for verhandeln über (acc)

bar'gain price' s Preisschlager m

bar'gain sale' s Sonderverkauf m

barge [bardʒ] s Lastkahn m; || intr—b. in hereinstürzen; b. into stürzen in (acc)

baritone ['berɪ,ton] s Bariton m

barium ['berɪ.əm] s Barium n

bark [bark] s (of a tree) Rinde f; (of a dog) Bellen n, Gebell n; (boat) Barke f; || tr—b. out bellend hervorstoßen || intr bellen; b. at anbellen

barker ['barkər] s Anreißer m

barley ['barlɪ] s Gerste f; grain of b. Graupe f

bar'maid' s Schankmädchen n, Bardame f

barn [barn] s Scheune f; (for animals) Stall m

barnacle ['barnəkəl] s Entenmuschel f

barn'storm' intr auf dem Lande Theateraufführungen versanstalten; (pol) auf dem Lande Wahlreden halten

barn'yard' s Scheunenhof m

barometer [bə'ramɪtər] s Barometer n

barometric [,bærə'metrɪk] adj barometrisch

baron ['bærən] s Baron m

baroness ['bærənɪs] s Baronin f

baroque [bə'rok] adj barock || s (style, period) Barock m & n

barracks ['bærəks] s (temporary wooden structure) Baracke f; (mil) Kaserne f

barrage [bə'raʒ] s Sperrfeuer n; moving b. Sperrfeuerwalze f

barrel ['bærəl] s Faß n, Tonne f; (of a gun) Lauf m; (of money, fun) große Menge f; have over the b. (sl) in der Gewalt haben || intr (coll) rasen, sausen

barren ['bærən] adj dürr, unfruchtbar; (landscape) kahl

barricade ['bærɪ,ked] s Barrikade f || tr verbarrikadieren

barrier ['bærɪ.ər] s Schranke f, Schlagbaum m; (e.g., on a street) Sperre f

bar'room' s Schenkstube f, Bar f

bartend ['bar,tend] intr Getränke ausschenken

bar'tend'er s Schankwirt m, Barmixer m

barter ['bartər] s Tauschhandel m || tr tauschen || intr Tauschhandel treiben

basalt [bə'sɔlt], ['bæsɔlt] s Basalt m

base [bes] adj gemein, niedrig; (metal) unedel || s (cosmetic) Schminkunterlage f; (fig) Grundlage f; (archit) Basis f, Fundament n; (baseball) Mal n; (chem) Base f; (geom) Grundlinie f, Grundfläche f; (math) Basis f; (mil) Stützpunkt m || tr (mil) stationieren; b. on stützen auf (acc), gründen auf (acc)

base'ball' s Baseball m

base'board' s Wandleiste f

basement ['besmənt] s Kellergeschoß n

bash [bæʃ] s heftiger Schlag m

bashful ['bæʃfəl] adj schüchtern

basic ['besɪk] adj grundsätzlich; (e.g., salary) Grund-; (chem) basisch

basically ['besɪkəlɪ] adv grundsätzlich

ba'sic train'ing s Grundausbildung f

basilica [bə'sɪlɪkə] s Basilika f

basin ['besɪn] s Becken n; (geol) Mulde f; (naut) Bassin n

ba·sis ['besɪs] s (-ses [siz]) Basis f, Grundlage f; **b. of comparison** Vergleichsgrundlage f; **put on a firm b.** (fin) sanieren

bask [bæsk] intr (& fig) sich sonnen

basket ['bæskɪt] s (& sport) Korb m

bas'ketball' s Basketball m, Korbball m

bas-relief [,bɑrɪ'lif] s Flachrelief n

bass [bes] adj Baß– || s (mus) Baß m || [bæs] s (ichth) Flußbarsch m, Seebarsch m

bass' clef' s Baßschlüssel m

bass' drum' s große Trommel f

bass' fid'dle s Baßgeige f

bassoon [bə'sun] s Fagott n

bass viol ['bes'vaɪ·əl] s Gambe f

bastard ['bæstərd] adj Bastard–; (illegitimate in birth) unehelich || s Bastard m; (vulg) Schweinehund m

baste [best] tr (thrash) verprügeln; (scold) schelten; (culin) begießen; (sew) lose (an)heften

bastion ['bæstʃən] s Bastion f

bat [bæt] s (sport) Schläger m; (zool) Fledermaus f; **go to bat for s.o.** (fig) für j–n eintreten || v (pret & pp batted; ger batting) tr schlagen; **without batting an eye** ohne mit der Wimper zu zucken

batch [bætʃ] s Satz m, Haufen m; (of bread) Schub m; (of letters) Stoß m

bated ['betɪd] adj—**with b. breath** mit verhaltenem Atem

bath [bæθ] s Bad n; **take a b.** ein Bad nehmen

bathe [beð] tr & intr baden

bather ['beðər] s Badende mf

bath'house' s Umkleideräume pl

bath'ing s Baden n, Bad n

bath'ing cap' s Badehaube f

bath'ing suit' s Badeanzug m

bath'ing trunks' spl Badehose f

bath'robe' s Bademantel m

bath'room' s Badezimmer n

bath'room fix'tures spl Armaturen pl

bath'room scales spl Personenwaage f

bath' tow'el s Badetuch n

bath' tub' s Badewanne f

baton [bæ'tɑn] s (mil) Kommandostab m; (mus) Taktstock m

battalion [bə'tæljən] s Bataillon n

batter ['bætər] s Teig m; (baseball) Schläger –in mf || tr zerschlagen; (aer) bombardieren; **b. down** niederschlagen; **b. in** einschlagen

bat'tering ram' s Sturmbock m

battery ['bætərɪ] s Batterie f; (secondary cell) Akkumulator m; (arti) Batterie f; (nav) Geschützgruppe f

battle ['bætəl] s Schlacht f; (& fig) Kampf m; **do b.** kämpfen; **in b.** im Felde || tr bekämpfen || intr kämpfen

bat'tle array' s Schlachtordnung f

bat'tleax' s Streitaxt f; (fig) Drachen m

bat'tle cruis'er s Schlachtkreuzer m

bat'tle cry' s Schlachtruf m; (fig) Schlagwort n

bat'tle fatigue' s Kriegsneurose f

bat'tlefield' s Schlachtfeld n

bat'tlefront' s Front f, Hauptkampflinie f

bat'tleground' s Kampfplatz m

battlement ['bætəlmənt] s Zinne f

bat'tle scar' s Kampfmal n

bat'tleship' s Schlachtschiff n

bat'tle wag'on s (coll) Schlachtschiff n

batty ['bætɪ] adj (sl) doof

bauble ['bɔbəl] s Tand m; (jester's staff) Narrenstab m

Bavaria [bə'verɪ·ə] s Bayern n

Bavarian [bə'verɪ·ən] adj bayerisch || s Bayer –in mf

bawd [bɔd] s Dirne f

bawdy ['bɔdɪ] adj unzüchtig

bawl [bɔl] s Geplärr n || tr—**b. out** (names, etc.) ausschreien; (scold) anschnauzen || intr (coll) plärren

bay [be] adj kastanienbraun || s Bucht f; (horse) Rotfuchs m; (bot) Lorbeer m; **keep at bay** in Schach halten || intr laut bellen; **bay at** anbellen

bayo·net ['be·ənɪt] s Bajonett n, Seitengewehr n; **with fixed bayonets** mit aufgepflanztem Bajonett || v (pret & pp –net(t)ed; ger –net(t)ing) tr mit dem Bajonett erstechen

bay' win'dow s Erkerfenster n

bazaar [bə'zɑr] s Basar m, Markt m

bazooka [bə'zukə] s Panzerfaust f

be [bi] v (pres am [æm], is [ɪz], are [ɑr]; pret was [wɑz], [wʌz], were [wʌr]; pp been [bɪn]) intr sein; **be about** in der Nähe sein; **be about to** (inf) im Begriff sein zu (inf); **be after s.o.** hinter j–m her sein; **be along** hier sein; **be behind** im Rückstand sein; **be behind s.o.** j–m den Rücken decken; **be from** (a country) stammen aus, sein aus; **be in** zu Hause sein; **be in for** zu erwarten haben; **be in for it** in der Patsche sitzen; **be in on** dabei sein bei; **be off** weggehen; **be on to s.o.** j–m auf die Schliche kommen; **be out** nicht zu Hause sein, aus sein; **be out for s.th.** auf der Suche nach etw sein; **be up** auf sein; **be up to s.th.** etw im Sinn haben; **how are you?** wie geht es Ihnen?, wie befinden Sie sich?; **how much is that?** wieviel kostet das?; **there are, there is** es gibt (acc) || aux—**he is studying** er studiert; **he is to go** er soll gehen; **he was hit** er ist getroffen worden || impers—**how is it that...?** wie kommt es, daß...?; **it is cold** es ist kalt; **it is to be seen that** es ist darauf zu sehen, daß

beach [bitʃ] s Strand m; **on the b.** am Strand, an der See || tr auf den Strand ziehen; **be beached** stranden

beach'comb'er s Strandgutjäger m; (wave) Strandwelle f

beach'head' s Landekopf m

beach' tow'el s Badetuch n

beach' umbrel'la s Strandschirm m

beacon ['bikən] s Leuchtfeuer n, Bake f; (lighthouse) Leuchtturm m; (aer)

Scheinwerfer *m* ‖ *tr* lenken ‖ *intr* leuchten

bead [bid] (*of glass, wood, sweat*) Perle *f*; (*of a gun*) Korn *n*; beads (eccl) Rosenkranz *m*; draw a b. on zielen auf (*acc*)

beagle ['bigəl] *s* Spürhund *m*

beak [bik] *s* Schnabel *m*; (*nose*) (sl) Rübe *f*

beam [bim] *s* (*of wood*) Balken *m*; (*of light, heat, etc.*) Strahl *m*; (*fig*) Glanz *m*; (aer) Leitstrahl *m*; (*width of a vessel*) (naut) größte Schiffsbreite *f*; (*horizontal structural member*) (naut) Deckbalken *m*; b. of light Lichtkegel *m*; off the b. (sl) auf dem Holzweg; on the b. (sl) auf Draht ‖ *intr* strahlen; b. at anstrahlen

bean [bin] *s* Bohne *f*; (*head*) (sl) Birne *f*; spill the beans (sl) alles ausquatschen

bean'pole' *s* (& coll) Bohnenstange *f*

bear [ber] *adj* (*market*) flau, Baisse– ‖ *s* Bär *m*; (st. exch.) Baissier *m* ‖ *v* (*pret* bore [bor]; *pp* borne [born]) *tr* (*carry*) tragen; (*endure*) dulden, ertragen; (*children*) gebären; (*date*) tragen; (*a name, sword*) führen; (*a grudge, love*) hegen; (*a message*) überbringen; (*the consequences*) auf sich [*acc*] nehmen; **bear in mind** bedenken, beachten; **bear fruit** Früchte tragen; (fig) Frucht tragen; **bear out** bestätigen ‖ *intr*—**bear down on** losgehen auf (*acc*); (naut) zufahren auf (*acc*); **bear left** sich links halten; **bear on** sich beziehen auf (*acc*); **bear up (well) against** gut ertragen; **bear with** Geduld haben mit

bearable ['berəbəl] *adj* erträglich

beard [bɪrd] *s* Bart *m*

beard'ed *adj* bärtig

beardless ['bɪrdlɪs] *adj* bartlos

bearer ['berər] *s* Träger –in *mf*; (*of a message*) Überbringer –in *mf*; (com) Inhaber –in *mf*

bear' hug' *s* (coll) Knutsch *m*

bear'ing *s* Körperhaltung *f*; (mach) Lager *n*; (on) Beziehung *f* (auf *acc*); **bearings** (aer, naut) Lage *f*, Richtung *f*, Peilung *f*; lose one's bearings die Richtung verlieren

bear'skin' *s* Bärenfell *n*

beast [bist] *s* Tier *n*; (fig) Bestie *f*

beastly ['bistlɪ] *adj* bestialisch; b. weather Hundewetter *n*

beast' of bur'den *s* Lasttier *n*

beat [bit] *adj* (sl) erschöpft ‖ *s* (*of the heart*) Schlag *m*; (*of a policeman*) Runde *f*, Revier *n*; (mus) Takt *m* ‖ *v* (*pret* beat; *pp* beat & beaten) *tr* (*eggs, a child, record, team, etc.*) schlagen; (*a carpet*) ausklopfen; (*metal*) hämmern; (*a path*) treten; b. it! hau ab!; b. one's brains out sich [*dat*] den Kopf zerbrechen; b. s.o. to it j–m zuvorkommen; b. up verprügeln ‖ *intr* schlagen, klopfen; b. against peitschen gegen; b. down niederprallen

beati·fy [bɪ'ætɪ ˌfaɪ] *v* (*pret* & *pp* –fied) *tr* seligsprechen

beat'ing *s* Prügel *pl*

beatitude [bɪ'ætɪ ˌt(j)ud] *s* Seligpreisung *f*

beau [bo] *s* (beaus & beaux [boz]) Liebhaber *m*

beautician [bju'tɪʃən] *s* Kosmetiker –in *mf*; (*hairdresser*) Friseuse *f*

beautiful ['bjutɪfəl] *adj* schön

beauti·fy ['bjutɪ ˌfaɪ] *v* (*pret* & *pp* –fied) *tr* verschönern

beauty ['bjutɪ] *s* (*quality; woman*) Schönheit *f*; (coll) Prachtexemplar *n*

beau'ty queen' *s* Schönheitskönigin *f*

beau'ty shop' *s* Frisiersalon *m*

beau'ty sleep' *s* Schönheitsschlaf *m*

beau'ty spot' *s* Schönheitsmal *n*

beaver ['bivər] *s* Biber *m*

because [bɪ'kɔz] *conj* weil, da ‖ *interj* darum!

because' of' *prep* wegen (*genit*)

beck [bek] *s* Wink *m*; be at s.o.'s b. and call j–m ganz zu Diensten sein

beckon ['bekən] *tr* zuwinken (*dat*); (*summon*) heranwinken ‖ *intr* winken; b. to s.o. j–m zuwinken

become [bɪ'kʌm] *v* (*pret* –came; *pp* –come) *tr* (*said of clothes*) gut anstehen (*dat*); (*said of conduct*) sich schicken für ‖ *intr* werden; what has b. of him? was ist aus ihm geworden?

becom'ing *adj* (*said of clothes*) kleidsam; (*said of conduct*) schicklich

bed [bed] *s* (*for sleeping; of a river*) Bett *n*; (*of flowers*) Beet *n*; (*of straw*) Lager *n*; (geol) Lager *n*; (rr) Unterbau *m*; put to bed zu Bett bringen

bed'bug' *s* Wanze *f*

bed'clothes' *spl* Bettwäsche *f*

bed'ding *s* Bettzeug *n*; (*for animals*) Streu *f*

bed'fel'low *s*—strange bedfellows ein seltsames Paar *n*

bedlam ['bedləm] *s* (fig) Tollhaus *n*; there was b. es ging zu wie im Tollhaus

bed' lin'en *s* Bettwäsche *f*

bed'pan' *s* Bettschüssel *f*

bed'post' *s* Bettpfosten *m*

bedraggled [bɪ'drægəld] *adj* beschmutzt

bedridden ['bed ˌrɪdən] *adj* bettlägerig

bed'rock' *s* Grundgestein *n*; (fig) Grundlage *f*

bed'room' *s* Schlafzimmer *n*

bed'side' *s*—at s.o.'s b. an j–s Bett

bed'sore' *s* wundgelegene Stelle *f*; get bedsores sich wundliegen

bed'spread' *s* Bettdecke *f*, Tagesdecke *f*

bed'spring' *s* (*one coil*) Sprungfeder *f*; (*framework of springs*) Sprungfedermatratze *f*

bed'stead' *s* Bettgestell *n*

bed'time' *s* Schlafenszeit *f*; it's past b. es ist höchste Zeit, zu Bett zu gehen

bee [bi] *s* Biene *f*

beech [bitʃ] *s* Buche *f*

beech'nut' *s* Buchecker *f*

beef [bif] *s* Rindfleisch *n*; (*brawn*) (coll) Muskelkraft *f*; (*human flesh*) (coll) Fleisch *n*; (*complaint*) (sl) Gemecker *n* ‖ *tr*—b. up (coll) verstärken || *intr (complain)* (sl) meckern

beef' broth' *s* Kraftbrühe *f*

beef'steak' *s* Beefsteak *n*

beefy ['bifi] *adj* muskulös

bee'hive' *s* Bienenstock *m*, Bienenkorb *m*

bee'line' *s*—**make a b. for** schnurstracks losgehen auf *(acc)*

beer [bɪr] *s* Bier *n*

bee' sting' *s* Bienenstich *m*

beeswax ['biz‚wæks] *s* Bienenwachs *n*

beet [bit] *s* Rübe *f*

beetle ['bitəl] *s* Käfer *m*

be·fall [bɪ'fɔl] *v (pret* –**fell** ['fel]; *pp* –**fallen** ['fɔlən]) *tr* betreffen, zustoßen || *intr* sich ereignen

befit'ting *adj* passend

before [bɪ'for] *adv* vorher, früher || *prep (position or time)* vor *(dat)*; *(direction)* vor *(acc)*; **b. long** binnen kurzem; **b. now** schon früher || *conj* bevor, ehe

before'hand' *adv* zuvor, vorher

befriend [bɪ'frɛnd] *tr* sich *[dat]* *(j–n)* zum Freund machen, sich anfreunden mit

befuddle [bɪ'fʌdəl] *tr* verwirren

beg [beg] *v (pret & pp* begged; *ger* begging) *tr* bitten um; *(a meal)* betteln um; **beg s.o. to** *(inf)* j–n bitten zu *(inf)*; **I beg your pardon** (ich bitte um) Verzeihung! || *intr* betteln; *(said of a dog)* Männchen machen; **beg for** bitten um, flehen um; **beg off** absagen

be·get [bɪ'gɛt] *v (pret* –**got** ['gɑt]; *pp* –**gotten** & –**got**; *ger* –**getting**) *tr* erzeugen

beggar ['begər] *s* Bettler –in *mf*

be·gin [bɪ'gɪn] *v (pret* –**gan** ['gæn]; *pp* –**gun** ['gʌn]; *ger* –**ginning** ['gɪnɪŋ]) *tr* beginnen, anfangen || *intr* beginnen, anfangen; **to b. with** zunächst

beginner [bɪ'gɪnər] *s* Anfänger –in *mf*

begin'ning *s* Beginn *m*, Anfang *m*

begrudge [bɪ'grʌdʒ] *tr*—**b. s.o. s.th.** j–m etw mißgönnen

beguile [bɪ'gaɪl] *tr (mislead)* verleiten; *(charm)* betören

behalf [bɪ'hæf] *s*—**on b. of** zugunsten *(genit)*, für; *(as a representative of)* im Namen *(genit)*, im Auftrag von

behave [bɪ'hev] *intr* sich benehmen

behavior [bɪ'hevjər] *s* Benehmen *n*

behead [bɪ'hɛd] *tr* enthaupten

behind [bɪ'haɪnd] *adj (in arrears)* (in) im Rückstand (mit); **the clock is ten minutes b.** die Uhr geht zehn Minuten nach || *adv (in the rear)* hinten, hinterher; *(to the rear)* nach hinten, zurück; **from b.** von hinten || *s* (sl) Hintern *m*, Popo *m* || *prep (position)* hinter *(dat)*; *(direction)* hinter *(acc)*; **be b. schedule** sich verspäten; **b. time** zu spät sein; **b. the times** hinter dem Mond

be·hold [bɪ'hold] *v (pret & pp* –**held** ['hɛld]) *tr* betrachten || *interj* schau!

behoove [bɪ'huv] *impers*—**it behooves me** es geziemt mir

beige [beʒ] *adj* beige || *s* Beige *n*

be'ing *adj*—**for the time b.** einstweilen

|| *s* Dasein *n*; *(creature)* Wesen *n*; **come into b.** entstehen

belabor [bɪ'lebər] *tr* herumreiten auf *(dat)*

belated [bɪ'letɪd] *adj* verspätet

belch [bɛltʃ] *s* Rülpser *m* || *tr (fire)* ausspeien || *intr* rülpsen

beleaguer [bɪ'ligər] *tr* belagern

belfry ['bɛlfri] *s* Glockenturm *m*

Belgian ['bɛlʒən] *adj* belgisch || *s* Belgier –in *mf*

Belgium ['bɛldʒəm] *s* Belgien *n*

belief [bɪ'lif] *s* (in) Glaube(n) *m* (an *acc*)

believable [bɪ'livəbəl] *adj* glaublich

believe [bɪ'liv] *tr (a thing)* glauben; *(a person)* glauben *(dat)* || *intr* glauben; **b. in** glauben an *(acc)*; **I don't b. in war** ich halte nicht viel vom Kriege

believer [bɪ'livər] *s* Gläubige *mf*

belittle [bɪ'lɪtəl] *tr* herabsetzen

bell [bɛl] *s* Glocke *f*; *(small bell)* Klingel *f*; *(of a wind instrument)* Schalltrichter *m*; *(box)* Gong *m*

bell'boy' *s* Hotelpage *m*

bell'hop' *s* (sl) Hotelpage *m*

belligerent [bə'lɪdʒərənt] *adj* streitlustig || *s* kriegführender Staat *m*

bell' jar' *s* Glasglocke *f*

bellow ['bɛlo] *s* Gebrüll *n*; **bellows** Blasebalg *m*; *(phot)* Balgen *m* || *tr & intr* brüllen

bell' tow'er *s* Glockenturm *m*

bel·ly ['bɛli] *s* Bauch *m*; *(of a sail)* Bausch *m* || *v (pret & pp* –**lied**) *intr* bauschen

bel'lyache' *s* (coll) Bauchweh *n* || *intr* (sl) jammern

bel'ly but'ton *s* Nabel *m*

bel'ly danc'er *s* Bauchtänzerin *f*

bel'ly flop' *s* Bauchklatscher *m*

bellyful ['bɛlɪ‚ful] *s*—**have a b. of** die Nase voll haben von

bel'ly-land'ing *s* Bauchlandung *f*

belong [bɪ'lɔŋ] *intr* **b. to** *(designating ownership)* gehören *(dat)*; *(designating membership)* gehören zu; **where does this table b.?** wohin gehört dieser Tisch?

belongings [bɪ'lɔŋɪŋz] *spl* Sachen *pl*

beloved [bɪ'lʌvɪd], [bɪ'lʌvd] *adj* geliebt || *s* Geliebte *mf*

below [bɪ'lo] *adv (position)* unten; *(direction)* nach unten, hinunter || *prep (position)* unter *(dat)*, unterhalb *(genit)*; *(direction)* unter *(acc)*

belt [bɛlt] *s* Riemen *m*, Gurt *m*, Gürtel *m*; *(geol)* Gebiet *n*; *(mach)* Treibriemen *m*; **tighten one's b.** den Riemen enger schnallen || *tr* (sl) e–n heftigen Schlag versetzen *(dat)*

belt' buck'le *s* Gürtelschnalle *f*

belt'way' *s* Verkehrsgürtel *m*

bemoan [bɪ'mon] *tr* betrauern, beklagen

bench [bɛntʃ] *s* Bank *f*; *(jur)* Gerichtshof *m*; *(sport)* Reservebank *f*, Bank *f*

bend [bɛnd] *s* Biegung *f*; *(in a road)* Kurve *f*; **bends** (pathol) Tauchkrankheit *f* || *v (pret & pp* bent [bɛnt]) *tr* biegen, beugen; *(a bow)* spannen ||

intr sich biegen, sich beugen; **b. down** sich bücken; **b. over backwards** (fig) sich [*dat*] übergroße Mühe geben

beneath [bɪ'niːθ] *adv* unten ‖ *prep* (*position*) unter (*dat*), unterhalb (*genit*); (*direction*) unter (*acc*); **b. me** unter meiner Würde

benediction [ˌbenɪ'dɪkʃən] *s* Segen *m*

benefactor ['benɪˌfæktər] *s* Wohltäter –in *mf*

beneficence [bɪ'nefɪsəns] *s* Wohltätigkeit *f*

beneficent [bɪ'nefɪsənt] *adj* wohltätig

beneficial [ˌbenɪ'fɪʃəl] *adj* heilbringend, gesund; **(to)** nützlich (*dat*)

beneficiary [ˌbenɪ'fɪʃərɪ] *s* Begünstigte *mf*; (ins) Bezugsberechtigte *mf*

benefit ['benɪfɪt] *s* Nutzen *m*; (*fundraising performance*) Benefiz *n*; (ins) Versicherungsleistung *f*

benevolence [bɪ'nevələns] *s* Wohlwollen *n*

benevolent [bɪ'nevələnt] *adj* wohlwollend

benign [bɪ'naɪn] *adj* gütig; (pathol) gutartig

bent [bent] *adj* krumm, verbogen; **b. on** versessen auf (*acc*) ‖ *s* Hang *m*

benzene ['benˈziːn] *s* Benzol *n*

bequeath [bɪ'kwiːð] *tr* vermachen

bequest [bɪ'kwest] *s* Vermächtnis *n*

berate [bɪ'reɪt] *tr* ausschelten, rügen

be·reave [bɪ'riːv] *v* (*pret & pp* **-reaved & -reft** ['reft]) *tr* (**of**) berauben (*genit*)

bereavement [bɪ'riːvmənt] *s* Trauerfall *m*

beret [bə'reɪ] *s* Baskenmütze *f*

Berlin [bər'lɪn] *s* Berliner, berlinerisch ‖ *s* Berlin *n*

Berliner [bər'lɪnər] *s* Berliner –in *mf*

berry ['berɪ] *s* Beere *f*

berserk [bʌr'sʌrk] *adj* wütend ‖ *adv*—**go b.** wütend werden

berth [bʌrθ] *s* Schlafkoje *f*; (naut) Liegeplatz *m*; (rr) Bett *n*; **give s.o. wide b.** um j–n e–n weiten Bogen machen ‖ *tr* am Kai festmachen

be·seech [bɪ'siːt∫] *v* (*pret & pp* **-sought** ['sɔt] **& -seeched**) *tr* anflehen

be·set [bɪ'set] *v* (*pret & pp* **-set**; *ger* **-setting**) *tr* bedrängen, umringen

beside [bɪ'saɪd] *prep* (*position*) neben (*dat*), bei (*dat*); (*direction*) neben (*acc*); **be b. oneself with** außer sich [*dat*] sein vor (*dat*)

besides [bɪ'saɪdz] *adv* überdies, außerdem ‖ *prep* außer (*dat*)

besiege [bɪ'siːdʒ] *tr* belagern

besmirch [bɪ'smʌrt∫] *tr* beschmutzen

be·speak [bɪ'spiːk] *v* (*pret* **-spoke** ['spok]; *pp* **-spoken** ['spokən]) *tr* bezeigen

best [best] *adj* beste; **b. of all, very b.** allerbeste ‖ *adv* am besten; **had b. es wäre am besten, wenn** ‖ *s*—**at b.** bestenfalls; **be at one's b.** in bester Form sein; **for the b.** zum Besten; **make the b. of** sich abfinden mit; **to the b. of one's ability** nach bestem Vermögen

bestial ['best∫əl] *adj* bestialisch

best′ man′ *s* Brautführer *m*

bestow [bɪ'sto] *tr* verleihen

bestowal [bɪ'sto·əl] *s* Verleihung *f*

best′ sel′ler *s* (book) Bestseller *m*

bet [bet] *s* Wette *f*; **make a bet** e–e Wette abschließen (or eingehen) ‖ *v* (*pret & pp* **bet & betted**; *ger* **betting**) *tr* (**on**) wetten (auf *acc*) ‖ *intr* wetten; **you bet!** aber sicher!

betray [bɪ'tre] *tr* verraten; (*a secret*) preisgeben; (*ignorance*) offenbaren; (*a trust*) mißbrauchen

betrayal [bɪ'tre·əl] *s* Verrat *m*

betrayer [bɪ'tre·ər] *s* Verräter –in *mf*

better ['betər] *adj* besser; **the b. part of** der größere Teil (*genit*) ‖ *s*—**change for the b.** sich zum Besseren wenden; **get the b. of** übervorteilen; **one's betters** die Höherstehenden *pl*; ‖ *adv* besser; **all the b.** um so besser; **so much the b.** desto besser; **you had b. do it at once** am besten tust du es sofort; **you had b. not** das will ich dir nicht geraten haben ‖ *tr* verbessern; **b. oneself** sich verbessern

bet′ter half′ *s* (coll) bessere Hälfte *f*

betterment ['betərmənt] *s* Besserung *f*

bettor ['betər] *s* Wettende *mf*

between [bɪ'twin] *adv*—**in b.** dazwischen ‖ *prep* (*position*) zwischen (*dat*); (*direction*) zwischen (*acc*); **just b. you and me** ganz unter uns gesagt

bev·el ['bevəl] *adj* schräg ‖ *s* schräge Kante *f* ‖ *v* (*pret & pp* **-el(l)ed**; *ger* **-el(l)ing**) *tr* abschrägen

beverage ['bevərɪdʒ] *s* Getränk *n*

bevy ['bevɪ] *s* Schar *f*

bewail [bɪ'wel] *tr* beklagen

beware [bɪ'wer] *intr* sich hüten; **b.! gib acht!; b. of** sich hüten vor (*dat*); **b. of imitations** vor Nachahmungen wird gewarnt

bewilder [bɪ'wɪldər] *tr* verblüffen

bewilderment [bɪ'wɪldərmənt] *s* Verblüffung *f*

bewitch [bɪ'wɪt∫] *tr* (fig) bezaubern

beyond [bɪ'jɑnd] *adv* jenseits ‖ *s*—**the b.** das Jenseits ‖ *prep* jenseits (*genit*), über (*acc*) hinaus; (fig) über (*acc*), außer (*dat*); **he is b. help** ihm ist nicht mehr zu helfen; **that's b. me** das geht über meinen Verstand

B′-girl′ *s* (coll) Animiermädchen *n*

bias ['baɪ·əs] *s* Voreingenommenheit *f* ‖ *tr* (**against**) einnehmen (gegen)

bi′ased *adj* voreingenommen

bib [brb] *s* Latz *m*, Lätzchen *n*

Bible ['baɪbəl] *s* Bibel *f*

Biblical ['brbɪkəl] *adj* biblisch

bibliographer [ˌbrblɪ'ɑɡrəfər] *s* Bibliograph –in *mf*

bibliography [ˌbrblɪ'ɑɡrəfɪ] *s* Bücherverzeichnis *n*; (science) Bücherkunde *f*

bi·ceps ['baɪseps] *s* (**-cepses** [sepsɪz] **& -ceps**) Bizeps *m*

bicker ['brkər] *intr* (sich) zanken

bick′ering *s* Gezänk *n*

bicuspid [baɪ'kʌspɪd] *s* kleiner Backenzahn *m*

bicycle ['baɪsɪkəl] s Fahrrad n
bid [bɪd] s Angebot n; (cards) Meldung f; (com) Kostenvoranschlag m || v (pret **bade** [bæd] & **bid**; pp **bidden** ['bɪdən]) tr (ask) heißen; (at auction) bieten; (cards) melden, reizen || intr (cards) reizen; (com) ein Preisangebot machen; **bid for** sich bewerben um
bidder ['bɪdər] s (at an auction) Bieter –in mf; **highest b.** Meistbietende m
bid'ding s (at an auction) Bieten n; (request) Geheiß n; (cards) Reizen n
bide [baɪd] tr—b. one's time seine Gelegenheit abwarten
biennial [baɪ'ɛnɪəl] adj zweijährig
bier [bɪr] s Totenbahre f
bifocals [baɪ'fokəlz] spl Zweistärkenbrille f
big [bɪg] adj (bigger; biggest) groß
bigamist ['bɪgəmɪst] s Bigamist m
bigamous ['bɪgəməs] adj bigamisch
bigamy ['bɪgəmi] s Bigamie f
big'-boned' adj starkknochig
Big' Dip'per s Großer Bär m
big' game' s Hochwild n
big'-heart'ed adj großherzig
big'mouth' s (sl) Großmaul n
bigot ['bɪgət] s Fanatiker –in mf
bigoted ['bɪgətɪd] adj bigott, fanatisch
bigotry ['bɪgətri] s Bigotterie f
big' shot' s (coll) hohes Tier n, Bonze m
big'-time' adj groß, erstklassig; **b. operator** Großschieber –in mf
big' toe' s große Zehe f
big' top' s (coll) großes Zirkuszelt n
big' wheel' s (coll) hohes Tier n
big' wig' s (coll) Bonze m
bike [baɪk] s (coll) Rad n
bikini [bɪ'kini] s Bikini m
bilateral [baɪ'lætərəl] adj beiderseitig verbindlich
bile [baɪl] s Galle f
bilge [bɪldʒ] s Bilge f, Kielraum m
bilge' wat'er s Bilgenwasser n
bilingual [baɪ'lɪŋgwəl] adj zweisprachig
bilk [bɪlk] tr (out of) prellen (um)
bill [bɪl] s Rechnung f; (paper money) Geldschein m, Schein m; (of a bird) Schnabel m; (parl) Gesetzesvorlage f; **pass a b.** ein Gesetz verabschieden || tr in Rechnung stellen
bill'board' s Anschlagtafel f
bill' collec'tor s Einkassierer –in mf
billet ['bɪlɪt] s (mil) Quartier n || tr (mil) einquartieren, unterbringen
bill'fold' s Brieftasche f
bil'liard ball' s Billardkugel f
billiards ['bɪljərdz] s Billard n
bil'liard ta'ble s Billardtisch m
billion ['bɪljən] s Milliarde f; (Brit) Billion f (million million)
bill' of exchange' s Tratte f, Wechsel m
bill' of fare' s Speisekarte f
bill' of health' s Gesundheitszeugnis n; **he gave me a clean b.** (fig) er hat für einwandfrei befunden
bill' of lad'ing ['leɪdɪŋ] s Frachtbrief m

bill' of rights' s erste zehn Zusatzartikel pl zur Verfassung (der U.S.A.)
bill' of sale' s Kaufurkunde f
billow ['bɪlo] s Woge f || intr wogen
bil'ly club' ['bɪli] s Polizeiknüppel m
bil'ly goat' s (coll) Ziegenbock m
bind [baɪnd] s—**in a b.** in der Klemme || v (pret & pp **bound** [baʊnd]) tr binden; (obligate) verpflichten; (bb) einbinden
binder ['baɪndər] s Binder –in mf; (e.g., cement) Bindemittel n; (for loose papers) Aktendeckel m; (mach) Garbenbinder m
bindery ['baɪndəri] s Buchbinderei f
bind'ing adj (on) verbindlich (für) || s Binden n; (for skis) Bindung f; (bb) Einband m
binge [bɪndʒ] s (sl) Zechtour f; **go on a b.** (sl) e-e Zechtour machen
binoculars [bɪ'nɑkjələrz] spl Fernglas n
biochemistry [,baɪ·ə'kɛmɪstri] s Biochemie f
biographer [baɪ'ɑgrəfər] s Biograph –in mf
biographic(al) [,baɪ·ə'græfɪk(əl)] adj biographisch
biography [baɪ'ɑgrəfi] s Biographie f
biologic(al) [,baɪ·ə'lɑdʒɪk(əl)] adj biologisch
biologist [baɪ'ɑlədʒɪst] s Biologe m, Biologin f
biology [baɪ'ɑlədʒi] s Biologie f
biophysics [,baɪ·ə'fɪzɪks] s Biophysik f
biopsy ['baɪ·apsi] s Biopsie f
bipartisan [baɪ'partɪzən] adj Zweiparteien-
biped ['baɪped] s Zweifüßer m
bird [bɪrd] s Vogel m; **for the birds** für die Katz; **kill two birds with one stone** zwei Fliegen mit e-r Klappe schlagen
bird'cage' s Bauer n, Vogelkäfig m
bird' call' s Vogelruf m, Lockpfeife f
bird' dog' s Hühnerhund m
bird' of prey' s Raubvogel m
bird'seed' s Vogelfutter n
bird's'-eye view' s Vogelperspektive f
birth [bʌrθ] s Geburt f; (origin) Herkunft f; **give b. to** gebären
birth' certi'ficate s Geburtsurkunde f
birth' control' s Geburtenbeschränkung f
birth'day' s Geburtstag m
birth'day cake' s Geburtstagskuchen m
birth'day par'ty s Geburtstagsfeier f
birth'day pres'ent s Geburtstagsgeschenk n
birth'day suit' s (hum) Adamskostüm n
birth'mark' s Muttermal n
birth'place' s Geburtsort m
birth' rate' s Geburtenziffer f
birth'right' s Geburtsrecht n
biscuit ['bɪskɪt] s Keks m
bisect [baɪ'sɛkt] tr halbieren || intr sich teilen
bishop ['bɪ/əp] s Bischof m; (chess) Läufer m
bison ['baɪsən] s Bison m
bit [bɪt] s Bißchen n; (of food) Stück-

chen n; (of time) Augenblick m;
(part of a bridle) Gebiß n; (drill)
Bohrer m; a bit (somewhat) ein wenig; a little bit ein klein wenig; bit
by bit brockenweise: bits and pieces
Brocken pl; every bit as ganz genauso

bitch [brtʃ] s Hündin f; (vulg) Weibsbild n

bite [baɪt] s Biß m; (wound) Biß-
wunde f; (of an insect) Stich m; (of
a snake) Biß m; (snack) Imbiß m;
(fig) Bissigkeit f; **I have a b.** (in fishing) es beißt e-r an ‖ v (pret bit
[bɪt]; pp bit & bitten ['bɪtən]) tr
beißen; (said of insects) stechen;
(said of snakes) beißen; **b. one's
nails** an den Nägeln kauen ‖ intr
beißen; (said of fish) anbeißen; (said
of the wind) schneiden; **b. into** anbeißen

bit'ing adj (remark) bissig; (cold,
wind) schneidend

bit' part' s kleine Rolle f

bitter ['bɪtər] adj (& fig) bitter; (Person, Blick) bitterböse

bitterly ['bɪtərli] adv bitterlich

bitterness ['bɪtərnɪs] s Bitterkeit f

bitters ['bɪtərz] spl Magenbitter m

bitu'minous coal' [bɪ't(j)umɪnəs] s
Fettkohle f

bivouac ['bɪvwæk] s Biwak n ‖ intr
biwakieren

bizarre [bɪ'zar] adj bizarr

blab [blæb] v (pret & pp blabbed; ger
blabbing) tr ausplaudern ‖ intr plaudern

blabber ['blæbər] intr schwatzen

blab'bermouth' s Schwatzmaul n

black [blæk] adj schwarz ‖ s Schwarz
n; (black person) Neger –in mf,
Schwarze mf ‖ tr schwärzen; **b. out**
(mil) verdunkeln ‖ intr—**b. out** die
Besinnung verlieren

black'-and-blue' adj blau unterlaufen;
beat s.o. b. j-n grün und blau
schlagen

black' and white' s—**in b.** schwarz auf
weiß, schriftlich

black'-and-white' adj schwarzweiß

black'ball' tr (ostracize) ausschließen;
(vote against) stimmen gegen

black'ber'ry s Brombeere f

black'berry bush' s Brombeerstrauch m

black'bird' s Amsel f

black'board' s Tafel f, Wandtafel f

blacken ['blækən] tr schwärzen; (a
name) anschwärzen

black' eye' s blaues Auge n; **give s.o.
a b.** (fig) j-m Schaden zufügen

black'head' s Mitesser m

blackish ['blækɪʃ] adj schwärzlich

black'jack' s (club) Totschläger m;
(cards) Siebzehnundvier n ‖ tr nie-
derknüppeln

black'list' s schwarze Liste f ‖ tr auf
die schwarze Liste setzen

black' mag'ic s schwarze Kunst f

black'mail' s Erpressung f ‖ tr erpressen

blackmailer ['blæk,melər] s Erpresser
–in mf

black' mar'ket s Schwarzmarkt m

black' marketeer' s Schwarzhändler
–in mf

black'out' s (fainting) Bewußtlosigkeit
f; (of memory) kurze Gedächtnis-
störung f; (of news) Nachrichten-
sperre f; (mil) Verdunkelung f; (telv)
Sperre f; (theat) Auslöschen n aller
Rampenlichter

black' sheep' s (fig) schwarzes Schaf n

black'smith' s Grobschmied m; (person
who shoes horses) Hufschmied m

bladder ['blædər] s Blase f

blade [bled] s (of a sword, knife) Klinge f; (of grass) Halm m; (of a saw,
ax, shovel, oar) Blatt n; (of a propeller) Flügel m

blame [blem] s Schuld f ‖ tr die
Schuld geben (dat); **b. s.o. for** j-m
Vorwürfe machen wegen; **I don't b.
you for laughing** ich nehme es Ihnen
nicht übel, daß Sie lachen

blameless ['blemlɪs] adj schuldlos

blame'wor'thy adj tadelnswert, schuldig

blanch [blæntʃ] tr erbleichen lassen;
(celery) bleichen; (almonds) blan-
chieren ‖ intr erbleichen

bland [blænd] adj sanft, mild

blandish ['blændɪʃ] tr schmeicheln
(dat)

blank [blæŋk] adj (cartridge) blind;
(piece of paper, space, expression)
leer; (form) unausgefüllt; (tape) un-
bespielt; (nonplussed) verblüfft; **my
mind went b.** ich konnte mich an
nichts erinnern ‖ s (cartridge) Platz-
patrone f; (unwritten space) leere
Stelle f; (form) Formular n; (unfinished piece of metal) Rohling m
‖ tr (sport) auf Null halten

blank' check' s Blankoscheck m

blanket ['blæŋkɪt] adj generell, umfassend ‖ s Decke f

blank' verse' s Blankvers m

blare [bler] s Lärm m; (of trumpets)
Geschmetter n ‖ intr schmettern;
(aut) laut hupen

blasé [bla'ze] adj blasiert; **b. attitude**
Blasiertheit f

blaspheme [blæs'fim] tr & intr lästern

blasphemous ['blæsfɪməs] adj lästerlich

blasphemy ['blæsfɪmi] s Lästerung f

blast [blæst] s (of an explosion) Luft-
druck m; (of a horn, trumpet, air)
Stoß m; (of air) Luftzug m; **at full b.**
(fig) auf höchsten Touren ‖ tr (e.g.,
a tunnel) sprengen; (ruin) (fig) verderben; (criticize) wettern gegen;
(blight) versengen; **b. it!** verdammt!
‖ intr—**b. off** (rok) starten

blast' fur'nace s Hochofen m

blast'-off' s (rok) Start m

blatant ['bletənt] adj (lie, infraction)
eklatant; (nonsense) schreiend

blaze [blez] s Brand m; **b. of color**
Farbenpracht f; **b. of glory** Ruhmes-
glanz m; **b. of light** Lichterglanz m;
go to blazes! (sl) geh zum Teufel!;
like blazes wie verrückt ‖ tr—**b. a
trail** e-n Weg markieren; (fig) e-n
Weg bahnen ‖ intr lodern; **b. away
at** drauflosschießen auf (acc)

blazer ['bleɪzər] s Sportjacke f

blaz'ing adj (sun) prall

bleach [bliːtʃ] s Bleichmittel n || tr bleichen; (hair) blondieren || intr bleichen

bleachers ['bliːtʃərs] spl Zuschauersitze pl im Freien

bleak [bliːk] adj öde, trostlos

bleary-eyed ['blɪrɪ,aɪd] adj triefäugig

bleat [bliːt] s Blöken n || intr blöken; (said of a goat) meckern

bleed [bliːd] v (pret & pp bled [bled]) tr (brakes) entlüften; (med) zur Ader lassen; b. white (fig) zum Weißbluten bringen || intr bluten; b. to death verbluten

blemish ['blemɪʃ] s Fleck m, Makel m; (fig) Schandfleck m

blend [blend] s Mischung f; (liquor) Verschnitt m || v (pret & pp blended & blent [blent]) tr mischen; (wine, liquor) verschneiden || intr sich vermischen; (said of colors) zueinander passen, zusammenpassen

bless [bles] tr segnen; God b. you! (after a sneeze) Gesundheit!

blessed ['blesɪd] adj selig

bless'ing s Segen m, Gnade f; b. in disguise Glück n im Unglück

blight [blaɪt] s (fig) Gifthauch m; (agr) Brand m, Mehltau m || tr (fig) verderben; (agr) schädigen

blight'ed adj brandig

blimp [blɪmp] s unstarres Luftschiff n

blind [blaɪnd] adj blind; (curve) unübersichtlich; go b. erblinden || s Jalousie f; (hunt) Attrappe f || tr blenden; (fig) verblenden

blind' al'ley s (& fig) Sackgasse f

blind' date' s Verabredung f mit e-r (or e-m) Unbekannten

blinder ['blaɪndər] s Scheuklappe f

blind' fly'ing s Blindflug m

blind'fold' adj mit verbundenen Augen || adv blindlings || tr die Augen verbinden (dat)

blind' man' s Blinder m

blind'man's' bluff' s Blindekuhspiel n

blindness ['blaɪndnɪs] s Blindheit f

blink [blɪŋk] s Blinken n; (with the eyes) Blinzeln n; on the b. (sl) kaputt || tr—b. one's eyes mit den Augen zwinkern || intr (said of a light) blinken; (said of the eyes) blinzeln

blinker ['blɪŋkər] s (for horses) Scheuklappe f; (aut) Blinker m

blip [blɪp] s (radar) Leuchtfleck m

bliss [blɪs] s Wonne f

blissful ['blɪsfəl] adj glückselig

blister ['blɪstər] s Blase f; (from a burn) Brandblase f || intr (said of the skin) Blasen ziehen; (said of paint) Blasen werfen

blithe [blaɪð] adj fröhlich

blitzkrieg ['blɪts,kriːg] s Blitzkrieg m

blizzard ['blɪzərd] s Blizzard m

bloat [bloːt] tr aufblähen || intr anschwellen

bloc [blɑk] s (parl) Stimmblock m; (pol) Block m

block [blɑk] s (of wood) Klotz m; (toy) Bauklotz m; (for chopping) Hackklotz m; (of houses) Häuser-

block m; (of seats) Reihe f; (mach) Rolle f; (sport) Block m; five blocks from here fünf Straßen weiter || tr versperren; (traffic, a street, a player) blockieren; (a ball) abfangen; (a hat) aufdämpfen; be blocked sich stauen; b. off (a street) absperren; b. up verstopfen, versperren

blockade [blɑ'keːd] s Blockade f, Sperre f || tr blockieren, sperren

blockade' run'ner s Blockadebrecher m

blockage ['blɑkɪdʒ] s Stockung f

block' and tac'kle s Flaschenzug m

block'head' s Klotz m, Dummkopf m

blond [blɑnd] adj blond || s Blonde m

blonde [blɑnd] s Blondine f

blood [blʌd] s Blut n; (lineage) Geblüt n; in cold b. kaltblütig

blood' circula'tion s Blutkreislauf m

blood' clot' s Blutgerinnsel n

bloodcurdling ['blʌd,kʌrdlɪŋ] adj haarsträubend

blood' do'nor s Blutspender –in mf

blood'hound' s (& fig) Bluthund m

bloodless ['blʌdlɪs] adj blutlos; (revolution) unblutig

blood' poi'soning s Blutvergiftung f

blood' pres'sure s Blutdruck m

blood' rela'tion s Blutsverwandte mf

blood'shed' s Blutvergießen n

blood'shot' adj blutunterlaufen

blood'stain' s Blutfleck m, Blutspur f

blood'stained' adj blutbefleckt

blood'stream' s Blutstrom m

blood'suck'er s (& fig) Blutsauger m

blood' test' s Blutprobe f

blood'thirst'y adj blutdürstig

blood' transfu'sion s Blutübertragung f

blood' type' s Blutgruppe f

blood' ves'sel s Blutgefäß n

blood-y ['blʌdɪ] adj blutig; (bloodstained) blutbefleckt || v (pret & pp –ied) tr mit Blut beflecken

bloom [bluːm] s Blüte f || intr blühen

blossom ['blɑsəm] s Blüte f || intr blühen

blot [blɑt] s Fleck m; (fig) Schandfleck m || v (pret & pp blotted) ger blotting) tr (smear) beschmieren; (with a blotter) (ab)löschen; b. out ausstreichen; (fig) auslöschen || intr (said of ink) klecksen

blotch [blɑtʃ] s Klecks m; (on the skin) Ausschlag m

blotter ['blɑtər] s Löscher m

blot'ting pa'per s Löschpapier n

blouse [blaus] s Bluse f

blow [bloː] s Schlag m, Hieb m; (fig) Schlag m; come to blows handgemein werden || v (pret blew [bluː]; pp blown) tr blasen; (money) (sl) verschwenden; (a fuse) durchbrennen; b. a whistle pfeifen; b. off steam sich austoben; b. one's top (coll) hochgehen; b. out (a candle) ausblasen; b. up (inflate) aufblasen; (with explosives) sprengen; (phot) vergrößern || intr blasen; b. out (said of a candle) auslöschen; (said of a tire) platzen; blow over vorüberziehen; b. up (& fig) in die Luft gehen

blower ['bloːər] s Gebläse n, Bläser m

blow'out' s (sl) Gelage n; (aut) Reifen-panne f
blow'pipe' s Blasrohr n
blow'torch' s Lötlampe f
blubber ['blʌbər] s Tran m || intr (cry noisily) jaulen
bludgeon ['blʌdʒən] s Knüppel m || tr mit dem Knüppel bearbeiten
blue [blu] adj blau; (fig) bedrückt || s Blau n; blues (mus) Blues m; have the blues trüb gestimmt sein; out of the b. aus heiterem Himmel
blue'ber'ry s Heidelbeere f
blue'bird' s Blaukehlchen n
blue' chip' s (cards) blaue Spielmarke f; (fin) sicheres Wertpapier n
blue'-col'lar work'er s Arbeiter m
blue' jeans' spl Jeans pl
blue' moon' s—once in a b. alle Jubel-jahre einmal
blue'print' s Blaupause f
blue' streak' s—talk a b. (coll) in e-r Tour reden
bluff [blʌf] adj schroff; (person) derb || s (coll) Bluff m; (geol) Steilküste f; call s.o.'s b. j–m beim Wort neh-men || tr & intr bluffen
bluffer ['blʌfər] s Bluffer m
blu'ing s Waschblau n
bluish ['blu·ɪʃ] adj bläulich
blunder ['blʌndər] s Schnitzer m; || intr e–n Schnitzer machen; b. into stolpern in (acc); b. upon zufällig geraten auf (acc)
blunt [blʌnt] adj stumpf; (fig) plump, unverblümt || tr abstumpfen
bluntly ['blʌntli] adv unverblümt
blur [blʌr] s Verschwommenheit f || v (pret & pp blurred; ger blurring) tr verwischen || intr verschwommen werden
blurb [blʌrb] s Reklametext m
blurred adj verschwommen; (vision) unscharf
blurt [blʌrt] tr—b. out herausplatzen
blush [blʌʃ] s Röte f, Schamröte f || intr (at) erröten (über acc)
bluster ['blʌstər] s Prahlerei f || intr (said of a person) prahlen, poltern; (said of wind) toben
blustery ['blʌstəri] adj stürmisch
boa constrictor ['bo·ə kən'strɪktər] s Abgottschlange f, Königsschlange f
boar [bor] s Eber m; (wild boar) Wild-schwein n
board [bord] s Brett n; (of administra-tors) Ausschuß m, Behörde f, Rat m; (meals) Kost f; (educ) Schultafel f; above b. offen; on b. an Bord || tr (a ship) besteigen; (a plane, train) einsteigen in (acc); (paying guests) beköstigen; b. up mit Brettern ver-nageln || intr (with) in Kost sein (bei)
boarder ['bordər] s Kostgänger –in mf
board'inghouse' s Pension f
board'ing pass' s Bordkarte f
board'ing school' s Internat n
board'ing stu'dent s Interne mf
board' of direc'tors s Verwaltungsrat m, Aufsichtsrat m
board' of educa'tion s Unterrichtsmi-nisterium n

board' of health' s Gesundheitsbehörde f
board' of trade' s Handelskammer f
board' of trustees' s Verwaltungsrat m
board'walk' s Strandpromenade f
boast [bost] s Prahlerei f; (cause of pride) Stolz m || tr sich rühmen (genit) || intr (about) prahlen (mit)
boastful ['bostfəl] adj prahlerisch
boat [bot] s Boot n; in the same b. (fig) in der gleichen Lage
boat'house' s Bootshaus n
boat'ing s Bootsfahrt f; go b. e–e Boot-fahrt machen
boat'race' s Bootrennen n
boat' ride' s Bootsfahrt f
boatswain ['bosən] s Hochbootsmann m
bob [bab] s (jerky motion) Ruck m; (hairdo) Bubikopf m; (of a fishing line) Schwimmer m; (of a plumb line) Senkblei n || v (pret & pp bobbed; ger bobbing) tr (hair) kurz schneiden || intr sich hin und her be-wegen; bob up and down sich auf und ab bewegen
bobbin ['babɪn] s Klöppel m
bobble ['babəl] tr (coll) ungeschickt handhaben
bob'by pin' ['babi] s Haarklammer f
bob'sled' s Bob m, Rennschlitten m
bode [bod] tr bedeuten
bodily ['badɪli] adj leiblich; b. injury Körperverletzung f || adv leibhaftig
body ['badi] s Körper m; (of a person or animal) Körper m; (corpse) Leiche f; (collective group) Körperschaft f; (of a plane, ship) Rumpf m; (of a vehicle) Karosserie f; (of beer, wine) Schwere f; (of a letter) Text m; b. of water Gewässer n; in a b. geschlos-sen
bod'yguard' s Leibgarde f
bod'y o'dor s Körpergeruch m
bog [bag] s Sumpf m || v (pret & pp bogged; ger bogging) intr—bog down steckenbleiben
bogey-man ['bogi‚mæn] s (-men) Kin-derschreck m
bogus ['bogəs] adj schwindelhaft
Bohemia [bo'himi·ə] s Böhmen n
Bohemian [bo'himi·ən] adj böhmisch || s (person) Böhme m, Böhmin f; (fig) Bohemien m; (language) Böh-misch n
boil [bɔɪl] s (pathol) Geschwür n; bring to a b. zum Sieden bringen || tr kochen, sieden || intr kochen, sie-den; b. away verkochen; b. over überkochen
boiled' ham' s gekochter Schinken m
boiled' pota'toes spl Salzkartoffeln pl
boiler ['bɔɪlər] s (electrical water tank) Boiler m; (kettle) Kessel m
boil'ermak'er s Kesselschmied m
boil'er room' s Heizraum m
boil'ing adj siedend || adv—be b. mad vor Zorn kochen; b. hot siedeheiß
boil'ing point' s Siedepunkt m
boisterous ['bɔɪstərəs] adj ausgelassen
bold [bold] adj kühn, gewagt; (out-lines) deutlich
bold'face' s Fettdruck m

boldness ['bəʊldnɪs] *s* Kühnheit *f*

Bolshevik ['bɒlʃəvɪk] *adj* bolschewistisch ‖ *s* Bolschewik –in *mf*

bolster ['bəʊlstər] *s* Nackenrolle *f* ‖ *tr* unterstützen

bolt [bəʊlt] *s* Bolzen *m*; (*door lock*) Riegel *m*; (*of cloth*) Stoffballen *m*; (*of lightning*) Blitzstrahl *m*; **b. out of the blue** Blitz *m* aus heiterem Himmel ‖ *tr* (*a door*) verriegeln; (*a political party*) im Stich lassen; (*food*) hinunterschlingen ‖ *intr* davonstürzen; (*said of a horse*) durchgehen

bomb [bɒm] *s* (*dropped from the air*) Bombe *f*; (*planted*) Sprengladung *f*; (*fiasco*) (sl) Versager *m* ‖ *tr* (*from the air*) bombardieren; (*blow up*) sprengen ‖ *intr* (sl) versagen

bombard [bɒm'bɑrd] *tr* bombardieren, beschießen; (fig) bombardieren

bombardier [ˌbɒmbər'dɪr] *s* Bombenschütze *m*

bombardment [bɒm'bɑrdmənt] *s* Bombardement *n*, Beschießung *f*

bombast ['bɒmbæst] *s* Schwulst *m*

bombastic [bɒm'bæstɪk] *adj* schwülstig

bomb′ bay′ *s* Bombenschacht *m*

bomb′ cra′ter *s* Bombentrichter *m*

bomber ['bɒmər] *s* Bomber *m*

bomb′ ing *s* Bombenabwurf *m*

bomb′ ing run′ *s* Bomben(ziel)anflug *m*

bomb′ proof′ *adj* bombenfest, bombensicher

bomb′ shell′ *s* (& fig) Bombe *f*

bomb′ shel′ ter *s* Bombenkeller *m*

bomb′ sight′ *s* Bombenzielgerät *n*

bomb′ squad′ *s* Entschärfungskommando *n*

bona fide ['bɒnəˌfaɪd] *adj* ehrlich, echt; (*offer*) solide

bonanza [bɒ'nænzə] *s* Goldgrube *f*

bond [bɒnd] *s* Fessel *f*; (fin) Obligation *f*

bondage ['bɒndɪdʒ] *s* Knechtschaft *f*

bond′ hold′ er *s* Inhaber –in *mf* e-r Obligation

bonds′ man ['bɒndzmən] *s* (–men) Bürge *m*

bone [bɒn] *s* Knochen *m*, Bein *n*; (*of fish*) Gräte *f*; **bones** Gebein *n*; (*mortal remains*) Gebeine *pl*; **have a b. to pick with** ein Hühnchen zu rupfen haben mit; **make no bones about it** nicht viel Federlesens machen mit; **to the b.** bis ins Mark ‖ *tr* (*meat*) ausbeinen; (*fish*) ausgräten ‖ *intr*— **b. up for** (sl) büffeln für

bone′ dry′ *adj* knochentrocken

bone′ head′ *s* Dummkopf *m*

boneless ['bɒnlɪs] *adj* ohne Knochen; (*fish*) ohne Gräten

boner ['bɒnər] *s* (coll) Schnitzer *m*; **pull a b.** (coll) e-n Schnitzer machen

bonfire ['bɒnˌfaɪr] *s* Freudenfeuer *n*

bonnet ['bɒnɪt] *s* Haube *f*

bonus ['bɒnəs] *s* Gratifikation *f*

bony ['bɒnɪ] *adj* knochig; (*fish*) grätig

boo [bu] *s* Pfuiruf *m* ‖ *tr* niederbrüllen ‖ *intr* pfui rufen ‖ *interj* (*to jeer*) pfui!; (*to scare someone*) huh!

boob [bub] *s* (sl) Blödkopf *m*

booby ['bubɪ] *s* Blödkopf *m*

boo′ by hatch′ *s* (sl) Affenkasten *m*

boo′ by prize′ *s* Trostpreis *m*

boo′ by trap′ *s* Minenfalle *f*

boogey·man ['bugɪˌmæn], ['bogɪˌmæn] *s* (–men′) Schreckgespenst *n*

book [bʊk] *s* Buch *n*; (*of stamps, tickets, matches*) Heftchen *n*; **keep books** Bücher führen ‖ *tr* buchen; (*e.g., seats*) vorbestellen

book′ bind′ er *s* Buchbinder –in *mf*

book′ bind′ ery *s* Buchbinderei *f*

book′ bind′ ing *s* Buchbinderei *f*

book′ case′ *s* Bücherschrank *m*

book′ end′ *s* Bücherstütze *f*

bookie ['bʊkɪ] *s* (coll) Buchmacher –in *mf*

book′ ing *s* Buchung *f*

bookish ['bʊkɪʃ] *adj* lesefreudig

book′ keep′ er *s* Buchhalter –in *mf*

book′ keep′ ing *s* Buchhaltung *f*

book′ learn′ ing *s* Schulweisheit *f*

booklet ['bʊklɪt] *s* Büchlein *n*

book′ mak′ er *s* Buchmacher –in *mf*

book′ mark′ *s* Lesezeichen *n*

book′ rack′ *s* Büchergestell *n*

book′ review′ *s* Buchbesprechung *f*

book′ sel′ ler *s* Buchhändler –in *mf*

book′ shelf′ *s* (–shelves) Bücherregal *n*

book′ stand′ *s* Bücher(verkaufs)stand *m*

book′ store′ *s* Buchhandlung *f*

book′ worm′ *s* (& fig) Bücherwurm *m*

boom [bum] *s* (*noise*) dumpfes Dröhnen *n*; (*of a crane*) Ausleger *m*; (cin, telv) Galgen *m*; (econ) Boom *m*, Hochkonjunktur *f*; (naut) Baum *m*, Spiere *f*; (st.exch.) Hausse *f* ‖ *intr* dröhnen; (*said of an organ*) brummen

boomerang ['buməˌræŋ] *s* Bumerang *m*

boon [bun] *s* Wohltat *f*, Segen *m*

boon′ compan′ ion *s* Zechkumpan *m*

boor [bʊr] *s* Rüpel *m*, Flegel *m*

boorish ['bʊrɪʃ] *adj* flegelhaft

boost [bust] *s* (*push*) Auftrieb *m*; (*in pay*) Gehaltserhöhung *f* ‖ *tr* fördern; (*prices*) in die Höhe treiben; (elec) verstärken; **b. business** die Wirtschaft ankurbeln

booster ['bustər] *s* (*backer*) Förderer *m*, Förderin *f*

boost′ er rock′ et *s* Hilfsrakete *f*

boost′ er shot′ *s* (med) Nachimpfung *f*

boot [but] *s* Stiefel *m*; (*kick*) Fußtritt *m*; **to b. noch dazu; you can bet your boots on that** (sl) darauf kannst du Gift nehmen ‖ *tr* (sl) stoßen; (fb) kicken; **b. out** (sl) 'rausschmeißen

booth [buθ] *s* (*at a fair*) Marktbude *f*; (*for telephone, voting*) Zelle *f*

boot′ leg′ *adj* geschmuggelt ‖ *v* (*pret* & *pp* –legged; *ger* –legging) *tr* (*make illegally*) illegal brennen; (*smuggle*) schmuggeln

bootlegger ['butˌlegər] *s* Alkoholschmuggler *m*, Bootlegger *m*

bootlicker ['butˌlɪkər] *s* (sl) Kriecher *m*

booty ['butɪ] *s* Beute *f*

booze [buz] *s* (coll) Schnaps *m* ‖ *intr* (coll) saufen

booze′ hound′ *s* Saufbold *m*, Saufaus *m*

border ['bɔrdər] *s* Rand *m*; (*of a country*) Grenze *f*; (*of a dress, etc.*) Saum m, Borte f ‖ tr umranden, begrenzen; be bordered by grenzen an (acc) ‖ intr—b. on (& fig) grenzen an (acc)

bor'derline s Grenzlinie f

bor'derline case' s Grenzfall m

bore [bor] s (drill hole) Bohrloch n; (of a gun) Bohrung f; (of a cylinder) innerer Zylinderdurchmesser m; (fig) langweiliger Mensch m ‖ tr bohren; (fig) langweilen

boredom ['bordəm] s Langeweile f

bor'ing adj langweilig ‖ s Bohren n

born [bɔrn] adj geboren; he was b. (said of a living person) er ist geboren; (said of a deceased person) er war geboren

borough ['bʌro] s Städtchen n

borrow ['bɔro] tr leihen

borrower ['bɔro-ər] s Entleiher -in mf; (fin) Kreditnehmer -in mf

bor'rowing s Borgen n; (fin) Kreditaufnahme f; (ling) Lehnwort n

bosom ['buzəm] s Busen m; (fig) Schoß m

bos'om friend' s Busenfreund m

boss [bɔs] s (coll) Chef m, Boß m; (of a shield) Buckel m; (pol) Bonze m ‖ tr (around) herumkommandieren

bossy ['bɔsi] adj herrschsüchtig

botanical [bə'tænɪkəl] adj botanisch

botanist ['bɑtənɪst] s Botaniker -in mf

botany ['bɑtəni] s Botanik f

botch [bɑtʃ] tr (coll) verpfuschen

both [boθ] adj & pron beide ‖ conj—both... and sowohl... als auch

bother ['bɑðər] s Belästigung f, Mühe f ‖ tr (annoy) belästigen, stören; (worry) bedrücken; (said of a conscience) quälen ‖ intr sich bemühen; b. about sich bekümmern um; b. with (a thing) sich befassen mit; (a person) verkehren mit

bothersome ['bɑðərsəm] adj lästig

bottle ['bɑtəl] s Flasche f ‖ tr in Flaschen abfüllen; **bottled up** aufgestaut

bot'tleneck' s Flaschenhals m; (fig) Engpaß m, Stauung f

bot'tle o'pener s Flaschenöffner m

bottom ['bɑtəm] adj niedrigste, unterste ‖ s Boden m; (of a well, shaft, river, valley) Sohle f; (of a mountain) Fuß m; (of an affair) Grund m; (buttocks) Hintern m; at the b. of the page unten auf der Seite; bottoms up! prosit, ex!; get to the b. of a problem e-r Frage auf den Grund gehen; reach b. (fig) den Nullpunkt erreichen

bottomless ['bɑtəmlɪs] adj bodenlos

bough [bau] s Ast m

bouillon ['buljɑn] s Kraftbrühe f

bouil'lon cube' s Bouillonwürfel m

boulder ['boldər] s Felsblock m

bounce [bauns] s Aufprall m; (fig) Schwung m ‖ tr (a ball) aufprallen lassen; (throw out) (sl) 'rausschmeißen ‖ intr aufprallen, aufspringen; (said of a check) (coll) platzen

bouncer ['baunsər] s (sl) Rausschmeißer m

bounc'ing adj (baby) stramm

bound [baund] adj gebunden, gefesselt; (book) gebunden; (in duty) verpflichtet; be b. for unterwegs sein nach; be b. up with eng verbunden sein mit; I am b. to (inf) ich muß (inf) ‖ s Sprung m, Satz m; bounds Grenzen pl, Schranken pl; in bounds (sport) in; keep within bounds in Schranken halten; know no bounds weder Maß noch Ziel kennen; out of bounds (sport) aus; within the bounds of im Bereich (genit) ‖ tr begrenzen ‖ intr aufprallen, aufspringen

boundary ['baundəri] s Grenze f; (fig) Umgrenzung f

boun'dary line' s Grenzlinie f

boun'dary stone' s Grenzstein m

boundless ['baundlɪs] adj grenzenlos

bountiful ['bauntɪfəl] adj (generous) freigebig; (ample) reichlich

bounty ['baunti] s (generosity) Freigebigkeit f; (gift) Geschenk n; (reward) Prämie f

bouquet [bu'ke] s Strauß m; (aroma) Blume f

bout [baut] s (box) Kampf m; (fencing) Gang m; (pathol) Anfall m

bow [bau] s Verbeugung f; (naut) Bug m ‖ intr sich verbeugen; bow and scrape before sich schmiegen und biegen vor (dat); bow down sich bücken; bow out sich geschickt zurückziehen; bow to sich (ver)neigen vor (dat) ‖ [bo] s (weapon) Bogen m; (of a violin) Geigenbogen m; (bowknot) Schleife f; bow and arrow Pfeil m und Bogen m ‖ intr (mus) geigen

bowel ['bau-əl] s Darm m; bowels Eingeweide pl; bowels of the earth Erdinnere n

bow'el move'ment s Stuhlgang m

bowl [bol] s Napf m, Schüssel f; (of a pipe) Kopf m; (washbowl, toilet bowl) Becken n; (of a spoon) Höhlung f; (sport) Stadion n ‖ tr umhauen; (fig) umwerfen ‖ intr kegeln

bowlegged ['bo,leg(r)d] adj O-beinig

bowler ['bolər] s Kegler -in mf

bowl'ing s Kegeln n

bowl'ing al'ley s Kegelbahn f

bowl'ing ball' s Kegelkugel f

bowl'ing pin' s Kegel m

bowstring ['bo,strɪŋ] s Bogensehne f

bow' tie' [bo] s Schleife f, Fliege f

bow' win'dow [bo] s Bogenfenster n

bowwow ['bau'wau] interj wauwau!

box [bɑks] s (small and generally of cardboard) Schachtel f; (larger and generally of cardboard) Karton m; (generally of wood) Kasten m; (larger and generally of wood) Kiste f; (of strips of wood) Spanschachtel f; (theat) Loge f; (typ) Kasten m; box of candy Bonbonniere f; box on the ear Ohrfeige f ‖ tr (sport) boxen; box in einschließen; box s.o.'s ears j-n ohrfeigen ‖ intr (sport) boxen

box'car' s geschlossener Güterwagen m

boxer ['bɑksər] s (sport, zool) Boxer m

box'ing s Boxen n, Boxsport m

box'ing glove' s Boxhandschuh m

box'ing match' s Boxkampf m
box' kite' s Kastendrachen m
box' of'fice s (cin, theat) Kasse f
box' seat' s Logenplatz m
box'wood' s Buchsbaum m
boy [bɔɪ] s Junge m; (servant) Boy m
boycott ['bɔɪkɑt] s Boykott m || tr
  boykottieren
boy'friend' s Freund m
boy'hood' s Knabenalter n
boyish ['bɔɪ·ɪʃ] adj jungenhaft
boy' scout' s Pfadfinder m
bra [brɑ] s (coll) BH m
brace [bres] s (carp) Strebe f, Stütze
  f; (dent) Zahnklammer f, Zahn-
  spange f; (hunt) Paar n; (med)
  Schiene f; (typ) geschweifte Klammer
  f || tr verstreben; (fig) stärken; b.
  oneself sich zusammenreißen; b. oneself against sich stemmen gegen; b.
  oneself for seinen Mut zusammen-
  nehmen für; b. up (fig) aufpulvern
brace' and bit' s Bohrwinde f
bracelet ['breslɪt] s Armband n
brac'ing adj (invigorating) erfrischend
bracket ['brækɪt] s Winkelstütze f,
  Konsole f; (wall bracket) Wandarm
  m; (mounting clip) Befestigungs-
  schelle f; (typ) eckige Klammer f ||
  tr einklammern; (arti) eingabeln
brackish ['brækɪʃ] adj brackig
brag [bræg] v (pret & pp bragged;
  ger bragging) intr (about) prahlen
  (mit)
braggart ['brægərt] s Prahler –in m f
brag'ging adj prahlerisch || s Prahlerei
  f
braid [bred] s (of hair) Flechte f; (flat
  trimming) Tresse f, Litze f; (round
  trimming) Kordel f || tr (hair, rope)
  flechten; (trim with braid) mit Tresse (or Borten) besetzen
braille [brel] s Blindenschrift f
brain [bren] s Hirn n; brains Hirn n;
  (fig) Grütze f || tr (coll) den Schädel
  einschlagen (dat)
brain'child' s Geistesfrucht f
brainless ['brenlɪs] adj hirnlos
brain'storm' s (coll) Geistesblitz m
brain'wash' tr Gehirnwäsche vornehmen bei
brain'wash'ing s Gehirnwäsche f
brain' wave' s Hirnwelle f; (fig) Geistesblitz m
brain'work' s Gehirnarbeit f
brainy ['breni] adj geistreich
braise [brez] tr schmoren, dünsten
brake [brek] s Bremse f || put on the
  brakes bremsen || intr bremsen
brake' drum' s Bremstrommel f
brake' light' s Bremslicht n
brake' lin'ing s Bremsbelag m
brake'man s (–men) Bremser m
brake'ped'al s Bremspedal n
brake' shoe' s (aut) Bremsbacke f
bramble ['bræmbəl] s Dornbusch m
bran [bræn] s Kleie f
branch [bræntʃ] s (of a tree) Ast m;
  (smaller branch; of lineage) Zweig
  m; (of river) Arm m; (of a road,
  railroad) Abzweigung f; (of science,
  work, a shop) Branche f, Unterabteilung f; (com) Filiale f, Nebenstelle

f || intr—b. off abzweigen; b. out
  sich verzweigen
branch' line' s Seitenlinie f
branch' of'fice s Zweigstelle f
branch' of serv'ice s Truppengattung
  f
brand [brænd] s (kind) Marke f;
  (trademark) Handelsmarke f; (on
  cattle) Brandmal n; (branding iron)
  Brandeisen n; (dishonor) Schand-
  fleck m || tr (& fig) brandmarken
brand'ing i'ron s Brandeisen n
brandish ['brændɪʃ] tr schwingen;
  (threateningly) schwenken
brand'-new' adj nagelneu
brandy ['brændi] s Branntwein m
brash [bræʃ] adj schnodd(e)rig, frech
brass [bræs] adj Messing– || s Messing
  n; (mil) hohe Offiziere pl; (mus)
  Blechinstrumente pl
brass' band' s Blechblaskapelle f
brassiere [brə'zɪr] s Büstenhalter m
brass' knuck'les spl Schlagring m
brass' tacks' spl—get down to b. (coll)
  zur Sache kommen
brat [bræt] s (coll) Balg m
bravado [brə'vɑdo] s Bravour f, Angabe f
brave [brev] adj tapfer, mutig || s indi-
  anischer Krieger m || tr trotzen (dat)
bravery ['brevəri] s Tapferkeit f
bra·vo ['brɑvo] s (–vos) Bravo n ||
  interj bravo!
brawl [brɔl] s Rauferei f || intr raufen
brawler ['brɔlər] s Raufbold m
brawn [brɔn] s Muskelkraft f
brawny ['brɔni] adj muskulös, kräftig
bray [bre] s Eselsschrei m || intr schrei-
  en, iahen
braze [brez] tr (brassplate) mit Messing überziehen; (solder) hartlöten
brazen ['brezən] adj Messing–, ehern;
  (fig) unverschämt || tr—b. it out
  unverschämt durchsetzen
Brazil [brə'zɪl] s Brasilien n
Brazilian [brə'zɪljən] adj brasilianisch,
  brasilisch || s Brasilier –in m f
Brazil' nut' s Paranuß f
breach [britʃ] s Bruch m; (mil)
  Bresche f || tr (mil) durchbrechen
breach' of con'tract s Vertragsbruch m
breach' of prom'ise s Verlöbnisbruch
  m
breach' of the peace' s Friedensbruch
  m
breach' of trust' s Vertrauensbruch m
bread [bred] s Brot n; (money) (sl)
  Pinke f || tr (culin) panieren
bread' and but'ter s Butterbrot n;
  (livelihood) Lebensunterhalt m
bread' box' s Brotkasten m
bread' crumb' s Brotkrume f
bread'ed adj paniert
bread'ed veal' cut'let s Wiener Schnitzel n
bread' knife' s Brotmesser n
breadth [bredθ] s Breite f
bread'win'ner s Brotverdiener –in m f
break [brek] s Bruch m; (split, tear)
  Riß m; (crack) Sprung m; (in relations) Bruch m; (in a forest) Lichtung f; (in the clouds) Lücke f;
  (recess) Pause f; (rest from work)

Arbeitspause *f;* (*luck*) Glück *n;* (*chance*) Chance *f;* (box) Lösen *n;* bad b. Pech *n;* b. in the weather Wetterumschlag *m;* give s.o. a b. j—m e—e Chance geben; make a b. for losstürzen auf (*acc*); take a b. e—e Pause machen; **tough** b. Pech *n;* **without** a b. ohne Unterbrechung ‖ *v* (*pret* **broke** [brok], *pp* **broken** ['brokən]) *tr* (& fig) brechen; (*snap*) zerreißen; (*a string*) durchreißen; (*a dish*) zerbrechen; (*an appointment* nicht einhalten; (*contact*) unterbrechen; (*an engagement*) auflösen; (*a law, limb*) verletzen; (*monotony*) auflockern; (*a record*) brechen; (*a seal*) erbrechen; (*a window*) einschlagen; (*one's word, promise*) nicht halten; **b. down** (*into constituents*) zerlegen; (*s.o.'s resistance*) überwinden; (*mach*) abmontieren; **b. in** (*a horse*) zureiten; (*a car*) einfahren; (*a person*) anlernen; **b. loose** losreißen; **b. off** abbrechen, losbrechen; (*an engagement*) auflösen; **b. open** aufbrechen; **b. s.o. from s.th.** j—m etw abgewöhnen; **b. the news (to)** die Nachricht eröffnen (*dat*), die Nachricht beibringen (*dat*); **b. to pieces** zerbrechen; (*a meeting*) auflösen; (*forcibly*) sprengen; **break wind** e—n Darmwind abgehen lassen ‖ *intr* brechen; (*snap*) reißen; (*said of the voice*) mutieren; (*said of waves*) sich brechen; (*said of large waves*) sich überschlagen; (*said of the weather*) umschlagen; **b. down** zusammenbrechen; (*mach*) versagen; **b. even** gerade die Unkosten decken; **b. loose** losbrechen, sich losreißen; **b. out** (*said of fire, an epidemic, prisoner*) ausbrechen; **b. up** (*said of a meeting*) sich auflösen

breakable ['brekəbəl] *adj* zerbrechlich
breakage ['brekɪdʒ] *s* Bruch *m;* (*cost of broken articles*) Bruchschaden *m*
break′down′ *s* (*of health, discipline, morals*) Zusammenbruch *m;* (*disintegration*) Zersetzung *f;* (*of costs, etc.*) Aufgliederung *f;* (aut) Panne *f;* (chem) Analyse *f;* (elec) Durchschlag *m;* (*of a piece of equipment*) (mach) Versagen *n;* (*e.g., of power supply, factory equipment*) Betriebsstörung *f*
breaker ['brekər] *s* Sturzwelle *f;* **breakers** Brandung *f*
breakfast ['brekfəst] *s* Frühstück *n* ‖ *intr* frühstücken
break′neck′ *adj* halsbrecherisch
break′ of day′ *s* Tagesanbruch *m*
break′through′ *s* Durchbruch *m*
break′up′ *s* Aufbrechen *n;* (*of a meeting*) Auflösung *f*
break′wa′ter *s* Wellenbrecher *m*
breast [brest] *s* Brust *f;* (*of a woman*) Brust *f,* Busen *m;* **beat one's b.** sich an die Brust schlagen; **make a clean b. of** sich [*dat*] vom Herzen reden
breast′bone′ *s* Brustbein *n*
breast′ feed′ing *s* Stillen *n*
breast′plate′ *s* Brustharnisch *m*
breast′stroke′ *s* Brustschwimmen *n*

breath [breθ] *s* Atem *m;* (*single inhalation*) Atemzug *m;* (fig) Hauch *m;* **b. of air** Lüftchen *n;* **gasp for b.** nach Luft schnappen; **have bad b.** aus dem Mund riechen; **in the same b.** im gleichen Atemzug; **save one's b.** sich [*dat*] seine Worte ersparen; **take a deep b.** tief Luft holen; **take one's b. away** j—m den Atem verschlagen; **waste one's b.** in den Wind reden
breathe [brið] *tr* atmen, schöpfen; **b. a sigh of relief** aufatmen; **b. life into** beseelen; **b. one's last** die Seele aushauchen; **b. out** ausatmen; **not b. a word about it** kein Wort davon verlauten lassen ‖ *intr* atmen, hauchen; **b. again** aufatmen; **on** anhauchen
breath′ing space′ *s* Atempause *f*
breathless ['breθlɪs] *adj* atemlos
breath′-tak′ing *adj* atemberaubend
breech [brit∫] *s* Verschlußstück *s*
breed [brid] *s* Zucht *f,* Stamm *m;* (*sort, group*) Schlag *m;* (*of animals*) Rasse *f* ‖ *v* (*pret & pp* **bred** [bred]) *tr* (*beget*) erzeugen; (*raise*) züchten; (fig) hervorrufen ‖ *intr* sich vermehren
breeder ['bridər] *s* Züchter –in *mf*
breed′ing *s* (*of animals*) Züchtung *f,* Aufzucht *f;* (fig) Erziehung *f*
breeze [briz] *s* Lüftchen *n,* Brise *f* ‖ *intr*—**b. by** vorbeiflitzen; **b. in** frisch und vergnügt hereinkommen
breezy ['brizi] *adj* luftig; (fig) keß
brevity ['brevɪti] *s* Kürze *f*
brew [bru] *s* Brühe *f;* (*of beer*) Bräu *m* ‖ *tr* (*tea, coffee*) aufbrühen; (*beer*) brauen ‖ *intr* ziehen; (*said of a storm*) sich zusammenbrauen; **something is brewing** etwas ist im Anzuge
brewer ['bru·ər] *s* Brauer –in *mf*
brewery ['bru·əri] *s* Brauerei *f*
bribe [braɪb] *s* Bestechungsgeld *n* ‖ *tr* bestechen
bribery ['braɪbəri] *s* Bestechung *f*
brick [brɪk] *s* Ziegelstein *m*
bricklayer ['brɪk ˌle·ər] *s* Maurer *m*
brick′work′ *s* Mauerwerk *n*
brick′yard′ *s* Ziegelei *f*
bridal ['braɪdəl] *adj* Braut-, Hochzeits-
brid′al gown′ *s* Brautkleid *n*
brid′al veil′ *s* Brautschleier *m*
bride [braɪd] *s* Braut *f*
bride′groom′ *s* Bräutigam *m*
brides′maid′ *s* Brautjungfer *f*
bridge [brɪdʒ] *s* (*over a river*) Brücke *f;* (*of eyeglasses*) Steg *m;* (*of a nose*) Nasenrücken *m;* (*cards*) Bridge *n;* (*dent*) Zahnbrücke *f;* (naut) Kommandobrücke *f* ‖ *tr* (& fig) überbrücken
bridge′head′ *s* Brückenkopf *m*
bridge′work′ *s* (*dent*) Brückenarbeit *f*
bridle ['braɪdəl] *s* Zaum *m,* Zügel *m* ‖ *tr* aufzäumen, zügeln
bri′dle path′ *s* Reitweg *m*
brief [brif] *adj* kurz; **be b.** sich kurz fassen ‖ *s* (jur) Schriftsatz *m* ‖ *tr* einweisen, orientieren
brief′ case′ *s* Aktentasche *f*

brief′ing s Einsatzbesprechung f

brier ['braɪ·ər] s Dornbusch m

brig [brɪg] s (naut) Brigg f; (nav) Knast m

brigade [brɪ'ged] s Brigade f

brigadier′ gen′eral [,brɪgə'dɪr] s Brigadegeneral m

brigand ['brɪgənd] s Brigant m

bright [braɪt] adj hell; (color) lebhaft; (face) strahlend; (weather) heiter; (smart) gescheit, aufgeweckt || adv —b. and early in aller Frühe

brighten ['braɪtən] tr aufhellen || intr sich aufhellen

bright′-eyed′ adj helläugig

brightness ['braɪtnɪs] s Helle f

bright′ side′ s (fig) Lichtseite f

bright′ spot′ s (fig) Lichtblick m

brilliance ['brɪljəns], **brilliancy** ['brɪljənsɪ] s Glanz m

brilliant ['brɪljənt] adj (& fig) glänzend

brim [brɪm] s Rand m; (of a hat) Krempe f; **to the b.** bis zum Rande || v (pret & pp **brimmed**; ger **brimming**) intr—**b. over (with)** (fig) überschäumen (vor dat)

brimful ['brɪm‚fʊl] adj übervoll

brim′stone′ s Schwefel m

brine [braɪn] s Salzwasser n, Sole f; (for pickling) Salzlake f

bring [brɪŋ] v (pret & pp **brought** [brɔt]) tr bringen; **b. about** zustande bringen; **b. back** zurückbringen; (memories) zurückrufen; **b. down** herunterbringen; (shoot down) abschießen; **b. down the house** (fig) Lachstürme entfesseln; **b. forth** (e.g., complaints) hervorbringen; **b. forward** vorbringen; **b. it about that** es durchsetzen, daß; **b. on** herbeiführen; **b. oneself to** (inf) sich überwinden zu (inf); **b. to** wieder zu sich bringen; **b. together** zusammenbringen; **b. up** (children) erziehen; (a topic) zur Sprache bringen

bring′ing-up′ s Erziehung f

brink [brɪŋk] s (& fig) Rand m

brisk [brɪsk] adj (pace, business) flott; (air) frisch, scharf

bristle ['brɪsəl] s Borste f || intr sich sträuben

bristly ['brɪslɪ] adj borstig

Britain ['brɪtən] s Britannien n

British ['brɪtɪʃ] adj britisch || **the B.** spl die Briten m

Britisher ['brɪtɪʃər] s Brite m, Britin f

Briton ['brɪtən] s Brite m, Britin f

Brittany ['brɪtənɪ] s die Bretagne f

brittle ['brɪtəl] adj brüchig, spröde

broach [brotʃ] tr zur Sprache bringen

broad [brɔd] adj breit; (daylight) hellicht; (outline) grob; (sense) weit; (view) allgemein, umfassend

broad′cast′ s Sendung f, Übertragung f || v (pret & pp **-cast**) tr (rumors, etc.) ausposaunen || (pret & pp **-cast** & **-casted**) tr & intr senden, übertragen

broadcaster ['brɔd‚kæstər] s Rundfunksprecher -in mf

broad′casting sta′tion s Sender m

broad′casting stu′dio s Senderaum m

broad′cloth′ s feiner Wäschestoff m

broaden ['brɔdən] tr verbreitern || intr sich verbreitern

broad′-gauge′ adj (rr) breitspurig

broad′-mind′ed adj großzügig

broad′-shoul′dered adj breitschultrig

broad′side′ s (guns on one side of ship) Breitseite f; (fig) Schimpfkanonade f

brocade [bro'ked] s Brokat m

broccoli ['brɑkəlɪ] s Spargelkohl m

brochure [bro'ʃʊr] s Broschüre f

broil [brɔɪl] tr am Rost braten, grillen

broiler ['brɔɪlər] s Bratrost m

broke [brok] adj (coll) abgebrannt, pleite; **go b.** (coll) pleite gehen

broken ['brokən] adj zerbrochen; (limb, spirit, English) gebrochen; (home) zerrüttet; (line) gestrichelt

bro′ken-down′ adj erschöpft; (horse) abgearbeitet

bro′ken-heart′ed adj mit gebrochenem Herzen

broker ['brokər] s Makler –in mf

brokerage ['brokərɪdʒ] s Maklergeschäft n; (fee) Maklergebühr f

bromide ['bromaɪd] s Bromid n; (coll) Binsenweisheit f

bromine ['bromin] s Brom n

bronchial ['brɑŋkɪ·əl] adj bronchial

bron′chial tube′ s Luftröhre f, Bronchie f

bronchitis [brɑŋ'kaɪtɪs] s Bronchitis f

bron·co ['brɑŋko] s (**-cos**) kleines halbwildes Pferd n

bronze [brɑnz] adj Bronze– || s Bronze f || tr bronzieren || intr sich bräunen

brooch [brotʃ], [brutʃ] s Brosche f

brood [brud] s Brut f, Junge pl || tr ausbrüten || intr brüten; (coll) sinnieren; **b. over** grübeln über (acc)

brook [brʊk] s Bach m || tr dulden

broom [brum] s Besen m

broom′stick′ s Besenstiel m

broth [brɔθ] s Brühe f

brothel ['brɑθəl] s Bordell n

brother ['brʌðər] s Bruder m; **brother(s) and sister(s)** Geschwister pl

broth′erhood′ s (& relig) Brüderschaft f

broth′er-in-law′ s (**brothers-in-law**) Schwager m

brotherly ['brʌðərlɪ] adj brüderlich

brow [brau] s Stirn f

brow′beat′ v (pret **-beat**; pp **-beaten**) tr einschüchtern

brown [braun] adj braun || s Bräune f || tr & intr bräunen

brownish ['braunɪʃ] adj bräunlich

brown′-nose′ tr (sl) kriechen (dat)

brown′ sug′ar s brauner Zucker m

browse [brauz] intr grasen, weiden; (through books) schmökern, stöbern; (through a store) herumsuchen

bruise [bruz] s Quetschung f || tr quetschen

brunette [bru'nɛt] adj brünett || s Brünette f

brunt [brʌnt] s Anprall m; **bear the b.** die Hauptlast tragen

brush [brʌʃ] s Bürste f; (of an artist; for shaving) Pinsel m; (brief encoun-

ter) kurzer Zusammenstoß *m*; (*light touch*) leichte Berührung *f*; (*bot*) Gebüsch *n*; (*elec*) Bürste *f*; || *tr* bürsten; **b. aside** beiseite schieben; **b. off** abbürsten; (*devour*) verschlingen; (*make light of*) abwimmeln || *intr*—**b. against** streifen; **b. up on** auffrischen

brush'-off' *s* (coll) Laufpaß *m*

brush'wood' *s* Unterholz *n*, Niederwald *m*

brusque [brʌsk] *adj* brüsk

Brussels ['brʌsəlz] *s* Brüssel *n*

Brus'sels sprouts' *spl* Rosenkohl *m*

brutal ['brutəl] *adj* brutal

brutality [bru'tælɪti] *s* Brutalität *f*

brute [brut] *adj* viehisch; (*strength*) roh || *s* Tier *n*; (fig) Unmensch *m*

brutish ['brutɪʃ] *adj* tierisch, roh

bubble ['bʌbəl] *s* Blase *f*, Bläschen *n* || *intr* sprudeln; **b. over** (with) übersprudeln (vor *dat*)

bub'ble bath' *s* Schaumbad *n*

bub'ble gum' *s* Knallkaugummi *m*

bubbly ['bʌbli] *adj* sprudelnd; (*Person*) lebhaft

buck [bʌk] *s* Bock *m*; (sl) Dollar *m*; **pass the b.** (coll) die Verantwortung abschieben || *tr* (fig) kämpfen gegen; **b. off** abwerfen || *intr* bocken; **b. for** (*a promotion*) sich bemühen um

bucket ['bʌkɪt] *s* Eimer *m*

buck'et seat' *s* Schalensitz *m*

buckle ['bʌkəl] *s* Schnalle *f*; (*bend*) Ausbuchtung *f* || *tr* zuschnallen || *intr* (*from heat, etc.*) zusammensacken; **b. down** sich auf die Hosen setzen

buck' pri'vate *s* gemeiner Soldat *m*

buckram ['bʌkrəm] *s* Buckram *n*

buck'shot' *s* Rehposten *m*

buck'tooth' *s* (-teeth) vorstehender Zahn *m*

buck'wheat' *s* Buchweizen *m*

bud [bʌd] *s* Knospe *f*, Keim *m*; **nip in the bud** (fig) im Keime ersticken || *v* (*pret & pp* budded; *ger* budding) *intr* knospen, keimen, ausschlagen

buddy ['bʌdi] *s* (coll) Kumpel *m*

budge [bʌdʒ] *tr* (von der Stelle) bewegen || *intr* sich (von der Stelle) bewegen

budget ['bʌdʒɪt] *s* Budget *n*, Haushaltsplan *m*; (*of a state*) Staatshaushalt *m* || *tr* einteilen, vorausplanen

budgetary ['bʌdʒɪ,teri] *adj* Budget-

buff [bʌf] *adj* lederfarben || *s* Lederfarbe *f*; (coll) Schwärmer –in *mf* || *tr* polieren

buffa·lo ['bʌfə,lo] *s* (-loes & -los) Büffel *m*

buffer ['bʌfər] *s* Puffer *m*; (*polisher*) Polierer *m*; (rr) Prellbock *m*

buff'er state' *s* Pufferstaat *m*

buffet [bu'fe] *s* (*meal*) Büfett *n*; (*furniture*) Kredenz *f* || ['bʌfɪt] *tr* herumstoßen

buffoon [bə'fun] *s* Hanswurst *m*

bug [bʌg] *s* Insekt *n*, Käfer *m*; (*defect*) (coll) Defekt *m*; (electron) Abhörgerät *n*, Wanze *f*; **bugs** Ungeziefer *n* || *v* (*pret & pp* bugged; *ger* bugging) *tr* (*annoy*) (sl) ärgern;

(electron) (sl) Abhörgeräte einbauen in (*dat*)

bug'-eyed' *adj* (sl) mit großen Augen

buggy ['bʌgi] *adj* verwanzt; (*crazy*) (sl) verrückt || *s* Wagen *m*

bugle ['bjugəl] *s* Signalhorn *n*

bu'gle call' *s* Signal *n*

bugler ['bjuglər] *s* Hornist –in *mf*

build [bɪld] *s* Bauart *f*, Gestalt *f*; (*of a person*) Körperbau *m* || *v* (*pret & pp* built [bɪlt]) *tr* bauen; (*a bridge*) schlagen; (*with stone or brick*) mauern; (*a fire*) anmachen; **b. up** aufbauen; (*an area*) ausbauen; (*hopes*) erwecken

builder ['bɪldər] *s* Baumeister *m*

build'ing *s* Gebäude *n*

build'ing and loan' associa'tion *s* Bausparkasse *f*

build'ing block' *s* Zementblock *m*; (*for children*) Bauklötzchen *n*

build'ing con'tractor *s* Bauunternehmer *m*

build'ing in'dustry *s* Bauindustrie *f*

build'ing lot' *s* Bauplatz *m*, Grundstück *n*

build'ing mate'rial *s* Baustoff *m*

build'-up' *s* (coll) Propaganda *f*

built'-in' *adj* Einbau-

built'-up' *adj* bebaut

bulb [bʌlb] *s* (bot) Knolle *f*, Zwiebel *f*; (elec) Glühbirne *f*; (phot) Blitzlampe *f*

Bulgaria [bʌl'gɑri·ə] *s* Bulgarien *n*

Bulgarian [bʌl'gɑri·ən] *adj* bulgarisch || *s* Bulgare *m*, Bulgarin *f*; (*language*) Bulgarisch *n*

bulge [bʌldʒ] *s* Ausbauchung *f*, Beule *f*; (*of a sail*) Bausch *m*; (mil) Frontvorsprung *m* || *intr* sich bauschen; (*said of eyes*) hervortreten

bulg'ing *adj* (*belly, muscles*) hervorspringend; (*eyes*) hervorquellend; (*sails*) gebläht; **b. with** bis zum Platzen gefüllt mit

bulk [bʌlk] *adj* Massen-, unverpackt || *s* Masse *f*; (*main part*) Hauptteil *m*; **in b.** unverpackt || *intr*—**b. large** e-e große Rolle spielen

bulk'head' *s* (aer) Spant *m*; (naut) Schott *n*

bulky ['bʌlki] *adj* sperrig

bull [bul] *s* Bulle *m*, Stier *m*; (sl) Quatsch *m*; (eccl) Bulle *f*; (st. exch.) Haussier *m*; **like a b. in a china shop** wie ein Elefant im Porzellanladen; **shoot the b.** (sl) quatschen; **take the b. by the horns** den Stier an den Hörnern packen; **throw the b.** (sl) aufschneiden

bull'dog' *s* Bulldogge *f*

bull'doze' *tr* planieren; (fig) überfahren

bulldozer ['bʌl,dozər] *s* Planierraupe *f*

bullet ['bulɪt] *s* Kugel *f*

bul'let hole' *s* Schußöffnung *f*

bulletin ['bulətɪn] *s* (*report*) Bulletin *n*; (*flyer*) Flugschrift *f*

bul'letin board' *s* Anschlagbrett *n*

bul'letproof' *adj* kugelsicher

bull'fight' *s* Stierkampf *m*

bull'fight'er *s* Stierkämpfer –in *mf*

bull'frog' *s* Ochsenfrosch *m*

bull'-head'ed *adj* dickköpfig

bull' horn' *s* Richtungslautsprecher *m*

bullion ['buljən] *s* Barren *m;* (mil, nav) Kordel *f*

bull' mar'ket *s* Spekulationsmarkt *m*

bullock ['bulʌk] *s* Ochse *m*

bull'pen' *s* Stierpferch *m;* (baseball) Übungsplatz *m* für Reservewerfer

bull'ring' *s* Stierkampfarena *f*

bull' ses'sion *s* (sl) zwanglose Diskussion *f*

bull's'-eye' *s* (of a target) Schwarze *n;* (round window) Bullauge *n;* **hit the b. ins Schwarze treffen**

bul·ly ['buli] *adj*—**b. for you!** großartig! || *s* Raufbold *m* || *v* (pret & pp -lied) *tr* tyrannisieren

bulrush ['bul‚rʌʃ] *s* Binse *f*

bulwark ['bulwərk] *s* Bollwerk *n*

bum [bʌm] (sl) *s* Strolch *m;* **give s.o. the bum's rush** j-n auf den Schub bringen || *v* (pret & pp bummed; ger bumming) *tr* (sl) schinden, schnorren || *intr*—**bum around** bummeln

bumblebee ['bʌmbəl‚bi] *s* Hummel *f*

bump [bʌmp] *s* Stoß *m,* Bums *m;* (swelling) Beule *f;* (in the road) holp(e)rige Stelle *f* || *tr* (an)stoßen; **b. off** (sl) abknallen; **b. one's head against s.th.** mit dem Kopf gegen etw stoßen || *intr* zusammenstoßen; **b. against** stoßen an (acc); **b. into** stoßen gegen; (meet unexpectedly) in die Arme laufen (dat)

bumper ['bʌmpər] *s* Stoßstange *f*

bumpkin ['bʌmpkɪn] *s* Tölpel *m*

bumpy ['bʌmpi] *adj* holperig; (aer) böig

bum' steer' *s*—**give s.o. a b.** (coll) nasführen

bun [bʌn] *s* Kuchenbrötchen *n;* (of hair) Haarknoten *m*

bunch [bʌntʃ] *s* Bündel *n;* (of grapes) Traube *f;* (group) Schar *f,* Bande *f;* **b. of flowers** Blumenstrauß *m;* **b. of grapes** Weintraube *f* || *tr*—**b. together** zusammenfassen || *intr*—**b. together** sich zusammendrängen

bundle ['bʌndəl] *s* Bündel *n;* (heap) Stoß *m;* (of straw) Schütte *f;* **b. of nerves** Nervenbündel *n* || *tr* bündeln; **b. off** (coll) verfrachten; **b. up** sich warm anziehen

bung [bʌŋ] *s* Spund *m* || *tr* verspunden

bungalow ['bʌŋgə‚lo] *s* Bungalow *m*

bung'hole' *s* Spundloch *n*

bungle ['bʌŋgəl] *s* Pfuscherei *f* || *tr* verpfuschen || *intr* pfuschen

bungler ['bʌŋglər] *s* Pfuscher -in *mf*

bun'gling *adj* stümperhaft || *s* Stümperei *f*

bunk [bʌŋk] *s* Schlafkoje *f;* (sl) Unsinn *m* || *intr* (with) schlafen (mit)

bunk' bed' *s* Etagenbett *n*

bunker ['bʌŋkər] *s* Bunker *m*

bunny ['bʌni] *s* Kaninchen *n*

bunt'ing *s* (cloth) Fahnentuch *n;* (decoration) Fahnenschmuck *m;* (orn) Ammer *f*

buoy [bɔɪ], ['bu·i] *s* Boje *f* || *tr*—**b. up** flott erhalten; (fig) Auftrieb geben (dat)

buoyancy ['bɔɪ·ənsi] *s* Auftrieb *m;* (fig) Spannkraft *f*

buoyant ['bɔɪ·ənt] *adj* schwimmend; (fig) lebhaft

burden ['bʌrdən] *s* Bürde *f,* Last *f;* (fig) Belastung *f* || *tr* belasten

bur'den of proof' *s* Beweislast *f*

burdensome ['bʌrdənsəm] *adj* lästig

bureau ['bjuro] *s* Kommode *f;* (office) Büro *n;* (department) Amt *n*

bureaucracy [bju'rɑkrəsi] *s* Bürokratie *f,* Beamtenschaft *f*

bureaucrat ['bjurə‚kræt] *s* Bürokrat -in *mf*

bureaucratic [‚bjurə'krætɪk] *adj* bürokratisch

burglar ['bʌrglər] *s* Einbrecher -in *mf*

bur'glar alarm' *s* Einbruchssicherung *f*

burglarize ['bʌrglə‚raɪz] *tr* einbrechen in (acc)

bur'glarproof' *adj* einbruchssicher

burglary ['bʌrgləri] *s* Einbruchdiebstahl *m*

Burgundy ['bʌrgəndi] *s* Burgund *n;* (wine) Burgunder *m*

burial ['beri·əl] *s* Beerdigung *f*

bur'ial ground' *s* Begräbnisplatz *m*

burlap ['bʌrlæp] *s* Sackleinwand *f*

burlesque [bər'lesk] *adj* burlesk || *s* Burleske *f* || *tr* burlesk behandeln

burlesque' show' *s* Varié té *n*

burly ['bʌrli] *adj* stämmig, beleibt

Burma ['bʌrmə] *s* Birma *n*

Bur·mese [bər'miz] *adj* birmanisch || *s* (-mese) (person) Birmane *m,* Birmanin *f;* (language) Birmanisch *n*

burn [bʌrn] *s* Brandwunde *f;* || *v* (pret & pp burned & pret & pp burnt) *tr* (ver)brennen; **be burned up** (coll) fauchen; **b. down** niederbrennen; **b. up** (coll) wütend machen || *intr* (ver)brennen; (said of food) anbrennen; **b. out** ausbrennen; (elec) durchbrennen; **b. up** ganz verbrennen; (during reentry) verglühen

burner ['bʌrnər] *s* Brenner *m*

burn'ing *adj* (& fig) brennend

burnish ['bʌrnɪʃ] *tr* polieren

burn'out' *s* (rok) Brennschluß *m*

burnt *adj* verbrannt; (smell) brenzlig

burp [bʌrp] *s* Rülpser *m* || *tr* rülpsen lassen || *intr* rülpsen

burr [bʌr] *s* (growth on a tree) Auswuchs *m;* (in metal) Grat *m;* (bot) Klette *f*

burrow ['bʌro] *s* Bau *m* || *tr* graben || *intr* sich eingraben, wühlen

bursar ['bʌrsər] *s* Schatzmeister *m*

burst [bʌrst] *s* Bersten *n;* (split) Riß *m;* Bruch *m;* **b. of gunfire** Feuerstoß *m* || *v* (pret & pp burst) *tr* (auf)-sprengen, zum Platzen bringen || *intr* bersten, platzen; (split) reißen; (said of a boil) aufgehen; **b. into** (e.g., a room) hereinstürzen in (acc); **b. into tears** in Tränen ausbrechen; **b. open** aufplatzen; **b. out laughing** losiachen

bur·y ['beri] *v* (pret & pp -ied) *tr* beerdigen, begraben; **be buried in thought** in Gedanken versunken sein; **b. alive** verschütten

bus [bʌs] *s* (busses & buses) Autobus *m,* Bus *m* || *v* (pret & pp) **bussed &**

bused; ger bussing & busing) tr & intr mit dem Bus fahren

bus′ boy′ s Pikkolo m

bus′ driv′er s Autobusfahrer –in mf

bush [buʃ] s Busch m; **beat around the b.** um die Sache herumreden

bushed adj (coll) abgeklappert

bushel [′buʃəl] s Scheffel m; **by the b.** scheffelweise

bush′ing s Buchse f

bushy [′buʃi] adj strauchbewachsen; (brows) buschig

business [′bɪznɪs] adj Geschäfts– ‖ s Geschäft n; (company) Firma f, Betrieb m; (employment) Beruf m, Gewerbe n; (duty) Pflicht f; (right) Recht n; (coll) Sache f; **be in b.** geschäftlich tätig sein; **do b. with** Geschäfte machen mit; **get down to b.** (coll) zur Sache kommen; **go about one's b.** seiner Arbeit nachgehen; **he means b.** (coll) er meint es ernst; **know one's b.** seine Sache verstehen; **make s.th. one's b.** sich [dat] etw angelegen sein lassen; **mind your own b.** kümmere dich um deine eigenen Sachen; **that's none of your b.** das geht dich gar nichts an; **the whole b.** die ganze Geschichte; **you have no b. here** du hast hier nichts zu suchen

busi′ness call′ s Dienstgespräch n

busi′ness card′ s Geschäftskarte f

busi′ness cen′ter s Geschäftszentrum n

busi′ness col′lege s Handelsschule f

busi′ness dis′trict s Geschäftsviertel n

busi′ness expens′es spl Geschäftsspesen pl

busi′ness hours′ s Geschäftszeit f

busi′ness let′ter s Geschäftsbrief m

busi′ness·like adj sachlich; (pej) geschäftsmäßig

busi′ness·man s (-men′) Geschäftsmann m

busi′ness reply′ card′ s Rückantwortkarte f

busi′ness suit′ s Straßenanzug m

busi′ness·wom′an s (-wom′en) Geschäftsfrau f

bus′ line′ s Autobuslinie f

bus′ stop′ s Autobushaltestelle f

bust [bʌst] s (chest) Busen m; (measurement) Oberweite f; (statue) Brustbild n; (blow) (sl) Faustschlag m; (failure) (sl) Platzen n; (binge) Sauftour f ‖ tr (sl) kaputtmachen; (mil) degradieren ‖ intr (break) (sl) kaputtgehen

bustle [′bʌsəl] s (activity) Hochbetrieb m, Trubel m ‖ intr umherhasten; **b. about** herumsausen

bus′tling adj geschäftig

bus·y [′bɪzi] adj tätig, beschäftigt; (day, life) arbeitsreich; (street) lebhaft, verkehrsstark; (telp) belegt, besetzt; **be b.** (be occupied) zu tun haben; (be unavailable) nicht zu sprechen sein ‖ v (pret & pp -ied) tr beschäftigen

bus′ybod′y s Wichtigtuer –in mf

bus′y sig′nal s (telp) Besetztzeichen n

but [bʌt] adv nur, lediglich, bloß; (just, only) erst; **all but** beinahe ‖

prep außer (dat); (after negatives) als; **all but one** alle bis auf einen ‖ conj aber; (after negatives) sondern

butcher [′butʃər] s Fleischer –in mf, Metzger –in mf; (fig) Schlächter –in mf ‖ tr schlachten; (fig) abschlachten

butch′er knife′ s Fleischermesser n

butch′er shop′ s Metzgerei f

butchery [′butʃəri] s (slaughterhouse) Schlachthaus n; (fig) Gemetzel n

butler [′bʌtlər] s Haushofmeister m

butt [bʌt] s (of a gun) Kolben m; (of a cigarette) Stummel m; (with the horns, head) Stoß m; (of ridicule) Zielscheibe f ‖ tr stoßen ‖ intr stoßen; **b. in** (sl) sich einmischen, dazwischenfahren

butter [′bʌtər] s Butter f ‖ tr mit Butter bestreichen; (bread) schmieren; **b. s.o. up** (coll) j–m Honig um den Mund schmieren

but′terball′ s Butterkugel f; (chubby child) Pummelchen n

but′tercup′ s Butterblume f, Hahnenfuß m

but′ter dish′ s Butterdose f

but′terfly′ s Schmetterling m; (sport) Schmetterlingsstil m

but′ter knife′ s Buttermesser n

but′termilk′ s Buttermilch f

buttocks [′bʌtəks] spl Hinterbacken pl

button [′bʌtən] s Knopf m ‖ tr knöpfen; **button up** zuknöpfen

but′tonhole′ s Knopfloch n ‖ tr im Gespräch festhalten

buttress [′bʌtrɪs] s Strebepfeiler m; (fig) Stütze f ‖ tr (durch Strebepfeiler) stützen; (fig) (unter)stützen

butt′-weld′ tr stumpfschweißen

buxom [′bʌksəm] adj beleibt

buy [bai] s Kauf m ‖ v (pret & pp bought [bɔt]) tr kaufen; (bus ticket, train ticket) lösen; (accept, believe) glauben; **buy off** (bribe) bestechen; **buy out** auskaufen; **buy up** aufkaufen

buyer [′baiər] s Käufer –in mf

buzz [bʌz] s Summen n, Surren n; (telp) (coll) Anruf m ‖ tr (coll) (aer) dicht vorbeisausen an (dat); (telp) (coll) anrufen ‖ intr summen, surren; **b. around** herumsausen

buzzard [′bʌzərd] s Bussard m

buzz′ bomb′ s Roboterbombe f, V-Waffe f

buzzer [′bʌzər] s Summer m; **did the b. sound?** ist der Summer ertönt

buzz′ saw′ s Kreissäge f, Rundsäge f

by [bai] adv vorüber, vorbei; **by and by** nach und nach; **by and large** im großen und ganzen ‖ prep (agency) von (dat), durch (acc); (position) bei (dat), an (dat), neben (dat); (no later than) bis spätestens; (in division) durch (acc); (indicating mode of transportation) mit (dat); (indicating authorship) von (dat); (according to) nach (dat); (past) an (dat) vorbei; (by means of) mit (dat); **by** (ger) indem (ind); **by an inch** um e–n Zoll; **by day** bei Tag; **by far** bei weitem; **by heart** auswendig; **by itself** (automatically) von selbst; **by land** zu Lande; **by mail**

per Post; **by myself** ganz allein; **by nature** von Natur aus; **by now** schon; **by the pound** per Pfund; **two by four** zwei mal vier

bye [baɪ] *s* (sport) Freilos *n*

bye/bye/ *interj* Wiedersehen!

bygone [ˈbaɪˌgɔn] *adj* vergangen ‖ *s—***let bygones be bygones** laß(t) das Vergangene ruhen

by/law/ *s* Satzung *f*; **bylaws** (*of an organization*) Statuten *pl*, Satzungen *pl*

by/'-line/ *s* (journ) Verfasserangabe *f*

by/pass/ *s* Umgehungsstraße *f*, Umleitung *f*; (elec) Nebenschluß *m* ‖ *tr* umgehen

by/prod/uct *s* Nebenprodukt *n*

bystander [ˈbaɪˌstændər] *s* Umstehende *mf*

by/way/ *s* Seitenweg *m*

by/word/ *s* Sprichwort *n*

Byzantine [ˈbɪzənˌtin] [bɪˈzæntin] *adj* byzantinisch ‖ *s* Byzantiner –in *mf*

Byzantium [bɪˈzænʃɪ·əm], [bɪˈzæntɪ·əm] *s* Byzanz *n*

C

C, c [si] *s* dritter Buchstabe des englischen Alphabets; (mus) C *n*; **C flat** Ces *n*; **C sharp** Cis *n*

cab [kæb] *s* Taxi *n*; (*of a truck*) Fahrerkabine *f*

cabaret [ˌkæbəˈre] *s* Kabarett *n*

cabbage [ˈkæbɪdʒ] *s* Kohl *m*, Kraut *n*

cab/driv/er *s* Taxifahrer –in *mf*

cabin [ˈkæbɪn] *s* Hütte *f*; (aer) Kabine *f*; (naut) Kajüte *f*, Kabine *f*

cab/in boy/ *s* Schiffsjunge *m*

cabinet [ˈkæbɪnɪt] *s* Kabinetts– ‖ *s* (*in a kitchen*) Küchenschrank *m*; (*for a radio*) Gehäuse *n*; (pol) Kabinett *n*, Ministerrat *m*

cab/inetmak/er *s* Tischler *m*

cable [ˈkebəl] *s* Kabel *n*, Seil *n*; (naut) Tau *m*; (telg) Kabelnachricht *f* ‖ *tr & intr* kabeln

ca/ble car/ *s* Seilbahn *f*, Schwebebahn *f*

ca/blegram/ *s* Kabelnachricht *f*

caboose [kəˈbus] *s* (rr) Dienstwagen *m*

cab/stand/ *s* Taxistand *m*

cache [kæʃ] *s* Geheimlager *n*, Versteck *n*; **c. of arms** Waffenlager *n*

cachet [kæˈʃe] *s* Siegel *n*; (fig) Stempel *m*; (pharm) Kapsel *f*

cackle [ˈkækəl] *s* (*of chickens*) Gegacker *n*; (*of geese*) Geschnatter *n* ‖ *intr* gackern, gackeln; schnattern

cac·tus [ˈkæktəs] *s* (*-tuses & -ti* [taɪ]) Kaktus *m*

cad [kæd] *s* (sl) Saukerl *m*, Schuft *m*

cadaver [kəˈdævər] *s* Kadaver *m*, Leiche *f*

caddie [ˈkædi] *s* Golfjunge *m* ‖ *intr* die Schläger tragen

cadence [ˈkedəns] *s* (*rhythm*) Rhythmus *m*; (*flow of language*) Sprechrhythmus *m*; (mus) Kadenz *f*

cadet [kəˈdet] *s* Offizier(s)anwärter –in *mf*

cadre [ˈkædri] *s* Kader *m*

Caesar/ean opera/tion [sɪˈzɛrɪ·ən] *s* Kaiserschnitt *m*

café [kæˈfe] *s* Cafe *n*

cafeteria [ˌkæfəˈtɪrɪ·ə] *s* Selbstbedienungsrestaurant *n*

caffeine [kæˈfin] *s* Koffein *n*

cage [kedʒ] *s* Käfig *m* ‖ *tr* in e–n Käfig sperren

cagey [ˈkedʒi] *adj* (coll) schlau

cahoots [kəˈhuts] *s*—**be in c.** (sl) unter e–r Decke stecken

Cain [ken] *s*—**raise C.** Krach schlagen

caisson [ˈkesən] *s* Senkkasten *m*

cajole [kəˈdʒol] *tr* beschwatzen

cake [kek] *s* Kuchen *m*; (*round cake*) Torte *f*; (*of soap*) Riegel *m*; **he takes the c.** (coll) er schießt den Vogel ab; **that takes the c.** (coll) das ist die Höhe ‖ *intr* zusammenbacken; **c. on** anbacken

calamitous [kəˈlæmɪtəs] *adj* unheilvoll

calamity [kəˈlæmɪti] *s* Unheil *n*

calci·fy [ˈkælsɪˌfaɪ] *v* (*pret & pp* *-fied*) *tr* verkalken

calcium [ˈkælsɪ·əm] *s* Kalzium *n*

calculate [ˈkælkjəˌlet] *tr* berechnen ‖ *intr* rechnen

cal/culated risk/ *s*—**take a c.** ein bewußtes Risiko eingehen

cal/culating *adj* berechnend

calculation [ˌkælkjəˈleʃən] *s* Berechnung *f*; **rough c.** Überschlagsrechnung *f*

calculator [ˈkælkjəˌletər] *s* Rechenmaschine *f*; (data proc) Rechner *m*

calcu·lus [ˈkælkjələs] *s* (*-luses & -li* [ˌlaɪ]) (math) Differenzial– und Integralrechnung *f*; (pathol) Stein *m*

caldron [ˈkɔldrən] *s* Kessel *m*

calendar [ˈkæləndər] *s* Kalender *m*

calf [kæf] *s* (calves [kævz]) (*of a cow*) Kalb *n*; (*of certain other mammals*) Junge *n*; (anat) Wade *f*

calf/skin/ *s* Kalbleder *n*

caliber [ˈkælɪbər] *s* (& fig) Kaliber *n*

calibrate [ˈkælɪˌbret] *tr* kalibrieren

cali·co [ˈkælɪˌko] *s* (*-coes & -cos*) Kaliko *m*

calisthenics [ˌkælɪsˈθɛnɪks] *spl* Leibesübungen *pl*

calk [kɔk] *tr* abdichten, kalfatern

calk/ing *s* Kalfaterung *f*

call [kɔl] *s* Ruf *m*; (*visit*) Besuch *m*; (*reason*) Grund *m*; (com) (for) Nachfrage *f* (nach); (naut) Anlaufen *n*; (telp) Anruf *m*; **on c.** auf Abruf ‖ *tr* rufen; (*name*) nennen; (*wake*) wecken; (*a meeting*) einberufen; (*a game*) absagen; (*a strike*) ausrufen; (*by phone*) anrufen; (*a witness*) vorladen; (*a doctor; taxi*) kommen lassen; **be called** heißen; **c. down** (coll) herunterputzen; **c. in** (*a doctor, specialist*) hinzuziehen; (*for advice*) zu Rate ziehen; (*currency*) einziehen; (*capital*) kündigen; **c. it a day** (coll) Schluß machen; **c. off** absagen; **c. out** ausrufen; (*the police*) einsetzen; **c. s.o. names** j–n beschimpfen; **c. up** (mil) einberufen; (telp) anrufen || *intr* rufen; (cards) ansagen; **c. for** (*require*) erfordern; (*fetch*) abholen; (*help*) rufen um; (*a person*) rufen nach; **c. on** (*a pupil*) aufrufen; (*visit*) e–n Besuch machen bei; **c. to s.o.** j–m zurufen; **c. upon** auffordern

call′ bell′ *s* Rufglocke *f*

call′ boy′ *s* Hotelpage *m*; (theat) Inspezientengehilfe *m*

caller [′kɔlər] *s* Besucher –in *mf*

call′ girl′ *s* Callgirl *n*

call′ing *s* Beruf *m*; (relig) Berufung *f*

call′ing card′ *s* Visitenkarte *f*

call′ing-down′ *s* (coll) Standpauke *f*

call′ num′ber *s* (libr) Standortnummer *f*

callous [′kæləs] *adj* schwielig; (fig) gefühllos, abgestumpft

call′up′ *s* (mil) Einberufung *f*

callus [′kæləs] *s* Schwiele *f*

calm [kɑm] *adj* ruhig || *s* Ruhe *f*; (naut) Flaute *f* || *tr* beruhigen; **c. down** beruhigen || *intr*—**c. down** sich beruhigen

calorie [′kæləri] *s* Kalorie *f*

calumny [′kæləmni] *s* Verleumdung *f*

Calvary [′kælvəri] *s* Golgatha *n*

calve [kæv] *intr* kalben

cam [kæm] *s* Nocken *m*

camel [′kæməl] *s* Kamel *n*

camellia [kə′miljə] *s* Kamelie *f*

came·o [′kæmɪ‚o] *s* (-os) Kamee *f*

camera [′kæmərə] *s* Kamera *f*

cam′era-man′ *s* (-men′) Kameramann *m*

camouflage [′kæmə‚flɑʒ] *s* Tarnung *f* || *tr* tarnen

camp [kæmp] *s* (& fig) Lager *n* || *intr* kampieren, lagern, campen

campaign [kæm′pen] *s* (& fig) Feldzug *m*; (pol) Wahlfeldzug *m* || *intr* an e–m Feldzug teilnehmen; **c. for** (pol) Wahlpropaganda machen für

campaigner [kæm′penər] *s* (*for a specific cause*) Befürworter –in *mf*; (pol) Wahlredner –in *mf*

campaign′ slo′gan *s* Wahlparole *f*

campaign′ speech′ *s* Wahlrede *f*

camper [′kæmpər] *s* Camper *m*

camp′fire′ *s* Lagerfeuer *m*

camp′ground *s* Campingplatz *m*

camphor [′kæmfər] *s* Kampfer *m*

camp′ing *s* Camping *n*

campus [′kæmpəs] *s* Universitätsgelände *n*

cam′shaft′ *s* Nockenwelle *f*

can [kæn] *s* Dose *f*, Büchse *f*; (*for gasoline, water*) Kanister *m* || *v* (*pret & pp* **canned**; *ger* **canning**) *tr* einmachen; (sl) 'rausschmeißen *f* || *v* (*pret & cond*) (**could**) *aux*—**I can come** ich kann kommen; **I cannot come** ich kann nicht kommen

Canada [′kænədə] *s* Kanada *n*

Canadian [kə′nedɪ‚ən] *adj* kanadisch || *s* Kanadier –in *mf*

canal [kə′næl] *s* Kanal *m*; (anat) Gang *m*

canary [kə′neri] *s* Kanarienvogel *m* || **the Canaries** *spl* die Kanarischen Inseln *pl*

can·cel [′kænsəl] *v* (*pret & pp* **-el(l)ed**; *ger* **-el(l)ing**) *tr* (*an event*) absagen; (*an order*) rückgängig machen; (*something written*) (aus)streichen, annulieren; (*stamps*) entwerten; (*a debt*) tilgen; (*a newspaper*) abbestellen; (math) streichen; **c. out** ausgleichen

cancellation [‚kænsə′leʃən] *s* (*of an event*) Absage *f*; (*of an order*) Annullierung *f*; (*of something written*) Streichung *f*; (*of a debt*) Tilgung *f*; (*of a stamp*) Entwertung *f*; (*of a newspaper*) Abbestellung *f*

cancer [′kænsər] *s* Krebs *m*

cancerous [′kænsərəs] *adj* krebsartig

candela·brum [‚kændə′lɑbrəm] *s* (-bra [brə] & -brums) Armleuchter *m*

candid [′kændɪd] *adj* offen

candidacy [′kændɪdəsi] *s* Kandidatur *f*

candidate [′kændɪ‚det] *s* (for) Kandidat –in *mf* (für)

candied [′kændɪd] *adj* kandiert

candle [′kændəl] *s* Kerze *f*

can′dlelight′ *s* Kerzenlicht *n*

can′dlepow′er *s* Kerzenstärke *f*

can′dlestick′ *s* Kerzenhalter *m*

candor [′kændər] *s* Offenheit *f*

can·dy [′kændi] *s* Süßwaren *pl*; **piece of c.** Bonbon *m* & *n* || *v* (*pret & pp* -died) *tr* glacieren, kandieren

can′dy store′ *s* Süßwarengeschäft *n*

cane [ken] *s* (plant; stem) Rohr *n*; (*walking stick*) Stock *m* || *tr* mit e–m Stock züchtigen

cane′ sug′ar *s* Rohrzucker *m*

canine [′kenaɪn] *adj* Hunde– || *s* (*tooth*) Eckzahn *m*, Reißzahn *m*

canister [′kænɪstər] *s* Dose *f*

canker [′kæŋkər] *s* (bot) Brand *m*; (pathol) Mundgeschwür *n*

canned′ goods′ *spl* Dosenkonserven *pl*

canned′ mu′sic *s* Konservenmusik *f*

canned′ veg′etables *spl* Gemüsekonserven *pl*

cannery [′kænəri] *s* Konservenfabrik *f*

cannibal [′kænɪbəl] *s* Kannibale *m*

can′ning *adj* Konserven– || *s* Konservenfabrikation *f*

cannon [′kænən] *s* Kanone *f*

cannonade [‚kænə′ned] *s* Kanonade *f*, Beschießung *f* || *tr* beschießen

can′nonball′ *s* Kanonenkugel *f*

can′non fod′der *s* Kanonenfutter *n*

canny [′kæni] *adj* (shrewd) schlau; (sagacious) klug

canoe [kə′nu] *s* Kanu *n*

canoe′ing *s* Kanufahren *n*

canoeist [kə′nu·ɪst] *s* Kanufahrer *m*

canon [′kænən] *s* Kanon *m*; (*of a cathedral*) Domherr *m*

canonical [kə′nɑnɪkəl] *adj* kanonisch || **canonicals** *spl* kirchliche Amtstracht *f*

canonize ['kænə,naɪz] *tr* heiligsprechen

can'on law' *s* kanonisches Recht *n*

can' o'pener *s* Dosenöffner *m*

canopy ['kænəpɪ] *s* Baldachin *m*; *(above a king or pope)* Thronhimmel *m*; *(of a bed)* Betthimmel *m*

cant [kænt] *s (insincere statements)* unaufrichtiges Gerede *n*; *(jargon of thieves)* Gaunersprache *f*; *(technical phraseology)* Jargon *m*

cantaloupe ['kæntə,lop] *s* Kantalupe *f*

cantankerous [kæn'tæŋkərəs] *adj* mürrisch, zänkisch

cantata [kən'tatə] *s* Kantate *f*

canteen [kæn'tin] *s (service club, service store)* Kantine *f*; *(flask)* Feldflasche *f*

canter ['kæntər] *s* kurzer Galopp *m* ‖ *intr* im kurzen Galopp reiten

canticle ['kæntɪkəl] *s* Lobgesang *m*

canton ['kæntən] *s* Kanton *m*

canvas ['kænvəs] *s* Leinwand *f*; *(naut)* Segeltuch *n*; *(a painting)* Gemälde *n*

canvass ['kænvəs] *s (econ)* Werbefeldzug *m*; *(pol)* Wahlfeldzug *m* ‖ *tr (a district)* (pol) bearbeiten; *(votes)* (pol) werben

canyon ['kænjən] *s* Schlucht *f*

cap [kæp] *s* Kappe *f*, Mütze *f*; *(of a jar)* Deckel *m*; *(twist-off type)* Kapsel *f*; *(for a toy pistol)* Knallblättchen *n*; *(typ)* großer Buchstabe *m*; use caps *(typ)* großschreiben ‖ *v (pret & pp capped; ger capping) tr (a bottle)* mit e-r Kapsel versehen; *(e.g., with snow)* bedecken; *(outdo)* übertreffen; *(success)* krönen

capability [,kepə'brlɪtɪ] *s* Fähigkeit *f*

capable ['kepəbəl] *adj* tüchtig; **c. of** fähig *(genit)*; *(ger)* fähig zu *(inf)*

capacious [kə'peʃəs] *adj* geräumig

capacity [kə'pæsɪtɪ] *adj* maximal, Kapazitäts— ‖ *s (ability)* Fähigkeit *f*; *(content)* Fassungsvermögen *n*; *(of a truck, bridge)* Tragfähigkeit *f*; *(tech)* Kapazität *f*; **in my c. as** in meiner Eigenschaft als

cap' and gown' *s* Barett *n* und Talar *m*

cape [kep] *s* Umhang *m*; *(geog)* Kap *n*

Cape' of Good' Hope' *s* Kap *n* der Guten Hoffnung

caper ['kepər] *s* Luftsprung *m*; *(prank)* Schabernack *m*; *(culin)* Kaper *f* ‖ *intr* hüpfen

capita ['kæpɪtə] *spl*—**per c.** pro Kopf, pro Person

capital ['kæpɪtəl] *adj (importance)* äußerste, höchste; *(city)* Haupt—; *(crime)* Kapital— ‖ *s (city)* Hauptstadt *f*; *(archit)* Kapitell *n*; *(fin)* Kapital *n*; *(typ)* Großbuchstabe *m*

cap'ital gains' *spl* Kapitalzuwachs *m*

capitalism ['kæpɪtə,lɪzəm] *s* Kapitalismus *m*

capitalist ['kæpɪtəlɪst] *s* Kapitalist –in *mf*

capitalistic [,kæpɪtə'lɪstɪk] *adj* kapitalistisch

capitalize ['kæpɪtə,laɪz] *tr* (fin) kapitalisieren; *(typ)* groß schreiben (or

drucken) ‖ *intr*—**c. on** Nutzen ziehen aus

cap'ital let'ter *s* Großbuchstabe *m*

cap'ital pun'ishment *s* Todesstrafe *f*

capitol ['kæpɪtəl] *s* Kapitol *n*

capitulate [kə'pɪt/ə,let] *intr* kapitulieren

capon ['kepən] *s* Kapaun *m*

caprice [kə'pris] *s* Grille *f*, Kaprice *f*

capricious [kə'prɪ/əs] *adj* kapriziös

capsize ['kæpsaɪz] *tr* zum Kentern bringen ‖ *intr* kentern

capsule ['kæpsəl] *s* Kapsel *f*

captain ['kæptən] *s (of police, of firemen, in the army)* Hauptmann *m*; *(naut, sport)* Kapitän *m*; *(nav)* Kapitän *m* zur See; *(sport)* Mannschaftsführer *m*

caption ['kæp/ən] *s (heading of an article)* Überschrift *f*; *(wording under a picture)* Bildunterschrift *f*; *(cin)* Untertitel *m*

captivate ['kæptɪ,vet] *tr* fesseln

captive ['kæptɪv] *adj* gefangen ‖ *s* Gefangene *mf*

cap'tive au'dience *s* unfreiwillige Zuhörerschaft *f*

captivity [kæp'tɪvɪtɪ] *s* Gefangenschaft *f*

captor ['kæptər] *s* Fänger –in *mf*

capture ['kæpt/ər] *s* Fangen *n*, Gefangennahme *f*; *(naut)* Kaperung *f* ‖ *tr (animals)* fangen; *(soldiers)* gefangennehmen; *(a ship)* kapern; *(a town)* erobern; *(a prize)* gewinnen

car [kar] *s (aut, rr)* Wagen *m*

carafe [kə'ræf] *s* Karaffe *f*

caramel ['kærəməl] *s* Karamelle *f*

carat ['kærət] *s* Karat *n*

caravan ['kærə,væn] *s* Karawane *f*

car'away seed' ['kærə,we] *s* Kümmelkorn *n*

carbide ['karbaɪd] *s* Karbid *n*

carbine ['karbaɪn] *s* Karabiner *m*

carbohydrate [,karbo'haɪdret] *s* Kohlenhydrat *n*

carbol'ic ac'id [kar'balɪk] *s* Karbolsäure *f*

carbon ['karbən] *s (chem)* Kohlenstoff *m*; *(elec)* Kohlenstift *m*

carbonated ['karbə,netɪd] *adj* kohlensäurehaltig, Brause—

car'bon cop'y *s* Durchschlag *m*; **make a c. of** durchschlagen

car'bon diox'ide *s* Kohlendioxyd *n*

car'bon monox'ide *s* Kohlenoxyd *n*

car'bon pa'per *s* Kohlepapier *n*

carbuncle ['karbʌŋkəl] *s (stone)* Karfunkel *m*; *(pathol)* Karbunkel *m*

carburetor ['karb(j)ə,retər] *s* Vergaser *m*

carcass ['karkəs] *s* Kadaver *m*, Aas *n*; *(without offal)* Rumpf *m*

car' coat' *s* Stutzer *m*

card [kard] *s* Karte *f*; *(person)* (coll) Kerl *m*; *(text)* Krempel *f* ‖ *tr* (text) kardätschen

card'board' *s* Kartonpapier *n*; *(thick pasteboard)* Pappe *f*; **piece of c.** Papp(en)deckel *m*

card'board box' *s* Pappkarton *m*, Pappschachtel *f*

card' cat'alogue *s* Kartothek *f*

card′ file′ s Kartei f
cardiac [′kɑrdɪ͵æk] adj Herz– || s (remedy) Herzmittel n; (patient) Herzkranke mf
cardinal [′kɑrdɪnəl] adj Kardinal– || s (eccl, orn) Kardinal m
card′ in′dex s Karthotek f, Kartei f
card′sharp′ s Falschspieler –in mf
card′ trick′ s Kartenkunststück n
care [ker] s (accuracy) Sorgfalt f; (worry) Sorge f, Kummer m; (prudence) Vorsicht f; (upkeep) Pflege f; **be under a doctor′s c.** unter der Aufsicht e-s Arztes stehen; **c. of** (on letters) bei; **take c.** aufpassen; **take c. not to** (inf) sich hüten zu (inf); **take c. of s.o.** (provide for s.o.) für j-n sorgen; (attend to) sich um j-n kümmern; **take c. of s.th.** etw besorgen; (e.g., one′s clothes) schonen || intr–c. about sich kümmern um; **c. for** (like) mögen, gern haben; (have concern for) sorgen für; (attend to) pflegen; **c. to** (inf) Lust haben zu (inf); **for all I c.** von mir aus
careen [kə′rin] tr auf die Seite legen || intr (aut) sich in die Kurve neigen
career [kə′rɪr] adj Berufs– || s Karriere f
career′ wo′man s berufstätige Frau f
care′free′ adj unbelastet, sorgenfrei
careful [′kerfəl] adj (cautious) vorsichtig; (accurate) sorgfältig; **b. c.!** gib acht!
careless [′kerlɪs] adj (incautious) unvorsichtig; (remark) unbedacht; (inaccurate) nachlässig
carelessness [′kerlɪsnɪs] s Unvorsichtigkeit f; Nachlässigkeit f
caress [kə′res] s Liebkosung f || tr liebkosen
caret [′kærət] s Auslassungszeichen n
caretaker [′ker͵tekər] s Verwalter m
care′worn′ adj abgehärmt, vergrämt
car′fare′ s Fahrgeld n
car′go [′kɑrgo] s (–goes & –gos) Fracht f
car′go compart′ment s Frachtraum m
car′go plane′ s Frachtflugzeug n
Caribbean [͵kærɪ′biən], [kə′rɪbɪən] adj karibisch || s Karibisches Meer n
caricature [′kærɪkət∫ər] s Karikatur f || tr karikieren
caries [′keriz] s (dent) Karies f
carillon [′kærɪ͵lɑn] s Glockenspiel n
car′ lift′s (aut) Hebebühne f
car′load′ s Wagenladung f
carnage [′kɑrnɪdʒ] s Blutbad n
carnal [′kɑrnəl] adj fleischlich
car′nal know′ledge s Geschlechtsverkehr m
carnation [kɑr′ne∫ən] s Nelke f
carnival [′kɑrnɪvəl] s Karneval m
carnivorous [kɑr′nɪvərəs] adj fleischfressend
car-ol [′kærəl] s Weihnachtslied n || v (pret & pp –ol(l)ed; ger –l(l)ing) intr Weihnachtslieder singen
carom [′kærəm] s (billiards) Karambolage f || intr (fig) zusammenstoßen; (billiards) karambolieren
carouse [kə′rauz] intr zechen

carp [kɑrp] s Karpfen m || intr nörgeln
carpenter [′kɑrpəntər] s Zimmermann m
carpentry [′kɑrpəntri] s Zimmerei f
carpet [′kɑrpɪt] s Teppich m || tr mit Teppichen belegen
car′pet sweep′er s Teppichkehrmaschine f
car′port′ s Autoschuppen m
car′-ren′tal serv′ice s Autovermietung f
carriage [′kærɪdʒ] s Kutsche f; (of a typewriter) Wagen m; (bearing) Körperhaltung f; (econ) Transportkosten pl
car′ ride′ s Autofahrt f
carrier [′kærɪ-ər] s Träger m; (company) Transportunternehmen n
car′rier pig′eon s Brieftaube f
carrion [′kærɪ-ən] s Aas n
carrot [′kærət] s Karotte f, Mohrrübe f
carrousel [͵kærə′zel] s Karussell n
car-ry [′kæri] v (pret & pp –ried) tr tragen; (wares) führen; (a message) überbringen; (a tune) halten; (said of transportation) befördern; (insurance) haben; (math) übertragen; (parl) durchbringen; **be carried** (said of a motion, bill) angenommen werden; **be carried away by** (& fig) mitgerissen werden von; **c. away** (an audience) mitreißen; **c. off** (a prize) davontragen; **c. on** weiterführen; (a business) betreiben, führen; **c. out** hinaustragen; (a duty) erfüllen; (measures) durchführen; (a sentence) vollstrecken; (an order) ausführen; **c. over** (acct) übertragen; **c. s.th. too far** etw übertreiben; **c. through** durchsetzen; || intr (said of sounds) tragen; (parl) durchgehen; **c. on** (continue) weitermachen; (act up) (coll) toben; **c. on with** ein Verhältnis haben mit
car′rying char′ges spl Kreditgebühren pl
car′ry-o′ver s Überbleibsel n; (acct) Übertrag m
cart [kɑrt] s Karren m || tr mit dem Handwagen befördern; **c. away** (or **c. off**) abfahren
cartel [kɑr′tel] s Kartell n
cartilage [′kɑrtɪlɪdʒ] s Knorpel m
carton [′kɑrtən] s Karton m; **a c. of cigarettes** e-e Stange Zigaretten
cartoon [kɑr′tun] s Karikatur f; (comic strip) Karikaturenreihe f; (cin) Zeichentrickfilm m; (paint) Entwurf m natürlicher Größe || tr karikieren
cartoonist [kɑr′tunɪst] s Karikaturenzeichner –in mf
cartridge [′kɑrtrɪdʒ] s Patrone f; (phot) Filmpatrone f
car′tridge belt′ s Patronengurt m
cart′wheel′ s Wagenrad n; **turn a c.** ein Rad schlagen
carve [kɑrv] tr (wood) schnitzen; (meat) tranchieren, vorschneiden; (stone) meißeln; **c. out** (e.g., a career) aufbauen

carver ['kɑrvər] s (at table) Vor-schneider –in mf

carv'ing knife' s Tranchiermesser n

car' wash' s Wagenwäsche f

cascade [kæs'ked] s Kaskade f || intr kaskadenartig herabstürzen

case [kes] s (instance) Fall m; (situation) Sache f; (box) Kiste f; (for a knife, etc.) Hülle f; (for cigarettes) Etui n; (for eyeglasses) Futteral m; (for shipping) Schutzkarton m; (of a watch) Gehäuse n; (of sickness) Krankheitsfall m; (sick person) Patient –in mf; (gram) Fall m; (jur) Fall m, Sache f, Prozeß m; (typ) Setzkasten m; **as the c. may be** je nachdem; **have a strong c.** schlüssige Beweise haben; **if that's the c.** wenn es sich so verhält; **in any c.** auf jeden Fall, jedenfalls; **in c.** falls; **in c. of** im Falle (genit); **in c. of emergency** im Notfall; **in no c.** keinesfalls || tr (sl) genau ansehen; **the c. at issue** der vorliegende Fall

case' his'tory s Vorgeschichte f; (med) Krankengeschichte f

casement ['kesmənt] s Fensterflügel m

case'ment win'dow s Flügelfenster n

cash [kæʃ] adj Bar– || s Bargeld n; (cash payment) Barzahlung f; **c. and carry** nur gegen Barzahlung und eigenen Transport; **in c.** per Kasse; **out of c.** nicht bei Kasse; **pay c. for** bar bezahlen || tr einlösen || intr–c. **in on** (coll) Nutzen ziehen aus

cash'box' s Schatulle f, Kasse f

cash' dis'count s Kassaskonto n

cashew' nut' [kæ'ʃu], ['kæʃu] s Kaschunuß f

cashier [kæ'ʃɪr] s Kassierer –in mf

cashmere ['kæʃmɪr] s Kaschmir m

cash' on deliv'ery adv per Nachnahme

cash' reg'ister m Registrierkasse f

cas'ing s (wrapping) Verpackung f; (housing) Gehäuse n; (of a window or door) Futter n; (of a tire) Mantel m; (of a sausage) Wurstdarm m

casi·no [kə'sino] s (–nos) Kasino n

cask [kæsk] s Faß n, Tonne f

casket ['kæskɪt] s Sarg m

casserole ['kæsə‚rol] s Kasserolle f

cassette [kæ'sɛt] s Kassette f

cassock ['kæsək] s (eccl) Soutane f

cast [kæst] s (throw) Wurf m; (act of molding) Guß m; (mold) Gußform f; (object molded) Abguß m; (hue) Abtönung f; (surg) Gipsverband m; (theat) Rollenbesetzung f || v (pret & pp **cast**) tr werfen; (a net, anchor) auswerfen; (a ballot) abgeben; (lots) ziehen; (skin, horns) abwerfen; (a shadow, glance) werfen; (metal) gießen; (a play or motion picture) die Rollen besetzen in (dat); **be c. down** niedergeschlagen sein; **c. aside** (reject) verwerfen; || intr (angl) die Angel auswerfen; **c. off** (naut) loswerfen

castanet [‚kæstə'nɛt] s Kastagnette f

cast'away' adj verworfen; (naut) schiffbrüchig || s (naut) Schiffbrüchige mf

caste [kæst] s Kaste f

caster ['kæstər] s (under furniture) Rolle f; (shaker) Streuer m

castigate ['kæstɪ‚get] tr züchtigen; (fig) geißeln

cast'ing s Wurf m; (act of casting) (metal) Guß m; (the object cast) (metal) Gußstück n; (theat) Rollenverteilung f

cast'ing rod' s Wurfangel f

cast' i'ron s Gußeisen n

cast'-i'ron adj gußeisern; (fig) eisern

castle ['kæsəl] s Schloß n, Burg, f; (chess) Turm m || intr (chess) rochieren

cast'off' adj abgelegt || s (e.g., dress) abgelegtes Kleidungsstück n; (person) Verstoßene mf

cas'tor oil' ['kæstər] s Rizinusöl n

castrate ['kæstret] tr kastrieren

casual ['kæʒʊ·əl] adj (cursory) beiläufig; (occasional) gelegentlich; (incidental) zufällig; (informal) zwanglos; (unconcerned) gleichgültig

casualty ['kæʒʊ·əltɪ] s (victim) Opfer n; (accident) Unfall m; (person injured) Verunglückte mf; (person killed) (mil) Gefallene mf; (person wounded) (mil) Verwundete mf; **casualties** (in an accident) Verunglückte pl; (in war) Verluste pl

cas'ualty list' s Verlustliste f

cat [kæt] s Katze f; (guy) (sl) Typ m; (malicious woman) (sl) falsche Katze f

catacomb ['kætə‚kom] s Katakombe f

catalog(ue) ['kætə‚lɔg] s Katalog m; (list) Verzeichnis n; (of a university) Vorlesungsverzeichnis n || tr katalogisieren

catalyst ['kætəlɪst] s Katalysator m

catapult ['kætə‚pʌlt] s Katapult m & n || tr katapultieren, abschleudern

cataract ['kætə‚rækt] s Katarakt m; (pathol) grauer Star m; **remove s.o.'s c.** j-m den Star stechen

catastrophe [kə'tæstrəfi] s Katastrophe f

cat'call' s Auspfeifen n || tr auspfeifen

catch [kætʃ] s Fang m; (of fish) Fischfang m; (device) Haken m, Klinke f; (desirable partner) Partie f; (fig) Haken m; || v (pret & pp **caught** [kɔt]) tr fangen; (s.o. or s.th. falling) auffangen; (by pursuing) abfangen; (s.o. or s.th. that has escaped) einfangen; (by surprise) ertappen, erwischen; (in midair) aufschnappen; (take hold of) fassen; (said of a storm) überraschen; (e.g., a train) erreichen; **c. a cold** sich erkälten; **c. fire** in Brand geraten; **c. hold of** ergreifen; **c. it** (coll) sein Fett kriegen; **c. one's breath** wieder Atem schöpfen; **c. one's eye** j-m ins Auge fallen; **get caught on** hängenbleiben an (dat) || intr (said of a bolt, etc.) einschnappen; **c. on** (said of an idea) Anklang finden; **c. on to** (fig) kapieren; **catch up** aufholen; **c. up on** nachholen; **c. up with** einholen

catch'ing adj (disease) ansteckend; (attractive) anziehend catch'word' s (slogan) Schlagwort n; (actor's cue) Stichwort n; (pol) Parteiparole f

catchy ['kætʃi] adj einschmeichelnd

catechism ['kætɪ,kɪzəm] s Katechismus m

category [,kætə'gori] s Kategorie f

cater ['ketər] tr Lebensmittel liefern für ‖ intr—c. to schmeicheln (dat); (deliver food to) Lebensmittel liefern für

cater-corner ['kætər,kɔrnər] adj & adv diagonal

caterer ['ketərər] s Lebensmittellieferant –in mf

caterpillar ['kætər,pɪlər] s (ent, mach) Raupe f

cat'fish' s Katzenwels m, Katzenfisch m

cat'gut' s (mus) Darmseite f; (surg) Katgut n

cathedral [kə'θidrəl] s Dom m

catheter ['kæθɪtər] s Katheter n

cathode ['kæθod] s Kathode f

catholic ['kæθəlɪk] adj universal; Catholic katholisch ‖ Catholic s Katholik –in mf

cat'nap' s Nickerchen n

catnip ['kætnɪp] s Baldrian m

catsup ['kætsəp], ['ketʃəp] s Ketschup m

cattle ['kætəl] spl Vieh n

cat'tle car' s (rr) Viehwagen m

cat'tle-man s (–men) Viehzüchter m

cat'tle ranch' s Viehfarm f

catty ['kæti] adj boshaft

cat'walk' s Steg m, Laufplanke f

Caucasian [kɔ'keʒən] adj kaukasisch ‖ s Kaukasier –in mf

caucus ['kɔkəs] s Parteiführerversammlung f

cauliflower ['kɔlɪ,flau·ər] s Blumenkohl m

cause [kɔz] s (origin) Ursache f; (reason) Grund m; (person) Urheber –in mf; (occasion) Anlaß m; for a good c. für e–e gute Sache ‖ tr verursachen; c. s.o. to (inf) j–n veranlassen zu (inf)

cause'way' s Dammweg m

caustic ['kɔstɪk] adj (& fig) ätzend

cauterize ['kɔtə,raɪz] tr verätzen

caution ['kɔʃən] s (carefulness) Vorsicht f; (warning) Warnung f ‖ tr (against) warnen (vor dat)

cautious ['kɔʃəs] adj vorsichtig

cavalcade ['kævəl,ked] s Kavalkade f

cavalier [,kævə'lɪr] adj hochmütig ‖ s Kavalier m

cavalry ['kævəlri] s Kavallerie f

cav'alry-man s (–men) Kavallerist m

cave [kev] s Höhle f ‖ intr—c. in (collapse) einstürzen

cave'-in' s Einsturz m

cave' man' s Höhlenmensch m

cavern ['kævərn] s (große) Höhle f

caviar ['kævɪ,ɑr] s Kaviar m

cav-il ['kævɪl] v (pret & pp –l(l)ed; ger –l(l)ing) intr (at, about) herumnörgeln (an dat)

cavity ['kævɪti] s Hohlraum m; (anat) Höhle f; (dent) Loch n

cavort [kə'vɔrt] intr (coll) herumtollen

caw [kɔ] s Krächzen n ‖ intr krächzen

cease [sis] s—without c. unaufhörlich ‖ tr einstellen; (ger) aufhören (zu inf); c. fire das Feuer einstellen ‖ intr aufhören

cease'fire' s Feuereinstellung f

ceaseless ['sislɪs] adj unaufhörlich

cedar ['sidər] s Zeder f

cede [sid] tr abtreten, überlassen

cedilla [sɪ'dɪlə] s Cedille f

ceiling ['silɪŋ] s Decke f; (fin) oberste Grenze f; hit the c. (coll) platzen

ceil'ing light' s Deckenlicht n

ceil'ing price' s Höchstpreis m

celebrant ['selɪbrənt] s Zelebrant m

celebrate ['selɪ,bret] tr (a feast) feiern; (mass) zelebrieren ‖ intr feiern; (eccl) zelebrieren

cel'ebrat'ed (for) berühmt (wegen)

celebration [,selɪ'bre/ən] s Feier f; (eccl) Zelebrieren n; in c. of zur Feier (genit)

celebrity [sɪ'lebrɪti] s Berühmtheit f; (person) Prominente mf

celery ['seləri] s Selleriestengel m

celestial [sɪ'lestʃəl] adj himmlisch; (astr) Himmels–

celibacy ['selɪbəsi] s Zölibat m & n

celibate ['selɪbɪt] adj ehelos

cell [sel] s Zelle f

cellar ['selər] s Keller m

cellist ['tʃelɪst] s Cellist –in mf

cel-lo ['tʃelo] s (–los) Cello n

cellophane ['selə,fen] s Zellophan n

celluloid ['seljə,lɔɪd] s Zelluloid n

Celt [selt], [kelt] s Kelte m, Keltin f

Celtic ['seltɪk], ['keltɪk] adj keltisch

cement [sɪ'ment] s (glue) Bindemittel n; (used in building) Zement m ‖ tr zementieren; (glue) kitten; (fig) (be)festigen

cement' mix'er s Betonmischmaschine f

cemetery ['semɪ,teri] s Friedhof m

censer ['sensər] s Räucherfaß n

censor ['sensər] s (of printed matter, films) Zensor m; (of morals) Sittenrichter m ‖ tr zensieren

cen'sorship' s Zensur f

censure ['senʃər] s Tadel m ‖ tr tadeln

census ['sensəs] s Volkszählung f

cent [sent] s Cent m

centaur ['sentɔr] s Zentaur m

centennial [sen'tenɪəl] adj hundertjährig ‖ s Hundertjahrfeier f

center ['sentər] s Zentrum n, Mittelpunkt m; (pol) Mitte f ‖ tr in den Mittelpunkt stellen; (tech) zentrieren ‖ intr—c. on sich konzentrieren auf (acc)

cen'ter aisle' s Mittelgang m

cen'ter cit'y s Stadtmitte f

cen'terpiece' s Tischaufsatz m

centigrade ['sentɪ,gred] s Celsius, e.g., one degree c. ein Grad Celsius

centimeter ['sentɪ,mitər] s Zentimeter m

centipede ['sentɪ,pid] s Hundertfüßler m

central ['sentrəl] adj zentral

Cen'tral Amer'ica s Mittelamerika n

centralize ['sentrə,laɪz] tr zentralisieren

centri′fugal force′ [sɛn′trɪfjəgəl] *s* Fliehkraft *f*

centrifuge [′sɛntrɪ‚fjudʒ] *s* Zentrifuge *f*

century [′sɛntʃərɪ] *s* Jahrhundert *n*

ceramic [sɪ′ræmɪk] *adj* keramisch ‖ **ceramics** *s* (art) Keramik *f*; *spl* Töpferwaren *pl*

cereal [′sɪrɪ-əl] *adj* Getreide– ‖ *s* (grain) Getreide *n*; (dish) Getreideflockengericht *n*

cerebral [′sɛrɪbrəl] *adj* Gehirn–

ceremonial [‚sɛrɪ′monɪ-əl] *adj* zeremoniell, feierlich

ceremonious [‚sɛrɪ′monɪ-əs] *adj* zeremoniös, umständlich

ceremony [′sɛrɪ‚monɪ] *s* Zeremonie *f*

certain [′sʌrtən] *adj* (sure) sicher, bestimmt; (particular but unnamed) gewiß; **be c.** feststehen; **for c.** gewiß; **make c. of** sich vergewissern (genit); **make c. that** sich vergewissern, daß

certainly [′sʌrtənlɪ] *adv* sicher(lich); (as a strong affirmative) allerdings

certainty [′sʌrtəntɪ] *s* Sicherheit *f*

certificate [sər′tɪfɪkɪt] *s* Schein *m*; (educ) Abgangszeugnis *n*

certification [‚sʌrtɪfɪ′keʃən] *s* Bescheinigung *f*, Beglaubigung *f*

cer′tified *adj* beglaubigt

cer′tified check′ *s* durch Bank bestätigter Scheck *m*

cer′tified pub′lic account′ant *s* amtlich zugelassener Wirtschaftsprüfer *m*

certi-fy [′sʌrtɪ‚faɪ] *v* (pret & pp –fied) bescheinigen, beglaubigen

cervix [′sʌrvɪks] *s* (cervices [sər′vaɪsɪz]) Genick *n*

cessation [sɛ′seʃən] *s* (of territory) Abtretung *f*; (of activities) Einstellung *f*

cesspool [′sɛs‚pul] *s* Senkgrube *f*

chafe [tʃef] *tr* (the skin) wundscheuern ‖ *intr* (rub) scheuern; (become sore) sich wundreiben; (be irritated) (at) sich ärgern über (acc)

chaff [tʃæf] *s* Spreu *f*

chaf′ing dish′ *s* Speisenwärmer *m*

chagrin [ʃə′grɪn] *s* Verdruß *m* ‖ *tr* verdrießen

chain [tʃen] *s* Kette *f* ‖ *tr* (to) anketten (an acc)

chain′ gang′ *s* Kettensträflinge *pl*

chain′ reac′tion *s* Kettenreaktion *f*

chain′ smok′er *s* Kettenraucher –in *mf*

chain′ store′ *s* Kettenladen *m*

chair [tʃɛr] *s* Stuhl *m*; (upholstered) Sessel *m*; (of the presiding officer) Vorsitz *m*; (presiding officer) Vorsitzende *mf*; (educ) Lehrstuhl *m* ‖ *tr* den Vorsitz führen von

chair′la′dy *s* Vorsitzende *f*

chair′ lift′ *s* Sessellift *m*

chair′man *s* (–men) Vorsitzende *m*

chair′manship′ *s* Vorsitz *m*

chalice [′tʃælɪs] *s* Kelch *m*

chalk [tʃɔk] *s* Kreide *f* ‖ *tr*—**c. up** ankreiden; (coll) verbuchen

challenge [′tʃælɪndʒ] *s* Aufforderung *f*; (to a duel) Herausforderung *f*; (jur) Ablehnung *f*; (mil) Anruf *m* ‖ *tr* auffordern; (to a duel) herausfordern; (a statement, right) bestreiten; (jur) ablehnen; (mil) anrufen

chamber [′tʃembər] *s* Kammer *f*; (parl) Sitzungssaal *m*

chamberlain [′tʃembərlɪn] *s* Kammerherr *m*

cham′bermaid′ *s* Stubenmädchen *n*

cham′ber of com′merce *s* Handelskammer *f*

chameleon [kə′milɪ-ən] *s* Chamäleon *n*

chamfer [′tʃæmfər] *s* Schrägkante *f* ‖ *tr* abschrägen; (furrow) auskehlen

cham-ois [′ʃæmɪ] *s* (-ois) Sämischleder *n*; (zool) Gemse *f*

champ [tʃæmp] *s* (coll) Meister *m* ‖ *tr* kauen; **champ the bit am Gebiß kauen**

champagne [ʃæm′pen] *s* Champagner *m*, Sekt *m*

champion [′tʃæmpɪ-ən] *s* (of a cause) Verfechter –in *mf*; (sport) Meister –in *mf* ‖ *tr* eintreten für

cham′pionship′ *s* Meisterschaft *f*

chance [tʃæns] *adj* zufällig ‖ *s* (accident) Zufall *m*; (opportunity) Chance *f*, Gelegenheit *f*; (risk) Risiko *n*; (possibility) Möglichkeit *f*; (lottery ticket) Los *n*; **by c.** zufällig; **c. of a lifetime** einmalige Gelegenheit *f*; **chances are (that)** aller Wahrscheinlichkeit nach; **on the c. that** für den Fall, daß; **take a c.** ein Risiko eingehen; **take no chances** nichts riskieren; ‖ *tr* riskieren ‖ *intr* geschehen; **c. upon** stoßen auf (acc)

chancel [′tʃænsəl] *s* Altarraum *m*

chancellery [′tʃænsələrɪ] *s* Kanzlei *f*

chancellor [′tʃænsələr] *s* Kanzler *m*; (hist) Reichskanzler *m*

chandelier [‚ʃændə′lɪr] *s* Kronleuchter *m*

change [tʃendʒ] *s* Veränderung *f*; (in times, styles, etc.) Wechsel *m*; (in attitude, relations, etc.) Wandel *m*; (small coins) Kleingeld *n*; (of weather) Umschlag *m*; **c. for the better** Verbesserung *f*; **c. for the worse** Verschlechterung *f*; **for a c.** zur Abwechslung; **give c. for a dollar** auf e–n Dollar herausgeben; **need a c.** Luftveränderung brauchen ‖ *tr* verändern; (plans) ändern; (money, subject, oil) wechseln; (a baby) trockenlegen; (stations, channels) umschalten; **c. around** umändern; **c. hands** den Besitzer wechseln; **c. one′s mind** sich anders besinnen; **c. trains (or buses, streetcars)** umsteigen ‖ *intr* sich verändern; (said of a mood, wind, weather) umschlagen; (said of a voice) mutieren; (change clothes) sich umziehen **change into** sich wandeln in (acc)

changeable [′tʃendʒəbəl] *adj* veränderlich

changeless [′tʃendʒlɪs] *adj* unveränderlich

change′ of heart′ *s* Sinnesänderung *f*

change′ of life′ *s* Wechseljahre *pl*

change′ of scen′ery *s* Ortsveränderung *f*

change′-o′ver *s* Umstellung *f*

chan·nel ['tʃænəl] *s* (*strait*) Kanal *m*; (*of a river*) Fahrrinne *f*; (*groove*) Rinne *f*; (*furrow*) Furche *f*; (fig) Weg *m*; (telv) Kanal *m*; **through official channels** auf dem Amtswege || *v* (*pret & pp* **-nel(l)ed**; *ger* **-nel-(l)ing**) *tr* lenken; (*furrow*) kanalisieren

chant [tʃænt] *s* Gesang *m*; (*singsong*) Singsang *m*; (eccl) Kirchengesang *m* || *tr* singen

chanter ['tʃæntər] *s* Kantor *m*

chaos ['ke·as] *s* Chaos *n*

chaotic [ke'atɪk] *adj* chaotisch

chap [tʃæp] *s* (*in the skin*) Riß *m*; (coll) Kerl *m* || *v* (*pret & pp* **chapped**; *ger* **chapping**) *tr* (*the skin*) rissig machen || *intr* rissig werden, aufspringen

chapel ['tʃæpəl] *s* Kapelle *f*

chaperon ['ʃæpə‚ron] *s* Begleiter –in *mf*; (*of a young couple*) Anstandsdame *f* || *tr* als Anstandsdame begleiten

chaplain ['tʃæplɪn] *s* Kaplan *m*

chapter ['tʃæptər] *s* Kapitel *n*; (*of an organization*) Ortsgruppe *f*

char [tʃɑr] *v* (*pret & pp* **charred**; *ger* **charring**) *tr* verkohlen

character ['kærɪktər] *s* Charakter *m*; (*letter*) Schriftzeichen *n*; (*typewriter space*) Anschlag *m*; (coll) Kauz *m*; (theat) handelnde Person *f*; **be out of c.** nicht passen

characteristic [‚kærɪktə'rɪstɪk] *adj* (*of*) charakteristisch (für) || *s* Charakterzug *m*, Kennzeichen *n*

characterize ['kærɪktə‚raɪz] *tr* charakterisieren, kennzeichnen

charade [ʃə'red] *s* Scharade *f*

charcoal ['tʃɑr‚kol] *s* Holzkohle *f*; (*for sketching*) Zeichenkohle *f*

charge [tʃɑrdʒ] *s* (*accusation*) Anklage *f*; (*fee*) Gebühr *f*; (*custody*) Obhut *f*; (*responsibility*) Pflicht *f*; (*ward*) Pflegebefohlene *mf*; (*of an explosive or electricity*) Ladung *f*; (*assault*) Ansturm *m*; (*of a judge to the jury*) Rechtsbelehrung *f*; **be in c. of** verantwortlich sein für; **charges** Spesen *pl*; **take c. of** die Verantwortung übernehmen für; **there is no c.** es kostet nichts; **under s.o.'s c.** unter j-s Aufsicht || *tr* (*a battery*) (auf)-laden; (**with**) anklagen (wegen); (*a jury*) belehren; (mil) stürmen; **c.s.o. ten marks for** j-m zehn Mark berechnen für; **c. s.o.'s account** auf j-s Rechnung setzen || *intr* (mil) anrechnen für; **c. to s.o.'s account** auf j-s Rechnung setzen || *intr* (mil) anstürmen

charge' account' *s* laufendes Konto *n*

charger ['tʃɑrdʒər] *s* (elec) Ladevorrichtung *f*; (hist) Schlachtroß *n*

chariot ['tʃærɪ-ət] *s* Kampfwagen *m*

charitable ['tʃærɪtəbəl] *adj* (*generous*) freigebig; (*lenient*) nachsichtig; **c. institution** wohltätige Stiftung *f*

charity ['tʃærɪti] *s* (*giving of alms*) Wohltätigkeit *f*; (*alms*) Almosen *n*; (*institution*) Wohlfahrtsinstitut *n*; (*love of neighbor*) Nächstenliebe *f*

charlatan ['ʃɑrlətən] *s* Scharlatan *m*

Charles [tʃɑrlz] *s* Karl *m*

char'ley horse' ['tʃɑrli] *s* (coll) Muskelkater *m*

charm [tʃɑrm] *s* Charme *m*; (*trinket*) Amulett *n* || *tr* verzaubern; (fig) entzücken

charm'ing *adj* scharmant, reizend

chart [tʃɑrt] *s* Karte *f*; (*table*) Tabelle *f*; (naut) Seekarte *f* || *tr* entwerfen, auf e-r Karte graphisch darstellen

charter ['tʃɑrtər] *adj* (*plane, etc.*) Charter– || *s* Freibrief *m*, Charter *m*; (*of an organization*) Gründungsurkunde *f* und Satzungen *pl* || *tr* chartern

char'ter mem'ber *s* gründendes Mitglied *n*

char·woman ['tʃɑr‚wumən] *s* (**-women** [‚wɪmɪn]) Putzfrau *f*

chase [tʃes] *s* (*pursuit*) Verfolgung *f*; (*hunt*) Jagd *f* || *tr* jagen; (*girls*) nachsteigen (dat); **c. away** verjagen; **c. out** vertreiben || *intr*—**c. after** nachlaufen (dat)

chasm ['kæzəm] *s* (& fig) Abgrund *m*

chas·sis ['tʃæsi] *s* (**-sis** [siz]) Chassis *n*; (aut) Fahrgestell *n*

chaste [tʃest] *adj* keusch

chasten ['tʃesən] *tr* züchtigen

chastise [tʃæs'taɪz] *tr* züchtigen

chastity ['tʃæstɪti] *s* Keuschheit *f*

chat [tʃæt] *s* Plauderei *f* || *v* (*pret & pp* **chatted**; *ger* **chatting**) *intr* plaudern

chattel ['tʃætəl] *s* Sklave *m*; **chattels** Hab und Gut *n*

chatter ['tʃætər] *s* (*talk*) Geplapper *n*; (*of teeth*) Klappern *n* || *intr* (*talk*) plappern; (*said of teeth*) klappern

chat'terbox' *s* (coll) Plappermaul *n*

chauffeur ['ʃofər], [ʃo'fʌr] *s* Chauffeur *m* || *tr* fahren

cheap [tʃip] *adj* (*inexpensive*) billig; (*shoddy*) minderwertig; (*base*) gemein; (*stingy*) geizig; **feel c.** sich verlegen fühlen || *adv* billig; **get off c.** mit e-m blauen Auge davonkommen

cheapen ['tʃipən] *tr* herabsetzen

cheat [tʃit] *s* Betrüger –in *mf* || *tr* (**out of**) betrügen (um) || *intr* schwindeln; (*at cards*) mogeln; **c. on** (e.g., *a wife*) betrügen

cheat'ing *s* Betrügerei *f*; (*at cards*) Mogelei *f*

check [tʃek] *s* (*of a bank*) Scheck *m*; (*for luggage*) Schein *m*; (*in a restaurant*) Rechnung *f*; (*inspection*) Kontrolle *f*; (*test*) Nachprüfung *f*; (*repulse*) Rückschlag *m*; (*restraint*) (**on**) Hemmnis *n* (für); (*square*) Karo *n*; (chess) Schach *n*; **hold in c.** in Schach halten || *tr* (*restrain*) hindern; (*inspect*) kontrollieren; (*test*) nachprüfen, überprüfen; (*a hat, coat*) abgeben; (*luggage*) aufgeben; (*figures*) nachrechnen; (chess) Schach bieten (dat); **c. off** abhaken || *intr* (*agree*) übereinstimmen; **c. out** (*of a hotel*) sich abmelden; **c. up on** überprüfen; (*a person*) sich erkundigen über (acc); **c. with** (correspond to) übereinstimmen mit; (consult) sich besprechen mit || interj Schach!

check′book′ s Scheckbuch n, Scheckheft n

checker ['tʃekər] s Kontrolleur m; (in checkers) Damestein m; **checkers** Damespiel n

check′erboard′ s Damebrett n

check′ered adj kariert; (life, career) wechselvoll

check′ing account′ s Scheckkonto n

check′ list′ s Kontrolliste f

check′mate′ s Schachmatt n; (fig) Niederlage f || tr (& fig) matt setzen || interj schachmatt!

check′-out coun′ter s Kasse f

check′point′ s Kontrollstelle f

check′room′ s Garderobe f

check′up′ s Überprüfung f; (med) ärztliche Untersuchung f

cheek [tʃik] s Backe f, Wange f; (coll) Frechheit f

cheek′bone′ s Backenknochen m

cheek′ by jowl′ adv Seite an Seite

cheeky ['tʃiki] adj (coll) frech

cheer [tʃɪr] s (applause) Beifallsruf m; (encouragement) Ermunterung f; (sport) Ermunterungsruf m; **three cheers for** ein dreifaches Hoch auf (acc) || tr zujubeln (dat); **c. on** anfeuern; **c. up** aufmuntern; **c. up!** nur Mut!

cheerful ['tʃɪrfəl] adj heiter; (room, surroundings) freundlich

cheer′lead′er s Anführer –in mf beim Beifallsrufen

cheerless ['tʃɪrlɪs] adj freudlos

cheese [tʃiz] s Käse m

cheeseburger ['tʃiz,bʌrgər] s belegtes Brot n mit Frikadelle und überbackenem Käse

cheese′ cake′ s Käsekuchen m

cheese′ cloth′ s grobe Baumwollgaze f

cheesy ['tʃizi] adj (sl) minderwertig

chef [ʃef] s Küchenchef m

chemical ['kemɪkəl] adj chemisch; (fertilizer) Kunst– || s Chemikalie f

chemist ['kemɪst] s Chemiker –in mf

chemistry ['kemɪstri] s Chemie f

cherish ['tʃerɪʃ] tr (hold dear) schätzen; (hopes, thoughts) hegen

cherry ['tʃeri] s Kirsche f

cher′ry tree′ s Kirschbaum m

cher·ub ['tʃerəb] s (–ubim [əbɪm]) Cherub m || s (–ubs) Engelskopf m

chess [tʃes] s Schach n

chess′board′ s Schachbrett n

chess′man′ s (–men′) Schachfigur f

chest [tʃest] s Truhe f; (anat) Brust f

chestnut ['tʃesnʌt] adj kastanienbraun || s Kastanie f; (tree) Kastanienbaum m; (horse) Rotfuchs m

chest′ of draw′ers s Kommode f

chevron ['ʃevrən] s (mil) Winkel m

chew [tʃu] s Kauen n; (stick of tobacco) Priem m || tr kauen; **c. the cud** wiederkauen; **c. the rag** (sl) schwatzen

chew′ing gum′ s Kaugummi m

chew′ing tobac′co s Kautabak m

chic [ʃik] adj schick || s Schick m

chicanery [ʃɪ'kenəri] s Schikane f

chick [tʃɪk] s Küken n; (girl) (sl) kesse Biene f

chicken ['tʃɪkən] adj Hühner–; (sl) feig(e) || s Huhn n, Hühnchen n

chick′en coop′ s Hühnerstall m

chick′en-heart′ed adj feig(e)

chick′en pox′ s Windpocken pl

chick′en wire′ s Maschendraht m

chick′pea′ s Kichererbse f

chicory ['tʃɪkəri] s Zichorie f

chide [tʃaɪd] v (pret & pp **chided** & **chid** [tʃɪd]; pp **chided**) tr tadeln

chief [tʃif] adj Haupt–, Ober–, oberste; (leading) leitend || s Chef m, Oberhaupt n; (of an Indian tribe) Häuptling m

chief′ exec′utive s Regierungsoberhaupt n

chief′ jus′tice s Vorsitzender m des obersten Gerichtshofes

chiefly ['tʃifli] adv vorwiegend

chief′ of police′ s Polizeipräsident m

chief′ of staff′ s Generalstabschef m

chief′ of state′ s Staatschef m

chieftain ['tʃiftən] s Häuptling m

chiffon [ʃɪ'fɑn] s Chiffon m

child [tʃaɪld] s (**children** ['tʃɪldrən]) Kind n; **with c.** schwanger

child′ abuse′ s Kindermißhandlung f

child′birth′ s Niederkunft f

child′hood′ s Kindheit f

childish ['tʃaɪldɪʃ] adj kindisch

childless ['tʃaɪldlɪs] adj kinderlos

child′like′ adj kindlich

child′ prod′igy s Wunderkind n

child′s′ play′ s (fig) Kinderspiel n

child′ support′ s Alimente pl

child′ wel′fare s Jugendfürsorge f

Chile ['tʃɪlɪ] s Chile n

chili ['tʃɪli] s Cayennepfeffer m

chil′i sauce′ s Chillisoße f

chill [tʃɪl] s (coldness) Kälte f; (sensation of cold or fear) Schau(d)er m; **chills** Fieberschau(d)er m || tr kühlen; (hopes, etc.) dämpfen; (metals) abschrecken; **be chilled to the bone** durchfrieren || intr abkühlen

chilly ['tʃɪli] adj (& fig) frostig; **feel chilly** frösteln

chime [tʃaɪm] s Geläut n; **chimes** Glockenspiel n || intr (said of bells) läuten; (said of a doorbell) ertönen; (said of a clock) schlagen; **c. in** (coll) beipflichten

chimera [kaɪ'mɪrə] s Hirngespinst n

chimney ['tʃɪmni] s Schornstein m; (of a lamp) Zylinder m

chimpanzee [tʃɪm'pænzi] s Schimpanse m

chin [tʃɪn] s Kinn n; **keep one's c. up** die Ohren steifhalten; **up to the c.** bis über die Ohren

china ['tʃɪnə] s Porzellan n || **China** s China n

chi′na clos′et s Porzellanschrank m

chi′na·man s (–men) (pej) Chinese m

chin′aware′ s Porzellanwaren pl

Chi·nese [tʃaɪ'niz] adj chinesisch || s (–nese) Chinese m, Chinesin f; (language) Chinesisch n

Chi′nese lan′tern s Lampion m

chink [tʃɪŋk] s Ritze f; (of coins or

glasses) Klang *m* ‖ *tr* (*glasses*) anstoßen

chin'-up' *s* Klimmzug *m*

chip [tʃɪp] *s* Span *m*, Splitter *m*; (*in china*) angestoßene Stelle *f*; (*in poker*) Spielmarke *f*; **a c. off the old block** (coll) ganz der Vater; **have a c. on one's shoulder** (coll) vor Zorn geladen sein ‖ *v* (*pret & pp* **chipped**; *ger* **chipping**) *tr* (*e.g., a cup*) anschlagen; **c. in** (coll) beitragen; **c. off** abbrechen ‖ *intr* (leicht) abbrechen; **c. in** (with) einspringen (mit); **c. off** (*said of paint*) abblättern

chipmunk ['tʃɪp‚mʌŋk] *s* Streifenhörnchen *n*

chipper ['tʃɪpər] *adj* (coll) munter

chiropodist [kaɪ'rɑpədɪst], [kɪ'rɑpədɪst] *s* Fußpfleger –in *mf*

chiropractor ['kaɪrə‚præktər] *s* Chiropraktiker –in *mf*

chirp [tʃʌrp] *s* Gezwitscher *n* ‖ *intr* zwitschern

chis·el ['tʃɪzəl] *s* Meißel *m* ‖ *v* (*pret & pp* **-el[l]ed**; *ger* **-el[l]ing**) *tr* meißeln; (sl) bemogeln ‖ *intr* meißeln; (sl) mogeln

chiseler ['tʃɪzələr] *s* (sl) Mogler *m*

chitchat ['tʃɪt‚tʃæt] *s* Schnickschnack *m*

chivalrous ['ʃɪvəlrəs] *adj* ritterlich

chivalry ['ʃɪvəlri] *s* Rittertum *n*; (*politeness*) Ritterlichkeit *f*

chive [tʃaɪv] *s* Schnittlauch *m*

chloride ['klɔraɪd] *s* Chlorid *n*

chlorine ['klɔrin] *s* Chlor *n*

chloroform ['klɔrə‚fɔrm] *s* Chloroform *n* ‖ *tr* chloroformieren

chlorophyll ['klɔrəfɪl] *s* Chlorophyll *n*

chock-full ['tʃak'ful] *adj* zum Bersten voll

chocolate ['tʃɔkəlɪt] *adj* Schokoladen–; (*in color*) schokoladenfarben ‖ *s* Schokolade *f*; (*chocolate-covered candy*) Praline *f*

choc'olate bar' *s* Schokoladentafel *f*

choice [tʃɔɪs] *adj* (aus)erlesen ‖ *s* Wahl *f*; (*selection*) Auswahl *f*

choir [kwaɪr] *s* Chor *m*; (archit) Chor *m*

choir'boy' *s* Chorknabe *m*

choir' loft' *s* Chorgalerie *f*

choir'mas'ter *s* Chordirigent *m*

choke [tʃok] *s* (aut) Starterklappe *f* ‖ *tr* erwürgen, ersticken; **c. back** (*tears*) herunterschlucken; **c. down** herunterwürgen; **c. up** verstopfen ‖ *intr* ersticken; **c. on** ersticken an (*dat*)

choker ['tʃokər] *s* enges Halsband *n*

cholera ['kalərə] *s* Cholera *f*

cholesterol [kə'lestə‚rol] *s* Blutfett *n*

choose [tʃuz] *v* (*pret* **chose** [tʃoz]; *pp* **chosen** ['tʃozən]) *tr & intr* wählen

choosy ['tʃuzi] *adj* (coll) wählerisch

chop [tʃap] *s* Hieb *m*; (culin) Kotelett *n*, Schnitzel *n*; **chops** (sl) Maul *n* ‖ *v* (*pret & pp* **chopped**; *ger* **chopping**) *tr* hacken; **c. down** niederhauen; **c. off** abhacken; **c. up** zerhacken

chopper ['tʃapər] *s* (ax) Hackbeil *n*; (coll) Hubschrauber *m*

chop'ping block' *s* Hackklotz *m*

choppy ['tʃapi] *adj* (sea) bewegt

chop'stick' *s* Eßstäbchen *n*

choral ['korəl] *adj* Chor–, Sänger–

chorale [ko'ral] *s* Choral *m*

chord [kɔrd] *s* (anat) Band *n*; (geom) Sehne *f*; (*combination of notes*) (mus) Akkord *m*; (mus & fig) Saite *f*

chore [tʃor] *s* Hausarbeit *f*

choreography [‚korɪ'agrəfɪ] *s* Choreographie *f*

chorus ['korəs] *s* Chor *m*; (*refrain*) Kehrreim *m*

cho'rus girl' *s* Revuetänzerin *f*

chowder ['tʃaudər] *s* Fischsuppe *f*

Christ [kraɪst] *s* Christus *m*

Christ' child' *s* Christkind *n*

christen ['krɪsən] *tr* taufen

Christendom ['krɪsəndəm] *s* Christenheit *f*

chris'tening *s* Taufe *f*; **c. of a ship** Schiffstaufe *f*

Christian ['krɪstʃən] *adj* christlich ‖ Christ –in *mf*

Chris'tian E'ra *s* christliche Zeitrechnung *f*

Christianity [‚krɪstɪ'æniti] *s* (*faith*) Christentum *n*; (*all Christians*) Christenheit *f*

Chris'tian name' *s* Taufname *m*

Christmas ['krɪsməs] *adj* Weihnachts– ‖ *s* Weihnachten *pl*, Weihnachtsfest *n*

Christ'mas card' *s* Weihnachtskarte *f*

Christ'mas car'ol *s* Weihnachtslied *n*

Christ'mas Eve' *s* Heiliger Abend *m*

Christ'mas gift' *s* Weihnachtsgeschenk *n*

Christ'mas tree' *s* Christbaum *m*

Christ'mas tree' lights' *spl* Weihnachtskerzen *pl*

Christopher ['krɪstəfər] *s* Christoph *m*

chromatic [kro'mætɪk] *adj* chromatisch

chrome [krom] *adj* Chrom– ‖ *s* Chrom *n* ‖ *tr* verchromen

chrome'plate' *tr* verchromen

chromium ['kromɪ-əm] *s* Chrom *n*

chromosome ['kromə‚som] *s* Chromosom *n*

chronic ['kranɪk] *adj* chronisch

chronicle ['kranɪkəl] *s* Chronik *f* ‖ *tr* aufzeichnen

chronicler ['kranɪklər] *s* Chronist –in *mf*

chronological [‚kranə'ladʒɪkəl] *adj* chronologisch

chronology [krə'nalədʒɪ] *s* Chronologie *f*

chronometer [krə'namɪtər] *s* Chronometer *n*

chrysanthemum [krɪ'sænθɪməm] *s* Chrysantheme *f*

chubby ['tʃʌbɪ] *adj* pummelig

chuck [tʃʌk] *s* (culin) Schulterstück *n*; (mach) Klemmfutter *n* ‖ *tr* schmeißen

chuckle ['tʃʌkəl] *s* Glucksen *n* ‖ *intr* glucksen

chug [tʃʌg] *s* Tuckern *n* ‖ *v* (*pret & pp* **chugged**; *ger* **chugging**) *intr* tuckern; **c. along** tuckernd fahren

chum [tʃʌm] s (coll) Kumpel m ‖ v
(pret & pp chummed; ger chumming)
intr—c. around with sich eng anschließen an (acc)

chummy ['tʃʌmi] adj eng befreundet

chump [tʃʌmp] s (coll) Trottel m

chunk [tʃʌŋk] s Klotz m, Stück n

church [tʃʌrtʃ] s (adj) Kirchen-, kirchlich
‖ s Kirche f

churchgoer ['tʃʌrtʃˌgo·ər] s Kirch-
gänger –in mf

church' pic'nic s Kirchweih f

church'yard' s Kirchhof m

churl [tʃʌrl] s Flegel m

churlish ['tʃʌrlɪʃ] adj flegelhaft

churn [tʃʌrn] s Butterfaß n ‖ tr
(cream) buttern; c. up aufwühlen ‖
intr sich heftig bewegen

chute [ʃut] s (for coal, etc.) Rutsche
f; (for laundry, etc.) Abwurfschacht
m; (sliding board) Rutschbahn f; (in
a river) Stromschnelle f; (aer) Fallschirm m

cider ['saɪdər] s Apfelwein m

cigar [sɪ'gɑr] s Zigarre f

cigarette [ˌsɪgə'rɛt] s Zigarette f

cigarette' cough' s Raucherhusten m

cigarette' light'er s Feuerzeug n

cigar' store' s Rauchwarenladen m

cinch [sɪntʃ] s Sattelgurt m; (sure
thing) totsichere Sache f; (snap) (sl)
Kinderspiel n; (likely candidate) tot-
sicherer Kandidat m ‖ tr (sl) sich
[dat] sichern

cinder ['sɪndər] s (ember) glühende
Kohle f; (slag) Schlacke f; cinders
Asche f

Cinderella [ˌsɪndə'rɛlə] s Aschenbrödel m

cin'der track' s (sport) Aschenbahn f

cinema ['sɪnəmə] s Kino n

cinematography [ˌsɪnəmə'tɑgrəfi] s
Kinematographie f

cinnamon ['sɪnəmən] s Zimt m

cipher ['saɪfər] s Ziffer f; (zero) Null
f; (code) Chiffre f ‖ tr chiffrieren

circle ['sʌrkəl] s Kreis m; circles under the eyes Ränder pl unter den
Augen ‖ tr einkreisen; (go around)
umkreisen ‖ intr kreisen

circuit ['sʌrkɪt] s (course) Kreislauf
m; (elec) Stromkreis m; (jur) Bezirk
m

cir'cuit break'er s Ausschalter m

cir'cuit court' s Bezirksgericht n

circuitous [sər'kju·ɪtəs] adj weitschweifig

circular ['sʌrkjələr] adj kreisförmig;
(saw) Kreis– ‖ s Rundschreiben n

circulate ['sʌrkjəˌlet] tr in Umlauf
setzen; (a rumor) verbreiten; (fin)
girieren ‖ intr umlaufen; (said of
blood) kreisen; (said of a rumor)
umgehen

circulation [ˌsʌrkjə'leʃən] s (of blood)
Kreislauf m; (of a newspaper) Auflage f; (of money) Umlauf m

circumcize ['sʌrkəmˌsaɪz] tr beschneiden

circumference [sər'kʌmfərəns] s Umfang m

circumflex ['sʌrkəmˌflɛks] s Zirkum-
flex m

circumlocution [ˌsʌrkəmlo'kjuʃən] s
Umschreibung f

circumscribe ['sʌrkəmˌskraɪb] tr
(geom) umschreiben; (fig) umgren-
zen

circumspect ['sʌrkəmˌspɛkt] adj umsichtig

circumstance ['sʌrkəmˌstæns] s Um-
stand m; circumstances (financial
situation) Verhältnisse pl

cir'cumstan'tial ev'idence [ˌsʌrkəm-
'stænʃəl] s Indizienbeweis m

circumvent [ˌsʌrkəm'vɛnt] tr umgehen

circus ['sʌrkəs] s Zirkus m

cistern ['sɪstərn] s Zisterne f

citadel ['sɪtədəl] s Burg f

citation [saɪ'teʃən] s Zitat n; (jur)
Vorladung f; (mil) Belobung f

cite [saɪt] tr (quote) anführen; (jur)
vorladen; (mil) belobigen

citizen ['sɪtɪzən] s Bürger –in mf

cit'izenship' s Staatsangehörigkeit f

cit'rus fruit' ['sɪtrəs] s Zitrusfrucht f

city ['sɪti] s Stadt f

cit'y coun'cil s Stadtrat m

cit'y fa'ther s Stadtrat m

cit'y hall' s Rathaus n

cit'y plan'ning s Stadtplanung f

civic ['sɪvɪk] adj bürgerlich, Bürger–
‖ civics s Staatsbürgerkunde f

civil ['sɪvɪl] adj (life, duty) bürgerlich; (service) öffentlich; (polite)
höflich; (jur) privatrechtlich

civ'il cer'emony s standesamtliche
Trauung f

civ'il defense' s zivile Verteidigung f

civ'il engineer'ing s Hoch- und Tief-
bau m

civilian [sɪ'vɪljən] adj bürgerlich,
Zivil– ‖ s Zivilist –in mf

civilization [ˌsɪvɪlɪ'zeʃən] s Zivilisation f, Kultur f

civilize ['sɪvɪˌlaɪz] tr zivilisieren

civ'il rights' spl Bürgerrechte pl

civ'il serv'ant s Staatsbeamte m,
Staatsbeamtin f

civ'il serv'ice s Staatsdienst m

civ'il war' s Bürgerkrieg m

claim [klem] s Anspruch m; (assertion) Behauptung f; (for public land)
beanspruchtes Land n ‖ tr beanspruchen; (assert) behaupten; (attention) erfordern; c. to be sich
ausgeben für

claim' check' s Aufgabeschein m

clairvoyance [klɛr'vɔɪ·əns] s Hellsehen
n

clairvoyant [klɛr'vɔɪ·ənt] adj hellse-
herisch; be c. hellsehen ‖ s Hellse-
her –in mf

clam [klæm] s eßbare Meermuschel f

clamber ['klæmər] intr klettern

clammy ['klæmi] adj feuchtkalt

clamor ['klæmər] s Geschrei n ‖ intr
(for) schreien (nach)

clamorous ['klæmərəs] adj schreiend

clamp [klæmp] s Klammer f; (surg)
Klemme f ‖ tr (ver)klammern ‖ intr
—c. down on einschreiten gegen

clan [klæn] s Stamm m; (pej) Sippschaft f

clandestine [klæn'dɛstɪn] adj heimlich

clang [klæŋ] s Geklirr n ‖ intr klirren

clank [klæŋk] s Geklirr n, Gerassel n || intr klirren, rasseln

clannish ['klænɪʃ] adj stammesbewußt

clap [klæp] s (of the hands) Klatschen n; (of thunder) Schlag m || v (pret & pp clapped; ger clapping) tr (a tax, fine, duty) (on) auferlegen (dat); **clap hands** in die Hände klatschen || intr Beifall klatschen

clapper ['klæpər] s Klöppel m

clap'trap' s Phrasendrescherei f

claque [klæk] s Claque f

clari-fy ['klærɪ͵faɪ] v (pret & pp -fied) tr erklären

clarinet [͵klærɪ'nɛt] s Klarinette f

clarity ['klærɪti] s Klarheit f

clash [klæʃ] s (sound) Geklirr n; (of interests, etc.) Widerstreit m || intr (conflict) kollidieren; (said of persons) aufeinanderstoßen; (said of ideas) im Widerspruch stehen; (said of colors) nicht zusammenpassen

clasp [klæsp] s (fastener) Schließe f, Spange f; (on a necktie) Klammer f; (embrace) Umarmung f; (of hands) Händedruck m || tr umklammern; **c. s.o.'s hand** j-m die Hand drücken

class [klæs] s (group) Klasse f; (period of instruction) Stunde f; (year) Jahrgang m; **have c.** (sl) Niveau haben || tr einstufen

classic ['klæsɪk] adj klassisch || s Klassiker m

classical ['klæsɪkəl] adj klassisch; **c. antiquity** Klassik f; **c. author** Klassiker m

classicist ['klæsɪsɪst] s Kenner -in mf der Klassik

classification [͵klæsɪfɪ'keʃən] s Klassifikation f, Anordnung f

clas'sified ad' s geheimzuhaltend

clas'sified ad' s kleine Anzeige f

classi-fy ['klæsɪ͵faɪ] v (pret & pp -fied) tr klassifizieren

class'mate' s Klassenkamerad m

class' reun'ion s Klassentreffen n

class'room' s Klassenzimmer n

classy ['klæsi] adj (sl) pfundig

clatter ['klætər] s Geklapper n || intr klappern

clause [klɔz] s Satzteil m; (jur) Klausel f

clavicle ['klævɪkəl] s Schlüsselbein n

claw [klɔ] s Klaue f, Kralle f; (of a crab) Schere f || tr zerkratzen; (a hole) scharren || intr kratzen

clay [kle] adj tönern || s Ton m, Lehm m

clay' pig'eon s Tontaube f

clean [klin] adj sauber, rein; (cut) glatt; (features) klar || adv (coll) völlig || tr reinigen, putzen; **c. out** (clear out by force) räumen; (empty) ausleeren; (sl) ausbeuten; **c. up** (a room) aufräumen || intr putzen; **c. up** sich zurechtmachen; (in gambling) (sl) schwer einheimsen

clean'-cut' adj (person) ordentlich; (clearly outlined) klar umrissen

cleaner ['klinər] s (person, device) Reiniger m; **cleaners** (establishment) Reinigungsanstalt f

clean'ing flu'id s flüssiges Reinigungsmittel n

clean'ing wo'man s Reinemachefrau f

cleanliness ['klɛnlɪnɪs] s Sauberkeit f

cleanse [klɛnz] tr reinigen

cleanser ['klɛnzər] s Reinigungsmittel n

clean'-shav'en adj glattrasiert

clean'up' s Reinemachen n; (e.g., of vice, graft) Säuberungsaktion f

clear [klɪr] adj klar; (sky, weather) heiter; (light) hell; (profit) netto; (conscience) rein; (proof) offenkundig || adv (coll) völlig; (fin) netto || tr klären; (streets) freimachen; (the table) abräumen; (a room) räumen; (a forest) roden; (the air) reinigen; (an obstacle without touching it) setzen über (acc); (a path) bahnen; (as profit) rein gewinnen; (at customs) zollamtlich abfertigen; (one's name) reinwaschen; **c. away** wegräumen; (doubts) beseitigen; **c. up** klarlegen || intr sich klären; **c. out** (coll) sich davonmachen; **c. up** sich aufklären

clearance ['klɪrəns] s (approval) Genehmigung f; (at customs) Zollabfertigung f; (of a bridge) lichte Höhe f; (aer) Starterlaubnis f; (mach) Spielraum m

clear'ance sale' s Räumungsverkauf m

clear'-cut' adj klar, eindeutig

clear'-head'ed adj verständig

clear'ing s (in a woods) Lichtung f

clear'ing house' s Abstimmungszentrale f; (fin) Verrechnungsstelle f

clear'-sight'ed adj scharfsichtig

cleat [klit] s Stollen m

cleavage ['klivɪdʒ] s Spaltung f

cleave [kliv] v (pret & pp cleft [klɛft] & cleaved) tr zerspalten || intr (split) sich spalten; (to) kleben an (dat)

cleaver ['klivər] s Hackbeil n

clef [klɛf] s Notenschlüssel m

cleft [klɛft] s Riß m, Spalt m

clemency ['klɛmənsi] s Milde f; (jur) Begnadigung f

clement ['klɛmənt] adj mild

clench [klɛntʃ] tr (a fist) ballen; (the teeth) zusammenbeißen

clerestory ['klɪr͵stori] s Lichtgaden m

clergy ['klɛrdʒi] s Geistlichkeit f

cler'gy·man s (-men) Geistliche m

cleric ['klɛrɪk] s Kleriker m

clerical ['klɛrɪkəl] adj Schreib-, Büro-; (eccl) geistlich

cler'ical er'ror s Schreibfehler m

cler'ical staff' s Schreibkräfte pl

cler'ical work' s Büroarbeit f

clerk [klʌrk] s (in a store) Verkäufer -in mf; (in an office) Büroangestellte mf; (in a post office) Schalterbeamte m; (jur) Gerichtsschreiber -in mf

clever ['klɛvər] adj (intelligent) klug; (adroit) geschickt; (witty) geistreich; (ingenious) findig

cleverness ['klɛvərnɪs] s (intelligence) Klugheit f; (adroitness) Geschicklichkeit f; (ingeniousness) Findigkeit f

cliché [kli'ʃe] s Klischee n

click [klɪk] s Klicken n; (of the tongue) Schnalzen n; (of a lock) Einschnappen n || tr klicken lassen; **c. one's heels** die Hacken zusammenschlagen || intr klicken; (said of heels) knallen; (said of a lock) einschnappen || impers—**it clicks** (coll) es klappt

client ['klaɪ-ənt] s (customer) Kunde m, Kundin f; (of a company) Auftraggeber –in mf; (jur) Klient –in mf

clientele [ˌklaɪ-ən'tel] s Kundschaft f; (com, jur) Klientel f

cliff [klɪf] s Klippe f, Felsen m

climate ['klaɪmɪt] s Klima n

climax ['klaɪmæks] s Höhepunkt m

climb [klaɪm] s Aufsteig m, Besteigung f; (aer) Steigungsflug m || tr ersteigen, besteigen; (stairs) hinaufsteigen; **climb a tree** auf e–n Baum klettern; || intr steigen, klettern; (said of a street) ansteigen

climber ['klaɪmər] s Kletterer –in mf; (of a mountain) Bergsteiger –in mf; (bot) Kletterpflanze f

clinch [klɪntʃ] s (box) Clinch m || tr (settle) entscheiden || intr clinchen

clincher ['klɪntʃər] s (coll) Trumpf m

cling [klɪŋ] v (pret & pp clung [klʌŋ]) intr haften; **c. to** sich anklammern an (acc); (said of a dress) sich anschmiegen an (acc); (fig) festhalten an (dat)

clinic ['klɪnɪk] s Klinik f

clinical ['klɪnɪkəl] adj klinisch

clink [klɪŋk] s Klirren n; (prison) (sl) Kittchen n || tr—**c. glasses** mit den Gläsern anstoßen || intr klirren

clip [klɪp] s Klammer f; **go at a good c.** ein scharfes Tempo gehen || v (pret & pp clipped; ger clipping) (a hedge) beschneiden; (hair) schneiden; (wings) stutzen; (sheep) scheren; (from newspapers, etc.) ausschneiden; (syllables) verschlucken; (sl) schröpfen; **c. together** zusammenklammern

clip′board′ s Manuskripthalter m

clip′ joint′ s (sl) Nepplokal n

clipper ['klɪpər] s (aer) Klipperflugzeug n; (naut) Klipper m; **clippers** Haarschneidemaschine f

clip′ping s (act) Stutzen n; (from newspapers) Ausschnitt m; **clippings** (of paper) Schnitzel pl; (scraps) Abfälle pl

clique [klik] s Sippschaft f

cliquish ['klikɪʃ] adj cliquenhaft

cloak [klok] s Umhang m; (fig) Deckmantel m; **under the c. of darkness** im Schutz der Dunkelheit || tr (fig) bemänteln

cloak′-and-dag′ger adj Spionage–

cloak′room′ s Garderobe f

clobber ['klabər] tr (coll) verwichsen

clock [klak] s Uhr f || tr (a runner) abstoppen

clock′mak′er s Uhrmacher –in mf

clock′ tow′er s Uhrturm m

clock′wise′ adv im Uhrzeigersinn

clock′work′ s Uhrwerk n; **like c.** wie am Schnürchen

clod [klad] s Klumpen m, Scholle f

clodhopper ['klad ˌhapər] s Bauerntölpel m

clog [klag] s Verstopfung f; (shoe) Holzschuh m || v (pret & pp clogged; ger clogging) tr verstopfen || intr sich verstopfen

cloister ['klɔɪstər] s Kloster n; (covered walk) Kreuzgang m

close [klos] adj (near) nahe; (tight) knapp; (air) schwül; (ties; friend) eng; (attention) gespannt; (game) beinahe gleich; (observer) scharf; (surveillance) streng; (supervision) genau; (inspection) eingehend; (resemblance; competition) stark; (shave) glatt; (translation) wortgetreu; (stingy) geizig; (order) (mil) geschlossen; **c. to** (position) nahe an (dat), neben (dat); (direction) nahe an (acc), neben (acc) || adv dicht, eng; **from c. up** in der Nähe || [kloz] s Schluß m, Ende n; **bring to a c.** zu Ende bringen; **draw to a c.** zu Ende gehen || tr schließen; (an account, deal) abschließen; **c. down** stillegen; **c. off** abschließen; (a road) sperren; **c. out** (com) ausverkaufen; **c. up** zumachen || intr sich schließen; **c. in** immer näher kommen; **c. in on** umschließen

close′-by′ ['klos′baɪ] adj nebenan

close′-cropped′ ['klos′krapt] adj kurz geschoren

closed [klozd] adj geschlossen; **c. today** (public sign) heute Betriebsruhe

closed′ shop′ s Unternehmen n mit Gewerkschaftszwang

closefisted ['klos′fɪstəd] adj geizig

close′-fitting ['klos′fɪtɪŋ] adj eng anliegend

close′-mouthed ['klos′mavðd] adj verschwiegen

close′ or′der drill′ [klos] s (mil) geschlosssenes Exerzieren n

closeout ['kloz ˌaut] s Räumungsausverkauf m

close′ shave′ [klos] s glatte Rasure f; (fig) knappes Entkommen n; **have a c.** mit knapper Not davonkommen

closet ['klazɪt] s Schrank m

close-up ['klos ˌʌp] s Nahaufnahme f

clos′ing adj Schluß–; (day) scheidend || s Schließung f; (of an account) Abschluß m; (of a factory) Stillegung f; (of a road) Sperrung f

clos′ing price′ s Schlußkurs m

clos′ing time′ s (of a shop) Geschäftsschluß m; (of bars) Polizeistunde f

clot [klat] s Klumpen m; (of blood) Gerinnsel n || v (pret & pp clotted; ger clotting) intr gerinnen

cloth [klɔθ] s Stoff m, Tuch n; (for cleaning, etc.) Lappen m; **the c.** die Geistlichkeit

clothe [kloð] v (pret & pp clothed & clad [klæd]) tr ankleiden, (be)kleiden; (fig) (in) einhüllen (in acc)

clothes [kloz], [kloðz] spl Kleider pl; **change one's clothes** sich umziehen; **put on one's clothes** sich anziehen

clothes′bas′ket s Wäschekorb m

clothes′brush′ s Kleiderbürste f

clothes′ clos′et s Kleiderschrank m

clothes′ dri′er *s* Wäschetrockner *m*
clothes′ hang′er *s* Kleiderbügel *m*
clothes′line′ *s* Wäscheleine *f*
clothes′pin′ *s* Wäscheklammer *f*
clothier [′kloðjər] *s* Kleiderhändler *m*; (*cloth maker*) Tuchmacher *m*; (*cloth dealer*) Tuchhändler *m*
clothing [′kloðɪŋ] *s* Kleidung *f*
cloud [klaud] *s* Wolke *f*; be up in the clouds (fig) in höheren Regionen schweben ‖ *tr* bewölken; (*a liquid*) trüben; (fig) verdunkeln ‖ *intr*—c. over (or up) sich bewölken
cloud′burst′ *s* Wolkenbruch *m*
cloud′-capped′ *adj* von Wolken bedeckt
cloudiness [′klaudɪnɪs] *s* Bewölktheit *f*
cloudless [′klaudlɪs] *adj* unbewölkt
cloudy [′klaudi] *adj* bewölkt; (*liquid*) trüb(e)
clout [klaut] *s* (*blow*) (coll) Hieb *m*; (*influence*) (coll) Einfluß *m* ‖ *tr*—c. s.o. (coll) j-m eins herunterhauen
clove [klov] *s* Gewürznelke *f*; c. of garlic Knoblauchzehe *f*
clo′ven hoof′ [′kloven] *s* (*as a sign of the devil*) Pferdefuß *m*
clover [′klover] *s* Klee *m*
clo′ver-leaf′ *s* (-leaves) Kleeblatt *n*
clown [klaun] *s* Clown *m*, Hanswurst *m*
clownish [′klaunɪʃ] *adj* närrisch
cloy [kloɪ] *tr* übersättigen
club [klʌb] *s* (*weapon*) Keule *f*; (*organization*) Klub *m*; (*cards*) Kreuz *n*; (*golf*) Schläger *m* ‖ (*pret & pp* clubbed) *ger* clubbing) *tr* verprügeln
club′ car′ *s* (rr) Salonwagen *m*
club′house′ *s* Klubhaus *n*
cluck [klʌk] *s* Glucken *n* ‖ *intr* glucken
clue [klu] *s* Schlüssel *m*, Anhaltspunkt *m*
clump [klʌmp] *s* (*of earth*) Klumpen *m*; (*of hair, grass*) Büschel *n*; (*of trees*) Gruppe *f*; (*heavy tramping sound*) schwerer Tritt *m*; c. of bushes Gebüsch *n* ‖ *intr*—c. along trapsen
clumsy [′klʌmzi] *adj* ungeschickt, plump; c. ox Tölpel *m*
cluster [′klʌstər] *s* (*bunch growing together*) Büschel *n*; (*of grapes*) Traube *f*; (*group*) Gruppe *f* ‖ *intr*—c. around sich zusammendrängen um
clutch [klʌtʃ] *s* Griff *m*; (aut) Kupplung *f*; fall into s.o.'s clutches j-m in die Klauen geraten; let out the c. einkuppeln; step on the c. auskuppeln ‖ *tr* packen
clutter [′klʌtər] *s* Durcheinander *n* ‖ *tr*—c. up vollstopfen
Co. *abbr* (Company) Gesellschaft *f*
c/o *abbr* (care of) per Adresse, bei
coach [kotʃ] *s* Kutsche *f*; (rr) Personenwagen *m*; (sport) Trainer *m* ‖ *tr* Nachhilfeunterricht geben (*dat*); (sport) trainieren ‖ *intr* (sport) trainieren
coach′ing *s* Nachhilfeunterricht *m*; (sport) Training *n*
coach′man *s* (-men) Kutscher *m*

coagulate [ko′ægjə‚let] *tr* gerinnen lassen ‖ *intr* gerinnen
coal [kol] *s* Kohle *f*
coal′bin′ *s* Kohlenkasten *m*
coal′-black′ *adj* kohlrabenschwarz
coal′ car′ *s* (rr) Kohlenwagen *m*
coal′deal′er *s* Kohlenhändler *m*
coalesce [‚ko·ə′les] *intr* zusammenwachsen, sich vereinigen
coalition [‚ko·ə′lɪʃən] *s* Koalition *f*
coal′ mine′ *s* Kohlenbergwerk *n*
coal′ min′ing *s* Kohlenbergbau *m*
coal′ oil′ *s* Petroleum *n*
coal′yard′ *s* Kohlenlager *n*
coarse [kors] *adj* (& fig) grob
coast [kost] *s* Küste *f*; the c. is clear (coll) die Luft ist rein ‖ *intr* im Leerlauf fahren; c. along (fig) sich mühelos fortbewegen
coastal [′kostəl] *adj* küstennah, Küsten-
coaster [′kostər] *s* (*for a glass*) Untersatz *m*; (naut) Küstenfahrer *m*
coast′guard′ *s* Küstenwachdienst *m*
coast′line′ *s* Küstenlinie *f*
coat [kot] *s* (*of a suit*) Jacke *f*, Rock *m*; (topcoat) Mantel *m*; (*of fur*) Fell *n*; (*of enamel, etc.*) Belag *m*; (*of paint*) Anstrich *m* ‖ *tr* (e.g., with teflon) beschichten; (e.g., with chocolate) überziehen; (e.g., with oil) beschmieren
coat′ed *adj* überzogen; (*tongue*) belegt
coat′ hang′er *s* Kleiderbügel *m*
coat′ing *s* Belag *m*, Überzug *m*
coat′ of arms′ *s* Wappen *n*
coat′rack′ *s* Kleiderständer *m*
coat′room′ *s* Garderobe *f*
coat′tail′ *s* Rockschoß *m*; (*of formal wear*) Frackschoß *m*
coauthor [′ko·‚oθər] *s* Mitautor *m*
coax [koks] *tr* schmeicheln (*dat*); c. s.o. to (*inf*) j-n überreden zu (*inf*)
cob [kab] *s* Kolben *m*
cobalt [′kobolt] *s* Kobalt *m*
cobbler [′kablər] *s* Flickschuster *m*
cobblestone [′kabəl‚ston] *s* Pflasterstein *m*, Kopfstein *m*
cobra [′kobrə] *s* Kobra *f*
cob′web′ *s* Spinn(en)gewebe *n*
cocaine [ko′ken] *s* Kokain *n*
cock [kak] *s* Hahn *m*; (faucet) Wasserhahn *m*; (*of a gun*) Gewehrhahn *m* ‖ *tr* (*one's ears*) spitzen; (*one's hat*) schief aufsetzen; (*the firing mechanism*) spannen
cock-a-doodle-doo [′kakə‚dudəl′du] *s* Kikeriki *n*
cock′-and-bull′ sto′ry *s* Lügengeschichte *f*
cockeyed [′kak‚aɪd] *adj* (*cross-eyed*) nach innen schielend; (*slanted to one side*) (sl) schief; (*drunk*) (sl) blau; (*absurd*) (sl) verrückt
cock′fight′ *s* Hahnenkampf *m*
cock′pit′ *s* Hahnenkampfplatz *m*; (aer) Kabine *f*, Kanzel *f*
cock′roach′ *s* Schabe *f*
cock′sure′ *adj* todsicher
cock′tail′ *s* Cocktail *m*
cock′tail dress′ *s* Cocktailkleid *n*
cock′tail par′ty *s* Cocktailparty *f*

cock'tail shak'er s Cocktailmischgefäß n
cocky ['kɑki] adj (coll) frech
cocoa ['koko] s Kakao m
coconut ['kokə,nʌt] s Kokosnuß f
co'conut palm', co'conut tree' s Kokospalme f
cacoon [kə'kun] s Kokon m
C.O.D., c.o.d. abbr (cash on delivery) per Nachnahme
cod [kɑd] s Kabeljau m
coddle ['kɑdəl] tr hätscheln
code [kod] s Geheimschrift f; (jur) Kodex m || tr verschlüsseln, chiffrieren
codefendant [,kodɪ'fendənt] s Mitangeklagte mf
code' name' s Deckname m
code' of hon'or s Ehrenkodex m
code' of laws' s Gesetzsammlung f
code' word' s Kennwort n
codex ['kodeks] s (codices ['kodɪ,siz]) Kodex m
cod'fish' s Kabeljau m
codicil ['kɑdɪsɪl] s Kodizill n
codi·fy ['kɑdɪ,faɪ] v (pret & pp -fied) tr kodifizieren
cod'-liver oil' s Lebertran m
coed, co-ed ['ko,ed] s Studentin f
coeducation [,ko,edʒə'keʃən] s Koedukation f
coeducational [,ko,edʒə'keʃənəl] adj Koedukations-
coefficient [,ko·ɪ'fɪʃənt] s Koeffizient m
coerce [ko'ʌrs] tr zwingen
coercion [ko'ʌrʃən] s Zwang m
coexist [,ko·ɪg'zɪst] intr koexistieren
coexistence [,ko·ɪg'zɪstəns] s Koexistenz f
coffee ['kɔfi] s Kaffee m
cof'fee bean' s Kaffeebohne f
cof'fee break' s Kaffeepause f
cof'fee fiend' s Kaffeetante f
cof'fee grounds' spl Kaffeesatz m
cof'fee pot' s Kaffeekanne f
cof'fee shop' s Kaffeestube f
coffer ['kɔfər] s Truhe f; (archit) Deckenfeld n; coffers Schatzkammer f
cof'ferdam' s (caisson) Kastendamm m; (naut) Kofferdamm m
coffin ['kɔfɪn] s Sarg m
cog [kɑg] s Zahn m; (cogwheel) Zahnrad n
cogency ['kodʒənsi] s Beweiskraft f
cogent ['kodʒənt] adj triftig
cognac ['konjæk], ['kɑnjæk] s Kognak m
cognizance ['kɑgnɪzəns] s Kenntnis f; take c. of s.th. etw zur Kenntnis nehmen
cognizant ['kɑgnɪzənt] adj—be c. of Kenntnis haben von
cog'wheel' s Zahnrad n
cohabit [ko'hæbɪt] intr in wilder Ehe leben
coheir [ko'er] s Miterbe m, Miterbin f
cohere [ko'hɪr] intr zusammenhängen
cohesion [ko'hiʒən] s Kohäsion f
coiffeur [kwɑ'fʌr] s Friseur m
coiffure [kwɑ'fjur] s Frisur f
coil [kɔɪl] s (something wound in a spiral) Spirale f, Rolle f; (of tubing) Schlange f; (single wind) Windung f; (elec) Spule f || tr aufrollen; (naut) aufschießen || intr—c. up sich zusammenrollen
coil' spring' s Spiralfeder f
coin [kɔɪn] s Münze f, Geldstück n || tr münzen, (& fig) prägen
coinage ['kɔɪnɪdʒ] s (minting) Prägen n; (coins collectively) Münzen pl; (fig) Prägung f
coincide [,ko·ɪn'saɪd] intr (with) zusammentreffen (mit); (in time) (with) gleichzeitig geschehen (mit)
coincidence [ko'ɪnsɪdəns] s Zufall m; by mere c. rein zufällig
coin' machine' s Münzautomat m
coin' slot' s Münzeinwurf m
coition [ko'ɪʃən], **coitus** ['ko·ɪtəs] s Koitus m, Beischlaf m
coke [kok] s Koks m; (coll) Coca-Cola n
colander ['kʌləndər] s Sieb n
cold [kold] adj kalt f || s Kälte f; (indisposition) Erkältung f
cold' blood'—s—in c. kaltblütig
cold'-blood'ed adj kaltblütig
cold' chis'el s Kaltmeißel m
cold' com'fort s (fig) geringer Trost m
cold' cream' s Cold Cream n
cold' cuts' spl kalter Aufschnitt m
cold' feet' spl—have c. (fig) Angst haben
cold' front' s Kaltfront f
cold'-heart'ed adj kaltherzig
coldness ['koldnɪs] s Kälte f
cold' shoul'der s—give s.o. the c. j—m die kalte Schulter zeigen
cold' snap' s plötzlicher Kälteeinbruch m
cold' stor'age s Lagerung f im Kühlraum
cold' war' s kalter Krieg m
cold' wave' s (meteor) Kältewelle f
coleslaw ['kol,slɔ] s Krautsalat m
colic ['kɑlɪk] s Kolik f
coliseum [,kɑlɪ'si·əm] s Kolosseum n
collaborate [kə'læbə,ret] intr mitarbeiten; (pol) kollaborieren
collaboration [kə,læbə're/ən] s Mitarbeit f; (pol) Kollaboration f
collaborator [kə'læbə,retər] s Mitarbeiter –in mf; (pol) Kollaborateur m
collapse [kə'læps] s (of a bridge, etc.) Einsturz m; (com) Krach m; (pathol) Zusammenbruch m, Kollaps m || intr einstürzen; (fig) zusammenbrechen
collapsible [kə'læpsɪbəl] adj zusammenklappbar
collaps'ible boat' s Faltboot n
collar ['kɑlər] s Kragen m; (of a dog) Halsband n; (of a horse) Kummet n; (mach) Ring m, Kragen m
col'larbone' s Schlüsselbein n
collate [kə'let] tr kollationieren
collateral [kə'lætərəl] adj kollateral, Seiten– || s (fin) Deckung f
collation [kə'le/ən] s Kollation f
colleague ['kɑlig] s Kollege m, Kollegin f
collect ['kɑlekt] s (eccl) Kollekte f || [kə'lekt] adj—make a c. call ein R-

Gespräch führen || *adv*—**call c.** ein R-Gespräch führen; **send c.** gegen Nachnahme schicken || *tr* (*money*) (ein)kassieren; (*stamps, coins*) sammeln; (*e.g., examination papers*) einsammeln; (*taxes*) abheben; (*one's thoughts*) zusammennehmen; **c. oneself** sich fassen || *intr* sich (ver)sammeln; (*pile up*) sich anhäufen

collect′ed *adj* (*works*) gesammelt; (*self-possessed*) gefaßt

collection [kə′lekʃən] *s* (*of stamps, etc.*) Sammlung *f*; (*accumulation*) Ansammlung *f*; (*of money*) Einziehung *f*; (*in a church*) Kollekte *f*; (*of mail*) Leerung *f* des Briefkastens; (*com*) Kollektion *f*

collec′tion a′gency *s* Inkassobüro *n*

collec′tion bas′ket *s* Klingelbeutel *m*

collective [kə′lektɪv] *adj* kollektiv, Sammel-, Gesamt- || *s* (*pol*) Kollektiv *n*

collec′tive bar′gaining *s* Tarifverhandlungen *pl*

collec′tive farm′ *s* Kolchose *f*

collector [kə′lektər] *s* (*e.g., of stamps*) Sammler –in *mf*; (*bill collector*) Einkassierer –in *mf*; (*of taxes*) Einnehmer –in *mf*; (*of tickets*) Fahrkartenabnehmer –in *mf*

college [′kɑlɪdʒ] *s* College *n*; (*e.g., of cardinals*) Kollegium *n*

collide [kə′laɪd] *intr* zusammenstoßen

collie [′kɑli] *s* Collie *m*

collision [kə′lɪʒən] *s* Zusammenstoß *m*

colloquial [kə′lokwɪ·əl] *adj* umgangssprachlich, Umgangs-

colloquialism [kə′lokwɪ·ə‚lɪzəm] *s* Ausdruck *m* der Umgangssprache

colloquy [′kɑləkwi] *s* Gespräch *n*

collusion [kə′luʒən] *s* Kollusion *f*; **be in c.** kolludieren

colon [′kolən] *s* (*anat*) Dickdarm *m*; (*gram*) Doppelpunkt *m*

colonel [′kʌrnəl] *s* Oberst *m*

colonial [kə′lonɪ·əl] *adj* Kolonial- || *s* Einwohner –in *mf* e-r Kolonie

colonialism [kə′lonɪ·ə‚lɪzəm] *s* Kolonialismus *m*

colonize [′kɑlə‚naɪz] *tr* besiedeln

colonnade [‚kɑlə′ned] *s* Säulengang *m*

colony [′kɑləni] *s* Kolonie *f*

color [′kʌlər] *adj* (*film, photo, photography, slide, television*) Farb- || *s* Farbe *f*; **lend c. to** beleben; **show one's colors** sein wahres Gesicht zeigen; **the colors** die Flagge; **with flying colors** glänzend || *tr* färben; (*fig*) (*schön*)färben || *intr* sich verfärben; (*become red*) erröten

col′or-blind′ *adj* farbenblind

col′ored *adj* farbig

col′or-fast′ *adj* farbecht

colorful [′kʌlərfəl] *adj* bunt, farbenreich; (*fig*) farbig

col′oring *s* Kolorit *n*, Färbung *f*

col′oring book′ *s* Malbuch *n*

colorless [′kʌlərlɪs] *adj* farblos

col′or ser′geant *s* Fahnenträger *m*

colossal [kə′lɑsəl] *adj* kolossal

colossus [kə′lɑsəs] *s* Koloß *m*

colt [kolt] *s* Füllen *n*

Columbus [kə′lʌmbəs] *s* Kolumbus *m*

column [′kɑləm] *s* Säule *f*; (*syndicated article*) Kolumne *f*; (*mil*) Kolonne *f*; (*typ*) Spalte *f*, Rubrik *f*; **c. of smoke** Rauchsäule *f*

columnist [′kɑləmɪst] *s* Kolumnist –in *mf*

coma [′komə] *s* Koma *n*

comb [kom] *s* Kamm *m*; (*honeycomb*) Wabe *f*; (*of a rooster*) Kamm *m* || *tr* kämmen; (*an area*) absuchen

com·bat [′kɑmbæt] *s* (*e.g., pilot, strength, unit, zone*) Kampf- || *s* Kampf *m*, Streit *m* || [′kɑmbæt], [kəm′bæt] *v* (*pret & pp* –bat[t]ed; *ger* –bat[t]ing) *tr* bekämpfen || *intr* kämpfen

combatant [′kɑmbətənt] *s* Kämpfer –in *mf*

com′bat fatigue′ *s* Kriegsneurose *f*

combative [′kɑmbətɪv] *adj* streitsüchtig

comber [′komər] *s* Sturzwelle *f*

combination [‚kɑmbɪ′neʃən] *s* Verbindung *f*; (*com*) Konzern *m*

combine [′kɑmbaɪn] *s* (*agr*) Mähdrescher *m*; (*com*) Interessengemeinschaft *f* || [kəm′baɪn] *tr* kombinieren, verbinden

combustible [kəm′bʌstɪbəl] *adj* (ver)brennbar || *s* Brennstoff *m*

combustion [kəm′bʌstʃən] *s* Verbrennung *f*

combus′tion cham′ber *s* Brennkammer *f*

combus′tion en′gine *s* Verbrennungsmaschine *f*

come [kʌm] *v* (*pret* came [kem]; *pp* come) *intr* kommen; **c. about** geschehen, sich ereignen; **c. across** (*discover*) stoßen auf (*acc*); (*said of a speech, etc.*) ankommen; **c. across with** (*coll*) blechen; **c. after** folgen (*dat*); (*fetch*) holen kommen; **c. along** mitkommen; (*coll*) vorwärtskommen; **c. apart** auseinanderfallen; **c. around** herumkommen; (*said of a special day*) wiederkehren; (*improve*) wieder zu sich kommen; (*change one's view*) von e-r Ansicht abgehen; **c. back** zurückkehren; (*recur to the mind*) wieder einfallen; **c. between** treten zwischen (*acc*); **c. by** vorbeikommen; (*acquire*) geraten an (*acc*); **c. clean** (*sl*) mit der Wahrheit herausrücken; **c. down** (*said of prices*) sinken; (*& fig*) herunterkommen; **c. down with** erkranken an (*dat*); **c. first** (*have priority*) zuerst an die Reihe kommen; **c. for** abholen; **c. forward** vortreten; **c. from** herkommen; (*e.g., a rich family*) stammen aus; (*e.g., school*) kommen aus; **c. in** hereinkommen; **c. in for** (*coll*) erhalten; **c. in second** den zweiten Platz belegen; **c. off** (*said of a button*) abgehen; (*come loose*) losgehen; (*said of an event*) verlaufen; **c. on!** los!; **c. out** herauskommen; (*said of a spot*) herausgehen; (*said of a publication*) erscheinen; **c. out against** (or **for**) sich erklären gegen (or für); **c. over** (*said of fear, etc.*) überlaufen; **c. to** (*amount to*) betragen; (after fainting) wieder zu sich kommen; **c. together** zusammenkommen; **c. true** in Erfüllung gehen; **c. up** (occur) vorkommen; (said of a number) herauskommen; (said of plants) aufgehen; (in conversation) zur Sprache kommen; (said of a storm) heranziehen; **c. upon** kommen auf (acc); **c. up to** entsprechen (dat); for years to c. auf Jahre hinaus; **how c.?** (coll) wieso?; **it comes easy to me** es fällt mir leicht

come′back′ s Comeback n
comedian [kəˈmidɪ·ən] s Komiker m; (pej) Komödiant –in mf
comedienne [kəˌmidɪˈɛn] s Komikerin f
come′down′ s (coll) Abstieg m
comedy [ˈkamədɪ] s Komödie f
comely [ˈkamlɪ] adj anmutig
come′-on′ s (sl) Lockmittel n
comet [ˈkamɪt] s Komet m
comfort [ˈkʌmfərt] s (solace) Trost m; (of a room, etc.) Behaglichkeit f; (person or thing that comforts) Tröster m; (bed cover) Steppdecke f || tr trösten
comfortable [ˈkʌmfərtəbəl] adj behaglich, bequem; (income) ausreichend; **be (or feel) c.** sich wohl fühlen
comforter [ˈkʌmfərtər] s Tröster m; (bed cover) Steppdecke f
com′forting adj tröstlich
com′fort sta′tion s Bedürfnisanstalt f
comic [ˈkamɪk] adj komisch || s Komiker m; **comics** Comics pl, Witzblatt n
comical [ˈkamɪkəl] adj komisch
com′ic op′era s Operette f
com′ic strip′ s Bildstreifen m
com′ing adj künftig, kommend; **c. soon** (notice at theater) demnächst || s Kommen n, Ankunft f; **c. of age** Mündigwerden n
comma [ˈkamə] s Komma n, Beistrich m
command [kəˈmænd] s (order) Befehl m; (of language) Beherrschung f; (mil) Kommando n; (jurisdiction) (mil) Kommandobereich m; **at s.o.'s c.** auf j-s Befehl; **be in c. of** (mil) das Kommando führen über (acc); **have a good c. of** gut beherrschen; **take c. of** (mil) das Kommando übernehmen über (acc) || tr (a person) befehlen (dat); (respect, silence) gebieten; (troops) führen; (a high price) erzielen || intr (mil) kommandieren
commandant [ˌkamənˈdænt] s Kommandant m
commandeer [ˌkamənˈdɪr] tr (coll) organisieren; (mil) requirieren
commander [kəˈmændər] s Truppenführer m; (of a company) Chef m; (of a military unit from battalion to corps) Kommandeur m; (of an army) Befehlshaber m; (nav) Fregattenkapitän m
comman′der in chief′ s Oberbefehlshaber m
command′ing adj (appearance) eindrucksvoll; (view) weit; (position)

beherrschend; (general) kommandierend
command′ing of′ficer s Einheitsführer m
commandment [kəˈmændmənt] s Gebot n
command′ post′ s Befehlsstand m
commemorate [kəˈmɛməˌret] tr gedenken (genit), feiern
commemoration [kəˌmɛməˈreʃən] s Gedenkfeier f; **in c. of** zum Gedächtnis von
commence [kəˈmɛns] tr & intr anfangen
commencement [kəˈmɛnsmənt] s Anfang m; (educ) Schulentlassungsfeier f
commend [kəˈmɛnd] tr (praise) (& mil) belob(ig)en; (entrust) empfehlen
commendable [kəˈmɛndəbəl] adj lobenswert
commendation [ˌkamənˈdeʃən] s Belobigung f
comment [ˈkamənt] s Bemerkung f, Stellungnahme f; **no c.!** kein Kommentar! || intr Bemerkungen machen; **c. on** kommentieren
commentary [ˈkamənˌtɛri] s Kommentar m
commentator [ˈkamənˌtetər] s Kommentator –in mf; (of a text) Erklärer –in mf
commerce [ˈkamərs] s Handel m
commercial [kəˈmʌrʃəl] adj Handels-, Geschäfts-, kommerziell || s (rad, telv) Werbesendung f
commer′cial art′ s Gebrauchsgraphik f
commercialism [kəˈmʌrʃəˌlɪzəm] s Handelsgeist m
commercialize [kəˈmʌrʃəˌlaɪz] tr kommerzialisieren
commiserate [kəˈmɪzəˌret] intr—**c. with** bemitleiden
commissar [ˈkamɪˌsar] s (pol) Kommissar m
commissary [ˈkamɪˌsɛri] s (deputy) Kommissar m; (store) Militärversorgungsstelle f
commission [kəˈmɪʃən] s (order) Auftrag m; (of a crime) Begehung f; (committee) Kommission f; (percentage) Provision f; (mil) Offizierspatent n; **out of c.** außer Betrieb; || tr beauftragen; (a work) bestellen; (a ship) in Dienst stellen; (mil) ein Offizierspatent verleihen (dat)
commis′sioned of′ficer s Offizier –in mf
commissioner [kəˈmɪʃənər] s Kommissar –in mf
com·mit [kəˈmɪt] v (pret & pp **-mitted;** ger **-mitting**) tr (a crime) begehen; (entrust) anvertrauen; (give over) übergeben; (to an institution) einweisen; **c. oneself** to sich festlegen auf (acc); **c. to memory** auswendig lernen; **c. to writing** zu Papier bringen
commitment [kəˈmɪtmənt] s (to) Festlegung f (auf acc); (to an asylum) Anstaltsüberweisung f
committee [kəˈmɪtɪ] s Ausschuß m
commode [kəˈmod] s Kommode f

commodious [kə'modɪ-əs] *adj* geräumig

commodity [kə'mɑdɪtɪ] *s* Ware *f*

common ['kɑmən] *adj* (*language, property, interest*) gemeinsam; (*general*) allgemein; (*people*) einfach; (*soldier*) gemein; (*coarse, vulgar*) gemein; (*frequent*) häufig ‖ *s*—in c. gemeinsam

com'mon denom'inator *s* gemeinsamer Nenner *m*; reduce to a c. auf e-n gemeinsamen Nenner bringen

commoner ['kɑmənər] *s* Bürger –in *mf*

com'mon-law mar'riage *s* wilde Ehe *f*

Com'mon Mar'ket *s* Gemeinsamer Markt *m*

com'mon noun' *s* Gattungsname *m*

com'monplace' *adj* alltäglich ‖ *s* Gemeinplatz *m*

com'mon sense' *s* gesunder Menschenverstand *m*

com'mon stock' *s* Stammaktien *pl*

commonweal ['kɑmən‚wil] *s* Gemeinwohl *n*

com'monwealth' *s* (*republic*) Republik *f*; (*state in U.S.A.*) Bundesstaat *m*

commotion [kə'moʃən] *s* Aufruhr *m*

commune ['kɑmjun] *s* Kommune *f* ‖ [kə'mjun] *intr* sich vertraulich besprechen

communicable [kə'mjunɪkəbəl] *adj* übertragbar

communicant [kə'mjunɪkənt] *s* Kommunikant –in *mf*

communicate [kə'mjunɪ‚ket] *tr* mitteilen; (*a disease*) (to) übertragen (auf *acc*) ‖ *intr* sich besprechen

communication [kə‚mjunɪ'keʃən] *s* Mitteilung *f*; (*message*) Nachricht *f*; **communications** Nachrichtenwesen *n*; (mil) Fernmeldewesen *n*

communicative [kə'mjunɪ‚ketɪv] *adj* mitteilsam

communion [kə'mjunjən] *s* Gemeinschaft *f*; (Prot) Abendmahl *n*; (R. C.) Kommunion *f*

commun'ion rail' *s* Altargitter *n*

communiqué [kə‚mjunɪ'ke] *s* Kommuniqué *n*

communism ['kɑmjə‚nɪzəm] *s* Kommunismus *m*

communist ['kɑmjənɪst] *s* kommunistisch ‖ *s* Kommunist –in *mf*

community [kə'mjunɪtɪ] *s* Gemeinschaft *f*; (*people living together*) Gemeinde *f*

communize ['kɑmjə‚naɪz] *tr* kommunistisch machen

commutation [‚kɑmjə'teʃən] *s* (jur) Umwandlung *f*

commuta'tion tick'et *s* Zeitkarte *f*

commutator ['kɑmjə‚tetər] *s* (elec) Kommutator *m*, Kollektor *m*

commute [kə'mjut] *tr* (jur) umwandeln ‖ *intr* pendeln

commuter [kə'mjutər] *s* Pendler –in *mf*

commut'er train' *s* Pendelzug *m*

compact [kəm'pækt] *adj* kompakt, dicht ‖ ['kɑmpækt] *s* (*for cosmetics*) Kompaktdose *f*; (*agreement*) Vertrag *m*; (aut) Kompaktwagen *m*

companion [kəm'pænjən] *s* Kumpan –in *mf*; (*one who accompanies*) Begleiter –in *mf*

companionable [kə'pænjənəbəl] *adj* gesellig

compan'ionship' *s* Gesellschaft *f*

compan'ionway' *s* Kajütstreppe *f*

company ['kʌmpəni] *s* (*companions*) Umgang *m*; (& com) Gesellschaft *f*; (mil) Kompanie *f*; (theat) Truppe *f*; keep c. with verkehren mit; keep s.o. c. j–m Gesellschaft leisten

com'pany command'er *s* Kompaniechef *m*

comparable ['kɑmpərəbəl] *adj* vergleichbar

comparative [kəm'pærətɪv] *adv* vergleichend; (gram) komparativ ‖ *s* (gram) Komparativ *m*

comparatively [kəm'pærətɪvlɪ] *adv* verhältnismäßig

compare [kəm'per] *s*—beyond c. unvergleichlich ‖ *tr* (with, to) vergleichen (mit); (gram) steigern; as compared with im Vergleich zu

comparison [kəm'pærɪsən] *s* Vergleich *m*; (gram) Steigerung *f*

compartment [kəm'pɑrtmənt] *s* Fach *n*; (rr) Abteil *n*

compass ['kʌmpəs] *s* Kompaß *m*; (geom) Zirkel *m*; within the c. of innerhalb (*genit*)

com'pass card' *s* Kompaßrose *f*

compassion [kəm'pæʃən] *s* Mitleid *n*

compassionate [kəm'pæʃənɪt] *adj* mitleidig

compatible [kəm'pætɪbəl] *adj* vereinbar

com·pel [kəm'pel] *v* (*pret & pp* –pelled; *ger* –pelling) *tr* zwingen, nötigen

compendious [kəm'pendɪ-əs] *adj* gedrängt

compendi·um [kəm'pendɪ-əm] *s* (–ums & –a [ə]) Abriß *m*, Kompendium *n*

compensate ['kɑmpən‚set] *tr* entschädigen ‖ *intr*—c. for Ersatz leisten (or bieten) für

compensation [‚kɑmpən'seʃən] *s* (*for damages*) Entschädigung *f*; (*remuneration*) Entgeld *n*

compete [kəm'pit] *intr* (with) konkurrieren (mit); (for) sich mitbewerben (um); (sport) am Wettkampf teilnehmen

competence ['kɑmpɪtəns] *s* (*mental state*) Zurechnungsfähigkeit *f*; (*ability*) (in) Fähigkeit *f* (zu)

competent ['kɑmpɪtənt] *adj* (*able*) fähig, tüchtig; (*witness*) zulässig

competition [‚kɑmpɪ'tɪʃən] *s* Wettbewerb *m*; (com) Konkurrenz *f*; (sport) Wettkampf *m*

competitive [kəm'petɪtɪv] *adj* (*bidding*) Konkurrenz–; (*prices*) konkurrenzfähig; (*person*) ehrgeizig; (*exam*) Auslese–

competitor [kəm'petɪtər] *s* Mitbewerber –in *mf*; (com) Konkurrent –in *mf*; (sport) Wettkämpfer –in *mf*

compilation [‚kɑmpɪ'leʃən] *s* Zusammenstellung *f*; (*book*) Sammelwerk *n*

compile [kəm'paɪl] *tr* zusammenstellen, kompilieren; *(Material)* zusammentragen

complacence [kəm'pleɪsəns], **complacency** [kəm'pleɪsənsɪ] *s* Selbstgefälligkeit *f*

complacent [kəm'pleɪsənt] *adj* selbstgefällig

complain [kəm'pleɪn] *intr* klagen; **c. to s.o. about** sich bei j-m beklagen über *(acc)*

complaint [kəm'pleɪnt] *s* Klage *f*; *(ailment)* Beschwerde *f*

complement ['kamplɪmənt] *s* (& gram) Ergänzung *f*; (geom) Komplement *n*; (nav) Bemannung *f* ‖ ['kamplɪ͵ment] *tr* ergänzen

complete [kəm'plit] *adj* ganz, vollkommen, vollständig; *(works)* sämtlich ‖ *tr (make whole)* vervollständigen; *(make perfect)* vollenden; *(finish)* beenden; *(a job)* erledigen

completely [kəm'plitlɪ] *adv* völlig

completion [kəm'plɪʃən] *s* Vollendung *f*

complex [kəm'pleks], ['kampleks] *adj* verwickelt ‖ ['kampleks] *s* Komplex *m*

complexion [kəm'plekʃən] *s* Gesichtsfarbe *f*; *(appearance)* Aussehen *n*

complexity [kəm'pleksɪtɪ] *s* Kompliziertheit *f*

compliance [kəm'plaɪəns] *s* Einwilligung *f*; **in c. with your wishes** Ihren Wünschen gemäß

complicate ['kamplɪ͵ket] *tr* komplizieren

com'plicat'ed *adj* kompliziert

complication [͵kamplɪ'keʃən] *s* Verwicklung *f*; (& pathol) Komplikation *f*

complicity [kəm'plɪsɪtɪ] *s* (in) Mitschuld *f* (an *dat*)

compliment ['kamplɪmənt] *s* Kompliment *n*; *(praise)* Lob *n*; **compliments** Empfehlungen *pl*; **pay s.o. a (high) c.** j-m ein (großes) Lob spenden ‖ *tr* (on) beglückwünschen (zu)

complimentary [͵kamplɪ'mentərɪ] *adj* *(remark)* schmeichelhaft; *(free)* Frei–

com·ply [kəm'plaɪ] *v* *(pret & pp* –plied) *intr* sich fügen; **c. with** einwilligen in *(acc)*; **c. with the rules** sich an die Vorschriften halten

component [kəm'ponənt] *adj* Teil– ‖ *s* Bestandteil *m*; (math, phys) Komponente *f*

compose [kəm'poz] *tr* *(writings)* verfassen; *(a sentence)* bilden; (mus) komponieren; (typ) setzen; **be composed of** bestehen aus; **c. oneself** sich fassen

composed' *adj* ruhig, gefaßt

composer [kəm'pozər] *s* Verfasser –in *mf*; (mus) Komponist –in *mf*

composite [kəm'pazɪt] *adj* zusammengesetzt ‖ *s* Zusammensetzung *f*

composition [͵kampə'zɪʃən] *s* (chem) Zusammensetzung *f*; *(educ)* Aufsatz *m*; (mus, paint) Komposition *f*; (typ) Schriftsatz *m*

composi'tion book' *s* Übungsheft *n*

compositor [kəm'pazɪtər] *s* Setzer –in *mf*

composure [kəm'pozər] *s* Fassung *f*

compote ['kampot] *s* *(stewed fruit)* Kompott *n*; *(dish)* Kompottschale *f*

compound ['kampaʊnd] *adj* zusammengesetzt; *(fracture)* kompliziert ‖ *s* Zusammensetzung *f*; *(enclosure)* umzäumtes Gelände *n*; (chem) Verbindung *f*; (gram) Kompositum *n*; (mil) Truppenlager *n* ‖ [kəm'paʊnd] *tr* zusammensetzen

com'pound in'terest *s* Zinseszinsen *pl*

comprehend [͵kamprɪ'hend] *tr* auffassen

comprehensible [͵kamprɪ'hensɪbəl] *adj* faßlich, begreiflich

comprehension [͵kamprɪ'henʃən] *s* Auffassung *f*; *(ability to understand)* Fassungskraft *f*

comprehensive [͵kamprɪ'hensɪv] *adj* umfassend

compress ['kampres] *s* (med) Kompresse *f* ‖ [kəm'pres] *tr* komprimieren

compressed' *adj* komprimiert; *(air)* Druck–; (fig) gedrängt

compression [kəm'preʃən] *s* Kompression *f*, Druck *m*

comprise [kəm'praɪz] *tr* umfassen; **be comprised of** bestehen aus

compromise ['kamprə͵maɪz] *s* Kompromiß *m* ‖ *tr* kompromittieren; *(principles)* preisgeben ‖ *intr* (on) e–n Kompromiß schließen (über *acc*)

comptroller [kəm'trolər] *s* Rechnungsprüfer *m*

compulsion [kəm'pʌlʃən] *s* Zwang *m*

compulsive [kəm'pʌlsɪv] *adj* triebhaft

compulsory [kəm'pʌlsərɪ] *adj* obligatorisch, Zwangs–; **c. military service** allgemeine Wehrpflicht *f*

compute [kəm'pjut] *tr* berechnen ‖ *intr* rechnen

computer [kəm'pjutər] *s* Computer *m*

comput'er lan'guage *s* Maschinensprache *f*

comrade ['kamræd] *s* Kamerad *m*

con [kan] *v (pret & pp* conned) *ger* conning) *tr* beschwindeln

concave [kan'kev] *adj* konkav

conceal [kən'sil] *tr* verheimlichen

concealment [kən'silmənt] *s* Verheimlichung *f*; *(place)* Versteck *n*

concede [kən'sid] *tr* zugestehen, zubilligen; **c. victory** (pol) den Wahlsieg überlassen ‖ *intr* nachgeben

conceit [kən'sit] *s* *(vanity)* Einbildung *f*, Dünkel *m*; *(witty expression)* Witz *m*

conceit'ed *adj* eingebildet

conceivable [kən'sivəbəl] *adj* denkbar

conceive [kən'siv] *tr* begreifen; *(a desire)* hegen; *(a child)* empfangen

concentrate ['kansən͵tret] *tr* konzentrieren; *(troops)* zusammenziehen ‖ *intr* (on) sich konzentrieren (auf *acc*); *(gather)* sich sammeln

concentration [͵kansən'treʃən] *s* Konzentration *f*

concentric [kən'sentrɪk] *adj* konzentrisch

concept ['kansept] *s* Begriff *m*

conception [kən'sepʃən] s (*idea*) Vorstellung *f*; (*design*) Entwurf *m*; (biol) Empfängnis *f*

concern [kən'sʌrn] s (*worry*) Besorgnis *f*; (*matter*) Angelegenheit *f*; (com) Firma *f*; **that is no c. of mine** das geht mich nichts an || *tr* betreffen, angehen; **as far as I am concerned** von mir aus; **c. oneself about** sich bekümmern um; **c. oneself with** sich befassen mit; **to whom it may c.** Bescheinigung

concern'ing *prep* betreffend (*acc*), betreffs (*genit*), über (*acc*)

concert ['kɑnsərt] s (mus) Konzert *n*; **in c.** (with) im Einvernehmen (mit) || [kən'sʌrt] *tr* zusammenfassen

concession [kən'seʃən] s Konzession *f*

conciliate [kən'sɪlɪˌet] *tr* versöhnen

conciliatory [kən'sɪlɪˌə,tori] *adj* versöhnlich

concise [kən'saɪs] *adj* kurz, bündig

conclude [kən'klud] *tr* schließen; **c. from s.th. that** aus etw schließen, daß; **to be concluded** Schluß folgt || *intr* (with) schließen (mit)

conclusion [kən'kluʒən] s Schluß *m*; **draw conclusions from** Schlüsse ziehen aus; **in c.** zum Schluß; **jump at conclusions** voreilige Schlüsse ziehen

conclusive [kən'klusɪv] *adj* (*decisive*) entscheidend; (*proof*) schlagkräftig

concoct [kən'kɑkt] *tr* (*brew*) zusammenbrauen; (*plans*) schmieden

concoction [kən'kɑkʃən] s Gebräu *n*

concomitant [kən'kɑmɪtənt] *adj* begleitend || s Begleitumstand *m*

concord ['kɑnkɔrd] s Eintracht *f*

concordance [kən'kɔrdəns] s Übereinstimmung *f*; (*book*) Konkordanz *f*

concourse ['kɑnkɔrs] s (*of people*) Zusammenlaufen *n*, Anlauf *m*; (*of rivers*) Zusammenfluß *m*; (rr) Bahnhofshalle *f*

concrete ['kɑnkrit], [kɑn'krit] *adj* (*not abstract*) konkret; (*solid*) fest; (*evidence*) schlüssig; (*of concrete*) Beton–; (math) benannt || s Beton *m* || *tr* betonieren

con'crete block' s Betonblock *m*

con'crete noun' s Konkretum *n*

concubine ['kɑnkjəˌbaɪn] s Nebenfrau *f*; (*mistress*) Konkubine *f*

con-cur [kən'kʌr] v (*pret & pp* –curred; *ger* –curring) *intr* (*agree*) übereinstimmen; (*coincide*) (with) zusammenfallen (mit); **c. in** (*an opinion*) beistimmen (*dat*)

concurrence [kən'kʌrəns] s (*agreement*) Einverständis *n*; (*coincidence*) Zusammentreffen *n*; (geom) Schnittpunkt *m*

condemn [kən'dem] *tr* verdammen; (& jur) verurteilen; (*a building*) für unbewohnlich erklären

condemnation [ˌkɑndem'neʃən] s Verurteilung *f*; (*of a building, ship, plane*) Untauglichkeitserklärung *f*

condense [kən'dens] *tr* (*make thicker*) verdichten; (*writing*) zusammendrängen; || *intr* kondensieren

condenser [kən'densər] s Kondensator *m*

condescend [ˌkɑndɪ'send] *intr* sich herablassen

condescend'ing *adj* herablassend

condescension [ˌkɑndɪ'senʃən] s Herablassung *f*

condiment ['kɑndɪmənt] s Würze *f*

condition [kən'dɪʃən] s (*state*) Zustand *m*; (*state of health*) Verfassung *f*; (*stipulation*) Bedingung *f*; **conditions** (*e.g. for working; of the weather*) Verhältnisse *pl*; **on c. that** unter der Bedingung, daß || *tr* (*impose stipulations on*) bedingen; (*accustom*) (**to**) gewöhnen (an *acc*); (sport) in Form bringen

conditional [kən'dɪʃənəl] *adj* bedingt

condi'tional clause' s Bedingungssatz *m*

conditionally [kən'dɪʃənəli] *adv* bedingungsweise

condole [kən'dol] *intr* (with) kondolieren (*dat*)

condolence [kən'doləns] s Beileid *n*

condom ['kɑndəm] s Präservativ *n*

condominium [ˌkɑndə'mɪnɪ-əm] s Eigentumswohnung *f*

condone [kən'don] *tr* verzeihen

conducive [kən'd(j)usɪv] *adj*—**c. to** förderlich (*dat*)

conduct ['kɑndʌkt] s (*behavior*) Betragen *n*; (*guidance*) Führung *f* || [kən'dʌkt] *tr* (*business, a campaign, a tour*) führen; (elec, phys) leiten; (mus) dirigieren; **c. oneself** sich betragen || *intr* (mus) dirigieren

conductor [kən'dʌktər] s (elec, phys) Leiter *m*; (mus) Dirigent *m*; (rr) Schaffner *m*

conduit ['kɑnd(U)ɪt] s Röhre *f*; (elec) Isolierrohr *n*

cone [kon] s (*ice cream cone; paper cone*) Tüte *f*; (bot) Zapfen *m*; (geom) Kegel *m*, Konus *m*

confection [kən'fekʃən] s Konfekt *n*

confectioner [kən'fekʃənər] s Zuckerbäcker –in *mf*

confec'tioner's sug'ar s Puderzucker *m*

confectionery [kən'fekʃəˌneri] s (*shop*) Konditorei *f*; (*sweets*) Zuckerwerk *n*

confederacy [kən'fedərəsi] s Bündnis *n*; (*conspiracy*) Verschwörung *f*

confederate [kən'fedərɪt] *adj* verbündet || s Bundesgenosse *m*, Bundesgenossin *f*; (*accomplice*) Helfershelfer –in *mf* || [kən'fedə,ret] *tr* verbünden || *intr* sich verbünden

confederation [kənˌfedə're/ən] s Bund *m*

con-fer [kən'fʌr] v (*pret & pp* –ferred; *ger* –ferring) *tr* (*on, upon*) verleihen (*dat*) || *intr* sich besprechen, konferieren

conference ['kɑnfərəns] s Konferenz *f*; (sport) Verband *m*

con'ference call' s Sammelverbindung *f*

confess [kən'fes] *tr* (*ein*)gestehen, bekennen; (*sins*) beichten || *intr* gestehen

confession [kən'feʃən] s Geständnis *n*, Bekenntnis *n*; (*of sins*) Beichte *f*; **go to c.** beichten

confessional [kən'feʃənəl] *s* Beicht-
stuhl *m*

confes'sion of faith' *s* Glaubensbekenntnis *n*

confessor [kən'fesər] *s* Beichtvater *m*

confidant [‚kɑnfɪ'dænt] *s* Vertraute
mf

confide [kən'faɪd] *tr* (**to**) anvertrauen
(*dat*) ‖ *intr*—**c. in** vertrauen (*dat*)

confidence ['kɑnfɪdəns] *s* (*trust*) (**in**)
Vertrauen *n* (auf *acc*, zu); (*assurance*) Zuversicht *f*; **in c.** im Vertrauen

con'fidence man' *s* Bauernfänger *m*

confident ['kɑnfɪdənt] *adj* zuversichtlich; **be c.** of sich [*dat*] sicher sein
(*genit*)

confidential [‚kɑnfɪ'denʃəl] *adj* vertraulich

confine ['kɑnfaɪn] *s*—**the confines** die
Grenzen *pl* ‖ *tr* [kən'faɪn] *tr* (*limit*)
(**to**) beschränken (auf *acc*); (*shut in*)
einsperren; **be confined** (*in pregnancy*) niederkommen; **be confined
to bed** bettlägerig sein

confinement [kən'faɪnmənt] *s* Beschränkung *f*; (*arrest*) Haft *f*; (*childbirth*) Niederkunft *f*

confirm [kən'fʌrm] *tr* bestätigen;
(Prot) konfirmieren; (R.C.) firmen;
confirm in writing verbriefen

confirmation [‚kɑnfər'meʃən] *s* Bestätigung *f*; (Prot) Konfirmation *f*;
(R.C.) Firmung *f*

confirmed' *adj* (*e.g., report*) bestätigt;
(*inveterate*) unverbesserlich; **c. bachelor** Hagestolz *m*

confiscate ['kɑnfɪs‚ket] *tr* beschlagnahmen, konfiszieren

confiscation [‚kɑnfɪs'keʃən] *s* Beschlagnahme *f*

conflagration [‚kɑnflə'greʃən] *s* Brand
m, Feuerbrunst *f*

conflict ['kɑnflɪkt] *s* (*of interests, of
evidence*) Konflikt *m*; (*fight*) Zusammenstoß *m* ‖ [kən'flɪkt] *intr*
(**with**) im Widerspruch stehen (zu)

conflict'ing *adj* einander widerspre-
chend

con'flict of in'terest *s* Interessenkon-
flikt *m*, Interessenkollision *f*

confluence ['kɑnfluəns] *s* Zusammenfluß *m*

conform [kən'fɔrm] *tr* anpassen ‖ *intr*
übereinstimmen; (**to**) sich anpassen
(*dat*)

conformity [kən'fɔrmɪti] *s* (*adaptation*) (**to**) Anpassung *f* (an *acc*);
(*agreement*) (**with**) Übereinstimmung
f (mit)

confound [kɑn'faʊnd] *tr* (*perplex*) verblüffen; (*throw into confusion*) verwirren; (*erroneously identify*) verwechseln (mit) ‖ ['kɑn'faʊnd]
tr—**c. it!** zum Donnerwetter!

confound'ed *adj* (coll) verwünscht

confrere ['kɑnfrer] *s* Kollege *m*

confront [kən'frʌnt] *tr* (*face*) gegenüberstehen (*dat*); (*a problem, an
enemy*) entgegentreten (*dat*); **be
confronted with** gegenüberstehen
(*dat*); **c. s.o. with** j-n konfrontieren
mit

confrontation [‚kɑnfrən'teʃən] *s* Konfrontation *f*; (*of witnesses*) Gegenüberstellung *f*

confuse [kən'fjuz] *tr* (*e.g., names*)
verwechseln; (*persons*) verwirren

confused' *adj* konfus, verwirrt, wirr

confusion [kən'fjuʒən] *s* Verwechslung *f*; (*disorder, chaos*) Verwirrung
f

confute [kən'fjut] *tr* widerlegen

congeal [kən'dʒil] *tr* erstarren lassen
‖ *intr* erstarren

congenial [kən'dʒinjəl] *adj* (*person*)
sympathisch; (*surroundings*) angenehm

congenital [kən'dʒenɪtəl] *adj* angeboren

congen'ital de'fect *s* Geburtsfehler *m*

congest [kən'dʒest] *tr* überfüllen

congest'ed *adj* überfüllt; (*area*) übervölkert; (*with traffic*) verkehrsreich

congestion [kən'dʒest/ən] *s* Über-
füllung *f*; (*of traffic*) Verkehrsstockung *f*; (*of population*) Übervölkerung *f*; (*pathol*) Blutandrang *m*

congratulate [kən'grætʃə‚let] *tr* gratulieren (*dat*); **c. s.o. on** j-m gratulieren zu

congratulations [kən‚grætʃə'leʃənz]
spl Glückwunsch *m*; **c.!** ich gratu-
liere!

congregate ['kɑngrɪ‚get] *intr* sich
(ver)sammeln, zusammenkommen

congregation [‚kɑngrɪ'geʃən] *s* Versammlung *f*; (eccl) Gemeinde *f*

congress ['kɑngres] *s* Kongreß *m*

congressional [kən'greʃənəl] *adj* Kon-
greß-

congress-man ['kɑngrɪsmən] *s* (**-men**)
Abgeordnete *m*

con'gress-wom'an *s* (**-wom'en**) Abgeordnete *f*

congruent ['kɑngruˌənt] *adj* kongruent

conical ['kɑnɪkəl] *adj* kegelförmig

conjecture [kən'dʒekʃər] *s* Vermutung
f, Mutmaßung *f* ‖ *tr & intr* vermuten

conjugal ['kɑndʒəgəl] *adj* ehelich

conjugate ['kɑndʒə‚get] *tr* abwandeln

conjugation [‚kɑndʒə'geʃən] *s* Ab-
wandlung *f*

conjunction [kən'dʒʌnkʃən] *s* Binde-
wort *n*; **in c. with** in Verbindung mit

conjure [kən'dʒur] *tr* (*appeal solemn-
ly to*) beschwören ‖ ['kɑndʒər] *tr*—
c. away wegzaubern; **c. up** heraufbeschwören

conk [kɑnk] *tr* (sl) hauen ‖ *intr*—**c.
out** (sl) versagen

connect [kə'nekt] *tr* verbinden; (&
fig) verknüpfen; (elec) (**to**) anschließen (an *acc*); (telp) (**with**) verbinden
(mit) ‖ *intr* verbunden sein; (*said of
trains, etc.*) (**with**) Anschluß haben
(an *acc*); (box) treffen

connect'ing *adj* Verbindungs-, Binde-;
(*trains, buses*) Anschluß-; (*rooms*)
mit Zwischentür

connect'ing rod' *s* Schubstange *f*

connection [kə'nek/ən] *s* (*e.g., of a
pipe*) Verbindung *f*; (*of ideas*) Ver-
knüpfung *f*; (*context*) Zusammenhang *m*; (*part that connects*) Ver-
bindungsteil *m*; (elec) Schaltung *f*;

(mach, rr, telp) Verbindung *f*; **con-nections** Beziehungen *pl*; **in c. with** in Zusammenhang mit

con'ning tow'er ['kɒnɪŋ] *s* Kommandoturm *m*

connive [kə'naɪv] *intr*—**c.** at ein Auge zudrücken bei; **c. with** im geheimen Einverständnis stehen mit

connotation [ˌkɒno'teʃən] *s* Nebenbedeutung *f*

connote [kə'not] *tr* mitbezeichnen

conquer ['kɒŋkər] *tr* (*win in war*) erobern; (*overcome*) überwinden

conquerer ['kɒŋkərər] *s* Eroberer *m*

conquest ['kɒŋkwest] *s* Eroberung *f*

conscience ['kɒnʃəns] *s* Gewissen *n*

conscientious [ˌkɒnʃɪ'enʃəs] *adj* gewissenhaft, pflichtbewußt

conscien'tious objec'tor [əb'dʒektər] *s* Wehrdienstverweigerer *m*

conscious ['kɒnʃəs] *adj* bei Bewußtsein; **c. of** bewußt (*genit*)

consciousness ['kɒnʃəsnɪs] *s* Bewußtsein *n*; (*awareness*) (**of**) Kenntnis *f* (*genit* or von); **regain c.** wieder zu sich kommen

conscript ['kɒnskrɪpt] *s* Dienstpflichtige *m*; (mil) Wehrdienstpflichtige *m* ‖ [kən'skrɪpt] *tr* ausheben

conscription [kən'skrɪpʃən] *s* Dienstpflicht *f*; (*draft*) Aushebung *f*

consecrate ['kɒnsɪˌkret] *tr* weihen

consecration [ˌkɒnsɪ'kreʃən] *s* Einweihung *f*; (*at Mass*) Wandlung *f*

consecutive [kən'sekjətɪv] *adj* aufeinanderfolgend

consensus [kən'sensəs] *s* allgemeine Übereinstimmung *f*; **the c. of opinion** die übereinstimmende Meinung

consent [kən'sent] *s* Zustimmung *f*; **by common c.** mit allgemeiner Zustimmung ‖ *intr* zustimmen; **c. to** (*inf*) sich bereit erklären zu (*inf*)

consequence ['kɒnsɪˌkwens] *s* Folge *f*; (*influence*) Einfluß *m*; **in c. of** infolge (*genit*); **it is of no c.** es hat nichts auf sich; **suffer the consequences** die Folgen tragen

consequently ['kɒnsɪˌkwentlɪ] *adv* folglich, infolgedessen, mithin

conservation [ˌkɒnsər'veʃən] *s* Bewahrung *f*; (*of energy, etc.*) Erhaltung *f*; (*supervision of natural resources*) Naturschutz *m*; (*ecology*) Umweltschutz *m*

conservatism [kən'sʌrvəˌtɪzəm] *s* Konservatismus *m*

conservative [kən'sʌrvətɪv] *adj* konservativ; (*estimate*) vorsichtig ‖ *s* Konservative *mf*

conservatory [kən'sʌrvəˌtori] *s* Treibhaus *n*; (mus) Konservatorium *n*

conserve [kən'sʌrv] *tr* sparsam umgehen mit

consider [kən'sɪdər] *tr* (*take into account*) berücksichtigen; (*show consideration for*) Rücksicht nehmen auf (*acc*); (*reflect on*) sich (*dat*) überlegen; (*regard as*) halten für, betrachten als; **all things considered** alles in allem

considerable [kən'sɪdərəbəl] *adj* beträchtlich, erheblich

considerate [kən'sɪdərɪt] *adj* (**towards**) rücksichtsvoll (gegen)

consideration [kənˌsɪdə'reʃən] *s* (*taking into account*) Berücksichtigung *f*; (*regard*) (**for**) Rücksicht *f* (auf *acc*); **be an important c.** e-e wichtige Rolle spielen; **be under c.** in Betracht gezogen werden; **for a c.** entgeltlich; **in c. of** in Anbetracht (*genit*); **take into c.** in Betracht ziehen; **with c.** rücksichtsvoll

consid'ering *adv* (coll) den Umständen nach ‖ *prep* in Anbetracht (*genit*)

consign [kən'saɪn] *tr* (*ship*) versenden; (*address*) adressieren

consignee [ˌkɒnsaɪ'ni] *s* Adressat –in *mf*

consignment [kən'saɪnmənt] *s* (*act of sending*) Versand *m*; (*merchandise sent*) Sendung *f*; **on c.** in Kommission

consist [kən'sɪst] *intr*—**c. in** bestehen in (*dat*); **c. of** bestehen aus

consistency [kən'sɪstənsɪ] *s* Konsequenz *f*; (*firmness*) Festigkeit *f*; (*viscosity*) Dickflüssigkeit *f*; (*agreement*) Übereinstimmung *f*; (*steadfastness*) (**in**) Beständigkeit *f* (in *dat*)

consistent [kən'sɪstənt] *adj* (*performer*) stetig; (*performance*) gleichmäßig; (*free from contradiction*) konsequent; **c. with** in Übereinstimmung mit

consistory [kən'sɪstərɪ] *s* Konsistorium *n*

consolation [ˌkɒnsə'leʃən] *s* Trost *m*

console ['kɒnsol] *s* (*for radio or record player*) Musiktruhe *f*; (*of an organ*) Spieltisch *m*; (television) Fernsehtruhe *f* ‖ [kən'sol] *tr* trösten

consolidate [kən'salɪˌdet] *tr* (a position) festigen; (*debts*) konsolidieren; (*combine*) zusammenlegen

consonant ['kɒnsənənt] *adj* (**with**) im Einklang (mit) ‖ *s* Mitlaut *m*

consort ['kɒnsɔrt] *s* (*male*) Gemahl *m*; (*female*) Gemahlin *f* ‖ [kən'sɔrt] *intr* (**with**) Umgang haben (mit)

consorti·um [kən'sɔrtɪ·əm] *s* (-a [ə]) Konsortium *n*

conspicuous [kən'spɪkju·əs] *adj* auffallend, auffällig; **c. for** bemerkenswert wegen

conspiracy [kən'spɪrəsɪ] *s* Verschwörung *f*

conspirator [kən'spɪrətər] *s* Verschwörer –in *mf*

conspire [kən'spaɪr] *intr* sich verschwören

constable ['kɒnstəbəl] *s* Gendarm *m*

constancy ['kɒnstənsɪ] *s* Beständigkeit *f*

constant ['kɒnstənt] *adj* (*continuous*) dauernd, ständig; (*faithful*) treu; (*resolute*) standhaft; (*element, time element*) fest; (fig & tech) konstant ‖ *s* (math, phys) Konstante *f*

constantly ['kɒnstəntlɪ] *adv* immerfort

constellation [ˌkɒnstə'leʃən] *s* Sternbild *n*

consternation [ˌkɒnstər'neʃən] *s* Bestürzung *f*

constipate ['kanstı ,pet] *tr* verstopfen
constipation [,kanstı'peʃən] *s* Verstopfung *f*
constituency [kən'stıt/u·ənsi] *s* Wählerschaft *f*
constituent [kən'stıt/u·ənt] *adj* wesentlich; **c. part** Bestandteil *m* ‖ *s* Komponente *f*; (pol) Wähler –in *mf*
constitute ['kanstı ,t(j)ut] *tr* (*make up*) ausmachen, bilden; (*found*) gründen
constitution [,kanstı't(j)uʃən] *s* (*of a country or organization*) Verfassung *f*; (*bodily condition*) Konstitution *f*; (*composition*) Zusammensetzung *f*
constitutional [,kanstı't(j)uʃənəl] *adj* (*according to a constitution*) konstitutionell; (*crisis, amendment, etc.*) Verfassungs–
constrain [kən'stren] *tr* zwingen
constraint [kən'strent] *s* Zwang *m*; (jur) Nötigung *f*
constrict [kən'strıkt] *tr* zusammenziehen
construct [kən'strʌkt] *tr* errichten; (eng, geom, gram) konstruieren
construction [kən'strʌkʃən] *s* (*act of building*) Errichtung *f*; (*manner of building*) Bauweise *f*; (*interpretation*) Auslegung *f*; (eng, geom, gram) Konstruktion *f*; **under c.** im Bau
constructive [kən'strʌktıv] *adj* konstruktiv
construe [kən'stru] *tr* (*interpret*) auslegen; (gram) konstruieren
consul ['kansəl] *s* Konsul *m*
consular ['kans(j)ələr] *adj* konsularisch
consulate ['kans(j)əlıt] *s* Konsulat *n*
con′sul gen′eral *s* Generalkonsul *m*
consult [kən'sʌlt] *tr* konsultieren, um Rat fragen; (*a book*) nachschlagen ‖ *intr*–**c.** with sich beraten mit
consultant [kən'sʌltənt] *s* Berater –in *mf*
consultation [,kansəl'teʃən] *s* Beratung *f*; (& med) Konsultation *f*
consume [kən's(j)um] *tr* verzehren; (*use up*) verbrauchen; (*time*) beanspruchen
consumer [kən's(j)umər] *s* Konsument –in *mf*, Verbraucher –in *mf*
consum′er goods′ *spl* Konsumgüter *pl*
consummate [kən'sʌmıt] *adj* vollendet; (pej) abgefeimt ‖ ['kansə ,met] *tr* vollziehen
consumption [kən'sʌmpʃən] *s* (*of food*) Verzehr *m*; (econ) (*of*) Verbrauch *m* (an *dat*); (pathol) Schwindsucht *f*
consumptive [kə'sʌmptıv] *adj* schwindsüchtig ‖ *s* Schwindsüchtige *mf*
contact ['kantækt] *s* Kontakt *m*, Berührung *f*; (fig) (**with**) Verbindung *f* (mit); (elec) Kontakt *m* ‖ *tr* (coll) sich in Verbindung setzen mit
con′tact lens′ *s* Haftschale *f*
contagion [kən'tedʒən] *s* Ansteckung *f*
contagious [kən'tedʒəs] *adj* ansteckend
contain [kən'ten] *tr* enthalten; (*an*

enemy) aufhalten; (*one's feelings*) verhalten; **c. oneself** sich beherrschen
container [kən'tenər] *s* Behälter *m*
containment [kən'tenmənt] *s* (mil, pol) Eindämmung *f*
contaminate [kən'tæmı ,net] *tr* verunreinigen; (fig) vergiften
contamination [kən ,tæmı'neʃən] *s* Verunreinigung *f*; (fig) Vergiftung *f*
contemplate ['kantəm ,plet] *tr* betrachten; (*intend*) beabsichtigen ‖ *intr* nachdenken
contemplation [,kantəm'pleʃən] *s* Betrachtung *f*; (*consideration*) Erwägung *f*
contemporaneous [kən ,tempə'reni·əs] *adj* (**with**) gleichzeitig (mit)
contemporary [kən'tempə ,reri] *adj* zeitgenössisch; (*modern*) modern ‖ *s* Zeitgenosse *m*, Zeitgenossin *f*
contempt [kən'tempt] *s* Verachtung *f*; **beneath c.** unter aller Kritik
contemptible [kən'temptıbəl] *adj* verachtungswürdig
contempt′ of court′ *s* Mißachtung *f* des Gerichtes
contemptuous [kən'temptʃu·əs] *adj* verachtungsvoll, verächtlich
contend [kən'tend] *tr* behaupten ‖ *intr* (**for**) sich bewerben (um); (**with**) kämpfen (mit)
contender [kən'tendər] *s* (**for**) Bewerber –in *mf* (um)
content [kən'tent] *adj* (**with**) zufrieden (mit); **c. to** (*inf*) bereit zu (*inf*) ‖ *s* Zufriedenheit *f*; **to one's heart's c.** nach Herzenslust ‖ ['kantənt] *s* Inhalt *m*; (chem) Gehalt *m*; **contents** Inhalt *m* ‖ [kən'tent] *tr* zufriedenstellen; **c. oneself with** sich begnügen mit
content′ed *adj* zufrieden
contention [kən'tenʃən] *s* (*strife*) Streit *m*; (*assertion*) Behauptung *f*
contest ['kantest] *s* (**for**) Wettkampf *m* (um); (*written competition*) Preisausschreiben *n* ‖ [kən'test] *tr* (*argue against*) bestreiten; (*a will*) anfechten; (mil) kämpfen um; **contested** umstritten
contestant [kən'testənt] *s* Bewerber –in *mf*; (sport) Wettkämpfer –in *mf*
context ['kantekst] *s* Zusammenhang *m*
contiguous [kən'tıgju·əs] *adj* einander berührend; (**to**) angrenzend (an *acc*)
continence ['kantınəns] *s* Enthaltsamkeit *f*
continent ['kantınənt] *adj* enthaltsam ‖ *s* Kontinent *m*
continental [,kantı'nentəl] *adj* kontinental, Kontinental–
contingency [kən'tındʒənsi] *s* Zufall *m*
contingent [kən'tındʒənt] *adj* (**upon**) abhängig (von) ‖ *s* (mil) Kontingent *n*
continual [kən'tınju·əl] *adj* immer wiederkehrend
continuation [kən ,tınju'eʃən] *s* Fortsetzung *f*; (*continued existence*) Fortdauer *f*
continue [kən'tınju] *tr* fortsetzen; **c.**

to (*inf*) fortfahren zu (*inf*); weiter-, e.g., **c. to read** weiterlesen; **to be continued** Fortsetzung folgt || *intr* fortfahren; (*said of things*) anhalten

continuity [ˌkɑntɪˈn(j)u·ɪti] *s* Stetigkeit *f*

continuous [kənˈtɪnju·əs] *adj* ununterbrochen, anhaltend

contortion [kənˈtɔrʃən] *s* Verzerrung *f*

contour [ˈkɑntur] *s* Kontur *f*

con'tour line' *s* Schichtlinie *f*

con'tour map' *s* Landkarte *f* mit Schichtlinien

contraband [ˈkɑntrəˌbænd] *adj* Schmuggel– || *s* Konterbande *f*, Schmuggelware *f*

contraceptive [ˌkɑntrəˈsɛptɪv] *adj* empfängnisverhütend || *s* Empfängnisverhütungsmittel *n*

contract [ˈkɑntrækt] *s* Vertrag *m*, Kontrakt *m*; (*order*) Auftrag *m* || [kənˈtrækt] *tr* (*marriage*) (ab)schließen; (*a disease*) sich [*dat*] zuziehen; (*e.g., a muscle*) zusammenziehen; (*debts*) geraten in (*acc*); (ling) kontrahieren || *intr* (*shrink*) sich zusammenziehen; **c. to** (*inf*) sich vertraglich verpflichten zu (*inf*)

contract'ing *adj* vertragsschließend

contraction [kənˈtrækʃən] *s* (& ling) Zusammenziehung *f*, Kontraktion *f*; (*contracted word*) Verkürzung *f*

contractor [ˈkɑntræktər] *s* (*supplier*) Lieferant *m*; (*builder*) Bauunternehmer *m*

contradict [ˌkɑntrəˈdɪkt] *tr* widersprechen (*dat*)

contradiction [ˌkɑntrəˈdɪkʃən] *s* Widerspruch *m*

contradictory [ˌkɑntrəˈdɪktəri] *adj* widerspruchsvoll

contrail [ˈkɑnˌtrel] *s* Kondensstreifen *m*

contral·to [kənˈtrælto] *s* (–tos) (*person*) Altistin *f*; (*voice*) Alt *m*

contraption [kənˈtræpʃən] *s* (coll) Vorrichtung *f*; (*car*) (coll) Kiste *f*

contrary [ˈkɑntreri] *adj* konträr, gegensätzlich; (*person*) querköpfig; **c. to** entgegen (*dat*); **c. to nature** naturwidrig || *s* Gegenteil *n*; **on the c.** im Gegenteil

contrast [ˈkɑntræst] *s* Gegensatz *m* || [kənˈtræst] *tr* (**with**) gegenüberstellen (*dat*) || *intr* (**with**) im Gegensatz stehen (zu)

contravene [ˌkɑntrəˈvin] *tr* zuwiderhandeln (*dat*)

contribute [kənˈtrɪbjut] *tr* beitragen, spenden || *intr* **c. to** beitragen zu; (*with help*) mitwirken an (*dat*)

contribution [ˌkɑntrɪˈbjuʃən] *s* Beitrag *m*; (*of money*) Spende *f*

contributor [kənˈtrɪbjutər] *s* Spender –in *mf*; (*to a periodical*) Mitarbeiter –in *mf*

contrite [kənˈtraɪt] *adj* reuig

contrition [kənˈtrɪʃən] *s* Reue *f*

contrivance [kənˈtraɪvəns] *s* (*device*) Vorrichtung *f*; (*expedient*) Kunstgriff *m*; (*act of contriving*) Aushecken *n*

contrive [kənˈtraɪv] *tr* (*invent*) erfinden; (*devise*) ersinnen; **c. to** (*inf*) es fertig bringen zu (*inf*) || *intr* Anschläge aushecken

con·trol [kənˈtrol] *s* Kontrolle *f*, Gewalt *f*; (mach) Steuerung *f*; (mach) (*devise*) Regler *m*; **be out of c.** nicht zu halten sein; **be under c.** in bester Ordnung sein; **controls** (aer) Steuerwerk *n*; **gain c. over** die Herrschaft gewinnen über (*acc*); **have c. over s.o.** über j–n Gewalt haben; **keep under c.** im Zaume halten || *v* (*pret & pp* –trolled; *ger* –trolling) *tr* (*dominate*) beherrschen; (*verify*) kontrollieren; (*contain*) eindämmen; (*steer*) steuern; (*regulate*) regeln; **c. oneself** sich beherrschen

control' pan'el *s* Schaltbrett *n*

control' room' *s* Kommandoraum *m*; (rad) Regierraum *m*

control' stick' *s* (aer) Steuerknüppel *m*

control' tow'er *s* (*at an airport*) Kontrollturm *m*; (*on an aircraft carrier*) Kommandoturm *m*

controversial [ˌkɑntrəˈvɑrʃəl] *adj* umstritten, strittig; **c. subject** Streitfrage *f*

controversy [ˈkɑntrəˌvɑrsi] *s* Kontroverse *f*, Auseinandersetzung *f*

controvert [ˌkɑntrəˈvɑrt] *tr* (*argue against*) bestreiten; (*argue about*) streiten über (*acc*)

contusion [kənˈt(j)uʒən] *s* Quetschung *f*

convalesce [ˌkɑnvəˈlɛs] *intr* genesen

convalescence [ˌkɑnvəˈlɛsəns] *s* Genesung *f*

convalescent [ˌkɑnvəˈlɛsənt] *s* Genesende *mf*

convales'cent home' *s* Genesungsheim *n*

convene [kənˈvin] *tr* versammeln || *intr* sich versammeln

convenience [kənˈvinjəns] *s* Bequemlichkeit *f*; **at one's c.** nach Belieben; **at your earliest c.** möglichst bald; **modern conveniences** moderner Komfort *m*

convenient [kənˈvinjənt] *adj* gelegen

convent [ˈkɑnvɛnt] *s* Nonnenkloster *n*

convention [kənˈvɛnʃən] *s* (*professional meeting*) Tagung *f*; (*political meeting*) Konvent *m*; (*accepted usage*) Konvention *f*

conventional [kənˈvɛnʃənəl] *adj* konventionell, herkömmlich

converge [kənˈvɑrdʒ] *intr* zusammenlaufen; **c. on** sich stürzen auf (*acc*)

conversation [ˌkɑnvərˈseʃən] *s* Gespräch *n*

conversational [ˌkɑnvərˈseʃənəl] *adj* Gesprächs–

converse [ˈkɑnvʌrs] *adj* gegenteilig || *s* (of) Gegenteil *n* (von) || [kənˈvʌrs] *intr* sich unterhalten

conversion [kənˈvʌrʒən] *s* (**into**) Umwandlung *f* (in *acc*); (*of a factory*) (**to**) Umstellung *f* (auf *acc*); (*of a building*) (**into**) Umbau *m* (zu); (*of currency*) (**into**) Umwechslung *f* (in *acc*); (elec) (**to**) Umformung *f* (in *acc*); (math) Umrechnung *f*; (phys) Umsetzung *f*; (relig) Bekehrung *f*

convert ['kɔnvʌrt] s (to) Bekehrte mf (zu) ǁ [kən'vʌrt] tr (into) umwandeln (in acc); (a factory) (to) umstellen (auf acc); (a building) (into) umbauen (zu); (currency) (into) umwechseln (in acc); (biochem) (into) umsetzen (in acc); (chem) (into) umwandeln (in acc), verwandeln (in acc); (elec) (to) umformen (in acc); (math) (to) umrechnen (in acc); (phys) (to) umsetzen (in acc); (relig) (to) bekehren (zu) ǁ intr (to) sich bekehren (zu)

converter [kən'vʌrtər] s (elec) Umformer m, Stromrichter m

convertible [kən'vʌrtɪbəl] adj umwandelbar; (fin) konvertierbar ǁ s (aut) Kabriolett n

convex ['kɔnveks], [kɔn'veks] adj konvex

convey [kən've] tr (transport) befördern; (greetings, message) übermitteln; (sound) fortpflanzen; (meaning) ausdrücken; (a property) abtreten

conveyance [kən've-əns] s (act) Beförderung f; (means) Transportmittel n; (jur) Abtretung f

conveyor [kən've-ər] s Beförderer –in mf

convey'or belt' s Förderband n

convict ['kɔnvɪkt] s Sträfling m ǁ [kən'vɪkt] tr (of) überführen (genit)

conviction [kən'vɪkʃən] s (of a crime) Verurteilung f; (certainty) Überzeugung f; **convictions** Gesinnung f

convince [kən'vɪns] tr (of) überzeugen (von)

convivial [kən'vɪvɪ-əl] adj gesellig

convocation [‚kɔnvə'keʃən] s Zusammenberufung f; (educ) Eröffnungsfeier f

convoke [kən'vok] tr zusammenberufen

convoy ['kɔnvɔɪ] s (of vehicles) Kolonne f, Konvoi m; (nav) Geleitzug m

convulse [kən'vʌls] tr erschüttern

convulsion [kən'vʌlʃən] s Krampf m; **go into convulsions** Krämpfe bekommen

coo [ku] intr girren

cook [kʊk] s Koch m, Köchin f ǁ tr braten, backen; (boil) kochen; **c. up** (fig) zusammenbrauen ǁ intr braten, backen; (boil) kochen

cook'book' s Kochbuch n

cookie ['kʊki] s Plätzchen n, Keks m & n; **cookies** pl Gebäck n

cook'ing s Kochen n; **do one's own c.** sich selbst beköstigen

cool [kul] adj (& fig) kühl; **keep c.!** ruhig Blut!; **keep one's c.** (coll) ruhig Blut bewahren ǁ s Kühle f ǁ tr kühlen; **c. down** (fig) beruhigen; **c. off** abkühlen ǁ intr (& fig) sich abkühlen

cooler ['kulər] s Kühler m; (sl) Kittchen n

cool'-head'ed adj besonnen

coolie ['kuli] s Kuli m

coolness ['kulnɪs] s (& fig) Kühle f

coon [kun] s (zool) Waschbär m

coop [kup] s (building) Hühnerstall m; (enclosure) Hühnerhof m; (jail) (sl) Kittchen n; **fly the c.** (sl) auskneifen ǁ tr—**c. up** einsperren

co-op ['ko‚ɑp] s Konsumverein m

cooper ['kupər] s Küfer m, Böttcher m

cooperate [ko'ɑpə‚ret] intr (in) mitwirken (an dat, bei); (with) mitarbeiten (mit)

cooperation [ko‚ɑpə'reʃən] s Mitwirkung f, Mitarbeit f

cooperative [ko'ɑpə‚retɪv] adj hilfsbereit

coordinate [ko'ɔrdɪnɪt] adj gleichrangig; (gram) beigeordnet ǁ s (math) Koordinate f ǁ [ko'ɔrdɪ‚net] tr koordinieren

coordination [ko‚ɔrdɪ'neʃən] s Koordination f; (gram) Beiordnung f

cootie ['kuti] s (sl) Laus f

co-owner ['ko‚onər] s Miteigentümer –in mf

cop [kɑp] s (sl) Bulle m ǁ v (pret & pp copped; ger copped) tr (catch) (sl) erwischen; (steal) (sl) klauen ǁ intr—**cop out** (coll) auskneifen

copartner [ko'pɑrtnər] s Mitinhaber –in mf

cope [kop] intr—**c. with** sich messen mit, aufkommen gegen

cope'stone' s Schlußstein m

copier ['kɑpi-ər] s Kopiermaschine f

copilot ['ko‚paɪlət] s Kopilot m

coping ['kopɪŋ] s Mauerkappe f

copious ['kopɪ-əs] adj reichlich

cop'-out' s (act) Kneifen n; (person) Drückeberger m

copper ['kɑpər] adj kupfern, Kupfer–; (color) kupferrot ǁ s Kupfer n; (coin) Kupfermünze f; (sl) Schupo m

cop'persmith' s Kupferschmied m

copter ['kɑptər] s (coll) Hubschrauber m

copulate ['kɑpjə‚let] intr sich paaren

cop-y ['kɑpi] s Kopie f; (of a book) Exemplar n; (typ) druckfertiges Manuskript n ǁ v (pret & pp –ied) tr kopieren; (in school) abschreiben

cop'ybook' s Schreibheft n, Heft n

cop'ycat' s (imitator) Nachäffer –in mf

cop'yright' s Urheberrecht n, Verlagsrecht n ǁ tr urheberrechtlich schützen, verlagsrechtlich schützen

cop'ywrit'er s Texter –in mf

coquette [ko'ket] s Kokette f

coquettish [ko'ketɪʃ] adj kokett

coral ['kɔrəl] adj Korallen– ǁ s Koralle f

cor'al reef' s Korallenriff n

cord [kɔrd] s Schnur f, Strick m; (of wood) Klafter n; (elec) Leitungsschnur f

cordial ['kɔrdʒəl] adj herzlich ǁ s Likör m; (med) Herzstärkung f

cordiality [kɔr'dʒælɪti] s Herzlichkeit f

cordon ['kɔrdən] s Kordon m, Absperrkette f ǁ tr—**c. off** absperren

corduroy ['kɔrdə‚rɔɪ] s Kordsamt m; **corduroys** Kordsamthose f

core [kor] s (of fruit) Kern m; (of a

cable) Seele *f*; (fig) Kern *m*, Mark *n*; (elec) Spulenkern *m*

cork [kɔrk] *s* Kork *m*; (*stopper*) Pfropfen *m*, Korken *m* || *tr* verkorken

corker ['kɔrkər] *s* (sl) Schlager *m*

cork'ing *adj* (sl) fabelhaft

cork'oak', cork' tree' *s* Korkeiche *f*

cork'screw' *s* Korkenzieher *m*

corn [kɔrn] *s* (*Indian corn*) Mais *m*; (*on a foot*) Hühnerauge *n*; (*joke*) (sl) Kalauer *m*

corn'bread' *s* Maisbrot *n*

corn'cob' *s* Maiskolben *m*

corn'cob pipe' *s* Maiskolbenpfeife *f*

corn'crib' *s* Maisspeicher *m*

cornea ['kɔrnɪ·ə] *s* Hornhaut *f*

corned' beef' ['kɔrnd] *s* Pökelfleisch *n*

corner ['kɔrnər] *adj* Eck– || *s* Ecke *f*; (*secluded spot*) Winkel *m*; (*curve*) Kurve *f*; **c. of the eye** Augenwinkel *m*; **from all corners of the world** von allen Ecken und Enden; **turn the c.** um die Ecke biegen || *tr* (*a person*) in die Zange nehmen; (*the market*) aufkaufen

cor'nerstone' *s* Eckstein *m*; (*of a new building*) Grundstein *m*

cornet [kɔr'nɛt] *s* (mus) Kornett *n*

corn' exchange' *s* Getreidebörse *f*

corn'field' *s* Maisfeld *n*; (*grain field*) (Brit) Kornfeld *n*

corn'flakes' *spl* Maisflocken *pl*

corn' flour' *s* Maismehl *n*

corn'flow'er *s* Kornblume *f*

corn' frit'ter *s* Maispfannkuchen *m*

corn'husk' *s* Maishülse *f*

cornice ['kɔrnɪs] *s* Gesims *n*

corn' liq'uor *s* Maisschnaps *m*

corn' meal' *s* Maismehl *n*

corn' on the cob' *s* Mais *m* am Kolben

corn' silk' *s* Maisfasern *pl*

corn'stalk' *s* Maisstengel *m*

corn'starch' *s* Maisstärke *f*

cornucopia [,kɔrnə'kopɪ·ə] *s* Füllhorn *n*

corny ['kɔrni] *adj* (*sentimental*) rührselig; (*joke*) blöd

corollary ['kɔrə,lɛri] *s* (**to**) Folge *f* (von)

coron·a [kə'ronə] *s* (–nas & –nae [ni]) (astr) Hof *m*, Korona *f*; (archit) Kranzleiste *f*

coronary ['kɔrə,nɛri] *adj* koronar

coronation [,kɔrə'neʃən] *s* Krönung *f*

coroner ['kɔrənər] *s* Gerichtsmediziner *m*

cor'oner's in'quest *s* Totenschau *f*

coronet ['kɔrə,nɛt] *s* Krönchen *n*; (*worn by the nobility*) Adelskrone *f*; (*worn by women*) Diadem *n*

corporal ['kɔrpərəl] *adj* körperlich || *s* (mil) Obergefreite *m*

corporate ['kɔrpərɪt] *adj* korporativ

corporation [,kɔrpə'reʃən] *s* (fin) Aktiengesellschaft *f*; (jur) Körperschaft *f*

corpora'tion law'yer *s* Syndikus *m*

corporeal [kɔr'porɪ·əl] *adj* körperlich

corps [kɔr] *s* (**corps** [kɔrz]) Korps *n*

corpse [kɔrps] *s* Leiche *f*, Leichnam *m*

corps'man *s* (–men) Sanitäter *m*

corpulent ['kɔrpjələnt] *adj* beleibt

corpuscle ['kɔrpəsəl] *s* Blutkörperchen *n*

cor·ral [kə'ræl] *s* Pferch *m* || *v* (*pret & pp* –ralled; *ger* –ralling) *tr* zusammenpferchen

correct [kə'rɛkt] *adj* richtig; (*manners*) korrekt; (*time*) genau; **be c.** (*said of a thing*) stimmen; (*said of a person*) recht haben || *tr* korrigieren; (*examination papers*) verbessern; (*beat*) züchtigen; (*scold*) zurechtweisen; (*an unjust situation*) ausgleichen

correction [kə'rɛkʃən] *s* Berichtigung *f*; (*of examination papers*) Verbesserung *f*, Korrektur *f*; (*punishment*) Bestrafung *f*

corrective [kə'rɛktɪv] *adj* (*measures*) Gegen–; (*lenses, shoes*) Ausgleichs–

correctness [kə'rɛktnɪs] *s* Richtigkeit *f*; (*in manners*) Korrektheit *f*

correlate ['kɔrə,let] *tr* in Wechselbeziehung bringen || *intr* in Wechselbeziehung stehen

correlation [,kɔrə'leʃən] *s* Wechselbeziehung *f*, Korrelation *f*

correlative [kə'rɛlətɪv] *adj* korrelativ || *s* Korrelat *n*

correspond [,kɔrɪ'spand] *intr* einander übereinstimmen; (**to, with**) entsprechen (*dat*); (*exchange letters*) (**with**) im Briefwechsel stehen (mit)

correspondence [,kɔrɪ'spandəns] *s* (*act of corresponding*) Übereinstimmung *f*; (*instance of correspondence*) Entsprechung *f*; (*exchange of letters; letters*) Korrespondenz *f*

correspon'dence course' *s* Fernkursus *m*

correspondent [,kɔrɪ'spandənt] *s* Briefpartner –in *mf*; (journ) Korrespondent –in *mf*

correspond'ing *adj* entsprechend

corridor ['kɔridər] *s* Korridor *m*

corroborate [kə'rabə,ret] *tr* bestätigen

corrode [kə'rod] *tr & intr* korrodieren

corrosion [kə'roʒən] *s* Korrosion *f*

corrosive [kə'rosɪv] *adj* ätzend; (*influence*) schädigend || *s* Ätzmittel *n*

cor'rugated card'board ['kɔrə,getɪd] *s* Wellpappe *f*

cor'rugated i'ron *s* Wellblech *n*

corrupt [kə'rʌpt] *adj* (*text*) verderbt; (*morally*) verdorben; (*open to bribes*) bestechlich || *tr* verderben; (*bribe*) bestechen

corruption [kə'rʌpʃən] *s* Verderbtheit *f*; (*bribery*) Korruption *f*

corsage [kɔr'saʒ] *s* Blumensträußchen *n* zum Anstecken

corsair ['kɔrsɛr] *s* Korsar *m*

corset ['kɔrsɪt] *s* Korsett *n*

Corsica ['kɔrsɪkə] *s* Korsika *n*

Corsican ['kɔrsɪkən] *adj* korsisch

cortege [kɔr'teʒ] *s* Gefolge *n*; (*at a funeral*) Leichenzug *m*

cor·tex ['kɔr,tɛks] *s* (–tices [tɪ,siz]) Rinde *f*, Kortex *m*

cortisone ['kɔrtɪ,son] *s* Cortison *f*

corvette [kɔr'vɛt] *s* (naut) Korvette *f*

cosmetic [kaz'mɛtɪk] *adj* kosmetisch || *s* Kosmetikum *n*; **cosmetics** Kosmetikartikel *pl*

cosmic ['kazmɪk] *adj* kosmisch
cosmonaut ['kazmə,nɔt] *s* Kosmonaut –in *mf*
cosmopolitan [,kazə'palɪtən] *adj* kosmopolitisch || *s* Kosmopolit –in *mf*
cosmos ['kazməs] *s* Kosmos *m*
cost [kɔst] *s* Preis *m*; **at all costs** (fig) um jeden Preis; **at c.** zum Selbstkostenpreis; **at the c. of** auf Kosten (*genit*); **costs** Kosten *pl*; (jur) Gerichtskosten *pl* || *v* (*pret & pp* **cost**) *intr* kosten
cost′ account′ing *s* Kostenrechnung *f*
costly ['kɔstlɪ] *adj* kostspielig; (*of great value*) kostbar
cost′ of liv′ing *s* Lebenshaltungskosten *pl*
costume ['kast(j)um] *s* Kostüm *n*; (*national dress*) Tracht *f*
cos′tume ball′ *s* Kostümball *m*
cos′tume jew′elry *s* Modeschmuck *m*
cot [kat] *s* Feldbett *n*
coterie ['kotərɪ] *s* Klüngel *m*, Koterie *f*
cottage ['katɪdʒ] *s* Hütte *f*; (*country house*) Landhaus *n*
cot′tage cheese′ *s* Quark *m*, Quarkkäse *m*
cot′ter pin′ ['katər] *s* Schließbolzen *m*
cotton ['katən] *s* (*fiber, yarn*) Baumwolle *f*; (*unspun cotton*) Watte *f*; (*sterilized cotton*) Verbandswatte *f*
cot′ton field′ *s* Baumwollfeld *n*
cot′ton gin′ *s* Entkörnungsmaschine *f*
cot′ton mill′ *s* Baumwollspinnerei *f*
cot′ton pick′er ['pɪkər] *s* Baumwollpflücker –in *mf*; (*machine*) Baumwollpflückmaschine *f*
cot′tonseed oil′ *s* Baumwollsamenöl *n*
cot′ton waste′ *s* Putzwolle *f*
couch [kaʊtʃ] *s* Couch *f*, Liege *f* || *tr* (*words*) fassen; (*thoughts*) ausdrücken
cougar ['kugər] *s* Puma *m*
cough [kɔf] *s* Husten *m* || *tr*—**c. up** aushusten; (*money*) (sl) blechen || *intr* husten; (*in order to attract attention*) sich räuspern
cough′ drop′ *s* Hustenbonbon *m & n*
cough′ syr′up *s* Hustentropfen *pl*
could [kʊd] *aux*—**he c.** (*was able*) er konnte; **if he c.** (*were able*) wenn er könnte
council ['kaʊnsəl] *s* Rat *m*; (eccl) Konzil *n*
coun′cil·man *s* (–men) Stadtratsmitglied *n*
councilor ['kaʊnsələr] *s* Rat *m*
coun·sel ['kaʊnsəl] *s* Rat *m*; (*for the defense*) Verteidiger –in *mf*; (*for the prosecution*) Anklagevertreter –in *mf* || *v* (*pret & pp* –sel[l]ed; *ger* –sel[l]ing) *tr* raten (*dat*) || *intr* Rat geben
counselor ['kaʊnsələr] *s* Berater –in *mf*
count [kaʊnt] *s* Zahl *f*; (*nobleman*) Graf *m*; (jur) Anklagepunkt *m*; **lose c.** sich verzählen || *tr* zählen; (*the costs*) berechnen; **c. in** einschließen; **c. off** abzählen; **c. out** (*money, a boxer*) auszählen || *intr* zählen; **c. for little** (*or* **much**) wenig (*or* viel)

gelten; **c. off** (mil) abzählen; **c. on** zählen auf (*acc*)
count′down′ *s* Countdown *m & n*
countenance ['kaʊntɪnəns] *s* Antlitz *n* || *tr* (*tolerate*) zulassen; (*approve*) billigen
counter ['kaʊntər] *adj* Gegen– || *adv*—**c. to** widern; **run c. to** zuwiderlaufen (*dat*) || *s* Zähler *m*; (*in games*) Spielmarke *f*; (*in a store*) Ladentisch *m*, Theke *f*; (*in a restaurant*) Büffet *n*; (*in a bank*) Schalter *m*; **under the c.** (fig) heimlich || *tr* widerstreben (*dat*); (*in speech*) widersprechen (*dat*) || *intr* Gegenmaßnahmen treffen; (box) kontern, nachschlagen
coun′teract′ *tr* entgegenwirken (*dat*)
coun′terattack′ *s* Gegenangriff *m* || **coun′terattack′** *tr* e–n Gegenangriff machen auf (*acc*) || *intr* e–n Gegenangriff machen
coun′terbal′ance *s* Gegengewicht *n* || **coun′terbal′ance** *tr* das Gegengewicht halten (*dat*)
coun′terclock′wise *adj* linksläufig || *adv* entgegen der Uhrzeigerrichtung
coun′teres′pionage *s* Gegenspionage *f*
counterfeit ['kaʊntərfɪt] *adj* gefälscht || *s* Fälschung *f*; (*money*) Falschgeld *n* || *tr* fälschen
counterfeiter ['kaʊntər,fɪtər] *s* Falschmünzer –in *mf*
coun′terfeit mon′ey *s* Falschgeld *n*
coun′terintel′ligence *s* Spionageabwehr *f*
countermand ['kaʊntər,mænd] *s* Gegenbefehl *m* || *tr* widerrufen
coun′termeas′ure *s* Gegenmaßnahme *f*
coun′teroffen′sive *s* Gegenoffensive *f*
coun′terpart′ *s* Gegenstück *n*; (*person*) Ebenbild *n*
coun′terpoint′ *s* (mus) Kontrapunkt *m*
coun′terrevolu′tion *s* Konterrevolution *f*
coun′tersign′ *s* Gegenzeichen *n* || *tr & intr* mitunterzeichnen
coun′tersink′ *v* (*pret & pp* –sunk) *tr* (*a screw*) versenken; (*a hole*) ausfräsen
coun′terspy′ *s* Gegenspion –in *mf*
coun′terstroke′ *s* Gegenstoß *m*
coun′terweight′ *s* Gegengewicht *n*
countess ['kaʊntɪs] *s* Gräfin *f*
countless ['kaʊntlɪs] *adj* zahllos
countrified ['kaʊntrɪ,faɪd] *adj* ländlich; (*boorish*) bäu(e)risch
country ['kaʊntrɪ] *adj* (*air, house, life, road*) Land– || *s* (*state; rural area*) Land *n*; (*land of birth*) Heimatland *n*; **in the c.** auf dem Lande; **to the c.** aufs Land
coun′try club′ *s* exklusiver Klub *m* auf dem Lande
coun′tryfolk′ *spl* Landvolk *n*
coun′try gen′tleman *s* Landedelmann *m*
coun′try·man *s* (–men) Landsmann *m*
coun′tryside′ *s* Landschaft *f*, Land *n*
coun′try-wide′ *adj* über das ganze Land verbreitet (*or* ausgedehnt)
county ['kaʊntɪ] *s* Kreis *m*
coun′ty seat′ *s* Kreisstadt *f*

coup [ku] *s* Coup *m*

coup d'état [ku de 'ta] *s* Staatsstreich *m*

coupe [ku'pe], [kup] *s* Coupé *n*

couple ['kʌpəl] *s* Paar *n*; (*of lovers*) Liebespaar *n*; (*man and wife*) Ehepaar *n*; (*phys*) Kräftepaar *n*; **a c. of** ein paar, e.g., **a c. of days ago** vor ein paar Tagen || *tr* koppeln || *intr* sich paaren

couplet ['kʌplɪt] *s* Verspaar *n*

coupling ['kʌplɪŋ] *s* Verbindungsstück *n*; (*rad*) Kopplung *f*; (*rr*) Kupplung *f*

coupon ['k(j)upɑn] *s* Gutschein *m*

courage ['kʌrɪdʒ] *s* Mut *m*, Courage *f*; **get up the c. to** (*inf*) sich [*dat*] ein Herz fassen zu (*inf*)

courageous [kə'redʒəs] *adj* mutig

courier ['kʌrɪ·ər] *s* Eilbote *m*; (*tour guide*) Reiseleiter –in *mf*

course [kors] *s* (*direction*) Richtung *f*, Kurs *m*; (*of a river, of time*) Lauf *m*; (*method of procedure*) Weg *m*, Weise *f*, Kurs *m*; (*in racing*) Bahn *f*; (*archit*) Schicht *f*; (*culin*) Gang *m*; (*educ*) Kurs *m*; **c. of action** Handlungsweise *f*; **go off c.** (*aer*) sich verfliegen; **in due c.** zur rechten Zeit; **in the c. of** im Verlaufe von (*or genit*); (*with expressions of time*) im Laufe (*genit*); **of c.** natürlich; **run its c.** seinen Verlauf nehmen

court [kort] *s* (*of a king*) Hof *m*; (*of justice*) Gericht *n*; (*yard*) Hof *m*; (*tennis*) Platz *m*; **in c.** (*or into c.* **or to c.**) vor Gericht; **out of c.** außergerichtlich || *tr* (*a girl*) werben um; (*danger*) suchen; (*disaster*) heraufbeschwören

courteous ['kʌrtɪ·əs] *adj* höflich

courtesan ['kortɪʒən] *s* Kurtisane *f*

courtesy ['kʌrtɪsɪ] *s* Höflichkeit *f*; **by c. of** freundlicherweise zur Verfügung gestellt von

court'house' *s* Gerichtsgebäude *n*

courtier ['kortɪ·ər] *s* Höfling *m*

court' jest'er *s* Hofnarr *m*

courtly ['kortlɪ] *adj* höfisch

court'-mar'tial *s* (*courts-martial*) Kriegsgericht *n* || *v* (*pret & pp* –tial[l]ed; *ger* –tial[l]ing) *tr* vor ein Kriegsgericht stellen

court'room' *s* Gerichtssaal *m*

court'ship' *s* Werbung *f*

court'yard' *s* Hof *m*

cousin ['kʌzɪn] *s* Vetter *m*; (*female*) Kusine *f*

cove [kov] *s* Bucht *f*

covenant ['kʌvənənt] *s* Vertrag *m*; (Bib) Bund *m*

cover ['kʌvər] *s* Decke *f*; (*lid*) Deckel *m*; (*wrapping*) Hülle *f*; (*e.g., of a bed*) Bezug *m*; (*of a book*) Einband *m*; (*protection*) Schutz *m*; (*mil*) Deckung *f*; **from c. to c.** von vorn bis hinten; **take c.** sich unterstellen; **under c.** im Geheimen; **under c. of night** im Schutz der Dunkelheit || *tr* bedecken, decken; (*conceal*) verdecken; (*distances*) zurücklegen; (*a sales territory*) bearbeiten; (*a bet*) die gleiche Summe setzen gegen; (*expenses, losses*) decken; (*upholstered furniture*) beziehen; (*deal with*) behandeln; (*include*) umfassen; (*material in class*) durchnehmen; (*said of a reporter*) berichten über (*acc*); (*said of plants*) bewachsen; (*with insurance*) versichern, decken; (*protect with a gun*) sichern; (*threaten with a gun*) in Schach halten; (*have within range*) beherrschen; **c. up** zudecken; (*conceal*) verheimlichen || *intr*—**c. for** einspringen für

coverage ['kʌvərɪdʒ] *s* (*area covered*) Verbreitungsgebiet *n*; (*of news*) Berichterstattung *f*; (*ins*) Versicherungsschutz *m*; (rad, telv) Sendebereich *m*

coveralls ['kʌvər,ɔlz] *spl* Monteuranzug *m*

cov'ered wag'on *s* Planwagen *m*

cov'er girl' *s* Covergirl *n*

cov'ering *s* Decke *f*, Bedeckung *f*

covert ['kovərt] *adj* verborgen

cov'erup' *s* Beschönigung *f*, Bemäntelung *f*

covet ['kʌvɪt] *tr* begehren

covetous ['kʌvɪtəs] *adj* begehrlich

covetousness ['kʌvɪtəsnɪs] *s* Begehrlichkeit *f*

covey ['kʌvɪ] *s* (*brood*) Brut *f*; (*small flock*) Schwarm *m*; (*bevy*) Schar *f*

cow [kau] *s* Kuh *f* || *tr* einschüchtern

coward ['kau·ərd] *s* Feigling *m*, Memme *f*

cowardice ['kau·ərdɪs] *s* Feigheit *f*

cowardly ['kau·ərdlɪ] *adj* feig(e)

cow'bell' *s* Kuhglocke *f*

cow'boy' *s* Cowboy *m*

cower ['kau·ər] *intr* kauern

cow'herd' *s* Kuhhirt *m*

cow'hide' *s* Rindsleder *n*

cowl [kaul] *s* (*on a chimney*) Schornsteinkappe *f*; (*aer*) Motorhaube *f*; (eccl) Kapuze *f*

cowling ['kaulɪŋ] *s* (aer) Motorhaube *f*

co-worker ['ko ,wʌrkər] *s* Mitarbeiter –in *mf*

cowpox ['kau ,pɑks] *s* Kuhpocken *pl*

coxswain ['kɑksən] *s* Steuermann *m*

coy [kɔɪ] *adj* spröde

coyote [kaɪ'otɪ], ['kaɪ·ot] *s* Kojote *m*, Präriewolf *m*, Steppenwolf *m*

cozy ['kozɪ] *adj* gemütlich

C.P.A. ['si'pi'e] *s* (**certified public accountant**) amtlich zugelassener Wirtschaftsprüfer *m*

crab [kræb] *s* Krabbe *f*; (*grouch*) Sauertopf *m*

crab' ap'ple *s* Holzapfel *m*

crabbed ['kræbɪd] *adj* mürrisch; (*handwriting*) unleserlich; (*style*) schwer verständlich, verworren

crabby ['kræbɪ] *adj* mürrisch, grämlich

crack [kræk] *adj* erstklassig; (*troops*) Elite– *s* Riß *m*, Sprung *m*; (*of a whip or rifle*) Knall *m*; (*blow*) (sl) Klaps *m*; (*opportunity*) (sl) Gelegenheit *f*; (*try*) (sl) Versuch *m*; (*cutting remark*) (sl) Seitenhieb *m*; **at the c. of dawn** bei Tagesanbruch; **take a c. at** (sl) versuchen || *tr* spalten; (*a nut, safe*) knacken; (*an egg*) aufschlagen;

(a code) entziffern; *(hit)* (sl) e-n Klaps geben *(dat)*; *(chem)* spalten; **c. a joke** e-n Witz reißen; **c. a smile** lächeln ‖ *intr (make a cracking sound)* knacken, krachen; *(develop a crack)* rissig werden; *(said of a whip or rifle)* knallen; *(said of a voice)* umschlagen; *(said of ice)* (zer) springen; **c. down on scharf vorgehen gegen; c. up** (coll) überschnappen; (aut) aufknallen

cracked *adj (split)* rissig; *(crazy)* (sl) übergeschnappt

cracker ['krækər] s Keks m & n

crack'erjack' *adj* (coll) erstklassig ‖ *s* (coll) Kanone *f*

crackle ['krækəl] s Krakelierung *f* ‖ *tr* krakelieren ‖ *intr* prasseln

crack'pot' *adj* (sl) verrückt ‖ *s* (sl) Verrückte *mf*

crack' shot' s Meisterschütze m

crack'-up' s (aut) Zusammenstoß m

cradle ['kredəl] s Wiege *f*; (telp) Gabel *f* ‖ *tr* in den Armen wiegen

craft [kræft] s Handwerk n, Gewerbe n; (naut) Fahrzeug n; **by c.** durch List ‖ *spl* Fahrzeuge *pl*, Schiffe *pl*; **small c.** kleine Schiffe *pl*

craftiness ['kræftɪnɪs] s List *f*

crafts·man ['kræftsmən] s (-men) Handwerker m

crafts'manship' s Kunstfertigkeit *f*

crafty ['kræftɪ] *adj* arglistig

crag [kræg] s Felszacke *f*

cram [kræm] v (pret & pp crammed; ger cramming) tr vollstopfen; **c. into** hineinstopfen in *(acc)* ‖ *intr* (educ) büffeln, ochsen; **c. into** sich hineinzwängen in *(acc)*

cram' course' s Presse *f*

cramp [kræmp] s Krampf m; *(clamp)* Klammer *f* ‖ *tr* einschränken, beengen

cramped *adj* eng

cranberry ['kræn‚berɪ] s Preiselbeere *f*

crane [kren] s (mach) Kran m; (orn) Kranich m ‖—**c. one's neck** den Hals recken

crani·um ['krenɪəm] s (-a [ə]) s Hirnschale *f*, Schädel m

crank [kræŋk] s Kurbel *f*; *(grouch)* (coll) Griesgram m; *(eccentric)* (coll) Sonderling m ‖ *tr* kurbeln; **c. up** ankurbeln

crank'case' s Kurbelgehäuse n

crank'shaft' s Kurbelwelle *f*

cranky ['kræŋkɪ] *adj* launisch

cranny ['krænɪ] s Ritze *f*

crap [kræp] s *(nonsense)* (sl) Unsinn m; **craps** Würfel *pl*; **shoot craps** Würfel spielen

crash [kræʃ] s Krach m; (aer) Absturz m; (aut) Zusammenstoß m; (econ) Zusammenbruch m ‖ *tr* zerschmettern; *(a party)* hineinplatzen in *(acc)*; (aer) zum Absturz bringen ‖ *intr (produce a crashing sound)* krachen; *(shatter)* zerbrechen; *(collapse)* zusammenstürzen; (aer) abstürzen; (aut) zusammenstoßen; **c.** into fahren gegen

crash' dive' s Schnelltauchen n

crash'-dive' *intr* schnelltauchen

crash' hel'met s Sturzhelm m

crash' land'ing s Bruchlandung *f*

crash' pro'gram s Gewaltkur *f*

crass [kræs] *adj* kraß

crate [kret] s Lattenkiste *f*; *(old car, old plane)* (coll) Kiste *f* ‖ *tr* in e-r Lattenkiste verpacken

crater ['kretər] s Krater m; *(of a bomb)* Trichter m

crave [krev] tr ersehnen ‖ *intr*—**c. for** verlangen nach

craven ['krevən] *adj* feige ‖ *s* Feigling m

crav'ing s (for) Verlangen n (nach)

craw [krɔ] s Kropf m

crawl [krɔl] s Kriechen n ‖ *intr* kriechen; *(said of the skin)* kribbeln; *(said of a swimmer)* kraulen; *(said of cars)* schleichen; **c. along** im Schneckentempo gehen (or fahren); **c. into a hole** (& fig) sich verkriechen; **c. with** wimmeln von

crayon ['kre·ən] s *(wax crayon)* Wachsmalkreide *f*; *(colored pencil)* Farbstift m; *(artist's crayon)* Zeichenkreide *f*

craze [krez] s Mode *f*, Verrücktheit *f* ‖ *tr* verrückt machen

crazy ['krezɪ] *adj* verrückt; *(senseless)* sinnlos; **c. about** verrückt nach; **c. idea** Wahnidee *f*; **drive c.** verrückt machen

cra'zy bone' s Musikantenknochen m

creak [krik] s *(high-pitched sound)* Quietschen n; *(low-pitched sound)* Knarren n ‖ *intr* quietschen; knarren

creaky ['krikɪ] *adj* quietschend; knarrend

cream [krim] *adj* Sahne-, Rahm-; *(color)* creme, cremefarben ‖ *s* Sahne *f*, Rahm m; *(cosmetic)* Creme *f*; *(color)* Cremefarbe *f*; (fig) Creme *f* ‖ *tr (milk)* abrahmen; *(trounce)* (sl) schlagen

cream' cheese' s Rahmkäse m, Sahnekäse m

creamery ['krimərɪ] s Molkerei *f*

cream' pit'cher s Sahnekännchen n

cream' puff' s Windbeutel m

cream' sep'arator s ['sepə‚retər] s Milchschleuder *f*, Milchzentrifuge *f*

creamy ['krimɪ] *adj* sahnig

crease [kris] s Falte *f*; *(in trousers)* Bügelfalte *f* ‖ *tr* falten; *(trousers)* bügeln ‖ *intr* knittern

create [krɪ'et] tr (er)schaffen; *(excitement, an impression)* hervorrufen; *(noise)* verursachen; *(appoint)* ernennen, machen zu; *(a role, fashions)* kreieren

creation [krɪ'eʃən] s Schaffung *f*; *(of the world)* Schöpfung *f*; *(in fashions)* Modeschöpfung *f*

creative [krɪ'etɪv] *adj* schöpferisch

creator [krɪ'etər] s Schöpfer m

creature ['kritʃər] s Kreatur *f*, Geschöpf n; **every living c.** jedes Lebewesen n

credence ['kridəns] s Glaube m

credentials [krɪ'denʃəlz] *spl* Beglaubigungsschreiben n, Akkreditiv n

credenza [krɪ'denzə] s Kredenz *f*

credibility [ˌkredɪ'bɪlɪti] s Glaubwürdigkeit f

credibil'ity gap' s Vertrauenslücke f

credible ['kredɪbəl] adj glaubwürdig

credit ['kredɪt] s (credence) Glaube m; (honor) Ehre f; (recognition) Anerkennung f; (educ) Anrechnungspunkt m; (fin) Kredit m; (credit balance) (fin) Guthaben n; be a c. to Ehre machen (dat); credits (cin) Vorspann m; give s.o. c. for s.th. j-m etw hoch anrechnen; on c. auf Kredit; on thirty days' c. auf dreißig Tage Ziel; take c. for sich [dat] als Verdienst anrechnen; to s.o.'s c. zu j-s Ehre || tr (believe) glauben (dat); (an account) gutschreiben (dat); c. s.o. with s.th. j-m etw hoch anrechnen

creditable ['kredɪtəbəl] adj ehrenwert

cre'dit card' s Kreditkarte f

cre'dit hour' s (educ) Anrechnungspunkt m

creditor ['kredɪtər] s Gläubiger -in mf

cre'dit rat'ing s Bonität f

credulous ['kredʒələs] adj leichtgläubig

creed [krid] s (& fig) Glaubensbekenntnis n

creek [krik] s Bach m

creep [krip] s Kriechen n; (sl) Spinner m; it gives me the creeps mir gruselt || v (pret & pp crept [krept]) intr kriechen, schleichen; (said of plants) kriechen; c. along dahinschleichen; c. up on heranschleichen an (acc); it makes my flesh c. es macht mich schaudern

creeper ['kripər] s Kletterpflanze f

creepy ['kripi] adj schaudererregend; (sensation) gruselig; have a c. feeling gruseln

cremate ['krimet] tr einäschern

cremation [krɪ'meʃən] s Einäscherung f

crematory ['krimə,tori] s Krematorium n

crepe [krep] s Krepp m; (mourning band) Trauerflor m

crepe' pa'per s Kreppapier n

crescent ['kresənt] s Mondsichel f

cres'cent roll' s Hörnchen n

cress [kres] s (bot) Kresse f

crest [krest] s (of a hill, wave, or rooster) Kamm m; (of a helmet) Helmbusch m; (of a bird) Federbüschel n

crestfallen ['krest,fɔlən] adj niedergeschlagen

Crete [krit] s Kreta n

crevice ['krevɪs] s Riß m

crew [kru] s Gruppe f; (aer, nav) Besatzung f; (of a boat) (sport) Mannschaft f; (rowing) (sport) Rudersport m

crew' cut' s Bürstenschnitt m

crib [krɪb] s (manger) Krippe f; (for children) Kinderbettstelle f; (bin) Speicher m; (student's pony) Eselsbrücke f || v (pret & pp cribbed; ger cribbing) tr & intr abbohren

cricket ['krɪkɪt] s (ent) Grille f;

(sport) Kricketspiel n; not c. (coll) nicht fair

crime [kraɪm] s Verbrechen n

criminal ['krɪmɪnəl] adj verbrecherisch; (act, case, code, court, law) Straf-; (investigation, trial, police) Kriminal- || s Verbrecher -in mf

crim'inal charge' s Strafanzeige f

crim'inal neg'ligence s grobe Fahrlässigkeit f

crim'inal offense' s strafbare Handlung f

crim'inal rec'ord s Strafregister n

crimp [krɪmp] s Welle f; put a c. in (coll) e-n Dämpfer aufsetzen (dat) || tr wellen, riffeln

crimson ['krɪmzən] adj karmesinrot || s Karmesin n

cringe [krɪndʒ] intr sich krümmen; (fawn) kriechen

crinkle ['krɪŋkəl] s Runzel f || tr runzeln; (one's nose) rümpfen

cripple ['krɪpəl] s Krüppel m || tr verkrüppeln; (fig) lähmen, lahmlegen

crisis ['kraɪsɪs] s (-ses [siz]) Krise f

crisp [krɪsp] adj (brittle) knusprig; (firm and fresh) mürb; (air, clothes) frisch; (manner) forsch

crisscross ['krɪs,krɔs] adj & adv kreuz und quer || tr kreuz und quer markieren || intr sich kreuzen

criterion [kraɪ'tɪrɪ-ən] s (-a [ə] & -ons) Kennzeichen n, Kriterium n

critic ['krɪtɪk] s Kritiker -in mf

critical ['krɪtɪkəl] adj kritisch

criticism ['krɪtɪ,sɪzəm] s Kritik f

criticize ['krɪtɪ,saɪz] tr kritisieren

critique [krɪ'tik] s (review) Rezension f; (critical discussion) Kritik f

croak [krok] s (of a frog) Quaken n; (of a raven) Krächzen n || intr quaken; krächzen; (die) (sl) verrecken

crochet [kro'ʃə] s Häkelarbeit f || v (pret & pp -cheted ['ʃed]; ger -cheting ['ʃe-ɪŋ]) tr & intr häkeln

crochet' nee'dle s Häkelnadel f

crock [krak] s irdener Topf m, Krug m

crockery ['krakəri] s irdenes Geschirr n

crocodile ['krakə,daɪl] s Krokodil n

croc'odile tears' spl Krokodilstränen pl

crocus ['krokəs] s (bot) Krokus m

crone [kron] s altes Weib n

crony ['kroni] s alter Kamerad m

crook [kruk] s (of a shepherd) Hirtenstab m; (sl) Gauner m || tr krümmen

crooked ['krukɪd] adj krumm; (dishonest) unehrlich

croon [krun] tr & intr schmalzig singen

crooner ['krunər] s Schnulzensänger m

crop [krap] s Ernte f; (whip) Peitsche f; (of a bird) Kropf m; (large number) Menge f; the crops die ganze Ernte || v (pret & pp cropped; ger cropping) tr stutzen; (said of an animal) abfressen || intr—c. up auftauchen

crop' fail'ure s Mißerte f

croquet [kro'ke] s Krocket n

croquette [kro'ket] s (culin) Krokette f

crosier ['kroʒər] s Bischofsstab m

cross [kros] adj Quer-, Kreuz-; (biol) Kreuzungs-; (angry) (with) ärgerlich (auf acc, über acc) || s (& fig) Kreuz n; (biol) Kreuzung f || tr (arms, legs, streets, plans, breeds) kreuzen; (a mountain) übersteigen; (oppose) in die Quere kommen (dat); **c. my heart!** Hand aufs Herz!; **c. oneself** sich bekreuzigen; **c. s.o.'s mind** j-m durch den Kopf gehen; **c. out** ausstreichen || intr sich kreuzen; **c. over** to hinübergehen zu

cross'bones' spl gekreuzte Skelettknochen pl

cross'bow' s (hist) Armbrust f

cross'breed' v (pret & pp -bred) tr kreuzen

cross'-coun'try adj (vehicle) geländegängig || **cross'-coun'try** s (sport) Langlauf m

cross'cur'rent s Gegenströmung f

cross'-exam'ine tr ins Kreuzverhör nehmen

cross'-examina'tion s Kreuzverhör n

cross'-eyed' adj schieläugig

cross'fire' s Kreuzfeuer n

cross'ing s (of streets) Kreuzung f; (of the ocean) Überfahrt f, Überquerung f; (rr) Übergang m

cross'piece' s Querstück n

cross'-pur'pose s—**be at cross-purposes** einander entgegenarbeiten

cross' ref'erence s Querverweis m

cross'road' s Querweg m; **crossroads** Straßenkreuzung f; (fig) Scheideweg m

cross' sec'tion s Querschnitt m

cross'wind' s Seitenwind m

cross'wise' adj & adv quer, in die Quere

cross'word puz'zle s Kreuzworträtsel n

crotch [krɑtʃ] s (of a tree) Gabelung f; (of a body or trousers) Schritt m

crotchety ['krɑtʃiti] adj verschroben

crouch [krautʃ] s Hocke f || intr hocken

croup [krup] s (of a horse) Kruppe f; (pathol) Halsbräune f

croupier ['krupiər] s Croupier -in mf

crouton ['krutɑn] s gerösteter Brotwürfel m

crow [kro] s (cry) Krähen n; (bird) Krähe f; **as the c.** flies schnurgrade; **eat c.** klein beigeben || intr krähen

crow'bar' s Stemmeisen n

crowd [kraud] s Menge f; (mob) Masse f; (set) Gesellschaft f || tr vollstopfen; (push) stoßen; **c. out** verdrängen || intr (around) sich drängen (um); **c. into** sich hineindrängen in (acc)

crowd'ed adj überfüllt; (street) belebt

crown [kraun] s Krone f; (dent) Zahnkrone f || tr krönen, bekränzen; (checkers) zur Dame machen; (sl) eins aufs Dach geben (dat); (dent) überkronen

crown' jew'els spl Kronjuwelen pl

crown' prince' s Kronprinz m

crown' prin'cess s Kronprinzessin f

crow's'-feet' spl (wrinkles) Krähenfüße pl

crow's'-nest' s (naut) Krähennest n

crucial ['kruʃəl] adj entscheidend; (point) springend; **c. question** Gretchenfrage f; **c. test** Feuerprobe f

crucible ['krusɪbəl] s Schmelztiegel m

crucifix ['krusɪfɪks] s Kruzifix n

crucifixion [,krusɪ'fɪkʃən] s Kreuzigung f

cruci•fy ['krusɪ,faɪ] v (pret & pp -fied) tr kreuzigen

crude [krud] adj (raw, unrefined) roh; (person) grob, ungeschliffen; **c. joke** plumper Scherz m

crudity ['krudɪti] s Roheit f

cruel ['kru•əl] adj (to) grausam (gegen)

cruelty ['kru•əlti] s Grausamkeit f; **c. to animals** Tierquälerei f

cruet ['kru•ɪt] s Fläschchen n; (relig) Meßkännchen n

cruise [kruz] s Kreuzfahrt f || intr (aer) mit Reisegeschwindigkeit fliegen; (aut) herumfahren; (naut) kreuzen

cruiser ['kruzər] s (nav) Kreuzer m

cruise' ship' s Vergnügungsdampfer m

cruller ['krʌlər] s Krapfen m

crumb [krʌm] s Krümel m; (& fig) Bröckchen n; (sl) Schweinehund m

crumble ['krʌmbəl] tr & intr zerbröckeln

crumbly ['krʌmbli] adj bröcklig

crummy ['krʌmi] adj (sl) schäbig

crumple ['krʌmpəl] tr zerknittern || intr (said of clothes) faltig werden; (collapse) zusammenbrechen

crunch [krʌntʃ] s Knacken n; (of snow) Knirschen n; (tight situation) Druck m || tr knirschend kauen || intr (said of snow) knirschen; **c. on** knirschend kauen

crusade [kru'sed] s Kreuzzug m

crusader [kru'sedər] s Kreuzfahrer m

crush [krʌʃ] s Gedränge n; **have a c. on s.o.** (coll) in j-n vernarrt sein || tr (zer)quetschen, zerdrücken; (grain) schroten; (stone) zerkleinern; (suppress) unterdrücken; (oppress) bedrücken; (hopes) knicken; (overwhelm) zerschmettern; (min) pochen; **c. out** (a cigarette) ausdrücken || intr zerdrückt werden

crush'ing adj (victory) entscheidend; (defeat) vernichtend; (experience) überwältigend

crust [krʌst] s Kruste f; (sl) Frechheit f

crustacean [krʌs'teʃən] s Krebstier n

crustaceous [krʌs'teʃəs] adj Krebs-

crusty ['krʌsti] adj krustig, rösch; (surly) mürrisch

crutch [krʌtʃ] s (& fig) Krücke f

crux [krʌks] s Kern m, Kernpunkt m

cry [kraɪ] s (cries) (shout) Schrei m, Ruf m; (weeping) Weinen n; **a far cry from** etw ganz anderes als; **cry for help** Hilferuf m; **have a good cry** sich ordentlich ausweinen || v (pret & pp cried) tr schreien, rufen; **cry one's eyes out** sich [dat] die Augen aus dem Kopf weinen || intr (weep) weinen; (*shout*) schreien; **cry for help** um Hilfe rufen; **cry on s.o.'s shoulder** j-m seine Not klagen; **cry out against** scharf verurteilen; **cry out in** (*pain*) schreien vor (*dat*); **cry over** nachweinen (*dat*)

cry'ba'by *s* (*-bies*) Schreihals *m*

cry'ing *adj*—**c. jag** Schreikrampf *m*; **c. shame** schreiende Ungerechtigkeit *f* ‖ *s* Weinen *n*; **for c. out loud!** um Himmels willen!

crypt [krɪpt] *s* Totengruft *f*, Krypta *f*

cryptic(al) [ˈkrɪptɪk(əl)] *adj* (*secret*) geheim; (*puzzling*) rätselhaft; (*coded*) verschlüsselt

crystal [ˈkrɪstəl] *adj* Kristall- ‖ *s* Kristall *m*; (*cut glass*) Kristallglas *n*; (*of a watch*) Uhrglas *n*

crys'tal ball' *s* Kristall *m*

crystalline [ˈkrɪstəlɪn], [ˈkrɪstəˌlaɪn] *adj* kristallinisch, kristallen

crystallize [ˈkrɪstəˌlaɪz] *tr* kristallisieren ‖ *intr* kristallisieren; (*fig*) feste Form annehmen

cub [kʌb] *s* Junge *n*

Cuba [ˈkjubə] *s* Kuba *n*

Cuban [ˈkjubən] *adj* kubanisch ‖ *s* Kubaner *-in* *mf*

cubbyhole [ˈkʌbɪˌhol] *s* gemütliches Zimmerchen *n*

cube [kjub] *s* Würfel *m*; (*math*) dritte Potenz *f* ‖ *tr* in Würfel schneiden; (*math*) kubieren

cubic [ˈkjubɪk] *adj* Raum-; (*math*) kubisch; **c. foot** Kubikfuß *m*

cub' report'er *s* unerfahrener Reporter *m*

cub' scout' *s* Wölfling *m*

cuckold [ˈkʌkəld] *s* Hahnrei *m* ‖ *tr* zum Hahnrei machen

cuckoo [ˈkuku] *adj* (sl) verrückt ‖ *s* Kuckuck *m*

cuck'oo clock' *s* Kuckucksuhr *f*

cucumber [ˈkjukʌmbər] *s* Gurke *f*

cud [kʌd] *s*—**chew the cud** wiederkäuen

cuddle [ˈkʌdəl] *tr* herzen ‖ *intr* sich kuscheln; **c. up** sich behaglich zusammenkuscheln

cudg·el [ˈkʌdʒəl] *s* Prügel *m* ‖ *v* (*pret & pp* -el[l]ed; *ger* -el[l]ing) *tr* verprügeln

cue [kju] *s* Hinweis *m*; (billiards) Billardstock *m*; (theat) Stichwort *n*; **take the cue from s.o.** sich nach j-m richten ‖ *tr* das Stichwort geben (*dat*)

cuff [kʌf] *s* (*of a shirt*) Manschette *f*; (*of trousers*) Aufschlag *m*; (*blow*) Ohrfeige *f*; **off the c.** aus dem Handgelenk

cuff' link' *s* Manschettenknopf *m*

cuisine [kwɪˈzin] *s* Küche *f*

culinary [ˈkjulɪˌnɛri] *adj* kulinarisch, Koch-; **c. art** Kochkunst *f*

cull [kʌl] *tr* (*choose*) auslesen; (*pluck*) pflücken

culminate [ˈkʌlmɪˌnet] *intr* (**in**) kulminieren (in *dat*), gipfeln (in *dat*)

culmination [ˌkʌlmɪˈneʃən] *s* Gipfel *m*

culpable [ˈkʌlpəbəl] *adj* schuldhaft

culprit [ˈkʌlprɪt] *s* Schuldige *mf*

cult [kʌlt] *s* Kult *m*, Kultus *m*

cultivate [ˈkʌltɪˌvet] *tr* (*soil*) bearbeiten; (*plants*) ziehen; (*activities*) betreiben; (*an art*) pflegen; (*friendship*) hegen

cul'tivat'ed *adj* kultiviert

cultivation [ˌkʌltɪˈveʃən] *s* (*of the soil*) Bearbeitung *f*; (*of the arts*) Pflege *f*; (*of friendship*) Hegen *n*; **under c.** bebaut

cultivator [ˈkʌltɪˌvetər] *s* (mach) Kultivator *m*

cultural [ˈkʌltʃərəl] *adj* kulturell, Kultur-

culture [ˈkʌltʃər] *s* Kultur *f*

cul'ture me'dium *s* Nährboden *m*

cul'tured *adj* kultiviert

culvert [ˈkʌlvərt] *s* Rinnstein *m*

cumbersome [ˈkʌmbərsəm] *adj* (*unwieldy*) unhandlich; (*slow-moving*) schwerfällig; (*burdensome*) lästig

cunning [ˈkʌnɪŋ] *adj* (arg)listig ‖ *s* List *f*, Arglist *f*, Schlauheit *f*

cup [kʌp] *s* Tasse *f*; (*of a bra*) Körbchen *n*; (fig, bot, relig) Kelch *m*; (sport) Pokal *m* ‖ *v* (*pret & pp* cupped; *ger* cupping) *tr* (*the hands*) wölben; (med) schröpfen

cupboard [ˈkʌbərd] *s* Schrank *m*

cupidity [kjuˈpɪdɪti] *s* Habgier *f*

cupola [ˈkjupələ] *s* Kuppel *f*

cur [kʌr] *s* Köter *m*; (pej) Halunke *m*

curable [ˈkjurəbəl] *adj* heilbar

curate [ˈkjurɪt] *s* Kaplan *m*

curative [ˈkjurətɪv] *adj* heilend, Heil-

curator [kjuˈretər] *s* Kustos *m*

curb [kʌrb] *s* (*of a street*) Randstein *m*; (*of a horse*) Kandare *f* *tr* (& fig) zügeln; (*a person*) an die Kandare nehmen

curb'stone' *s* Bordstein *m*

curd [kʌrd] *s* Quark *m*; **curds** Quark *m*

curdle [ˈkʌrdəl] *tr* gerinnen lassen; (fig) erstarren lassen ‖ *intr* gerinnen, stocken; (fig) erstarren

cure [kjur] *s* (*restoration to health*) Heilung *f*; (*remedy*) Heilmittel *n*; (*treatment*) Kur *f* ‖ *tr* (*a disease, evil*) heilen; (*by smoking*) räuchern; (*by drying*) trocknen; (*by salting*) einsalzen ‖ *intr* heilen

cure'-all' *s* Allheilmittel *n*

curfew [ˈkʌrfju] *s* Ausgehverbot *n*; (*enforced closing time*) Polizeistunde *f*

curi·o [ˈkjurɪˌo] *s* (*-os*) Kuriosität *f*

curiosity [ˌkjurɪˈɑsɪti] *s* Neugier *f*; (*strange article*) Kuriosität *f*

curious [ˈkjurɪ-əs] *adj* neugierig; (*odd*) kurios, merkwürdig

curl [kʌrl] *s* (*of hair*) Locke *f*; (*of smoke*) Rauchkringel *m* ‖ *tr* locken; (*lips*) verächtlich schürzen ‖ *intr* sich kräuseln; **c. up** sich zusammenrollen; (*said of an edge*) sich umbiegen

curler [ˈkʌrlər] *s* Haarwickler *m*

curlicue [ˈkʌrlɪˌkju] *s* Schnörkel *m*

curly [ˈkʌrli] *adj* lockig; (*leaves, etc.*) gekräuselt

currant [ˈkʌrənt] *s* (*raisin*) Korinthe *f*; (*genus Ribes*) Johannisbeere *f*

currency [ˈkʌrənsi] s (*money*) Währung *f*; (*circulation*) Umlauf *m*; for·eign **c.** Devisen *pl*; gain **c.** in Gebrauch kommen

current [ˈkʌrənt] adj (*year, prices, account*) laufend; (*events*) aktuell, Tages–; be **c.** Gültigkeit haben; (*said of money*) gelten ‖ s (& elec) Strom *m*

currently [ˈkʌrəntli] adv gegenwärtig

curricu·lum [kəˈrikjələm] s (**–lums** & **–la** [lə]) Lehrplan *m*

cur·ry [ˈkʌri] s Curry *m* ‖ v (*pret & pp* **–ried**) *tr* (*a horse*) striegeln; **c.** favor with s.o. sich bei j–m einzuschmeicheln suchen

cur′rycomb′ s Striegel *m*

cur′ry pow′der s Currypulver *n*

curse [kʌrs] s Fluch *m*; put a **c.** on verwünschen ‖ *tr* verfluchen ‖ *intr* (at) fluchen (auf *acc*)

cursed [ˈkʌrsid, kʌrst] adj verflucht

curse′ word′ s Fluchwort *n*, Schimpfwort *n*

cursive [ˈkʌrsiv] adj Kurrent–

cursory [ˈkʌrsəri] adj flüchtig

curt [kʌrt] adj barsch, schroff

curtail [kərˈtel] *tr* einschränken

curtain [ˈkʌrtin] s Gardine *f*; (*drape*) Vorhang *m*; (theat) Vorhang *m* ‖ *tr*—**c.** off mit Vorhängen abteilen

cur′tain call′ s Vorhang *m*, Hervorruf *m*

cur′tain rod′ s Gardinenstange *f*

curt·sy [ˈkʌrtsi] s Knicks *m* ‖ v (*pret & pp* **–sied**) *intr* (to) knicksen (vor *dat*)

curvaceous [kʌrˈveʃəs] adj kurvenreich

curvature [ˈkʌrvətʃər] s (*of the spine*) Verkrümmung *f*; (*of the earth*) Krümmung *f*

curved adj krumm

cushion [ˈkuʃən] s Kissen *n*, Polster *m* & *n*; (billiards) Bande *f* ‖ *tr* polstern; (*a shock*) abfedern

cuss [kʌs] s (sl) Kerl *m*; (*curse*) (sl) Fluch *m* ‖ *tr* (sl) verfluchen ‖ *intr* (sl) fluchen

cussed [ˈkʌsid] adj (sl) verflucht

cussedness [ˈkʌsidnis] s (sl) Bosheit *f*

custard [ˈkʌstərd] s Eierkrem *f*

custodian [kəsˈtodi·ən] s (e.g., *of records*) Verwalter *m*; (*of inmates*) Wärter *m*; (*caretaker*) Hausmeister *m*

custody [ˈkʌstədi] s Verwahrung *f*, Obhut *f*; (jur) Gewahrsam *m*; **c.** of (*children*) Sorgerecht für; in the **c.** of in der Obhut (*genit*); take into **c.** in Gewahrsam nehmen

custom [ˈkʌstəm] s Brauch *m*, Sitte *f*; (*habit*) Gewohnheit *f*; **customs** Zollkontrolle *f*; pay customs on s.th. für etw Zoll bezahlen

customary [ˈkʌstə‚meri] adj gebräuchlich

cus′tom-built′ adj nach Wunsch gebaut

customer [ˈkʌstəmər] s Kunde *m*, Kundin *f*; (*in a restaurant*) Gast *m*; (telp) Teilnehmer –in *mf*

cus′tom-made′ adj nach Maß angefertigt

cus′toms clear′ance s Zollabertigung *f*

cus′toms declara′tion s Zollerklärung *f*; (*form*) Abfertigungsschein *m*

cus′toms inspec′tion s Zollkontrolle *f*

cus′toms of′fice s Zollamt *n*

customs of′ficer s Zollbeamte *m*, Zollbeamtin *f*

cus′tom tai′lor s Maßschneider *m*

cut [kʌt] adj (*glass*) geschliffen; **cut flowers** Schnittblumen *pl*; **cut out for** wie geschaffen für (or zu) ‖ s Schnitt *m*; (*piece cut off*) Abschnitt *m*; (*slice*) Schnitte *f*; (*wound*) Schnittwunde *f*; (*of a garment*) Schnitt *m*, Fasson *f*; (*of the profits*) Anteil *m*; (*in prices, pay*) Kürzung *f*, Senkung *f*; (*absence from school*) Schwänzen *n*; (*of meat*) Stück *n*; (cards) Abheben *n*; (tennis) Drehschlag *m*; a **cut above** e–e Stufe besser als ‖ v (*pret & pp* **cut**; *ger* **cutting**) *tr* schneiden; (*glass, precious stones*) schleifen; (*grass*) mähen; (*hedges*) stutzen; (*hay*) machen; (*a tunnel*) bohren; (*a motor*) abstellen; (*production*) drosseln; (*pay*) kürzen, vermindern; (*class*) (coll) schwänzen; (*prices*) herabsetzen, kürzen; (*whiskey*) (coll) panschen; (*cards*) abheben; (*tennis*) schneiden; **cut back** (*plants*) stutzen; (fig) abbauen; **cut down** fällen; **cut it out!** Schluß damit!; **cut off** abschneiden; (*a tail*) kupieren; (*gas, telephone, electricity*) absperren; (*troops*) absprengen; **cut one's finger** sich in den Finger schneiden; **cut out the nonsense!** laß den Quatsch!; **cut short** (e.g., *a vacation*) abkürzen; (*a person*) das Wort abschneiden (*dat*); **cut up** zerstückeln ‖ *intr* schneiden; **cut down on** einschränken, verringern; **cut in** sich einmischen; (*at a dance*) ablösen; **cut in ahead of** s.o. vor j–m einbiegen; **cut up** (sl) wild darauf losschießen

cut-and-dried [ˈkʌtənˈdraɪd] adj fix und fertig

cut′away′ s Cut *m*

cut′back′ s Einschränkung *f*

cute [kjut] adj (*pretty*) niedlich; (*shrewd*) (coll) klug

cut′ glass′ s geschliffenes Glas *n*

cuticle [ˈkjutikəl] s Nagelhaut *f*

cutie [ˈkjuti] s (sl) flotte Biene *f*

cutlass [ˈkʌtləs] s Entermesser *n*

cutlery [ˈkʌtləri] s Schneidwerkzeuge *pl*

cutlet [ˈkʌtlit] s Schnitzel *n*

cut′-off′ s (*turn-off*) Abzweigung *f*; (*cut-off point*) (acct) gemeinsamer Endpunkt *m*; (elec) Ausschaltvorrichtung *f*; (mach) Absperrvorrichtung *f*

cut′-off date′ s Abschlußtag *m*

cut′-out′ s Ausschnitt *m*; (*design to be cut out*) Ausschneidemuster *n*; (aut) Auspuffklappe *f*

cut′-rate′ adj (*price*) Schleuder–

cutter [ˈkʌtər] s (naut) Kutter *m*

cut′throat′ adj halsabschneiderisch ‖ s Halsabschneider –in *mf*

cut′ting adj schneidend; (*tools*)

Schneide–; (remark) scharf ‖ s Abschnitt m; (of prices) Herabsetzung f; (hort) Steckling m; cuttings Abfälle pl

cut'ting board' s Schneidebrett n

cut'ting edge' s Schnittkante f

cut'ting room' s (cin) Schneideraum m

cuttlefish ['kʌtl,fiʃ] s Tintenfisch m

cyanamide [saɪ'ænə,maɪd] s (chem) Zyanamid n; (com) Kalkstickstoff m

cycle ['saɪkəl] s Kreis m; (of internal combustion engine) Takt m; (phys) Periode f ‖ intr radeln

cyclic(al) ['sɪklɪk(əl)] adj zyklisch, kreisförmig

cyclist ['saɪklɪst] s Radfahrer –in mf

cyclone ['saɪklon] s Zyklon m

cyclotron ['saɪklə,trɑn] s Zyklotron n, Beschleuniger m

cylinder ['sɪlɪndər] s Zylinder m

cyl'inder block' s Zylinderblock m

cyl'inder bore' s Zylinderbohrung f

cyl'inder head' s Zylinderkopf m

cylindric(al) [sɪ'lɪndrɪk(əl)] adj zylindrisch

cymbal ['sɪmbəl] s Becken n

cynic ['sɪnɪk] adj (philos) zynisch ‖ s Menschenverächter –in mf; (philos) Zyniker m

cynical ['sɪnɪkəl] adj zynisch

cynicism ['sɪnɪ,sɪzəm] s Zynismus m; (cynical remark) zynische Bemerkung f

cypress ['saɪprəs] s Zypresse f

Cyprus ['saɪprəs] s Zypern n

Cyrillic [sɪ'rɪlɪk] adj kyrillisch

cyst [sɪst] s Zyste f

czar [zɑr] s Zar m

czarina [zɑ'rinə] s Zarin f

Czech [tʃɛk] adj tschechisch ‖ s Tscheche m, Tschechin f; (language) Tschechisch n

Czechoslovakia [,tʃɛkəslo'vækɪə] s die Tschechoslowakei f

D

D, d [di] s vierter Buchstabe des englischen Alphabets; (mus) D; D flat Des n; D sharp Dis n

D.A. abb (District Attorney) Staatsanwalt m

dab [dæb] s (of color) Klecks m; (e.g., of butter) Stückchen n ‖ v (pret & pp dabbed; ger dabbing) tr betupfen ‖ intr—dab at betupfen

dabble ['dæbəl] tr bespritzen ‖ intr (splash about) plantschen; d. in herumstümpern in (dat)

dachshund ['dɑks,hund] s Dachshund m

dad [dæd] s (coll) Vati m

daddy ['dædi] s (coll) Vati m

dad'dy-long'legs' s (–legs) Weberknecht m

daffodil ['dæfədɪl] s gelbe Narzisse f

daffy ['dæfi] adj (coll) doof

dagger ['dægər] s Dolch m; (typ) Kreuzzeichen n; look daggers at s.o. j–n mit Blicken durchbohren

dahlia ['dæljə] s Georgine f, Dahlie f

daily ['deli] adj täglich, Tages– ‖ adv täglich ‖ s Tageszeitung f

dainty ['denti] adj zart; (food) lecker; (finiky) wählerisch

dairy ['dɛri] s Molkerei f

dair'y farm' s Meierei f

dair'y farm'er s Meier –in mf

dais ['de·ɪs] s Tribüne f

daisy ['dezi] s Gänseblümchen n

dal·ly ['dæli] v (pret & pp –lied) intr (delay) herumtrödeln; (play amorously) liebäugeln

dam [dæm] s Damm m; (female quadruped) Muttertier n ‖ v (pret & pp dammed; ger damming) tr eindämmen; dam up anstauen

damage ['dæmɪdʒ] s Schaden m; damages (jur) Schadenersatz m; do d. Schaden anrichten; sue for damages auf Schadenersatz klagen ‖ tr beschädigen; (a reputation) beeinträchtigen

dam'aging adj (influence) schädlich; (evidence) belastend

dame [dem] s Dame f; (sl) Weibsbild n

damn [dæm] adj (sl) verflucht ‖ s— I don't give a d. about it (sl) ich mache mir e–n Dreck daraus; not be worth a d. (sl) keinen Pfifferling wert sein ‖ tr verdammen; (curse) verfluchen; d. it! (sl) verflucht!

damnation [dæm'neʃən] s Verdammnis f

damned adj verdammt; (sl) verflucht ‖ adv (sl) verdammt ‖ the d. spl die Verdammten pl

damp [dæmp] adj feucht ‖ s Feuchtigkeit f ‖ tr (be)feuchten; (a fire; enthusiasm) dämpfen; (elec, mus, phys) dämpfen

dampen ['dæmpən] tr befeuchten; (fig) dämpfen

damper ['dæmpər] s (of a fireplace) Schieber m; (of a stove) Ofenklappe f; (mus) Dämpfer m; put a d. on e–n Dämpfer aufsetzen (dat)

dampness ['dæmpnɪs] s Feuchtigkeit f

damsel ['dæmzəl] s Jungfrau f

dance [dæns] s Tanz m ‖ tr & intr tanzen

dance' band' s Tanzkapelle f

dance' floor' s Tanzfläche f

dance' hall' s Tanzsaal m, Tanzlokal n

dancer ['dænsər] s Tänzer –in mf

dance' step' s Tanzschritt m

danc'ing part'ner s Tanzpartner –in mf

dandelion ['dændɪ,laɪ·ən] s Löwen

dandruff ['dændrəf] s Schuppen pl

dandy ['dændi] *adj* (coll) pfundig, nett ‖ *s* Stutzer *m*

Dane [den] *s* Däne *m*, Dänin *f*

danger ['dendʒər] *s* (to) Gefahr *f* (für)

dan'ger list' *s*—be on the d. in Lebensgefahr sein

dangerous ['dendʒərəs] *adj* gefährlich

dangle ['dæŋgəl] *tr* schlenkern, baumeln lassen ‖ *intr* baumeln

Danish ['deni] *adj* dänisch ‖ *s* (language) Dänisch *n*

Dan'ish pas'try *s* feines Hefegebäck *n*

dank [dæŋk] *adj* feucht

Danube ['dænjub] *s* Donau *f*

dapper ['dæpər] *adj* schmuck

dappled ['dæpəld] *adj* scheckig, bunt

dare [der] *s* Herausforderung *f* ‖ *tr* wagen; (a person) herausfordern; d. to (inf) es wagen zu (inf); **don't you** **d.** go unterstehen Sie sich, wegzugehen!; I d. say ich darf wohl behaupten ‖ *intr*—don't you d.! unterstehen Sie sich!

dare'dev'il *s* Waghals *m*, Draufgänger *m*

dar'ing *adj* (deed) verwegen; (person) wagemutig ‖ *s* Wagemut *m*

dark [dɑrk] *adj* finster; (color, beer, complexion) dunkel; (fig) düster ‖ *s* Finsternis *f*, Dunkel *n*; be in the d. about im unklaren sein über (acc)

Dark' A'ges *spl* frühes Mittelalter *n*

dark-complexioned ['dɑrkkəm'plekʃənd] *adj* dunkelhäutig

darken ['dɑrkən] *tr* (a room) verfinstern ‖ *intr* sich verfinstern; (fig) sich verdüstern

dark'-eyed' *adj* schwarzäugig

dark' horse' *s* Außenseiter *m*

darkly ['dɑrkli] *adv* geheimnisvoll

darkness ['dɑrknɪs] *s* Finsternis *f*

dark'room' *s* (phot) Dunkelkammer *f*

darling ['dɑrlɪŋ] *adj* lieb ‖ *s* Liebchen *n*

darn [dɑrn] *adj* (coll) verwünscht ‖ *adv* (coll) verdammt ‖ *s*—I don't give a d. about it ich pfeif drauf! ‖ *tr* (stockings) stopfen; **d. it!** (coll) verflixt!; I'll be darned if der Kuckuck soll mich holen, wenn

darn'ing nee'dle *s* Stopfnadel *f*

dart [dɑrt] *s* Wurfspieß *m*, Pfeil *m*; (sew) Abnäher *m*; darts (game) Pfeilwerfen *n*; play darts Pfeile werfen ‖ *intr* huschen; **d. ahead** vorschießen; **d. off** davonstürzen

dash [dæʃ] *s* (rush) Ansturm *m*; (smartness) Schneidigkeit *f*; (spirit) Schwung *m*; (of solids) Prise *f*; (of liquids) Schuß *m*; (sport) Kurzstreckenlauf *m*; (typ) Gedankenstrich *m*; **make a d.** for losstürzen auf (acc) ‖ *tr* (throw) schleudern; (hopes) niederschlagen, knicken; **d. off** (a letter) hinwerfen ‖ *intr* stürmen, stürzen

dash'board' *s* (aut) Armaturenbrett *n*

dash'ing *adj* schneidig, forsch

dastardly ['dæstərdli] *adj* feige

data ['detə] *s* or *spl* Daten *pl*, Angaben *pl*

da'ta proc'essing *s* Datenverarbeitung *f*

date [det] *s* Datum *n*; (fixed time) Termin *m*; (period) Zeitraum *m*; (appointment) (coll) Verabredung *f*; (person on a date) Freund –in *mf*; (bot) Dattel *f*; (jur) Termin *m*; have a d. with verabredet sein mit; make a d. with sich verabreden mit; out of d. veraltet; to d. bis heute; what is the d. today? der wievielte ist heute? ‖ *tr* datieren; (coll) ausgehen mit ‖ *intr*—d. back to zurückgehen auf (acc); d. from stammen aus

dat'ed *adj* (provided with a date) datiert; (out-of-date) zeitgebunden

date' line' *s* Datumsgrenze *f*

date'line' *s* (journ) Datumszeile *f*

date' palm' *s* Dattelpalme *f*

dative ['detɪv] *s* Dativ *m*, Wemfall *m*

daub [dɔb] *s* Bewurf *m* ‖ *tr* (a canvas) beschmieren; (a wall) bewerfen; (e.g. mud, plaster) (on) schmieren (auf acc) ‖ *intr* (paint) klecksen

daughter ['dɔtər] *s* Tochter *f*

daugh'ter-in-law' *s* (daughters-in-law) Schwiegertochter *f*

daunt [dɔnt] *tr* einschüchtern

dauntless ['dɔntlɪs] *adj* furchtlos

davenport ['dævən,pɔrt] *s* Diwan *m*

davit ['dævɪt] *s* (naut) Bootskran *m*

daw [dɔ] *s* (orn) Dohle *f*

dawdle ['dɔdəl] *intr* trödeln, bummeln

dawn [dɔn] *s* Morgendämmerung *f*; (fig) Anbeginn *m* ‖ *intr* dämmern; **d. on s.o.** j–m zum Bewußtsein kommen

day [de] *adj* Tage-, Tages- ‖ *s* Tag *m*; (specific date) Termin *m*; **all day long** den ganzen Tag; **by day** am Tage, bei Tage; **by the day** tageweise; **call it a day** (coll) Feierabend machen; **day after day** Tag für Tag; **day by day** Tag für Tag; **day in, day out** tagaus, tagein; **day off** Urlaubstag *m*, Ruhetag *m*; **every other day** jeden zweiten Tag; **in days of old** in alten Zeiten; **in his day** zu seiner Zeit; **in those days** damals; **one day** e–s Tages; **one of these days** demnächst; **the day after** am folgenden Tag; **the day after tomorrow** übermorgen; **the day before** am Vortag; **the day before yesterday** vorgestern; **the other day** neulich, unlängst; **these days** heutzutage; **to this very day** bis auf den heutigen Tag; **what day of the week is it?** welchen Wochentag haben wir?

day' bed' *s* Ruhebett *n*, Liege *f*

day' break' *s* Tagesanbruch *m*

day'-by-day' *adj* tagtäglich, Tag für Tag

day'-care cen'ter *s* Kindertagesstätte *f*, Kindergarten *m*

day' coach' *s* (rr) Personenwagen *m*

day' dream' *s* Träumerei *f*, Wachtraum *m*; (wild ideas) Phantasterei *f* ‖ *intr* mit offenen Augen träumen

day'dream'er *s* Träumer –in *mf*

day' la'borer *s* Tagelöhner –in *mf*

day'light' *s* Tageslicht– ‖ *s* Tageslicht *n*; **in broad d.** am hellichten Tag; **knock the daylights out of** (sl) zur Sau machen

day'light-sav'ing time' s Sommerzeit f
day' nurs'ery s Kleinkinderbewahranstalt f
day' of reck'oning s Jüngster Tag m
day' shift' s Tagschicht f
day'time' s Tageszeit f; **in the d.** bei Tage, am Tage
daze [dez] s Benommenheit f; **be in a d.** benommen sein || tr betäuben
dazzle ['dæzəl] s Blenden n || tr (& fig) blenden
dazz'ling adj blendend
D-day ['di‚de] s X-Tag m; (hist) Invasionstag m
deacon ['dikən] s Diakon m
deaconess ['dikənıs] s Diakonisse f
dead [ded] adj tot; (plant) abgestorben, dürr; (faint, sleep) tief; (numb) gefühllos; (volcano, fire) erloschen; (elec) stromlos; (sport) tot, nicht im Spiel; **d. as a doornail** mausetot; **d. shot** unfehlbarer Schütze m; **d. stop** völliger Stillstand m; **d. silence** Totenstille f || adv völlig, tod– || s— **in the d. of night** mitten in der Nacht; **in the d. of winter** im tiefsten Winter
dead' beat' s (sl) Nichtstuer –in mf
dead' bolt' s Absteller m
dead' calm' s Windstille f
dead' cen'ter s genaue Mitte f; (dead point) (mach) toter Punkt m
deaden ['dedən] tr (pain) betäuben; (a nerve) abtöten; (sound) dämpfen
dead' end' s (& fig) Sackgasse f
dead'head' s Dummkopf m
dead' heat' s totes Rennen n
dead'-let'ter of'fice s Abteilung f für unbestellbare Briefe
dead'line' s (letzter) Termin m; (journ) Redaktionsschluß m; **meet the d.** den Termin einhalten; **set a d. for** terminieren
dead'lock' s Stillstand m; **break the d.** den toten Punkt überwinden; **reach a d.** steckenbleiben || tr zum völligen Stillstand bringen; **become deadlocked** stocken
deadly ['dedlı] adj (fatal) tödlich; **d. enemy** Todfeind –in mf; **d. fear** Todesangst f || adv—**d. dull** sterbenlangweilig; **d. pale** leichenblaß
dead'ly sins' spl Todsünden pl
dead'pan' adj (look) ausdruckslos; (person) schafsgesicht
dead' pan' s (coll) Schafsgesicht n
dead' reck'oning s (naut) Koppelkurs m
dead' ring'er ['rıŋər] s (coll) Doppelgänger m
dead'wood' s (& fig) totes Holz n
deaf [def] adj taub; **d. and dumb** taubstumm; **d. to** (fig) taub gegen; **turn a d. ear to** taube Ohren haben für
deafen ['defən] tr betäuben
deaf'ening adj ohrenbetäubend
deaf'-mute' adj taubstumm || s Taubstumme mf
deafness ['defnıs] s Taubheit f
deal [dil] s (business transaction) Geschäft n; (underhanded agreement) Schiebung f; (cards) Austeilen n, Geben n; **a good d. of** (coll) ziemlich

viel; **a good d. worse** (coll) viel (or weit) schlechter; **a great d. of** (coll) sehr viel; **give s.o. a good d.** (be fair to s.o.) j–n fair behandeln; (make s.o. a good offer) j–m ein gutes Angebot machen; **give s.o. a raw d.** j–m übel mitspielen; **it is my d.** (cards) ich muß geben; **it's a d.!** abgemacht!; **make a d.** (coll) ein Abkommen treffen || v (pret & pp dealt [delt]) tr (a blow) versetzen; (cards) austeilen, geben || intr (cards) geben; **d. at** (a store) kaufen bei; **d. in** handeln mit; **d. with** (settle) erledigen; (occupy oneself or itself with) sich befassen mit; (treat, e.g., fairly) behandeln; (patronize) kaufen bei; (do business with) in Geschäftsbeziehungen stehen mit; **I'll d. with you later** mit Ihnen werde ich später abrechnen
dealer ['dilər] s Geber –in mf; (com) Händler –in mf
deal'ings spl (business dealings) Handel m; (relations) Umgang m; **I'll have no d. with** ich will nichts zu tun haben mit
dean [din] s (eccl, educ) Dekan m
dean'ship' s (eccl, educ) Dekanat n
dear [dır] adj lieb, traut; (expensive) teuer; **Dear Madam** Sehr verehrte gnädige Frau!; **Dear Mrs. X** Sehr geehrte Frau X; **Dear Mr. X** Sehr geehrter Herr X!; **Dear Sir** Sehr geehrter Herr! || s Liebling m, Schatz m || interj—**oh d.!** ach herrje!
dearie ['dırı] s (coll) Liebchen n
dearth [dʌrθ] s (of) Mangel m (an dat)
death [deθ] s Tod m; (in the family) Todesfall m; **at death's door** sterbenskrank; **catch a d. of a cold** sich [dat] den Tod holen; **he'll be the d. of me** yet er bringt mich noch ins Grab; **put to d.** hinrichten; **to the d.** bis aufs Messer; **work to d.** totarbeiten
death'bed' s Totenbett n, Sterbebett n
death'blow' s Gnadenstoß m; (fig) Todesstoß m
death' certif'icate s Totenschein m
death' house' s Todeshaus n
death' knell' s Grabgeläute n
deathless ['deθlıs] adj unsterblich
deathly ['deθli] adj tödlich, Todes–, Toten– || adv toten–
death' mask' s Totenmaske f
death' pen'alty s Todesstrafe f
death' rate' s Sterblichkeitsziffer f
death' rat'tle s Todesröcheln n
death' sen'tence s Todesurteil n
death' strug'gle s Todeskampf m
death' trap' s (fig) Mausefalle f
death' war'rant s Hinrichtungsbefehl m
debacle [de'bakəl] s Zusammenbruch m
de·bar [dı'bar] v (pret & pp –barred; ger –barring) tr (from) ausschließen (aus)
debark [dı'bark] tr ausschiffen || intr sich ausschiffen, an Land gehen
debarkation [‚dibar'keʃən] s Ausschiffung f

debase [dɪ'bes] tr entwürdigen; (currency) entwerten

debatable [dɪ'betəbəl] adj strittig

debate [dɪ'bet] s Debatte f || tr & intr debattieren

debauch [dɪ'bɔtʃ] s Schwelgerei f || tr verderben; (seduce) verführen; d. oneself verkommen

debauched' adj ausschweifend

debauchee [,debə'tʃi] s Wüstling m

debauchery [dɪ'bɔtʃəri] s Schwelgerei f

debenture [dɪ'bentʃər] s (bond) Obligation f; (voucher) Schuldschein m

debilitate [dɪ'bɪlɪ,tet] tr entkräften

debility [dɪ'bɪlɪti] s Schwäche f

debit ['debɪt] s Debet n, Soll n; (as entry) Belastung f

de'bit bal'ance s Sollsaldo n

de'bit side' s Soll n, Sollseite f

debonair [,debə'ner] adj (courteous) höflich; (carefree) heiter und sorglos

debris [de'bri] s Trümmer pl

debt [det] s Schuld f; be in s.o.'s d. j-m verpflichtet sein; run into d. in Schulden geraten

debtor ['detər] s Schuldner –in mf

de-bug [dɪ'bʌg] v pret & pp -bugged; ger -bugging) tr (remove defects from) bereinigen; (electron) Abhörgeräte entfernen aus

debut [de'bju], ['debju] s Debüt n; make one's d. debütieren

debutante ['debju,tɑnt] s Debütantin f

decade ['dɛked] s Jahrzehnt n, Dekade f

decadence ['dɛkədəns] s Dekadenz f

decadent ['dɛkədənt] adj dekadent; (art) entartet

decal ['dikæl] s Abziehbild n

decanter [dɪ'kæntər] s Karaffe f

decapitate [dɪ'kæpɪ,tet] tr enthaupten

decathlon [dɪ'kæθlɑn] s Zehnkampf m

decay [dɪ'ke] s (rotting) Verwesung f; (fig) Verfall m; (dent) Karies f; fall into d. (& fig) in Verfall geraten || intr verfaulen; (fig) verfallen

decease [dɪ'sis] s Ableben n

deceased' adj verstorben || s Verstorbene mf

deceit [dɪ'sit] s Betrügerei f

deceitful [dɪ'sitfəl] adj betrügerisch

deceive [dɪ'siv] tr betrügen || intr trügen

decelerate [dɪ'selə,ret] tr verlangsamen || intr seine Geschwindigkeit verringern

December [dɪ'sembər] s Dezember m

decency ['disənsi] s Anstand m; decencies Anstandsformen pl

decent ['disənt] adj anständig

decentralize [dɪ'sentrə,laɪz] tr dezentralisieren

deception [dɪ'sepʃən] s (act of deceiving) Betrug m; (state of being deceived) Täuschung f

deceptive [dɪ'septɪv] adj trügerisch; (misleading) irreführend; (similarity) täuschend

decide [dɪ'saɪd] tr entscheiden || intr (on) sich entscheiden, sich entschließen (über acc, für)

deciduous [dɪ'sɪdʒʊ·əs] adj blattabwerfend; d. tree Laubbaum m

decimal ['desɪməl] adj dezimal || s Dezimalzahl f

dec'imal place' s Dezimalstelle f

dec'imal point' s (in German the comma is used to separate the decimal fraction from the integer) Komma n

decimate ['desɪ,met] tr dezimieren

decipher [dɪ'saɪfər] tr entziffern

decision [dɪ'sɪʒən] s Entscheidung f, Entschluß m; (jur) Urteil n

decisive [dɪ'saɪsɪv] adj entscheidend

deck [dɛk] s (of cards) Spiel n; (data proc) Kartensatz m; (naut) Deck n, Verdeck n || tr (coll) so Boden schlagen; d. out ausschmücken

deck' chair' s Liegestuhl m

deck' hand' s gemeiner Matrose m

deck' land'ing s (aer) Trägerlandung f

declaim [dɪ'klem] tr & intr deklamieren

declaration [,dɛklə'reʃən] s Erklärung f; (at customs) Zollerklärung f

declarative [dɪ'klærətɪv] adj—d. sentence Aussagesatz m

declare [dɪ'kler] tr erklären; (tourist's belongings) verzollen; (commercial products) deklarieren; d. oneself against sich aussprechen gegen

declension [dɪ'klenʃən] s Deklination f

declinable [dɪ'klaɪnəbəl] adj deklinierbar

decline [dɪ'klaɪn] s (decrease) Abnahme f; (in prices) Rückgang m; (deterioration) Verschlechterung f; (slope) Abhang m; (fig) Niedergang m; be on the d. in Abnahme begriffen sein || tr (refuse) ablehnen; (gram) deklinieren || intr (refuse) ablehnen; (descend) sich senken; (sink) sinken; (draw to a close) zu Ende gehen

declivity [dɪ'klɪvɪti] s Abhang m

decode [di'kod] tr entschlüsseln

decompose [,dikəm'poz] tr zerlegen || intr sich zersetzen, verwesen

decomposition [,dikɑmpə'zɪʃən] s Zersetzung f, Verwesung f

decompression [,dikəm'preʃən] s Dekompression f

decontaminaiton [,dikən,tæmɪ'neʃən] s Entseuchung f

décor [de'kor] s Dekor m

decorate ['dɛkə,ret] tr dekorieren, (aus)schmücken; (a new room) einrichten; (e.g., with a badge) auszeichnen

decoration [,dɛkə'reʃən] s Schmuck m; (medal) Orden m, Ehrenzeichen n, Dekoration f

decorative ['dɛkərətɪv] adj dekorativ

decorator ['dɛkə,retər] s Dekorateur –in mf

decorous ['dɛkərəs] adj schicklich

decorum [dɪ'korəm] s Schicklichkeit f

decoy ['dikɔɪ] s (bird or person) Lockvogel m; (anything used as a lure) Lockmittel n || [dɪ'kɔɪ] tr locken

decrease ['dikris] s Abnahme f ||

[dɪ'kris] *tr* verringern ‖ *intr* abnehmen

decree [dɪ'kri] *s* Dekret *n*, Verordnung *f* ‖ *tr* dekretieren, verordnen

decrepit [dɪ'krepɪt] *adj* (*age-worn*) altersschwach; (*frail*) gebrechlich

de·cry [dɪ'kraɪ] *v* (*pret & pp* –**cried**) *tr* (*disparage*) herabsetzen; (*censure openly*) kritisieren

dedicate ['dedɪˌket] *tr* (*a book, one's life*) (**to**) widmen (*dat*); (*a building*) einweihen

dedication [ˌdedɪ'keʃən] *s* Widmung *f*; (*of a building, etc.*) Einweihung *f*; (**to**) Hingabe *f* (an *acc*)

deduce [dɪ'd(j)us] *tr* (**from**) schließen (aus)

deduct [dɪ'dʌkt] *tr* abziehen, abrechnen

deduction [dɪ'dʌkʃən] *s* Abzug *m*; (*conclusion*) Schluß *m*, Folgerung *f*

deed [did] *s* (*act*) Tat *f*; (*jur*) Besitzurkunde *f*

deem [dim] *tr* halten für; **d. s.o. worthy of my confidence** j-n meines Vertrauens für würdig halten

deep [dip] *adj* tief; (*recondite*) dunkel; (*impression*) tiefgehend; (*color, sound*) tief, dunkel; **be d. in debt** tief in Schulden stecken; **four (ranks) d.** in Viererreihen; **in d. water** (fig) in Schwierigkeiten; **that's too d. for me** das ist mir zu hoch ‖ *adv* tief; **d. down** tief innen in (*dat*) ‖ *s* Tiefe *f*, Meer *n*

deepen ['dipən] *tr* (& fig) vertiefen ‖ *intr* sich vertiefen

deep'-freeze' *v* (*pret* –**freezed & –froze**; *pp* –**freezed & –frozen**) *tr* tiefkühlen

deep'-fry' *v* (*pret & pp* –**fried**) *tr* fritieren

deep'-laid' *adj* schlau angelegt

deep' mourn'ing *s* tiefe Trauer *f*

deep'-root'ed *adj* tiefsitzend

deep'-set' adj (*eyes*) tiefliegend

deer [dɪr] *s* Hirsch *m*, Reh *n*, Rotwild *n*

deer'skin' *s* Hirschleder *n*, Wildleder *n*

deface [dɪ'fes] *tr* (*disfigure*) verunstalten; (*make illegible*) unleserlich machen

defacement [dɪ'fesmənt] *s* Verunstaltung *f*

de facto [di'fækto] *adj & adv* tatsächlich, de facto

defamation [ˌdefə'meʃən] *s* Verleumdung *f*

defame [dɪ'fem] *tr* verleumden

default [dɪ'folt] *s* (*in duties*) Unterlassung *f*; (fin) Verzug *m*; **by d.** (jur) durch Nichterscheinen; (sport) durch Nichtantreten; **in d. of** in Ermangelung (*genit*) ‖ *tr* nicht erfüllen; (fin) nicht zahlen ‖ *intr* seinen Verpflichtungen nicht nachkommen; (fin) in Verzug sein

defeat [dɪ'fit] *s* Niederlage *f*; (parl) Niederstimmen *n*; **admit d.** sich geschlagen geben ‖ *tr* besiegen, schlagen; (*frustrate*) hilflos machen; (*plans*) zunichte machen; (*a bill*) niederstimmen; **d. the purpose** den Zweck verfehlen

defeatism [dɪ'fitɪzəm] *s* Defätismus *m*

defeatist [dɪ'fitɪst] *s* Defätist –in *mf*

defecate ['defɪˌket] *intr* Stuhl haben

defect ['difekt] *s* Defekt *m*; (*physical or mental defect*) Gebrechen *n*; (*imperfection*) Mangel *m*; (*in manufacture*) Fabrikationsfehler *m* ‖ [dɪ'fekt] *intr* (**from**) (*a religion*) abfallen (von); (*a party*) abtrünnig werden (von); (**to**) überlaufen (zu)

defection [dɪ'fekʃən] *s* Abfall *m*; (**to**) Übertritt *m* (zu)

defective [dɪ'fektɪv] *adj* fehlerhaft; (gram) unvollständig; (tech) defekt

defector [dɪ'fektər] *s* (pol) Abtrünnige *mf*, Überläufer –in *mf*

defend [dɪ'fend] *tr* verteidigen

defendant [dɪ'fendənt] *s* (*in civil suit*) Beklagte *mf*; (*in criminal suit*) Angeklagte *mf*

defender [dɪ'fendər] *s* Verteidiger –in *mf*; (sport) Titelverteidiger –in *mf*

defense [dɪ'fens] *s* (& jur, sport) Verteidigung *f*; (*tactical*) (mil) Abwehr *f*; **d. against** (*e.g., disease*) Schutz *m* vor (*dat*)

defenseless [dɪ'fenslɪs] *adj* schutzlos

defensible [dɪ'fensɪbəl] *adj* verteidigungsfähig; (*argument, claim*) verfechtbar

defensive [dɪ'fensɪv] *adj* defensiv; (mil) Verteidigungs-, Abwehr- ‖ *s* Defensive *f*; (*tactical*) Abwehr *f*; **be on the d.** –sich in der Defensive befinden

de·fer [dɪ'fʌr] *v* (*pret & pp* –**ferred**; *ger* –**ferring**) *tr* verschieben; (mil) zurückschieben ‖ *intr*—**d. to** nachgeben (*dat*)

deference ['defərəns] *s* (*courteous regard*) Ehrerbietung *f*; (*yielding*) Nachgiebigkeit *f*; **in d.** to aus Rücksicht gegen; **with all due d.** to bei aller Achtung vor (*dat*)

deferential [ˌdefə'renʃəl] *adj* ehrerbietig, rücksichtsvoll

deferment [dɪ'fʌrmənt] *s* Aufschub *m*; (mil) Zurückstellung *f*

defiance [dɪ'faɪəns] *s* Trotz *m*; **in d. of s.o.** j-m zum Trotz

defiant [dɪ'faɪ.ənt] *adj* trotzig

deficiency [dɪ'fɪʃənsi] *s* (**of**) Mangel *m* (an *dat*); (*shortcoming*) Defekt *m*; (*deficit*) Defizit *n*

deficient [dɪ'fɪʃənt] *adj* mangelhaft; **be d. in** Mangel haben an (*dat*); **mentally d.** schwachsinnig

deficit ['defɪsɪt] *s* Defizit *n*

defilade [ˌdefɪ'led] *s* Deckung *f* ‖ *tr* gegen Feuer sichern

defile [dɪ'faɪl] *s* ['difaɪl] Hohlweg *m* ‖ [dɪ'faɪl] *tr* beflecken

defilement [dɪ'faɪlmənt] *s* Befleckung *f*

define [dɪ'faɪn] *tr* definieren, bestimmen; (*e.g., boundaries*) festlegen

definite ['defɪnɪt] *adj* bestimmt

definition [ˌdefɪ'nɪʃən] *s* Definition *f*, Bestimmung *f*; (opt) Bildschärfe *f*

definitive [dɪ'fɪnɪtɪv] *adj* endgültig

deflate [dɪ'flet] *tr* Luft ablassen aus; (*prices*) herabsetzen; (*s.o.'s ego, hopes*) e-n Stoß versetzen (*dat*)

deflation [dɪ'fleʃən] s (fin) Deflation f

deflect [dɪ'flekt] tr ablenken || intr (from) abweichen (von)

deflection [dɪ'flekʃən] s Ablenkung f; Abweichung f; (of an indicator) Ausschlag m; (of light rays) Beugung f; (radar, telv) Ablenkung f

deflower [dɪ'flau·ər] tr entjungfern

defoliate [di'folɪ‚et] tr entblättern

deforest [di'fɔrɪst] tr abholzen

deform [dɪ'fɔrm] tr entstellen

deformed adj verwachsen, mißförmig

deformity [dɪ'fɔrmɪti] s (state of being deformed) Mißgestalt f; (deformed part) Verwachsung f; (ugliness) Häßlichkeit f

defraud [dɪ'frɔd] tr (of) betrügen (um)

defray [dɪ'fre] tr tragen, bestreiten

defrock [di'frɑk] tr das Priesteramt entziehen (dat)

defrost [dɪ'frɔst] tr entfrosten

defroster [dɪ'frɔstər] s Entfroster m

deft [deft] adj flink, fingerfertig

defunct [dɪ'fʌŋkt] adj (person) verstorben; (no longer in operation) stillgelegt; (no longer in effect) außer Kraft (befindlich); (newspaper) eingegangen

de•fy [dɪ'faɪ] v (pret & pp -fied) tr trotzen (dat); (challenge) herausfordern; **d. description** sich nicht beschreiben lassen

degeneracy [dɪ'dʒenərəsi] s Entartung f

degenerate [dɪ'dʒenərɪt] adj entartet, verkommen || [dɪ'dʒenə‚ret] intr entarten; (into) ausarten (in acc)

degrade [dɪ'gred] tr degradieren; (bring into low esteem) entwürdigen

degrad′ing adj entwürdigend

degree [dɪ'gri] s Grad m; (gram) Steigerungsstufe f; **by degrees** gradweise; **d. of latitude** Breitengrad m; **d. of longitude** Längengrad m; **take one's d.** promovieren; **to a d.** einigermaßen; **to a high d.** in hohem Maße

dehumanize [dɪ'hjumə‚naɪz] tr entmenschlichen

dehumidifier [‚dihju'mɪdɪ‚faɪ·ər] s Luftentfeuchter m

dehumidi•fy [‚dihju'mɪdɪ‚faɪ] v (pret & pp -fied) entfeuchten

dehydrate [di'haɪdret] tr (vegetables) dörren, das Wasser entziehen (dat); (chem) dehydrieren || intr das Wasser verlieren

dehy′drated adj (vegetables) Trocken–; (body) dehydriert

deice [di'aɪs] tr enteisen

dei•fy ['di·ɪ‚faɪ] v (pret & pp -fied) tr (a man) zum Gott erheben; (a woman) zur Göttin erheben

deject′ed adj niedergeschlagen

dejection [dɪ'dʒekʃən] s Niederschlagenheit f, Mutlosigkeit f

delay [dɪ'le] s Aufschub m, Verzögerung f; **without d.** unverzüglich || tr (postpone) aufschieben; (detain) aufhalten || intr zögern

delectable [dɪ'lektəbəl] adj ergötzlich

delegate ['delɪ‚get], ['delɪgɪt] s Delegierte mf || ['delɪ‚get] tr delegieren; (authority) übertragen

delegation [‚delɪ'geʃən] s (persons delegated) Delegation f; (e.g., of authority) Übertragung f

delete [dɪ'lit] tr tilgen

deletion [dɪ'liʃən] s Tilgung f

deliberate [dɪ'lɪbərɪt] adj (intentional) vorsätzlich, bewußt; (slow) gemessen, bedächtig || [dɪ'lɪbə‚ret] intr überlegen; (said of several persons) beratschlagen; **d. on** sich beraten über (acc)

deliberately [dɪ'lɪbərɪtli] adv mit Absicht

deliberation [dɪ‚lɪbə'reʃən] s Überlegung f; (by several persons) Beratung f; (slowness) Bedächtigkeit f

delicacy ['delɪkəsi] s Zartheit f; (fine food) Delikatesse f

delicate ['delɪkɪt] adj fein, delikat; (situation) heikel; (health) zart

delicatessen [‚delɪkə'tesən] s (food) Delikatessen pl; (store) Delikatessengeschäft n

delicious [dɪ'lɪʃəs] adj köstlich

delight [dɪ'laɪt] s Freude f; (high degree of pleasure) Entzücken n; **take d.** in Freude finden an (dat) || tr entzücken, erfreuen; **be delighted by** sich freuen an (dat); **I'll be delighted to come** ich komme mit dem größten Vergnügen || intr—**d. in** sich ergötzen an (dat)

delightful [dɪ'laɪtfəl] adj entzückend

delimit [dɪ'lɪmɪt] tr abgrenzen

delineate [dɪ'lɪnɪ‚et] tr zeichnen

delinquency [dɪ'lɪŋkwənsi] s Pflichtvergessenheit f; (misdeed) Vergehen n

delinquent [dɪ'lɪŋkwənt] adj pflichtvergessen; (guilty) straffällig; (overdue) rückständig; (in default) säumig || s Straffällige mf

delirious [dɪ'lɪrɪ·əs] adj irre; (with) rasend (vor dat)

delirium [dɪ'lɪrɪ·əm] s Fieberwahn m

deliver [dɪ'lɪvər] tr liefern; (a message) überreichen; (free) befreien; (mail) zustellen; (a speech) halten; (a blow) versetzen; (a verdict) aussprechen; (a child) zur Welt bringen; (votes) bringen; (a ball) werfen; (relig) erlösen

deliverance [dɪ'lɪvərəns] s Erlösung f

delivery [dɪ'lɪvəri] s Lieferung f; (freeing) Befreiung f; (of mail) Zustellung f; (of a speaker, actor, singer) Vortragsweise f; (of a pitcher) Wurf m; (childbirth) Entbindung f

deliv′ery-man s (-men′) Austräger m

deliv′ery room′ s Kreißsaal m

deliv′ery truck′ s Lieferwagen m

dell [del] s enges Tal n

delouse [di'laus] tr entlausen

delta ['deltə] s Delta n

delude [dɪ'lud] tr täuschen

deluge ['deljudʒ] s Überschwemmung f; (fig) Hochflut f; **Deluge** (Bib) Sintflut f || tr überschwemmen; (with letters, etc.) überschütten

delusion [dɪ'luʒən] s (state of being deluded) Täuschung f; (misconcep-

tion) Wahnvorstellung *f*; (psychiatry) Wahn *m*; **delusions of grandeur** Größenwahn *m*

deluxe [dɪ'lʊks], [dɪ'lʌks] *adj* Luxus-

delve [dɛlv] *intr*—**d. into** sich vertiefen in (*acc*)

demagogue ['dɛmə,gag] *s* Volksverführer -in *mf*

demand [dɪ'mænd] *s* Verlangen *n*; (com) (**for**) Nachfrage *f* (nach); **in (great) d.** (sehr) gefragt; **make demands on** Ansprüche erheben auf (*acc*); **on d.** auf Verlangen ‖ *tr* (**from** *or* **of**) verlangen (von), fordern (von)

demand'ing *adj* anspruchsvoll; (*strict*) streng

demarca'tion line' [,dɪmɑr'keʃən] *s* Demarkationslinie *f*

demean [dɪ'min] *tr* erniedrigen

demeanor [dɪ'minər] *s* Benehmen *n*

demented [dɪ'mɛntɪd] *adj* wahnsinnig

demerit [di'mɛrɪt] *s* (*fault*) Fehler *m*; (*deficiency mark*) Minuspunkt *m*

demigod ['dɛmɪ,gad] *s* Halbgott *m*

demijohn ['dɛmɪ,dʒan] *s* Korbflasche *f*

demilitarize [di'mɪlɪtə,raɪz] *tr* entmilitarisieren

demise [dɪ'maɪz] *s* Ableben *n*

demitasse ['dɛmɪ,tæs], ['dɛmɪ,tas] *s* Mokkatasse *f*

demobilize [dɪ'mobɪ,laɪz] *tr & intr* demobilisieren

democracy [dɪ'makrəsɪ] *s* Demokratie *f*

democrat ['dɛmə,kræt] *s* Demokrat -in *mf*

democratic [,dɛmə'krætɪk] *adj* demokratisch

demolish [dɪ'malɪʃ] *tr* (*raze*) niederreißen; (*destroy*) zertrümmern; (*an argument*) vernichten; (*devour*) (coll) verschlingen

demolition [,dɛmə'lɪʃən], [,dimə-'lɪʃən] *s* (*act of razing*) Abbruch *m*; (*by explosives*) Sprengung *f*; **demolitions** Sprengstoff *m*

demoli'tion squad' *s* Sprengkommando *n*

demoli'tion work' *s* Sprengarbeiten *pl*

demon ['dimən] *s* Dämon *m*, böser Geist *m*

demonstrable [dɪ'manstrəbəl] *adj* beweisbar

demonstrate ['dɛmən,stret] *tr* (*prove*) beweisen; (*explain*) dartun; (*display*) zeigen; (*a product, process*) vorführen ‖ *intr* (pol) demonstrieren

demonstration [,dɛmən'streʃən] *s* (com) Vorführung *f*; (pol) Demonstration *f*

demonstrative [dɪ'manstrətɪv] *adj* (*showing emotions*) gefühlvoll; (*illustrative*) anschaulich; (gram) hinweisend

demonstrator ['dɛmən,stretər] *s* (*of products*) Vorführer -in *mf*; (*model used in demonstration*) Vorführmodell *n*; (pol) Demonstrant -in *mf*

demoralize [dɪ'mɔrə,laɪz] *tr* demoralisieren

demote [dɪ'mot] *tr* (*an employee*) her-

abstufen; (*a student*) zurückversetzen; (mil) degradieren

demotion [dɪ'moʃən] *s* (*of an employee*) Herabstufung *f*; (*of a student*) Zurückversetzung *f*; (mil) Degradierung *f*

de·mur [dɪ'mʌr] *v* (*pret & pp* -**murred;** *ger* -**murring**) *intr* Einwände erheben

demure [dɪ'mjur] *adj* zimperlich

den [dɛn] *s* (*of animals; of thieves*) Höhle *f*; (*comfortable room*) Freizeitraum *m*

denaturalize [di'nætjərə,laɪz] *tr* ausbürgern

denial [dɪ'naɪəl] *s* (*of an assertion*) Leugnung *f*; (*of guilt*) Leugnen *n*; (*of a request*) Ablehnung *f*; (*of faith*) Ableugnung *f*; (*of rights*) Verweigerung *f*; (*of a report*) Dementi *n*

denigrate ['dɛnɪ,gret] *tr* anschwärzen

denim ['dɛnɪm] *s* Drillich *m*

denizen ['dɛnɪzən] *s* Bewohner -in *mf*

Denmark ['dɛnmark] *s* Dänemark *n*

denomination [dɪ,namɪ'neʃən] *s* Bezeichnung *f*; (*class, kind*) Klasse *f*; (*of money*) Nennwert *m*; (*of shares*) Stückelung *f*; (relig) Konfession *f*, Bekenntnis *n*; **in denominations of five and ten dollars** in Fünf- und Zehndollarnoten

denotation [,dino'teʃən] *s* Bedeutung *f*

denote [dɪ'not] *tr* (*mean*) bedeuten; (*indicate*) anzeigen

dénouement [,denu'mã] *s* Auflösung *f*

denounce [dɪ'nauns] *tr* (*inform against*) denunzieren; (*condemn openly*) brandmarken, anprangern; (*a treaty*) kündigen

dense [dɛns] *adj* dicht; (coll) beschränkt

density ['dɛnsɪtɪ] *s* Dichte *f*

dent [dɛnt] *s* Beule *f* ‖ *tr* einbeulen

dental ['dɛntəl] *adj* Zahn-; (ling) dental ‖ *s* (ling) Zahnlaut *m*

den'tal hygiene' *s* Zahnpflege *f*

den'tal sur'geon *s* Zahnarzt *m*, Zahnärztin *f*

dentifrice ['dɛntɪfrɪs] *s* Zahnputzmittel *n*

dentist ['dɛntɪst] *s* Zahnarzt *m*, Zahnärztin *f*

dentistry ['dɛntɪstrɪ] *s* Zahnheilkunde *f*

denture ['dɛntʃər] *s* künstliches Gebiß *n*

denunciation [dɪ,nʌnsɪ'eʃən] *s* (*informing against*) Denunzierung *f*; (*public condemnation*) Brandmarkung *f*

de·ny [dɪ'naɪ] *v* (*pret & pp* -**nied**) *tr* (*a statement*) leugnen; (*officially*) dementieren; (*a request*) ablehnen; (*one's faith*) ableugnen; (*rights*) verweigern; **d. oneself s.th.** sich [*dat*] etw versagen; **d. s.o. s.th.** j-m etw aberkennen

deodorant [di'odərənt] *s* Deodorant *n*

deodorize [di'odə,raɪz] *tr* desodorieren

deoxidize [di'aksɪ,daɪz] *tr* desoxydieren

depart [dɪ'pɑrt] *intr (on foot)* fortgehen; *(in a vehicle or boat)* abfahren; *(by plane)* abfliegen; *(on horseback)* abreiten; *(on a trip)* abreisen; *(deviate)* abweichen

department [dɪ'pɑrtmənt] *s (subdivision)* Abteilung *f*; *(field)* Fach *n*; *(principal branch of government)* Ministerium *n*; *(government office)* Amt *n*; *(educ)* Abteilung *f*

depart'ment head' *s* Abteilungsleiter –in *m*

depart'ment store' *s* Kaufhaus *n*, Warenhaus *n*

departure [dɪ'pɑrtʃər] *s (on foot)* Weggehen *n*; *(by car, boat, train)* Abfahrt *f*, Abreise *f*; *(by plane)* Abflug *m*; *(deviation)* Abweichung *f*

depend [dɪ'pend] *intr (on)* abhängen (von); *(rely on)* sich verlassen (auf *acc*); **depending on** je nach; **depending on how** je nachdem; **it all depends** (coll) es kommt darauf an

dependable [dɪ'pendəbəl] *adj* zuverlässig

dependence [dɪ'pendəns] *s* Abhängigkeit *f*

dependency [dɪ'pendənsi] *s* Schutzgebiet *n*

dependent [dɪ'pendənt] *adj (on)* abhängig (von) ‖ *s* Abhängige *mf*; *(for tax purposes)* Unterhaltsberechtigte *mf*

depict [dɪ'pɪkt] *tr* schildern

deplete [dɪ'plit] *tr* entleeren; (fig) erschöpfen

deplorable [dɪ'plorəbəl] *adj (situation)* beklagenswert; *(regrettable)* bedauerlich; *(bad)* schlecht

deplore [dɪ'plor] *tr* bedauern

deploy [dɪ'plɔɪ] *tr* entfalten ‖ *intr* sich entfalten

deployment [dɪ'plɔɪmənt] *s* Entfaltung *f*

depolarize [dɪ'polə,raɪz] *tr* depolarisieren

deponent [dɪ'ponənt] *s* (gram) Deponens *n*; (jur) Deponent –in *mf*

depopulate [dɪ'pɑpjə,let] *tr* entvölkern

deport [dɪ'port] *tr* deportieren; **d. oneself** sich benehmen

deportation [,dipor'teʃən] *s* Deportation *f*

deportment [dɪ'portmənt] *s* Benehmen *n*

depose [dɪ'poz] *tr (from office)* absetzen; (jur) bezeugen ‖ *intr* (jur) unter Eid aussagen; *(in writing)* (jur) eidesstattlich versichern

deposit [dɪ'pɑzɪt] *s (partial payment)* Anzahlung *f*; *(at a bank)* Einlage *f*; *(for safekeeping)* Hinterlegung *f*; (geol) Ablagerung *f*; (min) Vorkommen *n*; **for d. only** nur zur Verrechnung ‖ *tr (set down)* niederlegen; *(money at a bank)* einlegen; *(a check)* verrechnen; *(a part payment)* anzahlen; *(for safekeeping)* deponieren; (geol) ablagern; *(a coin)* (telp) einwerfen

depositor [dɪ'pɑzɪtər] *s* Einzahler –in *mf*; *(of valuables)* Hinterleger –in *mf*

depos'it slip' *s* Einzahlungsbeleg *m*

depot ['dipo], ['depo] *s (bus station; storage place)* Depot *n*; *(train station)* Bahnhof *m*

depraved [dɪ'prevd] *adj* verworfen

depravity [dɪ'prævɪti] *s* Verworfenheit *f*

deprecate ['deprɪ,ket] *tr* mißbilligen

depreciate [dɪ'priʃɪ,et] *tr (money, stocks)* abwerten; *(for tax purposes)* abschreiben; *(value or price)* herabsetzen; *(disparage)* geringschätzen ‖ *intr* im Wert sinken

depreciation [dɪ,priʃɪ'eʃən] *s (decrease in value)* Wertminderung *f*; *(of currency or stocks)* Abwertung *f*; *(for tax purposes)* Abschreibung *f*

depress [dɪ'pres] *tr* niederdrücken; *(sadden)* deprimieren; *(cause to sink)* herunterdrücken

depressed' *adj (saddened)* niedergeschlagen; *(market)* flau

depressed' ar'ea *s* Notstandsgebiet *n*

depress'ing *adj* deprimierend

depression [dɪ'preʃən] *s (mental state; economic crisis)* Depression *f*; (geol) Vertiefung *f*

deprive [dɪ'praɪv] *tr*—**d. s.o. of s.th.** j-m etw entziehen; *(withhold)* j-m etw vorenthalten

depth [depθ] *s* Tiefe *f*; **go beyond one's d.** den Boden unter den Füßen verlieren; **in d.** gründlich

depth' charge' *s* Wasserbombe *f*

depth' of field' *s* (phot) Tiefenschärfe *f*

deputation [,depjə'teʃən] *s* Abordnung *f*

deputize ['depjə,taɪz] *tr* abordnen

deputy ['depjəti] *s* Vertreter –in *mf*; (pol) Abgeordnete *mf*

derail [dɪ'rel] *tr* zum Entgleisen bringen ‖ *intr* entgleisen

derailment [dɪ'relmənt] *s* Entgleisung *f*

deranged [dɪ'rendʒd] *adj* geistesgestört

derangement [dɪ'rendʒmənt] *s* Geistesstörtheit *f*

derby ['dɑrbi] *s (hat)* Melone *f*; *(race)* Derbyrennen *n*

derelict ['derɪlɪkt] *adj (negligent)* (**in**) nachlässig (in *dat*); *(abandoned)* herrenlos ‖ *s (ship; bum)* Wrack *n*

dereliction [,derɪ'lɪkʃən] *s (neglect)* Vernachlässigung *f*

deride [dɪ'raɪd] *tr* verspotten

derision [dɪ'rɪʒən] *s* Spott *m*

derivation [,derɪ'veʃən] *s* (gram, math) Ableitung *f*

derivative [dɪ'rɪvətɪv] *adj* abgeleitet ‖ *s* (chem) Derivat *n*; (gram, math) Ableitung *f*

derive [dɪ'raɪv] *tr (obtain)* gewinnen; (gram, math) ableiten; **d. pleasure from s.th.** Freude an etw finden ‖ *intr (from)* herstammen (von)

dermatologist [[,dɑrmə'tɑlədʒɪst] *s* Hautarzt *m*, Hautärztin *f*

derogatory [dɪ'rɑgə,tori] *adj* abfällig

derrick ['derɪk] *s (over an oil well)* Bohrturm *m*; (naut) Ladebaum *m*

dervish ['dɑrvɪʃ] *s* Derwisch *m*

desalinization [di,selɪnɪ'zeʃən] *s* Entsalzung *f*

desalt [di'sɔlt] tr entsalzen

descend [dɪ'send] tr hinuntergehen ‖ intr (dismount, alight) absteigen; (said of a plane) niedergehen; (from a tree, from heaven) herabsteigen; (said of a road) sich senken; (pass by inheritance) (to) übergehen (auf acc); **be descended from** abstammen von; **d. upon** hereinbrechen über (acc)

descendant [dɪ'sendənt] s Abkömmling m, Nachkomme m; **descendants** Nachkommenschaft f

descendent [dɪ'sendənt] adj absteigend

descent [dɪ'sent] s Abstieg m; (lineage) Herkunft f; (of a plane or parachute) Niedergehen n; (slope) Abhang m; (hostile raid) (on) Überfall m (auf acc)

describe [dɪ'skraɪb] tr beschreiben

description [dɪ'skrɪp/ən] s Beschreibung f; (type) Art f; **beyond d.** unbeschreiblich

descriptive [dɪ'skrɪptɪv] adj beschreibend

de•scry [dɪ'skraɪ] v (pret & pp –scried) tr erspähen, erblicken

desecrate ['desɪ,kret] tr entweihen

desecration [,desɪ'kre/ən] s Entweihung f

desegregate [di'segrɪ,get] tr die Rassentrennung aufheben in (dat)

desegregation [di,segrɪ'ge/ən] s Aufhebung f der Rassentrennung

desert ['dezərt] adj öde, wüst; (sand, warfare, etc.) Wüsten– ‖ s Wüste f; (fig) Öde f ‖ [dɪ'zʌrt] s Verdienst m; **get one's just deserts** seinen wohlverdienten Lohn empfangen ‖ tr verlassen ‖ intr (mil) desertieren; (to) überlaufen (zu)

deserter [dɪ'zʌrtər] s Deserteur m

desertion [dɪ'zʌr/ən] s Verlassen n; (of a party) Abfall m; (mil) Fahnenflucht f

deserve [dɪ'zʌrv] tr verdienen

deservedly [dɪ'zʌrvɪdli] adv mit Recht

deserv'ing adj (of) würdig (genit)

design [dɪ'zaɪn] s (outline) Entwurf m; (pattern) Muster n; (plan) Plan m; (plot) Anschlag m; (of a building, etc.) Bauart f; (aim) Absicht f; **designs on** böse Absichten auf (acc) ‖ tr (make a preliminary sketch of) entwerfen; (draw up detailed plans for) konstruieren; **designed for** gedacht für

designate ['dezɪg,net] tr (as) bezeichnen (als); (to) ernennen (zu)

designation [,dezɪg'ne/ən] s (act of designating) Kennzeichnung f; (title) Bezeichnung f; (appointment) Ernennung f

designer [dɪ'zaɪnər] s (of patterns) Musterzeichner –in mf; (of fashions) Modeschöpfer –in mf; (theat) Dekorateur –in mf

design'ing adj intrigant; (calculating) berechnend

desirable [dɪ'zaɪrəbəl] adj wünschenswert, begehrenswert

desire [dɪ'zaɪr] s (wish) Wunsch m; (interest) Lust f; (craving) Begierde f; (thing desired) Gewünschte n ‖ tr wünschen

desirous [dɪ'zaɪrəs] adj (of) begierig (nach)

desist [dɪ'zɪst] intr (from) ablassen (von)

desk [desk] s Schreibtisch m; (of a teacher) Pult n; (of a pupil) Schulbank f; (in a hotel) Kasse f (acc)

desk' cop'y s Freiexemplar n

desk' lamp' s Tischlampe f

desk' pad' s Schreibunterlage f

desolate ['desəlɪt] adj (barren) öde; (joyless) trostlos; (deserted) verlassen; (dilapidated) verfallen ‖ ['desə,let] tr verwüsten

desolation [,desə'le/ən] s (devastation) Verwüstung f; (dreariness) Trostlosigkeit f

despair [dɪs'per] s Verzweiflung f ‖ intr (of) verzweifeln (an dat)

despair'ing adj verzweifelt

despera•do [,despə'rado], [,despə'redo] s (–does & –dos) Desperado m

desperate ['despərɪt] adj verzweifelt

desperation [,despə're/ən] s Verzweiflung f

despicable ['despɪkəbəl] adj verächtlich, verachtungswürdig

despise [dɪ'spaɪz] tr verachten

despite [dɪ'spaɪt] prep trotz (genit)

despondency [dɪ'spandənsi] s Kleinmut m

despondent [dɪ'spandənt] adj kleinmütig

despot ['despat] s Despot –in mf

despotic [des'patɪk] adj despotisch

despotism ['despə,tɪzəm] s Despotie f; (as a system) Despotismus m

dessert [dɪ'zʌrt] s Nachtisch m

destination [,destɪ'ne/ən] s (of a trip) Bestimmungsort m, Reiseziel n; (purpose) Bestimmung f

destine ['destɪn] tr (for) bestimmen (zu or für)

destiny ['destɪni] s Schicksal n; (doom) Verhängnis n

destitute ['destɪ,t(j)ut] adj mittellos; **d. of** ohne

destitution [,destɪ't(j)u/ən] s äußerste Armut f

destroy [dɪ'strɔɪ] tr vernichten, zerstören; (animals, bacteria) töten

destroyer [dɪ'strɔɪ-ər] s (nav) Zerstörer m

destroy'er es'cort s Zerstörergeleitschutz m

destruction [dɪ'strʌk/ən] s Zerstörung f; (of species) Ausrottung f

destructive [dɪ'strʌktɪv] adj zerstörend; (criticism) vernichtend; (tendency) destruktiv

desultory ['desəl,tori] adj (without plan) planlos; (fitful) sprunghaft; (remark) deplaciert

detach [dɪ'tæt/] tr ablösen; (along a perforation) abtrennen; (mil) abkommandieren

detachable [dɪ'tæt/əbəl] tr abnehmbar, ablösbar

detached' adj (building) alleinstehend; (objective) objektiv; (aloof) distanziert

detachment [dɪˈtætʃmənt] s Objektivität f; (aloofness) Abstand m; (mil) Trupp m, Kommando n

detail [dɪˈtel], [ˈditel] s Enzelheit f, Detail n; (mil) Kommando n, Trupp m; details (pej) Kleinkram m; in d. ausführlich || [dɪˈtel] (relate in detail) ausführlich berichten; (list) einzeln aufzählen; (mil) abkommandieren

de'tail draw'ing s Detailzeichnung f

detailed' adj ausführlich; d. work Kleinarbeit f

detain [dɪˈten] tr zurückhalten; (jur) in Haft behalten

detect [dɪˈtekt] tr (discover) entdecken; (catch) ertappen

detection [dɪˈtekʃən] s Entdeckung f

detective [dɪˈtektɪv] s Detektiv m

detec'tive sto'ry s Kriminalroman m

detector [dɪˈtektər] s (e.g., of smoke) Spürgerät n; (of objects) Suchgerät n; (rad) Detektor m

détente [deˈtɑnt] s Entspannung f, Détente f

detention [dɪˈtenʃən] s (jur) Haft f

deten'tion camp' s Internierungslager n

deten'tion home' s Haftanstalt f

de-ter [dɪˈtʌr] v (pret & pp -terred; ger-terring) tr (from) abschrecken (von), abhalten (von)

detergent [dɪˈtɑrdʒənt] s Reinigungsmittel n; (in a washer) Waschmittel n

deteriorate [dɪˈtɪrɪ-əˌret] tr verschlechtern || intr sich verschlechtern

deterioration [dɪˌtɪrɪ-əˈreʃən] s Verschlechterung f, Verfall m

determination [dɪˌtʌrmɪˈneʃən] s Bestimmung f; (resoluteness) Entschlossenheit f; (of boundaries) Festlegung f

determine [dɪˈtʌrmɪn] tr (fix conclusively) bestimmen; (boundaries) festlegen; (decide) entscheiden

deter'mined adj entschlossen

deterrent [dɪˈtʌrənt] adj abschreckend || s Abschreckungsmittel n

detest [dɪˈtest] tr verabscheuen

detestable [dɪˈtestəbəl] adj abscheulich

dethrone [dɪˈθron] tr entthronen

detonate [ˈdetəˌnet] tr explodieren lassen || intr explodieren

detour [ˈditur] s (for cars) Umleitung f; (for pedestrians) Umweg m || tr umleiten || intr e-n Umweg machen

detract [dɪˈtrækt] tr ablenken || intr— d. from beeinträchtigen

detraction [dɪˈtrækʃən] s Beeinträchtigung f

detractor [dɪˈtræktər] s Verleumder –in mf

detrain [dɪˈtren] tr ausladen || intr aussteigen

detriment [ˈdetrɪmənt] s Nachteil m

detrimental [ˌdetrɪˈmentəl] adj (to) nachteilig (für), schädlich (für)

deuce [d(j)us] s (in cards or dice) Zwei f; (in tennis) Einstand m; what the d.? was zum Teufel?

devaluate [diˈvæljuˌet] tr abwerten

devaluation [diˌvæljuˈeʃən] s Abwertung f

devastate [ˈdevəsˌtet] tr verheeren

develop [dɪˈveləp] tr entwickeln; (one's mind) (aus)bilden; (a habit) annehmen; (a disease) sich [dat] zuziehen; (cracks) bekommen; (land) nutzbar machen; (a mine) ausbauen; (phot) entwickeln || intr sich entwickeln; (said of habits) sich herausbilden; d. into sich entwickeln zu

developer [dɪˈveləpər] s (of land) Spekulant –in mf; (phot) Entwickler m

development [dɪˈveləpmənt] s Entwicklung f; (of relations, of a mine) Ausbau m; (of land) Nutzbarmachung f; (of housing) Siedlung f; (an event) Ereignis n; (educ) Ausbildung f; (phot) Entwicklung f

deviate [ˈdivɪˌet] intr abweichen

deviation [ˌdivɪˈeʃən] s Abweichung f

device [dɪˈvaɪs] s Vorrichtung f, Gerät n; (means) Mittel n; (crafty scheme) Kniff m; (literary device) Kunstgriff m; (heral) Sinnbild n; leave s.o. to his own devices j-n sich [dat] selbst überlassen

dev-il [ˈdevəl] s Teufel m; a d. of a (coll) verteufelt; between the d. and the deep blue sea zwischen zwei Feuern; poor d. armer Teufel; the d. with you! (coll) scher dich zum Teufel; what (who, etc.) the d.? was (wer, etc.) zum Teufel? || v (pret & pp -il[l]ed; ger -il[l]ing) tr (culin) mit viel Gewürz zubereiten

devilish [ˈdev(ə)lɪʃ] adj teuflisch

dev'il-may-care' adj (informal) wurstig; (reckless) verwegen

devilment [ˈdevɪlmənt] s Unfug m

deviltry [ˈdevɪltri] s Unfug m

devious [ˈdivɪ-əs] adj abweichend; (tricky) unredlich; (reasoning) abwegig

devise [dɪˈvaɪz] tr ersinnen; (jur) vermachen

devoid [dɪˈvoɪd] adj—d. of ohne

devolve [dɪˈvɑlv] intr—d. on zufallen (dat)

devote [dɪˈvot] tr widmen

devot'ed adj (dedicated) ergeben; (affectionate) liebevoll

devotee [ˌdevəˈti] s Anhänger –in mf

devotion [dɪˈvoʃən] s Ergebenheit f; (devoutness) Frömmigkeit f; (special prayer) (to) Gebet n (zu); devotions Andacht f

devour [dɪˈvaur] tr verschlingen; (said of fire) verzehren

devout [dɪˈvaut] adj fromm; (e.g., hope) innig

dew [d(j)u] s Tau m; dew is falling es taut

dew'drop' s Tautropfen m

dew'lap' s Wamme f

dewy [ˈd(j)u-i] adj tauig

dexterity [deksˈterɪti] s Geschicklichkeit f, Handfertigkeit f

dexterous [ˈdekstərəs] adj handfertig

dextrose [ˈdekstroz] s Traubenzucker m

diabetes [ˌdaɪ-əˈbitɪs] s Zuckerkrankheit f

diabetic [ˌdaɪ·əˈbetɪk] *adj* zucker-krank *mf*

diabolic(al) [ˌdaɪ·əˈbɑlɪk(ə)l] *adj* teuf-lisch

diacritical [ˌdaɪ·əˈkrɪtɪkəl] *adj* dia-kritisch

diadem [ˈdaɪ·əˌdem] *s* Diadem *n*

diaere·sis [daɪˈerɪsɪs] *s* (**–ses** [ˌsiz] Diäresis *f*; (*mark*) Trema *n*

diagnose [ˌdaɪ·əgˈnos], [ˌdaɪ·əgˈnoz] *tr* diagnostizieren

diagno·sis [ˌdaɪ·əgˈnosɪs] *s* (**–ses** [siz]) Diagnose *f*

diagonal [daɪˈægənəl] *adj* diagonal || *s* Diagonale *f*

diagonally [daɪˈægənəli] *adv*—**d. across from** schräg gegenüber von

diagram [ˈdaɪ·əˌgræm] *s* Diagramm *n*

di·al [ˈdaɪ·əl] *s* Zifferblatt *n*; (tech) Skalenscheibe *f*; (telp) Wählscheibe *f* || *v* (*pret & pp* **–al[l]ed**; *ger* **–al[l]ing**) *tr & intr* (telp) wählen

di′aling *s* (telp) Wählen *n* der Nummer

dialogue [ˈdaɪ·əˌlɔg] *s* Dialog *m*

di′al tel′ephone *s* Selbstanschlußtele-fon *n*

di′al tone′ *s* Summton *m*, Amtszeichen *n*

diameter [daɪˈæmɪtər] *s* Durchmesser *m*

diamond [ˈdaɪmənd] *adj* diamanten; (*in shape*) rautenförmig || *s* Diamant *m*; (*cut diamond*) Brillant *m*; (*rhom-bus*) Raute *f*; (baseball) Spielfeld *n*; (cards) Karo *n*

dia′mond ring′ *s* Brillantring *m*

diaper [ˈdaɪpər] *s* Windel *f*; **change the diapers of** trockenlegen, wickeln

diaphanous [daɪˈæfənəs] *adj* durch-sichtig, durchscheinend

diaphragm [ˈdaɪ·əˌfræm] *s* (*for birth control*) Gebärmutterkappe *f*; (anat) Zwerchfell *n*; (phot) Blende *f*; (tech, telp) Membran *f*

diarrhea [ˌdaɪ·əˈri·ə] *s* Durchfall *m*

diary [ˈdaɪ·əri] *s* Tagebuch *n*

diastole [daɪˈæstəli] *s* Diastole *f*

diatribe [ˈdaɪ·əˌtraɪb] *s* Schmährede *f*

dice [daɪs] *spl* Würfel *pl* || *tr* in Wür-fel schneiden

dice′box′ *s* Würfelbecher *m*

dichotomy [daɪˈkɑtəmi] *s* Zweiteilung *f*; (bot) Gabelung *f*

dicker [ˈdɪkər] *intr* (*about*) feilschen (um)

dickey [ˈdɪki] *s* Hemdbrust *f*

dictaphone [ˈdɪktəˌfon] *s* Diktaphon *n*

dictate [ˈdɪktet] *s* Diktat *n*; **the dic-tates of conscience** das Gebot des Gewissens || *tr & intr* diktieren

dictation [dɪkˈteʃən] *s* Diktat *n*

dictator [ˈdɪktetər] *s* Diktator *m*

dictatorial [ˌdɪktəˈtɔrɪ·əl] *adj* dikta-torisch; (*power*) unumschränkt

dic′tator′ship *s* Diktatur *f*

diction [ˈdɪkʃən] *s* Ausdrucksweise *f*

dictionary [ˈdɪkʃəˌneri] *s* Wörterbuch *n*

dic·tum [ˈdɪktəm] *s* (**–ta** [tə]) (*saying*) Spruch *m*; (*pronouncement*) Aus-spruch *m*

didactic [daɪˈdæktɪk] *adj* lehrhaft

die [daɪ] *s* (**dice** [daɪs]) Würfel *m*; **the die is cast** die Würfel sind ge-fallen || *s* (**dies**) (*coining die*) Präge-stempel *m*; (*casting die*) Form *f*; (*forging die*) Gesenk *n*; (*threader*) Schneidkopf *m* || *v* (*pret & pp* **died**; *ger* **dying**) *tr*—**die a natural death** e–s natürlichen Todes sterben || *intr* sterben; (*said of plants and animals*) eingehen; **be dying for** (coll) sich sehnen nach; **die down** (*said of the wind*) sich legen; (*said of noise*) er-sterben; **die from** sterben an (*dat*); **die laughing** sich totlachen; **die of hunger** verhungern; **die of thirst** ver-dursten; **die out** aussterben; (*said of fire*) erlöschen; **I am dying to** (*inf*) (coll) ich würde schrecklich gern (*inf*)

die′-hard′ *s* Unentwegte *mf*

die′sel en′gine [ˈdizəl] *s* Dieselmotor *m*

die′sel oil′ *s* Dieselöl *n*

die′stock′ *s* Gewindeschneidkluppe *f*

diet [ˈdaɪ·ət] *s* Kost *f*; (*special menu*) Diät *f*; (parl) Reichstag *m*; **be on a d.** diät leben; **put on a d.** auf Diät setzen || *intr* diät leben

dietary [ˈdaɪ·əˌteri] *adj* Diät–; **d. laws** rituelle Diätvorschriften *pl*

dietetic [ˌdaɪ·əˈtetɪk] *adj* diätetisch || **dietetics** *spl* Diätetik *f*

dietitian [ˌdaɪ·əˈtɪʃən] *s* Diätspezialist *–in mf*

differ [ˈdɪfər] *intr* sich unterscheiden; (*said of opinions*) auseinandergehen; **d. from** abweichen von; **d. in** ver-schieden sein in (*dat*); **d. with** an-derer Meinung sein als

difference [ˈdɪfərəns] *s* Unterschied *m*; (*argument*) Streit *m*; (math) Diffe-renz *f*; **d. of opinion** Meinungsver-schiedenheit *f*; **it makes no d. to me** es ist mir gleich; **split the d.** den Rest teilen

different [ˈdɪfərənt] *adj* verschieden; **a d. kind of** e–e andere Art von; **d. from** anders als, verschieden von; **d. kinds of** verschiedene

differential [ˌdɪfəˈrenʃəl] *adj* (econ, elec, mach, math, phys) Differential– || *s* (*difference*) Unterschied *m*; (*mach*) Differentialgetriebe *n*; (math) Differential *n*

dif′feren′tial cal′culus *s* Differential-rechnung *f*

differentiate [ˌdɪfəˈrenʃɪˌet] *tr* unter-scheiden; (math) differenzieren || *intr* —**d. between** unterscheiden zwischen (*dat*)

difficult [ˈdɪfɪˌkʌlt] *adj* schwierig, schwer

difficulty [ˈdɪfɪˌkʌlti] *s* Schwierigkeit *f*; **I have d. in** (*ger*) es fällt mir schwer zu (*inf*); **with d.** mit Mühe

diffuse [dɪˈfjus] *adj* (weit) zerstreut; (*style*) diffus || [dɪˈfjuz] *tr* (*spread*) verbreiten; (*pour out*) ausgießen; (phys) diffundieren || *intr* sich zer-streuen

diffusion [dɪˈfjuʃən] *s* (*spread*) Ver-breitung *f*; (phys) Diffusion *f*

dig [dɪg] *s* (*jab*) Stoß *m*; (*sarcasm*)

Seitenhieb *m;* (archeol) Ausgrabung *f* ‖ *v* (*pret & pp* dug [dʌg] & digged; *ger* digging) *tr* graben; (*a ditch*) auswerfen; (*potatoes*) ausgraben; (*understand*) (sl) kapieren; (*look at*) (sl) anschauen; (*appreciate*) (sl) schwärmen für; **dig up** ausgraben; (*find*) auftreiben; (*information*) ausfindig machen; (*money*) aufbringen; ‖ *intr* graben, wühlen; **dig in** (*with the hands*) hineinfassen; (*work hard*) (coll) schuften; (mil) sich eingraben; **dig for** (*e.g., gold*) schürfen nach

digest [ˈdaɪdʒest] *s* Zusammenfassung *f;* (jur) Gesetzessammlung *f* ‖ [daɪˈdʒest] *tr* verdauen; (*in the mind*) verarbeiten ‖ *intr* verdauen

digestible [daɪˈdʒestɪbəl] *adj* verdaulich, verträglich

digestion [daɪˈdʒestʃən] *s* Verdauung *f*

digestive [daɪˈdʒestɪv] *adj* Verdauungs–; **d. tract** Verdauungsapparat *m*

digit [ˈdɪdʒɪt] *s* (math) Ziffer *f* (unter zehn); (math) Stelle *f*

digital [ˈdɪdʒɪtəl] *adj* digital, Digital–

dig′ital comput′er *s* digitale Rechenanlage *f*

digitalis [dɪdʒɪˈtælɪs] *s* Digitalis *n*

dignified [ˈdɪgnɪˌfaɪd] *adj* würdig

digni·fy [ˈdɪgnɪˌfaɪ] *v* (*pret & pp* –fied) *tr* ehren

dignitary [ˈdɪgnɪˌteri] *s* Würdenträger –in *mf*

dignity [ˈdɪgnɪti] *s* Würde *f;* **d. of man** Menschenwürde *f;* **stand on one's d.** sich [*dat*] nichts vergeben

digress [daɪˈgres] *intr* (**from**) abschweifen (von)

digression [daɪˈgreʃən] *s* Abschweifung *f*

dike [daɪk] *s* Deich *m*

dilapidated [dɪˈlæpɪˌdetɪd] *adj* baufällig

dilate [daɪˈlet] *tr* ausdehnen ‖ *intr* sich ausdehnen

dilation [daɪˈleʃən] *s* Ausdehnung *f*

dilatory [ˈdɪləˌtori] *adj* saumselig; (*tending to cause delay*) hinhaltend

dilemma [dɪˈlemə] *s* Dilemma *n*

dilettan·te [ˌdɪləˈtænti], [ˌdɪləˌtɑnt] *s* (–tes & –ti [ti]) Dilettant –in *mf*

diligence [ˈdɪlɪdʒəns] *s* Fleiß *m*

diligent [ˈdɪlɪdʒənt] *adj* fleißig

dill [dɪl] *s* Dill *m*

dillydal·ly [ˈdɪlɪˌdæli] *v* (*pret & pp* –lied) *intr* herumtrödeln

dilute [dɪˈlut], [daɪˈlut] *adj* verdünnt ‖ [dɪˈlut] *tr* verdünnen; (*with water*) verwässern ‖ *intr* sich verdünnen

dilution [dɪˈluʃən] *s* Verdünnung *f;* (*with water*) Verwässerung *f*

dim [dɪm] *adj* (dimmer; dimmest) *adj* (*light, eyesight*) schwach; (*poorly lighted*) schwach beleuchtet; (*dull*) matt; (*chances, outlook*) schlecht; (*indistinct*) undeutlich; **take a dim view of** (*disapprove of*) mißbilligen; (*be pessimistic about*) sich [*dat*] etw schwarz ausmalen ‖ *v* (*pret & pp* dimmed; *ger* dimming) *tr* trüben; (*lights*) abblenden ‖ *intr* sich ver-

dunkeln; (*said of lights, hopes*) verblassen

dime [daɪm] *s* Zehncentstück *n*

dime′ nov′el *s* Groschenroman *m*

dimension [dɪˈmenʃən] *s* Maß *n,* Ausdehnung *f;* **dimensions** Ausmaß *n*

diminish [dɪˈmɪnɪʃ] *tr* (ver)mindern, verringern ‖ *intr* sich vermindern

diminutive [dɪˈmɪnjətɪv] *adj* winzig; (gram) Verkleinerungs– ‖ *s* Verkleinerungsform *f*

dimmer [ˈdɪmər] *s* (aut) Abblendvorrichtung *f*

dimple [ˈdɪmpəl] *s* Grübchen *n*

dim′wit′ *s* Schwachsinnige *mf*

din [dɪn] *s* Getöse *n* ‖ *v* (*pret & pp* dinned; *ger* dinning) *tr* betäuben; **din s.th. into s.o.** j–m etw einhämmern

dine [daɪn] *intr* speisen; **d. out** auswärts speisen

diner [ˈdaɪnər] *s* Tischgast *m;* (*small restaurant*) speisewagenähnliches Speiselokal *n;* (rr) Speisewagen *m*

dinette [daɪˈnet] *s* Speisenische *f*

dingbat [ˈdɪŋˌbæt] *s* (sl) (*person*) Dingsda *m;* (*thing*) Dingsda *n*

ding-dong [ˈdɪŋˌdɒŋ] *interj* bimbaml, klingklangl

dinghy [ˈdɪŋgi] *s* Beiboot *n;* **rubber d.** Schlauchboot *n*

dingy [ˈdɪndʒi] *adj* (*gloomy*) düster; (*shabby*) schäbig

din′ing car′ *s* (rr) Speisewagen *m*

din′ing hall′ *s* Speisesaal *m*

din′ing room′ *s* Eßzimmer *n*

dinner [ˈdɪnər] *s* (*supper*) Abendessen *n;* (*main meal*) Hauptmahlzeit *f;* (*formal meal*) Diner *n;* **after d.** nach Tisch; **at d.** bei Tisch; **before d.** vor Tisch

din′ner guest′ *s* Tischgast *m*

din′ner jac′ket *s* Smoking *m*

din′ner mu′sic *s* Tafelmusik *f*

din′ner par′ty *s* Tischgesellschaft *f*

din′ner time′ *s* Tischzeit *f*

dinosaur [ˈdaɪnəˌsɔr] *s* Dinosaurier *m*

dint [dɪnt] *s*—**by d. of** kraft (*genit*)

diocesan [daɪˈɑsɪsən] *adj* Diözesan–

diocese [ˈdaɪəˌsɪs] *s* Diözese *f*

diode [ˈdaɪˌod] *s* (*electron*) Diode *f*

dioxide [daɪˈaksaɪd] *s* Dioxyd *n*

dip [dɪp] *s* (*in the road*) Neigung *f;* (*short swim*) kurzes Bad *n;* (*dunk*) Eintauchen *n;* (*sauce*) Tunke *f;* (*of ice cream*) Portion *f* ‖ *v* (*pret & pp* dipped; *ger* dipping) *tr* eintauchen; (*e.g., doughnuts*) eintunken; (*a flag*) senken ‖ *intr* sich senken; **dip into** (*e.g., reserves*) angreifen; **dip into one's pockets** (fig) in die Tasche greifen

diphtheria [dɪfˈθɪrɪə] *s* Diphtherie *f*

diphthong [ˈdɪfθɔŋ] *s* Doppelvokal *m*

diploma [dɪˈplomə] *s* Diplom *n*

diplomacy [dɪˈploməsi] *s* Diplomatie *f*

diplomat [ˈdɪpləˌmæt] *s* Diplomat –in *mf*

diplomatic [ˌdɪpləˈmætɪk] *adj* (& fig) diplomatisch

dipper [ˈdɪpər] *s* Schöpflöffel *m*

dipsomania [ˌdɪpsəˈmenɪə] *s* Trunksucht *f*

dip′ stick′ s (aut) Ölstandmesser m
dire [daɪr] adj (terrible) gräßlich;
(need) äußerste
direct [dɪˈrekt] adj direkt, unmittelbar; (frank) unverblümt; (quotation)
wörtlich || tr (order) beauftragen;
(a company) leiten; (traffic) regeln;
(a movie, play) Regie führen bei;
(an orchestra) dirigieren; (attention,
glance) (to) richten (auf acc); (a
person) (to) verweisen (an acc);
(words, letter) (to) richten (an acc)
direct′ call′ s Selbstwählverbindung f
direct′ cur′rent s Gleichstrom m
direct′ dis′course s direkte Rede f
direct′ hit′ s Volltreffer m
direction [dɪˈrekʃən] s Richtung f;
(order) Anweisung f; (leadership)
Leitung f, Führung f; (cin, theat)
Regie f; (mus) Stabführung f; **directions** Weisungen pl; (for use) Gebrauchsanweisung f; **in all directions**
nach allen Richtungen
directional [dɪˈrekʃənəl] adj Richt-
direc′tion find′er s Peilgerät n
direc′tion sig′nal s (aut) Richtungsanzeiger m
directive [dɪˈrektɪv] s Anweisung f
direct′ ob′ject s direktes Objekt n
direct′ op′posite s genaues Gegenteil n
director [dɪˈrektər] s Leiter –in mf,
Direktor –in mf; (cin, theat) Regisseur –in mf; (mus) Dirigent –in mf;
(rad, telv) Sendeleiter –in mf
direc′torship′ s Direktorat n
directory [dɪˈrektəri] s Verzeichnis n
dirge [dʌrdʒ] s Trauergesang m
dirigible [ˈdɪrɪdʒɪbəl] s lenkbares
Luftschiff n
dirt [dʌrt] s Schmutz m, Dreck m;
(moral filth) Schmutz m; (soil) Erde
f
dirt′-cheap′ adj spottbillig
dirt′ farm′er s kleiner Farmer m
dirt′ road′ s unbefestigte Straße f
dirt·y [ˈdʌrti] adj schmutzig, dreckig;
(morally) schmutzig; **d. business**
Schweinerei f; **d. dog** Sauhund m;
d. joke Zote f; **d. lie** gemeine Lüge
f; **d. linen** schmutzige Wäsche f; **d.
look** böser Blick m; **d. trick** übler
Streich m; **that′s a d. shame** das ist
e–e Gemeinheit! || v (pret & pp
–ied) tr beschmutzen
disability [ˌdɪsəˈbɪlɪti] s Invalidität f
disable [dɪsˈebəl] tr (e.g., a worker)
arbeitsunfähig machen; (make un-
suited for combat) kampfunfähig
machen; (jur) rechtsunfähig machen
disa′bled adj invalide; (mil) kampfunfähig; **d. veteran** Kriegsversehrte
mf; **d. person** Invalide mf
disabuse [ˌdɪsəˈbjuz] tr—**d. of** befreien von
disadvantage [ˌdɪsədˈvæntɪdʒ] s Nachteil m; **place at a d.** benachteiligen
disadvantageous [dɪsˌædvənˈtedʒəs]
adj nachteilig
disagree [ˌdɪsəˈgri] intr nicht übereinstimmen; (be contradictory) einander widersprechen; (quarrel) (sich)
streiten; **d. with** (said of food) nicht
bekommen (dat); **d. with s.o. on**

anderer Meinung über (acc) als j–d
sein
disagreeable [ˌdɪsəˈgri-əbəl] adj unangenehm
disagreement [ˌdɪsəˈgrimənt] s (un-
likeness) Verschiedenheit f; (dissention) Uneinigkeit f; (quarrel) Meinungsverschiedenheit f
disappear [ˌdɪsəˈpɪr] intr verschwinden
disappearance [ˌdɪsəˈpɪrəns] s Verschwinden n
disappoint [ˌdɪsəˈpoɪnt] tr enttäu-
schen; **be disappointed at** (or with)
enttäuscht sein über (acc)
disappointment [ˌdɪsəˈpoɪntmənt] s
Enttäuschung f
disapproval [ˌdɪsəˈpruvəl] s Mißbilli-
gung f
disapprove [ˌdɪsəˈpruv] tr mißbilligen; (e.g., an application) nicht ge-
nehmigen || intr—**d. of** mißbilligen
disarm [dɪsˈɑrm] tr (& fig) entwaffnen;
(a bomb) entschärfen || intr ab-
rüsten
disarmament [dɪsˈɑrməmənt] s Ab-
rüstung f
disarm′ing adj (fig) entwaffnend
disarray [ˌdɪsəˈre] s Unordnung f ||
tr in Unordnung bringen, verwirren
disassemble [ˌdɪsəˈsembəl] tr zerlegen
disaster [dɪˈzæstər] s Unheil n
disas′ter ar′ea s Katastrophengebiet n
disastrous [dɪˈzæstrəs] adj unheilvoll
disavow [ˌdɪsəˈvau] tr ableugnen
disavowal [ˌdɪsəˈvau-əl] s Ableugnung
f
disband [dɪsˈbænd] tr auflösen || intr
sich auflösen
dis·bar [dɪsˈbɑr] v (pret & pp –barred;
ger –barring) tr aus dem Anwalts-
stand ausschließen
disbelief [ˌdɪsbɪˈlif] s Unglaube m
disbelieve [ˌdɪsbɪˈliv] tr & intr nicht
glauben
disburse [dɪsˈbʌrs] tr auszahlen
disbursement [dɪsˈbʌrsmənt] s Aus-
zahlung f
disc [dɪsk] s var of **disk**
discard [dɪsˈkɑrd] s Ablegen n || tr
(clothes, cards, habits) ablegen; (a
plan) verwerfen
discern [dɪˈsʌrn] tr (perceive) wahrnehmen; **be able to d. right from
wrong** zwischen Gut und Böse unterscheiden können
discern′ing adj scharfsinnig
discernment [dɪˈsʌrnmənt] s Scharfsinn m
discharge [dɪsˈtʃɑrdʒ] s (of a gun)
Abfeuern n; (of a battery) Ent-
ladung f; (of water) Abfluß m; (of
smoke) Ausströmen n; (of duties)
Erfüllung f; (of debts) Tilgung f;
(of employees, patients, soldiers)
Entlassung f; (of a prisoner) Freilas-
sung f; (pathol) Ausfluß m || tr (a
gun) abfeuern; (e.g., water) ergießen; (smoke) ausstoßen; (debts) tilgen; (duties) erfüllen; (an office)
verwalten; (an employee, patient,
soldier) entlassen || intr (said of a
gun) losgehen; (said of a battery)

sich entladen; (pour out) abfließen; (pathol) eitern

disciple [dɪ'saɪpəl] s Jünger m

disciplinarian [ˌdɪsɪplɪ'nerɪ·ən] s Zuchtmeister m

disciplinary ['dɪsɪplɪ ˌneri] adj Disziplinar-

discipline ['dɪsɪplɪn] s Disziplin f; (punishment) Züchtigung f || tr disziplinieren; (punish) züchtigen

disclaim [dɪs'klem] tr leugnen; (jur) verzichten auf (acc)

disclose [dɪs'kloz] tr enthüllen

disclosure [dɪs'kloʒər] s Enthüllung f

discolor [dɪs'kʌlər] tr verfärben || intr sich verfärben

discoloration [dɪsˌkʌlə'reʃən] s Verfärbung f

discomfiture [dɪs'kʌmfɪtʃər] s (defeat) Niederlage f; (frustration) Enttäuschung f; (confusion) Verwirrung f

discomfort [dɪs'kʌmfərt] s Unbehagen n || tr Unbehagen verursachen (dat)

disconcert [ˌdɪskən'sʌrt] tr aus der Fassung bringen

dis'concert'ed adj fassungslos

disconnect [ˌdɪskə'nekt] tr trennen; (elec) ausschalten; (mach) auskuppeln; (telp) unterbrechen

disconsolate [dɪs'kɑnsəlɪt] adj trostlos

discontent [ˌdɪskən'tent] s Unzufriedenheit f || tr unzufrieden machen

dis'content'ed adj (with) mißvergnügt (über acc)

discontinue [ˌdɪskən'tɪnju] tr (permanently) einstellen; (temporarily) aussetzen; (a newspaper) abbestellen; d. (ger) aufhören zu (inf)

discord ['dɪskɔrd] s Mißklang m; (dissention) Zwietracht f

discordance [dɪs'kɔrdəns] s Uneinigkeit f

discotheque [ˌdɪsko'tek] s Diskothek f

discount ['dɪskaʊnt] s (in price) Rabatt m; (cash discount) Kassaskonto n; (deduction from nominal value) Diskont m; at a d. mit Rabatt; (st. exch.) unter pari || tr (disregard) außer acht lassen; (minimize) geringen Wert beimessen (dat); (for cash payment) e-n Abzug gewähren auf (acc); (e.g., a promissory note) diskontieren

dis'count store' s Rabattladen m

discourage [dɪs'kʌrɪdʒ] tr (dishearten) entmutigen; d. s.o. from (ger) (deter) j-n davon abschrecken zu (inf); (dissuade) j-m davon abraten zu (inf)

discour'aged adj mutlos

discouragement [dɪs'kʌrɪdʒmənt] s (act) Entmutigung f; (state) Mutlosigkeit f; (deterrent) Abschreckung f

discourse ['dɪskɔrs] s (conversation) Gespräch n; (formal treatment) Abhandlung f; (lecture) Vortrag m || [dɪs'kɔrs] intr (on) sich unterhalten (über acc)

discourteous [dɪs'kʌrtɪ·əs] adj unhöflich

discourtesy [dɪs'kʌrtəsi] s Unhöflichkeit f

discover [dɪs'kʌvər] tr entdecken

discovery [dɪs'kʌvəri] s Entdeckung f

discredit [dɪs'kredɪt] s (disrepute) Mißkredit m; (disbelief) Zweifel m || tr (destroy confidence in) in Mißkredit bringen; (disbelieve) anzweifeln; (disgrace) in Verruf bringen

discreditable [dɪs'kredɪtəbəl] adj schändlich

discreet [dɪs'krit] adj diskret

discrepancy [dɪs'krepənsi] s Unstimmigkeit f

discretion [dɪs'kreʃən] s Diskretion f, Besonnenheit f; at one's d. nach Belieben; leave to s.o.'s d. in j-s Belieben stellen

discriminate [dɪs'krɪmɪ ˌnet] tr voneinander unterscheiden || intr—d. against diskriminieren

discrimination [dɪsˌkrɪmɪ'neʃən] s (distinction) Unterscheidung f; (prejudicial treatment) Diskriminierung f

discriminatory [dɪs'krɪmɪnəˌtori] adj diskriminierend

discus ['dɪskʌs] s Diskus m

discuss [dɪs'kʌs] tr besprechen, diskutieren; (formally) erörtern

discussion [dɪs'kʌʃən] s Diskussion f; (formal consideration) Erörterung f

disdain [dɪs'den] s Geringschätzung f || tr geringschätzen

disdainful [dɪs'denfəl] adj geringschätzig; be d. of geringschätzen

disease [dɪ'ziz] s Krankheit f

diseased' adj krank, erkrankt

disembark [ˌdɪsem'bark] tr ausschiffen, landen || intr an Land gehen, landen

disembarkation [dɪsˌembar'keʃən] s Ausschiffung f

disembow·el [ˌdɪsem'baʊ·əl] v (pret & pp -el[l]ed; ger -el[l]ing) tr ausweiden

disenchant [ˌdɪsen'tʃænt] tr ernüchtern

disenchantment [ˌdɪsen'tʃæntmənt] s Ernüchterung f

disengage [ˌdɪsen'gedʒ] tr (a clutch) ausrücken; (the enemy) sich absetzen von; (troops) entflechten; d. the clutch auskuppeln || intr loskommen; (mil) sich absetzen

disengagement [ˌdɪsen'gedʒmənt] s Lösung f; (mil) Truppenentflechtung f

disentangle [ˌdɪsen'tæŋgəl] tr entwirren

disentanglement [ˌdɪsen'tæŋgəlmənt] s Entwirrung f

disfavor [dɪs'fevər] s Ungunst f

disfigure [dɪs'fɪgjər] tr entstellen

disfigurement [dɪs'fɪgjərmənt] s Entstellung f

disfranchise [dɪs'fræntʃaɪz] tr die Bürgerrechte entziehen (dat)

disgorge [dɪs'gɔrdʒ] tr ausspeien || intr sich ergießen

disgrace [dɪs'gres] s Schande f; (of a family) Schandfleck m || tr in Schande bringen; (a girl) schänden; be disgraced in Schande kommen

disgraceful [dɪs'gresfəl] *adj* schändlich, schimpflich
disgruntled [dɪs'grʌntəld] *adj* mürrisch
disguise [dɪs'gaɪz] *s* (*clothing*) Verkleidung *f*; (*insincere manner*) Ver-
stellung *f* ‖ *tr* (*by dress*) verkleiden;
(*e.g., the voice*) verstellen
disgust [dɪs'gʌst] *s* (at) Ekel *m* (vor
dat) ‖ *tr* anekeln
disgust′ing *adj* ekelhaft
dish [dɪʃ] *s* Schüssel *f*, Platte *f*; (*food*)
Gericht *n*; **do the dishes** das Geschirr spülen ‖ *tr*—**d. out** (coll) austeilen
dish′cloth′ *s* Geschirrlappen *m*
dishearten [dɪs'hɑrtən] *tr* entmutigen
disheveled [dɪ'ʃevəld] *adj* unordentlich
dishonest [dɪs'ɑnɪst] *adj* unehrlich
dishonesty [dɪs'ɑnɪsti] *s* Unehrlichkeit
f
dishonor [dɪs'ɑnər] *s* Unehre *f* ‖ *tr*
verunehren
dishonorable [dɪs'ɑnərəbəl] *adj* (*person*) ehrlos; (*action*) unehrenhaft
dishon′orable dis′charge *s* Entlassung
f wegen Wehrunwürdigkeit
dish′pan′ *s* Aufwaschschüssel *f*
dish′rack′ *s* Abtropfkörbchen *n*
dish′rag′ *s* Spüllappen *m*
dish′tow′el *s* Geschirrtuch *n*
dish′wash′er *s* (*person*) Aufwäscher
–in *mf*; (*appliance*) Geschirrspülmaschine *f*
dish′wa′ter *s* Spülwasser *n*
disillusion [ˌdɪsɪ'luʒən] *s* Ernüchterung *f* ‖ *tr* ernüchtern
disillusionment [ˌdɪsɪ'luʒənmənt] *s* Ernüchterung *f*
disinclination [dɪsˌɪnklɪ'neʃən] *s* Abneigung *f*, Abgeneigtheit *f*
disinclined [ˌdɪsɪn'klaɪnd] *adj* abgeneigt
disinfect [ˌdɪsɪn'fekt] *tr* desinfizieren
disinfectant [ˌdɪsɪn'fektənt] *adj* des-
infizierend ‖ *s* Desinfektionsmittel *n*
disinherit [ˌdɪsɪn'herɪt] *tr* enterben
disintegrate [dɪs'ɪntɪˌgret] *tr* (& fig)
zersetzen ‖ *intr* zerfallen
disintegration [dɪsˌɪntɪ'greʃən] *s* (&
fig) Zerfall *m*
disin·ter [ˌdɪsɪn'tʌr] *v* (*pret* & *pp*
–terred) *ger* –terring) *tr* ausgraben
disinterested [dɪs'ɪntəˌrestɪd] *adj* (*unbiased*) unparteiisch; (*uninterested*)
desinteressiert
disjunctive [dɪs'dʒʌŋktɪv] *adj* disjunk-
tiv
disk [dɪsk] *s* Scheibe *f*
disk′ brake′ *s* Scheibenbremse *f*
disk′ jock′ey *s* Schallplattenjockei *m*
dislike [dɪs'laɪk] *s* (of) Abneigung *f*
(gegen) ‖ *tr* nicht mögen
dislocate ['dɪslo̱ˌket] *tr* verschieben;
(*a shoulder*) verrenken; (fig) stören
dislocation [ˌdɪslo'keʃən] *s* Verschie-
bung *f*; (*of a shoulder*) Verrenkung
f; (fig) Störung *f*
dislodge [dɪs'lɑdʒ] *tr* losreißen; (mil)
aus der Stellung werfen
disloyal [dɪs'lɔɪ-əl] *adj* untreu
disloyalty [dɪs'lɔɪ-əlti] *s* Untreue *f*
dismal ['dɪzməl] *adj* trübselig, düster
dismantle [dɪs'mæntəl] *tr* demontieren

dismay [dɪs'me] *s* Bestürzung *f* ‖ *tr*
bestürzen
dismember [dɪs'membər] *tr* zerstük-
keln
dismiss [dɪs'mɪs] *tr* verabschieden; (*an
employee*) (from) entlassen (aus);
(*a case*) (jur) abweisen; (mil) wegtreten lassen; **d. as** abtun als; **dismissed!** (mil) wegtreten!
dismissal [dɪs'mɪsəl] *s* Entlassung *f*;
(jur) Abweisung *f*
dismount [dɪs'maunt] *tr* (*throw down*)
abwerfen; (mach) abmontieren ‖ *intr*
(*from a carriage*) herabsteigen; (*from
a horse*) absitzen
disobedience [ˌdɪsə'bidɪ-əns] *s* Ungehorsam *m*, Unfolgsamkeit *f*
disobedient [ˌdɪsə'bidɪ-ənt] *adj* ungehorsam, unfolgsam
disobey [ˌdɪsə'be] *tr* nicht gehorchen
(*dat*) ‖ *intr* nicht gehorchen
disorder [dɪs'ɔrdər] *s* Unordnung *f*;
(*public disturbance*) Unruhe *f*;
(pathol) Erkrankung *f*; **throw into
d.** in Unordnung bringen
disorderly [dɪs'ɔrdərli] *adj* unordentlich, liederlich
disor′derly con′duct *s* ungebührliches
Benehmen *n*
disor′derly house′ *s* Bordell *n*; (*gambling house*) Spielhölle *f*
disorganize [dɪs'ɔrgəˌnaɪz] *tr* zerrütten, desorganisieren
disown [dɪs'on] *tr* verleugnen
disparage [dɪ'spærɪdʒ] *tr* herabsetzen,
geringschätzen
disparate ['dɪspərɪt] *adj* ungleichartig
disparity [dɪ'spærɪti] *s* (*inequality*)
Ungleichheit *f*; (*difference*) Unterschied *m*
dispassionate [dɪs'pæʃənɪt] *adj* leidenschaftslos
dispatch [dɪ'spætʃ] *s* Abfertigung *f*;
(*message*) Depesche *f*; **with d.** in Eile
‖ *tr* (*send off*) absenden; (*e.g., a
truck*) abfertigen; (*e.g., a task*)
schnell erledigen; (*kill*) töten; (*eat
fast*) (coll) verputzen
dispatcher [dɪ'spætʃər] *s* (*of vehicles*)
Fahrbereitschaftsleiter –in *mf*
dis·pel [dɪ'spel] *v* (*pret* & *pp* –pelled;
ger –pelling) *tr* vertreiben; (*thoughts,
doubts*) zerstreuen
dispensary [dɪ'spensəri] *s* Arzneiaus-
gabestelle *f*; (mil) Krankenrevier *n*
dispensation [ˌdɪspen'seʃən] *s* (eccl)
(from) Dispens *m* (von); **by divine
d.** durch göttliche Fügung
dispense [dɪ'spens] *tr* (*exempt*) (from)
entbinden (von); (pharm) zubereiten
und ausgeben; **d. justice** Recht
sprechen ‖ *intr*—**d. with** verzichten
auf (*acc*)
dispersal [dɪ'spʌrsəl] *s* Auflockerung
f
disperse [dɪ'spʌrs] *tr* zerstreuen; (*a
crowd*) zersprengen; (*one's troops*)
auflockern; (*the enemy*) auseinander-
sprengen ‖ *intr* sich verziehen; (*said
of clouds, etc.*) sich verziehen; (*said of crowds*) auseinandergehen
dispirited [dɪ'spɪrɪtɪd] *adj* niedergeschlagen

displace [dɪs'ples] *tr* (*people in war*) verschleppen; (phys) verdrängen

displacement [dɪs'plesmənt] *s* Vertreibung *f*; (phys) Verdrängung *f*

display [dɪ'sple] *s* (*of energy, wealth*) Entfaltung *f*; (*of goods*) Ausstellung *f*; (*pomp*) Aufwand *m*; **on d.** zur Schau ‖ *tr* (*wares*) ausstellen; (*reveal*) entfalten; (*flaunt*) protzen mit

display' case' *s* Vitrine *f*

display' room' *s* Ausstellungsraum *m*

display' win'dow *s* Schaufenster *n*

displease [dɪs'pliz] *tr* mißfallen (*dat*); **be displeased with** Mißfallen finden an (*dat*) ‖ *intr* mißfallen

displeas'ing *adj* mißfällig

displeasure [dɪs'plɛʒər] *s* Mißfallen *n*

disposable [dɪ'spozəbəl] *adj* Einweg-

disposal [dɪ'spozəl] *s* (*riddance*) Beseitigung *f*; (*of a matter*) Erledigung *f*; (*distribution*) Anordnung *f*; **be at s.o.'s d.** j-m zur Verfügung stehen; **have at one's d.** verfügen über (*acc*); **put at s.o.'s d.** j-m zur Verfügung stellen

dispose [dɪ'spoz] *tr* (*incline*) (**to**) geneigt machen (zu); (*arrange*) anordnen ‖ *intr*—**d. of** (*a matter*) erledigen; (*get rid of*) loswerden

disposed' *adj* gesinnt; **d. to** (*ger*) geneigt zu (*inf*)

disposition [ˌdɪspə'zɪʃən] *s* (*settlement*) Erledigung *f*; (*nature*) Gemütsart *f*; (*inclination*) Neigung *f*

dispossess [ˌdɪspə'zɛs] *tr*—**d. s.o. of s.th.** j-m etw enteignen

disproof [dɪs'pruf] *s* Widerlegung *f*

disproportionate [ˌdɪsprə'porʃənɪt] *adj* unverhältnismäßig; **be d. to** im Mißverhältnis stehen zu

disprove [dɪs'pruv] *tr* widerlegen

dispute [dɪs'pjut] *s* (*quarrel*) Streit *m*; (*debate*) Wortgefecht *n*; **beyond d.** unstreitig; **in d.** umstritten ‖ *tr* bestreiten ‖ *intr* disputieren

disqualification [dɪsˌkwɑlɪfɪ'keʃən] *s* Disqualifizierung *f*

disquali·fy [dɪs'kwɑlɪˌfaɪ] *v* (*pret & pp* -**fied**) *tr* (*make unfit*) (**for**) untauglich machen (für); (*declare ineligible*) disqualifizieren

disquiet [dɪs'kwaɪ·ət] *tr* beunruhigen

disqui'eting *adj* beunruhigend

disregard [ˌdɪsrɪ'gɑrd] *s* (*lack of attention*) Nichtbeachtung *f*; (*disrespect*) Mißachtung *f* ‖ *tr* (*not pay attention to*) nicht beachten; (*treat without due respect*) mißachten

disrepair [ˌdɪsrɪ'per] *s* Verfall *m*; **fall into d.** verfallen

disreputable [dɪs'repjətəbəl] *adj* verrufen

disrepute [ˌdɪsrɪ'pjut] *s* Verruf *m*

disrespect [ˌdɪsrɪ'spekt] *s* Nichtachtung *f*, Mißachtung *f* ‖ *tr* nicht achten

disrespectful [ˌdɪsrɪ'spektfəl] *adj* respektlos, unehrerbietig

disrobe [dɪs'rob] *tr* entkleiden ‖ *intr* sich entkleiden

disrupt [dɪs'rʌpt] *tr* (*throw into confusion*) in Verwirrung bringen; (*interrupt*) unterbrechen; (*cause to break down*) zum Zusammenbruch bringen

dissatisfaction [ˌdɪssætɪs'fækʃən] *s* Unzufriedenheit *f*

dissatisfied [dɪs'sætɪsˌfaɪd] *adj* unzufrieden

dissatis·fy [dɪs'sætɪsˌfaɪ] *v* (*pret & pp* -**fied**) *tr* nicht befriedigen

dissect [dɪ'sekt] *tr* (fig) zergliedern; (anat) sezieren

dissection [dɪ'sekʃən] *s* (fig) Zergliederung *f*; (anat) Sektion *f*

dissemble [dɪ'sembəl] *tr* verbergen ‖ *intr* heucheln

disseminate [dɪ'semɪˌnet] *tr* verbreiten

dissension [dɪ'senʃən] *s* Uneinigkeit *f*

dissent [dɪ'sent] *s* abweichende Meinung *f* ‖ *intr* (**from**) anderer Meinung sein (als)

dissenter [dɪ'sentər] *s* Andersdenkende *mf*; (relig) Dissident -in *mf*

dissertation [ˌdɪsər'teʃən] *s* Dissertation *f*

disservice [dɪs'sʌrvɪs] *s* schlechter Dienst *m*; **do s.o. a d.** j-m e-n schlechten Dienst erweisen

dissidence [ˈdɪsɪdəns] *s* Meinungsverschiedenheit *f*

dissident [ˈdɪsɪdənt] *adj* andersdenkend ‖ *s* Dissident -in *mf*

dissimilar [dɪ'sɪmɪlər] *adj* unähnlich

dissimilate [dɪ'sɪmɪˌlet] *tr* (phonet) dissimilieren

dissimulate [dɪ'sɪmjəˌlet] *tr* verheimlichen ‖ *intr* heucheln

dissipate [ˈdɪsɪˌpet] *tr* (*squander*) vergeuden; (*scatter*) zerstreuen; (*dissolve*) auflösen ‖ *intr* (*scatter*) sich zerstreuen; (*dissolve*) sich auflösen

dis'sipat'ed *adj* ausschweifend

dissipation [ˌdɪsɪ'peʃən] *s* (*squandering*) Vergeudung *f*; (*dissolute mode of life*) Ausschweifung *f*; (phys) Dissipation *f*

dissociate [dɪ'soʃɪˌet] *tr* trennen; **d. oneself from** abrücken von

dissolute [ˈdɪsəˌlut] *adj* ausschweifend

dissolution [ˌdɪsə'luʃən] *s* Auflösung *f*

dissolve [dɪ'zɑlv] *s* (cin) Überblendung *f* ‖ *tr* auflösen; (cin) überblenden ‖ *intr* sich auflösen; (cin) überblenden

dissonance [ˈdɪsənəns] *s* Mißklang *m*

dissuade [dɪ'swed] *tr* (**from**) abbringen (von); **d. s.o. from** (*ger*) j-n davon abbringen zu (*inf*)

dissyllabic [ˌdɪsɪ'læbɪk] *adj* zweisilbig

distaff [ˈdɪstæf] *s* Spinnrocken *m*; (fig) Frauen *pl*

dis'taff side' *s* weibliche Linie *f*

distance [ˈdɪstəns] *s* Entfernung *f*; (*between two points*) Abstand *m*; (*stretch*) Strecke *f*; (*of a race*) Rennstrecke *f*; **from a d.** aus einiger Entfernung; **go the d.** bis zum Ende aushalten; **in the d.** in der Ferne; **keep one's d.** zurückhaltend sein; **keep your d.** bleib mir vom Leib!; **within easy d. of** nicht weit weg von; **within walking d. of** zu Fuß erreichbar von

distant [ˈdɪstənt] *adj* entfernt; (*reserved*) zurückhaltend

distaste [dɪs'test] s (**for**) Abneigung f (gegen), Ekel m (vor dat)

distasteful [dɪs'testfəl] adj (unpleasant) (**to**) unangenehm (dat); (offensive) (**to**) ekelhaft (dat)

distemper [dɪs'tempər] s (of dogs) Staupe f; (paint) Temperafarbe f

distend [dɪs'tend] tr (swell) aufblähen; (extend) ausdehnen || intr (swell) anschwellen; (extend) (aus)dehnen

distension [dɪs'tenʃən] s Aufblähung f; Ausdehnung f

distill [dɪ'stɪl] tr destillieren; (e.g., whiskey) brennen

distillation [ˌdɪstɪ'leʃən] s Destillation f; (of whiskey) Brennen n

distiller [dɪs'tɪlər] s Brenner m

distillery [dɪs'tɪləri] s Brennerei f

distinct [dɪ'stɪŋkt] adj (clear) deutlich; (different) verschieden; as **d. from** zum Unterschied von; **keep d.** auseinanderhalten

distinction [dɪs'tɪŋkʃən] s (difference) Unterschied m; (differentiation) Unterscheidung f; (honor) Auszeichnung f; (eminence) Vornehmheit f; **have the d. of** (ger) den Vorzug haben zu (inf)

distinctive [dɪs'tɪŋktɪv] adj (distinguishing) unterscheidend; (characteristic) kennzeichnend

distinguish [dɪs'tɪŋwɪʃ] tr (differentiate) unterscheiden; (classify) einteilen; (honor) auszeichnen; (characterize) kennzeichnen; (discern) erkennen || intr (between) unterscheiden (zwischen dat)

distin'guished adj (eminent) prominent; (for) berühmt (wegen)

distort [dɪs'tort] tr verzerren; (the truth) entstellen; **distorted picture** Zerrbild n

distortion [dɪs'torʃən] s Verzerrung f; (of the truth) Entstellung f

distract [dɪ'strækt] tr ablenken

distraction [dɪ'strækʃən] s (diversion of attention) Ablenkung f; (entertainment) Zerstreuung f; **drive s.o. to d.** j-n zum Wahnsinn treiben

distraught [dɪ'strɔt] adj (bewildered) verwirrt; (deeply agitated) (**with**) aufgewühlt (von); (crazed) (**with**) rasend (vor dat)

distress [dɪ'stres] s (anxiety) Kummer m; (mental pain) Betrübnis f; (danger) Notstand m, Bedrängnis f; (naut) Seenot f || tr betrüben

distress'ing adj betrüblich

distress' sig'nal s Notzeichen n

distribute [dɪ'strɪbjut] tr verteilen; (divide) einteilen; (apportion) (jur) aufteilen

distribution [ˌdɪstrɪ'bjuʃən] s Verteilung f; (geographic range) Verbreitung f; (of films) Verleih m; (marketing) Vertrieb m; (of dividends) Ausschüttung f; (jur) Aufteilung f

distributor [dɪ'strɪbjətər] s Verteiler –in mf; (of films) Verleiher –in mf; (dealer) Lieferant –in mf; (aut) Verteiler m

distri'butorship' s Vertrieb m

district ['dɪstrɪkt] s Bezirk m

dis'trict attor'ney s Staatsanwalt m

distrust [dɪs'trʌst] s Mißtrauen n || tr mißtrauen (dat)

distrustful [dɪs'trʌstfəl] adj (**of**) mißtrauisch (gegen)

disturb [dɪs'tʌrb] tr stören; (disquiet) beunruhigen; **d. the peace** die öffentliche Ruhe stören

disturbance [dɪs'tʌrbəns] s (interruption) Störung f; (breach of peace) Unruhe f

disunited [ˌdɪsju'naɪtɪd] adj uneinig

disunity [dɪs'junti] s Uneinigkeit f

disuse [dɪs'jus] s Nichtverwendung f; **fall into d.** außer Gebrauch kommen

ditch [dɪtʃ] s Graben m || tr (discard) (sl) wegschmeißen; (aer) (coll) auf dem Wasser notlanden mit || intr (aer) (coll) notwassern

dither ['dɪðər] s—**be in a d.** verdattert sein

dit·to ['dɪto] adj (coll) dito || s (–tos) Kopie f || tr vervielfältigen

dit'to mark' s Wiederholungszeichen n

ditty ['dɪti] s Liedchen n

diva ['divə] s (mus) Diva f

divan [dɪ'væn], ['daɪvæn] s Diwan m

dive [daɪv] s Kopfsprung m; (coll) Spelunke f; (aer) Sturzflug m; (nav) Tauchen n; (sport) Kunstsprung m; **make a d. for** (fig) sich stürzen auf (acc) || v (pret & pp **dived** & **dove** [dov]) intr (submerge) tauchen; (plunge head first) e–n Kopfsprung machen; (aer) e–n Sturzflug machen; (nav) (unter)tauchen; (sport) e–n Kunstsprung machen

dive'-bomb' & intr im Sturzflug mit Bomben angreifen

dive' bomb'er s Sturzkampfbomber m

diver ['daɪvər] s Taucher –in mf; (orn) Taucher m; (sport) Kunstspringer –in mf

diverge [daɪ'vɑrdʒ] intr (said of roads, views) sich teilen; (from the norm) abweichen; (geom, phys) divergieren

diverse [daɪ'vʌrs] adj (different) verschieden; (of various kinds) vielförmig

diversi·fy [daɪ'vʌrsɪˌfaɪ] v (pret & pp –fied) tr abwechslungsreich gestalten

diversion [daɪ'vʌrʒən] s Ablenkung f; (recreation) Zeitvertreib m; (mil) Ablenkungsmanöver n

diversity [daɪ'vʌrsɪti] s Mannigfaltigkeit f

divert [daɪ'vʌrt] tr (attention) ablenken; (traffic) umleiten; (a river) ableiten; (money) abzweigen; (entertain) zerstreuen

divest [daɪ'vest] tr—**d. oneself of** sich entäußern (genit); **d. s.o. of** (e.g., office, power) j–n entkleiden (genit); (e.g., rights, property) j–m (seine Rechte, etc.) entziehen

divide [dɪ'vaɪd] s (geol) Wasserscheide f || tr teilen; (cause to disagree) entzweien; (math) (by) teilen (durch); **d. into** einteilen in (acc); **d. off** (a room) abteilen; **d. up** (among) aufteilen (unter acc) || intr (*said of a road*) sich teilen; **d. into** sich teilen in (*acc*)

dividend ['dɪvɪ‚dend] *s* Dividende *f*; (math) Dividend *m*; **pay dividends** Dividenden ausschütten; (fig) sich lohnen

divid/ing line/ *s* Trennungsstrich *m*

divination [‚dɪvɪ'neʃən] *s* Weissagung *f*

divine [dɪ'vaɪn] *adj* göttlich || *s* Geistlicher *m* || *tr* (er)ahnen

divine/ prov/idence *s* göttliche Vorsehung *f*

divine/ right/ of kings/ *s* Königtum *n* von Gottes Gnaden

div/ing *s* Tauchen *n* (sport) Kunstspringen *n*

div/ing bell/ *s* Taucherglocke *f*

div/ing board/ *s* Sprungbrett *n*

div/ing suit/ *s* Taucheranzug *m*

divin/ing rod/ *s* Wünschelrute *f*

divinity [dɪ'vɪnɪti] *s* (*divine nature*) Göttlichkeit *f*; (*deity*) Gottheit *f*

divisible [dɪ'vɪzɪbəl] *adj* teilbar

division [dɪ'vɪʒən] *s* Teilung *f*; (*dissention*) Uneinigkeit *f*; (adm) Abteilung *f*; (math, mil) Division *f*; (sport) Sportklasse *f*

divisor [dɪ'vaɪzər] *s* (math) Teiler *m*; Divisor *m*

divorce [dɪ'vors] *s* Scheidung *f*; **apply for a d.** die Scheidungsklage einreichen; **get a d.** sich scheiden lassen || *tr* (*said of a spouse*) sich scheiden lassen von; (*said of a judge*) scheiden; (*separate*) trennen

divorcee [dɪvor'si] *s* Geschiedene *f*

divulge [dɪ'vʌldʒ] *tr* ausplaudern

dizziness ['dɪzɪnɪs] *s* Schwindel *m*

dizzy ['dɪzi] *adj* schwindlig; (*causing dizziness*) schwindelerregend; (*mentally confused*) benommen; (*foolish*) damisch; (*feeling, spell*) Schwindel-

do [du] *v* (*3d pers* **does** [dʌz]; *pret* **did** [dɪd]; *pp* **done** [dʌn]; *ger* **doing** ['du‚ɪŋ]) *tr* tun, machen; (*damage*) anrichten; (*one's hair*) frisieren; (*an injustice*) antun; (*a favor, disservice*) erweisen; (*time in jail*) absitzen; (*miles per hour*) fahren; (*tour*) (coll) besichtigen; (Shakespeare, etc., *in class*) durchnehmen; **do duty as** dienen als; **do in** (sl) umbringen; **do over** (*with paint*) neu anstreichen; (*with covering*) neu überziehen; **what can I do for you?** womit kann ich dienen? || *intr* tun, machen; (*suffice*) genügen; **do away with** abschaffen; (*persons*) aus dem Wege räumen; **do away with oneself** sich [*dat*] das Leben nehmen; **do without** auskommen ohne; **I am doing well** es geht mir gut; (*financially*) ich verdiene gut; (*e.g., in history*) ich komme gut voran; **I'll make it** do ich werde schon damit auskommen; **nothing doing!** ausgeschlossen! **that will do!** genug davon! **that won't do!** das geht nicht! || *aux* used in English but not specifically expressed in German: 1) in questions, e.g., **do you speak German?** sprechen Sie deutsch?; 2) in negative sentences,

e.g., **I do not live here** ich wohne hier nicht; 3) for emphasis, e.g., **I do feel better** ich fühle mich wirklich besser; 4) in imperative entreaties, e.g., **do come again** besuchen Sie mich doch wieder!; 5) in elliptical sentences, e.g., **I like Berlin. So do I** Mir gefällt Berlin. Mir auch.; **he drinks, doesn't he?** er trinkt, nicht wahr?; 6) in inversions after adverbs such as hardly, rarely, scarcely, little, e.g., **little did she realize that...** sie hatte keine Ahnung, daß... || *impers*—**it doesn't do to** (*inf*) es ist unklug zu (*inf*); **it won't do you any good to stay here** es wird Ihnen nicht viel nützen, hier zu bleiben

docile ['dɑsɪl] *adj* gelehrig; (*easy to handle*) fügsam, lenksam

dock [dɑk] *s* Anlegeplatz *m*; (jur) Anklagebank *f*; **docks** Hafenanlagen *pl*; **in the d.** (jur) auf der Anklagebank || *tr* (*a ship, space vehicle*) docken; (*a tail*) stutzen; (*pay*) kürzen; **d. an employee (for)** e-m Arbeitnehmer den Lohn kürzen (um) || *intr* (naut) (*am Kai*) anlegen; (rok) docken, koppeln

docket ['dɑkɪt] *s* (*agenda*) Tagesordnung *f*; (jur) Prozeßliste *f*

dock/ hand/ *s* Hafenarbeiter *m*

dock/ing *s* (naut) Anlegen *n*; (rok) Andocken *n*

dock/ work/er *s* Dockarbeiter *m*

dock/yard/ *s* Werft *f*

doctor ['dɑktər] *s* Doktor *m*; (*physician*) Arzt *m*, Ärztin *f* || *tr* (*records*) frisieren; (*adapt, e.g., a play*) zurechtmachen || *intr* (coll) in ärztlicher Behandlung stehen

doctorate ['dɑktərɪt] *s* Doktorwürde *f*

doctrine ['dɑktrɪn] *s* Doktrin *f*, Lehre *f*

document ['dɑkjəmənt] *s* Urkunde *f* || ['dɑkjə‚ment] *tr* dokumentieren

documentary [‚dɑkjə'mentəri] *adj* dokumentarisch || *s* Dokumentarfilm *m*

documentation [‚dɑkjəmen'teʃən] *s* Dokumentation *f*

doddering ['dɑdərɪŋ] *adj* zittrig

dodge [dɑdʒ] *s* Winkelzug *m* || *tr* (*e.g., a blow*) ausweichen (*dat*); (*e.g., a responsibility*) sich drücken vor (*dat*) || *intr* ausweichen

do-do ['dodo] *s* (**-does** & **-dos**) (coll) Depp *m*

doe [do] *s* Rehgeiß *f*, Damhirschkuh *f*

doer ['du‚ər] *s* Täter –in *mf*

doe/skin/ *s* Rehleder *n*

doff [dɑf] *tr* (*a hat*) abnehmen; (*clothes*) ausziehen; (*habits*) ablegen

dog [dɔg] *s* Hund *m*; **dog eats dog** jeder für sich; **go to the dogs** (coll) vor die Hunde gehen; **lucky dog!** (coll) Glückspilz!; **put on the dog** (coll) großtun || *v* (*pret* & *pp* **dogged**; *ger* **dogging**) *tr* nachspüren (*dat*)

dog/ bis/cuit *s* Hundekuchen *m*

dog/ days/ *spl* Hundstage *pl*

dog/-eared/ *adj* mit Eselsohren

dog/face/ *s* (mil) Landser *m*

dog'fight' s (aer) Kurbelei f
dogged ['dɔgɪd] adj verbissen
doggerel ['dɔgərəl] s Knittelvers m
doggone ['dɔg'gɔn] adj (sl) verflixt
dog'house' s Hundehütte f; **in the d.** (fig) in Ungnade
dog'ken'nel s Hundezwinger m
dogma ['dɔgmə] s Dogma n
dogmatic [dɔg'mætɪk] adj dogmatisch
do-gooder ['du'gudər] s Humanitäts-apostel m
dog'show' s Hundeschau f
dog's'life' s Hundeleben n
Dog' Star' s Hundestern m
dog' tag' s Hundemarke f; (mil) Er-kennungsmarke f
dog'-tired' adj hundemüde
dog'wood' s Hartriegel m
doily ['dɔɪlɪ] s Zierdeckchen n
do'ing s (work) doings Tun und Trei-ben n; (events) Ereignisse pl
doldrums ['dɔldrəmz] spl Kalmengür-tel m; **in the d.** (fig) deprimiert
dole [dol] s Spende f; **be on the d.** stempeln gehen || tr—d. out verteilen
doleful ['dolfəl] adj trübselig
doll [dɑl] s Puppe f || tr—d. up (coll) aufdonnern || intr (coll) sich aufdon-nern
dollar ['dɑlər] s Dollar m
doll' car'riage s Puppenwagen m
dolly ['dɑlɪ] s Püppchen n; (cart) Schiebkarren m
dolphin ['dɑlfɪn] s Delphin m
dolt [dolt] s Tölpel m
domain [do'men] s (& fig) Domäne f
dome [dom] s Kuppel f
dome' light' s (aut) Deckenlicht n
domestic [də'mɛstɪk] adj (of the home) Haus-, häuslich, Haushalts-; (pro-duced at home) einheimisch, inlän-disch, Landes-; (tame) Haus-; (e.g., policy) Innen-, innere || s Hausange-stellte mf
domesticate [də'mɛstɪ,ket] tr zähmen
domicile ['dɑmɪ,saɪl] s Wohnsitz m
dominance ['dɑmɪnəns] s Vorherr-schaft f
dominant ['dɑmɪnənt] adj vorherr-schend; (factor) entscheidend
dominate ['dɑmɪ,net] tr beherrschen || intr (over) herrschen (über acc)
domination [,dɑmɪ'neʃən] s Beherr-schung f, Herrschaft f
domineer [,dɑmɪ'nɪr] tr & intr tyran-nisieren
domineer'ing adj tyrannisch
dominion [də'mɪnjən] s (sovereignty) (over) Gewalt f (über acc); (domain) Domäne f; (of British Empire) Do-minion n
domi·no ['dɑmɪ,no] s (-noes & nos) Dominostein m; dominoes ssg Do-minospiel n
don [dɑn] s Universitätsprofessor m || v (pret & pp donned; ger donning) tr anlegen; (a hat) sich [dat] auf-setzen
donate ['donet] tr schenken, spenden
donation [do'neʃən] s Schenkung f; (small contribution) Spende f
done [dʌn] adj erledigt; (culin) gar, fertig; **d. for** kaputt; **d. with** (com-

pleted) fertig; **get** (s.th.) **d.** fertigbe-kommen; **well d.** (culin) durchge-braten
donkey ['dʌŋki] s Esel m
donor ['donər] s Spender –in mf
doodad ['dudæd] s (gadget) Dings n; (decoration) Tand m
doodle ['dudəl] s Gekritzel n || tr be-kritzeln || intr kritzeln
doom [dum] s Verhängnis n || tr ver-dammen, verurteilen
doomed adj todgeweiht
doomsday ['dumz,de] s der Jüngste Tag
door [dor] s Tür f; **from d. to d.** von Haus zu Haus; **out of doors** draußen, im Freien; **show s.o. the d.** j–m die Tür weisen; **two doors away** zwei Häuser weiter
door'bell' s Türklingel f; **the d. is ring-ing** es klingelt
door'bell but'ton s Klingelknopf m
door'frame' s Türrahmen m
door'han'dle s Türgriff m, Türklinke f
door'jamb' s Türpfosten m
door'knob' s Türknopf m
door'man' s (–men') Portier m
door'mat' s Abtreter m, Türmatte f
door'nail' s—dead as a d. mausetot
door'post' s Türpfosten m
door'sill' s Türschwelle f
door'step' s Türstufe f
door'stop' s Türanschlag m
door'-to-door' sales'man s Hausierer m
door'-to-door sel'ling s Hausieren n
door'way' s Türöffnung f; (fig) Weg m
dope [dop] s (drug) (sl) Rauschgift n; (information) (sl) vertraulicher Tip m; (fool) (sl) Trottel m; (aer) Lack m || tr (a racehorse) (sl) dopen; (a person) (sl) betäuben, verdrogen; (aer) lackieren; **d. out** (sl) heraus-finden, ausarbeiten; **d. up** (sl) ver-drogen
dope' ad'dict s (sl) Rauschgiftsüchtige mf
dope' push'er s (sl) Rauschgiftschieber –in mf
dope'sheet' s (sl) vertraulicher Bericht m
dope' traf'fic s (sl) Rauschgifthandel m
dopey ['dopi] adj (dopier; dopiest) (sl) dämlich; (from sleep) (coll) schlaftrunken
dormant ['dɔrmənt] adj ruhend, un-tätig; (bot) in der Winterruhe
dormer ['dɔrmər] s Bodenfenster n; (the whole structure) Mansarde f
dor'mer win'dow s Bodenfenster n
dormitory ['dɔrmɪ,tori] s (building) Studentenheim n; (room) Schlafsaal m
dormouse ['dor,maus] s (mice [,mais]) Haselmaus f
dor'sal fin' ['dɔrsəl] s Rückenflosse f
dosage ['dosɪdʒ] s Dosierung f
dose [dos] s (& fig) Dosis f
dossier ['dɑsɪ,e] s Dossier m
dot [dɑt] s Punkt m, Tupfen m; **on the dot** auf die Sekunde; **three o'clock on the dot** Punkt drei Uhr || v (pret

& *pp* **dotted;** *ger* **dotting**) *tr* punktieren; tüpfeln; **dot one's i's den Punkt aufs i setzen;** *(fig)* übergenau sein

dotage ['dotɪdʒ] *s*—**be in one's d.** senil sein

dotard ['dotərd] *s* kindischer Greis *m*

dote [dot] *intr*—**d. on** vernarrt sein in *(acc)*

dot'ing *adj* **(on)** vernarrt (in *acc*)

dots' and dash'es *spl* (telg) Punkte und Striche *pl*

dot'ted *adj (pattern)* getüpfelt; *(with flowers, etc.)* übersät; *(line)* punktiert

double ['dʌbəl] *adj* doppelt || *s* Doppelte *n; (person)* Doppelgänger *m* (cin, theat) Double *n;* **doubles** (tennis) Doppel *n;* **on the d.** im Geschwindschritt || *tr* (ver)doppeln; *(the fist)* ballen; *(cards)* doppeln; (naut) umsegeln || *intr* sich verdoppeln; *(cards)* doppeln; **d. back um- kehren; d. up** with sich biegen vor *(dat)*

dou'ble-bar'reled *adj (gun)* doppelläufig; *(fig)* mit zweifacher Wirkung

dou'ble bass' [bes] *s* Kontrabaß *m*

dou'ble bed' *s* Doppelbett *n*

dou'ble-breast'ed *adj* doppelreihig

dou'ble chin' *s* Doppelkinn *n*

dou'ble cross' *s* Schwindel *m*

dou'ble-cross' *tr* beschwindeln

dou'ble-cross'er *s* Schwindler –in *mf*

dou'ble date' *s* Doppelrendezvous *n*

dou'ble-deal'er *s* Betrüger –in *mf*

dou'ble-deal'ing *s* Doppelzüngigkeit *f*

dou'ble-deck'er *s (ship, bus)* Doppeldecker *m; (sandwich)* Doppelsandwich *n; (bed)* Etagenbett *n*

dou'ble-edged' *adj* *(& fig)* zweischneidig

double entendre ['dʌbələn'tɑndrə] *s (ambiguity)* Doppelsinn *m; (ambiguous term)* doppelsinniger Ausdruck *m*

dou'ble en'try *s* (com) doppelte Buchführung *f*

dou'ble expo'sure *s* Doppelbelichtung *f*

dou'ble fea'ture *s* Doppelprogramm *n*

dou'blehead'er *s* Doppelspiel *n*

dou'ble-joint'ed *adj* mit Gummigelenken

dou'blepark' *tr & intr* falsch parken

dou'ble-spaced' *adj* mit doppeltem Zeilenabstand

dou'ble stand'ard *s* zweierlei Maß *n*

doublet ['dʌblɪt] *s (duplicate; counterfeit stone)* Dublette *f;* (hist) Wams *m;* (ling) Doppelform *f*

dou'ble take' *s* (fig) Spätzündung *f*

dou'ble-talk' *s* zweideutige Rede *f*

dou'ble time' *s (wage rate)* doppelter Lohn *m;* (mil) Eilschritt *m*

dou'ble track' *s* (rr) doppelgleisige Bahnlinie *f*

doubly ['dʌblɪ] *adv* doppelt

doubt [daut] *s* Zweifel *m;* **be still in d.** *(said of things)* noch zweifelhaft sein; **beyond d.** ohne (jeden) Zweifel; **in case of d.** im Zweifelsfalle; **no d.** zweifellos; **raise doubts** Bedenken

erregen; **there is no d. that** es unterliegt keinem Zweifel, daß || *tr* bezweifeln || *intr* zweifeln

doubter ['dautər] *s* Zweifler –in *mf*

doubtful ['dautfəl] *adj* zweifelhaft

doubtless ['dautlɪs] *adj & adv* zweifellos

douche [duʃ] *s (device)* Irrigator *m; (act of cleansing)* Spülung *f* || *tr & intr* spülen

dough [do] *s* Teig *m;* (sl) Pinke *f*

dough'boy' *s* (sl) Landser *m*

dough'nut' *s* Krapfen *m*

doughty ['dauti] *adj* wacker

doughy ['do·i] *adj* teigig

dour [daur], [dur] *adj* mürrisch

douse [daus] *tr* eintauchen; **(with)** übergießen mit; *(a fire)* auslöschen

dove [dʌv] *s (& pol)* Taube *f*

dovecote ['dʌv‚kot] *s* Taubenschlag *m*

dove'tail' *s* (carp) Schwalbenschwanz *m* || *tr* verzinken; (fig) ineinanderfügen || *intr* ineinanderpassen

dowager ['dau·ədʒər] *s* Witwe *f* (von Stand); (coll) Matrone *f*

dowdy ['daudi] *adj* schlampig

dow•el ['dau·əl] *s* Dübel *m* || *v (pret & pp* -el[l]ed; *ger* -el[l]ing) *tr* (ein)dübeln

down [daun] *adj (prices)* gesunken; *(sun)* untergegangen; **be d. for** vorgemerkt sein für; **be d. on s.o.** auf j-m herumtrampeln; **be d. three points** (sport) drei Punkte zurück sein; **be d. with a cold** mit e-r Erkältung im Bett liegen; **d. and out** völlig erledigt; **d. in the mouth** niedergedrückt || *adv* herunter, hinunter; **d. from** von...herab; **d. there** da unten; **d. to** bis hinunter zu; **d. to the last man** bis zum letzten Mann; **d. with...!** nieder mit...! || *s (of fowl)* Daune *f; (fine hair)* Flaum *m;* **downs** grasbedecktes Hügelland *n* || *prep* (postpositive) *(acc)* herunter, hinunter; **a little way d. the road** etwas weiter auf der Straße; **d. the river** flußabwärts || *tr* niederschlagen; *(a glass of beer)* (coll) hinunterstürzen; (aer) abschießen

down'cast' *adj* niedergeschlagen

down'draft' *s* Abwind *m,* Fallwind *m*

down'fall' *s* Untergang *m*

down'grade' *s* Gefälle *n;* **on the d.** (fig) im Niedergang || *tr* herabsetzen; niedriger einstufen

down'heart'ed *adj* niedergeschlagen

down'hill' *adj* bergabgehend; *(in skiing)* Abfahrts– || *adv* bergab; **he's going d.** (coll) mit ihm geht es abwärts

down' pay'ment *s* Anzahlung *f*

down'pour' *s* Regenguß *m,* Sturzregen *m*

down'right' *adj* ausgesprochen; *(lie)* glatt; *(contradiction)* schroff || *adv* ausgesprochen

down'spout' *s* Fallrohr *n*

down'stairs' *adj* unten befindlich || *adv (position)* unten; *(direction)* nach unten

down'stream' *adv* stromabwärts

down′stroke′ s (*in writing*) Grundstrich m; (*of a piston*) Abwärtshub m
down′-the-line′ adj vorbehaltlos
down-to-earth′ adj nüchtern
down′town′ adj im Geschäftsviertel gelegen ‖ adv (*position*) im Geschäftsviertel; (*direction*) ins Geschäftsviertel, in die Stadt ‖ s Geschäftsviertel n
down′trend′ s Baissestimmung f
downtrodden [′daʊn͵trɑdən] adj unterdrückt
downward [′daʊnwərd] adj Abwärts- ‖ adv abwärts
downwards [′daʊnwərdz] adv abwärts
downy [′daʊni] adj flaumig; (*soft*) weich wie Flaum
dowry [′daʊri] s Mitgift f
dowser [′daʊzər] s (*rod*) Wünschelrute f; (*person*) Wünschelrutengänger m
doze [doz] s Schläfchen n ‖ intr dösen
dozen [′dʌzən] s Dutzend n; **a d. times** dutzendmal
Dr. abbr (**Doctor**) Dr.; (*in addresses:* **Drive**) Str.
drab [dræb] adj (**drabber; drabbest**) graubraun; (fig) trüb
drach·ma [′drækmə] s (**-mas & -mae** [mi]) Drachme f
draft [dræft] s (*of air; drink*) Zug m; (*sketch*) Entwurf m; (fin) Tratte f; (mil) Einberufung f; **on d.** vom Faß ‖ tr (*sketch*) entwerfen, abfassen; (mil) einberufen
draft′ age′ s wehrpflichtiges Alter n
draft′ beer′ s Schankbier n
draft′ board′ s Wehrmeldeamt n
draft′ dodg′er [′dɑdʒər] s Drückeberger m
draftee [͵dræf′ti] s Dienstpflichtige mf
draft′ing s (*of a document*) Abfassung f; (*mechanical drawing*) Zeichnen n; (mil) Aushebung f
draft′ing board′ s Zeichenbrett n
draft′ing room′ s Zeichenbüro n
drafts·man [′dræftsmən] s (**-men**) Zeichner m
drafty [′dræfti] adj zugig
drag [dræg] s (*sledge*) Lastschlitten m; (*in smoking*) (coll) Zug m; (*boring person*) langweiliger Mensch m; (s.th. *tedious*) etwas langweiliges; (*encumbrance*) (on) Hemmschuh m (für); (aer) Luftwiderstand m; (*for recovering objects*) (naut) Schleppnetz n; (*for retarding motion*) (naut) Schleppanker m ‖ v (pret & pp **dragged;** ger **dragging**) tr schleppen, schleifen; **d. one's feet** schlurfen; (fig) sich [*dat*] Zeit lassen; **d. out** dahinschleppen; (*protract*) verschleppen; **d. through the mud** (fig) in den Schmutz zerren; **d. up** (fig) aufwärmen ‖ intr schleppen; (*said of a long dress, etc.*) schleifen; (*said of time*) dahinschleichen; **d. on** (*be prolonged*) sich hinziehen
drag′net′ s Schleppnetz n
dragon [′drægən] s Drache m
drag′onfly′ s Libelle f

dragoon [drə′gun] s Dragoner m ‖ tr (*coerce*) zwingen
drag′ race′ s Straßenrennen n; (sport) Kurzstreckenrennen n
drain [dren] s (*sewer*) Kanal m; (*under a sink*) Abfluß m; (*genit*) Belastung f; (surg) Drain m; **down the d.** (fig) zum Fenster hinaus ‖ tr (*land*) entwässern; (*water*) ableiten; (*a cup, glass*) austrinken; (fig) verzehren ‖ intr ablaufen; (culin) abtropfen
drainage [′drenidʒ] s Ableitung f; (*e.g., of land*) Entwässerung f; (surg) Drainage f
drain′age ditch′ s Abflußgraben m
drain′ cock′ s Entleerungshahn m
drain′pipe′ s Abflußrohr n
drain′ plug′ s Abflußstöpsel m
drake [drek] s Enterich m
dram [dræm] s Dram n
drama [′drɑmə] s Drama n; (*art and genre*) Dramatik f
dra′ma crit′ic s Theaterkritiker –in mf
dramatic [drə′mætɪk] adj dramatisch ‖ **dramatics** s Dramatik f; spl (pej) Schauspielerei f
dramatist [′dræmətɪst] s Dramatiker –in mf
dramatize [′dræmə͵taɪz] tr dramatisieren
drape [drep] s Vorhang m; (*hang of a drape or skirt*) Faltenwurf m ‖ tr drapieren
drapery [′drepəri] s Vorhänge pl
dra′pery mate′rial s Vorhangstoff m
drastic [′dræstɪk] adj drastisch
draught [dræft] s & tr var of **draft**
draw [drɔ] s (*in a lottery*) Ziehen n; (*that which attracts*) Schlager m; (*power of attraction*) Anziehungskraft f; **end in a d.** unentschieden ausgehen ‖ v (pret **drew** [dru]; pp **drawn** [drɔn]) tr (*pictures*) zeichnen; (*a line, comparison, parallel, conclusion, lots, winner, sword, wagon*) ziehen; (*a crowd*) anlocken; (*a distinction*) machen; (*blood*) vergießen; (*curtains*) zuziehen; (*a check*) ausstellen; (*water*) schöpfen; (*cards*) nehmen; (*rations*) (mil) in Empfang nehmen; **d. a blank** (coll) e-e Niete ziehen; **d. aside** beiseiteziehen; **d. attention to die** Aufmerksamkeit lenken auf (acc); **d. into** (e.g., *an argument*) hineinziehen in (acc); **d. lots for** losen um; **d. out** (*protract*) in die Länge ziehen; (*money from a bank*) abheben; **d. s.o. out** j-n ausholen; **d. the line** (fig) e-e Grenze ziehen; **d. up** (*a document*) verfassen; (*plans*) entwerfen ‖ intr ziehen; **d. away** sich entfernen; **d. back** sich zurückziehen; **d. near** herannahen; **d. on** zurückgreifen auf (acc); **d. to a close** sich dem Ende zuneigen
draw′back′ s Nachteil m
draw′bridge′ s Zugbrücke f
drawee [drɔ′i] s Trassat –in mf
drawer [′drɔ·ər] s Zeichner –in mf; (com) Trassant –in m ‖ [drɔr] s Schublade f; **drawers** Unterhose f
draw′ing s (*of pictures*) Zeichnen n;

(*picture*) Zeichnung *f*; (*in a lottery*) Ziehung *f*, Verlosung *f*
draw'ing board' *s* Reißbrett *n*
draw'ing card' *s* Zugnummer *f*
draw'ing room' *s* Empfangszimmer *n*
drawl [drɔl] *s* gedehntes Sprechen *n* || *intr* gedehnt sprechen
drawn [drɔn] *adj* (*face*) (**with**) verzerrt (vor *dat*); (*sword*) blank
dray [dre] *s* niedriger Rollwagen *m*; (*sledge*) Schleife *f*
dread [drɛd] *adj* furchtbar || *s* Furcht *f* || *tr* fürchten
dreadful ['drɛdfəl] *adj* furchtbar
dream [drim] *s* Traum *m*; (*aspiration, ambition*) Wunschtraum *m*; (*ideal*) (*coll*) Gedicht *n* || *v* (*pret & pp* **dreamed & dreamt** [drɛmt]) *tr* träumen; **d. away** verträumen; **d. up** zusammenträumen || *intr* träumen; **d. of** (*long for*) sich [*dat*] entträumen; **I dreamt of her** mir träumte von ihr
dreamer ['drimər] *s* Träumer –in *mf*
dream'land' *s* Traumland *n*
dream'-like' *adj* traumhaft
dream'world' *s* Traumwelt *f*
dreamy ['drimɪ] *adj* (*place*) verträumt; (*eyes*) träumerisch
dreary ['drɪrɪ] *adj* trüb, trist
dredge [drɛdʒ] *s* Bagger *m* || *tr* (aus-) baggern || *intr* baggern
dredger ['drɛdʒər] *s* Bagger *m*
dredg'ing *s* Baggern *n*
dregs [drɛgz] *spl* Bodensatz *m*; (*of society*) Abschaum *m*, Auswurf *m*
drench [drɛntʃ] *tr* durchnässen
Dres'den chi'na ['drɛzdən] *s* Meißner Porzellan *n*
dress [drɛs] *s* Kleidung *f*; (*woman's dress*) Kleid *n* || *tr* anziehen; (*a store window*) dekorieren; (*skins*) gerben; (*a salad, goose, chicken*) zubereiten; (*vines*) beschneiden; (*stones*) behauen; (*ore*) aufbereiten; (*wounds*) verbinden; (*hair*) frisieren; (*tex*) appretieren; **d. down** (*coll*) ausschimpfen; **d. ranks** die Glieder ausrichten; **get dressed** sich anziehen || *intr* sich anziehen; **d. up** sich fein machen
dress' affair' *s* Galaveranstaltung *f*
dresser ['drɛsər] *s* Frisierkommode *f*; **be a good d.** sich gut kleiden
dress'ing *s* (*stuffing for fowl*) Füllung *f*; (*for salad*) Soße *f*; (*surg*) Verband *m*
dress'ing down' *s* Gardinenpredigt *f*
dress'ing room' *s* Umkleideraum *m*; (*theat*) Garderobe *f*
dress'ing sta'tion *s* Verbandsplatz *m*
dress'ing ta'ble *s* Frisierkommode *f*
dress'mak'er *s* Schneiderin *f*
dress'mak'ing *s* Modenschneiderei *f*
dress' rehear'sal *s* Kostümprobe *f*
dress' shirt' *s* Frackhemd *n*
dress' shop' *s* Modenhaus *n*, Modengeschäft *n*
dress' suit' *s* Frackanzug *m*, Frack *m*
dress' un'iform *s* Paradeuniform *f*
dressy ['drɛsɪ] *adj* (*showy*) geschniegelt; (*stylish*) modisch; (*for formal affairs*) elegant
dribble ['drɪbəl] *s* (*trickle*) Getröpfel

n; (*sport*) Dribbeln *n* || *tr & intr* tröpfeln; (*sport*) dribbeln
driblet ['drɪblɪt] *s* Bißchen *n*
dried [draɪd] *adj* Trocken–, Dörr–
dried' beef' *s* Dörrfleisch *n*
dried' fruit' *s* Dörrobst *n*
dried'-up' *adj* ausgetrocknet, verdorrt
drier ['draɪ·ər] *s* Trockner *m*; (*for the hair*) Haartrockenhaube *f*; (*hand model*) Fön *m*
drift [drɪft] *s* (*of sand, snow*) Wehe *f*; (*tendency*) Richtung *f*, Neigung *f*; (*intent*) Absicht *f*; (*meaning*) Sinn *m*; (aer, naut, rad) Abtrift *f*; (*flow of the ocean current*) (naut) Drift *f* || *intr* (*said of sand, snow*) sich anhäufen; (*said of a boat*) treiben; **d. away** (*said of sounds*) verwehen; (*said of a crowd*) sich verlaufen; **d. shut** verweht werden
drifter ['drɪftər] *s* zielloser Mensch *m*
drift' ice' *s* Treibeis *n*
drift'wood' *s* Treibholz *n*
drill [drɪl] *s* (*tool*) Bohrer *m*; (*exercise*) Drill *m*; (tex) Drillich *m* || *tr* bohren; (*exercise*) drillen; **d. s.th. into s.o.** j–m etw einpauken || *intr* bohren; (*exercise*) drillen
drill'mas'ter *s* (mil) Ausbilder *m*
drill' press' *s* Bohrpresse *f*
drink [drɪŋk] *s* Trunk *m* || *v* (*pret* **drank** [dræŋk]; *pp* **drunk** [drʌŋk]) *tr* trinken; (*said of animals*) saufen; (pej) saufen; **d. away** (*money*) versaufen; **d. down** hinunterkippen; **d. in** (*air*) einschlürfen; (*s.o.'s words*) verschlingen || *intr* trinken; (*excessively*) saufen; **d. to** trinken auf (*acc*); **d. up** austrinken
drinkable ['drɪŋkəbəl] *adj* trinkbar
drinker ['drɪŋkər] *s* Trinker –in *mf*; **heavy drinker** Zecher –in *mf*
drink'ing foun'tain *s* Trinkbrunnen *m*
drink'ing par'ty *s* Zechgelage *n*
drink'ing song' *s* Trinklied *n*
drink'ing straw' *s* Strohhalm *m*
drink'ing trough' *s* Viehtränke *f*
drink'ing wa'ter *s* Trinkwasser *n*
drip [drɪp] *s* Tröpfeln *n* || *v* (*pret & pp* **dripped**; *ger* **dripping**) *tr & intr* tröpfeln
drip' cof'fee *s* Filterkaffee *m*
drip'-dry' *adj* bügelfrei
drip' pan' *s* Bratpfanne *f*
drip'pings *spl* Bratenfett *n*
drive [draɪv] *s* (*in a car*) Fahrt *f*; (*road*) Fahrweg *m*; (*energy*) Schwungkraft *f*; (*inner urge*) Antrieb *m*; (*campaign*) Aktion *f*; (*for raising money*) Spendeaktion *f*; (*golf*) Treibschlag *m*; (*mach*) Antrieb *m*; (mil) Vorstoß *m*; (*tennis*) Treibschlag *m*; **go for a d.** spazierenfahren || *v* (*pret* **drove** [drov]; *pp* **driven** ['drɪvən]) *tr* (*a car, etc.*) fahren; (*e.g., cattle*) treiben; (*a tunnel*) vortreiben; **d. a hard bargain** zäh um den Preis feilschen; **d. away** abtreiben; **d.** (*oneself, a horse*) hard abjagen; **d. home** nahebringen; **d. in** (*a nail*) einschlagen; **d. off course** (naut) verschlagen; **d. on** antreiben; **d. out** austreiben; **d. s.o. to** (*inf*) j–n–

dazu bringen zu (inf); **d. to despair** zur Verzweiflung treiben ‖ *intr* fahren; **d. along** mitfahren; **d. at** abzielen auf (acc); **d. away** wegfahren; **d. by** vorbeifahren an (dat); **d. in** einfahren; **d. on** weiterfahren; **d. out** herausfahren; **d. up** anfahren

drive′ belt′ s Treibriemen m

drive′-in′ s Autorestaurant n; (cin) Autokino n

driv•el [′drɪvəl] s (slobber) Geifer m; (nonsense) Faselei f ‖ v (pret & pp **-el[l]ed;** ger **-el[l]ing**) intr sabbern; (fig) faseln

driver [′draɪvər] s (of a car) Fahrer –in mf; (of a locomotive, streetcar) Führer m; (golf) Treibschläger m; (mach) Treibhammer m

driv′er's li′cense s Führerschein m

drive′ shaft′ s Antriebswelle f

drive′way′ s Einfahrt f

drive′-yourself′ serv′ice s Autovermietung f an Selbstfahrer

driv′ing adj (rain) stürmisch ‖ s (aut) Steuerung f

driv′ing instruc′tor s Fahrlehrer –in mf

driv′ing les′son s Fahrstunde f

driv′ing school′ s Autofahrschule f

drizzle [′drɪzəl] s (of a car) Nieselregen m ‖ impers—**it is drizzling** es nieselt

droll [drol] adj drollig

dromedary [′drɑmə‚derɪ] s Dromedar n

drone [dron] s (bee; loafer) Drohne f; (buzz) Gesumme n; (monotonous speech) Geleier n ‖ tr (e.g., prayers) leiern ‖ intr summen; (fig) leiern

drool [drul] intr sabbern

droop [drup] s Herabhängen n; (stoop) gebeugte Haltung f ‖ intr herabhängen; (said of flowers) zu welken beginnen; (fig) den Kopf hängen lassen

droopy [′drupɪ] adj (saggy) schlaff herabhängend; (dejected) mutlos; (shoulders) abfallend; (flowers) welkend

drop [drɑp] s (of liquid) Tropfen m; (candy) Fruchtbonbon m & n; (golf) Fall m; (height differential) Gefälle n; (reduction) Abnahme f; (in prices) Rückgang m; (in temperature) Sturz m; (of bombs or supplies) Abwurf m; (of paratroopers) Absprung m; **a fifty-meter d.** ein Fall m aus e-r Höhe von fünfzig Metern; **d. by d.** tropfenweise; **d. in the bucket** Tropfen m auf e-n heißen Stein ‖ v (pret & pp **dropped;** ger **dropping**) tr (let fall) fallenlassen; (bombs, supplies) abwerfen; (a subject, remarks, hints) fallenlassen; (the eyes, voice) senken; (anchor; young of animals) werfen; (money in gambling) (sl) verlieren; (terminate) einstellen; (from membership roll) ausschließen; (paratroopers) absetzen; **d. it!** laß das!; **d. s.o. a line** j–m ein paar Zeilen schreiben ‖ intr fallen; (drip) tropfen; (said of prices, temperature) sinken, fallen; (keel over) umfallen; (said of a curtain) niedergehen; **d. behind** zurück-

fallen; **d. dead!** (sl) laß dich begraben!; **d. in on s.o.** auf e-n Sprung bei j–m vorbeikommen; **d. off to sleep** einschlafen; **d. out** sich zurückziehen; (sport) ausscheiden; **d. out of school** von der Schule abgehen

drop′ ar′ea s (aer) Abwurfraum m

drop′ cur′tain s (bemalter) Vorhang m

drop′ ham′mer s Fallhammer m

drop′-leaf ta′ble s Tisch m mit herunterklappbaren Flügeln

drop′light′ s Hängelampe f

drop′out′ s Gescheiterte mf; (educ) Abgänger –in mf

dropper [′drɑpər] s (med) Tropfer m

drop′ping adj (prices) rückgängig ‖ s (of bombs, supplies) Abwurf m; **droppings** tierischer Kot m

dropsy [′drɑpsɪ] s Wassersucht f

drop′ ta′ble s Klapptisch m

dross [drɔs] s (slag) Schlacke f; (waste) Abfall m

drought [draut] s Dürre f

drove [drov] s Herde f

drown [draun] tr (& fig) ertränken; **d. out** übertönen ‖ intr ertrinken

drowse [drauz] intr dösen

drowsiness [′drauzɪnɪs] s Schläfrigkeit f

drowsy [′drauzɪ] adj schläfrig, dösig

drub [drʌb] v (pret & pp **drubbed;** ger **drubbing**) tr (flog) verprügeln; (sport) entscheidend schlagen

drudge [drʌdʒ] s Packesel m ‖ intr sich placken, schuften

drudgery [′drʌdʒərɪ] s Plackerei f

drug [drʌg] s Droge f, Arznei f; (narcotic) Betäubungsmittel n; (addictive narcotic) Rauschgift n ‖ v (pret & pp **drugged;** ger **drugging**) tr betäuben

drug′ ad′dict s Rauschgiftsüchtige mf

drug′ addic′tion s Rauschgiftsucht f

druggist [′drʌgɪst] s Apotheker –in mf

drug′store′ s Apotheke f, Drogerie f

drug′ traf′fic s Rauschgifthandel m

druid [′dru·ɪd] s Druide m

drum [drʌm] s (musical instrument; container) Trommel f ‖ v (pret & pp **drummed;** ger **drumming**) tr trommeln; **d. s.th. into s.o.** j–m etw einpauken; **d. the table** auf den Tisch trommeln; **d. up** zusammentrommeln ‖ intr trommeln

drum′ and bu′gle corps′ s Musikzug m

drum′beat′ s Trommelschlag m

drum′fire′ s (mil) Trommelfeuer n

drum′head′ s Trommelfell n

drum′ ma′jor s Tambourmajor m

drum′ majorette′ s Tambourmajorin f

drummer [′drʌmər] s Trommler –in mf

drum′stick′ s Trommelschlegel m; (culin) Unterschenkel m

drunk [drʌŋk] adj betrunken ‖ s Säufer –in mf

drunkard [′drʌŋkərd] s Trunkenbold m

drunken [′drʌŋkən] adj betrunken

dry [draɪ] adj trocken; (boring) trokken; (wine) herb; (thirsty) durstig; (rainless) regenarm; (wood) dürr ‖ v (pret & pp **-dried**) tr (ab)trocknen;

(*e.g., fruit*) dörren; **dry off** abtrocknen; **dry out** austrocknen; **dry up** austrocknen; (fig) erschöpfen ‖ *intr* trocknen; **dry out** austrocknen; **dry up** vertrocknen; (*said of grass, flowers*) verdorren; (fig) versiegen; (*keep quiet*) (sl) die Klappe halten

dry' bat'tery s Trockenbatterie *f*

dry'.cell' s Tockenelement *n*

dry'-clean' *tr* (*chemically*) reinigen

dry' clean'er's s Reinigungsanstalt *f*

dry' clean'ing s chemische Reinigung *f*

dry' dock' s Trockendock *n*

dry'-eyed' *adj* ungerührt

dry' goods' *spl* Schnittwaren *pl*

dry' ice' s Trockeneis *n*

dry' land' s fester Boden *m*

dry' meas'ure s Trockenmaß *n*

dryness ['draɪnɪs] s Trockenheit *f*, Dürre *f*; (fig) Nüchternheit *f*

dry' nurse' s Säuglingsschwester *f*

dry' rot' s Trockenfäule *f*

dry' run' s Vorübung *f*; (*test run*) Probelauf *m*; (*with blank ammunition*) Zielübung *f*

dry' sea'son s Trockenzeit *f*

dual ['d(j)u·əl] *adj* Zwei-, doppelt; (tech) Doppel-

dualism ['d(j)u·ə‚lɪzəm] s Dualismus *m*

du'al-pur'pose *adj* e-m doppelten Zweck dienend

dub [dʌb] *v* (*pret & pp* **dubbed;** *ger* **dubbing**) *tr* (*nickname*) betiteln; (cin) synchronisieren; (golf) schlecht treffen; (hist) zum Ritter schlagen

dub'bing s (cin) Synchronisierung *f*

dubious ['d(j)ubɪ·əs] *adj* zweifelhaft

ducal ['d(j)ukəl] *adj* herzoglich

duchess ['dʌtʃɪs] s Herzogin *f*

duchy ['dʌtʃɪ] s Herzogtum *n*

duck [dʌk] s Ente *f* ‖ *tr* (*the head*) ducken; (*in water*) (unter)tauchen; (*evade*) sich drücken vor (*dat*) ‖ *intr* ducken; (*go under the surface*) untertauchen

duck'ing s—give s.o. a d. j-n untertauchen

duck' pond' s Ententeich *m*

duck' soup' s (sl) Kinderspiel *n*

ducky ['dʌki] *adj* (coll) nett, lieb

duct [dʌkt] s Rohr *n*, Kanal *m*, Leitung *f*; (anat, elec) Kanal *m*

duct'less gland' ['dʌktlɪs] s endokrine Drüse *f*

duct'work' s Rohrleitungen *pl*

dud [dʌd] s (sl & mil) Versager *m*, Blindgänger *m*; **duds** (coll) Klamotten *pl*

dude [d(j)ud] s (*dandy*) Geck *m*

dude' ranch' s Vergnügungsfarm *f*

due [d(j)u] *adj* (*payment; bus, train*) fällig; (*proper*) gehörig; (*consideration*) reiflich; **be due to** (*as a cause*) beruhen auf (*dat*); (*said of an honor*) gebühren (*dat*); (*said of money*) zustehen (*dat*); **be due to** (*inf*) sollen, müssen; **in due course** im gegebenen Moment; **in due time** zur rechten Zeit ‖ *adv* (naut) genau ‖ *s—***dues** Beitrag *m*; **get one's due** nach Verdienst behandelt werden; **give every-**

one his **due** jedem geben, was ihm gebührt

due' date' s (*of a payment*) Termin *m*

duel ['d(j)u·əl] s Duell *n*; **fight a d.** sich duellieren ‖ *v* (*pret & pp* **duel[l]ed;** *ger* **duel[l]ing**) *intr* sich duellieren

dues-paying ['d(j)uz‚pe·ɪŋ] *adj* beitragzahlend

duet [d(j)u·'ɛt] s Duett *n*

due' to' *prep* wegen (*genit*)

duf'fle bag' ['dʌfəl] s (mil) Kleidersack *m*

dug'out' s (*boat*) Einbaum *m*; (baseball, mil) Unterstand *m*

duke [d(j)uk] s Herzog *m*

dukedom ['d(j)ukdəm] s Herzogtum *n*

dull [dʌl] *adj* (*not sharp*) stumpf; (*pain*) dumpf; (*not shining*) glanzlos, matt; (*uninteresting*) nüchtern, geistlos; (*stupid*) stumpfsinnig; (com) flau ‖ *tr* stumpf machen; (fig) abstumpfen ‖ *intr* stumpf werden; (fig) abstumpfen

dullard ['dʌlərd] s Dummkopf *m*

dullness ['dʌlnɪs] s (*of a blade*) Stumpfheit *f*; (*of color*) Mattheit *f*; (*of a speech, etc.*) Stumpfsinn *m*

duly ['d(j)uli] *adv* ordnungsgemäß

dumb [dʌmb] *adj* stumm; (*stupid*) dumm ‖ *adv*—**play d.** sich unwissend stellen

dumb'bell' s Hantel *f*; (sl) Dummkopf *m*

dumbstruck ['dʌm‚strʌk] *adj* wie auf den Mund geschlagen

dumb' wait'er s (*elevator*) Speiseaufzug *m*; (*serving table*) Serviertisch *m*

dumdum ['dʌm‚dʌm] s Dumdumgeschoß *n*

dummy ['dʌmi] *adj* (*not real*) Schein-; (mil) blind, Übungs- ‖ s (*representation for display*) Attrappe *f*; (*clothes form*) Schneiderpuppe *f*; (*dolt*) Ölgötze *m*; (cards) Strohmann *m*; (mil) Übungspatrone *f*; (typ) Blindband *m*

dump [dʌmp] s (*trash heap*) Schuttabladeplatz *m*; (sl) Bude *f*; (mil) Lager *n*; **be down in the dumps** (coll) Trübsal blasen ‖ *tr* (aus)kippen; (*fling down*) hinplumpsen; (*garbage*) abladen; (com) verschleudern; **be dumped** (*be fired*) entlassen werden; **no dumping** (*public sign*) Schuttabladen verboten

dumpling ['dʌmplɪŋ] s Kloß *m*, Knödel *m*

dump' truck' s Kipper *m*

dumpy ['dʌmpi] *adj* rundlich

dun [dʌn] *adj* schwarzbraun ‖ *v* (*pret & pp* **dunned;** *ger* **dunning**) *tr* drängen

dunce [dʌns] s Schwachkopf *m*

dunce' cap' s Narrenkappe *f*

dune [d(j)un] s Düne *f*

dung [dʌŋ] s Dung *m*, Mist *m* ‖ *tr* düngen

dungarees [‚dʌŋgə'riz] *spl* Drillichhose *f*, Drillichanzug *m*

dungeon ['dʌndʒən] s Verlies *n*; (hist) Bergfried *m*

dung'hill' s Düngerhaufen m
dunk [dʌŋk] tr eintunken
duo ['d(j)u·o] s (duet) Duett n; (a pair) Duo n
duode·num [,d(j)u·ə'dinəm] s (-na [nə]) Zwölffingerdarm m
dupe [d(j)up] s Düpierte mf || tr düpieren, übertölpeln
duplex ['d(j)upleks] s Doppelhaus n
duplicate ['d(j)uplɪkɪt] adj Duplikat–; (parts) Ersatz–; **d. key** Nachschlüssel m || s Duplikat n, Abschrift f; **in d.** abschriftlich || ['d(j)uplɪ,ket] tr (make a copy of) kopieren; (make many copies of) vervielfältigen; (reproduce by writing) abschreiben; (repeat) wiederholen; (perform again) nachmachen
duplication [,d(j)uplɪ'keʃən] s Vervielfältigung f
duplicator ['d(j)uplɪ,ketər] s Vervielfältigungsapparat m
duplicity [d(j)u'plɪsɪti] s Duplizität f
durable ['d(j)urəbəl] adj dauerhaft
duration [d(j)u'reʃən] s Dauer f
duress ['d(j)ures] s (jur) Nötigung f
during ['d(j)urɪŋ] prep während (genit), bei (dat); **d. the meal** bei Tisch; **d. the day** tagsüber
dusk [dʌsk] s Abenddämmerung f
dust [dʌst] s Staub m; **cover with d.** bestauben; **make d.** stauben || tr (free of dust) abstauben; (sprinkle, spray with insecticides) bestäuben
dust' bowl' s Staubsturmgebiet n
dust' cloth' s Staubtuch n
dust' collec'tor s Staubfänger m
duster ['dʌstər] s (feather duster) Staubwedel m; (for insecticides) Zerstäuber m
dust'ing pow'der s Streupulver n
dust' jac'ket s Schutzumschlag m
dust' mop' s Mop m
dust'pan' s Kehrichtschaufel f
dust'proof' adj staubdicht
dust' rag' s Staublappen m
dusty ['dʌsti] adj staubig
Dutch [dʌtʃ] adj niederländisch; **go D.** (coll) getrennt bezahlen || s (language) Niederländisch n; **in D.** (coll)

in der Patsche; **the D.** die Niederländer
Dutch'man s (-men) Niederländer m
Dutch' treat' s (coll) Beisammensein n bei getrennter Kasse
dutiable ['d(j)utɪ·əbəl] adj steuerpflichtig
dutiful ['d(j)utɪfəl] adj pflichtgetreu
duty ['d(j)uti] s (to) Pflicht f (gegenüber dat); (service) Dienst m; (task) Aufgabe f; (tax) Zoll m, Abgabe f; **be in d. bound to** (inf) pflichtgemäß müssen (inf); **do d. as** (said of a thing) dienen als; (said of a person) Dienst tun als; **off d.** außer Dienst, dienstfrei; **on. d.** im Dienst; **pay d. on** verzollen
du'ty-free' adj zollfrei
du'ty ros'ter s (mil) Diensteinteilung f
dwarf [dwɔrf] adj zwergenhaft, Zwerg– || s Zwerg m || tr (stunt) in der Entwicklung behindern; (fig) in den Schatten stellen
dwell [dwel] v (pret & pp dwelled & dwelt [dwelt]) intr wohnen; **d. on** verweilen bei
dwell'ing s Wohnung f
dwell'ing house' s Wohnhaus n
dwindle ['dwɪndəl] intr schwinden, abnehmen; **d. away** dahinschwinden
dye [daɪ] s Farbe f || v (pret & pp dyed; ger dyeing) tr färben
dyed'-in-the-wool' adj (fig) in der Wolle gefärbt
dye'ing s Färben n
dyer ['daɪ·ər] s Färber –in mf
dy'ing adj (person) sterbend; (words) letzte || s Sterben n
dynamic [daɪ'næmɪk] adj dynamisch || **dynamics** s Dynamik f; **dynamics** spl (fig) Triebkraft f
dynamite ['daɪnə,maɪt] s Dynamit n || tr sprengen
dyna·mo ['daɪnə,mo] s (-mos) Dynamo m
dynastic [daɪ'næstɪk] adj dynastisch
dynasty ['daɪnəsti] s Dynastie f
dysentery ['dɪsən,teri] s Ruhr f
dyspepsia [dɪs'pepsɪ·ə] s Verdauungsstörung f

E

E, e [i] s fünfter Buchstabe des englischen Alphabets; (mus) E n; **E flat** Es n; **E sharp** Eis n
each [itʃ] indef adj jeder; **e. and every** jeder einzelne || adv je, pro Person, pro Stück || indef pron jeder; **e. other** einander, sich
eager ['igər] adj eifrig; **e. for** begierig nach; **e. to** (inf) begierig zu (inf)
ea'ger bea'ver s (coll) Streber –in mf
eagerness ['igərnɪs] s Eifer m
eagle ['igəl] s Adler m
ea'gle-eyed' adj adleräugig
ear [ɪr] s Ohr n; (of corn, wheat) Ähre f; (fig) Gehör n; **be all ears**

ganz Ohr sein; **bend s.o.'s ears** (sl) j–m die Ohren vollreden; **be up to one's ears** in bis über die Ohren stecken in (dat); **by ear** nach Gehör; **ear for music** musikalisches Gehör n; **fall on deaf ears** kein Gehör finden; **in one ear and out the other** zu e–m Ohr hinein und zum anderen hinaus; **turn a deaf ear to** taub sein gegen
ear'ache' s Ohrenschmerzen pl
ear'drops' spl (med) Ohrentropfen pl
ear'drum' s Trommelfell n
earl [ʌrl] s Graf m
ear'lobe' s Ohrläppchen n

early ['ʌrli] *adj* früh; (*reply*) baldig; (*far back in time*) Früh–; **at the earliest possible moment** baldigst; **at your earliest convenience** bei erster Gelegenheit; **be too e.** sich verfrühen ‖ *adv* früh, frühzeitig; (*too soon*) zu früh; **as e. as** schon

ear'ly bird' *s* Frühaufsteher –in *mf*

ear'ly ris'er *s* Frühaufsteher –in *mf*

ear'ly warn'ing sys'tem *s* Vorwarnungssystem *n*

ear'mark' *s* (fig) Kennzeichen *n* ‖ *tr* (*mark out*) kennzeichnen; (*e.g., funds*) (for) bestimmen (für)

ear'muffs' *spl* Ohrenschützer *m*

earn [ʌrn] *tr* (*money*) verdienen; (*a reputation*) sich [*dat*] erwerben; (*interest*) einbringen

earnest ['ʌrnɪst] *adj* ernst, ernsthaft ‖ *s*—**are you in e.?** ist das Ihr Ernst?; **be in e. about** es ernst meinen mit; **in e.** im Ernst

ear'phone' *s* Kopfhörer *m*

ear'piece' *s* (*earphone*) Hörer *m*; (*of eyeglasses*) Bügel *m*

ear'ring' *s* Ohrring *m*

ear'shot' *s*—**within e.** in Hörweite

ear'split'ting *adj* ohrenbetäubend

earth [ʌrθ] *s* Erde *f*; **come down to e.** auf den Boden der Wirklichkeit zurückkehren; **on e.** (coll) in aller Welt

earthen ['ʌrθən] *adj* irden

earth'enware' *s* Tonwaren *pl*

earthly ['ʌrθli] *adj* irdisch; **be of no e. use** völlig unnütz sein; **e. possessions** Glücksgüter *pl*

earth'quake' *s* Erdbeben *n*

earth'shak'ing *adj* welterschütternd

earth'work' *s* Schanze *f*

earth'worm' *s* Regenwurm *m*

earthy ['ʌrθi] *adj* erdig; (fig) deftig

ear'wax' *s* Ohrenschmalz *m*

ease [iz] *s* (*facility*) Leichtigkeit *f*; (*comfort*) Bequemlichkeit *f*; (*informality*) Zwanglosigkeit *f*; **at e.!** (mil) rührt euch!; **feel at e. with** s.o. in j–s Gegenwart wohl fühlen; **put at e.** beruhigen; **with e.** mühelos ‖ *tr* (*work*) erleichtern; (*pain*) lindern; (*move carefully*) lavieren; **e. out** (*of a job*) hinausmanövrieren ‖ *intr*—**e. up** nachlassen; **e. up on** (*work*) es sich [*dat*] leichter machen mit

easel ['izəl] *s* Staffelei *f*

easement ['izmənt] *s* (jur) Dienstbarkeit *f*

easily ['izəli] *adv* leicht, mühelos; **e. satisfied** genügsam

easiness ['izinɪs] *s* Leichtigkeit *f*

east [ist] *adj* Ost–, östlich ‖ *adv* ostwärts, nach Osten; **e. of** östlich von ‖ *s* Osten *m*; **the East** der Osten

east'bound' *adj* nach Osten fahrend

Easter ['istər] *adj* Oster– ‖ *s* Ostern *n* & *pl*

easterly ['istərli] *adj* österlich

eastern ['istərn] *adj* Ost–

East'ertide' *s* Osterzeit *f*

East'–Ger'man mark' *s* Ostmark *f*

eastward ['istwərd] *adv* ostwärts

easy ['izi] *adj* leicht; (*terms*) günstig; (*virtue*) locker; (*pace*) gemächlich; **e. on the eye** knusprig; **e. to digest** leichtverdaulich; **have an e. time of it** leichtes Spiel haben; **it's e. for you to talk** du hast gut reden!; **make e.** erleichtern ‖ *adv*—**e. come, e. go** wie gewonnen, so zerronnen; **get off e.** gnädig davonkommen; **take it e.** (*relax*) sich [*dat*] leicht machen; **take one'e time**) sich [*dat*] Zeit lassen; (*in parting*) mach's gut! (*remain calm*) reg dich nicht auf!; **take it e. on** (*a person*) schonend umgehen mit; (*a thing*) sparsam umgehen mit

eas'y chair' *s* Lehnsessel *m*

eas'ygo'ing *adj* ungeniert, ungezwungen

eas'y mark' *s* (coll) leichte Beute *f*

eat [it] *s*—**eats** *pl* (coll) Essen *n* ‖ *v* (*pret* **ate** [et]; *pp* **eaten** ['itən]) *tr* essen; (*said of animals*) fressen; **eat away** zerfressen; **eat one's fill** sich satt essen; **eat one's heart out** sich in Kummer verzehren; **eat one's words** das Gesagte zurücknehmen; **eat up** aufessen; **what's eating him?** was hat er denn? ‖ *intr* essen; **eat out** auswärts essen

eatable ['itəbəl] *adj* eßbar

eaves [ivz] *spl* Dachrinne *f*, Traufe *f*

eaves'drop' *v* (*pret* & *pp* **–dropped**; *ger* **–dropping**) *intr* horchen; **e. on** belauschen

eaves'drop'per *s* Horcher –in *mf*

ebb [eb] *s* Ebbe *f*; **at a low ebb** sehr heruntergekommen ‖ *intr* ebben; (fig) nachlassen

ebb' and flow' *s* Ebbe und Flut *f*

ebb' tide' *s* Ebbe *f*

ebony ['ebəni] *s* Ebenholz *n*

ebullient [ɪ'bʌljənt] *adj* überschwenglich, hochbegeistert

eccentric [ek'sentrɪk] *adj* (& fig) exzentrisch ‖ *s* Sonderling *m*, Kauz *m*; (mach) Exzenter *m*

eccentricity [,eksen'trɪsɪti] *s* Verschrobenheit *f*, Tick *m*

ecclesiastic [ɪ,klizɪ'æstɪk] *adj* kirchlich; (*law*) Kirchen– ‖ *s* Geistlicher *m*

echelon ['eʃə,lɑn] *s* (*level*) Befehlsebene *f*; (*group occupying a particular level*) Stabsführung *f*; (*flight formation*) Staffel *f*; **in echelons** staffelförmig ‖ *tr* staffeln

ech•o ['eko] *s* (–**oes**) Echo *n* ‖ *tr* (*sounds*) zurückwerfen; (fig) nachsprechen ‖ *intr* widerhallen, echoen

éclair [e'kler] *s* Eclair *n*

eclectic [ek'lektɪk] *adj* eklektisch ‖ *s* Eklektiker –in *mf*

eclipse [ɪ'klɪps] *s* Verfinsterung *f*; **go into e.** sich verfinstern; **in e.** im Schwinden ‖ *tr* verfinstern; (fig) in den Schatten stellen

eclogue ['eklog] *s* Ekloge *f*

ecological [,ɛkə'lɑdʒɪkəl] *adj* ökologisch

ecology [ɪ'kɑlədʒi] *s* Ökologie *f*

economic [,ikə'nɑmɪk], [,ɛkə'nɑmɪk] *adj* wirtschaftlich, Wirtschafts–

economical [,ikə'nɑmɪkəl], [,ɛkə'nɑmɪkəl] *adj* sparsam

economics [,ikə'nɑmɪks], [,ɛkə'nɑmɪks] *s* Wirtschaftswissenschaften *pl*

economist [ɪ'kɑnəmɪst] *s* Volkswirt-schaftler –in *mf*
economize [ɪ'kɑnə‚maɪz] *intr* sparen
economy [ɪ'kɑnəmi] *s* Wirtschaft *f*; (thriftiness) Sparsamkeit *f*; (a saving) Ersparnis *f*
ecstasy ['ɛkstəsi] *s* Verzückung *f*; go into e. in Verzückung geraten
ecstatic [ɛk'stætɪk] *adj* verzückt
ecumenic(al) [‚ɛkjə'mɛnɪk(əl)] *adj* ökumenisch
eczema [ɛg'zimə] *s* Ausschlag *m*
ed•dy ['ɛdi] *s* Strudel *m* || *v* (pret & pp –died) *intr* strudeln
edelweiss ['edəl‚vaɪs] *s* Edelweiß *n*
edge [ɛdʒ] *s* (of a knife) Schneide *f*; (of a forest, town, water, road) Rand *m*; (e.g., of a table) Kante *f*; (keenness) Schärfe *f*; (bb) Schnitt *m*; have an e. on s.o. den Vorteil gegenüber j–m haben; on e. (said of a person or teeth) kribbelig; (said of nerves) aufs äußerste gespannt; take the e. off abstumpfen; (fig) die Schärfe nehmen (dat) || *tr* (a lawn) beschneiden; (put a border on) einfassen; e. out (sport) knapp schlagen || *intr* —e. forward langsam vorrücken
edge'wise' *adv*—not get a word in e. nicht zu Worte kommen können
edg'ing *s* Umrandung *f*, Besatz *m*
edgy ['ɛdʒi] *adj* kribbelig
edible ['ɛdɪbəl] *adj* eßbar, genießbar
edict ['idɪkt] *s* Edikt *n*, Erlaß *m*
edification [‚ɛdɪfɪ'keʃən] *s* Erbauung *f*
edifice ['ɛdɪfɪs] *s* Bauwerk *n*, Gebäude *n*
edi•fy ['ɛdɪ‚faɪ] *v* (pret & pp –fied) *tr* erbauen; be edified by sich erbauen an (dat)
ed'ifying *adj* erbaulich
edit ['ɛdɪt] *tr* (a book) herausgeben; (a newspaper) redigieren; (cin) schneiden
edition [ɛ'dɪʃən] *s* Ausgabe *f*
editor ['ɛdɪtər] *s* (of a newspaper or magazine) Redakteur –in *mf*; (of a book) Herausgeber –in *mf*; (of editorials) Leitartikler –in *mf*; (cin) Schnittmeister –in *mf*
editorial [‚ɛdɪ'torɪ‚əl] *adj* redaktionell, Redaktions– || *s* Leitartikel *m*
editorialize [‚ɛdɪ'torɪ‚ə‚laɪz] *intr* (on) seine Meinung zum Ausdruck bringen (über *acc*); (report with a slant) tendenziös berichten
edito'rial of'fice *s* Redaktion *f*
edito'rial staff' *s* Redaktion *f*
ed'itor in chief' *s* Chefredakteur –in *mf*
educate ['ɛdʒu‚ket] *tr* bilden, erziehen
education [‚ɛdʒu'keʃən] *s* Bildung *f*, Erziehung *f*; (educ) Pädagogik *f*
educational [‚ɛdʒu'keʃənəl] *adj* Bildungs–; e. background Vorbildung *f*; e. film Lehrfilm *m*; e. institution Lehranstalt *f*
educator ['ɛdʒu‚ketər] *s* Erzieher –in *mf*
educe [ɪ'd(j)us] *tr* hervorholen
eel [il] *s* Aal *m*
eerie, eery ['ɪri] *adj* unheimlich

efface [ɪ'fes] *tr* austilgen; e. oneself sich zurückhalten
effect [ɪ'fɛkt] *s* (on) Wirkung *f* (auf *acc*); (consequence) (on) Auswirkung *f* (auf *acc*); (impression) Eindruck *m*; effects (movable property) Habe *f*; for e. zum Effekt; go into e. in Kraft treten; have an e. on wirken auf (*acc*); in e. praktisch; put into e. in Kraft setzen; take e. zur Geltung kommen; to the e. that des Inhalts, daß || *tr* bewirken
effective [ɪ'fɛktɪv] *adj* wirkungsvoll; (actual) effektiv; e. against wirksam gegen; e. date Tag *m* des Inkrafttretens; e. from mit Wirkung von; e. immediately mit sofortiger Wirkung; e. strength (mil) Iststärke *f*
effectual [ɪ'fɛktʃʊ‚əl] *adj* wirksam
effectuate [ɪ'fɛktʃʊ‚et] *tr* bewirken
effeminacy [ɪ'fɛmɪnəsi] *s* Verweichlichung *f*
effeminate [ɪ'fɛmɪnɪt] *adj* verweichlicht
effervesce [‚ɛfər'vɛs] *intr* aufbrausen
effervescence [‚ɛfər'vɛsəns] *s* Aufbrausen *n*, Moussieren *n*
effervescent [‚ɛfər'vɛsənt] *adj* (liquid; personality) aufbrausend
effete [ɪ'fit] *adj* entkräftet
efficacious [‚ɛfɪ'keʃəs] *adj* wirksam
efficacy ['ɛfɪkəsi] *s* Wirksamkeit *f*, Wirkungskraft *f*
efficiency [ɪ'fɪʃənsi] *s* Tüchtigkeit *f*; (phys) Nutzeffekt *m*; (tech) Leistungsfähigkeit *f*
efficient [ɪ'fɪʃənt] *adj* tüchtig; (tech) leistungsfähig
effigy ['ɛfɪdʒi] *s* Abbild *n*; hang in e. symbolisch hängen
effort ['ɛfərt] *s* (exertion) Mühe *f*; (attempt) Bestreben *n*; efforts Bemühungen *pl*; make an honest e. to (inf) sich redlich bemühen zu (inf)
effortless ['ɛfərtlɪs] *adj* mühelos
effrontery [ɪ'frʌntəri] *s* Frechheit *f*, Unverschämtheit *f*
effusion [ɪ'fjuʒən] *s* Erguß *m*
effusive [ɪ'fjusɪv] *adj* überschwenglich
egg [ɛg] *s* Ei *n*; bad egg (sl) übler Geselle *m*; good egg (sl) feiner Kerl *m*; lay an egg ein Ei legen; (fig) e-e völlige Niete sein || *tr*—egg on anstacheln
egg'beat'er *s* Schneeschläger *m*
egg'cup' *s* Eierbecher *m*
egg'head' *s* (coll) Intelligenzler –in *mf*
eggnog ['ɛg‚nɑg] *s* Eierlikör *m*, Egg-Nog *m*
egg'plant' *s* Eierfrucht *f*
egg'shell' *s* Eierschale *f*
egg' white' *s* Eiweiß *n*
egg' yolk' *s* Eigelb *n*, Eidotter *m*
ego ['igo] *s* Ego *n*, Ich *n*; (coll) Ichsucht *f*
egocentric [‚igo'sɛntrɪk] *adj* egozentrisch
egoism ['igo‚ɪzəm] *s* Selbstsucht *f*
egoist ['igo‚ɪst] *s* Egoist *m*
egotism ['igo‚tɪzəm] *s* Ichsucht *f*
egotistic(al) [‚igo'tɪstɪk(əl)] *adj* egotistisch, geltungsbedürftig

egregious [ɪ'griːdʒəs] adj unerhört

egress ['iːgres] s Ausgang m

Egypt ['iːdʒɪpt] s Ägypten m

Egyptian [ɪ'dʒɪp/ən] adj ägyptisch || s Ägypter -in mf; (language) Ägyptisch n

eiderdown ['aɪdər‚daun] s Eiderdaunen pl; (cover) Daunenbett n

eight [et] adj & pron acht || s Acht f

eight'ball' s—be behind the e. (sl) in der Klemme sitzen

eighteen ['et'tin] adj & pron achtzehn || s Achtzehn f

eighteenth ['et'tinθ] adj achtzehnte || s (fraction) Achtzehntel n; the e. (in dates or in a series) der Achtzehnte

eighth [etθ] adj achte || s (fraction) Achtel n; the e. (in dates or in a series) der Achte

eighth' note's (mus) Achtelnote f

eightieth ['etɪ·ɪθ] adj achtzigste || s (fraction) Achtzigstel n; the e. der Achtzigste

eighty ['etɪ] adj & pron achtzig || s Achtzig f; the eighties die achtziger Jahre pl

eigh'ty-one' adj & pron einundachtzig

either ['iːðər], ['aɪðər] adj—e. one is correct beides ist richtig; e. way auf die e-e oder andere Art; in e. case in jedem der beiden Fälle; on e. side auf beiden Seiten || adv—not...e. auch nicht || pron einer von beiden; e. of you einer von euch beiden; I didn't see e. ich habe beide nicht gesehen || conj—e....or entweder... oder

ejaculate [ɪ'dʒækjə‚let] tr ausstoßen; (physiol) ejakulieren

eject [ɪ'dʒekt] tr ausstoßen; (from a property) (from) hinauswerfen (aus)

ejection [ɪ'dʒek/ən] s Ausstoßung f

ejec'tion seat' s Schleudersitz m

eke [ik] tr—eke out a living das Leben fristen

el [el] s (coll) Hochbahn f

elaborate [ɪ'læbərɪt] adj (detailed) weitläufig; (ornate) kunstvoll; (idea) compliziert || [ɪ'læbə‚ret] tr ausarbeiten || intr—e. on sich verbreiten über (acc)

elaboration [ɪ‚læbə're/ən] s Ausarbeitung f

elapse [ɪ'læps] intr verrinnen

elastic [ɪ'læstɪk] adj elastisch; (conscience) weit || s Gummiband n

elasticity [‚ɪlæs'tɪsɪtɪ] s Elastizität f

elated [ɪ'letɪd] adj freudig erregt

elation [ɪ'le/ən] s Hochgefühl n

elbow ['elbo] s Ellbogen m; (of a pipe) Rohrknie n; at one's e. bei der Hand; rub elbows with s.o. mit j-m in nähere Berührung kommen || tr—e. one's way sich [dat] seinen Weg bahnen

el'bow grease' s (coll) Knochenschmalz n

el'bowroom' s Spielraum m

elder ['eldər] adj älter || s Ältere mf; (bot) Holunder m; (eccl) Kirchenälteste mf

el'derber'ry s Holunderbeere f

elderly ['eldərlɪ] adj ältlich

el'der states'man s profilierter Staatsmann m

eldest ['eldɪst] adj älteste

elect [ɪ'lekt] adj erlesen; (elected but not yet installed) zukünftig; (relig) auserwählt || the e. spl die Auserwählten || tr wählen; e. s.o. president j-n zum Präsidenten wählen

election [ɪ'lek/ən] adj Wahl- || s Wahl f

elec'tion campaign' s Wahlkampf m

elec'tion day' s Wahltag m

electioneer [ɪ‚lek/ə'nɪr] intr Stimmen werben

elective [ɪ'lektɪv] adj (educ) wahlfrei; (pol) Wahl- || s (educ) Wahlfach n

electoral [ɪ'lektərəl] adj Wahl-

elec'toral col'lege s Wahlmänner pl

electorate [ɪ'lektərɪt] s Wählerschaft f

electric(al) [ɪ'lektrɪk(əl)] adj elektrisch, Elektro-

elec'trical appli'ance s Elektrogerät n

elec'trical engineer' s Elektroingenieur m

elec'trical engineer'ing s Elektrotechnik f

elec'tric blan'ket s Heizdecke f

elec'tric bulb' s Glühbirne f

elec'tric chair' s elektrischer Stuhl m; (penalty) Hinrichtung f auf dem elektrischen Stuhl

elec'tric cir'cuit s Stromkreis m

elec'tric eel' s Zitteraal m

elec'tric eye' s Photozelle f

elec'tric fan' s Ventilator m

elec'tric fence' s elektrisch geladener Drahtzaun m

electrician [ɪ‚lek'trɪ/ən] s Elektriker -in mf

electricity [‚ɪlek'trɪsɪtɪ] s Elektrizität f; (current) Strom m

elec'tric light' s elektrisches Licht n

elec'tric me'ter s Stromzähler m

elec'tric saw' s Motorsäge f

elec'tric shav'er s elektrischer Rasierapparat m

elec'tric storm' s Gewittersturm m

elec'tric stove' s Elektroherd m

electri•fy [ɪ'lektrɪ‚faɪ] v (pret & pp -fied) tr (& fig) elektrisieren; (a streetcar, railroad) elektrifizieren

electrocute [ɪ'lektrə‚kjut] tr durch elektrischen Strom töten; (jur) auf dem elektrischen Stuhl hinrichten

electrode [ɪ'lektrod] s Elektrode f

electrolysis [ɪ‚lek'trɑlɪsɪs] s Elektrolyse f

electrolyte [ɪ'lektrə‚laɪt] s Elektrolyt m

electromagnet [ɪ‚lektrə'mægnət] s Elektromagnet m

electromagnetic [ɪ‚lektrəmæg'netɪk] adj elektromagnetisch

electron [ɪ'lektrɑn] s Elektron n

electronic [ɪ‚lek'trɑnɪk] adj elektronisch, Elektronen- || electronics s Elektronik f

electron'ic flash' s Röhrenblitz m; (device) Blitzgerät n

electronic [ɪ‚lek'trɑnɪk] adj elektroplattieren, galvanisieren

electrostatic [ɪ ˌlektrə 'stætɪk] *adj* elektrostatisch

electrotype [ɪ 'lektrə ˌtaɪp] *s* Galvano *n* ‖ *tr* galvanoplastisch vervielfältigen

elegance ['elɪgəns] *s* Eleganz *f*

elegant ['elə ˌgənt] *adj* elegant

elegiac [ˌelɪ 'dʒaɪ-æk] *adj* elegisch

elegy ['elɪdʒɪ] *s* Elegie *f*

element ['elɪmənt] *s* (& fig) Element *n*; (*e.g., of truth*) Körnchen *n*

elementary [ˌelɪ 'mentərɪ] *adj* elementar, grundlegend

elemen'tary school' *s* Grundschule *f*

elephant ['elɪfənt] *s* Elefant *m*

elevate ['elɪ ˌvet] *tr* erheben, erhöhen

el'evated *adj* (*eyes*) erhoben; (*style*) erhaben ‖ *s* (coll) Hochbahn *f*

elevation [ˌelɪ 've∫ən] *s* (*height*) Höhe *f*; (hill) Anhöhe *f*; (*above sealevel*) Seehöhe *f*; (*to the throne*) Erhebung *f*; (archit) Aufriß *m*; (arti) Richthöhe *f*; (astr, relig) Elevation *f*

elevator ['elɪ ˌvetər] *s* Aufzug *m*, Fahrstuhl *m*; (aer) Höhenruder *n*; (agr) Getreidespeicher *m*

el'evator op'erator *s* Fahrstuhlführer –in *mf*

el'evator shaft' *s* Fahrstuhlschacht *m*

eleven [ɪ 'levən] *adj & pron* elf ‖ *s* Elf *f*

eleventh [ɪ 'levənθ] *adj* elfte ‖ *s* (*fraction*) Elftel *n*; the e. (*in dates and in a series*) der Elfte

elev'enth hour' *s*—at the e. (fig) kurz vor Torschluß

elf [elf] *s* (elves [elvz]) Elf *m*, Elfe *f*

elicit [ɪ 'lɪsɪt] *tr* hervorlocken; (*an answer*) entlocken

elide [ɪ 'laɪd] *tr* elidieren

eligible ['elɪdʒɪbəl] *adj* qualifiziert; (*entitled*) berechtigt; (*for office*) wählbar; (*for marriage*) heiratsfähig

el'igible bach'elor *s* Heiratskandidat *m*

eliminate [ɪ 'lɪmɪ ˌnet] *tr* ausscheiden; (alg) eliminieren

elimination [ɪ ˌlɪmɪ 'ne∫ən] *s* Ausscheidung *f*

elimina'tion bout' *s* Ausscheidungskampf *m*

elision [ɪ 'lɪʒən] *s* Auslassung *f*

elite [e 'lit] *adj* Elite– ‖ *s* Elite *f*

elixir [ɪ 'lɪksər] *s* Elixier *n*

elk [elk] *s* Elch *m*

ellipse [ɪ 'lɪps] *s* (geom) Ellipse *f*

ellip-sis [ɪ 'lɪpsɪs] *s* (-ses [siz]) (gram) Ellipse *f*

elliptic(al) [ɪ 'lɪptɪk(əl)] *adj* elliptisch

elm [elm] *s* Ulme *f*

elocution [ˌelə 'kju∫ən] *s* (art) Vortragskunst *f*; (*style*) Vortragsweise *f*

elope [ɪ 'lop] *intr* ausreißen

elopement [ɪ 'lopmənt] *s* Ausreißen *n*

eloquence ['eləkwəns] *s* Beredsamkeit *f*

eloquent ['eləkwənt] *adj* beredt

else [els] *adj* sonst; someone else's house das Haus e–s anderen; what e.? was sonst?; (*in addition*) was noch? ‖ *adv* sonst, anders; nowhere e. sonst nirgends; or e. sonst, andernfalls; where e.? wo sonst?

else'where' *adv* (*position*) woanders;

(*direction*) sonstwohin; from e. anderswoher

elucidate [ɪ 'lusɪ ˌdet] *tr* erläutern

elucidation [ɪ ˌlusɪ 'de∫ən] *s* Erläuterung *f*

elude [ɪ 'lud] *tr* entgehen (*dat*)

elusive [ɪ 'lusɪv] *adj* schwer zu fassen; (*memory*) unzuverlässig

emaciated [ɪ 'me∫ɪ ˌetɪd] *adj* abgezehrt

emanate ['emə ˌnet] *intr*—e. from (*said of gases*) ausströmen aus; (*said of rays*) ausstrahlen aus; (fig) ausgehen von

emancipate [ɪ 'mænsɪ ˌpet] *tr* emanzipieren

emasculate [ɪ 'mæskjə ˌlet] *tr* (& fig) entmannen

embalm [em 'bam] *tr* einbalsamieren

embankment [em 'bæŋkmənt] *s* Damm *m*

embar-go [em 'bargo] *s* (-goes) Sperre *f*, Embargo *n* ‖ *tr* sperren

embark [em 'bark] *intr* (for) sich einschiffen (nach); **e. upon** sich einlassen auf (*acc*)

embarkation [ˌembar 'ke∫ən] *s* Einschiffung *f*

embarrass [em 'bærəs] *tr* in Verlegenheit bringen

embar'rassed *adj* verlegen; feel e. sich genieren

embar'rassing *adj* peinlich

embarrassment [em 'bærəsmənt] *s* Verlegenheit *f*

embassy ['embəsɪ] *s* Botschaft *f*

em-bed [em 'bed] *v* (*pret & pp* –bedded; *ger* –bedding) *tr* einbetten; **e. in concrete** einbetonieren

embellish [em 'belɪʃ] *tr* verschönern

embellishment [em 'belɪʃmənt] *s* Verschönerung *f*

ember ['embər] *s* glühende Kohle *f*; **embers** Glut *f*

Em'ber day' *s* Quatember *m*

embezzle [em 'bezəl] *tr* unterschlagen

embezzlement [em 'bezəlmənt] *s* Unterschlagung *f*, Veruntreuung *f*

embezzler [em 'bezlər] *s* Veruntreuer –in *mf*

embitter [em 'bɪtər] *tr* verbittern

emblazon [em 'blezən] *tr* (*decorate*) verzieren; (*extol*) verherrlichen; (heral) heraldisch darstellen

emblem ['embləm] *s* Sinnbild *n*

emblematic(al) [ˌemblə 'mætɪk(əl)] *adj* sinnbildlich

embodiment [em 'badɪmənt] *s* Verkörperung *f*

embod-y [em 'badɪ] *v* (*pret & pp* –ied) *tr* verkörpern

embolden [em 'boldən] *tr* ermutigen

embolism ['embə ˌlɪzəm] *s* Embolie *f*

emboss [em 'bɒs] *tr* bossieren

embossed' *adj* getrieben

embrace [em 'bres] *s* Umarmung *f* ‖ *tr* umarmen; (*include*) umfassen; (*a religion, idea*) annehmen ‖ *intr* sich umarmen

embrasure [em 'breʒər] *s* Schießscharte *f*

embroider [em 'brɔɪdər] *tr* sticken

embroidery [em 'brɔɪdərɪ] *s* Stickerei *f*

embroi'dery nee'dle *s* Sticknadel *f*

embroil [ɛm'brɔɪl] *tr* verwickeln
embroilment [ɛm'brɔɪlmənt] *s* Verwicklung *f*
embry·o ['ɛmbrɪ,o] *s* (**-os**) Embryo *m*
embryology [,ɛmbrɪ'alədʒi] *s* Embryologie *f*
embryonic [,ɛmbrɪ'anɪk] *adj* embryonal
emend [ɪ'mɛnd] *tr* berichtigen
emendation [,imɛn'deʃən] *s* Berichtigung *f*
emerald ['ɛmərəld] *adj* smaragdgrün || *s* Smaragd *m*
emerge [ɪ'mʌrdʒ] *intr* (*come forth*) hervortreten; (*surface*) auftauchen; (*result*) (*from*) herauskommen (bei)
emergence [ɪ'mʌrdʒəns] *s* Hervortreten *n*; (*surfacing*) Auftauchen *n*
emergency [ɪ'mʌrdʒənsi] *adj* Not– || *s* Notlage *f*; **in case of e.** im Notfall
emeritus [ɪ'mɛrɪtəs] *adj* emeritiert
emersion [ɪ'mʌrʒən] *s* Auftauchen *n*
emery ['ɛməri] *s* Schmirgel *m*
em'ery cloth' *s* Schmirgelleinwand *f*
em'ery wheel' *s* Schmirgelrad *n*
emetic [ɪ'mɛtɪk] *adj* Brech– || *s* Brechmittel *n*
emigrant ['ɛmɪgrənt] *s* Auswanderer –in *mf*
emigrate ['ɛmɪ,gret] *intr* auswandern
emigration [,ɛmɪ'greʃən] *s* Auswanderung *f*
eminence ['ɛmɪnəns] *s* (*height*) Anhöhe *f*; (*fame*) Berühmtheit *f*; **Eminence** (*title of a cardinal*) Eminenz *f*; **rise to e.** zu Ruhm und Würde gelangen
eminent ['ɛmɪnənt] *adj* hervorragend
emissary ['ɛmɪ,sɛri] *s* Abgesandte *mf*
emission [ɪ'mɪʃən] *s* (*biol*) Erguß *m*; (*phys*) Austrahlung *f*, Ausströmung *f*
emis'sion control' *s* Abgasentgiftung *f*
emit [ɪ'mɪt] *v* (*pret & pp* **emitted; ger emitting**) *tr* von sich geben; (*rays*) austrahlen; (*gases*) ausströmen; (*sparks*) sprühen
emolument [e'maljəmənt] *s* Vergütung *f*
emotion [ɪ'moʃən] *s* Gemütsbewegung *f*
emotional [ɪ'moʃənəl] *adj* (*e.g., disorder*) Gemüts–; (*person*) gefühlvoll; (*e.g., sermon*) ergreifend; (*mawkish*) rührselig
emperor ['ɛmpərər] *s* Kaiser *m*
empha·sis ['ɛmfəsɪs] *s* (**-ses** [,siz]) Betonung *f*
emphasize ['ɛmfə,saɪz] *tr* betonen
emphatic [ɛm'fætɪk] *adj* nachdrücklich
emphysema [,ɛmfɪ'simə] *s* Emphysem *n*
empire ['ɛmpaɪr] *s* Reich *n*; (*Roman period*) Kaiserzeit *f*
Em'pire fur'niture *s* Empiremöbel *n*
empiric(al) [ɛm'pɪrɪk(əl)] *adj* erfahrungsmäßig, empirisch
empiricist [ɛm'pɪrɪsɪst] *s* Empiriker –in *mf*
emplacement [ɛm'plesmənt] *s* Stellung *f*
employ [ɛm'plɔɪ] *s* Dienst *m* || *tr* (*hire*) anstellen; (*keep in employ-*

ment) beschäftigen; (*use*) verwenden; (*troops, police*) einsetzen
employee [ɛm'plɔɪ·i], [,ɛmplɔɪ'i] *s* Arbeitnehmer –in *mf*
employer [ɛm'plɔɪ·ər] *s* Arbeitgeber –in *mf*
employment [ɛm'plɔɪmənt] *s* (*work*) Beschäftigung *f*, Arbeit *f*; (*use*) Verwendung *f*; (*e.g., of troops*) Einsatz *m*; **out of e.** arbeitslos
employ'ment a'gency *s* Arbeitsvermittlung *f*
empower [ɛm'pau·ər] *tr* ermächtigen
empress ['ɛmprɪs] *s* Kaiserin *f*
emptiness ['ɛmptɪnɪs] *s* Leere *f*; (*fig*) Nichtigkeit *f*
emp·ty ['ɛmpti] *adj* leer; **e. talk** leere Worte *pl*; **on an e. stomach** auf nüchternen Magen || **empties** *spl* Leergut *n* || *v* (*pret & pp* **-tied**) *tr* (*aus*)leeren || *intr*–**e. into** münden in (*acc*)
emp'ty-hand'ed *adj* mit leeren Händen
emp'ty-head'ed *adj* hohlköpfig
emulate ['ɛmjə,let] *tr* nacheifern (*dat*)
emulation [,ɛmjə'leʃən] *s* Nacheiferung *f*
emulator [,ɛmjə'letər] *s* Nacheiferer –in *mf*
emulsi·fy [ɪ'mʌlsɪ,faɪ] *v* (*pret & pp* **-fied**) *tr* emulgieren
emulsion [ɪ'mʌlʃən] *s* Emulsion *f*; (*phot*) Schicht *f*
enable [ɛn'ebəl] *tr* befähigen
enact [ɛn'ækt] *tr* erlassen
enactment [ɛn'æktmənt] *s* Erlassen *n*
enam·el [ɪ'næməl] *s* Email *n*; (*dent*) Zahnschmelz *m* || *v* (*pret & pp* **-el[l]ed; ger -el[l]ing**) *tr* emaillieren
enam'el paint' *s* Emaillack *m*
enam'elware' *s* Emailwaren *pl*
enamored [ɛ'næmərd] *adj*—**be e. of** verliebt sein in (*acc*)
encamp [ɛn'kæmp] *tr* in e–m Lager unterbringen || *intr* lagern, sich lagern
encampment [ɛn'kæmpmənt] *s* (*camping*) Lagern *n*; (*campsite*) Lager *n*
encase [ɛn'kes] *tr* einschließen
enchant [ɛn't'ʃænt] *tr* verzaubern; (*fig*) bezaubern
enchanter [ɛn't'ʃæntər] *s* Zauberer –in *mf*
enchant'ing *adj* bezaubernd
enchantment [ɛn't'ʃæntmənt] *s* (*state*) Verzauberung *f*; (*cause of enchantment*) Zauber *m*
enchantress [ɛn't'ʃæntrɪs] *s* Zauberin *f*
encircle [ɛn'sʌrkəl] *tr* umgeben; (*mil*) einschließen
encirclement [ɛn'sʌrkəlmənt] *s* (*mil*) Einschließung *f*
enclave ['ɛnklev] *s* Enklave *f*
enclitic [ɛn'klɪtɪk] *adj* enklitisch || *s* Enklitikon *n*
enclose [ɛn'kloz] *tr* einschließen; (*land*) umzäunen; (*in a letter*) beilegen; **e. in parentheses** einklammern; **please find enclosed** in der Anlage erhalten Sie
enclosure [ɛn'kloʒər] *s* Umzäunung *f*; (*in a letter*) Anlage *f*

encomi·um [enˈkomɪ·əm] s (-ums & -a [ə]) Lobpreisung f, Enkomion n

encompass [enˈkʌmpəs] tr umfassen

encore [ˈɑnkor] s (performance) Zugabe f; (recall) Dakaporuf m ‖ interj da capo!; noch einmal

encounter [enˈkaʊntər] s Begegnung f; (hostile meeting) Zusammenstoß m; (mil) Gefecht n ‖ tr begegnen (dat)

encourage [enˈkʌrɪdʒ] tr ermutigen

encouragement [enˈkʌrɪdʒmənt] s Ermutigung f

encroach [enˈkrotʃ] intr—e. on übergreifen auf (acc); (rights) beeinträchtigen

encroachment [enˈkrotʃmənt] s Übergriff m

encrust [enˈkrʌst] tr überkrusten

encumber [enˈkʌmbər] tr belasten; (with debts) verschulden

encumbrance [enˈkrʌmbrəns] s Belastung f

encyclical [enˈsɪklɪkəl] s Enzyklika f

encyclopedia [enˌsaɪkləˈpidɪ·ə] s Enzyklopädie f

encyclopedic [enˌsaɪkləˈpidɪk] adj enzyklopädisch

end [end] s Ende n; (purpose) Zweck m; (goal) Ziel n; (closing) Schluß m; (outcome) Ausgang m, Ergebnis n; at the end of one's strength am Rande seiner Kraft; come to a bad end ein schlimmes Ende finden; come to an end zu Ende gehen; end in itself Selbstzweck m; gain one's ends seinen Vorsatz ausführen; go off the deep end sich unnötig aufregen; in the end schließlich; make both ends meet gerade auskommen; no end of unendlich viel(e); on end hochkant; (without letup) ununterbrochen; put an end to ein Ende machen (dat); that will be the end of me das überlebe ich nicht; to no end vergebens ‖ tr beenden ‖ intr enden; (gram) auslauten; end in a point spitz zulaufen; end up (in) (coll) landen (in dat); end up with beenden mit

end'-all' s Schluß m vom Ganzen

endanger [enˈdendʒər] tr gefährden

endear [enˈdɪr] tr—e. s.o. to j-n einschmeicheln bei

endear'ing adj gewinnend

endearment [enˈdɪrmənt] s Beliebtheit f

endeavor [enˈdevər] s Bestreben n ‖ intr—e. to (inf) sich bestreben zu (inf), versuchen zu (inf)

endemic [enˈdemɪk] adj endemisch ‖ s Endemie f, endemische Krankheit f

end'ing s Beendigung f, Abschluß m; (gram) Endung f

endive [ˈendaɪv] s Endivie f

endless [ˈendlɪs] adj endlos; an e. number of unendlich viele

end'most' adj entfernteste

endocrine [ˈendoˌkraɪn] adj endokrin

endorse [enˈdors] tr (confirm) bestätigen; (a check) indossieren

endorsee [ˌendorˈsi] s Indossat -in mf

endorsement [enˈdorsmənt] s Indossament n; (approval) Bestätigung f

endorser [enˈdorsər] s Indossant -in mf; (backer) Hintermann m

endow [enˈdaʊ] tr (provide with income) dotieren; (with talent) begaben

endowment [enˈdaʊmənt] s Dotierung f; (talent) Begabung f

endow'ment fund' s Stiftungsvermögen n

endurance [enˈd(j)ʊrəns] s Dauer f; (ability to hold out) Ausdauer f

endur'ance test' s Dauerprobe f

endure [enˈd(j)ʊr] tr aushalten ‖ intr fortdauern

endur'ing adj dauerhaft

enema [ˈenəmə] s Einlauf m

enemy [ˈenəmi] adj feindlich, Feind- ‖ s Feind m; become enemies sich verfeinden

energetic [ˌenərˈdʒetɪk] adj energisch

energy [ˈenərdʒi] s Energie f

enervate [ˈenərˌvet] tr entkräften

enfeeble [enˈfibəl] tr entkräften

enfilade [ˈenfɪˌled] s (mil) Flankenfeuer n ‖ tr mit Flankenfeuer bestreichen

enfold [enˈfold] tr einhüllen

enforce [enˈfors] tr durchsetzen; (obedience) erzwingen

enforcement [enˈforsmənt] s Durchsetzung f

enfranchise [enˈfræntʃaɪz] tr (admit to citizenship) einbürgern; (give the right to vote to) das Wahlrecht verleihen (dat)

engage [enˈgedʒ] tr (hire) anstellen; (reserve) vorbestellen; (attention) fesseln; (gears) einrücken; (one's own troops) einsetzen; (the enemy) angreifen; be engaged in beschäftigt sein mit; e. in verwickeln in (acc) ‖ intr (mach) (ein)greifen; e. in sich einlassen in (acc)

engaged' adj verlobt; get e. (to) sich verloben (mit)

engaged' cou'ple s Brautleute pl

engagement [enˈgedʒmənt] s (betrothal) Verlobung f; (appointment) Verabredung f; (obligation) Verpflichtung f; (mil) Gefecht n; have a previous e. verabredet sein

engage'ment ring' s Verlobungsring m

engag'ing adj gewinnend

engender [enˈdʒendər] tr hervorbringen

engine [ˈendʒɪn] s Maschine f; (aer, aut) Motor m; (rr) Lokomotive f

engineer [ˌendʒəˈnɪr] s Ingenieur m, Techniker m; (mil) Pionier m; (rr) Lokomotivführer m; engineers (mil) Pioniertruppe f ‖ tr errichten; (fig) bewerkstelligen

engineer'ing s Ingenieurwesen n

engineer'ing school' s Technikum n

en'gine house' s Spritzenhaus n

en'gine room' s Maschinenraum m

England [ˈɪŋglənd] s England n

English [ˈɪŋglɪʃ] adj englisch ‖ s (spin) Effet m; (language) Englisch n; in plain E. unverblümt; the E. die Engländer

Eng′lish Chan′nel s Ärmelkanal m
Eng′lish horn′ s Englischhorn n
Eng′lish-man s (-men) Engländer m
Eng′lish-speak′ing adj englischsprechend
Eng′lish-wom′an s (-wom′en) Engländerin f
engraft [en′græft] tr aufpropfen; (fig) einprägen
engrave [en′grev] tr gravieren
engraver [en′grevər] s Graveur m
engrav′ing s Kupferstich m
engross [en′gros] tr in Anspruch nehmen; (a document) mit großen Buchstaben schreiben; **become engrossed** in sich versenken in (acc)
engross′ing adj fesselnd
engulf [en′gʌlf] tr (fig) verschlingen
enhance [en′hæns] tr erhöhen; **be enhanced** sich erhöhen
enhancement [en′hænsmənt] s Erhöhung f
enigma [ɪ′nɪgmə] s Rätsel n
enigmatic(al) [ˌɪnɪg′mætɪk(əl)] adj rätselhaft
enjoin [en′dʒɔɪn] tr (forbid) (from ger) verbieten (dat) (zu inf); e. s.o. to (inf) j-m auferlegen zu (inf)
enjoy [en′dʒɔɪ] tr (take pleasure in) Gefallen finden an (dat); (have the advantage of) genießen, sich erfreuen (genit); e. doing s.th. gern etw tun; e. oneself sich gut unterhalten; e. to the full auskosten; I e. the wine mir schmeckt der Wein
enjoyable [en′dʒɔɪ-əbəl] adj erfreulich; **thoroughly e.** genußreich
enjoyment [en′dʒɔɪmənt] s Genuß m
enkindle [en′kɪndəl] tr entzünden
enlarge [en′lardʒ] tr vergrößern || intr sich vergrößern; e. upon näher eingehen auf (acc)
enlargement [en′lardʒmənt] s Vergrößerung f
enlarger [en′lardʒər] s (phot) Vergrößerungsapparat m
enlighten [en′laɪtən] tr aufklären
enlightenment [en′laɪtənmənt] s (act) Aufklärung f; (state) Aufgeklärtheit f
enlist [en′lɪst] tr (services) in Anspruch nehmen; (mil) anwerben; e. s.o. in a cause j-n für e-e Sache gewinnen || intr (in) sich freiwillig melden (zu)
enlist′ed man′ s Soldat m; **enlisted men** Mannschaften pl
enlistment [en′lɪstmənt] s Anwerbung f; (period of service) Militärdienstzeit f
enliven [en′laɪvən] tr beleben
enmesh [en′meʃ] tr verstricken
enmity [′enmɪti] s Feindschaft f
ennoble [en′nobəl] tr veredeln, adeln
ennui [′onwi] s Langeweile f
enormity [ɪ′nɔrmɪti] s Ungeheuerlichkeit f
enormous [ɪ′nɔrməs] adj enorm, ungeheuer
enough [ɪ′nʌf] adj & adv genug, genügend; **be e.** genügen; **I have e. of it** ich bin es satt; **it's e. to drive one crazy** ist zum Verrücktwerden

enounce [ɪ′naʊns] tr (declare) verkünden; (pronounce) aussprechen
enrage [en′redʒ] tr wütend machen
enraged adj (at) wütend (über acc)
enrapture [en′ræptʃər] tr hinreißen
enrich [en′rɪtʃ] tr (a person with money; the mind, a program) bereichern; (soil) fruchtbarer machen; (food, metals, gases) anreichern
enrichment [en′rɪtʃmənt] s Bereicherung f; (of food, metals, gases) Anreicherung f
enroll [en′rol] tr als Mitglied aufnehmen || intr (educ) sich immatrikulieren lassen
enrollment [en′rolmənt] s (in a course or school) Schülerzahl f; (of a society) Mitgliederzahl f
en route [an ′rut] adv unterwegs
ensconce [en′skans] tr verbergen
ensemble [an′sambəl] s Ensemble n
ensign [′ensɪn] s (flag) (mil) Fahne f; (flag) (nav) Flagge f; (emblem) Abzeichen n; (nav) Leutnant m zur See
enslave [en′slev] tr versklaven
enslavement [en′slevmənt] s Versklavung f
ensnare [en′sner] tr (fig) umgarnen
ensue [en′s(j)u] intr (from) (er)folgen (aus)
ensu′ing adj darauffolgend
ensure [en′ʃur] tr gewährleisten
entail [en′tel] tr mit sich bringen
entangle [en′tæŋgəl] tr verwickeln; **get entangled** sich verwickeln
entanglement [en′tæŋgəlmənt] s Verwicklung f; (mil) Drahtverhau m
enter [′entər] tr (a room) betreten, treten in (acc); (political office) antreten; (a university) beziehen; (a protest) erheben; (a career) einschlagen; (in the records) eintragen; e. the army Soldat werden || intr eintreten, hereinkommen; (by car) einfahren; (sport) melden; (theat) auftreten; e. into (an agreement) treffen; (a contract) abschließen; e. upon anfangen; (a career) einschlagen; (an office, inheritance) antreten; (year of life) eintreten in (acc)
enterprise [′entər-praɪz] s Unternehmen n; (spirit) Unternehmungsgeist m
en′terprising adj unternehmungslustig
entertain [ˌentər′ten] tr unterhalten; (guests) bewirten; (doubts, hopes, suspicions) hegen || intr Gäste haben
entertainer [ˌentər′tenər] s Unterhaltungskünstler -in mf
entertain′ing adj unterhaltsam || s—**do a lot of e.** ein großes Haus führen
entertainment [ˌentər′tenmənt] s Unterhaltung f
entertain′ment tax′ s Vergnügungssteuer f
enthrall [en′θrɔl] tr bezaubern, fesseln
enthrone [en′θron] tr auf den Thron setzen; **be enthroned** thronen
enthuse [en′θ(j)uz] tr (coll) begeistern
enthusiasm [en′θ(j)uzɪˌæzəm] s Begeisterung f, Schwärmerei f

enthusiast [en'θ(j)uzɪ,æst] s Schwärmer –in *mf*

enthusiastic [en,θ(j)uzɪ'æstɪk] *adj* (about) begeistert (über *acc* or von)

entice [en'taɪs] *tr* (ver)locken

enticement [en'taɪsmənt] s Verlockung *f*

entic'ing *adj* verlockend

entire [en'taɪr] *adj* ganz, gesamt; (*trust*) voll

entirely [en'taɪrlɪ] *adv* ganz, gänzlich

entirety [en'taɪrtɪ] s—**in its e.** in seiner Gesamtheit

entitle [en'taɪtəl] *tr* (*call*) betiteln; (**to**) berechtigen (zu); **be entitled to** Anspruch haben auf (*acc*); **be entitled to** (*inf*) berechtigt sein zu (*inf*)

entity ['entɪtɪ] s Wesen *n*

entomb [en'tum] *tr* bestatten

entombment [en'tummənt] s Bestattung *f*

entomology [,entə'mɑlədʒɪ] s Entomologie *f*

entourage [,ɑntu'rɑʒ] s Begleitung *f*

entrails ['entrelz] *spl* Eingeweide *pl*

entrain [en'tren] *tr* verladen ‖ *intr* einsteigen

entrance ['entrəns] s Eingang *m*; (*drive*) Einfahrt *f*; (*of a home*) Flur *m*; (*upon office*) Antritt *m*; (*theat*) Auftritt *m*; **make one's e.** eintreten ‖ [en'træns] *tr* mitreißen

en'trance examina'tion s Aufnahmeprüfung *f*

en'trance fee' s Eintrittspreis *m*

entrant ['entrənt] s (**in**) Teilnehmer –in *mf* (an *dat*)

en-trap [en'træp] *v* (*pret & pp* **-trapped;** *ger* **-trapping**) *tr* verleiten

entreat [en'trit] *tr* anflehen

entreaty [en'tritɪ] s dringende Bitte *f*; **at his e.** auf seine Bitte

entrée ['ɑntre] s (*access*) Zutritt *m*; (*before main course*) Vorspeise *f*; (*between courses*) Zwischengericht *n*; (*main course*) Hauptgericht *n*

entrench [en'trentʃ] *tr* verschanzen; **be entrenched in** (fig) eingewurzelt sein in (*dat*)

entrenchment [en'trentʃmənt] s (*activity*) Schanzbau *m*; (*the result*) Verschanzung *f*

entrepreneur [ɑntrəprə'nʌr] s Unternehmer –in *mf*

entrust [en'trʌst] *tr* (**to**) anvertrauen (*dat*)

entry ['entrɪ] s Eintritt *m*; (*by car*) Einfahrt *f*; (*door*) Eingang *m*, Eingangstür *f*; (*into a country*) Einreise *f*; (*into office*) Antritt *m*; (*in a dictionary*) Stichwort *n*; (*into a race*) Nennung *f*; (*contestant*) Bewerber –in *mf*; (com) Buchung *f*; (theat) Auftritt *m*; **unlawful e.** Hausfriedensbruch *m*

entwine [en'twaɪn] *tr* umwinden

enumerate [ɪ'n(j)umə,ret] *tr* aufzählen

enunciate [ɪ'nʌnsɪ,et] *tr* aussprechen ‖ *intr* deutlich aussprechen

envelop [en'veləp] *tr* (said of crowds, waves) verschlingen; (said of mist, clouds, darkness) umhüllen; (mil) umfassen

envelope ['envə,lop] s Umschlag *m*

envelopment [en'veləpmənt] s Umhüllung *f*; (mil) Umfassung *f*

envenom [en'venəm] *tr* vergiften

enviable ['envɪ·əbəl] *adj* beneidenswert

envious ['envɪ·əs] *adj* (of) neidisch (auf *acc*)

environment [en'vaɪrənmənt] s (*ecological condition*) Umwelt *f*; (*surroundings*) Umgebung *f*

environmental [en,vaɪrən'mentəl] *adj* Umwelt–; umgebend, Umgebungs–

environmentalist [en,vaɪrən'mentəlɪst] Umweltschützer –in *mf*

environs [en'vaɪrənz] *spl* Umgebung *f*

envisage [en'vɪzɪdʒ] *tr* ins Auge fassen

envoy ['envɔɪ] s Gesandte *mf*

en·vy ['envɪ] s Neid *m* ‖ *v* (*pret & pp* **-vied**) *tr* (for) beneiden (um)

enzyme ['enzaɪm] s Enzym *n*

epaulet, epaulette ['epə,let] s Epaulette *f*, Schulterstück *n*

ephemeral [ɪ'femərəl] *adj* flüchtig

epic ['epɪk] *adj* episch; e. **poetry** Epik *f* ‖ s Epos *n*, Heldengedicht *n*

epicure ['epɪ,kjur] s Feinschmecker –in *mf*

epicurean [,epɪkju'ri·ən] *adj* genußsüchtig; (philos) epikureisch ‖ s Genußmensch *m*; (philos) Epikureer *m*

epidemic [,epɪ'demɪk] *adj* epidemisch ‖ s Epidemie *f*, Seuche *f*

epidermis [,epɪ'dʌrmɪs] s Oberhaut *f*

epigram ['epɪ,græm] s Epigramm *n*

epigraph ['epɪ,græf] s Inschrift *f*

epigraphy [e'pɪgrəfɪ] s Inschriftenkunde *f*

epilepsy ['epɪ,lepsɪ] s Epilepsie *f*

epileptic [,epɪ'leptɪk] *adj* epileptisch ‖ s Epileptiker –in *mf*

epilogue ['epɪ,lɔg] s Nachwort *n*

Epiphany [ɪ'pɪfənɪ] s Dreikönigsfest *n*

episcopal [ɪ'pɪskəpəl] *adj* bischöflich

Episcopalian [ɪ,pɪskə'peli·ən] *adj* Episkopal– ‖ s Episkopale *m*, Episkopalin *f*

epis'copal see' s Bischofssitz *m*

episcopate [ɪ'pɪskə,pet] s Bischofsamt *n*

episode ['epɪ,sod] s Episode *f*

epistemology [ɪ,pɪstə'mɑlədʒɪ] s Epistemologie *f*, Erkenntnistheorie *f*

epistle [ɪ'pɪsəl] s Epistel *f*

epitaph ['epɪtæf] s Grabinschrift *f*

epithet ['epɪ,θet] s Beiwort *n*

epitome [ɪ'pɪtəmɪ] s Auszug *m*; (fig) Verkörperung *f*

epitomize [ɪ'pɪtə,maɪz] *tr*—e–n Auszug machen von or aus; (fig) verkörpern

epoch ['epək], ['ipɑk] s Epoche *f*

epochal ['epəkəl] *adj* epochal

e'poch-mak'ing *adj* bahnbrechend

Ep'som salts' ['epsəm] *spl* Bittersalz *n*

equable ['ekwəbəl] *adj* gleichmäßig; (*disposition*) gleichmütig

equal ['ikwəl] *adj* gleich; (*in birth or status*) ebenbürtig; (*in worth*) gleichwertig; (*in kind*) gleichartig; **be e. to** (e.g., a task) gewachsen sein (*dat*); **be on e. terms** (be on the same level) auf gleichem Fuß stehen; **other**

things being e. bei sonst gleichen Verhältnissen || *s* Gleiche *mfn;* her or their e.(s) ihresgleichen; my (your, *etc.*) e.(s) meines– (deines–, *etc.*) e.(s) meines– (deines–, *etc.*)

equal[l]ed; *ger* **equal[l]ing** *tr* gleichkommen (*dat*); (*a record*) erreichen; (*math*) ergeben

equality [ɪ'kwɑlɪti] *s* Gleichheit *f;* (*in standing*) Gleichberechtigung *f*

equalize ['ikwə,laɪz] *tr* gleichmachen

equally ['ikwəli] *adv* gleich, ebenso

equanimity [,ikwə'nɪmɪti] *s* Gleichmut *m*

equate [i'kwet] *tr* (to or with) gleichsetzen (*dat* or mit)

equation [i'kweʒən] *s* Gleichung *f*

equator [i'kwetər] *s* Äquator *m*

equatorial [,ikwə'tɔri·əl] *adj* äquatorial

equestrian [ɪ'kwestrɪ·ən] *adj* Reiter–; **e. statue** Reiterstandbild *n* || *s* Kunstreiter –in *mf*

equilateral [,ikwɪ'lætərəl] *adj* gleichseitig

equilibrium [,ikwɪ'lɪbrɪ·əm] *s* Gleichgewicht *n;* (*fig*) Gleichmaß *n*

equinox ['ikwɪ,nɑks] *s* Tagundnachtgleiche *f*

equip [ɪ'kwɪp] *v* (*pret & pp* equipped; *ger* equipping) *tr* ausrüsten, ausstatten

equipment [ɪ'kwɪpmənt] *s* Ausrüstung *f,* Ausstattung *f*

equipoise ['ikwɪ,pɔɪz] *s* Gleichgewicht *n*

equitable ['ɛkwɪtəbəl] *adj* gerecht

equity ['ɛkwɪti] *s* (*fairness*) Unparteilichkeit *f;* (*fin*) Nettowert *m*

equivalent [ɪ'kwɪvələnt] *adj* gleichwertig; (to) gleichbedeutend (mit) || *s* Gegenwert *m;* (of) Äquivalent *n* (für)

equivocal [ɪ'kwɪvəkəl] *adj* zweideutig

equivocate [ɪ'kwɪvə,ket] *intr* zweideutig reden

equivocation [ɪ'kwɪvə,keʃən] *s* Zweideutigkeit *f*

era ['ɪrə], ['irə] *s* Zeitalter *n*

eradicate [ɪ'rædɪ,ket] *tr* ausrotten

erase [ɪ'res] *tr* ausradieren; (*a tape recording*) löschen; (*a blackboard*) abwischen; (*fig*) auslöschen

eraser [ɪ'resər] *s* Radiergummi *m;* (*for a blackboard*) Tafelwischer *m*

erasure [ɪ'reʒər], [ɪ'reʒər] *s* (*action*) Ausradieren *n;* (*erased spot*) Rasur *f*

ere [ɛr] *prep* (poet) vor (*dat*) || *conj* (poet) ehe, bevor

erect [ɪ'rɛkt] *adj* aufrecht, straff; (*hair*) gesträubt; **with head e.** erhobenen Hauptes || *tr* errichten

erection [ɪ'rɛkʃən] *s* Errichtung *f;* (*of sexual organs*) Erektion *f*

erg [ʌrg] *s* Erg *n*

ermine ['ʌrmɪn] *s* Hermelinpelz *m*

erode [ɪ'rod] *tr* (*corrode*) zerfressen; (*fig*) unterhöhlen; (*geol*) erodieren || *intr* zerfressen werden

erosion [ɪ'roʒən] *s* (*corrosion*) Zerfressen *n;* (*fig*) Unterhöhlung *f;* (*geol*) Erosion *f*

erotic [ɪ'rɑtɪk] *adj* erotisch

err [ʌr] *intr* irren, sich irren

errand ['ɛrənd] *s* Bersorgung *f;* **run an e. e–e** Besorgung machen

errand boy' *s* Laufbursche *m*

erratic [ɪ'rætɪk] *adj* regellos, ziellos; (geol) erratisch

erroneous [ɪ'roni·əs] *adj* irrtümlich

erroneously [ɪ'roni·əsli] *adv* irrtümlicherweise, versehentlich

error ['ɛrər] *s* Fehler *m,* Irrtum *m*

erudite ['ɛr(j)ʊ,daɪt] *adj* gelehrt

erudition [,ɛr(j)ʊ'dɪʃən] *s* Gelehrsamkeit *f*

erupt [ɪ'rʌpt] *intr* ausbrechen

eruption [ɪ'rʌpʃən] *s* Ausbruch *m;* (pathol) Ausschlag *m*

escalate ['ɛskə,let] *tr & intr* eskalieren

escalation [,ɛskə'leʃən] *s* Eskalierung *f*

escalator ['ɛskə,letər] *s* Rolltreppe *f*

es'calator clause' *s* Indexklausel *f*

escapade ['ɛskə,ped] *s* Eskapade *f*

escape [ɛs'kep] *s* Flucht *f;* (*of gas or liquid*) Ausströmen *n;* **have a narrow e.** mit knapper Not davonkommen || *intr* (said of gas or liquid) ausströmen; (from) flüchten (aus)

escape' clause' *s* Ausweichklausel *f*

escapee [,ɛskə'pi] *s* Flüchtling *m*

escape' hatch' *s* Notausstieg *m*

escapement [ɛs'kepmənt] *s* (horol) Hemmung *f*

escape' wheel' *s* (horol) Hemmungsrad *n*

escapism [ɛs'kepɪzəm] *s* Wirklichkeitsflucht *f*

escarpment [ɛs'kɑrpmənt] *s* (geol) Steilabhang *m;* (mil) Abdachung *f*

eschew [ɛs't/u] *tr* (ver)meiden

escort ['ɛskɔrt] *s* Geleit *n,* Schutzgeleit *n;* (*person*) Begleiter *m;* (mil) Begleitmannschaft *f,* Bedeckung *f;* (nav) Geleitschutz *m* || [ɛs'kɔrt] *tr* begleiten; (mil, nav) geleiten

es'cort ves'sel *s* Geleitschiff *n*

escutcheon [ɛs'kʌtʃən] *s* Wappenschild *m;* (*doorplate*) Schlüssellochschild *n*

Eskimo ['ɛskɪ,mo] *adj* Eskimo– || *s* (–mos & –mo) Eskimo *m*

esophagus [i'sɑfəgəs] *s* (–gi [,dʒaɪ]) Speiseröhre *f*

esoteric [,ɛso'tɛrɪk] *adj* esoterisch

especial [ɛs'pɛʃəl] *adj* besondere

especially [ɛs'pɛʃəli] *adv* besonders

espionage [,ɛspɪ·ə'nɑʒ] *s* Spionage *f*

espousal [ɛs'pauzəl] *s* (of) Annahme *f* (von)

espouse [ɛs'pauz] *tr* annehmen

esprit de corps [ɛs'pri də 'kɔr] *s* Korpsgeist *m,* Gemeinschaftsgeist *m*

espy [ɛs'paɪ] *v* (*pret & pp* espied) *tr* erspähen

essay ['ɛse] *s* Aufsatz *m,* Essay *n* || [ɛ'se] *tr* probieren

essayist ['ɛse·ɪst] *s* Essayist –in *mf*

essence ['ɛsəns] *s* Wesenheit *f;* (*scent*) Duft *m;* (*extract*) Essenz *f;* (philos) inneres Wesen *n;* **in e.** im wesentlichen

essential [ɛ'sɛnʃəl] *adj* (to) wesentlich (für) || *s* Hauptsache *f;* **the essentials** die Grundzüge *pl* establish [es'tæblɪʃ] tr (found) gründen; (a business, an account) eröffnen; (relations, connections) herstellen; (order) schaffen; (a record) aufstellen; (a fact) feststellen

establishment [es'tæblɪʃmənt] s (act) Gründung f; (institution) Anstalt f; (business) Unternehmen n; the Establishment das Establishment

estate [es'tet] s (landed property) Landgut n; (possessions) Vermögen n; (property of deceased person) Nachlaß m; (social station) Stand m

esteem [es'tim] s Hochachtung f; hold in e. achten || tr achten

esthete ['esθit] s Ästhetiker –in mf

esthetic [es'θetɪk] adj ästhetisch || esthetics s Ästhetik f

estimable ['estɪməbəl] adj schätzenswert

estimate ['estɪ‚met], ['estɪmɪt] s Kostenanschlag m; (judgment of value) Schätzung f; rough e. Überschlag m || ['estɪ‚met] tr (costs) veranschlagen; (the value) abschätzen; (homes, damages) schätzen; (at) beziffern (auf acc); e. roughly überschlagen

estimation [‚estɪ'me/ən] s Schätzung f; in my e. nach meiner Schätzung

Estonia [es'tonɪ‚ə] s Estland n

estrangement [es'trendʒmənt] s Entfremdung f

estuary ['estʃu‚ɛri] s (of a river) Mündung f; (inlet) Meeresarm m

etch [etʃ] tr radieren, ätzen

etcher ['etʃər] s Radierer –in mf

etch·ing s Radierung f; (as an art) Radierkunst f

eternal [ɪ'tʌrnəl] adj ewig

eternity [ɪ'tʌrnɪti] s Ewigkeit f

ether ['iθər] s Äther m

ethereal [ɪ'θɪrɪ‚əl] adj ätherisch

ethical ['eθɪkəl] adj ethisch, sittlich

ethics ['eθɪks] s Ethik f, Sittenlehre f

Ethiopia [‚iθɪ'opɪ‚ə] s Äthiopien n

Ethiopian [‚iθɪ'opɪ‚ən] adj äthiopisch || s Äthiopier –in mf; (language) Äthiopisch n

ethnic(al) ['eθnɪk(əl)] adj völkisch; e. group Volksgruppe f

ethnography [eθ'nɑgrəfi] s Ethnographie f

ethnology [eθ'nɑlədʒi] s Völkerkunde f

ethyl ['eθɪl] s Äthyl m

ethylene ['eθɪ‚lin] s Äthylen n

etiquette ['etɪ‚ket] s Etikette f

etymology [‚etɪ'mɑlədʒi] s Etymologie f

ety·mon ['etɪ‚mɑn] s (-mons & -ma [mə]) Etymon n

eucalyp·tus [‚jukə'lɪptəs] s (-tuses & -ti [taɪ]) Eukalyptus m

Eucharist ['jukərɪst] s—the E. das heilige Abendmahl, die Eucharistie f

eugenics [ju'dʒenɪks] s Rassenhygiene f

eulogize ['julə‚dʒaɪz] tr lobpreisen

eulogy ['julədʒi] s Lobrede f

eunuch ['junək] s Eunuch m

euphemism ['jufɪ‚mɪzəm] s Euphemismus m

euphemistic [‚jufə'mɪstɪk] adj euphemistisch, verblümt

euphonic [ju'fɑnɪk] adj wohlklingend

euphony ['jufəni] s Wohlklang m

euphoria [ju'forɪ‚ə] s Euphorie f

euphoric [ju'forɪk] adj euphorisch

euphuism ['jufju‚ɪzəm] s gezierte Ausdrucksweise f

Europe ['jurəp] s Europa n

European [‚jurə'pi‚ən] adj europäisch || s Europäer –in mf

Europe'an plan' s Hotelpreis m ohne Mahlzeiten

euthanasia [‚juθə'neʒə] s Euthanasie f

evacuate [ɪ'vækju‚et] tr evakuieren; (med) entleeren; (an area) räumen || intr sich zurückziehen

evacuation [ɪ‚vækju'e/ən] s Evakuierung f; (med) Entleerung f

evade [ɪ'ved] tr ausweichen (dat); (duties) vernachlässigen; (laws) umgehen; (prosecution, responsibility) sich entziehen (dat); (taxes) hinterziehen

evaluate [ɪ'vælju‚et] tr (e.g., jewels) (ab)schätzen; (e.g., a performance) beurteilen

evaluation [ɪ‚vælju'e/ən] s Abschätzung f; (judgment) Beurteilung f

evangelic(al) [‚ivæn'dʒelɪk(əl), ‚evən'dʒelɪk(əl)] adj evangelisch

Evangelist [ɪ'vændʒəlɪst] s Evangelist m

evaporate [ɪ'væpə‚ret] tr eindampfen || intr (above boiling point) verdampfen; (below boiling point) verdunsten; (fig) sich verflüchtigen

eva'porated milk' s Kondensmilch f

evasion [ɪ'veʒən] s (dodge) Ausweichen n; (of the law) Umgehung f; (of responsibility) Vernachlässigung f; (in speech) Ausflucht f

evasive [ɪ'vesɪv] adj ausweichend

eve [iv] s Vorabend m

even ['ivən] adj (smooth) eben, gerade; (number) gerade; (uniform) gleichmäßig; (chance) gleich; (temperament) ruhig, ausgeglichen; an e. break gleiche Aussichten pl; an e. dozen genau ein Dutzend; be e. (coll) quitt sein; e. with auf gleicher Höhe mit; get e. with mit j–m abrechnen || adv selbst, sogar; (before comparatives) noch; (as intensifier before nouns and pronouns) selbst; break e. gerade auf seine Kosten kommen; e. if selbst wenn, wenn auch; e. so trotzdem; e. though obgleich; e. today noch heute; e. when selbst wenn || tr ebnen; e. up ausgleichen

e'ven-hand'ed adj unparteiisch

evening ['ivnɪŋ] adj Abend– || s Abend m; in the e. am Abend; this e. heute abend

eve'ning gown' s Abendkleid n

eve'ning pa'per s Abendblatt n

eve'ning school' s Abendschule f

evenly ['ivənli] adv gleichmäßig; e. matched (sport) gleichwertig

ev'en-mind'ed adj gleichmütig

evenness ['ivənnɪs] s (smoothness)

Ebenheit *f;* (*uniformity*) Gleich-
mäßigkeit *f*

event [ɪ'vent] *s* Ereignis *n;* (sport)
Veranstaltung *f;* **at all events, in any
e. auf** jeden Fall; **in the e. of** im
Falle (*genit*)

eventful [ɪ'ventfəl] *adj* ereignisvoll

eventual [ɪ'ventʃu‧əl] *adj* schließlich

eventuality [ɪ‚ventʃu'æliti] *s* Möglichkeit *f*

eventually [ɪ'ventʃu‚əli] *adj* schließlich

ever ['evər] *adv* je, jemals; (*before
comparatives*) immer; **did you e.!** hat
man schon sowas gehört!; **e. after**
die ganze Zeit danach; **e. so** noch
so; **e. so much** (coll) sehr; **hardly e.**
fast nie

ev'ergreen' *adj* immergrün ‖ *s* Immergrün *n*

ev'erlast'ing *adj* ewig; (*continual*)
fortwährend; (iron) ewig

ev'ermore' *adv* immer; **for e.** in Ewigkeit

every ['evri] *adj* jeder; (*confidence*)
voll; **e. bit** (coll) völlig; **e. now and
then** ab und zu; **e. once in a while**
dann und wann; **e. other day** alle
zwei Tage; **e. time (that)** jedesmal
(wenn)

ev'erybod'y *indef pron* jeder, jeder-
mann

ev'eryday' *adj* alltäglich, Alltags-

ev'eryone', ev'ery one' *indef pron* (of)
jeder (von); **e. else** alle anderen

ev'erything' *indef pron* alles

ev'erywhere' *adv* (*position*) überall;
(*direction*) überallhin

evict [ɪ'vɪkt] *tr* delogieren

eviction [ɪ'vɪkʃən] *s* Delogierung *f*

evidence ['evɪdəns] *s* Beweismaterial
n, Beweise *pl;* (*piece of evidence*)
Beweis *m;* **as e. of** zum Beweis
(*genit*); **for lack of e.** wegen Mangels
an Beweisen; **give e.** aussagen; **in e.**
sichtbar

evident ['evɪdənt] *adj* (*obvious*) offen-
sichtlich; (*visible*) ersichtlich; **be e.**
zutage liegen

evidently ['evɪdəntli] *adv* offenbar

evil ['ivəl] *adj* übel, böse ‖ *s* Übel *n*

e'vildo'er *s* Übeltäter –in *mf*

e'vildo'ing *s* Missetat *f*

e'vil eye' *s* böser Blick *m*

e'vil-mind'ed *adj* übelgesinnt

E'vil One' *s* Böse *m*

evince [ɪ'vɪns] *tr* bekunden

evoke [ɪ'vok] *tr* hervorrufen

evolution [‚evə'luʃən] *s* Evolution *f*

evolve [ɪ'vɑlv] *tr* entwickeln, entfalten
‖ *intr* sich entwickeln, sich entfalten

ewe [ju] *s* Mutterschaf *n*

ewer ['ju‧ər] *s* Wasserkanne *f*

exact [eg'zækt] *adj* genau ‖ *tr* (*e.g.,
money*) beitreiben; (*obedience*) erzwingen

exact'ing *adj* (*strict*) streng; (*task*)
aufreibend; (*picky*) anspruchsvoll

exactly [eg'zæktli] *adv* genau

exactness [eg'zæktnɪs] *s* Genauigkeit *f*

exact' sci'ences *spl* Realien *pl*

exaggerate [eg'zædʒə‚ret] *tr* übertreiben

exaggeration [eg‚zædʒə'reʃən] *s* Über-
treibung *f*

exalt [eg'zɔlt] *tr* erheben

exam [eg'zæm] *s* (coll) Prüfung *f*

examination [eg‚zæmɪ'neʃən] *s* Prüfung *f,* Examen *n;* (jur) Verhör *n,*
Vernehmung *f;* (med) Untersuchung
f; **direct e.** (jur) direkte Befragung
f; **fail an e.** bei e-r Prüfung durchfallen; **on closer e.** bei näherer Prüfung; **pass an e.** e-e Prüfung bestehen; **take an e.** e-e Prüfung ablegen

examine [eg'zæmɪn] *tr* prüfen; (jur)
verhören, vernehmen; (med) untersuchen

examinee [eg‚zæmɪ'ni] *s* Prüfling *m*

examiner [eg'zæmɪnər] *s* (educ) Prüfer –in *mf;* (med) Untersucher –in
mf

example [eg'zæmpəl] *s* Beispiel *n;* **for
e.** zum Beispiel; **make an e. of** ein
Exempel statuieren an (*dat*); **set a
good e.** mit gutem Beispiel vorangehen

exasperate [eg'zæspə‚ret] *tr* reizen

excavate ['ekskə‚vet] *tr* ausgraben

excavation [‚ekskə've∫ən] *s* Ausgrabung *f*

excavator ['ekskə‚vetər] *s* (archeol)
Ausgräber –in *mf;* (mach) Trockenbagger *m*

exceed [ek'sid] *tr* überschreiten

exceedingly [ek'sidɪŋli] *adv* außerordentlich

ex·cel [ek'sel] *v* (pret & pp –**celled;**
ger –**celling**) *tr* übertreffen ‖ *intr*
(**in**) sich auszeichnen (in *dat*)

excellence ['eksələns] *s* Vorzüglichkeit
f

excellency ['eksələnsi] *s* Vorzüglichkeit *f;* **Your Excellency** Eure Exzellenz

excellent ['eksələnt] *adj* ausgezeichnet

excelsior [ek'selsɪ‧ər] *s* Holzwolle *f*

except [ek'sept] *adv*—**e. for** abgesehen
von; **e. if** außer wenn; **e. that** außer
daß; **e. when** außer wenn ‖ *prep*
außer (*dat*), ausgenommen (*acc*) ‖
tr ausnehmen, ausschließen

exception [ek'sepʃən] *s* Ausnahme *f;*
by way of e. ausnahmsweise; **take e.
to** Anstoß nehmen an (*dat*); **without
e.** ausnahmslos; **with the e. of** mit
Ausnahme von

exceptional [ek'sepʃənəl] *adj* außergewöhnlich, Sonder-

excerpt ['eksʌrpt] *s* Auszug *m* ‖ [ek-
'sʌrpt] *tr* exzerpieren

excess [ek'ses], ['ekses] *adj* überschüssig ‖ [ek'ses] *s* (*surplus*)
Überschuß *m;* (*immoderate amount*)
(of) Übermaß *n* (von or an *dat*);
carry to e. übertreiben; **excesses**
Ausschreitungen *pl;* **in e. of** mehr
als; **to e.** übermäßig

ex'cess bag'gage *s* Überfracht *f*

excessive [ek'sesɪv] *adj* übermäßig

ex'cess-prof'its tax' *s* Mehrgewinnsteu-
er *f*

exchange [eks't∫endʒ] *s* Austausch *m;*
(*e.g., of purchases*) Umtausch *m;*
(*of words*) Wechselgespräch *n;* (of

money) Geldwechsel *m;* (fin) Börse *f;* (mil) Kantine *f;* (telp) Vermittlung *f;* e. of letters Briefwechsel *m;* in e. dafür; in e. for für ‖ *tr (trade)* tauschen; *(replace)* auswechseln; e. for umtauschen gegen; e. places with s.o. mit j-m tauschen

exchequer [ɛks'tʃɛkər] *s* Staatskasse *f;* *(department)* Schatzamt *n*

ex'cise tax' ['ɛksaɪz] *s* Verbrauchssteuer *f*

excitable [ɛk'saɪtəbəl] *adj* erregbar

excite [ɛk'saɪt] *tr* erregen, aufregen

excitement [ɛk'saɪtmənt] *s* Erregung *f,* Aufregung *f*

excit'ing *adj* erregend, aufregend

exclaim [ɛks'klem] *tr & intr* ausrufen

exclamation [ˌɛksklə'meʃən] *s* Ausruf *m*

exclama'tion point' *s* Ausrufungszeichen *n*

exclude [ɛks'klud] *tr* ausschließen

exclusion [ɛks'kluʒən] *s* Ausschließung *f,* Ausschluß *m;* to the e. of unter Ausschluß *(genit)*

exclusive [ɛks'klusɪv] *adj (rights, etc.)* alleinig, ausschließlich; *(club)* exklusiv; *(shop)* teuer; e. of ausschließlich *(genit)*

excommunicate [ˌɛkskə'mjunɪˌket] *tr* exkommunizieren

excommunication [ˌɛkskəˌmjunɪ'keʃən] *s* Exkommunikation *f,* Kirchenbann *m*

excoriate [ɛks'korɪˌet] *tr* (fig) heruntermachen

excrement ['ɛkskrəmənt] *s* Exkremente *pl*

excrescence [ɛks'krɛsəns] *s* Auswuchs *m*

excruciating [ɛks'kruʃɪˌetɪŋ] *adj* qualvoll

exculpate ['ɛkskʌlˌpet] *tr* entschuldigen

excursion [ɛks'kʌrʒən] *s (side trip)* Abstecher *m;* *(short trip)* Ausflug *m*

excusable [ɛks'kjuzəbəl] *adj* entschuldbar, verzeihlich

excuse [ɛks'kjus] *s* Ausrede *f;* give as an e. vorgeben; make excuses for sich ausreden ‖ [ɛks'kjuz] *tr* entschuldigen; e. me! entschuldigen Sie!; you may be excused now Sie können jetzt gehen

execute ['ɛksɪˌkjut] *tr (a condemned man)* hinrichten; *(by firing squad)* erschießen; *(perform)* durchführen, vollziehen; *(a will, a sentence)* vollstrecken; *(mus)* vortragen

execution [ˌɛksɪ'kjuʃən] *s* Hinrichtung *f;* *(by firing squad)* Erschießung *f;* *(performance)* Durchführung *f,* Vollziehung *f;* (mus) Vortrag *m*

executioner [ˌɛksɪ'kjuʃənər] *s* Scharfrichter *m*

executive [ɛg'zɛkjətɪv] *adj* vollziehend, exekutiv ‖ *s* (com) Manager *m,* leitender Angestellte *mf;* the Executive (pol) die Exekutive *f*

exec'utive commit'tee *s* Vollzugsausschuß *m,* Vorstand *m*

exec'utive or'der *s* Durchführungsverordnung *f*

executor [ɛg'zɛkjətər] *s* Vollstrecker *m*

executrix [ɛg'zɛkjətrɪks] *s* Vollstreckerin *f*

exemplary [ɛg'zɛmpləri] *adj* vorbildlich, mustergültig

exempli·fy [ɛg'zɛmplɪˌfaɪ] *v* (pret & pp -fied) *tr (demonstrate)* an Beispielen erläutern; *(embody)* als Beispiel dienen für

exempt [ɛg'zɛmpt] *adj* (from) befreit (von) ‖ *tr* befreien; (mil) freistellen

exemption [ɛg'zɛmpʃən] *s* Befreiung *f;* (mil) Freistellung *f*

exercise ['ɛksərˌsaɪz] *s* Übung *f;* (of the body) Bewegung *f;* (of power) Ausübung *f;* (mil) Exerzieren *n;* take e. sich [dat] Bewegung machen ‖ *tr* üben; (the body, a horse) bewegen; (power, influence) ausüben; (mil) exerzieren ‖ *intr* üben; (mil) exerzieren

exert [ɛg'zʌrt] *tr* ausüben; e. every effort alle Kräfte rühren; e. oneself sich anstrengen

exertion [ɛg'zʌrʃən] *s* Anstrengung *f;* (e.g., of power) Ausübung *f*

exhalation [ˌɛks·hə'leʃən] *s* Ausatmung *f;* (of gases) Gasabgabe *f*

exhale [ɛks'hel] *tr & intr* ausatmen

exhaust [ɛg'zɔst] *s* (aut) Auspuff *m* ‖ *tr* erschöpfen

exhaust'ed *adj* erschöpft

exhaust' fan' *s* Absaugventilator *m*

exhaust' gas' *s* Abgas *n*

exhaust'ing *adj* anstrengend, mühselig

exhaustion [ɛg'zɔstʃən] *s* Erschöpfung *f*

exhaustive [ɛg'zɔstɪv] *adj* erschöpfend

exhaust' pipe' *s* Auspuffrohr *n*

exhaust' valve' *s* Auspuffventil *n*

exhibit [ɛg'zɪbɪt] *s* (exhibition) Ausstellung *f;* (object exhibited) Ausstellungsstück *n;* (jur) Beleg *m* ‖ *tr* zur Schau stellen; (wares) ausstellen; (e.g., courage) zeigen

exhibition [ˌɛksɪ'bɪʃən] *s* Ausstellung *f*

exhilarating [ɛg'zɪləˌretɪŋ] *adj* erheiternd

exhort [ɛg'zɔrt] *tr* ermahnen

exhume [ɛks'hjum] *tr* exhumieren

exigency ['ɛksɪdʒənsi] *s* (demand, need) Erfordnis *n;* (state of urgency) Dringlichkeit *f*

exigent ['ɛksɪdʒənt] *adj* dringlich

exile ['ɛgzaɪl] *s* Exil *n;* (person) Verbannte *mf* ‖ *tr* verbannen

exist [ɛg'zɪst] *intr* existieren; (continue to be) bestehen; e. from day to day dahinleben

existence [ɛg'zɪstəns] *s* Existenz *f,* Dasein *n;* be in e. bestehen; come into e. entstehen

existential [ˌɛgzɪs'tɛnʃəl] *adj* existentiell

existentialism [ˌɛgzɪs'tɛnʃəˌlɪzəm] *s* Existentialismus *m*

exit ['ɛgzɪt] *s* Ausgang *m;* (by car) Ausfahrt *f;* (theat) Abgang *m* ‖ *intr* (theat) abtreten

exodus ['ɛksədəs] *s* Abwanderung *f*

exonerate [ɛg'zɑnəˌret] *tr* entlasten

exorbitant [egˈzɔrbɪtənt] *adj* schwindelhaft; **e. price** Wucherpreis *m*

exorcise [ˈeksɔrˌsaɪz] *tr* exorzieren

exotic [egˈzɑtɪk] *adj* exotisch

expand [eksˈpænd] *tr* (aus)dehnen; (*enlarge*) erweitern; (*math*) entwickeln ‖ *intr* sich ausdehnen

expanse [eksˈpæns] *s* Weite *f*, Fläche *f*

expansion [eksˈpænʃən] *s* Ausdehnung *f*; (*expanded part*) Erweiterung *f*

expansive [eksˈpænsɪv] *adj* expansiv; (fig) mitteilsam

expatiate [eksˈpeʃɪˌet] *intr* (**on**) sich verbreiten (über *acc*)

expatriate [eksˈpetrɪˌɪt] *adj* ausgebürgert ‖ *s* Ausgebürgerte *mf* ‖ [eksˈpetrɪˌet] *tr* ausbürgern

expect [eksˈpekt] *tr* erwarten ‖ *intr—* **she's expecting** (coll) sie ist in anderen Umständen

expectancy [eksˈpektənsi] *s* Ewartung *f*

expectant [eksˈpektənt] *adj* erwartungsvoll; (*mother*) werdende

expectation [ˌekspekˈteʃən] *s* Erwartung *f*

expectorate [eksˈpektəˌret] *tr & intr* spucken

expediency [eksˈpidɪˌənsi] *s* Zweckmäßigkeit *f*

expedient [eksˈpidɪˌənt] *adj* zweckmäßig ‖ *s* Mittel *n*, Hilfsmittel *f*

expedite [ˈekspɪˌdaɪt] *tr* beschleunigen; (*a document*) ausstellen

expedition [ˌekspɪˈdɪʃən] *s* Expedition *f*

expeditionary force' [ˌekspɪˈdɪʃəˌneri] *s* (mil) Expeditionsstreitkräfte *pl*

expeditious [ˌekspɪˈdɪʃəs] *adj* schleunig

ex-pel [eksˈpel] *v* (*pret & pp* **-pelled;** *ger* **-pelling**) *tr* (aus)treiben; (*a student*) (**from**) verweisen (**von**)

expend [eksˈpend] *tr* (*time, effort, etc.*) aufwenden; (*money*) ausgeben

expendable [eksˈpendəbəl] *adj* entbehrlich

expenditure [eksˈpendɪtʃər] *s* Aufwand *m*; (*of money*) Ausgabe *f*

expense [eksˈpens] *s* Ausgabe *f*; **at s.o.'s e.** (& fig) auf j-s Kosten; **expenses** Unkosten *pl*; **go to great e.** sich in Unkosten stürzen

expense' account' *s* Spesenkonto *n*

expensive [eksˈpensɪv] *adj* kostspielig

experience [eksˈpɪrɪˌəns] *s* Erfahrung *f*; (*an event*) Erlebnis *n*; **no previous e. necessary** Vorkenntnisse nicht erforderlich ‖ *tr* erfahren; (*pain*) erdulden; (*loss*) erleiden

experienced [eksˈpɪrɪˌənst] *adj* erfahren

experiment [eksˈperɪmənt] *s* Experiment *n*, Versuch *m* ‖ [eksˈperɪˌment] *intr* experimentieren, Versuche anstellen

experimental [eksˌperɪˈmentəl] *adj* experimentell, Versuchs-

expert [ˈekspərt] *adj* fachmännisch, erfahren; **e. advice** Gutachten *n* ‖ *s* Fachmann *m*; (jur) Sachverständige *mf*

expertise [ˌeksperˈtiz] *s* (*opinion*) Gutachten *n*; (*skill*) Sachkenntnis *f*

expiate [ˈekspɪˌet] *tr* sühnen, büßen

expiation [ˌekspɪˈeʃən] *s* Sühnung *f*

expiration [ˌekspɪˈreʃən] *s* Verfall *m*

expira'tion date' *s* Verfalltag *m*

expire [eksˈpaɪr] *tr* ausatmen ‖ *intr* verfallen; (*die*) verscheiden

explain [eksˈplen] *tr* erklären, erläutern; (*justify*) rechtfertigen

explanation [ˌekspləˈneʃən] *s* Erklärung *f*, Erläuterung *f*

explanatory [eksˈplænəˌtori] *adj* erklärend, erläuternd

expletive [ˈeksplɪtɪv] *s* Füllwort *n*

explicit [eksˈplɪsɪt] *adj* ausdrücklich

explode [eksˈplod] *tr* explodieren lassen; (*a theory*) verwerfen ‖ *intr* explodieren; (*said of a grenade*) krepieren; (**with**) platzen (vor *dat*)

exploit [ˈeksplɔɪt] *s* Heldentat *f*, Großtat *f* ‖ [eksˈplɔɪt] *tr* ausnutzen; (pej) ausbeuten; (min) abbauen

exploitation [ˌeksplɔɪˈteʃən] *s* Ausnutzung *f*; (pej) Ausbeutung *f*; (min) Abbau *m*

exploration [ˌekspləˈreʃən] *s* Erforschung *f*

explore [eksˈplor] *tr* erforschen

explorer [eksˈplorər] *s* Forscher *–in mf*

explosion [eksˈploʒən] *s* Explosion *f*

explosive [eksˈplosɪv] *adj* explosiv, Spreng- ‖ *s* (*explosive substance*) Sprengstoff *m*; (*device*) Sprengkörper *m*

explo'sive charge' *s* Sprengladung *f*

exponent [eksˈponənt] *s* Exponent *m*

export [ˈeksport] *adj* Ausfuhr- ‖ *s* Ausfuhr *m*, Export *m*; **exports** Ausfuhrgüter *pl* ‖ [eksˈport] *tr* ausführen

exportation [ˌeksporˈteʃən] *s* Ausfuhr *m*

exporter [ˈeksportər], [eksˈportər] *s* Ausfuhrhändler *–in mf*, Exporteur *–in mf*

expose [eksˈpoz] *tr* (*to danger, ridicule, sun*) aussetzen; (*bare*) entblößen; (*a person*) (**as**) bloßstellen (als), entlarven (als); (phot) belichten

exposé [ˌekspoˈze] *s* Enthüllung *f*

exposition [ˌekspoˈzɪʃən] *s* Ausstellung *f*; (rhet) Exposition *f*

expostulate [eksˈpɑstʃəˌlet] *intr* protestieren; **e. with s.o. about** j-m ernste Vorhaltungen machen über (*acc*)

exposure [eksˈpoʒər] *s* (*of a child*) Aussetzung *f*; (*laying bare*) Entblößung *f*; (*unmasking*) Entlarvung *f*; (*of a building*) Lage *f*; (phot) Belichtung *f*

expo'sure me'ter *s* Belichtungsmesser *m*

expound [eksˈpaund] *tr* erklären

express [eksˈpres] *adj* ausdrücklich ‖ *s* (rr) Expreß *m*; **by e.** als Eilgut ‖ *tr* ausdrücken; (*feelings*) zeigen; **e. oneself** sich äußern

express' com'pany *s* Paketpostgesellschaft *f*

expression [eksˈpreʃən] *s* Ausdruck *m*

expressive [eks'presɪv] *adj* ausdrucksvoll

express' train' *s* Expreßzug *m*

express' way' *s* Schnellverkehrsstraße *f*

expropriate [eks'proprɪ͵et] *tr* enteignen

expulsion [eks'pʌlʃən] *s* Austreibung *f*; (*from school or a game*) Verweisung *f*

expunge [eks'pʌndʒ] *tr* ausstreichen

expurgate ['ekspər͵get] *tr* säubern

exquisite ['ekskwɪzɪt], [eks'kwɪzɪt] *adj* exquisit, vorzüglich

ex-service-man [͵eks'sʌrvɪs͵mæn] *s* (**-men'**) ehemaliger Soldat *m*

extant [ekstænt] *adj* noch bestehend

extemporaneous [eks͵tempə'renɪ-əs] *adj* aus dem Stegreif, unvorbereitet

extempore [eks'tempəri] *adj* unvorbereitet ‖ *adv* aus dem Stegreif

extemporize [eks'tempə͵raɪz] *tr & intr* extemporieren

extend [eks'tend] *tr* (*expand*) ausdehnen; (*a line*) fortführen; (*time*) verlängern; (*congratulations, invitation*) aussprechen; (*one's hand*) ausstrecken; (*a building*) ausbauen ‖ *intr* (**to**) sich erstrecken (bis); **e. beyond** hinausgehen über (*acc*)

extension [eks'tenʃən] *s* Ausdehnung *f*; (*of time, credit*) Verlängerung *f*; (*archit*) Anbau *m*; (*telp*) Nebenanschluß *m*

exten'sion cord' *s* Verlängerungsschnur *f*

exten'sion lad'der *s* Ausziehleiter *f*

exten'sion ta'ble *s* Ausziehtisch *m*

extensive [eks'tensɪv] *adj* umfassend

extent [eks'tent] *s* Umfang *m*, Ausmaß *n*; **to some e.** eingermaßen; **to the full e.** in vollem Umfang; **to what e.** inwiefern

extenuating [eks'tenju͵etɪŋ] *adj* mildernd

exterior [eks'tɪrɪ-ər] *adj* Außen-, äußere ‖ *s* Äußere *n*

exterminate [eks'tʌrmɪ͵net] *tr* vertilgen, ausrotten

extermination [eks͵tʌrmɪ'neʃən] *s* Vertilgung *f*; (*of vermin*) Raumentwesung *f*

exterminator [eks'tʌrmɪ͵netər] *s* Raumentweser *m*

external [eks'tʌrnəl] *adj* Außen-, äußerlich ‖ **externals** *spl* Äußerlichkeiten *pl*

extinct [eks'tɪŋkt] *adj* (*volcano*) erloschen; (*animal*) ausgestorben; **become e.** aussterben

extinguish [eks'tɪŋgwɪʃ] *tr* auslöschen; **be extinguished** erlöschen

extinguisher [eks'tɪŋgwɪʃər] *s* Löschgerät *n*

extirpate ['ekstər͵pet] *tr* ausrotten

ex-tol [eks'tol] *v* (*pret & pp* **-tolled;** *ger* **-tolling**) *tr* erheben, lobpreisen

extort [eks'tort] *tr* erpressen

extortion [eks'torʃən] *s* Erpressung *f*

extortionate [eks'torʃənɪt] *adj* überhöht

extra ['ekstrə] *adj* übrig; (*special*) Sonder-, Extra-; **meals are e.** Mahlzeiten werden zusätzlich berechnet ‖ *adv* extra, besonders ‖ *s* (cin) Statist *m* *in* *mf*; (journ) Sonderausgabe *f*; (theat) Komparse *m*; **extras** (*expenses*) Nebenausgaben *pl*; (*accessories*) Zubehör *n*

extract ['ekstrækt] *s* Extrakt *m*, Auszug *m*; (*excerpt*) Ausschnitt *m* ‖ [eks'trækt] *tr* extrahieren, ausziehen; (dent, math) ziehen

extraction [eks'trækʃən] *s* (*lineage*) Abstammung *f*; (dent) Zahnziehen *n*; (min) Gewinnung *f*

extracurricular [͵ekstrəkə'rɪkjələr] *adj* außerplanmäßig

extradite ['ekstrə͵daɪt] *tr* ausliefern

extradition [͵ekstrə'dɪʃən] *s* Auslieferung *f*

ex'tra in'come *s* Nebeneinkünfte *pl*

ex'tramar'ital *adj* außerehelich

extramural [͵ekstrə'mjurəl] *adj* außerhalb der Schule stattfindend

extraneous [eks'trenɪ-əs] *adj* unwesentlich

extraordinary [͵eks'trordɪ͵neri] *adj* außerordentlich

ex'tra pay' *s* Zulage *f*

extrapolate [eks'træpə͵let] *tr & intr* extrapolieren

extrasensory [͵ekstrə'sensəri] *adj* übersinnlich

extravagance [eks'trævəgəns] *s* Verschwendung *f*

extravagant [eks'trævəgənt] *adj* verschwenderisch, extravagant; (*idea, plan*) überspannt

extreme [eks'trim] *adj* äußerst; (*radical*) extrem; (*old age*) höchst; (*necessity*) dringend ‖ *s* Äußerste *n*; **at the other e.** am entgegengesetzten Ende; **carry to extremes** auf die Spitze treiben; **in the e.** äußerst

extremely [eks'trimli] *adv* äußerst

extreme' unc'tion *s* die Letzte Ölung

extremist [eks'trimɪst] *s* Extremist *–in* *mf*

extremity [eks'tremɪti] *s* Äußerste *n*, äußerstes Ende *n*; **be reduced to extremities** aus dem letzten Loch pfeifen; **extremities** (*hands and feet*) Extremitäten *pl*

extricate ['ekstrɪ͵ket] *tr* befreien

extrinsic [eks'trɪnsɪk] *adj* äußerlich

extrovert ['ekstrə͵vʌrt] *s* Extravertierte *mf*

extrude [eks'trud] *tr* ausstoßen

exuberant [eg'z(j)ubərənt] *adj* (*luxuriant*) üppig; (*lavish*) überschwenglich

exude [eg'zud] *tr* ausschwitzen; (fig) ausstrahlen

exult [eg'zʌlt] *intr* jauchzen

exultant [eg'zʌltənt] *adj* jauchzend

eye [aɪ] *s* Auge *n*; (*of a needle*) Öhr *n*; **an eye for an eye** Auge um Auge; **be all eyes** große Augen machen; **by** eye nach dem Augenmaß; **close one's eyes to** die Augen schließen vor (*dat*); **have an eye for** Sinn haben für; **have good eyes** gut sehen; **in my eyes** nach meiner Ansicht; **in the eyes of the law** vom Standpunkt des Gesetzes aus; **keep a close eye on** s.o. j-m auf die Finger sehen; **keep an eye on s.th.** ein wachsames Auge

auf etw [*acc*] haben; **keep one's eyes peeled** scharf aufpassen; **lay eyes on** zu Gesicht bekommen; **makes eyes at** verliebte Blicke zuwerfen (*dat*); **see eye to eye with** völlig übereinstimmen mit; **with an eye to** mit Rücksicht auf (*acc*) || *v* (*pret & pp* **eyed;** *ger* **eying & eyeing**) *tr* mustern, schielen nach
eye'ball' *s* Augapfel *m*
eye'brow' *s* Augenbraue *f*
eye'brow pen'cil *s* Augenbrauenstift *m*
eye' cat'cher *s* Blickfang *m*
eye'cup' *s* Augenspülglas *n*
eye' drops' *spl* Augentropfen *pl*
eyeful ['aɪful] *s*—**get an e.** etw Hübsches sehen
eye'glass' *s* Augenglas *n;* **eyeglasses** Brille *f*
eye'lash' *s* Wimper *f*
eyelet ['aɪlɪt] *s* Öse *f*

eye'lid' *s* Lid *n*, Augenlid *n*
eye'o'pener *s* (*surprise*) Überraschung *f;* (*liquor*) Schnäpschen *n*
eye'piece' *s* Okular *n*
eye'shade' *s* Augenschirm *m*
eye' shad'ow *s* Lidschatten *m*
eye'shot' *s*—**within e.** in Schweite
eye'sight' *s* Augenlicht *n*, Sehkraft *f;* (*range*) Schweite *f;* **have bad (or good) e.** schlechte (or gute) Augen haben
eye' sock'et *s* Augenhöhle *f*
eye'sore' *s* (fig) Dorn *m* im Auge
eye'strain' *s* Überanstrengung *f* der Augen
eye'tooth' *s* (–**teeth**) Augenzahn *m;* **cut one's eyeteeth** (fig) erfahrener werden
eye'wash' *s* Augenwasser *n;* (sl) Schwindel *m*
eye'wit'ness *s* Augenzeuge *m*, Augenzeugin *f*

F

F, f [ɛf] *s* sechster Buchstabe des englischen Alphabets; (mus) F *n;* **F flat** Fes *n;* **F sharp** Fis *n*
fable ['febəl] *s* Fabel *f*, Märchen *n*
fabric ['fæbrɪk] *s* Gewebe *n;* (*cloth*) Stoff *m;* (fig) Gefüge *n*
fabricate ['fæbrɪ‚ket] *tr* herstellen; (*lies*) erfinden
fabrication [‚fæbrɪ'keʃən] *s* Herstellung *f;* (fig) Erfindung *f*
fabulous ['fæbjələs] *adj* fabelhaft
façade [fə'sad] *s* Fassade *f*
face [fes] *s* Gesicht *n;* (*dial*) Zifferblatt *n;* (tex) rechte Seite *f;* (typ) Satzspiegel *m;* **f. to f. with** Auge in Auge mit; **in the f. of** angesichts (*genit*); **lose f.** sich blamieren; **make faces at s.o.** j–m Gesichter schneiden; **on the f. of it** augenscheinlich; **save f.** das Gesicht wahren; **show one's f.** sich blicken lassen || *tr* (& fig) ins Auge sehen (*dat*); (*said of a building*) liegen nach; (e.g., *with brick*) verkleiden; **be faced with** stehen vor (*dat*); **have to f. the music** die Suppe löffeln müssen || *intr* (*in some direction*) liegen; **about f.!** (mil) kehrt!; **he faced up to it like a man** er stellte seinen Mann
face' card' *s* Bildkarte *f*, Figur *f*
face' cream' *s* Gesichtskrem *f*
face' lift'ing *s* Gesichtsstraffung *f;* (*of a building*) Schönheitsreparatur *f*
face' pow'der *s* Gesichtspuder *m*
facet ['fæsɪt] *s* Facette *f;* (fig) Aspekt *m*
facetious [fə'siʃəs] *adj* scherzhaft
face' val'ue *s* Nennwert *m;* **take at f.** (fig) für bare Münze nehmen
facial ['feʃəl] *adj* Gesichts–; **f. expression** Miene *f* || *s* Gesichtspflege *f*
facilitate [fə'sɪlɪ‚tet] *tr* erleichtern
facility [fə'sɪlɪti] *s* (*ease*) Leichtigkeit

f; (*skill*) Geschicklichkeit *f;* **facilities** Einrichtungen *pl*
fac'ing *s* (archit) Verkleidung *f;* (sew) Besatz *m*
facsimile [fæk'sɪmɪli] *s* Faksimile *n*
fact [fækt] *s* Tatsache *f;* **apart from the f. that** abgesehen davon, daß; **facts of the case** Tatbestand *m;* **in f.** tatsächlich; **it is a f. that** es steht fest, daß
fact'-find'ing *adj* Untersuchungs–
faction ['fækʃən] *s* Clique *f*
factional ['fækʃənəl] *adj* klüngelhaft
factor ['fæktər] *s* (& math) Faktor *m*
factory ['fæktəri] *s* Fabrik *f*
factual ['fækt/ʊ‚əl] *adj* sachlich
faculty ['fækəlti] *s* Vermögen *n;* (educ) Lehrkörper *m*
fad [fæd] *s* Mode *f;* **latest fad** letzter Schrei *m*
fade [fed] *tr* verblassen lassen; **f. in** einblenden; **f. out** ausblenden || *intr* (*said of colors, memories*) verblassen; (*said of cloth, wallpaper, etc.*) verschießen; (*said of flowers*) verwelken; **f. in** (cin, rad, telv) einblenden; **f. out** (cin, rad, telv) ausblenden
fade'-in' *s* (cin, rad, telv) Einblenden *n*
fade'-out' *s* (cin, rad, telv) Ausblenden *n*
fag [fæg] *s* (*cigarette*) (sl) Glimmstengel *m;* (*homosexual*) (sl) Schwuler *m* || *v* (*pret & pp* **fagged;** *ger* **fagging**) *tr*—**fag out** (sl) auspumpen
fagged *adj* (sl) erschöpft
fagot ['fægət] *s* Reisigbündel *n*
fail [fel] *s*—**without f.** ganz bestimmt || *tr* (*an examination*) durchfallen bei; (*a student*) durchfallen lassen; (*friends*) im Stich lassen; (*a father*) enttäuschen; **failing this** widrigensfalls; **I f. to see** ich kann nicht einsehen; **words f. me** mir fehlen die

Worte || *intr* (*said of a person or device*) versagen; (*said of a project, attempt*) fehlschlagen; (*said of crops*) schlecht ausfallen; (*said of strength*) abnehmen; (*said of health*) sich verschlechtern; (com) in Konkurs geraten

failure [ˈfeljər] *s* Versagen *n*; (*person*) Versager –in *mf*; (*lack of success, unsuccessful venture*) Mißerfolg *m*; (*omission*) Versäumnis *n*; (*deterioration*) Schwäche *f*; (educ) ungenügende Zensur *f*; (com) Konkurs *m*

faint [fent] *adj* schwach; (*slight*) leise; **feel f.** sich schwach fühlen || *s* Ohnmacht *f* || *intr* ohnmächtig werden

faint'-heart'ed *adj* kleinmütig

faint'ing spell' *s* Ohnmachtsanfall *m*

fair [fer] *adj* (*just*) gerecht, fair; (*blond*) blond; (*complexion*) hell; (*weather*) heiter; (*chance, knowledge*) mittelmäßig; (*warning*) rechtzeitig; **f. to middling** gut bis mäßig || *s* Jahrmarkt *m*, Messe *f*

fair' game' *s* (& fig) Freiwild *n*

fair'ground' *s* Jahrmarktplatz *m*

fairly [ˈferli] *adv* ziemlich

fair'-mind'ed *adj* unparteiisch

fairness [ˈfernɪs] *s* Gerechtigkeit *f*; **in f. to s.o.** um j–m Gerechtigkeit widerfahren zu lassen

fair' play' *s* fair Play *n*

fair' sex', **the** *s* das schöne Geschlecht

fair'way' *s* (golf) Spielbahn *f*; (naut) Fahrwasser *n*

fair'-weath'er *adj* (*friend*) unzuverlässig

fairy [ˈferi] *adj* Feen– || *s* Fee *f*; (sl) Schwule *mf*

fair'y god'mother *s* gute Fee *f*

fair'yland' *s* Märchenland *n*

fair'ytale' *s* (& fig) Märchen *n*

faith [feθ] *s* Glaube(n) *m*; (in) Vertrauen *n* (auf *acc* or zu); **on the f.** of im Vertrauen auf (*acc*); **put one's f. in** Glauben schenken (*dat*)

faithful [ˈfeθfəl] *adj* (to) (ge)treu (*dat*); (*exact*) genau, wahrheitsgemäß || **the f.** *spl* die Gläubigen

faith' heal'er *s* Gesundbeter –in *mf*

faithless [ˈfeθlɪs] *adj* treulos

fake [fek] *adj* verfälscht || *s* Fälschung *f*; (*person*) Simulant –in *mf* || *tr* vortäuschen, simulieren; (*forge*) fälschen

faker [ˈfekər] *s* Simulant –in *mf*

falcon [ˈfɔ(l)kən] *s* Falke *m*

falconer [ˈfɔ(l)kənər] *s* Falkner *m*

fall [fɔl] *adj* Herbst– || *s* Fall *m*; (*of prices, of a government*) Sturz *m*; (*moral*) Verfall *m*; (*of water*) Fall *m*; (*autumn*) Herbst *m*; (Bib) Sündenfall *m*; || *v* (*pret* fell [fel]; *pp* fallen [ˈfɔlən] *intr* (*said of a person, object, rain, snow, holiday, prices, temperature*) fallen; (*said of a town*) gestürzt werden; **f. apart** auseinanderfallen; **f. away** wegfallen; **f. back** zurückfallen; (mil) sich zurückziehen; **f. back on** zurückgreifen auf (*acc*); **f. behind** (in) zurückbleiben (mit); **f. below** unterschreiten; **f. down** umfallen; (*said only of per-*

sons) hinfallen; **f. down on the job** versagen; **f. due** fällig werden; **f. flat** (coll) flachfallen; **f. for** reinfallen auf (*acc*); **f. from** abfallen von; **f. from grace** in Ungnade fallen; **f. in** (*said of a roof*) einstürzen; (mil) antreten; **f. in love with** sich verlieben in (*acc*); **f. in step** Tritt fassen; **f. into** (*e.g., a hole*) hereinfallen in (*acc*); (*e.g., trouble*) geraten in (*acc*); **f. into ruin** zerfallen; **f. in with s.o.** in zufällig treffen; **f. off** abfallen; (com) zurückgehen; **f. out** (*said of hair*) ausfallen; **f. out with** sich verfeinden mit; **f. over** umfallen; **f. short** knapp werden; (arti) kurz gehen; **f. short of** zurückbleiben hinter (*dat*); **f. through** durchfallen; **f. to s.o.'s share** in–m zufallen; **f. under s.o.'s influence** unter j–s Einfluß geraten; **f. upon** herfallen über (*acc*)

fallacious [fəˈleʃəs] *adj* trügerisch

fallacy [ˈfæləsi] *s* Trugschluß *m*, Fehlschluß *m*

fall' guy' *s* (sl) Sündenbock *m*

fallible [ˈfælɪbəl] *adj* fehlbar

fall'ing off' *s* Rückschritt *m*

fall'ing rocks' *spl* (public sign) Steinschlag *m*

fall'ing star' *s* Sternschnuppe *f*

fall'out' *s* radioaktiver Niederschlag *m*

fallow [ˈfælo] *adj* (agr) brach; **lie f.** (& fig) brachliegen

false [fɔls] *adj* falsch, Miß–; (*start, step*) Fehl–; (*bottom*) doppelt; (*ceiling*) Zwischen–

false' alarm' *s* blinder Alarm *m*; (fig) Schreckschuß *m*

false' face' *s* Maske *f*

false' front' *s* (fig) (coll) Mache *f*

false'-heart'ed *adj* treulos

false'hood' *s* Unwahrheit *f*

false' preten'ses *spl* Hochstapelei *f*

false' teeth' *spl* (künstliches) Gebiß *n*

false·to [ˈfɔlˈseto] *s* (–tos) Falset *n*

falsi·fy [ˈfɔlsɪˌfaɪ] *v* (*pret* & *pp* –fied) *tr* (ver)fälschen

falsity [ˈfɔlsɪti] *s* Falschheit *f*

falter [ˈfɔltər] *intr* schwanken; (in *speech*) stocken

fame [fem] *s* Ruf, *m*, Ruhm *m*

famed *adj* (for) berühmt (wegen, durch)

familiar [fəˈmɪljər] *adj* bekannt; (*expression*) geläufig; (*e.g., sight*) gewohnt; (*close*) vertraut; **become f. with** sich bekannt machen mit

familiarity [fəˌmɪliˈærɪti] *s* Vertrautheit *f*; (*closeness*) Vertraulichkeit *f*

familiarize [fəˈmɪljəˌraɪz] *tr* bekannt machen

family [ˈfæm(ɪ)li] *adj* Familien–; **in a f. way** in anderen Umständen || *s* Familie *f*

fam'ily doc'tor *s* Hausarzt *m*

fam'ily man' *s* häuslicher Mann *m*

fam'ily name' *s* Familienname *m*

fam'ily tree' *s* Stammbaum *m*

famine [ˈfæmɪn] *s* Hungersnot *f*

famish [ˈfæmɪʃ] *tr* (ver)hungern lassen || *intr* verhungern

fam'ished *adj* ausgehungert

famous ['feməs] *adj* (for) berühmt (wegen, durch)

fan [fæn] *s* Fächer *m*, Wedel *m*; (*electric*) Ventilator *m*; (sl) Fan *m* ‖ *v* (*pret & pp* fanned; *ger* fanning) *tr* fächeln; (*a fire*) anfachen; (*passions*) entfachen ‖ *intr*—fan out (*said of roads*) fächerförmig auseinandergehen; (mil) ausschwärmen

fanatic [fə'nætɪk] *adj* fanatisch ‖ *s* Fanatiker –in *mf*

fanatical [fə'nætɪkəl] *adj* fanatisch

fanaticism [fə'nætɪ‚sɪzəm] *s* Fanatismus *m*

fan′ belt′ *s* (aut) Keilriemen *m*

fan′cied *adj* eingebildet

fancier ['fænsɪ‚ər] *s* Liebhaber –in *mf*

fanciful ['fænsɪfəl] *adj* phantastisch

fan‑cy ['fænsɪ] *adj* (extra)fein; (*e.g., dress*) Luxus-; (sport) Kunst-; f. price Phantasiepreis *m* ‖ *s* Phantasie *f*; passing f. vorübergehender Spleen *m*; take a f. to Gefallen finden an (*dat*) ‖ *v* (*pret & pp* –cied) *tr* sich [*dat*] vorstellen

fan′cy foods′ *spl* Feinkost *f*

fan′cy‑free′ *adj* ungebunden

fan′fare′ *s* Fanfare *f*; (*fuss*) Tamtam *s*

fang [fæŋ] *s* Fangzahn *m*; (*of a snake*) Giftzahn *m*

fan′ mail′ *s* Verehrerbriefe *pl*

fantastic(al) [fæn'tæstɪk(əl)] *adj* phantastisch, toll

fantasy ['fæntəsɪ] *s* Phantasie *f*

far [far] *adj* (& fig) weit; at the far end am anderen Ende; far cry from etw ganz anderes als; far side andere Seite *f*; in the far future in der fernen Zukunft ‖ *adv* weit; as far as soweit; (*up to*) bis zu, bis an (*acc*); as far as I am concerned was mich anbelangt; as far as I know soviel ich weiß; as far as that goes was das betrifft; by far weitaus, bei weitem; far and away weitaus; far away weit entfernt; far below tief unten; far better weit besser; far from it! weit gefehlt!; far from ready noch lange nicht fertig; far into the night tief in die Nacht hinein; far out (sl) ausgefallen; from far von weitem; (*from a distant place*) von weit her; go far es weit bringen; go far towards (*ger*) viel beitragen zu (*inf*); go too far das Maß überschreiten; not far from unweit von; so far soweit, bisher

far′away′ *adj* weit entfernt; (fig) träumerisch

farce [fars] *s* Possenspiel *n*, Farce *f*; (fig) Posse *f*, Schwank *m*

farcical ['farsɪkəl] *adj* possenhaft

fare [fer] *s* (*travel price*) Fahrpreis *m*; (*money for travel*) Fahrgeld *n*; (*passenger*) Fahrgast *m*; (*food*) Kost *f* ‖ *intr* (er)gehen; how did you f., well or ill? wie ist es Ihnen ergangen, gut oder schlecht?

Far′ East′, the *s* der Ferne Osten

Far′ East′ern *adj* fernöstlich

fare′well′ *s* Valet *n*, Lebewohl *n*; bid s.o. f. j–m Lebewohl sagen ‖ *interj* lebe wohl!; lebt wohl!

farewell′ din′ner *s* Abschiedsschmaus *m*

farewell′ par′ty *s* Abschiedsfeier *f*

far‑fetched ['far'fɛt/t] *adj* gesucht

far‑flung ['far'flʌŋ] *adj* weit ausgedehnt

farina [fə'rinə] *s* Grießmehl *n*

farm [farm] *adj* landwirtschaftlich ‖ *s* Farm *f*, Bauernhof *m* ‖ *tr* bebauen, bewirtschaften ‖ *intr* Landwirtschaft betreiben, Bauer sein

farm′ hand′ *s* Landarbeiter *m*

farm′house′ *s* Bauernhaus *n*

farm′ing *adj* landwirtschaftlich ‖ *s* Landwirtschaft *f*

farm′land′ *s* Ackerland *n*

farm′ machin′ery *s* Landmaschinen *pl*

farm′yard′ *s* Bauernhof *m*

far′‑off′ *adj* fernliegend

far′‑reach′ing *adj* weitreichend; (*decision*) folgenschwer

far′‑sight′ed *adj* weitsichtig; (fig) weitblickend

farther ['farðər] *adj & adv* weiter

farthest ['farðɪst] *adj* weiteste ‖ *adv* am weitesten

farthing ['farðɪŋ] *s*—not worth a f. keinen Pfifferling wert

fascinate ['fæsɪ‚net] *tr* faszinieren

fas′cinating *adj* faszinierend

fascination [‚fæsɪ'neʃən] *s* Faszination *f*

fascism ['fæʃɪzəm] *s* Faschismus *m*

fascist ['fæʃɪst] *s* Faschist –in *mf*

fashion ['fæʃən] *s* Mode *f*; (*manner*) Art *f*, Weise *f*; after a f. in gewisser Weise; in f. in Mode; out of f. aus der Mode ‖ *tr* gestalten, bilden

fashionable ['fæʃənəbəl] *adj* (*modern*) modisch; (*elegant*) elegant

fash′ion magazine′ *s* Modenzeitschrift *f*

fash′ion plate′ *s* Modedame *f*

fash′ion show′ *s* Mode(n)schau *f*

fast [fæst] *adj* schnell; (*dye*) dauerhaft; (*company*) flott; (*life*) locker; (phot) lichtstark; be f. (*said of a clock*) vorgehen; f. train Schnellzug *m*; pull a f. one on s.o. (coll) j–m ein Schnippchen schlagen ‖ *adv* schnell; (*firmly*) fest; as f. as possible schnellstens; be f. asleep im tiefen Schlaf liegen; hold f. festhalten; not so f.! nicht so stürmisch! ‖ *s* Fasten *n* ‖ *intr* fasten

fast′ day′ *s* Fasttag *m*

fasten ['fæsən] *tr* festmachen, sichern; (*a buckle*) schnallen; (*to*) befestigen (an *dat*); f. one's seat belt sich anschnallen; f. the blame on die Schuld zuschieben (*dat*) ‖ *intr*—f. upon sich heften an (*acc*)

fastener ['fæsənər] *s* Verschluß *m*

fastidious [fæs'tɪdɪ‑əs] *adj* wählerisch

fast′ing *s* Fasten *n*

fat [fæt] *adj* (*fatter*; *fattest*) fett; (*plump*) dick, fett; (*profits*) reich ‖ *s* Fett *n*; chew the fat (sl) schwatzen

fatal ['fetəl] *adj* tödlich; (*mistake*) verhängnisvoll; f. to verhängnisvoll für

fatalism ['fetə‚lɪzəm] *s* Fatalismus *m*

fatalist ['fetəlɪst] *s* Fatalist –in *mf*

fatality [fə'tælɪti] *s* Todesfall *m*; (*accident victim*) Todesopfer *n*; (*disaster*) Unglück *n*

fat' cat' *s* (sl) Geldgeber –in *mf*

fate [fet] *s* Schicksal *n*, Verhängnis *n*; **the Fates** die Parzen *pl*

fated ['fetɪd] *adj* vom Schicksal bestimmt

fateful ['fetfəl] *adj* verhängnisvoll

fat'head' *s* (coll) dummes Luder *n*

father ['faðər] *s* Vater *m*; (eccl) Pater *m* || *tr* (*beget*) erzeugen; (*originate*) hervorbringen

fa'therhood' *s* Vaterschaft *f*

fa'ther-in-law' *s* (*fathers-in-law*) Schwiegervater *m*

fa'therland' *s* Vaterland *n*

fatherless ['faðərlɪs] *adj* vaterlos

fatherly ['faðərli] *adj* väterlich

Fa'ther's Day' *s* Vatertag *m*

fathom ['fæðəm] *s* Klafter *f* || *tr* sondieren; (fig) ergründen

fathomless ['fæðəmlɪs] *adj* unergründlich

fatigue [fə'tig] *s* Ermattung *f*; (mil) Arbeitsdienst *m*; **fatigues** (mil) Arbeitsanzug *m* || *tr* abmatten

fat·so ['fætso] *s* (*-sos* & *-soes*) (coll) Fettkloß *m*

fatten ['fætən] *tr* mästen || *intr*—f. up (coll) sich mästen

fatty ['fæti] *adj* fettig, fett; **f. tissue** Fettgewebe *n* || *s* (coll) Dicke *mf*

fatuous ['fætʃʊ·əs] *adj* albern

faucet ['fɔsɪt] *s* Wasserhahn *m*

fault [fɔlt] *s* (*blame*) Schuld *f*; (*misdeed*) Vergehen *n*, Fehler *m*; (*defect*) Defekt *m*; (geol) Verwerfung *f*; (tennis) Fehlball *m*; **at f.** schuldig; **find f. with** etw zu tadeln finden an (*dat*); **to a f.** allzusehr || *intr* (geol) sich verwerfen

fault'find'er *s* Krittler –in *mf*

fault'find'ing *adj* tadelsüchtig || *s* KritteIei *f*

faultless ['fɔltlɪs] *adj* fehlerfrei

faulty ['fɔlti] *adj* fehlerhaft

faun [fɔn] *s* (myth) Faun *m*

fauna ['fɔnə] *s* Fauna *f*

favor ['fevər] *s* (*kind act*) Gefallen *m*; (*good will*) Gunst *f*; **in f. of** zugunsten (*genit*), für; **in s.o.'s f. zu j–s Gunsten; lose f. with** s.o. sich [*dat*] j–s Gunst verwirken; **speak in f. of s.th.** für etw aussprechen || *tr* begünstigen; (*prefer*) bevorzugen; (*a sore limb*) schonen

favorable ['fevərəbəl] *adj* günstig; (*criticism*) positiv; (*report*) beifällig

favorite ['fevərɪt] *adj* Lieblings– || *s* Liebling *m*; (sport) Favorit –in *mf*

favoritism ['fevərɪ‚tɪzəm] *s* Günstlingswirtschaft *f*

fawn [fɔn] *s* Rehkalb *n* || *intr*—f. on schmeicheln (*dat*)

fawn'ing *adj* schmeichlerisch

faze [fez] *tr* (coll) auf die Palme bringen

FBI [‚ɛf‚bi'aɪ] *s* (*Federal Bureau of Investigation*) Bundessicherheitspolizei *f*

fear [fɪr] *s* (*of*) Furcht *f* (vor *dat*), Angst *f* (vor *dat*); **for f. of** aus Angst

vor (*dat*); **for f. of** (*ger*) um nicht zu (*inf*); **stand in f. of** sich fürchten vor (*dat*) || *tr* fürchten, sich fürchten vor (*dat*); **f. the worst** das Schlimmste befürchten || *intr* sich fürchten; **f. for** besorgt sein um

fearful ['fɪrfəl] *adj* (*afraid*) furchtsam; (*terrible*) furchtbar

fearless ['fɪrlɪs] *adj* furchtlos

feasible ['fɪzɪbəl] *adj* durchführbar

feast [fist] *s* Fest *n*; (*sumptuous meal*) Schmaus *m* || *tr* bewirten; **f. one's eyes on** seine Augen weiden an (*dat*) || *intr* schwelgen; **f. on** sich gütlich tun an (*dat*)

feast'day' *s* Festtag *m*

feast'ing *s* Schmauserei *f*

feat [fit] *s* Kunststück *n*; **f. of arms** Waffentat *f*

feather ['fɛðər] *s* Feder *f*; **a f. in his cap** ein Triumph für ihn || *tr* mit Federn versehen; (aer) auf Segelstellung fahren; (crew) flach drehen; **f. one's nest** sich warm betten

feath'er bed' *s* Federbett *n*

feath'erbed'ding *s* Anstellung *f* unnötiger Arbeitskräfte

feath'erbrain' *s* Schwachkopf *m*

feath'er dust'er *s* Staubwedel *m*

feath'eredge' *s* feine Kante *f*

feath'erweight' *adj* Federgewichts– || *s* (boxer) Federgewichtler *m*

feathery ['fɛðəri] *adj* federartig; (*light as feathers*) federleicht

feature ['fitʃər] *s* (*of the face*) Gesichtszug *m*; (*characteristic*) Merkmal *n*; **f. film** Spielfilm *m*; **main f.** Grundzug *m*; (cin) Hauptfilm *m* || *tr* als Hauptschlager herausbringen; (cin) in der Hauptrolle zeigen

fea'ture wri'ter *s* Sonderberichterstatter –in *mf*

February ['fɛbrʊ‚ɛri] *s* Februar *m*

feces ['fisiz] *spl* Kot *m*, Stuhl *m*

feckless ['fɛklɪs] *adj* (*incompetent*) unfähig; (*ineffective*) unwirksam; (*without spirit*) geistlos

fecund ['fikənd] *adj* fruchtbar

federal ['fɛdərəl] *adj* Bundes-, bundesstaatlich; **f. government** Bundesregierung *f*

federate ['fɛdə‚ret] *adj* verbündet || *tr* zu e–m Bund vereinigen || *intr* sich verbünden

federation [‚fɛdə'reʃən] *s* Staatenbund *m*

fed' up' [fɛd] *adj*—**be f.** die Nase voll haben; **be f. with s.th.** etw satt haben

fee [fi] *s* Gebühr *f*; (*of a doctor*) Honorar *n*

feeble ['fibəl] *adj* schwächlich

fee'ble-mind'ed *adj* schwachsinnig

feed [fid] *s* Futter *n*; (mach) Zuführung *f* || *v* (*pret* & *pp* **fed** [fɛd]) *tr* (*animals*) füttern; (*persons*) zu Essen geben; (*in a restaurant*) verpflegen; (*e.g., a nation*) nähren; (*a fire*) unterhalten; (mach) zuführen || *intr* fressen; **f. on** sich ernähren von

feed'back' *s* Rückwirkung *f*; (electron) Rückkoppelung *f*

feed' bag' *s* Futtersack *m*; **put on the f.** (sl) futtern

feeder ['fidər] *s* (elec) Speiseleitung *f*; (mach) Zubringer *m*

feed'er line' *s* (aer, rr) Zubringerlinie *f*

feed'ing *s* (of animals) Fütterung *f*; (& mach) Speisung *f*

feed' trough' *s* Futtertrog *m*

feed' wire' *s* (elec) Zuleitungsdraht *m*

feel [fil] *s* Gefühl *n*; get the f. of sich gewöhnen an (acc) || *v* (pret & pp felt [felt]) *tr* fühlen; (a pain) spüren; f. one's way sich vortasten; (fig) sondieren; f. s.o. out bei j-m vorfühlen || *intr* (sick, tired, well) sich fühlen; f. about for herumtasten nach; f. for s.o. mit j-m fühlen; f. like (ger) Lust haben zu (inf); f. up to sich gewachsen fühlen (dat); his head feels hot sein Kopf fühlt sich heiß an; how do you f. about it? was halten Sie davon?; I don't quite f. myself fühle mich nicht ganz wohl; I f. as if es ist mir, als wenn; make itself felt sich fühlbar machen

feeler ['filər] *s* (ent) Fühler *m*; put out feelers to vorfühlen bei

feel'ing *s* Gefühl *n*; bad f. Verstimmung *f*; good f. Wohlwollen *n*; have a f. for Sinn haben für; have a f. that das Gefühl haben, daß; with f. gefühlvoll

feign [fen] *tr* vortäuschen; f. death sich totstellen

feint [fent] *s* Finte *f*, Scheinangriff *m*

feldspar ['feld,spar] *s* Feldspat *m*

feline ['filaɪn] *adj* katzenartig

fell [fel] *adj* grausam || *tr* fällen

fellow ['felo] *s* (coll) Kerl *m*; (of a society) Mitglied *n*

fel'low be'ing *s* Mitmensch *m*

fel'low cit'izen *s* Mitbürger –in *mf*

fel'low coun'tryman *s* Landsmann *m*

fel'low crea'ture *s* Mitgeschöpf *n*

fel'lowman' *s* (-men') Mitmensch *m*

fel'low mem'ber *s* Mitglied *n*

fel'lowship' *s* Kameradschaft *f*; (educ) Stipendium *n*

fel'low stu'dent *s* Kommilitone *m*

fel'low trav'eler *s* Mitreisende *mf*; (pol) Mitläufer –in *mf*

felon ['felən] *s* Schwerverbrecher –in *mf*

felony ['feləni] *s* Schwerverbrechen *n*

felt [felt] *adj* Filz– || *s* Filz *m*

felt' pen' *s* Filzschreiber *m*, Faserstift *m*

female ['fimel] *adj* weiblich || *s* (of animals) Weibchen *n*; (pej) Weibsbild *n*

feminine ['femɪnɪn] *adj* weiblich

feminism ['femɪ,nɪzəm] *s* Feminismus *m*

fen [fen] *s* Bruch *m* & *n*

fence [fens] *s* Zaun *m*; (of stolen goods) Hehler *m*; on the f. (fig) unentschlossen || *tr*–f. in einzäunen; f. off abzäunen || *intr* (sport) fechten

fence' post' *s* Zaunpfahl *m*

fenc'ing *s* Fechten *n*

fend [fend] *tr*–f. off abwehren || *intr* –f. for oneself für sich selbst sorgen

fender ['fendər] *s* (aut) Kotflügel *m*

fennel ['fenəl] *s* Fenchel *m*

ferment ['fʌrment] *s* Gärmittel *n*; (fig)

Unruhe *f* || [fər'ment] *tr* in Gärung bringen || *intr* gären

fermentation [,fʌrmən'teʃən] *s* Gärung *f*

fern [fʌrn] *s* Farn *m*

ferocious [fə'roʃəs] *adj* wild

ferocity [fə'rɑsɪti] *s* Wildheit *f*

ferret ['ferɪt] *s* Frettchen *n* || *tr*–f. out aufspüren

Fer'ris wheel' ['ferɪs] *s* Riesenrad *n*

ferrule ['ferul], ['ferəl] *s* Stockzwinge *f*, Zwinge *f*

fer·ry ['feri] *s* Fähre *f* || *v* (pret & pp –ried) *tr* übersetzen

fer'ryboat' *s* Fährboot *n*

fer'ry·man' *s* (-men') Fährmann *m*

fertile ['fʌrtɪl] *adj* fruchtbar

fertility [fər'tɪlɪti] *s* Fruchtbarkeit *f*

fertilization [,fʌrtɪlɪ'zeʃən] *s* Befruchtung *f*; (of soil) Düngung *f*

fertilize ['fʌrtɪ,laɪz] *tr* (a field) düngen; (an egg) befruchten

fertilizer ['fʌrtɪ,laɪzər] *s* Kunstdünger *m*

fervent ['fʌrvənt] *adj* inbrünstig

fervid ['fʌrvɪd] *adj* brennend

fervor ['fʌrvər] *s* Inbrunst *f*

fester ['festər] *intr* schwären, eitern; (fig) nagen

festival ['festɪvəl] *adj* festlich, Fest– || *s* Fest *n*; (mus, theat) Festspiele *pl*

festive ['festɪv] *adj* festlich

festivity [fes'tɪvɪti] *s* Feierlichkeit *f*

festoon [fes'tun] *s* Girlande *f* || *tr* mit Girlanden schmücken

fetch [fetʃ] *tr* holen, abholen

fetch'ing *adj* entzückend

fete [fet] *s* Fest *n*

fetid ['fetɪd], ['fitɪd] *adj* stinkend

fetish ['fetɪʃ], ['fitɪʃ] *s* Fetisch *m*

fetlock ['fetlɑk] *s* Köte *f*; (tuft of hair) Kötenzopf *m*

fetter ['fetər] *s* Fessel *f* || *tr* fesseln

fettle ['fetəl] *s*–in fine f. in Form

fetus ['fitəs] *s* Leibesfrucht *f*

feud [fjud] *s* Fehde *f*

feudal ['fjudəl] *adj* feudal

feudalism ['fjudə,lɪzəm] *s* Feudalismus *m*

fever ['fivər] *s* Fieber *n*

feverish ['fivərɪʃ] *adj* fieberig; be f. fiebern

few [fju] *adj* & *pron* wenige; a few ein paar

fiancé [,fi·ɑn'se] *s* Verlobte *m*

fiancée [,fi·ɑn'se] *s* Verlobte *f*

fias·co [fɪ'æsko] *s* (-cos & -coes) Fiasko *n*

fib [fɪb] *s* Flunkerei *f* || *v* (pret & pp fibbed; ger fibbing) *intr* flunkern

fibber ['fɪbər] *s* Flunkerer –in *mf*

fiber ['faɪbər] *s* Faser *f*

fibrous ['faɪbrəs] *adj* faserig

fickle ['fɪkəl] *adj* wankelmütig

fickleness ['fɪkəlnɪs] *s* Wankelmut *m*

fiction ['fɪkʃən] *s* Dichtung *f*, Romanliteratur *f*

fictional ['fɪkʃənəl] *adj* romanhaft

fic'tion writ'er *s* Romanschriftsteller –in *mf*

fictitious [fɪk'tɪʃəs] *adj* fingiert

fiddle ['fɪdəl] *s* Fiedel *f*, Geige *f* || *tr* fiedeln; f. away (time) vergeuden ||

intr fiedeln; **f. with** herumfingern an (*dat*)

fiddler ['fɪdlər] *s* Fiedler –in *mf*

fid'dlestick' *s* Fiedelbogen *m* || **fiddle-sticks** *interj* Quatsch!

fidelity [fɪ'delɪtɪ] *s* Treue *f*

fidget ['fɪdʒɪt] *intr* zappeln; **f. with** nervös spielen mit

fidgety ['fɪdʒɪtɪ] *adj* zappelig

fiduciary [fɪ'd(j)u/ɪ‚erɪ] *adj* treuhänderisch; (*note*) ungedeckt || *s* Treuhänder –in *mf*

fief [fif] *s* (hist) Lehen *n*

field [fild] *adj* (*artillery, jacket, hospital, kitchen*) Feld– || *s* Feld *n*; (*under cultivation*) Acker *m*; (*contestants collectively*) Wettbewerbsteilnehmer *pl*; (*specialty*) Gebiet *n*; (aer) Flugplatz *m*; (elec) Feld *n*; (*of a motor*) (elec) Magnetfeld *n*; (sport) Spielfeld *n*

field' am'bulance *s* Sanitätskraftwagen *m*

field' day' *s* (fig) großer Tag *m*

fielder ['fildər] *s* Feldspieler *m*

field' ex'ercise *s* Truppenübung *f*

field' glass'es *spl* Feldstecher *m*

field' hock'ey *s* Rasenhockey *n*

field'mar'shal *s* Feldmarschall *m*

field' mouse' *s* Feldmaus *f*

field' of vi'sion *s* Blickfeld *n*

field' pack' *s* (mil) Tornister *m*

field' piece' *s* Feldgeschütz *n*

field' trip' *s* Studienfahrt *f*

field' work' *s* praktische Arbeit *f*

fiend [find] *s* (*devil*) Teufel *m*; (*wicked person*) Unhold *m*; (*addict*) Süchtige *mf*

fiendish ['findɪʃ] *adj* teuflisch

fierce [fɪrs] *adj* wild, wütend; (*vehement*) heftig; (*menacing*) drohend; (*heat*) glühend

fiery ['faɪrɪ], ['faɪ‚ərɪ] *adj* feurig

fife [faɪf] *s* Querpfeife *f*

fifteen ['fɪf'tin] *adj* & *pron* fünfzehn || *s* Fünfzehn *f*

fifteenth ['fɪf'tinθ] *adj* & *pron* fünfzehnte *s* (*fraction*) Fünfzehntel *n*; **the f.** (*in dates or a series*) der Fünfzehnte

fifth [fɪfθ] *adj* & *pron* fünfte || *s* (*fraction*) Fünftel *n*; **the f.** (*in dates or a series*) der Fünfte

fifth' col'umn *s* (pol) Fünfte Kolonne *f*

fiftieth ['fɪftɪ‚θ] *adj* & *pron* fünfzigste || *s* (*fraction*) Fünfzigstel *n*

fifty ['fɪftɪ] *adj* & *pron* fünfzig || *s* Fünfzig *f*; **the fifties** die fünfziger Jahre

fif'ty-fif'ty *adv* halbpart; **go f. with** s.o. mit j–m halbpart machen

fig [fɪg] *s* Feige *f*; (fig) Pfifferling *m*

fight [faɪt] *s* Kampf *m*, Gefecht *n*; (*quarrel*) Streit *m*; (*brawl*) Rauferei *f*; (box) Boxkampf *m*; **pick a f.** Zank suchen || *tr* bekämpfen; (*a case*) durchkämpfen; **f. back** (*tears*) niederkämpfen; **f. it out** ausfechten; **f. one's way out** sich durchkämpfen || *intr* kämpfen; (*quarrel*) streiten; (*brawl*) raufen

fighter ['faɪtər] *adj* (aer) Jagd– || *s*

intr fiedeln; **f. with** herumfingern an (*dat*)

Kämpfer –in *mf*; (aer) Jäger *m*; (box) Boxkämpfer *m*

fight'er pi'lot *s* Jagdflieger *m*

fight'ing *s* Schlägerei *f*; (*quarreling*) Streiten *n*; (mil) Kampfhandlungen *pl*

fig' leaf' *s* Feigenblatt *n*

figment ['fɪgmənt] *s*—**f. of the imagination** Hirngespinst *n*

fig' tree' *s* Feigenbaum *m*

figurative ['fɪgjərətɪv] *adj* bildlich; (*meaning*) übertragen

figure ['fɪgjər] *s* Figur *f*; (*personage*) Persönlichkeit *f*; (*number*) Zahl *f*; **be good at figures** ein guter Rechner sein; **cut a fine** (or **poor**) **f.** e–e gute (or schlechte) Figur abgeben; **run into three figures** in die Hunderte gehen || *tr* (coll) glauben, meinen; **f. out** ausknobeln || *intr*—**f. large** e–e große Rolle spielen; **f. on** rechnen mit

fig'urehead' *s* Strohmann *m*; (naut) Bugfigur *f*; **a mere f.** e–e bloße Nummer

fig'ure of speech' *s* Redewendung *f*

fig'ure skat'ing *s* Kunstlauf *m*

figurine [‚fɪgjə'rin] *s* Figurine *f*

filament ['fɪləmənt] *s* Faser *f*, Faden *m*; (elec) Glühfaden *m*

filbert ['fɪlbərt] *s* Haselnuß *f*

filch [fɪltʃ] *tr* mausen

file [faɪl] *s* (tool) Feile *f*; (*record*) Akte *f*; (*cards*) Kartei *f*; (*row*) Reihe *f*; **put on f.** zu den Akten legen || *tr* (*with a tool*) feilen; (*letters, etc.*) ablegen, abheften; (*a complaint*) erheben; (*a report*) erstatten; (*a claim*) anmelden; (*a petition*) einreichen; **f. suit** e–n Prozeß anstrengen || *intr* —**f. for** sich bewerben um; **f. out** im Gänsemarsch herausmarschieren; **f. past** vorbeidefilieren (an *dat*)

file' cab'inet *s* Aktenschrank *m*

file' card' *s* Karteikarte *f*

filial ['fɪlɪ‚əl] *adj* kindlich

filibuster ['fɪlɪ‚bʌstər] *s* Obstruktion *f* || *intr* Obstruktion treiben

filigree ['fɪlɪ‚grɪ] *s* Filigran *n*

fil'ing *s* Feilen *n*; (*of records*) Ablegen *n* von Akten; (*of a claim*) Anmeldung *f*; (*of a complaint*) Erhebung *f*; (*of a petition*) Einreichung *f*; **filings** Feilspäne *pl*

Filipi'no [‚fɪlɪ'pino] *adj* filipinisch || *s* (**-nos**) Filipino *m*

fill [fɪl] *s* (*fullness*) Fülle *f*; (*land fill*) Aufschüttung *f*; **eat one's f.** sich satt essen; **I have had my f. of it** ich habe es satt || *tr* füllen; (*an order*) ausführen; (*a pipe*) stopfen; (*a position*) besetzen; (dent) plombieren, füllen; **f. full** vollfüllen; **f. in** (*empty space*) ausfüllen; (*one's name*) einsetzen; (*a hole, grave*) zuwerfen; **f. it up** (aut) volltanken; **f. up** auffüllen; (*a tank*) nachfüllen; (*a bag*) anfüllen; (*a glass*) vollschenken; **f. with smoke** verräuchern || *intr* sich füllen; (*said of sails*) sich blähen; **f. in for** einspringen für; **f. out** rund werden; **f. up** sich füllen

filler ['fɪlər] *s* Füller *m*; (*of a cigar*)

Einlage *f*; (journ) Lückenbüßer *m*; (paint) Grundierfirnis *m*

fillet ['frlət] *s* (*headband*) Kopfbinde *f*; (archit) Leiste *f* || [fr'le] *s* (culin) Filet *n* || *tr* filetieren

fillet' of beef' *s* Rinderfilet *n*

fillet' of sole' *s* Seezungenfilet *n*

fill'ing *s* (culin, dent) Füllung *f*

fill'ing sta'tion *s* Tankstelle *f*

fillip ['frlrp] *s* Schnippchen *n*; (*on the nose*) Nasenstüber *m*

filly ['frli] *s* Stutenfüllen *n*

film [frlm] *s* (*thin layer*) Schicht *f*; (cin, phot) Film *m*; **f. of grease** Fettschicht *f*

film' fes'tival *s* Filmfestspiele *pl*

film' li'brary *s* Filmarchiv *n*

film' speed' *s* Filmempfindlichkeit *f*

film' star' *s* Filmstar *m*

film'strip' *s* Bildstreifen *m*

filmy ['frlmi] *adj* trüb

filter ['frltər] *s* Filter *m*; (rad) Sieb *n* || *tr* filtern; (rad) sieben

fil'tering *s* Filtrierung *f*

fil'ter pa'per *s* Filterpapier *n*

fil'ter tip' *s* Filtermundstück *n*; (coll) Filterzigarette *f*

filth [frlθ] *s* Schmutz *m*; (fig) Unflätigkeit *f*, Zote *f*

filthy ['frlθi] *adj* schmutzig (*talk*) unflätig; (*lucre*) schnöd(e) || *adv*—**f. rich** (sl) klotzig reich

filtrate ['frltret] *s* Filtrat *n* || *tr & intr* filtrieren

filtration [frl'treʃən] *s* Filtrierung *f*

fin [frn] *s* Flosse *f*; (*of a shark or whale*) Finne *f*; (*of a bomb*) Steuerschwanz *m*; (aer) Flosse *f*

final ['farnəl] *adj* End–, Schluß–; (*definitive*) endgültig || *s* (educ) Abschlußprüfung *f*; **finals** (sport) Endrunde *f*, Endspiel *n*

finale [fr'nɑli] *s* Finale *n*

finalist ['farnəlrst] *s* Finalist –in *mf*

finality [far'nælrti] *s* Endgültigkeit *f*

finally ['farnəli] *adv* schließlich

finance ['farnæns], [fr'næns] *s* Finanz *f*; **finances** Finanzwesen *n* || *tr* finanzieren

financial [fr'næn∫əl], [far'næn∫əl] *adj* (e.g., *policy, situation, crisis, aid*) Finanz–; (e.g., *affairs, resources, embarrassment*) Geld–

financier [,frnən'srr], [,farnən'srr] *s* Finanzmann *m*

financ'ing, fi'nancing *s* Finanzierung *f*

finch [frnt∫] *s* Fink *m*

find [farnd] *s* Fund *m*; (archeol) Bodenfund *m* || *v* (pret & pp **found** [faʊnd]) *tr* finden; (math) bestimmen; **f. one's way** sich zurechtfinden; **f. one's way back** zurückfinden; **f. out** herausfinden; **f. s.o. guilty** j–n für schuldig erklären || *intr*—**f. out about s.th.** hinter etw [acc] kommen

finder ['farndər] *s* Finder –in *mf*

find'ing *s* Finden *n*; **findings** Tatbestand *m*

fine [farn] *adj* fein; (*excellent*) hervorragend; (*weather*) schön; **f.!** gut! || *s* Geldstrafe *f* || *tr* mit e–r Geldstrafe belegen

fine' arts' *spl* schöne Künste *pl*

fineness ['farnrs] *s* Feinheit *f*; (*of a coin or metal*) Feingehalt *m*

fine' point' *s* Feinheit *f*

fine' print' *s* Kleindruck *m*

finery ['farnəri] *s* Putz *m*, Staat *m*

fine-spun ['farn,spʌn] *adj* feingesponnen

finesse [fr'nes] *s* Finesse *f*; (cards) Impaß *m* || *tr & intr* impassieren

fine-toothed ['farn,tuθt] *adj* feingezahnt; **go over with a f. comb** unter die Lupe nehmen

fine' touch' *s* Feinheit *f*

fine' tun'ing *s* Feineinstellung *f*

finger ['frŋgər] *s* Finger *m*; **have a f. in the pie** die Hand im Spiel haben; **keep your fingers crossed** halten Sie mir den Daumen; **not lift a f.** keinen Finger rühren; **put the f. on s.o.** (sl) j–n verpetzen; **snap one's fingers** mit den Fingern schnellen; **twist around one's little f.** um den kleinen Finger wickeln || *tr* befingern

fin'ger bowl' *s* Fingerschale *f*

fin'gering *s* (mus) Fingersatz *m*

fin'gernail' *s* Fingernagel *m*

fin'gernail pol'ish *s* Nagellack *m*

fin'gerprint' *s* Fingerabdruck *m* || *tr*—**f. s.o.** j–m die Fingerabdrücke abnehmen

fin'gertip' *s* Fingerspitze *f*; **have at one's fingertips** parat haben

finicky ['frnrki] *adj* wählerisch

finish ['frnr∫] *s* Ende *n*, Abschluß *m*; (*polish*) Lack *m*, Politur *f*; **put a f. on** fertig bearbeiten || *tr* beenden; (*complete*) vollenden; (*put a finish on*) fertig bearbeiten; (*smooth*) glätten; (*polish*) polieren; (*ruin*) kaputt machen; **f. drinking** austrinken; **f. eating** aufessen; **f. off** (*supplies*) aufbrauchen; (*food*) aufessen; (*a drink*) austrinken; (*kill*) (sl) erledigen; **f. reading** (*a book*) auslesen

fin'ished *adj* beendet, fertig; **be all f.** fix und fertig sein

fin'ished pro'duct *s* Fertigprodukt *n*

fin'ishing coat' *s* Deckanstrich *m*

fin'ishing mill' *s* Nachwalzwerk *n*

fin'ishing school' *s* Mädchenpensionat *n*

fin'ishing touch'es *spl*—**put the f. to** die letzte Hand legen an (*acc*)

fin'ish line' *s* Ziel *n*, Ziellinie *f*

finite ['farnart] *adj* endlich

fi'nite verb' *s* Verbum *n* finitum

fink [frŋk] *s* (*informer*) (sl) Verräter –in *mf*; (*strikebreaker*) (sl) Streikbrecher –in *mf*

Finland ['frnlənd] *s* Finnland *n*

Finn [frn] *s* Finne *f*, Finnin *f*

Finnish ['frnr∫] *adj* finnisch || *s* (*language*) Finnisch *n*

fir [fʌr] *s* Tanne *f*

fir' cone' *s* Tannenzapfen *m*

fire [farr] *s* Feuer *n*; (*conflagration*) Brand *m*; (mil) Feuer *n*; **come under f.** unter Beschuß geraten; **on f.** in Brand; **open f.** Feuer eröffnen; **set on f.** in Brand stecken || *tr* (*a gun, pistol, shot*) abfeuern; (*bricks, ceramics*) brennen; (*an oven*) befeuern; (*an employee*) entlassen; (*throw* *hard*) feuern; **f. questions at s.o.** j-n mit Fragen bombardieren; **f. up** (& *fig*) anfeuern || *intr* feuern, schießen; **f. away!** schieß los!; **f. on** (*mil*) beschießen

fire′ alarm′ *s* Feuermeldung *f*; (*box*) Feuermelder *m*

fire′arm′ *s* Schußwaffe *f*

fire′ball′ *s* Feuerball *m*; (*hustler*) Draufgänger *m*

fire′bomb′ *s* Brandbombe *f* || *tr* mit Brandbomben belegen

fire′brand′ *s* (*fig*) Spritze *f*... Aufwiegler –in *mf*

fire′break′ *s* Feuerschneise *f*

fire′ brigade′ *s* Feuerwehr *f*

fire′bug′ *s* (*coll*) Brandstifter –in *mf*

fire′ chief′ *s* Branddirektor *m*

fire′ com′pany *s* Feuerwehr *f*

fire′crack′er *s* Knallfrosch *m*

fire′damp′ *s* Schlagwetter *pl*

fire′ depart′ment *s* Feuerwehr *f*

fire′ drill′ *s* Feueralarmübung *f*; (*by a fire company*) Feuerwehrübung *f*

fire′ en′gine *s* Spritze *f*

fire′ escape′ *s* Feuerleiter *f*

fire′ extin′guisher *s* Feuerlöscher *m*

fire′fly′ *s* Glühwurm *m*

fire′ hose′ *s* Spritzenschlauch *m*

fire′house′ *s* Feuerwache *f*

fire′ hy′drant *s* Hydrant *m*

fire′ insur′ance *s* Brandversicherung *f*

fire′ i′rons *spl* Kamingeräte *pl*

fire′lane′ *s* Feuer(schutz)schneise *f*

fire′man *s* (**–men**) Feuerwehrmann *m*; (*stoker*) Heizer *m*

fire′place′ *s* Kamin *m*, Herd *m*

fire′plug′ *s* Hydrant *m*

fire′ pow′er *s* (*mil*) Feuerkraft *f*

fire′proof′ *adj* feuerfest || *tr* feuerfest machen

fire′ sale′ *s* Ausverkauf *m* von feuerbeschädigten Waren

fire′ screen′ *s* Feuervorhang *m*

fire′side′ *s* Kamin *m*, Herd *m*

fire′trap′ *s* feuergefährdetes Gebäude *n*

fire′ wall′ *s* Brandmauer *f*

fire′wa′ter *s* (*coll*) Feuerwasser *n*

fire′wood′ *s* Brennholz *n*

fire′works′ *spl* Feuerwerk *n*

fir′ing *s* (*of a weapon*) Abfeuern *n*; (*of an employee*) Entlassung *f*

fir′ing line′ *s* Feuerlinie *f*

fir′ing range′ *s* Schießstand *m*

fir′ing squad′ *s* Erschießungskommando *n*; (*for ceremonies*) Ehrensalutkommando *n*; **put to the f. an die Wand stellen**

firm [fʌrm] *adj* fest || *s* (*com*) Firma *f*

firmament [′fʌrməmənt] *s* Firmament *n*

firmness [′fʌrmnɪs] *s* Festigkeit *f*

first [fʌrst] *adj* erste; **very f.** allererste || *adv* erst, erstens; **f. of all** zunächst || *s* (*aut*) erster Gang *m*; **at f.** zuerst; **f. come, f. served** wer zuerst kommt, mahlt zuerst; **from the f.** von vornherein; **the f.** (*in dates or in a series*) der Erste

first′ aid′ *s* Erste Hilfe *f*

first′-aid′ kit′ *s* Verbandpäckchen *n*

first′-aid′ sta′tion *s* Unfallstation *f*; (*mil*) Verbandplatz *m*

first′-born′ *adj* erstgeboren

first′-class′ *adj* erstklassig || *adv* erster Klasse

first′-class′ mail′ *s* Briefpost *f*

first′-class′ tic′ket *s* Fahrkarte *f* (or Flugkarte *f*) erster Klasse

first′ cous′in *s* leiblicher Vetter *m*, leibliche Cousine *f*

first′-degree′ *adj* ersten Grades

first′ draft′ *s* Konzept *n*

first′ fin′ger *s* Zeigefinger *m*

first′ floor′ *s* Parterre *n*, Erdgeschoß *n*

first′ fruits′ *spl* Erstlinge *pl*

first′ lieuten′ant *s* Oberleutnant *m*

firstly [′fʌrstli] *adv* erstens

first′ mate′ *s* Obersteuermann *m*

first′ name′ *s* Vorname *m*

first′ night′ *s* (*theat*) Erstaufführung *f*

first-nighter [′fʌrst′naɪtər] *s* (*theat*) Premierenbesucher –in *mf*

first′ offen′der *s* noch nicht Vorbestrafte *mf*

first′ of′ficer *s* erster Offizier *m*

first′ prize′ *s* Hauptgewinn *m*, Haupttreffer *m*

first′-rate′ *adj* erstklassig

first′ ser′geant *s* Hauptfeldwebel *m*

fir′ tree′ *s* Tannenbaum *m*

fiscal [′fɪskəl] *adj* (*period, year*) Rechnungs–; (*policy*) Finanz–

fish [fɪʃ] *s* Fisch *m*; **drink like a f.** wie ein Bürstenbinder saufen; **like a f. out of water** nicht in seinem Element || *tr* fischen || *intr* fischen; **f. for angeln nach**

fish′bone′ *s* Gräte *f*, Fischgräte *f*

fish′ bowl′ *s* Fischglas *n*

fisher [′fɪʃər] *s* Fischer –in *mf*

fish′er-man *s* (**–men**) Angler *m*

fishery [′fɪʃəri] *s* Fischerei *f*

fish′hook′ *s* Angelhaken *m*

fish′ing *adj* Fisch–, Angel– || *s* Fischen *n*

fish′ing line′ *s* Angelschnur *f*

fish′ing reel′ *s* Angelschnurrolle *f*

fish′ing rod′ *s* Angelrute *f*

fish′ing tack′le *s* Fischgerät *n*

fish′ mar′ket *s* Fischmarkt *m*

fishmonger [′fɪʃ͵mʌŋɡər] *s* Fischhändler –in *mf*

fish′pond′ *s* Fischteich *m*

fish′ sto′ry *s* Jägerlatein *n*

fish′tail′ *s* (*aer*) Abbremsen *n* || *intr* (aer) abbremsen

fishy [′fɪʃi] *adj* fischig; (*eyes, look*) ausdruckslos; (*suspicious*) anrüchig; **there's s.th. f. about it** das geht nicht mit rechten Dingen zu

fission [′fɪʃən] *s* (*phys*) Spaltung *f*

fissionable [′fɪʃənəbəl] *adj* spaltbar

fissure [′fɪʃər] *s* Riß *m*, Spalt *m*

fist [fɪst] *s* Faust *f*; **make a f.** die Faust ballen; **shake one's f. at s.o.** j-m mit der Faust drohen

fist′ fight′ *s* Handgemenge *n*

fisticuffs [′fɪstɪ͵kʌfs] *spl* Faustschläge *pl*

fit [fɪt] *adj* (**fitter; fittest**) gesund; (*for*) tauglich (für, zu); (*sport*) gut in Form; **be fit as a fiddle** kerngesund sein; **be fit to be tied** Gift und Galle spucken; **feel fit** auf der Höhe sein; **fit for military service**

diensttauglich; **fit to eat** genießbar; **fit to drink** trinkbar; **keep fit in Form bleiben; see fit to** (*inf*) es für richtig halten zu (*inf*) || *s* (*of clothes*) Sitz *m*; **by fits and starts** ruckweise; **fit of anger** Wutanfall *m*; **fit of laughter** Lachkrampf *m*; **give s.o. fits** j-n auf die Palme bringen; **it is a good** (or **a bad**) **fit** es sitzt gut (or schlecht); **throw a fit** e-n Wutanfall kriegen || *v* (*pret & pp* **fitted;** *ger* **fitting**) *tr* passen (*dat*); **fit in** (*for an appointment*) einschieben; **fit out** ausrüsten, ausstatten || *intr* passen; **fit into** sich einfügen in (*acc*); **fit in with** passen zu; **fit together** zusammenpassen

fitful ['fɪtfəl] *adj* unregelmäßig

fitness ['fɪtnɪs] *s* Tauglichkeit *f*; **physical f.** gute körperliche Verfassung *f*

fit'ting *adj* passend, angemessen || *s* (*of a garment*) Anprobe *f*; (*mach*) Montage *f*; **fittings** Armaturen *pl*

five [faɪv] *adj & pron* fünf || *s* Fünf *f*

five'-year plan' *s* Fünfjahresplan *m*

fix [fɪks] *s* (*determination of a position*) Standortbestimmung *f*; (*position*) Standort *m*; (*injection of heroin*) (sl) Schuß *m*; **be in a fix** (coll) in der Klemme sein || *tr* befestigen; (*a price, time*) festsetzen; (*repair*) reparieren, wieder in Ordnung bringen; (*get even with*) (sl) erledigen, das Handwerk legen (*dat*); (*one's glance*) (**on**) heften (auf *acc*); (*the blame*) (**on**) zuschreiben (*dat*); (*a game*) (sl) auf unehrliche Weise beeinflussen; (*bayonets*) aufpflanzen; (phot) fixieren

flare'-up' *s* Auflodern *n*; (*of anger*) Aufbrausen *n*

fixed *adj* (*unmovable*) unbeweglich; (*stare*) starr; (*income*) fest; (*idea, cost*) fix; **f. date** Termin *m*

fixer ['fɪksər] *s* (phot) Fixiermittel *n*

fix'ing *s* (*making fast*) Befestigung *f*; (*of a date, etc.*) Festsetzung *f*; **fixings** (culin) Zutaten *pl*

fix'ing bath' *s* (phot) Fixierbad *n*

fixture ['fɪkstʃər] *s* Installationsteil *m*; **he is a permanent f.** er gehört zum Inventar

fizz [fɪz] *s* Zischen *n* || *intr* zischen

fizzle ['fɪzəl] *s* (coll) Pleite *f* || *intr* aufzischen; **f. out** verpuffen

flabbergast ['flæbər‚gæst] *tr* verblüffen

flabby ['flæbi] *adj* schlaff, schlapp

flag [flæg] *s* Fahne *f*, Flagge *f* || *v* (*pret & pp* **flagged;** *ger* **flagging**) *tr* signalisieren || *intr* nachlassen

flag'pole' *s* Fahnenmast *m*

flagrant ['flegrənt] *adj* schreiend

flag'ship' *s* Flaggschiff *n*

flag'staff' *s* Flaggenmast *m*

flag'stone' *s* Steinfliese *f*

flag' stop' *s* (rr) Bedarfshaltestelle *f*

flail [flel] *s* Dreschflegel *m* || *tr* dreschen || *intr*—**f. about** um sich schlagen

flair [fler] *s* Spürsinn *m*, feine Nase *f*

flak [flæk] *s* Flak *f*, Flakfeuer *n*

flake [flek] *s* (*thin piece*) Schuppe *f*; (*of snow, soap*) Flocke *f* || *intr* Schuppen bilden; **f. off** abblättern

flaky ['fleki] *adj* (*skin*) schuppig; (*pastry*) blätterig; (sl) überspannt

flamboyant [flæm'bɔɪ‚ənt] *adj* (*person*) angeberisch; (*style*) überladen

flame [flem] *s* Flamme *f*; **be in flames** in Flammen stehen; **burst into flames** in Flammen aufgehen || *intr* flammen

flamethrower ['flem‚θro‚ər] *s* Flammenwerfer *m*

flam'ing *adj* flammend

flamin·go [flə'mɪŋgo] *s* (**-gos** & **-goes**) (orn) Flamingo *m*

flammable ['flæməbəl] *adj* brennbar

Flanders ['flændərz] *s* Flandern *n*

flange [flændʒ] *s* (*of a pipe*) Flansch *m*; (*of a wheel*) (rr) Spurkranz *m*

flank [flæŋk] *s* (anat, mil, zool) Flanke *f* || *tr* flankieren

flank'ing move'ment *s* (mil) Umgehung *f*

flannel ['flænəl] *adj* flanellen || *s* Flanell *m*

flap [flæp] *s* Klappe *f*; **f. of the wing** Flügelschlag *m* || *v* (*pret & pp* **flapped;** *ger* **flapping**) *tr*—**f. the wings** mit den Flügeln schlagen || *intr* flattern

flare [fler] *s* Leuchtsignal *n*; (*of anger, excitement*) Aufbrausen *n*; (*of a skirt*) Glocke *f*; (mil) Leuchtrakete *f*, Leuchtbombe *f* || *intr* flackern; (*said of a skirt*) glockenförmig abstehen; **f. up** auflodern; (fig) aufbrausen

flash [flæʃ] *s* Blitz *m*; (*of a gun*) Mündungsfeuer *n*; (phot) Blitzlicht *n*; **f. of genius** Geistesblitz *m*; **f. of light** Lichtstrahl *m*; **f. of lightning** Blitzstrahl *m*; **in a f. im Nu** || *tr* (*a glance*) zuwerfen; (*a message*) funkeln; **f. a light in s.o.'s face** j-m ins Gesicht leuchten || *intr* blitzen; (*said of eyes*) funkeln; **f. by** vorbeisausen; **f. on** aufleuchten; **f. through one's mind** j-m durch den Kopf schießen

flash'back' *s* (cin) Rückblende *f*

flash' bulb' *s* Blitzlichtbirne *f*

flash' cube' *s* Blitzlichtwürfel *m*

flash' flood' *s* plötzliche Überschwemmung *f*

flash' gun' *s* Blitzlichtgerät *n*

flash'light' *s* Taschenlampe *f*

flash' pic'ture, flash' shot' *s* Blitzlichtaufnahme *f*

flashy ['flæʃi] *adj* auffällig; (*clothes*) protzig; (*colors*) grell

flask [flæsk] *s* Taschenflasche *f*; (*for laboratory use*) Glaskolben *m*

flat [flæt] *adj* (*bottle; feet*) platt, flach; (*food*) fad(e); (*rate*) Pauschal–; (*tire*) platt; (*color*) matt; (*beer, soda*) schal; (*lie*) glatt; (*denial*) entschieden; (mus) erniedrigt; **be f.** (mus) zu tief singen || *adv* (*e.g., in exactly ten minutes*) genau; **fall f.** (fig) flachfallen; **go f.** schal werden; **lie f.** flach liegen || *s* (*apartment*) Wohnung *f*; (*tire*) Reifenpanne *f*

flat'boat' *s* Flachboot *n*

flat-broke ['flæt'brok] *adj* (coll) völlig pleite

flat′car′ *s* Plattformwagen *m*

flat′ feet′ *spl* Plattfüße *pl*

flat′-foot′ed *adj* plattfüßig; **catch f.** auf frischer Tat ertappen

flat′i′ron *s* Bügeleisen *n*

flatly ['flætli] *adv* rundweg, reinweg

flatten ['flætən] *tr* (*paper, cloth*) glatt-streichen; (*raze*) einebnen; **f. out** abplatten; (aer) abfangen || *intr* sich verflachen; (aer) ausschweben

flatter ['flætər] *tr* schmeicheln (*dat*); **be flattered** sich geschmeichelt füh-len; **f. oneself** sich [*dat*] einbilden

flatterer ['flætərər] *s* Schmeichler –in *mf*

flat′tering *adj* schmeichelhaft

flattery ['flætəri] *s* Schmeichelei *f*

flat′ tire′ *s* Reifenpanne *f*

flat′top′ *s* (coll) Flugzeugträger *m*

flat′ trajec′tory *s* Rasanz *f*

flatulence ['flætʃələns] *s* Blähung *f*

flat′ware′ *s* (*silverware*) Eßbestecke *pl*

flaunt [flɔnt] *tr* prunken mit

flavor ['flevər] *s* Aroma *n* || *tr* würzen

fla′voring *s* Würze *f*

flavorless ['flevərlɪs] *adj* fad(e)

flaw [flɔ] *s* Fehler *m*; (*crack*) Riß *m*; (*in glass, precious stone*) Blase *f*

flawless ['flɔlɪs] *adj* tadellos

flax [flæks] *s* Flachs *m*, Lein *m*

flaxen ['flæksən] *adj* flachsen

flax′seed′ *s* Leinsamen *m*

flay [fle] *tr* ausbalgen

flea [fli] *s* Floh *m*

flea′bag′ *s* (*sleeping bag*) (coll) Floh-kiste *f*; (*hotel*) (coll) Penne *f*

flea′bite′ *s* Flohbiß *m*

flea′mar′ket *s* Flohmarkt *m*

fleck [flek] *s* Fleck *m*

fledgling ['fledʒlɪŋ] *s* eben flügge ge-wordener Vogel *m*; (fig) Grün-schnabel *m*

flee [fli] *v* (*pret & pp* **fled** [fled]) *intr* fliehen

fleece [flis] *s* Vlies *n* || *tr* (coll) rupfen

fleecy ['flisi] *adj* wollig; **f. clouds** Schäfchenwolken *pl*

fleet [flit] *adj* flink || *s* Flotte *f*; (aer) Geschwader *n*; (nav) Kriegsflotte *f*; **f. of cars** Wagenpark *m*

fleet′ing *adj* flüchtig

Flemish ['flemɪʃ] *adj* flämisch || *s* Flämisch *n*

flesh [fleʃ] *s* Fleisch *n*; **in the f.** leib-haftig

flesh′-col′ored *adj* fleischfarben

fleshiness ['fleʃɪnɪs] *s* Fleischigkeit *f*

flesh′ wound′ *s* Fleischwunde *f*

fleshy ['fleʃi] *adj* fleischig

flex [fleks] *tr* biegen; (*muscles*) an-spannen

flexible ['fleksɪbəl] *adj* biegsam

flex(i)time ['fleks(ɪ),taɪm] *s* Gleitzeit *f*

flick [flɪk] *s* Schnippen *n* || *tr* (*away*) wegschnippen

flicker ['flɪkər] *s* (*of a flame*) Flak-kern *n*; (*of eyelids*) Zucken *n* || *intr* flackern

flier ['flaɪ-ər] *s* Flieger –in *mf*; (*hand-bill*) Flugblatt *n*

flight [flaɪt] *s* Flug *m*; (*fleeing*) Flucht *f*; (*of birds, geese*) Schar *f*; (*of stairs*) Treppe *f*; **f. of stairs** Trep-penflucht *f*; **f. of the imagination** Geistesschwung *m*; **live two flights up** zwei Treppen hoch wohnen; **put to f.** in die Flucht schlagen; **take to f.** sich davonmachen

flight′ bag′ *s* (aer) Reisetasche *f*

flight′ deck′ *s* (nav) Landedeck *n*

flight′ engineer′ *s* Bordmechaniker *m*

flight′ instruc′tor *s* Fluglehrer –in *mf*

flight′ path′ *s* Flugstrecke *f*

flighty ['flaɪti] *adj* leichtsinnig

flim-flam ['flɪm,flæm] *s* (*nonsense*) Unsinn *m*; (*deception*) Betrügerei *f* || *v* (*pret & pp* **-flammed**; *ger* **-flamming**) *tr* (coll) betrügen

flimsy ['flɪmzi] *adj* (*material*) hauch-dünn; (*excuse, construction*) schwach

flinch [flɪntʃ] *intr* (*at*) zurückweichen (vor *dat*), zusammenfahren (vor *dat*)

flinch′ing *s*—**without f.** ohne mit der Wimper zu zucken

fling [flɪŋ] *s* Wurf *m*; **go on** (*or* **have**) **a f.** sich austoben; **have a f. at** ver-suchen || *v* (*pret & pp* **flung** [flʌŋ]) *tr* schleudern; **f. off** abschleudern; **f. open** aufreißen

flint [flɪnt] *s* Feuerstein *m*

flinty ['flɪnti] *adj* steinhart; (fig) hart

flip [flɪp] *adj* leichtfertig || *s* (*of a coin*) Hochwerfen *n*; (*somersault*) Purzelbaum *m* || *v* (*pret & pp* **flipped**; *ger* **flipping**) *tr* schnellen; (*a coin*) hochwerfen; **f. one's lid** (sl) rasend werden; **f. over** umdrehen

flippancy ['flɪpənsi] *s* Leichtfertigkeit *f*

flippant ['flɪpənt] *adj* leichtfertig

flipper ['flɪpər] *s* Flosse *f*

flirt [flʌrt] *s* Flirt *m* || *intr* koket-tieren, flirten; (*with an idea*) lieb-äugeln

flirtation [flʌr'teʃən] *s* Liebelei *f*

flit [flɪt] *v* (*pret & pp* **flitted**; *ger* **flitting**) *intr* flitzen; **f. by** vorbeiflit-zen; (*said of time*) verfliegen

float [flot] *s* Schwimmkörper *m*; (*of a fishing line*) Schwimmer *m*; (*raft*) Floß *n*; (*in parades*) Festwagen *m* || *tr* (*logs*) flößen; (*a loan*) auflegen || *intr* schwimmen; (*in the air*) schwe-ben; **f. about** herumtreiben

float′ing kid′ney *s* Wanderniere *f*

float′ing mine′ *s* Treibmine *f*

flock [flɑk] *s* (*of sheep*) Herde *f*; (*of birds*) Schar *f*, Schwarm *m*; (*of peo-ple*) Menge *f* || *intr* herbeiströmen; **come flocking** herbeigeströmt kom-men; **f. around** sich scharen um; **f. into** strömen in (*acc*); **f. to** zulaufen (*dat*); **f. together** sich zusammen-scharen

floe [flo] *s* Eisscholle *f*

flog [flɑg] *v* (*pret & pp* **flogged**; *ger* **flogging**) *tr* prügeln

flood [flʌd] *s* Flut *f*; (*caused by heavy rains*) Überschwemmung *f*; (*sudden rise of a river*) Hochwasser *n*; (fig) Schwall *m*; (Bib) Sintflut *f* || *tr* (& fig) überschwemmen; (*e.g., with mail*) überschütten

flood′gate′ s (& fig) Schleusentor n

flood′light′ s Flutlicht n || tr anstrahlen

flood′ tide′ s Flut f; at f. zur Zeit der Flut

flood′ wa′ters spl Flutwasser n

floor [flor] s Fußboden m; (story) Stock m; (parl) Sitzungssaal m; have the f. das Wort haben; may I have the f.? ich bitte ums Wort; on the third f. im zweiten Stock || tr zu Boden strecken; (coll) verblüffen

floor′board′ s Diele f

floor′ing s Fußbodenbelag m

floor′ lamp′ s Stehlampe f

floor′ plan′ s Grundriß m

floor′ pol′ish s Bohnermasse f

floor′ sam′ple s Vorführungsmuster n

floor′ show′ s Kabarett n

floor′ tile′ s Bodenfliese f

floor′walk′er s Abteilungsaufseher –in mf

floor′ wax′ s Bohnerwachs n

flop [flɑp] s (coll) Mißerfolg m; (person) Niete f; (fall) (coll) Plumps m; take a f. (coll) plumpsen || v (pret & pp flopped; ger flopping) intr (fall) (coll) plumpsen; (fail) (coll) versagen; (theat) (coll) durchfallen; f. down in (coll) sich plumpsen lassen in (acc)

flora [′florə] s Pflanzenwelt f

floral [′florəl] adj Blumen-

Florence [′florəns] s Florenz n

florescence [flo′resəns] s Blüte f

florid [′florɪd] adj (ornate) überladen; (complexion) blühend

florist [′florɪst] s Blumenhändler –in mf

floss [flɔs] s Rohseide f; (of corn) Narbenfäden pl

floss′ silk′ s Florettseide f

flossy [′flɔsi] adj seidenweich

flotilla [flo′tɪlə] s Flotille f

flotsam [′flɑtsəm] s Wrackgut n

flot′sam and jet′sam s Treibgut n; (trifles) Kleinigkeiten pl

flounce [flauns] s Volant m || tr mit Volants besetzen || intr erregt stürmen

flounder [′flaundər] s Flunder f || intr taumeln; (fig) ins Schwimmen kommen

flour [flaur] s Mehl n

flourish [′flʌrɪ/] s (in writing) Schnörkel m; (in a speech) Floskel f; (gesture) große Geste f; (mus) Tusch m; f. of trumpets Trompetengeschmetter n || tr (banners) schwenken; (swords) schwingen || intr blühen, gedeihen

flour′ishing adj blühend; (business) schwunghaft

flour′ mill′ s Mühle f

floury [′flauri] adj mehlig

flout [flaut] tr verspotten || intr—f. at spotten über (acc)

flow [flo] s Fluß m || intr fließen, rinnen; (said of hair, clothes) wallen; f. by vorbeifließen; f. into zuströmen (dat)

flower [′flau·ər] s Blume f; cut flowers Schnittblumen pl || intr blühen

flow′er bed′ s Blumenbeet n

flow′er gar′den s Blumengarten m

flow′er girl′ s Blumenmädchen n

flow′erpot′ s Blumentopf m

flow′er shop′ s Blumenladen m

flow′er show′ s Blumenausstellung f

flow′er stand′ s Blumenstand m

flowery [′flau·əri] adj blumig; (fig) geziert; f. phrase Floskel f

flu [flu] s (coll) Grippe f

flub [flʌb] v (pret & pp flubbed; ger flubbing) tr verpfuschen || s (coll) verkorksen

fluctuate [′flʌkt/u‚et] intr schwanken

fluctuation [‚flʌkt/u′e/ən] s Schwankung f

flue [flu] s Rauchrohr n

fluency [′flu·ənsi] s Geläufigkeit f

fluent [′flu·ənt] adj (speaker) redegewandt; (speech) fließend

fluently [′flu·əntli] adv fließend

fluff [flʌf] s Staubflocke f; (blunder) Schnitzer m || tr verpfuschen; f. up (a pillow) schütteln; (a rug) aufrauhen

fluffy [′flʌfi] adj flaumig

fluid [′flu·ɪd] adj flüssig || s Flüssigkeit f

fluke [fluk] s Ankerflügel m; (coll) Dusel m

flunk [flʌŋk] s Durchfallen n || tr (a test) (coll) durchfallen in (dat); (a student) (coll) durchfallen lassen || intr (coll) durchfallen

flunky [′flʌŋki] s Schranze mf

fluorescent [flo′resənt] adj fluoreszierend

fluores′cent light′ s Leuchtstofflampe f

fluores′cent tube′ s Leuchtröhre f

fluoridate [′florɪ‚det] tr mit e–m Fluorid versetzen

fluoride [′florɑɪd] s Fluorid n

fluorine [′florin] s Fluor n

fluorite [′florɑɪt] s Fluorkalzium n

fluoroscope [′florə‚skop] s Fluoroskop n

flurry [′flʌri] s (of snow) Schneegestöber m; (st. exch.) kurzes Aufflakkern n; f. of activity fieberhafte Tätigkeit f

flush [flʌ/] adj (even) eben, glatt; (well-supplied) gut bei Kasse; (full to overflowing) übervoll || adv direkt || s (on the cheeks) Erröten n; (of youth) Blüte f; (of a toilet) Spülung f; (cards) Flöte f; f. of victory Siegesrausch m || tr (a toilet) spülen; (hunt) auftreiben; f. down hinunterspülen; f. out (animals) auftreiben || intr erröten

flush′ switch′ s Unterputzschalter m

flush′ tank′ s Spülkasten m

flush′ toi′let s Spülklosett n

fluster [′flʌstər] s Verwirrung f || tr verwirren

flute [flut] s (archit) Kannelüre f; (mus) Flöte f || tr riffeln

flut′ing s (archit) Kannelierung f

flutist [′flutɪst] s Flötist –in mf

flutter [′flʌtər] s Flattern n; (excitement) Aufregung f || tr—f. one's eyelashes mit den Wimpern klimpern || intr flattern

flux [flʌks] s (flow) Fließen n, Fluß m; (for fusing metals) Schmelzmittel n; **in f.** im Fluß

fly [flaɪ] s Fliege f; (of trousers) Schlitz m; (angl) künstliche Fliege f; **flies** (theat) Soffitten pl; **fly in the ointment** Haar n in der Suppe || v (pret **flew** [flu]; pp **flown** [flon]) tr fliegen || intr fliegen; (rush) stürzen; (said of rumors) schwirren; (said of time) verfliegen; **fly around** umherfliegen; (e.g., the globe) umfliegen; **fly at s.o.** auf j-n losgehen; **fly away** abfliegen; **fly in all directions** nach allen Seiten zerstieben; **fly low** tief fliegen; **fly off the handle** (fig) aus der Haut fahren; **fly open** aufspringen; **fly over** überfliegen; **fly past** vorbeifliegen (an dat); **let** (e.g., an arrow) **schnellen**

fly′ ball′ s (baseball) Flugball m

fly′-by-night′ adj unverläßlich || s (coll) Schwindelunternehmen n

fly′ cast′ing s Fischen n mit der Wurfangel

flyer ['flaɪ·ər] s var of **flier**

fly′-fish′ intr mit künstlichen Fliegen angeln

fly′ing adj fliegend; (boat, field, time) Flug-; (suit, club, school) Flieger- || s Fliegen n

fly′ing but′tress s Strebebogen m

fly′ing col′ors spl—**come through with f. e-n** glänzenden Sieg erringen

fly′ing sau′cer s fliegende Untertasse f

fly′leaf′ s (–leaves′) Vorsatzblatt n

fly′pa′per s Fliegenfänger m

fly′ rod′ s Angelrute f

fly′speck′ s Fliegendreck m

fly′ swat′ter [‚swatər] s Fliegenklappe f

fly′trap′ s Fliegenfalle f

fly′wheel′ s Schwungrad n

foal [fol] s Fohlen n || intr fohlen

foam [fom] s Schaum m; (of waves) Gischt m; (from the mouth) Geifer m || intr schäumen; (said of waves) branden

foam′ rub′ber s Schaumgummi m

foamy ['fomɪ] adj (full of foam) schaumig; (beer) schäumend; (foam-like) schaumartig

F.O.B., f.o.b. [‚ef‚o'bi] adv (free on board) frei an Bord

focal ['fokəl] adj fokal; **be the f. point** im Brennpunkt stehen; **f. point** (fig & opt) Brennpunkt m

fo·cus ['fokəs] s (–cuses & –ci [saɪ]) (math, opt) Brennpunkt m; (pathol) Herd m; **bring into f.** richtig (or scharf) einstellen; **in f.** scharf eingestellt; **out of f.** unscharf || v (pret & pp –cus[s]ed; ger –cus[s]ing) tr (a camera) einstellen; (attention, etc.) (on) richten (auf acc) || intr sich scharf einstellen

fo′cusing s Scharfeinstellung f

fodder ['fadər] s Futter n

foe [fo] s Feind –in mf

fog [fɔg] s Nebel m; (fig) Verwirrung f; (phot) Grauschleier m || v (pret & pp **fogged**; ger **fogging**) tr ver-

nebeln; (fig) umnebeln || intr (phot) verschleiern; **fog up** beschlagen

fog′ bank′ s Nebelbank f

fog′ bell′ s Nebelglocke f

fog′-bound′ adj durch Nebel festgehalten

fogey ['fogɪ] s Kauz m

foggy ['fɔgɪ] adj neblig, nebelhaft; (phot) verschleiert; **he hasn't the foggiest idea** er hat nicht die leiseste Ahnung

fog′horn′ s Nebelhorn n

fog′ light′ s (aut) Nebelscheinwerfer m

foible ['fɔɪbəl] s Schwäche f

foil [fɔɪl] s (of metal) Folie f; (of a mirror) Spiegelbelag m; (fig) (to) Hintergrund m (für); (fencing) Florett n || tr (a plan) durchkreuzen; (an attempt) vereiteln

foist [fɔɪst] tr—**f. s.th. on s.o.** j-m etw anhängen

fold [fold] s Falte f; (in stiff material) Falz m; (for sheep) Pferch m; (flock of sheep) Schafherde f; (relig) Herde f || tr falten; (stiff material) falzen; (e.g., a chair) zusammenklappen; (the arms) kreuzen; (the wash) zusammenlegen || intr sich (zusammen) falten; (com) zusammenbrechen

folder ['foldər] s (loose-leaf binder) Schnellhefter m; (manila folder) Mappe f; (brochure) Prospekt m

fold′ing adj (bed, chair, camera, wing) Klapp-

fold′ing door′ s Falttür f

fold′ing screen′ s spanische Wand f

foliage ['folɪ·ɪdʒ] s Laubwerk n, Laub n

foli·o ['folɪ‚o] adj Folio-, in Folio || s (–os) (page) Folioblatt n; (book) Foliant m || tr paginieren

folk [fok] adj Volks- || **folks** spl (people) Leute pl; (family) Angehörige pl

folk′ dance′ s Volkstanz m

folk′lore′ s Volkskunde f

folk′ mu′sic s Volksmusik f

folk′ song′ s Volkslied n

folksy ['foksɪ] adj (person) leutselig; (speech, expression) volkstümlich

folk′ tale′ s Volkssage f

folk′way′ s spl volkstümliche Lebensweise f

follicle ['falɪkəl] s Follikel n

follow ['falo] tr folgen (dat); (instructions) befolgen; (a stage, events, news) verfolgen; (in office) folgen auf (acc); (a profession) ausüben; (understand) folgen können (dat); **f. one another** aufeinanderfolgen; (said of events) sich überstürzen; **f. up** nachgehen (dat); **f. your nose!** immer der Nase nach! || intr (nach) folgen; **as follows** folgendermaßen; **f. after** nachfolgen (dat); **f. through** (sport) ganz durchziehen; **f. upon** folgen auf (acc); **it follows that** daraus folgt, daß

follower ['falo·ər] s Anhänger –in mf

fol′lowing adj nachstehend, folgend || s Gefolgschaft f

fol′low-up′ adj Nach- || s weitere Verfolgung f

folly [ˈfɔli] s Torheit f; **follies** (theat) Revue f

foment [foˈment] tr schüren, anstiften

fond [fɔnd] adj (hope, wish) sehnlich; **become f. of** lieb gewinnen; **be f. of** gern haben; **be f. of reading** gern lesen

fondle [ˈfɔndəl] tr liebkosen

fondness [ˈfɔndnɪs] s Verliebtheit f; (for) Hang m (zu), Vorliebe f (für)

font [fɔnt] s (for holy water) Weihwasserbecken n; (for baptism) Taufbecken n; (typ) Schriftart f

food [fud] adj Nähr-, Speise- ‖ s (on the table) Essen n; (in a store) Lebensmittel pl; (requirement for life) Nahrung f; (for animals) Futter n; (for plants) Nährstoff m; **f. and drink** Speis' und Trank; **f. for thought** Stoff m zum Nachdenken

food′ poi′soning s Nahrungsmittelvergiftung f

food′stuffs′ spl Nahrungsmittel pl

food′ val′ue s Nährwert m

fool [ful] s Narr m; **born f.** Mondkalb n; **make a f. of oneself** sich blamieren ‖ tr täuschen, anführen ‖ intr— **f. around** herumtrödeln; **f. around with** herumspielen mit; (romantically) sich herumtreiben mit

fool′har′dy adj tollkühn

fool′ing s Späße pl; **f. around** Firlefanz m; **no f.!** na, so was!

foolish [ˈfulɪʃ] adj töricht, albern

foolishness [ˈfulɪnɪs] s Torheit f

fool′-proof′ adj narrensicher

fools′cap′ s Narrenkappe f; (paper size) Kanzleipapier n

foot [fut] s (feet [fit]) Fuß m; **be (back) on one's feet** (wieder) auf den Beinen sein; **f. of the bed** Fußende n des Bettes; **on f. zu Fuß**; **put one's best f. forward** sich ins rechte Licht setzen; **put one's f. down** (fig) ein Machtwort sprechen; **put one's f. in it** (coll) ins Fettnäpfchen treten; **stand on one's own two feet** auf eigenen Füßen stehen ‖ tr—**f. the bill** blechen

footage [ˈfutɪdʒ] s Ausmaß n in Fuß

foot′-and-mouth′ disease′ s Maul- und Klauenseuche f

foot′ball′ s Fußball m

foot′board′ s (in a car) Trittbrett n; (of a bed) Fußbrett n

foot′bridge′ s Steg m

foot′fall′ s Schritt m

foot′hills′ spl Vorgebirge n

foot′hold′ s (& fig) Halt m; **gain a f.** festen Fuß fassen

foot′ing s Halt m; **lose one's f. ausgleiten**; **on an equal f. with** auf gleichem Fuße mit

foot′lights′ spl Rampenlicht n

foot′man s (—men) Lakai m

foot′note′ s Fußnote f

foot′path′ s Fußpfad m, Fußsteig m

foot′print′ s Fußstapfe f

foot′ race′ s Wettlauf m

foot′rest′ s Fußraste f

foot′ rule′ s Zollstock m

foot′ sol′dier s Infanterist m

foot′sore′ adj fußkrank

foot′step′ s Tritt m; **follow in s.o.'s footsteps** in j-s Fußstapfen treten

foot′stool′ s Schemel m

foot′wear′ s Schuhwerk n

foot′work′ s (sl) Lauferei f; (sport) Beinarbeit f

foot′worn′ adj abgetreten

fop [fɑp] s Geck m

for [fɔr] prep für; (a destination) nach (dat); (with an English present perfect tense) schon (acc), e.g., **I have been living here for a month** ich wohne hier schone e-n Monat (or seit e-m Monat; (with an English future tense) für or auf (acc); **for good** für immer; **for joy** vor Freude; **for years** jahrelang ‖ conj denn

forage [ˈfɔrɪdʒ] s Furage f ‖ intr furagieren

foray [ˈfɔre] s (raid) Raubzug m; (e.g., into politics) Streifzug m ‖ intr plündern

for·bear [fɔrˈber] v (pret –bore [ˈbor]; pp –borne [ˈborn]) tr unterlassen ‖ intr ablassen

forbearance [fɔrˈberəns] s (patience) Geduld f; (leniency) Nachsicht f

for·bid [fɔrˈbɪd] v (pret –bade [ˈbæd] & –bad [ˈbæd]; pp –bidden [ˈbɪdən]) tr verbieten

forbid′ding adj abschreckend; (dangerous) gefährlich

force [fɔrs] s (strength) Kraft f; (compulsion) Gewalt f; (phys) Kraft f; **be in f.** in Kraft sein; **by f.** gewaltsam; **come into f.** in Kraft treten; **forces** (mil) Streitkräfte pl; **have the f. of** gelten als; **resort to f.** zu Zwangsmaßnahmen greifen; **with full f.** mit voller Wucht ‖ tr zwingen; (plants) treiben; (a door) aufsprengen; (e.g., an issue) forcieren; (into) zwängen (in acc); **f. down** hinunterdrücken; (aer) zur Landung zwingen; **f. one's way** sich drängen; **f. s.th. on s.o.** j-m etw aufdrängen

forced′ land′ing s Notlandung f

forced′ march′ s Gewaltsmarsch m

forceful [ˈfɔrsfəl] adj eindrucksvoll

for·ceps [ˈfɔrseps] s (–ceps & –cipes [sɪ͵piz]) (dent, surg, zool) Zange f

forcible [ˈfɔrsɪbəl] adj (strong) kräftig; (violent) gewaltsam

ford [fɔrd] s Furt f ‖ tr durchwaten

fore [fɔr] adj Vorder- ‖ adv (naut) vorn ‖ s—**come to the f.** hervortreten ‖ interj (golf) Achtung!

fore′ and aft′ adv längsschiffs

fore′arm′ s Vorderarm m, Unterarm m

fore′bears′ spl Vorfahren pl

forebode [fɔrˈbod] tr vorbedeuten

forebod′ing s (omen) Vorzeichen n; (presentiment) Vorahnung f

fore′cast′ s Voraussage f ‖ v (pret & pp –cast & –casted) tr voraussagen

forecastle [ˈfoksəl] s Back f

foreclose tr (a mortgage) für verfallen erklären; (shut out) ausschließen

foredoom′ tr im voraus verurteilen

fore′fa′thers spl Vorfahren pl

fore′fin′ger s Zeigefinger m

fore′front′ s Spitze f

fore′go′ing adj vorhergehend

fore'gone' conclu'sion s ausgemachte Sache f

fore'ground' s Vordergrund m

forehead ['fɔrɪd] s Stirn(e) f

foreign ['fɔrɪn] adj (e.g., aid, product) Auslands–; (e.g., body, language, word, worker) Fremd–; (e.g., minister, office, policy, trade) Außen–; (e.g., affairs, service) auswärtig

foreigner ['fɔrɪnər] s Ausländer –in mf

for'eign exchange' s Devisen pl

fore'leg' s Vorderbein n

fore'lock' s Stirnlocke f

fore'man s (-men) Vorarbeiter m; (jur) Obmann m; (min) Steiger m

foremast ['fɔr,mæst] s Fockmast m

fore'most' adj vorderste || adv zuerst

fore'noon' s Vormittag m

fore'part' s vorderster Teil m

fore'paw' s Vorderpfote f

fore'quar'ter s Vorderviertel n

fore'run'ner s Vorbote m

fore'sail' s Focksegel n

fore-see' v (pret –saw') pp –seen') tr voraussehen

foreseeable [fɔr'si·əbəl] adj absehbar

foreshad'ow tr ahnen lassen

foreshort'en tr verkürzen

fore'sight' s Voraussicht f

fore'sight'ed adj umsichtig

fore'skin' s Vorhaut f

forest ['fɔrɪst] s Wald m, Forst m

forestall' tr zuvorkommen (dat)

for'est fire' s Waldbrand m

for'est rang'er s Forstbeamte m

forestry ['fɔrɪstri] s Forstwirtschaft f

fore'taste' s Vorgeschmack m

fore-tell' v (pret & pp –told') tr vorhersagen, weissagen

fore'thought' s Vorsorge f, Vorbedacht m

forev'er adv ewig, für immer; f. and ever auf immer und ewig

forewarn' tr (of) vorher warnen (vor dat)

fore'word' s Vorwort n

forfeit ['fɔrfɪt] s Einbuße f || tr einbüßen, verwirken

forfeiture ['fɔrfɪtʃər] s Verwirkung f

forgather [fɔr'gæðər] intr sich treffen

forge [fɔrdʒ] s Schmiede f || tr schmieden; (documents) fälschen || intr— forge ahead vordringen

forger ['fɔrdʒər] s Fälscher –in mf

forgery ['fɔrdʒəri] s Fälschung f; (coin) Falschgeld n

for-get [fər'gɛt] v (pret –got; pp –got & –gotten; ger –getting) tr vergessen; f. it! spielt keine Rolle!; f. oneself sich vergessen

forgetful [fər'gɛtfəl] adj vergeßlich

forgetfulness [fər'gɛtfəlnɪs] s Vergeßlichkeit f

forget'-me-not' s Vergißmeinnicht n

forgivable [fər'gɪvəbəl] adj verzeihlich

for-give [fər'gɪv] v (pret –gave; pp –given) tr (a person) vergeben (dat); (a thing) vergeben

forgiveness [fər'gɪvnɪs] s Vergebung f

forgiv'ing adj versöhnlich

for-go [fɔr'go] v (pret –went; pp –gone) tr verzichten auf (acc)

fork [fɔrk] s Gabel f; (in the road) Gabelung f; (of a tree) Astgabelung f || tr gabeln; f. over (coll) übergeben

forked adj gabelförmig; (tongue) gespalten

fork'lift truck' s Gabelstapler m

forlorn [fɔr'lɔrn] adj (forsaken) verlassen; (wretched) elend; (attempt) verzweifelt

forlorn' hope' s aussichtsloses Unternehmen n

form [fɔrm] s Form f, Gestalt f; (paper to be filled out) Formular n || tr formen, bilden; (a plan) fassen; (a circle, alliance) schließen; (suspicions) schöpfen; (a habit) annehmen; (blisters) werfen || intr sich bilden

formal ['fɔrməl] adj formell, förmlich

for'mal call' s Höflichkeitsbesuch m

for'mal educa'tion s Schulbildung f

formality [fɔr'mælɪti] s Formalität f; without f. ohne Umstände

format ['fɔrmæt] s Format n

formation [fɔr'meʃən] s Bildung f; (aer) Verband m; (geol, mil) Formation f

former ['fɔrmər] adj ehemalig, früher; the f. jener

formerly ['fɔrmərli] adv ehemals, früher

form'-fit'ting adj—be f. e–e gute Paßform haben

formidable ['fɔrmɪdəbəl] adj (huge) gewaltig; (dreadful) schrecklich

formless ['fɔrmlɪs] adj formlos

form' let'ter s Rundbrief m

formu-la ['fɔrmjələ] s (-las & -lae [,li]) Formel f; (baby food) Kindermilch f

formulate ['fɔrmjə,let] tr formulieren

formulation [,fɔrmjə'leʃən] s Formulierung f

fornicate ['fɔrnɪ,ket] intr Unzucht treiben

fornication [,fɔrnɪ'keʃən] s Unzucht f

for-sake [fɔr'sek] v (pret –sook ['suk]; pp –saken ['sekən]) tr verlassen

fort [fɔrt] s Burg f; (mil) Fort n

forte [fɔrt] s Stärke f

forth [fɔrθ] adv hervor; and so f. und so fort; from that day f. von dem Tag an

forth'com'ing adj bevorstehend

forth'right' adj ehrlich, offen

forth'with' adv sofort

fortieth ['fɔrtɪ·ɪθ] adj & pron vierzigste || s (fraction) Vierzigstel n; (in a series) Vierzigste mfn

fortification [,fɔrtɪfɪ'keʃən] s Befestigung f

forti-fy ['fɔrtɪ,faɪ] v (pret & pp –fied) tr (a place) befestigen; (e.g., with liquor) kräftigen; (encourage) ermutigen

fortitude ['fɔrtɪ,t(j)ud] s Seelenstärke f

fortnight ['fɔrtnaɪt] s vierzehn Tage pl

fortress ['fɔrtrɪs] s Festung f

fortuitous [fɔr't(j)u·ɪtəs] adj zufällig

fortunate ['fɔrt/ənɪt] adj glücklich

fortunately ['fɔrt/ənɪtli] adv glücklicherweise

fortune ['fɔrtʃən] *s* Glück *n*; (*money*) Vermögen *n*; **make a f.** sich [*dat*] ein Vermögen erwerben; **have one's f. told** sich [*dat*] wahrsagen lassen; **tell fortunes** wahrsagen

for'tune hunt'er *s* Mitgiftjäger –in *mf*

for'tunetell'er *s* Wahrsagerin *f*

forty ['fɔrti] *adj* & *pron* vierzig ‖ *s* Vierzig *f*; **the forties** die vierziger Jahre

fo·rum ['fɔrəm] *s* (–rums *el* –ra [rə]) (& *fig*) Forum *n*

forward ['fɔrwərd] *adj* vordere, Vorwärts–; (*person*) keck; (mil) vorgeschoben ‖ *adv* vorwärts, nach vorn; **bring f.** (*an idea*) vorschlagen; (*a proposal*) vorbringen; **come f.** sich melden; **look f. to** sich freuen auf (*acc*); **put f.** vorlegen ‖ *s* (fb) Stürmer *m* ‖ *tr* befördern; **please f.** bitte nachsenden ‖ *interj*—f., **march!** im Gleichschritt, marsch!

fossil ['fɑsɪl] *adj* versteinert ‖ *s* Fossil *n*

foster ['fɔstər] *adj* (*child, father, mother, home*) Pflege–; (*brother, sister*) Milch– ‖ *tr* pflegen

foul [faul] *adj* übel; (*in smell*) übelriechend; (*air, weather*) schlecht; (*language*) unflätig; (*means*) unfair ‖ *s* (sport) Foul *n* ‖ *tr* (*make dirty*) besudeln; (*the lines*) verwickeln; (sport) foulen; **f. up** durcheinanderbringen ‖ *intr* (sport) foulen

foul' line' *s* (*baseball*) Grenzlinie *f*; (*basketball*) Freiwurflinie *f*

foul-mouthed ['faul,mauðd], ['faul,mauθt] *adj* zotige Reden führend

foul' play' *s* unfaires Spiel *n*; (*crime*) Verbrechen *n*, Mord *m*

found [faund] *tr* gründen; (*cast*) gießen

foundation [faun'deʃən] *s* (*act*) Gründung *f*; (*of a structure*) Fundament *n*; (*fund*) Stiftung *f*; (fig) Grundlage *f*; **lay the foundation of** (& fig) den Grund legen zu

founda'tion gar'ments *spl* Miederwaren *pl*

founda'tion wall' *s* Grundmauer *f*

founder ['faundər] *s* Gründer –in *mf*; (metal) Gießer –in *mf* ‖ *intr* sinken (*said of a ship*) sinken; (*fail*) scheitern

foundling ['faundlɪŋ] *s* Findling *m*

foundry ['faundri] *s* Gießerei *f*

found'ry-man *s* (–men) Gießer *m*

fount [faunt] *s* Quelle *f*

fountain ['fauntən] *s* Springbrunnen *m*

foun'tainhead' *s* Urquell *m*

foun'tain pen' *s* Füller *m*

four [fɔr] *adj* & *pron* vier ‖ *s* Vier *f*; **on all fours** auf allen vieren

four'-cy'cle *adj* (mach) Viertakt–

four'-en'gine *adj* viermotorig

fourflusher ['fɔr,flʌʃər] *s* Angeber *m*

four'foot'ed *adj* vierfüßig

four' hun'dred *adj* & *pron* vierhundert ‖ *spl*—**the Four Hundred** die oberen Zehntausend

four'lane' *adj* Vierbahn–

four'-leaf' *adj* vierblättrig

four'-leg'ged *adj* vierbeinig

four'-letter word' *s* unanständiges Wort *n*

foursome ['fɔrsəm] *s* Viererspiel *n*; (*group of four*) Quartet *n*

fourteenth [fɔr'tinθ] *adj* & *pron* vierzehnte ‖ *s* (*fraction*) Vierzehntel *n*; **the f.** (*in dates and in a series*) der Vierzehnte

fourth [fɔrθ] *adj* & *pron* vierte ‖ *s* (*fraction*) Viertel *n*; **the f.** (*in dates and in a series*) der Vierte

fourth' estate' *s* Presse *f*

fowl [faul] *s* Huhn *n*, Geflügel *n*

fox [fɑks] *s* (& *fig*) Fuchs *m*

fox'glove' *s* (bot) Fingerhut *m*

fox'hole' *s* (mil) Schützenloch *n*

fox'hound' *s* Hetzhund *m*

fox' hunt' *s* Fuchsjagd *f*

fox' ter'rier *s* Foxterrier *m*

fox' trot' *s* Foxtrott *m*

foyer ['fɔɪ·ər] *s* (*of a theater*) Foyer *n*; (*of a house*) Diele *f*

fracas ['frekəs] *s* Aufruhr *m*

fraction ['frækʃən] *s* Bruchteil *m*, Bruch *m*

frac'tions Bruchrechnung *f*

fractional ['frækʃənəl] *adj* Bruch–

fracture ['fræktʃər] *s* Bruch *m* ‖ *tr* sich [*dat*] brechen

fragile ['frædʒɪl] *adj* zerbrechlich

fragment ['frægmənt] *s* Bruchstück *n*; (*of writing*) Fragment *n*

fragmentary ['frægmən,teri] *adj* bruchstückhaft; (*writing*) fragmentarisch

fragmenta'tion bomb' [,frægmən'te-ʃən] *s* Splitterbombe *f*

fragrance ['fregrəns] *s* Duft *m*

fragrant ['fregrənt] *adj* duftend; **be f.** duften

frail [frel] *adj* schwach, hinfällig; (*fragile*) zerbrechlich

frailty ['frelti] *s* Schwachheit *f*

frame [frem] *s* (*e.g., of a picture, door*) Rahmen *m*; (*of glasses*) Fassung *f*; (*of a house*) Balkenwerk *n*; (*structure*) Gestell *n*; (anat) Körperbau *m*; (cin, phot) Bild *n*; (naut) Spant *n* ‖ *tr* (*a picture*) einrahmen; (*a plan*) ersinnen; (sl) reinhängen

frame' house' *s* Holzhaus *n*

frame' of mind' *s* Gemütsverfassung *f*

frame' of ref'erence *s* Bezugspunkte *pl*

frame'-up' *s* abgekartete Sache *f*

frame'work' *s* Gebälk *n*, Fachwerk *n*; (fig) Rahmen *m*; (aer) Aufbau *m*

franc [fræŋk] *s* Franc *m*; (*Swiss*) Franken *m*

France [fræns] *s* Frankreich *n*

Frances ['frænsɪs] *s* Franziska *f*

franchise ['fræntʃaɪz] *s* Konzession *f*; (*right to vote*) Wahlrecht *n*

Francis ['frænsɪs] *s* Franz *m*

Franciscan [fræn'sɪskən] *adj* Franziskaner– ‖ *s* Franziskaner *m*

frank [fræŋk] *adj* offen ‖ *s* Freivermerk *m*; Frank (*masculine name*) Franz *m*; (*medieval German person*) Franke *m*, Franka *f* ‖ *tr* freimachen

frankfurter ['fræŋkfərtər] *s* Würstel *n*

frankincense ['fræŋkɪn,sens] *s* Weihrauch *m*

Frankish ['fræŋkɪʃ] *adj* fränkisch

frankness ['fræŋknɪs] *s* Offenheit *f*; (*bluntness*) Freimut *m*

frantic ['fræntɪk] *adj* (*with*) außer sich (*vor dat*); (*efforts*) krampfhaft

fraternal [frə'tʌrnəl] *adj* brüderlich; *(twins)* zweieiig

fraternity [frə'tʌrnɪti] *s* Bruderschaft *f*; *(educ)* Studentenverbindung *f*

fraternize ['frætər,naɪz] *intr* (with) sich anfreunden (mit)

fraud [frɔd] *s* Betrug *m*; *(person)* (coll) Betrüger –in *mf*

fraudulent ['frɔdjələnt] *adj* betrügerisch

fraught [frɔt] *adj*—f. with voll mit; f. with danger gefahrvoll

fray [fre] *s* Schlägerei *f*; *(battle)* Kampf *m* ‖ *tr* ausfransen; *(the nerves)* aufreiben ‖ *intr* (said of edges) sich ausfransen; *(become threadbare)* sich durchscheuern

freak [frik] *s* Mißbildung *f*; *(whimsy)* Laune *f*; *(enthusiast)* Enthusiast –in *mf*; *(abnormal person)* verrückter Kerl *m*; f. of nature Monstrum *n*

freakish ['frikɪʃ] *adj* grotesk; *(capricious)* launisch

freckle ['frekəl] *s* Sommersprosse *f*

freckled ['frekəld], **freckly** ['frekli] *adj* sommersprossig

Frederick ['fredərɪk] *s* Friedrich *m*

free [fri] *adj* (freer ['fri-ər]; freest ['fri-ɪst]) frei; *(off duty)* dienstfrei; for f. (coll) gratis; f. with *(e.g., money, praise)* freigebig mit; go f. frei ausgehen; he is f. to *(inf)* es steht ihm frei zu *(inf)*; set f. freilassen ‖ *adv* umsonst, kostenlos ‖ *v* (pret & pp freed [frid]; ger freeing ['fri-ɪŋ]) *tr* (liberate) befreien; *(untie)* losmachen

free' and ea'sy *adj* zwanglos

freebooter ['fri,butər] *s* Freibeuter *m*

free'born' *adj* freigeboren

freedom ['fridəm] *s* Freiheit *f*

free'dom of assem'bly *s* Versammlungsfreiheit *f*

free'dom of speech' *s* Redefreiheit *f*

free'dom of the press' *s* Pressefreiheit *f*

free'dom of wor'ship *s* Glaubensfreiheit *f*

free' en'terprise *s* freie Wirtschaft *f*

free'-for-all' *s* allgemeine Prügelei *f*

free' hand' *s* freie Hand *f*

free'-hand draw'ing *s* (activity) Freihandzeichnen *n*; *(product)* Freihandzeichnung *f*

free'hand'ed *adj* freigebig

free'hold'er *s* (jur) Freigut *n*

free' kick' *s* (fb) Freistoß *m*

free'-lance' *adj* freiberuflich ‖ *intr* freiberuflich tätig sein

free-lancer ['fri,lænsər] *s* Freiberufliche *mf*

free' li'brary *s* Volksbibliothek *f*

free'man *s* (-men) Ehrenbürger *m*

Free'ma'son *s* Freimaurer *m*

Free'ma'sonry *s* Freimaurerei *f*

free' of charge' *adj & adv* kostenlos

free' on board' *adv* frei an Bord

free' play' *s* (fig & mach) Spielraum *m*

free' port' *s* Freihafen *m*

free' sam'ple *s* *(of food)* Gratiskostprobe *f*; *(of products)* Gratismuster *n*

free' speech' *s* Redefreiheit *f*

free'-spo'ken *adj* freimütig

free'stone' *adj* mit leicht auslösbarem Kern

free'think'er *s* Freigeist *m*

free' thought' *s* Freigeisterei *f*

free' trade' *s* Freihandel *m*

free'way' *s* Autobahn *f*

free' will' *s* Willensfreiheit *f*; of one's own f. aus freien Stücken

freeze [friz] *s* Frieren *n* ‖ *v* (pret froze [froz]; pp frozen ['frozən]) *tr* frieren; *(assets)* einfrieren; *(prices)* stoppen; *(food)* tiefkühlen; (surg) vereisen ‖ *intr* (ge)frieren; *(e.g., with fear)* erstarren; f. over zufrieren; f. to death erfrieren; f. up vereisen

freeze'-dry' *v* (pret & pp –dried) *tr* gefriertrocknen

freezer ['frizər] *s* (chest) Tiefkühltruhe *f*; *(cabinet)* Tiefkühlschrank *m*

freez'er compart'ment *s* Gefrierfach *n*

freez'ing *s* Einfrieren *n*; below f. unter dem Gefrierpunkt

freight [fret] *s* (load) Fracht *f*; *(cargo)* Frachtgut *n*; *(fee)* Frachtgebühr *f*; by f. als Frachtgut ‖ *tr* beladen

freight' car' *s* Güterwagen *m*

freight' el'evator *s* Warenaufzug *m*

freighter ['fretər] *s* Frachter *m*

freight' of'fice *s* Güterabfertigung *f*

freight' train' *s* Güterzug *m*

freight' yard' *s* Güterbahnhof *m*

French [frentʃ] *adj* französisch ‖ *s* (language) Französisch *n*; the F. die Franzosen

French' doors' *spl* Glastüre *pl*

French' fries' *spl* Pommes frites *pl*

French' horn' *s* (mus) Waldhorn *n*

French' leave' *s*—take F. sich französisch empfehlen

French'man *s* (-men) Franzose *m*

French' roll' *s* Schrippe *f*

French' toast' *s* arme Ritter *pl*

French' win'dow *s* Flügelfenster *n*

French' wom'an *s* (-wom'en) Französin *f*

frenzied ['frenzid] *adj* rasend

frenzy ['frenzi] *s* Raserei *f*

frequency ['frikwənsi] *s* Häufigkeit *f*; (phys) Frequenz *f*

fre'quency modula'tion *s* Frequenzmodulation *f*

frequent ['frikwənt] *adj* häufig ‖ [fri-'kwent] *tr* besuchen, frequentieren

frequently ['frikwentli] *adv* häufig

fres·co ['fresko] *s* (-coes & -cos) Fresko *n*, Freskogemälde *n*

fresh [freʃ] *adj* frisch; (coll) frech ‖ *adv* neu, kürzlich

fresh'-baked' *adj* neugebacken

freshen ['freʃən] *tr* erfrischen; f. up auffrischen ‖ *intr*—f. up sich auffrischen

freshet ['freʃɪt] *s* Hochwasser *n*; *(fresh-water stream)* Fluß *m*

fresh'man *s* (-men) Fuchs *m*

freshness ['freʃnɪs] *s* Frische *f*; (coll) Naseweisheit *f*

fresh' wa'ter *s* Süßwasser *n*

fresh'-wa'ter *adj* Süßwasser-

fret [fret] *s* Verdruß *m*; (carp) Laubsägewerk *n*; (mus) Bund *n* ‖ *v* (pret

& *pp* **fretted;** *ger* **fretting)** *tr* gitterförmig verzieren ‖ *intr* sich ärgern
fretful ['frɛtfəl] *adj* verdrießlich
fret'work' *s* Laubsägewerk *n*
Freudian ['frɔɪdɪ·ən] *adj* Freudsch ‖ *s* Freudianer –in *mf*
friar ['fraɪ·ər] *s* Klosterbruder *m*
fricassee [,frɪkə'si] *s* Frikassee *n*
friction ['frɪkʃən] *s* Reibung *f;* (fig) Reiberei *f*, Mißhelligkeit *f*
fric'tion tape' *s* Isolierband *n*
Friday ['fraɪdɪ] *s* Freitag *m*
fried [fraɪd] *adj* gebraten, Brat-, Back-
fried' chick'en *s* Backhuhn *n*
fried' egg' *s* Spiegelei *n*
fried' pota'toes *spl* Bratkartoffeln *pl*
friend [frɛnd] *s* Freund –in *mf;* **be (close) friends** (eng) befreundet sein; **make friends (with)** sich anfreunden (mit)
friendliness ['frɛndlɪnɪs] *s* Freundlichkeit *f*
friendly ['frɛndli] *adj* freundlich; **on f. terms with** in freundschaftlichem Verhältnis mit
friend'ship' *s* Freundschaft *f*
frieze [friz] *s* Fries *m*
frigate ['frɪgɪt] *s* Fregatte *f*
fright [fraɪt] *s* Schrecken *m*
frighten ['fraɪtən] *tr* schrecken; **be frightened** erschrecken; **f. away** verscheuchen, vertreiben
frightful ['fraɪtfəl] *adj* schrecklich
frigid ['frɪdʒɪd] *adj* eiskalt; (pathol) Frigid
frigidity [frɪ'dʒɪdɪti] *s* Kälte *f;* (pathol) Frigidität *f*
Frig'id Zone' *s* kalte Zone *f*
frill [frɪl] *s* (*ruffle*) Volant *m*, Krause *f;* (*frippery*) Schnörkel *m;* **put on frills** sich aufgeblasen benehmen; **with all the frills** mit allen Schikanen
fringe [frɪndʒ] *s* Franse *f* ‖ *tr* mit Fransen besetzen; (fig) einsäumen
fringe' ar'ea *s* Randgebiet *n*
fringe' ben'efit *s* zusätzliche Sozialleistung *f*
frippery ['frɪpəri] *s* (*cheap finery, trifles*) Flitterkram *m*
frisk [frɪsk] *tr* (sl) durchsuchen ‖ *intr* **–f. about** herumtollen
frisky ['frɪski] *adj* ausgelassen
fritter ['frɪtər] *s* Beignet *m* ‖ *tr*–**f. away** vertrödeln, verzetteln
fritz [frɪts] *s* **—on the f.** kaputt
frivolous ['frɪvələs] *adj* leichtfertig; (*object*) geringfügig
friz [frɪz] *s* (**frizzes**) Kraushaar *n* ‖ *v* (*pret* & *pp* **frizzed**) *ger* **frizzing**) *tr* kräuseln ‖ *intr* sich kräuseln
frizzle ['frɪzəl] *s* Kraushaar *n* ‖ *tr* (*hair*) kräuseln; (*food*) knusprig braten ‖ *intr* sich kräuseln; (*sizzle*) zischen
frizzy ['frɪzi] *adj* kraus
fro [fro] *adv*—**to and fro** hin und her
frock [frɑk] *s* Kleid *n;* (eccl) Mönchskutte *f*
frog [frɑg] *s* (*animal; slight hoarseness*) Frosch *m*
frog'man' *s* (**-men**) Froschmann *m*
frol·ic ['frɑlɪk] *s* Spaß *m* ‖ *v* (*pret* &

pp **–icked;** *ger* **–icking)** *intr* Spaß machen; (*frisk about*) herumtollen
frolicsome ['frɑlɪksəm] *adj* ausgelassen
from [frʌm] *prep* von (dat), aus (*dat*), von (*dat*) aus; **f. afar** von weitem; **f. now on** künftig; **f. ... on** von ... an
front [frʌnt] *adj* Vorder-, vordere ‖ *s* (*façade*) Vorderseite *f;* (*of a shirt, dress*) Einsatz *m;* (*cover-up*) Aushängeschild *n;* (meteor, mil) Front *f;* **from the f.** von vorn; **in f.** vorn; **in f. of** vor (*dat or acc*); **in the f. of the book** vorn im Buch; **put on a bold f.** Mut zeigen; **they put on a big f.** alles Fassade! ‖ *tr* gegenüberliegen (*dat*) ‖ *intr*—**f. for s.o.** j-m als Strohmann dienen; **f. on** mit der Front liegen nach
frontage ['frʌntɪdʒ] *s* Straßenfront *f*
frontal ['frʌntəl] *adj* Frontal-; (anat) Stirn-
fron'tal view' *s* Vorderansicht *f*
front' door' *s* Haustür *f*
front' foot' *s* Vorderfuß *m*
frontier [frʌn'tɪr] *s* (*border*) Grenze *f;* (*area*) Grenzland *n;* (fig) Grenzbereich *m*
frontiers'man *s* (**-men**) Pionier *m*
frontispiece ['frʌntɪs,pis] *s* Titelbild *n*
front' line' *s* Front *f*, Frontlinie *f*
front'-line' *adj* Front-, Gefechts-
front' page' *s* Titelseite *f*
front' porch' *s* Veranda *f*
front' rank' *s* (mil) vorderes Glied *n;* **be in the f.** (fig) im Vordergrund stehen
front' row' *s* erste Reihe *f*
front' run'ner *s* (pol) Spitzenkandidat –in *mf*
front' seat' *s* Vordersitz *m*
front' steps' *spl* Vordertreppe *f*
front' yard' *s* Vorgarten *m*, Vorplatz *m*
frost [frɔst] *s* (*freezing*) Frost *m;* (*frozen dew*) Reif *m* ‖ *tr* mit Reif überziehen; (culin) glasieren
frost'bite' *s* Erfrierung *f*
frost'bit'ten *adj* erfroren
frost'ed glass' *s* Mattglas *n*
frost'ing *s* Glasur *f*
frost' line' *s* Frostgrenze *f*
frosty ['frɔsti] *adj* (& fig) frostig
froth [frɔθ] *s* (*foam*) Schaum *m;* (*slaver*) Geifer *m* ‖ *intr* schäumen; geifern
frothy ['frɔθi] *adj* schäumend
froward ['froward] *adj* eigensinnig
frown [fraun] *s* Stirnrunzeln *n* ‖ *intr* die Stirn runzeln; **f. at** böse anschauen; **f. on** mißbilligen
frowsy, frowzy ['frauzi] *adj* (*slovenly*) schlampig; (*ill-smelling*) muffig
froz'en as'sets ['frozən] *spl* eingefrorene Guthaben *pl*
froz'en foods' *spl* tiefgekühlte Lebensmittel *pl*
frugal ['frugəl] *adj* frugal
fruit [frut] *adj* (*tree*) Obst-, Südfrucht- ‖ *s* Frucht *f*, Obst *n*, Südfrüchte *pl;* (fig) Frucht *f*
fruit' cake' *s* Stolle *f*, Stollen *m*

fruit' cup' s gemischte Früchte pl
fruit' fly' s Obstfliege f
fruitful ['frutfəl] adj fruchtbar
fruition [fru'ɪʃən] s Reife f; come to f. zur Reife gelangen
fruit' jar' s Konservenglas n
fruit' juice' s Fruchtsaft m, Obstsaft m
fruitless ['frutlɪs] adj (& fig) fruchtlos
fruit' sal'ad s Obstsalat m
fruit' stand' s Obststand m
frump [frʌmp] s Scharteke f
frumpish ['frʌmpɪʃ] adj schlampig
frustrate ['frʌstret] tr (discourage) frustrieren; (an endeavor) vereiteln
frustration [frʌs'treʃən] s Frustration f; (of an endeavor) Vereitelung f
fry [fraɪ] s Gebratenes n || v (pret & pp fried) tr & intr braten
fry'ing pan' s Bratpfanne f; jump out of the f. into the fire vom Regen unter die Traufe kommen
fuchsia ['fjuʃə] s (bot) Fuchsie f
fudge [fʌdʒ] s weiches, milchhaltiges, mit Kakao versetztes Zuckerwerk n
fuel ['fjuəl] s Brennstoff m; (for engines) Treibstoff m; (fig) Nahrung f; add f. to the flames Öl ins Feuer gießen || v (pret & pp fuel[l]ed) ger fuel[l]ing) tr mit Brennstoff versorgen || intr tanken
fu'el dump' s Treibstofflager n
fu'el gauge' s Benzinuhr f
fu'el tank' s Treibstoffbehälter m
fugitive ['fjudʒɪtɪv] adj flüchtig || s Flüchtling m
fugue [fjug] s (mus) Fuge f
ful·crum ['fʌlkrəm] s (-crums & -cra [krə]) Stützpunkt m, Drehpunkt m
fulfill [ful'fɪl] tr erfüllen
fulfillment [ful'fɪlmənt] s Erfüllung f
full [ful] adj voll; (with food) satt; (clothes) weit; (hour) ganz; (life) inhaltsreich; (voice) wohlklingend; (professor) ordentlich; f. of voller, voll von; too f. übervoll; work f. time ganztägig arbeiten || adv—f. well sehr gut || s—in f. voll, ganz || tr (tex) walken
full'back' s (fb) Außenverteidiger m
full'-blood'ed adj vollblütig
full-blown ['ful'blon] adj (flower) voll aufgeblüht; (fig) voll erblüht
full' bod'ied adj (wine) stark, schwer
full' dress' s Gesellschaftsanzug m; (mil) Paradeanzug m
full'-dress' adj Gala-, formell
full'-faced' adj pausbackig; (portrait) mit voll zugewandtem Gesicht
full-fledged ['ful'fledʒd] adj richtiggehend
full-grown ['ful'gron] adj voll ausgewachsen
full' house' s (cards) Full house n; (theat) volles Haus n
full'-length' adj (dress) in voller Größe; (portrait) lebensgroß; (movie) abendfüllend
full' moon' s Vollmond m
full'-page' adj ganzseitig
full' pay' s volles Gehalt n
full' profes'sor s Ordinarius m
full'-scale' adj in voller Größe
full'-sized' adj in natürlicher Größe

full' speed' adv auf höchsten Touren
full' stop' s (gram) Punkt m; come to a f. völlig stillstehen
full' swing' s—in f. in vollem Gange
full' throt'tle s Vollgas n
full' tilt' adv auf höchsten Touren
full'-time' adj ganztägig
full' view' s—in f. direkt vor den Augen
fully ['ful(l)i] adj völlig; be f. booked ausverkauft sein
fulsome ['fulsəm] adj (excessive) übermäßig; (offensive) widerlich
fumble ['fʌmbəl] tr (a ball) fallen lassen || intr fummeln; f. for umherfühlen nach
fume [fjum] s Gas n, Dampf m || intr dampfen; (smoke) rauchen; f. with rage vor Wut schnauben
fumigate ['fjumɪ‚get] tr ausräuchern
fun [fʌn] s Spaß m; be (great) fun (viel) Spaß machen; for fun zum Spaß; for the fun of it spaßeshalber; have fun! viel Spaß!; make fun of sich lustig machen über (acc); poke fun at witzeln über (acc)
function ['fʌŋkʃən] s Funktion f; (office) Amt n; (formal occasion) Feier f || intr funktionieren; (officiate) fungieren
functional ['fʌŋkʃənəl] adj (practical) Zweck-, zweckmäßig; (disorder) funktionell, Funktions-
functionary ['fʌŋkʃə‚neri] s Funktionär –in mf
fund [fʌnd] s Fonds m; (fig) Vorrat m funds Geldmittel pl || tr fundieren
fundamental [‚fʌndə'mentəl] adj grundlegend, Grund- || s Grundbegriff m
fundamentalist [‚fʌndə'mentəlɪst] s Fundamentalist –in mf
fundamentally [‚fʌndə'mentəli] adv im Grunde, prinzipiell
funeral ['fjunərəl] adj Leichen-, Trauer-, Begräbnis– || s Begräbnis n
fu'neral direc'tor s Bestattungsunternehmer –in mf
fu'neral home' s Aufbahrungshalle f
fu'neral proces'sion s Trauergefolge n
fu'neral serv'ice s Trauergottesdienst m
fu'neral wreath' s Totenkranz m
funereal [fju'nɪrɪəl] adj düster
fungus ['fʌŋgəs] s (funguses & fungi ['fʌndʒaɪ]) Pilz m, Schwamm m
funicular [fju'nɪkjələr] s Drahtseilbahn f
funk [fʌŋk] s (fear) Mordsangst f; be in a f. niedergeschlagen sein
fun·nel ['fʌnəl] s Trichter m; (naut) Schornstein m || v (pret & pp -nel[l]ed; ger -nel[l]ing) tr durch e-n Trichter gießen; (fig) (into) konzentrieren (auf acc)
funnies ['fʌniz] spl Witzseite f
funny ['fʌni] adj komisch; (strange, suspicious) sonderbar; don't try anything f. mach mir keine Dummheiten!
fun'ny bone' s Musikantenknochen m
fun'ny bus'iness s dunkle Geschäfte pl
fun'ny ide'as spl Flausen pl

fun'ny pa'per s Witzblatt n
fur [fʌr] adj (coat, collar) Pelz– ‖ s Pelz m; (on the tongue) Belag m
furbish ['fɜrbiʃ] tr aufputzen
furious ['fjuri·əs] adj (at) wütend (auf acc); be f. wüten
furl [fʌrl] tr zusammenrollen
fur'-lined' adj pelzgefüttert
furlong ['fɜrlɔŋ] s Achtelmeile f
furlough ['fɜrlo] s (mil) Urlaub m; go on f. auf Urlaub kommen ‖ tr beurlauben
furnace ['fʌrnɪs] s Ofen m
furnish ['fɜrnɪʃ] tr (a room) möblieren; (e.g., an office) ausstatten; (proof) liefern; (supply) (with) versehen (mit)
fur'nished room' s möbliertes Zimmer n
furnishings ['fɜrnɪʃɪŋz] spl Ausstattung f
furniture ['fɜrnɪtʃər] s Möbel pl; piece of f. Möbelstück n
fur'niture store' s Möbelhandlung f
furor ['fjurɔr] s (rage) Wut f; (uproar) Furore f; (vogue) Mode f; cause a f. Furore machen
furrier ['fʌrɪ·ər] s Pelzhändler –in mf
furrow ['fʌro] s Furche f ‖ tr furchen
furry ['fʌri] adj pelzig
further ['fɜrðər] adj weiter; (particulars) näher ‖ adv weiter ‖ tr fördern
furtherance ['fʌrðərəns] s Förderung f
fur'thermore' adv überdies, außerdem
furthest ['fɜrðɪst] adj weiteste ‖ adv am weitesten
furtive ['fʌrtɪv] adj verstohlen

fury ['fjuri] s Wut f; Fury (myth) Furie f
fuse [fjuz] s (of an explosive) Zünder m; (elec) Sicherung f; blown f. durchgebrannte Sicherung f ‖ tr verschmelzen ‖ intr verschmelzen; (fig) sich vereinigen
fuse' box' s Sicherungskasten m
fuselage ['fjuzəlɪdʒ] s (aer) Rumpf m
fusible ['fjuzɪbəl] adj schmelzbar
fusillade ['fjusə‚led] s Feuersalve f; (fig) Hagel m
fusion ['fjuʒən] s Verschmelzung f; (pol, phys) Fusion f
fuss [fʌs] s Getue n; make a f. over viel Aufhebens machen von ‖ intr sich aufregen; f. around herumwirtschaften; f. over viel Aufhebens machen von; f. with herumspielen mit
fuss' bud'get, fuss'pot' s Umstandskrämer m
fussy ['fʌsi] adj (given to detail) umständlich; (fastidious) heikel; (irritable) reizbar; be f. Umstände machen
fustian ['fʌstʃən] s (bombast) Schwulst m; (tex) Barchent m
fusty ['fʌsti] adj (musty) muffig; (old-fashioned) veraltet
futile ['fjutəl] adj vergeblich, nutzlos
futility [fju'tɪlɪti] s Nutzlosigkeit f
future ['fjutʃər] adj (zu)künftig ‖ s Zukunft f; futures (econ) Termingeschäfte pl; in the f. künftig
fuzz [fʌz] s (from cloth) Fussel f; (on peaches) Flaum m
fuzzy ['fʌzi] adj flaumig; (unclear) unklar; (hair) kraus

G

G, g [dʒi] s siebenter Buchstabe des englischen Alphabets
gab [gæb] s (coll) Geschwätz n ‖ v (pret & pp gabbed; ger gabbing) intr schwatzen
gabardine ['gæbər‚din] s Gabardine m
gabble ['gæbəl] s Geschnatter n ‖ intr schnattern
gable ['gebəl] s Giebel m
ga'ble end' s Giebelwand f
ga'ble roof' s Giebeldach n
gad [gæd] v (pret & pp gadded; ger gadding) intr—gad about umherstreifen
gad'about' s Bummler –in mf
gad'fly' s Viehbremse f; (fig) Störenfried m
gadget ['gædʒɪt] s (coll) Gerät n
Gaelic ['gelɪk] adj gälisch ‖ s (language) Gälisch n
gaff [gæf] s Fischhaken m
gag [gæg] s (something put into the mouth) Knebel m; (joke) Witz m; (hoax, trick) amüsanter Trick m ‖ v (pret & pp gagged; ger gagging) tr knebeln; (said of a tight collar) würgen; (fig) mundtot machen ‖ intr (on food) würgen

gage [gedʒ] s (challenge) Fehdehandschuh m; (pawn) Pfand m
gaiety ['ge·ɪti] s Fröhlichkeit f
gaily ['geli] adv fröhlich
gain [gen] s Gewinn m; (advantage) Vorteil m; g. in weight Gewichtszunahme f ‖ tr gewinnen; (pounds) zunehmen; (a living) verdienen; (a victory) erringen; g. a footing festen Fuß fassen; g. ground (mil & fig) Terrain gewinnen; g. speed schneller werden; g. weight an Gewicht zunehmen ‖ intr (said of a car) aufholen; (said of a clock) vorgehen; g. from Gewinn haben von; g. in gewinnen an (dat); g. on s.o. j–m den Vorteil abgewinnen
gainful ['genfəl] adj einträglich
gainfully ['genfəli] adv—g. employed erwerbstätig
gain'say' v (pret & pp –said [‚sed], [‚sɛd]) tr (a thing) verneinen; (a person) widersprechen (dat)
gait [get] s Gang m, Gangart f
gala ['gælə], ['gelə] adj festlich ‖ s (celebration) Feier f; (dress) Gala f
galaxy ['gæləksi] s Galaxis f; (fig) glänzende Versammlung f

gale [gel] *s* Sturm *m*, Sturmwind *m*; **gales of laughter** Lachensalven *pl*

gale′ warn′ing *s* Sturmwarnung *f*

gall [gɔl] *s* Galle *f*; (*audacity*) Unverschämtheit *f* ‖ *tr* (*rub*) wundreiben; (*vex*) ärgern, belästigen

gallant ['gælənt] *adj* tapfer); (*stately*) stattlich ‖ [gə'lænt] *adj* galant ‖ *s* Galan *m*

gallantry ['gæləntri] *s* (*bravery*) Tapferkeit *f*; (*courteous behavior*) Ritterlichkeit *f*

gall′ blad′der *s* Gallenblase *f*

galleon ['gæli·ən] *s* Galeone *f*

gallery ['gæləri] *s* (*arcade*) Säulenhalle *f*; (art, theat) Galerie *f*; (min) Stollen *m*; **play to the g.** (coll) Effekthascherei treiben

galley ['gæli] *s* (*a ship*) Galeere *f*; (*a kitchen*) Kombüse *f*; (typ) Setzschiff *n*

gal′ley proof′ *s* (typ) Fahne *f*

gal′ley slave′ *s* Galeerensklave *m*

Gallic ['gælɪk] *adj* gallisch

gall′ing *adj* verdrießlich

gallivant ['gælɪˌvænt] *intr* bummeln

gallon ['gælən] *s* Gallone *f*

galloon [gə'lun] *s* Tresse *f*

gallop ['gæləp] *s* Galopp *m*; **at full g.** in gestrecktem Galopp ‖ *tr* in Galopp setzen ‖ *intr* galoppieren

gal·lows ['gæloz] *s* (–lows & –lowses) Galgen *m*

gal′lows bird′ *s* (coll) Galgenvogel *m*

gall′stone′ *s* Gallenstein *m*

galore [gə'lor] *adv* im Überfluß

galosh [gə'lɑʃ] *s* Galosche *f*

galvanize ['gælvəˌnaɪz] *tr* galvanisieren

gambit ['gæmbɪt] *s* (fig) Schachzug *m*; (chess) Gambit *n*

gamble ['gæmbəl] *s* Hasardspiel *n*; (*risk*) Risiko *n*; (com) Spekulationsgeschäft *n* ‖ *tr*—**g. away** verspielen ‖ *intr* spielen, hasardieren

gambler ['gæmblər] *s* Spieler –in *mf*; (fig) Hasardeur *m*, Hasardeuse *f*

gam′bling *s* Spielen *n*, Spiel *n*

gam′bling house′ *s* Spielhölle *f*

gam′bling ta′ble *s* Spieltisch *m*

gam·bol ['gæmbəl] *s* Luftsprung *m* ‖ *v* (*pret & pp* –bol[l]ed; *ger* –bol[l]ing) *intr* umhertollen

gambrel ['gæmbrəl] *s* (hock) Hachse *f*; (*in a butcher shop*) Spriegel *m*

gam′brel roof′ *s* Mansardendach *n*

game [gem] *adj* bereit; (*fight*) tapfer; (*leg*) lahm; (hunt) Wild–, Jagd– ‖ *s* Spiel *n*; (*e.g., of chess*) Partie *f*; (fig) Absicht *f*; (culin) Wildbret *n*; (hunt) Wild *n*, Jagdwild *n*; **have the g. in the bag** den Sieg in der Tasche haben; **play a losing g.** auf verlorenem Posten kämpfen; **the g. is up** das Spiel ist aus

game′ bird′ *s* Jagdvogel *m*

game′ board′ *s* Spielbrett *n*

game′cock′ *s* Kampfhahn *m*

gameness ['gemnɪs] *f* Tapferkeit *f*

game′ of chance′ *s* Glücksspiel *n*

game′ preserve′ *s* Wildpark *m*

game′ war′den *s* Jagdaufseher *m*

gamut ['gæmət] *s* Skala *f*

gamy ['gemi] *adj* nach Wild riechend; **g. flavor** Wildgeschmack *m*

gander ['gændər] *s* Gänserich *m*; **take a g. at** (coll) e–n Blick werfen auf (*acc*)

gang [gæŋ] *s* (*group of friends*) Gesellschaft *f*; (*antisocial group*) Bande *f*; (*of workers*) Kolonne *f* ‖ *intr*— **g. up** (**on**) sich zusammenrotten (gegen)

gangling ['gæŋglɪŋ] *adj* schlaksig

gangli·on ['gæŋgli·ən] *s* (–ons & –a [ə]) (*cystic tumor*) Überbein *n*; (*of nerves*) Nervenknoten *m*

gangly ['gæŋgli] *adj* schlaksig

gang′plank′ *s* Laufplanke *f*, Steg *m*

gangrene ['gæŋgrin] *s* Gangrän *n*, Brand *m* ‖ *intr* brandig werden

gangrenous ['gæŋgrɪnəs] *adj* brandig

gangster ['gæŋstər] *s* Gangster *m*

gang′way′ *s* (*passageway*) Durchgang *m*; (naut) Laufplanke *f* ‖ *interj* aus dem Weg!

gantlet ['gɔntlət] *s* (rr) Gleisverschlingung *f*

gantry ['gæntri] *s* (rok) Portalkran *m*; (rr) Signalbrücke *f*

gan′try crane′ *s* Portalkran *m*

gap [gæp] *s* Lücke *f*; (*in the mountains*) Schlucht *f*; (mil) Bresche *f*

gape [gep] *s* Riß *m*, Sprung *m*; (*gaping*) Gaffen *n* ‖ *intr* gaffen; (*said of wounds, etc.*) klaffen; **g. at** angaffen

garage [gə'rɑʒ] *s* Garage *f*; (*repair shop*) Reparaturwerkstatt *f*; **put into the g.** unterstellen

garb [gɑrb] *s* Tracht *f*

garbage ['gɑrbɪdʒ] *s* Müll *m*; (*nonsense*) Unsinn *m*

gar′bage can′ *s* Mülltonne *f*

gar′bage dispos′al *s* Müllabfuhr *f*

gar′bage dump′ *s* Müllplatz *m*

gar′bage man′ *s* Müllfahrer *m*

gar′bage truck′ *s* Müllabfuhrwagen *m*

garble ['gɑrbəl] *tr* verstümmeln

garden ['gɑrdən] *s* Garten *m*; **gardens** Gartenanlage *f*

gardener ['gɑrdənər] *s* Gärtner –in *mf*

gar′den hose′ *s* Gartenschlauch *m*

gardenia [gɑr'dini·ə] *s* Gardenie *f*

gar′dening *s* Gartenarbeit *f*

gar′den par′ty *s* Gartengesellschaft *f*

gargle ['gɑrgəl] *s* Mundwasser *n* ‖ *tr & intr* gurgeln

gargoyle ['gɑrgɔɪl] *s* Wasserspeier *m*

garish ['gerɪʃ], ['gærɪ] *adj* grell

garland ['gɑrlənd] *s* Girlande *f*

garlic ['gɑrlɪk] *s* Knoblauch *m*

garment ['gɑrmənt] *s* Kleidungsstück *n*

garner ['gɑrnər] *tr* (*grain*) aufspeichern; (*gather*) ansammeln

garnet ['gɑrnɪt] *s* Granat *m*

garnish ['gɑrnɪʃ] *s* Verzierung *f*; (culin) Garnierung *f* ‖ *tr* verzieren; (culin) garnieren

garret ['gærɪt] *s* Dachstube *f*

garrison ['gærɪsən] *s* (*troops*) Garnison *f*, Besatzung *f*; (*fort*) Festung *f* ‖ *tr* mit e–r Garnison versehen; (*troops*) in Garnison stationieren

gar′rison cap′ *s* Schiffchen *n*

garrote [gə'rɑt], [gə'rot] *s* Garrotte *f* ‖ *tr* garrottieren

garrulous ['gær(j)ələs] *adj* schwatzhaft
garter ['gartər] *s* Strumpfband *n*
gar'ter belt' *s* Strumpfhaltergürtel *m*
gas [gæs] *adj* (e.g., *generator, light, main, meter*) Gas– || *s* Gas *n*; (coll) Benzin *n*, Sprit *m*; (*empty talk*) (sl) leeres Geschwätz *n*; **get gas** (coll) tanken; **step on the gas** (coll) Gas geben || *v* (*pret & pp* **gassed; ger gassing**) *tr* vergasen || *intr* (sl) schwatzen; **gas up** (coll) volltanken
gas' attack' *s* Gasangriff *m*
gas' burn'er *s* Gasbrenner *m*
gas' en'gine *s* Gasmotor *m*
gaseous ['gæsɪ·əs], ['gæ/əs] *adj* gasförmig
gas' fit'ter *s* Gasinstallateur *m*
gash [gæʃ] *s* tiefe Schnittwunde *f* || e-e tiefe Schnittwunde beibringen (*dat*)
gas' heat' *s* Gasheizung *f*
gas'hold'er *s* Gasbehälter *m*
gasi·fy ['gæsɪ‚faɪ] *v* (*pret & pp* –**fied**) *tr* in Gas verwandeln || *intr* zu Gas werden
gas' jet' *s* Gasflamme *f*
gasket ['gæskɪt] *s* Dichtung *f*
gas' mask' *s* Gasmaske *f*
gasoline [‚gæsə'lin] *s* Benzin *n*
gasoline' pump' *s* Benzinzapfsäule *f*
gasp [gæsp] *s* Keuchen *n* || *tr* (out) hervorstoßen || *intr* keuchen; **g. for air** nach Luft schnappen; **g. for breath** nach Atem ringen
gas' range' *s* Gasherd *m*
gas' sta'tion *s* Tankstelle *f*
gas' sta'tion attend'ant *s* Tankwart *m*
gas' stove' *s* Gasherd *m*
gas' tank' *s* Benzinbehälter *m*
gastric ['gæstrɪk] *adj* gastrisch
gas'tric juice' *s* Magensaft *m*
gastronomy [gæs'trɑnəmi] *s* Gastronomie *f*
gas'works' *spl* Gasanstalt *f*
gate [get] *s* Tor *n*, Pforte *f*; (rr) Sperre *f*; (sport) eingenommenes Eintrittsgeld *n*; **crash the g.** ohne Eintrittskarte durchschlupfen
gate' crash'er [‚kræʃər] *s* unberechtigter Zuschauer *m*
gate'keep'er *s* Pförtner –in *mf*
gate'post' *s* Torpfosten *m*
gate'way' *s* Tor *n*, Torweg *m*
gather ['gæðər] *tr* (things) sammeln; (*people*) versammeln; (*flowers, fruit, peas*) pflücken; (*courage*) aufbringen; (*the impression*) gewinnen; (*information*) einziehen; (*strength, speed*) zunehmen an (*dat*); (*conclude*) (from) schließen (aus); **g. together** versammeln; **g. up** aufheben; (*curtains, dress*) raffen || *intr* sich (an)sammeln; (*said of clouds*) sich zusammenziehen; **g. around** sich scharen um
gath'ered *adj* (skirt) gerafft
gath'ering *s* Versammlung *f*; (sew) Kräuselfalten *pl*
gaudy ['gɔdi] *adj* (overdone) überladen; (color) grell
gauge [gedʒ] *s* (instrument) Messer *m*, Anzeiger *m*; (measurement) Eichmaß *n*; (of wire) Stärke *f*; (of a shot-

gun) Kaliber *n*; (fig) Maß *n*; (mach) Lehre *f*; (rr) Spurweite *f* || *tr* messen; (*check for accuracy*) eichen; (fig) abschätzen
Gaul [gɔl] *s* Gallien *n*; (native) Gallier –in *mf*
Gaulish ['gɔlɪʃ] *adj* gallisch
gaunt [gɔnt] *adj* hager
gauntlet ['gɔntlɪt] *s* Panzerhandschuh *m*; (fig) Fehdehandschuh *m*; **run the g.** Spießruten laufen
gauze [gɔz] *s* Gaze *f*
gavel ['gævəl] *s* Hammer *m*
gawk [gɔk] *s* (coll) Depp *m* || *intr*—g. **at** (coll) blöde anstarren
gawky ['gɔki] *adj* schlaksig
gay [ge] *adj* lustig; (homosexual) schwul
gay' blade' *s* lebenslustiger Kerl *m*
gaze [gez] *intr* starren; **g. at** anstarren; (*in astonishment*) anstaunen
gazelle [gə'zɛl] *s* Gazelle *f*
gazetteer [‚gæzə'tɪr] *s* Ortslexikon *n*
gear [gɪr] *s* (equipment) Ausrüstung *f*; (aut) Schaltgetriebe *n*, Gang *m*; (mach) Zahnrad *n*; **gears** Räderwerk *n*; **in g.** eingeschaltet; **in high g.** im höchsten Gang; (fig) auf Touren; **shift gears** umschalten; **throw into g.** einschalten; **throw out of g.** (fig) aus dem Gleichgewicht bringen || *tr*—g. **to** anpassen (*dat*)
gear'box' *s* Schaltgetriebe *n*
gear'shift' *s* Gangschaltung *f*; (lever) Schalthebel *m*
gear'wheel' *s* Zahnrad *n*
gee [dʒi] *interj* nanu!
Geiger counter ['gargər‚kauntər] *s* Geigerzähler *m*
gel [dʒɛl] *s* Gel *n* || *v* (*pret & pp* **gelled; ger gelling**) *intr* gelieren; (coll) klappen
gelatin ['dʒɛlətɪn] *s* Gelatine *f*
geld [gɛld] *v* (*pret & pp* **gelded & gelt** [gɛlt]) *tr* kastrieren
geld'ing *s* Wallach *m*
gem [dʒɛm] *s* Edelstein *m*; (fig) Perle *f*
Gemini ['dʒɛmɪ‚naɪ] *s* (astr) Zwillinge *pl*
gender ['dʒɛndər] *s* Geschlecht *n*
gene [dʒin] *s* Gen *n*, Erbanlage *f*
genealogical [‚dʒini·ə'lɑdʒɪkəl] *adj* genealogisch, Stamm–
genealog'ical ta'ble *s* Stammtafel *f*
genealog'ical tree' *s* Stammbaum *m*
genealogy [‚dʒini'ælədʒi] *s* Genealogie *f*
general ['dʒɛnərəl] *adj* allgemein, Gesamt– || *s* General *m*; **in g.** im allgemeinen
Gen'eral Assem'bly *s* Vollversammlung *f*
gen'eral deliv'ery *adv* postlagernd
gen'eral head'quarters *spl* Oberkommando *n*
generalissi·mo [‚dʒenərə'lɪsɪmo] *s* (–mos) Generalissimus *m*
generality [‚dʒenə'rælɪti] *s* Allgemeingültigkeit *f*; **generalities** Gemeinplätze *pl*
generalization [‚dʒenərəlɪ'zeʃən] *s* Verallgemeinerung *f*

generalize ['dʒenərə,laɪz] *tr & intr* verallgemeinern

generally ['dʒenərəli] *adv* im allgemeinen; (*usually*) gewöhnlich; (*mostly*) meistens

gen'eral man'ager *s* Generaldirektor –in *mf*

gen'eral plan' *s* Übersichtsplan *m*

gen'eral post' of'fice *s* Oberpostamt *n*

gen'eral practi'tioner *s* praktischer Arzt *m*

gen'eralship' *s* Führereigenschaften *pl*

gen'eral staff' *s* Generalstab *m*

gen'eral store' *s* Gemischtwarenhandlung *f*

gen'eral strike' *s* Generalstreik *m*

generate ['dʒenə,ret] *tr* (*procreate*) zeugen; (fig) verursachen; (elec) erzeugen; (geom) bilden

gen'erating sta'tion *s* Kraftwerk *n*

generation [,dʒenə'reʃən] *s* Generation *f*; **present g.** Mitwelt *f*; **younger g.** junge Generation *f*

genera'tion gap' *s* Generationsproblem *n*

generator ['dʒenə,retər] *s* Erzeuger *m*; (chem, elec) Generator *m*; (elec) Stromerzeuger *m*

generic [dʒɪ'nerɪk] *adj* generisch, Gattungs–; **g. name** Gattungsname *m*

generosity [,dʒenə'rɑsɪti] *s* Freigebigkeit *f*

generous ['dʒenərəs] *adj* freigebig

gene·sis ['dʒenɪsɪs] *s* (**–ses** [,sɪz]) Genese *f*, Entstehung *f*; **Genesis** (Bib) Genesis *f*

genetic [dʒɪ'netɪk] *adj* genetisch

genet'ic engineer' *s* Gen-Ingineur *m*

genet'ic engineer'ing *s* Gen-Manipulation *f*

genetics [dʒɪ'netɪks] *s* Genetik *f*, Vererbungslehre *f*

Geneva [dʒɪ'nivə] *adj* Genfer ‖ *s* Genf *n*

Genevieve ['dʒenə,viv] *s* Genoveva *f*

genial ['dʒinɪ·əl] *adj* freundlich

genie ['dʒini] *s* Kobold *m*

genital ['dʒenɪtəl] *adj* Genital– ‖ **genitals** *spl* Genitalien *pl*

genitive ['dʒenɪtɪv] *s* Genitiv *m*, Wesfall *m*

genius ['dʒinɪ·əs] *s* (**geniuses**) Genie *n* ‖ *s* (**genii** [dʒɪnɪ,aɪ]) Genius *m*

Genoa ['dʒeno·ə] *s* Genua *n*

genocidal [,dʒenə'saɪdəl] *adj* rassenmörderisch

genocide ['dʒenə,saɪd] *s* Rassenmord *m*

genre ['ʒɑnrə] *s* Genre *n*

genteel [dʒen'til] *adj* vornehm

gentile ['dʒentaɪl] *adj* nichtjüdisch; (*pagan*) heidnisch ‖ *s* Nichtjude *m*, Nichtjüdin *f*; (*pagan*) Heide *m*, Heidin *f*

gentility [dʒen'tɪlɪti] *s* Vornehmheit *f*

gentle ['dʒentəl] *adj* sanft, mild; (*tame*) zahm

gen'tle·man *s* (**–men**) Herr *m*, Gentleman *m*

gentlemanly ['dʒentəlmənli] *adj* weltmännisch

gen'tleman's agree'ment *s* Kavaliersab-

kommen *n*, **Gentleman's Agreement** *n*

gentleness ['dʒentəlnɪs] *s* Sanftmut *f*

gen'tle sex' *s* zartes Geschlecht *n*

gentry ['dʒentri] *s* feine Leute *pl*

genuflection [,dʒenju'flekʃən] *s* Kniebeugung *f*

genuine ['dʒenju·ɪn] *adj* echt

genus ['dʒinəs] *s* (**genera** ['dʒenərə] & **genuses**) (biol, log) Gattung *f*

geographer [dʒɪ'ɑgrəfər] *s* Geograph –in *mf*

geographic(al) [,dʒɪ·ə'græfɪk(əl)] *adj* geographisch

geography [dʒɪ'ɑgrəfi] *s* Geographie *f*

geologic(al) [,dʒɪ·ə'lɑdʒɪk(əl)] *adj* geologisch

geolog'ical e'ra *s* Erdalter *n*

geologist [dʒɪ'ɑlədʒɪst] *s* Geologe *m*, Geologin *f*

geology [dʒɪ'ɑlədʒi] *s* Geologie *f*

geometric(al) [,dʒɪ·ə'metrɪk(əl)] *adj* geometrisch

geometrician [dʒɪ,ɑmɪ'trɪʃən] *s* Geometer –in *mf*

geometry [dʒɪ'ɑmɪtri] *s* Geometrie *f*

geophysics [,dʒɪ·ə'fɪzɪks] *s* Geophysik *f*

geopolitics [,dʒɪ·ə'pɑlɪtɪks] *s* Geopolitik *f*

George [dʒɔrdʒ] *s* Georg *m*

geranium [dʒɪ'renɪ·əm] *s* Geranie *f*

geriatrics [,dʒerɪ'ætrɪks] *s* Geriatrie *f*

germ [dʒʌrm] *s* Keim *m*

German ['dʒʌrmən] *adj & adv* deutsch ‖ *s* Deutsche *mf*; (*language*) Deutsch *n*; **in G.** auf deutsch

germane [dʒer'men] *adj* (to) passend (zu)

Germanize ['dʒʌrmə,naɪz] *tr* eindeutschen

Ger'man mea'sles *s & spl* Röteln *pl*

Ger'man shep'herd *s* deutscher Schäferhund *m*

Ger'man sil'ver *s* Alpaka *n*, Neusilber *n*

Germany ['dʒʌrməni] *s* Deutschland *n*

germ' cell' *s* Keimzelle *f*

germicidal [,dʒʌrmɪ'saɪdəl] *adj* keimtötend

germicide ['dʒʌrmɪ,saɪd] *s* Keimtöter *m*

germinate ['dʒʌrmɪ,net] *intr* keimen

germ' war'fare *s* bakteriologische Kriegsführung *f*

gerontology [,dʒerɑn'tɑlədʒi] *s* Gerontologie *f*

gerund ['dʒerənd] *s* Gerundium *n*

gerundive [dʒɪ'rʌndɪv] *s* Gerundiv *n*

gestation [dʒes'teʃən] *s* Schwangerschaft *f*; (*in animals*) Trächtigkeit *f*

gesticulate [dʒes'tɪkjə,let] *intr* gestikulieren, sich gebärden

gesticulation [dʒes,tɪkjə'leʃən] *s* Gebärdenspiel *n*, Gestikulation *f*

gesture ['dʒestʃər] *s* Geste *f* ‖ *intr* Gesten machen

get [get] *v* (*pret* **got** [gɑt]; *pp* **got** & **gotten** ['gɑtən]; *ger* **getting**) *tr* (*acquire*) bekommen; (*receive*) erhalten; (*procure*) beschaffen, besorgen; (*fetch*) holen; (*understand*) (coll) kapieren; (*s.o. to do s.th.*) dazu bringen; (*reach by telephone*) erreichen; (*make, e.g., dirty*) machen; (*convey, e.g., a message*) übermitteln; **get across** klarmachen; **get back** zurückbekommen; **get down** (*depress*) verdrießen; (*swallow*) hinunterwürgen; **get going** in Gang setzen; **get hold of** (*a person*) erwischen; (*a thing*) erlangen; (*grip*) ergreifen; **get off** (*e.g., a lid*) abbekommen; **get one's way** sich durchsetzen; **get out** (*e.g., a spot*) herausbekommen; **get s.o. used to** j-n gewöhnen an (*acc*); **get s.th. into one's head** sich [*dat*] etw in den Kopf setzen; **get the hang of** (coll) wegbekommen; **get the jump on s.o.** j-m zuvorkommen; **get the worst of it** am schlechtesten dabei wegkommen; **get** (*s.th.*) **wrong** falsch verstehen; **you're going to get it!** (coll) du wirst es kriegen! ‖ *intr* (*become*) werden; **get about** sich fortbewegen; **get ahead in the world** in der Welt fortkommen; **get along** auskommen; **get along with** zurechtkommen mit; **get around** herumkommen; **get around to it** dazu kommen; **get at** herankommen an (*acc*); (*e.g., the real reason*) herausfinden; **get away** (*run away*) entlaufen; (*escape*) entkommen; **get away from me!** geh weg von mir!; **get away with** davonkommen mit; **get back at s.o.** es j-m heimzahlen; **get by** (*e.g., the guards*) vorbeikommen an (*dat*); (*on little money*) durchkommen; **get down** (*step down*) absteigen; **get down to brass tacks** (or **business**) zur Sache kommen; **get going** sich auf den Weg machen; **get going!** mach, daß du weiter kommst!; **get into** (*a vehicle*) einsteigen in (*acc*); (*trouble, etc.*) geraten in (*acc*); **get loose** sich losmachen; **get lost** verloren gehen, abhanden kommen; (*lose one's way*) sich verirren; **get lost!** (sl) hau ab!; **get off** aussteigen; **get off with** (*a light sentence*) davonkommen mit; **get on** (*e.g., a train*) einsteigen (in *acc*); **get on one's feet again** sich hochrappeln; **get on with** (*s.o.*) zurechtkommen mit; **get out** aussteigen; **get out of a tight spot** sich aus der Schlinge ziehen; **get over** (*a hurdle*) nehmen; (*a misfortune*) überwinden; (*a sickness*) überstehen; **get ready** sich fertig machen; **get through** durchkommen; **get through to s.o.** sich verständlich machen (*dat*); (telp) erreichen; **get to be** werden; **get together** (*meet*) sich treffen; (*agree*) (on) sich einig werden (über *acc*); **get to the bottom of** ergründen; **get up** aufstehen; **get used to** sich gewöhnen an (*acc*); **get well** gesund werden; **get with it!** (coll) zur Sache!

get'away' *s* Entkommen *n*; (sport) Start *m*; **make one's g.** entkommen
get'away car' *s* Fluchtwagen *m*
get'-togeth'er *s* zwangloses Treffen *n*
get'up' *s* (coll) Aufzug *m*

get' up' and go' *s* Unternehmungsgeist *m*
gewgaw ['g(j)ugɔ] *s* Plunder *m*
geyser ['gaɪzər] *s* Geiser *m*
ghastly ['gæstlɪ] *adj* (*ghostly*) gespenstisch; (*e.g., crime*) grausig; (*intensely unpleasant*) schrecklich
gherkin ['gɑrkɪn] *s* Essiggurke *f*
ghet·to ['gɛto] *s* (-*tos*) Getto *n*
ghost [gost] *s* Gespenst *n*, Geist *m*; (telv) Doppelbild *n*; **give up the g.** den Geist aufgeben; **not a g. of a chance** nicht die geringsten Aussichten
ghostly ['gostlɪ] *adj* gespenstisch
ghost' sto'ry *s* Spukgeschichte *f*
ghost' town' *s* Geisterstadt *f*
ghost' writ'er *s* Ghostwriter *m*
ghoul [gul] *s* (& fig) Unhold *m*
ghoulish ['gulɪʃ] *adj* teuflisch
GHQ ['dʒɪ'et͡ʃ'kju] *s* (General Headquarters) Oberkommando *n*
GI ['dʒɪ'aɪ] *s* (GI's) (coll) Landser *m*
giant ['dʒaɪ·ənt] *adj* riesig, Riesen– ‖ *s* Riese *m*, Riesin *f*
giantess ['dʒaɪ·əntɪs] *s* Riesin *f*
gibberish ['dʒɪbərɪʃ], ['gɪbərɪʃ] *s* Kauderwelsch *n*
gibbet ['dʒɪbɪt] *s* Galgen *m* ‖ *tr* hängen
gibe [dʒaɪb] *s* Spott *m* ‖ *intr* spotten; **g. at** verspotten
giblets ['dʒɪblɪts] *spl* Gänseklein *n*
giddiness ['gɪdɪnɪs] *s* Schwindelgefühl *n*; (*frivolity*) Leichtsinn *m*
giddy ['gɪdɪ] *adj* (*dizzy*) schwindlig; (*height*) schwindelerregend; (*frivolous*) leichtsinnig
gift [gɪft] *s* Geschenk *n*; (*natural ability*) Begabung *f*
gift'ed *adj* begabt
gift' horse' *s*—**never look a g. in the mouth** e-m geschenkten Gaul schaut man nicht ins Maul
gift' of gab' *s* (coll) gutes Mundwerk *n*
gift' shop' *s* Geschenkartikelladen *m*
gift'-wrap' *v* (*pret* & *pp* **-wrapped**; *ger* **-wrapping**) *tr* als Geschenk verpacken
gift'wrap'ping *s* Geschenkverpackung *f*
gigantic [dʒaɪ'gæntɪk] *adj* riesig
giggle ['gɪgəl] *s* Gekicher *n* ‖ *intr* kichern
gigly ['gɪglɪ] *adj* allezeit kichernd
gigo·lo ['dʒɪgə‚lo] *s* (-*los*) Gigolo *m*
gild [gɪld] *v* (*pret* & *pp* **gilded** & **gilt** [gɪlt]) *tr* vergolden
gild'ing *s* Vergoldung *f*
gill [gɪl] *s* (*of a fish*) Kieme *f*; (*of a cock*) Kehllappen *m*
gilt [gɪlt] *adj* vergoldet ‖ *s* Vergoldung *f*
gilt' edge' *s* Goldschnitt *m*
gilt'-edged' *adj* mit Goldschnitt versehen; (*first-class*) (coll) erstklassig
gimlet ['gɪmlɪt] *s* Handbohrer *m*
gimmick ['gɪmɪk] *s* (sl) Trick *m*
gin [dʒɪn] *s* Wacholderbranntwein *m*, Gin *m*; (*snare*) Schlinge *f* ‖ *v* (*pret* & *pp* **ginned**; *ger* **ginning**) *tr* entkörnen
ginger ['dʒɪndʒər] *s* Ingwer *m*

gin′ger ale′ s Ingwerlimonade f
gin′gerbread′ s Pfefferkuchen m
gingerly [′dʒɪndʒərli] adv sacht(e)
gin′gersnap′ s Ingwerplätzchen n
gingham [′ɡɪŋəm] s Gingham m
giraffe [dʒɪ′ræf] s Giraffe f
gird [ɡʌrd] v (pret & pp girt [ɡʌrt] & girded) tr gürten; g. oneself with a sword sich [dat] ein Schwert umgürten
girder [′ɡʌrdər] s Tragbalken m
girdle [′ɡʌrdəl] s Gürtel m
girl [ɡʌrl] s Mädchen n, Mädel n
girl′ friend′ s Freundin f, Geliebte f
girl′hood′ s Mädchenzeit f
girlish [′ɡʌrlɪʃ] adj mädchenhaft
girl′ scout′ s Pfadfinderin f
girth [ɡʌrθ] s Umfang m; (for a horse) Sattelgurt m
gist [dʒɪst] s Kernpunkt m; g. of the matter des Pudels Kern
give [ɡɪv] s Elastizität f; (yielding) Nachgeben n ‖ v (pret gave [ɡev]; pp given [′ɡɪvən]) tr geben; (a gift, credence) schenken; (free of charge) verschenken; (contribute) spenden; (hand over) übergeben; (a report) erstatten; (a reason, the time) angeben; (attention, recognition) zollen; (a lecture) halten; (an award) zusprechen; (homework) aufgeben; (a headache, etc.) verursachen; (joy) machen; (a reception) veranstalten; (a blow) versetzen; g. away weggeben; (divulge) verraten; g. away the bride Brautvater sein; g. back zurückgeben; g. ground zurückweichen; g. it to ′em! (coll) hau zu!; g. off von sich geben; (steam) ausströmen lassen; g. oneself away sich verplappern; g. oneself up sich stellen; g. or take mehr oder weniger; g. out ausgeben; g. rise to Anlaß geben zu; g. up aufgeben; (a business) schließen; g. up for lost verlorengeben; g. way weichen; g. way to sich überlassen (dat) ‖ intr (yield) nachgeben; (collapse) einstürzen; g. in to nachgeben (dat), welchen (dat); g. out (said of the voice, legs) versagen; (said of strength) nachlassen; g. up aufgeben; (mil) die Waffen strecken; g. up on verzagen an (dat)
give′-and-take′ s Kompromiß m & n; (exchange of opinion) Meinungsaustausch m
give′away′ s (betrayal of a secret) unbeabsichtigte Preisgabe f; (promotional article) Gratisprobe f
give′away show′ s Preisrätselsendung f
given [′ɡɪvən] adj gegeben; (time) festgesetzt; (math, philos) gegeben; g. to drinking dem Trunk ergeben
giv′en name′ s Vorname m
giver [′ɡɪvər] s Geber –in m f; (of a contribution) Spender –in m f
gizzard [′ɡɪzərd] s Geflügelmagen m
gla′cial per′iod [′ɡleʃəl] s Eiszeit f
glacier [′ɡleʃər] s Gletscher m
glad [ɡlæd] adj (gladder; gladdest) froh; be g. (about) sich freuen (über acc); g. to (inf) erfreut zu (inf); g. to meet you sehr erfreut!, sehr ange-

nehm!; I'll be g. to do it for you ich werde das gern für Sie tun
gladden [′ɡlædən] tr erfreuen
glade [ɡled] s Waldwiese f, Waldlichtung f
gladiator [′ɡlædɪ‚etər] s Gladiator m
gladiola [‚ɡlædɪ′olə] s Gladiole f
gladly [′ɡlædli] adv gern(e)
gladness [′ɡlædnɪs] s Freude f
glad′ rags′ spl (sl) Sonntagsstaat m
glad′ tid′ings spl Freudenbotschaft f
glamorous [′ɡlæmərəs] adj bezaubernd
glamour [′ɡlæmər] s (of a girl) Zauber m; (of an event) Glanz m
glam′our girl′ s gefeierte Schönheit f; (pej) Zierpuppe f
glance [ɡlæns] s Blick m; at a g., at first g. auf den ersten Blick; ‖ intr (at) blicken (auf acc or nach); g. around umherblicken; g. off abgleiten an (dat); g. through (or over) flüchtig durchsehen; g. up aufblicken
gland [ɡlænd] s Drüse f
glanders [′ɡlændərz] spl Rotskrankheit f
glare [ɡler] s grelles Licht n; (look) böser Blick m ‖ intr blenden; (look) böse starren; g. at böse anstarren
glar′ing adj (light) grell; (fig) schreiend, aufdringlich
glass [ɡlæs] adj gläsern, Glas– ‖ s Glas n; glasses Brille f
glass′ bead′ s Glasperle f
glass′ blow′er [′blo‚ər] s Glasbläser –in m f
glass′ blow′ing s Glasbläserei f
glass′ case′ s Schaukasten m
glass′ cut′ter s Glasschleifer –in m f; (tool) Glasschneider m
glassful [′ɡlæsful] s Glas n
glass′ware′ s Glaswaren pl
glass′ wool′ s Glaswolle f
glass′works′ s Glasfabrik f, Glashütte f
glassy [′ɡlæsi] adj (surface) spiegelglatt; (eyes) glasig
glaucoma [ɡlau′komə] s Glaukom n, grüner Star m
glaze [ɡlez] s (on ceramics) Glasur f; (on paintings) Lasur f; (of ice) Glatteis n ‖ tr (ceramics, baked goods) glasieren; (a window) verglasen; (a painting) lasieren
glazed adj (ceramics, baked goods) glasiert; (eyes) glasig; g. tile Kachel f
glazier [′ɡleʒər] s Glaser –in m f
gleam [ɡlim] s Lichtstrahl m; g. of hope Hoffnungsschimmer m ‖ intr strahlen
glean [ɡlin] tr & intr auflesen; (fig) zusammentragen
gleanings [′ɡlinɪŋz] spl Nachlese f
glee [ɡli] s Frohsinn m
glee′ club′ s Gesangverein m
glen [ɡlen] s Bergschlucht f
glib [ɡlɪb] adj (glibber; glibbest) (tongue) beweglich; (person) zungenfertig
glide [ɡlaɪd] s Gleiten n; (aer) Gleitflug m; (with a glider) (aer) Segelflug m; (ling) Gleitlaut m; (mus) Glissando n ‖ intr gleiten

glider ['glaɪdər] s (porch swing) Schaukelbett n; (aer) Segelflugzeug n

glid'er pi'lot s Segelflieger -in mf

glid'ing s Segelfliegen n

glimmer ['glɪmər] s Schimmer m; g. of hope Hoffnungsschimmer m ‖ intr schimmern

glim'mering adj flimmernd ‖ s Flimmern n

glimpse [glɪmps] s flüchtiger Blick m; catch a g. of flüchtig zu sehen bekommen ‖ tr flüchtig erblicken ‖ intr—g. at e-n flüchtigen Blick werfen auf (acc)

glint [glɪnt] s Lichtschimmer m ‖ intr schimmern

glisten ['glɪsən] s Glanz m ‖ intr glänzen

glitter ['glɪtər] s Glitzern n, Glanz m ‖ intr glitzern, glänzen

gloat [glot] intr schadenfroh sein; g. over sich weiden an (dat)

gloat'ing s Schadenfreude f

global ['globəl] adj global, Welt-

globe [glob] s Erdkugel f, Globus m

globe'-trot'ter s Weltenbummler -in mf

globule ['glabjul] s Kügelchen n

glockenspiel ['glakən ,spil] s Glockenspiel n

gloom [glum] s Düsternis f; (fig) Trübsinn m

gloominess ['glumɪnɪs] s Düsterkeit f; (fig) Trübsinn m

gloomy ['glumɪ] adj düster; (depressing) bedrückend; (depressed) trübsinning

glorification ['glorɪfɪ ,keʃən] s Verherrlichung f

glori·fy ['glorɪ ,faɪ] v (pret & pp -fied) tr verherrlichen

glorious ['glorɪ-əs] adj (full of glory) glorreich; (magnificent) herrlich

glo·ry ['glorɪ] s Ruhm m; (magnificence) Herrlichkeit f; be in one's g. im siebenten Himmel sein ‖ v (pret & pp -ried) intr—g. in frohlocken über (acc)

gloss [glɔs] s (shine) Glanz m; (notation) Glosse f ‖ tr glossieren; g. over verschleiern

glossary ['glɔsərɪ] s Glossar n

glossy ['glɔsɪ] adj glänzend

glottis ['glatɪs] s Stimmritze f

glove [glʌv] s Handschuh m; fit like a g. wie angegossen passen

glove' compart'ment s Handschuhfach n

glow [glo] s Glühen n ‖ intr glühen; g. with (fig) (er)glühen vor (dat)

glower ['glau·ər] s finsterer Blick m ‖ intr finster blicken; g. at finster anblicken

glow'ing adj glühend; (account) begeistert

glow'worm' s Glühwurm m

glucose ['glukos] s Glukose f

glue [glu] s Leim m, Klebemittel n ‖ tr (wood) leimen; (paper) kleben

gluey ['glu·ɪ] adj leimig

glum [glʌm] adj (glummer; glummest) verdrießlich

glut [glʌt] s Übersättigung f; a g. on the market e-e Überschwemmung des Marktes ‖ v (pret & pp glutted; ger glutting) tr übersättigen; (com) überschwemmen

glutton ['glʌtən] s Vielfraß m

gluttonous ['glʌtənəs] adj gefräßig

gluttony ['glʌtənɪ] s Gefräßigkeit f

glycerine ['glɪsərɪn] s Glyzerin n

gnarled [narld] adj knorrig

gnash [næʃ] tr—g. one's teeth mit den Zähnen knirschen

gnat [næt] s Mücke f

gnaw [nɔ] tr zernagen; g. off abnagen ‖ intr (on) nagen (an dat)

gnome [nom] s Gnom m, Berggeist m

go [go] s—be on the go auf den Beinen sein; have a lot of go viel Mumm in den Knochen haben; it's no go es geht nicht; let's have a go at it probieren wir's mal; make a go of it es zu e—m Erfolg machen ‖ v (pret went [went]; pp gone [gɔn]) tr—go it alone es ganz allein(e) machen ‖ intr gehen; (depart) weggehen; (travel) fahren, reisen; (operate) arbeiten; (belong) gehören; (turn out) verlaufen; (collapse) zusammenbrechen; (fail, go out of order) kaputtgehen; (said of words) lauten; (said of bells) läuten; (said of a buzzer) ertönen; (said of awards) zugeteilt werden; (said of a road) führen; be going to, e.g., I am going to study ich werde studieren; go about umhergehen; (a task) in Angriff nehmen; go about it darangehen; go after (run after) nachlaufen; (strive for) streben nach; go against the grain gegen den Strich gehen; go ahead vorausgehen; go ahead! voran!; go along with (accompany) mitgehen mit; (agree with) zustimmen mit; go and see for yourself überzeugen Sie sich selbst davon!; go around herumgehen; (suffice) (aus)reichen; (an obstacle) umgehen; go at (a person) losgehen auf (acc); (a thing) herangehen an (acc); go away weggehen; go bad schlecht werden; go back zurückkehren; (ride back) zurückfahren; go back on (one's word) brechen; go beyond überschreiten; go by (pass by) vorbeigehen (an dat); (said of time) vergehen; (act according to) sich richten nach; go down niedergehen; (said of the sun or a ship) untergehen; (said of a swelling) zurückgehen; (said of a fever or a price) sinken; go down in history in die Geschichte eingehen; go for (fetch) holen; (apply to) gelten für; (be enthusiastic about) schwärmen für; (have a crush on) verknallt sein in (acc); (be sold for) verkauft werden für; (attack) losgehen auf (acc); go in hineingehen; (said of the sun) verschwinden; go in for schwärmen für; (sport) treiben; go into eintreten in (acc); (arith) enthalten sein in (dat); go

into detail ins Detail gehen; **go in with** s.o. on sich beteiligen mit j-m an (dat); **go off** (depart) weggehen; (said of a gun) losgehen; (said of a bomb) explodieren; **go on** (happen) vorgehen; (continue) weitergehen; (with) fortfahren (mit); (theat) auftreten; **go on!** (expressing encouragement) nur zu!; (expressing disbelief) ach was!; **go on reading** weiterlesen; **go on to** (another theme) übergehen auf (acc); **go over** (check) überprüfen; (review) noch einmal durchgehen; (figures) nachrechnen; (be a success) einschlagen; **go over to** hinübergehen zu; (the enemy) übergehen zu; **go out** (e.g., of the house) hinausgehen; (on an errand or socially; said of a light) ausgehen; **go out of one's way** sich besonders anstrengen; **go out to dinner** auswärts essen; **go through** (penetrate) durchdringen; (a traffic signal) überfahren; (endure) durchmachen; **go through with** zu Ende führen; **go to** (said of a prize) zugeteilt werden (dat); **go together** zueinanderpassen; **go to it!** los!; **go to show** ein Beweis sein für; **go with** (fit, match) passen zu; (associate with) verkehren mit; **go without** entbehren; **go under an assumed name** e-n angenommenen Namen führen; **go up to** s.o. auf j-n zugehen
goad [god] s Stachel m || tr antreiben; **g. on** (fig) anstacheln
go'-ahead sig'nal n freie Bahn f
goal [gol] s Ziel n; (sport) Tor n; **make a goal** (sport) ein Tor schießen
goalie ['goli] s Torwart m
goal'keep'er s Torwart m
goal' line' s Torlinie f
goal' post' s Torpfosten m
goat [got] s Ziege f, Geiß f; (male goat) Ziegenbock m; **get s.o.'s g.** (sl) j-n auf die Palme bringen
goatee [go'ti] s Ziegenbart m, Spitzbart m
goat' herd' s Ziegenhirt m
goat'skin' s Ziegenfell n
gob [gab] s (coll) Klumpen m; (sailor) (coll) Blaujacke f; **gobs of money** (coll) ein Haufen m Geld
gobble ['gabəl] s Kollern n || tr verschlingen; **g. up** (food) herunterschlingen; (e.g., land) zusammenraffen || intr (said of a turkey) kollern
gobbledegook ['gabəldɪ‚guk] s (coll) Amtssprache f
gobbler ['gablər] s (coll) Fresser –in mf; (orn) (coll) Puter m, Truthahn m
go'-between' s Vermittler –in mf, Unterhändler –in mf
goblet ['gablɪt] s Kelchglas n
goblin ['gablɪn] s Kobold m
go'cart' s (walker) Laufstuhl m; (stroller) Sportwagen m; (small racer) Go-Kart m; (handcart) Handwagen m
god [gad] s Gott m; **God forbid!** Gott bewahre!; **God knows** weiß Gott; **my God!** du lieber Gott!; **so help**

me God! so wahr mir Gott helfe!; **ye gods!** heiliger Strohsack!
god'child' s (–chil'dren) Patenkind n
goddess ['gadɪs] s Göttin f
god'fa'ther s Pate m; **be a g. Pate stehen**
God'-fear'ing adj gottesfürchtig
god'forsak'en adj gottverlassen
god'head' s Göttlichkeit f; **Godhead** Gott m
godless ['gadlɪs] adj gottlos
god'like' adj göttlich
godly ['gadli] adj gottselig
god'moth'er s Patin f; **be a g. Patin stehen**
god'send' s Segen m
God'speed' s—**wish s.o. G.** j-m Lebewohl sagen
go-getter ['go‚gɛtər] s Draufgänger m
goggle ['gagəl] intr glotzen
gog'gle-eyed' adj glotzäugig
goggles ['gagəlz] spl Schutzbrille f
go'ing adj (rate) gültig, üblich; **g. on** (e.g., six o'clock) gegen; **I'm g. to do it** ich werde es tun
go'ing concern' s schwunghaftes Geschäft n
go'ing-o'ver s Überprüfung f; (beating) Prügel pl
go'ings on' spl Treiben n, Wirtschaft f
goiter ['gɔrtər] s Kropf m
gold [gold] adj Gold– || s Gold n
gold' bar' s Goldbarren m
gold'brick' s (mil) Drückeberger m
gold'-brick' intr faulenzen
gold'brick'ing s (mil) Drückebergerei f
gold'crest' s Goldhähnchen n
gold' dig'ger ['dɪgər] s Goldgräber m; (sl) Vamp m
golden ['goldən] adj golden; (opportunity) günstig
gold'en age' s Glanzzeit f, Goldenes Zeitalter n
gold'en calf', **the** s das Goldene Kalb
gold'en ea'gle s Goldadler m
Gold'en Fleece', **the** (myth) das Goldene Vlies
gold'en mean' s goldene Mitte f
gold'en rule' s goldene Regel f
gold'en wed'ding s goldene Hochzeit f
gold'-filled' adj vergoldet
gold' fill'ing s (dent) Goldplombe f
gold'finch' s Goldfink m, Stieglitz m
gold'fish' s Goldfisch m
goldilocks ['goldɪ‚laks] s (bot) Hahnenfuß m
gold' leaf' s Blattgold n
gold'mine' s Goldbergwerk n
gold' nug'get s Goldklumpen m
gold' plate' s Goldgeschirr n
gold'-plate' tr vergolden
gold'smith' s Goldschmied –in mf
gold' stand'ard s Goldwährung f
golf [galf] s Golf n || intr Golf spielen
golf' bag' s Köcher m
golf' club' s Golfschläger m; (organization) Golfklub m
golf' course' s Golfplatz m
golfer ['galfər] s Golfspieler –in mf
golf' links' spl Golfplatz m
gondola ['gandələ] s Gondel f

gon'dola car' s offener Güterwagen m
gondolier [ˌgʌndəˈlɪr] s Gondelführer m
gone [gɔn] adj hin, weg; (ruined) futsch; all g. ganz weg; (sold out) ausverkauft; **he is g.** er ist fort
goner [ˈgɔnər] s (coll) verlorener Mensch m
gong [gɔŋ] s Gong m, Tamtam n
gonorrhea [ˌgɑnəˈriˌə] s Tripper m
goo [gu] s (sl) klebrige Masse f
good [gud] adj (better; best) gut; (well behaved) brav, artig; (in health) gesund; (valid) gültig; as g. as so gut wie; be g. enough to (inf) so gut sein und; g. and recht, e.g., g. and cheap recht billig; g. at gut in (dat); g. for (suited to) geeignet zu; (effective against) wirksam für; (valid for) gültig für; g. for you! (serves you right!) das geschieht dir recht!; (expressing congratulations) ich gratuliere!, bravo! make g. wiedergutmachen; (losses) vergüten; (a promise) erfüllen; || s Gut n; (welfare) Wohl n; (advantage) Nutzen m; (philos) Gut n, das Gute; be up to no g. nichts Gutes im Schilde führen; catch with the goods auf frischer Tat ertappen; do g. wohltun; for g. für immer; goods Waren pl; to the g. als Nettogewinn; what g. is it?, what's the g. of it? was nutzt es?
good'-by', **good'-bye'** s Lebewohl n; say g. (to) sich verabschieden (von) || interj auf Wiedersehen!; (on the telephone) auf Wiederhören!
good' day' interj guten Tag!
good' deed' s Wohltat f
good' egg' s (sl) feiner Kerl m
good' eve'ning interj guten Abend!
good' fel'low s netter Kerl m
good'-fel'lowship s gute Kameradschaft f
good'-for-noth'ing adj nichtsnutzig || s Taugenichts m, Nichtsnutz m
Good' Fri'day s Karfreitag m
good' grac'es spl—be in s.o.'s g. in j-s Gunst stehen
good'-heart'ed adj gutherzig
good'-hu'mored adj gutgelaunt, gutmütig
good'-look'ing adj gutaussehend, hübsch
goodly [ˈgudli] adj beträchtlich; a g. number of viele
good' morn'ing interj guten Morgen!
good'-na'tured adj gutmütig
goodness [ˈgudnɪs] s Güte f; for g. sake! um Himmels willen!; g. knows weiß Gott; thank g. Gott sei Dank!
good' night' interj gute Nacht!
good' sense' s Sinn m; (common sense) gesunder Menschenverstand m; make g. Sinn haben
good'-sized' adj ziemlich groß
good'-tem'pered adj ausgeglichen
good' time' s—have a g. sich gut unterhalten; keep g. taktfest sein
good' turn' s Gefallen m; one g. deserves another e-e Hand wäscht die andere

good' will' s Wohlwollen n; (com) Geschäftswert m
goody [ˈgudi] s Näscherei f || interj pfundig!
gooey [ˈgu-i] adj klebrig
goof [guf] s (person) (sl) Depp m; (mistake) (sl) Schnitzer m || tr (sl) verpfuschen || intr (sl) e-n Schnitzer machen; g. off (sl) faulenzen
goof'ball' s (pill) (sl) Beruhigungspille f; (eccentric person) (sl) Sonderling m
goofy [ˈgufi] adj (sl) dämlich; g. about (sl) vernarrt in (acc)
goon [gun] s (sl) Dummkopf m; (in strikes) bestellter Schläger m
goose [gus] s (geese [gis]) Gans f; (culin) Gänsebraten m; cook s.o.'s g. j-n erledigen
goose'ber'ry s Stachelbeere f
goose' egg' s (sl) Null f
goose' flesh' s Gänsehaut f
goose' neck' s Schwanenhals m
goose' pim'ples spl Gänsehaut f
goose' step' s Stechschritt m
goose'-step' v (pret & pp –stepped; ger –stepping) intr im Stechschritt marschieren
gopher [ˈgofər] s Taschenratte f
gore [gor] s geronnenes Blut n || tr aufspießen
gorge [gɔrdʒ] s Schlucht f || tr vollstopfen || intr schlingen
gorgeous [ˈgɔrdʒəs] adj prachtvoll
gorilla [gəˈrɪlə] s Gorilla m
gorse [gɔrs] s Stechginster m
gory [ˈgori] adj blutig
gosh [gɑʃ] interj herrjeh!
Gospel [ˈgɑspəl] s Evangelium n
gos'pel truth' s reine Wahrheit f
gossamer [ˈgɑsəmər] s Sommerfäden pl
gossip [ˈgɑsɪp] s Klatsch m; (woman) Klatschweib n; (man) Schwätzer m || intr klatschen, tratschen
gos'sip col'umn s Klatschspalte f
gossipmonger [ˈgɑsɪpˌmʌŋgər] s Klatschbase f
gossipy [ˈgɑsɪpi] adj tratschsüchtig
Goth [gɑθ] s Gote m, Gotin f
Gothic [ˈgɑθɪk] adj gotisch || s (language) Gotisch n
Goth'ic arch' s Spitzbogen m
gouge [gaudʒ] s (tool) Hohlmeißel m; (hole made by a gouge) ausgemeißelte Vertiefung f || tr aushöhlen; (overcharge) übervorteilen; g. out (eyes) herausdrücken
gouger [ˈgaudʒər] s Wucherer –in mf
goulash [ˈgulɑʃ] s Gulasch n
gourd [gord], [gurd] s Kürbis m
gourmand [ˈgurmənd] s (glutton) Schlemmer –in mf; (gourmet) Feinschmecker m
gourmet [ˈgurme] s Feinschmecker m
gout [gaut] s Gicht f
govern [ˈgʌvərn] tr regieren; (fig) beherrschen; (gram) regieren || intr regieren
governess [ˈgʌvərnɪs] s Gouvernante f
government [ˈgʌvərnmənt] adj Regierungs–, Staats– || s Regierung f

gov′ernment con′tract s Staatsauftrag m

gov′ernment control′ s Zwangsbewirtschaftung f

gov′ernment employ′ee s Staatsbeamte m, Staatsbeamtin f

gov′ernment grant′ s Staatszuschuß m

gov′ernment-in-ex′ile s Exilregierung f

governor [′gʌvərnər] s Statthalter m, Gouverneur m; (mach) Regler m

gov′ernorship′ s Statthalterschaft f

gown [gaʊn] s Damenkleid n; (of a judge, professor) Robe f, Talar m

grab [græb] s—make a g. for grapschen nach ‖ v (pret & pp grabbed; ger grabbing) tr schnappen; g. hold of anpacken ‖ intr—g. for greifen nach

grab′ bag′ s Glückstopf m

grace [gres] s (mercy, divine favor) Gnade f; (charm) Grazie f; (table prayer) Tischgebet n; (charm) Grazie f; Graces (myth) Grazien pl

graceful [′gresfəl] adj graziös, anmutig

gracious [′gre∫əs] adj gnädig; (living) angenehm ‖ interj lieber Himmel!

gradation [gre′de∫ən] s Stufenfolge f

grade [gred] s (level) Stufe f, Grad m; (quality) Qualität f; (class year) Schulklasse f; (mark in a course, test) Zensur f; (slope) Steigung f; (mil) Dienstgrad m ‖ tr (sort) einstufen; (evaluate) bewerten; (make level) planieren; (educ) zensieren

grade′ cross′ing s (rr) Schienenübergang m

grade′ school′ s Grundschule f

gradient [′gredɪ·ənt] s Neigung f

gradual [′grædʒʊ·əl] adj allmählich

graduate [′grædʒʊ·ɪt] adj (student) graduiert; (course) Graduierten- ‖ s Promovierte mf; (from a junior college) Abiturient -in mf; (from a university) Absolvent –in mf ‖ [′grædʒʊ‚et] tr & intr graduieren, promovieren; g. from absolvieren

grad′uated adj (tax) abgestuft; (marked by divisions of measurement) graduiert; g. scale Gradmesser m

graduation [‚grædʒʊ′e∫ən] s Graduierung f, Promotion f; (marking on a vessel or instrument) Gradeinteilung f

gradua′tion ex′ercises spl Schlußfeier f

graft [græft] s (illegal gain) Schiebung f; (money involved in graft) Schmiergeld n; (twig) (hort) Pfropfreis n; (place where scion is inserted) (hort) Propfstelle f; (organ transplanted) (surg) verpflanztes Gewebe n; (transplanting) (surg) Gewebeverpflanzung f ‖ tr (hort) pfropfen; (surg) verpflanzen

gra′ham bread′ [′gre·əm] s Grahambrot n

gra′ham crack′er s Grahamplätzchen n

gra′ham flour′ s Grahammehl n

grain [gren] s Korn n; (of leather) Narbe f; (in wood, marble) Maserung f; (unit of weight) Gran n; (cereals) Getreide n; (phot) Korn n; against the g. (& fig) gegen den Strich; g. of truth Körnchen n Wahrheit

grain′ el′evator s Getreidesilo m

grain′field′ s Saatfeld n, Kornfeld n

gram [græm] s Gramm n

grammar [′græmər] s Grammatik f

gram′mar school′ s Grundschule f

grammatical [grə′mætɪkəl] adj grammatisch, grammatikalisch

gramophone [′græmə‚fon] s Grammophon n

granary [′grenəri] s Getreidespeicher m

grand [grænd] adj großartig; (large and striking) grandios; (lofty) erhaben; (wonderful) (coll) herrlich

grand′aunt′ s Großtante f

grand′child′ s (–chil′dren) Enkelkind n

grand′daugh′ter s Enkelin f

grand′ duch′ess s Großfürstin f, Großherzogin f

grand′ duch′y s Großfürstentum n, Großherzogtum n

grand′ duke′ s Großfürst m, Großherzog m

grandee [græn′di] s Grande m

grandeur [′grændʒər], [′grændʒʊr] s Großartigkeit f, Erhabenheit f

grand′fath′er s Großvater m

grand′father's clock′ s Standuhr f

grandiose [′grændɪ‚os] adj grandios

grand′ ju′ry s Anklagekammer f

grand′ lar′ceny s schwerer Diebstahl m

grand′ lodge′ s Großloge f

grandma [′grɑn(d)‚mɑ], [′græm‚mɑ] s (coll) Oma f

grand′moth′er s Großmutter f

grand′neph′ew s Großneffe m

grand′niece′ s Großnichte f

grandpa [′grɑn(d)‚pɑ], [′græm‚pɑ] s (coll) Opa m

grand′par′ents spl Großeltern pl

grand′ pian′o s Konzertflügel m

grand′ slam′ s Schlemm m

grand′son′ s Enkel m

grand′stand′ s Tribüne f

grand′ to′tal s Gesamtsumme f

grand′un′cle s Großonkel m

grand′ vizier′ s Großwesir m

grange [grendʒ] s Farm f; (organization) Farmervereinigung f

granite [′grænɪt] adj Granit- ‖ s Granit m

granny [′græni] s (coll) Oma f

grant [grænt] s (of money) Beihilfe f; (of a pardon) Gewährung f; (of an award) Verleihung f ‖ tr (permission) geben; (credit) bewilligen; (a favor) gewähren; (a request) erfüllen; (a privilege, award) verleihen; (admit) zugeben; granted that angenommen, daß; take for granted als selbstverständlich hinnehmen

grantee [græn′ti] s Empfänger –in mf

grant′-in-aid′ s (grants-in-aid) (by the government) Subvention f; (educ) Stipendium n

grantor [′græntər] s Verleiher –in mf

granular [′grænjələr] adj körnig

granulate [′grænjə‚let] tr körnen

gran'ulated sug'ar s Streuzucker m

granule ['grænjul] s Körnchen n

grape [grep] s Weintraube f

grape' ar'bor s Weinlaube f

grape'fruit' s Pampelmuse f

grape' juice' s Most m, Traubensaft m

grape' pick'er s Weinleser –in mf

grape'vine' s Weinstock m; **through the g.** gerüchteweise

graph [græf] s Diagramm n

graphic(al) ['græfɪk(əl)] adj graphisch; (description) anschaulich, bildhaft

graphite ['græfaɪt] s Graphit m

graph' pa'per s Millimeterpapier n

grapnel ['græpnəl] s Wurfanker m

grapple ['græpəl] s Enterhaken m; (fight) Handgemenge n || tr packen || intr (use a grapple) (naut) e-n Enterhaken gebrauchen; **g. with** (& fig) ringen mit

grap'pling hook', grap'pling i'ron s Wurfanker m; (naut) Enterhaken m

grasp [græsp] s Griff m; (control) Gewalt f; (comprehension) Verständnis n; (reach) Reichweite f; **have a good g. of** gut beherrschen || tr (& fig) fassen || intr—**g. at** schnappen nach

grasp'ing adj habgierig, geldgierig

grass [græs] s Gras n; (lawn) Rasen m; (pasture land) Weide f

grass' court' s Rasenspielplatz m

grass'hop'per s Grashüpfer m

grass' land' s Weideland n, Grasland n

grass'-roots' adj (coll) volkstümlich

grass' seed' s Grassamen m

grass' wid'ow s Strohwitwe f

grassy ['græsi] adj grasig

grate [gret] s (on a window) Gitter n; (of a furnace) Rost m || tr (e.g., cheese) reiben; **g. the teeth** mit den Zähnen knirschen || intr knirschen; **g. on one's nerves** an den Nerven reißen

grateful ['gretfəl] adj dankbar

grater ['gretər] s (culin) Reibeisen n

grati-fy ['grætɪ‚faɪ] v (pret & pp -fied) tr befriedigen; **be gratified by** sich freuen über (acc)

grat'ifying adj erfreulich

grat'ing adj knirschend || s Gitter n

gratis ['grætɪs], ['gretɪs] adj & adv unentgeltlich

gratitude ['grætɪ‚t(j)ud] s Dankbarkeit f

gratuitious [grə't(j)u‑ɪtəs] adj unentgeltlich; (undeserving) unverdient

gratuity [grə't(j)u‑ɪti] s Trinkgeld n

grave [grev] adj (face) ernst; (condition) besorgniserregend; (mistake) folgenschwer; (sound) tief || s Grab n; (accent) Gravis m

gravedigger ['grev‚dɪgər] s Totengräber m

gravel ['grævəl] s (rounded stones) Kies m; (crushed stones) Schotter m; (pathol) Harngrieß m || tr mit Kies (od Schotter) bestreuen

gravelly ['grævəli] adj heiser

grav'el pit' s Kiesgrube f

grav'el road' s Schotterstraße f

grave'stone' s Grabstein m

grave'yard' s Friedhof m

gravitate ['grævɪ‚tet] intr gravitieren; **g. towards** (fig) neigen zu

gravitation [‚grævɪ'te/ən] s Gravitation f, Massenanziehung f

gravitational [‚grævɪ'te/ənəl] adj Gravitations-, Schwer-

gravita'tional force' s Schwerkraft f

gravita'tional pull' s Anziehungskraft f

gravity ['grævɪti] s (seriousness) Ernst m; (of a situation) Schwere f; (phys) Schwerkraft f

gravy ['grevi] s Soße f; (coll) leichter Gewinn m

gra'vy boat' s Soßenschüssel f

gra'vy train' s (sl) Futterkrippe f

gray [gre] adj grau || s Grau n || intr ergrauen

gray'beard' s Graubart m

gray'-haired' adj grauhaarig

grayish ['gre‑ɪ/] adj gräulich

gray' mat'ter s graue Substanz f

graze [grez] tr (said of a bullet) streifen; (cattle) weiden lassen || intr weiden

graz'ing land' s Weide f

grease [gris] s Fett n, Schmiere f || [gris], [griz] tr (aut) schmieren

grease' gun' [gris] s Schmierpresse f

grease' paint' s Schminke f

grease' pit' s (aut) Schmiergrube f

grease' spot' s Fettfleck m

greasy ['grisi], ['grizi] adj fett(ig)

great [gret] adj groß; (wonderful) (coll) großartig; **a g. many** (of) e–e große Anzahl von; **g. fun** Heidenspaß m; **g. guy** Prachtkerl m

great'-aunt' s Großtante f

Great' Bear' s Großer Bär m

Great' Brit'ain s Großbritannien n

Great' Dane' s deutsche Dogge f

great'-grand'child' s (-chil'dren) Urenkel m

great'-grand'daugh'ter s Urenkelin f

great'-grand'fa'ther s Urgroßvater m

great'-grand'moth'er s Urgroßmutter f

great'-grand'par'ents spl Urgroßeltern pl

great'-grand'son' s Urenkel m

greatly ['gretli] adv sehr, stark

great'-neph'ew s Großneffe m

greatness ['gretnɪs] s Größe f

great'-niece' s Großnichte f

great'-un'cle s Großonkel m

Grecian ['gri/ən] adj griechisch

Greece [gris] s Griechenland n

greed [grid] s Habgier f, Gier f

greediness ['gridɪnɪs] s Gierigkeit f

greedy ['gridi] adj (for) gierig (nach)

Greek [grik] adj griechisch || s (person) Grieche m, Griechin f; (language) Griechisch n; **that's G. to me** das kommt mir spanisch vor

green [grin] adj grün; (unripe) unreif; (inexperienced) unerfahren, neu; **become g.** grünen; **turn g. with envy** grün vor Neid werden || s (& golf) Grün n; **greens** Blattgemüse n

green'back' s (coll) Geldschein m

greenery ['grinəri] s Grün n

green'-eyed' adj grünäugig; (fig) neidisch

green'gro'cer s Obst– und Gemüsehändler –in mf

green'horn' s Ausländer –in mf

green'house' s Gewächshaus n

greenish ['grinɪʃ] adj grünlich

Green'land s Grönland n

green' light' s (fig) freie Fahrt f

greenness ['grinnɪs] s Grün n; (inexperience) Unerfahrenheit f

green' pep'per s Paprikaschote f

green'room' s (theat) Aufenthaltsraum m

greensward ['grin‚swɔrd] s Rasen m

green' thumb' s—have a g. gärtnerisches Geschick besitzen

greet [grit] tr grüßen; (welcome) begrüßen

greet'ing s Gruß m; (welcoming) Begrüßung f; greetings Grüße pl

greet'ing card' s Glückwunschkarte f

gregarious [grɪ'gɛrɪ-əs] adj gesellig

Gregor'ian cal'endar [grɪ'gɔrɪ-ən] s Gregorianischer Kalender m

Gregor'ian chant' s Gregorianischer Gesang m

grenade [grɪ'ned] s Granate f

grenade' launch'er s Gewehrgranatgerät n

grey [gre] adj, s, & intr var of gray

grey'hound's Windhund m

grid [grɪd] s (on a map) Gitternetz n; (culin) Bratrost m; (electron) Gitter n

griddle ['grɪdəl] s Bratpfanne f; (cookie sheet) Backblech n

grid'dlecake' s Pfannkuchen m

grid'i'ron s Bratrost m; (sport) Spielfeld n; (theat) Schnürboden m

grid' leak' s (electron) Gitterwiderstand m

grief [grif] s Kummer m; come to g. zu Fall (or Schaden) kommen, scheitern

grief'-strick'en adj gramgebeugt

grievance ['grivəns] s Beschwerde f

grieve [griv] tr bekümmern || intr (over) sich grämen (über acc)

grievous ['grivəs] adj (causing grief) schmerzlich; (serious) schwerwiegend

griffin ['grɪfɪn] s Greif m

grill [grɪl] s Grill m || tr grillen; (an accused person) scharf verhören

grille [grɪl] s Gitter n

grim [grɪm] adj (grimmer; grimmest) grimmig; g. humor Galgenhumor m

grimace ['grɪməs], [grɪ'mes] s Grimasse f || intr Grimassen schneiden

grime [graɪm] s Schmutz m, Ruß m

grimness ['grɪmnɪs] s Grimmigkeit f

grimy ['graɪmɪ] adj schmutzig, rußig

grin [grɪn] s Grinsen n, Schmunzeln n || v (pret & pp grinned; ger grinning) intr grinsen, schmunzeln; I had to g. and bear it ich mußte gute Miene zum bösen Spiel machen

grind [graɪnd] s (of coffee, grain) Mahlen n; (hard work) Schinderei f; (a student) (coll) Streber –in mf; the daily g. der graue Alltag || v (pret & pp ground [graʊnd]) tr (coffee,

grain) mahlen; (glass, tools) schleifen; (meat) zermahlen; (in a mortar) stampfen; g. down zerreiben; g. one's teeth mit den Zähnen knirschen; g. out (e.g., articles) ausstoßen; (tunes) leiern

grinder ['graɪndər] s (molar) (dent) Backenzahn m; (mach) Schleifmaschine f

grind'stone' s Schleifstein m

grip [grɪp] s Griff m; (handle) Handgriff m; (handbag) Reisetasche f; (power) Gewalt f; come to grips with in Angriff nehmen; have a good g. on (fig) sicher beherrschen; lose one's g. (fig) den Halt verlieren || v (pret & pp gripped; ger gripping) tr (& fig) packen

gripe [graɪp] s Meckerei f || intr (about) meckern (über acc)

grippe [grɪp] s (pathol) Grippe f

grip'ping adj fesselnd, packend

grisly ['grɪzlɪ] adj gräßlich

grist [grɪst] s Mahlkorn n; that's g. for his mill das ist Wasser auf seine Mühle

gristle ['grɪsəl] s Knorpel m

gristly ['grɪslɪ] adj knorpelig

grist'mill' s Getreidemühle f

grit [grɪt] s (abrasive particles) Grieß m; (pluck) (coll) Mumm m; grits Schrotmehl n || v (pret & pp gritted; ger gritting) tr (one's teeth) zusammenbeißen

gritty ['grɪtɪ] adj grießig

grizzly ['grɪzlɪ] adj gräulich

griz'zly bear' s Graubär m

groan [gron] s Stöhnen n; groans Geächze n || intr stöhnen; (grumble) (coll) brumen

grocer ['grosər] s Lebensmittelhändler –in mf

grocery ['grosərɪ] s (store) Lebensmittelgeschäft n; groceries Lebensmittel pl

gro'cery store' s Lebensmittelgeschäft n

grog [grɑg] 's Grog m

groggy ['grɑgɪ] adj benommen

groin [grɔɪn] s (anat) Leiste f, Leistengegend f; (archit) Rippe f

groom [grum] s Bräutigam m; (stableboy) Reitknecht m || tr (a person, animal) pflegen; (for a position) heranziehen

groove [gruv] s Kerbe f; (for letting off water) Rinne f; (of a record) Rille f; (in a barrel) Zug m; in the g. (fig) im richtigen Fahrwasser

grope [grop] tr—g. one's way sich vorwärtstasten || intr tappen; g. about herumtappen; g. for tappen nach, tasten nach

gropingly ['gropɪŋlɪ] adv tastend

gross [gros] adj (coarse, vulgar) roh, derb; (mistake) grob; (crass, extreme) kraß; (without deductions) Brutto– || s Gros n || tr e-n Bruttogewinn haben von

grossly ['groslɪ] adv sehr, stark

gross' na'tional prod'uct s Bruttosozialprodukt n

gross' receipts' *spl* Bruttoeinnahmen *pl*

grotesque [gro'tesk] *adj* grotesk

grot·to ['grato] *s* (-toes & -tos) Grotte *f*, Höhle *f*

grouch [graut∫] *s* (coll) Brummbär *m*, Griesgram *m* ‖ *intr* brummen

grouchy ['graut∫i] *adj* (coll) brummig

ground [graund] *s* Grund *m*, Boden *m*; (*reason*) Grund *m*; (elec) Erde *f*; every inch of g. jeder Fußbreit Boden; **grounds** (*e.g., of an estate*) Anlagen *pl*; (*reasons*) Gründe *pl*; (*of coffee*) Satz *m*; **break g.** mit dem Bau beginnen; **gain g.** (an) Boden gewinnen; **hold one's g.** seinen Standpunkt behaupten; **level to the g.** dem Erdboden gleichmachen; **lose g.** (an) Boden verlieren; **low g.** Niederung *f*; **new g.** (fig) Neuland *n*; **on the grounds that** mit der Begründung, daß; **run into the g.** (fig) bis zum Überdruß wiederholen; **stand one's g.** standhalten; **yield g.** (fig) nachgeben ‖ *tr* (a pilot) Startverbot erteilen (*dat*); (a ship) auflaufen lassen; (elec) erden; **be grounded by bad weather** wegen schlechten Wetters am Starten gehindert werden

ground' connec'tion *s* (elec) Erdung *f*

ground' crew' *s* (aer) Bodenmannschaft *f*

ground' floor' *s* Parterre *n*, Erdgeschoß *n*

ground' glass' *s* Mattglas *n*

ground' hog' *s* Murmeltier *n*

groundless ['graundlɪs] *adj* grundlos

ground' meat' *s* Hackfleisch *n*

ground' plan' *s* Grundriß *m*; (fig) Entwurf *m*

ground' speed' *s* Geschwindigkeit *f* über Grund

ground' swell' *s* Dünung *f*; (fig) wogende Erregung *f*

ground'-to-air' *adj* Boden-Bord-

ground' wa'ter *s* Grundwasser *n*

ground' wire' *s* (elec) Erdleitung *f*

ground'work' *s* Grundlage *f*

group [grup] *adj* Gruppen- ‖ *s* Gruppe *f*; (*consisting of 18 aircraft*) Geschwader *n* ‖ *tr* gruppieren ‖ *intr* sich gruppieren

group'ing *s* Gruppierung *f*

group' insur'ance *s* Gruppenversicherung *f*

group' ther'apy *s* Gruppentherapie *f*

grouse [graus] *s* Waldhuhn *n* ‖ *intr* (sl) meckern

grout [graut] *s* dünner Mörtel *m* ‖ *tr* verstreichen

grove [grov] *s* Gehölz *n*, Hain *m*

grov·el ['grʌvəl], ['grɑvəl] *v* (*pret & pp* -el[l]ed; *ger* -el[l]ing) *intr* (& fig) kriechen; **g. in filth** in Schmutz wühlen

grow [gro] *v* (*pret* grew [gru]; *pp* grown [gron]) *tr* (*plants*) pflanzen, züchten; (*grain*) anbauen; (a beard) sich [*dat*] wachsen lassen; **the ram grows horns** dem Widder wachsen Hörner ‖ *intr* wachsen; (*become*) werden; (*become bigger*) größer werden; **g. fond of** liebgewinnen; **g. luxuriantly** wuchern; **g. older** an Jahren zunehmen; **g. on s.o.** j-m ans Herz wachsen; **g. out of** (*clothes*) herauswachsen aus; (fig) entstehen aus; **g. pale** erblassen; **g. together** zusammenwachsen; (*close*) zuwachsen; **g. up** aufwachsen; **g. wild** (*luxuriantly*) wuchern; (*in the wild*) wild wachsen

grower ['gro·ər] *s* Züchter –in *mf*

growl [graul] *s* (*of a dog, stomach*) Knurren *n*; (*of a bear*) Brummen *n* ‖ *tr* (*words*) brummen ‖ *intr* knurren; (*said of a bear*) brummen; **g. at** anknurren

grown [gron] *adj* erwachsen

grown'-up' *adj* erwachsen ‖ *s* (grownups) Erwachsene *mf*

growth [groθ] *s* Wachstum *n*; (*increase*) Zuwachs *m*; (pathol) Gewächs *n*; **full g.** volle Größe *f*

grub [grʌb] *s* Larve *f*, Made *f*; (sl) Fraß *m* ‖ *v* (*pret & pp* grubbed; *ger* grubbing) *tr* ausjäten ‖ *intr* wühlen; **g. for** graben nach

grubby ['grʌbi] *adj* (*dirty*) schmutzig

grudge [grʌdʒ] *s* Mißgunst *f*, Groll *m*; **bear (or have) a g. against s.o.** j-m grollen ‖ *tr* mißgönnen

grudg'ing *adj* mißgünstig

grudg'ingly *adv* (nur) ungern

gruel ['gru·əl] *s* Haferschleim *m*

gruel'ing *adj* strapaziös

gruesome ['grusəm] *adj* grausig

gruff [grʌf] *adj* barsch

grumble ['grʌmbəl] *s* Murren *n* ‖ *intr* (*over*) murren (über *acc*)

grumbler ['grʌmblər] *s* Brummbär *m*

grumpy ['grʌmpi] *adj* übellaunig

grunt [grʌnt] *s* Grunzen *n* ‖ *tr & intr* grunzen

G'-string' *s* (*of a dancer*) letzte Hülle *f*; (*of a native*) Lendenschurz *m*

guarantee [,gærən'ti] *s* Garantie *f* ‖ *tr* garantieren für

guarantor ['gærən,tɔr] *s* Garant –in *mf*

guaranty ['gærənti] *s* Garantie *f* ‖ *v* (*pret & pp* -tied) *tr* garantieren

guard [gɑrd] *s* (*watch*; *watchman*) Wache *f*; (*person*) Wächter –in *mf*; (fb) Verteidiger *m*; (mach) Schutzvorrichtung *f*; (*soldier*) (mil) Posten *m*; (*soldiers*) (mil) Wachmannschaft *f*, Wache *f*; **be on g. against** sich hüten vor (*dat*); **be on one's g.** auf der Hut sein; **keep under close g.** scharf bewachen; **mount g.** Wache beziehen; **relieve the g.** die Wache ablösen; **stand g.** Posten (or Wache) stehen; (*during a robbery*) Schmiere stehen ‖ *tr* bewachen; (fig) hüten; **g. one's tongue** seine Zunge im Zaum halten ‖ *intr*—**g. against** sich vorsehen gegen; **g. over** wachen über (*acc*)

guard' de'tail *s* Wachmannschaft *f*

guard' du'ty *s* Wachdienst *m*; **pull g.** Wache schieben

guard'house' *s* (*building used by guards*) Wache *f*; (*military jail*) Arrestlokal *n*

guardian ['gɑrdɪ·ən] s (custodian) Wächter –in mf; (jur) Vormund m
guard'ian an'gel s Schutzengel m
guard'lanship s Obhut f; (jur) Vormundschaft f
guard'rail' s Geländer n
guard'room' s Wachstube f, Wachlokal n
guerrilla [gəˈrɪlə] s Guerillakämpfer –in mf
gueril'la war'fare s Guerillakrieg m
guess [ges] s Vermutung f; anybody's g. reine Vermutung f; take a good g. gut raten ‖ tr vermuten; you guessed it! geraten! ‖ intr raten; g. at schätzen
guesser ['gesər] s Rater –in mf
guess'work' s Raten n, Mutmaßung f
guest [gest] adj Gast–, Gäste– ‖ s Gast m; be a g. of zu Gaste sein bei
guest' book' s Gästebuch n
guest' perform'ance s Gastspiel n; give a g. (theat) gastieren
guest' perform'er s Gast m
guest' room' s Gästezimmer n
guest' speak'er s Gastredner –in mf
guffaw [gəˈfɔ] s Gewieher n ‖ intr wiehern
guidance ['gaɪdəns] s Leitung f, Führung f; (educ) Studienberatung f; for your g. zu Ihrer Orientierung
guid'ance coun'selor s Studienberater –in mf
guide [gaɪd] s Führer –in mf; (book) Reiseführer m; (tourist escort) Reiseführer –in mf; (for gardening, etc.) Leitfaden m ‖ tr führen; (rok) lenken
guide'book' s Reiseführer m, Führer m
guid'ed mis'sile s Fernlenkkörper m
guid'ed tour' s Führung f
guide'line' s Richtlinie f
guide'post' s Wegweiser m
guide' word' s Stichwort n
guild [gɪld] s Zunft f, Gilde f
guile [gaɪl] s Arglist f
guileful ['gaɪlfəl] adj arglistig
guileless ['gaɪllɪs] adj arglos
guillotine ['gɪlə͵tin] s Fallbeil n, Guillotine f ‖ tr mit dem Fallbeil (or mit der Guillotine) hinrichten
guilt [gɪlt] s Schuld f
guilt'-rid'den adj schuldbeladen
guilty ['gɪlti] adj (of) schuldig (genit); (conscience) schlecht; plead g. sich schuldig bekennen; plead not g. sich für nicht schuldig erklären
guil'ty par'ty s Schuldige mf
guil'ty ver'dict s Schuldspruch m
guinea fowl' ['gɪni], **guin'ea hen'** s Perlhuhn n
guin'ea pig' s Meerschweinchen n; (fig) Versuchskaninchen n
guise [gaɪz] s Verkleidung f; under the g. of unter dem Schein (genit)
guitar [gɪˈtɑr] s Gitarre f
guitarist [gɪˈtɑrɪst] s Gitarrenspieler –in mf
gulch [gʌltʃ] s Bergschlucht f
gulf [gʌlf] s Golf m; (fig) Kluft f
Gulf' Stream' s Golfstrom m
gull [gʌl] s Möwe f; (coll) Tölpel m ‖ tr übertölpeln

gullet ['gʌlɪt] s Gurgel f, Schlund m
gullible ['gʌlɪbəl] adj leichtgläubig
gully ['gʌli] s Wasserrinne f
gulp [gʌlp] s Schluck m, Zug m; at one g. in e–m Zuge ‖ tr schlucken; g. down schlingen ‖ intr schlucken
gum [gʌm] s Gummi m & n; (chewing gum) Kaugummi m & n; (anat) Zahnfleisch n ‖ v (pret & pp gummed; ger gumming) tr (e.g., labels) gummieren; **gum up the works** (coll) die Arbeit (or das Spiel) vermasseln
gum' ar'abic s Gummiarabikum n
gum'boil' s (pathol) Zahngeschwür n
gum'drop' s Gummibonbon m & n
gummy ['gʌmi] adj klebrig
gumption ['gʌmpʃən] s Unternehmungsgeist m, Mumm m
gun [gʌn] s Gewehr n; (handgun) Handfeuerwaffe f; (arti) Geschütz n; stick to one's guns bei der Stange bleiben ‖ v (pret & pp gunned; ger gunning) tr—gun down niederschießen; gun the engine Gas geben ‖ intr auf die Jagd gehen; be out gunning for auf dem Korn haben; gun for game auf die Jagd gehen
gun' bar'rel s Gewehrlauf m; (arti) Geschützrohr n
gun' bat'tle s Feuergefecht n
gun' belt' s Wehrgehänge n
gun'boat' s Kanonenboot n
gun' car'riage s Lafette f
gun'cot'ton s Schießbaumwolle f
gun' crew' s Bedienungsmannschaft f
gun' emplace'ment s Geschützstand m
gun' fight' s Schießerei f
gun'fire' s Geschützfeuer n
gun'man s (–men) bewaffneter Bandit m
gun' met'al s Geschützlegierung f
gun' mount' s Lafette f; (of swivel type) Schwenklafette f
gunner ['gʌnər] s Kanonier m; (aer) Bordschütze m
gunnery ['gʌnəri] s Geschützwesen n
gun'nery prac'tice s Übungsschießen n
gunnysack ['gʌni͵sæk] s Jutesack m
gun' per'mit s Waffenschein m
gun'point' s—at g. mit vorgehaltenem Gewehr
gun'pow'der s Schießpulver n
gun'run'ning s Waffenschmuggel m
gun'shot' s Schuß m; (range) Schußweite f
gun'shot wound' s Schußwunde f
gun'-shy' adj schußscheu
gun'sight' s Visier n
gun'smith' s Büchsenmacher m
gun'stock' s Gewehrschaft m
gun' tur'ret s Geschützturm m; (aer) Schwalbennest n
gunwale ['gʌnəl] s Schandeckel m
guppy ['gʌpi] s Millionenfisch m
gurgle ['gʌrgəl] s Glucksen n, Gurgeln n ‖ intr glucksen, gurgeln
gush [gʌʃ] s Guß m; (fig) Erguß m ‖ intr sich ergießen; g. out hervorströmen; g. over (fig) viel Aufhebens machen von
gusher ['gʌʃər] s Schwärmer –in mf; (oil well) sprudelnde Ölquelle f

gush'ing adj (fig) überschwenglich
gushy ['gʌʃi] adj schwärmerisch
gusset ['gʌsɪt] s Zwickel m
gust [gʌst] s Stoß m; (of wind) Windstoß m, Bö f
gusto ['gʌsto] s Gusto m
gusty ['gʌsti] adj böig
gut [gʌt] s Darm m; **guts** Eingeweide pl; (coll) Schneid m ‖ v (pret & pp **gutted**; ger **gutting**) tr ausbrennen; **be gutted** ausbrennen
gutter ['gʌtər] s Gosse f; (of a roof) Dachrinne f
gut'tersnipe' s (coll) Straßenjunge m
guttural ['gʌtərəl] adj kehlig; (ling) Kehl- ‖ s (ling) Kehllaut m
guy [gaɪ] s Halteseil n; (of a tent) Spannschnur f; (coll) Kerl m; **dirty guy** (coll) Saugel m; **great guy** Prachtkerl m ‖ tr verspannen
guy' wire' s Spanndraht m
guzzle ['gʌzəl] tr & intr saufen
guzzler ['gʌzlər] s Säufer -in mf
gym [dʒɪm] adj (coll) Turn- ‖ s (coll) Turnhalle f
gym' class' s (coll) Turnstunde f

gymnasi•um [dʒɪm'nezɪ•əm] s (-ums & -a [ə]) Turnhalle f
gymnast ['dʒɪmnæst] s Turner -in mf
gymnastic [dʒɪm'næstɪk] adj Turn-, gymnastisch; g. exercise Turnübung f ‖ **gymnastics** spl Gymnastik f, Turnen n
gynecologist [ˌgaɪnə'kalədʒɪst] s Gynäkologe m, Gynäkologin f
gynecology [ˌgaɪnə'kalədʒi] s Gynäkologie f
gyp [dʒɪp] s (sl) Nepp m; (person) Nepper m; **that's a gyp** das ist Nepp! ‖ v (pret & pp **gypped**; ger **gypping**) tr neppen
gyp' joint' s Nepplokal n
gypper ['dʒɪpər] s Nepper m
gypsy ['dʒɪpsi] adj Zigeuner- ‖ s Zigeuner -in mf
gyp'sy moth' s Großer Schwammspinner m
gyrate ['dʒaɪret] intr sich drehen; kreiseln
gyration [dʒaɪ'reʃən] s Kreiselbewegung f
gyroscope ['dʒaɪrə‚skop] s Kreisel m

H

H, h [etʃ] s achter Buchstabe des englischen Alphabets
haberdasher ['hæbər‚dæʃər] s Inhaber -in mf e-s Herrenmodengeschäfts
haberdashery ['hæbər‚dæʃəri] s Herrenmodengeschäft n
habit ['hæbɪt] s Gewohnheit f; (eccl) Ordenskleid n; **be in the h. of** (ger) pflegen zu (inf); **break s.o. of that h. of smoking** j-m das Rauchen abgewöhnen; **from h.** aus Gewohnheit; **get into the h. of smoking sich** [dat] das Rauchen angewöhnen; **make a h. of it** es zur Gewohnheit werden lassen
habitat ['hæbɪ‚tæt] s Wohngebiet n
habitation [ˌhæbɪ'teʃən] s Wohnort m
habitual [hə'bɪtʃʊ•əl] adj gewohnheitsmäßig, Gewohnheits-
hack [hæk] s (blow) Hieb m; (notch) Kerbe f; (rasping cough) trockener Husten m; (worn-out horse) Schindmähre f; (hackney) Droschke f; (taxi) (coll) Taxi n; (writer) Schreiberling m ‖ tr hacken, hauen; (basketball) auf den Arm schlagen ‖ intr Taxi fahren
hackney ['hækni] s (carriage) Droschke f; (horse) gewöhnliches Gebrauchspferd n
hackneyed ['hæknid] adj abgedroschen
hack'saw' s Metallsäge f, Bügelsäge f
haddock ['hædək] s Schellfisch m
haft [hæft] s Griff m
hag [hæg] s Vettel f; (witch) Hexe f
haggard ['hægərd] adj hager
haggle ['hægəl] intr (over) feilschen (um)

hag'gling s Feilschen n
Hague, the [heg] s den Haag m
hail [hel] s Hagel m; **h. of bullets** Kugelhagel m ‖ tr (a taxi, ship) anrufen; (acclaim) preisen; (as) begrüßen (als) ‖ intr hageln; **h. from** stammen aus (or von) ‖ interj Heil!
Hail' Mar'y s Ave Maria n
hail'stone' s Hagelkorn n, Schloße f
hail'storm' s Hagelschauer m
hair [her] s (single hair) Haar n; (collectively) Haare pl; **by a h.** um ein Haar; **do s.o.'s h.** j-n frisieren; **get in s.o.'s h.** j-m auf die Nerven gehen lassen; **split hairs** Haarspalterei treiben
hair'breadth' s—**by a h.** um Haaresbreite
hair'brush' s Haarbürste f
hair' clip' s Spange f, Klammer f
hair'cloth' s Haartuch n
hair'curl'er s Lockenwickler m
hair'cut' s Haarschnitt m; **get a h.** sich [dat] die Haare schneiden lassen
hair'do' s (-dos) Frisur f
hair'dress'er s Friseur m, Friseuse f
hair'dri'er s Haartrockner m
hair' dye' s Haarfärbemittel n
hairiness ['herɪnɪs] s Behaartheit f
hairless ['herlɪs] adj haarlos
hair'line' s Haaransatz m
hair' net' s Haarnetz n
hair' oil' s Haaröl n
hair'piece' s Haarteil m
hair'pin' s Haarnadel f
hair'-pin curve' s Haarnadelkurve f
hair'-rais'ing adj haarsträubend
hair' rinse' s Spülmittel n

hair'roll'er s Haarwickler m
hair' set' s Wasserwelle f
hair' shirt' s Büßerhemd n
hair'split'ting s Haarspalterei f
hair' spray' s Haarspray n
hair'spring' s Haarfeder f, Spirale f
hair'style' s Frisur f
hair' ton'ic s Haarwasser n
hairy ['heri] adj haarig, behaart
Haiti ['heti] s Haiti n
halberd ['hælbərd] s Hellebarde f
hal'cyon days' ['hælsı-ən] spl (fig) glückliche Zeit f
hale [hel] adj gesund; **h. and hearty** gesund und munter
half [hæf] adj halb; **at h. price** zum halben Preis; **have h. a mind to** (inf) halb und halb entschlossen sein zu (inf); **one and a h.** eineinhalb || adv halb; **h. as much as nur halb so wie; h. as much again** um die Hälfte mehr; **h. past three** halb vier; **not h.** durchaus nicht || s (halves [hævz]) Hälfte f; **cut in h.** in die Hälfte schneiden; **go halves with** halbpart machen mit
half'-and-half' adj & adv halb und halb || s Halb-und-halb-Mischung f
half'back' s (fb) Läufer m
half'-baked' adj halb gebacken; (plans, etc.) halbfertig; (person) unerfahren
half'-blood' s Halbblut n
half'-breed' s Halbblut n, Mischling m
half' broth'er s Halbbruder m
half'-cocked' adv (coll) nicht ganz vorbereitet
half'-day' adj halbtags
half'-full' adj halbvoll
half'-heart'ed adj zaghaft
half'-hour' adj halbstündig || s halbe Stunde f; **every h.** halbstündlich
half' leath'er s (bb) Halbleder n
half'-length' adj halblang; (portrait) in Halbfigur
half'-length por'trait s Brustbild n
half'-light' s Halbdunkel n
half-mast' s—**at h.** auf halbmast
half'-meas'ure s Halbheit f
half'-moon' s Halbmond m
half' note' s (mus) halbe Note f
half' pay' s (sl) Wartegeld n; **be on h.** Wartegeld beziehen
half' pint' s (sl) Zwerg m
half' sis'ter s Halbschwester f
half' sleeves' spl halblange Ärmel pl
half' sole' s Halbsohle f
half'-staff' s—**at h.** auf halbmast
half'-tim'bered adj Fachwerk–
half' time' s (sport) Halbzeit f
half'-time' adj Halbzeit–
half' ti'tle s Schmutztitel m
half'tone' s (mus, paint, typ) Halbton m
half'-track' s Halbkettenfahrzeug n
half'-truth' s halbe Wahrheit f
half'way' adj auf halbem Wege liegend || adv halbwegs, auf halbem Wege; **meet s.o. h.** j-m auf dem halben Wege entgegenkommen
half'way meas'ure s Halbheit f
half'-wit' s Schwachkopf m
half'-wit'ted adj blöd
halibut ['hælıbət] s Heilbutt m

halitosis [,hælı'tosıs] s Mundgeruch m
hall [hɔl] s (entranceway) Diele f, Flur m; (passageway) Gang m; (large meeting room) Saal m; (building) Gebäude n
hall'mark' s Kennzeichen n
hal·lo [hə'lo] s (–los) Hallo n || interj hallo!
hall' of fame' s Ruhmeshalle f
hallow ['hælo] tr heiligen
hallucination [hə,lusı'neʃən] s Sinnestäuschung f, Halluzination f
hall'way' s Flur m, Diele f; (passageway) Gang m
ha·lo ['helo] s (–los) Glorienschein m; (astr) Ring m, Hof m
halogen ['hælədʒən] s Halogen n
halt [hɔlt] s Halt m, Stillstand m; (rest) Rast f; **bring to a h.** zum Stillstand bringen; **call a h.** to halten lassen; **come to a h.** stehenbleiben || tr anhalten || intr halten; (rest) rasten || interj halt!
halter ['hɔltər] s (for a horse) Halfter m; (noose) Strick m
halt'ing adj (gait) hinkend; (voice) stockend
halve [hæv] tr halbieren
halyard ['hæljərd] s Fall n
ham [hæm] s (pork) Schinken m; (back of the knee) Kniekehle f; (actor) (sl) Schmierenschauspieler –in mf; (rad) (sl) Funkamateur m
hamburger ['hæm,bʌrgər] s Hackfleisch n, deutsches Beefsteak n
hamlet ['hæmlıt] s Dörfchen n
hammer ['hæmər] s Hammer m; (of a bell) Klöppel m; (sport) Wurfhammer m || tr hämmern; **h. in** (a nail) einschlagen; (e.g., rules) einhämmern; **h. out** aushämmern || intr hämmern; **h. away at** (fig) herumarbeiten an (dat)
hammock ['hæmək] s Hängematte f
hamper ['hæmpər] s Wäschebehälter m || tr behindern
hamster ['hæmstər] s Hamster m
ham'string' s Kniesehne f || v (pret & pp –strung) tr (fig) lähmen
hand [hænd] s Hand f; (applause) Beifall m; (handwriting) Handschrift f; (of a clock) Zeiger m; (help) Hilfe f; **all hands on deck!** alle Mann an Deck!; **at first h.** aus erster Hand; **at h.** vorhanden, zur Hand; **at the hands of** von seiten (genit); **be on h.** zur Stelle sein; **by h.** mit der Hand; **change hands** in andere Hände übergehen; **fall into s.o.'s hands** in j-s Hände fallen; **from h. to mouth** von der Hand in den Mund; **get one's hands on** in die Hände bekommen; **get the upper h.** die Oberhand gewinnen; **give s.o. a free h.** j-m freies Spiel lassen; **give s.o. a h.** (help s.o.) j-m helfen; (applaud s.o.) j-m Beifall spenden; **go h. in h. with** (fig) Hand in Hand gehen mit; **h. and foot** eifrig; **h. in h.** Hand in Hand; **hands off!** Hände weg!; **hands up!** Hände hoch!; **have a good h.** (cards) gute Karten haben; **have a h.**

in die Hand im Spiel haben bei; **have one's hands full** alle Hände voll zu tun haben; **have well in h.** gut in der Hand haben; **hold hands** sich bei den Händen halten; **in one's own h.** eigenhändig; **I wash my hands of it** ich wasche meine Hände in Unschuld; **join hands** (fig) sich zusammenschließen; **new h.** Neuling m; **on all hands** auf allen Seiten; **on h.** (com) vorrätig; **on one h. ... on the other einerseits ... andererseits; out of h.** außer Rand und Band; **play into s.o.'s hands** j-m in die Hände spielen; **put one's h. on** (fig) finden; **show one's h.** (fig) seine Karten aufdecken; **take a h. in** mitarbeiten an (dat); **throw up one's hands** verzweifelt die Hände hochwerfen; **try one's h. at** versuchen; **win hands down** spielend gewinnen; **with a heavy h.** streng || tr (zu)reichen; **h. down** (to s.o. below) herunterreichen; (e.g., traditions) überliefern; **h. in** (e.g., homework) abgeben; (an application) einreichen; **h. out** austeilen; **h. over** übergeben; (relinquish) aushändigen, hergeben; **I have to h. it to you** (coll) ich muß dir recht geben

hand'bag' s Handtasche f, Tasche f
hand'ball' s Handball m
hand'bill' s Handzettel m
hand'book' s Handbuch n
hand' brake' s (aut) Handbremse f
hand'breadth' s Handbreit f
hand' cart' s Handkarren m
hand'clasp' s Händedruck m
hand'cuff' s Handschelle f || tr Handschellen anlegen (dat)
-handed [ˌhændɪd] suf -händig
hand'ful [ˈhændˌful] s Handvoll f; (a few) ein paar; (fig) Nervensäge f
hand'glass' s Leselupe f
hand' grenade' s Handgranate f
handi·cap [ˈhændɪˌkæp] s Handikap n, Benachteiligung f || v (pret & pp -capped; ger -capping) tr handikapen, benachteiligen
hand'icap race' s Vorgaberennen n
handicraft [ˈhændɪˌkræft] s Handwerk n
handily [ˈhændɪlɪ] adv (dexterously) geschickt; (easily) mit Leichtigkeit
handiwork [ˈhændɪˌwɜrk] s Handarbeit f; (fig) Werk n, Schöpfung f
handkerchief [ˈhæŋkərtʃɪf] s Taschentuch n
handle [ˈhændəl] s Griff m; (of a pot) Henkel m; (of a frying pan, broom, etc.) Stiel m; (of a crank) Handkurbel f; (of a pump) Schwengel m; (of a door) Drücker m; (name) (coll) Name m; (title) (coll) Titelkram m; **fly off the h.** vor Wut platzen || tr (touch) berühren; (tools, etc.) handhaben; (operate) bedienen; (fig) erledigen; (com) handeln mit; **h. with care!** Vorsicht!; **know how to h. customers** es verstehen, mit Kunden umzugehen || intr—**h. well** sich leicht lenken lassen

han'dlebars' spl Lenkstange f, (mustache) (coll) Schnauzbart m
handler [ˈhændlər] s (sport) Trainer m
han'dling s (e.g., of a car) Lenkbarkeit f; (of merchandise, theme, ball) Behandlung f; (of a tool) Handhabung f
han'dling charg'es spl Umschlagspesen pl
hand' lug'gage s Handgepäck n
hand'made' adj handgemacht
hand'-me-downs' spl getragene Kleider pl
hand' mir'ror s Handspiegel m
hand'-op'erated adj mit Handbetrieb
hand' or'gan s Drehorgel f
hand'out' s milde Gabe f; (sheet) Handzettel m
hand'-picked' adj handgepflückt; (fig) ausgesucht
hand'rail' s Geländer n
hand'saw' s Handsäge f
hand'shake' s Handschlag m, Händedruck m
handsome [ˈhænsəm] adj schön
hand'-to-hand' fight'ing s Nahkampf m
hand'-to-mouth' adj von der Hand in den Mund
hand'work' s Handarbeit f
hand'writ'ing s Handschrift f
handwritten [ˈhænd ˌrɪtən] adj handschriftlich; **h. letter** Handschreiben n
handy [ˈhændɪ] adj handlich; (practical) praktisch; (person) geschickt; **come in h.** gelegen kommen; **have h.** zur Hand haben
hand'y·man' s (-men') Handlanger m
hang [hæŋ] s (of curtains, clothes) Fall m; **get the h. of** (coll) sich einarbeiten in (acc); **I don't give a h. about it** (coll) es ist mir Wurst || v (pret & pp hung [hʌŋ]) tr hängen; (a door) einhängen; (wallpaper) ankleben; **h. one's head** den Kopf hängen lassen; **h. out** heraushängen; **h. up** aufhängen; (the receiver) (telp) auflegen; **I'll be hanged if I will** mich hängen lassen, wenn || intr hängen; (float) schweben; **h. around** herumlungern; **h. around the bar** sich in der Bar herumtreiben; **h. around with** umgehen mit; **h. back** sich zurückhalten; **h. by** (a thread, rope) hängen an (dat); **h. down** niederhängen; **h. in the balance** in der Schwebe sein; **h. on** durchhalten; **h. on s.o.'s words** an j-s Worten hängen; **h. on to** festhalten; (retain) behalten; **h. together** zusammenhalten; **h. up** (telp) einhängen || v (pret & pp hanged & hung) tr hängen
hangar [ˈhæŋər] s Hangar m
hang'-dog look' s Armesündergesicht n
hanger [ˈhæŋər] s Kleiderbügel m
hang'er-on' s (hangers-on) Mitläufer -in mf
hang'ing adj (herab)hängend || s Hängen n
hang'man s (-men) Henker m
hang'nail' s Niednagel m

hang′out′ s Treffpunkt m
hang′o′ver s (coll) Kater m
hank [hæŋk] s Strähne f
hanker [′hæŋkər] intr (for) sich sehnen (nach)
hanky-panky [′hæŋkɪ′pæŋkɪ] s (coll) Schwindel m
haphazard [‚hæp′hæzərd] adj wahllos
haphazardly [‚hæp′hæzərdlɪ] adv aufs Geratewohl
hapless [′hæplɪs] adj unglücklich
happen [′hæpən] intr geschehen; **h. to see** zufällig sehen; **h. upon** zufällig stoßen auf (acc); **what happens now?** was soll nun werden?
hap′pening s Ereignis n.
happily [′hæpɪlɪ] adv glücklich
happiness [′hæpɪnɪs] s Glück n
happy [′hæpɪ] adj glücklich; **be h. about s.th.** über etw erfreut sein; **be h. to** (inf) sich freuen zu (inf); **h. as a lark** quietschvergnügt
Hap′py Birth′day interj Herzlichen Glückwunsch zum Geburtstag!
hap′py-go-luck′y adj unbekümmert
hap′py me′dium s—strike a h. e-n glücklichen Ausgleich treffen
Hap′py New′ Year′ interj Glückliches Neujahr!
harangue [hə′ræŋ] s leidenschaftliche Rede f || tr e-e leidenschaftliche Rede halten an (acc)
harass [hə′ræs], [′hærəs] tr schikanieren; (mil) stören
harass′ing fire′ s (mil) Störungsfeuer n
harassment [hə′ræsmənt], [′hærəsmənt] s Schikane f; (mil) Störung f
harbinger [′hɑrbɪndʒər] s Vorbote m || tr anmelden
harbor [′hɑrbər] adj Hafen– || s Hafen m || tr (give refuge to) beherbergen; (hide) verbergen; (thoughts) hegen
har′bor mas′ter s Hafenmeister m
hard [hɑrd] adj (substance, water, words) hart; (problem) schwierig; (worker) fleißig; (blow, times, work) schwer; (life) mühsam; (fact) nackt; (rain) heftig; (winter) streng; (drinks) alkoholisch; **be h. on s.o.** j-m schwer zusetzen; **have a h. time** Schwierigkeiten haben; **h. to believe** kaum zu glauben; **h. to please** anspruchsvoll; **h. to understand** schwer zu verstehen || adv hart; (energetically) fleißig; **he was h. put to** (inf) es fiel ihm schwer zu (inf); **rain h.** stark regnen; **take h.** schwer nehmen; **try h.** mit aller Kraft versuchen
hard′-and-fast′ adj fest
hard-bitten [′hɑrd‚bɪtn] adj verbissen
hard′-boiled′ adj (egg) hartgekocht; (coll) hartgesotten
hard′ can′dy s Bonbons pl
hard′ cash′ s bare Münze f
hard′ ci′der s Apfelwein m
hard′ coal′ s Steinkohle f
hard′-earned′ adj schwer verdient
harden [′hɑrdən] tr & intr (er)härten
hard′ened adj (criminal) hartgesotten
hard′ening s Verhärtung f
hard′-head′ed adj nüchtern
hard′-heart′ed adj hartherzig

hardihood [′hɑrdɪ‚hʊd] s Kühnheit f; (insolence) Frechheit f
hardiness [′hɑrdɪnɪs] s Ausdauer f, Widerstandsfähigkeit f
hard′ la′bor s Zwangsarbeit f
hard′ luck′ s Pech n
hardly [′hɑrdlɪ] adv kaum, schwerlich; **h. ever** fast gar nicht
hardness [′hɑrdnɪs] s Härte f
hard′-of-hear′ing adj schwerhörig
hard′-pressed′ adj schwer bedrängt
hard′-shell′ adj hartschalig; (coll) unnachgiebig
hard′ship′ s Mühsal f
hard′top′ s (aut) Hardtop n
hard′ up′ adj (for money) schlecht bei Kasse; **h. for** in Verlegenheit um
hard′ware′ s Eisenwaren pl; (e.g., on doors, windows) Beschläge pl; military h. militärische Ausrüstung f
hard′ware store′ s Eisenwarenhandlung f
hard′wood′ s Hartholz n
hard′wood floor′ s Hartholzboden m
hard′-work′ing adj fleißig
hardy [′hɑrdɪ] adj (plants) winterfest; (person) widerstandsfähig
hare [her] s Hase m
hare′-brained′ adj unbesonnen
hare′lip′ s Hasenscharte f
harem [′herəm] s Harem m
hark [hɑrk] intr horchen; **h. back to** zurückgehen auf (acc)
harlequin [′hɑrləkwɪn] s Harlekin m
harlot [′hɑrlət] s Hure f
harm [hɑrm] s Schaden m; **do h.** Schaden anrichten; **I meant no h. by it** ich meinte es nicht böse; **out of harm's way** in Sicherheit; **there's no h. in trying** ein Versuch kann nicht schaden || tr beschädigen; (e.g., a reputation, chances) schaden (dat); **h. s.o.** (physically) j-m etw zuleide tun; (fig) schaden (dat)
harmful [′hɑrmfəl] adj schädlich
harmless [′hɑrmlɪs] adj unschädlich
harmonic [hɑr′mɑnɪk] adj harmonisch || s (mus) Oberton m
harmonica [hɑr′mɑnɪkə] s Harmonika f
harmonious [hɑr′monɪ·əs] adj harmonisch
harmonize [′hɑrmə‚naɪz] intr harmonieren
harmony [′hɑrmənɪ] s Harmonie f; **be in h. with** im Einklang stehen mit
harness [′hɑrnɪs] s Geschirr n; **die in the h.** in den Sielen sterben || tr anschirren; (e.g., a river, power) nutzbar machen
har′ness mak′er s Sattler m
har′ness rac′ing s Trabrennen n
harp [hɑrp] s Harfe f || intr—**h. on** herumreiten auf (dat)
harpist [′hɑrpɪst] s Harfner –in mf
harpoon [hɑr′pun] s Harpune f || tr harpunieren
harpsichord [′hɑrpsɪ‚kɔrd] s Cembalo n
harpy [′hɑrpɪ] s (myth) Harpyie f
harrow [′hæro] s Egge f || tr eggen
har′rowing adj schrecklich

har·ry ['hæri] v (pret & pp **-ried**) tr martern

Harry ['hæri] s Heinz m

harsh [harʃ] adj (conditions) hart; (tone) schroff; (light) grell; (treatment) rauh

harshness ['harʃnɪs] s Härte f; Schroffheit f; Grelle f; Rauheit f

hart [hart] s Hirsch m

harum-scarum ['herəm'skerəm] adj wild || adv wie ein Wilder

harvest ['harvɪst] s Ernte f; bad h. Mißernte f || tr & intr ernten

harvester ['harvɪstər] s Schnitter –in mf; (mach) Mähmaschine f

har'vest moon' s Erntemond m

has-been ['hæz,bɪn] s (coll) Gestrige mf

hash [hæʃ] s Gehacktes n; make h. of (coll) verwursteln || tr zerhacken

hashish ['hæʃiʃ] s Haschisch n

hasp [hæsp] s Haspe f

hassle ['hæsəl] s (coll) Streit m

hassock ['hæsək] s Hocker m

haste [hest] s Hast f, Eile f; in (all) h. in (aller) Eile; make h. sich beeilen

hasten ['hesən] tr beschleunigen || intr hasten, eilen

hasty ['hesti] adj eilig; (rash) hastig

hat [hæt] s Hut m; keep under one's h. für sich behalten

hat'band' s Hutband n

hat'block' s Hutform f

hat'box' s Hutschachtel f

hatch [hætʃ] s (opening) (aer, naut) Luke f; (cover) (naut) Lukendeckel m || tr (eggs) ausbrüten; (a scheme) aushecken; (mark with strokes) schraffieren || intr Junge ausbrüten; (said of chicks) aus dem Ei kriechen

hat'check girl' s Garderobe(n)fräulein n

hatchet ['hætʃɪt] s Beil n; bury the h. die Streitaxt begraben

hatch'ing s Schraffierung f

hatch'way' s (naut) Luke f

hate [het] s Haß m || tr hassen; I h. to (inf) es widerstrebt mir zu (inf)

hateful ['hetfəl] adj verhaßt

hatless ['hætlɪs] adj hutlos

hat'pin' s Hutnadel f

hat'rack' s Hutständer m

hatred ['hetrɪd] s Haß m

haughtiness ['hotɪnɪs] s Hochmut m

haughty ['hoti] adj hochmütig

haul [hol] s Schleppen n; (hauling distance) Transportstrecke f; (amount caught) Fang m; make a big h. (fig) reiche Beute machen; over the long h. auf die Dauer || tr (tug) schleppen; (transport) transportieren; h. ashore an Land ziehen; h. down (a flag) einholen; h. into court vor Gericht stellen; h. out of bed aus dem Bett herausholen || intr—h. off (naut) abdrehen; h. off and hit ausholen um zu schlagen

haulage ['holɪdʒ] s Transport m; (costs) Transportkosten pl

haunch [hontʃ] s (hip) Hüfte f; (hind quarter of an animal) Keule f

haunt [hont] s Aufenthaltsort m || tr

verfolgen; **h. a place** an e–m Ort umgehen; **this place is haunted** es spukt hier

haunt'ed house' s Haus n in dem es spukt

have [hæv] s—**the haves** und **the have-nots** die Besitzenden und die Besitzlosen || v (pret & pp **had** [hæd]) tr haben; (a baby) bekommen; (a drink) trinken; (food) essen; **h. back** zurückhaben; **h. in mind** vorhaben; **h. it in for s.o.** j–n auf dem Strich haben; **h. it out with s.o.** sich mit j–m aussprechen; **h. it your way** meinetwegen machen Sie es, wie Sie wollen; **h. left** übrig haben; **h. on** (clothes) anhaben; (a hat) aufhaben; (e.g., a program) vorhaben; **h. on one's person** bei sich tragen; **h. to do with s.o.** mit j–m zu tun haben; **h. what it takes** das Zeug dazu haben; **I've had it!** jetzt langt's mir aber!; **I will not h. it!** ich werde es nicht dulden!; **you had better** es wäre besser, wenn Sie; **what would you h. me do?** was soll ich machen? || intr—**h. done with it** fertig sein damit; **h. off** frei haben || aux (to form compound past tenses) haben, e.g., **he has paid the bill** er hat die Rechnung bezahlt; (to form compound past tenses of certain intransitive verbs of motion and change of condition, of the verb **bleiben**, and of the transitive verb **eingehen**) sein, e.g., **she has gone to the theater** sie ist ins Theater gegangen; **they h. become rich** sie sind reich geworden; **you h. stayed too long** Sie sind zu lange geblieben; **I h. assumed an obligation** ich bin e–e Verpflichtung eingegangen; (to express causation) lassen, e.g., **I am having a new suit made** ich lasse mir e–n neuen Anzug machen; (to express necessity) müssen, e.g., **I h. to study now** jetzt muß ich studieren; **that will h. to do** das wird genügen müssen

haven ['hevən] s Hafen m

haversack ['hævər,sæk] s Brotbeutel m

havoc ['hævək] s Verwüstung f; wreak h. on verwüsten

haw [ho] s (bot) Mehlbeere f; (in speech) Äh n || tr nach links lenken || intr nach links gehen || interj (to a horse) hü!

Hawaii [hə'waɪ·i] s Hawaii n

Hawaiian [hə'waɪjən] adj hawaiisch

Hawai'ian Is'lands spl Hawaii-Inseln pl

hawk [hok] s Habicht m || tr (wares) verhökern; **h. up** aushusten || intr sich räuspern

hawker ['hokər] s Straßenhändler –in mf

hawse [hoz] s (hole) (naut) Klüse f; (prow) (naut) Klüsenwand f

hawse'hole' s (naut) Klüse f

hawser ['hozər] s (naut) Trosse f, Tau n

hawthorn ['hɔθɔrn] s Weißdorn m

hay [he] s Heu n; **hit the hay** (sl) sich

in die Falle hauen; **make hay** Heu machen

hay′fe′ver s Heufieber n
hay′field′ s Kleefeld n
hay′fork′ s Heugabel f
hay′loft′ s Heuboden m
hay′mak′er s (box) Schwinger m
hay′rack′ s Heuraufe f
hayrick [′he͵rɪk] s Heuschober m
hay′ride′ s Ausflug m in e-m teilweise mit Heu gefüllten Wagen
hay′seed′ s (coll) Bauerntölpel m
hay′stack′ s Heuschober m
hay′wire′ adj (sl) übergeschnappt; **go h.** (go wrong) schiefgehen; (go insane) überschnappen
hazard [′hæzərd] s (danger) Gefahr f; (risk) Risiko n || tr riskieren
hazardous [′hæzərdəs] adj gefährlich
haze [hez] s Dunst m; (fig) Unklarheit f || tr (students) piesacken
hazel [′hezəl] adj (eyes) nußbraun || s (bush) Hasel f
ha′zelnut′ s Haselnuß f
haziness [′hezɪnɪs] s Dunstigkeit f; (fig) Verschwommenheit f
haz′ing s (of students) Piesacken n
hazy [′hezɪ] adj dunstig; (recollection) verschwommen
H-bomb [′etʃ͵bɑm] s Wasserstoffbombe f
he [hi] pers pron er; **he who** wer || s Männchen n
head [hed] adj Kopf-; (chief) Haupt-, Ober-, Chef- || s (of a body, cabbage, nail, lettuce, pin) Kopf m; (of a gang, family) Haupt m; (of a firm) Chef m; (of a school) Direktor -in mf; (of a department) Leiter -in mf; (of a bed) Kopfende n; (of a coin) Bildseite f; (of a glass of beer) Blume f; (of cattle) Stück n; (of stairs) oberer Absatz m; (of a river) Quelle f; (of a parade, army) Spitze f; (toilet) Klo n; **a h.** pro Person, pro Kopf; **at the h. of** an der Spitze (genit); **be at the h. of** vorstehen (dat); **be h. and shoulders above s.o.** haushoch über j-m stehen; (be far superior to s.o.) j-m haushoch überlegen sein; **be over one's h.** über j-s Verstand gehen; **bring to a h.** zur Entscheidung bringen; **by a h.** um e-e Kopflänge; **from h. to foot** von Kopf bis Fuß; **go over s.o.'s h.** über j-s Verstand gehen; (adm) über j-s Kopf hinweg handeln; **go to s.o.'s h.** j-m zu Kopfe steigen; **have a good h. for** begabt sein für; **h. over heels** kopfüber; (in love) bis über die Ohren; (in debt) bis über den Hals; **heads or tails?** Kopf oder Wappen?; **heads up!** aufpassen!; **keep one's h.** kaltes Blut behalten; **keep one's h. above water** sich über Wasser halten; **lose one's h.** den Kopf verlieren; **my h. is spinning** es schwindelt mir; **not be able to make h. or tail of** nicht klug werden aus; **out of one's h.** nicht ganz richtig im Kopf; **per h.** pro Kopf; **put heads together** die Köpfe zusammenstecken; **talk over**

s.o.'s h. über j-s Kopf hinwegreden; **talk s.o.'s h. off** j-n dumm und dämlich reden; **take it into one's h. es** sich [dat] in den Kopf setzen || tr (be in charge of) leiten; (a parade, army, expedition) anführen; (steer, guide) lenken; **h. a list** als erster auf e-r Liste stehen; **h. off** abwehren; **h. up** (a committee) vorsitzen (dat) || intr— **h. back** zurückkehren; **h. for** auf dem Wege sein nach; (aer) anfliegen; (naut) ansteuern; **h. home** sich heimbegeben; **where are you heading?** wo wollen Sie hin?
head′ache′ s Kopfweh n, Kopfschmerzen pl
head′band′ s Kopfband n
head′board′ s Kopfbrett n
head′cold′ s Schnupfen m
head′ doc′tor s Chefarzt m, Chefärztin f
head′dress′ s Kopfputz m
-headed [͵hedɪd] suf –köpfig
head first adv kopfüber; (fig) Hals über Kopf
head′gear′ s Kopfbedeckung f
head′hunt′er s Kopfjäger m
head′ing s Überschrift f; (aer) Steuerkurs m
headland [′hedlənd] s Landspitze f
headless [′hedlɪs] adj kopflos; (without a leader) führerlos
head′light′ s (aut) Scheinwerfer m
head′line′ s (in a newspaper) Schlagzeile f; (at the top of a page) Überschrift f; **hit the headlines** (coll) Schlagzeilen liefern
head′lin′er s Hauptdarsteller -in mf
head′long′ adj stürmisch || adv kopfüber
head′man s (–men) Häuptling m, Chef m
head′mas′ter s Direktor m
head′mis′tress s Direktorin f
head′ nurse′ s Oberschwester f
head′ of′fice s Hauptgeschäftsstelle f
head′ of gov′ernment s Regierungschef m
head′ of hair′ s—**beautiful h.** schönes volles Haar n
head′ of the fam′ily s Familienoberhaupt n
head′-on′ adj Frontal- || adv frontal
head′phones′ spl Kopfhörer pl
head′piece′ s Kopfbedeckung f; (brains) (coll) Kopf m; (typ) Zierleiste f
head′quar′ters s Hauptquartier n; (of police) Polizeidirektion f; (mil) Hauptquartier n, Stabsquartier n
head′quarters com′pany s Stabskompanie f
head′rest′ s Kopflehne f; (aut) Kopfstütze f
head′ restrain′er s (aut) Kopfstütze f
head′set′ s Kopfhörer m
head′ shrink′er s (coll) Psychiater –in mf
head′stand′ s Kopfstand m
head′start′ s Vorsprung m
head′stone′ s Grabstein m
head′strong′ adj starrköpfig

head′ wait′er s Oberkellner m

head′ wa′ters spl Quellflüsse pl

head′way′ s Vorwärtsbewegung f; (fig) Fortschritte pl

head′ wear′ s Kopfbedeckung f

head′wind′ s Gegenwind m

head′work′ s Kopfarbeit f

heady [′hɛdi] adj (wine) berauschend; (news) spannend; (impetuous) unbesonnen

heal [hil] tr & intr heilen; **h. up** zuheilen

healer [′hilər] s Heilkundige mf

heal′ing s Heilung f

health [hɛlθ] s Gesundheit f; **drink to s.o.'s h.** auf j–s Wohl trinken; **in good h.** gesund; **in poor h.** kränklich; **to your h.!** auf Ihr Wohl!

health′ certi′ficate s Gesundheitspaß m

healthful [′hɛlθfəl] adj heilsam; (climate) bekömmlich

health′ insur′ance s Krankenversicherung f

health′ resort′ s Kurort m

healthy [′hɛlθi] adj gesund; (respect) gehörig; **keep h.** sich gesund halten

heap [hip] s Haufen m; **in heaps** haufenweise || tr beladen; h. (e.g., praise) **on s.o.** j–n überhäufen mit; **h. up** anhäufen

hear [hɪr] v (pret & pp heard [hʌrd] tr hören; (find out) erfahren; (get word) Bescheid bekommen; **h. s.o.'s lessons** j–n überhören; **h. s.o. out** j–n ganz ausreden lassen || intr hören; **h. about** hören über (acc) or von; **h. from** Nachricht bekommen von; **h. of** hören von; **h. wrong** sich verhören; **he wouldn't h. of it** er wollte nichts davon hören

hearer [′hɪrər] s Hörer –in mf; **hearers** Zuhörer pl

hear′ing s Hören n, Gehör n; (jur) Verhör n; **within h.** in Hörweite

hear′ing aid′ s Hörgerät n, Hörapparat m

hear′say′ s Hörensagen n; **know sth. by h.** etw nur vom Hörensagen kennen; **that's mere h.** das ist bloßes Gerede

hearse [hʌrs] s Leichenwagen m

heart [hɑrt] s Herz n; **after my own h.** nach meinem Herzen; **at h.** im Grunde genommen; **be the h. and soul of** die Seele sein (genit); **by h.** auswendig; **cross my h.!** Hand aufs Herz!; **cry one's h. out** sich ausweinen; **eat one's h. out** sich vor Kummer verzehren; **get to the h. of** auf den Grund kommen (dat); **have a h.** (coll) ein Herz haben; **have one's h. in s.th.** mit dem Herzen bei etw sein; **have the h. to** (inf) es übers Herz bringen zu (inf); **h. and soul** mit Leib und Seele; **hearts** (cards) Herz n; **lose h.** den Mut verlieren; **lose one's h. to** sein Herz verlieren an (acc); **set one's h. on** sein Herz hängen an (acc); **take h.** Mut fassen; **take to h.** beherzigen; **to one's heart's content** nach Herzenslust; **wear one's h. on one's sleeve** das Herz auf der

Zunge tragen; **with all one's h.** mit ganzem Herzen

heart′ache′ s Herzweh n

heart′ attack′ s Herzanfall m

heart′beat′ s Herzschlag m

heart′break′ s Herzeleid n

heart′break′er s Herzensbrecher –in mf

heartbroken [′hɑrt‚brokən] adj trostlos

heart′burn′ s Sodbrennen n

heart′ disease′ s Herzleiden n

–hearted [‚hɑrtɪd] suf –herzig

hearten [′hɑrtən] tr ermutigen

heart′ fail′ure s Herzschlag m

heartfelt [′hɑrt‚fɛlt] adj herzinnig, tiefempfunden; (wishes) herzlich

hearth [hɑrθ] s Herd m

hearth′stone′ s Kaminplatte f

heartily [′hɑrtɪli] adv (with zest) herzhaft; (sincerely) von Herzen

heartless [′hɑrtlɪs] adj herzlos

heart′ mur′mur s Herzgeräusch n

heart′-rend′ing adj herzzerreißend

heart′sick′ adj tief betrübt

heart′ strings′ spl–**pull at s.o.'s h.** j–m ans Herz greifen

heart′ throb′ s Schwarm m

heart′ trans′plant s Herzverpflanzung f

heart′ trou′ble s Herzbeschwerden pl

heart′wood′ s Kernholz n

hearty [′hɑrti] adj herzhaft; (meal) reichlich; (eater) stark; (appetite) gut

heat [hit] s Hitze f, Wärme f; (heating) Heizung f; (sexual) Brunst f; (in the case of dogs) Läufigkeit f; (of battle) Eifer m; (sport) Rennen n, Einzelrennen n; **be in h.** brunsten; (said of dogs) läufig sein; **final h.** Schlußrennen n; **put the h. on** (sl) unter Druck setzen; **qualifying h.** Vorlauf m || tr (e.g., food) wärmen; (fluids) erhitzen; (a house) heizen; **h. up** aufwärmen || intr–**h. (up)** warm (or heiß) werden

heat′ed adj erhitzt; (fig) erregt

heater [′hitər] s Heizkörper m; (oven) Heizofen m

heath [hiθ] s Heide f

hea·then [′hiðən] adj heidnisch || s (–then & –thens) Heide m, Heidin f

heathendom [′hiðəndəm] s Heidentum n

heather [′hɛðər] s Heiderkraut n

heat′ing s Heizung f

heat′ing pad′ s Heizkissen n

heat′ing sys′tem s Heizanlage f

heat′ light′ning s Wetterleuchten n

heat′ prostra′tion s Hitzekollaps m

heat′-resis′tant adj hitzebeständig

heat′ shield′ s (rok) Hitzeschild m

heat′stroke′ s Hitzschlag m

heat′ treat′ment s Wärmebehandlung f

heat′ wave′ s Hitzewelle f

heave [hiv] s Hub m; (throw) Wurf m; **heaves** (vet) schweres Atmen n || v (pret & pp heaved & hove [hov]) tr heben; (throw) werfen; (a sigh) ausstoßen; (the anchor) lichten || intr (said of the breast or sea) wogen; (retch) sich übergeben; **h. in sight** auftauchen; **h. to** (naut) stoppen

heaven ['hevən] *s* Himmel *m;* **for heaven's sake** um Himmels willen; **good heavens!** ach du lieber Himmel!; **the heavens** der Himmel

heavenly ['hevənli] *adj* himmlisch

hea'venly bod'y *s* Himmelskörper *m*

heavenwards ['hevənwərdz] *adv* himmelwärts

heavily ['hevɪli] *adv* schwer; **h. in debt** überschuldet

heavy ['hevɪ] *adj* schwer; *(food)* schwer verdaulich; *(fine, price)* hoch; *(walk)* schwerfällig; *(heart)* bedrückt, schwer; *(traffic, frost, rain)* stark; *(fog)* dicht; *(theat)* ernst, düster; **h. drinker** Gewohnheitstrinker –in *mf;* **h. seas** Sturzsee *f;* **h. with sleep** schlaftrunken

heavy'-armed' *adj* schwerbewaffnet

heav'y-du'ty *adj* Hochleistungs-, Schwerlast-

heav'y-du'ty truck' *s* Schwerlastwagen *m*

heav'y-heart'ed *adj* bedrückt

heav'y in'dustry *s* Schwerindustrie *f*

heav'yset' *adj* untersetzt

heav'y weight' *adj* Schwergewicht- ‖ *s* Schwergewichtler *m*

Hebrew ['hibru] *adj* hebräisch ‖ *s* Hebräer –in *mf;* *(language)* Hebräisch *n*

hecatomb ['hekə‚tom] *s* Hekatombe *f*

heck [hek] *s*—**give s.o. h.** (sl) j-m tüchtig einheizen; **what the h. are you doing?** (sl) was zum Teufel tust du? ‖ *interj* (sl) verflixt!

heckle ['hekəl] *tr* durch Zwischenrufe belästigen

heckler ['heklər] *s* Zwischenrufer –in *mf*

hectic ['hektɪk] *adj* hektisch

hectograph ['hektə‚græf] *s* Hektograph *m* ‖ *tr* hektographieren

hedge [hedʒ] *s* Hecke *f* ‖ *tr*—**h. in** (or **h. off**) einhegen ‖ *intr* sich den Rücken decken

hedge'hog' *s* Igel *m*

hedge'hop' *v* (*pret & pp* **-hopped**; *ger* **hopping**) *intr* (aer) heckenspringen

hedge'hop'ping *s* (aer) Heckenhüpfen *n*

hedge'row' *s* Hecke *f*

hedonism ['hidə‚nɪzəm] *s* Hedonismus *m*

hedonist ['hidənɪst] *s* Hedonist –in *mf*

heed [hid] *s* Acht *f;* **pay h. to** achtgeben auf *(acc);* **take h.** achtgeben ‖ *tr* beachten ‖ *intr* achtgeben

heedful ['hidfəl] *adj* (of) achtsam (auf *acc*)

heedless ['hidlɪs] *adj* achtlos; **h. of** ungeachtet (*genit*)

heehaw ['hi‚hɔ] *s* Iah *n* ‖ *interj* iah!

heel [hil] *s* *(of the foot)* Ferse *f;* *(of a shoe)* Absatz *m;* *(of bread)* Brotende *n;* (sl) Schurke *m;* **down at the h.** abgerissen; **cool one's heels** sich [*dat*] die Beine in den Bauch stehen; **take to one's heels** Fersengeld geben ‖ *intr* (*said of a dog*) auf den Fersen folgen

hefty ['hefti] *adj* *(heavy)* schwer; *(muscular)* stämmig; *(blow)* zünftig

heifer ['hefər] *s* Färse *f*

height [haɪt] *s* Höhe *f;* *(e.g., of power)* Gipfel *m;* **h. of the season** Hochsaison *f*

heighten ['haɪtən] *tr* erhöhen; (fig) verschärfen

heinous ['henəs] *adj* abscheulich

heir [ɛr] *s* Erbe *m;* **become h. to** erben; **become s.o.'s h.** j-n beerben

heir' appar'ent *s* (heirs apparent) Thronerbe *m*

heiress ['ɛrɪs] *s* Erbin *f*

heir'loom' *s* Erbstück *n*

heir' presump'tive *s* (heirs presumptive) mutmaßlicher Erbe *m*

Helen ['helən] *s* Helene *f*

helicopter ['helɪ‚kaptər] *s* Hubschrauber *m*

heliport ['helɪ‚pɔrt] *s* Hubschrauberlandeplatz *m*

helium ['hilɪəm] *s* Helium *n*

helix ['hilɪks] *s* (helixes & helices ['helɪ‚siz]) Spirale *f;* (archit) Schnecke *f*

hell [hel] *s* Hölle *f*

hell'bent' *adj*—**h. on** (sl) erpicht auf *(acc)*

hell'cat' *s* (*shrew*) Hexe *f*

Hellene ['helin] *s* Hellene *m*, Hellenin *f*

Hellenic [he'lenɪk] *adj* hellenisch

hell'fire' *s* Höllenfeuer *n*

hellish ['helɪʃ] *adj* höllisch

hel-lo [he'lo] *s* (-los) Hallo *n* ‖ *interj* guten Tag!; (in southern Germany and Austria) Grüß Gott!; (to get s.o.'s attention and in answering the telephone) hallo!

helm [helm] *s* (& fig) Steuerruder *n*

helmet ['helmɪt] *s* Helm *m*

helms'man *s* (-men) Steuermann *m*

help [help] *s* Hilfe *f;* *(domestic)* Hilfe *f,* Hilfskraft *f;* *(temporary)* Aushilfe *f;* **h. wanted** (in newspapers) Stellenangebot *n;* **there's no h. for it** da ist nicht zu helfen; **with the h. of** mit Hilfe (*genit*) ‖ *tr* helfen (*dat*); **can I h. you?** womit kann ich (Ihnen) dienen?; **h. along** nachhelfen (*dat*); **h. down from** herunterhelfen (*dat*) von (*dat*); **h. oneself** sich bedienen; (*at table*) zugreifen; **h. oneself to** sich [*dat*] nehmen; **h. out** aushelfen (*dat*); **h. s.o. on** (or **off**) **with the coat** j-m in den (or aus dem) Mantel helfen; **I cannot h.** (*ger*), **I cannot h. but** (*inf*) ich kann nicht umhin zu (*inf*); **sorry, that can't be helped** es tut mir leid, aber es geht nicht anders ‖ *intr* helfen ‖ *interj* Hilfe!

helper ['helpər] *s* Gehilfe *m*, Gehilfin *f*

helpful ['helpfəl] *adj* (*person*) hilfsbereit; *(e.g., suggestion)* nützlich

help'ing *s* Portion *f*

help'ing hand' *s* hilfreiche Hand *f*

helpless ['helplɪs] *adj* hilflos, ratlos

helter-skelter ['heltər'skeltər] *adj* wirr ‖ *adv* holterdiepolter

hem [hem] *s* Saum *m* ‖ *v* (*pret & pp* **hemmed**; *ger* **hemming**) *tr* säumen; **hem in** umringen ‖ *intr* stocken; **hem**

and haw nicht mit der Sprache her- auswollen || *interj* hm!
hemisphere ['hemı,sfır] *s* Halbkugel *f*
hemistich ['hemı,stık] *s* Halbvers *m*
hem'line' *s* Rocklänge *f*
hem'lock' *s* (*conium*) Schierling *m;* (*poison*) Schierlingsgift *n;* (*Tsuga canadensis*) Kanadische Hemmlock- tanne *f*
hemoglobin [,hımə'globın] *s* Blutfarb- stoff *m*, Hämoglobin *n*
hemophilia [,hımə'fılı·ə] *s* Bluter- krankheit *f*, Hämophilie *f*
hemorrhage ['hemərıdʒ] *s* Blutung *f*
hemorrhoids ['hemə,rɔıdz] *spl* Hämor- rhoiden *pl*
hemostat ['hımə,stæt] *s* Unterbin- dungssklemme *f*
hemp [hemp] *s* Hanf *m*
hem'stitch' *s* Hohlsaum *m* || *tr* mit e-m Hohlsaum versehen
hen [hen] *s* Henne *f*, Huhn *n*
hence [hens] *adv* von hier; (*therefore*) daher, daraus; a year h. in e-m Jahr
hence'forth' *adv* hinfort, von nun an
hench·man ['hent/mən] *s* (-men) An- hänger *m;* (*gang member*) Helfers- helfer *m*
hen'house' *s* Hühnerstall *m*
henna ['henə] *s* Henna *f*
hen' par'ty *s* (coll) Damengesellschaft *f*
hen'peck' *tr* unter dem Pantoffel ha- ben; **be henpecked** unter dem Pan- toffel stehen; **henpecked husband** Pantoffelheld *m*
Henry ['henrı] *s* Heinrich *m*
hep [hep] *adj* (to) eingeweiht (in *acc*)
her [hʌr] *poss adj* ihr; (if the antece- dent is neuter, e.g., Fräulein) sein || *pers pron* sie; (if the antecedent is neuter) es; (indirect object) ihr; (if the antecedent is neuter) ihm
herald ['herəld] *s* Herold *m;* (fig) Vor- bote *m* || *tr* ankündigen; h. in ein- führen
heraldic [he'rældık] *adj* heraldisch; h. figure Wappenbild *n;* h. motto Wappenspruch *n*
heraldry ['herəldrı] *s* Wappenkunde *f*
herb [(h)ʌrb] *s* Kraut *n*, Gewürz *n;* (pharm) Arzneikraut *n*
herculean [hʌrkju'li·ən] *adj* herkulisch
herd [hʌrd] *s* Herde *f;* (of game) Rudel *n;* the common h. der Pöbel *m* || *tr* hüten; **h. together** zusammenpfer- chen || *intr* in e-r Herde gehen (or leben)
herds'man *s* (-men) Hirt *m*
here [hır] *adv* (position) hier; (direc- tion) hierher, her; h. and there hie(r) und da; h. below in diesem Leben; h. goes! jetzt gilt's!; here's to you! auf Ihr Wohl!; neither h. nor there belanglos || *interj* hier!
hereabouts ['hırə,bauts] *adv* hier in der Nähe
hereaf'ter *adv* hiernach || *s* Jenseits *n*
hereby' *adv* hierdurch
hereditary [hı'redı,terı] *adj* erblich, Erb-; be h. sich vererben
heredity [hı'redıtı] *s* Vererbung *f*

herein' *adv* hierin
hereof' *adv* hiervon
hereon' *adv* hierauf
heresy ['herəsı] *s* Ketzerei *f*
heretic ['herətık] *s* Ketzer –in *mf*
heretical [hı'retıkəl] *adj* ketzerisch
heretofore [,hırtu'fɔr] *adv* zuvor
hereupon' *adv* daraufhin
herewith' *adv* hiermit; (in a letter) an- bei, in der Anlage
heritage ['herıtıdʒ] *s* Erbe *n*
hermet'ically sealed' [hʌr'metıkəlı] *adj* hermetisch verschlossen
hermit ['hʌrmıt] *s* Einsiedler –in *mf;* (eccl) Eremit *m*
hermitage ['hʌrmıtıdʒ] *s* Eremitage *f*
herni·a ['hʌrnı·ə] *s* (-as & -ae [,ı]) Bruch *m*
he·ro ['hıro] *s* (-roes) Held *n*
heroic [hı'ro·ık] *adj* heldenhaft, Helden-; (pros) heroisch || **heroics** *spl* Heldentaten *pl*
hero'ic age' *s* Helden(zeit)alter *n*
hero'ic coup'let *s* heroisches Reim- paar *n*
hero'ic verse' *s* heroisches Vermaß *n*
heroin ['hero·ın] *s* Heroin *n*
heroine ['hero·ın] *s* Heldin *f*
heroism ['hero,ızəm] *s* Heldenmut *m*
heron ['herən] *s* (orn) Fischreiher *m*
he'ro wor'ship *s* Heldenverehrung *f*
herring ['herıŋ] *s* Hering *m*
her'ringbone' *s* (pattern) Grätenmuster *n;* (parquetry) Riemenparkett *n*
hers [hʌrz] *poss pron* der ihre (or ihrige), ihrer
herself' *reflex pron* sich; she's not h. today sie ist heute gar nicht wie sonst || *intens pron* selbst, selber
hesitancy ['hezıtənsı] *s* Zaudern *n*
hesitant ['hezıtənt] *adj* zögernd
hesitate ['hezı,tet] *intr* zögern
hesitation [,hezı'te/ən] *s* Zögern *n*
heterodox ['hetərə,daks] *adj* anders- gläubig, heterodox
heterodyne ['hetərə,daın] *adj* Über- lagerungs– || *tr* & *intr* überlagern
heterogeneous [,hetərə'dʒını·əs] *adj* heterogen
hew [hju] *v* (pret **hewed;** pp **hewed** & **hewn**) *tr* (stone) hauen; (trees) fäl- len; **hew down** umhauen
hex [heks] *s* (spell) Zauber *m;* (witch) Hexe *f;* put a hex on (coll) behexen || *tr* (coll) behexen
hexagon ['heksəgən] *s* Hexagon *n*
hey [he] *interj* heil; **hey there!** heda!
hey'day' *s* Hochblüte *f*, Glanzzeit *f*
H'-hour' *s* (mil) X-Zeit *f*
hi [haı] *interj* heil; **hi there!** heda!
hia·tus [haı'etəs] *s* (-tuses & -tus) Lücke *f;* (ling) Hiatus *m*
hibernate ['haıbər,net] *intr* (& fig) Winterschlaf halten
hibernation [,haıbər'ne/ən] *s* Winter- schlaf *m*
hibiscus [haı'bıskəs] *s* Hibiskus *m*
hiccough, hiccup ['hıkəp] *s* Schluckauf *m*
hick [hık] *s* Tölpel *m*
hickory ['hıkərı] *s* Hickorybaum *m*
hick' town' *s* Kuhdorf *n*

hidden ['hɪdən] adj verborgen, versteckt; (secret) geheim

hide [haɪd] s Haut f, Fell n || v (pret **hid** [hɪd]; pp **hid & hidden** ['hɪdən] tr verstecken; (a view) verdecken; (fig) verbergen; **h. from** verheimlichen vor (dat) || intr (out) sich verstecken

hide'-and-seek' s Versteckspiel n; **play h.** Versteck spielen

hide'away' s Schlupfwinkel m

hide'bound' adj engherzig

hideous ['hɪdɪ‧əs] adj gräßlich

hide'out' s (coll) Versteck n

hid'ing s Verstecken n; **be in h.** sich versteckt halten; **get a h.** (coll) Prügel bekommen

hid'ing place' s Versteck n

hierarchy ['haɪ‧ə‧rɑrki] s Hierarchie f

hieroglyphic ['haɪ‧ərə'glɪfɪk] adj Hieroglyphen- || s Hieroglyphe f

hi-fi ['haɪ'faɪ] adj Hif-fi- || s Hi-Fi n

high [haɪ] adj hoch; (wind) stark; (hopes) hochgespannt; (fever) heftig (spirits) gehoben; **h. and dry** auf dem Trockenen; **h. and mighty** hochfahrend; **it is h. time** es ist höchste Zeit || adv hoch; **h. and low** weit und breit || s (e.g., in prices) Hochstand m; (aut) höchster Gang m; (meteor) Hoch n; **on h.** oben; **shift into h.** den höchsten Gang einschalten

high'al'tar s Hochaltar m

high'ball' s Highball m

high'born' adj hochgeboren

high'boy' s hochbeinige Kommode f

high'brow' adj intellektuell || s Intellektuelle m

high'chair' s Kinderstuhl m

High'Church' s Hochkirche f

high'-class' adj vornehm, herrschaftlich

high'command' s Oberkommando n

high'cost' of liv'ing s hohe Lebenshaltungskosten pl

high'div'ing s Turmspringen n

high'er educa'tion s Hochschulbildung f

high'er-up' s (coll) hohes Tier n

high'est bid' ['haɪ‧ɪst] s Meistgebot n

high'est bid'der s Meistbietende mf

high'explo'sive s hochexplosiver Sprengstoff m

highfalutin [‚haɪfə'lutən] adj hochtönend

high'fidel'ity s äußerst getreue Tonwiedergabe f, High Fidelity f

high'-fidel'ity adj klanggetreu

high'fre'quency s Hochfrequenz f

high'-fre'quency adj hochfrequent

high'gear' s höchster Gang m; **shift into h.** den höchsten Gang einschalten; (fig) auf Hochtouren gehen

High'Ger'man s Hochdeutsch n

high'-grade' adj hochfein, Qualitäts-

high'-grade steel' s Edelstahl m

high'-hand'ed adj anmaßend

high'heel' s Stöckel m

high'-heeled shoe' s Stöckelschuh m

high'horse' s—come off one's **h.** klein beigeben; **get up on one's h.** sich aufs hohe Roß setzen

high'jinks' [‚dʒɪŋks] spl Ausgelassenheit f

high'jump' s (sport) Hochsprung m

highland ['haɪlənd] s Hochland n; **highlands** Hochland n

highlander ['haɪləndər] s Hochländer –in mf

high'life' s Prasserei f, Highlife n

high'light' s (big moment) Höhepunkt m; (in a picture) Glanzlicht n || tr hervorheben; (in a picture) Glanzlichter aufsetzen (dat)

highly ['haɪli] adv hoch, hoch-, höchst; **h. sensitive** hochempfindlich; **speak h. of** in den höchsten Tönen sprechen von; **think h. of** große Stücke halten auf (acc)

High'Mass' s Hochamt n

high'-mind'ed adj hochgesinnt

high'-necked' adj hochgeschlossen

highness ['haɪnɪs] s Höhe f; **Highness** (title) Hoheit f

high'noon' s—at h. am hellen Mittag

high'-oc'tane adj mit hoher Oktanzahl

high'-pitched' adj (voice) hoch; (roof) steil

high'-pow'ered adj starkmotorig; **h. engine** Hochleistungsmotor m

high'pres'sure s Hochdruck m

high'-pres'sure adj Hochdruck-; **h. area** Hochdruckgebiet n || tr (com) bearbeiten

high'-priced' adj kostspielig

high'priest' s Hohe(r)priester m

high'-qual'ity adj Qualitäts-, hochwertig

high'-rank'ing adj hochgestellt

high'rise' s Hochbau m, Hochhaus n

high'road' s (fig) sicherer Weg m

high'school' s Oberschule f

high'sea' s—on the high seas auf offenem Meer

high'soci'ety s vornehme Welt f, High Society f

high'-sound'ing adj hochtönend

high'-speed' adj Schnell-; (phot) lichtstark

high'-speed steel' s Schnelldrehstahl m

high'-spir'ited adj hochgemut; (horse) feurig

high-strung ['haɪ'strʌŋ] adj überempfindlich

high'ten'sion s Hochspannung f

high'-ten'sion adj Hochspannungs-

high'-test' gas'oline s Superbenzin n

high'tide' s Flut f

high'time' s höchste Zeit f; (sl) Heidenspaß m

high'trea'son s Hochverrat m

high'volt'age s Hochspannung f

high'-volt'age adj Hochspannungs-

high'-wa'ter mark' s Hochwassermarke f; (fig) Höhepunkt m

high'way' s Landstraße f, Chaussee f

high'way'man s (–men) Straßenräuber m

high'way patrol' s Straßenstreife f

high'way rob'bery s Straßenraub m

hijack ['haɪ‚dʒæk] tr (a truck) überfallen und rauben; (a plane) entführen hijacker ['haɪ‚dʒækər] s (of a truck) Straßenräuber –in mf; (of a plane) Entführer –in mf

hi'jack'ing s Entführung f

hike [haɪk] s Wanderung f; (in prices) Erhöhung f || tr (prices) erhöhen || intr wandern

hiker ['haɪkər] s Wanderer –in mf

hik'ing s Wandern n

hilarious [hɪ'lerɪ-əs] adj heiter

hill [hɪl] s Hügel m; go over the h. (mil) ausbüxen; over the h. (coll) auf dem absteigenden Ast || tr häufeln

hill'bil'ly adj hinterwäldlerisch || s Hinterwäldler –in mf

hill' coun'try s Hügelland n

hillock ['hɪlək] s Hügelchen n

hill'side' s Hang m

hilly ['hɪli] adj hügelig

hilt [hɪlt] s Griff m; armed to the h. bis an die Zähne bewaffnet; to the h. (fig) gründlich

him [hɪm] pers pron (dative) ihm; (accusative) ihn

himself' reflex pron sich; he is not h. today er ist heute gar nicht wie sonst || intens pron selbst, selber

hind [haɪnd] adj Hinter– || s Hirsch-kuh f

hinder ['hɪndər] tr (ver)hindern

hind'most' adj hinterste

hind'quar'ter s Hinterviertel n; (of a horse) Hinterhand f; (of venison) Ziemer m

hindrance ['hɪndrəns] s (to) Hindernis n (für)

hind'sight' s späte Einsicht f

Hindu ['hɪndu] adj Hindu– || s Hindu m

hinge [hɪndʒ] s Scharnier n; (of a door) Angel f || intr—h. on abhängen von

hint [hɪnt] s Wink m, Andeutung f; give a broad h. e–n Wink mit dem Zaunpfahl geben; take the h. den Wink verstehen || intr—h. at andeuten

hinterland ['hɪntər‚lænd] s Hinterland n

hip [hɪp] adj (sl) im Bild || s Hüfte f; (of a roof) Walm m

hip'bone' s Hüftbein n

hip'joint' s Hüftgelenk n

hipped adj—h. on (coll) erpicht auf (acc)

hippopota·mus [‚hɪpə'pɑtəməs] s (–muses & –mi [‚maɪ]) Nilpferd n

hip' roof' s Walmdach n

hire [haɪr] s Miete f; (salary) Lohn m; for h. zu vermieten || tr (workers) anstellen; (rent) mieten; h. oneself out to sich verdingen bei; h. out vermieten

hired' hand' s Lohnarbeiter –in mf

hireling ['haɪrlɪŋ] s Mietling m

his [hɪz] poss adj sein || poss pron seiner, der seine (or seinige)

Hispanic [hɪs'pænɪk] adj hispanisch

hiss [hɪs] s Zischen n || tr auszischen || intr zischen

hiss'ing s Zischen n, Gezisch n

hiss'ing sound' s Zischlaut m

hist [hɪst] interj st!

historian [hɪs'torɪ-ən] s Historiker –in mf

historic [hɪs'torɪk] adj historisch bedeutsam

historical [hɪs'torɪkəl] adj historisch, geschichtlich

history ['hɪstəri] s Geschichte f

historionic [‚hɪstrɪ'ɑnɪk] adj schauspielerisch; (fig) übertrieben || histrionics spl theatralisches Benehmen n

hit [hɪt] s Schlag m, Stoß m; (a success) Schlager m; (sport) Treffer m; (theat) Zugstück n || v (pret & pp hit; ger hitting) tr (e.g., with the fist) schlagen; (a note, target) treffen; hit bottom (fig) auf den Nullpunkt angekommen sein; hit it off gut miteinander auskommen; hit one's head against mit dem Kopf stoßen gegen; hit s.o. hard (said of misfortunes, etc.) schwer treffen; hit the road sich auf den Weg machen; hit the sack sich hinhauen || intr schlagen; hit on (or upon) kommen auf (acc)

hit'-and-run' adj (driver) flüchtig; h. accident Unfall m mit Fahrerflucht; h. attack Zerstörangriff m

hitch [hɪtʃ] s (difficulty) Haken m; (knot) Stich m; (term of service) Dienstzeit f; that's the h. das ist ja gerade der Haken; without a h. reibungslos || tr spannen; h. a ride (to) per Anhalter fahren (nach); h. to the wagon vor (or an) den Wagen spannen; h. up (horses) anspannen; (trousers) hochziehen

hitch'hike' intr per Anhalter fahren

hitch'ing post' s Pfosten m (zum Anbinden von Pferden)

hither ['hɪðər] adv her, hierher; h. and thither hierhin und dorthin

hitherto' adv bisher

hit' or miss' adv aufs Geratewohl

hit'-or-miss' adj planlos

hitter ['hɪtər] s Schläger m

hive [haɪv] s Bienenstock m; hives (pathol) Nesselausschlag m

hoard [hord] s Hort m || tr & intr horten; (food) hamstern

hoarder ['hordər] s Hamsterer –in mf

hoard'ing s Horten n; (of food) Hamstern n

hoarfrost ['hor‚frɔst] s Rauhreif m

hoarse [hors] adj heiser

hoarseness ['horsnɪs] s Heiserkeit f

hoary ['hori] adj ergraut; (fig) altersgrau

hoax [hoks] s Schnabernack m || tr anführen

hob [hɑb] s Kamineinsatz m

hobble ['hɑbəl] s Humpeln n || intr humpeln

hobby ['hɑbi] s Hobby n

hob'byhorse' s (stick with horse's head) Steckenpferd n; (rocking horse) Schaukelpferd n

hob'gob'lin s Kobold m; (bogy) Schreckgespenst n

hob'nail' s grober Schuhnagel m

hob·nob ['hɔb‚nɔb] v (pret & pp
-nobbed; ger -nobbing) intr—h. with
freundschaftlich verkehren mit

ho·bo ['hobo] s (-bos & -boes) Landstreicher m

hock [hɔk] s (of a horse) Sprunggelenk
n; **in h.** verpfändet ‖ tr (hamstring)
lähmen; (pawn) (coll) verpfänden

hockey ['hɔki] s Hockey n

hoc′key stick′ s Hockeystock m

hock′shop′ s (coll) Leihhaus n

hocus-pocus ['hokəs'pokəs] s Hokuspokus m

hod [hɔd] s Mörteltrog m

hodgepodge ['hɔdʒ‚pɔdʒ] s Mischmasch m

hoe [ho] s Hacke f, Haue f ‖ tr hacken

hog [hɔg] s Schwein n ‖ v (pret & pp
hogged; ger hogging) tr (sl) gierig
an sich reißen; **hog the road** rücksichtslos fahren

hog′back′ s scharfer Gebirgskamm m

hog′ bris′tle s Schweinsborste f

hoggish ['hɔgiʃ] adj schweinisch, gefräßig

hog′wash′ s (nonsense) Quatsch m

hoist [hɔist] s (apparatus for lifting)
Hebezeug n; (act of lifting) Hochwinden n ‖ tr hochwinden; (a flag,
sail) hissen

hokum ['hokəm] s (nonsense) (coll)
Quatsch m; (flimflam) (coll) Effekthascherei f

hold [hold] s Halt m, Griff m; (naut)
Raum m; (sport) Griff m; **get h. of**
(catch) erwischen; (acquire) erwerben; **get h. of oneself** sich fassen;
take h. of anfassen ‖ v (pret & pp
held [held] tr halten; (contain) enthalten; (regard as) halten für; (one's
breath) anhalten; (an audience) fesseln; (a meeting, election, court) abhalten; (an office, position) bekleiden, innehaben; (talks) führen; (a
viewpoint) vertreten; (a meet) (sport)
veranstalten; **able to h. one's liquor**
trinkfest; **h. back** zurückhalten;
(news) geheimhalten; **h. dear** wert-
halten; **h. down** niederhalten; **h. in
contempt** verachten; **h. it! halt!; h.
off** abhalten; **h. office** amtieren; **h.
one's ground** die Stellung halten;
h. one's own seinen Mann stehen;
h. one's own against sich behaupten
gegen; **h. one's tongue** den Mund
halten; **h. open** (a door) aufhalten;
h. out (a hand) hinhalten; (proffer)
vorhalten; **h. over** (e.g., a play) verlängern; **h. s.th. against s.o.** j–m
etw nachtragen; **h. sway** walten; **h.
under** niederhalten; **h. up** (raise)
hochhalten; (detain) aufhalten; (traffic) behindern; (rob) räuberisch
überfallen; **h. up to ridicule** dem
Spott preisgeben; **h. the line** (telp) am
Apparat bleiben; **h. the road well**
e–e gute Straßenlage haben; **h. together** zusammenhalten; **h. water**
(fig) stichhaltig sein ‖ intr (said of
a knot) halten; **h. back** sich zurückhalten; **h. forth** (coll) dozieren; **h. on**
warten; **h. on to** festhalten, sich

festhalten an (dat); **h. out** aushalten;
h. out for abwarten; **h. true** gelten;
h. true for zutreffen auf (acc); **h. up**
(wear well) halten

holder ['holdər] s (device) Halter m;
(e.g., of a title) Inhaber –in mf

hold′ing s (of a meeting) Abhaltung f;
(of an office) Bekleidung f; **holdings**
Besitz m, Bestand m

hold′ing com′pany s Holdinggesell-
schaft f

hold′ing pat′tern s (aer) Platzrunde f

hold′-o′ver s Überbleibsel n

hold′up′ s (delay) Aufenthalt m; (robbery) Raubüberfall m; (in traffic)
Verkehrsstauung f

hold′up man′ s Räuber m

hole [hol] s Loch n; (of animals) Bau
m; **h. in the wall** Loch n; **in a h. in
der Patsche; in the h.** hängengeblie-
ben, e.g., **I am ten dollars in the h.**
ich bin mit zehn Dollar hängenge-
blieben; **pick holes in** (fig) herum-
kritisieren an (dat); **wear holes in**
völlig abtragen ‖ intr—**h. out** (golf)
ins Loch spielen; **h. up** sich vergra-
ben; (fig) sich verstecken

holiday ['hɑli‚de] s Feiertag m; (vacation) Ferien pl; **take a h.** e–n
freien Tag machen, Urlaub nehmen

hol′iday mood′ s Ferienstimmung f

holiness ['holinis] s Heiligkeit f; **His
Holiness** Seine Heiligkeit

Holland ['hɑlənd] s Holland n

Hollander ['hɑləndər] s Holländer –in
mf

hollow ['hɑlo] adj hohl ‖ s Höhle f,
Höhlung f; (geol) Talmulde f ‖ tr—
h. out aushöhlen

hol′low-cheeked′ adj hohlwangig

hol′low-eyed′ adj hohläugig

holly ['hɑli] s Stechpalme f

holm′ oak′ [hom] s Steineiche f

holocaust ['hɑlə‚kɔst] s Brandopfer n;
(disaster) Brandkatastrophe f

holster ['holstər] s Pistolentasche f

holy ['holi] adj heilig; **h. smokes!**
(coll) heiliger Strohsack!

Ho′ly Commun′ion s Kommunion f,
das Heilige Abendmahl

ho′ly day′ s Feiertag m

Ho′ly Ghost′ s Heiliger Geist m

Ho′ly of Ho′lies s Allerheiligste n

ho′ly or′ders spl Priesterweihe f

Ho′ly Scrip′ture s die Heilige Schrift

Ho′ly See′ s Heiliger Stuhl m

Ho′ly Sep′ulcher s Heiliges Grab n

Ho′ly Spir′it s Heiliger Geist m

ho′ly wa′ter s Weihwasser n

Ho′ly Week′ s Karwoche f

Ho′ly Writ′ s die Heilige Schrift

homage ['(h)ɑmidʒ] s Huldigung f;
pay h. to huldigen (dat)

home [hom] adj inländisch, Innen– ‖
adv nach Hause, heim; **bring h. to
s.o.** j–m beibringen ‖ s Heim n; (house) Haus n, Wohnung f; (place
of residence) Wohnort m; (institu-
tion) Heim n; **at h.** zu Hause, daheim; **at h. and abroad** im In– und
Ausland; **feel at h.** sich zu Hause
fühlen; **for the h.** für den Hausbe-

darf; **from h.** von zu Hause; **h. for the aged** Altersheim *n*; **h. for the blind** Blindenheim *n*; **h. of one's own** Zuhause *n*
home′ address′ *s* Privatadresse *f*
home′-baked′ *adj* hausbacken
home′ base′ *s* (aer) Heimatflughafen *m*
home′bod′y *s* Stubenhocker –in *mf*
homebred [′hom₁bred] *adj* einheimisch
home′-brew′ *s* selbstgebrautes Getränk *n*
home′-brewed′ *adj* selbstgebraut
home′com′ing *s* Heimkehr *f*
home′ comput′er *s* Heimcomputer *m*
home′ coun′try *s* Heimatstaat *m*
home′ econom′ics *s* Hauswirtschafts-lehre *f*
home′-fried pota′toes *spl*, **home′ fries′** [′fraɪz] *spl* Bratkartoffeln *pl*
home′ front′ *s* Heimatfront *f*
home′-grown′ *adj* selbstgezogen
home′ guard′ *s* Landsturm *m*
home′land′ *s* Heimatland *n*
homeless [′homlɪs] *adj* obdachlos ‖ *s* Obdachlose *mf*
home′like′ *adj* anheimelnd
homely [′homli] *adj* unschön
home′made′ *adj* selbstgemacht; (culin) selbstgebacken
home′mak′er *s* Hausfrau *f*
home′ of′fice *s* Hauptbüro *n*
home′ own′er *s* Hausbesitzer –in *mf*
home′ plate′ *s* Schlagmal *n*
home′ rem′edy *s* Hausmittel *n*
home′ rule′ *s* Selbstverwaltung *f*
home′ run′ *s* (baseball) Vier-Mal-Lauf *m*
home′sick′ *adj*—**be h.** Heimweh haben
home′sick′ness *s* Heimweh *n*
homespun [′hom₁spʌn] *adj* selbstge-macht; (fig) einfach
home′stead′ *s* Siedlerstelle *f*
home′stretch′ *s* Zielgerade *f*
home′ team′ *s* Ortsmannschaft *f*
home′town′ *adj* Heimat– ‖ *s* Heimat-stadt *f*
homeward [′homwərd] *adv* heimwärts
home′ward jour′ney *s* Heimreise *f*
home′work′ *s* Hausaufgabe *f*
homey [′homi] *adj* anheimelnd
homicidal [,hɑmɪ′saɪdəl] *adj* mörde-risch
homicide [′hɑmɪ,saɪd] *s* (act) Tot-schlag *m*; (person) Totschläger –in *mf*
hom′icide squad′ *s* Mordkommission *f*
homily [′hɑmɪli] *s* Homilie *f*
hom′ing device′ [′homɪŋ] *s* Zielsucher *m*
hom′ing pi′geon *s* Brieftaube *f*
homogeneous [,homə′dʒɪnɪ·əs] *adj* ho-mogen
homogenize [hə′mɑdʒə,naɪz] *tr* homo-genisieren
homonym [′hɑmənɪm] *s* Homonym *n*
homosexual [,homə′sɛk[v·ə]l] *adj* ho-mosexuell ‖ *s* Homosexuelle *mf*
hone [hon] *s* Wetzstein *m* ‖ *tr* honen
honest [′ɑnɪst] *adj* ehrlich, aufrecht
honestly [′ɑnɪstli] *adv* ehrlich; **to tell you h.** offengestanden ‖ *interj* auf mein Wort!

honesty [′ɑnɪsti] *s* Ehrlichkeit *f*
hon·ey [′hʌni] *s* Honig *m*; (as a term of endearment) Schatz *m*, Liebling *m* ‖ *v* (pret & pp –eyed & –ied) *tr* versüßen; (speak sweetly to) schmeicheln (dat)
hon′eybee′ *s* Honigbiene *f*
hon′eycomb′ *s* Honigwabe *f* ‖ *tr* (e.g., a hall) wabenartig durchlöchern
hon′eyed *adj* mit Honig gesüßt; (fig) honigsüß
hon′ey lo′cust *s* Honigdorn *m*
hon′eymoon′ *s* Flitterwochen *pl* ‖ *intr* die Flitterwochen verbringen
hon′eysuck′le *s* Geißblatt *n*
honk [hɑŋk] *s* (aut) Hupensignal *n* ‖ *tr*—**h. the horn** hupen ‖ *intr* hupen
honkytonk [′hɑŋkɪ,tɑŋk] *s* (sl) Tingel-tangel *m* & *n*
honor [′ɑnər] *s* Ehre *f*; (award) Aus-zeichnung *f*; (chastity) Ehre *f*; **be held in h.** in Ehren gehalten werden; **consider it an h.** es sich [dat] zur Ehre anrechnen; **do the honors** die Honneurs machen; **have the h. of** (ger) sich beehren zu (inf); **in s.o.'s h.** j–m zu Ehren; **your Honor** Euer Gnaden ‖ *tr* ehren; (favor) beehren; (a check) honorieren; **feel honored** sich geehrt fühlen
honorable [′ɑnərəbəl] *adj* (person) ehr-bar; (intentions) ehrlich; (peace treaty) ehrenvoll
honorari·um [,ɑnə′rɛrɪ·əm] *s* (–ums & –a [ə]) Honorar *n*; **give an h. to** honorieren
hon′orary degree′ *s* Ehrendoktorat *n*
honorific [,ɑnə′rɪfɪk] *adj* ehrend, Ehren– ‖ *s* Ehrentitel *m*
hooch [hutʃ] *s* (sl) Fusel *m*, Schnaps *m*
hood [hud] *s* Haube *f*; (of a monk) Kapuze *f*; (of a baby carriage) Ver-deck *n*; (sl) Gangster *m*; (aut) Motorhaube *f*; (culin) Rauchabzug *m*; (educ) Talarüberwurf *m* ‖ *tr* mit e–r Haube versehen; (fig) verhüllen
hoodlum [′hudləm] *s* Ganove *m*
hoodoo [′hudu] *s* Unglücksbringer *m* ‖ *tr* Unglück bringen (dat)
hood′wink′ *tr* täuschen
hooey [′hu·i] *s* (sl) Quatsch *m*
hoof [huf], [huf] *s* Huf *m* ‖ *tr*—**h. it** auf Schusters Rappen reiten
hoof′beat′ *s* Hufschlag *m*
hook [huk] *s* Haken *m*; (angl) Angel-haken *m*; (baseball) Kurvball *m*; (box) Haken *m*; (golf) Hook *m*; **by h. or by crook** so oder so; **h., line, and sinker** mit allem Drum und Dran; **off the h.** (coll) aus der Schlinge; **on one's own h.** (coll) auf eigene Faust ‖ *tr* festhaken, ein-haken; (e.g., a boyfriend) angeln; (steal) schnappen; (box) e–n Haken versetzen (dat); (golf) nach links verziehen; **h. up** zuhaken; (elec) an-schließen ‖ *intr* sich krümmen; **h. up with s.o.** sich j–m anschließen
hook′ and eye′ *s* Haken *m* und Öse *f*
hook′-and-lad′der truck′ *s* Feuerwehr-fahrzeug *n* mit Drehleiter

hooked *adj* hakenförmig; **h. on drugs** rauschgiftsüchtig
hooker [′hukər] *s* (sl) Nutte *f*
hook′nose′ *s* Hakennase *f*
hook′up′ *s* (elec, electron) Schaltung *f*; (electron) Schaltbild *n*; (rad, telv) Gemeinschaftsschaltung *f*
hook′worm′ *s* Hakenwurm *m*
hooky [′huki] *s*—**play h.** schwänzen
hooligan [′huligən] *s* Straßenlümmel *m*
hoop [hup] *s* Reifen *m* || *tr* binden
hoop′ skirt′ *s* Reifrock *m*
hoot [hut] *s* Geschrei *n*; **not give a h. about** keinen Pfifferling geben für || *intr* schreien; **h. at** anschreien
hoot′ owl′ *s* Waldkauz *m*
hop [hap] *s* Hopser *m*; *(dance)* Tanz *m*; hops (bot) Hopfen *m* || *v* (*pret & pp* hopped; *ger* hopping) *tr* (*e.g., a train*) aufspringen auf (*acc*); **hop a ride** (coll) mitfahren || *intr* hüpfen; **hop around** herumhüpfen
hope [hop] *s* (of) Hoffnung *f* (auf *acc*); **beyond h.** hoffnungslos; **not get up one's hopes** sich [*dat*] keine Hoffnungen machen || *tr* hoffen || *intr* hoffen; **h. for** hoffen auf (*acc*); **h. for the best** das Beste hoffen; **I h.** (parenthetical) hoffentlich
hope′ chest′ *s* Aussteuertruhe *f*
hopeful [′hopfəl] *adj* hoffnungsvoll || *s* (pol) Kandidat –in *mf*
hopefully [′hopfəli] *adv* hoffentlich
hopeless [′hoplɪs] *adj* hoffnungslos
hopper [′hapər] *s* Fülltrichter *m*; (in *a toilet*) Spülkasten *m*; (*storage container*) Vorratsbehälter *m*; (data proc) Kartenmagazin *n*
hop′per car′ *s* (rr) Selbstentladewagen *m*
hop′ping mad′ *adj* fuchsteufelswild
hop′scotch′ *s* Himmel und Hölle
horde [hord] *s* Horde *f*
horehound [′hor‚haund] *s* (*lozenge*) Hustenbonbon *m*; (bot) Andorn *m*
horizon [hə′raɪzən] *s* Horizont *m*
horizontal [‚hɑrɪ′zɑntəl] *adj* horizontal, waagrecht || *s* Horizontale *f*
horizon′tal bar′ *s* (gym) Reck *n*
horizon′tal controls′ *spl* (aer) Seitenleitwerk *n*
horizon′tal sta′bilizer *s* (aer) Höhenflosse *f*
hormone [′hormon] *s* Hormon *n*
horn [horn] *s* (*of an animal; wind instrument*) Horn *n*; (aut) Hupe *f*; **blow one's own h.** (coll) ins eigene Horn stoßen; **blow the h.** (aut) hupen; **horns** (*of an animal*) Geweih *n* || *intr*—**h. in** (on) (coll) sich eindrängen (in *acc*)
hornet [′hornɪt] *s* Hornisse *f*
hor′net's nest′ *s*—**stir up a h.** in ein Wespennest stechen
horn′ of plen′ty *s* Füllhorn *n*
horn′-rimmed glass′es *spl* Hornbrille *f*
horny [′horni] *adj* (*callous*) schwielig; (*having horn-like projections*) verhornt; (sl) geil
horoscope [′hɔrə‚skop] *s* Horoskop *n*; **cast s.o.'s h.** j-m das Horoskop stellen

horrible [′hɔrɪbəl] *adj* (& coll) schrecklich
horrid [′hɔrɪd] *adj* abscheulich
horri·fy [′hɔrɪ‚faɪ] *v* (*pret & pp* –fied) *tr* erschrecken, entsetzen
horror [′hɔrər] *s* Schrecken *m*, Entsetzen *n*
hor′ror sto′ry *s* Schaudergeschichte *f*
hors d'oeuvre [ɔr′dʌrv] *s* (hors d'oeuvres [ɔr′dʌrvz]) Vorspeise *f*
horse [hors] *s* Pferd *n*; (carp) Sägebock *m*; **back the wrong h.** (fig) auf's falsche Pferd setzen; **bet on a h.** auf ein Pferd setzen; **hold your horses** immer mit der Ruhe!; **h. of another color** e–e andere Sache; **mount a h.** zu Pferd steigen; **straight from the horse's mouth** direkt von der Quelle || *intr*—**h. around** (sl) herumalbern; **stop horsing around** laß den Unsinn!
horse′back′ *s*—**on h.** zu Pferd || *adv*—**ride h.** reiten
horse′back rid′ing *s* Reiten *n*
horse′ blan′ket *s* Pferdedecke *f*
horse′ chest′nut *s* Roßkastanie *f*
horse′ col′lar *s* Kummet *n*
horse′ doc′tor *s* (coll) Roßarzt *m*
horse′fly′ *s* Pferdebremse *f*
horse′hair′ *s* Roßhaar *n*, Pferdehaar *n*
horse′laugh′ *s* wieherndes Gelächter *n*
horse′man *s* (–men) Reiter *m*
horse′manship′ *s* Reitkunst *f*
horse′ meat′ *s* Pferdefleisch *n*
horse′ op′era *s* (coll) Wildwestfilm *m*
horse′play′ *s* grober Unfug *m*
horse′pow′er *s* Pferdestärke *f*
horse′ race′ *s* Pferderennen *n*
horse′rad′ish *s* Meerrettich *m*, Kren *m*
horse′ sense′ *s* gesunder Menschenverstand *m*
horse′ shoe′ *s* Hufeisen *n* || *tr* beschlagen
horse′shoe mag′net *s* Hufeisenmagnet *m*
horse′ show′ *s* Pferdeschau *f*
horse′ tail′ *s* Pferdeschwanz *m*
horse′ trad′er *s* Pferdehändler *m*; (fig) Kuhhändler *m*
horse′ trad′ing *s* Pferdehandel *m*; (fig) Kuhhandel *m*
horse′whip′ *s* Reitpeitsche *f* || *v* (*pret & pp* –whipped; *ger* –whipping) *tr* mit der Reitpeitsche schlagen
horse′wom′an *s* (–wom′en) Reiterin *f*
horsy [′hɔrsi] *adj* pferdeartig; (*horseloving*) pferdeliebend
horticultural [‚hɔrtɪ′kʌltʃərəl] *adj* Gartenbau–
horticulture [′hɔrtɪ‚kʌltʃər] *s* Gartenbau *m*, Gärtnerei *f*
hose [hoz] *s* Schlauch *m* || *s* (hose) Strumpf *m*; (*collectively*) Strümpfe *pl*
hosiery [′hoʒəri] *s* Strumpfwaren *pl*; (*mill*) Strumpffabrik *f*
hospice [′haspɪs] *s* Hospiz *n*
hospitable [′haspɪtəbəl], [has′pɪtəbəl] *adj* gastlich, gastfreundlich
hospital [′haspɪtəl] *s* Hospital *n*, Krankenhaus *n*; (mil) Lazarett *n*
hospitality [‚haspɪ′tælɪti] *s* Gast-

freundschaft *f;* **show s.o. h.** j–m Gastfreundschaft gewähren

hospitalize ['hɑspɪtə͵laɪz] *tr* ins Krankenhaus einweisen

hos'pital ship' *s* Lazarettschiff *f*

hos'pital train' *s* Sanitätszug *m*

hos'pital ward' *s* Kranken(haus)station *f*

host [host] *s* Gastgeber *m; (at an inn)* Wirt *m; (in a television show)* Leiter *m; (multitude)* Heerschar *f; (army)* Heer *n;* **Host** (relig) Hostie *f*

hostage ['hɑstɪdʒ] *s* Geisel *m f*

hostel ['hɑstəl] *s* Herberge *f*

hostelry ['hɑstəlrɪ] *s* Gasthaus *n*

hostess ['hostɪs] *s* Gastgeberin *f; (at an inn)* Wirtin *f; (on an airplane)* Stewardeß *f; (in a restaurant)* Empfangsdame *f; (on a television show)* Leiterin *f*

hostile ['hɑstɪl] *adj* feindlich; **(to)** feindselig (gegen)

hostility [hɑs'tɪlɪtɪ] *s* Feindseligkeit *f;* **hostilities** Feindseligkeiten *pl*

hot [hɑt] *adj* heiß; *(spicy)* scharf; *(meal)* warm; *(stolen, sought by the police, radioactive; jazz, tip)* heiß; *(trail, scent)* frisch; *(in heat)* geil; **be hot** *(said of the sun)* stechen; **get into hot water** in die Patsche geraten; **hot and bothered** aufgeregt; **hot from the press** frisch von der Presse; **hot on s.o.'s trail** j–m dicht auf der Spur; **hot stuff** *(sl)* toller Kerl *m;* **I am hot** mir ist heiß; **I don't feel so hot** (coll) ich fühle mich nicht besonders; **she's not so hot** (coll) sie ist nicht so toll

hot' air' *s* Heißluft *f; (sl)* blauer Dunst *m*

hot'-air heat' *s* Heißluftheizung *f*

hot'bed' *s* Frühbeet *n; (fig)* Brutstätte *f*

hot'-blood'ed *adj* heißblütig

hot' cake' *s* Pfannkuchen *m;* **sell like hot cakes** wie warme Semmeln weggehen

hotchpotch ['hɑtʃ͵pɑtʃ] *s* (coll) Mischmasch *m*

hot' dog' *s* warmes Würstel *n*

hotel [ho'tel] *adj* Hotel– || *s* Hotel *n; (small hotel)* Gasthof *m*

hotel' busi'ness *s* Hotelgewerbe *n*

hotel'keep'er *s* (–men) Hotelbesitzer *m*

hot'foot' *adv* in aller Eile || *tr*—**h. it** schleunigst eilen; **h. it after s.o.** j–m nacheilen

hot'head' *s* Hitzkopf *m*

hot'-head'ed *adj* hitzköpfig

hot'house' *s* Treibhaus *n,* Gewächshaus *n*

hot' line' *s* (telp) heißer Draht *m*

hot' mon'ey *s* (sl) Fluchtkapital *n*

hot' pep'per *s* scharfe Paprikaschote *f*

hot' plate' *s* Heizplatte *f*

hot' pota'to *s* (coll) schwieriges Problem *n*

hot' rod' *s* (sl) frisiertes altes Auto *n*

hot' rod'der [͵rɑdər] *s* (sl) Fahrer *m* e–s frisierten Autos

hot' seat' *s* (sl) elektrischer Stuhl *m*

hot' springs' *spl* Thermalquellen *pl*

hot' tem'per *s* hitziges Temperament *n*

hot'-tem'pered *adj* hitzig, hitzköpfig

hot' war' *s* Schießkrieg *m*

hot' wa'ter *s* Heißwasser *n;* **be in h.** (fig) in der Tinte sitzen; **get into h.** (fig) in die Patsche geraten

hot'-wa'ter bot'tle *s* Gummiwärmflasche *f*

hot'-wa'ter heat'er *s* Heißwasserbereiter *m*

hot'-wa'ter heat'ing *s* Heißwasserheizung *f*

hot'-wa'ter tank' *s* Heißwasserspeicher *m*

hound [haund] *s* Jagdhund *m* || *tr* hetzen

hour [aur] *s* Stunde *f;* **after hours** nach Arbeitsschluß; **at any h.** zu jeder Tageszeit; **by the h.** stundenweise; **every h.** stündlich; **for an h.** e–e Stunde lang; **for a solid h.** e–e geschlagene Stunde lang; **for hours** stundenlang; **h. of death** Todesstunde *f;* **h. overtime** Überstunde *f;* **in the small hours** in den frühen Morgenstunden; **keep late hours** spät zu Bett gehen; **keep regular hours** zur Zeit aufstehen und schlafengehen; **on the h.** zur vollen Stunde

–hour *suf* –stündig

hour'glass' *s* Stundenglas *n*

hour' hand' *s* Stundenzeiger *m*

hourly ['aurlɪ] *adj* stündlich; **h. rate** Stundensatz *m;* **h. wages** Stundenlohn *m* || *adv* stündlich

house [haus] *adj (boat, dress)* Haus– || *s* **(houses** ['hauzɪz]) Haus *n;* **h. and home** Haus und Hof; **h. for rent** Haus *n* zu vermieten; **keep h.** (for s.o.) (j–m) den Haushalt führen; **on the h.** auf Kosten des Wirts; **put one's h. in order** (fig) seine Angelegenheiten in Ordnung bringen || [hauz] *tr* unterbringen

house' arrest' *s* Hausarrest *m*

house'boat' *s* Hausboot *n*

house'break'ing *s* Einbruchsdiebstahl *m*

housebroken ['haus͵brokən] *adj* stubenrein

house' clean'ing *s* Hausputz *m; (fig)* Säuberungsaktion *f*

house'fly' *s* Stubenfliege *f*

houseful ['haus͵ful] *s* Hausvoll *n*

house' guest' *s* Logiergast *m*

house'hold' *adj* Haushalts– || *s* Haushalt *m*

house'hold'er *s* Haushaltsvorstand *m*

house'hold fur'nishings *spl* Hausrat *m*

house'hold needs' *spl* Hausbedarf *m*

house'hold word' *s* Alltagswort *n*

house' hunt'ing *s* Wohnungssuche *f*

house'keep'er *s* Haushälterin *f*

house'keep'ing *s* Hauswirtschaft *f*

house'maid' *s* Dienstmädchen *n*

house'moth'er *s* Hausmutter *f*

house' of cards' *s* Kartenhaus *n*

House' of Com'mons *s* Unterhaus *n*

house' of correc'tion *s* Zuchthaus *n,* Besserungsanstalt *f*

house' of ill' repute' *s* öffentliches Haus *n*

House' of Lords' *s* Oberhaus *n*

house′ physi′cian s Krankenhausarzt m; (in a hotel) Hausarzt m

house′-to-house′ adv von Haus zu Haus; **sell h.** hausieren

house′warm′ing s Einzugsfest n

house′wife′ s (wives′) Hausfrau f

house′work′ s Hausarbeit f

hous′ing s Unterbringung f, Wohnung f; (mach) Gehäuse n

hous′ing devel′opment s Siedlung f

hous′ing pro′ject s Sozialsiedlung f

hous′ing short′age s Wohnungsnot f

hous′ing un′it s Wohneinheit f

hovel [′hʌvəl], [′hʌvəl] s Hütte f

hover [′hʌvər] intr schweben; (fig) pendeln; **h. about** sich herumtreiben in der Nähe von

Hov′ercraft′ s (trademark) Schwebefahrzeug n

how [hau] adv wie; **and how!** und wie!; **how about …?** (would you care for …?) wie wäre es mit …?; (what's the progress of …?) wie steht es mit …?; (what do you think of …?) was halten Sie von …?; **how are you?** wie befinden Sie sich?; **how beautiful!** wie schön!; **how come?** wieso?, wie kommt es?; **how do you do?** (as a greeting) guten Tag!; (at an introduction) freut mich sehr!; **how many** wie viele; **how much** wieviel; **how on earth** wie in aller Welt; **how the devil** wie zum Teufel || s Wie n

how-do-you-do [′haudəjə′du] s—**that's a fine h.!** (coll) das ist e-e schöne Geschichte!

however adv jedoch, aber; (with adjectives and adverbs) wie … auch immer; **h. it may be** wie es auch sein mag

howitzer [′hau·ɪtsər] s Haubitze f

howl [haul] s Geheul n, Gebrüll n || tr heulen, brüllen; **h. down** (a speaker) niederschreien; **h. out** hinausbrüllen || intr (said of a dog, wolf, wind, etc.) heulen; (in pain, anger) brüllen; **h. with laughter** vor Lachen brüllen

howler [′haulər] s (coll) Schnitzer m

hub [hʌb] s Nabe f, Radnabe f

hubbub [′hʌbʌb] s Rummel m

hubby [′hʌbi] s (coll) Mann m

hub′cap′ s Radkappe f

huckleberry [′hʌkəl‚bɛri] s Heidelbeere f

huckster [′hʌkstər] s (hawker) Straßenhändler m; (peddler) Hausierer m; (adman) Reklamefachmann m || tr verhökern

huddle [′hʌdəl] s (fb) Zusammendrängen n; **go into a h.** die Köpfe zusammenstecken || intr sich zusammendrängen; (fb) sich um den Mannschaftsführer drängen

hue [hju] s Farbton m

hue′ and cry′ s Zetergeschrei n

huff [hʌf] s Aufbrausen n; **in a h.** beleidigt

huffy [′hʌfi] adj übelnehmerisch

hug [hʌg] s Umarmung f; **give s.o. a hug** j-n an sich drücken || v (pret & pp **hugged**) ger **hugging**) tr umar-

men; **hug the road** gut auf der Straße liegen; **hug the shore** sich dicht an der Küste halten || intr einander herzen

huge [hjudʒ] adj riesig, ungeheuer; **h. success** (theat) Bombenerfolg m

hulk [hʌlk] s (body of an old ship) Schiffsrumpf m; (old ship used as a warehouse, etc.) Hulk m & f; **h. of a man** Koloß m

hulk′ing adj ungeschlacht

hull [hʌl] s (of seed) Schale f; (naut) Schiffsrumpf m || tr schälen

hullabaloo [‚hʌləbə′lu] s Heidenlärm m

hum [hʌm] s Summen n || v (pret & pp **hummed**) ger **humming**) tr summen; **hum** (e.g., a tune) **to oneself** vor sich hin summen || intr summen; (fig) in lebhafter Bewegung sein

human [′hjumən] adj menschlich, Menschen-

hu′man be′ing s Mensch m, menschliches Wesen n

humane [hju′men] adj human

humaneness [hju′mennɪs] s Humanität f

humanistic [hjumə′nɪstɪk] adj humanistisch

humanitarian [hju‚mænɪ′tɛrɪ·ən] adj menschenfreundlich || s Menschenfreund –in mf

humanity [hju′mænɪti] s (mankind) Menschheit f; (humaneness) Humanität f, Menschlichkeit f; **humanities** Geisteswissenschaften pl; (Greek and Latin studies) klassische Philologie f

humanize [′hjumə‚naɪz] tr zivilisieren

hu′mankind′ s Menschengeschlecht n

humanly [′hjumənli] adv menschlich; **h. possible** menschenmöglich; **h. speaking** nach menschlichen Begriffen

hu′man na′ture s menschliche Natur f

hu′man race′ s Menschengeschlecht n

humble [′(h)ʌmbəl] adv demütig; (origens) niedrig; **in my h. opinion** nach meiner unmaßgeblichen Meinung || tr demütigen

hum′ble pie′ s—**eat h.** sich demütigen

hum′bug′ s Humbug m

hum′drum′ adj eintönig

humer·us [′hjumərəs] s (–i [‚aɪ]) Oberarmknochen m

humid [′hjumɪd] adj feucht

humidifier [hju′mɪdɪ‚faɪ·ər] s Verdunster m

humidity [hju′mɪdɪti] s Feuchtigkeit f

humiliate [hju′mɪlɪ‚et] tr erniedrigen

humil′iating adj schmachvoll

humiliation [hju‚mɪlɪ′eʃən] s Erniedrigung f

hum′mingbird′ s Kolibri m

humor [′(h)jumər] s (comic quality) Komik f; (frame of mind) Laune f; **in bad** (or **good**) **humor** bei schlechter (or guter) Laune || tr bei guter Laune

humorist [′(h)jumərɪst] s Humorist –in mf

humorous [′(h)jumərəs] adj humorvoll

hump [hʌmp] s Buckel m; (of a camel)

Höcker m; (slight elevation) kleiner Hügel m; over the h. (fig) über den Berg || tr—h. its back (said of an animal) e-n Buckel machen
hump′back′ s Buckel m; (person) Bucklige mf
Hun [hʌn] s (hist) Hunne m, Hunnin f
hunch [hʌntʃ] s (hump) Buckel m; (coll) Ahnung f || intr—h. over sich bücken über (acc)
hunch′back′ s Bucklige mf
hunch′backed′ adj bucklig
hunched adj—h. up zusammengekauert
hundred [′hʌndrəd] adj & pron hundert || s Hundert n; by the h.(s) hundertweise; hundreds (and hundreds) of Hunderte (und aber Hunderte) von
hun′dredfold′ adj & adv hundertfach
hundredth [′hʌndrədθ] adj & pron hundertste; for the h. time (fig) zum X-ten Male; h. anniversary Hundertjahrfeier f || s (fraction) Hundertstel n
hun′dredweight′ s Zentner n
Hungarian [hʌŋ′gerɪ-ən] adj ungarisch || s (person) Ungar -in mf; (language) Ungarisch n
Hungary [′hʌŋgərɪ] s Ungarn n
hunger [′hʌŋgər] s Hunger m || intr hungern; h. for hungern nach
hun′ger strike′ s Hungerstreik m
hungry [′hʌŋgrɪ] adj hungrig; be h. Hunger haben; be h. for (fig) begierig sein nach; go h. am Hungertuch nagen; I feel h. es hungert mich
hunk [hʌŋk] s großes Stück n
hunt [hʌnt] s Jagd f; (search) (for) Suche f (nach); on the h. for auf der Suche nach || tr jagen; (a horse) jagen mit; (look for) suchen; h. down erjagen || intr jagen; h. for suchen; (game) jagen; (a criminal) fahnden nach; go hunting auf die Jagd gehen
hunter [′hʌntər] s Jäger -in mf; (horse) Jagdpferd n
hunt′ing adj (e.g., dog, knife, season) Jagd- || s Jägerei f; (on horseback) Parforcejagd f
hunt′ing ground′ s Jagdrevier n
hunt′ing li′cense s Jagdschein m
hunt′ing lodge′ s Jagdhütte f
huntress [′hʌntrɪs] s Jägerin f
hunts′man s (-men) Weidmann m
hurdle [′hʌrdəl] s Hürde f; (fig) Hindernis n; hurdles (sport) Hürdenlauf m || tr überspringen; (fig) überwinden
hurdygurdy [′hʌrdɪ′gɑrdɪ] s Drehorgel f
hurl [hʌrl] s Wurf m || tr scheudern; h. abuse at s.o. j–m Beleidigungen ins Gesicht schleudern; h. down zu Boden werfen
hurrah [hə′rɑ], **hurray** [hə′re] s Hurra n || interj hurra!
hurricane [′hʌrɪ‚ken] s Orkan m
hur′ricane lamp′ s Sturmlaterne f
hurried [′hʌrɪd] adj eilig, flüchtig
hurriedly [′hʌrɪdlɪ] adv eilig, eilends
hur·ry [′hʌrɪ] s Eile f; be in too much of a h. sich übereilen; in a h. in Eile; there's no h. es hat keine Eile || v

(pret & pp –ried) tr (prod) antreiben; (expedite) beschleunigen; (an activity) zu schnell tun; (to overhasty action) drängen || intr eilen; h. away wegeilen; h. over s.th. etw flüchtig erledigen; h. up sich beeilen
hurt [hʌrt] adj (injured, offended) verletzt; feel h. (about) sich verletzt (or gekränkt) fühlen (durch) || s Verletzung f || v (pret & pp hurt) tr (a person, animal, feelings) verletzen; (e.g., a business) schaden (dat); it hurts him to think of it es schmerzt ihn, daran zu denken || intr (& fig) weh tun, schmerzen; my arm hurts mir tut der Arm weh; that won't h. das schadet nichts; will it h. if I'm late? macht es etw aus, wenn ich zu spät komme?
hurtle [′hʌrtəl] tr schleudern || intr stürzen
husband [′hʌzbənd] s Ehemann m; my h. mein Mann m || tr haushalten mit
hus′bandman s (-men) Landwirt m
husbandry [′hʌzbəndrɪ] s Landwirtschaft f
hush [hʌʃ] s Stille f || tr zur Ruhe bringen; h. up (suppress) vertuschen || intr schweigen || interj still!
hush′-hush′ adj streng vertraulich und geheim
hush′ mon′ey s Schweigegeld n
husk [hʌsk] s Hülse f; (of corn) Maishülse f || tr enthülsen
husky [′hʌskɪ] adj stämmig; (voice) belegt || s Eskimohund m
hussy [′hʌsɪ] s (prostitute) Dirne f; (saucy girl) Fratz m
hustle [′hʌsəl] s (coll) Betriebsamkeit f; h. and bustle Getriebe n || tr (jostle, rush) drängen; (wares, girls) an den Mann bringen; (customers) bearbeiten; (money) betteln || intr rührig sein; (shove) sich drängen; (hasten) hasten; (make money by fraud) Betrügereien verüben; (engage in prostitution) Prostitution betreiben
hustler [′hʌslər] s rühriger Mensch m
hut [hʌt] s Hütte f; (mil) Baracke f
hutch [hʌtʃ] s Stall m
hyacinth [′haɪ‚əsɪnθ] s Hyazinthe f
hybrid [′haɪbrɪd] adj hybrid || s Kreuzung f
hydrant [′haɪdrənt] s Hydrant m
hydrate [′haɪdret] s Hydrat n || tr hydratisieren, hydrieren
hydraulic [haɪ′drɔlɪk] adj hydraulisch || hydraulics s Hydraulik f
hydrau′lic brakes′ spl Öldruckbremsen pl
hydrocarbon [‚haɪdrə′kɑrbən] s Kohlenwasserstoff m
hydrochlor′ic ac′id [‚haɪdrə′klorɪk] s Salzsäure f
hydroelectric [‚haɪdro‚ɪ′lektrɪk] adj hydroelektrisch
hydroelec′tric plant′ s Wasserkraftwerk n
hydrofluo′ric ac′id [‚haɪdrəflu′orɪk] s Flußsäure f
hydrofoil [′haɪdrə‚fɔɪl] s Tragflügelboot n

hydrogen ['haɪdrədʒən] s Wasserstoff *m*

hy'drogen bomb' s Wasserstoffbombe *f*

hy'drogen perox'ide s Wasserstoffsuperoxyd *n*

hydrometer [haɪ'drɑmɪtər] s Hydrometer *m*

hydrophobia [,haɪdrə'fobɪ·ə] s Wasserscheu *f*; (*rabies*) Tollwut *f*

hydrophone ['haɪdrə ,fon] s Unterwasserhorchgerät *n*, Hydrophon *n*

hydroplane ['haɪdrə ,plen] s (aer) Wasserflugzeug *n*; (aer) Gleitfläche *f*; (naut) Gleitboot *n*; (in a submarine) (nav) Tiefenruder *n*

hydroxide [haɪ'drɑksaɪd] s Hydroxyd *n*

hyena [haɪ'inə] s Hyäne *f*

hygiene ['haɪdʒin] s Hygiene *f*; (educ) Gesundheitslehre *f*

hygienic [haɪ'dʒinɪk] adj hygienisch

hymn [hɪm] s Hymne *f*; (eccl) Kirchenlied *n*

hymnal ['hɪmnəl] s Gesangbuch *n*

hymn'book' s Gesangbuch *n*

hyperacidity [,haɪpərə'sɪdɪti] s Übersäuerung *f*

hyperbola [haɪ'pʌrbələ] s Hyperbel *f*

hyperbole [haɪ'pʌrbəli] s Hyperbel *f*

hypersensitive [,haɪpər'sensɪtɪv] adj (to) überempfindlich (gegen)

hypertension [,haɪpər'tenʃən] s Hypertonie *f*

hyphen ['haɪfən] s Bindestrich *m*

hyphenate ['haɪfə ,net] tr mit Bindestrich schreiben

hypnosis [hɪp'nosɪs] s Hypnose *f*

hypnotic [hɪp'nɑtɪk] adj hypnotisch

hypnotism ['hɪpnə ,tɪzəm] s Hypnotismus *m*

hypnotist ['hɪpnətɪst] s Hypnotiseur *m*

hypnotize ['hɪpnə ,taɪz] tr hypnotisieren

hypochondriac [,haɪpə'kɑndrɪ ,æk] s Hypochonder *m*

hypocrisy [hɪ'pɑkrəsi] s Heuchelei *f*

hypocrite ['hɪpəkrɪt] s Heuchler –in *mf*; be a h. heucheln

hypocritical [,hɪpə'krɪtɪkəl] adj heuchlerisch

hypodermic [,haɪpə'dʌrmɪk] adj subkutan || s (injection) subkutane Spritze

hypoderm'ic nee'dle s Injektionsnadel *f*

hypotenuse [haɪ'pɑtɪ ,n(j)us] s Hypotenuse *f*

hypothe·sis [haɪ'pɑθɪsɪs] s (–ses [,siz]) Hypothese *f*

hypothetic(al) [,haɪpə'θetɪk(əl)] adj hypothetisch

hysterectomy [,hɪstə'rektəmi] s Hysterektomie *f*

hysteria [hɪs'tɪrɪ·ə] s Hysterie *f*

hysteric [hɪs'terɪk] adj hysterisch || hysterics spl Hysterie *f*; go into hysterics e–n hysterischen Anfall bekommen

hysterical [hɪs'terɪkəl] adj hysterisch

I

I, i [aɪ] s elfter Buchstabe des englischen Alphabets

I pers pron ich

iambic [aɪ'æmbɪk] adj jambisch

Iberian [aɪ'bɪrɪ·ən] adj iberisch

ibex ['aɪbeks] s (ibexes & ibices ['ɪbɪ ,siz]) Steinbock *m*

ice [aɪs] s Eis *n*; break the ice (coll) das Eis brechen; cut no ice (coll) nicht ziehen || tr (a cake) glasieren || intr—ice up vereisen

ice' age' s Eiszeit *f*

iceberg ['aɪs ,bʌrg] s Eisberg *m*

ice'boat' s (sport) Segelschlitten *m*

ice'bound' adj (boat) eingefroren; (port, river) zugefroren

ice'box' s Eisschrank *m*; (refrigerator) Kühlschrank *m*

ice'break'er s Eisbrecher *m*

ice' buck'et s Sektkübel *m*

ice'cap' s Eiskappe *f*

ice' cream' s Eis *n*, Eiskrem *f*

ice'-cream cone' s Tüte *f* Eis

ice' cube' s Eiswürfel *m*

ice'-cube tray' s Eiswürfelschale *f*

iced' tea' s Eistee *m*

ice' floe' s Eisscholle *f*

ice' hock'ey s Eishockey *n*

Iceland ['aɪslənd] s Island *n*

Icelander ['aɪs ,lændər] s Isländer –in *mf*

Icelandic [aɪs'lændɪk] adj isländisch || s (language) Isländisch *n*

ice'man' s (–men) Eismann *m*

ice' pack' s (geol) Packeis *n*; (med) Eisbeutel *m*

ice' pick' s Eispfriem *m*; (mount) Eispickel *m*

ice' skate' s Schlittschuh *m*

ice'-skate' intr eislaufen

ichthyology [,ɪkθɪ'ɑlədʒi] s Ichthyologie *f*, Fischkunde *f*

icicle ['aɪsɪkəl] s Eiszapfen *m*

icing ['aɪsɪŋ] s Glasur *f*, Zuckerguß *m*; (aer) Vereisung *f*

icon ['aɪkɑn] s Ikone *f*

iconoclast [aɪ'kɑnə ,klæst] s Bilderstürmer –in *mf*

icy ['aɪsi] adj (& fig) eisig

id [ɪd] s (psychol) Es *n*

I.D. card ['aɪ'di'kard] s Ausweis *m*

idea [aɪ'di·ə] s Idee *f*, Vorstellung *f*; (intimation) Ahnung *f*; crazy i. Schnapsidee *f*; have big ideas große Rosinen im Kopf haben; that's the i.! so ist's richtig!; the i.! na so was!; what's the i.? wie kommen Sie darauf?

ideal [aɪ'di·əl] *adj* ideal || *s* Ideal *n*

idealism [aɪ'di·ə,lɪzəm] *s* Idealismus *m*

idealist [aɪ'di·əlɪst] *s* Idealist –in *mf*

idealistic [aɪ,di·ə'lɪstɪk] *adj* idealistisch

idealize [aɪ'di·ə,laɪz] *tr* idealisieren

identical [aɪ'dɛntɪkəl] *adj* identisch

identification [aɪ'dɛntɪfɪ'keʃən] *s* Identifizierung *f*

identifica'tion tag' *s* Erkennungsmarke *f*

identi·fy [aɪ'dɛntɪ,faɪ] *v* (*pret* & *pp* –fied) *tr* identifizieren; **i. oneself** sich ausweisen || *intr*—**i. with** sich einfühlen in (*acc*)

identity [aɪ'dɛntɪti] *s* Identität *f*; **prove one's i.** sich ausweisen

iden'tity card' *s* Ausweis *m*

ideological [,aɪdɪ·ə'lɑdʒɪkəl] *adj* ideologisch

ideology [,aɪdɪ'ɑlədʒi] *s* Ideologie *f*

idiocy ['ɪdɪ·əsɪ] *s* Idiotie *f*

idiom ['ɪdɪ·əm] *s* (*phrase*) Redewendung *f*; (*language, style*) Idiom *n*

idiomatic [,ɪdɪ·ə'mætɪk] *adj* idiomatisch; **i. expression** (idiomatische) Redewendung *f*

idiosyncrasy [,ɪdɪ·ə'sɪnkrəsi] *s* Idiosynkrasie *f*

idiot ['ɪdɪ·ət] *s* Idiot *m*, Trottel *m*

idiotic [,ɪdɪ'ɑtɪk] *adj* idiotisch

idle ['aɪdəl] *adj* (*person, question, hours*) müßig; (*machine, factory*) stillstehend; (*capital*) tot; (*fears*) grundlos; (*talk, threats*) leer; **lie i.** stilliegen; **stand i.** stillstehen || *s* (aut) Leerlauf *m* || *tr* arbeitslos machen; **i. away** vertrödeln || *intr* (aut) leerlaufen

idleness ['aɪdəlnɪs] *s* Müßiggang *m*

idler ['aɪdlər] *s* Müßiggänger *m*

i'dling s (aut) Leerlauf *m*

idol ['aɪdəl] *s* Abgott *m*; (fig) Idol *n*

idolatry [aɪ'dɑlətrɪ] *s* Abgötterei *f*

idolize ['aɪdə,laɪz] *tr* verhimmeln

idyll ['aɪdəl] *s* Idyll *n*, Idylle *f*

idyllic [aɪ'dɪlɪk] *adj* idyllisch

if [ɪf] *s* Wenn *n* || *conj* wenn; (*whether*) ob

igloo ['ɪglu] *s* Schneehütte *f*, Iglu *m* & *n*

ignite [ɪg'naɪt] *tr* & *intr* zünden

ignition [ɪg'nɪʃən] *adj* Zünd– || *s* Entzünden *n*; (aut) Zündung *f*

igni'tion key' *s* Zündschlüssel *m*

igni'tion switch' *s* Zündschloß *n*

ignoble [ɪg'nobəl] *adj* unedel

ignominious [,ɪgnə'mɪnɪ·əs] *adj* schmachvoll, schändlich

ignoramus [,ɪgnə'reməs] *s* Ignorant –in *mf*

ignorance ['ɪgnərəns] *s* Unwissenheit *f*; (of) Unkenntnis *f* (*genit*)

ignorant ['ɪgnərənt] *adj* unwissend; **be i. of** nicht wissen

ignore [ɪg'nor] *tr* ignorieren; (*words*) überhören; (*rules*) nicht beachten

ilk [ɪlk] **s—of that ilk** derselben Art

ill [ɪl] *adj* (*worse* [wʌrs]; *worst* [wʌrst]) krank; (*repute*) schlecht; (*feelings*) feindselig; **fall** (*or* **take**)

ill krank werden || *adv* schlecht; **he can ill afford to** (*inf*) er kann es sich [*dat*] kaum leisten zu (*inf*); **take s.th. ill** etw übelnehmen

ill'-advised' *adj* (*person*) schlecht beraten; (*action*) unbesonnen

ill'-at-ease' *adj* unbehaglich

ill'-bred' *adj* ungezogen

ill'-consid'ered *adj* unbesonnen

ill'-disposed' *adj*—**be i. towards** übelgesinnt sein (*dat*)

illegal [ɪ'ligəl] *adj* illegal

illegible [ɪ'lɛdʒɪbəl] *adj* unlesbar

illegitimate [,ɪlɪ'dʒɪtɪmɪt] *adj* unrechtmäßig; (*child*) illegitim

ill'-fat'ed *adj* unglücklich

illgotten ['ɪl,gɑtən] *adj* unrechtmäßig erworben

ill' health' *s* Kränklichkeit *f*

ill'-hu'mored *adj* übelgelaunt

illicit [ɪ'lɪsɪt] *adj* unerlaubt

illiteracy [ɪ'lɪtərəsɪ] *s* Analphabetentum *n*

illiterate [ɪ'lɪtərɪt] *adj* analphabetisch || *s* Analphabet –in *mf*

ill'-man'nered *adj* ungehobelt

ill'-na'tured *adj* bösartig

illness ['ɪlnɪs] *s* (& fig) Krankheit *f*

illogical [ɪ'lɑdʒɪkəl] *adj* unlogisch

ill'-spent' *adj* verschwendet

ill'-starred' *adj* unglücklich

ill'-suit'ed *adj* (to) unpassend (*dat*)

ill'-tem'pered *adj* schlechtgelaunt

ill'-timed' *adj* unpassend

ill'-treat' *tr* mißhandeln

illuminate [ɪ'lumɪ,net] *tr* beleuchten; (*public buildings, manuscripts*) illuminieren; (*enlighten*) erleuchten; (*explain*) erklären

illumination [ɪ,lumɪ'neʃən] *s* Beleuchten *n*; Erleuchtung *f*; Illuminierung *f*

illusion [ɪ'luʒən] *s* Illusion *f*

illusive [ɪ'lusɪv] *adj* trügerisch

illusory [ɪ'lusərɪ] *adj* illusorisch

illustrate ['ɪləs,tret] *tr* (*exemplify*) erläutern; (*a book*) illustrieren; **illustrated lecture** Lichtbildervortrag *m*; **richly illustrated** bilderreich

illustration [,ɪləs'treʃən] *s* Erläuterung *f*; (*in a book*) Abbildung *f*

illustrative [ɪ'lʌstrətɪv] *adj* erläuternd; **i. material** Anschauungsmaterial *n*

illustrator ['ɪləs,tretər] *s* Illustrator *m*

illustrious [ɪ'lʌstrɪ·əs] *adj* berühmt

ill' will' *s* Feindschaft *f*

image ['ɪmɪdʒ] *s* Bild *n*; (*reflection*) Spiegelbild *n*; (*statue*) Standbild *n*; (*before the public*) Image *n*; (opt, phot, telv) Bild *n*; **the spitting i. of his father** ganz der Vater

imagery ['ɪmɪdʒ(ə)rɪ] *s* Bildersprache *f*

imaginable [ɪ'mædʒɪnəbəl] *adj* erdenklich

imaginary [ɪ'mædʒɪ,nerɪ] *adj* imaginär

imagination [ɪ,mædʒɪ'neʃən] *s* Phantasie *f*, Einbildungskraft *f*; **that's pure i.** das ist pure Einbildung

imaginative [ɪ'mædʒɪnətɪv] *adj* phantasievoll

imagine [ɪ'mædʒɪn] *tr* sich [*dat*] vorstellen, sich [*dat*] denken; **i. oneself**

in sich hineindenken in (acc); **you're only imagining things** das bilden Sie sich [dat] nur ein. || intr—**I can i.** das läßt sich denken; **I i.** so ich glaube schon; **just i.** denken Sie nur mal!

imbecile ['ɪmbɪsɪl] adj geistesschwach || s Geistesschwache mf

imbecility [ˌɪmbɪ'sɪlɪti] s Geistesschwäche f, Blödheit f

imbibe [ɪm'baɪb] tr aufsaugen; (coll) trinken; (fig) (geistig) aufnehmen

imbue [ɪm'bju] tr durchfeuchten; (fig) (with) durchdringen (mit)

imitate ['ɪmɪˌtet] tr nachahmen, nachmachen; **i. s.o. in everything** j–m alles nachmachen

imitation [ˌɪmɪ'teʃən] adj unecht, nachgemacht || s Nachahmung f; **in i. of** nach dem Muster (genit)

imita'tion leath'er s Kunstleder n

imitator ['ɪmɪˌtetər] s Nachahmer –in mf

immaculate [ɪ'mækjəlɪt] adj makellos; (sinless) unbefleckt

immaterial [ˌɪmə'tɪrɪ·əl] adj immateriell, unkörperlich; (unimportant) unwesentlich; **it's i. to me** es is mir gleichgültig

immature [ˌɪmə'tjʊr] adj unreif

immaturity [ˌɪmə'tjʊrɪti] s Unreife f

immeasurable [ɪ'mɛʒərəbəl] adj unermeßlich

immediacy [ɪ'midɪ·əsi] s Unmittelbarkeit f

immediate [ɪ'midɪ·ɪt] adj sofortig; (direct) unmittelbar

immediately [ɪ'midɪ·ɪtli] adv sofort; **i. afterwards** gleich darauf

immemorial [ˌɪmɪ'morɪ·əl] adj uralt; **since time i.** seit Menschengedenken

immense [ɪ'mɛns] adj unermeßlich

immensity [ɪ'mɛnsɪti] s Unermeßlichkeit f

immerse [ɪ'mʌrs] tr (unter)tauchen; **immersed in** (books, thought, work) vertieft in (acc); **i. oneself in** sich vertiefen in (acc)

immersion [ɪ'mʌrʒən] s Untertauchen n; (fig) Versunkenheit f

immigrant ['ɪmɪgrənt] adj einwandernd || s Einwanderer –in mf

immigrate ['ɪmɪˌgret] intr einwandern

immigration [ˌɪmɪ'greʃən] s Einwanderung f

imminent ['ɪmɪnənt] adj drohend

immobile [ɪ'mobɪl] adj unbeweglich

immobilize [ɪ'mobɪˌlaɪz] tr unbeweglich machen; (tanks) bewegungsunfähig machen; (troops) fesseln; (med) ruhigstellen

immoderate [ɪ'modərɪt] adj unmäßig

immodest [ɪ'modɪst] adj unbescheiden

immolate ['ɪməˌlet] tr opfern

immoral [ɪ'morəl] adj unsittlich

immorality [ˌɪmə'rælɪti] s Unsittlichkeit f

immortal [ɪ'mortəl] adj unsterblich

immortality [ˌɪmor'tælɪti] s Unsterblichkeit f

immortalize [ɪ'mortəˌlaɪz] tr unsterblich machen

immovable [ɪ'muvəbəl] adj unbeweglich

immune [ɪ'mjun] adj (free, exempt) (from) immun (gegen); (not responsive) (to) gefeit (gegen); (med) (to) immun (gegen)

immunity [ɪ'mjunɪti] s Immunität f

immunization [ˌɪmjunɪ'zeʃən] s Schutzimpfung f, Immunisierung f

immunize ['ɪmjəˌnaɪz] tr (against) immunisieren (gegen)

immutable [ɪ'mjutəbəl] adj unwandelbar

imp [ɪmp] s Schlingel m

impact ['ɪmpækt] s Anprall m; (of a shell) Aufschlag m; (fig) Einwirkung f

impair [ɪm'pɛr] tr beeinträchtigen

impale [ɪm'pel] tr pfählen

impanel [ɪm'pænəl] v (pret & pp -el[l]ed; ger -el[l]ing) tr in die Geschworenenliste eintragen

impart [ɪm'part] tr mitteilen

impartial [ɪm'parʃəl] adj unparteiisch

impassable [ɪm'pæsəbəl] adj (on foot) ungangbar; (by car) unbefahrbar

impasse [ɪm'impæs] s Sackgasse f; **reach an i.** in e–e Sackgasse geraten

impassible [ɪm'pæsɪbəl] adj (to) unempfindlich (für)

impassioned [ɪm'pæʃənd] adj leidenschaftlich

impassive [ɪm'pæsɪv] adj (person) teilnahmslos; (expression) ausdruckslos

impatience [ɪm'peʃəns] s Ungeduld f

impatient [ɪm'peʃənt] adj ungeduldig

impeach [ɪm'pitʃ] tr (an official) wegen Amtsmißbrauchs unter Anklage stellen; (a witness, motives) in Zweifel ziehen

impeachment [ɪm'pitʃmənt] s (of an official) öffentliche Anklage f; (of a witness, motives) Anzweiflung f

impeccable [ɪm'pɛkəbəl] adj makellos

impecunious [ˌɪmpɪ'kjunɪ·əs] adj mittellos

impede [ɪm'pid] tr behindern, erschweren

impediment [ɪm'pɛdɪmənt] s Behinderung f; (of speech) Sprachfehler m

im-pel [ɪm'pɛl] v (pret & pp -pelled; ger -pelling) tr antreiben

impending [ɪm'pɛndɪŋ] adj nahe bevorstehen; (threatening) drohend

impenetrable [ɪm'pɛnətrəbəl] adj undurchdringlich; (fig) unergründlich

impenitent [ɪm'pɛnɪtənt] adj unbußfertig

imperative [ɪm'pɛrətɪv] adj dringend nötig || s Imperativ m

imper'ative mood' s Befehlsform f

imperceptible [ˌɪmpər'sɛptɪbəl] adj nicht wahrnehmbar, unmerklich

imperfect [ɪm'pʌrfɪkt] adj unvollkommen || s (gram) Imperfekt(um) n

imperfection [ˌɪmpər'fɛkʃən] s Unvollkommenheit f; (flaw) Fehler m

imperial [ɪm'pɪrɪ·əl] adj kaiserlich

imperialism [ɪm'pɪrɪ·əˌlɪzəm] s Imperialismus m

imperialist [ɪm'pɪrɪ·əlɪst] adj imperialistisch || s Imperialist –in mf

imper·il [ɪm'perɪl] v (pret & pp
 -il[l]ed; ger **-il[l]ing**) tr gefährden
imperious [ɪm'perɪ·əs] adj herrisch, anmaßend
imperishable [ɪm'perɪʃəbəl] adj unver-
 gänglich
impersonal [ɪm'pʌrsənəl] adj unpersönlich
impersonate [ɪm'pʌrsə‚net] tr (imitate) nachmachen; (e.g., an officer)
 sich ausgeben als; (theat) darstellen
impersonator [ɪm'pʌrsə‚netər] s Imitator -in mf
impertinence [ɪm'pʌrtɪnəns] s Ungezogenheit f
impertinent [ɪm'pʌrtɪnənt] adj ungezogen
imperturbable [‚ɪmpʌr'tʌrbəbəl] adj
 unerschütterlich
impetuous [ɪm'petʃʊ·əs] adj ungestüm
impetus ['ɪmpɪtəs] s (& fig) Antrieb
 m
impiety [ɪm'paɪ·əti] s Gottlosigkeit f
impinge [ɪm'pɪndʒ] intr—**i. on** (an)
 stoßen an (acc); (said of rays) fallen
 auf (acc); (fig) eingreifen in (acc)
impious ['ɪmpɪ·əs] adj gottlos
impish ['ɪmpɪʃ] adj spitzbübisch
implant [ɪm'plænt] tr einpflanzen
implement ['ɪmplɪmənt] s Werkzeug
 n, Gerät n || ['ɪmplɪ‚ment] tr durch-
 führen
implicate ['ɪmplɪ‚ket] tr (in) verwickeln (in acc)
implication [‚ɪmplɪ'keʃən] s (involvement) Verwicklung f; (implying) Andeutung f; **implications** Folgerungen
 pl
implicit [ɪm'plɪsɪt] adj (approval) stillschweigend; (trust) unbedingt
implied [ɪm'plaɪd] adj stillschweigend
implore [ɪm'plor] tr anflehen
im·ply [ɪm'plaɪ] v (pret & pp **-plied**)
 tr (express indirectly) andeuten; (involve) in sich schließen; (said of
 words) besagen
impolite [‚ɪmpə'laɪt] adj unhöflich
import ['ɪmport] s Import m, Einfuhr
 f; (meaning) Bedeutung f; **imports**
 Einfuhrwaren pl || [ɪm'port], ['ɪm-
 port] tr importieren, einführen
importance [ɪm'portəns] s Wichtigkeit
 f; **a man of i.** ein Mann m von Bedeutung; **of no i.** unwichtig
important [ɪm'portənt] adj wichtig
im'port du'ty s Einfuhrzoll m
importer [ɪm'portər] s Importeur m
importune [‚ɪmpor't(j)un] adj auf-
 dringlich || tr bestürmen
impose [ɪm'poz] tr (on, upon) auf-
 erlegen (dat) || intr—**i. on** über Ge-
 bühr beanspruchen
impos'ing adj imposant
imposition [‚ɪmpə'zɪʃən] s (of hands,
 of an obligation) Auferlegung f; (taking unfair advantage) Zumutung f
impossible [ɪm'pɑsɪbəl] adj unmöglich
impostor [ɪm'pɑstər] s Hochstapler m
imposture [ɪm'pɑstʃər] s Hochstapelei
 f
impotence ['ɪmpətəns] s Machtlosig-
 keit f; (pathol) Impotenz f

impotent ['ɪmpətənt] adj machtlos;
 (pathol) impotent
impound [ɪm'paʊnd] tr beschlagnahmen
impoverish [ɪm'pɑvərɪʃ] tr arm machen; **become impoverished** verarmen
impracticable [ɪm'præktɪkəbəl] adj unausführbar
impractical [ɪm'præktɪkəl] adj un-
 praktisch
impregnable [ɪm'pregnəbəl] adj unein-
 nehmbar
impregnate [ɪm'pregnet] tr (saturate)
 imprägnieren; (& fig) schwängern
impresari·o [‚ɪmprɪ'sarɪ‚o] s (**-os**)
 Impresario m
impress [ɪm'pres] tr (affect) imponieren (dat), beeindrucken; (imprint,
 emphasize) einprägen; **i. s.th. on s.o.**
 j-m etw einprägen
impression [ɪm'preʃən] s Eindruck m;
 (stamp) Gepräge n; **try to make an i.**
 Eindruck schinden
impressive [ɪm'presɪv] adj eindrucksvoll
imprint ['ɪmprɪnt] s Aufdruck m; (fig)
 Eindruck m || [ɪm'prɪnt] tr (on) auf-
 drucken (auf acc); **i. on s.o.'s** memory j-m ins Gedächtnis einprägen
imprison [ɪm'prɪzən] tr einsperren
imprisonment [ɪm'prɪzənmənt] s Haft
 f; (penalty) Freiheitsstrafe f; (captivity) Gefangenschaft f
improbable [ɪm'prɑbəbəl] adj unwahrscheinlich
impromptu [ɪm'prɑmpt(j)u] adj & adv
 aus dem Stegreif || s Stegreifstück n
improper [ɪm'prɑpər] adj ungehörig,
 unschicklich; (use) unzulässig
improve [ɪm'pruv] tr verbessern; (relations) ausbauen; (land) kultivieren;
 (a salary) aufbessern; **i. oneself** sich
 bessern; (financially) sich verbessern
 || intr bessern; (com) sich erholen;
 i. on Verbesserungen vornehmen an
 (dat)
improvement [ɪm'pruvmənt] s Verbesserung f; (reworking) Umarbeitung
 f; (of money value) Erholung f; (of
 a salary) Aufbesserung f; (in health)
 Besserung f; **be an i. on** ein Fortschritt sein gegenüber
improvident [ɪm'prɑvɪdənt] adj unbedacht
improvise ['ɪmprə‚vaɪz] tr improvisie-
 ren || intr improvisieren; (mus) phan-
 tasieren
imprudence [ɪm'prudəns] s Unklugheit
 f
imprudent [ɪm'prudənt] adj unklug
impudence ['ɪmpjədəns] s Unverschämtheit f
impudent ['ɪmpjədənt] adj unverschämt
impugn [ɪm'pjun] tr bestreiten
impulse ['ɪmpʌls] s Impuls m; **act on i.**
 impulsiv handeln
impulsive [ɪm'pʌlsɪv] adj impulsiv
impunity [ɪm'pjunɪti] s Straffreiheit
 f; **with i.** ungestraft
impure [ɪm'pjur] adj (& fig) unrein

impurity [ɪmˈpjuːrɪtɪ] s (& fig) Unreinheit f

impute [ɪmˈpjuːt] tr (to) unterstellen (dat)

in [ɪn] adv (position) drin, drinnen; (direction away from the speaker) hinein; (direction toward the speaker) herein; **be all in** ganz erschöpft sein; **be in** da sein; (said of a political party) an der Macht sein; (be in style) in Mode sein; **be in for** zu erwarten haben; **have it in for** auf dem Strich haben ‖ s—**the ins and outs of** die Einzelheiten (genit) ‖ prep (position) in (dat); (direction) in (acc); (e.g., the morning, afternoon, evening) am; (a field, the country; one eye) auf (dat); (one's opinion; all probability) nach (dat); (circumstances; a reign) unter (dat); (ink; one stroke) mit (dat); (because of pain, joy, etc.) vor (dat); **he doesn't have it in him to** (inf) er hat nicht das Zeug dazu zu (inf); **in German** auf deutsch

inability [ˌɪnəˈbɪlɪtɪ] s Unfähigkeit f; **i. to pay** Zahlungsunfähigkeit f

inaccessible [ˌɪnækˈsesɪbəl] adj unzugänglich

inaccuracy [ɪnˈækjərəsɪ] s Ungenauigkeit f

inaccurate [ɪnˈækjərɪt] adj ungenau

inaction [ɪnˈækʃən] s Untätigkeit f

inactive [ɪnˈæktɪv] adj untätig; (chem) unwirksam; (mil) ruhig; lustlos

inactivity [ˌɪnækˈtɪvɪtɪ] s Untätigkeit f

inadequate [ɪnˈædɪkwɪt] adj unangemessen

inadmissible [ˌɪnədˈmɪsɪbəl] adj unstatthaft, unzulässig

inadvertent [ˌɪnədˈvʌrtənt] adj versehentlich

inadvisable [ɪnədˈvaɪzəbəl] adj nicht ratsam

inalienable [ɪnˈeljənəbəl] adj unveräußerlich

inane [ɪnˈen] adj leer, unsinnig

inanimate [ɪnˈænɪmɪt] adj unbeseelt

inappropriate [ˌɪnəˈproprɪ·ɪt] adj unangemessen

inarticulate [ˌɪnɑrˈtɪkjəlɪt] adj unartikuliert, undeutlich

inartistic [ˌɪnɑrˈtɪstɪk] adj unkünstlerisch, kunstlos

inasmuch as [ˌɪnəzˈmʌtʃ ˌæz] conj da

inattentive [ˌɪnəˈtentɪv] adv (to) unaufmerksam (or unachtsam) (gegenüber)

inaudible [ɪnˈɔdɪbəl] adj unhörbar

inaugural [ɪnˈɔg(j)ərəl] adj Antritts—

inaugurate [ɪnˈɔg(j)ə·ˌret] tr feierlich eröffnen; (a new policy) einleiten

inauguration [ɪnˌɔg(j)əˈreʃən] s Eröffnung f; (of an official) Amtsantritt m

inauspicious [ˌɪnɔˈspɪəs] adj ungünstig

inborn [ˈɪn ˌbɔrn] adj angeboren

inbred [ˈɪn ˌbred] adj angeboren, ererbt

in'breed'ing s Inzucht f

incalculable [ɪnˈkælkjələbəl] adj unberechenbar

incandescent [ˌɪnkənˈdesənt] adj Glühend

incantation [ˌɪnkænˈteʃən] s Beschwörung f

incapable [ɪnˈkepəbəl] adj untüchtig; **i. of** (ger) nicht fähig zu (inf)

incapacitate [ˌɪnkəˈpæsɪˌtet] tr unfähig machen; (jur) für geschäftsunfähig erklären

incarcerate [ɪnˈkɑrsə·ˌret] tr einkerkern

incarnate [ɪnˈkɑrnet] adj—**God i.** Gottmensch m; **the devil i.** der Teufel in Menschengestalt

incarnation [ˌɪnkɑrˈneʃən] s (fig) Verkörperung f; (eccl) Fleischwerdung f

incendiary [ɪnˈsendɪ ˌerɪ] adj Brand—; (fig) aufhetzend ‖ s Brandstifter –in mf

incense [ˈɪnsɛns] s Weihrauch m ‖ tr (eccl) beräuchern ‖ [ɪnˈsɛns] tr erzürnen

in'cense burn'er s Räuchergefäß n

incentive [ɪnˈsɛntɪv] s Anreiz m

inception [ɪnˈsepʃən] s Anfang m

incessant [ɪnˈsesənt] adj unaufhörlich

incest [ˈɪnsɛst] s Blutschande f

incestuous [ɪnˈsɛst/u·əs] adj blutschänderisch

inch [ɪntʃ] s Zoll m; **beat within an i. of one's life** fast zu Tode prügeln; **by inches** nach und nach; **not yield an i.** keinen Fußbreit nachgeben ‖ intr—**i. along** dahinschleichen; **i. forward** langsam vorrücken

incidence [ˈɪnsɪdəns] s Vorkommen n

incident [ˈɪnsɪdənt] s Vorfall m; (adverse event) Zwischenfall m

incidental [ˌɪnsɪˈdentəl] adj zufällig; **i. to** gehörig zu ‖ **incidentals** spl Nebenausgaben pl

incidentally [ˌɪnsɪˈdɛntəlɪ] adv übrigens

incinerate [ɪnˈsɪnə·ˌret] tr einäschern

incinerator [ɪnˈsɪnə·ˌretər] s Verbrennungsofen m

incipient [ɪnˈsɪpɪ·ənt] adv beginnend

incision [ɪnˈsɪʒən] s Schnitt m

incisive [ɪnˈsaɪsɪv] adj (biting) beißend; (penetrating) durchdringend; (sharp) scharf

incisor [ɪnˈsaɪzər] s Schneidezahn m

incite [ɪnˈsaɪt] tr aufreizen, aufhetzen

inclement [ɪnˈklemənt] adj ungünstig

inclination [ˌɪnklɪˈneʃən] s (& fig) Neigung f

incline [ˈɪnklaɪn] s Abhang m ‖ [ɪnˈklaɪn] tr neigen ‖ intr (towards) sich neigen (nach or zu); (fig) (towards) neigen (zu); **the roof inclines sharply** das Dach fällt steil ab

include [ɪnˈklud] tr einschließen; **i. among** rechnen unter (acc); **i. in** einrechnen in (acc)

includ'ed adj (mit) inbegriffen

includ'ing prep einschließlich (genit)

inclusive [ɪnˈklusɪv] adj umfassend, gesamt; **all i.** alles inbegriffen; **from ... to ... i.** von ... zu ... einschließlich (or inklusive); **i. of** einschließlich (genit)

incognito [ɪn'kɒgnɪ,to] *adv* inkognito
incoherent [,ɪnko'hɪrənt] *adj* unzusammenhängend; **be i.** (*said of a person*) nicht ganz bei sich sein
incombustible [,ɪnkəm'bʌstɪbəl] *adj* unverbrennbar
income ['ɪnkʌm] *s* (**from**) Einkommen *n* (aus)
in'come tax' *s* Einkommensteuer *f*
in'come-tax return' *s* Einkommensteuererklärung *f*
in'com'ing *adj* (*e.g., tide*) hereinkommend; (*bus, train*) ankommend; (*official*) neu eintretend; **i. goods, i. mail** Eingänge *pl*
incomparable [ɪn'kɒmpərəbəl] *adj* unvergleichlich
incompatible [,ɪnkəm'pætɪbəl] *adj* (**with**) unvereinbar (mit); (*persons*) unverträglich
incompetent [ɪn'kɒmpɪtənt] *adj* untauglich; (*not legally qualified*) nicht zuständig; (*not legally capable*) geschäftsunfähig; (*inadmissible*) unzulässig ‖ *s* Nichtkönner –in *mf*
incomplete [,ɪnkəm'plit] *adj* unvollständig
incomprehensible [,ɪnkɒmprɪ'hɛnsɪbəl] *adj* unbegreiflich
inconceivable [,ɪnkən'sivəbəl] *adj* undenkbar
inconclusive [,ɪnkən'klusɪv] *adj* (*not convincing*) nicht überzeugend; (*leading to no result*) ergebnislos
incongruous [ɪn'kɒŋgru·əs] *adj* nicht übereinstimmend
inconsequential [ɪn,kɒnsɪ'kwɛnʃəl] *adj* belanglos
inconsiderate [,ɪnkən'sɪdərɪt] *adj* unüberlegt; (*towards*) rücksichtslos (gegen)
inconsistency [,ɪnkən'sɪstənsi] *s* (*lack of logical connection*) Inkonsequenz *f*; (*contradiction*) Unstimmigkeit *f*; (*instability*) Unbeständigkeit *f*
inconsistent [,ɪnkən'sɪstənt] *adj* inkonsequent; (*uneven*) unbeständig
inconspicuous [,ɪnkən'spɪkju·əs] *adj* unauffällig
inconstant [ɪn'kɒnstənt] *adj* unbeständig
incontinent [ɪn'kɒntɪnənt] *adj* zügellos
incontrovertible [,ɪnkɒntrə'vʌrtɪbəl] *adj* unwiderlegbar
inconvenience [,ɪnkən'vini·əns] *s* Ungelegenheit *f* ‖ *tr* bemühen, belästigen
inconvenient [,ɪnkən'vini·ənt] *adj* ungelegen
incorporate [ɪn'kɒrpə,ret] *tr* einverleiben; (*an organization*) zu e–e Körperschaft machen ‖ *intr* e–e Körperschaft werden
incorporation [ɪn,kɒrpə'reʃən] *s* Einverleibung *f*; (*jur*) Körperschaftsbildung *f*
incorrect [,ɪnkə'rɛkt] *adj* unrichtig, falsch; (*conduct*) unschicklich
incorrigible [ɪn'kɒrɪdʒɪbəl] *adj* unverbesserlich
increase ['ɪnkris] *s* Zunahme *f*; **be on the i.** steigen; **i. in costs** Kostensteigerung *f*; **i. in pay** Gehaltser-

höhung *f*; (*mil*) Solderhöhung *f*; **i. in population** Bevölkerungszunahme *f*; **i. in prices** Preiserhöhung *f*; **i. in rent** Mieterhöhung *f*; **i. in taxes** Steuererhöhung *f*; **i. in value** Wertsteigerung *f*; **i. in weight** Gewichtszunahme *f* ‖ [ɪn'kris] *tr* (*in size*) vergrößern; (*in height*) erhöhen; (*in quantity*) vermehren; (*in intensity*) verstärken; (*prices*) heraufsetzen ‖ *intr* zunehmen, sich vergrößern; (*rise*) sich erhöhen; (*in quantity*) sich vermehren; (*in intensity*) sich verstärken; **i. in** zunehmen an (*dat*)
increasingly [ɪn'krisɪŋli] *adv* immer mehr; **i. more difficult** immer schwieriger
incredible [ɪn'krɛdɪbəl] *adj* unglaublich
incredulous [ɪn'krɛdʒələs] *adj* ungläubig
increment ['ɪnkrɪmənt] *s* Zunahme *f*, Zuwachs *m*; (*in pay*) Gehaltszulage *f*
incriminate [ɪn'krɪmɪ,net] *tr* belasten
incrust [ɪn'krʌst] *tr* überkrusten
incubate ['ɪnkjə,bet] *tr & intr* brüten
incubator ['ɪnkjə,betər] *s* Brutapparat *m*
inculcate [ɪn'kʌlket], ['ɪnkʌl,ket] *tr* (**in**) einprägen (*dat*)
incumbency [ɪn'kʌmbənsi] *s* (*obligation*) Obliegenheit *f*; (*term of office*) Amtszeit *f*
incumbent [ɪn'kʌmbənt] *adj*—**be i. on** obliegen (*dat*) ‖ *s* Amtsinhaber –in *mf*
incunabula [,ɪnkju'næbjələ] *spl* (*typ*) Wiegendrucke *pl*
in·cur [ɪn'kʌr] *v* (*pret & pp* –**curred**; *ger* –**curring**) *tr* sich [*dat*] zuziehen; (*debts*) machen; (*a loss*) erleiden; (*a risk*) eingehen
incurable [ɪn'kjurəbəl] *adj* unheilbar ‖ *s* unheilbarer Kranke *m*
incursion [ɪn'kʌrʒən] *s* Einfall *m*
indebted [ɪn'dɛtɪd] *adj* (**to**) verschuldet (bei); **be i. to s.o. for s.th.** j–m etw zu verdanken haben
indecency [ɪn'disənsi] *s* Unsittlichkeit *f*
indecent [ɪn'disənt] *adj* unsittlich; **i. assault** Sittlichkeitsvergehen *n*
indecision [,ɪndɪ'sɪʒən] *s* Unentschlossenheit *f*
indecisive [,ɪndɪ'saɪsɪv] *adj* (*person*) unentschlossen; (*battle*) nicht entscheidend
indeclinable [,ɪndɪ'klaɪnəbəl] *adj* undeklinierbar
indeed [ɪn'did] *adv* ja, zwar ‖ *interj* jawohl!
indefatigable [,ɪndɪ'fætɪgəbəl] *adj* unermüdlich
indefensible [,ɪndɪ'fɛnsɪbəl] *adj* nicht zu verteidigen(d); (*argument*) unhaltbar; (*behavior*) unentschuldbar
indefinable [,ɪndɪ'faɪnəbəl] *adj* undefinierbar
indefinite [ɪn'dɛfɪnɪt] *adj* (*unlimited*) unbegrenzt; (*not exact*) unbestimmt; (*answer*) ausweichend; (*vague*) undeutlich; (*gram*) unbestimmt

indelible [ɪnˈdelɪbəl] *adj (ink, pencil)* wasserfest; *(fig)* unauslöschlich

indelicate [ɪnˈdelɪkɪt] *adj* unzart

indemnification [ɪnˌdemnɪfɪˈkeʃən] *s* Schadenersatzleistung *f*

indemni·fy [ɪnˈdemnɪˌfaɪ] *v (pret & pp –fied) tr* entschädigen

indemnity [ɪnˈdemnɪtɪ] *s* Schadenersatz *m*

indent [ɪnˈdent] *tr (notch)* einkerben; *(the coast)* tiefe Einschnitte bilden in *(dat)*; *(typ)* einrücken ‖ *intr (typ)* einrücken

indentation [ˌɪndənˈteʃən] *s* Kerbe *f*; *(typ)* Absatz *m*

indenture [ɪnˈdentʃər] *s (service contract)* Arbeitsvertrag *m*; *(apprentice contract)* Lehrvertrag *m* ‖ *tr* vertraglich binden

independence [ˌɪndɪˈpendəns] *s* Unabhängigkeit *f*

independent [ˌɪndɪˈpendənt] *adj (of)* unabhängig (von) ‖ *s* Unabhängige *mf*

indescribable [ˌɪndɪˈskraɪbəbəl] *adj* unbeschreiblich

indestructible [ˌɪndɪˈstrʌktɪbəl] *adj* unzerstörbar

index [ˈɪndeks] *s (indexes & indices* [ˈɪndɪˌsiz]*) (in a book)* Register *n*; *(fig) (to)* Hisweis *m* (auf *acc*); **Index** *m* ‖ *tr* registrieren; *(a book)* mit e–m Register versehen

in′dex card′ *s* Karteikarte *f*

in′dex fin′ger *s* Zeigefinger *m*

India [ˈɪndɪ-ə] *s* Indien *n*

In′dia ink′ *s* chinesische Tusche *f*

Indian [ˈɪndɪ-ən] *adj* indisch; *(e.g., chief, tribe)* Indianer– ‖ *s (of India)* Inder –in *mf*; *(of North America)* Indianer –in *mf*; *(of Central or South America)* Indio *m*

In′dian corn′ *s* Mais *m*

In′dian file′ *adv* in Gänsemarsch

In′dian O′cean *s* Indischer Ozean *m*

In′dian sum′mer *s* Altweibersommer *m*

indicate [ˈɪndɪˌket] *tr* angeben, anzeigen

indication [ˌɪndɪˈkeʃən] *s* Angabe *f*; *(of s.th. imminent)* (of) Anzeichen *n (für)*; **give i. of** anzeigen

indicative [ɪnˈdɪkatɪv] *adj (gram)* indikativ; **be i. of** hindeuten auf *(acc)* ‖ *s (gram)* Wirklichkeitsform *f*, Indikativ *m*

indicator [ˈɪndɪˌketər] *s* Zeiger *m*

indict [ɪnˈdaɪt] *tr (for)* anklagen (wegen)

indictment [ɪnˈdaɪtmənt] *s* Anklage *f*

indifference [ɪnˈdɪfərəns] *s (to)* Gleichgültigkeit *f* (gegen or gegenüber)

indifferent [ɪnˈdɪfərənt] *adj (mediocre)* mittelmäßig; *(to)* gleichgültig (gegen)

indigenous [ɪnˈdɪdʒɪnəs] *adj (to)* einheimisch (in *dat*)

indigent [ˈɪndɪdʒənt] *adj* bedürftig

indigestible [ˌɪndɪˈdʒestɪbəl] *adj* unverdaulich

indigestion [ˌɪndɪˈdʒestʃən] *s* Verdauungsstörung *f*, Magenverstimmung *f*

indignant [ɪnˈdɪgnənt] *adj (at)* empört *(über acc)*

indignation [ˌɪndɪgˈneʃən] *s (at)* Empörung *f (über acc)*

indignity [ɪnˈdɪgnɪtɪ] *s* Beleidigung *f*

indigo [ˈɪndɪˌgo] *adj* Indigo– ‖ *s* Indigo *m & n*

indirect [ˌɪndɪˈrekt] *adj* indirekt

in′direct dis′course *s* indirekte Rede

in′direct ques′tion *s* indirekter Fragesatz *m*

indiscreet [ˌɪndɪsˈkrit] *adj* indiskret

indiscretion [ˌɪndɪsˈkreʃən] *s* Indiskretion *f*

indiscriminate [ˌɪndɪsˈkrɪmɪnɪt] *adj* unterschiedslos

indispensable [ˌɪndɪsˈpensəbəl] *adj* unentbehrlich

indisposed *adj (ill)* unpäßlich; **i. to** abgeneigt *(dat)*

indissoluble [ˌɪndɪˈsɑljəbəl] *adj* unauflösbar

indistinct [ˌɪndɪˈstɪŋkt] *adj* undeutlich

individual [ˌɪndɪˈvɪdʒu-əl] *adj* individuell, Einzel–, einzeln ‖ *s* Individuum *n*

individ′ual case′ *s* Einzelfall *m*

individuality [ˌɪndɪˌvɪdʒuˈælɪtɪ] *s* Individualität *f*

individually [ˌɪndɪˈvɪdʒu-əlɪ] *adv* einzeln

indivisible [ˌɪndɪˈvɪzɪbəl] *adj* unteilbar

Indochina [ˈɪndoˈtʃaɪnə] *s* Indochina *n*

indoctrinate [ɪnˈdɑktrɪˌnet] *tr (in)* schulen (in *dat*), unterweisen (in *dat*)

indoctrination [ˌɪndɑktrɪˈneʃən] *s* Schulung *f*, Unterweisung *f*

Indo-European [ˈɪndoˌjurəˈpi-ən] *adj* indogermanisch ‖ *s (language)* Indogermanisch *n*

indolence [ˈɪndələns] *s* Trägheit *f*

indolent [ˈɪndələnt] *adj* träge

Indonesia [ˌɪndoˈniʒə] *s* Indonesien *n*

Indonesian [ˌɪndoˈniʒən] *adj* indonesisch ‖ *s* Indonesier –in *mf*

indoor [ˈɪnˌdor] *adj* Haus–, Zimmer–, Innen–; *(sport)* Hallen–

indoors [ɪnˈdorz] *adv* innen, drin(nen)

in′door shot′ *s (phot)* Innenaufnahme *f*

induce [ɪnˈd(j)us] *tr* veranlassen, bewegen; *(bring about)* verursachen; *(elec, phys)* induzieren

inducement [ɪnˈd(j)usmənt] *s* Anreiz *m*

induct [ɪnˈdʌkt] *tr (into)* einführen (in *acc*); *(mil) (into)* einberufen (zu)

inductee [ˌɪnˈdʌkti] *s* Einberufene *mf*

induction [ɪnˈdʌkʃən] *s* Einführung *f*; *(elec, log)* Induktion *f*; *(mil)* Einberufung *f*

induc′tion coil′ *s* Induktionsspule *f*

indulge [ɪnˈdʌldʒ] *tr (a desire)* frönen *(dat)*; *(a person)* befriedigen; *(children)* verwöhnen; **i. oneself** in schwelgen in *(dat)* ‖ *intr (coll)* trinken; **i. in s.th.** sich *(dat)* etw gestatten

indulgence [ɪnˈdʌldʒəns] *s (of a desire)* Frönen *n*; *(tolerance)* Duldung *f*; *(relig)* Ablaß *m*; **ask s.o.'s i.** j–n um Nachsicht bitten

indulgent [ɪnˈdʌldʒənt] *adj* schonend; *(toward)* nachsichtig (gegen)

industrial [ɪnˈdʌstrɪ-əl] *adj (e.g., bank,*

center, alcohol, product, worker)
Industrie–; (e.g., accident, medicine)
Betriebs–; (e.g., revolution) industri-
ell; (e.g., school, engineering) Gewerbe–

industrialist [ɪn'dʌstrɪ·əlɪst] s In-
dustrielle mf

industrialize [ɪn'dʌstrɪ·ə‚laɪz] tr industrialisieren

indus'trial man'agement s Betriebs-
wirtschaft f

industrious [ɪn'dʌstrɪ·əs] adj fleißig

industry ['ɪndəstri] s Industrie f; (energy) Fleiß m

inebriated [ɪn'ibrɪ‚etɪd] adj betrunken

inedible [ɪn'edɪbəl] adj ungenießbar

ineffable [ɪn'efəbəl] adj unaussprechlich

ineffective [‚ɪnɪ'fektɪv] adj unwirksam; (person) untüchtig

ineffectual [‚ɪnɪ'fekt/ʊ·əl] adj unwirksam

inefficient [‚ɪnɪ'fɪʃənt] adj untüchtig;
(process, procedure) unrationell;
(mach) nicht leistungsfähig

ineligible [ɪn'elɪdʒɪbəl] adj nicht wählbar; (not suitable) ungeeignet

inept [ɪn'ept] adj ungeschickt

inequality [‚ɪnɪ'kwɑlɪti] s Ungleichheit f

inequity [ɪn'ekwɪti] s Ungerechtigkeit
f

inertia [ɪn'ʌrʃə] s Trägheit f

inescapable [‚ɪnes'kepəbəl] adj unentrinnbar, unabwendbar

inevitable [ɪn'evɪtəbəl] adj unvermeid-
lich, unausweichlich

inexact [‚ɪneg'zækt] adj ungenau

inexcusable [‚ɪneks'kjuzəbəl] adj unentschuldbar

inexhaustible [‚ɪneg'zɔstɪbəl] adj unerschöpflich

inexorable [ɪn'eksərəbəl] adj unerbittlich

inexpensive [‚ɪnek'spensɪv] adj billig

inexperience [‚ɪnek'spɪrɪ·əns] s Unerfahrenheit f

inexpe'rienced adj unerfahren

inexplicable [ɪn'eksplɪkəbəl] adj uner-
klärlich

inexpressible [‚ɪnek'spresɪbəl] adj unaussprechlich

infallibility [‚ɪnfælɪ'bɪlɪti] s Unfehl-
barkeit f

infallible [ɪn'fælɪbəl] adj unfehlbar

infamous ['ɪnfəməs] adj schändlich

infamy ['ɪnfəmi] s Schändlichkeit f

infancy ['ɪnfənsi] s Kindheit f; be still
in its i. (fig) noch in den Kinder-
schuhen stecken

infant ['ɪnfənt] adj Säuglings– ‖ s
Kleinkind n, Säugling m

infantile ['ɪnfən‚taɪl] adj infantil

in'fantile paral'ysis s Kinderlähmung f

infantry ['ɪnfəntri] s Infanterie f

in'fantry·man s (-men) Infanterist m

infatuated [ɪn'fæt/ʊ‚etɪd] adj betört

infatuation [ɪn‚fæt/ʊ'eʃən] s Betörung
f

infect [ɪn'fekt] tr anstecken, infizieren; **become infected** sich anstecken

infection [ɪn'fekʃən] s Ansteckung f

infectious [ɪn'fekʃəs] adj (& fig) ansteckend

in-fer [ɪn'fʌr] v (pret & pp –ferred;
ger –ferring) tr folgern

inference ['ɪnfərəns] s Folgerung f

inferior [ɪn'fɪrɪ·ər] adj (in rank) niedriger; (in worth) minderwertig; (to)
unterlegen (dat)

inferiority [ɪn‚fɪrɪ'ɑrɪti] s Unterlegen-
heit f; (in worth) Minderwertigkeit f

inferior'ity com'plex s Minderwertig-
keitskomplex m

infernal [ɪn'fʌrnəl] adj höllisch

infest [ɪn'fest] tr in Schwärmen überfallen; **be infested with** wimmeln von

infidel ['ɪnfɪdəl] adj ungläubig ‖ s
Ungläubige mf

infidelity [‚ɪnfɪ'delɪti] s Untreue f

in'field s (baseball) Innenfeld n

infiltrate [ɪn'fɪltret], ['ɪnfɪl‚tret] tr
(filter through) infiltrieren; (mil)
durchsickern durch; (pol) unterwan-
dern ‖ intr infiltrieren

infinite ['ɪnfɪnɪt] adj unendlich

infinitive [ɪn'fɪnɪtɪv] s (gram) Nennform f, Infinitiv m

infinity [ɪn'fɪnɪti] s Unendlichkeit f;
to i. endlos

infirm [ɪn'fʌrm] adj schwach; (from
age) altersschwach

infirmary [ɪn'fʌrməri] s Krankenstube
f; (mil) Revier n

infirmity [ɪn'fʌrmɪti] s Schwachheit f

inflame [ɪn'flem] tr (fig & pathol) entzünden; **become inflamed** sich entzünden

inflammable [ɪn'flæməbəl] adj entzündbar, feuergefährlich

inflammation [‚ɪnflə'meʃən] s Entzündung f

inflammatory [ɪn'flæmə‚tori] adj aufrührerisch; (pathol) Entzündungs–

inflate [ɪn'flet] tr aufblasen; (tires)
aufpumpen

inflation [ɪn'fleʃən] s (econ) Inflation
f

inflationary [ɪn'fleʃə‚neri] adj infla-
tionistisch

inflect [ɪn'flekt] tr (the voice) modulieren; (gram) flektieren

inflection [ɪn'flekʃən] s (of the voice)
Tonfall m; (gram) Flexion f

inflexible [ɪn'fleksɪbəl] adj unbiegsam;
(person) unbeugsam; (law) unabänderlich

inflict [ɪn'flɪkt] tr (punishment) (on)
auferlegen (dat); (a defeat) (on) zufügen (dat); (a wound) (on) beibringen (dat)

influence ['ɪnflu·əns] s (on) Einfluß m
(auf acc) ‖ tr beeinflussen

influential [‚ɪnflu'enʃəl] adj einfluß-
reich, maßgebend

influenza [‚ɪnflu'enzə] s Grippe f

influx ['ɪnflʌks] s Zufluß m

inform [ɪn'fɔrm] tr (of) benachrichtigen (von) ‖ intr—**i. against** anzeigen

informal [ɪn'fɔrməl] adj zwanglos

informant [ɪn'fɔrmənt] s Gewährsmann m

information [‚ɪnfər'meʃən] s Nachricht
f, Auskunft f; (items of information)

Informationen *pl;* **a piece of i.** e-e Auskunft *f;* **for your i.** zu Ihrer Information

informa'tion desk' *s* Auskunftsstelle *f*

informative [ɪn'fɔrmətɪv] *adj* belehrend

informed' *adj* unterrichtet

informer [ɪn'fɔrmər] *s* Denunziant –in *mf*

infraction [ɪn'frækʃən] *s* **(of)** Verstoß *m* **(gegen)**

infrared [ˌɪnfrə'red] *adj* infrarot

infrequent [ɪn'dʒiːnɪ.əs] *adj* selten

infringe [ɪn'frɪndʒ] *tr* verletzen ‖ *intr* **—i. on** eingreifen in *(acc)*

infringement [ɪn'frɪndʒmənt] *s (of a law)* Verletzung *f;* **(of a right)** Eingriff *m* (in *acc)*

infuriate [ɪn'fjʊrɪˌet] *tr* wütend machen

infuse [ɪn'fjuz] *tr* (& fig) **(into)** einflößen *(dat)*

infusion [ɪn'fjuʒən] *s* (& fig) Einflößung *f;* (med) Infusion *f*

ingenious [ɪn'dʒiːnɪ.əs] *adj* erfinderisch

ingenuity [ˌɪndʒɪ'n(j)uːɪti] *s* Erfindungsgabe *f,* Scharfsinn *m*

ingenuous [ɪn'dʒenju.əs] *adj* aufrichtig; *(naive)* naiv

ingest [ɪn'dʒest] *tr* zu sich nehmen

inglorious [ɪn'glɔrɪ.əs] *adj (shameful)* unrühmlich; *(without honor)* ruhmlos

ingot ['ɪŋgət] *s* Block *m; (of gold or silver)* Barren *m*

ingrained', **in'grained** *adj* eingewurzelt

ingrate ['ɪngret] *s* Undankbare *mf*

ingratiate [ɪn'greʃɪˌet] *tr—i.* **oneself with** sich einschmeicheln bei

ingra'tiating *adj* einschmeichelnd

ingratitude [ɪn'grætɪˌt(j)ud] *s* Undankbarkeit *f,* Undank *m*

ingredient [ɪn'gridɪ.ənt] *s* Bestandteil *m;* (culin) Zutat *f*

in'grown' *adj* eingewachsen

inhabit [ɪn'hæbɪt] *tr* bewohnen

inhabitant [ɪn'hæbɪtənt] *s* Bewohner –in *mf,* Einwohner –in *mf*

inhale [ɪn'hel] *tr* & *intr* einatmen; inhalieren

inherent [ɪn'hɪrənt] *adj* innewohnend; *(right)* angeboren

inherit [ɪn'herɪt] *tr* (biol, jur) erben

inheritance [ɪn'herɪtəns] *s* Erbschaft *f*

inher'itance tax' *s* Erbschaftssteuer *f*

inheritor [ɪn'herɪtər] *s* Erbe *m,* Erbin *f*

inhibit [ɪn'hɪbɪt] *tr* hemmen, inhibieren

inhibition [ˌɪnɪ'bɪʃən] *s* Hemmung *f*

inhospitable [ɪn'hɑspɪtəbəl] *adj* ungastlich; *(place)* unwirtlich

inhuman [ɪn'hjumən] *adj* unmenschlich

inhumane [ˌɪnju'men] *adj* inhuman

inhumanity [ˌɪnhju'mænɪti] *s* Unmenschlichkeit *f*

inimical [ɪ'nɪmɪkəl] *adj* **(to)** abträglich *(dat)*

iniquity [ɪ'nɪkwɪti] *s* Niederträchtigkeit *f,* Ungerechtigkeit *f*

ini·tial [ɪn'ɪʃəl] *adj* anfänglich ‖ *s* Anfangsbuchstabe *m,* Initiale *f* ‖ *v*

(pret & pp **–tial[l]ed;** *ger* **–tial[l]ing)** *tr* mit den Initialen unterzeichnen

initially [ɪ'nɪʃəli] *adv* anfangs

initiate [ɪ'nɪʃɪˌet] *tr* einführen; *(reforms)* einleiten; **(into)** aufnehmen in *(acc)*

initiation [ɪˌnɪʃɪ'eʃən] *s* Einführung *f;* **(into)** Aufnahme *f* (in *acc)*

initiative [ɪ'nɪʃ(ɪ)ətɪv] *s* Unternehmungsgeist *m;* **take the i.** die Initiative ergreifen

inject [ɪn'dʒekt] *tr (a needle)* einführen; *(a word)* dazwischenwerfen; *(e.g., bigotry into a campaign)* einfließen lassen; *(a liquid)* (med) injizieren

injection [ɪn'dʒekʃən] *s* (mach) Einspritzung *f;* (med) Injektion *f*

injudicious [ˌɪndʒu'dɪʃəs] *adj* unverständig

injunction [ɪn'dʒʌŋkʃən] *s* Gebot *n;* (jur) gerichtliche Verfügung *f*

injure ['ɪndʒər] *tr* verletzen; (fig) schädigen

injurious [ɪn'dʒʊrɪ.əs] *adj* schädlich

injury ['ɪndʒəri] *s* Verletzung *f;* **(to)** Schädigung *f (genit)*

injustice [ɪn'dʒʌstɪs] *s* Ungerechtigkeit *f*

ink [ɪŋk] *s* Tinte *f* ‖ *tr* schwärzen

inkling ['ɪŋklɪŋ] *s* leise Ahnung *f*

ink' pad' *s* Stempelkissen *n*

ink' spot' *s* Tintenklecks *m*

inky ['ɪŋki] *adj* tiefschwarz

inlaid ['ɪn,led] *adj* eingelegt

in'laid floor' *s* Parkettfußboden *m*

inland ['ɪnlənd] *adj* Binnen– ‖ *adv* landeinwärts ‖ *s* Binnenland *n*

in'-laws' *spl* angeheiratete Verwandte *pl*

inlay ['ɪn,le] *s* Einlegearbeit *f;* (dent) gegossene Plombe *f*

inlet *s* Meeresarm *m; (opening)* Öffnung *f*

in'mate *s* Insasse *m,* Insassin *f*

inn [ɪn] *s* Gasthaus *n,* Wirtshaus *n*

innards ['ɪnərdz] *spl* (coll) Innere *n*

innate [ɪ'net] *adj* angeboren

inner ['ɪnər] *adj* innere, inwendig, Innen–

in'nermost' *adj* innerste

in'nerspring mat'tress *s* Federkernmatratze *f*

in'ner tube' *s* Schlauch *m*

inning ['ɪnɪŋ] *s* Runde *f*

inn'keep'er *s* Wirt *m,* Wirtin *f*

innocence ['ɪnəsəns] *s* Unschuld *f; (of a crime)* Schuldlosigkeit *f*

innocent ['ɪnəsənt] *adj* **(of)** unschuldig **(an** *dat);* *(harmless)* harmlos; *(guileless)* arglos ‖ *s* Unschuldige *mf*

innocuous [ɪ'nɑkju.əs] *adj* harmlos

innovation [ˌɪnə've·ʃən] *s* Neuerung *f*

innovative ['ɪnə,vetɪv] *adj (person)* neuerungssüchtig; *(thing)* Neuerungs–

innuen·do [ˌɪnju'endo] *s* **(–does)** Unterstellung *f*

innumerable [ɪ'n(j)umərəbəl] *adj* unzählbar, unzählig

inoculate [ɪn'ɑkjəˌlet] *tr* impfen

inoculation [ɪnˌɑkjə'leʃən] *s* Impfung *f*

inoffensive [ˌɪnəˈfɛnsɪv] adj unschädlich

inopportune [ɪnˌɑpərˈt(j)un] adj ungelegen

inordinate [ɪnˈɔrdɪnɪt] adj übermäßig

inorganic [ˌɪnɔrˈgænɪk] adj unorganisch; (chem) anorganisch

in'put' adj (data proc) Eingabe- || s (in production) Aufwand m; (data proc) Eingabe f, Eingangsinformation f; (elec) Stromzufuhr f

inquest [ˈɪnkwɛst] s Untersuchung f

inquire [ɪnˈkwaɪr] intr anfragen; i. about sich erkundigen nach; i. into untersuchen; i. of sich erkundigen bei

inquiry [ɪnˈkwaɪri], [ˈɪnkwɪri] s Anfrage f; (investigation) Untersuchung f; make inquiries (about) Erkundigungen einziehen (über acc)

inquisition [ˌɪnkwɪˈzɪʃən] s Inquisition f

inquisitive [ɪnˈkwɪzɪtɪv] adj wißbegierig

in'road s (raid) Einfall m; (fig) Eingriff m

ins' and outs' spl alle Kniffe pl

insane [ɪnˈsen] adj wahnsinnig; (absurd) unsinnig

insane' asy'lum s Irrenanstalt f

insanity [ɪnˈsænɪti] s Wahnsinn m

insatiable [ɪnˈseʃəbəl] adj unersättlich

inscribe [ɪnˈskraɪb] tr (a name) einschreiben; (a book) widmen; (a monument) mit e-r Inschrift versehen

inscription [ɪnˈskrɪpʃən] s Inschrift f; (of a book) Widmung f

inscrutable [ɪnˈskrutəbəl] adj unerforschlich

insect [ˈɪnsɛkt] s Insekt n, Kerbtier n

insecticide [ɪnˈsɛktɪˌsaɪd] s Insektenvertilgungsmittel n, Insektizid n

insecure [ˌɪnsɪˈkjur] adj unsicher

insecurity [ˌɪnsɪˈkjurɪti] s Unsicherheit f

insensitive [ɪnˈsɛnsɪtɪv] adj (to) unempfindlich (gegen)

inseparable [ɪnˈsɛpərəbəl] adj untrennbar; (friends) unzertrennlich

insert [ˈɪnsʌrt] s Einsatzstück n || [ɪnˈsʌrt] tr einfügen; (a coin) einwerfen

insertion [ɪnˈsʌrʃən] s Einfügung f; (of a coin) Einwurf m

in'set' (of a map) Nebenkarte f; (inserted piece) Einsatz m

in'shore' adj Küsten- || adv auf die Küste zu

in'side' adj innere, Innen- || s; (information) vertraulich || adv innen, drinnen; come i. hereinkommen; i. of innerhalb von; i. out verkehrt; know i. out in- und auswendig kennen; turn i. out umdrehen || s Innenseite f, Innere n; on the i. innen || prep innerhalb (genit)

insider [ɪnˈsaɪdər] s Eingeweihte mf

in'side track' s (sport) Innenbahn f; have the i. (fig) im Vorteil sein

insidious [ɪnˈsɪdɪəs] adj hinterlistig

in'sight' s Einsicht f

insignia [ɪnˈsɪgnɪə] s (-a & -as) Abzeichen n; i. of office Amtsabzeichen pl; i. of rank Rangabzeichen pl

insignificant [ˌɪnsɪgˈnɪfɪkənt] adj bedeutungslos, geringfügig

insincere [ˌɪnsɪnˈsɪr] adj unaufrichtig

insincerity [ˌɪnsɪnˈsɛrɪti] s Unaufrichtigkeit f

insinuate [ɪnˈsɪnjuˌet] tr andeuten

insipid [ɪnˈsɪpɪd] adj (a fig) fad(e)

insist [ɪnˈsɪst] intr—i. on bestehen auf (dat); i. on (ger) darauf bestehen zu (inf)

insistent [ɪnˈsɪstənt] adj beharrlich

insofar as [ˌɪnsoˈfar ˌæz] conj insoweit als

insolence [ˈɪnsələns] s Unverschämtheit f

insolent [ˈɪnsələnt] adj unverschämt

insoluble [ɪnˈsaljəbəl] adj unlösbar

insolvency [ɪnˈsalvənsi] s Zahlungsunfähigkeit f, Insolvenz f

insolvent [ɪnˈsalvənt] adj zahlungsunfähig

insomnia [ɪnˈsamnɪ-ə] s Schlaflosigkeit f

insomuch as [ˌɪnsoˈmʌtʃəz] conj insofern als

inspect [ɪnˈspɛkt] tr (view closely) besichtigen; (check) kontrollieren; (aut) untersuchen; (mil) besichtigen

inspection [ɪnˈspɛkʃən] s Besichtigung f; Kontrolle f; (aut) Untersuchung f; (mil) Truppenbesichtigung f

inspector [ɪnˈspɛktər] s Kontrolleur m; (of police) Inspektor m

inspiration [ˌɪnspɪˈreʃən] s Begeisterung f

inspire [ɪnˈspaɪr] tr begeistern; (feelings) erwecken

inspir'ing adj begeisternd

instability [ˌɪnstəˈbɪlɪti] s Unbeständigkeit f

install [ɪnˈstɔl] tr (appliances) installieren; (in office) einführen

installation [ˌɪnstəˈleʃən] s (of appliances) Installation f; (mil) Anlage f

installment [ɪnˈstɔlmənt] s Installation f; (in a serialized story) Fortsetzung f; (partial payment) Rate f; in installments ratenweise

install'ment plan' s Teilzahlungsplan m

instance [ˈɪnstəns] s (case) Fall m; (example) Beispiel n; (jur) Instanz f; for i. zum Beispiel

instant [ˈɪnstənt] adj augenblicklich; (foods) gebrauchsfertig || s Augenblick m; this i. sofort

instantaneous [ˌɪnstənˈtenɪ-əs] adj augenblicklich, sofortig

instead [ɪnˈstɛd] adv statt dessen

instead' of prep (an)statt (genit); (ger) anstatt zu (inf)

in'step' s Rist m

instigate [ˈɪnstɪˌget] tr anstiften

instigation [ˌɪnstɪˈgeʃən] s Anstiftung f

instigator [ˈɪnstɪˌgetər] s Anstifter –in mf

instill [ɪnˈstɪl] tr einflößen

instinct [ˈɪnstɪŋkt] s Trieb m, Instinkt m; by i. instinktiv

instinctive [ɪnˈstɪŋktɪv] adj instinktiv

institute ['Insti,t(j)ut] *s* Institut *n* || *tr* einleiten

institution [,Insti't(j)uʃən] *s* Anstalt *f*

instruct [In'strʌkt] *tr* anweisen, beauftragen; (*teach*) unterrichten

instruction [In'strʌkʃən] *s* (*teaching*) Unterricht *m*; **instructions** Anweisungen *pl*; **instructions for use** Gebrauchsanweisung *f*

instructive [In'strʌktIv] *adj* lehrreich

instructor [In'strʌktər] *s* Lehrer –in *mf*; (*at a university*) Dozent –in *mf*

instrument ['Instrəmənt] *s* Instrument *n*; (*tool*) Werkzeug *n*; (jur) Dokument *n*

instrumental [,Instrə'mentəl] *adj* (mus) instrumental; **he was i. in my getting an award** er war mir behilflich, e–n Preis zu erhalten

instrumentality [,Instrəmən'tælIti] *s* Vermittlung *f*

in'strument land'ing *s* Instrumentenlandung *f*

in'strument pan'el *s* Armaturenbrett *n*

insubordinate [,Insə'bɔrdInIt] *adj* widersetzlich

insubordination [,InsəbɔrdI'neʃən] *s* Widersetzlichkeit *f*

insufferable [In'sʌfərəbəl] *adj* unausstehlich

insufficient [,Insə'fIʃənt] *adj* ungenügend, unzureichend

insular ['Ins(j)ələr] *adj* insular

insulate ['Insə,let] *tr* isolieren

insulation [,Insə'leʃən] *s* Isolierung *f*; (*insulating material*) Isolierstoff *m*

insulator ['Insə,letər] *s* Isolator *m*

insulin ['InsəlIn] *s* Insulin *n*

insult ['InsʌIt] *s* Beleidigung *f* || [In-'sʌIt] *tr* beleidigen, beschimpfen

insurance [In'ʃʊrəns] *adj* Versicherungs– || *s* Versicherung *f*

insure [In'ʃʊr] *tr* versichern

insured *adj* (*letter, package*) Wert– || *s* Versicherungsnehmer –in *mf*

insurer [In'ʃʊrər] *s* Versicherer –in *mf*

insurgent [In'sʌrdʒənt] *adj* aufständisch || *s* Aufständische *mf*

insurmountable [,Insər'mauntəbəl] *adj* unübersteigbar; (fig) unüberwindlich

insurrection [,Insə'rekʃən] *s* Aufstand *m*

intact [In'tækt] *adj* unversehrt

in'take *s* (aut) Einlaß *m*; **i. of food** Nahrungsaufnahme *f*

in'take valve *s* Einlaßventil *n*

intangible [In'tændʒIbəl] *adj* immateriell

integer ['IntIdʒər] *s* ganze Zahl *f*

integral ['IntIgrəl] *adj* wesentlich; (math) Integral– || *s* Integral *n*

integrate ['IntI,gret] *tr* eingliedern; (*a school*) die Rassentrennung aufheben in (*dat*); (& math) integrieren

integration [,IntI'greʃən] *s* Integration *f*; (*of schools*) Aufhebung *f* der Rassentrennung

integrity [In'tegrIti] *s* Redlichkeit *f*

intellect ['Intə,lekt] *s* Intellekt *m*

intellectual [,Intə'lektʃʊ·əl] *adj* intellektuell; (*freedom, history*) Geistes– || *s* Intellektuelle *mf*

intelligence [In'telIdʒəns] *s* Intelligenz *f*, Klugheit *f*; (*information*) Nachricht *f*; (*department*) Nachrichtendienst *m*; **gather i.** Nachrichten einziehen

intel'ligence quo'tient *s* Intelligenz-Quotient *m*

intel'ligence test' *s* Begabungsprüfung *f*

intelligent [In'telIdʒənt] *adj* intelligent, klug

intelligentsia [In,telI'dʒentsI·ə] *s* Intelligenz *f*, geistige Oberschicht *f*

intelligible [In'telIdʒIbəl] *adj* (to) verständlich (*dat*)

intemperate [In'tempərIt] *adj* unmäßig; (*in drink*) trunksüchtig

intend [In'tend] *tr* beabsichtigen; **be intended for** bestimmt sein für, gemünzt sein auf (*acc*) **i. by** bezwecken mit; **i. for s.o.** j–m zudenken

intend'ed *s* (coll) Verlobte *mf*

intense [In'tens] *adj* intensiv, stark

intensi·fy [In'tensI,faI] *v* (*pret & pp* **–fied**) *tr* steigern, verstärken || *intr* sich steigern, stärker werden

intensity [In'tensIti] *s* Stärke *f*

intensive [In'tensIv] *adj* intensiv; (gram) verstärkend

inten'sive care' *s* Intensivstation *f*

intent [In'tent] *adj* (on) erpicht (auf *acc*) || *s* Absicht *f*; **to all intents and purposes** praktisch genommen

intention [In'tenʃən] *s* Absicht *f*; **good i.** guter Wille *m*; **have honorable intentions** es ehrlich meinen; **with the i. of** (*ger*) in der Absicht zu (*inf*)

intentional [In'tenʃənəl] *adj* absichtlich

intently [In'tentli] *adv* gespannt

in·ter [In'tʌr] *v* (*pret & pp* **–terred**; *ger* **–terring**) *tr* beerdigen

interact [,Intər'ækt] *intr* zusammenwirken, aufeinander wirken

interaction [,Intər'ækʃən] *s* Wechselwirkung *f*

inter·breed [,Intər'brid] *v* (*pret & pp* **–bred**) *tr* kreuzen || *intr* sich kreuzen

intercede [,Intər'sid] *intr* Fürsprache einlegen; **i. for s.o.** with Fürsprache einlegen für j–n bei

intercept [,Intər'sept] *tr* (*a letter, aircraft*) abfangen; (*a radio message*) abhören; (*cut off, check*) den Weg abschneiden (*dat*)

interceptor [,Intər'septər] *s* (aer) Abfangjäger *m*

intercession [,Intər'seʃən] *s* Fürsprache *f*; (relig) Fürbitte *f*

interchange ['Intər,tʃendʒ] *s* Wechsel *m*; (*on a highway*) Anschlußstelle *f* || [,Intər'tʃendʒ] *tr* auswechseln || *intr* (with) abwechseln (mit)

interchangeable [,Intər'tʃendʒəbəl] *adj* auswechselbar, austauschbar

intercom ['Intər,kʌm] *s* Wechselsprachanlage *f*

intercourse ['Intər,kɔrs] *s* Verkehr *m*; (*sexual*) Geschlechtsverkehr *m*

interdependent [,Intərdɪ'pendənt] *adj* voneinander abhängig

interdict ['Intər,dɪkt] *s* Verbot *n*; (eccl) Interdikt *n* || [,Intər'dɪkt] *tr* verbieten; **i. s.o. from** (*ger*) j-m verbieten zu (*inf*)

interest ['ɪnt(ə)rɪst] *s* (**in**) Interesse *n* (**an** *dat*, für); (fin) Zinsen *pl*; **at i. gegen Zinsen; be in s.o.'s i.** in j-s Interesse liegen; **have an i. in** beteiligt sein an (*dat*) or bei; **interests** Belange *pl*; **pay i.** (*bring in interest*) Zinsen abwerfen; (*pay out interest*) Zinsen zahlen; **take an i. in** sich interessieren für; **with l.** (& fig) mit Zinsen ‖ *tr* (**in**) interessieren (für)

in'terested *adj*—**i. in** interessiert an (*dat*); **the i. parties** die Beteiligten *pl*

in'teresting *adj* interessant

in'terest rate' *s* Zinsfuß *m*, Zinssatz *m*

interfere [,ɪntər'fɪr] *intr* (*said of a thing*) dazwischenkommen; (*said of a person*) eingreifen; (**in** or **with**) sich (ein)mengen (**in** *acc*); **i. with** (rad, telv) stören; **i. with s.o.'s work** j-n bei seiner Arbeit stören

interference [,ɪntər'fɪrəns] *s* Einmischung *f*; (phys) Interferenz *f*; (rad, telv) Störung *f*

interim ['ɪntərɪm] *adj* Zwischen- ‖ *s* Zwischenzeit *f*

interior [ɪn'tɪrɪ-ər] *adj* innere, Innen- ‖ *s* Innere *n*; (*of a building*) Innenraum *m*; (*of a country*) Inland *n*

inte'rior dec'orator *s* Innenarchitekt –in *mf*

interject [,ɪntər'dʒekt] *tr* dazwischenwerfen

interjection [,ɪntər'dʒekʃən] *s* Zwischenwurf *m*; (gram) Interjektion *f*

interlard [,ɪntər'lard] *tr* (& fig) spicken

interlinear [,ɪntər'lɪnɪ-ər] *adj* Interlinear-

interlock [,ɪntər'lak] *tr* miteinander verbinden ‖ *intr* sich ineinanderschließen

interloper [,ɪntər'lopər] *s* Eindringling *m*

interlude ['ɪntər,lud] *s* (*interval*) Pause *f*; (fig, mus, theat) Zwischenspiel *n*

intermediary [,ɪntər'midɪ,erɪ] *adj* vermittelnd ‖ *s* Vermittler –in *mf*

intermediate [,ɪntər'midɪ-ɪt] *adj* zwischenliegend, Zwischen-

interment [ɪn'tarmənt] *s* Beerdigung *f*

intermezzo [,ɪntər'metso] *s* (**-zos** & **zi** [tsɪ]) Intermezzo *n*

intermingle [,ɪntər'mɪŋɡəl] *tr* vermischen ‖ *intr* sich vermischen

intermission [,ɪntər'mɪʃən] *s* Unterbrechung *f*; (theat) Pause *f*

intermittent [,ɪntər'mɪtənt] *adj* intermittierend

intermix [,ɪntər'mɪks] *tr* vermischen ‖ *intr* sich vermischen

intern ['ɪntʌrn] *s* Assistenzarzt *m*, Assistenzärztin *f*

internal [ɪn'tʌrnəl] *adj* innere, intern; (*domestic*) einheimisch; (*trade, rhyme*) Binnen-

inter'nal-combus'tion en'gine *s* Verbrennungsmotor *m*

inter'nal med'icine *s* innere Medizin *f*

inter'nal rev'enue *s* Steueraufkommen *n*

international [,ɪntər'næʃənəl] *adj* international

interna'tional date' line' *s* internationale Datumsgrenze *f*

interna'tional law' *s* Völkerrecht *n*

interne'cine war' [,ɪntər'nisɪn] *s* gegenseitiger Vernichtungskrieg *m*

internee [,ɪntər'ni] *s* Internierte *mf*

internment [ɪn'tʌrnmənt] *s* Internierung *f*

in'ternship' *s* Pflichtzeit *f* als Assistenzarzt (or Assistenzärztin)

interoffice [,ɪntər'ɔfɪs] *adj* Haus-

interplanetary [,ɪntər'plænɪ,terɪ] *adj* interplanetarisch

interplay [,ɪntər,ple] *s* Wechselspiel *n*

interpolate [ɪn'tʌrpə,let] *tr* interpolieren

interpose [,ɪntər'poz] *tr* (*an obstacle*) dazwischensetzen; (*a remark*) einwerfen

interpret [ɪn'tʌrprɪt] *tr* (& mus) interpretieren; (*translate*) verdolmetschen ‖ *intr* dolmetschen

interpretation [ɪn,tʌrprɪ'teʃən] *s* (& mus) Interpretation *f*

interpreter [ɪn'tʌrprɪtər] *s* Dolmetscher –in *mf*; **act as i.** dolmetschen

interrogate [ɪn'terə,get] *tr* ausfragen; (jur) verhören, vernehmen

interrogation [ɪn,terə'geʃən] *s* Verhör *n*

interrogative [,ɪntər'rɑɡətɪv] *adj* Frage-

interrupt [,ɪntə'rʌpt] *tr* unterbrechen

interruption [,ɪntə'rʌpʃən] *s* Unterbrechung *f*; (*in industry*) Betriebsstörung *f*

intersect [,ɪntər'sekt] *tr* durchschneiden ‖ *ref* sich kreuzen

intersection [,ɪntər'sekʃən] *s* Straßenkreuzung *f*; (math) Schnittpunkt *m*

intersperse [,ɪntər'spʌrs] *tr* durchsetzen

interstate ['ɪntər,stet] *adj* zwischenstaatlich

interstellar [,ɪntər'stelər] *adj* interstellar

interstice [ɪn'tʌrstɪs] *s* Zwischenraum *m*

intertwine [,ɪntər'twaɪn] *tr* verflechten ‖ *intr* sich verflechten

interval ['ɪntərvəl] *s* Abstand *m*; (mus) Stufe *f*, Intervall *n*

intervene [,ɪntər'vin] *intr* dazwischenkommen; (*interfere*) eingreifen; (*intercede*) intervenieren

intervention [,ɪntər'venʃən] *s* Dazwischenkommen *n*; Eingreifen *n*; Intervention *f*

interview ['ɪntər,vju] *s* Interview *n* ‖ *tr* interviewen

inter·weave [,ɪntər'wiv] *v* (*pret* **-wove** & **-weaved**; *pp* **-wove**, **-woven** & **-weaved**) *tr* durchweben, durchflechten

intestate [ɪn'testet] *adj* ohne Testament

intestine [ɪn'testɪn] *s* Darm *m*; **intestines** Gedärme *pl*

intimacy ['ɪntɪməsɪ] *s* Vertraulichkeit *f*; **intimacies** Intimitäten *pl*

intimate ['ɪntɪmɪt] *adj* intim, vertraut

|| *s* Vertraute *mf* || ['ɪntɪ,met] *tr* andeuten

intimation [,ɪntɪ'meʃən] *s* Andeutung *f*

intimidate [ɪn'tɪmɪ,det] *tr* einschüchtern

intimidation [,ɪntɪmɪ'deʃən] *s* Einschüchterung *f*

into ['ɪntu], ['ɪntu] *prep* in (*acc*)

intolerable [ɪn'tɑlərəbəl] *adj* unerträglich

intolerance [ɪn'tɑlərəns] *s* (of) Intoleranz *f* (gegen)

intolerant [ɪn'tɑlərənt] *adj* (of) intolerant (gegen)

intonation [,ɪnto'neʃən] *s* Tonfall *m*

intone [ɪn'ton] *tr* intonieren

intoxicate [ɪn'tɑksɪ,ket] *tr* berauschen; (*poison*) vergiften

intoxication [ɪn,tɑksɪ'keʃən] *s* (& fig) Rausch *m*; (*poisoning*) Vergiftung *f*

intractable [ɪn'træktəbəl] *adj* (*person*) störrisch; (*thing*) schwer zu bearbeiten(d)

intransigent [ɪn'trænsɪdʒənt] *adj* unversöhnlich

intransitive [ɪn'trænsɪtɪv] *adj* intransitiv

intravenous [,ɪntrə'vinəs] *adj* intravenös

intrepid [ɪn'trepɪd] *adj* unerschrocken

intricate ['ɪntrɪkɪt] *adj* verwickelt

intrigue [ɪn'trig, 'ɪntrig] *s* Intrige *f* || [ɪn'trig] *tr* fesseln || *intr* intrigieren

intrigu'ing *adj* fesselnd

intrinsic(al) [ɪn'trɪnsɪk(əl)] *adj* innere, innerlich; (*value*) wirklich

introduce [,ɪntrə'd(j)us] *tr* einführen; (*strangers*) vorstellen

introduction [,ɪntrə'dʌkʃən] *s* Einführung *f*; (*of strangers*) Vorstellung *f*; (*in a book*) Einleitung *f*

introductory [,ɪntrə'dʌktəri] *adj* (*offer, price*) Einführungs-; (*remarks*) einleitend

introspection [,ɪntrə'spekʃən] *s* Selbstbeobachtung *f*

introspective [,ɪntrə'spektɪv] *adj* introspektiv

introvert ['ɪntrə,vʌrt] *s* Introvertierte *mf*

intrude [ɪn'trud] *intr* (on) sich aufdrängen (dat); **am I intruding?** störe ich?

intruder [ɪn'trudər] *s* Eindringling *m*

intrusion [ɪn'truʒən] *s* Eindrängen *n*, Stören *n*

intrusive [ɪn'trusɪv] *adj* störend, lästig

intuition [,ɪnt(j)u'ɪʃən] *s* Intuition *f*

inundate ['ɪnən,det] *tr* überschwemmen

inundation [,ɪnən'deʃən] *s* Überschwemmung *f*

inure [ɪn'jʊr] *tr* (to) abhärten (gegen)

invade [ɪn'ved] *tr* (*a country*) eindringen in (*acc*); (*rights*) verletzen; (*privacy*) stören

invader [ɪn'vedər] *s* Eindringling *m*; (mil) Angreifer *m*

invalid [ɪn'vælɪd] *adj* ungültig || ['ɪnvəlɪd] *adj* kränklich || *s* Invalide *m*

invalidate [ɪn'vælɪ,det] *tr* ungültig machen; (*a law*) außer Kraft setzen

invalidity [,ɪnvə'lɪdɪti] *s* Ungültigkeit *f*

invaluable [ɪn'væljʊ-əbəl] *adj* unschätzbar

invariable [ɪn'verɪ-əbəl] *adj* unveränderlich

invasion [ɪn'veʃən] *s* Invasion *f*

invective [ɪn'vɛktɪv] *s* Schmähung *f*

inveigh [ɪn've] *intr*—**i. against** schimpfen über (*acc*) or auf (*acc*)

inveigle [ɪn'vigəl] *tr* verleiten; **i. s.o. into** (*ger*) j–n verleiten zu (*inf*)

invent [ɪn'vent] *tr* erfinden; (*a story*) sich (*dat*) ausdenken

invention [ɪn'venʃən] *s* Erfindung *f*

inventive [ɪn'ventɪv] *adj* erfinderisch

inventiveness [ɪn'ventɪvnɪs] *s* Erfindungsgabe *f*

inventor [ɪn'ventər] *s* Erfinder –in *mf*

inven·to·ry ['ɪnvən,tori] *s* (stock) Inventar *n*; (*act*) Inventur *f*; (*list*) Bestandsverzeichnis *n*; **take i.** Inventur machen || *v* (*pret & pp* **-ried**) *tr* inventarisieren

inverse [ɪn'vʌrs] *adj* umgekehrt

inversion [ɪn'vʌrʒən] *s* Umkehrung *f*; (gram) Umstellung *f*

invert [ɪn'vʌrt] *tr* umkehren; (gram) umstellen

invertebrate [ɪn'vʌrtɪ,bret] *adj* wirbellos || *s* wirbelloses Tier *n*

invest [ɪn'vest] *tr* (in) investieren (in *acc*); (mil) belagern; **i. with** ausstatten mit

investigate [ɪn'vestɪ,get] *tr* untersuchen

investigation [ɪn,vestɪ'geʃən] *s* Untersuchung *f*

investigator [ɪn'vestɪ,getər] *s* Untersucher –in *mf*

investment [ɪn'vestmənt] *s* Anlage *f*, Investition *f*; (*with an office*) Amtseinführung *f*; (mil) Belagerung *f*

investor [ɪn'vestər] *s* Investor –in *mf*

inveterate [ɪn'vetərɪt] *adj* (*habitual*) eingefleischt; (*firmly established*) eingewurzelt

invidious [ɪn'vɪdɪ-əs] *adj* haßerregend

invigorate [ɪn'vɪgə,ret] *tr* beleben

invig'orating *adj* belebend

invincible [ɪn'vɪnsɪbəl] *adj* unbesiegbar

invisible [ɪn'vɪzɪbəl] *adj* unsichtbar

invis'ible ink' *s* Geheimtinte *f*

invitation [,ɪnvɪ'teʃən] *s* Einladung *f*

invite [ɪn'vart] *tr* einladen; **i. in** hereinbitten

invit'ing *adj* lockend

invocation [,ɪnvo'keʃən] *s* Anrufung *f*; (relig) Bittgebet *n*

invoice ['ɪnvoɪs] *s* Faktura *f*, Warenrechnung *f*; **as per i.** laut Rechnung || *tr* fakturieren

invoke [ɪn'vok] *tr* anrufen; (*cite*) zitieren

involuntary [ɪn'vɑlən,teri] *adj* (*against one's will*) unfreiwillig; (*without one's will*) unwillkürlich

invol'untary man'slaughter *s* unbeabsichtigte Tötung *f*

involve [ɪn'vɑlv] *tr* verwickeln; (*include*) einschließen; (*affect*) betreffen; (*entail*) zur Folge haben

involved' *adj* verwickelt, kompliziert; **be i. in** (*e.g., construction*) beschäftigt sein bei; (*e.g., a crime*) verwickelt sein in (*acc*); **be i. with** (*e.g., a married person*) e-e Affäre haben mit

involvement [ɪn'vɑlʌmənt] *s* Verwicklung *f*

invulnerable [ɪn'vʌlnərəbəl] *adj* unverwundbar

inward ['ɪnwərd] *adj* inner(lich) ‖ *adv* nach innen

inwardly ['ɪnwərdli] *adv* innerlich

iodine ['aɪ·ə‚dɪn] *s* (chem) Jod *n* ‖ ['aɪ·ə‚daɪn] *s* (pharm) Jodtinktur *f*

ion ['aɪ·ən], ['aɪ·ɑn] *s* Ion *n*

ionize ['aɪ·ə‚naɪz] *tr* ionisieren

IOU ['aɪ‚o'ju] *s* (**I owe you**) Schuldschein *m*

I.Q. ['aɪ'kju] *s* (**intelligence quotient**) Intelligenz-Quotient *m*

Iran [ɪ'rɑn], [ɪ'ræn] *s* Iran *m*

Iranian [aɪ'renɪ·ən] *adj* iranisch ‖ *s* Iran(i)er –in *mf*

Iraq [ɪ'rɑk] *s* Irak *m*

Iraqi [ɪ'rɑki] *adj* irakisch ‖ *s* (**–qis**) Iraker –in *mf*

irascible [ɪ'ræsɪbəl] *adj* jähzornig

irate ['aɪret], [aɪ'ret] *adj* zornig

ire [aɪr] *s* Zorn *m*

Ireland ['aɪrlənd] *s* Irland *n*

iris ['aɪrɪs] *s* (anat, bot) Iris *f*

Irish ['aɪrɪʃ] *adj* irisch ‖ *s* (*language*) Irisch *n*; **the I.** die Iren *pl*

Irishman *s* (**–men**) Ire *m*

Irishwoman *s* (**–women**) Irin *f*

irk [ʌrk] *tr* ärgern

irksome ['ʌrksəm] *adj* ärgerlich

iron ['aɪ·ərn] *adj* (& fig) eisern ‖ *s* Eisen *n*; (*for pressing clothes*) Bügeleisen *n* ‖ *tr* bügeln; **i. out** ausbügeln; (fig) ins Reine bringen

ironclad ['aɪ·ərn‚klæd] *adj* (fig) unumstößlich

iron cur'tain *s* eiserner Vorhang *m*

ironic(al) [aɪ'rɑnɪk(əl)] *adj* ironisch

i'roning *s* (*act*) Bügeln *n*; (*clothes*) Bügelwäsche *f*

i'roning board' *s* Bügelbrett *n*

i'ron lung' *s* eiserne Lunge *f*

i'ron ore' *s* Eisenerz *n*

irony ['aɪrənɪ] *s* Ironie *f*

irradiate [ɪ'redɪ‚et] *tr* bestrahlen; (*light*) ausstrahlen; (*a face*) aufheitern

irrational [ɪ'ræʃənəl] *adj* irrational

irreconcilable [ɪ‚rekən'saɪləbəl] *adj* unversöhnlich

irredeemable [‚ɪrɪ'dɪməbəl] *adj* (*loan, bond*) nicht einlösbar; (*hopeless*) hoffnungslos

irrefutable [‚ɪrɪ'fjutəbəl] *adj* unwiderlegbar

irregular [ɪ'regjələr] *adj* unregelmäßig

irregularity [ɪ‚regjə'lærɪti] *s* Unregelmäßigkeit *f*

irrelevant [ɪ'reləvənt] *adj* (**to**) nicht anwendbar (auf *acc*)

irreligious [‚ɪrɪ'lɪdʒəs] *adj* irreligiös

irreparable [ɪ'repərəbəl] *adj* unersetzlich

irreplaceable [‚ɪrɪ'plesɪbəl] *adj* unersetzlich

irrepressible [‚ɪrɪ'presɪbəl] *adj* unbezähmbar

irreproachable [‚ɪrɪ'protʃəbəl] *adj* untadelig

irresistible [‚ɪrɪ'zɪstɪbəl] *adj* unwiderstehlich

irresolute [ɪ'rezəlut] *adj* unentschlossen, unschlüssig

irrespective [‚ɪrɪ'spektɪv] *adj—***i. of** ohne Rücksicht auf (*acc*)

irresponsible [‚ɪrɪ'spɑnsɪbəl] *adj* unverantwortlich

irretrievable [‚ɪrɪ'trivəbəl] *adj* unwiederbringlich, unrettbar

irreverent [ɪ'revərənt] *adj* unehrerbietig

irrevocable [ɪ'revəkəbəl] *adj* unwiderruflich

irrigate ['ɪrɪ‚get] *tr* verwässern; (med) irrigieren

irrigation [‚ɪrɪ'geʃən] *s* Bewässerung *f*

irritable ['ɪrɪtəbəl] *adj* reizbar

irritant ['ɪrɪtənt] *s* Reizstoff *m*

irritate ['ɪrɪ‚tet] *tr* reizen, irritieren

ir'ritating *adj* ärgerlich

irritation [‚ɪrɪ'teʃən] *s* Reizung *f*

irruption ['ɪrʌpʃən] *s* Einbruch *m*

isinglass ['aɪzɪŋ‚glæs] *s* Fischleim *m*; (*mica*) Glimmer *m*

Islam ['ɪsləm] *s* Islam *m*

island ['aɪlənd] *s* Insel *f*

islander ['aɪləndər] *s* Insulaner –in *mf*

isle [aɪl] *s* kleine Insel *f*

isolate ['aɪsə‚let] *tr* isolieren

isolation [‚aɪsə'leʃən] *s* Isolierung *f*

isolationist [‚aɪsə'leʃənɪst] *s* Isolationist –in *mf*

isola'tion ward' *s* Isolierstation *f*

isometric [‚aɪsə'metrɪk] *adj* isometrisch

isosceles [aɪ'sɑsə‚liz] *adj* gleichschenklig

isotope ['aɪsə‚top] *s* Isotop *n*

Israel ['ɪzrɪ·əl] *s* Israel *n*

Israeli [ɪz'reli] *adj* israelisch ‖ *s* (**–lis**) Israeli *m*

Israelite ['ɪzrɪ·ə‚laɪt] *adj* israelitisch ‖ *s* Israelit –in *mf*

issuance ['ɪʃu·əns] *s* Ausgabe *f*

issue ['ɪʃu] *s* (*of a magazine*) Nummer *f*; (*result*) Ausgang *m*; (*e.g., of securities*) Ausgabe *f*, Emission *f*; (*under discussion*) Streitpunkt *m*; (*offspring*) Nachkommenschaft *f*; **avoid the i.** der Frage ausweichen; **be at i.** zur Debatte stehen; **make an i. of it** e-e Streitfrage daraus machen; **take i.** with anderer Meinung sein als ‖ *tr* (*orders, supplies, stamps, stocks*) ausgeben; (*a pass*) ausstellen ‖ *intr* (**from**) herauskommen (aus)

isthmus ['ɪsməs] *s* Landenge *f*

it [ɪt] *pron* es; **about it** darüber, davon; **it is I** ich bin es

Italian [ɪ'tælɪ·ən] *adj* italienisch ‖ *s* (*person*) Italiener –in *mf*; (*language*) Italienisch *n*

italicize [ɪ'tælɪ‚saɪz] *tr* kursiv drucken

italics [ɪˈtælɪks] *spl* Kursivschrift *f*

Italy [ˈɪtəli] *s* Italien *n*

itch [ɪtʃ] *s* Jucken *n*; (pathol) Krätze *f* || *intr* jucken; **I am itching to** (*inf*) es reizt mich zu (*inf*); **my nose itches me** es juckt mich in die Nase

itchy [ˈɪtʃi] *adj* juckend; (pathol) krätzig

item [ˈaɪtəm] *s* Artikel *m*; (*in a list*) Punkt *m*; (com) Posten *m*; (journ) Nachricht *f*; **hot i.** (coll) Schlager *m*

itemize [ˈaɪtəˌmaɪz] *tr* einzeln aufführen

itinerant [aɪˈtɪnərənt], [ɪˈtɪnərənt] *adj* Wander-, reisend || *s* Reisende *mf*

itinerary [aɪˈtɪnəˌreri] *s* Reiseplan *m*

its [ɪts] *poss adj* sein

itself *reflex pron* sich; **in i.** an und für sich || *intens pron* selbst, selber

ivied [ˈaɪvid] *adj* efeubewachsen

ivory [ˈaɪvəri] *adj* elfenbeinern, Elfenbein-; (*color*) kremfarben || *s* Elfenbein *n*; **tickle the ivories** in die Tasten greifen

i'vory tow'er *s* (fig) Elfenbeinturm *m*

ivy [ˈaɪvi] *s* Efeu *m*

J

J, j [dʒe] *s* zehnter Buchstabe des englischen Alphabets

jab [dʒæb] *s* Stoß *m*; (box) Gerade *f* || *v* (*pret & pp* **jabbed**; *ger* **jabbing**) *tr* stoßen; (box) mit der Gerade stoßen

jabber [ˈdʒæbər] *tr & intr* plappern

jack [dʒæk] *s* (*money*) (sl) Pinke *f*; (aut) Wagenheber *m*; (*cards*) Bube *m*; (telp) Klinke *f*; **Jack Hans m** || *tr—j. up* (aut) heben; (*prices*) hinaufschrauben

jackal [ˈdʒækəl] *s* Schakal *m*

jack'ass' *s* Esel *m*

jacket [ˈdʒækɪt] *s* Jacke *f*; (*of a book*) Umschlag *m*; (*of a potato*) Schale *f*

Jack' Frost' *s* Herr Winter *m*

jack'ham'mer *s* Preßlufthammer *m*

jack'-in-the-box' *s* Kastenteufel *m*

jack'knife' *s* (**-knives**) Klappmesser *n*; (*dive*) Hechtbeuge *f* || *intr* zusammenklappen

jack'-of-all'-trades' *s* Hansdampf *m* in allen Gassen

jack'pot' *s* Jackpot *m*; **hit the j.** das Große Los gewinnen

jack' rab'bit *s* Hase *m*

Jacob [ˈdʒekəb] *s* Jakob *m*

jade [dʒed] *adj* jadegrün || *s* (*stone*) Jade *f*; (*color*) Jadegrün *n*; (*horse*) Schindmähre *f*

jad'ed *adj* ermattet

jag [dʒæg] *s* Zacke *f*; **have a jag on** (sl) e-n Schwips haben

jagged [ˈdʒægɪd] *adj* zackig, schartig

jaguar [ˈdʒægwɑr] *s* Jaguar *m*

jail [dʒel] *s* Gefängnis *n*, Untersuchungsgefängnis *n*; **be in j.** sizten || *tr* einsperren

jail'bird' *s* Knastbruder *m*

jailer [ˈdʒelər] *s* Gefängniswärter *m*

jalopy [dʒəˈlɑpi] *s* Rumpelkasten *m*

jal'ousie win'dow [ˈdʒæləsi] *s* Glasjalousie *f*

jam [dʒæm] *s* Marmelade *f*; **be in a jam** (coll) in der Patsche sitzen || *v* (*pret & pp* **jammed**; *ger* **jamming**) *tr* (*a room*) überfüllen; (*a street*) verstopfen; (*a finger*) quetschen; (rad) stören; **be jammed** in eingezwängt sein; **jam on the brakes** auf die Bremsen drücken; **jam s.th. into** etw stopfen in (*acc*) || *intr* (*said of a window*) klemmen; (*said of gears*) sich verklemmen; (*said of a gun*) Ladehemmung haben; **jam into** sich hineinquetschen in (*acc*)

jamb [dʒæm] *s* Pfosten *m*

jamboree [ˌdʒæmbəˈri] *s* Trubel *m*; (*of scouts*) Pfadfindertreffen *n*

James [dʒemz] *s* Jakob *m*

Jane [dʒen] *s* Johanna *f*

Janet [ˈdʒænɪt] *s* Hanna *f*

jangle [ˈdʒæŋgəl] *s* Rasseln *n* || *tr* rasseln lassen; **j. s.o.'s nerves** j-m auf die Nerven gehen || *intr* rasseln

janitor [ˈdʒænɪtər] *s* Hausmeister *m*

January [ˈdʒænjuˌeri] *s* Januar *m*

Japan [dʒəˈpæn] *s* Japan *n*

Japanese [ˌdʒæpəˈniz] *adj* japanisch || *s* Japaner -in *mf*; (*language*) Japanisch *n*

Jap'anese bee'tle *s* Japankäfer *m*

jar [dʒɑr] *s* Krug *m*; (*e.g., of jam*) Glas *n*; (*jolt*) Stoß *m* || *v* (*pret & pp* **jarred**; *ger* **jarring**) *tr* (*jolt*) anstoßen; (fig) erschüttern || *intr* nicht harmonieren; **jar on the nerves** auf die Nerven gehen

jargon [ˈdʒɑrgən] *s* Jargon *m*

jasmine [ˈdʒæzmɪn] *s* Jasmin *m*

jaundice [ˈdʒɔndɪs] *s* Gelbsucht *f*

jaun'diced *adj* gelbsüchtig

jaunt [dʒɔnt] *s* Ausflug *m*

jaunty [ˈdʒɔnti] *adj* (*sprightly*) lebhaft; (*clothes*) fesch

javelin [ˈdʒæv(ə)lɪn] *s* Speer *m*

jaw [dʒɔ] *s* Kiefer *m*; **the jaws of death** die Klauen des Todes

jaw'bone' *s* Kiefer *m* || *intr* (sl) sich stark machen

jay [dʒe] *s* (orn) Häher *m*

jay'walk' *intr* verkehrswidrig die Straße überqueren

jazz [dʒæz] *s* Jazz *m* || *tr—j. up* (coll) aufmöbeln

jazz' band' *s* Jazzband *f*

jazzy [ˈdʒæzi] *adj* bunt, grell

jealous [ˈdʒeləs] *adj* (*of*) eifersüchtig (auf *acc*)

jealousy [ˈdʒeləsi] *s* Eifersucht *f*

jeans [dʒinz] *spl* Jeans *pl*

jeep [dʒip] s Jeep m

jeer [dʒɪr] s Hohn m ‖ tr verhöhnen ‖ intr höhnen; **j. at** verhöhnen

Jeffrey ['dʒɛfri] s Gottfried m

Jehovah [dʒɪ'hovə] s Jehova m

jell [dʒɛl] s Gelee n ‖ intr gelieren; (fig) zum Klappen kommen

jellied ['dʒɛlɪd] adj geliert

jelly ['dʒɛli] s Gallerte f

jel′lyfish′ s Qualle f; (pej) Waschlappen m

jeopardize ['dʒɛpər‚daɪz] tr gefährden

jeopardy ['dʒɛpərdi] s Gefahr f

jerk [dʒʌrk] s Ruck m; (sl) Knülch m ‖ tr ruckweise ziehen ‖ intr zucken

jerky ['dʒʌrki] adj ruckartig

jersey ['dʒʌrzi] s (material) Jersey m; (shirt) Jersey m; (sport) Trikot n

jest [dʒɛst] s Scherz m; **in j.** scherzweise ‖ intr scherzen

jester ['dʒɛstər] s Hofnarr m; (joker) Spaßvogel m

Jesuit ['dʒɛʒʊ‚ɪt] adj Jesuiten– ‖ s Jesuit m

Jesus ['dʒizəs] s Jesus m

jet [dʒɛt] adj Düsen– ‖ s (stream) Strahl m; (nozzle) Düse f; (plane) Jet m, Düsenflugzeug n ‖ v (pret & pp **jetted;** ger **jetting**) herausströmen; (aer) jetten

jet′-black′ adj rabenschwarz

jet′ propul′sion s Düsenantrieb m

jetsam ['dʒɛtsəm] s Seewurfgut n

jet′ stream′ s Strahlströmung f

jettison ['dʒɛtɪsən] s Seewurf m ‖ tr (aer) abwerfen; (naut) über Bord werfen

jetty ['dʒɛti] s (warf) Landungsbrücke f; (breakwater) Hafendamm m

Jew [dʒu] s Jude m, Jüdin f

jewel ['dʒu‚əl] s (& fig) Juwel n; (in a watch) Stein m

jew′el box′ s Schmuckkästchen n

jewel(l)er ['dʒu‚ələr] s Juwelier –in mf

jewelry ['dʒu‚əlri] s Juwelen pl; **piece of j.** Schmuckstück n

jew′elry store′ s Juweliergeschäft n

Jewish ['dʒu‚ɪʃ] adj jüdisch

Jew′s′ harp′ s Maultrommel f

jib [dʒɪb] s Ausleger m; (naut) Klüver m

jibe [dʒaɪb] intr (coll) übereinstimmen

jiffy ['dʒɪfi] s—**in a j.** im Nu

jig [dʒɪg] s (dance) Gigue f; (tool) Spannvorrichtung f; **the jig is up** (sl) das Spiel ist aus

jigger ['dʒɪgər] s Schnapsglas n; (gadget) Dingsbums n; (naut) Besan m

jiggle ['dʒɪgəl] tr & intr rütteln

jig′saw′ s Laubsäge f

jig′saw puz′zle s Puzzelspiel n

jilt [dʒɪlt] tr (a girl) sitzenlassen; (a boy) dem Laufpaß geben (dat)

jim·my ['dʒɪmi] s Brecheisen n ‖ v (pret & pp **-mied**) tr mit dem Brecheisen aufbrechen

jingle ['dʒɪŋgəl] s (of coins) Klimpern n; (bell) Schelle f; (verse) Verseklingel n ‖ tr klimpern mit ‖ intr klimpern; (said of verses) klingeln

jin·go ['dʒɪŋgo] s (-goes) Chauvinist –in mf; **by j.!** alle Wetter!

jinx [dʒɪŋks] s Unglücksrabe m ‖ tr Pech bringen (dat); **be jinxed** vom Pech verfolgt sein

jitters ['dʒɪtərz] spl—**have the j.** wahnsinnig nervös sein; **give s.o. the j.** j-n wahnsinnig nervös machen

jittery ['dʒɪtəri] adj durchgedreht

Joan [dʒon] s Johanna f

job [dʒab] s (employment) Job m; (task, responsibility) Aufgabe f; **bad job** Machwerk n; **do a good job** gute Arbeit leisten; **fall down on the job** seine Pflicht nicht erfüllen; **know one's job** seine Sache verstehen; **on the job** bei der Arbeit; (fig) auf Draht; **out of a job** arbeitslos

jobber ['dʒabər] s (middleman) Zwischenhändler –in mf; (pieceworker) Akkordarbeiter –in mf

job′hold′er s Stelleninhaber –in mf

jobless ['dʒablɪs] adj stellungslos

jockey ['dʒaki] s Jockei m ‖ tr manövrieren

jog [dʒag] s Dauerlauf m; (of a horse) Trott m ‖ v (pret & pp **jogged;** ger **jogging**) tr (shake) rütteln; (the memory) auffrischen ‖ intr trotten; (for exercise) langsam rennen, Dauerlauf machen

John [dʒan] s Johann m; **john** (sl) Klo n

Johnny ['dʒani] s Hans m

John′ny-come′-late′ly s Neuling m, Nachzügler m

join [dʒɔɪn] tr verbinden; (a club) beitreten (dat); (a person) sich anschließen (dat); (two parts) zusammenfügen; **j. the army** zum Militär gehen ‖ intr sich verbinden; **j. in** sich beteiligen an (dat); **j. up** (mil) einrücken

joiner ['dʒɔɪnər] s (coll) Vereinsmeier m; (carp) Tischler m

joint [dʒɔɪnt] adj (account, venture) gemeinschaftlich; (return) gemeinsam; (committee) gemischt; (heir, owner) Mit– ‖ s Verbindungspunkt m; (in plumbing) Naht f; (sl) Bumslokal n; (anat, bot, mach) Gelenk n; (carp) Fuge f; (culin) Bratenstück n; **throw out of j.** auskugeln

jointly ['dʒɔɪntli] adv gemeinsam

joint′-stock′ com′pany s Aktiengesellschaft f

joist [dʒɔɪst] s Tragbalken m

joke [dʒok] s Witz m; **he can't take a j.** er versteht keinen Spaß; **make a j. of** ins Lächerliche ziehen; **play a j. on** e-n Streich spielen (dat) ‖ intr Spaß machen; **j. about** witzeln über (acc); **j. around** schäkern; **joking aside** Spaß beiseite

joker ['dʒokər] s Spaßvogel m; (pej) Knülch m; (cards) Joker m

jolly ['dʒali] adj lustig

jolt [dʒolt] s Stoß m ‖ tr stoßen ‖ intr holpern; **j. along** dahinholpern

Jordan ['dʒɔrdən] s (country) Jordanien n; (river) Jordan m

josh [dʒaʃ] tr & intr hänseln

jostle ['dʒasəl] tr & intr drängeln

jot [dʒat] s—**not a jot** kein Jota ‖ v

(pret & pp **jotted**; ger **jotting**) tr— **jot down** notieren

journal ['dʒʌrnəl] s (daily record) Tagebuch n; (magazine) Zeitschrift f

journalism ['dʒʌrnə‚lızəm] s Journalismus m, Zeitungswesen n

journalist ['dʒʌrnəlıst] s Journalist –in mf

journey ['dʒʌrni] s Reise f; **go on a j.** verreisen || intr reisen

jour'ney·man adj tüchtig || s (–men) Geselle m

joust [dʒaust] s Tjost f || intr turnieren

jovial ['dʒovı·əl] adj jovial

jowls [dʒaulz] spl Hängebacken pl

joy [dʒɔɪ] s Freude f

joyful ['dʒɔɪfəl] adj froh, freudig

joyless ['dʒɔɪlıs] adj freudlos

joy' ride' s (coll) Schwarzfahrt f

joy' stick' s (aer) Steuerknüppel m

Jr. abbr (Junior) jr., jun.

jubilant ['dʒubılənt] adj frohlockend

jubilation [‚dʒubı'leʃən] s Jubel m

jubilee ['dʒubı‚li] s Jubiläum n

Judaea [dʒu'di·ə] s Judäa n

Judaic [dʒu'de·ık] adj jüdisch

Judaism ['dʒudə‚ızəm] s Judaismus m

judge [dʒʌdʒ] s (in a competition) Preisrichter –in mf; (box) Punktrichter m; (jur) Richter –in mf || tr (by) beurteilen (nach); (distances) abschätzen; (jur) richten || intr urteilen; (jur) richten; **judging by his words** seinen Worten nach zu urteilen

judge' ad'vocate s Kriegsgerichtsrat m

judgment ['dʒʌdʒmənt] s (& jur) Urteil n; **in my j.** meines Erachtens; **show good j.** ein gutes Urteilsvermögen haben; **sit in j. over** zu Gericht sitzen über (acc)

Judg'ment Day' s Tag m des Gerichts

judicial [dʒu'dıʃəl] adj Rechts–

judiciary [dʒu'dıʃı‚eri] adj richterlich || s (branch) richterliche Gewalt f; (judges) Richterstand m

judicious [dʒu'dıʃəs] adj klug

judo ['dʒudo] s Judo n

jug [dʒʌg] s Krug m; (jail) Kittchen n

juggle ['dʒʌgəl] tr jonglieren; (accounts) frisieren || intr jonglieren

juggler ['dʒʌglər] s Gaukler –in mf

Jugoslav ['jugo‚slav] adj jugoslawisch || s Jugoslawe m, Jugoslawin f

Jugoslavia [‚jugo'slavı·ə] s Jugoslawien n

jug'ular vein' ['dʒʌgjələr] s Halsader f

juice [dʒus] s Saft m

juicy ['dʒusi] adj saftig

jukebox ['dʒuk‚baks] s Musikautomat m

July [dʒu'laɪ] s Juli m

jumble ['dʒʌmbəl] s Wust m || tr durcheinanderwerfen

jumbo ['dʒʌmbo] adj Riesen–

jump [dʒʌmp] s Sprung m; (aer) Absprung m; **get the j. on** zuvorkommen (dat) || tr überspringen; (attack) überfallen; (a hurdle) nehmen; (in checkers) schlagen; **j. bail** die Kaution verfallen lassen; **j. channels** den amtlichen Weg nicht einhalten; **j. rope** seilspringen; **j. ship** vom Schiff weglaufen; **j. the gun** übereilt handeln; (sport) zu früh starten; **j. the track** entgleisen || intr springen; (be startled) auffahren; **j. at** (a chance) stürzen auf (acc); **j. down s.o.'s throat** j–n anfahren

jump' ball' s (basketball) Sprungball m

jumper ['dʒʌmpər] s (dress) Jumper m; (elec) Kurzschlußbrücke f

jump'-off' s Beginn m; (sport) Start m

jump' rope' s Springseil n

jumpy ['dʒʌmpi] adj unruhig, nervös

junction ['dʒʌŋkʃən] s Verbindung f; (of roads, rail lines) Knotenpunkt m

juncture ['dʒʌŋktʃər] s Verbindungsstelle f; **at this j.** in diesem Augenblick

June [dʒun] s Juni m

June' bug' s Maikäfer m

jungle ['dʒʌŋgəl] s Dschungel m, n & f

junior ['dʒunjər] adj jünger || s Student –in mf im dritten Studienjahr

juniper ['dʒunıpər] s Wacholder m

junk [dʒʌŋk] s Altwaren pl; (scrap iron) Schrott m; (useless stuff) Plunder m; (naut) Dschunke f

junket ['dʒʌŋkıt] s Vergnügungsreise f auf öffentliche Kosten

junk' mail' s Wurfsendung f

junk'yard' s Schrottplatz m

junta ['hʌntə], ['dʒʌntə] s Junta f

jurisdiction [‚dʒurıs'dıkʃən] s Zuständigkeit f; **have j. over** zuständig sein für

jurisprudence [‚dʒurıs'prudəns] s Rechtswissenschaft f

jurist ['dʒurıst] s Jurist –in mf

juror ['dʒurər] s Geschworene mf

jury ['dʒuri] s Geschworene pl

ju'ry box' s Geschworenenbank f

ju'ry tri'al s Schwurgerichtsverfahren n

just [dʒʌst] adj gerecht || adv gerade; (only) nur; (simply) einfach

justice ['dʒʌstıs] s Gerechtigkeit f; (of a claim) Berechtigung f; (judge) Richter m; **bring to j.** vor Gericht bringen; **do j. to** (a meal) wacker zusprechen (dat); (said of a picture) gerecht werden (dat)

jus'tice of the peace' s Friedensrichter m

justification [‚dʒʌstıfı'keʃən] s Rechtfertigung f

justi·fy ['dʒʌstı‚faɪ] v (pret & pp –fied) tr rechtfertigen

justly ['dʒʌstli] adv mit Recht

jut [dʒʌt] v (pret & pp **jutted**; ger **jutting**) intr—**jut out** hervorragen

juvenile ['dʒuvə‚naɪl] adj (books, court) Jugend–; (childish) unreif

ju'venile delin'quency s Jugendkriminalität f

ju'venile delin'quent s jugendlicher Verbrecher m

juxtapose [‚dʒʌkstə'poz] tr nebeneinanderstellen

K

K, k [ke] *s* elfter Buchstabe des englischen Alphabets
kale [kel] *s* Grünkohl *m*
kaleidoscopic [kə‚laɪdə'skɑpɪk] *adj* (& *fig*) kaleidoskopisch
kangaroo [‚kæŋgə'ru] *s* Känguruh *n*
kangaroo court' *s* Scheingericht *n*
kashmir ['kae'mɪr] *s* (tex) Kaschmir *m*
kayo ['ke'o] *s* K.o. *m* ∥ *tr* k.o. schlagen
keel [kil] *s* Kiel *m*; on an even k. (fig) gleichmäßig ∥ *intr*—k. over umkippen; (naut) kentern
keen [kin] *adj* (*sharp*) scharf; (*interest*) lebhaft; k. on scharf auf (*acc*)
keenness ['kinnɪs] *s* Schärfe *f*
keep [kip] *s* Unterhalt *m*; (*of a castle*) Bergfried *m*; for keeps (*forever*) für immer; (*seriously*) im Ernst ∥ *v* (*pret & pp* kept [kept]) *tr* (*retain*) behalten; (*detain*) aufhalten; (*save for s.o.*) aufbewahren; (*a secret*) bewahren; (*a promise*) (ein)halten; (*animals*) halten; (*books*) (acct) führen; be kept in school nachsitzen müssen; k. at arm's length vom Leibe halten; k. at bay sich erwehren (*genit*); k. away fernhalten; k. back zurückhalten; (*retain*) zurückbehalten; k. ... (*s.o.*) company Gesellschaft leisten (*dat*); k. down (*one's head*) niederhalten; (*one's voice*) verhalten; (*prices*) niedrig halten; k. from abhalten von; k. from (*ger*) daran hindern zu (*inf*); k. going im Gange halten; k. good time gut gehen; k. guard Wache halten; k. house den Haushalt führen; k. in good condition instand halten; k. in mind sich [*dat*] merken; k. it up! nur so weiter; k. on (*a garment*) anbehalten; (*a hat*) aufbehalten; k. oneself from (*ger*) es fertigbringen nicht zu (*inf*); k. one's temper sich beherrschen; k. out ausschließen; (*light*) nicht durchlassen; (*rain*) abhalten; k. posted auf dem laufenden halten; k. score die Punktliste führen; k. secret geheimhalten; k. step Tritt halten; k. s.th. from s.o. j-m etw verschweigen; k. track of sich [*dat*] merken; k. under wraps (coll) totschweigen; k. up instand halten; (*appearances*) wahren; (*correspondence*) unterhalten; k. up the good work! arbeiten Sie weiter so gut!; k. waiting warten lassen; k. warm warm halten; k. your shirt on! (coll) daß du die Nase im Gesicht behältst! ∥ *intr* (*said of food*) sich halten; k. at beharren bei; k. at it! bleib dabei!; k. away sich fernhalten; k. cool (fig) die Nerven behalten; k. cool! ruhig Blut!; k. from sich enthalten (*genit*); k. from (*ger*) es unterlassen zu (*inf*); k. from laughing sich das Lachen verkneifen;

k. going weitermachen; k. moving weitergehen; k. on (*ger*) weiter (*inf*), e.g., k. on driving weiterfahren; k. out! Eintritt verboten! k. out of sich fernhalten von; k. quiet sich ruhig verhalten; k. quiet! sei still!; k. to the right sich rechts halten; k. up with (*work*) nachkommen mit; k. up with the Joneses mit den Nachbarn Schritt halten; k. within bleiben innerhalb (*genit*)
keeper ['kipər] *s* (*of animals*) Halter –in *mf*; (*at a zoo*) Tierwärter –in *mf*; (*watchman*) Wächter *m*
keep'ing *s* Verwahrung *f*; in k. with in Einklang mit
keep'sake' *s* Andenken *n*
keg [keg] *s* Faß *n*
ken [ken] *s* Gesichtskreis *m*
kennel ['kenəl] *s* Hundezwinger *m*
kep·i ['kepi], ['kepi] *s* (-is) Kappi *n*
kerchief ['kʌrtʃɪf] *s* (*for the head*) Kopftuch *n*; (*for the neck*) Halstuch *n*
kernel ['kʌrnəl] *s* (*of fruit*) Kern *m*; (*of grain*) Korn *n*; (fig) Kern *m*
kerosene [‚kerə'sin] *s* Petroleum *n*
kerplunk [kər'plʌŋk] *interj* bums!
ketchup ['ketʃəp] *s* Ketchup *m* & *n*
kettle ['ketəl] *s* Kessel *m*
ket'tledrum' *s* Kesselpauke *f*
key [ki] *adj* (*ring, hole, industry, position*) Schlüssel– ∥ *s* (& *fig*) Schlüssel *m*; (*of a map*) Zeichenerklärung *f*; (*of a typewriter, piano, organ*) Taste *f*; (*of windinstrument*) Klappe *f*; (*reef*) Riff *n*; (*low island*) Insel *f*; (mus) Tonart *f*; key of C major C-dur; off key falsch ∥ *tr* (mach) festkeilen
key'board' *s* Tastatur *f*
keyed *adj*—k. to gestimmt auf (*acc*); k. up in Hochspannung
key' man' *s* Schlüsselfigur *f*
key'note *s* Grundgedanke *m*; (mus) Tonika *f*
key'note address' *s* programmatische Rede *f*
keynoter ['kɪ‚notər] *s* Programmatiker –in *mf*
keypuncher ['ki‚pʌntʃər] *s* Locher –in *mf*
key'stone' *s* Schlußstein *m*; (fig) Grundlage *f*
key' word' *s* Stichwort *n*
kha·ki ['kæki] *adj* Khaki– ∥ *s* (-kis) Khaki *m*; khakis Khakiuniform *f*
kibitz ['kɪbɪts] *intr* (coll) kiebitzen
kibitzer ['kɪbɪtsər] *s* (coll) Kiebitz *m*
kick [kɪk] *s* Fußtritt *m*; (*of a rifle*) Rückstoß *m*; (*of a horse*) Schlag *m*; (*final spurt*) (sport) Endspurt *m*; give s.o. a k. j-m e-n Fußtritt versetzen; I get a (great) k. out of him er macht mir (riesigen) Spaß ∥ *tr* treten, stoßen; (fb) kicken; be kicked upstairs (coll) die Treppe hinauffallen;

I could k. myself ich könnte mich ohrfeigen; **k. a goal** (fb) ein Tor schießen; **k.** (s.o.) **around** schlecht behandeln; (e.g., an idea) beschwatzen; **k. in** (money) beisteuern; **k. open** (a door) aufstoßen; **k. out** (coll) rausschmeißen; **k. s.o. in the shins** j-n gegen das Schienbein treten; **k. the bucket** (sl) krepieren; **k. up a storm** Krach schlagen || intr (said of a gun) stoßen; (said of a horse) ausschlagen; (complain) (about) meckern (über acc); **k. around** Europe in Europa herumbummeln; **k. off** (fb) anspielen

kick'back' s Schmiergeld n

kick'off' s (commencement) Beginn m; (fb) Anstoß m

kid [kɪd] s Zicklein n; (coll) Kind n || v (pret & pp kidded; ger kidding) tr necken || intr scherzen; **no kidding!** mach keine Witze!

kid' gloves' spl Glacéhandschuhe pl; **handle with k.** (fig) mit Glacéhandschuhen anfassen

kid'nap' v (pret & pp -nap(p)ed; ger -nap(p)ing) tr kidnappen, entführen

kidnap(p)er ['kɪd,næpər] s Kidnapper m

kid'nap(p)ing s Kidnapping s

kidney ['kɪdnɪ] s Niere f

kid'ney bean' s rote Bohne f

kid'ney-shaped' adj nierenförmig

kid'ney stone' s Nierenstein m

kid'ney trans'plant s Nierenverpflanzung f; (transplanted kidney) verpflanzte Niere f

kid'ney trou'ble s Nierenleiden n

kid' stuff' s (coll) Kinderei f

kill [kɪl] s (aer) Abschuß m; (hunt) Jagdbeute f; (nav) Versenkung f || tr töten; (murder) ermorden, killen; (plants) zum Absterben bringen; (time) totschlagen; (a proposal, plans, competition) zu Fall bringen; (the motor) abwürgen; (the ball) stark schlagen; (a bottle) austrinken; **be killed in action** (mil) im Felde) fallen; **it won't k. you** (coll) es wird dich nicht umbringen; **k. off** abschlachten; **k. oneself** sich umbringen; **k. two birds with one stone** zwei Fliegen mit e-r Klappe schlagen; **she is dressed to k.** sie ist totschick angezogen

killer ['kɪlər] s Totschläger –in mf, Killer m

kill'er whale' s Schwertwal m

kill'ing s Tötung f; **make a k.** e-n unerhofften Gewinn erzielen

kill'joy' s Spaßverderber m

kiln ['kɪl(n)] s Brennofen m

kil·o ['kɪlo], ['kilo] s (-os) Kilo n

kilocycle ['kɪlə,saɪkəl] s Kiloherz n

kilogram ['kɪlə,græm] s Kilogramm n

kilohertz ['kɪlə,hʌrts] s Kiloherz n

kilometer [kɪ'lɑmɪtər] s Kilometer m; **kilometers per hour** Stundenkilometer pl

kilowatt ['kɪlə,wɑt] s Kilowatt n

kil'owatt-hour' s Kilowattstunde f

kilt [kɪlt] s Kilt m

kilter ['kɪltər] s—**out of k.** nicht in Ordnung

kimo·no [kɪ'mono] s (-nos) Kimono m

kin [kɪn] s Sippe f; **the next of kin** die nächsten Angehörigen

kind [kaɪnd] adj liebenswürdig; (to) gütig (zu), freundlich (zu); **would you be so k. as to** (inf)? würden Sie so gefällig sein zu (inf)?; **with k. regards** mit freundlichen Grüßen || s Art f, Sorte f; **all kinds of** allerlei; **another k. of** ein anderer; **any k. of** irgendwelcher; **every k. of** jede Art von; **in k.** (fig) auf gleiche Weise; **k. of** (coll) etwas; **nothing of the k.** nichts dergleichen; **that k. of** derartig; **two** (three) **kinds of** zweierlei (dreierlei); **what k. of** was für ein

kindergarten ['kɪndər,gɑrtən] s Vorschule f, Vorschuljahr n

kind'-heart'ed adj gutmütig

kindle ['kɪndəl] tr anzünden; (fig) erwecken || intr sich entzünden

kindling ['kɪndlɪŋ] s Entzündung f; (wood) Kleinholz n

kindly ['kaɪndli] adj gütig, freundlich || adv freundlich; (please) bitte

kindness ['kaɪndnɪs] s Freundlichkeit f; (deed) Gefälligkeit f

kindred ['kɪndrɪd] adj verwandschaftlich; (fig) verwandt || s Verwandtschaft f

kinescope ['kɪnɪ,skop] s (trademark) Fernsehempfangsröhre f

kinetic [kɪ'netɪk] adj kinetisch || **kinetics** s Kinetik f

king [kɪŋ] s König m; (cards, chess) König m; (checkers) Dame f

kingdom ['kɪŋdəm] s Königreich n; (of animals, etc.) Reich n; **k. of heaven** Himmelreich n

king'fish'er s Königsfischer m

kingly ['kɪŋli] adj königlich

king'pin' s (coll) Boß m; (bowling) König m

king'ship' s Königtum n

king'-size' adj übergroß

kink [kɪŋk] s (in a wire) Knick m; (in the hair) Kräuselung f; (in a muscle) Muskelkrampf m; (flaw) Fehler m

kinky ['kɪŋki] adj gekräuselt

kin'ship' s Verwandtschaft f

kins'man s (-men) Blutsverwandte m

kins'wom'an s (-wom'en) Blutsverwandte f

kipper ['kɪpər] s Räucherhering m || tr einsalzen und räuchern

kiss [kɪs] s Kuß m || tr & intr küssen

kisser ['kɪsər] s (sl) Fresse f

kit [kɪt] s (equipment) Ausrüstung f; (tool kit) Werkzeugkasten m; (for models) Modellsatz m; (e.g., for a convention) Mappe f; **the whole kit and caboodle** (things) der ganze Kram; (persons) die ganze Sippschaft

kitchen ['kɪtʃən] s Küche f

kitchenette [,kɪtʃə'net] s Kochnische f

kit'chen knife' s Küchenmesser n

kit'chen police' s (mil) Küchendienst m

kit'chen range' s Herd m, Kochherd m

kit′chen sink′ s Ausguß m
kit′chenware′ s Küchengeschirr n
kite [kaɪt] s Drachen m; (orn) Weih m; **fly a k.** e-n Drachen steigen lassen; **go fly a k.!** (coll) scher dich zum Kuckuck!
kith′ and kin′ [kɪθ] spl Freunde and Verwandte pl
kitten ['kɪtən] s Kätzchen n
kitty ['kɪti] s Kätzchen n; (cards) gemeinsame Kasse f; **Kitty** Käthchen n
kleptomaniac [‚klɛptə'meni‚æk] s Kleptomane m, Kleptomanin f
knack [næk] s—**have a k. for** Talent haben für; **have the k. of** it den Griff heraus haben
knapsack ['næp‚sæk] s Rucksack m
knave [nev] s Schelm m; (cards) Bube m
knavery ['nevəri] s Schelmenstreich m
knead [nid] tr kneten
knead′ing trough′ s Teigmulde f
knee [ni] s Knie n; **bring s.o. to his knees** j–n auf die Knie zwingen; **go down on one's knees** niederknien; **on bended knees** kniefällig
knee′ bend′ s Kniebeuge f
knee′ breech′es spl Kniehose f
knee′cap′ s Kniescheibe f
knee′-deep′ adj knietief
knee′-high′ adj kniehoch
knee′ jerk′ s Patellarreflex m
kneel [nil] v (pret & pp **knelt** [nelt] & **kneeled**) intr knien
knee′-length′ adj kniefreit
knee′pad′ s (sport) Knieschützer m
knee′pan′ s Kniescheibe f
knee′ swell′ s (of organ) Knieschweller m
knell [nel] s Totengeläute n
knickers ['nɪkərz] spl Knickerbockerhosen pl
knicknack ['nɪk‚næk] s Nippsache f
knife [naɪf] s (knives [naɪvz]) Messer n || tr erstechen
knife′ sharp′ener s Messerschleifer m
knife′ switch′ s (elec) Messerschalter m
knight [naɪt] s Ritter m; (chess) Springer m || tr zum Ritter schlagen
knight′hood′ s Ritterschaft f
knightly ['naɪtli] adj ritterlich
knit [nɪt] v (pret & pp **knitted** & **knit**; ger **knitting**) tr stricken; **k. one's brows** die Brauen runzeln || intr stricken; (said of bones) zusammenheilen
knit′ goods′ spl Trikotwaren pl
knit′ted dress′ s Strickkleid n
knit′ting s (act) Strickerei f; (materials) Strickzeug n
knit′ting machine′ s Strickmaschine f
knit′ting nee′dle s Stricknadel f
knit′ting yarn′ s Strickgarn n
knit′wear′ s Strickwaren pl
knob [nɑb] s (of a door) Drücker m; (lump) Auswuchs m; (in wood) Knorren m; (of a radio) Knopf m
knock [nɑk] s (& aut) Klopfen n || tr (criticize) tadeln; **k. a hole through** durchbrechen; **k. around** herumstoßen; (mistreat) unsanft behandeln;

k. down niederschlagen; (with a car) umfahren; (trees) umbrechen; (at auctions) zuschlagen; **k. it off!** (sl) hör mal auf!; **k. oneself out over** sich [dat] die Zähne ausbeißen an (dat); **k. one's head against the wall** mit dem Kopf gegen die Wand rennen; **k. out** ausschlagen; (exhaust) (coll) strapazieren; (a tank) abschießen; (box) k.o. schlagen; **k. over** umwerfen; **k. together** (build hurriedly) schnell zusammenhauen; **k. to the ground** zu Boden schlagen; **k. up a girl** (sl) e-m Mädchen ein Kind anhängen || intr (an)klopfen; (aut) klopfen; **k. about** herumbummeln; **k. against** stoßen an (acc); **k. off** (from) (coll) aufhören (mit)
knock′down′ s (box) Niederschlag m
knocker ['nɑkər] s Türklopfer m; **knockers** (sl) Brüste pl
knock-kneed ['nɑk ‚nid] adj x-beinig
knock′-knees′ spl X-beine pl
knock′out′ s (woman) (coll) Blitzmädel n; (box) Knockout m
knock′out drops′ spl Betäubungsmittel n
knock′-out punch′ s K.o.-Schlag m
knoll [nol] s Hügel m
knot [nɑt] s Knoten m; (in wood) Knorren m; (of people) Gruppe f; (naut) Knoten m; **tie a k.** e-n Knoten machen; **tie the k.** (coll) sich verheiraten || tr e-n Knoten machen in (acc); (two ends) zusammenknoten
knot′hole′ s Astloch n
knotty ['nɑti] adj knorrig; (problem) knifflig
know [no] s—**be in the k.** Bescheid wissen || v (pret **knew** [n(j)u]; pp **known**) tr (facts) wissen; (be familiar with) kennen; (a language) können; **come to k.** erfahren; **get to k.** kennenlernen; **known** bekannt; **k. one's way around** sich auskennen; **k. the ropes** (coll) Bescheid wissen; **k. what's what** (coll) den Rummel kennen || intr wissen; **he ought to k. better** er sollte mehr Verstand haben; **k. about** wissen über (acc); **k. of** wissen von; **not that I k. of** (coll) nicht, daß ich wüßte; **you k.** (coll) wissen Sie
knowable ['no·əbəl] adj kenntlich
know′-how′ s Sachkenntnis f
know′ing adj (glance) vielsagend
knowingly ['no·ɪŋli] adv wissentlich; (intentionally) absichtlich
know′-it-all′ s Naseweis m
knowledge ['nɑlɪdʒ] s Wissen n, Kenntnisse pl; (information) (of) Kenntnis f (von); **basic k. of** Grundkenntnisse pl in (dat); **come to s.o.'s k.** j–m zur Kenntnis kommen; **to my k.** soweit ich weiß; **to the best of my k.** nach bestem Wissen; **without my k.** ohne mein Mitwissen; **working k.** of praktisch verwertbare Kenntnisse pl (genit)
knowledgeable ['nɑlɪdʒəbəl] adj kenntnisreich
known [non] adj bekannt; **become k.**

kundwerden; **k. all over town** stadtbekannt; **make k.** bekanntgeben

know'-noth'ing s Nichtswisser m

knuckle ['nʌkəl] s Knöchel m, Fingerknöchel m; (mach) Gelenkstück n; **k. of ham** Eisbein n || intr—**k. down to work** sich ernsthaft an die Arbeit machen; **k. under** klein beigeben

k.o. ['keʼo] s K.o. m || tr k.o.-schlagen

Koran [koʼræn] s Koran m

Korea [koʼri·ə] s Korea n

Korean [koʼri·ən] adj koreanisch || s Koreaner –in mf; (language) Koreanisch n

kosher ['koʃər] adj (& coll) koscher

kowtow ['kauʼtau] intr e–n Kotau machen; **k. to** kriechen vor (dat)

K.P. ['keʼpi] s **(kitchen police)** (mil) Küchendienst m

Kremlin ['kremlɪn] s Kreml m

kudos ['k(i)udɑs] s (coll) Ruhm m, Renommee n

L

L, l [ɛl] s zwölfter Buchstabe des englischen Alphabets

lab [læb] s (coll) Labor n

la·bel ['lebəl] s Etikett n; (brand) Marke f; (fig) Bezeichnung f || v (pret & pp –bel[l]ed; ger —bel[l]ing) tr etikettieren; (fig) bezeichnen

labial ['lebɪ·əl] adj Lippen– || s Lippenlaut m, Labial m

labor ['lebər] adj Arbeits–, Arbeiter– || s Arbeit f; (toil) Mühe f; **be in l.** in den Wehen liegen || tr (a point) ausführlich eingehen auf (acc) || intr sich abmühen; (at) arbeiten (an dat); (exert oneself) sich anstrengen; (said of a ship) stampfen; **l. under** zu leiden haben unter (dat)

la'bor and man'agement spl Arbeitnehmer und Arbeitgeber pl

laboratory ['læbərə,tori] s Laboratorium n

lab'oratory techni'cian s Laborant –in mf

la'bor camp' s Zwangsarbeitslager n

la'bor con'tract s Tarifvertrag m

la'bor dis'pute s Arbeitsstreitigkeit f

la'bored adj (e.g., breathing) mühsam; (style) gezwungen

laborer ['lebərər] s Arbeiter –in mf; (unskilled) Hilfsarbeiter –in mf

la'bor force' s Arbeitskräfte pl

laborious [ləʼborɪ·əs] adj mühsam, schwierig

la'bor law' s Arbeitsrecht n

la'bor lead'er s Arbeiterführer –in mf

la'bor mar'ket s Arbeitsmarkt m

la'bor move'ment s Arbeiterbewegung f

la'bor pains' spl Geburtswehen pl

la'bor-sav'ing adj arbeitssparend; **l. device** Hilfsgerät n

la'bor short'age s Mangel m an Arbeitskräften

la'bor sup'ply s Arbeitsangebot n

la'bor un'ion s Gewerkschaft f

laburnum [ləʼbʌrnəm] s Goldregen m

labyrinth ['læbɪrɪnθ] s Labyrinth n

lace [les] s (collar, dress) Spitzen– || s Spitze f; (shoestring) Schnürsenkel m || tr (e.g., shoes) schnüren; (braid) flechten; (drinks) (coll) mit e–m Schuß Branntwein versetzen; (beat) (coll) prügeln; **l. up** zuschnüren

lacerate ['læsə,ret] tr zerfleischen

laceration [,læsəʼreʃən] s Fleischwunde f

lace' trim'ming s Spitzenbesatz m

lace'work' s Spitzenarbeit f

lachrymose ['lækrɪ,mos] adj tränenreich

lac'ing s Schnürung f; (coll) Prügel pl

lack [læk] s (of) Mangel m (an dat); **for l. of** aus Mangel an (dat); **l. of space** Raummangel m; **l. of time** Zeitmangel m || tr—**I l.** es mangelt mir an (dat) || intr—**be lacking** fehlen; **he is lacking in courage** ihm fehlt der Mut

lackadaisical [,lækəʼdezɪkəl] adj teilnahmslos, gleichgültig

lackey ['læki] s Lakai m

lack'ing prep mangels (genit)

lack'lus'ter adj glanzlos

laconic [ləʼkɑnɪk] adj lakonisch

lacquer ['lækər] s Lack m || tr lackieren

lac'quer ware' s Lackwaren pl

lacrosse [ləʼkrɔs] s Lacrosse n

lacu·na [ləʼkjunə] s (–nas & –nae [ni]) Lücke f, Lakune f

lacy ['lesi] adj spitzenartig

lad [læd] s Bube m

la'dies' man' s Weiberheld m, Salonlöwe m

la'dies' room' s Damentoilette f

ladle ['ledəl] s Schöpflöffel m || tr ausschöpfen

lady ['ledi] s Dame f; **ladies and gentlemen** meine Damen und Herren!

la'dybird', la'dybug' s Marienkäfer m

la'dy compan'ion s Gesellschaftsdame f

la'dyfin'ger s Löffelbiskuit m & n

la'dy-in-wait'ing s (ladies-in-waiting) Hofdame f

la'dy-kil'ler s Schwerenöter m

la'dylike' adj damenhaft

la'dylove' s Geliebte f

la'dy of the house' s Hausherrin f

la'dy's maid' s Zofe f

la'dy's man' s var of **ladies' man**

lag [læg] s Zurückbleiben n; (aer) Rücktrift f; (phys) Verzögerung f || v (pret & pp **lagged**; ger **lagging**) intr (behind) zurückbleiben (hinter dat)

la'ger beer' ['lɑgər] s Lagerbier n

laggard ['lægərd] s Nachzügler m

lagoon [lə'guːn] *s* Lagune *f*
laid' up' *adj* (with) bettlägerig (infolge von); **be l. in bed** auf der Nase liegen
lair [ler] *s* Höhle *f*, Lager *n*
laity ['leːɪti] *s* Laien *pl*
lake [lek] *s* See *m*
Lake' Con'stance ['kɑnstəns] *s* der Bodensee
lamb [læm] *s* Lamm *n*; (culin) Lammfleisch *n*
lambaste [læm'best] *tr* (berate) (coll) herunterputzen; (beat) (coll) verdreschen
lamb' chop' *s* Hammelrippchen *n*
lambkin ['læmkɪn] *s* Lammfell *n*
lame [lem] *adj* (person, leg; excuse) lahm; **be l. in one leg** auf e—m Bein lahm sein ‖ *tr* lähmen
lament [lə'ment] *s* Jammer *m*; (dirge) Klagelied *n* ‖ *tr* beklagen ‖ *intr* wehklagen
lamentable ['læməntəbəl] *adj* beklagenswert; (pej) jämmerlich
lamentation [ˌlæmə'teːən] *s* Wehklage *f*
laminate ['læmɪˌnet] *tr* schichten
lamp [læmp] *s* Lampe *f*
lamp' chim'ney *s* Lampenzylinder *m*
lamp'light' *s* Lampenlicht *n*
lamp'light'er *s* Laternenanzünder *m*
lampoon [læm'puːn] *s* Schmähschrift *f* ‖ *tr* mit e—r Schmähschrift verspotten
lamp'post' *s* Laternenpfahl *m*
lamp'shade' *s* Lampenschirm *m*
lance [læns] *s* Lanze *f*; (surg) Lanzette *f* ‖ *tr* (surg) aufstechen
lance' cor'poral *s* (Brit) Hauptgefreite *m*
lancet ['lænsɪt] *s* Lanzette *f*
land [lænd] *s* (dry land; country) Land *n*; (ground) Boden *m*; **by l.** zu Lande ‖ *tr* (a plane, troops, punch) landen; (a ship, fish) an Land bringen; (a job) (coll) kriegen; **l. s.o. in trouble** j—n in Schwierigkeiten bringen ‖ *intr* (aer, naut, & fig) landen; (said of a blow) treffen; **l. on s.o.'s head** j—m auf den Kopf fallen; **l. on water** auf dem Wasser aufsetzen
land' breeze' *s* Landwind *m*
land'ed prop'erty *s* Landbesitz *m*
land'fall' *s* (sighting of land) Sichten *n* von Land; **make l.** landen
land' forc'es *spl* Landstreitkräfte *pl*
land'ing *s* Landung *f*; (of a staircase) Absatz *m*; **l. on the moon** Mondlandung *f*
land'ing craft' *s* Landungsboot *n*
land'ing field' *s* Landeplatz *m*
land'ing force' *s* Landekorps *n*
land'ing gear' *s* Fahrgestell *n*
land'ing par'ty *s* Landeabteilung *f*
land'ing stage' *s* Landungssteg *m*
land'ing strip' *s* Start- und Landestreifen *m*
land'la'dy *s* (of an apartment) Hauswirtin *f*; (of an inn) Gastwirtin *f*
land'locked' *adj* landumschlossen
land'lord' *s* (of an apartment) Hauswirt *m*; (of an inn) Gastwirt *m*
landlubber ['lænd,lʌbər] *s* Landratte *f*

land'mark' *s* Landmarke *f*; (cardinal event) Markstein *m*
land' of'fice *s* Grundbuchamt *n*
land'-office bus'iness *s* (fig) Bombengeschäft *n*
land'own'er *s* Grundbesitzer –in *mf*
landscape ['lænd,skep] *s* Landschaft *f*; (paint) Landschaftsbild *n* ‖ *tr* landschaftlich gestalten
land'scape ar'chitect *s* Landschaftsarchitekt –in *mf*
land'scape paint'er *s* Landschaftsmaler –in *mf*
land'slide' *s* Bergrutsch *m*; (pol) Stimmenrutsch *m*
landward ['lændwərd] *adv* landwärts
land' wind' [wɪnd] *s* Landwind *m*
lane [len] *s* Bahn *f*; (country road) Feldweg *m*; (aer) Flugschneise *f*; (aut) Fahrbahn *f*; (naut) Fahrtroute *f*; (sport) Laufbahn *f*; (sport) Schwimmbahn *f*
language ['læŋgwɪdʒ] *s* Sprache *f*
lan'guage instruc'tion *s* Sprachunterricht *m*
lan'guage teach'er *s* Sprachlehrer –in *mf*
languid ['læŋgwɪd] *adj* schlaff
languish ['læŋgwɪʃ] *intr* schmachten
languor ['læŋgər] *s* Mattigkeit *f*
languorous ['læŋgərəs] *adj* matt
lank [læŋk] *adj* schlank; (hair) glatt
lanky ['læŋki] *adj* schlaksig
lanolin ['lænəlɪn] *s* Lanolin *n*
lantern ['læntərn] *s* Laterne *f*
lan'tern slide' *s* Diapositiv *n*
lanyard ['lænjərd] *s* (around the neck) Halsschnur *f*; (naut) Taljereep *n*
Laos ['leːɑs] *s* Laos *n*
Laotian [le'oʃən] *adj* laotisch ‖ *s* Laote *m*, Laotin *f*; (language) Laotisch *n*
lap [læp] *s* (of the body or clothing) Schoß *m*; (of the waves) Plätschern *n*; (sport) Runde *f* ‖ *v* (pret & pp lapped; ger lapping) *tr* schlappen; (sport) überrunden; **lap up** auf(sch)lecken ‖ *intr*—**lap against** (e.g., a boat, shore) plätschern gegen; **lap over** hinausragen über (acc)
lap' dog' *s* Schoßhund *m*
lapel [lə'pel] *s* Aufschlag *m*
Lap'land' *s* Lappland *n*
Laplander ['læp,lændər] *s* Lappländer –in *mf*
Lapp [læp] *s* Lappe *m*, Lappin *f*; (language) Lappisch *n*
lapse [læps] *s* (error) Versehen *n*; (of time) Ablauf *m*; **after a l. of** nach Ablauf von; **l. of duty** Pflichtversäumnis *f*; **l. of memory** Gedächtnislücke *f* ‖ *intr* (said of a right, an insurance policy) verfallen; (said of time) ablaufen; **l. into** verfallen in (acc); **l. into unconsciousness** das Bewußtsein verlieren
lap'wing' *s* Kiebitz *m*
larceny ['lɑrsəni] *s* Diebstahl *m*
larch [lɑrtʃ] *s* (bot) Lärche *f*
lard [lɑrd] *s* Schmalz *n* ‖ *tr* spicken
larder ['lɑrdər] *s* Speisekammer *f*
large [lɑrdʒ] *adj* groß; **at l.** (as a whole) gesamt; (at liberty) auf freiem

Fuß; (*said of an official*) zur besonderen Verfügung; **become larger** sich vergrößern; **on a l. scale** in großem Umfang

large′ intes′tine *s* Dickdarm *m*

largely [′lɑrdʒli] *adv* größtenteils

largeness [′lɑrdʒnɪs] *s* Größe *f*

large′-scale′ *adj* Groß–; (*map*) in großem Maßstab; (*production*) Serien–

largesse [′lɑrdʒes] *s* (*generosity*) Freigebigkeit *f*; (*handout*) Geldverteilung *f*

lariat [′lærɪ-ət] *s* Lasso *m & n*; (*for grazing animals*) Halteseil *n*

lark [lɑrk] *s* (orn) Lerche *f*; **for a l.** zum Spaß

lark′spur′ *s* (bot) Rittersporn *m*

lar·va [′lɑrvə] *s* (–vae [vi]) Larve *f*

laryngitis [ˌlærɪn′dʒaɪtɪs] *s* Kehlkopfentzündung *f*, Laryngitis *f*

larynx [′lærɪŋks] *s* (**larynxes & larynges** [ləˈrɪndʒiz]) Kehlkopf *m*

lascivious [ləˈsɪvɪ-əs] *adj* wollüstig

lasciviousness [ləˈsɪvɪ-əsnɪs] *s* Wollüstigkeit *f*

laser [′lezər] *s* Laser *m*

lash [læʃ] *s* Peitsche *f*; (*as a punishment*) Peitschenhieb *m*; (*of the eye*) Wimper *f* ‖ *tr* (*whip*) peitschen; (*bind*) (*to*) anbinden (an *acc*); (*said of rain, storms*) peitschen ‖ *intr*— **l. out** (*at*) ausschlagen (nach)

lass [læs] *s* Mädel *n*

lassitude [′læsɪˌt(j)ud] *s* Mattigkeit *f*

last [læst] *adj* letzte; **very l.** allerletzte ‖ *adv* zuletzt; **l. of all** zuallerletzt ‖ *s* Letzte *mfn*; (*of a cobbler*) Schuhleisten *m*; **at l.** schließlich; **at long l.** zu guter Letzt; **look one's l. on** zum letzten Mal blicken auf (*acc*); **see the l. of s.o.** j–n nicht mehr wiedersehen; **to the l.** bis zum Letzten ‖ *intr* (*remain unchanged*) anhalten; (*for a specific time*) dauern; (*said of money, supplies*) reichen; (*said of a person*) aushalten

last′ing *adj* dauerhaft, andauernd; **l. effect** Dauerwirkung *f*; **l. for months** monatelang

Last′ Judg′ment *s* Jüngstes Gericht *n*

lastly [′læstli] *adv* zuletzt

last′-min′ute *adj* in letzter Minute

last′-minute news′ *s* neueste Nachrichten *pl*

last′ night′ *adv* gestern abend

last′ quar′ter *s* (astr) abnehmendes Mondviertel *n*; (com) letztes Quartal *n*

last′ resort′ *s* letztes Mittel *n*

last′ sleep′ *s* Todesschlaf *m*

last′ straw′ *s*—**that's the l.** das schlägt dem Faß den Boden aus

Last′ Sup′per, the *s* das Letzte Abendmahl

last′ week′ *adv* vorige Woche

last′ will′ and test′ament *s* letztwillige Verfügung *f*

last′ word′ *s* letztes Wort *n*; **the l.** (fig) der letzte Schrei

latch [lætʃ] *s* Klinke *f* ‖ *tr* zuklinken ‖ *intr* einschnappen; **l. on to** (coll) spitzkriegen

latch′key′ *s* Hausschlüssel *m*

late [let] *adj* (*after the usual time*) spät; (*at a late hour*) zu später Stunde; (*deceased*) verstorben; **be l.** sich verspäten; (*said of a train*) Verspätung haben; **keep l. hours** spät aufbleiben ‖ *adv* spät; **come l.** zu spät kommen; **of l.** kürzlich; **see you later** (coll) bis später!

latecomer [′letˌkʌmər] *s* Nachzügler *m*

lateen′ sail′ [læ′tin] *s* Lateinsegel *n*

lateen′ yard′ *s* Lateinrah *f*

lately [′letli] *adv* neulich, unlängst

lateness [′letnɪs] *s* Verspätung *f*

latent [′letənt] *adj* latent, verborgen

later [′letər] *adj* später ‖ *adv* später, nachher; **l. on** späterhin

lateral [′lætərəl] *adj* seitlich, Seiten–

lath [læθ] *s* Latte *f* ‖ *tr* belatten

lathe [leθ] *s* Drehbank *f*; **turn on a l.** drechseln

lather [′læðər] *s* Seifenschaum *m*; (*of a horse*) schäumender Schweiß *m* ‖ *tr* einseifen ‖ *intr* schäumen

lathing [′læθɪŋ] *s* Lattenwerk *n*

Latin [′lætɪn] *adj* lateinisch ‖ *s* (*Romance-speaking person*) Romane *m*, Romanin *f*; (*language*) Lateinisch *n*

La′tin Amer′ica *s* Lateinamerika *n*

La′tin-Amer′ican *adj* lateinamerikanisch ‖ *s* Lateinamerikaner –in *mf*

latitude [′lætɪˌt(j)ud] *s* Breite *f*; (fig) Spielraum *m*

latrine [ləˈtrin] *s* Latrine *f*

latter [′lætər] *adj* (*later*) später; (*final*) End–; (*recent*) letzte; **in the l. part of** (*e.g., the year*) in der zweiten Hälfte (*genit*); **the l.** dieser

lat′ter-day′ *adj* (*later*) später; (*recent*) letzte

Lat′ter-day Saint′ *s* Heilige *mf* der Jüngsten Tage

lattice [′lætɪs] *s* Gitter *n* ‖ *tr* vergittern

lat′ticework′ *s* Gitterwerk *n*

Latvia [′lætvɪ-ə] *s* Lettland *n*

Latvian [′lætvɪ-ən] *adj* lettisch ‖ *s* Lette *m*, Lettin *f*; (*language*) Lettisch *n*

laud [lɔd] *tr* loben, preisen

laudable [′lɔdəbəl] *adj* löblich

laudanum [′lɔd(ə)nəm] *s* Opiumtinktur *f*

laudatory [′lɔdəˌtɔri] *adj* Lob–

laugh [læf] *s* Lachen *n*, Gelächter *n*; **for laughs** zum Spaß; **have a good l.** sich auslachen ‖ *tr*—**l. off** sich lachend hinwegsetzen über (*acc*) ‖ *intr* lachen; **it's easy for you to l.** Sie haben leicht lachen!; **l. about** lachen über (*acc*); **l. at** (*deride*) auslachen; (*find amusement in*) lachen über (*acc*)

laughable [′læfəbəl] *adj* lächerlich

laugh′ing *adj* lachend; **it's no l. matter** es ist nichts zum Lachen

laugh′ing gas′ *s* Lachgas *n*

laugh′ingstock′ *s* Gespött *n*

laughter [′læftər] *s* Gelächter *n*, Lachen *n*; **roar with l.** vor Lachen brüllen

launch [lɔntʃ] *s* (*open boat*) Barkasse

f ‖ *tr* (*a boat*) aussetzen; (*a ship*) vom Stapel laufen lassen; (*a plane*) katapultieren; (*a rocket*) starten; (*a torpedo*) abschießen; (*an offensive*) beginnen; **be launched** (naut) vom Stapel laufen; (rok) starten ‖ *intr*—**l. into** sich stürzen in (*acc*)

launch′ing *s* (*of a ship*) Stapellauf *m*; (*of a torpedo*) Ausstoß *m*; (*of a rocket*) Abschuß *m*, Start *m*

launch′ pad′ *s* (rok) Startrampe *f*

launder [′lɔndər] *tr* waschen

laundress [′lɔndrɪs] *s* Wäscherin *f*

laundry [′lɔndrɪ] *s* (*clothes*) Wäsche *f*; (*room*) Waschküche *f*; (*business*) Wäscherei *f*

laun′drybag′ *s* Wäschebeutel *m*

laun′drybas′ket *s* Wäschekorb *m*

laun′dry list′ *s* Waschzettel *m*

laun′dry·man′ *s* (**–men′**) Wäscher *m*

laun′dry·wom′an *s* (**–wom′en**) Wäscherin *f*

laurel [′lɔrəl] *s* Lorbeer *m*

lau′rel tree′ *s* Lorbeerbaum *m*

lava [′lɑvə] *s* Lava *f*

lavatory [′lævə‚torɪ] *s* Waschraum *m*; (*toilet*) Toilette *f*

lavender [′lævəndər] *adj* lavendelfarben ‖ *s* (bot) Lavendel *m*

lavish [′lævɪʃ] *adj* (*person*) verschwenderisch; (*dinner*) üppig ‖ *tr*—**l. care on** hegen und pflegen; **l. sth. on s.o.** j-n mit etw überhäufen

lavishness [′lævɪ‚nɪs] *s* Üppigkeit *f*

law [lɔ] *s* Gesetz *n*; (*system*) Recht *n*; (*as a science*) Rechtswissenschaft *f*; (relig) Gebot *n*; **according to law** dem Recht entsprechend; **act within the law** sich ans Gesetz halten; **against the law** gesetzwidrig; **become law** Gesetzkraft erlangen; **by law** gesetzlich; **go against the law** gegen das Gesetz handeln; **lay down the law** gebieterisch auftreten; **practice law** den Anwaltsberuf ausüben; **study law** Jura studieren; **take the law into one's own hands** sich [*dat*] selbst sein Recht verschaffen; **under the law** nach dem Gesetz

law′-abid′ing *adj* friedlich

law′ and or′der *s* Ruhe und Ordnung *pl*

law′-and-or′der *adj* für Ruhe und Ordnung

law′break′er *s* Rechtsbrecher *–in mf*

law′break′ing *s* Rechtsbruch *m*

law′court′ *s* Gerichtshof *m*, Gericht *n*

lawful [′lɔfəl] *adj* gesetzmäßig

lawless [′lɔlɪs] *adj* gesetzlos

lawlessness [′lɔlɪsnɪs] *s* Gesetzlosigkeit *f*

law′mak′er *s* Gesetzgeber *m*

lawn [lɔn] *s* Rasen *m*; (tex) Batist *m*

lawn′ mow′er *s* Rasenmäher *m*

lawn′ par′ty *s* Gartenfest *n*

lawn′ sprin′kler *s* Rasensprenger *m*

law′ of dimin′ishing returns′ *s* Gesetz *n* der abnehmenden Erträge

law′ of′fice *s* Anwaltsbüro *n*

law′ of na′tions *s* Völkerrecht *n*

law′ of na′ture *s* Naturgesetz *n*

law′ of probabil′ity *s* Wahrscheinlichkeitsgesetz *n*

law′ of supply′ and demand′ *s* Gesetz *n* von Angebot und Nachfrage

law′ of the land′ *s* Landesgesetz *n*

law′ school′ *s* juristische Fakultät *f*

law′ stu′dent *s* Student *–in mf* der Rechtswissenschaft

law′suit′ *s* Klage *f*, Prozeß *m*

lawyer [′lɔjər] *s* Advokat *–in m*, Anwalt *–in mf*

lax [læks] *adj* lax, nachlässig

laxative [′læksətɪv] *s* Abführmittel *n*

laxity [′læksɪtɪ] *s* Laxheit *f*

lay [le] *adj* (*not of the clergy*) Laien-, weltlich; (*non-expert*) laienhaft ‖ *s* (*poem*) Lied *n* ‖ *v* (*pret & pp* laid [led]) *tr* legen; (*eggs; foundation, bricks, lineoleum*) legen; (*cables, pipes, tracks*) verlegen; (vulg) umlegen; **be laid up with** das Bett hüten müssen wegen (*genit*); **I'll lay you two to one** ich wette mit dir zwei zu eins; **lay aside** beiseite legen; (*save*) sparen; **lay bare** bloßlegen; **lay down** niederlegen; (*principles*) aufstellen; **lay claim to** Anspruch erheben auf (*acc*); **lay it on thick** dick auftragen; **lay low** (*said of an illness*) bettlägerig machen; **lay off** (*workers*) vorübergehend entlassen; **lay open** freilegen; **lay out** auslegen; (*a garden*) anlegen; (*money*) aufwenden; (*a corpse*) aufbahren; (surv) abstecken; **lay siege to** belagern; **lay waste** verwüsten ‖ *intr* (*said of hens*) legen; **lay for** auflauern (*dat*); **lay into** (*beat*) (coll) verdreschen; (*scold*) (coll) heruntermachen; **lay off** (*abstain from*) sich enthalten (*genit*); (*let alone*) in Ruhe lassen; **lay over** (*on a trip*) sich aufhalten; **lay to** (naut) stilliegen

lay′ broth′er *s* Laienbruder *m*

layer [′le·ər] *s* Schicht *f*; (bot) Ableger *m*; **in layers** schichtenweise; **l. of fat** Fettschicht *f*; **thin l.** Hauch *m*

lay′er cake′ *s* Schichttorte *f*

layette [le′ɛt] *s* Babyausstattung *f*

lay′ fig′ure *s* Gliederpuppe *f*

lay′man *s* (**–men**) Laie *m*; **layman's** laienhaft

lay′off′ *s* vorübergehende Entlassung *f*

lay′ of the land′ *s* Gestaltung *f* des Terrains; (fig) Gesichtspunkt *m* der Angelegenheit

lay′out′ *s* Anlage *f*, Anordnung *f*; (typ) Layout *n*; **l. of rooms** Raumverteilung *f*

laziness [′lezɪnɪs] *s* Faulheit *f*

lazy [′lezɪ] *adj* faul

la′zybones′ *s* (coll) Faulpelz *m*

la′zy Su′san *s* drehbares Tablett *n*

lea [li] *s* (poet) Aue *f*

lead [led] *adj* Blei– ‖ *s* Blei *n*; (*in a pencil*) Mine *f*; (*plumb line*) Bleilot *n* ‖ *v* (*pret & pp* leaded; *ger* leading) *tr* verbleien; (typ) durchschießen ‖ [lid] *s* Führung *f*; (cards) Vorhand *f*; (elec) Zuführung *f*; (sport) Vorsprung *m*; (theat) Hauptrolle *f*; **be in the l.** an der Spitze stehen; **have the l.** die Führung haben; **take the l.** die Führung übernehmen ‖ *v* (*pret & pp* led [led]) *tr* führen, leiten; *(to error, drinking, etc.)* verleiten; *(a parade)* anführen; *(a life)* führen; **l. astray** verführen; **l. away** wegführen; *(e.g., a criminal)* abführen; **l. back** zurückführen; **l. by the nose** an der Nase herumführen; **l. on** weiterführen; *(deceive)* täuschen; **l. the way** vorangehen || *intr* führen; *(cards)* anspielen; **l. nowhere** zu nichts führen; **l. off** den Anfang machen; **l. to** hinausgehen auf *(acc)*; **l. up to** hinauswollen auf *(acc)* **where will all this l. to?** wo soll das alles hinführen?

leaden ['ledən] *adj* bleiern; *(in color)* bleifarbig; *(sluggish)* schwerfällig; **l. sky** bleierner Himmel *m*

leader ['lidər] *s* Führer –in *mf*; *(of a band)* Dirigent –in *mf*; *(of a film)* Vorspann *m*; *(lead article)* Leitartikel *m*

lead′ership′ *s* Führung *f*

leading ['lidɪŋ] *adj* *(person, position, power)* führend

lead′ing i′de′a *s* Leitgedanke *m*

lead′ing la′dy *s* Hauptdarstellerin *f*

lead′ing man′ *s* Hauptdarsteller *m*

lead′ing ques′tion *s* Suggestivfrage *f*

lead′ing role′ *s* Hauptrolle *f*

lead′-in wire′ *s* Zuleitungsdraht *m*

lead′ pen′cil [led] *s* Bleistift *m*

lead′ pipe′ [led] *s* Bleirohr *n*

lead′ poi′soning [led] *s* Bleivergiftung *f*

leaf [lif] *s* **(leaves** [livz] **)** Blatt *n*; *(of a folding door)* Flügel *m*; *(of a folding table)* Tischklappe *f*; *(insertable table board)* Einlegebrett *n*; **turn over a new l.** ein neues Leben anfangen || *intr*—**l. through** durchblättern

leafage ['lifɪdʒ] *s* Laubwerk *n*

leafless ['liflɪs] *adj* blattlos

leaflet ['liflɪt] *s* Werbeprospekt *m*, Flugblatt *n*; *(bot)* Blättchen *n*

leafy ['lifi] *adj* *(abounding in leaves)* belaubt; *(e.g., vegetables)* Blatt–

league [lig] *s* Bund *m*; *(unit of distance)* Meile *f*; *(sport)* Liga *f*; **in l. with** verbündet mit || *tr* verbünden || *intr* sich verbünden

League′ of Na′tions *s* Völkerbund *m*

leak [lik] *s* Leck *n*; **spring a l.** ein Leck bekommen; **take a l.** (vulg) schiffen || *tr* *(e.g., a story to the press)* durchsickern lassen || *intr* *(said of a container)* leck sein; *(said of a boat)* lecken; *(said of a fluid)* auslaufen; *(said of a spigot)* tropfen; **l. out** (& fig) durchsickern

leakage ['likɪdʒ] *s* Lecken *n*; (& fig) Durchsickern *n*; *(com)* Schwund *m*; *(elec)* Streuung *f*

leaky ['liki] *adj* leck

lean [lin] *adj* mager || *v* *(pret & pp* **leaned** & **leant** [lent]) *tr (against)* lehnen (an *acc* or gegen) || *intr* lehnen; **l. against** sich anlehnen an *(acc)*; **l. back** sich zurücklehnen; **l. forward** sich vorbeugen; **l. on** sich stützen auf *(acc)*; **l. over** *(e.g., a railing)* sich neigen über *(acc)*; **l. toward** (fig) neigen zu

lean′ing *adj* sich neigend; *(tower)* schief || *s* **(toward)** Neigung *f* (zu)

leanness ['linnɪs] *s* Magerkeit *f*

lean′-to′ *s* **(–tos)** Anbau *m* mit Pultdach

lean′ years′ *spl* magere Jahre *pl*

leap [lip] *s* Sprung *m*, Satz *m*; **by leaps and bounds** sprungweise; **l. in the dark** (fig) Sprung *m* ins Ungewisse || *v* *(pret & pp* **leaped** & **leapt** [lept]) *tr* überspringen || *intr* springen; **l. at** anspringen; **l. at an opportunity** e-e Gelegenheit beim Schopf ergreifen; **l. forward** vorspringen; **l. up** emporschnellen

leap′frog′ *s* Bockspringen *m*; **play l.** Bocksprünge machen

leap′ year′ *s* Schaltjahr *n*

learn [lʌrn] *v* *(pret & pp* **learned** & **learnt** [lʌrnt]) *tr* lernen; *(find out)* erfahren; **l. s.th. from s.o.**

learned ['lʌrnɪd] *adj* *(person, word)* gelehrt; *(for or of scholars)* Gelehrten–

learn′ed jour′nal *s* Gelehrtenzeitschrift *f*

learn′ed soci′ety *s* Gelehrtenvereinigung *f*

learn′ed world′ *s* Gelehrtenwelt *f*

learn′ing *s* *(act)* Lernen *n*; *(erudition)* Gelehrsamkeit *f*

lease [lis] *s* Mietvertrag *m*; *(of land)* Pachtvertrag *m* || *tr (in the role of landlord)* vermieten; *(land)* verpachten; *(in the role of tenant)* mieten; *(land)* pachten

lease′hold′ *adj* Pacht– || *s* Pachtbesitz *m*

leash [liʃ] *s* Leine *f*, Hundeleine *f*; **keep on the l.** an der Leine führen; **strain at the l.** (fig) an der Leine zerren || *tr* an die Leine nehmen

leas′ing *s* Miete *f*; *(of land)* Pachtung *f*; **l. out** Vermietung *f*; *(of land)* Verpachtung *f*

least [list] *adj* mindeste, wenigste || *adv* am wenigsten; **l. of all** am wenigsten von allen || *s* Geringste *mfn*; **at l.** mindestens, wenigstens; **at the very l.** zum mindesten; **not in the l.** nicht im mindesten

leather ['lɛðər] *adj* ledern || *s* Leder *n*

leath′er bind′ing *s* Ledereinband *m*

leath′erbound′ *adj* ledergebunden

leath′erneck′ *s* (sl) Marineinfanterist *m*

leathery ['lɛðəri] *adj* *(e.g., steak)* (coll) lederartig

leave [liv] *s* *(permission)* Erlaubnis *f*; (mil) Urlaub *m*; **on l.** auf Urlaub; **take l. (from)** Abschied nehmen (von); **take l. of one's senses** (coll) den Verstand verlieren || *v* *(pret & pp* **left** [left]) *tr (go away from)* verlassen; *(undone, open, etc.)* lassen; *(a message, bequest)* hinterlassen; *(a job)* aufgeben; *(a scar)* zurücklassen; *(forget)* liegenlassen, stehenlassen; *(e.g., some food for s.o.)* übriglassen; **be left** übrig sein; **l. alone** *(a thing)* bleibenlassen; *(a person)* in Frieden lassen; **l. behind** *(said of a deceased person)* hinterlassen; *(forget)* liegenlassen; **l. home** von zu Hause fortgehen; **l. it at that!** überlaß es mir!; **l. lying about** herumliegen lassen; **l. nothing to chance** nichts dem Zufall überlassen; **l. nothing undone** nichts unversucht lassen; **l. open** offen lassen; **l. out** auslassen; **l. standing** stehenlassen; **l.** *(e.g., work)* **undone** liegenlassen || *intr* fortgehen; *(on travels)* abreisen; *(said of vehicles)* abfahren; (aer) abfliegen; **l. off** *(e.g., from reading)* aufhören

leaven ['lɛvən] *s* Treibmittel *n* || *tr* säuern

leav'ening *s* Treibstoff *m*

leave' of ab'sence *s* Urlaub *m*

leave'-tak'ing *s* Abschiednehmen *n*

leavings ['livɪŋz] *spl* Überbleibsel *pl*

Leba·nese [ˌlɛbə'niz] *adj* libanesisch || *s (-nese)* Libanese *m*, Libanesin *f*

Lebanon ['lɛbənən] *s* Libanon *n*

lecher ['lɛtʃər] *s* Lüstling *m*

lecherous ['lɛtʃərəs] *adj* wollüstig

lechery ['lɛtʃəri] *s* Wollust *f*

lectern ['lɛktərn] *s* Lesepult *n*

lector ['lɛktər] *s* (eccl) Lektor *m*

lecture ['lɛktʃər] *s* Vorlesung *f*, Vortrag *m*; (coll) Standpauke *f*; **give a l. on** e-n Vortrag halten über *(acc)*; **give s.o. a l.** j-m den Text lesen || *tr* (coll) abkanzeln || *intr* lesen

lecturer ['lɛktʃərər] *s* Vortragende *mf*; *(at a university)* Dozent –in *mf*

lec'ture room' *s* Hörsaal *m*

ledge [lɛdʒ] *s* Sims *m & n*; *(of a cliff)* Felsenriff *n*

ledger ['lɛdʒər] *s* (acct) Hauptbuch *n*

lee [li] *s* Lee *f*

leech [litʃ] *s* Blutegel *m*; (fig) Blutsauger –in *mf*

leek [lik] *s* (bot) Porree *m*, Lauch *m*

leer [lɪr] *s* lüsterner Seitenblick *m* || *intr* (at) lüstern schielen (nach)

leery ['lɪri] *adj* mißtrauisch; **be l. of** mißtrauen *(dat)*

lees [liz] *spl* Hefe *f*

lee' side' *s* Leeseite *f*

leeward ['liwərd] *adv* leewärts || *s* Leeseite *f*

Lee'ward Is'lands *spl* Inseln *pl* unter dem Winde

lee'way' *s* (coll) Spielraum *m*; (aer, naut) Abtrift *f*

left [lɛft] *adj* linke; *(left over)* übrig || *adv* links; **l. face!** (mil) links um! || *s (left hand)* Linke *f*; **on our l.** zu unserer Linken; **the l.** (pol) die Linke; **the third street to the l.** die dritte Querstraße links; **to the l.** nach links; **to the l. of** links von

left' field' *s* (baseball) linkes Außenfeld *n*

left' field'er *s* Spieler *m* im linken Außenfeld

left'-hand drive' *s* Linkssteuerung *f*

left'-hand'ed *adj* linkshändig; *(compliment)* fragwürdig; *(counterclockwise)* linksgängig; *(clumsy)* linkisch

left-hander ['lɛft'hændər] *s* Linkshänder –in *mf*

leftish ['lɛftɪʃ] *adj* linksgerichtet

leftist ['lɛftɪst] *s* Linksradikaler *m*; (pol) Linkspolitiker –in *mf*

left'o'ver *adj* übriggeblieben || **leftovers** *spl* Überbleibsel *pl*

left'-wing' *adj* Links-

left' wing' *s* (pol) linker Flügel *m*; (sport) Linksaußen *m*

left-winger ['lɛft'wɪŋər] *s* (coll) Linkspolitiker –in *mf*

lefty ['lɛfti] *adj* (coll) linkshändig || *s* (coll) Linkshänder –in *mf*

leg [lɛg] *s* *(of a body, of furniture, of trousers)* Bein *n*; *(stretch)* Etappe *f*; *(of a compass)* Schenkel *m*; *(of a boot)* Schaft *m*; **be on one's last legs** auf dem letzten Loche pfeifen; **pull s.o.'s leg** (coll) j-n auf die Schippe nehmen; **run one's legs off** sich abrennen; **you don't have a leg to stand on** Sie haben keinerlei Beweise

legacy ['lɛgəsi] *s* Vermächtnis *n*

legal ['ligəl] *adj (according to the law)* gesetzlich, legal; *(pertaining to or approved by law)* Rechts-, juristisch; **take l. action** den Rechtsweg beschreiten; **take l. steps against s.o.** gerichtlich gegen j-n vorgehen

le'gal advice' *s* Rechtsberatung *f*

le'gal advis'er *s* Rechtsberater –in *mf*

le'gal age' *s* Volljährigkeit *f*; **of l.** großjährig

le'gal aid' *s* Rechtshilfe *f*

le'gal ba'sis *s* Rechtsgrundlage *f*

le'gal case' *s* Rechtsfall *m*

le'gal claim' *s* Rechtsanspruch *m*

le'gal en'tity *s* juristische Person *f*

le'gal force' *s* Rechtskraft *f*

le'gal grounds' *spl* Rechtsgrund *m*

le'gal hol'iday *s* gesetzlicher Feiertag *m*

legality [lɪ'gælɪti] *s* Gesetzlichkeit *f*, Rechtlichkeit *f*

legalize ['ligəˌlaɪz] *tr* legalisieren

le'gal jar'gon *s* Kanzleisprache *f*

le'gal profes'sion *s* Rechtsanwaltsberuf *m*

le'gal rem'edy *s* Rechtsmittel *n*

le'gal ten'der *s* gesetzliches Zahlungsmittel *n*; **be l.** gelten

le'gal ti'tle *s* Rechtsanspruch *m*

legate ['lɛgɪt] *s* Legat –in *mf*

legatee [ˌlɛgə'ti] *s* Legatar –in *mf*

legation [lɪ'geʃən] *s* Gesandtschaft *f*

legend ['lɛdʒənd] *s* Legende *f*

legendary ['lɛdʒənˌdɛri] *adj* legendär

legerdemain [ˌlɛdʒərdɪ'men] *s* Taschenspielerei *f*

leggings ['lɛgɪŋz] *spl* hohe Gamaschen *pl*

leggy ['lɛgi] *adj* langbeinig

Leg'horn' *s* (chicken) Leghorn *n*; *(town in Italy)* Livorno *n*

legibility [ˌlɛdʒɪ'bɪlɪti] *s* Lesbarkeit *f*

legible ['lɛdʒɪbəl] *adj* lesbar

legion ['lidʒən] *s* Legion *f*; (fig) Heerschar *f*

legionnaire [ˌlidʒə'nɛr] *s* Legionär *m*

legislate ['lɛdʒɪsˌlet] *tr* durch Gesetzgebung bewirken || *intr* Gesetze geben

legislation [ˌlɛdʒɪs'leʃən] *s* Gesetzgebung *f*

legislative ['ledʒɪs,letɪv] *adj* gesetzgebend

legislator ['ledʒɪs,letər] *s* Gesetzgeber –in *mf*

legislature ['ledʒɪs,letʃər] *s* Legislatur

legitimacy [lɪ'dʒɪtɪməsɪ] *s* Rechtmäßigkeit *f*

legitimate [lɪ'dʒɪtɪmɪt] *adj* gesetzmäßig, legitim; (*child*) ehelich || [lɪ'dʒɪtɪ,met] *tr* legitimieren

legit'imate the'ater *s* literarisch wertvolles Theater *n*

legitimize [lɪ'dʒɪtɪ,maɪz] *tr* legitimieren

leg' of lamb' *s* Lammkeule *f*

leg' of mut'ton *s* Hammelkeule *f*

leg' room' *s* Beinfreiheit *f*

leg'work' *s* Vorarbeiten *pl*

leisure ['liʒər] *s* Muße *f*; at l. mit Muße; at s.o.'s l. wenn es j–m paßt

lei'sure class' *s* wohlhabende Klasse *f*

lei'sure hours' *spl* Mußestunden *pl*

leisurely ['liʒərlɪ] *adj & adv* gemächlich

lei'sure time' *s* Freizeit *f*

lemon ['lemən] *adj* Zitronen– || *s* Zitrone *f*; (sl) Niete *f*

lemonade [,lemɪ'ned] *s* Zitronenlimonade *f*

lem'on squeez'er *s* Zitronenpresse *f*

lend [lend] *v* (*pret & pp* lent [lent]) *tr* leihen, borgen; l. at five percent interest zu fünf Prozent Zinsen anlegen; l. itself to sich eignen zu or für; l. oneself to sich hergeben zu; l. out ausleihen, verborgen; l. s.o. a hand j–m zur Hand gehen

lender ['lendər] *s* Verleiher –in *mf*

lend'ing li'brary *s* Leihbücherei *f*

length [leŋθ] *s* Länge *f*; (*of time*) Dauer *f*; (*in horse racing*) Pferdelänge *f*; at great l. sehr ausführlich; at l. ausführlich; (*finally*) schließlich; at some l. ziemlich ausführlich; go to any l. alles Erdenkliche tun; go to great lengths sich sehr bemühen; keep s.o. at arm's l. zu j–m Abstand wahren; stretch out full l. sich der Länge nach ausstrecken

lengthen ['leŋθən] *tr* verlängern; (*a vowel*) dehnen

length'ening *s* Verlängerung *f*; (ling) Dehnung *f*

length'wise' *adj & adv* der Länge nach

lengthy ['leŋθɪ] *adj* langwierig

leniency ['linɪ-ənsɪ] *s* Milde *f*

lens [lenz] *s* Linse *f*; (*combination of lenses*) Objektiv *n*

Lent [lent] *s* Fastenzeit *f*

Lenten ['lentən] *adj* Fasten–

lentil ['lentɪl] *s* (bot) Linse *f*

leopard ['lepərd] *s* Leopard *m*

leper ['lepər] *s* Aussätzige *mf*

leprosy ['lepräsɪ] *s* Aussatz *m*, Lepra *f*

lesbian ['lezbɪ-ən] *adj* lesbisch || *s* Lesbierin *f*

lesbianism ['lezbɪ-ə,nɪzəm] *s* lesbische Liebe *f*

lesion ['liʒən] *s* Wunde *f*

less [les] *comp adj* weniger, geringer;

l. and l. immer weniger || *adv* weniger, minder; l. than weniger als || *s*—do with l. mit weniger auskommen; for l. billiger; in l. than no time in Null Komma nichts || *prep* abzüglich (*genit or acc*); (arith) weniger (*acc*), minus (*acc*)

lessee [le'si] *s* Mieter –in *mf*; (*of land*) Pächter –in *mf*

lessen ['lesən] *tr* vermindern || *intr* sich vermindern, abnehmen

lesser ['lesər] *comp adj* minder, geringer

lesson ['lesən] *s* Unterrichtsstunde *f*, Stunde *f*; (*in a textbook*) Lektion *f*; (*warning*) Lehre *f*; learn a l. from e–e Lehre ziehen aus; let that be l. to you! lassen Sie sich das e–e Lehre sein

lessor ['lesər] *s* Vermieter –in *mf*; (*of land*) Verpächter –in *mf*

lest [lest] *conj* damit nicht; (after expressions of fear) daß

let [let] *v* (*pret & pp* let; *ger* letting) *tr* lassen; I really let him have it! (coll) ich hab's ihm ordentlich gegeben!; let alone in Ruhe lassen; (*not to mention*) geschweige denn; let down herunterlassen; (*disappoint*) enttäuschen; let fly fliegen lassen; (coll) loslassen; let go fortlassen, loslassen; let go ahead vorlassen; let in hereinlassen; (*water*) zuleiten; let in on (*e.g., a secret*) einweihen in (*acc*); let it go, e.g., I'll let it go this time diesmal werde ich es noch hingehen lassen; let lie liegenlassen; let know wissen lassen, Bescheid geben (*dat*); let off (*e.g., at the next corner*) absetzen; let off easy noch so davonkommen lassen; let off scot-free straflos laufen lassen; let one's hair down (fig) sich gehenlassen; let out (*seams, air, water*) auslassen; (*e.g., a yell*) von sich geben; let pass durchlassen; let s.o. have s.th. j–m etw zukommen lassen; let stand (fig) gelten lassen; let through durchlassen; let things slide die Dinge laufen lassen; let things take their course den Dingen ihren Lauf lassen; let's go! los!; let us (or let's) (*inf*), e.g., let's (or let us) sing singen wir || *intr* (*be rented out*) (for) vermietet werden (für); let fly with (coll) loslegen mit; let go of loslassen; let on that sich [*dat*] anmerken lassen, daß; let up nachlassen; let up on (coll) ablassen von

let'down' *s* Hereinfall *m*

lethal ['liθəl] *adj* tödlich

lethargic [lɪ'θärdʒɪk] *adj* lethargisch

lethargy ['leθərdʒɪ] *s* Lethargie *f*

letter ['letər] *s* Brief *m*, Schreiben *n*; (*of the alphabet*) Buchstabe *m*; by l. brieflich, schriftlich; to the l. aufs Wort || *tr* beschriften

let'ter box' *s* Briefkasten *m*

let'ter car'rier *s* Briefträger –in *mf*

let'ter drop' *s* Briefeinwurf *m*

let'tered *adj* gelehrt

let'ter file' *s* Briefordner *m*

let′terhead′ *s* Briefkopf *m*
let′tering *s* (*act*) Beschriften *n*; (*inscription*) Beschriftung *f*
let′ter of condol′ence *s* Beileidsbrief *m*
let′ter of cred′it *s* Kreditbrief *m*
let′ter of recommenda′tion *s* Empfehlungsbrief *m*
letter o′pener *s* Brieföffner *m*
let′terper′fect *adj* buchstabengetreu
let′terpress′ *s* (*typ*) Hochdruck *m*
let′ter scales′ *spl* Briefwaage *f*
let′ter to the ed′itor *s* Leserbrief *m*
lettuce [′letɪs] *s* Salat *m*
let′up′ *s* Nachlassen *n*; **without l.** ohne Unterlaß
leukemia [lu′kimi·ə] *s* Leukämie *f*
Levant [lɪ′vænt] *s* Levante *f*
Levantine [lɪ′væntin] *adj* levantinisch || *s* Levantiner –in *mf*
levee [′levɪ] *s* Uferdamm *m*
lev·el [′levəl] *adj* eben, gerade; (*flat*) flach; (*spoonful*) gestrichen; **be l. with** so hoch sein wie; **do one's l. best** sein Möglichstes tun; **have a l. head** ausgeglichen sein; **keep a l. head** e–n klaren Kopf behalten || *s* (& *fig*) Niveau *n*; (*tool*) Wasserwaage *f*; **at higher levels** höheren Ortes; **be up to the usual l.** (*fig*) auf der gewöhnlichen Höhe sein; **on a l. with** (& *fig*) auf gleicher Höhe mit; **on the l.** (*fig*) ehrlich || *v* (*pret & pp* **-el[l]ed;** *ger* **-el[l]ing** *tr* (*a street, ground*) planieren; **l.** (*e.g., a rifle*) **at** richten auf (*acc*); (*e.g., complaints*) richten gegen; **l. off** nivellieren; (*aer*) abfangen; **l. to the ground** dem Erdboden gleichmachen || *intr*— **l. off** sich verflachen; (*said of prices*) sich stabilisieren; (*aer*) **in** Horizontalflug übergehen; **l. with s.o.** mit j–m offen sein
lev′elhead′ed *adj* besonnen, vernünftig
lever [′livər] *s* Hebel *m*, Brechstange *f* || *tr* mit e–r Brechstange fortbewegen
leverage [′livərɪdʒ] *s* Hebelkraft *f*; (*fig*) Einfluß *m*
leviathan [lɪ′vaɪ·əθən] *s* Leviathan *m*
levitate [′levɪ‚tet] *tr* schweben lassen || *intr* frei schweben
levitation [‚levɪ′teʃən] *s* Schweben *n*
levity [′levɪti] *s* Leichtsinn *m*
lev·y [′levɪ] *s* Truppenaushebung *f*; (*of taxes*) Erhebung *f*; (*tax*) Steuer *f* || *v* (*pret & pp* **-vied**) *tr* (*troops*) ausheben; (*taxes*) erheben; **l. war on** Krieg führen gegen
lewd [lud] *adj* unzüchtig
lewdness [′ludnɪs] *s* Unzucht *f*
lexical [′leksɪkəl] *adj* lexikalisch
lexicographer [‚leksɪ′kagrəfər] *s* Lexikograph –in *mf*
lexicographic(al) [‚leksɪkə′græfɪk(əl)] *adj* lexikographisch
lexicography [‚leksɪ′kagrəfi] *s* Lexikographie *f*
lexicology [‚leksɪ′kalədʒi] *s* Wortforschung *f*, Lexikologie *f*
lexicon [′leksɪkən] *s* Wörterbuch *n*
liability [‚laɪ·ə′bɪlɪti] *s* (ins) Haftpflicht *f*; (jur) Haftung *f*; **liabilities** Schulden *pl*; (acct) Passiva *pl*

liabil′ity insur′ance *s* Haftpflichtversicherung *f*
liable [′laɪ·əbəl] *adj* (jur) (**for**) haftbar (**für**); **be l. to** (*inf*) (coll) leicht können (*inf*); **l. for damages** schadenersatzpflichtig
liaison [li′ezɑn] *s* Verbindung *f*; (*illicit affair*) Liaison *f*; (ling) Bindung *f*
liai′son of′ficer *s* Verbindungsoffizier *m*
liar [′laɪ·ər] *s* Lügner –in *mf*
libation [laɪ′beʃən] *s* Opfertrank *m*
li·bel [′laɪbəl] *s* Verleumdung *f*; (*in writing*) Schmähschrift *f* || *v* (*pret & pp* **-bel[l]ed;** *ger* **-bel[l]ing**) *tr* verleumden
libelous [′laɪbələs] *adj* verleumderisch
li′bel suit′ *s* Verleumdungsklage *f*
liberal [′lɪbərəl] *adj* (*views*) liberal, freisinnig; (*with money*) freigebig; (*gift*) großzügig; (*interpretation*) weitherzig; (*education*) allgemeinbildend; (pol) liberal || *s* Liberale *mf*
lib′eral arts′ *spl* Geisteswissenschaften *pl*
liberalism [′lɪbərə‚lɪzəm] *s* Liberalismus *m*
liberality [‚lɪbə′rælɪti] *s* Freigebigkeit *f*, Großzügigkeit *f*
liberate [′lɪbə‚ret] *tr* befreien; (chem) freimachen
liberation [‚lɪbə′reʃən] *s* Befreiung *f*; (chem) Freimachen *n*
liberator [′lɪbə‚retər] *s* Befreier –in *mf*
libertine [′lɪbər‚tin] *s* Wüstling *m*
liberty [′lɪbərti] *s* Freiheit *f*; **take liberties** sich [*dat*] Freiheiten herausnehmen; **you are at l. to** (*inf*) es steht Ihnen frei zu (*inf*)
libidinous [lɪ′bɪdɪnəs] *adj* wollüstig
libido [lɪ′bido] *s* Libido *f*
librarian [laɪ′brerɪ·ən] *s* Bibliothekar –in *mf*
library [′laɪ‚brerɪ] *s* Bibliothek *f*
li′brary card′ *s* Benutzerkarte *f*
libret·to [lɪ′breto] *s* (**-tos**) Operntext *m*, Libretto *n*
Libya [′lɪbɪ·ə] *s* Libyen *n*
Libyan [′lɪbɪ·ən] *adj* libysch || *s* Libyer –in *mf*
license [′laɪsəns] *s* Lizenz *f*, Genehmigung *f*; (*document*) Zulassungsschein *m*; (*for a business, restaurant*) Konzession *f*; (*to drive*) Führerschein *m*; (*excessive liberty*) Zügellosigkeit *f* || *tr* konzessionieren; (aut) zulassen
li′cense num′ber *s* (aut) Kennzeichen *n*
li′cense plate′ or **tag′** *s* Nummernschild *n*
licentious [laɪ′senʃəs] *adj* unzüchtig
lichen [′laɪkən] *s* (bot) Flechte *f*
lick [lɪk] *s* Lecken *n* || *tr* lecken; (*thrash*) (coll) wichsen; (*defeat*) (coll) schlagen; (*said of a flame*) züngeln an (*dat*); **l. clean** auslecken; **l. into shape** auf Hochglanz bringen; **l. off** ablecken; **l. one's chops** sich [*dat*] die Lippen lecken; **l. s.o.'s boots** vor j–m kriechen; **l. up** auflecken
lick′ing *s* Prügel *pl*; **give s.o. a good l.** j–n versohlen

licorice [ˈlɪkərɪs] s Lakritze f
lid [lɪd] s Deckel m
lie [laɪ] s Lüge f; **give the lie to s.o. (or s.th.)** j–n (or etw) Lügen strafen; **tell a lie** lügen ‖ v (pret & pp **lied; ger lying**) tr—**lie one's way out of sich** herauslügen aus ‖ intr lügen; **lie like mad** das Blaue vom Himmel herunter lügen; **lie to** belügen ‖ v (pret **lay** [le]; pp **lain** [len]; ger **lying**) intr liegen; **lie down** sich hinlegen; **lie down!** (to a dog) leg dich!; **lie in wait** auf der Lauer liegen; **lie in wait for** auflauern (dat); **lie low** sich versteckt halten; (bide one's time) abwarten; **take s.th. lying down** etw widerspruchslos hinnehmen
lie' detec'tor s Lügendetektor m
lien [lin] s Pfandrecht n
lieu [lu] s—**in l. of** statt (genit)
lieutenant [luˈtɛnənt] s Leutnant m; (nav) Kapitänleutnant m
lieuten'ant colo'nel s Oberstleutnant m
lieuten'ant comman'der s Korvettenkapitän m
lieuten'ant gen'eral s Generalleutnant m
lieuten'ant gov'ernor s Vizegouverneur m
lieuten'ant jun'ior grade' s (nav) Oberleutnant m zur See
lieuten'ant sen'ior grade' s (nav) Kapitänleutnant m
life [laɪf] adj (imprisonment) lebenslänglich ‖ s (lives [laɪvz]) Leben n; (e.g., of a car) Lebensdauer f; **all my l.** mein ganzes Leben lang; **as big as l.** in voller Lebensgröße; **bring back to l.** wieder zum Bewußtsein bringen; **bring to l.** ins Leben bringen; **for dear l.** ums liebe Leben; **for l.** auf Lebenszeit; **full of l.** voller Leben; **I can't for the l. of me** ich kann beim besten Willen nicht; **lives lost** Menschenleben pl; **not on your l.** auf keinen Fall; **put l. into** beleben; **such is l.!** so ist nun mal das Leben; **take one's l.** sich [dat] das Leben nehmen; **upon my l!** so wahr ich lebe!; **you can bet your l. on that!** darauf kannst du Gift nehmen!
life'-and-death' adj auf Leben und Tod
life' annu'ity s Lebensrente f
life' belt' s Schwimmgürtel m
life'blood' s Lebensblut n
life'boat' s Rettungsboot n
life' buoy' s Rettungsboje f
life' expect'ancy s Lebenserwartung f
life' guard' s (at a pool) Bademeister –in mf; (at the shore) Strandwärter –in mf
life' impris'onment s lebenslängliche Haft f
life' insur'ance s Lebensversicherung f
life' jack'et s Schwimmweste f
lifeless [ˈlaɪflɪs] adj leblos; (fig) schwunglos
life'-like' adj naturgetreu, lebensecht
life' line' s Rettungsleine f; (for a diver) Signalleine f; (supply line) Lebensader f
life'long' adj lebenslänglich

life' mem'ber s Mitglied n auf Lebenszeit
life' of lei'sure s Wohlleben n
life' of plea'sure s Wohlleben n
life' of Ri'ley [ˈraɪli] s Herrenleben n
life' of the par'ty s—**be the l.** die ganze Gesellschaft unterhalten
life' preserv'er [prɪ͵zɑrvər] s Rettungsring m
lifer [ˈlaɪfər] s (sl) Lebenslängliche mf
life' raft' s Rettungsfloß n
lifesaver [ˈlaɪf͵sevər] s Rettungsschwimmer –in mf; (fig) rettender Engel m
life' sen'tence s Verurteilung f zu lebenslänglicher Haft
life'-size(d)' adj lebensgroß
life' span' s Lebensdauer f
life' style' s Lebensweise f
life'time' adj lebenslänglich ‖ s Leben n; **for a l.** auf Lebenszeit; **once in a l.** einmal im Leben
life' vest' s Schwimmweste f
life'work' s Lebenswerk n
lift [lɪft] s (elevator) Aufzug m; (aer & fig) Auftrieb m; **give s.o. a l.** j–n im Wagen mitnehmen ‖ tr heben; (gently) lüpfen; (with effort) wuchten; (weights) stemmen; (the receiver) abnehmen; (an embargo) aufheben; (steal) (sl) klauen; **l. up** aufheben; (the eyes) erheben; **not l. a finger** keinen Finger rühren ‖ intr (said of a mist) steigen; **l. off** (rok) starten
lift'-off' s (rok) Start m
lift' truck' s Lastkraftwagen m mit Hebevorrichtung
ligament [ˈlɪgəmənt] s Band n
ligature [ˈlɪgətʃər] s (mus) Bindung f; (act) (surg) Abbinden n; (filament) (surg) Abbindungsschnur f; (typ) Ligatur f
light [laɪt] adj (clothing, meal, music, heart, wine, sleep, punishment, weight) leicht; (day, beer, color, complexion, hair) hell; **as l. as day** tageshell; **l. as a feather** federleicht; **make l. of** auf die leichte Schulter nehmen; (belittle) als bedeutungslos hinstellen ‖ s Licht n; **according to his lights** nach dem Maß seiner Einsicht; **bring to l.** ans Licht bringen; **come to l.** ans Licht kommen; **do you have a l.?** haben Sie Feuer?; **in the l. of** im Lichte (genit), angesichts (genit); **put in a false l.** in ein falsches Licht stellen; **see the l. of day** (be born) das Licht der Welt erblicken; **shed l. on** Licht werfen auf (acc); **throw quite a different l. on** ein ganz anderes Licht werfen auf (acc) ‖ v (pret & pp **lighted** & **lit** [lɪt]) tr (a fire, cigarette) anzünden; (an oven) anheizen; (a street) beleuchten; (a hall) erleuchten; (a face) aufleuchten lassen ‖ intr sich entzünden; **l. up** (said of a face) aufleuchten; (light a cigarette) sich [dat] e-e Zigarette anstecken
light'-blue' adj lichtblau, hellblau
light' bulb' s Glühbirne f

light-complexioned ['laɪtkəm'plɛkʃənd] *adj* von heller Hautfarbe

lighten ['laɪtən] *tr (in weight)* leichter machen; *(brighten)* erhellen; *(fig)* erleichtern ‖ *intr (become brighter)* sich aufhellen; *(during a storm)* blitzen

lighter ['laɪtər] *s* Feuerzeug *n; (naut)* Leichter *m*

ligh'ter flu'id *s* Feuerzeugbenzin *n*

light'-fin'gered *adj* geschickt; *(thievish)* langfingerig

light'-foot'ed *adj* leichtfüßig

light'-head'ed *adj* leichtsinnig; *(dizzy)* schwindlig

light'-heart'ed *adj* leichtherzig

light'-heavy'weight' *adj* (box) Halbschwergewichts– ‖ *s* Halbschwergewichtler *m*

light'house' *s* Leuchtturm *m*

light'ing *s* Beleuchtung *f*

light'ing effects' *spl* Lichteffekte *pl*

light'ing fix'ture *s* Beleuchtungskörper *m*

lightly ['laɪtli] *adv* leicht; *(without due consideration)* leichthin; *(disparagingly)* geringschätzig

light' me'ter *s* Lichtmesser *m*

lightness ['laɪtnɪs] *s (in weight)* Leichtigkeit *f; (in shade)* Helligkeit *f*

lightning ['laɪtnɪŋ] *s* Blitz *m* ‖ *impers* —it is l. es blitzt

light'ning arrest'er [ə‚rɛstər] *s* Blitzableiter *m*

light'ning bug' *s* Leuchtkäfer *m*

light'ning rod' *s* Blitzableiter *m*

light'ning speed' *s* Windeseile *f*

light' op'era *s* Operette *f*

light' read'ing *s* Unterhaltungslektüre *f*

light'ship' *s* Leuchtschiff *n*

light' sleep' *s* Dämmerschlaf *m*

light' switch' *s* Lichtschalter *m*

light' wave' *s* Lichtwelle *f*

light'weight' *adj* (box) Leichtgewichts– ‖ *s (coll)* geistig Minderbemittelter *m;* (box) Leichtgewichtler *m*

light'-year' *s* Lichtjahr *n*

likable ['laɪkəbəl] *adj* sympathisch, lieb

like [laɪk] *adj* gleich, ähnlich; **be l.** gleichen *(dat)* ‖ *adv*—l. **crazy** (coll) wie verrückt ‖ *s*—**and the l.** und dergleichen; **likes and dislikes** Neigungen und Abneigungen *pl* ‖ *tr* gern haben, mögen; **I l. him** er ist mir sympathisch; **I l. the picture** das Bild gefällt mir; **I l. the food** das Essen schmeckt mir; **l. to** *(inf)*, e.g., **I l. to read** ich lese gern ‖ *intr*—**as you l.** wie Sie wollen; **if you l.** wenn Sie wollen ‖ *prep* wie; **feel l.** *(ger)* Lust haben zu *(inf);* **feel l. hell** (sl) sich elend fühlen; **it looks l.** es sieht nach ... aus; **it greased lightning** wie geschmiert; **that's just l. him** das sieht ihm ähnlich; **there's nothing l. traveling** es geht nichts übers Reisen

likelihood ['laɪklɪ‚hʊd] *s* Wahrscheinlichkeit *f*

likely ['laɪkli] *adj* wahrscheinlich; **a l. story!** (iron) e-e glaubhafte Ge-

schichte; **it's l. to rain** es wird wahrscheinlich regen

like'-mind'ed *adj* gleichgesinnt

liken ['laɪkən] *tr* (to) vergleichen (mit)

likeness ['laɪknɪs] *s* Ähnlichkeit *f;* **a good l.** of ein gutes Porträt *(genit)*

like'wise' *adv* gleichfalls, ebenso

lik'ing *s* (for) Zuneigung *f (zu);* **not to my l.** nicht nach meinem Geschmack; **take a l. to** Zuneigung fassen zu

lilac ['laɪlək] *adj* lila ‖ *s* Flieder *m*

lilt [lɪlt] *s* rhythmischer Schwung *m; (lilting song)* lustiges Lied *n*

lily ['lɪli] *s* Lilie *f*

lil'y of the val'ley *s* Maiglöckchen *n*

lil'y pad' *s* schwimmendes Seerosenblatt *n*

lil'y-white' *adj* lilienweiß

li'ma bean' ['laɪmə] *s* Limabohne *f*

limb [lɪm] *s* Glied *n; (of a tree)* Ast *m;* **go out on a l.** (fig) sich exponieren; **limbs** Gliedmaßen *pl*

limber ['lɪmbər] *adj* geschmeidig ‖ *tr* —l. **up** geschmeidig machen ‖ *intr*— sich geschmeidig machen

lim·bo ['lɪmbo] *s (-bos)* Vorhölle *f;* (fig) Vergessenheit *f*

lime [laɪm] *s* Kalk *m;* (bot) Limonelle *f*

lime'kiln' *s* Kalkofen *m*

lime'light' *s (fig)* Rampenlicht *n*

limerick ['lɪmərɪk] *s* Limerick *m*

lime'stone' *adj* Kalkstein– ‖ *s* Kalkstein *m*

limit ['lɪmɪt] *s* Grenze *f;* **go the l.** zum Äußersten gehen; **off limits** Zutritt verboten; **set a l. to** e-e Grenze ziehen *(dat);* **that's the l.!** das ist denn doch die Höhe!; **there's a l. to every- thing** alles hat seine Grenzen; **within limits** in Grenzen; **without l.** schrankenlos ‖ *tr* begrenzen; (to) beschränken (auf *acc*)

limitation [‚lɪmɪ'teʃən] *s* Begrenzung *f*, Beschränkung *f*

lim'ited *adj* (to) beschränkt (auf *acc*)

lim'ited-ac'cess high'way *s* Autobahn *f*

lim'ited mon'archy *s* konstitutionelle Monarchie *f*

limitless ['lɪmɪtlɪs] *adj* grenzenlos

limousine ['lɪmə‚zin], [‚lɪmə'zin] *s* Limousine *f*

limp [lɪmp] *adj* (& fig) schlaff ‖ *s* Hinken *n;* **walk with a l.** hinken ‖ *intr* (& fig) hinken

limpid ['lɪmpɪd] *adj* durchsichtig

linchpin ['lɪntʃ‚pɪn] *s* Achsnagel *m*

linden ['lɪndən] *s* Linde *f*, Lindenbaum *m*

line [laɪn] *s* Linie *f*, Strich *m; (boundary)* Grenze *f; (of a page)* Zeile *f; (of verse)* Verszeile *f; (of a family)* Zweig *m; (sphere of activity)* Fach *n; (e.g., of a streetcar)* Linie *f*, Strecke *f; (wrinkle)* Furche *f; (of articles for sale)* Sortiment *n; (for wash)* Leine *f; (queue)* Schlange *f;* (sl) zungenfertiges Gerede *n;* (angl) Schnur *f;* (mil) Linie *f*, Front *f;* (telp) Leitung *f;* **all along the l.** (fig) auf der ganzen Linie; **along the lines**

of nach dem Muster von; **draw the l. (at)** (fig) e-e Grenze ziehen (bei); **fall into l.** sich einfügen; **forget one's lines** (theat) steckenbleiben; **form a l.** sich in e-r Reihe aufstellen; **get a l. on** (coll) herausklamüsern; **give s.o. a l.** (sl) j-m schöne Worte machen; **hold the l.** die Stellung halten; (telp) am Apparat bleiben; **in l. of duty** im Dienst; **in l. with** in Übereinstimmung mit; **keep in l.** in der Reihe bleiben; **keep s.o. in l.** j-n im Zaum halten; **stand in l.** Schlange stehen; **the l. is busy** (telp) Leitung besetzt || *tr* linieren; (*e.g., a coat*) füttern; (*a face*) furchen; (*a drawer*) ausschlagen; (*a wall*) verkleiden; **l. one's purse** sich [*dat*] den Beutel spicken; **l. the streets** in den Straßen Spalier bilden; **l. up** ausrichten; (mil) aufstellen || *intr*—**l. up** Schlange stehen; (mil) antreten; **l. up for** sich anstellen nach

lineage ['lɪnɪ·ɪdʒ] *s* Abkunft *f*, Abstammung *f*

lineal ['lɪnɪ·əl] *adj* (*descent*) direkt; (*linear*) geradlinig

lineaments ['lɪnɪ·əmənts] *spl* Gesichtszüge *pl*

linear ['lɪnɪ·ər] *adj* (*arranged in a line*) geradlinig; (*involving a single dimension*) Längen-; (*using lines*) Linien-; (math) linear

lined' pa'per *s* Linienpapier *n*

line'man *s* (**-men**) (rr) Streckenwärter *m*; (telp) Telephonarbeiter *m*

linen ['lɪnən] *adj* Leinen- || *s* Leinen *n*; (*in the household*) Wäsche *f*; (*of the bed*) Bettwäsche *f*; **linens** Weißzeug *n*; **put fresh l. on the bed** das Bett überziehen

lin'en clos'et *s* Wäscheschrank *m*

lin'en cloth' *s* Leinwand *f*

lin'en goods' *s* Weißwaren *pl*

line' of approach' *s* (aer) Anflugschneise *f*

line' of bus'iness *s* Geschäftszweig *m*

line' of communica'tion *s* Verbindungslinie *f*

line' of fire' *s* Schußlinie *f*

line' of sight' *s* (*of a gun*) Visierlinie *f*; (astr) Sichtlinie *f*

liner ['laɪnər] *s* Einsatz *m*; (naut) Linienschiff *n*

lines'man *s* (**-men**) (sport) Linienrichter *m*

line'up' *s* (*at a police station*) Gegenüberstellung *f*; (sport) Aufstellung *f*

linger ['lɪŋgər] *intr* (*tarry*) verweilen; (*said of memories*) nachwirken; (*said of a melody*) nachtönen; **l. over** verweilen bei

lingerie [ˌlænzə'ri] *s* Damenunterwäsche *f*

lin'gering *adj* (*disease*) schleichend; (*tune*) nachklingend; (*memory, taste, feeling*) nachwirkend

lingo ['lɪŋgo] *s* Kauderwelsch *n*

linguist ['lɪŋgwɪst] *s* Sprachwissenschaftler -in *mf*

linguistic [lɪŋ'gwɪstɪk] *adj* (*e.g., skill*) sprachlich; (*of linguistics*) sprach-

wissenschaftlich || **linguistics** *s* Sprachwissenschaft *f*

liniment ['lɪnɪmənt] *s* Einreibemittel *n*

lin'ing *s* (*of a coat*) Futter *n*; (*of a brake*) Bremsbelag *m*; (*e.g., of a wall*) Verkleidung *f*

link [lɪŋk] *s* Glied *n*; (fig) Bindeglied *n* || *tr* verbinden; (fig) verketten; **l. to** verbinden mit; (fig) in Verbindung bringen mit || *intr*—**l. up** (rok) docken; **l. up with** sich anschließen an (*acc*)

linnet ['lɪnɪt] *s* (orn) Hänfling *m*

linoleum [lɪ'nolɪ·əm] *s* Linoleum *n*

linotype ['laɪnə,taɪp] *s* (trademark) Linotype *f*

lin'seed oil' ['lɪn,sid] *s* Leinöl *n*

lint [lɪnt] *s* Fussel *f*

lintel ['lɪntəl] *s* Sturz *m*

lion ['laɪ·ən] *s* Löwe *m*

li'on cage' *s* Löwenzwinger *m*

lioness ['laɪ·ənɪs] *s* Löwin *f*

lionize ['laɪ·ə,naɪz] *tr* zum Helden des Tages machen

li'ons' den' *s* Löwengrube *f*

li'on's share' *s* Löwenanteil *m*

li'on tam'er *s* Löwenbändiger -in *mf*

lip [lɪp] *s* Lippe *f*; (*edge*) Rand *m*; **bite one's lips** sich auf die Lippen beißen; **smack one's lips** sich [*dat*] die Lippen lecken

lip' read'ing *s* Lippenlesen *n*

lip' serv'ice *s* Lippenbekenntnis *n*; **pay l. to** ein Lippenbekenntnis ablegen zu

lip'stick' *s* Lippenstift *m*

lique·fy ['lɪkwɪ,faɪ] *v* (*pret & pp* **-fied**) *tr* verflüssigen || *intr* sich verflüssig

liqueur [lɪ'kʌr] *s* Likör *m*

liquid ['lɪkwɪd] *adj* flüssig; (*clear*) klar || *s* Flüssigkeit *f*

liq'uid as'sets *spl* flüssige Mittel *pl*

liquidate ['lɪkwɪ,det] *tr* (*a debt*) tilgen; (*an account*) abrechnen; (*a company*) liquidieren

liquidation [ˌlɪkwɪ'deʃən] *s* (*of a debt*) Tilgung *f*; (*of an account*) Abrechnung *f*; (*of a company*) Liquidation *f*

liquidity [lɪ'kwɪdɪti] *s* flüssiger Zustand *m*; (fin) Liquidität *f*

liq'uid meas'ure *s* Hohlmaß *m*

liquor ['lɪkər] *s* Spirituosen *pl*, Schnaps *m*; **have a shot of l.** einen zwitschern

liquorice ['lɪkərɪs] *s* Lakritze *f*

li'quor li'cense *s* Schankerlaubnis *f*

Lisbon ['lɪzbən] *s* Lissabon *n*

lisp [lɪsp] *s* Lispeln *n* || *tr & intr* lispeln

lissome ['lɪsəm] *adj* biegsam, gelenkig

list [lɪst] *s* Liste *f*, Verzeichnis *n*; (naut) Schlagseite *f*; **enter the lists** (& fig) in die Schranken treten; **make a l. of** verzeichnen || *tr* verzeichnen || *intr* (naut) Schlagseite haben

listen ['lɪsən] *intr* horchen, zuhören; **l. closely** die Ohren aufsperren; **l. for** achten auf (*acc*); **l. in** mithören; **l. to** zuhören (*dat*); (*a thing*) horchen auf (*acc*); (*obey*) gehorchen (*dat*); (*take advice from*) hören auf (*acc*); **l. to reason** auf e-n Rat hören; **l. to the radio** Radio hören

listener ['lɪsənər] *s* Zuhörer –in *mf;* (rad) Rundfunkhörer –in *mf*

lis'tening *adj* Abhör-, Horch-

lis'tening post' *s* Horchposten *m*

listless ['lɪstlɪs] *adj* lustlos

list' price' *s* Listenpreis *m*

litany ['lɪtəni] *s* (& fig) Litanei *f*

liter ['litər] *s* Liter *m & n*

literacy ['lɪtərəsi] *s* Kenntnis *f* des Lesens und Schreibens

literal ['lɪtərəl] *adj* buchstäblich; (*person*) pedantisch; **l. sense** wörtlicher Sinn *m*

literally ['lɪtərəli] *adv* buchstäblich

literary ['lɪtə‚reri] *adj* literarisch; **l. language** Literatursprache *f;* **l. reference** Schrifttumsangabe *f*

literate ['lɪtərɪt] *adj* des Lesens und des Schreibens kundig; (*educated*) gebildet || *s* Gebildete *mf*

literati [‚lɪtə'rɑti] *spl* Literaten *pl*

literature ['lɪtərət/ər] *s* Literatur *f;* (com) Drucksachen *pl*

lithe [laɪð] *adj* gelenkig

lithia ['lɪθɪ·ə] *s* (chem) Lithiumoxyd *n*

lithium ['lɪθɪ·əm] *s* Lithium *n*

lithograph ['lɪθə‚græf] *s* Steindruck *m* || *tr* lithographieren

lithographer [lɪ'θɑgrəfər] *s* Lithograph –in *mf*

lithography [lɪ'θɑgrəfi] *s* Steindruck *m,* Lithographie *f*

Lithuania [‚lɪθu'eni·ə] *s* Litauen *n*

Lithuanian [‚lɪθu'eni·ən] *adj* litauisch || *s* Litauer –in *mf;* (*language*) Litauisch *n*

litigant ['lɪtɪgənt] *adj* prozessierend; **the l. parties** die streitenden Parteien || *s* Prozeßführer –in *mf*

litigate ['lɪtɪ‚get] *tr* prozessieren gegen || *intr* prozessieren

litigation [‚lɪtɪ'geʃən] *s* Rechsstreit *m*

lit'mus pa'per ['lɪtməs] *s* Lackmuspapier *n*

litter ['lɪtər] *s* (*stretcher*) Tragbahre *f;* (*bedding for animals*) Streu *f;* (*of pigs, dogs*) Wurf *m;* (*trash*) herumliegender Abfall *m;* (hist) Sänfte *f* || *tr* verunreinigen || *intr* (*bear young*) werfen; (*strew litter*) Abfälle wegwerfen; **no littering!** das Wegwerfen von Abfällen ist verboten!

lit'terbug *s*—don't be a l. wirf keine Abfälle weg

little ['lɪtəl] *adj* (*in size*) klein; (*in amount*) wenig || *adv* wenig; **l. by l.** nach und nach || *s*—after a l. nach kurzer Zeit; **a l.** ein wenig, ein bißchen; **make l. of** wenig halten von

Lit'tle Bear' *s* Kleiner Bär *m*

Lit'tle Dip'per *s* Kleiner Wagen *m,* Kleiner Bär *m*

lit'tle fin'ger *s* kleiner Finger *m*

lit'tle peo'ple *s* kleine Leute *pl;* (myth) Heinzelmännchen *pl*

Lit'tle Red Rid'inghood' *s* Rotkäppchen *n*

lit'tle slam' *s* (cards) Klein-Schlemm *m*

liturgic(al) [lɪ'tʌrdʒɪk(əl)] *adj* liturgisch

liturgy ['lɪtərdʒi] *s* Liturgie *f*

livable ['lɪvəbəl] *adj* (*place*) wohnlich; (*life*) erträglich

live [laɪv] *adj* lebendig; (*coals*) glühend; (*ammunition*) scharf; (elec) stromführend; (rad, telv) live; **l. program** Originalsendung *f* || *adv* (rad, telv) live || [lɪv] *tr* leben; (*a life*) führen; **l. down** durch einwandfreien Lebenswandel vergessen machen; **l. it up** (coll) das Leben genießen; **l. out** (*survive*) überleben || *intr* leben; (*reside*) wohnen; (*reside temporarily*) sich aufhalten; **l. and learn!** man lernt nie aus!; **l. for the moment** in den Tag hineinleben; **l. high off the hog** in Saus und Braus leben; **l. off s.o.** j–m auf der Tasche liegen; **l. on** (*subsist on*) sich nähren von; (*continue to live*) fortleben; **l. through** durchmachen; **l. to see** erleben; **l. up to** gerecht werden (*dat*)

livelihood ['laɪvlɪ‚hud] *s* Lebensunterhalt *m*

liveliness ['laɪvlinɪs] *s* Lebhaftigkeit *f*

livelong ['lɪv‚lɔŋ] *adj*—all the l. day den lieben langen Tag

lively ['laɪvli] *adj* lebhaft; (*street*) belebt

liven ['laɪvən] *tr* aufmuntern || *intr* munter werden

liver ['lɪvər] *s* (anat) Leber *f*

liverwurst ['lɪvər‚wʌrst] *s* Leberwurst *f*

livery ['lɪvəri] *s* Livree *f*

liv'ery sta'ble *s* Mietstallung *f*

live' show' [laɪv] *s* Originalsendung *f,* Livesendung *f*

livestock ['laɪv‚stɑk] *s* Viehstand *m*

live' wire' [laɪv] *s* geladener Draht *m;* (coll) energiegeladener Mensch *m*

livid ['lɪvɪd] *adj* bleifarben; (*enraged*) wütend

living *adj* (*alive*) lebend, lebendig; (*for living*) Wohn-; **not a l. soul** keine Mutterseele *f* || *s* Unterhalt *n;* **good l.** Wohlleben *n;* **make a l.** (as) sein Auskommen haben (als); **what do you do for a l.?** wie verdienen Sie Ihren Lebensunterhalt?

liv'ing accommoda'tions *spl* Unterkunft *f*

liv'ing be'ing *s* Lebewesen *n*

liv'ing condi'tions *spl* Lebensbedingungen *pl*

liv'ing expens'es *spl* Unterhaltskosten *pl*

liv'ing quar'ters *spl* Unterkunft *f*

liv'ing room' *s* Wohnzimmer *n*

liv'ing-room set' (or **suite'**) *s* Polstergarnitur *f*

liv'ing space' *s* Lebensraum *m*

liv'ing wage' *s* Existenzminimum *n*

lizard ['lɪzərd] *s* Eidechse *f*

load [lod] *s* Last *f,* Belastung *f;* (*in a truck*) Fuhre *f;* **get a l. of that!** schau dir das mal an!; **have a l. on** (sl) einen sitzen haben; **loads of** (coll) Mengen von; **that's a l. off my mind** mir ist dabei ein Stein vom Herzen gefallen || *tr* (*a truck, gun*) laden; (*cargo on a ship*) einladen; (*with work*) überladen; (*with worries*) belasten; **l. down** belasten; **l. the cam-**

era den Film einlegen; **l. up** aufladen || *intr* das Gewehr laden

load'ed *adj* (*rifle*) scharf geladen; (*dice*) falsch; (*question*) verfänglich; (*very rich*) (sl) steinreich; (*drunk*) (sl) sternhagelvoll; **fully l.** (aut) mit allen Schikanen

loader ['lodər] *s* (*worker*) Ladearbeiter –in *mf*; (*device*) Verladevorrichtung *f*

load'ing *s* Ladung *f*, Verladung *f*

load'ing plat'form *s* Ladebühne *f*

load'ing ramp' *s* Laderampe *f*

load' lim'it *s* Tragfähigkeit *f*; (elec) Belastungsgrenze *f*

load'stone' *s* Magneteisenstein *m*

loaf [lof] *s* (loaves [lovz]) Laib *m* || *intr* faulenzen; **l. around** herumlungern

loafer ['lofər] *s* Faulenzer *m*

loaf'ing *s* Faulenzen *n*

loam [lom] *s* Lehm *m*

loamy ['lomi] *adj* lehmig

loan [lon] *s* Anleihe *f*, Darlehe(n) *n* || *tr* (ver)leihen, borgen; **l. out** leihen

loan' com'pany *s* Leihanstalt *f*

loan' shark' *s* (coll) Wucherer *m*

loan' word' *s* Lehnwort *n*

loath [loθ] *adj*—**be l. to** (inf) abgeneigt sein zu (inf)

loathe [loð] *tr* verabscheuen

loathing ['loðɪŋ] *s* (for) Abscheu *m* (vor *dat*)

loathsome ['loðsəm] *adj* abscheulich

lob [lɑb] *s* (tennis) Lobball *m* || *v* (pret & pp **lobbed**; ger **lobbing**) *tr* lobben, hochschlagen

lob·by ['lɑbi] *s* (*of a hotel or theater*) Vorhalle *f*, Foyer *n*; (pol) Interessengruppe *f* || *v* (pret & pp **–bied**) *intr* antichambrieren

lob'bying *s* Beeinflussung *f* von Abgeordneten, Lobbying *n*

lobbyist ['lɑbɪɪst] *s* Lobbyist –in *mf*

lobe [lob] *s* (anat) Lappen *m*

lobster ['lɑbstər] *s* Hummer *m*; **red as a l.** (fig) krebsrot

local ['lokəl] *adj* örtlich, Orts–; (*produce*) heimisch || *s* (*group*) Ortsgruppe *f*; (rr) Personenzug *m*

lo'cal anesthe'sia *s* Lokalanästhese *f*

lo'cal call' *s* (telp) Ortsgespräch *n*

lo'cal col'or *s* Lokalkolorit *n*

lo'cal deliv'ery *s* Ortszustellung *f*

locale [lo'kæl] *s* Ort *m*

lo'cal gov'ernment *s* Gemeindeverwaltung *f*

locality [lo'kælɪti] *s* Örtlichkeit *f*

localize ['lokə,laɪz] *tr* lokalisieren

lo'cal news' *s* Lokalnachrichten *pl*

lo'cal pol'itics *s* Kommunalpolitik *f*

lo'cal show'er *s* Strichregen *m*

lo'cal tax' *s* Gemeindesteuer *f*

lo'cal time' *s* Ortszeit *f*

lo'cal traf'fic *s* Nahverkehr *m*, Ortsverkehr *m*

locate [lo'ket] *tr* (*find*) ausfindig machen; (*a ship, aircraft*) orten; (*the trouble*) finden, feststellen; (*set up, e.g., an office*) errichten; **be located** liegen, gelegen sein || *intr* sich niederlassen

location [lo'keʃən] *s* Lage *f*; **on l.** (cin) auf Außenaufnahme

lock [lɑk] *s* Schloß *n*; (*of hair*) Locke *f*; (*of a canal*) Schleuse *f*; **l., stock, and barrel** mit allem Drum und Dran; **under l. and key** unter Verschluß || *tr* zusperren; (*arms*) verschränken; **l. in** einsperren; **l. out** aussperren; **l. up** (*a house*) zusperren; (*imprison*) einsperren || *intr* (*said of a lock*) zuschnappen; (*said of brakes*) sperren; **l. together** (*said of bumpers*) sich ineinander verhaken

locker ['lɑkər] *s* (*as in a gym or barracks*) Spind *m* & *n*; (*for luggage*) Schließfach *n*

lock'er room' *s* Umkleideraum *m*

locket ['lɑkɪt] *s* Medaillon *n*

lock'jaw' *s* Maulsperre *f*

lock'nut' *s* Gegenmutter *f*

lock'out' *s* Aussperrung *f*

lock'smith' *s* Schlosser –in *mf*

lock'smith shop' *s* Schlosserei *f*

lock' step' *s* Marschieren *n* in dicht geschlossenen Gliedern

lock' stitch' *s* Kettenstich *m*

lock'up' *s* (coll) Gefängnis *n*

lock' wash'er *s* Sicherungsring *m*

locomotion [,lokə'moʃən] *s* (*act*) Fortbewegung *f*; (*power*) Fortbewegungsfähigkeit *f*

locomotive [,lokə'motɪv] *s* Lokomotive *f*

lo·cus ['lokəs] *s* (**–ci** [saɪ]) Ort *m*; (geom) geometrischer Ort *m*

locust ['lokəst] *s* (*black locust*) (bot) Robinie *f*; (*carob*) (bot) Johannisbrotbaum *m*; (*Cicada*) (ent) Zikade *f*

lode [lod] *s* (min) Gang *m*

lode'star' *s* Leitstern *m*

lodge [lɑdʒ] *s* (*of Masons*) Loge *f*; (*for hunting*) Jagdhütte *f*; (*for weekending*) Wochenendhäuschen *n*; (*summer house*) Sommerhäuschen *n* || *tr* unterbringen; **l. a complaint** e–e Beschwerde einreichen || *intr* wohnen; (*said of an arrow, etc.*) steckenbleiben

lodger ['lɑdʒər] *s* Untermieter –in *mf*

lodg'ing *s* Unterkunft *f*; **lodgings** Logis *n*

loft [lɔft] *s* Speicher *m*; (*for hay*) Heuboden *m*; (*of a church*) Chor *m*; (*of a golf club*) Hochschlaghaltung *f* || *tr* (*a golf club*) in Hochschlaghaltung bringen; (*a golf ball*) hochschlagen

loftiness ['lɔftɪnɪs] *s* Erhabenheit *f*

lofty ['lɔfti] *adj* (*style*) erhaben; (*high*) hochragend; (*elevated in rank*) gehoben; (*haughty*) anmaßend

log [lɔg] *s* (*trunk*) Baumstamm *m*; (*for the fireplace*) Holzklotz *m*; (*record book*) Tagebuch *n*; (aer, naut) Log *n*; **sleep like a log** wie ein Klotz schlafen || *v* (pret & pp **logged**; ger **logging**) *tr* (*trees*) fällen und abästen; (*cut into logs*) in Klötze schneiden; (*an area*) abholzen; (*enter into a logbook*) in das Logbuch eintragen; (*traverse*) zurücklegen

logarithm ['lɔgə,rɪðəm] *s* Logarithmus *m*

log'book' s (aer, naut) Logbuch n
log' cab'in s Blockhaus n, Blockhütte f
logger ['lɔgər] s Holzfäller m
log'gerhead' s—**at loggerheads** auf Kriegsfuß
log'ging s Holzarbeit f
logic ['lɑdʒɪk] s Logik f
logical ['lɑdʒɪkəl] adj logisch
logician [lo'dʒɪʃən] s Logiker –in mf
logistic(al) [lo'dʒɪstɪk(əl)] adj logistisch
logistics [lo'dʒɪstɪks] s Logistik f
log'jam' s aufgestaute Baumstämme pl; (fig) völlige Stockung f
log'wood' s Kampescheholz n
loin [lɔɪn] s (of beef) Lendenstück n; (anat) Lende f; **gird up one's loins** (fig) sich rüsten
loin'cloth' s Lendentuch n
loin' end' s (of pork) Rippenstück n
loiter ['lɔɪtər] tr—**l. away** vertrödeln || intr trödeln; (hang around) herumlungern
loiterer ['lɔɪtərər] s Bummler –in mf
loi'tering s Trödelei f; **no l. Herumlungern verboten!**
loll [lɑl] intr sich bequem ausstrecken
lollipop ['lɑlɪ,pɑp] s Lutschbonbon m & n
Lombardy ['lʌmbərdi] s die Lombardei
London ['lʌndən] adj Londoner || s London n
Londoner ['lʌndənər] s Londoner –in mf
lone [lon] adj (sole) alleinig; (solitary) einzelstehend
loneliness ['lonlinɪs] s Einsamkeit f
lonely ['lonli] adj einsam; **become l. vereinsamen**
loner ['lonər] s Einzelgänger m
lonesome ['lonsəm] adj einsam; **be l. for sich sehnen nach**
lone' wolf' s (fig) Einzelgänger m
long [lɔŋ] adj (longer ['lɔŋgər]; longest ['lɔŋgɪst]) lang; (way, trip) weit; (detour) groß; **a l. time** lange; **a l. time since** schon lange her, daß; **in the l. run** auf die Dauer || adv lange; **as l. as** so lange wie; **but not for l.** aber nicht lange; **l. after** lange nach; **l. ago** vor langer Zeit; **l. live ...!** es lebe ...!; **l. since** längst; **so l.!** bis dann! || intr—**l. for** sich sehnen nach; **l. to** (inf) sich danach sehnen zu (inf)
long'boat' s Pinasse f
long' dis'tance s (telp) Ferngespräch n; **call l.** ein Ferngespräch anmelden
long'-dis'tance adj (sport) Langstrecken-
long'-dis'tance call' s Ferngespräch n
long'-dis'tance flight' s Langstreckenflug m
long'-drawn'-out' adj ausgedehnt; (story) langatmig
longevity [lɑn'dʒevɪti] s Langlebigkeit f
long' face' s langes Gesicht n
long'hair' adj (fig) intellektuell || s (fig) Intellektueller m; (mus) (coll) konservativer Musiker m
long'hand' s Langschrift f; **in l.** mit der Hand geschrieben

long'ing adj sehnsüchtig || s (for) Sehnsucht f (nach)
longitude ['lɑndʒɪ,t(j)ud] s Länge f
longitudinal [,lɑndʒɪ't(j)udɪnəl] adj Longitudinal–
long' jump' s Weitsprung m
long-lived ['lɔŋ 'laɪvd] adj langlebig
long'-play'ing rec'ord s Langspielplatte f
long'-range' adj (plan) auf lange Sicht; (aer) Langstrecken–
long'shore'man s (–men) Hafenarbeiter m
long' shot' s (coll) riskante Wette f; **by l.** bei weitem
long'stand'ing adj althergebracht, alt
long'-suf'fering adj langmütig
long' suit' s (fig) Stärke f; (cards) lange Farbe f
long'-term' adj langfristig
long-winded ['lɔŋ 'wɪndɪd] adj langatmig
look [lʊk] s (glance) Blick m; (appearance) Aussehen n; (expression) Ausdruck m; **from the looks of things** wie die Sache aussieht; **give a second l.** sich (dat) genauer ansehen; **have a l. around** Umschau halten; **have a l. at s.th.** sich (dat) etw ansehen; **I don't like the looks of it** die Sache gefällt mir nicht; **looks** Aussehen n; **new l.** verändertes Aussehen n; (latest style) neueste Mode f; **take a l. at s.th.** sich (dat) etw ansehen || tr—**he looks his age** man sieht ihm sein Alter an; **l. one's best** sich in bester Verfassung zeigen; **l. one's last** at zum letzten Mal ansehen; **l. s.o. in the eye** j–m in die Augen sehen; **l. s.o. over** j–n mustern; **l. s.th. over** etw (über)prüfen (or durchsehen); **l. up** (e.g., a word) nachschlagen; (e.g., a friend) aufsuchen; **l. up and down** von oben bis unten mustern || intr schauen; (appear, seem) aussehen; **l. after** (e.g., children) betreuen; (a household, business) besorgen; (a departing person) nachblicken (dat); **l. ahead** vorausschauen; **l. around** (for) sich (dat) umsehen (nach); **l. at** anschauen; **l. back (on)** zurücksehen (auf acc); **l. down** herabsehen; (cast the eyes down) die Augen niederschlagen; **l. down on** herabsehen auf (acc); (in contempt) über die Achseln ansehen; **l. for** suchen; (e.g., a criminal) fahnden nach; **l. forward to** sich freuen auf (acc); **l. hard at** scharf ansehen; **l. into** (a mirror, the future) blicken in (acc); (a matter) nachgehen (dat); **l. like** gleichen (dat); (e.g., rain) aussehen nach; **l. on** zuschauen; **l. on s.o. as** j–n betrachten als; **l. out** aufpassen; **l. out for** aussehen nach; **l. out on** (a view) hinausgehen auf (acc); **l. over** hinwegsehen über (acc); **l. sharp!** jetzt aber hoppla!; **l. through** (e.g., a window) blicken durch; (s.o. or s.o.'s motives) durchschauen; **l. up** (raise one's gaze) aufschauen; **l. up to s.o.** zu j–m hinaufsehen; **things**

are beginning to l. up es wird langsam besser; things don't l. so good for est steht übel mit; what does he l. like? wie sieht er aus?

look'ing glass' s Spiegel m

look'out' s (watchman) Wachposten m; (observation point) Ausguck m; (matter of concern) Sache f; be a l. Schmiere stehen; be on the l. (for) Auschau halten (nach)

look'out man' s—be the l. Schmiere stehen

look'out tow'er s Aussichtsturm m

loom [lum] s Webstuhl m || intr undeutlich und groß auftauchen; l. large von großer Bedeutung scheinen

loon [lun] s (orn) Taucher m

loony ['luni] adj verrückt; be l. spinnen

loop [lup] s Schleife f, Schlinge f; (e.g., on a dress for a hook) Öse f; (aer) Looping m; do a l. (aer) e-n Looping drehen || tr schlingen || intr Schlingen (or Schleifen) bilden

loop'hole' s Guckloch n; (in a fortification) Schießscharte f; (in a law) Lücke f

loose [lus] adj locker, los; (wobbly) wackelig; (morally) locker, unsolid; (unpacked) unverpackt; (translation) frei; (interpretation) dehnbar; (dress, tongue) lose; (skin) schlaff; l. connection (elec) Wackelkontakt m || adv—break l. (from an enclosure) ausbrechen; (e.g., from a hitching) sich losmachen; (said of a storm, hell) losbrechen; come l. losgehen; cut l. (act up) (coll) außer Rand und Band geraten; turn l. befreien; work l. sich lockern; (said of a button) abgehen; (said of a brick, stone, shoestring) sich lösen || tr schlagen; l.—on the l. ungehemmt, frei || tr (a boat) losmachen; (a knot) lösen

loose' change' s Kleingeld n

loose' end' s (fig) unerledigte Kleinigkeit f; at loose ends im ungewissen

loose'-leaf note'book s Loseblattbuch n

loosen ['lusən] tr lockern, locker machen || intr locker werden

looseness ['lusnɪs] s Lockerheit f

loot [lut] s Beute f || tr erbeuten; (plunder) plündern; (e.g., art treasures) verschleppen

lop [lɑp] v (pret & pp lopped; ger lopping) tr—lop off abhacken

lope [lop] s Trab m || intr—l. along in großen Schritten laufen

lop'sid'ed adj schief; (score) einseitig

loquacious [lo'kweʃəs] adj geschwätzig

lord [lɔrd] s Herr m; (Brit) Lord m; **Lord** Herrgott m || tr—l. it over sich als Herr aufspielen über (acc)

lordly ['lɔrdli] adj würdig; (haughty) hochmütig

Lord's' Day' s Tag m des Herrn

lord'ship' s Herrschaft f

Lord's' Prayer' s Vaterunser n

Lord's' Sup'per s heiliges Abendmahl n

lore [lor] s Kunde f; (traditional wisdom) überlieferte Kunde f

lorry ['lɔri] s (Brit) Lastkraftwagen m

lose [luz] v (pret & pp lost [lɔst]) tr verlieren; (several minutes, as a clock does) zurückbleiben; (in betting) verwetten; (in gambling) verspielen; (the page in a book) verblättern; l. one's way sich verirren; (on foot) sich verlaufen; (by car) sich verfahren || intr verlieren; (sport) geschlagen werden; l. to (sport) unterliegen (dat)

loser ['luzər] s Unterlegene mf; be the l. mit langer Nase abziehen

los'ing adj verlierend; (com) verlustbringend || **losings** spl Verluste pl

los'ing game' s aussichtsloses Spiel n

loss [lɔs] s (in) Verlust m (an dat); at a l. in Verlegenheit; (com) mit Verlust; be at a l. for words nach Worten suchen; inflict l. on s.o. j-m Schaden zufügen; l. of appetite Appetitlosigkeit f; l. of blood Blutverlust m; l. of face Blamage f; l. of life Verluste pl an Menschenleben; l. of memory Gedächtnisverlust m; l. of sight Erblindung f; l. of time Zeitverlust m; straight l. Barverlust m

lost [lɔst] adj verloren; be l. (said of a thing) verlorengehen; (not know one's way) sich verirrt haben; be l. on s.o. auf j-n keinen Eindruck machen; get l. in Verlust geraten; get l.! hau ab!; l. in thought in Gedanken versunken

lost'-and-found' depart'ment s Fundbüro n

lost' cause' s aussichtslose Sache f

lot [lɑt] s (fate) Los n, Schicksal n; (in a drawing) Los n; (portion of land) Grundstück n; (cin) Filmgelände n; (com) Posten m, Partie f; a lot viel, sehr; a lot of (or lots of) viel(e); the lot das Ganze

lotion ['loʃən] s Wasser n

lottery ['lɑtəri] s Lotterie f

lot'tery tick'et s Lotterielos n

lotto ['lɑto] s Lotto n

lotus ['lotəs] s Lotos m

loud [laud] adj laut; (colors) schreiend

loud-mouthed ['laud‚mauðd] adj laut

loud'speak'er s Lautsprecher m

lounge [laundʒ] s Aufenthaltsraum m || intr sich recken; l. around herumlungern

lounge' chair' s Klubsessel m

lounge' liz'ard s (sl) Salonlöwe m

louse [laus] s (lice [laɪs]) Laus f; (sl) Sauhund m || tr—l. up (sl) versauen

lousy ['lauzi] adj verlaust; (sl) lausig; l. with (people) wimmelnd von; l. with money stinkreich

lout [laut] s Lümmel m

louver ['luvər] s Jalousie f

lovable ['lʌvəbəl] adj liebenswürdig

love [lʌv] adj Liebes– || s (for, of) Liebe f (zu); be in l. with verliebt sein in (acc); for the l. of God um Gottes willen; fall (madly) in l. with sich (heftig) verlieben in (acc); Love (at the end of a letter) herzliche Grüße; l. at first sight Liebe f auf den ersten Blick; make l. to herzen;

(sl) geschlechtlich verkehren mit; not for l. or money nicht für Gold und gute Worte; **there's no** l. lost between them sie schätzen sich nicht || *tr* lieben; *(like)* gern haben; **l. to dance** sehr gern tanzen
love′ affair′ *s* Liebeshandel *m*, Liebesverhältnis *n*
love′birds′ *spl* **(coll)** Unzertrennlichen *pl*
love′ child′ *s* Kind *n* der Liebe
love′ feast′ *s* **(eccl)** Liebesmahl *n*
love′ game′ *s* (tennis) Nullpartie *f*
love′ knot′ *s* Liebesschleife *f*
loveless [′lʌvlɪs] *adj* lieblos
love′ let′ter *s* Liebesbrief *m*
lovelorn [′lʌv ‚lɔrn] *adj* vor Liebe vergehend
lovely [′lʌvli] *adj* lieblich
love′-mak′ing *s* Geschlechtsverkehr *m*
love′ match′ *s* Liebesheirat *f*
love′ po′em *s* Liebesgedicht *n*
love′ po′tion *s* Liebestrank *m*
lover [′lʌvər] *s* Liebhaber *m*; **lovers** Liebespaar *n*
love′ scene′ *s* Liebesszene *f*
love′ seat′ *s* Sofasessel *m*
love′sick′ *adj* liebeskrank
love′ song′ *s* Liebeslied *n*
love′ to′ken *s* Liebespfand *n*
lov′ing *adj* liebevoll; **Your l. ...** Dich liebender ...
lov′ing-kind′ness *s* Herzensgüte *f*
low [lo] *adj* (building, mountain, forehead, birth, wages, estimate, prices, rent) niedrig; *(number)* nieder; *(altitude, speed)* gering; *(not loud)* leise; *(vulgar)* gemein; *(grades, company)* schlecht; *(fever)* leicht; *(pulse, pressure)* schwach; *(ground)* tiefgelegen; *(bow, voice)* tief; *(almost empty)* fast leer; *(supplies, funds)* knapp; **be low** *(said of the sun, water)* niedrigstehen; **be low in funds** knapp bei Kasse sein; **feel low** niedergeschlagen sein; **have a low opinion of** e-e geringe Meinung haben von || *adv* niedrig; **lay low** über den Haufen werfen; **lie low** sich versteckt halten; *(bide one's time)* abwarten; **run low** knapp werden; **sing low** tief singen; **sink low** tief sinken || *s* (low point) (fig) Tiefstand *m*; (meteor) Tief *n* || *intr* muhen, brüllen
low′ blow′ *s* (box) Tiefschlag *m*
low′born′ *adj* von niederer Herkunft
low′brow′ *s* Spießbürger *m*
low′-cost hous′ing *s* sozial geförderter Wohnungsbau *m*
Low′ Coun′tries, the *spl* die Niederlande
low′-cut′ *adj* tiefausgeschnitten
low′-down′ *adj* schurkisch || *s* *(unadorned facts)* unverblümte Wahrheit *f*; *(inside information)* Geheimnachrichten *pl*
lower [′lo·ər] *comp adj* untere; *(e.g., deck, house, jaw, lip)* Unter– || *tr* herunterlassen; *(the eyes, voice, water level, temperature)* senken; *(prices)* herabsetzen; *(a flag, sail)* streichen; *(lifeboats)* aussetzen; **l.**

oneself sich herablassen || [′lau·ər] *intr* finster blicken; **l. at** finster anblicken
low′er ab′domen [′lo·ər] *s* Unterbauch *m*
low′er berth′ [′lo·ər] *s* untere Koje *f*
low′er case′ [′lo·ər] *s* Kleinbuchstaben *pl*
lower-case [′lo·ər′kes] *adj* klein
low′er course′ [′lo·ər] *s (of a river)* Unterlauf *m*
low′er mid′dle class′ [′lo·ər] *s* Kleinbürgertum *n*
lowermost [′lo·ər ‚most] *adj* niedrigste
low′er world′ [′lo·ər] *s* Unterwelt *f*
low′-fly′ing *adj* tieffliegend
low′-fre′quency *s* Niederfrequenz *f*
low′-fre′quency *adj* Niederfrequenz–
low′ gear′ *s* erster Gang *m*
low′-grade′ *adj* minderwertig
low′ing *s* Gebrüll *n*
lowland [′loland] *s* Flachland *n*; **Lowlands** *(in Scotland)* Unterland *n*
low′ lev′el *s* Tiefstand *m*
low′-lev′el attack′ *s* Tiefangriff *m*
low′-lev′el flight′ *s* Tiefflug *m*
lowly [′loli] *adj* bescheiden; *(humble in spirit)* niederträchtig
low′-ly′ing *adj* tiefliegend
Low′ Mass′ *s* stille Messe *f*
low′-mind′ed *adj* niedrig gesinnt
low′ neck′ *s (of a dress)* Ausschnitt *m*
low′-necked′ *adj* tief ausgeschnitten
low′-pitched′ *adj* (sound) tief; *(roof)* mit geringer Neigung
low′-pres′sure *adj* Tiefdruck–, Unterdruck–
low′-priced′ *adj* billig
low′ shoe′ *s* Halbschuh *m*
low′-speed′ *adj* mit geringer Geschwindigkeit; *(film)* unempfindlich
low′-spir′ited *adj* niedergeschlagen
low′ spir′its *spl* Niedergeschlagenheit *f*; **be in l.** niedergeschlagen sein
low′ tide′ *s* Ebbe *f*; (fig) Tiefstand *m*
low′ wa′ter *s* Niedrigwasser *n*
low′-wa′ter mark′ *s* (fig) Tiefpunkt *m*
loyal [′lɔɪ·əl] *adj* treu, loyal
loyalist [′lɔɪ·əlɪst] *s* Regierungstreue *mf*
loyalty [′lɔɪ·əlti] *s* Treue *f*
lozenge [′lazɪndʒ] *s* Pastille *f*
LP [′el′pi] *s* (trademark) **(long-playing record)** Langspielplatte *f*
Ltd. *abbr* (Brit) **(Limited)** Gesellschaft *f* mit beschränkter Haftung
lubricant [′lubrɪkənt] *s* Schmiermittel *n*
lubricate [′lubrɪ ‚ket] *tr* (ab)schmieren
lubrication [‚lubrɪ′keʃən] *s* Schmierung *f*
lucerne [lu′sʌrn] *s* (bot) Luzerne *f*; **Lucerne** Luzern *n*
lucid [′lusɪd] *adj* (clear) klar, deutlich; *(bright)* hell
luck [lʌk] *s* Glück *n*; *(chance)* Zufall *m*; **as l. would have it** wie es der Zufall wollte; **be down on one's l.** an seinem Glück verzagen; **be out of l.** Unglück haben; **dumb l.** (coll) Sauglück *n*; **have tough l.** (coll) Pech haben;

rotten l. (coll) Saupech n; try one's l. sein Glück versuchen; with l. you should win wenn Sie Glück haben, werden Sie gewinnen

luckily ['lʌkɪlɪ] adv zum Glück

luckless ['lʌklɪs] adj glücklos

lucky ['lʌki] adj glücklich; be l. Glück haben; l. dog (coll) Glückspilz m; l. penny Glückspfennig m

luck'y shot' s Glückstreffer m

lucrative ['lukrətɪv] adj gewinnbringend

ludicrous ['ludɪkrəs] adj lächerlich

lug [lʌg] s (pull, tug) Ruck m; (lout) (sl) Lümmel m; (elec) Öse f ‖ v (pret & pp lugged; ger lugging) tr schleppen

luggage ['lʌgɪdʒ] s Gepäck n; excess l. Mehrgepäck n; piece of l. Gepäckstück n

lug'gage car'rier s Gepäckträger m

lug'gage compart'ment s (aer) Frachtraum m

lug'gage rack' s Gepäckablage f; (on the roof of a car) Dachgepäckträger m

lug'gage receipt' s Aufgabeschein m

lugubrious [lu'g(j)ubrɪ·əs] adj tieftraurig

lukewarm ['luk,wɔrm] adj lau, lauwarm

lull [lʌl] s Windstille f; (com) Flaute f ‖ tr einlullen; (e.g., fears) beschwichtigen; l. to sleep einschläfern ‖ intr nachlassen

lullaby ['lʌlə,baɪ] s Wiegenlied n

lumbago [lʌm'bego] s Hexenschluß m

lumber ['lʌmbər] s Bauholz n ‖ intr sich schwerfällig fortbewegen

lum'berjack' s Holzfäller m

lum'ber-man' s (-men') (dealer) Holzhändler m; (lumberjack) Holzfäller m

lum'beryard' s Holzplatz m

luminary ['lumɪ,nerɪ] s Leuchtkörper m; (fig) Leuchte f

luminescent [,lumɪ'nesənt] adj lumineszierend

luminous ['lumɪnəs] adj leuchtend, Leucht–

lu'minous di'al s Leuchtzifferblatt n

lu'minous paint' s Leuchtfarbe f

lummox ['lʌməks] s Lümmel m

lump [lʌmp] s (e.g., of clay) Klumpen m; (on the body) Beule f; have a l. in one's throat e–n Kloß (or Knödel) im Hals haben; l. of sugar Würfel m Zucker ‖ tr—l. together (fig) zusammenwerfen

lumpish ['lʌmpɪʃ] adj klumpig

lump' sug'ar s Würfelzucker m

lump' sum' s Pauschalbetrag m

lumpy ['lʌmpi] adj klumpig; (sea) bewegt

lunacy ['lunəsi] s Irrsinn m

lu'nar eclipse' ['lunər] s Mondfinsternis f

lu'nar land'ing s Mondlandung f

lu'nar mod'ule s (rok) Mondfähre f

lu'nar year' s Mondjahr n

lunatic ['lunətɪk] s Irre mf

lu'natic asy'lum s Irrenhaus n

lu'natic fringe' s Extremisten pl

lunch [lʌntʃ] s (at noon) Mittagessen n, Lunch m; (light meal) Zwischenmahlzeit f; eat l. zu Mittag essen; have (s.th.) for l. zum Mittagessen haben ‖ intr zu Mittag essen, lunchen

lunch' coun'ter s Theke f

luncheon ['lʌntʃən] s gemeinsames Mittagessen n

luncheonette [,lʌntʃə'nɛt] s Imbißstube f

lunch' hour' s Mittagsstunde f

lunch'room' s Imbißhalle f

lunch'time' s Mittagszeit f

lung [lʌŋ] s Lunge f; at the top of one's lungs aus voller Kehle

lunge ['lʌndʒ] s Sprung m vorwärts; (fencing) Ausfall m ‖ tr (a horse) an der Longe laufen lassen ‖ intr—e–n Sprung vorwärts machen; (with a sword) (at) e–n Ausfall machen (gegen); l. at losstürzen auf (acc)

lurch [lʌrtʃ] s Torkeln n, Taumeln n; leave in a l. im Stich lassen ‖ intr torkeln; (said of a ship) zur Seite rollen

lure [lur] s Köder m ‖ tr ködern; (fig) verlocken; l. away weglocken

lurid ['lurɪd] adj (light) gespenstisch; (sunset) düsterrot; (gruesome) grausig; (pallid) fahl

lurk [lʌrk] intr lauern

luscious ['lʌʃəs] adj köstlich; a l. doll (coll) ein tolles Weib

lush [lʌʃ] adj üppig

lust [lʌst] s Wollust f; (for) Begierde f (nach) ‖ intr (after, for) gieren (nach)

luster ['lʌstər] s Glanz m; (e.g., chandelier) Lüster m

lusterless ['lʌstərlɪs] adj matt

lus'terware' s Tongeschirr n mit Lüster

lustful ['lʌstfəl] adj lüstern, geil

lustrous ['lʌstrəs] adj glänzend

lusty ['lʌsti] adj kräftig

lute [lut] s Laute f

Lutheran ['luθərən] adj lutherisch ‖ s Lutheraner –in mf

luxuriance [lʌg'ʒurɪ·əns] s Üppigkeit f

luxuriant [lʌg'ʒurɪ·ənt] adj üppig

luxuriate [lʌg'ʒurɪ,et] intr (thrive) gedeihen; (delight) (in) schwelgen (in dat)

luxurious [lʌg'ʒurɪ·əs] adj luxuriös; l. living Prasserei f

luxury ['lʌgʒərɪ] s Extravaganz f, Luxus m; (object of luxury) Luxusartikel m; live a life of l. im vollen leben

lye [laɪ] s Lauge f

ly'ing adj lügenhaft ‖ s Lügen n

ly'ing-in' hos'pital s Entbindungsanstalt f

lymph [lɪmf] s Lymphe f

lymphatic [lɪm'fætɪk] adj lymphatisch

lynch [lɪntʃ] tr lynchen

lynch'ing s Lynchen n

lynch' law' s Lynchjustiz f

lynx [lɪŋks] s Luchs m

lynx'-eyed' adj luchsäugig

lyre [laɪr] *s* (mus) Leier *f*
lyric ['lɪrɪk] *adj* lyrisch; **l. poetry** Lyrik *f* ‖ *s* lyrisches Gedicht *n*; *(of a song)* Text *m*

lyrical ['lɪrɪkəl] *adj* lyrisch
lyricism ['lɪrɪˌsɪzəm] *s* Lyrik *f*
lyricist ['lɪrɪsɪst] *s* *(of a song)* Texter –in *mf*; *(poet)* lyrischer Dichter *m*

M

M, m [ɛm] *s* dreizehnter Buchstabe des englischen Alphabets
ma [mɑ] *s* (coll) Mama *f*
ma'am [mæm] *s* (coll) gnädige Frau *f*
macadam [mə'kædəm] *s* Makadamdecke *f*
macadamize [mə'kædəˌmaɪz] *tr* makadamisieren
maca'dam road' *s* Straße *f* mit Makadamdecke
macaroni [ˌmækə'roni] *spl* Makkaroni *pl*
macaroon [ˌmækə'run] *s* Makrone *f*
macaw [mə'kɔ] *s* (orn) Ara *m*
mace [mes] *s* Stab *m*, Amtsstab *m*
mace'bear'er *s* Träger *m* des Amtsstabes
machination [ˌmækɪ'neʃən] *s* Intrige *f*; **machinations** Machenschaften *pl*
machine [mə'ʃin] *s* Maschine *f*; (pol) Apparat *m*; **by m.** maschinell ‖ *tr* spannabhebend formen
machine'-driv'en *adj* mit Maschinenantrieb
machine' gun' *s* Maschinengewehr *n*
machine'-gun' *v* *(pret & pp* **-gunned;** *ger* **-gunning)** *tr* unter Maschinengewehrfeuer nehmen
machine' gun'ner *s* Maschinengewehrschütze *m*
machine'-made' *adj* maschinell hergestellt
machinery [mə'ʃinəri] *s* (& fig) Maschinerie *f*
machine' screw' *s* Maschinenschraube *f*
machine' shop' *s* Maschinenhalle *f*
machine' tool' *s* Werkzeugmaschine *f*
machinist [mə'ʃinɪst] *s* *(maker and repairer of machines)* Maschinenbauer *m*; *(machine operator)* Maschinenschlosser –in *mf*
mackerel ['mækərəl] *s* Makrele *f*
mad [mæd] *adj* (madder; maddest) verrückt; *(angry)* böse; **be mad about** vernarrt sein in *(acc)*; **be mad at** böse sein auf *(acc)*; **drive mad** verrückt machen; **go mad** verrückt werden
madam ['mædəm] *s* gnädige Frau *f*; *(of a brothel)* (sl) Bordellmutter *f*
mad'cap' *adj* ausgelassen ‖ *s* Wildfang *m*
madden ['mædən] *tr* verrückt machen; *(make angry)* zornig machen
made'-to-or'der *adj* nach Maß angefertigt
made'-up' *adj* *(story)* erfunden; *(artificial)* künstlich; *(with cosmetics)* geschminkt

mad'house' *s* Irrenhaus *n*, Narrenhaus *n*
madly ['mædli] *adv* (coll) wahnsinnig
mad'man' *s* (-men') Verrückter *m*
madness ['mædnɪs] *s* Wahnsinn *m*
Madonna [mə'dɑnə] *s* Madonna *f*
maelstrom ['melstrəm] *s* (& fig) Strudel *m*
magazine [ˌmægə'zin] *s* *(periodical)* Zeitschrift *f*; *(illustrated)* Illustrierte *f*; *(warehouse for munitions; cartridge container)* Magazin *n*; *(for a camera)* Kassette *f*
magazine' rack' *s* Zeitschriftenständer *m*
Maggie ['mægi] *s* Gretchen *n*
maggot ['mægət] *s* Made *f*
Magi ['medʒaɪ] *spl*—**the three M.** (Bib) die drei Weisen *pl* aus dem Morgenland
magic ['mædʒɪk] *adj* *(enchanting)* zauberhaft; *(trick, word, wand)* Zauber– ‖ *s* Zauberkunst *f*
magician [mə'dʒɪʃən] *s* Zauberer –in *mf*
ma'gic lan'tern *s* Laterna magica *f*
magisterial [ˌmædʒɪs'tɪrɪəl] *adj* *(of a magistrate)* obrigkeitlich; *(authoritative)* autoritativ; *(pompous)* anmaßend
magistrate ['mædʒɪs,tret] *s* Polizeirichter *m*
magnanimous [mæg'nænɪməs] *adj* großmütig
magnate ['mægnet] *s* Magnat *m*
magnesium [mæg'nizɪ·əm] *s* Magnesium *n*
magnet ['mægnɪt] *s* Magnet *m*
magnetic [mæg'netɪk] *adj* magnetisch; *(personality)* fesselnd
magnetism ['mægnɪˌtɪzəm] *s* Magnetismus *m*; (fig) Anziehungskraft *f*
magnetize ['mægnɪˌtaɪz] *tr* magnetisieren
magnificence [mæg'nɪfɪsəns] *s* Pracht *f*
magnificent [mæg'nɪfɪsənt] *adj* prächtig
magnifier ['mægnɪˌfaɪ·ər] *s* (electron) Verstärker *m*
magni·fy ['mægnɪˌfaɪ] *v* *(pret & pp* **-fied)** *tr* vergrößern; (fig) übertreiben
mag'nifying glass' *s* Lupe *f*
magnitude ['mægnɪˌt(j)ud] *s* (& astr) Größe *f*
magno'lia tree' [mæg'noli·ə] *s* Magnolia *f*
magpie ['mæg,paɪ] *s* (& fig) Elster *f*
mahlstick ['mɑlˌstɪk] *s* Malerstock *m*

mahogany [mə'hʊgəni] s Mahagoni n
mahout [mə'haut] s Elefantentreiber m
maid [med] s Dienstmädchen n
maiden ['medən] s Jungfer f; (poet) Maid f
maid′enhair′ s (bot) Jungfernhaar n
maid′enhead′ s Jungfernhäutchen n
maid′enhood′ s Jungfräulichkeit f
maidenly ['medənli] adj jungfräulich
maid′en name′ s Mädchenname m
maid′en voy′age s Jungfernfahrt f
maid′-in-wait′ing s (maids-in-waiting) Hofdame f
maid′ of hon′or s erste Brautjungfer f
maid′serv′ant s Dienstmädchen n
mail [mel] adj Post— || s Post f; (armor) Kettenpanzer m; by m. brieflich; by return m. postwendend || tr (put into the mail) aufgeben; (send) abschicken; m. to zuschicken (dat)
mail′bag′ s Postsack m
mail′boat′ s Postschiff n
mail′box′ s Briefkasten m
mail′ car′rier s Briefträger –in mf
mail′ deliv′ery s Postzustellung f
mail′ drop′ s Briefeinwurf m
mailer ['melər] s (phot) Versandbeutel m
mail′ing s Absendung f
mail′ing list′ s Postversandliste f
mail′ing per′mit s Zulassung f zum portofreien Versand
mail′man′ s (–men′) Briefträger m
mail′ or′der s Bestellung f durch die Post
mail′-order house′ s Versandhaus n
mail′ plane′ s Postflugzeug n
mail′ train′ s Postzug m
mail′ truck′ s Postauto n
maim [mem] tr verstümmeln
main [men] adj Haupt— || s Hauptleitung f; in the main hauptsächlich
main′ clause′ s (gram) Hauptsatz m
main′ course′ s Hauptgericht n
main′ deck′ s Hauptdeck n
main′ floor′ s Erdgeschoß n
mainland ['men,lænd] s Festland n
main′ line′ s (rr) Hauptstrecke f
mainly ['menli] adv größtenteils
mainmast ['men,mæst] s Großmast m
main′ of′fice s Hauptbüro n, Zentrale f
main′ point′ s springender Punkt m
mainsail ['men,sel] s Großsegel m
main′spring′ s (horol & fig) Triebfeder f
main′stay′ s (fig) Hauptstütze f; (naut) Großstag n
main′ street′ s Hauptstraße f
maintain [men'ten] tr aufrechterhalten; (e.g., a family) unterhalten; (assert) behaupten; (one's reputation) wahren; (e.g., in good condition) bewahren; (order, silence) halten; (a road) instand halten
maintenance ['mentinəns] s (upkeep) Instandhaltung f; (support) Unterhalt m; (e.g., of an automobile) Wardirektor m
maître d'hôtel [,metərdo'tel] s (head waiter) Oberkellner m; (owner) Hotelbesitzer m; (manager) Hoteltung f
majestic [mə'dʒestɪk] adj majestätisch
majesty ['mædʒɪsti] s Majestät f
major ['medʒər] adj Haupt–; (mus) –Dur || s (educ) Hauptfach n; (mil) Major m || intr—m. in als Hauptfach studieren
majordomo ['medʒər'domo] s Haushofmeister m
ma′jor gen′eral s Generalmajor m
majority [mə'dʒɔrɪti] adj Mehrheits– || s Mehrheit f; (full age) Mündigkeit f; (mil) Majorsrang m; (parl) Stimmenmehrheit f; be in the m. in der Mehrheit sein; in the m. of cases in der Mehrzahl der Fälle; the m. of people die meisten Menschen
major′ity vote′ s Mehrheitsbeschluß m
ma′jor league′ s Oberliga f
make [mek] s Fabrikat n, Marke f || tr machen; (in a factory) herstellen; (cause) lassen; (force) zwingen; (clothes) anfertigen; (money) verdienen; (a reputation, name) erwerben; (a choice) treffen; (a confession) ablegen; (a report) erstatten; (plans) schmieden; (changes) vornehmen; (a movie) drehen; (contact) herstellen; (a meal) (zu)bereiten; (conditions) stellen; (rules, assertions) aufstellen; (a bet, compromise, peace) schließen; (excuses, requests, objections) vorbringen; (a protest) erheben; (a goal) schießen (or erzielen); (a comparison) ziehen; (a speech) halten; (e.g., a good father) abgeben; (be able to fit through, e.g., a window) gehen durch; (e.g., a train, bus, destination) erreichen; (e.g., ten miles) zurücklegen; (a girl) (sl) verführen; (arith) machen; m. (s.o.) believe weismachen (dat); m. into verarbeiten zu; m. of halten von; m. out (e.g., writing) entziffern; (e.g., a person at a distance) erkennen; (understand) kapieren; (a blank or form) ausfüllen; (a check, receipt) ausstellen; m. over to (jur) überschreiben auf (acc); m. s.o. out to be a liar j–n als Lügner hinstellen; m. s.th. of oneself es weit bringen; m. the most of ausnutzen; m. time Zeit gewinnen; m. time with (a woman) (coll) flirten mit; m. up (e.g., a list) zusammenstellen; (a bill) ausstellen; (a sentence) bilden; (a story) sich [dat] ausdenken; m. up one's mind (about) sich [dat] schlüssig werden (über acc); m. way! Platz da!; m. way for ausweichen vor (dat) || intr—m. believe schauspielern; m. believe that nur so tun, als ob; m. do with sich behelfen mit; m. for lossteuern auf (acc); m. off with durchbrennen mit; m. out well gut auskommen; m. sure of sich vergewissern (genit); m. sure that vergewissern, daß; m. up (after a quarrel) sich versöhnen; m. up for (past mistakes) wieder gutmachen; (lost time) wieder einbringen

make'-believe' *adj* Schein-, vorgetäuscht ‖ *s* Schein *m*, Mache *f*
maker ['mekər] *s* Hersteller –in *mf*; **Maker** Schöpfer *m*
make'shift' *adj* behelfsmäßig, Behelfs- ‖ *s* Notbehelf *m*
make'-up' *s* Aufmachung *f*; (*cosmetic*) Make-up *n*, Schminke *f*; (*of a team*) Aufstellung *f*; (*theat*) Maske *f*; (*typ*) Umbruch *m*; **apply m.** sich schminken
make'weight' *s* Gewichtszugabe *f*
mak'ing *s* Herstellung *f*; **be in the m.** im Werden sein; **have the makings of das** Zeug haben zu; **this is of his own m.** dies ist sein eigenes Werk
maladjusted [,mælə'dʒʌstɪd] *adj* unausgeglichen
maladroit [,mælə'drɔɪt] *adj* ungeschickt
malady ['mælədi] *s* (& fig) Krankheit *f*
malaise [mæ'lez] *s* (*physical*) Unwohlsein *n*; (*mental*) Unbehagen *n*
malaria [mə'lerɪ·ə] *s* Malaria *f*
Malaya [mə'le·ə] *s* Malaya *n*
Malaysia [mə'leʒɪ·ə] *s* Malaysia *n*
malcontent ['mælkən,tent] *adj* unzufrieden ‖ *s* Unzufriedene *mf*
male [mel] *adj* männlich ‖ *s* Mann *m*; (*bot*) männliche Pflanze *f*; (*zool*) Männchen *n*
malediction [,mælɪ'dɪkʃən] *s* Verwünschung *f*
malefactor ['mælɪ,fæktər] *s* Übeltäter –in *mf*
male' nurse' *s* Pfleger *m*
malevolence [mæ'levələns] *s* Böswilligkeit *f*
malevolent [mə'levələnt] *adj* böswillig
malfeasance [,mæl'fizəns] *s* strafbare Handlung *f*; **m. in office** Amtsvergehen *n*
malfunction [mæl'fʌŋkʃən] *s* technische Störung *f*
malice ['mælɪs] *s* Bosheit *f*
malicious [mə'lɪʃəs] *adj* boshaft
malign [mə'laɪn] *adj* böswillig ‖ *tr* verleumden
malignancy [mə'lɪgnənsi] *s* (pathol) Bösartigkeit *f*
malignant [mə'lɪgnənt] *adj* böswillig; (pathol) bösartig
malinger [mə'lɪŋgər] *intr* simulieren
malingerer [mə'lɪŋgərər] *s* Simulant –in *mf*
mall [mɔl] *s* (*promenade*) Laubenpromenade *f*; (*shopping center*) überdachtes Einkaufszentrum *n*, Mall *f*
mallard ['mælərd] *s* Stockente *f*
malleable ['mælɪ·əbəl] *adj* schmiedbar
mallet ['mælɪt] *s* Schlegel *m*
mallow ['mælo] *s* Malve *f*
malnutrition [,mæln(j)u'trɪʃən] *s* Unterernährung *f*
malodorous [mæl'odərəs] *adj* übelriechend
malpractice [mæl'præktɪs] *s* ärztlicher Kunstfehler *m*
malt [mɔlt] *s* Malz *n*
maltreat [mæl'trit] *tr* mißhandeln
mamma ['mɑmə] *s* Mama *f*, Mutti *f*

mammal ['mæməl] *s* Säugetier *n*
mammalian [mæ'melɪ·ən] *adj* Säugetier- ‖ *s* Säugetier *n*
mam'mary gland' ['mæməri] *s* Milchdrüse *f*
mam'ma's boy' *s* Muttersöhnchen *n*
mammoth ['mæməθ] *adj* ungeheuer (groß) ‖ *s* (zool) Mammut *n*
man [mæn] *s* (**men** [men]) (*adult male*) Mann *m*; (*human being*) Mensch *m*; (*servant*) Diener *m*; (*worker*) Arbeiter *m*; (*mankind*) die Menschheit *f*; (checkers) Stein *m*; **man alive!** Menschenskind! ‖ *v* (*pret* & *pp* **manned**; *ger* **manning**) *tr* besetzen; (nav, rok) bemannen
man' about town' *s* weltgewandter Mann *m*
manacle ['mænəkəl] *s* Handschelle *f* ‖ *tr* fesseln
manage ['mænɪdʒ] *tr* (*a business, household*) leiten; (*an estate*) verwalten; (*tools, weapons*) handhaben; (*e.g., a boat, car*) völlig in der Gewalt haben; (*children*) fertig werden mit; **I'll m. it** ich werde es schon schaffen; **m. the situation** die Sache deichseln ‖ *intr* zurechtkommen; (**with, on**) auskommen (mit); **m. to** (*inf*) es fertigbringen zu (*inf*)
manageable ['mænɪdʒəbəl] *adj* handlich; (hair) fügsam
management ['mænɪdʒmənt] *s* Unternehmensführung *f*; (*group which manages*) Direktion *f*; (*as opposed to labor*) Management *n*
man'agement consult'ant *s* Unternehmungsberater –in *mf*
manager ['mænədʒər] *s* Manager *m*, Geschäftsführer –in *mf*; (*of a bank or hotel*) Direktor –in *mf*; (*of an estate*) Verwalter –in *mf*; (*of a department*) Abteilungsleiter –in *mf*; (*of a star, theater, athlete*) Manager *m*
managerial [,mænə'dʒɪrɪ·əl] *adj* Leitungs-, Führungs-
man'aging *adj* geschäftsführend
man'aging direc'tor *s* Geschäftsführer –in *mf*
Manchuria [mæn'tʃʊrɪ·ə] *s* Mandschurei *f*
man'darin or'ange ['mændərɪn] *s* Mandarine *f*
mandate ['mændet] *s* Mandat *n* ‖ *tr* (**to**) zuweisen (*dat*)
mandatory ['mændə,tori] *adj* verbindlich
mandolin ['mændəlɪn] *s* Mandoline *f*
mandrake ['mændrek] *s* (bot) Alraune *f*
mane [men] *s* Mähne *f*
maneuver [mə'nuvər] *s* Manöver *n*; **go on maneuvers** (mil) ins Manöver ziehen ‖ *tr* manövrieren; **m. s.o. into** (*ger*) j–n dazubringen zu (*inf*)
maneuverability [mə,nuvərə'bɪlɪti] *s* Manövrierbarkeit *f*
maneuverable [mə'nuvərəbəl] *adj* manövrierfähig
manful ['mænfəl] *adj* mannhaft
manganese ['mæŋgə,niz] *s* Mangan *n*

mange [mendʒ] s Räude f
manger ['mendʒər] s Krippe f
mangle ['mæŋgəl] s Mangel f || tr (tear apart) zerfleischen; (wash) mangeln
mangy ['mendʒi] adj räudig; (fig) schäbig
man'han'dle tr grob behandeln
man'hole' s Kanalschacht m, Mannloch n
man'hole cov'er s Schachtdeckel m
man'hood' s (virility) Männlichkeit f; (age) Mannesalter n
man'-hour' s Arbeitsstunde f pro Mann
man'hunt' s Fahndung f
mania ['menɪ·ə] s Manie f
maniac ['menɪˌæk] s Geisteskranke mf
maniacal [mə'naɪ·əkəl] adj manisch
manicure ['mænɪˌkjur] s Maniküre f, Handpflege f || tr maniküren
manicurist ['mænɪˌkjurɪst] s Maniküre f
manifest ['mænɪˌfest] adj offenkundig, offenbar || s (aer, naut) Manifest n || tr bekunden, bezeigen
manifestation [ˌmænɪfes'te/ən] s (manifesting) Offenbarung f; (indication) Anzeichen n
manifes·to [ˌmænɪ'festo] s (-toes) Manifest n
manifold ['mænɪˌfold] adj mannigfaltig || s (aut) Rohrverzweigung f
manikin ['mænɪkɪn] s Männchen n; (for teaching anatomy) anatomisches Modell n; (mannequin) Mannequin n
man' in the moon' s Mann m im Mond
man' in the streets' s Durchschnittsmensch m
manipulate [mə'nɪpjəˌlet] tr manipulieren
man'kind' s Menschheit f
manliness ['mænlɪnɪs] s Männlichkeit f
manly ['mænli] adj mannhaft, männlich
man'-made' adj künstlich
manna ['mænə] s Manna n, Himmelsbrot n
manned' space'craft s bemanntes Raumfahrzeug n
mannequin ['mænɪkɪn] s (clothes model) Mannequin n; (in a display window) Schaufensterpuppe f
manner ['mænər] s Art f, Weise f; (custom) Sitte f; after the m. of nach der Art von; by all m. of means auf jeden Fall; by no m. of means auf keinen Fall; in a m. gewissermaßen; in a m. of speaking sozusagen; in like m. gleicherweise; in the following m. folgendermaßen; in this m. auf diese Weise; it's bad manners to (inf) es schickt sich nicht zu (inf); m. of death Todesart f; manners Manieren pl
mannerism ['mænəˌrɪzəm] s Manieriertheit f
mannerly ['mænərli] adj manierlich
mannish ['mænɪ/] adj männisch; (woman) unweiblich
man' of let'ters s Literat m

man' of the world' s Weltmann m
man' of war' s Kriegsschiff n
manor ['mænər] s Herrengut n
man'or house' s Herrenhaus n
man'pow'er s Arbeitskräfte pl; (mil) Kriegsstärke f
man'serv'ant s (menservants) Diener m
mansion ['mæn/ən] s Herrenhaus n
man'slaugh'ter s Totschlag m
mantel ['mæntəl] s Kaminsims m & n
man'telpiece' s Kaminsims m & n
mantilla [mæn'tɪlə] s Mantille f
mantle ['mæntəl] s (& fig) Mantel m; (of a gaslight) Glühstrumpf m; (geol) Mantel m || tr verhüllen
manual ['mænju·əl] adj manuell, Hand– || s (book) Handbuch n, Leitfaden m; (mus) Manual n
man'ual control' s Handbedienung f
man'ual dexter'ity s Handfertigkeit f
man'ual la'bor s Handarbeit f
man'ual of arms' s (mil) Dienstvorschrift f
man'ual train'ing s Werkunterricht m
manufacture [ˌmænjə'fækt/ər] s Herstellung f; (production) Erzeugnis n || tr herstellen; (clothes) konfektionieren
manufac'tured goods' spl Fertigwaren pl
manufacturer [ˌmænjə'fækt/ərər] s Hersteller –in mf
manure [mə'n(j)ur] s Mist m || tr misten
manuscript ['mænjəˌskrɪpt] adj handschriftlich || s Manuskript n
many ['meni] adj viele; a good (or great) m. sehr viele; how m. wieviele; in so m. words ausdrücklich; m. a mancher, manch ein; m. a person manch einer; m. a time manchmal; twice as m. noch einmal so viele || pron viele; as m. as ten nicht weniger als zehn; how m. wieviele
man'y-sid'ed adj vielseitig
map [mæp] s Karte f, Landkarte f; (of a city) Plan m; (of a local area) Spezialkarte f; map of the world Weltkarte f; put on the map (coll) ausposaunen || v (pret & pp mapped; ger mapping) tr kartographisch aufnehmen; map out planen
maple ['mepəl] s Ahorn m
ma'ple sug'ar s Ahornzucker m
ma'ple syr'up s Ahornsirup m
mar [mar] v (pret & pp marred; ger marring) tr (detract from the beauty of) verunzieren; (e.g., a reputation) beeinträchtigen
marathon ['mærəˌθən] s Dauerwettbewerb m
mar'athon race' s Marathonlauf m
maraud [mə'rɔd] tr & intr plündern
marauder [mə'rɔdər] s Plünderer m
marble ['marbəl] adj marmorn || s Marmor m; (little glass ball) Murmel f; marbles (game) Murmelspiel n || tr marmorieren
mar'ble quar'ry s Marmorbruch m
march [mart/] s Marsch m; (festive parade) Umzug m; March März m; on the m. auf dem Marsch; steal a

m. on s.o. j—m den Rang ablaufen;
the m. of time der Lauf der Zeit ‖ *tr*
marschieren ‖ *intr* marschieren; m.
by vorbeimarschieren (an *dat*); m.
off abmarschieren ‖ *interj* marsch!
marchioness ['mɑrʃənɪs] *s* Marquise *f*
mare [mɛr] *s* Stute *f*
Margaret ['mɑrgərɪt] *s* Margarete *f*
margarine ['mɑrdʒərɪn] *s* Margarine *f*
margin ['mɑrdʒɪn] *s* (*of a page*) Rand
m; (*leeway*) Spielraum *m*; (fin)
Spanne *f*; by a narrow m. mit knappem Abstand; leave a m. am Rande
Raum lassen; m. of profit Gewinn-
spanne *f*; m. of safety Sicherheits-
faktor *m*; win by a ten-second m.
mit zehn Sekunden Abstand gewinnen; write in the m. an dem Rand
schreiben
marginal ['mɑrdʒɪnəl] *adj* (*costs, profits, case*) Grenz—; (*in the margin*)
Rand—
mar'ginal note' *s* Randbemerkung *f*
mar'gin release' *s* Randauslöser *m*
mar'gin set'ter *s* Randsteller *m*
marigold ['mærɪˌgold] *s* Ringelblume
f
marijuana [ˌmɑrɪ'hwɑnə] *s* Marihuana
n
marinate ['mærɪˌnet] *tr* marinieren
marine [mə'rin] *adj* See—, Meer(es)— ‖
s (*fleet*) Marine *f*; (*fighter*) Marineinfanterist *m*; **marines** Marinetruppen
pl
Marine' Corps' *s* Marineinfanterie-
korps *n*
mariner ['mærɪnər] *s* Seemann *m*
marionette [ˌmærɪ·ə'nɛt] *s* Marionette
f
marital ['mærɪtəl] *adj* ehelich, Gatten—
mar'ital sta'tus *s* Familienstand *m*
maritime ['mærɪˌtaɪm] *adj* See—
marjoram ['mɑrdʒərəm] *s* Majoran *m*
mark [mɑrk] *s* (& fig) Zeichen *n*;
(*stain, bruise*) Fleck *m*, Mal *n*; (*German unit of currency*) Mark *f*; (educ)
Zensur *f*; be an easy m. (coll) leicht
reinzulegen sein; hit the m. ins
Schwarze treffen; make one's m. sich
durchsetzen; m. of confidence Ver-
trauensbeweis *m*; m. of favor Gunst-
bezeichnung *f*; m. of respect Zeichen
n der Hochachtung; on your marks!
auf die Plätze!; wide of the m. am
Ziel vorbei ‖ *tr* (aus)zeichnen, bezeichnen; (*student papers*) zensieren;
(*cards*) zinken; (*labels*) beschriften;
(*laundry*) zeichnen; (*the score*) notieren; m. down aufschreiben,
niederschreiben; (com) im Preis herabsetzen; m. my words! merken Sie
sich, was ich sage!; m. off abgrenzen;
(surv) abstecken; m. time (mil & fig)
auf der Stelle treten; (mus) den Takt
schlagen; m. up (*e.g., a wall*) beschmieren; (com) im Preis heraufsetzen
mark'down' *s* Preisnachlaß *m*
marked *adj* (*difference*) merklich; a m.
man ein Gezeichneter *m*
marker ['mɑrkər] *s* (*of scores*) Anschreiber —in *mf*; (*commemorative*

marker) Gedenktafel *f*; (*on a firing
range*) Anzeiger *m*; (*bombing marker*) Leuchtbombe *f*; (*felt pen*) Filzschreiber *m*
market ['mɑrkɪt] *s* Markt *m*; (*grocery
store*) Lebensmittelgeschäft *n*; (*stock
exchange*) Börse *f*; (*ready sale*) Absatz *m*; be in the m. for Bedarf haben
an (*dat*); be on the m. zum Verkauf
stehen; put on the m. auf den Markt
bringen ‖ *tr* verkaufen
marketable ['mɑrkɪtəbəl] *adj* markt-
fähig
mar'ket anal'ysis *s* Marktanalyse *f*
mar'keting *s* (econ) Marketing *n*; do
the m. Einkäufe machen
mar'keting research' *s* Absatzforschung
f
mar'ketplace' *s* Marktplatz *m*
mar'ket price' *s* Marktpreis *m*
mar'ket town' *s* Marktflecken *m*
mar'ket val'ue *s* Marktwert *m*; (st.
exch.) Kurswert *m*
mark'ing *s* Kennzeichen *n*
marks·man ['mɑrksmən] *s* (—men)
Schütze *m*
marks'manship' *s* Schießkunst *f*
mark'up' *s* (com) Gewinnaufschlag *m*
marl [mɑrl] *s* Mergel *m* ‖ *tr* mergeln
marmalade ['mɑrməˌled] *s* Marmelade
f
maroon [mə'run] *adj* rotbraun, kastanienbraun ‖ *s* Kastanienbraun *n* ‖ *tr*
aussetzen; be marooned von der Au-
ßenwelt abgeschnitten sein
marquee [mɑr'ki] *s* Schutzdach *n*
marquess ['mɑrkwɪs] *s* Marquis *m*
marquis ['mɑrkwɪs] *s* Marquis *m*
marquise [mɑr'kiz] *s* Marquise *f*
marriage ['mærɪdʒ] *s* Heirat *f*; (*state*)
Ehe *f*, Ehestand *m*; by m. angeheiratet, schwägerlich; give in m. verheiraten
marriageable ['mærɪdʒəbəl] *adj* heiratsfähig; m. age (of a girl) Mannbarkeit
f
mar'riage brok'er *s* Heiratsvermittler
—in *mf*
mar'riage cer'emony *s* Trauung *f*
mar'riage li'cense *s* Heiratsurkunde *f*
mar'riage of conven'ience *s* Vernunft-
ehe *f*
mar'riage por'tion *s* Mitgift *f*
mar'riage propos'al *s* Heiratsantrag *m*
mar'riage vow' *s* Ehegelöbnis *n*
mar'ried cou'ple *s* Ehepaar *n*
mar'ried state' *s* Ehestand *m*
marrow ['mæro] *s* Knochenmark *n*;
(fig) Mark *n*
mar·ry ['mærɪ] *v* (*pret & pp* —ried) *tr*
heiraten; (*said of a priest or minister*)
trauen; m. off (to) verheiraten (mit)
‖ *intr* heiraten; m. rich e—e gute
Partie machen
Mars [mɑrz] *s* Mars *m*
marsh [mɑrʃ] *s* Sumpf *m*
mar·shal ['mɑrʃəl] *s* Zeremonienmeister *m*; (*police officer*) Bezirkspoli-
zeichef *m*; (mil) Marschall *m* ‖ *v*
(*pret & pp* —shal[l]ed; *ger* —shal[l]ing)
tr (*troops*) ordnungsgemäß aufstellen; (*strength*) zusammenraffen

marsh**'**land**'** s Sumpfland n
marsh**'** mal**'**low s (bot) Eibisch m
marsh**'**mal**'**low s (candy) Konfekt n aus Stärkesirup, Zucker, Stärke, Gelatine, und geschlagenem Eiweiß
marshy ['marʃi] adj sumpfig
mart [mart] s Markt m
marten ['martən] s (zool) Marder m
Martha ['marθə] s Martha f
martial ['marʃəl] adj Kriegs-
mar**'**tial law**'** s Standrecht n; declare m. das Standrecht verhängen; under m. standrechtlich
martin ['martɪn] s Mauerschwalbe f; Martin Martin m
martinet [,martɪ'nɛt] s Pauker –in mf; (mil) Schleifer m
martyr ['martər] s Märtyrer –in mf ‖ tr martern
martyrdom ['martərdəm] s Märtyrertum n
mar•vel ['marvəl] s Wunder n ‖ v (pret & pp –vel[l]ed; ger –vel[l]ing) intr (at) sich wundern (über acc)
marvelous ['marvələs] adj wundervoll; (coll) pfundig
Marxist ['marksɪst] adj marxistisch ‖ Marxist –in mf
marzipan ['marzɪ ,pæn] s Marzipan n
mascara [mæs'kærə] s Lidtusche f
mascot ['mæskət] s Maskotte f
masculine ['mæskjəlɪn] adj männlich
mash [mæʃ] s Brei m; (in brewing) Maische f ‖ tr zerquetschen; (potatoes) zerdrücken
mashed**'** pota**'**toes spl Kartoffelbrei m
mask [mæsk] s Maske f ‖ tr maskieren
masked**'** ball**'** s Maskenball m
mason ['mesən] s Maurer m; Mason Freimaurer m
Masonic [mə'sanɪk] adj Freimaurer-
masonite ['mesə ,naɪt] s Holzfaserplatte f
masonry ['mesənri] s Mauerwerk n; Masonry Freimaurerei f
masquerade [,mæskə'red] s (& fig) Maskerade f ‖ intr (& fig) sich maskieren; m. as sich ausgeben als
mass [mæs] adj Massen– ‖ s Masse f; (eccl) Messe f; the masses die breite Masse f ‖ tr massieren ‖ intr sich ansammeln
massacre ['mæsəkər] s Massaker n ‖ tr massakrieren, niedermetzeln
massage [mə'saʒ] s Massage f ‖ tr massieren
masseur [mə'sʌr] s Masseur m
masseuse [mə'suz] s Masseuse f
massif ['mæsɪf] s Gebirgsstock m
massive ['mæsɪv] adj massiv
mass**'** me**'**dia ['mɪdɪ-ə] spl Massenmedien pl
mass**'** meet**'**ing s Massenversammlung f
mass**'** mur**'**der s Massenmord m
mass**'**-produce**'** tr serienmäßig herstellen
mass**'** produc**'**tion s Serienherstellung f
mast [mæst] s Mast m; (food for swine) Mast f
master ['mæstər] adj (bedroom, key, switch, cylinder) Haupt– ‖ s Herr m,

Meister m; (male head of a household) Hausherr m; (of a ship) Kapitän m ‖ tr beherrschen
mas**'**ter build**'**er s Baumeister m
mas**'**ter car**'**penter s Zimmermeister m
mas**'**ter cop**'**y s Originalkopie f
masterful ['mæstərfəl] adj herrisch; (masterly) meisterhaft
masterly ['mæstərli] adj meisterhaft
mas**'**ter mechan**'**ic s Schlossermeister m
mas**'**termind**'** s führender Geist m ‖ tr planen und überwachen
Mas**'**ter of Arts**'** s Magister m der freien Künste
mas**'**ter of cer**'**emonies s Zeremonienmeister m
mas**'**ter of the house**'** s Hausherr m
mas**'**terpiece**'** s Meisterstück n
mas**'**ter ser**'**geant s Oberfeldwebel m
mas**'**ter stroke**'** s Meisterstreich m
mas**'**terwork**'** s Meisterwerk n
mastery ['mæstəri] s (of) Beherrschung f (genit); gain m. over die Oberhand gewinnen über (acc)
mast**'**head**'** s (naut) Topp m; (typ) Impressum n
masticate ['mæstɪ ,ket] tr zerkauen ‖ intr kauen
mastiff ['mæstɪf] s Mastiff m
masturbate ['mæstər ,bet] intr onanieren
masturbation [,mæstər'beʃən] s Onanie f
mat [mæt] s (for a floor) Matte f; (before the door) Türvorleger m; (under cups, vases, etc.) Zierdeckchen n ‖ v (pret & pp matted; ger matting) (cover with matting) mit Matten belegen; (the hair) verfilzen ‖ intr sich verfilzen
match [mætʃ] s Streichholz n; (for marriage) Partie f; (sport) Match n; be a good m. zueinanderpassen; be a m. for gewachsen sein (dat); be no m. for sich nicht messen können mit; meet one's m. seinen Mann finden ‖ tr (fit together) zusammenstellen; (harmonize with) passen zu; (equal) (in) gleichkommen (in dat); (funds) in gleicher Höhe aufbringen; (adapt) in Übereinstimmung bringen mit; be well matched auf gleicher Höhe sein; m. up zusammenpassen; m. wits mit sich geistig messen mit ‖ intr zueinanderpassen
match**'**book**'** s Streichholzbrief m
match**'** box**'** s Streichholzschachtel f
match**'**ing adj (clothes) passend; (funds) in gleicher Höhe ‖ s Paarung f
match**'**mak**'**er s Heiratsvermittler –in mf; (sport) Veranstalter m
mate [met] s Genosse m, Kamerad m; (in marriage) Ehepartner m; (one of a pair, e.g., of gloves) Gegenstück n; (especially of birds) Männchen n, Weibchen n; (naut) Maat m ‖ tr paaren ‖ intr sich paaren
material [mə'tɪrɪ ,əl] adj materiell; (important) wesentlich ‖ s Material n, Stoff m; (tex) Stoff m

materialist [mə'tırı-əlıst] s Materialist –in mf

materialistic [mə,tırı-ə'lıstık] adj materialistisch

materialize [mə'tırı-ə,laız] intr sich verwirklichen

materiel [mə,tırı'ɛl] s Material n; (mil) Kriegsmaterial n

maternal [mə'tʌrnəl] adj mütterlich; (relatives) mütterlicherseits

maternity [mə'tʌrnıti] s Mutterschaft f

mater′nity dress′ s Umstandskleid n

mater′nity hos′pital s Wöchnerinnenheim n

mater′nity ward′ s Wöchnerinnenstation f

math [mæθ] s (coll) Mathe f

mathematical [,mæθı'mætıkəl] adj mathematisch

mathematician [,mæθımə'tıʃən] s Mathematiker –in mf

mathematics [,mæθı'mætıks] s Mathematik f

matinée [,mætı'ne] s Nachmittagsvorstellung f

mat′ing sea′son s Paarungszeit f

matins [mætınz] spl Frühmette f

matriarch [metrı,ark] s Stammesmutter f

matriarchal [,metrı'arkəl] adj matriarchalisch

matriarchy [metrı,arki] s Matriarchat n

matricide [mætrı,saıd] s (act) Muttermord m; (person) Muttermörder –in mf

matriculate [mə'trıkjə,let] tr immatrikulieren ‖ intr sich immatrikulieren

matriculation [mə,trıkjə'leʃən] s Immatrikulation f

matrimonial [,mætrı'monı-əl] adj Ehe–

matrimony [mætrı,moni] s Ehestand m

ma·trix [metrıks] s (–trices [trı,siz] & –trixes) (mold) Gießform f; (math) Matrix f; (typ) Matrize f

matron [metrən] s Matrone f

matronly [metrənli] adj matronenhaft, gesetzt

matt [mæt] adj (phot) matt

matter [mætər] s Stoff m; (affair) Sache f, Angelegenheit f; (pus) Eiter m; (phys) Materie f; as a m. of course routinemäßig; as matters now stand wie die Sache jetzt liegt; for that m. was das betrifft; it's a m. of es handelt sich um; it's a m. of life and death es geht um Leben und Tod; m. of opinion Ansichtssache f; m. of taste Geschmackssache f; something is the m. with his heart er hat was am Herz; no laughing m. nichts zum Lachen; no m. ganz gleich; what's the m. (with)? was ist los (mit)? ‖ intr von Bedeutung sein; it doesn't m. es macht nichts (aus); it doesn't m. to me es liegt mir nichts daran; it matters a great deal to me es liegt mir sehr viel daran

mat′ter of fact′ s Tatsache f; as a m. tatsächlich

mat′ter-of-fact′ adj sachlich, nüchtern

Matthew [mæθju] s Matthäus m

mattock [mætək] s Breithacke f

mattress [mætrıs] s Matratze f

mature [mə't/ʊr] adj (& fig) reif ‖ tr reifen lassen ‖ intr reifen; (fin) fällig werden

maturity [mə't/ʊrıti] s Reife f; (fin) Verfall m

maudlin [mɔdlın] adj rührselig

maul [mɔl] tr schlimm zurichten

maulstick [mɔl,stık] s Mahlstock m

mausole·um [,mɔsə'li-əm] s (–ums & –a [ə]) Mausoleum n

maw [mɔ] s (mouth of an animal) Rachen m; (stomach of an animal) Tiermagen m; (of birds) Kropf m

mawkish [mɔkıʃ] adj rührselig

maxim [mæksım] s Maxime f, Lehrspruch m

maximum [mæksıməm] adj Höchst–; m. load Höchstbelastung f ‖ s Maximum n

May [me] s Mai m ‖ **may** v (pret might [maıt] aux (expressing possibility) mögen, können; (expressing permission) dürfen; (expressing a wish) mögen; be that as it may wie dem auch sei; come what may komme, was da wolle; it may be too late es ist vielleicht zu spät; that may be das kann (or mag) sein

maybe [mebi] adv vielleicht

May′ Day′ s der erste Mai

mayhem [mehəm] s Körperverletzung f

mayonnaise [,me-ə'nez] s Mayonnaise f

mayor [mer] s Bürgermeister m; (of a large city) Oberbürgermeister m

May′pole′ s Maibaum m

May′ queen′ s Maikönigin f

maze [mez] s Irrgarten m; (fig) Gewirr n

me [mi] pers pron (direct object) mich; (indirect object) mir; this one is on me das geht auf meine Rechnung

mead [mid] s (hist) Met m; (poet) Aue f

meadow [medo] s Wiese f

mead′owland′ s Wiesenland n

meager [migər] adj karg, kärglich

meal [mil] s Mahl n, Mahlzeit f; (grain) grobes Mehl n

meal′ tick′et s Gutschein m für e–e Mahlzeit

meal′time′ s Essenszeit f

mealy [mili] adj mehlig

mealy-mouthed [mili,maʊðd] adj zurückhaltend

mean [min] adj (nasty) bösartig; (lowly) gemein, niedrig; (shabby) schäbig; (in statistics) mittlere; no m. kein schlechter ‖ s (log) Mittelbegriff m; (math) Mittel n; by all means unbedingt; by every means mit allen Mitteln; by fair means or foul ganz gleich wie; by lawful means auf dem Rechtswege; by means of mittels (*genit*); **by no means keineswegs**; **live beyond one's means** über seine Verhältnisse leben; **live within one's means** seinen Verhältnissen entsprechend leben; **means** (*way*) Mittel *n*; (*resources*) Mittel *pl*, Vermögen *n*; **means of transportation** Verkehrsmittel *n*; **means to an end** Mittel *pl* zum Zweck; **of means** bemittelt ‖ *v* (*pret & pp* **meant** [mɛnt]) *tr* (*intend, intend to say*) meinen; (*signify*) bedeuten; **be meant for** (*said, e.g., of a remark*) gelten (*dat*); (*said, e.g., of a gift*) bestimmt sein für; **it means a lot to me to** (*inf*) mir liegt viel daran zu (*inf*); **m. business** es ernst meinen; **m. little** (or **much**) wenig (or viel) gelten; **m. no harm** es nicht böse meinen; **m. s.o. no harm** j-n nicht verletzen wollen; **m. the world to s.o.** j-m alles bedeuten; **what is meant by ...?** was versteht man unter ...? ‖ *intr*—**m. well** es gut meinen

meander [mɪˈændər] *intr* sich winden
mean'ing *s* Bedeutung *f*; **take on m.** e-n Sinn bekommen; **what's the m. of this?** was soll das heißen?
meaningful [ˈminɪŋfəl] *adj* sinnvoll
meaningless [ˈminɪŋlɪs] *adj* sinnlos
mean'-look'ing *adj* bösartig aussehend
meanness [ˈminnɪs] *s* Gemeinheit *f*; (*nastiness*) Bösartigkeit *f*
mean'time', mean'while' *adv* mittlerweile ‖ *s*—**in the m.** mittlerweile, in der Zwischenzeit
measles [ˈmizəlz] *s* Masern *pl*; (*German measles*) Röteln *pl*
measly [ˈmizli] *adj* kümmerlich, lumpig
measurable [ˈmɛʒərəbəl] *adj* meßbar
measure [ˈmɛʒər] *s* Maß *n*; (*step*) Maßnahme *f*; (*law*) Gesetz *n*; (*mus*) Takt *m*; **beyond m.** übermäßig; **for good m.** obendrein; **in a great m.** in großem Maß; **to some m.** gewissermaßen; **take drastic measures** durchgreifen; **take measures to** (*inf*) Maßnahmen ergreifen um zu (*inf*); **take s.o.'s m.** (*fig*) j-n einschätzen ‖ *tr* messen; **m. off** abmessen; **m. out** ausmessen ‖ *intr* messen; **m. up to** gewachsen sein (*dat*)
measurement [ˈmɛʒərmənt] *s* (*measured dimension*) Maß *n*; (*measuring*) Messung *f*; **measurements** Maße *pl*; **take s.o.'s measurements for** j-m Maß nehmen zu
meas'uring cup' *s* Meßbecher *m*
meas'uring tape' *s* Meßband *n*
meat [mit] *s* Fleisch *n*; (*of a nut, of the matter*) Kern *m*
meat'ball' *m* Fleischklößchen *n*
meat' grind'er *s* Fleischwolf *m*
meat'hook' *s* Fleischhaken *m*
meat'mar'ket *s* Fleischmarkt *m*
meat' pie' *s* Fleischpastete *f*
meaty [ˈmiti] *adj* fleischig; (*fig*) kernig
Mecca [ˈmɛkə] *s* Mekka *n*
mechanic [məˈkænɪk] *s* Mechaniker *m*, Schlosser *m*; (*aut*) Autoschlosser *m*; **mechanics** Mechanik *f*

mechanical [məˈkænɪkəl] *adj* mechanisch
mechan'ical engineer' *s* Maschinenbauingenieur *m*
mechan'ical engineer'ing *s* Maschinenbau *m*
mechanism [ˈmɛkəˌnɪzəm] *s* Mechanismus *m*
mechanize [ˈmɛkəˌnaɪz] *tr* mechanisieren
medal [ˈmɛdəl] *s* Medaille *f*, Orden *m*
medallion [mɪˈdæljən] *s* Medaillon *n*
meddle [ˈmɛdəl] *intr* sich einmischen; **m. with** sich abgeben mit
meddler [ˈmɛdlər] *s* zudringliche Person *f*
meddlesome [ˈmɛdəlsəm] *adj* zudringlich
media [ˈmidɪ-ə] *spl* Medien *pl*
median [ˈmidɪ-ən] *adj* mittlere, Mittel- ‖ *s* (*arith*) Mittelwert *m*; (*geom*) Mittellinie *f*
me'dian strip' *s* Mittelstreifen *m*
mediate [ˈmidɪˌet] *tr & intr* vermitteln
mediation [ˌmidɪˈeʃən] *s* Vermittlung *f*
mediator [ˈmidɪˌetər] *s* Vermittler –in *mf*
medic [ˈmɛdɪk] *s* (*mil*) Sanitäter *m*
medical [ˈmɛdɪkəl] *adj* (*of a doctor*) ärztlich; (*of medicine*) medizinisch; (*of the sick*) Kranken-
med'ical bul'letin *s* Krankheitsbericht *m*
med'ical corps' *s* Sanitätstruppe *f*
med'ical profes'sion *s* Arztberuf *m*
med'ical school' *s* medizinische Fakultät *f*
med'ical sci'ence *s* Heilkunde *f*
med'ical stu'dent *s* Medizinstudent –in *mf*
medication [ˌmɛdɪˈkeʃən] *s* Medikament *n*
medicinal [məˈdɪsɪnəl] *adj* medizinisch
medicine [ˈmɛdɪsən] *s* Medizin *f*, Arznei *f*; (*profession*) Medizin *f*; **practice m.** den Arztberuf ausüben
med'icine cab'inet *s* Hausapotheke *f*
med'icine kit' *s* Reiseapotheke *f*
med'icine man' *s* Medizinmann *m*
medic-o [ˈmɛdɪˌko] *s* (**–cos**) (*coll*) Mediziner –in *mf*
medieval [ˌmidɪˈivəl], [ˌmɛdɪˈivəl] *adv* mittelalterlich
mediocre [ˌmidɪˈokər] *adj* mittelmäßig
mediocrity [ˌmidɪˈɑkrɪti] *s* Mittelmäßigkeit *f*
meditate [ˈmɛdɪˌtet] *tr* vorhaben ‖ *intr* (*on*) meditieren (über *acc*)
meditation [ˌmɛdɪˈteʃən] *s* Meditation *f*
Mediterranean [ˌmɛdɪtəˈreni-ən] *adj* Mittelmeer- ‖ *s* Mittelmeer *n*
medi-um [ˈmidɪ-əm] *adj* Mittel-, mittlere ‖ *s* (**–ums & –a** [ə]) Mitte *n*; (*culture*) Nährboden *n*; (*in spiritualism, communications*) Medium *n*; **through the m. of** vermittels (*genit*)
me'dium of exchange' *s* Tauschmittel *n*
me'dium-rare' *adj* halb durchgebraten
me'dium size' *s* Mittelgröße *f*

med′ium-sized′ *adj* mittelgroß

medley [′medli] *s* Mischmasch *m;* (mus) Potpourri *n*

medul·la [mɪ′dʌlə] *s* (**-las** & **-lae** [li]) Knochenmark *n*, Mark *n*

meek [mik] *adj* sanftmütig; **m. as a lamb** lammfromm

meekness [′miknɪs] *s* Sanftmut *m*

meerschaum [′mɪrʃəm] *s* Meerschaum *m*

meet [mit] *adj* passend ‖ *s* (sport) Treffen *n*, Veranstaltung *f* ‖ *v* (*pret* & *pp* **met** [mɛt]) *tr* begegnen (*dat*), treffen; (*make the acquaintance of*) kennenlernen; (*demands*) befriedigen; (*obligations*) nachkommen (*dat*); (*wishes*) erfüllen; (*a deadline*) einhalten; **m. s.o. at the train** j–n von der Bahn abholen; **m. s.o. halfway** j–m auf halbem Wege entgegenkommen; **m. the train** zum Zug gehen; **pleased to m. you** freut mich sehr, sehr angenehm ‖ *intr* (*said of persons, of two ends*) zusammenkommen; (*said of persons*) sich treffen; (*in conference*) tagen; (*said of roads, rivers*) sich vereinigen; **make both ends m.** gerade mit dem Geld auskommen; **m. again** sich wiedersehen; **m. up with s.o.** j–n einholen; **m. with** zusammentreffen mit; **m. with an accident** verunglücken; **m. with a refusal** e–e Fehlbitte tun; **m. with approval** Beifall finden; **m. with success** Erfolg haben

meet′ing *s* (*of an organization*) Versammlung *f;* (*e.g., of a committee*) Sitzung *f;* (*of individuals*) Zusammenkunft *f*

meet′ing place′ *s* Treffpunkt *m*

megacycle [′megə‚sarkəl], **megahertz** [′megə‚hʌrts] *s* (elec) Megahertz *n*

megalomania [‚megəlo′menɪ·ə] *s* Größenwahn *m*

megaphone [′megə‚fon] *s* Sprachrohr *n*

megohm [′meg‚om] *s* Megohm *n*

melancholy [′melən‚kɑli] *adj* schwermütig ‖ *s* Schwermut *f*

melee [′mele], [′mele] *s* Gemenge *n*

mellow [′melo] *adj* (*very ripe*) mürb(e); (*wine*) abgelagert; (*voice*) schmelzend; (*person*) gereift ‖ *tr zur* Reife bringen; (fig) mildern ‖ *intr* mürb(e) werden; (fig) mild werden

melodic [mɪ′lɑdɪk] *adj* melodisch

melodious [mɪ′lodɪ·əs] *adj* melodisch

melodrama [′melo‚dramə] *s* (& fig) Melodrama *n*

melody [′meladi] *s* Melodie *f*

melon [′melən] *s* Melone *f*

melt [melt] *tr* & *intr* schmelzen

melt′ing point′ *s* Schmelzpunkt *m*

melt′ing pot′ *s* (& fig) Schmelztiegel *m*

member [′membər] *s* Glied *n;* (*person*) Mitglied *n*, Angehörige *mf;* **m. of the family** Familienangehörige *mf*

mem′bership′ *s* Mitgliedschaft *f;* (*collectively*) Mitglieder *pl;* (*number of members*) Mitgliederzahl *f*

mem′bership card′ *s* Mitgliedskarte *f*

membrane [′membren] *s* Häutchen *n*, Membran(e) *f*

memen·to [mɪ′mento] *s* (**-tos** & **-toes**) Erinnerung *f*, Memento *n*

mem·o [′memo] *s* (**-os**) (coll) Notiz *f*

mem′o book′ *s* Notizbuch *n*, Agenda *f*

memoirs [′memwɑrz] *spl* Memoiren *pl*

mem′o pad′ *s* Notizblock *m*, Agenda *f*

memorable [′memərəbəl] *adj* denkwürdig

memoran·dum [‚memə′rændəm] *s* (**-dums** & **-da** [də]) Notiz *f*, Vermerk *m;* (dipl) Memorandum *n*

memorial [mɪ′morɪ·əl] *adj* Gedächtnis–. Erinnerungs– ‖ *s* Denkmal *n*

Memor′ial Day′ *s* Gefallenengedenktag *m*

memorialize [mɪ′morɪ·ə‚laɪz] *tr* gedenken (*genit*)

memorize [′memə‚raɪz] *tr* auswendig lernen

memory [′meməri] *s* (*faculty*) Gedächtnis *n;* (*of*) Gedenken *n* (an *acc*), Erinnerung *f* (an *acc*); **commit to m.** auswendig lernen; **escape one's m.** seinem Gedächtnis entfallen; **from m.** aus dem Gedächtnis; **in m. of** zur Erinnerung an (*acc*); **of blessed m.** seligen Angedenkens; **within the m. of men** seit Menschengedenken

menace [′menɪs] *s* (**to**) Drohung *f* (*genit*) ‖ *tr* bedrohen

menagerie [mə′nædʒəri] *s* Menagerie *f*

mend [mend] *s* Besserung *f;* **on the m.** auf dem Wege der Besserung ‖ *tr* (*clothes*) ausbessern; (*socks*) stopfen; (*repair*) reparieren

mendacious [men′deʃəs] *adj* lügnerisch

mendicant [′mendɪkənt] *adj* Bettel– ‖ *s* Bettelmönch *m*

menfolk [′men‚fok] *spl* Mannsleute *pl*

menial [′minɪ·əl] *adj* niedrig ‖ *s* Diener –in *mf*

menopause [′menə‚pɔz] *s* Wechseljahre *pl*

menses [′mensiz] *spl* Monatsfluß *m*

men′s room′ *s* Herrentoilette *f*

men′s′ size′ *s* Herrengröße *f*

men′s′ store′ *s* Herrenbekleidungsgeschäft *n*

menstruate [′menstru‚et] *intr* menstruieren

menstruation [‚menstru′eʃən] *s* Menstruation *f*

men′s′ wear′ *s* Herrenbekleidung *f*

mental [′mentəl] *adj* geistig, Geistes–

men′tal an′guish *s* Seelenpein *f*

men′tal arith′metic *s* Kopfrechnen *n*

men′tal capac′ity *s* Fassungskraft *f*

men′tal disor′der *s* Geistesstörung *f*

men′tal institu′tion *s* Nervenheilanstalt *f*

mentality [men′tælɪti] *s* Mentalität *f*

mentally [′mentəli] *adv* geistig, Geistes–; **m. alert** geistesgegenwärtig; **m. disturbed** geistesgestört; **m. lazy** denkfaul

men′tal reserva′tion *s* geistiger Vorbehalt *m*

men′tal teleʹpathy *s* Gedankenübertragung *f*

mention [′menʃən] *s* Erwähnung *f;*

make m. of erwähnen ‖ *tr* erwähnen, nennen; **be mentioned** zur Sprache kommen; **don't m. it!** keine Ursache!; **not worth mentioning** nicht der Rede wert

menu ['menju] *s* Speisekarte *f*

meow ['mi'au] *s* Miauen *n* ‖ *intr* miauen

mercantile ['mʌrkən,til], ['mʌrkən,tail] *adj* Handels-, kaufmännisch

mercenary ['mʌrsə,neri] *adj* gewinnsüchtig ‖ *s* Söldner *m*

merchandise ['mʌrt/ən,daiz] *s* Ware *f* ‖ *tr* handeln

mer'chandising *s* Verkaufspolitik *f*

merchant ['mʌrt/ənt] *s* Händler, Kaufmann *m*

mer'chant·man *s* (-men) Handelsschiff *n*

mer'chant marine' *s* Handelsmarine *f*

mer'chant ves'sel *s* Handelsschiff *n*

merciful ['mʌrsifəl] *adj* barmherzig

merciless ['mʌrsilis] *adj* erbarmungslos

mercurial [mer'kjuri·əl] *adj* quecksilbrig

mercury ['mʌrkjəri] *s* Quecksilber *n*

mercy ['mʌrsi] *s* Barmherzigkeit *f*; **be at s.o.'s m.** in j-s Gewalt sein; **be at the m. of** (*e.g., the wind, waves*) preisgegeben sein (*dat*); **beg for m.** um Gnade flehen; **show no m.** keine Gnade walten lassen; **show s.o. m.** sich j-s erbarmen; **throw oneself on the m. of** sich auf Gnade und Ungnade ergeben (*dat*); **without m.** ohne Gnade

mere [mir] *adj* bloß, rein

merely ['mirli] *adv* nur, lediglich

meretricious [,meri'tri/əs] *adj* (*tawdry*) flitterhaft; (*characteristic of a prostitute*) dirnenhaft

merge [mʌrdʒ] *tr* verschmelzen ‖ *intr* sich verschmelzen

merger ['mʌrdʒər] *s* (com) Fusion *f*; (jur) Verschmelzung *f*

meridian [mə'ridi·ən] *s* (astr) Meridian *m*; (geog) Meridian *m*, Längenkreis *m*

meringue [mə'ræŋ] *s* (*topping*) Eierschnee *m*; (*pastry*) Schaumgebäck *n*

merit ['merit] *s* Verdienst *n*; **of great m.** hochverdient ‖ *tr* verdienen

meritorious [,meri'tori·əs] *adj* verdienstvoll

merlin ['mʌrlin] *s* (orn) Merlinfalke *m*

mermaid ['mʌr,med] *s* Seejungfer *f*

merriment ['merimənt] *s* Fröhlichkeit *f*

merry ['meri] *adj* fröhlich, heiter

Mer'ry Christ'mas *s* fröhliche Weihnachten *pl*

mer'ry-go-round' *s* Karussell *n*

mer'rymak·er *s* Zecher –in *mf*

mesh [me/] *s* Masche *f*; (*network*) Netzwerk *n*; (mach) Ineinandergreifen *n*; **meshes** (fig) Schlingen *pl* ‖ *intr* ineinandergreifen

mesmerize ['mesmə,raiz] *tr* hypnotisieren

mess [mes] *s* (*disorder*) Durcheinander

n; (*dirty condition*) Schweinerei *f*; (*for officers*) Messe *f*; **a nice m.!** e–e schöne Wirtschaft!; **get into a m.** in die Klemme geraten; **make a m.** Schmutz machen; **make a m. of** verpfuschen; **what a m.!** nette Zustände! ‖ *tr*—**m. up** (*dirty*) beschmutzen; (*put into disarray*) in Unordnung bringen ‖ *intr*—**m. around** herumtrödeln; **m. around with** herummurksen an (*dat*)

message ['mesidʒ] *s* Botschaft *f*

messenger ['mesəndʒər] *s* Bote *m*, Botin *f*

mess' hall' *s* Messe *f*

Messiah [mə'sai·ə] *s* Messias *m*

mess' kit' *s* Eßgeschirr *n*

messy ['mesi] *adj* (*disorderly*) unordentlich; (*dirty*) dreckig

metabolism [mə'tæbə,lizəm] *s* Stoffwechsel *m*

metal ['metəl] *s* Metall *n*

metallic [mi'tælik] *adj* metallisch

metallurgy ['metə,lʌrdʒi] *s* Hüttenwesen *n*, Metallurgie *f*

met'alwork' *s* Metallarbeit *f*

metamorpho·sis [,metə'mɔrfəsis] *s* (-ses [,siz]) Verwandlung *f*

metaphor ['metə,fɔr] *s* Metapher *f*

metaphorical [,metə'fɔrikəl] *adj* bildlich

metaphysical [,metə'fizikəl] *adj* metaphysisch

metaphysics [,metə'fiziks] *s* Metaphysik *f*

metathe·sis [mi'tæθisis] *s* (-ses [,siz]) Metathese *f*, Lautversetzung *f*

mete [mit] *tr*—**m. out** austeilen

meteor ['miti·ər] *s* Meteor *m*

meteoric [,miti'ɔrik] *adj* meteorisch; (fig) kometenhaft

meteorite ['miti·ə,rait] *s* Meteorit *m*

meteorologist [,miti·ə'ralədʒist] *s* Meteorologe *m*, Meteorologin *f*

meteorology [,miti·ə'ralədʒi] *s* Meteorologie *f*, Wetterkunde *f*

meter ['mitər] *s* Meter *m* & *n*; (*instrument*) Messer *m*, Zähler *m*; (pros) Versmaß *n*

me'ter read'er *s* Zählerableser –in *mf*

methane ['meθen] *s* Methan *n*, Sumpfgas *n*

method ['meθəd] *s* Methode *f*

methodic(al) [mi'θadik(əl)] *adj* methodisch

Methodist ['meθədist] *s* Methodist –in *mf*

methodology [,meθə'dalədʒi] *s* Methodenlehre *f*

Methuselah [mi'θuzələ] *s* Methusalem *m*

meticulous [mi'tikjələs] *adj* übergenau

metric(al) ['metrik(əl)] *adj* metrisch

metrics ['metriks] *s* Metrik *f*

metronome ['metrə,nom] *s* Metronom *n*

metropolis [mi'trapəlis] *s* Metropole *f*

metropolitan [,metrə'palitən] *adj* großstädtisch ‖ *s* (eccl) Metropolit *m*

mettle ['metəl] *s* (*temperament*) Veranlagung *f*; (*courage*) Mut *m*

mettlesome ['metəlsəm] *adj* mutig

mew [mju] s Miau n || intr miauen
Mexican ['mɛksɪkən] adj mexikanisch || s Mexikaner –in mf
Mexico ['mɛksɪ,ko] s Mexiko n
mezzanine ['mɛzə,nin] s Zwischengeschoß n
mica ['maɪkə] s Glimmer m, Marienglas n
Michael ['maɪkəl] s Michel m
microbe ['maɪkrob] s Mikrobe f
microbiology [,maɪkrəbaɪ'alədʒi] s Mikrobiologie f
microcosm ['maɪkrə,kɑzəm] s Mikrokosmos m
microfilm ['maɪkrə,fɪlm] s Mikrofilm m || tr mikrofilmen
microgroove ['maɪkrə,gruv] s Mikrorille f
mic'rogroove rec'ord s Schallplatte f mit Mikrorillen
microphone ['maɪkrə,fon] s Mikrophon n
microscope ['maɪkrə,skop] s Mikroskop n
microscopic [,maɪkrə'skɑpɪk] adj mikroskopisch
microwave ['maɪkrə,wev] s Mikrowelle f
mid [mɪd] adj mittlere
midair' s—in m. mitten in der Luft
mid'day' adj mittäglich, Mittags– || s Mittag m
middle ['mɪdəl] adj mittlere || s Mitte f, Mittel n; in the m. of inmitten (genit), mitten in (dat)
mid'dle age' s mittleres Lebensalter n; Middle Ages Mittelalter n
middle-aged ['mɪdəl,edʒd] adj mittleren Alters
mid'dle class' s Mittelstand m
mid'dle-class' adj bürgerlich
mid'dle dis'tance s Mittelgrund m
mid'dle ear' s Mittelohr n
Mid'dle East', the s der Mittlere Osten
mid'dle fin'ger s Mittelfinger m
Mid'dle High' Ger'man s Mittelhochdeutsch n
Mid'dle Low' Ger'man s Mittelniederdeutsch n
mid'dle-man' s (–men') Mittelsmann m, Zwischenhändler m
mid'dleweight box'er s Mittelgewichtler m
mid'dleweight divi'sion s Mittelgewicht n
middling ['mɪdlɪŋ] adj mittelmäßig || adv leidlich, ziemlich
middy ['mɪdi] s (nav) Fähnrich m zur See
midget ['mɪdʒɪt] s Zwerg m
mid'get rail'road s Liliputbahn f
mid'get submarine' s Kleinst-U-Boot n
midland ['mɪdlənd] adj binnenländisch
mid'night' adj mitternächtlich; burn the m. oil bis in die tiefe Nacht arbeiten || s Mitternacht f; at m. um Mitternacht
midriff ['mɪdrɪf] s (of a dress) Mittelteil m; (diaphragm) Zwerchfell n; (middle part of the body) Magengrube f; have a bare m. die Taille frei lassen

mid'shipman' s (–men') Fähnrich m zur See
midst [mɪdst] s Mitte f; from our m. aus unserer Mitte; in the m. of mitten in (dat)
mid'stream' s—in m. in der Mitte des Stromes
mid'sum'mer s Mittsommer m
mid'-term' adj mitten im Semester || midterms spl Prüfungen pl mitten im Semester
mid'way' adj in der Mitte befindlich || adv auf halbem Weg || s Mitte f des Weges; (at a fair) Mittelstraße f
mid'week' s Wochenmitte f
mid'wife' s (–wives') Hebamme f
mid'win'ter s Mittwinter m
mid'year' adj in der Mitte des Studienjahres || midyears spl Prüfungen pl in der Mitte des Studienjahres
mien [min] s Miene f
miff [mɪf] s kleine Auseinandersetzung f || tr ärgern
might [maɪt] s Macht f, Kraft f; with m. and main mit aller Kraft || aux used to form the potential mood, e.g., she m. lose her way sie könnte sich verirren; we m. as well go es ist wohl besser, wenn wir gehen
mightily ['maɪtəli] adv gewaltig; (coll) enorm
mighty ['maɪti] adj mächtig || adv (coll) furchtbar
migraine ['maɪgren] s Migräne f
mi'grant work'er ['maɪgrənt] s Wanderarbeiter –in mf
migrate ['maɪgret] intr wandern, ziehen
migration [maɪ'greʃən] s Wanderung f; (e.g., of birds) Zug m
migratory ['maɪgrə,tori] adj Wander-
mi'gratory bird' s Zugvogel m
Milan [mɪ'læn] s Mailand n
mild [maɪld] adj mild, lind
mildew ['mɪl,d(j)u] s Mehltau m
mildly ['maɪldli] adv leicht, schwach; to put it m. gelinde gesagt
mildness ['maɪldnɪs] s Milde f
mile [maɪl] s Meile f; for miles meilenweit; miles apart meilenweit auseinander; miles per hour Stundengeschwindigkeit
mileage ['maɪlɪdʒ] s Meilenzahl f; (charge) Meilengeld n
mile'post' s Wegweiser m mit Entfernungsangabe
mile'stone' s (& fig) Meilenstein m
militancy ['mɪlɪtənsi] s Kampfgeist m
militant ['mɪlɪtənt] adj militant || s Kämpfer –in mf
militarism ['mɪlɪtə,rɪzəm] s Militarismus m
militarize ['mɪlɪtə,raɪz] tr auf den Krieg vorbereiten
military ['mɪlə,teri] adj militärisch; (academy, band, government) Militär– || s Militär n
mil'itary campaign' s Feldzug m
mil'itary cem'etery s Soldatenfriedhof m
mil'itary obliga'tions spl Wehrpflicht f
mil'itary police' s Militärpolizei f

mil'itary police'man s (–men) Militär-
polizist m

mil'itary sci'ence s Kriegswissenschaft
f

militate ['mɪlɪ‚tet] intr (against) entgegenwirken (dat)

militia [mɪ'lɪʃə] s Miliz f

mili'tia-man s (–men) Milizsoldat m

milk [mɪlk] s Milch f || tr (& fig)
melken

milk' bar' s Milchbar f

milk' car'ton s Milchtüte f

milk'maid' s Milchmädchen n

milk'man' s (–men') Milchmann m

milk' pail' s Melkeimer m

milk'shake' s Milchmischgetränk n

milk'sop' s Milchbart m

milk' tooth' s Milchzahn m

milk'weed' s Wolfsmilch f, Seiden-
pflanze f

milky ['mɪlkɪ] adj milchig

Milk'y Way' s Milchstraße f

mill [mɪl] s Mühle f; (factory) Fabrik
f, Werk n; put through the m. (coll)
durch e-e harte Schule schicken || tr
(grain) mahlen; (coins) rändeln;
(with a milling machine) fräsern;
(chocolate) quirlen || intr—m. around
durcheinanderlaufen

millenial [mɪ'lɛnɪ‚əl] adj tausendjährig

millenni-um [mɪ'lɛnɪ‚əm] s (–ums &
–a [ə]) Jahrtausend n

miller ['mɪlər] s Müller m

millet ['mɪlɪt] s Hirse f

milligram ['mɪlɪ‚græm] s Milligramm
n

millimeter ['mɪlɪ‚mitər] s Millimeter
n

milliner ['mɪlɪnər] s Putzmacher –in
mf

mil'linery shop' ['mɪlɪ‚nɛrɪ] s Damen-
hutgeschäft n

mill'ing s (of grain) Mahlen n; (of
wood or metal) Fräsen n

mill'ing machine' s Fräsmaschine f

million ['mɪljən] adj—one m. people
e-e Million Menschen; two m. people
zwei Millionen Menschen || s Million
f

millionaire [‚mɪljən'ɛr] s Millionär –in
mf

millionth ['mɪljənθ] adj & pron mil-
lionste || s (fraction) Millionstel n

mill'pond' s Mühlteich m

mill'stone' s Mühlstein m

mill' wheel' s Mühlrad n

mime [maɪm] s Mime m, Mimin f || tr
mimen

mimeograph ['mɪmɪ‚ə‚græf] s Verviel-
fältigungsapparat m || tr vervielfäl-
tigen

mim-ic ['mɪmɪk] s Mimiker –in mf ||
v (pret & pp –icked; ger –icking) tr
nachäffen

mimicry ['mɪmɪkrɪ] s Nachäffen n;
(zool) Mimikry f

mimosa [mɪ'mosə] s Mimose f

minaret [‚mɪnə'rɛt] s Minarett n

mince [mɪns] tr (meat) zerhacken; not
m. words kein Blatt vor den Mund
nehmen

mince'meat' s Pastetenfüllung f;

(chopped meat) Hackfleisch n; make
m. of (fig) in die Pfanne hauen

mind [maɪnd] s Geist m; bear in m.
denken an (acc); be of one m. ein
Herz und e–e Seele sein; be of two
minds geteilter Meinung sein; be out
of one's m. nicht bei Trost sein;
call to m. erinnern; (remember) sich
erinnern; change one's m. sich anders besinnen; give s.o. a piece of
one's m. j–m gründlich die Meinung
sagen; have a good m. to (inf) große
Lust haben zu (inf); have in m. im
Sinn haben zu (inf); have one's m.
on s.th. ständig an etw denken
müssen; I can't get her out of my m.
sie will mir nicht aus dem Sinn;
know one's own m. wissen, was man
will; of sound m. zurechnungsfähig;
put s.th. out of one's m. sich [dat]
etw aus dem Sinn schlagen; set one's
m. on sein Sinnen und Trachten
richten auf (acc); slip s.o.'s m. j–m
entfallen; to my m. meines Erach-
tens || tr (watch over) aufpassen auf
(acc); (obey) gehorchen (dat); (be
troubled by; take care of) sich kümmern um; do you m. if I smoke?
macht es Ihnen etw aus, wenn ich
rauche?; do you m. the smoke? macht
Ihnen der Rauch etw aus?; I don't
m. your smoking ich habe nichts dagegen, daß (or wenn) Sie rauchen;
m. your own business! kümmere dich
um deine Angelegenheit!; m. you!
wohlgemerkt! || intr—I don't m. es
macht mir nichts aus; I don't m. if
I do (coll) ja, recht gern; never m.!
schon gut!

-minded [‚maɪndɪd] suf –mütig. –gesinnt, –sinnig

mindful ['maɪndfəl] adj (of) eingedenk
(genit); be m. of achten auf (acc)

mind' read'er s Gedankenleser –in mf

mind' read'ing s Gedankenlesen n

mine [maɪn] s Bergwerk n, Mine f;
(fig) Fundgrube f; (mil) Mine f ||
poss pron meiner || tr (e.g., coal)
abbauen; (mil) verminen || intr—m.
for graben nach

mine' detec'tor s Minensuchgerät n

mine'field' s Minenfeld n

minelayer ['maɪn‚le‚ər] s Minenleger
m

miner ['maɪnər] s Bergarbeiter m

mineral ['mɪnərəl] adj mineralisch,
Mineral– || s Mineral n

mineralogy [‚mɪnə'rɑlədʒɪ] s Mineralogie f

min'eral resour'ces spl Bodenschätze
pl

min'eral wa'ter s Mineralwasser n

mine'sweep'er s Minenräumboot n

mingle ['mɪŋgəl] tr vermengen || intr
(with) sich mischen (unter acc)

miniature ['mɪnɪ‚ət/ər], ['mɪnɪt/ər]
adj Miniatur–, Klein– || s Miniatur f

minimal ['mɪnɪməl] adj minimal, Mindest–

minimize ['mɪnə‚maɪz] tr auf das
Minimum herabsetzen; (fig) bagatellisieren

minimum ['mɪnɪməm] *adj* minimal, Mindest– ‖ *s* Minimum *n; (lowest price)* untere Preisgrenze *f*

min'imum wage' *s* Mindestlohn *m*

min'ing *adj* Bergbau– ‖ *s* Bergbau *m*, Bergwesen *n; (mil)* Minenlegen *n*

minion ['mɪnjən] *s* Günstling *m*

miniskirt ['mɪni ‚skɑrt] *s* Minirock *m*

minister ['mɪnɪstər] *s* (eccl) Geistlicher *m; (pol)* Minister *m* ‖ *intr*—m. to dienen *(dat); (aid)* Hilfe leisten *(dat)*

ministerial [‚mɪnɪs'tɪrɪ·əl] *adj* (eccl) geistlich; (pol) ministeriell

ministry ['mɪnɪstri] *s (office)* (eccl) geistliches Amt *n; (the clergy)* (eccl) geistlicher Stand *m; (pol)* Ministerium *n*

mink [mɪŋk] *s* (zool) Nerz *m; (fur)* Nerzfell *n*

mink' coat' *s* Nerzmantel *m*

minnow ['mɪno] *s* Pfrille *f*, Elritze *f*

minor ['maɪnər] *adj* minder, geringer, Neben– ‖ *s (person)* Minderjährige *mf; (educ)* Nebenfach *n; (log)* Untersatz *m; (mus)* Moll *n* ‖ *intr*—m. in als Nebenfach studieren

minority [mɪ'nɔrɪti] *adj* Minderheits– ‖ *s* Minderheit *f; (of votes)* Stimmenminderheit *f; (ethnic group)* Minorität *f*

mi'nor key' *s* Molltonart *f*; in a m. in Moll

minstrel ['mɪnstrəl] *s* (hist) Spielmann *m*

mint [mɪnt] *s* Münzanstalt *f; (bot)* Minze *f* ‖ *tr* münzen

mintage ['mɪntɪdʒ] *s* Prägung *f*

minuet [‚mɪnju'et] *s* Menuett *n*

minus ['maɪnəs] *adj* negativ ‖ *prep* minus, weniger; *(without)* (coll) ohne *(acc)*

mi'nus sign' *s* Minuszeichen *n*

minute [maɪ'n(j)ut] *adj* winzig ‖ ['mɪnɪt] *s* Minute *f*; **minutes** Protokoll *n*; **take the minutes** das Protokoll führen

–minute [mɪnɪt] *suf* –minutig

min'ute hand' *s* Minutenzeiger *m*

minutiae [mɪ'n(j)uʃɪ·i] *spl* Einzelheiten *pl*

minx [mɪŋks] *s* Range *f*

miracle ['mɪrəkəl] *s* Wunder *n*

mir'acle play' *s* Mirakelspiel *n*

miraculous [mɪ'rækjələs] *adj* wunderbar; *(e.g., power)* Wunder–

mirage [mɪ'rɑʒ] *s* Luftspiegelung *f*; (fig) Luftbild *n*, Täuschung *f*

mire [maɪr] *s* Morast *m*, Schlamm *m*

mirror ['mɪrər] *s* Spiegel *m* ‖ *tr* spiegeln

mirth [mʌrθ] *s* Fröhlichkeit *f*

miry ['maɪri] *adj* sumpfig, schlammig

misadventure [‚mɪsəd'ventʃər] *s* Mißgeschick *n*

misanthrope ['mɪsən ‚θrop] *s* Menschenfeind *m*

misapprehension [‚mɪsæprɪ'henʃən] *s* Mißverständnis *n*

misappropriate [‚mɪsə'propri ‚et] *tr* sich *[dat]* widerrechtlich aneignen

misbehave [‚mɪsbɪ'hev] *intr* sich schlecht benehmen

misbehavior [‚mɪsbɪ'hevɪ·ər] *s* schlechtes Benehmen *n*

miscalculate [mɪs'kælkjə ‚let] *tr* falsch berechnen ‖ *intr* sich verrechnen

miscalculation [‚mɪskælkjə'leʃən] *s* Rechenfehler *m*

miscarriage [mɪs'kærɪdʒ] *s* Fehlgeburt *f; (fig)* Fehlschlag *m*

miscar'riage of jus'tice *s* Justizirrtum *m*

miscar-ry [mɪs'kæri] *v (pret & pp* –ried) *intr* ə–ə Fehlgeburt haben; *(said of a plan)* scheitern, fehlschlagen

miscellaneous [‚mɪsə'leni·əs] *adj* vermischt

miscellany ['mɪsə ‚leni] *s* Gemisch *n; (of literary works)* Sammelband *m*

mischief ['mɪstʃɪf] *s* Unfug *m*; be up to m. ə–n Unfug im Kopf haben; cause m. Unfug treiben; get into m. etw anstellen

mis'chief-mak'er *s* Störenfried *m*

mischievous ['mɪstʃɪvəs] *adj* mutwillig

misconception [‚mɪskən'sepʃən] *s* falsche Auffassung *f*

misconduct [mɪs'kɑndʌkt] *s* schlechtes Benehmen *n*; m. in office Amtsvergehen *n* ‖ [‚mɪskən'dʌkt] *tr* schlecht verwalten; m. oneself sich schlecht benehmen

misconstrue [‚mɪskən'stru] *tr* falsch auffassen

miscount [mɪs'kaunt] *s* Rechenfehler *m* ‖ *tr* falsch zählen ‖ *intr* sich verzählen

miscreant ['mɪskrɪ·ənt] *s* Schurke *m*

miscue [mɪs'kju] *s* (fig) Fehler *m; (billiards)* Kicks *m* ‖ *intr* (billiards) kicksen; (theat) den Auftritt verpassen

mis-deal ['mɪs ‚dil] *s* falsches Geben *n* ‖ [mɪs'dil] *v (pret & pp* –dealt [delt]) *tr* falsch geben ‖ *intr* sich vergeben

misdeed [mɪs'did] *s* Missetat *f*

misdemeanor [‚mɪsdɪ'minər] *s* Vergehen *n*

misdirect [‚mɪsdɪ'rekt], [‚mɪsdaɪ'rekt] *tr* (& fig) fehlleiten

misdoing [mɪs'du·ɪŋ] *s* Missetat *f*

miser ['maɪzər] *s* Geizhals *m*

miserable ['mɪzərəbəl] *adj* elend; feel m. sich elend fühlen; make life m. for s.o. j–m das Leben sauer machen

miserly ['maɪzərli] *adj* geizig

misery ['mɪzəri] *s* Elend *n*

misfeasance [mɪs'fizəns] *s* (jur) Amtsmißbrauch *m*

misfire [mɪs'faɪr] *s* Versagen *n* ‖ *intr* versagen

misfit ['mɪsfɪt] *s (clothing)* schlecht sitzendes Kleidungsstück *n; (person)* Gammler *m*

misfortune [mɪs'fɔrtʃən] *s* Unglück *n*

misgiving [mɪs'gɪvɪŋ] *s* böse Ahnung *f*; full of misgivings ahnungsvoll

misgovern [mɪs'gʌvərn] *tr* schlecht verwalten

misguidance [mɪs'gaɪdəns] *s* Irreführung *f*

misguide [mɪs'gaɪd] *tr* irreleiten

misguid'ed *adj* irregeleitet

mishap [ˈmɪʃæp] *s* Unfall *m*

mishmash [ˈmɪʃˌmæʃ] *s* Mischmasch *m*

misinform [ˌmɪsɪnˈfɔrm] *tr* falsch informieren, falsch unterrichten

misinterpret [ˌmɪsɪnˈtʌrprɪt] *tr* mißdeuten, falsch auffassen

misjudge [mɪsˈdʒʌdʒ] *tr* (e.g., a person, situation) falsch beurteilen; (distance) falsch schätzen

mis·lay [mɪsˈle] *v* (pret & pp –laid) *tr* verlegen, verkramen

mis·lead [mɪsˈlid] *v* (pret & pp –led) *tr* irreführen

mislead'ing *adj* irreführend

mismanage [mɪsˈmænɪdʒ] *tr* schlecht verwalten; (funds) verwirtschaften

mismanagement [mɪsˈmænɪdʒmənt] *s* Mißwirtschaft *f*, schlechte Verwaltung *f*

mismarriage [mɪsˈmærɪdʒ] *s* Mißheirat *f*

misnomer [mɪsˈnomər] *s* Felhbezeichnung *f*

misplace [mɪsˈples] *tr* verlegen

misprint [ˈmɪsˌprɪnt] *s* Druckfehler *m* || [mɪsˈprɪnt] *tr* verdrucken

mispronounce [ˌmɪsprəˈnauns] *tr* falsch aussprechen

mispronunciation [ˌmɪsprənʌnsɪˈeʃən] *s* falsche Aussprache *f*

misquote [mɪsˈkwot] *tr* falsch zitieren

misread [mɪsˈrid] *v* (pret & pp –read [ˈred]) *tr* falsch lesen || *intr* sich verlesen

misrepresent [ˌmɪsreprɪˈzent] *tr* falsch darstellen; **m. the facts to s.o.** j–m falsche Tatsachen vorspiegeln

miss [mɪs] *s* Fehlschlag *m*, Versager *m*; **Miss** Fräulein *n*; **Miss America** die Schönheitskönigin von Amerika || *tr* (a target; one's calling; a person, e.g., at the station; a town along the road; one's way) verpassen; (feel the lack of) verpassen; (school, a train, an opportunity) versäumen; **m. one's step** fehltreten; **m. the mark** vorbeischießen; (fig) sein Ziel verfehlen; **m. the point** die Pointe nicht verstanden haben || *intr* fehlen; (in shooting) vorbeischießen

missal [ˈmɪsəl] *s* Meßbuch *n*

misshapen [mɪsˈʃepən] *adj* mißgestaltet

missile [ˈmɪsɪl] *s* Geschoß *n*; (rok) Rakete *f*

missing [ˈmɪsɪŋ] *adj*—**be m.** fehlen; (said, e.g., of a child) vermißt werden; **m. in action** vermißt

miss'ing per'son *s* Vermißte *mf*

miss'ing-per'sons bu'reau *s* Suchdienst *m*

mission [ˈmɪʃən] *s* Mission *f*; **m. in life** Lebensaufgabe *f*

missionary [ˈmɪʃənˌɛri] *adj* Missions– || *s* Missionar –in *mf*

missis [ˈmɪsɪz] *s*—**the m.** (the wife) die Frau; (of the house) (coll) die Frau des Hauses

missive [ˈmɪsɪv] *s* Sendschreiben *n*

mis·spell [mɪsˈspel] *v* (pret & pp –spelled & –spelt) *tr & intr* falsch schreiben

misspell'ing *s* Schreibfehler *m*

misspent [mɪsˈspent] *adj* vergeudet

misstate [mɪsˈstet] *tr* falsch angeben

misstatement [mɪsˈstetmənt] *s* falsche Angabe *f*

misstep [mɪsˈstep] *s* (& fig)Fehltritt *m*

mist [mɪst] *s* feiner Nebel *m* || *tr* umnebeln || *intr* (said of the eyes) sich trüben; **mist over** nebeln

mis·take [mɪsˈtek] *s* Fehler *m*; **by m.** aus Versehen || *v* (pret –took [ˈtuk]; pp –taken) *tr* verkennen; **m. s.o. for s.o. else** j–n mit e–m anderen verwechseln

mistaken [mɪsˈtekən] *adj* falsch, irrig; **be m. (about)** sich irren (in dat); **unless I'm m.** wenn ich mich nicht irre

mistak'en iden'tity *s* Personenverwechslung *f*

mistakenly [mɪsˈtekənli] *adv* versehentlich

mister [ˈmɪstər] *s* Herr *m* || *interj* (pej) Herr!

mistletoe [ˈmɪsəlˌto] *s* Mistel *f*

mistreat [mɪsˈtrit] *tr* mißhandeln

mistreatment [mɪsˈtritmənt] *s* Mißhandlung *f*

mistress [ˈmɪstrɪs] *s* Herrin *f*; (lover) Mätresse *f*, Geliebte *f*

mistrial [mɪsˈtraɪ·əl] *s* fehlerhaft geführter Prozeß *m*

mistrust [mɪsˈtrʌst] *s* Mißtrauen *n* || *tr* mißtrauen (dat)

misty [ˈmɪsti] *adj* neblig; (eyes) umflort; (fig) unklar

misunder·stand [ˌmɪsʌndərˈstænd] *v* (pret & pp –stood) *tr & intr* mißverstehen

misunderstanding [ˌmɪsʌndərˈstændɪŋ] *s* Mißverständnis *n*

misuse [mɪsˈjus] *s* Mißbrauch *m* || [mɪsˈjuz] *tr* mißbrauchen; (mistreat) mißhandeln

misword [mɪsˈwʌrd] *tr* in falsche Worte fassen

mite [maɪt] *s* (ent) Milbe *f*

miter [ˈmaɪtər] *s* Bischofsmütze *f* || *tr* auf Gehrung verbinden

mi'ter box' *s* Gehrlade *f*

mitigate [ˈmɪtɪˌget] *tr* lindern

mitigation [ˌmɪtɪˈgeʃən] *s* Linderung *f*

mitt [mɪt] *s* Fausthandschuh *m*; (sl) Flosse *f*; (baseball) Fängerhandschuh *m*

mitten [ˈmɪtən] *s* Fausthandschuh *m*

mix [mɪks] *s* Mischung *f*, Gemisch *n* || *tr* (ver)mischen; (a drink) mixen; (a cake) anrühren; **mix in** beimischen; **mix up** vermischen; (confuse) verwirren || *intr* sich (ver)mischen; **mix with** vekehren mit

mixed *adj* vermischt; (feelings, company, doubles) gemischt

mixed' drink' *s* Mixgetränk *n*

mixed' mar'riage *s* Mischehe *f*

mixer [ˈmɪksər] *s* Mischer –in *mf*; (of cocktails) Mixer –in *mf*; (mach) Mischmaschine *f*; **a good m.** ein guter Gesellschafter

mixture [ˈmɪkstʃər] *s* (e.g., of gases)

Gemisch *n*; (*e.g., of tobacco, coffee*) Mischung *f*; (pharm) Mixtur *f*

mix'-up' *s* Wirrwar *m*, Verwechslung *f*

mizzen ['mɪzən] *s* Besan *m*

mnemonic [nə'manɪk] *s* Gedächtnishilfe *f*

moan [mon] *s* Stöhnen *n* ‖ *intr* stöhnen; **m. about** jammern über (*acc*) or um

moat [mot] *s* Schloßgraben *m*

mob [mab] *s* (*populace*) Pöbel *m*; (*crush of people*) Andrang *m*; (*gang of criminals*) Verbrecherbande *f* ‖ *v* (*pret & pp* mobbed; *ger* mobbing) *tr* (*crowd into*) lärmend eindringen in (*acc*); (*e.g., a consulate*) angreifen; (*a celebrity*) umringen

mobile ['mobɪl] *adj* fahrbar; (mil) motorisiert

mo'bile home' *s* Wohnwagen *m*

mobility [mo'bɪlɪti] *s* (& mil) Beweglichkeit *f*

mobilization [,mobɪlɪ'zeʃən] *s* Mobilisierung *f*

mobilize ['mobɪ ,laɪz] *tr* mobilisieren; (*strength*) aufbieten

mob' rule' *s* Pöbelherrschaft *f*

mobster ['mabstər] *s* Gangster *m*

moccasin ['makəsɪn] *s* Mokassin *m*; (*snake*) Mokassinschlange *f*

Mo'cha cof'fee ['mokə] *s* Mokka *m*

mock [mak] *adj* Schein– ‖ *tr* verspotten; (*imitate*) nachäffen ‖ *intr* spotten; **m. at** sich lustig machen über (*acc*); **m. up** improvisieren

mocker ['makər] *s* Spötter –in *mf*

mockery ['makəri] *s* Spott *m*, Spötterei *f*; **make a m. of** hohnsprechen (*dat*)

mock'ing-bird' *s* spöttisch

mock'ingbird' *s* Spottdrossel *f*

mock' tri'al *s* Schauprozeß *m*

mock' tur'tle soup' *s* falsche Schildkrötensuppe *f*

mock'-up' *s* Schaumodell *n*

modal ['modəl] *adj* modal, Modal–

mode [mod] *s* Modus *m*; (mus) Tonart *f*

mod·el ['madəl] *adj* vorbildlich; (*student, husband*) Muster– ‖ *s* (*e.g., of a building*) Modell *n*; (*at a fashion show*) Vorführdame *f*; (*for art or photography*) Modell *n*; (*example for imitation*) Vorbild *n*, Muster *n*; (*make*) Typ *m*, Bauart *f* ‖ *v* (*pret & pp* –el[l]ed; *ger* –el[l]ing) *tr* (*clothes*) vorführen; **m. oneself on** sich (*dat*) ein Muster nehmen an (*dat*); **m. s.th. on** etw formen nach; (fig) etw gestalten nach ‖ *intr* (for) Modell stehen (zu *dat*)

mod'el air'plane *s* Flugzeugmodell *n*

mod'el num'ber *s* (aut) Typennummer *f*

moderate ['madərɪt] *adj* (*climate*) gemäßigt; (*demand*) maßvoll; (*price*) angemessen; (*e.g., in drinking*) mäßig; **of m. means** minderbemittelt ‖ ['madə ,ret] *tr* mäßigen; (*a meeting*) den Vorsitz führen über (*acc*) or bei; (*a television show*) moderieren ‖ *intr* sich mäßigen

moderation [,madə'reʃən] *s* Mäßigung

f, Maß *n*; **in m. mit Maß; observe m.** Maß halten

moderator ['madə ,retər] *s* Moderator *m*

modern ['madərn] *adj* modern, zeitgemäß

mod'ern Eng'lish *s* Neuenglisch *n*

mod'ern his'tory *s* Neuere Geschichte *f*

modernize ['madər ,naɪz] *tr* modernisieren

mod'ern lan'guages *spl* neuere Sprachen *pl*

mod'ern times' *spl* die Neuzeit *f*

modest ['madɪst] *adj* bescheiden

modesty ['madɪsti] *s* Bescheidenheit *f*

modicum ['madɪkəm] *s* bißchen; **a m. of truth** ein Körnchen Wahrheit

modification [,madɪfɪ'keʃən] *s* Abänderung *f*

modifier ['madɪ ,faɪər] *s* (gram) nähere Bestimmung *f*

modi-fy ['madɪ ,faɪ] *v* (*pret & pp* –fied) *tr* abändern; (gram) näher bestimmen

modish ['modɪʃ] *adj* modisch

modulate ['madjə ,let] *tr & intr* modulieren

modulation [,madjə'leʃən] *s* Modulation *f*

mohair ['mo ,her] *s* Mohair *m*

Mohammedan [mo'hæmɪdən] *adj* mohammedanisch ‖ *s* Mohammedaner –in *mf*

Mohammedanism [mo'hæmɪdə ,nɪzəm] *s* Mohammedanismus *m*

moist [mɔɪst] *adj* feucht; (*eyes*) tränenfeucht

moisten ['mɔɪsən] *tr* anfeuchten; (*lips*) befeuchten ‖ *intr* feucht werden

moisture ['mɔɪstʃər] *s* Feuchtigkeit *f*

molar ['molər] *s* Backenzahn *m*

molasses [mə'læsɪz] *s* Melasse *f*

mold [mold] *s* Form *f*; (*mildew*) Schimmel *m*; (*typ*) Matrize *f* ‖ *tr* formen ‖ *intr* (ver)schimmeln

molder ['moldər] *s* Former –in *mf*; (fig) Bildner –in *mf* ‖ *intr* modern

mold'ing *s* Formen *n*; (carp) Gesims *n*

moldy ['moldi] *adj* mod(e)rig, schimmlig

mole [mol] *s* (*breakwater*) Hafendamm *m*; (*blemish*) Muttermal *n*; (zool) Maulwurf *m*

molecular [mə'lekjələr] *adj* molekular

molecule ['malı ,kjul] *s* Molekül *n*

mole'skin' *s* (*fur*) Maulwurfsfell *n*; (tex) Englischleder *n*

molest [mə'lest] *tr* belästigen

molli-fy ['malı ,faɪ] *v* (*pret & pp* –fied) *tr* besänftigen

mollusk ['maləsk] *s* Weichtier *n*

mollycoddle ['malı ,kadəl] *s* Weichling *m* ‖ *tr* verweichlichen

Mol'otov cock'tail ['malətəf] *s* Flaschengranate *f*

molt [molt] *s* *intr* sich mausern

molten ['moltən] *adj* schmelzflüssig

molybdenum [mə'lɪbdɪnəm] *s* Molybdän *n*

mom [mam] *s* (coll) Mama *f*, Mutti *f*

moment ['momənt] *s* Moment *m*, Augenblick *m*; **a m. ago** nur eben; **at a moment's notice** jeden Augenblick; **at any m.** jederzeit; **at the m.** im Augenblick, zur Zeit; **of great m.** von großer Tragweite; **the very m. I spotted her** sobald ich sie erblickte

momentarily ['moman͵terɪli] *adv* momentan; (*in a moment*) gleich

momentary ['momən͵teri] *adj* vorübergehend

momentous [mo'mɛntəs] *adj* folgenschwer

momen·tum [mo'mɛntəm] *s* (**-tums &** **-ta** [tə]) (phys) Moment *n;* (fig) Schwung *m;* **gather m.** Schwung bekommen

monarch ['monərk] *s* Monarch *m*

monarchical [mə'narkɪkəl] *adj* monarchisch

monarchy ['monərki] *s* Monarchie *f*

monastery ['monəs͵teri] *s* Kloster *n*

monastic [mə'næstɪk] *adj* Kloster–, Mönchs–

monasticism [mə'næstɪ͵sɪzəm] *s* Mönchswesen *n*

Monday ['mʌndi], ['mʌnde] *s* Montag *m;* **on M.** am Montag

monetary ['monɪ͵teri] *adj* (*e.g., crisis, unit*) Währungs–; (*e.g., system, value*) Geld–

mon'etary stand'ard *s* Münzfuß *m*

money ['mʌni] *adj* Geld– ‖ *s* Geld *n;* **big m.** schweres Geld; **get one's money's worth** reell bedient werden; **make m.** (on) Geld verdienen (an *dat*); **put m. on** Geld setzen auf (*acc*)

mon'eybag' *s* Geldbeutel *m;* **moneybags** (coll) Geldsack *m*

mon'ey belt' *s* Geldgürtel *m*

moneychanger ['monɪ͵tʃendʒər] *s* Wechsler –in *mf*

moneyed ['mʌnid] *adj* vermögend

mon'ey exchange' *s* Geldwechsel *m*

mon'eylend'er *s* Geldverleiher –in *mf*

mon'eymak'er *s* (fig) Goldgrube *f*

mon'ey or'der *s* Postanweisung *f*

Mongol ['moŋgəl] *adj* mongolid ‖ *s* Mongole *m,* Mongolin *f*

Mongolian [moŋ'golɪ·ən] *adj* mongolisch ‖ *s* (*language*) Mongolisch *n*

mon·goose ['moŋgus] *s* (**-gooses**) Mungo *m*

mongrel ['mʌŋgrəl] *s* Bastard *m*

monitor ['monɪtər] *s* (*at school*) Klassenordner *m;* (rad, telv) Überwachungsgerät *n,* Monitor *m* ‖ *tr* überwachen

monk [mʌŋk] *s* Mönch *m*

monkey ['mʌŋki] *s* Affe *m;* (*female*) Äffin *f;* **make a m. of** zum Narren halten ‖ *intr*—**m. around** (*trifle idly*) herumalbern; **m. around with s.o.** es mit j–m treiben; **m. around with s.th.** an etw [*dat*] herummurksen

mon'keybusi'ness *s* (*underhanded conduct*) Gaunerei *f;* (*frivolous behavior*) (sl) Unfug *m*

mon'keyshine' *s* (sl) Possen *m*

mon'key wrench' *s* Engländer *m*

monocle ['monəkəl] *s* Monokel *n*

monogamous [mə'nagəməs] *adj* monogam

monogamy [mə'nagəmi] *s* Einehe *f*

monogram ['monə͵græm] *s* Monogramm *n*

monograph ['monə͵græf] *s* Monographie *f*

monolithic [͵monə'lɪθɪk] *adj* (& fig) monolithisch

monologue ['monə͵log] *s* Monolog *m*

monomania [͵monə'meni·ə] *s* Monomanie *f*

monoplane ['monə͵plen] *s* Eindecker *m*

monopolize [mə'napə͵laɪz] *tr* monopolisieren

monorail ['monə͵rel] *s* Einschienenbahn *f*

monosyllable ['monə͵sɪləbəl] *s* einsilbiges Wort *n*

monotheism [͵monə'θi·ɪzəm] *s* Monotheismus *m*

monotonous [mə'natənəs] *adj* eintönig

monotony [mə'natəni] *s* Eintönigkeit *f*

monotype ['monə͵taɪp] *s* Monotype *f*

monoxide [mə'naksaɪd] *s* Monoxyd *n*

monsignor [mon'sinjər] *s* (**monsignors** **& monsignori** [͵monsi'njori]) (eccl) Monsignore *m*

monsoon [mon'sun] *s* Monsun *m*

monster ['monstər] *s* (& fig) Ungeheuer *n*

monstrance ['monstrəns] *s* Monstranz *f*

monstrosity [mons'trasɪti] *s* Monstrosität *f,* Ungeheuerlichkeit *f*

monstrous ['monstrəs] *adj* ungeheuer(lich)

month [mʌnθ] *s* Monat *m*

monthly ['mʌnθli] *adj & adv* monatlich ‖ *s* Monatszeitschrift *f*

monument ['monjəmənt] *s* Denkmal *n*

monumental [͵monjə'mɛntəl] *adj* monumental

moo [mu] *s* Muhen *n* ‖ *intr* muhen

mood [mud] *s* Laune *f,* Stimmung *f;* (gram) Aussageweise *f,* Modus *m;* **be in a bad m.** schlechtgelaunt sein; **be in the m. for s.th.** zu etw gelaunt sein

moody ['mudi] *adj* launisch

moon [mun] *s* Mond *m* ‖ *intr*—**m. about** herumlungern

moon'beam' *s* Mondstrahl *m*

moon'light' *s* Mondschein *m* ‖ *intr* schwarzarbeiten

moon'light'er *s* Doppelverdiener –in *mf*

moon'light'ing *s* Schwarzarbeit *f*

moon'lit' *adj* mondhell

moon'shine' *s* Mondschein *m;* (sl) schwarz gebrannter Whisky *m*

moonshiner ['mun͵ʃaɪnər] *s* Schwarzbrenner –in *mf*

moon'shot' *s* Mondgeschoß *n*

moor [mur] *s* Moor *n,* Heidemoor *n,* Moor Mohr *m* ‖ *tr* (naut) vertäuen ‖ *intr* (naut) festmachen

moor'ing *s* (act) Festmachen *n;* **moorings** (*cables*) Vertäuung *f;* (*place*) Liegeplatz *m*

Moorish ['murɪʃ] *adj* maurisch

moose [mus] *s* (**moose**) amerikanischer Elch *m*

moot [mut] *adj* umstritten

mop [map] *s* Mop *m*; *(of hair)* Wust *m* ‖ *v* *(pret & pp* **mopped**; *ger* **mopping**) *tr* mit dem Mop wischen; **mop up** mit dem Mop aufwischen; *(mil)* säubern

mope [mop] *intr* Trübsal blasen

moped ['moped] *s* Moped *n*

mop'ping-up' opera'tion *s* (mil) Säuberungsaktion *f*

moral ['mɔrəl] *adj* moralisch ‖ *s* Moral *f*; **morals** Sitten *pl*

morale [mə'ræl] *s* Moral *f*

morality [mə'rælti] *s* Sittlichkeit *f*

moralize ['mɔrə‚laɪz] *intr* moralisieren

morass [mə'ræs] *s* Morast *m*

morator·um [‚mɔrə'tɔri‚əm] *s* (**-ums** & a– [ə]) Moratorium *n*

Moravia [mə'revɪ·ə] *s* Mähren *n*

morbid ['mɔrbɪd] *adj* krankhaft, morbid

mordacious [mɔr'deʃəs] *adj* bissig

mordant ['mɔrdənt] *adj* beißend

more [mɔr] *comp adj* mehr; **one m. minute** noch e–e Minute ‖ *comp adv* mehr; **all the m.** erst recht; **all the m. because** zumal, da; **m. and m.** immer mehr; **m. and m. expensive** immer teurer; **m. or less** gewissermaßen; **m. than anything** über alles; **no m.** nicht mehr; **not any m.** nicht mehr; **once m.** noch einmal; **the more ... the** (expressing quantity) je mehr ... desto; (expressing frequency) je öfter ... desto ‖ *s* mehr; **see m. of s.o.** j–n noch öfter sehen; **what's m.** außerdem ‖ *pron* mehr

more'o'ver *adv* außerdem, übrigens

morgue [mɔrg] *s* Leichenschauhaus *n*; (journ) Archiv *n*, Zeitungsarchiv *n*

morning ['mɔrnɪŋ] *adj* Morgen– ‖ *s* Morgen *m*; **from m. till night** von früh bis spät; **in the early m.** in früher Morgenstunde; **in the m.** am Morgen; **this m.** heute morgen; **to-morrow m.** morgen früh

morn'ing-af'ter pill' *s* Pille *f* danach

morn'ing-glo'ry *s* Trichterwinde *f*

morn'ing sick'ness *s* morgendliches Erbrechen *n*

morn'ing star' *s* Morgenstern *m*

Moroccan [mə'rakən] *adj* marokkanisch ‖ *s* Marokkaner –in *mf*

morocco [mə'rako] *s* (leather) Saffian *m*; **Morocco** Marokko *n*

moron ['mɔran] *s* Schwachsinnige *mf*

morose [mə'ros] *adj* mürrisch

morphine ['mɔrfin] *s* Morphium *n*

morphology [mɔr'falədʒi] *s* Morphologie *f*

morrow ['mɔro] *s*—**on the m.** am folgenden Tag

Morse' code' [mɔrs] *s* Morsealphabet *n*

morsel ['mɔrsəl] *s* Bröckchen *n*

mortal ['mɔrtəl] *adj* sterblich ‖ *s* Sterbliche *mf*

mor'tal dan'ger *s* Lebensgefahr *f*

mor'tal en'emy *s* Todfeind *m*

mor'tal fear' *s* Heidenangst *f*

mortality [mɔr'tælti] *s* Sterblichkeit *f*

mortally ['mɔrtəli] *adv* tödlich

mor'tal remains' *spl* irdische Überreste *pl*

mor'tal sin' *s* Todsünde *f*

mor'tal wound' *s* Todeswunde *f*

mortar ['mɔrtər] *s* (vessel) Mörser *m*; (archit) Mörtel *m*; (mil) Granatwerfer *m*

mor'tarboard' *s* Mörtelbrett *n*

mor'tar fire' *s* Granatwerferfeuer *n*

mor'tar shell' *s* Granate *f*

mortgage ['mɔrgɪdʒ] *s* Hypothek *f* ‖ *tr* mit e–r Hypothek belasten

mortgagee [‚mɔrgɪ'dʒi] *s* Hypothekengläubiger –in *mf*

mortgagor ['mɔrgɪdʒər] *s* Hypothekenschuldner –in *mf*

mortician [mɔr'tɪʃən] *s* Leichenbestatter –in *mf*

morti·fy ['mɔrtɪ‚faɪ] *v* (pret & pp **-fied**) *tr* (the flesh) abtöten; (humiliate) demütigen; **m. oneself** sich kasteien

mortise ['mɔrtɪs] *s* (carp) Zapfenloch *n* ‖ *tr* (carp) verzapfen

mortuary ['mɔrtʃu‚eri] *s* Leichenhalle *f*

mosaic [mo'ze·ɪk] *adj* mosaisch ‖ *s* Mosaik *n*

Moscow ['mɑsko], ['mɑskau] *s* Moskau *n*

Moses ['moziz], ['mozis] *s* Moses *m*

mosey ['mozi] *intr* (coll) dahinschlürfen

Mos·lem ['mɑzləm] *adj* muselmanisch ‖ *s* (**-lems** & **-lem**) Moslem –in *mf*

mosque [mɑsk] *s* Moschee *f*

mosqui·to [mɑs'kito] *s* (**-toes** & **-tos**) Moskito *m*, Mücke *f*

mosqui'to net' *s* Moskitonetz *n*

moss [mɑs] *s* Moos *n*

mossy ['mɑsi] *adj* bemoost

most [most] *super adj* meist ‖ *super adv* am meisten; (very) höchst; **m. of all** allermeisten ‖ *s*—**at (the) m.** höchstens; **make the m. of** möglichst gut ausnützen; **m. of** die meisten; **m. of the day** der größte Teil des Tages; **the m.** das meiste, das Höchste ‖ *pron* die meisten

mostly ['mostli] *adv* meistens

motel [mo'tel] *s* Motel *n*

moth [mɔθ] *s* Nachtfalter *m*; (clothes moth) Motte *f*

moth'ball' *s* Mottenkugel *f*; **put into mothballs** (nav) stillegen, einmotten ‖ *tr* (& fig) einmotten

moth-eaten ['mɔθ‚itən] *adj* mottenzerfressen

mother ['mʌðər] *s* Mutter *f* ‖ *tr* (produce) gebären; (take care of as a mother) bemuttern

moth'er coun'try *s* Mutterland *n*

moth'erhood' *s* Mutterschaft *f*

moth'er-in-law' *s* (mothers-in-law) Schwiegermutter *f*

motherless ['mʌðərlɪs] *adj* mutterlos

motherly ['mʌðərli] *adj* mütterlich

mother-of-pearl ['mʌðərəv'pʌrl] *adj* perlmuttern ‖ *s* Perlmutter *f*

Moth'er's Day' *s* Muttertag *m*

moth'er's help'er *s* Stütze *f* der Hausfrau

moth'er supe'rior s (Schwester) Oberin f

moth'er tongue' s Muttersprache f

moth' hole' s Mottenfraß m

mothy ['mɔθɪ] adj mottenzerfressen

motif [mo'tif] s (mus, paint) Motiv n

motion ['moʃən] s Bewegung f; (parl) Antrag m; **make a m. e-n Antrag stellen; set in m.** in Bewegung setzen || tr zuwinken (dat); **m. s.o. to** (inf) j-n durch e-n Wink auffordern zu (inf)

motionless ['moʃənlɪs] adj bewegungslos

mo'tion pic'ture s Film m; **be in motion pictures** beim Film sein

mo'tion-pic'ture adj Film-

mo'tion-pic'ture the'ater s Kino n

motivate ['motɪ,vet] tr begründen, motivieren

motive ['motɪv] s Anlaß m, Beweggrund m

mo'tive pow'er s Triebkraft f

motley ['motlɪ] adj bunt zusammengewürfelt

motor ['motər] adj Motor- || s Motor m

motorcade ['motər,ked] s Wagenkolonne f

mo'torcy'cle s Motorrad n

mo'torcy'list s Motorradfahrer -in mf

mo'toring s Autofahren n

motorist ['motərɪst] s Autofahrer -in mf

motorize ['motə,raɪz] tr motorisieren

mo'tor launch' s Motorbarkasse f

mo'tor-man s (–men) Straßenbahnführer m

mo'tor pool' s Fahrbereitschaft f

mo'tor scoot'er s Motorroller m

mo'tor ve'hicle s Kraftfahrzeug n

mottle ['motəl] tr sprenkeln

mot-to ['moto] s (–toes & –tos) Motto n

mound [maʊnd] s Wall m, Erdhügel m

mount [maʊnt] s (mountain) Berg m; (riding horse) Reittier n || tr (a horse, mountain) besteigen; (stairs) hinaufgehen; (e.g., a machinegun) in Position bringen; (a precious stone) fassen; (photographs in an album) einkleben; (photographs on a backing) aufkleben; m. (e.g., a gun) on montieren auf (acc)

mountain ['maʊntən] s Berg m; **down the m.** bergab; **up the m.** bergauf

moun'tain climb'er s Bergsteiger -in mf

moun'tain climb'ing s Bergsteigen n

mountaineer [,maʊntə'nɪr] s Bergbewohner -in mf

mountainous ['maʊntənəs] adj gebirgig

moun'tain pass' s Gebirgspaß m, Paß m

moun'tain rail'road s Bergbahn f

moun'tain range' s Gebirge n

moun'tain scen'ery s Berglandschaft f

mountebank ['maʊntə,bæŋk] s Quacksalber m; (charlatan) Scharlatan m

mount'ing s Montage f; (of a precious stone) Fassung f

mourn [morn] tr betrauren || intr

trauern; **mourn for** betrauern, trauern um

mourner ['mornər] s Leidtragende mf

mournful ['mornfəl] adj traurig

mourn'ing s Trauer f; **be in m.** Trauer tragen

mourn'ing band' s Trauerflor m

mourn'ing clothes' spl Trauerkleidung f; **wear m.** Trauer tragen

mouse [maʊs] s (mice [maɪs]) Maus f

mouse'hole' s Mauseloch n

mouse'trap' s Mausefalle f

moustache [məs'tæʃ] s Schnurbart m

mouth [maʊθ] s (mouths [maʊðz]) Mund m; (of an animal) Maul n; (of a gun, bottle, river) Mündung f; (sl) Maul n; **keep one's m. shut** den Mund halten; **make s.o.'s m. water** j-m das Wasser im Munde zusammenlaufen lassen

mouthful ['maʊθ,fʊl] s Mundvoll m; (sl) großes Wort n

mouth' or'gan s Mundharmonika f

mouth'piece' s (of an instrument) Ansatz m; (box) Mundstück n; (fig) Sprachrohr n

mouth'wash' s Mundwasser n

movable ['muvəbəl] adj beweglich, mobil || **movables** spl Mobilien pl

move [muv] s (movement) Bewegung f; (step, measure) Maßnahme f; (resettlement) Umzug m; (checkers) Zug m; (parl) Vorschlag m; **be on the m.** unterwegs sein; **don't make a m.!** keinen Schritt!; **get a m. on** (coll) sich rühren; **it's your m.** (& fig) du bist am Zug; **she won't make a m. without him** sie macht keinen Schritt ohne ihn || tr bewegen; (emotionally) rühren; (shove) rücken; (checkers) e-n Zug machen mit; (parl) beantragen; **m. the bowels** abführen; **m. up** (mil) vorschieben || intr (stir) sich bewegen; (change residence) umziehen; (in society) verkehren; (checkers) ziehen; (com) Absatz haben; **m. away** wegziehen; **m. back** zurückziehen; **m. for** (e.g., a new trial) beantragen; **m. in** zuziehen; **m. into** (a home) beziehen; **m. on** fortziehen; **m. out (of)** ausziehen (aus); **m. over** (make room) zur Seite rücken; **m. up** (to a higher position) vorrücken; (into a vacated position) nachrücken; (said of a team) aufsteigen

movement ['muvmənt] s (& fig) Bewegung f; (mus) Satz m

mover ['muvər] s Möbeltransporteur m; (parl) Antragsteller -in mf

movie ['muvɪ] adj (actor, actress, camera, projector) Film- || s (coll) Film m; **movies** Kino n; **go to the movies** ins Kino gehen

mov'ie cam'era s Filmkamera f

moviegoer ['muvɪ,go·ər] s Kinobesucher -in mf

mov'ie house' s Kino n

mov'ie screen' s Filmleinwand f

mov'ie set' s Filmkulisse f

mov'ie the'ater s Kino n

mov'ing adj beweglich; (force) treibend; (fig) herzergreifend ‖ s (change of residence) Umzug m

mov'ing pic'ture s Lichtspiel n, Film m

mov'ing spir'it s führender Kopf m

mow [mo] v (pret **mowed**; pp **mowed** & **mown**) tr mähen; **mow down** (enemies) niedermähen

mower ['mo·ər] s Mäher m

m.p.h. ['em'pi'et∫] spl (miles per hour) Stundenmeilen; **drive sixty m.p.h.** mit sechzig Stundenmeilen fahren

Mr. [ˈmɪstər] s Herr m

Mrs. [ˈmɪsɪz] s Frau f

Ms. [mɪz] s Fräulein n

much [mʌt∫] adj, adv & pron viel; as m. again noch einmal soviel; how m. wieviel; m. less (not to mention) geschweige denn; not so m. as nicht einmal; so m. so so sehr; so m. the better um so besser; very m. sehr

mucilage [ˈmjusɪlɪdʒ] s Klebstoff m

muck [mʌk] s (& fig) Schmutz m

muck'rake' intr (coll) Korruptionsfälle enthüllen

muckraker [ˈmʌk‚rekər] s (coll) Korruptionsschnüffler -in mf

mucky [ˈmʌki] adj schmutzig

mucous [ˈmjukəs] adj schleimig

muc'ous mem'brane s Schleimhaut f

mucus [ˈmjukəs] s Schleim m

mud [mʌd] s Schlamm m; drag through the mud (fig) in den Schmutz ziehen

mud' bath' s Schlammbad n, Moorbad n

muddle [ˈmʌdəl] s Durcheinander n ‖ tr durcheinanderbringen ‖ intr—m. through sich durchwursteln

mud'dlehead' s Wirrkopf m

mud·dy [ˈmʌdi] adj schlammig; (fig) trüb ‖ v (pret & pp -died) trüben

mud'hole' s Schlammloch n

mudslinging [ˈmʌd‚slɪŋɪŋ] s (fig) Verleumdung f

muff [mʌf] s Muff m ‖ tr (coll) verpfuschen

muffin [ˈmʌfɪn] s Teekuchen m aus Backpulverteig

muffle [ˈmʌfəl] tr (sounds) dämpfen; m. up (wrap up) einhüllen

muf'fled adj dumpf

muffler [ˈmʌflər] s (scarf) Halstuch n; (aut) Auspufftopf m

mufti [ˈmʌfti] s Zivil n

mug [mʌg] s Krug m; (for beer) Seidel n; (thug) (sl) Rocker m; (face) (sl) Fratze f ‖ v (pret & pp **mugged**; ger **mugging**) tr (sl) photographieren; (assault) (sl) überfallen ‖ intr (sl) Gesichter schneiden

muggy [ˈmʌgi] adj schwül

mug' shot' s (sl) Polizeiphoto n

mulat·to [məˈlæto] s (-toes) Mulatte m, Mulattin f

mulberry [ˈmʌl‚beri] s Maulbeere f

mul'berry tree' s Maulbeerbaum m

mulch [mʌlt∫] s Streu n

mulct [mʌlkt] tr (of) betrügen (um)

mule [mjul] s Maulesel m, Maultier n

mulish [ˈmjulɪ∫] adj störrisch

mull [mʌl] intr—m. over nachgrübeln über (acc)

mullion [ˈmʌljən] s Mittelpfosten m

multicolored [ˈmʌlti‚kələrd] adj bunt

multigraph [ˈmʌlti‚græf] s (trademark) Vervielfältigungsmaschine f ‖ tr vervielfältigen

multilateral [‚mʌltiˈlætərəl] adj mehrseitig

multimillionaire [ˈmʌlti‚mɪljəˈner] s vielfacher Millionär m

multiple [ˈmʌltɪpəl] adj mehrfach, Vielfach- ‖ s (math) Vielfaches n

multiplication [‚mʌltɪplɪˈke∫ən] s Vermehrung f; (arith) Multiplikation f

multiplica'tion ta'ble s Einmaleins n

multiplicity [‚mʌltɪˈplɪsɪti] s Vielfältigkeit f

multi·ply [ˈmʌlti‚plaɪ] v (pret & pp -plied) tr vervielfältigen; (biol) vermehren; (math) multiplizieren ‖ intr sich vervielfachen; (biol) sich vermehren

multistage [ˈmʌlti‚stedʒ] adj mehrstufig

multistory [ˈmʌlti‚stori] adj mehrstöckig

multitude [ˈmʌlti‚t(j)ud] s (large number) Vielheit f; (of people) Masse f

mum [mʌm] adj still; keep mum about Stillschweigen beobachten über (acc); mum's the word! Mund halten!

mumble [ˈmʌmbəl] tr & intr murmeln

mummery [ˈmʌməri] s Hokuspokus m

mummy [ˈmʌmi] s Mumie f

mumps [mʌmps] s Ziegenpeter m, Mumps m

munch [mʌnt∫] tr & intr geräuschvoll kauen

mundane [mʌnˈden] adj irdisch

municipal [mjuˈnɪsɪpəl] adj städtisch

munic'ipal bond' s Kommunalobligation f

municipality [mju‚nɪsɪˈpælɪti] s Stadt f, Gemeinde f; (governing body) Stadtverwaltung f

munificent [mjuˈnɪfɪsənt] adj freigebig

munificence [mjuˈnɪfɪsəns] s Freigebigkeit f

munitions [mjuˈnɪ∫əns] s Kriegsmaterial n, Munition f

muni'tions dump' s Munitionsdepot n

muni'tions fac'tory s Rüstungsfabrik f

mural [ˈmjurəl] s Wandgemälde n

murder [ˈmʌrdər] s Mord m ‖ tr (er)morden; (a language) radebrechen

murderer [ˈmʌrdərər] s Mörder m

murderess [ˈmʌrdərɪs] s Mörderin f

mur'der mys'tery s Krimi m

murderous [ˈmʌrdərəs] adj mörderisch

mur'der plot' s Mordanschlag m

murky [ˈmʌrki] adj düster

murmur [ˈmʌrmər] s Gemurmel n ‖ tr & intr murmeln

muscle [ˈmʌsəl] s Muskel m; muscles Muskulatur f

muscular [ˈmʌskjələr] adj muskulös

Muse [mjuz] s Muse f ‖ muse intr (over) nachsinnen (über acc)

museum [mjuˈzi·əm] s Museum n

mush [mʌ∫] s (corn meal) Maismehlbrei m; (soft mass) Matsch m; (sentimental talk) Süßholzraspeln n

mush'room' s Pilz m, Champignon m

‖ *intr* wie Pilze aus dem Boden schießen

mushy ['mʌ/i] *adj* matschig; (*sentimental*) rührselig

music ['mjuːsɪk] *s* Musik *f*; (*score*) Noten *pl*; **face the m.** die Sache ausbaden; **set to m.** vertonen

musical ['mjuːzɪkəl] *adj* musikalisch ‖ *s* (*cin*) Singspielfilm *m*; (*theat*) Musical *n*, Singspiel *n*

mu'sical in'strument *s* Musikinstrument *n*

musicale [ˌmjuːzɪ'kæl] *s* Musikabend *m*

mu'sic box' *s* Spieldose *f*

musician [mjuː'zɪ/ən] *s* Musikant –in *mf*; (*accomplished artist*) Musiker –in *mf*

musicology [ˌmjuːzɪ'kɑlədʒi] *s* Musikwissenschaft *f*

mu'sic stand' *s* Notenständer *m*

mus'ing *s* Grübelei *f*

musk [mʌsk] *s* Moschus *m*

musket ['mʌskɪt] *s* Muskete *f*

musk'rat' *s* Bisamratte *f*

muslin ['mʌzlɪn] *s* Musselin *m*

muss [mʌs] *tr* (*hair*) zerzausen; (*dirty*) schmutzig machen; (*rumple*) zerknittern

mussel ['mʌsəl] *s* Muschel *f*

mussy ['mʌsi] *adj* (*hair*) zerzaust; (*clothes*) zerknittert

must [mʌst] *s* (*a necessity*) Muß *n*; (*new wine*) Most *m*; (*mold*) Moder *m* ‖ *mod*—**I m.** (*inf*) ich muß (*inf*)

mustache [məs'tæ/] *s* Schnurrbart *m*

mustard ['mʌstərd] *s* Senf *m*

mus'tard plas'ter *s* Senfpflaster *n*

muster ['mʌstər] *s* Appell *m*; **pass m.** die Prüfung bestehen ‖ *tr* (*troops*) antreten lassen; (*courage, strength*) aufbringen; **m. out** ausmustern

musty ['mʌsti] *adj* mod(e)rig

mutation [mjuː'te/ən] *s* (biol) Mutation *f*

mute [mjuːt] *adj* (& *ling*) stumm ‖ *s* (*ling*) stummer Buchstabe *m*; (mus) Dämpfer ‖ *tr* (mus) dämpfen

mutilate ['mjuːtɪˌlet] *tr* verstümmeln

mutineer [ˌmjuːtɪ'nɪr] *s* Meuterer *m*

mutinous ['mjuːtɪnəs] *adj* meuterisch

muti•ny ['mjuːtɪni] *s* Meuterei *f* ‖ *v* (*pret & pp* –**nied**) *intr* meutern

mutt [mʌt] *s* (coll) Köter *m*

mutter ['mʌtər] *s* Gemurmel *n* ‖ *tr & intr* murmeln

mutton ['mʌtən] *s* (culin) Hammel *m*

mut'ton-head' *s* (sl) Hammel *m*

mutual ['mjuːt/u•əl] *adj* gegenseitig; (*friends*) gemeinsam

mu'tual fund' *s* Investmentfond *m*

mu'tual insur'ance com'pany *s* Versicherungsgesellschaft *f* auf Gegenseitigkeit

mutually ['mjuːt/u•əli] *adv* gegenseitig

muzzle ['mʌzəl] *s* Maulkorb *m*; (*of a gun*) Rohrmündung *f*; (*snout*) Schnauze *f* ‖ *tr* (*an animal*) e–n Maulkorb anlegen (*dat*); (*e.g., the press*) mundtot machen

muz'zle flash' *s* Mündungsfeuer *n*

my [maɪ] *poss adj* mein

myopic [maɪ'ɑpɪk] *adj* kurzsichtig

myriad ['mɪrɪ•əd] *adj* Myriade *f*

myrrh [mʌr] *s* Myrrhe *f*

myrtle ['mʌrtəl] *s* Myrte *f*

myself [maɪ'self] *reflex pron* mich; (*indirect object*) mir ‖ *intens pron* selbst, selber

mysterious [mɪs'tɪrɪ•əs] *adj* mysteriös

mystery ['mɪstəri] *s* Geheimnis *n*; (*fi*) Rätsel *n*; (relig) Mysterium *n*

mys'tery nov'el *s* Kriminalroman *m*

mys'tery play' *s* Mysterienspiel *n*

mystic ['mɪstɪk] *adj* mystisch ‖ *s* Mystiker –in *mf*

mystical ['mɪstɪkəl] *adj* mystisch

mysticism ['mɪstɪˌsɪzəm] *s* Mystik *f*

mystification [ˌmɪstɪfɪ'ke/ən] *s* Verwirrung *f*

mysti•fy ['mɪstɪˌfaɪ] *v* (*pret & pp* –**fied**) *tr* verwirren

myth [mɪθ] *s* Mythe *f*, Mythos *m*; (*ill-founded belief*) Märchen *n*

mythical ['mɪθɪkəl] *adj* mythisch

mythological [ˌmɪθə'lɑdʒɪkəl] *adj* mythologisch

mythology [mɪ'θɑlədʒi] *s* Mythologie *f*

N

N, n [ɛn] *s* vierzehnter Buchstabe des englischen Alphabets

nab [næb] *v* (*pret & pp* **nabbed**; *ger* –**nabbing**) *tr* (coll) schnappen

nadir ['nedɪr] *s* (fig) Tiefpunkt *m*; (astr) Nadir *m*

nag [næg] *s* Gaul *m*; **old nag** Schindmähre *f* ‖ *v* (*pret & pp* **nagged**; *ger* **nagging**) *tr* zusetzen (*dat*) ‖ *intr* nörgeln; **nag at** herumnörgeln an (*dat*)

nag'ging *adj* nörgelnd ‖ *s* Nörgelei *f*

naiad ['naɪˌæd] *s* Najade *f*

nail [nel] *s* Nagel *m*; **hit the n. on the head** den Nagel auf den Kopf treffen ‖ *tr* (**to**) annageln (an *acc*); (*catch*) (coll) erwischen; (box) (coll) treffen; **n. down** (fig) festnageln; **n. shut** zunageln

nail' clip'pers *spl* Nagelzange *f*

nail' file' *s* Nagelfeile *f*

nail' pol'ish *s* Nagellack *m*

nail' scis'sors *s & spl* Nagelschere *f*

naïve [nɑ'iv] *adj* naiv

naked ['nekɪd] *adj* nackt; (*eye*) bloß

nakedness ['nekɪdnɪs] *s* Nacktheit *f*

name [nem] *s* Name *m*; (*reputation*) Name *m*, Ruf *m*; **by n.** dem Namen nach; **by the n. of** namens; **in n. only** nur dem Namen nach; **of the same n.** gleichnamig; **spell one's n.** sich

schreiben; **what is your n.?** wie hei-
ßen Sie? || *tr* nennen; (*nominate*)
ernennen; **be named after** heißen
nach; **n. after** nennen nach; **named**
namens
name'-call'ng *s* Beschimpfung *f*
name' day' *s* Namenstag *m*
nameless ['nemlɪs] *adj* namenlos
namely ['nemlɪ] *adv* nämlich, und
zwar
name'plate' *s* Namensschild *n*
name'sake' *s* Namensvetter *m*
nanny ['nænɪ] *s* Kindermädchen *n*
nan'ny goat' *s* (coll) Ziege *f*
nap [næp] *s* Schläfchen *n*; (tex) Noppe
f; **take a nap** ein Schläfchen machen
|| *v* (*pret & pp* napped; *ger* napping)
intr schlummern; **catch s.o. napping**
(fig) j-n überrumpeln
napalm ['nepɑm] *s* Napalm *n*
nape [nep] *s*—**n. of the neck** Nacken
m
naphtha ['næfθə] *s* Naphtha *f & n*
napkin ['næpkɪn] *s* Serviette *f*
nap'kin ring' *s* Serviettenring *m*
narcissism ['nɑrsɪ‚sɪzəm] *s* Narzißmus
m
narcissus [nɑr'sɪsəs] *s* (bot) Narzisse *f*
narcotic [nɑr'kɑtɪk] *adj* narkotisch ||
s (med) Betäubungsmittel *n*, Narko-
tikum *n*; (*addictive drug*) Rauschgift
n; (*addict*) Rauschgiftsüchtige *mf*
narrate [næ'ret] *tr* erzählen
narration [næ'reʃən] *s* Erzählung *f*
narrative ['nærətɪv] *adj* erzählend || *s*
Erzählung *f*
narrator [næ'retər] *s* Erzähler *m*; (telv)
Moderator *m*
narrow ['næro] *adj* eng, schmal; (*e.g.,*
margin) knapp || **narrows** *spl*
Meerenge *f* || *tr* verengen || *intr* sich
verengen
nar'row escape' *s*—**have a n.** mit
knapper Not entkommen
nar'row-gauge rail'road *s* Schmalspur-
bahn *f*
narrowly ['nærolɪ] *adv* mit knapper
Not
nar'row-mind'ed *adj* engstirnig
nasal ['nezəl] *adj* (*of the nose*) Nasen-;
(*sound*) näselnd || *s* (phonet) Nasen-
laut *m*
nasalize ['nezə‚laɪz] *tr* nasalieren ||
intr näseln
na'sal twang' *s* Näseln *n*
nascent ['nesənt] *adj* werdend
nastiness ['næstɪnɪs] *s* Ekligkeit *f*
nasturtium [nə'stʌr/əm] *s* Kapuziner-
kresse *f*
nasty ['næstɪ] *adj* (*person, smell, taste*)
ekelhaft; (*weather*) scheußlich; (*dog,*
accident, tongue) böse; **n. to** garstig
zu or gegen
nation ['ne/ən] *s* Nation *f*, Volk *n*
national ['næ/ənəl] *adj* national, Lan-
des- || *s* Staatsangehörige *mf*
na'tional an'them *s* Nationalhymne *f*
na'tional defense' *s* Landesverteidigung
f
nationalism ['næ/ənə‚lɪzəm] *s* Nationalismus *m*
nationality [‚næ/ə'nælɪtɪ] *s* (*citizen-*

ship) Staatsangehörigkeit *f*; (*ethnic*
identity) Nationalität *f*
nationalization [‚næ/ənəlɪ'ze/ən] *s*
Verstaatlichung *f*
nationalize ['næ/ənə‚laɪz] *tr* verstaatlichen
na'tional park' *s* Naturschutzpark *m*
na'tional so'cialism *s* Nationalsozialis-
mus *m*
na'tionwide *adj* im ganzen Land
native ['netɪv] *adj* eingeboren; (*prod-*
ucts) heimisch, Landes- || *s* Eingebo-
rene *mf*; **be a n. of** beheimatet sein
in (*dat*)
na'tive coun'try *s* Vaterland *n*
na'tive land' *s* Heimatland *n*
na'tive tongue' *s* Muttersprache *f*
nativity [nə'tɪvɪtɪ] *s* Geburt *f*; (astrol)
Nativität *f*; **the Nativity** die Geburt
Christi
NATO ['neto] *s* (**North Atlantic Treaty**
Organization) NATO *f*
natty ['nætɪ] *adj* elegant
natural ['næt/ərəl] *adj* natürlich; (*be-*
havior) ungezwungen || *s* (mus)
weiße Taste *f*; (*symbol*) (mus) Auf-
lösungszeichen *n*; (*person*) (coll)
ein Naturtalent *n*; (*thing*) (coll) e-e
totsichere Sache *f*
na'tural his'tory *s* Naturgeschichte *f*
naturalism ['næt/ərə‚lɪzəm] *s* Natura-
lismus *m*
naturalist ['næt/ərəlɪst] *s* (*student of*
natural history) Naturforscher –in
mf; (paint, philos) Naturalist –in *mf*
naturalization [‚næt/ərəlɪ'ze/ən] *s* Ein-
bürgerung *f*
naturalize ['næt/ərə‚laɪz] *tr* einbürgern
na'tural law' *s* Naturgesetz *n*
na'tural phenom'enon *s* (*occurring in*
nature) Naturereignis *n*; (*not super-*
natural) natürliche Erscheinung *f*
na'tural re'sources *spl* Bodenschätze *pl*
na'tural sci'ence *s* Naturwissenschaft *f*
na'tural state' *s* Naturzustand *m*
nature ['net/ər] *s* die Natur; (*quali-*
ties) Natur *f*, Beschaffenheit *f*; **by n.**
von Natur aus
naught [nɔt] *s* Null *f*; **all for n.** ganz
umsonst; **bring to n.** zuschanden machen; **come to n.** zunichte werden
naughty ['nɔtɪ] *adj* unartig, ungezogen
nausea ['nɔ/ɪ‚ə], ['nɔsɪ‚ə] *s* Übelkeit *f*
nauseate ['nɔ/ɪ‚et], ['nɔsɪ‚et] *tr* Übelkeit erregen (*dat*)
naus'eating *adj* Übelkeit erregend
nauseous ['nɔ/ɪ‚əs], ['nɔsɪ‚əs] *adj*
(*causing nausea*) Übelkeit erregend;
I feel n. mir ist übel
nautical ['nɔtɪkəl] *adj* See-; nautisch
nau'tical mile' ['nɔtɪkəl] *s* Seemeile *f*
nau'tical term' *s* Ausdruck *m* der See-
mannssprache *f*
naval ['nevəl] *adj* (*e.g., battle, block-*
ade, cadet, victory) See-; (*unit*)
Flotten-; (*academy, officer*) Marine-
na'val base' *s* Flottenstützpunkt *m*
na'val engage'ment *s* Seegefecht *n*
na'val cap'tain *s* Kapitän *m* zur See
na'val forc'es *s* Seestreitkräfte *pl*
na'val suprem'acy *s* Seeherrschaft *f*

nave [nev] *s* (*of a church*) Schiff *n*; (*of a wheel*) Nabe *f*

navel ['nevəl] *s* Nabel *m*

na'vel or'ange *s* Navelorange *f*

navigable ['nævigəbəl] *adj* schiffbar

navigate ['nævɪ,get] *tr* (*traverse*) befahren; (*steer*) steuern ‖ *intr* (aer, naut) navigieren

navigation [,nævɪ'geʃən] *s* (*plotting courses*) Navigation *f*; (*sailing*) Schiffahrt *f*

naviga'tion chart' *s* Navigationskarte *f*

naviga'tion light' *s* (aer, naut) Positionslicht *n*

navigator ['nævɪ,getər] *s* Seefahrer *m*; (aer) Navigator *m*

navy ['nevi] *adj* Marine– ‖ *s* Kriegsmarine *f*

na'vy bean' *s* Weiße Bohne *f*

na'vy blue' *adj* marineblau ‖ *s* Marineblau *n*

na'vy yard' *s* Marinewerft *f*

nay [ne] *adv* nein ‖ *s* Nein *n*; (parl) Neinstimme *f*; **the nays have it** die Mehrheit stimmt dagegen

Nazarene [,næzə'rin] *adj* aus Nazareth ‖ *s* Nazarener *m*

Nazi ['natsi] *adj* Nazi– ‖ *s* Nazi *m*

Nazism ['natsızəm] *s* Nazismus *m*

N.C.O. ['en'si'o] *s* (**noncommissioned officer**) Unteroffizier *m*

neap' tide' [nip] *s* Nippflut *f*

near [nɪr] *adj* nahe(liegend); (*escape*) knapp; **n. at hand** zur Hand ‖ *adv* nahe; **draw n. (to)** sich nähern (*dat*); **live n.** (*e.g., a church*) in der Nähe wohnen (*genit*) ‖ *prep* nahe (*dat*), nahe an (*dat*), bei (*dat*); **n. here** hier in der Nähe

near'by' *adj* nahe(gelegen) ‖ *adv* in der Nähe

Near' East', the *s* der Nahe Osten

nearly ['nɪrli] *adv* beinahe, fast

nearness ['nɪrnɪs] *s* Nähe *f*

near'-sight'ed *adj* kurzsichtig

near'-sight'edness *s* Kurzsichtigkeit *f*

neat [nit] *adj* sauber, ordentlich; (*simple but tasteful*) nett; (*cute*) niedlich; (*tremendous*) (coll) prima

neatness ['nitnɪs] *s* Sauberkeit *f*

nebu·la ['nɛbjələ] *s* (**-lae** [,li] & **-las**) (astr) Nebelfleck *m*

nebulous ['nɛbjələs] *adj* nebelhaft; (astr) Nebel–

necessarily [,nɛsɪ'sɛrɪli] *adv* notwendigerweise, unbedingt

necessary ['nɛsɪ,sɛri] *adj* notwendig, nötig; (*consequence*) zwangsläufig; **if n.** notfalls

necessitate [nɪ'sɛsɪ,tet] *tr* notwendig machen, enfordern

necessity [nɪ'sɛsɪti] *s* (*state of being necessary*) Notwendigkeit *f*; (*something necessary*) Bedürfnis *n*; (*poverty*) Not *f*; **in case of n.** im Notfall; **necessities of life** Lebensbedürfnisse *pl*; **of n.** notwendigerweise

neck [nɛk] *s* Hals *m*; (*of a dress*) Halsausschnitt *m*; **break one's n.** (& fig) sich [*dat*] den Hals brechen; **get it in the n.** (sl) eins aufs Dach kriegen; **get s.o. off one's n.** sich [*dat*] j–n

vom Halse schaffen; **n. and n.** Seite an Seite ‖ *intr* (coll) sich knutschen

–necked [,nɛkt] *suf* –halsig, –nackig

neckerchief ['nɛkərtʃɪf] *s* Halstuch *n*

neck'ing *s* Abknutscherei *f*

necklace ['nɛklɪs] *s* Halsband *n*; (*metal chain*) Halskette *f*

neck'line' *s* Halsausschnitt *m*; **with a low n.** tief ausgeschnitten

neck'tie' *s* Krawatte *f*, Schlips *m*

necrology [nɛ'kralədʒi] *s* (*list of the dead*) Totenliste *f*; (*obituary*) Nekrolog *m*

necromancer ['nɛkrə,mænsər] *s* Geistesbeschwörer –in *mf*

necromancy ['nɛkrə,mænsi] *s* Geistesbeschwörung *f*

necropolis [nɛ'krapəlɪs] *s* Nekropolis *f*

nectar ['nɛktər] *s* (bot, myth) Nektar *m*

nectarine [,nɛktə'rin] *s* Nektarine *f*

nee [ne] *adj* geborene, e.g., **Mrs. Mary Schmidt, nee Müller Frau Maria Schmidt, geborene Müller**

need [nid] *s* Bedarf *m*, Bedürfnis *n*; **be in n.** in Not sein; **be in n. of repair** reparaturbedürftig sein; **be in n. of s.th.** etw nötig haben; **if n. be** erforderlichenfalls; **meet s.o.'s needs** j–s Bedarf decken; **needs** Bedarfsartikel *pl* ‖ *tr* benötigen, brauchen; **as needed** nach Bedarf

needful ['nidfəl] *adj* nötig

needle ['nidəl] *s* Nadel *f* ‖ *tr* (*prod*) anstacheln; **n. s.o. about** gegen j–n sticheln wegen

nee'dlepoint', nee'dlepoint lace' *s* Nadelspitze *f*

needless ['nidlɪs] *adj* unnötig; **n. to say** es erübrigt sich zu sagen

nee'dlework' *s* Näharbeit *f*

needy ['nidi] *adj* bedürftig

ne'er [nɛr] *adv* nie

ne'er-do-well' *s* Tunichtgut *m*

nefarious [nɪ'fɛri-əs] *adj* ruchlos

negate [nɪ'get] *tr* verneinen

negation [nɪ'geʃən] *s* Verneinung *f*

negative ['nɛgətɪv] *adj* negativ ‖ *s* Verneinung *f*; (elec) negativer Pol *m*; (gram) Verneinungswort *n*; (phot) Negativ *n*

neglect [nɪ'glɛkt] *s* Vernachlässigung *f* ‖ *tr* vernachlässigen; **n. to** (*inf*) unterlassen zu (*inf*)

négligée, negligee [,nɛglɪ'ʒe] *s* Negligé *n*

negligence ['nɛglɪdʒəns] *s* Fahrlässigkeit *f*

negligent ['nɛglɪdʒənt] *adj* fahrlässig

negligible ['nɛglɪdʒɪbəl] *adj* geringfügig

negotiable [nɪ'goʃ1·əbəl] *adj* diskutierbar; (fin) übertragbar, bankfähig

negotiate [nɪ'goʃi,et] *tr* (*a contract*) abschließen; (*a curve*) nehmen ‖ *intr* verhandeln

negotiation [nɪ,goʃi'eʃən] *s* Verhandlung *f*; **carry on negotiations with** in Verhandlungen stehen mit; **enter negotiations with** in Verhandlungen treten mit

negotiator [nɪ'goʃɪ,etər] s Unterhändler –in mf

Ne·gro ['nigro] s (–groes) Neger –in mf

neigh [ne] s Wiehern n || intr wiehern

neighbor ['nebər] s Nachbar –in mf; (fellow man) Nächste m || tr angrenzen an (acc) || intr—n. on angrenzen an (acc)

neigh'borhood' s Nachbarschaft f; (vicinity) Umgebung f; in the n. of (coll) etwa

neigh'boring adj benachbart, Nachbar–, angrenzend

neighborliness ['nebərlɪnɪs] s gutnachbarliche Beziehungen pl

neighborly ['nebərli] adj (gut)nachbarlich

neither ['niðər] indef adj keiner || indef pron (of) keiner (von); n. of them keiner von beiden || conj noch, ebensowenig; auch nicht, e.g., n. do I ich auch nicht; neither ... nor weder ... noch; that's n. here nor there das hat nichts zu sagen

neme·sis ['nɛməsɪs] s (–ses [,siz]) Nemesis f

Neolith'ic Age' [,ni·ə'lɪθɪk] s Neusteinzeit f

neologism [ni'ɑlə,dʒɪzəm] s Neubildung f, Neologismus m

neon ['ni·ɑn] s Neon n

ne'on light' s Neonröhre f

ne'on sign' s Neonreklame f

neophyte ['ni·ə,faɪt] s Neuling m; (relig) Neubekehrte mf

nephew ['nɛfju] s Neffe m

nepotism ['nɛpə,tɪzəm] s Nepotismus m

Neptune ['nɛpt(j)un] s Neptun m

neptunium [nɛp't(j)unɪ·əm] s Neptunium n

nerve [nʌrv] adj Nerven– || s Nerv m; (courage) Wagemut m; (gall) (coll) Unverfrorenheit f; get on s.o.'s nerves j–m auf die Nerven gehen; lose one's n. die Nerven verlieren; nerves of steel Nerven pl wie Drahtseile

nerve' cen'ter s Nervenzentrum n

nerve'-rack'ing adj nervenaufreibend

nervous ['nʌrvəs] adj nervös; (system) Nerven–; (horse) kopfscheu; be a n. wreck mit den Nerven herunter sein

ner'vous break'down s Nervenzusammenbruch m

nervousness ['nʌrvəsnɪs] s Nervosität f

nervy ['nʌrvi] adj (brash) unverschämt; (courageous) mutig

nest [nɛst] s Nest n || intr nisten

nest' egg' s (fig) Sparpfennig m

nestle ['nɛsəl] intr (up to) sich anschmiegen (an acc)

net [nɛt] adj Rein– || adv netto, rein || s Netz m; (for fire victims) Sprungtuch n || v (pret & pp netted; ger netting) tr (e.g., fish, butterflies) mit dem Netz fangen; (said of an enterprise) netto einbringen; (said of a person) rein verdienen

net'ball' s (tennis) Netzball m

Netherlander ['nɛðər,lændər] s Niederländer –in mf

Netherlands, the ['nɛðərləndz] s & spl die Niederlande

net'ting s Netzwerk n

nettle ['nɛtəl] s Nessel f || tr reizen

net'work' s Netzwerk n; (rad, telv) Sendergruppe f

neuralgia [n(j)u'rældʒə] s Neurologie f

neuritis [n(j)u'raɪtɪs] s Nervenentzündung f

neurologist [n(j)u'rɑlədʒɪst] s Nervenarzt m, Nervenärztin f

neurology [n(j)u'rɑlədʒi] s Nervenheilkunde f, Neurologie f

neuron ['n(j)urɑn] s Neuron n

neuro·sis [n(j)u'rosɪs] s (–ses [siz]) Neurose f

neurotic [n(j)u'rɑtɪk] adj neurotisch || s Neurotiker –in mf

neuter ['n(j)utər] adj (gram) sächlich || s (gram) Neutrum n

neutral ['n(j)utrəl] adj neutral || s Neutrale mf; (aut) Leerlauf m

neutrality [n(j)u'trælɪti] s Neutralität f

neutralize ['n(j)utrə,laɪz] tr (a bomb) entschärfen; (& chem) neutralisieren; (troops) lahmlegen; (an attack) unterbinden

neutron ['n(j)utrɑn] s Neutron n

never ['nɛvər] adv nie(mals); n. again nie wieder; n. before noch nie; n. mind! spielt keine Rolle!

ne'vermore' adv nimmermehr

ne'vertheless' adv nichtsdestoweniger

new [n(j)u] adj neu; (wine) jung; (inexperienced) unerfahren; what's new? was gibt's Neues?

new' arriv'al s Neuankömmling m

new'born' adj neugeboren

New'cas'tle s—carry coals to N. Eulen nach Athen tragen

newcomer ['n(j)u,kʌmər] s Neuankömmling m

newel ['n(j)u·əl] s Treppenspindel f

new'el post' s Geländerpfosten m

newfangled ['n(j)u,fæŋgəld] adj neumodisch

Newfoundland ['n(j)ufənd,lænd] s Neufundland n || [n(j)u'faundlənd] s (dog) Neufundländer m

newly ['n(j)uli] adv neu, Neu–

new'lyweds' spl Neuvermählten pl

new' moon' s Neumond m

new-mown ['n(j)u,mon] adj frischgemäht

newness ['n(j)unɪs] s Neuheit f

news [n(j)uz] s Nachricht f; (rad, telv) Nachrichten pl; that's not n. to me das ist mir nicht neu; piece of n. Neuigkeit f

news' a'gency s Nachrichtenagentur f

news'boy' s Zeitungsjunge m

news' bul'letin s Kurznachricht f

news'cast' s Nachrichtensendung f

news'cast'er s Nachrichtensprecher –in mf

news'deal'er s Zeitungshändler –in mf

news' ed'itor s Nachrichtenredakteur –in mf

news'let'ter s Rundschreiben n

news'man' s (-men') Journalist m; (dealer) Zeitungshändler m

news'pa'per adj Zeitungs- || s Zeitung f

news'paper clip'ping s Zeitungsausschnitt m

news'paper-man' s (-men') Journalist m; (dealer) Zeitungshändler m

news'paper se'rial s Zeitungsroman m

news'print' s Zeitungspapier n

news'reel' s Wochenschau f

news' report' s Nachrichtensendung f

news' report'er s Zeitungsreporter -in mf

news' room' s Nachrichtenbüro n

news'stand' s Zeitungskiosk m

news'wor'thy adj berichtenswert

New' Tes'tament s Neues Testament n

New' World' s Neue Welt f

New' Year' s Neujahr n; happy N.! glückliches Neues Jahr!

New' Year's' Eve' s Silvesterabend m

New' Zea'land ['ziland] s Neuseeland n

next [nɛkst] adj nächste; be n. an der Reihe sein; come n. folgen; in the n. place darauf; n. best nächstbeste; n. time das nächste Mal; n. to (locally) gleich neben (dat); (almost) sogut wie; the n. day am nächsten Tag || adv dann, danach; what should I do n.? was soll ich als Nächstes tun?

next'-door' adj—n. neighbor unmittelbarer Nachbar m || next'-door' adv nebenan; n. to direkt neben (dat)

next' of kin' s (pl: next of kin) nächster Angehöriger m

niacin ['naɪ-əsɪn] s Niacin n

Niag'ara Falls' [naɪˈægrə] s Niagarafall m

nib [nɪb] s Spitze f; (of a pen) Federspitze f

nibble ['nɪbəl] tr knabbern || intr (on) knabbern (an dat)

Nibelung ['nibəluŋ] s (myth) Nibelung m

nice [naɪs] adj nett; (pretty) hübsch; (food) lecker; (well-behaved) artig; (distinction) fein; have a n. time sich gut unterhalten; n. and warm schön warm

nicely ['naɪslɪ] adv nett; he's doing n. es geht ihm recht gut; that will do n. das paßt gut

nicety ['naɪsətɪ] s Feinheit f; niceties of life Annehmlichkeiten pl des Lebens

niche [nɪtʃ] s Nische f; (fig) rechter Platz m

nick [nɪk] s Kerbe f, Scharte f; in the n. of time gerade im rechten Augenblick || tr kerben

nickel ['nɪkəl] s Nickel n; (coin) Fünfcentstück n || tr vernickeln

nick'el-plate' tr vernickeln

nick'name' s Spitzname m || tr e-n Spitznamen geben (dat)

nicotine ['nɪkə,tin] s Nikotin n; low in n. nikotinarm

niece [nis] s Nichte f

nifty ['nɪftɪ] adj (coll) fesch, prima

niggard ['nɪgərd] s Knauser –in mf

niggardly ['nɪgərdlɪ] adj knauserig

night [naɪt] adj (light, shift, train, watch) Nacht- || s Nacht f; all n. (long) die ganze Nacht (über); at n. nachts; last n. gestern abend; n. after n. Nacht für Nacht; n. before last vorgestern abend

night' cap' s Nachtmütze f; (drink) Schlummertrunk m

night' club' s Nachtklub m

night'fall' s Anbruch m der Nacht; at n. bei Anbruch der Nacht

night'gown' s Damennachthemd n

nightingale ['naɪtən,gel] s Nachtigall f

night'light' s Nachtlicht n

night'long' adj & adv die ganze Nacht dauernd

nightly ['naɪtlɪ] adj & adv allnächtlich

night'mare' s Alptraum m

nightmarish ['naɪt,merɪʃ] adj alpartig

night' owl' s (coll) Nachteule f

night' school' s Abendschule f

night'time' s Nachtzeit f; at n. zur Nachtzeit

night' watch'man s Nachtwächter m

nihilism ['naɪ-ɪ,lɪzəm] s Nihilismus m

nil [nɪl] s Nichts n, Null f

Nile [naɪl] s Nil m

nimble ['nɪmbəl] adj flink

nincompoop ['nɪnkəm,pup] s Trottel m

nine [naɪn] adj & pron neun || s Neun f

nineteen ['naɪn'tin] adj & pron neunzehn || s Neunzehn f

nineteenth ['naɪn'tinθ] adj & pron neunzehnte || s (fraction) Neunzehntel n; the nineteenth (in dates or in a series) der Neunzehnte

ninetieth ['naɪntɪ-ɪθ] adj & pron neunzigste || s (fraction) Neunzigstel n

ninety ['naɪntɪ] adj & pron neunzig || s Neunzig f; the nineties die neunziger Jahre

nine'ty-first' adj & pron einundneunzigste

nine'ty-one' adj & pron einundneunzig

ninny ['nɪnɪ] s (coll) Trottel m

ninth [naɪnθ] adj & pron neunte || s (fraction) Neuntel n; the n. (in dates or in a series) der Neunte

nip [nɪp] s (pinch) Kneifen n; (of cold weather) Schneiden n; (of liquor) Schluck m || v (pret & pp nipped; ger nipping) tr (pinch) kneifen; (alcohol) nippen; nip in the bud im Keime ersticken

nippers ['nɪpərz] spl Zwickzange f

nipple ['nɪpəl] s (of a nursing bottle) Lutscher m; (anat) Brustwarze f; (mach) Schmiernippel m

nippy ['nɪpɪ] adj schneidend

nirvana ['nɪr'vɑnə] s Nirwana n

nit [nɪt] s (ent) Nisse f

niter ['naɪtər] s Salpeter m

nit'pick'er s (coll) Pedant –in mf

nitrate ['naɪtret] s Nitrat n || tr nitrieren

ni'tric ac'id ['naɪtrɪk] s Salpetersäure f

nitride ['naɪtraɪd] s Nitrid n
nitrogen ['naɪtrədʒən] s Stickstoff m
nitroglycerin [ˌnaɪtrə'glɪsərɪn] s Nitroglyzerin n
ni'trous ac'id ['naɪtrəs] s salpetrige Säure f
ni'trous ox'ide s Stickstoffoxydul n
nit'wit' s Trottel m
no [no] adj kein; **no admittance** Zutritt verboten; **no ... of any kind** keinerlei; **no offense!** nichts für ungut!; **no parking** Parkverbot; **no smoking** Rauchen verboten; **no thoroughfare** Durchgang verboten; **no ... whatever** überhaupt kein || adv nein; **no?** nicht wahr?; **no longer** (or **no more**) nicht mehr || s Nein n; **give no for an answer** mit (e–m) Nein antworten
No'ah's Ark' ['no·əz] s Arche f Noah(s)
nobility [no'bɪlɪti] s (nobleness; aristocracy) Adel m; (noble rank) Adelsstand m; n. of mind Seelenadel m
noble ['nobəl] adj (rank) ad(e)lig; (character, person) edel || s Adliger m; **nobles** Edelleute pl
no'ble-man s (-men) Edelmann m
no'blemind'ed adj edelgesinnt
nobleness ['nobəlnɪs] s Vornehmheit f
no'ble-wom'an s (-wom'en) Edelfrau f
nobody ['no ˌbadi] s indef pron niemand, keiner; **n. else** sonst keiner || s (coll) Null f
nocturnal [nak'tʌrnəl] adj nächtlich
nod [nad] s Kopfnicken n || v (pret & pp **nodded**; ger **nodding**) tr—**nod one's head** mit dem Kopf nicken || intr nicken; **nod to** zunicken (dat)
node [nod] s (anat, astr, math, phys) Knoten m
module ['nadʒul] s Knötchen n; (bot) Knollen m
noise [nɔɪz] s Geräusch n; (disturbingly loud) Lärm m || tr—**n. abroad** ausposaunen
noiseless ['nɔɪzlɪs] adj geräuschlos
noisy ['nɔɪzi] adj lärmend, geräuschvoll
nomad ['nomæd] s Nomade m, Nomadin f
no' man's' land' s Niemandsland n
nomenclature ['nomən ˌkletʃər] s Nomenklatur f
nominal ['namɪnəl] adj nominell
nominate ['namɪ ˌnet] tr ernennen; **n. as candidate** als Kandidaten aufstellen
nomination [ˌnamɪ'neʃən] s Ernennung f; (of a candidate) Aufstellung f
nominative ['namɪnətɪv] s Nominativ m
nominee [ˌnamɪ'ni] s Designierte mf
non– [nan] pref Nicht–, nicht–
non'accept'ance s Nichtannahme f
non'belli'gerent adj nicht am Krieg teilnehmend
non'break'able adj unzerbrechlich
non'-Cath'olic adj nichtkatholisch || s Nichtkatholik –in mf
nonchalant [ˌnanʃə'lant] adj zwanglos

noncom ['nan ˌkam] s (coll) Kapo m
non'com'batant s Nichtkämpfer m
non'commis'sioned of'ficer s Unteroffizier m
noncommittal [ˌnankə'mɪtəl] adj nichtssagend; (person) zurückhaltend
nondescript ['nandɪ ˌskrɪpt] adj unbestimmbar
none [nʌn] adv—**n. too** keineswegs zu || indef pron keiner; **that's n. of your business** das geht dich nichts an
nonen'tity s Nichts n; (fig) Null f
non'exis'tent adj nichtexistent
nonfic'tion s Sachbücher pl
nonfulfill'ment s Nichterfüllung f
non'interven'tion s Nichteinmischung f
non'met'al s Nichtmetall n, Metalloid n
non'nego'tiable adj unübertragbar; (demands) unabdingbar
nonpar'tisan adj überparteilich
nonpay'ment s Nichtbezahlung f
non'polit'ical adj unpolitisch
non–plus ['nan'plʌs] s Verlegenheit f || v (pret & pp **–plus[s]ed**; ger **–plus[s]ing**) tr verblüffen
nonprof'it adj gemeinnützig
nonres'ident adj nich ansässig || s Nichtansässige mf
non'return'able adj (bottles, etc.) Einweg–; (merchandise) nicht rücknehmbar
non'scienti'fic adj nichtwissenschaftlich
non'sectar'ian adj keiner Sekte angehörend
nonsense ['nansəns] s Unsinn m
nonsen'sical adj unsinnig, widersinnig
non'skid' adj rutschsicher
nonsmok'er s Nichtraucher –in mf
non'stop' adj & adv ohne Zwischenlandung
nonvi'olence s Gewaltlosigkeit f
nonvi'olent adj gewaltlos
noodle ['nudəl] s Nudel f; (head) (coll) Birne f
noo'dle soup' s Nudelsuppe f
nook [nʊk] s Ecke f; (fig) Winkel m
noon [nun] s Mittag m; **at n.** zu Mittag
no' one', no'-one' indef pron niemand, keiner; **n. else** kein anderer
noon' hour' s Mittagsstunde f
noon'time' adj mittäglich || s Mittagszeit f
noose [nus] s Schlinge f
nor [nɔr] conj (after **neither**) noch; auch nicht, e.g., **nor do I** ich auch nicht
Nordic ['nɔrdɪk] adj nordisch
norm [nɔrm] s Norm f
normal ['nɔrməl] adj normal
normalcy ['nɔrməlsi] s Normalzustand m
normalize ['nɔrmə ˌlaɪz] tr normalisieren
Norman ['nɔrmən] adj normannisch || s Normanne m, Normannin f
Normandy ['nɔrməndi] s die Normandie
Norse [nɔrs] adj altnordisch || s (language) Altnordisch n; **the N.** die Skandinavier pl
Norse'man s (–men) Nordländer m

north [norθ] *adj* nördlich, Nord– ‖ *adv* nach Norden ‖ *s* Norden *m*; **to the n. of** im Norden von

North′ Amer′ica *s* Nordamerika *n*

North′ Amer′ican *adj* nordamerikanisch ‖ *s* Nordamerikaner –in *mf*

north′east′ *adj & adv* nordöstlich ‖ *s* Nordosten *m*

north′east′er *s* Nordostwind *m*

northerly [′norðərli] *adj* nördlich

northern [′norðərn] *adj* (*direction*) nördlich; (*race*) nordisch

north′ern expo′sure *s* Nordseite *f*

North′ern Hem′isphere *s* nördliche Halbkugel *f*

north′ern lights′ *spl* Nordlicht *n*

nor′thernmost′ *adj* nördlichst

North′ Pole′ *s* Nordpol *m*

North′ Sea′ *s* Nordsee *f*

northward [′norθwərd] *adv* nach Norden

north′west′ *adj & adv* nordwestlich ‖ *s* Nordwesten *m*

north′ wind′ *s* Nordwind *m*

Norway [′norwe] *s* Norwegen *n*

Norwegian [nor′widʒən] *adj* norwegisch ‖ *s* Norweger –in *mf*; (*language*) Norwegisch *n*

nose [noz] *s* Nase *f*; (aer) Nase *f*, Bug *m*; by a n. (sport) um e-e Nasenlänge; **blow one's n.** sich schneuzen; **lead around by the n.** an der Nase herumführen; **pay through the n.** e-n zu hohen Preis bezahlen; **turn one's n. up at** die Nase rümpfen über (*acc*) ‖ *tr*—**n. out** (fig) mit knappem Vorsprung besiegen; (sport) um e-e Nasenlänge schlagen ‖ *intr*—**n. about** herumschnüffeln; **n. over** (aer) sich überschlagen

noseable [′notisəbəl] *adj* wahrnehmbar

nose′bleed′ *s* Nasenbluten *n*

nose′ cone′ *s* (rok) Raketenspitze *f*

nose′ dive′ *s* (aer) Sturzflug *m*

nose′-dive′ *intr* e-n Sturzflug machen

nose′ drops′ *spl* Nasentropfen *pl*

nose′gay′ *s* Blumenstrauß *m*

nose′-heav′y *adj* (aer) vorderlastig

nostalgia [na′stældʒə] *s* Heimweh *n*

nostalgic [na′stældʒik] *adj* wehmütig

nostril [′nastril] *s* (anat) Nasenloch *n*; (zool) Nüster *f*

nostrum [′nastrəm] *s* Allheilmittel *n*

nosy [′nozi] *adj* neugierig

not [nat] *adv* nicht; **not at all** überhaupt nicht; **not even** nicht einmal; **not one** keiner; **not only . . . but also** nicht nur . . . sondern auch

notable [′notəbəl] *adj* bemerkenswert ‖ *s* Standesperson *f*

notarial [no′teri·əl] *adj* notariell

notarize [′notə‚raiz] *tr* notariell beglaubigen

no′tary pub′lic [′notəri] *s* (**notaries public**) Notar *m*, Notarin *f*

notation [no′teʃən] *s* (*note*) Aufzeichnung *f*; (*system of symbols*) Bezeichnung *f*; (*method of noting*) Schreibweise *f*

notch [natʃ] *s* Kerbe *f*; (*in a belt*) Loch *n*; (*degree, step*) Grad *m*; (*of a wheel*) Zahn *m* ‖ *tr* einkerben

note [not] *s* Notiz *f*; (*to a text*) Anmerkung *f*; (*slip*) Zettel *m*; (*e.g., of doubt*) Ton *m*; (mus) Note *f*; **jot down notes** sich [*dat*] Notizen machen; **make a n. of** sich [*dat*] notieren; **take n. of** zur Kenntnis nehmen; **take notes** sich [*dat*] Notizen machen ‖ *tr* beachten; **n. down** notieren; **n. in passing** am Rande bemerken

note′book′ *s* Heft *n*, Notizbuch *n*

note′ pad′ *s* Schreibblock *m*

note′wor′thy *adj* beachtenswert

nothing [′nʌθiŋ] *indef pron* nichts; **be for n.** vergebens sein; **come to n.** platzen; **for n.** (*gratis*) umsonst; **have n. to go on** keine Unterlagen haben; **next to n.** soviel wie nichts; **n. at all** gar nichts; **n. but** lauter; **n. doing!** kommt nicht in Frage!; **n. else** sonst nichts; **n. new** nichts Neues; **there is n. like** es geht nichts über (*acc*)

nothingness [′nʌθiŋnis] *s* (*non-existence*) Nichts *n*; (*utter insignificance*) Nichtigkeit *f*

notice [′notis] *s* (*placard*) Anschlag *m*; (*in the newspaper*) Anzeige *f*; (*attention*) Beachtung *f*; (*announcement*) Ankündigung *f*; (*notice of termination*) Kündigung *f*; **at a moment's n.** jeden Moment; **escape s.o.'s n.** j–m entgehen; **give s.o. a week's n.** j–m acht Tage vorher kündigen; **take n. of** Notiz nehmen von; **until further n.** bis auf weiteres ‖ *tr* (be)merken, wahrnehmen; **be noticed by s.o.** j–m auffallen; **n. s.th. about s.o.** j–m etw anmerken

noticeable [′notisəbəl] *adj* wahrnehmbar

notification [‚notifi′keʃən] *s* Benachrichtigung *f*

noti·fy [′noti‚fai] *v* (*pret & pp* **–fied**) *tr* (*about*) benachrichtigen (von)

notion [′noʃən] *s* (*idea*) Vorstellung *f*; **I have a good n. to** (*inf*) ich habe gute Lust zu (*inf*); **notions** Kurzwaren *pl*

notoriety [‚notə′rai·iti] *s* Verruf *m*

notorious [no′tori·əs] *adj* (**for**) notorisch (wegen)

no′-trump′ *adj* ohne Trumpf ‖ *s* Ohne Trumpf-Ansage *f*

notwithstanding [‚natwiθ′stændiŋ] *adv* trotzdem ‖ *prep* trotz (genit)

noun [naun] *s* Hauptwort *n*

nourish [′nʌriʃ] *tr* (er)nähren

nour′ishing *adj* nahrhaft, Nähr–

nourishment [′nʌriʃmənt] *s* (*feeding*) Ernährung *f*; (*food*) Nahrung *f*

Nova Scotia [′novə′skoʃə] *s* Neuschottland *n*

novel [′navəl] *adj* neuartig ‖ *s* Roman *m*

novelist [′navəlist] *s* Romanschriftsteller –in *mf*

novelty [′navəlti] *s* Neuheit *f*

November [no′vembər] *s* November *m*

novena [no′vinə] *s* Novene *f*

novice [′navis] *s* Neuling *m*; (eccl) Novize *m*, Novizin *f*

novitiate [no′viʃi·it] *s* Noviziat *n*

novocaine [′novə‚ken] *s* Novokain *n*

now [nau] *adv* jetzt; (*without tem-*

poral force) nun; **before now** schon früher; **by now** nachgerade; **from now on** von nun ab, fortan; **now and then** dann und wann; **now ... now** bald ... bald; **now or never** jetzt oder nie

nowadays ['nau·ə‚dez] *adv* heutzutage

no′way′, no′ways′ *adv* keineswegs

no′where′ *adv* nirgends

noxious ['nɔk/əs] *adj* schädlich

nozzle ['nɔzəl] *s* Düse *f*; (*on a can*) Schnabel *m*

nth [enθ] *adj*—**nth times** zig mal; **to the nth degree** (fig) im höchsten Maße

nuance ['n(j)u·ɑns] *s* Nuance *f*

nub [nʌb] *s* Knoten *m*; (*gist*) Kernpunkt *m*

nuclear ['n(j)ukli·ər] *adj* nuklear; (*energy, fission, fusion, physics, reactor, weapon*) Kern—

nu′clear pow′er *s* Atomkraft *f*

nu′clear pow′er plant′ *s* Atomkraftwerk *n*

nucleolus [n(j)u'kli·ələs] *s* Nukleolus *m*

nucleon ['n(j)ukli·ɑn] *s* Nukleon *n*

nucle·us ['n(j)ukli·əs] *s* (—uses & i—[‚aɪ]) Kern *m*

nude [n(j)ud] *adj* nackt || *s* (*nude figure*) Akt *m*; **in the n.** nackt

nudge [nʌdʒ] *s* Stups *m* || *tr* stupsen

nudist ['n(j)udɪst] *s* Nudist —in *mf*

nudity ['n(j)udɪti] *s* Nacktheit *f*

nugget ['nʌgɪt] *s* Klumpen *m*

nuisance ['n(j)usəns] *s* Ärgernis *n*; **be a n.** lästig sein

nui′sance raid′ *s* Störungsangriff *m*

null′ and void′ [nʌl] *adj* null und nichtig

nulli·fy ['nʌlɪ‚faɪ] *v* (*pret & pp* —fied) *tr* (*e.g., a law*) für ungültig erklären; (*e.g., the effects*) aufheben

numb [nʌm] *adj* taub; (*with*) starr (vor *dat*); (fig) betäubt; **grow n.** erstarren || *tr* (& fig) betäuben; (*said of cold*) starr machen

number ['nʌmbər] *s* Nummer *f*; (*count*) Zahl *f*, Anzahl *f*; (*article*) (com) Artikel *m*; (gram) Zahl *f*; (mus) Stück *n*; **in n. der Zahl nach**; **get s.o.'s n.** (coll) j—m auf die Schliche kommen || *tr* (*e.g., pages*) numerieren; (*amount to*) zählen; **be numbered among** zählen zu; **n. among** zählen zu

numberless ['nʌmbərlɪs] *adj* zahllos

num′bers game′ *s* Zahlenlotto *n*

numbness ['nʌmnɪs] *s* Taubheit *f*; (*from cold*) Starrheit *f*

numeral ['n(j)umərəl] *adj* Zahl— || *s* Zahl *f*, Ziffer *f*; (gram) Zahlwort *n*

numerator ['n(j)umə‚retər] *s* Zähler *m*

numerical [n(j)u'merɪkəl] *adj* numerisch; **n. order** Zahlenfolge *f*; **n. superiority** Überzahl *f*; **n. value** Zahlenwert *m*

numerous ['n(j)umərəs] *adj* zahlreich

numismatic [‚n(j)umɪz'mætɪk] *adj* numismatisch || **numismatics** *s* Münzkunde *f*

numskull ['nʌm‚skʌl] *s* Dummkopf *m*

nun [nʌn] *s* Nonne *f*

nunci·o ['nʌn/ɪ·o] *s* (—os) Nuntius *m*

nuptial ['nʌp/əl] *adj* Braut—, Hochzeits— || **nuptials** *spl* Trauung *f*

Nuremberg ['n(j)urəm‚bʌrg] *s* Nürnberg *n*

nurse [nʌrs] *s* Krankenschwester *f*; (*male*) Krankenpfleger *m*; (*wet nurse*) Amme *f* || *tr* (*the sick*) pflegen; (*a child*) stillen; (*hopes*) hegen; **n. a cold** e—e Erkältung kurieren

nurse′maid′ *s* Kindermädchen *n*

nursery ['nʌrsəri] *s* Kinderstube *f*; (*for day care*) Kindertagesstätte *f*; (hort) Baumschule *f*, Pflanzschule *f*

nurs′ery-man *s* (—men) Kunstgärtner *m*

nurs′ery rhyme′ *s* Kinderlied *n*

nurs′ery school′ *s* Kindergarten *m*

nurse′′s aide′ *s* Schwesternhelferin *f*

nurs′ing *s* (*as a profession*) Krankenpflege *f*; (*of a person*) Pflege *f*; (*of a baby*) Stillen *n*

nurs′ing home′ *s* Pflegeheim *n*

nurture ['nɑrt/ər] *s* Nahrung *f* || *tr* (er)nähren

nut [nʌt] *s* Nuß *f*; (sl) verrückter Kerl *m*; (mach) Mutter *f*, Schraubenmutter *f*; **be nuts** (sl) verrückt sein; **be nuts about** (sl) vernarrt sein in (*acc*); **go nuts** (sl) e—n Klaps kriegen

nut′crack′er *s* Nußknacker *m*

nutmeg ['nʌt‚meg] *s* (*spice*) Muskatnuß *f*; (*tree*) Muskat *m*

nutrient ['n(j)utri·ənt] *s* Nährstoff *m*

nutriment ['n(j)utrɪmənt] *s* Nährstoff *m*

nutrition [n(j)u'trɪ/ən] *s* Ernährung *f*

nutritious [n(j)u'trɪ/əs] *adj* nahrhaft

nutritive ['n(j)utrɪtɪv] *adj* nahrhaft, Nähr—

nut′shell′ *s* Nußschale *f*; **in a n.** mit wenigen Worten

nutty ['nʌti] *adj* nußartig; (sl) spleenig, verrückt

nuzzle ['nʌzəl] *tr* sich mit der Schnauze (or Nase) reiben an (*dat*) || *intr* (*burrow*) mit der Schnauze wühlen; **n. up to** sich anschmiegen an (*acc*)

nylon ['naɪlən] *s* Nylon *n*

nymph [nɪmf] *s* Nymphe *f*

nymphomaniac [‚nɪmfə'meni·æk] *s* Nymphomanin *f*

O

O, o [o] fünfzehnter Buchstabe des englischen Alphabets

oaf [of] *s* Tölpel *m*

oak [ok] *adj* eichen || *s* Eiche *f*

oak′ leaf′ clus′ter *s* Eichenlaub *n*

oak′ tree′ *s* Eichbaum *m*

oakum ['okəm] *s* Werg *n*

oar [or], [ər] *s* Ruder *n*, Riemen *m*

oar'lock' s Ruderdolle f

oars'man' s (-men') Ruderer m

oa·sis [o'esɪs] s (-ses [siz] Oase f

oath [oθ] s (oaths [oðz]) Eid m; o. of allegiance Treueid m; o. of office Amtseid m; under o. eidlich

oat'meal' s Hafergrütze f, Hafermehl n

oats [ots] spl Hafer m; he's feeling his o. (coll) ihn sticht der Hafer; sow one's wild o. (coll) sich [dat] die Hörner ablaufen

obbligato [,ɑblɪ'gato] adj hauptstimmig || s Obligato m

obdurate ['ɑbdjərɪt] adj verstockt

obedience [o'bidɪəns] s (to) Gehorsam m (gegenüber dat, gegen); blind o. Kadavergehorsam m

obedient [o'bidɪənt] adj (to) gehorsam (dat)

obeisance [o'bisəns] s Ehrerbietung f

obelisk ['ɑbəlɪsk] s Obelisk m

obese [o'bis] adj fettleibig

obesity [o'bisɪti] s Fettleibigkeit f

obey [o'be] tr gehorchen (dat); (a law, order) befolgen || intr gehorchen

obfuscate [ɑb'fʌsket] tr verdunkeln

obituary [o'bɪtʃu,ɛri] adj Todes- || s Todesanzeige f, Nachruf m

object ['ɑbdʒɪkt] s Gegenstand m; (aim) Ziel n, Zweck m; (gram) Ergänzung f, Objekt n; money is no o. Geld spielt keine Rolle || [ɑb'dʒɛkt] intr (to) Einwände erheben (gegen)

objection [ɑb'dʒɛkʃən] s Einwand m; I have no o. to his staying ich habe nichts dagegen (einzuwenden), daß er bleibe

objectionable [ɑb'dʒɛkʃənəbəl] adj nicht einwandfrei

objective [ɑb'dʒɛktɪv] adj sachlich, objektiv || s Ziel n

objec'tive case' s Objektsfall m

ob'ject les'son s Lehre f

obligate ['ɑblɪ,get] tr verpflichten; be obligated to s.o. j-m zu Dank verbunden sein

obligation [,ɑblɪ'geʃən] s Verpflichtung f

obligatory ['ɑblɪgə,tori], [ə'blɪgə,tori] adj verpflichtend, obligatorisch

oblige [ə'blaɪdʒ] tr (bind) verpflichten; (do a favor to) gefällig sein (dat); be obliged to (inf) müssen (inf); feel obliged to (inf) sich bemüßigt fühlen zu (inf); I'm much obliged to you ich bin Ihnen sehr verbunden

oblig'ing adj gefällig

oblique [ə'blik] adj schief

obliterate [ə'blɪtə,ret] tr auslöschen; (traces) verwischen; (writing) unleserlich machen

oblivion [ə'blɪvɪ-ən] s Vergessenheit f

oblivious [ə'blɪvɪ-əs] adj—be o. of sich [dat] nicht bewußt sein (genit)

oblong ['ɑblɒŋ] adj länglich || s Rechteck n

obnoxious [ɑb'nɑkʃəs] adj widerlich

oboe ['obo] s Oboe f

oboist ['obo-ɪst] s Oboist -in mf

obscene [ɑb'sin] adj obszön

obscenity [ɑb'sɛnɪti] s Obszönität f

obscure [əb'skjur] adj dunkel, obskur || tr verdunkeln

obscurity [əb'skjurɪti] s Dunkelheit f

obsequies ['ɑbsɪkwiz] spl Totenfeier f

obsequious [əb'sikwɪ-əs] adj unterwürfig

observance [əb'zʌrvəns] s Beachtung f, Befolgung f; (celebration) Feier f

observant [əb'zʌrvənt] adj beobachtend

observation [,ɑbzər've/ən] s Beobachtung f; keep under o. beobachten

observa'tion tow'er s Aussichtsturm m

observatory [əb'zʌrvə,tori] s Sternwarte f, Observatorium n

observe [əb'zʌrv] tr (a person, rules) beobachten; (a holiday) feiern; o. silence Stillschweigen bewahren

obsess [əb'sɛs] tr verfolgen; obsessed (by) besessen (von)

obsession [əb'sɛʃən] s Besessenheit f

obsolescent [,ɑbsə'lɛsənt] adj veraltend

obsolete ['ɑbsə,lit] adj veraltet; become o. veralten

obstacle ['ɑbstəkəl] s Hindernis n

ob'stacle course' s Hindernisbahn f

obstetrical [ɑb'stetrɪkəl] adj Geburtshilfe-, Entbindungs-

obstetrician [,ɑbstə'trɪʃən] s Geburtshelfer –in mf

obstetrics [ɑb'stetrɪks] s Geburtshilfe f

obstinacy ['ɑbstɪnəsi] s Starrheit f

obstinate ['ɑbstɪnɪt] adj starr

obstreperous [əb'strepərəs] adj (clamorous) lärmend; (unruly) widerspenstig

obstruct [əb'strʌkt] tr (e.g., a pipe) verstopfen; (a view, way) versperren; (traffic) behindern; o. justice die Rechtspflege behindern

obstruction [əb'strʌkʃən] s (of a view, way) Versperrung f; (of traffic) Behinderung f; (obstacle) Hindernis n; (parl, pathol) Obstruktion f

obtain [əb'ten] tr erhalten, erlangen || intr bestehen

obtrusive [əb'trusɪv] adj aufdringlich

obtuse [əb't(j)us] adj (& fig) stumpf

obviate ['ɑbvɪ,et] tr erübrigen

obvious ['ɑbvɪ-əs] adj naheliegend; it is o. es liegt auf der Hand

occasion [ə'keʒən] s Gelegenheit f; (reason) Anlaß m; on o. gelegentlich; on the o. of anläßlich (genit) || tr veranlassen

occasional [ə'keʒənəl] adj gelegentlich

occasionally [ə'keʒənəli] adv gelegentlich, zuweilen

occident ['ɑksɪdənt] s Abendland n

occidental [,ɑksɪ'dɛntəl] adj abendländisch || s Abendländer –in mf

occlusion [ə'kluʒən] s Okklusion f

occult [ə'kʌlt] adj geheim, okkult

occupancy ['ɑkjəpənsi] s Besitz m, Besitzergreifung f; (of a home) Einzug m

occupant ['ɑkjəpənt] s Besitzer –in mf; (of a home) Insasse –in mf; (of a car) Insasse m, Insassin f

occupation [,ɑkjə'peʃən] s (employment) Beruf *m*, Beschäftigung *f*; (mil) Besetzung *f*, Besatzung *f*

occup'ational disease' [,ɑkjə'peʃənəl] *s* Berufskrankheit *f*

occupa'tional ther'apy *s* Beschäftigungstherapie *f*

occupa'tion troops' *spl* Besatzungstruppen *pl*

occu·py ['ɑkjə,paɪ] *v* (*pret & pp* -pied) *tr* in Besitz nehmen; (*a house*) bewohnen; (*time*) in Anspruch nehmen; (*keep busy*) beschäftigen; (mil) besetzen; **occupied** (*said of a seat or toilet*) besetzt; (*said of a person*) beschäftigt; **o. oneself with** sich befassen mit

oc·cur [ə'kʌr] *v* (*pret & pp* -curred; *ger* -curring) *intr* sich ereignen; (*come to mind*) (**to**) einfallen (*dat*)

occurrence [ə'kʌrəns] *s* Ereignis *n*; (*e.g., of a word*) Vorkommen *n*

ocean ['oʃən] *s* Ozean *m*

oceanic [,oʃɪ'ænɪk] *adj* Ozean-, ozeanisch

o'cean lin'er *s* Ozeandampfer *m*

oceanography [,oʃən'ɑɡrəfi] *s* Ozeanographie *f*

ocher ['okər] *s* Ocker *m & f*

o'clock [ə'klɑk] *adv* Uhr; **at ... o'clock** um ... Uhr

octane ['ɑkten] *s* Oktan *n*

oc'tane num'ber *s* Oktanzahl *f*

octave ['ɑktɪv], ['ɑktev] *s* Oktave *f*

October [ɑk'tobər] *s* Oktober *m*

octogenarian [,ɑktədʒɪ'nerɪ·ən] *s* Achtzige *mf*

octo·pus ['ɑktəpəs] *s* (-puses & -pi [,paɪ]) Seepolyp *m*

ocular ['ɑkjələr] *adj* Augen-

oculist ['ɑkjəlɪst] *s* Augenarzt *m*, Augenärztin *f*

odd [ɑd] *adj* (*strange*) seltsam, eigenartig; (*number*) ungerade; (*e.g., glove*) einzeln; **two hundred odd pages** etwas über zweihundert Seiten || **odds** *spl* (*probability*) Wahrscheinlichkeit *f*; (*advantage*) Vorteil *m*; (*in gambling*) Vorgabe *f*; **at odds** uneinig; **lay** (*or* **give**) **odds** vorgeben; **the odds are two to one** die Chancen stehen zwei zu eins

odd' ball' *s* (sl) Sonderling *m*

oddity ['ɑdɪti] *s* Seltsamkeit *f*

odd' jobs' *spl* Gelegenheitsarbeit *f*; (*chores*) kleine Aufgaben *pl*

odds' and ends' *spl* Kleinkram *m*

ode [od] *s* Ode *f*

odious ['odɪ·əs] *adj* verhaßt

odor ['odər] *s* Duft *m*, Geruch *m*; **be in bad o.** in schlechtem Ruf stehen

odorless ['odərlɪs] *adj* geruchlos

odyssey ['ɑdɪsi] *s* Irrfahrt *f*; **Odyssey** Odyssee *f*

of [ɑv], [əv] *prep* von (*dat*); *genit*, e.g., **the name of the dog** der Name des Hundes

off [ɔf] *adj* (*free from work*) dienstfrei; (*poor, bad*) schlecht; (*electric current*) ausgeschaltet, abgeschaltet; **be badly off** in schlechten Verhältnissen sein; **be off** (*said of a clock*) nachgehen; (*said of a measurement*)

falsch sein; (*said of a person*) im Irrtum sein; (*be crazy*) nicht ganz richtig im Kopf sein; **be well off** in guten Verhältnissen sein; **the deal** (or **party**) **is off** es ist aus mit dem Geschäft (or mit der Party) || *adv* (*distant*) weg; **he was off in a flash** er war im Nu weg; **I must be off** ich muß fort || *prep* von (*dat*); **off duty** außer Dienst; **off limits** Zutritt verboten

offal ['ɔfəl] *s* (*refuse*) Abfall *m*; (*of butchered meat*) Innereien *pl*

off' and on' *adv* ab und zu

off'beat' *adj* (sl) ungewöhnlich

off' chance' *s* geringe Chance *f*

off'-col'or *adj* schlüpfrig

off'-du'ty *adj* außerdienstlich

offend [ə'fend] *tr* beleidigen || *intr*—**o. against** verstoßen gegen

offender [ə'fendər] *s* Missetäter -in *mf*; **first o.** nicht Vorbestrafte *mf*; **second o.** Vorbestrafte *mf*

offense [ə'fens] *s* (**against**) Vergehen *n* (gegen); **give o.** Anstoß geben; **no o.!** nichts für ungut!; **take o.** (**at**) Anstoß nehmen (an *dat*)

offensive [ə'fensɪv] *adj* anstößig; (*odor*) ekelhaft; (*action*) offensiv || *s* Offensive *f*; **take the o.** die Offensive ergreifen

offer ['ɔfər] *s* Angebot *n* || *tr* anbieten; (*a price*) bieten; (*help, resistance*) leisten; (*friendship*) schenken; **o. an excuse** e-e Entschuldigung vorbringen; **o. as an excuse** als Entschuldigung vorbringen; **o. for sale** feilbieten; **o. one's services** sich anbieten; **o. up** aufopfern || *intr*—**o. to** (*inf*) sich erbieten zu (*inf*)

of'fering *s* (*act*) Opferung *f*; (*gift*) Opfergabe *f*

offertory ['ɔfər,tori] *s* Offertorium *n*

off'hand' *adj* (*excuse*) unvorbereitet; (*manner*) lässig || *adv* kurzerhand

office ['ɔfɪs] *s* (*room*) Büro *n*, Amt *n*; (*position*) Amt *n*; (*of a doctor*) Sprechzimmer *n*; **be in o.** amtieren; **through the good offices of** durch die freundliche Vermittlung (*genit*); **run for o.** für ein Amt kandidieren

of'fice boy' *s* Bürojunge *m*

of'fice build'ing *s* Bürogebäude *n*

of'ficehold'er *s* Amtsträger -in *mf*

of'fice hours' *spl* Dienststunden *pl*; (*of a doctor, lawyer*) Sprechstunde *f*

officer ['ɔfɪsər] *s* (adm) Beamte *m*, Beamtin *f*; (com) Direktor -in *mf*; (mil) Offizier -in *mf*

of'ficer can'didate *s* Offiziersanwärter -in *mf*

of'ficers' mess' *s* Offizierskasino *n*; (nav) Offiziersmesse *f*

of'fice seek'er *s* Amtsbewerber -in *mf*

of'fice supplies' *spl* Bürobedarf *m*

of'fice work' *s* Büroarbeit *f*

official [ə'frɪʃəl] *adj* amtlich; (*in line of duty*) Dienst-; (*visit*) offiziell; (*document*) öffentlich; **on o. business** dienstlich || *s* Beamte *m*, Beamtin *f*; **top officials** Spitzenkräfte *pl*

offi'cial busi'ness *s* Dienstsache *f*

offi′cial call′ s (telp) Dienstgespräch n

officialdom [ə′fɪʃəldəm] s Beamtentum n

officialese [ə‚fɪʃə′liz] s Amtssprache f

officially [ə′fɪʃəli] adv offiziell

offi′cial use′ s Dienstgebrauch m

officiate [ə′fɪʃɪ‚et] intr amtieren; **o. at a marriage** e-n Traugottesdienst halten

officious [ə′fɪʃəs] adj dienstbeflissen

offing [′ɔfɪŋ] s—**in the o.** in Aussicht

off′-lim′its adj gesperrt

off′print′ s Abdruck m, Sonderdruck m

off′-seas′on adj—**o.** prices Preise pl während der Vor- und Nachsaison ‖ s Vor- und Nachsaison f

off′set′ s (compensation) Ausgleich m; (typ) Offsetdruck m ‖ **off′set′** v (pret –set; ger –setting) tr ausgleichen

off′set press′ s Offsetdruck m

off′shoot′ s Ableger m

off′shore′ adj küstennah

off′side′ adv (sport) abseits

off′spring′ s Sprößling m

off′stage′ adj hinter der Bühne befindlich ‖ adv hinter der Bühne

off′-the-cuff′ adj aus dem Stegreif

off′-the-rec′ord adj im Vertrauen

often [′ɔfən] adv oft, häufig; **every so o.** von Zeit zu Zeit; **quite o.** öfters

of′tentimes′ adv oftmals

ogive [′odʒaɪv] s (diagonal vaulting rib) Gratrippe f; (pointed arch) Spitzbogen m

ogle [′ogəl] tr liebäugeln mit ‖ intr liebäugeln

ogre [′ogər] s Scheusal n; (myth) Menschenfresser m

oh [o] interj oh!; **oh, dear!** o weh!

ohm [om] s Ohm n

oil [ɔɪl] s Öl n; **strike oil** auf Öl stoßen ‖ tr ölen

oil′ burn′er s Ölbrenner m

oil′can′ s Ölkanne f

oil′cloth′ s Wachsleinwand f

oil′ col′or s Ölfarbe f

oil′ drum′ s Ölfaß n

oil′ field′ s Ölfeld n

oil′ gauge′ s Ölstandsanzeiger m

oil′ heat′ s Ölheizung f

oil′ lev′el s Ölstand m

oil′man′ s (-men′) Ölhändler m

oil′ paint′ing s Ölgemälde n

oil′ pres′sure s Öldruck m

oil′ rig′ s Ölbohrinsel f

oil′ shale′ s Ölschiefer m

oil′ slick′ s Öllache f

oil′ tank′ s Ölbehälter m

oil′ tank′er s Öltanker m

oil′ well′ s Ölquelle f

oily [′ɔɪli] adj ölig; (unctious) salbungsvoll

ointment [′ɔɪntmənt] s Salbe f

O.K. [′o′ke] adj in Ordnung, okay ‖ s Billigung f ‖ v (pret & pp **O.K.′d**; ger **O.K.′ing**) tr billigen ‖ intr okay!

old [old] adj alt; **as old as the hills** uralt; (said of a person) steinalt

old′ age′ s Alter n, Greisenalter n

old′-age′ home′ s Altersheim f

old′ coun′try s Heimatland n

olden [′oldən] adj alt

old′-fash′ioned adj altmodisch

old′ fog′(e)y [′fogi] s alter Kauz m

Old′ Glo′ry s Sternenbanner n

old′ hand′ s alter Hase m

old′ hat′ adj bärtig

old′ la′dy s Greisin f; (wife) (pej) Alte f

old′ maid′ s alte Jungfer f

old′ man′ s Greis m; (mil) Alter m

old′ mas′ter s (paint) alter Meister m

old′ moon′ s letztes Viertel n

old′ salt′ s alter Seebär m

oldster [′oldstər] s alter Knabe m

Old′ Tes′tament s Altes Testament n

old′-time′ adj altväterisch

old′-tim′er s (coll) alter Hase m

old′ wives′′ tale′ s Altweibergeschichte f

Old′ World′ s alte Welt f

oleander [‚olɪ′ændər] s Oleander m

olfactory [al′fæktəri] adj Geruchs–

oligarchy [′alɪ‚gɑrɪ] s Oligarchie f

olive [′alɪv] s Olive f

ol′ive branch′ s Ölzweig m

ol′ive grove′ s Olivenhain m

ol′ive oil′ s Olivenöl n

ol′ive tree′ s Ölbaum m, Olivenbaum m

olympiad [o′lɪmpɪ‚æd] s Olympiade f

Olympian [o′lɪmpɪ‚ən] adj olympisch

Olympic [o′lɪmpɪk] adj olympisch ‖ **the Olympics** spl die Olympischen Spiele

omelet, omelette [′amə‚let] s Eierkuchen m, Omelett n

omen [′omən] s Omen n, Vorzeichen n

ominous [′amɪnəs] adj ominös, unheilvoll

omission [o′mɪʃən] s Auslassung f; (of a deed) Unterlassung f

omit [o′mɪt] v (pret & pp **omitted**; ger **omitting**) tr (a word) auslassen; (a deed) unterlassen; **be omitted** ausfallen; **o. (ger)** es unterlassen zu (inf)

omnibus [′amnɪ‚bʌs] adj Sammel–, Mantel– ‖ s Omnibus m, Autobus m

omnipotent [am′nɪpətənt] adj allmächtig

omnipresent [‚amnɪ′prezənt] adj allgegenwärtig

omniscient [am′nɪʃənt] adj allwissend

on [ɔn] adj (in progress) im Gange; (light, gas, water) an; (radio, television) angestellt; (switch) eingeschaltet; (brakes) angezogen; **be on to s.o.** j–n durchsehen; **be on to s.th.** über etw [acc] im Bilde sein ‖ adv weiter; **on and off** dann und wann; **on and on** in e–m fort ‖ prep auf (dat or acc), an (dat or acc); (concerning) über (acc)

once [wʌns] adv einmal; (formerly) einst; **at o.** auf einmal; (immediately) sofort; **not o.** nicht ein einziges Mal; **o. and for all** ein für allemal; **o. before** früher einmal; **o. in a while** ab und zu; **o. more** noch einmal; **o. upon a time there was** es war einmal ‖ s—**this o.** dieses (eine) Mal n ‖ conj sobald

once′-o′ver s—**give** (s.o. or s.th.) **the o.** rasch mustern

one [wʌn] adj ein; (one certain, e.g.,

Mr. Smith) ein gewisser; **for one thing** zunächst; her one care ihre einzige Sorge; **it's all one to me** es ist mir ganz gleich; **one and a half hours** anderthalb Stunden; **one day** e-s Tages; **one more** noch ein; **one more thing** noch etwas; **one o'clock** ein Uhr, eins; **on the one hand** ... on the other einerseits ... andererseits || *s* Eins *f* || *pron* einer; **I for one** was mich betrifft, ich jedenfalls; **one after another** einer nach dem anderen; **one after the other** nacheinander; **one another** einander, sich; **one at a time, please!** einer nach dem anderen, bitte!; **one behind the other** hintereinander; **one by one** einer nach dem anderen; **one of these days** früher oder später; **one on top of the other** übereinander, aufeinander; **one to nothing** eins zu Null; **this one** dieser da, der da; **with one another** miteinander || *indef pron* man; **one's** sein

one'-armed' *adj* einarmig
one'-eyed' *adj* einäugig
one'-horse town' *s* Kuhdorf *n*
one'-leg'ged *adj* einbeinig
onerous ['ɑnərəs] *adj* lästig
oneself' *reflex pron* sich; **be o.** sein, wie man immer ist; **by o.** allein; **to o.** vor sich [*acc*] hin
one'-sid'ed *adj* (& fig) einseitig
one'-track' *adj* eingleisig; (fig) einseitig
one'-way street' *s* Einbahnstraße *f*
one'-way tick'et *s* einfache Fahrkarte *f*
one'-week' *adj* achttägig
onion ['ʌnjən] *s* Zwiebel *f*; **know one's onions** (coll) Bescheid wissen
on'lonskin' *s* Durchschlagpapier *n*
on'look'er *s* Zuschauer –in *mf*
only ['onli] *adj* (son, hope) einzig || *adv* nur; **not only** ... but also nicht nur ... sondern auch; **o. too** nur (all)zu; **o. too well** zur Genüge; **o. yesterday** erst gestern || *conj* aber; **o. that** nur daß
on'ly-begot'ten *adj* eingeboren
onomatopoeia [ˌɑnəˌmætə'pi·ə] *s* Lautmalerei *f*
on'-ramp' *s* Zufahrtsrampe *f*
on'rush' *s* Ansturm *m*
on'set' *s* Anfang *m*; (attack) Angriff *m*
onslaught ['ɔnˌslɔt] *s* Angriff *m*
on'to *prep* auf (*acc*) hinauf; **be o. s.o.** hinter j-s Schliche kommen; **be o. s.th.** über etw [*acc*] im Bilde sein
onus ['onəs] *s* Last *f*; **o. of proof** Beweislast *f*
onward(s) ['ɑnwərd(z)] *adv* vorwärts
onyx ['ɑnɪks] *s* Onyx *m*
oodles ['udəlz] *spl* (coll) (of) Unmengen *pl* (von)
ooze [uz] *s* Sickern *n*; (mud) Schlamm *m* || *tr* ausschwitzen || *intr* sickern; **o. out** durchsickern
opal ['opəl] *s* Opal *m*
opaque [o'pek] *adj* undurchsichtig; (stupid) stumpf
open ['opən] *adj* (window, position, sea, question, vowel) offen; (air, field, seat) frei; (business, office)

geöffnet; (seam) geplatzt; (account) laufend; (meeting) öffentlich; **be o.** offenstehen; **get o.** aufbekommen; **have an o. mind about s.th.** sich noch nicht auf etw [*acc*] festgelegt haben; **keep o.** offenhalten; **lay oneself o. to** sich aussetzen (*dat*); **o. to** (the public) zugänglich (*dat*); (criticism) ausgesetzt (*dat*); (doubt) unterworfen (*dat*); **o. to bribery** bestechlich; **o. to question** strittig || *s*—**come out into the o.** (fig) mit seinen Gedanken herauskommen; **in the o.** im Freien || *tr* öffnen, aufmachen; (a business, account, meeting, hostilities, fire) eröffnen; (a book) aufschlagen; (eyes in surprise) aufreißen; (a box, bottle) anbrechen; (an umbrella) aufspannen; **o. the attack** losschlagen; **o. to traffic** dem Verkehr übergeben; **o. wide** weit aufreißen || *intr* sich öffnen, aufgehen; (said of a school, speech, play) beginnen; **o. onto** hinausgehen auf (*acc*); **o. up** sich auftun; **o. with hearts** (cards) Herz ausspielen

o'pen-air' *adj* Freiluft–; (theat) Freilicht–; **o. concert** Konzert *n* im Freien
opener ['opənər] *s* Öffner *m*, **for openers** (coll) für den Anfang
o'pen-eyed' *adj* mit offenen Augen
o'pen-hand'ed *adj* freigebig
o'pen-heart'ed *adj* offenherzig
o'pen house' *s* allgemeiner Besuchstag *m*
o'pening *adj* (scene) erste; (remarks) Eröffnungs– || *s* Öffnung *f*; (of a speech, play) Anfang *m*; (of a store, etc.) Eröffnung *f*; (vacant job) freie (or offene) Stelle *f*; (in the woods) Lichtung *f*; (good opportunity) günstige Gelegenheit *f*; (theat) Erstaufführung *f*
o'pening night' *s* Eröffnungsvorstellung *f*, Premiere *f*
o'pening num'ber *s* erstes Stück *n*
o'pen-mind'ed *adj* aufgeschlossen
openness ['opənnɪs] *s* Offenheit *f*
o'pen sea'son *s* Jagdzeit *f*
o'pen se'cret *s* offenes Geheimnis *n*
o'pen shop' *s* offener Betrieb *m* (für den kein Gewerkschaftszwang besteht)
opera ['ɑprə] *s* Oper *f*
op'era glass'es *spl* Opernglas *n*
op'era house' *s* Opernhaus *n*
operate ['ɑpəˌret] *tr* (a machine, gun) bedienen; (a tool) handhaben; (a business) betreiben; **be operated by electricity** elektrisch betrieben werden || *intr* (said of a device, machine) funktionieren, laufen; (surg) operieren; **o. on** (surg) operieren
operatic [ˌɑpə'rætɪk] *adj* opernhaft
op'erating costs' *spl* Betriebskosten *pl*
op'erating instruc'tions *spl* Bedienungsanweisung *f*
op'erating room' *s* Operationssaal *m*
op'erating ta'ble *s* Operationstisch *m*
operation [ˌɑpə'reʃən] *s* (process) Verfahren *n*; (of a machine) Bedie-

nung f; (of a business) Leitung f; (mil) Operation f, Aktion f; (surg) Operation f; be in o. (said of a machine) in Betrieb sein; (said of a law) in Kraft sein; have (or undergo) an o. sich e-r Operation unterziehen; in a single o. in e-m einzigen Arbeitsgang; put into o. in Betrieb setzen

operational [ˌɑpəˈreʃənəl] adj (ready to be used) betriebsbereit; (pertaining to operations) Betriebs– Arbeits–; (mil) Einsatz–, Operations–

opera'tions room' s (aer) Bereitschaftsraum m

operative [ˈɑpərətɪv] adj funktionsfähig, wirkend; become o. in Kraft treten || s Agent –in mf

operator [ˈɑpəˌretər] s (of a machine) Bedienende mf; (of an automobile) Fahrer –in mf; (sl) Schieber –in mf; (telp) Telephonist –in mf; o.! (telp) Zentrale!

op'erator's li'cense s Führerschein m

operetta [ˌɑpəˈretə] s Operette f

ophthalmologist [ˌɑfθəlˈmɑlədʒɪst] s Augenarzt m, Augenärztin f

ophthalmology [ˌɑfθəlˈmɑlədʒi] s Augenheilkunde f, Ophthalmologie f

opiate [ˈopɪˌet] s Opiat n; (fig) Betäubungsmittel n

opinion [əˈpɪnjən] s Meinung f; be of the o. der Meinung sein; give an o. on begutachten; have a high o. of große Stücke halten auf (acc); in my o. meiner Meinung nach, meines Erachtens

opinionated [əˈpɪnjəˌnetɪd] adj von sich eingenommen

opin'ion poll' s Meinungsumfrage f

opium [ˈopɪəm] s Opium n

o'pium den' s Opiumhöhle f

o'pium pop'py s Schlafmohn m

opossum [əˈpɑsəm] s Opossum n

opponent [əˈponənt] s Gegner –in mf

opportune [ˌɑpərˈt(j)un] adj gelegen

opportunist [ˌɑpərˈt(j)unɪst] s Opportunist –in mf

opportunity [ˌɑpərˈt(j)unɪti] s Gelegenheit f

oppose [əˈpoz] tr sich widersetzen (dat); (for comparison) gegenüberstellen; be opposed to s.th. gegen etw sein

oppos'ing adj (team, forces) gegnerisch; (views) entgegengesetzt

opposite [ˈɑpəsɪt] adj (side, corner) gegenüberliegend; (meaning) entgegengesetzt; (view) gegenteilig; o. angle (geom) Gegenwinkel m; o. to gegenüber (dat) || s Gegensatz m, Gegenteil n || prep gegenüber (dat)

op'posite num'ber s Gegenstück n, Gegenspieler –in mf

opposition [ˌɑpəˈzɪʃən] s Widerstand m; (pol) Opposition f; meet with stiff o. auf heftigen Widerstand stoßen; offer o. Widerstand leisten

oppress [əˈpres] tr unterdrücken

oppression [əˈpreʃən] s Unterdrückung f

oppressive [əˈpresɪv] adj bedrückend

oppressor [əˈpresər] s Unterdrücker –in mf

opprobrious [əˈprobrɪ-əs] adj schändlich

opprobrium [əˈprobrɪ-əm] s Schande f

opt [ɑpt] intr—opt for optieren für

optic [ˈɑptɪk] adj Augen– || **optics** s Optik f

optical [ˈɑptɪkəl] adj optisch

op'tical illus'ion s optische Täuschung f

optician [ɑpˈtɪʃən] s Optiker –in mf

op'tic nerve' s Augennerv m

optimism [ˈɑptɪˌmɪzəm] s Optimismus m

optimist [ˈɑptɪmɪst] s Optimist –in mf

optimistic [ˌɑptɪˈmɪstɪk] adj optimistisch

option [ˈɑpʃən] s (choice) Wahl f; (alternative) Alternative f; (ins) Option f

optional [ˈɑpʃənəl] adj wahlfrei; be o. freistehen

optometrist [ɑpˈtɑmɪtrɪst] s Augenoptiker –in mf

optometry [ɑpˈtɑmɪtri] s Optometrie f

opulent [ˈɑpjələnt] adj (wealthy) reich; (luxurious) üppig

or [ɔr] conj oder

oracle [ˈɔrəkəl] s Orakel n

oracular [oˈrækjələr] adj orakelhaft

oral [ˈɔrəl] adj mündlich

o'ral hygiene' s Mundpflege f

orange [ˈɔrɪndʒ] adj orange || s Orange f, Apfelsine f

orangeade [ˌɔrɪndʒˈed] s Orangeade f

or'ange blos'som s Orangenblüte f

or'ange grove' s Orangenhain m

or'ange tree' s Orangenbaum m

orang-outang [oˈræŋuˌtæŋ] s Orang-Utan m

oration [oˈreʃən] s Rede f

orator [ˈɔrətər] s Redner –in mf

oratorical [ˌɔrəˈtɔrɪkəl] adj rednerisch

oratorio [ˌɔrəˈtɔriˌo] s (–os) Oratorium n

oratory [ˈɔrəˌtori] s Redekunst f

orb [ɔrb] s Kugel f; (of the moon or sun) Scheibe f

orbit [ˈɔrbɪt] s Umlaufbahn f; send into o. in die Umlaufbahn schicken || tr umkreisen

orbital [ˈɔrbɪtəl] adj Kreisbahn–

orchard [ˈɔrtʃərd] s Obstgarten m

orchestra [ˈɔrkɪstrə] s Orchester n

or'chestra pit' s Orchesterraum m

orchestrate [ˈɔrkɪˌstret] tr orchestrieren

orchid [ˈɔrkɪd] s Orchidee f

ordain [ɔrˈden] tr verordnen; (eccl) ordinieren, zum Priester weihen

ordeal [ɔrˈdil] s Qual f; (hist) Gottesurteil n; o. by fire Feuerprobe f

order [ˈɔrdər] s (command) Befehl m; (decree) Verordnung f; (order, arrangement) Ordnung f; (medal) Orden m; (sequence) Reihenfolge f; (archit, bot, zool) Ordnung f; (com) (for) Auftrag m (auf acc), Bestellung f (auf acc); (eccl) Orden m; (jur) Beschluß m; according to orders befehlsgemäß; be in good o. in gutem

Zustand sein; **be the o. of the day** (coll) an der Tagesordnung sein; **be under orders** to (inf) Befehl haben zu (inf); **by o. of** auf Befehl von (or genit); **call to o.** (a meeting) für eröffnet erklären; (reestablish order) zur Ordnung rufen; **in o.** (functioning) in Ordnung; (proper, in place) angebracht; **in o. of** geordnet nach; **in o. that** damit; **in o. to** (inf) um ... zu (inf); **make to o.** nach Maß machen; **of a high o.** von ausgezeichneter Art; **on o.** (com) in Auftrag; **o.!, o.!** zur Ordnung! **out of o.** (defective) außer Betrieb; (not functioning at all) nicht in Ordnung; (disarranged) in Unordnung; (parl) im Widerspruch zur Geschäftsordnung, unzulässig; **put in o.** in Ordnung bringen; **restore to o.** die Ordnung wiederherstellen; **you are out of o.** Sie haben nicht das Wort ‖ tr (command) befehlen, anordnen; (decree) verordnen; (com) bestellen; **as ordered** auftragsgemäß; **o. around** herumkommandieren; **o. in advance** vor(her)bestellen; **o. more of** nachbestellen; **o. s.o. off** (e.g., the premises) j-n weisen von

or'der blank' s Auftragsformular n

orderliness ['ɔrdərlɪnɪs] s (of a person) Ordnungsliebe f; (of a room, etc.) Ordnung f

orderly ['ɔrdərli] adj ordentlich ‖ s (med) Krankenwärter m; (mil) Bursche m

or'derly room' s (mil) Schreibstube f

or'der slip' s Bestellzettel m

ordinal ['ɔrdɪnəl] adj Ordnungs– ‖ s Ordnungszahl f

ordinance ['ɔrdɪnəns] s Verfügung f; (of a city) Verordnung f

ordinary ['ɔrdɪˌneri] adj gewöhnlich; (member) ordentlich; **o. person** Alltagsmensch m ‖ s Gewöhnliche n; (eccl) Ordinarius m; **nothing out of the o.** nichts Ungewöhnliches; **out of the o.** außerordentlich

ordination [ˌɔrdɪ'neʃən] s Priesterweihe f

ordnance ['ɔrdnəns] s Waffen und Munition pl; (arti) Geschützwesen n

ore [or] s Erz n

organ ['ɔrgən] s (means) Werkzeug n; (publication) Organ n; (adm, biol) Organ n; (mus) Orgel f

organdy ['ɔrgəndi] s Organdy m

or'gan grind'er s Drehorgelspieler m

organic [ɔr'gænɪk] adj organisch

organism ['ɔrgəˌnɪzəm] s Organismus m

organist ['ɔrgənɪst] s Organist –in f

organization [ˌɔrgənɪ'zeʃən] s Organisation f

organizational [ˌɔrgənɪ'zeʃənəl] adj organisatorisch

organize ['ɔrgəˌnaɪz] tr organisieren

organizer ['ɔrgəˌnaɪzər] s Organisator –in f

or'gan loft' s Orgelbühne f

orgasm ['ɔrgæzəm] s Orgasmus m

orgy ['ɔrdʒi] s Orgie f

Orient ['ɔri·ənt] s Orient m ‖ **orient** ['ɔriˌɛnt] tr orientieren

oriental [ˌɔri'ɛntəl] adj orientalisch ‖ **Oriental** s Orientale m, Orientalin f

orientation [ˌɔri·ən'teʃən] s Orientierung f; (of new staff members) Einführung f

orifice ['ɔrɪfɪs] s Öffnung f

origin ['ɔrɪdʒɪn] s Ursprung m; (of a person or word) Herkunft f

original [ə'rɪdʒɪnəl] adj ursprünglich; (first) Ur–; (novel, play) originell; (person) erfinderisch ‖ s Original n

originality [əˌrɪdʒɪ'mælɪti] s Originalität f

ori'ginal research' s Quellenstudium n

ori'ginal sin' s Erbsünde f, Sündenfall m

originate [ə'rɪdʒɪˌnet] tr hervorbringen ‖ intr (from) entstehen (aus); **o. in** seinen Ursprung haben in (dat)

originator [ə'rɪdʒɪˌnetər] s Urheber –in mf

oriole ['ɔri·ol] s Goldamsel f, Pirol m

ormolu ['ɔrməˌlu] s Malergold n

ornament ['ɔrnəmənt] s Verzierung f, Schmuck m ‖ ['ɔrnəˌment] tr verzieren

ornamental [ˌɔrnə'mentəl] adj Zier–

ornamentation [ˌɔrnəmən'teʃən] s Verzierung f

ornate [ɔr'net] adj überladen; (speech) bilderreich

ornery ['ɔrnəri] adj (cantankerous) mürrisch; (vile) gemein

ornithology [ˌɔrnɪ'θalədʒi] s Vogelkunde f, Ornithologie f

orphan ['ɔrfən] s Waise f; **become an o.** verwaisen

orphanage ['ɔrfənɪdʒ] s Waisenhaus n

or'phaned adj verwaist; **be o.** verwaisen

or'phans' court' s Vormundschaftsgericht n

orthodox ['ɔrθəˌdaks] adj orthodox

orthography [ɔr'θagrəfi] s Orthographie f, Rechtschreibung f

orthopedist [ˌɔrθə'pidɪst] s Orthopäde m, Orthopädin f

oscillate ['ɑsɪˌlet] intr schwingen

oscillation [ˌɑsɪ'leʃən] s Schwingung f

oscillator ['ɑsɪˌletər] s Oszillator m

osier ['oʒər] s Korbweide f

osmosis [ɑs'mosɪs] s Osmose f

osprey ['ɑspri] s Fischadler m

ossi·fy ['ɑsɪˌfaɪ] v (pret & pp –fied) tr verknöchern lassen ‖ intr verknöchern

ostensible [ɑs'tensɪbəl] adj vorgeblich

ostentation [ˌɑstən'teʃən] s Zurschaustellung f, Prahlerei f

ostentatious [ˌɑstən'teʃəs] adj prahlerisch, prunksüchtig

osteopath ['ɑstɪ·əˌpæθ] s Osteopath –in mf

osteopathy [ˌɑstɪ'apəθi] s Osteopathie f

ostracism ['ɑstrəˌsɪzəm] s Ächtung f; (hist) Scherbengericht n

ostracize ['ɑstrəˌsaɪz] tr verfemen

ostrich ['ɑstrɪtʃ] s Strauß m

Ostrogoth ['ɑstrəˌgɑθ] s Ostgote m

other [ˈʌðər] *adj* andere, sonstig; among o. **things** unter anderem; every o. **day** jeden zweiten Tag; none o. **than** he kein anderer als er; **on the o. hand** andererseits; o. **things being equal** unter gleichen Voraussetzungen; **someone** or o. irgend jemand; **some ... or** o. irgendein; **the o. day** unlängst || *adv*—o. **than** anders als || *indef pron* andere; **the others** die anderen

otherwise [ˈʌðərˌwaɪz] *adj* sonstig || *adv* sonst; I **can't do** o. ich kann nicht umhin; o. **engaged** anderweitig beschäftigt; **think** o. anders denken

otter [ˈɑtər] *s* Otter *m*; (*snake*) Otter *f*

Ottoman [ˈɑtəmən] *adj* osmanisch || **ottoman** *s* (*couch*) Ottomane *m*; (*cushioned stool*) Polsterschemel *m*; **O. Osmane** *m*

ouch [aʊtʃ] *interj* au!

ought [ɔt] *aux* used to express obligation, e.g., **you** o. **to tell her** Sie sollten es ihr sagen; **they** o. **to have been here** sie hätten hier sein sollen

ounce [aʊns] *s* Unze *f*

our [aʊr] *poss adj* unser

ours [aʊrz] *poss pron* der uns(e)rige, der uns(e)re, uns(e)rer; **a friend of** o. ein Freund von uns; **this is** o. das gehört uns

ourselves [aʊrˈsɛlvz] *reflex pron* uns; **we are by** o. wir sind doch unter uns || *intens pron* selbst, selber

oust [aʊst] *tr* (*from*) verdrängen (aus); o. **from office** seines Amtes entheben

ouster [ˈaʊstər] *s* Amtsenthebung *f*

out [aʊt] *adj*—**an evening out** ein Ausgehabend *m*; **be out** (*of the house*) ausgegangen sein; (*said of a light, fire*) aus sein; (*said of a new book*) erschienen sein; (*said of a secret*) enthüllt sein; (*said of flowers*) aufgeblüht sein; (*said of a dislocated limb*) verrenkt sein; (*be out of style*) aus der Mode sein; (*be at an end*) aus sein; (*be absent from work*) der Arbeit fernbleiben; (*be on strike*) streiken; **be out after** s.o. hinter j–m her sein; **be out for a good time** dem Vergnügen nachgehen; **be out on one's feet** (coll) erledigt sein; **be out ten marks** zehn Mark eingebüßt haben; **be out to** (*inf*) darauf ausgehen (or aus sein) zu (*inf*); **that's out** das kommt nicht in Frage; **the best thing out** das Beste, was es gibt || *adv* (*gone forth; ended, terminated*) aus, out of (*curiosity, pity, etc.*) aus (*dat*); (*fear*) vor (*dat*); (*a certain number*) von (*dat*); (*deprived of*) beraubt (*genit*); **out of breath** außer Atem; **out of money** ohne Geld; **out of place** verlegt; (*not appropriate or proper*) unpassend; **out of the window** zum Fenster hinaus || *s* (*pretext*) Ausrede *f*; **be on the outs with** s.o. mit j–m auf gespanntem Fuße sein || *prep* aus (*dat*) || *interj* (sport) aus!; **out with it!** heraus damit!

out′ and away′ *adv* bei weitem

out′-and-out′ *adj* abgefeimt

out′-ar′gue *tr* in Grund und Boden argumentieren

out′bid′ *v* (*pret* –bid; *pp* –bid & –bidden; *ger* –bidding) *tr* überbieten

out′board mo′tor *s* Außenbordmotor *m*

out′bound′ *adj* nach auswärts bestimmt; (*traffic*) aus der Stadt fließend

out′break′ *s* Ausbruch *m*

out′build′ing *s* Nebengebäude *n*

out′burst′ *s* Ausbruch *m*; o. **of anger** Zornausbruch *m*

out′cast′ *adj* ausgestoßen || *s* Ausgestoßene *mf*

out′come′ *s* Ergebnis *n*

out′cry′ *s* Ausruf *m*; **raise an** o. ein Zetergeschrei erheben

out′dat′ed *adj* zeitlich überholt

out′dis′tance *tr* hinter sich [*dat*] lassen

out′do′ *v* (*pret* –did; *pp* –done) *tr* überbieten, übertreffen; **not to be outdone by** s.o. im Eifer zu j–m nichts an Eifer nachgeben; o. **oneself** in sich überbieten in (*dat*)

out′door′ *adj* Außen–

out′doors′ *adv* draußen, im Freien || *s*—**in the outdoors** im Freien

out′door shot′ *s* (*phot*) Außenaufnahme *f*

out′door swim′ming pool′ *s* Freibad *n*

out′door the′ater *s* Naturtheater *n*

out′door toil′et *s* Abtritt *m*

outer [ˈaʊtər] *adj* äußere, Außen–

out′er ear′ *s* Ohrmuschel *f*

out′er gar′ment *s* Oberkleid *n*

out′ermost′ *adj* äußerste

out′er space′ *s* Weltall *n*, Weltraum *m*

out′field′ *s* (baseball) Außenfeld *n*

out′fit′ *s* (*equipment*) Ausrüstung *f*; (*set of clothes*) Ausstattung *f*; (*uniform*) Kluft *f*; (*business firm*) Gesellschaft *f*; (mil) Einheit *f* || *v* (*pret* –fitted; *ger* –fitting) *tr* (*with equipment*) ausrüsten; (*with clothes*) neu ausstaffieren

out′flank′ *tr* überflügeln, umfassen

out′flow′ *s* Ausfluß *m*

out′go′ing *adj* (*sociable*) gesellig; (*officer*) bisherig; (*tide*) zurückgehend; (*train, plane*) abgehend

out′grow′ *v* (*pret* –grew; *pp* –grown) *tr* herauswachsen aus; (fig) entwachsen (*dat*)

out′growth′ *s* Auswuchs *m*; (fig) Folge *f*

out′ing *s* Ausflug *m*

outlandish [aʊtˈlændɪʃ] *adj* fremdartig; (*prices*) überhöht

out′last′ *tr* überdauern

out′law′ *s* Geächtete *mf* || *tr* ächten

out′lay′ *s* Auslage *f*, Kostenaufwand *m* || **out′lay′** *v* (*pret* & *pp* –laid) *tr* auslegen

out′let′ *s* (*for water*) Abfluß *m*, Ausfluß *m*; (fig) (*for*) Ventil *n* (für); (com) Absatzmarkt *m*; (elec) Steckdose *f*; **find an** o. **for** (fig) Luft machen (*dat*); **no** o. Sackgasse *f*

out′line′ *s* (*profile*) Umriß *m*; (*sketch*) Umrißzeichnung *f*; (*summary*) Grundriß *m*; **rough** o. knapper Umriß *m* || *tr* umreißen

out'live' *tr* überleben

out'look' *s* (*place giving a view*) Ausguck *m*; (*view from a place*) Ausblick *m*; (*point of view*) Anschauung *f*; (*prospects*) Aussichten *pl*

out'ly'ing *adj* Außen–

out'maneu'ver *tr* ausmanövrieren; (fig) überlisten

outmoded [ˌautˈmodɪd] *adj* unmodern

out'num'ber *tr* an Zahl übertreffen

out'-of-bounds' *adj* (fig) nicht in den Schranken; (sport) im Aus

out'-of-court' set'tlement *s* außergerichtlicher Vergleich *m*

out'-of-date' *adj* veraltet

out'-of-door' *adj* Außen–

out'-of-doors' *adj* Außen– || *adv* im Freien, draußen || *s*—in the o. im Freien

out'-of-pock'et *adj*—o. expenses Barauslagen *pl*

out' of print' *adj* vergriffen

out'-of-the-way' *adj* abgelegen

out' of tune' *adj* verstimmt

out' of work' *adj* arbeitslos, erwerbslos

out'pace' *tr* überholen

out'pa'tient *s* ambulant Behandelte *mf*

out'patient clin'ic *s* Ambulanz *f*

out'play' *tr* überspielen

out'point' *tr* (sport) nach Punkten schlagen

out'post' *s* (mil) Vorposten *m*

out'pour'ing *s* (& fig) Erguß *m*

out'put' *s* (*of a machine or factory*) Arbeitsleistung *f*; (*of a factory*) Produktion *f*; (mech) Nutzleistung *f*; (min) Förderung *f*

out'rage' *s* Unverschämtheit *f*; (*against*) Verletzung *f* (*genit*) || *tr* gröblich beleidigen

outrageous [autˈredʒəs] *adj* unverschämt

out'rank' *tr* im Rang übertreffen

out'rid'er *s* Vorreiter *m*

outrigger [ˈautˌrɪɡər] *s* Ausleger *m*; (*of a racing boat*) Outrigger *m*

out'right' *adj* (*lie, refusal*) glatt; (*loss*) total; (*frank*) offen || *adv* (*completely*) völlig; (*without reserve*) ohne Vorbehalt; (*at once*) auf der Stelle; **buy o.** per Kasse kaufen; **refuse o.** glatt ablehnen

out'run' *v* (pret **–ran;** pp **–run;** ger **–running**) *tr* hinter sich [*dat*] lassen

out'sell' *v* (pret & pp **–sold**) *tr* e-n größeren Umsatz haben als

out'set' *s* Anfang *m*

out'shine' *v* (pret & pp **–shone**) *tr* überstrahlen

out'side' *adj* (*help, interference*) von außen; (*world, influence, impressions*) äußere; (*lane, work*) Außen– || *adv* draußen || *s* Außenseite *f*, Äußere *n*; **at the** (**very**) **o.** (aller–) höchstens; **from the o.** von außen || *prep* außerhalb (*genit*)

outsider [ˌautˈsaɪdər] *s* Außenstehende *mf*; (sport) Außenseiter *m*

out'size' *adj* übergroß || *s* Übergröße *f*

out'skirts' *spl* Randgebiet *n*, Stadtrand *m*

out'smart' *tr* überlisten

out'spo'ken *adj* freimütig

out'spread' *adj* (legs) gespreizt; (*arms, wings*) ausgebreitet

out'stand'ing *adj* hervorragend, profiliert; (*money, debts*) ausstehend

out'strip' *v* (pret & pp **–stripped;** ger **–stripping**) *tr* (& fig) hinter sich [*dat*] lassen

out'vote' *tr* überstimmen

outward [ˈautwərd] *adj* äußerlich, äußere || *adv* auswärts, nach außen

outwardly [ˈautwərdli] *adv* äußerlich

outwards [ˈautwərdz] *adv* auswärts

out'weigh' *tr* an Gewicht übertreffen; (fig) überwiegen

out'wit' *v* (pret & pp **–witted;** ger **–witting**) *tr* überlisten

oval [ˈovəl] *adj* oval || *s* Oval *n*

ovary [ˈovəri] *s* Eierstock *m*

ovation [oˈveʃən] *s* Huldigung *f*, Ovation *f*

oven [ˈʌvən] *s* Ofen *m*; (*for baking*) Backofen *m*

over [ˈovər] *adj* (*ended*) vorbei, aus; **it's all o. with him** es ist vorbei mit ihm; **o. and done with** total erledigt || *adv*—**all o.** (*everywhere*) überall; (*on the body*) über und über; **children of twelve and o.** Kinder von zwölf Jahren und darüber; **come o.!** komm herüber!; **o.!** (*turn the page*) bitte wenden!; **o. again** noch einmal; **o. against** gegenüber (*dat*); **o. and above** obendrein; **o. and out!** (rad) Ende!; **o. and o. again** immer wieder; **o. in Europe** drüben in Europa; **o. there** dort, da drüben || *prep* (*position*) über (*dat*); (*motion*) über (*acc*); (*because of*) wegen (*genit*); (*in the course of, e.g., a cup of tea*) bei (*dat*); (*during; more than*) über (*acc*); **all o. town** (*position*) in der ganzen Stadt; (*direction*) durch die ganze Stadt; **be o. s.o.** über j-m stehen; **b. o. s.o.'s head** j-m zu hoch sein; **from all o. Germany** aus ganz Deutschland; **o. and above** außer (*genit*); **o. the radio** im Radio

o'veract' *tr* & *intr* (theat) übertreiben

o'verac'tive *adj* übermäßig tätig

overage [ˈovəredʒ] *adj* über das vorgeschriebene Alter hinaus

o'verall' *adj* Gesamt– || **o'veralls'** *spl* Monteuranzug *m*; (*trousers*) Überziehhose *f*

o'verambi'tious *adj* allzu ehrgeizig

o'veranx'ious *adj* überängstlich; (*overeager*) übereifrig

o'verawe' *tr* einschüchtern

o'verbear'ing *adj* überheblich

o'verboard' *adv* über Bord; **go o. about** sich übermäßig begeistern für

o'vercast' *adj* bewölkt, bedeckt; **become o.** sich bewölken || *s* Bewölkung *f*

o'vercharge' *s* Überteuerung *f*; (elec) Überladung *f* || **o'vercharge'** *tr* e-n Überpreis abverlangen (*dat*); (elec) überladen

o'vercoat' *s* Mantel *m*, Überrock *m*

o'ver·come' *v* (pret **–came;** pp **–come**)

tr überwältigen; **be o. with joy** vor Freude hingerissen sein

o'vercon'fidence *s* zu großes Selbstvertrauen *n*

o'vercon'fident *adj* zu vertrauensvoll

o'vercook' *tr* (*overboil*) zerkochen; (*overbake*) zu lange backen, zu lange braten

o'vercrowd' *tr* überfüllen; (*a room, hotel, hospital*) überbelegen

o'ver·do' *v* (*pret* –did; *pp* –done) *tr* übertreiben; **o. it** sich überanstrengen

o'verdone' *adj* (culin) übergar

o'verdose' *s* Überdosis *f*

o'verdraft' *s* Überziehung *f*

o'ver·draw' *v* (*pret* –drew; *pp* –drawn) *tr* überziehen

o'verdress' *intr* sich übertrieben kleiden

o'verdrive' *s* (aut) Schongang *m*

o'verdue' *adj* überfällig

o'ver·eat' *v* (*pret* –ate; *pp* –eaten) *intr* sich überessen

o'verem'phasis *s* Überbetonung *f*

o'verem'phasize *tr* überbetonen

o'veres'timate *tr* überschätzen

o'verexcite' *tr* überreizen

o'verexert' *tr* überanstrengen

o'verexer'tion *s* Überanstrengung *f*

o'verexpose' *tr* (phot) überbelichten

o'verexpo'sure *s* Überbelichtung *f*

o'verextend' *tr* übermäßig ausweiten

o'verflow' *s* (*inundation*) Überschwemmung *f*; (*surplus*) Überschuß *m*; (*outlet for surplus liquid*) Überlauf *m*; **filled to o.** bis zum Überfließen gefüllt || o'verflow' *tr* überfluten; **o. the banks** über die Ufer treten || *intr* überfließen

o'ver·fly' *v* (*pret* –flew; *pp* –flown) *tr* überfliegen

o'verfriend'ly *adj* katzenfreundlich

o'vergrown' *adj* überwachsen; (*child*) lang aufgeschossen; **become o.** (*said of a garden*) verwildern; **become o. with** überwuchert werden von

o'verhang' *s* Überhang *m* || o'ver·hang' *v* (*pret* & *pp* –hung) *tr* hervorragen über (*acc*); (*threaten*) bedrohen || *intr* überhängen

o'verhaul' *s* Überholung *f* || o'verhaul' *tr* (*repair; overtake*) überholen

o'verhead' *adj* (*line*) oberirdisch; (*valve*) obengesteuert || *adv* droben || *s* (econ) Gemeinkosten *pl*, laufende Unkosten *pl*

o'verhead door' *s* Federhubtor *n*

o'verhead line' *s* (*of a trolley*) Oberleitung *f*

o'ver·hear' *v* (*pret* & *pp* –heard) *tr* mithören; **be o.** belauscht werden

o'verheat' *tr* überhitzen; (*a room*) überheizen || *intr* heißlaufen

o'verindulge' *tr* verwöhnen || *intr* (in) sich allzusehr ergehen (in *dat*)

o'verkill' *s* Overkill *m*

overjoyed [‚ovər'dʒɔɪd] *adj* überglücklich

overland [‚ovər‚lænd] *adj* Überland–; **o. route** Landweg *m* || *adv* über Land

o'verlap' *s* Überschneiden *n* || o'verlap' *v* (*pret* & *pp* –lapped; *ger* –lapping)

tr sich überschneiden mit || *intr* (& fig) sich überschneiden

o'verlap'ping *s* (& fig) Überschneidung *f*

o'verlay' *s* Auflage *f*; (*for a map*) Planpause *f*; **o. of gold** Goldauflage *f*

o'verload' *s* Überbelastung *f*; (elec) Überlast *f* || o'verload' *tr* überlasten; (*a truck*) überladen; (in radio communications) übersteuern; (elec) überlasten

o'verlook' *tr* (by mistake) übersehen; (*a mistake*) hinwegsehen über (*acc*); (*a view*) überblicken

overly ['ovərli] *adv* übermäßig

o'vernight' *adj*—**o. stop** Aufenthalt *m* von e–r Nacht; **o. things** Nachtzeug *n* || *adv* über Nacht; **stay o.** übernachten

o'vernight' bag' *s* Nachtzeugtasche *f*

o'verpass' *s* Überführung *f*

o'ver·pay' *v* (*pret* & *pp* –paid) *tr* & *intr* überbezahlen

o'verpay'ment *s* Überbezahlung *f*

o'verpop'ulat'ed *adj* übervölkert

o'verpop'ula'tion *s* Übervölkerung *f*

o'verpow'er *tr* (& fig) überwältigen

o'verproduc'tion *s* Überproduktion *f*

o'verrate' *tr* zu hoch schätzen

o'verreach' *tr* (*extend beyond*) hinausragen über (*acc*); (*an arm*) zu weit ausstrecken; **o. oneself** sich übernehmen

o'verrefined' *adj* überspitzt

o'verripe' *adj* überreif

o'verrule' *tr* (*an objection*) zurückweisen; (*a proposal*) verwerfen; (*a person*) überstimmen

o'verrun' *s* Überproduktion *f* || o'ver·run' *v* (*pret* –ran; *pp* –run; *ger* –running) *tr* überrennen; (*said of a flood*) überschwemmen; **o. with** (*weeds*) überwuchert von; (*tourists*) überlaufen von; (*vermin*) wimmeln von

o'versalt' *tr* versalzen

o'versea(s) *adj* Übersee– || *adv* nach Übersee

o'ver·see' *v* (*pret* & *pp* –saw; *pp* –seen) *tr* beaufsichtigen

o'verse'er *s* Aufseher –in *mf*

o'versen'sitive *adj* überempfindlich

o'vershad'ow *tr* überschatten; (fig) **in den Schatten stellen**

o'vershoe' *s* Überschuh *m*

o'ver·shoot' *v* (*pret* & *pp* –shot) *tr* (& fig) hinausschießen über (*acc*)

o'versight' *s* Versehen *n*; **through an o.** aus Versehen

o'versimplifica'tion *s* allzu große Vereinfachung *f*

o'versize' *adj* übergroß || *s* Übergröße *f*

o'ver·sleep' *v* (*pret* & *pp* –slept) *tr* & *intr* verschlafen

o'verspe'cialized *adj* überspezialisiert

o'verstaffed' *adj* (mit Personal) übersetzt

o'verstay' *tr* überschreiten

o'ver·step' *v* (*pret* & *pp* –stepped; *ger* –stepping) *tr* überschreiten o'verstock' tr überbevorraten

o'verstrain' tr überanstrengen

o'verstuffed' adj überfüllt; (furniture) überpolstert

o'versupply' s zu großer Vorrat m; (com) Überangebot n || o'versup•ply' v (pret & pp –plied) tr überreichlich versehen; (com) überreichlich anbieten

overt ['ovərt], [o'vʌrt] adj offenkundig

o'ver•take' v (pret –took; pp –taken) tr (catch up to) einholen; (pass) überholen; (suddenly befall) überfallen

o'vertax' tr überbesteuern; (fig) überfordern, übermäßig in Anspruch nehmen

o'ver-the-coun'ter adj (pharm) rezeptfrei; (st. exch.) freihändig

o'verthrow' s Sturz m || o'ver•throw' (pret –threw; pp –thrown) tr stürzen

o'vertime' adj Überstunden- || adv—work o. Überstunden arbeiten; work five hours o. fünf Überstunden machen || s Überstunden pl; (sport) Spielverlängerung f

o'vertired' adj übermüdet

o'vertone' s (fig) Nebenbedeutung f; (mus) Oberton m

o'vertrump' tr überstechen

overture ['ovərt/ər] s Antrag m; (mus) Ouvertüre f

o'verturn' tr umstürzen || intr umkippen; (aut) sich überschlagen

overweening [,ovər'winiŋ] adj hochmütig

o'verweight' adj zu schwer || s Übergewicht n; (of freight) Überfracht f

overwhelm [,ovər'whelm] tr (with some feeling) überwältigen; (e.g., with questions, gifts) überschütten; (with work) überbürden

o'verwhelm'ing adj überwältigend

overwind [,ovər'waind] v (pret & pp –wound) tr überdrehen

o'verwork' s Überarbeitung f, Überanstrengung f || o'verwork' tr überfordern || intr sich überarbeiten

o'verwrought' adj überreizt

o'verzeal'ous adj übereifrig

ow [au] interj au!

owe [o] tr schulden (dat), schuldig sein (dat); he owes her everything er verdankt ihr alles

ow'ing adj—it is o. to you that es ist dein Verdienst, daß; o. to infolge (genit)

owl [aul] s Eule f; (barn owl, screech owl) Schleiereule f

own [on] adj eigen || s—be left on one's own sich (dat) selbst überlassen sein; be on one's own auf eigenen Füßen stehen; come into one's own zu seinem Recht kommen; hold one's own sich behaupten; of one's own für sich allein; on one's own (initiative) aus eigener Initiative; (responsibility) auf eigene Faust || tr besitzen; (acknowledge) anerkennen; who owns this house? wem gehört dieses Haus? || intr—own to sich bekennen zu; own up to zugeben (dat)

own'ership' s Eigentum n; (legal right of possession) Eigentumsrecht n; under new o. unter neuer Leitung

ox [aks] s (oxen ['aksən]) Ochse m

ox'cart' s Ochsenkarren m

oxfords ['aksfərdz] spl Halbschuhe pl

oxide ['aksaid] s Oxyd n

oxidize ['aksi,daiz] tr & intr oxydieren

oxydation [,aksi'defən] s Oxydation f

oxygen ['aksidʒən] s Sauerstoff m

oxygenate ['aksidʒə,net] tr mit Sauerstoff anreichern

ox'ygen mask' s Sauerstoffmaske f

ox'ygen tank' s Sauerstofflasche f

ox'ygen tent' s Sauerstoffzelt n

oxytone ['aksi,ton] adj oxytoniert || s Oxytonon n

oyster ['ɔistər] s Auster f

oys'ter bed' s Austernbank f

oys'ter farm' s Austernpark m

oys'ter•man s (–men) Austernfischer m

oys'tershell' s Austernschale f

oys'ter stew' s Austernragout n

ozone ['ozon] s Ozon n

O'zone layer' s Ozonschicht f

P

P, p [pi] s sechzehnter Buchstabe des englischen Alphabets

pace [pes] s Schritt m; (speed) Tempo n; at a fast p. in schnellem Tempo; keep p. with Schritt halten mit; put s.o. through his paces j-n auf Herz und Nieren prüfen; set the p. das Tempo angeben; (sport) Schrittmacher sein || tr (the room, floor) abschreiten; p. off abschreiten || intr—p. up and down (in) auf und ab schreiten (in dat)

pace'mak'er s Schrittmacher m

pacific [pə'sifik] adj pazifisch; the

Pacific Ocean der Pazifische (or Stille) Ozean || s—the Pacific der Pazifik

pacifier ['pæsi,fai•ər] s Friedensvermittler –in mf; (for a baby) Schnuller m

pacifism ['pæsi,fizəm] s Pazifismus m

pacifist ['pæsifist] s Pazifist –in mf

paci•fy ['pæsi,fai] v (pret & pp –fied) tr (a country) befrieden; (a person) beruhigen

pack [pæk] s Pack m, Packen m; (of a soldier) Gepäck n; (of wolves, submarines) Rudel n; (of hounds) Meute *f*; (*of cigarettes*) Päckchen *n*, Schachtel *f*; (*on pack animals*) Last *f*; (med) Packung *f*; **p. of cards** Spiel *n* Karten; **p. of lies** Lug und Trug ‖ *tr* (*a trunk*) packen; (*clothes*) einpacken; (*seal*) abdichten; **p. in** (*above normal capacity*) einpferchen; **p. up** zusammenpacken ‖ *intr* packen; **send s.o. packing** j-m Beine machen

package ['pækɪdʒ] *adj* (*price, tour, agreement*) Pauschal– ‖ *s* Paket *n* ‖ *tr* (ver)packen

pack'age deal' *s* Koppelgeschäft *n*

pack' an'imal *s* Packtier *n*

packet ['pækɪt] *s* Paket *n*, Päckchen *n*; (naut) Postschiff *n*

pack'ing *s* (*act*) Packen *n*; (*seal*) Dichtung *f*; (*wrapper*) Verpackung *f*

pack'ing case' *s* Packkiste *f*

pack'ing house' *s* Konservenfabrik *f*

pack'sad'dle *s* Packsattel *m*

pact [pækt] *s* Pakt *m*; **make a p.** paktieren

pad [pæd] *s* (*of writing paper*) Block *m*; (*ink pad*) Stempelkissen *n*; (*cushion*) Kissen *n*; (*of butter*) Stück *n*; (*under a rug*) Unterlage *f*; (*living quarters*) Bude *f*; (rok) Abschußrampe *f*; (sport) Schützer *m*; (surg) Bausch *m* ‖ *v* (*pret & pp* **padded**; *ger* **padding**) *tr* (*e.g., the shoulders*) wattieren; (*writing*) ausbauschen

pad'ded cell' *s* Gummizelle *f*

pad'ding *s* Wattierung *f*; (coll) Ballast *m*

paddle ['pædəl] *s* (*of a canoe*) Paddel *n*; (*for table tennis*) Schläger *m* ‖ *tr* paddeln; (*spank*) prügeln ‖ *intr* paddeln

pad'dle wheel' *s* Schaufelrad *n*

paddock ['pædək] *s* Pferdekoppel *f*; (*at the races*) Sattelplatz *m*

pad'dy wag'on *s* ['pædi] (sl) Grüne Minna *f*

pad'lock' *s* Vorhängeschloß *n* ‖ *tr* mit e-m Vorhängeschloß verschließen

paean ['pi·ən] *s* Siegeslied *n*

pagan ['pegən] *adj* heidnisch ‖ *s* Heide *m*, Heidin *f*

paganism ['pegə‚nɪzəm] *s* Heidentum *n*

page [pedʒ] *s* Seite *f*; (*in a hotel or club; at court*) Page *m* ‖ *tr* (*summon*) über den Lautsprecher (od durch Pagen) holen lassen ‖ *intr*— **p. through** durchblättern

pageant ['pædʒənt] *s* Festspiel *n*; (*procession*) Festzug *m*

pageantry ['pædʒəntri] *s* Schaugepränge *n*

page'boy' *s* Pagenfrisur *f*

page' proof' *s* Umbruchabzug *m*

pagoda [pə'godə] *s* Pagode *f*

paid' in full' [ped] *adj* voll bezahlt

paid'-up' *adj* (*debts*) abgezahlt; (*policy, capital*) voll eingezahlt

pail [pel] *s* Eimer *m*

pain [pen] *s* Schmerz *m*; **on p. of death** bei Todesstrafe; **take pains sich bemühen** ‖ *tr & intr* schmerzen ‖ *impers*—**it pains me to** (*inf*) es fällt mir schwer zu (*inf*)

painful ['penfəl] *adj* schmerzhaft; (fig) peinlich

pain' in the neck' *s* (coll) Nervensäge *f*

pain'kill'er *s* schmerzstillendes Mittel *n*

painless ['penlɪs] *adj* schmerzlos

pains'tak'ing *adj* (*work*) mühsam; (*person*) sorgfältig

paint [pent] *s* Farbe *f*; (*for a car*) Lack *m* ‖ *tr* (be)malen; (*e.g., a house*) (an) streichen; (*a car*) lackieren; (*with watercolors*) aquarellieren; (fig) schildern; **p. the town red** tüchtig auf die Pauke hauen ‖ *intr* malen; (*with house paint*) überstreichen

paint'box' *s* Malkasten *m*

paint'brush' *s* Pinsel *m*

paint' can' *s* Farbendose *f*

painter ['pentər] *s* Maler –in *mf*; (*of houses, etc.*) Anstreicher –in *mf*

paint'ing *s* Malerei *f*; (*picture*) Gemälde *n*

paint' remov'er *s* Farbenabbeizmittel *n*

paint' spray'er *s* Farbspritzpistole *f*

pair [per] *s* Paar *n*; **a p. of glasses** e–e Brille *f*; **a p. of gloves** ein Paar *n* Handschule; **a p. of pants** e–e Hose *f*; **a p. of scissors** e–e Schere *f*; **a p. of twins** ein Zwillingspaar *n*; **in pairs** paarweise ‖ *tr* paaren; **p. off** paarweise ordnen; (coll) verheiraten ‖ *intr*—**p. off** sich paarweise absondern

pajamas [pə'dʒaməz] *s* Pyjama *m*

Pakistan ['pækɪ‚stæn] *s* Pakistan *n*

Pakista·ni [‚pækɪ'stæni] *adj* pakistanisch ‖ *s* (–nis) Pakistaner –in *mf*

pal [pæl] *s* Kamerad *m* ‖ *v* (*pret & pp* **palled**; *ger* **palling**) *intr*—**pal around with** dick befreundet sein mit

palace ['pælɪs] *s* Palast *m*

palatable ['pælətəbəl] *adj* (& fig) mundgerecht

palatal ['pælətəl] *adj* Gaumen– ‖ *s* (phonet) Gaumenlaut *m*

palate ['pælɪt] *s* Gaumen *m*

palatial [pə'leʃəl] *adj* palastartig

Palatinate [pə'lætɪ‚net] *s* Rheinpfalz *f*

pale [pel] *adj* (*face, colors, recollection*) blaß; **turn pale** erblassen, erbleichen ‖ *s* Pfahl *m* ‖ *intr* erblassen; **pale beside** (fig) verblassen neben (*dat*)

pale'face' *s* Bleichgesicht *n*

Palestine ['pælɪs‚taɪn] *s* Palästina *n*

palette ['pælɪt] *s* Palette *f*

palisade [‚pælɪ'sed] *s* Palisade *f*; (*line of cliffs*) Flußklippen *pl*

pall [pɔl] *s* Bahrtuch *n*; (*of smoke, gloom*) Hülle *f* ‖ *intr* (**on**) zuviel werden (*dat*)

pall'bear'er *s* Sargträger *m*

pallet ['pælɪt] *s* Lager *n*

palliate ['pælɪ‚et] *tr* lindern; (fig) bemänteln

pallid ['pælɪd] *adj* blaß, bleich

pallor ['pælər] *s* Blässe *f*

palm [pɑm] *s* (*of the hand*) Handfläche *f*; (*tree*) Palme *f*; **grease s.o.'s palm** j-n schmieren; **palm of victory** Siegespalme *f* ‖ *tr* (*a card*) in der Hand verbergen; **palm s.th. off on s.o.** j-m etw andrehen

palmette [pæl'met] *s* Palmette *f*

palmet·to [pæl'meto] *s* (-tos & -toes) Fächerpalme *f*

palmist ['pɑmɪst] *s* Wahrsager –in *mf*

palmistry ['pɑmɪstrɪ] *s* Handlesekunst *f*

palm' leaf' *s* Palmblatt *n*

Palm' Sun'day *s* Palmsonntag *m*

palm' tree' *s* Palme *f*

palpable ['pælpəbəl] *adj* greifbar

palpitate ['pælpɪ͵tet] *intr* klopfen

palsied ['pɔlzid] *adj* lahm, gelähmt

palsy ['pɔlzi] *s* Lähmung *f*

paltry ['pɔltri] *adj* armselig

pamper ['pæmpər] *tr* verwöhnen

pamphlet ['pæmflɪt] *s* Flugschrift *f*

pan [pæn] *s* Pfanne *f*; (sl) Visage *f* ‖ *tr* (*gold*) waschen; (*a camera*) schwenken; (*criticize sharply*) (coll) verreißen ‖ *intr* (cin) panoramieren; **pan out** glücken, klappen

panacea [͵pænə'si·ə] *s* Allheilmittel *n*

Panama ['pænəmɑ] *s* Panama *n*

Pan'ama Canal' *s* Panamakanal *m*

Pan-American [͵pænə'merɪkən] *adj* panamerikanisch

pan'cake' *s* (flacher) Pfannkuchen *m* ‖ *intr* (aer) absacken, bumslanden

pan'cake land'ing *s* Bumslandung *f*

panchromatic [͵pænkro'mætɪk] *adj* panchromatisch

pancreas ['pænkrɪ·əs] *s* Bauchspeicheldrüse *f*

pandemic [pæn'demɪk] *adj* pandemisch

pandemonium [͵pændə'moni·əm] *s* Höllenlärm *m*

pander ['pændər] *s* Kuppler *m* ‖ *intr* kuppeln; **p. to** Vorschub leisten (*dat*)

pane [pen] *s* Scheibe *f*

panegyric [͵pænɪ'dʒɪrɪk] *s* Lobrede *f*

pan·el ['pænəl] *s* Tafel *f*, Feld *n*; (*in a door*) Füllung *f*; (*for instruments*) Schlattafel *f*; (*of experts*) Diskussionsgruppe *f*; (archit) Paneel *n*; (jur) Geschworenenliste *f* ‖ *v* (*pret & pp* -el[l]ed; *ger* -el[l]ing) *tr* täfeln

pan'el discus'sion *s* Podiumsdiskussion *f*

pan'eling *s* Täfelung *f*

panelist ['pænəlɪst] *s* Diskussionsteilnehmer –in *mf*

pang [pæŋ] *s* stechender Schmerz *m*; (fig) Angst *f*; **pangs of conscience** Gewissensbisse *pl*; **pangs of hunger** nagender Hunger *m*

pan'han'dle *s* Pfannenstiel *m*; (geog) Landzunge *f* ‖ *intr* (sl) betteln

pan'han'dler *s* (sl) Bettler –in *mf*

pan·ic ['pænɪk] *s* Panik *f* ‖ *v* (*pret & pp* -icked; *ger* -icking) *tr* in Panik versetzen ‖ *intr* von panischer Angst erfüllt werden

pan'ic-strick'en *adj* von panischem Schrecken erfaßt

panicky ['pænɪki] *adj* übernervös

panoply ['pænəpli] *s* Pracht *f*; (*full suit of armor*) vollständige Rüstung *f*

panorama [͵pænə'ræmə] *s* Panorama *n*

pansy ['pænzi] *s* Stiefmütterchen *n*

pant [pænt] *s* Keuchen *n*; **pants** Hose *f*, Hosen *pl* ‖ *intr* keuchen; **p. for** or **after** gieren nach

pantheism ['pænθɪ͵ɪzəm] *s* Pantheismus *m*

pantheon ['pænθɪ͵ɑn] *s* Pantheon *n*

panther ['pænθər] *s* Panther *m*

panties ['pæntiz] *spl* Schlüpfer *m*

pantomime ['pæntə͵maɪm] *s* Pantomime *f*

pantry ['pæntri] *s* Speisekammer *f*

pap [pæp] *s* Brei *m*, Kleister *m*

papa ['pɑpə] *s* Papa *m*, Vati *m*

papacy ['pepəsi] *s* Papsttum *n*

papal ['pepəl] *adj* päpstlich

Pa'pal State' *s* Kirchenstaat *m*

paper ['pepər] *adj* (*money, plate, towel*) Papier– ‖ *s* Papier *n*; (*before a learned society*) Referat *n*; (*newspaper*) Zeitung *f*; **papers** (*documents*) Papiere *pl* ‖ *tr* tapezieren

pa'perback' *s* Taschenbuch *n*, Pappband *m*

pa'per bag' *s* Papiertüte *f*, Tüte *f*

pa'perboy' *s* Zeitungsjunge *m*

pa'per clip' *s* Büroklammer *f*

pa'per cone' *s* Tüte *f*

pa'per cup' *s* Papierbecher *m*

pa'per cut'ter *s* Papierschneidemaschine *f*

pa'perhang'er *s* Tapezierer –in *mf*

pa'perhang'ing *s* Tapezierarbeit *f*

pa'per mill' *s* Papierfabrik *f*

pa'per nap'kin *s* Papierserviette *f*

pa'perweight' *s* Briefbeschwerer *m*

pa'perwork' *s* Schreibarbeit *f*

papier-mâché [͵pepərmɑ'ʃe] *s* Papier-maché *n*, Pappmaché *n*

paprika [pæ'prikə] *s* Paprika *m*

papy·rus [pə'paɪrəs] *s* (-ri [raɪ]) Papyrus *m*

par [pɑr] *s* (fin) Pari *n*; (golf) festgesetzte Schlagzahl *f*; **at par** pari, auf Pari; **on a par with** auf gleicher Stufe mit; **up to par** (coll) auf der Höhe

parable ['pærəbəl] *s* Gleichnis *n*

parabola [pə'ræbələ] *s* Parabel *f*

parachute ['pærə͵ʃut] *s* Fallschirm *m* ‖ *tr* mit dem Fallschirm abwerfen ‖ *intr* abspringen

par'achute jump' *s* Fallschirmabsprung *m*

parachutist ['pærə͵ʃutɪst] *s* Fallschirmspringer –in *mf*

parade [pə'red] *s* Parade *f* ‖ *tr* zur Schau stellen ‖ *intr* paradieren; (mil) aufmarschieren

paradigm ['pærədɪm], ['pærə͵daɪm] *s* Musterbeispiel *n*, Paradigma *n*

paradise ['pærə͵daɪs] *s* Paradies *n*

paradox ['pærə͵dɑks] *s* Paradox *n*

paradoxical [͵pærə'dɑksɪkəl] *adj* paradox

paraffin ['pærəfɪn] *s* Paraffin *n*

paragon ['pærə͵gɑn] *s* Musterbild *n*

paragraph ['pærə͵græf] *s* Absatz *m*, Paragraph *m*

parakeet ['pærə͵kit] *s* Sittich *m*

paral·lel ['pærə͵lel] *adj* parallel; **be** (or **run**) **p. to** parallel verlaufen zu ‖ *s* Parallele *f*; (*of latitude*) Breitenkreis *m;* (fig) Gegenstück *n;* **without p.** ohnegleichen ‖ *v (pret & pp* **-lel[l]ed;** *ger* **-lel[l]ing)** *tr* parallel verlaufen zu; *(match)* gleichkommen *(dat);* *(correspond to)* entsprechen *(dat)*

par′allel bars′ *spl* Barren *m*

paraly·sis [pə′rælɪsɪs] *s* (**-ses** [ˌsiz]) Lähmung *f,* Paralyse *f*

paralytic [ˌpærə′lɪtɪk] *adj* paralytisch ‖ *s* Paralytiker **-in** *mf*

paralyze [′pærəˌlaɪz] *tr* lähmen, paralysieren; *(traffic)* lahmlegen

parameter [pə′ræmɪtər] *s* Parameter *m*

paramilitary [ˌpærə′mɪlɪˌteri] *adj* halbmilitärisch

paramount [′pærəˌmaunt] *adj* oberste; **be p. an erster Stelle stehen; of p. importance** von äußerster Wichtigkeit

paranoia [ˌpærə′nɔɪ·ə] *s* Paranoia *f*

paranoiac [ˌpærə′nɔɪ·æk] *adj* paranoisch ‖ *s* Paranoiker **-in** *mf*

paranoid [′pærəˌnɔɪd] *adj* paranoid

parapet [′pærəˌpet] *s (of a wall)* Brustwehr *f; (of a balcony)* Geländer *n*

paraphernalia [ˌpærəfər′nelɪ·ə] *s* Zubehör *n,* Ausrüstung *f*

paraphrase [′pærəˌfrez] *s* Umschreibung *f* ‖ *tr* umschreiben

parasite [′pærəˌsaɪt] *s (& fig)* Parasit *m*

parasitic(al) [ˌpærə′sɪtɪk(əl)] *adj* parasitisch

parasol [′pærəˌsɔl] *s* Sonnenschirm *m*

paratrooper [′pærəˌtrupər] *s* Fallschirmjäger *m*

par·cel [′parsəl] *s* Paket *n;* (com) Posten *m* ‖ *v (pret & pp* **-cel[l]ed;** *ger* **-cel[l]ing)** *tr*—**p. out** aufteilen

par′cel post′ *s* Paketpost *f*

parch [partʃ] *tr* ausdörren; **my throat is parched** mir klebt die Zunge am Gaumen

parchment [′partʃmənt] *s* Pergament *n*

pardon [′pardən] *s* Verzeihung *f;* (jur) Begnadigung *f;* **I beg your p.** ich bitte um Entschuldigung; **p.?** wie, bitte? ‖ *tr (a person)* verzeihen *(dat); (an act)* verzeihen; *(officially)* begnadigen

pardonable [′pardənəbəl] *adj* verzeihlich

pare [per] *tr (nails)* schneiden; *(e.g., potatoes)* (ab)schälen; *(costs)* beschneiden

parent [′perənt] *s* Elternteil *m;* **parents** Eltern *pl*

parentage [′perəntɪdʒ] *s* Abstammung *f*

parental [pə′rentəl] *adj* elterlich

parenthe·sis [pə′renθɪsɪs] *s* (**-ses** [ˌsiz]) Klammer *f; (expression in parentheses)* Parenthese *f*

parenthetic(al) [ˌperən′θetɪk(əl)] *adj* parenthetisch

parenthood [′perəntˌhud] *s* Elternschaft *f*

pariah [pə′raɪ·ə] *s* Paria *m*

par′ing knife′ *s* Schälmesser *n*

Paris [′pærɪs] *s* Paris *n*

parish [′pærɪʃ] *adv* Pfarr- ‖ *s* Pfarrgemeinde *f*

parishioner [pə′rɪʃənər] *s* Gemeindemitglied *n,* Pfarrkind *n*

Parisian [pə′rɪʒən] *adj* Pariser ‖ *s* Pariser **-in** *mf*

parity [′pærɪti] *s* Parität *f*

park [park] *s* Park *m* ‖ *tr* abstellen, parken ‖ *intr* parken

park′ing *s* Parken *n;* **no p.** (public sign) Parken verboten

park′ing light′ *s* Parklicht *n*

park′ing lot′ *s* Parkplatz *m*

park′ing lot′ atten′dant′ *s* Parkplatzwärter **-in** *mf*

park′ing me′ter *s* Parkuhr *f*

park′ing place′, park′ing space *s* Parkplatz *m,* Parkstelle *f*

park′ing tick′et *s* gebührenpflichtige Verwarnung *f* (wegen falschen Parkens)

park′way′ *s* Aussichtsautobahn *f*

parley [′parli] *s* Unterhandlung *f* ‖ *intr* unterhandeln

parliament [′parləmənt] *s* Parlament *n*

parliamentary [ˌparlə′mentəri] *adj* parlamentarisch

parlor [′parlər] *s* Salon *m; (living room)* Wohnzimmer *n*

par′lor game′ *s* Gesellschaftsspiel *n*

parochial [pə′roki·əl] *adj* Pfarr-; (fig) beschränkt

paro′chial school′ *s* Pfarrschule *f*

paro·dy [′pærədi] *s* Parodie *f* ‖ *v (pret & pp* **-died)** *tr* parodieren

parole [pə′rol] *s* bedingte Strafaussetzung *f;* **be out on p.** bedingt entlassen sein ‖ *tr* bedingt entlassen

par·quet [par′ke], [par′ket] *v (pret & pp* **-queted** [′ked]; *ger* **-queting** [′ke·ɪŋ])** *tr* parkettieren

parquetry [′parkɪtri] *s* Parkettfußboden *m*

parrot [′pærət] *s* Papagei *m* ‖ *tr* nachplappern

par·ry [′pæri] *s* Parade *f* ‖ *v (pret & pp* **-ried)** *tr* parieren

parse [pars] *tr* zergliedern

parsimonious [ˌparsɪ′monɪ·əs] *adj* sparsam

parsley [′parsli] *s* Petersilie *f*

parsnip [′parsnɪp] *s* Pastinak *m*

parson [′parsən] *s* Pfarrer *m*

parsonage [′parsənɪdʒ] *s* Pfarrhaus *n*

part [part] *adv*—**p.** ... **p.** zum Teil ... zum Teil ‖ *s* Teil *m & n; (section)* Abschnitt *m; (spare part)* Ersatzteil *m; (of a machine, etc.)* Bestandteil *m; (share)* Anteil *m; (of the hair)* Scheitel *m;* (mus) Partie *f;* (theat) Rolle *f;* **do one's p.** das Seinige tun; **for his p.** seinerseits; **for the most p.** größtenteils; **have a p. in** Anteil haben an *(dat);* **in p.** zum Teil, teilweise; **make a p.** *(in the hair)* e-n Scheitel ziehen; **on his p.** seinerseits; **p. and parcel** ein wesentlicher Bestandteil *m;* **take p. (in)** teilnehmen *(an dat);* **take s.o.'s p.** j-s Partei ergreifen ‖ *tr* (ab)scheiden; *(the hair)* scheiteln; **p. company** von einander scheiden || *intr* sich trennen; **p. with** hergeben

par·take [pɑr'tek] *v* (*pret* **–took**; *pp* **taken**) *intr*—**p. in** teilnehmen an (*dat*); **p. of** zu sich nehmen

partial ['pɑrʃəl] *adj* Teil-, partiell; (*prejudiced*) parteiisch; **be p. to** bevorzugen

partiality [‚pɑrʃɪ'ælɪti] *s* Parteilichkeit *f*, Befangenheit *f*

partially ['pɑrʃəli] *adv* teilweise

participant [pɑr'tɪsɪpənt] *s* Teilnehmer –in *mf*

participate [pɑr'tɪsɪ‚pet] *intr* (**in**) teilnehmen (an *dat*)

participation [pɑɪ‚tɪsɪ'peʃən] *s* (**in**) Teilnahme *f* (*an dat*)

participle ['pɑrtɪ‚sɪpəl] *s* Mittelwort *n*, Partizip *n*

particle ['pɑrtɪkəl] *s* Teilchen *n*; (gram, phys) Partikel *f*

particular [pɑr'tɪkjələr] *adj* (*specific*) bestimmt; (*individual*) einzeln; (*meticulous*) peinlich genau; (*especial*) peinlich genau; (*choosy*) heikel || *s* Einzelheit *f*; **in p.** insbesondere

partisan ['pɑrtɪzən] *adj* parteiisch || *s* (mil) Partisan –in *mf*; (pol) Parteigänger –in *mf*

partition [pɑr'tɪʃən] *s* Teilung *f*; (*wall*) Scheidewand *f* || *tr* (auf)teilen; **p. off** abteilen

partly ['pɑrtli] *adv* teils, teilweise

partner ['pɑrtnər] *s* Partner –in *mf*

part′nership′ *s* Partnerschaft *f*

part′ of speech′ *s* Wortart *f*

partridge ['pɑrtrɪdʒ] *s* Rebhuhn *n*

part′-time′ *adj* & *adv* nicht vollzeitlich

part′-time work′ *s* Teilzeitarbeit *f*

party ['pɑrti] *s* Gesellschaft *f*, Party *f*; (jur) Partei *f*; (mil) Kommando *n*; (pol) Partei *f*; (telp) Teilnehmer –in *mf*; **be a p. to** sich hergeben zu

par′ty affilia′tion *s* Parteizugehörigkeit *f*

par′ty line′ *s* (pol) Parteilinie *f*; (telp) Gemeinschaftsanschluß *m*

par′ty mem′ber *s* Parteigenosse *m*, Parteigenossin *f*

par′ty pol′itics *s* Parteipolitik *f*

paschal ['pæskəl] *adj* Oster-

pass [pæs] *s* (*over a mountain*; *permit*) Paß *m*; (*erotic advance*) Annäherungsversuch *m*; (fencing) Stoß *m*; (fb) Paßball *m*; (mil) Urlaubsschein *m*; (theat) Freikarte *f*; **make a p. at** (*flirt with*) e-n Annäherungsversuch machen bei; (aer) vorbeifliegen an (*dat*) || *tr* (*go by*) vorbeigehen an (*dat*), passieren; (*a test*) bestehen; (*a student in a test*) durchlassen; (*a bill*) verabschieden; (*hand over*) reichen; (*judgment*) abgeben; (*sentence*) sprechen; (*time*) verbringen; (*counterfeit money*) in Umlauf bringen; (*a car*) überholen; (*e.g., a kidney stone*) ausscheiden; (*a ball*) weitergeben; (*to*) zuspielen (*dat*); **p. around** herumgehen lassen; **p. away** (*time*) vertreiben; **p. in** einhändigen; **p. off** as ausgeben als; **p. on** weiterleiten; (*e.g., news*) weitersagen; **p.**

out ausgeben; **p. over in silence** unerwähnt lassen; **p. up** verzichten auf (*acc*) || *intr* (by) vorbeikommen (an *dat*), vorbeigehen (an *dat*); (*in a car*) (by) vorbeifahren (an *dat*); (*in a test*) durchkommen; (*e.g., from father to son*) übergehen; (cards) passen; (parl) zustandekommen; **bring to p.** herbeiführen; **come to p.** geschehen; **p.¹** (cards) passe!; **p. away** verscheiden; **p. for** gelten als; **p. on** abscheiden; **p. out** ohnmächtig werden; **p. over** (*disregard*) hinweggehen über (*acc*); **p. through** durchgehen (*durch*); (*said of an army*) durchziehen (*durch*); (*said of a train*) berühren

passable ['pæsəbəl] *adj* (*road*) gangbar; (*by car*) befahrbar; (*halfway good*) leidlich, passabel

passage ['pæsɪdʒ] *s* Korridor *m*, Gang *m*; (*crossing*) Überfahrt *f*; (*in a book*) Stelle *f*; (*of a law*) Annahme *f*; (*of time*) Ablauf *m*; **book p. for** e-e Schiffskarte bestellen nach

pas′sageway′ *s* Durchgang *m*, Passage *f*

pass′book′ *s* Sparbuch *n*

passenger ['pæsəndʒər] *s* Passagier –in *mf*; (*in public transportation*) Fahrgast *m*; (*in a car*) Insasse *m*, Insassin *f*

pas′senger car′ *s* Personenkraftwagen *m*

pas′senger plane′ *s* Passagierflugzeug *n*

pas′senger train′ *s* Personenzug *m*

passer-by ['pæsər‚baɪ] *s* (**passers-by**) Passant –in *mf*

pass′ing *adj* vorübergehend; **a p. grade** die Note „befriedigend" || *s* (*act of passing*) Vorbeigehen *n*; (*of a law*) Verabschiedung *f*; (*of time*) Verstreichen *n*; (*dying*) Hinscheiden *n*; **in p.** im Vorbeigehen; (*as understatement*) beiläufig; **no p.** (public sign) Überholen verboten

passion ['pæʃən] *s* Leidenschaft *f*; (*of Christ*) Passion *f*; **fly into a p. in** Zorn geraten; **have a p. for** e-e Vorliebe haben für

passionate ['pæʃənɪt] *adj* leidenschaftlich

pas′sion play′ *s* Passionsspiel *n*

passive ['pæsɪv] *adj* (& gram) passiv || *s* Passiv(um) *n*

pass′key′ *s* (*master key*) Hauptschlüssel *m*; (*skeleton key*) Nachschlüssel *m*

Pass′o′ver *s* Passah *n*

pass′port′ *s* Paß *m*, Reisepaß *m*

pass′port of′fice *s* Paßamt *n*

pass′word′ *s* (mil) Kennwort *n*

past [pæst] *adj* (*e.g., week*) vergangen; (*e.g., president*) ehemalig, früher; (*gone*) vorbei; **for some time p.** seit einiger Zeit || *s* Vergangenheit *f* || *prep* (*e.g., one o'clock*) nach; (*beyond*) über (*acc*) hinaus; **get p.** (*an opponent*) (sport) umspielen; **go p.** vorbeigehen an (*dat*); **it's way p. bedtime** es ist schon längst Zeit zum Schlafengehen

paste [pest] *s* (*glue*) Kleister *m*; (culin) Brei *m*, Paste *f* || *tr* (*e.g., a wall*) (**with**) bekleben (mit); **p. on** aufkleben auf (acc); **p. together** zusammen-kleben

paste′board′ s Pappe f

pastel [pæs′tɛl] adj pastellfarben || s Pastell n

pastel′ col′or s Pastellfarbe f

pasteurize [′pæstə‚raɪz] tr pasteurisieren

pastime [′pæs‚taɪm] s Zeitvertreib m

past′ mas′ter s Experte m

pastor [′pæstər] s Pastor m

pastoral [′pæstərəl] adj Schäfer-, Hirten-; (eccl) Hirten-, pastoral || s Schäfergedicht n

pas′toral let′ter s Hirtenbrief m

pastorate [′pæstərɪt] s Pastorat n

pastry [′pestri] s Gebäck n; **pastries** Backwaren pl

pas′try shop′ s Konditorei f

past′ tense′ s Vergangenheit f

pasture [′pæst/ər] s Weide f || tr & intr weiden

pas′ture land′ s Weideland n

pasty [′pesti] adj (sticky) klebrig; (complexion) bläßlich

pat [pæt] adj (answer) treffend; **have s.th. down pat** etw in- und auswendig wissen || adv—**stand pat** bei der Stange bleiben || s Klaps m; (of butter) Klümpchen n || tr tätscheln; **pat s.o. on the back** j-m auf die Schulter klopfen; (fig) j-n beglückwünschen

patch [pæt∫] s (of clothing, land, color) Fleck m; (garden bed) Beet n; (for clothing, inner tube) Flicken m; (over the eye) Binde f; (for a wound) Pflaster n || tr flicken; **p. together** (& fig) zusammenflicken; **p. up** (a friendship) kitten; (differences) beilegen

patch′work′ s Flickwerk n; (fig) Stückwerk n

patch′work quilt′ s Flickendecke f

pate [pet] s (coll) Schädel m

patent [′pɛtənt] adj öffentlich || [′pætənt] adj Patent-, e.g., **p. lawyer** Patentanwalt m || s Patent n; **p. pending** Patent angemeldet || tr patentieren

pa′tent leath′er [′pætənt] s Lackleder n

pa′tent-leath′er shoe′ s Lackschuh m

pat′ent med′icine [′pætənt] s rezeptfreies Medikament n

pat′ent rights′ [′pætənt] spl Schutzrechte pl

paternal [pə′tʌrnəl] adj väterlich

paternity [pə′tʌrnɪti] s Vaterschaft f

path [pæθ] s Pfad m; (astr) Lauf m; **clear a p.** m n Weg bahnen; **cross s.o.'s p.** j-s Weg kreuzen

pathetic [pə′θɛtɪk] adj (moving) rührend; (evoking contemptuous pity) kläglich

path′find′er s Pfadfinder m; (aer) Beleuchter m

pathologist [pə′θɑlədʒɪst] s Pathologe m, Pathologin f

pathology [pə′θɑlədʒi] s Pathologie f

pathos [′peθɑs] s Pathos n

path′way′ s Weg m, Pfad m

patience [′pe∫əns] s Geduld f

patient [′pe∫ənt] adj geduldig || s Patient –in mf

pati·o [′pæti·o] s (–os) Terasse f

patriarch [′petri‚ɑrk] s Patriarch m

patrician [pə′trɪ∫ən] adj patrizisch || s Patrizier –in mf

patricide [′pætri‚saɪd] s (act) Vatermord m; (person) Vatermörder –in mf

patrimony [′pætri‚moni] s väterliches Erbe n

patriot [′petri·ət] s Patriot –in mf

patriotic [‚petri′ɑtɪk] adj patriotisch

patriotism [′petri·ə‚tɪzəm] s Patriotismus m

pa·trol [pə′trol] s Patrouille f, Streife f || v (pret & pp –trolled; ger –trolling) tr & intr patrouillieren

patrol′ car′ s Streifenwagen m

patrol′man s (–men) Polizeistreife f

patrol′ wag′on s Gefangenenwagen m

patron [′petrən] s Schutzherr m; (com) Kunde m, Kundin f; (eccl) Schutzpatron m

patronage [′petrənɪdʒ] s Patronat n

patroness [′petrənɪs] s Schutzherrin f; (eccl) Schutzpatronin f

patronize [′petrə‚naɪz] tr beschützen, protegieren; (com) als Kunde besuchen; (theat) regelmäßig besuchen

pa′tronizing adj gönnerhaft

pa′tron saint′ s Schutzheilige mf

patter [′pætər] s (of rain) Prasseln n; (of feet) Getrappel n || intr (said of rain) prasseln; (said of feet) trappeln

pattern [′pætərn] s Muster n; (sew) Schnittmuster n

patty [′pæti] s Pastetchen n

paucity [′pɔsɪti] s Knappheit f

paunch [pɔnt∫] s Wanst m

paunchy [′pɔn∫i] adj dickbäuchig

pauper [′pɔpər] s Arme mf; (person on welfare) Unterstützte mf

pause [pɔz] s Pause f; (mus) Fermate f || intr pausieren

pave [pev] tr pflastern; **p. the way for** (fig) anbahnen

pavement [′pevmənt] s Pflaster n; (sidewalk) Bürgersteig m, Trottoir n

pavilion [pə′vɪljən] s Pavillon m

pav′ing s Pflasterung f

pav′ing stone′ s Pflasterstein m

paw [pɔ] s Pfote f || tr (scratch) kratzen; (coll) befummeln; **paw the ground** auf den Boden scharren || intr (said of a horse) mit dem Huf scharren

pawl [pɔl] s Sperrklinke f

pawn [pɔn] s Pfand n; (fig) Schachfigur f; (chess) Bauer m || tr verpfänden

pawn′brok′er s Pfandleiher –in mf

pawn′shop′ s Pfandhaus n

pawn′ tick′et s Pfandschein m

pay [pe] s Lohn m; (mil) Sold m || v (pret & pp paid [ped]) tr bezahlen; (a visit) abstatten; (a dividend) ausschütten; (a compliment) machen; **pay back** zurückzahlen; **pay damages** Schadenersatz leisten; **pay down** anzahlen; **pay extra** nachzahlen; **pay in advance** vorausbezahlen; **pay in full**

begleichen; **pay interest on** verzinsen; **pay off** (*a debt*) abbezahlen; (*a person*) entlohnen; **pay one's way** ohne Verlust arbeiten; **pay out** auszahlen; **pay s.o. back for s.th.** j-m etw heimzahlen; **pay taxes on** versteuern; **pay up** (*a debt*) abbezahlen; (ins) voll einzahlen ‖ *intr* zahlen; (*be worthwhile*) sich lohnen; **pay extra** zuzahlen; **pay for** (*a purchase*) (be)zahlen für; (*suffer for*) büßen

payable ['pe·əbəl] *adj* fällig, zahlbar

pay' check' *s* Lohnscheck *m*

pay' day' *s* Zahltag *m*

pay' dirt' *s*—**hit p.** sein Glück machen

payee [pe'i] *s* (*of a draft*) Zahlungsempfänger –in *mf*; (*of a check*) Wechselnehmer –in *mf*

pay' en'velope *s* Lohntüte *f*

payer ['pe·ər] *s* Zahler –in *mf*

pay' load' *s* Nutzlast *f*; (*explosive energy*) Sprengladung *f*

pay' mas'ter *s* Zahlmeister *m*

payment ['pemənt] *s* Zahlung *f*; **in p. of** zur Bezahlung (*genit*)

pay' phone' *s* Münzfernsprecher *m*

pay' raise' *s* Gehaltserhöhung *f*

pay' rate' *s* Lohnsatz *m*

pay' roll' *s* Lohnliste *f*; (*money paid*) gesamte Lohnsumme *f*

pay' sta'tion *s* Telephonautomat *m*

pea [pi] *s* Erbse *f*

peace [pis] *s* Friede(n) *m*; (*quiet*) Ruhe *f*; **be at p. with** in Frieden leben mit; **keep the p.** die öffentliche Ruhe bewahren

peaceable ['pisəbəl] *adj* friedfertig

Peace' Corps' *s* Friedenskorps *n*

peace'-lov'ing *adj* friedliebend

peace'mak'er *s* Friedensstifter –in *mf*

peace' negotia'tions *spl* Friedensverhandlungen *pl*

peace' of mind' *s* Seelenruhe *f*

peace'pipe' *s* Friedenspfeife *f*

peace'time' *adj* Friedens– ‖ *s*—**in p.** in Friedenszeiten

peace' trea'ty *s* Friedensvertrag *m*

peach [pit/] *s* Pfirsich *m*

peach' tree' *s* Pfirsichbaum *m*

peachy ['pit/i] *adj* (coll) pfundig

pea'cock' *s* Pfau *m*

pea'hen' *s* Pfauenhenne *f*

pea' jack'et *s* (nav) Matrosenjacke *f*

peak [pik] *adj* Spitzen– ‖ *s* (& fig) Gipfel *m*; (*of a cap*) Mützenschirm *m*; (elec) Leistungsspitze *f*; (phys) Scheitelwert *m*

peak' hours' *spl* (*of traffic*) Hauptverkehrszeit *f*; (elec) Stoßzeit *f*

peak' load' *s* (elec) Spitzenlast *f*

peak' vol'tage *s* Spitzenspannung *f*

peal [pil] *s* Geläute *n* ‖ *intr* erschallen

peal' of laugh'ter *s* Lachsalve *f*

peal' of thun'der *s* Donnergetöse *n*

pea'nut' *s* Erdnuß *f*; **peanuts** (coll) kleine Fische *pl*

pea'nut but'ter *s* Erdnußbutter *f*

pear [per] *s* Birne *f*

pearl [pʌrl] *adj* Perlen– ‖ *s* Perle *f*

pearl' neck'lace *s* Perlenkette *f*

pearl' oys'ter *s* Perlenauster *f*

pear' tree' *s* Birnbaum *m*

peasant ['pɛzənt] *adj* Bauern–, bäuerlich ‖ *s* Bauer *m*, Bäuerin *f*

peasantry ['pɛzəntri] *s* Bauernstand *m*

pea'shoot'er *s* Blasrohr *n*

pea' soup' *s* Erbsensuppe *f*; (fig) Waschküche *f*

peat [pit] *s* Torf *m*

peat' moss' *s* Torfmull *m*

pebble ['pɛbəl] *s* Kiesel *m*; **pebbles** Geröll *n*

peck [pɛk] *s* (*measure*) Viertelscheffel *m*; (*e.g., of a bird*) Schnabelhieb *m*; (*kiss*) (coll) flüchtiger Kuß *m*; (*of trouble*) (coll) Menge *f* ‖ *tr* hacken; (*food*) aufpicken ‖ *intr* hacken, picken; (*eat food*) picken; **p. at** hacken nach; (*food*) (coll) herumstochern in (*dat*)

peculation [ˌpɛkjə'lɛʃən] *s* Geldunterschlagung *f*

peculiar [pɪ'kjuljər] *adj* eigenartig, absonderlich; **p. to eigen** (*dat*)

peculiarity [pɪˌkjuli'ɛriti] *s* Eigenheit *f*, Absonderlichkeit *f*

pedagogic(al) [ˌpɛdə'gadʒɪk(əl)] *adj* pädagogisch, erzieherisch

pedagogue ['pɛdəˌgag] *s* Pädagoge *m*, Erzieher *m*

pedagogy ['pɛdəˌgadʒi] *s* Pädagogik *f*, Erziehungskunde *f*

ped-al ['pɛdəl] *s* Pedal *n* ‖ *v* (*pret & pp* **-al[l]ed**; *ger* **-al[l]ing**) *tr* fahren ‖ *intr* die Pedale treten

pedant ['pɛdənt] *s* Pedant –in *mf*

pedantic [pɪ'dæntɪk] *adj* pedantisch

pedantry ['pɛdəntri] *s* Pedanterie *f*

peddle ['pɛdəl] *tr* hausieren mit ‖ *intr* hausieren

peddler ['pɛdlər] *s* Hausierer –in *mf*

pedestal ['pɛdɪstəl] *s* Sockel *m*, Postament *n*; **put s.o. on a p.** (fig) j–n aufs Podest erheben

pedestrian [pɪ'dɛstri·ən] *adj* Fußgänger–; (fig) schwunglos ‖ *s* Fußgänger –in *mf*

pediatrician [ˌpidi·ə'trɪʃən] *s* Kinderarzt *m*, Kinderärztin *f*

pediatrics [ˌpidi'ætrɪks] *s* Kinderheilkunde *f*

pediment ['pɛdɪmənt] *s* Giebelfeld *n*

peek [pik] *s* schneller Blick *m* ‖ *intr* gucken; **p. at** angucken

peekaboo ['pikəˌbu] *adj* durchsichtig ‖ *interj* guck, guck!

peel [pil] *s* Schale *f* ‖ *tr* schälen; **p. off** abschälen ‖ *intr* sich schälen; (*said of paint*) abbröckeln; **p. off** (aer) sich aus dem Verband lösen

peep [pip] *s* schneller Blick *m*; heimlicher Blick *m*; **not another p. out of you!** kein Laut mehr aus dir! ‖ *intr* gucken; (*look carefully*) lugen; **p. out** hervorlugen

peep'hole' *s* Guckloch *n*

peep' show' *s* Fleischbeschau *f*

peer [pɪr] *s* Gleichgestellte *mf* ‖ *intr* blicken; **p. at** mustern

peerless ['pɪrlɪs] *adj* unvergleichlich

peeve [piv] *s* (coll) Beschwerde *f* ‖ *tr* (coll) ärgern

peeved *adj* verärgert

peevish ['pivɪʃ] *adj* sauertöpfisch

peg [pɛg] *s* Pflock *m*; *(for clothes)* Haken *m*; *(e.g., of a violin)* Wirbel *m*; **take down a peg or two** ducken || *v* *(pret & pp* pegged; *ger* pegging) *tr* festpflocken; *(prices)* festlegen; *(throw)* (sl) schmeißen; *(identify)* (sl) erkennen

peg'board' *s* Klammerplatte *f*

Peggy ['pɛgɪ] *s* Gretchen *n*, Gretl *f & n*

peg' leg' *s* Stelzbein *n*

Pekin-ese [ˌpikɪ'niz] *s* (**-ese**) Pekinese *m*

pelf [pɛlf] *s* (pej) Mammon *m*

pelican ['pɛlɪkən] *s* Pelikan *m*

pellet ['pɛlɪt] *s* Kügelchen *n*; *(bullet)* Schrotkugel *f*, Schrotkorn *n*

pell-mell ['pɛl'mɛl] *adj* verworren || *adv* durcheinander

pelt [pɛlt] *s* Fell *n*, Pelz *m*; *(whack)* Schlag *m* || *tr (with)* bewerfen (mit); *(with questions)* bombardieren

pelvis ['pɛlvɪs] *s* Becken *n*

pen [pɛn] *s* Feder *f*; *(fountain pen)* Füllfederhalter *m*; *(enclosure)* Pferch *m*; *(prison)* (sl) Kittchen *n* || *v* *(pret & pp* penned; *ger* penning) *tr (a letter)* verfassen || *(pret & pp* penned & pent; *ger* penning) *tr*—**pen** in pferchen

penal ['pinəl] *adj* strafrechtlich, Straf-

pe'nal code' *s* Strafgesetzbuch *n*

penalize ['pinəˌlaɪz] *tr* bestrafen; *(box)* mit Strafpunkten belegen

penalty ['pɛnəltɪ] *s* Strafe *f*; *(point deducted)* (sport) Strafpunkt *m*; **under p. of death** bei Todesstrafe

pen'alty ar'ea *s* (sport) Strafraum *m*

pen'alty box' *s* Strafbank *f*

pen'alty kick' *s* Strafstoß *m*

penance ['pɛnəns] *s* Buße *f*

penchant ['pɛnʃənt] *s (for)* Hang *m* (zu)

pen·cil ['pɛnsəl] *s* Bleistift *m* || *v* *(pret & pp* -cil[l]ed; *ger* -cil[l]ing) *tr* mit Bleistift anzeichnen

pen'cil push'er *s* (coll) Schreiberling *m*

pen'cil sharp'ener *s* Bleistiftspitzer *m*

pendant ['pɛndənt] *s* Anhänger *m*; *(electrical fixture)* Hängeleuchter *m*

pendent ['pɛndənt] *adj* (herab)hängend

pend'ing *adj* schwebend; **be p.** in (der) Schwebe sein || *prep (during)* während *(genit)*; *(until)* bis zu *(dat)*

pendulum ['pɛndʒələm] *s* Pendel *n*

pen'dulum bob' *s* Pendelgewicht *n*

penetrate ['pɛnɪˌtret] *tr* eindringen in *(acc)* || *intr* eindringen

penetration [ˌpɛnɪ'treʃən] *s* Durchdringen *n*; *(of, e.g., a country)* Eindringen *n* (in *acc*); *(in ballistics)* Durchschlagskraft *f*

penguin ['pɛŋgwɪn] *s* Pinguin *m*

penicillin [ˌpɛnɪ'sɪlɪn] *s* Penizillin *n*

peninsula [pə'nɪnsələ] *s* Halbinsel *f*

pe·nis ['pinɪs] *s* (**-nes** [niz] **& -nises**) Penis *m*

penitence ['pɛnɪtəns] *s* Bußfertigkeit *f*

penitent ['pɛnɪtənt] *adj* bußfertig || *s* Büßer -in *mf*; *(eccl)* Beichtkind *n*

penitentiary [ˌpɛnɪ'tɛnʃərɪ] *s* Zuchthaus *n*

pen'knife' *s* (**-knives'**) Federmesser *n*

penmanship ['pɛnmən ˌʃɪp] *s* Schreibkunst *f*

pen' name' *s* Schriftstellername *m*

pennant ['pɛnənt] *s* Wimpel *m*; *(nav)* Stander *m*

penniless ['pɛnɪlɪs] *adj* mittellos

penny ['pɛni] *s* Pfennig *m*; *(U.S.A.)* Cent *m*

pen'ny pinch'er [ˌpɪntʃər] *s* Pfennigfuchser *m*

pen' pal' *s* Schreibfreund -in *mf*

pension ['pɛnʃən] *s* Pension *f*, Rente *f*; **put on p.** pensionieren || *tr* pensionieren

pensioner ['pɛnʃənər] *s* Pensionär -in *mf*; *(ins)* Rentenempfänger -in *mf*

pen'sion fund' *s* Pensionskasse *f*

pensive ['pɛnsɪv] *adj* sinnend

pentagon ['pɛntəˌgɑn] *s* Fünfeck *n*; **the Pentagon** das Pentagon

Pentecost ['pɛntɪˌkɔst] *s* Pfingsten *n*

penthouse ['pɛntˌhaʊs] *s* Wetterdach *n*; *(exclusive apartment)* Penthouse *n*

pent-up ['pɛnt'ʌp] *adj* verhalten

penult ['pinʌlt] *s* vorletzte Silbe *f*

penurious [pɪ'nʊrɪəs] *adj* karg

penury ['pɛnjərɪ] *s* Kargheit *f*

peony ['pi·ənɪ] *s* Pfingstrose *f*

people ['pipəl] *spl* Leute *pl*, Menschen *pl*; **his p.** die Seinen; **p. like him** seinesgleichen; **p. say** man sagt, die Leute sagen || *s* (**peoples**) Volk *n* || *tr* bevölkern

pep [pɛp] *s* (coll) Schwungkraft *f* || *v* *(pret & pp* pepped; *ger* pepping) *tr*—**pep up** aufpulvern

pepper ['pɛpər] *s (spice)* Pfeffer *m*; *(plant)* Paprika *f*; *(vegetable)* Paprikaschote *f* || *tr* pfeffern

pep'per mill' *s* Pfeffermühle *f*

pep'permint' *adj* Pfefferminz- || *s* Pfefferminze *f*

pep'per shak'er *s* Pfefferstreuer *m*

peppery ['pɛpərɪ] *adj* pfefferig

per [pʌr] *prep* pro *(acc)*; **as per** laut *(genit & dat)*

perambulator [pər'æmbjəˌletər] *s* Kinderwagen *m*

per capita [pər'kæpɪtə] pro Kopf

perceivable [pər'sivəbəl] *adj* wahrnehmbar

perceive [pər'siv] *tr* wahrnehmen

percent [pər'sɛnt] *s* Prozent *n*

percentage [pər'sɛntɪdʒ] *s* Prozentsatz *m*; **p. of** *(e.g., the profit)* Anteil *m* an *(dat)*; *(e.g., of a group)* Teil *m* *(genit)*

perceptible [pər'sɛptəbəl] *adj* wahrnehmbar

perception [pər'sɛpʃən] *s* Wahrnehmung *f*

perch [pʌrtʃ] *s* Stange *f*; *(ichth)* Barsch *m* || *tr* setzen || *intr* sitzen

percolate ['pʌrkəˌlet] *tr* durchseihen; *(coffee)* perkolieren || *intr* durchsickern

percolator ['pʌrkəˌletər] *s* Perkolator *m*

percussion [pər'kʌʃən] *s* Schlag *m*; *(med)* Perkussion *f*

percus'sion in'strument *s* Schlaginstrument *n*

per di'em allow'ance [pər 'daɪ-əm] s Tagegeld n

perdition [pər'dɪʃən] s Verdammnis f

perennial [pə'rɛnɪ-əl] adj immerwährend; (bot) ausdauernd || s ausdauernde Pflanze f

perfect ['pʌrfɪkt] adj perfekt, vollkommen; **he is a p. stranger to me** er ist mir völlig fremd || s (gram) Perfekt(um) n || [pər'fɛkt] tr vervollkommen

perfection [pər'fɛkʃən] s Vollkommenheit f; **to p.** vollkommen

perfectionist [pər'fɛkʃənɪst] s Perfektionist –in mf

perfectly ['pʌrfɪktlɪ] adv völlig, durchaus; **p. well** ganz genau

perfidious [pər'fɪdɪ-əs] adj treulos

perfidy ['pʌrfɪdɪ] s Treubruch m

perforate ['pʌrfə,ret] tr durchlöchern

per'forated line' s durchlochte Linie f

perforation [,pʌrfə'reʃən] s gelochte Linie f

perforce [pər'fors] adv notgedrungen

perform [pər'form] tr ausführen; (an operation) vornehmen; (theat) aufführen || intr (öffentlich) auftreten; (mach) funktionieren

performance [pər'forməns] s Ausführung f; (mach) Leistung f; (theat) Aufführung f

performer [pər'formər] s Künstler –in mf

perform'ing arts' spl darstellende Künste pl

perfume [pər'fjum] s Parfüm n || tr parfümieren

perfunctorily [pər'fʌŋktərɪlɪ] adv oberflächlich

perfunctory [pər'fʌŋktərɪ] adj oberflächlich

perhaps [pər'hæps] adv vielleicht

per hour' pro Stunde, in der Stunde

peril ['pɛrɪl] s Gefahr f; **at one's own p.** auf eigene Gefahr

perilous ['pɛrɪləs] adj gefährlich

perimeter [pə'rɪmɪtər] s (math) Umfang m; (mil) Rand m

period ['pɪrɪ-əd] s Periode f, Zeitabschnitt m; (menstrual period) Periode f; (educ) Stunde f; (gram) Punkt m; (sport) Viertel n; **extra p.** (sport) Verlängerung f; **for a p. of** für die Dauer von; **p.l** und damit punktum!; **p. of grace** Frist f; **p. of life** Lebensalter n; **p. of time** Zeitdauer pl

pe'riod fur'niture s Stilmöbel pl

periodic [,pɪrɪ'ɑdɪk] adj zeitweilig

periodical [,pɪrɪ'ɑdɪkəl] s Zeitschrift f

peripheral [pə'rɪfərəl] adj peripher

periphery [pə'rɪfərɪ] s Peripherie f

periscope ['pɛrɪ,skop] s Periskop n

perish ['pɛrɪʃ] intr umkommen; (said of wares) verderben

perishable ['pɛrɪʃəbəl] adj vergänglich; (food) leicht verderblich

perjure ['pʌrdʒər] tr—**p. oneself** Meineid begehen

perjury ['pʌrdʒərɪ] s Meineid m; **commit p.** e-n Meineid leisten

perk [pʌrk] tr—**p. up** (the head) aufwerfen; (the ears) spitzen || intr

(percolate) (coll) perkolieren; **p. up** lebhaft werden

permanence ['pʌrmənəns] s Dauer f

permanent ['pʌrmənənt] adj (fort)-dauernd, bleibend || s Dauerwelle f

per'manent address' s ständiger Wohnort m

per'manent job' s Dauerstellung f

per'manent wave' s Dauerwelle f

permeable ['pʌrmɪ-əbəl] adj durchlässig

permeate ['pʌrmɪ,et] tr durchdringen || intr durchsickern

permissible [pər'mɪsɪbəl] adj zulässig

permission [pər'mɪʃən] s Erlaubnis f; **with your p.** mit Verlaub

permissive [pər'mɪsɪv] adj nachsichtig

per·mit ['pʌrmɪt] s Erlaubnis f; (document) Erlaubnisschein m || [pər'mɪt] v (pret & pp —mitted; ger —mitting) tr erlauben, gestatten; **be permitted to** (inf) dürfen (inf)

permute [pər'mjut] tr umsetzen; (math) permutieren

pernicious [pər'nɪʃəs] adj (to) schädlich

perox'ide blonde' [pə'rɑksaɪd] s Wasserstoffblondine f

perpendicular [,pʌrpən'dɪkjələr] adj senkrecht || s Senkrechte f

perpetrate ['pʌrpɪ,tret] tr verüben

perpetual [pər'pɛtʃʊ-əl] adj (everlasting) ewig; (continual) unaufhörlich

perpetuate [pər'pɛtʃʊ,et] tr verewigen

perplex [pər'plɛks] tr verblüffen

perplexed' adj verblüfft

perplexity [pər'plɛksɪtɪ] s Verblüffung f

persecute ['pʌrsɪ,kjut] tr verfolgen

persecution [,pʌrsɪ'kjuʃən] s Verfolgung f

persecutor ['pʌrsɪ,kjutər] s Verfolger –in mf

perseverance [,pʌrsɪ'vɪrəns] s Ausdauer f, Beharrlichkeit f

persevere [,pʌrsɪ'vɪr] intr ausdauern; **p. in** (cling to) beharren auf (acc); (e.g., efforts, studies) fortfahren mit

Persia ['pʌrʒə] s Persien n

Persian ['pʌrʒən] adj persisch || s Perser –in mf; (language) Persisch n

Per'sian rug' s Perserteppich m

persimmon [pər'sɪmən] s Persimone f

persist [pər'sɪst] intr andauern; **p. in** verbleiben bei

persistent [pər'sɪstənt] adj andauernd

person ['pʌrsən] s Person f; **in p.** persönlich; **per p.** pro Person

personable ['pʌrsənəbəl] adj (attractive) ansehnlich; (good-natured) verträglich

personage ['pʌrsənɪdʒ] s Persönlichkeit f

personal ['pʌrsənəl] adj persönlich; (private) Privat–; **become p.** anzüglich werden

per'sonal da'ta spl Personalien pl

per'sonal hygiene' s Körperpflege f

per'sonal in'jury s Personenschaden m

personality [,pʌrsə'nælɪtɪ] s Persönlichkeit f

personally ['pʌrsənəlɪ] adv persönlich

per'sonal pro'noun s Personalpronomen n

personi•fy [pər'sɑnɪ,faɪ] v (pret & pp –fied) tr personifizieren, verkörpern

personnel [,pɑrsə'nel] s Personal n

per'son-to-per'son call' s Gespräch n mit Voranmeldung

perspective [pər'spektɪv] s Perspektive f

perspicacious [,pɑrspɪ'keʃəs] adj scharfsinnig

perspiration [,pɑrspɪ'reʃən] s Schweiß m; (perspiring) Schwitzen n

perspire [pər'spaɪr] intr schwitzen

persuade [pər'swed] tr überreden

persuasion [pər'sweʒən] s Überredung f

persuasive [pər'swesɪv] adj redegewandt

pert [pʌrt] adj keck; (sprightly) lebhaft

pertain [pər'ten] intr—p. to betreffen, sich beziehen auf (acc)

pertinacious [,pʌrtɪ'neʃəs] adj beharrlich

pertinent ['pʌrtɪnənt] adj einschlägig; be p. to sich beziehen auf (acc)

perturb [pər'tʌrb] tr beunruhigen

peruse [pə'ruz] tr sorgfältig durchlesen

pervade [pər'ved] tr durchdringen

perverse [pər'vʌrs] adj (abnormal) pervers; (obstinate) verstockt

perversion [pər'vʌrʒən] s Perversion f; (of truth) Verdrehung f

perversity [pər'vʌrsɪti] s Perversität f

pervert ['pʌrvərt] s perverser Mensch m ‖ [pər'vʌrt] tr (corrupt) verderben; (twist) verdrehen; (misapply) mißbrauchen

pesky ['peski] adj (coll) lästig

pessimism ['pesɪ,mɪzəm] s Pessimismus m

pessimist ['pesɪmɪst] s Pessimist –in mf

pessimistic [,pesɪ'mɪstɪk] adj pessimistisch

pest [pest] s (insect) Schädling m; (annoying person) Plagegeist m; (pestilence) Pest f

pest' control' s Schädlingsbekämpfung f

pester ['pestər] tr piesacken; (with questions) belästigen

pesticide ['pestɪ,saɪd] s Pestizid n

pestilence ['pestɪləns] s Pestilenz f

pestle ['pesəl] s Stößel m

pet [pet] adj Lieblings– ‖ s (animal) Haustier n; (person) Liebling m; (favorite child) Schoßkind n ‖ v (pret & pp petted); ger petting) tr streicheln ‖ intr sich abknutschen

petal ['petəl] s Blumenblatt n

Peter ['pitər] s Peter m ‖ intr—peter out im Sande verlaufen

pet' ide'a s Lieblingsgedanke m

petition [pɪ'tɪʃən] s Eingabe f; (jur) Gesuch n ‖ tr (s.o.) ersuchen

pet' name' s Kosename m

petri•fy ['petrɪ,faɪ] v (pret & pp –fied) tr (& fig) versteinern; be petrified versteinern; (fig) zu Stein werden

petroleum [pə'trolɪ-əm] s Petroleum n

pet' shop' s Tierhandlung f

petticoat ['petɪ,kot] s Unterrock m

pet'ting s Petting n

petty ['peti] adj klein, geringfügig; (narrow) engstirnig

pet'ty cash' s Handkasse f

pet'ty lar'ceny s geringer Diebstahl m

pet'ty of'ficer s (nav) Bootsmann m

petulant ['petʃələnt] adj verdrießlich

petunia [pə't(j)unɪ-ə] s Petunie f

pew [pju] s Bank f, Kirchenstuhl m

pewter ['pjutər] s Weißmetall n

Pfc. ['pi'ef'si] s (private first class) Gefreiter m

phalanx ['fælæŋks] s Phalanx f

phantasm ['fæntæzəm] s Trugbild n

phantom ['fæntəm] s Phantom n

Pharaoh ['fero] s Pharao m

Pharisee ['færɪ,si] s Pharisäer m

pharmaceutical [,fɑrmə'sutɪkəl] adj pharmazeutisch

pharmacist ['fɑrməsɪst] s Apotheker –in mf

pharmacy ['fɑrməsi] s Apotheke f; (science) Pharmazie f

pharynx ['færɪŋks] s Rachenhöhle f

phase [fez] s Phase f ‖ tr in Phasen einteilen; p. out abwickeln

pheasant ['fezənt] s Fasan m

phenobarbital [,fino'bɑrbɪ,tæl] s Phenobarbital n

phenomenal [fɪ'nɑmɪnəl] adj phänomenal

phenome•non [fɪ'nɑmɪ,nɑn] s (–na [nə]) (& fig) Phänomen n, Erscheinung f

phial ['faɪ-əl] s Phiole f

philanderer [fɪ'lændərər] s Schürzenjäger m

philanthropist [fɪ'lænθrəpɪst] s Menschenfreund –in mf, Philanthrop –in mf

philanthropy [fɪ'lænθrəpi] s Menschenliebe f, Philanthropie f

philately [fɪ'lætəli] s Briefmarkenkunde f

Philippine ['fɪlɪ,pin] adj philippinisch ‖ the Philippines spl die Philippinen

Philistine ['fɪlɪstin] adj (& fig) philisterhaft ‖ s (& fig) Philister m

philologist [fɪ'lɑlədʒɪst] s Philologe m, Philologin f

philology [fɪ'lɑlədʒi] s Philologie f

philosopher [fɪ'lɑsəfər] s Philosoph m

philosophic(al) [,fɪlə'sɑfɪk(əl)] adj philosophisch

philosophy [fɪ'lɑsəfi] s Philosophie f

phlebitis [flɪ'baɪtɪs] s Venenentzündung f

phlegm [flem] s Schleim m

phlegmatic(al) [fleg'mætɪk(əl)] adj phlegmatisch

phobia ['fobɪ-ə] s Phobie f

Phoenicia [fɪ'nɪʃə] s Phönizien n

Phoenician [fɪ'nɪʃən] adj phönizisch ‖ s Phönizier m

phoenix ['finɪks] s Phönix m

phone [fon] s (coll) Telephon n; on the p. am Apparat ‖ tr (coll) anrufen ‖ intr telephonieren

phone' call' s (coll) Anruf m

phonetic [fo'netɪk] *adj* phonetisch, Laut– || **phonetics** *s* Lautlehre *f*, Phonetik *f*

phonograph ['fonə͵græf] *s* Grammophon *n*

pho'nograph rec'ord *s* Schallplatte *f*

phonology [fə'nɑlədʒi] *s* Lautlehre *f*

phony ['foni] *adj* falsch, Schein– || *s* Schwindler –in *mf*

phosphate ['fɑsfet] *s* Phosphat *n*

phosphorescent [͵fɑsfə'resənt] *adj* phosphoreszierend

phospho·rus ['fɑsfərəs] *s* (–ri [͵raɪ]) Phosphor *m*

pho·to ['foto] *s* (–tos) (coll) Photo *n*

pho'tocop'y *s* Photokopie *f* || *v* (*pret & pp* –ied) *tr* photokopieren

pho'toengrav'ing *s* Lichtdruckverfahren *n*

pho'to fin'ish *s* Zielphotographie *f*

photogenic [͵foto'dʒenɪk] *adj* photogen

photograph ['fotə͵græf] *s* Photographie *f* || *tr & intr* photographieren

photographer [fə'tɑgrəfər] *s* Photograph –in *mf*

photography [fə'tɑgrəfi] *s* Photographie *f*

photostat ['fotə͵stæt] *s* (trademark) Photokopie *f* || *tr* photokopieren

phrase [frez] *s* Sinngruppe *f* || *tr* formulieren; (mus) phrasieren

phrenology [frə'nɑlədʒi] *s* Schädellehre *f*

physic ['fɪzɪk] *s* Abführmittel *n*; **physics** *s* Physik *f*

physical ['fɪzɪkəl] *adj* körperlich, physisch || *s* (*examination*) ärztliche Untersuchung *f*

phys'ical condi'tion *s* Gesundheitszustand *m*

phys'ical de'fect *s* körperliches Gebrechen *n*

phys'ical educa'tion *s* Leibeserziehung *f*

phys'ical ex'ercise *s* Leibesübungen *pl*; (*calisthenics*) Bewegung *f*

phys'ical hand'icap *s* Körperbehinderung *f*

physician [fɪ'zɪ/ən] *s* Arzt *m*, Ärztin *f*

physicist ['fɪzɪsɪst] *s* Physiker –in *mf*

physics ['fɪzɪks] *s* Physik *f*

physiognomy [͵fɪzɪ'ɑgnəmi] *s* Gesichtsbildung *f*, Physiognomie *f*

physiological [͵fɪzɪ·ə'lɑdʒɪkəl] *adj* physiologisch

physiology [͵fɪzɪ'ɑlədʒi] *s* Physiologie *f*

physique [fɪ'zik] *s* Körperbau *m*

pi [paɪ] *s* (math) Pi *n* || *tr* (typ) zusammenwerfen

pianist ['pi·ənɪst] *s* Pianist –in *mf*

pian·o [pɪ'æno] *s* (–os) Klavier *n*

pian'o stool' *s* Klavierschemel *m*

picayune [͵pɪkə'jun] *adj* (*paltry*) geringfügig; (*person*) kleinlich

picco·lo ['pɪkəlo] *s* (–los) Pikkoloflöte *f*

pick [pɪk] *s* (*tool*) Spitzhacke *f*; (*choice*) Auslese *f*; **the p. of the crop** das Beste von allem || *tr* (*choose*) sich [*dat*] aussuchen; (*e.g., fruit*)

pflücken; (*one's teeth*) stochern in (*dat*); (*one's nose*) bohren in (*dat*); (*a lock*) mit e–m Dietrich öffnen; (*a quarrel*) suchen; (*a bone*) abnagen; **p. off** abpflücken; (*shoot*) (coll) abknallen; **p. out** auswählen; **p. s.o.'s brains** j–s Ideen klauen; **p. s.o.'s pocket** j–m die Tasche ausräumen; **p. up** (*lift up*) aufheben; (*a girl*) (coll) aufgabeln; (*a suspect*) aufgreifen; (*with a car*) abholen; (*passengers; the scent*) aufnehmen; (*a language; news*) aufschnappen; (*a habit*) annehmen; (*a visual object*) erkennen; (*strength*) wieder erlangen; (*weight*) zunehmen an (*dat*); **p. up speed** in Fahrt kommen || *intr*—**p. and choose** wählerisch suchen; **p. at** herumstochern in (*dat*); **p. on** herumreiten auf (*dat*); **p. up** (*improve in health or business*) sich (wieder) erholen

pick'ax' *s* Picke *f*, Pickel *m*

picket ['pɪkɪt] *s* Holzpfahl *m*; (*of strikers*) Streikposten *m* || *tr* durch Streikposten absperren, Streikposten stehen vor (*dat*) || *intr* Streikposten stehen

pick'et fence' *s* Lattenzaun *m*

pick'et line' *s* Streikkette *f*

pickle ['pɪkəl] *s* Essiggurke *f*; **be in a p.** (coll) im Schlamassel sitzen || *tr* (ein)pökeln

pick'led *adj* (sl) blau

pick'led her'ring *s* Rollmops *m*

pick'pock'et *s* Taschendieb *m*

pick'up' *s* (*of a car*) Beschleunigungsvermögen *n*; (*girl*) Straßenbekanntschaft *f*; (*restorative*) Stärkungsmittel *n*, Erfrischung *f*; (*a stop to pick up*) Abholung *f*; (*of a phonograph*) Schalldose *f*

pick'up truck' *s* offener Lieferwagen *m*

picky ['pɪki] *adj* wählerisch

pic·nic ['pɪknɪk] *s* Picknick *n* || *v* (*pret & pp* –nicked; *ger* –nicking) *intr* picknicken

pictorial [pɪk'torɪ·əl] *adj* illustriert || *s* Illustrierte *f*

picture ['pɪktʃər] *s* Bild *n*; (fig) Vorstellung *f*; **look the p. of health** kerngesund aussehen || *tr* sich [*dat*] vorstellen

pic'ture gal'lery *s* Gemäldegalerie *f*

pic'ture post'card *s* Ansichtspostkarte *f*

picturesque [͵pɪktʃə'resk] *adj* malerisch, pittoresk; (*language*) bilderreich

pic'ture tube' *s* Bildröhre *f*

pic'ture win'dow *s* Panoramafenster *n*

piddling ['pɪdlɪŋ] *adj* lumpig

pie [paɪ] *s* Torte *f*; (*meat-filled*) Pastete *f*; **pie in the sky** Luftschloß *n*

piece [pis] *s* Stück *n*; (checkers) Stein *m*; (chess) Figur *f*; (mil) Geschütz *n*; (mus; theat) Stück *n*; **a p. of advice** ein Rat *m*; **a p. of bad luck** ein unglückliche Zufall *m*; **a p. of furniture** ein Möbelstück *n*; **a p. of luggage** ein Gepäckstück *n*; **a p. of**

news e–e Neuigkeit *f;* **a p. of paper** ein Blatt Papier; **a p. of toast** e–e geröstete Brotscheibe *f;* **say one's p.** seine Meinung sagen
piece'meal' *adv* stückweise
piece'work' *s* Akkordarbeit *f;* **do p. in Akkord arbeiten**
piece'work'er *s* Akkordarbeiter –*in mf*
pier [pɪr] *s* Landungsbrücke *f,* Pier *m & f;* (*of a bridge*) Pfeiler *m*
pierce [pɪrs] *tr* durchstechen, durchbohren
pierc'ing *adj* (*look, pain*) scharf, stechend; (*cry*) gellend; (*cold*) schneidend
piety ['paɪ-əti] *s* Frömmigkeit *f*
pig [pɪg] *s* Schwein *n*
pigeon ['pɪdʒən] *s* Taube *f*
pi'geonhole' *s* Fach *n* ‖ *tr* auf die lange Bank schieben
pi'geon loft' *s* Taubenschlag *m*
pi'geon-toed' *adj & adv* mit einwärts gerichteten Zehen
piggish ['pɪgɪʃ] *adj* säuisch
piggyback ['pɪgɪ‚bæk] *adv* huckepack
pig'gy bank' *s* Sparschweinchen *n*
pig'head'ed *adj* dickköpfig
pig' i'ron *s* Roheisen *n*
pigment ['pɪgmənt] *s* Pigment *n*
pig'pen' *s* Schweinekoben *m*
pig'skin' *s* Schweinsleder *n;* (sport) (coll) Fußball *m*
pig'sty' *s* Schweinestall *m*
pig'tail' *s* (*hair style*) Rattenschwanz *m*
pike [paɪk] *s* Pike *f,* Spieß *m;* (*highway*) Landstraße *f;* (ichth) Hecht *m*
piker ['paɪkər] *s* (coll) Knicker *m*
pilaster [pɪ'læstər] *s* Wandpfeiler *m*
pile [paɪl] *s* (*heap*) Haufen *m;* (*e.g., of papers*) Stoß *m;* (*stake*) Pfahl *m;* (*fortune*) (coll) Menge *f;* (atom. phys) Meiler *m,* Reaktor *m;* (elec, phys) Säule *f;* (tex) Flor *m;* **piles** (pathol) Hämorrhoiden *pl;* **piles of money** (coll) Heidengeld *n* ‖ *tr* anhäufen, aufhäufen; **p. it on** (coll) dick auftragen ‖ *intr*—**p. into** sich drängen in (*acc*); **p. on** sich übereinander stürzen; **p. out of** sich hinausdrängen aus; **p. up** sich (an)häufen
pile' driv'er *s* Pfahlramme *f,* Rammbär *m*
pilfer ['pɪlfər] *tr* mausen, stibitzen
pilgrim ['pɪlgrɪm] *s* Pilger –*in mf*
pilgrimage ['pɪlgrɪmɪdʒ] *s* Pilgerfahrt *f;* **go on a p.** pilgern
pill [pɪl] *s* (& fig) Pille *f*
pillar ['pɪlər] *s* Pfeiler *m,* Säule *f*
pill'box' *s* Pillenschachtel *f;* (mil) Bunker *m*
pillo•ry ['pɪləri] *s* Pranger *m* ‖ *v* (*pret & pp* –ried) *tr* an den Pranger stellen; (fig) anprangern
pillow ['pɪlo] *s* Kopfkissen *n*
pil'lowcase' *s* Kopfkissenbezug *m*
pilot ['paɪlət] *adj* (*experimental*) Versuchs– ‖ *s* (aer) Pilot *m,* Flugzeugführer –*in mf;* (naut) Lotse *m* ‖ *tr* (aer) steuern, führen; (naut) steuern, lotsen
pi'lothouse' *s* (naut) Ruderhaus *n*
pi'lot light' *s* Sparflamme *f*

pi'lot's li'cense *s* Flugzeugführerschein *m*
pimp [pɪmp] *s* Zuhälter *m* ‖ *intr* kuppeln
pimp'ing *s* Zuhälterei *f*
pimple ['pɪmpəl] *s* Pickel *m*
pimply ['pɪmpli] *adj* pickelig
pin [pɪn] *s* Stecknadel *f;* (*ornament*) Ansteknadel *f;* (bowling) Kegel *m;* (mach) Pinne *f,* Zapfen *m;* **be on pins and needles** wie auf Nadeln sitzen ‖ *v* (*pret & pp* **pinned;** *ger* **pinning**) *tr* (*fasten with a pin*) mit e–r Nadel befestigen; (*e.g., a dress*) abstecken; (*e.g., under a car*) einklemmen; (*e.g., against the wall*) drücken; (*in wrestling*) auf die Schultern legen; **pin down** (*a person*) festlegen; (*troops*) niederhalten; **pin one's hopes on** seine Hofnungen setzen auf (*acc*); **pin s.th. on s.o.** (fig) j–m etw anhängen; **pin up** (*a sign*) anschlagen; (*the hair, a dress*) aufstecken
pinafore ['pɪnə‚for] *s* Latz *m*
pin'ball machine' *s* Spielautomat *m*
pin' boy' *s* Kegeljunge *m*
pincers ['pɪnsərs] *s & spl* Kneifzange *f*
pinch [pɪntʃ] *s* Kneifen *n;* (*of salt*) Prise *f;* **give s.o. a p.** j–n kneifen; **in a p.** zur Not, in der Not ‖ *tr* kneifen, zwicken; (*steal*) (sl) klauen; (*arrest*) (coll) schnappen; **I got my finger pinched in the door** ich habe mir den Finger in der Tür geklemmt; **p. and scrape every penny** sich [*dat*] jeden Groschen vom Munde absparen; **p. off** abzwicken ‖ *intr* (*said of shoe*) (& fig) drücken
pinchers ['pɪntʃərz] *s & spl* Kneifzange *f*
pinch'-hit' *v* (*pret & pp* –hit; *ger* –hitting) *intr* einspringen
pinch' hit'ter *s* Ersatzmann *m*
pin'cush'ion *s* Nadelkissen *n*
pine [paɪn] *adj* Kiefern– ‖ *s* Kiefer *f* ‖ *intr*—**p. away** sich abzehren; **p. for** sich sehnen nach
pine'ap'ple *s* Ananas *f*
pine' cone' *s* Kiefernzapfen *m*
pine' nee'dle *s* Kiefernnadel *f*
ping [pɪŋ] *s* Päng *n;* (*of a motor*) Klopfen *n* ‖ *intr* (aut) klopfen
ping-pong ['pɪŋ‚pɑŋ] *s* Ping-pong *n*
pin'head' *s* (& fig) Stechnadelkopf *m*
pink [pɪŋk] *adj* rosa ‖ *s* Rosa *n*
pin' mon'ey *s* Nadelgeld *n*
pinnacle ['pɪnəkəl] *s* Zinne *f*
pin'point' *adj* haarscharf; **p. landing** Ziellandung *f* ‖ *tr* markieren
pin'prick' *s* Nadelstich *m*
pint [paɪnt] *s* Schoppen *m,* Pinte *f*
pin'up girl' *s* Pin-up-Girl *n*
pin'wheel' *s* (*toy*) Windmühle *f;* (*fireworks*) Feuerrad *n*
pioneer [‚paɪ-ə'nɪr] *s* Bahnbrecher –*in mf;* (fig & mil) Pionier *m* ‖ *tr* (fig) den Weg freimachen für ‖ *intr* (fig) Pionierarbeit leisten
pious ['paɪ-əs] *adj* fromm
pip [pɪp] *s* (*in fruit*) Kern *m;* (*on dice*) Punkt *m;* (*on a radarscope*) Leuchtpunkt *m;* (*of chickens*) Pips *m*

pipe [paɪp] s Rohr n; (for smoking; of an organ) Pfeife f || tr durch ein Rohr (weiter)leiten || intr pfeifen; **p. down** (sl) das Maul halten; **p. up** (coll) anfangen zu sprechen, loslegen

pipe′ clean′er s Pfeifenreiniger m

pipe′ dream′ s Wunschtraum m

pipe′ joint′ s Rohranschluß m

pipe′ line′ s Rohrleitung f, Pipeline f; (of information) Informationsquelle f

pipe′ or′gan s Orgel f

piper [′paɪpər] s Pfeifer –in mf

pipe′ wrench′ s Rohrzange f

piping [′paɪpɪŋ] adv—**p. hot** siedend heiß || s Rohrleitung f; (on uniforms) Biese f; (sew) Paspel f

piquancy [′pikənsi] s Pikanterie f

piquant [′pikənt] adj pikant

pique [pik] s Pik m || tr verärgern; **be piqued at** pikiert sein über (acc)

piracy [′paɪrəsi] s Seeräuberei f

pirate [′paɪrɪt] s Seeräuber m || tr (a book) (ungesetzlich) nachdrucken

pirouette [,pɪru′ɛt] s Pirouette f

pista′chio nut′ [pɪs′tæʃı‧o] s Pistaziennuß f

pistol [′pɪstəl] s Pistole f

pis′tol point′ s—at p. mit vorgehaltener Pistole

piston [′pɪstən] s Kolben m

pis′ton ring′ s Kolbenring m

pis′ton rod′ s Kolbenstange f

pis′ton stroke′ s Kolbenhub m

pit [pɪt] s Grube f; (in fruit) Kern m; (trap) Fallgrube f; (in the skin) Narbe f; (from corrosion) Rostgrübchen n; (in auto racing) Box f; (for cockfights) Kampfplatz m; (min) Schacht m; (theat) Parkett n; (mus) Orchester n; **pit of the stomach** Magengrube f || v (pret & pp pitted; ger pitting) tr (a face) mit Narben bedecken; (fruit) entkernen; (through corrosion) anfressen; **pit A against B** A gegen B ausspielen; **pit one′s strength against s.th.** seine Kraft mit etw messen

pitch [pɪtʃ] s Pech n; (of a roof) Dachschräge f; (downward slope) Gefälle n; (of a ship) Stampfen n; (of a screw, thread) Teilung f; (of a propeller) Steigung f; (throw) Wurf m; (sales talk) Verkaufsgespräch n; (mus) Tonhöhe f || tr (seal with pitch) verpichen; (a tent) aufschlagen; (a ball) dem Schläger zuwerfen; (hay) mit der Heugabel werfen || intr (naut) stampfen; **p. and toss** schlingern; **p. in** mithelfen

pitch′ ac′cent s musikalischer Tonakzent m

pitch′-black′ adj pechrabenschwarz

pitcher [′pɪtʃər] s (jug) Krug m

pitch′fork′ s Heugabel f

pitch′ing s (naut) Stampfen n

pit′fall′ s Fallgrube f; (fig) Falle f

pith [pɪθ] s (& fig) Mark n

pithy [′pɪθɪ] adj (& fig) markig

pitiable [′pɪtɪ‧əbl] adj erbarmenswert

pitiful [′pɪtɪfəl] adj erbärmlich

pitiless [′pɪtɪlɪs] adj erbarmungslos

pit′ted adj (by corrosion) angefressen; (fruit) entkernt

pit·y [′pɪti] s Erbarmen n, Mitleid n; **have p. on** Mitleid haben mit; **it′s a p. that** (es ist) schade, daß; **move to p.** jammern; **what a p.!** wie schade! || v (pret & pp –ied) tr sich erbarmen (genit), bemitleiden

pivot [′pɪvət] s Drehpunkt m || intr (on) sich drehen (um); (mil) schwenken

placard [′plækərd] s Plakat n

placate [′pleket] tr begütigen

place [ples] s (seat; room) Platz m; (area, town, etc.) Ort m, Ortschaft f; (in a book; in a room) Stelle f; (situation) Lage f; (spot to eat in, dance in, etc.) Lokal n; **all over the p.** überall; **at your p.** (coll) bei Ihnen; **in my p.** an meiner Stelle; **in p. of** anstelle von (or genit); **in the first p.** erstens; **know one′s p.** wissen, wohin man gehört; **out of p.** (& fig) nicht am Platz; **p. to stay** Unterkunft f; **put s.o. in his p.** j–n in seine Schranken verweisen; **take one′s p.** antreten; **take p.** stattfinden; **take s.o.′s p.** an j–s Stelle treten || tr setzen, stellen; (an advertisement) aufgeben; (an order) erteilen; (find a job for) unterbringen; **I can′t p. him** ich weiß nicht, wo ich ihn hintun soll; **p. a call** (telp) ein Gespräch anmelden || intr (in horseracing) sich als Zweiter placieren; (sport) sich placieren

place·bo [plə′sibo] s (–bos & –boes) Placebo n

place′ card′ s Tischkarte f

place′ mat′ s Tischmatte f

placement [′plesmənt] s Unterbringung f

place′-name′ s Ortsname m

place′ of birth′ s Geburtsort m

place′ of employ′ment s Arbeitsstätte f

place′ of res′idence s Wohnsitz m

placid [′plæsɪd] adj ruhig, sanftmütig

plagiarism [′pledʒə,rɪzəm] s Plagiat n

plagiarist [′pledʒərɪst] s Plagiator –in mf

plagiarize [′pledʒə,raɪz] intr ein Plagiat begehen

plague [pleg] s Seuche f || tr heimsuchen

plaid [plæd] adj buntkariert || s Schottenkaro n

plain [plen] adj (simple) einfach; (clear) klar; (fabric) einfarbig; (homely) unschön; (truth) rein; (food) bürgerlich; (paper) unlin(i)iert; (speech) unverblümt; (alcohol) unverdünnt || s Ebene f

plain′ clothes′ spl—**in p.** in Zivil

plain′-clothes′ man′ s Geheimpolizist m

plaintiff [′plentɪf] s Kläger –in mf

plaintive [′plentɪv] adj Klage-, klagend

plait [plet], [plæt] s Flechte f; **p. of hair** Zopf m || tr flechten

plan [plæn] s Plan m; (intention) Vorhaben n; **according to p.** planmäßig;

what are your plans for this evening?
was haben Sie für heute abend vor?
|| v (pret & pp **planned**; ger **planning**) tr planen; (one's time) einteilen; **p. to** (inf) vorhaben zu (inf) || intr—**p. for** Pläne machen für; **p. on** rechnen mit

plane [plen] s (airplane) Flugzeug n, Maschine f; (airfoil) Tragfläche f; (carp) Hobel n; (geom) Ebene f; **on a high p.** (fig) auf e-m hohen Niveau || tr hobeln; **p. down** abhobeln

plane' connec'tion s Fluganschluß m
plane' geom'etry s Planimetrie f
planet ['plænɪt] s Planet m
planetari·um [ˌplænɪ'terɪ·əm] s (-a [ə] & -ums) Planetarium n
planetary ['plænəˌteri] adj Planeten-
plane' tick'et s Flugkarte f
plane' tree' s Platane f
plank [plæŋk] s Brett n, Planke f; (pol) Programmpunkt m
planned' par'enthood s Familienplanung f
plant [plænt] s (factory) Anlage f; (spy) Spion –in mf; (bot) Pflanze f || tr (an)pflanzen; (a field) bepflanzen; (a colony) gründen; (as a spy) als Falle unterschieben; (a bomb) verstecken; **p. oneself** sich hinstellen
plantation [plæn'teʃən] s Plantage f
planter ['plæntər] s (person who plants; plantation owner) Pflanzer –in mf; (decorative container) Blumentrog m; (mach) Pflanzmaschine f
plasma ['plæzmə] s Plasma n
plaster ['plæstər] s Verputz m; (med) Pflaster n || tr verputzen; (e.g., with posters) bepflastern; **be plastered** (sl) besoffen sein
plas'terboard' s Gipsdiele f
plas'ter cast' s (med) Gipsverband m; (sculp) Gipsabguß m
plasterer ['plæstərər] s Stukkateur m
plas'tering s Verputz m
plas'ter of Par'is s Gips m
plastic ['plæstɪk] adj Plastik– || s Plastik n
plas'tic sur'gery s Plastik f
plas'tic wood' s Holzpaste f
plate [plet] s (dish) Teller m; (of metal) Platte f; (in a book) Tafel f; (elec, phot, typ) Platte f; (electron) Plattenelektrode f || tr plattieren
plateau [plæ'to] s Plateau n
plate' glass' s Tafelglas n
platen ['plætən] s Schreibmaschinenwalze f
platform ['plætˌfɔrm] s Plattform f; (for a speaker) Bühne f; (for loading) Rampe f; (pol) Programm n; (rr) Bahnsteig m
plat'form shoes' spl Plateauschuhe pl
plat'ing s (e.g., of gold) Plattierung f; (armor) Panzerung f
platinum ['plætɪnəm] s Platin n
plat'inum blonde' s Platinblondine f
platitude ['plætɪˌt(j)ud] s Gemeinplatz m
Plato ['pleto] s Plato m

Platonic [plə'tɑnɪk] adj platonisch
platoon [plə'tun] s Zug m
platter ['plætər] s Platte f
plausible ['plɔzɪbəl] adj plausibel
play [ple] s Spiel n; (mach) Spielraum m; (sport) Spielzug m; (theat) Stück n; **in p.** im Spiel; **out of p.** aus dem Spiel || tr spielen; (a card) ausspielen; (an opponent) spielen gegen; **p. back** (a tape, record) abspielen; **p. down** bagatellisieren; **p. the horses** bei Pferderennen wetten || intr spielen; (records, tapes) abspielen; **p. about** (the lips) umspielen; **p. along** mitspielen; **p. around with** herumspielen mit; **p. for** (stakes) spielen um; (a team) spielen für; **p. into s.o.'s hands** j–m in die Hände spielen; **p. safe** auf Nummer Sicher gehen; **p. up to** schmeicheln (dat)
play'back' s (reproduction) Wiedergabe f; (device) Abspielgerät n
play'boy' s Playboy m
player ['ple·ər] s Spieler –in mf; (sport) Sportler –in mf; (theat) Schauspieler –in mf
playful ['plefəl] adj spielerisch
play'ground' s Spielplatz m
play'house' s Theater n; (for children) Spielhaus n
play'ing card' s Spielkarte f
play'ing field' s Spielfeld n
play'mate' s Spielkamerad –in mf
play'-offs' spl Vorrunde f
play' on words' s Wortspiel n
play'pen' s Laufgitter n
play'room' s Spielzimmer n
play'-school' s Kindergarten m
play'thing' s (& fig) Spielzeug n
playwright ['pleˌraɪt] s Schauspieldichter –in mf
plea [pli] s Bitte f; (jur) Plädoyer n
plead [plid] v (pret & pp **pleaded** & **pled** [pled]) tr (ignorance) vorschützen || intr plädieren; **p. guilty** sich schuldig bekennen; **p. not guilty** sich als nichtschuldig erklären; **p. with s.o.** j–n anflehen
pleasant ['plezənt] adj angenehm
pleasantry ['plezəntri] s Heiterkeit f; (remark) Witz m
please [pliz] tr gefallen (dat); **be pleased to** (inf) sich freuen zu (inf); **be pleased with** sich freuen über (acc); **pleased to meet you!** sehr angenehm || intr gefallen; **as one pleases** nach Gefallen; **do as you p.** tun Sie, wie Sie wollen; **if you p.** wenn ich bitten darf; (iron) gefälligst; **p.!** bitte!
pleas'ing adj angenehm, gefällig
pleasure ['pleʒər] s Vergnügen n
pleas'ure trip' s Vergnügungsreise f
pleat [plit] s Plissee n || tr plissieren
pleat'ed skirt' s Plisseerock m
plebeian [plɪ'bi·ən] adj plebejisch || s Plebejer –in mf
plectrum ['plɛktrəm] s (-rums & -ra [rə]) Plektron n; (for zither) Schlagring m
pledge [plɛdʒ] s (solemn promise) Gelübde n; (security for a payment)

Pfand *n*; (fig) Unterpfand *n* || *tr* geloben; (*money*) zeichnen

plenary ['pli:nəri] *adj* Plenar-, Voll-

ple'nary indul'gence *s* vollkommener Ablaß *m*

ple'nary ses'sion *s* Plenum *n*

plenipotentiary [,plenipə'tenʃi ,eri] *adj* bevollmächtigt || *s* Bevollmächtigte *mf*

plentiful ['plentifəl] *adj* reichlich

plenty ['plenti] *s* Fülle *f*; **have p. of** Überfluß haben an (*dat*); **have p. to do** vollauf zu tun haben || *adv* (coll) reichlich

pleurisy ['plurisi] *s* Brustfellentzündung *f*

plexiglass ['pleksi ,glæs] *s* Plexiglas *n*

pliant ['plaɪ-ənt] *adj* biegsam; (fig) gefügig

pliers ['plaɪ-ərz] *s & spl* Zange *f*

plight [plaɪt] *s* Notlage *f*

plod [plad] *v* (*pret & pp* **plodded;** *ger* **plodding**) *intr* stapfen; **p. along** mühsam weitermachen

plop [plap] *v* (*pret & pp* **plopped;** *ger* **plopping**) *tr* plumpsen lassen || *intr* plumpsen || *interj* plumps!

plot [plat] *s* (*conspiracy*) Komplott *n*; (*of a story*) Handlung *f*; (*of ground*) Grundstück *n* || *v* (*pret & pp* **plotted;** *ger* **plotting**) *tr* (*a course*) abstecken; (*intrigues*) schmieden; (*e.g., murder*) planen || *intr* sich verschwören

plough [plaʊ] *s, tr & intr* var of **plow**

plow [plaʊ] *s* Pflug *m* || *tr* pflügen; **p. up** umpflügen; **p. under** unterpflügen || *intr* pflügen; **p. through the waves** durch die Wellen streichen

plow'man *s* (**-men**) Pflüger *m*

plow'share *s* Pflugschar *f*

pluck [plʌk] *s* (*tug*) Ruck *m*; (fig) Schneid *m* || *tr* (*e.g., a chicken*) rupfen; (*flowers, fruit*) pflücken; (*eyebrows*) auszupfen; (*mus*) zupfen || *intr*—**p. up** Mut fassen

plug [plʌg] *s* (*for a sink*) Pfropfen *m*; (*of tobacco*) Priem *m*; (*old horse*) alter Klepper *m*; (*advertising*) Befürwortung *f*; (aut) Zündkerze *f*; (elec) Stecker *m* || *v* (*pret & pp* **plugged;** *ger* **plugging**) *tr* (*a hole*) zustopfen; **p. in** an die Steckdose anschließen || *intr*—**p. away** (*work hard*) schuften; (*study hard*) pauken

plum [plʌm] *s* Pflaume *f*

plumage ['plu:mɪdʒ] *s* Gefieder *n*

plumb [plʌm] *adj* lotrecht || *adv* (coll) völlig || *s* Lot *n*; **out of p.** aus dem Lot || *tr* loten, sondieren

plumb' bob' *s* Lot *n*

plumber ['plʌmər] *s* Installateur *m*

plumb'ing *s* (*plumbing work*) Installateurarbeit *f*; (*pipes*) Rohrleitung *f*

plumb' line' *s* Lotschnur *f*

plume [plum] *s* Feder *f*; (*on a helmet*) Helmbusch *m*; **p. of smoke** Rauchfahne *f* || *tr* (*adorn with plumes*) mit Federn schmücken; **p. itself** sich putzen

plummet ['plʌmɪt] *s* Lot *n* || *intr* stürzen

plump [plʌmp] *adj* rundlich || *tr* plumpsen; **p. oneself down** sich schwerfällig hinwerfen

plum' tree' *s* Pflaumenbaum *m*

plunder ['plʌndər] *s* (*act*) Plünderung *f*; (*booty*) Beute *f* || *tr & intr* plündern

plunderer ['plʌndərər] *s* Plünderer *m*

plunge [plʌndʒ] *s* Sturz *m* || *tr* stürzen || *intr* (*fall*) stürzen; (*throw oneself*) sich stürzen

plunger ['plʌndʒər] *s* Saugglocke *f*

plunk [plʌŋk] *adv* (*squarely*) (coll) genau || *tr* (*e.g., a guitar*) zupfen; **p. down** klirrend auf den Tisch legen

pluperfect [,plu'pɑrfekt] *s* Vorvergangenheit *f*, Plusquamperfekt(um) *n*

plural ['plurəl] *adj* Plural- || *s* Mehrzahl *f*, Plural *m*

plurality [plu'rælɪti] *s* Mehrheit *f*; (pol) Stimmenmehrheit *f*

plus [plʌs] *adj* Plus-; (elec) positiv *f* || *s* Plus *n* || *prep* plus (*acc*)

plush [plʌʃ] *adj* (coll) luxuriös

plus' sign' *s* Pluszeichen *n*

plutonium [plu'toni-əm] *s* Plutonium *n*

ply [plaɪ] *s* (*of wood, etc.*) Schicht *f*; (*of yarn*) Strähne *f* || *v* (*pret & pp* **plied**) *tr* (*e.g., a needle*) (eifrig) handhaben; (*a trade*) betreiben; (*with questions*) bestürmen; (*a waterway*) regelmäßig befahren || *intr* (*between*) verkehren (zwischen *dat*)

ply'wood' *s* Sperrholz *n*

pneumatic [n(j)u'mætɪk] *adj* pneumatisch

pneumat'ic drill' *s* Preßluftbohrer *m*

pneumonia [n(j)u'moni-ə] *s* Lungenentzündung *f*

poach [potʃ] *tr* (*eggs*) pochieren || *intr* wildern

poached' egg' *s* verlorenes Ei *n*

poacher ['potʃər] *s* Wilderer *m*

pock [pak] *s* Pocke *f*, Pustel *f*

pocket ['pakɪt] *adj* (*comb, flap, knife, money, watch*) Taschen- || *s* Tasche *f*; (billiards) Loch *n*; (mil) Kessel *m* || *tr* in die Tasche stecken; (billiards) ins Loch spielen

pock'etbook' *s* Handtasche *f*; (*book*) Taschenbuch *n*

pock'et cal'culator *s* Taschenrechner *m*

pock'mark' *s* Pockennarbe *f*

pock'marked' *adj* pockennarbig

pod [pad] *s* Hülse *f*

podi·um ['podi-əm] *s* (**-ums & -a** [ə]) Podium *n*

poem ['po-ɪm] *s* Gedicht *n*

poet ['po-ɪt] *s* Dichter *m*, Poet *m*

poetaster ['po-ɪt ,æstər] *s* Dichterling *m*

poetess ['po-ɪtɪs] *s* Dichterin *f*

poetic [po'etɪk] *adj* dichterisch, poetisch || **poetics** *s* Poetik *f*

poetry ['po-ɪtri] *s* Dichtung *f*; **write p.** dichten, Gedichte schreiben

poignant ['pɔɪn(j)ənt] *adj* (*touching*) ergreifend; (*pungent*) scharf; (*cutting*) beißend

point [pɔɪnt] *s* (*dot, score*) Punkt *m*;

(*tip*) Spitze *f*; (*of a joke*) Pointe *f*; (*of a statement*) Hauptpunkt *m*; (*side of a character*) Seite *f*; (*purpose*) Sinn *m*; (*matter, subject*) Sache *f*; (*of a compass*) Kompaßstrich *m*; (*to show decimals*) Komma *n*; (aut) Zündkontakt *m*; (geog) Landspitze *f*; (typ) Punkt *m*; **at this p.** in diesem Augenblick; **be on the p. of** (ger) gerade im Begriff sein zu (*inf*); **come to the p.!** zur Sache!; **get the p.** verstehen; **in p. of fact** tatsächlich; **make a p. of** bestehen auf (*dat*); **make it a p. to** (*inf*) es sich [*dat*] zur Pflicht machen zu (*inf*); **not to the p.** nicht zur Sache gehörig; **off the p.** unzutreffend; **on points** (sport) nach Punkten; **p. at issue** strittiger Punkt *m*; **p. of order!** zur Tagesordnung!; **p. of time** Zeitpunkt *m*; **score a p.** (fig) e-n Punkt für sich buchen; **that's beside the p.** darum handelt es sich nicht; **there's no p. to it** es hat keinen Zweck; **to the p.** zutreffend; **up to a certain p.** bis zu e-m gewissen Grade ‖ *tr* (*e.g., a gun*) (at) richten (*acc*); **p. out** (auf)zeigen; **p. s.th. out to s.o.** j-n auf etw [*acc*] hinweisen; **p. the finger at** mit dem Finger zeigen auf (*acc*) ‖ *intr* mit dem Finger zeigen; **p. to** deuten auf (*acc*); (fig) hinweisen auf (*acc*)

point'-blank' *adj* (*refusal*) glatt; (*shot*) rasant, Kernschuß–; **at p. range** auf Kernschußweite ‖ *adv* (*at close range*) aus nächster Nähe; (fig) glatt; (arti) auf Kernschußweite

point'ed *adj* spitzig; (*remark*) anzüglich; (*gun*) gerichtet; (*arch, nose*) Spitz–

pointer ['pɔɪntər] *s* (*of a meter*) Zeiger *m*; (*stick*) Zeigestock *m*; (*advice*) Tip *m*; (*hunting dog*) Vorstehhund *m*

pointless ['pɔɪntlɪs] *adj* zwecklos

point' of hon'or *s* Ehrensache *f*

point' of law' *s* Rechtsfrage *f*

point' of view' *s* Gesichtspunkt *m*

poise [pɔɪz] *s* sicheres Auftreten *n* ‖ *tr* im Gleichgewicht halten ‖ *intr* schweben

poison ['pɔɪzən] *s* Gift *n* ‖ *tr* (& fig) vergiften

poi'son gas' *s* Giftgas *n*

poi'son i'vy *s* Giftsumach *m*

poisonous ['pɔɪzənəs] *adj* giftig

poke [pok] *s* Stoß *m*, Knuff *m* ‖ *tr* stoßen, knuffen; (*the fire*) schüren; (*head, nose*) stecken; **p. fun at** sich lustig machen über (*acc*); **p. out** (*an eye*) ausstechen; **p. s.o. in the ribs** j-m e-n Rippenstoß geben ‖ *intr* bummeln; **p. around** herumstochern; (*be slow*) herumbummeln; (*in another's business*) herumstöbern

poker ['pokər] *s* Schürhaken *m*; (cards) Poker *n*

pok'er face' *s* Pokergesicht *n*

poky ['poki] *adj* bummelig

Poland ['polənd] *s* Polen *n*

polar ['polər] *adj* Polar–

po'lar bear' *s* Eisbär *m*

polarity [po'lærɪti] *s* Polarität *f*

polarize ['polə ‚raɪz] *tr* polarisieren

pole [pol] *s* (*rod*) Stange *f*; (*for telephone lines, flags, etc.*) Mast *m*; (astr, geog, phys) Pol *m*; **Pole Pole** *m*, Polin *f* ‖ *tr* (*a raft, boat*) staken

pole'cat' *s* Iltis *m*

polemic(al) [pə'lemɪk(əl)] *adj* polemisch

polemics [pə'lemɪks] *s* Polemik *f*

pole'star' *s* Polarstern *m*

pole'-vault' *intr* stabhochspringen

pole' vault'ing *s* Stabhochsprung *m*

police [pə'lis] *adj* polizeilich ‖ *s* Polizei *f* ‖ *tr* polizeilich überwachen; (*clean up*) (mil) säubern

police' es'cort *s* Polozeibedeckung *f*

police'man *s* (–men) Polizist *m*

police' of'ficer *s* Polizeibeamte *m*, Polizeibeamtin *f*

police' pre'cinct *s* Polizeirevier *n*

police' state' *s* Polizeistaat *m*

police' sta'tion *s* Polizeiwache *f*

police'wom'an *s* (–wom'en) Polizistin *f*

policy ['palɪsi] *s* Politik *f*; (ins) Police *f*

polio ['polɪ ‚o] *s* Polio *f*

polish ['palɪ] *s* (*material; shine*) Politur *f*; (*for shoes*) Schuhcreme *f*; (fig) Schliff *m* ‖ *tr* polieren; (*fingernails*) lackieren; (*shoes, silver, etc.*) putzen; (*floors*) bohnern; (fig) abschleifen; **p. off** (*eat*) (sl) verdrücken; (*an opponent*) (sl) erledigen; (*work*) (sl) hinhauen ‖ *intr*—**p. up on** aufpolieren ‖ **Polish** ['polɪʃ] *adj* polnisch ‖ *s* Polnisch *n*

polite [pə'laɪt] *adj* höflich

politeness [pə'laɪtnɪs] *s* Höflichkeit *f*

politic ['palɪtɪk] *adj* diplomatisch

political [pə'lɪtɪkəl] *adj* politisch

poli'tical econ'omy *s* Volkswirtschaft *f*

poli'tical sci'ence *s* Staatswissenschaften *pl*

politician [‚palɪ'tɪʃən] *s* Politiker –in *mf*

politics ['palɪtɪks] *s* Politik *f*; **be in p.** sich politisch betätigen; **talk p.** politisieren

polka ['po(l)kə] *s* Polka *f*

pol'ka-dot' *adj* getupft

poll [pol] *s* (*voting*) Abstimmung *f*; (*of public opinion*) Umfrage *f*; **be defeated at the polls** e-e Wahlniederlage erleiden; **go to the polls** zur Wahl gehen; **polls** (*voting place*) Wahllokal *n*; **take a p.** e-e Umfrage halten ‖ *tr* befragen

pollen ['palən] *s* Pollen *m*

poll'ing booth' *s* Wahlzelle *f*

pollster ['polstər] *s* Meinungsforscher –in *mf*

poll' tax' *s* Kopfsteuer *f*

pollute [pə'lut] *tr* verunreinigen

pollution [pə'luʃən] *s* Verunreinigung *f*

polo ['polo] *s* (sport) Polo *n*

po'lo shirt' *s* Polohemd *n*

polygamist [pə'lɪgəmɪst] *s* Polygamist *m*

polygamy [pə'lɪgəmi] *s* Polygamie *f*

polyglot ['palɪ ‚glat] *s* Polyglott *m*

polygon ['palı ,gan] *s* Vieleck *n*
polyp ['palıp] *s* Polyp *m*
polytheism [,palı'θi ,ızem] *s* Vielgötterei *f*, Polytheismus *m*
polytheistic [,palıθi'ıstık] *adj* polytheistisch
pomade [pə'med] *s* Pomade *f*
pomegranate ['pam ,grænıt] *s* Granatapfel *m*; *(tree)* Granatapfelbaum *m*
Pomerania [,pamə'renı·ə] *s* Pommern *n*
pom•mel ['pʌməl] *s (of a sword)* Degenkopf *m*; *(of a saddle)* Sattelknopf *m* ‖ *v (pret & pp* -mel[l]ed; *ger* -el[l]ing) *tr* mit der Faust schlagen
pomp [pamp] *s* Pomp *m*, Prunk *m*
pompous ['pampəs] *adj* hochtrabend
pon•cho ['pant/o] *s* (-chos) Poncho *m*
pond [pand] *s* Teich *m*
ponder ['pandər] *tr* erwägen; *(words)* abwägen ‖ *intr* (over) nachsinnen (über *acc*)
ponderous ['pandərəs] *adj* schwerfällig
pontiff ['pantıf] *s* (eccl) Papst *m*; (hist) Pontifex *m*
pontifical [pan'tıfıkəl] *adj* pontifikal
pontoon [pan'tun] *s* Ponton *m*; (aer) Schwimmer *m*
pony ['poni] *s (small horse; hair style)* Pony *n*; *(crib)* Eselsbrücke *f*
poodle ['pudəl] *s* Pudel *m*
pool [pul] *s (small pond)* Tümpel *m*; *(of blood)* Lache *f*; *(swimming pool)* Schwimmbecken *n*; *(in betting)* Pool *m*; *(game)* Billiard *n*; *(fin)* Pool *m* ‖ *tr* zusammenlegen
pool′room′ *s* Billardsalon *m*
pool′ ta′ble *s* Billardtisch *m*
poop [pup] *s* Heck *n* ‖ *tr* (sl) erschöpfen; **be pooped (out)** erschöpft sein
poor [pur] *adj* arm; *(e.g., in spelling)* schwach; *(soil, harvest)* schlecht; *(miserable)* armselig; **p. in arm an** *(dat)*
poor′ box′ *s* Opferstock *m*
poor′house′ *s* Armenhaus *n*
poorly ['purlı] *adv* schlecht
pop [pap] *adj (concert, singer, music)* Pop- ‖ *s* Puff *m*, Knall *m*; *(dad)* Vati *m*; *(soda)* Brauselimonade *f*; *(mus)* Popmusik *f* ‖ *v (pret & pp* popped; *ger* popping) *tr (corn)* rösten; *(cause to pop)* knallen lassen; **pop the question** (coll) e-n Heiratsantrag machen ‖ *intr (make a popping noise)* knallen; *(said of popcorn)* aufplatzen; **pop in** *(visit unexpectedly)* (coll) hereinplatzen; **pop off** (sl) das Maul aufreißen; **pop up** *(appear)* (coll) auftauchen; *(jump up)* hochfahren
pop′corn′ *s* Puffmais *m*
pope [pop] *s* Papst *m*
pop′-eyed′ *adj* glotzäugig
pop′gun′ *s* Knallbüchse *f*
poplar ['paplər] *s* Pappel *f*
poppy ['papi] *s* Mohnblume *f*, Mohn *m*
pop′pycock′ *s* (coll) Quatsch *m*
pop′pyseed′ *s* Mohn *m*
popsicle ['pap ,sıkəl] *s* Eis *n* am Stiel
populace ['papjəlıs] *s* Pöbel *m*

popular ['papjələr] *adj* populär; *(e.g., music, expression)* volkstümlich; **p. with** beliebt bei
popularity [,papjə'lærıti] *s* Popularität *f*, Beliebtheit *f*
popularize ['papjələ ,raız] *tr* popularisieren
populate ['papjə ,let] *tr* bevölkern
population [,papjə'le/ən] *s* Bevölkerung *f*
popula′tion explo′sion *s* Bevölkerungsexplosion *f*
populous ['papjələs] *adj* volkreich
porcelain ['pors(ə)lın] *s* Porzellan *n*
porch [port/] *s* Vorbau *m*, Veranda *f*
porcupine ['pɔrkjə ,paın] *s* Stachelschwein *n*
pore [por] *s* Pore *f* ‖ *intr*—**p. over** eifrig studieren
pork [pork] *adj* Schweine- ‖ *s* Schweinefleisch *n*
pork′chop′ *s* Schweinekotelett *n*
pornography [pɔr'nagrəfi] *s* Pornographie *f*
porous ['porəs] *adj* porös
porphyry ['pɔrfıri] *s* Porphyr *m*
porpoise ['pɔrpəs] *s* Tümmler *m*
porridge ['pɔrıdʒ] *s* Brei *m*
port [port] *s* Hafen *m*; *(wine)* Portwein *m*; *(slit for shooting)* Schießscharte *f*; (naut) Backbord *m* & *n*; **to p.** (naut) backbord
portable ['portəbəl] *adj* tragbar; *(radio, television, typewriter)* Koffer-
portal ['pɔrtəl] *s* Portal *n*
portend [pɔr'tend] *tr* vorbedeuten
portent ['pɔrtənt] *s* schlimmes Vorzeichen *n*, böses Omen *n*
portentous [pɔr'tentəs] *adj* unheildrohend
porter ['portər] *s (in a hotel)* Hausdiener *m*; *(at a station)* Gepäckträger *m*; *(doorman)* Portier *m*
portfoli•o [pɔrt'folı ,o] *s* (-os) Aktenmappe *f*; (fin) Portefeuille *n*; **without p.** ohne Geschäftsbereich
port′hole′ *s (for shooting)* Schießscharte *f*; (naut) Bullauge *n*
porti•co ['pɔrtı ,ko] *s* (-coes & -cos) Säulenvorbau *m*, Portikus *m*
portion ['pɔr/ən] *s* Anteil *m*; *(serving)* Portion *f*; *(dowry)* Heiratsgut *n* ‖ *tr*—**p. out** austeilen, einteilen
portly ['portli] *adj* wohlbeleibt
port′ of call′ *s* Anlaufhafen *m*
port′ of en′try *s* Einfuhrhafen *m*
portrait ['portret] *s* Porträt *n*
portray [pɔr'tre] *tr* porträtieren; (fig) beschreiben; (theat) darstellen
portrayal [pɔr'tre·əl] *s* Porträtieren *n*; (fig) Beschreibung *f*; (theat) Darstellung *f*
port′side′ *s* Backbord *m* & *n*
Portugal ['port/əgəl] *s* Portugal *n*
Portuguese ['port/ə ,giz] *adj* portugiesisch ‖ *s* Portugiese *m*, Portugiesin *f*; *(language)* Portugiesisch *n*
port′ wine′ *s* Portwein *m*
pose [poz] *s* Haltung *f*, Pose *f* ‖ *tr (a question, problem)* stellen ‖ *intr* posieren; **p. as** sich ausgeben als; **p. for an artist** e-m Künstler Modell ste-

hen; **p. for a picture** sich e-m Photographen stellen
posh [pɑʃ] *adj* (sl) großartig
position [pə'ziʃən] *s* Stellung *f*; (*situation, condition*) Lage *f*; (*job; place of defense*) Stellung *f*; (*point of view*) Standpunkt *m*; (aer, naut) Standort *m*; (astr, mil, naut) Position *f*; **be in a p.** to (*inf*) in der Lage sein zu (*inf*); **in p.** am rechten Platz; **p. wanted** (*as in an ad*) Stelle gesucht; **take a p. on** Stellung nehmen zu; **take one's p.** sich aufstellen
positive ['pɑzɪtɪv] *adj* (*reply, result, attitude*) positiv; (*answer*) zustimmend; (*sure*) sicher; (*offer*) fest; (elec, math, med, phot, phys) positiv ‖ *s* (gram) (phot) Positiv *n*
posse ['pɑsi] *s* Polizeiaufgebot *n*
possess [pə'zɛs] *tr* besitzen; **be possessed by the devil** von dem Teufel besessen sein
possession [pə'zɛʃən] *s* Besitz *m*; (*property*) Eigentum *n*; **be in p. of s.th.** etw besitzen; **take p. of s.th.** etw in Besitz nehmen
possessive [pə'zɛsɪv] *adj* eifersüchtig; (gram) besitzanzeigend, Besitz-
possibility [,pɑsɪ'bɪlɪti] *s* Möglichkeit *f*
possible ['pɑsɪbəl] *adj* möglich; **make p.** ermöglichen
possibly ['pɑsɪbli] *adv* möglicherweise
possum ['pɑsəm] *s* Opossum *n*; **play p.** sich verstellen; (*play dead*) sich tot stellen
post [post] *s* (*pole*) Pfahl *m*; (*job; of a sentry*) Posten *m*; (*military camp*) Standort *m* ‖ *tr* (*a notice*) anschlagen; (*a guard*) aufstellen; **p. bond** Kaution stellen; **p. no bills** Plakatankleben verboten
postage ['postɪdʒ] *s* Porto *n*
post'age due' *s* Nachporto *n*
post'age stamp' *s* Briefmarke *f*
postal ['postəl] *adj* Post-
post'al mon'ey or'der *s* Postanweisung *f*
post'card' *s* Ansichtskarte *f*
post'date' *tr* nachdatieren
post'ed *adj*—**keep s.o. p.** j-n auf dem laufenden halten
poster ['postər] *s* Plakat *n*
posterity [pɑs'tɛrɪti] *s* Nachkommenschaft *f*, Nachwelt *f*
postern ['postərn] *s* Hintertür *f*
post' exchange' *s* Marketenderei *f*
post'haste' *adv* schnellstens
posthumous ['pɑstʃuməs] *adj* posthum
post'man *s* (**-men**) Briefträger *m*
post'mark' *s* Poststempel *m* ‖ *tr* abstempeln
post'mas'ter *s* Postmeister *m*
post'master gen'eral *s* Postminister *m*
post-mortem [,post'mortəm] *s* Obduktion *f*
post' of'fice *s* Post *f*, Postamt *n*
post'-office box' *s* Postschließfach *n*
post'paid' *adj* frankiert
postpone [post'pon] *tr* (**till, to**) aufschieben (auf *acc*)

postponement [post'ponmənt] *s* Aufschub *m*
post'script' *s* Nachschrift *f*
posture ['pɑstʃər] *s* Haltung *f*
post'war' *adj* Nachkriegs-
posy ['pozi] *s* Sträußchen *n*
pot [pɑt] *s* Topf *m*; (*for coffee, tea*) Kanne *f*; (*in gambling*) Einsatz *m*; **go to pot** (sl) hops gehen; **pots and pans** Kochgeschirr *n*
potash ['pɑtˌæʃ] *s* Pottasche *f*, Kali *n*
potassium [pə'tæsɪəm] *s* Kalium *n*
pota-to [pə'teto] *s* (**-toes**) Kartoffel *f*
pota'to chips' *spl* Kartoffelchips *pl*
potbellied ['pɑt,belɪd] *adj* dickbäuchig
pot'bel'ly *s* Spitzbauch *m*
potency ['potənsi] *s* Stärke *f*; (physiol) Potenz *f*
potent ['potənt] *adj* (*powerful*) mächtig; (*persuasive*) überzeugend; (*e.g., drugs*) wirksam; (physiol) potent
potentate ['potənˌtet] *s* Potentat *m*
potential [pə'tenʃəl] *adj* möglich; (phys) potentiell ‖ *s* (& elec, math, phys) Potential *n*
pot'hold'er *s* Topflappen *m*
pot'hole' *s* Schlagloch *n*
potion ['poʃən] *s* Trank *m*
pot'luck' *s*—**take p.** mit dem vorliebnehmen, was es gerade gibt
pot' roast' *s* Schmorbraten *m*
pot'sherd' *s* Topfscherbe *f*
pot' shot' *s* müheloser Schuß *m*; **take a p. at** unfair bekritteln
pot'ted *adj* Topf-
potter ['pɑtər] *s* Töpfer *m*
pot'ter's clay' *s* Töpferton *m*
pot'ter's wheel' *s* Töpferscheibe *f*
pottery ['pɑtəri] *s* Tonwaren *pl*
potty ['pɑti] *s* (coll) Töpfchen *n*
pouch [pautʃ] *s* Beutel *m*
poultice ['poltɪs] *s* Breiumschlag *m*
poultry ['poltri] *s* Geflügel *n*
poul'try-man *s* (**-men**) Geflügelzüchter *m*; (*dealer*) Geflügelhändler *m*
pounce [pauns] *intr*—**p. on** sich stürzen auf (*acc*)
pound [paund] *s* Pfund *n*; (*for animals*) Pferch *m* ‖ *tr* (zer)stampfen; (*meat*) klopfen; **p. the sidewalks** Pflaster treten ‖ *intr* (*said of the heart*) klopfen; **p. on** (*e.g., a door*) hämmern an (*acc*)
-pound *suf* -pfündig
pound' ster'ling *s* Pfund *n* Sterling
pour [por] *tr* gießen; (*e.g., coffee*) einschenken; **p. away** wegschütten ‖ *intr* (meteor) gießen; **p. out of** (*e.g., a theater*) strömen aus ‖ *impers*—**it's pouring** es gießt
pout [paut] *s* Schmollen *n* ‖ *intr* schmollen
pout'ing *adj* (*lips*) aufgeworfen ‖ *s* Schmollen *n*
poverty ['pɑvərti] *s* Armut *f*
pov'erty-strick'en *adj* verarmt
POW ['pi'o'dʌbl,ju] *s* (**prisoner of war**) Kriegsgefangener *m*
powder ['paudər] *s* Pulver *n*; (*cosmetic*) Puder *m* ‖ *tr* (*e.g., the face*) pudern; (*plants*) stäuben; (*a cake*) bestreuen ‖ *intr* zu Pulver werden

pow'der box' s Puderdose f
pow'dered milk' s Milchpulver n
pow'dered sug'ar s Staubzucker m
pow'der keg' s Pulverfaß n
pow'der puff' s Puderquaste f
pow'der room' s Damentoilette f
powdery ['paʊdəri] adj pulverig
power ['paʊ·ər] s Macht f; (personal control) Gewalt f; (electricity) Strom m; (math) Potenz f; (opt) Vergrößerungskraft f; (phys) Leistung f; (pol) Macht f; **be in p.** an der Macht sein; **be in s.o.'s p.** in j-s Gewalt sein; **be within s.o.'s p.** in j-s Macht liegen; **come to p.** an die Macht gelangen; **have the p. to** (inf) vermögen zu (inf); **more p. to you!** viel Erfolg!; **the powers that be** die Obrigkeit f || tr antreiben
pow'er brake' s (aut) Servobremse f
pow'er dive' s (aer) Vollgassturzflug m
pow'er drill' s Elektrobohrer m
pow'er-driv'en adj mit Motorantrieb
pow'er fail'ure s Stromausfall m
powerful ['paʊ·ərfəl] adj mächtig; (opt) stark
pow'erhouse' s Kraftwerk n; (coll) Kraftprotz m
pow'erhun'gry adj herrschsüchtig
powerless ['paʊ·ərlɪs] adj machtlos
pow'er line' s Starkstromleitung f
pow'er mow'er s Motorrasenmäher m
pow'er of attor'ney s Vollmacht f
pow'er plant' s (powerhouse) Kraftwerk n; (aer, aut) Triebwerk n
pow'er shov'el s Löffelbagger m
pow'er sta'tion s Kraftwerk n
pow'er steer'ing s Servolenkung f
pow'er supply' s Stromversorgung f
practicable ['præktɪkəbəl] adj praktikabel, durchführbar
practical ['præktɪkəl] adj praktisch
prac'tical joke' s Streich m
practically ['præktɪkəli] adv praktisch; (almost) fast, so gut wie
prac'tical nurse' s praktisch ausgebildete Krankenschwester f
practice ['præktɪs] s (exercise) Übung f; (habit) Gewohnheit f; (of medicine, law) Praxis f; **in p.** (in training) in der Übung; (in reality) in der Praxis; **make it a p. to** (inf) es sich [dat] zur Gewohnheit machen zu (inf); **out of p.** aus der Übung || tr (a profession) tätig sein als; (patience, reading, dancing, etc.) sich üben in (dat); (music, gymnastics) treiben; (piano, etc.) üben || intr üben; (said of a doctor) praktizieren; **p. on** (e.g., the violin, piano, parallel bars) üben auf (dat)
prac'tice game' s Übungsspiel n
prac'tice teach'er s Studienreferendar –in mf
practitioner [præk'tɪʃənər] s Praktiker –in mf
pragmatic [præg'mætɪk] adj pragmatisch
pragmatism ['prægmə,tɪzəm] s Sachlichkeit f; (philos) Pragmatismus m
Prague [prɑg] s Prag n
prairie ['preri] s Steppe f, Prärie f

praise [prez] s Lob n || tr (for) loben (wegen); **p. to the skies** verhimmeln
praise'wor'thy adj lobenswert
prance [præns] intr tänzeln
prank [præŋk] s Schelmenstreich m
prate [pret] intr schwätzen
prattle ['prætəl] s Geplapper n || intr plappern, schwätzen
prawn [prɔn] s Garnele f
pray [pre] tr & intr beten
prayer [prer] s Gebet n; **say a p.** ein Gebet sprechen
prayer' book' s Gebetbuch n
preach [pritʃ] tr & intr predigen
preacher ['pritʃər] s Prediger m
preamble ['pri,æmbəl] s Präambel f
precarious [prɪ'kerɪ·əs] adj prekär
precaution [prɪ'kɔʃən] s Vorsichtsmaßnahme f; **as a p.** vorsichtshalber; **take precautions** Vorkehrungen treffen
precede [prɪ'sid] tr vorausgehen (dat) || intr vorangehen
precedence ['presɪdəns] s Vorrang m; **take p. over** den Vorrang haben vor (dat)
precedent ['presɪdənt] s Präzedenzfall m; **set a p.** e–n Präzedenzfall schaffen
preced'ing adj vorhergehend
precept ['prisept] s Vorschrift f
precinct ['prisɪŋkt] s Bezirk m
precious ['preʃəs] adj (expensive) kostbar; (valuable) wertvoll; (excessively refined) geziert; (child) lieb || adv **p. few** (coll) herzlich wenige
pre'cious stone' s Edelstein m
precipice ['presɪpɪs] s Abgrund m
precipitate [prɪ'sɪpɪ,tet] adj steil abfallend || s (chem) Niederschlag m || tr (hurl) hinein stürzen in (acc); (bring about) heraufbeschwören; (vapor) (chem) niederschlagen; (from a solution) (chem) ausfällen || intr (chem, meteor) sich niederschlagen
precipitation [prɪ,sɪpɪ'teʃən] s (meteor) Niederschlag m
precipitous [prɪ'sɪpɪtəs] adj jäh
precise [prɪ'saɪs] adj präzis, genau
precision [prɪ'sɪʒən] s Präzision f
preclude [prɪ'klud] tr ausschließen
precocious [prɪ'koʃəs] adj frühreif
preconceived [,prikən'sivd] adj vorgefaßt
predatory ['predə,tori] adj Raub–
predecessor ['predɪ,sesər] s Vorgänger –in mf
predestination [,pridɛstɪ'neʃən] s Prädestination f
predicament [prɪ'dɪkəmənt] s Mißliche Lage f
predicate ['predɪkɪt] s (gram) Aussage f, Prädikat n || ['predɪ,ket] tr (of) aussagen (über acc); (base) (on) gründen (auf acc)
predict [prɪ'dɪkt] tr voraussagen
prediction [prɪ'dɪkʃən] s Voraussage f
predispose [,pridɪs'poz] tr (to) im voraus geneigt machen (zu); (pathol) empfänglich machen (für)
predominant [prɪ'dɑmɪnənt] adj vorwiegend

preeminent [prɪ'emɪnənt] *adj* hervorragend
preempt [prɪ'empt] *tr (a program)* ersetzen; *(land)* durch Vorkaufsrecht
erwerben
preen [priːn] *tr* putzen
prefabricated [pri'fæbrɪ,ketɪd] *adj*
Fertig–
preface ['prefɪs] *s* Vorwort *n*, Vorrede
f || *tr* einleiten
prefer [prɪ'fʌr] *v (pret & pp* –ferred;
ger –ferring) *tr* bevorzugen; *(charges)*
vorbringen; **I p. to wait** ich warte
lieber
preferable ['prefərəbəl] *adj* (to) vorzu-
ziehen(d) *(dat)*
preferably ['prefərəbli] *adv* vorzugs-
weise
preferred' stock' *s* Vorzugsaktie *f*
prefix ['priːfɪks] *s* Vorsilbe *f*, Präfix *n*
|| *tr* vorsetzen
pregnancy ['pregnənsi] *s* Schwangerschaft *f*; *(of animals)* Trächtigkeit *f*
pregnant ['pregnənt] *adj* schwanger;
(animals) trächtig; *(fig)* inhalts-
schwer
prehistoric [,priːhɪs'tɔrɪk] *adj* vorge-
schichtlich, prähistorisch
prejudice ['predʒədɪs] *s* Voreingeno-
menheit *f*; *(detriment)* Schaden *m* ||
tr beeinträchtigen; **p. s.o. against**
j–n einnehmen gegen
prejudiced *adj* voreingenommen
prejudicial [,predʒə'dɪʃəl] *adj* (to)
schädlich (für)
prelate ['prelɪt] *s* Prälat *m*
preliminary [prɪ'lɪmɪ,neri] *adj* ein-
leitend, Vor– || *s* Vorbereitung *f*
prelude ['prel(j)ud] *s* (fig, mus, theat)
Vorspiel *n*
premarital [pri'mærɪtəl] *adj* vorehelich
premature [,primə't(j)ʊr] *adj* verfrüht;
p. birth Frühgeburt *f*
premeditated [pri'medɪ,tetɪd] *adj* vorbedacht; *(murder)* vorsätzlich
premier [prɪ'mɪr] *s* Premier *m*
premiere [prɪ'mɪr] *s* Erstaufführung *f*
premise ['premɪs] *s* Voraussetzung *f*;
on the premises an Ort und Stelle;
the premises das Lokal
premium ['primɪ·əm] *s* Prämie *f*; **at a
p.** *(in demand)* sehr gesucht; *(at a
high price)* über pari
premonition [,primə'nɪʃən] *s* Vorahnung *f*
preoccupation [pri,akjə'peʃən] *s* **(with)**
Beschäftigtsein *n* (mit)
preoccupied [pri'akjə,paɪd] *adj* ausschließlich beschäftigt
preparation [,prepə're ʃən] *s* Vorberei-
tung *f*; (med) Präparat *n*
preparatory [prɪ'pærə,tori] *adj* vorbe-
reitend; **p. to** vor *(dat)*
prepare [prɪ'per] *tr* vorbereiten; *(a
meal)* zubereiten; *(a prescription)*
anfertigen; *(a document)* abfassen
preparedness [prɪ'perɪdnɪs] *s* Bereitschaft *f*; (mil) Einsatzbereitschaft *f*
pre-pay [pri'pe] *v (pret & pp* –paid)
tr im voraus bezahlen
preponderant [prɪ'pandərənt] *adj* überwiegend

preposition [,prepə'zɪʃən] *s* Präposition *f*, Verhältniswort *n*
prepossessing [,pripə'zesɪŋ] *adj* ein-
nehmend
preposterous [prɪ'pastərəs] *adj* lächerlich
prep' school' [prep] *s* Vorbereitungs-
schule *f*
prerecorded [,prirɪ'kɔrdɪd] *adj* vorher aufgenommen
prerequisite [pri'rekwɪzɪt] *s* Voraussetzung *f*, Vorbedingung *f*
prerogative [prɪ'rɑgətɪv] *s* Vorrecht *n*
presage ['presɪdʒ] *s* Vorzeichen *n* ||
[prɪ'sedʒ] *tr* ein Vorzeichen sein für
Presbyterian [,prezbɪ'tɪrɪ·ən] *adj*
presbyterianisch || *s* Presbyterianer
–in *mf*
prescribe [prɪ'skraɪb] *tr* vorschreiben;
(med) verordnen
prescription [prɪ'skrɪpʃən] *s* Vorschrift
f; (med) Rezept *n*, Verordnung *f*
presence ['prezəns] *s* Anwesenheit *f*
pres'ence of mind' *s* Geistesgegenwart
f
present ['prezənt] *adj (at this place)*
anwesend; *(of the moment)* gegen-
wärtig || *s (gift)* Geschenk *n*; *(pres-
ent time or tense)* Gegenwart *f*; **at p.**
zur Zeit; **for the p.** vorläufig ||
[prɪ'zent] *tr* bieten; *(facts)* darstellen; *(introduce)* vorstellen; (theat)
vorführen; **p. s.o. with s.th.** j–m etw
verehren
presentable [prɪ'zentəbəl] *adj* presen-
tabel
presentation [,prezən'teʃən] *s* Vorstellung *f*; (theat) Aufführung *f*
pres'ent-day' *adj* heutig, aktuell
presentiment [prɪ'zentɪmənt] *s* Ahnung
f
presently ['prezəntli] *adv* gegenwärtig;
(soon) alsbald
preservation [,prezər'veʃən] *s* Erhaltung *f*; *(from)* Bewahrung *f* (vor *dat*)
preservative [prɪ'zɑrvətɪv] *s* Konser-
vierungsmittel *n*
preserve [prɪ'zɑrv] *s* Revier *n*; pre-
serves Konserven *pl* || *tr* konservie-
ren; **p. from** schützen vor *(dat)*
preside [prɪ'zaɪd] *intr* **(over)** den Vorsitz führen (über *acc* or bei)
presidency [prɪ'prezɪdənsi] *s* Präsident-
schaft *f*
president ['prezɪdənt] *s* Präsident –in
mf; *(of a university)* Rektor –in *mf*;
(of a board) Vorsitzende *mf*
presidential [,prezɪ'dentʃəl] *adj* Prä-
sidenten–
press [pres] *adj (agency, agent, conference, gallery, report, secretary)*
Presse– || *s (wine press; printing
press; newspapers)* Presse *f*; **go to p.**
in Druck gehen || *tr* drucken; *(a
suit)* (auf)bügeln; *(a person)* bedrängen; *(fruit)* ausdrücken; **be
pressed for** knapp sein an *(dat)*; **p.
s.o. to** *(inf)* j–n dringend bitten zu
(inf); **p. the button** auf den Knopf
drücken || *intr (said of time)* drän-
gen; **p. for** drängen auf *(acc)*; **p.
forward** sich vorwärtsdrängen

press′ box′ *s* Pressekabine *f*

press′ card′ *s* Presseausweis *m*

press′ing *adj* dringend, dringlich

press′ release′ *s* Pressemitteilung *f*

pressure [ˈpreʃər] *s* Druck *m*; *(of work)* Andrang *m*; *(aut)* Reifendruck *m*; put p. on unter Druck setzen ‖ *tr* drängen

pres′sure cook′er *s* Schnellkochtopf *m*

pres′sure group′ *s* Interessengruppe *f*

pressurize [ˈpreʃəˌraɪz] *tr* druckfest machen

prestige [presˈtiʒ] *s* Prestige *n*

presumably [prɪˈz(j)uməblɪ] *adv* vermutlich

presume [prɪˈz(j)um] *tr* vermuten ‖ *intr* vermuten; p. on pochen auf *(acc)*

presumption [prɪˈzʌmpʃən] *s* Vermutung *f*; *(presumptuousness)* Anmaßung *f*

presumptuous [prɪˈzʌmptʃu·əs] *adj* anmaßend

presuppose [ˌprisəˈpoz] *tr* voraussetzen

pretend [prɪˈtend] *tr* vorgeben; he pretended that he was a captain er gab sich für e-n Hauptmann aus ‖ *intr* so tun, als ob

pretender [prɪˈtendər] *s* Quaksalber *m*; p. to the throne Thronbewerber *m*

pretense [prɪˈtens], [ˈpritəns] *s* Schein *m*; under false pretenses unter Vorspiegelung falscher Tatsachen; under the p. of unter dem Vorwand *(genit)*

pretentious [prɪˈtenʃəs] *adj* *(person)* anmaßend; *(home)* protzig

pretext [ˈpritekst] *s* Vorwand *m*

pretty [ˈprɪtɪ] *adj* hübsch ‖ *adv* (coll) ziemlich

pretzel [ˈpretsəl] *s* Brezel *f*

prevail [prɪˈvel] *intr* *(predominate)* (vor)herrschen; *(triumph)* (against) sich behaupten (gegen); p. on überreden

prevail′ing *adj* *(fashion, view)* (vor)herrschend; *(situation)* obwaltend

prevalence [ˈprevələns] *s* Vorherrschen *n*

prevalent [ˈprevələnt] *adj* vorherrschend; be p. herrschen

prevaricate [prɪˈværɪˌket] *intr* Ausflüchte machen

prevent [prɪˈvent] *tr* verhindern; *(war, danger)* abwenden; p. s.o. from j-n hindern an *(dat)*; p. s.o. from *(ger)* j-n daran hindern zu *(inf)*

prevention [prɪˈvenʃən] *s* Verhütung *f*

preventive [prɪˈventɪv] *adj* vorbeugend ‖ *s* Schutzmittel *n*

preview [ˈpriˌvju] *s* Vorschau *f*

previous [ˈprivɪ·əs] *adj* vorhergehend, vorig; Vor-, e.g., p. conviction Vorstrafe *f*; p. day Vortag *m*; p. record Vorstrafenregister *n*

previously [ˈprivɪ·əslɪ] *adv* vorher

prewar [ˈpriˌwɔr] *adj* Vorkriegs-

prey [pre] *s* Beute *f*, Raub *m*; (fig) Opfer *n*; fall p. to (& fig) zum Opfer fallen *(dat)* ‖ *intr*—p. on erbeuten; *(exploit)* ausbeuten; p. on s.o.'s mind an j-s Gewissen nagen

price [praɪs] *s* Preis *m*; (st. exch.) Kurs *m*; at any p. um jeden Preis; at the p. of im Wert von ‖ *tr* mit Preisen versehen; *(inquire about the price of)* nach dem Preis fragen *(genit)*

price′ control′ *s* Preiskontrolle *f*

price′ fix′ing *s* Preisbindung *f*

price′ freeze′ *s* Preisstopp *m*

priceless [ˈpraɪslɪs] *adj* unbezahlbar; (coll) sehr komisch

price′ range′ *s* Preislage *f*

price′ rig′ging *s* Preistreiberei *f*

price′ tag′ *s* Preiszettel *m*, Preisschild *n*

price′-wage′ spi′ral *s* Preis-Lohn-Spirale *f*

price′ war′ *s* Preiskrieg *m*

prick [prɪk] *s* (& fig) Stich *m* ‖ *tr* stechen; p. up *(ears)* spitzen

prickly [ˈprɪklɪ] *adj* stachelig, Stech-

prick′ly heat′ *s* Hitzepickel *pl*

pride [praɪd] *s* Stolz *m*; (pej) Hochmut *m*; swallow one's p. seinen Stolz in die Tasche stecken; take p. in stolz sein auf *(acc)* ‖ *tr*—p. oneself on sich viel einbilden auf *(acc)*

priest [prist] *s* Priester *m*

priestess [ˈprɪstɪs] *s* Priesterin *f*

priest′hood *s* Priestertum *n*

priestly [ˈpristlɪ] *adj* priesterlich

prig [prɪg] *s* Tugendbold *m*

prim [prɪm] *adj* (primmer; primmest) spröde

primacy [ˈpraɪməsɪ] *s* Primat *m* & *n*

primarily [praɪˈmerɪlɪ] *adv* vor allem

primary [ˈpraɪˌmerɪ] *adj* primär, Haupt-; *(e.g., color, school)* Grund- ‖ *s* (pol) Vorwahl *f*

primate [ˈpraɪmet] *s* (zool) Primat *m*

prime [praɪm] *adj* *(chief)* Haupt-; *(best)* erstklassig ‖ *s* Blüte *f*; (math) Primzahl *f*; p. of life Lenz *m* des Lebens ‖ *tr* *(a pump)* ansaugen lassen; *(ammunition)* scharfmachen; *(a surface for painting)* grundieren; *(with information)* vorher informieren

prime′ min′ister *s* Ministerpräsident *m*; *(in England)* Premierminister *m*

primer [ˈprɪmər] *s* Fibel *f* ‖ [ˈpraɪmər] *s* *(for painting)* Grundierfarbe *f*; *(of an explosive)* Zündsatz *m*; (aut) Einspritzpumpe *f*

prime′ time′ *s* schönste Zeit *f*

primeval [praɪˈmivəl] *adj* urweltlich, Ur-; p. world Urwelt *f*

primitive [ˈprɪmɪtɪv] *adj* primitiv ‖ *s* Primitive *mf*, Urmensch *m*

primp [prɪmp] *tr* aufputzen ‖ *intr* sich aufputzen, sich zieren

prim′rose′ *s* Himmelschlüssel *m*

prince [prɪns] *s* Prinz *m*, Fürst *m*

Prince′ Al′bert *s* Gehrock *m*

princely [ˈprɪnslɪ] *adj* prinzlich

princess [ˈprɪnsɪs] *s* Prinzessin *f*, Fürstin *f*

principal [ˈprɪnsɪpəl] *adj* Haupt- ‖ *s* (educ) Schuldirektor -in *mf*; (fin) Kapitalbetrag *m*, Kapital *n*

principality [ˌprɪnsɪˈpælɪtɪ] *s* Fürstentum *n*

principally ['prɪnsɪpəli] *adv* größtenteils
principle ['prɪnsɪpəl] *s* Grundsatz *m*,
Prinzip *n;* **in p.** im Prinzip
print [prɪnt] *s* (*lettering; design on
cloth*) Druck *m;* (*printed dress*) be-
drucktes Kleid *n;* (*phot*) Abzug *m;*
in cold p. schwarz auf weiß; **out of
p.** vergriffen ‖ *tr* drucken; (*e.g.,
one's name*) in Druckschrift schreiben; (*phot*) kopieren; (*tex*) bedrucken
print'ed mat'ter *s* Drucksache *f*
printer ['prɪntər] *s* Drucker *m;* (*phot*)
Kopiermaschine *f*
prin'ter's ink' *s* Druckerschwärze *f*
print'ing *s* Drucken *n;* (*of a book*)
Buchdruck *m;* (*subsequent printing*)
Abdruck *m;* (*phot*) Kopieren *n*, Abziehen *n*
print'ing press' *s* Druckerpresse *f*
print' shop' *s* Druckerei *f*
prior ['praɪ·ər] *adj* vorherig; **p. to** vor
(*dat*) ‖ *s* (eccl) Prior *m*
priority [praɪ'ɔrɪti] *s* Priorität *f*
prism ['prɪzəm] *s* Prisma *n*
prison ['prɪzən] *s* Gefängnis *n*
pris'on camp' *s* Gefangenenlager *n*
prisoner ['prɪz(ə)nər] *s* Gefangene
mf; (*in a concentration camp*) Häftling *m;* **be taken p.** in Gefangenschaft
geraten; **take p.** gefangennehmen
pris'oner of war' *s* Kriegsgefangene *mf*
prissy ['prɪsi] *adj* zimperlich
privacy ['praɪvəsi] *s* Zurückgezogenheit *f;* **disturb s.o.'s p.** j-s Ruhe
stören
private ['praɪvɪt] *adj* privat; (*personal*) persönlich; **keep p.** geheimhalten ‖ *s* (mil) Gemeine *mf;* **in p.**
privat(im); **privates** Geschlechtsteile
pl
pri'vate cit'izen *s* Privatperson *f*
pri'vate eye' *s* (coll) Privatdetektiv *m*
pri'vate first' class' *s* Gefreite *mf*
privately ['praɪvɪtli] *adv* privat(im)
privet ['prɪvɪt] *s* Liguster *m*
privilege ['prɪvɪlɪdʒ] *s* Privileg *n*
privy ['prɪvi] *adj*—**p. to** eingeweiht in
(*acc*) ‖ *s* Abtritt *m*
prize [praɪz] *s* Preis *m*, Prämie *f;* (nav)
Prise *f* ‖ *tr* schätzen
prize' fight' *s* Preisboxkampf *m*
prize' fight'er *s* Berufsboxer *m*
prize' ring' *s* Boxring *m*
pro [pro] *s* (pros) (coll) Profi *m;* **the
pros and the cons** das Für und Wider
‖ *prep* für (*acc*)
probability [,prɑbə'bɪlɪti] *s* Wahrscheinlichkeit *f;* **in all p.** aller Wahrscheinlichkeit nach
probable ['prɑbəbəl] *adj* wahrscheinlich
probate ['probet] *s* Testamentsbestäti-
gung *f* ‖ *tr* bestätigen
pro'bate court' *s* Nachlaßgericht *n*
probation [pro'beʃən] *s* Probe *f;* (jur)
Bewährungsfrist *f;* **on p.** auf Probe;
(jur) mit Bewährung
proba'tion of'ficer *s* Bewährungshelfer
–in *mf*
probe [prob] *s* (jur) Untersuchung *f;*

(mil) Sondierungsangriff *m;* (rok)
Versuchsrakete *f;* (surg) Sonde *f* ‖
tr (*with the hands*) abtasten; (fig &
surg) sondieren
problem ['prɑbləm] *s* Problem *n;*
(math) Aufgabe *f*
prob'lem child' *s* Sorgenkind *n*
procedure [pro'sidʒər] *s* Verfahren *n*
proceed [pro'sid] *intr* (*go on*) fortfahren; (*act*) verfahren; **p. against** (jur)
vorgehen gegen; **p. from** kommen
von; **p. to** (*inf*) darangehen zu (*inf*)
proceed'ing *s* Vorgehen *n;* **proceedings**
(*of a society*) Sitzungsberichte *pl;*
(jur) Verfahren *n*
proceeds ['prosidz] *spl* Erlös *n*
process ['prɑses] *s* Verfahren *n*, Prozeß *m;* **be in p.** im Gang sein; **in the
p. dabei** ‖ *tr* (*raw materials*) verarbeiten; (*applications*) bearbeiten;
(*persons*) abfertigen; (phot) entwickeln und vervielfältigen
procession [pro'seʃən] *s* Prozession *f*
proclaim [pro'klem] *tr* ankündigen; (*a
law*) bekanntmachen; **p. (as)** a holiday zum Feiertag erklären
proclamation [,prɑklə'meʃən] *s* Auf-
ruf *m*, Proklamation *f*
procrastinate [pro'kræstɪ,net] *intr*
zaudern
proctor ['prɑktər] *s* Aufsichtsführende
mf ‖ *tr* beaufsichtigen
procure [pro'kjur] *tr* besorgen, verschaffen; (*said of a pimp*) verkup-
peln
procurement [pro'kjurmənt] *s* Besorgung *f*
procurer [pro'kjurər] *s* Kuppler *m*
prod [prɑd] *s* Stoß *m;* (*stick*) Stachel-
stock *m* ‖ *v* (*pret & pp* **prodded**) *ger*
prodding) *tr* stoßen; **prod s.o. into**
(*ger*) j-n dazu anstacheln zu (*inf*)
prodigal ['prɑdɪgəl] *adj* verschwenderisch
prod'igal son' *s* verlorener Sohn *m*
prodigious [pro'dɪdʒəs] *adj* großartig
prodigy ['prɑdɪdʒi] *s* Wunderzeichen
n; (*talented child*) Wunderkind *n*
produce ['prɑd(j)us] *s* (*product*) Erzeugnis *n;* (*amount produced*) Ertrag
m; (*fruits and vegetables*) Boden-
produkte *pl* ‖ [pro'd(j)us] *tr* produzieren; (*manufacture*) herstellen;
(*said of plants, trees*) hervorbringen;
(*interest, profit*) abwerfen; (*proof*)
beibringen; (*papers*) vorlegen; (cin)
produzieren; (theat) inszenieren ‖
intr (bot) tragen; (econ) Gewinne
abwerfen
producer [pro'd(j)usər] *s* Hersteller
m; (cin, theat) Produzent –in *mf*
product ['prɑdʌkt] *s* Erzeugnis *n*, Produkt *n*
production [pro'dʌkʃən] *s* Erzeugung
f, Produktion *f;* (fa, lit) Werk *n*
productive [pro'dʌktɪv] *adj* produktiv
profane [pro'fen] *adj* profan; **p. language** Fluchen *n* ‖ *tr* profanieren
profanity [pro'fænɪti] *s* Fluchen *n;*
profanities Flüche *pl*

profess [pro'fes] *tr* gestehen

profession [pro'feʃən] *s* Beruf *m*; (*of faith*) Bekenntnis *n*; by p. von Beruf

professional [pro'feʃənəl] *adj* berufsmäßig, professionell || *s* (*expert*) Fachmann *m*; (sport) Profi *m*

profes'sional jea'lousy *s* Brotneid *m*

professor [pro'fesər] *s* Professor –in *mf*

profes'sorship' *s* Professur *f*

proffer ['prɔfər] *s* Angebot *n* || *tr* anbieten

proficient [pro'fiʃənt] *adj* tüchtig

profile ['profaɪl] *s* Profil *n*; (*biographical sketch*) Kurzbiographie *f*

profit ['prɔfɪt] *s* Gewinn *m*; show a p. e–n Gewinn abwerfen || *tr* nutzen || *intr* (by) Nutzen ziehen aus

profitable ['prɔfɪtəbəl] *adj* einträglich

profiteer [,prɔfɪ'tɪr] *s* Wucherer *m*, Schieber *m* || *intr* wuchern, schieben

prof'it shar'ing *s* Gewinnbeteiligung *f*

profligate ['prɔflɪgɪt] *adj* verkommen; (*extravagant*) verschwenderisch || *s* verkommener Mensch *m*; (*spendthrift*) Verschwender –in *mf*

profound [pro'faund] *adj* (*knowledge*) gründlich; (*change*) tiefgreifend

profuse [prə'fjus] *adj* überreichlich

progeny ['prɔdʒəni] *s* (& bot) Nachkommenschaft *f*; (*of animals*) Junge *pl*

prog·no·sis [prɑg'nosɪs] *s* (–ses [siz]) Prognose *f*

prognosticate [prɑg'nɑstɪ,ket] *tr* voraussagen

pro·gram ['progræm] *s* Programm *n*; (*radio or television show*) Sendung *f* || *v* (*pret & pp* –grammed; *ger* –gramming) *tr* programmieren

progress ['progres] *s* Fortschritt *m*; be in progress im Gang sein || [prə'gres] *intr* (*make progress*) fortschreiten; (*develop*) sich fortentwickeln

progressive [prə'gresɪv] *adj* fortschrittlich; (*party*) Fortschritts– || *s* Fortschrittler –in *mf*

prog'ress report' *s* Tätigkeitsbericht *m*

prohibit [pro'hɪbɪt] *tr* verbieten

prohibition [,pro·ə'bɪʃən] *s* Verbot *n*; (hist) Prohibition *f*

prohibitive [pro'hɪbɪtɪv] *adj* (*costs*) unertragbar; (*prices*) unerschwinglich

project ['prɑdʒɛkt] *s* Project *n*, Vorhaben *n* || [prə'dʒɛkt] *tr* (*light, film*) projizieren; (*plan*) vorhaben || *intr* vorspringen, vorragen

projectile [prə'dʒɛktɪl] *s* (*fired from a gun*) Projektil *n*; (*thrown object*) Wurfgeschoß *n*

projection [prə'dʒɛkʃən] *s* (*jutting out*) Vorsprung *m*, Vorbau *m*; (cin) Projektion *f*

projector [prə'dʒɛktər] *s* Projektor *m*

proletarian [,prolɪ'tɛrɪ·ən] *adj* proletarisch || *s* Proletarier –in *mf*

proletariat [,prolɪ'tɛrɪ·ət] *s* Proletariat *n*

proliferate [prə'lɪfə,ret] *intr* sich stark vermehren

prolific [prə'lɪfɪk] *adj* fruchtbar

prolix [pro'lɪks] *adj* weitschweifig

prologue ['prolɔg] *s* Prolog *m*

prolong [pro'lɔŋ] *tr* verlängern

promenade [,prɑmɪ'ned] *s* Promenade *f* || *intr* promenieren

promenade' deck' *s* Promenadendeck *n*

prominent ['prɑmɪnənt] *adj* hervorragend, prominent; (*chin*) vorstehend

promiscuity [,prɑmɪs'kju·ɪti] *s* Promiskuität *f*

promiscuous [pro'mɪskju·əs] *adj* unterschiedslos; (*sexually*) locker

promise ['prɑmɪs] *s* Versprechen *n* || *tr* versprechen

prom'ising *adj* (*thing*) aussichtsreich; (*person*) vielversprechend

prom'issory note' ['prɑmɪ,sori] *s* Eigenwechsel *m*

promontory ['prɑmən,tori] *s* Landspitze *f*

promote [prə'mot] *tr* (*in rank*) befördern; (*a cause*) fördern; (*a pupil*) versetzen; (*wares*) werben für

promoter [prə'motər] *s* Förderer –in *mf*; (sport) Veranstalter –in *mf*

promotion [prə'moʃən] *s* (*in rank*) Beförderung *f*; (*of a cause*) Förderung *f*; (*of a pupil*) Versetzung *f*

prompt [prɑmpt] *adj* prompt || *tr* veranlassen; (theat) soufflieren (*dat*)

prompter ['prɑmptər] *s* Souffleur *m*, Souffleuse *f*

promp'ter's box' *s* Souffleurkasten *m*

promptness ['prɑmptnɪs] *s* Pünktlichkeit *f*

promulgate [pro'mʌlget] *tr* bekanntmachen

prone [pron] *adj*—be p. to neigen zu; in the p. position auf Anschlag liegend

prong [prɔŋ] *s* (*of a fork*) Zinke *f*; (*of a deer*) Sprosse *f*

pronoun ['pronaun] *s* Fürwort *n*

pronounce [prə'nauns] *tr* (*enunciate*) aussprechen; p. sentence das Strafausmaß festsetzen; p. s.o. (*e.g., guilty, insane, man and wife*) erklären für

pronouncement [prə'naunsmənt] *s* (*announcement*) Erklärung *f*; (*of a sentence*) (jur) Verkündung *f*

pronunciation [prə,nʌnsɪ'eʃən] *s* Aussprache *f*

proof [pruf] *adj*—p. against (fig) gefeit gegen; 90 p. 45 prozentig || *s* Beweis *m*; (phot) Probebild *n*; (typ) Korrekturbogen *m*

proof'read'er *s* Korrektor –in *mf*

prop [prɑp] *s* Stütze *f*; props (coll) Beine *pl*; (theat) Requisiten *pl* || *v* (*pret & pp* propped; *ger* propping) *tr* stützen; p. oneself up sich aufstemmen; p. up abstützen

propaganda [,prɑpə'gændə] *s* Propaganda *f*

propagate ['prɑpə,get] *tr* fortpflanzen; (fig) propagieren || *intr* sich fortpflanzen

pro·pel [prə'pɛl] *v* (*pret & pp* –pelled; *ger* –pelling) *tr* antreiben

propeller [prə'pɛlər] *s* (aer) Propeller *m*; (naut) Schraube *f*

propensity [prə'pɛnsɪti] *s* Neigung *f*

proper ['prɑpər] *adj* passend; (*way, time*) richtig; (*authority*) zuständig; (*strictly so-called*) selbst, e.g., Germany p. Deutschland selbst

properly ['prɑpərli] *adj* gehörig

prop'er name' *s* Eigenname *m*

property ['prɑpərti] *s* Eigentum *n*; (*land*) Grundstück *n*; (*quality*) Eigenschaft *f*

prop'erty dam'age *s* Sachschaden *m*

prop'erty tax' *s* Grundsteuer *f*

prophecy ['prɑfɪsi] *s* Prophezeiung *f*

prophe•sy ['prɑfɪ,saɪ] *v* (*pret & pp -sied*) *tr* prophezeien

prophet ['prɑfɪt] *s* Prophet *m*

prophetess ['prɑfɪtɪs] *s* Prophetin *f*

prophylactic [,prɑfɪ'læktɪk] *adj* prophylaktisch || *s* Prophylaktikum *n*; (*condom*) Präservativ *n*

propitiate [prə'pɪʃɪ,et] *tr* versöhnen

propitious [prə'pɪʃəs] *adj* günstig

prop'jet' *s* Flugzeug *n* mit Turboprop

proportion [prə'porʃən] *s* Verhältnis *n*; in p. to im Verhältnis zu; out of p. to in keinem Verhältnis zu; proportions Proportionen *pl* || *tr* bemessen; well proportioned gut proportioniert

proposal [prə'pozəl] *s* Vorschlag *m*; (*of marriage*) Heiratsantrag *m*

propose [prə'poz] *tr* vorschlagen; (*intend*) beabsichtigen; p. a toast to e-n Toast ausbringen auf (*acc*) || *intr* (to) e-n Heiratsantrag machen (*dat*)

proposition [,prɑpə'zɪʃən] *s* Vorschlag *m*; (log, math) Lehrsatz *m* || *tr* ansprechen

propound [prə'paund] *tr* vortragen

proprietor [prə'praɪ-ətər] *s* Inhaber *m*

proprietress [prə'praɪ-ətrɪs] *s* Inhaberin *f*

propriety [prə'praɪ-əti] *s* Anstand *m*; **proprieties** Anstandsformen *pl*

propulsion [prə'pʌlʃən] *s* Antrieb *m*

prorate [pro'ret] *tr* anteilmäßig verteilen

prosaic [pro'ze-ɪk] *adj* prosaisch

proscribe [pro'skraɪb] *tr* proskribieren

prose [proz] *adj* Prosa- || *s* Prosa *f*

prosecute ['prɑsɪ,kjut] *tr* verfolgen

prosecutor ['prɑsɪ,kjutər] *s* Ankläger -in *mf*

proselytize ['prɑsəlɪ,taɪz] *intr* Anhänger gewinnen

prose' writ'er *s* Prosaiker -in *mf*

prosody ['prɑsədi] *s* Silbenmessung *f*

prospect ['prɑspekt] *s* Aussicht *f*; (*person*) Interessent -in *mf*; hold out the p. of s.th. etw in Aussicht stellen || *intr* (for) schürfen (nach)

prospector ['prɑspektər] *s* Schürfer *m*

prospectus [prə'spektəs] *s* Prospekt *m*

prosper ['prɑspər] *intr* gedeihen

prosperity [prɑs'perɪti] *s* Wohlstand *m*

prosperous ['prɑspərəs] *adj* wohlhabend

prostitute ['prɑstɪ,t(j)ut] *s* Prostituierte *f* || *tr* prostituieren

prostrate ['prɑstret] *adj* hingestreckt; (*exhausted*) erschöpft || *tr* niederwerfen; (fig) niederzwingen

prostration [prɑs'treʃən] *s* Niederwerfen *n*; (*abasement*) Demütigung *f*

protagonist [pro'tægənɪst] *s* Protagonist *m*, Hauptfigur *f*

protect [prə'tekt] *tr* (be)schützen; (*interests*) wahrnehmen; p. from schützen vor (*dat*)

protection [prə'tekʃən] *s* (**from**) Schutz *m* (vor *dat*)

protector [prə'tektər] *s* Beschützer *m*

protein ['protin] *s* Protein *n*

protest ['protest] *s* Protest *m* || [pro'test] *tr & intr* protestieren

Protestant ['prɑtɪstənt] *adj* protestantisch || *s* Protestant -in *mf*

protocol ['protə,kɑl] *s* Protokoll *n*

proton ['protɑn] *s* Proton *n*

protoplasm ['protə,plæzəm] *s* Protoplasma *n*

prototype ['protə,taɪp] *s* Prototyp *m*

protozo•an [,protə'zo-ən] *s* (**-a** [ə]) Einzeller *m*

protract [pro'trækt] *tr* hinziehen

protrude [pro'trud] *intr* hervorstehen

proud [praud] *adj* (of) stolz (auf *acc*)

prove [pruv] *v* (*pret* **proved**; *pp* **proved** & **proven** ['pruvən]) *tr* beweisen; p. a failure sich nicht bewähren; p. one's worth sich bewähren || *intr*—p. right zutreffen; p. to be sich erweisen als

proverb ['prɑvərb] *s* Sprichwort *n*

proverbial [prə'vʌrbɪ-əl] *adj* sprichwörtlich

provide [prə'vaɪd] *tr* (*s.th.*) besorgen; p. s.o. with s.th. j-n mit etw versorgen || *intr*—p. for (*e.g., a family*) sorgen für; (*e.g., a special case*) vorsehen; (*the future*) voraussehen

provid'ed *adj* (with) versehen (mit) || *conj* vorausgesetzt, daß

Providence ['prɑvɪdəns] *s* Vorsehung *f*

providential [,prɑvɪ'dentʃəl] *adj* von der Vorsehung beschlossen

provid'ing *conj* vorausgesetzt, daß

province ['prɑvɪns] *s* (*district*) Provinz *f*; (*special field*) Ressort *n*

provision [prə'vɪʒən] *s* (*providing*) Versorgung *f*; (*stipulation*) Bestimmung *f*; make p. for Vorsorge treffen für; **provisions** Lebensmittelvorräte *pl* || *tr* (mil) verpflegen

provisional [prə'vɪʒənəl] *adj* vorläufig

provi•so [prə'vaɪzo] *s* (**-sos** & **-soes**) Vorbehalt *m*

provocation [,prɑvə'keʃən] *s* Provokation *f*

provocative [prə'vɑkətɪv] *adj* aufreizend

provoke [prə'vok] *tr* (*a person*) provozieren; (*e.g., laughter*) erregen

provok'ing *adj* ärgerlich

prow [prau] *s* Bug *m*

prowess ['prau-ɪs] *s* Tapferkeit *f*

prowl [praul] *intr* herumschleichen

prowl' car' *s* Streifenwagen *m*

prowler ['praulər] *s* mutmaßlicher Einbrecher *m*

proximity [prɑk'sɪmɪti] *s* Nähe *f*

proxy ['prɑksi] *s* Stellvertreter -in *mf*; by p. in Vertretung

prude [prud] *s* prüde Person *f*
prudence ['prudəns] *s* Klugheit *f*; (*caution*) Vorsicht *f*
prudent ['prudənt] *adj* klug; (*cautious*) umsichtig
prudish ['prudɪʃ] *adj* prüde
prune [prun] *s* Zwetschge *f* || *tr* stuzen
Prussia ['prʌʃə] *s* Preußen *n*
Prussian ['prʌʃən] *adj* preußisch || *s* Preuße *m*, Preußin *f*
pry [praɪ] *v* (*pret & pp* pried) *tr*—pry open aufbrechen; pry s.th. out of s.o. etw aus j—m herauspressen || *intr* herumschnüffeln; pry into seine Nase stecken in (*acc*)
P.S. ['pi'es] *s* (postscript) NS
psalm [sɑm] *s* Psalm *m*
pseudo· ['sudo] *adj* Pseudo-, falsch
pseudonym ['sudənɪm] *s* Deckname *m*
psyche ['saɪkɪ] *s* Psyche *f*
psychiatrist [saɪ'kaɪ·ətrɪst] *s* Psychiater –in *mf*
psychiatry [saɪ'kaɪ·ətrɪ] *s* Psychiatrie *f*
psychic ['saɪkɪk] *adj* psychisch || *s* Medium *n*
psychoanalysis [ˌsaɪko·ə'nælɪsɪs] *s* Psychoanalyse *f*
psychoanalyze [ˌsaɪko'ænə,laɪz] *tr* psychoanalytisch behandeln
psychologic(al) [ˌsaɪko'lɑdʒɪk(əl)] *adj* psychologisch
psychologist [saɪ'kɑlədʒɪst] *s* Psychologe *m*, Psychologin *f*
psychology [saɪ'kɑlədʒɪ] *s* Psychologie *f*
psychopath ['saɪkə,pæθ] *s* Psychopath –in *mf*
psycho·sis [saɪ'kosɪs] *s* (–ses [siz]) Psychose *f*
psychotic [saɪ'kɑtɪk] *adj* psychotisch || *s* Psychosekranke *mf*
pto'main poi'soning ['tomen] *s* Fleischvergiftung *f*
pub [pʌb] *s* Kneipe *f*
puberty ['pjubərtɪ] *s* Pubertät *f*
public ['pʌblɪk] *adj* öffentlich || *s* Öffentlichkeit *f*, Publikum *n*
pub'lic address' sys'tem *s* Lautsprecheranlage *f*
publication [ˌpʌblɪ'keʃən] *s* Veröffentlichung *f*
pub'lic domain' *n*—in the p. d. gemeinfrei
publicity [pʌb'lɪsɪtɪ] *s* Publizität *f*
publicize ['pʌblɪ,saɪz] *tr* bekanntmachen
pub'lic opin'ion *s* öffentliche Meinung *f*
pub'lic-opin'ion poll' *s* öffentliche Meinungsumfrage *f*
pub'lic pros'ecutor *s* Staatsanwalt *m*
pub'lic rela'tions *spl* Kontaktpflege *f*
pub'lic serv'ant *s* Staatsangestellte *mf*
pub'lic util'ity *s* öffentlicher Versorgungsbetrieb *m*
publish ['pʌblɪʃ] *tr* veröffentlichen
publisher ['pʌblɪʃər] *s* Verleger –in *mf*
pub'lishing house' *s* Verlag *m*
puck [pʌk] *s* Puck *m*
pucker ['pʌkər] *tr* (*the lips*) spitzen || *intr*—p. up den Mund spitzen
pudding ['pudɪŋ] *s* Pudding *m*

puddle ['pʌdəl] *s* Pfütze *f*, Lache *f*
pudgy ['pʌdʒɪ] *adj* dicklich
puerile ['pju·ərɪl] *adj* knabenhaft
puff [pʌf] *s* (*on a cigarette*) Zug *m*; (*of smoke*) Rauchwölkchen *n*; (*on sleeves*) Puff *m* || *tr* (*e.g., a cigar*) paffen; p. oneself up sich aufblähen; p. out ausblasen (*weeds*) || *intr* keuchen; p. on (*a pipe, cigar*) paffen an (*dat*)
pugilist ['pjudʒɪlɪst] *s* Faustkämpfer *m*
pugnacious [pʌg'neʃəs] *adj* kampflustig
pug-nosed ['pʌg,nozd] *adj* stupsnasig
puke [pjuk] *s* (sl) Kotze *f* || *intr* (sl) kotzen
pull [pul] *s* Ruck *m*; (*influence*) Beziehungen *pl*; (*of gravity*) Anziehungskraft *f* || *tr* ziehen; (*a muscle*) zerren; (*proof*) (typ) abziehen; p. down (*e.g., a shade*) herunterziehen; (*a building*) niederreißen; p. off (coll) zuwegebringen; p. oneself together sich zusammennehmen; p. out (*weeds*) herausreißen; p. up (*e.g., a chair*) heranrücken || *intr* (on) ziehen (an *dat*); p. back sich zurückziehen; p. in (*arrive*) ankommen; p. out (*depart*) abfahren; p. over to the side an den Straßenrand heranfahren; p. through durchkommen; p. up (*e.g., in a car*) vorfahren
pullet ['pulɪt] *s* Hühnchen *n*
pulley ['pulɪ] *s* Rolle *f*; (*pulley block*) Flaschenzug *m*
pull'o'ver *s* Pullover *m*
pulmonary ['pʌlmə,nerɪ] *adj* Lungen-
pulp [pʌlp] *s* Brei *m*; (*to make paper*) Papierbrei *m*; beat to a p. windelweich schlagen
pulpit ['pulpɪt] *s* Kanzel *f*
pulsate ['pʌlset] *intr* pulsieren
pulsation [pʌl'seʃən] *s* Pulsieren *n*
pulse [pʌls] *s* Puls *m*; take s.o.'s p. j—m den Puls fühlen
pulverize ['pʌlvə,raɪz] *tr* pulverisieren
pum'ice stone' ['pʌmɪs] *s* Bimsstein *m*
pum·mel ['pʌməl] *v* (*pret & pp* –mel[l]ed; *ger* –mel[l]ing) *tr* mit der Faust schlagen
pump [pʌmp] *s* Pumpe *f*; (*shoe*) Pump *m* || *tr* pumpen; (*for information*) ausfragen; p. up (*a tire*) aufpumpen
pump'han'dle *s* Pumpenschwengel *m*
pumpkin ['pʌmpkɪn] *s* Kürbis *m*
pun [pʌn] *s* Wortspiel *n* || *v* (*pret & pp* punned; *ger* punning) *intr* ein Wortspiel machen
punch [pʌntʃ] *s* Faustschlag *m*; (*to make holes*) Locher *m*; (*drink*) Punsch *m* || *tr* mit der Faust schlagen; (*a card*) lochen; (*a punch clock*) stechen
punch' bowl' *s* Punschschüssel *f*
punch' card' *s* Lochkarte *f*
punch' clock' *s* Kontrolluhr *f*
punch'-drunk' *adj* von Faustschlägen betäubt
punch'ing bag' *s* Punchingball *m*
punch' line' *s* Pointe *f*
punctilious [pʌŋk'tɪlɪ·əs] *adj* förmlich
punctual ['pʌŋktʃu·əl] *adj* pünktlich
punctuate ['pʌŋkt∫u,et] *tr* interpunktieren

punctuation [ˌpʌŋktʃuˈeʃən] s Interpunktion f
punctua'tion mark' s Satzzeichen n
puncture [ˈpʌŋktʃər] s Loch n || tr durchstechen; **p.** a tire e–e Reifenpanne haben
punc'ture-proof' adj pannensicher
pundit [ˈpʌndɪt] s Pandit m
pungent [ˈpʌndʒənt] adj beißend, scharf
punish [ˈpʌnɪʃ] tr (be)strafen
punishment [ˈpʌnɪʃmənt] s Strafe f, Bestrafung f; (educ) Strafarbeit f
punk [pʌŋk] adj (sl) mies; **I feel p.** mir ist mies || s (sl) Rocker m
punster [ˈpʌnstər] s Wortspielmacher m
puny [ˈpjuni] adj kümmerlich, winzig
pup [pʌp] s junger Hund m
pupil [ˈpjupəl] s Schüler –in mf; (of the eye) Pupille f
puppet [ˈpʌpɪt] s Marionette f
pup'pet gov'ernment s Marionettenregierung f
pup'pet show' s Marionettentheater n
puppy [ˈpʌpi] s Hündchen n
pup'py love' s Jugendliebe f
purchase [ˈpʌrtʃəs] s Kauf m; (leverage) Hebelwirkung f || tr kaufen
pur'chasing pow'er s Kaufkraft f
pure [pjur] adj (& fig) rein
purgative [ˈpʌrgətɪv] s Abfuhrmittel n
purgatory [ˈpʌrgəˌtori] s Fegefeuer n
purge [pʌrdʒ] s (pol) Säuberungsaktion f || tr reinigen; (pol) säubern
puri·fy [ˈpjuriˌfai] v (pret & pp –fied) tr reinigen, läutern
puritan [ˈpjuritən] adj puritanisch || **Puritan** s Puritaner –in mf
purity [ˈpjurɪti] s Reinheit f
purloin [pərˈlɔin] tr entwenden
purple [ˈpʌrpəl] adj purpurn || s Purpur m
purport [ˈpʌrport] s Sinn m || [pərˈport] tr vorgeben; (imply) besagen
purpose [ˈpʌrpəs] s Absicht f; (goal) Zweck m; **on p.** absichtlich; **to no p.** ohne Erfolg
purposely [ˈpʌrpəsli] adv absichtlich
purr [pʌr] s Schnurren n || intr schnurren
purse [pʌrs] s Beutel m; (handbag) Handtasche f || tr—**p.** one's lips den Mund spitzen
purse' strings' spl—**hold the p.** über das Geld verfügen
pursue [pərˈs(j)u] tr (a person; a plan, goal) verfolgen; (studies, profession) betreiben; (pleasures) suchen
pursuit [pərˈs(j)ut] s Verfolgung f; **in hot p.** hart auf den Fersen
pursuit' plane' s Jäger m
purvey [pərˈve] tr liefern, versorgen
pus [pʌs] s Eiter m
push [puʃ] s Schub m; (mil) Offensive f || tr (e.g., a cart) schieben; (jostle) stoßen; (a button) drücken auf (acc); **p. around** (coll) schlecht behandeln; **p. aside** beiseite schieben; (curtains) zurückschlagen; **p. one's way through** sich durchdrängen; **p. through** durchsetzen || intr drängen

push' but'ton s Druckknopf m
push' cart' s Verkaufskarren m
push'o'ver s (snap) (coll) Kinderspiel n; (sucker) Gimpel m; (easy opponent) leicht zu besiegender Gegner m
push'-up' s (gym) Liegestütz m
pushy [ˈpuʃi] adj zudringlich
puss [pus] s (cat) Mieze f; (face) (sl) Fresse f
pussy [ˈpʌsi] adj eit(e)rig || [ˈpusi] s Mieze f
puss'y wil'low s Salweide f
put [put] v (pret & pp **put**; ger putting) tr (stand) stellen; (lay) legen; (set) setzen; **feel put out** ungehalten sein; **put across** to beibringen (dat); **put aside** beiseite legen; **put down** (a load) abstellen; (a rebellion) niederschlagen; (in writing) aufschreiben; **put in** (e.g., a windowpane) einsetzen; (e.g., a good word) einlegen; (time) (on) verwenden (auf acc); **put off** (a person) hinhalten; (postpone) aufschieben; **put on** (clothing) anziehen; (a hat) aufsetzen; (a ring) anstecken; (an apron) umbinden; (the brakes) betätigen; (to cook) ansetzen; (a play) aufführen; **put on an act** sich in Szene setzen; **put oneself into** sich hineindenken in (acc); **put oneself out** sich [dat] Umstände machen; **put on its feet again** (com) auf die Beine stellen; **put s.o. on to** s.th. j-m auf etw [acc] bringen; **put out** (a fire) löschen; (lights) auslöschen; (throw out) herauswerfen; (a new book) herausbringen; **put out of action** kampfunfähig machen; **put over on** s.o. j-n übers Ohr hauen; **put through** durchsetzen; (a call) (telp) herstellen; (s.o.) through to (telp) j-n verbinden mit; **put to good use** gut verwenden; **put up** (erect) errichten; (bail) stellen; (for the night) unterbringen; **put up a fight** sich zur Wehr setzen; **put up to** anstiften zu; **to put it mildly** gelinde gesagt || intr —**put on** sich verstellen; **put out to sea** (said of a ship) in See gehen; **put up with** sich abfinden mit
put'-on' adj vorgetäuscht || s (affectation) Affektiertheit f; (parody) Jux m
put-put [ˈpʌtˌpʌt] s Tacktack n || intr —**p.** along knattern
putrid [ˈpjutrɪd] adj faul(ig)
putt [pʌt] tr & intr (golf) putten
putter [ˈpʌtər] s (golf) Putter m || intr—**p.** around herumwursteln
put·ty [ˈpʌti] s Kitt m || v (pret & pp –tied) tr (ver)kitten
put'ty knife' s Spachtel m & f
put'-up job' s abgekartete Sache f
puzzle [ˈpʌzəl] s Rätsel n; (game) Geduldspiel n || tr verwirren; **be puzzled** verwirrt sein; **p. out** enträtseln || intr—**p.** over tüfteln an (dat)
puzzler [ˈpʌzlər] s Rätsel n
puz'zling adj rätselhaft
PW [ˈpiˈdʌbəlˌju] s (prisoner of war) Kriegsgefangene mf

pygmy ['pıgmi] s Pygmäe m, Pygmäin f

pylon ['paılɑn] s (entrance to Egyptian temple) Pylon m; (aer) Wendemarke f; (elec) Leitungsmast m

pyramid ['pırəmɪd] s Pyramide f

pyre [paır] s Scheiterhaufen m

Pyrenees ['pırı,niz] spl Pyrenäen pl

pyrotechnics [,paırə'teknıks] spl Feuerwerkskunst f, Pyrotechnik f

python ['paıθən] s Pythonschlange f

pyx [pıks] s (eccl) Pyxis f

Q

Q, q [kju] s siebzehnter Buchstabe des englischen Alphabets

quack [kwæk] s Quacksalber m, Kurpfuscher m || intr schnattern

quadrangle ['kwɑd,ræŋgəl] s Viereck n; (inner yard) Innenhof m, Lichthof m

quadrant ['kwɑdrənt] s Quadrant m

quadratic [kwɑd'rætɪk] adj quadratisch

quadruped ['kwɑdrʊ,ped] s Vierfüßer m

quadruple [kwɑd'rupəl] adj vierfach; s Vierfache n || tr vervierfachen || intr sich vervierfachen

quadruplets [kwɑd'ruplɛts] spl Vierlinge pl

quaff [kwɑf] tr in langen Zügen trinken

quagmire ['kwæg,maır] s Morast m

quail [kwel] s Wachtel f || intr verzagen

quaint [kwent] adj seltsam

quake [kwek] s Zittern n; (geol) Beben n || intr zittern; (geol) beben

Quaker ['kwekər] s Quäker –in mf

qualification [,kwɑlıfı'keʃən] s (for) Qualifikation f (für)

quali·fy ['kwɑlı,faı] v (pret & pp –fied) tr qualifizieren; (modify) einschränken || intr sich qualifizieren

quality ['kwɑltı] s (characteristic) Eigenschaft f; (grade) Qualität f

qualm [kwɑm] s Bedenken n

quandary ['kwɑndərı] s Dilemma n

quantity ['kwɑntıtı] s Menge f, Quantität f; (math) Größe f; (pros) Silbenmaß n; buy in q. auf Vorrat kaufen

quan'tum the'ory ['kwɑntəm] s Quantentheorie f

quarantine ['kwɔrən,tin] s Quarantäne f || tr unter Quarantäne stellen

quar·rel ['kwɔrəl] s Streit m; pick a q. Händel suchen || v (pret & pp –rel[l]ed; ger –el[l]ing) intr (over) streiten (über acc or um)

quarrelsome ['kwɔrəlsəm] adj streitsüchtig, händelsüchtig

quar·ry ['kwɔrı] s Steinbruch m; (hunt) Jagdbeute f || v (pret & pp –ried) tr brechen

quart [kwɔrt] s Quart n

quarter ['kwɔrtər] s Viertel n; (of a city) Stadtviertel n; (of the moon) Mondviertel n; (of the sky) Himmelsrichtung f; (coin) Vierteldollar m; (econ) Quartal n; (sport) Viertelzeit f; a q. after one (ein) Viertel nach

eins; a q. of an hour e–e Viertelstunde f; a q. to eight dreiviertel acht, (ein) viertel vor acht; at close quarters im Nahkampf; from all quarters von überall; give no q. keinen Pardon geben; quarters (& mil) Unterkunft f, Quartier n || tr (lodge) einquartieren; (divide into four, tear into quarters) vierteilen || intr im Quartier liegen

quar'ter-deck' s Quarterdeck n

quar'terfi'nal s Zwischenrunde f

quar'ter-hour' s Viertelstunde f

quarterly ['kwɔrtərlı] adj vierteljährig; (econ) Quartals– || s Vierteljahresschrift f

quar'termas'ter s Quartiermeister m

Quar'termaster Corps' s Versorgungstruppen pl

quar'ter note' s (mus) Viertelnote f

quar'ter rest' s (mus) Viertelpause f

quartet [kwɔr'tet] s Quartett n

quartz [kwɔrts] s Quarz m

quash [kwɑʃ] tr niederschlagen

quatrain ['kwɑtren] s Vierzeiler m

quaver ['kwevər] s Zittern n; (mus) Triller m || intr zittern; (mus) trillern, tremolieren

queasy ['kwizi] adj übel

queen [kwin] s Königin f; (cards) Dame f

queen' bee' s Bienenkönigin f

queen' dow'ager s Königinwitwe f

queenly ['kwinli] adj königlich

queen' moth'er s Königinmutter f

queer [kwır] adj sonderbar; (homosexual) schwul || s (homosexual) Schwule mf

queer' duck' s (coll) Unikum n

quell [kwel] tr unterdrücken

quench [kwɛntʃ] tr (thirst) löschen; (a fire) (aus)löschen

que·ry ['kwırı] s Frage f || v (pret & pp –ried) tr befragen; (cast doubt on) bezweifeln

quest [kwɛst] s Suche f; in q. of auf der Suche nach

question ['kwɛstʃən] s Frage f; ask (s.o.) a q. (j–m) e–e Frage stellen; be out of the q. außer Frage stehen; beyond q. außer Frage; call into q. in Frage stellen; call the q. (parl) um Abstimmung bitten; in q. betreffend; it is a q. of (ger) es handelt sich darum zu (inf); q. of time Zeitfrage f; that's an open q. darüber läßt sich streiten; there's no q. about it darüber besteht kein Zweifel || tr befragen; (*said of the police*) verhören; (*cast doubt on*) bezweifeln

questionable ['kwestʃənəbl] *adj* fraglich, fragwürdig; (*doubtful*) zweifelhaft; (*character*) bedenklich

ques'tioning *s* Verhör *n*, Vernehmung *f*

ques'tion mark' *s* Fragezeichen *n*

questionnaire [,kwestʃə'ner] *s* Fragebogen *m*

queue [kju] *s* Schlange *f* || *intr*—q. up sich anstellen

quibble ['kwɪbəl] *s* Deutelei *f* || *intr* (*about*) deuteln (an *dat*)

quibbler ['kwɪblər] *s* Wortklauber *m*

quick [kwɪk] *adj* schnell, fix || *s*—cut to the q. bis ins Mark treffen

quicken ['kwɪkən] *tr* beschleunigen || *intr* sich beschleunigen

quick'lime' *s* gebrannter ungelöschter Kalk *m*

quick' lunch' *s* Schnellimbiß *m*

quick'sand' *s* Treibsand *m*

quick'sil'ver *s* Quecksilber *n*

quick'-tem'pered *adj* jähzornig

quick'-wit'ted *adj* scharfsinnig

quiet ['kwaɪ.ət] *adj* ruhig; (*person*) schweigsam; (*still*) still; (*street*) unbelebt; **be q.!** sei still!; **keep q.** schweigen || *s* Stille *f* || *tr* beruhigen || *intr*—q. down sich beruhigen; (*said of excitement, etc.*) sich legen

quill [kwɪl] *s* Feder *f*, Federkiel *m*; (*of a porcupine*) Stachel *m*

quilt [kwɪlt] *s* Steppdecke *f* || *tr* steppen

quince [kwɪns] *s* Quitte *f*

quince' tree' *s* Quittenbaum *m*

quinine ['kwaɪnaɪn] *s* Chinin *n*

quintessence [kwɪn'tesəns] *s* Inbegriff *m*

quintet [kwɪn'tet] *s* Quintett *n*

quintuplets [kwɪn'tʌplets] *spl* Fünflinge *pl*

quip [kwɪp] *s* witziger Seitenhieb *m* || *v* (*pret & pp* quipped; *ger* quipping) *tr* witzig sagen || *intr* witzeln

quire [kwaɪr] *s* (bb) Lage *f*

quirk [kwʌrk] *s* Eigenart *f*; (*subterfuge*) Ausflucht *f*; (*sudden change*) plötzliche Wendung *f*

quit [kwɪt] *adj* quitt; **let's call it quits!** (coll) Strich drunter! || *v* (*pret & pp* quit & quitted; *ger* quitting) *tr* aufgeben; (*e.g., a gang*) abspringen von; **q. it!** hören Sie damit auf! || *intr* aufhören; (*at work*) seine Stellung aufgeben

quite [kwaɪt] *adv* recht, ganz; **q. a disappointment** e-e ausgesprochene Enttäuschung *f*; **q. recently** in jüngster Zeit; **q. the reverse** genau das Gegenteil

quitter ['kwɪtər] *s* Schlappmacher *m*

quiver ['kwɪvər] *s* Zittern *n*; (*to hold arrows*) Köcher *m* || *intr* zittern

quixotic [kwɪks'ɑtɪk] *adj* überspannt

quiz [kwɪz] *s* Prüfung *f*; (*game*) Quiz *n* || *v* (*pret & pp* quizzed; *ger* quizzing) *tr* ausfragen; **q. s.o. on s.th.** j-n etw abfragen

quiz'mas'ter *s* Quizonkel *m*

quiz' show' *s* Quizshow *f*

quizzical ['kwɪzɪkəl] *adj* (*puzzled*) verwirrt; (*strange*) seltsam; (*mocking*) spöttisch

quoit [kwɔɪt] *s* Wurfring *m*

quondam ['kwɑndæm] *adj* ehemalig

Quon'set hut' ['kwɑnset] *s* Nissenhütte *f*

quorum ['kworəm] *s* beschlußfähige Anzahl *f*

quota ['kwotə] *s* Quote *f*, Anteil *m*; (*work*) Arbeitsleistung *f*

quotation [kwo'teʃən] *s* Zitat *n*; (*price*) Notierung *f*

quota'tion marks' *spl* Anführungszeichen *pl*

quote [kwot] *s* Zitat *n*; (*of prices*) Notierung *f* || *tr* zitieren; (*prices*) notieren || *interj*—q. ... unquote Beginn des Zitats! ... Ende des Zitats!

quotient ['kwoʃənt] *s* Quotient *m*

R

R, r [ɑr] *s* achtzehnter Buchstabe des englischen Alphabets

rabbet ['ræbɪt] *s* Falz *m* || *tr* falzen

rabbi ['ræbaɪ] *s* Rabbiner *m*

rabbit ['ræbɪt] *s* Kaninchen *n*

rabble ['ræbəl] *s* Pöbel *m*

rab'ble-rous'er *s* Volksaufwiegler *-in mf*

rabid ['ræbɪd] *adj* rabiat; (*dog*) tollwütig

rabies ['rebiz] *s* Tollwut *f*

raccoon [ræ'kun] *s* Waschbär *m*

race [res] *s* Rasse *f*; (*contest*) Wettrennen *n*; (fig) Wettlauf *m* || *tr* um die Wette laufen mit; (*in a car*) um die Wette fahren mit; (*a horse*) rennen lassen; (*an engine*) hochjagen || *intr* rennen; (*on foot*) um die Wette laufen; (*in a car*) um die Wette fahren

race' driv'er *s* Rennfahrer *-in mf*

race' horse' *s* Rennpferd *n*

racer ['resər] *s* (*person*) Wettfahrer *-in mf*; (*car*) Rennwagen *m*; (*in speed skating*) Schnelläufer *-in mf*

race' ri'ot *s* Rassenaufruhr *m*

race' track' *s* Rennbahn *f*

racial ['reʃəl] *adj* rassisch, Rassen-

rac'ing *s* Rennsport *m*

racism ['resɪzəm] *s* Rassenhaß *m*

rack [ræk] *s* (shelf) Regal *n*, Ablage *f*; (*for clothes, bicycles, hats*) Ständer *m*; (*for luggage*) Gepäcknetz *n*; (*for fodder*) Futterraufe *f*; (*for torture*) Folter *f*; (*toothed bar*) Zahnstange *f*;

go to r. and ruin völlig zugrunde gehen; **put to the r.** auf die Folter spannen ‖ *tr (with pain)* quälen; **r. one's brains** *(over)* sich *[dat]* den Kopf zerbrechen (über *acc*)

racket ['rækɪt] *s (noise)* Krach *m; (illegal business)* Schiebergeschäft *n; (tennis)* Rakett *n*

racketeer [,rækɪ'tɪr] *s* Schieber –in *mf*

racketeer'ing *s* Schiebertum *n*

rack' rail'way *s* Zahnradbahn *f*

racy ['resɪ] *adj (off-color)* schlüpfrig; *(vivacious, pungent)* rassig

radar ['redər] *s* Radar *n*

ra'darscope' *s* Radarschirm *m*

radial ['redɪ·əl] *adj* radial

radiance ['redɪ·əns] *s* Strahlung *f*

radiant ['redɪ·ənt] *adj (with)* strahlend (vor *dat*); *(phys)* Strahlungs-

radiate ['redɪ,et] *tr & intr* ausstrahlen

radiation [,redɪ'eʃən] *s* Strahlung *f*

radia'tion belt' *s* Strahlungsgürtel *m*

radia'tion treat'ment *s* Bestrahlung *f;* **give r. treatment to** bestrahlen

radiator ['redɪ,etər] *s* Heizkörper *m; (aut)* Kühler *m*

ra'diator cap' *s* Kühlerverschluß *m*

radical ['rædɪkəl] *adj* radikal ‖ *s* Radikale *mf*

radically ['rædɪkəlɪ] *adv* von Grund auf

radi·o ['redɪ,o] *s (-os)* Radio *n,* Rundfunk *m;* **go on the r.** im Rundfunk sprechen ‖ *tr* funken

ra'dioac'tive *adj* radioaktiv

ra'dio announc'er *s* Rundfunkansager –in *mf*

ra'dio bea'con *s (aer)* Funkfeuer *n*

ra'dio beam' *s* Funkleitstrahl *m*

ra'dio broad'cast *s* Rundfunksendung *f*

radiocar'bon dat'ing *s* Radiokarbonmethode *f*

ra'diofre'quency *s* Hochfrequenz *f*

radiogram ['redɪ·o,græm] *s* Radiogramm *n*

radiologist [,redɪ'ɑlədʒɪst] *s* Röntgenologe *m,* Röntgenologin *f*

radiology [redɪ'ɑlədʒɪ] *s* Röntgenologie *f*

ra'dio net'work *s* Rundfunknetz *n*

ra'dio op'erator *s* Funker –in *mf*

radioscopy [,redɪ'ɑskəpɪ] *s* Durchleuchtung *f*

ra'dio set' *s* Radioapparat *m*

ra'dio sta'tion *s* Rundfunkstation *f*

radish ['rædɪʃ] *s* Radieschen *n*

radium ['redɪ·əm] *s* Radium *n*

radi·us ['redɪ·əs] *s (-i [,aɪ] & -uses)** Halbmesser *m; (anat)* Speiche *f;* **within a r. of** in e–m Umkreis von

raffish ['ræfɪʃ] *adj* gemein, niedrig

raffle ['ræfəl] *s* Tombola *f* ‖ *tr—***r. off** in e–r Tombola verlosen

raft [ræft] *s* Floß *n;* **a r. of** *(coll)* ein Haufen *m*

rafter ['ræftər] *s* Dachsparren *m;* **rafters** Sparrenwerk *n*

rag [ræg] *s* Lumpen *m;* **chew the rag** *(sl)* quasseln

ragamuffin ['rægə,mʌfɪn] *s* Lump *m*

rag' doll' *s* Stoffpuppe *f*

rage [redʒ] *s* Wut *f;* **all the r.** letzter

Schrei *m;* **be the r.** die große Mode sein; **fly into a r.** in Wut geraten ‖ *intr* wüten, toben

ragged ['rægɪd] *adj* zerlumpt, lumpig

rag'man *s (-men)* Lumpenhändler *m*

ragout [ræ'gu] *s* Ragout *n*

rag'weed' *s* Ambrosiapflanze *f*

raid [red] *s* Beutezug *m; (by police)* Razzia *f; (mil)* Überfall *m* ‖ *tr* überfallen; **e–e Razzia machen auf** *(acc)*

raider ['redər] *s (naut)* Kaperkreuzer *m;* **raiders** (mil) Kommandotruppe *f*

rail [rel] *s (rr)* Geländerstange *f; (naut)* Reling *f; (rr)* Schiene *f;* **by r.** per Bahn ‖ *intr***—r. at** beschimpfen

rail'head' *s* Schienenkopf *m*

rail'ing *s* Geländer *n; (naut)* Reling *f*

rail'road' *s* Eisenbahn *f* ‖ *tr (a bill)* durchpeitschen

rail'road cross'ing *s* Bahnübergang *m*

rail'road embank'ment *s* Bahndamm *m*

rail'road sta'tion *s* Bahnhof *m*

rail'road tie' *s* Schwelle *f*

rail'way' *adj* Eisenbahn- ‖ *s* Eisenbahn *f*

raiment ['remənt] *s* Kleidung *f*

rain [ren] *s* Regen *m;* **it looks like r.** es sieht nach Regen aus; **r. or shine** bei jedem Wetter ‖ *tr—***r. cats and dogs** Bindfäden regnen; **r. out** verregnen ‖ *intr* regnen

rainbow ['ren,bo] *s* Regenbogen *m*

rain'coat' *s* Regenmantel *m*

rain'drop' *s* Regentropfen *m*

rain'fall' *s* Regenfall *m; (amount of rain)* Regenmenge *f*

rain' gut'ter *s* Dachrinne *f*

rain' pipe' *s* Fallrohr *n*

rain'proof' *adj* regenfest, regendicht

rainy ['renɪ] *adj* regnerisch; *(e.g., day, weather)* Regen–; **save money for a r. day** sich *[dat]* e–n Notpfennig aufsparen

rain'y sea'son *s* Regenzeit *f*

raise [rez] *s* Lohnerhöhung *f; (in poker)* Steigerung *f* ‖ *tr (lift)* heben, erheben; *(increase)* erhöhen, steigern; *(erect)* aufstellen; *(children)* großziehen; *(a family)* ernähren; *(grain, vegetables)* anbauen; *(animals)* züchten; *(dust)* aufwirbeln; *(money, troops)* aufbringen; *(blisters)* ziehen; *(a question)* aufwerfen; *(hopes)* erwecken; *(a laugh, smile)* hervorrufen; *(the ante)* steigern; *(a siege)* aufheben; *(from the dead)* auferwecken; **r. Cain (or hell)** Krach schlagen; **r. the arm** *(before striking)* mit dem Arm ausholen; **r. the price of** verteuern; **r. to a higher power** potenzieren ‖ *intr (in poker)* höher wetten

raisin ['rezən] *s* Rosine *f*

rake [rek] *s* Rechen *m; (person)* Wüstling *m* ‖ *tr* rechen; *(with gunfire)* bestreichen; **r. in** *(money)* kassieren; **r. together (or up)** zusammenrechen

rake'-off' *s (coll)* Gewinnanteil *m*

rakish ['rekɪʃ] *adj (dissolute)* liederlich; *(jaunty)* schmissig

ral·ly ['rælɪ] *s (meeting)* Massenversammlung *f; (recovery)* Erholung *f;*

(mil) Umgruppierung f ‖ v (pret & pp –lied) tr (wieder) sammeln ‖ intr sich (wieder) sammeln; (recover) sich erholen

ram [ræm] s Schafbock m ‖ v (pret & pp rammed; ger ramming) tr rammen; ram s.th. down s.o.'s throat j–m etw aufdrängen

ramble ['ræmbəl] intr—r. about herumwandern; r. on daherreden

ramification [ˌræmɪfɪ'keʃən] s Verzweigung f

ramp [ræmp] s Rampe f

rampage ['ræmpedʒ] s Toben n, Wüten n; go on a r. toben, wüten

rampant ['ræmpənt] adj—be r. grassieren

rampart ['ræmpɑrt] s Wall m, Ringwall m

ram'rod' s Ladestock m; (cleaning rod) Reinigungsstock m

ram'shack'le adj baufällig

ranch [ræntʃ] s Ranch f

rancid ['rænsɪd] adj ranzig

random ['rændəm] adj zufällig, Zufalls–; at r. aufs Geratewohl

range [rendʒ] s (row) Reihe f; (mountains) Bergkette f; (stove) Herd m; (for firing practice) Schießplatz m; (of a gun) Schießweite f; (distance) Reichweite f; (mus) Umfang m; at a r. of in e–r Entfernung von; at close r. auf kurze Entfernung; come within s.o.'s r. j–m vor den Schuß kommen; out of r. außer Reichweite; (in shooting) außer Schußweite; within r. in Reichweite; (in shooting) in Schußweite ‖ tr reihen ‖ intr—r. from ... to sich bewegen zwischen (dat) ... und

range' find'er s Entfernungsmesser m

ranger ['rendʒər] s Förster m; rangers Stoßtruppen pl

rank [ræŋk] adj (rancid) ranzig; (smelly) stinkend; (absolute) kraß; (excessive) übermäßig; (growth) üppig ‖ s Rang m; according to r. standesgemäß; person of r. Standesperson f ‖ tr einreihen, rangieren; be ranked as gelten als ‖ intr rangieren; r. above stehen über (dat); r. among zählen zu; r. below stehen unter (dat); r. with mitzählen zu

rank' and file' s die breite Masse

rank'ing of'ficer s Rangälteste mf

rankle ['ræŋkəl] tr nagen an (dat) ‖ intr nagen

ransack ['rænsæk] tr durchstöbern

ransom ['rænsəm] s Lösegeld n ‖ tr auslösen

rant [rænt] intr schwadronieren

rap [ræp] s (on the door) Klopfen n; (blow) Klaps m; not give a rap for husten auf (acc); take the rap den Kopf hinhalten; there was a rap on the door es klopfte an der Tür ‖ v (pret & pp rapped; ger rapping) tr (strike) schlagen; (criticize) tadeln ‖ intr (talk freely) offen reden; (on) klopfen (an dat)

rapacious [rə'peʃəs] adj raffgierig; (animal) raubgierig

rape [rep] s Vergewaltigung f ‖ tr vergewaltigen

rapid ['ræpɪd] adj rapid(e); (river) reißend ‖ rapids spl Stromschnelle f

rap'id-fire' adj Schnell–; (mil) Schnellfeuer–

rap'id trans'it s Nahschnellverkehr m

rapier ['repɪ·ər] s Rapier n

rapist ['repɪst] s sexueller Gewaltverbrecher m

rap' ses'sion s zwanglose Diskussion f

rapt [ræpt] adj (attention) gespannt; (in thought) vertieft

rapture ['ræptʃər] s Entzückung f; go into raptures in Entzücken geraten

rare [rer] adj selten; (culin) halbgar

rare' bird' s (fig) weißer Rabe m

rare-fy ['rerɪˌfaɪ] v (pret & pp –fied) tr verdünnen

rarely ['rerlɪ] adv selten

rarity ['rerɪtɪ] s Rarität f

rascal ['ræskəl] s Bengel m

rash [ræʃ] adj vorschnell, unbesonnen ‖ s Ausschlag m

rasp [ræsp] s (sound) Kratzlaut m; (tool) Raspel f ‖ tr raspeln

raspberry ['ræzˌberɪ] s Himbeere f

rat [ræt] s Ratte f; (deserter) (sl) Überläufer –in mf; (informer) (sl) Spitzel m; (scoundrel) (sl) Gauner m; smell a rat (coll) den Braten riechen ‖ intr—rat on (sl) verpetzen

ratchet ['rætʃɪt] s (wheel) Sperrad n; (pawl) Sperrklinke f

rate [ret] s Satz m; (for mail, freight) Tarif m; at any r. auf jeden Fall; at the r. of (a certain speed) mit der Geschwindigkeit von; (a certain price) zum Preis von; at the r. of a dozen per week ein Dutzend pro Woche; at this (or that) r. bei diesem Tempo ‖ tr bewerten ‖ intr (coll) hochgeschätzt sein

rate' of exchange' s Kurs m

rate' of in'terest s Zinssatz m

rather ['ræðər] adv ziemlich; I would r. wait ich würde lieber warten; r. ... than lieber ... als ‖ interj na obl

rati-fy ['rætɪˌfaɪ] v (pret & pp –fied) tr ratifizieren, bestätigen

rat'ing s Beurteilung f; (mach) Leistung f; (mil) Dienstgrad m; (sport) Bewertung f

ra-tio ['reʃ(ɪ)ˌo] s (–tios) Verhältnis n

ration ['ræʃən], ['reʃən] s Ration f; rations (mil) Verpflegung f ‖ tr rationieren

ra'tion card' s Bezugsschein m

ra'tioning s Rationierung f

rational ['ræʃənəl] adj vernünftig

rationalize ['ræʃənəˌlaɪz] tr & intr rationalisieren

rat' poi'son s Rattengift n

rat' race' s (fig) Hetzjagd f

rattle ['rætəl] s Geklapper n; (toy) Klapper f, Schnarre f ‖ tr (confuse) verwirren; get s.o. rattled j–n aus dem Konzept bringen; r. off herunterschnarren; r. the dishes mit dem Geschirr klappern ‖ intr klappern; (said of a machine gun) knattern;

(said of windows) klirren; **r. on** daherplappern

rat'tlebrain' *s* Hohlkopf *m*

rat'tlesnake' *s* Klapperschlange *f*

rat'tletrap' *s* (coll) Kiste *f*, Karre *f*

rat'trap' *s* Rattenfalle *f*

raucous ['rɔkəs] *adj* heiser

ravage ['rævɪdʒ] *s* Verwüstung *f*, Verheerung *f* ∥ *tr* verwüsten, verheeren

rave [rev] *s (coll)* Modeschrei *m* ∥ *intr* irrereden; **r. about** schwärmen von

raven ['revən] *adj (black)* rabenschwarz ∥ *s* Kolkrabe *m*, Rabe *m*

ravenous ['rævənəs] *adj* rasend

ravine [rə'vin] *s* Bergschlucht *f*

rav'ing *adj (coll)* toll ∥ *adv*—**r. mad** tobsüchtig

ravish ['rævɪʃ] *tr* vergewaltigen

rav'ishing *adv* entzückend

raw [rɔ] *adj* roh; *(weather)* naßkalt; *(throat)* rauh; *(recruit)* unausgebildet; *(skin)* wundgerieben; *(leather)* ungegerbt; *(wool)* ungesponnen

raw'-boned' *adj* hager

raw' deal' *s (sl)* unfaire Behandlung *f*

raw'hide' *s* Rohhaut *f*

raw' mate'rial *s* Rohstoff *m*

ray [re] *s* Strahl *m*; (ichth) Rochen *m*; **ray of hope** Hoffnungsstrahl *m*

rayon ['re·ɑn] *adj* kunstseiden ∥ *s* Kunstseide *f*, Rayon *n*

raze [rez] *tr* abtragen; **r. to the ground** dem Erdboden gleichmachen

razor ['rezər] *s* Rasiermesser *n*; *(safety razor)* Rasierapparat *m*

ra'zor blade' *s* Rasierklinge *f*

razz [ræz] *tr (sl)* aufziehen

re [ri] *prep* betreffs *(genit)*

reach [rit∫] *s* Reichweite *f*; **beyond the r. of s.o.** für j—n unerreichbar; **out of r.** unerreichbar; **within easy r.** leicht zu erreichen; **within r. in** Reichweite ∥ *tr* (a goal, person, city, advanced age, an understanding) erreichen; *(a certain amount)* sich belaufen auf *(acc)*; *(a compromise)* schließen; *(an agreement)* treffen; *(e.g., the ceiling)* heranreichen an *(acc)*; **r. out** ausstrecken ∥ *intr (extend)* reichen, sich erstrecken; **r. for** greifen nach; **r. into one's pocket** in die Tasche greifen

react [rɪ'ækt] *intr (to)* reagieren (auf *acc*); **r. upon** zurückwirken auf *(acc)*

reaction [rɪ'æk∫ən] *s* Reaktion *f*

reactionary [rɪ'æk∫ən‚erɪ] *adj* reaktionär ∥ *s* Reaktionär –in *mf*

reac'tion time' *s* Reaktionszeit *f*

reactor [rɪ'æktər] *s* Reaktor *m*

read [rid] *v (pret & pp read* [red]*) tr* lesen; **a paper on** referieren über *(acc)*; **r. off** verlesen; **r. over** durchlesen; **r. to** vorlesen *(dat)* ∥ *intr* lesen; *(said of a passage)* lauten; *(said of a thermometer)* zeigen; **r. up on** studieren

readable ['ridəbəl] *adj* lesbar

reader ['ridər] *s (person)* Leser –in *mf*; *(book)* Lesebuch *n*

readily ['redɪlɪ] *adv* gern(e)

readiness ['redɪnɪs] *s* Bereitwilligkeit *f*; *(preparedness)* Bereitschaft *f*

read'ing *s (act)* Lesen *n*; *(material)* Lektüre *f*; *(version)* Lesart *f*; *(eccl, parl)* Lesung *f*

read'ing glass'es *spl* Lesebrille *f*

read'ing lamp' *s* Leselampe *f*

read'ing room' *s* Lesesaal *m*

readjustment [‚ri·ə'dʒʌstmənt] *s* Umstellung *f*

read-y ['redɪ] *adj (done)* fertig; **be r.** *(stand in readiness)* in Bereitschaft stehen; **get r.** sich fertig *(be bereit)* machen; **get s.th. r.** etw fertigstellen; **r. for** bereit zu; **r. for take-off** startbereit; **r. for use** gebrauchsfertig; **r. to** *(inf)* bereit zu *(inf)* ∥ *v (pret & pp –ied) tr* fertigmachen

read'y cash' *s* flüssiges Geld *n*

read'y-made' *adj* von der Stange

read'y-made' clothes' *spl* Konfektion *f*

reaffirm [‚ri·ə'fʌrm] *tr* nochmals beteuern

real ['ri·əl] *adj* wirklich; *(genuine)* echt; *(friend)* wahr

re'al estate' *s* Immobilien *pl*

re'al-estate' a'gent *s* Immobilienmakler –in *mf*

re'al-estate tax' *s* Grundsteuer *f*

realist ['ri·əlɪst] *s* Realist –in *mf*

realistic [ri·ə'lɪstɪk] *adj* wirklichkeitsnah, realistisch

reality [ri'ælɪtɪ] *s* Wirklichkeit *f*; **in r.** wirklich; **realities** *(facts)* Tatsachen *pl*

realize ['ri·ə‚laɪz] *tr (*einsehen; *(a profit)* erzielen; *(a goal)* verwirklichen; *(a good)* realisieren

really ['ri·əlɪ] *adv* wirklich; **not r.** eigentlich nicht

realm [relm] *s* Königreich *n*; (fig) Reich *n*, Gebiet *n*; **within the r. of possibility** im Rahmen des Möglichen

Realtor ['ri·əltər] *s* Immobilienmakler –in *mf*

ream [rim] *s* Ries *n* ∥ *tr* ausbohren

reamer ['rimər] *s* Reibahle *f*

reap [rip] *tr (cut)* mähen; *(& fig)* ernten

reaper ['ripər] *s* Mäher –in *mf*; (mach) Mähmaschine *f*

reappear [‚ri·ə'pɪr] *intr* wiederauftauchen, wiedererscheinen

rearmament [ri'ɑrməmənt] *s* Wiederscheinen *s*

reappoint [‚ri·ə'pɔɪnt] *tr* wieder anstellen

rear [rɪr] *adj* hintere, rückwärtig ∥ *s* Hinterseite *f*; *(of an army)* Nachhut *f*; (sl) Hintern *m*; **bring up the r.** den Schluß bilden; (mil) den Zug beschließen; **from the r.** von hinten; **to the r.** nach hinten; **to the r., march!** kehrt, marsch! ∥ *tr (children)* aufziehen; *(animals)* züchten; *(a structure, one's head)* aufrichten ∥ *intr* sich bäumen

rear' ad'miral *s* Konteradmiral *m*

rear' ax'le *s* Hinterachse *f*

rear' end' *s (sl)* Hintern *m*

rear' guard' *s (mil)* Nachhut *f*

rear' gun'ner *s* Heckschütze *m*

rearm [ri'ɑrm] *tr* wieder aufrüsten
rearmament [ri'ɑrməmənt] *s* Wieder-
aufrüstung *f*
rearrange [,ri·ə'rendʒ] *tr* umstellen
rear′ seat′ *s* Hintersitz *m*
rear′-view mir′ror *s* Rückspiegel *m*
rear′-wheel drive′ *s* Hinterradantrieb
m
rear′ win′dow *s* (aut) Heckfenster *n*
reason ['rizən] *s* Vernunft *f*; (*cause*)
Grund *m*; **by r.** of auf Grund (*genit*);
for this r. aus diesem Grund; **listen
to r.** sich belehren lassen; **not listen
to r.** sich [*dat*] nichts sagen lassen;
not without good r. nicht umsonst ||
tr—**r.** out durchdenken || *intr*—**r.**
with vernünftig reden mit
reasonable ['rizənəbəl] *adj* (*person*)
vernünftig; (*price*) solid; (*wares*)
preiswert
reassemble [,ri·ə'sembəl] *tr* (*people*)
wieder versammeln; (mach) wieder
zusammenbauen || *intr* sich wieder
sammeln
reassert [,ri·ə'sert] *tr* wieder behaupten
reassurance [,ri·ə'ʃurəns] *s* Beruhigung
f
reassure [ri·ə'ʃur] *tr* beruhigen
reawaken [,ri·ə'wekən] *tr* wieder er-
wecken || *intr* wieder erwachen
rebate ['ribet] *s* Rabatt *m*
re·bel ['rebəl] *adj* Rebellen– || *s* Rebell
–in *mf* || [ri'bel] *v* (*pret* & *pp*
–**belled**; *ger* –**belling**) *intr* rebellieren
rebellion [ri'beljən] *s* Aufstand *m*,
Rebellion *f*
rebellious [ri'beljəs] *adj* aufständisch
rebirth ['ribʌrθ] *s* Wiedergeburt *f*
rebore [ri'bor] *tr* nachbohren
rebound ['ri,baund] *s* Rückprall *m* ||
[ri'baund] *intr* zurückprallen
rebroad·cast [ri'brɔd,kæst] *s* Wieder-
holungssendung *f* || *v* (*pret* & *pp*
–**cast** & –**casted**) *tr* nochmals übertragen
rebuff [ri'bʌf] *s* Zurückweisung *f* || *tr*
schroff abweisen
re·build [ri'bild] *v* (*pret* & *pp* –**built**)
tr wiederaufbauen; (mach) über-
holen; (*confidence*) wiederherstellen
rebuke [ri'bjuk] *s* Verweis *m* || *tr* ver-
weisen
re·but [ri'bʌt] *v* (*pret* & *pp* –**butted**;
ger –**butting**) *tr* widerlegen
rebuttal [ri'bʌtəl] *s* Widerlegung *f*
recall [ri'kɔl], ['rikɔl] *s* (*recollection*)
Erinnerungsvermögen *n*; (com) Zurücknahme *f*; (dipl, pol) Abberufung
f; **beyond r.** unwiderruflich || [ri'kɔl]
tr (*remember*) sich erinnern an (*dat*);
(*an ambassador*) abberufen; (*workers*) zurückrufen; (mil) wiederein-
berufen
recant [ri'kænt] *tr* & *intr* (öffentlich)
widerrufen
re·cap ['ri,kæp] *s* Zusammenfassung
f || *v* (*pret* & *pp* –**capped**; *ger* –**cap-
ping**) *tr* zusammenfassen; (*a tire*)
runderneuern
recapitulate [,rikə'pitʃə,let] *tr* zusammenfassen

recapitulation [,rikə,pitʃə'leʃən] *s*
Rekapitulation *f*, Zusammenfassung
f
re·cast ['ri,kæst] *s* Umguß *m* ||
[ri'kæst] *v* (*pret* & *pp* –**cast**) *tr* um-
gießen; (*a sentence*) umarbeiten;
(theat) neubesetzen
recede [ri'sid] *intr* zurückgehen; (*become more distant*) zurückweichen
reced′ing *adj* (*forehead*, *chin*) fliehend
receipt [ri'sit] *s* Quittung *f*; acknowledge r. of den Empfang bestätigen
(*genit*); **receipts** Eingänge *pl* || *tr*
quittieren
receive [ri'siv] *tr* bekommen, erhalten;
(*a guest*) empfangen; (*pay*) beziehen;
(rad) empfangen
receiver [ri'sivər] *s* Empfänger –in *mf*;
(jur) Zwangsverwalter –in *mf*; (telp)
Hörer *m*
receiv′ership′ *s* Zwangsverwaltung *f*
recent ['risənt] *adj* neu, jung; **in r.
years** in den letzten Jahren; **of r. date**
neueren Datums
recently ['risəntli] *adv* kürzlich
receptacle [ri'septəkəl] *s* Behälter *m*;
(elec) Steckdose *f*
reception [ri'sepʃən] *s* (& rad) Empfang *m*
recep′tion desk′ *s* Empfang *m*
receptionist [ri'sepənɪst] *s* Empfangsdame *f*; (med) Sprechstundenhilfe *f*
receptive [ri'septɪv] *adj* (**to**) aufgeschlossen (für)
recess [ri'ses], ['rises] *s* (*alcove*)
Nische *f*; (*cleft*) Einschnitt *m*; (at
school) Pause *f*; (jur) Unterbrechung
f; (parl) Ferien *pl* || [ri'ses] *tr*
(*place in a recess*) versenken || *intr*
(*until*) sich vertagen (auf *acc*)
recession [ri'seʃən] *s* Rezession *f*,
Rückgang *m*
recharge [ri'tʃɑrdʒ] *tr* wieder aufladen
recipe ['resɪ,pi] *s* Rezept *n*
recipient [ri'sɪpɪ·ənt] *s* Empfänger –in
mf
reciprocal [ri'sɪprəkəl] *adj* gegenseitig
reciprocate [ri'sɪprə,ket] *tr* sich er-
kenntlich zeigen für || *intr* sich er-
kenntlich zeigen
reciprocity [,resɪ'prɑsɪti] *s* Gegenseitigkeit *f*
recital [ri'saɪtəl] *s* Vortrag *m*
recite [ri'saɪt] *tr* vortragen
reckless ['reklɪs] *adj* (*careless of consequences*) unbekümmert; (*lacking
caution*) leichtsinnig; (*negligent*)
fahrlässig
reck′less driv′ing *s* rücksichtsloses Fahren *n*
reckon ['rekən] *tr* (*count*) rechnen;
(*compute*) (coll) schätzen || *intr*
rechnen; (coll) schätzen; **r. on** rechnen auf (*acc*); **r. with** (*deal with*)
abrechnen mit; (*take into consideration*) rechnen mit
reck′oning *s* (*accounting*) Abrechnung
f; (*computation*) Berechnung *f*; (aer,
naut) Besteck *n*
reclaim [ri'klem] *tr* (*demand back*)
zurückfordern; (*from wastes*) rück-
gewinnen; (*land*) urbar machen

reclamation [ˌreklə'meʃən] s (of land) Urbarmachung f

recline [rɪ'klaɪn] intr ruhen; **r. against** sich lehnen an (acc); **r. in** (a chair) sich zurücklehnen in (dat)

recluse ['reklus] s Einsiedler –in mf

recognition [ˌrekəg'nɪʃən] s Wiedererkennung f; (acknowledgement) Anerkennung f; **gain r.** zur Geltung kommen

recognizable [ˌrekəg'naɪzəbəl] adj erkennbar

recognize ['rekəgˌnaɪz] tr (by) erkennen an (dat); **r.** as anerkennen als

recoil ['rikɔɪl] s (of a rifle) Rückstoß m; (arti) Rücklauf m ‖ [rɪ'kɔɪl] intr (in fear) zurückfahren; (from, e.g., a challenge) zurückschrecken vor (dat); (said of a rifle) zurückstoßen; (arti) zurücklaufen

recoilless [rɪ'kɔɪllɪs] adj rückstoßfrei

recollect [ˌrekə'lekt] tr sich erinnern an (acc)

recollection [ˌrekə'lekʃən] s Erinnerung f

recommend [ˌrekə'mend] tr empfehlen

recommendation [ˌrekəmən'deʃən] s Empfehlung f

recompense ['rekəmˌpens] s (for) Vergütung f (für) ‖ tr vergüten

reconcile ['rekənˌsaɪl] tr (with) versöhnen (mit); **become reconciled** sich versöhnen; **r. oneself to** sich abfinden mit

reconciliation [ˌrekənˌsɪlɪ'eʃən] s Versöhnung f, Aussöhnung f

recondite ['rekənˌdaɪt] adj (deep) tiefgründig; (obscure) dunkel

recondition [ˌrikən'dɪʃən] tr wiederinstandsetzen

reconnaissance [rɪ'kɑnɪsəns] s Aufklärung f

reconnoiter [ˌrekə'nɔɪtər] tr erkunden ‖ intr aufklären

reconquer [rɪ'kɑŋkər] tr zurückerobern

reconquest [rɪ'kɑŋkwest] s Zurückeroberung f

reconsider [ˌrikən'sɪdər] tr noch einmal erwägen

reconstruct [ˌrikən'strʌkt] tr (rebuild) wiederaufbauen; (make over) umbauen; (e.g., events of a case) rekonstruieren

record ['rekərd] adj Rekord– ‖ s (highest achievement) Rekord m; (document) Akte f, Protokoll n; (documentary evidence) Aufzeichnung f; (mus) Schallplatte f; **have a criminal r.** vorbestraft sein; **keep a r. of** Buch führen über (acc); **make a r. of** zu Protokoll nehmen; **off the r.** inoffiziell; **on r.** bisher registriert; **set a r.** e-n Rekord aufstellen ‖ [rɪ'kɔrd] tr (in writing) aufzeichnen; (officially) protokollieren; (on tape or disk) aufnehmen ‖ intr Schallplatten aufnehmen

rec'ord chang'er s Plattenwechsler m

recorder [rɪ'kɔrdər] s Protokollführer –in mf; (device) Zähler m; (on tape

or disk) Aufnahmegerät; (mus) Blockflöte f

rec'ord hold'er s Rekordler –in mf

record'ing adj aufzeichnend; (on tape or disk) Aufnahme– ‖ s Aufzeichnung f; (on tape or disk) Tonaufnahme f

record'ing sec'retary s Protokollführer –in mf

rec'ord play'er s Plattenspieler m

recount [rɪ'kaʊnt] s Nachzählung f ‖ [rɪ'kaʊnt] tr (count again) nachzählen ‖ [rɪ'kaʊnt] tr (relate) im einzelnen erzählen

recoup [rɪ'kup] tr (losses) wieder einbringen; (a fortune) wiedererlangen; (reimburse) entschädigen

recourse [rɪ'kɔrs], ['rikɔrs] s (to) Zuflucht f (zu); (jur) Regreß m; **have r. to** seine Zuflucht nehmen zu

recover [rɪ'kʌvər] tr (get back) wiedererlangen; (losses) wiedereinbringen; (e.g., a spent rocket) wiederfinden; (one's balance) wiederfinden; (e.g., a chair) neu beziehen ‖ intr (from) sich erholen (von)

recovery [rɪ'kʌvəri] s Wiedererlangung f, Rückgewinnung f; (of health) Genesung f; (of a rocket) Bergung f

recreation [ˌrekrɪ'eʃən] s Erholung f

recrea'tion room' s Unterhaltungsraum m

recruit [rɪ'krut] s Rekrut m ‖ (& mil) rekrutieren; **be recruited from** sich rekrutieren aus

recruit'ing of'ficer s Werbeoffizier m

recruitment [rɪ'krutmənt] s Rekrutierung f; (mil) Rekrutenaushebung f

rectangle ['rekˌtæŋgəl] s Rechteck n

rectangular [rek'tæŋgjələr] adj rechteckig

rectifier ['rektəˌfaɪ·ər] s Berichtiger m; (elec) Gleichrichter m

recti•fy ['rektɪˌfaɪ] v (pret & pp –fied) tr berichtigen; (elec) gleichrichten

rector ['rektər] s Rektor m

rectory ['rektəri] s Pfarrhaus n

rec•tum ['rektəm] s (–ta [tə]) Mastdarm m

recumbent [rɪ'kʌmbənt] adj liegend

recuperate [rɪ'k(j)upəˌret] intr sich (wieder) erholen

re•cur [rɪ'kʌr] v (pret & pp –curred; ger –curring) intr wiederkehren

recurrence [rɪ'kʌrəns] s Wiederkehr f

red [red] adj (redder; reddest) rot ‖ s Rot n, Röte f; **be in the red** in den Roten Zahlen stecken; **Red** (pol) Rote mf; **see red** wild werden

red' ant' s rote Waldameise f

red'bird' s Kardinal m

red'blood'ed adj lebensprühend

red'breast' s Rotkehlchen n

red' cab'bage s Rotkohl m

red' car'pet s (fig) roter Teppich m

red' cent' s—not give a r. for keinen roten Heller geben für

red'-cheeked' adj rotbäckig

Red' Cross', the s das Rote Kreuz

redden ['redən] tr röten, rot machen ‖ intr erröten, rot werden

reddish ['redɪʃ] adj rötlich

redecorate [rɪˈdɛkəˌret] *tr* neu dekorieren

redeem [rɪˈdim] *tr* zurückkaufen; (*a pawned article, promise*) einlösen; **r. oneself** seine Ehre wiederherstellen

redeemable [rɪˈdiməbəl] *adj* (fin) ablösbar, kündbar

Redeemer [rɪˈdimər] *s* Erlöser *m*

redemption [rɪˈdɛmpʃən] *s* Rückkauf *m*, Wiedereinlösung *f*; (relig) Erlösung *f*

red′-haired′ *adj* rothaarig

red′-hand′ed *adj*—**catch s.o. r.** j-n auf frischer Tat ertappen

red′head′ *s* Rotkopf *m*

red′ her′ring *s* Bückling *m*; (fig) Ablenkungsmanöver *n*

red′-hot′ *adj* glühend heiß, rotglühend

redirect [ˌrɪdɪˈrɛkt] *tr* umdirigieren

rediscover [ˌrɪdɪsˈkʌvər] *tr* wiederentdecken

red′-let′ter day′ *s* Glückstag *m*

red′ light′ *s* rotes Licht *n*

red′-light′ dis′trict *s* Bordellviertel *n*

red′ man′ *s* Rothaut *f*

redness [ˈrɛdnɪs] *s* Röte *f*

re·do [riˈdu] *v* (*pret* –**did**; *pp* –**done**) *tr* neu machen; (*redecorate*) renovieren

redolent [ˈrɛdələnt] *adj* (**with**) duftend (**nach**)

redoubt [rɪˈdaut] *s* Redoute *f*

redound [rɪˈdaund] *intr*—**r. to** gereichen zu

red′ pep′per *s* spanischer Pfeffer *m*

redress [rɪˈdrɛs] *s* Wiedergutmachung *f* ‖ *tr* wiedergutmachen

Red′ Rid′inghood′ *s* Rotkäppchen *n*

red′skin′ *s* Rothaut *f*

red′ tape′ *s* Amtsschimmel *m*

reduce [rɪˈd(j)us] *tr* reduzieren, verringern; (*prices*) herabsetzen; (math) (ab)kürzen

reduction [rɪˈdʌkʃən] *s* Verminderung *f*; (*gradual reduction*) Abbau *m*; (*in prices*) Absetzung *f*; (*in weight*) Abnahme *f*

redundant [rɪˈdʌndənt] *adj* überflüssig

red′ wine′ *s* Rotwein *m*

red′wing′ *s* Rotdrossel *f*

red′wood′ *s* Rotholz *n*

reecho [riˈɛko] *tr* wiederhallen lassen ‖ *intr* wiederhallen

reed [rid] *s* Schilf *n*; (*in mouthpiece*) Rohrblatt *n*; (*of metal*) Zunge *f*; (*pastoral pipe*) Hirtenflöte *f*

reedit [riˈɛdɪt] *tr* neu herausgeben

reeducate [riˈɛdʒʊˌket] *tr* umerziehen

reef [rif] *s* Riff *n*; (naut) Reff *n* ‖ *tr* (naut) reffen

reek [rik] *intr* (**of**) riechen (**nach**)

reel [ril] *s* (*sway*) Taumeln *n*; (*for cables*) Trommel *f*; (angl, cin) Spule *f*; (min, naut) Haspel *f* ‖ *tr* (angl, cin) spulen; (min, naut) haspeln; **r. in** (*a fish*) einholen; **r. off** abhaspeln; (fig) herunterrasseln ‖ *intr* taumeln

reelect [ˌri·ɪˈlɛkt] *tr* wiederwählen

reelection [ˌri·ɪˈlɛkʃən] *s* Wiederwahl *f*

reenlist [ˌri·ɛnˈlɪst] *tr* wieder anwerben ‖ *intr* sich weiterverpflichten

reenlistment [ˌri·ɛnˈlɪstmənt] *s* Weiterverpflichtung *f*

reentry [riˈɛntri] *s* Wiedereintritt *m*

reexamination [ˌri·ɛgˌzæmɪˈneʃən] *s* Nachprüfung *f*

re·fer [rɪˈfʌr] *v* (*pret* & *pp* –**ferred**; *ger* –**ferring**) *tr*—**r. s.o. to** j-n verweisen an (*acc*) ‖ *intr*—**r. to** hinweisen auf (*acc*); (*e.g., to an earlier correspondence*) sich beziehen auf (*acc*)

referee [ˌrɛfəˈri] *s* (box) Ringrichter *m*; (sport) Schiedsrichter *m* ‖ *tr* als Schiedsrichter fungieren bei ‖ *intr* als Schiedsrichter fungieren

reference [ˈrɛfərəns] *s* (**to**) Hinweis *m* (auf *acc*); (*person or document*) Referenz *f*; **in r. to** in Bezug auf (*acc*); **make r. to** hinweisen auf (*acc*)

ref′erence lib′rary *s* Handbibliothek *f*

ref′erence work′ *s* Nachschlagewerk *n*

referen·dum [ˌrɛfəˈrɛndəm] *s* (–**da** [də]) Volksentscheid *m*

referral [rɪˈfʌrəl] *s* (**to**) Zuweisung *f* (**an** *acc*, **auf** *acc*); **by r.** auf Empfehlung

refill [ˈrɪfɪl] *s* Nachfüllung *f*; (*for a pencil, ball-point pen*) Ersatzmine *f* ‖ [rɪˈfɪl] *tr* nachfüllen

refine [rɪˈfaɪn] *tr* (metal) läutern; (*oil, sugar*) raffinieren; (fig) verfeinern

refinement [rɪˈfaɪnmənt] *s* Läuterung *f*; (*of oil, sugar*) Raffination *f*; (fig) Verfeinerung *f*

refinery [rɪˈfaɪnəri] *s* Raffinerie *f*

reflect [rɪˈflɛkt] *tr* (& fig) widerspiegeln ‖ *intr* (*throw back rays*) reflektieren; (**on**) nachdenken (über *acc*); **r. on** (*comment on*) sich äußern über (*acc*); (*bring reproach on*) ein schlechtes Licht werfen auf (*acc*)

reflection [rɪˈflɛkʃən] *s* (*e.g., of light*) Reflexion *f*; (*reflected image*) Spiegelbild *n*; (*thought*) Überlegung *f*; **that's no r. on you** das färbt nicht auf Sie ab

reflector [rɪˈflɛktər] *s* Reflektor *m*

reflex [ˈriflɛks] *s* Reflex *m*

reflexive [rɪˈflɛksɪv] *adj* (gram) reflexiv ‖ *s* Reflexivform *f*

reforestation [ˌrifɔrɪsˈteʃən] *s* Aufforstung *f*

reform [rɪˈfɔrm] *s* Reform *f* ‖ *tr* reformieren, verbessern ‖ *intr* sich bessern

reformation [ˌrɛfərˈmeʃən] *s* Besserung *f*; **Reformation** Reformation *f*

reformatory [rɪˈfɔrməˌtori] *s* Besserungsanstalt *f*

reformer [rɪˈfɔrmər] *s* Reformator –in *mf*

reform′ school′ *s* Besserungsanstalt *f*

refraction [rɪˈfrækʃən] *s* Ablenkung *f*

refrain [rɪˈfren] *s* Kehrreim *m* ‖ *intr*—**r. from** sich enthalten (*genit*); **r. from** (*ger*) es unterlassen zu (*inf*)

refresh [rɪˈfrɛʃ] *tr* erfrischen; (*the memory*) auffrischen

refresh′er course′ [rɪˈfrɛʃər] *s* Auffrischungskurs *m*

refresh′ing *adj* erfrischend

refreshment [rɪˈfreʃmənt] *s* Erfrischung *f*

refresh'ment stand' *s* Erfrischungsstand *m*

refrigerant [rɪˈfrɪdʒərənt] *s* Kühlmittel *n*

refrigerate [rɪˈfrɪdʒəˌret] *tr* kühlen

refrigerator [rɪˈfrɪdʒəˌretər] *s* Kühlschrank *m*; (*walk-in type*) Kühlraum *m*

refrig'erator car' *s* (rr) Kühlwagen *m*

re·fuel [riˈfjul] *v* (*pret & pp* –fuel[l]ed; *ger* –fuel[l]ing) *tr* auftanken ‖ *intr* tanken

refuge [ˈrefjudʒ] *s* Zuflucht *f*; take r. in (sich) flüchten in (*acc*)

refugee [ˌrefjuˈdʒi] *s* Flüchtling *m*

refugee' camp' *s* Flüchtlingslager *n*

refund [ˈrifʌnd] *s* Zurückzahlung *f* ‖ [rɪˈfʌnd] *tr* (*pay back*) zurückzahlen ‖ [riˈfʌnd] *tr* (*fund again*) neu fundieren

refurnish [riˈfʌrnɪʃ] *tr* neu möblieren

refusal [rɪˈfjuzəl] *s* Ablehnung *f*

refuse [ˈrefjus] *s* Abfall *m* ‖ [rɪˈfjuz] *tr* ablehnen; r. to (*inf*) sich weigern zu (*inf*)

refutation [ˌrefjuˈteʃən] *s* Widerlegung *f*

refute [rɪˈfjut] *tr* widerlegen

regain [rɪˈgen] *tr* zurückgewinnen

regal [ˈrigəl] *adj* königlich

regale [rɪˈgel] *tr* (*delight*) ergötzen; (*entertain*) reichlich bewirten

regalia [rɪˈgelɪ·ə] *spl* Insignien *pl*

regard [rɪˈgɑrd] *s* (for) Rücksicht *f* (auf *acc*); best regards to herzlichster Gruß an (*acc*); have little r. for wenig achten; in every r. in jeder Hinsicht; in (or with) r. to in Hinsicht auf (*acc*); in this r. in dieser Hinsicht; without r. for ohne Rücksicht auf (*acc*) ‖ *tr* betrachten; as regards in Bezug auf (*acc*)

regard'ing *prep* hinsichtlich (*genit*)

regardless [rɪˈgɑrdlɪs] *adv* (coll) ungeniert; r. of ungeachtet (*genit*)

regatta [rɪˈgætə] *s* Regatta *f*

regency [ˈridʒənsi] *s* Regentschaft *f*

regenerate [rɪˈdʒenəˌret] *tr* regenerieren

regent [ˈridʒənt] *s* Regent –in *mf*

regicide [ˈredʒɪˌsaɪd] *s* (*act*) Königsmord *m*; (*person*) Königsmörder –in *mf*

regime [reˈʒim] *s* Regime *n*

regiment ‖ [ˈredʒɪmənt] *s* (mil) Regiment *n* ‖ [ˈredʒɪˌment] *tr* reglementieren

regimental [ˌredʒɪˈmentəl] *adj* Regiments–

region [ˈridʒən] *s* Gegend *f*, Region *f*

regional [ˈridʒənəl] *adj* regional

register [ˈredʒɪstər] *s* Register *n*, Verzeichnis *n* ‖ *tr* registrieren; (*students*) immatrikulieren; (*feelings*) erkennen lassen ‖ *intr* sich einschreiben lassen; (*at a hotel*) sich eintragen lassen

reg'istered let'ter *s* eingeschriebener Brief *m*

reg'istered nurse' *s* (staatlich) geprüfte Krankenschwester *f*

registrar [ˈredʒɪstrɑr] *s* Registrator –in *mf*

registration [ˌredʒɪsˈtreʃən] *s* (e.g., of firearms) Registrierung *f*; (for a course; at a hotel) Anmeldung *f*; (of a trademark) Eintragung *f*; (aut) Zulassung *f*; (educ) Einschreibung *f*

registra'tion blank' *s* Meldeformular *n*

registra'tion fee' *s* Anmeldegebühr *f*

registra'tion num'ber *s* Registriernummer *f*

regression [rɪˈgreʃən] *s* Rückgang *m*

regret [rɪˈgret] *s* (over) Bedauern *n* (über *acc*) ‖ *v* (*pret & pp* –regretted; *ger* regretting) *tr* bedauern; I r. to say es tut mir leid, sagen zu müssen

regrettable [rɪˈgretəbəl] *adj* bedauerlich

regroup [riˈgrup] *tr* umgruppieren

regular [ˈregjələr] *adj* (*usual*) gewöhnlich; (*pulse, breathing, features, intervals*) regelmäßig; r. army stehendes Heer *n*; r. guy (coll) Pfundskerl *m*; r. officer Berufsoffizier –in *mf*

regularity [ˌregjəˈlærɪti] *s* Regelmäßigkeit *f*

regulate [ˈregjəˌlet] *tr* regeln

regulation [ˌregjəˈleʃən] *s* Regelung *f*; (*rule*) Vorschrift *f*, Bestimmung *f*; against regulations vorschriftswidrig

regulator [ˈregjəˌletər] *s* Regler *m*

rehabilitate [ˌrihəˈbɪlɪˌtet] *tr* rehabilitieren

rehash [riˈhæʃ] *tr* (coll) aufwärmen

rehearsal [rɪˈhɑrsəl] *s* Probe *f*

rehearse [rɪˈhɑrs] *tr & intr* proben

rehire [riˈhaɪr] *tr* wiedereinstellen

reign [ren] *s* Regierung *f*; (*period of rule*) Regierungszeit *f* ‖ *intr* regieren; r. over herrschen über (*acc*)

reimburse [ri·ɪmˈbʌrs] *tr* (*costs*) rückerstatten; r. s.o. for s.th. j–m etw vergüten

rein [ren] *s* Zügel *m*; give free r. to die Zügel schießen lassen (*dat*) ‖ *tr* —r. in (*a horse*) parieren

reincarnation [ˌri·ɪnkɑrˈneʃən] *s* Reinkarnation *f*, Wiedergeburt *f*

rein'deer' *s* Rentier *n*

reinforce [ˌri·ɪnˈfors] *tr* verstärken

reinforced' concrete' *s* Stahlbeton *m*

reinforcement [ˌri·ɪnˈforsmənt] *s* Verstärkung *f*; reinforcements (mil) Verstärkungen *pl*

reinstate [ˌri·ɪnˈstet] *tr* (in) wiedereinsetzen (in *acc*)

reiterate [riˈɪtəˌret] *tr* wiederholen

reject [ˈridʒekt] *s* Ausschußware *f* ‖ [rɪˈdʒekt] *tr* ablehnen, zurückweisen; (*a request, appeal*) abweisen

rejection [rɪˈdʒekʃən] *s* Ablehnung *f*; (*of a request, appeal*) Abweisung *f*

rejoice [rɪˈdʒɔɪs] *intr* frohlocken

rejoin [rɪˈdʒɔɪn] *tr* (*answer*) erwidern; (*a group*) sich wieder anschließen (*dat*)

rejoinder [rɪˈdʒɔɪndər] *s* Erwiderung *f*; (jur) Duplik *f*

rejuvenate [rɪˈdʒuvɪˌnet] *tr* verjüngen

rekindle [riˈkɪndəl] *tr* wieder anzünden; (fig) wieder entzünden

relapse [rɪˈlæps] *s* (& pathol) Rückfall

m ‖ *intr* **(into)** wieder verfallen (in *acc*)

relate [rɪ'let] *tr* **(a story)** erzählen; **(connect)** verknüpfen; **r. s.th. to s.th.** etw auf etw **[acc]** beziehen ‖ *intr*—**r. to** in Beziehung stehen mit

relat'ed *adj* **(by blood)** verwandt; **(by marriage)** verschwägert; **(subjects)** benachbart

relation [rɪ'leʃən] *s* Beziehung *f*, Verhältnis *n*; **(relative)** Verwandte *mf*; **in r. to** in Bezug auf **(acc)**; **relations (sex)** Verkehr *m*

rela'tionship' *s* **(connection)** Beziehung *f*; **(kinship)** Verwandschaft *f*

relative ['relətɪv] *adj* relativ, verhältnismäßig; **r. to** bezüglich **(genit)** ‖ *s* Verwandte *mf*

rel'ative clause' *s* Relativsatz *m*

rel'ative pro'noun *s* Relativpronomen *n*

relativity [‚relə'tɪvɪti] *s* Relativität *f*

relax [rɪ'læks] *tr* auflockern; **(muscles)** entspannen ‖ *intr* sich entspannen

relaxation [‚rɪlæk'seʃən] *s* Entspannung *f*; **r. of tension** Entspannung *f*

relay ['rile] *s* Relais *n*; **(sport)** Staffel *f* ‖ [ri'le] *v* (*pret* & *pp* **-layed**) *tr* übermitteln; **(through relay stations)** übertragen

re'lay race' *s* Staffellauf *m*

re'lay team' *s* Staffel *f*

release [rɪ'lis] *s* **(from)** Entlassung *f* **(aus)**; **(of bombs)** Abwurf *m*; **(of news)** Mitteilung *f* ‖ *tr* entlassen; **(a film, book)** freigeben; **(bombs)** abwerfen; **(energy)** freisetzen; **(brakes)** lösen; **r. the clutch** auskuppeln

relegate ['reli‚get] *tr* **(to)** verweisen **(an acc)**; **r. to second position** auf den zweiten Platz verweisen

relent [rɪ'lent] *intr* **(let up)** nachlassen; **(yield)** sich erweichen lassen

relentless [rɪ'lentlɪs] *adj* **(tireless)** unermüdlich; **(unappeasable)** unerbittlich; **(never-ending)** unaufhörlich

relevant ['reləvənt] *adj* sachdienlich

reliable [rɪ'laɪ‚əbəl] *adj* zuverlässig

reliance [rɪ'laɪ‚əns] *s* Vertrauen *n*

relic ['relɪk] *s* Reliquie *f*; **r. of the past** Zeuge *m* der Vergangenheit

relief [rɪ'lif] *s* Erleichterung *f*; **(for the poor)** Armenunterstützung *f*; **(replacement)** Ablösung *f*; **(sculpture)** Relief *n*; **on r.** von Sozialhilfe lebend; **bring r.** Linderung schaffen; **go on r.** stempeln gehen

relief' map' *s* Reliefkarte *f*

relieve [rɪ'liv] *tr* erleichtern; **(from guard duty)** ablösen; **r. oneself** seine Notdurft verrichten

religion [rɪ'lɪdʒən] *s* Religion *f*

religious [rɪ'lɪdʒəs] *adj* religiös; **(order)** geistlich

relinquish [rɪ'lɪŋkwɪʃ] *tr* aufgeben; **r. the right to s.th. to s.o.** j-m das Recht auf etw **[acc]** überlassen

relish ['relɪʃ] *s* **(for)** Genuß *m* **(an acc)**; **(condiment)** Würze *f* ‖ *tr* genießen

reluctance [rɪ'lʌktəns] *s* Widerstreben *n*

reluctant [rɪ'lʌktənt] *adj* widerstrebend; **be r. to do s.th.** etw ungern tun

reluctantly [rɪ'lʌktəntli] *adv* ungern

re·ly [rɪ'laɪ] *v* (*pret* & *pp* **-lied**) *intr*—**r. on** sich verlassen auf **(acc)**

remain [rɪ'men] *s*—**remains** Überreste *pl*; **(corpse)** sterbliche Reste *pl* ‖ *intr* bleiben; **(at end of letter)** verbleiben; **r. behind** zurückbleiben; **r. seated** sitzenbleiben; **r. steady (said of prices)** sich behaupten

remainder [rɪ'mendər] *s* Restbestand *m*, Rest *m* ‖ *tr* verramschen

remark [rɪ'mark] *s* Bemerkung *f* ‖ *tr* bemerken

remarkable [rɪ'markəbəl] *adj* markant, bemerkenswert

remar·ry [rɪ'mæri] *v* (*pret* & *pp* **-ried**) *tr* sich wiederverheiraten mit ‖ *intr* sich wiederverheiraten

reme·dy ['remidi] *s* **(for)** Heilmittel *n* **(für)**; **(fig) (for)** Gegenmittel *n* **(gegen)** ‖ *v* (*pret* & *pp* **-died**) *tr* abhelfen **(dat)**; **(damage, shortage)** abheben

remember [rɪ'membər] *tr* sich erinnern an **(acc)**; **r. me to** empfehlen Sie mich **(dat)** ‖ *intr* sich erinnern

remembrance [rɪ'membrəns] *s* Erinnerung *f*; **in r. of** zum Andenken an **(acc)**

remind [rɪ'maɪnd] *tr* **(of)** erinnern **(an acc)**; **r. s.o. to** **(inf)** j-n mahnen zu **(inf)**

reminder [rɪ'maɪndər] *s* **(note)** Zettel *m*; **(from a creditor)** Mahnung *f*

reminisce [‚remɪ'nɪs] *intr* in Erinnerungen schwelgen

remiss [rɪ'mɪs] *adj* nachlässig

remission [rɪ'mɪʃən] *s* Nachlaß *m*

re·mit [rɪ'mɪt] *v* (*pret* & *pp* **-mitted;** *ger* **-mitting**) *tr* **(in cash)** übersenden; **(by check)** überweisen; **(forgive)** vergeben

remittance [rɪ'mɪtəns] *s* **(in cash)** Übersendung *f*; **(by check)** Überweisung *f*

remnant ['remnənt] *s* Rest *m*; **(of cloth)** Stoffrest *m*

remod·el [rɪ'madəl] *v* (*pret* & *pp* **-el[l]ed;** *ger* **-el[l]ing**) *tr* umgestalten; **(a house)** umbauen

remonstrate [rɪ'manstret] *intr* protestieren; **r. with s.o.** j-m Vorwürfe machen

remorse [rɪ'mɔrs] *s* Gewissensbisse *pl*

remorseful [rɪ'mɔrsfəl] *adj* reumütig

remote [rɪ'mot] *adj* fern; **(possibility)** vage; **(idea)** blaß; **(resemblance)** entfernt; **(secluded)** abgelegen

remote' control' *s* Fernsteuerung *f*; **(telv)** Fernbedienung *f*; **guide by r.** fernlenken

removable [rɪ'muvəbəl] *adj* entfernbar

removal [rɪ'muvəl] *s* Entfernung *f*; **(by truck)** Abfuhr *f*; **(from office)** Absetzung *f*

remove [rɪ'muv] *tr* entfernen; **(clothes)** ablegen; **(one's hat)** abnehmen; **(e.g., dishes from the table)** abräumen; **(a stain)** entfernen; **(from office)** absetzen; **(furniture)** ausräumen

remuneration [rɪ‚mjunə'reʃən] s Vergütung f

renaissance [‚renə'sɑns] s Renaissance f

rend [rend] v (pret & pp **rent** [rent]) tr (& fig) zerreißen

render ['rendər] tr (give) geben; (a service) leisten; (honor) erweisen; (thanks) abstatten; (a verdict) fällen; (translate; play, e.g., on the piano) wiedergeben; **r. harmless** unschädlich machen

rendez·vous ['rɑndə‚vu] s (-vous [‚vuz]) Rendezvous n, Treffpunkt m; (mil) Sammelplatz m || v (pret & pp -voused ['vud]; ger -vousing [‚vu·ɪŋ]) intr sich treffen; (mil) sich versammeln

rendition [ren'dɪʃən] s Wiedergabe f

renegade ['renɪ‚ged] s Renegat –in mf

renege [rɪ'nɪg] s Renonce f || intr (cards) nicht bedienen; **r. on** nicht einhalten

renew [rɪ'n(j)u] tr erneuern; (e.g., a passport) verlängern lassen

renewable [rɪ'n(j)u·əbəl] adj erneuerbar

renewal [rɪ'n(j)u·əl] s Erneuerung f; (e.g., of a passport) Verlängerung f

renounce [rɪ'nauns] tr verzichten auf (acc)

renovate ['renə‚vet] tr renovieren; (fig) erneuern

renovation [‚renə've ʃən] s Renovierung f

renown [rɪ'naun] s Ruhm m

renowned [rɪ'naund] adj (for) berühmt (wegen)

rent [rent] adj zerrissen || s Miete f; (tear) Riß m || tr mieten; **r. out** vermieten

rental ['rentəl] s Miete f

rent′al serv′ice s Verleih m

rent′ed car′ s Mietwagen m, Mietauto n

renter ['rentər] s Mieter –in mf

renunciation [rɪ‚nʌnsɪ'eʃən] s (of) Verzicht m (auf acc)

reopen [ri'opən] tr wieder öffnen; (a business) wieder eröffnen; (an argument; school year) wieder beginnen || intr (said of a shop or business) wieder geöffnet werden; (said of a school year) wieder beginnen

reopening [ri'opənɪŋ] s (of a business) Wiedereröffnung f; (of school) Wiederbeginn m; (jur) Wiederaufnahme f

reorder [ri'ɔrdər] tr nachbestellen

reorganization [‚ri·ɔrgənɪ'zeʃən] s Reorganisation f, Neuordnung f

reorganize [ri'ɔrgə‚naɪz] tr reorganisieren; (an administration) umbilden

repack [ri'pæk] tr umpacken

repair [rɪ'per] s Ausbesserung f, Reparatur f; **in bad r.** in schlechtem Zustand; **keep in good r.** im Stande halten || tr ausbessern, reparieren || intr (to) sich begeben (nach, zu)

repair′ gang′ s Störungstrupp m

repair′ shop′ s Reparaturwerkstatt f

repaper [ri'pepər] tr neu tapezieren

reparation [‚repə'reʃən] s Wiedergutmachung f; **reparations** Reparationen pl, Kriegsentschädigung f

repartee [‚repɑr'ti] s schlagfertige Antwort f

repast [rɪ'pæst] s Mahl n

repatriate [ri'petrɪ‚et] tr repatriieren

re·pay [rɪ'pe] v (pret & pp –paid) tr (e.g., a loan) zurückzahlen; (a person) entschädigen; **r. a favor** e–n Gefallen erwidern

repayment [rɪ'pemənt] s Rückzahlung f; (reprisal) Vergeltung f

repeal [rɪ'pil] s Aufhebung f || tr aufheben, außer Kraft setzen

repeat [rɪ'pit] tr wiederholen; (a story, gossip) weitererzählen; **r. s.th. after s.o.** j–m etw nachsagen

repeat′ed adj abermalig, mehrmalig

repeatedly [rɪ'pitɪdli] adv wiederholt

re·pel [rɪ'pel] v (pret & pp –pelled; ger –pelling) tr (an enemy, an attack) zurückschlagen; (e.g., water) abstoßen

repellent [rɪ'pelənt] s Bekämpfungsmittel n

repent [rɪ'pent] tr bereuen || intr Reue empfinden; **r. of** bereuen

repentance [rɪ'pentəns] s Reue f

repentant [rɪ'pentənt] adj reuig

repercussion [‚rɪpər'kʌʃən] s Rückwirkung f

repertory ['repər‚tori] s Repertoire n

repetition [‚repɪ'tɪʃən] s Wiederholung f

replace [rɪ'ples] tr (with) ersetzen (durch)

replaceable [rɪ'plesəbəl] adj ersetzbar

replacement [rɪ'plesmənt] s (act) Ersetzen n; (substitute part) Ersatz m; (person) Ersatzmann m

replay ['riple] s (sport) Wiederholungsspiel n || [ri'ple] tr nochmals spielen

replenish [rɪ'plenɪʃ] tr wieder auffüllen

replete [rɪ'plit] adj angefüllt

replica ['replɪkə] s Replik f

re·ply [rɪ'plaɪ] s Erwiderung f; (letter) Antwortschreiben n; **in r. to your letter** in Beantwortung Ihres Schreibens || v (pret & pp –plied) tr & intr erwidern

report [rɪ'port] s Bericht m; (rumor) Gerücht n; (e.g., of a gun) Knall m || tr (give an account of) berichten; (give notice of) melden; **r. s.o. to the police** j–n bei der Polizei anzeigen || intr (to) sich melden (bei); **r. in** sich anmelden

report′ card′ s Zeugnis n

reportedly [rɪ'portɪdli] adv angeblich

reporter [rɪ'portər] s Reporter –in mf

repose [rɪ'poz] s Ruhe f || intr ruhen

repository [rɪ'pazɪ‚tori] s Verwahrungsort m; (of information) Fundgrube f

represent [‚reprɪ'zent] tr vertreten; (depict) darstellen

representation [‚reprɪzen'teʃən] s Vertretung f; (depiction) Darstellung f

representative [‚reprɪ'zentətɪv] adj (function) stellvertretend; (government) parlamentarisch; (typical) (of) typisch (für) ‖ s Vertreter -in mf; (pol) Abgeordnete mf

repress [rɪ'pres] tr unterdrücken; (psychoanal) verdrängen

repression [rɪ'preʃən] s Unterdrückung f; (psychoanal) Verdrängung f

reprieve [rɪ'priv] s Strafaufschub m; (fig) Gnadenfrist f, Atempause f

reprimand ['reprɪ͵mænd] s Verweis m; **give s.o. a r.** j-m e-n Verweis erteilen ‖ tr (for) zurechtweisen (wegen, für), rügen (wegen, für)

reprint ['riprɪnt] s Nachdruck m ‖ [ri'prɪnt] tr nachdrucken

reprisal [rɪ'praɪzəl] s Vergeltung f; **take reprisals against or on** Repressalien ergreifen gegen

reproach [rɪ'protʃ] s Vorwurf m ‖ tr (for) tadeln (wegen); **r. s.o. with s.th.** j-m etw vorwerfen

reproduce [͵riprə'd(j)us] tr reproduzieren; (copies) vervielfältigen; (an experiment) wiederholen; (a play) neuaufführen; (a sound) wiedergeben; (a lost limb) regenerieren ‖ intr sich fortpflanzen

reproduction [͵riprə'dʌkʃən] s Reproduktion f; (making copies) Vervielfältigung f; (of sound) Wiedergabe f; (biol) Fortpflanzung f

reproductive [͵riprə'dʌktɪv] adj Fortpflanzungs-

reproof [rɪ'pruf] s Rüge f

reprove [rɪ'pruv] tr rügen

reptile ['reptaɪl] s Kriechtier n

republic [rɪ'pʌblɪk] s Republik f

republican [rɪ'pʌblɪkən] adj republikanisch ‖ s Republikaner -in mf

repudiate [rɪ'pjudɪ͵et] tr (disown) verleugnen; (a charge) zurückweisen; (a debt) nicht anerkennen; (a treaty) für unverbindlich erklären; (a woman) verstoßen

repugnant [rɪ'pʌgnənt] adj widerwärtig

repulse [rɪ'pʌls] s (refusal) Zurückweisung f; (setback) Rückschlag m ‖ tr zurückweisen; (mil) zurückschlagen

repulsive [rɪ'pʌlsɪv] adj abstoßend

reputable ['repjətəbəl] adj anständig

reputation [͵repjə'teʃən] s Ruf m, Ansehen n; **have the r. of being** im Rufe stehen zu sein

repute [rɪ'pjut] s—**be held in high r.** hohes Ansehen genießen; **bring into bad r.** in üble Nachrede bringen; **of r.** von Ruf ‖ tr—**she is reputed to be a beauty** sie soll e-e Schönheit sein

reputedly [rɪ'pjutɪdli] adv angeblich

request [rɪ'kwest] s Bitte f, Gesuch n; **at his r.** auf seine Bitte; **on r.** auf Wunsch ‖ tr (a person) bitten; (a thing) bitten um, ersuchen

Requiem ['rekwɪ͵em] s (Mass) Seelenmesse f; (chant, composition) Requiem n

require [rɪ'kwaɪr] tr erfordern; **if required** erforderlichenfalls

requirement [rɪ'kwaɪrmənt] s Anforderung f

requisite ['rekwɪzɪt] adj erforderlich ‖

s Erfordernis n; (required article) Requisit n

requisition [͵rekwɪ'zɪʃən] s Anforderung f; (mil) Requisition f ‖ tr anfordern; (mil) beschlagnahmen

requital [rɪ'kwaɪtəl] s (retaliation) Vergeltung f; (for a kindness) Belohnung f

requite [rɪ'kwaɪt] tr vergelten; **r. s.o. for a favor** sich j-m für e-n Gefallen erkenntlich zeigen

re-read [ri'rid] v (pret & pp -read [red]) tr nachlesen

rerun ['riran] s (cin) Reprise f

resale ['ri͵sel] s Wiederverkauf m

rescind [rɪ'sɪnd] tr (an order) rückgängig machen; (a law) aufheben

rescue ['reskju] s Rettung f, Bergung f ‖ tr retten, bergen

rescuer ['reskju·ər] s Retter -in mf

research [rɪ'sʌrtʃ], ['risʌrtʃ] s Forschung f; **do r. on** Forschungen betreiben über (acc) ‖ intr forschen

researcher ['risʌrtʃər] s Forscher -in mf

re-sell [ri'sel] v (pret & pp -sold) tr wiederverkaufen, weiterverkaufen

resemblance [rɪ'zembləns] s (to) Ähnlichkeit f (mit); **bear a close r. to s.o.** große Ähnlichkeit mit j-m haben

resemble [rɪ'zembəl] tr ähneln (dat)

resent [rɪ'zent] tr—**I r. your remark** Ihre Bemerkung paßt mir nicht

resentful [rɪ'zentfəl] adj grollend

resentment [rɪ'zentmənt] s Groll m; **feel r. toward** Groll hegen gegen

reservation [͵rezər've(ə)n] s Vorbestellung f; (Indian land) Reservation f; **do you have a r.?** haben Sie vorbestellt?; **make reservations** vorbestellen

reserve [rɪ'zʌrv] s (discretion) Zurückhaltung f; (econ, mil) Reserve f; **without r.** rückhaltlos ‖ tr (e.g., seats) reservieren, belegen; **r. judgment** mit seinem Urteil zurückhalten

reserved adj (place) belegt; (person) zurückhaltend

reserve officer s Reserveoffizier m

reservist [rɪ'zʌrvɪst] s Reservist -in mf

reservoir ['rezər͵vwɑr] s Staubecken m

re-set [ri'set] v (pret & pp -set; ger -setting) tr (a gem) neu fassen; (mach) nachstellen; (typ) neu setzen

resettle [ri'setəl] tr & intr umsiedeln

reshape [ri'ʃep] tr umformen

reshuffle [rɪ'ʃʌfəl] tr (cards) neu mischen; (pol) umgruppieren

reside [rɪ'zaɪd] intr wohnen

residence ['rezɪdəns] s Wohnsitz m; (for students) Studentenheim n

resident ['rezɪdənt] adj wohnhaft ‖ s Einwohner -in mf

residential [͵rezɪ'dentʃəl] adj Wohn-

residue ['rezɪ͵d(j)u] s Rest m; (chem) Rückstand m

resign [rɪ'zaɪn] tr (an office) niederlegen; **r. oneself to** sich ergeben in (acc) ‖ intr zurücktreten

resignation [͵rezɪg'neʃən] s (from an office) Rücktritt m; (submissive *state*) Ergebung *f*; **hand in one's r.** sein Entlassungsgesuch einreichen

resilience [rɪ'zɪlɪ-əns] *s* Elastizität *f*; (fig) Spannkraft *f*

resilient [rɪ'zɪlɪ-ənt] *adj* elastisch; (fig) unverwüstlich

resin ['rezɪn] *s* Harz *m*

resist [rɪ'zɪst] *tr* widerstehen (*dat*) || *intr* Widerstand leisten

resistance [rɪ'zɪstəns] *s* (& elec) Widerstand *m*

resole [ri'sol] *tr* neu besohlen

resolute ['rezə ˌlut] *adj* entschlossen

resolution [rezə'luʃən] *s* (*resoluteness*) Entschlossenheit *f*; (parl) Beschluß *m*; **make good resolutions** gute Vorsätze fassen

resolve [rɪ'zɒlv] *s* Vorsatz *m* || *tr* auflösen; (*a question, problem*) lösen; **r. to** (*inf*) beschließen zu (*inf*) || *intr* —**r. into** sich auflösen in (*acc*); **r. upon s.th.** sich [*dat*] etw vornehmen

resonance ['rezənəns] *s* Resonanz *f*

resort [rɪ'zɔrt] *s* (*refuge*) Zuflucht *f*; (*for health*) Kurort *m*; (*for vacation*) Ferienort *m*, Sommerfrische *f*; **as a last r.** als letztes Mittel || *intr*—**r. to** greifen zu

resound [rɪ'zaund] *intr* widerhallen

resource ['risors] *s* Mittel *n*; **resources** (fin) Geldmittel *pl*

resourceful [rɪ'sorsfəl] *adj* findig

respect [rɪ'spekt] *s* (*esteem*) Achtung *f*, Respekt *m*; (*reference*) Hinsicht *f*; **in every r.** in jeder Hinsicht; **pay one's respects to s.o.** j-m seine Aufwartung machen; **with r. to** mit Bezug auf (*acc*) || *tr* achten

respectable [rɪ'spektəbəl] *adj* achtbar; (*e.g., firm*) angesehen

respect'ed *adj* angesehen

respectful [rɪ'spektfəl] *adj* ehrerbietig

respectfully [rɪ'spektfəli] *adv*—**r. yours** hochachtungsvoll, Ihr ... or Ihre ...

respective [rɪ'spektɪv] *adj* jeweilig

respectively [rɪ'spektɪvli] *adv* beziehungsweise

respiration [ˌrespɪ'reʃən] *s* Atmung *f*

respirator ['respɪ ˌretər] *s* Atemgerät *n*

respiratory ['respɪrə ˌtori] *adj* Atmungs-

respite ['respɪt] *s* (*pause*) Atempause *f*; (*reprieve*) Aufschub *m*; **without r.** ohne Unterlaß

resplendent [rɪ'splendənt] *adj* glänzend

respond [rɪ'spɒnd] *tr* antworten || *intr* (*reply*) (**to**) antworten (auf *acc*); (*react*) (**to**) ansprechen (auf *acc*)

response [rɪ'spɒns] *s* Antwort *f*; (*reaction*) Reaktion *f*; (fig) Widerhall *m*; **in r. to** als Antwort auf (*acc*)

responsibility [rɪ ˌspɒnsɪ'brlɪti] *s* Verantwortung *f*

responsible [rɪ'spɒnsɪbəl] *adj* (*position*) verantwortlich; (*person*) verantwortungsbewußt; **be held r.** for verantwortlich gemacht werden für; **be r. for** (*be answerable for*) verantwortlich sein für; (*be to blame for*) schuld sein an (*dat*); (*be the cause of*) die Ursache sein (*genit*); (*be liable for*) haften für

responsive [rɪ'spɒnsɪv] *adj*—**be r. to** ansprechen auf (*acc*)

rest [rest] *s* (*repose*) Ruhe *f*; (*from work*) Ruhepause *f*; (*e.g., from walking*) Rast *f*; (*remainder*) Rest *m*; (*support*) Stütze *f*; (mus) Pause *f*; **all the r.** (*in number*) alle andern; (*in quantity*) alles übrige; **be at r.** (*be calm*) beruhigt sein; (*be dead*) ruhen; (*not be in motion*) sich in Ruhelage befinden; **come to r.** stehenbleiben; **put one's mind to r.** sich beruhigen; **take a r.** sich ausruhen; **the r. of the boys** die übrigen (or andern) Jungen || *tr* ruhen lassen, ausruhen; (*support, e.g., one's elbow*) stützen || *intr* sich ausruhen; **r. on** lasten auf (*dat*); (*be based on*) beruhen auf (*dat*); **r. with** liegen bei

restaurant ['restərənt] *s* Restaurant *n*

restful ['restfəl] *adj* ruhig

rest' home' *s* Erholungsheim *n*

rest'ing place' *s* Ruheplatz *m*; **final r.** letzte Ruhestätte *f*

restitution [ˌrestɪ'(j)uʃən] *s* Wiedergutmachung *f*; **make r.** Genugtuung leisten

restive ['restɪv] *adj* (*restless*) unruhig; (*balky*) störrisch

restless ['restlɪs] *adj* ruhelos

restock [ri'stɑk] *tr* wieder auffüllen; (*waters*) wieder mit Fischen besetzen

restoration [ˌrestə'reʃən] *s* (*of a work of art or building*) Restaurierung *f*

restore [rɪ'stor] *tr* (*order*) wiederherstellen; (*a painting, building*) restaurieren; (*stolen goods*) zurückerstatten; **r. to health** wiederherstellen

restrain [rɪ'stren] *tr* zurückhalten; (*feelings; a horse*) zügeln; (*e.g., trade*) einschränken; **r. s.o. from** (*ger*) j-n davon abhalten zu (*inf*)

restrain'ing or'der *s* Unterlassungsurteil *n*

restraint [rɪ'strent] *s* Zurückhaltung *f*; (*force*) Zwang *m*

restrict [rɪ'strɪkt] *tr* begrenzen; **r. to** beschränken auf (*acc*)

restrict'ed ar'ea *s* Sperrgebiet *n*

rest' room' *s* Abort *m*, Toilette *f*

result [rɪ'zʌlt] *s* Ergebnis *n*, Resultat *n*; (*consequence*) Folge *f*; **as a r. of** als Folge (*genit*); **without r.** ergebnislos || *intr*—**r. from** sich ergeben aus; **r. in** führen zu

result' clause' *s* Folgesatz *m*

resume [rɪ'zum] *tr* wieder aufnehmen; (*a journey*) fortsetzen

résumé ['rezu ˌme] *s* Zusammenfassung *f*

resumption [rɪ'zʌmpʃən] *s* Wiederaufnahme *f*

resurface [ri'sʌrfɪs] *tr*—**r. the road** die Straßendecke erneuern von || *intr* (naut & fig) wiederauftauchen

resurrect [ˌrezə'rekt] *tr* (*the dead*) wieder zum Leben erwecken; (fig) wieder aufleben lassen

resurrection [ˌrezə'rekʃən] *s* Auferstehung *f*

resuscitate [rɪ'sʌsɪ ˌtet] *tr* wiederbeleben

retail ['ritel] *adj* Kleinhandels- ‖ *adv* im Kleinhandel ‖ *tr* im Kleinhandel verkaufen ‖ *intr*—r. at two dollars im Kleinverkauf zwei Dollar kosten

re'tail busi'ness *s* Kleinhandel *m*

retailer ['ritelər] *s* Kleinhändler –in *mf*

retain [rɪ'ten] *tr* (zurück)behalten; (a *lawyer*) sich [*dat*] nehmen

retainer [rɪ'tenər] *s* (hist) Gefolgsmann *m*; (jur) Honorarvorschuß *m*

retain'ing wall' *s* Stützmauer *f*

retake ['ritek] *s* (cin) Neuaufnahme *f* ‖ [ri'tek] *tr* (a *town*) zurückerobern; (cin) nochmals aufnehmen

retaliate [rɪ'tælɪ,et] *intr* (**against**) Vergeltung üben (an *dat*)

retaliation [rɪ,tælɪ'eʃən] *s* Vergeltung *f*

retaliatory [rɪ'tælɪ-ə,tori] *adj* Vergeltungs-

retard [rɪ'tard] *tr* verzögern

retard'ed *adj* zurückgeblieben

retch [retʃ] *intr* würgen

retch'ing *s* Würgen *n*

retell [ri'tel] *tr* wiedererzählen

retention [rɪ'tenʃən] *s* Beibehaltung *f*

re·think [rɪ'θɪŋk] *v* (*pret* & *pp* –thought*) *tr* umdenken

reticence ['retɪsəns] *s* Verschwiegenheit *f*

reticent ['retɪsənt] *adj* verschwiegen

retina ['retɪnə] *s* Netzhaut *f*, Retina *f*

retinue ['retɪ,n(j)u] *s* Gefolge *n*

retire [rɪ'taɪr] *tr* pensionieren ‖ *intr* (*from employment*) in den Ruhestand treten; (*withdraw*) sich zurückziehen; (*go to bed*) sich zur Ruhe begeben

retired' *adj* pensioniert

retirement [rɪ'taɪrmənt] *s* Ruhestand *m*; go into r. in den Ruhestand treten, sich pensionieren lassen

retire'ment pay' *s* Pension *f*

retire'ment plan' *s* Pensionsplan *m*

retir'ing *adj* zurückhaltend

retort [rɪ'tort] *s* schlagfertige Erwiderung *f*; (chem) Retorte *f* ‖ *tr* & *intr* erwidern

retouch [ri'tʌtʃ] *tr* retuschieren

retrace [rɪ'tres] *tr* zurückverfolgen

retract [rɪ'trækt] *tr* (a *statement*) widerrufen; (*claws*; *landing gear*) einziehen

retract'able land'ing gear' [rɪ'træktəbəl] *s* Verschwindfahrgestell *n*

retrain [ri'tren] *tr* umschulen

retread ['ri,tred] *s* (aut) runderneuerter Reifen *m* ‖ *tr* runderneuern

retreat [rɪ'trit] *s* (*quiet place*) Ruhesitz *m*; (mil) Rückzug *m*; (rel) Exerzitien *pl*; beat a hasty r. eilig den Rückzug antreten ‖ *intr* sich zurückziehen

retrench [rɪ'trentʃ] *tr* einschränken ‖ *intr* sich einschränken

retribution [,retrɪ'bjuʃən] *s* Vergeltung *f*

retrieval [rɪ'trivəl] *s* Wiedererlangung *f*

retrieve [rɪ'triv] *tr* wiedererlangen; (a *loss*) wettmachen; (hunt) apportieren

retriever [rɪ'trivər] *s* Apportierhund *m*

retroactive [,retro'æktɪv] *adj* (**from**) rückwirkend von ... an

retrogressive [,retro'gresɪv] *adj* rückläufig

retrorocket ['retro,rakɪt] *s* Bremsrakete *f*

retrospect ['retrə,spekt] *s*—in r. rückblickend

re·try [ri'traɪ] *v* (*pret* & *pp* –tried) *tr* (jur) nochmals verhandeln

return [rɪ'tʌrn] *s* Rückkehr *f*; (*giving back*) Rückgabe *f*; (*the way back*) Rückweg *m*; (*tax form*) Steuererklärung *f*; (*profit*) Umsatz *m*; (tennis) Rückschlag *m*; in r. dafür; in r. for als Entgelt für; returns (*profits*) Ertrag *m*; (*of an election*) Ergebnisse *pl* ‖ *tr* zurückgeben; (*send back*) zurücksenden; (*put back*) zurückstellen; (*thanks*) abstatten; (a *verdict*) fällen; (a *favor, love, gun fire*) erwidern; (tennis) zurückschlagen ‖ *intr* zurückkehren; r. to (*e.g., a topic*) zurückkommen auf (*acc*)

return' address' *s* Rückadresse *f*

return' flight' *s* Rückflug *m*

return' match' *s* Revanchepartie *f*

return' tick'et *s* Rückfahrkarte *f*; (aer) Rückflugkarte *f*

reunification [ri,junɪfɪ'keʃən] *s* (pol) Wiedervereinigung *f*

reunion [ri'junjən] *s* Treffen *n*

rev [rev] *v* (*pret* & *pp* revved; *ger* revving) *tr* (**up**) auf Touren bringen ‖ *intr* auf Touren kommen

revamp [ri'væmp] *tr* umgestalten

reveal [rɪ'vil] *tr* offenbaren

reveille ['revəli] *s* Wecken *n*

rev·el ['revəl] *s* Gelage *n* ‖ *v* (*pret* & *pp* –el[l]ed; *ger* –el[l]ing) *intr* ein Gelage halten; r. in (fig) schwelgen in (*dat*)

revelation [,revə'leʃən] *s* Offenbarung *f*; Revelations (Bib) Offenbarung *f*

reveler ['revələr] *s* Zecher –in *mf*

revelry ['revəlri] *s* Zechgelage *n*

revenge [rɪ'vendʒ] *s* Rache *f*; take r. on s.o. for s.th. sich an j–m für etw rächen ‖ *tr* rächen

revengeful [rɪ'vendʒfəl] *adj* rachsüchtig

revenue ['revə,n(j)u] *s* (*yield*) Ertrag *m*; (*internal revenue*) Steueraufkommen *n*

rev'enue stamp' *s* Banderole *f*

reverberate [rɪ'vʌrbə,ret] *intr* widerhallen

revere [rɪ'vɪr] *tr* verehren

reverence ['revərəns] *s* (*respect given or received*) Ehrerbietung *f*; (*respect felt*) Ehrfurcht *f*

reverend ['revərənd] *adj* ehrwürdig; the Reverend ... Hochwürden ...

reverie ['revəri] *s* Träumerei *f*; be lost in r. in Träumen versunken sein

reversal [rɪ'vʌrsəl] *s* Umkehrung *f*; (*of opinion*) Umschwung *m*

reverse [rɪ'vʌrs] *adj* umgekehrt; (*side*) linke ‖ *s* (*back side*) Rückseite *f*; (*opposite*) Gegenteil *n*; (*setback*) Rückschlag *m*; (*of a coin*) Revers *m*;

(aut) Rückwärtsgang m || tr umkehren, umdrehen; (a decision) umstoßen || intr sich rückwärts bewegen

reverse′ side′ s Rückseite f, Kehrseite f

reversible [rɪ'vʌrsɪbəl] adj (decision) umstoßbar; (material) zweiseitig; (chem, phys) umkehrbar; (mach) umsteuerbar

revert [rɪ'vʌrt] intr—r. to zurückkommen auf (acc); (jur) zurückfallen an (acc)

review [rɪ'vju] s (of) Überblick m (über acc); (of a lesson) Wiederholung f; (of a book) Besprechung f; (periodical) Rundschau m; (mil) Besichtigung f; pass in r. mustern || tr (a lesson) wiederholen; (a book) besprechen; (e.g., the events of the day) überblicken; (mil) besichtigen

reviewer [rɪ'vju·ər] s Besprecher –in mf

revile [rɪ'vaɪl] tr schmähen

revise [rɪ'vaɪz] tr (a book) umarbeiten; (one's opinion) revidieren

revised′ edi′tion s verbesserte Auflage f

revision [rɪ'vɪʒən] s Neubearbeitung f

revival [rɪ'vaɪvəl] s Wiederbelebung f; (rel) Erweckung f; (theat) Reprise f

reviv′al meet′ing s Erweckungsversammlung f

revive [rɪ'vaɪv] tr wieder aufleben lassen; (memories) aufrühren; (a victim) wieder zu Bewußtsein bringen || intr wieder aufleben

revoke [rɪ'vok] tr widerrufen

revolt [rɪ'volt] s Aufstand m || tr abstoßen || intr revoltieren

revolt′ing adj abstoßend

revolution [ˌrevə'luʃən] s Revolution f; (turn) Umdrehung f; revolutions per minute Drehzahl f

revolutionary [ˌrevə'luʃəˌneri] adj revolutionär || s Revolutionär –in mf

revolve [rɪ'vɑlv] intr (around) sich drehen (um)

revolver [rɪ'vɑlvər] s Revolver m

revolv′ing adj Dreh-

revue [rɪ'vju] s (theat) Revue f

revulsion [rɪ'vʌlʃən] s Abscheu m

reward [rɪ'wɔrd] s Belohnung f || tr belohnen

reward′ing adj lohnend

re-wind [ri'waɪnd] v (pret & pp -wound) tr (a tape, film) umspulen; (a clock) wieder aufziehen

rewire [ri'waɪr] tr Leitungen neu legen in (dat)

rework [ri'wʌrk] tr umarbeiten

re-write [ri'raɪt] v (pret –wrote; pp –written) tr umschreiben

rhapsody ['ræpsədi] s Rhapsodie f

rheostat ['ri·ə‚stæt] s Rheostat m

rhetoric ['retərɪk] s Redekunst f

rhetorical [rɪ'tɔrɪkəl] adj rhetorisch

rheumatic [ru'mætɪk] adj rheumatisch

rheumatism ['rumə‚tɪzəm] s Rheumatismus m

Rhine [raɪn] s Rhein m

Rhineland ['raɪn‚lænd] s Rheinland n

rhine′stone′ s Rheinkiesel m

rhinoceros [raɪ'nɑsərəs] s Nashorn n

rhubarb ['rubɑrb] s Rhabarber m; (sl) Krach m

rhyme [raɪm] s Reim m || tr & intr reimen

rhythm ['rɪðəm] s Rhythmus m

rhythmic(al) ['rɪðmɪk(əl)] adj rhythmisch

rib [rɪb] s Rippe f || v (pret & pp ribbed; ger ribbing) tr (coll) sich lustig machen über (acc)

ribald ['rɪbəld] adj zotig

ribbon ['rɪbən] s Band n; (decoration) Ordensband n; (for a typewriter) Farbband n

rice [raɪs] s Reis m

rich [rɪtʃ] adj reich; (voice) volltönend; (soil) fruchtbar; (funny) (coll) köstlich; r. in reich an (dat) || riches spl Reichtum s

rickets ['rɪkɪts] s Rachitis f

rickety ['rɪkɪti] adj (building) baufällig; (furniture) wackelig

rid [rɪd] v (pret & pp rid; ger ridding) tr (of) befreien (von); get rid of loswerden

riddance ['rɪdəns] s Befreiung f; good r.! den (or die or das) wäre ich glücklich los!

riddle ['rɪdəl] s Rätsel n

ride [raɪd] s Fahrt f; give s.o. a r. j-n im Auto mitnehmen; take for a r. (murder) entführen und umbringen; (dupe) hochnehmen || v (pret rode [rod]; pp ridden ['rɪdən]) tr (a bicycle) fahren; (a horse) reiten; (a train, bus) fahren mit; (harass) hetzen; r. out (a storm) gut überstehen || intr (e.g., in a car) fahren; (on a horse) reiten; let s.th. r. sich mit etw abfinden

rider ['raɪdər] s (on horseback) Reiter –in mf; (on a bicycle) Radfahrer –in mf; (in a vehicle) Fahrer –in mf; (to a document) Zusatzklausel f

ridge [rɪdʒ] s (of a hill; of the nose) Rücken m; (of a roof) Dachfirst m

ridge′pole′ s Firstbalken m

ridicule ['rɪdɪ‚kjul] s Spott m || tr verspotten

ridiculous [rɪ'dɪkjələs] adj lächerlich; look r. lächerlich wirken

rid′ing acad′emy s Reitschule f

rid′ing boot′ s Reitstiefel m

rid′ing breech′es spl Reithose f

rid′ing hab′it s Reitkostüm n

rife [raɪf] adj häufig; r. with voll von

riffraff ['rɪf‚ræf] s Gesindel n

rifle ['raɪfəl] s Gewehr n || tr ausplündern

rift [rɪft] s (& fig) Riß m

rig [rɪg] s (gear) Ausrüstung f; (horse and carriage) Gespann n; (truck) Laster m; (oil drill) Bohrturm m; (getup) (coll) Aufmachung f; (naut) Takelung f || v (pret & pp rigged; ger rigging) tr (auf)takeln; (prices, elections, accounts) manipulieren

rig′ging s Takelung f

right [raɪt] adj (side, glove, angle) recht; (just) gerecht; (correct) richtig; (moment) richtig; do you have the r. time? können Sie mir die genaue Uhrzeit sagen?; **be in one's r. mind** bei klarem Verstand sein; **it is all r.** es ist schon gut; **r.?** nicht wahr?; **that's r.!** ebent; **the r. thing** das Richtige; **you are r.** Sie haben recht || *adj* direkt; (*to the right*) rechts; **r. along** durchaus; **r. away** sofort, gleich; **r. behind the door** gleich hinter der Tür; **r. glad** (coll) recht froh; **r. here** gleich hier; **r. now** (*at the moment*) momentan; (*immediately*) sofort; **r. through** durch und durch || *s* Recht *n*; (box) Rechte *f*; **all rights reserved** alle Rechte vorbehalten; **by rights von Rechts wegen; in the r.** im Recht; **on the r.** rechts, zur Rechten || *tr* aufrichten; (*an error*) berichtigen; (*a wrong*) wiedergutmachen || *interj* stimmt!

righteous ['raɪtʃəs] *adj* gerecht, rechtschaffen; (*smug*) selbstgerecht

rightful ['raɪtfəl] *adj* (*owner*) rechtmäßig; (*claim, place*) berechtigt

right'-hand' *adj* zur Rechten; (*glove*) recht

right'-hand'ed *adj* rechtshändig

right-hander ['raɪt'hændər] *s* Rechtshänder –in *mf*

right'-hand man' *s* rechte Hand *f*

rightist ['raɪtɪst] *adj* rechtsstehend || *s* Rechtspolitiker –in *mf*

rightly ['raɪtli] *adv* richtig; (*rightfully*) rechtmäßig

right' of way' *s* (*in traffic*) Vorfahrtsrecht *n*; (*across another's land*) Grunddienstbarkeit *f*

right' wing' *s* rechter Flügel *m*

rigid ['rɪdʒɪd] *adj* steif, starr

rigmarole ['rɪgmə͵rol] *s* (*meaningless talk*) Geschwafel *n*; (*fuss*) Getue *n*

rigorous ['rɪgərəs] *adj* hart, streng

rile [raɪl] *tr* aufbringen

rill [rɪl] *s* Bächlein *n*

rim [rɪm] *s* Rand *m*; (*of eyeglasses*) Fassung *f*; (*of a wheel*) Felge *f*

rind [raɪnd] *s* Rinde *f*

ring [rɪŋ] *s* (*for the fingers; for boxing; of criminals or spies; of a circus; circle under the eyes*) Ring *m*; (*of a bell, voice, laughter*) Klang *m*; **give s.o. a r.** (telp) j–n anrufen; **run rings around s.o.** j–n in die Tasche stecken || *v* (*pret & pp ringed*) *tr* umringen; **r. in** einschließen || *v* (*pret rang* [ræŋ]; *pp rung* [rʌŋ]) *tr* läuten; **r. the bell** läuten, klingeln; **r. out** ausläuten; **r. up** anrufen || *intr* läuten, klingeln; **my ears are ringing** mir klingen die Ohren; **r. for s.o.** nach j–m klingeln; **r. out** laut schallen; **the bell is ringing** es läutet

ring'ing *adj* schallend || *s* Läuten *n*; (*in the ears*) Klingen *n*

ring'lead'er *s* Rädelsführer *m*

ring'mas'ter *s* Zirkusdirektor *m*

ring'side' *s* Ringplatz *m*

ring'worm' *s* Scherpilzflechte *f*

rink [rɪŋk] *s* Eisbahn *f*; (*for roller-skating*) Rollschuhbahn *f*

rinse [rɪns] *s* Spülen *n* || *tr* ausspülen

riot ['raɪət] *s* Aufruhr *m*; **r. of colors**

Farbengemisch *n*; **run r.** sich austoben; (*said of plants*) wuchern || *intr* sich zusammenrotten

ri'ot act' *s*—**read the r. to s.o.** j–m die Leviten lesen

rioter ['raɪətər] *s* Aufrührer –in *mf*

rip [rɪp] *s* Riß *m* || *v* (*pret & pp ripped; ger ripping*) *tr* (zer)reißen; **rip off** abreißen; (*the skin*) abziehen; (*cheat*) betrügen || *intr* reißen

rip' cord' *s* Reißlinie *f*

ripe [raɪp] *adj* reif

ripen ['raɪpən] *tr* (& fig) reifen lassen || *intr* (& fig) reifen

rip' off' *s* (sl) Wucher *m*

ripple ['rɪpəl] *s* leichte Welle *f* || *intr* leichte Wellen schlagen

rise [raɪz] *s* Aufsteigen *n*; (*in prices*) Steigerung *f*; (*of heavenly bodies*) Aufgang *m*; (*increase, e.g., in population*) Zunahme *f*; (*in the ground*) Erhebung *f*; **get a r. out of s.o.** j–n zu e–r Reaktion veranlassen; **give r. to** veranlassen || *v* (*pret rose* [roz]; *pp risen* ['rɪzən]) *intr* (*said of the sun, of a cake*) aufgehen; (*said of a river, prices, temperature, barometer*) steigen; (*said of a road*) ansteigen; (*get out of bed*) aufstehen; (*stand up*) sich erheben; (*from the dead*) auferstehen; (*said of anger*) hochsteigen; **r. to the occasion** sich der Lage gewachsen zeigen; **r. up from the ranks** von der Pike auf dienen

riser ['raɪzər] *s* (*of a staircase*) Futterbrett *n*; **early r.** Frühaufsteher –in *mf*; **late r.** Langschläfer –in *mf*

risk [rɪsk] *s* Risiko *n*; **run the r. of** (ger) Gefahr laufen zu (inf) || *tr* wagen, aufs Spiel setzen

risky ['rɪski] *adj* riskant, gewagt

risque ['rɪske] *adj* schlüpfrig

rite [raɪt] *s* Ritus *m*; **last rites** Sterbesakramente *pl*

ritual ['rɪtʃu͵əl] *adj* rituell || *s* Ritual *n*

ri·val ['raɪvəl] *adj* rivalisierend || *s* Rivale *m*, Rivalin *f* || *v* (*pret & pp –val[l]ed; ger –val[l]ing*) *tr* rivalisieren, wetteifern mit

rivalry ['raɪvəlri] *s* Rivalität *f*

river ['rɪvər] *adj* Fluß– || *s* Fluß *m*

riv'er ba'sin *s* Flußgebiet *n*

riv'erfront' *s* Flußufer *n*

riv'erside' *adj* am Flußufer gelegen || *s* Flußufer *n*

rivet ['rɪvɪt] *s* Niet *m* || *tr* nieten

riv'et gun' *s* Nietmaschine *f*

riv'eting *s* (*act*) Vernieten *n*; (*connection*) Nietnaht *f*

rivulet ['rɪvjəlɪt] *s* Flüßchen *n*

R.N. ['ar'en] *s* (registered nurse) staatlich geprüfte Krankenschwester *f*

roach [rotʃ] *s* (ent) Schabe *f*; (ichth) Plötze *f*

road [rod] *s* (& fig) Weg *m*; **be (much) on the r.** (viel) auf Reisen sein; **go on the r.** auf Tour gehen; (theat) auf Tournee gehen

road'bed' *s* Bahnkörper *m*

road'block' *s* Straßensperre *f*

road' hog' s rücksichtsloser Autofahrer m

road' house' s Wirtshaus n, Rasthaus n

road' map' s Straßenkarte f, Autokarte f

road'side' adj Straßen– || s Straßenrand m

road'side inn' s Rasthaus n

road'sign' s Wegweiser m

road'stead' s Reede f

road' test' s (aut) Probefahrt f

road'way' s Fahrweg m

roam [rom] tr durchstreifen || intr herumstreifen

roar [ror] s Gebrüll n; (of a waterfall, sea, wind) Brausen n; (of an engine) Dröhnen n; (laughter) schallendes Gelächter n || intr brüllen; (said of a waterfall, sea, wind) brausen; **r. at** anbrüllen; (e.g., a joke) schallend lachen über (acc); **r. by** vorbeibrausen; **r. with** brüllen vor (dat)

roast [rost] adj gebraten || s Braten m || tr (meat, fish) braten, rösten; (coffee, chestnuts) rösten; (a person) (coll) durch den Kakao ziehen || intr braten

roast' beef' s Roastbeef n

roaster ['rostər] s (appliance) Röster m, Röstapparat m; (fowl) Brathuhn n

roast' pork' s Schweinsbraten m

rob [rab] v (pret & pp robbed; ger robbing) tr (a thing) rauben; (a person) (of) berauben (genit)

robber ['rabər] s Räuber –in mf

robbery ['rabəri] s Raubüberfall m

robe [rob] s Robe f; (house robe) Hausrock m || tr feierlich ankleiden || intr sich feierlich ankleiden

robin ['rabɪn] s Rotkehlchen n

robot ['robat] s Roboter m

robust [ro'bʌst] adj robust

rock [rak] adj (mus) Rock– || s Fels m; (one that is thrown) Stein m; (mus) Rockmusik f; **on the rocks** mit Eiswürfeln; (ruined) kaputt || tr schaukeln, wiegen; **r. the boat** (fig) die Sache ins Wanken bringen; **r. to sleep** in den Schlaf wiegen || intr schwanken, wanken; (said of a boat) schaukeln

rock'-bot'tom adj äußerst niedrig || s Tiefpunkt m

rock' can'dy s Kandiszucker m

rock' crys'tal s Bergkristall m

rocker ['rakər] s Schaukelstuhl m; **go off one's r.** (coll) den Verstand verlieren

rocket ['rakɪt] s Rakete f

rock'et launch'er s Raketenwerfer m

rocketry ['rakətri] s Raketentechnik f

rock'et ship' s Rakentenflugkörper m

rock' gar'den s Steingarten m

rock'ing chair' s Schaukelstuhl m

rock'ing horse' s Schaukelpferd n

rock-'n'-roll ['rakən'rol] s Rock 'n Roll m

rock' salt' s Steinsalz n

rocky ['raki] adj felsig; (shaky) wacklig

rod [rad] s Stab m, Stange f; (whip)

Zuchtrute f; (of the retina; of a microorganism) Stäbchen n; (revolver) (sl) Schießeisen n; (angl) Angelrute f; (Bib) Reis n; (mach) Pleuelstange f; (surg) Absteckpfahl m

rodent ['rodənt] s Nagetier n

roe [ro] s (deer) Reh n; (ichth) Rogen m

rogue [rog] s Schuft m, Schurke m

rogues' gal'lery s Verbrecheralbum n

roguish ['rogɪʃ] adj schurkisch

role, rôle [rol] s Rolle f

roll [rol] s Rolle f; (bread) Brötchen n; (of thunder, of a ship) Rollen n; (of drums) Wirbel m; (of fat) Wulst m; **call the r.** die Namen verlesen; (mil) Appell halten || tr rollen; (cigarettes) drehen; (metals, roads) walzen; **r. over** überrollen; **r. up** zusammenrollen; (sleeves) zurückstreifen || intr sich wälzen; **be rolling in money** im Geld wühlen

roll'back' s (com) Senkung f

roll'call' s Namensverlesung f; (mil) Appell m

roll'er bear'ing s Rollenlager n

roll'er coast'er s Berg-und-Tal-Bahn f

roll'er skate' s Rollschuh m

roll'er-skate' intr rollschuhlaufen

roll'er tow'el s Rollhandtuch n

roll'ing mill' s Walzwerk n

roll'ing pin' s Nudelholz n, Teigrolle f

roll'ing stock' s (rr) rollendes Material n

roly-poly ['roli'poli] adj dick und rund

roman ['romən] adj (typ) Antiqua–; **Roman** römisch || s (typ) Antiqua f; **Roman** Römer –in mf

Ro'man can'dle s Leuchtkugel f

Ro'man Cath'olic adj römisch-katholisch || s Katholik –in mf

romance [ro'mæns] adj (ling) romanisch || s Romanze f

Romanesque [,romə'nesk] adj romanisch || s das Romanische

Ro'man nose' s Römernase f

Ro'man nu'meral s römische Ziffer f

romantic [ro'mæntɪk] adj romantisch

romanticism [ro'mæntɪ,sɪzəm] s Romantik f

romp [ramp] intr umhertollen

rompers ['rampərz] spl Spielanzug m

roof [ruf] s Dach n; (aut) Verdeck n; **raise the r.** (coll) Krach machen; **r. of the mouth** Gaumendach n

roofer ['rufər] s Dachdecker m

roof' gar'den s Dachgarten m

roof' tile' s Dachziegel m

rook [ruk] s (chess) Turm m; (orn) Saatkrähe f || tr (coll) (out of) beschwindeln (um)

rookie ['ruki] s (coll) Neuling m

room [rum] s Zimmer n; (space) Raum m, Platz m; **make r.** Platz machen; **r. for complaint** Anlaß m zur Klage; **take up too much r.** zu viel Platz in Anspruch nehmen || intr wohnen

room' and board' s Kost und Quartier

room' clerk' s Empfangschef m

roomer ['rumər] s Mieter –in mf

room'ing house' s Pension f
room'mate' s Zimmergenosse m
room' serv'ice s Bedienung f aufs Zimmer
roomy ['rumɪ] adj geräumig
roost [rust] s Hühnerstange f; **rule the r.** Hahn im Korb sein || intr auf der Stange sitzen
rooster ['rustər] s Hahn m
root [rut] s Wurzel f; **get to the r. of s.th.** etw [dat] auf den Grund gehen; **take r.** Wurzel schlagen; (fig) sich einbürgern || tr—**be rooted in** wurzeln in (dat); **rooted to the spot** festgewurzelt; **r. out** ausrotten || intr —**r. about** wühlen; **r. for** zujubeln (dat)
rope [rop] s Strick m, Seil n; **know the ropes** alle Kniffe kennen || tr mit e–m Seil festbinden; (a steer) mit e–m Lasso einfangen; **r. in** (coll) einwickeln; **r. off** absperren
rosary ['rozərɪ] s Rosenkranz m
rose [roz] adj rosenrot || s Rose f
rose'bud' s Rosenknospe f
rose'bush' s Rosenstock m
rose'-col'ored adj rosenfarbig; (fig) rosa(rot)
rosemary ['roz‚merɪ] s Rosmarin m
rosin ['razɪn] s Harz n; (for violin bow) Kolophonium n
roster ['rustər] s Namenliste f; (educ) Stundenplan m; (mil, naut) Dienstplan m
rostrum ['rustrəm] s Rednerbühne f
rosy ['rozɪ] adj (& fig) rosig
rot [rat] s Fäulnis f; (sl) Quatsch m || v (pret & pp rotted; ger rotting) tr faulen lassen || intr verfaulen
rotate ['rotet] tr rotieren lassen; (tires) auswechseln; (agr) wechseln || intr rotieren; (take turns) sich abwechseln
rotation [ro'teʃən] s Rotation f; **in r.** wechselweise; **r. of crops** Wechselwirtschaft f
rote [rot] s—**by r.** mechanisch
rotisserie [ro'tɪsərɪ] s Fleischbraterei f
rotten ['ratən] adj faul; (trick) niederträchtig; **feel r.** (sl) sich elend fühlen
rotund [ro'tʌnd] adj rundlich
rotunda [ro'tʌndə] s Rotunde f
rouge [ruʒ] s Rouge n || tr schminken
rough [rʌf] adj (hands, voice, person) rauh; (piece of wood) roh; (work, guess, treatment) grob; (water, weather) stürmisch; (road) uneben; **have it r.** viel durchmachen || tr— **r. in** roh entwerfen; (carp) grob bearbeiten; **r. it** primitiv leben; **r. up** grob behandeln
rough' draft' s Konzept n
roughen ['rʌfən] tr aufrauhen
rough'house' s Radau m || intr Radau machen
roughly ['rʌflɪ] adv grob; (about) etwa
rough'neck' s (coll) Rauhbein n
roulette [ru'lɛt] s Roulett n
round [raund] adj rund || s Runde f; (of applause) Salve f; (shot) Schuß m; (of drinks) Lage f; (of a sentinel,

policeman, inspector, mailman) Rundgang m; **daily r.** Alltag m || prep um (acc) herum || tr (make round) runden; (a corner) herumgehen (or herumfahren) um (acc); **r. off** abrunden; (finish) vollenden; **r. up** (animals) zusammentreiben; (persons) zusammenbringen; (criminals) ausheben
round'house' s (rr) Lokomotivschuppen m
round'-shoul'dered adj mit runden Schultern
round' steak' s Kugel f
round'ta'ble adj am runden Tisch
round' trip' s Hin-und Rückfahrt f; (aer) Hin- und Rückflug m
round'-trip' tick'et s Rückfahrkarte f
round'up' s (of cattle) Zusammentreiben n; (of criminals) Aushebung f
rouse [rauz] tr (from) aufwecken (aus)
rout [raut] s völlige Niederlage f; (mil) wilde Flucht f; **put to r.** in die Flucht schlagen || tr (mil) zersprengen
route [rut], [raut] s Route f, Weg m || tr leiten
routine [ru'tin] adj routinemäßig || s Routine f; **be r.** die Regel sein
rove [rov] intr umherwandern
row [rau] s Krach m; **raise a row** (coll) Krach machen || s [ro] Reihe f; **in a row** hintereinander || tr rudern
rowboat ['ro‚bot] s Ruderboot n
rowdy ['raudɪ] adj flegelhaft || s Flegel m
rower ['ro·ər] s Ruderer –in mf
rowing ['ro·ɪŋ] s Rudersport m
royal ['rɔɪ·əl] adj königlich
royalist ['rɔɪ·əlɪst] adj königstreu || s Königstreue mf
royalty ['rɔɪ·əltɪ] s (royal status) Königswürde f; (personage) fürstliche Persönlichkeit f; (collectively) fürstliche Persönlichkeiten pl; (author's compensation) Tantieme f; (inventor's compensation) Lizenzgebühr f
r.p.m. ['ar‚pi'ɛm] spl (revolutions per minute) Drehzahl f
R.S.V.P. abbr u.A.w.g. (um Antwort wird gebeten)
rub [rʌb] s Reiben n; **there's the rub** (coll) da sitzt der Haken || v (pret & pp rubbed; ger rubbing) tr reiben; **rub down** abreiben; **rub elbows with** verkehren mit; **rub in** einreiben; **rub it in** (sl) es (j–m) unter die Nase reiben; **rub out** ausradieren; (sl) umbringen; **rub s.o. the wrong way** j–m auf die Nerven gehen || intr reiben; **rub against** sich reiben an (dat); **rub off on** (fig) abfärben auf (acc)
rubber ['rʌbər] adj Gummi– || s Gummi m & n; (cards) Robber m; **rubbers** Gummischuhe pl
ru'ber band' s Gummiband n
rubberize ['rʌbə‚raɪz] tr gummieren
rub'ber plant' s Kautschukpflanze f
rub'ber stamp' s Gummistempel m
rub'ber-stamp' tr abstempeln; (coll) automatisch genehmigen
rubbery ['rʌbərɪ] adj gummiartig
rub'bing al'cohol s Franzbranntwein m

rubbish [ˈrʌbɪʃ] s (trash) Abfall m; (nonsense) dummes Zeug n

rubble [ˈrʌbəl] s Schutt m; (used in masonry) Bruchstein m

rub´down´ s Abreibung f

rubric [ˈrubrɪk] s Rubrik f

ruby [ˈrubi] adj rubinrot || s Rubin m

ruckus [ˈrʌkəs] s (coll) Krawall m

rudder [ˈrʌdər] s (aer) Seitenruder n; (naut) Steuerruder n

ruddy [ˈrʌdi] adj rosig

rude [rud] adj grob

rudeness [ˈrudnɪs] s Grobheit f

rudiments [ˈrudɪmənts] spl Grundlagen pl

rue [ru] tr bereuen

rueful [ˈrufəl] adj reuig; (pitiable) kläglich; (mournful) wehmütig

ruffian [ˈrʌfɪ-ən] s Raufbold m

ruffle [ˈrʌfəl] s Rüsche f; (in water) Kräuseln n; (of a drum) gedämpfter Trommelwirbel m || tr kräuseln; (feathers, hair) sträuben

rug [rʌg] s Teppich m

rugged [ˈrʌgɪd] adj (country) wild; (robust) kräftig; (life) hart

ruin [ˈru-ɪn] s Ruine f; (undoing) Ruin m; go to r. zugrunde gehen; lie in ruins in Trümmern liegen; ruins (debris) Trümmer pl || tr ruinieren

rule [rul] s (reign) Herrschaft f; (regulation) Regel f; as a r. in der Regel; become the r. zur Regel werden || tr beherrschen; (paper) linieren; r. out ausschließen || intr (over) herrschen (über acc)

rule´ of law´ s Rechtsstaatlichkeit f

rule´ of thumb´ s Faustregel f; by r. über den Daumen gepeilt

ruler [ˈrulər] s Herrscher –in mf; (for measuring) Lineal n

rul´ing adj herrschend || s Regelung f

rum [rʌm] s Rum m

Rumania [ruˈmenɪ-ə] s Rumänien n

Rumanian [ruˈmenɪ-ən] adj rumänisch || s Rumäne m, Rumänin f; (language) Rumänisch n

rumble [ˈrʌmbəl] s (of thunder) Rollen n; (of a truck) Rumpeln n || intr rollen; rumpeln

ruminate [ˈrumɪˌnet] tr & intr wiederkäuen

rummage [ˈrʌmɪdʒ] intr—r. through durchsuchen

rum´mage sale´ s Ramschverkauf m

rumor [ˈrumər] s Gerücht n || tr—it is rumored that es geht das Gerücht, daß

rump [rʌmp] s (of an animal) Hinterteil m & n; (buttocks) Gesäß n

rumple [ˈrʌmpəl] tr (clothes) zerknittern; (hair) zerzausen

rump´ steak´ s Rumpsteak n

rumpus [ˈrʌmpəs] s (coll) Krach m; raise a r. (coll) Krach machen

rum´pus room´ s Spielzimmer n

run [rʌn] s Lauf m; (in stockings) Laufmasche f; (fin) Run m; (theat) Laufzeit f; be on the run auf der Flucht sein; in the long run auf die Dauer; run of bad luck Pechsträhne f; run of good luck Glücksträhne f ||

v (pret ran [ræn]; pp run; ger running) tr (a machine) bedienen; (a business, household) führen; (a distance) laufen; (a blockade) brechen; (a cable) verlegen; **run a race** um die Wette laufen; **run down** (with a car) niederfahren; (clues) nachgehen (dat); (a citation) aufspüren; (through gossip) schlechtmachen; **run off** (typ) Abzüge machen von; **run over** (with a vehicle) überfahren; (rehearse) nochmal durchgehen; **run through** (with a sword) erstechen; **run up** (bills) auflaufen lassen; (prices) in die Höhe treiben; (a flag) hissen || intr laufen, rennen; (flow) fließen; (said of buses, etc.) verkehren; (said of the nose) laufen, e.g., **ihm läuft die Nase** his nose is running; (said of colors) auslaufen; (said of a meeting) dauern; (said of a lease) gelten (auf acc); **run across** zufällig treffen; **run after** nachlaufen (dat); **run around** herumlaufen; **run around with** sich herumtreiben mit; **run away** weglaufen; (said of a spouse) durchgehen; **run down** (said of a clock) ablaufen; **run dry** austrocknen; **run for** kandidieren für; **run high**, e.g., **feelings ran high** die Gemüter waren erhitzt; **run in the family** in der Familie liegen; **run into** (e.g., a tree) fahren gegen; (e.g., trouble, debt) geraten in (acc); (e.g., a friend) unerwartet treffen; **run into the thousands** in die Tausende gehen; **run low** knapp werden; **run out** (said of liquids) ausgehen; (said of supplies, time) zu Ende gehen; **run out of** ausgehen, e.g., **they ran out of supplies** die Vorräte gingen ihnen aus; **run over** (said of a pot) überlaufen; **run up against** stoßen auf (acc); **run up to** s.o. j-m entgegenlaufen; **run wild** verwildern

run´-around´ s—give s.o. the r. j-n von Pontius zu Pilatus schicken

run´away´ adj flüchtig; (horse) durchgegangen || s Ausreißer m; (horse) Durchgänger m

run´down´ s kurze Zusammenfassung f

run´-down´ adj (condition) heruntergekommen; (clock) abgelaufen; (battery) entladen

rung [rʌŋ] s (of a ladder) Sprosse f; (of a chair) Querleiste f

run-in´ s (coll) Zusammenstoß m

runner [ˈrʌnər] s Läufer –in mf; (of a sled or skate) Kufe f; (of a sliding door) Laufschiene f; (rug) Läufer m; (bot) Ausläufer m; (mil) Meldegänger m

run´ner-up´ s (runners-up) Zweitbeste mf; (sport) Zweite mf

run´ning adj (water) fließend; (debts, expenses, sore) laufend || s Laufen n, Lauf m; be in the r. gut im Rennen liegen; be out of the r. (out of the race) aus dem Rennen ausgeschlossen sein; (not among the front runners) keine Aussichten haben

run'ning board' s Trittbrett n
run'ning start' s fliegender Start m
run'off' s (sport) Entscheidungslauf m
run'off elec'tion s entscheidende Vorwahl f
run'-of-the-mill' adj Durchschnitts-
runt [rʌnt] s Dreikäsehoch m
run'way' s Startbahn f
rupture ['rʌptʃər] s Bruch m || tr (relations) abbrechen; **be ruptured** e-n Bruch (or Riß) bekommen; **r. oneself** sich [dat] e-n Bruch zuziehen || intr platzen
rural ['rʊrəl] adj ländlich
ruse [ruz] s List f
rush [rʌʃ] adj dringend || s Eile f; (for) Ansturm m (auf acc); (bot) Binse f; **be in a r.** es eilig haben; **what's your r.?** wozu die Eile? || tr (a person) hetzen; (a defensive position) im Sturm nehmen; (work) schnell erledigen; (goods) schleunigst schicken; (e.g., to a hospital) schleunigst schaffen; **be rushed for time** sehr wenig Zeit haben; **r. through** (a bill) durchpeitschen; **r. up** (reinforcements) schnell herbeischaffen || intr eilen, sich stürzen; **r. at** zustürzen auf (acc); **r. forward** vorstürmen; **r. into** stürzen in (acc); **r. up to** zuschießen auf (acc); **the blood rushed to his head** ihm stieg das Blut in den Kopf
rush' hour' s spl Hauptverkehrszeit f
rush' or'der s Eilauftrag m
russet ['rʌsɪt] adj rotbraun
Russia ['rʌʃə] s Rußland n
Russian ['rʌʃən] adj russisch || s Russe m, Russin f; (language) Russisch n
rust [rʌst] s Rost m || tr rostig machen || intr (ver)rosten
rustic ['rʌstɪk] adj (rural) ländlich; (countryish) bäuerlich || s Bauer m
rustle ['rʌsəl] s Rauschen n; (of silk) Knistern n || tr rascheln mit; (cattle) stehlen || intr rauschen; (said of silk) knistern
rust'proof' adj rostfrei
rusty ['rʌsti] adj rostig; (fig) eingerostet
rut [rʌt] s Geleise n, Spur f; (fig) alter Trott m
ruthless ['ruθlɪs] adj erbarmungslos
rye [raɪ] s (grain) Roggen m; (whiskey) Roggenwhisky m
rye' bread' s Roggenbrot n
rye' grass' s Raigras n

---

s

S, s [es] s neunzehnter Buchstabe des englischen Alphabets
Sabbath ['sæbəθ] s Sabbat m
sabbat'ical year' [sə'bætɪkəl] s einjähriger Urlaub m (e-s Professors)
saber ['sebər] s Säbel m
sable ['sebəl] adj schwarz || s (fur) Zobelpelz m; (zool) Zobel m
sabotage ['sæbə‚taʒ] s Sabotage f || tr sabotieren
saboteur [‚sæbə'tʌr] s Saboteur –in mf
saccharin ['sækərɪn] s Saccharin n
sachet [sæ'ʃe] s Duftkissen n
sack [sæk] s Sack m; (bed) (coll) Falle f; **hit the s.** (coll) in die Falle gehen || tr einsacken; (dismiss) (coll) an die Luft setzen; (mil) ausplündern
sack'cloth' s Sacktuch n; **in s. and ashes** in Sack und Asche
sacrament ['sækrəmənt] s Sakrament n
sacramental [‚sækrə'mentəl] adj sakramental
sacred ['sekrəd] adj heilig; **s. to** geweiht (dat)
sacrifice ['sækrɪ‚faɪs] s Opfer n; **at a s.** mit Verlust || tr opfern
sacrilege ['sækrɪlɪdʒ] s Sakrileg n
sacrilegious [‚sækrɪ'lɪdʒəs] adj frevelhaft, gotteslästerlich
sacristan ['sækrɪstən] s Sakristan m
sacristy ['sækrɪsti] s Sakristei f
sad [sæd] adj traurig; (plight) schlimm
sadden ['sædən] s traurig machen
saddle ['sædəl] s Sattel m || tr satteln; **be saddled with** auf dem Halse haben
sad'dlebag' s Satteltasche f
sadism ['sedɪzəm] s Sadismus m
sadistic [se'dɪstɪk] adj sadistisch
sadness ['sædnɪs] s Traurigkeit f
sad' sack' s (sl) Trauerkloß m
safe [sef] adj (from) sicher (vor dat); (arrival) glücklich; **s. and sound** heil und gesund; (said of a thing) unversehrt; **to be on the s. side** vorsichtshalber || s Geldschrank m
safe'-con'duct s sicheres Geleit n
safe'-depos'it box' s Schließfach n
safe' dis'tance s Sicherheitsabstand m
safe'guard' s Schutz m || tr schützen
safe'keep'ing s sicherer Gewahrsam m
safety ['sefti] adj Sicherheits- || s Sicherheit f
safe'ty belt' s Sicherheitsgurt m
safe'ty pin' s Sicherheitsnadel f
safe'ty ra'zor s Rasierapparat m
safe'ty valve' s Sicherheitsventil n
saffron ['sæfrən] adj safrangelb || s Safran m
sag [sæg] s Senkung f || v (pret & pp sagged; ger sagging) intr sich senken; (said of a cable) durchhängen; (fig) sinken
sagacious [sə'geʃəs] adj scharfsinnig
sage [sedʒ] adj weise, klug || s Weise m; (plant) Salbei f
sage'brush' s Beifuß m
sail [sel] s Segel n; **set s. for** in See stechen nach || tr (a boat) fahren; (the sea) segeln über (acc) || intr segeln; (depart) abfahren; **s. across** übersegeln; **s. along the coast** an der

Küste entlangsegeln; **s. into** (coll) herunterputzen

sail'boat' s Segelboot n

sail'cloth' s Segeltuch n

sail'ing s Segelfahrt f; (sport) Segelsport m; **it will be smooth s.** (fig) es wird alles glattgehen

sail'ing ves'sel s Segelschiff n

sailor ['selər] s Matrose m

Saint [sent] s Heilige mf; **S. George** der heilige Georg, Sankt Georg

Saint' Bernard' s (dog) Bernhardiner m

sake [sek] s—**for her s.** ihretwegen; **for his s.** seinetwegen; **for my s.** meinetwegen; **for our s.** unsertwegen; **for their s.** ihretwegen; **for the s. of** um (genit) willen; **for your s.** deinetwegen, Ihretwegen

salable ['seləbəl] adj verkäuflich

salacious [sə'leʃəs] adj (person) geil; (writing, pictures) obszön

salad ['sæləd] s Salat m

sal'ad bowl' s Salatschüssel f

sal'ad dress'ing s Salatsoße f

sal'ad oil' s Salatöl n

salami [sə'lɑmi] s Salami f

salary ['sæləri] s Gehalt n

sale [sel] s Verkauf m; (special sale) Ausverkauf m; **be up for s.** zum Kauf stehen; **for s.** zu verkaufen; **sales** (com) Absatz m, Umsatz m; **put up for s.** zum Verkauf anbieten

sales' clerk' s Verkäufer –in mf

sales'girl' s Ladenmädchen n

sales'la'dy s Verkäuferin f

sales'man s (–men) Verkäufer m

sales'man'ship s Verkaufstüchtigkeit f

sales' promo'tion s Verkaufsförderung f

sales' slip' s Kassenzettel m, Bon m

sales' tax' s Umsatzsteuer f

saliva [sə'laɪvə] s Speichel m

sallow ['sælo] adj bläßlich

sal·ly ['sæli] s (side trip) Abstecher m; (mil) Ausfall m ‖ v (pret & pp –lied) intr (mil) ausfallen; **s. forth** sich aufmachen

salmon ['sæmən] adj lachsfarben ‖ s Lachs m

saloon [sə'lun] s Kneipe f; (naut) Salon m

salt [sɔlt] s Salz n ‖ tr salzen; **s. away** (coll) auf die hohe Kante legen

salt'cel'lar s Salzfaß n

salt'ed meat' s Salzfleisch n

salt' mine' s Salzbergwerk n; **back to the salt mines** zurück zur Tretmühle

salt'pe'ter s Salpeter m

salt' shak'er s Salzfaß n

salty ['sɔlti] adj salzig

salutary ['sæljə,teri] adj heilsam

salute [sə'lut] s Salut m ‖ tr & intr salutieren

salvage ['sælvɪdʒ] s (saving by ship) Bergung n; (property saved by ship) Bergungsgut n; (discarded material) Altmaterial n ‖ tr bergen; (discarded material) verwerten

salvation [sæl've/ən] s Heil n

Salva'tion Ar'my s Heilsarmee f

salve [sæv] s Salbe f ‖ tr (one's conscience) beschwichtigen

sal·vo ['sælvo] s (–vos & –voes) Salve f

Samaritan [sə'mærɪtən] s Samariter –in mf; **good S.** barmherziger Samariter m

same [sem] adj—**at the s. time** gleichzeitig; **it's all the s. to me** es ist mir ganz gleich; **just the s.** trotzdem; **thanks, s. to you!** danke, gleichfalls!; **the s.** derselbe

sameness ['semnɪs] s Eintönigkeit f

sample ['sæmpəl] s Muster n, Probe f ‖ tr (aus)probieren

sancti·fy ['sæŋktɪ,faɪ] v (pret & pp –fied) tr heiligen

sanctimonious [,sæŋktɪ'moniəs] adj scheinheilig

sanction ['sæŋkʃən] s Sanktion f ‖ tr sanktionieren

sanctity ['sæŋktɪti] s Heiligkeit f

sanctuary ['sæŋktʃu,eri] s (shrine) Heiligtum n; (of a church) Altarraum m; (asylum) Asyl n

sand [sænd] s Sand m ‖ tr mit Sandpapier abschleifen; (a road, sidewalk) mit Sand bestreuen

sandal ['sændəl] s Sandale f

san'dalwood' s Sandelholz n

sand'bag' s Sandsack m

sand'bank' s Sandbank f

sand' bar' s Sandbank f

sand'blast' tr sandstrahlen

sand'box' s Sandkasten m

sand' cas'tle s Strandburg f

sand' dune' s Sanddüne f

sand'glass' s Sanduhr f

sand'man s (–men) (fig) Sandmann m

sand'pa'per s Sandpapier n ‖ tr mit Sandpapier abschleifen

sand'stone' s Sandstein m

sand'storm' s Sandsturm m

sandwich ['sændwɪtʃ] s belegtes Brot n, Sandwich n ‖ tr (in between) einzwängen (zwischen dat)

sandy ['sændi] adj sandig; (color) sandfarben

sane [sen] adj geistig gesund; (e.g., advice) vernünftig

sanguine ['sæŋgwɪn] adj (about) zuversichtlich (in Bezug auf acc)

sanitarium [,sænɪ'teriəm] s Heilanstalt f, Sanatorium n

sanitary ['sænɪ,teri] adj sanitär

san'itary nap'kin s Damenbinde f

sanitation [,sænɪ'teʃən] s Gesundheitswesen n; (in a building) sanitäre Einrichtungen pl

sanity ['sænɪti] s geistige Gesundheit f

Santa Claus ['sæntə,klɔz] s der Weihnachtsmann m, der Nikolaus

sap [sæp] s Saft m; (coll) Schwachkopf m ‖ v (pret & pp sapped; ger sapping) tr (strength) erschöpfen

sapling ['sæplɪŋ] s junger Baum m

sapphire ['sæfaɪr] s Saphir m

Saracen ['særəsən] adj sarazenisch ‖ s Sarazene m, Sarazenin f

sarcasm ['sɑrkæzəm] s Sarkasmus m

sarcastic [sɑr'kæstɪk] adj sarkastisch

sarcophagus [sɑr'kɑfəgəs] s Sarkophag m

sardine [sɑr'din] s Sardine f; **packed**

in like sardines zusammengedrängt wie die Heringe
Sardinia [sɑr'dɪnɪ-ə] s Sardinien n
Sardinian [sɑr'dɪnɪ-ən] adj sardinisch || s Sardinier –in mf; (language) Sardinisch n
sash [sæʃ] s Schärpe f; (of a window) Fensterrahmen m
sass [sæs] s (coll) Revolverschnauze f || tr (coll) (off) patzig antworten (dat)
sassy ['sæsɪ] adj (coll) patzig
Satan ['setən] s Satan m
satanic(al) [sə'tænɪk(əl)] adj satanisch
satchel ['sætʃəl] s Handtasche f
sate [set] tr übersättigen
satellite ['sætə,laɪt] s Satellit m
sat′ellite coun′try s Satellitenstaat m
satiate ['seʃɪ,et] tr sättigen
satin ['sætɪn] s Seidenatlas m
satire ['sætaɪr] s Satire f
satiric(al) [sə'tɪrɪk(əl)] adj satirisch
satirize ['sætɪ,raɪz] tr verspotten
satisfaction [,sætɪs'fækʃən] s Befriedigung f, Genugtuung f
satisfactory [,sætɪs'fæktərɪ] adj friedenstellend, genügend
satis·fy ['sætɪs,faɪ] v (pret & pp –fied) tr (desires, needs) befriedigen; (requirements) genügen (dat); (a person) zufriedenstellen; **be satisfied with** zufrieden sein mit || intr befriedigen
saturate ['sætʃə,ret] tr (& chem) sättigen, saturieren
satura′tion bomb′ing s Bombenteppich m
satura′tion point′ s Sättigungspunkt m
Saturday ['sætər,de] s Samstag m; **on S. am Samstag**
sauce [sɔs] s Soße f; (coll) Frechheit f || tr mit Soße zubereiten; (season) würzen
sauce′pan′ s Stielkasserolle f
saucer ['sɔsər] s Untertasse f
saucy ['sɔsɪ] adj (impertinent) frech; (amusingly flippant) keß; (trim) flott
sauerkraut ['saʊr,kraʊt] s Sauerkraut n
saunter ['sɔntər] s Schlendern n || intr schlendern
sausage ['sɔsɪdʒ] s Wurst f
saute [so'te] v (pret & pp sauteed) tr sautieren
savage ['sævɪdʒ] adj wild || s Wilde mf
savant ['sævənt] s Gelehrte m
save [sev] tr (rescue) retten; (money, fuel) sparen; (keep, preserve) aufheben; (trouble) ersparen; (time) gewinnen; (stamps) sammeln; **s. face** das Gesicht wahren; **s. from** bewahren vor (dat) || prep außer (dat)
sav′ing adj (grace) seligmachend; (quality) ausgleichend || s (of souls) Rettung f; (in) Ersparnis f (an dat); **savings** Ersparnisse pl
sav′ings account′ s Sparkonto n
sav′ings bank′ s Sparkasse f
sav′ings certi′ficate s Sparbon m
sav′ings depos′it s Spareinlage f
savior ['sevjər] s Retter –in mf; **Saviour Heiland** m

savor ['sevər] s Wohlgeschmack m || tr auskosten || intr—s. of (smell of) riechen nach; (taste of) schmecken nach
savory ['severɪ] adj wohschmeckend
saw [sɔ] s Säge f; (saying) Sprichwort n || tr sägen; **saw up** zersägen
saw′dust′ s Sägespäne pl
saw′horse′ s Sägebock m
saw′mill′ s Sägemühle f
Saxon ['sæksən] adj sächsisch || s Sachse m, Sachsin f
Saxony ['sæksənɪ] s Sachsen n
saxophone ['sæksə,fon] s Saxophon n
say [se] s—have a (or no) say in etw (or nichts) zu sagen haben bei; **have one's say (about)** seine Meinung äußern (über acc) || v (pret & pp said [sed]) tr sagen; (Mass) lesen; (a prayer) sprechen; (one's prayers) verrichten; (said of a newspaper article, etc.) besagen; **it says in the papers** in der Zeitung steht; **(let's) say** sagen wir; **no sooner said than done** gesagt, getan; **say!** (to draw attention) sag mal!; (to elicit agreement) gelt!; **say s.th. behind s.o.'s back** j–m etw nachsagen; **she is said to be clever** sie soll klug sein; **that is not to say** das will nicht sagen; **that is to say** das heißt; **they say man sagt; to say nothing of ganz zu schweigen von; you don't say so!** tatsächlich!
say′ing s Sprichwort n; **as the s. goes** wie man zu sagen pflegt; **it goes without s.** das versteht sich von selbst
say′-so′ s (assertion) Behauptung f; (order) Anweisung f; (final authority) letztes Wort n
scab [skæb] s Schorf m; (sl) Streikbrecher –in mf
scabbard ['skæbərd] s Schwertscheide f
scabby ['skæbɪ] adj schorfig
scads [skædz] spl (sl) e–e Menge f
scaffold ['skæfəld] s Gerüst n; (for executions) Schafott n
scaf′folding s Baugerüst n
scald [skɔld] tr verbrühen; (milk) aufkochen
scale [skel] s (on fish, reptiles) Schuppe f; (pan of a balance) Waagschale f; (of a thermometer, wages) Skala f; (mus) Tonleiter f; **on a grand s.** im großen Stil; **on a large (or small) s.** in großem (or kleinem) Maßstab; **s. 1:1000** Maßstab 1:1000; **scales** Waage f; **to s.** maßstabgerecht || tr erklettern; **s. down** maßstäblich verkleinern; (prices) herabsetzen
scallop ['skæləp] s Kammuschel f; (sew) Zacke f || tr auszacken; (culin) überbacken
scalp [skælp] s Kopfhaut f; (Indian trophy) Skalp m || tr skalpieren
scalpel ['skælpəl] s Skalpell n
scaly ['skelɪ] adj schuppig
scamp [skæmp] s Fratz m, Wildfang m
scamper ['skæmpər] intr herumtollen; **s. away** davonlaufen
scan [skæn] v (pret & pp scanned; ger

scanning) tr (a page) überfliegen; (a verse) skandieren; (examine) genau prüfen; (radar, telv) abtasten

scandal ['skændəl] s Skandal m

scandalize ['skændə͵laɪz] tr schockieren

scandalmonger ['skændəl͵mʌŋgər] s Lästermaul n

scandalous ['skændələs] adj skandalös

scan'dal sheet' s Sensationsblatt n

Scandinavia [͵skændɪ'nevɪ·ə] s Skandinavien n

Scandinavian [͵skændɪ'nevɪ·ən] adj skandinavisch ‖ s Skandinavier -in mf; (language) Skandinavisch n

scansion ['skænʃən] s Skandieren n

scant [skænt] adj gering; a s. two hours knapp zwei Stunden

scantily ['skæntɪlɪ] adv—s. clad leicht bekleidet

scanty ['skæntɪ] adj kärglich, knapp

scapegoat ['skep͵got] s Sündenbock m

scar [skar] s Narbe f; (fig) Makel m ‖ v (pret & pp scarred; ger scarring) tr (e.g., a face) entstellen; (e.g., a tabletop) verschrammen; (fig) beinträchtigen

scarce [skers] adj knapp, rar; make oneself s. (coll) das Weite suchen

scarcely ['skerslɪ] adv kaum; be s. able to (inf) Not haben zu (inf)

scarcity ['skersɪtɪ] s (of) Knappheit f (an dat), Mangel m (an dat)

scare [sker] s Schrecken m; be scared erschrecken; be scared stiff e-e Hundeangst haben; give s.o. a s. j-m e-n Schrecken einjagen ‖ tr erschrecken; s. away verscheuchen; s. up (money) auftreiben ‖ intr erschrecken

scare'crow' s Vogelscheuche f

scarf [skarf] s (scarfs & scarves [skarvz]) Schal m

scarlet ['skarlɪt] adj scharlachrot ‖ s Scharlachrot n

scar'let fe'ver s Scharlach m

scarred adj narbig, schrammig

scary ['skerɪ] adj schreckerregend

scat [skæt] interj weg!

scathing ['skeðɪŋ] adj vernichtend

scatter ['skætər] tr zerstreuen ‖ intr sich zerstreuen

scat'terbrain' s Wirrkopf m

scat'tered show'ers spl einzelne Schauer pl

scenari·o [sɪ'nerɪ·o] s (-os) Drehbuch n

scene [sin] s Szene f; be on the s. zur Stelle sein; behind the scenes hinter den Kulissen; make a s. e-e Szene machen; s. of the crime Tatort m

scenery ['sinarɪ] s Landschaft f; (theat) Bühnenausstattung f

scenic ['sinɪk] adj landschaftlich; (theat) szenisch

scent [sent] s Duft m; (of a dog) Witterung f; (hunt) Spur f; have a s. of adj schmecken ‖ tr wittern

scepter ['septər] s Zepter n

sceptic ['skeptɪk] s Skeptiker -in mf

scepticism ['skeptɪ͵sɪzəm] s (doubt) Skepsis f; (doctrine) Skeptizismus m

schedule ['skedjul] s Plan m; (for work) Arbeitsplan m; (in travel) Fahrplan m; (at school) Stundenplan m; (appendix to a tax return) Einkommensteuerformular n; (table) Einkommensteuertabelle f; on s. fahrplanmäßig ‖ tr ansetzen; the plane is scheduled to arrive at six nach dem Flugplan soll die Maschine um sechs Uhr ankommen

scheme [skim] s (schematic) Schema n; (plan, program) Plan m; (intrigue) Intrige f ‖ tr planen ‖ intr Ränke schmieden

schemer ['skimər] s Ränkeschmied m

schilling ['ʃɪlɪŋ] s (Aust) Schilling m

schism ['sɪzəm] s (fig) Spaltung f; (eccl) Schisma n

schizophrenia [͵skɪtso'frinɪ·ə] s Schizophrenie f, Bewußtseinsspaltung f

schizophrenic [͵skɪtso'frenɪk] adj schizophren

schmaltzy ['ʃmɔltsɪ] adj schmalzig

scholar ['skalər] s Gelehrte mf

scholarly ['skalərlɪ] adj gelehrt

schol'arship' s Gelehrsamkeit f; (award) Stipendium n

scholastic [skə'læstɪk] adj Schul-, Bildungs-; (hist) scholastisch

school [skul] adj (book, house, master, room, teacher, yard, year) Schul- ‖ s Schule f; (of a university) Fakultät f; (of fish) Schwarm m; s. is over die Schule ist aus ‖ tr schulen

school' age' s schulpflichtiges Alter n; of s. schulpflichtig

school'bag' s Schulranzen m

school' board' s Schulausschuß m

school'boy' s Schüler m

school'girl' s Schülerin f

school'ing s (formal education) Schulbildung f; (training) Schulung f

school'mate' s Mitschüler -in mf

schooner ['skunər] s Schoner m

sciatica [saɪ'ætɪkə] s Hüftschmerz m

science ['saɪ·əns] s Wissenschaft f; the sciences die Naturwissenschaften pl

sci'ence fic'tion s Science-fiction f

scientific [͵saɪ·ən'tɪfɪk] adj wissenschaftlich

scientist ['saɪ·əntɪst] s Wissenschaftler -in mf

scimitar ['sɪmɪtər] s Türkensäbel m

scintillate ['sɪntɪ͵let] intr funkeln

scion ['saɪ·ən] s Sprößling m; (bot) Pfropfreis n

scissors ['sɪzərz] s & spl Schere f; (in wrestling) Zangengriff m

scoff [skɔf] s Spott m ‖ intr (at) spotten (über acc)

scold [skold] tr & intr schelten

scold'ing s Schelte f; get a s. Schelte bekommen

sconce [skans] s Wandleuchter m

scoop [skup] s (ladle) Schöpfkelle f; (for sugar, flour) Schaufel f; (amount scooped) Schlag m; (journ) Knüller m ‖ tr schöpfen; s. out ausschaufeln; s. up scheffeln

scoot [skut] intr (coll) flitzen

scooter ['skutər] s Roller m

scope [skop] s (extent) Umfang m;

(range) Reichweite *f*; **give free s. to the imagination** der Phatasie freien Lauf lassen; **give s.o. free s.** j—m freie Hand geben; **within the s. of** im Rahmen *(genit)* or von

scorch [skɔrtʃ] *tr* versengen

scorched'-earth' pol'icy *s* Politik *f* der verbrannten Erde

scorch'ing *adj & adv* sengend

score [skor] *s (of a game)* Punktzahl *f*; *(final score)* Ergebnis *n*; *(notch)* Kerbe *f*; *(mus)* Partitur *f*; **s. of** zwanzig; **have an old s. to settle with s.o.** mit j—m e—e alte Rechnung zu begleichen haben; **keep s.** die Punktzahl anschreiben; **know the s.** (coll) auf Draht sein; **on that s.** diesbezüglich; **what's the s.?** wie steht das Spiel? || *tr (points)* erzielen; *(goals)* schießen; *(notch)* einkerben; *(mus)* in Partitur setzen || *intr* e—n Punkt erzielen

score'board' *s* Anzeigetafel *f*

score'card' *s* Punktzettel *m*

score'keep'er *s* Anschreiber –in *mf*

score'sheet' *s* Spielberichtsbogen *m*

scorn [skɔrn] *s* Verachtung *f*; **laugh to s.** auslachen || *tr* verachten

scornful ['skɔrnfəl] *adj* verächtlich

scorpion ['skɔrpɪ·ən] *s* Skorpion *m*

Scot [skɑt] *s* Schotte *m*, Schottin *f*

Scotch [skɑtʃ] *adj* schottisch; *(sl)* geizig || *s* schottischer Whisky *m*; *(dialect)* Schottisch *n* || *tr (a rumor)* ausrotten; *(with a chock)* blockieren; *(render harmless)* unschädlich machen

Scotch'man *s* (–men) Schotte *m*

Scotch' pine' *s* gemeine Kiefer *f*

Scotch' tape' *s* (trademark) durchsichtiger Klebstreifen *m*

scot'-free' *adj* ungestraft

Scotland ['skɑtlənd] *s* Schottland *n*

Scottish ['skɑtɪʃ] *adj* schottisch || *s (dialect)* Schottisch *n*; **the S.** die Schotten *pl*

scoundrel ['skaundrəl] *s* Lump *m*

scour [skaur] *tr* scheuern; *(the city)* absuchen

scourge [skʌrdʒ] *s* Geißel *f* || *tr* geißeln

scout [skaut] *s* Pfadfinder *m*; *(mil, sport)* Kundschafter *m* || *tr* aufklären || *intr* kundschaften

scout'mas'ter *s* Pfadfinderführer *m*

scowl [skaul] *s* finsterer Blick *m* || *intr* finster blicken; **s. at** grollend ansehen

scram [skræm] *v (pret & pp* **scrammed;** *ger* **scramming)** *intr* (coll) abhauen

scramble ['skræmbəl] *s (for)* Balgerei *f* (um) || *tr (mix up)* durcheinandermischen; *(a message)* unverständlich machen; **s. eggs** Rührei machen || *intr (e.g., over rocks)* klettern; **s. for s.th.** sich um etw reißen; **s. to one's feet** sich aufrappeln

scram'bled eggs' *spl* Rührei *n*

scrap [skræp] *s (of metal)* Schrott *m*; *(of paper)* Fetzen *m*; *(of food)* Rest *m*; *(refuse)* Abfall *m*; *(quarrel)* (coll) Zank *m*; *(fight)* (coll) Rauferei *f* || *v (pret & pp* **scrapped;** *ger*

scrapping) *tr* ausrangieren || *intr (quarrel)* (coll) zanken; *(fight)* (coll) raufen

scrap'book' *s* Einklebebuch *n*

scrape [skrep] *s* Kratzer *m*; (coll) Patsche *f* || *tr* schaben; *(the skin)* abscheuern; **s. off** abschaben; **s. together (or up)** zusammenkratzen

scrap'heap' *s* Schrotthaufen *m*; *(refuse heap)* Abfallhaufen *m*

scrap'i'ron *s* Schrott *m*, Alteisen *n*

scrapper ['skræpər] *s* Zänker –in *mf*

scrappy ['skræpɪ] *adj (made of scraps)* zusammengestoppelt; (coll) rauflustig

scratch [skrætʃ] *s* Kratzer *m*, Schramme *f*; **start from s.** wieder ganz von vorne anfangen || *tr* kratzen; *(sport)* streichen; **s. open** aufkratzen; **s. out** *(a line)* ausstreichen; *(eyes)* aushacken; **s. the surface of** nur streifen || *intr* kratzen; *(scratch oneself)* sich kratzen

scratch' pad' *s* Notizblock *m*

scratch' pa'per *s* Schmierpapier *n*

scrawl [skrɔl] *s* Gekritzel *n* || *tr & intr* kritzeln

scrawny ['skrɔnɪ] *adj* spindeldürr

scream [skrim] *s* Aufschrei *m*; **he's a s.!** er ist zum Schreien! || *tr & intr* schreien

screech [skritʃ] *s* Kreischen *n* || *intr (said of tires, brakes)* kreischen; *(said of an owl)* schreien

screech' owl' *s* Kauz *m*

screen [skrin] *s* Wandschirm *m*; *(for a window)* Fliegengitter *n*; *(camouflage)* Tarnung *f*; *(aer) (of)* Abschirmung *f (durch)*; *(cin)* Leinwand *f*; *(nav)* Geleitschutz *m*; *(radar, telv)* Leinwand *f* || *tr (sand, gravel, coal; applications)* durchsieben; *(applicants)* überprüfen; *(a porch, windows)* mit Fliegengittern versehen; *(mil)* verschleiern; **s. off** abschirmen

screen'play' *s* Filmdrama *n*; *(scenario)* Drehbuch *n*

screen' test' *s* Probeaufnahme *f*

screw [skru] *s* Schraube *f*; **he has a s. loose** (coll) bei ihm ist e—e Schraube locker || *tr* schrauben; *(cheat)* (sl) hereinlegen; *(vulg)* vögeln; **s. tight** festschrauben; **s. up** *(courage)* aufbringen; *(bungle)* (coll) verpfuschen

screw'ball' *adj* (coll) verrückt || *s* (coll) Wirrkopf *m*

screw'driv'er *s* Schraubenzieher *m*

screw'-on cap' *s* Schraubendeckel *m*

screwy ['skru·ɪ] *adj* (sl) verrückt

scribble ['skrɪbəl] *s* Gekritzel *n* || *tr & intr* kritzeln

scribe [skraɪb] *s* Schreiber *m*; (Bib) Schriftgelehrte *m*

scrimmage ['skrɪmɪdʒ] *s* (fb) Übungsspiel *n*

scrimp [skrɪmp] *tr* knausern mit || *intr* (on) knausern (mit)

scrimpy ['skrɪmpɪ] *adj* knapp

script [skrɪpt] *s (handwriting)* Handschrift *f*; *(cin)* Drehbuch *n*; *(rad)* Textbuch *n*; *(typ)* Schreibschrift *f*

scriptural ['skrɪptʃərəl] *adj* biblisch; **s. passage** Bibelstelle *f*

Scripture ['skrɪptʃər] s die Heilige Schrift; *(Bible passage)* Bibelzitat n

script'writ'er s (cin) Drehbuchautor m

scrofula ['skrɒfjələ] s Skrofeln pl

scroll [skrol] s Schriftrolle f; *(archit)* Schnörkel m

scroll'work' s Schnörkelverzierung f

scro·tum ['skrotəm] s (-ta [tə] or -tums) Hodensack m

scrounge [skraʊndʒ] tr stibitzen || intr —s. around for herumstöbern nach

scrub [skrʌb] s Schrubben n; *(shrubs)* Buschwerk n; *(sport)* Ersatzmann m || v *(pret & ger scrubbed; ger scrubbing)* tr schrubben

scrub'bing brush' s Scheuerbürste f

scrub'wom'an s (-wom'en) Scheuerfrau f

scruff [skrʌf] s—s. of the neck Genick n

scruple ['skrupəl] s Skrupel m

scrupulous ['skrupjələs] adj skrupulös

scrutinize ['skrutɪ,naɪz] tr genau prüfen; *(a person)* mustern

scrutiny ['skrutɪni] s genaue Prüfung f

scud [skʌd] s Wolkenfetzen m

scuff [skʌf] tr *(a shoe, waxed floor)* abschürfen || intr *(shuffle)* schlurfen

scuffle ['skʌfəl] s Rauferei f || intr raufen

scuff' mark' s Schmutzfleck m

scull [skʌl] s *(sport)* Skull m || intr *(sport)* skullen

scullery ['skʌləri] s Spülküche f

scul'lery maid' s Spülerin f

sculptor ['skʌlptər] s Bildhauer m

sculptress ['skʌlptrɪs] s Bildhauerin f

sculptural ['skʌlptərəl] adj bildhauerisch

sculpture ['skʌlptʃər] s *(art)* Bildhauerei f; *(work of art)* Skulptur f || tr meißeln || intr bildhauern

scum [skʌm] s *(& fig)* Abschaum m

scummy ['skʌmi] adj schaumig; *(fig)* niederträchtig

scurrilous ['skʌrɪləs] adj skurril

scur·ry ['skʌri] v *(pret & pp -ried)* intr huschen

scurvy ['skʌrvi] adj gemein || s Skorbut m

scuttle ['skʌtəl] s *(naut)* Springluke f || tr *(hopes, plans)* vernichten; *(naut)* selbst versenken

scut'tlebutt' s *(coll)* Latrinenparole f

scut'tling s Selbstversenkung f

scythe [saɪð] s Sense f

sea [si] s See f, Meer n; at sea auf See; go to sea zur See gehen; heavy seas hoher (or schwerer) Seegang m

sea'board' s Küstenstrich m

sea' breeze' s Seebrise f

sea'coast' s Seeküste f, Meeresküste f

seafarer ['si,ferər] s Seefahrer m

seafaring ['si,ferɪŋ] s Seefahrt f

sea'food' s Fischgerichte pl

sea'go'ing adj seetüchtig

sea' gull' s Seemöwe f, Möwe f

seal [sil] s Siegel n; *(zool)* Seehund m || tr *(a document)* siegeln; *(a deal, s.o.'s fate)* besiegeln; *(against leakage)* verschließen, abdichten; **s. off** absperren; *(mil)* abriegeln; **s. up** abdichten

sea' legs' spl—get one's s. seefest werden

sea'lev'el s Meereshöhe f

seal'ing wax' s Siegellack m

seal'skin' s Seehundsfell n

seam [sim] s *(groove)* Fuge f; *(geol)* Lager n; *(min)* Flöz n; *(sew)* Naht f

sea'man s (-men) Seemann m; *(nav)* Matrose m

sea' mile' s Seemeile f

seamless ['simlɪs] adj nahtlos

sea' mon'ster s Meeresungeheuer n

seamstress ['simstrɪs] s Näherin f

seamy ['simi] adj verrufen; **s. side** *(fig)* Schattenseite f

séance ['se,ɑns] s Séance f

sea'plane' s Seeflugzeug n

sea'port' s Seehafen m

sea'port town' s Hafenstadt f

sea' pow'er s Seemacht f

sear [sɪr] tr versengen

search [sʌrtʃ] s Durchsuchung f; *(for a person)* (for) Fahndung f (nach); in s. of auf der Suche nach || tr durchsuchen || intr suchen; **s. for** suchen, fahnden nach

search'ing adj gründlich; *(glance)* forschend

search'light' s Scheinwerfer m

search' war'rant s Haussuchungsbefehl m

seascape ['si,skep] s Seegemälde n

sea' shell' s Muschel f

sea'shore' s Strand m

sea'shore resort' s Seebad n

sea'sick' adj seekrank

sea'sick'ness s Seekrankheit f

sea'side' adj Meeres—, See—

season ['sizən] s Jahreszeit f; *(appropriate period)* Saison f; closed s. (hunt) Schonzeit f; dry s. Trockenzeit f; in and out of s. jederzeit; in s. zur rechten Zeit; out of s. *(game)* außerhalb der Saison; *(fruits, vegetables)* nicht auf dem Markt; peak s. Hochsaison f || tr *(food)* würzen; *(wine)* lagern; *(wood)* austrocknen lassen; *(tobacco)* reifen lassen; *(soldiers)* abhärten || intr *(e.g., said of wine)* (ab)lagern

seasonal ['sizənəl] adj jahreszeitlich; *(caused by seasons)* saisonbedingt

sea'sonal work' s Saisonarbeit f

sea'soned adj erfahren; *(troops)* kampfgewohnt, fronterfahren

sea'soning s Würze f

sea'son's greet'ings spl Festgrüße pl

sea'son tick'et s Dauerkarte f

seat [sit] s Sitz m, Platz m; *(of trousers)* Gesäß n; have a s. Platz nehmen; keep one's s. sitzenbleiben || tr *(a person)* e-n Platz anweisen *(dat)*; *(said of a room)* Sitzplätze bieten für; be seated sich hinsetzen

seat' belt' s (aer, aut) Sicherheitsgurt m; fasten seat belts! bitte anschnallen!

seat' cov'er s (aut) Auto-Schonbezug m

seat'ing capac'ity s (for) Sitzgelegenheit f (für); have a s. of fassen

seat' of gov'ernment s Regierungssitz m

sea'wall' s Strandmauer f

sea'way' s Seeweg m; (heavy sea) schwerer Seegang m

sea'weed' s Alge f, Seetang m

sea'wor'thy adj seetüchtig

secede [sɪ'sid] intr sich trennen

secession [sɪ'sɛʃən] s Sezession f

seclude [sɪ'klud] tr abschließen

seclud'ed adj abgeschieden; (life) zurückgezogen; (place) abgelegen

seclusion [sɪ'kluʒən] s Zurückgezogenheit f, Abgeschiedenheit f

second ['sɛkənd] adj zweite; **be s. to none** niemandem nachstehen; **in the s. place** zweitens; **s. in command** stellvertretender Kommandeur m || s (unit of time) Sekunde f; (moment) Augenblick m; (in boxing or dueling) Sekundant m; **George the Second** Georg der Zweite; **the s.** (of the month) der zweite || pron zweite || tr unterstützen

secondary ['sɛkən,dɛri] adj sekundär, Neben– || s (elec) Sekundärwicklung f; (fb) Spieler pl in der zweiten Reihe

sec'ondary school' s Oberschule

sec'ondary-school' teach'er s Oberlehrer –in mf

sec'ondary sourc'es spl Sekundärliteratur f

sec'ondary tar'get s Ausweichziel n

sec'ond best' s Zweitbeste mfn

sec'ond-best' adj zweitbeste; **come off s.** den kürzeren ziehen

sec'ond-class' adj zweitklassig; **s. ticket** Fahrkarte f zweiter Klasse

sec'ond cous'in s Cousin m (or Kusine f) zweiten Grades

sec'ond fid'dle s—**play s.** die zweite Geige spielen

sec'ond hand' s (horol) Sekundenzeiger m

sec'ondhand' adj (car) gebraucht (information) aus zweiter Hand; (books) antiquarisch

sec'ondhand book'store s Antiquariat n

sec'ondhand deal'er s Altwarenhändler –in mf

sec'ond lieuten'ant s Leutnant m

secondly ['sɛkəndli] adv zweitens

sec'ond mate' s (naut) zweiter Offizier m

sec'ond na'ture s zweite Natur f

sec'ond-rate' adj zweitklassig

sec'ond sight' s zweites Gesicht n

sec'ond thought' s—**have second thoughts** Bedenken hegen; **on s.** bei weiterem Nachdenken

sec'ond wind' s—**get one's s.** wieder zu Kräften kommen

secrecy ['sikrəsi] s Heimlichkeit f

secret ['sikrɪt] adj geheim || s Geheimnis n; **in s.** insgeheim; **keep no secrets from** keine Geheimnisse haben vor (dat); **keep sth. secret** geheimhalten; **make no s. of** kein Hehl machen aus

secretary ['sɛkrə,tɛri] s (man, desk, bird) Sekretär m; (female) Sekretärin f; (in government) Minister m

sec'retary-gen'eral s Generalsekretär m

sec'retary of com'merce s Handelsminister m

sec'retary of defense' s Verteidigungsminister m

sec'retary of la'bor s Arbeitsminister m

sec'retary of state' s Außenminister m

sec'retary of the inter'ior s Innenminister m

sec'retary of the treas'ury s Finanzminister n

se'cret bal'lot s geheime Abstimmung f

secrete [sɪ'krit] tr (hide) verstecken; (physiol) absondern, ausscheiden

secretive ['sikrɪtɪv] adj verschwiegen

se'cret police' s Geheimpolizei f

se'cret serv'ice s Geheimdienst m

sect [sɛkt] s Sekte f

sectarian [sɛk'tɛri·ən] adj sektiererisch; (school) Konfessions–

section ['sɛkʃən] s (segment, part) Teil m; (of a newspaper, chapter) Abschnitt m; (of a city) Viertel n; (group) Abteilung f; (cross section; thin slice, e.g., of tissue) Schnitt m; (jur) Paragraph m; (mil) Halbzug m; (rr) Strecke f; (surg) Sektion f || tr— **s. off** abteilen

sectional ['sɛkʃənəl] adj (view) Teil–; (pride) Lokal–

sec'tional fur'niture s Anbaumöbel n

sec'tion hand' s Schienenleger m

sector ['sɛktər] s Sektor m

secular ['sɛkjələr] adj weltlich || s Weltpriester m, Weltgeistlicher m

secularism ['sɛkjələ,rɪzəm] s Weltlichkeit f, Säkularismus m

secure [sɪ'kjur] adj sicher || tr (make fast) sichern; (obtain) sich [dat] beschaffen

security [sɪ'kjurɪti] s (& jur) Sicherheit f; **securities** Wertpapiere pl

sedan [sɪ'dæn] s Limousine f

sedan' chair' s Sänfte f

sedate [sɪ'det] adj gesetzt

sedation [sɪ'deʃən] s Beruhigung f

sedative ['sɛdətɪv] s Beruhigungsmittel n

sedentary ['sɛdən,tɛri] adj sitzend

sedge [sɛdʒ] s (bot) Segge f

sediment ['sɛdɪmənt] s Bodensatz m; (geol) Ablagerung f, Sediment n

sedition [sɪ'dɪʃən] s Aufruhr m

seditious [sɪ'dɪʃəs] adj aufrührerisch

seduce [sɪ'd(j)us] tr verführen

seducer [sɪ'd(j)usər] s Verführer –in mf

seduction [sɪ'dʌkʃən] s Verführung f

seductive [sɪ'dʌktɪv] adj verführerisch

sedulous ['sɛdʒələs] adj emsig

see [si] s (eccl) (erz)bischöflicher Stuhl m || v (pret saw [sɔ]; pp seen [sin]) tr sehen; (comprehend) verstehen; (realize) einsehen; (a doctor) gehen zu; **see red** rasend werden; **see s.o. off** j–n an den Zug (aus Flugzeug) bringen; **see s.o. to the door** j–n zur Tür geleiten; **see s.th. through** etw durchstehen; **that remains to be seen** das wird man erst sehen || intr sehen; **see through** (fig) durchschauen; **see to** sich kümmern um; **see to it that** sich darum kümmern, daß; **you see** (*parenthetical*) wissen Sie

seed [sid] *s* Samen *m*; (*collective & fig*) Saat *f*; (*in fruit*) Kern *m*; (*physiol*) Samen *m*: **go to s.** in Samen schießen; **seeds** (fig) Keim *m* || *tr* besäen

seed'bed' *s* Samenbeet *n*

seed'ed rye' bread' *s* Kümmelbrot *n*

seedless ['sidlɪs] *adj* kernlos

seedling ['sidlɪŋ] *s* Sämling *m*

seedy ['sidi] *adj* (*person*) heruntergekommen; (*thing*) schäbig

see'ing *s* Sehen *n* || *conj*—**s. that** in Anbetracht dessen, daß

See'ing Eye' dog' *s* Blindenhund *m*

seek [sik] *v* (*pret & pp* **sought** [sɔt]) *tr* suchen; **s. s.o.'s advice** j-s Rat erbitten; **s. to** (*inf*) versuchen zu (*inf*) || *intr*—**s. after** suchen nach

seem [sim] *intr* scheinen || *impers*—**it seems to me** es kommt mir vor

seemingly ['simɪŋli] *adv* anscheinend

seemly ['simli] *adj* schicklich

seep [sip] *intr* sickern

seepage ['sipɪdʒ] *s* Durchsickern *n*

seer [sɪr] *s* Seher *m*

seeress ['sɪrɪs] *s* Seherin *f*

see'saw' *s* Schaukelbrett *n*, Wippe *f* || *intr* wippen; (fig) schwanken

seethe [sið] *intr* sieden; **s. with** (fig) sieden vor (*dat*)

segment ['sɛgmənt] *s* Abschnitt *m*

segregate ['sɛgrɪˌget] *tr* trennen, absondern

segregation [ˌsɛgrɪ'geʃən] *s* Absonderung *f*; (*of races*) Rassentrennung *f*

seismograph ['saɪzməˌgræf] *s* Erdbebenmesser *m*, Seismograph *m*

seismology [saɪz'malədʒi] *s* Erdbebenkunde *f*, Seismologie *f*

seize [siz] *tr* anfassen; (*a criminal*) festnehmen; (*a town, fortress*) einnehmen; (*an opportunity*) ergreifen; (*power*) an sich reißen; (*confiscate*) beschlagnahmen

seizure ['siʒər] *s* Besitzergreifung *f*; (*confiscation*) Beschlagnahme *f*; (*pathol*) plötzlicher Anfall *m*

seldom ['sɛldəm] *adv* selten

select [sɪ'lɛkt] *adj* erlesen || *tr* auslesen, auswählen

select'ed *adj* ausgesucht

selection [sɪ'lɛkʃən] *s* Auswahl *f*

selective [sɪ'lɛktɪv] *adj* Auswahl-; (rad) trennscharf

selec'tive serv'ice *s* allgemeine Wehrpflicht *f*

self [sɛlf] *s* (**selves** [sɛlvz]) Selbst *n*, Ich *n*; **be one's old s.** again wieder der alte sein; **his better s.** sein besseres Ich || *pron*—**payable to s.** auf Selbst ausgestellt

self'-addressed' en'velope *s* mit Anschrift versehene Freiumschlag *m*

self'-assur'ance *s* Selbstbewußtsein *n*

self'-cen'tered *adj* ichbezogen

self'-conceit'ed *adj* eingebildet

self'-con'fident *adj* selbstsicher

self'-con'scious *adj* befangen

self'-control' *s* Selbstbeherrschung *f*

self'-decep'tion *s* Selbsttäuschung *f*

self'-defense' *s* Selbstverteidigung *f*; **in s.** aus Notwehr

self'-deni'al *s* Selbstverleugnung *f*

self'-destruc'tion *s* Selbstvernichtung *f*

self'-determina'tion *s* Selbstbestimmung *f*

self'-dis'cipline *s* Selbstzucht *f*

self'-ed'ucated per'son *s* Autodidakt –in *mf*

self'-employed' *adj* selbständig

self'-esteem' *s* Selbsteinschätzung *f*

self'-ev'ident *adj* selbstverständlich

self'-explan'ator'y *adj* keiner Erklärung bedürftig

self'-gov'ernment *s* Selbstverwaltung *f*

self'-impor'tant *adj* eingebildet

self'-indul'gence *s* Genußsucht *f*

self'-in'terest *s* Eigennutz *m*

selfish ['sɛlfɪʃ] *adj* eigennützig

selfishness ['sɛlfɪnɪs] *s* Eigennutz *m*

selfless ['sɛlflɪs] *adj* selbstlos

self'-love' *s* Selbstliebe *f*

self'-made man' *s* Selfmademan *m*

self'-por'trait *s* Selbstbildnis *n*

self'-possessed' *adj* selbstbeherrscht

self'-praise' *s* Eigenlob *n*

self'-preserva'tion *s* Selbsterhaltung *f*

self'-reli'ant *adj* selbstsicher

self'-respect' *s* Selbstachtung *f*

self'-right'eous *adj* selbstgerecht

self'-sac'rifice *s* Selbstaufopferung *f*

self'-same' *adj* ebenderselbe

self'-sat'isfied *adj* selbstzufrieden

self'-seek'ing *adj* selbstsüchtig

self'-serv'ice *adj* mit Selbstbedienung || *s* Selbstbedienung *f*

self'-styled' *adj* von eigenen Gnaden

self'-suffi'cient *adj* selbstgenügsam

self'-support'ing *adj* finanziell unabhängig

self'-taught' *adj* autodidaktisch

self'-willed' *adj* eigenwillig

self'-wind'ing *adj* automatisch

sell [sɛl] *v* (*pret & pp* **sold** [sold]) *tr* verkaufen; (*at auction*) versteigern; (*wares*) führen; **be sold on** (coll) begeistert sein von; **s. dirt cheap** verramschen; **s. s.o. on s.th.** (coll) j-n zu etw überreden; **s. out** ausverkaufen; (*betray*) verraten; **s. short** (st. exch.) in blanko verkaufen || *intr* sich verkaufen; **s. for** verkauft werden für; **s. short** fixen

seller ['sɛlər] *s* Verkäufer –in *mf*; **good s.** (com) Reißer *m*

Seltzer ['sɛltsər] *s* Selterswasser *n*

selvage ['sɛlvɪdʒ] *s* (*of fabric*) Salleiste *f*; (*of a lock*) Eckplatte *f*

semantic [sɪ'mæntɪk] *adj* semantisch || **semantics** *s* Wortbedeutungslehre *f*

semaphore ['sɛməˌfor] *s* Winkzeichen *n*; (rr) Semaphor *m* || *intr* winken

semblance ['sɛmbləns] *s* Anschein *m*

semen ['simən] *s* Samen *m*

semicircle ['sɛmɪˌsʌrkəl] *s* Halbkreis *m*

semicolon ['sɛmɪˌkolən] *s* Strichpunkt *m*

semiconductor [ˌsɛmɪkən'dʌktər] *s* Halbleiter *m*

semiconscious [ˌsɛmɪ'kanʃəs] *adj* halbbewußt

semifinal [‚semɪ'faɪnəl] *adj* Halbfinale– ‖ *s* Halbfinale *n*, Vorschlußrunde *f*

seminar ['semɪ ‚nɑr] *s* Seminar *n*

seminarian [‚semɪ'nerɪ·ən] *s* Seminarist *m*

seminary ['semɪ ‚neri] *s* Seminar *n*

semiprecious [‚semɪ'preʃəs] *adj* halbedel

Semite ['semaɪt] *s* Semit –in *mf*

Semitic [sɪ'mɪtɪk] *adj* semitisch

semitrailer ['semɪ ‚treɪlər] *s* Schleppanhänger *m*

senate ['senɪt] *s* Senat *m*

senator ['senətər] *s* Senator *m*

senatorial [‚senə'torɪ·əl] *adj* (*of one senator*) senatorisch; (*of the senate*) Senats–

send [send] *v* (*pret & pp* **sent** [sent]) *tr* schicken, senden; (*rad, telv*) senden; **s. back** zurückschicken; **s. back word** zurücksagen lassen; **s. down** (*box*) niederschlagen; **s. forth** (*leaves*) treiben; **s. off** absenden; **s. on** (*forward*) weiterbefördern; **s. word** that benachrichtigen, daß ‖ *intr*—**s. for** (*e.g., free samples*) bestellen; (*e.g., a doctor*) rufen lassen

sender ['sendər] *s* Absender –in *mf*; (*telg*) Geber –in *mf*

send'-off' *s* Abschiedsfeier *f*

senile ['sinaɪl] *adj* senil

senility [sɪ'nɪlɪti] *s* Senilität *f*

senior ['sinjər] *adj* (*in age*) älter; (*in rank*) ranghöher; (*class*) oberste; **Mr. John Smith Senior** Herr John Smith senior ‖ *s* Älteste *mf*; (*student*) Student –in *mf* im letzten Studienjahr

sen'ior cit'izen *s* bejahrter Mitbürger *m*

seniority [sin'jɑrɪti] *s* Dienstalter *n*

sen'ior of'ficer *s* Vorgesetzte *mf*

sen'ior part'ner *s* geschäftsführender Partner *m*

sen'ior year' *s* letztes Studienjahr *n*

sensation [sen'seʃən] *s* (*feeling*) Gefühl *n*; (*cause of interest*) Sensation *f*

sensational [sen'seʃənəl] *adj* sensationell

sensationalism [sen'seʃənə ‚lɪzəm] *s* Sensationsgier *f*

sense [sens] *s* (*e.g., of sight; meaning*) Sinn *m*; (*feeling*) Gefühl *n*; (*common sense*) Verstand *m*; **be out of one's senses** von Sinnen sein; **bring s.o. to his senses** j–n zur Vernunft bringen; **in a s.** in gewissem Sinne; **in the broadest s.** im weitesten Sinne; **make s.** Sinn haben; **there's no s. to it** da steckt kein Sinn drin ‖ *tr* spüren, fühlen

senseless ['senslɪs] *adj* sinnlos; (*from a blow*) bewußtlos

sense' of direc'tion *s* Ortssinn *m*

sense' of du'ty *s* Pflichtgefühl *n*

sense' of guilt' *s* Schuldgefühl *n*

sense' of hear'ing *s* Gehör *n*

sense' of hon'or *s* Ehrgefühl *n*

sense' of hu'mor *s* Humor *m*

sense' of jus'tice *s* Gerechtigkeitsgefühl *n*

sense' of responsibil'ity *s* Verantwortungsbewußtsein *n*

sense' of sight' *s* Gesichtssinn *m*

sense' of smell' *s* Geruchssinn *m*

sense' of taste' *s* Geschmackssinn *m*

sense' of touch' *s* Tastsinn *m*

sense' or'gan *s* Sinnesorgan *n*

sensibility [‚sensɪ'bɪlɪti] *s* Empfindlichkeit *f*

sensible ['sensɪbəl] *adj* vernünftig

sensitive ['sensɪtɪv] *adj* (to, *e.g., cold*) empfindlich (gegen); (*touchy*) überempfindlich; **s. post** Vertrauensposten *m*; **very s.** überempfindlich

sensitize ['sensɪ ‚taɪz] *tr* (phot) lichtempfindlich machen

sensory ['sensəri] *adj* Sinnes–

sen'sory depriva'tion *s* Reizentzug *m*

sensual ['sen/ʊ·əl] *adj* sinnlich

sensuality [‚sen/ʊ'ælɪti] *s* Sinnlichkeit *f*, Sinnenlust *f*

sensuous ['sen/ʊ·əs] *adj* sinnlich

sentence ['sentəns] *s* (gram) Satz *m*; (jur) Urteil *n*; **pronounce s.** das Urteil verkünden ‖ *tr* verurteilen

sentiment ['sentɪmənt] *s* Empfindung *f*

sentimental [‚sentɪ'mentəl] *adj* sentimental, rührselig

sentinel ['sentɪnəl] *s* Posten *m*; **stand s.** Wache stehen

sentry ['sentri] *s* Wachposten *m*

sen'try box' *s* Schilderhaus *n*

separable ['sepərəbəl] *adj* trennbar

separate ['sepəret] *adj* getrennt; **under s. cover** separat ‖ ['sepə ‚ret] *tr* trennen; (*segregate*) absondern; (*scatter*) zerstreuen; (*discharge*) entlassen; **s. into** teilen in (*acc*) ‖ *intr* sich trennen, sich scheiden

sep'arated *adj* (*couple*) getrennt

separation [‚sepə'reʃən] *s* Trennung *f*

September [sep'tembər] *s* September *m*

sep'tic tank' ['septɪk] *s* Kläranlage *f*

sepulcher ['sepəlkər] *s* Grabmal *n*

sequel ['sikwəl] *s* Fortsetzung *f*; (fig) Nachspiel *n*

sequence ['sikwəns] *s* Reihenfolge *f*

se'quence of tens'es *s* Zeitenfolge *f*

sequester [sɪ'kwestər] *tr* (*remove*) entfernen; (*separate*) absondern; (jur) sequestrieren

sequins ['sikwɪnz] *spl* Flitter *m*

seraph ['serəf] *s* (–aphs & –aphim [əfɪm]) Seraph *m*

Serb [sʌrb] *adj* serbisch ‖ *s* Serbe *m*, Serbin *f*

Serbia ['sʌrbɪ·ə] *s* Serbien *n*

serenade [‚serə'ned] *s* Ständchen *n* ‖ *tr* ein Ständchen bringen (*dat*)

serene [sɪ'rin] *adj* heiter; (*sea*) ruhig

serenity [sɪ'renɪti] *s* Heiterkeit *f*

serf [sʌrf] *s* Leibeigene *mf*

serfdom ['sʌrfdəm] *s* Leibeigenschaft *f*

serge [sʌrdʒ] *s* (tex) Serge *f*

sergeant ['sɑrdʒənt] *s* Feldwebel *m*

ser'geant-at-arms' *s* (sergeants-at-arms) Ordnungsbeamter *m*

ser'geant first' class' *s* Oberfeldwebel *m*

ser'geant ma'jor s (sergeant majors) Hauptfeldwebel m

serial ['sɪrɪ-əl] s Fortsetzungsroman m, Romanfolge f

serialize ['sɪrɪ-ə‚laɪz] tr in Fortsetzungen veröffentlichen

se'rial num'ber s laufende Nummer f; (of a product) Fabriknummer f

se-ries ['sɪrɪz] s (-ries) Serie f, Reihe f; **in s.** reihenweise; (elec) hintereinandergeschaltet

serious ['sɪrɪ-əs] adj ernst; (mistake) schwerwiegend; (illness) gefährlich

seriously ['sɪrɪ-əsli] adv ernstlich; **s. wounded** schwerverwundet; **take s. ernst** nehmen

seriousness ['sɪrɪ-əsnɪs] s Ernst m

sermon ['sɜrmən] s Predigt f

sermonize ['sɜrmə‚naɪz] intr e-e Moralpredigt halten

serpent ['sɜrpənt] s Schlange f

serrated ['sɛretɪd] adj sägeartig

se-rum ['sɪrəm] s (-rums & -ra [rə]) Serum n

servant ['sɜrvənt] s Diener –in mf; (domestic) Hausdiener –in mf

serv'ant girl' s Dienstmädchen n

serve [sɜrv] s (tennis) Aufschlag m || tr (a master, God) dienen (dat); (food) servieren; (a meal) anrichten; (guests) bedienen; (time in jail) verbüßen; (one's term in the service) abdienen; (the purpose) erfüllen; (tennis) aufschlagen; **s. mass** (eccl) zur Messe dienen; **s. notice on s.o. j-n** vorladen; **s. up** (food) auftragen || intr (& mil) dienen; (at table) servieren; **s. as** dienen als; **s. on a committe e-m** Ausschuß angehören

server ['sɜrvər] s (eccl) Ministrant m; (tennis) Aufschläger m

service ['sɜrvɪs] s (diplomatic, secret, foreign, public, etc.) Dienst m; (in a restaurant) Bedienung f; (set of table utensils) Besteck n; (set of dishes) Service n; (assistance at a repair shop) Service m; (maintenance) Wartung f; (transportation) Verkehr m; (relig) Gottesdienst m; (tennis) Aufschlag m; **at your s. zu Ihren Diensten; be in s.** (mach) in Betrieb sein; **be in the s.** (mil) beim Militär sein; **be of s.** behilflich sein; **do s.o. a s.** j-m e-n Dienst erweisen; **essential services** lebenswichtige Betriebe pl; **fit for active s.** kriegerverwendungsfähig; see s. Kriegsdienst tun; **the services** die Waffengattungen pl || tr (mach) warten

serviceable ['sɜrvɪsəbəl] adj (usable) verwendungsfähig; (helpful) nützlich; (durable) haltbar

serv'ice club' s (mil) Soldatenklub m

serv'ice en'trance s Dienstboteneingang m

serv'ice-man' s (–men') Monteur m; (at a gas station) Tankwart m; (mil) Soldat m

serv'ice rec'ord s Wehrpaß m

serv'ice sta'tion s Tankstelle f

serv'ice-station atten'dant s Tankwart m

serv'ice troops' spl Versorgungstruppen pl

servile ['sʌrvaɪl] adj kriecherisch

serv'ing cart' s (e.g., of a subpoena) Zustellung f

serv'ing cart' s Servierwagen m

servitude ['sʌrvɪ‚t(j)ud] s Knechtschaft f

ses'ame seed' ['sɛsəmi] s Sesamsamen m

session ['sɛʃən] s Sitzung f, Tagung f; (educ) Semester n; **be in session** tagen

set [sɛt] adj (price, time) festgesetzt; (rule) festgelegt; (speech) wohlüberlegt; **be all set** fix und fertig sein; **be set in one's ways** festgefahren sein || s (group of things belonging together) Satz m, Garnitur f; (of chess or checkers) Spiel n; (clique) Sippschaft f; (rad, telv) Apparat m; (tennis) Satz m; (theat) Bühnenbild n; **younger set** Nachwuchs m || v (pret & pp set; ger setting) tr (put) setzen; (stand) stellen; (lay) legen; (a clock, a trap) stellen; (the hair) legen; (a record) aufstellen; (an example) geben; (a time, price) festsetzen; (the table) decken; (jewels) (ein)fassen; (a camera) einstellen; (surg) einrenken; (typ) setzen; **set ahead** (a clock) vorstellen; **set back** (a clock) nachstellen; (a patient) zurückwerfen; **set down** niedersetzen; **set down in writing** schriftlich niederlegen; **set foot in** (or on) betreten; **set forth** (explain) erklären; **set free** freilassen; **set in order** in Ordnung bringen; **set limits to** Schranken setzen (dat); **set off** (a bomb) sprengen lassen; **set (s.o.) over** (j–n) überordnen (dat); **set right** wieder in Ordnung bringen; **set store by Gewicht** beimessen (dat); **set straight** (on) aufklären (über acc); **set the meeting for two die** Versammlung auf zwei Uhr ansetzen; **set up** (at the bar) (coll) zu e–m Gläschen einladen; (mach) montieren; (typ) (ab)setzen; **set up housekeeping** Wirtschaft führen; **set up in business** etablieren || intr (said of cement) abbinden; (astr) untergehen; **set about** (ger) darangehen zu (inf); **set in** einsetzen; **set out** (for) sich auf den Weg machen (nach); **set out on** (a trip) antreten; **set to work** sich an die Arbeit machen

set'back' s Rückschlag m, Schlappe f

set'screw' s Stellschraube f

settee [sɛ'ti] s Polsterbank f

setter ['sɛtər] s Vorstehhund m

set'ting s (of the sun) Niedergang m; (of a story) Ort m der Handlung; (of a gem) Fassung f; (theat) Bühnenbild n

settle ['sɛtəl] tr (conclude) erledigen; (decide) entscheiden; (an argument) schlichten; (a problem) erledigen; (an account) begleichen; (one's affairs) in Ordnung bringen; (a creditor's claim) befriedigen; (a lawsuit) durch Vergleich beilegen; (a region) besiedeln; (*people*) ansiedeln ‖ *intr* (*in a region*) sich niederlassen; (*said of a building*) sich senken; (*said of a ship*) absacken; (*said of dust*) sich legen; (*said of a liquid*) sich klären; (*said of suspended particles*) sich setzen; (*said of a cold*) (in) sich festsetzen (in *dat*); **s. down** (*in a chair*) sich niederlassen; (*calm down*) sich beruhigen; **s. down to** (*e.g., work*) sich machen an (*acc*); **s. for** sich einigen auf (*acc*); **s. on** sich entscheiden für; **s. up** (fin) die Verbindlichkeit vergleichen

settlement ['setəlmənt] *s* (*colony*) Siedlung *f*; (*agreement*) Abkommen *n*; (*of an argument*) Beilegung *f*; (*of accounts*) Abrechnung *f*; (*of a debt*) Begleichung *f*; **reach a s.** e-n Vergleich schließen

settler ['setlər] *s* Ansiedler –in *mf*

set′up′ *s* Aufbau *m*, Anlage *f*

seven ['sevən] *adj & pron* sieben ‖ *s* Sieben *f*

seventeen ['sevən'tin] *adj & pron* siebzehn ‖ *s* Siebzehn *f*

seventeenth ['sevən'tinθ] *adj & pron* siebzehnte ‖ *s* (*fraction*) Siebzehntel *n*; **the s.** (*in dates or a series*) der Siebzehnte

seventh ['sevənθ] *adj & pron* sieb(en)te ‖ *s* (*fraction*) Sieb(en)tel *n*; **the s.** (*in dates or a series*) der Sieb(en)te

seventieth ['sevənti‧iθ] *adj & pron* siebzigste ‖ *s* (*fraction*) Siebzigstel *n*

seventy ['sevənti] *adj & pron* siebzig ‖ *s* Siebzig *f*; **the seventies** die siebziger Jahre

sev′enty-first′ *adj & pron* einundsiebzigste

sev′enty-one′ *adj* einundsiebzig

sever ['sevər] *tr* (ab)trennen; (*relations*) abbrechen

several ['sevərəl] *adj & indef pron* mehrere; **s. times** mehrmals

severance ['sevərəns] *s* Trennung *f*; (*of relations*) Abbruch *m*

sev′erance pay′ *s* (& mil) Abfindungsentschädigung *f*

severe [sɪ'vɪr] *adj* (*judge, winter, cold*) streng; (*blow, sentence, winter*) hart; (*illness, test*) schwer; (*criticism*) scharf

severity [sɪ'verɪti] *s* Strenge *f*; Härte *f*; Schärfe *f*

sew [so] *v* (*pret* sewed; *pp* sewed & sewn) *tr & intr* nähen

sewage ['su‧ɪdʒ] *s* Abwässer *pl*

sew′age-dispos′al plant′ *s* Kläranlage *f*

sewer ['su‧ər] *s* Kanal *m* ‖ ['so‧ər] *s* Näher –in *mf*

sewerage ['su‧ərɪdʒ] *s* Kanalisation *f*

sew′er pipe′ ['su‧ər] *s* Abwasserleitung *f*

sew′ing *s* Näharbeit *f*

sew′ing bas′ket *s* Nähkasten *m*

sew′ing kit′ *s* Nähzeug *n*

sew′ing machine′ *s* Nähmaschine *f*

sex [seks] *s* (*crime, education, harmone*) Sexual– ‖ *s* Geschlecht *n*; (*intercourse*) Sex *m*

sex appeal′ *s* Sex-Appeal *m*

sex′ pot′ *s* (coll) Sexbombe *f*

sextent ['sekstənt] *s* Sextant *m*

sexton ['sekstən] *s* Küster *m*

sexual ['sek/u‧əl] *adj* geschlechtlich, Geschlechts–, sexuell

sex′ual in′tercourse *s* Geschlechtsverkehr *m*

sexuality [sek/u‧ælɪti] *s* Sexualität *f*

sexy ['seksi] *adj* sexy

shabbily ['s/æbɪli] *adv* schäbig; (*in treatment*) stiefmütterlich

shabby ['/æbi] *adj* schäbig

shack [/æk] *s* Bretterbude *f*

shackle ['/ækəl] *s* (naut) Schäkel *m*; **shackles** Fesseln *pl* ‖ *tr* fesseln

shad [/æd] *s* Shad *m*, Alse *f*

shade [/ed] *s* Schatten *m*; (*for a window*) Rollo *n*; (*of a lamp*) Schirm *m*; (*hue*) Schattierung *f*; **throw into the s.** (fig) in den Schatten stellen ‖ *tr* beschatten; (paint) schattieren

shad′ing *s* Schattierung *f*

shadow ['/ædo] *s* Schatten *m* ‖ *tr* (*a person*) beschatten

shad′ow box′ing *s* Schattenboxen *n*

shadowy ['/ædo‧i] *adj* (*like a shadow*) schattenhaft; (*indistinct*) verschwommen; (*shady*) schattig

shady ['/edi] *adj* schattig; (coll) dunkel; **s. character** Dunkelmann *m*; **s. deal** Lumperei *f*; **s. side** (& fig) Schattenseite *f*

shaft [/æft] *s* Schaft *m*; (*of an elevator*) Schacht *m*; (*handle*) Stiel *m*; (*of a wagon*) Deichsel *f*; (*of a column*) Säulenschaft *m*; (*of a transmission*) Welle *f*

shaggy ['/ægi] *adj* zottig, struppig

shake [/ek] *s* Schütteln *n*; **he's no great shakes** mit ihm ist nicht viel los ‖ *v* (*pret* shook [/ʊk]; *pp* shaken) *tr* schütteln; **s. a leg!** (coll) rühr dich ein bißchen; **s. before using** vor Gebrauch schütteln; **s. down** (sl) erpressen; **s. hands** sich [*dat*] die Hand geben; **s. hands with** s.o. j–m die Hand drücken; **s. off** (& fig) abschütteln; **s. one's head** mit dem Kopf schütteln; **s. out** (*a rug*) ausschütteln; **s. up** aufschütteln; (fig) aufrütteln ‖ *intr* (with) zittern (vor *dat*), beben (vor *dat*)

shake′down′ *s* (sl) Erpressung *f*

shake′down cruise′ *s* Probefahrt *f*

shaker ['/ekər] *s* (*for salt*) Streuer *m*; (*for cocktails*) Shaker *m*

shake′-up′ *s* Umgruppierung *f*

shaky ['/eki] *adj* (& fig) wacklig

shale [/el] *s* Schiefer *m*

shale′ oil′ *s* Schieferöl *n*

shall [/æl] *v* (*pret* should [/ʊd]) *aux* (*to express future tense*) werden, e.g., **I s.** go ich werde gehen; (*to express obligation*) sollen, e.g., **s. I stay?** soll ich bleiben?

shallow ['/ælo] *adj* (*river, person*) seicht; (*water, bowl*) flach ‖ **shallows** *spl* Untiefe *f*

sham [/æm] *adj* Schein– ‖ *s* Schein *m* ‖ *v* (*pret & pp* shammed; *ger* shamming) *tr* vortäuschen

sham′ bat′tle s Scheingefecht n

shambles [ˈʃæmbəlz] s Trümmerhaufen m

shame [ʃem] s Schande f; (feeling of shame) Scham f; **put s.o. to s.** (outdo s.o.) }–n in den Schatten stellen; **s. on you! schäm dich!; what a s.! wie schade!** || tr beschämen

shame′faced′ adj verschämt

shameful [ˈʃemfəl] adj schändlich

shameless [ˈʃemlɪs] adj unverschämt

shampoo [ʃæmˈpu] s Shampoo n || tr shampoonieren

shamrock [ˈʃæmrɑk] s Kleeblatt n

Shanghai [ʃænˈhaɪ] s Schanghai n ||

shanghai [ʃænˈhaɪ] tr schanghaien

shank [ʃæŋk] s Unterschenkel m; (of an anchor, column, golf club) Schaft m; (cut of meat) Schenkel m

shanty [ˈʃænti] s Bude f

shan′tytown′ s Bretterbudensiedlung f

shape [ʃep] s Form f, Gestalt f; **in bad s.** (coll) in schlechter Form; **in good s.** in gutem Zustand; **out of s.** aus der Form; **take s.** sich gestalten || tr formen, gestalten || intr—**s. up** (coll) sich zusammenfassen

shapeless [ˈʃeplɪs] adj formlos

shapely [ˈʃepli] adj wohlgestaltet

share [ʃer] s Anteil m; (st. exch.) Aktie f; **do one's s.** das Seine tun || tr teilen || intr—**s. in** teilhaben an (dat)

share′hold′er s Aktionär –in mf

shark [ʃɑrk] s Hai m, Haifisch m

sharp [ʃɑrp] adj scharf; (pointed) spitzig; (keen) pfiffig || adv pünktlich || s (mus) Kreuz n

sharpen [ˈʃɑrpən] tr schärfen; (a pencil) spitzen

sharply [ˈʃɑrpli] adv scharf

sharp′shoot′er s Scharfschütze m

shatter [ˈʃætər] tr zersplittern; (the nerves) zerrütten; (dreams) zerstören || intr zersplittern

shat′terproof′ adj splittersicher

shave [ʃev] s—**get a s.** sich rasieren lassen || tr rasieren || intr sich rasieren

shav′ing brush′ s Rasierpinsel m

shav′ing cream′ s Rasierkrem m

shav′ing mug′ s Rasiernapf m

shawl [ʃɔl] s Schal m

she [ʃi] s Weibchen n || pers pron sie

sheaf [ʃif] s (sheaves [ʃivz]) Garbe f

shear [ʃɪr] s—**shears** Schere f || v (pret sheared; pp sheared & shorn [ʃorn]) tr scheren; **s. off** abschneiden

sheath [ʃiθ] s Scheide f

sheathe [ʃið] tr in die Scheide stecken

shed [ʃed] s Schuppen m || v (pret & pp shed; ger shedding) tr (leaves) abwerfen; (tears) vergießen; (hair, leaves) verlieren; (peace) verbreiten; **s. light on** (fig) Licht werfen auf (acc)

sheen [ʃin] s Glanz m

sheep [ʃip] s (sheep) Schaf n

sheep′dog′ s Schäferhund m

sheep′fold′ s Schafhürde f, Schafpferch m

sheepish [ˈʃipɪʃ] adj (embarrassed) verlegen; (timid) schüchtern

sheep′skin′ s Schaffell n; (coll) Diplom n

sheep′skin coat′ s Schafpelz m

sheer [ʃɪr] adj rein; (tex) durchsichtig; **by s. force** durch bloße Gewalt || intr—**s. off** abscheren

sheet [ʃit] s (for the bed) Leintuch n; (of paper) Blatt n, Bogen m; (of metal) Blech n; (naut) Segelleine f; **come down in sheets** (fig) in Strömen regnen; **s. of ice** Glatteis n; **s. of flame** Feuermeer n

sheet′ i′ron s Eisenblech n

sheet′ mu′sic s Notenblatt n

she′-goat′ s Ziege f

sheik [ʃik] s Scheich m

shelf [ʃelf] s (shelves [ʃelvz]) Regal n; **put on the s.** (fig) auf die lange Bank schieben

shell [ʃel] s Schale f; (conch) Muschel f; (of a snail) Gehäuse n; (of a tortoise) Panzer m; (bullet) Patrone f || tr (eggs) schälen; (nuts) aufknacken; (mil) beschießen; **s. out money** (coll) mit dem Geld herausrücken || intr—**s. out** (coll) blechen

shel·lac [ʃəˈlæk] s Schellack m || v (pret & pp -lacked; ger -lacking) tr mit Schellack streichen; (sl) verdreschen

shell′fish′ s Schalentier n

shell′ hole′ s Granattrichter m

shell′ shock′ s Bombenneurose f

shelter [ˈʃeltər] s Obdach n; (fig) Schutz m || tr schützen

shelve [ʃelv] tr auf ein Regal stellen; (fig) auf die lange Bank schieben

shenanigans [ʃɪˈnænɪgənz] spl Possen pl

shepherd [ˈʃepərd] s Hirt m; (fig) Seelenhirt m || tr hüten

shep′herd dog′ s Schäferhund m

shepherdess [ˈʃepərdɪs] s Hirtin f

sherbet [ˈʃɑrbət] s Speiseeis n

sheriff [ˈʃerɪf] s Sheriff m

sherry [ˈʃeri] s Sherry m

shield [ʃild] s Schild m; (fig) Schutz m; (rad) Röhrenabschirmung f || tr (from) schützen (vor dat); (elec, mach) abschirmen

shift [ʃɪft] adj (worker, work) Schicht– || s Schicht f; (change) Verschiebung f; (loose-fitting dress) Kittelkleid n || tr (a meeting) verschieben; (the blame) (on) abschieben (auf acc); **s. gears** umschalten || intr (said of the wind) umspringen; **s. for oneself** sich allein durchschlagen; **s. into second gear** in den zweiten Gang umschalten

shift′ key′ s Umschalttaste f

shiftless [ˈʃɪftlɪs] adj träge

shifty [ˈʃɪfti] adj schlau, gerissen

shimmer [ˈʃɪmər] s Schimmer m || intr schimmern, flimmern

shin [ʃɪn] s Schienbein n

shin′bone′ s Schienbein n

shine [ʃaɪn] s Schein m, Glanz m || v (pret & pp shined) tr polieren; (shoes) wichsen || v (pret & pp shone [ʃon]) intr scheinen; (said of the *eyes*) leuchten; (*be outstanding*) (in) glänzen (in *dat*)

shiner ['ʃaɪnər] *s* (sl) blaues Auge *n*

shingle ['ʃɪŋgəl] *s* (*for a roof*) Schindel *f*; (*e.g., of a doctor*) Aushängeschild *n* || *tr* mit Schindeln decken

shin'ing *adj* (*eyes*) leuchtend, strahlend; (*example*) glänzend

shiny ['ʃaɪni] *adj* blank, glänzend

ship [ʃɪp] *s* Schiff *n* || *v* (*pret & pp* shipped; *ger* shipping) *tr* senden; **s. water** e-e Sturzsee bekommen || *intr*—**s. out** absegeln

ship'board' *s* Bord *m*; **on s.** an Bord

ship'build'er *s* Schiffbauer *m*

ship'build'ing *s* Schiffbau *m*

shipment ['ʃɪpmənt] *s* Lieferung *f*

ship'ping *s* Absendung *f*, Verladung *f*; (*ships*) Schiffe *pl*

ship'ping clerk' *s* Expedient –in *mf*

ship'ping depart'ment *s* Versandabteilung *f*

ship'shape' *adj* ordentlich

ship'wreck' *s* Schiffbruch *m* || *tr* scheitern lassen; **be s.** schiffbrüchig sein || *intr* Schiffbruch erleiden

ship'yard' *s* Werft *f*

shirk [ʃɪrk] *tr* sich drücken vor (*dat*) || *intr* (from) sich drücken vor (*dat*)

shirt [ʃʌrt] *s* Hemd *n*; **keep your s. on!** (sl) regen Sie sich nicht auf!

shirt'col'lar *s* Hemdkragen *m*

shirt'sleeve' *s* Hemdsärmel *m*

shirttail' *s* Hemdschoß *m*

shit [ʃɪt] *s* (vulg) Scheiße *f* || *v* (*pret & pp* shit) *tr & intr* (vulg) scheißen

shiver ['ʃɪvər] *s* Schauder *m* || *intr* (at) schaudern (vor *dat*); (with) zittern (vor *dat*)

shoal [ʃol] *s* Untiefe *f*

shock [ʃɑk] *s* Schock *m*; (*of hair*) Schopf *m*; (agr) Schober *m*; (elec) Schlag *m* || *tr* schockieren; (elec) e–n Schlag versetzen (*dat*)

shock' absorb'er [æb'sɔrbər] *s* Stoßdämpfer *m*

shock'ing *adj* schockierend

shock' troops' *spl* Stoßtruppen *pl*

shock' wave' *s* Stoßwelle *f*

shoddy ['ʃɑdi] *adj* schäbig

shoe [ʃu] *s* Schuh *m* || *v* (*pret & pp* shod [ʃɑd]) *tr* beschlagen

shoe'horn' *s* Schuhlöffel *m*

shoe'lace' *s* Schuhband *n*, Schnürsenkel *m*

shoe'mak'er *s* Schuster *m*

shoe' pol'ish *s* Schuhwichse *f*

shoe'shine' *s* Schuhputzen *n*

shoe' store' *s* Schuhladen *m*

shoe' string' *s* Schuhband *m*; **on a s.** mit ein paar Groschen

shoe'tree' *s* Schuhspanner *m*

shoo [ʃu] *tr* (away) wegscheuchen || *interj* sch!

shook-up ['ʃʊk'ʌp] *adj* (coll) verdattert

shoot [ʃut] *s* Schößling *m* || *v* (*pret & pp* shot [ʃɑt]) *tr* (an)schießen, (ab)schießen; (*kill*) erschießen; (*dice*) werfen; (cin) drehen; (phot) aufnehmen; **s. down** (aer) abschießen; **s. the breeze** zwanglos plaudern; **s. up** (*e.g., a town*) zusammenschie-

ßen || *intr* schießen; **s. at** schießen auf (*acc*); **s. by** vorbeisausen an (*dat*); **s. up** (*in growth*) aufschießen; (*said of flames*) emporschlagen; (*said of prices*) emporschnellen

shoot'ing *s* Schießerei *f*; (*execution*) Erschießung *f*; (*of a film*) Drehen *n*

shoot'ing gal'lery *s* Schießbude *f*

shoot'ing match' *s* Preisschießen *n*

shoot'ing star' *s* Sternschnuppe *f*

shoot'ing war' *s* heißer Krieg *m*

shop [ʃɑp] *s* Laden *m*, Geschäft *n*; **talk s.** fachsimpeln || *v* (*pret & pp* shopped; *ger* shopping) *intr* einkaufen; **go shopping** einkaufen gehen; **s. around** for sich in einigen Läden umsehen nach

shop'girl' *s* Ladenmädchen *n*

shop'keep'er *s* Ladeninhaber –in *mf*

shoplifter ['ʃɑp,lɪftər] *s* Ladendieb –in *mf*

shop'lift'ing *s* Ladendiebstahl *m*

shopper ['ʃɑpər] *s* Einkäufer –in *mf*

shop'ping *s* Einkaufen *n*; (*purchases*) Einkäufe *pl*

shop'ping bag' *s* Einkaufstasche *f*

shop'ping cen'ter *s* Einkaufcenter *n*

shop'ping dis'trict *s* Geschäftsviertel *n*

shop'ping spree' *s* Einkaufsorgie *f*

shop'talk' *s* Fachsimpelei *f*

shop'win'dow *s* Schaufenster *n*

shop'worn' *adj* (fig) abgerissen

shore [ʃor] *s* Küste *f*; (*beach*) Strand *m*; (*of a river*) Ufer *n*; **go to the s.** ans Meer fahren || *tr*—**s. up** abstützen

shore' leave' *s* Landurlaub *m*

shore'line' *s* Küstenlinie *f*; (*of a river*) Uferlinie *f*

shore' patrol' *s* Küstenstreife *f*

short [ʃort] *adj* kurz; (*person*) klein; (*loan*) kurzfristig; **a s. time ago** vor kurzem; **be s. of**, e.g., **I am s. of bread** das Brot geht mir aus; **be s. with s.o.** j–n kurz abfertigen; **cut s.** abbrechen; **fall s. of** zurückbleiben hinter (*dat*); **get the s. end** das Nachsehen haben; **I am three marks s.** es fehlen mir drei Mark; **in s.** kurzum; **s. of breath** außer Atem; **s. of cash** knapp bei Kasse || *s* (cin) Kurzfilm *m*; (elec) Kurzschluß *m* || *tr* (elec) kurzschließen

shortage ['ʃortɪdʒ] *s* (of) Mangel *m* (an *dat*); (com) Minderbetrag *m*

short'cake' *s* Mürbekuchen *m*

short'change' *tr* zu wenig Wechselgeld herausgeben (*dat*); (fig) betrügen

short' cir'cuit *s* Kurzschluß *m*

short'-cir'cuit *tr* kurzschließen

short'com'ing *s* Fehler *m*, Mangel *m*

short'cut' *s* Abkürzung *f*; **take a s.** den Weg abkürzen

shorten ['ʃortən] *tr* abkürzen

short'ening *s* Abkürzung *f*; (culin) Backfett *n*

short'hand' *adj* stenographisch || *s* Stenographie *f*; **in s.** stenographisch; **take down in s.** stenographieren

short-lived ['ʃort'laɪvd] *adj* kurzlebig

shortly ['ʃortli] *adv* in kurzem; **s. after** kurz nach

short'-or'der cook' s Schnellimbißkoch m, Schnellimbißköchin f
short'-range' adj Nah-, auf kurze Sicht
shorts [ʃɔrts] s (underwear) Unterhose f; (walking shorts) kurze Hose f; (sport) Sporthose f
short'-sight'ed adj kurzsichtig
short' sto'ry s Novelle f
short'-tem'pered adj leicht aufbrausend
short'-term' adj kurzfristig
short'wave' adj Kurzwellen-|| s Kurzwelle f
short'wind'ed adj kurzatmig
shot [ʃat] adj (sl) kaputt; (drunk) (sl) besoffen; **my nerves are s.** ich bin mit meinen Nerven ganz herunter || s Schuß m; (shooter) Schütze m; (pellets) Schrot m; (injection) Spritze f; (snapshot) Aufnahme f; (of liquor) Gläschen n; **be a good s.** gut schießen; **s. in the arm** (fig) Belebungsspritze f; **s. in the dark** Sprung m ins Ungewisse; **take a s. at** e-n Schuß abgeben auf (acc); (fig) versuchen; **wild s.** Schuß m ins Blaue
shot'gun' s Schrotflinte f
shot'gun wed'ding s Mußehe f
shot'-put' s (sport) Kugelstoßen n
should [ʃʊd] aux (to express softened affirmation) **I s.** like to know ich möchte wissen; **I s. think so** das will ich meinen; (to express obligation) **how s. I know?** wie sollte ich das wissen?; **you shouldn't do that** Sie sollten das nicht tun; (in conditional clauses) **if it s. rain tomorrow** wenn es morgen regnen sollte
shoulder ['ʃoldər] s Schulter f, Achsel f; (of a road) Bankett n; **have broad shoulders** e-n breiten Rücken haben || tr (a rifle) schultern; (responsibility) auf sich nehmen
shoul'der bag' s Umhängetasche f
shoul'der blade' s Schulterblatt n
shoul'der strap' s (of underwear) Trägerband n; (mil) Schulterriemen m
shout [ʃaʊt] s Schrei m, Ruf m || tr schreien, rufen; **s. down** (coll) niederschreien || intr schreien, rufen
shove [ʃʌv] s Stoß m; **give s.o. a s.** j-m e-n Stoß versetzen || tr stoßen; (e.g., furniture) rücken; **s. around** (coll) herumschubsen; **s. forward** vorschieben || intr drängeln; **s. off** (coll) abschieben; (naut) vom Land abstoßen
shov·el ['ʃʌvəl] s Schaufel f || v (pret & pp -el[l]ed; ger -el[l]ing) tr schaufeln
show [ʃo] s (exhibition) Ausstellung f; (outer appearance) Schau f; (spectacle) Theater n; (cin, theat) Vorstellung f; **by s. of hands** durch Handzeichen; **make a s. of s.th.** mit etw Staat machen; **only for s.** nur zur Schau || v (pret showed; pp shown [ʃon] & showed) tr zeigen; (prove) beweisen, nachweisen; (said of evidence, tests) weisen; (tickets, passport, papers) vorweisen; **s. around** (a person) herumführen; (a thing) herumzeigen || intr zu sehen sein;

(said of a slip) vorgucken; **s. off** (with) großtun (mit); **s. up** erscheinen
show' busi'ness s Unterhaltungsindustrie f
show'case' s ein Schaukasten m, Vitrine f
show'down' s entscheidender Wendepunkt m; (e.g., in a western) Kraftprobe f; (cards) Aufdecken n der Karten
shower ['ʃaʊ·ər] s (rain) Schauer m; (bath) Dusche f; (shower room) Duschraum m; (of stones, arrows) Hagel m; (of bullets, sparks) Regen m; (for a bride) Party f zur Überreichung der Brautgeschenke; **take a s.** (sich) duschen || intr (with gifts) überschütten || intr duschen; (meteor) schauern
show'er bath' s Dusche f, Brausebad n
show' girl' s Revuegirl n
show'ing s Zeigen n; (cin) Vorführung f
show'ing off' s Großtuerei f
show'man s (-men) s Schauspieler m
show'-off' s Protz m
show'piece' s Schaustück n
show'room' s Ausstellungsraum m
show' win'dow s Schaufenster n
showy ['ʃo·i] adj prunkhaft
shrapnel ['ʃræpnəl] s Schrapnell n
shred [ʃred] s Fetzen m; (least bit) Spur f; **tear to shreds** in Fetzen reißen; (an argument) gründlich widerlegen || v (pret & pp shredded & shred; ger shredding) tr zerfetzen; (paper) in Streifen schneiden; (culin) schnitzeln
shredder ['ʃredər] s (of paper) Reißwolf m; (culin) Schnitzelmaschine f
shrew [ʃru] s böse Sieben f
shrewd [ʃrud] adj schlau
shriek [ʃrik] s Gekreische n, gellender Schrei m || intr kreischen
shrill [ʃrɪl] adj schrill
shrimp [ʃrɪmp] s Garnele f; (coll) Knirps m
shrine [ʃraɪn] s Heiligtum n
shrink [ʃrɪŋk] v (pret shrank [ʃræŋk] & shrunk [ʃrʌŋk]; pp shrunk & shrunken) tr einlaufen lassen || intr schrumpfen; **s. back from** zurückschrecken vor (dat); **s. from** sich scheuen vor (dat); **s. up** einschrumpfen
shrinkage ['ʃrɪŋkɪdʒ] s Schrumpfung f
shriv·el ['ʃrɪvəl] s (pret & pp -el[l]ed; ger -el[l]ing) intr schrumpfen; **s. up** zusammenschrumpfen
shriv'eled adj schrumpelig
shroud [ʃraʊd] s Leichentuch n; (fig) Hülle f; (naut) Want f || tr (in) einhüllen (in acc)
shrub [ʃrʌb] s Strauch m
shrubbery ['ʃrʌbəri] s Strauchwerk n
shrug [ʃrʌg] s Zucken n || v (pret & pp shrugged; ger shrugging) tr zucken; **s. off** mit e-m Achselzucken abtun; **s. one's shoulders** mit den Achseln zucken || intr mit den Achseln zucken
shuck [ʃʌk] tr enthülsen
shudder ['ʃʌdər] s Schau(d)er m ||

intr (at) schau(d)ern (vor *dat*); s. at the thought of s.th. bei dem Gedanken an etw [*acc*] zittern

shuffle [ˈʃʌfəl] *s* Schlurfen *n*; (cards) Mischen *n*; get lost in the s. (fig) unter den Tisch fallen ‖ *tr* (cards) mischen; (the feet) schleifen; ‖ *intr* die Karten mischen; (walk) schlurfen; s. along latschen

shun [ʃʌn] *v* (pret & pp shunned; ger shunning) *tr* (a person) meiden; (a thing) (ver)meiden

shunt [ʃʌnt] *s* (elec) Nebenschluß *m* ‖ *tr* (shove aside) beiseite schieben; (across) parallelschalten (zu); (rr) rangieren

shut [ʃʌt] *adj* zu ‖ (pret & pp shut; ger shutting) *tr* schließen, zumachen; be s. down stilliegen; s. down stillegen; s. off absperren; s. one's eyes to hinwegsehen über (acc); s. out ausperren; s. s.o. up j-m den Mund stopfen ‖ *intr* sich schließen; s. up! (coll) halt's Maul!

shut′down′ *s* Stillegung *f*

shutter [ˈʃʌtər] *s* Laden *m*; (phot) Verschluß *m*

shuttle [ˈʃʌtəl] *s* Schiffchen *n* ‖ *intr* pendeln, hin- und herfahren

shut′tle bus′ *s* Pendelbus *m*

shut′tlecock′ *s* Federball *m*

shut′tle serv′ice *s* Pendelverkehr *m*

shut′tle train′ *s* Pendelzug *m*

shy [ʃaɪ] *adj* (shyer; shyest) schüchtern; be a dollar shy e-n Dollar los sein ‖ *intr* (said of a horse) stutzen; shy at zurückscheuen vor (dat); shy away from sich scheuen vor (dat)

shyness [ˈʃaɪnɪs] *s* Scheu *f*

shyster [ˈʃaɪstər] *s* Winkeladvokat *m*

Siamese′ twins′ [ˌsaɪəˈmiz] *spl* Siamesische Zwillinge *pl*

Siberia [saɪˈbɪriə] *s* Sibirien *n*

Siberian [saɪˈbɪriən] *adj* sibirisch ‖ *s* Sibirier –in *mf*

sibilant [ˈsɪbɪlənt] *s* Zischlaut *m*

siblings [ˈsɪblɪŋz] *spl* Geschwister *pl*

sibyl [ˈsɪbɪl] *s* Sibylle *f*

sic [sɪk] *adv* sic ‖ *v* (pret & pp sicked; ger sicking) *tr*—sic 'em! (coll) faß!; sic the dog on s.o. den Hund auf j-n hetzen

Sicilian [sɪˈsɪljən] *adj* sizilianisch ‖ *s* Sizilianer –in *mf*

Sicily [ˈsɪsɪli] *s* Sizilien *n*

sick [sɪk] *adj* krank; be s. and tired of s.th. etw gründlich satt haben; be s. as a dog sich hundeelend fühlen; I am s. to my stomach mir ist übel; play s. krankfeiern

sick′ bay′ *s* Schiffslazarett *n*

sick′bed′ *s* Krankenbett *n*

sicken [ˈsɪkən] *tr* krank machen; (disgust) anekeln ‖ *intr* krank werden

sick′ening [ˈsɪ] *adj* ekelhaft

sick′ head′ache *s* Kopfschmerzen *pl* mit Übelkeit

sickle [ˈsɪkəl] *s* Sichel *f*

sick′ leave′ *s* Krankenurlaub *m*

sickly [ˈsɪkli] *adj* kränklich; (smile) erzwungen

sickness [ˈsɪknɪs] *s* Krankheit *f*

sick′ room′ *s* Krankenzimmer *n*

side [saɪd] *adj* Neben-, Seiten– ‖ *s* Seite *f*; (of a team, government) Partei *f*; (edge) Rand *m*; at my s. mir zur Seite; dark s. Schattenseite *f*; off sides (sport) abseits; on the father's s. väterlicherseits; on the s. (coll) nebenbei; ‖ *intr* s. up Vorsicht, nicht stürzen; to be on the safe s. um ganz sicher zu gehen ‖ *intr*—s. with s.o. j-s Partei ergreifen

side′ aisle′ *s* Seitengang *m*; (of a church) Seitenschiff *n*

side′ al′tar *s* Nebenaltar *m*

side′arm′ *s* Seitengewehr *n*

side′board′ *s* Anrichte *f*, Büffet *n*

side′burns′ *spl* Koteletten *pl*

side′ dish′ *s* Nebengericht *n*

side′ door′ *s* Seitentür *f*

side′ effect′ *s* Nebenwirkung *f*

side′ en′trance *s* Seiteneingang *m*

side′ glance′ *s* Seitenblick *m*

side′ is′sue *s* Nebenfrage *f*

side′ job′ *s* Nebenverdienst *m*

side′kick′ *s* (coll) Kumpel *m*

side′line′ *s* (occupation) Nebenbeschäftigung *f*; (fb) Seitenlinie *f* ‖ *tr* (coll) an der aktiven Teilnahme hindern

side′ of ba′con *s* Speckseite *f*

side′ road′ *s* Seitenweg *m*

side′sad′dle *adv*—ride s. im Damensattel reiten

side′ show′ *s* Nebenvorstellung *f*; (fig) Episode *f*

side′split′ting *adj* zwerchfellerschütternd

side′-step′ *v* (pret & pp –stepped; ger –stepping) *tr* ausweichen (dat)

side′ street′ *s* Seitenstraße *f*

side′stroke′ *s* Seitenschwimmen *n*

side′track′ *s* Seitengeleise *n* ‖ *tr* (& fig) auf ein Seitengeleise schieben

side′ trip′ *s* Abstecher *m*

side′ view′ *s* Seitenansicht *f*

side′walk′ *s* Bürgersteig *m*, Gehsteig *m*

sideward [ˈsaɪdwərd] *adj* nach der Seite gerichtet ‖ *adv* seitwärts

side′ways′ *adv* seitlich, seitwärts

sid′ing *s* (of a house) Verkleidung *f*; (rr) Nebengeleise *n*

sidle [ˈsaɪdəl] *intr*—s. up to s.o. sich heimlich an j-n heranmachen

siege [sidʒ] *s* Belagerung *f*; lay s. to belagern

siesta [siˈestə] *s* Mittagsruhe *f*

sieve [sɪv] *s* Sieb *n* ‖ *tr* durchsieben

sift [sɪft] *tr* (durch)sieben; (fig) sichten; s. out aussieben

sigh [saɪ] *s* Seufzer *m*; with a s. seufzend ‖ *intr* seufzen

sight [saɪt] *s* Anblick *m*; (faculty) Sehvermögen *n*; (on a weapon) Visier *n*; at first s. auf den ersten Blick; at s. sofort; be a s. (coll) unmöglich aussehen; by s. vom Sehen; catch s. of erblicken; in s. in Sicht; lose s. of aus den Augen verlieren; out of s. außer Sicht; s. for sore eyes Augentrost *m*; sights Sehenswürdigkeiten *pl*; s. unseen unbesehen; within s. in Sehweite ‖ *tr* sichten

sight'see'ing s Besichtigung f; go s. sich [dat] die Sehenswürdigkeiten ansehen

sight'seeing tour' s Rundfahrt f

sightseer ['saɪt,si·ər] s Tourist –in mf

sign [saɪn] s (signboard) Schild n; (symbol, omen, signal) Zeichen n; (symptom, indication) Kennzeichen n; (trace) Spur f; (math, mus) Vorzeichen n; s. of life Lebenszeichen n || tr unterschreiben; s. away aufgeben; s. over (to) überschreiben (auf acc) || intr unterschreiben; s. for zeichnen für; s. in sich eintragen; s. off (rad) die Sendung beenden; s. out sich austragen; s. up (mil) sich anwerben lassen; s. up for (e.g., courses, work) sich anmelden für

sig·nal ['sɪgnəl] adj auffallend || s (by gesture) Zeichen n, Wink m; (aut, rad, rr, telv) Signal n || v (pret & pp –nal[l]ed; ger –nal[l]ing) tr signalisieren; (a person) ein Zeichen geben (dat)

sig'nal corps' s Fernmeldetruppen pl

sig'nal·man s (–men) (nav) Signalgast m; (rr) Bahnwärter m

signatory ['sɪgnə,tori] s Unterzeichner –in mf

signature ['sɪgnət∫ər] s Unterschrift f

sign'board' s Aushängeschild n

signer ['saɪnər] s Unterzeichner –in mf

sig'net ring' ['sɪgnɪt] s Siegelring m

significance [sɪg'nɪfɪkəns] s Bedeutung f

significant [sɪg'nɪfɪkənt] adj bedeutsam

signi·fy ['sɪgnɪ,faɪ] v (pret & pp –fied) bedeuten, bezeichnen

sign' language s Zeichensprache f

sign' of the cross' s Kreuzzeichen n; make the s. sich bekreuzigen

sign'post' s Wegweiser m

silence ['saɪləns] s Ruhe f, Stille f; (reticence) Schweigen n; in s. schweigend || tr zum Schweigen bringen; (a conscience) beschwichtigen

silent ['saɪlənt] adj (night, partner) still; (movies) stumm; (person) schweigend; be s. stillschweigen; keep s. schweigen

silhouette [,sɪlu'et] s Schattenbild n, Silhouette f || tr silhouettieren

silicon ['sɪlɪkən] s Silizium n

silicone ['sɪlɪkon] s Silikon n

silk [sɪlk] adj seiden || s Seide f

silken ['sɪlkən] adj seiden

silk' hat' s Zylinder m

silk' mill' s Seidenfabrik f

silk' worm' s Seidenraupe f

silky ['sɪlki] adj seiden, seidenartig

sill [sɪl] s (of a window) Sims m & n; (of a door) Schwelle f

silliness ['sɪlɪnɪs] s Albernheit f

silly ['sɪli] adj albern, blöd(e)

si·lo ['saɪlo] s (–los) Getreidesilo m; (rok) Raketenbunker m, Silo m

silt [sɪlt] s Schlick m || intr—s. up verschlammen

silver ['sɪlvər] adj silbern || s Silber n; (for the table) Silberzeug n; (money) Silbergeld n

sil'verfish' s Silberfischchen n

sil'ver foil' s Silberfolie f

sil'ver lin'ing s (fig) Silberstreifen m

sil'ver plate' s Silbergeschirr n

sil'ver-plat'ed adj versilbert

sil'versmith' s Silberschmied m

sil'ver spoon' s—be born with a s. in one's mouth ein Sonntagskind sein

sil'verware' s Silbergeschirr n

silvery ['sɪlvəri] adj silbern

similar ['sɪmɪlər] adj (to) ähnlich (dat)

similarity [,sɪmɪ'lærɪti] s Ähnlichkeit f

simile ['sɪmɪli] s Gleichnis n

simmer ['sɪmər] tr leicht kochen lassen || intr brodeln; s. down (coll) sich abreagieren

simper ['sɪmpər] s selbstgefälliges Lächeln n || intr selbstgefällig lächeln

simple ['sɪmpəl] adj einfach; (truth) rein; (fact) bloß

sim'ple-mind'ed adj einfältig

simpleton ['sɪmpəltən] s Einfaltspinsel m

simpli·fy ['sɪmplɪ,faɪ] v (pret & pp –fied) tr vereinfachen

simply ['sɪmpli] adv einfach

simulate ['sɪmjə,let] tr (illness) simulieren; (e.g., a rocket flight) am Modell vorführen

sim'ulated adj unecht

simultaneous [,saɪməl'teni·əs] adj gleichzeitig, simultan

sin [sɪn] s Sünde f || v (pret & pp sinned; ger sinning) intr sündigen; sin against sich versündigen an (dat)

since [sɪns] adv seitdem, seither || prep seit (dat); s. then seither; s. when seit wann || conj (temporal) seit(dem); (causal) da

sincere [sɪn'sɪr] adj aufrichtig

sincerely [sɪn'sɪrli] adv aufrichtig, ehrlich; **Sincerely yours** Ihr ergebener, Ihre ergebene

sincerity [sɪn'serɪti] s Aufrichtigkeit f

sinecure ['saɪnɪ,kjʊr] s Sinekure f

sinew ['sɪnju] s Sehne f, Flechse f; (fig) Muskelkraft f

sinewy ['sɪnju·i] adj sehnig; (fig) kräftig, nervig

sinful ['sɪnfəl] adj sündhaft

sing [sɪŋ] v (pret sang [sæŋ] & sung [sʌŋ]; pp sung) tr & intr singen

singe [sɪndʒ] v (singeing) tr sengen; (the hair) versengen

singer ['sɪŋər] s Sänger –in mf

single ['sɪŋgəl] adj einzeln; (unmarried) ledig; not a s. word kein einziges Wort || tr—s. out herausgreifen

sin'gle bed' s Einzelbett n

sin'gle-breast'ed adj einreihig

sin'gle file' s Gänsemarsch m

sin'gle-hand'ed adj einhändig

sin'gle-lane' adj einbahnig

sin'gle life' s Ledigenstand m

sin'gle-mind'ed adj zielstrebig

sin'gle room' s Einzelzimmer n

sin'gle-track' adj (& fig) eingleisig

sing'song' adj eintönig || s Singsang m

singular ['sɪŋgjələr] adj (outstanding) ausgezeichnet; (unique) einzig; (odd) seltsam || s (gram) Einzahl f

sinister ['sınıstər] *adj* unheimlich

sink [sıŋk] *s* (*in the kitchen*) Ausguß *m*; (*in the bathroom*) Waschbecken *n* || *v* (*pret* sank [sæŋk] & sunk [sʌŋk]; *pp* sunk) *tr* (*a ship; a post*) versenken; (*money*) investieren; (*min*) abteufen; **s. a well** e-n Brunnen bohren || *intr* sinken; (*said of a building*) sich senken; **he is sinking fast** seine Kräfte nehmen rapide ab; **s. in** (*coll*) einleuchten; **s. into** (*an easychair*) sich fallen lassen in (*acc*); (*poverty*) geraten in (*acc*); (*unconsciousness*) fallen in (*acc*)

sink'ing feel'ing *s* Beklommenheit *f*

sink'ing fund' *s* Schuldentilgungsfonds *m*

sinless ['sınlıs] *adj* sünd(en)los

sinner ['sınər] *s* Sünder –in *mf*

sinuous ['sınjʊ‧əs] *adj* gewunden

sinus ['saınəs] *s* Stirnhöhle *f*

sip [sıp] *s* Schluck *m* || *v* (*pret* & *pp* sipped; *ger* sipping) *tr* schlürfen

siphon ['saıfən] *s* Siphon *m*, Saugheber *m* || *tr* entleeren; **s. off** absaugen; (*profits*) abschöpfen

sir [sʌr] *s* Herr *m*; yes sir! jawohl!; **Dear Sir** Sehr geehrter Herr

sire [saır] *s* (& zool) Vater *m* || *tr* zeugen

siren ['saırən] *s* (& myth) Sirene *f*

sirloin ['sʌrlɔın] *s* Lendenbraten *m*

sissy ['sısi] *s* Schlappschwanz *m*

sister ['sıstər] *s* Schwester *f*

sis'ter-in-law' *s* (sisters-in-law) Schwägerin *f*

sisterly ['sıstərli] *adj* schwesterlich

sit [sıt] *v* (*pret* & *pp* sat [sæt]; *ger* sitting) *intr* sitzen; **sit down** sich (hin)setzen; **sit for a painter** e-m Maler Modell stehen; **sit in on** (*a meeting*) dabeisein bei; **sit up and beg** Männchen machen

sit'down strike' *s* Sitzstreik *m*

site [saıt] *s* (*position, location*) Lage *f*; (*piece of ground*) Gelände *n*

sit'ting—**at one s.** auf e-n Sitz

sit'ting duck' *s* wehrloses Ziel *n*

sit'ting room' *s* Gemeinschaftsraum *m*

situated ['sıtʃʊ‚etıd] *adj* gelegen; **be s.** liegen

situation [‚sıtʃʊ'eʃən] *s* Lage *f*; **s. wanted** Stelle gesucht

six [sıks] *adj* & *pron* sechs || *s* Sechs *f*

sixteen ['sıks'tin] *adj* & *pron* sechzehn || *s* Sechzehn *f*

sixteenth ['sıks'tinθ] *adj* & *pron* sechzehnte || *s* (*fraction*) Sechzehntel *n*; **the s.** (*in dates or in series*) der Sechzehnte

sixth [sıksθ] *adj* & *pron* sechste || *s* (*fraction*) Sechstel *n*; **the s.** (*in dates or in series*) der Sechste

sixtieth ['sıkstı‧ıθ] *adj* & *pron* sechzig || *s* (*fraction*) Sechzigstel *n*

sixty ['sıksti] *adj* & *pron* sechzig || *s* Sechzig *f*; **the sixties** die sechziger Jahre

six'ty-four dol'lar ques'tion *s* Preisfrage *f*

sizable ['saızəbəl] *adj* beträchtlich

size [saız] *s* Größe *f*; (*of a book,*

paper) Format *n* || *tr* grundieren; **s. up** einschätzen

sizzle ['sızəl] *s* Zischen *n* || *intr* zischen

skate [sket] *s* Schlittschuh *m* || *intr* Schlittschuh laufen

skat'ing rink' *s* Eisbahn *f*

skein [sken] *s* Strähne *f*

skeleton ['skelıtən] *s* Gerippe *n*

skel'eton crew' *s* Minimalbelegschaft *f*

skel'eton key' *s* Dietrich *m*

skeptic ['skeptık] *s* Zweifler –in *mf*

skeptical ['skeptıkəl] *adj* skeptisch

skepticism ['skeptı‚sızəm] *s* (*doubt*) Skepsis *f*; (philos) Skeptizismus *m*

sketch [sketʃ] *s* Skizze *f*; (theat) Sketch *m* || *tr & intr* skizzieren

sketch'book' *s* Skizzenbuch *n*

sketchy ['sketʃi] *adj* skizzenhaft

skewer ['skjʊ‧ər] *s* Fleischspieß *m*

ski [ski] *s* Schi *m* || *intr* schilaufen

ski' boot' *s* Schistiefel *m*

skid [skıd] *s* Rutschen *n*, Schleudern *n*; **go into a s.** ins Schleudern geraten || *v* (*pret* & *pp* skidded; *ger* skidding) *intr* rutschen, schleudern

skid'mark' *s* Bremsspur *f*

skid'proof' *adj* bremssicher

skid'row' [ro] *s* Elendsviertel *n*

skiff [skıf] *s* Skiff *n*

ski'ing *s* Schilaufen *n*

ski'jack'et *s* Anorak *m*

ski' jump' *s* Schisprung *m*; (*chute*) Sprungschanze *f*

ski' jump'ing *s* Schispringen *n*

ski' lift' *s* Schilift *m*

skill [skıl] *s* Fertigkeit *f*

skilled *adj* gelernt

skillet ['skılıt] *s* Bratpfanne *f*

skillful ['skılfəl] *adj* geschickt

skim [skım] *v* (*pret* & *pp* skimmed; *ger* skimming) *tr* (*milk*) abrahmen; (*a book*) überfliegen; **s. off** abschöpfen || *intr*—**s. over the water** über das Wasser streichen; **s. through** (*a book*) flüchtig durchblättern

skim' milk' *s* entrahmte Milch *f*

skimp [skımp] *intr* (**on**) knausern (mit)

skimpy ['skımpi] *adj* (*person*) knauserig; (*thing*) knapp, dürftig

skin [skın] *s* Haut *f*; (*fur*) Fell *n*; (*of fruit*) Schale *f*; **by the s. of one's teeth** mit knapper Not; **get under s.o.'s s.** j–m auf die Nerven gehen || *v* (*pret* & *pp* skinned; *ger* skinning) *tr* (*an animal*) enthäuten; (*a knee*) aufschürfen; (*fleece*) das Fell über die Ohren ziehen (*dat*); (*defeat*) schlagen; **s. alive** zur Sau machen

skin'-deep' *adj* oberflächlich

skin' div'er *s* Schwimmtaucher –in *mf*

skin'flint' *s* Geizhals *m*

skin' graft' *s* Hautverpflanzung *f*

skinny ['skını] *adj* spindeldürr, mager

skin'tight' *adj* hauteng

skip [skıp] *s* Sprung *m* || *v* (*pret* & *pp* skipped; *ger* skipping) *tr* (*omit*) auslassen; (*a page*) überblättern; **s. it!** Schwamm drüber!; **s. rope** Seil springen; **s. school** Schule schwänzen || *intr* springen; **s. out** abhauen

ski' pole' *s* Schistock *m*

skipper ['skɪpər] s Kapitän m

skirmish ['skɑrmɪʃ] s Scharmützel n ‖ intr scharmützeln

skir'mish line' s (mil) Schützenlinie f

skirt [skɑrt] s Rock m ‖ tr (border) umsäumen; (pass along) sich entlangziehen (an dat)

ski' run' s Schipiste f

skit [skɪt] s Sket(s)ch m

skittish ['skɪtɪʃ] adj (lively) lebhaft; (horse) scheu

skull [skʌl] s Schädel m

skull' and cross'bones s Totenkopf m

skull'cap' s Käppchen n

skunk [skʌŋk] s Stinktier n; (sl) Saukerl m

sky [skaɪ] s Himmel m; out of the clear blue sky wie aus heiterem Himmel; praise to the skies über den grünen Klee loben

sky'-blue' adj himmelblau

sky'div'er s Fallschirmspringer –in mf

sky'div'ing s Fallschirmspringen n

sky'lark' s Feldlerche f

sky'light' s Dachluke f

sky'line' s Horizontlinie f; (of a city) Stadtsilhouette f

sky'rock'et s Rakete f ‖ intr in die Höhe schießen

sky'scrap'er s Wolkenkratzer m

sky'writ'ing s Himmelsschrift f

slab [slæb] s Platte f, Tafel f

slack [slæk] adj schlaff; (period) flau ‖ s Spielraum m; **slacks** Herrenhose f, Damenhose f ‖ intr—**s. off** nachlassen

slacken ['slækən] tr (slow down) verlangsamen; (loosen) lockern ‖ intr nachlassen

slack' pe'riod s Flaute f

slack' sea'son s Sauregurkenzeit f

slag [slæg] s Schlacke f

slag' pile' s Schlackenhalde f

slake [slek] tr (thirst, lime) löschen

slalom ['slɑləm] s Slalom m

slam [slæm] s Knall m; (cards) Schlemm m ‖ v (pret & pp **slammed**; ger **slamming**) tr zuknallen; **s. down** hinknallen ‖ intr knallen

slander ['slændər] s Verleumdung f ‖ tr verleumden

slanderous ['slændərəs] adj verleumderisch

slang [slæŋ] s Slang m

slant [slænt] s Schräge f; (view) Einstellung f; (personal point of view) Tendenz f ‖ tr abschrägen; (fig) färben

slap [slæp] s Klaps m; **s. in the face** Ohrfeige f ‖ v (pret & pp **slapped**; ger **slapping**) tr schlagen; (s.o.'s face) ohrfeigen; **s. together** zusammenhauen

slap'stick' adj Radau– ‖ s Radaukomödie f

slash [slæʃ] s Schnittwunde f ‖ tr aufschlitzen; (prices) drastisch herabsetzen

slat [slæt] s Stab m

slate [slet] s Schiefer m; (to write on) Schiefertafel f; (of candidates) Vorschlagsliste f ‖ tr (a roof) mit Schie-

fer decken; (schedule) planen; **he is slated to speak** er soll sprechen

slate' roof' s Schieferdach n

slattern ['slætərn] s (slovenly woman) Schlampe f; (slut) Dirne f

slaughter ['slɔtər] s Schlachten n; (massacre) Metzelei f ‖ tr schlachten; (massacre) niedermetzeln

slaugh'terhouse' s Schlachthaus n

Slav [slɑv], (slæv) adj slawisch ‖ s (person) Slawe m, Slawin f

slave [slev] s Sklave m, Sklavin f ‖ intr (coll) schuften; **s. at a job** sich mit e–r Arbeit abquälen

slave' driv'er s (fig) Leuteschinder m

slaver ['slævər] s Geifer m

slavery ['slevəri] s Sklaverei f

slave' trade' s Sklavenhandel m

Slavic ['slɑvɪk], ['slævɪk] adj slawisch

slavish ['slevɪʃ] adj slawisch

slay [sle] v (pret **slew** [slu]; pp **slain** [slen]) tr erschlagen

slayer ['sle·ər] s Totschläger –in mf

sled [sled] s Schlitten m ‖ v (pret & pp **sledded**; ger **sledding**) intr Schlitten fahren

sledge [sledʒ] s Schlitten m

sledge' ham'mer s Vorschlaghammer m

sleek [slik] adj (hair) glatt; (cattle) fett ‖ tr glätten

sleep [slip] s Schlaf m; **get enough s.** sich ausschlafen ‖ v (pret & pp **slept** [slept]) tr (accommodate) Schlafgelegenheiten bieten für; **s. off a hangover** seinen Kater ausschlafen ‖ intr schlafen; **I didn't s. a wink** ich habe kein Auge zugetan; **s. like a log** wie ein Murmeltier schlafen; **s. with (a woman)** schlafen mit

sleeper ['sliper] s Schläfer –in mf; (sleeping car) Schlafwagen m; (fig) überraschender Erfolg m

sleepiness ['slipinɪs] s Schläfrigkeit f

sleep'ing bag' s Schlafsack m

Sleep'ing Beau'ty s Dornröschen n

sleep'ing car' s Schlafwagen m

sleep'ing compart'ment s Schlafabteil n

sleep'ing pill' s Schlaftablette f

sleep'ing sick'ness s Schlafkrankheit f

sleepless ['sliplɪs] adj schlaflos

sleep'walk'er s Nachtwandler –in mf

sleepy ['slipi] adj schläfrig

sleep'yhead' s Schlafmütze f

sleet [slit] s Schneeregen m; (on the ground) Glatteis n ‖ impers—**it is sleeting** es gibt Schneeregen, es graupelt

sleeve [sliv] s Ärmel m; (mach) Muffe f; **have s.th. up one's s.** etw im Schilde führen; **roll up one's sleeves** die Ärmel hochkrempeln

sleeveless ['slivlɪs] adj ärmellos

sleigh [sle] s Schlitten m

sleigh' bell' s Schlittenschelle f

sleigh' ride' s Schlittenfahrt f; **go for sleight' of hand'** [slart] s Taschenspielertrick m

slender ['slɛndər] adj schlank; (means) gering

sleuth [sluθ] s Detektiv m

slice [slaɪs] s Scheibe f, Schnitte f;

slice (tennis) Schnittball *m* || *tr* aufschneiden

slicer ['slaisər] *s* Schneidemaschine *f*

slick [slik] *adj* glatt; (*talker*) raffiniert

slicker ['slikər] *s* Regenmantel *m*

slide [slaid] *s* (*slip*) Rutsch *m*; (*chute*) Rutschbahn *f*; (*of a microscope*) Objektträger *m*; (*phot*) Diapositiv *n* || *v* (*pret & pp* **slid** [slid]) *tr* schieben *intr* rutschen; **let things s. die** Dinge laufen lassen

slide′ rule′ *s* Rechenschieber *m*

slide′ valve′ *s* Schieberventil *n*

slide′ view′er *s* Bildbetrachter *m*

slid′ing door′ *s* Schiebetür *f*

slid′ing scale′ *s* gleitende Skala *f*

slight [slait] *adj* gering(fügig); (*illness*) leicht; (*petite*) zart || *tr* mißachten (*said of a road*) abfallen

slim [slim] *adj* schlank; (*chance*) gering || *intr*—**s. down** abnehmen

slime [slaim] *s* Schlamm *m*; (*e.g., of fish, snakes*) Schleim *m*

slimy ['slaimi] *adj* schleimig; (*muddy*) schlammig

sling [slin] *s* (*to hurl stones*) Schleuder *f*; (*for a broken arm*) Schlinge *f* || *v* (*pret & pp* **slung** [slʌn]) *tr* schleudern; **s. over the shoulders** umhängen

sling′shot′ *s* Schleuder *f*

slink [slink] *v* (*pret & pp* **slunk** [slʌnk]) *intr* schleichen; **s. away** wegschleichen

slip [slip] *s* (*slide*) Ausrutschen *n*; (*cutting*) Ableger *m*; (*underwear*) Unterrock *m*; (*paper*) Zettel *m*; (*pillowcase*) Kissenbezug *m*; (*error*) Flüchtigkeitsfehler *m*; (*for ships*) Schlipp *m*; **give s.o. the s.** j-m entwischen; **s. of the pen** Schreibfehler *m*; **s. of the tongue** Sprechfehler *m* || *v* (*pret & pp* **slipped**; *ger* **slipping**) *tr*—**s. in** (*a remark*) einfließen lassen; (*poison*) heimlich schütten; **s. on** (*a glove*) überstreifen; (*a coat*) überziehen; (*a ring*) auf den Finger streifen; **s. s.o. money** j-m etw Geld zustecken; **s.o.'s mind** j-m entfallen || *intr* rutschen; (*e.g., out of or into a room*) schlüpfen; (*lose one's balance*) ausgleiten; **let s.** sich [*dat*] entgehen lassen; **s. by** verstreichen; **s. in** (*said of errors*) unterlaufen; **s. through one's fingers** durch die Finger gleiten; **s. out on s.o.** j-m entschlüpfen; **s. up (on)** danebenhauen (bei); **you are slipping** (coll) Sie lassen in der Leistung nach

slip′cov′er *s* Schonbezug *m*

slip′knot′ *s* Schleife *f*

slipper ['slipər] *s* Pantoffel *m*

slippery ['slipəri] *adj* glatt

slipshod ['slip‚ʃad] *adj* schlampig; **do s. work** schludern

slip′stream′ *s* Luftschraubenstrahl *m*

slip′-up′ *s* (coll) Flüchtigkeitsfehler *m*

slit [slit] *s* Schlitz *m* || *v* (*pret & pp* **slit**; *ger* **slitting**) *tr* schlitzen; **s. open** aufschlitzen

slit′-eyed′ *adj* schlitzäugig

slither ['sliðər] *intr* gleiten

slit′ trench′ *s* (mil) Splittergraben *m*

sliver ['slivər] *s* Splitter *m*, Span *m*

slob [slab] *s* (sl) Schmutzfink *m*

slobber ['slabər] *s* Geifer *m* || *intr* geifern

sloe [slo] *s* (bot) Schlehe *f*

sloe′-eyed′ *adj* schlitzäugig

slog [slag] *v* (*pret & pp* **slogged**; *ger* **slogging**) *intr* stapfen

slogan ['slogən] *s* Schlagwort *n*

sloop [slup] *s* Schaluppe *f*

slop [slap] *s* Spülicht *n*; (*bad food*) (sl) Fraß *m* || *v* (*pret & pp* **slopped**; *ger* **slopping**) *tr* (*hogs*) füttern; (*spill*) verschütten

slope [slop] *s* Abhang *m*; (*of a road*) Gefälle *n*; (*of a roof*) Neigung *f* || *tr* abschrägen || *intr* sich neigen; (*said of a road*) abfallen

sloppy ['slapi] *adj* schlampig; (*weather*) matschig

slosh [slaʃ] *intr* schwappen

slot [slat] *s* Schlitz *m*

sloth [sloθ] *s* Faulheit *f*, Trägheit *f*; (zool) Faultier *n*

slothful ['sloθfəl] *adj* faul, träge

slot′ machine′ *s* Spielautomat *m*

slouch [slautʃ] *s* nachlässige Haltung *f*; (*person*) Schlappschwanz *m* || *intr* in schlechter Haltung sitzen; **s. along** latschen

slouch′ hat′ *s* Schlapphut *m*

slough [slau] *s* Sumpf *m* || [sləf] *s* (*of a snake*) abgestreifte Haut *f*; (pathol) Schorf *m* || *tr* (& fig) abstreifen || *intr* (*said of a snake*) sich häuten

Slovak ['slovak], ['slovæk] *adj* slowakisch || *s* (*person*) Sklowake *m*, Slowakin *f*; (*language*) Slowakisch *n*

slovenly ['slʌvənli] *adj* schlampig

slow [slo] *adj* langsam; (*dawdling*) bummelig; (*mentally*) schwer von Begriff; (com) flau; **be s.** (horol) nachgehen || *adv* langsam || *tr*—**s. down** verlangsamen || *intr*—**s. down** (in driving) langsamer fahren; (in working) nachlassen; **s. down** (public sign) Schritt fahren

slow′down′ *s* Bummelstreik *m*

slow′ mo′tion *s* (cin) Zeitlupe *f*; **in s.** (cin) im Zeitlupentempo

slow′-mo′tion *adj* Zeitlupen-

slow′poke′ *s* (coll) langsamer Mensch *m*

slow′-wit′ted *adj* schwer von Begriff

slug [slʌg] *s* Rohling *m*; (*drink*) Zug *m* (zool) Wegschnecke *f* || *v* (*pret & pp* **slugged**; *ger* **slugging**) *tr* (coll) hart mit der Faust treffen

sluggard ['slʌgərd] *s* Faulpelz *m*

sluggish ['slʌgiʃ] *adj* träge

sluice [slus] *s* Schleuse *f*

sluice′ gate′ *s* Schleusentor *n*

slum [slʌm] *s* Elendsviertel *n*

slumber ['slʌmbər] *s* Schlummer *m* || *intr* schlummern

slum′ dwell′ing *s* Elendsquartier *n*

slump [slʌmp] *s* (st. exch.) Baisse *f*; **s. in sales** Absatzstockung *f* || *intr* zusammensacken; (*said of prices*) stürzen

slur [slʌr] *s* (*insult*) Verleumdung *f*; (mus) Bindezeichen *n* || *v* (*pret & pp* **slurred**; *ger* **slurring**) *tr* (*words*) verschleifen; (mus) binden; **s. over** hinweggehen über (acc)

slurp [slʌrp] s Schlürfen n || tr & intr schlürfen

slush [slʌʃ] s Matsch m, Schneematsch m

slush' fund' s Schmiergeld n

slushy ['slʌʃi] adj matschig

slut [slʌt] s Nutte f

sly [slaɪ] adj (**slyer & slier; slyest & sliest**) schlau || s—**on the sly** im Verborgenen

sly' fox' s Pfiffikus m

smack [smæk] s (blow) Klaps m; (sound) Klatsch m; (kiss) Schmatz m; **s. in the face** Backpfeife f || tr klapsen; **s. one's lips** schmatzen || intr—**s.** of riechen nach

small [smɔl] adj klein; (difference) gering; (comfort) schlecht; (petty) kleinlich

small' arms' spl Handwaffen pl

small' busi'ness s Kleinbetrieb m

small' cap'ital s (typ) Kapitälchen n

small' change' s Kleingeld n

small' fry' s kleine Fische pl

small' intes'tine s Dünndarm m

small'-mind'ed adj engstirnig

small' of the back' s Kreuz n

smallpox ['smɔl͵pɑks] s Pocken pl

small' print' s Kleindruck m

small' talk' s Geplauder n

small'-time' adj klein

small'-town' adj kleinstädtisch

smart [smɑrt] adj (bright) klug; (neat, trim) schick; (car) schneidig; (pej) überklug || s Schmerz m || intr weh tun; (burn) brennen

smart' al'eck s [͵ælɪk] s Neunmalkluge mf

smart'-look'ing adj schnittig

smart' set' s elegante Welt f

smash [smæʃ] s (hit) (coll) Bombe f; (tennis) Schmetterschlag m || tr zerschmettern; (e.g., a window) einschlagen; (sport) schmettern; **s. up** zerknallen || intr zerbrechen; **s. into** krachen gegen

smash' hit' s (theat) Bombenerfolg m

smash'-up' s (aut) Zusammenstoß m

smattering ['smætərɪŋ] s (of) oberflächliche Kenntnis f (genit)

smear [smɪr] s Schmiere f; (smudge) Schmutzfleck m; (vilification) Verunglimpfung f; (med) Abstrich m || tr (spread) schmieren; (make dirty) beschmieren; (vilify) verunglimpfen; (trounce) vollständig fertigmachen

smear' campaign' s Verleumdungsfeldzug m

smell [smɛl] s Geruch m; (aroma) Duft m; (sense) Geruchssinn m || v (pret & pp smelled & smelt [smɛlt]) tr riechen; (danger, trouble) wittern || intr (of) riechen (nach)

smell'ing salts' pl Riechsalz n

smelly ['smɛli] adj übelriechend

smelt [smɛlt] s (fish) Stint m || tr schmelzen, verhütten

smile [smaɪl] s Lächeln n || intr lächeln; **s. at** anlächeln; (clandestinely) zulächeln (dat); **s. on** lächeln (dat)

smirk [smɪrk] s Grinsen n || intr grinsen

smite [smaɪt] v (pret **smote** [smot]; pp **smitten** ['smɪtən] & **smit** [smɪt]) tr schlagen; (said of a plague) befallen; **smitten with** hingerissen von

smith [smɪθ] s Schmied m

smithy ['smɪθi] s Schmiede f

smock [smɑk] s Kittel m, Bluse f

smog [smɑg] s Smog m

smoke [smok] s Rauch m; (heavy smoke) Qualm m; **go up in s.** (fig) in Dunst und Rauch aufgehen || tr rauchen; (meat) räuchern || intr rauchen; (said of a chimney) qualmen

smoke' bomb' s Rauchbombe f

smoked' ham' s Räucherschinken m

smoker ['smokər] s Raucher –in mf; (sl) obszöner Film m

smoke' screen' s Rauchvorhang m

smoke'stack' s Schornstein m

smok'ing s Rauchen n; **no s.** (public sign) Rauchen verboten

smok'ing car' s Raucherwagen m

smok'ing jack'et s Hausjacke f

smoky ['smoki] adj rauchig

smolder ['smoldər] intr (& fig) schwelen

smooch [smutʃ] intr sich abknutschen

smooth [smuð] adj (surface; talker; landing, operation) glatt; (wine) mild || tr glätten; **s. away** (difficulties) beseitigen; **s. out** glätten; **s. over** beschönigen

smooth'-faced' adj glattwangig

smooth-shaven ['smuð'ʃevən] adj glattrasiert

smooth-talk'ing adj schönrednerisch

smoothy ['smuði] s Schönredner –in mf

smother ['smʌðər] tr ersticken; **s. with** kisses abküssen

smudge [smʌdʒ] s Schmutzfleck m || tr beschmutzen || intr schmutzig werden

smug [smʌg] adj (smugger; smuggest) selbstgefällig

smuggle ['smʌgəl] tr & intr schmuggeln

smuggler ['smʌglər] s Schmuggler –in mf

smug'gling s Schmuggel m

smut [smʌt] s Schmutz m

smutty ['smʌti] adj schmutzig, obszön

snack [snæk] s Imbiß m

snack' bar' s Imbißstube f, Snack Bar f

snaffle ['snæfəl] s Trense f

snag [snæg] s—**hit a s.** auf Schwierigkeiten stoßen || v (pret & pp snagged; ger snagging) tr hängenbleiben mit

snail [snel] s Schnecke f; **at a snail's pace** im Schneckentempo

snake [snek] s Schlange f || intr sich schlängeln

snake'bite' s Schlangenbiß m

snake' in the grass' s heimtückischer Mensch m

snap [snæp] s (sound) Knacks m; (on clothes) Druckknopf m; (of a dog) Biß m; (liveliness) Schwung m; (easy work) Kinderspiel n || v (pret & pp snapped; ger snapping) tr (break) zerreißen, entzweibrechen; (a picture) knipsen; **s. a whip** mit der

Peitsche knallen; **s. back** (*words*) hervorstoßen; (*the head*) zurückwerfen; **s. off** abbrechen; **s. one's fingers** mit den Fingern schnalzen; **s. s.o.'s head off** j-n zusammenstauchen; **s. up** gierig an sich reißen; (*buy up*) aufkaufen || *intr* (*tear*) zerreißen; (*break*) entzweibrechen; **s. at** schnappen nach; (*fig*) anfahren; **s. out of it!** komm zu dir!; **s. shut** zuschnappen; **s. to it!** mach zu!

snap'drag'on s (bot) Löwenmaul n

snap' fas'tener s Druckknopf m

snap' judg'ment s vorschnelles Urteil n

snap'per soup' ['snæpər] s Schildkrötensuppe f

snappish ['snæpɪʃ] adj bissig

snappy ['snæpɪ] adj (*caustic*) bissig; (*lively*) energisch; **make it s.!** mach schnell!

snap'shot' s Schnappschuß m

snare [sner] s Schlinge f || tr mit e-r Schlinge fangen; (fig) fangen

snare' drum' s Schnarrtrommel f

snarl [snɑrl] s (*tangle*) Verwicklung f; (*sound*) Knurren n || tr verwickeln; **s. traffic** e-e Verkehrsstockung verursachen || intr knurren

snatch [snætʃ] s—in **snatches** ruckweise; **snatches** (*of conversation*) Bruchstücke pl || tr schnappen; **s. away from** entreißen (dat); **s. up** schnappen

snazzy ['snæzi] adj (sl) schmissig

sneak [snik] s Schleicher –in mf || tr (*e.g., a drink*) heimlich trinken; **s. in** einschmuggeln || intr schleichen; **s. away** sich davonschleichen; **s. in** sich einschleichen; **s. out** sich herausschleichen; **s. up on s.o.** an j-n heranschleichen

sneaker ['snikər] s Tennisschuh m

sneaky ['sniki] adj heimtückisch

sneer [snɪr] s Hohnlächeln n || intr höhnisch grinsen; **s. at** spötteln über (acc)

sneeze [sniz] s Niesen n || tr—**not to be sneezed at** nicht zu verachten || intr niesen

snicker ['snɪkər] s Kichern n || intr kichern

snide' remark' [snaɪd] s Anzüglichkeit f

sniff [snɪf] s Schnüffeln n || tr (be)riechen; **s. out** ausschnüffeln || intr (at) schnüffeln (an dat)

sniffle ['snɪfəl] s Geschnüffel n; **sniffles** Schnupfen m || intr schniefen

snip [snɪp] s (cut) Einschnitt m; (small piece snipped off) Schnippel m || v (pret & pp **snipped**; ger **snipping**) tr & intr schnippeln

snipe [snaɪp] intr—**s. at** aus dem Hinterhalt schießen auf (acc)

sniper ['snaɪpər] s Heckenschütze m

snippet ['snɪpɪt] s Schnippelchen n; (small person) Knirps m

snippy ['snɪpi] adj schroff, barsch

snitch [snɪtʃ] tr (coll) klauen || intr (coll) petzen; **s. on** (coll) verpfeifen

sniv•el ['snɪvəl] s (whining) Gewimmer n; (mucus) Nasenschleim m || v

(pret & pp –el[l]ed; ger –el[l]ing) intr (whine) wimmern; (cry with sniffling) schluchzen; (have a runny nose) e-e tropfende Nase haben

snob [snɑb] s Snob m

snob' appeal' s Snobappeal m

snobbery ['snɑbəri] s Snobismus m

snobbish ['snɑbɪʃ] adj snobistisch

snoop [snup] s (coll) Schnüffler –in mf || intr (coll) schnüffeln

snoopy ['snupi] adj schnüffelnd

snoot [snut] s (sl) Rüssel m; **make a s.** e-e Schnute ziehen

snooty ['snuti] adj hochnäsig

snooze [snuz] s (coll) Nickerchen n || intr (coll) ein Nickerchen machen

snore [snor] s Schnarchen n || intr schnarchen

snort [snɔrt] s Schnauben n || tr wütend schnauben || intr prusten; (said of a horse) schnauben; (with laughter) vor Lachen prusten

snot [snɑt] s (sl) Rotz m

snotty ['snɑti] adj (sl & fig) rotzig

snout [snaut] s Schnauze f, Rüssel m

snow [sno] s Schnee m || tr (sl) einwickeln; **s. in** einschneien; **s. under** mit Schnee bedecken || impers—**it is snowing** es schneit

snow'ball' s Schneeball m || intr (fig) lawinenartig anwachsen

snow'bank' s Schneeverwehung f

snow'bird' s Schneefink m

snow' blind'ness s Schneeblindheit f

snow' blow'er s Schneefräse f

snow'bound' adj eingeschneit

snow'-capped' adj schneebedeckt

snow' chain' s (aut) Schneekette f

snow'-clad' adj verschneit

snow'drift' s Schneeverwehung f

snow'fall' s Schneefall m

snow'flake' s Schneeflocke f

snow' flur'ry s Schneegestöber n

snow' job' s—**give s.o. a s.** (sl) j-n hereinlegen

snow'man' s (–men) Schneemann m

snow'mobile' s Motorschlitten m

snow'plow' s Schneepflug m

snow'shoe' s Schneeteller m

snow'shov'el s Schneeschaufel f

snow'storm' s Schneesturm m

snow' tire' s Winterreifen m

Snow' White' s Schneewittchen n

snow'-white' adj schneeweiß

snowy ['sno-i] adj schneeig

snub [snʌb] s verächtliche Behandlung f || v (pret & pp **snubbed**; ger **snubbing**) tr (ignore) schneiden; (treat contemptuously) verächtlich behandeln

snubby ['snʌbi] adj (nose) etwas abgestumpft; (person) abweisend

snub'-nosed' adj stupsnasig

snuff [snʌf] s Schnupftabak m; (of a candle) Schnuppe f; **up to s.** (sl) auf Draht || tr—**s. out** (a candle) auslöschen; (suppress) unterdrücken

snuff'box' s Schnupftabakdose f

snug [snʌg] adj (snugger; snuggest) behaglich; (fit) eng angeschmiegt; **s. as a bug in a rug** wie die Made im Speck

snuggle ['snʌgəl] *intr*—**s. up (to)** sich schmiegen (an *acc*)

so [so] *adv* (with adjectives or adverbs) so; (*thus*) so; (*for this reason*) daher; (*then*) also; **and so forth** und so weiter; **or so** etwa, e.g., **ten miles or so** etwa zehn Meilen; **so as to** (*inf*) um zu (*inf*); **so far** bisher; **so far as** soviel; **so far, so good** soweit ganz gut; **so I see!** das seh' ich!; **so long!** (coll) bis bald!; **so much** soviel; **so much the better** um so besser; **so that** damit; **so what?** na, und?

soak [sok] *s* Einweichen *n* || *tr* einweichen; (*soak through and through*) durchnässen; (*overcharge*) (sl) schröpfen; **soaked to the skin** bis auf die Haut durchnäßt || *intr* weichen

so'-and-so' *s* (-sos) Soundso *mf*

soap [sop] *s* Seife *f* || *tr* einseifen

soap'box der'by *s* Seifenkistenrennen *n*

soap'box or'ator *s* Straßenredner –in *mf*

soap' bub'ble *s* Seifenblase *f*

soap' dish' *s* Seifenschale *f*

soap' flakes' *spl* Seifenflocken *pl*

soap' op'era *s* (rad) rührselige Hörspielreihe *f*; (telv) rührselige Fernsehspielreihe *f*

soap' pow'der *s* Seifenpulver *n*

soap'stone' *s* Seifenstein *m*

soap'suds' *spl* Seifenlauge *f*

soapy ['sopi] *adj* seifig; (*like soap*) seifenartig

soar [sor] *intr* schweben, (auf)steigen; (*prices*) steigen

sob [sab] *s* Schluchzen *n* || *v* (*pret & pp* **sobbed**; *ger* **sobbing**) *intr* schluchzen

sober ['sobər] *adj* nüchtern || *tr* (up) ernüchtern || *intr*—**s. up** wieder nüchtern werden

sobriety [so'braɪ·əti] *s* Nüchternheit *f*

sob' sto'ry *s* Schmachtfetzen *m*

so'-called' *adj* sogenannt

soccer ['sakər] *s* Fußball *m*

soc'cer play'er *s* Fußballer *m*

sociable ['soʃəbəl] *adj* gesellig

social ['soʃəl] *adj* gesellschaftlich || *s* geselliges Beisammensein *n*

so'cial climb'er *s* Streber –in *mf*

socialism ['soʃə‚lɪzəm] *s* Sozialismus *m*

socialist ['soʃəlɪst] *s* Sozialist –in *mf*

socialistic [‚soʃə'lɪstɪk] *adj* sozialistisch

socialite ['soʃə‚laɪt] *s* Prominente *mf*

socialize ['soʃə‚laɪz] *intr* (with) verkehren (mit)

so'cialized med'icine *s* staatliche Gesundheitspflege *f*

so'cial reg'ister *s* Register *n* der prominenten Mitglieder der oberen Gesellschaftsklasse

so'cial sci'ence *s* Sozialwissenschaft *f*

so'cial secu'rity *s* Sozialversicherung *f*

so'cial wel'fare *s* Sozialfürsorge *f*

so'cial work'er *s* Sozialfürsorger –in *mf*

society [sə'saɪ·əti] *s* Gesellschaft *f*; (*an organization*) Verein *m*

soci'ety col'umn *s* Gesellschaftsspalte *f*

soci'ety for the preven'tion of cru'elty to an'imals *s* Tierschutzverein *m*

sociological [‚sosɪ·ə'lɑdʒɪkəl] *adj* sozialwissenschaftlich, soziologisch

sociologist [‚sosɪ'alədʒɪst] *s* Soziologe *m*, Soziologin *f*

sociology [‚sosɪ'alədʒi] *s* Soziologie *f*

sock [sak] *s* Socke *f*; (sl) Faustschlag *m* || *tr*—**s. it to him!** gib's ihm!; **s.o.** j-m eine 'runterhauen

socket ['sakɪt] *s* (anat) Höhle *f*; (elec) Steckdose *f*; (mach) Muffe *f*

sock'et joint' *s* (anat) Kugelgelenk *n*

sock'et wrench' *s* Steckschlüssel *m*

sod [sad] *s* Rasenstück *n* || *v* (*pret & pp* **sodded**; *ger* **sodding**) *tr* mit Rasen bedecken

soda ['sodə] *s* (*refreshment*) Limonade *f*; (*in mixed drinks*) Selterswasser *n*; (chem) Soda *f & n*

so'da crack'er *s* Keks *m*

so'da wa'ter *s* Sodawasser *n*

sodium ['sodɪ·əm] *s* Natrium *n*

sofa ['sofə] *s* Sofa *n*

soft [sɔft] *adj* (*not hard or tough*) weich; (*not loud*) leise; (*light, music*) sanft; (*sleep, breeze*) leicht; (*effeminate*) verweichlicht; (*muscles*) schlaff; **be s. on** weich sein gegenüber (*dat*)

soft'-boiled egg' *s* weichgekochtes Ei *n*

soft' coal' *s* Braunkohle *f*

soft' drink' *s* alkoholfreies Getränk *n*

soften ['sɔfən] *tr* aufweichen; (*palliate*) lindern; (*water*) enthärten; **s. up** (mil) zermürben || *intr* (& fig) weich werden

soft'-heart'ed *adj* weichherzig

soft' job' *s* Druckposten *m*

soft' land'ing *s* (rok) weiche Landung *f*

soft' pal'ate *s* Hintergaumen *m*

soft'-ped'al *v* (*pret & pp* **-al[l]ed**; *ger* **-al[l]ing**) *tr* zurückhaltender vorbringen

soft'-soap' *tr* (coll) schmeicheln (*dat*)

soggy ['sagi] *adj* (*soaked*) durchnäßt; (*ground*) sumpfig

soil [sɔɪl] *s* Boden *m* || *tr* beschmutzen || *intr* schmutzen

soil' pipe' *s* Abflußrohr *n*

sojourn ['sodʒʌrn] *s* Aufenthalt *m* || *intr* sich vorübergehend aufhalten

solace ['salɪs] *s* Trost *m* || *tr* trösten

solar ['solər] *adj* Sonnen-

so'lar plex'us ['plɛksəs] *s* (anat) Sonnengeflecht *n*

solder ['sadər] *s* Lötmetall *n* || *tr* löten

sol'dering i'ron *s* Lötkolben *m*

soldier ['sodʒər] *s* Soldat *m*

sole [sol] *s* einzig, alleinig || *s* (*of a shoe, foot*) Sohle *f*; (*fish*) Scholle *f* || *tr* (be)sohlen

solely ['soli] *adv* einzig und allein

solemn ['saləm] *adj* feierlich; (*expression*) ernst

solemnity [sə'lɛmnɪti] *s* Feierlichkeit *f*

solicit [sə'lɪsɪt] *tr* (*beg for*) dringend bitten um; (*accost*) ansprechen; (*new members, customers*) werben

solicitor [sə'lɪsɪtər] *s* (com) Agent –in *mf*; (jur) Rechtsanwalt *m*

solicitous [sə'lısıtəs] *adj* fürsorglich

solid ['salıd] *adj (hard, firm, e.g., ice, ground)* fest; *(sturdy, e.g., person, furniture; firm, e.g., foundation, learning; financially sound)* solid(e); *(compact)* kompakt, massiv; *(durable)* dauerhaft; *(gold)* gediegen; *(meal, blow)* kräftig; *(hour)* ganz, geschlagen; *(of one color)* einfarbig; *(color)* getönt; *(of one mind)* einmütig; *(grounds, argument)* stichhaltig; *(row of houses)* geschlossen; *(clouds, fog)* dicht; *(geom)* Raum- ‖ *s* (geom, phys) Körper *m*

solidarity [salı'dærıtı] *s* Solidarität *f*, Verbundenheit *f*

sol'id food' *s* feste Nahrung *f*

sol'id geo'metry *s* Stereometrie *f*

solidi·fy [sə'lıdı,faı] *v (pret & pp -fied) tr* fest werden lassen; *(fig)* konsolidieren ‖ *intr* fest werden

solidity [sə'lıdıtı] *s (state)* Festigkeit *f; (soundness)* Solidität *f*

solidly ['salıdlı] *adv*—**be s. behind s.o.** sich mit j-m solidarisch erklären

sol'id-state' *adj* Transistor-

soliloquy [sə'lıləkwı] *s* Selbstgespräch *n*

solitaire ['salı,ter] *s* Solitär *m*

solitary ['salı,terı] *adj* allein; *(life)* zurückgezogen; *(exception)* einzig; *(lonely)* einsam

sol'itary confine'ment *s* Einzelhaft *f*

solitude ['salı,t(j)ud] *s* Einsamkeit *f; (lonely spot)* abgelegener Ort *m*

so·lo ['solo] *adj & adv* solo ‖ *s* (-los) Solo *n*

so'lo flight' *s* Soloflug *m*

soloist ['solo·ıst] *s* Solist –in *mf*

so'lo part' *s* (mus) Solostimme *f*

solstice ['salstıs] *s* Sonnenwende *f*

soluble ['saljəbəl] *adj* (fig) (auf)lösbar; (chem) löslich

solution [sə'luʃən] *s* Lösung *f*

solvable ['salvəbəl] *adj* (auf)lösbar

solve [salv] *tr* (auf)lösen

solvency ['salvənsı] *s* Zahlungsfähigkeit *f*

solvent ['salvənt] *adj* zahlungsfähig; (chem) (auf)lösend ‖ *s* Lösungsmittel *n*

somber ['sambər] *adj* düster, trüb(e)

some [sʌm] *indef adj* (with singular nouns) etwas; (with plural nouns) manche; (sometimes not translated) e.g., **I am buying s. stockings** ich kaufe Strümpfe; (coll) toll, e.g., **s. girl!** tolles Mädchen!; **at s. time or other** irgendeinmal, irgendwann; **s. ... or other** irgendein; **s. other way** sonstwie ‖ *adv* (with numerals) etwa, ungefähr ‖ *indef pron* manche; (part of) ein Teil *m*; **s. of these people** einige Leute; **s. of us** manche von uns

some'bod'y *indef pron* jemand, irgendwer; **s. else** jemand anderer ‖ *s*—**be a s.** etwas Besonderes sein

some'day' *adv* e-s Tages

some'how' *adv* irgendwie; (for some reason or other) aus irgendeinem Grunde

some'one' *indef pron* jemand, irgendwer; **s. else** jemand anderer; **s. else's** fremd, e.g., **s. else's property** fremdes Eigentum

some'place' *adv* irgendwo; (direction) irgendwohin

somersault ['sʌmər,salt] *s* Purzelbaum *m*; (gym) Überschlag *m*; **do a s.** e-n Purzelbaum schlagen ‖ *intr* sich überschlagen

some'thing' *indef pron* etwas; **he is s. of an expert** er ist e-e Art Experte; **s. else** etwas anderes; **s. or other** irgend etwas

some'time' *adv* einmal; **s. today** irgendwann heute

some'times' *adv* manchmal; **sometimes ... sometimes ... mal ... mal ...**

some'way', **some'ways'** *adv* irgendwie

some'what' *adv* etwas

some'where' *adv* irgendwo; (direction) irgendwohin; **from s. else** sonstwoher; **s. else** sonstwo

somnambulist [sam'næmbjəlıst] *s* Nachtwandler –in *mf*

somnolent ['samnələnt] *adj* schläfrig

son [sʌn] *s* Sohn *m*

sonar ['sonar] *s* Sonar *n*

sonata [sə'natə] *s* Sonate *f*

song [saŋ] *s* Lied *n*; (of birds) Gesang *m*; **for a s.** (coll) um ein Spottgeld

Song' of Songs' *s* (Bib) Hohelied *n*

sonic ['sanık] *adj* Schall-

son'ic boom' *s* Kopfwellenknall *m*

son'-in-law' *s* (sons-in-law) Schwiegersohn *m*

sonnet ['sanıt] *s* Sonett *n*

sonny ['sʌnı] *s* Söhnchen *n*, Kleiner *m*

Son' of Man', **the** *s* (Bib) der Menschensohn

sonorous [sə'norəs] *adj* sonor

soon [sun] *adv* bald; **as s. as** sobald; **as s. as possible** sobald wie möglich; **just as s.** (expressing preference) genauso gern(e); **no sooner said than done** gesagt, getan; **sooner** (expressing time) früher, eher; (expressing preference) lieber, eher; **sooner or later** über kurz oder lang; **the sooner the better** je eher, je besser; **too s.** zu früh

soot [sut] *s* Ruß *m*

soothe [suð] *tr* beschwichtigen, beruhigen; **have a soothing effect on** beruhigend wirken auf (acc)

soothsayer ['suθ,se·ər] *s* Wahrsager *m*

sooty ['sutı] *adj* rußig

sop [sap] *s* eingetunktes Stück *n* Brot; (something given to pacify) Beschwichtigungsmittel *n*; (bribe) Schmiergeld *n*; (spineless person) Waschlappen *m* ‖ *v* (pret & pp sopped) *tr* (dip) eintunken; **sop up** aufsaugen

sophist ['safıst] *s* Sophist –in *mf*

sophisticated [sə'fıstı,ketıd] *adj* (person) weltklug; (way of life) verfeinert; (highly developed) hochentwickelt

sophistication [sə,fıstı'keʃən] *s* Weltklugheit *f*

sophistry ['safıstrı] *s* Sophisterei *f*

sophomore ['sɔfə‚mɔr] *s* Student –in *mf* im zweiten Studienjahr

sop'ping *adj* klatschnaß ‖ *adv—s.* wet klatschnaß

sopran‧o [sə'præno] *adj* Sopran– ‖ *s* (-os) (*uppermost voice*) Sopran *m*; (*soprano part*) Sopranpartie *f*; (*singer*) Sopranist –in *mf*

sorcerer ['sɔrsərər] *s* Zauberer *m*

sorceress ['sɔrsərɪs] *s* Zauberin *f*

sorcery ['sɔrsərɪ] *s* Zauberei *f*

sordid ['sɔrdɪd] *adj* schmutzig; (*improper*) unlauter

sore [sor] *adj* wund; (*sensitive*) empfindlich; (*coll*) (*at*) bös (auf *acc*); be s. weh tun; s. spot (& fig) wunder Punkt *m* ‖ *s* Wunde *f*

sore'head' *s* (coll) Verbitterte *mf*

sorely ['sorlɪ] *adv* sehr

soreness ['sornɪs] *s* Empfindlichkeit *f*

sore' throat' *s* Halsweh *n*

sorority [sə'rɔrɪtɪ] *s* Studentinnenvereinigung *f*

sorrel ['sɔrəl] *adj* fuchsrot ‖ *s* Fuchs *m*; (bot) Sauerampfer *m*

sorrow ['sɔro] *s* Kummer *m* ‖ *intr* (for or over) Kummer haben (um)

sorrowful ['sɔrəfəl] *adj* betrübt

sorry ['sɔrɪ] *adj* traurig, betrübt; (*appearance*) armselig; I am s. es tut mir leid; I am (or feel) s. for him er tut mir leid

sort [sɔrt] *s* Art *f*, Sorte *f*; all sorts of alle möglichen; nothing of the s. nichts dergleichen; out of sorts unpäßlich; s. of (coll) (with adjectives) etwas; (with verbs) irgendwie; (with nouns) so 'n, e.g., I had a s. of feeling that ich hatte so 'ne Ahnung, daß; these sorts of derartige; what s. of was für ein ‖ *tr* sortieren; s. out aussortieren; (fig) sichten

sortie ['sɔrtɪ] *s* (from a fortress) Ausfall *m*; (aer) Einzeleinsatz *m* ‖ *intr* e-n Ausfall machen

so'-so' *adj & adv* soso, leidlich

sot [sɑt] *s* Trunkenbold *m*

soul [sol] *s* (spiritual being; inhabitant) Seele *f*; not a s. (coll) keine Seele *f*; upon my s.! meiner Seele!

sound [saʊnd] *adj* Schall–, Ton–; (*healthy*) gesund; (*valid*) einwandfrei; (*basis*) tragfähig; (*sleep*) fest; (*beating*) (coll) tüchtig; (*business*) solid; (*judgment*) treffsicher ‖ *s* Laut *m*, Ton *m*; (*noise*) Geräusch *n*; (of one's voice) Klang *m*; (narrow body of water) Sund *m*; (phys) Schall *m*; (surg) Sonde *f* ‖ *adv*—be s. asleep fest schlafen ‖ *tr* ertönen lassen; (med) sondieren; (naut) loten; s. s.o. out (coll) j–m auf den Zahn fühlen; s. the alarm Alarm schlagen; s. the all-clear entwarnen ‖ *intr* (er)klingen, (er)tönen; (seem) klingen; (naut) loten; it sounds good to me es kommt mir gut vor; s. off (coll) sich laut beschweren

sound' bar'rier *s* Schallgrenze *f*, Schallmauer *f*

sound' effects' *spl* Klangeffekte *pl*

sound' film' *s* Tonfilm *m*

sound'ing *s* Lotung *f*; take soundings loten

sound'ing board' *s* (on an instrument) Resonanzboden *m*; (over an orchestra or speaker) Schallmuschel *f*; (board for damping sounds) Schalldämpfungsbrett *n*

soundly ['saʊndlɪ] *adv* tüchtig

sound'proof' *adj* schalldicht ‖ *tr* schalldicht machen

sound' stu'dio *s* (cin) Tonatelier *n*

sound' techni'cian *s* Tontechniker *m*

sound' track' *s* (cin) Tonstreifen *m*

sound' truck' *s* Lautsprecherwagen *m*

sound' wave' *s* Schallwelle *f*

soup [sup] *s* Suppe *f*; (thick fog) (coll) Waschküche *f*; in the s. (coll) in der Patsche ‖ *tr*—s. up (aut) frisieren

soup' kitch'en *s* Volksküche *f*

soup'meat' *s* Suppenfleisch *n*

soup' plate' *s* Suppenteller *m*

soup'spoon' *s* Suppenlöffel *m*

sour [saʊr] *adj* (& fig) sauer ‖ *tr* säuern; (fig) verbittern ‖ *intr* säuern; (fig) versauern

source [sors] *s* Quelle *f*

source' lan'guage *s* Ausgangssprache *f*

source' mate'rial *s* Quellenmaterial *n*

sour' cher'ry *s* Weichsel *f*

sour' grapes' *spl* saure Trauben *pl*

sour' note' *s* (& fig) Mißklang *m*

sour'puss' *s* (sl) Sauertopf *m*

souse [saʊs] *s* (sl) Säufer –in *mf*

soused *adj* (sl) besoffen

south [saʊθ] *adj* Süd–, südlich ‖ *adv* (direction) nach Süden; s. of südlich von ‖ *s* Süd(en) *m*

South' Amer'ica *s* Südamerika *n*

south'east' *adj* Südost– ‖ *adv* (direction) südöstlich; s. of südöstlich von ‖ *s* Südost(en) *m*

south'east'ern *adj* südöstlich

southerly ['sʌðərlɪ] *adj* südlich

southern ['sʌðərn] *adj* südlich

southerner ['sʌðərnər] *s* Südländer –in *mf*; (in the U.S.A.) Südstaatler –in *mf*

south'paw' *adj* (coll) linkshändig ‖ *s* (coll) Linkshänder –in *mf*

South' Pole' *s* Südpol *m*

South' Seas' *spl* Südsee *f*

southward ['saʊθwərd] *adv* südwärts

south'west' *adj* Südwest– ‖ *adv* südwestlich; s. of südwestlich von ‖ *s* Südwest(en) *m*

south'west'ern *adj* südwestlich

souvenir [‚suvə'nɪr] *s* Andenken *n*

sovereign ['savrɪn] *adj* souverän ‖ *s* Souverän *m*, Landesfürst *m*

sov'ereign rights' *spl* Hoheitsrechte *pl*

sovereignty ['savrɪntɪ] *s* Souveränität *f*

soviet ['sovɪ‚et] *adj* sowjetisch ‖ *s* Sowjet *m*; the Soviets die Sowjets *pl*

So'viet Rus'sia *s* Sowjetrußland *n*

So'viet Un'ion *s* Sowjetunion *f*

sow [saʊ] *s* Sau *f* ‖ [so] *v* (pret sowed; pp sowed & sown) *tr & intr* säen

soybean ['sɔɪ‚bin] *s* Sojabohne *f*

spa [spɑ] *s* Bad *n*, Badekurort *m*

space [spes] *s* Raum *m*; (between ob-

fects) Zwischenraum *m*; (typ) Spa-
tium *n*; **take up** s. Platz einnehmen
|| *tr* in Abständen anordnen; (typ)
spationieren
space′ age′ *s* Weltraumzeitalter *n*
space′ bar′ *s* (typ) Leertaste *f*
space′ cap′sule *s* (rok) Raumkapsel *f*
space′craft′ *s* Weltraumfahrzeug *n*
space′ flight′ *s* Raumflug *m*
space′man′ *s* (-men′) Raumfahrer *m*
space′ probe′ *s* Sonde *f*
space′ship′ *s* Raumschiff *n*
space′ shot′ *s* Weltraumabschuß *m*
space′ shut′tle *s* Raumfähre *f*
space′ suit′ *s* Raumanzug *m*
space′ trav′el *s* Raumfahrt *f*
spacious [′speʃəs] *adj* geräumig
spade [sped] *s* Spaten *m*; (cards) Pik
n; **call a** s. **a** s. das Kind beim richtigen Namen nennen
spade′work′ *s* (fig) Pionierarbeit *f*
spaghetti [spə′getɪ] *s* Spahetti *pl*
Spain [spen] *s* Spanien *n*
span [spæn] *s* (& fig) Spanne *f*; (*of
a bridge*) Joch *n*; s. **of time** Zeit-
spanne *f* || *v* (*pret & pp* spanned;
ger spanning) *tr* (*e.g., the waist*) umspannen; (*a river*) überbrücken; (*said
of a bridge*) überspannen
spangle [′spæŋgəl] *s* Flitter *m* || *tr* mit
Flitter besetzen
Spaniard [′spænjərd] *s* Spanier -in *mf*
spaniel [′spænjəl] *s* Wachtelhund *m*
Spanish [′spænɪʃ] *adj* spanisch || *s*
Spanisch *n*; **the S.** die Spanier
Span′ish-Amer′ican *adj* spanisch-
amerikanisch || *s* Amerikaner -in *mf*
mit spanischer Muttersprache
Span′ish moss′ *s* Moosbärte *pl*
spank [spæŋk] *tr* (ver)hauen
spank′ing *adj* (*quick*) flink; (*breeze*)
frisch || *adv*—s. **new** funkelnagelneu
|| *s* Schläge *pl*
spar [spar] *s* (aer) Holm *m*; (mineral)
Spat *m*; (naut) Spiere *f* || *v* (*pret &
pp* sparred; *ger* sparring) *intr* sparren
spare [sper] *adj* Ersatz-; (*thin*) mager;
(*time*) frei; (*leftover*) übrig || *s* (aut)
Ersatzreifen *m* || *tr* (*a person*) scho-
nen; (*time, money*) erübrigen; (*expense*) scheuen; (*do without*) entbehren; **have to** s. übrig haben;
s. **s.o. s.th.** j-m etw ersparen
spare′ bed′ *s* Gastbett *n*
spare′ part′ *s* Ersatzteil *n*
spare′rib′ *s* Rippenspeer *m*
spare′ time′ *s* Freizeit *f*
spare′-time′ *adj* nebenberuflich
spare′ tire′ *s* Ersatzreifen *m*
spar′ing *adj* sparsam; **be** s. **with** sparsam umgehen mit
spark [spark] *s* Funke(n) *m* || *tr* (*set
off*) auslösen; (*stimulate*) anregen ||
intr Funken sprühen
spark′ gap′ *s* Funkenstrecke *f*
sparkle [′sparkəl] *s* Funkeln *n* || *intr*
funkeln; (*said of wine*) moussieren
spark′ plug′ *s* Zündkerze *f*
spar′ring part′ner *s* Übungspartner *m*
sparrow [′spæro] *s* Spatz *m*, Sperling
m

spar′row hawk′ *s* Sperber *m*
sparse [spars] *adj* spärlich
Spartan [′spartən] *adj* spartanisch ||
s Spartaner -in *mf*
spasm [′spæzəm] *s* Krampf *m*, Zuk-
kung *f*
spasmodic [spæz′madɪk] *adj* sprunghaft; (pathol) krampfartig
spastic [′spæstɪk] *adj* spastisch
spat [spæt] *s* (coll) Wortwechsel *m*
spatial [′speʃəl] *adj* räumlich
spatter [′spætər] *s* Spritzen *n*; (*stain*)
Spritzfleck *m* || *tr* verspritzen
spatula [′spætʃələ] *s* Spachtel *m & f*
spawn [spɔn] *s* Fischlaich *m* || *tr* her-
vorbringen || *intr* (*said of fish*) laichen
spay [spe] *tr* die Eierstöcke entfernen
aus
speak [spik] *v* (*pret* spoke [spok]; *pp*
spoken) *tr* sprechen; s. **one′s mind**
sich aussprechen || *intr* (**about**) spre-
chen (über *acc*, von); **generally
speaking** im allgemeinen; **so to** s.
sozusagen; **speaking!** (telp) am Apparat!; s. **to** sprechen mit; (*give a
speech to*) sprechen zu; s. **up** lauter
sprechen; (*say something*) den Mund
aufmachen; s. **up!** heraus mit der
Sprache!; s. **up for** eintreten für
speak′-eas′y *s* Flüsterkneipe *f*
speaker [′spikər] *s* Sprecher -in *mf*;
(*before an audience*) Redner -in *mf*;
(parl) Sprecher -in *mf*; (rad) Lautsprecher *m*
spear [spɪr] *s* Speer *m* || *tr* durchboh-
ren; (*a piece of meat*) aufspießen;
(*fish*) mit dem Speer fangen
spear′head′ *s* Speerspitze *f*; (mil) Stoß-
keil *m* || *tr* an der Spitze stehen von
spear′mint′ *s* Krauseminze *f*
special [′speʃəl] *adj* besonder, Sonder-
|| *s* (rr) Sonderzug *m*; **today′s** s.
Stammgericht *n*
spe′cial deliv′ery *s* Eilzustellung *f*;
(*tab on envelope*) Eilsendung *f*
spe′cial-deliv′ery let′ter *s* Eilbrief *m*
specialist [′speʃəlɪst] *s* Spezialist -in
mf
specialization [,speʃəlɪ′zeʃən] *s* Spe-
zialisierung *f*
specialize [′speʃə,laɪz] *intr* sich spezialisieren; **specialized knowledge**
Fachkenntnisse *pl*
spe′cial of′fer *s* (com) Sonderangebot
n
specialty [′speʃəlti] *s* Spezialität *f*;
(*special field*) Spezialfach *n*
spe′cialty shop′ *s* Spezialgeschäft *n*
specie [′spisi] *s*—**in** s. der Art nach
spe·cies [′spisiz] *s* (-cies) Gattung *f*
specific [spɪ′sɪfɪk] *adj* spezifisch
specification [,spesɪfɪ′keʃən] *s* Spe-
zifizierung *f*; **specifications** (tech)
technische Beschreibung *f*
specif′ic grav′ity *s* spezifisches Gewicht *n*
speci·fy [′spesɪ,faɪ] *v* (*pret & pp*
-fied) *tr* spezifizieren; (*stipulate*)
bestimmen
specimen [′spesɪmən] *s* (*example*)
Exemplar *n*; (*test sample*) Probe *f*
specious [′spiʃəs] *adj* Schein-

speck [spek] *s* Fleck *m; (in the distance)* Pünktchen *n;* **s. of dust** Stäubchen *n;* **s. of grease** Fettauge *n*

speckle ['spekəl] *s* Sprenkel *m* ‖ *tr* sprenkeln

spectacle ['spektəkəl] *s* Schauspiel *n,* Anblick *m;* **spectacles** Brille *f*

spec'tacle case' *s* Brillenfutteral *n*

spectacular [spek'tækjələr] *adj* sensationell ‖ *s* (cin) Monsterfilm *m*

spectator ['spektetər] *s* Zuschauer –in *mf*

specter ['spetər] *s* Gespenst *n*

spec·trum ['spektrəm] *s* (-tra [trə]) Spektrum *n*

speculate ['spekjə‚let] *intr* spekulieren; **s.** in spekulieren in (*dat*); **s.** on Überlegungen anstellen über (*acc*)

speculation [‚spekjə'leʃən] *s* Spekulation *f*

speculative ['spekjələtɪv] *adj* (com) Spekulations–; (philos) spekulativ

speculator ['spekjə‚letər] *s* Spekulant –in *mf*

speech [spitʃ] *s* Sprache *f; (address)* Rede *f;* **give a s.** e–e Rede halten

speech' defect' *s* Sprachfehler *m*

speech' imped'iment *s* Sprachstörung *f*

speechless ['spitʃlɪs] *adj* sprachlos

speed [spid] *s* Geschwindigkeit *f; (gear)* Gang *m;* **at top s.** mit Höchstgeschwindigkeit; **pick up s.** auf Touren kommen ‖ *v (pret & pp speeded & sped* [sped]) *tr* beschleunigen; **s. up** forcieren; **s. it up** (coll) ein scharfes Tempo vorlegen ‖ *intr* (aut) rasen; *(above the speed limit)* (aut) zu schnell fahren

speed'boat' *s* Schnellboot *n*

speed'ing *s* (aut) Schnellfahren *n;* **be arrested for s.** wegen Überschreitung der Höchstgeschwindigkeit verhaftet werden; **no s.** *(public sign)* Schnellfahren verboten

speed' lim'it *s* Geschwindigkeitsgrenze *f*

speed' of light' *s* Lichtgeschwindigkeit *f*

speed' of sound' *s* Schallgeschwindigkeit *f*

speedometer [spi'dɑmɪtər] *s* Tachometer *n; (mileage indicator)* Meilenzähler *m,* Kilometerzähler *m*

speed' rec'ord *s* Geschwindigkeitsrekord *m*

speed' trap' *s* Autofalle *f*

speed'way' *s* (aut) Rennstrecke *f*

speedy ['spidi] *adj* schnell, schleunig; *(reply)* baldig

speed' zone' *s* Geschwindigkeitsbeschränkung *f*

spell [spel] *s (short period)* Zeitlang *f; (attack)* Anfall *m; (magical influence)* Bann *m;* **be under s.o.'s s.** in j–s Bann stehen; **cast a s.** bannen ‖ *v (pret & pp spelled & spelt* [spelt]) *tr* buchstabieren; *(in writing)* schreiben; **s. out** Buchstaben für Buchstaben lesen; (fig) auseinanderklamüsern; **s. trouble** Schwie-

rigkeiten bedeuten ‖ *intr* buchstabieren

spell'bind'er *s* faszinierender Redner *m*

spell'bound' *adj* gebannt

spell'ing *s* Schreibweise *f; (orthography)* Rechtschreibung *f*

spell'ing bee' *s* orthographischer Wettbewerb *m*

spelt [spelt] *s* Spelz *m*

spelunker [spɪ'lʌŋkər] *s* Höhlenforscher –in *mf*

spend [spend] *v (pret & pp spent* [spent]) *tr (money)* ausgeben; *(time)* verbringen; **s. the night** übernachten; **s. time and effort on** Zeit und Mühe verwenden auf (*acc*)

spend'thrift' *s* Verschwender –in *mf*

spent [spent] *adj (exhausted)* erschöpft; *(cartridge)* leergeschossen

sperm [spʌrm] *s* Sperma *n*

sperm' whale' *s* Pottwal *m*

spew [spju] *tr* erbrechen; (fig) ausspeien ‖ *intr* sich erbrechen; (fig) herausströmen

sphere [sfɪr] *s* Kugel *f,* Sphäre *f;* (fig) Bereich *m;* **s. of influence** Einflußsphäre *f*

spherical ['sferɪkəl] *adj* sphärisch, kugelförmig

sphinx [sfɪŋks] *s* (**sphinxes & sphinges** ['sfɪndʒiz]) Sphinx *f*

spice [spaɪs] *s* Gewürz *n,* Würze *f;* (fig) Würze *f* ‖ *tr* würzen

spick-and-span ['spɪkənd'spæn] *adj* blitzblank

spicy ['spaɪsi] *adj* würzig; (fig) pikant

spider ['spaɪdər] *s* Spinne *f*

spi'derweb' *s* Spinnengewebe *n*

spiffy ['spɪfi] *adj* (sl) fesch

spigot ['spɪgət] *s* Wasserhahn *m*

spike [spaɪk] *s (nail)* langer Nagel *m; (in volleyball)* Schmetterball *m;* (bot) Ähre *f;* (rr) Schwellenschraube *f;* (sport) Dorn *m* ‖ *tr (a drink)* e–n Schuß Alkohol tun in (*acc*); *(in volleyball)* schmettern

spill [spɪl] *s (spilling)* Vergießen *n; (stain)* Fleck *m,* Klecks *m; (fall)* Sturz *m;* **take a s.** stürzen ‖ *v (pret & pp spilled & spilt* [spɪlt]) *tr* verschütten; *(a rider)* abwerfen; **s. out** ausschütten; **s. the beans** (sl) alles ausplaudern ‖ *intr* überlaufen; **s. over into** (fig) übergreifen auf (*acc*)

spill'way' *s* Überlauf *m*

spin [spɪn] *s (rotation)* Umdrehung *f; (short ride)* kurze Fahrt *f;* (aer) Trudeln *n;* **go for a s.** e–e Spritztour machen; **go into a s.** (aer) ins Trudeln kommen ‖ *v (pret & pp spun* [spʌn]) *ger spinning) tr (rotate)* drehen; (tex) spinnen; **s. out** *(a story)* ausspinnen; **s. s.o. around** j–n im Kreise herumwirbeln ‖ *intr* kreiseln, sich drehen; (tex) spinnen; **my head is spinning** mir dreht sich alles im Kopf

spinach ['spɪnɪtʃ] *s* Spinat *m*

spi'nal col'umn ['spaɪnəl] *s* Wirbelsäule *f*

spi'nal cord' *s* Rückenmark *n*

spi'nal flu'id s Rückenmarksflüssigkeit f

spindle ['spɪndəl] s Spindel f

spin'-dry' v (pret & pp **–dried**) tr schleudern

spin'-dry'er s Trockenschleuder m

spine [spaɪn] s Rückgrat n, Wirbelsäule f; (bb) Buchrücken m

spineless ['spaɪnlɪs] adj (& fig) rückgratlos

spinet ['spɪnɪt] s Spinett n

spinner ['spɪnər] s Spinner –in mf; (mach) Spinnmaschine f

spin'ning adj (rotating) sich drehend; (tex) Spinn– ‖ s (tex) Spinnen n

spin'ning wheel' s Spinnrad n

spinster ['spɪnstər] s alte Jungfer f

spi'ral ['spaɪrəl] adj spiralig ‖ s Spirale f; **s. of rising prices and wages** Lohn-Preis-Spirale f ‖ v (pret & pp **–ral[l]ed**; ger **–ral[l]ing**) intr sich in die Höhe schrauben

spi'ral stair'case s Wendeltreppe f

spire [spaɪr] s Spitze f

spirit ['spɪrɪt] s Geist m; (enthusiasm) Schwung m; (ghost) Geist m; **in high spirits** in gehobener Stimmung; **in low spirits** in gedrückter Stimmung; **spirits** Spirituosen pl; **that's the right s.!** das ist die richtige Einstellung! ‖ tr—**s. away** wegzaubern

spir'ited adj lebhaft; (horse) feurig

spiritless ['spɪrɪtlɪs] adj schwunglos

spiritual ['spɪrɪt/ʊ-əl] adj (incorporeal) geistig; (of the soul) seelisch; (religious) geistlich ‖ s geistliches Negerlied n

spiritualism ['spɪrɪt/ʊə ˌlɪzəm] s Spiritismus m

spiritualist ['spɪrɪt/ʊ-əlɪst] s Spiritist –in mf

spir'itual life' s Seelenleben n

spit [spɪt] s Spucke f; (culin) Spieß m ‖ v (pret & pp spat [spæt] & spit; ger **spitting**) tr & intr spucken

spite [spaɪt] s Trotz m; **for s.** aus Trotz; **in s. of** trotz (genit) ‖ tr kränken; **he did it to s. me** er hat es mir zum Trotz getan

spiteful ['spaɪtfəl] adj gehässig

spit'fire s (coll) Sprühteufel m

spit'ting im'age s (coll) Ebenbild n

spittoon [spɪ'tun] s Spucknapf m

splash [splæʃ] s Platschen n; (noise of falling into water) Klatschen n; **make a s.** (coll) Aufsehen erregen ‖ tr (a person, etc.) bespritzen; (e.g., water) spritzen ‖ intr klatschen, patschen; **s. about** planschen; **s. down** (rok) wassern ‖ interj schwaps!, platsch!

splash'down' s (rok) Wasserung f

splatter ['splætər] tr & intr kleckern

spleen [splin] s Milz f; (fig) schlechte Laune f; **vent one's s. on** seiner schlechten Laune Luft machen gegenüber (dat)

splendid ['splendɪd] adj prächtig, herrlich; (coll) großartig

splendor ['splendər] s Herrlichkeit f

splice [splaɪs] s Spleiß m ‖ tr (a rope) spleißen; (film) zusammenkleben

splint [splɪnt] s Schiene f; **put in splints** schienen

splinter ['splɪntər] s Splitter m ‖ tr (zer)splittern

splin'ter group' s Splittergruppe f

split [splɪt] adj rissig ‖ s Riß m, Spalt m; (fig) Spaltung f; (gym) Spagat m ‖ v (pret & pp split; ger **splitting**) tr spalten; (pants) platzen; (profits, the difference) sich teilen in (acc); **s. hairs** Haarspalterei treiben; **s. one's sides laughing** vor Lachen platzen; **s. open** aufbrechen ‖ intr (into) sich spalten (in acc); **splitting headache** rasende Kopfschmerzen pl; **s. up** (said of a couple) sich trennen

split' infin'itive s gespaltener Infinitiv m

split'-lev'el adj mit Zwischenstockwerk versehen

split' personal'ity s gespaltene Persönlichkeit f

split' sec'ond s Sekundenbruchteil m

splotch [splɑt/] s Klecks m ‖ tr kleckern

splotchy ['splɑt/i] adj fleckig

splurge [splʌrdʒ] s—**go on a s.** verschwenderischen Aufwand treiben ‖ tr verschwenden ‖ intr (on) verschwenderische Ausgaben machen (für)

splutter ['splʌtər] s Geplapper n ‖ tr (words) heraussprudeln; (besplatter) bespritzen ‖ intr plappern; (said, e.g., of grease) spritzen

spoil [spoɪl] s—**spoils** Beute f ‖ v (pret & pp spoiled & spoilt [spoɪlt]) tr (perishable goods; fun) verderben; (a child) verziehen, verwöhnen ‖ intr verderben, schlecht werden; **spoiling for a fight** zanksüchtig

spoilage ['spoɪlɪdʒ] s Verderb m

spoil'sport' s Spielverderber –in mf

spoils' sys'tem s Futterkrippensystem n

spoke [spok] s Speiche f

spokes'man s (–men) Wortführer –in mf

sponge [spʌndʒ] s Schwamm m ‖ tr schnorren ‖ intr schnorren; **s. on** (coll) schmarotzen bei

sponge' cake' s Sandtorte f

sponger ['spʌndʒər] s Schmarotzer –in mf

sponge' rub'ber s Schaumgummi m & n

spongy ['spʌndʒi] adj schwammig

sponsor ['spɑnsər] s Förderer –in mf; (of a program) Sponsor m; (of an immigrant) Bürge m, Bürgin f; (at baptism or confirmation) Pate m, Patin f ‖ tr fördern; (a program) finanziell fördern

spontaneity [spɑntə'ni-ɪti] s Spontaneität f

spontaneous [spɑn'teni-əs] adj spontan

sponta'neous combus'tion s Selbstverbrennung f

spontaneously [spɑn'teni-əsli] adv von selbst, unaufgefordert

spoof [spuf] *s* (*hoax*) Jux *m*; (*parody*)
(on) Parodie *f* (auf *acc*) ‖ *intr*
albern

spook [spuk] *s* (coll) Spuk *m*

spooky ['spukɪ] *adj* spukhaft

spool [spul] *s* Spule *f*, Rolle *f*

spoon [spun] *s* Löffel *m*; **wooden s.**
Kochlöffel *m* ‖ *tr* (out) löffeln

spoonerism ['spunə‚rɪzəm] *s* Schüttelreim *m*

spoon'-feed' *v* (*pret & pp* –fed) *tr* (fig)
es leicht machen (*dat*)

spoonful ['spunful] *s* Löffel *m*

sporadic [spə'rædɪk] *adj* vereinzelt

spore [spor] *s* Spore *f*

sport [sport] *s* Sport– ‖ *s* Sport *m*;
(biol) Spielart *f*; **a good s.** ein
Pfundskerl *m*; **go in for sports** sporteln; **in s. im** Spaß; **make s. of** sich
lustig machen über (*acc*); **play
sports** Sport treiben; **poor s.** Spielverderber –in *mf*; **sports** Sport *m*;
(sportscast) Sportbericht *m* ‖ *intr*
sich belustigen

sport'ing event' *s* Sportveranstaltung *f*

sport'ing goods' *spl* Sportwaren *pl*

sport' jac'ket *s* Sportjacke *f*

sports' car' *s* Sportwagen *m*

sports'cast' *s* Sportbericht *m*

sports'cast'er *s* Sportberichterstatter *m*

sports' fan' *s* Sportfreund –in *mf*

sport' shirt' *s* Sporthemd *n*

sports'man *s* (–men) Sportsmann *m*

sports'manlike *adj* sportlich

sports'manship' *s* sportliches Verhalten
n

sports' news' *s* Sportnachrichten *pl*

sports'wear' *s* Sportkleidung *f*

sports' world' *s* Sportwelt *f*

sports' writ'er *s* Sportjournalist –in *mf*

sporty ['sportɪ] *adj* auffallend

spot [spat] *s* (stain) Fleck(en) *m*;
(place) Platz *m*, Ort *m*; (as on a
leopard) Tüpfel *m & n*; **be on the s.**
(be present) zur Stelle sein; (be in
difficulty) in der Klemme sein; **hit
the s.** gerade das Richtige sein; **on
the s.** auf der Stelle; **put on the s.**
in Verlegenheit bringen ‖ *v* (*pret &
pp* **spotted; ger** spotting) *tr* (stain)
beflecken; (espy) erblicken; (points
in betting) vorgeben

spot' announce'ment *s* Durchsage *f*

spot' cash' *s* ungebundene Barmittel
pl

spot' check' *s* Stichprobe *f*

spot'-check' *tr* stichprobenweise prüfen

spotless ['spatlɪs] *adj* makellos

spot'light' *s* Scheinwerfer *m*; **in the s.**
(fig) im Rampenlicht der Öffentlichkeit ‖ *tr* (fig) in den Vordergrund
stellen

spot' remov'er [rɪ‚muvər] *s* Fleckputzmittel *n*

spotty ['spatɪ] *adj* fleckig; (uneven)
ungleichmäßig

spot' weld'ing *s* Punktschweißung *f*

spouse [spaus] *s* Gatte *m*, Gattin *f*

spout [spaut] *s* (of a pot) Tülle *f*;
(jet of water) Strahl *m* ‖ *tr* (& fig)
hervorsprudeln ‖ *intr* spritzen; (coll)
große Reden schwingen

sprain [spren] *s* Verstauchung *f* ‖ *tr*
verstauchen; **s. one's ankle** sich [*dat*]
den Fuß vertreten

sprat [spræt] *s* (ichth) Sprotte *f*

sprawl [sprɔl] *intr* (out) alle viere von
sich ausstrecken; (said of a city)
sich weit ausbreiten

spray [spre] *s* (of ocean) Gischt *m*;
(from a can) Spray *n*; (from a fountain) Sprühwasser *n*; **s. of flowers**
Blütenzweig *m* ‖ *tr* spritzen; (liquids)
zerstäuben; (plants) besprühen

sprayer ['spre‑ər] *s* Zerstäuber *m*; (for
a garden) Gartenspritze *f*

spray' gun' *s* Spritzpistole *f*

spray' paint' *s* Spritzfarbe *f*

spread [spred] *s* (act of spreading)
Ausbreitung *f*; (extent) Verbreitung
f; (e.g., of a tree) Umfang *m*; (on
bread) Aufstrich *m*; (bedspread) Bettdecke *f*; (large piece of land) weite
Fläche *f*; (of a shot) Streubereich
m & n; (sumptuous meal) Gelage *n*
‖ *v* (*pret & pp* spread) *tr* (warmth,
light, news, rumors) verbreiten; (mortar, glue) auftragen; (e.g., butter)
aufstreichen; (the legs) spreizen;
(manure) streuen; **s. oneself too thin**
sich verzetteln; **s. out over a year**
über ein Jahr verteilen ‖ *intr* sich
verbreiten; (said of margarine) sich
aufstreichen lassen

spree [spri] *s* Bummel *m*; (carousal)
Zechgelage *n*; **go on a buying s.**
in e-e Kauforgie stürzen

sprig [sprɪg] *s* Zweiglein *n*

sprightly ['spraɪtlɪ] *adj* lebhaft; (gait)
federnd

spring [sprɪŋ] *adj* Frühlings– ‖ *s* (of
water) Quelle *f*; (season) Frühling
m; (resilience) Sprungkraft *f*; (of
metal) Feder *f*; (jump) Sprung *m*;
springs (aut) Federung *f* ‖ *v* (*pret*
sprang [spræŋ] *& sprung* [sprʌŋ];
pp **sprung** [sprʌŋ]) *tr* (a trap) zuschnappen lassen; (a leak) bekommen; (a question) (on) plötzlich
stellen (*dat*); (a surprise) (on) bereiten (*dat*); **s. the news on s.o.** j-n
mit der Nachricht überraschen ‖ *intr*
springen; **s. back** zurückschnellen;
s. from entspringen (*dat*); **s. up** aufspringen; (said of industry, towns)
aus dem Boden schießen

spring'board' *s* (& fig) Sprungbrett *n*

spring' chic'ken *s* Hähnchen *n*; **she's
no s.** (sl) sie ist nicht die Jüngste

spring' fe'ver *s* Frühlingsmüdigkeit *f*

spring'time' *s* Frühlingszeit *f*

spring' wa'ter *s* Quellwasser *n*

springy ['sprɪŋɪ] *adj* federnd

sprinkle ['sprɪŋkəl] *s* Spritzen *n*;
(light rain) Sprühregen *m* ‖ *tr*
(water, streets, lawns, laundry)
sprengen; (e.g., sugar) streuen ‖ *intr*
sprühen

sprinkler ['sprɪŋklər] *s* (truck) Sprengwagen *m*; (for the lawn) Rasensprenger *m*; (eccl) Sprengwedel *m*

sprin'kling *s* Sprengung *f*; **a s. of** (e.g.,
sugar) ein bißchen; (e.g., of people)
ein paar

sprin′kling can′ *s* Gießkanne *f*
sprin′kling sys′tem *s* Feuerlöschanlage *f*
sprint [sprɪnt] *s* Sprint *m* ‖ *intr* sprinten
sprinter [′sprɪntər] *s* Sprinter –in *mf*
sprite [spraɪt] *s* Kobold *m*, Elfe *f*
sprocket [′sprɑkɪt] *s* Zahnrad *n*
sprout [spraut] *s* Sproß *m* ‖ *intr* sprießen
spruce [sprus] *adj* schmuck ‖ *s* (bot) Fichte *f* ‖ *intr*—s. up sich schmücken
spry [spraɪ] *adj* (spryer & sprier; spryest & spriest) flink
spud [spʌd] *s* (for weeding) Jäthacke *f*; (potatoe) (coll) Kartoffel *f*
spume [spjum] *s* Schaum *m*
spun′ glass′ *s* Glasfaser *f*
spunk [spʌŋk] *s* (coll) Mumm *m*
spunky [′spʌŋki] *adj* (coll) feurig
spur [spʌr] *s* (on riding boot; on a rooster) Sporn *m*; (of a mountain) Ausläufer *m*; (fig) Ansporn *m*; (archit) Strebe *f*; (bot) Stachel *m*; (rr) Seitengleis *n*; **on the s. of the moment** der Eingebung des Augenblicks folgend ‖ *v* (pret & pp spurred; ger spurring) *tr* die Sporen geben (dat); s. on anspornen
spurious [′spjurɪ-əs] *adj* unecht
spurn [spʌrn] *tr* verschmähen
spurt [spʌrt] *s* Ruck *m*; (sport) Spurt *m*; **in spurts** ruckweise ‖ *tr* speien ‖ *intr* herausspritzen; (sport) spurten
sputnick [′spʌtnɪk] *s* Sputnik *m*
sputter [′spʌtər] *s* Stottern *n* ‖ *tr* umherspritzen; (words) hervorsprudeln ‖ *intr* (said of a person, engine) stottern; (said of a candle, fire) flackern
sputum [′spjutəm] *s* Sputum *n*
spy [spaɪ] *s* Spion –in *mf* ‖ *v* (pret & pp spied) *tr*—spy out ausspionieren ‖ *intr* spionieren
spy′glass′ *s* Fernglas *n*
spy′ing *s* Spionage *f*
spy′ ring′ *s* Spionageorganization *f*
squabble [′skwɑbəl] *s* Zank *m* ‖ *intr* zanken
squad [skwɑd] *s* (gym) Riege *f*; (mil) Gruppe *f*; (sport) Mannschaft *f*
squad′ car′ *s* Funkstreifenwagen *m*
squad′ lead′er *s* (mil) Gruppenführer *m*
squadron [′skwɑdrən] *s* (aer) Staffel *f*; (nav) Geschwader *n*
squalid [′skwɑlɪd] *adj* verkommen
squall [skwɔl] *s* Bö *f*
squander [′skwɑndər] *tr* verschwenden
square [skwer] *adj* quadratisch; (mile, meter, foot) Quadrat–; (fellow; meal) anständig; (even) quitt; **ten meters s.** zehn Meter im Quadrat; **ten s. meters** zehn Quadratmeter ‖ *s* Quadrat *n*; (city block) Häuserblock *m*; (open area) Platz *m*; (of a checkerboard or chessboard) Feld *n*; (carp) Winkel *m*; (math) zweite Potenz *f* ‖ *tr* quadrieren; (a number) ins Quadrat erheben; (accounts) abrechnen ‖ *intr*—s. off in Kampfstellung gehen; s. with (agree with)

übereinstimmen mit; (be frank with) aufrichtig sein zu
square′ dance′ *s* Reigen *m*
square′ deal′ *s* reelles Geschäft *n*
square′ root′ *s* Quadratwurzel *f*
squash [skwɑʃ] *s* (bot) Kürbis *m* ‖ *tr* (a hat) zerdrücken; (a finger, grape) quetschen; (fig) unterdrücken ‖ *intr* zerdrückt (or zerquetscht) werden
squashy [′skwɑʃi] *adj* weich, matschig
squat [skwɑt] *adj* gedrungen, untersetzt ‖ *s* Hocken *n* ‖ *v* (pret & pp squatted; ger squatting) *intr* hocken; s. down sich (hin)hocken
squatter [′skwɑtər] *s* Ansiedler –in *mf* ohne Rechtstitel
squaw [skwɔ] *s* Indianerin *f*
squawk [skwɔk] *s* Geschrei *n*; (sl) Schimpferei *f* ‖ *intr* schreien; (sl) schimpfen
squeak [skwik] *s* (of a door) Quietschen *n*; (of a mouse) Pfeifen *n* ‖ *intr* quietschen; (said of a mouse) pfeifen
squeal [skwil] *s* Quieken *n* ‖ *intr* (said of a pig) quieken; (said of a mouse) pfeifen; (sl) petzen; s. for joy vor Vergnügen quietschen; s. on (sl) (a pupil) verpetzen; (to the police) verpfeifen
squealer [′skwilər] *s* (sl) Petze *f*
squeamish [′skwimɪʃ] *adj* zimperlich
squeeze [skwiz] *s* Druck *m*; s. of the hand Händedruck *m* ‖ *tr* drücken; (oranges) auspressen; s. into (e.g., a trunk) hineinquetschen; s. out auspressen; s. together zusammenpressen; (e.g., people) zusammenpferchen ‖ *intr*—s. in sich eindrängen; s. through sich durchzwängen (durch)
squelch [skweltʃ] *s* schlagfertige Antwort *f* ‖ *tr* niederschmettern
squid [skwɪd] *s* Tintenfisch *m*
squill [skwɪl] *s* (bot) Meerzwiebel *f*; (zool) Heuschreckenkrebs *m*
squint [skwɪnt] *s* Schielen *n* ‖ *intr* (look with eyes partly closed) blinzeln; (be cross-eyed) schielen; (look askance) (at) argwöhnisch blicken (auf acc)
squint′-eyed′ *adj* schielend
squire [skwaɪr] *s* (hist) Knappe *m*; (jur) Friedensrichter *m*
squirm [skwʌrm] *intr* (through) sich winden (durch); (be restless) zappeln; s. out of sich herauswinden aus
squirrel [′skwʌrəl] *s* Eichhörnchen *n*
squirt [skwʌrt] *s* Spritzer *m*; (boy) (coll) Stöpsel *m* ‖ *tr* (ver)spritzen ‖ *intr* spritzen; s. out herausspritzen
S′S′ troops′ [′es′es] *spl* Schutzstaffel *f*
stab [stæb] *s* Stich *m*; (wound) Stichwunde *f*; make a s. at (coll) probieren ‖ *v* (pret & pp stabbed; ger stabbing) *tr* stechen; (kill) erstechen; (a pig) abstechen; s. s.o. in the back j–m in den Rücken fallen
stability [stə′bɪlɪti] *s* Stabilität *f*
stabilization [ˌstebɪlɪ′zeʃən] *s* (e.g., of prices) Stabilisierung *f*; (aer) Dämpfung *f*

stabilize ['stebɪ͵laɪz] *tr* stabilisieren

stabilizer ['stebɪ͵laɪzər] *s* (aer) Flosse *f*

stab' in the back' *s* Stoß *m* aus dem Hinterhalt

stable ['stebəl] *adj* stabil || *s* Stall *m* || *tr* unterbringen

sta'ble boy' *s* Stalljunge *m*

stack [stæk] *s* (*of papers, books*) Stapel *m*; (*of wheat*) Schober *m*; (*of a ship*) Schornstein *m*; (*of rifles*) Pyramide *f*; **stacks** (libr) Bücherregale *pl* || *tr* (*wood, wheat*) aufstapeln; (*rifles*) zusammensetzen; (*cards*) packen

stadi-um ['stedɪ-əm] *s* (**-ums** & **-a** [ə]) Stadion *n*

staff [stæf] *s* (*rod*) Stab *m*; (*personnel*) Personal *n*; (*of a newspaper*) Redaktion *f*; (mil) Stab *m*; (mus) Notensystem *n* || *tr* mit Personal besetzen

staff' of'ficer *s* Stabsoffizier *m*

staff' ser'geant *s* Feldwebel *m*

stag [stæg] *adj* Herren– || *adv*—**go s.** ohne Damenbegleitung sein || *s* Hirsch *m*

stage [stedʒ] *s* (*of a theater*) Bühne *f*; (*phase*) Stadium *n*; (*stretch*) Strecke *f*; (*of life*) Etappe *f*; (*of a rocket*) Stufe *f*; (*scene*) Szene *f*; **at this s. in diesem Stadium; by easy stages** etappenweise; **final stages** Endstadien *pl* || *tr* (*a play*) inszenieren; (*a comeback*) veranstalten

stage'coach' *s* Postkutsche *f*

stage'craft' *s* Bühnenkunst *f*

stage' direc'tion *s* Bühnenanweisung *f*

stage' door' *s* Bühneneingang *m*

stage' effect' *s* Bühnenwirkung *f*

stage' fright' *s* Lampenfieber *n*

stage' hand' *s* Bühnenarbeiter –in *mf*

stage' light'ing *s* Bühnenbeleuchtung *f*

stage' man'ager *s* Bühnenleiter –in *mf*

stage' play' *s* Bühnenstück *n*

stage' prop'erties *spl* Theaterrequisiten *pl*

stagestruck ['stedʒ͵strʌk] *adj* theaterbegeistert

stagger ['stægər] *s* Taumeln *n* || *tr* (*e.g., lunch hours*) staffeln; (& fig) erschüttern || *intr* taumeln

stag'gering *adj* taumelnd; (*blow, loss*) vernichtend; (*news*) erschütternd

stagnant ['stægnənt] *adj* (*water*) stillstehend; (*air*) schlecht; (fig) träge

stagnate ['stægnet] *intr* stagnieren

stag' par'ty *s* Herrenabend *m*

staid [sted] *adj* gesetzt

stain [sten] *s* Fleck *m*; (*paint*) Beize *f* || *tr* beflecken; (*wood*) beizen

stained'-glass win'dow *s* buntes Glasfenster *n*

stainless ['stenlɪs] *adj* rostfrei

stair [ster] *s* Stufe *f*; **stairs** Treppe *f*

stair'case' *s* Treppenhaus *n*

stair'way' *s* Treppenaufgang *m*

stair'well' *s* Treppenschacht *m*

stake [stek] *s* Pfahl *m*; (*bet*) Einsatz *m*; **be s. auf dem Spiel stehen; die at the s.** auf dem Scheiterhaufen sterben; **play for high stakes** viel riskieren; **pull up stakes** (coll) ab-

hauen || *tr* (*plants*) mit e–m Pfahl stützen; **s. off** abstecken; **s. out a claim** (fig) e–e Forderung umreißen

stake'-out' *s* polizeiliche Überwachung *f*

stalactite ['stælæktaɪt] *s* Stalaktit *m*

stalagmite [stə'lægmaɪt] *s* Stalagmit *m*

stale [stel] *adj* (*baked goods*) altbacken; (*e.g., beer*) schal; (*air*) verbraucht; (*joke*) abgedroschen; **get s.** abstehen

stale'mate' *s* (fig) Sackgasse *f*; (chess) Patt *n* || *tr* (fig) in e–e Sackgasse treiben; (chess) patt setzen

stalk [stɔk] *s* (*of grain*) Halm *m*; (*of a plant*) Stiel *m* || *tr* beschleichen; **s. game** pirschen

stall [stɔl] *s* (*for animals*) Stall *m*; (*booth*) Bude *f*; (sl) Vorwand *m* || *tr* (*a motor*) abwürgen; (*a person*) aufhalten || *intr* ausweichen; (aut) absterben; **s. for time** Zeit zu gewinnen suchen

stallion ['stæljən] *s* Hengst *m*

stalwart ['stɔlwərt] *adj* stämmig; (*supporter*) treu

stamen ['stemən] *s* Staubfaden *m*

stamina ['stæmɪnə] *s* Ausdauer *f*

stammer ['stæmər] *s* Stammeln *n* || *tr* & *intr* stammeln

stammerer ['stæmərər] *s* Stammler –in *mf*

stamp [stæmp] *s* (*mark*) Gepräge *n*; (*device for stamping*) Stempel *m*; (*for postage*) Briefmarke *f* || *tr* (*e.g., a document*) stempeln; (*a letter*) freimachen; (*the earth*) stampfen; **s. one's foot** mit dem Fuß aufstampfen; **s. out** (*a fire*) austreten; (*a rebellion*) niederschlagen

stampede [stæm'pid] *s* panische Flucht *f* || *tr* in die Flucht jagen || *intr* in wilder Flucht davonrennen

stamped' en'velope *s* Freiumschlag *m*

stamp'ing grounds' *spl* Lieblingsplatz *m*

stamp' machine' *s* Briefmarkenautomat *m*

stamp' pad' *s* Stempelkissen *n*

stance [stæns] *s* Haltung *f*, Stellung *f*

stanch [stɑntʃ] *tr* stillen

stand [stænd] *s* (*booth*) Stand *m*; (*platform*) Tribüne *f*; (*e.g., for bicycles*) Ständer *m*; (*view, position*) Standpunkt *m*; (*piece of furniture*) Ständer *m*; **take a s.** (on) Stellung nehmen (zu); **take one's s.** (*e.g., near the door*) sich stellen; **s. of timber** Waldbestand *m*; **stands** (sport) Tribüne *f*; **take the s.** (jur) als Zeuge auftreten || *v* (*pret* & *pp* **stood** [stʊd]) *tr* (*put*) stellen; (*the cold, hardships*) aushalten; (*a person*) leiden; **s. a chance** e–e Chance haben; **s. guard** Posten stehen; **s. one's ground** sich behaupten; **s. s.o. up** j–n aufsitzen lassen; **s. the test** sich bewähren || *intr* stehen; (*have validity*) gelten; **she wants to know where she stands** sie will wissen, wie sie daran ist; **s. aside** auf die Seite treten; **s. at attention** stillstehen; **s.**

back zurückstehen; **s. behind** s.o. (fig) hinter j–m stehen; **s. by** (in *readiness*) in Bereitschaft stehen; (a *decision*) bleiben bei; (e.g., *for the latest news*) am Apparat bleiben; **s. by** s.o. j–m beistehen; **s. firm** fest bleiben; **s. for** (*champion*) eintreten für; (*tolerate*) sich [*dat*] gefallen lassen; (*mean*) bedeuten; **s. good for** gutstehen für; **s. idle** stillstehen; **s. on end** sich sträuben, e.g., **my hair stood on end** mir sträubten sich die Haare; **s. on one's head** kopfstehen; **s. out** (*project*) abstehen; (*be conspicuous*) hervorstechen; **s. out against** sich abzeichnen gegen; **s. s.o. in good stead** j–m zugute kommen; **s. up** aufstehen; **s. up against** aufkommen gegen; **s. up for** (a *thing*) verfechten; (a *person*) die Stange halten (*dat*); **s. up to** s.o. j–m die Stirn bieten; **s. up under** aushalten

standard ['stændərd] *adj* Standard–, Normal– ‖ *s* Standard *m*; (*banner*) Banner *n*

stand'ard-bear'er *s* Bannerträger *m*

stand'ard-gauge track' *s* Normalspur *f*

standardize ['stændər‚daɪz] *tr* normen

stand'ard of liv'ing *s* Lebensstandard *m*

stand'ard time' *s* Normalzeit *f*

stand'-by' *adj* Reserve– ‖ *s*—**on s. in** Bereitschaft

standee [stæn'di] *s* Stehplatzinhaber –in *mf*

stand'in' *s* (coll) Ersatzmann *m*; (cin, theat) Double *n*

stand'ing *adj* (army, water, rule) stehend; (*committee*) ständig; (*jump*) aus dem Stand ‖ *s* Stehen *n*; (*social*) Stellung *f*; (of a *team*) Stand *m*; **in good s.** treu; **of long s.** langjährig

stand'ing or'der *s* (com) Dauerauftrag *m*

stand'ing room' *s* Stehplatz *m*; **s. only** nur noch Stehplätze

stand'-off' *s* Unentschieden *n*

stand-offish ['stænd'ofɪʃ] *adj* zurückhaltend

stand'out' *s* Blickfang *m*

stand'point' *s* Standpunkt *m*

stand'still' *s* Stillstand *m*; **come to a s.** zum Stillstand kommen

stanza ['stænzə] *s* Strophe *f*

staple ['stepəl] *adj* Haupt–, Stapel– ‖ *s* (*food*) Hauptnahrungsmittel *n*; (*product*) Hauptprodukt *n*; (*clip*) Heftklammer *f* ‖ *tr* mit Draht heften

stapler ['steplər] *s* Heftmaschine *f*

star [star] *adj* Spitzen–; (astr) Stern– ‖ *s* Stern *m*; (cin, rad, telv, theat) Star *m*; **I saw stars** (fig) Sterne tanzten mir vor den Augen ‖ *v* (*pret & pp* **starred**) *ger* **starring**) *tr* (cin, rad, sport, telv, theat) als Star herausstellen; (*typ*) mit Sternchen kennzeichnen ‖ *intr* Star sein

starboard ['starbərd] *adj* Steuerbord– ‖ *s* Steuerbord *n*

starch [startʃ] *s* Stärke *f* ‖ *tr* stärken

starchy ['startʃi] *adj* stärkenhaltig

stare [ster] *s* starrer Blick *m* ‖ *tr*—

s. down durch Anstarren aus der Fassung bringen ‖ *intr* starren; **s. at** anstarren; **s. into space** ins Leere blicken, ins Blaue starren

star'fish' *s* Seestern *m*

stargazer ['star‚gezər] *s* Sterngucker –in *mf*

stark [stark] *adj* (landscape) kahl; (*sheer*) völlig ‖ *adv* völlig

stark'-na'ked *adj* splitter(faser)nackt

starlet ['starlet] *s* Sternchen *n*

star'light' *s* Sternenlicht *n*

starling ['starlɪŋ] *s* (orn) Star *m*

star'lit' *adj* sternhell

Star of Da'vid *s* David(s)stern *m*

starry ['stari] *adj* gestirnt; (night) sternklar; (sky) Sternen–

star'ry-eyed' *adj* verträumt

Stars' and Stripes' *spl* Sternenbanner *n*

Star'-Spangled Ban'ner *s* Sternenbanner *n*

start [start] *s* Anfang *m*; (*sudden springing movement*) plötzliches Hochfahren *n*; (lead, advantage) Vorgabe *f*, Vorsprung *m*; (of a *race*) Start *m*; **give s.o. a s.** j–m auf die Beine helfen ‖ *tr* anfangen; (a *motor*) anlassen; (a *rumor*) in die Welt setzen; (a *conversation*) anknüpfen; **s. a fire** ein Feuer anmachen; (*said of an arsonist*) e–n Brand legen ‖ *intr* anfangen; **s. in** to (*inf*) anfangen zu (*inf*); **s. out** (*begin*) anfangen; (*start walking*) losgehen; **s. out on** (a *trip*) antreten; **to s. with** zunächst

start'ing gate' *s* Startmaschine *f*

start'ing gun' *s* Startpistole *f*; **at the s.** beim Startschuß

start'ing point' *s* Ausgangspunkt *m*

startle ['startəl] *tr* erschrecken; **be startled** zusammenfahren

starvation [star've/ən] *s* Hunger *m*; **die of s.** verhungern

starva'tion di'et *s* Hungerkur *f*

starva'tion wag'es *spl* Hungerlohn *m*

starve [starv] *tr* verhungern lassen; **s. out** aushungern ‖ *intr* hungern; (coll) furchtbaren Hunger haben; **s. to death** verhungern

state [stet] *adj* staatlich, Staats–; (as *opposed to federal*) bundesstaatlich ‖ *s* (*condition*) Zustand *m*; (*government*) Staat *m*; (of the *U.S.A.*) Bundesstaat *m* ‖ *tr* angeben; (a *rule, problem*) aufstellen; **as stated above** wie oben angegeben

State' Depart'ment *s* Außenministerium *n*

stateless ['stetlɪs] *adj* staatenlos

stately ['stetli] *adj* stattlich

statement ['stetmənt] *s* Angabe *f*; (*from a bank*) Abrechnung *f*; (jur) Aussage *f*

state' of affairs' *s* Lage *f*

state' of emer'gency *s* Notstand *m*

state' of health' *s* Gesundheitszustand *m*

state' of mind' *s* Geisteszustand *m*

state' of war' *s* Kriegszustand *m*

state'-owned' *adj* staatseigen; (*in communistic countries*) volkseigen

state' police' *s* Staatspolizei *f*

state′room′ s (*in a palace*) Prunkzimmer n; (*on a ship*) Passagierkabine f
states′man s (-men) Staatsmann m
states′manlike′ adj staatsmännisch
states′manship′ s Staatskunst f
static ['stætɪk] adj statisch || s (rad) Nebengeräusche pl
station ['steɪʃən] s (*social*) Stellung f; (*of a bus, rail line*) Bahnhof m; (mil) Standort m || tr aufstellen; (mil) stationieren
stationary ['steɪʃə‚nɛri] adj stationär
sta′tion break′ s Werbepause f
stationer ['steɪʃənər] s Schreibwarenhändler –in mf
stationery ['steɪʃə‚nɛri] s Briefpapier n
sta′tionery store′ s Schreibwarenhandlung f
sta′tion house′ s Polizeiwache f
sta′tion identifica′tion s (rad) Pausenzeichen n
sta′tionmas′ter s Bahnhofsvorsteher m
sta′tions of the cross′ spl Kreuzweg m
sta′tion wag′on s Kombiwagen m
statistic [stə′tɪstɪk] s Angabe f; **statistics** (*science*) Statistik f || spl (*data*) Statistik f
statistical [stə′tɪstɪkəl] adj statistisch
statistician [‚stætɪs′tɪʃən] s Statistiker –in mf
statue ['stætʃu] s Statue f
statuesque [‚stætʃʊ′ɛsk] adj statuenhaft
stature ['stætʃər] s Gestalt f; (fig) Format m
status ['steɪtəs] s (*in society*) Stellung f; (e.g., *mental*) Stand m
sta′tus quo′ [kwo] s Status m quo
sta′tus sym′bol s Statussymbol n
statute ['stætʃut] s Satzung f, Statut n
statutory ['stætʃu‚tori] adj statutenmäßig
staunch [stɔntʃ] adj unentwegt
stave [stev] s (*of a barrel*) Daube f; (*of a chair*) Steg m; (*of a ladder*) Sprosse f; (mus) Notensystem n || tr—s. off abwenden
stay [ste] s (*visit*) Aufenthalt m; (*prop*) Stütze f; (*of execution*) Aufschub m || intr bleiben; **have to s. in** (*after school*) nachsitzen müssen; **s. away** wegbleiben; **s. behind** zurückbleiben; (*in school*) sitzenbleiben
stay′-at-home′ s Stubenhocker –in mf
stead [sted] s Statt f; **in s.o.'s s.** an j–s Statt
stead′fast′ adj standhaft
stead·y ['stedi] adj fest, beständig; (*hands*) sicher; (*ladder*) fest; (*pace*) gleichmäßig; (*progress*) ständig; (*nerves*) stark; (*prices*) stabil; (*work*) regelmäßig; **s. customer** Stammkunde m, Stammkundin f; **s. now!** immer langsam! || v (*pret & pp* –ied) tr festigen
steak [stek] s Beefsteak n
steal [stil] s—**it's a s.** (coll) das ist geschenkt || v (*pret* stole [stol]; *pp* stolen) tr stehlen; (*a kiss*) rauben; **s. s.o.'s thunder** j–m den Wind aus den Segeln nehmen; **s. the show** den Vogel abschießen || intr stehlen; **s.**

away wegstehlen; **s. up on s.o.** sich an j–n heranschleichen
stealth [stelθ] s—**by s.** heimlich
stealthy ['stelθi] adj verstohlen
steam [stim] s Dampf m; (*vapor*) Dunst m; (fig) Kraft f; **full s. ahead!** Volldampf voraus!; **let off s.** Dampf ablassen; (fig) sich [dat] Luft machen; **put on s.** (fig) Dampf dahinter machen || tr dämpfen; (culin) dünsten; **s. up beschlagen** || intr dampfen; (culin) dünsten; **s. up sich beschlagen**
steam′ bath′ s Dampfbad n
steam′boat′ s Dampfer m
steam′ en′gine s Dampfmaschine f
steamer ['stimər] s Dampfer m
steam′ heat′ s Dampfheizung f
steam′ i′ron s Dampfbügeleisen n
steam′ roll′er s (& fig) Dampfwalze f || tr glattwalzen; (fig) niederwalzen
steam′ship′ s Dampfschiff n
steam′ship line′ s Dampfschiffahrtslinie f
steam′ shov′el s Dampflöffelbagger m
steamy ['stimi] adj dampfig, dunstig
steed [stid] s Streitroß n
steel [stil] adj stählern, Stahl- || s Stahl m || tr stählen; **s. oneself against s.th.** sich gegen etw wappnen
steel′ wool′ s Stahlwolle f
steel′works′ spl Stahlwerk n
steely ['stili] adj (fig) stählern
steelyard ['stiljərd] s Schnellwaage f
steep [stip] adj steil; (*prices*) happig || tr (*immerse*) eintauchen; (*soak*) einweichen; **be steeped in** (e.g., *prejudice*) durchdrungen sein von; (*be expert in*) ein Kenner sein (*genit*); **s. oneself in** sich versenken in (*acc*)
steeple ['stipəl] s Kirchturm m
stee′plechase′ s Hindernisrennen n
steer [stɪr] s Stier m || tr lenken, steuern; **s. a middle course** e–n Mittelweg einschlagen || intr lenken, steuern; **s. clear of** vermeiden
steerage ['stɪrɪdʒ] s Zwischendeck n
steer′ing wheel′ s Steuerrad n
stellar ['stelər] adj (*role*) Star-; (*attraction*) Haupt–; (astr) Stern(en)–
stem [stem] s (*of a plant*) Halm m; (*of a word; of a tree*) Stamm m; (*of a leaf, fruit; of a glass; of a smoke pipe*) Stiel m; (*of a watch*) Aufziehwelle f; (naut) Steven m; **from s. to stern** von vorn bis achtern || v (*pret & pp* stemmed; *ger* stemming) tr (*check*) hemmen; (*fruit*) entstielen; (*the flow*) (an)stauen; (*the blood*) stillen; (*in skiing*) stemmen || intr— **s. from** (ab)stammen von
stench [stentʃ] s Gestank m
sten·cil ['stensɪl] s (*for printing*) Schablone f; (*for typing*) Matrize f || v (*pret & pp* –cil[l]ed; *ger* –cil[l]ing) tr mittels Schablone aufmalen
stenographer [stə′nɑgrəfər] s Stenograph –in mf
stenography [stə′nɑgrəfi] s Stenographie f
step [step] s Schritt m; (*of a staircase*) Stufe f; (*footprint*) Fußtritt m;

(*measure*) Maßnahme *f*; **be out of s.** nicht Schritt halten; **in. s.** im Takt; **keep in s. with the times** mit der Zeit Schritt halten; **s. by s.** schrittweise; **watch your s.!** Vorsicht! ‖ *v* (*pret & pp* stepped; *ger* stepping) *tr*—**s. down** (elec) heruntertransformieren; **s. off** abschreiten ‖ *intr* schreiten, treten; **s. aside** beiseitetreten; **s. back** zurücktreten; **s. forward** vortreten; **s. on** betreten; **s. on it** (coll) sich beeilen; **s. on s.o.'s toes** (fig) j—m auf die Zehen treten; **s. out** hinausgehen; **s. out on** (*a marriage partner*) betrügen

step'broth'er *s* Stiefbruder *m*

step'child' *s* (–chil'dren) Stiefkind *n*

step'daugh'ter *s* Stieftochter *f*

step'fa'ther *s* Stiefvater *m*

step'lad'der *s* Stehleiter *f*

step'moth'er *s* Stiefmutter *f*

steppe [step] *s* Steppe *f*

step'ping stone' *s* Trittstein *m*; (fig) Sprungbrett *n*

step'sis'ter *s* Stiefschwester *f*

step'son' *s* Stiefsohn *m*

stere·o ['stɛrɪ,o] *adj* Stereo– ‖ *s* (–os) (*sound*) Stereoton *m*, Raumton *m*; (*reproduction*) Raumtonwiedergabe *f*; (*set*) Stereoapparat *m*

stereotyped ['stɛrɪ·ə,taɪpt] *adj* (& fig) stereotyp

sterile ['stɛrɪl] *adj* keimfrei

sterility [stɛ'rɪlɪti] *s* Sterilität *f*

sterilize ['stɛrɪ,laɪz] *tr* sterilisieren

sterling ['stʌrlɪŋ] *adj* (fig) gediegen ‖ *s* (*currency*) Sterling *m*; (*sterling silver*) Sterlingsilber *n*; (*articles of sterling silver*) Sterlingsilberwaren *pl*

stern [stʌrn] *adj* streng; (*look*) finster ‖ *s* (naut) Heck *n*

stethoscope ['stɛθə,skop] *s* Stethoskop *n*

stevedore ['stivə,dor] *s* Stauer *m*

stew [st(j)u] *s* Ragout *n*, Stew *n* ‖ *tr* & *intr* dünsten; (& fig) schmoren

steward ['st(j)u·ərd] *s* (aer, naut) Steward *m*; (*of an estate*) Gutsverwalter *m*; (*of a club*) Tafelmeister *m*

stewardess ['st(j)u·ərdɪs] *s* (aer, naut) Stewardeß *f*

stewed' fruit' *s* Kompott *n*

stick [stɪk] *s* Stecken *m*, Stock *m*; (*for punishment*) Prügel *pl*; (*of candy or gum*) Stange *f*; **the sticks** (coll) die Provinz *f* ‖ *tr* (*with a sharp point; into one's pocket*) stecken; (*paste*) (on) ankleben (an *acc*); **s. it out** durchhalten; **s. one's finger** sich in den Finger stechen; **s. out** herausstrecken; **s. up** (sl) überfallen und berauben ‖ *intr* (*adhere*) kleben; (*be stuck, be tight*) klemmen; **nothing sticks in his mind** (coll) bei ihm bleibt nichts haften; **s. around** (coll) in der Nähe bleiben; **s. by** (coll) Stange halten; **s. close to** sich heften an (*acc*); **s. out** (*said of ears*) abstehen; (*be visible*) heraushängen; **s. to** (fig) beharren auf (*dat*); **s. together** zusammenkleben; (fig) zusammenhalten; **s. up for** sich einsetzen für

sticker ['stɪkər] *s* Klebezettel *m*

stick'-in-the-mud' *s* (coll) Schlafmütze *f*

stickler ['stɪklər] *s* (for) Pedant *m* (in *dat*)

stick'pin' *s* Krawattennadel *f*

stick'-up' *s* (sl) Raubüberfall *m*

sticky ['stɪki] *adj* klebrig; (*air*) schwül; (*ticklish*) heikel

stiff [stɪf] *adj* steif; (*difficult*) schwer; (*drink*) stark; (*opposition*) hartnäckig; (*sentence*) streng; (*bearing*) steif; (*price*) hoch; **s. as a board** stocksteif ‖ *s* (*corpse*) (sl) Leiche *f*; **big s.** (sl) blöder Kerl *m*

stiffen ['stɪfən] *tr* versteifen ‖ *intr* sich versteifen

stiffly ['stɪfli] *adv* gezwungen

stiff'-necked' *adj* mit steifem Hals; (fig) eigensinnig

stifle ['staɪfəl] *tr* (*a yawn*) unterdrücken; (*a person*) ersticken

stig·ma ['stɪgmə] *s* (–mas & mata [mətə]) Brandmal *n*; **stigmata** Wundmale *pl* Christi

stigmatize ['stɪgmə,taɪz] *tr* brandmarken

stile [staɪl] *s* Stiege *f*

stiletto [stɪ'lɛto] *s* (–os) Stilett *n*

still [stɪl] *adj* still, ruhig ‖ *adv* (*up to this time, as yet, even*) noch; (*yet, nevertheless*) dennoch; **keep s.** stillbleiben ‖ *s* (*stillness*) Stille *f*; (*for whiskey*) Brennapparat *m*; (cin) Einzelphotographie *f*; (phot) Standphoto *n* ‖ *tr* stillen

still'born' *adj* totgeboren

still' life' *s* (still lifes & still lives) Stilleben *n*

stilt [stɪlt] *s* Stelze *f*

stilt'ed *adj* (*style*) geschraubt; (archit) auf Pfeilern ruhend

stimulant ['stɪmjələnt] *s* Reizmittel *n*; **act as a s.** anregend wirken

stimulate ['stɪmjə,let] *tr* anregen

stimulation [,stɪmjə'leʃən] *s* Anregung *f*

stimu·lus ['stɪmjələs] *s* (–li [,laɪ]) (& fig) Reizmittel *n*; (fig) Ansporn *m*

sting [stɪŋ] *s* Biß *m*, Stich *m*; (*stinging organ*) Stachel *m* ‖ *v* (*pret & pp* stung [stʌŋ]) *tr* & *intr* stechen

stingy ['stɪndʒi] *adj* geizig

stink [stɪŋk] *s* Gestank *m*; (sl) Krach *m* ‖ *v* (*pret* stank [stæŋk]; *stunk* [stʌŋk]) *tr*—**s. up** verstänkern ‖ *intr* stinken

stinker ['stɪŋkər] *s* (sl) Stinker *m*

stinky ['stɪŋki] *adj* stinkend, stinkig

stint [stɪnt] *s* bestimmte Arbeit *f*; **without s.** freigebig ‖ *tr* einschränken ‖ *intr* (on) knausern (mit)

stipend ['staɪpənd] *s* (*salary*) Gehalt *n*; (*of a scholarship*) Zuwendung *f*

stipple ['stɪpəl] *tr* punktieren

stipulate ['stɪpjə,let] *tr* bedingen; **as stipulated** wie vertraglich festgelegt

stipulation [,stɪpjə'leʃən] *s* Bedingung *f*

stir [stʌr] *s* (*movement*) Bewegung *f*; (*unrest*) Unruhe *f*; (*commotion, ex-*

citement) Aufsehen *n;* **create quite a s.** großes Aufsehen erregen ‖ *v* (*pret & pp* **stirred;** *ger* **stirring**) *tr* e.g., **with a spoon**) (um)rühren; (*said of a breeze*) bewegen; (*the fire*) schüren; **s. up** (*hatred*) entfachen; (*trouble*) stiften; (*people*) aufhetzen ‖ *intr* sich rühren

stir'ring *adj* erregend; (*times*) bewegt; (*speech*) mitreißend; (*song*) schwungvoll

stirrup ['stʌrəp] *s* Steigbügel *m*

stitch [stɪtʃ] *s* Stich *m;* (*in knitting*) Masche *f;* **stitches** (*surg*) Naht *f;* **s. in the side** Seitenstechen *n* ‖ *tr* heften; (*surg*) nähen

stock [stak] *s* (*supplies*) Lager *n;* (*of a gun*) Schaft *m;* (*lineage*) Zucht *f;* (*of paper*) Papierstoff *m;* (*culin*) Fond *m;* (*st. exch.*) Aktie *f;* **in s.** vorrätig, auf Lager; **not put much s. in** nicht viel Wert legen auf (*acc*); **out of s.** nicht (mehr) vorrätig, (*books*) vergriffen; **stocks** (*hist*) Stock *m;* **take s.** den Bestand aufnehmen; **take s. of** (fig) in Betracht ziehen ‖ *tr* auf Lager halten; (*a stream*) (mit Fischen) besetzen; (*a farm*) ausstatten ‖ *intr*—**s. up** (on) sich eindecken (mit)

stockade [sta'ked] *s* Palisade *f;* (mil) Gefängnis *n*

stock'breed'er *s* Viehzüchter –in *mf*

stock'brok'er *s* Börsenmakler –in *mf*

stock' car' *s* (aut) Serienwagen *m;* (sport) als Rennwagen hergerichteter Personenkraftwagen *m*

stock' com'pany *s* (com) Aktiengesellschaft *f;* (theat) Repertoiregruppe *f*

stock' div'idend *s* Aktiendividende *f*

stock' exchange' *s* Börse *f*

stock'hold'er *s* Aktionär –in *mf*

stock'ing *s* Strumpf *m*

stock' in trade' *s* Warenbestand *m;* (fig) Rüstzeug *n*

stock'pile' *s* Vorrat *m* ‖ *tr* aufstapeln

stock'room' *s* Lagerraum *m*

stocky ['staki] *adj* untersetzt

stock'yard' *s* Viehhof *m*

stodgy ['stadʒi] *adj* gezwungen

stogy ['stogi] *s* (coll) Glimmstengel *m*

stoic ['sto·ɪk] *adj* stoisch ‖ *s* Stoiker *m*

stoke [stok] *tr* (*a fire*) schüren; (*a furnace*) heizen

stoker ['stokər] *s* Heizer *m*

stole [stol] *s* (*woman's fur piece*) Pelzstola *f;* (eccl) Stola *f*

stolid ['stalɪd] *adj* unempfindlich

stomach ['stʌmək] *s* Magen *m;* (fig) (**for**) Lust *f* (zu) ‖ *tr* (*food*) verdauen; (fig) vertragen

stom'ach ache' *s* Magenschmerzen *pl*

stone [ston] *adj* steinern ‖ *s* Stein *m;* (*of fruit*) Kern *m;* (pathol) Stein *m* ‖ *tr* steinigen; (*fruit*) entsteinen

stone' age' *s* Steinzeit *f*

stone'-broke' *adj* (coll) völlig abgebrannt

stone'-deaf' *adj* stocktaub

stone' ma'son *s* Steinmetz *m*

stone' quar'ry *s* Steinbruch *m*

stone's' throw' *s* Katzensprung *m*

stony ['stoni] *adj* steinig

stooge [studʒ] *s* Lakai *m*

stool [stul] *s* Schemel *m;* (e.g., **at a bar**) Hocker *m;* (*bowel movement*) Stuhl *m*

stool' pi'geon *s* Polizeispitzel *m*

stoop [stup] *s* Beugung *f;* (*condition of the body*) gebeugte Körperhaltung *f;* (*porch*) kleine Verande *f* ‖ *intr* sich bücken; (*demean oneself*) sich erniedrigen

stoop'-shoul'dered *adj* gebeugt

stop [stap] *s* (*for a bus or streetcar*) Haltestelle *f;* (*layover*) Aufenthalt *m;* (*station*) Station *f;* (*of an organ*) Register *n;* (ling) Verschlußlaut *m;* **bring to a s.** zum Halten bringen; **come to a s.** anhalten; **put a s. to** ein Ende machen (*dat*) ‖ *v* (*pret & pp* **stopped;** *ger* **stopping**) *tr* (*an activity*) aufhören mit; (*ger*) aufhören (zu *inf*); (e.g., **a thief, car**) anhalten; (*bring to a stop with difficulty*) zum Halten bringen; (*delay, detain*) aufhalten; (*a leak*) stopfen; (*a check*) sperren; (*payment*) einstellen; (*the blood*) stillen; (*traffic*) lahmlegen; **s. down** (phot) abblenden; **s. s.o. from** (*ger*) j-n davonhalten zu (*inf*) ‖ *intr* (*cease*) aufhören; (*come to a stop; break down*) stehenbleiben; (*said of a person stopping for a short time or of a vehicle at an unscheduled stop*) anhalten; (*said of a vehicle at a scheduled stop*) halten; **s. at nothing** vor nichts zurückschrecken; **s. dead** plötzlich stehenbleiben; **s. in** vorbeikommen; **s. off at** e-n kurzen Halt machen bei

stop'gap' *adj* Not-, Behelfs- ‖ *s* Notbehelf *m*

stop'light' *s* (*on a car*) Bremslicht *n;* (*traffic light*) Verkehrsampel *f*

stop'o'ver *s* Fahrtunterbrechung *f;* (aer) Zwischenlandung *f*

stoppage ['stapɪdʒ] *s* (*of a pipe*) Verstopfung *f;* (*of payment, of work*) Einstellung *f;* (pathol) Verstopfung *f*

stopper ['stapər] *s* Stöpsel *m;* (*made of cork*) Korken *m*

stop' sign' *s* Haltezeichen *n*

stop'watch' *s* Stoppuhr *f*

storage ['storɪdʒ] *s* Lagerung *f*

stor'age bat'tery *s* Akkumulator *m*

stor'age charge' *s* Lagergebühr *f*

stor'age room' *s* Rumpelkammer *f;* (com) Lagerraum *m*

stor'age tank' *s* Sammelbehälter *m*

store [stor] *s* (*small shop*) Laden *m;* (*large shop*) Geschäft *n;* (*supply*) Vorrat *m;* **be in s. for** bevorstehen (*dat*); **have in s. for** bereithalten für; **set great s. by** viel Wert legen auf (*acc*); **s. of knowledge** Wissenschatz *m* ‖ *tr* einlagern; (*in the attic*) auf den Speicher stellen; **s. up** aufspeichern

store'house' *s* Lagerhaus *n;* (fig) Schatz *m,* Fundgrube *f*

store'keep'er *s* Ladeninhaber –in *mf*

store'room' *s* Lagerraum *m*, Vorratsraum *m*

stork [stɔrk] *s* Storch *m*

storm [stɔrm] *s* Sturm *m*; *(thunderstorm)* Gewitter *n*; *(fig)* Sturm *m*; **take by s.** (& fig) im Sturm nehmen || *tr* (er)stürmen || *intr* stürmen

storm' cloud' *s* Gewitterwolke *f*

storm' door' *s* Doppeltür *f*

storm' warn'ing *s* Sturmwarnung *f*

storm' win'dow *s* Doppelfenster *n*

stormy ['stɔrmi] *adj* stürmisch

story ['stori] *s* Geschichte *f*; *(floor)* Stock *m*, Stockwerk *n*; **that's another s.** das ist e–e Sache für sich

sto'rybook' *s* Geschichtenbuch *n*

sto'rytell'er *s* Erzähler –in *mf*

stout [staut] *adj* beleibt; *(heart)* tapfer || *s* Starkbier *n*

stout'-heart'ed *adj* beherzt

stove [stov] *s* Ofen *m*, Küchenherd *m*

stove'pipe' *s* Ofenrohr *n*; (coll) Angströhre *f*

stow [sto] *tr* stauen; **s. away** verstauen || *intr*—**s. away** als blinder Passagier mitreisen

stowage ['sto·ɪdʒ] *s* Stauen *n*; *(costs)* Staugebühr *f*

stow'away' *s* blinder Passagier *m*

straddle ['strædəl] *tr* mit gespreizten Beinen sitzen auf *(dat)*

strafe [stref] *tr* im Tiefflug mit Bordwaffen angreifen

straggle ['strægəl] *intr* abschweifen

straggler ['stræglər] *s* Nachzügler –in *mf*; (mil) Versprengte *m*

straight [stret] *adj* gerade; *(honest)* aufrecht; *(candid)* offen; *(hair)* glatt; *(story)* wahr; *(uninterrupted)* ununterbrochen; *(whiskey)* unverdünnt || *adv (directly)* direkt; *(without interruption)* ununterbrochen; **give it to s.o.** s. j–m die ungeschminkte Wahrheit sagen; **go s.** (fig) seinen geraden Weg gehen; **is my hat on s.?** sitzt mein Hut richtig?; **make s. for** zuhalten auf *(acc)*; **set the record s.** den Sachverhalt klarstellen; **s. ahead** (immer) geradeaus; **s. as an arrow** pfeilgerade; **s. from the horse's mouth** (coll) aus erster Hand; **s. home** schnurstracks nach Hause; **s. off** ohne weiteres || *s* (cards) Buch *n*

straight'away' *adv* geradewegs, sofort || *s* (sport) Gerade *f*

straighten ['stretən] *tr* gerade machen; *(e.g., a tablecloth)* glattziehen; **s. out** (fig) wieder in Ordnung bringen; **s. s.o.'s tie** j–m die Krawatte zurechtrücken; **s. up** *(a room)* aufräumen || *intr* gerade werden; **s. up** sich aufrichten

straight' face' *s*—**keep a s.** keine Miene verziehen

straight'for'ward *adj* aufrichtig

straight' left' *s* (box) linke Gerade *f*

straight' man' *s* Stichwortgeber *m*

straight' ra'zor *s* Rasiermesser *n*

straight' right' *s* (box) rechte Gerade *f*

straight'way' *adv* auf der Stelle

strain [stren] *s* Belastung *f*; *(of a muscle or tendon)* Zerrung *f*; *(task requiring effort)* (coll) Strapaze *f*; *(stock, family)* Linie *f*; *(trait)* Erbeigenschaft *f*; (bot) Art *f*; **without s.** mühelos || *tr (filter)* durchseihen; *(the eyes, nerves)* überanstrengen; **s. oneself** *(make a great effort)* sich überanstrengen; *(in lifting)* sich überheben; **s. the truth** übertreiben || *intr* sich anstrengen; **s. after s.** abmühen um; **s. at** ziehen an *(dat)*, zerren an *(dat)*

strained *adj (smile)* gezwungen; *(relations)* gespannt

strainer ['strenər] *s* Seiher *m*, Filter *m*

strait [stret] *s* Straße *f*; **financial straits** finanzielle Schwierigkeiten *pl*; **straits** Meerenge *f*

strait'jack'et *s* Zwangsjacke *f*

strait'-laced' *adj* sittenstreng

strand [strænd] *s* Strähne *f*; *(beach)* Strand *m*; **s. of pearls** Perlenschnur *f* || *tr* auf den Strand setzen; **be stranded** (fig) in der Patsche sitzen; **get stranded** auflaufen; **leave s.o. stranded** j–n im Stich lassen

strange [strendʒ] *adj (quaint)* sonderbar; *(foreign)* fremd; **s. character** Sonderling *m* || *adv*—**s. to say** merkwürdigerweise

stranger ['strendʒər] *s* Fremde *mf*

strangle ['stræŋgəl] *tr* erwürgen || *intr* ersticken

stran'glehold' *s* Würgegriff *m*

strap [stræp] *s* Riemen *m*, Gurt *m*; *(of metal)* Band *n* || *v (pret & pp* **strapped;** *ger* **strapping)** *tr* (to) anschnallen (an *acc*); *(a razor)* abziehen

strap'ping *adj* stramm

stratagem ['strætədʒəm] *s* Kriegslist *f*

strategic(al) [strə'tidʒɪk(əl)] *adj* strategisch

strategist ['strætɪdʒɪst] *s* Stratege *m*

strategy ['strætɪdʒɪ] *s* Strategie *f*

stratification [ˌstrætɪfɪ'keʃən] *s* Schichtung *f*

strati·fy ['strætɪˌfaɪ] *v (pret & pp* **–fied)** *tr* schichten || *intr* Schichten bilden

stratosphere ['strætəˌsfɪr] *s* Stratosphäre *f*

stra·tum ['stretəm], ['strætəm] *s* (**–ta** [tə] & **–tums**) Schicht *f*

straw [stro] *adj (e.g., hat, man, mat)* Stroh– || *s* Stroh *n*; *(single stalk; for drinking)* Strohhalm *m*; **that's the last s.!** das schlägt dem Faß den Boden aus!

straw'ber'ry *s* Erdbeere *f*

straw'berry blond' *adj* rotblond

straw' mat'tress *s* Strohsack *m*

straw' vote' *s* Probeabstimmung *f*

stray [stre] *adj (e.g., bullet)* verirrt; *(cat, dog)* streunend; **s. shell** (mil) Ausreißer *m* || *s* verirrtes Tier *n* || *intr* herumirren; (fig) abschweifen

streak [strik] *s* Streifen *m*; **like a s.** wie der Blitz; **s. of bad luck** Pechsträhne *f*; **s. of luck** Glückssträhne *f*; **s. of light** Lichtstreifen *m* || *tr* streifen || *intr* streifig werden; **s. along** vorbeisausen

streaky ['striki] *adj* gestreift; (*uneven*) (coll) ungleich(mäßig)

stream [strim] *s* Fluß *m; (of people, cars, air, blood, lava)* Strom *m; (of words)* Schwall *m; (of tears)* Flut *f; (of a liquid)* Strahl *m* || *intr* (aus)-strömen

streamer ['strimǝr] *s (pennant)* Wimpel *m; (ribbon)* herabhängendes Band *n; (rolled crepe paper)* Papierschlange *f*

stream'line' *tr* in Stromlinienform bringen; (fig) reorganizieren

stream'lined' *adj* stromlinienförmig

street [strit] *s* Straße *f*

street'car' *s* Straßenbahn *f*

street' clean'er *s* Straßenkehrer –in *mf; (truck)* Straßenkehrmaschine *f*

street' fight' *s* Straßenschlacht *f*

street'light' *s* Straßenlaterne *f*

street' sign' *s* Straßenschild *n*

street' ven'dor *s* Straßenhändler –in *mf*

street'walk'er *s* Straßendirne *f*

strength [streŋθ] *s* Kraft *f; (strong point; potency of alcohol; moral or mental power)* Stärke *f; (mil)* Kopfstärke *f; bodily s.* Körperkraft *f;* on the s. of auf Grund (*genit*)

strengthen ['streŋθǝn] *tr* stärken; (fig) bestärken || *intr* stärker werden

strenuous ['strenjʊ-ǝs] *adj* anstrengend; s. effort Kraftanstrengung *f*

stress [stres] *s (emphasis, weight)* Nachdruck *m; (mental)* Belastung *f;* (mus, pros) Ton *m,* Betonung *f;* (phys) Beanspruchung *f,* Spannung *f* || *tr (& mus, pros)* betonen

stress' ac'cent *s* Betonungsakzent *m*

stress' mark' *s* Betonungszeichen *n*

stretch [stretʃ] *s (of road)* Strecke *f; (of the limbs)* Strecken *n; (of water)* Fläche *f; (of a racetrack)* Gerade *f; (of years)* Zeitspanne *f;* do a s. (sl) brummen; in one's s. in e–m Zug || *tr (a rope)* spannen; *(one's neck)* recken; *(shoes, gloves)* ausdehnen; *(wire)* ziehen; *(strings of an instrument)* straffziehen; s. a point ist es nicht allzu genau nehmen; s. oneself sich strecken; s. one's legs sich *[dat]* die Beine vertreten; s. out *(e.g., hands)* ausstrecken || *intr* sich (aus)-dehnen; *(said of a person)* sich strecken; s. out so sich ausstrecken auf *(dat)*

stretcher ['stretʃǝr] *s* Tragbahre *f*

stretch'erbear'er *s* Krankenträger *m*

strew [stru] *v (pret* strewed; *pp* strewed & strewn) *tr* (aus)streuen; s. with bestreuen mit

stricken ['strikǝn] *adj* (with e.g., misfortune) heimgesucht (von); (with e.g., fear, grief) ergriffen (von); (with a disease) befallen (von)

strict [strikt] *adj* streng; in s. confidence streng vertraulich

strictly ['striktli] *adv* streng; s. speaking genau genommen

stricture ['striktʃǝr] *s (on)* kritische Bemerkung *f* (über *acc*)

stride [straɪd] *s* Schritt *m;* hit one's s. auf Touren kommen; make great

strides große Fortschritte machen; take in s. ruhig hinnehmen || *v (pret* strode [strod]; *pp* stridden ['strɪdǝn]) *intr* schreiten; s. along tüchtig ausschreiten

strident ['straɪdǝnt] *adj* schrill

strife [straɪf] *s* Streit *m,* Hader *m*

strike [straɪk] *s (work stoppage)* Streik *m; (blow)* Schlag *m; (discovery, e.g., of oil)* Fund *m; (baseball)* Fehlschlag *m;* go on s. in Streik treten || *v (pret & pp* struck [strʌk]) *tr (a person, the hours, coins, strings of an instrument)* schlagen; *(a match)* anstreichen; *(a bargain)* schließen; *(a note)* greifen; *(go on strike against)* bestreiken; *(a tent)* abbrechen; *(oil)* stoßen auf *(acc); (run into)* auffahren auf *(acc); (s.o. blind, dumb)* machen; *(s.o. with fear)* erfüllen; *(a blow)* versetzen; *(a pose)* einnehmen; *(seem to s.o.)* erscheinen *(dat);* s. it rich auf e–e Goldader stoßen; s. fear into s.o. j–m e–n Schrecken einjagen; s. up *(a conversation, an acquaintance)* anknüpfen; *(a song)* anstimmen || *intr (said of a person or clock)* schlagen; *(said of workers)* streiken; *(said of lightning)* einschlagen; s. home Eindruck machen; s. out *(& fig)* fehlschlagen

strike'break'er *s* Streikbrecher –in *mf*

striker ['straɪkǝr] *s* Streikende *mf*

strik'ing *adj* auffallend; *(example)* treffend; *(workers)* streikend

strik'ing pow'er *s* Schlagkraft *f*

string [strɪŋ] *s* Bindfaden *m; (row, series)* Reihe *f; (of a bow)* Sehne *f; (of a musical instrument)* Saite *f;* pull strings (fig) der Drahtzieher sein; s. of pearls Perlenkette *f;* strings (mus) Streicher *pl;* with no strings attached ohne einschränkende Bedingungen || *v (pret & pp* strung [strʌŋ]) *tr (pearls)* auf e–e Schnur (auf)reihen; *(a bow)* spannen; s. along hinhalten; s. up (coll) aufknüpfen

string' band' *s* Streichorchester *n*

string' bean' *s* grüne Bohne *f; (tall, thin person)* Bohnenstange *f*

stringed' in'strument *s* Saiteninstrument *n*

stringent ['strɪndʒǝnt] *adj* streng

string' quartet' *s* Streichquartett *n*

stringy ['strɪŋi] *adj (vegetables)* holzig; *(meat)* sehnig; *(hair)* zottelig

strip [strɪp] *s* Streifen *m* || *v (pret & pp* stripped; *ger* stripping) *tr (off)* abziehen; *(clothes) (off)* abstreifen; *(a thread)* überdrehen; *(gears)* beschädigen; s. down abmontieren; s.o. of office j–n seines Amtes entkleiden || *intr* sich ausziehen

stripe [straɪp] *s* Streifen *m; (elongated welt)* Striemen *m; (mil)* Tresse *f* || *tr* streifen

strip' mine' *s* Tagebau *m*

stripper ['strɪpǝr] *s* Stripperin *f*

strip'tease' *s* Entkleidungsnummer *f*

stripteaser ['strɪp͵tizǝr] *s* Stripperin *f*

strive [straɪv] *v (pret* strove [strov];

pp **striven** ['strɪvən]) *intr* (for) streben (nach); **s. to** (*inf*) sich bemühen zu (*inf*)

stroke [strok] *s* Schlag *m*; (*caress with the hand*) Streicheln *n*; (*of a piston*) Hub *m*; (*of a pen, brush*) Strich *m*; (*of a sword*) Hieb *m*; (*in swimming*) Schwimmstoß *m*; (*of the leg*) Beinstoß *m*; (*of an oar*) Schlag *m*; (*pathol*) Schlaganfall *m*; **at a single s.** mit e-m Schlag; **at the s. of twelve** Schlag zwölf Uhr; **not do a s. of work** keinen Strich tun; **she'll have a s.** (coll) dann trifft sie der Schlag; **s. of genius** Genieblitz *m*; **s. of luck** Glücksfall *m*; **with a s. of the pen** mit e-m Federstrich || *tr* streicheln

stroll [strol] *s* Spaziergang *m* || *intr* spazieren

stroller ['strolər] *s* Spaziergänger –in *mf*; (*for a baby*) Kindersportwagen *m*

strong [strɔŋ] *adj* kräftig; (*firm*) fest; (*drink, smell, light, wind, feeling*) stark; (*glasses*) scharf; (*wine*) schwer; (*suspicion*) dringend; (*memory*) gut; (*candidate*) aussichtsreich; (*argument*) triftig

strong'-arm' *adj* (e.g., *methods*) Zwangs–

strong'box' *s* Geldschrank *m*

strong'hold *s* Feste *f*; (fig) Hochburg *f*

strong' lan'guage *s* Kraftausdrücke *pl*

strongly ['strɔŋli] *adv* nachdrücklich; **feel s. about** sich sehr einsetzen für

strong'-mind'ed *adj* willensstark

strontium ['strɑnʃɪ·əm] *s* Strontium *n*

strop [strɑp] *s* Streichriemen *m* || *v* (*pret & pp* **stropped**; *ger* **stropping**) *tr* abziehen

strophe ['strofi] *s* Strophe *f*

structural ['strʌktʃərəl] *adj* strukturell, Bau–

structure ['strʌktʃər] *s* Struktur *f*; (*building*) Bau *m*

struggle ['strʌgəl] *s* Kampf *m* || *intr* (for) kämpfen (um); **s. against** ankämpfen gegen; **s. to one's feet** sich mit Mühe erheben

strum [strʌm] *v* (*pret & pp* **strummed**; *ger* **strumming**) *tr* klimpern auf (dat)

strumpet ['strʌmpɪt] *s* Dirne *f*

strut [strʌt] *s* (*brace*) Strebebalken *m*; (*haughty walk*) stolzer Gang *m* || *v* (*pret & pp* **strutted**; *ger* **strutting**) *intr* stolzieren

strychnine ['strɪknaɪn] *s* Strychnin *n*

stub [stʌb] *s* (*of a checkbook*) Abschnitt *m*; (*of a ticket*) Kontrollabschnitt *m*; (*of a candle, pencil, cigarette*) Stummel *m* || *v* (*pret & pp* **stubbed**; *ger* **stubbing**) *tr*–**s. one's toe** sich an der Zehe stoßen

stubble ['stʌbəl] *s* Stoppel *f*; (*facial hair*) Bartstoppeln *pl*

stubbly ['stʌbli] *adj* stopp(e)lig

stubborn ['stʌbərn] *adj* eigensinnig; (e.g., *resistance*) hartnäckig; (*hair*) widerspenstig

stubby ['stʌbi] *adj* **kurz und dick**; (*person*) untersetzt

stuc·co ['stʌko] *s* (**-coes** & **-cos**) Verputz *m* || *tr* verputzen

stuc'co work' *s* Verputzarbeit *f*

stuck [stʌk] *adj*—**be s.** feststecken; (*said, e.g., of a lock*) klemmen; **be s. on** vernarrt sein in (acc); **get s.** steckenbleiben

stuck'-up' *adj* (coll) hochnäsig

stud [stʌd] *s* (*ornament*) Ziernagel *m*; (*horse*) Zuchthengst *m*; (*archit*) Wandpfosten *m* || *v* (*pret & pp* **studded**; *ger* **studding**) *tr* mit Ziernägeln verzieren

stud' bolt' *s* Schraubenbolzen *m*

student ['st(j)udənt] *adj* Studenten– || *s* (*in college*) Student –in *mf*; (*in grammar or high school*) Schüler –in *mf*; (*scholar*) Gelehrte *mf*

stu'dent bod'y *s* Studentenschaft *f*

stu'dent nurse' *s* Krankenpflegerin *f* in Ausbildung

stud' farm' *s* Gestüt *n*

stud'horse' *s* Zuchthengst *m*

stud'ied *adj* gesucht

studi·o ['st(j)udɪˌo] *s* (**-os**) (fa, phot) Atelier *n*; (cin, fa, phot, telv) Studio *n*

studious ['st(j)udɪ·əs] *adj* fleißig

stud·y ['stʌdi] *s* Studium *n*; (*room*) Studierzimmer *n*; (*paint*) Studie *f* || *v* (*pret & pp* **-ied**) *tr & intr* studieren

stuff [stʌf] *s* Stoff *m*; (coll) Kram *m*; **do your s.!** (coll) schieß los!; **know one's s.** (coll) sich auskennen || *tr* (*animals*) ausstopfen; (*a cushion*) polstern; (e.g., *cotton in the ears*) sich [dat] stopfen; (culin) füllen; **s. oneself** sich vollstopfen

stuffed' shirt' *s* steifer, eingebildeter Mensch *m*

stuff'ing *s* Polstermaterial *n*; (culin) Fülle *f*

stuffy ['stʌfi] *adj* (*room*) stickig; (*nose*) verstopft; (*person*) steif

stumble ['stʌmbəl] *intr* stolpern; (*in reading*) holpern; **s. across** stoßen auf (acc)

stum'bling block' *s* Stein *m* des Anstoßes

stump [stʌmp] *s* (*of an arm, tree, cigarette, pencil*) Stummel *m* || *tr* (*a cigarette*) ausdrücken; (*nonplus*) verblüffen; (*a district, state*) als Wahlredner bereisen

stump' speak'er *s* Wahlredner –in *mf*

stun [stʌn] *v* (*pret & pp* **stunned**; *ger* **stunning**) *tr* betäuben

stun'ning *adj* (coll) phantastisch

stunt [stʌnt] *s* Kunststück *n*; **do stunts** Kunststücke vorführen || *tr* hemmen

stunt'ed *adj* verkümmert

stunt' fly'ing *s* Kunstflug *m*

stunt' man' *s* (**men'**) Sensationsdarsteller *m*

stupe·fy ['st(j)upɪˌfaɪ] *v* (*pret & pp* **-fied**) *tr* verblüffen

stupendous [st(j)u'pɛndəs] *adj* erstaunlich

stupid ['st(j)upɪd] *adj* dumm, blöd

stupidity [st(j)u'pɪdɪti] *s* Dummheit *f*

stupor ['st(j)upər] *s* Stumpfsinn *m*

sturdy ['stʌrdi] *adj* (*person*) kräftig;

(thing) stabil; *(resolute)* standhaft; *(plant)* widerstandsfähig

sturgeon ['stɜːdʒən] *s* Stör *m*

stutter ['stʌtər] *s* Stottern *n* || *tr & intr* stottern

sty [staɪ] *s* Schweinestall *m*; *(pathol)* Gerstenkorn *n*

style [staɪl] *s* Stil *m*; *(manner)* Art *f*; *(fashion)* Mode *f*; *(cut of suit)* Schnitt *m*; **be in s.** in Mode sein; **go out of s.** veralten; **live in s.** auf großem Fuße leben || *tr (title)* betiteln; *(e.g., clothes)* gestalten; *(hair)* nach der Mode frisieren

stylish ['staɪlɪʃ] *adj* modisch; *(person)* modisch gekleidet

stylistic [staɪ'lɪstɪk] *adj* stilistisch

stymie ['staɪmi] *tr* vereiteln

styp'tic pen'cil ['stɪptɪk] *s* Alaunstift *m*

suave [swɑv] *adj* verbindlich

sub [sʌb] *s* (naut) U-boot *n*; (sport) Ersatzspieler –in *mf*

sub'chas'er *s* U-bootjäger *m*

sub'com·mit'tee *s* Unterausschuß *m*

subconscious [səb'kɑnʃəs] *adj* unterbewußt || *s* Unterbewußtsein *n*

sub'con'tinent *s* Subkontinent *m*

sub'con'tract *s* Nebenvertrag *m* || *tr* e–n Nebenvertrag abschließen über *(acc)*

sub'con'tractor *s* Unterlieferant –in *mf*

sub'divide', sub'divide' *tr* unterteilen || *intr* sich unterteilen

sub'divi'sion *s* *(act)* Unterteilung *f*; *(unit)* Unterabteilung *f*

subdue [səb'd(j)u] *tr (an enemy)* unterwerfen; *(one who is struggling)* überwältigen; *(light, sound)* dämpfen; *(feelings, impulses)* bändigen

sub'floor' *s* Blindboden *m*

sub'head' *s* Untertitel *m*

subject ['sʌbdʒɪkt] *adj (to)* untertan *(dat)*; **be s. to** *(e.g., approval, another country)* abhängig sein von; *(e.g., colds)* neigen zu; *(e.g., laws of nature, change)* unterworfen sein *(dat)*; **s. to change without notice** Änderungen vorbehalten || *s* Thema *n*; *(of a kingdom)* Untertan –in *mf*; *(educ)* Fach *n*; *(fa)* Vorwurf *m*; *(gram)* Satzgegenstand *m*, Subjekt *n*; *(libr)* Stichwort *n*; **change the s.** das Thema wechseln; **get off the s.** vom Thema abkommen || [səb'dʒɛkt] *tr (& fig)* unterwerfen *(dat)*

subjection [səb'dʒɛkʃən] *s* Unterwerfung *f*

subjective [səb'dʒɛktɪv] *adj* subjektiv; **s. case** Werfall *m*

sub'ject mat'ter *s* Inhalt *m*

subjugate ['sʌdʒə‚get] *tr* unterjochen

subjunctive [səb'dʒʌŋktɪv] *adj* konjunktiv(isch) || *s* Konjunktiv *m*

sub'lease' *s* Untermiete *f* || **sub'lease'** *tr & intr (to s.o.)* untervermieten; *(from s.o.)* untermieten

sublet [sʌb'lɛt] *v (pret & pp –let; ger –letting) tr & intr (to s.o.)* untervermieten; *(from s.o.)* untermieten

sublimate ['sʌblɪmət] *s* (chem) Sublimat *n* || ['sʌblɪ‚met] *tr* sublimieren

sublime [sə'blaɪm] *adj* erhaben || *s* Erhabene *n*

submachine' gun' *s* Maschinenpistole *f*

sub'marine' *adj* U-boot– || *s* U-boot *n*

sub'marine' base' *s* U-bootstützpunkt *m*

submerge [səb'mʌrdʒ] *tr & intr* untertauchen; **ready to s.** tauchklar

submersion [səb'mʌrʒən] *s* Untertauchen *n*

submission [səb'mɪʃən] *s* **(to)** Unterwerfung *f* (unter *acc*); *(of a document)* Vorlage *f*; *(of a question)* Unterbreitung *f*

submissive [səb'mɪsɪv] *adj* unterwürfig

sub·mit [səb'mɪt] *v (pret & pp –mitted; ger –mitting) tr (a question)* unterbreiten; *(a document)* vorlegen; *(suggest)* der Ansicht sein || *intr* **(to)** sich unterwerfen *(dat)*

subordinate [səb'ɔrdɪnɪt] *adj (lower in rank)* untergeordnet; *(secondary)* Neben– || *s* Untergebene *mf* || [səb'ɔrdɪ‚net] *tr* (to) unterordnen *(dat)*

subor'dinate clause' *s* Nebensatz *m*

suborn [sə'bɔrn] *tr* verleiten; *(bribe)* bestechen

sub'plot' *s* Nebenhandlung *f*

subpoena [sʌb'pina] *s* Vorladung *f* || *tr* (unter Strafandrohung) vorladen

subscribe [səb'skraɪb] *tr* unterschreiben; *(money)* zeichnen || *intr*—**s. to** *(a newspaper)* abonnieren; *(to a series of volumes)* subskribieren; *(an idea)* billigen

subscriber [səb'skraɪbər] *s* Abonnent –in *mf*

subscription [səb'skrɪpʃən] *s* **(to)** Abonnement *n* (auf *acc*); *(to a series of volumes)* Subskription *f* (auf *acc*); **take out a s. to** sich abonnieren auf *(acc)*

sub'sec'tion *s* Unterabteilung *f*

subsequent ['sʌbsɪkwənt] *adj* (nach)folgend; **s. to** anschließend an *(acc)*

subsequently ['sʌbsɪkwəntli] *adv* anschließend

subservient [səb'sʌrvi‚ənt] *adj* **(to)** unterwürfig (gegenüber *dat*)

subside [səb'saɪd] *intr* nachlassen; (geol) sich senken

subsidiary [səb'sɪdi‚ɛri] *adj* Tochter– || *s* Tochtergesellschaft *f*

subsidize ['sʌbsɪ‚daɪz] *tr* subventionieren

subsidy ['sʌbsɪdi] *s* Subvention *f*

subsist [səb'sɪst] *intr (exist)* existieren; **s. on** leben von

subsistence [səb'sɪstəns] *s* *(existence)* Dasein *n*; *(livelihood)* Lebensunterhalt *m*; *(philos)* Subsistenz *f*

subsist'ence allow'ance *s* Unterhaltszuschuß *m*

sub'soil' *s* Untergrund *m*

subsonic [səb'sɑnɪk] *adj* Unterschall–

sub'spe'cies *s* Unterart *f*

substance ['sʌbstəns] *s* Substanz *f*, Stoff *m*; **in s.** im wesentlichen

substand'ard *adj* unter dem Niveau

substantial [səb'stænʃəl] *adj (sum, amount)* beträchtlich; *(difference)* wesentlich; (*meal*) kräftig; **be in s. agreement** im wesentlichen übereinstimmen

substantiate [səb'stænʃɪ‚et] *tr* begründen, nachweisen

substantive ['sʌbstəntɪv] *adj* wesentlich || *s* (gram) Substantiv *m*

sub'sta'tion *s* Nebenstelle *f*; (*postoffice*) Zweigpostamt *n*; (elec) Umspannwerk *n*

substitute ['sʌbstɪ‚t(j)ut] *s* (*person*) Stellvertreter –in *mf*; (*material*) Austauschstoff *m*; (pej) Ersatz *m*; (sport) Ersatzspieler –in *mf*; **act as a s. for** vertreten; **beware of substitutes** vor Nachamung wird gewarnt || *tr*—s. **A for B** B durch A ersetzen || *intr*— **s. for** einspringen für

sub'stitute teach'er *s* Aushilfslehrer –in *mf*

substitution [‚sʌbstɪ't(j)uʃən] *s* Einsetzung *f*; (chem, math, ling) Substitution *f*; (sport) Auswechseln *n*

sub'stra'tum *s* (-ta [tə] & -tums) Unterlage *f*; (biol) Nährboden *m*

sub'struc'ture *s* Unterbau *m*

subsume [sʌb'sjum] *tr* unterordnen

subterfuge ['sʌbtər‚fjudʒ] *s* Winkelzug *m*

subterranean [‚sʌbtə'reni‚ən] *adj* unterirdisch

sub'ti'tle *s* Untertitel *m*

subtle ['sʌtəl] *adj* fein; (*poison*) schleichend; (*cunning*) raffiniert

subtlety ['sʌtəlti] *s* Feinheit *f*

subtract [səb'trækt] *tr* subtrahieren

subtraction [səb'trækʃən] *s* Subtraktion *f*

suburb ['sʌbʌrb] *s* Vorstadt *f*, Vorort *m*; **the suburbs** der Stadtrand

suburban [sə'bʌrbən] *adj* Vorstadt–

suburbanite [sə'bʌrbə‚naɪt] *s* Vorstadtbewohner –in *mf*

subvention [səb'venʃən] *s* Subvention *f*

subversion [səb'vʌrʒən] *s* Umsturz *m*

subversive [səb'vʌrsɪv] *adj* umstürzlerisch || *s* Umstürzler –in *mf*

subver'sive activ'ity *s* Wühlarbeit *f*

subvert [səb'vʌrt] *tr* (a government) stürzen; (*the law*) umstoßen; (*corrupt*) (sittlich) verderben

sub'way' *s* U-Bahn *f*, Untergrundbahn *f*

succeed [sək'sid] *tr* folgen (*dat*) || *intr* (*said of persons*) (in) Erfolg haben (mit); (*said of things*) gelingen; **I succeeded in** (*ger*) es gelang mir zu (*inf*); **not s.** mißglücken; **s. to the throne** die Thronfolge antreten

success [sək'ses] *s* Erfolg *m*; (*play, song, piece of merchandise*) Knüller *m*; **be a s.** Erfolg haben; **without s.** erfolglos

successful [sək'sesfəl] *adj* erfolgreich

succession [sək'seʃən] *s* Reihenfolge *f*; (*as heir*) Erbfolge *f*; **in s.** nacheinander; **s. to** (e.g., *an office, estate*) Übernahme *f* (*genit*)

successive [sək'sesɪv] *adj* aufeinanderfolgend

successor [sək'sesər] *s* Nachfolger –in *mf*; **s. to the throne** Thronfolger –in *mf*

succor ['sʌkər] *s* Beistand *m* || *tr* beistehen (*dat*)

succotash ['sʌkə‚tæʃ] *s* Gericht *n* aus Süßmais und grünen Bohnen

succulent ['sʌkjələnt] *adj* saftig

succumb [sə'kʌm] *intr* (to) erliegen (*dat*)

such [sʌtʃ] *adj* solch; **as s.** als solcher; **no s. thing** nichts dergleichen; **some s. thing** irgend so (et)was; **s. and s.** der und der; **s. as we** wie (etwa); **s. a long time** so lange; **s. as it is** wie es nun einmal ist

suck [sʌk] *s* Saugen *n*; (*licking*) Lutschen *n* || *tr* saugen; **s. in** einsaugen; (sl) reinlegen || *intr* saugen; **s. on** (e.g., *candy*) lutschen

sucker ['sʌkər] *s* (coll) Gimpel *m*; (*carp*) Karpfenfisch *m*; (bot) Wurzelschößling *m*; (zool) Saugröhre *f*

suckle ['sʌkəl] *tr* stillen; (*animals*) säugen

suck'ling *s* Säugling *m*

suck'ling pig' *s* Spanferkel *n*

suction ['sʌkʃən] *s* Saugen *n*, Sog *m*

suc'tion cup' *s* Saugnapf *m*

suc'tion pump' *s* Saugpumpe *f*

sudden ['sʌdən] *adj* plötzlich, jäh; **all of a s.** (ganz) plötzlich

suddenly ['sʌdənli] *adv* plötzlich

suds [sʌdz] *spl* Seifenschaum *m*

sudsy ['sʌdzi] *adj* schaumig

sue [s(j)u] *tr* (for) verklagen (auf *acc*) || *intr* (for) klagen (auf *acc*)

suede [swed] *adj* Wildleder– || *s* Wildleder *n*

suet ['s(j)u‚ɪt] *s* Talg *m*

suffer ['sʌfər] *tr* erleiden; (*damage*) nehmen; (*put up with*) ertragen || *intr* (from) leiden (an *dat*)

sufferance ['sʌfərəns] *s* stillschweigende Einwilligung *f*

suf'fering *s* Leiden *n*

suffice [sə'faɪs] *intr* ausreichen

sufficient [sə'fɪʃənt] *adj* (for) ausreichend (zu)

suffix ['sʌfɪks] *s* Nachsilbe *f*

suffocate ['sʌfə‚ket] *tr* & *intr* ersticken

suffrage ['sʌfrɪdʒ] *s* Stimmrecht *n*

suffuse [sə'fjuz] *tr* übergießen

sugar ['ʃugər] *s* Zucker *m* || *tr* zuckern

sug'ar beet' *s* Zuckerrübe *f*

sug'ar bowl' *s* Zuckerdose *f*

sug'ar cane' *s* Zuckerrohr *n*

sug'ar-coat' *tr* (& fig) überzuckern

sug'ar dad'dy *s* Geldonkel *m*

sug'ar ma'ple *s* Zuckerahorn *m*

sug'ar tongs' *spl* Zuckerzange *f*

sugary ['ʃugəri] *adj* zuckerig

suggest [səg'dʒest] *tr* vorschlagen; (*hint*) andeuten

suggestion [səg'dʒestʃən] *s* Vorschlag *m*

suggestive [səg'dʒestɪv] *adj* (*remark*) zweideutig; (*thought-provoking*) anregend; (*dress*) hauteng; **be s. of** erinnern an (*acc*)

suicidal [‚su·ɪ'saɪdəl] *adj* selbstmörderisch

suicide ['su·ɪ‚saɪd] *s* Selbstmord *m*;

(*person*) Selbstmörder –in *mf*; commit s. Selbstmord begehen
suit [sut] *s* (*men's*) Anzug *m*;
(*women's*) Kostüm *n*; (*cards*) Farbe
f; (*jur*) Prozeß *m*; bring s. (*against*)
e–e Klage einbringen (gegen); follow
s. Farbe bekennen; (*fig*) sich nach
den anderen richten || *tr* (*please*)
passen (*dat*); (*correspond to*) entsprechen (*dat*); (*said, e.g., of colors,
style*) gut passen (*dat*); be suited for
sich eignen für; s. s.th. to etw anpassen (*dat*); s. yourself! wie Sie wollen!
suitable ['sutəbəl] *adj* (to) geeignet
(für)
suit'case' *s* Handkoffer *m*
suit' coat' *s* Sakko *m* & *n*
suite [swit] *s* (*series of rooms*) Zim-
merflucht *f*; (*set of furniture*) Zim-
mergarnitur *f*; (*mus*) Suite *f*
suitor ['sutər] *s* Freier *m*
sul'fa drug' *s* Sulfonamid *n*
sulfate ['sʌlfet] *s* Sulfat *n*
sulfide ['sʌlfaɪd] *s* Sulfid *n*
sulfur ['sʌlfər] *adj* Schwefel– || *s*
Schwefel *m* || *tr* einschwefeln
sulfur'ic ac'id [sʌl'f(j)urɪk] *s* Schwe-
felsäure *f*
sul'fur mine' *s* Schwefelgrube *f*
sulk [sʌlk] *intr* trotzen
sulky ['sʌlki] *adj* trotzend, mürrisch
|| *s* (*sport*) Traberwagen *m*
sulk'y race' *s* Trabrennen *n*
sullen ['sʌlən] *adj* mißmutig
sul·ly ['sʌli] *v* (*pret & pp* –lied) *tr*
besudeln
sulphur ['sʌlfər] *var of* **sulfur**
sultan ['sʌltən] *s* Sultan *m*
sultry ['sʌltri] *adj* schwül
sum [sʌm] *s* Summe *f*, Betrag *m*; in
sum kurz gesagt || *v* (*pret & pp*
summed; *ger* summing)—sum up
summieren; (*summarize*) zusammenfassen; (*make a quick estimate of*)
kurz abschätzen
sumac, sumach ['(s)umæk] *s* Sumach *m*
summarize ['sʌmə‚raɪz] *tr* zusammenfassen
summary ['sʌməri] *adj* summarisch ||
s Zusammenfassung *f*
sum'mary court'-martial *s* summari-
sches Militärgericht *n*
summer ['sʌmər] *s* Sommer *m*
sum'mer cot'tage *s* Sommerwohnung *f*
sum'mer resort' *s* Sommerfrische *f*
sum'mer school' *s* Sommerkurs *m*
sum'mertime' *s* Sommerzeit *f*
summery ['sʌməri] *adj* sommerlich
summit ['sʌmɪt] *s* (& *fig*) Gipfel *m*
sum'mit con'ference *s* Gipfelkonferenz
f
sum'mit talks' *spl* Gipfelgespräche *pl*
summon ['sʌmən] *tr* (e.g., a doctor)
kommen lassen; (*a conference*) einberufen; (*jur*) vorladen; s. up (*courage, strength*) aufbieten
summons ['sʌmənz] *s* (*jur*) Vorladung
f
sumptuous ['sʌmptʃu-əs] *adj* üppig
sun [sʌn] *s* Sonne *f* || *v* (*pret & pp*
sunned; *ger* sunning) *tr* sonnen; sun
oneself sich sonnen

sun' bath' *s* Sonnenbad *n*
sun'beam' *s* Sonnenstrahl *m*
sun'burn' *s* Sonnenbrand *m*
sun'burned' *adj* sonnverbrannt
sundae ['sʌnde] *s* Eisbecher *m* mit
Sirup, Nüssen, Früchten und Schlagsahne
Sunday ['sʌnde] *adj* sonntäglich;
dressed in one's S. best sonntäglich
gekleidet || *s* Sonntag *m*; on S. am
Sonntag
Sun'day driv'er *s* Sonntagsfahrer –in
mf
Sun'day school' *s* Sonntagsschule *f*
sunder ['sʌndər] *tr* trennen
sun'di'al *s* Sonnenuhr *f*
sun'down' *s* Sonnenuntergang *m*
sun'-drenched' *adj* sonnenüberflutet
sundries ['sʌndriz] *pl* Diverses *n*
sundry ['sʌndri] *adj* verschiedene
sun'fish' *s* Sonnenfisch *m*
sun'flow'er *s* Sonnenblume *f*
sun'glass'es *pl* Sonnenbrille *f*
sun' hel'met *s* Tropenhelm *m*
sunken ['sʌŋkən] *adj* (*ship*) gesunken;
(*eyes; garden*) tiefliegend; (*treasure*)
versunken; (*cheeks*) eingefallen; s.
rocks blinde Klippe *f*
sun' lamp' *s* Höhensonne *f*
sun'light' *s* Sonnenlicht *n*
sunny ['sʌni] *adj* sonnig
sun'ny side' *s* Sonnenseite *f*
sun' par'lor *s* Glasveranda *f*
sun'rise' *s* Sonnenaufgang *m*
sun' roof' *s* (*aut*) Schiebedach *n*
sun'set' *s* Sonnenuntergang *m*
sun'shade' *s* Sonnenschirm *m*; (*awning*)
Sonnendach *n*; (*phot*) Gegenlicht-
blende *f*
sun'shine' *s* Sonnenschein *m*
sun'spot' *s* Sonnenfleck *m*
sun'stroke' *s* Sonnenstich *m*
sun'tan' *s* Sonnenbräune *f*
sun'tanned' *adj* sonnengebräunt
sun' vis'or *s* (*aut*) Sonnenblende *f*
sup [sʌp] *v* (*pret & pp* supped; *ger*
supping) *intr* zu Abend essen
super ['supər] *adj* (*oversized*) Super–;
(sl) prima || *s* (*theat*) Komparse *m*
su'perabun'dance *s* (of) Überfülle *f*
(*an dat*)
su'perabun'dant *adj* überreichlich
superannuated [‚supər'ænju‚etɪd] *adj*
(*person*) pensioniert; (*thing*) veraltet
superb [su'pɜrb] *adj* prachtvoll, herrlich
su'perbomb' *s* Superbombe *f*
su'perbomb'er *s* Riesenbomber *m*
supercilious [‚supər'sɪlɪ-əs] *adj* hochnäsig
superficial [‚supər'fɪʃəl] *adj* oberflächlich
superfluous [su'pʌrflu-əs] *adj* überflüssig
su'perhigh'way' *s* Autobahn *f*
su'perhu'man *adj* übermenschlich
su'perimpose' *tr* darüberlegen; (*elec,
phys*) überlagern
su'perintend' *tr* die Aufsicht führen
über (*acc*), beaufsichtigen
superintendent [‚supərɪn'tɛndənt] *s*
Oberaufseher –in *mf*; (*in industry*)

Betriebsleiter –in *mf;* (*of a factory*) Werksleiter –in *mf;* (*of a building*) Hausverwalter –in *mf;* (*educ*) Schulinspektor –in *mf*

superior [sə'pɪrɪ-ər] *adj* (*physically*) höher; (*in rank*) übergeordnet; (*quality*) hervorragend; **s. in** überlegen an (*dat*); **s. to** überlegen (*dat*) || *s* Vorgesetzte *mf*

supe'rior court' *s* Obergericht *n*

superiority [sə‚pɪrɪ'ɔrɪti] *s* (**in**) Überlegenheit *f* (*in dat,* an *dat*); (*mil*) Übermacht *f*

superlative [su'pʌrlətɪv] *adj* hervorragend; (*gram*) superlativisch, Superlativ– || *s* (*gram*) Superlativ *m*

su'perman' *s* (**–men'**) Übermensch *m*

su'permar'ket *s* Supermarkt *m*

su'pernat'ural *adj* übernatürlich || *s* Übernatürliche *n*

supersede [‚supər'sid] *tr* ersetzen

su'persen'sitive *adj* überempfindlich

su'person'ic *adj* Überschall–

superstition [‚supər'stɪʃən] *s* Aberglaube *m;* (*superstitious idea*) abergläubische Vorstellung *f*

superstitious [‚supər'stɪʃəs] *adj* abergläubisch

su'perstruc'ture *s* Überbau *m;* (*of a bridge*) Oberbau *m;* (*of a building or ship*) Aufbauten *pl*

supervise ['supər‚vaɪz] *tr* beaufsichtigen

supervision [‚supər'vɪʒən] *s* Beaufsichtigung *f*

supervisor ['supər‚vaɪzər] *s* Vorgesetzte *mf*

su'pine posi'tion ['supaɪn] *s* Rückenlage *f*

supper ['sʌpər] *s* Abendessen *n;* **eat s.** zu Abend essen

sup'pertime' *s* Abendbrotzeit *f*

supplant [sə'plænt] *tr* ersetzen

supple ['sʌpəl] *adj* geschmeidig; (*mind*) beweglich

supplement ['sʌplɪmənt] *s* (*e.g.,* **to a** *diet*) (**to**) Ergänzung *f* (*genit*); (*to a writing*) Anhang *m;* (*to a newspaper*) Beilage *f* || ['sʌplɪ‚ment] *tr* ergänzen

supplementary [‚sʌplɪ'mentəri] *adj* ergänzend

suppliant ['sʌplɪ-ənt] *adj* flehend || *s* Bittsteller –in *mf*

supplicant ['sʌplɪkənt] *s* Bittsteller –in *mf*

supplicate ['sʌplɪ‚ket] *tr* flehen

supplication [‚sʌplɪ'keʃən] *s* Flehen *n*

supplier [sə'plaɪ-ər] *s* Lieferant –in *mf*

sup•ply [sə'plaɪ] *s* (*supplying*) Versorgung *f;* (*stock*) (**of**) Vorrat *m* (an *dat*); (*com*) Angebot *n;* **supplies** Vorräte *pl;* (*e.g., office supplies, dental supplies*) Bedarfsartikel *pl;* (*mil*) Nachschub *m* || *v* (*pret & pp* **–plied**) *tr* (**with**) versorgen (mit); (*deliver*) liefern; (*procure*) beschaffen; (*with a truck*) zuführen; (*equip*) (**with**) versehen (mit); (*a demand*) befriedigen; (*a loss*) ausgleichen; (*missing words*) ergänzen; (*mil*) mit Nachschub versorgen

supply' and demand' *spl* Angebot *n* und Nachfrage *f*

supply' base' *s* Nachschubstützpunkt *m*

supply' line' *s* Versorgungsweg *m;* (*mil*) Nachschubweg *m*

support [sə'port] *adj* Hilfs– || *s* (*prop, brace, stay; person*) Stütze *f;* (*of a family*) Unterhalt *m;* **in s.** of zur Unterstützung (*genit*); **without s.** (*unsubstantiated*) haltlos; (*unprovided*) unversorgt; **with the s. of** mit dem Beistand von || *tr* stützen, tragen; (*back*) unterstützen; (*a family*) erhalten; (*a charge*) erhärten; (*a claim*) begründen

supporter [sə'portər] *s* (*of a family*) Ernährer –in *mf;* (*backer*) Förderer –in *mf;* (*jockstrap*) Suspensorium *n*

support'ing role' *s* Nebenrolle *f*

suppose [sə'poz] *tr* annehmen; **be supposed to sollen; I s. so** ich glaube schon; **s. it rains** gesetzt den Fall (or angenommen), es regnet; **s. we take a walk** wie wäre es, wenn wir e–n Spaziergang machten?; **what is that supposed to mean?** was soll das bedeuten? || *intr* vermuten

supposed' *adj* mutmaßlich

supposedly [sə'pozɪdli] *adv* angeblich

supposition [‚sʌpə'zɪʃən] *s* Annahme *f*

suppository [sə'pazɪ‚tori] *s* Zäpfchen *n*

suppress [sə'pres] *tr* unterdrücken; (*news, scandal*) verheimlichen

suppression [sə'preʃən] *s* Unterdrückung *f;* (*of news, truth, scandal*) Verheimlichung *f*

suppurate ['sʌpjə‚ret] *intr* eitern

supremacy [sə'preməsi] *s* Oberherrschaft *f*

supreme [sə'prim] *adj* Ober–, höchste

supreme' author'ity *s* Obergewalt *f*

Supreme' Be'ing *s* höchstes Wesen *n*

supreme' command' *s* Oberkommando *n;* **have s. an** den Oberbefehl führen

supreme' command'er *s* oberster Befehlshaber *m*

Supreme' Court' *s* Oberster Gerichtshof *m*

surcharge ['sʌr‚tʃardʒ] *s* (**on**) Zuschlag *m* (zu)

sure [ʃur] *adj* sicher, gewiß; (*shot, cure*) unfehlbar; (*shot, footing, ground, way, proof*) sicher; **are you s. you won't come?** kommen Sie wirklich nicht?; **be s. of** sicher sein (*genit*); **be s. to** (*inf*) vergiß nicht zu (*inf*); **feel s. of oneself** s–r selbst sicher sein; **for s.** sicherlich; **she is s. to come** sie wird sicher(lich) kommen; **s. enough** wirklich; **to be s.** (*parenthetically*) zwar

sure'-foot'ed *adj* trittsicher

surely ['ʃurli] *adv* sicher(lich), gewiß

surety ['ʃur(ɪ)ti] *s* Bürgschaft *f;* **stand s.** (**for**) bürgen (für)

surf [sʌrf] *s* Brandung *f* || *intr* wellenreiten

surface ['sʌrfɪs] *adj* (*superficial*) oberflächlich; (*apparent rather than real*)

Schein– ‖ s Oberfläche f; (of a road) Belag m; (aer) Tragfläche f; on the s. oberflächlich (betrachtet) ‖ tr (a road) mit e–m Belag versehen ‖ intr auftauchen

sur'face mail' s gewöhnliche Post f

sur'face-to-air' mis'sile s Boden-Luft-Rakete f

sur'face-to-sur'face mis'sile s Boden-Boden-Rakete f

surf'board' s Wellenreiterbrett n

surf'board'ing s Wellenreiten n

surfeit ['sʌrfɪt] s Übersättigung f ‖ tr übersättigen

surfer ['sʌrfər] s Wellenreiter –in mf

surf'ing s Wellenreiten n

surge [sʌrdʒ] s (forward rush of a wave or crowd) Wogen n; (swelling wave) Woge f; (swelling sea) Wogen n; (elec) Stromstoß m ‖ intr (said of waves or a crowd) wogen; (said of emotions, blood) (up) (auf)wallen

surgeon ['sʌrdʒən] s Chirurg –in mf

surgery ['sʌrdʒəri] s Chirurgie f; (room) Operationssaal m; undergo s. sich e–r Operation unterziehen

surgical ['sʌrdʒɪkəl] adj chirurgisch; (resulting from surgery) Operations–

surly ['sʌrli] adj bärbeißig

surmise [sər'maɪz] s Vermutung f ‖ tr & intr vermuten

surmount [sər'maunt] tr überwinden

surname ['sʌr‚nem] s (family name) Zuname m; (epithet) Beiname m ‖ tr e–n Zunamen (or Beinamen) geben (dat)

surpass [sər'pæs] tr (in) übertreffen (an dat)

surplice ['sʌrplɪs] s Chorhemd n

surplus ['sʌrpləs] adj überschüssig, Über– ‖ s (of) Überschuß m (an dat)

surprise [sər'praɪz] adj Überraschungs– ‖ s Überraschung f; take by s. überraschen; to my (great) s. zu meiner (großen) Überraschung ‖ tr überraschen; be surprised at sich wundern über (acc); be surprised to see how staunen, wie; I am surprised that es wundert mich, daß

surpris'ing adj überraschend

surrealism [sə'ri·ə‚lɪzəm] s Surrealismus m

surrender [sə'rendər] s (e.g., of a fortress) Übergabe f; (of an army or unit) Kapitulation f; (of rights) Aufgabe f; (of a prisoner) Auslieferung f ‖ tr übergeben; (rights) aufgeben; (a prisoner) ausliefern ‖ intr sich ergeben

surren'der val'ue s (ins) Rückkaufswert m

surreptitious [‚sʌrep'tɪʃəs] adj heimlich; (glance) verstohlen

surround [sə'raund] tr umgeben; (said of a crowd, police) umringen; (mil) einschließen

surround'ing adj umliegend ‖ surroundings spl Umgebung f

surtax ['sʌr‚tæks] s Steuerzuschlag m

surveillance [sər'vel(j)əns] s Überwachung f; keep under s. unter Polizeiaufsicht halten

survey ['sʌrve] s (of) Überblick m (über acc); (of opinions) Umfrage f; (of land) Vermessung f; (plan or description of the survey) Lageplan m ‖ [sʌr've] tr überblicken; (a person) mustern; (land) vermessen; (people for their opinion) befragen

sur'vey course' s Einführungskurs m

survey'ing s Landvermessung f

surveyor [sər've·ər] s Landmesser m

survival [sər'varvəl] s Überleben n; (after death) Weiterleben n

surviv'al of the fit'test s Überleben n des Tüchtigsten

survive [sər'vaɪv] tr (a person) überleben; (a thing) überstehen; be survived by hinterlassen ‖ intr am Leben bleiben

surviv'ing adj überlebend

survivor [sər'vaɪvər] s Überlebende mf

susceptible [sə'septɪbəl] adj (impressionable) eindrucksfähig; be s. of zulassen; be s. to (disease, infection) anfällig sein für; (flattery) empfänglich sein für

suspect ['sʌspekt] adj verdächtig ‖ s Verdächtige mf ‖ [sə'spekt] tr in Verdacht haben; (surmise) vermuten; (have a hint of) ahnen; s. s.o. of j–n verdächtigen (genit)

suspend [sə'spend] tr (from a job, office) suspendieren; (payment, hostilities, proceedings, a game) einstellen; (a rule) zeitweilig aufheben; (a sentence) aussetzen; (a player) sperren; (from a club) zeitweilig ausschließen; (from) hängen (an dat)

suspenders [səs'pendərz] spl Hosenträger pl

suspense [səs'pens] s Spannung f; hang in s. in der Schwebe sein; keep in s. im ungewissen lassen

suspension [səs'penʃən] s Aufhängung f; (of a sentence) Aussetzung f; (of work) Einstellung f; (e.g., of telephone service) Sperrung f; (aut) Federung f; (chem) Suspension f; s. of driver's license Führerscheinentzug m

suspen'sion bridge' s Hängebrücke f

suspen'sion points' spl (indicating unfinished thoughts) Gedankenpunkte pl; (indicating omission) Auslassungspunkte pl

suspicion [səs'pɪʃən] s Verdacht m; above s. über jeden Verdacht erhaben; be under s. unter Verdacht stehen; on s. of murder unter Mordverdacht

suspicious [səs'pɪʃəs] adj (person) verdächtig; (e.g., glance) argwöhnisch; (character) zweifelhaft

sustain [səs'ten] tr aufrechterhalten; (a loss, defeat, injury) erleiden; (a family) ernähren; (an army) verpflegen; (a motion, an objection) stattgeben (dat); (a theory, position) erhärten; (a note) dehnen

sustenance ['sʌstɪnəns] s (nourishment) Nahrung f; (means of livelihood) Unterhalt m

swab [swab] s (med, surg) Tupfer m;

(matter collected on a swab) Abstrich *m*; *(naut)* Schwabber *m* ‖ *v (pret & pp* **swabbed;** *ger* **swabbing)** *tr (med,* surg*)* abtupfen; *(naut)* schrubben

Swabia ['swebɪ·ə] *s* Schwaben *n*

Swabian ['swebɪ·ən] *adj* schwäbisch ‖ *s* **Schwabe** *m*, Schwäbin *f*; *(dialect)* Schwäbisch *n*

swad'dling clothes' ['swɑdlɪŋ] *spl* Windeln *pl*

swagger ['swægər] *s (strut)* Stolzieren *n*; *(swaggering manner)* Prahlerei *f* ‖ *intr* stolzieren; *(show off)* prahlen

swain [swen] *s (lover)* Liebhaber *m*; *(country lad)* Bauernbursche *m*

swallow ['swɑlo] *s* Schluck *m*; *(orn)* Schwalbe *f* ‖ *tr* schlucken; *(fig)* hinunterschlucken ‖ *intr* schlucken; **s. the wrong way** sich verschlucken

swamp [swɑmp] *s* Sumpf *m*, Moor *n* ‖ *tr* überfluten; *(with work)* überhäufen

swamp'land' *s* Moorland *n*

swampy ['swɑmpi] *adj* sumpfig

swan [swɑn] *s* Schwan *m*

swan' dive' *s* Schwalbensprung *m*

swank [swæŋk], **swanky** ['swæŋki] *adj (luxurious)* schick; *(ostentatious)* protzig

swan's'-down' *s* Schwanendaunen *pl*

swan' song' *s* Schwanengesang *n*

swap [swɑp] *s (coll)* Tauschgeschäft *n* ‖ *v (pret & pp* **swapped;** *ger* **swapping)** *tr & intr (coll)* tauschen

swarm [swɑrm] *s* Schwarm *m*; *(of children)* Schar *f* ‖ *intr* schwärmen; **s. around** umschwärmen; **s. into** sich drängen in *(acc)*; **s. with** *(fig)* wimmeln von

swarthy ['swɔrði] *adj* dunkelhäutig

swashbuckler ['swɑʃ ˌbʌklər] *s* Eisenfresser *m*

swastika ['swɑstɪkə] *s* Hakenkreuz *n*

swat [swɑt] *s* Schlag *m* ‖ *v (pret & pp* **swatted;** *ger* **swatting)** *tr* schlagen

swath [swɔθ] *s* Schwaden *m*

swathe [sweð] *tr* umwickeln, einwickeln

sway [swe] *s* Schwanken *n*, Schwingen *n*; *(domination)* Herrschaft *f* ‖ *tr (e.g., tree)* hin- und herbewegen; *(influence)* beeinflussen; *(cause to vacillate)* ins Wanken bringen ‖ *intr* schwanken

sway'-back' *s* Senkrücken *m*

swear [swer] *v (pret* **swore** [swor]; *pp* **sworn** [sworn]) *tr* schwören; **s. in** vereidigen; **s. s.o. to secrecy** j–n auf Geheimhaltung vereidigen ‖ *intr* schwören; *(coll)* fluchen; **s. at** schimpfen über *(acc) or* auf *(acc)*; **s. by** schwören bei; **s. off** abschwören *(dat)*; **s. on a stack of Bibles** Stein und Bein schwören; **s. to** *(a statement)* beschwören; **s. to it** darauf schwören

swear'ing-in' *s* Vereidigung *f*

swear'word' *s* Fluchwort *n*

sweat [swet] *s* Schweiß *m*; **break out in s.** in Schweiß geraten ‖ *v (pret & pp* **sweat & sweated)** *tr (blood)* schwitzen; *(metal)* seigern; *(a horse)* in Schweiß bringen; **s. off** abschwitzen; **s. out** (sl) geduldig abwarten; **s. up** durchschwitzen ‖ *intr* schwitzen

sweater ['swetər] *s* Sweater *m*, Pullover *m*

sweat'er girl' *s* vollbusiges Mädchen *n*

sweat' shirt' *s* Trainingsbluse *f*

sweat' shop' *s* (sl) Knochenmühle *f*

sweaty ['sweti] *adj* verschwitzt; *(hand)* schweißig

Swede [swid] *s* Schwede *m*, Schwedin *f*

Swedish ['swidɪʃ] *adj* schwedisch ‖ *s* Schwedisch *n*

sweep [swip] *s (sweeper)* Kehrer –in *mf*; *(of the arm, scythe, weapon)* Schwung *m*; *(of an oar)* Schlag *m*; *(range)* Reichweite *f*; *(continuous stretch)* ausgedehnte Strecke *f*; **in one clean s.** mit e–m Schlag; **make a clean s. of it** reinen Tisch machen ‖ *v (pret & pp* **swept** [swept]) *tr* kehren, fegen; *(mines)* räumen; *(with machine-gun fire)* bestreichen; *(with a searchlight)* absuchen; **he swept her off her feet** er hat sie im Sturm erobert; **s. clean** reinemachen ‖ *intr* kehren, fegen

sweeper ['swipər] *s* Kehrer –in *mf*; *(carpet sweeper)* Teppichkehrer *m*

sweep'ing *adj* weitreichend ‖ **sweepings** *spl* Kehricht *m & n*

sweep'-sec'ond *s* Zentralsekundenzeiger *m*

sweep'stakes' *s & spl* Lotterie *f*; (sport) Toto *m & n*

sweet [swit] *adj* süß; *(person)* lieb; *(butter)* ungesalzen; **be s. on** scharf sein auf *(acc)* ‖ **sweets** *spl* Süßigkeiten *pl*

sweet'bread' *s* Bries *n*

sweet'bri'er *s* Heckenrose *f*

sweet' corn' *s* Zuckermais *m*

sweeten ['switən] *tr* süßen; *(fig)* versüßen ‖ *intr* süß(er) werden

sweet'heart' *s* Liebste *mf*, Schatz *m*

sweetish ['switɪʃ] *adj* süßlich

sweet' mar'joram *s* Gartenmajoran *m*

sweet'meats' *spl* Zuckerwerk *n*

sweetness ['switnɪs] *s* Süßigkeit *f*

sweet' pea' *s* Gartenwicke *f*

sweet' pep'per *s* grüner Paprika *m*

sweet' pota'to *s* Süßkartoffel *f*

sweet'-scent'ed *adj* wohlriechend

sweet' tooth' *s*—**have a s.** gern naschen

sweet' wil'liam *s* Fleischnelke *f*

swell [swel] *adj* (coll) prima ‖ *s (of the sea)* Wellengang *m*; *(of an organ)* Schweller *m* ‖ *v (pret* **swelled;** *pp* **swelled & swollen** ['swolən]) *tr* zum Schwellen bringen; *(the number)* vermehren; *(a musical tone)* anschwellen lassen ‖ *intr* schwellen

swell'ing *s* Schwellung *f*

swelter ['sweltər] *intr* unter der Hitze leiden

swept'-back' *adj* (aer) keilförmig

swerve [swʌrv] *s* Abweichung *f* ‖ *tr* ablenken ‖ *intr* scharf abbiegen

swift [swɪft] *adj* geschwind, rasch

swig [swɪg] *s* (coll) kräftiger Schluck

$m \parallel v$ (*pret & pp* **swigged;** *ger* **swig-ging**) *tr* in langen Zügen trinken

swill [swɪl] *s* Spülicht *n;* (*for swine*) Schweinefutter *n;* (*deep drink*) tüchtiger Schluck *m* ‖ *tr & intr* gierig trinken

swim [swɪm] *s* Schwimmen *n;* **take a s.** schwimmen ‖ *v* (*pret* **swam** [swæm]; *pp* **swum** [swʌm]; *ger* **swimming**) *tr* (*e.g., a lake*) durchschwimmen; (*cause to swim*) schwimmen lassen; (*challenge in swimming*) um die Wette schwimmen mit ‖ *intr* schwimmen; **my head is swimming** mir schwindelt der Kopf

swimmer ['swɪmər] *s* Schwimmer –in *mf*

swim'ming *adj* Schwimm– ‖ *s* Schwimmen *n;* (*sport*) Schwimmsport *m*

swim'ming pool *s* Schwimmbecken *n*

swim'ming suit *s* Badeanzug *m*

swim'ming trunks *spl* Badehose *f*

swindle ['swɪndəl] *s* Schwindel *m* ‖ *tr* gaunern; **s. s.th. out of** etw erschwindeln von

swindler ['swɪndlər] *s* Schwindler –in *mf*

swind'ling *s* Schwindelei *f*

swine [swaɪn] *s* Schwein *n*

swine'herd' *s* Schweinehirt *m*

swing [swɪŋ] *s* (*for children*) Schaukel *f;* (*swinging movement*) Hin– und Herschwingen *n;* (*box*) Schwinger *m;* (*mus*) Swing *m;* **in full s.** in vollem Gang; **take a s. at** s.o. nach j–m schlagen ‖ *v* (*pret & pp* **swung** [swʌŋ]) *tr* schwingen; (*children on a swing*) schaukeln; (*an election*) entscheidend beeinflussen; **s.** (*e.g., a car*) **around** herumdrehen; **we'll s. it somehow** (coll) wir werden es schon schaffen ‖ *intr* pendeln; (*on a swing*) schaukeln; **s. around** sich umdrehen; **s. into action** in Schwung kommen; **things are swinging around here** (coll) hier geht es lustig zu

swing'ing door' *s* Pendeltür *f*

swinish ['swaɪnɪʃ] *adj* schweinisch

swipe [swaɪp] *s* (coll) Hieb *m;* **take a s. at** (coll) schlagen nach ‖ *tr* (*hit with full force*) (coll) kräftig schlagen; (*steal*) (sl) mausen

swirl [swʌrl] *s* Wirbel *m* ‖ *tr* (**about**) herumwirbeln ‖ *intr* wirbeln; (*said of water*) Strudel bilden

swish [swɪʃ] *s* (*e.g., of a whip*) Sausen *n;* (*of a dress*) Rauschen *n* ‖ *tr* (*a whip*) sausen lassen; **s. its tail** mit dem Schwanz wedeln ‖ *intr* (*said of a whip*) sausen; (*said of a dress*) rauschen

Swiss [swɪs] *adj* schweizerisch ‖ *s* Schweizer –in *mf*

Swiss' cheese' *s* Schweizer Käse *m*

Swiss' franc' *s* Schweizerfranken *m*

Swiss' Guard' *s* Schweizergarde *f*

switch [swɪtʃ] *s* (*exchange*) Wechsel *m,* Umschwung *m;* (*stick*) Rute *f;* (elec) Schalter *m;* (rr) Weiche *f* ‖ *tr* wechseln; (*e.g., coats by mistake*) verwechseln; (rr) rangieren; **s. off** (elec, rad, telv) ausschalten; **s. on**

(elec, rad, telv) einschalten ‖ *intr* Plätze wechseln

switch'-blade knife' *s* feststellbares Messer *n*

switch'board' *s* Schaltbrett *n,* Zentrale *f*

switch'board op'erator *s* Telephonist –in *mf*

switch' box' *s* Schaltkasten *m*

switch'man *s* (**–men**) (rr) Weichensteller *m*

switch' tow'er *s* (rr) Blockstation *f*

switch'yard' *s* Rangierbahnhof *m*

Switzerland ['swɪtsərlənd] *s* die Schweiz

sviv·el ['swɪvəl] *s* Drehlager *n* ‖ *v* (*pret & pp* **–el[l]ed;** *ger* **–el[l]ing**) *tr* herumdrehen ‖ *intr* sich drehen

sviv'el chair' *s* Drehstuhl *m*

swiz'zle stick' ['swɪzəl] *s* Rührstäbchen *n*

swollen ['swolən] *adj* (an)geschwollen; (*eyes*) verquollen

swoon [swun] *s* Ohnmacht *f* ‖ *intr* ohnmächtig werden

swoop [swup] *s* Herabstoßen *n;* **in one fell s.** mit e–m Schlag ‖ *intr*—**s. down** (**on**) herabstoßen (auf *acc*)

sword [sɔrd] *s* Schwert *n;* **put to the s.** mit dem Schwert hinrichten

sword' belt' *s* Schwertgehenk *n*

sword'fish' *s* Schwertfisch *m*

swords'man *s* (**–men**) Fechter *m*

sworn [sɔrn] *adj* (*statement*) eidlich; **s. enemy** Todfeind *m*

sycamore ['sɪkəmɔr] *s* Platane *f*

sycophant ['sɪkəfənt] *s* Sykophant *m*

syllabary ['sɪlə‚beri] *s* Silbenschrift *f*

syllabification [sɪ‚læbɪfɪ'keʃən] *s* Silbentrennung *f*

syllable ['sɪləbəl] *s* Silbe *f*

sylla·bus ['sɪləbəs] *s* (**–bai** [‚baɪ] & **–buses**) Lehrplan *m*

syllogism ['sɪlə‚dʒɪzəm] *s* Syllogismus *m*

sylvan ['sɪlvən] *adj* Wald–

symbol ['sɪmbəl] *s* Sinnbild *n,* Symbol *n*

symbolic(al) [sɪm'bɑlɪk(əl)] *adj* sinnbildlich, symbolisch

symbolism ['sɪmbə‚lɪzəm] *s* Symbolik *f*

symbolize ['sɪmbə‚laɪz] *tr* symbolisieren

symmetric(al) [sɪ'metrɪk(əl)] *adj* symmetrisch

symmetry ['sɪmɪtri] *s* Symmetrie *f*

sympathetic [‚sɪmpə'θetɪk] *adj* mitfühlend; (physiol) sympathisch

sympathize ['sɪmpə‚θaɪz] *intr*—**s. with** mitfühlen mit; (*be in accord with*) sympathisieren mit

sympathizer ['sɪmpə‚θaɪzər] *s* Sympathisant –in *mf*

sympathy ['sɪmpəθi] *s* Mitleid *n;* **be in s. with** im Einverständnis sein mit; **offer one's sympathies to** s.o. j–m sein Beileid bezeigen

sym'pathy card' *s* Beileidskarte *f*

sym'pathy strike' *s* Sympathiestreik *m*

symphonic [sɪm'fɑnɪk] *adj* sinfonisch

symphony ['sɪmfəni] *s* Sinfonie *f*

symposi·um [sɪm'pozɪ·əm] *s* (**-a** [ə] & **-ums**) Symposion *n*

symptom ['sɪmptəm] *s* (**of**) Symptom *n* (für)

symptomatic [ˌsɪmtə'mætɪk] *adj* (**of**) symptomatisch (für)

synagogue ['sɪnə.ɡɔɡ] *s* Synagoge *f*

synchronize ['sɪŋkrə.naɪz] *tr* synchronisieren

synchronous ['sɪŋkrənəs] *adj* synchron; (elec) Synchron-

syncopate ['sɪŋkə.pet] *tr* synkopieren

syncopation [ˌsɪŋkə'pefən] *s* Synkope *f*

syncope ['sɪŋkə.pi] *s* Synkope *f*

syndicate ['sɪndɪkɪt] *s* Interessengemeinschaft *f*, Syndikat *n* ‖ ['sɪndɪ.ket] *tr* zu e-m Syndikat zusammenschließen; (*a column*) in mehreren Zeitungen zugleich veröffentlichen ‖ *intr* ein Syndikat bilden

synod ['sɪnəd] *s* Synode *f*

synonym ['sɪnənɪm] *s* Synonym *n*

synonymous [sɪ'nɑnəməs] *adj* sinnverwandt; **s. with** gleichbedeutend mit

synop·sis [sɪ'nɑpsɪs] *s* (**-ses** [siz]) Zusammenfassung *f*

synoptic [sɪ'nɑptɪk] *adj* synoptisch

syntax ['sɪntæks] *s* Satzlehre *f*, Syntax *f*

synthe·sis ['sɪnθɪsɪs] *s* (**-ses** [ˌsiz]) Synthese *f*

synthesize ['sɪnθɪ.saɪz] *tr* (& chem) zusammenfügen

synthetic [sɪn'θetɪk] *adj* künstlich, Kunst- ‖ *s* Kunststoff *m*

syphilis ['sɪfɪlɪs] *s* Syphilis *f*

Syria ['sɪrɪ·ə] *s* Syrien *n*

Syrian ['sɪrɪ·ən] *adj* syrisch ‖ *s* Syrer –in *mf*; (*language*) Syrisch *n*

syringe [sɪ'rɪndʒ] *s* Spritze *f* ‖ *tr* (*inject*) einspritzen; (*wash*) ausspritzen

syrup ['sɪrəp] *s* Sirup *m*

system ['sɪstəm] *s* System *n*; (*bodily system*) Organismus *m*

systematic(al) [ˌsɪstə'mætɪk(əl)] *adj* systematisch, planmäßig

systematize ['sɪstəmə.taɪz] *tr* systematisieren, systematisch ordnen

systole ['sɪstəlɪ] *s* Systole *f*

T, t [ti] *s* zwanzigster Buchstabe des englischen Alphabets

tab [tæb] *s* (*label*) Etikett *n*; (*on file cards*) Karteireiter *m*; **keep tabs on** (coll) genau kontrollieren; **pick up the tab** (coll) die Zeche bezahlen ‖ *v* (*pret* & *pp* **tabbed**; *ger* **tabbing**) *tr* (*designate*) ernennen

tabby ['tæbɪ] *s* getigerte Katze *f*

tabernacle ['tæbər.nækəl] *s* Tabernakel *n*

table ['tebəl] *s* Tisch *m*; (*list, chart*) Tafel *f*, Tabelle *f*; (geol) Tafel *f*; **at t. bei** Tisch; **the tables have turned** das Blatt hat sich gewendet ‖ *tr* (parl) verschieben

tab·leau ['tæblo] *s* (**-leaus** & **leaux** [loz]) Tableau *n*

ta'blecloth' *s* Tischtuch *n*

ta'bieland' *s* Tafelland *n*

ta'ble man'ners *spl* Tischmanieren *pl*

ta'ble of con'tents *s* Inhaltsverzeichnis *n*

ta'ble salt' *s* Tafelsalz *n*

ta'ble set'ting *s* Gedeck *n*

ta'blespoon' *s* Eßlöffel *m*

tablespoonful ['tebəl.spun.ful] *s* Eßlöffel *m*

tablet ['tæblɪt] *s* (*writing pad*) Schreibblock *m*; (med) Tablette *f*

ta'ble talk' *s* Tischgespräch *n*

ta'ble ten'nis *s* Tischtennis *n*

ta'bletop' *s* Tischplatte *f*

ta'bleware' *s* Tafelgeschirr *n*

ta'ble wine' *s* Tafelwein *m*

tabloid ['tæblɔɪd] *adj* konzentriert ‖ *s* Bildzeitung *f*; (pej) Sensationsblatt *n*

taboo [tə'bu] *adj* tabu ‖ *s* Tabu *n* ‖ *tr* für Tabu erklären

tabular ['tæbjələr] *adj* tabellarisch

tabulate ['tæbjə.let] *tr* tabellarisieren

tabulator ['tæbjə.letər] *s* Tabelliermaschine *f*

tacit ['tæsɪt] *adj* stillschweigend

taciturn ['tæsɪtɜrn] *adj* schweigsam

tack [tæk] *s* (*nail*) Zwecke *f*, Stift *m*; (*stitch*) Heftstich *m*; (*stickiness*) Klebrigkeit *f*; (*course of action*) Kurs *m*; (*gear for a riding horse*) Reitgeschirr *n*; (*course run obliquely to the wind*) Schlag *m*; **be on the wrong t.** (fig) auf dem Holzweg sein ‖ *tr* (**down**) mit Zwecken befestigen; (sew) heften; **t. on** (**to**) anfügen (an *acc*) ‖ *intr* (fig & naut) lavieren

tackle ['tækəl] *s* (*gear*) Ausrüstung *f*; (*for lifting*) Flaschenzug *m*; (fb) Halbstürmer *m*; (naut) Takelwerk *n* ‖ *tr* (*a problem*) anpacken; (fb) packen

tacky ['tækɪ] *adj* klebrig; (*gaudy*) geschmacklos

tact [tækt] *s* Takt *m*, Feingefühl *n*

tactful ['tæktfəl] *adj* taktvoll

tactical ['tæktɪkəl] *adj* taktisch

tac'tical u'nit *s* Kampfeinheit *f*

tactician [tæk'tɪʃən] *s* Taktiker *m*

tactics ['tæktɪks] *spl* (& fig) Taktik *f*

tactless ['tæktlɪs] *adj* taktlos

tadpole ['tæd.pol] *s* Kaulquappe *f*

taffeta ['tæfɪtə] *s* Taft *m*

taffy ['tæfɪ] *s* Sahnebonbon *n*

tag [tæɡ] *s* (*label*) Etikett *n*; (*loose end*) loses Ende *n*; (*on a shoestring*) Stift *m*; (*loop for hanging up a coat*) Aufhänger *m*; (*on a fish hook*) Glitzerschmuck *m*; (*game*) Haschen *n*; **play tag** sich haschen; **tags** (aut)

Nummernschild n ‖ v (pret & pp
tagged; ger tagging) tr (mark with
a tag) mit e-m Etikett versehen;
(touch) haschen; (hit solidly) heftig
schlagen; (give a traffic ticket to)
e-n Strafzettel geben (dat) ‖ intr—
tag after s.o. sich an j-s Sohlen
heften

tag′ line′ s (e.g., of a play) Schlußworte
pl; (favorite phrase) stehende Redensart f

tail [tel] s Schwanz m; (of a horse,
comet) Schweif m; (of a shirt) Schoß
m; (aer) Heck n; tails ein Frack m;
(of a coin) Rückseite f; turn t. ausreißen; wag its t. mit dem Schwanz
wedeln ‖ tr (coll) beschatten ‖ intr
—t. after nachlaufen (dat); t. off
abflauen

tail′ end′ s (e.g., of a conversation)
Schlußteil n; come in at the t. end als
letzter durchs Ziel gehen

tail′gate′ s (of a station wagon) Heck-
tür f; (of a truck) Ladeklappe f ‖
intr dicht hinter e-m anderen fahren

tail′ gun′ner s (aer) Heckschütze m

tail′-heav′y adj schwanzlastig

tail′light′ s (aer) Hecklicht n; (aut)
Rücklicht n

tailor ['telər] s Schneider m ‖ tr &
intr schneidern

tai′loring s Schneiderarbeit f

tai′lor-made suit′ s Maßanzug m

tai′lor shop′ s Schneiderei f

tail′piece′ s (appendage) Anhang m;
(of a stringed instrument) Saiten-
halter m; (typ) Zierleiste f

tail′ pipe′ s (aut) Auspuffrohr n

tail′skid′ s (aer) Sporn m

tail′spin′ s—go into a t. abtrudeln

tail′ wheel′ s (aer) Spornrad n

tail′wind′ s Rückenwind m

taint [tent] s Fleck m; (fig) Schandfleck m ‖ tr beflecken; (food) verderben

take [tek] s (income) (sl) Einnahmen
pl; (loot) (sl) Beute f; (angl) Fang
m; (cin) Szenenaufnahme f; be on
the t. (sl) sich bestechen lassen ‖ v
(pret took [tuk]; pp taken) tr nehmen; (in a car) mitnehmen; (bring,
carry) bringen; (subtract) abziehen;
(require) erfordern; (insults, criticism) hinnehmen; (bear, stand) ertragen; (with a camera) aufnehmen;
(food, pills) einnehmen; (s.o.'s temperature) messen; (courage) schöpfen; (a deep breath) holen; (precautions) treffen; (responsibility) übernehmen; (an oath, test) ablegen;
(inventory) aufnehmen; (a walk, trip,
examination, turn, notes) machen;
(the consequences) tragen; (measures) ergreifen; (a certain amount
of time to travel) in Anspruch nehmen; (a step) tun; (advice) befolgen;
(a game) gewinnen; (e.g., third
place) belegen; (a trick) (cards)
stechen; (gram) regieren; be able to
t. a lot e-n breiten Rücken haben;
be taken in by s.o. j-m auf den
Leim gehen; I'm not going to t. that

das lasse ich nicht auf mir sitzen;
t. along mitnehmen; t. aside bei-
seitenehmen; t. at one's word beim
Wort nehmen; t. away wegschaffen;
t. away from wegnehmen (dat); t.
back zurücknehmen; t. (e.g., s.o.'s
hat) by mistake verwechseln; t. down
herunternehmen; (in writing) aufschreiben; (dictation) aufnehmen;
(minutes) zu Protokoll nehmen; t. in
(money) einnehmen; (washing) ins
Haus nehmen; (as guest) beherbergen; (deceive) täuschen; (encompass)
umfassen; (observe) beobachten;
(sightsee) besichtigen; (sew) enger
machen; t. it out on s.o. seinen Zorn
an j-m auslassen; t. it that annehmen, daß; taken (occupied) besetzt;
t. off (subtract) abziehen; (clothes)
ausziehen; (a coat) ablegen; (gloves)
abstreifen; (a hat) abnehmen; (a
tire, wheel) abmontieren; (e.g., a
day from work) sich [dat] freineh-
men; t. (e.g., wares) off s.o.'s hands
j-m abnehmen; t. on (hire) anstellen; (passengers) aufnehmen; t. out
(from a container) herausnehmen; (a
spot) entfernen; (a girl) ausführen;
(a mortgage, loan) aufnehmen; (ins)
abschließen; (libr) sich [dat] ausleihen; t. over übernehmen; t. s.o.
for j-n halten für; t. up aufnehmen;
(absorb) aufsaugen; (a profession)
ergreifen; (room, time) wegnehmen;
(a collection) veranstalten; (a skirt)
kürzer machen; t. upon oneself auf
sich nehmen; t. up (a matter) with
besprechen mit ‖ intr (said of an
injection) anschlagen; (said of seed-
lings, skin transplants) anwachsen;
how long does it t.? wie lange dauert
es?; how long does it t. to (inf)?;
wie lange braucht man, um zu (inf)?;
t. after nachgeraten (dat); t. off
(depart) (coll) abhauen; (from work)
wegbleiben; (aer, rok) starten; (aut)
abfahren; t. over for s.o. für j-n
einspringen; t. to (a person) warm
werden mit; (an idea) aufgreifen; t.
up with sich abgeben mit

take′-home pay′ s Nettolohn m

take′-off′ s Karikatur f; (aer) Start m

take′-off ramp′ s (in skiing) Schanzen-
tisch m

take′o′ver s Übernahme f

tal′cum pow′der ['tælkəm] s Feder-
weiß n

tale [tel] s Geschichte f; tell tales out
of school aus der Schule plaudern

tale′bear′er s Zuträger –in mf

talent ['tælənt] s Talent n

tal′ented adj talentiert, begabt

talisman ['tælɪsmən] s Talisman m

talk [tɔk] s Gespräch n; (gossip) Geschwätz n; (lecture) Vortrag m;
(speech) Rede f; cause t. von sich
reden machen; give a t. on e-n Vortrag halten über (acc); t. of the town
Stadtgespräch n ‖ tr reden; (business, politics, etc.) sprechen über
(acc); t. down zum Schweigen bringen; (aer) heruntersprechen; t. one-

self hoarse sich heiser reden; **t. one's way** out of sich herausreden aus; **t. over** besprechen; **t. sense** vernünftig reden; **t. s.o. into** (ger) j-n überreden zu (inf); **t. up** Reklame machen für ‖ intr reden; (chat) schwätzen; **t. back** scharf erwidern; **t. big** große Töne reden; **t. dirty** Zoten reißen; **t. down to** herablassend reden zu; **talking of food à propos** Essen; **t. on** (a topic) e-n Vortrag halten über (acc); **t. to the walls** in den Wind reden

talkative ['tɔkətɪv] adj redselig

talker ['tɔkər] s Plauderer –in mf; **big t.** Schaumschläger m

talkie ['tɔki] s (cin) Sprechfilm m

talk'ing-to' s Denkzettel m

tall [tɔl] adj hoch; (person) hochgewachsen; **t. story** Mordsgeschichte f

tallow ['tælo] s Talg m

tal·ly ['tæli] s (reckoning) Rechnung f; (game score) Punktzahl f ‖ v (pret & pp –lied) tr (up) berechnen ‖ intr (with) übereinstimmen (mit)

tallyho [‚tælɪ'ho] interj hallo!

tal'ly sheet' s Zählbogen m

talon ['tælən] s Klaue f

tambourine [‚tæmbə'rin] s Tamburin n

tame [tem] adj zahm; (docile) gefügig; (dull) langweilig ‖ tr zähmen; (e.g., lions) bändigen ‖ intr—**t. down** (said of a person) gesetzter werden

tamp [tæmp] tr (a tobacco pipe) stopfen; (earth, cement) stampfen; (a drill hole) zustopfen

tamper ['tæmpər] s Stampfer m ‖ intr —**t. with** sich einmischen in (acc); (machinery) herumbasteln an (dat); (documents) frisieren

tampon ['tæmpɑn] s Damenbinde f; (surg) Tampon m ‖ tr (surg) tamponieren

tan [tæn] adj gelbbraun ‖ s Sonnenbräunung f ‖ v (pret & pp tanned; ger tanning) tr (the skin) bräunen; (leather) gerben ‖ intr sich bräunen

tandem ['tændəm] adj & adv hintereinander (geordnet) ‖ s Tandem n; **in t.** hintereinander

tang [tæŋ] s Herbheit f; (sound) Geklingel n

tangent ['tændʒənt] adj—**be t. to** tangieren ‖ s Tangente f; **fly off on a t.** plötzlich vom Thema abschweifen

tangerine [‚tændʒə'rin] s Mandarine f

tangible ['tændʒɪbəl] adj (& fig) greifbar

tangle ['tæŋgəl] s Verwicklung f; (twisted strands; confused jumble) Gewirr n; (conflict) Auseinandersetzung f ‖ tr verwirren; **get tangled** sich verfilzen ‖ intr sich verwirren; **t. with** sich mit j-m in e-n Kampf einlassen mit

tango ['tæŋgo] s Tango m ‖ intr Tango tanzen

tangy ['tæŋi] adj herb

tank [tæŋk] s Behälter m; (of a toilet) Spülkasten m; (mil) Panzer m

tank' attack' s Panzerangriff m

tank' car' s (rr) Kesselwagen m, Tankwagen m

tanker ['tæŋkər] s (truck) Tankwagen m; (ship) Tanker m; (plane) Tankflugzeug n

tank' trap' s Panzersperre f

tank' truck' s Tankwagen m

tanned adj gebräunt

tanner ['tænər] s Gerber –in mf

tannery ['tænəri] s Gerberei f

tantalize ['tæntə‚laɪz] tr quälen

tantamount ['tæntə‚maunt] adj—**be t. to** gleichkommen (dat)

tantrum ['tæntrəm] s Koller m; **throw a t.** e-n Koller kriegen

tap [tæp] s (light blow) Klaps m; (on a window or door) Klopfen n; (faucet) Wasserhahn m; (in a cask) Faßhahn m; (elec) Anzapfung f; (mach) Gewindebohrer m; (surg) Punktion f; **on tap** vom Faß; **play taps** (mil) den Zapfenstreich blasen ‖ v (pret & pp tapped; ger tapping) tr (a cask, powerline, telephone) anzapfen; (fluids) abzapfen; (a person on the shoulder) antippen; (a hole) mit e-m Gewinde versehen; **tap one's foot** (to mark time) Takt treten; **tap s.o. for** (money) (coll) j-n anpumpen um; **tap s.o.'s spine** j-n punktieren; **tap the window** am Fenster klopfen ‖ intr tippen

tap' dance' s Steptanz m

tap'-dance' intr steppen

tap' dan'cer s Stepper –in mf

tape [tep] s Band n; (electron) Tonband n; (friction tape) Isolierband n; (of paper) Papierstreifen m; (med) Klebstreifen m; (sport) Zielband n ‖ tr (mit Band) umwickeln; (electron) auf Tonband aufnehmen

tape' meas'ure s Meßband n

taper ['tepər] s Wachsfaden m ‖ tr zuspitzen ‖ intr spitz zulaufen; **t. off** langsam abnehmen

tape' record'er s Tonbandgerät n

ta'pered adj kegelförmig, Keil–

tapestry ['tæpɪstri] s Wandteppich m

tape'worm' s Bandwurm m

tapioca [‚tæpɪ'okə] s Tapioka f

tap'room' s Ausschank m

tap'root' s Pfahlwurzel f

tap' wa'ter s Leitungswasser n

tap' wrench' s Gewindeschneidkluppe f

tar [tɑr] s Teer m ‖ v (pret & pp tarred; ger tarring) tr teeren

tardy ['tɑrdi] adj säumig

target ['tɑrgɪt] s Ziel n; (on a firing range; of ridicule) Zielscheibe f

tar'get ar'ea s Zielraum m

tar'get date' s Zieltag m

tar'get lan'guage s Zielsprache f

tar'get prac'tice s Scheibenschießen n

tariff ['tærɪf] s Tarif m

tarnish ['tɑrnɪʃ] tr matt (or blind) machen; (fig) beflecken ‖ intr matt (or blind) werden

tar' pa'per s Teerpappe f

tarpaulin ['tɑrpəlɪn] s Plane f

tar·ry ['tɑri] adj teerig ‖ ['tæri] v

(pret & pp **-ried**) *intr* verweilen; *(stay)* bleiben

tart [tɑrt] *adj* sauer; *(reply)* scharf ‖ *s* Tortelett *n*

tartar ['tɑrtər] *s* (dent) Zahnstein *m*

tar'tar sauce' *s* pikante Soße *f*

task [tæsk] *s* Aufgabe *f;* take to t. zur Rede stellen

task' force' *s* Sonderverband *m*

task'mas'ter *s* Zuchtmeister *m*

tassel ['tæsəl] *s* Quaste *f; (on corn)* Narbenfäden *pl*

taste [test] *s* (& *fig)* Geschmack *m;* develop a t. for Geschmack gewinnen an *(dat);* have a bad t. schlecht ‖ *intr*—t. like (or of) schmecken schmecken; have bad t. e-n schlechten Geschmack haben; in bad t. geschmacklos; in good t. geschmackvoll; to t. (culin) nach Gutdünken ‖ *tr* schmecken; *(try out)* kosten; *(e.g.,* the pepper in soup) herausschmecken; t. blood (fig) Blut lecken nach

taste' bud' *s* Geschmacksknospe *f*

tasteful ['testfəl] *adj* geschmackvoll

tasteless ['testlɪs] *adj* (& *fig)* geschmacklos

tasty ['testi] *adj* schmackhaft

tatter ['tætər] *s* Lumpen *m* ‖ *tr* zerfetzen

tat'tered *adj* zerlumpt

tattle ['tætəl] *intr* petzen

tattler ['tætlər] *s* Petze *f*

tat'tletale' *s* Petze *f*

tattoo [tæ'tu] *s* Tätowierung *f* ‖ *tr* tätowieren

taunt [tɔnt] *s* Stichelei *f* ‖ *tr* sticheln gegen

taut [tɔt] *adj* straff, prall

tavern ['tævərn] *s* Schenke *f*

tawdry ['tɔdri] *adj* aufgedonnert

tawny ['tɔni] *adj* gelbbraun

tax [tæks] *s* Steuer *f* ‖ *tr* besteuern; (fig) beanspruchen; tax s.o. with j-n rügen wegen

taxable ['tæksəbəl] *adj* steuerpflichtig

tax' assess'ment *s* Steuereinschätzung *f*

taxation [tæk'seʃən] *s* Besteuerung *f*

tax' brac'ket *s* Steuerklasse *f*

tax' collec'tor *s* Steuereinnehmer –in *mf*

tax' cut' *s* Steuersenkung *f*

tax' eva'sion *s* Steuerhinterziehung *f*

tax' exemp'tion *s* steuerfreier Betrag *m*

tax·i ['tæksi] *s* Taxi *n;* go by t. mit e-m Taxi fahren ‖ *v (pret & pp* **-ied**) *ger* **-iing** & **-ying**) *tr* (aer) rollen lassen ‖ *intr* mit e-m Taxi fahren; (aer) rollen

tax'icab' *s* Taxi *n*

tax'i danc'er *s* Taxigirl *n*

taxidermist ['tæksɪ‚dʌrmɪst] *s* Tierpräparator –in *mf*

tax'i driv'er *s* Taxifahrer –in *mf*

tax'ime'ter *s* Taxameter *m*

tax'i stand' *s* Taxistand *m*

tax'pay'er *s* Steuerzahler –in *mf*

tax' rate' *s* Steuersatz *m*

tax' return' *s* Steuererklärung *f*

tea [ti] *s* Tee *m*

tea' bag' *s* Teebeutel *m*

tea' cart' *s* Teewagen *m*

teach [tit∫] *v (pret & pp* **taught** [tɔt]) *tr* lehren; *(instruct)* unterrichten; t. school an e-r Schule unterrichten; t. s.o. manners j-m Manieren beibringen; t. s.o. music j-n in Musik unterrichten; t. s.o. (to play) tennis j-m das Tennisspielen beibringen ‖ *intr* lehren, unterrichten

teacher ['tit∫ər] *s* Lehrer –in *mf*

teach'er's pet' *s* Liebling *m* des Lehrers (or der Lehrerin)

teach'ing *s* Lehren *n; (profession)* Lehrberuf *m*

teach'ing aid' *s* Lehrmittel *n*

teach'ing staff' *s* Lehrkörper *m*

tea'cup' *s* Teetasse *f*

teak [tik] *s* Teakholz *n*

tea'ket'tle *s* Teekessel *m*

tea' leaves' *spl* Teesatz *m*

team [tim] *s* Team *n; (of draught animals)* Gespann *n;* (sport) Mannschaft *f* ‖ *tr (draft animals)* zusammenspannen ‖ *intr*—t. up with sich vereinigen mit

team' cap'tain *s* Spielführer –in *mf*

team'mate' *s* Mannschaftskamerad –in *mf*

teamster ['timstər] *s* Fuhrmann *m; (trucker)* Lastwagenfahrer *m*

team'work' *s* Gemeinschaftsarbeit *f;* (sport) Zusammenspiel *n*

tea'pot' *s* Teekanne *f*

tear [tɪr] *s* Träne *f;* bring tears to the eyes Tränen in die Augen treiben; burst into tears in Tränen ausbrechen ‖ [ter] *s* Riß *m* ‖ *v (pret* **tore** [tor]; *pp* **torn** [torn]) *tr* (zer)reißen; t. apart *(meat)* zerreißen; *(a speech)* zerpflücken; t. away wegreißen; t. down *(a building)* abreißen; (mach) zerlegen; *(a person)* sich [dat] das Maul zerreißen über *(acc);* t. off abreißen; t. open aufreißen; t. oneself away sich losreißen; t. out ausreißen; t. up *(a street)* aufreißen; *(e.g., letter)* zerreißen ‖ *intr* (zer)reißen; t. along *(at high speed)* dahinsausen

teardrop ['tɪr‚drɑp] *s* Träne *f*

tear' gas' [tɪr] *s* Tränengas *n*

tear-jerker ['tɪr‚dʒʌrkər] *s* (sl) Schnulze *f*

tea'room' *s* Teestube *f*

tease [tiz] *tr* necken; *(e.g., a dog)* quälen; *(hair)* auflockern

teas'ing *s* Neckerei *f*

tea'spoon' *s* Teelöffel *m*

teaspoonful ['ti‚spun‚ful] *s* Teelöffel *m*

teat [tit] *s* Zitze *f*

technical ['tɛknɪkəl] *adj* technisch, Fach-

tech'nical in'stitute *s* technische Hochschule *f*

technicality [‚tɛknɪ'kælɪti] *s* technische Einzelheit *f*

tech'nical school' *s* Technikum *n*

tech'nical term' *s* Fachausdruck *m*

technician [tɛk'nɪʃən] *s* Techniker –in *mf*

technique [tɛk'nik] *s* Technik *f*

technocrat ['tɛknə‚kræt] s Technokrat m

technological [‚tɛknə'lɑdʒɪkəl] adj technologisch

technology [tek'nɑlɪdʒi] s Technologie f

ted'dy bear' ['tedi] s Teddybär m

tedious ['tidɪ‚əs] adj langweilig

tee [ti] s (mound) Abschlagplatz m; (wooden or plastic peg) Aufsatz m; to a tee aufs Haar || tr—tee off (sl) aufregen; tee up (golf) auf den Aufsatz stellen || intr—tee off (golf) abschlagen

teem [tim] intr (with) wimmeln (von)

teem'ing adj wimmelnd; (rain) strömend

teen-age ['tin‚edʒ] adj halbwüchsig

teen-ager ['tin‚edʒər] s Teenager m

teens [tinz] spl Jugendalter n (vom dreizehnten bis neunzehnten Lebensjahr); in one's t. in den Jugendjahren

teeny ['tini] adj (coll) winzig

tee' shot' s (golf) Abschlag m

teeter ['titər] s Schaukeln n || intr schaukeln

teethe [tið] intr zahnen

teeth'ing ring' s Beißring m

teetotaler [ti'totələr] s Abstinenzler –in mf

tele-cast ['tɛlɪ‚kæst] s Fernsehsendung f || v (pret & pp –cast & –casted) tr im Fernsehen übertragen

telecommunications [‚tɛlɪkə‚mjunɪ'keʃəns] spl Fernmeldewesen n

telegram ['tɛlɪ‚græm] s Telegramm n

telegraph ['tɛlɪ‚græf] s Telegraph m || tr & intr telegraphieren

telegrapher [tɪ'lɛgrəfər] s Telegraphist –in mf

tel'egraph pole' s Telegraphenstange f

telemeter [tɪ'lɛmɪtər] s Telemeter n

telepathy [tɪ'lɛpəθi] s Telepathie f

telephone ['tɛlɪ‚fon] s Telephon n, Fernsprecher m; be on the t. am Apparat sein; by t. telephonisch; speak on the t. with telephonieren mit || tr & intr anrufen

tel'ephone booth' s Telephonzelle f

tel'ephone call' s Telephonanruf m

tel'ephone direc'tory s Teilnehmerverzeichnis n

tel'ephone exchange' s Telephonzentrale f

tel'ephone num'ber s Telephonnummer f

tel'ephone op'erator s Telephonist –in mf

tel'ephone receiv'er s Telephonhörer m

tel'ephoto lens' ['tɛlɪ‚foto] s Teleobjektiv n

telescope ['tɛlɪ‚skop] s Fernrohr n, Perspektiv n || tr ineinanderschieben; (fig) verkürzen || intr sich ineinanderschieben

telescopic [‚tɛlɪ'skɑpɪk] adj teleskopisch

telescop'ic sight' s Zielfernrohr n

Teletype ['tɛlɪ‚taɪp] s (trademark) Fernschreiber m || teletype tr durch Fernschreiber übermitteln || intr fernschreiben

tel'etype'writ'er s Fernschreiber m

televiewer ['tɛlɪ‚vju‚ər] s Fernsehteilnehmer –in mf

televise ['tɛlɪ‚vaɪz] tr im Fernsehen übertragen (or senden)

television ['tɛlɪ‚vɪʒən] adj Fernseh– || s Fernsehen n; watch t. fernsehen

tel'evision net'work s Fernsehnetz n

tel'evision screen' s Bildschirm m

tel'evision set' s Fernsehapparat m; color t. Farbfernsehapparat m

tel'evision show' s Fernschau f

telex ['tɛleks] s Fernschreiber m; (message) Telex n || tr fernschreiben

tell [tɛl] v (pret & pp told [told]) tr (the truth, a lie) sagen; (relate) erzählen; (a secret) anvertrauen; (let know) Bescheid sagen (dat); (inform) bestellen; (express) ausdrücken; (the reason) angeben; (distinguish) auseinanderhalten; be able to t. time die Uhr lesen können; t. apart auseinanderhalten; t. me another! (sl) das machst du mir nicht weis!; t. s.o. off j–n abkanzeln; t. s.o. that (assure s.o. that) j–m versichern, daß; t. s.o. to (inf) j–m sagen, daß er (inf) soll; t. s.o. where to get off (sl) j–m e–e Zigarre verpassen; to t. the truth ehrlich gesagt; you can t. by looking at her that man sieht es ihr an, daß || intr—don't t. me! na, so was!; t. on (betray) verraten; (produce a marked effect on) sehr mitnehmen; you're telling me! wem sagst du das!

teller ['tɛlər] s (of a bank) Kassierer –in mf; (of votes) Zähler –in mf

tell'ing adj (blow) wirksam

tell'-tale' adj verräterisch

temper ['tɛmpər] s (anger) Zorn m; (of steel) Härtegrad m; bad t. großer Zorn m; even t. Gleichmut m; lose one's t. in Wut geraten || tr (with) mildern (durch); (steel) härten; (mus) temperieren

temperament ['tɛmpərəmənt] s Temperament n

temperamental [‚tɛmpərə'mɛntəl] adj launisch, temperamentvoll

temperance ['tɛmpərəns] s Mäßigkeit f

temperate ['tɛmpərɪt] adj mäßig; (climate) gemäßigt

Tem'perate Zone' s gemäßigte Zone f

temperature ['tɛmərət/ər] s Temperatur f

tempest ['tɛmpɪst] s Sturm m; a t. in a teapot ein Sturm im Wasserglas

tempestuous [tɛm'pest/ʊ‚əs] adj stürmisch

temple ['tɛmpəl] s Tempel m; (of glasses) Bügel m; (anat) Schläfe f

tem-po ['tɛmpo] s (–pos & –pi [pi]) Tempo n

temporal ['tɛmpərəl] adj zeitlich

temporary ['tɛmpə‚reri] adj zeitweilig; (credit, solution) Zwischen–

temporize ['tɛmpə‚raɪz] intr Zeit zu gewinnen suchen

tempt [tɛmpt] tr versuchen; (said of things) reizen, locken

temptation [temp'teʃən] s Versuchung f

tempter ['temptər] s Versucher m

tempt'ing adj verlockend

temptress ['temptris] s Versucherin f

ten [ten] adj & pron zehn || s Zehn f

tenable ['tenəbəl] adj haltbar

tenacious [tɪ'neʃəs] adj (obstinate) nartnäckig; (memory) verläßlich

tenacity [tɪ'næsɪti] s Hartnäckigkeit f

tenant ['tenənt] s Mieter –in mf

ten'ant farm'er s Pächter –in mf

tend [tend] tr (flocks) hüten; (the sick) pflegen; (a machine) bedienen || intr—t. to (attend to) sich kümmern um; (inf) dazu neigen zu (inf); t. toward(s) neigen zu

tendency ['tendənsi] s Tendenz f

tender ['tendər] adj zart || s Angebot n; (nav, rr) Tender m || tr anbieten

ten'derfoot' s Neuankömmling m; (boy-scout) neu aufgenommener Pfadfinder m

ten'derheart'ed adj zartfühlend

ten'derloin' s Rindslendenstück n

tenderness ['tendərnɪs] s Zartheit f

tendon ['tendən] s Sehne f

tendril ['tendrɪl] s Ranke f

tenement ['tenɪmənt] s (dwelling) Wohnung f; (rented dwelling) Mietwohnung f

ten'ement house' s Mietskaserne f

tenet ['tenɪt] s Grundsatz m, Lehrsatz m

ten'fold' adj & adv zehnfach

tennis ['tenɪs] s Tennis n

ten'nis court' s Tennisplatz m

ten'nis rack'et s Tennisschläger m

tenor ['tenər] s (drift, meaning; singer; voice range) Tenor m

ten'pin' s Kegel m

tense [tens] adj gespannt, straff; make t. spannen || s (gram) Tempus n, Zweitform f

tension ['tenʃən] s (& elec) Spannung f; (phys) Spannkraft f

tent [tent] s Zelt n

tentacle ['tentəkəl] s Fühler m; (bot) Tentakel m

tentative ['tentətɪv] adj vorläufig

tenth [tenθ] adj & pron zehnte || s (fraction) Zehntel n; the t. (in dates and in series) der Zehnte

tent' pole' s Zeltstange f

tenuous ['tenjʊ·əs] adj (thin) dünn; (rarefied) verdünnt; (insignificant) unbedeutend; (weak) schwach

tenure ['tenjər] s (possession) Besitz m; (educ) Anstellung f auf Lebenszeit; t. of office Amtsdauer f

tepid ['tepɪd] adj lauwarm

term [tʌrm] s (expression) Ausdruck m; (time period) Frist f; (of office) Amtszeit f; (jur) Sitzungsperiode f; (math) Glied n; (log) Begriff m; be on good terms with in guten Beziehungen stehen mit; come to terms with handelseinig werden mit; in plain terms unverblümt; in terms of im Sinne von; in terms of praise mit lobenden Worten; on easy terms zu günstigen Bedingungen; on equal terms auf gleichem Fuß; on t. (com) auf Zeit; not be on speaking terms with nicht sprechen mit; tell s.o. in no uncertain terms j–m gründlich die Meinung sagen; terms (of a contract, treaty, payment) Bedingungen pl || tr bezeichnen

termagant ['tʌrməgənt] s Xanthippe f

terminal ['tʌrmɪnəl] adj End–; (disease) unheilbar || s (aer) Flughafenempfangsgebäude n; (pole) (elec) Pol m; (rr) Kopfbahnhof m

terminate ['tʌrmɪ,net] tr (end) beenden; (limit) begrenzen || intr enden, endigen; (gram) (in) auslauten (auf acc)

termination [,tʌrmɪ'neʃən] s Beendigung f; (gram) Endung f

terminology [,tʌrmɪ'nɑlɪdʒi] s Terminologie f

term' insur'ance s Versicherung f auf Zeit

terminus ['tʌrmɪnəs] s (end) Endpunkt m; (boundary) Grenze f; (rr) Endstation f

termite ['tʌrmaɪt] s Termite f

term' pa'per s Referat n

terrace ['terəs] s Terrasse f || tr abstufen, terrassieren

terra cotta ['terə'kɑtə] s Terrakotta f

ter'ra-cot'ta adj Terrakotta–

terrain [te'ren] s Gelände n, Terrain n

terrestrial [tə'restrɪ·əl] adj irdisch

terrible ['terɪbəl] adj furchtbar

terribly ['terɪbli] adv (coll) furchtbar

terrier ['terɪ·ər] s Terrier m

terrific [tə'rɪfɪk] adj (frightful) fürchterlich; (intense) (coll) gewaltig; (splendid) (coll) prima

terri•fy ['terɪ,faɪ] v (pret & pp –fied) tr Entsetzen einjagen (dat)

ter'rifying adj schrecklich

territorial [,terɪ'torɪ·əl] adj territorial; t. waters Hoheitsgewässer pl

territory ['terɪ,tori] s Gebiet n, Territorium n; (of a salesman) Absatzgebiet n; (pol) Hoheitsgebiet n; (sport) Spielhälfte f

terror ['terər] s Schrecken m; in t. vor Schrecken

terrorism ['terə,rɪzəm] s Terrorismus m

terrorist ['terərɪst] s Terrorist –in mf

terrorize ['terə,raɪz] tr terrorisieren

ter'ror-strick'en adj schreckerfüllt

ter'ry cloth' ['teri] s Frottee m & n

terse [tʌrs] adj knapp

tertiary ['tʌrʃɪ,eri] adj Tertiär–

test [test] s Probe f, Prüfung f; (criterion) Prüfstein m; (med) Probe f; put to the t. auf die Probe stellen || tr (for) prüfen (auf acc); (chem) (for) analysieren (auf acc); t. out (coll) ausprobieren

testament ['testəmənt] s Testament n

testator [tes'tetər] s Erblasser –in mf

test' ban' s Atomstopp m

test' case' s Probefall m; (jur) Präzedenzfall m

test'flight' s Probeflug m

testicle ['testɪkəl] s Hoden m

testi•fy ['testɪ,faɪ] v (pret & pp –fied)

intr (**against**) zeugen (gegen), aussagen (gegen); **t. to** bezeugen

testimonial [ˌtestɪ'monɪəl] *adj* (*dinner*) Ehren- || *s* Anerkennungsschreiben *n*

testimony ['testɪˌmonɪ] *s* Zeugnis *n*

test′ pa′per *s* Prüfungsarbeit *f*

test′ pi′lot *s* Versuchsflieger –in *mf*

test′ tube′ *s* Reagenzglas *n*

testy ['testɪ] *adj* reizbar

tetanus ['tetənəs] *s* Starrkrampf *m*

tether ['teðər] *s* Haltestrick *m*; **be at the end of one's t.** nicht mehr weiter wissen || *tr* anbinden

Teuton ['t(j)utən] *s* Teutone *m*, Teutonin *f*

Teutonic [t(j)u'tɑnɪk] *adj* teutonisch

text [tekst] *s* Text *m*

text′book′ *s* Lehrbuch *n*

textile ['tekstaɪl] *adj* Textil- || *s* Webstoff *m*; **textiles** Textilien *pl*

textual ['tekst/ʊ‑əl] *adj* textlich

texture ['tekst/ər] *s* (*structure*) Gefüge *n*; (*of a fabric*) Gewebe *n*; (*of a play*) Aufbau *m*

Thai [taɪ] *adj* Thai- || *s* (*person*) Thai –in *mf*; (*language*) Thai *n*

Thailand ['taɪlənd] *s* Thailand *n*

Thames [temz] *s* Themse *f*

than [ðæn] *conj* als; **t. ever** denn je

thank [θæŋk] *adj* (*offering*) Dank- || **thanks** *spl* Dank *m*; **give thanks to** danken (*dat*); **many thanks!** vielen Dank!; **return thanks** danksagen; **thanks a lot!** danke vielmals!; **thanks to her,** I ich verdanke es ihr, daß ich || *tr* danken (*dat*). **t. God!** Gott sei Dank!; **t. goodness!** gottlob!; **t. you!** danke schön!; **t. you ever so much!** verbindlichsten Dank!; **you have only yourself to t. for** das hast du dir nur selbst zu verdanken

thankful ['θæŋkfəl] *adj* dankbar

thankless ['θæŋklɪs] *adj* undankbar

Thanksgiv′ing Day′ *s* Danksagungstag *m*

that [ðæt] *adj* jener, der; **t. one** der da, jener || *adv* (*coll*) so, derart || *rel pron* der, welcher; (*after indefinite pronouns*) was || *dem pron* das; **about t.** darüber; **after t.** danach; **and that's t.** und damit punktum!; **at t.** so, dabei; **by t.** dadurch; **for all t.** trotz alledem; **for t.** dafür; **from t.** daraus; **in t.** darin, daran; **on t.** darauf, drauf; **t. is** das heißt; **that's out** das kommt nicht in Frage!; **t. will do!** das reicht! || *conj* daß

thatch [θæt/] *s* Dachstroh *n*

thatched′ roof′ *s* Strohdach *n*

thaw [θɔ] *s* Tauwetter *n* || *tr & intr* (auf)tauen

the [ðə], [ði] *def art* der, die, das || *adv*—**so much the better** um so besser; **the … the** je … desto, je … um so

theater ['θiˌətər] *s* Theater *n*

the′atergo′er *s* Theaterbesucher –in *mf*

the′ater of war′ *s* Kriegsschauplatz *m*

theatrical [θi'ætrɪkəl] *adj* (& *fig*) theatralisch

thee [ði] *pers pron* dich; **to t.** dir

theft [θeft] *s* Diebstahl *m*

their [ðer] *poss adj* ihr

theirs [ðerz] *poss pron* ihrer

them [ðem] *pron* sie; **to t.** ihnen

theme [θim] *s* Thema *n*; (*essay*) Aufsatz *m*; (*mus*) Thema *n*

theme′ song′ *s* Kennmelodie *f*

themselves′ *intens pron* selbst, selber || *reflex pron* sich

then [ðen] *adv* (*next; in that case*) dann; (*at that time*) damals; **by t. bis** dahin; **from t. on** von da an; **t. and there** auf der Stelle; **till t.** bis dahin; **what t.?** was dann?

thence [ðens] *adv* von da, von dort; (*from that fact*) daraus

thence′forth′ *adv* von da an

theologian [ˌθiə'lodʒən] *s* Theologe *m*, Theologin *f*

theological [ˌθiə'lɑdʒɪkəl] *adj* theologisch

theology [θi'ɑlədʒi] *s* Theologie *f*

theorem ['θiərəm] *s* Lehrsatz *m*

theoretical [ˌθiə'retɪkəl] *adj* theoretisch

theorist ['θiərɪst] *s* Theoretiker –in *mf*

theorize ['θiəˌraɪz] *intr* theoretisieren

theory ['θiəri] *s* Theorie *f*, Lehre *f*

the′ory of relativ′ity *s* Relativitätstheorie *f*

therapeutic [ˌθerə'pjutɪk] *adj* therapeutisch || **therapeutics** *s* Therapeutik *f*

therapy ['θerəpi] *s* Therapie *f*

there [ðer] *adv* (*position*) da; (*direction*) dahin; **down t.** da unten; **not be all t.** (coll) nicht ganz richtig sein; **over t.** da drüben; **t. are** es gibt, es sind; **t. is** es gibt, es ist; **t., t.!** sachte, sachte!; **up t.** da (or dort) oben

there′abouts′ *adv* daherum; **ten people or t.** so ungefähr zehn Leute

there′af′ter *adv* danach

there′by′ *adv* dadurch, damit

therefore ['ðer‚for] *adv* deshalb, darum

there′in′ *adv* darin

there′of′ *adv* davon

there′to′ *adv* dazu

there′upon′ *adv* daraufhin, danach

there′with′ *adv* damit

thermal ['θʌrməl] *adj* Thermal-, Wärme-

thermodynamic [ˌθʌrmodaɪ'næmɪk] *adj* thermodynamisch || **thermodynamics** *s* Thermodynamik *f*, Wärmelehre *f*

thermometer [θər'mɑmɪtər] *s* Thermometer *n*

thermonuclear [ˌθɜrmo'n(j)uklɪ‑ər] *adj* thermonuklear

ther′mos bot′tle ['θʌrməs] *s* Thermosflasche *f*

thermostat ['θʌrmə‚stæt] *s* Thermostat *m*

thesaurus [θɪ'sɔrəs] *s* (**-ri** [raɪ]) Thesaurus *m*

these [ðiz] *dem adj & pron* diese

the·sis ['θisɪs] *s* (**-ses** [siz]) These *f*

they [ðe] *pers pron* sie; **t. say** man sagt

thick [θɪk] *adj* dick; (*dense*) dicht;

(*stupid*) stumpfsinnig; (*lips*) wulstig; (*intimate*) (coll) dick; **t. with dust** dick bedeckt mit Staub || *adv*—**be in t. with** (coll dicke Beziehungen haben mit; **come t. and fast** Schlag auf Schlag gehen; **lay it on t.** (coll) dick auftragen || *s*—**in the t. of** mitten in (*dat*); **through t. and thin** durch dick und dünn

thicken ['θɪkən] *tr* verdicken; (*make denser*) verdichten; (*a sauce*) eindicken || *intr* sich verdicken; (*become denser*) sich verdichten; (*said of liquids*) sich verfestigen; (*said of a sauce*) eindicken; **the plot thickens** der Knoten schürzt sich

thicket ['θɪkɪt] *s* Dickicht *n*

thick'head' *s* (coll) Dickkopf *m*

thick'-head'ed *adj* (coll) dickköpfig

thickness ['θɪknɪs] *s* Dicke *f*

thick'-set' *adj* stämmig

thick'-skinned' *adj* (coll) dickfellig

thief [θif] *s* (thieves [θivz]) Dieb –in *mf*

thieve [θiv] *intr* stehlen

thievery ['θivəri] *s* Dieberei *f*

thievish ['θivɪʃ] *adj* diebisch

thigh [θaɪ] *s* Schenkel *m*, Oberschenkel *m*

thighbone' *s* Oberschenkelknochen *m*

thimble ['θɪmbəl] *s* Fingerhut *m*

thin [θɪn] *adj* (thinner; thinnest) dünn; (*hair*) schütter; (*lean*) mager; (*excuse*) schwach; (*soup*) wäßrig || *v* (*pret & pp* thinned; *ger* thinning) *tr* (*a liquid*) verdünnen; (*a forest*) lichten; **t. out** (*plants*) vereinzeln || *intr* (*said of hair*) sich lichten; **t. out** (*said of a crowd*) sich verlaufen

thing [θɪŋ] *s* Ding *n*, Sache *f*; **among other things** unter anderem; **first t.** zu allerest; **how are things?** wie geht's?; **I'll do no such t.!** ich werde mich schön hüten; **of all things!** na sowas!; **the real t.** das Richtige; **things** (*the situation*) die Lage *f*; (*belongings*) Sachen *pl*

think [θɪŋk] *v* (*pret & pp* thought [θɔt]) *tr* denken; (*regard*) halten; (*believe*) glauben, denken; **he thinks he's clever** er hält sich für klug; **that's what you t.!** ja, denkste!; **t. better of it** sich e–s Besseren besinnen; **t. it best to** (*inf*) es für das Beste halten zu (*inf*); **t. little of** nicht viel halten von; **t. nothing of it!** es ist nicht der Rede wert!; **t. over** sich [*dat*] überlegen; **t. up** sich [*dat*] ausdenken; **what do you t. you're doing?** was soll das? || *intr* denken; **be thinking of** (*ger*) beabsichtigen zu (*inf*); **do you t. so?** meinen Sie?; **t. about** (*call to consciousness*) denken an (*acc*); (*reflect on*) nachdenken über (*acc*); (*be concerned about*) bedacht sein auf (*acc*); **t. twice before** es sich [*dat*] zweimal überlegen, bevor

thinker ['θɪŋkər] *s* Denker –in *mf*

thin'-lipped' *adj* dünnlippig

thinner ['θɪnər] *s* Verdünnungsmittel *n*

third [θɪrd] *adj & pron* dritte || *s* (frac-

tion) Drittel *n;* (mus) Terz *f;* **the third** (*in dates and in series*) der Dritte

third'-class' *adj & adv* dritter Klasse

third' degree' *s*—**give s.o. the t.** j–n e–m Folterverhör unterwerfen

third' par'ty *s* Dritter *m*, dritte Seite *f*

third'-rate' *adj* drittrangig

thirst [θʌrst] *s* (for) Durst *m* (nach); **t. for knowledge** Wissensdurst *m;* **t. for power** Herrschsucht *f* || *intr* (for) dürsten (nach)

thirsty ['θʌrsti] *adj* durstig; **be t.** Durst haben

thirteen ['θʌr'tin] *adj & pron* dreizehn || *s* Dreizehn *f*

thirteenth ['θʌr'tinθ] *adj & pron* dreizehnte || *s* (fraction) Dreizehntel *n;* **the t.** (*in dates and in series*) der Dreizehnte

thirtieth ['θʌrtɪ·ɪθ] *adj & pron* dreißigste || *s* (fraction) Dreißigstel *n;* **the t.** (*in dates and in series*) der Dreißigste

thirty ['θʌrti] *adj & pron* dreißig || *s* Dreißig *f;* **the thirties** die dreißiger Jahre

thir'ty-one' *adj & pron* einunddreißig

this [ðɪs] *dem adj* dieser; **t. afternoon** heute nachmittag; **t. evening** heute abend; **t. minute** augenblicklich; **t. one** dieser || *adv* (coll) so || *dem pron* dieser, der; **about t.** hierüber; (*concerning this*) davon; **t. and that** dies und jenes

thistle ['θɪsəl] *s* Distel *f*

thither ['θɪðər] *adv* dorthin, hinzu

thong [θɔŋ] *s* Riemen *m;* (*sandal*) Sandale *f*

tho·rax ['θoræks] *s* (–raxes & –races [rə͵siz]) Brustkorb *m*

thorn [θɔrn] *s* Dorn *m;* **t. in the side** Dorn *m* im Fleisch

thorny ['θɔrni] *adj* dornig; (fig) heikel

thorough ['θʌro] *adj* gründlich; (coll) tüchtig

thor'oughbred' *adj* reinrassig || *s* Vollblut *n;* (*horse*) Vollblutpferd *n*, Rassepferd *n*

thor'oughfare' *s* Durchgang *m;* **no t.** (public sign) Durchgang verboten

thor'oughgo'ing *adj* gründlich

thoroughly ['θʌroli] *adv* gründlich

those [ðoz] *dem adj & pron* jene, die da

thou [ðaʊ] *pers pron* du

though [ðo] *adv* immerhin || *conj* obwohl

thought [θɔt] *s* Gedanke(n) *m;* **be lost in t.** in Gedanken versunken sein; **give some t. to** sich [*dat*] Gedanken machen über (*acc*); **have second thoughts** sich [*dat*] eines Besseren besinnen; **on second t.** nach reiflicher Überlegung; **the mere t.** schon der Gedanke

thoughtful ['θɔtfəl] *adj* (reflective) nachdenklich; (*e.g., essay*) gedankenvoll; (*considerate*) aufmerksam; (*gift*) sinnig; **t. of** bedacht auf (*acc*)

thoughtless ['θɔtlɪs] *adj* gedankenlos

thought'-provok'ing *adj* anregend

thousand ['θauzənd] *adj & pron* tausend; **a t. times** tausendmal || *s* Tausend *f*; **by the t.** zu Tausenden

thousandth ['θauzəndθ] *adj & pron* tausendste || *s* (*fraction*) Tausendstel *n*

thrash [θræʃ] *tr* (& *fig*) dreschen; **t. out** (*debate*) gründlich erörtern || *intr* dreschen; **t. about** sich hin- und herwerfen

thrash'ing *s* Dreschen *n*; (*beating*) Dresche *f*

thread [θred] *s* Faden *m*; (*of a screw*) Gewinde *n*; (*of a story*) Faden *m*; **hang by a t.** an e-m Faden hängen || *tr* (*a needle*) einfädeln; (*pearls*) aufreihen; (*mach*) Gewinde schneiden in (*acc*)

thread'bare' *adj* fadenscheinig

threat [θret] *s* Drohung *f*

threaten ['θretən] *tr* drohen (*dat*), bedrohen; **t. so. with s.th.** j-m etw androhen || *intr* drohen

three [θri] *adj & pron* drei || *s* Drei *f*; **in threes** zu dritt

three' cheers' *spl* ein dreimaliges Hoch

three'-dimen'sional *adj* dreidimensional

three'-en'gine *adj* dreimotorig

three'-piece' *adj* (*suit*) dreiteilig

three'-ply' *adj* dreischichtig

three'-point' land'ing *s* Dreipunktlandung *f*

threnody ['θrenədi] *s* Klagelied *n*

thresh [θreʃ] *tr* dreschen; **t. out** (*debate*) gründlich erörtern || *intr* dreschen

thresh'ing floor' *s* Dreschtenne *f*

thresh'ing machine' *s* Dreschmaschine *f*

threshold ['θreʃold] *s* Türschwelle *f*; (*psychol*) Schwelle *f*

thrice [θrais] *adv* dreimal

thrift [θrift] *s* Sparsamkeit *f*

thrifty ['θrifti] *adj* sparsam

thrill [θril] *s* Nervenkitzel *m* || *tr* erregen, packen

thriller ['θrilər] *s* Thriller *m*

thrill'ing *adj* packend, spannend

thrive [θraiv] *v* (*pret* **thrived** & **throve** [θrov]; *pp* **thrived** & **thriven** ['θrivən]) *intr* gedeihen

throat [θrot] *s* Kehle *f*; **clear one's t.** sich räuspern; **cut one another's t.** (fig) sich gegenseitig kaputt machen; **cut one's own t.** (fig) sich [*dat*] sein eigenes Grab schaufeln; **jump down s.o.'s t.** j-m an die Gurgel fahren; **sore t.** Halsweh *n*

throb [θrab] *s* Schlagen *n*; (*of a motor*) Dröhnen *n* || *v* (*pret & pp* **throbbed**; *ger* **throbbing**) *intr* schlagen; (*said of a motor or head*) dröhnen

throes [θroz] *spl* Schmerzen *pl*; **in the t. of death** im Todeskampf liegen

thrombosis [θram'bosis] *s* Thrombose *f*

throne [θron] *s* Thron *m*

throng [θrɔŋ] *s* Menschenmenge *f* || *tr* umdrängen; (*the streets*) sich drängen in (*acc*) || *intr* (**around**) sich drängen (um)

throttle ['θratəl] *s* Drossel(klappe) *f*

|| *tr* drosseln; (*a person*) erwürgen || *intr*—**t. back** (*aut*) das Gas zurücknehmen

through [θru] *adj* (*traffic, train*) Durchgangs—; (*street*) durchgehend; (*finished*) fertig; (*coll*) quitt || *adv*—**t. and t.** durch und durch || *prep* durch (*acc*)

throughout' *adv* durch und durch || *prep* hindurch (*acc*) (postpositive), e.g., **t. the summer** den ganzen Sommer hindurch; **t. the world** in der ganzen Welt

throw [θro] *s* Wurf *m*; (*scarf*) Überwurf *m* || *v* (*pret* **threw** [θru]; *pp* **thrown** [θron]) *tr* werfen; (*a rider*) abwerfen; (*sparks*) sprühen; (*a party, banquet*) geben; (*a game*) absichtlich verlieren; (*into confusion*) bringen; **t. away** wegwerfen; **t. down** niederwerfen; (*overturn*) umwerfen; **t. in** (*e.g., a few extras*) als Zugabe geben; **t. off** (*fig*) aus dem Gleichgewicht bringen; **t. out** hinauswerfen; (*a person*) vor die Tür setzen; (*the chest*) herausdrücken; **t. out of the game** vom Platz verweisen; **t. the book at s.o.** (fig) j—n zur Höchststrafe verurteilen; **t. up to s.o.** j—m vorwerfen || *intr* werfen; **t. up** sich erbrechen

throw'away' *adj* Einweg—

throw'back' *s* (**to**) Rückkehr *f* (zu)

throw' rug' *s* Vorleger *m*

thrum [θram] *v* (*pret & pp* **thrummed**; *ger* **thrumming**) *intr* (**on**) mit den Fingern trommeln (auf *acc*)

thrush [θraʃ] *s* (orn) Drossel *f*

thrust [θrast] *s* (*shove*) Stoß *m*; (*stab*) Hieb *m*; (aer, archit, geol, rok) Schub *m*; (mil) Vorstoß *m* || *v* (*pret & pp* **thrust**) *tr* stoßen

thud [θad] *s* Bums *m* || *v* (*pret & pp* **thudded**; *ger* **thudding**) *tr* & *intr* bumsen || *interj* bums!

thug [θag] *s* Rocker *m*

thumb [θam] *s* Daumen *m*; **be all thumbs** zwei linke Hände haben; **be under s.o.'s t.** unter j—s Fuchtel stehen; **thumbs down!** pfui!; **thumbs up!** Kopf hoch! || *tr* (*a book*) abgreifen; **t. a ride** per Anhalter fahren; **t. one's nose at s.o.** j—m e—e lange Nase machen || *intr*—**t. through** durchblättern

thumb' in'dex *s* Daumenindex *m*

thumb'print' *s* Daumenabdruck *m*

thumb'screw' *s* Flügelschraube *f*

thumb'tack' *s* Reißnagel *m*

thump [θamp] *s* Bums *m* || *tr* & *intr* bumsen || *interj* bums!

thump'ing *adj* (coll) enorm

thunder ['θandər] *s* Donner *m* || *tr* & *intr* donnern

thun'derbolt' *s* Donnerkeil *m*

thun'derclap' *s* Donnerschlag *m*

thunderous ['θandərəs] *adj* donnernd

thun'dershow'er *s* Gewitterregen *m*

thun'derstorm' *s* Gewitter *n*

thunderstruck ['θandər‚strak] *adj* (fig) wie vom Schlag getroffen

Thursday ['θarzde] *s* Donnerstag *m*; **on T.** am Donnerstag

thus [ðʌs] *adv* so; (*consequently*) also; t. far soweit

thwack [θwæk] *s* heftiger Schlag *m* || *tr* klatschen

thwart [θwɔrt] *adj* Quer– || *s* (naut) Ruderbank *f* || *tr* (*plans*) durchkreuzen; (*a person*) in die Quere kommen (*dat*)

thy [ðaɪ] *poss adj* dein

thyme [taɪm] *s* Thymian *m*

thy′roid gland′ [′θaɪrɔɪd] *s* Schilddrüse *f*

thyself [ðaɪ′self] *intens pron* selbst, selber || *reflex pron* dich

tiara [taɪ′erə] *s* Tiara *f*; (*lady's headdress*) Diadem *n*

tibia [′tɪbɪ·ə] *s* Schienbein *n*

tic [tɪk] *s* (pathol) Tick *m*

tick [tɪk] *s* (*of a clock*) Ticken *n*; (*mattress case*) Überzug *m*; (ent) Zecke *f*; on t. (coll) auf Pump || *tr*– be ticked off (at) (sl) verärgert sein (über *acc*); **t. off** (*names, items*) abhaken; (*the minutes*) ticken || *intr* ticken; **t. by** vergehen

ticker [′tɪkər] *s* (*watch*) (sl) Uhr *f*, Armbanduhr *f*; (*heart*) (sl) Herz *n*; (st. exch.) Börsentelegraph *m*

tick′er tape′ *s* Papierstreifen *m* (des Börsentelegraphen)

tick′er-tape parade′ *s* Konfettiregenparade *f*

ticket [′tɪkɪt] *s* Karte *f*; (*for travel*) Fahrkarte *f*; (*by air*) Flugkarte *f*; (*for admission*) Eintrittskarte *f*; (*in a lottery*) Los *n*; (*for a traffic violation*) Strafzettel *m*; (pol) Wahlliste *f* || *tr* etikettieren; (*aut*) mit e-m Strafzettel versehen

tick′et a′gency *s* Vorverkaufsstelle *f*

tick′et a′gent *s* Fahrkartenverkäufer –in *mf*

tick′et of′fice *s* Kartenverkaufsstelle *f*

tick′et win′dow *s* Schalter *m*

tick′ing *s* Ticken *n*

tickle [′tɪkəl] *s* Kitzel *m* || *tr* kitzeln || *intr* jucken

ticklish [′tɪklɪʃ] *adj* kitzlig; (*touchy*) heikel

ticktock [′tɪk‚tɑk] *adv*—go t. ticktack machen || *s* Ticken *n*

tid′al wave′ [′taɪdəl] *s* Flutwelle *f*

tidbit [′tɪd‚bɪt] *s* Leckerbissen *m*

tiddlywinks [′tɪdlɪ‚wɪŋks] *s* Flohhüpfspiel *n*

tide [taɪd] *s* Gezeiten *pl*; **against the t.** (fig) gegen den Strom; **the t. is coming in** die Flut steigt; **the t. is going out** die Flut fällt || *tr*—t. s.o. over j–n über Wasser halten

tide′land′ *s* Watt *n*

tide′wa′ter *s* Flutwasser *n*

tidings [′taɪdɪŋz] *spl* Botschaft *f*

ti·dy [′taɪdɪ] *adj* ordentlich; (*sum*) hübsch || *v* (*pret & pp* –died) *tr* in Ordnung bringen; **t. up** aufräumen || *intr*—t. up aufräumen

tie [taɪ] *adj* (sport) unentschieden || *s* (*cord*) Schnur *f*; (*ribbon*) Band *n*; (*necktie*) Krawatte *f*; (*knot*) Schleife *f*; (mus) Ligatur *f*; (parl) Stimmengleichheit *f*; (rr) Schwelle *f*; (sport)

Unentschieden *n*; **end in a tie** punktgleich enden; **ties** (*e.g., of friendship*) Bande *pl* || *v* (*pret & pp* tied; *ger* tying) *tr* binden; **be tied up** (*said of a person or telephone*) besetzt sein; **get tied up** (*in traffic*) steckenbleiben; **my hands are tied** mir sind die Hände gebunden; **tie in with** verknüpfen mit; **tie oneself down** sich festlegen; **tie to** festbinden an (*dat*); **tie up** (*a wound*) verbinden; (*traffic*) lahmlegen; (*money*) fest anlegen; (*production*) stillegen; (*the telephone*) blockieren; (*a boat*) festmachen

tie′back′ *s* Gardinenhalter *m*

tie′clasp′ *s* Krawattenhalter *m*

tie′pin′ *s* Krawattennadel *f*

tier [tɪr] *s* Reihe *f*; (theat) Rang *m*

tie′rod′ *s* (aut) Zugstange *f*

tie′-up′ *s* (*of traffic*) Stockung *f*

tiger [′taɪgər] *s* Tiger *m*

ti′ger shark′ *s* Tigerhai *m*

tight [taɪt] *adj* (*firm*) fest; (*clothes*) eng; (*taut*) straff; (*scarce*) knapp; (*container*) dicht; (*drunk*) beschwipst; (*with money*) knaus(e)rig; **feel t. in the chest** sich beengt fühlen || *adv* fest; **hold t.** festhalten; **sit t.** sich nicht rühren; **pull t.** strammziehen || **tights** *spl* Trikot *m* & *n*

tighten [′taɪtən] *tr* (*a rope*) straff spannen; (*a belt*) enger schnallen; (*a jar lid*) festziehen; (*a screw*) anziehen; (*a spring*) spannen; (*a knot*) zuziehen

tight′-fist′ed *adj* knaus(e)rig

tight′-fit′ting *adj* eng anliegend

tight′-lipped′ *adj* verschlossen

tight′rope′ *s* Drahtseil *n*; **walk a t.** auf e–m festgespannten Drahtseil gehen

tight′ spot′ *s* (coll) Klemme *f*

tight′ squeeze′ *s* (coll) Zwickmühle *f*

tight′wad′ *s* Geizkragen *m*

tigress [′taɪgrɪs] *s* Tigerin *f*

tile [taɪl] *s* (*for the floor or wall*) Fliese *f*; (*for the roof*) Dachziegel *m*; (*glazed tile*) Kachel *f* || *tr* (*a roof*) mit Ziegeln decken; (*a floor*) mit Fliesen auslegen; (*a bathroom*) kacheln

tile′ roof′ *s* Ziegeldach *n*

till [tɪl] *s* Kasse *f* || *tr* ackern || *prep* bis (*acc*); **t. now bisher** || *conj* bis

tiller [′tɪlər] *s* (naut) Pinne *f*

tilt [tɪlt] *s* Kippen *n*; **full t.** mit voller Wucht || *tr* kippen; (*a bottle, the head*) neigen; **t. back** (*e.g., a chair*) zurücklehnen; **t. over** umkippen || *intr* kippen; **t. over** umkippen

timber [′tɪmbər] *s* Holz *n*; (*for structural use*) Bauholz *n*; (*rafter*) Balken *m*

tim′berland′ *s* Waldland *n*

tim′ber line′ *s* Baumgrenze *f*

timbre [′tɪmbər] *s* Klangfarbe *f*

time [taɪm] *s* Zeit *f*; (*limited period*) Frist *f*; (*instance*) Mal *n*; (mus) Takt *m*; **all the t.** ständig; **all this t.** die ganze Zeit; **any number of times** x–mal; **at no t.** nie; **at one t.** einst; **at some t.** irgendwann; **at that t.**

damals; **at the present t.** derzeit; **at times** manchmal; **at what t.?** um wieviel Uhr?; **by this t.** nunmehr; **do t.** (sl) sitzen; **do you have the t.?** können Sie mir sagen, wie spät es ist?; **for a t.** e-e Zeitlang; **for the last t.** zum letzten Mal; **for the t. being** vorläufig; **give s.o. a hard t.** j-m das Leben schwer machen; **have a good t.** sich gut unterhalten; **have a hard t.** (ger) es schwer haben zu (inf); **in no t.** im Nu; **in t.** zur rechten Zeit; (in the course of time) mit der Zeit; **make good t.** Fortschritte machen; **on one's own t.** in der Freizeit; **on t.** pünktlich; (on schedule) fahrplanmäßig; (com) auf Raten; **several times** mehrmals; **take one's t.** sich [dat] Zeit lassen; **there's t. for that** das hat Zeit; **this t. tomorrow** morgen um diese Zeit; **t.!** (sport) Zeit!; **t. is up!** die Zeit ist um!; **t. of life** Lebensalter n; **times** Zeiten pl; (math) mal, e.g., **two times two** zwei mal zwei; **t. will tell** die Zeit wird es lehren; **what t. is it?** wieviel Uhr ist es? || tr (mit der Uhr) messen; **t. s.th. right** die richtige Zeit wählen für
time′ bomb′ s Zeitbombe f
time′ card′ s Stechkarte f
time′ clock′ s Stechuhr f
time′-consum′ing adj zeitraubend
time′ expo′sure s (phot) Zeitaufnahme f
time′ fuse′ s Zeitzünder m
time′-hon′ored adj altehrwürdig
time′keep′er s Zeitnehmer –in mf
time′-lag′ s Verzögerung f
timeless ['taɪmlɪs] adj zeitlos
time′ lim′it s Frist f; **set a t. on** befristen
timely ['taɪmli] adj zeitgerecht; (topic) aktuell
time′ pay′ment s Ratenzahlung f
time′piece′ s Uhr f
timer ['taɪmər] s (person) Zeitnehmer –in mf; (device) Schaltuhr f; (aut) Zündunterbrecher m; (phot) Zeitauslöser m
time′ sig′nal s Zeitzeichen n
time′ stud′y s Zeitstudien pl
time′ta′ble s Zeittabelle f; (aer) Flugplan m; (rr) Fahrplan m
time′work′ s Zeitlohnarbeit f
time′worn′ adj abgenutzt
time′ zone′ s Zeitzone f
timid ['tɪmɪd] adj ängstlich
tim′ing s genaue zeitliche Berechnung f; (aut) Zündeinstellung f
timorous ['tɪmərəs] adj furchtsam
tin [tɪn] s Zinn– || s (element) Zinn n; (tin plate) Weißblech n
tin′ can′ s Blechdose f
tincture ['tɪŋktʃər] s Tinktur f
tinder ['tɪndər] s Zunder m
tin′derbox′ s (fig) Pulverfaß n
tin′ foil′ s Zinnfolie f
ting-a-ling ['tɪŋəˌlɪŋ] s Klingeling m
tinge [tɪndʒ] s (of color) Stich m; (fig) Spur f || v (pret tingeing & tinging) tr leicht färben

tingle ['tɪŋɡəl] s Kribbeln n, Prickeln n || intr kribbeln, prickeln
tinker ['tɪŋkər] s (bungler) Pfuscher m || intr basteln
tinkle ['tɪŋkəl] s Klingeln n || intr klingeln
tin′ mine′ s Zinnbergwerk n
tinsel ['tɪnsəl] s Lametta f; (fig) Flitterkram m
tin′smith′ s Klempner m
tin′ sol′dier s Zinnsoldat m
tint [tɪnt] s Farbton m || tr tönen, leicht färben
tint′ed glass′ s (aut) blendungsfreies Glas n
tiny ['taɪni] adj winzig
tip [tɪp] s Spitze f; (gratuity) Trinkgeld n; (hint) Tip m; **it's on the tip of my tongue** es schwebt mir auf der Zunge || v (pret & pp tipped; ger tipping) tr schief halten; (a waiter) ein Trinkgeld geben (dat); **tip off** e-n Tip geben (dat); **tip one's hat** auf den Hut tippen || intr—**tip over** umtippen
tip′-off′ s Tip m, rechtzeitiger Wink m
tipple ['tɪpəl] tr & intr süffeln
tippler ['tɪplər] s Säufer –in mf
tipster ['tɪpstər] s Wettberater m
tipsy ['tɪpsi] adj beschwipst
tip′toe′ s—**on t.** auf den Zehenspitzen || v (pret & pp -toed; ger -toeing) intr auf den Zehenspitzen gehen
tip′top′ adj tipptopp
tirade ['taɪred] s Tirade f
tire [taɪr] s Reifen m || tr ermüden; **t. out** strapazieren || intr ermüden
tired adj müde; **be t. of** (ger) es satt haben zu (inf); **be t. of coffee** den Kaffee satt haben; **t. out** abgespannt
tire′ gauge′ s Reifendruckmesser m
tireless ['taɪrlɪs] adj unermüdlich
tire′ pres′sure s Reifendruck m
tiresome ['taɪrsəm] adj (tiring) ermüdend; (boring) langweilig
tissue ['tɪʃju] s Gewebe n; (thin paper) Papiertaschentuch n; **t. of lies** Lügengewebe n
tis′sue pa′per s Seidenpapier n
tit [tɪt] s (sl) Brust f; **tit for tat wie** du mir, so ich dir
Titan ['taɪtən] s Titan(e) m
titanic [taɪ'tænɪk] adj titanisch
titanium [taɪ'tɛni-əm] s Titan n
tithe [taɪð] s Kirchenzehnt m || tr (pay one tenth of) den Zehnten bezahlen von; (exact a tenth from) den Zehnten erheben von
Titian ['tɪʃən] adj tizianrot
titillate ['tɪtɪˌlet] tr & intr kitzeln, (angenehm) reizen
title ['taɪtəl] s Titel m; (to a property) Eigentumsrecht n; (claim) Rechtstitel m; (of a chapter) Überschrift f; (honor) Würde f; (aut) Kraftfahrzeugbrief m || tr titulieren
ti′tle bout′ s (box) Titelkampf m
ti′tled ad(e)lig
ti′tle deed′ s Eigentumsurkunde f
ti′tle hold′er s Titelverteidiger –in mf
ti′tle page′ s Titelblatt n
ti′tle role′ s Titelrolle f

titter ['tɪtər] s Gekicher n || intr kichern

titular ['tɪtjələr] adj Titular–

to [tu], [tu] adv—**to and fro** hin und her || prep zu (dat); (a city, country, island) nach (dat); (as far as) bis (acc); (in order to) um ... zu (inf); (against, e.g., a wall) an (dat or acc); **a quarter to eight** viertel vor acht; **how far is it to the town?** wie weit ist es bis zur Stadt?; **to a T** haargenau

toad [tod] s Kröte f

toad'stool' s Giftpilz m

toad·y ['todɪ] s Schranze m & f || v (pret & pp –ied) intr (to) scharwenzeln (um)

to-and-fro ['tu·ənd'fro] adj Hin- und Her– || adv hin und her

toast [tost] s (bread; salutation) Toast m; **drink a t.** to e-n Toast ausbringen auf (acc) || tr (bread) rösten

toaster ['tostər] s Toaster m

toast'mas'ter s Toastmeister m

tobac·co [tə'bæko] s (–cos) Tabak m

tobac'co pouch' s Tabaksbeutel m

toboggan [tə'bagən] s Rodel m & f || intr rodeln

tocsin ['taksɪn] s Alarmglocke f

today [tu'de] adv heute; **t.—from t.** on von heute an; **today's** heutig

toddle ['tadəl] s Watscheln n || intr watscheln

toddler ['tadlər] s Kleinkind n

toddy ['tadɪ] s Toddy m

to-do [tə'du] s Getue n

toe [to] s Zehe f; **be on one's toes** on Draht sein; **step on s.o.'s toes** j–m auf die Zehen treten || v (pret & pp **toed;** ger **toeing**) tr—**toe the line** nicht aus der Reihe tanzen

toe' dance' s Spitzentanz m

toe'-in' s (aut) Spur f

toe'nail' s Zehennagel m

together [tu'gɛðər] adv zusammen; **t. with** mitsamt (dat), samt (dat)

togetherness [tu'gɛðərnɪs] s Zusammengehörigkeit f

tog'gle switch' ['tagəl] s (elec) Kippschalter m

togs [tagz] spl Klamotten pl

toil [tɔɪl] s Mühe f; **toils** Schlingen pl || intr sich mühen

toilet ['tɔɪlɪt] s (room) Toilette f; (bathroom fixture) Klosett n

toi'let ar'ticle s Toilettenartikel m

toi'let bowl' s Klosettschüssel f

toi'let pa'per s Klosettpapier n

toi'let seat' s Toilettenring m

token ['tokən] adj (payment) symbolisch; (strike) Warn– || s Zeichen n; (proof) Beweis m; **by the same t.** aus dem gleichen Grund; **as** (or **in**) **t. of** zum Beweis (genit)

tolerable ['talərəbəl] adj erträglich

tolerably ['talərəbli] adv leidlich

tolerance ['talərəns] s Duldsamkeit f; (mach) Toleranz f

tolerant ['talərənt] adj (of) duldsam (gegen), tolerant (gegen)

tolerate ['talə‚ret] tr dulden

toleration [‚talə're/ən] s Duldung f

toll [tol] adj (road) gebührenpflichtig || s Wegezoll m; (at a bridge) Brückenzoll m; (of bells) Läuten n; (number of victims) Zahl f der Opfer; (fig) Tribut m; (telp) Gebühr f für ein Ferngespräch; **take a heavy t. of life** viele Menschenleben kosten || tr & intr läuten

toll' booth' s Zahlkasse f

toll' bridge' s Zollbrücke f

toll' call' s Ferngespräch n

toll' collec'tor s Zolleinnehmer –in mf

toma·to [tə'meto] s (–toes) Tomate f

toma'to juice' s Tomatensaft f

tomb [tum] s Grab n, Grabmal n

tomboy ['tam ‚bɔɪ] s Wildfang m

tomb'stone' s Grabstein m

tomcat ['tam ‚kæt] s Kater m

tome [tom] s Band m

tomfoolery [tam'fuləri] s Albernheit f

Tom'my gun' ['tami] s Maschinenpistole f

tom'myrot' s Blödsinn m

tomorrow [tu'mɔro] adv morgen; **t. evening** morgen abend; **t. morning** morgen früh; **t. night** morgen abend; **t. noon** morgen mittag || s morgen; **tomorrow's** morgig

tom-tom ['tam ‚tam] s Hindutrommel f

ton [tʌn] s Tonne f

tone [ton] s Ton m; (of color) Farbton m; (phot) Tönung f || tr tönen; (phot) tönen; **t. down** dämpfen || intr milder werden

tone'-control knob' s (rad) Klangregler m

tongs [taŋz] spl Zange f

tongue [tʌŋ] s Zunge f; (language) Sprache f; (of a shoe) Zunge f; (of a buckle) Dorn m; (of a bell) Klöppel m; (of a wagon) Deichsel f; (carp) Feder f; **hold one's t.** den Mund halten

tongue'-tied' adj zungenlahm; (fig) sprachlos

tongue' twist'er s Zungenbrecher m

tonic ['tanɪk] adj tonisch || s (med) Tonikum n; (mus) Tonika f

tonight [tu'naɪt] adv heute nacht; (this evening) heute abend

tonnage ['tʌnɪdʒ] s Tonnage f

tonsil ['tansɪl] s Mandel f

tonsilitis [‚tansɪ'laɪtɪs] s Mandelentzündung f

tonsure ['tan/ər] s Tonsur f

too [tu] adv (also) auch; (excessively) zu; **too bad!** Schade!

tool [tul] s (& fig) Werkzeug n || tr (with tools) bearbeiten

tool'box' s Werkzeugkasten m

tool'mak'er s Werkzeugmacher m

tool' shed' s Geräteschuppen m

toot [tut] s (aut) Hupen n || tr (a trumpet) blasen; **t. the horn** (aut) hupen || intr (aut) hupen

tooth [tuθ] s (teeth [tiθ]) Zahn m; (of a rake) Zinke f; **t. and nail** mit aller Gewalt

tooth'ache' s Zahnschmerz m, Zahnweh n

tooth'brush' s Zahnbürste f
tooth' decay' s Zahnfäule f
toothless ['tuθlɪs] adj zahnlos
tooth'paste' s Zahnpaste f
tooth'pick' s Zahnstocher m
tooth' pow'der s Zahnpulver m
top [tap] adj oberste; (speed, price, form) Höchst–; (team) Spitzen–; (first-class) erstklassig || s Spitze f; (of a mountain) Gipfel m; (of a tree) Wipfel m; (of a car) Verdeck n; (of a box) Deckel m; (of a garment) Oberteil m & n; (of a bottle) Verschluß m; (of an object) obere Seite f; (of the water) Oberfläche f; (of a turnip) Kraut n; (toy) Kreisel m; at the top of one's voice aus voller Kehle; at the top of the page oben auf der Seite; be tops with s.o. (coll) bei j–m ganz groß angeschrieben sein; from top to bottom von oben bis unten; on top (& fig) obenauf; on top of (position) auf (dat); (direction) auf (acc); on top of that obendrein || v (pret & pp topped; ger topping) tr (a tree) kappen; (surpass) übertreffen; that tops everything das übersteigt alles; top off (a meal, an evening) abschließen; to top it off zu guter Letzt
topaz ['topæz] s Topas m
top' brass' s (mil) hohe Tiere pl
top'coat' s Überzieher m
top' dog' s (coll) Erste mf
top' ech'elon s Führungsspitze f
top' hat' s Zylinder m
top'-heav'y adj oberlastig
topic ['tapɪk] s Gegenstand m, Thema n
topical ['tapɪkəl] adj aktuell
top' kick' s (mil) Spieß m
topless ['taplɪs] adj Oben-ohne–
topmast ['tap,mæst] s Toppmast m
top'most adj oberste
top'notch' adj erstklassig
top' of the head' s Scheitel m
topography [tə'pɑɡrəfi] s Topographie f
topple ['tapəl] tr & intr stürzen
topsail ['tapsəl] s Toppsegel n
top'-se'cret adj streng geheim
top' ser'geant s Hauptfeldwebel m
top'side' adv auf Deck || s Oberseite f
top'soil' s Mutterboden m
topsy-turvy ['tapsɪ'tʌrvɪ] adj drunter und drüber || adv—turn t. durcheinanderbringen
torch [tɔrtʃ] s Fackel f; (Brit) Taschenlampe f; carry the t. for (coll) verknallt sein in (acc)
torch'bear'er s (& fig) Fackelträger m
torch'light' s Fackelschein m
torch'light parade' s Fackelzug m
torment ['tɔrment] s Qual f || [tɔr'ment] tr quälen
tormentor [tɔr'mentər] s Quäler –in mf
torn [tɔrn] adj zerrissen, rissig
torna·do [tɔr'nedo] s (–does & –dos) Tornado m, Windhose f
torpe·do [tɔr'pido] s (–does) Torpedo m || tr torpedieren

torpe'do boat' s Torpedoboot n
torpe'do tube' s Ausstoßrohr n
torpid ['tɔrpɪd] adj träge
torque [tɔrk] s Drehmoment n
torrent ['tɔrənt] s Sturzbach m; (of words) Schwall m; in torrents stromweise
torrential [tɔ'rentʃəl] adj—t. rain Wolkenbruch m
torrid ['tɔrɪd] adj brennend
Tor'rid Zone' s heiße Zone f
tor·so ['tɔrso] s (–sos) (of a statue) Torso m; (of a human body) Rumpf m
tortoise ['tɔrtəs] s Schildkröte f
tor'toise shell' s Schildpatt n
torture ['tɔrtʃər] s Folter f, Qual f || tr foltern, quälen
toss [tɔs] s Wurf m; (of the head) Zurückwerfen n; (of a ship) Schlingern n; (of a coin) Loswurf m || tr (throw) werfen; (the head) zurückwerfen; (a ship) hin- und herwerfen; (a coin) hochwerfen; t. off (work) hinhauen; t. s.o. for mit j–m losen um || intr (naut) schlingern; t. for e–e Münze hochwerfen um; t. in bed sich im Bett hin –und herwerfen
toss'up' s Loswurf m; it's a t. whether es hängt ganz vom Zufall ab, ob
tot [tat] s Knirps m
to·tal ['totəl] adj Gesamt–, total || s Gesamtsumme f || v (pret & pp –tal[l]ed; ger –tal[l]ing) tr (add up) zusammenrechnen; (amount to) sich belaufen auf (acc); (sl) (Wagen) ganz kaputt machen
totalitarian [to,tælɪ'terɪ·ən] adj totalitär
tote [tot] tr schleppen
totem ['totəm] s Totem n
totter ['tatər] intr schwanken
touch [tʌtʃ] s Berührung f; (sense of touch) Tastsinn m; (e.g., of a fever) Anflug m; (trace, small bit) Spur f; (of a pianist) Anschlag m; get in t. with in Verbindung treten mit; keep in t. with in Verbindung bleiben mit; put in t. with in Verbindung setzen mit; with sure t. mit sicherer Hand || tr berühren; (fig) rühren; he's a little touched (coll) er hat e–n kleinen Klaps; t. bottom anstoßen; t. glasses mit den Gläsern anstoßen; t. off auslösen; t. s.o. for (coll) j–n anpumpen um; t. up (with cosmetics) auffrischen; (paint, phot) retuschieren || intr sich berühren; t. down (aer) aufsetzen; t. on (a topic) berühren; (e.g., arrogance) grenzen an (acc)
touch' and go' s—be t. auf der Kippe stehen
touch'ing adj rührend, herzergreifend
touch'stone' s (fig) Prüfstein m
touch'-type' intr blindschreiben
touchy ['tʌtʃi] adj (spot, person) empfindlich; (situation) heikel
tough [tʌf] adj (strong) derb; (meat) zäh; (life) mühselig; (difficult) schwierig || s Gassenjunge m
toughen ['tʌfən] tr zäher machen; t.

up (*through training*) ertüchtigen ‖ *intr* (up) zäher werden

tough' luck' *s* Pech *n*

tour [tʊr] *s* (*of a country*) Tour *f*; (*of a city*) Rundfahrt *f*; (*of a museum*) Führung *f*; (*mus, theat*) Tournee *f*; go on t. auf Tournee gehen ‖ *tr* besichtigen; (*a country*) bereisen ‖ *intr* auf der Reise sein; (theat) auf Tournee sein

tour' guide' *s* Reiseführer –in *mf*

tourism ['tʊrɪzəm] *s* Touristik *f*

tournament ['tʊrnəmənt] *s* Turnier *n*

tourney ['tʊrni] *s* Turnier *f*

tourniquet ['tʊrnɪ͵ket] *s* Aderpresse *f*

tousle ['taʊzəl] *tr* (zer)zausen

tow [to] *s*—have in tow im Schlepptau haben; take in tow ins Schlepptau nehmen ‖ *tr* schleppen; tow away abschleppen

toward(s) [tord(z)] *prep* (*with respect to*) gegenüber (*dat*); (*a goal, direction*) auf (*acc*), zu; (*shortly before*) gegen (*acc*); (*for*) für (*acc*); (*facing*) zugewandt (*dat*)

tow'boat' *s* Schleppschiff *n*

tow·el ['taʊ·əl] *s* Handtuch *n* ‖ *v* (*pret & pp* –el[l]ed; *ger* –el[l]ing) *tr* mit e–m Handtuch abtrocknen

tow'el rack' *s* Handtuchhalter *m*

tower ['taʊ·ər] *s* Turm *m*; t. of strength starker Hort *m* ‖ *intr* ragen; t. over überragen

tow'ering *adj* hochragend; (*rage*) rasend

tow'ing serv'ice *s* Schleppdienst *m*

tow'line' *s* Schlepptau *n*

town [taʊn] *s* städtisch, Stadt– ‖ *s* Stadt *f*; in t. in der Stadt; out of t. verreist; go to t. on Feuer und Flamme sein für

town' coun'cil *s* Stadtrat *m*

town' hall' *s* Rathaus *n*

town' house' *s* Stadthaus *n*

town'ship' *s* Gemeinde *f*

tow'rope' *s* Schlepptau *n*; (*for a glider*) Startseil *n*

tow' truck' *s* Abschleppwagen *m*

toxic ['taksɪk] *adj* Gift–, toxisch ‖ *s* Giftstoff *m*

toy [tɔɪ] *adj* Spielzeug– ‖ *s* Spielzeug *n*; toys Spielsachen *pl*; (com) Spielwaren *pl* ‖ *intr* spielen; toy with (fig) herumspielen mit

toy' dog' *s* Schoßhund *m*

toy' shop' *s* Spielwarengeschäft *n*

toy' sol'dier *s* Spielzeugsoldat *m*

trace [tres] *s* Spur *f*; (*of a harness*) Strang *m*; without a t. spurlos ‖ *tr* (*a drawing*) durchpausen; (*lines*) nachziehen; (*track*) ausfindig machen; t. (back) to zurückführen auf (*acc*)

tracer ['tresər] *s* Suchzettel *m*

trac'er bul'let *s* Leuchtspurgeschoß *n*

trac'ing pa'per *s* Pauspapier *n*

track [træk] *s* Spur *f*; (*of a foot*) Fußspur *f*; (*of a wheel*) Radspur *f*; (*chain of a tank*) Raupenkette *f*; (*parallel rails*) Geleise *n*; (*single rail*) Gleis *n*, Schiene *f*; (*station platform*) Bahnsteig *m*; (*path*) Pfad *m*; (*course*

for running) Laufbahn *f*; (*course for motor and horse racing*) Rennbahn *f*; (*running as a sport*) Laufen *n*; be off the t. (fig) auf dem Holzweg sein; go off the t. (*derail*) entgleisen; in one's tracks mitten auf dem Weg; jump the t. aus den Schienen springen ‖ *tr* verfolgen; t. down (*game, a criminal*) zur Strecke bringen; (*a rumor, reference*) nachgehen (*dat*); t. up (*a rug*) schmutzig treten

track'-and-field' *adj* Leichtathletik–

trackless ['træklɪs] *adj* pfadlos; (*vehicle*) schienenlos

track' meet' *s* Leichtathletikwettkampf *m*

tract [trækt] *s* Strich *m*; (*treatise*) Traktat *n*; t. of land Grundstück *n*

traction ['trækʃən] *s* (med) Ziehen *n*; (*of the road*) Griffigkeit *f*

tractor ['træktər] *s* Traktor *m*; (*of a tractor-trailer*) Zugmaschine *f*

trac'tor-trail'er *s* Sattelschlepper *m* mit e–m Anhänger

trade [tred] *s* Handel *m*; (*calling, job*) Gewerbe *n*; (*exchange*) Tausch *m*; by t. von Beruf ‖ *tr* (aus)tauschen; t. in (e.g., *a used car*) in Zahlung geben ‖ *intr* Handel treiben

trade' agree'ment *s* Handelsabkommen *n*

trade' bar'riers *spl* Handelsschranken *pl*

trade'-in val'ue *s* Handelswert *m*

trade'mark' *s* Warenzeichen *n*

trade' name' *s* (*of products*) Handelsbezeichnung *f*; (*of a firm*) Firmenname *m*

trader ['tredər] *s* Händler –in *mf*

trade' school' *s* Gewerbeschule *f*

trade' se'cret *s* Geschäftsgeheimnis *n*

trades'man *s* (–men) Handelsmann *m*

trade' un'ion *s* Gewerkschaft *f*

trade'wind' *s* Passatwind *m*

trad'ing post' *s* Handelsniederlassung *f*

trad'ing stamp' *s* Rabattmarke *f*

tradition [trə'dɪʃən] *s* Tradition *f*

traditional [trə'dɪʃənəl] *adj* herkömmlich, traditionell

traf·fic ['træfɪk] *s* Verkehr *m*; (*trade*) (in) Handel *m* (in *dat*) ‖ *v* (*pret & pp* –ficked; *ger* –ficking) *intr*—t. in handeln in (*dat*)

traf'fic ac'cident *s* Verkehrsunfall *m*

traf'fic cir'cle *s* Kreisverkehr *m*

traf'fic is'land *s* Verkehrsinsel *f*

traf'fic jam' *s* Verkehrsstockung *f*

traf'fic lane' *s* Fahrbahn *f*

traf'fic light' *s* Verkehrsampel *f*; go through a t. bei Rot durchfahren

traf'fic sign' *s* Verkehrszeichen *n*

traf'fic tick'et *s* Strafzettel *m*

traf'fic viola'tion *s* Verkehrsdelikt *n*

tragedian [trə'dʒɪd·ən] *s* Tragiker *m*

tragedy ['trædʒɪdi] *s* (& *fig*) Tragödie *f*

tragic ['trædʒɪk] *adj* tragisch

trail [trel] *s* (*path*) Fährte *f*; be on s.o.'s t. j–m auf der Spur sein; t. of smoke Rauchfahne *f* ‖ *tr* (*on foot*) nachgehen (*dat*); (*in a vehicle*) nachfahren (*dat*); (*in a race*) nachhinken (*dat*) ‖ *intr* (*said of a robe*) schleifen

trailer ['treilər] s Anhänger m; (mobile home) Wohnwagen m

trail'er camp' s Wohnwagenparkplatz m

train [tren] s (of railway cars) Zug m; (of a dress) Schleppe f; (following) Gefolge n; (of events) Folge f; go by t. mit dem Zug fahren; **t. of thought** Gedankengang m || tr ausbilden; (for a particular job) anlernen; (the memory) üben; (plants) am Spalier aufziehen; (an animal) dressieren; (a gun) (on) zielen (auf acc); (sport) trainieren || intr üben; (sport) trainieren

trained adj geschult, ausgebildet

trainee [tre'ni] s Anlernling m

trainer ['trenər] s (of domestic animals) Dresseur m, Dresseuse f; (of wild animals) Dompteur m, Dompteuse f; (aer) Schulflugzeug n; (sport) Sportwart –in mf

train'ing s Ausbildung f; (of animals) Dressur f; (sport) Training n

train'ing school' s (vocational school) Berufsschule f; (reformatory) Erziehungsanstalt f

trait [tret] s Charakterzug m

traitor ['tretər] s Verräter –in mf; (of a country) Hochverräter –in mf

trajectory [trə'dʒektəri] s Flugbahn f

tramp [træmp] s Landstreicher –in mf; (loose woman) Frauenzimmer n || tr trampeln; (traverse on foot) durchstreifen || intr vagabundieren; **t. on** herumtrampeln auf (dat)

trample ['træmpəl] s Getrampel n || tr trampeln; **t. to death** tottreten; **t. under foot** (fig) mit Füßen treten || intr—**t. on** herumtrampeln auf (dat); (fig) mit Füßen treten

trampoline ['træmpə,lin] s Trampolin n

trance [træns] s Trance f

tranquil ['træŋkwil] adj ruhig

tranquilize ['træŋkwɪ,laɪz] tr beruhigen

tranquilizer ['træŋkwɪ,laɪzər] s Beruhigungsmittel n

tranquillity [træn'kwɪlɪti] s Ruhe f

transact [træn'zækt] tr abwickeln

transaction [træn'zækʃən] s Abwicklung f; **transactions** (of a society) Sitzungsbericht m

transatlantic [,trænsət'læntɪk] adj transatlantisch

transcend [træn'send] tr übersteigen

transcendental [,trænsen'dentəl] adj übersinnlich; (philos) transzendental

transcribe [træn'skraɪb] tr (copy) umschreiben; (dictated or recorded material) übertragen; (mus) transkribieren; (phonet) in Lautschrift wiedergeben; (rad) auf Band aufnehmen

transcript ['trænskrɪpt] s Transkript n

transcription [træn'skrɪpʃən] s Umschrift f; (mus) Transkription f

transept ['trænsept] s Querschiff n

trans•fer ['trænsfər] s (of property) Übertragung f (of money) Überweisung f; (of an employee) Versetzung f; (of a passenger) Umsteigen n; (ticket) Umsteigefahrschein

m || [træns'fʌr], ['trænsfər] v (pret & pp –ferred; ger –ferring) tr (property) übertragen; (money) überweisen; (to another account) umbuchen; (an employee) versetzen || intr (to) versetzt werden (nach, zu); (said of a passenger) umsteigen

transfix [træns'fɪks] tr durchbohren

transform [træns'form] tr (a person) verwandeln; (into) umwandeln (in acc); (elec) umspannen

transformer [træns'formər] s (elec) Stromwandler m, Transformator m

transfusion [træns'fjuʒən] s (med) Übertragung f, Transfusion f

transgress [træns'gres] tr überschreiten

transgression [træs'grɛʃən] s Vergehen n

transient ['trænʃənt] adj vorübergehend; (fleeting) flüchtig || s Durchreisende mf

transistor [træn'sɪstər] adj Transistor– || s Transistor m

transistorize [træn'sɪstə,raɪz] tr transistorisieren

transit ['trænzɪt] s (astr) Durchgang m; (com) Transit m; **in t.** unterwegs

transition [træn'zɪʃən] s Übergang m

transitional [træn'zɪʃənəl] adj Übergangs–

transitive ['trænsɪtɪv] adj transitiv

transitory ['trænsɪ,tori] adj vergänglich

translate [træns'let] tr übersetzen; **t. into action** in die Tat umsetzen

translation [træns'leʃən] s Übersetzung f

translator [træns'letər] s Übersetzer –in mf

transliterate [træns'lɪtə,ret] tr transkribieren

translucent [træns'lusənt] adj durchscheinend, lichtdurchlässig

transmigration [,trænsmaɪ'greʃən] s— **t. of the soul** Seelenwanderung f

transmission [træns'mɪʃən] s (of a text) Textüberlieferung f; (of news, information) Übermittlung f; (aut) Getriebe n; (rad, telv) Sendung f

trans•mit [træns'mɪt] v (pret & pp –mitted; ger –mitting) tr (send forward) übersenden; (disease, power, light, heat) übertragen; (e.g., customs) überliefern; (by inheritance) vererben; (rad, telp, telv) senden

transmitter [træns'mɪtər] s (rad, telg, telv) Sender m

transmutation [,trænsmʊ'teʃən] s Umwandlung f; (biol) Transmutation f; (chem, phys) Umwandlung f

transmute [træns'mjut] tr umwandeln

transoceanic [,trænzo/ɪ'ænɪk] adj überseeisch, Übersee–

transom ['trænsəm] s (crosspiece) Querbalken m; (window over a door) Oberlicht n mit Kreuzsprosse; (of a boat) Spiegel m

transparency [træns'perənsi] s Durchsichtigkeit f, Transparenz f; (phot) Diapositiv n

transparent [træns'perənt] adj durchsichtig, transparent

transpire [træns'paɪr] *intr* (*happen*) sich ereignen; (*leak out*) (fig) durchsickern

transplant ['træns‚plænt] *s* (bot, surg) Verpflanzung *f* || [træns'plænt] *tr* (bot, surg) verpflanzen

transport ['trænsport] *s* Beförderung *f*, Transport *m*; (nav) Truppentransporter *m* || [træns'port] *tr* befördern

transportation [‚trænspor'teʃən] *s* Beförderung *f*; (*public transportation*) Verkehrsmittel *n*; do you need t.? brauchen Sie e-e Fahrgelegenheit?

trans'port plane' *s* Transportflugzeug *n*

transpose [træns'poz] *tr* umstellen; (math, mus) transponieren

trans•ship [træns'ʃɪp] *v* (*pret & pp* -shipped; *ger* -shipping) *tr* (com, naut) umladen

trap [træp] *s* (& fig) Falle *f*; (*snare*) Schlinge *f*; (*pit*) Fallgrube *f*; (*under a sink*) Geruchsverschluß *m*; (*mouth*) (sl) Klappe *f*; (chem) Abscheider *m*; (golf) Sandbunker *m*; fall (or walk) into a t. in die Falle gehen; set a trap e-e Falle stellen || *v* (*pret & pp* trapped; *ger* trapping) *tr* mit e-r Falle fangen; (fig) erwischen; (mil) einfangen

trap' door' *s* Falltür *f*, Klapptür *f*; (theat) Versenkung *f*

trapeze [trə'piz] *s* Trapez *n*; (gym) Schwebereck *n*

trapezoid ['træpɪ‚zɔɪd] *s* Trapez *n*

trapper ['træpər] *s* Fallensteller *m*

trappings ['træpɪŋz] *spl* Staat *m*; (*caparison*) Staatsgeschirr *n*

trap'shoot'ing *s* Tontaubenschießen *n*

trash [træʃ] *s* Abfälle *pl*; (*junk*) Schund *m*; (*artistically inferior material*) Kitsch *m*; (*worthless people*) Gesindel *n*

trash' can' *s* Mülleimer *m*, Abfalleimer *m*

trashy ['træʃi] *adj* kitschig; (*literature*) Schund–

travail [trə'vel] *s* Plackerei *f*; (*labor of childbirth*) Wehen *pl*

trav•el ['trævəl] *s* Reisen *n*; (*trip*) Reise *f*; (*e.g., of a bullet, rocket*) Bewegung *f*; (*of moving parts*) Lauf *m*; travels Reiseerlebnisse *pl* || *v* (*pret & pp* -el[l]ed; *ger* -el[l]ing) *tr* bereisen || *intr* reisen; (*said of a vehicle or passenger*) fahren; (astr, aut, mach, phys) sich bewegen

trav'el a'gency *s* Reisebüro *n*

traveler ['trævələr] *s* Reisende *mf*

trav'eler's check' *s* Reisescheck *m*

trav'el fold'er *s* Reiseprospekt *m*

trav'eling bag' *s* Reisetasche *f*

trav'eling sales'man *s* (-men) Geschäftsreisende *m*

travelogue ['trævə‚log] *s* Reisebericht *m*; (cin) Reisefilm *m*

traverse [trə'vʌrs] *tr* durchqueren || *intr* (*said of a gun*) sich drehen

traves•ty ['trævɪsti] *s* Travestie *f* || *v* (*pret & pp* -tied) *tr* travestieren

trawl [trɔl] *s* Schleppnetz *n* || *tr* mit dem Schleppnetz fangen || *intr* mit dem Schleppnetz fischen

trawler ['trɔlər] *s* Schleppnetzboot *n*

tray [tre] *s* Tablett *n*; (phot) Schale *f*

treacherous ['tretʃərəs] *adj* verräterisch; (*e.g., ice*) trügerisch

treachery ['tretʃəri] *s* Verrat *m*

tread [tred] *s* (*step*) Tritt *m*; (*imprint*) Spur *f*; (*on a tire*) Profil *n* || *v* (*pret* trod [trɑd]; *pp* trodden ['trɑdən] & trod) *tr* betreten || *intr* (on) treten (auf *acc*)

treadle ['tredəl] *s* Trittbrett *n*

tread'mill' *s* (& fig) Tretmühle *f*

treason ['trizən] *s* Verrat *m*

treasonable ['trizənəbəl] *adj* verräterisch

treasure ['treʒər] *s* Schatz *m* || *tr* sehr schätzen

treasurer ['treʒərər] *s* Schatzmeister –in *mf*

treasury ['treʒəri] *s* Schatzkammer *f*; (*chest*) Tresor *m*; (*public treasury*) Staatsschatz *m*; Treasury Finanzministerium *n*

treat [trit] *s* Hochgenuß *m* || *tr* behandeln; (*regard*) (as) betrachten (als); t. oneself to s.th. sich [*dat*] etw genehmigen; t. s.o. to s.th j–n bewirten mit

treatise ['tritɪs] *s* Abhandlung *f*

treatment ['tritmənt] *s* Behandlung *f*

treaty ['triti] *s* Vertrag *m*

treble ['trebəl] *adj* (*threefold*) dreifach; (mus) Diskant– || *s* Diskant *m*; (*voice*) Diskantstimme *f* || *tr* verdreifachen || *intr* sich verdreifachen

tre'ble clef' *s* Violinschlüssel *m*

tree [tri] *s* Baum *m*

treeless ['trilɪs] *adj* baumlos

tree'top' *s* Baumwipfel *m*

tree' trunk' *s* Baumstamm *m*

trellis ['trelɪs] *s* Spalier *n*; (*gazebo*) Gartenhäuschen *n*

tremble ['trembəl] *s* Zittern *n* || *intr* zittern; (geol) beben; t. all over am ganzen Körper zittern

tremendous [trɪ'mendəs] *adj* ungeheuer

tremor ['tremər] *s* Zittern *n*; (geol) Beben *n*

trench [trentʃ] *s* Graben *m*; (mil) Schützengraben *m*

trenchant ['trentʃənt] *adj* schneidend; (*policy*) durchschlagend

trench' war'fare *s* Stellungskrieg *m*

trend [trend] *s* Richtung *f*, Trend *m*

trespass ['trespəs] *s* unbefugtes Betreten *n*; (*sin*) Sünde *f* || *intr* unbefugt fremdes Eigentum betreten; no trespassing (public sign) Betreten verboten; t. on unbefugt betreten

trespasser ['trespəsər] *s* Unbefugte *mf*

tress [tres] *s* Flechte *f*

trestle ['tresəl] *s* Gestell *n*; (*of a bridge*) Brückenbock *m*

trial ['traɪəl] *s* (*attempt*) Versuch *m*; (*hardship*) Beschwernis *f*; (jur) Prozeß *m*; a week's t. e–e Woche Probezeit; be on t. for vor Gericht stehen wegen; be brought up (or come up) for t. zur Verhandlung kommen; new t. Wiederaufnahmeverfahren *n*; on t. (com) auf Probe; put on t. vor Gericht bringen

tri'al and er'ror s—**by t.** durch Ausprobieren
tri'al balloon' s Versuchsballon m
tri'al by ju'ry s Verhandlung f vor dem Schwurgericht
tri'al or'der s Probeauftrag m
tri'al run' s Probelauf m
triangle ['traɪˌæŋgəl] s Dreieck n
triangular [traɪˈæŋgjələr] adj dreieckig
tribe [traɪb] s Stamm m; (pej) Sippschaft f
tribunal [traɪˈbjunəl] s Tribunal n
tributary ['trɪbjəˌteri] adj zinspflichtig || s Nebenfluß m
tribute ['trɪbjut] s Tribut m, Zins m; **pay t. to** Anerkennung zollen (dat)
trice [traɪs] s—**in a t.** im Nu
trick [trɪk] s Trick m; (prank) Streich m; (technique) Kniff m; (artifice) Schlich m; (cards) Stich m; **be on to s.o.'s tricks** j-s Schliche kennen; **be up to one's old tricks** sein Unwesen treiben; **do the t.** die Sache schaffen; **play a dirty t. on s.o.** j-m e-n gemeinen Streich spielen || tr reinlegen; **t. s.o. into** (ger) j-n durch Kniffe dazu bringen zu (inf)
trickery ['trɪkəri] s Gaunerei f
trickle ['trɪkəl] s Tröpfeln n || intr tröpfeln, rieseln
trickster ['trɪkstər] s Gauner m
tricky ['trɪki] adj (wily) listig; (touchy) heikel; (difficult) verzwickt
trident ['traɪdənt] s Dreizack m
tried [traɪd] adj bewährt, probat
trifle ['traɪfəl] s Kleinigkeit f; **a t.** (e.g., too big) ein bißchen || tr—**t. away** vertändeln || intr tändeln
trif'ling adj geringfügig || s Tändelei f
trigger ['trɪgər] s Abzug m; **pull the t.** abdrücken || tr auslösen
trig'ger-hap'py adj schießwütig
trigonometry [ˌtrɪgəˈnɑmətri] s Trigonometrie f
trill [trɪl] s Triller m || tr & intr trillern
trillion ['trɪljən] s Billion f; (Brit) Trillion f
trilogy ['trɪlədʒi] s Trilogie f
trim [trɪm] adj (trimmer; trimmest) (figure) schick; (well-kept) gepflegt || s (e.g., of a hat) Zierleiste f; (naut) Trimm m; **be in t.** in Form sein || v (pret & pp trimmed; ger trimming) tr (clip) stutzen; (decorate) dekorieren; (a Christmas tree) schmücken; (beat) (coll) schlagen; (naut) trimmen
trim'ming s (e.g., of a dress) Besatz m; (of hedges) Stutzen n; **take a t.** (coll) e-e Niederlage erleiden; **trimmings** (decorations) Verzierungen pl; (food) Zutaten pl; (scraps) Abfälle pl; **with all the trimmings** (fig) mit allen Schikanen
trinity ['trɪnɪti] s Dreiheit f; **Trinity** Dreifaltigkeit f
trinket ['trɪŋkɪt] s Schmuckgegenstand m
tri·o ['tri·o] s (-os) (& mus) Trio n
trip [trɪp] s Reise f; (on drugs) Trip m; **go on** (or **take**) **a t.** e-e Reise machen || v (pret & pp tripped; ger tripping) tr ein Bein stellen (dat); **t. up** (fig) zu Fall bringen || intr stolpern
tripartite [traɪˈpartaɪt] adj Dreiparteien—; (of three powers) Dreimächte—
tripe [traɪp] s Kutteln pl; (sl) Schund m
trip'ham'mer s Schmiedehammer m
triple ['trɪpəl] adj dreifach || s Dreifache n || tr verdreifachen
triplet ['trɪplɪt] s (offspring) Drilling m; (mus) Triole f
triplicate ['trɪplɪkɪt] adj dreifach || s—**in t.** in dreifacher Ausfertigung
tripod ['traɪpɑd] s Dreifuß m; (phot) Stativ n
triptych ['trɪptɪk] s Triptychon n
trite [traɪt] adj abgedroschen
triumph ['traɪ·əmf] s Triumph m || intr (over) triumphieren (über acc)
triumphal [traɪˈʌmfəl] adj Sieges—
triumphant [traɪˈʌmfənt] adj triumphierend
trivia ['trɪvɪ·ə] spl Nichtigkeiten pl
trivial ['trɪvɪ·əl] adj trivial, alltäglich; (person) oberflächlich
triviality [ˌtrɪvɪˈælɪti] s Trivialität f, Nebensächlichkeit f
Trojan ['trodʒən] adj trojanisch || s Trojaner —in mf
troll [trol] s (myth) Troll m || tr & intr mit der Schleppangel fischen
trolley ['trali] s Straßenbahn f
trollop ['traləp] s (slovenly woman) Schlampe f; (prostitute) Dirne f
trombone ['trambon] s Posaune f
troop [trup] s Trupp m; (mil) Truppe f
trooper ['trupər] s Kavallerist m; **swear like a t.** fluchen wie ein Kutscher
troop'ship' s Truppentransporter m
trophy ['trofi] s Trophäe f; (sport) Pokal m
tropical ['trapɪkəl] adj Tropen—
tropics ['trapɪks] spl Tropen pl
trot [trat] s Trab m || v (pret & pp trotted; ger trotting) tr—**t. out** (coll) zur Schau stellen || intr traben
troubadour ['trubəˌdor] s Minnesänger m
trouble ['trʌbəl] s (inconvenience, bother) Mühe f; (difficulty) Schwierigkeit f; (physical distress) Leiden n; (civil disorder) Unruhe f; **ask for t.** das Schicksal herausfordern; **be in t. in Schwierigkeiten sein; (be pregnant)** schwanger sein; **cause s.o. a lot of t.** j-m viel zu schaffen machen; **get into t.** in Schwierigkeiten geraten; **go to a lot of t.** sich (dat) viel Mühe machen; **it was no t. at all!** gern geschehen!; **make t.** Geschichten machen; **take the t. to** (inf) sich der Mühe unterziehen zu (inf); **that's the t.** da liegt die Schwierigkeit; **what's the t.?** was ist los? || tr (worry) beunruhigen; (bother) belästigen; (disturb) stören; (said of ills) plagen
trou'blemak'er s Unruhestifter —in mf
troubleshooter ['trʌbəlˌʃutər] s Stö-

rungssucher –in *mf;* (*in disputes*) Friedensstifter –in *mf*

troublesome ['trʌbəlsəm] *adj* lästig

trough [trɔf] *s* Trog *m;* (*of a wave*) Wellental *n*

troupe [trup] *s* Truppe *f*

trousers ['trauzərz] *spl* Hose *f*

trous·seau [tru'so] *s* (–seaux & –seaus) Brautausstattung *f*

trout [traut] *s* Forelle *f*

trowel ['trau·əl] *s* Kelle *f*

truant ['tru·ənt] *adj* schwänzend ‖ *s—* **play** t. die Schule schwänzen

truce [trus] *s* Waffenruhe *f*

truck [trʌk] *s* Last(kraft)wagen *m;* (*for luggage*) Gepäckwagen *m* ‖ *tr* mit Lastkraftwagen befördern

truck′driv′er *s* Lastwagenfahrer *m*

trucker ['trʌkər] *s* (*driver*) Lastwagenfahrer *m;* (*owner of a trucking firm*) Fuhrunternehmer –in *mf*

truck′ farm′ing *s* Gemüsebau *m*

truculent ['trʌkjələnt] *adj* gehässig

trudge [trʌdʒ] *intr* stapfen

true [tru] *adj* wahr; (*loyal*) (ge)treu; (*genuine*) echt; (*sign*) sicher; **come t.** sich verwirklichen; **prove t.** sich als wahr erweisen; **that′s t.** das stimmt

truffle ['trʌfəl] *s* Trüffel *f*

truism ['tru·ɪzm] *s* Binsenwahrheit *f*

truly ['truli] *adv* wirklich; **Yours t.** Hochachtungsvoll

trump [trʌmp] *s* Trumpf *m* ‖ *tr* trumpfen; **t. up** erdichten ‖ *intr* trumpfen

trumpet ['trʌmpɪt] *s* Trompete *f* ‖ *intr* (*said of an elephant*) trompeten

truncheon ['trʌntʃən] *s* Gummiknüppel *m*

trunk [trʌŋk] *s* (*chest*) Koffer *m;* (*of a tree*) Stamm *m;* (*of a living body*) Rumpf *m;* (*of an elephant*) Rüssel *m;* (*aut*) Kofferraum *m;* **trunks** (sport) Sporthose *f*

trunk′ line′ *s* Fernverkehrsweg *m*

truss [trʌs] *s* (*archit*) Tragwerk *n;* (*med*) Bruchband *n* ‖ *tr* (*archit*) stützen; (*bind*) festbinden

trust [trʌst] *s* (*in*) Vertrauen *n* (auf *acc*); (*com*) Trust *m;* (*jur*) Treuhand *f* ‖ *tr* trauen (*dat*); (*hope*) hoffen ‖ *intr*—**t. in** vertrauen auf (*acc*)

trust′ com′pany *s* Treuhandgesellschaft *f*

trustee [trʌs'ti] *s* Aufsichtsrat *m;* (*jur*) Treuhänder –in *mf*

trustee′ship *s* Treuhandverwaltung *f*

trustful ['trʌstfəl] *adj* zutraulich

trust′ fund′ *s* Treuhandfonds *m*

trust′wor′thy *adj* vertrauenswürdig

trusty ['trʌsti] *adj* treu ‖ *s* Kalfaktor *m*

truth [truθ] *s* Wahrheit *f;* **in t.** wahrlich

truthful ['truθfəl] *adj* (*person*) ehrlich; (*e.g., account*) wahrheitsgemäß

try [traɪ] *s* Versuch *m* ‖ *v* (*pret & pp tried*) *tr* versuchen; (*one′s patience*) auf e-e harte Probe stellen; (*a case*) verhandeln; **be tried for** vor Gericht kommen wegen; **try on** anprobieren; (*a hat*) aufprobieren; **try out** erproben; (*new food*) kosten; **try s.o. for**

gegen j–n verhandeln wegen ‖ *intr* versuchen

try′ing *adj* anstrengend

try′out′ *s* (sport) Ausscheidungskampf *m*

T′-shirt′ *s* T-Shirt *n*

tub [tʌb] *s* Wanne *f;* (*boat*) Kasten *m*

tubby ['tʌbi] *adj* (coll) kugelrund

tube [t(j)ub] *s* (*pipe*) Rohr *n,* Röhre *f;* (*e.g., of toothpaste*) Tube *f;* (*of rubber*) Schlauch *m;* (rad) Röhre *f*

tuber ['t(j)ubər] *s* (bot) Knolle *f*

tubercle ['t(j)ubərkəl] *s* Tuberkel *m*

tuberculosis [t(j)u‚bʌrkjə'losɪs] *s* Lungenschwindsucht *f*

tuck [tʌk] *s* (sew) Abnäher *m* ‖ *tr* (*into one′s pocket, under a mattress*) stecken; (*under one′s arm*) klemmen; (*into bed*) packen; **t. in** reinstecken; **t. up** (*trousers*) hochkrempeln; (*a skirt, dress*) hochschürzen

Tuesday ['t(j)uzde] *s* Dienstag *m;* **on T.** am Dienstag

tuft [tʌft] *s* Büschel *m* & *n* ‖ *tr* (*e.g., a mattress*) durchheften

tug [tʌg] *s* (*pull*) Zug *m;* (*boat*) Schlepper *m* ‖ *v* (*pret & pp tugged; ger tugging*) *tr* schleppen ‖ *intr* (*at*) zerren (an *dat*)

tug′boat′ *s* Schleppdampfer *m*

tug′ of war′ *s* Tauziehen *n*

tuition [t(j)u'rʃən] *s* Schulgeld *n*

tulip ['t(j)ulɪp] *s* Tulpe *f*

tumble ['tʌmbəl] *s* (*fall*) Sturz *m;* (gym) Purzelbaum *m* ‖ *intr* (*fall*) stürzen; (gym) Saltos machen; **t. down the stairs** die Treppe herunterpurzeln

tum′ble-down′ *adj* baufällig

tumbler ['tʌmblər] *s* (*glass*) Trinkglas *n;* (*of a lock*) Zuhaltung *f;* (*acrobat*) Akrobat –in *mf*

tumor ['t(j)umər] *s* Geschwulst *f*

tumult ['t(j)umʌlt] *s* Getümmel *n*

tuna ['tunə] *s* Thunfisch *m*

tune [t(j)un] *s* Melodie *f;* **be in t.** richtig gestimmt sein; **be out of t.** falsch singen; (*said of a piano*) verstimmt sein; **change one′s t.** e–n anderen Ton anschlagen ‖ *tr* stimmen; **t. up** (aut) neu einstellen ‖ *intr*— **t. in on** (rad) einstellen; **t. up** (*said of an orchestra*) stimmen

tungsten ['tʌŋstən] *s* Wolfram *n*

tunic ['t(j)unɪk] *s* Tunika *f*

tun′ing fork′ *s* Stimmgabel *f*

tun·nel ['tʌnəl] *s* Tunnel *m;* (min) Stollen *m* ‖ *v* (*pret & pp –nel[l]ed; ger –nel[l]ing*) *intr* e–n Tunnel bohren

turban ['tʌrbən] *s* Turban *m*

turbid ['tʌrbɪd] *adj* trüb(e)

turbine ['tʌrbɪn] *s* Turbine *f*

turboprop ['tʌrbo‚prɑp] *s* Turboprop *m*

turbulence ['tʌrbjələns] *s* Turbulenz *f*

tureen [t(j)u'rin] *s* Terrine *f*

turf [tʌrf] *s* Rasendecke *f;* (*of a gang*) (sl) Gebiet *n;* **the t. der** Turf

Turk [tʌrk] *s* Türke *m,* Türkin *f*

turkey ['tʌrki] *s* Truthahn *m;* (*female*) Truthenne *f;* **Turkey** die Türkei

Turkish ['tʌrkɪʃ] *adj* türkisch ‖ *s* Türkisch *n*

Tur'kish tow'el *s* Frottiertuch *n*

turmoil ['tʌrmɔɪl] *s* Getümmel *n*

turn [tʌrn] *s* (*rotation*) Drehung *f*; (*change of direction or condition*) Wendung *f*; (*curve*) Kurve *f*; (*by a driver*) Abbiegen *n*; (*of a century*) Wende *f*; (*of a spool*) Windung *f*; **at every t.** bei jeder Gelegenheit; **good t.** Gunst *f*; **it's his t.** er ist dran; **out of t.** außer der Reihe; **take turns** sich abwechseln ‖ *tr* drehen; (*the page*) umblättern; (*one's head*) wenden; **t. down** (*refuse*) ablehnen; (*a radio*) leiser stellen; (*a bed*) aufdecken; (*a collar*) umschlagen; (*an appeal*) (jur) verwerfen; **t. in** (*application, resignation*) einreichen; (*lost articles*) abgeben; (*a person*) anzeigen; **t. into** verwandeln in (*acc*); **t. loose** frei lassen; **t. off** (*light, gas*) abdrehen; (rad, telv) abstellen; **t. on** (*gas, light*) andrehen; (*excite*) (coll) in Erregung versetzen; (rad, telv) anstellen; **t. out** produzieren; (*pockets*) umkehren; (*eject*) vor die Tür setzen; **t. over** (*property*) abtreten; (*a business*) übertragen; (*e.g., weapons*) abliefern; **t. up** (*a card, sleeve*) aufschlagen ‖ *intr* (*rotate*) sich drehen; (*in some direction*) sich wenden; **it turned out that** es stellte sich heraus, daß; **t. against** (fig) sich wenden gegen; **t. around** sich herumdrehen; **t. back** umdrehen; **t. down** (*a street*) einbiegen in (*acc*); **t. in** (*go to bed*) zu Bett gehen; **t. into** werden zu; **t. out** ausfallen; **t. out for** sich einfinden zu; **t. out for the best** sich zum Guten wenden; **t. out in force** vollzählig erscheinen; **t. out to be** sich erweisen als; **t. over** (*tip over*) umkippen; (aut) anspringen; **t. to s.o. for help** sich an j-n um Hilfe wenden; **t. towards** sich wenden gegen; **t. up** auftauchen

turn'coat' *s* Überläufer –in *mf*

turn'ing point' *s* Wendepunkt *m*

turnip ['tʌrnɪp] *s* Steckrübe *f*

turn'out' *s* Beteiligung *f*

turn'o'ver *s* Umsatz *m*

turn'pike' *s* Autobahn *f*

turnstile ['tʌrn‚staɪl] *s* Drehkreuz *n*

turn'ta'ble *s* Plattenteller *m*; (rr) Drehscheibe *f*

turpentine ['tʌrpən‚taɪn] *s* Terpentin *n*

turpitude ['tʌrpɪ‚t(j)ud] *s* Verworfenheit *f*

turquoise ['tʌrk(w)ɔɪz] *adj* türkisfarben ‖ *s* Türkis *m*

turret ['tʌrɪt] *s* Turm *m*

turtle ['tʌrtəl] *s* Schildkröte *f*

tur'tledove' *s* Turteltaube *f*

tur'tleneck' *s* Rollkragen *m*

tusk [tʌsk] *s* (*of an elephant*) Stoßzahn *m*; (*of a boar*) Hauer *m*

tussle ['tʌsəl] *s* Rauferei *f* ‖ *intr* raufen

tutor ['t(j)utər] *s* Hauslehrer –in *mf*

tuxe•do [tʌk'sido] *s* (–dos) Smoking *m*

twang [twæŋ] *s* (*of a musical instrument*) Schwirren *n*; (*of the voice*) Näseln *n* ‖ *intr* schwirren; näseln

tweed [twid] *adj* aus Tweed ‖ *s* Tweed *m*

tweet [twit] *s* Gezwitscher *n* ‖ *intr* zwitschern

tweezers ['twizərz] *spl* Pinzette *f*

twelfth [twelfθ] *adj & pron* zwölfte ‖ *s* (*fraction*) Zwölftel *n*; **the t.** (*in dates or in series*) der Zwölfte

twelve [twelv] *adj & pron* zwölf ‖ *s* Zwölf *f*

twentieth ['twentɪ‚ɪθ] *adj & pron* zwanzigste ‖ *s* (*fraction*) Zwanzigstel *n*; **the t.** (*in dates or in series*) der Zwanzigste

twenty ['twenti] *adj & pron* zwanzig ‖ *s* Zwanzig *f*; **the twenties** die zwanziger Jahre

twen'ty-one' *adj & pron* einundzwanzig

twice [twaɪs] *adv* zweimal

twiddle ['twɪdəl] *tr* müßig herumdrehen; **t. one's thumbs** Daumen drehen

twig [twɪg] *s* Zweig *m*

twilight ['twaɪ‚laɪt] *adj* dämmerig ‖ *s* Abenddämmerung *f*

twin [twɪn] *adj* (*brother, sister*) Zwillings–; (*double*) Doppel– ‖ *s* Zwilling *m*

twine [twaɪn] *s* (*for a package*) Bindfaden *m*; (*sew*) Zwirn *m* ‖ *tr*—**t. around** winden um

twin'-en'gine *adj* zweimotorig

twinge [twɪndʒ] *s* stechender Schmerz *m*

twinkle ['twɪŋkəl] *s* Funkeln *n*; **in a t.** im Nu ‖ *intr* funkeln

twirl [twʌrl] *s* Wirbel *m* ‖ *tr* herumwirbeln ‖ *intr* wirbeln

twist [twɪst] *s* (*turn*) Drehung *f*; (*distortion*) Verdrehung *f*; (*strand*) Flechte *f*; (*bread roll*) Zopf *m*; (*dance*) Twist *m* ‖ *tr* (*revolve*) drehen; (*wind*) winden; (*an arm, words*) verdrehen; **t. one's ankle** sich [*dat*] den Knöchel vertreten ‖ *intr* sich drehen; (*wind*) sich winden

twister ['twɪstər] *s* (coll) Windhose *f*

twit [twɪt] *s* (sl) Depp *m* ‖ *v* (*pret & pp* twitted; *ger* twitting) *tr* verspotten; (*upbraid*) rügen

twitch [twɪtʃ] *s* Zucken *n* ‖ *intr* zucken

twitter ['twɪtər] *s* Zwitschern *n* ‖ *intr* zwitschern

two [tu] *adj & pron* zwei ‖ *s* Zwei *f*; **by twos** zu zweit; **in two** entzwei; **put two and two together** Schlußfolgerungen ziehen

two'-edged' *adj* zweischneidig

two'-faced' *adj* doppelzüngig

two' hun'dred *adj & pron* zweihundert

two'-piece' *adj* (*suit*) zweiteilig

twosome ['tusəm] *s* (*of lovers*) Liebespaar *n*; (golf) Einzelspiel *n*

two'-time' *tr* untreu sein (*dat*)

two'-tone' *adj* zweifarbig

two'-way traf'fic *s* Gegenverkehr *m*

tycoon [taɪ'kun] *s* Industriekapitän *m*

type [taɪp] *s* (*kind*) Art *f*; (*of person*; *of manufacture*) Typ *m*; (typ) Drucktype *f*, Letter *f* ‖ *tr & intr* tippen

type'face' s Schriftbild n
type'script' s Maschinenschrift f
type'set'ter s Schriftsetzer –in mf
type'write' v (pret –wrote; pp –written) tr & intr mit der Maschine schreiben
type'writ'er s Schreibmaschine f
type'writer rib'bon s Farbband n
ty'phoid fe'ver ['taɪfoɪd] s Typhus m
typhoon [taɪ'fun] s Taifun m
typical ['tɪpɪkəl] adj (of) typisch (für)
typi·fy ['tɪpɪ‚faɪ] v (pret & pp –fied) tr (characterize) typisch sein für; (exemplify) ein typisches Beispiel sein für
typ'ing er'ror s Tippfehler m

typist ['taɪpɪst] s Maschinenschreiber –in mf
typographic(al) [‚taɪpə'græfɪk(əl)] adj typographisch; (error) Druck–
typography [taɪ'pɑgrəfi] s (the skill) Buchdruckerkunst f; (the work) Buchdruck m
tyrannical [tɪ'rænɪkəl] adj tyrannisch
tyrannize ['tɪrə‚naɪz] tr tyrannisieren
tyranny ['tɪrəni] s Tyrannei f
tyrant ['taɪrənt] s Tyrann m
ty·ro ['taɪro] s (-ros) Neuling m
Tyrol [tɪ'rol] s Tirol n
Tyrolean [tɪ'roli·ən] adj tirolerisch ‖ s Tiroler –in mf

U

U, u [ju] s einundzwanzigster Buchstabe des englischen Alphabets
ubiquitous [ju'bɪkwɪtəs] adj allgegenwärtig
udder ['ʌdər] s Euter n
ugliness ['ʌglɪnɪs] s Häßlichkeit f
ugly ['ʌgli] adj häßlich
Ukraine [ju'kren] s Ukraine f
Ukrainian [ju'kreni·ən] adj ukrainisch ‖ s (person) Ukrainer –in mf; (language) Ukrainisch n
ulcer ['ʌlsər] s Geschwür n
ulcerate ['ʌlsə‚ret] intr eitern
ulte'rior mo'tive [ʌl'tɪrɪ·ər] s Hintergedanke m
ultimate ['ʌltɪmɪt] adj äußerste; (goal) höchst; (result) End– ‖ s Letzte n
ultima·tum [‚ʌltɪ'metəm] s (-tums & –ta [tə]) Ultimatum n
ul'trahigh fre'quency ['ʌltrə‚haɪ] s Ultrahochfrequenz f
ultramodern [‚ʌltrə'mɑdərn] adj ultramodern
ultraviolet [‚ʌltrə'vaɪ·əlɪt] adj ultraviolett ‖ s Ultraviolett n
ultravi'olet lamp' s Höhensonne f
umbil'ical cord' [ʌm'bɪlɪkəl] adj Nabelschnur f
umbrage ['ʌmbrɪdʒ] s—take u. at Anstoß nehmen an (dat)
umbrella [ʌm'brelə] s Regenschirm m; (aer) Abschirmung f
umlaut ['umlaut] s Umlaut m ‖ tr umlauten
umpire ['ʌmpaɪr] s Schiedsrichter –in mf ‖ tr als Schiedsrichter leiten ‖ intr Schiedsrichter sein
umpteen [ʌmp'tin] adj zig; u. times zigmal
UN ['ju'en] s (United Nations) UNO f
unable [ʌn'ebəl] adj unfähig
unabridged [‚ʌnə'brɪdʒd] adj ungekürzt
unaccented [‚ʌnæk'sentɪd] adj unbetont
unacceptable [‚ʌnæk'septɪbəl] adj unannehmbar
unaccountable [‚ʌnə'kauntəbəl] adj

nicht verantwortlich; (strange) seltsam
unaccounted-for [‚ʌnə'kauntɪd‚fər] adj unerklärt; (acct) nicht belegt
unaccustomed [‚ʌnə'kʌstəmd] adj (to) nicht gewöhnt (an acc)
unaffected [‚ʌnə'fektɪd] adj nicht affektiert; u. by unbeeinflusst von
unafraid [‚ʌnə'fred] adj—be u. (of) sich nicht fürchten (vor dat)
unalterable [ʌn'ɔltərəbəl] adj unabänderlich
unanimity [‚junə'nɪmɪti] s Stimmeneinheit f
unanimous [ju'nænɪməs] adj (persons) einmütig; (vote) einstimmig
unannounced [‚ʌnə'naunst] adj unangemeldet
unanswered [ʌn'ænsərd] adj (question) unbeantwortet; (claim, statement) unwiderlegt; (request) nicht erhört
unappreciative [‚ʌnə'priʃɪ·ətɪv] adj (of) unempfänglich (für)
unapproachable [‚ʌnə'protʃəbəl] adj unzugänglich
unarmed [ʌn'ɑrmd] adj unbewaffnet
unasked [ʌn'æskt] adj (advice) unerbeten; (uninvited) ungeladen
unassailable [‚ʌnə'seləbəl] adj unangreifbar
unassuming [‚ʌnə's(j)umɪŋ] adj nicht anmaßend
unattached [‚ʌnə'tætʃt] adj (to) nicht befestigt (an dat); (person) ungebunden; (mil) zur Verfügung stehend
unattainable [‚ʌnə'tenəbəl] adj unerreichbar
unattended [‚ʌnə'tendɪd] adj unbeaufsichtigt
unattractive [‚ʌnə'træktɪv] adj reizlos
unauthorized [ʌn'əθəraɪzd] adj unberechtigt
unavailable [‚ʌnə'veləbəl] adj (person) unabkömmlich; (thing) nicht verfügbar
unavenged [‚ʌnə'vendʒd] adj ungerächt
unavoidable [‚ʌnə'vɔɪdəbəl] adj unvermeidlich

unaware [ˌʌnəˈwer] adj (of) nicht bewußt (genit)

unawares [ˌʌnəˈwerz] adv (unexpectedly) unversehens; (unintentionally) versehentlich; **catch u.** überraschen

unbalanced [ʌnˈbælənst] adj nicht im Gleichgewicht; (fig) unausgeglichen

un·bar [ʌnˈbɑr] v (pret & pp –barred; ger –barring) tr aufriegeln

unbearable [ʌnˈberəbəl] adj unerträglich

unbeaten [ʌnˈbitən] adj (& fig) ungeschlagen

unbecoming [ˌʌnbɪˈkʌmɪŋ] adj (improper) ungeziemend; (clothing) unkleidsam

unbelievable [ˌʌnbɪˈlivəbəl] adj unglaublich

unbeliever [ˌʌnbɪˈlivər] s Ungläubige mf

unbending [ʌnˈbendɪŋ] adj unbeugsam

unbiased [ʌnˈbaɪəst] adj unvoreingenommen

unbidden [ʌnˈbɪdən] adj ungebeten

un·bind [ʌnˈbaɪnd] v (pret & pp –bound) tr losbinden

unbleached [ʌnˈblitʃt] adj ungebleicht

unbolt [ʌnˈbolt] tr aufriegeln

unborn [ˈʌnˈbɔrn] adj ungeboren

unbosom [ʌnˈbuzəm] tr—**u. oneself to** sich offenbaren (dat)

unbowed [ʌnˈbaud] adj ungebeugt

unbreakable [ʌnˈbrekəbəl] adj unzerbrechlich

unbridled [ʌnˈbraɪdəld] adj ungezügelt

unbroken [ʌnˈbrokən] adj (intact) ungebrochen; (line, series) ununterbrochen; (horse) nicht zugeritten

unbuckle [ʌnˈbʌkəl] tr aufschnallen

unburden [ʌnˈbɑrdən] tr entlasten; **u. oneself** sein Herz ausschütten

unburied [ʌnˈberɪd] adj unbeerdigt

unbutton [ʌnˈbʌtən] adj aufknöpfen

uncalled-for [ʌnˈkɔld‚fɔr] adj unangebracht

uncanny [ʌnˈkæni] adj unheimlich

uncared-for [ʌnˈkerd‚fɔr] adj verwahrlost

unceasing [ʌnˈsisɪŋ] adj unaufhörlich

unceremonious [ˌʌnserɪˈmoni‚əs] adj (informal) ungezwungen; (rude) unsanft

uncertain [ʌnˈsʌrtən] adj unsicher

uncertainty [ʌnˈsʌrtənti] s Unsicherheit f

unchain [ʌnˈtʃen] tr losketten; (fig) entfesseln

unchangeable [ʌnˈtʃendʒəbəl] adj unveränderlich

uncharacteristic [ˌʌnkærɪktəˈrɪstɪk] adj wesensfremd

uncharted [ʌnˈtʃɑrtɪd] adj auf keiner Karte verzeichnet

unchaste [ʌnˈtʃest] adj unkeusch

unchecked [ʌnˈtʃɛkt] adj ungehemmt

unchristian [ʌnˈkrɪstʃən] adj unchristlich

uncivilized [ʌnˈsɪvɪˌlaɪzd] adj unzivilisiert

unclad [ʌnˈklæd] adj unbekleidet

unclaimed [ʌnˈklemd] adj nicht abgeholt

unclasp [ʌnˈklæsp] tr loshaken; (the arms, hands) öffnen

unclassified [ʌnˈklæsɪˌfaɪd] adj nicht klassifiziert; (not secret) nicht geheim

uncle [ˈʌnkəl] s Onkel m

unclean [ʌnˈklin] adj unsauber; (relig) unrein

unclear [ʌnˈklɪr] adj unklar

un·clog [ʌnˈklɑg] v (pret & pp –clogged; ger –clogging) tr von e–m Hindernis befreien

uncombed [ʌnˈkomd] adj ungekämmt

uncomfortable [ʌnˈkʌmfərtəbəl] adj unbequem; **feel u.** sich nicht recht wohl fühlen

uncommitted [ˌʌnkəˈmɪtɪd] adj (troops) nicht eingesetzt; (delegates, nations) unentschieden

uncommon [ʌnˈkɑmən] adj ungewöhnlich; (outstanding) außergewöhnlich

uncomplaining [ˌʌnkəmˈplenɪŋ] adj klaglos

uncompromising [ʌnˈkɑmprəˌmaɪzɪŋ] adj unbeugsam

unconcealed [ˌʌnkənˈsild] adj unverholen

unconcerned [ˌʌnkənˈsʌrnd] adj (about) unbesorgt (um)

unconditional [ˌʌnkənˈdɪʃənəl] adj bedingslos

unconfirmed [ˌʌnkənˈfɪrmd] adj unbestätigt, unverbürgt

unconquerable [ʌnˈkɑŋkərəbəl] adj unüberwindlich

unconquered [ʌnˈkɑŋkərd] adj unbezwungen

unconscious [ʌnˈkɑnʃəs] adj bewußtlos; (of) nicht bewußt (genit) || s—**the u.** das Unbewußte

unconstitutional [ˌʌnkɑnstɪˈt(j)uʃənəl] adj verfassungswidrig

uncontested [ˌʌnkənˈtestɪd] adj unbestritten

uncontrollable [ˌʌnkənˈtroləbəl] adj unkontrollierbar; (fig) unbändig

unconventional [ˌʌnkənˈventʃənəl] adj unkonventionell

uncork [ʌnˈkɔrk] tr entkorken

uncouple [ʌnˈkʌpəl] tr abkoppeln

uncouth [ʌnˈkuθ] adj ungehobelt; (appearance) ungeschlacht

uncover [ʌnˈkʌvər] tr aufdecken

unctuous [ˈʌŋkt/ʊ‚əs] adj salbungsvoll

uncultivated [ʌnˈkʌltɪˌvetɪd] adj unbebaut

uncultured [ʌnˈkʌltʃərd] adj (fig) unkultiviert

uncut [ʌnˈkʌt] adj nicht abgeschnitten; (gem) ungeschliffen; (grain) ungemäht

undamaged [ʌnˈdæmɪdʒd] adj unbeschädigt, unversehrt

undaunted [ʌnˈdɔntɪd] adj unverzagt

undecided [ˌʌndɪˈsaɪdɪd] adj (person) unschlüssig; (thing) unentschieden

undefeated [ˌʌndɪˈfitɪd] adj unbesiegt

undefended [ˌʌndɪˈfendɪd] adj unverteidigt

undefiled [ˌʌndɪˈfaɪld] adj unbefleckt

undefined [ˌʌndɪˈfaɪnd] adj unklar

undeliverable [ˌʌndɪˈlɪvərəbəl] adj unbestellbar

undeniable [‚ʌndɪ'naɪ·əbəl] *adj* unleugbar

under ['ʌndər] *adj* Unter– ‖ *adv* unter–, e.g., go u. untergehen ‖ *prep* unter (*position*) (*dat*); (*direction*) unter (*acc*)

un'derage' *adj* unmündig

un'der·bid' *v* (*pret & pp* –bid; *ger* –bidding) *tr* unterbieten

un'derbrush' *s* Unterholz *n*

un'dercar'riage *s* Fahrgestell *n*

un'derclothes' *spl* Unterwäsche *f*

un'dercov'er *adj* Geheim–; u. agent Spitzel *m*

un'dercur'rent *s* (& *fig*) Unterströmmung *f*

un'dercut' *v* (*pret & pp* –cut; *ger* –cutting) *tr* unterbieten

un'derdevel'oped *adj* unterentwickelt

un'derdog' *s* (*coll*) Unterlegene *mf*

un'derdone' *adj* nicht durchgebraten

un'deres'timate *tr* unterschätzen

un'derexpose' *tr* (*phot*) unterbelichten

un'dergar'ment *s* Unterkleidung *f*

un'der·go' *v* (*pret* –went; *pp* –gone) durchmachen; (*an operation*) sich unterziehen (*dat*)

un'dergrad'uate *s* Collegestudent –in *mf*

un'derground' *adj* unterirdisch; (*fig*) Untergrund–; (*water*) Grund–; (*min*) unter Tage ‖ un'derground' *s* (*secret movement*) Untergrundbewegung *f*; go u. untertauchen

un'dergrowth' *s* Buschholz *n*, Unterholz *n*

un'derhand' *adj* (*throw*) unter Schulterhöhe (ausgeführt)

un'derhand'ed *adj* hinterhältig

un'derline', un'derline' *tr* unterstreichen

underling ['ʌndərlɪŋ] *s* Handlanger *m*

un'dermine' *tr* (& *fig*) untergraben

underneath [‚ʌndər'niθ] *adj* Unter– ‖ *adv* unten ‖ *s* Unterseite *f* ‖ *prep* (*position*) unter (*dat*), unterhalb (*genit*); (*direction*) unter (*acc*)

un'dernour'ished *adj* unterernährt

un'dernour'ishment *s* Unterernährung *f*

un'derpad' *s* (*of a rug*) Unterlage *f*

un'derpaid' *adj* unterbezahlt

un'derpass' *s* Straßenunterführung *f*

un'der·pin' *v* (*pret & pp* –pinned; *ger* –pinning) *tr* untermauern

un'derplay' *tr* unterspielen

un'derpriv'ileged *adj* benachteiligt

un'derrate' *tr* unterschätzen

un'derscore' *tr* (& *fig*) unterstreichen

un'dersea' *adj* Unterwasser–

un'dersec'retar'y *s* Untersekretär –in *mf*

un'der·sell' *v* (*pret & pp* –sold; *ger* –selling) *tr* (*a person*) unterbieten; (*goods*) verschleudern

un'dershirt' *s* Unterhemd *n*

un'derside' *s* Unterseite *f*

un'dersigned' *adj* unterschrieben ‖ un'dersigned *s* Unterzeichnete *mf*

un'der·stand' *v* (*pret & pp* –stood) *tr* verstehen; it's understood that es ist selbstverständlich, daß; make oneself understood sich verständlich machen

understandable [‚ʌndər'stændəbəl] *adj* verständlich

understandably [‚ʌndər'stændəbli] *adv* begreiflicherweise

un'derstand'ing *adj* verständnisvoll ‖ *s* (*of*) Verständnis *n* (für); (*between persons*) Einvernehmen *n*; (*agreement*) Übereinkommen *n*; come to an u. with s.o. sich mit j–m verständigen; it is my u. that wie ich verstehe

un'derstud'y *s* Ersatzmann *m*; (*cin*, *theat*) Ersatzschauspieler –in *mf*

un'der·take' *v* (*pret* –took; *pp* –taken) *tr* unternehmen

undertaker ['ʌndər‚tekər] *s* Leichenbestatter –in *mf*

un'dertak'ing *s* Unternehmen *n*

un'dertone' *s* leise Stimme *f*; (*fig*) Unterton *m*

un'dertow' *s* Sog *m*

un'derwa'ter *adj* Unterwasser–

un'derwear' *s* Unterwäsche *f*

un'derweight' *adj* untergewichtig

un'derworld' *s* (*of criminals*) Unterwelt *f*; (*myth*) Totenreich *n*

un'der·write', un'der·write' *v* (*pret* –wrote; *pp* –written) *tr* unterschreiben; (*ins*) versichern

un'derwrit'er *s* Unterzeichner –in *mf*; (*ins*) Versicherer –in *mf*; (*st. exch.*) Wertpapiermakler –in *mf*; underwriters Emissionsfirma *f*

undeserved [‚ʌndɪ'zɑrvd] *adj* unverdient

undeservedly [‚ʌndɪ'zɑrvidli] *adv* unverdientermaßen

undesirable [‚ʌndɪ'zaɪrəbəl] *adj* unerwünscht ‖ *s* Unerwünschte *mf*

undeveloped [‚ʌndɪ'veləpt] *adj* unentwickelt; (*land*) unerschlossen

undies ['ʌndiz] *spl* (*coll*) Unterwäsche *f*

undigested [‚ʌndɪ'dʒestɪd] *adj* (& *fig*) unverdaut

undignified [ʌn'dɪgnɪ‚faɪd] *adj* würdelos

undiluted [‚ʌndɪ'lutɪd] *adj* unverdünnt

undiminished [‚ʌndɪ'mɪnɪʃt] *adj* unvermindert

undisciplined [ʌn'dɪsəplɪnd] *adj* undiszipliniert, zuchtlos

undisputed [‚ʌndɪs'pjutɪd] *adj* unbestritten, unangefochten

undisturbed [‚ʌndɪs'tɑrbd] *adj* ungestört

undivided [‚ʌndɪ'vaɪdɪd] *adj* ungeteilt

un-do [ʌn'du] *v* (*pret* –did; *pp* –done) *tr* (*a knot*) aufschnüren; (*a deed*) ungeschehen machen

undo'ing *s* Ruin *m*

undone [ʌn'dʌn] *adj* (*not done*) ungetan; (*ruined*) ruiniert; come u. sich lösen; leave nothing u. nichts unversucht lassen

undoubtedly [ʌn'dautɪdli] *adv* zweifellos

undramatic [‚ʌndrə'mætɪk] *adj* undramatisch

undress [ʌn'dres] *s*—in a state of u. (*nude*) in unbekleidetem Zustand; (*in a negligee*) im Negligé ‖ *tr* ausziehen ‖ *intr* sich ausziehen

undrinkable [ʌn'drɪŋkəbəl] *adj* nicht trinkbar

undue [ʌn'd(j)u] *adj (inappropriate)* unangemessen; *(excessive)* übermäßig

undulate ['ʌndjə,let] *intr* wogen

undulating ['ʌndjə,letɪŋ] *adj* wellenförmig

unduly [ʌn'd(j)uli] *adv* übermäßig

undying [ʌn'daɪ·ɪŋ] *adj* unsterblich

un'earned in'come ['ʌnɜrnd] *s* Kapitalrente *f*

unearth [ʌn'ʌrθ] *tr* ausgraben; *(fig)* aufstöbern

unearthly [ʌn'ʌrθli] *adj* unirdisch; *(cry)* schauerlich; **at an u. hour** *(early)* in aller Herrgottsfrühe

uneasy [ʌn'izi] *adj (worried)* ängstlich; *(ill at ease)* unbehaglich

uneatable [ʌn'itəbəl] *adj* ungenießbar

uneconomic(al) [,ʌnekə'nɑmɪk(əl)] *adj* unwirtschaftlich

uneducated [ʌn'edʒə,ketɪd] *adj* ungebildet

unemployed [,ʌnem'plɔɪd] *adj* arbeitslos ‖ *s* Arbeitslose *mf*

unemployment [,ʌnem'plɔɪmənt] *s* Arbeitslosigkeit *f*

unemploy'ment compensa'tion *s* Arbeitslosenunterstützung *f;* **collect u.** (sl) Stempeln gehen

unencumbered [,ʌnən'kʌmbərd] *adj* unbelastet

unending [ʌn'endɪŋ] *adj* endlos

unequal [ʌn'ikwəl] *adj* ungleich; **u. to** nicht gewachsen *(dat)*

unequaled [ʌn'ikwəld] *adj* ohnegleichen

unequivocal [,ʌnə'kwɪvəkəl] *adj* eindeutig

unerring [ʌn'ɜrɪŋ] *adj* unfehlbar

UNESCO [ju'nesko] *s* (United Nations Educational, Scientific, and Cultural Organization) UNESCO *f*

unessential [,ʌnɛ'senʃəl] *adj* unwesentlich

uneven [ʌn'ivən] *adj (not smooth)* uneben; *(unbalanced)* ungleich; *(not uniform)* ungleichmäßig; *(number)* ungerade

uneventful [,ʌnɪ'ventfəl] *adj* ereignislos

unexceptional [,ʌnek'sepʃənəl] *adj* nicht außergewöhnlich

unexpected [,ʌnek'spektɪd] *adj* unerwartet

unexplained [,ʌnek'splend] *adj* unerklärt

unexplored [,ʌnek'splord] *adj* unerforscht

unexposed [,ʌnek'spozd] *adj* (phot) unbelichtet

unfading [ʌn'fedɪŋ] *adj* unverwelklich

unfailing [ʌn'felɪŋ] *adj* unfehlbar

unfair [ʌn'fer] *adj* unfair; *(competition)* unlauter

unfaithful [ʌn'feθfəl] *adj* treulos

unfamiliar [,ʌnfə'mɪljər] *adj* unbekannt

unfasten [ʌn'fæsən] *tr* losbinden; *(e.g., a seat belt)* aufschnallen

unfathomable [ʌn'fæðəməbəl] *adj* unergründlich

unfavorable [ʌn'fevərəbəl] *adj* ungünstig

unfeasible [ʌn'fizəbəl] *adj* unausführbar

unfeeling [ʌn'filɪŋ] *adj* unempfindlich

unfilled [ʌn'fɪld] *adj* ungefüllt; *(post)* unbesetzt

unfinished [ʌn'fɪnɪʃt] *adj* unfertig; *(business)* unerledigt

unfit [ʌn'fɪt] *adj (for)* ungeeignet (für); *(not qualified)* (for) untauglich (für); **u. for military service** wehrdienstuntauglich

unfold [ʌn'fold] *tr (a chair)* aufklappen; *(cloth, paper)* entfalten; *(ideas, plans)* offenbaren

unforeseeable [,ʌnfor'si·əbəl] *adj* unabsehbar

unforeseen [,ʌnfor'sin] *adj* unvorhergesehen

unforgettable [,ʌnfor'getəbəl] *adj* unvergeßlich

unfortunate [ʌn'fortʃənɪt] *adj* unglücklich

unfortunately [ʌn'fortʃənɪtli] *adv* leider

unfounded [ʌn'faundɪd] *adj* unbegründet

un-freeze [ʌn'friz] *v (pret* –**froze;** *pp* –**frozen)** *tr* auftauen; *(prices)* freigeben

unfriendly [ʌn'frendli] *adj* unfreundlich

unfruitful [ʌn'frutfəl] *adj* unfruchtbar

unfulfilled [,ʌnfəl'fɪld] *adj* unerfüllt

unfurl [ʌn'fɜrl] *tr (a flag)* entrollen; *(sails)* losmachen

unfurnished [ʌn'fɜrnɪʃt] *adj* unmöbliert

ungainly [ʌn'genli] *adj* plump

ungentlemanly [ʌn'dʒentəlmənli] *adj* unfein, unedel

ungodly [ʌn'gɑdli] *adj (hour)* ungehörig

ungracious [ʌn'greʃəs] *adj* ungnädig

ungrammatical [,ʌngrə'mætɪkəl] *adj* ungrammatisch

ungrateful [ʌn'gretfəl] *adj* undankbar

ungrudgingly [ʌn'grʌdʒɪŋli] *adv* gern

unguarded [ʌn'gɑrdɪd] *adj* unbewacht; *(moment)* unbedacht

unguent ['ʌŋgwent] *s* Salbe *f*

unhandy [ʌn'hændi] *adj* unhandlich; *(person)* unbeholfen

unhappy [ʌn'hæpi] *adj* unglücklich

unharmed [ʌn'hɑrmd] *adj* unversehrt

unharness [ʌn'hɑrnɪs] *tr* abschirren

unhealthful [ʌn'helθfəl] *adj* ungesund

unhealthy [ʌn'helθi] *adj* ungesund

unheard-of [ʌn'hɑrd,ʌv] *adj* unerhört

unheated [ʌn'hitɪd] *adj* ungeheizt

unhesitating [ʌn'hezɪ,tetɪŋ] *adj (immediate)* unverzüglich; *(unswerving)* unbeirrbar; *(support)* bereitwillig

unhinge [ʌn'hɪndʒ] *tr* (fig) aus den Angeln heben

unhitch [ʌn'hɪtʃ] *tr (horses)* ausspannen; *(undo)* losmachen

unholy [ʌn'holi] *adj* unheilig

unhook [ʌn'huk] *tr* losmachen; *(a dress)* aufhaken; *(the receiver)* abnehmen

unhoped-for [ʌn'hopt ,fɔr] adj unverhofft

unhurt [ʌn'hʌrt] adj unbeschädigt; (person) unversehrt

unicorn ['juni ,kɔrn] s Einhorn n

unification [,junifɪ'keʃən] s Vereinigung f

uniform ['juni ,fɔrm] adj gleichförmig || s Uniform f

uniformity [,juni'fɔrmiti] s Gleichförmigkeit f

uni·fy ['juni ,fai] v (pret & pp –fied) tr vereinigen

unilateral [,juni'lætərəl] adj einseitig

unimpaired [,ʌnim'perd] adj ungeschwächt

unimpeachable [,ʌnim'pitʃəbəl] adj unantastbar

unimportant [,ʌnim'pɔrtənt] adj unwichtig

uninflected [,ʌnin'flektid] adj (gram) unflektiert

uninhabited [,ʌnin'hæbitid] adj unbewohnt

uninspired [,ʌnin'spaird] adj schwunglos

unintelligible [,ʌnin'telidʒəbəl] adj unverständlich

unintentional [,ʌnin'tenʃənəl] adj unabsichtlich

uninterested [ʌn'intə ,restid] adj (in) uninteressiert (an dat)

uninteresting [ʌn'intə ,restiŋ] adj uninteressant

uninterrupted [,ʌnintə'rʌptid] adj ununterbrochen

uninvited [,ʌnin'vaitid] adj ungeladen

union ['junjən] adj Gewerkschafts– || s Vereinigung f; (harmony) Eintracht f; (of workers) Gewerkschaft f; (pol) Union f

unionize ['junjə ,naiz] tr gewerkschaftlich organisieren || intr sich gewerkschaftlich organisieren

un'ion shop' s Betrieb m, der nur Gewerkschaftsmitglieder beschäftigt

unique [ju'nik] adj einzigartig

unison ['junisən] s Einklang m

unit ['junit] s (& mil) Einheit f

unite [ju'nait] tr vereinigen; (chem) verbinden || intr sich vereinigen; (chem) sich verbinden

Unit'ed King'dom s Vereinigtes Königreich n

Unit'ed Na'tions spl Vereinte Nationen pl

Unit'ed States' s Vereinigte Staaten pl

unity ['juniti] s (harmony) Einigkeit f; (e.g., of a nation) Einheit f; (fa) Einheitlichkeit f

universal [,juni'vʌrsəl] adj universal, allgemein || s Allgemeine n; (philos) Allgemeinbegriff m

u'niver'sal joint' s Kardangelenk n

u'niver'sal mil'itary train'ing s allgemeine Wehrpflicht f

universe ['juni ,vʌrs] s Universum n

university [,juni'vʌrsiti] adj Universitäts– || s Universität f

unjust [ʌn'dʒʌst] adj ungerecht

unjustified [ʌn'dʒʌsti ,faid] adj ungerechtfertigt

unjustly [ʌn'dʒʌstli] adv zu Unrecht

unkempt [ʌn'kempt] adj ungekämmt; (fig) verwahrlost

unkind [ʌn'kaind] adj unfreundlich

unknown [ʌn'non] adj unbekannt

un'known quan'tity s Unbekannte f

Un'known Sol'dier s Unbekannter Soldat m

unlatch [ʌn'lætʃ] tr aufklinken

unlawful [ʌn'lɔfəl] adj gesetzwidrig

unleash [ʌn'liʃ] tr losbinden; (fig) entfesseln

unleavened [ʌn'levənd] adj ungesäuert

unless [ʌn'les] conj wenn ... nicht

unlettered [ʌn'letərd] adj ungebildet

unlicensed [ʌn'laisənst] adj unerlaubt

unlike [ʌn'laik] adj (unequal) ungleich; (dissimilar) unähnlich || prep im Gegensatz zu (dat); be u. s.o. anders als jemand sein

unlikely [ʌn'laikli] adj unwahrscheinlich

unlimited [ʌn'limitid] adj unbeschränkt

unlined [ʌn'laind] adj (clothes) ungefüttert; (paper) unliniert; (face) faltenlos

unload [ʌn'lod] tr & intr ausladen

unload'ing s Ausladen n; (naut) Löschen n

unlock [ʌn'lak] tr aufsperren

unloose [ʌn'lus] tr lösen

unloved [ʌn'lʌvd] adj ungeliebt

unlucky [ʌn'lʌki] adj unglücklich

un·make [ʌn'mek] v (pret & pp –made) tr rückgängig machen; (a bed) abdecken

unmanageable [ʌn'mænidʒəbəl] adj (person, animal) widerspenstig; (thing) unhandlich

unmanly [ʌn'mænli] adj unmännlich

unmanned [ʌn'mænd] adj (rok) unbemannt

unmannerly [ʌn'mænərli] adj unmännlich

unmarketable [ʌn'markitəbəl] adj nicht marktgängig

unmarriageable [ʌn'mæridʒəbəl] adj nicht heiratsfähig

unmarried [ʌn'mærid] adj unverheiratet

unmask [ʌn'mæsk] tr (& fig) demaskieren || intr sich demaskieren

unmatched [ʌn'mætʃt] adj (not matched) ungleichartig; (unmatchable) unvergleichlich

unmerciful [ʌn'mʌrsifəl] adj unbarmherzig

unmesh [ʌn'meʃ] tr (mach) ausrücken

unmindful [ʌn'maindfəl] adj uneingedenk

unmistakable [,ʌnmis'tekəbəl] adj unmißverständlich

unmitigated [ʌn'miti ,getid] adj ungemildert; (liar) Erz–

unmixed [ʌn'mikst] adj ungemischt

unmoor [ʌn'mur] tr losmachen || intr sich losmachen

unmoved [ʌn'muvd] adj (fig) ungerührt

unmuzzle [ʌn'mʌzəl] tr den Maulkorb abnehmen (dat)

unnatural [ʌnˈnætʃərəl] *adj* unnatürlich; *(forced)* gezwungen

unnecessary [ʌnˈnesəˌseri] *adj* unnötig

unneeded [ʌnˈnidid] *adj* nutzlos

unnerve [ʌnˈnʌrv] *tr* entnerven

unnoticeable [ʌnˈnotisəbəl] *adj* unbemerkbar

unnoticed [ʌnˈnotist] *adj* unbemerkt

unobserved [ˌʌnəbˈzʌrvd] *adj* unbeobachtet

unobtainable [ˌʌnəbˈtenəbəl] *adj* nicht erhältlich

unobtrusive [ˌʌnəbˈtrusɪv] *adj* unaufdringlich

unoccupied [ʌnˈɑkjəˌpaɪd] *adj (room, house)* leerstehend; *(seat)* unbesetzt; *(person)* unbeschäftigt

unofficial [ˌʌnəˈfɪʃəl] *adj* inoffiziell

unopened [ʌnˈopənd] *adj* ungeöffnet

unopposed [ˌʌnəˈpozd] *adj (without opposition)* widerspruchslos; *(unresisted)* unbehindert

unorthodox [ʌnˈɔrθəˌdɑks] *adj* unorthodox; *(relig)* nicht orthodox

unpack [ʌnˈpæk] *tr* auspacken

unpalatable [ʌnˈpælətəbəl] *adj* unschmackhaft; *(fig)* widerlich

unparalleled [ʌnˈpærəˌleld] *adj* unvergleichlich

unpardonable [ʌnˈpɑrdənəbəl] *adj* unverzeihlich

unpatriotic [ˌʌnpetriˈɑtɪk] *adj* unpatriotisch

unpaved [ʌnˈpevd] *adj* ungepflastert

unperceived [ˌʌnpərˈsivd] *adj* unbemerkt

unpleasant [ʌnˈplezənt] *adj* unangenehm; *(person)* unsympathisch

unpopular [ʌnˈpɑpjələr] *adj* unbeliebt

unpopularity [ʌnˌpɑpjəˈlærɪti] *s* Unbeliebtheit *f*

unprecedented [ʌnˈpresɪˌdentɪd] *adj* unerhört; *(jur)* ohne Präzedenzfall

unpredictable [ˌʌnprɪˈdɪktəbəl] *adj* unberechenbar; *(weather)* wechselhaft

unprejudiced [ʌnˈpredʒədɪst] *adj* unvoreingenommen

unprepared [ˌʌnprɪˈperd] *adj* unvorbereitet

unpresentable [ˌʌnprɪˈzentəbəl] *adj* nicht präsentabel

unpretentious [ˌʌnprɪˈtenʃəs] *adj* anspruchslos

unprincipled [ʌnˈprɪnsɪpəld] *adj* haltlos

unproductive [ˌʌnprəˈdʌktɪv] *adj* unproduktiv; *(of)* unergiebig (an *dat*)

unprofessional [ˌʌnprəˈfeʃənəl] *adj (work)* unfachmännisch; *(conduct)* berufswidrig

unprofitable [ʌnˈprɑfɪtəbəl] *adj (useless)* nutzlos; *(fin)* unrentabel

unpronounceable [ˌʌnprəˈnaʊnsəbəl] *adj* unaussprechlich

unprotected [ˌʌnprəˈtektɪd] *adj (place)* ungeschützt; *(person)* unbeschützt

unpropitious [ˌʌnprəˈpɪʃəs] *adj* ungünstig

unpublished [ʌnˈpʌblɪʃt] *adj* unveröffentlicht

unpunished [ʌnˈpʌnɪʃt] *adj* ungestraft

unqualified [ʌnˈkwɑləˌfaɪd] *adj* unqualifiziert; *(full, complete)* unbedingt

unquenchable [ʌnˈkwentʃəbəl] *adj* unstillbar

unquestionably [ʌnˈkwestʃənəbli] *adv* fraglos, unbezweifelbar

unquestioning [ʌnˈkwestʃənɪŋ] *adj (obedience)* bedingungslos

unquiet [ʌnˈkwaɪət] *adj* unruhig

unravel [ʌnˈrævəl] *v (pret & pp* -el[l]ed; *ger* -el[l]ling) *tr (a knitted fabric)* auftrennen; *(fig)* entwirren || *intr* sich fasern; *(fig)* sich entwirren

unreachable [ʌnˈritʃəbəl] *adj* unerreichbar

unreal [ʌnˈriəl] *adj* unwirklich

unreality [ˌʌnriˈælɪti] *s* Unwirklichkeit *f*

unreasonable [ʌnˈrizənəbəl] *adj* unvernünftig

unrecognizable [ʌnˈrekəgˌnaɪzəbəl] *adj* unerkennbar

unreel [ʌnˈril] *tr* abspulen

unrefined [ˌʌnriˈfaɪnd] *adj* roh

unrelated [ˌʌnriˈletɪd] *adj (to)* ohne Beziehung (zu)

unrelenting [ˌʌnriˈlentɪŋ] *adj* unerbittlich

unreliable [ˌʌnriˈlaɪəbəl] *adj* unzuverlässig; *(fin)* unsolid(e)

unremitting [ˌʌnriˈmɪtɪŋ] *adj* unablässig

unrepentant [ˌʌnriˈpentənt] *adj* unbußfertig

unrequited [ˌʌnriˈkwaɪtɪd] *adj* unerwidert

unreserved [ˌʌnriˈzʌrvd] *adj* vorbehaltlos

unresponsive [ˌʌnriˈspɑnsɪv] *adj (to)* unempfänglich (für)

unrest [ʌnˈrest] *s* Unruhe *f*

unrestricted [ˌʌnriˈstrɪktɪd] *adj* uneingeschränkt

unrewarded [ˌʌnriˈwɔrdɪd] *adj* unbelohnt

unrhymed [ʌnˈraɪmd] *adj* ungereimt

unrig [ʌnˈrɪg] *v (pret & pp* -rigged; *ger* -rigging) *tr* abtakeln

unripe [ʌnˈraɪp] *adj* unreif

unrivaled [ʌnˈraɪvəld] *adj* unübertrefflich

unroll [ʌnˈrol] *tr* aufrollen; *(e.g., a cable)* abrollen || *intr* sich aufrollen; sich abrollen

unromantic [ˌʌnroˈmæntɪk] *adj* unromantisch

unruffled [ʌnˈrʌfəld] *adj* unerschüttert

unruly [ʌnˈruli] *adj* ungebärdig

unsaddle [ʌnˈsædəl] *tr (a horse)* absatteln; *(a rider)* aus dem Sattel werfen

unsafe [ʌnˈsef] *adj* unsicher

unsaid [ʌnˈsed] *adj* ungesagt

unsalable [ʌnˈseləbəl] *adj* unverkäuflich

unsanitary [ʌnˈsænɪˌteri] *adj* unhygienisch

unsalted [ʌnˈsɔltɪd] *adj* ungesalzen

unsatisfactory [ʌnˌsætɪsˈfæktəri] *adj* unbefriedigend

unsatisfied [ʌnˈsætɪsˌfaɪd] *adj* unbefriedigt

unsavory [ʌn'sevəri] *adj* unschmackhaft; (fig) widerlich
unscathed [ʌn'skeðd] *adj* unversehrt
unscientific [ˌʌnsaɪ-ən'tɪfɪk] *adj* un-
wissenschaftlich
unscramble [ʌn'skræmbəl] *tr* (*a message*) entziffern; (fig) entflechten
unscrew [ʌn'skru] *tr* aufschrauben
unscrupulous [ʌn'skrupjələs] *adj* skru-
pellos
unseal [ʌn'sil] *tr* entsiegeln; (*eyes,
lips*) öffnen
unseasonable [ʌn'sizənəbəl] *adj* unzei-
tig; (*weather*) nicht der Jahreszeit
entsprechend
unseasoned [ʌn'sizənd] *adj* ungewürzt
unseat [ʌn'sit] *tr* (*a rider*) aus dem
Sattel heben; (*an official*) aus dem
Posten verdrängen
unseemly [ʌn'simli] *adj* ungehörig
unseen [ʌn'sin] *adj* ungesehen
unselfish [ʌn'selfɪʃ] *adj* selbstlos
unsettle [ʌn'setəl] *tr* beunruhigen
unsettled [ʌn'setəld] *adj* (*matter, bill*)
unerledigt; (*without a residence*)
ohne festen Wohnsitz; (*restless*) unruhig; (*life*) unstet
unshackle [ʌn'ʃækəl] *tr* die Fesseln
abnehmen (*dat*)
unshakable [ʌn'ʃekəbəl] *adj* unerschütterlich
unshapely [ʌn'ʃepli] *adj* mißgestaltet
unshaven [ʌn'ʃevən] *adj* unrasiert
unsheathe [ʌn'ʃið] *tr* aus der Scheide
ziehen
unshod [ʌn'ʃɑd] *adj* unbeschuht
unsightly [ʌn'saɪtli] *adj* unansehnlich
unsinkable [ʌn'sɪŋkəbəl] *adj* nicht ver-
senkbar
unskilled [ʌn'skɪld] *adj* ungelernt; **u.
laborer** Hilfsarbeiter –in *mf*
unskillful [ʌn'skɪlfəl] *adj* ungewandt
unsnarl [ʌn'snɑrl] *tr* entwirren
unsociable [ʌn'soʃəbəl] *adj* ungesellig
unsolicited [ˌʌnsə'lɪsɪtɪd] *adj* unverlangt
unsold [ʌn'sold] *adj* unverkauft
unsophisticated [ˌʌnsə'fɪstɪˌketɪd] *adj*
unverfälscht; (*naive*) arglos
unsound [ʌn'saʊnd] *adj* ungesund;
(*sleep*) unruhig; **of u. mind** geistes-
krank
unspeakable [ʌn'spikəbəl] *adj* unsagbar
unspoiled [ʌn'spɔɪld] *adj* unverdorben
unsportsmanlike [ʌn'sportsmən,laɪk]
adj unsportlich
unstable [ʌn'stebəl] *adj* unbeständig;
(*e.g., ladder*) wacklig; (*hand*) zittrig;
(*market, walk*) schwankend; (*inconstant*) unbeständig; (chem) unbeständig
unstinted [ʌn'stɪntɪd] *adj* uneingeschränkt
unstinting [ʌn'stɪntɪŋ] *adj* freigebig
unstitch [ʌn'stɪtʃ] *tr* auftrennen
unstressed [ʌn'strest] *adj* unbetont
unsuccessful [ˌʌnsək'sesfəl] *adj* erfolglos
unsuitable [ʌn'sutəbəl] *adj* ungeeignet;
(*inappropriate*) unangemessen
unsullied [ʌn'sʌlid] *adj* unbefleckt

unsung [ʌn'sʌŋ] *adj* unbesungen
unsuspected [ˌʌnsəs'pektɪd] *adj* unver-
dächtig; (*not known to exist*) ungeahnt
unsuspecting [ˌʌnsəs'pektɪŋ] *adj* arglos
unswerving [ʌn'swʌrvɪŋ] *adj* unentwegt
unsympathetic [ˌʌnsɪmpə'θetɪk] *adj*
teilnahmslos
unsystematic(al) [ˌʌnsɪstə'mætɪk(əl)]
adj unsystematisch
untactful [ʌn'tæktfəl] *adj* taktlos
untalented [ʌn'tæləntɪd] *adj* unbegabt
untamed [ʌn'temd] *adj* ungezähmt
untangle [ʌn'tæŋgəl] *tr* (& fig) entwirren
untenable [ʌn'tenəbəl] *adj* unhaltbar
untested [ʌn'testɪd] *adj* ungeprüft
unthankful [ʌn'θæŋkfəl] *adj* undankbar
unthinking [ʌn'θɪŋkɪŋ] *adj* gedankenlos
untidy [ʌn'taɪdi] *adj* unordentlich
un-tie [ʌn'taɪ] *v* (*pret & pp* –tied; *ger*
–tying) *tr* aufbinden; (*a knot*) lösen;
my shoe is untied mein Schuh ist auf-
gegangen
until [ʌn'tɪl] *prep* bis (*acc*); **u. further
notice** bis auf weiteres || *conj* bis
untimely [ʌn'taɪmli] *adj* frühzeitig; (*at
the wrong time*) unzeitgemäß
untiring [ʌn'taɪrɪŋ] *adj* unermüdlich
untold [ʌn'told] *adj* (*suffering*) unsäglich; (*countless*) zahllos
untouched [ʌn'tʌtʃt] *adj* unangetastet;
(fig) ungerührt
untoward [ʌn'tord] *adj* (*unfavorable*)
ungünstig; (*unruly*) widerspenstig
untrained [ʌn'trend] *adj* unausgebildet; (*eye*) ungeschult; (sport) un-
trainiert
untried [ʌn'traɪd] *adj* (*unattempted*)
unversucht; (*untested*) unerprobt;
(*case*) (jur) nicht verhandelt
untroubled [ʌn'trʌbəld] *adj* (*mind,
times*) ruhig; (*peace*) ungestört
untrue [ʌn'tru] *adj* unwahr; (*unfaithful*) un(ge)treu; (*not exact*) ungenau
untrustworthy [ʌn'trʌst,wʌrði] *adj* un-
glaubwürdig
untruth [ʌn'truθ] *s* Unwahrheit *f*
untruthful [ʌn'truθfəl] *adj* (*statement*)
unwahr; (*person*) unaufrichtig
untwist [ʌn'twɪst] *tr* aufflechten || *intr*
aufgehen
unusable [ʌn'juzəbəl] *adj* nicht verwendbar; (*unconsumable*) unbenutzbar
unusual [ʌn'juʒʊ-əl] *adj* ungewöhnlich
unutterable [ʌn'ʌtərəbəl] *adj* unaussprechlich
unvarnished [ʌn'vɑrnɪʃt] *adj* nicht ge-
firnißt; (*truth*) ungeschminkt
unveil [ʌn'vel] *tr* (*a monument*) enthüllen; (*a face*) entschleiern
unventilated [ʌn'ventɪ,letɪd] *adj* un-
gelüftet
unvoiced [ʌn'vɔɪst] *adj* (ling) stimmlos
unwanted [ʌn'wɑntɪd] *adj* unerwünscht
unwarranted [ʌn'wɑrəntɪd] *adj* ungerechtfertigt
unwary [ʌn'weri] *adj* unvorsichtig

unwavering [ʌn'wevərɪŋ] *adj* standhaft
unwelcome [ʌn'welkəm] *adj* unwillkommen
unwell [ʌn'wel] *adj* unwohl
unwept [ʌn'wept] *adj* unbeweint
unwholesome [ʌn'holsəm] *adj* schädlich; (& fig) unbekömmlich
unwieldy [ʌn'wildi] *adj* (*person*) schwerfällig; (*thing*) unhandlich
unwilling [ʌn'wɪlɪŋ] *adj* (*involuntary*) unfreiwillig; (*reluctant*) widerwillig; (*obstinate*) eigensinnig; **be u. to** (*inf*) nicht (*inf*) wollen
unwillingly [ʌn'wɪlɪŋli] *adv* ungern
un·wind [ʌn'waɪnd] *v* (*pret & pp -wound*) *tr* abwickeln || *intr* sich abwickeln; (fig) sich entspannen
unwise [ʌn'waɪz] *adj* unklug
unwished-for [ʌn'wɪʃ,fər] *adj* unerwünscht
unwitting [ʌn'wɪtɪŋ] *adj* unwissentlich
unworkable [ʌn'wʌrkəbəl] *adj* (*plan*) unausführbar; (*material*) nicht zu bearbeiten(d)
unworldly [ʌn'wʌrldli] *adj* nicht weltlich; (*naïve*) weltfremd
unworthy [ʌn'wʌrði] *adj* unwürdig
un·wrap [ʌn'ræp] *v* (*pret & pp -wrapped*; *ger -wrapping*) *tr* auspacken || *intr* aufgehen
unwrinkled [ʌn'rɪŋkəld] *adj* faltenlos
unwritten [ʌn'rɪtən] *adj* ungeschrieben; (*agreement*) mündlich
unyielding [ʌn'jildɪŋ] *adj* unnachgiebig
up [ʌp] *adj & adv* (*at a height*) oben; (*to a height*) hinauf; **be up** (*be out of bed*; *said of a shade*) aufsein; (*baseball*) am Schlag sein; **be up and around again** wieder am Damm sein; **be up to** (*be ready for*) gewachsen sein (*dat*); (e.g., *mischief*) vorhaben; **from ten dollars and up** von zehn Dollar aufwärts; **it's up to you** es hängt von Ihnen ab; **prices are up** die Preise sind gestiegen; **up and down** (*back and forth*) auf und ab; (*from head to toe*) von oben bis unten; **up there** da oben; **up to** (e.g., *one hour*) bis zu; **up to the ears in debt** bis über die Ohren in Schulden || *v* (*pret & pp upped*; *ger upping*) *tr* erhöhen || *prep* (*acc*) hinauf (*postpositive*)
up-and-coming [ʌpən'kʌmɪŋ] *adj* (coll) unternehmungslustig
up-and-up [ʌpən'ʌp] *s*—**be on the u.** aufrichtig sein
upbraid' *tr* Vorwürfe machen (*dat*)
upbringing [ʌp,brɪŋɪŋ] *s* Erziehung *f*
update' *tr* aufs laufende bringen
up'draft' *s* Aufwind *m*
upend' *tr* hochkant stellen
up'grade' *s* Steigung *f*; **on the u.** (fig) im Aufsteigen || **up'grade'** *tr* (*reclassify*) höher einstufen; (*improve*) verbessern
upheaval [ʌp'hivəl] *s* Umbruch *m*
up'hill' *adj* ansteigend; (fig) mühsam; **u. struggle** harter Kampf *m* || *adv* bergauf
uphold' *v* (*pret & pp -held*) *tr* (*the law*) unterstützen; (*a verdict*) bestätigen

upholster [ʌp'holstər] *tr* (auf)polstern
upholsterer [ʌp'holstərər] *s* Polsterer –in *mf*
upholstery [ʌp'holstəri] *s* Polsterung *f*
up'keep' *s* Instandhaltung *f*; (*maintenance costs*) Instandhaltungskosten *pl*
upland ['ʌplənd] *adj* Hochlands–, Berg– || **the uplands** *spl* das Hochland
up'lift' *s* (fig) Aufschwung *m*; **moral u.** moralischer Auftrieb *m* || **up'lift'** *tr* (fig) geistig (*or* moralisch) erheben
upon [ə'pɑn] *prep* (*position*) an (*dat*), auf (*dat*); (*direction*) an (*acc*), auf (*acc*); **u. my word!** auf mein Wort!
upper ['ʌpər] *adj* obere, Ober– || **uppers** *spl* Oberleder *n*
up'per-case' *adj* in Großbuchstaben gedruckt (*or* geschrieben)
up'per class'es *spl* Oberschicht *f*
up'percut' *s* (box) Aufwärtshaken *m*
up'per deck' *s* Oberdeck *n*
up'per hand' *s* Oberhand *f*
up'per lip' *s* Oberlippe *f*
up'permost' *adj* oberste
uppish ['ʌpɪʃ] *adj* (coll) hochnäsig
uppity ['ʌpɪti] *adj* (coll) eingebildet
upraise' *tr* erheben
up'right' *adj* aufrecht; (fig) redlich || *s* (fb) Torpfosten *m*
up'ris'ing *s* Aufstand *m*
up'roar' *s* Aufruhr *m*
uproarious [ʌp'rori-əs] *adj* (*noisy*) lärmend; (*laughter*) schallend; (*applause*) tosend; (*very funny*) zwerchfellerschütternd
uproot' *tr* entwurzeln
ups' and downs' *spl* Auf und Ab *n*
upset' *adj* (*over*) verstimmt (über *acc*) || **up'set'** *s* unerwartete Niederlage *f* || **up'set'** *v* (*pret & pp -set*; *ger -setting*) *tr* (*throw over*) umwerfen; (*tip over*) umkippen; (*plans*) umstoßen; (*a person*) aufregen; (*the stomach*) verderben
up'shot' *s* Ergebnis *n*
up'side down' *adv* verkehrt; **turn u.** auf den Kopf stellen
up'stage' *adv* in den (*or* im) Hintergrund der Bühne || *tr* (coll) ausstechen
up'stairs' *adj* im oberen Stockwerk || *adv* (*position*) oben; (*direction*) nach oben || *s* oberes Stockwerk *n*
upstand'ing *adj* aufrecht; (*sincere*) aufrichtig
up'start' *s* Emporkömmling *m*
up'stream' *adj* weiter stromaufwärts gelegen || *adv* stromaufwärts
up'stroke' *s* Aufstrich *m*; (mach) Hub *m*
up'surge' *s* Aufwallung *f*
up'sweep' *s* Hochfrisur *f*
up'swing' *s* (fig) Aufschwung *m*
upsy-daisy ['ʌpsi'dezi] *interj* hopsasa!
up-to-date ['ʌptə'det] *adj* (*modern*) zeitgemäß; (*with latest information*) auf dem neuesten Stand
up'-to-the-min'ute news' ['ʌptəðə'mɪnɪt] *s* Zeitfunk *m*
up'trend' *s* steigende Tendenz *f*

up'turn' s Aufschwung m
upturned' adj nach oben gebogen; **u. nose** Stupsnase f
upward ['ʌpwərd] adj nach oben gerichtet; (tendency) steigend || adv aufwärts
U'ral Moun'tains ['jurəl] spl Ural m
uranium [ju'reni·əm] adj Uran– || s Uran n
urban ['ʌrbən] adj städtisch, Stadt–
urbane [ʌr'ben] adj weltgewandt
urbanite ['ʌrbə‚naɪt] s Städter –in mf
urbanize ['ʌrbə‚naɪz] tr verstädtern
ur'ban renew'al s Altstadtsanierung f
urchin ['ʌrtʃɪn] s Bengel m
ure·thra [ju'riθrə] s (-thras & -thrae [θri]) Harnröhre f
urge [ʌrdʒ] s Drang m, Trieb m || tr drängen; **u. on** antreiben
urgency ['ʌrdʒənsi] s Dringlichkeit f
urgent ['ʌrdʒənt] adj dringend
urinal ['jurɪnəl] s (in a toilet) Urinbecken n; (in a sick bed) Urinflasche f
urinary ['jurɪ‚neri] adj Harn–, Urin–
urinate ['jurɪ‚net] intr harnen
urine ['jurɪn] s Harn m, Urin m
urn [ʌrn] s Urne f; (for coffee) Kaffeemaschine f
urology [jɪ'rɑlədʒi] s Urologie f
us [ʌs] per pron uns
U.S.A. ['ju'es'e] s (United States of America) USA pl
usable ['juzəbəl] adj (consumable items) verwendbar; (non-consumable items) benutzbar
usage ['jusɪdʒ] s (using) Gebrauch m; (treatment) Behandlung f; (ling) Sprachgebrauch m; **rough u.** starke Beanspruchung f
use [jus] s (of consumable items) Verwendung f, Gebrauch m; (of non-consumable items) Benutzung f; (application) Anwendung f; (advantage) Nutzen m; (purpose) Zweck m; (consumption) Verbrauch m; **I have no use for him** ich habe nichts für ihn übrig; **in use** in Gebrauch; **it's no use** es nützt nichts; **make use of** ausnutzen; **of use** von Nutzen; **there's no use** (ger) es hat keinen Zweck zu (inf) || [juz] tr (ge)brauchen, verwenden; (non-consumable items) benutzen; (apply) anwenden; (e.g.,

troops) einsetzen; **use up** verbrauchen || intr—**he used to live here** er wohnte früher hier
used [juzd] adj gebraucht; (car) Gebraucht–; **be u. to** gewöhnt sein an (acc); **be u. to** (ger) gewöhnt sein zu (inf); **get s.o. u. to** j–n gewöhnen an (acc); **get u. to** sich gewöhnen an (acc)
useful ['jusfəl] adj nützlich
usefulness ['jusfəlnɪs] s Nützlichkeit f; (usability) Brauchbarkeit f
useless ['juslɪs] adj nutzlos; (not usable) unbrauchbar
user ['juzər] s (of gas, electric) Verbraucher –in f; (e.g., of a book) Benutzer –in mf
usher ['ʌʃər] s Platzanweiser –in mf || tr—**u. in** hereinführen; (a new era) einleiten
U.S.S.R. ['ju'es'es'ar] s (Union of Soviet Socialist Republics) UdSSR f
usual ['juʒu·əl] adj gewöhnlich; **as u.** wie gewöhnlich
usually ['juʒu·əli] adv gewöhnlich
usurp [ju'zʌrp] tr usurpieren
usurper [ju'zʌrpər] s Usurpator –in mf
usury ['juʒəri] s Wucher m
utensil [ju'tensɪl] s Gerät n; **utensils** Utensilien pl
uter·us ['jutərəs] s (-i [‚aɪ]) Gebärmutter f
utilitarian [‚jutɪlɪ'teri·ən] adj utilitaristisch, Nützlichkeits–
utility [ju'tɪlɪti] s (usefulness) Nützlichkeit f; (company) öffentlicher Versorgungsbetrieb m; **apartment with all utilities** Wohnung f mit allem Zubehör; **utilities** Gas, Wasser, Strom pl
utilize ['jutɪ‚laɪz] tr verwerten
utmost ['ʌt‚most] adj äußerste, höchste || s—**do one's u.** sein Äußerstes tun; **to the u.** auf äußerste; **to the u. of one's power** nach besten Kräften
utopia [ju'topɪ·ə] s Utopie f
utopian [ju'topɪ·ən] adj utopisch
utter ['ʌtər] adj völlig, Erz– || tr (a sigh) ausstoßen; (a sound) hervorbringen; (feelings) ausdrücken; (words) äußern
utterance ['ʌtərəns] s Äußerung f
utterly ['ʌtərli] adv ganz und gar, völlig

V

V, v [vi] s zweiundzwanzigster Buchstabe des englischen Alphabets
vacancy ['vekənsi] s (emptiness) Leere f; (unfilled job) freie Stelle f; **no v.** (public sign) kein freies Zimmer
vacant ['vekənt] adj frei; (stare) geistesabwesend; (lot) unbebaut
vacate [ve'ket] tr (a home) räumen; (a seat) freimachen || intr ausziehen
vacation [ve'keʃən] s Urlaub m; (educ)

Ferien pl; **on v.** auf Urlaub || intr Urlaub machen
vacationer [ve'keʃənər] s Urlauber –in mf
vaccinate ['væksɪ‚net] tr impfen
vaccination [‚væksɪ'neʃən] s Impfung f
vaccina'tion certif'icate s Impfschein m
vaccine [væk'sin] s Impfstoff m

vacillate ['væsɪ‚let] *intr* schwanken
vacuous ['vækju-əs] *adj* nichtssagend
vacu·um ['vækju-əm] *s* (-ums & -a [ə]) Vakuum *n* ‖ *tr* & *intr* staubsaugen
vac'uum clean'er *s* Staubsauger *m*
vac'uum pump' *s* Absaugepumpe *f*
vac'uum tube' *s* Vakuumröhre *f*
vagabond ['vægə‚bɑnd] *s* Landstreicher –in *mf*
vagary ['vegərɪ] *s* Laune *f*
vagina [və'dʒaɪnə] *s* Scheide *f*
vagrancy ['vegrənsɪ] *s* Landstreicherei *f*
vagrant ['vegrənt] *adj* vagabundierend ‖ *s* Landstreicher –in *mf*
vague [veg] *adj* unbestimmt, vage
vain [ven] *adj* (*proud*) eitel; (*pointless*) vergeblich; **in v.** vergebens
vainglo'rious *adj* prahlerisch
valance ['veləns] *s* Quervolant *m*
vale [vel] *s* Tal *n*
valedictory [‚vælɪ'dɪktərɪ] *s* Abschiedsrede *f*
valence ['veləns] *s* Wertigkeit *f*
valentine ['vælən‚taɪn] *s* Valentinsgruß *m*
vale' of tears' *s* Jammertal *n*
valet ['vælɪt] *s* Kammerdiener *m*
valiant ['væljənt] *adj* tapfer
valid ['vælɪd] *adj* (*law, ticket*) gültig; (*argument, objection*) wohlbegründet; (*e.g., contract*) rechtsgültig; **be v.** gelten
validate ['vælɪ‚det] *tr* bestätigen
validation [‚vælɪ'deʃən] *s* Bestätigung *f*
validity [və'lɪdɪtɪ] *s* Gültigkeit *f*
valise [və'lis] *s* Reisetasche *f*
valley ['vælɪ] *s* Tal *n*
valor ['vælər] *s* Tapferkeit *f*
valorous ['vælərəs] *adj* tapfer
valuable ['vælju·əbəl] *adj* wertvoll ‖ **valuables** *spl* Wertsachen *pl*
value ['vælju] *s* Wert *m* ‖ *tr* (at) schätzen (auf *acc*)
val'ue judg'ment *s* Werturteil *n*
valueless ['væljulɪs] *adj* wertlos
valve [vælv] *s* (anat, mach, zool) Klappe *f*; (mach, mus) Ventil *n*
vamp [væmp] *s* (coll) Vamp *m*
vampire ['væmpaɪr] *s* Vampir *m*
van [væn] *s* Möbelwagen *m*; (*panel truck*) Kastenwagen *m*; (fig) Avantgarde *f*; (mil) Vorhut *f*
vandal ['vændəl] *s* Vandale *m*; **Vandal** Vandale *m*
vandalism ['vændə‚lɪzəm] *s* Vandalismus *m*
vane [ven] *s* (*of a windmill, fan, propeller*) Flügel *m*; (*in a turbine*) Schaufel *f*
vanguard ['væn‚gɑrd] *s* (fig) Spitze *f*; (mil) Vorhut *f*
vanilla [və'nɪlə] *s* Vanille *f*
vanish ['vænɪʃ] *intr* (ver)schwinden; **v. into thin air** sich in blauen Dunst auflösen
van'ishing cream' *s* Tagescreme *f*
vanity ['vænɪtɪ] *s* (*arrogance*) Anmaßung *f*; (*emptiness*) Nichtigkeit *f*; (*furniture*) Frisiertisch *m*

van'ity case' *s* Kosmetikköfferchen *n*
vanquish ['væŋkwɪʃ] *tr* besiegen
van'tage point' ['væntɪdʒ] *s* (*advantage*) günstiger Ausgangspunkt *m*; (*view*) Aussichtspunkt *m*
vapid ['væpɪd] *adj* schal, fad(e)
vapor ['vepər] *s* Dampf *m*, Dunst *m*
vaporize ['vepə‚raɪz] *tr* & *intr* verdampfen
vaporizer ['vepə‚raɪzər] *s* Inhalationsapparat *m*
va'por trail' *s* Kondensstreifen *m*
variable ['verɪ·əbəl] *adj* veränderlich; (*wind*) aus wechselnden Richtungen ‖ *s* (math) Veränderliche *f*
variance ['verɪ·əns] *s* Veränderung *f*; (*difference*) Abweichung *f*; (*argument*) Streit *m*; **be at v. with** (*a person*) in Zwiespalt sein mit; (*a thing*) in Widerspruch stehen zu
variant ['verɪ·ənt] *adj* abweichend ‖ *s* Variante *f*
variation [‚verɪ'eʃən] *s* Veränderung *f*; (alg, biol, mus) Variation *f*
var'icose vein' ['verɪ‚kos] *s* Krampfader *f*
varied ['verɪd] *adj* abwechslungsreich; (*diverse*) verschieden
variegated ['verɪ·ə‚getɪd] *adj* (*diverse*) verschieden; (*in color*) bunt
variety [və'raɪ·ətɪ] *s* (*choice*) Auswahl *f*; (*difference*) Verschiedenheit *f*; (*sort*) Art *f*; (biol) Spielart *f*; **for a v. of reasons** aus verschiedenen Gründen
vari'ety show' *s* Varietévorstellung *f*
various ['verɪ·əs] *adj* verschieden; (*several*) mehrere
varnish ['vɑrnɪʃ] *s* Firnis *m*, Lack *m* ‖ *tr* firnissen
varsity ['vɑrsɪtɪ] *adj* Auswahl– ‖ *s* Auswahlmannschaft *f*
var·y ['verɪ] *v* (*pret* & *pp* **–ied**) *tr* & *intr* abwechseln, variieren
vase [ves], [vez] *s* Vase *f*
vaseline ['væsə‚lin] *s* (trademark) Vaseline *f*
vassal ['væsəl] *s* Lehensmann *m*
vast [væst] *adj* riesig; (*majority*) überwiegend; **v. amount** Unmasse *f*
vastness ['væstnɪs] *s* Unermeßlichkeit *f*
vat [væt] *s* Bottich *m*
Vatican ['vætɪkən] *adj* vatikanisch; (*city*) Vatikan– ‖ *s* Vatikan *m*
Vat'ican Coun'cil *s* Vatikanisches Konzil *n*
vaudeville ['vɔdvɪl] *s* Varieté *n*
vaude'ville show' *s* Varietévorstellung *f*
vault [vɔlt] *s* (*underground chamber*) Gruft *f*; (*of a bank*) Tresor *m*; (*archit*) Gewölbe *n*; **v. of heaven** Himmelsgewölbe *n* ‖ *tr* überspringen
vaunt [vɔnt] *s* Prahlerei *f* ‖ *tr* sich rühmen (genit) ‖ *intr* sich rühmen
veal [vil] *s* Kalbfleisch *n*
veal' cut'let *s* Kalbskotelett *n*
veer [vɪr] *intr* drehen, wenden
vegetable ['vedʒɪtəbəl] *adj* pflanzlich; (*garden, soup*) Gemüse–; (*kingdom, life, oil, dye*) Pflanzen– ‖ *s* Gemüse *n*; **vegetables** Gemüse *n*

vegetarian [ˌvedʒɪ'terɪ-ən] *adj* vegetarisch ‖ *s* Vegetarier –in *mf*
vegetate ['vedʒɪ,tet] *intr* vegetieren
vegetation [ˌvedʒɪ'teʃən] *s* Vegetation *f*

vehemence ['vi-ɪməns] *s* Heftigkeit *f*
vehement ['vi-ɪmənt] *adj* heftig
vehicle ['vi-ɪkəl] *s* Fahrzeug *n*
veil [vel] *s* Schleier *m* ‖ *tr* (& *fig*) verschleiern
veiled *adj* verschleiert; (*threat*) verhüllt
vein [ven] *s* Vene *f*; (*geol, min*) Ader *f*
vellum ['veləm] *s* Velin *n*
velocity [vɪ'lɑsɪti] *s* Geschwindigkeit *f*
velvet ['velvɪt] *adj* Samt– ‖ *s* Samt *m*
velveteen [ˌvelvɪ'tin] *s* Baumwollsamt *m*
velvety ['velvɪti] *adj* samtartig
vend [vend] *tr* verkaufen
vend′ing machine′ *s* Automat *m*
vendor ['vendər] *s* Verkäufer –in *mf*
veneer [və'nɪr] *s* Furnier *n*; (*fig*) Tünche *f* ‖ *tr* furnieren
venerable ['venərəbəl] *adj* ehrwürdig
venerate ['venə,ret] *tr* verehren
veneration [ˌvenə'reʃən] *s* Verehrung *f*
Venetian [vɪ'niʃən] *adj* venezianisch ‖ *s* Venezianer –in *mf*
Vene′tian blind′ *s* Fensterjalousie *f*
vengeance ['vendʒəns] *s* Rache *f*; **take v. on** sich rächen an (*dat*); **with a v.** mit Gewalt
vengeful ['vendʒfəl] *adj* rachsüchtig
venial ['vinɪ-əl] *adj* (*sin*) läßlich
Venice ['venɪs] *s* Venedig *n*
venison ['venɪsən] *s* Wildbret *n*
venom ['venəm] *s* Gift *n*; (*fig*) Geifer *m*
venomous ['venəməs] *adj* giftig
vent [vent] *s* Öffnung *f*; **give v. to** Luft machen (*dat*) ‖ *tr* auslassen
ventilate ['ventɪ,let] *tr* ventilieren
ventilation [ˌventɪ'leʃən] *s* Ventilation *f*
ventilator ['ventɪ,letər] *s* Ventilator *m*
ventricle ['ventrɪkəl] *s* Ventrikel *m*
ventriloquist [ven'trɪləkwɪst] *s* Bauchredner –in *mf*
venture ['ventʃər] *s* Unternehmen *n* ‖ *tr* wagen ‖ *intr* (**on**) sich wagen (an *acc*); **v. out** sich hinauswagen; **v. to** (*inf*) sich vermessen zu (*inf*)
venturesome ['ventʃərsəm] *adj* (*person*) wagemutig; (*deed*) gewagt
venue ['venju] *s* zuständiger Gerichtsort *m*; **change of v.** Änderung *f* des Gerichtsstandes
Venus ['vinəs] *s* Venus *f*
veracity [vɪ'ræsɪti] *s* Wahrhaftigkeit *f*
veranda [və'rændə] *s* Veranda *f*
verb [verb] *s* Verb *n*, Zeitwort *n*
verbal ['verbal] *adj* (*oral*) mündlich; (*gram*) verbal
verbatim [vər'betɪm] *adj* wortgetreu
verbiage ['verbɪ-ɪdʒ] *s* Wortschwall *m*
verbose [vər'bos] *adj* weitschweifig
verdant ['verdənt] *adj* grün
verdict ['verdɪkt] *s* Urteilsspruch *m* (der Geschworenen); **give a v.** e-n Spruch fällen

verdigris ['vɑrdɪ,gris] *s* Grünspan *m*
verge [vɑrdʒ] *s* (*fig*) Rand *m*; **on the v. of** (*ger*) nahe daran zu (*inf*) ‖ *intr*—**v. on** grenzen an (*acc*)
verifiable [ˌverɪ'faɪ-əbəl] *adj* nachprüfbar
verification [ˌverɪfɪ'keʃən] *s* Nachprüfung *f*
veri-fy ['verɪ,faɪ] *v* (*pret* & *pp* **-fied**) *tr* nachprüfen
verily ['verɪli] *adv* (*Bib*) wahrlich
veritable ['verɪtəbəl] *adj* echt
vermilion [vər'mɪljən] *adj* zinnoberrot
vermin ['vɑrmɪn] *s* (*objectionable person*) Halunke *m*; **v. spl** Schädlinge *pl*; (*objectionable persons*) Gesindel *n*
vermouth [vər'muθ] *s* Wermut *m*
vernacular [vər'nækjələr] *adj* volkssprachlich ‖ *s* Volkssprache *f*
ver′nal e′quinox ['vɑrnəl] *s* Frühlingstagundnachtgleiche *f*
versatile ['vɑrsətɪl] *adj* beweglich
verse [vɑrs] *s* (& *Bib*) Vers *m*; (*stanza*) Strophe *f*
versed [vɑrst] *adj* (**in**) bewandert in (*dat*)
versification [ˌvɑrsɪfɪ'keʃən] *s* (*metrical structure*) Versbau *m*; (*versifying*) Verskunst *f*; (*metrical version*) Versfassung *f*
versifier ['vɑrsɪ,faɪ-ər] *s* Verseschmied *m*
version ['vɑrʒən] *s* Version *f*
ver-so ['vɑrso] *s* (**-sos**) (*of a coin*) Revers *m*; (*typ*) Verso *n*
versus ['vɑrsəs] *prep* gegen (*acc*)
verte-bra ['vɑrtɪbrə] *s* (**-brae** [,brɪ] & **-bras**) Rückenwirbel *m*, Wirbel *m*
vertebrate ['vɑrtɪ,bret] *s* Wirbeltier *n*
ver-tex ['vɑrteks] *s* (**-texes** & **-tices** [tɪ,siz]) Scheitelpunkt *m*
vertical ['vɑrtɪkəl] *adj* senkrecht ‖ *s* Vertikale *f*
ver′tical hold′ *s* (telv) Vertikaleinstellung *f*
ver′tical take′off *s* Senkrechtstart *m*
vertigo ['vɑrtɪ,go] *s* Schwindel *m*, Schwindelgefühl *n*
very ['veri] *adj*—**that v. day** an demselben Tag; **the v. thought** der bloße Gedanke; **the v. truth** die reine Wahrheit; **the v. man** genau der Mann ‖ *adv* sehr; **the v. best** der allerbeste; **the v. same** ebenderselbe
vesicle ['vesɪkəl] *s* Bläschen *n*
vespers ['vespərz] *spl* Vesper *f*
vessel ['vesəl] *s* (*ship*) Schiff *n*; (*container*) Gefäß *n*
vest [vest] *s* Weste *f*; (*for women*) Leibchen *n* ‖ *tr* (**with**) bekleiden (mit); **be vested in** zustehen (*dat*)
vest′ed in′terest *s* (*for personal benefits*) persönliches Interesse *n*; (*jur*) rechtmäßiges Interesse *n*
vestibule ['vestɪ,bjul] *s* Vestibül *n*
vestige ['vestɪdʒ] *s* Spur *f*
vestment ['vestmənt] *s* Gewand *n*
vest′-pock′et *adj* Westentaschen–
vestry ['vestri] *s* Sakristei *f*; (*committee*) Gemeindevertretung *f*
vetch [vetʃ] *s* Wicke *f*

veteran ['vetərən] s Veteran m; (sport) Senior m

veterinarian [,vetərɪ'nerɪ·ən] s Tierarzt m, Tierärztin f

veterinary ['vetərɪ,nerɪ] adj (college) tierärztlich; v. medicine Tierheilkunde f

ve·to ['vito] s (–toes) Veto n || tr ein Veto einlegen gegen

vex [veks] tr ärgern

vexation [vek'seʃən] s Ärger m

V'-forma'tion s (aer) Staffelkeil m

via ['vi·ə] prep über (acc)

viable ['vaɪ·əbəl] adj lebensfähig

viaduct ['vaɪ·ə,dʌkt] s Viadukt m

vial ['vaɪ·əl] s Phiole f

viands ['vaɪ·əndz] spl Lebensmittel pl

vibrate ['vaɪbret] intr vibrieren; cause to v. in Schwingung versetzen

vibration [vaɪ'breʃən] s Schwingung f

vicar ['vɪkər] s Vikar m

vicarage ['vɪkərɪdʒ] s Pfarrhaus n

vicarious [vaɪ'kerɪ·əs] adj (pleasure) nachempfunden; (taking the place of another) stellvertretend; v. experience Ersatzbefriedigung f

vice [vaɪs] s Laster n

vice'-ad'miral s Vizeadmiral m

vice'-con'sul s Vizekonsul m

vice'-pres'ident s Vizepräsident –in mf

viceroy ['vaɪsrɔɪ] s Vizekönig m

vice' squad's Sittenpolizei f

vice versa ['vaɪsə'vʌrsə] adv umgekehrt

vicinity [vɪ'sɪnɪti] s Umgebung f; in the v. of in der Nähe (genit)

vicious ['vɪʃəs] adj (temper) bösartig; (dog) bissig; (person, gossip) heimtückisch

vi'cious cir'cle s Zirkelschluß m

vicissitudes [vɪ'sɪsɪ,tjudz] spl Wechselfälle pl

victim ['vɪktɪm] s Opfer n; (animal) Opfertier n; fall v. to zum Opfer fallen (dat)

victimize ['vɪktɪ,maɪz] tr (make a victim of) benachteiligen; (dupe) hereinlegen

victor ['vɪktər] s Sieger –in mf

victorious [vɪk'torɪ·əs] adj siegreich

victory ['vɪktərɪ] adj Sieges– || s Sieg m; (myth) Siegesgöttin f; flushed with v. siegestrunken

victuals ['vɪt·əlz] spl Viktualien pl

vid'eo sig'nal ['vɪdɪ,o] s Bildsignal n

vid'eo tape' s Bildband n

vid'eo tape' record'er s Bildbandgerät n

vid'eo tape' record'ing s Bildbandaufnahme f

vie [vaɪ] v (pret & pp vied; ger vying) intr (with) wetteifern (mit)

Vienna [vɪ'enə] s Wien n

Vien·nese [,vɪ·ə'niz] adj wienerisch || s (–nese) Wiener –in mf

Vietnam [vɪ'et'nɑm] s Vietnam n

Vietnam·ese [vɪ,etnə'miz] adj vietnamesisch || s (–se) Vietnamese m, Vietnamesin f

view [vju] s Aussicht f; (opinion) Ansicht f; come into v. in Sicht kommen; in my v. meiner Ansicht nach;

in v. of angesichts (genit); with a v. to (ger) in der Absicht zu (inf) || tr betrachten; (sights) besichtigen

viewer ['vju·ər] s Zuschauer –in mf

view'find'er s Bildsucher m

view'point' s Standpunkt m

vigil ['vɪdʒɪl] s Nachtwache f; keep v. wachen

vigilance ['vɪdʒɪləns] s Wachsamkeit f

vigilant ['vɪdʒɪlənt] adj wachsam

vignette [vɪn'jet] s Vignette f

vigor ['vɪgər] s (physical) Kraft f; (mental) Energie f; (intensity) Wucht f

vigorous ['vɪgərəs] adj (strong) kräftig; (act) energisch

vile [vaɪl] adj gemein; (coll) scheußlich

vileness ['vaɪlnɪs] s Gemeinheit f

vili·fy ['vɪlɪ,faɪ] v (pret & pp –fied) tr verleumden

villa ['vɪlə] s Villa f

village ['vɪlɪdʒ] s Dorf n, Ort m

villager ['vɪlɪdʒər] s Dorfbewohner –in mf

villain ['vɪlən] s Bösewicht m, Schurke m

villainous ['vɪlənəs] adj schurkisch

villainy ['vɪlənɪ] s Schurkerei f

vim [vɪm] s Mumm m

vindicate ['vɪndɪ,ket] tr rechtfertigen

vindictive [vɪn'dɪktɪv] adj rachsüchtig

vine [vaɪn] s Rebe f; (creeper) Ranke f

vinegar ['vɪnɪgər] s Essig m

vine' grow'er [,gro·ər] s Winzer m

vineyard ['vɪnjərd] s Weinberg m

vintage ['vɪntɪdʒ] adj Qualitäts– || s Weinernte f

vint'age year' s Weinjahr n

vintner ['vɪntnər] s Weinbauer –in mf

vinyl ['vaɪnɪl] adj Vinyl–

viola [vaɪ'olə] s Bratsche f, Viola f

violate ['vaɪ·ə,let] tr (a law) verletzen; (a promise) brechen; (the peace) stören; (a custom, shrine) entweihen; (a girl) vergewaltigen

violation [,vaɪ·ə'leʃən] s (of the law) Verletzung f; (of a shrine) Entweihung f; (of a girl) Vergewaltigung f

violence ['vaɪ·ələns] s Gewalt f

violent ['vaɪ·ələnt] adj (person) gewalttätig; (deed) gewaltsam; (anger, argument) heftig

violet ['vaɪ·əlɪt] adj violett || s Veilchen n

violin [,vaɪ·ə'lɪn] s Geige f

violinist [,vaɪ·ə'lɪnɪst] s Geiger –in mf

violoncel·lo [,vaɪ·ələn't'ʃelo] s (–los) Violoncello n

viper ['vaɪpər] s Natter f, Viper f

virgin ['vʌrdʒɪn] adj Jungfern–; (land) unberührt || s Jungfrau f

virginity [vər'dʒɪnɪtɪ] s Jungfräulichkeit f

virile ['vɪrɪltɪ] s Zeugungskraft f

virology [vaɪ'rolədʒɪ] s Virusforschung f

virtual ['vʌrtʃu·əl] adj faktisch; (opt, tech) virtuell

virtue ['vʌrtʃu] s Tugend f; by v. of kraft (genit), vermöge (genit)

virtuosity [ˌvɑrtʃʊ'ɑsɪtɪ] s Virtuosität f

virtu·so [ˌvɑrtʃʊ'oso] s (-sos & -si [si]) Virtuose m, Virtuosin f

virtuous ['vɑrtʃʊ·əs] adj tugendhaft

virulence ['vɪrjələns] s Virulenz f

virulent ['vɪrjələnt] adj virulent

virus ['vaɪrəs] s Virus n

visa ['vizə] s Visum n

visage ['vɪzɪdʒ] s Antlitz n

viscera ['vɪsərə] s Eingeweide pl

viscosity [vɪs'kɑsɪtɪ] s Viskosität f

viscount ['vaɪkaunt] s Vicomte m

viscountess ['vaɪkauntɪs] s Vicomtesse f

viscous ['vɪskəs] adj zähflüssig

vise [vaɪs] s Schraubstock m

visibility [ˌvɪzɪ'brlɪtɪ] s Sichtbarkeit f; (meteor) Sicht f

visible ['vɪzɪbəl] adj sichtbar

visibly ['vɪzɪblɪ] adv zusehends

vision ['vɪʒən] s (faculty) Sehvermögen n; (appearance) Vision f; of great v. von großem Weitblick

visionary ['vɪʒə‚nerɪ] adj visionär || s Visionär –in m f

visit ['vɪzɪt] s Besuch m; (official) Visite f || tr besuchen; (a museum, town) besichtigen

visitation [ˌvɪzɪ'teʃən] s Visitation f; Visitation of our Lady Heimsuchung f Mariä

vis'iting hours' spl Besuchszeit f

vis'iting nurse' s Fürsorgerin f

visitor ['vɪzɪtər] s Besucher –in m f; have visitors Besuch haben

visor ['vaɪzər] s Schirm m; (on a helmet) Visier n

vista ['vɪstə] s (& fig) Ausblick m

Vistula ['vɪstʃʊlə] s Weichsel f

visual ['vɪʒʊ·əl] adj visuell

vis'ual aids' spl Anschauungsmaterial n

visualize ['vɪʒʊ·ə‚laɪz] tr sich [dat] vorstellen

vital ['vaɪtəl] adj (lebens)wichtig; (signs, functions) Lebens– || **vitals** spl edle Teile pl

vitality [var'tælɪtɪ] s Lebenskraft f

vitalize ['vaɪtə‚laɪz] tr beleben

vitamin ['vaɪtəmɪn] s Vitamin n

vi'tamin defi'ciency s Vitaminmangel m

vitiate ['vɪʃɪ‚et] tr verderben

vitreous ['vɪtrɪ·əs] adj glasartig

vitriolic [ˌvɪtrɪ'ɑlɪk] adj (fig) beißend; (chem) Vitriol–

vituperate [vaɪ't(j)upə‚ret] tr schelten

vivacious [vɪ've ʃəs] adj lebhaft

vivid ['vɪvɪd] adj lebhaft

vivi·fy ['vɪvɪ‚faɪ] v (pret & pp –fied) tr beleben

vivisection [ˌvɪvɪ'sɛkʃən] s Vivisektion f

vixen ['vɪksən] s Füchsin f

viz. abbr nämlich

vizier [vɪ'zɪr] s Vezier m, Wesir m

vocabulary [vo'kæbjə‚lerɪ] s (word range) Wortschatz m; (list) Wörterverzeichnis n

vocal ['vokəl] adj stimmlich, Stimm–; (outspoken) redselig

voc'al cord' s Stimmband n

vocalist ['vokəlɪst] s Sänger –in m f

vocalize ['vokə‚laɪz] tr (phonet) vokalisieren || intr singen; (phonet) in e–n Vokal verwandelt werden

vocation [vo'keʃən] s Beruf m; (relig) Berufung f

voca'tional guid'ance [vo'keʃənəl] s Berufsberatung f

voca'tional school' s Berufsschule f

voca'tional train'ing s Berufsausbildung f

vocative ['vokətɪv] s Vokativ m

vociferous [vo'sɪfərəs] adj laut

vodka ['vadkə] s Wodka m

vogue [vog] s (herrschende) Mode f; be in v. Mode sein

voice [vɔɪs] s Stimme f; in a low v. mit leiser Stimme || tr äußern; (phonet) stimmhaft aussprechen

voiced adj (phonet) stimmhaft

voiceless ['vɔɪslɪs] adj stimmlos

void [vɔɪd] adj leer; (invalid) ungültig || s Leere f || tr für ungültig erklären; (the bowels) entleeren

volatile ['valətɪl] adj (explosive) jähzornig; (changeable) unbeständig; (chem) flüchtig

volcanic [val'kænɪk] adj vulkanisch

volca·no [val'keno] s (-noes & -nos) Vulkan m

volition [vo'lɪʃən] s Wollen n; of one's own v. aus eigenem Antrieb

volley ['valɪ] s (of gunfire) Salve f; (of stones) Hagel m; (sport) Flugschlag m

vol'leyball' s Volleyball m

volt [volt] s Volt n

voltage ['voltɪdʒ] s Spannung f

voluble ['valjəbəl] adj redegewandt

volume ['valjəm] s (book) Band m; (of a magazine series) Jahrgang m; (of sound) Lautstärke f; (amount) Ausmaß n; (of a container) Rauminhalt m; speak volumes Bände sprechen; v. of sales Umsatz m

vol'ume control' s Lautstärkeregler m

voluminous [və'lumɪnəs] adj (writer) produktiv; (of great extent or size) umfangreich

voluntary ['valən‚terɪ] adj freiwillig

volunteer [ˌvalən'tɪr] adj Freiwilligen– || s Freiwillige m f || tr freiwillig anbieten || intr (for) sich freiwillig erbieten (für, zu)

voluptuary [və'lʌptʃʊ‚erɪ] s Wollüstling m

voluptuous [və'lʌptʃʊ·əs] adj wollüstig

vomit ['vamɪt] s Erbrechen n || tr (er)brechen; (smoke) ausstoßen; (fire) speien; (lava) auswerfen || intr sich erbrechen

voodoo ['vudu] adj Wudu– || s Wudu m

voracious [və're ʃəs] adj gefräßig

voracity [və'ræsɪtɪ] s Gefräßigkeit f

vor·tex ['vorteks] s (-texes & -tices [tɪ‚siz]) (& fig) Wirbel m

votary ['votərɪ] s Verehrer –in m f

vote [vot] s Stimme f; (act of voting) Abstimmung f; (right to vote) Stimmrecht n; put to a v. zur Abstimmung bringen || *tr* (*approve of, e.g., money*) (**for**) bewilligen (für); **v. down niederstimmen** || *intr* niederstimmen; **v. by acclamation** durch Zuruf stimmen; **v. for wählen; v. on** abstimmen über (*acc*)

vote' get'ter [ˌgetər] *s* Wahllokomotive *f*

vote' of con'fidence *s* Vertrauensvotum *n*

vote' of no' con'fidence *s* Mißvertrauensvotum *n*

voter ['votər] *s* Wähler –in *mf*

vot'ing booth' *s* Wahlzelle *f*

vot'ing machine' *s* Stimmenzählapparat *m*

votive ['votɪv] *adj* Votiv-, Weih-

vo'tive of'fering *s* Weihgabe *f*

vouch [vaʊt͡ʃ] *tr* bezeugen || *intr*—**v. for** bürgen für

voucher ['vaʊt͡ʃər] *s* Beleg *m*

vouchsafe' *tr* gewähren

vow [vaʊ] *s* Gelübde *n*; **take a vow of** geloben || *tr* geloben; (*revenge*) schwören; **vow to** (*inf*) sich [*dat*] geloben zu (*inf*)

vowel ['vaʊ-əl] *s* Selbstlaut *m*, Vokal *m*

voyage ['vɔɪ-ɪd͡ʒ] *s* Reise *f*; (*by sea*) Seereise *f* || *intr* reisen

voyager ['vɔɪ-ɪd͡ʒər] *s* Reisende *mf*; (*by sea*) Seereisende *mf*

V'-shaped' *adj* keilförmig

V'-sign' *s* Siegeszeichen *n*

vulcanize ['vʌlkə ˌnaɪz] *tr* vulkanisieren

vulgar ['vʌlgər] *adj* vulgär

vulgarity [vʌl'gærɪti] *s* Gemeinheit *f*

Vul'gar Lat'in *s* Vulgärlatein *n*

Vulgate ['vʌlget] *s* Vulgata *f*

vulnerable ['vʌlnərəbəl] *adj* verwundbar; (*position*) ungeschützt; (*fig*) angreifbar; **v. to** anfällig für

vulture ['vʌlt͡ʃər] *s* Geier *m*

W

W, w ['dʌbəl ˌju] *s* dreiundzwanzigster Buchstabe des englischen Alphabets

wad [wɑd] *s* (*of cotton*) Bausch *m*; (*of money*) Bündel *m*; (*of papers*) Stoß *m*; (*of tobacco*) Priem *m*

waddle ['wɑdəl] *s* Watscheln *n* || *intr* watscheln

wade [wed] *intr* waten; **w. into** (fig) anpacken; **w. through** (fig) sich mühsam durcharbeiten durch

wafer ['wefər] *s* Oblate *f*

waffle ['wɑfəl] *s* Waffel *f*

waf'fle i'ron *s* Waffeleisen *n*

waft [wæft], [wɑft] *tr* & *intr* wehen

wag [wæg] *s* (*nod*) Nicken *n*; (*shake*) Schütteln *n*; (*of the tail*) Wedeln *n*; (*mischievous person*) Schalk *m* || *v* (*pret* & *pp* **wagged**; *ger* **wagging**) *tr* (*the tail*) wedeln mit; (*nod*) nicken mit; (*shake*) schütteln || *intr* (*said of a tail*) wedeln; (*said of tongues*) nicht still sein

wage [wed͡ʒ] *adj* Lohn– || *s* Lohn *m*; **wages** Lohn *m* || *tr* (*war*) führen

wage' cut' *s* Lohnabbau *m*

wage' freeze' *s* Lohnstopp *m*

wager ['wed͡ʒər] *s* Wette *f*; **lay a w.** e-e Wette eingehen || *tr* & *intr* wetten

waggish ['wægɪʃ] *adj* schalkhaft

wagon ['wægən] *s* Wagen *m*

wag'on load' *s* Wagenladung *f*

waif [wef] *s* (*child*) verwahrlostes Kind *n*; (*animal*) verwahrlostes Tier *n*

wail [wel] *s* Wehklage *f* || *intr* (*over*) wehklagen (über *acc*)

wain-scot ['wenskət] *s* Täfelung *f* || *v* (*pret* & *pp* **–scot[t]ed**; *ger* **–scot[t]ing**) *tr* täfeln

waist [west] *s* Taille *f*; **strip to the w.** den Oberkörper freimachen

waist'-deep' *adj* bis an die Hüften (reichend)

waist'line' *s* Taille *f*; **watch one's w.** auf die schlanke Linie achten

wait [wet] *s* Warten *n*; **an hour's w.** e-e Stunde Wartezeit || *intr* warten; **that can w.** das hat Zeit; **w. for** (*a person*) warten auf (*acc*); (*e.g., an answer*) abwarten; **w. on** bedienen; **w. up for** aufbleiben und warten auf (*acc*)

wait'-and-see' *pol'icy* *s* Politik *f* des Abwartens

waiter ['wetər] *s* Kellner *m*; **w.!** Herr Ober!

wait'ing line' *s* Schlange *f*

wait'ing list' *s* Warteliste *f*

wait'ing room' *s* Warteraum *m*; (*e.g., in a railroad station*) Wartesaal *m*

waitress ['wetrɪs] *s* Kellnerin *f*

waive [wev] *tr* verzichten auf (*acc*)

waiver ['wevər] *s* Verzicht *m*

wake [wek] *s* (*at a funeral*) Totenwache *f*; (*naut*) Kielwasser *n*; **in the w. of** im Gefolge (*genit*) || *v* (*pret* **waked** & **woke** [wok]; *pp* **waked**) *tr* wecken; **w. up** aufwecken || *intr* erwachen; **w. up** aufwachen; **w. up to** (fig) bewußt werden (*genit*)

wakeful ['wekfəl] *adj* wachsam

waken ['wekən] *tr* (auf)wecken || *intr* erwachen

walk [wɔk] *s* Spaziergang *m*; (*gait*) Gang *m*; (*path*) Spazierweg *m*; **a five-minute w.** to fünf Minuten zu Fuß zu; **from all walks of life** aus allen Ständen; **go for a w.** spazierengehen; **take a w.** spazierenführen || *tr* (*a dog*) spazierenführen; (*a person*) begleiten; (*a horse*) führen; (*the streets*) ablaufen || *intr* (zu Fuß) gehen, laufen; **w. off with** klauen; **w. out on** sitzenlassen; **w. up to** zugehen auf (*acc*)

walk'-away' *s* (coll) leichter Sieg *m*

walker ['wɔkər] s Fußgänger –in mf
walkie-talkie ['wɔki'tɔki] s Sprechfunkgerät n
walk'-in' adj (closet) begehbar
walk'ing pa'pers spl Laufpaß m
walk'ing shoes' spl Straßenschuhe pl
walk'ing stick' s Spazierstock m
walk'-on' s (theat) Statist –in mf
walk'out' s Ausstand m
walk'-o'ver s (sport) leichter Sieg m
walk'-up' s Mietwohnung f ohne Fahrstuhl
wall [wɔl] s Mauer f; (between rooms) Wand f || tr—w. up vermauern
wall' brack'et s Konsole f
wall' clock' s Wanduhr f
wallet ['wɑlɪt] s Brieftasche f
wall'flow'er s (coll) Wandblümchen n
wall' map' s Wandkarte f
wallop ['wɑləp] s Puff m; have a w. Schlagkraft haben || tr verprügeln; (defeat) schlagen
wal'loping adj (sl) mordsgroß
wallow ['wɑlo] intr sich wälzen; w. in (fig) schwelgen in (dat)
wall'pa'per s Tapete f || tr tapezieren
walnut ['wɔlnət] s Walnuß f; (wood) Walnußholz n; (tree) Walnußbaum m
walrus ['wɔlrəs] s Walroß n
waltz [wɔlts] s Walzer m || intr Walzer tanzen
wan [wɑn] adj (wanner; wannest) bleich; (smile) schwach, matt
wand [wɑnd] s Stab m; (in magic) Zauberstab m
wander ['wɑndər] intr wandern; (from a subject) abschweifen
wanderer ['wɑndərər] s Wanderer –in mf
wan'derlust' s Wanderlust f
wane [wen] s—be on the w. abnehmen || intr abnehmen
wangle ['wæŋgəl] tr sich [dat] erschwindeln
want [wɑnt] s Bedürfnis n; for w. of mangels (genit) || tr wollen; wanted (sought, desired) gesucht
want' ad' s Kleinanzeige f
want'ing adj—be w. in ermangeln (genit)
war [wɔr] s Krieg m; at war im Kriege; go to war with e–n Krieg beginnen gegen; make war on Krieg führen gegen || v (pret & pp warred; ger warring) intr kämpfen
warble ['wɔrbəl] s Trillern n || intr trillern
war' bond' s Kriegsanleihe f
war' cry' s Schlachtruf m
ward [wɔrd] s (in a hospital) Station f; (of a city) Bezirk m; (person under protection) Schützling m; (person under guardianship) Mündel m; (guardianship) Vormundschaft f || tr—w. off abwehren
warden ['wɔrdən] s Gefängnisdirektor m
ward'robe' s Garderobe f
ward'room' s (nav) Offiziersmesse f
ware [wer] s Ware f
ware'house' s Lagerhaus n, Warenlager n

ware'house'man s (–men) Lagerist m
war'fare' s Kriegsführung f, Krieg m
war' foot'ing s Kriegsbereitschaft f
war'head' s Gefechtskopf m
war'-horse' s (coll) alter Kämpe m
war'like' adj kriegerisch
war' lord' s Kriegsherr m
warm [wɔrm] adj warm; (friends) intim || tr wärmen; w. up aufwärmen || intr—w. up warm werden; (sport) in Form kommen
warm'-blood'ed adj warmblütig
warm'front' s Warmfront f
warm'-heart'ed adj warmherzig
warmonger ['wɔr,mʌŋgər] s Kriegshetzer –in mf
warmth [wɔrmθ] s Wärme f
warm'-up' s (sport) Lockerungsübungen pl
warn [wɔrn] tr (against) warnen (vor dat)
warn'ing s Warnung f; let this be a w. to you lassen Sie sich das zur Warnung dienen
warn'ing shot' s Warnschuß m
war' of attri'tion s Zermürbungskrieg m
warp [wɔrp] s (of a board) Verziehen n || tr (wood) verziehen; w. s.o.'s mind j–n verschroben machen || intr sich verziehen
war'path' s Kriegspfad m
warped adj (wood) verzogen; (mind, opinion) verschroben
war'plane' s Kampfflugzeug n
warrant ['wɔrənt] s (justification) Rechtfertigung f; (authorization) Berechtigung f; w. for arrest Haftbefehl m || tr (justify) rechtfertigen; (guarantee) garantieren
war'rant of'ficer s (mil) Stabsfeldwebel m; (nav) Deckoffizier m
warranty ['wɔrənti] s Gewährleistung f
war'ranty serv'ice s Kundendienst m
warren ['wɔrən] s Kaninchengehege n
war'ring adj kriegsführend
warrior ['wɔri.ər] s Krieger m
Warsaw ['wɔrsɔ] s Warschau n
war'ship' s Kriegsschiff n
wart [wɔrt] s Warze f
war'time' adj Kriegs– || s Kriegszeit f
war'-torn' adj vom Krieg verwüstet
wary ['weri] adj vorsichtig
war' zone' s Kriegsgebiet n
wash [wɔʃ] adj Wasch– || s Wäsche f; (aer) Luftstrudel m; (paint) dünner Farbüberzug m; do the w. die Wäsche waschen || tr waschen; (metal) schlämmen; (paint) tuschen; (phot) wässern; w. ashore anschwemmen; w. away wegspülen; w. off abwaschen; w. out auswaschen; (a bridge) wegreißen; w. up aufwaschen || intr waschen; w. ashore ans Land spülen
washable ['wɔʃəbəl] adj waschbar
wash'-and-wear' adj bügelfrei
wash'ba'sin s Waschbecken n
wash'bas'ket s Wäschekorb m
wash'board' s Waschbrett n
wash'bowl' s Waschbecken n
wash'cloth' s Waschlappen m

wash'day' *s* Waschtag *m*

washed'-out' *adj* verwaschen; *(tired)* schlapp

washer ['wɔʃər] *s* Waschmaschine *f;* *(of rubber)* Dichtungsring *m;* *(of metal)* Unterlegscheibe *f*

washed'-up' *adj* (coll) erledigt

wash'er-wom'an *s* (-wom'en) Waschfrau *f*

wash'ing *s* Waschen *n;* *(clothes)* Wäsche *f*

wash'ing machine' *s* Waschmaschine *f*

wash'out' *s* Auswaschung *f;* *(failure)* Pleite *f;* *(person who fails)* Versager -in *mf*

wash'rag' *s* Waschlappen *m*

wash'room' *s* Waschraum *m*

wash'stand' *s* Waschtisch *m*

wash'tub' *s* Waschtrog *m*

wasp [wɑsp] *s* Wespe *f*

wasp'waist' *s* Wespentaille *f*

waste [west] *adj (superfluous)* überflüssig; *(land)* öde ‖ *s (of material goods, time, energy)* Verschwendung *f;* *(waste material)* Müll *m;* *(wilderness)* Wildnis *f;* go to w. vergeudet werden ‖ *tr* verschwenden, vergeuden ‖ *intr*—w. away verfallen

waste'bas'ket *s* Papierkorb *m*

wasteful ['westfəl] *adj* verschwenderisch

waste'land' *s* Ödland *n*

waste'pa'per *s* Makulatur *f*

waste'pipe' *s* Abflußrohr *n*

waste'pro'duct *s* Abfallprodukt *n*

wastrel ['westrəl] *s* Verschwender -in *mf*

watch [wɑtʃ] *s* Uhr *f;* *(lookout)* Wache *f;* be on the w. for acht haben auf *(acc)* ‖ *tr (observe)* beobachten; *(guard)* bewachen; *(oversee)* aufpassen auf *(acc);* w. how I do it passen Sie auf, wie ich es mache; w. your step! Vorsicht, Stufe! ‖ *intr (keep guard)* wachen; *(observe)* zuschauen; w. for abwarten; w. over überwachen; w. out! Vorsicht!; w. out for ausschauen nach; *(some danger)* sich hüten vor *(dat);* w. out for oneself sich vorsehen

watch'band' *s* Uhrarmband *n*

watch'case' *s* Uhrgehäuse *n*

watch' crys'tal *s* Uhrglas *n*

watch'dog' *s* Wachhund *m*

watch'dog commit'tee *s* Überwachungsausschuß *m*

watchful ['wɑtʃfəl] *adj* wachsam

watchfulness ['wɑtʃfəlnɪs] *s* Wachsamkeit *f*

watch'mak'er *s* Uhrmacher -in *mf*

watch'man *s* (-men) Wächter *m*

watch' pock'et *s* Uhrtasche *f*

watch' strap' *s* Uhrarmband *n*

watch'tow'er *s* Wachturm *m*

watch'word' *s* Kennwort *n*, Parole *f*

water ['wɔtər] *s* Wasser *n;* *(body of water)* Gewässer *n;* pass w. Wasser lassen ‖ *tr* (e.g., *flowers*) begießen; *(fields)* bewässern; *(animals)* tränken; *(the garden, streets)* sprengen; w. down (& fig) verwässern ‖ *intr* *(said of the eyes)* tränen; my mouth

waters das Wasser läuft mir im Mund zusammen

wa'ter boy' *s* Wasserträger *m*

wa'ter clos'et *s* Wasserklosett *n*

wa'tercol'or *s* *(paint)* Aquarellfarbe *f;* *(painting)* Aquarell *n*

wa'tercourse' *s* Wasserlauf *m*

wa'tercress' *s* Brunnenkresse *f*

wa'terfall' *s* Wasserfall *m*

wa'terfront' *s* Hafenviertel *n*

wa'ter heat'er *s* Warmwasserbereiter *m*

wa'tering can' *s* Wasserkanne *f*

wa'tering place' *s* *(for cattle)* Tränke *f;* *(for tourists)* Badeort *m*

wa'ter lev'el *s* Wasserstand *m*

wa'terlogged' *adj* vollgesogen

wa'ter main' *s* Wasserleitung *f*

wa'termark' *s* Wasserzeichen *n*

wa'ter mat'tress *s* Wasserbett *n*

wa'termel'on *s* Wassermelone *f*

wa'ter me'ter *s* Wasserzähler *m*

wa'ter pipe' *s* Wasserrohr *n*

wa'ter po'lo *s* Wasserball *m*

wa'ter pow'er *s* Wasserkraft *f*

wa'terproof' *adj* wasserdicht ‖ *tr* imprägnieren

wa'ter-repel'lent *adj* wasserabstoßend

wa'tershed' *s* Wasserscheide *f*

wa'ter-ski' *intr* wasserschifahren

wa'terspout' *s* *(orifice)* Wasserspeier *m;* *(pipe)* Ablaufrohr *n*

wa'ter supply' *s* Wasserversorgung *f*

wa'ter ta'ble *s* Grundwasserspiegel *m*

wa'ter tank' *s* Wasserbehälter *m*

wa'tertight' *adj* wasserdicht; *(fig)* eindeutig

wa'ter wag'on *s*—be on the w. Abstinenzler sein

wa'terway' *s* Wasserstraße *f*

wa'ter wheel' *s* *(for raising water)* Schöpfwerk *n;* *(water-driven)* Wasserrad *n*

wa'ter wings' *spl* Schwimmkissen *n*

wa'terworks' *s* Wasserwerk *n*

watery ['wɔtəri] *adj* wäss(e)rig

watt [wɑt] *s* Watt *n*

wattage ['wɑtɪdʒ] *s* Wattleistung *f*

wattles ['wɑtəlz] *spl* Flechtwerk *s*

watt'me'ter *s* Wattmeter *n*

wave [wev] *s* (fig, meteor, mil, phys, rad) Welle *f;* w. of the hand Wink *m* mit der Hand ‖ *tr* *(a hat, flag)* schwenken; *(a hand, handkerchief)* winken mit; *(hair)* wellen; w. one's hands about mit den Händen herumfuchteln; w. s.o. away j-n abwinken ‖ *intr* *(said of a flag)* wehen; *(said of grain)* wogen; *(with the hand)* winken; w. to zuwinken *(dat)*

wave'length' *s* Wellenlänge *f*

waver ['wevər] *intr* schweben, wanken

wavy ['wevi] *adj* wellenförmig; w. line Wellenlinie *f*

wax [wæks] *adj* Wachs- ‖ *s* Wachs *n* ‖ *tr* *(the floor)* bohnern; *(skis)* wachsen ‖ *intr* werden; *(said of the moon)* zunehmen; wax and wane zu- und abnehmen

wax' muse'um *s* Wachsfigurenkabinett *n*

wax' pa'per *s* Wachspapier *n*

way [we] *adv* weit; way ahead weit

voraus ‖ *s* Weg *m*; *(manner)* Art *f*; *(means)* Mittel *n*; *(condition)* Verfassung *f*; *(direction)* Richtung *f*; **across the way** gegenüber; **a long way from** weit weg von; **a long way off** weit weg; **by the way** übrigens; **by way of über** *(acc)*; **by way of comparison** vergleichsweise; **get s.th. out of the way** etw aus dem Wege schaffen; **get under way** in Gang kommen; **go all the way** aufs Ganze gehen; **go one's own way** aus der Reihe tanzen; **have a way with s.o.** mit j—m umzugehen verstehen; **have in the way of** *(merchandise)* haben an *(dat)*; **have it both ways** es sich *[dat]* aussuchen können; **have one's own way** seinen Willen durchsetzen; **I'm on my way!** ich komme schon!; **in a way** gewissermaßen; **in no way** keineswegs; **in the way** im Weg; **in this way** auf diese Weise; **in what way** in welcher Hinsicht; **make one's way through the crowd** sich *[dat]* e-n Weg durch die Menge bahnen; **one way or another** irgendwie; **on the way** unterwegs; **on the way out** *(fig)* im Begriff unmodern zu werden; **see one's way clear** bereit sein; **that way** auf diese Weise; *(in that direction)* in jener Richtung; **the way it looks** voraussichtlich; **way back** Rückweg *m*; **way here** Herweg *m*; **way out** Ausgang *m*; *(fig)* Ausweg *m*; **way there** Hinweg *m*

wayfarer ['we‚fɛrər] *s* Wanderer *m*

way'lay' *v* *(pret & pp* **-laid)** *tr* auflauern *(dat)*

way' of life' *s* Lebensweise *f*

way' of think'ing *s* Denkweise *f*

ways' and means' *spl* Mittel und Wege *pl*

way'side' *adj* an der Straße gelegen ‖ *s* Wegrand *m*; **fall by the w.** dem Untergang anheimfallen

wayward ['wewərd] *adj* ungeraten

we [wi] *pers pron* wir

weak [wik] *adj* schwach

weaken ['wikən] *tr* (ab)schwächen ‖ *intr* schwach werden

weakling ['wiklɪŋ] *s* Schwächling *m*

weak'-mind'ed *adj* willenlos

weakness ['wiknɪs] *s* *(& fig)* Schwäche *f*

weak' spot' *s* schwache Stelle *f*

weal [wil] *s* Strieme *f*, Striemen *m*

wealth [welθ] *s (of)* Reichtum *m* *(an (dat)*

wealthy ['welθi] *adj* wohlhabend

wean [win] *tr (from)* entwöhnen *(genit)*

weapon ['wepən] *s* Waffe *f*

weaponry ['wepənri] *s* Bewaffnung *f*

wear [wer] *s (use)* Gebrauch *m*; *(durability)* Haltbarkeit *f*; *(clothing)* Kleidung *f*; *(wearing down)* Verschleiß *m* ‖ *v* *(pret wore* [wor]; *pp* **worn** [worn])*tr* tragen; **w. down** *(a heel)* abtreten; *(a person)* zermürben; **w. out** abnützen; *(tires)* abfahren; *(a person)* erschöpfen; **w. the pants in the family** die Hosen anhaben ‖ *intr* sich tragen; **w. off** sich abtragen; **w. out** sich abnützen; **w. thin** *(said of clothes)* fadenscheinig werden; *(said of patience)* zu Ende gehen

wearable ['werəbəl] *adj* tragbar

wear' and tear' [ter] *s* Verschleiß *m*; **takes a lot of w.** strapazierfähig sein

weariness ['wirinis] *s* Müdigkeit *f*

wearisome ['wirisəm] *adj* mühsam

wea‧ry ['wiri] *adj* müde ‖ *v* *(pret & pp* **-ried)** *tr* ermüden ‖ *intr (of)* müde werden *(genit)*

weasel ['wizəl] *s* Wiesel *n* ‖ *intr*—**w. out of** sich herauswinden aus

weather ['weðər] *s* Wetter *n*; **be under the w.** unpäßlich sein; **w. permitting** bei günstiger Witterung ‖ *tr* dem Wetter aussetzen; *(the storm)* (fig) überstehen ‖*intr* verwittern

weath'erbeat'en *adj* verwittert

weath'er bu'reau *s* Wetterdienst *m*

weath'er condi'tions *spl* Wetterverhältnisse *pl*

weath'er fore'cast *s* Wettervoraussage *f*

weath'erman' *s* *(-men')* Wetteransager *m*

weath'er report' *s* Wetterbericht *m*

weath'erstrip'ping *s* Dichtungsstreifen *pl*

weath'er vane' *s* *(& fig)* Wetterfahne *f*

weave [wiv] *s* Webart *f* ‖ *v* *(pret wove* [wov] *& weaved*; *pp* **woven** ['wovən]) *tr* weben; *(a rug)* wirken; *(a basket)* flechten; *(a wreath)* winden; **w. one's way through traffic** sich durch den Verkehr schlängeln ‖ *intr* weben

weaver ['wivər] *s* Weber –in *mf*

web [web] *s (of a spider)* Spinngewebe *n*; *(of ducks)* Schwimmhaut *f*; **web of lies** Lügengewebe *n*

web'-foot'ed *adj* schwimmfüßig

wed [wed] *v* *(pret & pp wed & wedded*; *ger wedding)* *tr & intr* heiraten

wed'ding *adj* *(cake, present, day, reception)* Hochzeits–; *(ring)* Trau– ‖ *s* Hochzeit *f*; *(ceremony)* Trauung *f*

wedge [wedʒ] *s* Keil *m* ‖ *tr*—**w. in** einkeilen

wed'lock' *s* Ehestand *m*; **out of w.** unehelich

Wednesday ['wenzde] *s* Mittwoch *m*; **on W.** am Mittwoch

wee [wi] *adj* winzig; **a wee bit** ein klein wenig

weed [wid] *s* Unkraut *n*; *(marijuana)* (sl) Marihuana *n*; *(cigarette)* (sl) Zigarette *f*; **pull weeds** jäten ‖ *tr* jäten; **w. out** (fig) aussondern

weed' kill'er *s* Unkrautvertilgungsmittel *n*

week [wik] *s* Woche *f*; **a w. from today** heute in e–r Woche; **a w. ago today** heute vor acht Tagen; **for weeks** wochenlang

week'day' *s* Wochentag *m*

week'end' *s* Wochenende *n*

weekender ['wik‚ɛndər] *s* Wochenendausflügler –in *mf*

weekly ['wikli] *adj* wöchentlich; *(wages)* Wochen– ‖ *s* Wochenblatt *n*

weep [wip] *v* *(pret & pp wept* [wept]) *tr & intr* weinen

weep'ing wil'low s Trauerweide f

weevil ['wiːvəl] s Rüsselkäfer m

weft [weft] s (tex) Schußfaden m

weigh [wel] tr wiegen; (ponder) wägen; (anchor) lichten || intr wiegen; **w. heavily on** schwer lasten auf (dat)

weight [wet] s Gewicht n; (burden) Last f; (influence) Einfluß m; (importance) Bedeutung f; **carry great w.** sehr ins Gewicht fallen; **lift weights** Gewichte heben; **pull one's w.** das Seine tun; **throw one's w. about** sich breitmachen

weightless ['wetlɪs] adj schwerelos

weightlessness ['wetlɪsnɪs] s Schwerelosigkeit f

weighty ['wetɪ] adj (& fig) gewichtig

weird [wɪrd] adj unheimlich

weir-do ['wɪrdo] s (-dos) (sl) Kauz m

welcome ['welkəm] adj willkommen; (news) erfreulich; **you're w.!** bitte sehr!; **you're w. to** (inf) es steht Ihnen frei zu (inf) || s Empfang m, Willkomm m || tr empfangen; (an opportunity) mit Freude begrüßen || interj (to) willkommen! (in dat)

weld [weld] s Schweißnaht n || tr & intr schweißen

welder ['weldər] s Schweißer –in mf

weld'ing ['weldɪŋ] s Schweißung f, Schweißarbeit f

welfare ['welˌfer] s Wohlfahrt f

wel'fare work'er s Wohlfahrtspfleger –in mf

well [wel] adj gesund; **all is w.** alles ist in Ordnung; **feel w.** sich wohl fühlen || adv gut, wohl; **as w.** ebenso; **as w. as** so gut wie; (in addition to) sowohl ... als auch; **he is doing w.** es geht ihm gut; **his company is doing w.** seine Firma geht gut; **leave w. enough alone** es gut sein lassen; **w. on in years** schon bejahrt; **w. on the way** mitten auf dem Wege; (fig) **on the best way** auf dem besten Wege; **w. over** well über || s Brunnen m; (hole) Bohrloch n; (source) Quelle f || intr— **w. up** hervorquellen || interj na!; (in surprise) nanu!

well'-behaved' adj artig

well'-be'ing s Wohlergehen n

well'born' adj aus guter Familie

wellbred ['wel'bred] adj wohlerzogen

well'-deserved' adj wohlverdient

well'-disposed' adj (toward) wohlgesinnt (dat)

well-done ['wel'dʌn] adj (culin) durchgebraten || interj gut gemacht!

well'-dressed' adj gut angezogen

well'-found'ed adj wohlbegründet

well'-groomed' adj gut gepflegt

well'-heeled' adj (coll) steinreich

well'-informed' adj wohlunterrichtet

well'-inten'tioned adj wohlmeinend

well-kept ['wel'kept] adj gut gepflegt; (secret) gut gehütet

well'-known' adj wohlbekannt

well'-mean'ing adj wohlmeinend

well'-nigh' adv fast

well'-off' adj wohlhabend, vermögend

well'-preserved' adj gut erhalten

well-read ['wel'red] adj belesen

well'-spent' adj (money) gut verwendet; (time) gut verbracht

well'spring' s Brunnquell m

well'-thought'-of' adj angesehen

well'-timed' adj wohl berechnet

well-to-do ['weltə'du] adj wohlhabend

well'-wisher ['wel'wɪʃər] s Gratulant –in mf

well'-worn' adj (clothes) abgetragen; (phrase, subject) abgedroschen

Welsh [welʃ] adj walisisch || s Walisisch n; **the W.** die Waliser pl || welsh intr—**welsh on** (a promise) brechen

Welsh' rab'bit or **rare'bit** ['rerbɪt] s geröstete Käseschnitte f

welt [welt] s Striemen m

welter ['weltər] s Durcheinander n || intr sich wälzen

wel'terweight' s Weltergewichtler m

we'lterweight divi'sion s Weltergewicht n

wench [wentʃ] s Dirne f, Weibsbild n

wend [wend] tr—**w. one's way** seinen Weg nehmen

werewolf ['werˌwʌlf] s Werwolf m

west [west] adj westlich || adv nach Westen || s Westen m

western ['westərn] adj westlich || s (cin) Wildwestfilm m

West' Ger'many s Westdeutschland n

West' In'dies s, the ['ɪndiz] spl Westindien n

Westphalia [ˌwestˈfeliˌə] s Westfalen n

westward ['westwərd] adv westwärts

wet [wet] adj (wetter; wettest) naß; **all wet** (coll) auf dem Holzwege || v (pret & pp wet & wetted; ger wetting) tr naß machen

wet' blan'ket s (fig) Miesepeter m

wet' nurse s Amme f

whack [wæk] s (coll) Klaps m || tr (coll) klapsen

whale [wel] s Wal(fisch) m; **have a w. of a time** sich großartig unterhalten

whaler ['welər] s Walfänger m

wharf [wɔrf] s (wharves [wɔrvz]) Kaianlage f

what [wɑt] interr adj welcher, was für ein || interr pron was; **so w.?** na und?; **w. about me?** und was geschieht mit mir?; **w. if** was geschieht, wenn; **w. is more** außerdem; **w. next?** was noch?; **w. of it?** was ist da schon dabei?; **what's new?** was gibt es Neues? **what's that to you?** was geht Sie das an? || interj was für ein

whatev'er adj welch ... auch immer; **no ... w.** überhaupt kein || pron was auch immer; **w. I have** alles, was ich habe; **w. you please** was Sie wollen

what'not' s—**and w.** und was weiß ich noch (alles)

what's-his-name' s (coll) Dingsda m

wheal [wil] s Pustel f; (welt) Striemen m

wheat [wit] s Weizen m

wheedle ['hwidəl] tr—**w. s.o. into** (ger) j-n beschwatzen zu (inf); **w. s.th. out of s.o.** j-m etw abschwatzen

wheel [wil] *s* Rad *n*; **at the w.** (aut) am Steuer || *tr* fahren || *intr* sich drehen; **w. around** sich umdrehen

wheelbarrow ['wil,bæro] *s* Schubkarre *f*

wheel'chair' *s* Krankenfahrstuhl *m*

wheeler-dealer ['wilər'dilər] *s* Drahtzieher –in *mf*

wheeze [wiz] *s* Schnaufen *n* || *intr* schnaufen

whelp [welp] *s* Welpe *m* || *tr* werfen

when [wen] *adv* wann || *conj* (once in the past) als; (whenever; at a future time) wenn

whence [wens] *adv & conj* woher

whenev'er *conj* wenn, wann immer

where [wer] *adv & conj* wo; (whereto) wohin; **from w.** woher

whereabouts ['werə,bauts] *adv* wo ungefähr || *s & spl* Verbleib *m*

whereas' *conj* während, wohingegen

whereby' *conj* wodurch

where'fore' *adv & conj* weshalb

wherefrom' *adv* woher

wherein' *adv & conj* worin

whereof' *adv & conj* wovon

whereto' *adv* wohin

where'upon' *adv* worauf, wonach

wherever [wer'evər] *conj* wo auch

wherewith' *adv* womit

wherewithal ['werwið,ol] *s* Geldmittel *pl*

whet [wet] *v* (pret & pp whetted; ger whetting) *tr* wetzen, schleifen; (the appetite) anregen

whether ['weðər] *conj* ob

whet'stone' *s* Wetzstein *m*, Schleifstein *m*

whew [hwju] *interj* hui!; ui!

which [wɪtʃ] *interr adj* welcher || *interr pron* welcher || *rel pron* der, welcher

whichev'er *rel adj & rel pron* welcher

whiff [wɪf] *s* Geruch *m*, Nasevoll *f*

while [waɪl] *s* Weile *f* || *conj* während || *tr*—**w. away** sich [dat] vertreiben

whim [wɪm] *s* Laune *f*, Grille *f*

whimper ['wɪmpər] *s* Wimmern *n* || *tr & intr* wimmern

whimsical ['wɪmzɪkəl] *adj* schrullig

whine [waɪn] *s* Wimmern *n*; (of a siren, engine, storm) Heulen *n* || *intr* wimmern; heulen

whin·ny ['wɪni] *s* Wiehern *n* || *v* (pret & pp -nied) *intr* wiehern

whip [wɪp] *s* Peitsche *f* || *v* (pret & pp whipped; ger whipping) *tr* peitschen; (egg whites) zu Schaum schlagen; (defeat) schlagen; **w. out** blitzschnell ziehen; **w. up** (a meal) hervorzaubern; (enthusiasm) erregen

whip'lash' *s* Peitschenhieb *m*; (fig) Peitschenhiebeffekt *n*

whipped' cream' *s* Schlagsahne *f*

whipper-snapper ['wɪpər,snæpər] *s* Frechdachs *m*

whip'ping *s* Prügel *pl*

whip'ping boy' *s* Prügelknabe *m*

whip'ping post' *s* Schandpfahl *m*

whir [wʌr] *s* Schnurren *n* || *v* (pret & pp whirred; ger whirring) *intr* schnurren

whirl [wʌrl] *s* Wirbel *m*; **give s.th. a w.** (coll) etw ausprobieren || *tr* wirbeln || *intr* wirbeln; **my head is whirling** mir ist schwindlig

whirl'pool' *s* Strudel *m*, Wirbel *m*

whirl'wind' *s* Wirbelwind *m*

whirlybird ['wʌrli,bʌrd] *s* (coll) Hubschrauber *m*

whisk [wɪsk] *s* Wedel *m*; (culin) Schneebesen *m* || *tr* wischen; **w. away** (fig) eilends mitnehmen; **w. off** wegfegen

whisk' broom' *s* Kleiderbesen *m*

whiskers ['wɪskərz] *spl* Bart *m*; (on the cheeks) Backenbart *m*; (of a cat) Barthaare *pl*

whiskey ['wɪski] *s* Whisky *m*

whisper ['wɪspər] *s* Flüsterton *m* || *tr & intr* flüstern

whistle ['wɪsəl] *s* (sound) Pfiff *m*; (device) Trillerpfeife *f*; **wet one's w.** sich [dat] die Nase begießen || *tr* pfeifen || *intr* pfeifen; (said of the wind, bullet) sausen; **w. for** (coll) vergeblich warten auf (acc)

whit [wɪt] *s*—**not care a w. about** sich keinen Deut kümmern um

white [waɪt] *adj* weiß; **w. as a sheet** kreidebleich || *s* Weiß *n*; (of the eye) Weiße *f*

white'caps' *spl* Schaumkronen *pl*

white'-col'lar work'er *s* Angestellte *mf*

white'fish' *s* Weißfisch *m*

white'-haired' *adj* weißhaarig

white'-hot' *adj* weißglühend

white' lie' *s* Notlüge *f*

white' meat' *s* weißes Fleisch *n*

whiten ['waɪtən] *tr* weiß machen || *intr* weiß werden

whiteness ['waɪtnɪs] *s* Weiße *f*

white' slav'ery *s* Mädchenhandel *m*

white' tie' *s* Frackschleife *f*; (formal) Frack *m*

white'wash' *s* Tünche *f*; (fig) Beschönigung *f* || *tr* tünchen; (fig) beschönigen

whither ['wɪðər] *adv* wohin

whitish ['waɪtɪʃ] *adj* weißlich

whittle ['wɪtəl] *tr* schnitzeln; **w. away** (or **down**) verringern || *intr*—**w. away at** herumschnitzeln an (dat); (fig) verringern

whiz(z) [wɪz] *s* Zischen *n*; (fig) Kanone *f* || *v* (pret & pp whizzed; ger whizzing) *intr* zischen; **w. by** flitzen

who [hu] *interr pron* wer; **who the devil** wer zum Teufel || *rel pron* der; he who wer

whoa [wo] *interj* halt!

whoever *rel pron* wer, wer auch immer

whole [hol] *adj* ganz || *s* Ganze *n*; **as a w.** im großen und ganzen

whole'-heart'ed *adj* ernsthaft

whole' note' *s* (mus) ganze Note *f*

whole' rest' *s* (mus) ganze Pause *f*

whole'sale' *adj* Massen–; (com) Großhandels– || *adv* en gros || *s* Großhandel *m* || *tr* en gros verkaufen || *intr* im großen handeln

wholesaler ['hol,selər] *s* Großhändler –in *mf*

wholesome ['holsəm] *adj* gesund; *(food)* zuträglich
whole'-wheat' bread' *s* Vollkornbrot *n*
wholly ['holi] *adv* ganz, völlig
whom [hum] *interr pron* wen; **to w. wem** || *rel pron* den, welchen; **to w. dem, welchem**
whomev'er *rel pron* wen auch immer; **to w.** wem auch immer
whoop [hup], [hwup] *s* Ausruf *m* || *tr—w.* **it up** Radau machen
whoop'ing cough' *s* Keuchhusten *m*
whopper ['wapər] *s* Mordsding *n*; *(lie)* (coll) faustdicke Lüge *f*
whop'ping *adj* (coll) enorm, Riesen-
whore [hor] *s* Hure *f* || *intr—w.* **around** huren
whose [huz] *interr adj* wessen || *rel pron* dessen
why [waɪ] *adv* warum; **that's why deswegen; why, there you are!** da sind Sie ja!; **why, yes!** aber ja! || *s* Warum *n*; **the whys and the wherefores** das Warum und Weshalb
wick [wɪk] *s* Docht *m*
wicked ['wɪkɪd] *adj* *(evil)* böse; *(roguish)* boshaft; *(vicious)* bösartig; *(unpleasant)* ekelhaft; *(cold, pain, storm, wound)* (coll) schlimm; *(fantastic)* (coll) großartig
wicker ['wɪkər] *adj* *(basket, chair)* Weiden- || *s* *(wickerwork)* Flechtwerk *n*
wide [waɪd] *adj* breit; *(selection)* reich || *adv* weit
wide'-an'gle lens' *s* Weitwinkelobjektiv *n*
wide'-awake' *adj* hellwach
wide'-eyed' *adj* mit weit aufgerissenen Augen; *(innocence)* naiv
widely ['waɪdli] *adv* weit
widen ['waɪdən] *tr* ausweiten, verbreiten || *intr* sich ausweiten
wide'-o'pen *adj* weit geöffnet
wide' screen' *s* (cin) Breitleinwand *f*
wide'spread' *adj* weitverbreitet; *(damage)* weitgehend
widow ['wɪdo] *s* Witwe *f*
widower ['wɪdo-ər] *s* Witwer *m*
wid'owhood' *s* Witwenstand *m*
width [wɪdθ] *s* Breite *f*; **in w.** breit
wield [wild] *tr* *(a weapon)* führen; *(power, influence)* ausüben
wife [waɪf] *s* (**wives** [waɪvz]) Frau *f*
wig [wɪg] *s* Perücke *f*
wiggle ['wɪgəl] *s* Wackeln *n* || *tr* wackeln mit
wigwag ['wɪg‚wæg] *s* Winksignal *n*
wigwam ['wɪgwam] *s* Wigwam *m* & *n*
wild [waɪld] *adj* wild; **w. about** scharf auf *(acc)*; **go w.** verwildern; **grow w.** *(become neglected)* verwildern; **make s.o. w.** (coll) j-n rasend machen || *adv—grow w.* *(grow in the wild)* wild wachsen; **run w.** verwildern
wild' boar' *s* Wildschwein *n*
wild' card' *s* wilde Karte *f*
wild'cat' *s* Wildkatze *f*
wild'cat strike' *s* wilder Streik *m*
wilderness ['wɪldərnɪs] *s* Wildnis *f*
wild'fire' *s—like w.* wie Lauffeuer
wild' flow'er *s* Feldblume *f*

wild'-goose' chase' *s—go on a w.* sich [*dat*] vergeblich Mühe machen
wild'life' *s* Wild *n*
wild' oats' *spl—sow one's w.* sich [*dat*] die Hörner abstoßen
wile [waɪl] *s* List *f* || *tr—w.* **away** sich [*dat*] vertreiben
will [wɪl] *s* Wille(n) *m*; (jur) Testament *n*; **at w.** nach Belieben || *tr* *(bequeath)* vermachen || *v* *(pret & cond* **would** [wʊd]) *aux* werden
willful ['wɪlfəl] *adj* absichtlich; *(stubborn)* eigensinnig
William ['wɪljəm] *s* Wilhelm *m*
will'ing *adj* bereitwillig; **be w. to** *(inf)* bereit sein zu *(inf)*
willingly ['wɪlɪŋli] *adv* gern
willingness ['wɪlɪŋnɪs] *s* Bereitwilligkeit *f*
will-o'-the-wisp ['wɪlədə‚wɪsp] *s* (& fig) Irrlicht *n*
willow ['wɪlo] *s* Weide *f*
willowy ['wɪlo-i] *adj* biegsam
will' pow'er *s* Willenskraft *f*
willy-nilly ['wɪli'nɪli] *adv* wohl oder übel
wilt [wɪlt] *tr* verwelken lassen || *intr* verwelken
wilt'ed *adj* welk
wily ['waɪli] *adj* schlau, listig
wimple ['wɪmpəl] *s* Kinntuch *n*
win [wɪn] *s* Gewinn *m*; (sport) Sieg *m* || *v* *(pret & pp* **won** [wʌn]; *ger* **winning**) *tr* gewinnen; **win over to one's side** auf seine Seite ziehen || *intr* gewinnen, siegen
wince [wɪns] *s* Zucken *n* || *intr* zucken
winch [wɪntʃ] *s* *(windlass)* Winde *f*; *(handle)* Kurbel *f*; (min, naut) Haspel *f* & *m*
wind [wɪnd] *s* Wind *m*; **break w.** e-n Darmwind lassen; **get w. of** Wind bekommen von; **take the w. out of s.o.'s sails** j-m den Wind aus den Segeln nehmen; **there is s.th. in the w.** es liegt etw in der Luft || [waɪnd] *v* *(pret & pp* **wound** [waʊnd]) *tr* wickeln, winden; *(a timepiece)* aufziehen; **w. up** aufwickeln; *(affairs)* abwickeln; *(a speech)* abschließen || *intr* *(said of a river, road)* sich winden; **w. around** *(said of a plant)* sich ranken um
windbag ['wɪnd‚bæg] *s* (coll) Schaumschläger -in *mf*
windbreak ['wɪnd‚brek] *s* Windschutz *m*
windbreaker ['wɪnd‚brekər] *s* Windjacke *f*
winded ['wɪndɪd] *adj* außer Atem, atemlos
windfall ['wɪnd‚fɔl] *s* *(fallen fruit)* Fallobst *n*; (fig) Glücksfall *m*
wind'ing road' ['waɪndɪŋ] *s* Serpentinenstraße *f*; *(public sign)* kurvenreiche Straße *f*
wind'ing sheet' ['waɪndɪŋ] *s* Leichentuch *n*
wind' in'strument [wɪnd] *s* Blasinstrument *n*
windlass ['wɪndləs] *s* Winde *f*
windmill ['wɪnd‚mɪl] *s* Windmühle *f*

window ['wɪndo] s Fenster n; (of a ticket office) Schalter m; (for display) Schaufenster n

win'dow display' s Schaufensterauslage f

win'dow dress'er s Schaufensterdekorateur –in mf

win'dow dress'ing s Schaufensterdekoration f

win'dow en'velope s Fensterumschlag m

win'dow frame' s Fensterrahmen m

win'dowpane' s Fensterscheibe f

win'dow screen' s Fliegengitter n

win'dow shade' s Rollvorhang m, Rollo n

win'dow-shop' v (pret & pp –shopped; ger –shopping) intr e–n Schaufensterbummel machen

win'dow shut'ter s Fensterladen m

win'dow sill' s Fensterbrett n

windpipe ['wɪnd,paɪp] s Luftröhre f

windshield ['wɪnd,ʃild] s Windschutzscheibe f

wind'shield wash'er s Scheibenwäscher m

wind'shield wip'er s Scheibenwischer m

windsock ['wɪnd,sɑk] s Windsack m

windstorm ['wɪnd,stɔrm] s Sturm m

wind' tun'nel [wɪnd] s Windkanal m

wind-up ['wɪnd,ʌp] s (of affairs) Abwicklung f; (of a speech) Schluß m

windward ['wɪndwərd] adj (side) Wind– || adv windwärts || s Windseite f; **turn to w.** anluven

windy ['wɪndi] adj windig; (speech) weitschweifig; (person) redselig

wine [waɪn] s Wein m || tr mit Wein bewirten

wine' cel'lar s Weinkeller m

wine' glass' s Weinglas n

winegrower ['waɪn,gro·ər] s Weinbauer –in mf

wine'grow'ing s Weinbau m

wine' list' s Weinkarte f

wine' press' s Weinpresse f

winery ['waɪnəri] s Weinkellerei f

wine'skin' s Weinschlauch m

wing [wɪŋ] s (of a bird, building, party) Flügel m; (unit of three squadrons) Geschwader n; (theat) Kulisse f || tr (shoot) in den Flügel treffen; **w. one' way** dahinfliegen

wing' chair' s Ohrensessel m

wing' nut' s Flügelmutter f

wing'spread' s Spannweite f

wink [wɪŋk] s Augenwink m; **quick as a w.** im Nu || intr blinzeln; **w. at** zublinzeln (dat); (overlook) ein Auge zudrücken bei (dat)

winner ['wɪnər] s Gewinner –in mf, Sieger –in mf; (e.g., winning ticket) Treffer m

win'ning adj (e.g., smile) gewinnend; (sport) siegreich || **winnings** spl Gewinn m

winsome ['wɪnsəm] adj reizend

winter ['wɪntər] s Winter m || intr überwintern

winterize ['wɪntə,raɪz] tr winterfest machen

wintry ['wɪntri] adj winterlich; (fig) frostig

wipe [waɪp] tr wischen; **w. clean** abwischen; **w. out** auswischen; (e.g., a debt) tilgen; (destroy) vernichten; (fin) ruinieren; **w. up** aufwischen

wire [waɪr] s Draht m; (telg) Telegramm n; **get in under the w.** es gerade noch schaffen || tr mit Draht versehen; (a house) (elec) elektrische Leitungen legen in (dat); (a message) drahten; (a person) telegraphieren (dat)

wire' cut'ter s Drahtschere f

wire'draw' v (pret –drew; pp –drawn) tr drahtziehen

wire' entan'glement s Drahtverhau m

wire' gauge' s Drahtlehre f

wire'-haired' adj drahthaarig

wireless ['waɪrlɪs] adj drahtlos

wire' nail' s Drahtnagel m

Wire'pho'to s (–tos) (trademark) Bildtelegramm n

wire' record'er s Drahttonaufnahmegerät n

wire'tap' s Abhören n || v (pret & pp –tapped; ger –tapping) tr abhören

wir'ing s Leitungen pl; **do the w.** die elektrischen Leitungen legen

wiry ['waɪri] adj drahtig

wisdom ['wɪzdəm] s Weisheit f

wis'dom tooth' s Weisheitszahn m

wise [waɪz] adj (person, decision) klug; (impertinent) naseweis; **be w. to** sich [dat] klar werden über (acc); **put s.o. w. to** j–n einweihen in (acc) || **–in no w.** keineswegs || intr—**w. up** endlich mal vernünftig werden

wise'a'cre s Neunmalkluge mf

wise'crack' s schnippische Bemerkung f

wise' guy' s (sl) Naseweis m

wisely ['waɪzli] adv wohlweislich

wish [wɪʃ] s Wunsch m || tr wünschen || intr—**w. for** sich [dat] wünschen

wish'bone' s Gabelbein n

wish'ful think'ing ['wɪʃfəl] s ein frommer Wunsch m

wishy-washy ['wɪʃi,waʃi] adj charakterlos; **be w. ein** Waschlappen sein

wisp [wɪsp] s (of hair) Strähne f

wistful ['wɪstfəl] adj versonnen

wit [wɪt] s Geist m; (person) geistreicher Mensch m; **be at one's wit's end** sich [dat] keinen Rat mehr wissen; **keep one's wits about one** e–n klaren Kopf behalten; **live by one's wits** sich durchschlagen

witch [wɪtʃ] s Hexe f

witch'craft' s Hexerei f

witch' doc'tor s Medizinmann m

witch' ha'zel s Zaubernuß f; (ointment) Präperat n aus Zaubernuß

witch' hunt' s Hexenjagd f

with [wɪð], [wɪθ] prep mit (dat); (at the house of) bei (dat); (because of) vor (dat), e.g., **green w. envy** grün vor Neid; (despite) trotz (genit); **not be w. it** nicht bei der Sache sein

with'draw' v (pret –drew; pp –drawn) tr zurückziehen; (money) abheben || intr sich zurückziehen

withdrawal [wɪð'drɔ·əl] *s* Zurückziehung *f*; *(retraction)* Zurücknahme *f*; *(from a bank)* Abhebung *f*; *(mil)* Rückzug *m*

withdraw'al slip' *s* Abhebungsformular *n*

wither ['wɪðər] *intr* verwelken

with·hold' *v (pret & pp* –held) *tr (pay)* einbehalten; *(information) (from)* vorenthalten *(dat)*

withhold'ing tax' *s* einbehaltene Steuer *f*

within' *adv* drin(nen); **from w.** von innen || *prep (time)* binnen *(dat)*, innerhalb von *(dat)*; *(place)* innerhalb *(genit)*; **w. walking distance** in Gehweite

without' *adv* draußen || *prep* ohne *(acc)*; **w.** (*ger*) ohne zu (*inf*), ohne daß; **w. reason** ohne allen Anlaß

with·stand' *v (pret & pp* –stood) *tr* widerstehen *(dat)*

witness ['wɪtnɪs] *s* Zeuge *m*, Zeugin *f*; *(evidence)* Zeugnis *n*; **bear w.** to Zeugnis ablegen von; **in w. whereof** zum Zeugnis dessen; **w. for the defense** Entlastungszeuge *m*; **w. for the prosecution** Belastungszeuge *m* || *tr (an event)* anwesend sein bei; *(an accident, crime)* Augenzeuge sein *(genit)*; *(e.g., a contract, will)* als Zeuge unterschreiben

wit'ness stand' *s* Zeugenstand *m*

witticism ['wɪtɪˌsɪzəm] *s* Witzelei *f*

wittingly ['wɪtɪŋlɪ] *adv* wissentlich

witty ['wɪtɪ] *adj* geistreich, witzig

wizard ['wɪzərd] *s* Hexenmeister *m*

wizardry ['wɪzərdrɪ] *s* (& fig) Hexerei *f*

wizend ['wɪzənd] *adj* runzelig

wobble ['wɑbəl] *intr* wackeln

wobbly ['wɑblɪ] *adj* wackelig

woe [wo] *s* Weh *n* || *interj*—**woe is me!** weh mir!

woebegone ['wobɪˌgɔn] *adj* jammervoll

woeful ['wofəl] *adj* jammervoll

wolf [wʊlf] *s* (wolves [wʊlvz]) Wolf *m*; *(coll)* Schürzenjäger *m*; **cry w. blinden Alarm schlagen**; **keep the w. from the door** sich über Wasser halten || *tr*—**w. down** verschlingen

wolf'pack' *s* Wolfsrudel *n*; *(nav)* U-bootrudel *n*

wolfram ['wʊlfrəm] *s* (chem) Wolfram *n*; *(mineral)* Wolframit *n*

woman ['wʊmən] *s* (women ['wɪmən]) Frau *f*

wom'an doc'tor *s* Ärztin *f*

wom'anhood' *s* Frauen *pl*; **reach w. e-e Frau werden**

womanish ['wʊmənɪʃ] *adj* weibisch

wom'ankind' *s* Frauen *pl*

womanly ['wʊmənlɪ] *adj* fraulich

womb [wum] *s* Mutterleib *m*

wom'enfolk' *spl* Weibsvolk *n*

wom'en's dou'bles *spl* (tennis) Damendoppelspiel *n*

wom'en's sin'gles *spl* (tennis) Dameneinzelspiel *n*

wonder ['wʌndər] *s* Wunder *n* || *intr (be surprised)* sich wundern; *(ask*

oneself) sich fragen; *(reflect)* überlegen; **wonder at** sich verwundern über *(acc)*

wonderful ['wʌndərfəl] *adj* wunderbar

won'derland' *s* Wunderland *n*

won'der work'er *s* Wundertäter –in *mf*

wont [wʌnt], [wont] *adj*—**be w. to** (*inf*) pflegen zu (*inf*) || *s* Gepflogenheit *f*

wont'ed *adj* gewöhnlich, üblich

woo [wu] *tr* den Hof machen *(dat)*

wood [wʊd] *s* Holz *n*; **out of the woods** (fig) über den Berg; **woods** Wald *m*

wood' al'cohol *s* Methylalkohol *m*

woodbine ['wʊdˌbaɪn] *s* Geißblatt *n*; *(Virginia creeper)* wilder Wein *m*

wood' carv'ing *s* Holzschnitzerei *f*

wood'chuck' *s* Murmeltier *n*

wood'cock' *s* Holzschnepfe *f*

wood'cut' *s (block)* Holzplatte *f*; *(print)* Holzschnitt *m*

wood'cut'ter *s* Holzfäller *m*

wood'ed *adj* bewaldet

wooden ['wʊdən] *adj* (& fig) hölzern

wood' engrav'ing *s* Holzschnitt *m*

wood'en leg' *s* Stelzbein *n*

wood'en shoe' *s* Holzschuh *m*

woodland ['wʊdlənd] *adj* Wald– || *s* Waldland *n*

wood'man *s* (–men) Holzhauer *m*

woodpecker ['wʊdˌpekər] *s* Specht *m*

wood' pi'geon *s* Ringeltaube *f*

wood'pile' *s* Holzhaufen *m*

wood'pulp' *s* Holzfaserstoff *m*

wood' screw' *s* Holzschraube *f*

wood'shed' *s* Holzschuppen *m*

woods'man *s* (–men) Förster *m*; *(lumberman)* Holzhauer *m*

wood'winds' *spl* Holzblasinstrumente *pl*

wood'work' *s* Holzarbeit *f*; *(structure in wood)* Gebälk *n*

wood'work'er *s* Holzarbeiter –in *mf*

wood'worm' *s* (ent) Holzwurm *m*

woody ['wʊdɪ] *adj* waldig; *(woodlike)* holzig

wooer ['wu·ər] *s* Verehrer *m*

woof [wʊf] *s (of a dog)* unterdrücktes Bellen *n*; *(tex)* Gewebe *n*

woofer ['wʊfər] *s* (rad) Tieftöner *m*

wool [wʊl] *adj* wollen || *s* Wolle *f*

woolen ['wʊlən] *adj* wollen, Woll– || **woolens** *spl* Wollwaren *pl*

woolly ['wʊlɪ] *adj* wollig; *(e.g., thinking)* verschwommen

woozy ['wuzɪ] *adj* benebelt

word [wʌrd] *s* Wort *n*; **be as good as one's w.** zu seinem Wort stehen; **by w. of mouth** mündlich; **get w. from** Nachricht haben von; **give one's w.** sein Wort geben; **have a w. with** ein ernstes Wort sprechen mit; **have words** e-n Wortwechsel haben; **in a w.** mit e-m Wort; **in other words** mit anderen Worten; **in so many words** ausdrücklich; **leave w.** Bescheid hinterlassen; **not another w.!** kein Wort mehr!; **not a w. of truth in it** kein wahres Wort daran; **put in a good w. for s.o.** ein gutes Wort für j-n einlegen; **put into words** in

Worte kleiden; **put words in s.o.'s mouth** j-m Worte in den Mund legen; **send w. to s.o.** j-n benachrichtigen; **take s.o.'s w. for it** j-n beim Wort nehmen; **w. for w.** Wort für Wort || *tr* formulieren

word'-for-word' *adj* wörtlich

word'ing *s* Formulierung *f*

word' of hon'or *s* Ehrenwort *n*; **w.!** auf mein Wort!

word' or'der *s* Wortfolge *f*

wordy ['wʌrdɪ] *adj* wortreich

work [wʌrk] *s* Arbeit *f*; (*production, book*) Werk *n*; **be in the works** (coll) im Gang sein; **get to w.** sich an die Arbeit machen; (*travel to work*) zum Arbeitsplatz kommen; **give s.o. the works** (coll) j-n fertigmachen; **have one's w. cut out** zu tun haben; **it took a lot of w.** to (*inf*) es hat viel Arbeit gekostet zu (*inf*); **make short w. of** kurzen Prozeß machen mit; **out of w.** arbeitslos; **works** (horol) Uhrwerk *n* || *tr* (*a machine*) bedienen; (*a pedal*) treten; (*a mine*) abbauen; (*the soil*) bearbeiten; (*metal*) treiben; (*dough*) kneten; (*wonders*) wirken; **w. in** einarbeiten; **w. off** (*a debt*) abarbeiten; **w. oneself to death** sich totarbeiten; **w. one's way up** sich hocharbeiten; **w. out** (*a solution*) ausarbeiten; (*a problem*) lösen; **w. to death** abhetzen; **w. up an appetite** sich [*dat*] Appetit machen || *intr* arbeiten; (*junction*) funktionieren; (*succeed*) klappen; **w. against** wirken gegen; **w. away at** losarbeiten auf (*acc*); **w. at** (*a trade*) ausüben; **w. both ways** für beide Fälle gelten; **w. loose** sich lockern; **w. on** (*a person*) bearbeiten; (*a patient, car*) arbeiten an (*dat*); **w. out** (sport) trainieren; **w. out well** gut aussehen

workable ['wʌrkəbəl] *adj* brauchbar; (*plan*) durchführbar

work'bench' *s* Werkbank *f*

work'book' *s* Übungsheft *n*

work' camp' *s* Arbeitslager *n*

work'day' *s* Arbeitstag *m*

work' detail' *s* (mil) Arbeitskommando *n*

worked'-up' *adj* erregt; **get s.o. w.** j-n erregen; **get w.** sich erregen

worker ['wʌrkər] *s* Arbeiter –in *mf*

work' force' *s* Belegschaft *f*

work'horse' *s* Arbeitspferd *n*

work'ing day' *s* Arbeitstag *m*

work'ing girl' *s* Arbeiterin *f*

work'ing hours' *spl* Arbeitsstunden *pl*

work'ingman' *s* (–men') Arbeiter *m*

work'ing or'der *s*—**in w.** betriebsfähig

work'ingwom'an *s* (–wom'en) Arbeiterin *f*; (*professionally*) berufstätige Frau *f*

work'man *s* (–men) Arbeiter *m*

work'manship' *s* Ausführung *f*

work'men's compensa'tion insur'ance *s* Arbeitsunfallversicherung *f*

work' of art' *s* Kunstwerk *n*

work'out' *s* Training *n*

work' per'mit *s* Arbeitsgenehmigung *f*

work'room' *s* Arbeitszimmer *n*

work' sche'dule *s* Dienstplan *m*

work'shop' *s* Werkstatt *f*

work' stop'page *s* Arbeitseinstellung *f*

world [wʌrld] *adj* Welt– || *s* Welt *f*; **a w. of** groß; **from all over the w.** aus aller Herren Ländern; **not for all the w.** nicht um die Welt; **see the w.** in der Welt herumkommen; **they are worlds apart** es liegen Welten zwischen den beiden; **think the w. of** große Stücke halten auf (*acc*); **who (where) in the w.** wer (wo) in aller Welt

world' affairs' *spl* internationale Angelegenheiten *pl*

world'-fa'mous *adj* weltberühmt

worldly ['wʌrldlɪ] *adj* (*goods, pleasures*) irdisch; (*person*) weltlich; (*wisdom*) Welt–

world'ly-wise' *adj* weltklug

world's fair' *s* Weltausstellung *f*

world'-shak'ing *adj* weltbewegend

world'-wide' *adj* weltweit

worm [wʌrm] *s* Wurm *m* || *tr*—**w. one's way** sich schlängeln; **w. secrets out of s.o.** j-m die Würmer aus der Nase ziehen

worm-eaten ['wʌrm,itən] *adj* (& fig) wurmstichig

wormy ['wʌrmɪ] *adj* wurmig

worn [wɔrn] *adj* (*clothes*) getragen; (*tires*) abgenutzt; (*wearied*) müde

worn'-out' *adj* (*clothes*) abgetragen; (*tires*) abgenutzt; (*exhausted*) erschöpft

worrisome ['wʌrɪsəm] *adj* (*causing worry*) beunruhigend; (*inclined to worry*) sorgenvoll

wor·ry ['wʌri] *s* Sorge *f*; (*source of worry*) Ärger *m* || *v* (*pret & pp* –ried) *tr* beunruhigen; **be worried** besorgt sein || *intr* (*about*) sich [*dat*] Sorgen machen (um); **don't w.!** keine Sorge!

worse [wʌrs] *comp adj* schlechter, schlimmer; **be w. off** schlimmer daran sein; **he's none the w. for it** es hat ihm nichts geschadet; **what's w.** was noch schlimmer ist

worsen ['wʌrsən] *tr* verschlimmern || *intr* sich verschlimmern

wor·ship ['wʌr/ɪp] *s* Anbetung *f*; (*services*) Gottesdienst *m* || *v* (*pret & pp* –shiped; *ger* –ship[p]ing) *tr* (& fig) anbeten || *intr* seine Andacht verrichten

worship(p)er ['wʌr/ɪpər] *s* Anbeter –in *mf*; (*in church*) Andächtige *mf*

worst [wʌrst] *super adj* schlimmste || *super adv* am schlimmsten || *s* Schlimmste *n*; **at the w.** schlimmstenfalls; **get the w. of** den kürzeren ziehen bei; **if w. comes to w.** wenn alle Stricke reißen; **the w. is yet to come** das dicke Ende kommt noch || *tr* schlagen

worsted ['wʊstɪd] *adj* Kammgarn–

worth [wʌrθ] *adj* wert; **it is w.** (*ger*) es lohnt sich zu (*inf*); **it is w. the trouble** es ist der Mühe wert; **ten dollars' w. of meat** für zehn Dollar Fleisch; **w. seeing** sehenswert || *s* Wert *m*

worthless ['wʌrθlɪs] *adj* wertlos; (*person*) nichtsnutzig

worth'while' *adj* lohnend

worthy ['wʌrði] *adj* (**of**) würdig (*genit*)

would [wʊd] *aux* used to express 1) indirect statements, e.g., **he said he w. come** er sagte, er würde kommen; 2) the present conditional, e.g., **he w. do it if he could** er würde es tun, wenn er könnte; 3) past conditional, e.g., **he w. have paid, if he had had the money** er würde gezahlt haben, wenn er das Geld gehabt hätte; 4) habitual action in the past, e.g., **he w. always buy the morning paper** er kaufte immer das Morgenblatt; 5) polite requests, e.g., **w. you please pass me the butter?** würden Sie mir bitte die Butter reichen; 6) a wish, e.g., **w. that I had never seen it** wenn ich es nur nie gesehen hätte!; **w. rather** möchte lieber, e.g., **I w. rather go on foot** ich möchte lieber zu Fuß gehen

would'-be' *adj* angeblich, Möchtegern-

wound [wuːnd] *s* Wunde *f* ‖ *tr* verwunden

wound'ed *adj* verwundet ‖ **the w.** *spl* die Verwundeten *pl*

wow [waʊ] *s* (coll) Bombenerfolg *m* ‖ *tr* (coll) erstaunen ‖ *interj* nanu!

wrack [ræk] *s*—**go to w. and ruin** untergehen, in Brüche gehen

wraith [reθ] *s* (*apparition*) Erscheinung *f*; (*spirit*) Geist *m*

wrangle ['ræŋgəl] *s* Streit *m* ‖ *intr* streiten

wrap [ræp] *s* Überwurf *m* ‖ *v* (*pret & pp* **wrapped**; *ger* **wrapping**) *tr* wickeln; (*a package*) einpacken; **be wrapped up in** (*e.g., thoughts*) versunken sein in (*dat*); **wrapped in darkness** in Dunkelheit gehüllt; **w. up** (*a deal*) abwickeln

wrapper ['ræpər] *s* Verpackung *f*; (*for mailing newspapers*) Streifband *n*

wrap'ping *s* Verpackung *f*

wrap'ping pa'per *s* Packpapier *n*

wrath [ræθ] *s* Zorn *m*, Wut *f*

wrathful ['ræθfəl] *adj* zornig, wütend

wreak [riːk] *tr* (*vengeance*) üben; **w. havoc** schlimm hausen

wreath [riθ] *s* (**wreaths** [riðz]) Kranz *m*; **w. of smoke** Rauchfahne *f*

wreathe [riːð] *tr* bekränzen, umwinden

wreck [rɛk] *s* (*of a car or train*) Unglück *n*; (**wrecked ship, car, person**) Wrack *n* ‖ *tr* (*e.g., a car*) zertrümmern; (*a building*) in Trümmer legen; (*a marriage*) zerrütten; (fig) zum Scheitern bringen; **be wrecked** (fig & naut) scheitern

wreckage ['rɛkɪdʒ] *s* Wrackgut *n*; (*of an accident*) Trümmer *pl*

wrecker ['rɛkər] *s* Abschleppwagen *m*

wren [rɛn] *s* (orn) Zaunkönig *m*

wrench [rɛntʃ] *s* (*tool*) Schraubenschlüssel *m*; (*of a muscle*) Verrenkung *f* ‖ *tr* verrenken

wrest [rɛst] *tr* (**from**) entreißen (*dat*)

wrestle ['rɛsəl] *tr* ringen mit ‖ *intr* ringen

wrestler ['rɛslər] *s* Ringer *m*; (*professional wrestler*) Catcher *m*

wrestling ['rɛslɪŋ] *s* Ringen *n*; (*professional wrestling*) Catchen *n*

wres'tling match' *s* Ringkampf *m*

wretch [rɛtʃ] *s* armer Kerl *m*; (*vile person*) Schuft *m*

wretched ['rɛtʃɪd] *adj* elend; (*terrible*) scheußlich

wriggle ['rɪgəl] *s* Krümmung *f*; (*of a worm*) schlängelnde Bewegung *f* ‖ *tr* hin- und herbewegen; **w. one's way** sich dahinschlängeln ‖ *intr* sich winden

wring [rɪŋ] *v* (*pret & pp* **wrung** [rʌŋ]) *tr* (*the hands*) ringen; **w. out** (*the wash*) auswinden; **w. s.o.'s neck** j-m den Hals umdrehen

wringer ['rɪŋər] *s* Wringmaschine *f*

wrinkle ['rɪŋkəl] *s* Falte *f*; **new w.** (fig) neuer Kniff *m*; **take out the wrinkles** (fig) den letzten Schliff geben ‖ *tr* falten, runzeln; (*paper, clothes*) zerknittern ‖ *intr* Falten werfen

wrin'kle-proof' *adj* knitterfrei

wrinkly ['rɪŋkli] *adj* faltig, runzelig

wrist [rɪst] *s* Handgelenk *n*

wrist'band' *s* Armband *n*

wrist' watch' *s* Armbanduhr *f*

writ [rɪt] *s* gerichtlicher schriftlicher Befehl *m*

write [raɪt] *v* (*pret* **wrote** [rot]; *pp* **written** ['rɪtən]) *tr* schreiben; (*compose*) verfassen; **it is written** (*in the Bible*) es steht geschrieben; **it is written all over his face** es steht ihm im Gesicht geschrieben; **w. down** aufschreiben; **w. off** abschreiben; **w. out** ausschreiben; (*a check*) ausstellen ‖ *intr* schreiben; **w. for information** Informationen anfordern

write'-off' *s* Abschreibung *f*

writer ['raɪtər] *s* Schreiber –in *mf*; (*author*) Schriftsteller –in *mf*

writ'er's cramp' *s* Schreibkrampf *m*

writ'e-up' *s* Pressebericht *m*

writhe [raɪð] *intr* (in) sich krümmen (vor *dat*)

writ'ing *s* Schreiben *n*; (*handwriting*) Schrift *f*; **in w.** schriftlich; **put in w.** niederschreiben

writ'ing desk' *s* Schreibtisch *m*

writ'ing pad' *s* Schreibblock *m*

writ'ing pa'per *s* Schreibpapier *n*; (*stationery*) Briefpapier *n*

written ['rɪtən] *adj* schriftlich; (*law*) geschrieben; (*language*) Schrift–

wrong [rɔŋ] *adj* (*incorrect*) falsch; (*unjust*) unrecht; **be w.** (*be incorrect*) nicht stimmen; (*be in error*) Unrecht haben; (*said of a situation*) nicht in Ordnung sein; **be. w. with** fehlen (*dat*); **sorry, w. number!** (telp) falsch verbunden! ‖ *s* Unrecht *n*; **be in the w.** im Unrecht sein; **do w.** ein Unrecht begehen; **do w. to s.o.** j-m ein Unrecht zufügen; **get in w. with s.o.** es sich (*dat*) mit j-m verderben ‖ *adv* falsch, unrecht; **go w.** (*morally*) auf Abwege geraten; (*in walking*) sich verirren; (*in reckoning*) irregehen; (in driving) sich verfahren; (said of plans) schief gehen

wrong'doer ['rɔŋ‚du‧ər] s Missetäter –in mf

wrong'do'ing s Missetat f

wrought' i'ron [rɔt] s Schmiedeeisen n

wrought'-up' adj aufgebracht

wry [raɪ] adj schief

X

X, x [eks] s vierundzwanzigster Buchstabe des englischen Alphabets

xenophobia [‚zɛnə'fobɪ‧ə] s Fremdenhaß m

Xerox ['zɪrɑks] s (trademark) Xerographie f || xerox tr ablichten

Xer'ox-cop'y s Ablichtung f

Xmas ['krɪsməs] adj Weihnachts– || s Weihnachten pl

x'-ray' adj Röntgen– || s (picture) Röntgenbild n; x-rays Röntgenstrahlen pl || tr röntgen

x'-ray ther'apy s Röntgentherapie f

xylophone ['zaɪlə‚fon] s Xylophon n

Y

Y, y [waɪ] s fünfundzwanzigster Buchstabe des englischen Alphabets

yacht [jɑt] s Jacht f

yacht' club' s Jachtklub m

yam [jæm] s Yamwurzel f

yank [jæŋk] s Ruck m; Yank Ami m || tr—y. s.th. out of reißen aus || intr —y. on heftig ziehen an (dat)

Yankee ['jæŋki] s Yankee m

yap [jæp] s (talk) (sl) Geschwätz n; (mouth) (sl) Maul n; (bark) Gekläff n || v (pret & pp yapped; ger yapping) intr (bark) kläffen; (talk) (sl) schwätzen

yard [jɑrd] s (measure) Yard n; (ground adjoining a building) Hof m; (naut) Rahe f; (rr) Rangierbahnhof m

yard'arm' s (naut) Nock f & n

yard' mas'ter s (rr) Rangiermeister m

yard'stick' s Yardmaß n; (fig) Maßstab m

yarn [jɑrn] s (thread; story) Garn n; spin yarns (fig) Garne spinnen

yaw [jɔ] s (aer, rok) Schwanken n; (naut) Gieren n || intr (aer, rok) schwanken; (naut) gieren

yawl [jɔl] s (naut) Jolle f

yawn [jɔn] s Gähnen n || intr gähnen; (said, e.g., of a gorge) klaffen

ye [ji] pers pron ihr

yea [je] s Jastimme f || adv ja

yeah [je] adv ja

year [jɪr] s Jahr n; all y. round das ganze Jahr hindurch; a y. from today heute übers Jahr; for years seit Jahren; jahrelang; in years seit Jahren; y. in, y. out jahraus jahrein

year'book' s Jahrbuch n

yearling ['jɪrlɪŋ] s Jährling m

yearly ['jɪrli] adj & adv jährlich

yearn [jɑrn] intr—y. for sich sehnen nach; y. to (inf) sich danach sehnen zu (inf)

yearn'ing s Sehnsucht f

yeast [jist] s Hefe f

yell [jel] s Ruf m, Aufschrei m; (sport) Kampfruf m || tr (gellend) schreien; y. one's lungs out sich tot schreien || intr schreien; y. at anschreien

yellow ['jelo] adj gelb; (sl) feige || s Gelb n || tr gelb machen || intr vergilben

yellowish ['jelo‧ɪʃ] adj gelblich

yel'lowjack'et s Wespe f

yel'low jour'nalism s Sensationspresse f

yel'low streak' s Zug m von Feigheit

yelp [jelp] s Gekläff n || intr kläffen

yen [jen] s (Japanese money) Yen m; (for) brennendes Verlangen n (nach)

yeo·man ['jomən] s (–men) (nav) Verwaltungsunteroffizier m

yeo'man's serv'ice s großer Dienst m

yes [jes] adv ja; yes, Sir jawohl || s Ja n; say yes to bejahen

yes' man' s Jasager m

yesterday ['jestər‚de] adv gestern; y. morning gestern früh || s Gestern n; yesterday's gestrig

yet [jet] adv (still) noch; (however) doch; (already) schon; and yet trotzdem, dennoch; as yet schon; not yet noch nicht || conj aber

yew [ju] s Eibe f

Yiddish ['jɪdɪʃ] adj jiddisch || s Jiddisch n

yield [jild] s Ertrag m || tr (profit) einbringen; (interest) tragen; (crops) hervorbringen; (give up) überlassen || intr (to) nachgeben (dat)

yo·del ['jodəl] s Jodler m || v (pret & pp –del[l]ed; ger –del[l]ing) intr jodeln

yodeler ['jodələr] s Jodler –in mf

yogurt ['jogurt] s Yoghurt m & n

yoke [jok] s (part of harness; burden) Joch n; pass under the y. sich in ein Joch fügen; y. of oxen Ochsengespann n || tr ins Joch spannen

yokel ['jokəl] *s* Bauerntölpel *m*

yolk [jok] *s* Dotter *m & n*

yonder ['jandər] *adv* dort drüben

yore [jor] *s*—of y. vormals

you [ju] *pers pron* du; *(plural form)* ihr; *(polite form)* Sie; **to you** dir; *(plural form)* euch; *(polite form)* Ihnen; **you of all people!** ausgerechnet Sie! ‖ *indef pron* man

young [jʌŋ] *adj* (younger ['jʌŋgər]; youngest ['jʌŋgɪst]) jung; **y. for one's age** jugendlich für sein Alter ‖ *spl (of animals)* Jungen *pl;* **the y.** die Jungen, die Jugend; **with y.** *(pregnant)* trächtig

young' la'dy *s* Fräulein *n*

young' man' *s* junger Mann *m;* (boyfriend) Freund *m*

youngster ['jʌŋstər] *s* Jugendliche *mf*

your [jur] *poss adj* dein; *(plural form)* euer; *(polite form)* Ihr

yours [jurz] *poss pron* deiner; *(plural*

form) euerer; *(polite form)* Ihrer; **y. truly** hochachtungsvoll

your·self [jur'self] *intens pron* (–selves ['selvz]) selbst, selber ‖ *reflex pron* dich; *(plural form)* euch; *(polite form)* Sich; **to y.** dir; *(polite form)* Sich; **to yourselves** euch; *(polite form)* Sich

youth [juθ] *s* (youths [juθs], [juðz]) *(age)* Jugend *f; (person)* Jugendliche *mf*

youthful ['juθfəl] *adj* jugendlich

youth' hos'tel *s* Jugendherberge *f*

yowl [jaul] *s* Gejaule *n* ‖ *tr & intr* jaulen

Yugoslav ['jugo'slav] *adj* jugoslawisch ‖ *s* Jugoslawe *m,* Jugoslawin *f*

Yugoslavia ['jugo'slavɪ·ə] *s* Jugoslavien *n*

yule' log' [jul] *s* Weihnachtsscheit *n*

yule'tide' *s* Weihnachtszeit *f*

Z

Z, z [zi] *s* sechsundzwanzigster Buchstabe des englischen Alphabets

zany ['zeni] *adj* närrisch ‖ *s* Hanswurst *m*

zeal [zil] *s* Eifer *m*

zealot ['zelət] *s* Zelot –in *mf*

zealous ['zeləs] *adj* eifrig

zebra ['zibrə] *s* Zebra *n*

zenith ['ziniθ] *s* Scheitelpunkt *m,* Zenit *m*

zephyr ['zefər] *s* Zephir *m*

zeppelin ['zepəlɪn] *s* Zeppelin *m*

ze·ro ['ziro] *s* (–ros & –roes) Null *f* ‖ *tr*—z. in a rifle Visier e–s Gewehrs justieren ‖ *intr*—z. in on zielen auf (acc)

ze'ro hour' *s* Stunde *f* Null

zest [zest] *s* Würze *f*

Zeus [zus] *s* Zeus *m*

zig·zag ['zɪg,zæg] *adj* Zickzack– ‖ *adv* im Zickzack ‖ *s* Zickzack *m* ‖ *(pret & pp* –zagged; *ger* –zagging) *intr* im Zickzack fahren

zinc [zɪŋk] *s* Zink *n*

Zionism ['zaɪ·ə,nɪzəm] *s* Zionismus *m*

zip [zɪp] *s* (coll) Schmiß *m* ‖ *v (pret & pp* zipped; *ger* zipping) *tr (convey with speed)* mit Schwung befördern; *(fasten with a zipper)* mit e–m Reißverschluß schließen ‖ *intr* sausen; **zip by** vorbeisausen ‖ *interj* wuppdich!

zip' code' *s* Postleitzahl *f*

zipper ['zɪpər] *s* Reißverschluß *m*

zircon ['zʌrkan] *s* Zirkon *m*

zither ['zɪθər] *s* Zither *f*

zodiac ['zodɪ,æk] *s* Tierkreis *m*

zombie ['zombi] *s* (sl) Depp *m*

zone [zon] *s* (& geol) Zone *f; (postal zone)* Postbezirk *m;* (mil) Bereich *m*

zoo [zu] *s* Zoo *m,* Tiergarten *m*

zoologic(al) [,zo·ə'ladʒɪk(əl)] *adj* zoologisch

zoologist [zo'alədʒɪst] *s* Zoologe *m,* Zoologin *f*

zoology [zo'alədʒi] *s* Zoologie *f*

zoom [zum] *s* lautes Summen *n;* (aer) Hochreißen *n* ‖ *intr* laut summen; **z. up** (aer) hochreißen

zoom' lens' *s* Gummilinse *f*

METRIC CONVERSIONS

Multiply:	By:	To Obtain:
acres	43,560	sq. ft.
	0.4047	hectares
	0.0015625	sq. mi.
ampere-hours	3600	coulombs
atmospheres	76.0	cm. of mercury
	33.90	ft. of water
	14.70	lbs./sq. in.
British thermal units	1054	joules
	777.5	ft.-lbs.
	252.0	gram calories
	0.0003927	horsepower-hrs.
	0.0002928	kilowatt-hrs.
B.T.U./hr.	0.2928	watts
B.T.U./min.	12.96	ft.-lbs./sec.
	0.02356	horsepower
bushels	3523.8	hectoliters
	2150.42	cu. ins.
	35.238	liters
°C + 17.78	1.8	°F
centimeters	0.3937	inches
cm-grams	980.1	cm.-dynes
chains	66	ft.
circumference	6.2832	radians
cubic centimeters	0.0610	cu. ins.
cu. feet	1728	cu. ins.
	62.43	lbs. of water
	7.481	gals. (liq.)
	0.0283	cu. m.
cu. ft./min.	62.43	lbs. water/min.
cu. ft./sec.	448.831	gals./min.
cu. inches	16.387	cu. cm.
	0.0005787	cu. ft.
cu. meters	264.2	gals. (liq.)
	35.3147	cu. ft.
	1.3079	cu. yds.
cu. yards	27	cu. ft.
	0.765	cu. m.
days	86,400	seconds
degrees/sec.	0.1667	revolutions/min.
°F − 32	0.5556	°C
faradays/sec.	96,500	amperes
feet	30.48	cm.
	0.3048	meters
	0.0001894	mi. (stat.)
	0.0001645	mi. (Brit. naut.)

Multiply:	By:	To Obtain:
ft. of water	62.43	lbs./sq. ft.
	0.4335	lbs./sq. in.
ft./min.	0.5080	cm./sec.
ft./sec.	0.6818	mi./hr.
	0.5921	knots
fluid ounces	29.573	milliliters
furlongs	660	feet
	0.125	mi.
gallons	231	cu. ins.
	8.345	lbs. of water
	8	pts.
	4	qts.
	3.785	liters
	0.003785	cu. m.
gals./min.	8.0208	cu. ft./hr.
grains	0.0648	grams
grams	980.1	dynes
	15.43	grains
	0.0353	oz. (avdp.)
	0.0022	lbs. (avdp.)
hectares	107,600	sq. ft.
	2.47	acres
hectoliters	2.838	bushels
horsepower	33,000	ft.-lbs./min.
	2545	B.T.U./hr.
	745.7	watts
	42.44	B.T.U./min.
	0.7457	kilowatts
inches	25.40	mm.
	2.540	cm.
	0.00001578	mi.
ins. of water	0.03613	lbs./sq. in.
kilograms	980,100	dynes
	2.2046	lbs. (avdp.)
kg. calories	3086	ft.-lbs.
	3.968	B.T.U.
kg. cal./min.	51.43	ft.-lbs./sec.
	0.06972	kilowatts
kilometers	3280.8	ft.
	0.621	mi.
km./hr.	0.621	mi./hr.
	0.5396	knots
kilowatts	737.6	ft.-lbs./sec.
	56.92	B.T.U./min.
	1.341	horsepower
kilowatt-hrs.	2,655,000	ft.-lbs.
	3415	B.T.U.
	1.341	horsepower-hrs.
knots	6080	ft./hr.
	1.151	stat. mi./hr.
	1	(Brit.) naut. mi./hr.
liters	61.02	cu. ins.
	2.113	pts. (liq.)
	1.057	qts. (liq.)
	0.264	gals. (liq.)
	1.816	pts. (dry)
	0.908	qts. (dry)
	0.1135	pecks
	0.0284	bushels

Multiply:	By:	To Obtain:
meters	39.37	inches
	3.2808	ft.
	1.0936	yds.
	0.0006215	mi. (stat.)
	0.0005396	mi. (Brit. naut.)
miles		
statute	5280	ft.
	1.609	km.
	0.8624	mi. (Brit. naut.)
nautical (Brit.)	6080	ft.
	1.151	mi. (stat.)
mi./hr.	1.467	ft./sec.
milligrams/liter	1	parts/million
milliliters	0.0338	fluid oz.
millimeters	0.03937	inches
ounces		
avoirdupois	28.349	grams
	0.9115	oz. (troy)
	0.0625	lbs. (avdp.)
troy	31.103	grams
	1.0971	oz. (avdp.)
pecks	8.8096	liters
pints		
liquid	473.2	cu. cm.
	28.875	cu. ins.
	0.473	liters
dry	0.550	liters
pounds		
avoirdupois	444,600	dynes
	453.6	grams
	32.17	poundals
	14.58	oz. (troy)
	1.21	lbs. (troy)
	0.4536	kg.
troy	0.373	kg.
lbs. (avdp.)/sq. in.	70.22	g./sq. cm.
	2.307	ft. of water
quarts		
liquid	57.75	cu. ins.
	32	fluid oz.
	2	pts.
	0.946	liters
dry	67.20	cu. ins.
	1.101	liters
quires	25	sheets
radians	3437.7	minutes
	57.296	degrees
reams	500	sheets
revolutions/min.	6	degrees/sec.
rods	16.5	ft.
	5.5	yds.
	5.029	meters
slugs	32.17	lbs. (mass)
square centimeters	0.155	sq. ins.
sq. feet	0.093	sq. m.
sq. inches	6.451	sq. cm.
sq. kilometers	247.1	acres
	0.3861	sq. mi.

Multiply:	By:	To Obtain:
sq. meters	10.76	sq. ft.
	1.1960	sq. yds.
sq. miles	27,878,400	sq. ft.
	640	acres
	2.5889	sq. km.
sq. yards	0.8361	sq. m.
tons		
long	2240	lbs. (avdp.)
	1.12	short tons
	1.0160	metric tons
metric	2204.6	lbs. (avdp.)
	1000	kg.
	1.1023	short tons
	0.9842	long tons
short	2000	lbs. (avdp.)
	0.9072	metric tons
	0.8929	long tons
watts	3.415	B.T.U./hr.
	0.001341	horsepower
yards	36	inches
	3	ft.
	0.9144	meters
	0.0005682	mi. (stat.)
	0.0004934	mi. (Brit. naut.)

LABELS AND ABBREVIATIONS

BEZEICHNUNGEN DER SACHGEBIETE UND ABKÜRZUNGEN

abbr abbreviation—Abkürzung
acc accusative—Akkusativ
(acct) accounting—Rechnungswesen
adj adjective—Adjektiv
(adm) administration—Verwaltung
adv adverb—Adverb
(aer) aeronautics—Luftfahrt
(agr) agriculture—Landwirtschaft
(alg) algebra—Algebra
(Am) American—amerikanisch
(anat) anatomy—Anatomie
(angl) angling—Angeln
(archeol) archeology—Archäologie
(archit) architecture—Architektur
(arith) arithmetic—Rechnen
art article—Artikel
(arti) artillery—Artillerie
(astr) astronomy—Astronomie
(atom. phys.) Atomic physics—Atomphysik
(Aust) Austrian—österreichisch
(aut) automobile—Automobile
aux auxiliary verb—Hilfsverb
(bact) bacteriology—Bakteriologie
(baseball) Baseball
(basketball) Korbball
(bb) bookbinding—Buchbinderei
(Bib) Biblical—biblisch
(billiards) Billard
(biochem) biochemistry—Biochemie
(biol) biology—Biologie
(bowling) Kegeln
(bot) botany—Botanik
(box) boxing—Boxen
(Brit) British—britisch
(cards) Kartenspiel
(carp) carpentry—Zimmerhandwerk
(checkers) Damespiel

(chem) chemistry—Chemie
(chess) Schachspiel
(cin) cinematography—Kinematographie
(coll) colloquial—umgangssprachlich
(com) commercial—Handels-
comb.fm. combining form—Wortbildungselement
comp comparative—Komparativ
conj conjunction—Konjunktion
(crew) Rudersport
(culin) culinary—kulinarisch
(data proc.) data processing—Datenverarbeitung
dem demonstrative—hinweisend
(dent) dentistry—Zahnheilkunde
(dial) dialectical—dialektisch
(dipl) diplomacy—Diplomatie
(eccl) ecclesiastical—kirchlich
(econ) economics—Wirtschaft
(educ) education—Schulwesen
e–e a(n)—eine
e.g. for example—zum Beispiel
(elec) electricity—Elektrizität
(electron) electronics—Elektronik
e–m to a(n)—einem
e–n a(n)—einen
(eng) engineering—Technik
(ent) entomology—Entomologie
e–r of a(n), to a(n)—einer
e–s of a(n)—eines
etw something—etwas
f feminine noun—Femininum
(fa) fine arts—schöne Künste
fem feminine—weiblich
(fencing) Fechtkunst
(fig) figurative—bildlich
(& fig) literal and figurative—buchstäblich und bildlich
(fin) finance—Finanzwesen
(fb) football, soccer—Fußball
fut future—Zukunft
genit genitive—Genitiv
(geog) geography, Geographie
(geol) geology—Geologie
(geom) geometry—Geometrie
ger gerund—Gerundium
(golf) Golf
(gram) grammar—Grammatik
(gym) gymnastics—Gymnastik
(heral) heraldry—Wappenkunde
(hist) history—Geschichte
(horol) horology—Zeitmessung
(hort) horticulture—Gartenbau
(hum) humorous—scherzhaft
(hunt) hunting—Jagdwesen
(ichth) ichthyology—Ichthyologie

imperf imperfect—Imperfekt
impers impersonal—unpersönlich
ind indicative—Indikativ
indecl indeclinable—undeklinierbar
indef indefinite—unbestimmt
(indust) industry—Industrie
inf infinitive—Infinitiv
(ins) insurance—Versicherungswesen
insep inseparable—untrennbar
intens intensive—verstärkend
interj interjection—Interjektion
interr interrogative—Frage-
intr intransitive—intransitiv
invar invariable—unveränderlich
(iron) ironical—ironisch
j-m to someone—jemandem
j-n someone—jemanden
(journ) journalism—Zeitungswesen
j-s someone's—jemand(e)s
(jur) jurisprudence—Rechtswissenschaft
(libr) library science—Bibliothekswissenschaft
(ling) linguistics—Linguistik
(lit) literary—literarisch
(log) logic—Logik
m masculine noun—Maskulinum
(mach) machinery—Maschinen
(mech) mechanics—Mechanik
(med) medicine—Medizin
(metal) metallurgy—Metallurgie
(meteor) meteorology—Meteorologie
mf masculine or feminine noun according to sex—Maskulinum
    oder Femininum je nach Geschlecht
(mil) military—Militär-
(min) mining—Bergwerkswesen
(mineral) mineralogy—Mineralogie
mod aux modal auxiliary—Modalverb
(mount) mountain climbing—Bergsteigerei
(mus) music—Musik
(myth) mythology—Mythologie
m & f masculine and feminine noun without regard to sex—
    Maskulinum oder Femininum ohne Rücksicht auf Geschlecht
(naut) nautical—nautisch
(nav) navy—Kriegsmarine
neut neuter—sächlich
(obs) obsolete—veraltet
(obstet) obstetrics—Geburtshilfe
(opt) optics—Optik
(orn) ornithology—Ornithologie
(paint) painting—Malerei
(parl) parliamentary—parlamentarisch
(pathol) pathology—Pathologie
(pej) pejorative—pejorativ
   personal—Personal-

(pharm) pharmacy—Pharmazie
(philos) philosophy—Philosophie
(phonet) phonetics—Phonetik
(phot) photography—Photographie
(phys) physics—Physik
(physiol) physiology—Physiologie
pl plural—Plural
(poet) poetical—dichterisch
(pol) politics—Politik
poss possessive—besitzanzeigend
pp past participial—Partizip Perfekt
pref prefix—Präfix
prep preposition—Präposition
pres present—Gegenwart
pret preterit—Präteritum
pron pronoun—Pronomen
pros prosody—Prosodie
(Prot) Protestant—protestantisch
(psychol) psychology—Psychologie
(public sign) Hinweisschild
(rad) radio—Radio
(radar) Radar
recip reciprocal—wechselseitig
ref reflexive verb—Reflexivverb
reflex reflexive—reflexiv
rel relative—relativ
(relig) religion—Religion
(rhet) rhetoric—Rhetorik
(rok) rocketry—Raketen
(rr) railroad—Eisenbahn
s substantive—Substantiv
(sculp) sculpture—Bildhauerkunst
sep separable—trennbar
(sewing) Näherei
sg singular—Einzahl
(sl) slang—Slang
s.o. someone—jemand
s.o.'s someone's—jemand(e)s
spl substantive plural—pluralisches Substantiv
(sport) sports—Sports
(st. exch.) stock exchange—Börse
subj subjunctive—Konjunktiv
suf suffix—Suffix
super superlative—Superlativ
(surg) surgery—Chirurgie
(surv) surveying—Vermessungswesen
(tech) technical—Fachsprache
(telg) telegraphy—Telegraphie
(telp) telephone—Fernsprechwesen
(telv) television—Fernsehen
(tennis) Tennis
(tex) textiles—Textilien
(theat) theater—Theater

(theol) theology—Theologie
tr transitive—transitiv
(typ) typography—Typographie
usw. and so forth—und so weiter
v verb—Verb
var variant—Variante
(vet) veterinary medicine—Veterinärmedizin
(vulg) vulgar—vulgär
(zool) zoology—Zoologie